W9-CPX-878

FUNK & WAGNALLS STANDARD DESK DICTIONARY

VOLUME 1

A

M

FUNK & WAGNALLS, INC., NEW YORK
1975

Funk & Wagnalls
Standard Desk Dictionary
Library of Congress Catalog Card No. 66-25079

Manufactured in the United States of America
fge

TABLE OF CONTENTS

PREFACE

This dictionary contains over 100,000 entries, offering comprehensive coverage of the general vocabulary and including many scientific and technical terms seldom found in dictionaries of comparable size. Based upon the considerably larger Standard College Dictionary, it represents an up-to-date survey of the English language, and includes, apart from the main body of vocabulary words, a wide selection of idioms and figurative expressions, as well as many common slang terms and meanings. It also includes a large number of usage notes, marked off in the dictionary proper by this symbol [◆], which give helpful information and counsel on a variety of traditionally troublesome words, such as *can* and *may*, *lay* and *lie*, *infer* and *imply*.

Following the main vocabulary section is *A Pronouncing Gazetteer*, including all places in the United States and Canada having a population of 5000 or over, as well as all the countries of the world and the major foreign cities, and indicating political status, location, and, if appropriate, ZIP Code number. A separate section, *Abbreviations*, is a comprehensive list of abbreviations and acronyms that one is most likely to encounter, whether in business practice or in everyday affairs. *Biographies*, which immediately follows the abbreviations section, lists and pronounces the names of, and gives information about, people of the past and present who have distinguished themselves in the arts and sciences, in world affairs, or in other areas of endeavor.

Finally, the *Secretarial Handbook* includes sections on usage, punctuation, business correspondence, and forms of address that should be of considerable help not only to secretaries but to anyone who is sometimes puzzled by the complexities of English grammar and usage, or who is called upon to write an important business letter.

For a more complete account of these sections as well as other features of this book, and for valuable discussions of pronunciation, restrictive labels, etymologies, and synonyms and antonyms, the reader is urged to read the *Guide to This Dictionary* beginning on p. v.

The Editors

EDITORIAL STAFF

Funk & Wagnalls' Editorial Board for Dictionaries consists of Albert H. Marckwardt, Chairman, Professor of English and Linguistics, Princeton University; Frederic G. Cassidy, Professor of English, University of Wisconsin; S. I. Hayakawa, Professor of English, San Francisco State College; and James B. McMillan, Professor of English, University of Alabama. Each of these scholars has contributed an essay in his field of special competence to the *Guide to This Dictionary*. In addition, many other authorities in a variety of fields have given us the benefit of their specialized knowledge and advice in formulating the definitions that appear in this book.

Editor in Chief:	Sidney I. Landau
General Editors:	Sheila C. Brantley, Samuel Davis, Ruth Koenigsberg
Science Editor:	Harold Ward
Geography Editor:	Harold A. Rodgers, Jr.
Production Editor:	Jack Doenias
Associate Editors:	Veronica P. Collings, Alma E. Graham
Office Staff:	Maxine Edelstein, Bruce Chalnick, Wendy Duveen, Seth Malin
Illustrations:	Stephen J. Voorhies

GUIDE TO THIS DICTIONARY

The following explanatory material deals with the different kinds of information given in this dictionary and with their arrangement within each entry. A careful reading of the fourteen items discussed below, and of the essays on **Pronunciations, Level and Style Labels, Etymologies,** and **Synonyms** that begin on page vii, will help the reader use this dictionary effectively. Items 1–14 are listed in roughly the same order in which the information they describe appears in most individual entries:

1. The Main Entry
2. Pronunciations
3. Parts of Speech
4. Inflected Forms
5. Definitions
6. Restrictive Labels
7. Collateral Adjectives
8. Variant Forms
9. Cross-references
10. Etymologies
11. Run-on Derivatives
12. Usage Notes
13. Synonyms and Antonyms
14. Geographical Entries

The Main Entry

The main entry word or words have been printed in rge, boldface type, set slightly into the left-hand argin so as to be easily found. General vocabulary ords and phrases, prefixes and suffixes, foreign terms, ographical and geographical entries, etc., are arranged one alphabetic list. Thus, the entry for **harlequin** ecedes that for **Harlequin.** Biographical entries, ographical entries, and abbreviations appear in parate alphabetical lists following the main vocabury section.

A center period is used to indicate division in main try words, as **par·ti·cip·i·al.** In other boldface tries, such as run-on derivatives and variant forms, e center period is eliminated wherever the primary d secondary syllable stresses are marked, as **par'ti·p'i·al·ly.** Phrasal entries, as **intelligence quoent,** are not divided when the elements are indidually entered elsewhere.

Pronunciations

Pronunciations are shown in parentheses immediately llowing the boldface main entry, as **di·chot·o·my** (dī·kot'ə·mē). The pronunciation system used in this dictionary utilizes, with a few exceptions, the letters of the alphabet, combined with certain standard diacritical marks, such as the macron for the so-called "long vowels" (ā, ē, ī, ō, yōō). The "short vowels" have no diacritical marks. The breve is retained in the one symbol (ŏŏ), the vowel in *book,* to avoid confusion with the vowel in *pool,* for which the macron is used (ōō). The dieresis is used for one symbol (ä), and the circumflex for three (â, ô, û). The schwa (ə) is used for the unstressed neutral vowel, however spelled. This pronunciation key is based on phonemic principles to the extent that each symbol represents a single sound or closely associated cluster of sounds, and no sound is transcribed with more than one symbol.

The pronunciation key appears in full on p. xv; an abbreviated key is given at the foot of every odd-numbered page in the main vocabulary section. For a fuller discussion of the treatment given pronunciation in this dictionary, see p.vii.

3. Parts of Speech

These are shown in italics following the pronunciation for main entries, and are abbreviated as follows: *n.* (noun), *v.* (verb), *pron.* (pronoun), *adj.* (adjective), *adv.* (adverb), *prep.* (preposition), *conj.* (conjunction), *interj.* (interjection). When more than one part of speech is entered under a main entry, the additional designations are run in and preceded by a boldface dash, as **cor·ner** (kôr′nər) *n.* . . . **—** *v.t.* . . . **—** *v.i.* . . . **—** *adj.* . . .

Verbs used transitively are identified as *v.t.*, those intransitively as *v.i.*; those used both transitively and intransitively in all senses are designated *v.t. & v.i.*

4. Inflected Forms

These include the past tense, past participle, and present participle of verbs, the plural of nouns, and the comparative and superlative of adjectives and adverbs. Inflected forms are entered wherever there is some irregularity in spelling or form. They are shown in boldface type, with syllabication, immediately after the part-of-speech designation. Only the syllable affected is shown, unless ambiguity may occur, as **com·pute** (kəm·pyo͞ot′) *v.t. & v.i.* **·put·ed, ·put·ing.** An inflected form that requires pronunciation or is alphabetically distant from the main entry will also be separately entered and pronounced in its proper vocabulary place.

Principal parts of verbs The order in which the principal parts are shown is past tense, past participle, and present participle, as **come** (kum) *v.i.* **came, come, com·ing.** Where the past tense and past participle are identical, only two forms are entered, as **bake** (bāk) *v.* **baked, bak·ing.** When alternative forms are given, the first form indicated is usually the one preferred, as **grov·el** (gruv′əl, grov′-) *v.i.* **grov·eled** or **·elled, grov·el·ing** or **·el·ling.** Principal parts entirely regular in formation — those that add *-ed* and *-ing* directly to the infinitive without spelling modification — are not shown.

Plurals of nouns Irregular forms are here preceded by the designation *pl.*, as **a·lum·nus** (ə·lum′nəs) *n. pl.* **·ni** (-nī); **co·dex** (kō′deks) *n. pl.* **co·di·ces** (kō′də·sēz, kod′ə-); **deer** (dir) *n. pl.* **deer.** When alternative plurals are given, the first shown is the preferred form, as **buf·fa·lo** (buf′ə·lō) *n. pl.* **·loes** or **·los; chrys·a·lis** (kris′ə·lis) *n. pl.* **chrys·a·lis·es** or **chry·sal·i·des** (kri·sal′ə·dēz).

Comparison of adjectives and adverbs The comparatives and superlatives of adjectives and adverbs are shown immediately after the part of speech when there is some spelling modification or a complete change of form, as **mer·ry** (mer′ē) *adj.* **·ri·er, ·ri·est; bad**[1] (bad) *adj.* **worse, worst; well**[2] (wel) *adv.* **bet·ter, best.**

5. Definitions

In entries for words having several senses, the definition appearing first is the one most frequently used. Successive definitions are listed, wherever possible, in order of declining frequency of use rather than according to semantic evolution. Each such definition is distinguished by a boldface numeral, the numbering starting anew after each part-of-speech designation when more than one sense follows. Closely related meanings, especially those within a specific field or area of study, are defined under the same number and set apart by boldface letters.

6. Restrictive Labels

No restrictive label is required for those genera purpose words and meanings, usable in any contex which make up the bulk of the English language as is spoken and written throughout the world. Words c particular senses of words, however, which have an restriction of use are labeled. A number of differer types of labels are used in this dictionary to indica where, by whom, or in what context a particular wo or expression is most commonly used. For a full di cussion of **Level and Style Labels,** including th labels *Informal, Dial.* (for *dialectal*), *Slang,* and *Illi* (for *illiterate*), see p. ix. The following are other typ of labels found in this dictionary:

Currency Labels Both standard and nonstanda words may be in less than general currency. If these a included they are labeled *Rare, Archaic,* or *Obs.* (obs lete). (See the definitions of these words in the body the dictionary.)

Locality Labels These identify the geographic region of the English-speaking world in which a wo or meaning, either standard or nonstandard, is use exclusively or more characteristically than it is in oth regions. (For example, *elevator* is labeled *U.S.*, while t synonymous *lift* is labeled *Brit.*)

Field Labels These identify the field of learning of activity in which a word or sense belongs. (Sor common examples are *Bot., Chem., Mil., Photog.* — s the list of abbreviations.) Because of the frequent ove lapping between fields, however, these labels can applied only broadly.

Foreign-language Labels These identify t source of words or phrases not fully naturalized in English. Because these retain the foreign spelling a pronunciation, though used in English context, th should be italicized when written. (Examples are *joie vivre* labeled *French, Weltschmerz* labeled *German.*)

7. Collateral Adjectives

Because of extensive borrowing in English fro Norman French and Medieval Latin, we find a go many English nouns which have adjectives closely co nected with them in meaning, but not in form, su as *arm* and *brachial, horse* and *equine, dog* and *canin day* and *diurnal,* etc. These functionally related a jectives are defined in this dictionary in their alphabet place, but as an added convenience many of them a also shown with their associated nouns. Collateral a jectives follow the sense or senses of the noun to whi they apply, and are introduced with a diamond symb

arm (ärm) *n.* **1.** *Anat.* **a** The upper limb of the hum body. . . . ◆ Collateral adjective: *brachial.*

8. Variant Forms

Some words have more than one standard spelli or form, as *center, centre; algebraic, algebraical.* Som times, completely different forms have the same mea ing, as *bachelor's-button* and *cornflower.* These varian are listed in two ways: (1) When the variant form alphabetically close to the commoner form, it is enter with the main entry in boldface type, syllabicate stressed, and, where necessary, pronounced; (2) Wh the variant is alphabetically distant, it is shown italic print under the main entry, and is also listed in proper alphabetic place with a cross-reference to t main entry.

bach·e·lor (bach′ə·lər, bach′lər) *n.* . . . . **3.** A young knight serving under another's banner: also **bach′e·lor-at-arms′** . . . .
bas-re·lief (bä′ri·lēf′, bas′-) *n.* That type of sculpture in which the figures project . . . : also called *low relief.*

ɔrms that have some restricted usage are labeled ac-ɾdingly, as **hon·or** . . . . Also *Brit.* **hon′our.**

. Cross-references

Cross-references are directions to see another entry r additional information. The entry to be sought is ·nerally indicated in small capital letters, as **car·a·cul** . See KARAKUL; **cor·po·ra** . . . Plural of CORPUS; **ulgar Latin** See under LATIN.

Some entries are defined by citing another form:

cach·a·lot (kash′ə·lot, -lō) *n.* The sperm whale.
cou·gar (kōō′gər) *n.* The puma.
fog chamber *Physics* A cloud chamber.

omplete information will be found under the word or ·rm used in the definition.

Cross-references are also used to indicate where more formation may be found, or when an important se-antic distinction might otherwise be missed, as **etit mal** . . .: distinguished from *grand mal*; **Brun-ild.** . . . Compare BRUNNHILDE.

For information about cross-references used in the ymologies, see p. x.

0. Etymologies

Etymologies are given in brackets at the end of each ·try. For a full discussion of the treatment given ymology in this dictionary, see p. x.

1. Run-on Derivatives

Words that are actually or apparently derived from her words by the addition or replacement of a suffix, ·d whose sense can be inferred from the meaning of ·e main word, are run on, in smaller boldface type, at the end of the appropriate main entries. The run-on entries are preceded by a heavy dash and followed by a part-of-speech designation. They are syllabicated and stressed, and, when necessary, a full or partial pronunciation is indicated:

in·sip·id (in·sip′id) *adj.* . . . **— in·si·pid·i·ty** (in′si·pid′ə·tē), **in·sip′id·ness** *n.* **— in·sip′id·ly** *adv.*

12. Usage Notes

Special points of grammar and idiom, when essential to correct usage, are included, following a colon, after the particular sense of a word to which they apply, as **anx·ious** . . . **3.** Intent; eagerly desirous: with *for* or the infinitive. . . . More extensive notes consisting of supplementary information on grammar, accepted usage, the relative status of variant forms, etc., are entered at the end of the relevant entries and prefaced with the symbol ◆. Examples may be found under the entries **Asiatic, gotten,** and **me.**

13. Synonyms and Antonyms

Extended discussions of the differentiation in shades of meaning within a group of related words are given at the end of relevant entries in paragraphed form. They are introduced by the abbreviation **Syn.** Since a word may have distinct synonyms for each of several senses, the discussions are numbered, where necessary, to accord with the numbering of relevant definitions in the preceding entry. In addition to the discussions, lists of synonyms and antonyms are entered in cases where the distinctions between the words in question are easily ascertained from the definitions. For a full discussion of the treatment given synonyms in this dictionary, see p. xi.

14. Geographical Entries

Population figures for places in the United States are based on the 1960 census, and those for Canada on the 1961 census. Population figures for foreign places are dated to show the time of census or estimate.

ʼRONUNCIATIONS by James B. McMillan

A pronunciation is correct when it is normally and ·affectedly used by cultivated people. Strictly, any onunciation is correct when it serves the purposes of mmunication and does not call unfavorable attention the speaker, but the user of a desk dictionary does ·t need or expect to find every pronunciation of every ɔrd that may be heard in the smallest, most isolated mmunities. He expects to find the pronunciations at he can use comfortably before educated audiences.

We do not have in the English-speaking world a andard of pronunciation like the standard specimens meters, liters, feet, and gallons that national bureaus standards keep to preserve and enforce uniformity. would be technically simple to have a professional eaker record on magnetic tape his pronunciation of ery word in a dictionary and to store the tapes in raries where they could be heard, even in distant ·ies, by dialing the telephone number of a computer at would select and play back the pronunciation of ·y desired word. But choosing the model speaker uld not be simple. Should he pronounce *forest* as it sounds in Boston? Or Chicago? Or Atlanta? Or Spokane? If he pronounced *dew* and *do* differently, would educated people who pronounce the two words alike change to conform? Or if he pronounced both (dōō), would educated people who distinguish the two words be willing to give up their distinction? Simple inanimate quart jars and foot rulers can easily be taken to a government bureau and compared with a standard measure, but pronunciations are articulations of sounds by individual human vocal organs, with all the diversity of human beings. One standard of correctness is impractical, unenforceable, impossible.

Correctness in pronunciation is so flexible and pronunciations are so varied that a desk dictionary cannot list nearly all the acceptable forms of even common words; for this reason the absence of a pronunciation, for example *said* as (sād), rhyming with *laid*, does not mean that the pronunciation is necessarily "incorrect," but simply that there is not space to record every minority practice. The editors do not include (bûr′ē) for *bury* (rhyming with *hurry*) because they have heard it very rarely, and not usually in cultivated speech. On the other hand, when a pronunciation is listed the dictionary user can be confident that the pronunciation is in actual use among educated people. Disagreements that arise because two people do not pronounce the key words alike cannot be settled; the fact that every user has to interpret the pronunciation symbols in terms of his own pronunciation of the key words makes each one, in a sense, his own standard.

Because words are listed in a dictionary as separate items, not as segments of a flow of speech, the pronunciations given are for words pronounced in isolation; for example the pronunciation (fāt) is what one would say in answering "How do you pronounce the word spelled *f-e-t-e*?" In the stream of speech, many words, particularly pronouns, articles, and auxiliaries, occur in shortened or changed form when they are weakly stressed. Thus the words (tel), (him), (hē), (haz), (to͞o), (sē), (hûr) may appear in sentence form as (tel·im·ē·has·tə·sē·ər). The changed pronunciations that actual utterance produces are not normally listed.

Syllabication in pronunciation follows, in general, the breaks heard in speech, rather than the conventional division of the boldface entry, as **hid·ing** (hī′ding), **lat·er** (lā′tər), **of·fi·cial** (ə·fish′əl). Syllable boundaries are sometimes impossible to set with certainty and are sometimes variable. Thus words like **met·ric** (met′rik) and **cad·re** (kad′rē) are divided between the consonants, although many people pronounce both consonants in the second syllable (me′trik) and (ka′drē), as the contrast between *metric* and *met Rick* will show.

Three levels of stress are indicated in the pronunciations. Syllables with weakest stress are not marked; every word with two or more syllables has one primary stress marked, as *editor* (ed′it·ər); and words with three or more syllables frequently have a secondary stress marked by a light symbol, as *acceleration* (ak·sel′ə·rā′·shən), or a secondary stress indicated simply by a vowel, as in the final syllable of *ameliorate* (ə·mēl′yə·rāt). These three levels correspond to the primary, tertiary (*not* secondary), and weak levels in the four-stress system commonly used by linguists. The secondary level of the four-stress system is not used here because it occurs only in phrases or other word groups, not in single words.

Because a dictionary records and reports the pronunciations of educated people, and all educated people do not pronounce identically, a dictionary must list variant forms of thousands of words. When two or more pronunciations are indicated for a word, the one that the editors believe must frequent in the northern and western sections of the United States is listed first, but other pronunciations are equally reputable. (The dictionary does not list socially substandard pronunciations, no matter how common they may be.)

Pronunciation differences are of seven principal kinds:

(1) Different consonants may be used in the same word; e.g. some people pronounce *exit* (ek′sit), others (eg′zit); some pronounce *blouse* (blous), others (blouz).

(2) Different vowels may be used in the same word; e.g. for some people the word *lever* rhymes with *clever* (klev′ər), for others it rhymes with *beaver* (bē′vər); the first syllable of *economics* may rhyme with *peck* (ek·ə·nom′iks) or with *peak* (ē·kə·nom′iks).

(3) A word may have different syllables stressed; e.g. *altimeter* (al·tim′ə·tər) or (al′tə·mē′tər), and *abdomen* (ab′də·mən) or (ab·dō′mən).

(4) The same consonant may be used in a word, but it may be articulated very differently; e.g. the /t/* in *metal*, or *writer*, or *winter*, or the /r/ in *very* (sometimes humorously written *veddy*).

(5) The same vowel may be used in a word, but it may be articulated very differently; e.g. the /ô/ in *raw*, the /ou/ in *house*, the /ī/ in *ice*, and the /ä/ in *park*, whic have wide regional variations.

(6) Although all dialects of American English seem t have the same twenty-four consonants, some have fewe vowels than others; e.g., the contrasts made in some re gions between *morning* and *mourning*, *cot* and *caugh* *burred* and *bird*, and *Cary*, *Kerry*, and *Carrie* are nc made in other regions.

(7) The same vowel or consonant may not occur i the same positions in all varieties; e.g., some speake pronounce /y/ before /o͞o/ in *cute* (kyo͞ot) but not i *new* (no͞o) or *due* (do͞o) or *tune* (to͞on), while others equal education pronounce these words (nyo͞o), (dyo͞o and (tyo͞on). Some speakers have /zh/ normally be tween vowels, as in *pleasure* (plezh′ər) and *vision* (vizh ən) but not at the ends of words, so that *garage* is bot (gə·räzh′) and (gə·raj′).

Some differences in pronunciation can be correlate with geography, and others are purely personal. N dictionary can pick one pronunciation of *dog*, or *eithe* or *room* and ignore other pronunciations of equal reput The principal variants must be acknowledged. For ra words, such as terms in the arts and sciences that are nc learned vernacularly, analogy and the pattern of sour languages provide the pronunciations listed.

Two methods of providing variants are used, (1 multiple pronunciations, as *fog* (fog, fôg), and (2) var able symbols keyed to common words, such as /â/ as i *dare, fair;* it is assumed that when a dictionary user look up *parterre* and finds (pär·târ′) he will pronounce th first syllable to rhyme with *bar* and the second syllab to rhyme with *dare, air,* since /ä/ is keyed to the wor *father*, and /â/ is keyed to the words *dare, air*. The di tionary does not tell the user how to pronounce the ke words, assuming that they represent stable basic pa terns.

When a variant pronunciation differs only in pa from the first pronunciation recorded, only the differir syllable or syllables are shown, provided there is r possibility of misinterpretation, as **eq·ua·ble** (ek′w bəl, ē′kwə-).

Phrasal entries of two or more words are not pr nounced if the individual elements are separately e tered in proper alphabetic place.

Sometimes a word will differ in its pronunciation d pending on its use as a noun, verb, etc., or in son particular sense. The differing pronunciations are show immediately after the entry word, with the applicatio clearly indicated, as follows:

ad·dress (ə·dres′; *for n. defs. 2, 3, also* ad′res)
re·ject (*v.* ri·jekt′; *n.* rē′jekt)

A few foreign words occur with sufficient frequen in English to require dictionary entry; as their use i creases they usually become adapted to English pr nunciation patterns. For the dictionary user who spea the language from which a word is imported, no pr nunciation is necessary; he recognizes the word or c pronounce it from his knowledge of the spelling of t foreign language. However, the dictionary user w does not speak the foreign language may wish to pr nounce a word in a recognizable approximation of i native form. Such words are respelled with the Engli vowels and consonants that are closest to the forei phonemes, plus a handful of symbols for French a German sounds that have no counterparts in Englis Thus the French word *chef-d'oeuvre* is respelled (sh doe′vr′), which warns that a non-English vowel occu in the second syllable and that the /r/ at the end is voic less. It is assumed that the consonants /sh/, /d/, a /v/, and the vowel /e/ will be reasonably similar to t corresponding (but not identical) French sounds, a that the stress on the second syllable will be lighter th English primary stress.

*The symbols printed between virgules represent phonemes.

EVEL AND STYLE LABELS by Frederic G. Cassidy

The language is often thought of as existing on two evels of usage," the standard and the nonstandard. his distinction rests on the fact that, though there is othing intrinsically higher or lower, better or worse in e word than in another *considered as words* (language gnals), every speech community nevertheless responds ore or less favorably toward individual words and nses on the basis of association, habit, imposed value dgments, and the like. The language of cultivation, ing that normally used by the leading part of the com- unity, and that most widely understood within the nglish-speaking world, has high prestige and is con- dered to be of the "upper" level. This is *Standard Eng- sh.* In contrast, the language of limited, local, or uncul- vated use is nonstandard and of "lower" level. The llowing scheme represents the relative positions of rious types of discourse and the corresponding labels ed in this dictionary.

andard glish
- Throughout the English-speaking world
  (No label)
- Characteristic of a national division of English
  Labels: *U.S., Brit., Scot., Austral.*, etc.
- Characteristic of a broad region of a national division
  Labels: *Southern U.S., SW U.S.*, etc.
- Characteristic of general informal use
  Label: *Informal*

nstandard glish
- Used within a small geographical area, and often rural and traditional
  Label: *Dial.*
- Used to express a humorous, racy, and irreverent attitude, often within a particular group
  Label: *Slang*
- Used within a group in connection with a common activity, trade, or profession
  (No label or a field label)
- Used by the least educated, and considered incorrect by most users of Standard English
  Label: *Illit.*

The dictionary concentrates on standard words and eanings; only those nonstandard ones are included hich have wide currency or which deserve notice for me other reason (e.g., their relationship to standard ords). Lines of distinction cannot always be sharply awn between the various types of nonstandard words meanings. It is sometimes necessary also to combine e labels (e.g., *Brit. Dial., U.S. Slang*) for precise dis- iminations.

In addition, since the response to words depends in rt upon the stylistic context in which they are used, e dictionary maker must take this response into con- deration in applying labels. Two distinct styles are nerally recognized: Formal and Informal.*

Formal style is that appropriate to all public and rious expression; to spoken use in legislative assem- ies, in courts, in the pulpit; to "belles lettres" or tistic literature; to legal and scientific writing. Because users belong to the cultivated and literate part of the blic it tends to be more deliberate, precise, discrim- ating, and orderly than the casual usage normal to eryday discourse, even that carried on by this same ltivated group.

Informal style, that employed by most people a great rt of the time in both speaking and writing, differs from the formal in being less consciously controlled, less precise, less complex and compact, less careful in diction — though quite acceptable within its sphere, and more appropriate to relaxed situations than formal style would be.

In pronunciation the formal style is more controlled, with conscious use of prosodic features (pitch, pause, stress) and with clear articulation and syllabication (though without restressing, spelling-pronunciation, or other distortions). In grammar it is conservative; in sentence form it has more variety and range than everyday discourse has. Its vocabulary is far broader and richer, demanding sharper distinctions and more sensitive choice. In overall structure it is orderly, consciously articulated, intellectually directed.

In pronunciation the informal style is easy, relaxed; it admits a degree of slurring and ellipsis, though not to the point of becoming unclear. It makes fuller use of voice qualifiers (indicating emotional attitudes) than does formal style; it is therefore far more personal. In grammar it is less conservative, reflecting contemporary tendencies in the development of the language. In sentence form it is less complex and varied, and in vocabulary less discriminating, than is formal style: it experiments with neologisms, slang, and the livelier words of current vogue. It is given to abbreviation and contraction. In overall structure it is likely to be casual, not closely knit, additive rather than integral.

New scientific and literary words are apt to enter the sphere of standard usage at once; new popular words, by contrast, tend to remain nonstandard for a time — perhaps always; but they may and sometimes do rapidly gain status and enter the standard sphere.

Since "formal" and "informal" properly describe *styles* of discourse, the application of one of these terms to an individual word or meaning indicates only that such an item is appropriate to the one style or the other. If a word of one style is employed in a context not its own, it will give some effect of its own style to that context. Further, since no meaning is irrevocably fixed, the connotation of a word repeatedly used in a stylistic context not its own may change.

A word or meaning labeled *Informal* is therefore one which, though as well known as any other standard one, is less acceptable (i.e., less accepted at any given time) for formal use than for informal. The actual usage of cultivated writers and speakers is the only valid test of such status. Words not labeled are appropriate to formal use.

The "levels" and "styles" do not coincide exactly. Their relationship may best be expressed by the following diagram, in which the sphere of Standard English is represented by a circle, the nonstandard lying outside it.

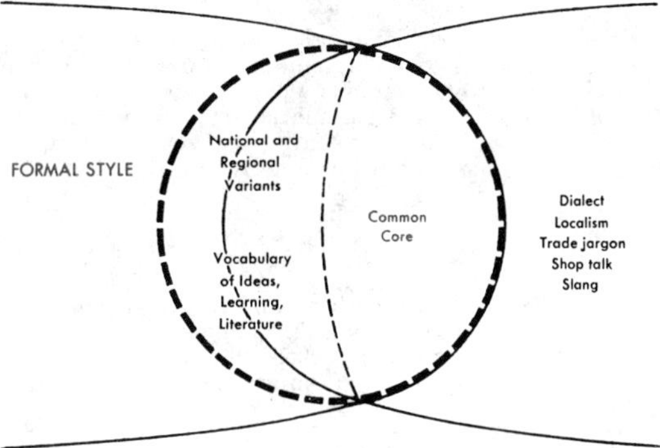

THE CIRCLE OF STANDARD ENGLISH

*The label *Colloq.* (colloquial — see its definition in the body the dictionary) is now so widely misunderstood by the public to be no longer serviceable and is therefore not used in this ctionary.

The circle is broken to indicate that nonstandard usages sometimes enter and become standard, and that formerly standard words also drop out into nonstandard usage or disappear altogether. Elliptical lines to left and right, drawn through the circle of Standard English, set off those parts that are appropriate respectively to formal and informal style. The Common Core comprises those words and senses which are used in all types of English.

Distinctions within the levels of language can be made nowadays with a considerable degree of obj tivity. Distinctions of style, on the other hand, a partly esthetic and subjective. In every case an accura application of labels must rest on the investigation the situations in which any word or sense is actua used, the kind of people who do or do not use it, and t kind of response (apart from that of its denotati meaning) which it is likely to elicit in any linguis community. Ultimately, however, it must also depe to some extent upon the judgment of the lexicograph

ETYMOLOGIES by Albert H. Marckwardt

Etymology is the systematic study of word origins, or in a particular sense the facts relating to the derivation or formation of a word. To illustrate, *etymology* is a borrowing of French *étymologie*, which developed from Latin *etymologia*, itself a borrowing from the Greek. The Greek form may be divided into two parts, *etymon* a form of the adjective "true" and *logos* "word, study, account." Thus we have the elements which entered into the formation of this word and the languages through which it passed into English.

The etymology of a word is given after the definition. It appears in square brackets, and precedes the boldface listing of derivative forms. The following three symbols are used: < "derived from"; + "and" or "combined with"; ? "possible."

Native words that were present in the earliest period of the language (450–1050) are shown in their Old English form.

bed·rid·den . . . [Earlier *bedrid* < OE *bedrida* < *bed* bed + *rida* rider]

For borrowed words, the immediate source is given first, followed by those intermediate forms and languages which show significant changes.

pi·ra·nha . . . [< Pg. (Brazilian) < Tupi, toothed fish]

If the specific language of origin cannot be determined but the general provenance is known, a linguistic family or a geographical area is indicated as the source.

ba·nan·a . . . [< Sp. < native African name]

Words of unknown or uncertain origin are so marked. If there is a Middle English form for a word of obscure origin, it is cited. Even though the origin of a word cannot be determined, it is sometimes possible to give cognate forms from related languages. Be careful to note the difference between the mark < which means "derived from" and the abbreviation *cf.* which indicates a cognate relationship but not a derivation.

bud . . . [ME *budde*; origin uncertain]
gloat . . . [Cf. ON *glotta* to grin]

In order to avoid repetition and to present as much information as possible within a limited space, cross-references are occasionally used to direct attention to main entries where detailed information may be found.

de·cep·tion . . . [See DECEIVE.]
de·ceive . . . [< OF < L < *de-* away, down + *capere* to take]

The etymologies of words representing various typ of combinations of free and bound forms (*wildcat, p judge, goodness*) may be found under the main entr for *wild, cat; pre-, judge; good, -ness.*

Etymologies of a somewhat unusual character, esp cially those connecting words with particular peop places, or events are recorded with additional notes e plaining the historic background of the word. For exa ples of this see *buncombe, gerrymander, knickerbock* Acronyms and blends are shown by placing the portic of the source words which have survived in the n formation in distinctive type. Back formations a instances of folk etymology are so labeled. See *dona legislate, woodchuck.*

A knowledge of etymology can be useful in ma ways. If, for example, those words which have come in English from any one language are considered as group, they often reveal much about the nature of t cultural impact of that language and the people w speak it upon English. The fact that so many of o mineralogical terms come from German suggests t preeminence of that nation in the development of t science and our indebtedness to its scientists. The sa might be said with respect to the Italian origin of o musical terminology. The common and intimate cha acter of many of the Scandinavian borrowings in Engli tells us something of the nature of the relationship b tween the Norse and the English during the tenth a eleventh centuries.

It may also be true that in certain instances a kno edge of the etymology of a word may give the individ speaker or writer a surer sense of its meaning and use. word like *supercilious* would seem, at least, to be m vivid to someone who can connect it with raised e brows than to the person for whom it is merely a po syllable with a general implication of superiority attitude. The word *equinox* will be employed with greater feeling of certainty by one who connects t component parts of the word with the simple facts b hind them.

A note of warning is called for, however. Etymolo informative and interesting though it may be, is no valid criterion of present meaning or determiner of u Meaning is determined by present usage; the meani assigned to the words included in this dictionary w determined by a careful and systematic examination their use in actual context.

The fact that *dilapidated* contains a form of *la* "stone" does not signify that this word can be appl only to stone structures. The word *etymology* itself is excellent illustration of this point. Despite the fact t its first element is the neuter form of *etymos* "true," etymology of a word is not the sole determiner of a sin "true" or correct meaning, however much light it m shed upon aspects of its significance.

;YNONYMS by S. I. Hayakawa

The English language is unusually rich in synonyms ıd near-synonyms. This richness is due to the fact that .e vocabulary of English, a language especially hospi-ble to loan-words, is drawn from many sources. The)cabulary of Anglo-Saxon, already containing loan-ords from Celtic, Latin, and Scandinavian, was just ›out doubled after the Norman Conquest by borrow-gs from French, to form the Middle English vocabu-ry. From the sixteenth century on, with the revival of assical learning, there was vast borrowing from Latin ıd Greek. Wherever English-speaking people have ıbsequently gone, in war, travel, or colonization, they ıve added new words to the language, and they con-nue to do so today. Thus, one may give a *speech* or *talk* .nglo-Saxon words), a *lecture* or *address* or *harangue* 'rench words), an *oration* (Latin), or a *homily* (Greek). ne may live on a wide and open *plain* (Old French), *eppe* (Russian), *prairie* (French), *tundra* (Lapp), *pam-ıs* (South American Indian), or *savanna* (Spanish). A ırson may adhere to a *teaching* (Anglo-Saxon), a *doc-ine* (French), a *tenet* (Latin), a *dogma* (Greek). Some ›rds were borrowed more than once, at different times ıd in different forms, like *warden* and *warranty* (Nor-an French) as compared with *guardian* and *guarantee* ;entral French); like *loyal* and *legal*, *royal* and *regal*, *ncy* and *fantasy*, *count* and *compute*, *gentle* and *genteel*, *iest* and *presbyter*. Some of these "doublets" are alike meaning, some are quite different.

Often the borrowings were in a strict sense unneces-ry; many that remain today are simply relics of the xteenth-century fad of embellishing one's speech and :iting with Latinisms. Certainly it is possible to talk ›out *kissing* without using the word *osculatory*, about *:y* without *diurnal*. Nevertheless, the availability of reign and learned vocabularies, even if they partly ıplicate the native vocabulary, is a tremendous asset any language. An advanced civilization needs, in ldition to a language of everyday life (from which ıerges the language of poetry), a language for law and cial organization and the discussion of policy, and an 'en more abstract language for scientific and philo-phical discourse. These many distinct needs are more sily met by a language that has had a long history of ›rrowing than by a language (like Gaelic) whose speak-s insist on a fanatical "purity" of vocabulary, such as .n only result in a poverty of things to talk about.

Are there any *exact* synonyms? The general semanti-ıts, who assert that "no word ever has exactly the me meaning twice," would seem to assert that a word nnot even be synonymous with itself. What they mean that the word *apple*, for example, cannot be applied *r*ice to *exactly* the same referent, because every apple is different from every other apple, and because each apple is itself changing from moment to moment. However, in a dictionary we are concerned not so much with referents as with *verbal* equivalences: what word or phrase or circumlocution can serve as an equivalent for the word defined. Thus, *entire* means "having no part missing; whole; complete." Insofar as certain words can be substituted for others without affecting the meaning of a sentence, one can indeed speak of exact synonyms. "The *entire* (*whole*, *complete*) cast was invited to the party." The test for exact synonymy, then, is interchangeability. Despite Hilaire Belloc's haughty distinction, "what Anglo-Saxons call a *foreword*, but gentlemen a *preface*," these terms are also genuinely interchangeable in most contexts. But interchangeability in certain contexts does not mean interchangeability in all. "The cast is now *complete*" — not *whole*, or *entire*. A skirmish may be a *preface* to a battle, but not a *foreword*.

Hence interchangeability is by no means the whole story on synonyms. What are treated as synonyms in this dictionary are more often words that point to the same facts but convey different attitudes on the part of the speaker. An individual's regard for himself may be termed *egotism*, *conceit*, or *self-esteem*, depending on whether or not the speaker approves of it. Other synonyms point to similar actions or events, but in different contexts or applications: a *journey* is usually by land, a *voyage* by water; a short journey, whether by land or water, is a *trip*; an *excursion* is a short trip (usually for pleasure) from which one soon returns to a starting point; a military excursion is a *sortie*. We *accompany* our equals, *attend* those whom we serve, *conduct* those whom we guide, *escort* those whom we protect, except for merchant ships, which we *convoy*. It would be simpler if *go with* could be used in all these contexts. But the language would be infinitely poorer if these shades of meaning, expressive of innumerable nuances of human relationships, attitudes, and perceptions, were to be lost.

Occupational and regional differences also account for many synonyms. Is a *loch* a *lake*? Is an *arroyo* a *dry wash*? Is a *billabong* the same as an *oxbow*? What is the difference between the *headmaster* of a school and a *principal*, between a *dining room* and a *mess*, between being *cashiered*, *disbarred*, *unfrocked*, and *drummed out*? Words not only point to things and events and ideas; they also advertise our social affiliations and reinforce our self-concepts. It is as important for a sailor to refer to a privy as a *head* as it is for him to wear his uniform; indeed, his nautical vocabulary is part of his uniform. The richness of English synonymy attests to the variety of adventures of both body and mind encountered by speakers of English in many climes over many centuries.

WEIGHTS AND MEASURES

METRIC SYSTEM

LENGTH

Unit		Metric Equivalent		U.S. Equivalent	
millimeter	(mm)	0.001	meter	0.03937	inch
centimeter	(cm)	0.01	meter	0.3937	inch
decimeter	(dm)	0.1	meter	3.937	inches
METER	(m)	1.0	meter	39.37	inches
dekameter	(dkm)	10.0	meters	10.93	yards
hectometer	(hm)	100.0	meters	328.08	feet
kilometer	(km)	1000.0	meters	0.6214	mile

WEIGHT OR MASS

Unit		Metric Equivalent		U.S. Equivalent	
milligram	(mg)	0.001	gram	0.0154	grain
centigram	(cg)	0.01	gram	0.1543	grain
decigram	(dg)	0.1	gram	1.543	grains
GRAM	(g)	1.0	gram	15.43	grains
dekagram	(dkg)	10.0	grams	0.3527	ounce avoirdupois
hectogram	(hg)	100.0	grams	3.527	ounces avoirdupois
kilogram	(kg)	1000.0	grams	2.2	pounds avoirdupois

CAPACITY

Unit		Metric Equivalent		U.S. Equivalent	
milliliter	(ml)	0.001	liter	0.034	fluid ounce
centiliter	(cl)	0.01	liter	0.338	fluid ounce
deciliter	(dl)	0.1	liter	3.38	fluid ounces
LITER	(l)	1.0	liter	1.05	liquid quarts
dekaliter	(dkl)	10.0	liters	0.284	bushel
hectoliter	(hl)	100.0	liters	2.837	bushels
kiloliter	(kl)	1000.0	liters	264.18	gallons

AREA

Unit		Metric Equivalent		U.S. Equivalent	
square millimeter	(mm^2)	0.000001	centare	0.00155	square inch
square centimeter	(cm^2)	0.0001	centare	0.155	square inch
square decimeter	(dm^2)	0.01	centare	15.5	square inches
CENTARE *also* square meter	(ca) (m^2)	1.0	centare	10.76	square feet
are *also* square dekameter	(a) (dkm^2)	100.0	centares	0.0247	acre
hectare *also* square hectometer	(ha) (hm^2)	10,000.0	centares	2.47	acres
square kilometer	(km^2)	1,000,000.0	centares	0.386	square mile

VOLUME

Unit		Metric Equivalent		U.S. Equivalent	
cubic millimeter	(mm^3)	0.001	cubic centimeter	0.016	minim
cubic centimeter	(cc, cm^3)	0.001	cubic decimeter	0.061	cubic inch
cubic decimeter	(dm^3)	0.001	cubic meter	61.023	cubic inches
STERE *also* cubic meter	(s) (m^3)	1.0	cubic meter	1.308	cubic yards
cubic dekameter	(dkm^3)	1000.0	cubic meters	1307.943	cubic yards
cubic hectometer	(hm^3)	1,000,000.0	cubic meters	1,307,942.8	cubic yards
cubic kilometer	(km^3)	1,000,000,000.0	cubic meters	0.25	cubic mile

SYMBOLS

g	10^9 times (a unit) giga-
m	10^6 times (a unit) mega-
k	10^3 times (a unit) kilo-
h	10^2 times (a unit) hecto-
dk	10 times (a unit); deka-
d	10^{-1} times (a uni deci-
c	10^{-2} times (a uni centi-
m	10^{-3} times (a uni milli-
μ	10^{-6} times (a uni micro-
n	10^{-9} times (a uni nano-
μμ	10^{-12} times (a uni micromicro-
Å, λ	Angstrom unit
μμ	micromicron
μ	micron

U.S. SYSTEM

LIQUID MEASURE

4	gills	= 1 pint (pt.)
2	pints	= 1 quart (qt.)
4	quarts	= 1 gallon (gal.)
31.5	gallons	= 1 barrel (bbl.)
2	barrels	= 1 hogshead
60	minims	= 1 fluid dram (fl. dr.)
8	fluid drams	= 1 fluid ounce (fl. oz.)
16	fluid ounces	= 1 pint

LINEAR MEASURE

1	mil	= 0.001 inch (in.)
12	inches	= 1 foot (ft.)
3	feet	= 1 yard (yd.)
6	feet	= 1 fathom
5.5	yards	= 1 rod (rd.)
40	rods	= 1 furlong
5280	feet	= 1 mile (mi.)
1760	yards	= 1 mile

SQUARE MEASURE

144	square inches (sq. in.)	= 1 square foot (sq. ft.)
9	square feet	= 1 square yard (sq. yd.)
30.25	square yards	= 1 square rod (sq. rd.)
160	square rods	= 1 acre (A.)
640	acres	= 1 square mile (sq. mi.)

APOTHECARIES' WEIGHT

20	grains (gr.)	= 1 scruple
3	scruples	= 1 dram (dr.)
8	drams	= 1 ounce (oz.)
12	ounces	= 1 pound (lb.)

AVOIRDUPOIS WEIGHT

27.34	grains (gr.)	= 1 dram (dr. av.)
16	drams	= 1 ounce (oz. av.)
16	ounces	= 1 pound (lb. av.)
2000	pounds	= 1 short ton (sh. tn.)
2240	pounds	= 1 long ton (l. tn.)

TROY WEIGHT

24	grains	= 1 pennyweight (dwt.)
20	pennyweight	= 1 ounce (oz. t.)
12	ounces	= 1 pound (lb. t.)

CUBIC MEASURE

144	cubic inches (cu. in.)	= 1 board foot (bd. ft.)
1728	cubic inches	= 1 cubic foot (cu. ft.)
27	cubic feet	= 1 cubic yard (cu. yd.)
128	cubic feet	= 1 cord (cd.)

DRY MEASURE

2	pints	= 1 quart (qt.)
8	quarts	= 1 peck (pk.)
4	pecks	= 1 bushel (bu.)
3.28	bushels	= 1 barrel (bbl.)

SYMBOLS

lb., #	pound(s)
′	foot, feet
″	inch(es)

Apothecaries' Measure

℔	pound(s)
ʒ	dram(s)
℥	ounce(s)
℈	scruple(s)
m, ♍, ♏	minim
i, j	one: used as a coefficient
ij	two
	one half
iss	one and one h

TABLE OF ENGLISH SPELLINGS

OLLOWING is a list of words exemplifying the possible spellings for the sounds of English. The sounds epresented by these spellings are shown in the pronunciation symbols used in this dictionary, followed by heir equivalents in the International Phonetic Alphabet.

CTIONARY KEY	IPA SYMBOL	EXAMPLES
a	æ	cat, plaid, calf, laugh
ā	eɪ,e	mate, bait, gaol, gauge, pay, steak, skein, weigh, prey
â(r)	ɛ,ɛr	dare, fair, prayer, where, bear, their
ȧ	a	bar, ask, cot (a vowel midway in quality between [æ] and [ɑ], used in some regional American speech)
ä	ɑ	dart, ah, sergeant, heart
b	b	boy, rubber
ch	tʃ	chip, batch, righteous, bastion, structure
d	d	day, ladder, called
e	ɛ	many, aesthete, said, says, bet, steady, heifer, leopard, friend, foetid
ē	i	Caesar, quay, scene, meat, see, seize, people, key, ravine, grief, phoebe, city
f	f	fake, coffin, cough, half, phase
g	g	gate, beggar, ghoul, guard, vague
h	h	hot, whom
hw	hw, ʍ	whale
i	ɪ	pretty, been, tin, sieve, women, busy, guilt, lynch
ī	aɪ	aisle, aye, sleight, eye, dime, pie, sigh, guile, buy, try, lye
j	dʒ	edge, soldier, modulate, rage, exaggerate, joy
k	k	can, accost, saccharine, chord, tack, acquit, king, talk, liquor
l	l	let, gall
m	m	drachm, phlegm, palm, make, limb, grammar, condemn
n	n	gnome, know, mnemonic, note, banner, pneumatic
ng	ŋ	sink, ring, meringue
o	ɑ, ɒ	watch, pot
ō	oʊ,o	beau, yeoman, sew, over, soap, roe, oh, brooch, soul, though, grow
ô	ɔ	ball, balk, fault, dawn, cord, broad, ought
oi	ɔɪ	poison, toy
ou	aʊ	out, bough, cow
o͞o	u	rheum, drew, move, canoe, mood, group, through, fluke, sue, fruit
o͝o	ʊ	wolf, foot, could, pull
p	p	map, happen
r	r	rose, rhubarb, marry, diarrhea, wriggle
s	s	cite, dice, psyche, saw, scene, schism, mass
sh	ʃ	ocean, chivalry, vicious, pshaw, sure, schist, prescience, nauseous, shall, pension, tissue, fission, potion
t	t	walked, thought, phthisic, ptarmigan, tone, Thomas, butter
th	θ	thick
t͟h	ð	this, bathe
u	ʌ	some, does, blood, young, sun
yo͞o	ju,ɪu	beauty, eulogy, queue, pew, ewe, adieu, view, fuse, cue, youth, yule
û(r)	ɜr, ɝ	yearn, fern, err, girl, worm, journal, burn, guerdon, myrtle
v	v	of, Stephen, vise, flivver
w	w	choir, quilt, will
y	j	onion, hallelujah, yet
z	z	was, scissors, xylophone, zoo, muzzle
zh	ʒ	rouge, pleasure, incision, seizure, glazier
ə	ə	above, fountain, darken, clarity, parliament, cannon, porpoise, vicious, locus
ər	ər, ɚ	mortar, brother, elixir, donor, glamour, augur, nature, zephyr

SPECIAL SIGNS AND SYMBOLS

ASTRONOMY

Astronomical Bodies

☉ **1.** the sun **2.** Sunday

☿ **1.** Mercury **2.** Wednesday

♀ **1.** Venus **2.** Friday

⊕, ♁, ⊖ the earth

☾, ☽, ◐ **1.** the moon **2.** Monday

○, ◎ full moon

☽, ◐, ☽, ◗, ☽ the moon, first quarter

☾, ◑, ☾, ☾, ☾ the moon, last quarter

● new moon

♂ **1.** Mars **2.** Tuesday

①, ②, ③, etc. asteroids: in order of discovery, as ① Ceres, ② Pallas, etc.

♃ **1.** Jupiter **2.** Thursday

♄ **1.** Saturn **2.** Saturday

♅, ♅, ♅ Uranus

♆ Neptune

♇, P Pluto

☄ comet

✳, ✳ star; fixed star

α, β, γ, etc. stars (of a constellation): in order of brightness, the Greek letter followed by the Latin genitive of the name of the constellation, as α Centauri

Position and Notation

☌ in conjunction; having the same longitude or right ascension

⚹ sextile; 60° apart in longitude or right ascension

□ quadrature; 90° apart in longitude or right ascension

△ trine; 120° apart in longitude or right ascension

☍ opposition; 180° apart in longitude or right ascension

☊ ascending node

☋ descending node

♈ vernal equinox

♎ autumnal equinox

α right ascension

β celestial latitude

δ declination

λ celestial or geographical longitude

Δ distance

θ sidereal time

a mean distance

v, ☊ longitude of ascending node

ϕ **1.** angle of eccentricity **2.** geographical latitude

Signs of the Zodiac

♈ Aries, the Ram ♉ Taurus, the Bull ♊, Π Gemini, the Twins	Spring Signs
♋, ♋ Cancer, the Crab ♌ Leo, the Lion ♍ Virgo, the Virgin	Summer Signs
♎ Libra, the Balance ♏ Scorpio, the Scorpion ♐, ♐ Sagittarius, the Archer	Autumn Signs
♑, ♑ Capricorn, the Goat ♒ Aquarius, the Water Bearer ♓, ♓ Pisces, the Fishes	Winter Signs

BIOLOGY

○, ☉, ① annual plant

☉, ☉, ♂ biennial plant

♃ perennial herb

△ evergreen plant

☉ monocarpic plant

W plant useful to wildlife

♂, ♁ **1.** male organism or cell **2.** staminate plant or flower

♀ **1.** female organism or cell **2.** pistillate plant or flower

☿ hermaphroditic or perfect plant or flower

⚲ neuter organism or cell

○ individual organism, especially female

□ individual organism, especially male

∞ indefinite number

P parental generation

F filial generation

F_1, F_2, F_3, etc. first, second, third, etc., filial generation

BOOKS

f°	folio
4mo, 4°	quarto
8vo, 8°	octavo
12mo, 12°	duodecimo
18mo, 18°	octodecimo
32mo, 32°	thirty-twomo

CHEMISTRY

Elements

See table of ELEMENTS.

Compounds

Compounds are represented by the symbols for their constituent elements, each element followed by a subscript numeral if the number of atoms of it appearing in the compound is greater than one, as NaCl, H_2O, H_2SO_4, etc. If a radical appears more than once in a compound, the radical is enclosed in parentheses followed by a subscript numeral, as $Ca(OCl)_2$, $Al_2(SO_4)_3$, etc. Molecules consisting entirely of one element are represented by the symbol for the element followed by a subscript numeral indicating the number of atoms in the molecule, as H_2, O_2, O_3, etc. In addition: · denotes water of crystallization or hydration, as $CaSO_4 \cdot 5H_2O$.

α, β, γ, etc., *or* 1, 2, 3, etc. (in names of compounds), indicate different positions of substituted atoms or radicals.

+ denotes dextrorotation, as + 120°.

− denotes levorotation, as − 113°.

[ ] include parentheses if one radical contains another, as $Fe_3[Fe(CN)_6]_2$.

In structural formulas:

—, =, ≡, etc., *or* ., :, ⋮, etc., denotes a single, double, or triple bond, etc.

R— denotes any alkyl radical.

⬡ *or* ⌬ denotes a benzene ring.

Ions

Ions are represented by the symbols for their respective elements or by the symbols for the elements composing them, followed by a superscript symbol indicating the electric charge, as H^+, Cl^-, SO_4^{--}, etc. Thus:

$^-$, $^{--}$, $^{---}$ etc., *or* $^{-1}$, $^{-2}$, $^{-3}$, etc., denote a single, double, triple, etc., negative charge.

+, ++, +++, etc., *or* $^{+1}$, $^{+2}$, $^{+3}$, etc., denote a single, double, triple, etc., positive charge.

′, ″, ‴, etc., denote single, double, triple, etc., valence or charge (especially negative), as S″.

Chemical Reactions

Chemical reactions are written in a form resembling equations, with reactants on the left and products on the right. If more than one equivalent of a compound appears, it is preceded by a coefficient. Conditions of temperature, pressure, catalysis, etc., are indicated above the arrow that shows direction. The following symbols are used:

→ *or* ← denotes "yields"; also indicates the direction of the reaction.

⇌ indicates a reversible reaction.

+ denotes "added to; together with."

↓ (written after a compound) denotes appearance as a precipitate.

↑ (written after a compound) denotes appearance as a gas.

△ denotes the presence of heat.

= *or* ⇌ denotes equivalence of amounts in a quantitative equation.

COMMERCE AND FINANCE

@ **1.** at: peaches @ $.39 per pound **2.** to: nails per pound $.50 @ $.60

$, $ dollar(s); peso(s): $100

¢ cent(s): 37¢

₱ peso(s) (Philippines)

/ shilling(s) (British): 3/

£ pound(s): £25

d penny, pence (British): 4d

¥, Y yen

₨, R rupee(s)

Rs rupees

℔ per: 50¢ ℔ dozen

number: #60 thread

MATHEMATICS

See table at MATHEMATICS.

MISCELLANEOUS

&, & and See AMPERSAND.

&c et cetera

7ber, 8ber, etc. September, October, et

† died

% percent

× by: used in expressing dimensions, a sheet of paper 8½″ × 11″

© copyright; copyrighted

♠ spade

♥ heart

♦ diamond

♣ club

MUSIC

Music is generally written on one or mo staves. The pitch of each staff is indicate by a clef. The forms of the various not and their corresponding rests indica relative duration. In addition the follow ing are used:

♭ flat

♯ sharp

♭♭ double flat

※ double sharp

♮ natural

C common time; 4/4 meter

₵ alla breve; 2/2 or 4/2 meter

∾ turn

∾ inverted turn

𝆗 mordent

𝆖 inverted mordent

>, <, ∧ accent

· ˈ staccato

– tenuto

tr trill

⌒, ⌣ slur or tie

’ phrase or breath mark

𝆔 grace note

< crescendo

> diminuendo; decrescendo

⊓ down-bow

V up-bow

8va all' ottava; at the octave (raises pitch of a staff one octave when writt above it, lowers it when written belo

𝄐, 𝄑 hold

PHYSICS

α alpha particle

β beta particle

c velocity of light

g acceleration due to gravity

h Planck's constant

λ wavelength

ν frequency

j square root of minus one

∽ cycles (of alternating current or v tage)

RELIGION

✠, + **1.** a sign of the cross used bishops before their names **2.** in so service books, an indication that t sign of the cross is to be made

* in some service books, a mark used divide psalm verses into two parts

℟ response

℣, V', V, versicle

☧, ☧, ☧ a monogram for Christ [G Χρ(ιστός)]

PRONUNCIATION KEY

ıe primary stress mark (′) is placed after the syllable bearing the heavier stress or accent; the secondary stress mark (′) .lows a syllable having a somewhat lighter stress, as in **com·men·da·tion** (kom′ən·dā′shən).

a	add, map	m	move, seem	u	up, done
ā	ace, rate	n	nice, tin	û(r)	urn, term
â(r)	care, air	ng	ring, song	yōō	use, few
ä	palm, father				
b	bat, rub	o	odd, hot	v	vain, eve
ch	check, catch	ō	open, so	w	win, away
d	dog, rod	ô	order, jaw	y	yet, yearn
e	end, pet	oi	oil, boy	z	zest, muse
ē	even, tree	ou	out, now	zh	vision, pleasure
f	fit, half	ōō	pool, food		
g	go, log	ŏŏ	took, full	ə	the schwa, an unstressed vowel representing the sound spelled *a* in *above*, *e* in *sicken*, *i* in *clarity*, *o* in *melon*, *u* in *focus*
h	hope, hate	p	pit, stop		
i	it, give	r	run, poor		
ī	ice, write	s	see, pass		
j	joy, ledge	sh	sure, rush		
k	cool, take	t	talk, sit		
l	look, rule	th	thin, both		
		t͟h	this, bathe		

ıe schwa (ə) varies widely in quality from a sound close to the (u) in *up* to a sound close to the (i) in *it* as heard in pronuncia-ıns of such words as *ballot, custom, landed, horses.*

ıe (r) in final position as in *star* (stär) and before a consonant as in *heart* (härt) is regularly indicated in the respellings, but onunciations without (r) are unquestionably reputable. Standard British is much like the speech of Eastern New England and e Lower South in this feature.

a few words, such as *button* (but′n) and *sudden* (sud′n), no vowel appears in the unstressed syllable because the (n) consti-tes the whole syllable.

Foreign Sounds

as in French *ami, patte.* This is a vowel midway in quality between (a) and (ä).

as in French *peu,* German *schön.* Round the lips for (ō) and pronounce (ā).

as in French *vue,* German *grün.* Round the lips for (ōō) and pronounce (ē).

h as in German *ach,* Scottish *loch.* Pronounce a strongly aspirated (h) with the tongue in position for (k) as in *cool* or *keep.*

ṅ This symbol indicates that the preceding vowel is nasal. The nasal vowels in French are œṅ (*brun*), aṅ (*main*), äṅ (*chambre*), ôṅ (*dont*).

’ This symbol indicates that a preceding (l) or (r) is voiceless, as in French *fin-de-siècle* (faṅ·de·sye′kl’) or *fiacre* (fyȧ′kr’); that a preceding (y) is pronounced consonantly in a separate syllable followed by a slight schwa sound, as in French *fille* (fē′y’); or that a consonant preceding a (y) is palatalized, as in Russian *oblast* (ô′bləsty’).

Note on the accentuation of foreign words

any languages do not employ stress in the manner of English; only an approximation can be given of the actual situation such languages. As it is not possible to reproduce the tones of Chinese in a work of this kind, Chinese names have been here corded with primary stress on each syllable and may be so pronounced. Japanese and Korean have been shown without ress and may be pronounced with a level accent throughout. French words are shown conventionally with a primary stress the last syllable; however, this stress tends to be evenly divided among the syllables (except for those that are completely stressed), with slightly more force and higher pitch on the last syllable.

ABBREVIATIONS USED IN THIS BOOK

A.D.	year of our Lord
adj.	adjective
adv.	adverb
Aeron.	Aeronautics
AF	Anglo-French
Agric.	Agriculture
Alg.	Algebra
alter.	alteration
Am. Ind.	American Indian
Anat.	Anatomy
Ant.	Antonyms
Anthropol.	Anthropology
appar.	apparently
Archeol.	Archeology
Archit.	Architecture
assoc.	association
Astron.	Astronomy
aug.	augmentative
Austral.	Australian
Bacteriol.	Bacteriology
B.C.	Before Christ
Biochem.	Biochemistry
Biol.	Biology
Bot.	Botany
Brit.	British
c.	century
cap.	capitalized
cf.	compare
Chem.	Chemistry
Chron.	Chronicles
Col.	Colossians
compar.	comparative
conj.	conjunction
contr.	contraction
Cor.	Corinthians
Crystall.	Crystallography
Dan.	Daniel, Danish
def.	definition
Dent.	Dentistry
Deut.	Deuteronomy
Dial.	Dialect, Dialectal
dim.	diminutive
Du.	Dutch
E	English
Eccl.	Ecclesiastical
Eccles.	Ecclesiastes
Ecclus.	Ecclesiasticus
Ecol.	Ecology
Econ.	Economics
Electr.	Electricity
Engin.	Engineering
Entomol.	Entomology
Eph.	Ephesians
esp.	especially
est.	estimate
Esth.	Esther
Ex.	Exodus
Ezek.	Ezekiel
F, Fr.	French
fem.	feminine
freq.	frequentative
G, Ger.	German
Gal.	Galatians
Gen.	Genesis
Geog.	Geography
Geol.	Geology
Geom.	Geometry
Gk.	Greek (Homer — A.D. 200)
Gmc.	Germanic
Govt.	Government
Gram.	Grammar
Hab.	Habakkuk
Hag.	Haggai
Heb.	Hebrews
HG	High German
Hind.	Hindustani
Hos.	Hosea
Hung.	Hungarian
Icel.	Icelandic
Illit.	Illiterate
imit.	imitative
infl.	influence, influenced
intens.	intensive
interj.	interjection
Isa.	Isaiah
Ital.	Italian
Jas.	James
Jer.	Jeremiah
Jon.	Jonah
Josh.	Joshua
Judg.	Judges
L, Lat.	Latin (Classical, 80 B.C.–A.D. 200)
Lam.	Lamentations
Lev.	Leviticus
LG	Low German
LGk.	Late Greek (200–600)
Ling.	Linguistics
lit.	literally
LL	Late Latin (200–600)
M	Middle
Mal.	Malachi
masc.	masculine
Math.	Mathematics
Matt.	Matthew
MDu.	Middle Dutch
ME	Middle English (1050–1475)
Mech.	Mechanics
Med.	Medicine, Medieval
Med. Gk.	Medieval Greek (600–1500)
Med. L	Medieval Latin (600–1500)
Metall.	Metallurgy
Meteorol.	Meteorology
MF	Middle French (1400–1600)
MHG	Middle High German (1100–1450)
Mic.	Micah
Mil.	Military
Mineral.	Mineralogy
MLG	Middle Low German (1100–1450)
n.	noun
Nah.	Nahum
N. Am. Ind.	North American Indian
Naut.	Nautical
NE	Northeast
Neh.	Nehemiah
neut.	neuter
NL	New Latin (after 1500)
Norw.	Norwegian
Num.	Numbers
NW	Northwest
O	Old
Obad.	Obadiah
Obs.	Obsolete
OE	Old English (before 1050)
OF	Old French (before 1400)
OHG	Old High German (before 1100)
OIrish	Old Irish
ON	Old Norse (before 1500)
orig.	original, originally
Ornithol.	Ornithology
OS	Old Saxon (before 1100)
Paleontol.	Paleontology
Pathol.	Pathology
Pet.	Peter
Pg.	Portuguese
Phil.	Philippians
Philem.	Philemon
Philos.	Philosophy
Phonet.	Phonetics
Photog.	Photography
Physiol.	Physiology
pl.	plural
pop.	population
pp.	past participle, pages
ppr.	present particip
prep.	preposition
prob.	probably
pron.	pronoun
pronun.	pronunciation
Prov.	Proverbs
Ps.	Psalms
Psychoanal.	Psychoanalysis
Psychol.	Psychology
pt.	preterit
ref.	reference
Rev.	Revelation
Rom.	Romans
Russ.	Russian
Sam.	Samuel
S. Am. Ind.	South American Indian
Scand.	Scandinavian
Scot.	Scottish
SE	Southeast
sing.	singular
Skt.	Sanskrit
Sociol.	Sociology
S. of Sol.	Song of Solomo
Sp.	Spanish
Stat.	Statistics
superl.	superlative
Surg.	Surgery
Sw.	Swedish
SW	Southwest
Syn.	Synonyms
Telecom.	Telecommunication
Theol.	Theology
Thess.	Thessalonians
Tim.	Timothy
Tit.	Titus
trans.	translation
Trig.	Trigonometry
ult.	ultimate, ultimately
U.S.	American (adj.)
v.	verb
var.	variant
Vet.	Veterinary medicine
v.i.	intransitive ver
v.t.	transitive verb
WGmc.	West Germanic
Zech.	Zechariah
Zeph.	Zephaniah
Zool.	Zoology

< from   + plus   ? possibly

A

a, A (ā) *n.* *pl.* **a's** or **as, A's** or **As, aes** (āz) **1.** The first letter of the English alphabet. **2.** Any sound represented by the letter *a.* — *symbol* **1.** Primacy in class. **2.** A substitute for the numeral 1. **3.** *Music* **a** One of a series of tones, the sixth in the natural diatonic scale of C, or the first note in the related minor scale. **b** A written note representing this tone. **c** The scale built upon A. **4.** *Chem.* Argon (symbol A).

a[1] (ə, *stressed* ā) *indefinite article* or *adj.* In each; to each; for each: one dollar *a* bushel. [OE *on, an* in, on, at]

a[2] (ə, *stressed* ā) *indefinite article* or *adj.* One; any; some; each: expressing singleness, unity, etc., more or less indefinitely. It is used: **1.** Before a noun expressing an individual object or idea: *a* bird; *a* hope. **2.** Before an abstract noun used concretely: to show *a* kindness. **3.** Before a collective noun: *a* crowd. **4.** Before a proper noun denoting a type: He is *a* Hercules in strength. **5.** Before plural nouns with *few, great many,* or *good many*: *a* few books. **6.** After *on, at,* or *of,* denoting oneness, sameness: birds of *a* feather. ◆ Before vowel sounds the form becomes *an.* See note under AN[1]. [Reduced form of AN[1] used before consonant sounds]

a-[1] *prefix* In; on; at: *aboard, asleep, agog, agoing.* [OE *on, an* in, on, at]

a-[2] *prefix* Up; on; away: *arise, abide.* [OE *ā-* up, on, away]

a-[3] *prefix* Of; from: *athirst, akin, anew.* [OE *of* off, of]

a-[4] *prefix* **1.** Without; not: *achromatic.* **2.** Apart from; unconcerned with: *amoral.* [Reduced form of AN-[1]]

a-[5] Reduced var. of AB-[1].

a-[6] Reduced var. of AD-.

aard·vark (ärd′värk′) *n.* A burrowing, ant-eating African mammal. [< Afrikaans < Du. *aarde* earth + *vark* pig]

aard·wolf (ärd′wŏŏlf′) *n.* A hyenalike mammal of Africa. [< Afrikaans < Du. *aarde* earth + *wolf* wolf]

Aar·on (âr′ən, ar′ən) The first high priest of the Hebrews, older brother of Moses. *Ex.* xxviii 1–4.

ab-[1] *prefix* Off; from; away: *absolve, abduct, abrogate.* Also: *a-* before *m, p, v,* as in *avocation*; *abs-* before *c, t,* as in *abscess, abstract.* [< L < *ab* from]

ab-[2] Var. of AD-.

Ab (ab, äb) *n.* The eleventh month of the Hebrew year. See (Hebrew) CALENDAR.

ab·a·ca (ab′ə·kä, ä′bə·kä′) *n.* **1.** A banana plant of the Philippines. **2.** The inner fiber of this plant, used for cordage. Also **ab′a·ka.** [< Tagalog]

a·back (ə·bak′) *adv.* *Naut.* Back against the mast: said of sails so blown by the wind. — **taken aback** Disconcerted, as by a sudden check. [OE *on bæc* on or to the back]

ab·a·cus (ab′ə·kəs) *n.* *pl.* **·cus·es** or **·ci** (-sī) **1.** A calculator with sliding counters. **2.** *Archit.* A slab forming the top of a capital. [< L < Gk. *abax* counting table]

CHINESE ABACUS
The counters in the upper compartment have five times the value of those below.

a·baft (ə·baft′, ə·bäft′) *Naut.* *adv.* Toward the stern; aft. — *prep.* Further aft than; astern of. [OE < *on* on, at + *be* by + *æftan* behind, back]

ab·a·lo·ne (ab′ə·lō′nē) *n.* An edible shellfish having a shell lined with mother-of-pearl. [< Am. Sp.]

a·ban·don (ə·ban′dən) *v.t.* **1.** To give up wholly; desert; forsake. **2.** To surrender or give over: with *to.* **3.** To yield (oneself) without restraint, as to an emotion. — *n.* Utter surrender to one's feelings or natural impulses. [< OF *abandoner* < *a bandon* under one's control] — **a·ban′don·er** *n.* — **a·ban′don·ment** *n.*

a·ban·doned (ə·ban′dənd) *adj.* **1.** Deserted; forsaken. **2.** Unrestrained. **3.** Profligate; shameless.

a·base (ə·bās′) *v.t.* **a·based, a·bas·ing** To lower in position, rank, prestige, or estimation; cast down; humble. [< OF < LL *abassare* to lower] — **a·bas·ed·ly** (ə·bā′sid·lē) *adv.* — **a·bas′ed·ness** *n.* — **a·base′ment** *n.* — **a·bas′er** *n.*

a·bash (ə·bash′) *v.t.* To deprive of self-possession; disconcert; make ashamed or confused. [< AF < OF *esbaïr* to astonish] — **a·bash·ed·ly** (ə·bash′id·lē) *adv.* — **a·bash′ment** *n.*

a·bate (ə·bāt′) *v.* **a·bat·ed, a·bat·ing** *v.t.* **1.** To make less; reduce in quantity, value, force, or intensity. **2.** To deduct. **3.** *Law* To do away with (a nuisance); annul (a writ). — *v.i.* **4.** To become less, as in strength or degree. **5.** *Law* To fail; become void. — **Syn.** See ANNUL, DECREASE. [< OF *abatre* to beat down] — **a·bat·a·ble** (ə·bā′tə·bəl) *adj.* — **a·bat′er** *n.* — **a·bate′ment** *n.*

ab·ba·cy (ab′ə·sē) *n.* *pl.* **·cies** The office, term of office, dignity, or jurisdiction of an abbot.

ab·bé (ab′ā, *Fr.* à·bā′) *n.* **1.** In France, a title given to a priest or other cleric. **2.** An abbot. [< F]

ab·bess (ab′is) *n.* The female superior of a community of nuns connected with an abbey. [ME < OF *abbesse*]

ab·bey (ab′ē) *n.* *pl.* **·beys** **1.** A monastery or convent under the jurisdiction of an abbot or abbess. **2.** A church or building attached to an abbey. [ME < OF < LL < Gk. < Aramaic *abbā* father]

ab·bot (ab′ət) *n.* The superior of a community of monks. [OE < LL < Gk. < Aramaic *abbā* father] — **ab′bot·cy, ab′bot·ship** *n.*

ab·bre·vi·ate (ə·brē′vē·āt) *v.t.* **·at·ed, ·at·ing** **1.** To condense or make briefer. **2.** To shorten, as a word or expression, esp. by omission or contraction. [< L < *ad-* to + *breviare* to shorten] — **ab·bre′vi·a′tor** *n.*

— **Syn.** shorten, curtail, abridge, contract.

ab·bre·vi·a·tion (ə·brē′vē·ā′shən) *n.* **1.** A shortened form of a word or phrase, used to represent the full form: Mr. is an *abbreviation* of Mister. **2.** The act of abbreviating, or the state of being abbreviated.

— **Syn. 1.** An *abbreviation* is a shortening by any method. A *contraction* is made by omitting certain medial elements (whether sounds or letters) and bringing together the first and last elements. *Rec't* for *receipt* is a written *contraction* as well as *abbreviation*; *Am.* for *American* is a written *abbreviation,* but not a *contraction.*

ABC (ā′bē′sē′) *pl.* **ABC's** **1.** *Usually pl.* The alphabet. **2.** The rudiments, elements, or basic facts (of a subject).

Ab·di·as (ab·dī′əs) The Douai Bible name for OBADIAH.

ab·di·cate (ab′də·kāt) *v.* **·cat·ed, ·cat·ing** *v.t.* **1.** To give up formally; renounce, as a throne, power, or rights. — *v.i.* **2.** To relinquish power, sovereignty, or rights. [< L *abdicare* to renounce] — **ab·di·ca·ble** (ab′di·kə·bəl) *adj.* — **ab′di·ca′tion** *n.* — **ab′di·ca′tive** *adj.* — **ab′di·ca′tor** *n.*

ab·do·men (ab′də·mən, ab·dō′mən) *n.* **1.** In mammals, the body cavity between the diaphragm and the pelvic floor containing the viscera. **2.** In other vertebrates, the region or cavity that contains the viscera. **3.** In insects and other arthropods, the hindmost of the main body divisions. [< L] — **ab·dom·i·nal** (ab·dom′ə·nəl) — **ab·dom′i·nal·ly** *adv.*

ab·duct (ab·dukt′) *v.t.* **1.** To carry away wrongfully, as by force or fraud; kidnap. **2.** *Physiol.* To draw aside or away from the original position. [< L < *ab-* away + *ducere* to lead] — **ab·duc′tion** *n.* — **ab·duc′tor** *n.*

a·beam (ə·bēm′) *adv.* *Naut.* **1.** At right angles to the keel of a vessel. **2.** At or off the side of a vessel: with *of.*

a·bed (ə·bed′) *adv.* In bed; on a bed; to bed.

A·bel (ā′bəl) Second son of Adam. *Gen.* iv 2.

ab·er·rant (ab·er′ənt, ab′ər·ənt) *adj.* **1.** Straying from the right way or usual course; wandering. **2.** Varying from type; abnormal; exceptional. [< L < *ab-* from + *errare* to wander] — **ab·er′rance, ab·er′ran·cy** *n.*

ab·er·ra·tion (ab′ə·rā′shən) *n.* **1.** Deviation from a right, customary, prescribed, or natural course or condition. **2.** Partial mental derangement.

a·bet (ə·bet′) *v.t.* **a·bet·ted, a·bet·ting** To encourage and support; esp., to support wrongdoing or a wrongdoer. [< OF < *a-* to + *beter* to tease, bait] — **a·bet′ment, a·bet′tal** *n.*

a·bet·tor (ə·bet′ər) *n.* One who abets. Also **a·bet′ter.**

a·bey·ance (ə·bā′əns) *n.* **1.** Suspension or temporary inaction. **2.** *Law* An undetermined condition, as of an estate not legally assigned. Also **a·bey′an·cy.** [< AF < OF < *a-* to, at + *bair* to gape] — **a·bey′ant** *adj.*

ab·hor (ab·hôr′) *v.t.* **·horred, ·hor·ring** To regard with repugnance; detest; loathe. — **Syn.** See HATE. [< L *ab-* from + *horrere* to shudder] — **ab·hor′rer** *n.*

ab·hor·rence (ab·hôr′əns, -hor′-) *n.* **1.** A feeling of utter loathing. **2.** Something loathsome or repugnant.

ab·hor·rent (ab·hôr′ənt, -hor′-) *adj.* **1.** Repugnant or detestable. **2.** Opposed: with *to*. **3.** Feeling repulsion. — **ab·hor′rent·ly** *adv.*

a·bide (ə·bīd′) *v.* **a·bode** or **a·bid·ed, a·bid·ing** *v.i.* **1.** To continue in a place; remain. — *v.t.* **2.** To look for; wait for. **3.** To endure; put up with. — **to abide by 1.** To behave in accordance with; adhere to, as a promise or rule. **2.** To accept the consequences of; submit to. [OE *ābīdan*] — **a·bi′·dance** *n.* — **a·bid′er** *n.* — **a·bid′ing·ly** *adv.*

a·bil·i·ty (ə·bil′ə·tē) *n. pl.* **·ties 1.** The state or quality of being able; capacity. **2.** *pl.* Talents. **3.** Competence or skill. [< OF < L < *habilis* suitable < *habere* to have, hold]

ab·ir·ri·tant (ab·ir′ə·tənt) *n.* A soothing agent; medicine that eases irritation. — *adj.* Relieving irritation; soothing.

ab·ir·ri·tate (ab·ir′ə·tāt) *v.t.* **·tat·ed, ·tat·ing** *Med.* To diminish sensibility or irritation in. — **ab·ir′ri·ta′tion** *n.*

ab·ject (ab′jekt, ab·jekt′) *adj.* **1.** Sunk to a low condition; groveling; mean; despicable. **2.** Hopelessly low; disheartening. [< L < *ab-* away + *jacere* to throw] — **ab·jec′tive** *adj.* — **ab′ject·ly** *adv.* — **ab′ject·ness, ab·jec′tion** *n.*

ab·jure (ab·jŏŏr′) *v.t.* **·jured, ·jur·ing 1.** To renounce under oath; forswear. **2.** To retract or recant, as an opinion. — **Syn.** See RENOUNCE. [< L < *ab-* away + *jurare* to swear] **ab′ju·ra′tion** *n.* — **ab·jur·a·to·ry** (ab·jŏŏr′ə·tôr′ē, -tō′rē) *adj.* — **ab·jur′er** *n.*

ab·la·tive (ab′lə·tiv) *adj. Gram.* In some inflected languages, as Latin and Sanskrit, pertaining to a case expressing separation, position, motion from, instrumentality, etc. — *n.* **1.** The ablative case. **2.** A word in this case. [< L, *ablatus*, pp. of *auferre* < *ab-* away + *ferre* to carry]

a·blaze (ə·blāz′) *adv.* On fire. — *adj.* **1.** Flaming. **2.** Zealous; ardent.

a·ble (ā′bəl) *adj.* **a·bler** (ā′blər), **a·blest** (ā′blist) **1.** Having adequate power. **2.** Having or exhibiting superior abilities; skillful: an *able* writer. [< OF < L *habilis* suitable, fit < *habere* to have, hold] — **a′bly** *adv.*

-able *suffix* **1.** Given to; tending to; likely to: *changeable.* **2.** Fit to; able to; capable of; worthy of: *eatable, solvable.* Also spelled *-ble, -ible.* [< F < L *-abilis, -ibilis, -bilis*]

a·ble-bod·ied (ā′bəl·bod′ēd) *adj.* Having a sound, strong body; competent for physical service; robust.

able-bodied seaman An experienced and skilled seaman.

able seaman *pl.* **·men 1.** In the Royal Canadian Navy the fourth lowest grade. **2.** One who holds this grade.

a·bloom (ə·blōōm′) *adj.* & *adv.* Blooming; in blossom.

ab·lu·tion (ab·lōō′shən) *n.* **1.** A washing or cleansing of the body; a bath. **2.** *Eccl.* **a** A ceremonial washing of the priest's hands or of the chalice and paten during the Eucharist. **b** The liquid used for this. [< L < *ab-* away + *luere* to wash] — **ab·lu′tion·ar′y** *adj.*

-ably *suffix* Like; in the manner of: *peaceably*: used to form adverbs from adjectives ending in *-able.*

ab·ne·gate (ab′nə·gāt) *v.t.* **·gat·ed, ·gat·ing** To deny; renounce. [< L < *ab-* away + *negare* to deny] — **ab′ne·ga′tion** *n.* — **ab′ne·ga′tor** *n.*

ab·nor·mal (ab·nôr′məl) *adj.* Not according to rule; different from the average; unusual; irregular. [< F < Med.L < L < *ab-* from + *norma* rule] — **ab·nor′mal·ly** *adv.*

ab·nor·mal·i·ty (ab′nôr·mal′ə·tē) *n. pl.* **·ties 1.** The state of being abnormal. **2.** An abnormal thing.

a·board (ə·bôrd′, ə·bōrd′) *adv.* **1.** On board; into, in, or on a ship, train, etc. **2.** Alongside. — **all aboard!** Get on board! Get in!: a warning to passengers. — *prep.* **1.** On board of; upon or within. **2.** Alongside of.

a·bode (ə·bōd′) Past tense and past participle of ABIDE. — *n.* **1.** A place of abiding; dwelling; home. **2.** The state or act of abiding; sojourn; stay. [OE *ābād*]

a·bol·ish (ə·bol′ish) *v.t.* To do away with; put an end to; annul; destroy. [< F < L *abolere* to destroy] — **a·bol′·ish·a·ble** *adj.* — **a·bol′ish·er** *n.* — **a·bol′ish·ment** *n.*

ab·o·li·tion (ab′ə·lish′ən) *n.* **1.** The act of abolishing, or the state of being abolished. **2.** *Sometimes cap.* The abolishing of slavery in the United States. — **ab′o·li′tion·al, ab′o·li′tion·ar′y** *adj.* — **ab′o·li′tion·ism** *n.* — **ab′o·li′tion·ist** *n.*

ab·o·ma·sum (ab′ə·mā′səm) *n. pl.* **·sa** (-sə) The fourth or true digestive stomach of a ruminant: also called *reed.* Also **ab·o·ma·sus** (ab′ə·mā′səs). [< NL < L *ab-* away from + *omasum* bullock's tripe]

A–bomb (ā′bom′) *n.* An atomic bomb.

a·bom·i·na·ble (ə·bom′in·ə·bəl) *adj.* **1.** Very hateful; loathsome. **2.** Extremely disagreeable; bad. — **a·bom′i·na·ble·ness** *n.* — **a·bom′i·na·bly** *adv.*

a·bom·i·nate (ə·bom′ə·nāt) *v.t.* **·nat·ed, ·nat·ing 1.** To regard with loathing; abhor. **2.** To dislike strongly. — **Syn.** See HATE. [< L *abominari* to abhor as an ill omen] — **a·bom′i·na′tion** *n.* — **a·bom′i·na′tor** *n.*

ab·o·rig·i·nal (ab′ə·rij′ə·nəl) *adj.* **1.** Of or pertaining to aborigines. **2.** Native; indigenous. — *n. Austral.* An aborigine. — **ab′o·rig′i·nal·ly** *adv.*

ab·o·rig·i·ne (ab′ə·rij′ə·nē) *n.* **1.** One of the original native inhabitants of a country. **2.** *pl.* Flora and fauna indigenous to a geographical area. [< L *ab origine* from the beginning]

a·bort (ə·bôrt′) *v.i.* **1.** To bring forth young prematurely; miscarry. **2.** To fail of complete development. — *v.t.* **3.** To cause to have a miscarriage. **4.** To bring to a premature or unsuccessful conclusion. [< L *aboriri* to miscarry]

a·bor·tion (ə·bôr′shən) *n.* **1.** *Law* A miscarriage produced artificially, esp. as an illegal operation. **2.** The expulsion of a fetus prematurely; miscarriage. **3.** The defective result of a premature birth. **4.** Partial or complete arrest of development in anything. — **a·bor′tion·al** *adj.*

a·bor·tion·ist (ə·bôr′shən·ist) *n.* One who causes abortion.

a·bor·tive (ə·bôr′tiv) *adj.* **1.** Coming to naught; failing. **2.** Brought forth or born prematurely. **3.** Imperfectly developed; rudimentary. **4.** *Med.* Causing abortion. — **Syn.** See FUTILE. — **a·bor′tive·ly** *adv.* — **a·bor′tive·ness** *n.*

a·bound (ə·bound′) *v.i.* **1.** To be in abundance; be plentiful. **2.** To have plenty; be rich. **3.** To be full; teem. [< OF < L < *ab-* from + *undare* to flow in waves]

a·bout (ə·bout′) *adv.* **1.** Approximately; nearly. **2.** *Informal* Almost; not quite. **3.** Nearby; in the vicinity. **4.** To a reversed position; around. **5.** In rotation; around and around. **6.** In every direction; to all sides. **7.** Here and there, as without direction. **8.** Astir; in motion; active. **9.** On every side; around. — *prep.* **1.** On every side of; encircling. **2.** Near; within; on some side of. **3.** Here and there in or upon. **4.** Near; close to. **5.** Engaged in. **6.** Concerning; in reference to. **7.** In one's possession. **8.** Attached to (a person) as an attribute. **9.** On the point of; ready to. [OE < *on, a* on + *būtan* outside]

a·bout-face (*n.* ə·bout′fās′; *v.* ə·bout′fās′) *n.* **1.** *Mil.* A pivoting turn to the rear executed when halted. **2.** Any turning around or reversal, as of opinion or point of view. — *v.i.* **-faced, -fac·ing** To perform an about-face.

a·bove (ə·buv′) *adv.* **1.** In or to a higher place; overhead; up. **2.** Superior in rank or position. **3.** In an earlier section of something written. **4.** In heaven. — *adj.* Given, said, named, etc., in what is above; preceding: The *above* men were acquitted. — *n.* That which is higher up or just before: preceded by *the.* — *prep.* **1.** Directly over; on top of. **2.** Higher than; rising beyond. **3.** Farther north than. **4.** More than, in number, quantity, degree, etc.; beyond. **5.** Superior to in authority or power. **6.** Beyond the influence or reach of. [ME *abofen* < OE *onbufan*]

a·bove·board (ə·buv′bôrd′, -bōrd′) *adj.* & *adv.* In open sight; without concealment, fraud, or trickery.

ab·ra·ca·dab·ra (ab′rə·kə·dab′rə) *n.* **1.** Any spell or incantation. **2.** Jargon or nonsensical words. [< L]

a·brade (ə·brād′) *v.t.* **a·brad·ed, a·brad·ing** To rub or wear off by friction; scrape away. [< L < *ab-* away + *radere* to scrape] — **a·bra′dant** *adj.* & *n.* — **a·brad′er** *n.*

A·bra·ham (ā′brə·ham) The progenitor of the Hebrews; first called **A·bram** (ā′brəm). *Gen.* xvii 5.

a·bran·chi·al (ā·brang′kē·əl) *adj. Zool.* Without gills. Also **a·bran·chi·ate** (ā·brang′kē·it, -āt). [< A-[4] without + Gk. *branchia* gills]

a·bra·sion (ə·brā′zhən) *n.* **1.** A wearing or rubbing away, as of rocks by glaciers. **2.** An abraded area, as on the skin.

a·bra·sive (ə·brā′siv, -ziv) *adj.* Abrading or tending to abrade. — *n.* An abrading substance, as emery or sand.

a·breast (ə·brest′) *adv.* & *adj.* Side by side. — **abreast of** (or **with**) Side by side with.

a·bridge (ə·brij′) *v.t.* **a·bridged, a·bridg·ing 1.** To give the substance of in fewer words; condense. **2.** To shorten, as in time. **3.** To curtail or lessen, as rights. **4.** To deprive. [< OF < L *abbreviare* < *ad-* to + *brevis* short] — **a·bridg′a·ble** or **a·bridge′a·ble** *adj.* — **a·bridg′er** *n.*

a·bridg·ment (ə·brij′mənt) *n.* **1.** The act of abridging, or the state of being abridged. **2.** A condensation, as of a book; epitome; abstract. Also **a·bridge′ment.**

— **Syn. 2.** An *abridgment* gives the most important portions of a work substantially as they stand. An *abstract, digest,* or *précis* is an independent statement of what a book or an article contains, the *abstract* closely following the main heads, the *digest* or *précis* giving careful consideration of all the contents.

a·broad (ə·brôd′) *adv.* **1.** Out of one's home or abode; out-of-doors. **2.** In or to foreign lands. **3.** At large; in circulation. **4.** Broadly; widely. **5.** Wide of the mark. [ME]

ab·ro·gate (ab′rə·gāt) *v.t.* **·gat·ed, ·gat·ing** To annul by authority, as a law; abolish; repeal. — **Syn.** See ANNUL. [< L < *ab-* away + *rogare* to propose a law] — **ab·ro·ga·ble** (ab′rə·gə·bəl) *adj.* — **ab′ro·ga′tion** *n.* — **ab′ro·ga′tive** *adj.* — **ab′ro·ga′tor** *n.*

a·brupt (ə·brupt′) *adj.* **1.** Beginning, ending, or changing suddenly; unexpected. **2.** Unceremonious; rude, as in speech or departure. **3.** Unconnected, as literary style. **4.** Steep, as a cliff. — **Syn.** See BLUNT. [< L < *ab-* off + *rumpere* to break] — **a·brupt′ly** *adv.* — **a·brupt′ness** *n.*

abs- Var. of AB-[1].

Ab·sa·lom (ab′sə·ləm) The favorite and rebellious son of David. II *Sam.* xiii–xix.

ab·scess (ab′ses) *Pathol. n.* A collection of pus in any part of the body, often inflamed —*v.i.* To form an abscess. [< L < *ab-* away + *cedere* to go] —**ab′scessed** *adj.*

ab·scis·sa (ab·sis′ə) *n. pl.* **ab·scis·sas** or **ab·scis·sae** (-sis′ē) *Math.* The distance of any point from the vertical or Y-axis in a coordinate system, measured on a line parallel to the horizontal or X-axis. [< L (*linea*) *abscissa* (line) cut off < *ab-* off + *scindere* to cut]

C d f A e B

ABSCISSA
AB: x axis.
AC: y axis.
Ae abscissa of point *f*.

ab·scis·sion (ab·sizh′ən, -sish′ən) *n.* **1.** The act of cutting off or removing. **2.** In rhetoric, an abrupt breaking off for effect, as in the middle of a sentence. [< L < *ab-* off + *scindere* to cut]

ab·scond (ab·skond′) *v.i.* To depart suddenly and secretly, esp. to escape the law. [< L < *ab-* away + *condere* to store away, conceal] —**ab·scond′er** *n.*

ab·sence (ab′səns) *n.* **1.** The state of being absent. **2.** The period of being away. **3.** Lack.

ab·sent (*adj.* ab′sənt; *v.* ab·sent′) *adj.* **1.** Not present; away. **2.** Lacking; nonexistent. **3.** Inattentive; absent-minded. —*v.t.* To take or keep (oneself) away. [< L < *ab-* away + *esse* to be] —**ab·sent′er** *n.* —**ab′sent·ly** *adv.* —**ab′sent·ness** *n.*

ab·sen·tee (ab′sən·tē′) *n.* One who is absent, as from a job. —*adj.* Temporarily absent. —**ab′sen·tee′ism** *n.*

ab·sent-mind·ed (ab′sənt·mīn′did) *adj.* Inattentive to one's immediate surroundings or business because of preoccupation of the mind; forgetful. —**ab′sent-mind′ed·ly** *adv.* —**ab′sent·mind′ed·ness** *n.*

absent without leave *Mil.* Absent without authorization but not intending to desert. Abbr. *a.w.o.l., A.W.O.L.*

ab·sinthe (ab′sinth) *n.* **1.** A green, bitter liqueur having the flavor of licorice and wormwood. **2.** Wormwood. Also **ab′sinth.** [< F < L *absinthium* wormwood]

ab·so·lute (ab′sə·lo͞ot) *adj.* **1.** Free from restriction; unlimited; unconditional. **2.** Complete; perfect. **3.** Unadulterated; pure. **4.** Not relative to anything else; independent. **5.** Positive; certain. **6.** *Gram.* **a** Free from the usual relations of syntax or construction with other words in the sentence, as *It being late* in *It being late, we started home.* **b** Of a transitive verb, having no object expressed, as *That professor inspires and stimulates.* **c** Of an adjective standing without a noun, as *the brave and the fair.* —*n.* That which is absolute or perfect. —**the Absolute** *Philos.* The ultimate basis of all thought, reasoning, or being. [< L < *ab-* from + *solvere* to loosen] —**ab′so·lute′ness** *n.*

ab·so·lute·ly (ab′sə·lo͞ot′lē, *emphatic* ab′sə·lo͞ot′lē) *adv.* **1.** Completely; unconditionally. **2.** Positively. **3.** *Gram.* So as not to take an object: to use a verb *absolutely.*

absolute pitch *Music* The ability to produce or name the pitch of any note sounded or asked for: also *perfect pitch.*

absolute zero That temperature at which a body contains no heat, and at which a perfect gas exerts no pressure, equivalent to about −273.16° C. or −459.7° F.

ab·so·lu·tion (ab′sə·lo͞o′shən) *n.* **1.** The act of absolving, as from guilt. **2.** *Eccl.* **a** A remission of sin and its penalties pronounced by a priest. **b** A formula declaring the forgiveness of sin. [< L < *ab-* from + *solvere* to loosen]

ab·so·lut·ism (ab′sə·lo͞o·tiz′əm) *n.* In government, the doctrine or practice of unlimited authority and control; despotism. —**ab′so·lut′ist** *n.* —**ab′so·lu·tis′tic** *adj.*

ab·solve (ab·solv′, -zolv′, əb-) *v.t.* **·solved, ·solv·ing 1.** To free from the penalties or consequences of an action. **2.** To release, as from an obligation. **3.** *Eccl.* To grant a remission of sin. [< L < *ab-* from + *solvere* to loosen.] —**ab·solv′a·ble** *adj.* —**ab·sol′vent** *adj. & n.* —**ab·solv′er** *n.*

ab·sorb (ab·sôrb′, -zôrb′) *v.t.* **1.** To drink in or suck up, as through or into pores. **2.** To engross completely. **3.** To take up or in by chemical or molecular action, as gases, heat, liquid, light, etc.: distinguished from *adsorb.* **4.** To take in and incorporate. **5.** To receive the force or action of; intercept. [< L < *ab-* from + *sorbere* to suck in] —**ab·sorb′a·bil′i·ty** *n.* —**ab·sorb′a·ble** *adj.* —**ab·sorb′er** *n.* —**ab·sorb′ing** *adj.* —**ab·sorb′ing·ly** *adv.*

ab·sor·bent (ab·sôr′bənt, -zôr′-) *adj.* Absorbing or tending to absorb. —*n.* A substance, duct, etc., that absorbs. —**ab·sor′ben·cy** *n.*

absorbent cotton Cotton from which all fatty matter has been removed, used in surgical dressings, etc.

ab·sorp·tion (ab·sôrp′shən, -zôrp′-) *n.* **1.** The act of absorbing, or the condition of being absorbed. **2.** Assimilation, as by the digestive process. **3.** Preoccupation of the mind. —**ab·sorp′tive** *adj.* —**ab·sorp′tive·ness, ab′sorp·tiv′i·ty** *n.*

ab·stain (ab·stān′) *v.i.* To keep oneself back; refrain voluntarily: with *from.* [< OF < L *abstinere* to hold back < *ab-* from + *tenere* to hold] —**ab·stain′er** *n.*

ab·ste·mi·ous (ab·stē′mē·əs) *adj.* Eating and drinking sparingly; abstinent; temperate. [< L < *ab-* from + root of *temetum* intoxicating drink] —**ab·ste′mi·ous ly** *adv.* —**ab·ste′mi·ous·ness** *n.*

ab·sten·tion (ab·sten′shən) *n.* An abstaining. —**ab·sten′·tious** *adj.*

ab·sti·nence (ab′stə·nəns) *n.* **1.** The act or practice of abstaining, as from food, pleasure, etc. **2.** Abstention from alcoholic beverages. [< F < L *abstinere* < *ab-* from + *tenere* to hold] —**ab′sti·nent** *adj.* —**ab′sti·nent·ly** *adv.*

ab·stract (*adj.* ab·strakt′, ab′strakt; *n.* ab′strakt; *v. defs. 1–4* ab·strakt′; *v. def.* 5 ab′strakt) *adj.* **1.** Considered apart from matter or from specific examples; not concrete. **2.** Theoretical; ideal, as opposed to practical. **3.** Abstruse. **4.** Considered or expressed without reference to particular example, as numbers, attributes, or qualities. **5.** In art, generalized or universal, as opposed to concrete, specific, or representational. —*n.* **1.** A summary or epitome, as of a document. **2.** The essence of some larger object or whole. **3.** An abstract idea or term. Abbr. *abs.* —**Syn.** See ABRIDGMENT. —**in the abstract** Apart from concrete relation or embodiment; abstractly. —*v.t.* **1.** To take away; remove. **2.** To take away secretly; purloin. **3.** To withdraw or disengage (the attention, interest, etc.). **4.** To consider apart from particular or material instances. **5.** To make an abstract of; summarize. [< L < *ab-* away + *trahere* to draw] —**ab·stract′er** *n.* —**ab·stract′ly** *adv.* —**ab·stract′ness** *n.*

ab·stract·ed (ab·strak′tid) *adj.* **1.** Lost in thought; absent-minded. **2.** Separated from all else; apart. —**ab·stract′·ed·ly** *adv.* —**ab·stract′ed·ness** *n.*

ab·strac·tion (ab·strak′shən) *n.* **1.** The process of abstracting. **2.** A product of this process; a concept. **3.** A visionary or impractical theory. **4.** The act of withdrawing; separation. **5.** Absence of mind; preoccupation. **6.** An art form or work of art in which the qualities are abstract.

ab·strac·tive (ab·strak′tiv) *adj.* **1.** Of, pertaining to, or tending to abstraction. **2.** Having the power of abstraction; epitomizing. —**ab·strac′tive·ly** *adv.* —**ab·strac′tive·ness** *n.*

abstract noun *Gram.* A noun that names a quality, idea, etc., as *goodness, democracy, reputation.*

ab·struse (ab·stro͞os′) *adj.* Hard to understand. —**Syn.** See COMPLEX, MYSTERIOUS. [< L < *ab-* away + *trudere* to thrust] —**ab·struse′ly** *adv.* —**ab·struse′ness** *n.*

ab·surd (ab·sûrd′, -zûrd′) *adj.* Irrational; ridiculous. [< F < L < *ab-* completely + *surdus* deaf, dull] —**ab·surd′ly** *adv.* —**ab·surd′ness** *n.*

ab·surd·i·ty (ab·sûr′də·tē, -zûr′-) *n. pl.* **·ties 1.** The quality of being absurd. **2.** Something absurd.

a·bun·dance (ə·bun′dəns) *n.* **1.** A plentiful or overflowing supply. **2.** Wealth; affluence.

a·bun·dant (ə·bun′dənt) *adj.* **1.** Existing in plentiful supply; ample. **2.** Abounding. —**Syn.** See PLENTIFUL. [< OF < L *abundare.* See ABOUND.] —**a·bun′dant·ly** *adv.*

a·buse (*v.* ə·byo͞oz′; *n.* ə·byo͞os′) *v.t.* **a·bused, a·bus·ing 1.** To use improperly or injuriously; misuse. **2.** To hurt by treating wrongly; injure. **3.** To speak in coarse or bad terms of or to; revile. —*n.* **1.** Improper or injurious use; misuse. **2.** Ill-treatment; injury. **3.** Vicious conduct, practice, or action. **4.** Abusive language; slander. [< F < L < *ab-* away + *uti* to use] —**a·bus′er** *n.*

a·bu·sive (ə·byo͞o′siv) *adj.* **1.** Mistreating. **2.** Insulting; vituperative. —**a·bu′sive·ly** *adv.* —**a·bu′sive·ness** *n.*

a·but (ə·but′) *v.i.* **a·but·ted, a·but·ting** To touch, join, or adjoin at the end or side; border: with *on, upon,* or *against.* [< OF < *a-* to + *bout* end] —**a·but′ter** *n.*

a·but·ment (ə·but′mənt) *n.* **1.** The act of abutting. **2.** Something that abuts, the thing abutted upon, or the point of junction. **3.** A supporting or buttressing structure.

a·bys·mal (ə·biz′məl) *adj.* Unfathomable; immeasurable; extreme: an *abysmal* ignorance. —**a·bys′mal·ly** *adv.*

a·byss (ə·bis′) *n.* **1.** A bottomless gulf; chasm. **2.** Any profound depth or void. **3.** The depths of the sea. [< L < Gk. < *a-* without + *byssos* bottom] —**a·bys′sal** *adj.*

Ab·ys·sin·i·an (ab′ə·sin′ē·ən) *adj. & n.* Ethiopian.

ac- Assimilated var. of AD-.

-ac *suffix* **1.** Having; affected by: *demoniac.* **2.** Pertaining to; of: *cardiac.* [< Gk. *-akos* or L *-acus* or F *-aque*]

a·ca·cia (ə·kā′shə) *n.* **1.** Any of various flowering, leguminous trees and shrubs of the tropics and warm temperate regions. **2.** The locust tree. **3.** Gum arabic. [< L < Gk. *akakia,* a thorny tree < *akē* point]

ac·a·dem·ic (ak′ə·dem′ik) *adj.* **1.** Pertaining to an academy, college, or university; scholarly. **2.** *U.S.* Offering or having to do with liberal rather than vocational or technical studies. **3.** Theoretical, as opposed to practical. **4.** Pedantic. Also **ac′a·dem′i·cal.** — *n.* A college or university student or faculty member. — **ac′a·dem′i·cal·ly** *adv.*

a·cad·e·mi·cian (ə·kad′ə·mish′ən, ak′ə·də-) *n.* A member of an academy of art, science, or literature.

ac·a·dem·i·cism (ak′ə·dem′ə·siz′əm) *n.* Pedantic formalism, as in art. Also **a·cad·e·mism** (ə·kad′ə·miz′əm).

a·cad·e·my (ə·kad′ə·mē) *n. pl.* **·mies 1.** A secondary school, usually a private one. **2.** A school giving instruction in some science or art. **3.** A learned society for the advancement of arts or sciences. [< F < L < Gk. *Akadēmeia* the grove where Plato taught]

A·ca·di·a (ə·kā′dē·ə) A former name for a region in eastern Canada, including Nova Scotia and New Brunswick.

A·ca·di·an (ə·kā′dē·ən) *adj.* Of or pertaining to Acadia or Nova Scotia. — *n.* One of the early French settlers of Acadia or their descendants. See CAJUN.

acantho- *combining form* Thorn or thorny; spine, point. Also, before vowels, **acanth-.** [< Gk. *akantha* thorn]

a·can·thus (ə·kan′thəs) *n. pl.* **·thus·es** or **·thi** (-thī) **1.** A plant having large spiny leaves, common in the Mediterranean region. **2.** *Archit.* A decorative representation of its leaf, characteristic of the Corinthian capital. [< L < Gk. *akē* thorn] — **a·can′thine** (-thin) *adj.*

ACANTHUS (*def.* 2)

a cap·pel·la (ä′ kə·pel′ə, *Ital.* ä′ käp·pel′lä) *Music* Sung without accompaniment. [< Ital., in chapel style]

ac·cede (ak·sēd′) *v.i.* **·ced·ed, ·ced·ing 1.** To give one's consent or adherence; agree; assent: with *to.* **2.** To come into or enter upon an office or dignity: with *to.* [< L < *ad-* to + *cedere* to yield]

ac·cel·er·an·do (ak·sel′ə·ran′dō, *Ital.* ät·chā′lā·rän′dō) *Music adj.* Gradually quickening in time. — *adv.* In gradually quickening tempo. [< Ital.]

ac·cel·er·ant (ak·sel′ər·ənt) *n.* That which accelerates.

ac·cel·er·ate (ak·sel′ə·rāt) *v.* **·at·ed, ·at·ing** *v.t.* **1.** To cause to act or move faster. **2.** To hasten the natural or usual course of. **3.** To cause to happen ahead of time. — *v.i.* **4.** To move or become faster. [< L < *ad-* to + *celerare* to hasten] — **ac·cel′er·a·ble** *adj.* — **ac·cel′er·a′tive** *adj.*

ac·cel·er·a·tion (ak·sel′ə·rā′shən) *n.* **1.** The act of accelerating or being accelerated. **2.** *Physics* The rate at which the velocity of a body increases per unit of time.

ac·cel·er·a·tor (ak·sel′ə·rā′tər) *n.* **1.** One who or that which accelerates. **2.** *Physics* Any of various devices for accelerating the velocity of atomic particles: also called *atom smasher.* **3.** *Mech.* The foot throttle of an automobile.

ac·cent (*n.* ak′sent; *v.* ak′sent, ak·sent′) *n.* **1.** The prominence given in speech to a particular sound, syllable, or word. **2.** A mark used to indicate the place of accent in a word. The **primary accent** notes the chief stress, and the **secondary accent** a somewhat weaker stress. **3.** A mark used in some languages to show the quality of a vowel. In French, the accents are acute (´), grave (`), and circumflex (ˆ). **4.** A modulation of the voice. **5.** Mode of utterance; pronunciation: a Southern *accent.* **6.** In prosody, the stress determining the rhythm of poetry. **7.** *Music* An emphasis given to one tone or chord. **8.** *pl.* Speech; words. — *v.t.* **1.** To speak, pronounce, play, or sing with an accent; stress. **2.** To write a mark indicating accent. **3.** To accentuate or emphasize. [< L < *ad-* to + *cantus* a singing]

ac·cen·tu·al (ak·sen′chōō·əl) *adj.* **1.** Of or pertaining to accent. **2.** In prosody, having a stress accent. — **ac·cen′tu·al·ly** *adv.*

ac·cen·tu·ate (ak·sen′chōō·āt) *v.t.* **·at·ed, ·at·ing 1.** To strengthen or heighten the effect of; emphasize. **2.** To mark or pronounce with an accent. — **ac·cen′tu·a′tion** *n.*

ac·cept (ak·sept′) *v.t.* **1.** To receive with favor, willingness, or consent. **2.** To give an affirmative answer to. **3.** To receive as satisfactory or sufficient. **4.** To take with good grace; submit to. **5.** In commerce, to agree to pay, as a draft. **6.** To believe in. [< L < *ad-* to + *capere* to take] — **ac·cept′er** *n.*

ac·cept·a·ble (ak·sep′tə·bəl) *adj.* Worthy of acceptance. — **ac·cept′a·ble·ness, ac·cept′a·bil′i·ty** *n.* — **ac·cept′a·bly** *adv.*

ac·cep·tance (ak·sep′təns) *n.* **1.** The act of accepting. **2.** The state of being accepted or acceptable. **3.** Favorable reception; approval. **4.** Assent; belief. **5.** In commerce, an agreement to pay a bill of exchange, etc.; also, the paper showing this. Also **ac·cep′tan·cy.** — **ac·cep′tant** *adj.*

ac·cep·ta·tion (ak′sep·tā′shən) *n.* The accepted meaning of a word or expression.

ac·cept·ed (ak·sep′tid) *adj.* Commonly recognized, believed, or approved; popular.

ac·cess (ak′ses) *n.* **1.** The act of coming to or near. **2.** A passage; path. **3.** The state or quality of being approachable; accessibility. **4.** A sudden attack of a disease. **5.** An outburst of emotion, etc. [< L *accedere* to yield]

ac·ces·si·ble (ak·ses′ə·bəl) *adj.* **1.** Easy of access; approachable. **2.** Attainable; obtainable. **3.** Open to the influence of. — **ac·ces′si·bil′i·ty** *n.* — **ac·ces′si·bly** *adv.*

ac·ces·sion (ak·sesh′ən) *n.* **1.** The act of attaining ar office, dignity, or right. **2.** An increase by something added. **3.** Assent; agreement. — *v.t.* To record, as additions to a library or museum. — **ac·ces′sion·al** *adj.*

ac·ces·so·ry (ak·ses′ər·ē) *n. pl.* **·ries 1.** Something added for convenience, display, etc., as to an automobile or to one's attire. **2.** *Law* A person who, though absent during the perpetration of a felony, instigates, aids, or encourages another to commit the felony (**accessory before the fact**), or knowingly comforts, conceals, or assists the felon (**accessory after the fact**). — *adj.* **1.** Aiding the principal design, or assisting subordinately the chief agent, as in the commission of a crime. **2.** Contributory; supplemental; additional. Also **ac·ces′sa·ry.** [< LL < L *accedere* to yield] — **ac′ces·so′ri·al** *adj.* — **ac·ces′so·ri·ly** *adv.* — **ac·ces′so·ri·ness** *n.*

— **Syn.** (noun) **2.** In law, an *accessory* assists in planning or concealing a crime, though he is not present when it is committed. An *accomplice* is actively or constructively present during the act itself. *Confederate* is a general term for one who assists another.

ac·ci·dent (ak′sə·dənt) *n.* **1.** Anything occurring unexpectedly, or without known cause. **2.** Any unpleasant or unfortunate occurrence involving injury, loss, or death. **3** Chance; fortune. **4.** Any nonessential attribute. [< L < *ad-* upon + *cadere* to fall]

ac·ci·den·tal (ak′sə·den′təl) *adj.* **1.** Happening or coming by chance. **2.** Nonessential; subordinate; incidental. **3** *Music* Pertaining to or indicating a sharp, natural, flat, etc. elsewhere than in the signature. — **ac′ci·den′tal·ly** *adv.*

ac·claim (ə·klām′) *v.t.* **1.** To proclaim with applause; hail They *acclaimed* him victor. **2.** To shout approval of. — *v.i.* **3.** To applaud; shout approval. — *n.* A shout of applause. — **Syn.** See PRAISE. [< L < *ad-* to + *clamare* to shout] — **ac·claim′a·ble** *adj.* — **ac·claim′er** *n.*

ac·cla·ma·tion (ak′lə·mā′shən) *n.* **1.** The act of acclaiming or of being acclaimed. **2.** A shout of applause or welcome. **3.** An oral vote, as in public assembly. **4.** *Canadian* Election without opposition. — **ac·clam·a·to·ry** (ə·klam′ə·tôr′ē, -tō′rē) *adj.*

ac·cli·mate (ə·klī′mit, ak′lə·māt) *v.t. & v.i.* **·mat·ed, ·mat·ing** *Chiefly U.S.* To adapt or become adapted to a new climate or environment. [< F < *à-* to + *climat* climate] — **ac·cli·ma·ta·ble** (ə·klī′mə·tə·bəl) *adj.* — **ac·cli·ma·tion** (ak′lə·mā′shən), **ac·cli·ma·ta·tion** (ə·klī′mə·tā′shən) *n.*

ac·cli·ma·tize (ə·klī′mə·tīz) *v.t. & v.i.* **·tized, ·tiz·ing** To acclimate. — **ac·cli′ma·ti·za′tion** *n.*

ac·cliv·i·ty (ə·kliv′ə·tē) *n. pl.* **·ties** An upward slope: opposed to *declivity.* [< L < *ad-* to + *clivus* hill] — **ac·cliv′i·tous, ac·cli·vous** (ə·klī′vəs) *adj.*

ac·co·lade (ak′ə·lād′, -läd′) *n.* **1.** The salutation (at first an embrace, now a light blow with a sword) in conferring knighthood. **2.** A conferring of praise; an honor. [< F < Ital. *accollare* to embrace about the neck]

ac·com·mo·date (ə·kom′ə·dāt) *v.* **·dat·ed, ·dat·ing** *v.t.* **1** To do a favor for; oblige; help. **2.** To provide for; give lodging to. **3.** To be suitable for; contain comfortably. **4** To adapt or modify, as to new conditions. **5.** To reconcile or settle, as conflicting opinions. — *v.i.* **6.** To be or become adjusted, as the eye to distance. [< L < *ad-* to + *commodare* to make fit, suit] — **ac·com′mo·da′tive** *adj.* — **ac·com′mo·da′tive·ness** *n.*

ac·com·mo·dat·ing (ə·kom′ə·dā′ting) *adj.* Disposed to make adjustment; obliging. — **ac·com′mo·dat′ing·ly** *adv.*

ac·com·mo·da·tion (ə·kom′ə·dā′shən) *n.* **1.** The act of accommodating, or the state of being accommodated; adjustment; adaptation. **2.** Reconciliation; compromise. **3.** Anything that supplies a need; convenience. **4.** *Usu. pl. U.S.* Lodging, board, etc. **5.** Willingness to please or help.

ac·com·pa·ni·ment (ə·kum′pə·ni·mənt, ə·kump′ni-) *n.* **1** Anything that accompanies something. **2.** *Music* A subordinate part supporting a leading part.

ac·com·pa·nist (ə·kum′pə·nist, ə·kump′nist) *n.* One who plays or sings the accompaniment. Also **ac·com′pa·ny·ist**

ac·com·pa·ny (ə·kum′pə·nē) *v.t.* **·nied, ·ny·ing 1.** To go with; attend; escort. **2.** To be or coexist with. **3.** To supplement. **4.** To play a musical accompaniment to or for [< F < *à-* to + *compagne* companion]

ac·com·plice (ə·kom′plis) *n.* An associate in wrongdoing partner in crime. — **Syn.** See ACCESSORY. [< *a,* indefinite article + F *complice* accomplice]

ac·com·plish (ə·kom′plish) *v.t.* To bring to pass or to completion. [< OF < LL < L *ad-* to + *complere* to fill up complete] — **ac·com′plish·a·ble** *adj.*

ac·com·plished (ə·kom′plisht) *adj.* **1.** Completed; done **2.** Proficient; skilled. **3.** Trained in the social graces.

ac·com·plish·ment (ə·kom′plish·mənt) *n.* **1.** The act of accomplishing. **2.** Something accomplished; achievement **3.** An acquirement or attainment, esp. a social skill. — **Syn.** See ATTAINMENT.

ac·cord (ə·kôrd′) *v.t.* **1.** To render as due; grant. **2.** To make harmonize or agree. — *v.i.* **3.** To agree; harmonize. — *n.* **1.** Harmony, as of sentiment, colors, sounds, etc.; agreement. **2.** A settlement of any difference, as between governments. — **Syn.** See HARMONY. — **of one's own accord** By one's own choice. [< OF < LL < L < *ad-* to + *cor* heart] — **ac·cord′a·ble** *adj.* — **ac·cord′er** *n.*

c·cord·ance (ə·kôr′dəns) *n.* Agreement; conformity. — **ac·cord′ant** *adj.* — **ac·cord′ant·ly** *adv.*

c·cord·ing (ə·kôr′ding) *adj.* Being in accordance or agreement; harmonizing. — *adv.* Accordingly. — **according as** **1.** In proportion as; just as. **2.** Depending on whether. — **according to** **1.** In accordance with. **2.** As stated by; on the authority of. **3.** In proportion to.

c·cord·ing·ly (ə·kôr′ding·lē) *adv.* **1.** In accord; correspondingly. **2.** Consequently; so.

c·cor·di·on (ə·kôr′dē·ən) *n.* A portable musical wind instrument with metallic reeds and a keyboard, the air for which is furnished by a bellows operated by the performer. [< Ital. *accordare* to harmonize] — **ac·cor′di·on·ist** *n.*

c·cost (ə·kôst′, ə·kost′) *v.t.* To speak to first; address; greet. [< F < L < *ad-* to + *costa* rib]

c·couche·ment (ə·ko͞osh′mənt, *Fr.* à·ko͞osh·mäṅ′) *n.* Confinement; childbirth. [< F *accoucher* to put to bed]

c·count (ə·kount′) *v.t.* **1.** To hold to be; consider; estimate. — *v.i.* **2.** To provide a reckoning, as of funds paid or received: with *to* or *with* (someone), *for* (something). **3.** To give a rational explanation: with *for.* **4.** To be responsible; answer: with *for.* **5.** To cause death, capture, or incapacitation: with *for.* — *n.* **1.** A record of events; narrative; description. **2.** A statement of causes; explanation. **3.** A record of monetary transactions. **4.** Worth; importance. **5.** Judgment; estimation. **6.** Profit; advantage. — **on account of** Because of. — **on no account** Under no circumstances. [< OF < LL < L *ad-* to + *computare* to reckon together]

c·count·a·ble (ə·koun′tə·bəl) *adj.* **1.** Liable to be called to account; responsible. **2.** Capable of being explained. — **ac·count′a·bil′i·ty** *n.* — **ac·count′a·bly** *adv.*

c·count·ant (ə·koun′tənt) *n.* One whose business is to keep or examine books, as of a mercantile or banking house. — **ac·count′an·cy** *n.*

c·count·ing (ə·koun′ting) *n.* The art or system of recording, classifying, and summarizing commercial transactions.

c·cou·ter (ə·ko͞o′tər) *v.t.* To furnish with dress or trappings; equip, as for military service. Also *Brit.* **ac·cou′tre.** [< F *accoutrer*; ult. origin uncertain]

c·cou·ter·ment (ə·ko͞o′tər·mənt) *n.* **1.** *pl.* Equipment; trappings; especially, the equipment of a soldier other than arms and dress. **2.** The act of accoutering.

c·cred·it (ə·kred′it) *v.t.* **1.** To give credit to as the owner, author, or creator of; attribute to: with *with.* **2.** To accept as true; believe. **3.** To bring into credit; vouch for. **4.** To furnish or send with credentials. **5.** To certify as fulfilling official requirements. [< F < L < *ad-* to + *credere* to believe, trust]

c·cred·i·ta·tion (ə·kred′ə·tā′shən) *n.* *U.S.* The granting of approved status to an academic institution.

c·cre·tion (ə·krē′shən) *n.* **1.** Growth by external additions or by adhesion or inclusion. **2.** An external addition; something added. **3.** Increase by natural growth.

c·crue (ə·kro͞o′) *v.i.* **·crued, ·cru·ing** **1.** To come as a natural result or increment, as by growth: with *to.* **2.** To accumulate, as the interest on money: with *from.* [< F < L < *ad-* to + *crescere* to grow] — **ac·cru′al, ac·crue′ment** *n.*

c·cu·mu·late (ə·kyo͞om′yə·lāt) *v.* **·lat·ed, ·lat·ing** *v.t.* **1.** To heap or pile up; amass; collect. — *v.i.* **2.** To become greater in quantity or number; increase. [< L < *ad-* to + *cumulare* to heap] — **ac·cu′mu·la·ble** (-lə·bəl) *adj.*

c·cu·mu·la·tion (ə·kyo͞om′yə·lā′shən) *n.* **1.** The act or process of accumulating. **2.** That which is accumulated. **3.** The addition of earnings or profits to capital.

c·cu·mu·la·tive (ə·kyo͞om′yə·lā′tiv, -lə·tiv) *adj.* **1.** Tending to accumulate. **2.** Arising from accumulation. — **ac·cu′mu·la′tive·ly** *adv.* — **ac·cu′mu·la′tive·ness** *n.*

c·cu·mu·la·tor (ə·kyo͞om′yə·lā′tər) *n.* **1.** A person or thing that accumulates. **2.** *Brit.* A storage battery.

c·cu·ra·cy (ak′yər·ə·sē) *n.* The condition or quality of being accurate; exactness; precision; correctness.

c·cu·rate (ak′yər·it) *adj.* Conforming exactly to truth or to a standard; without error; precise; exact. [< L < *ad-* to + *cura* care] — **ac′cu·rate·ly** *adv.* — **ac′cu·rate·ness** *n.*

c·curs·ed (ə·kûr′sid, ə·kûrst′) *adj.* **1.** Lying under a curse; doomed. **2.** Deserving a curse; detestable. Also **ac·curst′.** — **ac·curs′ed·ly** *adv.* — **ac·curs′ed·ness** *n.*

c·cu·sa·tion (ak′yo͞o·zā′shən) *n.* **1.** The act of accusing or the state of being accused. **2.** The crime or act charged. Also **ac·cu·sal** (ə·kyo͞o′zəl). — **ac·cu·sa·to·ry** (ə·kyo͞o′zə·tôr′ē, -tō′rē) *adj.*

ac·cu·sa·tive (ə·kyo͞o′zə·tiv) *Gram. adj.* Denoting, in inflected languages, the case or relation of the direct object of a verb or preposition, or the goal toward which an action is directed; objective. Also **ac·cu·sa·ti·val** (ə·kyo͞o′zə·tī′vəl). — *n.* **1.** The case of Latin and Greek nouns corresponding to the English objective. **2.** A word in this case. [< L *accusativus,* trans. of Gk. (*ptōsis*) *aitiatikē* (the case) of the effect < *aitiatos* effected] — **ac·cu′sa·tive·ly** *adv.*

ac·cuse (ə·kyo͞oz′) *v.* **·cused, ·cus·ing** *v.t.* **1.** To charge with fault or error; blame; censure. **2.** To bring charges against: with *of.* — *v.i.* **3.** To make accusation; utter charges. [< OF < L < *ad-* to + *causa* a cause, lawsuit] — **ac·cus′er** *n.* — **ac·cus′ing·ly** *adv.*

— **Syn. 2.** *Accuse* is a general word for declaring a person guilty of a fault; *charge* is more formal and stresses the serious or criminal nature of an act: to *accuse* a man of lying, to *charge* him with perjury. An *accused* man is *indicted* by a grand jury, and *arraigned* before a court to answer the indictment. *Incriminate* implies involvement in a serious crime.

ac·cused (ə·kyo͞ozd′) *n.* *Law* The defendant or defendants in a criminal case: preceded by *the.*

ac·cus·tom (ə·kus′təm) *v.t.* To familiarize by custom or use; habituate or inure: with *to*: to *accustom* oneself to noise.

ac·cus·tomed (ə·kus′təmd) *adj.* **1.** Habitual; usual. **2.** Wont; used: *accustomed* to hard work.

ace (ās) *n.* **1.** A playing card, die, etc., having a single spot. **2.** A very small amount, distance, or degree: within an *ace* of death. **3.** One who excels in a particular field, especially a combat flyer. **4.** In tennis and similar games, a point won by a single stroke, as upon the service. — **ace in the hole** *U.S. Slang* A hidden advantage. — *v.t.* **aced** (āst), **ac·ing** To score a point against in a single stroke, as in tennis. [< OF < L *as* unity, unit]

-acea *suffix Zool.* Used in forming names of classes and orders of animals. [< L, neut. pl. of *-aceus*]

-aceae *suffix Bot.* Used in forming names of families of plants. [< L, fem. pl. of *-aceus*]

a·ce·di·a (ə·sē′dē·ə) *n.* **1.** Extreme mental or spiritual torpor. **2.** Sloth regarded as one of the seven deadly sins. [< LL < Gk. < *a-* without + *kēdos* care]

a·cen·tric (ā·sen′trik) *adj.* Without a center; off center.

-aceous *suffix* Of the nature of; belonging or pertaining to; like: used to form adjectives corresponding to nouns in *-acea, -aceae.* [< L *-aceus* of the nature of]

ac·er·bate (as′ər·bāt) *v.t.* **·bat·ed, ·bat·ing** **1.** To make sour; embitter. **2.** To exasperate. [< L *acerbus* sharp]

a·cer·bi·ty (ə·sûr′bə·tē) *n. pl.* **·ties** **1.** Sourness, bitterness, as that of unripe fruit. **2.** Severity, as of temper, etc.; harshness. Also **a·cer·bi·tude** (ə·sûr′bə·to͞od, -tyo͞od).

acet- Var. of ACETO-.

ac·e·tab·u·lum (as′ə·tab′yə·ləm) *n. pl.* **·la** (-lə) *Anat.* The socket in the hip in which the head of the femur rests and revolves. [< L, a vinegar cup < *acetum* vinegar]

ac·e·tal (as′ə·tal) *n.* *Med.* A volatile, colorless liquid, $C_6H_{14}O_2$, having hypnotic properties.

ac·et·an·i·lide (as′ə·tan′ə·līd, -lid) *n.* *Chem.* A derivative of aniline, C_8H_9ON, used as a sedative and antipyretic.

ac·e·tate (as′ə·tāt) *n.* *Chem.* A salt or ester of acetic acid.

a·ce·tic (ə·sē′tik, ə·set′ik) *adj.* Pertaining to or like vinegar; sour. [< L *acetum* vinegar + -IC]

acetic acid *Chem.* A colorless, pungent liquid, $C_2H_4O_2$, occurring in a dilute form in vinegar.

a·cet·i·fy (ə·set′ə·fī) *v.t. & v.i.* **·fied, ·fy·ing** To change into acid or vinegar. — **a·cet′i·fi·ca′tion** *n.* — **a·cet′i·fi′er** *n.*

aceto- *combining form* Of, pertaining to, or from acetic acid or acetyl. Also, before vowels, *acet-.* [< L *acetum* vinegar]

ac·e·tone (as′ə·tōn) *n.* *Chem.* A clear, flammable liquid, C_3H_6O, used as a solvent for fats, camphor, and resins. — **ac·e·ton·ic** (as′ə·ton′ik) *adj.*

a·cet·y·lene (ə·set′ə·lēn) *n.* *Chem.* A colorless hydrocarbon gas, C_2H_2, used as an illuminant and for cutting metals.

ac·e·tyl·sal·i·cyl·ic acid (as′ə·til·sal′ə·sil′ik, ə·sē′təl-) Aspirin.

ace·y-deuc·y (ā′sē·do͞o′sē, -dyo͞o′sē) *n.* A variety of backgammon.

A·chae·an (ə·kē′ən) *adj.* Pertaining to Achaea, its people, or their culture. — *n.* **1.** A member of one of the four major tribes of ancient Greece. **2.** A Greek. Also **A·cha·ian** (ə·kā′ən, -kī-).

ache (āk) *v.i.* **ached** (ākt), **ach·ing** **1.** To suffer dull, continued pain; be in pain or distress. **2.** *Informal* To yearn; be eager; with *for* or the infinitive. — *n.* A local, dull, and protracted pain. [OE *acan*] — **ach′ing·ly** *adv.*

a·chene (ā·kēn′) *n.* *Bot.* A small, dry, one-seeded pericarp, as in the dandelion, buttercup, etc.: also spelled *akene.* [< NL < A-[4] not + Gk. *chainein* to gape] — **a·che′ni·al** *adj.*

Ach·e·ron (ak′ə·ron) **1.** In Greek and Roman mythology, the river of woe, one of the rivers surrounding Hades. 2. Hades. [< L < Gk. *Acherōn*]

a·chieve (ə·chēv′) *v.* **a·chieved, a·chiev·ing** *v.t.* 1. To accomplish; do successfully. 2. To win or attain, as by effort or skill. — *v.i.* 3. To accomplish something. [< OF < LL *ad caput* (*venire*) (to come) to a head, finish] — **a·chiev′a·ble** *adj.* — **a·chiev′er** *n.*

a·chieve·ment (ə·chēv′mənt) *n.* 1. Something accomplished. 2. The act of achieving. — **Syn.** See ACT.

A·chil·les (ə·kil′ēz) In the *Iliad,* the foremost Greek hero of the Trojan War, who killed Hector and was killed by an arrow Paris shot into his right heel, his only vulnerable spot. — **Ach·il·le·an** (ak′ə·lē′ən) *adj.*

Achilles' heel A vulnerable point.

Achilles' tendon *Anat.* The tendon connecting the calf muscles to the heel bone.

ach·ro·mat·ic (ak′rə·mat′ik) *adj.* 1. *Optics* Free from color or iridescence; transmitting light without separating it into its constituent colors, as a lens. 2. *Music* Diatonic; without accidentals. [< Gk. < *a-* without + *chrōma* color] — **ach′ro·mat′i·cal·ly** *adv.* — **a·chro·ma·tism** (ā·krō′mə·tiz′·əm), **a·chro·ma·tic·i·ty** (ā·krō′mə·tis′ə·tē) *n.*

a·chro·ma·tin (ā·krō′mə·tin) *n. Biol.* The substance in the cell nucleus that does not readily take color from stains.

a·chro·ma·tize (ā·krō′mə·tīz) *v.t.* **·tized, ·tiz·ing** To make achromatic.

a·chro·mic (ā·krō′mik) *adj.* Colorless. Also **a·chro′mous.**

ac·id (as′id) *adj.* 1. Sharp and biting to the taste, as vinegar; sour. 2. *Chem.* Pertaining to or like an acid. 3. *Geol.* Acidic. 4. Sharp-tempered; biting. — *n.* 1. Any sour substance. 2. *Chem.* A compound containing hydrogen in which all or a part of the hydrogen may be exchanged for a metal or a basic radical, forming a salt. Aqueous solutions of acids are sour, and redden litmus. — **Syn.** See SOUR. [< L *acidus*] — **ac′id·ly** *adv.* — **ac′id·ness** *n.*

ac·id-fast (as′id·fast′, -fäst′) *adj.* Not readily decolorized by acids when stained: said of bacteria, epithelial tissue, etc.

a·cid·ic (ə·sid′ik) *adj.* 1. *Geol.* Containing a high percentage of silica: said of rocks. 2. *Chem.* Acid.

a·cid·i·fy (ə·sid′ə·fī) *v.t. & v.i.* **·fied, ·fy·ing** To make or become acid; change into an acid. — **a·cid′i·fi′a·ble** *adj.* — **a·cid′i·fi·ca′tion** *n.* — **a·cid′i·fi′er** *n.*

a·cid·i·ty (ə·sid′ə·tē) *n.* 1. The state or quality of being acid. 2. Degree of acid strength. 3. *Chem.* The combining power of a base with reference to an acid. 4. Hyperacidity.

ac·i·do·sis (as′ə·dō′sis) *n. Pathol.* Acid intoxication due to faulty metabolism. — **ac·i·dot·ic** (as′ə·dot′ik) *adj.*

acid test A final, decisive test, as of worth or integrity.

a·cid·u·late (ə·sij′o͞o·lāt) *v.t.* **·lat·ed, ·lat·ing** To make somewhat acid or sour. — **a·cid′u·la′tion** *n.*

a·cid·u·lous (ə·sij′o͞o·ləs) *adj.* Slightly acid; sour. Also **a·cid′u·lent.** [< L *acidulus* slightly sour]

ac·i·nus (as′ə·nəs) *n. pl.* **·ni** (-nī) 1. *Bot.* One of the small parts of a fruit, as of the raspberry. 2. A berry, as a grape, growing in bunches; a bunch of such berries. [< L, grape]

-acious *suffix of adjectives* Abounding in; characterized by; given to: *pugnacious, vivacious.* [< L *-ax, -acis* + -OUS]

-acity *suffix* Quality or state of: used to form abstract nouns corresponding to adjectives in *-acious.* [< L *-acitas*]

ack-ack (ak′ak′) *n.* Antiaircraft fire. [British radio operator's code for *A.A.* (antiaircraft)]

ac·knowl·edge (ak·nol′ij) *v.t.* **·edged, ·edg·ing** 1. To admit the truth or fact of; confess. 2. To recognize as or avow to be. 3. To admit the validity of, as a claim or right. 4. To show appreciation of or admit obligation for; express thanks for. 5. To report receipt or arrival of. — **Syn.** See CONFESS. [Earlier *aknowledge* < obs. *aknow* to admit, confess] — **ac·knowl′edge·a·ble** *adj.* — **ac·knowl′edg·er** *n.*

ac·knowl·edg·ment (ak·nol′ij·mənt) *n.* 1. The act of admitting; confession. 2. Recognition of the existence or truth of something. 3. Something done or given in return. 4. *Law* A formal certificate. Also **ac·knowl′edge·ment.**

ac·me (ak′mē) *n.* The highest point. [< Gk. *akmē* point]

ac·ne (ak′nē) *n. Pathol.* A skin disease marked by pimples, chiefly on the face. [? Alter. of Gk. *akmē* point]

ac·o·lyte (ak′ə·līt) *n.* 1. An attendant or assistant. 2. An altar boy. 3. In the Roman Catholic Church, a member of the highest minor order. [< Med.L < Gk. *akolouthos* follower, attendant]

ac·o·nite (ak′ə·nīt) *n.* 1. The monkshood, or any similar plant. 2. An extract of this plant, used as a sedative. Also **ac·o·ni·tum** (ak′ə·nī′təm). [< F < L < Gk. *akoniton*]

a·corn (ā′kôrn, ā′kərn) *n.* The fruit of the oak, a one-seeded nut, fixed in a woody cup. [OE *æcern*]

a·cous·tic (ə·ko͞os′tik) *adj.* 1. Pertaining to the act or sense of hearing, heard sound, or the science of sound. 2. Adapted for conveying sound or aiding hearing. Also **a·cous′ti·cal.** [< F < Gk. *akouein* to hear] — **a·cous′ti·cal·ly** *adv.*

a·cous·tics (ə·ko͞os′tiks) *n.pl.* (*construed as sing. in def. 1*) 1. The branch of physics that treats of sound. 2. The sound-transmitting qualities of an auditorium, room, etc.

ac·quaint (ə·kwānt′) *v.t.* 1. To make familiar or conversant 2. To cause to know; inform. [< OF < LL < L *ad-* to + *cognitus*, pp. of *cognoscere* to know]

ac·quain·tance (ə·kwān′təns) *n.* 1. Knowledge of any per son or thing. 2. A person or persons with whom one is ac quainted. — **ac·quain′tance·ship** *n.*

ac·quaint·ed (ə·kwān′tid) *adj.* Having acquaintance; hav ing personal knowledge: with *with.*

ac·qui·esce (ak′wē·es′) *v.i.* **·esced** (-est′), **·esc·ing** To con sent or concur tacitly; assent; comply. [< MF < L < *ad-* t + *quiescere* to rest] — **ac′qui·esc′ing·ly** *adv.*

ac·qui·es·cence (ak′wē·es′əns) *n.* Quiet submission; pas sive consent. — **ac′qui·es′cent** *adj.* — **ac′qui·es′cent·ly** *adv*

ac·quire (ə·kwīr′) *v.t.* **·quired, ·quir·ing** 1. To obtain b one's own endeavor or action. 2. To come to possess; re ceive. — **Syn.** See GET, RECEIVE. [< L < *ad-* to + *quaerer* to seek] — **ac·quir′a·ble** *adj.* — **ac·quir′er** *n.*

acquired character *Biol.* A noninheritable change in a organism resulting from environmental influences.

ac·quire·ment (ə·kwīr′mənt) *n.* 1. The act of acquiring 2. Something acquired, as a skill; an attainment.

ac·qui·si·tion (ak′wə·zish′ən) *n.* 1. The act of acquiring 2. Anything gained or acquired.

ac·quis·i·tive (ə·kwiz′ə·tiv) *adj.* Able or inclined to acquir (money, property, etc.); grasping. — **ac·quis′i·tive·ly** *adv* — **ac·quis′i·tive·ness** *n.*

ac·quit (ə·kwit′) *v.t.* **·quit·ted, ·quit·ting** 1. To free or clea as from an accusation. 2. To relieve, as of an obligatio 3. To repay or return. 4. To conduct (oneself); behave. [< OF < L *ad-* to + *quietare* to settle, quiet] — **ac·quit′tal** *n* — **ac·quit′ter** *n.*

ac·quit·tance (ə·kwit′ns) *n.* 1. A release, as from a deb 2. Satisfaction of indebtedness or obligation. 3. A receip

a·cre (ā′kər) *n.* 1. A measure of land, equal to 43,560 squar feet. 2. *pl.* Lands; estate. [OE *æcer* field]

a·cre·age (ā′kər·ij, -krij) *n.* Area in acres; acres collectivel

a·cred (ā′kərd) *adj.* Comprising or owning acres of lan

ac·rid (ak′rid) *adj.* 1. Cutting or burning to the taste c smell. 2. Sharp and satirical, as speech. [< L *acer, acri* — **a·crid·i·ty** (ə·krid′ə·tē), **ac′rid·ness** *n.* — **ac′rid·ly** *adv.*

ac·ri·mo·ny (ak′rə·mō′nē) *n. pl.* **·nies** Sharpness or bi terness of speech or temper; acridity. [< L < *acer* sharp — **ac·ri·mo·ni·ous** (ak′rə·mō′nē·əs) *adj.* — **ac′ri·mo′ni·ou ly** *adv.* — **ac′ri·mo′ni·ous·ness** *n.*

acro- *combining form* 1. At the tip or end of. 2. *Me* Pertaining to the extremities. [< Gk. *akros* at the end]

ac·ro·bat (ak′rə·bat) *n.* One skilled in feats requiring mu cular coordination, as in tightrope walking, tumbling, tr peze performing, etc.; a gymnast. [< F < Gk. *akrobat* walking on tiptoe < *akros* at the tip + *bainein* to walk, g — **ac′ro·bat′ic** or **·i·cal** *adj.* — **ac′ro·bat′i·cal·ly** *adv.*

ac·ro·bat·ics (ak′rə·bat′iks) *n.pl.* The skills or activities an acrobat, as in gymnastics.

ac·ro·gen (ak′rə·jən) *n. Bot.* A plant growing at the t only, as ferns, mosses, etc. — **ac·ro·gen·ic** (ak′rə·jen′ik **a·crog·e·nous** (ə·kroj′ə·nəs) *adj.* — **a·crog′e·nous·ly** *adv.*

ac·ro·meg·a·ly (ak′rō·meg′ə·lē) *n. Pathol.* A disorder the pituitary gland characterized by an enlargement of t extremities, thorax, and face, including both soft and bon parts. [< F < Gk. *akros* at the tip + *megas, megalou* big — **ac·ro·me·gal·ic** (ak′rō·mi·gal′ik) *adj. & n.*

ac·ro·nym (ak′rə·nim) *n.* A word formed by combining in tial letters (*Eniac, UNESCO*) or syllables and letters (*rada sonar*) of a series of words or a compound term. [< ACR + *-nym* name, as in *homonym*]

a·crop·o·lis (ə·krop′ə·lis) *n.* The citadel of an ancient Gree city. — **the Acropolis** The citadel of Athens. [< G < *akros* at the top + *polis* city]

a·cross (ə·krôs′, ə·kros′) *adv.* 1. From one side to the othe 2. On or at the other side. 3. Crosswise; crossed, as arm — *prep.* 1. On or from the other side of; beyond; over. Through or over the surface of. 3. From side to side o [< A-[1] on, in + CROSS]

a·cros·tic (ə·krôs′tik, ə·kros′-) *n.* A poem or other comp sition in which initial or other letters, taken in order, form word or phrase. — *adj.* Of or resembling an acrostic. [< < Gk. < *akros* at the end + *stichos* line of verse] — **a·cros ti·cal·ly** *adv.*

A·crux (ā′kruks) *n.* One of the 20 brightest stars, 1.05 ma nitude; Alpha in the constellation Crux.

a·cryl·ic acid (ə·kril′ik) *Chem.* Any of a series of aci having a sharp, acrid odor, and used in plastics.

act (akt) *v.t.* 1. To play the part of; impersonate, as in drama. 2. To perform on the stage, as a play. 3. To pe form as if on a stage; feign the character of. 4. To behave suitable to. — *v.i.* 5. To behave or conduct oneself. 6. T carry out a purpose or function; perform. 7. To produce a effect: often with *on.* 8. To serve temporarily or as a su stitute, as in some office or capacity. 9. To perform on t stage; be an actor. 10. To pretend; play a part so as to a pear. 11. To serve for theatrical performance or use: Th scene *acts* well. **— to act on** (or **upon**) To order one's conduct in accordance with; obey: to *act on* someone's advice. **— to act up** *Informal* To behave mischievously; appear troublesome. **— *n.* 1.** The exertion of mental or physical power; the performance of a function or process; a doing: taken in the very *act.* **2.** Something done; a deed; action. **3.** An enactment or edict, as of a legislative body. **4.** *Often pl.* A formal written record or statement of a transaction, action taken, etc. **5.** One of the main divisions of a play or opera. **6.** A short theatrical performance. **7.** *Informal* Something feigned; a pose. [< L *actum* a thing done]

— Syn. (noun) **2.** *Act* and *deed* are both used for something done, while *action* refers more to the doing of it. *Acts* and *deeds* may be good or bad, but a *deed* is commonly great or notable. A *feat* requires daring and skill, and usually involves physical *action. Achievement* is usually notable and distinguished.

act·a·ble (ak′tə·bəl) *adj.* That can be acted, as a role in a play. **— act′a·bil′i·ty** *n.*

ACTH A pituitary hormone that stimulates the secretion of cortisone by the adrenal cortex.

act·ing (ak′ting) *adj.* **1.** Operating or officiating, especially in place of another: *acting* secretary. **2.** Functioning; working. **— *n.* 1.** The occupation of an actor. **2.** Pretense or simulation.

ac·tin·i·a (ak·tin′ē·ə) *n.* A sea anemone. Also **ac·tin′i·an.** [< NL < Gk. *aktis, aktinos* ray]

ac·tin·ic (ak·tin′ik) *adj.* Of, pertaining to, or having actinism. Also **ac·tin′i·cal. — ac·tin′i·cal·ly** *adv.*

actinic rays Those wavelengths of violet and ultraviolet light capable of effecting chemical changes.

ac·ti·nide series (ak′ti·nīd) *Physics* A series of radioactive elements beginning with actinium, atomic number 89, and ending with lawrencium, atomic number 103.

ac·tin·ism (ak′tin·iz′əm) *n.* **1.** The property of radiant energy that effects chemical changes. **2.** The production of such change.

ac·tin·i·um (ak·tin′ē·əm) *n.* A radioactive element (symbol Ac), isolated from pitchblende, and having a half life of about 13 years. See ELEMENT.

ac·ti·noid (ak′ti·noid) *adj.* Having the form of rays; radiate, as a starfish.

ac·ti·non (ak′ti·non) *n. Chem.* A radioactive isotope of radon, with a half life of nearly four seconds. [< NL]

ac·ti·no·zo·an (ak′ti·nə·zō′ən) *n. Zool.* An anthozoan. [< Gk. *aktis* ray + *zōion* animal] **— ac′ti·no·zo′al** *adj.*

ac·tion (ak′shən) *n.* **1.** The process of acting, doing, or working; operation. **2.** The result of putting forth power; a deed; act. **3.** *pl.* Habitual behavior; conduct. **4.** Activity; energy. **5.** The exertion of power; influence. **6.** *Physiol.* The performance by an organ of its proper function. **7.** *Mech.* **a** The mechanism by which a machine operates. **b** The movement of the parts of a machine. **8.** *Mil.* A battle; combat. **9.** *Law* A lawsuit. **10.** The posture and gestures of an actor or orator. **11.** In literature, the series of connected events that form the plot in a story or play. **12.** In sculpture or painting, gesture or attitude intended to express passion or sentiment. **— Syn.** See ACT, BATTLE. [< F < L < *agere* to do]

ac·tion·a·ble (ak′shən·ə·bəl) *adj.* Affording ground for prosecution, as a trespass or a libel. **— ac′tion·a·bly** *adv.*

ac·ti·vate (ak′tə·vāt) *v.t.* **·vat·ed, ·vat·ing 1.** To make active. **2.** To organize (a military unit) for its assigned function. **3.** *Physics* To make radioactive. **4.** *Chem.* To promote or hasten a reaction in, as by heat. **5.** To purify by aeration, as sewage. **— ac′ti·va′tion** *n.* **— ac′ti·va′tor** *n.*

ac·tive (ak′tiv) *adj.* **1.** Abounding in or exhibiting action; busy. **2.** Being in or pertaining to a state of action; not extinct or quiescent. **3.** Agile; quick; nimble. **4.** Characterized by much activity; brisk; lively. **5.** Causing or promoting action or change; not contemplative. **6.** Bearing interest: *active* investments. **7.** In business, busy; productive: *active* accounts. **8.** *Gram.* Designating a voice of the verb that indicates that the subject of the sentence is performing the action. **— *n.* *Gram.*** The active voice. Abbr. *a.* [< F < L *activus* < *agere* to do] **— ac′tive·ly** *adv.* **— ac′tive·ness** *n.*

ac·tiv·i·ty (ak·tiv′ə·tē) *n. pl.* **·ties 1.** The state of being active; action. **2.** Brisk or vigorous movement or action; liveliness; energy. **3.** A particular action or sphere of action.

act of God *Law* An event caused by the operations of nature unmixed with human agency or human negligence.

ac·tor (ak′tər) *n.* **1.** A player on the stage, in motion pictures, etc. **2.** One who does something.

ac·tress (ak′tris) *n.* A woman or girl who acts, as on the stage.

Acts of the Apostles The fifth book of the New Testament. Also **Acts.**

ac·tu·al (ak′chōō·əl) *adj.* **1.** Existing in fact; real. **2.** Being in existence or action now; existent; present. [< F < LL < L *actus* a doing] **— ac′tu·al·ness** *n.*

ac·tu·al·i·ty (ak′chōō·al′ə·tē) *n. pl.* **·ties 1.** The state or quality of being actual; reality; realism. **2.** *pl.* Actual circumstances or conditions.

ac·tu·al·ize (ak′chōō·əl·īz′) *v.t.* **·ized, ·iz·ing 1.** To make real; realize in action, as a possibility. **2.** To make seem real; represent realistically. **— ac′tu·al·i·za′tion** *n.*

ac·tu·al·ly (ak′chōō·əl·ē) *adv.* As a matter of fact; really.

ac·tu·ar·y (ak′chōō·er′ē) *n. pl.* **·ar·ies** A statistician who calculates and states risks, premiums, etc., for insurance purposes. [< L *actuarius* clerk] **— ac·tu·ar·i·al** (ak′chōō·âr′ē·əl) *adj.* **— ac′tu·ar′i·al·ly** *adv.*

ac·tu·ate (ak′chōō·āt) *v.t.* **·at·ed, ·at·ing 1.** To set into action or motion, as a mechanism. **2.** To incite or influence to action: *actuated* by motives of kindness. [< Med.L < L *actus* a doing] **— ac′tu·a′tion** *n.* **— ac′tu·a′tor** *n.*

— Syn. 2. *Actuate* and *impel* both imply mental or moral reasons for acting, while *urge* more often involves persuasion by others or from without.

acu- *combining form* Needle; point. [< L *acus*]

a·cu·i·ty (ə·kyōō′ə·tē) *n.* Acuteness; sharpness. [< MF < Med.L < L *acus* needle]

a·cu·men (ə·kyōō′mən, ak′ yōō·mən) *n.* Quickness of insight or discernment. [< L < *acuere* to sharpen]

— Syn. 1. *Sharpness, acuteness,* and *insight,* however keen, and *perception,* however deep, fall short of the meaning of *acumen,* which belongs to an astute and discriminating mind.

a·cu·mi·nate (ə·kyōō′mə·nāt; *for adj., also* ə·kyōō′mə·nit) *v.t.* **·nat·ed, ·nat·ing** To sharpen; make pointed. **— *adj.*** Ending in a long, tapering point, as a leaf, feather, fin, etc.: also **a·cu′mi·nat′ed** [< L *acuminatus,* pp. of *acuminare* to point, sharpen] **— a·cu′mi·na′tion** *n.*

a·cute (ə·kyōōt′) *adj.* **1.** Coming to a crisis quickly; violent: said of a disease: opposed to *chronic.* **2.** Of the greatest importance; crucial. **3.** Affecting keenly; poignant; intense. **4.** Keenly discerning or sensitive. **5.** *Music* High in pitch; shrill. [< L *acutus,* pp. of *acuere* to sharpen] **— a·cute′ly** *adv.* **— a·cute′ness** *n.*

acute accent See ACCENT (def. 3).

acute angle *Geom.* An angle less than a right angle.

-acy *suffix of nouns* Forming nouns of quality, state, or condition from adjectives in *-acious,* and nouns and adjectives in *-ate*: *fallacy, celibacy, curacy.* [< F *-atie* < L *-acia, -atia* < Gk. *-ateia*; or directly < L or < Gk.]

ad (ad) *n.* **1.** *Informal* An advertisement. **2.** In tennis, advantage.

ad- *prefix* To; toward; near: *adhere*: also spelled *a-, ab-, ac-, af-, ag-, al-, an-, ap-, ar-* before various consonants. [< L *ad-* < *ad* to]

-ad *suffix of nouns* Of or pertaining to; used to form: **a** Collective numerals: *triad.* **b** Names of poems: *Iliad.* [< Gk. *-as, -ados*]

ad·age (ad′ij) *n.* A maxim; proverb. **— Syn.** See PROVERB. [< F < L < *ad-* to + root of *aio* I say]

a·da·gio (ə·dä′jō, -zhē·ō, -zhō) *Music adj.* Slow. **— *adv.*** Slowly. **— *n.*** A composition in adagio time. [< Ital.]

Ad·am (ad′əm) In the Bible, the first man, progenitor of the human race. *Gen.* ii 7. **— *n.*** Mankind collectively. **— the old Adam** Unregenerate human nature.

ad·a·mant (ad′ə·mant, -mənt) *n.* A very hard legendary mineral, later identified with the diamond or lodestone. **— *adj.* 1.** Immovable; unyielding. **2.** Very hard. [< OF < L < Gk. < *a-* not + *damaein* to conquer] **— ad·a·man·tine** (ad′ə·man′tin, -tēn, -tīn) *adj.*

Adam's apple The prominence made by the thyroid cartilage at the front of the human throat, conspicuous in males.

a·dapt (ə·dapt′) *v.t.* **1.** To fit for a new use; make suitable: with *for.* **2.** To adjust (oneself or itself) to a new situation or environment. **— *v.i.* 3.** To become adjusted to a circumstance or environment. [< F < L *ad* to + *aptare* to fit]

a·dapt·a·ble (ə·dap′tə·bəl) *adj.* **1.** Capable of being adapted. **2.** Able to change easily to meet new circumstances. **— a·dapt′a·bil′i·ty, a·dapt′a·ble·ness** *n.*

ad·ap·ta·tion (ad′əp·tā′shən) *n.* **1.** The act of adapting or the state of being adapted. **2.** Anything produced by adapting. **— ad′ap·ta′tion·al** *adj.* **— ad′ap·ta′tion·al·ly** *adv.*

a·dapt·er (ə·dap′tər) *n.* **1.** A person or thing that adapts. **2.** *Mech.* **a** A device that connects parts not designed to fit together. **b** A device that extends or alters the function of an apparatus. Also **a·dap′tor.** Abbr. *ad.*

a·dap·tive (ə·dap′tiv) *adj.* Capable of, fit for, or manifesting adaptation. **— a·dap′tive·ly** *adv.* **— a·dap′tive·ness** *n.*

A·dar (ə·där′, ā′där) *n.* The sixth month of the Hebrew year. See (Hebrew) CALENDAR.

add (ad) *v.t.* **1.** To join or unite, so as to increase the importance, size, quantity, or scope: with *to.* **2.** To find the sum of, as a column of figures. **3.** To say or write further.

— *v.i.* **4.** To make or be an addition: with *to.* **5.** To perform the arithmetical process of addition. — **to add up 1.** To accumulate to a total. **2.** *Informal* To make sense. [< L *ad-* to + *dare* to give, put] — **add′a·ble** or **add′i·ble** *adj.*

— **Syn. 1.** *Add* denotes the joining of one thing to another to increase it. To *append* is to add something supplemental; *annex* indicates that the addition is subordinate, and often remains distinct. Compare INCREASE.

ad·dend (ad′ənd, ə·dend′) *n. Math.* A quantity or number that is to be added to another.

ad·den·dum (ə·den′dəm) *n. pl.* **·da** (-də) **1.** A thing added, or to be added. **2.** A supplement, as to a book; appendix. [< L, neut. gerundive of *addere* to add]

ad·der (ad′ər) *n.* **1.** A viper, esp. the common European viper. **2.** Any of various other snakes, as the puff adder. [OE *næ̅dre* (*a nadder* in ME becoming *an adder*)]

ad·der's-tongue (ad′ərz·tung′) *n.* **1.** A fern with a narrow spike. **2.** The dogtooth violet.

ad·dict (*v.* ə·dikt′; *n.* ad′ikt) *v.t.* To apply or devote (oneself) habitually: with *to.* — *n.* One who is given to some habit, esp. to the use of narcotic drugs. [< L *ad-* to + *dicere* to say] — **ad·dic′tion, ad·dict′ed·ness** *n.*

ad·dict·ed (ə·dik′tid) *adj.* Given over to a pursuit, practice, or habit: with *to*: *addicted* to drugs.

— **Syn.** *Addicted* suggests a pathological weakness; *given,* a tendency or usual practice. Both words may apply to good or bad things, but usually to bad: *addicted* to alcohol, *given* to lying.

ad·di·tion (ə·dish′ən) *n.* **1.** The act of adding. **2.** That which is added. **3.** The uniting of two or more quantities in one sum. — **ad·di′tion·al** *adj.* — **ad·di′tion·al·ly** *adv.*

ad·di·tive (ad′ə·tiv) *n.* Something added or to be added to a product or device. — *adj.* That is to be added; serving or tending to increase. — **ad′di·tive·ly** *adv.*

ad·dle (ad′l) *v.t. & v.i.* **·dled, ·dling 1.** To become or cause to become confused. **2.** To spoil, as eggs. — *adj.* **1.** Confused; mixed up: now generally in compounds: *addlepated.* **2.** Spoiled, as eggs; rotten. [OE *adela* liquid filth]

ad·dle·brained (ad′l·brānd′) *adj.* Confused; mixed up. Also **ad′dle·head′ed, ad′dle·pat′ed, ad′dle·wit′ted.**

ad·dress (ə·dres′; *for n. defs. 2, 3, also* ad′res) *v.t.* **·dressed, ·dress·ing 1.** To speak to. **2.** To deliver a set discourse to. **3.** To direct, as spoken or written words, to the attention of: with *to*: to *address* prayers to God. **4.** To devote the energy or force of (oneself): with *to*: to *address* oneself to a task. **5.** To mark with a destination, as a letter. **6.** To consign, as a cargo to a merchant. **7.** To aim or direct. **8.** To pay court to, as a lover; woo. **9.** To assume a preparatory stance toward (a golf ball, etc.). — *n.* **1.** A set or formal discourse. **2.** The writing on an envelope, etc., indicating its destination. **3.** The name, place, residence, etc., of a person. **4.** The manner of a person; bearing. **5.** *Chiefly pl.* Any courteous or devoted attention; wooing. **6.** Adroitness; tact. [< OF < L *ad-* to + *directus* straight] — **ad·dress′er, ad·dress′or** *n.*

ad·dress·ee (ad′res·ē′, ə·dres′ē′) *n.* One to whom mail, etc., is addressed.

ad·duce (ə·do͞os′, ə·dyo͞os′) *v.t.* **·duced, ·duc·ing** To present for proof or consideration, as an example; cite; allege. [< L *ad-* to + *ducere* to lead] — **ad·duce′a·ble** or **ad·duc′i·ble** *adj.*

ad·duct (ə·dukt′) *v.t. Physiol.* To draw toward the axis: said of muscles. — **ad·duc′tion** *n.* — **ad·duc′tive** *adj.*

ad·duc·tor (ə·duk′tər) *n.* An adducting muscle.

-ade[1] *suffix of nouns* **1.** Act or action: *cannonade.* **2.** A person or group concerned in an action or process: *cavalcade.* **3.** That which is produced by an action or process: *pomade.* **4.** A beverage made with or containing a fruit juice: *lemonade.* [< F < L *-ata,* fem. pp. ending]

-ade[2] *suffix of nouns* Relating to; pertaining to: *decade.* See -AD[1]. [< F *-ade* < Gk. *-as, -ados*]

adeno- *combining form* Gland. Also, before vowels, **aden-.** [< Gk. *adēn* gland]

ad·e·noid (ad′ə·noid) *adj.* Of or like a gland; glandular. Also **ad′e·noi′dal.** — *n. Usually pl. Pathol.* An enlarged lymphoid growth behind the pharynx.

ADENOIDS (*a*)

ad·e·no·ma (ad′ə·nō′mə) *n. Pathol.* A tumor of glandular origin or structure. — **ad·e·nom·a·tous** (ad′ə·nom′ə·təs) *adj.*

a·dept (ə·dept′; *for n., also* ad′ept) *adj.* Highly skilled; proficient: an *adept* worker. — *n.* One fully skilled in any art; an expert. [< L < *ad-* to + *apisci* to get] — **a·dept′ly** *adv.* — **a·dept′ness** *n.*

ad·e·quate (ad′ə·kwit) *adj.* **1.** Equal to what is required; fully sufficient. **2.** Barely sufficient. [< L < *ad-* to + *aequus* equal] — **ad′e·qua·cy** *n.* — **ad′e·quate·ness** *n.* — **ad′e·quate·ly** *adv.*

— **Syn. 1.** *Adequate* is applied to ability or power; *sufficient,* to quantity or number. A man is *adequate* to a situation; a supply is *sufficient* for a need. A thing is *satisfactory* if it measures up, more or less; it is *equal* if it is exactly commensurate. The connotation of these terms varies widely in contexts. An actor called *adequate* is usually regarded as mediocre. A *sufficient* reason may range from the flimsiest pretext to the surest demonstration. *Satisfactory* is a term in many grading systems, varying from passing to good.

ad·here (ad·hir′) *v.i.* **·hered, ·her·ing 1.** To stick fast or together. **2.** To be attached or devoted to a party or faith. **3.** To follow closely or without deviation. [< L < *ad-* to + *haerere* to stick] — **ad·her′ence** *n.* — **ad·her′er** *n.*

ad·her·ent (ad·hir′ənt) *adj.* Clinging or sticking fast. — *n.* One who is devoted or attached, as to a cause or leader; a follower. — **ad·her′ent·ly** *adv.*

— **Syn.** (noun) *Adherent* is the weakest term. A *follower* is more fervid in his attachment. A *disciple* has a pupil-teacher relationship with the one he follows. A *supporter* is one who aids in any way, while a *partisan* is militant in his support.

ad·he·sion (ad·hē′zhən) *n.* **1.** The act of adhering, or the state of being joined. **2.** Firm attachment, as to a cause; fidelity. **3.** *Physics* The binding force exerted by molecules of unlike substances in contact: distinguished from *cohesion.* **4.** *Med.* Abnormal surface union of dissimilar tissues as a result of inflammation, etc. [See ADHERE.]

ad·he·sive (ad·hē′siv) *adj.* **1.** Tending to adhere; sticky. **2.** Prepared to adhere; gummed. — *n.* A substance that causes adhesion. — **ad·he′sive·ly** *adv.* — **ad·he′sive·ness** *n.*

adhesive tape A piece or strip of fabric coated with adhesive material, used for bandages, dressings, etc.

ad hoc (ad hok′) *Latin* For this purpose.

ad·i·a·bat·ic (ad′ē·ə·bat′ik, ā′dē·ə-) *adj. Physics* Pertaining to a thermodynamic system in which changes are effected without gain or loss of heat. [< Gk. < *a-* not + *dia* through + *bainein* to go + -IC]

a·dieu (ə·do͞o′, ə·dyo͞o′; *Fr.* à·dyœ′) *n. pl.* **a·dieus,** *Fr.* **adieux** (à·dyœ′) A farewell. — *interj.* Good-by; farewell: literally, to God (I commend you). [< F]

ad in·fi·ni·tum (ad in′fə·nī′təm) *Latin* Endlessly; forever.

ad in·ter·im (ad in′tə·rim) *Latin* In the meantime.

a·di·os (ä′dē·ōs′, ad′ē·ōs′; *Sp.* ä·thyōs′) *interj.* Farewell; good-by: literally, to God (I commend you). [< Sp.]

ad·i·pose (ad′ə·pōs) *adj.* Of or pertaining to fat; fatty: also **ad·i·pous** (ad′ə·pəs). — *n.* Fat. [< NL < L *adeps, adipis* fat] — **ad′i·pose′ness, ad·i·pos·i·ty** (ad′ə·pos′ə·tē) *n.*

ad·ja·cen·cy (ə·jā′sən·sē) *n. pl.* **·cies 1.** The state of being adjacent; contiguity. **2.** That which is adjacent.

ad·ja·cent (ə·jā′sənt) *adj.* Lying near or close at hand; adjoining; contiguous. Abbr. *adj.* [< L < *ad-* near + *jacere* to lie] — **ad·ja′cent·ly** *adv.*

adjacent angle *Geom.* An angle having a common side with another angle and the same vertex.

ad·jec·tive (aj′ik·tiv) *n. Gram.* Any of a class of words used to limit or qualify a noun: one of the eight traditional parts of speech. — *adj. Gram.* Functioning as an adjective; depending upon or standing in adjunct relation to a noun. Abbr. *a., adj.* [< L *adjicere* to add to < *ad-* to + *jacere* to throw] — **ad·jec·ti·val** (aj′ik·tī′vəl, aj′ik·ti·vəl) *adj.* — **ad′jec·ti′val·ly** *adv.*

adjective clause *Gram.* A dependent clause usually introduced by a relative pronoun and qualifying its antecedent, as *who painted my house* in *the man who painted my house*: also called *relative clause.* Also **adjectival clause.**

ad·join (ə·join′) *v.t.* **1.** To be next to; border upon. **2.** To join to; append; unite: with *to.* — *v.i.* **3.** To lie close together; be in contact. [< OF < L < *ad-* to + *jungere* to join]

ad·join·ing (ə·joi′ning) *adj.* Lying next; contiguous.

ad·journ (ə·jûrn′) *v.t.* **1.** To put off to another day or place, as a meeting or session; postpone. — *v.i.* **2.** To postpone or suspend proceedings for a specified time. **3.** *Informal* To move or go to another place. — **Syn.** See POSTPONE. [< OF < LL < L *ad-* to + *diurnus* daily < *dies* day] — **ad·journ′ment** *n.*

ad·judge (ə·juj′) *v.t.* **·judged, ·judg·ing 1.** To determine or decide judicially, as a case. **2.** To pronounce or order by law: His testimony was *adjudged* perjury. **3.** To condemn or sentence: with *to.* **4.** To award by law, as damages. [< OF < L < *ad-* to + *judicare* to judge]

ad·ju·di·cate (ə·jo͞o′də·kāt) *v.* **·cat·ed, ·cat·ing** *v.t.* **1.** To determine judicially, as a case; adjudge. — *v.i.* **2.** To act as a judge. — **ad·ju′di·ca′tion** *n.* — **ad·ju′di·ca′tor** *n.*

ad·junct (aj′ungkt) *n.* **1.** Something joined to something else, but in an auxiliary or subordinate position. **2.** A helper; assistant. **3.** *Gram.* A modifier. **4.** *Logic* Any nonessential quality of a thing. — *adj.* Joined subordinately; auxiliary. [See ADJOIN.] — **ad·junc·tive** (ə·jungk′tiv) *adj.* — **ad·junc′tive·ly** *adv.*

ad·jure (ə·jo͝or′) *v.t.* **·jured, ·jur·ing 1.** To charge or entreat solemnly, as under oath or penalty. **2.** To appeal to earnestly. [< L < *ad-* to + *jurare* to swear] — **ad·ju·ra·tion** (aj′o͞o·rā′shən) *n.* — **ad·jur·a·to·ry** (ə·jo͝or′ə·tôr′ē, -tō′rē) *adj.* — **ad·jur′er** or **ad·ju′ror** *n.*

ad·just (ə·just′) *v.t.* **1.** To arrange so as to fit or match. **2.** To harmonize or compose, as differences. **3.** To regulate or make accurate. **4.** To determine the amount to be paid in settlement of (an insurance claim). **5.** To arrange in order. — *v.i.* **6.** To adapt oneself; conform, as to a new environ ient. [< OF < L *ad-* to + *juxta* near; refashioned on F *juste* ight < L *justus*] — **ad·just′a·ble** *adj.* — **ad·just′er** or **.d·jus′tor** *n.* — **ad·jus′tive** *adj.*

.·just·ment (ə·just′mənt) *n.* **1.** The act of adjusting or he state of being adjusted. **2.** An instrument or means of .djusting. **3.** The amount to be paid in settling a claim.

.·ju·tant (aj′ōō·tənt) *n.* **1.** *Mil.* A staff officer who assists . commanding officer in administrative duties. Abbr. *adj.* :. A carrion-eating East Indian stork: also called *marabou:* .lso **adjutant stork, adjutant crane.** [< L *adjutare* to ssist] — **ad′ju·tan·cy, ad′ju·tant·ship** *n.*

ljutant general *pl.* **adjutants general** The adjutant of a ıilitary unit having a general staff. — **The Adjutant Gen·ral** The major general in charge of the administrative ıranch of the United States Army.

l-lib (ad′lib′) *Informal v.t. & v.i.* **-libbed, -lib·bing** To im·rovise, as words or gestures not called for in the script. — :. An instance of this. [< AD LIBITUM]

l lib·i·tum (ad lib′ə·təm) **1.** *Latin* As one pleases. **2.** *Ausic* Freely: a direction indicating that a section may be ılayed as the performer wishes.

l·meas·ure (ad·mezh′ər) *v.t.* **·ured, ·ur·ing** To apportion. < OF < LL < *ad-* to + *mensurare* to measure] — **ad·ıeas′ur·er** *n.* — **ad·meas′ure·ment** *n.*

l·min·is·ter (ad·min′is·tər) *v.t.* **1.** To have the charge or irection of; manage. **2.** To supply or provide with; apply, s medicine or treatment. **3.** To inflict; mete out; dispense. *. Law* To act as executor or trustee of. **5.** To tender, as an ıath. — *v.i.* **6.** To contribute help; minister: with *to.* **7.** 'o carry out the functions of an administrator. [< OF < L < *ad-* to + *ministrare* to serve] — **ad·min·is·te·ri·al** (ad·ıin′is·tir′ē·əl) *adj.* — **ad·min′is·tra·ble** *adj.*

l·min·is·trate (ad·min′is·trāt) *v.t.* **·trat·ed, ·trat·ing** To dminister.

l·min·is·tra·tion (ad·min′is·trā′shən) *n.* **1.** The act of ad·ıinistering, or the state of being administered. **2.** The ex·cutive personnel of a government, institution, etc.: also, heir policies. **3.** The term of office of such a government. *. Law* The legal management of an estate.

l·min·is·tra·tive (ad·min′is·trā′tiv) *adj.* Pertaining to dministration; executive. — **ad·min′is·tra′tive·ly** *adv.*

l·min·is·tra·tor (ad·min′is·trā′tər) *n.* **1.** One who admin·sters something; an executive. **2.** *Law* One commissioned y a competent court to administer the personal property of deceased or incompetent person. [< L] — **ad·min′is·ra′tor·ship** *n.*

l·min·is·tra·trix (ad·min′is·trā′triks) *n.* *pl.* **·tra·trix·es** r **·tra·tri·ces** (-trā′trə·sēz, -trə·trī′sēz) A woman adminis·rator. Also **ad·min·is·tra′tress.**

l·mi·ra·ble (ad′mər·ə·bəl) *adj.* Worthy of admiration; ex·'ellent. — **ad′mi·ra·ble·ness, ad′mi·ra·bil′i·ty** *n.* — **ad′mi·a·bly** *adv.*

l·mi·ral (ad′mər·əl) *n.* **1.** The supreme commander of a ıavy or fleet. **2.** In the U.S. Navy and Royal Canadian Navy, an officer of the next to highest rank, equivalent to a eneral; also, loosely, a rear admiral or a vice admiral. [<)F < Arabic *amīr-al* commander of the]

dmiral of the Fleet The highest rank in the U.S. and Royal Canadian Navies, corresponding to General of the ırmy or Field Marshal. Also *Fleet Admiral.*

l·mi·ral·ty (ad′mər·əl·tē) *n.* *pl.* **·ties** **1.** The office or unctions of an admiral. **2.** *Law* Maritime law or courts.

d·mi·ral·ty (ad′mər·əl·tē) *n.* **1.** A department of the British government having charge of naval affairs. **2.** The uilding in London housing this department.

l·mi·ra·tion (ad′mə·rā′shən) *n.* **1.** A feeling of wonder nd approbation, as at the sight of anything rare, excellent, r sublime. **2.** High esteem. **3.** That which is admired.

l·mire (ad·mīr′) *v.* **·mired, ·mir·ing** *v.t.* **1.** To regard with vonder, pleasure, and approbation. **2.** To have respect or steem for. — *v.i.* **3.** To feel or express admiration. [< F < L < *ad-* at + *mirari* to wonder] — **ad·mir′er** *n.* — **ad·ıir′ing** *adj.* — **ad·mir′ing·ly** *adv.*

l·mis·si·ble (ad·mis′ə·bəl) *adj.* **1.** Worthy of being con·idered; allowable. **2.** Such as may be admitted. — **ad·ıis′si·bil′i·ty, ad·mis′si·ble·ness** *n.* — **ad·mis′si·bly** *adv.*

l·mis·sion (ad·mish′ən) *n.* **1.** The act of admitting, or the tate of being admitted. **2.** Authority to enter. **3.** An en·rance fee. **4.** A confession. **5.** Anything conceded.

l·mis·sive (ad·mis′iv) *adj.* Characterized by, implying, r granting admission. Also **ad·mis·so·ry** (ad·mis′ər·ē).

l·mit (ad·mit′) *v.* **·mit·ted, ·mit·ting** *v.t.* **1.** To allow to nter. **2.** To be the means or channel of admission to; let in. **.** To allow to join. **4.** To have room for; contain. **5.** To eave room for; permit: His impatience *admits* no delay. **6.** 'o concede or grant as valid. **7.** To acknowledge or avow. — *v.i.* **8.** To afford possibility or opportunity: This problem *dmits* of several solutions. **9.** To afford entrance; open on: with *to*: This gate *admits* to the garden. — **Syn.** See CONFESS. [< OF < L < *ad-* to + *mittere* to send]

ad·mit·tance (ad·mit′ns) *n.* **1.** The act of admitting, or the state or fact of being admitted; entrance. **2.** Right or permission to enter. **3.** Actual entrance; admission. **4.** *Electr.* The ability of a circuit to carry an alternating current, combining the effects of conductance and susceptance.

ad·mit·ted·ly (ad·mit′id·lē) *adv.* By admission; confessedly.

ad·mix (ad·miks′) *v.t. & v.i.* **·mixed** or **·mixt, ·mix·ing** To mingle or mix with something else. [ME < L *ad-* to + *miscere* to mix]

ad·mix·ture (ad·miks′chər) *n.* **1.** The act of mixing, or the state of being mixed. **2.** Anything added in mixing.

ad·mon·ish (ad·mon′ish) *v.t.* **1.** To administer mild reproof to. **2.** To caution against danger or error; warn. **3.** To charge authoritatively; exhort; urge. [< OF < LL < L < *ad-* to + *monere* to warn] — **ad·mon′ish·er** *n.*

ad·mo·ni·tion (ad′mə·nish′ən) *n.* **1.** The act of admonishing. **2.** A gentle reproof. Also **ad·mon′ish·ment.**

ad·mon·i·tor (ad·mon′ə·tər) *n.* One who admonishes. [< L] — **ad·mon·i·to·ry** (ad·mon′ə·tôr′ē, -tō′rē) *adj.*

ad nau·se·am (ad nô′zē·əm, -sē-, -zhē-, -shē-; äd) *Latin* To the point of nausea or disgust.

a·do (ə·dōō′) *n.* Activity; bustle; fuss. [ME *at do* to do]

a·do·be (ə·dō′bē) *n.* **1.** An unburnt, sun-dried brick. **2.** The mixed earth or sandy, calcareous clay of which such bricks are made. **3.** A structure made of such bricks. [< Sp.]

ad·o·les·cence (ad′ə·les′əns) *n.* **1.** The period of growth from puberty to adulthood. **2.** The quality or condition of being adolescent. Also **ad′o·les′cen·cy.**

ad·o·les·cent (ad′ə·les′ənt) *adj.* **1.** Approaching adulthood. **2.** Characteristic of or pertaining to youth. — *n.* A person in the period of adolescence. — **Syn.** See YOUTHFUL. [< L < *ad-* to + *alescere* to grow]

A·don·is (ə·don′is, ə·dō′nis) In Greek mythology, a youth beloved by Aphrodite for his beauty and killed by a wild boar. — *n.* Any man of rare beauty.

a·dopt (ə·dopt′) *v.t.* **1.** To take into some new relationship, as that of son, heir, etc. **2.** To take into one's family or as one's child by legal measures. **3.** To take and follow as one's own, as a course of action. **4.** To take up from someone else and use as one's own. **5.** To vote to accept, as a motion. [< MF < L < *ad-* to + *optare* to choose] — **a·dopt′a·ble** *adj.* — **a·dopt′er** *n.* — **a·dop′tion** *n.*

a·dop·tive (ə·dop′tiv) *adj.* **1.** Of or characterized by adoption. **2.** Related by adoption. — **a·dop′tive·ly** *adv.*

a·dor·a·ble (ə·dôr′ə·bəl, ə·dōr′-) *adj.* **1.** Worthy of adoration. **2.** *Informal* Delightful; lovable. — **a·dor′a·ble·ness, a·dor′a·bil′i·ty** *n.* — **a·dor′a·bly** *adv.*

ad·o·ra·tion (ad′ə·rā′shən) *n.* **1.** The act of adoring, as in worship. **2.** A feeling of profound admiration and devotion. **3.** An act of homage to a person or object.

a·dore (ə·dôr′, ə·dōr′) *v.* **a·dored, a·dor·ing** *v.t.* **1.** To render divine honors to; worship as divine. **2.** To love or honor with intense devotion. **3.** *Informal* To like especially. — *v.i.* **4.** To worship. — **Syn.** See VENERATE. [< OF < L < *ad-* to + *orare* to speak, pray] — **a·dor′er** *n.*

a·dorn (ə·dôrn′) *v.t.* **1.** To increase the beauty of; enhance. **2.** To furnish or decorate with or as with ornaments. [< OF < L < *ad-* to + *ornare* to deck out] — **a·dorn′er** *n.* — **a·dorn′ment** *n.*

ad·re·nal (ə·drē′nəl) *Physiol.* *n.* An adrenal gland. — *adj.* **1.** Near or upon the kidneys. **2.** Of or from the adrenal glands. [< AD- + L *renes* kidneys + -AL[3]]

adrenal gland One of a pair of small ductless glands situated on the kidneys of most vertebrates, in man secreting epinephrine and cortin: also called *suprarenal gland.*

Ad·ren·a·lin (ə·dren′ə·lin) *n.* Proprietary name for a brand of epinephrine. Also **ad·ren·a·lin** (ə·dren′ə·lin).

ad·re·no·cor·ti·co·tro·pic hormone (ə·drē′nō·kôr′ti·kō·trō′pik) *Physiol.* ACTH.

A·dri·at·ic (ā′drē·at′ik) *adj.* Of or pertaining to the Adriatic Sea or to the inhabitants of its coastal regions.

a·drift (ə·drift′) *adv. & adj.* Without moorings; drifting.

a·droit (ə·droit′) *adj.* Skillful; expert. [< F < *à* to + *droit* right] — **a·droit′ly** *adv.* — **a·droit′ness** *n.*

ad·sorb (ad·sôrb′, -zôrb′) *v.t.* *Chem.* To condense and hold by adsorption: distinguished from *absorb.* [< AD- + L *sorbere* to suck in] — **ad·sor′bent** *n. & adj.*

ad·sorp·tion (ad·sôrp′shən, -zôrp′-) *n.* *Chem.* The action of a body, as charcoal, in condensing and holding a gas or soluble substance upon its surface. — **ad·sorp′tive** *adj.*

ad·u·late (aj′ōō·lāt) *v.t.* **·lat·ed, ·lat·ing** To flatter or praise extravagantly. [< L *adulari* to fawn] — **ad′u·la′tion** *n.* — **ad′u·la′tor** *n.* — **ad·u·la·to·ry** (aj′ōō·lə·tôr′ē, -tō′rē) *adj.*

a·dult (ə·dult′, ad′ult) *n.* **1.** A person who has attained the age of maturity or legal majority. **2.** *Biol.* A fully developed animal or plant. — *adj.* **1.** Pertaining to mature life;

full-grown. **2.** Of or for mature people. [< L < *ad-* to + *alescere* to grow] **— a·dult′ness** *n.* **— a·dult′hood** *n.*

a·dul·ter·ant (ə·dul′tər·ənt) *n.* An adulterating substance. — *adj.* Adulterating.

a·dul·ter·ate (ə·dul′tə·rāt; *for adj., also* ə·dul′tər·it) *v.t.* **·at·ed, ·at·ing** To make impure or inferior by admixture of other ingredients; corrupt. — *adj.* Corrupted; debased. [< L < *ad-* to + *alter* other, different] **— a·dul′ter·a′tion** *n.* **— a·dul′ter·a′tor** *n.*

a·dul·ter·er (ə·dul′tər·ər) *n.* One who commits adultery. **— a·dul′ter·ess** (-tər·is, -tris) *n. fem.*

a·dul·ter·ous (ə·dul′tər·əs) *adj.* Of, pertaining to, or given to adultery; illicit. **— a·dul′ter·ous·ly** *adv.*

a·dul·ter·y (ə·dul′tər·ē) *n. pl.* **·ter·ies** The voluntary sexual intercourse of a married person with someone not the spouse; unfaithfulness. [< L *adulterium*]

ad·um·brate (ad·um′brāt, ə·dum′-) *v.t.* **·brat·ed, ·brat·ing** **1.** To represent the mere shadow of; outline sketchily. **2.** To overshadow; darken. [< L < *ad-* to + *umbrare* to shade] **— ad′um·bra′tion** *n.* **— ad·um′bra·tive** *adj.*

ad va·lo·rem (ad və·lôr′əm, -lō′rəm) *Latin* According or in proportion to the value. Abbr. *adv., ad val.*

ad·vance (ad·vans′, -väns′) *v.* **·vanced, ·vanc·ing** *v.t.* **1.** To move or cause to go forward or upward. **2.** To offer; propose. **3.** To further; promote. **4.** To put in a better or more advantageous rank, position, or situation. **5.** To make occur earlier; accelerate. **6.** To raise (a rate, price, etc.). **7.** To pay, as money or interest, before legally due. **8.** To lend, as money. **9.** *Law* To provide an advancement for. — *v.i.* **10.** To move or go forward. **11.** To make progress; rise or improve. — *adj.* **1.** Being before in time; early. **2.** Being or going before; in front. — *n.* **1.** The act of going forward; progress. **2.** Improvement; promotion. **3.** An increase or rise, as of prices. **4.** *pl.* Personal approaches; overtures. **5.** The supplying of goods, money, etc., on credit. **6.** The goods or money so supplied; a loan. **7.** The payment of money before it is legally due. **8.** *U.S.* The front or foremost part. Abbr. *adv.* **— in advance 1.** In front. **2.** Before due; beforehand. [ME < OF *avancier* < L < *ab-* away + *ante* before] **— ad·vanc′er** *n.*

ad·vanced (ad·vanst′, -vänst′) *adj.* **1.** In advance of others, as in progress or thought. **2.** In front; moved forward. **3.** At a late or forward stage, as of life, time, etc.

ad·vance·ment (ad·vans′mənt, -väns′-) *n.* **1.** The act of advancing, or the state of being advanced. **2.** Progression; promotion; preferment. **3.** An advance of property or money.

ad·van·tage (ad·van′tij, -vän′-) *n.* **1.** Any circumstance, state, or condition favoring success. **2.** Benefit or gain; profit. **3.** A better state or position; superiority. **4.** In tennis, the first point scored after deuce. **— to advantage** To good effect; favorably. **— to take advantage of 1.** To avail oneself of. **2.** To impose upon; use selfishly. — *v.t.* **·taged, ·tag·ing** To give advantage or profit to. [< OF < *avant* before < L *ab ante* from before]

ad·van·ta·geous (ad′vən·tā′jəs) *adj.* Affording advantage; profitable; favorable; beneficial. **— ad′van·ta′geous·ly** *adv.* **— ad′van·ta′geous·ness** *n.*

ad·vec·tion (ad·vek′shən) *n.* *Meteorol.* Heat transfer by the horizontal motion of air. [< L < *ad-* to + *vehere* to carry] **— ad·vec′tive** *adj.*

ad·vent (ad′vent) *n.* A coming or arrival. [< L < *ad-* to + *venire* to come]

Ad·vent (ad′vent) *n.* **1.** The birth of Christ. **2.** The Second Advent. **3.** The season prior to Christmas.

Ad·vent·ist (ad′ven·tist, ad·ven′-) *n.* A member of a denomination that believes the Second Advent is imminent. The largest U.S. Adventist bodies are the **Advent Christian Church** and the **Seventh-Day Adventists.**

ad·ven·ti·tious (ad′ven·tish′əs) *adj.* Not inherent; accidentally acquired; extrinsic. **— ad′ven·ti′tious·ly** *adv.* **— ad′ven·ti′tious·ness** *n.*

ad·ven·tive (ad·ven′tiv) *adj.* Occurring away from the natural habitat; exotic.

ad·ven·ture (ad·ven′chər) *n.* **1.** A hazardous or perilous undertaking. **2.** A stirring or thrilling experience. **3.** Risky or exciting activity. **4.** A commercial venture; speculation. — *v.* **·tured, ·tur·ing** *v.t.* **1.** To venture upon; take the chance of. — *v.i.* **2.** To venture upon daring or dangerous undertakings. [< OF < L *adventura* about to happen]

ad·ven·tur·er (ad·ven′chər·ər) *n.* **1.** One who seeks after or takes part in adventures. **2.** One who seeks his fortune in war; a soldier of fortune. **3.** A speculator in commerce. **4.** A person who seeks advancement by questionable means. **— ad·ven′tur·ess** *n. fem.*

ad·ven·tur·ous (ad·ven′chər·əs) *adj.* **1.** Disposed to seek adventures or take risks; venturesome. Also **ad·ven′ture·some** (-səm). **2.** Attended with risk; hazardous. **— ad·ven′tur·ous·ly** *adv.* **— ad·ven′tur·ous·ness** *n.*

ad·verb (ad′vûrb) *n.* *Gram.* Any of a class of words used to modify the meaning of a verb, adjective, or other adverb, in regard to time, place, manner, means, cause, degree, etc. [< L < *ad-* to + *verbum* verb] **— ad·ver′bi·al** *adj.* **— ad·ver′bi·al·ly** *adv.*

adverb clause *Gram.* A dependent clause that functio[n]s as an adverb in a sentence, as *when the guests arrive* in *W[e] will eat when the guests arrive*: also **adverbial clause.**

ad·ver·sar·y (ad′vər·ser′ē) *n. pl.* **·sar·ies** One actively ho[s]tile to another; an opponent; enemy. **— Syn.** See ENEM[Y].

ad·ver·sa·tive (ad·vûr′sə·tiv) *adj.* Expressing oppositi[on] or antithesis. — *n.* An antithetic word or proposition. [< L *adversatus* opposite] **— ad·ver′sa·tive·ly** *adv.*

ad·verse (ad·vûrs′, ad′vûrs) *adj.* **1.** Opposed; antagonisti[c]. **2.** Unpropitious; detrimental. **3.** Opposite. [< L < *a[d-]* to + *vertere* to turn] **— ad·verse′ly** *adv.* **— ad·verse′ness** *n.*

ad·ver·si·ty (ad·vûr′sə·tē) *n. pl.* **·ties** **1.** A condition [of] hardship or affliction. **2.** *Often pl.* A misfortune.

ad·vert (ad·vûrt′) *v.i.* To call attention; refer: with *to.* [< L *advertere* < *ad-* to + *vertere* to turn]

ad·ver·tent (ad·vûr′tənt) *adj.* Giving attention; heedfu[l]. **— ad·ver′tence, ad·ver′ten·cy** *n.* **— ad·ver′tent·ly** *adv.*

ad·ver·tise (ad′vər·tīz, ad′vər·tīz′) *v.* **·tised, ·tis·ing** *v.t.* [1.] To make known by public notice; proclaim the qualities [of], as by publication or broadcasting, generally in order to se[ll]. — *v.i.* **2.** To inquire by public notice, as in a newspaper: [to] *advertise* for a house. **3.** To distribute or publish advertise[]ments. Also **ad′ver·tize.** [< MF < L *advertere* to dire[ct] one's attention to] **— ad′ver·tis′er** *n.*

ad·ver·tise·ment (ad′vər·tīz′mənt, ad·vûr′tis·mənt, -tiz-) A public notice, as in a newspaper or on a radio progra[m]. Also **ad′ver·tize′ment.** Abbr. *ad., adv., advt.*

ad·ver·tis·ing (ad′vər·tī′zing) *n.* **1.** Advertisements co[l]lectively. **2.** The business of writing and publicizing a[d]vertisements. Also **ad′ver·tiz′ing.**

ad·vice (ad·vīs′) *n.* **1.** Counsel given to encourage or di[s]suade; suggestion. **2.** *Often pl.* Information; notificatio[n]. [< OF < LL < L *ad-* to + *videre* to see]

ad·vis·a·ble (ad·vī′zə·bəl) *adj.* Proper to be advised or re[c]ommended; sensible. **— Syn.** See EXPEDIENT. **— ad·vis′a·bil′i·ty, ad·vis′a·ble·ness** *n.* **— ad·vis′a·bly** *adv.*

ad·vise (ad·vīz′) *v.* **·vised, ·vis·ing** *v.t.* **1.** To give advice t[o]; counsel. **2.** To recommend. **3.** To notify; inform, as of [a] transaction: with *of.* — *v.i.* **4.** To take counsel: with *wit[h].* **5.** To give advice. Abbr. *adv.* [< OF < LL < L *ad-* to + *videre* to see]

ad·vised (ad·vīzd′) *adj.* **1.** Planned; deliberate: chiefly i[n] *ill-advised, well-advised.*

ad·vis·ed·ly (ad·vī′zid·lē) *adv.* With forethought or advic[e].

ad·vise·ment (ad·vīz′mənt) *n.* Consultation; deliberatio[n].

ad·vis·er (ad·vī′zər) *n.* **1.** One who advises. **2.** A teach[er] in a school or college who counsels students about the[ir] studies, careers, etc. Also **ad·vi′sor.**

ad·vi·so·ry (ad·vī′zər·ē) *adj.* **1.** Having power to advise. **2.** Containing or given as advice; not mandatory.

ad·vo·ca·cy (ad′və·kə·sē) *n.* The act of advocating or plea[d]ing a cause; vindication; defense.

ad·vo·cate (*v.* ad′və·kāt; *n.* ad′və·kit, -kāt) *v.t.* **·cat·ed, ·ca[t]·ing** To speak or write in favor of; defend; recommend. — [*n.*] **1.** One who pleads the cause of another; an intercessor. **2.** One who espouses or defends a cause by argument: an *a[d]vocate* of slavery. [< OF < L < *ad-* to + *vocare* to call] **— ad′vo·ca′tor** *n.* **— ad·voc·a·to·ry** (ad·vok′ə·tôr′ē, -tō′rē) *ad[j].*

adz (adz) *n.* A hand cutting tool with its blade at right a[n]gles to its handle and usually curved inward, used for dressing timber, etc. Also **adze.** [OE *adesa*]

ADZES *a* Sculptor's. *b* Cooper's. *c* Carpenter's.

ae- For those words not entered below see under E-.

æ 1. A ligature of Latin origin, equivalent to Greek *ai*: usually printed *ae.* It is sometimes retained in the spelling of Greek and Latin proper names and in certain scientific terms, but, in modern use, is generally reduced to *e.* **2.** A character in Old English, representing the sound of *a* in modern *hat.*

a·e·des (ā·ē′dēz) *n.* A mosquito that carries yellow fever: formerly called *stegomyia.* [< NL < Gk. *a-* not + *hēdys* sweet]

Ae·ge·an (i·jē′ən) *adj.* Of or pertaining to the Aege[an] Islands or the Aegean Sea.

Æ·gir (ē′jər, ā′jər) The Norse god of the sea. Also **Æ′ge[r].**

ae·gis (ē′jis) *n.* **1.** In Greek mythology, the breastplate [of] Zeus and Athena. **2.** Any shield or armor. **3.** A protecti[ng] influence. Also spelled *egis.* [< Gk. *aigis* goatskin]

-aemia See -EMIA.

Ae·ne·as (i·nē′əs) In classical legend, a Trojan warrior a[nd] hero of the *Aeneid.* After the sack of Troy he wandered f[or] seven years before reaching Latium.

Ae·ne·id (i·nē′id) A Latin epic poem by Vergil, narrating t[he] adventures of Aeneas.

ae·o·li·an (ē·ō′lē·ən) *adj.* Pertaining to or caused by t[he] winds; wind-borne: also spelled *eolian.*

eolian harp A stringed instrument so constructed as to ›roduce musical sounds when exposed to a current of air.

e·o·lus (ē′ə·ləs) In Greek mythology, the god of the winds.

›·on (ē′ən, ē′on), **ae·o·ni·an** (ē·ō′nē·ən) See EON, etc.

›r- Var. of AERO-.

›r·ate (âr′āt, ā′ə·rāt) *v.t.* **·at·ed, ·at·ing 1.** To supply or harge with air or gas. **2.** To purify by exposure to air. — **.er·a′tion** *n.* — **aer′a·tor** *n.*

›ri- Var. of AERO-.

›r·i·al (âr′ē·əl, ā·ir′ē·əl) *adj.* **1.** Of or in the air. **2.** Living r moving in the air. **3.** Extending into the air; lofty. **4.** ,ight as air; airy. **5.** Unsubstantial; intangible; imaginary. **.** Of, by, or pertaining to aircraft, or to flying. — *n.* An ntenna, as in television. [< L *aer* air] — **aer′i·al·ly** *adv.*

›r·i·al·ist (âr′ē·əl·ist, ā·ir′ē·əl-) *n.* One who performs on a ightrope, trapeze, etc.

›r·ie (âr′ē, ir′ē) *n.* **1.** The nest of a predatory bird, as the agle, on a crag. **2.** The brood or young of such a bird. **3.** . house or stronghold situated on a height. Also spelled *ery, eyrie, eyry.* [< Med.L < OF < L *area* open space]

›r·i·fy (âr′ə·fī, ā′ər·ə·fī) *v.t.* **·fied, ·fy·ing 1.** To aerate. **2.** 'o change into a gaseous form. — **aer′i·fi·ca′tion** *n.*

›ro- *combining form* **1.** Air; of the air. **2.** Of aircraft or ,ying. **3.** Gas; of gases. Also *aer-, aeri-.* [< Gk. *aēr* air]

›r·obe (âr′ōb, ā′ər·ōb) *n.* A microorganism that can live nly in air or free oxygen. [< AERO- + Gk. *bios* life] — **.er·o′bic** *adj.*

›r·o·drome (âr′ə·drōm, ā′ər·ə-) *n.* An airdrome.

›r·o·dy·nam·ics (âr′ō·dī·nam′iks, ā′ər·ō-) *n.pl.* (*construed s sing.*) The branch of physics that treats of the laws of moion of gases, under the influence of gravity and other orces. — **aer′o·dy·nam′ic** *adj.*

›r·o·gramme (âr′ə·gram, ā′ər·ə-) *n.* An international airnail letter consisting of a single folded sheet. [< Fr.]

›r·o·lite (âr′ə·līt, ā′ər·ə-) *n.* A meteorite containing more tone than iron. Also **aer′o·lith** (-lith). [< AERO- + Gk. *thos* stone] — **aer′o·lit′ic** (-lit′ik) *adj.*

›r·ol·o·gy (âr·ol′ə·jē, ā′ə·rol′-) *n. pl.* **·gies** The scientific tudy of the atmosphere and its phenomena. — **aer·o·log·ic** âr′ə·loj′ik, ā′ər·ə-) or **·i·cal** *adj.* — **aer·ol′o·gist** *n.*

›r·o·me·chan·ics (âr′ō·mə·kan′iks, ā′ər·ō-) *n.pl.* (*construed s sing.*) The science that treats of equilibrium and motion f air and gases. — **aer′o·me·chan′ic** *adj.* & *n.*

›r·o·naut (âr′ə·nôt, ā′ər·ə-) *n.* One who pilots a balloon r dirigible. [< F < Gk. *aēr* air + *nautēs* sailor]

›r·o·nau·tics (âr′ə·nô′tiks, ā′ər·ə-) *n.pl.* (*construed as sing.*) .. The science or art of navigating aircraft. **2.** That branch f engineering that deals with the design, construction, peration, and performance of aircraft. — **aer′o·nau′tic, .er′o·nau′ti·cal** *adj.*

›r·o·pause (âr′ə·pôz, ā′ər·ə-) *n.* *Meteorol.* The region of he atmosphere near outer space.

›r·o·phyte (âr′ə·fīt, ā′ər·ə-) *n.* An epiphyte.

›r·o·plane (âr′ə·plān, ā′ər·ə-) *n.* *Brit.* Airplane.

›r·o·sol (âr′ə·sōl, -sol, ā′ər·ə-) *n.* A suspension of solid or iquid particles in a gas.

›rosol bomb A small spraying can holding a liquid, as an nsecticide, etc., under gas pressure.

›r·o·space (âr′ō·spās, ā′ər·ō-) *n.* **1.** The earth's atmosphere nd outer space, considered as a single region in the operaion of spacecraft. **2.** The study of this region.

›rospace medicine The branch of medicine that deals vith conditions and disorders associated with space flight.

›r·o·sphere (âr′ə·sfir, ā′ər·ə-) *n.* The entire atmosphere onsidered as a single gaseous shell surrounding the earth.

›r·o·stat (âr′ə·stat, ā′ər·ə-) *n.* Any lighter-than-air craft, .s a balloon or dirigible. [< F < Gk. *aēr* air + *statos* standng] — **aer′o·stat′ic** or **·i·cal** *adj.*

›r·o·stat·ics (âr′ə·stat′iks, ā′ər·ə-) *n.pl.* (*construed as sing.*) 'he branch of physics that treats of the mechanical properies of air and gases in equilibrium.

›r·y (âr′ē, ir′ē) See AERIE.

es·cu·la·pi·us (es′kyə·lā′pē·əs) In Roman mythology, he god of medicine: identified with the Greek *Asclepius.* — **Aes′cu·la′pi·an** *adj.* & *n.*

:·sir (ā′sir, ē′-) *n. pl. of* **As** (äs) The gods of the Norse antheon collectively.

›s·thete (es′thēt), **aes·thet·ic** (es·thet′ik), etc. See ES-'HETE, etc.

›s·ti·val (es′tə·vəl, es·tī′-), **aes·ti·vate** (es′tə·vāt), etc. ›ee ESTIVAL, etc.

›·ther (ē′thər) See ETHER (defs. 3 and 4).

›·ti·ol·o·gy (ē′tē·ol′ə·jē) See ETIOLOGY.

f- Assimilated var. of AD-.

far (ə·fär′) *adv.* At, from, or to a distance; remotely.

f·fa·ble (af′ə·bəl) *adj.* Easy to approach and speak to; riendly; courteous. [< F < L < *ad-* to + *fari* to speak] — **af′fa·bil′i·ty, af′fa·ble·ness** *n.* — **af′fa·bly** *adv.*

af·fair (ə·fâr′) *n.* **1.** Anything done or to be done; business; concern. **2.** *pl.* Matters of business or concern. **3.** A thing or occurrence. **4.** A love affair. [< OF < L *ad* to + *facere* to do]

af·fect[1] (*v.* ə·fekt′; *n.* af′ekt) *v.t.* **1.** To act upon or have an effect upon; influence. **2.** To touch or move emotionally. **3.** To attack or attaint, as a part of the body. — *n.* *Psychol.* Emotion; feeling. [< L < *ad-* to + *facere* to do; noun < G *affekt*]

af·fect[2] (ə·fekt′) *v.t.* **1.** To show a preference for by wearing, using, etc.; fancy: to *affect* large hats. **2.** To imitate or assume: to *affect* a British accent. [< F < L *affectare* to aim at. See AFFECT[1].] — **af·fect′er** *n.*

af fec·ta·tion (af′ek·tā′shən) *n.* **1.** A studied pretense; display: with *of.* **2.** Artificiality of manner or behavior.

af·fec·ted[1] (ə·fek′tid) *adj.* **1.** Acted upon, as by a drug. **2.** Moved emotionally. **3.** Attacked, as by disease.

af·fect·ed[2] (ə·fek′tid) *adj.* **1.** Artificial; feigned. **2.** Showing affectation. [pp. of AFFECT[2]] — **af·fect′ed·ly** *adv.* — **af·fect′ed·ness** *n.*

af·fect·ing (ə·fek′ting) *adj.* Having power to move the feelings; touching; pathetic. — **af·fect′ing·ly** *adv.*

af·fec·tion (ə·fek′shən) *n.* **1.** Fond attachment or kind feeling. **2.** *Often pl.* A mental state brought about by any influence; an emotion or feeling. **3.** An abnormal state of the body; disease. **4.** The act of affecting or the state of being affected.

af·fec·tion·ate (ə·fek′shən·it) *adj.* Having or expressing affection; loving; fond. — **af·fec′tion·ate·ly** *adv.* — **af·fec′tion·ate·ness** *n.*

af·fer·ent (af′ər·ənt) *adj.* *Physiol.* Conducting inward, or toward the center, as nerves that transmit sensory stimuli to the central nervous system: opposed to *efferent.* [< L < *ad-* to + *ferre* to bear]

af·fi·ance (ə·fī′əns) *v.t.* **·anced, ·anc·ing** To promise in marriage; betroth. — *n.* A betrothal; pledge of faith. [< OF *afiance* trust, confidence] — **af·fi′an·cer** *n.*

af·fi·da·vit (af′ə·dā′vit) *n.* *Law* A sworn, written declaration, made before competent authority. — **Syn.** See TESTIMONY. [< Med.L, he has stated on oath]

af·fil·i·ate (*v.* ə·fil′ē·āt; *n.* ə·fil′ē·it) *v.* **·at·ed, ·at·ing** *v.t.* **1.** To associate or unite, as a member or branch to a larger or principal body: with *to* or *with.* **2.** To join or associate (oneself): with *with.* **3.** To determine the source or relations of. — *v.i.* **4.** To associate or ally oneself: with *with.* — *n.* An affiliated person, company, etc. [< L *affiliare* to adopt < *ad-* to + *filius* son] — **af·fil′i·a′tion** *n.*

af·fin·i·ty (ə·fin′ə·tē) *n. pl.* **·ties 1.** A natural attraction or inclination. **2.** Any close relation or agreement; kinship in general; similarity. **3.** Relationship by marriage. **4.** An attraction between certain persons, esp. of opposite sexes; also, the person exerting such attraction. **5.** *Chem.* The property by which differing chemical elements or groups of elements unite to form a new compound. [< L *affinis* adjacent, related < *ad-* to + *finis* end]

af·firm (ə·fûrm′) *v.t.* **1.** To declare or state positively. **2.** To confirm or ratify. — *v.i.* **3.** *Law* To make a formal judicial declaration, but not under oath. [< OF < L < *ad-* to + *firmare* to make firm] — **af·firm′a·ble** *adj.* — **af·firm′a·bly** *adv.* — **af·firm′ance** *n.* — **af·firm′ant** *adj* & *n.* — **af·firm′er** *n.*

af·fir·ma·tion (af′ər·mā′shən) *n.* **1.** The act of affirming; assertion. **2.** That which is affirmed or asserted. **3.** A solemn declaration made before a competent officer, in place of a judicial oath. — **Syn.** See OATH.

af·firm·a·tive (ə·fûr′mə·tiv) *adj.* **1.** Characterized by affirmation; asserting that the fact is so. **2.** Positive. Also **af·firm·a·to·ry** (ə·fûr′mə·tôr′ē, -tō′rē). — *adv.* Yes; that is so: a military usage. — *n.* **1.** A word or expression of affirmation or assent. **2.** The side in a debate that affirms the proposition debated. — **af·firm′a·tive·ly** *adv.*

af·fix (*v.* ə·fiks′; *n.* af′iks) *v.t.* **1.** To fix or attach; fasten; append. **2.** To connect with or lay upon, as blame, responsibility, etc. — *n.* **1.** That which is attached, appended, or added. **2.** A prefix, suffix, or infix. [< L *affigere* < *ad-* to + *figere* to fasten]

af·fla·tus (ə·flā′təs) *n.* Any creative inspiration or impulse. [< L < *ad-* to + *flare* to blow]

af·flict (ə·flikt′) *v.t.* To distress with continued suffering; trouble greatly. [< L < *ad-* to + *figere* to dash, strike] — **af·flict′er** *n.* — **af·flic′tive** *adj.* — **af·flic′tive·ly** *adv.*

af·flic·tion (ə·flik′shən) *n.* **1.** The state of being afflicted; sore distress of body or mind. **2.** A misfortune; calamity.

af·flu·ence (af′lo͞o·əns) *n.* Riches; wealth.

af·flu·ent (af′lo͞o·ənt) *adj.* **1.** Abounding; abundant. **2.** Wealthy; opulent. — *n.* A stream that flows into another. [< L < *ad-* to + *fluere* to flow] — **af′flu·ent·ly** *adv.*

af·ford (ə·fôrd′, ə·fōrd′) *v.t.* **1.** To have sufficient means for;

be able to meet the expense of. **2.** To incur without detriment. **3.** To spare. **4.** To provide, yield, or furnish. [OE *geforthian* to further, promote] — **af·ford′a·ble** *adj.*

af·fray (ə·frā′) *n.* A public brawl or fight; a disturbance of the peace. [< OF, *effrei, esfrei*]

af·fri·cate (af′ri·kit) *n. Phonet.* A sound consisting of a stop followed by the fricative release of breath at the point of contact, as *ch* in *match.* [< L < *ad-* against + *fricare* to rub] — **af·fric·a·tive** (ə·frik′ə·tiv) *n. & adj.*

af·front (ə·frunt′) *v.t.* **1.** To insult openly; treat with insolence. **2.** To confront in defiance; accost. — *n.* An open insult or indignity. — **Syn.** See OFFEND. [< OF < LL *affrontare* to strike against] — **af·front′er** *n.* — **af·fron′·tive** *adj.*

af·ghan (af′gən, -gan) *n.* A soft wool coverlet, knitted or crocheted, often in many-colored geometrical patterns.

Af·ghan (af′gən, -gan) *n.* A native of Afghanistan. — *adj.* Of or pertaining to Afghanistan, its inhabitants, etc.

a·field (ə·fēld′) *adv.* **1.** In or to the field; abroad. **2.** Off the track; astray.

a·fire (ə·fīr′) *adv. & adj.* On fire. [ME]

a·flame (ə·flām′) *adv. & adj.* Flaming; glowing.

a·float (ə·flōt′) *adv. & adj.* **1.** Floating. **2.** Not aground or ashore; at sea. **3.** In circulation: Rumors were *afloat.* **4.** Overflowed; flooded, as the deck of a ship. **5.** Adrift.

a·foot (ə·fo͝ot′) *adv.* **1.** On foot. **2.** In motion or progress; on the move; astir. [ME *on flote*]

a·fore·men·tioned (ə·fôr′men′shənd, ə·fōr′-) *adj.* Mentioned previously.

a·fore·said (ə·fôr′sed′, ə·fōr′-) *adj.* Mentioned before.

a·fore·thought (ə·fôr′thôt′, ə·fōr′-) *adj.* Intended beforehand: now chiefly in the phrase *malice aforethought.*

a·fore·time (ə·fôr′tīm′, ə·fōr′-) *adv.* At a previous time.

a·foul (ə·foul′) *adv. & adj.* In entanglement or collision; entangled. — **to run** (or **fall**) **afoul of** To become entangled with; get into difficulties with.

a·fraid (ə·frād′) *adj.* Filled with fear or apprehension; apprehensive; fearful: often used to soften an unpleasant statement: I'm *afraid* you're wrong. [Orig. pp. of AFFRAY]

a·fresh (ə·fresh′) *adv.* Once more; anew; again.

Af·ri·can (af′ri·kən) *adj.* Of or pertaining to Africa, or its inhabitants. — *n.* **1.** A native inhabitant of Africa. **2.** A member of one of the African peoples; a Negro or Negrito.

Af·ri·kaans (af′ri·käns′, -känz′) *n.* The Dutch dialect spoken in South Africa.

Af·ri·kan·er (af′ri·kä′nər) *n.* An Afrikaans-speaking South African of Dutch ancestry. Also **Af′ri·kan′der** (-kan′dər).

Afro- *combining form* Africa; African.

Af·ro-A·mer·i·can (af′rō·ə·mer′ə·kən) *adj.* Of or pertaining to Americans of black African descent. — *n.* An Afro-American person.

aft (aft, äft) *Naut. adj.* Of or near the stern of a vessel. — *adv.* At, toward, or near the stern. [OE *æftan* behind]

af·ter (af′tər, äf′-) *prep.* **1.** In the rear of; farther back than; following: He came *after* me. **2.** In search or pursuit of: Strive *after* wisdom. **3.** In relation to; concerning: to inquire *after* one's health. **4.** Subsequently to; at a later period than. **5.** In succession to; following repeatedly: day *after* day. **6.** As a result of; subsequently to and because of. **7.** Notwithstanding; subsequently to and in spite of: *After* the best endeavors, one may fail. **8.** Next below in order or importance: *after* the king in power. **9.** According to the nature, wishes, or customs of; in conformity with: a man *after* my own heart. **10.** In imitation of; in the manner of. **11.** In honor, remembrance, or observance of. **12.** *U.S.* Of time by the clock, past. — *adv.* **1.** In the rear; behind. **2.** At a later time; subsequently. — *adj.* **1.** Following in time or place; later; subsequent: In *after* years they lived as friends. **2.** *Naut.* Toward the stern; farther aft. — *conj.* Following the time that: *After* I went home, I ate. [OE *æfter*]

af·ter·birth (af′tər·bûrth′, äf′-) *n.* The placenta and fetal membranes expelled from the uterus after childbirth.

af·ter·bod·y (af′tər·bod′ē, äf′-) *n. Aerospace* A section of a rocket or missile that continues to trail the nose cone or satellite from which it was separated in flight.

af·ter·brain (af′tər·brān′, äf′-) *n. Anat.* The metencephalon.

af·ter·burn·er (af′tər·bûr′nər, äf′-) *n. Aeron.* A device for injecting extra fuel into the exhaust system of a jet engine as a means of increasing the thrust. — **af′ter·burn′ing** *n.*

af·ter·damp (af′tər·damp′, äf′-) *n. Mining* A mixture of dangerous gases resulting from a fire or explosion in a mine.

af·ter·deck (af′tər·dek′, äf′-) *n. Naut.* That part of a deck aft of amidships.

af·ter·ef·fect (af′tər·ə·fekt′, äf′-) *n.* An effect succeeding its cause after an interval.

af·ter·glow (af′tər·glō′, äf′-) *n.* A glow after a light has disappeared, as in the western sky after sunset.

af·ter·im·age (af′tər·im′ij, äf′-) *n. Physiol.* The persistence or renewal of the image of an object after the direct stimulation has been withdrawn.

af·ter·math (af′tər·math, äf′-) *n.* Result; consequence.

af·ter·most (af′tər·mōst, äf′-) *adj.* **1.** *Naut.* Nearest t stern: also **aft′most.** **2.** Last.

af·ter·noon (af′tər·no͞on′, äf′-) *n.* **1.** The part of the d between noon and sunset. **2.** The closing part: the *afterno* of life. — *adj.* Of, for, or occurring in the afternoon.

af·ter·taste (af′tər·tāst′, äf′-) *n.* A taste persisting in t mouth, as after a meal.

af·ter·thought (af′tər·thôt′, äf′-) *n.* **1.** An expedient, e planation, etc., that occurs to one after decision or actic **2.** A subsequent or second thought.

af·ter·ward (af′tər·wərd, äf′-) *adv.* In time following; su sequently. Also **af′ter·wards.** [OE *æfterweard*]

ag- Assimilated var. of AD-.

a·gain (ə·gen′, *esp. Brit.* ə·gān′) *adv.* **1.** Another time; or more; anew. **2.** Once repeated. **3.** To the same place over the same course; back, as in a previous condition. Further; moreover. **5.** On the other hand. [OE *ongegn*

a·gainst (ə·genst′, *esp. Brit.* ə·gānst′) *prep.* **1.** In the opp site direction to; counter to. **2.** In contact or collision wit upon. **3.** In contact with and pressing upon. **4.** In opp sition to; contrary to. **5.** In contrast or comparison wit **6.** In preparation for. **7.** In hostility to. **8.** In resistan to. **9.** To the debit of. **10.** Directly opposite; facing: n usu. *over against.* [OE *ongegn* + *-es*, adverbial suffix]

Ag·a·mem·non (ag′ə·mem′non, -nən) In Greek legend, ki of Mycenae and chief of the Greek army in the Trojan Wa

a·gape (ə·gāp′, ə·gap′) *adv. & adj.* In a gaping state; gapir

a·gar-a·gar (ä′gär·ä′gär, ā′gər-, ä′gär-, ag′ər-) *n.* A gel inous substance obtained from seaweeds, used as a laxati and in the cultivation of bacteria. Also **a′gar.** [< Mala

ag·a·ric (ag′ə·rik, ə·gar′ik) *n.* Any of several mushroon esp. the common edible variety. [< L < Gk. *Agaria,* town in Sarmatia] — **a·gar·i·ca·ceous** (ə·gar′i·kā′shəs) *a*

ag·ate (ag′it) *n.* **1.** A variegated waxy quartz or chalce ony, in which the colors are usually in bands. **2.** A chil playing marble. **3.** *Printing* A size of type, 5½ points. [F < L < Gk. *Achatēs,* a river in Sicily]

a·ga·ve (ə·gā′vē) *n.* Any desert plant of the amaryllis fa ily, as the century plant. [< Gk. *Agauē,* a proper name]

a·gaze (ə·gāz′) *adv.* Gazing.

age (āj) *n.* **1.** The period of existence of a person, thing, n tion, etc., particularly as measured by the time past. The entire span of life of any being or thing. **3.** The time life marked by maturity and discretion; adulthood; es that age when full civil rights or certain personal rights c be legally exercised, usually 18 or 21 years: also called *le age.* **4.** Any period of life which, by reason of natural d velopment or custom, fits or unfits for anything. **5.** A distinct stage of life. **6.** The closing period of life; the sta of being old. **7.** Any great period of time in the history man, of the earth, etc., marked off by certain distincti features or characters. **8.** The people alive at a given tim a generation. **9.** *Informal* A long time. — **mental a** *Psychol.* The level of mental development as measur against the chronological age at which this level is reach by the average child. Abbr. *MA, M.A.* — *v.* **aged, ag·i** or **age·ing** *v.t.* **1.** To make or cause to grow mature or ol — *v.i.* **2.** To assume or show some characteristics of ag ripen. [< OF < L *aetas* age, a span of life]

-age *suffix of nouns* **1.** Collection or aggregate of: *leafa* **2.** Condition, office, service, or other relation or connecti of: *haulage.* [< OF < L *-aticum,* neut. adj. suffix]

a·ged (ā′jid *for defs. 1 & 2;* ājd *for def. 3*) *adj.* **1.** Advanc in years; old. **2.** Of, like, or characteristic of old age. **3.** or at the age of: a child, *aged* six. — **Syn.** See OLD. — t **aged** Those who are old. — **a′ged·ly** *adv.* — **a′ged·ness**

age·ing (ā′jing) See AGING.

age·less (āj′lis) *adj.* **1.** Not seeming to grow old. **2.** Ha ing no limits of duration; eternal.

age·long (āj′lông′, -long′) *adj.* Lasting for a long time.

a·gen·cy (ā′jən·sē) *n. pl.* **·cies 1.** Active power or operatio activity. **2.** Means; instrumentality. **3.** A firm or esta lishment where business is done for others. **4.** The office function of an agent. [< L < *agere* to do]

a·gen·da (ə·jen′də) *n. pl. of* **a·gen·dum** (ə·jen′dəm) (*us construed as sing.*) A list of things to be done; esp., a pr gram of business at a meeting. [< L *agere* to do]

◆ *Agenda,* originally the plural of the Latin *agendum,* nc has a regular English plural *agendas.*

a·gent (ā′jənt) *n.* **1.** One who or that which acts or has pow to act; an efficient cause of anything. **2.** One who acts f or by the authority of a government, company, etc. **3.** A force, substance, or organism that causes a material chang **4.** A means by which something is done; instrument. *Informal* A traveling salesman. [< L *agens, agentis,* p of *agere* to do] — **a·gen·tial** (ā·jen′shəl) *adj.*

a·gent pro·vo·ca·teur (á·zhän′ prô·vô·ká·tœr′) *pl.* **a·gen pro·vo·ca·teurs** (á·zhän′ prô·vô·ká·tœr′) *French* A secr agent planted in a trade union, political party, etc., to inci actions or declarations that will incur punishment.

;·ge·us (ə·gē′us) The Douai Bible name for HAGGAI.

:·glom·er·ate (ə·glom′ə·rāt; *for adj. & n., also* -ər·it) *v.t. & i.* **·at·ed, ·at·ing** To gather, form, or grow into a ball or ɔunded mass. — *adj.* Gathered into a mass or heap; clus-ɜred densely. — *n.* A heap or mass of things thrown to-ether indiscriminately. [< L < *ad-* to + *glomerare* to ather into a ball] — **ag·glom′er·a′tion** *n.* — **ag·glom′er·′tive** *adj.*

:·glu·ti·nant (ə·glōō′tə·nənt) *adj.* Tending to cause ad-esion; uniting. — *n.* Any sticky substance.

:·glu·ti·nate (ə·glōō′tə·nāt; *for adj., also* -nit) *v.t. & v.i.* **·at·ed, ·nat·ing 1.** To unite, as with glue; join by adhesion. . *Ling.* To form (words) by agglutination. **3.** *Physiol.* To ıass together, as bacteria. — *adj.* Joined by adhesion. [< < *ad-* to + *glutinare* to glue] — **ag·glu′ti·na′tive** *adj.*

:·glu·ti·na·tion (ə·glōō′tə·nā′shən) *n.* **1.** Adhesion of dis-nct parts; also, a mass formed by adhesion. **2.** *Ling.* A ɔmbining of words into compounds in which the constituent ements retain their characteristic forms.

:·glu·ti·nin (ə·glōō′tə·nin) *n.* *Biochem.* An antibody in lood serum that causes the red corpuscles or any bacteria touches to coalesce into floccules.

:·gran·dize (ə·gran′dīz, ag′rən·dīz) *v.t.* **·dized, ·diz·ing 1.** 'o make great or greater; enlarge or intensify. **2.** To make ppear greater; exalt. [< F < L *ad-* to + *grandire* to make reat] — **ag·gran·dize·ment** (ə·gran′diz·mənt) *n.* — **ag·ran′diz·er** *n.*

·gra·vate (ag′rə·vāt) *v.t.* **·vat·ed, ·vat·ing 1.** To make 'orse; intensify, as an illness. **2.** To make heavier or more urdensome, as a duty. **3.** *Informal* To provoke or exasper-te. [< L < *ad-* to + *gravare* to make heavy] — **ag′gra·at′ing** *adj.* — **ag′gra·vat′ing·ly** *adv.* — **ag·gra·va·tion** ıg′rə·vā′shən) *n.* — **ag′gra·va′tive** *adj.*

·gre·gate (*v.* ag′rə·gāt; *adj. & n.*·-git) *v.t.* **·gat·ed, ·gat·ing** . To bring or gather together, as into a mass, sum, or body. . To amount to; form a total of. — *adj.* Collected into a ım or mass; gathered into a whole. — *n.* The entire num-ɜr, mass, or quantity of anything; amount; total. — **in the ggregate** Collectively; as a whole. [< L < *ad-* to + *·egare* to collect] — **ag·gre·ga·tion** (ag′rə·gā′shən) *n.* — **g′gre·ga′tive** *adj.* — **ag′gre·ga′tor** *n.*

·gress (ə·gres′) *v.i.* To undertake an attack; begin a quar-ɜl. [< L < *ad-* to + *gradi* to step, go]

·gres·sion (ə·gresh′ən) *n.* **1.** An unprovoked attack or ıcroachment. **2.** Habitual aggressive action or practices.

·gres·sive (ə·gres′iv) *adj.* **1.** Of or characterized by ag-ɜession or attack. **2.** Disposed to vigorous activity; asser-ve. — **ag·gres′sive·ly** *adv.* — **ag·gres′sive·ness** *n.*

·gres·sor (ə·gres′ər) *n.* One who commits an aggression.

·grieve (ə·grēv′) *v.t.* **·grieved, ·griev·ing 1.** To cause sor-ɔw to; distress or afflict. **2.** To give cause for just com-laint, as by injustice. [< OF < L *aggravare*]

;hast (ə·gast′, ə·gäst′) *adj.* Struck dumb with horror. ME < OE *ā* + *gǣstan* to terrify; spelling infl. by *ghost*]

·ile (aj′əl, aj′il) *adj.* Able to move or act quickly and eas-y; active. [< F < L *agere* to move] — **ag′ile·ly** *adv.*

;il·i·ty (ə·jil′ə·tē) *n.* Quickness in movement.

·ing (ā′jing) *n.* **1.** The process or the effects of growing ıature or old. **2.** Any artificial process for producing the fects of age. Also, *Brit., ageing.*

·i·tate (aj′ə·tāt) *v.* **·tat·ed, ·tat·ing** *v.t.* **1.** To disturb or ıake irregularly. **2.** To set or keep moving. **3.** To excite stir up; perturb. **4.** To keep before the public, as a con-'oversial issue. — *v.i.* **5.** To excite, or endeavor to excite, ublic interest and action. [< L *agitare* to set in motion]

·i·ta·tion (aj′ə·tā′shən) *n.* **1.** Violent motion; commo-on. **2.** Strong emotional disturbance.

·i·ta·tor (aj′ə·tā′tər) *n.* One who or that which agitates; ɜp., one who persists in political or social agitation.

;leam (ə·glēm′) *adv. & adj.* Bright; gleaming.

;lit·ter (ə·glit′ər) *adv. & adj.* Glittering.

;low (ə·glō′) *adv. & adj.* In a glow; glowing.

·no·men (ag·nō′mən) *n.* *pl.* **ag·nom·i·na** (ag·nom′ə·nə) . nickname. [< L < *ad-* to + (*g*)*nomen* name] — **ag·om′i·nal** *adj.*

·nos·tic (ag·nos′tik) *adj.* Of or pertaining to agnostics or gnosticism. — *n.* One who holds the theory of agnosti-sm. — **Syn.** See SKEPTIC. [< Gk. < *a-* not + *gignōskein* know]

·nos·ti·cism (ag·nos′tə·siz′əm) *n.* The doctrine and hilosophical theory that man cannot know God, first 'uths, or anything beyond material phenomena.

;·nus De·i (ag′nəs dē′ī, dā′ē) **1.** *Eccl.* A figure of a lamb, an emblem of Christ, often bearing a cross and banner. **2.** *'ccl.* **a** A Eucharistic prayer beginning with *Agnus Dei.* **b** ts music. [< LL, Lamb of God. See *John* i 29.]

;o (ə·gō′) *adv.* In the past; since: long *ago.* — *adj.* Gone y; past: a year *ago.* [OE *āgān* past, gone away]

a·gog (ə·gog′) *adv. & adj.* In a state of eager curiosity; ex-cited; expectant. [< MF *en gogues* in a merry mood]

-agogue *combining form* Leading, promoting, or inciting: *demagogue, pedagogue.* Also **-agog.** [< Gk. *agein* to lead]

ag·o·nize (ag′ə·nīz) *v.* **·nized, ·niz·ing** *v.i.* **1.** To be in or suf-fer extreme pain or anguish. **2.** To make convulsive efforts; strive. — *v.t.* **3.** To subject to agony; torture. [< F < Med.L < Gk. *agōnizesthai* to contend, strive]

ag·o·ny (ag′ə·nē) *n.* *pl.* **·nies 1.** Intense suffering of body or mind; anguish. **2.** Any intense or sudden emotion. **3.** The suffering that precedes death. **4.** Violent striving. [< L < Gk. *agōn* contest]

ag·o·ra (ag′ər·ə) *n.* *pl.* **ag·o·rae** (-ər·ē) or **ag·o·ras 1.** In ancient Greece, a popular assembly. **2.** Any place of popu-lar assembly, esp. a market place. [< Gk.]

a·gou·ti (ə·gōō′tē) *n.* *pl.* **·tis** or **·ties** A tropical American rodent of grayish color, with slender limbs and three hind toes. Also **a·gou′ty.** [< F < Sp. *aguti* < Tupi]

a·grar·i·an (ə·grâr′ē·ən) *adj.* **1.** Pertaining to land or the distribution of lands. **2.** Organizing or furthering agricul-tural interests. — *n.* One who advocates equal distribution of lands or equalizing farm income. [< L < *ager* field] — **a·grar′i·an·ism** *n.*

a·gree (ə·grē′) *v.* **a·greed, a·gree·ing** *v.i.* **1.** To give con-sent; accede: with *to* or the infinitive. **2.** To come into or be in harmony. **3.** To be of one mind; concur: often with *with.* **4.** To come to terms, as in the details of a transaction: with *about* or *on.* **5.** To be acceptable; suit: with *with.* **6.** *Gram.* To correspond in person, number, case, or gender. — *v.t.* **7.** To grant as a concession: with a noun clause. [< OF < L *ad* to + *gratus* pleasing]

a·gree·a·ble (ə·grē′ə·bəl) *adj.* **1.** Pleasant to the mind or senses. **2.** Being in accordance or conformity. **3.** Ready or willing to agree. — **a·gree′a·bil′i·ty, a·gree′a·ble·ness** *n.* — **a·gree′a·bly** *adv.*

a·greed (ə·grēd′) *adj.* **1.** In agreement. **2.** Settled by con-sent, bargain, or contract. **3.** Granted: used as a rejoinder.

a·gree·ment (ə·grē′mənt) *n.* **1.** The act of coming into ac-cord. **2.** The state of being in accord; conformity. **3.** A contract. **4.** *Gram.* Correspondence in person, number, case, or gender.

ag·ri·cul·ture (ag′rə·kul′chər) *n.* The science and art of the cultivation of the soil, the breeding and raising of live-stock, etc.; tillage; farming. Abbr. *agr., agric.* — **Depart-ment of Agriculture** An executive department of the U.S. government headed by the Secretary of Agriculture, that administers loans and grants in aid to farmers and assists in production, irrigation, etc. [< F < L *ager* field + *cultura* cultivation] — **ag′ri·cul′tur·al** *adj.* — **ag′ri·cul′tur·al·ly** *adv.*

ag·ri·cul·tur·ist (ag′rə·kul′chər·ist) *n.* **1.** An expert in agri-culture. **2.** A farmer: also **ag′ri·cul′tur·al·ist.**

agro- *combining form* Of or pertaining to fields or agricul-ture: *agronomy.* [< Gk. < *agros* field]

ag·ro·bi·ol·o·gy (ag′rō·bī·ol′ə·jē) *n.* The quantitative study of plant life, esp. in relation to the yields of cultivated plants. — **ag·ro·bi·o·log·ic** (ag′rō·bī′ə·loj′ik) or **·i·cal** *adj.* — **ag′ro·bi′o·log′i·cal·ly** *adv.* — **ag′ro·bi·ol′o·gist** *n.*

ag·ro·nom·ics (ag′rə·nom′iks) *n.pl.* (*construed as sing.*) Agronomy.

a·gron·o·my (ə·gron′ə·mē) *n.* The application of scientific principles to the cultivation of land. [< Gk. < *agros* field + *nemein* to distribute, manage] — **ag·ro·nom·ic** (ag′rə·nom′ik) or **·i·cal** *adj.* — **a·gron′·o·mist** *n.*

a·ground (ə·ground′) *adv. & adj.* On the shore or bottom, as a vessel; stranded.

a·gue (ā′gyōō) *n.* **1.** *Pathol.* A periodic malarial fever marked by intermittent chills. **2.** A chill or paroxysm. [< OF < L (*febris*) *acuta* acute (fever)] — **a′gu·ish** *adj.*

ah (ä) *interj.* An exclamation expressive of various emotions, as surprise, triumph, satisfaction, contempt, etc. [ME]

a·ha (ä·hä′) *interj.* An exclamation expressing surprise, tri-umph, or mockery. [ME]

a·head (ə·hed′) *adv.* **1.** At the head or front. **2.** In advance. **3.** Onward; forward. — **ahead of** In advance of, as in time, rank, achievement, etc. — **to be ahead** *U.S. Informal* To have as profit or advantage; be winning. — **to get ahead** To make one's way socially, financially, etc.

a·hem (ə·hem′) *interj.* An exclamation similar to the sound of clearing the throat, made to attract attention.

a·hoy (ə·hoi′) *interj.* Ho there!: a call used in hailing.

aid (ād) *v.t. & v.i.* To render assistance (to); help. — *n.* **1.** Assistance; help. **2.** A person or thing that affords assist-ance. **3.** An aide. [< OF < L < *ad-* to + *juvare* to help] — **aid′er** *n.*

aide (ād) *n.* **1.** An aide de camp. **2.** An assistant. [< F]

aide-de-camp (ād′də·kamp′) *n.* *pl.* **aides-de-camp** A mili-tary or naval officer on the personal staff of a superior officer

in a high command as his confidential assistant and secretary: also *aide*. Also *U.S.* **aid′-de-camp′.** [< F *aide de camp*, lit., field assistant]
ai·grette (ā′gret, ā·gret′) *n.* **1.** The tail plume of the egret. **2.** A tuft of feathers or gems, worn on a helmet, headdress, etc. Also **ai′gret.** [< F, a heron]
ail (āl) *v.t.* **1.** To cause uneasiness or pain to; trouble; make ill. **—*v.i.*** **2.** To be somewhat ill; feel pain. [OE *eglan*]
ai·lan·thus (ā·lan′thəs) *n.* A large, deciduous tree of the quassia family, having malodorous, greenish flowers. [< NL, genus name] **— ai·lan′thic** *adj.*
ai·le·ron (ā′lə·ron) *n.* *Aeron.* Any of several movable surfaces of an airplane wing, used to bank the airplane. [< F]
ail·ing (ā′ling) *adj.* Sick; ill. **— Syn.** See SICK.
ail·ment (āl′mənt) *n.* A slight illness.
aim (ām) *v.t.* **1.** To direct, as a weapon, remark, or act, toward or against some object or person. **—*v.i.*** **2.** To have a purpose; try: with the infinitive. **3.** To direct a missile, weapon, etc. **—*n.*** **1.** The act of aiming. **2.** The line of direction of anything aimed. **3.** Design; purpose. [< OF < L *aestimare* to estimate]
aim·less (ām′lis) *adj.* Wanting in aim or purpose. **— aim′·less·ly** *adv.* **— aim′less·ness** *n.*
ain't (ānt) *Illit. & Dial.* Am not: also used for *are not, is not, has not,* and *have not.*
◆ **ain't, aren't I?** *Ain't* is now nonstandard, although users of standard English sometimes say or write it for amusing effect when they are sure it will not be taken as their normal usage. *Aren't I?* is an ungrammatical locution used to avoid *Ain't I?* when one means *Am I not?*
air (âr) *n.* **1.** The mixture of gases that forms the atmosphere of the earth, consisting chiefly of oxygen and nitrogen very nearly in the proportions one to four. **2.** The open space around and above the earth; sky. **3.** An atmospheric movement or current; wind; breeze. **4.** Utterance abroad; publicity: to give *air* to one's feelings. **5.** Peculiar or characteristic appearance; mien; manner: an honest *air.* **6.** *pl.* Assumed manner; affectation: to put on *airs.* **7.** *Music* A melody; tune. **8.** The medium through which radio signals are sent. **— in the air 1.** Prevalent; abroad, as gossip. **2.** In the making, as plans. **— on the air** Now broadcasting or transmitting, as by radio; being broadcast. **— up in the air** *Informal* Undecided. **—*v.t.*** **1.** To expose to the air; admit air into so as to purify or dry; ventilate. **2.** To make public; display; exhibit. [< OF < L < Gk. *aēr* air, mist]
air base A base for operations by aircraft.
air bladder 1. *Zool.* In fishes, a sac filled with air, aiding them to maintain an equilibrium in the water: also called *sound, swimming bladder.* **2.** Any vesicle filled with air.
air·borne (âr′bôrn′, -bōrn′) *adj.* **1.** Carried through the air, as bacteria, pollen, etc. **2.** Transported in aircraft: *airborne* infantry. **3.** In flight; flying.
air brake A brake operated by compressed air.
air·brush (âr′brush′) *n.* A kind of atomizer for spraying paint or other liquids by compressed air. Also **air brush.**
air·bus (âr′bus′) *n.* A large passenger airplane designed to accommodate hundreds of people. [< AIR(PLANE) + BUS]
air castle A visionary project; a daydream.
air chamber An enclosed space containing, or designed to contain, air, esp. in hydraulics.
air chief marshal In the Royal, Royal Canadian, and other Commonwealth air forces, an officer of the next to highest rank. See table at GRADE.
air coach *U.S.* The second-best and cheaper class of accommodations in commercial aircraft. Also **air·coach** (âr′cōch′).
air commodore In the Royal, Royal Canadian, and other Commonwealth air forces, an officer ranking next above group captain. See table at GRADE.
air-con·di·tion (âr′kən·dish′ən) *v.t.* To equip with or ventilate by air conditioning. **— air′-con·di′tioned** *adj.*
air conditioner Any of various air-conditioning devices.
air conditioning A system for treating air in buildings, etc., so as to maintain those conditions of temperature, humidity, and purity best adapted to personal comfort, etc.
air·cool (âr′kōōl′) *v.t.* To cool, as the cylinders of an engine, with a flow of air instead of liquid. **— air′-cooled′** *adj.*
air·craft (âr′kraft′, -kräft′) *n.* *pl.* **·craft** Any form of craft designed for flight through or navigation in the air.
aircraft carrier *Naval* A large ship designed to carry aircraft, having a flight deck for landing and taking off.
air·craft·man (âr′kraft′mən, kräft′-) *n.* *pl.* **·men** *Brit.* Any of the four lower grades in the Royal or Royal Canadian Air Force. See table at GRADE.
air·drome (âr′drōm′) *n.* *Chiefly Brit.* An airport.
air·drop (âr′drop′) *n.* Aerial delivery of supplies and equipment from an aircraft in flight. **—*v.t. & v.i.*** **·dropped, ·drop·ping** To drop (supplies, etc.) from an aircraft.
Aire·dale (âr′dāl) *n.* A large terrier with a wiry tan coat. [after *Airedale*, the Aire river valley, England]
air·field (âr′fēld′) *n.* An airport.
air·foil (âr′foil′) *n.* *Aeron.* A surface, as a wing, ai ron, etc., designed to provide the maximum aerodynamic advantage for an airplane in flight.
air force The air arm of a country's defense forces. **— United States Air Force** The air force of the United States.
air gun A gun impelling a charge by compressed air.
air hole 1. A hole containing, or made by or for, gas or air. **2.** A flaw in a casting. **3.** An opening in the ice over a body of water. **4.** *Aeron.* An air pocket.

AIREDALE
(About 23 inche
high at shoulde

air·i·ly (âr′ə·lē) *adv.* In a light or airy manner; jauntily.
air·ing (âr′ing) *n.* **1.** An exposure to air, as for drying. Public exposure or discussion. **3.** Exercise in the air.
air lane A route regularly used by airplanes.
air·less (âr′lis) *adj.* Destitute of air or of fresh air.
air letter 1. An airmail letter. **2.** A sheet of lightweig paper for airmail letters. **3.** *Brit.* An aérogramme.
air·lift (âr′lift′) *n.* The transporting of passengers and ca by aircraft. **—*v.t. & v.i.*** To transport by airplane.
air·line (âr′līn′) *n.* A business organization that transpo passengers and freight by air. **— air′lin′er** *n.*
air lock An airtight antechamber, as of a caisson, for mai taining the air pressure.
air mail 1. Mail carried by airplane. **2.** A system of car ing mail by airplane. **— air′-mail′, air′mail′** *adj.*
air·man (âr′mən) *n.* *pl.* **·men** (-mən) An aviator; fly
air marshal In the Royal, Royal Canadian, and ot Commonwealth air forces, an officer ranking next below chief marshal. See table at GRADE.
air mass *Meteorol.* A body of air having essentially u form conditions of temperature, humidity, etc.
Air Medal A decoration awarded by the U.S. Air Force meritorious achievement during flight. See DECORATION.
air·plane (âr′plān′) *n.* A heavier-than-air, powered fly craft having fixed wings. Also, *Brit., aeroplane.*
air pocket *Aeron.* A sinking mass of cooled air.
air·port (âr′pôrt′, -pōrt′) *n.* A field laid out as a base aircraft, including all structures and appurtenances nec sary for operation, housing, storage, and maintenance.
air power The strength of a nation in terms of its comma of the air in peace and war.
air·proof (âr′prōōf′) *adj.* Impenetrable by air. **—*v.t.*** make airproof.
air raid An attack by military aircraft, esp. by bombe
air-raid shelter A place set aside and equipped for the p tection of people during an air raid.
air sac *Ornithol.* One of the membranous sacs filled w air in different parts of the body in birds and communicat with the lungs.
air shaft An open shaft intended to provide ventilation.
air·ship (âr′ship′) *n.* A lighter-than-air, powered fly craft.
air·sick·ness (âr′sik′nis) *n.* Motion sickness caused by travel. **— air′sick′** *adj.*
air·space (âr′spās′) *n.* That portion of the atmosph overlying a designated area, considered as subject to ter torial jurisdiction or international law.
air speed The speed of an airplane with relation to the a
air·strip (âr′strip′) *n.* A flat surface used as an airfield.
air·tight (âr′tīt′) *adj.* **1.** Not allowing air to escape or ter. **2.** Having no weak places; flawless: an *airtight* cas
air vice-marshal (vīs′mär′shəl) In the Royal, Royal Ca dian, and other Commonwealth air forces, an officer ra ing next below air marshal. See table at GRADE.
air·way (âr′wā′) *n.* **1.** Any passageway for air, as the v tilating passage of a mine. **2.** *Aeron.* An air lane.
air·wor·thy (âr′wûr′thē) *adj.* Being in fit condition to f said of aircraft. **— air′wor′thi·ness** *n.*
air·y (âr′ē) *adj.* **air·i·er, air·i·est 1.** Of or pertaining to t air. **2.** Like or resembling air; immaterial. **3.** Thin or lig as air; delicate. **4.** Light or buoyant in manner; lively; g **5.** Unsubstantial as air; unreal; empty. **6.** Dealing w fancies; visionary; speculative. **7.** Open to the air; bree **8.** Performed in the air; aerial. **9.** *Informal* Giving ones airs; affected. **— air′i·ness** *n.*
aisle (īl) *n.* **1.** A passageway between rows of seats. **2.** division of a church, usu. divided from the nave by a ra of columns or piers. [< MF < L *ala* wing]
a·jar[1] (ə·jär′) *adv. & adj.* Partly open, as a door. [ME on + *char*, OE *cerr* turn]
a·jar[2] (ə·jär′) *adv. & adj.* Not in harmony.
a·kim·bo (ə·kim′bō) *adv. & adj.* With hands on hips and bows outward. [ME *in kenebowe* in a sharp bow]
a·kin (ə·kin′) *adj. & adv.* **1.** Of the same kin; related blood. **2.** Of similar nature or qualities. [< A-[3] + KIN
al-[1] *prefix* The Arabic definite article, seen in words of A bic origin, as *Alkoran, algebra.*

l-[2] Assimilated var. of AD-.

l[1] *suffix of adjectives and nouns* Of or pertaining to; characterized by: *personal, musical.* [< L *-alis*]

l[2] *suffix of nouns* The act or process of, used in nouns ormed from verbs: *betrayal, refusal.* [< OF < L *-alis*]

l[3] *suffix Chem.* Denoting a compound having the properties f or derived from an aldehyde: *chloral.* [< AL(DEHYDE)]

la (ā′lə) *n. pl.* **a·lae** (ā′lē) A wing or a winglike part. < L, wing]

la (ä′ lä, ä′ lə; *Fr.* à là) After the manner or in the style of. Also **a la.** [< F]

l·a·bam·ine (al′ə·bam′ēn, -in) *n.* A hypothetical element f atomic number 85; replaced by astatine. [*Alabama*]

l·a·bas·ter (al′ə·bas′tər, -bäs′-) *n.* **1.** A white or tinted ne-grained gypsum. **2.** A banded variety of calcite. — *dj.* Made of or like alabaster; smooth and white: also **al′a·as′trine** (-trin). [< L < Gk. *alabast(r)os* alabaster box]

la carte (ä′ lə kärt′) By the bill of fare; each item havng a separate price. Compare TABLE D'HÔTE. [< F]

lac·ri·ty (ə·lak′rə·tē) *n.* Cheerful willingness and promptitude; liveliness. [< L *alacer* lively] — **a·lac′ri·tous** *adj.*

lad·din (ə·lad′n) In the *Arabian Nights*, a boy who can ummon a jinni by rubbing a magic lamp or a magic ring.

la king (ä′ lə king′) Cooked in a cream sauce, with pimiento or green pepper, mushrooms, etc.

l·a·mo (al′ə·mō) A Franciscan mission building, San Antonio, Texas; besieged and taken by Mexicans, 1836.

la mode (ä′ lə mōd′, al′ ə mōd′) **1.** In style; fashionable. **2.** In cookery: **a** Served with ice cream: said of pie. **b** Braised with vegetables and served in a rich gravy. [< F]

la New·burg (ä′ lə no͞o′bûrg, nyo͞o′bûrg) Cooked with a auce made of egg yolks, cream, sherry, and butter.

lar (ā′lər) *adj.* Having or pertaining to an ala or wing; ving-shaped. [< L *ala* wing]

larm (ə·lärm′) *n.* **1.** Sudden fear or apprehension caused y awareness of danger. **2.** Any sound or signal intended to waken or apprise of danger; a warning. **3.** Any device, as a ell, for giving such a signal. **4.** A call to arms, to meet anger or attack. — *v.t.* **1.** To strike with sudden fear. **2.** To arouse to a sense of danger; give warning to. [< OF < Ital. *all' arme* to arms] — **a·larm′a·ble** *adj.*

larm clock A clock fitted with a device to sound a bell or uzzer when the hands reach a predetermined hour.

larm·ing (ə·lär′ming) *adj.* Exciting alarm; causing fear nd apprehension; disturbing. — **a·larm′ing·ly** *adv.*

larm·ist (ə·lär′mist) *n.* **1.** One who needlessly excites or ries to excite alarm. **2.** One who is easily alarmed.

las (ə·las′, ə·läs′) *interj.* An exclamation of regret, sorrow, tc. [< OF *a* ah! + *las* wretched]

late (ā′lāt) *adj. Bot.* Winged, as a stem, petiole, or fruit. Also **a′lat·ed.** [< L *ala* wing]

lb (alb) *n. Eccl.* A white linen eucharistic vestment reaching to the ankles, close-sleeved and girded at the waist. [OE < L *alba (vestis)* white garment]

l·ba·core (al′bə·kôr, -kōr) *n.* Any of various tunas or large elated fishes of the Atlantic. [< Pg. < Arabic *al* the + *bukr* young camel]

l·ba·ni·an (al·bā′nē·ən, -bān′yən) *adj.* Of or pertaining to Albania, its people, or their language. — *n.* **1.** A native or nhabitant of Albania. **2.** The language of Albania.

l·ba·tross (al′bə·trôs, -tros) *n. pl.* **·tross·es** or **tross** A arge, web-footed sea bird, with long, narow wings and a hooked beak. [Orig. *alcaras* frigate bird < Sp., Pg. *alcatraz*]

l·be·it (ôl·bē′it) *conj.* Even though; lthough. [ME *al be it* although it be]

l·bes·cent (al·bes′ənt) *adj.* Growing white or moderately white; becoming whitsh. [< L *albescens, -entis*, ppr. of *albescere* o become white] — **al·bes′cence** *n.*

l·bi·gen·ses (al′bə·jen′sēz) *n.pl.* A sect f religious reformers during the 11th to 3th centuries in the south of France, supressed as heretics. [< Med.L, after *Albi*, town in southern France] — **Al′bi·gen′·i·an** (-sē·ən, -shən) *adj. & n.*

ALBATROSS
(About 40 inches long; wingspread 10 to 12 feet)

l·bi·no (al·bī′nō) *n. pl.* **·nos** **1.** A person acking pigment in the skin, hair, and eyes. **2.** Any plant or animal lacking normal pigmentation. [< Pg. < L *albus* white] — **al·bin·ic** (al·bin′ik) *adj.* — **al·bin·ism** al′bə·niz′əm) *n.*

l·bum (al′bəm) *n.* **1.** A booklike container for stamps, picures, phonograph records, etc. **2.** A set of phonograph ecords stored in such a container. [< L, blank tablet]

l·bu·men (al·byo͞o′mən) *n.* **1.** The white of an egg. **2.** *Bot.* The nutritive material in a seed between the embryo nd the seed coats. **3.** Albumin. [< L < *albus* white]

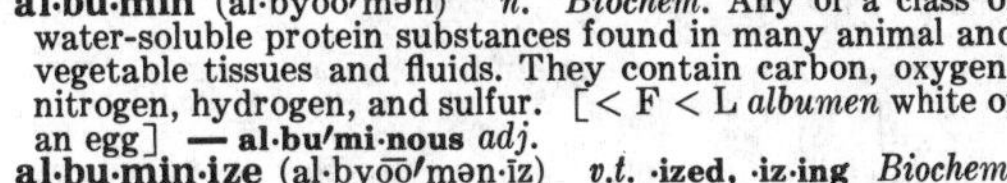

al·bu·min (al·byo͞o′mən) *n. Biochem.* Any of a class of water-soluble protein substances found in many animal and vegetable tissues and fluids. They contain carbon, oxygen, nitrogen, hydrogen, and sulfur. [< F < L *albumen* white of an egg] — **al·bu′mi·nous** *adj.*

al·bu·min·ize (al·byo͞o′mən·īz) *v.t.* **·ized, ·iz·ing** *Biochem.* To convert into or coat with albumin.

al·caz·ar (al′kə·zär; *Sp.* äl·kä′thär) *n.* A Moorish castle in Spain. — **the Alcazar** A Moorish palace in Seville, later used by the Spanish kings. [< Sp. < Arabic *al-qasr* the castle]

al·che·mist (al′kə·mist) *n.* One skilled in or practicing alchemy. — **al′che·mis′tic** or **·ti·cal** *adj.*

al·che·mize (al′kə·mīz) *v.t.* **·mized, ·miz·ing** To transmute by or as by alchemy.

al·che·my (al′kə·mē) *n.* **1.** The chemistry of the Middle Ages, concerned primarily with the transmutation of base metals into gold. **2.** Any power or process of transmutation. Also **al′chy·my.** [< OF < Med.L *alchimia* < Gk. *cheein* to pour] — **al·chem·ic** (al·kem′ik) *adj.* — **al·chem′·i·cal·ly** *adv.*

al·co·hol (al′kə·hôl, -hol) *n.* **1.** Either of two volatile, flammable, pungent liquids, ethanol, the intoxicating principle of wines and liquors, and methanol, or wood alcohol. **2.** Any drink containing alcohol. **3.** *Chem.* Any of a group of organic compounds derived from the alkanes by the substitution of one hydroxyl radical for one hydrogen atom. [< Med.L < Arabic *al-kohl* the fine powder (of antimony)]

al·co·hol·ic (al′kə·hôl′ik, -hol′-) *adj.* **1.** Containing or using alcohol. **2.** Caused by alcohol or alcoholism. **3.** Suffering from alcoholism. — *n.* One who suffers from alcoholism.

al·co·hol·ism (al′kə·hôl′iz·əm, -hol′-) *n. Pathol.* A diseased condition resulting from the excessive or persistent use of alcoholic beverages.

al·co·hol·ize (al′kə·hôl·īz′, -hol-) *v.t.* **·ized, ·iz·ing** **1.** To change into alcohol. **2.** To mix or saturate with alcohol. — **al′co·hol′i·za′tion** *n.*

Al·co·ran (al′kō·rän′, -ran′) *n.* The Koran.

al·cove (al′kōv) *n.* **1.** A recess at the side of a larger room. **2.** Any secluded spot. [< F < Sp. < Arabic *al-qobbah* the vaulted chamber]

Al·deb·a·ran (al·deb′ə·rən) *n.* A red star, one of the 20 brightest, 1.06 magnitude, Alpha in the constellation Taurus.

al·de·hyde (al′də·hīd) *n.* **1.** *Chem.* Any of a group of compounds derived from the alcohols, and intermediate between the alcohols and the acids. **2.** Acetaldehyde.

al·der (ôl′dər) *n.* A shrub or small tree of the birch family, growing in wet ground and bearing small catkins. [OE *alor*]

al·der·man (ôl′dər·mən) *n. pl.* **·men** **1.** *U.S.* In many municipalities, a member of the governing body. **2.** In England and Ireland a member of the higher branch of a municipal or borough council. [OE *eald* old, senior + *man*] — **al′der·man·ship′** *n.* — **al′der·man′ic** (-man′ik) *adj.*

Al·der·ney (ôl′dər·nē) *n.* One of a breed of cattle originally peculiar to the island of Alderney.

ale (āl) *n.* A fermented malt flavored with hops, resembling beer but generally having more body. [OE *ealu*]

a·le·a·to·ry (ā′lē·ə·tôr′ē, -tō′rē) *adj.* Dependent on gambling or luck. [< L *aleator* gambler]

a·lee (ə·lē′) *adv. Naut.* At, on, or to the lee side. [< ON]

ale·house (āl′hous′) *n.* A public place where ale is sold.

a·lem·bic (ə·lem′bik) *n.* **1.** An apparatus of glass or metal formerly used in distilling. **2.** Anything that tests, purifies, or transforms. [< OF ult. < Arabic < Gk. *ambix* a cup]

A·len·çon lace (ə·len′sən, *Fr.* à·län·sôn′) A fine needlepoint lace. [after *Alençon*, France]

a·lert (ə·lûrt′) *adj.* **1.** Keenly watchful; ready for sudden action; vigilant. **2.** Lively; nimble. **3.** Intelligent; bright. — *n.* **1.** A warning against attack; esp., a signal to prepare for an air raid. **2.** The time during which such a warning is in effect. — **on the alert** On the lookout; vigilant. — *v.t.* To warn, as of a threatened attack or raid. [< Ital. *all'erta* on the watch] — **a·lert′ly** *adv.* — **a·lert′ness** *n.*

-ales *suffix Bot.* A feminine plural used to form the scientific names of plant orders. [< L, pl. of *-alis*]

Al·e·ut (al′ē·o͞ot) *n. pl.* **Al·e·uts** or **Al·e·ut** **1.** A native of the Aleutian Islands. **2.** The language of the Aleuts. — **A·leu·tian** (ə·lo͞o′shən), **A·leu′tic** *adj.*

ale·wife (āl′wīf′) *n. pl.* **·wives** A small North American herring-like fish. [Origin unknown]

Al·ex·an·dri·an (al′ig·zan′drē·ən, -zän′-) *adj.* **1.** Of Alexandria in Egypt. **2.** Of Alexander the Great, his reign, or his conquests. **3.** In prosody, Alexandrine. — *n.* **1.** An inhabitant of Alexandria. **2.** An Alexandrine verse.

Al·ex·an·drine (al′ig·zan′drin, -drēn, -zän′-) *n.* In prosody, a line of verse having six iambic feet with the caesura generally after the third. — *adj.* Of, composed of, or characterized by Alexandrines. Also *Alexandrian.*

al·fal·fa (al·fal′fə) *n.* A cloverlike plant of the bean family, used as forage. Also, *Brit., lucerne.* [< Sp. < Arabic *al-fasfasah,* the best kind of fodder]

al·fres·co (al·fres′kō) *adv.* In the open air. — *adj.* Occurring outdoors, as a meal. Also **al fresco.** [< Ital.]

al·ga (al′gə) *n. pl.* **·gae** (-jē) Any of various primitive, chlorophyll-bearing plants widely distributed in fresh and salt water and moist lands, including the seaweeds and kelps. [< L, seaweed] — **al·gal** (al′gəl) *adj.*

al·ge·bra (al′jə·brə) *n.* The branch of mathematics that treats of quantity and the relations of numbers in the abstract, and in which calculations are performed by means of letters and symbols. [< Ital. < Arabic *al-jebr* the reunion of broken parts, bonesetting] — **al·ge·bra·ic** (al′jə·brā′ik) or **·i·cal** *adj.* — **al′ge·bra′i·cal·ly** *adv.* — **al′ge·bra′ist** *n.*

Al·ge·ri·an (al·je′ri·an) *adj.* Of or pertaining to Algeria or its people. — *n.* A citizen or inhabitant of Algeria.

-algia *suffix* Pain: *neuralgia.* [< Gk. *algos* pain]

al·gid (al′jid) *adj.* Cold. [< F < L *algere* to be cold]

al·gin (al′jin) *n.* The dried, gelatinous form of various seaweeds, used as an emulsifier, etc. [< ALGA]

Al gon·ki·an (al·gong′kē·ən) *adj. & n.* Algonquian.

Al·gon·kin (al·gong′kin) *n. pl.* **·kin** or **·kins** Algonquin.

Al·gon·qui·an (al·gong′kē·ən, -kwē·ən) *n. pl.* **·qui·an** or **·qui·ans** 1. A family of North American Indian languages, including Arapaho, Blackfoot, Cheyenne, Cree, Ojibwa, Micmac, Delaware, and Massachusett. 2. A member of an Algonquian-speaking tribe. — *adj.* Of or pertaining to the Algonquian family of languages.

Al·gon·quin (al·gong′kin, -kwin) *n. pl.* **·quin** or **·quins** 1. A member of certain Algonquian tribes formerly living along the Ottawa River. 2. The Algonquian language.

Al·ham·bra (al·ham′brə) The palace of the Moorish kings at Granada, Spain, built in the 13th and 14th centuries. [< Sp. < Arabic *al-hamrā'* the red (house)]

a·li·as (ā′lē·əs) *n. pl.* **a·li·as·es** An assumed name. — **Syn.** See PSEUDONYM. — *adv.* Called by an assumed name: Miller, *alias* Brown. [< L, at another time]

al·i·bi (al′ə·bī) *n. pl.* **·bis** 1. *Law* A form of defense by which an accused person attempts to show that he was elsewhere when the crime was committed. 2. *U.S. Informal* An excuse. — *v.i.* **·bied, ·bi·ing** *U.S. Informal* To make excuses for oneself. [< L, elsewhere]

al·ien (āl′yən, ā′lē·ən) *adj.* 1. Owing allegiance to another country; unnaturalized; foreign. 2. Of or related to aliens. 3. Not one's own; strange. 4. Not consistent with; incongruous; opposed: with *to.* — *n.* 1. An unnaturalized foreign resident. 2. A member of a foreign nation, tribe, people, etc. 3. One estranged or excluded. [< L *alius* another]

— **Syn.** (adj.) 4. extrinsic, extraneous, irrelevant. — (noun) 1. An *alien* is not a citizen of the country in which he resides. A *foreigner* is not a native of the country where he lives, but he may become a naturalized citizen.

al·ien·a·ble (āl′yən·ə·bəl, ā′lē·ən-) *adj. Law* Capable of being transferred in ownership. — **al′ien·a·bil′i·ty** *n.*

al·ien·ate (āl′yən·āt, ā′lē·ən-) *v.t.* **·at·ed, ·at·ing** 1. To make indifferent or unfriendly; estrange. 2. To cause to feel estranged or withdrawn from society. 3. To turn away: to *alienate* the affections. 4. *Law* To transfer, as property. [< L *alienare* to estrange] — **al′ien·a′tor** *n.*

al·ien·a·tion (āl′yən·ā′shən, ā′lē·ən-) *n.* 1. The act of alienating, or the state of being alienated; estrangement: the growing *alienation* of students. 2. Insanity.

al·ien·ee (āl′yən·ē′, ā′lē·ən·ē′) *n. Law* One to whom property is transferred.

al·ien·ist (āl′yən·ist, ā′lē·ən-) *n.* A doctor skilled in the treatment of mental disorders: used chiefly in medical jurisprudence. [< F < L *alienus* insane] — **al′ien·ism** *n.*

al·ien·or (āl′yən·ər, ā′lē·ən·ôr′) *n. Law* One who alienates property to another; a vendor. Also **al′ien·er.** [< AF]

al·i·form (al′ə·fôrm, ā′lə·fôrm) *adj.* Wing-shaped; alar. [< F *ala* wing + -FORM]

a·light[1] (ə·līt′) *v.i.* **a·light·ed** or **a·lit, a·light·ing** 1. To descend and come to rest; settle, as after flight. 2. To dismount. 3. To come by accident: with *on* or *upon.* [OE *ālihtan* < *ā-* out, off + *lihtan* to alight]

a·light[2] (ə·līt′) *adj. & adv.* Lighted; burning.

a·lign (ə·līn′) *v.t.* 1. To bring into a straight line. 2. To put (oneself, one's party, etc.) on one side of an issue, controversy, etc. — *v.i.* 3. To fall into line. Also spelled *aline.* [< F *aligner* < *a-* to + *ligner* to place in line]

a·lign·ment (ə·līn′mənt) *n.* 1. Position, place, or arrangement in a straight line. 2. A line or lines so made. 3. The state of being on one side of an issue, controversy, etc.

a·like (ə·līk′) *adj.* Having resemblance; like one another: used predicatively: The family are all *alike.* — *adv.* In the same or like manner; equally. [Fusion of ON *ālīkr* and OE *gelīc, anlīc*] — **a·like′ness** *n.*

al·i·ment (al′ə·mənt) *n.* 1. Food for body or mind; nutriment. 2. That which sustains or supports. — *v.t.* To furnish with food; nourish. [< L *alere* to nourish] — **al·i·men·tal** (al′ə·men′təl) *adj.* — **al′i·men′tal·ly** *adv.*

al·i·men·ta·ry (al′ə·men′trē, -tə·rē) *adj.* 1. Supplyi nourishment. 2. Connected with food or the function nutrition. 3. Providing support; sustaining.

alimentary canal The food canal between the mouth a the anus, including esophagus, stomach, and intestines.

al·i·men·ta·tion (al′ə·men·tā′shən) *n.* 1. The act or pr ess of supplying or receiving nourishment. 2. Maintenan support. — **al·i·men·ta·tive** (al′ə·men′tə·tiv) *adj.*

al·i·mo·ny (al′ə·mō′nē) *n. Law* The allowance made tc woman from her husband's estate or income after a divor or legal separation. [< L < *alere* to nourish]

a·line (ə·līn′), **a·line·ment** (ə·līn′mənt) See ALIGN, etc.

al·i·quant (al′ə·kwənt) *adj. Math.* Not dividing evenly ir another number: 4 is an *aliquant* part of 11. [< L *ali* other + *quantus* how large, how much]

al·i·quot (al′ə·kwət) *adj. Math.* Dividing evenly into a other number: 4 is an *aliquot* part of 12. [< L *alius* other *quot* how many]

a·lit (ə·lit′) Alternative past tense and past participle ALIGHT[1].

a·live (ə·līv′) *adj.* 1. In a living or functioning state; havi life. 2. In existence or operation: to keep hope *alive.* 3. lively action; animated: *alive* with enthusiasm. 4. Awa sensitive: with *to.* 5. Abounding. [OE *on līfe* in life]

a·liz·a·rin (ə·liz′ə·rin) *n. Chem.* An orange-red compour $C_{14}H_8O_4$, formerly prepared from madder, used as a d Also **a·liz·a·rine** (ə·liz′ə·rin, -rēn). [< F < Arabic *al-asār* juice]

al·ka·li (al′kə·lī) *n. pl.* **·lis** or **·lies** *Chem.* 1. A hydrox of any of the alkali metals, soluble in water and capable neutralizing acids and of turning red litmus paper blue. Any compound that will neutralize an acid, as lime, m nesia, etc. [< MF < Arabic *al-galiy* the ashes of saltwo

al·ka·li·fy (al′kə·lə·fī′, al·kal′ə·fī) *v.t. & v.i.* **·fied, ·fy·ing** change into or become alkaline or an alkali.

alkali metals *Chem.* A group of elements including lit ium, sodium, potassium, rubidium, cesium, and franciu

al·ka·line (al′kə·līn, -lin) *adj.* Of, like, or containing alkali. Also **al′ka·lin.** — **al′ka·lin′i·ty** *n.*

alkaline earths *Chem.* The oxides of calcium, strontiu barium, and sometimes magnesium.

al·ka·lize (al′kə·līz) *v.t. & v.i.* **·lized, ·liz·ing** To convert ir or become alkali or alkaline. — **al′ka·li·za′tion** *n.*

al·ka·loid (al′kə·loid) *n. Chem.* Any of a class of nitr enous organic bases, especially one of vegetable origin, ha ing a physiological effect on animals and man, as strychni or morphine. — **al′ka·loi′dal** *adj.*

Al·ko·ran (al′kō·rän′, -ran′) *n.* The Koran. — **Al′ko·ran** (-ran′ik) *adj.* [< Arabic *al-qurān* the reading]

al·kyl (al′kil) *n. Chem.* A univalent radical obtained by moving one hydrogen atom from an aliphatic compour

al·kyl·a·tion (al′kə·lā′shən) *n. Chem.* The introducti of an alkyl group into an organic compound.

all (ôl) *adj.* 1. The entire substance or extent of: *all* Euro 2. The entire number of: known to *all* men. 3. The gre est possible: in *all* haste. 4. Any whatever: beyond *all* dou 5. Every: used in phrases with *manner, sorts,* and *kinds:* manner of men. 6. Nothing except: He was *all* skin a bones. — *n.* 1. Everything that one has: to give one's 2. Whole being; totality. — *pron.* 1. Everyone: *All* condemned. 2. Everything: *All* is lost. 3. Every part, of a whole: *All* of it is gone. — **above all** Primarily. **after all** Everything else being considered; neverthele — **all in all** Taken as a whole. — **at all** 1. In any way can't come *at all.* 2. To any degree or extent: no luck *at* — **for all** To the degree that: *For all* I care, you can alone. — **for all of** As for: You can leave now, *for all of* — **in all** Including everything; all told: ten books *in all.* *adv.* 1. Wholly; entirely: fallen *all* to bits. 2. Exclusive only: This desk is *all* for me. 3. For each; on each side score of three *all.* — **all but** 1. Almost; on the verge of. Every one except. — **all in** *Informal* Wearied. — **all** Making every effort: *all out* for victory. — **all the** (**bett more,** etc.) So much the (better, more, etc.). [OE]

Al·lah (al′ə, ä′lə) In Islam, the one supreme being; G [< Arabic]

all-A·mer·i·can (ôl′ə·mer′ə·kən) *adj.* 1. Composed of t best in the United States: an *all-American* football team. Of or composed of Americans or American products exc sively. — *n.* A player selected for an all-American tea

all-a·round (ôl′ə·round′) *adj.* All-round.

al·lay (ə·lā′) *v.t.* **·layed, ·lay·ing** 1. To lessen the violer or reduce the intensity of. 2. To lay to rest, as fears; paci calm. [OE < *ā-* away + *lecgan* to lay] — **al·lay′er** *n.*

all clear The signal indicating that an air raid is over..

al·le·ga·tion (al′ə·gā′shən) *n.* 1. The act of alleging. That which is alleged. 3. Something alleged without pro 4. *Law* The assertion that a party to a suit undertakes prove. [< L < *ad-* to + *legare* to commission]

al·lege (ə·lej′) *v.t.* **·leged, ·leg·ing** 1. To assert to be tr without proving; affirm. 2. To plead as an excuse, in su ort of or in opposition to a claim or accusation. [< AF ; OF < L *ex-* out + *litigare* to sue] **— al·lege′a·ble** *adj.* **– al·leged′** (ə·lejd′, ə·lej′id) *adj.* **— al·leg′er** *n.*

·leg·ed·ly (ə·lej′id·lē) *adv.* According to allegation.

·le·giance (ə·lē′jəns) *n.* **1.** Fidelity, or an obligation of delity, to a government or sovereign. **2.** Fidelity in gen-ral, as to a principle. [ME < *a-* to + OF *liege* liege]

·le·gor·ic (al′ə·gôr′ik, -gor′-) *adj.* Pertaining to, appear-ıg in, or containing allegory; figurative. Also **al′le·gor′i·al.** **— al′le·gor′i·cal·ly** *adv.*

·le·go·rist (al′ə·gôr′ist, -gō′rist, al′ə·gər·ist) *n.* One who omposes or uses allegories.

·le·go·ris·tic (al′ə·gə·ris′tik) *adj.* Allegorizing.

·le·go·rize (al′ə·gə·rīz′) *v.* **·rized, ·riz·ing** *v.t.* **1.** To turn ıto an allegory; relate in the manner of an allegory. **2.** To xplain or interpret as an allegory. **—** *v.i.* **3.** To make or se allegory. **— al·le·go·ri·za·tion** (al′ə·gôr′ə·zā′shən, -gor′-) . **— al′le·go·riz′er** *n.*

·le·go·ry (al′ə·gôr′ē, -gō′rē) *n.* *pl.* **·ries 1.** A story or arrative, as a fable, in which a moral principle or truth is resented by means of fictional characters, events, etc. **2.** 'he presentation of a truth or moral by such stories. **3.** oosely, any symbolic representation in literature or art. < L < Gk. *allos* other + *agoreuein* to speak publicly]

·le·gret·to (al′ə·gret′ō, *Ital.* äl′lā·gret′tō) *Music adj. & dv.* Rather fast. **—** *n.* *pl.* **·tos** A composition, movement, tc., in such tempo. [< Ital., dim. of *allegro* lively]

·le·gro (ə·lā′grō, ə·leg′rō; *Ital.* äl·lā′grō) *Music adj. & adv.* ively. **—** *n.* *pl.* **·gros** A composition, movement, etc., in ıch tempo. [< Ital.]

·lele (ə·lēl′) *n.* *Genetics* One of a series of hereditary char-cters alternative to each other. Also **al·le·lo·morph** (ə·lē′·-môrf, ə·lel′ə-). [< Gk. *allēlōn* of one another + *morphē* ›rm] **— al·le′lo·mor′phic** *adj.* **— al·le·lo·mor′phism** *n.*

·le·lu·ia (al′ə·lōō′yə) *n. & interj.* Hallelujah: the Latin pelling and more common liturgic form. Also **al′le·lu′iah.**

·ler·gen (al′ər·jən) *n.* Any substance capable of producing llergy. Also **al′ler·gin.** **— al·ler·gen·ic** (al′ər·jen′ik) *adj.*

·ler·gic (ə·lûr′jik) *adj.* **1.** Of, pertaining to, or having an llergy. **2.** *Informal* Having an aversion: *allergic* to work.

·ler·gist (al′ər·jist) *n.* A specialist in the diagnosis and eatment of allergies.

·ler·gy (al′ər·jē) *n.* *pl.* **·gies** *Med.* A condition of eightened sensitivity to a substance, as food, pollen, dust, tc. [< NL < Gk. *allos* other + *ergon* work]

·le·vi·ate (ə·lē′vē·āt) *v.t.* **·at·ed, ·at·ing** To make lighter r easier to bear. [< L < *ad-* to + *levis* light, not heavy]

·le·vi·a·tive (ə·lē′vē·ā′tiv, ə·lē′vē·ə·tiv) *adj.* Tending to lleviate. Also **al·le·vi·a·to·ry** (ə·lē′vē·ə·tôr′ē, -tō′rē), **—** *n.* nything that alleviates.

·ley (al′ē) *n.* **1.** A narrow passageway; esp., a narrow ay between or behind city buildings. **2.** A bowling alley. . A walk bordered with trees or shrubbery. [< OF *alee* a oing, passage < *aler* to go]

·ley·way (al′ē·wā′) *n.* A passageway between buildings.

l Fools' Day The first of April, a day on which jokes and icks are commonly practiced: also *April Fools' Day.*

l fours The four legs of a quadruped, or the arms and gs of a person. **— to go** (or **be**) **on all fours** To rest or awl on all four limbs.

l·hal·low·mas (ôl′hal′ō·məs) *n.* All Saints' Day. Also **ll·hal·lows** (ôl·hal′ōz).

·li·ance (ə·lī′əns) *n.* **1.** The state or condition of being al-ed. **2.** The relationship or union brought about by mar-age. **3.** Any union, coalition, or agreement between par-es, sovereigns, nations, etc., in their common interest. **4.** elationship in qualities or characteristics; affinity. [< OF ; L < *ad-* to + *ligare* to bind]

·lied (ə·līd′, al′īd) *adj.* **1.** United, confederated, or leagued. . Closely related: *allied* interests.

·lies (al′īz, ə·līz′) *n.pl.* **1.** The twenty-seven nations al-ed against the Central Powers in World War I; esp., Rus-a, France, Great Britain, Italy, and the United States. **2.** 'he nations and governments-in-exile known as the United lations in World War II. **— Al·lied** (ə·līd′, al′īd) *adj.*

·li·ga·tor (al′ə·gā′tər) *n.* **1.** A large crocodilian reptile ›und only in the southern United States and in the Yangtze ver, China, having shorter, blunter nout than the croco-ile. **2.** Leather made om the skin of the lligator. [< Sp. *el* ıgarto < L *lacertus* zard]

ALLIGATOR
(To 16 feet long)

ligator pear The fruit of the avocado.

l-im·por·tant (ôl′im·pôr′tənt) *adj.* Very important.

l-in·clu·sive (ôl′in·klōō′siv) *adj.* Including everything.

al·lit·er·ate (ə·lit′ə·rāt) *v.* **·at·ed, ·at·ing** *v.i.* **1.** To use allit-eration. **2.** To contain alliteration. **—** *v.t.* **3.** To make al-literative. [< AL-[2] to + L *littera* a letter (of the alphabet)]

al·lit·er·a·tion (ə·lit′ə·rā′shən) *n.* The occurrence, in a phrase or line, of two or more words having the same initial sound or sound cluster, as in "A fair field full of folk."

al·lit·er·a·tive (ə·lit′ə·rā′tiv, -ər·ə·tiv) *adj.* Of or like allit-eration. **— al·lit′er·a′tive·ly** *adv.* **— al·lit′er·a′tive·ness** *n.*

allo- *combining form* **1.** Other; alien. **2.** Extraneousness; difference from or opposition to the normal: *allopathy.* [< Gk. *allos* other]

al·lo·cate (al′ə·kāt) *v.t.* **·cat·ed, ·cat·ing 1.** To set apart for a special purpose, as funds. **2.** To apportion; assign as a share or in shares. **3.** To locate or localize, as a person or event. [< Med.L < L *ad-* to + *locare* to place] **— al·lo·ca·ble** (al′ə·kə·bəl) *adj.* **— al′lo·ca′tion** *n.*

al·lom·er·ism (ə·lom′ər·iz′əm) *n.* *Crystall.* Constancy of crystalline form with variation in chemical constitution. [< ALLO- + Gk. *meros* a part] **— al·lom′er·ous** *adj.*

al·lo·path (al′ə·path) *n.* One who practices or favors allop-athy. Also **al·lop·a·thist** (ə·lop′ə·thist).

al·lop·a·thy (ə·lop′ə·thē) *n.* A system of treatment that seeks to cure a disease by producing a condition different from the effects of the disease. **— al·lo·path·ic** (al′ə·path′·ik) *adj.* **— al′lo·path′i·cal·ly** *adv.*

al·lot (ə·lot′) *v.t.* **·lot·ted, ·lot·ting 1.** To assign by lot; dis-tribute. **2.** To apportion or assign: with *to.* [< OF < *a-* to + *loter* to apportion]

al·lot·ment (ə·lot′mənt) *n.* **1.** The act of allotting, or that which is allotted. **2.** *U.S. Mil.* A portion of a serviceman's pay regularly assigned, as to a member of his family.

al·lo·trope (al′ə·trōp) *n.* *Chem.* One of the forms assumed by an allotropic substance.

al·lot·ro·py (ə·lot′rə·pē) *n.* *Chem.* The variation in proper-ties shown by elements or their compounds without change of chemical composition. Also **al·lot·ro·pism** (ə·lot′rə·piz′·əm). [< Gk. *allos* other + *tropos* turn, manner] **— al·lo·trop·ic** (al′ə·trop′ik) or **·i·cal** *adj.* **— al′lo·trop′i·cal·ly** *adv.*

al·lot·tee (ə·lot′ē) *n.* One to whom anything is allotted.

all-out (ôl′out′) *adj.* Complete and entire; total.

all·o·ver (*adj.* ôl′ō′vər; *n.* ôl′ō′vər) *adj.* Extending over the whole or surface of anything: the *allover* effect. **—** *n.* A fabric or other substance having an allover pattern.

al·low (ə·lou′) *v.t.* **1.** To permit to occur or do. **2.** To con-cede; admit. **3.** To make allowance or provision for: to *allow* an hour for lunch. **4.** To make concession of: to *allow* a month to pay. **5.** To grant; allot. **6.** *U.S. Dial* To say; declare. **—** *v.i.* **7.** To permit or admit: with *of*: Your re-mark *allows* of several interpretations. **8.** To make conces-sion or due allowance: with *for.* [< OF *alouer* to place, use, assign < Med.L < L < *ad-* to + *laudare* to praise]

al·low·a·ble (ə·lou′ə·bəl) *adj.* Permissible; admissible. **— al·low′a·ble·ness** *n.* **— al·low′a·bly** *adv.*

al·low·ance (ə·lou′əns) *n.* **1.** That which is allowed. **2.** A definite sum of money given at regular intervals. **3.** A discount, as for a purchase in volume, a trade-in, etc. **4.** The act of allowing; toleration; sanction. **5.** Admission; acceptance. **— to make allowance(s) for** To take into ac-count or to excuse because of modifying circumstances. **—** *v.t.* **·anced, ·anc·ing 1.** To put on an allowance; limit to a regular amount. **2.** To supply in limited quantities.

al·low·ed·ly (ə·lou′id·lē) *adv.* Admittedly.

al·loy (*n.* al′oi, ə·loi′; *v.* ə·loi′) *n.* **1.** *Metall.* **a** A mixture or combination formed by the fusion of two or more metals or of a metal and a nonmetal. **b** A baser metal mixed or com-bined with a finer one. **2.** Anything that reduces purity. **—** *v.t.* **1.** To reduce the purity of, as a metal, by mixing with an alloy. **2.** To mix (metals) so as to form into an alloy. **3.** To modify or debase, as by mixture with something in-ferior. [< F < OF < L < *ad-* to + *ligare* to bind]

all-pur·pose (ôl′pûr′pəs) *adj.* Generally useful.

all-right (ôl′rīt′) *adj.* *Slang* **1.** Dependable; honest; loyal. **2.** Good; excellent.

all right 1. Satisfactory. **2.** Correct, as a sum in addi-tion. **3.** Uninjured. **4.** Certainly. **5.** Yes. See ALRIGHT.

all-round (ôl′round′) *adj.* **1.** *U.S.* Of comprehensive range or scope; complete in action or effect. **2.** Excelling in all or many aspects; many-sided; versatile. Also *all-around.*

All Saints' Day *Eccl.* November 1, a festival commemora-tive of all saints and martyrs. Also **All Saints.**

All Souls' Day *Eccl.* November 2, a day of commemora-tion on which intercession is made for the souls of all the faithful departed. Also **All Souls.**

all·spice (ôl′spīs′) *n.* **1.** The aromatic dried berry of the pimento. **2.** The sharply flavored spice made from it.

al·lude (ə·lōōd′) *v.i.* **·lud·ed, ·lud·ing** To refer without ex-press mention; make indirect or casual reference: with *to.* [< L < *ad-* to + *ludere* to play]

ONUNCIATION KEY: **add, āce, câre, pälm; end, ēven; it, īce; odd, ōpen, ôrder; tŏŏk, pōōl; up, bûrn; ə** = a in *above,* e in *sicken,* i in *flex-e,* o in *melon,* u in *focus;* **yōō** = u in *fuse;* **oil; pout; check; go; ring; thin; this; zh,** vision.

al·lure (ə·lo͝or′) *v.t. & v.i.* **·lured, ·lur·ing** To draw with or as with a lure; attract; entice. — *n.* That which allures. [< OF < *a-* to + *leurre* lure] — **al·lure′ment** *n.* — **al·lur′er** *n.*

al·lur·ing (ə·lo͝or′ing) *adj.* Attractive; fascinating. — **al·lur′ing·ly** *adv.* — **al·lur′ing·ness** *n.*

al·lu·sion (ə·lo͞o′zhən) *n.* The act of alluding; indirect reference; suggestion. [< L *alludere* to play with, joke]

al·lu·sive (ə·lo͞o′siv) *adj.* Making allusion; suggestive. — **al·lu′sive·ly** *adv.* — **al·lu′sive·ness** *n.*

al·lu·vi·al (ə·lo͞o′vē·əl) *adj.* Pertaining to or composed of earth deposited by water. — *n.* Alluvial soil.

al·lu·vi·um (ə·lo͞o′vē·əm) *n. pl.* **·vi·a** (-vē·ə) or **·vi·ums** A deposit, as of sand or mud, transported and laid down by flowing water in river beds, flood plains, lakes, etc. [< L]

al·ly (ə·lī′, al′ī) *v.* **·lied, ·ly·ing** *v.t.* **1.** To connect by some relationship or bond: with *to* or *with.* — *v.i.* **2.** To enter into alliance; become allied. — *n. pl.* **·lies 1.** A person or country connected with another, as by treaty or common action. **2.** Any friendly associate or helper. **3.** An organism or substance associated with another by similarity. [< OF < L < *ad-* to + *ligare* to bind]

al·ma ma·ter (al′mə mä′tər, al′mə mā′tər, äl′mə mä′tər) The institution of learning that one has attended. Also **Al′ma Ma′ter.** [< L, fostering mother]

al·ma·nac (ôl′mə·nak) *n.* A yearly calendar giving weather forecasts, astronomical information, times of high and low tides, etc. [< Med.L < Sp. < Arabic *al-manākh*]

al·might·y (ôl·mīt′ē) *adj.* **1.** Able to do all things; omnipotent. **2.** *U.S. Informal* Great; extreme: an *almighty* noise. — *adv. U.S. Informal* Exceedingly: *almighty* mad. — **the Almighty** God; the Supreme Being. [OE *eal* all + *mihtig* mighty] — **al·might′i·ly** *adv.* — **al·might′i·ness** *n.*

al·mond (ä′mənd, am′ənd) *n.* **1.** A small tree of the rose family, widely cultivated in the warmer temperate regions. **2.** The kernel of the fruit of the almond tree. **3.** Anything having the pointed, oval shape of an almond. [< OF < LL < L < Gk. *amygdalē*]

al·mon·er (al′mən·ər, ä′mən-) *n.* An official dispenser of alms. Also **alm·ner** (alm′nər, äm′nər). [< OF < LL < L < Gk. *eleēmosynē* alms < *eleos* pity]

al·most (ôl′mōst, ôl·mōst′) *adv.* Approximately; very nearly; all but: *almost* complete. [OE *ealmǣst*]

alms (ämz) *n. sing. & pl.* A gift or gifts for the poor. ◆ Collateral adjective: *eleemosynary.* Some self-explanatory compounds have *alms* as their first element: **almsgiver, almsgiving, almsmoney,** etc. [OE < LL < Gk. *eleēmosynē* alms < *eleos* pity]

alms·house (ämz′hous′) *n.* A poorhouse.

al·oe (al′ō) *n. pl.* **·oes 1.** An Old World plant of the lily family, some species of which furnish a drug, and others valuable fiber. **2.** *pl.* (*construed as sing.*) A cathartic made from the juice of certain aloes. [OE < L < Gk. *aloē*] — **al·o·et·ic** (al′ō·et′ik) or **·i·cal** *adj.*

a·loft (ə·lôft′, ə·loft′) *adv.* **1.** In or to a high or higher place; on high; high up. **2.** *Naut.* At or to the higher parts of a ship's rigging. [< ON *ā lopt* in (the) air]

a·lo·ha (ə·lō′ə, ä·lō′hä) *n. & interj. Hawaiian* Love: used as a salutation and a farewell.

Aloha State Nickname of HAWAII.

a·lone (ə·lōn′) *adv. & adj.* **1.** Without company; solitary. **2.** Excluding all others; only: He *alone* survived. **3.** Without equal; unique; unparalleled: As an artist, he stands *alone.* [ME *al one* solitary]

a·long (ə·lông′, ə·long′) *adv.* **1.** Following the length or course of; lengthwise: usually with *by.* **2.** Progressively onward in a course; forward: The years roll *along* quickly. **3.** In company or association; together: usually with *with.* **4.** *U.S.* As a companion: Bring a friend *along.* **5.** *U.S. Informal* Advanced in its natural course. **6.** *U.S. Informal* Approaching a time, age, number, etc.: usually with *about.* — **all along** From the outset; throughout. — **to be along** *U.S. Informal* To arrive at a place; come. — **right along** *U.S. Informal* Without interruption. — *prep.* Throughout or over the length or course of. [OE *andlang* continuous]

a·long·shore (ə·lông′shôr′, ə·long′-, -shōr′) *adv.* Along the shore, either on the water or on the land.

a·long·side (ə·lông′sīd′, ə·long′-) *adv.* Close to or along the side. — *prep.* Side by side with; at the side of.

a·loof (ə·lo͞of′) *adj.* Distant, esp. in manner; unsympathetic. — *adv.* At a distance; apart: to stand *aloof.* [< A-[1] + *loof* < Du. *loef* windward] — **a·loof′ly** *adv.* — **a·loof′·ness** *n.*

a·loud (ə·loud′) *adv.* Loudly or audibly.

alp (alp) *n.* **1.** A lofty mountain. **2.** Any peak of the Alps. [Back formation < L *Alpes* the Alps]

al·pac·a (al·pak′ə) *n.* **1.** A domesticated ruminant of South America, related to the llama and vicuña. **2.** Its long silky wool. **3.** A thin cloth made of or containing this wool. **4.** A glossy black fabric of cotton and wool. [< Sp. < Arabic *al* the + Peruvian *paco,* name of the animal]

al·pen·horn (al′pən·hôrn′) *n.* A long, slightly curved ho made of wood and used in the Alps for signaling over lo distances. Also **alp′horn′.** [< G]

al·pen·stock (al′pən·stok′) *n.* A long, iron-pointed st used by mountain climbers. [< G]

al·pha (al′fə) *n.* **1.** The first letter in the Greek alphal (Α, α), corresponding to English *a.* See table for ALPHABI **2.** The first of anything. [< Gk. < Hebrew *āleph* ox]

al·pha·bet (al′fə·bet) *n.* **1.** The letters that form the e ments of written language, in an order fixed by usage. Any system of characters or symbols representing t sounds of speech. **3.** The simplest elements of anythi [< L < Gk. < Hebrew *āleph* ox + *beth* house]

al·pha·bet·i·cal (al′fə·bet′i·kəl) *adj.* **1.** Arranged in t order of the alphabet. **2.** Pertaining to or expressed by alphabet. Also **al′pha·bet′ic.** — **al′pha·bet′i·cal·ly** *adv.*

al·pha·bet·ize (al′fə·bə·tīz′) *v.t.* **·ized, ·iz·ing 1.** To put alphabetical order. **2.** To express by or furnish with an phabet or alphabetic symbols. — **al·pha·bet·i·za·tion** (fə·bet′ə·zā′shən) *n.* — **al′pha·bet·iz′er** *n.*

alpha particle *Physics* The positively charged nucleus the helium atom.

alpha ray *Physics* A stream of alpha particles.

alpha rhythm *Physiol.* The recurring cycles of electri change in the brain, each cycle known as an **alpha wave.**

al·pine (al′pīn, -pin) *adj.* **1.** Like an alp; lofty and tow ing. **2.** *Biol.* Inhabiting or growing in mountain region

Al·pine (al′pīn, -pin) *adj.* Pertaining to or characteristic the Alps. [< L *Alpes* the Alps]

al·pi·nist (al′pə·nist) *n.* A climber of alps; a mountaine Also **Al′pi·nist.** — **al′pi·nism, Al′pi·nism** *n.*

al·read·y (ôl·red′ē) *adv.* Before or by the time mention

al·right (ôl·rīt′) *adv.* All right: a spelling not yet conside acceptable.

Al·sa·tian (al·sā′shən) *adj.* **1.** Of or pertaining to Alsa **2.** Of or pertaining to Alsatia. — *n.* **1.** A native or inha tant of Alsace. **2.** A German shepherd dog.

al·so (ôl′sō) *adv.* In addition; besides; likewise. [OE *als ealswā* all (wholly) so]

al·so-ran (ôl′sō·ran′) *n. U.S. Informal* **1.** A horse that f to win, place, or show in a race. **2.** Any unsuccessful co petitor.

Al·ta·ic (al·tā′ik) *adj.* Of the Altai Mountains or the l guages spoken there. Also **Al·tai·an** (al·tā′ən, -tī′-) *adj.*

al·tar (ôl′tər) *n.* **1.** Any raised place or structure on wh sacrifices may be offered or incense burned as an act of w ship. **2.** *Eccl.* The structure of wood or stone on which elements are consecrated in the Eucharist. [OE < L *altus* hi

altar boy An attendant at the altar; acolyte.

al·tar·piece (ôl′tər·pēs′) *n.* A painting, mosaic, or b relief over and behind the altar; a reredos.

al·ter (ôl′tər) *v.t.* **1.** To cause to be different. **2.** *U.S.* castrate or spay. — *v.i.* **3.** To change. [< MF < Me < L *alter* other]

al·ter·a·ble (ôl′tər·ə·bəl) *adj.* Capable of alteration. — **ter·a·bil′i·ty, al′ter·a·ble·ness** *n.* — **al′ter·a·bly** *adv.*

al·ter·a·tion (ôl′tə·rā′shən) *n.* **1.** The act or process of tering. **2.** Any change. [< MF < Med.L < L *alter* oth

al·ter·a·tive (ôl′tə·rā′tiv) *adj.* **1.** Tending to prod change. **2.** *Med.* Tending to change gradually the bod condition to a normal state. — *n. Med.* An alterative me cine or treatment. Also **al·ter·ant** (ôl′tər·ənt).

al·ter·cate (ôl′tər·kāt, al′-) *v.i.* **·cat·ed, ·cat·ing** To disp vehemently. [< L *alter* other]

al·ter·ca·tion (ôl′tər·kā′shən, al′-) *n.* A heated dispute

al·ter e·go (ôl′tər ē′gō, al′tər eg′ō) **1.** Another self; a do le. **2.** An intimate friend. [< L, lit., other I]

al·ter·nant (ôl·tûr′nənt, ôl′tər·nənt, al-) *adj.* Alternati

al·ter·nate (*v.* ôl′tər·nāt, al′-; *adj. & n.* ôl′tər·nit, al′-) **·nat·ed, ·nat·ing** *v.i.* **1.** To follow one another by tur **2.** To change from one place, condition, etc., to another back again repeatedly. **3.** *Electr.* To reverse direction flow repeatedly: said of a current. — *v.t.* **4.** To do or p form by turns. **5.** To cause to follow one another by tur — *adj.* **1.** Existing, occurring, or following by turns. Referring or pertaining to every other of a series. **3.** Alt native: *alternate* plans. — *n.* A substitute or second. [< *alternus* every second one] — **al′ter·nate·ly** (-nit·lē) *a* — **al′ter·nate·ness** *n.*

alternate angle *Geom.* Either of two nonadjacent inter or exterior angles formed on opposite sides of a line t crosses two other lines.

al·ter·na·tion (ôl′tər·nā′shən, al′-) *n.* Occurrence or act of two things in turn; passage from one place or state to other and back again.

al·ter·na·tive (ôl·tûr′nə·tiv, al-) *n.* **1.** A choice betw two things: often loosely applied to more than two. Either of the two or more things to be chosen. **3.** The maining choice. — *adj.* Affording or implying a choice tween two (or sometimes more) things. — **al·ter′na·tive** *adv.* — **al·ter′na·tive·ness** *n.* [< Med.L *alternativus*]

ter·na·tor (ôl′tər·nā′tər, al′-) *n. Electr.* A generator giv-g an alternating current. Also **al′ter·nat′er.**
the·a (al·thē′ə) *n.* Any of several plants of the mallow mily, including the rose of Sharon. Also **al·thae′a.** [< L Gk. *althainein* to heal]
·horn (alt′hôrn′) *n.* An alto flügelhorn or saxhorn.
though (ôl·thō′) *conj.* Notwithstanding the fact that; pposing that; though. Also **al·tho′.**
i- *combining form* High. Also *alto-*. [< L < *altus* high]
tim·e·ter (al·tim′ə·tər, al′tə·mē′tər) *n.* **1.** An aneroid rometer for determining altitudes. **2.** Any instrument r determining altitude. — **al·tim·e·try** (al·tim′ə·trē) *n.*
ti·tude (al′tə·to͞od, -tyo͞od) *n.* **1.** Elevation above any ven point, esp. above mean sea level; height. **2.** *Astron.* ngular elevation above the horizon. **3.** *Geom.* The vertical stance from the base of a figure to its highest point. **4.** A gh place or rank. [< L *altus* high] — **al′ti·tu′di·nal** *adj.*
to (al′tō) *Music n. pl.* **·tos 1.** The lowest female voice; ntralto. **2.** The highest male voice; countertenor. **3.** A nger who has an alto voice. **4.** A musical part for this voice. – *adj.* Of or for the alto. [< Ital. < L *altus* high]
to- Var. of ALTI-.
to·geth·er (ôl′tə·geth′ər, ôl′tə·geth′ər) *adv.* **1.** Com-etely; wholly; entirely. **2.** With everything included. – *n.* A whole. — **in the altogether** *Informal* Nude.
tru·ism (al′tro͞o·iz′əm) *n.* Selfless devotion to the wel-re of others. [< F < L *alter* other] — **al′tru·ist** *n.* — **al·u·is·tic** (al′tro͞o·is′tik) *adj.* — **al′tru·is′ti·cal·ly** *adv.*
um (al′əm) *n. Chem.* An astringent, crystalline, double sulfate of aluminum and potassium, $K_2SO_4Al_2(SO_4)_3 \cdot 24H_2O$, used in medicine and industry. [< OF < L *alumen* alum]
a·lu·mi·na (ə·lo͞o′mə·nə) *n. Chem.* Aluminum oxide, Al_2O_3, occurring in the silicate minerals and as corundum in the sapphire and ruby. Also **al·u·min** (al′yə·min), **al·u·mine** (al′yə·mēn, -min). [< NL < L *alumen* alum]
a·lu·mi·nize (ə·lo͞o′mə·nīz) *v.t.* **·nized, ·niz·ing** To cover or treat with aluminum. Also **a·lu·me·tize** (ə·lo͞o′mə·tīz).
a·lu·mi·num (ə·lo͞o′mə·nəm) *n.* A light, bluish white, malleable and ductile metallic element (symbol Al) found only in combination. It is widely used in alloys. Also *Brit.* **al·u·min·i·um** (al′yə·min′ē·əm). See ELEMENT. [< NL < L *alumen* alum] — **a·lu′mi·nous** *adj.*
a·lum·na (ə·lum′nə) *n. pl.* **·nae** (-nē) *U.S.* A female graduate or former student of a college or school. [< L]
a·lum·nus (ə·lum′nəs) *n. pl.* **·ni** (-nī) *Chiefly U.S.* A male graduate or former student of a college or school. [< L, foster son, pupil < *alere* to nourish]
al·ve·o·lar (al·vē′ə·lər) *adj.* **1.** *Anat.* Denoting that part of the jaws in which the teeth are set. **2.** *Phonet.* Formed with the tongue tip touching or near the alveolar ridge, as (t), (d), and (s) in English. — *n. Phonet.* A sound so produced.
al·ve·o·late (al·vē′ə·lit, al′vē·ə-) *adj.* Having alveoli arranged like the cells of a honeycomb; deeply pitted. Also **al·ve·o·lat·ed** (al·vē′ə·lā′tid). — **al·ve′o·la′tion** *n.*
al·ve·o·lus (al·vē′ə·ləs) *n. pl.* **·li** (-lī) *Anat.* **1.** A small cavity or pit, as an air cell of the lung. **2.** The socket in which a tooth is set. **3.** *pl.* The bony ridge holding the upper front teeth. [< L, dim. of *alveus* a hollow]

TABLE OF FOREIGN ALPHABETS

(1) ARABIC

ا	alif	–[1]
ب	ba	b
ت	ta	t
ث	sa	th
ج	jim	j
ح	ha	h
خ	kha	kh
د	dal	d
ذ	zal	th
ر	ra	r
ز	za	z
س	sin	s
ش	shin	sh
ص	sad	s
ض	ḍad	d
ط	ta	t
ظ	za	z
ع	ain	–[2]
غ	ghain	gh[3]
ف	fa	f
ق	qaf	k[4]
ك	kaf	k[5]
ل	lam	l
م	mim	m
ن	nun	n
ه	ha	h
و	waw	w
ي	ya	y

(2) HEBREW

א	aleph	–[6]
בּ, ב	beth	b, v
גּ, ג	gimel	g, gh[3]
דּ, ד	daleth	d, th
ה	he	h
ו	vav	v
ז	zayin	z
ח	ḥeth	kh
ט	ṭeth	t
י	yod	y
ך[8], כ, כּ	kaph	k[5], kh
ל	lamed	l
ם[8], מ	mem	m
ן[8], נ	nun	n
ס	samek	s
ע	ayin	–[7]
ף[8], פ, פּ	pe	p, f
ץ[8], צ	sade	s
ק	ḳoph	k[4]
ר	resh	r
שׂ, שׁ	sin, shin	s, sh
ת, תּ	tav	t, th

(3) GREEK

Α	α	alpha	ä
Β	β	beta	b
Γ	γ	gamma	g
Δ	δ	delta	d
Ε	ϵ	epsilon	e
Ζ	ζ	zeta	z
Η	η	eta	ā
Θ	θ	theta	th[9]
Ι	ι	iota	ē
Κ	κ	kappa	k
Λ	λ	lambda	l
Μ	μ	mu	m
Ν	ν	nu	n
Ξ	ξ	xi	ks
Ο	ο	omicron	o
Π	π	pi	p
Ρ	ρ	rho	r
Σ	σ, ς[8]	sigma	s
Τ	τ	tau	t
Υ	υ	upsilon	ü, o͞o
Φ	φ	phi	f[10]
Χ	χ	chi	kh[11]
Ψ	ψ	psi	ps
Ω	ω	omega	ō

(4) RUSSIAN

А	а	ä	ä
Б	б	be	b
В	в	ve	v
Г	г	ge	g
Д	д	de	d
Е	е	ye	ye, e[12]
Ё	ё	yô	yô, ô[12, 13]
Ж	ж	zhe	zh[14]
З	з	ze	z
И	и	ē	ē[15]
Й	й	ē krät′·kə·yə	ē[16]
К	к	kä	k
Л	л	el	l
М	м	em	m
Н	н	en	n
О	о	ô	ô
П	п	pe	p
Р	р	er	r
С	с	es	s
Т	т	te	t
У	у	o͞o	o͞o
Ф	ф	ef	f
Х	х	khä	kh
Ц	ц	tse	ts[14]
Ч	ч	che	ch[17]
Ш	ш	shä	sh[14]
Щ	щ	shchä	shch[17]
Ъ	ъ	tvyôr′dē znäk	–[18]
Ы	ы	i[19]	i[19]
Ь	ь	myäkh′·kyē znäk	–[20]
Э	э	e	e
Ю	ю	yo͞o	yo͞o, o͞o[12]
Я	я	yä	yä, ä[12]

(5) GERMAN

𝔄	𝔞	ä	A	a
𝔄̈	𝔞̈	e[21]	Ä	ä
𝔅	𝔟	bā	B	b
ℭ	𝔠	tsā	C	c
𝔇	𝔡	dā	D	d
𝔈	𝔢	ā[22]	E	e
𝔉	𝔣	ef	F	f
𝔊	𝔤	gā	G	g
ℌ	𝔥	hä	H	h
ℑ	𝔦	ē	I	i
𝔍	𝔧	yôt	J	j
𝔎	𝔨	kä	K	k
𝔏	𝔩	el	L	l
𝔐	𝔪	em	M	m
𝔑	𝔫	en	N	n
𝔒	𝔬	ō[22]	O	o
𝔒̈	𝔬̈	œ[21]	Ö	ö
𝔓	𝔭	pā	P	p
𝔔	𝔮	ko͞o	Q	q
ℜ	𝔯	er	R	r
𝔖	ſ, 𝔰[8]	es	S	s
—	ß[23]	es′tset	—	ß[23], ss
𝔗	𝔱	tā	T	t
𝔘	𝔲	o͞o	U	u
𝔘̈	𝔲̈	ü[21]	Ü	ü
𝔙	𝔳	fou	V	v
𝔚	𝔴	vā	W	w
𝔛	𝔵	iks	X	x
𝔜	𝔶	üp′si·lōn	Y	y
ℨ	𝔷	tset	Z	z

In each column the characters of the alphabet are given first, followed by their names. columns 4 (Russian) and 5 (German) the names are printed in the phonetic system used this dictionary. The last rows of columns 1 through 4 show the approximate sound resented by each character. Columns 3 through 5 show the upper- and lower-case forms.

The Arabic characters are given in their final, unconnected forms. The German style letter, called *fraktur*, has been gradually replaced by the Latin letter. The last row of column 5 gives the Latin equivalents.

[1] Functions as the bearer of *hamza* (the glottal stop), as a lengthener of short *a*. [2] A voiced pharyngeal frica-. [3] A voiced velar fricative. [4] A uvular stop. [5] A voice- velar stop. [6] A glottal stop, now usually silent, or nounced according to the accompanying vowel points. pharyngeal fricative, now usually silent, or pronounced ording to the accompanying vowel points. [8] The alter-e form is restricted to the ends of words. [9, 10, 11] In classical Greek these were pronounced as aspirated stops similar to the sounds in foot*h*ill, ha*ph*azard, and blo*ckh*ouse. [12] Preceded by a *y* glide when initial, following a vowel, or following a previously palatalized consonant. The glide is otherwise omitted and the preceding consonant palatalized. [13] The diacritical mark is most often omitted. [14] Never palatalized. [15] Palatalizes the consonant preceding it. [16] A short vowel, as *y* in *boy*, used only as the second element of diphthongs. [17] Always palatalized. [18] No phonetic value, used to separate parts of compounds and indicate that the consonant preceding it is not palatalized; a hard sign. [19] No English equivalent, similar to *i* as in *kick* with the tongue drawn back. [20] Indicates that the preceding consonant is to be palatalized. [21] See UMLAUT in vocabulary section. [22] In German this vowel is not a diphthong. [23] Restricted to the ends of words.

al·ways (ôl′wāz, -wiz) *adv.* **1.** Perpetually; for all time; ceaselessly. **2.** At every time; on all occasions. [ME *alles weyes* < OE *aelne weg*]

a·lys·sum (ə·lis′əm) *n.* **1.** Any plant of the mustard family, bearing white or yellow flowers. **2.** The sweet alyssum. [< NL < Gk. < *a-* not + *lyssa* madness]

am (am, *unstressed* əm) Present indicative, first person singular, of BE. [OE *eom, am*]

a·mah (ä′mə, am′ə) *n.* In India and the Orient, a female attendant for children; esp., a wet nurse. Also **a′ma.** [< Anglo-Indian < Pg. *ama* nurse]

a·mal·gam (ə·mal′gəm) *n.* **1.** An alloy or union of mercury with another metal. **2.** A silver-white, brittle compound of mercury and silver. **3.** Any combination of two or more things. [< MF < Med.L < Gk. *malagma* an emollient < *malassein* to soften]

a·mal·ga·mate (ə·mal′gə·māt) *v.t. & v.i.* **·mat·ed, ·mat·ing** **1.** To form an amalgam. **2.** To unite or combine. — **a·mal·ga·ma·ble** (ə·mal′gə·mə·bəl) *adj.* — **a·mal·ga·ma·tive** (ə·mal′gə·mā′tiv) *adj.* — **a·mal′ga·ma′tor** or **a·mal′ga·mat′er** *n.* — **a·mal′ga·ma′tion** *n.*

a·man·u·en·sis (ə·man′yo͞o·en′sis) *n. pl.* **·ses** (-sēz) One who copies manuscript or takes dictation; a secretary. [< L < (*servus*) *a manu* hand (servant), secretary]

am·a·ranth (am′ə·ranth) *n.* **1.** Any of various allied plants, as the love-lies-bleeding. **2.** *Poetic* An imaginary nonfading flower. [< L < Gk. < *a-* not + *marainein* to wither] — **am′a·ran′thine** *adj.*

am·a·ryl·lis (am′ə·ril′is) *n.* A bulbous plant, producing large, lily-like flowers. [< L < Gk. *Amaryllis*, fem. personal name]

a·mass (ə·mas′) *v.t.* To heap up, esp. wealth or possessions for oneself. [< OF < *a-* to + *masser* to pile up] — **a·mass′a·ble** *adj.* — **a·mass′er** *n.* — **a·mass′ment** *n.*

am·a·teur (am′ə·cho͝or, -to͝or, -tyo͝or, am′ə·tûr′) *n.* **1.** One who practices an art or science for his own pleasure, rather than as a profession. **2.** An athlete who has not engaged in contests for money. **3.** One who does something without professional skill or ease. — *adj.* **1.** Of, pertaining to, or done by an amateur. **2.** Not expert. [< F < L *amare* to love] — **am′a·teur·ism** *n.*

— **Syn.** (noun) **1.** In present usage, *amateur* is often used to indicate lack of skill, while *connoisseur* implies the ability to make discriminating judgments. A *dilettante* loves the arts, and often possesses great esthetic sensitivity, but lacks technical mastery.

am·a·teur·ish (am′ə·cho͝or′ish, -to͝or′-, -tyo͝or′-, -tûr′-) *adj.* Lacking the skill or perfection of an expert or professional. — **am′a·teur′ish·ly** *adv.* — **am′a·teur′ish·ness** *n.*

am·a·to·ry (am′ə·tôr′ē, -tō′rē) *adj.* Pertaining to, expressing, or exciting love, especially sexual love. — **Syn.** See AMOROUS. [< L *amare* to love]

a·maze (ə·māz′) *v.t.* **a·mazed, a·maz·ing** To overwhelm, as by wonder or surprise; astonish greatly. [OE *āmasian*] — **a·maz·ed·ly** (ə·mā′zid·lē) *adv.* — **a·maz′ed·ness** *n.*

a·maze·ment (ə·māz′mənt) *n.* Extreme wonder or surprise; astonishment.

a·maz·ing (ə·mā′zing) *adj.* Causing amazement; astonishing; wonderful. — **a·maz′ing·ly** *adv.*

Am·a·zon (am′ə·zon, -zən) *n.* **1.** In Greek mythology, one of a race of female warriors. **2.** Any large, strong or athletic woman or girl: also **am′a·zon.** [< L < Gk. *Amazōn* < Gk. *a-* without + *mazōs* breast, because of the fable that they cut off the right breast to facilitate the use of the bow] — **Am′a·zo′ni·an** (-zō′nē·ən) *adj.*

am·bas·sa·dor (am·bas′ə·dər, -dôr) *n.* **1.** An accredited diplomatic agent of the highest rank, appointed as the representative of one government to another. **2.** Any personal representative or messenger. — **ambassador-at-large** An ambassador accredited to no specific government. [< F, ult. < LL *ambactus* servant, goer about, prob. < Celtic] — **am·bas·sa·do·ri·al** (am·bas′ə·dôr′ē·əl, -dō′rē-) *adj.* — **am·bas′·a·dress** (-dris) *n.fem.* — **am·bas′sa·dor·ship** *n.*

— **Syn. 1.** A diplomatic representative of highest rank is an *ambassador*; one of lower rank is a *minister*. A *minister* sent on a special mission is called an *envoy*. A *nuncio* is a papal *ambassador*; a papal *envoy* is a *legate*.

am·ber (am′bər) *n.* **1.** A yellow or brownish-yellow fossilized vegetable resin, hard, brittle, and translucent, used in jewelry, etc. **2.** The color of amber. — *adj.* Pertaining to or like amber. [< OF < Arabic *anbar* ambergris]

am·ber·gris (am′bər·grēs, -gris) *n.* An opaque, grayish secretion of the sperm whale, sometimes found floating on the ocean, used in perfumery. [< F *ambre gris* gray amber]

ambi- *combining form* Both: *ambidextrous.* [< L *ambo* both]

am·bi·dex·trous (am′bə·dek′strəs) *adj.* **1.** Able to use both hands equally well. **2.** Very dexterous or skillful. **3.** Dissembling; double-dealing. — **am′bi·dex′trous·ly** *adv.* — **am′bi·dex·ter′i·ty** (-dek·ster′ə·tē), **am′bi·dex′trous·ness** *n.*

am·bi·ent (am′bē·ənt) *adj.* **1.** Surrounding; encircling; encompassing. **2.** Circulating. [< L < *ambi-* around + *ire* to go] — **am′bi·ence** *n.*

am·bi·gu·i·ty (am′bə·gyo͞o′ə·tē) *n. pl.* **·ties 1.** The qual of being ambiguous; doubtfulness. **2.** An expression, sta ment, situation, etc., that can be variously interpreted.

am·big·u·ous (am·big′yo͞o·əs) *adj.* **1.** Capable of being u derstood in more senses than one; having a double meani **2.** Doubtful or uncertain. [< L < *ambi-* around + *ag* to go] — **am·big′u·ous·ly** *adv.* — **am·big′u·ous·ness** *n.*

am·bi·tion (am·bish′ən) *n.* **1.** Eager desire to succeed, achieve power, wealth, fame, etc. **2.** The object of aspi tion or desire. — *v.t.* To desire and seek eagerly. [< *ambitio, -onis* a going about (to solicit votes) < *ambi-* arou + *ire* to go] — **am·bi′tion·less** *adj.*

am·bi·tious (am·bish′əs) *adj.* **1.** Actuated or characteri by ambition. **2.** Greatly desiring; eager for: with *of* or infinitive. **3.** Challenging; difficult: an *ambitious* proje — **am·bi′tious·ly** *adv.* — **am·bi′tious·ness** *n.*

am·biv·a·lent (am·biv′ə·lənt) *adj.* **1.** Uncertain or chan ful, esp. because affected by contradictory emotions. *Psychol.* Experiencing contradictory emotions, as love a hate, toward the same object. [< AMBI- + L *valens, -en* ppr. of *valere* to be strong, be worth] — **am·biv′a·lence**

am·ble (am′bəl) *v.i.* **·bled** (-bəld), **·bling 1.** To move, a horse, by lifting the two feet on one side together, alternat with the two feet on the other. **2.** To walk or proceed surely. — *n.* **1.** The gait of a horse when ambling. **2.** A movement resembling this. [< OF < L *ambulare* to wa — **am′bler** *n.* — **am′bling·ly** *adv.*

am·bro·sia (am·brō′zhə, -zhē·ə) *n.* **1.** In classical myth ogy, the food of the gods, giving immortality. **2.** Any very delicious food or drink. [< L < Gk. < *a-* not + *brotos* mortal]

am·bro·sial (am·brō′zhəl, -zhē·əl) *adj.* **1.** Of or like ambrosia; fragrant; delicious. **2.** Worthy of the gods; heavenly. Also **am·bro·sian** (am·brō′zhən, -zhē·ən) — **am·bro′sial·ly** *adv.*

AMBROS (*def.* 4 Commo ragwee (3 to 6 feet hig

am·bu·lance (am′byə·ləns) *n.* **1.** A special vehicle equipped for conveying the sick and wounded. **2.** A moving or field hospital. [< F < L *ambulare* to walk]

am·bu·lant (am′byə·lənt) *adj.* Walking or moving about.

am·bu·late (am′byə·lāt) *v.i.* **·lat·ed, ·lat·ing** To walk about; move from place to place. [< L *ambulare* to walk] — **am′bu·la′tion** *n.*

am·bu·la·to·ry (am′byə·lə·tôr′ē, -tō′rē) *adj.* **1.** Of or for walking. **2.** Able to walk, as an invalid. Shifting; not fixed or stationary. **4.** *Law* Alterable; chan able. — *n.pl.* **·ries** A sheltered place for walking, as a cloist

am·bus·cade (am′bəs·kād′) *n.* An ambush. — *v.t.* **·cad·** **·cad·ing** To ambush. [See AMBUSH.] — **am′bus·cad′er**

am·bush (am′bo͝osh) *n.* **1.** A lying in wait to attack awares; also, the attackers. **2.** Any unseen peril or sna **3.** A secret position for surprise attack. Also **am′bush·me** — *v.t.* To attack from a hidden place; waylay. [< OF Ital. < L *in-* in + *boscus* a wood] — **am′bush·er** *n.*

a·me·ba (ə·mē′bə) *n. pl.* **·bas** or **·bae** (-bē) A unicellu protozoan found in stagnant water or as a parasite, of definite shape, and reproducing by simple division: a spelled *amoeba.* [< NL < Gk. *amoibē* change] — **a·me·** (ə·mē′bik) *adj.*

a·me·boid (ə·mē′boid) *adj.* Resembling an ameba, as in change of form: also spelled *amoeboid.*

a·meer (ə·mir′) See AMIR.

a·mel·io·rate (ə·mēl′yə·rāt) *v.t. & v.i.* **·rat·ed, ·rat·ing** make or become better; meliorate; improve. [< F < L to + *meliorare* to better] — **a·mel·io·ra·ble** (ə·mēl′yə bəl) *adj.* — **a·mel′io·rant** (-rənt) *n.* — **a·mel′io·ra′tion** — **a·mel·io·ra·tive** (ə·mēl′yə·rā′tiv, -rə·tiv) *adj.* — **a·m io·ra′tor** *n.*

a·men (ā′men′, ä′-) *interj.* So it is; so be it: used at the e of a prayer or statement to express agreement. — *n.* T word *amen* or any use of it. — *adv.* Verily; truly. [< L Gk. < Hebrew *āmēn* verily]

a·me·na·ble (ə·mē′nə·bəl, ə·men′ə-) *adj.* **1.** Capable of ing persuaded; submissive. **2.** Liable to be called to count; responsible to authority. **3.** Capable of being tes or judged by rule or law. [< AF < *a-* to + *mener* to lead L *minare* to drive (with threats)] — **a·me′na·bil′i·ty, a·m na·ble·ness** *n.* — **a·me′na·bly** *adv.*

a·mend (ə·mend′) *v.t.* **1.** To change for the better; impro correct. **2.** To change or alter by authority. — *v.i.* **3.** become better in conduct. [< OF < L *emendare* to f from faults] — **a·mend′a·ble** *adj.* — **a·mend′a·ble·ness** — **a·mend′er** *n.*

a·mend·a·to·ry (ə·men′də·tôr′ē, -tō′rē) *adj.* Tending amend; corrective.

a·mend·ment (ə·mend′mənt) *n.* **1.** Change for the bett **2.** A removal of faults; correction. **3.** The changing, as o law, bill, or motion. **4.** The statement of such a change

a·mends (ə·mendz′) *n.pl.* Reparation, as in satisfaction compensation for loss, etc. [< OF < L *mendum* fault]

nen·i·ty (ə·men′ə·tē) *n. pl.* **·ties 1.** Agreeableness; pleas-ntness. **2.** *Usu. pl.* An act or expression of courtesy; vility. [< L *amoenitas, -tatis* < *amoenus* pleasant]

nerce (ə·mûrs′) *v.t.* **a·merced, a·merc·ing 1.** To punish y an assessment or arbitrary fine. **2.** To punish, as by dep-vation. [< AF < *a merci* at the mercy of] **— a·merce′·ble** *adj.* **— a·merce′ment** *n.* **— a·merc′er** *n.*

mer·i·can (ə·mer′ə·kən) *adj.* **1.** Pertaining to the nited States of America, its history, government, people, c. **2.** Pertaining to the continent or people of North or outh America, or of the Western Hemisphere. **—** *n.* **1.** A tizen of the United States. **2.** An inhabitant of America.

mer·i·ca·na (ə·mer′ə·kä′nə, -kan′ə, -kā′nə) *n.pl.* Any ollection of American literary papers, sayings, etc., that re-te to America.

nerican eagle The bald eagle. See under EAGLE.

nerican English The English language as used or oken in the United States.

nerican Expeditionary Forces United States troops nt to Europe in World War I.

nerican Federation of Labor A federation of trade nions, founded in 1886, in 1955 merged with the Congress Industrial Organizations. Abbr. *AFL, A.F.L., A.F. of L.*

mer·i·can·ism (ə·mer′ə·kən·iz′əm) *n.* **1.** A trait, custom, tradition especially characteristic of the people of the nited States or of some of them. **2.** A word, phrase, or us-ge especially characteristic of American English. **3.** Devo-on to the United States, its institutions, etc.

mer·i·can·ize (ə·mer′ə·kən·īz′) *v.t. & v.i.* **·ized, ·iz·ing** To ake or become American in spirit, methods, speech, etc. **- A·mer′i·can·i·za′tion** *n.*

nerican League See under MAJOR LEAGUE.

nerican Revolution See under REVOLUTION.

nerican Standard Version or **American Revised ersion** See under KING JAMES BIBLE.

ı·er·ic·i·um (am′ə·rish′ē·əm) *n.* An unstable radioactive ement (symbol Am), resulting from the bombardment of anium and plutonium by high-energy helium ions. See LEMENT. [< NL, after *America*]

n·er·in·di·an (am′ə·rin′dē·ən) *adj.* Of or pertaining to e American Indians or the Eskimos. Also **Am′er·in′dic.** **-** *n.* An American Indian or Eskimo. Also **Am·er·ind** (am′·rind).

ı·e·thyst (am′ə·thist) *n.* **1.** Quartz with clear purple or iolet color, a semiprecious stone. **2.** A purple variety of pphire or corundum used as a gem: also called *Oriental nethyst.* **3.** A purplish violet. [< OF < L < Gk. < *a-* ot + *methystos* drunken < *methy* wine; from the ancient be-ef that a wearer of the stone would be unaffected by wine]

ı·e·thys·tine (am′ə·this′tin, -tīn) *adj.* Violet; purple.

ni (à·mē′) *n.masc. pl.* **a·mis** (à·mē′) *French* A friend. **- a·mie** (à·mē′) *n.fem.*

ni·a·ble (ā′mē·ə·bəl) *adj.* **1.** Pleasing in disposition; kind- . **2.** Free from irritation; friendly: an *amiable* rivalry. [< F < L *amicabilis* friendly < *amicus* friend] **— a′mi·a·bil′·ty, a′mi·a·ble·ness** *n.* **— a′mi·a·bly** *adv.*

ı·i·ca·ble (am′i·kə·bəl) *adj.* Friendly; peaceable. [< L *nicabilis* friendly] **— am·i·ca·bil·i·ty** (am′i·kə·bil′ə·tē), **n′i·ca·ble·ness** *n.* **— am′i·ca·bly** *adv.*

ni·cus cu·ri·ae (ə·mē′kəs kyŏŏr′ē·ī) *Law* One who advises is asked to advise a court upon a pending cause to which e is not a party. [< L, friend of the court]

nid (ə·mid′) *prep.* In the midst of; among. Also *amidst, ıidst.* [ME < OE *on middan* in the middle]

ı·ide (am′īd, -id) *n. Chem.* **1.** Any compound of the type ormula $RCONH_2$. **2.** A derivative of ammonia in which a etal replaces a hydrogen atom. Also **am·id** (am′id). **— ·mid·ic** (ə·mid′ik) *adj.*

ıido- *combining form Chem.* **1.** Pertaining to or containing oth the NH_2 radical and an acid radical. **2.** Less frequently, mino-. [< AMIDE]

ı·i·dol (am′ə·dol, -dōl) *n.* A white crystalline powder, $_6H_8N_2O{\cdot}2HCl$, used in photography as a developer.

nid·ships (ə·mid′ships′) *adv. Naut.* Halfway between ow and stern; toward the middle of a ship: also *midships.*

nidst (ə·midst′) *prep.* Amid. [ME *amidde* + -s³ + *t*]

ni·go (ə·mē′gō) *n. pl.* **·gos** A friend; comrade. [< Sp.]

mine (ə·mēn′, am′in) *n. Chem.* One of a class of organic ompounds derived from ammonia by replacement of one or ore of its hydrogen atoms by an alkyl radical. Also **am′in.**

ni·no (ə·mē′nō, am′ə·nō) *adj. Chem.* Of or pertaining to e NH_2 group combined with a nonacid radical. [< AMINE]

nino acid *Biochem.* Any of a group of organic compounds ontaining the amino group combined with the carboxyl idical and forming an essential part of the protein molecule.

mir (ə·mir′) *n.* **1.** A sovereign of Afghanistan. **2.** A Mos-m prince or governor. Also spelled *ameer.* [< Arabic *amīr*]

ı·ish (am′ish, ä′mish) *adj.* Relating to or designating the adherents of Jacob Ammann, a 17th-century Mennonite. **—** *n.pl.* A sect of Mennonites, founded by Jacob Ammann.

a·miss (ə·mis′) *adj.* Out of order or relation; wrong; improper: used predicatively: Something is *amiss.* **—** *adv.* In a wrong or defective way; erroneously. **— to take amiss** To take offense at. [ME < *a-* at + *mis* failure]

am·i·to·sis (am′ə·tō′sis) *n. Biol.* Cell division without the formation and splitting of chromosomes; direct division. [< NL < A-⁴ without + MITOSIS] **— am·i·tot·ic** (am′ə·tot′ik) *adj.* **— am′i·tot′i·cal·ly** *adv.*

am·i·ty (am′ə·tē) *n. pl.* **·ties** Peaceful relations, as between nations; friendship. [< MF < L *amicus* friend]

am·me·ter (am′mē′tər) *n. Electr.* An instrument for measuring amperage.

am·mo·nia (ə·mōn′yə, ə·mō′nē·ə) *n.* **1.** A colorless, pungent, suffocating gas, NH_3, obtained chiefly by the synthesis of nitrogen and hydrogen. **2.** Spirits of hartshorn. [< NL < SAL AMMONIAC] **— am·mo′ni·ac** *adj.*

am·mo·ni·ac (ə·mō′nē·ak) *n.* The resinous gum of a tree found in Persia and western India, used in medicine: also *gum ammoniac.* [< F < L < Gk. *ammōniakon*, a resinous gum]

am·mo·ni·ate (*v.* ə·mō′nē·āt; *n.* ə·mō′nē·it) *v.t.* **·at·ed, ·at·ing** To treat or combine with ammonia.

am·mon·ite (am′ən·īt) *n. Paleontol* A curved or spiral fossil cephalopod shell, commonly found in Mesozoic rocks. [< NL *ammonites* < L *(cornu) Ammonis* (horn) of Ammon]

am·mo·ni·um (ə·mō′nē·əm) *n. Chem.* The univalent radical NH_4, that in compounds formed from ammonia acts as an alkali metal.

ammonium hydroxide *Chem.* A compound, NH_4OH, formed in ordinary aqueous or caustic ammonia.

am·mu·ni·tion (am′yə·nish′ən) *n.* **1.** Any one of various articles used in the discharge of firearms and ordnance, as cartridges, shells, rockets, etc. **2.** Any resources for attack or defense. [< F < L *munire* to fortify]

am·ne·sia (am·nē′zhə, -zhē·ə) *n. Psychiatry* Partial or total loss or impairment of memory. [< NL < Gk. < *a-* not + *mnasthai* to remember] **— am·ne·sic** (am·nē′sik, -zik), **am·nes·tic** (am·nes′tik) *adj.*

am·nes·ty (am′nəs·tē) *n. pl.* **·ties 1.** A general pardon by which a government absolves offenders. **2.** Intentional overlooking, esp. of wrongdoing; forgetfulness. **—** *v.t.* **·tied, ·ty·ing** To pardon; grant amnesty to. [< F < L < Gk. < *a-* not + *mnasthai* to remember]

am·ni·on (am′nē·ən) *n. pl.* **·ni·ons** or **·ni·a** (-nē·ə) *Biol.* A membranous sac enclosing the embryo and fetus in mammals, birds, and reptiles. [< Gk. *amnion* the fetal envelope] **— am·ni·ot·ic** (am′nē·ot′ik), **am·ni·on·ic** (am′nē·on′ik) *adj.*

a·moe·ba (ə·mē′bə), **a·moe·bic** (ə·mē′bik), **a·moe·boid** (ə·mē′boid), etc. See AMEBA, etc.

am·oe·bae·an, am·oə·be·an (am′ə·bē′ən) See AMEBEAN.

amok (ə·muk′, ə·mok′) See AMUCK.

a·mong (ə·mung′) *prep.* **1.** In the midst of. **2.** In the class or number of: He was *among* the dead. **3.** Within or by the group of: a practice *among* the French. **4.** By the joint or concerted action of: *Among* us, we can build the wall. **5.** In portions for each of: to distribute money *among* the poor. **6.** Reciprocally between: disputes *among* friends. Also **a·mongst′.** ◆ See note under BETWEEN. [OE *on gemonge* in the crowd]

a·mon·til·la·do (ə·mon′tə·lä′dō, *Sp.* ä·môn′tē·lyä′thō) *n.* A pale dry sherry. [< Sp., after *Montilla*, a town in Spain]

a·mor·al (ā·môr′əl, ā·mor′əl) *adj.* **1.** Not subject to or concerned with moral or ethical distinctions. **2.** Lacking a sense of right and wrong. **— Syn.** See IMMORAL. **— a·mo·ral·i·ty** (ā′mə·ral′ə·tē) *n.* **— a·mor′·al·ly** *adv.*

am·o·rous (am′ər·əs) *adj.* **1.** Tending to fall in love; affectionate; loving. **2.** Of or related to love. **3.** Showing or arising from love or sexual desire; ardent. **4.** In love; enamored: often with *of*: *amorous* of the truth. [< OF < LL < L *amor* love] **— am′o·rous·ly** *adv.* **— am′o·rous·ness** *n.*

— Syn. 1, 2. *Amorous* is applied to persons and emotions; *amatory* refers to literature and other things that deal with love.

a·mor·phous (ə·môr′fəs) *adj.* **1.** Without definite form or shape. **2.** Of no fixed character; anomalous; unorganized. **3.** *Chem.* Uncrystallized. [< Gk. < *a-* without + *morphē* form] **— a·mor′phism** *n.* **— a·mor′phous·ly** *adv.* **— a·mor′phous·ness** *n.*

am·or·tize (am′ər·tīz, ə·môr′tīz) *v.t.* **·tized, ·tiz·ing** To extinguish gradually, as a debt or liability, by installment payments or by a sinking fund. Also *Brit.* **am′or·tise.** [< OF < *amortir* to extinguish < L *ad-* to + *mors, mortis* death] **— am·or·tiz·a·ble** (am′ər·tīz′ə·bəl, ə·môr′tiz·ə·bəl) *adj.* **— am′or·ti·za′tion, a·mor·tize·ment** (ə·môr′tiz·mənt) *n.*

A·mos (ā′məs) Eighth-century B.C. Hebrew minor prophet. **—** *n.* A book of the Old Testament containing his prophecies.

a·mount (ə·mount′) *n.* **1.** A sum total of two or more

ONUNCIATION KEY: **add, āce, câre, pälm; end, ēven; it, īce; odd, ōpen, ôrder; tŏŏk, pōōl; up, bûrn; ə** = a in *above*, e in *sicken*, i in *flex-*, o in *melon*, u in *focus*; **yōō** = u in *fuse*; **oil; pout; check; go; ring; thin; this; zh,** vision.

quantities. **2.** The value of the principal with the interest upon it, as in a loan. **3.** The entire significance, value, or effect. **4.** Quantity: a considerable *amount* of discussion. — *v.i.* **1.** To reach in number or quantity: with *to*: to *amount* to ten dollars. **2.** To be equivalent in effect or importance: with *to*: It *amounts* to treason. [< OF < L *ad* to + *mons, montis* mountain]

a·mour (ə·mŏŏr′) *n.* A love affair, esp. an illicit one. [< F]

a·mour-pro·pre (ȧ·mōōr′prôpr′) *n. French* Self-respect.

am·per·age (am·pir′ij, am′pər·ij) *n. Electr.* The strength of a current in amperes.

am·pere (am′pir, am·pir′) *n. Electr.* The practical unit of current strength; such a current as would be given by one volt through a wire having a resistance of one ohm. [after A. M. *Ampère*, 1775-1836, French physicist]

am·per·sand (am′pər·sand, am′pər·sand′) *n.* The character & or *&* or & meaning *and.* [< *and per se and*, lit., & by itself = and]

am·phet·a·mine (am·fet′ə·mēn, -min) *n.* An acrid liquid compound, $C_9H_{13}N$, used as a nasal spray. [< *a(lpha)-m(ethyl)-ph(enyl)-et(hyl)-amine*]

amphi- *prefix* **1.** On both or all sides; at both ends. **2.** Around: *amphitheater.* **3.** Of both kinds; in two ways. [< Gk. < *amphi* around]

am·phib·i·an (am·fib′ē·ən) *adj.* **1.** *Zool.* Of or pertaining to a class of cold-blooded, chiefly egg-laying vertebrates adapted for life both on land and in water, as frogs, newts, salamanders, etc. **2.** Amphibious. — *n.* **1.** An amphibian animal or plant. **2.** An airplane constructed to rise from and alight on either land or water. **3.** A vehicle capable of self-propulsion upon land and upon water.

am·phib·i·ous (am·fib′ē·əs) *adj.* **1.** Living or adapted to life on land or in water. **2.** Capable of operating or landing on land or water. **3.** Of a mixed nature. [< Gk. < *amphi-* of two kinds + *bios* life] — **am·phib′i·ous·ly** *adv.* — **am·phib′i·ous·ness** *n.*

am·phi·bole (am′fə·bōl) *n. Mineral.* Any of a class of variously colored hydrous silicates, consisting chiefly of calcium, magnesium, iron, aluminum, and sodium, as asbestos. [< F < L < Gk. < *amphi-* around + *ballein* to throw]

am·phi·bol·ic (am′fə·bol′ik) *adj.* Ambiguous; equivocal.

am·phi·ox·us (am′fē·ok′səs) *n. Zool.* The most primitive of the chordates, a lancelet. [< AMPHI- + Gk. *oxys* sharp]

am·phi·the·a·ter (am′fə·thē′ə·tər) *n.* **1.** An oval structure having tiers of seats built around an open space or arena. **2.** A level area surrounded by slopes. **3.** A place of contest. Also *Brit.* **am′phi·the′a·tre.** [< L < Gk. < *amphi-* around + *theatron* theater]

am·pho·ra (am′fə·rə) *n. pl.* **·rae** (-rē) In ancient Greece and Rome, a tall, two-handled earthenware jar for wine or oil, narrow at the neck and the base. [< L < Gk. < *amphi-* on both sides + *phoreus* bearer] — **am′pho·ral** *adj.*

AMPHORAE

am·pho·ter·ic (am′fə·ter′ik) *adj. Chem.* Exhibiting the characteristics of both an acid and a base. [< Gk. *amphoteros* both]

am·ple (am′pəl) *adj.* **1.** Of great dimension, capacity, amount, degree, etc.; large. **2.** More than enough; abundant. **3.** Fully sufficient; adequate. — **Syn.** See PLENTIFUL. [< F < L *amplus* large, abundant] — **am′ple·ness** *n.* — **am·ply** (am′plē) *adv.*

am·pli·fi·ca·tion (am′plə·fi·kā′shən) *n.* **1.** The act of extending or enlarging; also, that which is added. **2.** An extended statement, phrase, etc.

am·pli·fi·er (am′plə·fī′ər) *n.* **1.** One who or that which amplifies or increases. **2.** *Electronics* Any of a class of devices for reinforcing a signal by means of power supplied to the output from a source other than the input.

am·pli·fy (am′plə·fī) *v.* **·fied, ·fy·ing** *v.t.* **1.** To enlarge or increase in scope, significance, or power. **2.** To add to so as to make more complete, as by illustrations. **3.** To exaggerate; magnify. **4.** *Electronics* To increase the strength or amplitude of, as electromagnetic impulses. — *v.i.* **5.** To make additional remarks. [< F < L < *amplus* large + *facere* to make] — **am·pli·fi·ca·tive** (am′plə·fi·kā′tiv, am·plif′i·kə·tiv), **am·plif·i·ca·to·ry** (am·plif′i·kə·tôr′ē, -tō′rē) *adj.*

am·pli·tude (am′plə·tōōd, -tyōōd) *n.* **1.** Greatness of extent; largeness; breadth. **2.** Fullness; abundance. **3.** Scope or range, as of mind. **4.** *Physics* **a** The extent of the swing of a vibrating body on each side of the mean position. **b** The peak value attained by a wave or an alternating current during one complete cycle. [< L *amplus* large]

amplitude modulation *Telecom.* That form of radio transmission in which the carrier wave is modulated by varying the amplitude above and below a standard value in accordance with the signals to be transmitted. Compare FREQUENCY MODULATION. Abbr. *AM, a-m, a.m., A.M.*

am·pule (am′pyōōl) *n. Med.* A sealed glass vial used as a container for one dose of a hypodermic solution. Also **am·poule** (am′pōōl), **am·pul** (am′pul, am′pōōl). [< F < L *ampulla* ampulla (def. 1)]

am·pul·la (am·pul′ə) *n. pl.* **·pul·lae** (-pul′ē) **1.** An anci Roman bottle or vase with slender neck and flattened mou used for oil, wine, or perfume. **2.** *Eccl.* **a** A cruet for wine water at the Eucharist. [< L, dim. of *amphora* jar]

am·pu·tate (am′pyōō·tāt) *v.t. & v.i.* **·tat·ed, ·tat·ing** To off (a limb, etc.) by surgical means. [< L < *ambi-* arou + *putare* to trim] — **am′pu·ta′tion** *n.* — **am′pu·ta′tor** *n*

am·pu·tee (am′pyōō·tē′) *n.* One who has had a limb limbs removed by amputation.

a·muck (ə·muk′) *adv.* In a murderous or frenzied mann only in the phrase **to run amuck.** Also *amok.* [< Ma *amoq* engaging furiously in battle]

am·u·let (am′yə·lit) *n.* Anything worn about the person protection against accident, evil, etc.; a charm. [< L *am letum* charm; ult. origin unknown]

a·muse (ə·myōōz′) *v.t.* **a·mused, a·mus·ing 1.** To occu pleasingly. **2.** To cause to laugh or smile. [< MF < *d* + OF *muser* to stare] — **a·mus′a·ble** *adj.* — **a·mus′er** *n*

a·muse·ment (ə·myōōz′mənt) *n.* **1.** The state of be amused. **2.** That which diverts or entertains.

amusement park A park having various devices for tertainment, as roller coasters, shooting galleries, etc.

a·mus·ing (ə·myōō′zing) *adj.* **1.** Entertaining, or dive ing. **2.** Arousing laughter or mirth. — **a·mus′ing·ly** *a*

a·myg·da·la (ə·mig′də·lə) *n. pl.* **·lae** (-lē) **1.** *Anat.* A almond-shaped structure or part; esp., a tonsil. **2.** almond. [< L < Gk. *amygdalē* almond] — **a·myg′de·l** (-lit, -lāt), **a·myg′da·line** (-lin, -līn) *adj.*

am·yl (am′il) *n. Chem.* The univalent alcohol radic C_5H_{11}, derived from pentane. [< Gk. *amylon* starch + - — **a·myl·ic** (ə·mil′ik) *adj.*

am·y·la·ceous (am′ə·lā′shəs) *adj.* Of or like starch.

am·y·lase (am′ə·lās) *n. Biochem.* An enzyme, found plant and animal tissue, that promotes the conversion starch and glycogen into maltose.

am·y·loid (am′ə·loid) *n.* **1.** A gummy or starchlike s stance formed in certain diseased plant and animal tissu — *adj.* Like or containing starch: also **am′y·loi′dal.**

am·y·lum (am′ə·ləm) *n.* Starch (def. 1) [< L < Gk.]

Am·y·tal (am′ə·tal, -tôl) *n.* Proprietary name for a col less, crystalline compound, $C_{11}H_{18}N_2O_3$, used as a sedati

an (an, *unstressed* ən) *indefinite article* or *adj.* Equivalent the article *a*, but used before words beginning with a vow as *an* eagle and sometimes before words beginning with *h* an unstressed syllable, as *an* hotel. [OE *ān* one]

an-[1] *prefix* Without; not: *anarchy.* Also, before consona (except *h*) *a-.* [< Gk.]

an-[2] Var. of ANA-.

an-[3] Assimilated var. of AD-.

-an *suffix* Used to form adjectives and nouns denoting c nection with a country, person, group, doctrine, etc., as f lows: **1.** Pertaining to; belonging to: *human, sylvan.* Originating in; living in: *Italian.* **3.** Adhering to; followi *Lutheran.* **4.** *Zool.* Belonging to a class or order: *amphibi* See -IAN. [< L *-anus*]

ana- *prefix* **1.** Up; upward: *anadromous.* **2.** Back; ba ward: *anapest.* **3.** Anew: sometimes capable of being r dered *re-*, as *anabaptism*, rebaptism. **4.** Thoroughly: *an ysis.* Also, before vowels or *h*, *an-.* [< Gk. < *ana* up, ba

-ana *suffix* Pertaining to: added to the names of nota persons, places, etc., to indicate a collection of materi such as writings or anecdotes, about the subject: *America* Also *-iana.* [< L, neut. pl. of *-anus.* See -AN.]

An·a·bap·tist (an′ə·bap′tist) *n.* One of a sect that arose Switzerland about 1520, who rejected infant baptism a limited church membership to adults baptized after a c fession of faith. [< NL < LL < Gk. < *ana-* new + *b tizein* to baptize] — **An′a·bap′tism** *n.*

an·a·bi·o·sis (an′ə·bī·ō′sis) *n.* A return to life; resusci tion. [< NL < ANA- + Gk. *bios* life] — **an·a·bi·ot·ic** (a ə·bī·ot′ic) *adj.*

a·nab·o·lism (ə·nab′ə·liz′əm) *n. Biol.* The process which food is built up into protoplasm: opposed to *cata lism.* [< Gk. *anabolē* a heaping up] — **an·a·bol·ic** (an bol′ik) *adj.*

a·nach·ro·nism (ə·nak′rə·niz′əm) *n.* **1.** The assigning an event, person, etc., to a wrong, esp. an earlier, date. Something out of its proper time. [< F < L < Gk. < *a* against + *chronos* time] — **a·nach′ro·nis′tic, a·nach′ nis′ti·cal, a·nach′ro·nous** *adj.*

an·a·con·da (an′ə·kon′də) *n.* **1.** A very large, nonveno ous tropical serpent that crushes its prey in its coils. **2.** A boa constrictor. [? < Singhalese]

a·nad·ro·mous (ə·nad′rə·məs) *adj. Zool.* Of fishes, as t salmon, going from the sea up rivers to spawn. [< Gk. *ana-* up + *dromos* a running, course]

a·nae·mi·a (ə·nē′mē·ə), **a·nae·mic** (ə·nē′mik), etc. S ANEMIA, etc.

an·aer·obe (an·âr′ōb, an·ā′ə·rōb) *n.* An anaerobic org ism. [See ANAEROBIC]

an·aer·o·bic (an′âr·ō′bik, -ob′ik) *adj.* Living or functioni

a the absence of free oxygen. [< NL < AN-[1] without + ERO- + Gk. *bios* life] **— an/aer·o/bi·cal·ly** *adv.*
·aes·the·sia (an/is·thē/zhə, -zhē·ə), **an·aes·thet·ic** (an/·thet/ik), etc. See ANESTHESIA, etc.
·a·gram (an/ə·gram) *n.* **1.** A word or phrase formed by ansposing the letters of another word or phrase. **2.** *pl. construed as sing.*) A game in which the players make words y transposing or adding letters. [< MF < LGk < Gk. < *na-* backwards + *gramma* letter] **— an·a·gram·mat·ic** (an/·grə·mat/ik) or **·i·cal** *adj.* **— an/a·gram·mat/i·cal·ly** *adv.*
·a·gram·ma·tize (an/ə·gram/ə·tīz) *v.t.* **·tized, ·tiz·ing** To rrange as an anagram.
al (ā/nəl) *adj. Anat.* Of, pertaining to, or situated in the gion of the anus. [< L *anus* + -AL[1]]
·a·lects (an/ə·lekts) *n.pl.* Selections or fragments from a terary work or group of works. Also **an·a·lec·ta** (an/ə·lek/·) [< L < Gk. < *ana-* up + *legein* to gather]
·al·ge·si·a (an/əl·jē/zē·ə, -sē·ə) *n. Pathol.* Inability to el pain. Also **an·al·gi·a** (an·al/jē·ə). [< NL < Gk. < *an-* ithout + *algos* pain]
·al·ge·sic (an/əl·jē/zik, -sik) *Med. n.* A drug for the al-viation of pain. **—** *adj.* Promoting analgesia.
alog computer A computer that solves problems by ubstituting analogous quantities, as voltage, etc., for the ariables of the problems. Compare DIGITAL COMPUTER.
al·o·gous (ə·nal/ə·gəs) *adj.* **1.** Resembling or compara-e in certain respects. **2.** *Biol.* Having a similar function ut differing in origin and structure, as the wings of birds nd insects: distinguished from *homologous.* **— a·nal/o·ous·ly** *adv.* **— a·nal/o·gous·ness** *n.*
·a·logue (an/ə·lôg, -log) *n.* Anything analogous to some-ing else. Also **an/a·log.**
al·o·gy (ə·nal/ə·jē) *n. pl.* **·gies 1.** Agreement or resem-ance in certain aspects. **2.** *Biol.* A similarity in function nd appearance, but not in origin. **4.** *Logic* Reasoning in hich relations or resemblances are inferred from others at are known or observed. Abbr. *anal.* [< L < Gk. < *na-* according to + *logos* proportion]
— Syn. 1, 2. In careful usage, an *analogy* is drawn only between ings clearly unlike in kind, form, or appearance, and refers to eir similar properties, relations, behavior, etc. A *resemblance* is most always a likeness in appearance, while *similarity* is usually likeness in some external or superficial aspect or characteristic.
al·y·sis (ə·nal/ə·sis) *n. pl.* **·ses** (-sēz) **1.** The separation f a whole into its parts or elements: opposed to *synthesis.* . A statement of the results of this; logical synopsis. **3.** A ethod of determining or describing the nature of a thing by parating it into its parts. **4.** *Chem.* The determination of e kind, quantity, and proportions of constituents forming compound or substance. **5.** Psychoanalysis. [< Med.L. Gk. < *ana-* throughout + *lyein* to loosen]
·a·lyst (an/ə·list) *n.* **1.** One who analyzes or is skilled in nalysis. **2.** A psychoanalyst.
·a·lyt·ic (an/ə·lit/ik) *adj.* **1.** Pertaining to or proceeding y analysis. **2.** Separating into constituent parts or first inciples. Also **an/a·lyt/i·cal. — an/a·lyt/i·cal·ly** *adv.*
·a·lyt·ics (an/ə·lit/iks) *n.pl.* (*construed as sing.*) **1.** The ience or use of analysis. **2.** The part of logic concerned ith analysis.
·a·lyze (an/ə·līz) *v.t.* **·lyzed, ·lyz·ing 1.** To separate into onstituent parts or elements, especially so as to determine e nature, form, etc., of the whole by examination of the arts. **2.** To examine critically or minutely. **3.** To psycho-nalyze. Also, *Brit., analyse.* See ANALYSIS. **— an/a·lyz/a·le** *adj.* **— an/a·ly·za/tion** *n.* **— an/a·lyz/er** *n.*
·a·pest (an/ə·pest) *n.* **1.** In prosody, a metrical foot con-sting of two short or unaccented syllables followed by one ng or accented syllable (˘˘¯). **2.** A line of verse made up f such feet: Then the rāin \| ănd thĕ trēē \| wĕre ălōne. Also **n/a·paest.** [< L < Gk. < *ana-* back + *paiein* to strike, so alled because it is a reversed dactyl] **— an/a·pes/tic** *adj.*
·ar·chic (an·är/kik) *adj.* **1.** Pertaining to or like anarchy. . Advocating anarchy. **3.** Inducing anarchy; lawless. Also **n·ar/chi·cal. — an·ar/chi·cal·ly** *adv.*
·ar·chism (an/ər·kiz/əm) *n.* **1.** The theory that all forms f government are incompatible with individual and social berty and should be abolished. **2.** The methods of anar-nists. **— an·ar·chis·tic** (an/ər·kis/tik) *adj.*
·ar·chist (an/ər·kist) *n.* **1.** One who believes in and advo-ates anarchism. **2.** One who encourages or furthers anar-hy. Also **an·arch** (an/ärk).
·ar·chy (an/ər·kē) *n.* **1.** Absence of government. **2.** Law-ss confusion and political disorder. **3.** General disorder. < Gk. < *an-* without + *archos* leader]
·as·tig·mat·ic (an·as/tig·mat/ik) *adj. Optics* Not astig-atic; esp., corrected for astigmatism, as a lens.
nas·to·mose (ə·nas/tə·mōz) *v.i.* **·mosed, ·mos·ing** To onnect by anastomosis.
a·nas·to·mo·sis (ə·nas/tə·mō/sis) *n. pl.* **·ses** (-sēz) **1.** *Physiol.* A union, interlacing, or running together, as of veins, nerves, or canals of animal bodies. **2.** Any intercom-munication, as of two or more rivers. [< NL < Gk. *anas-tomōsis* opening] **— a·nas/to·mot/ic** (-mot/ik) *adj.*
a·nath·e·ma (ə·nath/ə·mə) *n. pl.* **·mas** or **·ma·ta** (-mə·tə) **1.** A formal ecclesiastical ban or curse, excommunicating a person or damning something, as a book or doctrine. **2.** Any curse or imprecation. **3.** One who or that which is excom-municated or damned. **4.** One who or that which is greatly disliked. [< L < Gk. *anathema* a thing devoted (to evil)]
a·nath·e·ma·tize (ə·nath/ə·mə·tīz/) *v.* **·tized, ·tiz·ing** *v.t.* **1.** To pronounce an anathema against. **—** *v.i.* **2.** To utter or express anathemas. **— a·nath/e·ma·ti·za/tion** *n.*
an·a·tom·i·cal (an/ə·tom/i·kəl) *adj.* Of or pertaining to anatomy. Also **an/a·tom/ic. — an/a·tom/i·cal·ly** *adv.*
a·nat·o·mist (ə·nat/ə·mist) *n.* One skilled in anatomy.
a·nat·o·mize (ə·nat/ə·mīz) *v.t.* **·mized, ·miz·ing 1.** To dis-sect (an animal or plant) for the purpose of investigating the structure, position, and interrelationships of its parts. **2.** To examine minutely; analyze. **a·nat/o·mi·za/tion** *n.*
a·nat·o·my (ə·nat/ə·mē) *n. pl.* **·mies 1.** The structure of a plant or animal, or of any of its parts. **2.** The science of the structure of plants or animals. **3.** The art or practice of anatomizing. [< F < L < Gk. < *ana-* up + *temnein* to cut]
-ance *suffix of nouns* Used to form nouns of action, quality, state, or condition from adjectives in *-ant*, and also directly from verbs, as in *abundance, forbearance.* Compare -ANCY. [< F *-ance* < L *-antia, -entia,* a suffix used to form nouns]
an·ces·tor (an/ses·tər) *n.* **1.** One from whom a person is descended; progenitor; forbear. **2.** *Biol.* An organism from which later organisms have been derived. [< OF < L < *ante-* before + *cedere* to go] **— an·ces·tress** (an/ses·tris) *n.fem.*
an·ces·tral (an·ses/trəl) *adj.* Of, pertaining to, or descend-ing from an ancestor. Also **an·ces·to·ri·al** (an/ses·tôr/ē·əl, -tō/rē-). **— an·ces/tral·ly** *adv.*
an·ces·try (an/ses·trē) *n. pl.* **·tries 1.** A line or body of ancestors; ancestors collectively. **2.** Ancestral lineage.
an·chor (ang/kər) *n.* **1.** A heavy implement, usu. of iron or steel, with hooks or flukes to grip the bottom, attached to a cable and dropped from a ship or boat to hold it in place. **2.** Any object used for a similar purpose. **3.** Anything that makes stable or secure. **— at anchor** Anchored, as a ship. **— to drop** (or **cast**) **anchor** To put down the anchor in order to hold fast a vessel. **— to ride at anchor** To be anchored, as a ship. **— to weigh anchor** To take up the anchor so as to sail away. **—** *v.t.* **1.** To secure or make secure by an anchor. **2.** To fix firmly. **—** *v.i.* **3.** To lie at anchor, as a ship. [OE < L < Gk. *ankyra*]
an·chor·age (ang/kər·ij) *n.* **1.** A place for anchoring. **2.** A coming to or lying at anchor. **3.** A source or place of sta-bility or security. **4.** A fee charged for anchoring.
an·cho·rite (ang/kə·rīt) *n.* One who has withdrawn from the world for religious reasons; hermit. Also **an/cho·ret** (-rit, -ret). [< L < Gk. < *ana-* back + *chōreein* to with-draw] **— an/cho·rit/ic** (-rit/ik) *adj.*
an·cho·vy (an/chō·vē, -chə·vē, an·chō/vē) *n. pl.* **·vies** or **·vy 1.** A very small, herringlike fish inhabiting warm seas, valued as a delicacy. **2.** *U.S.* Smelt. [< Sp., Pg. *anchova*]
an·chy·lose (ang/kə·lōs), **an·chy·lo·sis** (ang/kə·lō/sis) See ANKYLOSE, etc.
an·cien ré·gime (äṅ·syaṅ/rā·zhēm/) *French* A former po-litical and social system; esp., the system in France before the revolution of 1789. Also **Ancient Regime.**
an·cient (ān/shənt) *adj.* **1.** Existing or occurring in times long past, esp. before the fall of the Western RomanEmpire, in A.D. 476. **2.** Having existed from remote antiquity; of great age. **3.** Very old: said of persons. Abbr. *anc.* **—** *n.* **1.** One who lived in ancient times. **2.** An aged or venerable person. **— the ancients 1.** The ancient Greeks, Romans, Hebrews, or other civilized nations of antiquity. **2.** The ancient authors of Greece and Rome. [< OF < LL < L *ante* before] **— an/cient·ness** *n.* **— an/cient·ly** *adv.*
an·cil·lar·y (an/sə·ler/ē) *adj.* Subordinate; auxiliary. [< L *ancilla* maid]
an·con (ang/kon) *n. pl.* **an·co·nes** (ang·kō/nēz) **1.** *Anat.* The point of the elbow. **2.** *Archit.* An elbow-shaped projec-tion, as for an ornament on a keystone. Also **an·cone** (ang/·kōn). [< L < Gk. *ankōn* a bend, the elbow] **— an·co·nal** (ang/kə·nəl), **an·co·ne·al** (ang·kō/nē·əl) *adj.*
-ancy *suffix of nouns* A modern variant of -ANCE: used to form new words expressing quality, state, or condition (*in-fancy, vacancy*), or to refashion older nouns of quality in *-ance* (*constancy*). [< L *-antia*]
an·cy·los·to·mi·a·sis (an/sə·lōs/tə·mī/ə·sis) *n.* A progres-sive anemia caused by nematode worms that suck the blood from the small intestine. Also called *hookworm disease.* [< NL < Gk. *ankylos* crooked + *stoma* mouth + -IASIS]

and (and, *unstressed* ənd, ən, 'n) *conj.* **1.** Also; added to; as well as: a particle denoting addition, emphasis, or union, used as a connective between words, phrases, clauses, and sentences: shoes *and* ships *and* sealing wax. **2.** As a result or consequence: Make one move *and* you are dead! **3.** To: with *come, go, try,* etc.: Try *and* stop me. [OE *ond, and*]

an·dan·te (an·dan′tē, än·dän′tā) *Music adj. & adv.* Moderately slow; slower than allegretto but faster than larghetto. — *n.* An andante movement or passage. [< Ital., walking]

an·dan·ti·no (an′dan·tē′nō, än′dän-) *Music adj. & adv.* Slightly quicker than andante; originally, slower than andante. — *n.* An andantino movement or passage. [< Ital., dim. of *andante*]

An·de·an (an·dē′ən, an′dē·ən) *adj.* Of the Andes.

and·i·ron (and′ī′ərn) *n.* One of two metal supports for holding wood in an open fireplace: also called *firedog.* [< OF *andier*; infl. by *iron*]

and/or Either *and* or *or*, according to the meaning intended.

andro- *combining form* **1.** Man in general. **2.** The male sex. **3.** *Bot.* Stamen; anther. [< Gk. *anēr, andros* man]

an·droe·ci·um (an·drē′shē·əm, -sē·əm) *n. pl.* **·ci·a** (-shē·ə, -sē·ə) *Bot.* The stamens of a flower collectively. [< NL < ANDRO- + Gk. *oikos* house] — **an·droe′cial** (-shəl) *adj.*

an·dro·gen (an′drə·jən) *n. Biochem.* Any of various hormones that control the development of masculine characteristics. — **an·dro·gen·ic** (an′drə·jen′ik) *adj.*

an·drog·y·nous (an·droj′ə·nəs) *adj.* **1.** Uniting the characteristics of both sexes; hermaphroditic. **2.** *Bot.* Having the male and female flowers in the same cluster. Also **an·drog·y·nal** (an·droj′ə·nəl), **an·dro·gyn·ic** (an′drə·jin′ik). [< L < Gk. < *anēr*, man + *gynē* woman] — **an·drog′y·ny** *n.*

An·drom·a·che (an·drom′ə·kē) In Greek legend, the wife of Hector, taken captive to Greece after the fall of Troy.

An·drom·e·da (an·drom′ə·də) In Greek mythology, a princess rescued from a sea monster by Perseus, who then married her. — *n.* A constellation containing the bright star Alpheratz.

an·dros·ter·one (an·dros′tə·rōn) *n. Biochem.* A male sex hormone, $C_{19}H_{30}O_2$.

-androus *suffix* **1.** *Bot.* Having a (specified) number or kind of stamens. **2.** Having a (given) number of husbands. [< Gk. *anēr, andros* man]

-ane[1] *suffix* Used primarily to differentiate words that have a corresponding form in -AN, as *human, humane.* [< L *-anus*]

-ane[2] *suffix Chem.* Denoting a hydrocarbon compound of the methane series: *pentane.* [An arbitrary formation]

an·ec·do·tal (an′ik·dōt′l) *adj.* Pertaining to, characterized by, or consisting of anecdotes.

an·ec·dote (an′ik·dōt) *n.* A brief account of an interesting or entertaining nature. [< Med.L < Gk. < *an-* not + *ekdotos* published < *ekdidonai* to give out, publish]

an·ec·dot·ic (an′ik·dot′ik) *adj.* **1.** Anecdotal. **2.** Habitually telling or given to anecdotes. Also **an′ec·dot′i·cal.**

an·ec·dot·ist (an′ik·dō′tist) *n.* One who collects, publishes, or is given to telling anecdotes.

a·ne·mi·a (ə·nē′mē·ə) *n. Pathol.* A deficiency in hemoglobin or the number of red corpuscles in the bood, characterized by pallor, loss of energy, etc. [< NL < Gk. < *an-* without + *haima* blood] — **a·ne′mic** *adj.*

a·nem·o·graph (ə·nem′ə·graf, -gräf) *n. Meteorol.* An instrument that makes a record of the velocity and direction of the wind. — **a·nem′o·graph′ic** *adj.*

an·e·mom·e·ter (an′ə·mom′ə·tər) *n. Meteorol.* An instrument for measuring the velocity of the wind. — **an·e·mo·met·ric** (an′ə·mō·met′rik) or **·ri·cal** *adj.*

ANEMOMETER

an·e·mom·e·try (an′ə·mom′ə·trē) *n. Meteorol.* The technique of determining the velocity of the wind.

a·nem·o·ne (ə·nem′ə·nē) *n.* **1.** A plant having flowers with no petals but showy, multicolored sepals: also called *windflower.* **2.** *Zool.* The sea anemone. [< Gk. *anemos* wind]

an·er·oid (an′ə·roid) *adj.* Not using liquid. — *n.* An aneroid barometer. [< F < Gk. *a-* not + *nēros* wet + -OID]

aneroid barometer An instrument for measuring atmospheric pressure through its effect upon the flexible top of a partially evacuated chamber.

an·es·the·sia (an′is·thē′zhə, -zhē·ə) *n.* Partial or total loss of physical sensation, particularly of pain, due to disease or certain drugs. Also **an·es·the·sis** (an′is·thē′sis). [< NL < Gk. < *an-* without + *aisthēsis* sensation]

an·es·thet·ic (an′is·thet′ik) *n.* A drug, gas, etc., that causes anesthesia. — *adj.* **1.** Pertaining to or like anesthesia. **2.** Producing anesthesia. Also spelled *anaesthetic.*

an·es·the·tist (ə·nes′thə·tist) *n.* A person trained to administer anesthetics: also spelled *anaesthetist.*

an·es·the·tize (ə·nes′thə·tīz) *v.t.* **·tized, ·tiz·ing** To render insensible, esp. to pain, by means of an anesthetic: also spelled *anaesthetize.* — **an·es′the·ti·za·tion** *n.*

an·eu·rysm (an′yə·riz′əm) *n. Pathol.* A dilatation of t wall of an artery, forming a sac. Also **an′eu·rism.** [< G < *ana-* up + *eurys* wide] — **an·eu·rys·mal** (an′yə·riz′mə or **·ris′mal** *adj.*

a·new (ə·nōō′, ə·nyōō′) *adv.* **1.** Again. **2.** Over again in different way. [OE *of nīwe*]

an·ga·ry (ang′gə·rē) *n.* In international law, the right of belligerent, in case of need, to seize, use, or destroy neutr property, esp. ships, subject to claim for full compensatio [< F < LL < Gk. *angaros* courier]

an·gel (ān′jəl) *n.* **1.** *Theol.* **a** A spiritual being attenda upon the Deity; a heavenly messenger. **b** A fallen spiritu being, also immortal. **2.** A conventional representation an angel, usually a youthful winged human figure in wh robes and with a halo. **3.** A person of real or fancied ange qualities, as of character or beauty. **4.** *Informal* The fina cial backer of a play, etc. **5.** A former English gold co [OE < L < Gk. *angelos* messenger]

an·gel·fish (ān′jəl·fish′) *n. pl.* **·fish** or **·fish·es** **1.** A ra like shark having very large, winglike pectoral fins. **2.** fish of warm seas having brilliant coloration, as the porg

angel food cake A delicate, spongy cake made witho shortening or egg yolks. Also **angel cake.**

an·gel·ic (an·jel′ik) *adj.* **1.** Pertaining to, of, or consisti of angels; celestial. **2.** Like an angel; pure; beautiful. A **an·gel′i·cal.** — **an·gel′i·cal·ly** *adv.*

an·gel·i·ca (an·jel′i·kə) *n.* **1.** A fragrant plant of the pa ley family. **2.** The stalks of one species of this plant, oft candied and used as a flavoring and an aromatic. [< Med (*herba*) *angelica* the angelic (herb)]

an·ge·lus (an′jə·ləs) *n. Eccl.* **1.** A devotional prayer us to commemorate the Annunciation. **2.** A bell rung at mo ing, noon, and night as a call to recite this prayer: also call **angelus bell.** Also **An′ge·lus.** [< L]

an·ger (ang′gər) *n.* A feeling of sudden and strong d pleasure and antagonism directed against the cause of an sumed wrong or injury; wrath; ire. — *v.t.* To make angr enrage. [< ON *angr* grief]

An·ge·vin (an′jə·vin) *adj.* **1.** Of or from Anjou. **2.** Of pertaining to the Plantagenet kings of England. — *n.* **1.** native or inhabitant of Anjou. **2.** A member of the ro house of Anjou. Also **An′ge·vine** (-vin, -vīn). [< F]

an·gi·na (an·jī′nə, an′jə·nə) *n. Pathol.* **1.** Any disease ch acterized by spasmodic suffocation, as croup. **2.** Angi pectoris. [< L, quinsy < *angere* to choke]

angina pec·to·ris (pek′tə·ris) *Pathol.* A defect of corona circulation, characterized by paroxysmal pain below t sternum. [< NL, angina of the chest]

angio- *combining form* **1.** *Bot.* Seed vessel. **2.** *Med.* Blo vessel; lymph vessel. Also, before vowels, **angi-.** [< G *angeion* case, vessel, capsule]

an·gi·o·ma (an′jē·ō′mə) *n. pl.* **·mas** or **·ma·ta** (-mə· *Pathol.* A tumor consisting of dilated blood or lymph v sels. — **an·gi·om·a·tous** (an′jē·om′ə·təs) *adj.*

an·gi·o·sperm (an′jē·ə·spûrm′) *n.* Any of a class of plar having the seeds in a closed seed vessel. — **an′gi·o·sper′m an′gi·o·sper′ma·tous** (-spûr′mə·təs), **an′gi·o·sper′mous** *a*

an·gle[1] (ang′gəl) *v.i.* **·gled, ·gling** **1.** To fish with a ho and line. **2.** To try to get something slyly or artfully: w *for.* [< OE *angel* fishhook]

an·gle[2] (ang′gəl) *n.* **1.** *Geom.* **a** The figure formed by t divergence of two straight lines from a common point or of two or more planes from a common straight line. **b** The space between these lines or surfaces. **c** The amount of divergence of these lines or surfaces, measured in degrees. **2.** A projecting corner, as of a building. **3.** The point of view or aspect from which som thing is regarded. **4.** *U.S. Slang* Special selfish motive interest. — *v.* **an·gled, an·gling** *v.t.* **1.** To move or turn an angle or by angles. **2.** *Informal* To impart a particu bias or interpretation to, as a story or report. — *v.i.* **3.** proceed or turn itself at an angle or by angles. [< F < *angulus* a corner, angle]

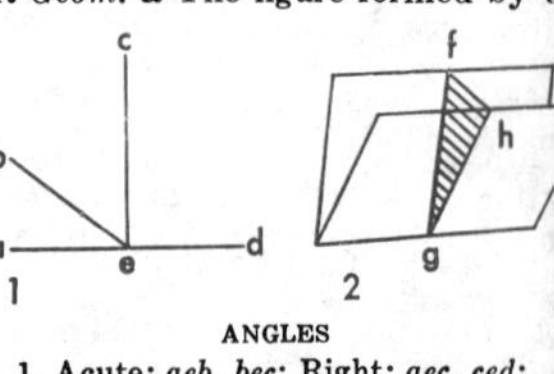

ANGLES
1. Acute: *aeb, bec;* Right: *aec, ced;* Obtuse: *bed.* 2. Dihedral.

An·gle (ang′gel) *n.* A member of a Germanic tribe th migrated to Britain in the fifth century. [< L *Anglus,* si of *Angli* < Gmc.] — **An′gli·an** *adj. & n.*

angle iron A piece of iron in the form of an angle, for jo ing or strengthening beams, girders, etc.

angle of incidence *Physics* The angle relative to the p pendicular drawn from the point of impact at which object, beam of light, etc., strikes a surface.

an·gler (ang′glər) *n.* **1.** One who fishes with rod, hook, a line. **2.** A fish having antennalike filaments on its head.

·gle·worm (ang′gəl·wûrm′) *n.* An earthworm, commonly sed as bait on fishhooks.
·gli·can (ang′glə·kən) *adj.* Pertaining to or characteristic of the Church of England, or of the churches that agree ith it in faith and order. — *n.* **1.** A member of an Anglican Church. [< Med.L *Anglicanus* < L *Angli* the Angles]
nglican Church **1.** The Church of England. **2.** A body f churches, including the Protestant Episcopal Church, ostly derived from the Church of England and in comunion with it. — **An·gli·can·ism** (ang′glə·kən·iz′əm) *n.*
·gli·cism (ang′glə·siz′əm) *n.* **1.** An idiom or turn of hrase peculiar to the English language. **2.** A Briticism. . The state or quality of being English.
·gli·cize (ang′glə·sīz) *v.* **·cized, ·ciz·ing** *v.t.* **1.** To give n English form, style, or idiom to. — *v.i.* **2.** To acquire ome English trait or peculiarity; become like the English. lso *Brit.* **An′gli·cise.** — **An′gli·ci·za′tion** *n.*
·gli·fy (ang′glə·fī) *v.t. & v.i.* **·fied, ·fy·ing** To Anglicize.
·gling (ang′gling) *n.* The act or art of fishing with a ook, line, and rod.
glo- *combining form* English; English and: *Anglophile, nglo-Norman.*
·glo·ma·ni·a (ang′glō·mā′nē·ə) *n.* Overfondness for or nitation of English manners, speech, institutions, etc.
·glo-Nor·man (ang′glō·nôr′mən) *adj.* Pertaining to the ormans who settled in England after the Norman Conuest, their descendants, or their language. — *n.* **1.** One of he Norman settlers in England after the Norman Conquest. . The dialect of Old French of these settlers.
·glo·phile (ang′glə·fīl, -fil) *n.* A lover of England or its eople, customs, institutions, or manners. — *adj.* Of or like nglophiles. Also **An′glo·phil** (fil).
·glo·pho·bi·a (ang′glə·fō′bē·ə) *n.* Hatred or dread of England, its customs, people, or institutions. — **An′glo·phobe** . & *adj.* — **An′glo·pho′bic** (-fō′bik, -fob′ik) *adj.*
·glo-Sax·on (ang′glō·sak′sən) *n.* **1.** A member of one of he Germanic tribes (Angles, Saxons, and Jutes) that domiated England until the Norman Conquest. **2.** Their West ermanic language; Old English. **3.** A person of English ationality or descent. — *adj.* Of or pertaining to the nglo-Saxons, their language or descendants.
·go·ra (ang·gôr′ə, -gō′rə) *n.* **1.** A goat, originally from nkara, having long, silky hair. **2.** A shawl, cloth, etc., ade of Angora wool or its imitations. **3.** An Angora cat.
gora cat A variety of cat with long, silky hair.
·gos·tu·ra bark (ang′gəs·to͝or′ə, -tyo͝or′ə) A bark from a outh American tree, used in the preparation of a tonic and avoring. Also **an′gos·tu′ra.** [after *Angostura,* former name Ciudad Bolívar, Venezuela]
·gry (ang′grē) *adj.* **ang·ri·er, an·gri·est** **1.** Feeling, showg, or excited by anger; indignant. **2.** Showing signs of nger; wrathful. **3.** Seeming to be in anger. **4.** Badly inamed. — **an·gri·ly** (ang′grə·lē) *adv.* — **an′gri·ness** *n.*
g·strom (ang′strəm) *n.* A linear unit equal to 10^{-8} cenmeter or 3.937×10^{-9} inch, used for minute measureents, as of wavelengths of light. Also **angstrom unit.** [after . J. Ångström, 1814–75, Swedish physicist]
·guish (ang′gwish) *n.* Excruciating mental or bodily pain; gony; torture. — *v.t. & v.i.* To affect or suffer with anguish. < OF *anguisse* < L *angustia* tightness, difficulty]
·gu·lar (ang′gyə·lər) *adj.* **1.** Having, forming, or constiting an angle or angles; sharp-cornered. **2.** Measured by n angle. **3.** Pertaining to angles. **4.** Bony; gaunt. **5.** wkward or ungraceful. [< L < *angulus* corner, angle] — **n′gu·lar·ly** *adv.*
·gu·lar·i·ty (ang′gyə·lar′ə·tē) *n.* *pl.* **·ties** **1.** The state f being angular: also **an′gu·lar·ness.** **2.** *pl.* Angular outnes or parts.
·hy·dride (an·hī′drīd, -drid) *n.* *Chem.* **1.** Any organic r inorganic compound that has been dehydrated. **2.** A comound formed from another compound, especially an acid or ase, by the removal of one or more molecules of water, the rocess being generally reversible. [See ANHYDROUS]
·hy·drous (an·hī′drəs) *adj.* *Chem.* Pertaining to or desigating a compound that has no water of crystallization in its omposition. [< Gk. < *an-* without + *hydōr* water]
·il (an′il) *n.* **1.** A West Indian indigo plant. **2.** The ingo dye made from this plant. [< F < Pg. < Arabic *al-il* the blue < Skt.]
·i·line (an′ə·lin, -līn) *n.* *Chem.* A colorless oily, poisonus compound, $C_6H_5NH_2$, the base of many coal-tar dyes, hiefly made from nitrobenzene. Also called *phenylamine.* - *adj.* Made of, derived from, or pertaining to aniline. lso **an·i·lin** (an′ə·lin). [< ANIL + -INE[2]]
·i·ma (an′ə·mə) *n.* The vital principle; soul. [< L]
·i·mad·ver·sion (an′ə·mad·vûr′zhən, -shən) *n.* A cenrious comment or reflection: with *on* or *upon.*
·i·mad·vert (an′ə·mad·vûrt′) *v.i.* To comment critically, usu. in an adverse sense: with *on* or *upon.* [< L < *animus* mind + *advertere* to turn to]
an·i·mal (an′ə·məl) *n.* **1.** A sentient living organism typically capable of voluntary motion and sensation: distinguished from *plant.* **2.** Any such creature as distinguished from man. **3.** A bestial human being. — *adj.* **1.** Of, characteristic of, derived from, or resembling animals. **2.** Carnal; sensual: *animal* appetites. [< L, < *anima* breath, soul, life]
an·i·mal·cule (an′ə·mal′kyo͞ol) *n.* An animal of microscopic smallness, as an ameba. Also **an′i′mal′cu·lum** (-kyə·ləm). [< L *animalculum,* dim. of *animal* animal] — **an′i·mal′cu·lar** (-kyə·lər) *adj.*
animal husbandry The branch of agriculture specializing in the breeding, raising, and care of farm animals.
an·i·mal·ism (an′ə·məl·iz′əm) *n.* **1.** The state or condition of a mere animal. **2.** Animal activity. **3.** The doctrine that man is entirely animal, having no soul. — **an′i·mal·ist** *n.* — **an′i·mal·is′tic** *adj.*
an·i·mal·i·ty (an′ə·mal′ə·tē) *n.* **1.** The nature or qualities of an animal. **2.** Animal life; the animal kingdom.
an·i·mal·ize (an′ə·məl·īz′) *v.t.* **·ized, ·iz·ing** To render brutal; sensualize. — **an·i·mal·i·za·tion** (an′ə·mel·ə·zā′shən, -ī·zā′-) *n.*
animal kingdom Animal organisms collectively, as distinguished from plants.
an·i·mal·ly (an′ə·məl·ē) *adv.* Physically, as distinguished from spiritually or mentally.
animal magnetism Mesmerism.
an·i·mate (*v.* an′ə·māt; *adj.* an′ə·mit) *v.t.* **·mat·ed, ·mat·ing** **1.** To impart life to; make alive. **2.** To move to action; incite; inspire. **3.** To produce activity or energy in. — *adj.* **1.** Possessing animal life; living. **2.** Full of life; vivacious; lively: also **an′i·mat′ed** (-mā′tid). [< L *anima* breath, soul] — **an′i·mat′ed·ly** *adv.* — **an′i·ma′tor, an′i·ma′ter** *n.*
animated cartoon See CARTOON.
an·i·ma·tion (an′ə·mā′shən) *n.* **1.** The act of imparting life, or the state of possessing life. **2.** The quality of being lively or quick; vivacity. **3.** The process and technique of preparing animated cartoons.
a·ni·ma·to (ä′nē·mä′tō) *adj. & adv.* *Music* With animation. [< Ital.]
an·i·mism (an′ə·miz′əm) *n.* **1.** The belief in the existence of spirit or soul, as distinct from matter. **2.** The doctrine that natural objects and phenomena possess a soul. [< L *anima* soul] — **an′i·mist** *n.* — **an′i·mis′tic** *adj.*
an·i·mos·i·ty (an′ə·mos′ə·tē) *n.* *pl.* **·ties** Active and vehement enmity; hatred. [< L *animositas, -tatis* high spirit]
an·i·mus (an′ə·məs) *n.* **1.** Hostile feeling; animosity. **2.** The animating thought or purpose; intention. [< L]
an·i·on (an′ī′ən) *n.* *Chem.* A negative ion: opposed to *cation.* [< Gk. *anienai* to go up] — **an′i·on′ic** (-on′ik) *adj.*
an·ise (an′is) *n.* **1.** A small South European and North African plant that furnishes aniseed. **2.** Aniseed. [< OF < L < Gk. *anison*]
an·i·seed (an′i·sēd′) *n.* The fragrant seed of the anise plant.
an·i·sette (an′ə·zet′, -set′) *n.* A cordial made from or flavored with aniseed. [< F.]
an·kle (ang′kəl) *n.* **1.** The joint connecting the foot and the leg. **2.** The part of the leg between the foot and the calf near the ankle joint. [ME *ankel* < OE *ancléow*]
an·kle·bone (ang′kəl·bōn′) *n.* The talus. Also **ankle bone.**
an·klet (ang′klit) *n.* **1.** An ornament or fetter for the ankle. **2.** A short sock reaching just above the ankle.
ankylo- *combining form* Bent; crooked: in anatomy, referring to adhesion of bones. [< Gk. *ankylos* crooked]
an·ky·lose (ang′kə·lōs) *v.t. & v.i.* **·losed, ·los·ing** To unite or join by ankylosis: also spelled *anchylose.*
an·ky·lo·sis (ang′kə·lō′sis) *n.* **1.** *Anat.* The fusing of bones or parts of bones. **2.** *Pathol.* The abnormal adhesion of bones, especially those forming a joint; stiffening of a joint. Also spelled *anchylosis.* [< NL < Gk. *ankylōsis* < *ankyloein* to bend < *ankylos* crooked] — **an′ky·lot′ic** (-lo t′ik) *adj.*
an·nal·ist (an′əl·ist) *n.* A writer of annals; a historian. — **an′nal·is′tic** *adj.*
an·nals (an′əlz) *n.pl.* **1.** A record of events in their chronological order, year by year. **2.** History or records. **3.** A periodical publication of discoveries, transactions, etc. [< L *annus* year]
An·na·mese (an′ə·mēz′, -mēs′) *n.* *pl.* **An·na·mese** **1.** A native or inhabitant of Annam. **2.** Formerly, the Vietnamese language. — *adj.* Of Annam or the Annamese.
Anne, Saint Traditionally, the mother of the Virgin Mary.
an·neal (ə·nēl′) *v.t.* **1.** To reduce the brittleness of, as glass and various metals, by heating and then slowly cooling. **2.** To toughen, as the will. [OE *onælan* to burn]
an·ne·lid (an′ə·lid) *Zool.* *adj.* Belonging to a phylum of segmented worms, including the earthworm and leeches. — *n.* An annelid worm. [< NL < F < L *annellus* a ring]

an·nex (*v.* ə·neks′; *n.* an′eks) *v.t.* **1.** To add or append, as an additional or minor part, to existing possessions; affix. **2.** To attach, as an attribute, condition, or consequence. — **Syn.** See ADD. — *n.* **1.** An addition to a building. **2.** An addition to a document; addendum. [< F < L < *ad-* to + *nectere* to tie] — **an·nex′a·ble** *adj.*

an·nex·a·tion (an′ek·sā′shən) *n.* **1.** The act of annexing. **2.** That which is added or attached. Also **an·nex′ment.**

an·ni·hi·late (ə·nī′ə·lāt) *v.t.* **·lat·ed, ·lat·ing** To destroy utterly. [< L *ad-* to + *nihil* nothing] — **an·ni′hi·la·ble** *adj.* — **an·ni′hi·la′tive** *adj.* — **an·ni·hi·la·tion** (ə·nī′ə·lā′shən) *n.* — **an·ni′hi·la′tor** *n.*

an·ni·ver·sa·ry (an′ə·vûr′sər·ē) *n. pl.* **·ries 1.** A day in the year on the date of which an event occurred in some preceding year. **2.** A celebration on such occasion. — *adj.* **1.** Recurring annually or at the same date every year. **2.** Pertaining to or occurring on an anniversary. [< L < *annus* year + *versus*, pp. of *vertere* to turn]

an·no Dom·i·ni (an′ō dom′ə·nī) *Latin* In the year of our Lord or of the Christian era. Abbr. *A.D.*

an·no·tate (an′ō·tāt) *v.t. & v.i.* **·tat·ed, ·tat·ing** To provide (a text, etc.) with explanatory or critical notes. [< L < *ad-* to + *notare* to note, mark] — **an′no·ta′tion** *n.* — **an′no·ta′tive** *adj.* — **an′no·ta′tor** *n.*

an·nounce (ə·nouns′) *v.t.* **·nounced, ·nounc·ing 1.** To make known publicly or officially; proclaim. **2.** To give notice of the approach or appearance of: to *announce* guests. **3.** To make known to the senses. **4.** To serve as the announcer for, as a radio program. [< OF < L < *ad-* to + *nuntiare* to report] — **an·nounce′ment** *n.*

an·nounc·er (ə·noun′sər) *n.* **1.** One who announces. **2.** A person who identifies the station from which a radio or television program is broadcast, introduces the performers, etc.

an·noy (ə·noi′) *v.t.* **1.** To be troublesome to; bother; irritate. **2.** To do harm to or injure. [< OF *anuier, anoier*, ult. < L *in odio* in hatred] — **an·noy′er** *n.*

an·noy·ance (ə·noi′əns) *n.* **1.** One who or that which annoys. **2.** The act of annoying or of being annoyed.

an·noy·ing (ə·noi′ing) *adj.* Vexatious; troublesome. — **an·noy′ing·ly** *adv.* — **an·noy′ing·ness** *n.*

an·nu·al (an′yōō·əl) *adj.* **1.** Returning, performed, or occurring every year. **2.** Reckoned by the year. — *n.* **1.** A book or pamphlet issued once a year. **2.** *Bot.* A plant living for a single year or season. Abbr. *ann.* [< L *annualis* yearly] — **an′nu·al·ly** *adv.*

an·nu·i·tant (ə·nōō′ə·tənt, ə·nyōō′-) *n.* One receiving, or entitled to receive, an annuity.

an·nu·i·ty (ə·nōō′ə·tē, ə·nyōō′-) *n. pl.* **·ties 1.** An income paid yearly. **2.** The right to receive such an allowance, or the duty of paying it. **3.** Interest from an investment in yearly payments. [< OF < Med.L *annuitas, -tatis*]

an·nul (ə·nul′) *v.t.* **·nulled, ·nul·ling** To put an end to; nullify, esp. a marriage. [< OF < LL < L *ad-* to + *nullus* none] — **an·nul′ment** *n.* — **an·nul′la·ble** *adj.*

— **Syn. 1.** *Annul* and *nullify* are general terms; *nullify* may also be used in an extralegal sense. A marriage is *annulled*; a law may be *nullified* by a new law, or by the effects of popular defiance. *Cancel, abate, void, vacate, quash, abrogate, repeal, rescind,* and *revoke* differ chiefly in technical usage. Typically, we *cancel* a lease, *abate* or *void* a writ, *vacate* an injunction, *quash* an indictment, *abrogate* a treaty, *repeal* a law, *rescind* a ruling, and *revoke* a will.

an·nu·lar (an′yə·lər) *adj.* Formed like a ring; ring-shaped. [< L *annularis* < *annulus, anulus* ring] — **an′nu·lar·ly** *adv.*

annular eclipse *Astron.* A solar eclipse in which a narrow ring of the sun is visible beyond the dark mass of the moon.

an·nu·late (an′yə·lit, -lāt) *adj.* Furnished with rings; ringed. [< L *annulatus* < *annulus* a ring] — **an′nu·la′tion** *n.*

an·nu·lus (an′yə·ləs) *n. pl.* **·li** (-lī) or **·lus·es** A ringlike part, body, or space. [< L, a ring]

an·nun·ci·ate (ə·nun′shē·āt, -sē-) *v.t.* **·at·ed, ·at·ing** To announce. [< L *annuntiare* to report]

an·nun·ci·a·tion (ə·nun′sē·ā′shən, -shē-) *n.* The act of announcing, or that which is announced; proclamation.

An·nun·ci·a·tion (ə·nun′sē·ā′shən, -shē-) *n. Eccl.* **1.** The announcement of the Incarnation to the Virgin Mary by an angel. *Luke* i 28–38. **2.** The festival (March 25) commemorating this event.

an·nun·ci·a·tor (ə·nun′shē·ā′tər, -sē-) *n.* **1.** An announcer. **2.** An electrical indicator used in hotels, etc., that shows a number or name when a bell is rung.

an·ode (an′ōd) *n. Electr.* **1.** The positive electrode toward which anions migrate in an electrolytic cell. **2.** The plate of an electron tube toward which electrons are attracted. [< Gk. *anodos* a way up] — **an·od·ic** (an·od′ik) *adj.*

an·o·dyne (an′ə·dīn) *adj.* Having power to allay pain; soothing. — *n. Med.* Anything that relieves pain or soothes. [< L < Gk. < *an-* without + *odynē* pain]

a·noint (ə·noint′) *v.t.* **1.** To smear with oil or ointment. **2.** To put oil on in a religious ceremony. [< OF < L < *in-* on + *ungere* to smear] — **a·noint′er** *n.* — **a·noint′ment** *n.*

a·nom·a·lous (ə·nom′ə·ləs) *adj.* Deviating from the common rule; exceptional; abnormal. [< L < Gk. < *an-* not + *homalos* even] — **a·nom′a·lous·ly** *adv.* — **a·nom′a·lou ness** *n.*

a·nom·a·ly (ə·nom′ə·lē) *n. pl.* **·lies 1.** Deviation from ru type, or form; irregularity. **2.** Anything anomalous. **a·nom′a·lism** *n.* — **a·nom·a·lis·tic** (ə·nom′ə·lis′tik) or cal *adj.*

a·non (ə·non′) *adv.* **1.** In a little while; soon. **2.** At anoth time; again. [OE *on ān* in one]

an·o·nym (an′ə·nim) *n.* **1.** An anonymous person or writ **2.** A pseudonym.

a·non·y·mous (ə·non′ə·məs) *adj.* **1.** Having or bearing name. **2.** Of unknown authorship or agency. [< Gk. < *a* without + *onoma* name] — **an·o·nym·i·ty** (an′ə·nim′ə·t **a·non′y·mous·ness** *n.* — **a·non′y·mous·ly** *adv.*

a·noph·e·les (ə·nof′ə·lēz) *n.* A mosquito carrying t malaria parasite. [< NL < Gk. *anōphelēs* harmful] **a·noph·e·line** (ə·nof′ə·līn, -lin) *adj.*

an·o·rex·i·a (an′ə·rek′sē·ə) *n. Med.* Loss of appetite. A **an′o·rex′y.** [< NL < Gk. < *an-* without + *orexis* appeti — **an·o·rec·tic** (an′ə·rek′tik), **an′o·rec′tous** *adj.*

an·oth·er (ə·nuth′ər) *adj.* **1.** An additional; one more. Not the same; different: *another* man. — *pron.* **1.** An ad tional one; one more. **2.** A different one. **3.** A similar identical one. [< *an other*]

an·ox·i·a (an·ok′sē·ə) *n. Pathol.* An insufficient oxyg supply to the body tissues.

An·schluss (än′shlōōs) *n. German* Political union.

an·swer (an′sər, än′-) *v.i.* **1.** To reply or respond, as words or actions. **2.** To be responsible or accountable: w *for.* **3.** To serve the purpose. **4.** To correspond or mat as in appearance: with *to.* — *v.t.* **5.** To speak, write, or in response or reply to. **6.** To be sufficient for; fulfill. To pay for: to *answer* damages. **8.** To conform or cor spond to; match. **9.** *Law* To reply favorably to, as a pe tion or petitioner. — **to answer back** To talk back, as contradiction. — *n.* **1.** A reply. **2.** Any action in retu or in kind; retaliation. **3.** The result of a calculation solution. **4.** *Law* The defense of a defendant. **5.** *Mu* The restatement of a musical theme or phrase. [OE *a swarian*] — **an′swer·er** *n.*

an·swer·a·ble (an′sər·ə·bəl, än′-) *adj.* **1.** Accountable; sponsible. **2.** That may be answered. — **an·swer·a·b ness** *n.* — **an′swer·a·bly** *adv.*

ant (ant) *n.* A small insect, usu. wingless, and living colonies. [OE *ǣmete*]

ant- Var. of ANTI-.

-ant *suffix* **1.** Forming adjectives that mean in the act process of doing (what is denoted by the stem): *milita litigant*, etc. **2.** One who or that which does (what is in cated by the stem): *servant*, one who serves. [< F < L *-a -ens*, present participial suffixes]

ant·ac·id (ant·as′id) *adj.* Correcting acidity. — *n.* An kaline remedy for stomach acidity.

an·tag·o·nism (an·tag′ə·niz′əm) *n.* **1.** Mutual opposit or resistance; hostility. **2.** An opposing principle or for

an·tag·o·nist (an·tag′ə·nist) *n.* **1.** An adversary; oppone **2.** *Anat.* A muscle that acts counter to another muscle. **Syn.** See ENEMY.

an·tag·o·nis·tic (an·tag′ə·nis′tik) *adj.* Opposed; hostile. **an·tag′o·nis′ti·cal·ly** *adv.*

an·tag·o·nize (an·tag′ə·nīz) *v.* **·nized, ·niz·ing** *v.t.* **1.** make unfriendly; make an enemy of. **2.** To struggle again oppose. — *v.i.* **3.** To act antagonistically. [< Gk. < *ar* against + *agōnizesthai* to struggle, strive]

ant·al·ka·li (ant·al′kə·lī) *n. pl.* **·lis** or **·lies** Any substar able to neutralize alkalis.

Ant·arc·tic (ant·ärk′tik, -är′tik) *adj.* Of or relating to South Pole, or the regions within the Antarctic Crcle. [< < Gk. < *anti-* opposite + *arktos* the Bear (a northern c stellation), the north]

An·tar·es (an·târ′ēz) *n.* A giant red star, one of the brightest; Alpha in the constellation Scorpio. [< Gk.]

ant bear A mammal of tropical America feeding on an

an·te (an′tē) *v.t. & v.i.* **·ted** or **·teed, ·te·ing 1.** In poker, to put up (one's stake). **2.** *Slang* To pay (one's share). — *n.* **1.** In poker, the stake put up before receiving the hand. **2.** *Slang* One's share. [< L, before]

ANT BEAR
(8 feet long; 2 feet high)

ante- *prefix* **1.** Before in time or order: *antemeridiem.* **2.** Before in position; in front of: *antechamber.* [< L *ante* before]

ant·eat·er (ant′ē′tər) *n.* **1.** The ant bear. **2.** One of seve other mammals that feed partly on ants, as the aardvar

an·te·bel·lum (an′tē·bel′əm) *adj.* Before the war; esp., fore the Civil War in the United States. [< L]

an·te·cede (an′tə·sēd′) *v.t. & v.i.* **·ced·ed, ·ced·ing** To go come before. [< L < *ante-* before + *cedere* to go]

an·te·ce·dence (an′tə·sēd′ns) *n.* **1.** A going before; pre ence; priority. **2.** *Astron.* The apparent retrograde motion f a planet. Also **an′te·ce′den·cy.**

·te·ce·dent (an′tə·sēd′nt) *adj.* **1.** Prior; preceding. — . **1.** One who or that which precedes. **2.** *Gram.* The word, hrase, or clause to which a pronoun refers. **3.** *pl.* The past vents, circumstances, etc., of a person's life; also, anestry. **4.** *Math.* The first term of a ratio; in a proportion, he first and third terms. **5.** *Logic* The condition on which a ypothetical proposition depends. [< L < *ante-* before + *edere* to go] — **an′te·ce′dent·ly** *adv.*

·te·cham·ber (an′ti·chām′bər) *n.* A room serving as an ntranceway to another room

·te·date (an′ti·dāt′) *v.t.* **·dat·ed, ·dat·ing** **1.** To precede time. **2.** To assign to a date earlier than the actual one. . To cause to happen at an earlier date.

·te·di·lu·vi·an (an′ti·di·lo͞o′vē·ən) *adj.* **1.** Before the lood. **2.** Antiquated; primitive. — *n.* **1.** A person, aniaal, or plant that lived before the Flood. **2.** An old or oldashioned person. [< ANTE- + L *diluvium* deluge]

·te·lope (an′tə·lōp) *n.* *pl.* **·lope** or **·lopes** **1.** Any of arious swift, hollow-horned animals, as the gazelle, chams, gnu, etc. **2.** Leather made from its hide. **3.** *U.S.* The ronghorn. [< OF < Med.L < LGk. *antholops*]

·te me·rid·i·em (an′tē mə·rid′ē·em) *Latin* Before noon. bbr. *a.m., A.M.* — **an′te·me·rid′i·an** *adj.*

·ten·na (an·ten′ə) *n.* *pl.* **·ten·nae** (-ten′ē) *for def. 1* **·ten·as** *for def. 2* **1.** *Entomol.* One of the paired, movable sense rgans on the head of an insect or other arthropod. **2.** *Telem.* A system of wires, etc., for transmitting or receiving ectromagnetic waves. [< NL < L, a yard for a sail]

·te·pe·nult (an′ti·pē′nult, -pi·nult′) *n.* The last syllable ut two in a word, as *te* in *antepenult.* [< L]

·te·pe·nul·ti·mate (an′ti·pi·nul′tə·mit) *adj.* Pertaining the last but two of any series. — *n.* The antepenult.

·te·ri·or (an·tir′ē·ər) *adj.* **1.** Antecedent in time; prior. . Farther front or forward in space. [< L, compar. of *ante* efore] — **an·te′ri·or·ly** *adv.*

tero- *combining form* Anterior; placed in front. [< L *anrus* (assumed form)]

·te·room (an′ti·ro͞om′, -ro͝om′) *n.* A waiting room.

th- Var. of ANTI-.

·them (an′thəm) *n.* **1.** A hymn of gladness or praise: a ational *anthem.* **2.** A musical composition, usually set to ords from the Bible. — *v.t.* To celebrate with an anthem. OE < LL < Gk., < *anti-* against + *phōnē* voice]

·ther (an′thər) *n.* *Bot.* The pollen-bearing part of a amen. For illustration see FLOWER. [< F < L < Gk. *nthos* flower]

·ther·id·i·um (an′thə·rid′ē·əm) *n.* *pl.* **·ther·id·i·a** (-thəid′ē·ə) *Bot.* The male sexual organ in cryptogams. [< NL, im. of Gk. *antheros* flowery] — **an′ther·id′i·al** *adj.*

tho- *combining form* Flower. [< Gk. *anthos* a flower]

·thol·o·gize (an·thol′ə·jīz) *v.* **·gized, ·giz·ing** *v.i.* **1.** To ake an anthology or anthologies. — *v.t.* **2.** To put into an nthology or make an anthology of.

·thol·o·gy (an·thol′ə·jē) *n.* *pl.* **·gies** A collection of choice representative literary extracts. [< L < Gk. < *anthos* ower + *legein* to gather] — **an·tho·log·i·cal** (an′thə·loj′iəl) *adj.* — **an·thol′o·gist** *n.*

·tho·zo·an (an′thə·zō′ən) *Zool. adj.* Of or belonging to a ass of marine animals including the sea anemones and orals. — *n.* An anthozoan animal. [< NL < ANTHO- + k. *zōion* animal] — **an′tho·zo′ic** *adj.*

·thra·cene (an′thrə·sēn) *n.* *Chem.* A crystalline comound, $C_{14}H_{11}$, obtained from coal tar and used in manuacturing dyes. [< Gk. *anthrax, -akos* coal + -ENE]

·thra·cite (an′thrə·sīt) *n.* Coal that burns slowly and ith great heat: also called *hard coal.* [< L < Gk. *anthrax* oal] — **an·thra·cit·ic** (an′thr·sit′ik) *adj.*

·thrax (an′thraks) *n.* *pl.* **·thra·ces** (-thrə·sēz) *Pathol.* n infectious, malignant disease of man and some animals, ften with carbuncles; also, the carbuncle. [< Gk., coal]

thropo- *combining form* Man; human: *anthropology.* lso, before vowels, **anthrop-.** [< Gk. *anthrōpos* man]

·thro·po·cen·tric (an′thrə·pō·sen′trik) *adj.* Regarding an as the central fact or final aim of the universe.

·thro·pog·e·ny (an′thrə·poj′ə·nē) *n.* The branch of anhropology that treats of the origin and development of man. lso **an·thro·po·gen·e·sis** (an′thrə·pō·jen′ə·sis).

·thro·poid (an′thrə·poid) *adj.* Like a human being in orm or other characteristics, as the gorilla, chimpanzee, nd orang-utan. Also **an′thro·poi′dal.** — *n.* An ape.

·thro·pol·o·gy (an′thrə·pol′ə·jē) *n.* **1.** The science treatg of the physical, social, material, and cultural developent of man, including his origin, evolution, distribution, ustoms, beliefs, folkways, etc. — **an·thro·po·log·i·cal** (an′hrə·pə·loj′i·kəl) or **·log′ic** *adj.* — **an′thro·po·log′i·cal·ly** *dv.* — **an′thro·pol′o·gist** *n.*

an·thro·pom·e·try (an′thrə·pom′ə·trē) *n.* The science and technique of human anatomical measurements. — **an·thro·po·met·ric** (an′thrə·pō·met′rik) or **·ri·cal** *adj.*

an·thro·po·mor·phic (an′thrə·pō·môr′fik) *adj.* Of or characterized by anthropomorphism.

an·thro·po·mor·phism (an′thrə·pō·môr′fiz·əm) *n.* The ascription of human form or characteristics to a deity, or to any being or thing not human. — **an′thro·po·mor′phist** *n.*

an·thro·po·mor·phize (an′thrə·pō·môr′fīz) *v.t.* & *v.i.* **·phized, ·phiz·ing** To ascribe human characteristics (to).

an·thro·po·mor·phous (an′thrə·pō·môr′fəs) *adj.* Having or resembling human form. [< Gk. < *anthrōpos* man + *morphē* form, shape]

an·ti (an′tī, an′tē) *n.* *pl.* **·tis** *Informal* One opposed to some policy, group, etc.

anti- A prefix having the following meanings: **1.** Against; opposed to, as in: **antitobacco, anti-Fascist. 2.** Opposite to; reverse, as in: **anticyclic, antilogic. 3.** *Med.* Counteracting; curative, as in: **antianemic, antivirus.** *Anti-* usu. changes to *ant-* before words beginning with a vowel, as in *antacid.* [< Gk. *anti* against]

an·ti·air·craft (an′tē·âr′kraft′, -âr′kräft′, an′tī-) *adj.* Used for defense against enemy aircraft. Abbr. *AA, A.A.*

an·ti·bi·o·sis (an′ti·bī·ō′sis) *n.* *Biol.* The condition of associated organisms in which one is detrimental to the other.

an·ti·bi·ot·ic (an′ti·bī·ot′ik, an′ti-, an′ti·bē·ot′ik) *n.* *Biochem.* Any of a large class of substances, as penicillin, streptomycin, etc., having the power of destroying or arresting the growth of microorganisms. [< ANTI- + Gk. *bios* life]

an·ti·bod·y (an′ti·bod′ē) *n.* *pl.* **·bod·ies** *Biochem.* Any of a class of proteins serving to immunize the body against specific antigens.

an·tic (an′tik) *n.* **1.** *Usually pl.* A prank; caper. **2.** A clown; buffoon. — *adj.* Odd; fantastic; ludicrous. — *v.i.* **an·ticked, an·tick·ing** To play the clown; perform antics. [< Ital. *antico* old, grotesque] — **an′tic·ly** *adv.*

an·ti·christ (an′ti·krīst′) *n.* *Often cap.* A denier or opponent of Christ or Christianity. — **an′ti·chris′tian** *adj.* & *n.*

An·ti·christ (an′ti·krīst′) *n.* The blasphemous antagonist of Christ. I *John* ii 18.

an·tic·i·pant (an·tis′ə·pənt) *adj.* Coming or acting in advance; anticipating; expectant. — *n.* One who anticipates.

an·tic·i·pate (an·tis′ə·pāt) *v.t.* **·pat·ed, ·pat·ing** **1.** To experience or realize beforehand. **2.** To look forward to. **3.** To act or arrive sooner than, especially so as to forestall. **4.** To foresee and fulfill beforehand, as desires. **5.** To make use of beforehand. **6.** To discharge, as a debt, before it is due. **7.** To cause to happen earlier. [< L < *ante-* before + *capere* to take] — **an·tic′i·pa′tor** *n.*

an·tic·i·pa·tion (an·tis′ə·pā′shən) *n.* **1.** The act of anticipating; also, that which is anticipated. **2.** An expectation. **3.** An intuitive prevision.

an·tic·i·pa·tive (an·tis′ə·pā′tiv) *adj.* Anticipating, or characterized by anticipation. — **an·tic′i·pa′tive·ly** *adv.*

an·tic·i·pa·to·ry (an·tis′ə·pə·tôr′ē, -tō′rē) *adj.* Of, showing, or embodying anticipation. — **an·tic′i·pa·to′ri·ly** *adv.*

an·ti·cler·i·cal (an′ti·kler′i·kəl) *adj.* Opposed to clerical influence in political and civic affairs. — **an′ti cler′i·cal ism** *n.*

an·ti·cli·max (an′ti·klī′maks) *n.* **1.** In rhetoric, a ludicrous decrease in the importance or impressiveness of what is said. **2.** Any sudden descent or fall contrasted with a previous rise. — **an′ti·cli·mac′tic** (-klī·mak′tik) *adj.*

an·ti·cline (an′ti·klīn) *n.* *Geol.* A system of roughly parallel folds in stratified rock in which the folds slope downward from the crest in opposite directions. Compare SYNCLINE. [< ANTI- + Gk. *klinein* to slope] — **an′ti·cli′nal** *adj.*

ANTICLINE

an·ti·cy·clone (an′ti·sī′klōn) *n.* *Meteorol.* An atmospheric condition in which winds spiral outward from a central point of high pressure. — **an′ti·cy·clon′ic** (-klon′ik) *adj.*

an·ti·dote (an′ti·dōt) *n.* Anything that will counteract or remove the effects of poison, disease, or any evil. [< L < Gk. < *anti-* against + *didonai* to give] — **an′ti·do′tal** *adj.* — **an′ti·do′tal·ly** *adv.*

An·ti·fed·er·al·ist (an′ti·fed′ər·əl·ist, -fed′rəl-) *n.* A member of the political party that opposed the ratification of the U.S. Constitution. — **An′ti·fed′er·al** *adj.*

an·ti·freeze (an′ti·frēz′) *n.* A liquid of low freezing point, added to or substituted for the cooling agent in combustion-engine radiators, to prevent freezing.

an·ti·gen (an′tə·jən) *n.* *Biochem.* Any of several substances

that cause the development of antibodies. Also **an′ti·gene** (-jēn). — **an·ti·gen·ic** (an′tə·jen′ik) *adj.*
An·tig·o·ne (an·tig′ə·nē) In Greek legend, a daughter of Oedipus and Jocasta, who was sentenced to death for illegally burying her brother.
an·ti·his·ta·mine (an′ti·his′tə·mēn, -min) *n. Med.* Any of certain drugs that neutralize the action of histamine in the treatment of hay fever, asthma, etc. — **an′ti·his′ta·min′ic** (-min′ik) *adj.*
an·ti·knock (an′ti·nok′) *n.* An agent that prevents premature combustion when added to the fuel of an internal-combustion engine.
an·ti·log·a·rithm (an′ti·lôg′ə·rith′əm, -log′-) *n. Math.* The number corresponding to a given logarithm. Also, in shortened form, **an·ti·log** (an′ti·lôg, -log).
an·ti·ma·cas·sar (an′ti·mə·kas′ər) *n.* A covering for the backs and arms of chairs and sofas to prevent soiling; a tidy.
an·ti·mat·ter (an′ti·mat′ər) *n. Physics* A form of matter composed of antiparticles.
an·ti·mo·ni·al (an′tə·mō′nē·əl) *adj.* Of or containing antimony. — *n.* A medicine containing antimony.
an·ti·mo·ny (an′tə·mō′nē) *n.* A silver-white, crystalline, metallic element (symbol Sb) used in chemistry, medicine, in alloys, etc.: also called *stibium.* See ELEMENT. ◆ Collateral adjective: *stibial.* [< Med.L *antimonium*]
an·ti·par·ti·cle (an′ti·pär′ti·kəl) *n. Physics* Any of a group of atomic particles having masses equal to the electron, proton, neutron, etc., but with opposite charges and magnetic characteristics.
an·ti·pas·to (än′tē·päs′tō) *n.* A course of smoked or salted meat, fish, vegetables, etc., served as an appetizer. [< Ital.]
an·tip·a·thet·ic (an·tip′ə·thet′ik, an′ti·pə-) *adj.* Having a natural aversion; constitutionally opposed: often with *to.* Also **an·tip′a·thet′i·cal.** — **an·tip′a·thet′i·cal·ly** *adv.*
an·tip·a·thy (an·tip′ə·thē) *n. pl.* **·thies 1.** An instinctive feeling of aversion or dislike. **2.** The object of such a feeling. [< L < Gk. < *anti-* against + *pathein* to feel, suffer]
an·ti·per·son·nel (an′ti·pûr′sə·nel′, an′tī-) *adj. Mil.* Designating weapons that are employed against troops rather than against defenses or mechanized equipment.
an·ti·per·spi·rant (an′ti·pûr′spə·rənt, an′tī-) *n.* A skin astringent that prevents or diminishes perspiration.
an·ti·phlo·gis·tic (an′ti·flō·jis′tik) *Med. adj.* Capable of reducing inflammation. — *n.* A remedy for inflammation. [< ANTI- + Gk. *phlogizein* to burn]
an·ti·phon (an′tə·fon) *n.* A verse of a psalm or hymn said or chanted in response to another. [< LL < Gk. < *anti-* against + *phōnē* voice]
an·tiph·o·nal (an·tif′ə·nəl) *adj.* Of or like an antiphon; sung responsively. Also **an·ti·phon·ic** (an′tə·fon′ik). — *n.* An antiphonary. — **an·tiph′o·nal·ly** *adv.*
an·tiph·o·nar·y (an·tif′ə·ner′ē) *n. pl.* **·nar·ies** A book of antiphons. — *adj.* Of or pertaining to a book of antiphons.
an·tip·o·dal (an·tip′ə·dəl) *adj.* **1.** Pertaining to or situated on the opposite side of the earth. **2.** Diametrically opposed. Also **an·tip·o·de·an** (an·tip′ə·dē′ən).
an·ti·pode (an′ti·pōd) *n.* An exact opposite.
an·tip·o·des (an·tip′ə·dēz) *n.* (*construed as sing. or pl.*) A place or region on the opposite side of the earth, or its inhabitants. [< L < Gk. < *anti-* opposite + *pous* foot]
an·ti·py·ret·ic (an′ti·pī·ret′ik) *Med. adj.* Reducing fever. — *n.* A medicine to reduce fever. [< ANTI- + Gk. *pyretos* fever]
an·ti·quar·i·an (an′ti·kwâr′ē·ən) *adj.* Pertaining to antiques or antiquaries. — *n.* An antiquary. — **an′ti·quar′i·an·ism** *n.*
an·ti·quar·y (an′ti·kwer′ē) *n. pl.* **·quar·ies** One who collects, deals in, or studies antiques or antiquities.
an·ti·quate (an′ti·kwāt) *v.t.* **·quat·ed, ·quat·ing 1.** To make old or out-of-date. **2.** To cause to look antique. [< L *antiquare* to make old] — **an′ti·qua′tion** *n.*
an·ti·quat·ed (an′ti·kwā′tid) *adj.* **1.** Out-of-date; old-fashioned; obsolete. **2.** Ancient; very old.
an·tique (an·tēk′) *adj.* **1.** Of or pertaining to ancient times. **2.** Of an earlier period: an *antique* chair. **3.** Old-fashioned; out-of-date. — *n.* **1.** The style of ancient art, or a specimen of it. **2.** Any old object, usually prized for its rarity, style or craft, etc. **3.** *Printing* A style of type with all the lines of nearly equal thickness. — *v.t.* **an·tiqued, an·ti·quing** To give the appearance of antiquity to. [< F < L *antiquus* ancient] — **an·tique′ly** *adv.* — **an·tique′ness** *n.*
an·tiq·ui·ty (an·tik′wə·tē) *n. pl.* **·ties 1.** The quality of being ancient. **2.** Ancient times, esp. before the Middle Ages. **3.** The people of ancient times collectively; the ancients. **4.** *Usually pl.* Ancient relics.
an·ti-Sem·i·tism (an′ti·sem′ə·tiz′əm, an′tī-) *n.* Opposition to, discrimination against, or intolerance of Jews, Jewish culture, etc. — **an′ti-Sem′ite** (-sem′īt) *n.* — **an′ti-Se·mit′ic** (-sə·mit′ik) *adj.* — **an′ti-Se·mit′i·cal·ly** *adv.*
an·ti·sep·sis (an′tə·sep′sis) *n.* The condition of being free of pathogenic bacteria; also, the method of obtaining this.
an·ti·sep·tic (an′tə·sep′tik) *adj.* **1.** Of, pertaining to, used in antisepsis. **2.** Preventing or counteracting infectic Also **an′ti·sep′ti·cal.** — *n.* Any antiseptic substance. [ANTI- + Gk. *sēpsis* putrefaction] — **an′ti·sep′ti·cal·ly** *ad*
an·ti·se·rum (an′ti·sir′əm) *n.* A serum that provides i munity from specific diseases.
an·ti·slav·er·y (an′ti·slā′vər·ē, -slāv′rē, an′tī-) *adj.* Oppos to human slavery.
an·ti·so·cial (an′ti·sō′shəl, an′tī-) *adj.* **1.** Unsociable. Opposed to or disruptive of society or the general good.
an·ti·spas·mod·ic (an′ti·spaz·mod′ik) *Med. adj.* Relievi or checking spasms. — *n.* An antispasmodic agent.
an·tis·tro·phe (an·tis′trə·fē) *n.* In ancient Greek dran the verses sung by the chorus while returning from left right, in answer to the previous strophe. [< L < Gk. *anti-* against, opposite + *strephein* to turn] — **an·ti·stro ic** (an′ti·strof′ik) *adj.*
an·ti·tank (an′ti·tangk′) *adj. Mil.* Designed to comb tanks and other armored vehicles: *antitank* guns. Abbr.
an·tith·e·sis (an·tith′ə·sis) *n. pl.* **·ses** (-sēz) **1.** The b ancing of two contrasted words, ideas, or phrases agai each other. Example: *My prayers go up; my thoughts remc below.* **2.** Opposition; contrast: the *antithesis* of peace a war. **3.** The direct opposite. **4.** One of the three categor found in the dialectic systems of Hegel, Marx, etc. [< < Gk. < *anti-* against + *tithenai* to place] — **an·ti·the cal** (an′tə·thet′i·kəl) *adj.* — **an′ti·thet′i·cal·ly** *adv.*
an·ti·tox·in (an′ti·tok′sin) *n. Biochem.* A substan formed in the living tissues of an animal, that neutralize specific bacterial poison; also, serum containing this. A **an′ti·tox′ine** (-tok′sin, -sēn). — **an′ti·tox′ic** *adj.*
an·ti·trade (an′ti·trād′) *n.* One of the upper air currents the tropics, moving contrary to the trade winds.
an·ti·trust (an′ti·trust′) *adj.* Pertaining to the regulati of or opposition to trusts, cartels, monopolies, etc.
ant·ler (ant′lər) *n. Usu. pl.* Either of the branched hor on the head of members of the deer family. [< OF < *ante-* before + *oculus* eye] — **ant′lered** *adj.*
ant lion An insect resembling a dragonfly, whose lar preys on ants and other insects.
an·to·nym (an′tə·nim) *n.* A word that is the opposite of a other in meaning: opposed to *synonym.* Abbr. *ant.* [< G < *anti-* opposite + *onoma, onyma* name]
an·trum (an′trəm) *n. pl.* **·tra** (-trə) *Anat.* A cavity, us ally in a bone; esp., the cavity in the upper jaw opening in the nose. [< L < Gk. *antron* cave]
a·nus (ā′nəs) *n. Anat.* The excretory opening at the lov extremity of the alimentary canal. [< L, orig., a ring]
an·vil (an′vil, -vəl) *n.* **1.** A heavy block of iron or steel which metal may be forged. **2.** *Anat.* The incus. — *v.t. & v.i.* **an·viled** or **·villed, an·vil·ing** or **·vil·ling** To work at or shape on an anvil. [OE *anfilt*]

DOUBLE-BEAK ANVIL
a Rounded beak. **b** Flat beak. **c** Hardy hole, cutter, or chisel hole.

anx·i·e·ty (ang·zī′ə·tē) *n. pl.* **·ties 1.** Disturbance of mind regarding some uncertain event; misgiving; worry. **2.** Strained or solicitous desire; eagerness. **3.** *Psychiatry* A tense emotional state characterized by fear and apprehension without apparent cause.
anx·ious (angk′shəs, ang′-) *adj.* **1.** Troubled in mind specting some uncertain matter. **2.** Causing anxiety; d tressing: an *anxious* matter. **3.** Intent; eagerly desiro with *for* or the infinitive. [< L *angere* to choke, distre — **anx′ious·ly** *adv.* — **anx′ious·ness** *n.*
an·y (en′ē) *adj.* **1.** One, no matter which; a or an, or (plur some: Have we *any* choice? **2.** Some, however much little: Did he eat *any* supper? **3.** Every: *Any* fool kno that. — *pron.* One or more persons or things of a numb Have *any* of the guests arrived? — *adv.* At all; to any e tent: Are they *any* nearer? [OE *ǣnig* < *ān* one]
an·y·bod·y (en′i·bod′ē, -bud′ē) *pron.* Any person whatev anyone. — *n. pl.* **·bod·ies** A person of importance.
an·y·how (en′i·hou′) *adv.* **1.** In any way whatever; by a means. **2.** Notwithstanding; in any case. **3.** Carelessly
an·y·one (en′i·wun′, -wən) *pron.* Any person. ◆ **any o anyone** *Any one* is used to distinguish one person from ot ers in the same group or class: *Any one* of these men may guilty. *Anyone* (indefinite pronoun) means any person at a
an·y·thing (en′i·thing′) *pron.* Any thing, event, or matt whatever. — *n.* A thing of any kind. — *adv.* To any d gree; in any way: now only in the expression **anything lik**
anything but By no means; far from: *anything but* safe
an·y·way (en′i·wā′) *adv.* **1.** In any manner. **2.** Nevertl less; anyhow. **3.** Carelessly; haphazardly.
an·y·where (en′i·hwâr′) *adv.* In, at, or to any place.
an·y·wise (en′i·wīz′) *adv.* In any manner.
An·zac (an′zak) *adj.* Pertaining to the Australian and N Zealand Army Corps during World War I. — *n.* Any s dier from Australia or New Zealand.

one (ā′wun′) *adj.* *Informal* Excellent. Also **A-1.**
)r·ta (ā·ôr′tə) *n.* *pl.* **·tas** or **·tae** (-tē) *Anat.* The great
ırtery springing from the left ventricle of the heart and form-
ıg the main arterial trunk that distributes blood to all of the
ody except the lungs. [< NL < Gk. < *aeirein* to raise,
eave] **— a·or′tal, a·or′tic** *adj.*
ı-[1] Assimilated var. of AD-.
ı-[2] Var. of APO-.
pace (ə·pās′) *adv.* Rapidly; quickly. [< A-[1] on + PACE]
pache (ə·päsh′, ə·pash′; *Fr.* à·pàsh′) *n.* A ruffian or gang-
;er of Paris. [< F < APACHE]
pach·e (ə·pach′ē) *n.* *pl.* **A·pach·es** or **A·pach·e** One of a
roup of Indians, inhabiting the southern and SW U.S.
ache State Nickname of ARIZONA.
part (ə pärt′) *adv.* **1.** Separated; not together. **2.** One
om another. **3.** Separately for some use or purpose. **4.**
ıdependently in logic or thought: Let us view this matter
part. **5.** Aside; to one side. **6.** In pieces or to pieces: The
ıip broke *apart.* **—** *adj.* Separate; distinct. [< MF < L
l to + *pars, partis* part]
part·heid (ə·pärt′hīt) *n.* In the Republic of South Africa,
ıe official policy of political, social, and economic discrimi-
ation and segregation enforced against nonwhites. [< Af-
ikaans, apartness, separation]
part·ment (ə·pärt′mənt) *n.* **1.** Any of several suites of
ooms in a building, each equipped for housekeeping; a flat.
. A room. Abbr. *apt.* (pl. *apts.*). [< F < Ital., ult. < L *ad*
) + *pars, partis* part]
artment house *U.S.* A multiple-dwelling building di-
ided into a number of apartments.
·a·thet·ic (ap′ə·thet′ik) *adj.* **1.** Lacking emotion. **2.**
ıdifferent; unconcerned. Also **ap′a·thet′i·cal.** [< APATHY,
n analogy with *sympathetic*] **— ap′a·thet′i·cal·ly** *adv.*
·a·thy (ap′ə·thē) *n.* *pl.* **·thies** **1.** Lack of emotion. **2.**
ıdifference. [< L < Gk. < *a-* without + *pathos* feeling]
— Syn. 1, 2. *Apathy* may refer to a habitual lack of feeling,
it may be used in the sense of *indifference* to describe a tem-
orary lack of interest caused by depression, sorrow, ignorance,
espair, etc. *Insensibility* is a lack of feeling for other persons.
e (āp) *n.* **1.** A large, tailless, Old World primate, as a go-
lla or chimpanzee. **2.** Loosely, any monkey. **3.** A mimic.
— *v.t.* **aped, ap·ing** To imitate; mimic. [OE *apa*]
)e·ri·ent (ə·pir′ē·ənt) *Med.* *adj.* Laxative. **—** *n.* A gen-
e purgative. Also **a·per·i·tive** (ə·per′ə·tiv). [< L *aperire*
) open]
pé·ri·tif (à.pā·rē·tēf′) *n.* *French* A drink of alcoholic liq-
or or wine taken as an appetizer.
·er·ture (ap′ər·chŏŏr, -chər) *n.* **1.** An opening; orifice.
. *Optics* An opening, often adjustable in diameter, through
hich light enters the lens of a camera, etc. [< L *aperire* to
pen] **— ap′er·tur·al** *adj.* **— ap′er·tured** *adj.*
et·al·ous (ā·pet′l·əs) *adj.* *Bot.* Without petals.
)ex (ā′peks) *n.* *pl.* **a·pex·es** or **ap·i·ces** (ap′ə·sēz, ā′pə-)
. The highest point; tip; top. **2.** *Geom.* The vertex of an
ıgle. **3.** Climax. [< L]
h- Var. of APO-.
ha·sia (ə·fā′zhə, -zhē·ə) *n.* *Pathol.* Any partial or total
ss of the power of articulate speech, usu. due to a brain
sion. [< NL < Gk. < *a-* not + *phanai* to speak] **— a·pha·**
c (ə·fā′zik, -sik), **a·pha·si·ac** (ə·fā′zē·ak) *adj.* & *n.*
)he·li·on (ə·fē′lē·ən) *n.* *pl.* **·li·a** (-lē·ə) *Astron.* The point
an orbit, as of a planet, farthest from the
ın: opposed to *perihelion.* [< APH (APO-)
way from + Gk. *hēlios* sun] **— a·phe′li·**
n (-ən) *adj.*
)hid (ā′fid, af′id) *n.* A small, juice-
ıcking insect, injurious to plants: also
alled *plant louse.* Also **a′phis.** [Origin un-
ertain] **— a·phid·i·an** (ə·fid′ē·ən) *adj.*
h·o·rism (af′ə·riz′əm) *n.* **1.** A brief
atement of a truth or principle. **2.** A
roverb; maxim. [< MF < Med.L < Gk.
apo- from + *horizein* to divide] **—**
ph′o·rist *n.* **— aph·o·ris·tic** (af′ə·ris′tik) or **·i·cal** *adj.* **—**
ph′o·ris′ti·cal·ly *adv.*

P S A

APHELION
P Perihelion. *S* Sun. *A* Aphelion.

h·ro·dis·i·ac (af′rə·diz′ē·ak) *adj.* Arousing or increasing
exual desire or potency. **—** *n.* An aphrodisiac drug, food,
tc. [< Gk. *aphrodisiakos* < *Aphroditē*, goddess of love]
)h·ro·di·te (af′rə·dī′tē) In Greek mythology, the goddess
love and beauty, the daughter of Zeus: identified with the
oman *Venus.* [< Gk. *Aphroditē* the foam-born]
)i·ar·i·an (ā′pē·âr′ē·ən) *adj.* Of or relating to bees or the
eeping of bees. **—** *n.* An apiarist.
)i·a·rist (ā′pē·ə·rist) *n.* A beekeeper.
)i·a·ry (ā′pē·er′ē) *n.* *pl.* **·ar·ies** A place where bees are
ept; a set of hives, bees, etc. [< L *apiarium* < *apis* bee]
·i·cal (ap′i·kəl, ā′pi-) *adj.* Situated at or belonging to the
pex or top. [< L *apex, apicis* tip]

ap·i·ces (ap′ə·sēz, ā′pə-) Alternative plural of APEX.
a·pi·cul·ture (ā′pi·kul′chər) *n.* The raising and care of bees. [< L *apis* bee + CULTURE] **— a′pi·cul′tur·ist** *n.*
a·piece (ə·pēs′) *adv.* For or to each one; each.
ap·ish (ā′pish) *adj.* Like an ape; servilely imitative; foolish and tricky. **— ap′ish·ly** *adv.* **— ap′ish·ness** *n.*
a·plomb (ə·plom′, *Fr.* à·plôṅ′) *n.* Assurance; self-confidence. [< F < *à* according to + *plomb* plumb bob]
apo- *prefix* Off; from; away: *apostasy.* Also *ap-* before vowels; *aph-* before an aspirate. [< Gk. < *apo* from, off]
a·poc·a·lypse (ə·pok′ə·lips) *n.* A prophecy or revelation. [< L < Gk. < *apo-* from + *kalyptein* to cover]
A·poc·a·lypse (ə·pok′ə·lips) The book of Revelaton, the last book of the New Testament. Abbr. *Apoc.*
a·poc·a·lyp·tic (ə·pok′ə·lip′tik) *adj.* **1.** Of or of the nature of a revelation. **2.** Pertaining to the Apocalypse. Also **a·poc′·a·lyp′ti·cal.** **— a·poc′a·lyp′ti·cal·ly** *adv.*
a·poc·o·pe (ə·pok′ə·pē) *n.* A cutting off or elision of the last sound or syllable of a word. [< Gk. *apokopē* < *apokoptein* to cut off < *apo-* off + *koptein* to cut]
A·poc·ry·pha (ə·pok′rə·fə) *n.pl.* (*often construed as sing.*) Those books of the Septuagint included in the Vulgate but rejected by Protestants as uncanonical because not in the Hebrew Scriptures. [< LL < Gk. *apokryphos* hidden]
a·poc·ry·phal (ə·pok′rə·fəl) *adj.* Having little or no authenticity. **— a·poc′ry·phal·ly** *adv.* **— a·poc′ry·phal·ness** *n.*
ap·o·gee (ap′ə·jē) *n.* **1.** *Astron.* That point in the orbit of a celestial body which is farthest from the earth: opposed to *perigee.* **2.** The highest point; climax. [< MF < L < Gk. < *apo-* away from + *gē, gaia* earth] **— ap·o·ge·al** (ap′ə·jē′əl), **ap′o·ge′an** *adj.*
A·pol·lo (ə·pol′ō) In Greek and Roman mythology, the god of music, poetry, prophecy, and medicine, and later of the sun. **—** *n.* Any handsome young man.

P E A

APOGEE
P Moon at perigee. *E* Earth. *A* Moon at apogee.

a·pol·o·get·ic (ə·pol′ə·jet′ik) *adj.* **1.** Of the nature of an apology; excusing. **2.** Defending or explaining. Also **a·pol′o·get′i·cal.** **—** *n.* An apology or defense. [< F < L < Gk. < *apologia* a speech in defense] **— a·pol′o·get′i·cal·ly** *adv.*
a·pol·o·get·ics (ə·pol′ə·jet′iks) *n.pl.* (*construed as sing.*) The branch of theology that defends Christianity.
a·pol·o·gist (ə·pol′ə·jist) *n.* One who argues in defense of any person or cause.
a·pol·o·gize (ə·pol′ə·jīz) *v.i.* **·gized, ·giz·ing** **1.** To offer an excuse; acknowledge, with regret, any offense. **2.** To make a formal defense in speech or writing. **— a·pol′o·giz′er** *n.*
ap·o·logue (ap′ə·lôg, -log) *n.* A fable or tale having a moral. Also **ap′o·log.** [< L < Gk. < *apo-* from + *logos* speech]
a·pol·o·gy (ə·pol′ə·jē) *n.* *pl.* **·gies** **1.** A statement or explanation expressing regret for some error or offense. **2.** A poor substitute. [< L < Gk. *apologia* a speech in defense]
ap·o·phthegm (ap′ə·them) See APOTHEGM.
ap·o·plec·tic (ap′ə·plek′tik) *adj.* Pertaining to, affected with, or tending toward apoplexy. Also **ap′o·plec′ti·cal.** **—** *n.* A person subject to apoplexy.
ap·o·plex·y (ap′ə·plek′sē) *n.* *Pathol.* Sudden paralysis and loss of sensation caused by a bloodclot or hemorrhage in the brain. [< Gk. < *apo-* from, off + *plēssein* to strike]
a·port (ə·pôrt′, ə·pōrt′) *adj.* *Naut.* On or toward the port side.
a·pos·ta·sy (ə·pos′tə·sē) *n.* *pl.* **·sies** Desertion of one's faith, religion, party, or principles. Also **a·pos′ta·cy.** [< L < Gk. < *apo-* away + *stasis* a standing] **— a·pos·tate** (ə·pos′·tāt, -tit) *adj.* & *n.*
a·pos·ta·tize (ə·pos′tə·tīz) *v.i.* **·tized, ·tiz·ing** To forsake one's faith or principles; become an apostate.
a pos·te·ri·o·ri (ā′ pos·tir′ē·ôr′ī, -ō′rī) **1.** *Logic* Reasoning from facts to principles or from effect to cause. **2.** Inductive; empirical. [< L, from the later]
a·pos·tle (ə·pos′əl) *n.* **1.** One of the twelve disciples originally commissioned by Christ to preach the gospel (*Matt.* x 2–4). **2.** One of a class of missionaries in the early church (I *Cor.* xii 28). **3.** A Christian missionary who first evangelizes a nation or place. **4.** The earliest or foremost advocate of a cause. [OE *apostol* < L < Gk. a messenger]
Apostles' Creed A traditional and still widely accepted Christian confession of faith.
a·pos·to·late (ə·pos′tə·lit, -lāt) *n.* The dignity or office of an apostle. Also **a·pos′tle·ship.**
ap·os·tol·ic (ap′ə·stol′ik) *adj.* **1.** Of or pertaining to an apostle, the apostles, or their times. **2.** According to the doctrine or practice of the apostles. **3.** *Often cap.* Papal. Also **ap′os·tol′i·cal.** **— ap′os·tol′i cism** *n.* **— a·pos·to·lic·i·ty** (ə·pos′tə·lis′ə·tē) *n.*
Apostolic See **1.** The Church of Rome, regarded as having been founded by St. Peter. **2.** The papacy.

a·pos·tro·phe[1] (ə·pos′trə·fē) *n.* A symbol (') written above the line to mark the omission of a letter or letters from a word, to indicate the possessive case, and to denote certain plurals, as *5's*, cross your *t's*. [< F < L < Gk. < *apo-* away + *strephein* to turn] — **ap·os·troph·ic** (ap′ə·strof′ik) *adj.*

a·pos·tro·phe[2] (ə·pos′trə·fē) *n.* A digression from a discourse; esp., a turning aside to speak to an absent person. — **ap·os·troph·ic** (ap′ə·strof′ik) *adj.*

a·pos·tro·phize[1] (ə·pos′trə·fīz) *v.t. & v.i.* **·phized, ·phiz·ing** To shorten (a word) by the omission of a letter or letters.

a·pos·tro·phize[2] (ə·pos′trə·fīz) *v.t. & v.i.* **·phized, ·phiz·ing** To speak or write an apostrophe (to).

apothecaries' measure A system of liquid measure used in pharmacy. See table front of book. Abbr. *ap.*

apothecaries' weight A system of weights used in pharmacy. See table front of book. Abbr. *ap.*

a·poth·e·car·y (ə·poth′ə·ker′ē) *n. pl.* **·car·ies** A druggist. [< OF < L < Gk. < *apo-* away + *tithenai* to put]

ap·o·thegm (ap′ə·them) *n.* A terse, instructive, practical saying; maxim: also spelled *apophthegm.* [< Gk. < *apo-* from + *phthengesthai* to utter] — **ap·o·theg·mat·ic** (ap′ə·theg·mat′ik) or **·i·cal** *adj.*

a·poth·e·o·sis (ə·poth′ē·ō′sis, ap′ə·thē′ə·sis) *n. pl.* **·ses** (-sēz) **1.** Exaltation to divine rank; deification. **2.** Supreme exaltation of any person, principle, etc. [< L < Gk. < *apo-* from + *theos* a god]

a·poth·e·o·size (ə·poth′ē·ə·sīz′, ap′ə·thē′ə·sīz) *v.t.* **·sized, ·siz·ing 1.** To deify. **2.** To glorify; exalt.

ap·pal (ə·pôl′) *v.t.* **·palled, ·pal·ling** *Brit.* Appall.

ap·pall (ə·pôl′) *v.t.* To fill with dismay or horror; shock: also, *Brit., appal.* [< OF *apallir* to pale < L *pallidus*]

ap·pal·ling (ə·pô′ling) *adj.* Causing dismay or terror; frightful. — **ap·pal′ling·ly** *adv.*

ap·pa·ra·tus (ap′ə·rā′təs, -rat′əs) *n. pl.* **·tus** or (rarely) **·tus·es 1.** A device, machine, or assembly of tools, instruments, etc., for a particular purpose. **2.** *Physiol.* Those organs and parts of the body by means of which natural processes are carried on. [< L < *ad-* to + *parare* to prepare]

ap·par·el (ə·par′əl) *n.* **1.** Clothing; attire. **2.** Equipment or furnishings, especially for a ship. — *v.t.* **·eled** or **·elled, ·el·ing** or **·el·ling.** To clothe; dress. [< OF *apareiller* to prepare, ult. < L *ad-* to + *par* equal]

ap·par·ent (ə·par′ənt, ə·pâr′-) *adj.* **1.** Readily perceived by the mind; evident; obvious. **2.** Easily seen; visible. **3.** Seeming, in distinction from real or actual. [< OF < L *apparere*] — **ap·par′ent·ness** *n.*

ap·par·ent·ly (ə·par′ənt·lē, ə·pâr′-) *adv.* **1.** Obviously; plainly. **2.** Seemingly.

ap·pa·ri·tion (ap′ə·rish′ən) *n.* **1.** A visual appearance of a disembodied spirit; phantom; ghost. **2.** Anything that appears, esp. if remarkable or startling. [< MF < L *apparitio, -onis* < *apparere* to appear] — **ap′pa·ri′tion·al** *adj.*

ap·peal (ə·pēl′) *n.* **1.** An earnest entreaty for aid, sympathy, or the like; prayer; supplication. **2.** The quality of being attractive. **3.** A resort to some higher power or final means, for sanction, proof, or aid. **4.** *Law* **a** The carrying of a case from a lower to a higher tribunal for a rehearing. **b** A case so carried. — *v.t.* **1.** *Law* To refer or remove, as a case, to a higher court. — *v.i.* **2.** To make an earnest supplication or request, as for sympathy, corroboration, or aid. **3.** To awaken a favorable response; be interesting. **4.** *Law* To remove a case, or request that a case be moved, to a higher court. **5.** To resort or have recourse: with *to.* [< OF < L *appellare* to accost, call upon] — **ap·peal′a·ble** *adj.* — **ap·peal′er** *n.* — **ap·peal′ing·ly** *adv.*

ap·pear (ə·pir′) *v.i.* **1.** To come into view; become visible. **2.** To seem, or seem likely. **3.** To be clear to the mind; be obvious. **4.** To come before the public; also, to be published, as a book. **5.** *Law* To come formally into court. [< OF < L < *ad-* to + *parere* to come forth, appear]

ap·pear·ance (ə·pir′əns) *n.* **1.** The act of appearing or coming into view. **2.** External or physical aspect; presence: a commanding *appearance.* **3.** *pl.* Circumstances or indications: *Appearances* are against him. **4.** Outward show; pretense. **5.** An apparition; phenomenon.

ap·pease (ə·pēz′) *v.t.* **·peased, ·peas·ing 1.** To placate by making concessions or yielding to demands. **2.** To satisfy or allay. [< OF *apaisier* < L *pax*] — **ap·peas′a·ble** *adj.* — **ap·peas′a·bly** *adv.* — **ap·peas′er** *n.* — **ap·peas′ing·ly** *adv.*

ap·pease·ment (ə·pēz′mənt) *n.* **1.** The act of appeasing or being appeased. **2.** The policy of making concessions to potential aggressors in order to maintain peace.

ap·pel·lant (ə·pel′ənt) *adj.* *Law* Of or pertaining to an appeal; appellate. — *n.* One who appeals, in any sense.

ap·pel·late (ə·pel′it) *adj.* *Law* Pertaining to or having jurisdiction of appeals: an *appellate* court.

ap·pel·la·tion (ap′ə·lā′shən) *n.* **1.** A name or title. **2.** The act of calling or naming.

ap·pel·la·tive (ə·pel′ə·tiv) *adj.* **1.** Serving to designate or name. **2.** *Gram.* Denoting a class: said of common nouns. — *n.* **1.** A title; appellation. **2.** A common noun. — **a pel′la·tive·ly** *adv.* — **ap·pel′la·tive·ness** *n.*

ap·pend (ə·pend′) *v.t.* **1.** To add, as something subordina or supplemental. **2.** To hang or attach: to *append* a seal. **Syn.** See ADD. [< L < *ad-* to + *pendere* to hang]

ap·pend·age (ə·pen′dij) *n.* **1.** Anything appended. *Zool.* Any part joined to or diverging from the axial trun as a limb.

ap·pen·dant (ə·pen′dənt) *adj.* **1.** Attached; adjunct. Hanging attached. **3.** Attendant; consequent. — *n.* Son thing appended or attached. Also **ap·pen′dent.**

ap·pen·dec·to·my (ap′ən·dek′tə·mē) *n. pl.* **·mies** *Surg.* T removal of the vermiform appendix.

ap·pen·di·ces (ə·pen′də·sēz) Alternative plural of APPEND

ap·pen·di·ci·tis (ə·pen′də·sī′tis) *n.* *Pathol.* Inflammation the vermiform appendix.

ap·pen·dix (ə·pen′diks) *n. pl.* **·dix·es** or **·di·ces** (-də·sēz) An addition or appendage, as of supplementary matter the end of a book. **2.** *Anat.* **a** The vermiform appendix. An outgrowth of an organ. [< L, an appendage]

ap·per·cep·tion (ap′ər·sep′shən) *n.* *Psychol.* Conscio perception. [< F *apercevoir* to see, recognize] — **ap′p cep′tive** *adj.*

ap·per·tain (ap′ər·tān′) *v.i.* To pertain or belong as by cu tom, function, nature, right, or fitness; relate: with *to.* [OF < LL < L *ad-* to + *pertinere* to reach to]

ap·pe·tence (ap′ə·təns) *n.* **1.** Strong craving or propensi **2.** Instinct or tendency. Also **ap′pe·ten·cy.** [< L < *ap tere* to seek] — **ap′pe·tent** *adj.*

ap·pe·tite (ap′ə·tīt) *n.* **1.** A desire for food or drink. **2.** A physical craving or natural desire. **3.** A strong liking. OF < L < *ad-* to + *petere* to seek] — **ap′pe·ti′tive** *adj.*

ap·pe·tiz·er (ap′ə·tī′zər) *n.* Anything that excites appet or gives relish before a meal. Also *Brit.* **ap′pe·tis′er.**

ap·pe·tiz·ing (ap′ə·tī′zing) *adj.* Stimulating or tempting the appetite. Also *Brit.* **ap′pe·tis′ing.** [Orig. ppr. of ra *appetize*] — **ap′pe·tiz′ing·ly** *adv.*

ap·plaud (ə·plôd′) *v.t. & v.i.* **1.** To express approval (by clapping the hands. **2.** To commend; praise. — **Sy** See PRAISE. [< L < *ad-* to + *plaudere* to clap han strike] — **ap·plaud′er** *n.* — **ap·plaud′ing·ly** *adv.*

ap·plause (ə·plôz′) *n.* Approval or commendation, esp. shown by clapping the hands, shouting, etc. — **ap·pla sive** (ə·plô′siv) *adj.* — **ap·plau′sive·ly** *adv.*

ap·ple (ap′əl) *n.* **1.** The fleshy, edible fruit of a widely d tributed tree of the rose family, usually of a roundish conical shape. **2.** The similar fruit of several allied speci as the crab apple. **3.** One of several fruits or plants wi little or no resemblance to the apple. [OE *æppel*]

apple cart A handcart used for peddling apples, etc. — **upset the apple cart** To ruin someone's plans.

ap·ple·jack (ap′əl·jak′) *n.* Brandy made from cider.

ap·ple·sauce (ap′əl·sôs′) *n.* **1.** Apples stewed to a pulp. *U.S. Slang* Nonsense; bunk.

Ap·ple·ton layer (ap′əl·tən) A region of the ionosph about 150 miles above sea level that acts as a reflector certain frequencies of radio waves: also called *F layer.* [af Sir E. V. *Appleton*, born 1892, English physicist.]

ap·pli·ance (ə·plī′əns) *n.* A device or instrument; esp., electrically powered device for household work.

ap·pli·ca·ble (ap′li·kə·bəl, ə·plik′ə-) *adj.* Capable of or su able for application; relevant; fitting. [< L *applicare* to a ply + -ABLE] — **ap′pli·ca·bil′i·ty, ap′pli·ca·ble·ness** *n.* **ap′pli·ca·bly** *adv.*

ap·pli·cant (ap′li·kənt) *n.* One who applies, as for a jo

ap·pli·ca·tion (ap′li·kā′shən) *n.* **1.** The act of applying. That which is applied, especially as a remedial agent. Employment for a special purpose or use. **4.** Capacity being used; relevance. **5.** Close attention. **6.** A form written request, esp. for employment.

ap·pli·ca·tive (ap′li·kā′tiv) *adj.* Applicatory.

ap·pli·ca·tor (ap′li·kā′tər) *n.* An instrument or utensil applying medication, etc.

ap·pli·ca·to·ry (ap′li·kə·tôr′ē, -tō′rē) *adj.* Fit for appli tion; practical; applicative.

ap·plied (ə·plīd′) *adj.* Put in practice; utilized: opposed *abstract, theoretical,* or *pure*: *applied* science.

ap·pli·qué (ap′li·kā′) *adj.* Applied: said of ornaments, as needlework, sewn to the surface of another. — *n.* Deco tion or ornaments so applied. — *v.t.* **·quéd** (-kād′), **·q ing** (-kā′ing) To decorate by appliqué work. [< F]

ap·ply (ə·plī′) *v.* **·plied, ·ply·ing** *v.t.* **1.** To bring into conta with something; put on or to. **2.** To devote or put to a pa ticular use: to *apply* steam to navigation. **3.** To connect, an epithet, with a particular person or thing. **4.** To gi (oneself) wholly to; devote. — *v.i.* **5.** To make a request petition; ask: with *for.* **6.** To be relevant: This order *appl* to all. [< OF < L < *ad-* to + *plicare* to fold]

ap·point (ə·point′) *v.t.* **1.** To name or select, as a perso a time and place, etc. **2.** To ordain, as by decree; comman prescribe. **3.** To fit out; equip: used chiefly in combinati

ı the past participle: a *well-appointed* yacht. [< OF < LL ; L *ad-* to + *punctum* a point]
›point·ee (ə·poin′tē′) *n.* One appointed to an office.
›poin·tive (ə·poin′tiv) *adj.* Filled by appointment.
›point·ment (ə·point′mənt) *n.* **1.** The act of appointing r placing in office. **2.** A position held by someone appointed. . An agreement to meet someone or to be somewhere at a pecified time; engagement. **4.** *Usually pl.* Furniture.
›po·mat·tox (ap′ə·mat′əks) A village in central Virginia. t **Appomattox Court House** Lee surrendered to Grant, pril 9, 1865, virtually ending the Civil War.
›por·tion (ə·pôr′shən, ə·pōr′-) *v.t.* To divide and assign roportionally; allot. [< OF < *a-* to + *portionner* to ivide] — **ap·por′tion·ment** *n.*
›pose (ə·pōz′) *v.t.* **·posed, ·pos·ing** **1.** To apply or put, as ıe thing to another: with *to*: to *appose* a seal to a document. . To arrange side by side. [< OF < *a-* to + *poser* to put]
›po·site (ap′ə·zit) *adj.* Fit for or appropriate. [< L *pponere* to put near to] — **ap′po·site·ly** *adv.* — **ap′po·ite·ness** *n.*
›po·si·tion (ap′ə·zish′ən) *n.* **1.** *Gram.* **a** The placing of ıe word beside another so that the second adds to or exlains the first, and both have the same grammatical form, s *John, president* of the class. **b** The syntactical relationship etween such words. **2.** An apposing or being apposed. - **ap′po·si′tion·al** *adj.* — **ap′po·si′tion·al·ly** *adv.*
›pos·i·tive (ə·poz′ə·tiv) *adj.* Of or in apposition. — *n.* . word or phrase in apposition. — **ap·pos′i·tive·ly** *adv.*
›prais·al (ə·prā′zəl) *n.* **1.** An appraising. **2.** An official aluation, as for sale, taxation, etc. Also **ap·praise′ment.**
›praise (ə·prāz′) *v.t.* **·praised, ·prais·ing** **1.** To make an fficial valuation of; set a price or value on. **2.** To estimate he amount, quality, or worth of; judge. — **ap·prais′a·ble** *dj.* — **ap·prais′er** *n.*
— **Syn. 1.** evaluate, value, assess, assay.
·pre·ci·a·ble (ə·prē′shē·ə·bəl, -shə·bəl) *adj.* Capable of eing valued or estimated. — **ap·pre′ci·a·bly** *adv.*
·pre·ci·ate (ə·prē′shē·āt) *v.* **·at·ed, ·at·ing** *v.t.* **1.** To be ılly aware of the value, importance, magnitude, etc., of. . To esteem adequately or highly. **3.** To be keenly ensible of or sensitive to. **4.** To show gratitude for. . To increase the price or value of. **6.** To estimate the orth of. — *v.i.* **7.** To rise in value. [< LL < *ad-* to + *retium* price] — **ap·pre′ci·a′tor** *n.*
·pre·ci·a·tion (ə·prē′shē·ā′shən) *n.* **1.** The act of placg an estimate on persons or things; judgment. **2.** Percepon or awareness, as of qualities, values, etc. **3.** Gratiıde. **4.** Increase in value.
›pre·ci·a·tive (ə·prē′shē·ā′tiv, -shə·tiv) *adj.* Capable of ıowing appreciation; manifesting appreciation. — **ap·re′ci·a′tive·ly** *adv.* — **ap·pre′ci·a′tive·ness** *n.*
›pre·ci·a·to·ry (ə·prē′shē·ə·tôr′ē, -tō′rē, -shə-) *adj.* Apreciative. — **ap·pre′ci·a·to′ri·ly** *adv.*
›pre·hend (ap′rə·hend) *v.t.* **1.** To lay hold of or grasp ıentally; understand; perceive. **2.** To expect with anxious oreboding; dread. **3.** To arrest; take into custody. **4.** *Obs.* 'o take hold of. — *v.i.* **5.** To understand. [< L < *ad-* › + *prehendere* to seize] — **ap′pre·hend′er** *n.*
— **Syn. 1.** To *apprehend* is merely to perceive, while to *comrehend* something is to grasp its meaning in its entirety. *Underand* is close in meaning to *comprehend*, but can also mean to have ısight into or sympathy with.
›pre·hen·si·ble (ap′rə·hen′sə·bəl) *adj.* Capable of being pprehended. — **ap′pre·hen′si·bil′i·ty** *n.*
›pre·hen·sion (ap′rə·hen′shən) *n.* **1.** Foreboding; ıisgiving. **2.** The power of apprehending; understanding. . An estimate; opinion. **4.** Arrest; capture. — **Syn.** See NOWLEDGE.
›pre·hen·sive (ap′rə·hen′siv) *adj.* **1.** Fearful; anxious. . Quick to apprehend or perceive. — **ap′pre·hen′sive·ly** *dv.* — **ap′pre·hen′sive·ness** *n.*
›pren·tice (ə·pren′tis) *n.* **1.** One who is bound by a ɜgal agreement to serve another for a fixed period of time ı order to learn a trade or business. **2.** Any learner or beinner. — *v.t.* **·ticed, ·tic·ing** To bind or take on as an pprentice. [< OF < L *apprehendere* to comprehend] - **ap·pren′tice·ship** *n.*
›prise (ə·prīz′) *v.t.* **·prised, ·pris·ing** To notify, as of an vent; inform. Also **ap·prize′.** [< F < L *apprehendere* to omprehend] — **ap·prise′ment** *n.* — **ap·pris′er** *n.*
›prize (ə·prīz′) *v.t.* **·prized, ·priz·ing** To appraise. Also **p·prise′.** [Prob. < OF < *a-* on, to + *prisier* to value]
›proach (ə·prōch′) *v.i.* **1.** To come near or nearer in ime or space. — *v.t.* **2.** To come near or nearer to. **3.** To ome close to; approximate. **4.** To make advances to; ffer a proposal, or bribe to. **5.** To cause to move nearer. . To start to deal with: to *approach* a problem. — *n.* . The act of approaching; a coming near. **2.** An approximation; nearness. **3.** A way or means of approaching; access. **4.** A method of beginning or accomplishing something. **5.** *Often pl.* An overture of friendship, etc.; advance. **6.** In golf, a stroke made after the tee shot, intended to land the ball on the putting green. [< OF < LL < L *ad-* to + *prope* near] — **ap·proach′a·ble** *adj.* — **ap·proach′a·bil′i·ty, ap·proach′a·ble·ness** *n.*
ap·pro·ba·tion (ap′rə·bā′shən) *n.* **1.** The act of approving; approval. **2.** Sanction. — **ap·pro·ba′tive, ap·pro·ba·to·ry** (ə·prō′bə·tôr′ē, -tō′rē) *adj.*
ap·pro·pri·ate (*adj.* ə·prō′prē·it; *v.* ə·prō′prē·āt) *adj.* Suitable; fit; proper; relevant. — *v.t.* **·at·ed, ·at·ing** **1.** To set apart for a particular use. **2.** To take for one's own use. [< L < *ad-* to + *proprius* one's own] — **ap·pro′pri·ate·ly** *adv.* — **ap·pro′pri·ate·ness** *n.* — **ap·pro′pri·a′tor** *n.*
ap·pro·pri·a·tion (ə·prō′prē·ā′shən) *n.* **1.** The act of appropriating or setting apart. **2.** Anything, esp. money, set apart for a special use. — **ap·pro′pri·a′tive** *adj.*
ap·prov·al (ə·prōō′vəl) *n.* **1.** The act of approving; approbation. **2.** Official consent; sanction. **3.** Favorable opinion; praise, commendation. — **on approval** For (a customer's) examination without obligation to purchase.
ap·prove (ə·prōōv′) *v.* **·proved, ·prov·ing** *v.t.* **1.** To regard as worthy, proper, or right. **2.** To confirm formally or authoritatively; sanction; ratify. — *v.i.* **3.** To show or state approval: often with *of.* [< OF < L < *ad-* to + *probare* to approve, prove] — **ap·prov′a·ble** *adj.* — **ap·prov′er** *n.* — **ap·prov′ing·ly** *adv.*
ap·prox·i·mate (*adj.* ə·prok′sə·mit; *v.* ə·prok′sə·māt) *adj.* **1.** Nearly exact, accurate, or complete. **2.** Like; resembling. **3.** Near; close together. — *v.* **·mat·ed, ·mat·ing** *v.t.* **1.** To come close to, as in quality, degree, or quantity. **2.** To cause to come near. — *v.i.* **3.** To come near in quality, degree, etc. [< L < *ad-* to + *proximus*, superl. of *prope* near] — **ap·prox′i·mate·ly** *adv.*
ap·prox·i·ma·tion (ə·prok′sə·mā′shən) *n.* **1.** The act or result of approximating. **2.** *Math.* A result sufficiently exact for a specified purpose.
ap·pur·te·nance (ə·pûr′tə·nəns) *n.* **1.** Something attached to another, more important thing. **2.** *pl.* Apparatus. **3.** *Law* Something passing as an incident to a principal thing. [< AF, OF < LL < L *ad-* to + *pertinere* to reach to]
ap·pur·te·nant (ə·pûr′tə·nənt) *adj.* Appertaining or belonging, as by right; accessory. — *n.* An appurtenance.
a·pri·cot (ā′pri·kot, ap′ri·kot) *n.* **1.** A yellow fruit of a tree, similar to a small peach. **2.** The tree bearing this fruit. **3.** A pinkish yellow color. [Earlier *apricock* (prob. directly < Pg.) < F < Pg. or Sp. < L *praecoquus* early ripe]
A·pril (ā′prəl) *n.* The fourth month of the year, containing 30 days. [< L *Aprilis*]
April fool The victim of a practical joke on April 1, known as **April** (or **All**) **Fools' Day.**
a pri·o·ri (ā′ prī·ō′rī, ä′ prē·ôr′ē) **1.** *Logic* Proceeding from cause to effect, or from an assumption to its logical conclusion. **2.** Based on theory rather than on experience or examination. [< L, from what is before] — **a·pri·or·i·ty** (ā′prī·ôr′ə·tē, -or′-) *n.*
a·pron (ā′prən, ā′pərn) *n.* **1.** A garment of cloth, leather, etc., worn to protect or adorn the front of a person's clothes. **2.** *Mech.* Any of various overlapping pieces protecting parts of machines. **3.** *Engin.* **a** The platform or sill at the entrance to a dock. **b** The platform below a dam or in a sluiceway. **4.** *Aeron.* A hard-surfaced area in front of and around a hangar or aircraft shelter. **5.** The part of a theater stage in front of the curtain. — *v.t.* To cover or furnish with an apron. [< OF < L *mappa* cloth, napkin]
ap·ro·pos (ap′rə·pō′) *adj.* Suited to the occasion; opportune: an *apropos* remark. — *adv.* **1.** With reference or regard; in respect: with *of*: *apropos* of spring. **2.** To the purpose; pertinently. **3.** By the way; incidentally: used to introduce a remark. [< F < *à* to + *propos* purpose]
apse (aps) *n.* *Archit.* An extending portion of an edifice, usually semicircular with a half dome; especially, the eastern or altar end of a church. [< L *apsis* arch]
apt (apt) *adj.* **1.** Inclined; liable; likely. **2.** Quick to learn; intelligent. **3.** Pertinent; relevant. [< L *aptus* fitted, suited] — **apt′ly** *adv.* — **apt′ness** *n.*
ap·ter·ous (ap′tər·əs) *adj.* *Biol.* Without wings; wingless.
ap·ter·yx (ap′tər·iks) *n.* A New Zealand bird with undeveloped wings, now nearly extinct: also called *kiwi.* [< NL < Gk. *a-* without + *pteryx* wing]
ap·ti·tude (ap′tə·tōōd, -tyōōd) *n.* **1.** Natural or acquired ability or bent. **2.** Quickness of understanding; intelligence. **3.** The state or quality of being apt or fitting. [< F < LL < L *aptus* fitted, suited]
aq·ua (ak′wə, ā′kwə) *n.* *pl.* **aq·uae** (ak′wē, ā′kwē) or **aq·uas** Water: in Latin phrases applied to different kinds of water. — *adj.* & *n.* Bluish green. [< L]

aqua for·tis (fôr′tis) Commercial nitric acid.
Aq·ua-Lung (ak′wə·lung′) *n.* A scuba: a trade name. Also **aq′ua·lung′.**
aq·ua·ma·rine (ak′wə·mə·rēn′) *n.* **1.** A sea-green variety of precious beryl. **2.** A bluish green color. — *adj.* Bluish green. [< L *aqua marina* sea water]
aq·ua·naut (ak′wə·nôt) *n.* One who is trained to live and work underwater over a period of time. [< L *aqua* water + *-naut* (< Gk. *nautēs* sailor), after *aeronaut, astronaut*]
aq·ua·plane (ak′wə·plān) *n.* A board on which one stands while being towed by a motorboat. — *v.i.* **·planed, ·plan·ing** To ride an aquaplane. [< L *aqua* water + PLANE[4]]
aqua re·gi·a (rē′jē·ə) A mixture of nitric and hydrochloric acid, a solvent for gold and platinum. [< L, royal water]
a·quar·i·um (ə·kwâr′ē·əm) *n. pl.* **a·quar·i·ums** or **a·quar·i·a** (ə·kwâr′ē·ə) **1.** A tank, pond, or the like for the exhibition or study of aquatic animals or plants. **2.** A public building containing such an exhibition. [< L < *aqua* water]
A·quar·i·us (ə·kwâr′ē·əs) *n.* A constellation, the Water Bearer; also, a sign of the zodiac. See ZODIAC. [< L]
a·quat·ic (ə·kwat′ik, ə·kwot′-) *adj.* **1.** Living or growing in or near water. **2.** Performed on or in water. — *n.* An aquatic animal or plant. [< L < *aqua* water]
aq·ua·tint (ak′wə·tint′) *n.* **1.** A technique of engraving by treating the surface of a copper plate with an acid to give the effect of a water color. **2.** Such an engraving. — *v.t.* To etch by aquatint. [< F < Ital. < L *aqua tincta*]
aqua vi·tae (vī′tē) **1.** Alcohol. **2.** Whisky; brandy. [< L]
aq·ue·duct (ak′wə·dukt) *n.* **1.** A water conduit, esp. one for supplying water to a community from a distance. **2.** A structure supporting a canal carried across a river or over low ground. [< L < *aqua* water + *ducere* to lead]
a·que·ous (ā′kwē·əs, ak′wē-) *adj.* **1.** Of or like water; watery. **2.** Composed of matter deposited by water.
aqueous humor *Physiol.* A clear fluid filling the space in the eye between the cornea and the lens.
aqui- *combining form* Water. [< L *aqua*]
aq·ui·line (ak′wə·līn, -lin) *adj.* **1.** Of or like an eagle. **2.** Curving or hooked: an *aquiline* nose. [< L *aquila* eagle]
ar- Assimilated var. of AD-.
-ar[1] *suffix* **1.** Pertaining to; like: *regular, singular.* **2.** The person or thing pertaining to: *scholar.* [< OF *-er, -ier* < L *-aris* (in nouns *-are*), var. of *-alis*, suffix of adjectives; or directly < L]
-ar[2] *suffix* A form of -ARY, -ER[2], refashioned in imitation of -AR[1]: *vicar*, in ME *vicary, viker.*
-ar[3] *suffix* A form of -ER[1], refashioned in imitation of -AR[2]: *pedlar.*
Ar·ab (ar′əb) *n.* **1.** A native or inhabitant of Arabia. **2.** Any of a Semitic-speaking people inhabiting Arabia. **3.** A horse of a graceful, intelligent breed originally native to Arabia. — *adj.* Arabian.
ar·a·besque (ar′ə·besk′) *n.* **1.** An ornament or design, as used in Moorish architecture, of intertwined scrollwork, leaves or flowers, etc. **2.** In ballet, a position in which the dancer extends one leg straight backward, one arm forward, and the other arm backward. — *adj.* Relating to, executed in, or resembling arabesque; fanciful; ornamental. [< F < Ital. *Arabo* Arab]

ARABESQUE (*def.* 1)

A·ra·bi·an (ə·rā′bē·ən) *adj.* Of or pertaining to Arabia or the Arabs. — *n.* An Arab (defs. 1 and 3).
Arabian Nights A collection of stories from Arabia, India, Persia, etc., from the tenth century.
Ar·a·bic (ar′ə·bik) *adj.* Of or pertaining to Arabia, the Arabs, their language, culture, etc. — *n.* The Southwest Semitic language of the Arabs.
Arabic numerals The symbols 1, 2, 3, 4, 5, 6, 7, 8, 9, and 0, in general use in Europe since about the tenth century.
ar·a·ble (ar′ə·bəl) *adj.* Capable of being plowed. — *n.* Arable land. [< L *arare* to plow] — **ar′a·bil′i·ty** *n.*
Arab League A confederation, established 1945, of the states of Iraq, Jordan (then Trans-Jordan), Lebanon, Saudi Arabia, the United Arab Republic (Egypt), Syria, and Yemen, joined by 1959 by Libya, Morocco, Sudan, and Tunisia, and in 1961 by Kuwait.
a·rach·nid (ə·rak′nid) *n.* Any of a class of arthropods, including the spiders, scorpions, mites, etc. [< NL < Gk. *arachnē* spider] — **a·rach·ni·dan** (ə·rak′nə·dən) *adj.* & *n.*
Ar·a·gon (ar′ə·gon) A former kingdom in Spain. — **Ar·a·go·nese** (ar′ə·gə·nēz′, -nēs′) *adj.* & *n.*
Ar·am (âr′əm) The Biblical name of ancient Syria. Also **Ar·a·me·a** (ar′ə·mē′ə).
Ar·a·ma·ic (ar′ə·mā′ik) *n.* Any of a group of Semitic languages, including Syriac and the language spoken by Christ.
Ar·a·me·an (ar′ə·mē′ən) *adj.* Of or pertaining to ancient Aram or Aramea, or its peoples, languages, etc. — *n.* **1.** An inhabitant of Aram. **2.** Aramaic. Also **Ar′a·mae′an.**
A·rap·a·ho (ə·rap′ə·hō) *n. pl.* **·ho** or **·hoes** A member of a nomadic Algonquian tribe, now dwelling primarily in Ok homa and Wyoming. Also **A·rap′a·hoe.**
ar·ba·lest (är′bə·list) *n.* A medieval crossbow requiring mechanical appliance to bend it. Also **ar′ba·list.** [< (< L *arcus* a bow + *ballista* to throw] — **ar′ba·lest′er** *n.*
ar·bi·ter (är′bə·tər) *n.* **1.** A chosen or appointed judge umpire, as between parties in a dispute. **2.** One who h matters under his sole control; an absolute and final judg — **Syn.** See JUDGE. [< L < *ad-* to + *bitere, betere* to g — **ar′bi·tress** *n.fem.* — **ar′bi·tral** (-trəl) *adj.*
ar·bi·tra·ble (är′bə·trə·bəl) *adj.* Subject to, capable of, suitable for arbitration.
ar·bit·ra·ment (är·bit′rə·mənt) *n.* **1.** Arbitration. The decision of an arbitrator; an award. **3.** The power right to make such decision. Also **ar·bit′re·ment.**
ar·bi·trar·y (är′bə·trer′ē) *adj.* **1.** Based on or subject one's opinion, judgment, prejudice, etc. **2.** Absolute; d potic. **3.** *Law* Not determined by statute. [See ARBITE — **ar′bi·trar′i·ly** *adv.* — **ar′bi·trar′i·ness** *n.*
ar·bi·trate (är′bə·trāt) *v.* **·trat·ed, ·trat·ing** *v.t.* **1.** To cide as arbitrator. **2.** To submit to or settle by arbitratic — *v.i.* **3.** To act as arbitrator. **4.** To submit a dispute arbitration. — **ar′bi·tra′tive** *adj.*
ar·bi·tra·tion (är′bə·trā′shən) *n.* The settlement of dispute by the decision of a third party or court.
ar·bi·tra·tor (är′bə·trā′tər) *n.* A person chosen to decid dispute. — **Syn.** See JUDGE. [< L]
ar·bor[1] (är′bər) *n.* A bower, as of latticework, supporti vines or trees. Also *Brit.* **ar′bour.** [Earlier *erber, herber* AF < L < *herba* grass, herb]
ar·bor[2] (är′bər) *n. pl.* **ar·bo·res** (är′bər·ēz) *for def. 1;* **bors** *for def. 2.* **1.** A tree: used chiefly in botanical nam **2.** *Mech.* **a** A shaft, mandrel, spindle, or axle. **b** A princip support of a machine. [< L, tree]
ar·bo·re·al (är·bôr′ē·əl, -bō′rē-) *adj.* **1.** Of or like a tr **2.** Inhabiting trees, or adapted to life in trees.
ar·bo·res·cent (är′bə·res′ənt) *adj.* Treelike; branching.
ar·bo·re·tum (är′bə·rē′təm) *n. pl.* **·tums** or **·ta** (-tə) A l tanical garden exhibiting trees for display or study.
arbori- *combining form* Tree. [< L *arbor* tree]
ar·bor·vi·tae (är′bər·vī′tē) *n.* An evergreen shrub or t of the pine family. [< L *arbor vitae* tree of life]
ar·bu·tus (är·byōō′təs) *n.* **1.** An evergreen tree or shrub the heath family. **2.** The trailing arbutus. [< L, stra berry tree]
arc (ärk) *n.* **1.** Anything in the shape of an arch, a curve, a part of a circle; a bow; arch. **2.** *Geom.* A part of any cur **3.** *Electr.* The bow of flame formed by the passage of electric current across the gap between two conducto **4.** *Astron.* A part of the apparent path of a heavenly bo — *v.i.* **arced** (ärkt) or **arcked, arc·ing** (är′king] or **arck·i** *Electr.* To form an arc. [< L *arcus* bow, arch]
ar·cade (är·kād′) *n.* **1.** *Archit.* A series of arches w supporting columns or piers, standing against the face o wall or free. **2.** A roofed passageway or street, esp. c having shops, etc., opening from it. — *v.t.* **·cad·ed, ·cad·i** To furnish with or form into an arcade or arcades. [< < Med.L < L *arcus* bow, arch]
Ar·ca·di·a (är·kā′dē·ə) Any region of ideal rustic simplici and contentment. Also **Ar·ca·dy** (är′kə·dē).
Ar·ca·di·an (är·kā′dē·ən) *adj.* **1.** Of or pertaining to A cadia. **2.** Rural or simple; pastoral. — *n.* **1.** A native or dweller in Arcadia. **2.** One with simple, pastoral tast
ar·cane (är·kān′) *adj.* Secret; hidden. [< L *arcanus* hidde
ar·ca·num (är·kā′nəm) *n. pl.* **·na** (-nə) An inner secr
arch[1] (ärch) *n.* **1.** A curved structure spanning an openir formed of wedge-shaped parts resting on supports at t two extremities. **2.** Any similar structure or object. **3.** bowlike curve. **4.** *Anat.* A curved or archlike part, as of t foot. — *v.t.* **1.** To cause to form an arch or arches. To furnish with an arch or arches. **3.** To span; extend ov as an arch. — *v.i.* **4.** To form an arch or arches. [< OF Med.L < L *arcus* bow, arch]
arch[2] (ärch) *adj.* **1.** Cunning; roguish; sly. **2.** M eminent; chief. [< ARCH-] — **arch′ly** *adv.* — **arch′ness**
arch- *prefix* **1.** Chief; principal. **2.** Very great; extren Also *archi-.* [OE < L < Gk. *archos* ruler]
archaeo- See ARCHEO-.
ar·chae·ol·o·gy (är′kē·ol′ə·jē), etc. See ARCHEOLOGY, etc
ar·cha·ic (är·kā′ik) *adj.* **1.** Old-fashioned; antiquate **2.** Characterizing a word, an inflectional form, or a phra no longer in current use. Also **ar·cha′i·cal.** — **Syn.** S OBSOLETE. [< Gk. *archaios* ancient]
ar·cha·ism (är′kē·iz′əm, -kā-) *n.* An archaic word, idio or style. — **ar′cha·ist** *n.* — **ar′cha·is′tic** *adj.*
arch·an·gel (ärk′ān′jəl) *n.* **1.** An angel of highest ran **2.** The angelica. — **the Archangel** In Christian legen usually Michael. [< LL < Gk. < *arch-* chief + *angel* angel] — **arch·an·gel·ic** (ärk′an·jel′ik) or **·i·cal** *adj.*
arch·bish·op (ärch′bish′əp) *n. Eccl.* The chief bishop o province. — **arch′bish′op·ric** *n.*

arch·dea·con (ärch′dē′kən) *n. Eccl.* A chief deacon, ranking just below a bishop.

arch·dea·con·ry (ärch′dē′kən·rē) *n. pl.* **·ries 1.** The jurisdiction or office of an archdeacon. Also **arch′dea′con·ate** (-it), **arch′dea′con·ship. 2.** An archdeacon's residence.

arch·di·o·cese (ärch′dī′ə·sēs, -sis) *n.* The diocese or jurisdiction of an archbishop.

arch·du·cal (ärch′dōō′kəl, -dyōō′-) *adj.* Of or pertaining to an archduke or an archduchy.

arch·duch·ess (ärch′duch′is) *n.* **1.** The wife or widow of an archduke. **2.** A princess of the former royal family of Austria.

arch·duch·y (ärch′duch′ē) *n. pl.* **·duch·ies** The territory ruled by an archduke. Also **arch′duke′dom.**

arch·duke (ärch′dōōk′, -dyōōk′) *n.* A chief duke, especially a prince of the former royal family of Austria. Abbr. *Archd.*

arched (ärcht) *adj.* **1.** Having the form of an arch. **2.** Covered or furnished with arches.

ar·che·go·ni·um (är′kə·gō′nē·əm) *n. pl.* **·ni·a** (-nē·ə) *Bot.* The female sexual organ of the higher cryptogams. Also **ar·che·gone** (är′kə·gōn). [< NL < Gk. < *archos* chief, first + *gonos* race, offspring] **— ar′che·go′ni·al** *adj.* **— ar′che·go′ni·ate** *adj.*

archeo- *combining form* Ancient: *Archeozoic.* Also *archaeo-.* [< Gk. *archaios* ancient]

ar·che·ol·o·gy (är′kē·ol′ə·jē) *n.* The science or study of history from the remains of early human cultures as discovered chiefly by systematic excavations: also, *esp. Brit., archaeology.* **— ar·che·o·log·i·cal** (är′kē·ə·loj′i·kəl) or **·log′ic** *adj.* **— ar′che·ol′o·gist** *n.*

ar·che·o·zo·ic (är′kē·ə·zō′ik) *adj. Geol.* Of or pertaining to the oldest of the eras making up the geological record. See chart for GEOLOGY. Also spelled *Archaeozoic.* [< ARCHEO- + Gk. *zōion* animal]

arch·er (är′chər) *n.* One who shoots with a bow and arrow. [< AF < L *arcus* bow]

Arch·er (är′chər) *n.* The constellation and sign of the zodiac Sagittarius.

arch·er·y (är′chər·ē) *n.* **1.** The art or sport of shooting with bow and arrows. **2.** The weapons and outfit of an archer.

ar·che·type (är′kə·tīp) *n.* An original or standard pattern or model; a prototype. [< L < Gk. < *arche-* first + *typos* stamp, pattern] **— ar′che·typ′al** (-tī′pəl), **ar′che·typ′ic** (-tip′ik) or **·i·cal** *adj.*

archi- *prefix* **1.** Var. of ARCH-. **2.** *Biol.* Original; primitive: *archicarp.* [See ARCH-.]

ar·chi·e·pis·co·pate (är′kē·i·pis′kə·pit, -pāt) *n.* The office or tenure of an archbishop. **— ar′chi·e·pis′co·pal** *adj.*

Ar·chi·me·de·an (är′kə·mē′dē·ən, mə·dē′ən) *adj.* Of, discovered by, or pertaining to Archimedes.

ar·chi·pel·a·go (är′kə·pel′ə·gō) *n. pl.* **·goes** or **·gos 1.** A sea with many islands. **2.** The islands in such a sea. [< Ital. < Gk. *archi-* chief + *pelagos* sea] **— ar·chi·pe·lag·ic** (är′kə·pə·laj′ik) *adj.*

ar·chi·tect (är′kə·tekt) *n.* **1.** One whose profession is to design and draw up the plans for buildings, etc., and supervise their construction. **2.** One who devises or creates anything. [< F < L < Gk. < *archi-* chief + *tektōn* worker]

ar·chi·tec·ton·ic (är′kə·tek·ton′ik) *adj.* **1.** Pertaining to an architect or architecture; constructive. **2.** Having architectural qualities of design and structure.

ar·chi·tec·ton·ics (är′kə·tek·ton′iks) *n.pl.* (*construed as sing.*) **1.** The science of architecture. **2.** Structural design, as in works of music or art.

ar·chi·tec·ture (är′kə·tek′chər) *n.* **1.** The science, art, or profession of designing and constructing buildings or other structures. **2.** A style or system of building: Gothic *architecture.* **3.** Construction or structure generally. **4.** A building, or buildings collectively. Abbr. *arch., archit.* **— ar′chi·tec′tur·al** *adj.* **— ar′chi·tec′tur·al·ly** *adv.*

ar·chi·trave (är′kə·trāv) *n. Archit.* **1.** The part of an entablature that rests upon the column heads and supports the frieze. For illus. see COLUMN. **2.** A molded ornament skirting the head and sides of a door or window. [< F < Ital. < Gk. < *archi-* chief + Ital. *trave* beam]

ar·chives (är′kīvz) *n.pl.* **1.** A place where public records and historical documents are kept. **2.** Public records, documents, etc., as kept in such a depository. [< F < LL < Gk. *archeion* a public office] **— ar·chi·val** (är·kī′vəl) *adj.*

ar·chi·vist (är′kə·vist) *n.* A keeper of archives.

arch·priest (ärch′prēst′) *n.* **1.** Formerly, the senior priest of a cathedral chapter, serving as assistant to a bishop: later called *dean.* **2.** A chief priest. **— arch′priest′hood.**

arch·way (ärch′wā′) *n.* A passage under an arch.

-archy *combining form* Rule; government: *monarchy.* [< Gk. *-archia* < *archos* ruler]

arc light A lamp in which light of high intensity is produced between two adjacent electrodes. Also **arc lamp.**

arc·tic (ärk′tik, är′tik) *adj.* Characteristic of the Arctic; extremely cold; frigid. [Earlier *artik* < OF < L < Gk. < *arktos* a bear]

Arctic Circle The parallel at 66°33′ north latitude; the boundary of the North Frigid Zone.

Arc·tu·rus (ärk·tŏŏr′əs, -tyŏŏr′-) *n.* An orange-red star, one of the 20 brightest, 0.24 magnitude; Alpha in the constellation Boötes. [< L < Gk. *arktos* a bear + *ouros* a guard]

-ard *suffix of nouns* One who does something to excess or who is to be disparaged: *drunkard, coward;* sometimes changed to *-art: braggart.* [< OF *-ard, -art* < G *-hard, -hart* hardy]

ar·den·cy (är′dən·sē) *n.* Intensity of emotion; ardor.

ar·dent (är′dənt) *adj.* **1.** Passionate; zealous; intense. **2.** Glowing; flashing. **3.** Hot; burning. [< L *ardere* to burn] **— ar′dent·ly** *adv.* **— ar′dent·ness** *n.*

ar·dor (är′dər) *n.* **1.** Warmth or intensity of passion or affection; eagerness; vehemence; zeal. **2.** Great heat, as of fire. Also *Brit.* **ar′dour.** [< L *ardere* to burn]

ar·du·ous (är′jōō·əs) *adj.* **1.** Involving great labor or hardship; difficult. **2.** Toiling strenuously; energetic. **3.** Steep; hard to climb or surmount. [< L *arduus* steep] **— ar′du·ous·ly** *adv.* **— ar′du·ous·ness** *n.*

are[1] (är, *unstressed* ər, r, ə) *v.* First, second, and third person plural, present indicative, of BE: also used as second person singular. [OE (Northumbrian) *aron*]

are[2] (âr, är) *n.* In the metric system, a surface measure equal to one hundred square meters; also spelled *ar.* See table inside back cover. [< F < L *area* area]

ar·e·a (âr′ē·ə) *n. pl.* **ar·e·as 1.** A particular portion of the earth's surface; region. **2.** The surface included within a bounding line. **3.** The extent or scope of anything. **4.** The yard of a building. **5.** Any flat, open space. [< L, an open space] **— ar′e·al** *adj.*

ar·e·a·way (âr′ē·ə·wā′) *n.* **1.** A small sunken court before a basement door. **2.** A passageway.

a·re·na (ə·rē′nə) *n.* **1.** The oval space in a Roman amphitheater, where contests and shows were held. **2.** Any place of this nature: a football *arena.* **3.** A scene or sphere of action or contest: the political *arena.* [< L, sand, sandy place]

arena theater A stage in the center of an auditorium, surrounded by seats: also called *theater-in-the-round.*

aren't (ärnt) Are not.

aren't I ◆ See note under AIN'T.

areo- *combining form* Mars. [< Gk. *Arēs*]

a·re·o·la (ə·rē′ə·lə) *n. pl.* **·lae** (-lē) or **·las 1.** *Bot.* An interstice in a network of leaf veins. **2.** *Anat.* The colored circle about a nipple or about a vesicle. Also **ar·e·ole** (âr′ē·ōl). [< L, dim. of *area* open space] **— a·re′o·lar, a·re·o·late** (ə·rē′ə·lit, -lāt) *adj.* **— ar·e·o·la·tion** (är′ē·ə·lā′shən) *n.*

Ar·e·op·a·gus (ar′ē·op′ə·gəs) **1.** A hill NW of the Acropolis on which the highest court of ancient Athens held its sessions; also, the court itself. **2.** Any high law court. [< L < Gk. *Areios* of Ares + *pagos* hill]

Ar·es (âr′ēz) In Greek mythology, the god of war: identified with the Roman *Mars.*

ar·ga·li (är′gə·lē) *n. pl.* **·lis** or **·li 1.** An Asian wild sheep with large horns curved spirally outward. **2.** Any of several other wild sheep. Also **ar·gal** (är′gəl). [< Mongolian]

ARGALI
(4 feet high at shoulder)

ar·gent (är′jənt) *n. Archaic & Poetic* Silver. *— adj.* Like or made of silver; white; silvery: also **ar·gen·tal** (är·jen′təl). [< F < L *argentum* silver]

ar·gen·tine (är′jən·tin, -tīn) *adj.* Silvery. [< F < L *argentum* silver]

Ar·gen·tine (är′jən·tēn, -tīn) *adj.* Of or pertaining to Argentina. *— n.* A native or citizen of Argentina: also **Ar·gen·tin·e·an** (är′jən·tin′ē·ən).

ar·gen·tum (är·jen′təm) *n. Chem.* Silver. [< L]

ar·gil (är′jil) *n.* Potters' clay; white clay. [< MF < L < Gk. < *argos* white]

ar·gi·nine (är′jə·nēn, -nin, -nīn) *n. Biochem.* One of the amino acids essential to nutrition, $C_6H_{14}O_2N_4$. [< NL *argin-* + -INE[2]]

Ar·give (är′jīv, -gīv) *adj. & n.* Greek.

Ar·go (är′gō) *n.* In Greek legend, the ship in which Jason and the Argonauts sailed for the Golden Fleece.

ar·gol (är′gəl) *n.* Crude potassium bitartrate, the base of tartaric acid. [ME < AF *argoil*]

ar·gon (är′gon) *n.* A colorless, gaseous element (symbol Ar) present in the atmosphere, used in electric display signs and as a filter for incandescent electric lamps. [< NL < Gk. neut. of *argos* idle, inert + -ON]

Ar·go·naut (är′gə·nôt) *n.* **1.** In Greek legend, one who sailed with Jason in the ship Argo to find the Golden Fleece. **2.** One who went to California in 1849 to hunt gold. [< L

PRONUNCIATION KEY: add, āce, câre, pälm; end, ēven; it, īce; odd, ōpen, ôrder; tŏŏk, pōōl; up, bûrn; ə = a in *above,* e in *sicken,* i in *flexible,* o in *melon,* u in *focus;* yōō = u in *fuse;* oil; pout; check; go; ring; thin; this; zh, vision.

< Gk. < *Argō*, the ship + *nautēs* sailor] — **ar′go·nau′tic** *adj.*

ar·go·sy (är′gə·sē) *n. pl.* **·sies** 1. A large merchant ship. 2. A fleet of merchant vessels. [Earlier *ragusy*, after *Ragusa*, Italian name of Dubrovnik, Yugoslav port]

ar·got (är′gō, -gət) *n.* The specialized vocabulary or jargon of any class or group, as that of the underworld. [< F] — **ar·got·ic** (är·got′ik) *adj.*

ar·gue (är′gyōō) *v.* **·gued, ·gu·ing** *v.i.* 1. To present reasons to support or contest a measure or opinion. 2. To contend in argument; quarrel. — *v.t.* 3. To present reasons for or against; discuss, as a proposal. 4. To contend or maintain, by reasoning. 5. To prove or indicate, as from evidence. 6. To influence or convince, as by argument. [< OF < L *arguere* to prove] — **ar′gu·a·ble** *adj.* — **ar′gu·er** *n.*

ar·gu·ment (är′gyə·mənt) *n.* 1. An angry discussion or quarrel. 2. A reason or reasons offered for or against something. 3. Discourse intended to persuade or to convince. 4. A short summary of a piece of subject matter.

ar·gu·men·ta·tion (är′gyə·men·tā′shən) *n.* 1. The methodical setting forth of premises and the drawing of conclusions therefrom. 2. Discussion; debate.

ar·gu·men·ta·tive (är′gyə·men′tə·tiv) *adj.* 1. Controversial. 2. Given to argumentation; disputatious. — **ar′gu·men′ta·tive·ly** *adv.* — **ar′gu·men′ta·tive·ness** *n.*

Ar·gus (är′gəs) 1. In Greek mythology, a giant with a hundred eyes, killed by Hermes. 2. Any vigilant watchman.

Ar·gus-eyed (är′gəs·īd′) *adj.* Sharp-sighted; vigilant.

a·ri·a (ä′rē·ə, âr′ē·ə) *n.* 1. An air; melody. 2. An elaborate melody for single voice, as in an opera or oratorio, often with instrumental accompaniment. [< Ital. < L *aer* air]

-aria *suffix* Used in forming new Latin names, esp. in zoological and botanical classifications. [< NL < L *-arius*]

Ar·i·ad·ne (ar′ē·ad′nē) In Greek mythology, the daughter of Minos, who gave Theseus the thread by which he found his way out of the Labyrinth.

-arian *suffix* Used in forming adjectives and adjectival nouns denoting occupation, age, sect, beliefs, etc.: *nonagenarian, predestinarian.* [< L *-arius* -ary + -AN]

Ar·i·an (âr′ē·ən, ar′-, är′yən) See ARYAN.

Ar·i·an·ism (âr′ē·ən·iz′əm) *n. Theol.* The doctrine denying that Christ is of one substance with God the Father. [after *Arius*, 250?–336, Greek theologian] — **Ar′i·an** *adj. & n.*

ar·id (ar′id) *adj.* 1. Parched with heat; dry. 2. Without interest or feeling; dull. [< L *arere* to be dry] — **a·rid·i·ty** (ə·rid′ə·tē), **ar′id·ness** *n.* — **ar′id·ly** *adv.*

Ar·ies (âr′ēz, âr′i·ēz) *n.* A constellation, the Ram; also, the first sign of the zodiac. See ZODIAC. [< L]

a·right (ə·rīt′) *adv.* In a right way; correctly; rightly.

a·rio·so (ä·ryō′sō) *adj. Music* Characteristic of an aria. — *adv.* In the manner of an aria. — *n.* A passage, composition, etc., resembling an aria. [< Ital.]

-arious *suffix of adjectives* Connected with; pertaining to: *gregarious.* [< L *-arius* -ary + -OUS]

a·rise (ə·rīz′) *v.i.* **a·rose** (ə·rōz′), **a·ris·en** (ə·riz′ən), **a·ris·ing** 1. To get up, as from a prone position. 2. To rise; ascend. 3. To come into being; originate; issue. 4. To result; proceed. [OE < *ā-* up + *rīsan* to rise]

aristo- *combining form* Best; finest. [< Gk. *aristos*]

ar·is·toc·ra·cy (ar′is·tok′rə·sē) *n. pl.* **·cies** 1. A hereditary nobility or privileged class. 2. A state ruled by a privileged upper class, or by the nobility. 3. Government by an upper class or the nobility. 4. Originally, government by its best citizens or a state governed by its best citizens. 5. Any preeminent group: the *aristocracy* of talent. [< L < Gk. < *aristos* best + *krateein* to rule]

a·ris·to·crat (ə·ris′tə·krat, ar′is·tə·krat′) *n.* 1. A member of an aristocracy. 2. A proud and exclusive person. 3. One who prefers an aristocratic form of government. — **a·ris′to·crat′ic** or **·i·cal** *adj.* — **a·ris′o·crat′i·cal·ly** *adv.*

Ar·is·to·te·li·an (ar′is·tə·tē′lē·ən, -tēl′yən, ə·ris′tə-) *adj.* Pertaining to or characteristic of Aristotle or his philosophy. — *n.* An adherent of Aristotle's teachings; one who tends to be empirical or scientific in his method, rather than speculative. Also **Ar′is·to·te′le·an.** — **Ar′is·to·te′li·an·ism** *n.*

Aristotelian logic The deductive method of logic of Aristotle, characterized by the syllogism.

a·rith·me·tic (*n.* ə·rith′mə·tik; *adj.* ar′ith·met′ik) *n.* The science of computing with numbers by the operations of addition, subtraction, multiplication, and division. — *adj.* Of or pertaining to arithmetic: also **ar′ith·met′i·cal.** [< L < Gr. *arithmos* number] — **ar′ith·met′i·cal·ly** *adv.*

a·rith·me·ti·cian (ə·rith′mə·tish′ən, ar′ith-) *n.* One who uses or is skilled in arithmetic.

arithmetic mean (ar′ith·met′ik) *Math.* The sum of a set of numbers, divided by the number of terms in the set.

arithmetic progression (ar′ith·met′ik) *Math.* A sequence of terms in which each, except the first, differs from the preceding one by a constant quantity, as 2, 4, 6, 8.

-arium *suffix of nouns* 1. A place for: *herbarium.* 2. Connected with: *honorarium.* [< L < *-arius.* See -ARY[1].]

ark (ärk) *n.* 1. In the Bible: **a** The ship of Noah. *Gen.* vi viii. **b** The chest containing the stone tablets bearing th Ten Commandments: also called **ark of the covenant.** *Ex* xxv 10. 2. A large, flat-bottomed or awkward boat; scow [OE *arc* < L *arca* chest]

arm[1] (ärm) *n.* 1. *Anat.* An upper limb of the human body from the shoulder to the hand or wrist. ◆ Collatera adjective: *brachial.* 2. The forelimb of certain other verte brates. 3. An armlike part or appendage. 4. Something in tended to support or cover the human arm. 5. Anythin branching out like an arm from a main body, as the end of spar. — **at arm's length** At a distance. — **with open arm** Cordially; warmly. [OE *earm, arm*]

arm[2] (ärm) *n.* 1. A weapon. 2. A distinct branch of th military service: the air *arm.* — *v.t.* 1. To supply wit weapons. 2. To make secure, as with a protective covering — *v.i.* 3. To supply or equip oneself with weapons. [< OF < L *arma* weapons] — **arm′er** *n.*

ar·ma·da (är·mä′də, -mā′-) *n.* A fleet of war vessels. — th **Armada** The fleet sent against England by Spain in 1588 defeated by the English navy: also **Invincible Armada Spanish Armada.** [< Sp. < L *armare* to arm]

ar·ma·dil·lo (är′mə·dil′ō) *n. pl.* **·los** An American burrow ing nocturnal mammal having an armorlike covering of jointed plates. [< Sp. < L *armare* to arm]

ARMADILLO (30 inches long; tail 12 inches)

Ar·ma·ged·don (är′mə·ged′n) *n.* 1. In Biblical prophecy, the scene of a great battle between the forces of good and evil, to occur at the end of the world. *Rev.* xvi 16. 2. Any great or decisive conflict.

ar·ma·ment (är′mə·mənt) *n.* 1. *Often pl.* The guns and other military equipment of a fortification, military unit, warship, etc. 2. The act o arming or equipping for war. [< L *armare* to arm]

ar·ma·ture (är mə·chŏŏr) *n.* 1. A piece of soft iron joinin the poles of a magnet to prevent the loss of magnetic powe 2. *Electr.* **a** In a dynamo or motor, the cylindrical, lami nated iron core carrying the coils of insulated wire to be re volved through the magnetic field. **b** The part of a relay, a a buzzer or bell, that vibrates when activated. 3. *Biol.* Pro tective covering, as the shells of animals. 4. In sculpture a framework to support the clay or other substance in model ing. 5. Arms; armor. [< MF < L *armare* to arm]

arm·chair (ärm′châr′) *n.* A chair with supports for the arms

armed (ärmd) *adj.* 1. Provided with weapons. 2. Havin upper limbs: used in combination: *strong-armed.*

armed forces The military and naval forces of a nation.

Ar·me·ni·an (är·mē′nē·ən, -mēn′yən) *adj.* Of or pertainin to the country, people, or language of Armenia. — *n.* 1. A native of Armenia. 2. The language of the Armenians.

arm·ful (ärm′fŏŏl′) *n. pl.* **·fuls** That which is held, or a much as can be held, in the arm or arms.

Ar·min·i·an·ism (är·min′ē·ən·iz′əm) *n. Theol.* The doc trines holding a less rigorous view of predestination tha Calvinism. [after Jacobus *Arminius*, 1560–1609, Dutc Protestant theologian] — **Ar·min′i·an** *adj. & n.*

ar·mi·stice (är′mə·stis) *n.* A temporary cessation of hos tilities by mutual agreement; a truce. [< F < L < *arm* arms + *sistere* to stop, stand still]

Armistice Day See VETERANS DAY.

arm·let (ärm′lit) *n.* 1. A little arm, as of the sea. 2. band worn around the arm. 3. A small, short sleeve.

ar·moire (är·mwär′) *n.* A large, movable, often ornate cab inet or cupboard. [< F < OF < L *armarium* a chest]

ar·mor (är′mər) *n.* 1. A defensive covering, as of metalli plates for a war vessel, a tank, etc. 2. The armored vehicle of an army. 3. Any protective covering, as the shell of turtle. — *v.t. & v.i.* To furnish with or put on armor. Als *Brit.* **ar′mour.** [< OF *armeür* < L *armare* to arm]

ar·mored (är′mərd) *adj.* 1. Protected by armor. 2 Equipped with armored vehicles, as a military unit.

ar·mor·er (är′mər·ər) *n.* 1. A maker or repairer, of arm or armor. 2. A manufacturer of arms. 3. *Mil.* An enliste man in charge of small arms. Also *Brit.* **ar′mour·er.**

ar·mo·ri·al (är·môr′ē·əl, -mō′rē-) *adj.* Pertaining to heraldry

armor plate A covering of very hard steel plating, used o warships, tanks, etc. — **ar·mor-plat·ed** (är′mər·plā′tid) *ad*

ar·mor·y (är′mər·ē) *n. pl.* **·mor·ies** 1. A place where arm are kept; arsenal. 2. *U.S.* A building for the use of a bod of militia, including storage for arms and equipment, dri rooms, etc. 3. *U.S.* A factory for making firearms. Als *Brit.* **ar′mour·y.** [Prob. < ARMOR]

arm·pit (ärm′pit′) *n.* The cavity under the arm at the shoul der; axilla.

arms (ärmz] *n.pl.* 1. Weapons collectively. 2. Warfare 3. The official insignia of a state, etc. 4. Heraldic symbols — **to arms!** Make ready for battle! — **to bear arms** 1. T carry weapons. 2. To serve in the armed forces. — **unde arms** Provided with weapons; ready for war. — **up i arms** Aroused and ready to fight. [< F < L *arma* weapons

r·my (är′mē) *n. pl.* **·mies** **1.** A large organized body of men armed for military service on land. **2.** The total military land forces of a country. **3.** Any large body of people, animals, etc.; host; multitude. [< OF < L *armare* to arm]
r·ni·ca (är′ni·kə) *n.* **1.** A widely distributed herbaceous perennial of the composite family. **2.** A tincture prepared from this herb, used for sprains and bruises. [< NL]
·ro·ma (ə·rō′mə) *n.* **1.** Fragrance, as from appetizing food, spices, etc.; agreeable odor. **2.** Characteristic quality or style. **— Syn.** See SMELL. [< L < Gk. *arōma, -atos* spice] **— a·ro·ma·tous** (ə·rō′mə·təs) *adj.*
r·o·mat·ic (ar′ə·mat′ik) *adj.* Having an aroma; fragrant; spicy. Also **ar′o·mat′i·cal.** **—** *n.* Any vegetable or drug of agreeable odor. **— ar′o·mat′i·cal·ly** *adv.*
·ro·ma·tize (ə·rō′mə·tīz) *v.t.* **·tized, ·tiz·ing** To make fragrant or aromatic.
·rose (ə·rōz′) Past tense of ARISE.
·round (ə·round′) *adv.* **1.** On all sides; in various directions: It is raining all *around.* **2.** In the opposite direction: to turn *around.* **3.** *U.S.* From place to place; here and there: to walk *around.* **4.** *U.S. Informal* Nearby; in the vicinity: Wait *around* until I call. **5.** In or to a particular place: Come *around* to see us again. **— to get around** *U.S. Informal* **1.** To be experienced and up to date. **2.** To overcome or cope with (someone or something). **— to get around to** *U.S. Informal* To give attention to or accomplish. **— to have been around** *U.S. Informal* To be experienced in the ways of the world. **—** *prep.* **1.** About the circumference or circuit of. **2.** On all sides of; surrounding or enveloping. **3.** *U.S. Informal* Here and there in: He wandered *around* the city. **4.** *U.S. Informal* Somewhere near or within. **5.** *U.S. Informal* Somewhere near in time, amount, etc.; about.
·rouse (ə·rouz′) *v.* **a·roused, a·rous·ing** *v.t.* **1.** To awaken. **2.** To excite, as to a state of high emotion. **—** *v.i.* **3.** To arouse oneself. [< A-[2] + ROUSE] **— a·rous′al** (-zəl) *n.*
r·peg·gi·o (är·pej′ē·ō, -pej′ō) *n. pl.* **·gi·os** *Music* **1.** The sounding or playing of the notes of a chord in rapid succession. **2.** A chord so played. [< Ital. *arpa* a harp]
r·que·bus (är′kwə·bəs) *n.* A harquebus.
r·raign (ə·rān′) *v.t.* **1.** *Law* To call into court and cause to answer to an indictment. **2.** To call upon for an answer; accuse. **— Syn.** See ACCUSE. [< AF < LL *arrationare* to call to account] **— ar·raign′er** *n.* **— ar·raign′ment** *n.*
r·range (ə·rānj′) *v.* **·ranged, ·rang·ing** *v.t.* **1.** To put in definite or proper order. **2.** To plan the details of; prepare for. **3.** To adjust, as a conflict or dispute; settle. **4.** *Music* To change or adapt for other instruments or voices. **—** *v.i.* **5.** To come to an agreement or understanding. **6.** To see about the details; make plans. [< OF *arangier* < *a-* to + *rangier* to put in order] **— ar·rang′er** *n.*
r·range·ment (ə·rānj′mənt) *n.* **1.** The act of arranging, or the state of being arranged; disposition. **2.** That which is arranged. **3.** The style in which something is arranged; order. **4.** A settlement, as of a dispute; adjustment. **5.** *Usually pl.* The plans or preparations made, or measures taken, for a particular purpose. **6.** *Music* The adaptation of a composition to other voices or instruments.
r·rant (ar′ənt) *adj.* Notoriously bad; unmitigated. [Var. of ERRANT] **— ar′rant·ly** *adv.*
r·ras (ar′əs) *n.* **1.** A tapestry. **2.** A wall hanging, esp. of tapestry. [after *Arras,* France]
rray (ə·rā′) *n.* **1.** Regular or proper order, esp. of troops. **2.** The persons or things arrayed. **3.** Clothing; fine dress. **—** *v.t.* **1.** To draw up in order of battle; set in order. **2.** To adorn; dress, as for display. [< AF < OF *arei* < *a-* to + *rei* order]
r·ray·al (ə·rā′əl) *n.* **1.** The act or process of arraying. **2.** Anything arrayed; an array.
r·rear·age (ə·rir′ij) *n.* **1.** The state of being in arrears. **2.** The amount in arrears. **3.** A thing kept in reserve.
r·rears (ə·rirz′) *n.pl.* That which is behindhand; a part, as of a debt, overdue and unpaid. **— in arrears** (or **arrear**) Behind in meeting payment, completing work, etc. [< OF < L *ad-* to + *retro* backward]
r·rest (ə·rest′) *v.t.* **1.** To stop suddenly; check. **2.** To take into legal custody. **3.** To attract and fix, as the attention. **—** *n.* **1.** The act of arresting, or the state of being arrested. **2.** Seizure by legal authority. Also **ar·rest′ment.** **3.** A device for arresting motion. **— under arrest** In custody; arrested. [< OF < LL < L *ad-* to + *restare* to stop, remain] **— ar·rest′er, ar·rest′or** *n.*
r·ri·val (ə·rī′vəl) *n.* **1.** The act of arriving. **2.** One who or that which arrives or has arrived.
r·rive (ə·rīv′) *v.i.* **·rived, ·riv·ing** **1.** To reach a destination or place. **2.** To come to a desired object, state, etc.: often with *at.* **3.** To attain success or fame. **4.** To come at length: The hour has *arrived.* [< OF < LL < L *ad-* to + *ripa* shore]
ar·ro·gance (ar′ə·gəns) *n.* The quality or state of being arrogant or haughty. Also **ar′ro·gan·cy, ar′ro·gant·ness.**
ar·ro·gant (ar′ə·gənt) *adj.* **1.** Overbearing; haughty. **2.** Characterized by or due to arrogance. [< OF < L < *ad-* to + *rogare* to ask] **— ar′ro·gant·ly** *adv.*
ar·ro·gate (ar′ə·gāt) *v.t.* **·gat·ed, ·gat·ing** **1.** To claim or take without right. **2.** To ascribe to another without reason. [< L < *ad-* to + *rogare* to ask] **— ar′ro·ga′tion** *n.* **— ar′ro·ga′tive** *adj.*
ar·row (ar′ō, -ə) *n.* **1.** A slender shaft, generally feathered at one end and with a pointed head at the other, to be shot from a bow. **2.** Anything resembling an arrow in shape, speed, etc. **3.** A sign or figure in the shape of an arrow, used to indicate directions. [OE *earh, arwe*] **— ar·row·y** (ar′ō·ē) *adj.*
ar·row·head (ar′ō·hed′, -ə-) *n.* **1.** The sharp-pointed head of an arrow. **2.** Something resembling an arrowhead, as a mark used to point direction, etc. **3.** *Bot.* An aquatic plant with arrow-shaped leaves.
ar·row·root (ar′ō·ro͞ot′, -ə-, -ro͝ot′) *n.* **1.** A nutritious starch obtained from a tropical American plant. **2.** The plant itself. [Plant so called because used to treat arrow wounds]
ar·roy·o (ə·roi′ō) *n. pl.* **·os** (-ōz) *SW U.S.* **1.** A deep, dry gully. **2.** A brook. [< Sp., ult. < L *arrugia* pit, shaft]
ar·se·nal (är′sə·nəl) *n.* **1.** A government facility for manufacturing and storing arms and munitions. **2.** A store of arms. [< Ital. < Arabic *dār aṣ-ṣin'ah* workshop]
ar·se·nic (är′sə·nik) *n.* A grayish white, brittle metallic element (symbol As), forming many poisonous compounds and used in medicine, industry, and the arts. [< OF < L < Gk. *arsenikon* yellow orpiment]
ar·sen·i·cal (är·sen′i·kəl) *adj.* Of or containing arsenic. Also **ar·sen′ic.** **—** *n.* Any arsenical insecticide or drug.
ar·son (är′sən) *n. Law* The crime of setting fire to a building or other property. [< OF < LL < L *ardere* to burn]
ars po·et·i·ca (ärz pō·et′i·kə) *Latin* The art of poetry.
art[1] (ärt) *n.* **1.** An esthetically pleasing and meaningful arrangement of elements, as words, sounds, colors, shapes, etc. **2.** Literature, music, and esp. painting, sculpture, drawing, etc. **3.** Any system of rules and principles that facilitates skilled human accomplishment. **4.** A pursuit or occupation that depends upon the skilled application of such a system of rules and principles. **5.** Practical skill; dexterity: the *art* of a craftsman. **6.** *pl.* The liberal arts. **7.** *Usu. pl.* Cunning. [< OF < L *ars, artis* skill]
art[2] (ärt) *Archaic* or *Poetic* Second person singular present tense of BE: used with *thou.* [OE *eart*]
-art *suffix* Var. of -ARD.
Ar·te·mis (är′tə·mis) In Greek mythology, the goddess identified with the Roman *Diana.*
ar·te·ri·al (är·tir′ē·əl) *adj.* **1.** Of or pertaining to the arteries or an artery. **2.** *Physiol.* Pertaining to the bright red blood that has undergone aeration in the lungs. **3.** Resembling an artery: an *arterial* highway.
ar·te·ri·al·ize (är·tir′ē·əl·īz′) *v.t.* **·ized, ·iz·ing** *Physiol.* To convert (venous blood) into arterial blood by oxygenation. Also *Brit.* **ar·te′ri·al·ise′.** **— ar·te′ri·al·i·za′tion** *n.*
arterio- *combining form* Artery. Also, before vowels, **arter-.** [< Gk. *artēria*]
ar·te·ri·o·scle·ro·sis (är·tir′ē·ō·sklə·rō′sis) *n. Pathol.* The thickening and hardening of the walls of an artery. **— ar·te′ri·o·scle·rot′ic** (-rot′ik) *adj.*
ar·ter·y (är′tər·ē) *n. pl.* **·ter·ies** **1.** *Anat.* Any of a large number of muscular vessels conveying blood away from the heart to every part of the body. **2.** Any main channel or route. [< L *arteria* artery, windpipe]
ar·te·sian well (är·tē′zhən) A well that penetrates to a water-bearing stratum from a surface lower than the source of the water supply, so that the water pressure forces a flow of water out at the surface. [< F, after *Artois,* town in France)
art·ful (ärt′fəl) *adj.* **1.** Crafty; cunning. **2.** Skillful; ingenious. **3.** Artificial. **— art′ful·ly** *adv.* **— art′ful·ness** *n.*
ar·thri·tis (är·thrī′tis) *n. Pathol.* Inflammation of a joint or joints. [< L < Gk. *arthron* joint] **— ar·thrit·ic** (är·thrit′ik) *adj.* & *n.*

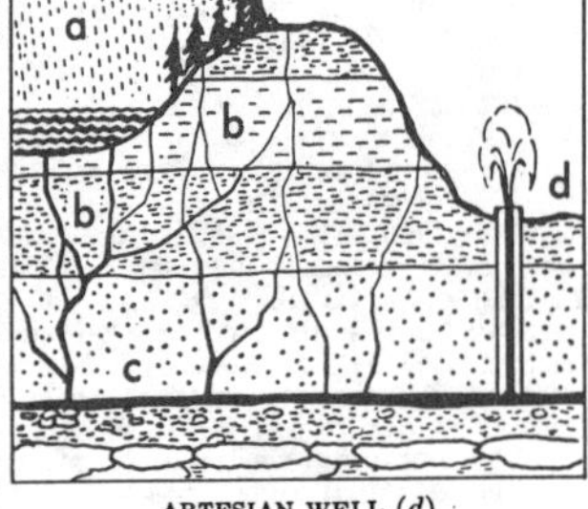

ARTESIAN WELL (*d*)
a Precipitation. *b* Seepage.
c Water table.

arthro- *combining form* Joint. Also, before vowels, **arthr-**. [< Gk. *arthron*]

ar·thro·pod (är′thrə·pod) *Zool. n.* Any of a large phylum of invertebrate animals having jointed legs and segmented body parts, including insects, spiders, and crabs. [< ARTHRO- + Gk. *pous, podos* foot] **— ar·throp·o·dous** (är·throp′ə·dəs), **ar·throp′o·dal** *adj.*

Ar·thur (är′thər) Legendary sixth-century British king; hero of the Round Table. [? < Celtic, high, admirable] **— Ar·thu′ri·an** (-thŏŏr′ē·ən) *adj.*

ar·ti·choke (är′tə·chōk) *n.* **1.** A thistlelike garden plant. **2.** Its flower head, used as a vegetable. **3.** The Jerusalem artichoke. [< Ital. ult. < Arabic *al-kharshūf*]

ar·ti·cle (är′ti·kəl) *n.* **1.** A particular object or substance; a thing. **2.** An individual item in a class: an *article* of food. **3.** A literary composition forming an independent part of a newspaper, magazine, etc. **4.** A separate section in a document, as in a treaty, contract, statute, etc. **5.** *Gram.* One of a class of auxiliary words inserted before a noun to limit or modify it in some way, as English *a, an* (**indefinite article**) and *the* (**definite article**). **—** *v.* **·cled, ·cling** *v.t.* **1.** To bind to service by a written contract. **2.** To accuse by formal articles. **—** *v.i.* **3.** To make accusations: with *against.* [< F < L *artus* a joint]

ar·tic·u·lar (är·tik′yə·lər) *adj.* Pertaining to a joint or the joints. [< L *articularis*]

ar·tic·u·late (*adj.* är·tik′yə·lit; *v.* är·tik′yə·lāt) *adj.* **1.** Able to speak, esp. well or expressively. **2.** Clearly enunciated. **3.** Coherent; well presented: an *articulate* thesis. **4.** Jointed; segmented, as limbs. Also **ar·tic′u·lat′ed.** **— ·lat·ed, ·lat·ing** *v.t.* **1.** To utter distinctly; enunciate. **2.** To give utterance to; express in words. **3.** To joint together; unite by joints. **—** *v.i.* **4.** To speak distinctly. **5.** *Phonet.* To produce a speech sound. [< L *articulare* to divide into joints, utter distinctly] **— ar·tic′u·late·ly** *adv.* **— ar·tic′u·late·ness** *n.*

ar·tic·u·la·tion (är·tik′yə·lā′shən) *n.* **1.** A jointing or being jointed together. **2.** The manner or method of jointing. **3.** *Anat.* The union forming a joint, as of bones. **4.** The utterance of speech sounds; enunciation. **5.** *Phonet.* **a** A speech sound. **b** The movements of the organs of speech in producing a speech sound. **6.** *Bot.* A node or the space between two nodes. **— ar·tic·u·la·tive** (är·tik′yə·lā′tiv, -lə·tiv), **ar·tic·u·la·to·ry** (är·tik′yə·lə·tôr′ē, -tō′rē) *adj.*

ar·tic·u·la·tor (är·tik′yə·lā′tər) *n.* One who or that which articulates.

ar·ti·fact (är′tə·fakt) *n.* Anything made by human work or art. Also **ar′te·fact.** [< L *ars, artis* art, skill + *facere* to make]

ar·ti·fice (är′tə·fis) *n.* **1.** An ingenious expedient; stratagem; maneuver. **2.** Subtle or deceptive craft; trickery. **3.** Skill; ingenuity. [< F < L *ars, artis* art + *facere* to make]

ar·tif·i·cer (är·tif′ə·sər) *n.* **1.** One who constructs with skill. **2.** *Mil.* A skilled mechanic. **3.** An inventor.

ar·ti·fi·cial (är′tə·fish′əl) *adj.* **1.** Produced by human art. **2.** Made in imitation of something natural. **3.** Feigned; fictitious. **4.** Not genuine or natural; affected. [See ARTIFICE.] **— ar′ti·fi′cial·ly** *adv.* **— ar′ti·fi′cial·ness** *n.*

artificial horizon *Aeron.* An instrument that shows the deviations of an aircraft from level flight.

artificial insemination Impregnation of the female without direct sexual contact.

ar·ti·fi·ci·al·i·ty (är′tə·fish′ē·al′ə·tē) *n. pl.* **·ties** **1.** The quality or state of being artificial. **2.** Something artificial.

ar·til·ler·y (är·til′ə·rē) *n.* **1.** Guns of larger caliber than machine guns. **2.** Military units armed with such guns. **3.** A branch of the U.S. Army. **4.** The science of gunnery. **5.** *U.S. Slang* A firearm. [< OF *artiller* to fortify]

ar·til·ler·y·man (är·til′ə·rē·mən) *n. pl.* **·men** (-mən) A soldier in the artillery. Also **ar·til′ler·ist.**

ar·ti·san (är′tə·zən) *n.* A trained or skilled workman. [< F < Ital. < L *ars, artis* art]

ar·tist (är′tist) *n.* **1.** One skilled in any of the fine arts, esp. the graphic arts. **2.** One whose work exhibits artistic qualities and skill; a craftsman. **3.** An artiste. [< F < Ital. < L *ars, artis* art]

ar·tiste (är·tēst′) *n.* **1.** An entertainer, as a dancer or singer. **2.** An artist: often used ironically.

ar·tis·tic (är·tis′tik) *adj.* **1.** Of or pertaining to art or artists. **2.** Conforming or conformable to the principles of art; tastefully executed. **3.** Fond of or sensitive to art. Also **ar·tis′ti·cal.** **— ar·tis′ti·cal·ly** *adv.*

art·ist·ry (är′tis·trē) *n.* **1.** Artistic workmanship or ability. **2.** The pursuits or occupation of an artist.

art·less (ärt′lis) *adj.* **1.** Lacking craft or deceit; guileless; naive. **2.** Natural; simple. **3.** Devoid of art or skill; clumsy. **4.** Uncultured; ignorant. **— Syn.** See INGENUOUS. **— art′less·ly** *adv.* **— art′less·ness** *n.*

art·y (är′tē) *adj.* Ostentatiously claiming artistic worth or interest. **— art′i·ness** *n.*

ar·um (âr′əm) *n.* Any of a genus of Old World herbs, including the philodendron. [< L < Gk. *aron*]

-ary[1] *suffix of adjectives and nouns* **1.** Connected with or per taining to what is expressed in the root word: *elementary* **2.** A person employed as or engaged in: *apothecary.* **3.** A thing connected with or a place dedicated to: *dictionary* [< L *-arius, -arium*]

-ary[2] *suffix of adjectives* Of or pertaining to; belonging to *military, salutary.* See -AR[1]. [< L *-aris*]

Ar·y·an (âr′ē·ən, ar′-, är′yən) *n.* **1.** A member or descend ant of a prehistoric people who spoke Indo-European. **2.** In Nazi ideology, a Caucasian gentile, esp. one of Nordic stock **—** *adj.* **1.** Of or pertaining to the Aryans or their languages **2.** In Nazi ideology, of or pertaining to Caucasian gentiles Also spelled *Arian.* [< Skt. *ārya* noble]

Ar·y·an·ize (âr′ē·ən·īz′, ar′-, är′yən-) *v.t.* **·ized, ·iz·ing** In Nazi ideology, to make characteristically Aryan or to fre from (so-called) non-Aryan influences, control, etc.

as[1] (az, *unstressed* əz) *adv.* To the same degree; equally **—** *conj.* **1.** To the same degree or extent that: often use in correlative constructions with *as* or *so* to denote equalit or identity: *as* fair *as* the sun. **2.** In the way that; in th same manner that: Do *as* I do. **3.** In proportion that; t the degree in which: He became gentler *as* he grew olde **4.** At the same time that; while. **5.** Because; since. ◆ Thi sense, though standard, often involves an ambiguity i meaning, and should be used with care. In the sentenc *As it was raining, we stayed at home, as* may mean *while when,* or *because.* **6.** With the result or purpose that: Spea louder, so *as* to make yourself heard. **7.** For instance: use to introduce examples or illustrations: Some animals ar cunning, *as* the fox. **8.** Though; however: Bad *as* it was it might have been worse. **— as for** (or **as to**) In the matte of; concerning. **— as if** (or **as though**) The same, or in th same manner, that it would be if. **— as is** *Informal* Jus as it is; in its present condition. **—** *pron.* **1.** That; whc which: after *same* and *such*: He lived in the same city *as* did. **2.** A fact which: He is dead, *as* everyone knows **—** *prep.* **1.** In the role or character of: to act *as* umpire **2.** In the manner of; like: to use a board *as* a hammer. [M *as, als, alse,* OE *ealswā* entirely so, just as]

as- Assimilated var. of AD-.

As (äs) Singular of ÆSIR.

as·a·fet·i·da (as′ə·fet′ə·də) *n.* A fetid substance prepare from certain plants of the parsley family, formerly used i medicine as an antispasmodic. Also **as′a·foet′i·da.** [< Med.L *asa* gum + L *foetida,* fem., ill-smelling]

as·bes·tos (as·bes′təs, az-) *n.* **1.** A white or light gra silicate mineral, occurring in long slender needles or fibrou masses that may be woven or shaped into acid-resisting nonconducting, and fireproof articles. **2.** A fireproof cur tain, as in a theater. **—** *adj.* Of or made of asbestos. Als **as·bes′tus.** [< L < Gk., < *a-* not + *sbennynai* to quench **— as·bes·tine** (as·bes′tin, az-), **as·bes′tic** *adj.*

as·ca·rid (as′kə·rid) *n. Zool.* A nematode worm parasiti in the intestines. [< Gk. *askaris, -idos*]

as·cend (ə·send′) *v.i.* **1.** To go or move upward; rise. **2** To lie along an ascending slope. **—** *v.t.* **3.** To mount; climb [< L *ad-* to + *scandere* to climb] **— as·cend′a·ble** o **as·cend′i·ble** *adj.* **— as·cen′sive** *adj.* **— as·cen′der** *n.*

as·cen·dan·cy (ə·sen′dən·sē) *n.* The quality, fact, or stat of being in the ascendant; domination; sway. Also **as·cen dance, as·cen′dence, as·cen′den·cy.**

as·cen·dant (ə·sen′dənt) *adj.* **1.** Ascending; rising. **2.** Su perior; dominant. **3.** *Astron.* Coming to or above the hori zon. **—** *n.* A position of preeminence; domination. Als **as·cen′dent.** **— to be in the ascendant** To approach o occupy a predominating position.

as·cen·sion (ə·sen′shən) *n.* The act of ascending. **— the Ascension** *Theol.* The bodily assent of Christ into heave after the Resurrection, commemorated on **Ascension Day** the fortieth day after Easter. **— as·cen′sion·al** *adj.*

as·cent (ə·sent′) *n.* **1.** The act of ascending in space; a ris ing, soaring, or climbing. **2.** A rise in state, rank, o station; advancement. **3.** A way or means of ascending upward slope. **4.** The degree of acclivity: an *ascent* of 30°

as·cer·tain (as′ər·tān′) *v.t.* To learn with certainty; fin out by experiment or investigation. [< OF < *a-* to (< *ad-*) + *certain*] **— as′cer·tain′a·ble** *adj.* **— as′cer·tain′a ble·ness** *n.* **— as′cer·tain′a·bly** *adv.* **— as′cer·tain′ment** *n*

as·cet·ic (ə·set′ik) *n.* One who leads a very austere an self-denying life, esp. for religious purposes. **—** *adj.* **1** Pertaining to ascetics or asceticism. **2.** Rigidly abstinent austere. Also **as·cet′i·cal** *adj.* [< Gk. *askētēs* one wh practices (self-denial), a monk] **— as·cet′i·cal·ly** *adv.*

as·cet·i·cism (ə·set′ə·siz′əm) *n.* Ascetic belief or conduct

as·cid·i·an (ə·sid′ē·ən) *Zool. n.* One of a class of marin animals having a leathery sac; a tunicate. **—** *adj.* Of o pertaining to this class of animals. [< NL < ASCIDIUM]

as·cid·i·um (ə·sid′ē·əm) *n. pl.* **·cid·i·a** (-sid′ē·ə) *Bot.* A flask-shaped plant appendage. [< NL < Gk. *askos* bag]

As·cle·pi·us (as·klē′pē·əs) In Greek mythology, the god o medicine: identified with the Roman *Aesculapius.*

s·co·my·ce·tous (as′kə·mī·sē′təs) *adj. Bot.* Belonging to a large class of fungi, including mildews and yeasts. [< NL *Ascomycetes*]
·scor·bic (ə·skôr′bik) *adj.* Antiscorbutic.
scorbic acid *Biochem.* The scurvy-preventing vitamin C, a white, odorless, crystalline compound, $C_6H_8O_6$, present in citrus and other fresh fruits, tomatoes, potatoes, and green leafy vegetables, and also made synthetically.
s·cot (as′kət, -kot) *n.* A kind of necktie knotted so that the broad ends are laid one across the other. [after *Ascot,* a village in England.]
s·cribe (ə·skrīb′) *v.t.* **·cribed, ·crib·ing** **1.** To attribute or impute, as to a cause or source: I *ascribe* his conduct to insanity. **2.** To consider or declare as belonging (to); assign as a quality or attribute. — **Syn.** See ATTRIBUTE. [< L < *ad-* to + *scribere* to write] — **as·crib′a·ble** *adj.*
s·crip·tion (ə·skrip′shən) *n.* **1.** The act of ascribing. **2.** That which ascribes; esp., a text or sentence of praise to God.
ase *suffix Chem.* Used in naming enzymes: *amylase, casease.*
·sea (ə·sē′) *adv.* To or toward the sea; at sea.
·sep·sis (ə·sep′sis, ā-) *n. Med.* **1.** Absence of pathogenic organisms. **2.** The prevention of infection by the use of sterilized instruments, dressings, etc. [< A-[4] + SEPSIS]
·sep·tic (ə·sep′tik, ā-) *adj.* Free of pathogenic microorganisms. — **a·sep′ti·cal·ly** *adv.*
·sex·u·al (ā·sek′shōō·əl) *adj. Biol.* **1.** Having no distinct sexual organs; without sex. **2.** Occurring or performed without union of male and female gametes. — **a·sex·u·al·i·ty** (ā·sek′shōō·al′ə·tē) *n.* — **a·sex′u·al·ly** *adv.*
s·gard (as′gärd, äs′-) In Norse mythology, the home of the gods and of heroes slain in battle. Also **As·garth** (äs′gärth). [< ON < *āss* god + *gardhr* yard, dwelling]
sh[1] (ash) *n.* The powdery, whitish gray residue of a substance that has been burned. [OE *æsce, asce*]
sh[2] (ash) *n.* **1.** A tree of the olive family. **2.** The light, tough, elastic wood of this tree. — *adj.* Made of ash wood. [OE *æsc*]
·shamed (ə·shāmd′) *adj.* **1.** Feeling shame. **2.** Deterred by fear of shame. [OE *āscamod,* pp. of *āscamian*] — **a·sham·ed·ly** (ə·shā′mid·lē) *adv.* — **a·sham′ed·ness** *n.*
sh·en[1] (ash′ən) *adj.* **1.** Of, pertaining to, or like ashes. **2.** Pale in color; gray.
sh·en[2] (ash′ən) *adj.* Pertaining to or made of ash wood.
sh·es (ash′iz) *n.pl.* **1.** The grayish white, powdery particles remaining after something has been burned. **2.** The remains of the human body after cremation. **3.** Mortal remains. **4.** Volcanic lava. [pl. of ASH[1]]
sh·lar (ash′lər) *n.* **1.** In masonry, a roughhewn block of stone. **2.** A thin, dressed, squared stone, used for facing a wall. **3.** Masonry made of such stones. Also **ash′ler.** [< OF < L *axis* board, plank]
·shore (ə·shôr′, ə·shōr′) *adv. & adj.* **1.** To or on the shore. **2.** On land; aground.
sh Wednesday The first day of Lent: from the sprinkling of ashes on the heads of penitents.
sh·y (ash′ē) *adj.* **ash·i·er, ash·i·est** **1.** Of, pertaining to, or like ashes; ash-covered. **2.** Ash-colored; ashen.
·sian (ā′zhən, ā′shən) *adj.* Of or characteristic of Asia or its peoples. — *n.* A native or inhabitant of Asia.
·si·at·ic (ā′zhē·at′ik, ā′shē-) *adj. & n.* Asian. ◆ In most cases, esp. in the ethnic sense, *Asian* is now preferred.
·side (ə·sīd′) *adv.* **1.** On or to one side; apart. **2.** Out of thought or use: to put grief *aside.* **3.** Away from the general company; in seclusion: He drew me *aside.* **4.** Away from one's person; down. **5.** In reserve. — **aside from** *U.S.* **1.** Apart from. **2.** Excepting. — *n.* Lines spoken privately by an actor and supposed to be heard by the audience but not by the other actors.
s·i·nine (as′ə·nīn) *adj.* Pertaining to or like an ass, considered a stupid, obstinate animal. [< L *asinus* ass] — **as′·i·nine′ly** *adv.* — **as·i·nin·i·ty** (as′ə·nin′ə·tē) *n.*
sk (ask, äsk) *v.t.* **1.** To put a question to: Don't *ask* me. **2.** To put a question about: to *ask* the time. **3.** To make a request of or for; solicit. **4.** To need or require: This job *asks* too much time. **5.** To state the price of; demand. **6.** To invite. — *v.i.* **7.** To make inquiries: with *for, after,* or *about.* **8.** To make a request: often with *for:* He *asked* for aid. [OE *āscian*] — **ask′er** *n.*
— **Syn. 1.** *Ask* is the most direct and inclusive term of putting a question to a person. *Query* suggests the effort to settle a doubt. To *question* is to put a series of questions; to *interrogate* is to *question* formally or by right of authority. We *quiz* as a test of knowledge. *Inquire* suggests the effort to ascertain facts or the truth. **3.** *Ask* and *request* mean to urge that something desired be granted or handed over. *Ask* suggests the expectation of compliance; *request* is more formal, and allows for refusal.
·skance (ə·skans′) *adv.* **1.** With a side glance; sidewise. **2.** Disdainfully; distrustfully. Also **a·skant′.** [Origin unknown]
a·skew (ə·skyōō′) *adj.* Oblique. — *adv.* In an oblique position or manner; to one side; awry.
a·slant (ə·slant′, ə·slänt′) *adj.* Slanting; oblique. — *adv.* At a slant; obliquely. — *prep.* Slantingly across or over.
a·sleep (ə·slēp′) *adj.* **1.** In a state of sleep; sleeping. **2.** Dormant; inactive. **3.** Benumbed, as an arm or leg. **4.** Dead. — *adv.* Into a sleeping condition: to fall *asleep.*
a·slope (ə·slōp′) *adj.* Sloping. — *adv.* At a slope.
a·so·cial (ā·sō′shəl) *adj.* **1.** Avoiding society; not gregarious. **2.** Heedless of one's fellow beings; self-centered.
asp (asp) *n.* The common European viper. [< L < Gk.]
as·par·a·gus (ə·spar′ə·gəs) *n.* **1.** The succulent, edible shoots of a cultivated variety of a perennial herb of the lily family. **2.** Any related plant. [< L < Gk. *aspharagos*]
as·pect (as′pekt) *n.* **1.** The look of a person; facial expression. **2.** Appearance to the eye; look: the pleasant *aspect* of a lake. **3.** Appearance presented to the mind by circumstances, etc.; interpretation: all *aspects* of a problem. **4.** A looking or facing in a given direction: the southern *aspect* of a house. **5.** The side or surface facing in a certain direction: ventral *aspect.* **6.** In astrology: **a** Any configuration of the planets. **b** The supposed influence of this for good or evil. — **Syn.** See PHASE. [< L < *ad-* at + *specere* to look]
asp·en (as′pən) *n.* Any of several species of poplar of North America or Europe with leaves that tremble in the slightest breeze. — *adj.* **1.** Of the aspen. **2.** Shaking, like aspen leaves. [OE *æspe*]
as·per·i·ty (as·per′ə·tē) *n. pl.* **·ties** **1.** Roughness or harshness, as of surface, sound, etc. **2.** Sharpness of temper; acrimony. [< OF < L *asper* rough]
as·perse (ə·spûrs′) *v.t.* **as·persed** (ə·spûrst′), **as·pers·ing** To spread false charges against; slander. [< L < *ad-* to + *spargere* to sprinkle] — **as·pers′er** or **as·per′sor** *n.* — **as·per′sive** (-siv) *adj.*
as·per·sion (ə·spûr′zhən, -shən) *n.* **1.** A slandering; defamation. **2.** A slanderous or damaging report; calumny.
as·phalt (as′fôlt, -falt) *n.* **1.** A solid, brownish black, combustible mixture of bituminous hydrocarbons, found native in various parts of the world and also obtained as a residue in the refining of petroleum. **2.** A mixture of this with sand or gravel, used for paving, etc. Also **as·phal·tum** (as·fal′·təm), **as·phal′tus.** — *v.t.* To pave with asphalt. [< LL < Gk. *asphalton*] — **as·phal·tic** (as·fôl′tik, -fal′-) *adj.*
as·pho·del (as′fə·del) *n.* A plant of the lily family, bearing white, pink, or yellow flowers. [< L < Gk. *asphodelos*]
as·phyx·i·a (as·fik′sē·ə) *n. Pathol.* Unconsciousness caused by too little oxygen and too much carbon dioxide in the blood. [< NL < Gk. < *a-* not + *sphyzein* to beat] — **as·phyx′i·al** *adj.* — **as·phyx′i·ant** *adj. & n.*
as·phyx·i·ate (as·fik′sē·āt) *v.* **·at·ed, ·at·ing** *v.t.* **1.** To cause asphyxia in; suffocate. — *v.i.* **2.** To undergo asphyxia. — **as·phyx′i·a′tion** *n.* — **as·phyx′i·a′tor** *n.*
as·pic (as′pik) *n.* A jelly of meat or vegetable juices, served as a relish or as a mold for meat, vegetables, etc. [< F]
as·pi·dis·tra (as′pə·dis′trə) *n.* A stemless, Asian herb of the lily family, with large, glossy, evergreen leaves. [< NL < Gk. *aspis, aspidos* shield + *astron* star]
as·pir·ant (ə·spīr′ənt, as′pər·ənt) *n.* One who aspires, as after honors or place; a candidate. — *adj.* Aspiring.
as·pi·rate (*v.* as′pə·rāt; *n. & adj.* as′pər·it) *v.t.* **·rat·ed, ·rat·ing** **1.** To utter with a puff of breath or as if preceded by an *h* sound. **2.** To follow with a puff of breath, as (p), (t), and (k) when before a vowel. **3.** *Med.* To draw out with an aspirator. — *n.* An aspirated sound. — *adj. Phonet.* Uttered with an aspirate: also **as′pi·rat′ed** (-rā′tid). [See ASPIRE.]
as·pi·ra·tion (as′pə·rā′shən) *n.* **1.** Exalted desire; high ambition. **2.** The act of breathing; breath. **3.** *Med.* The use of an aspirator. **4.** *Phonet.* An aspirate.
as·pi·ra·tor (as′pə·rā′tər) *n. Med.* A device for drawing off fluid matter or gases from the body by suction.
as·pir·a·to·ry (ə·spīr′ə·tôr′ē, -tō′rē) *adj.* Of, pertaining to, or adapted for breathing or suction.
as·pire (ə·spīr′) *v.i.* **·spired, ·spir·ing** To have an earnest desire or ambition. [< L < *ad-* to + *spirare* to breathe] — **as·pir′er** *n.* — **as·pir′ing** *adj.* — **as·pir′ing·ly** *adv.*
as·pi·rin (as′pər·in, -prin) *n.* A white crystalline compound, the acetyl derivative of salicylic acid, $C_9H_8O_4$, used for the relief of fever, pain, etc. [< A(CETYL) + SPIR(AEIC ACID), former name of salicylic acid, + -IN]
a·squint (ə·skwint′) *adj. & adv.* With sidelong glance.
ass (as, äs) *n. pl.* **ass·es** **1.** A long-eared quadruped smaller than the ordinary horse, used as a beast of burden; the donkey. **2.** A stupid person; fool. [OE *assa* ? < OIrish < L *asinus*]
as·sail (ə·sāl′) *v.t.* To attack violently, as by force, argument, etc. — **Syn.** See ATTACK. [< OF < LL < L *ad-* to + *salire* to leap] — **as·sail′a·ble** *adj.* — **as·sail′a·ble·ness** *n.*

as·sail·ant (ə·sā′lənt) *n.* One who assails. Also **as·sail′er.** — *adj.* Attacking; hostile.

as·sas·sin (ə·sas′in) *n.* One who kills; esp., one who murders a political figure from fanaticism or for a price.

as·sas·si·nate (ə·sas′ə·nāt) *v.t.* **·nat·ed, ·nat·ing 1.** To kill by secret or surprise assault. **2.** To destroy or injure by treachery, as a reputation. — **Syn.** See KILL. — **as·sas′si·na′tion** *n.* — **as·sas′si·na′tor** *n.*

as·sault (ə·sôlt′) *n.* **1.** Any violent attack, as an act, speech, or writing. **2.** *Law* An unlawful attempt or offer to do bodily injury to another. **3.** A rape. **4.** *Mil.* **a** An attack upon a fortified place. **b** A closing with the enemy. — *v.t. & v.i.* To attack with violence. — **Syn.** See ATTACK. [< OF < L *ad-* to + *salire* to leap]

assault and battery *Law* The carrying out of an assault with force and violence; a beating.

as·say (*n.* ə·sā′, as′ā; *v.* ə·sā′) *n.* **1.** The analysis or testing of an alloy or ore to ascertain the ingredients and their proportions. **2.** The substance to be so examined. **3.** The result of such a test. **4.** Any examination or testing. — *v.t.* **1.** To subject to chemical analysis; make an assay of. **2.** To prove; test. — *v.i.* **3.** *U.S.* To show by analysis a certain value or proportion, as of a precious metal. [< OF *assai*, var. of *essai* trial] — **as·say′er** *n.*

as·sem·blage (ə·sem′blij, *for def. 4, also Fr.* à·säṅ·bläzh′) *n.* **1.** The act of assembling, or the state of being assembled. **2.** Any gathering of persons or things; collection; assembly. **3.** A fitting together, as of the parts of a machine. **4.** A work of art created by assembling materials and objects; also, the technique of making such works: compare COLLAGE. — **Syn.** See COMPANY. [< F]

as·sem·ble (ə·sem′bəl) *v.t. & v.i.* **·bled, ·bling 1.** To come or bring together; collect or congregate. **2.** To fit or join together, as the parts of a mechanism. [< OF < L < *ad-* to + *simul* together] — **as·sem′bler** *n.*

as·sem·bly (ə·sem′blē) *n. pl.* **·blies 1.** The act of assembling, or the state of being assembled. **2.** A number of persons met together for a common purpose. **3.** The act or process of fitting together the parts of a machine, etc.; also, the parts themselves. **4.** *Mil.* The signal calling troops to form ranks.

assembly line An arrangement of industrial equipment and workers in which the product passes from one specialized operation to another until completed.

as·sem·bly·man (ə·sem′blē·mən) *n. pl.* **·men** (-men′, -mən) *U.S. & Canadian* A member of a legislative assembly, esp. of a State or Provincial legislature.

as·sent (ə·sent′) *v.i.* To express agreement; acquiesce; concur: usually with *to.* — *n.* **1.** Mental concurrence or agreement. **2.** Consent; sanction. [< OF < L < *ad-* to + *sentire* to feel] — **as′sen·ta′tion** *n.* — **as·sent′er** *n.*

as·sert (ə·sûrt′) *v.t.* **1.** To state positively; affirm; declare. **2.** To maintain as a right or claim, as by words or force. — **to assert oneself** To put forward and defend one's own rights or claims. [< L < *ad-* to + *serere* to bind] — **as·sert′a·ble** or **as·sert′i·ble** *adj.* — **as·sert′er** or **as·ser′tor** *n.*

as·ser·tion (ə·sûr′shən) *n.* **1.** The act of asserting. **2.** A positive declaration without attempt at proof.

as·ser·tive (ə·sûr′tiv) *adj.* Confident; aggressive. — **as·ser′tive·ly** *adv.* — **as·ser′tive·ness** *n.*

as·sess (ə·ses′) *v.t.* **1.** To charge with a tax, fine, or other payment, as a person or property. **2.** To determine the amount of, as a tax or other fine on a person or property. **3.** To evaluate, as property, for taxation. [< OF < LL < L *assidere* to sit by (as a judge in court)] — **as·sess′a·ble** *adj.*

as·sess·ment (ə·ses′mənt) *n.* **1.** The act of assessing. **2.** An amount assessed.

as·ses·sor (ə·ses′ər) *n.* One who makes assessments, as for taxation. — **as·ses·so·ri·al** (as′ə·sôr′ē·əl, -sō′rē-) *adj.*

as·set (as′et) *n.* **1.** An item of property. **2.** A useful or valuable thing or quality.

as·sets (as′ets) *n.pl.* **1.** In accounting, a balance sheet showing all the property or resources of a person or business, and money owed: opposed to *liabilities.* **2.** *Law* All the property, real and personal, of a person, corporation, or partnership, that is or may be chargeable with their debts or legacies. [< OF < LL *ad-* to + *satis* enough]

as·sev·er·ate (ə·sev′ə·rāt) *v.t.* **·at·ed, ·at·ing** To affirm or declare emphatically or solemnly. [< L < *ad-* to + *severus* serious] — **as·sev′er·a′tion** *n.*

as·si·du·i·ty (as′ə·do͞o′ə·tē, -dyo͞o′-) *n. pl.* **·ties** Close and continuous application or effort; diligence.

as·sid·u·ous (ə·sij′o͞o·əs) *adj.* **1.** Devoted; attentive. **2.** Unremitting; persistent: *assiduous* study. [< L < *ad-* to + *sedere* to sit] — **as·sid′u·ous·ly** *adv.* — **as·sid′u·ous·ness** *n.*

as·sign (ə·sīn′) *v.t.* **1.** To set apart, as for a particular function; designate: to *assign* a day for trial. **2.** To appoint, as to or for a post or duty. **3.** To allot as a task: to *assign* a lesson. **4.** To ascribe or attribute; refer: to *assign* a monument to Roman times. **5.** *Law* To transfer, as personal property, rights, or interests. — *v.i.* **6.** To transfer property, especially for the benefit of creditors. — **Syn.** See ATTRIBUT — *n. Law Usually pl.* Assignee. [< OF < L < *ad-* to - *signare* make a sign] — **as·sign′a·bil′i·ty** *n.* — **as·sign′** **ble** *adj.* — **as·sign′a·bly** *adv.* — **as·sign′er,** *Law* **as·sign·o** (ə·sī′nôr′, as′ə·nôr′) *n.*

as·sig·na·tion (as′ig·nā′shən) *n.* **1.** An appointment fo meeting, esp. a secret or illicit one as made by lovers. **2.** A assignment. [See ASSIGN.]

as·sign·ee (ə·sī′nē′, as′ə·nē′) *n. Law* A person to whon property, rights, or powers are transferred.

as·sign·ment (ə·sīn′mənt) *n.* **1.** The act of assigning. **2** Anything assigned, as a lesson or task. **3.** *Law* **a** The trans fer of a claim, right, or property, or the instrument or writin of transfer. **b** The claim, right, or property transferred.

as·sim·i·la·ble (ə·sim′ə·lə·bəl) *adj.* Capable of being as similated. — **as·sim′i·la·bil′i·ty** *n.*

as·sim·i·late (ə·sim′ə·lāt) *v.* **·lat·ed, ·lat·ing** *v.t.* **1.** *Biol.* T take up and incorporate into living organisms, as food. **2** To make into a homogeneous part, as of a substance (system. **3.** To make alike or similar; cause to resemble. - *v.i.* **4.** To become alike or similar. **5.** To become absorbe or assimilated. [< L < *ad-* to + *similare* to make like — **as·sim′i·la·tive, as·sim·i·la·to·ry** (ə·sim′ə·lə·tôr′ē, -tō′r *adj.*

as·sim·i·la·tion (ə·sim′ə·lā′shən) *n.* **1.** The act or proces of assimilating. **2.** *Biol.* The transformation of nutrimer into an integral part of a plant or animal. **3.** *Phonet.* Th process whereby a sound is influenced by a neighborin sound, as when *horseshoe* is pronounced (hôrsh′sho͞o′).

as·sist (ə·sist′) *v.t.* **1.** To give or render help to; reliev succor. **2.** To act as subordinate or deputy to. — *v.i.* **3.** T give help or support. **4.** In baseball, to aid a teammate in put-out. — **to assist at** To be present at (a ceremony, etc. — *n.* **1.** An act of helping. **2.** In baseball, a play that help to put out a runner. [< MF < L < *ad-* to + *sistere* to caus to stand] — **as·sist′er,** *Law* **as·sis′tor** *n.*

as·sis·tance (ə·sis′təns) *n.* The act of helping, or the hel given; aid; support.

as·sis·tant (ə·sis′tənt) *n.* One who assists; a subordinate (helper. — *adj.* **1.** Holding a subordinate or auxiliary plac office, or rank. **2.** Affording aid; assisting.

as·size (ə·sīz′) *n.* **1.** Originally, a session of a legislative (judicial body. **2.** *pl.* In England, one of the regular cou sessions held in each county for the trial of civil and crimin cases by jury; also, the time and place of such sessions. [OF < L *assidere* to sit by (as a judge at court)]

as·so·ci·ate (*n. & adj.* ə·sō′shē·it, -āt, -sē-; *v.* ə·sō′shē·ā -sē-) *n.* **1.** A companion. **2.** A partner, colleague, or fe low employee. **3.** Anything that habitually accompanie something else; a concomitant. **4.** One admitted to parti membership in an association, society, or institution. - *adj.* **1.** Joined with another or others in a common pursu or office. **2.** Having subordinate or secondary status: a *associate* professor. **3.** Existing or occurring together; co comitant. — *v.* **·at·ed, ·at·ing** *v.t.* **1.** To ally; unite. **2.** T combine. **3.** To connect mentally. — *v.i.* **4.** To unite for common purpose. **5.** To keep or be in company: with *wit* [< L < *ad-* to + *sociare* to join]

Associated Press An organization for collecting news an distributing it to member newspapers.

as·so·ci·a·tion (ə·sō′sē·ā′shən, -shē-) *n.* **1.** The act of ass ciating. **2.** The state of being associated; fellowship; con panionship. **3.** A body of persons associated for some cor mon purpose; society; league. Abbr. *ass., assn., assoc.* *Ecol.* A group of plants or animals sharing a common hab tat and similar geographic conditions. **5.** The connection (relation of ideas, feelings, etc. — **as·so′ci·a′tion·al** *adj.*

association football Soccer.

as·so·ci·a·tive (ə·sō′shē·ā′tiv, -shē·ə-) *adj.* **1.** Of or chara terized by association. **2.** Causing association. — **as·so ci·a′tive·ly** *adv.*

as·so·nance (as′ə·nəns) *n.* **1.** Resemblance in sound; esp cially, in prosody, correspondence of accented vowels, b not of consonants, as in *main, came.* **2.** Rough likeness; a proximation. [< F, ult. < L < *ad-* to + *sonare* to soun — **as′so·nant** *adj. & n.*

as·sort (ə·sôrt′) *v.t.* **1.** To distribute into groups accordi to kinds; classify. **2.** To furnish, as a warehouse, with variety of goods, etc. — *v.i.* **3.** To fall into groups or class of the same kind. **4.** To associate: with *with.* [< OF < *a-* + *sorte* sort] — **as·sort′er** *n.*

as·sort·ed (ə·sôr′tid) *adj.* **1.** Containing or arranged in va ious sorts or kinds; miscellaneous. **2.** Classified. **3.** Matche

as·sort·ment (ə·sôrt′mənt) *n.* **1.** The act of assortin classification. **2.** A varied collection; miscellany.

as·suage (ə·swāj′) *v.t.* **·suaged, ·suag·ing 1.** To make le harsh or severe; alleviate. **2.** To satisfy, as thirst. **3.** calm; pacify. [< OF < L *ad-* to + *suavis* sweet] — **a suage′ment** *n.*

as·sume (ə·so͞om′) *v.t.* **·sumed, ·sum·ing 1.** To take on adopt, as a style of dress, aspect, or character. **2.** To unde take, as an office or duty. **3.** To usurp, as powers of state. **4.** To take for granted. **5.** To affect; feign. [< L < *ad-* to + *sumere* to take] — **as·sum·a·ble** (ə·sōō′mə·bəl) *adj.*

as·sump·tion (ə·sump′shən) *n.* **1.** The act of assuming, or that which is assumed. **2.** That which is taken for granted; a supposition. **3.** Presumption; arrogance. **4.** *Logic* A minor premise. — **Syn.** See HYPOTHESIS. — **the Assumption** A church feast, observed on August 15, commemorating the bodily ascent of the Virgin Mary into heaven. — **as·sump′·tive** *adj.* — **as·sump′tive·ly** *adv.*

as·sur·ance (ə·shŏŏr′əns) *n.* **1.** The act of assuring, or the state of being assured. **2.** A positive statement, intended to give confidence, encouragement, etc. **3.** Self-confidence. **4.** Boldness; effrontery. **5.** *Chiefly Brit.* Insurance.

as·sure (ə·shŏŏr′) *v.t.* **·sured, ·sur·ing 1.** To make sure or secure; establish firmly. **2.** To make (something) certain; guarantee. **3.** To cause to feel certain; convince. **4.** To promise; make positive declaration to. **5.** To encourage; reassure. **6.** To insure, as against loss. [< OF < LL < L *ad-* to + *securus* safe] — **as·sur′a·ble** *adj.* — **as·sur′er** *n.*

as·sured (ə·shŏŏrd′) *adj.* **1.** Made certain; undoubted; sure: His defeat is *assured.* **2.** Self-possessed; confident. **3.** Insured. — *n.* An insured person. — **as·sur·ed·ly** (ə·shŏŏr′·id·lē) *adv.* — **as·sur′ed·ness** *n.*

As·syr·i·a (ə·sir′ē·ə) An ancient empire of western Asia; capital, Nineveh. — **As·syr′i·an** *adj. & n.*

as·ta·tine (as′tə·tēn, -tin) *n.* An unstable chemical element (symbol At) of atomic number 85, related to the halogens and occupying the place formerly assigned to alabamine. [< Gk. *astatos* unstable + -INE[2]]

as·ter (as′tər) *n.* A plant of the composite family, having flowers with white, purple, or blue rays and yellow disc. [< L < Gk. *astēr* star]

-aster *suffix* Little; inferior: *poetaster.* [< L *-aster*, dim. suffix]

as·ter·isk (as′tər·isk) *n.* *Printing* A starlike figure (*) used to indicate omissions, footnotes, references, etc. — *v.t.* To mark with an asterisk. [< L < Gk. *astēr* star]

a·stern (ə·stûrn′) *adv. & adj.* *Naut.* **1.** In the rear; at any point behind a vessel. **2.** To the rear; backward.

astero- *combining form* Of or related to a star. Also *aster-* (before vowels): also **asteri-**. [< Gk. *astēr* a star]

as·ter·oid (as′tə·roid) *adj.* Star-shaped. — *n.* **1.** *Astron.* Any of several hundred small planets between Mars and Jupiter: also called *planetoid.* **2.** A starfish. [< Gk. *astēr* a star] — **as′ter·oi′dal** *adj.*

asth·ma (az′mə, as′-) *n.* *Pathol.* A chronic respiratory disorder characterized by recurrent paroxysmal coughing and constriction of the chest. [< Gk. *azein* to breathe hard]

asth·mat·ic (az·mat′ik, as-) *adj.* Of, pertaining to, or affected with asthma. Also **asth·mat′i·cal.** — *n.* A person suffering from asthma. — **asth·mat′i·cal·ly** *adv.*

as·tig·mat·ic (as′tig·mat′ik) *adj.* Of, having, or correcting astigmatism.

a·stig·ma·tism (ə·stig′mə·tiz′əm) *n.* A defect of the eye or of a lens such that the rays of light from an object do not converge to a focus, thus causing imperfect vision or images. [< A-[4] without + Gk. *stigma, -atos* mark, spot + -ISM]

a·stir (ə·stûr) *adv. & adj.* Stirring; moving about.

a·ston·ish (ə·ston′ish) *v.t.* To affect with wonder and surprise; amaze; confound. [OF *estoner* < L *ex-* out + *tonare* to thunder] — **a·ston′ish·er** *n.* — **a·ston′ish·ing** *adj.* — **a·ston′ish·ing·ly** *adv.*

a·ston·ish·ment (ə·ston′ish·mənt) *n.* **1.** The state of being astonished. **2.** A cause of such emotion.

a·stound (ə·stound′) *v.t.* To overwhelm with wonder; confound. [ME < OF *estoner* < L *ex-* out + *tonare* to thunder] — **a·stound′ing** *adj.* — **a·stound′ing·ly** *adv.*

as·trag·a·lus (as·trag′ə·ləs) *n. pl.* **·li** (-lī) *Anat.* The talus. [< L < Gk. *astragalos*] — **as·trag′a·lar** (-lər) *adj.*

as·tra·khan (as′trə·kan, -kən) *n.* **1.** The black or gray, loosely curled fur made from the pelt of lambs raised near Astrakhan. **2.** A fabric with a curled pile imitative of this. Also **as′tra·chan.**

as·tral (as′trəl) *adj.* **1.** Of, pertaining to, coming from, or like the stars; starry. **2.** Of or designating a supposedly supernatural substance. — *n.* An astral body. [< LL < L < Gk. *astron* star] — **as′tral·ly** *adv.*

a·stray (ə·strā′) *adv. & adj.* Away from the right path; wandering. [< OF < L *extra-* beyond + *vagare* to wander]

a·stride (ə·strīd′) *adv. & adj.* **1.** With one leg on each side. **2.** With the legs far apart. — *prep.* With one leg on each side of: *astride* a horse.

as·trin·gent (ə·strin′jənt) *adj.* **1.** *Med.* Tending to contract or draw together organic tissues; binding; styptic. **2.** Harsh; stern; austere. — *n.* An astringent substance. [< L < *ad-* to + *stringere* to bind fast] — **as·trin′gen·cy** *n.* — **as·trin′gent·ly** *adv.*

astro- *combining form* **1.** Star. **2.** Of, pertaining to, occurring in, or characteristic of outer space: *astronautics.* [< Gk. *astron* star]

as·tro·dy·nam·ics (as′trō·dī·nam′iks) *n.pl.* (*construed as sing.*) The branch of dynamics concerned with the motions of celestial bodies.

as·tro·labe (as′trə·lāb) *n.* An instrument formerly used for obtaining the altitudes of planets and stars. [< OF < Med.L < Gk. *astron* star + *lambanein* to take]

as·trol·o·gy (ə·strol′ə·jē) *n.* The study professing to foretell the future and interpret the influence of the heavenly bodies upon the destinies of men. [< L < Gk. < *astron* star + *logos* discourse] — **as·trol′o·ger** *n.* — **as·tro·log·ic** (as′trə·loj′ik) or **·i·cal, as·trol′o·gous** (-gəs) *adj.* — **as′tro·log′i·cal·ly** *adv.*

as·tro·naut (as′trə·nôt) *n.* One who travels in space. [< ASTRO- + *-naut* (< Gk. *nautēs* sailor), after *aeronaut*]

as·tro·nau·tics (as′trə·nô′tiks) *n.pl.* (*construed as sing.*) The science and art of space travel. — **as′tro·nau′tic** or **·ti·cal** *adj.* — **as′tro·nau′ti·cal·ly** *adv.*

as·tron·o·mer (ə·stron′ə·mər) *n.* One learned or expert in astronomy. Abbr. *astr., astron.*

as·tro·nom·i·cal (as′trə·nom′i·kəl) *adj.* **1.** Of or pertaining to astronomy. **2.** Enormously or inconceivably large. Also **as′tro·nom′ic.** — **as′tro·nom′i·cal·ly** *adv.*

astronomical unit A space unit for expressing the distances of the stars, equal to the mean distance of the earth from the sun.

astronomical year The period between two passages of the sun through the same equinox, equal to about 365 days, 5 hours, 48 minutes, and 46 seconds.

as·tron·o·my (ə·stron′ə·mē) *n.* The science that treats of the heavenly bodies, their motions, magnitudes, distances, and constitution. [< OF < L < Gk. *astron* star + *nomos* law]

as·tro·phys·ics (as′trō·fiz′iks) *n.pl.* (*construed as sing.*) The branch of astronomy that treats of the physical constitution and properties of the heavenly bodies. — **as′tro·phys′i·cal** *adj.* — **as·tro·phys·i·cist** (as′trō·fiz′ə·sist) *n.*

as·tute (ə·stōōt′, ə·styōōt′) *adj.* Keen in discernment; acute; shrewd; cunning. [< L *astus* cunning] — **as·tute′ly** *adv.* — **as·tute′ness** *n.*

a·sun·der (ə·sun′dər) *adv.* **1.** Apart; into pieces. **2.** In or into a different place or direction. — *adj.* Separated; apart. [OE *on sundran*]

a·sy·lum (ə·sī′ləm) *n. pl.* **·lums** or **·la** (-lə) **1.** An institution for the care of the mentally ill, the aged, the destitute, etc. **2.** A place of refuge. **3.** An inviolable shelter from arrest or punishment, as a temple or church in ancient times. [< L < Gk. < *a-* without + *sylon* right of seizure]

a·sym·met·ric (ā′si·met′rik, as′i-) *adj.* **1.** Not symmetrical. **2.** *Chem.* Designating an unbalanced spatial arrangement of atoms and radicals within a molecule. Also **a′sym·met′ri·cal.** — **a′sym·met′ri·cal·ly** *adv.*

a·sym·me·try (ā·sim′ə·trē) *n.* Lack of symmetry.

as·ymp·tote (as′im·tōt) *n.* *Math.* A straight line that an indefinitely extended curve continually approaches as a tangent. [< Gk. < *a-* not + *syn-* together + *piptein* to fall] — **as′ymp·tot′ic** or **·i·cal** *adj.* — **as′ymp·tot′i·cal·ly** *adv.*

at (at, *unstressed* ət) *prep.* **1.** In or on the position of: *at* the center of the circle. **2.** Of time, on or upon the point or stroke of: *at* noon. **3.** During the course or lapse of: *at* night. **4.** In contact with; on; upon: *at* sea. **5.** To or toward: Look *at* that sunset! **6.** Through; by way of: Smoke came out *at* the windows. **7.** Within the limits of; present in: *at* home. **8.** Engaged or occupied in: *at* work. **9.** Attending: *at* a party. **10.** In the state or condition of: *at* war. **11.** In the region or vicinity of: *at* the door. **12.** With an interval of: *at* sixty paces. **13.** Having reference to; in connection with: He winced *at* the thought. **14.** In the manner of: *at* a trot. **15.** In pursuit or quest of; in the direction of; against: to catch *at* straws. **16.** Dependent upon: *at* an enemy's mercy. **17.** According to: Proceed *at* your discretion. **18.** Amounting to: interest *at* two percent. **19.** From; out of: to draw water *at* a well. **20.** On the occasion of. [OE *æt*]

— **Syn. 2.** *At, in,* and *on* may be used with reference to time. An event occurs *at* an hour of the day, *in* a month or year, *on* a day of the week, a date, or a precise division of time: to arrive *on* the hour. **7.** *At, in,* and *on* may be used of spatial location. Something is *at* a place regarded as a point: *at* a city, displayed *at* the museum. It is *in* a place regarded as embracing it: *in* a country, *in* a suburb. A building is said to be *on* a street.

At·a·brine (at′ə·brin, -brēn) *n.* Proprietary name for a brand of quinacrine. Also **at′a·brine.**

at·a·rac·tic (at′ə·rak′tik) *n.* *Med.* A drug having the power to tranquilize and to lessen nervous tension. Also **at′a·rax′ic** (-rak′sik). [< NL < Gk. *atarakteein* to be calm]

at·a·vism (at′ə·viz′əm) *n.* **1.** Reversion to an earlier or primitive type. **2.** *Biol.* Reversion. [< F < L < *at-* beyond + *avus* grandfather] **— at′a·vist** *n.* **— at′a·vis′tic** *adj.*

a·tax·i·a (ə·tak′sē·ə) *n. Pathol.* Loss or failure of muscular coordination. Also **a·tax·y** (ə·tak′sē). [< NL < Gk. < *a-* not + *tattein* to arrange] **— a·tax′ic** *adj. & n.*

ate (āt, *chiefly Brit.* et) Past tense of EAT.

-ate[1] *suffix* Forming: **1.** Participial adjectives equivalent to those in *-ated.* **2.** Adjectives from nouns with the meaning "possessing or characterized by": *caudate.* **3.** Verbs, originally from stems of Latin verbs of the first conjugation, and, by analogy, extended to other stems: *fascinate.* **4.** *Chem.* Verbs with the meaning "combine or treat with": *chlorinate.* [< L *-atus*, pp. ending of 1st conjugation verbs]

-ate[2] *suffix* Forming: **1.** Nouns denoting office, function, or agent: *magistrate.* **2.** Nouns denoting the object or result of an action: *mandate.* [< L *-atus*, suffix of nouns]

at·el·ier (at′əl·yā, *Fr.* à·tə·lyā′) *n.* A workshop, esp. of an artist; studio. [< F]

a·the·ism (ā′thē·iz′əm) *n.* The belief that there is no God. [< MF < Gk. < *a-* without + *theos* god]

a·the·ist (ā′thē·ist) *n.* One who denies or disbelieves in the existence of God. **— a′the·is′tic** or **·tic·al** *adj.* **— a′the·is′·ti·cal·ly** *adv.*

A·the·na (ə·thē′nə) In Greek mythology, the goddess identified with the Roman *Minerva.* Also **Athena Parthenos, A·the·ne** (ə·thē′nē). [< Gk. *Athēnē*]

ath·e·ne·um (ath′ə·nē′əm) *n.* **1.** A literary club, academy, or other institution for the promotion of learning. **2.** A reading room, library, etc. Also **ath′e·nae′um.**

A·the·ni·an (ə·thē′nē·ən) *adj.* Of or pertaining to Athens, or to its art or culture. **—** *n.* A native or citizen of Athens.

ath·er·o·scle·ro·sis (ath′ər·ō·sklə·rō′sis) *n. Pathol.* Hardening of the arteries, accompanied by the deposit of fat in the inner arterial walls. [< NL < Gk. *athērē* gruel + *sklēros* hard]

a·thirst (ə·thûrst′) *adj.* Keenly desirous; longing; eager: with *for.* [OE < *of-*, intensive + *thyrstan* to thirst]

ath·lete (ath′lēt) *n.* One trained in acts or feats of physical strength and agility, as in sports. [< L < Gk. *athleein* to contend for a prize]

athlete's foot Ringworm of the foot, caused by a fungus.

ath·let·ic (ath·let′ik) *adj.* **1.** Of, pertaining to, or befitting an athlete or athletics. **2.** Strong; vigorous; muscular. **— ath·let′i·cal·ly** *adv.* **— ath·let·i·cism** (ath·let′ə·siz′əm) *n.*

ath·let·ics (ath·let′iks) *n.pl.* Athletic games and exercises, as rowing, wrestling, etc.

ath·o·dyd (ath′ō·did) *n.* A jet engine consisting of a pipe to which air is admitted, heated, and expelled from the rear at high velocity.

at-home (ət·hōm′) *n.* An informal party or reception given at one's home.

a·thwart (ə·thwôrt′) *adv.* **1.** From side to side; across. **2.** So as to thwart; perversely. **—** *prep.* **1.** From side to side of. **2.** Contrary to. **3.** *Naut.* Across the course of.

-atic *suffix* Of; of the kind of: *erratic.* [< F < L < Gk. *-atikos*]

a·tilt (ə·tilt′) *adv. & adj.* In a tilted manner; tilted up.

-ation *suffix of nouns* **1.** Action or process of: *creation.* **2.** Condition or quality of: *affectation.* **3.** Result of: *reformation.* Also *-ion, -tion.* [< F *-ation* or L *-atio, -ationis*]

-ative *suffix* Denoting relation, tendency, or characteristic: *remunerative.* [< F *-atif*, masc., *-ative*, fem. or < L *-ativus*]

At·lan·tic (at·lan′tik) *adj.* Of, near, in, or pertaining to the Atlantic Ocean. [< L < Gk. *Atlantikos* pertaining to Atlas]

Atlantic Charter A statement issued in August, 1941, by Churchill and Roosevelt, setting forth the basic aims of the Allied Nations for the peace after World War II.

At·lan·tis (at·lan′tis) A mythical island west of Gibraltar, said by Plato to have been engulfed by the sea.

at·las (at′ləs) *n.* **1.** A volume of maps usu. bound together. **2.** Any book of tables or charts on a given subject.

At·las (at′ləs) *n.* **1.** In Greek mythology, a Titan who supported the heavens on his shoulders. **2.** An intercontinental ballistic missile of the U.S. Air Force.

at·man (ät′mən) *n.* In Hinduism, the soul; the divine life principle in man. **— Atman** The supreme soul, the source and goal of all individual souls. [< Skt.]

atmo- *combining form* Vapor. [< Gk. *atmos*]

at·mos·phere (at′məs·fir) *n.* **1.** The body of gases surrounding the earth or a celestial body. **2.** The particular climatic condition of any place or region. **3.** Any surrounding or pervasive element or influence. **4.** *Informal* A quality regarded as especially characteristic or interesting: This café has *atmosphere.* **5.** *Physics* A unit of pressure, equal to 14.69 pounds per square inch. [< NL < Gk. *atmos* vapor + *sphaira* sphere]

at·mos·pher·ic (at′məs·fer′ik) *adj.* **1.** Of or in the atmosphere. **2.** Dependent on or resulting from the atmosphere. Also **at′mos·pher′i·cal.** **— at′mos·pher′i·cal·ly** *adv.*

at·mos·pher·ics (at′məs·fer′iks) *n.pl.* (*construed as sing.*) In radio transmission, static.

at·oll (at′ôl, -ol, ə·tol′) *n.* A ring-shaped coral island and i associated reef, nearly or completely enclosing a lagoon. [< Malayalam *adal* closing, uniting]

a·tom (at′əm) *n.* **1.** *Chem.* The smallest part of an element capable of existing alone or in combination, and that cannot be changed or destroyed in any chemical reaction. **2.** *Physics* One of the particles of which all matter is formed, regarded as an aggregate of nucleons and electrons variously organized within and around a central nucleus, and exhibiting complex mass-energy characteristics. **3.** A hypothetical entity admitting of no division into smaller parts. **4.** The smallest quantity or particle; iota. [< L < Gk. < *a-* not + *temnein* to cut]

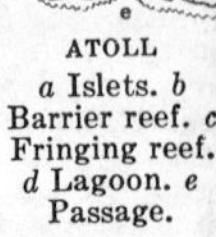

ATOLL
a Islets. *b* Barrier reef. *c* Fringing reef. *d* Lagoon. *e* Passage.

a·tom·ic (ə·tom′ik) *adj.* **1.** Of or pertaining to an atom atoms. Also **a·tom′i·cal.** **2.** Very minute; infinitesima **— a·tom′i·cal·ly** *adv.*

atomic age The era characterized by the use and growir importance of atomic energy.

atomic bomb A bomb of formidable destructive power u ing the energy released by the fission of atomic nuclei, es those of radioactive elements, as uranium: also called *bomb.* Also **atom bomb.**

atomic clock A high-precision instrument for the measur ment of time by the vibration rate of suitable molecules.

atomic energy The energy contained within the nucleus the atom, esp. when made available for human use by co trolled nuclear fission or thermonuclear reactions.

atomic number *Physics* A number that represents the un positive charges (protons) in the atomic nucleus of each el ment and corresponds to the number of extranuclear ele trons. Hydrogen is assigned an atomic number of 1.

atomic power Atomic energy as a source of power.

atomic reactor Reactor (def. 4).

a·tom·ics (ə·tom′iks) *n.pl.* (*construed as sing.*) Nucle physics, esp. in its practical applications.

atomic structure *Physics* The conception of the atom a system of particles consisting of a central positive nucle and a cluster of negatively charged electrons, the numb and arrangement of the particles determining the energy rel tions within and between atoms.

atomic theory **1.** *Chem.* The doctrine that elements uni with one another, atom by atom, and in definite simple pr portions by weight. **2.** *Physics* The modern concept of ator ic structure as a complex of mass-energy relationships.

atomic weight *Chem.* **a** Since 1961, the weight of an ato of an element relative to that of an atom of carbon, taken 12. **b** Formerly, the weight of an atom of an element relati to that of an atom of oxygen, taken as 16.

at·om·ize (at′əm·īz) *v.t.* **·ized, ·iz·ing** **1.** To reduce atoms. **2.** To spray or reduce to a spray, as by an atomiz Also *Brit.* **at′om·ise.** **— at′om·i·za′tion** *n.*

at·om·iz·er (at′əm·ī′zər) *n.* An apparatus for reducing liquid, esp. medicine or perfume, to a spray.

atom smasher *Physics* An accelerator.

a·to·nal (ā·tō′nəl) *adj. Music* Without tonality; lacking k or tonal center. **— a·to′nal·ly** *adv.*

a·to·nal·i·ty (ā′tō·nal′ə·tē) *n. Music* The use of a syste of tones, especially the chromatic scale, so that each tone equal in its relation to the others and no one tone holds a ce tral or primary position; absence of key or tonal center.

a·tone (ə·tōn′) *v.i.* **a·toned, a·ton·ing** To make expiatio as for sin or wrongdoing. [< earlier adverbial phrase *at o* in accord, short for *to set at one*, i.e., reconcile] **— a·ton′ ble** or **a·tone′a·ble** *adj.* **— a·ton′er** *n.*

a·tone·ment (ə·tōn′mənt) *n.* **1.** Satisfaction, reparation, expiation made for wrong or injury. **2.** *Usually cap. The* The reconciliation between God and man effected by Chris

a·ton·ic (ə·ton′ik, ā-) *adj.* **1.** Not accented, as a word or sy lable. **2.** Lacking tone or vigor. [< Med.L < Gk. < not + *teinein* to stretch]

a·top (ə·top′) *adv. & adj.* On or at the top. **—** *prep. Chie U.S.* On the top of.

-ator *suffix of nouns* An agent; doer; actor; one who or th which: *arbitrator, mediator.* [< L]

-atory *suffix of adjectives* Characterized by; producing produced by: *conciliatory.* [< L *-atorius*, adj. suffix]

at·ra·bil·ious (at′rə·bil′yəs) *adj.* Disposed to hypocho dria; melancholy; splenetic. Also **at′ra·bil′i·ar** (-bil′ē·ə [< L *atra bilis* black bile] **— at′ra·bil′ious·ness** *n.*

a·tri·um (ā′trē·əm) *n. pl.* **a·tri·a** (ā′trē·ə) **1.** The entran hall or central open court of an ancient Roman house. **2.** court or hall. **3.** *Anat.* One of the upper chambers of t heart: also called *auricle.* [< L, a hall] **— a′tri·al** *adj.*

a·tro·cious (ə·trō′shəs) *adj.* **1.** Very wicked, cruel, etc. *Informal* Very bad, or in bad taste. [< L *atrox, atro* harsh, cruel] **— a·tro′cious·ly** *adv.* **— a·tro′cious·ness**

a·troc·i·ty (ə·tros′ə·tē) *n. pl.* **·ties** **1.** The state or quali f being atrocious. **2.** An atrocious deed or act. **3.** *Infor-ɩal.* Something in very bad taste.

·ro·phy (at′rə·fē) *n. pl.* **·phies** *Pathol.* A wasting or ailure in development of the body or any of its parts. **— v. ·phied, ·phy·ing** *v.t.* **1.** To cause to waste away or wither. **—** *v.i.* **2.** To waste away; wither. [< F < L < Gk. < *a-* ot + *trephein* to nourish] **— a·troph·ic** (ə·trof′ik) *adj.* **— at′ro·phied** *adj.*

·ro·pine (at′rə·pēn, -pin) *n.* A crystalline, poisonous alka-ɔid, $C_{17}H_{23}O_3N$, found in the deadly nightshade and in cer-ain other plants, used as an antispasmodic and to enlarge he pupil of the eye. Also **at′ro·pin** (-pin). [See ATROPOS.]

:·ro·pos (at′rə·pos) One of the three Fates. [< Gk., in-exible < *a-* not + *trepein* to turn]

·tach (ə·tach′) *v.t.* **1.** To make fast to something; fasten n; affix. **2.** To join on as a part or adjunct. **3.** To add or ppend, as a signature. **4.** To connect by personal ties, as f affection. **5.** To ascribe: with *to.* **6.** To appoint offi-ally; assign. **7.** *Law* To secure for legal jurisdiction; seize y legal process: to *attach* an employee's salary. **—** *v.i.* **8.** 'o be attached; connect. [< OF < *a-* to + *tache* nail] **— t·tach′a·ble** *adj.*

·ta·ché (at′ə·shā′, *esp. Brit.* ə·tash′ā) *n.* A person official-ʳ attached to a diplomatic mission or staff in a specified ca-acity: military *attaché.* [< F, pp. of *attacher* to attach]

taché case A boxlike hinged briefcase.

·tach·ment (ə·tach′mənt) *n.* **1.** The act of attaching, or ne state of being attached. **2.** A bond; band; tie. **3.** Affec-on; devoted regard. **4.** An appendage or adjunct. **5.** *Law* eizure of a person or property.

·tack (ə·tak′) *v.t.* **1.** To set upon violently; begin battle ʳ conflict with. **2.** To assail with hostile words; criticize. . To begin work on; set about, as an undertaking. **4.** To egin to affect injuriously. **—** *v.i.* **5.** To make an attack; egin battle. **—** *n.* **1.** The act of attacking; assault; onset. . The first movement toward any undertaking. **3.** A izure, as by disease. [< F, ult. < same source as ATTACH] **— Syn.** (verb) **1.** *Attack* is applied loosely to any offensive :tion, but strictly means to begin hostilities. *Assault* always ggests close physical contact and extreme violence. To *assail* to belabor with repeated words or blows. **—** (noun) **1.** assault, ıslaught, onset, invasion, incursion, raid.

·tain (ə·tān′) *v.t.* **1.** To gain by exertion of body or ind; achieve. **2.** To come to, as in time; arrive at: He *at-ined* old age. **— to attain to** To arrive at with effort; suc-ed in reaching. [< OF < L < *ad-* to + *tangere* to touch]

·tain·a·ble (ə·tā′nə·bəl) *adj.* That can be attained. **— t·tain′a·bil′i·ty, at·tain′a·ble ness** *n.*

·tain·der (ə·tān′dər) *n.* The loss of all civil rights con-equent to a sentence of death or of outlawry for a capital ffense. **— bill of attainder** Formerly, a legislative act in-icting attainder upon a person guilty of a capital offense. < OF *ataindre* to attain, strike]

tain·ment (ə·tān′mənt) *n.* **1.** The act of attaining. **2.** hat which is attained; an acquisition, as of skill.

·taint (ə·tānt′) *v.t.* **1.** To inflict attainder upon; condemn. . To touch or affect injuriously; disgrace; taint. **—** *n.* . Imputation; stigma. **2.** Attainder. [See ATTAIN.]

·tar (at′ər) *n.* The fragrant essential oil extracted from ne petals of flowers, esp. roses. [< Arabic *itr* perfume]

·tempt (ə·tempt′) *v.t.* **1.** To make an effort to do or ac-omplish; try. **2.** To try to take by force; attack: to *attempt* ne life of someone. **—** *n.* **1.** A putting forth of effort; a ial; endeavor. **2.** An attack; assault. [< OF < L < *ad-* ɔward + *tendere* to stretch] **— at·tempt′a·bil′i·ty** *n.* **— t·tempt′a·ble** *adj.* **— at·tempt′er** *n.*

·tend (ə·tend′) *v.t.* **1.** To be present at, as a meeting. **2.** 'o wait upon or go with as an attendant; escort. **3.** To visit ʳ minister to (a sick person). **4.** To accompany as a result. . To give heed to; listen to. **—** *v.i.* **6.** To be present. **7.** 'o give heed; listen. **— to attend to 1.** To apply oneself to. . To take care of; tend to. [< OF < L < *ad-* toward + *ndere* to stretch]

·ten·dance (ə·ten′dəns) *n.* **1.** The act of attending. **2.** 'hose who attend; an audience or retinue.

·ten·dant (ə·ten′dənt) *n.* **1.** One who attends, esp. as a ervant. **2.** One who is present. **3.** A concomitant; conse-uence. **—** *adj.* Following or accompanying.

·ten·tion (ə·ten′shən) *n.* **1.** Close or earnest attending. . The power or faculty of mental concentration. **3.** Prac-ical consideration; care: *attention* to one's appearance. **4.** *'su. pl.* Acts of courtesy, esp. on the part of a lover. **5.** *Mil.* 'he prescribed position of readiness: to stand at *attention;* lso, the order to take this position.

·ten·tive (ə·ten′tiv) *adj.* **1.** Observant. **2.** Courteous or allant. **— at·ten′tive·ly** *adv.* **— at·ten′tive·ness** *n.*

·ten·u·ate (*v.* ə·ten′yōō·āt; *adj.* ə·ten′yōō·it) *v.* **·at·ed, ·at·ıg** *v.t.* **1.** To make thin, small, or fine; draw out, as a wire. **2.** To weaken; lessen. **3.** To reduce in density; rarefy, as a liquid or gas. **4.** *Bacteriol.* To weaken the virulence of (a microorganism). **—** *v.i.* **5.** To become thin, weak, rarefied, etc. **—** *adj.* Attenuated. [< L < *ad-* (intensive) + *tenuare* to make thin] **— at·ten′u·a·ble** *adj.*

at·ten·u·a·tion (ə·ten′yōō·ā′shən) *n.* The act or process of attenuating, or the state of being attenuated.

at·test (ə·test′) *v.t.* **1.** To confirm as accurate, true, or gen-uine; vouch for. **2.** To certify, as by signature or oath. **3.** To be proof of. **4.** To put upon oath. **—** *v.i.* **5.** To bear witness; testify: with *to.* **—** *n.* Attestation. [< MF < L < *ad-* to + *testari* to bear witness]

at·tes·ta·tion (at′es·tā′shən) *n.* **1.** The act of attesting. **2.** Testimony.

at·tic (at′ik) *n.* **1.** A low story beneath the roof of a build-ing; a garret. **2.** *Archit.* A low structure, above a cornice or entablature. [< F < L *Atticus,* architectural term]

At·tic (at′ik) *adj.* **1.** Of Attica. **2.** Of or characteristic of Athens or the Athenians. **3.** Simple and graceful; delicate; refined: also **at′tic.** **—** *n.* The dialect of Attica. [< L < Gk. *Attikē* Attica]

At·ti·ca (at′i·kə) In ancient times, the region of Greece sur-rounding Athens.

Attic salt Delicate, refined, graceful wit. Also **Attic wit.**

at·tire (ə·tīr′) *v.t.* **·tired, ·tir·ing** To dress; array; adorn. **—** *n.* Dress or clothing. [< OF *atirer* to arrange, adorn]

at·ti·tude (at′ə·tōōd, -tyōōd) *n.* **1.** Position of the body, as suggesting some thought or feeling. **2.** State of mind, behavior, or conduct regarding some matter, as indicating opinion or purpose. [< F < Ital. < LL < L *aptus* fitted, suited] **— at·ti·tu·di·nal** (at′ə·tōō′də·nəl, -tyōō′-) *adj.*

at·ti·tu·di·nize (at′ə·tōō′də·nīz, -tyōō′-) *v.i.* **·nized, ·niz·ing** To take a pose for effect. Also *Brit.* **at′ti·tu′di·nise.**

atto- *combining form* One quintillionth (10^{-18}) of a specific quantity or dimension.

at·tor·ney (ə·tûr′nē) *n.* A person empowered by another to act in his stead; esp., a lawyer. **— by attorney** By proxy. [< OF *atorner* to turn to, appoint] **— at·tor′ney·ship** *n.*

attorney at law A lawyer.

attorney general *pl.* **attorneys general, attorney generals** The chief law officer of a government. Abbr. *A.G., Atty. Gen.*

at·tract (ə·trakt′) *v.t.* **1.** To draw to or cause to come near by some physical force, as magnetism. **2.** To draw, as the admiration or attention of. **—** *v.i.* **3.** To exert attractive influence. [< L < *ad-* toward + *trahere* to draw, drag] **— at·tract′a·ble** *adj.* **— at·tract′a·ble·ness, at·tract′a·bil′i·ty** *n.* **— at·trac′tile** *adj.* **— at·trac′tor** or **at·tract′er** *n.*

at·trac·tion (ə·trak′shən) *n.* **1.** The act or power of attract-ing. **2.** Attractive quality or characteristic; enticement; charm. **3.** Something that attracts. **4.** *Physics* A force that, exerted between or among bodies, tends to make them approach each other or prevents their separating.

at·trac·tive (ə·trak′tiv) *adj.* **1.** Pleasing; winning; charm-ing. **2.** Having the power to attract. **— at·trac′tive·ly** *adv.* **— at·trac′tive·ness** *n.*

at·trib·ute (ə·trib′yōōt) *v.t.* **·ut·ed, ·ut·ing** To ascribe as belonging to or resulting from: to *attribute* wisdom to old age. **— at·tri·bute** (at′rə·byōōt) *n.* **1.** A quality or characteristic of a person or thing. **2.** *Gram.* An adjective or its equivalent. **3.** In art and mythology, a distinctive mark or symbol. [< L < *ad-* to + *tribuere* to allot, give over] **— at·trib′ut·a·ble** *adj.* **— at·trib′u·ter** or **at·trib′u·tor** *n.*

— Syn. (verb) *Attribute, impute,* and *ascribe* are largely inter-changeable, but usually we *attribute* good things, *impute* bad, and *ascribe* either. We usually *assign* or *refer* a thing to a category, as time, place, cause, etc., rather than to a person.

at·tri·bu·tion (at′rə·byōō′shən) *n.* **1.** The act of attribut-ing. **2.** An ascribed characteristic or quality; attribute.

at·trib·u·tive (ə·trib′yə·tiv) *adj.* **1.** Pertaining to or of the nature of an attribute. **2.** Ascribed, as a work of art: an *attributive* Vermeer. **3.** *Gram.* Designating an adjective or its equivalent that stands before the noun it modifies. **—** *n.* *Gram.* An attributive word or phrase. **— at·trib′u·tive·ly** *adj.* **— at·trib′u·tive·ness** *n.*

at·tri·tion (ə·trish′ən) *n.* **1.** A rubbing out or grinding down, as by friction. **2.** A gradual wearing down or weakening. [< L < *ad-* to, against + *terere* to rub]

at·tune (ə·tōōn′, ə·tyōōn′) *v.t.* **·tuned, ·tun·ing 1.** To bring into accord; harmonize. **2.** To tune.

a·typ·i·cal (ā·tip′i·kəl) *adj.* Not typical; differing from the type; irregular. Also **a·typ′ic.** **— a·typ′i·cal·ly** *adv.*

au·burn (ô′bûrn) *adj. & n.* Reddish brown. [< OF < LL < L *albus* white; infl. in meaning by ME *brun* brown]

au cou·rant (ō kōō·räṅ′) *French* Up to date; well informed.

auc·tion (ôk′shən) *n.* **1.** A public sale in which the price is increased by bids until the highest bidder becomes the pur-chaser. **2.** The bidding in bridge. **—** *v.t.* To sell by or at auction: usually with *off.* [< L *augere* to increase]

auction bridge A variety of the game of bridge in which tricks made by the declarer in excess of the contract count toward game. Compare CONTRACT BRIDGE.

auc·tion·eer (ôk′shən·ir′) *n.* One who conducts an auction, usu. as a business. — *v.t.* To sell at aucton.

au·da·cious (ô·dā′shəs) *adj.* **1.** Showing no fear; daring; bold. **2.** Shameless; impudent. [< L *audere* to dare + -OUS] — **au·da′cious·ly** *adv.* — **au·da′cious·ness** *n.*

au·dac·i·ty (ô·das′ə·tē) *n.* **1.** Boldness; daring. **2.** Impudence; shamelessness. — **Syn.** See TEMERITY.

au·di·ble (ô′də·bəl) *adj.* Perceptible by the ear; loud enough to be heard. [< Med.L < L *audire* to hear] — **au′di·bil′i·ty, au′di·ble·ness** *n.* — **au′di·bly** *adv.*

au·di·ence (ô′dē·əns) *n.* **1.** An assembly of listeners or spectators, as at a concert. **2.** Those who are reached by a book, television program, etc. **3.** A formal hearing, interview, or conference. **4.** Opportunity to be heard. [<OF < L *audire* to hear]

au·di·o (ô′dē·ō) *adj.* **1.** Of or pertaining to characteristics associated with sound waves. **2.** *Electronics* Designating devices used in transmission or reception of sound waves: in television, distinguished from *video.* [< L *audire* to hear]

audio- *combining form* Pertaining to hearing: Also **audi-.** [< L *audire* to hear]

audio frequency *Physics* A frequency of electrical, sound, or other wave vibrations within the range of normal human hearing, or from about 20 to 20,000 cycles a second.

au·di·o·vis·u·al aids (ô′dē·ō·vizh′ōō·əl) Motion pictures, photographs, recordings, etc., used as teaching devices.

au·dit (ô′dit) *v.t.* **1.** To examine, adjust, and certify, as accounts. **2.** *U.S.* To attend (a college course) as a listener and without earning credit. — *v.i.* **2.** To make an audit. — *n.* **1.** An examination of an accounting document and of the evidence in support of its correctness. **2.** A final statement of such an account. **3.** An adjustment and settling of accounts. [< L *audire* to hear]

au·di·tion (ô·dish′ən) *n.* **1.** The act or sense of hearing. **2.** A test or hearing, as of an actor or singer. — *v.t.* & *v.i.* To give an audition. [< L *audire* to hear]

au·di·tor (ô′də·tər) *n.* **1.** One who audits accounts. **2.** A listener. **3.** *U.S.* One who audits classes [< L]

au·di·to·ri·um (ô′də·tôr′ē·əm, -tō′rē·əm) *n.* *pl.* **·to·ri·ums** or **·to·ri·a** (-tôr′ē·ə, -tō′rē·ə) **1.** The room or part of a school, church, theater, etc., occupied by the audience. **2.** A building for concerts, public meetings, etc. [< L, lecture room]

au·di·to·ry (ô′də·tôr′ē, -tō′rē) *adj.* Of or pertaining to hearing or the organs or sense of hearing. — *n.* *pl.* **·ries** **1.** An audience. **2.** The nave of a church. [< L *audire* to hear]

auditory canal *Anat.* The passage leading from the auricle to the tympanic membrane. For illustration see EAR.

auf Wie·der·seh·en (ouf vē′dər·zā′ən) *German* Till we meet again; good-by for now.

Au·ge·an stables (ô·jē′ən) In Greek mythology, the stables that were cleaned in a day by Hercules.

au·gend (ô′jend) *n.* *Math.* A number to which another is to be added. See ADDEND. [< L *augere* to increase]

au·ger (ô′gər) *n.* Any of various tools for boring wood. [OE *nafugār,* < *nafu* nave of a wheel + *gār* borer, spear]

aught[1] (ôt) *n.* Anything; any part or item. — *adv.* By any chance; at all. [OE *āwiht, ōwiht* < *ā* ever + *wiht* thing]

aught[2] (ôt) *n.* The figure 0; cipher; a naught; nothing. [*a naught* taken as *an aught*]

aug·ment (*v.* ôg·ment′; *n.* ôg′ment) *v.t.* **1.** To make greater, as in size, number, or amount; enlarge; intensify. — *v.i.* **2.** To become greater, as in size. — **Syn.** See INCREASE. — *n.* Increase; enlargement. [< F < L *augere* to increase] — **aug·ment′a·ble** *adj.*

aug·men·ta·tion (ôg′men·tā′shən) *n.* **1.** The act of augmenting, or the state of being augmented. **2.** An addition.

aug·men·ta·tive (ôg·men′tə·tiv) *adj.* **1.** Having the quality or power of augmenting. **2.** *Gram.* Denoting greater size or intensity, as a suffix. — *n.* *Gram.* An augmentative form. Also **aug·men′tive.** Abbr. *aug.*

aug·ment·er (ôg·men′tər) *n.* One who or that which augments. **2.** *Aeron.* Afterburner.

au gra·tin (ō grät′n, grat′n; *Fr.* ō grȧ·taṅ′) Sprinkled with bread crumbs or grated cheese and baked until brown. [< F]

au·gur (ô′gər, -gyər) *n.* A prophet; soothsayer. — *v.t.* & *v.i.* **1.** To prophesy. **2.** To betoken; be an omen of. [< L *augere* to increase] — **au′gu·ral** *adj.*

au·gu·ry (ô′gyə·rē) *n.* *pl.* **·ries** **1.** The art or practice of divination. **2.** A portent or omen.

au·gust (ô·gust′) *adj.* Inspiring awe, admiration, or reverence; majestic; imposing. [< L *augere* to increase, exalt] — **au·gust′ly** *adv.* — **au·gust′ness** *n.*

Au·gust (ô′gəst) *n.* The eighth month of the year, containing 31 days. Abbr. *Ag., Aug, Aug.* [< L *Augustus Caesar*]

Au·gus·tan (ô·gus′tən) *adj.* **1.** Of or pertaining to Augustus Caesar or to his times. **2.** Pertaining to any similar era. — *n.* A writer or artist of an Augustan age.

Augustan age **1.** The period of the reign of Augustus Caesar, the golden age of Roman literature. **2.** A similar perio[d] in English literature during the reign of Queen Anne.

auk (ôk) *n.* A short-winged, web-footed diving bird [of] northern seas; the **razor-billed auk** of the North Atlantic. [< ON *ālka*]

auld lang syne (ōld′ lang sīn′, zīn′) *Scot.* Literally, old long since; long ago.

au na·tu·rel (ō nȧ·tü·rel′) *French* **1.** Plainly cooked; ungarnished. **2.** In the natural condition; nude.

aunt (ant, änt) *n.* A sister of one's father or mother, or the wife of one's uncle. [< OF *aunte, ante*]

au pair (ō pâr) *Chiefly Brit.* **1.** An arrangement whereby one receives room and board in a foreign household in exchange for doing certain chores, as caring for children: often used attributively: *au pair* girls. **2.** *Informal* An au pair girl. [< F, lit., at par, even (with)]

RAZOR–BILLED AUK (About 16 inches high)

au·ra (ôr′ə) *n.* *pl.* **au·ras** or **au·rae** (ôr′ē) **1.** An invisible emanation or exhalation. **2.** A distincti[ve] air or quality enveloping or characterizing a person or thin[g]. **3.** *Pathol.* The sensory, motor, or psychic manifestatio[n] preceding an epileptic attack or other paroxysm. [< breeze < Gk. *aurē* breath] — **au′ral** *adj.*

au·ral (ôr′əl) *adj.* Pertaining to the ear or the sense [of] hearing; auricular. [< L *auris* ear + -AL]

au·re·ate (ôr′ē·it) *adj.* **1.** Of the color of gold; golden. Splendid. [< L *aureus* < *aurum* gold]

au·re·ole (ôr′ē·ōl) *n.* **1.** In art, a halo. **2.** Any radiance halo around a body. Also **au·re·o·la** (ô·rē′ə·lə). [< *aureola (corona)* golden (crown) < *aurum* gold]

Au·re·o·my·cin (ôr′ē·ō·mī′sin) *n.* Proprietary name for type of antibiotic. Also **au′re·o·my′cin.** [< L *aureus* gold + Gk. *mykes* fungus]

au re·voir (ō rə·vwȧr′) *French* Good-by; till we meet agai[n]

au·ri·cle (ôr′i·kəl) *n.* **1.** *Anat.* **a** An atrium of the hea[rt] **b** The external ear; pinna. **2.** An ear-shaped part. [< *auricula,* dim. of *auris* ear] — **au′ri·cled** *adj.*

au·ric·u·lar (ô·rik′yə·lər) *adj.* **1.** Of or pertaining to the e[ar] or the sense of hearing. **2.** Intended for the ear. **3.** Ea[r-] shaped. **4.** Of or pertaining to an auricle.

au·rif·er·ous (ô·rif′ər·əs) *adj.* Containing gold. [< L *aurum* gold + *ferre* to bear]

au·ri·form (ôr′ə·fôrm) *adj.* Ear-shaped.

Au·ri·ga (ô·rī′gə) *n.* A constellation, the Charioteer or Wa[g]oner, containing the bright star Capella. [< L]

au·ro·ra (ô·rôr′ə, ô·rō′rə) *n.* **1.** *Meteorol.* A display of ar[cs,] bands, streamers, etc., of light occasionally seen in the sk[y] of polar latitudes. **2.** The dawn. [< L, dawn]

Au·ro·ra (ô·rôr′ə, ô·rō′rə) In Roman mythology, the go[d]dess of the dawn: identified with the Greek *Eos.*

aurora aus·tra·lis (ôs·trā′lis) *Meteorol.* The aurora se[en] in far southern latitudes: also called *southern lights.* [< N[L,] southern aurora < L *auster* south wind]

aurora bo·re·al·is (bôr′ē·al′is, -ā′lis, bō′rē-) *Meteorol.* T[he] aurora seen in high northern latitudes: also called *northe[rn] lights.* [< NL, northern aurora < Gk. *boreas* north win[d]

au·ro·ral (ô·rôr′əl, ô·rō′rəl) *adj.* **1.** Pertaining to or like t[he] dawn; roseate. **2.** *Meteorol.* Of, like, or caused by an auro[ra]

au·rum (ôr′əm) *n.* Gold. [< L]

aus·cul·tate (ôs′kəl·tāt) *v.t.* & *v.i.* **·tat·ed, ·tat·ing** *Med.* examine by auscultation. [< L *auscultare* to listen, give [ear] to] — **aus′cul·ta′tor** *n.*

aus·cul·ta·tion (ôs′kəl·tā′shən) *n.* **1.** *Med.* The act of l[is]tening, as with a stethoscope. **2.** A listening.

aus·pice (ôs′pis) *n.* *pl.* **aus·pi·ces** (ôs′pə·sēz) **1.** *Usu.* Patronage. **2.** An omen, or sign. [< F < L *auspex*]

aus·pi·cious (ôs·pish′əs) *adj.* **1.** Of good omen; propitio[us] **2.** Prosperous; fortunate. — **Syn.** See PROPITIOUS. **aus·pi′cious·ly** *adv.* — **aus–pi′cious·ness** *n.*

aus·tere (ô·stir′) *adj.* **1.** Severe, grave, or stern, as in asp[ect] or conduct. **2.** Morally strict; abstemious; ascetic. **3.** So[ur] and astringent. **4.** Severely simple; unadorned. [< OF L < Gk. *austēros* harsh, bitter] — **aus·tere′ly** *adv.*

aus·ter·i·ty (ô·ster′ə·tē) *n.* *pl.* **·ties** **1.** The quality of [be]ing austere; severity of demeanor, way of life, etc.: also **a[us]tere′ness.** **2.** *Usually pl.* Severe or ascetic acts.

aus·tral (ôs′trəl) *adj.* Southern; torrid. [< L southern *auster* south wind]

Aus·tral·a·sian (ôs′tral·ā′zhən, -ā′shən) *n.* A native inhabitant of Australasia. — *adj.* Of Australasia.

Aus·tral·ian (ô·strāl′yən) *n.* A native or naturalized [in]habitant of Australia. — *adj.* Of or pertaining to Austra[lia] or to its people.

Australian English The English language as spoken a[nd] written in Australia.

Aus·tri·an (ôs′trē·ən) *n.* An inhabitant or citizen of A[us]tria. — *adj.* Of Austria or its people.

Austro- *combining form* **1.** Austrian. **2.** Australian.

us·tro·ne·sian (ôs′trō·nē′zhən, -shən) *adj.* Of or pertaining to Austronesia, its inhabitants, or their languages. — *n.* A family of languages of the Pacific comprising the Indonesian, Oceanic (including Melanesian and Micronesian), and Polynesian subfamilies. Also *Malayo-Polynesian.*
ut- Var. of AUTO-[1].
u·tar·chy (ô′tär·kē) *n.* *pl.* **·chies 1.** Absolute rule or sovereignty, or a country under such rule. **2.** Self-government. **3.** Autarky. [< Gk. < *autos* self + *archein* to rule] — **au·tar·chic** (ô·tär′kik) or **·chi·cal** *adj.*
u·tar·ky (ô′tär·kē) *n.* National economic self-sufficiency. [< Gk. *autarkeia* self-sufficiency] — **au·tar·kik** (ô·tär′kik) or **·ki·kal** *adj.*
u·then·tic (ô·then′tik) *adj.* **1.** Authoritative; reliable. **2.** Of undisputed origin; genuine. **3.** *Law* Duly executed before the proper officer. Also **au·then′ti·cal.** [< OF < L < Gk. < *authentēs* the doer of a deed] — **au·then′ti·cal·ly** *adv.*
— **Syn. 1.** true, veritable. **2.** real, legitimate, authorized, accredited. — **Ant.** spurious, counterfeit, fictitious, false.
u·then·ti·cate (ô·then′ti·kāt) *v.t.* **·cat·ed, ·cat·ing 1.** To make authentic or authoritative. **2.** To give legal validity to. **3.** To establish the authenticity of. — **au·then′ti·ca′·tion** *n.* — **au·then′ti·ca′tor** *n.*
u·then·tic·i·ty (ô′thən·tis′ə·tē) *n.* The state or quality of being authentic, authoritative, or genuine.
u·thor (ô′thər) *n.* **1.** The writer of a book, treatise, etc.; also, one who makes literary composition his profession. **2.** One who begins or originates; creator. **3.** An author's writings collectively. — *v.t. Informal* To be the author of; write. [< AF < L *auctor* originator, producer] — **au′thor·ess** *n.fem.* — **au·tho·ri·al** (ô·thôr′ē·əl, ô·thō′rē-) *adj.*
u·thor·i·tar·i·an (ə·thôr′ə·târ′ē·ən, ə·thor′-) *adj.* Favoring subjection to authority as opposed to individual freedom. — *n.* One who favors the principle of authority. — **au·thor′i·tar′i·an·ism** *n.*
u·thor·i·ta·tive (ə·thôr′ə·tā′tiv, ə·thor′-) *adj.* **1.** Possessing or proceeding from proper authority; duly sanctioned. **2.** Exercising authority; commanding; dictatorial. — **au·thor′i·ta′tive·ly** *adv.* — **au·thor′i·ta′tive·ness** *n.*
u·thor·i·ty (ə·thôr′ə·tē, ə·thor′-) *n.* *pl.* **·ties 1.** The right to command and to enforce obedience; the right to act, decide, etc. **2.** Delegated right or power; authorization. **3.** *pl.* Those having the power to govern or command. **4.** Title to respect, confidence, etc.; personal influence. **5.** A person, volume, etc., appealed to in support of action or belief. **6.** One who has special knowledge; an expert. **7.** An official or group having administrative control in a specified area. **8.** An authoritative opinion, decision, or precedent. Abbr. *auth.* [< OF < L < *augere* to increase]
u·thor·ize (ô′thə·rīz) *v.t.* **·ized, ·iz·ing 1.** To confer authority upon; empower; commission. **2.** To warrant; justify. **3.** To sanction. [< OF < Med.L < L *auctor* originator] — **au′thor·i·za′tion** *n.* — **au′thor·iz′er** *n.*
u·thor·ized (ô′thə·rīzd) *adj.* **1.** Endowed with authority; accepted as authoritative. **2.** Formally or legally sanctioned.
u·thor·ship (ô′thər·ship) *n.* **1.** The profession or occupation of an author. **2.** Origin or source.
u·to (ô′tō) *U.S. Informal n.* An automobile. — *v.i.* **au·toed, au·to·ing** To ride in or travel by an automobile.
uto-[1] *combining form* **1.** Arising from some process or action within the object; not induced by any stimulus from without; as in:

autoagglutination	**autodiffusion**	**autoinduction**

2. Acting, acted, or directed upon the self; as in:

autoanalysis	**autodiagnosis**	**autolavage**

Also, before vowels, *aut-*. [< Gk. *autos* self]
uto-[2] *combining form* Self-propelled. [< Gk. *autos* self]
u·to·bi·og·ra·phy (ô′tə·bī·og′rə·fē, -bē·og′-) *n.* *pl.* **·phies** The story of a person's life written by that person. — **au′to·bi·og′ra·pher** *n.* — **au·to·bi·o·graph·ic** (ô′tə·bī′ə·graf′ik) or **·cal** *adj.* — **au′to·bi′o·graph′i·cal·ly** *adv.*
u·to·clave (ô′tə·klāv) *n.* **1.** An enclosed chamber for the sterilization of drugs, vaccines, instruments, etc. **2.** A pressure cooker. [< F < *auto-* self + L *clavis* a key]
u·toc·ra·cy (ô·tok′rə·sē) *n.* *pl.* **·cies 1.** Absolute government by an individual; rule or authority of an autocrat. **2.** A state ruled by an autocrat.
u·to·crat (ô′tə·krat) *n.* **1.** A supreme ruler of unrestricted power. **2.** An arrogant, dictatorial person. [< F < Gk. < *autos* self + *kratos* power] — **au′to·crat′ic** or **·i·cal** *adj.* — **au′to·crat′i·cal·ly** *adv.*
u·to-da-fé (ô′tō·də·fā′, ou′-) *n.* *pl.* **au·tos-da-fé** (ô′tōz-, ou′tōz-) The public announcement and execution of a sentence of the Inquisition; esp., the burning of heretics at the stake. [< Pg., lit., act of the faith]
u·tog·e·nous (ô·toj′ə·nəs) *adj.* Self-produced or self-generated. Also **au·to·gen·ic** (ô′tō·jen′ik). [< Gk. *autogenēs* self-produced]

au·to·gi·ro (ô′tō·jī′rō) *n.* *pl.* **·ros** An airplane that is supported in the air chiefly by freely-turning rotors but is drawn forward by a conventional propeller. Also **au′to·gy′ro.** [< AUTO-[1] + Gk. *gyros* a circle]
au·to·graph (ô′tə·graf, -gräf) *n.* **1.** One's own signature or handwriting. **2.** A manuscript in the author's handwriting. — *v.t.* **1.** To write one's name in or affix one's signature to. **2.** To write in one's own handwriting. — *adj.* Written by one's own hand, as a will. [< L < Gk. < *autos* self + *graphein* to write] — **au′to·graph′ic** or **·i·cal** *adj.* — **au′to·graph′i·cal·ly** *adv.*
au·to·in·tox·i·ca·tion (ô′tō·in·tok′sə·kā′shən) *n.* Poisoning from noxious secretions of one's own body.
au·to·mat (ô′tə·mat) *n.* *U.S.* A restaurant in which food is automatically made available from a receptacle when coins are deposited in a slot alongside.
au·to·mate (ô′tə·māt) **·mat·ed, ·mat·ing** *v.t.* To adapt, as a machine, factory, or process, for automation. [Back formation < AUTOMATION]
au·to·mat·ic (ô′tə·mat′ik) *adj.* **1.** Acting from forces inherent in itself; self-moving. **2.** Self-acting and self-regulating, as machinery; mechanical. **3.** *Psychol.* Done from force of habit or without volition. **4.** Of firearms, extracting and ejecting the empty case and chambering the next round, using the force of recoil or of part of the exploding gas, and firing continuously until the trigger is released. Also (*except for def. 4*) **au′to·mat′i·cal, au·tom·a·tous** (ô·tom′ə·təs) — *n.* An automatic device, pistol, etc. [< Gk. *automatos* acting of oneself] — **au′to·mat′i·cal·ly** *adv.*
automatic pilot *Aeron.* An automatic-control mechanism designed to keep an aircraft level and on an even course.
automatic pistol A pistol using the force of recoil to extract and eject used shells and chamber the next round.
automatic rifle A rifle capable of automatic fire.
au·to·ma·tion (ô′tə·mā′shən) *n.* The automatic transfer of one unit of a complex industrial assembly to a succession of machines, each of which completes another stage in manufacture. — **au·to·ma·tive** (ô′tə·mā′tiv) *adj.*
au·tom·a·tism (ô·tom′ə·tiz′əm) *n.* **1.** The state or quality of being automatic or of having no voluntary action. **2.** *Physiol.* The functioning or power of functioning of muscular or other processes in response to external stimuli but independent of conscious control. — **au·tom′a·tist** *n.*
au·tom·a·ton (ô·tom′ə·ton, -tən) *n.* *pl.* **·tons** or **·ta** (-tə) **1.** An apparatus that appears to function of itself by the action of a concealed mechanism. **2.** Any living being whose actions are or appear to be involuntary or mechanical. **3.** Anything capable of spontaneous movement or action. [< Gk. *automaton*, neut. of *automatos* acting of oneself, independent]
au·to·mo·bile (*n.* & *v.* ô′tə·mə·bēl′, ô′tə·mə·bēl′, ô′tə·mō′·bēl; *adj.* ô′tə·mō′bil) *n.* A four-wheeled passenger vehicle that carries its own source of power and travels on roads or streets; motorcar. — *v.i.* **·biled, ·bil·ing** To ride in or drive an automobile. — *adj.* Automotive. [< F < Gk. *auto-* + *mobile* moving] — **au·to·mo·bil·ist** (ô′tə·mə·bēl′ist, -mō′·bil·ist) *n.*
au·to·mo·tive (ô′tə·mō′tiv) *adj.* **1.** Self-propelling. **2.** Of or for automobiles.
au·to·nom·ic (ô′tə·nom′ik) *adj.* **1.** Autonomous. **2.** *Physiol.* Pertaining to the autonomic nervous system. Also **au′to·nom′i·cal.** — **au′to·nom′i·cal·ly** *adv.*
autonomic nervous system A plexus of nerve ganglia and fibers originating in the spinal column and acting to innervate and control the efferent functions of all body tissues and organs not subject to voluntary control, as the heart, blood vessels, smooth muscle, glands, stomach, and intestines.
au·ton·o·mous (ô·ton′ə·məs) *adj.* **1.** Independent; self-governing. **2.** *Biol.* Independent. [< Gk. < *autos* self + *nomos* law, rule] — **au·ton′o·mous·ly** *adv.*
au·ton·o·my (ô·ton′ə·mē) *n.* *pl.* **·mies 1.** The condition or quality of being autonomous; esp., the power or right of self-government. **2.** A self-governing community or group. **3.** Self-determination. — **au·ton′o·mist** *n.*
au·top·sy (ô′top·sē, ô′təp-) *n.* *pl.* **·sies** Post-mortem examination of a human body, esp. when ordered by a coroner. [< NL < Gk. < *autos* self + *opsis* a seeing]
au·to·sug·ges·tion (ô′tō·səg·jes′chən) *n.* *Psychol.* Suggestion emanating from one's self only. — **au′to·sug·gest′i·bil′·i·ty** *n.* — **au′to·sug·ges′tive** *adj.*
au·tumn (ô′təm) *n.* **1.** The season of the year occurring between summer and winter. Often called *fall.* **2.** A time of maturity and incipient decline. [< OF < L *autumnus*]
au·tum·nal (ô·tum′nəl) *adj.* **1.** Of, pertaining to, or like autumn. **2.** Ripening or harvested in autumn. **3.** Past maturity; declining. — **au·tum′nal·ly** *adv.*
autumnal equinox See under EQUINOX.
aux·il·ia·ry (ôg·zil′yər·ē, -zil′ər-) *adj.* **1.** Giving or furnishing aid. **2.** Subsidiary; accessory. **3.** Supplementary; re-

serve. — *n.* *pl.* **·ries** 1. One who or that which aids or helps; assistant; associate. 2. *Gram.* A verb that helps to express tense, mood, etc., as *have* in *We have gone:* also **auxiliary verb.** 3. *pl.* Foreign troops associated with those of a nation at war. [< L < *auxilium* help]

a·vail (ə·vāl′) *v.t.* 1. To assist or aid; profit. — *v.i.* 2. To be of value or advantage; suffice. — **to avail oneself of** To take advantage of; utilize. — *n.* 1. Utility for a purpose; benefit; good: His efforts were of no *avail.* 2. *pl.* Proceeds. [< OF < L *ad-* to + *valere* to be strong]

a·vail·a·ble (ə·vā′lə·bəl) *adj.* 1. Capable of being used; at hand; usable. 2. *Law* Valid. — **a·vail′a·bil′i·ty, a·vail′·a·ble·ness** *n.* — **a·vail′a·bly** *adv.*

av·a·lanche (av′ə·lanch, -länch) *n.* A large mass of snow or ice falling down a slope. 2. Something like an avalanche, as in power, destructiveness, etc. — *v.* **·lanched, ·lanch·ing** *v.i.* 1. To fall or slide like an avalanche. — *v.t.* 2. To fall or come down upon like an avalanche. [< F < dial. F (Swiss) *lavenche* < L *ad vallem*]

a·vant-garde (ə·vänt′gärd′, *Fr.* à·väṅ·gård′) *n.* The vanguard; esp., in art, the group regarded as most advanced or daring in technique and ideas. — *adj.* Of or pertaining to this group. [< F, lit., advance guard]

av·a·rice (av′ə·ris) *n.* Passion for acquiring and hoarding riches; greed. [< OF < L < *avere* to desire, crave]

av·a·ri·cious (av′ə·rish′əs) *adj.* Greedy of gain; grasping; miserly. — **av′a·ri′cious·ly** *adv.* — **av′a·ri′cious·ness** *n.*

a·vast (ə·vast′, ə·väst′) *interj. Naut.* Stop! hold! cease! [< Du. *hou' vast, houd vast* hold fast]

av·a·tar (av′ə·tär′) *n.* 1. In Hindu mythology, the incarnation of a god. 2. Any incarnation. [< Skt. *avatāra* descent]

a·ve (ā′vē, ä′vā) *interj.* 1. Hail! 2. Farewell! — *n.* The salutation *ave.* [< L, hail, farewell]

A·ve Ma·ri·a (ä′vā mə·rē′ə, ā′vē) A Roman Catholic prayer to the Virgin Mary: also called *Hail Mary.* Also **A′ve, Mar·y** (ā′vē mâr′ē). [< L, Hail, Mary]

a·venge (ə·venj′) *v.* **a·venged, a·veng·ing** *v.t.* 1. To take vengeance or exact exemplary punishment for or in behalf of. — *v.i.* 2. To take vengeance. [< OF < L < *ad-* to + *vindicare* to avenge] — **a·veng′er** *n.* — **a·veng′ing·ly** *adv.*

av·e·nue (av′ə·nōō, -nyōō) *n.* 1. A broad street. 2. A way of approach, as to a building, often bordered with trees. 3. A mode of access or attainment. [< F *avenue* < L < *ad-* toward + *venire* to come]

a·ver (ə·vûr′) *v.t.* **a·verred, a·ver·ring** 1. To declare confidently as fact; affirm. 2. *Law* To assert formally; prove or justify (a plea). [< OF < L *ad-* to + *verus* true] — **a·ver′·ment** *n.* — **a·ver′ra·ble** *adj.*

av·er·age (av′rij, av′ər·ij) *n.* 1. *Math.* An arithmetic mean. 2. A mean, ratio, etc., showing a specific standing or accomplishment: batting *average*; B *average.* 3. The ordinary rank, degree, or amount; general type. 4. In marine law: **a** The loss arising by damage to a ship or cargo. **b** The proportion of such loss falling to a single person in an equitable distribution among those interested. — *adj.* 1. Obtained by calculating the mean of several. 2. Medium; ordinary. — *v.* **·aged, ·ag·ing** *v.t.* 1. To fix or calculate as the mean. 2. To amount to or obtain an average of: He *averages* three dollars an hour. 3. To apportion on the average. — *v.i.* 4. To be or amount to an average. 5. To buy or sell more goods, shares, etc., in order to get a better average price. [< F *avarie* damage to a ship] — **av′er·age·ly** *adv.*

A·ver·nus (ä·ver′nəs) In Roman mythology, hell; Hades. — **A·ver′nal** *adj.*

a·verse (ə·vûrs′) *adj.* Opposed; unfavorable; reluctant: with *to.* [< L *aversus*, pp. of *avertere* to turn aside] — **a·verse′ly** *adv.* — **a·verse′ness** *n.*

a·ver·sion (ə·vûr′zhən, -shən) *n.* 1. Extreme dislike; opposition; antipathy. 2. A cause of repugnance or dislike.

a·vert (ə·vûrt′) *v.t.* 1. To turn or direct away or aside, as one's regard. 2. To prevent or ward off, as a danger. — **Syn.** See PREVENT. [< OF *avertir* < L *avertere* to turn aside < *ab-* away + *vertere* to turn] — **a·vert′ed·ly** *adv.* — **a·vert′i·ble** or **a·vert′a·ble** *adj.*

A·ves·ta (ə·ves′tə) The sacred writings of Zoroastrianism, written in **A·ves·tan,** (ə·ves′tən), an ancient Iranian language. See ZEND–AVESTA. — **A·ves′tan** *adj.*

avi- *combining form* Bird; of or related to birds. [< L *avis* bird]

a·vi·ar·y (ā′vē·er′ē) *n.* *pl.* **·ar·ies** An enclosure or large cage for live birds. [< L < *avis* bird] — **a·vi·ar·ist** (ā′vē·er′ist, -ə·rist) *n.*

a·vi·a·tion (ā′vē·ā′shən, av′ē-) *n.* The act, science, or art of flying heavier-than-air aircraft. [< F < L *avis* bird]

a·vi·a·tor (ā′vē·ā′tər, av′ē-) *n.* An airplane pilot. — **a′vi·a′tress** (-tris) or **a·vi·a·trix** (ā′vē·ā′triks, av′ē-) *n.fem.*

av·id (av′id) *adj.* Very desirous; eager; greedy. [< L < *avere* to crave] — **a·vid·i·ty** (ə·vid′ə·tē) *n.* — **av′id·ly** *adv.*

a·vi·on·ics (ā′vē·on′iks, av′ē-) *n.pl.* (*construed as sing.*) The applications of electronics to aviation, astronautics, etc.

av·o·ca·do (av′ə·kä′dō, ä′və-) *n.* *pl.* **·dos** 1. The pear-shaped fruit of a West Indian tree: also called *alligator pe*[ar]. 2. The tree bearing this fruit. [< Sp. < Nahuatl *ahuaca*[tl]]

av·o·ca·tion (av′ə·kā′shən) *n.* A casual or occasional [oc]cupation; diversion; hobby. — **Syn.** See OCCUPATION. [< L < *ab-* away + *vocare* to call]

av·o·cet (av′ə·set) *n.* A long-legged shore bird havi[ng] webbed feet and an upcurved bill. Also **av′o·set.** [< F < Ital. *avocetta*]

a·void (ə·void′) *v.t.* 1. To keep away or at a distance fro[m]; shun; evade. 2. *Law* To make void. [< OF < L *ex-* o[ut] + *viduare* to empty, deprive] — **a·void′a·ble** *adj.* — **void′a·bly** *adv.* — **a·void′ance** *n.*

av·oir·du·pois (av′ər·də·poiz′) *n.* 1. The ordinary syste[m] of weights of the U.S. and Great Britain in which 16 ounc[es] avoirdupois make a pound. Abbr. *av., avdp., avoir.* See tab[le in] front of book. 2. *Informal* Weight; corpulence. [< O[F] *avoir de pois* goods of (i.e., sold by) weight]

a·vouch (ə·vouch′) *v.t.* 1. To vouch for; guarantee. 2. [To] affirm positively; proclaim. 3. To acknowledge; avow. [< OF < L < *ad-* to + *vocare* to call]

a·vow (ə·vou′) *v.t.* To declare openly, as facts; own; [ac]knowledge. [< OF < L *advocare* to summon] — **a·vow[′a]·ble** *adj.* — **a·vow′a·bly** *adv.* — **a·vow′er** *n.*

a·vow·al (ə·vou′əl) *n.* Frank admission or acknowledgme[nt].

a·vowed (ə·voud′) *adj.* Openly acknowledged; plainly [de]clared. — **a·vow·ed·ly** (ə·vou′id·lē) *adv.* — **a·vow′ed·ness**

a·vun·cu·lar (ə·vung′kyə·lər) *adj.* Of or pertaining to [an] uncle. [< L *avunculus* maternal uncle]

a·wait (ə·wāt′) *v.t.* 1. To wait for; expect. 2. To be rea[dy] or in store for. [< OF *awaitier* to watch for < *a-* to (< *ad-*) + *waitier* to watch < OHG *wahtēn* to watch]

a·wake (ə·wāk′) *adj.* Not asleep; alert; vigilant. [< v.] *v.* **a·woke** (*Rare* **a·waked**), **a·waked** (*Rare* **a·woke**), **a·wa[k]·ing** *v.t.* 1. To arouse from sleep. 2. To stir up; excite. *v.i.* 3. To cease to sleep; become awake. 4. To beco[me] alert or aroused. [OE *onwæcnan* rise from sleep]

a·wak·en (ə·wā′kən) *v.t. & v.i.* To awake. — **a·wa[k]·en·er** *n.*

a·wak·en·ing (ə·wā′kən·ing) *adj.* Stirring; exciting. — 1. The act of waking. 2. A reviving, as of interest.

a·ward (ə·wôrd′) *v.t.* 1. To adjudge as due, as by legal de[ci]sion. 2. To bestow as the result of a contest or examinati[on], as a prize. — *n.* 1. A decision, as by a judge or arbitrat[or]. 2. The document containing it. 3. That which is award[ed], as a medal. [< AF, OF < *es-* out (< L *ex-*) + *guarder* watch] — **a·ward′a·ble** *adj.* — **a·ward′er** *n.*

a·ware (ə·wâr′) *adj.* Conscious; cognizant: often with [of]. [OE *gewær* watchful] — **a·ware′ness** *n.*

a·wash (ə·wosh′, ə·wôsh′) *adv. & adj.* 1. Level with or j[ust] above the surface of the water. 2. Tossed or washed ab[out] by waves. 3. Covered or overflowed by water.

a·way (ə·wā′) *adv.* 1. From a given place; off. 2. Far; at to a distance. 3. In another direction; aside. 4. Out [of] existence; at or to an end: to waste *away.* 5. On and [on]; continuously: to peg *away* at a task. 6. From one's keepi[ng], attention, or possession: to give food *away.* 7. At on[ce]; without hesitation: Fire *away!* — **to do away with** 1. [To] get rid of. 2. To kill. — *adj.* 1. Absent. 2. At a distan[ce]. — *interj.* Begone! [OE *on weg* on (one's) way]

awe (ô) *n.* Reverential fear; dread mingled with venerati[on]. — *v.t.* **awed, aw·ing** or **awe·ing** To impress with reverent fear. [< ON *agi* fear]

a·weigh (ə·wā′) *adv. Naut.* Hanging with the flukes j[ust] clear of the bottom: said of an anchor.

awe·some (ô′səm) *adj.* 1. Inspiring awe. 2. Characteriz[ed] by or expressing awe; reverential. — **awe′some·ly** *adv.* **awe′some·ness** *n.*

aw·ful (ô′fəl) *adj.* 1. *Informal* Exceedingly bad or unple[as]ant; ugly. 2. Inspiring awe; majestically or solemnly i[m]pressive. 3. Causing fear or dread. 4. *Informal* Ve[ry] great. — **aw′ful·ness** *n.*

aw·ful·ly (ô′fəl·ē *for def. 1*; ô′flē *for def. 2*) *adv.* 1. In an a[w]ful manner. 2. *Informal* Excessively; very: *awfully* rich

a·while (ə·hwīl′) *adv.* For a brief time. [OE *ānē hwīle* a whi[le]]

awk·ward (ôk′wərd) *adj.* 1. Ungraceful in bearing. 2. U[n]skillful in action; bungling. 3. Embarrassing or perplexi[ng]. 4. Difficult or dangerous to deal with. 5. Inconvenient [for] use; uncomfortable. [< ON *öfugr* turned the wrong way -WARD] — **awk′ward·ly** *adv.* — **awk′ward·ness** *n.*

awl (ôl) *n.* A pointed instrument for making small hol[es], as in wood or leather. [ME *awel* < OE *æl*]

awn (ôn) *n. Bot.* A bristlelike appendage of certain grass[es], beard, as of wheat or rye. [ME < ON *ögn* chaff] — **awn[ed]** (ônd) *adj.* — **awn′less** *adj.* — **awn′y** *adj.*

awn·ing (ô′ning) *n.* A rooflike cover, as of canvas, for p[ro]tection from sun or rain. [Origin unknown]

a·woke (ə·wōk′) Past tense of AWAKE.

AWOL (*as an acronym pronounced* ā′wôl) *Mil.* Absent or [ab]sence without leave. Also **awol, A.W.O.L., a.w.o.l.**

a·wry (ə·rī′) *adj. & adv.* 1. Toward one side; askew. 2. O[ut] of the right course; amiss; wrong.

ɛ (aks) *n.* *pl.* **ax·es** A tool with a bladed head mounted on , handle, used for chopping, hewing, etc. **— to have an ax o grind** *Informal* To have a private purpose or interest to ursue. — *v.t.* **1.** To cut or trim with an ax. **2.** To behead vith an ax. Also *Brit.* **axe.** [OE *æx*] **— ax′like′** *adj.*

:·es¹ (ak′sēz) Plural of AXIS¹.

:·es² (ak′siz) Plural of AX.

:i·al (ak′sē·əl) *adj.* **1.** Of, pertaining to, or forming an xis. **2.** Situated on or along an axis. Also **ax·ile** (ak′sil, -sīl).

:il (ak′sil) *n.* *Bot.* The cavity or angle formed by the ınction of the upper side of a leafstalk, branch, etc., with a tem or branch. [< L *axilla* armpit]

:il·la (ak·sil′ə) *n.* *pl.* **ax·il·lae** (-sil′ē) **1.** *Anat.* The armit. **2.** An axil. [< L]

:il·lar (ak′sə·lər) *adj.* Axillary.

:il·lar·y (ak′sə·ler′ē) *adj.* **1.** *Bot.* Of, pertaining to, or situated in an axil. **2.** *Anat.* Pertaining to the axilla.

.i·om (ak′sē·əm) *n.* **1.** A self-evident or universally recgnized truth. **2.** An established principle or rule. **3.** *Logic : Math.* A self-evident proposition accepted as true without roof. [< L < Gk. < *axioein* to think worthy]

.i·o·mat·ic (ak′sē·ə·mat′ik) *adj.* **1.** Of, pertaining to, or esembling an axiom; self-evident. **2.** Aphoristic. Also **ax′·ɔ·mat′i·cal.** **— ax′i·o·mat′i·cal·ly** *adv.*

.is¹ (ak′sis) *n.* *pl.* **ax·es** (ak′sēz) **1.** A line around which turning body rotates or may be supposed to rotate. **2.** *eom.* **a** A straight line through the center of a plane or solid gure, esp. the line in relation to which the figure is symetrical. **b** A fixed line, as in a graph, along which distances e measured or to which positions are referred. **3.** The cenal line about which the parts of a body or thing are regurly arranged. **4.** An affiliation of two or more nations to romote and ensure mutual interest, cooperation, and soliarity in their foreign relations. [< axis, axle]

·le (ak′səl) *n.* **1.** A crossbar on which a wheel or wheels ırn. **2.** An axletree. [< AXLETREE] **— ax′led** *adj.*

·le·tree (ak′səl·trē′) *n.* A bar or beam on the ends of which e opposite wheels of a carriage or wagon revolve. [< ON *öxull* axle + *trē* tree, beam]

·man (aks′mən) *n.* *pl.* **·men** (-mən) One who wields an ɛ; a woodsman. Also **axe′man.**

Ax·min·ster (aks′min·stər) *n.* **1.** A carpet with a long, soft pile. **2.** A carpet made in imitation of this. [after *Axminster*, England, where first made]

ax·o·lotl (ak′sə·lot′l) *n.* A North American tailed amphibian that retains its external gills and breeds in a larval state. [< Sp. < Nahuatl, lit., servant of water]

ax·on (ak′son) *n.* *Physiol.* The central process of a neuron, usu. carrying impulses away from the cells. Also **ax·one** (ak′·sōn). [< NL < Gk. *axōn* axis]

a·yah (ä′yə) *n.* *Anglo-Indian* A native nurse or lady's maid. [< Hind. *āyā* < Pg. *aia* nurse]

aye (ī) *n.* An affirmative vote or voter. — *adv.* Yes; yea. Also **ay.** [Origin unknown]

a·zal·ea (ə·zāl′yə) *n.* A flowering shrub of the heath family, esp. the **flame azalea,** with showy scarlet or orange flowers. [< NL < Gk. < *azein* to parch, dry up]

az·i·muth (az′ə·məth) *n.* **1.** The angular distance in a horizontal plane measured clockwise from true north to a given course or celestial object. **2.** In celestial navigation, the angle measured at the zenith, clockwise, from true north to a vertical plane passing through a heavenly body; in astronomy, measured clockwise from the south point. [< OF < Arabic *as-sumūt* the ways, pl. of *samt* way] **— az·i·muth·al** (az′ə·muth′əl) *adj.* **— az′i·muth′al·ly** *adv.*

az·o (az′ō, ā′zō) *adj.* *Chem.* Containing nitrogen. [< *azote*, former name for nitrogen]

a·zo·ic (ə·zō′ik) *adj.* *Geol.* Of or pertaining to those periods on earth before life appeared; without organic remains. [< Gk. < *a-* without + *zōē* life]

Az·tec (az′tek) *n.* **1.** One of a tribe of Indians of Nahuatlan stock, founders of an empire that was at its height when Cortés invaded Mexico in 1519. **2.** Nahuatl. — *adj.* Of or pertaining to the Aztec Indians, their language, culture, or empire: also **Az·tec·an** (az′tek·ən).

az·ure (azh′ər, ā′zhər) *adj.* Sky blue. — *n.* **1.** A clear, sky-blue color or pigment. **2.** *Poetic* The sky. [< OF < Arabic < Persian *lāzhward* lapis lazuli]

az·u·rite (azh′ə·rīt) *n.* A vitreous, monoclinic, azure-blue, basic copper carbonate, often used as a gemstone.

az·y·gous (az′i·gəs) *adj.* *Biol.* Occurring singly; not paired. [< Gk. < *a-* without + *zygon* a yoke]

B

B (bē) *n.* *pl.* **b's** or **bs, B's** or **Bs, bees** (bēz) **1.** The econd letter of the English alphabet. **2.** The sound represnted by the letter *b.* — *symbol* **1.** *Music* **a** One of a series tones, the seventh in the natural diatonic scale of C. **b** A ritten note representing it. **c** A scale built upon B. **2.** *hem.* Boron (symbol B). **3.** The second in sequence, etc.

a (bä, ba) *v.i.* **baaed, baa·ing** To bleat, as a sheep. — *n.* bleat, as of a sheep. [Imit.]

ı·al (bā′əl, bāl) *n.* *pl.* **Ba·al·im** (bā′əl·im) **1.** Any of veral ancient Semitic gods of fertility and flocks; esp., the ın god of the Phoenicians. **2.** An idol or false god. [< ebrew *ba'al* lord] **— Ba′al·ish** *adj.* **— Ba′al·ist, Ba′al·ite — Ba′al·ism** *n.*

b·bitt (bab′it) *v.t.* To line, fill, etc., with Babbitt metal.

ıb·bitt (bab′it) *n.* A type of conventional American busissman who is mediocre and smug; philistine. [after Sinair Lewis's novel *Babbitt* (1922)] **— Bab′bitt·ry** *n.*

.bbitt metal **1.** A soft, white, antifriction alloy of tin, pper, and antimony. **2.** Any of a group of similar alloys. fter Isaac *Babbitt*, 1799–1862, U.S. metallurgist]

b·ble (bab′əl) *v.* **·bled, ·bling** *v.i.* **1.** To utter inarticute or meaningless sounds. **2.** To make a murmuring or opling sound, as a stream. **3.** To talk unwisely or foolishly. · *v.t.* **4.** To utter unintelligibly. **5.** To blurt out thoughtssly. — *n.* **1.** Inarticulate or confused speech. **2.** Prattle, of an infant. **3.** A murmuring or rippling sound. [ME *:belen;* ult. origin unknown] **— bab′bler** *n.*

be (bāb) *n.* **1.** An infant; baby. **2.** *U.S. Informal* An tless or inexperienced person. **3.** *U.S. Slang* A girl. [ME]

·bel (bā′bəl, bab′əl) *n.* A confusion of many voices or nguages; tumult. Also **Ba′bel.** [after (*Tower of*) *Babel*]

.·bel (bā′bəl, bab′əl) In the Bible, an ancient city in Shiır, now identified with Babylon. **— Tower of Babel** **1.** A tower begun in Babel by the descendants of Noah and intended to reach heaven, but abandoned. *Gen.* xi 9. **2.** Any impractical scheme or structure.

ba·bies'-breath (bā′bēz·breth′) See BABY'S-BREATH.

ba·boon (ba·bōōn′) *n.* **1.** A large, terrestrial monkey of Africa and Asia, having a doglike muzzle and usu. a short tail. **2.** *Slang* A coarse or stupid person. [< OF *babuin*]

ba·bush·ka (bə·bōōsh′kə) *n.* A woman's scarf, worn over the head. [< Russian, grandmother]

ba·by (bā′bē) *n.* *pl.* **·bies** **1.** A very young child of either sex; an infant. **2.** The youngest or smallest member of a family or group. **3.** One who looks or acts like a child. **4.** Any young animal. **5.** *Slang* A girl. — *adj.* **1.** For a baby. **2.** Childish; infantile. **3.** Small; diminutive; miniature. — *v.t.* **·bied, ·by·ing** To treat as a baby; pamper. [ME *baby*, dim. of *babe*] **— ba′by·hood** *n.* **— ba′by·like′** *adj.*

ba·by-blue-eyes (bā′bē·blōō′īz′) *n.* An annual plant with showy, sky-blue flowers. Also **baby blue-eyes.**

ba·by·ish (bā′bē·ish) *adj.* Childish; infantile. **— ba′by·ish·ly** *adv.* **— ba′by·ish·ness** *n.*

Bab·y·lon (bab′ə·lən, -lon) **1.** An ancient city of Mesopotamia on the Euphrates, capital of Babylonia from about 2100 B.C.; celebrated as a seat of wealth, luxury, and vice. **2.** Any city or place of great wealth, luxury, or vice.

Bab·y·lo·ni·a (bab′ə·lō′nē·ə) An ancient empire of Mesopotamia; capital, Babylon; conquered by Persia, 538 B.C. **— Bab′y·lo′ni·an** *adj.* & *n.*

ba·by's-breath (bā′bēz·breth′) *n.* **1.** An Old World perennial with numerous clusters of small, white or pink, fragrant flowers. **2.** Any of certain other fragrant herbs, as the wild madder. Also spelled *babies'-breath.*

baby-sit (bā′bē·sit′) *v.i.* **-sat, -sit·ting** To act as a baby sitter.

---

baby sitter A person employed to take care of young children while the parents are absent: also called *sitter.*

bac·ca·lau·re·ate (bak′ə·lôr′ē·it) *n.* **1.** The degree of bachelor of arts, bachelor of science, etc. **2.** An address to a graduating class at commencement: also **baccalaureate sermon.** [< Med.L < *baccalaureus,* var. of *baccalaris,* a young farmer; infl. in form by L *bacca lauri* laurel berry]

bac·ca·rat (bak′ə·rä′, bak′ə·rä) *n.* A gambling game in which winnings are decided by comparing cards held by the banker with those held by the players. Also **bac·ca·ra** (bak′·ə·rä′, bak′ə·rä). [< F *baccara,* a game of cards]

bac·cha·nal (bak′ə·nəl) *n.* **1.** A votary of Bacchus. **2.** A drunken reveler. **3.** *pl.* Bacchanalia. — *adj.* Bacchanalian. [< L *bacchanalis* of Bacchus]

bac·cha·na·li·a (bak′ə·nā′lē·ə, -nāl′yə) *n.pl.* Drunken revelries; orgies. [< L, neut. pl. of *bacchanalis* of Bacchus] — **bac′cha·na′li·an** *adj.* — **bac′cha·na′li·an·ism** *n.*

bac·chant (bak′ənt) *n. pl.* **bac·chants** or **bac·chan·tes** (bə·kan′tēz) **1.** A votary of Bacchus. **2.** A carouser; reveler. — *adj.* Given to drunkenness. — **bac·chan·te** (bə·kan′tē, bə·kant′, bak′ənt) *n. fem.*

bac·chic (bak′ik) *adj.* Riotous; orgiastic; drunken.

Bac·chus (bak′əs) In classical mythology, the god of wine and revelry: identified with *Dionysus.* — **Bac·chic** *adj.*

bacci- *combining form* Berry or berries. [< L *bacca* berry]

bach·e·lor (bach′ə·lər, bach′lər) *n.* **1.** An unmarried man. **2.** One who has taken his first university or college degree. **3.** A young knight serving under another's banner: also **bach′e·lor-at-arms′.** [< OF < Med.L *baccalaris,* a young farmer] — **bach′e·lor·hood′, bach′e·lor·ship′** *n.*

Bachelor of Arts **1.** A degree usu. given by a college or university to a person who has completed a four-year course in the humanities. **2.** One who has received this degree.

Bachelor of Science **1.** A degree given by a college or university to a person who has completed a four-year course in the sciences. **2.** One who has received this degree.

bach·e·lor's-but·ton (bach′ə·lərz·but′n, bach′lərz-) *n.* **1.** Any of several plants with button-shaped flowers or flower heads. **2.** The cornflower.

bac·il·lar·y (bas′ə·ler′ē) *adj.* **1.** Rod-shaped. **2.** Pertaining to or caused by bacilli. Also **ba·cil·lar** (bə·sil′ər).

ba·cil·lus (bə·sil′əs) *n. pl.* **·cil·li** (-sil′ī) **1.** *Bacteriol.* Any of a large class of straight, rod-shaped bacteria including both beneficial and pathogenic species. **2.** A bacterium. — **Syn.** See MICROBE. [< NL < L *baculus* stick]

back[1] (bak) *n.* **1.** The part of the body nearest the spine; in man the hinder, in quadrupeds the upper part, extending from the neck to the base of the spine. ◆ Collateral adjective: *dorsal.* **2.** The backbone. **3.** The rear or posterior part of anything. **4.** The farther or other side; the reverse. **5.** The part behind or opposite to the part used: the *back* of a knife. **6.** Anything to cover or support the back. **7.** The part of a garment covering the back. **8.** Physical strength: Put your *back* into it. **9.** In football, a player in a position behind the line of scrimmage. **10.** *Phonet.* The part of the tongue directly behind the front and below the velum. — **at one's back** Following closely. — **behind one's back** **1.** Secretly. **2.** Treacherously. — **in back of** Behind; at or to the rear of. — **to be (flat) on one's back** To be helplessly ill. — **to turn one's back on** **1.** To show contempt or ill feeling toward by ignoring. **2.** To renounce. — *v.t.* **1.** To cause to move backward; reverse the action of. **2.** To furnish with a back. **3.** To support, as by financing or by endorsing: to *back* a candidate; to *back* a business. **4.** To bet on. **5.** To form a background for. **6.** To mount, as a horse. **7.** To write on the back of. — *v.i.* **8.** To move backward. **9.** To shift counterclockwise: said of the wind. — **to back down** To withdraw from a position, abandon a claim, etc. — **to back off** To retreat, as from contact. — **to back out (of)** To withdraw from or refuse to carry out a promise, contest, etc. — *adj.* **1.** In the rear; behind. **2.** Distant; remote: the *back* country. **3.** Of or for a date earlier than the present: a *back* issue. **4.** In arrears; overdue: *back* taxes. **5.** In a backward direction. [OE *bæc*]

back[2] (bak) *adv.* **1.** At, to, or toward the rear. **2.** In, to, or toward a former place or condition. **3.** Into time past. **4.** In return or retort. **5.** In reserve or concealment. **6.** In check or hindrance. **7.** In withdrawal or repudiation. — **back and forth** First in one direction and then in the opposite. — **back of** *U.S.* Behind. — **to go back on** *Informal* **1.** To fail to keep (an engagement, promise, etc.). **2.** To desert or betray. [< ABACK]

back·bite (bak′bīt′) *v.t. & v.i.* **·bit, ·bit·ten** (*Informal* **·bit**), **·bit·ing** To revile behind one's back; slander. — **back′bit′·er** *n.*

back·board (bak′bôrd′, -bōrd′) *n.* **1.** A board forming or supporting the back of something. **2.** In basketball, the vertical board behind the basket.

back·bone (bak′bōn′) *n.* **1.** The spine or vertebral column. **2.** Something likened to a backbone in function or appearance. **3.** Strength of character. — **back′boned′** *adj.*

back·break·ing (bak′brā′king) *adj.* Physically exhaustir

back·door (bak′dôr′, -dōr′) *adj.* Clandestine; underhar

back·drop (bak′drop′) *n.* The curtain hung at the rear o stage, often representing a scene. Also **back cloth.**

backed (bakt) *adj.* Having a (specified kind of) back backing: used in combination: *low-backed; cardboard-back*

back·er (bak′ər) *n.* **1.** One who supports with money patron. **2.** One who bets on a contestant.

back·field (bak′fēld′) *n.* In football, the players behind t line of scrimmage, usu. the fullback, two halfbacks, and t quarterback.

back·fire (bak′fīr′) *n.* **1.** A fire built to check an adva ing forest or prairie fire by creating a barren area in its pa **2.** Premature explosion in the cylinder of an internal-co bustion engine. **3.** An explosion of unburned fuel in t muffler of an internal combustion engine. **4.** An explosi in the back part of a gun. — *v.i.* **·fired, ·fir·ing** **1.** To set use a backfire. **2.** To explode in a backfire. **3.** To react an unexpected and unwelcome manner: His scheme *backfir*

back formation *Ling.* **1.** The creation by analogy o new word from an existing word. **2.** A word so formed, *enthuse* from *enthusiasm.*

back·gam·mon (bak′gam′ən, bak′gam′ən) *n.* **1.** A ga played by two persons, on a special board, the moves of pieces being determined by dice throws. **2.** A victory in t game. — *v.t.* To win a backgammon from. [ME *back ga en* back game]

back·ground (bak′ground′) *n.* **1.** That part in a pict against which the principal elements, motifs, or subjects represented. **2.** Ground in the rear or distance. **3.** A s ordinate position; obscurity; retirement. **4.** The aggreg of one's experiences, education, etc. **5.** The events lead up to or causing a situation, event, etc. **6.** Music or sou effects employed in a motion picture, radio program, etc

back·hand (bak′hand′) *n.* **1.** Handwriting that slopes ward the left. **2.** The hand turned backward in makin stroke, as with a racket. **3.** A stroke made with the ha turned backward, as in tennis. — *adj.* Backhanded. — *a* With a backhand stroke.

back·hand·ed (bak′han′did) *adj.* **1.** Delivered or made w the back of the hand turned forward, as a stroke in ten **2.** Insincere; equivocal: a *backhanded* compliment. **3.** Sl ing to the left, as handwriting. — **back′hand′ed·ly** *adv.* **back′hand′ed·ness** *n.*

back·ing (bak′ing) *n.* **1.** Support or assistance. **2.** Supp ers or promoters collectively. **3.** Endorsement. **4.** Mot backward. **5.** The back of anything, as for support.

back·lash (bak′lash′) *n.* **1.** *Mech.* **a** A jarring recoil, as the parts of a machine when poorly fitted. **b** The amo of loose play in such parts. **2.** In angling, a snarl or tan of line on a reel, caused by a faulty cast.

back·log (bak′lôg′, -log′) *n.* *U.S.* **1.** A large log at the b of an open fireplace to maintain and concentrate the he **2.** Any reserve supply, as of funds, business orders, etc.

back·most (bak′mōst) *adj.* Farthest to the rear; hindm

back number **1.** An old issue of a magazine or newspap **2.** *U.S. Informal* An old-fashioned person or thing.

back·rest (bak′rest′) *n.* A support for or at the back.

back seat **1.** A seat in the rear, as of a vehicle, hall, e **2.** An inconspicuous or subordinate position.

back-seat driver (bak′sēt′) A passenger in an automol who persists in directing and advising the driver.

back·side (bak′sīd′) *n.* **1.** The hind part. **2.** The rur

back·slide (bak′slīd′) *v.i.* **·slid, ·slid** or **·slid·den, ·slid·** To return to wrong or sinful ways. — **back′slid′er** *n.*

back·spin (bak′spin′) *n.* Reverse rotation of a round obj that is moving forward, as a golf ball, baseball, etc.

back·stage (*n., adv.* bak′stāj′; *adj.* bak′stāj′) *adv.* **1.** In toward the portion of a theater behind the stage, includ the wings, dressing rooms, etc. **2.** To or toward the b portion of the stage. — *n.* The back portion of the sta — *adj.* Situated or occurring backstage.

back·stairs (bak′stârz′) *adj.* Indirect; underhand. A **back′stair′.**

back·stay (bak′stā′) *n. Naut.* A stay supporting a mast the aft side.

back·stitch (bak′stich′) *n.* A stitch made by carrying thread back half the length of the preceding stitch. — *v.t. v.i.* To sew with backstitches.

back·stop (bak′stop′) *n. U.S.* A fence, wire screen, or to stop the ball from going too far, as in baseball, tennis, e

back·stretch (bak′strech′) *n.* That part of a racecourse f thest from the spectators, usually a straightaway.

back·stroke (bak′strōk′) *n.* **1.** A backhanded stro **2.** In swimming, a stroke executed while on one's ba — *v.* **·stroked, ·strok·ing** *v.t.* **1.** To strike, as a ball, wit backstroke. — *v.i.* **2.** To swim with a backstroke.

back talk Impudent retort; insolent answering back.

back·track (bak′trak′) *v.i. U.S.* **1.** To retrace one's ste **2.** To withdraw from a position, undertaking, etc.

back·ward (bak′wərd) *adv.* **1.** Toward the back; to

ear. **2.** With the back foremost. **3.** In reverse order. **4.** 'rom better to worse. **5.** To or into time past. Also **back′-**
'ards. — *adj.* **1.** Turned to the back or rear; reversed.
. Done the reverse or wrong way. **3.** Behind in growth or evelopment; retarded; slow. **4.** Hesitating; reluctant; ashful. — **back′ward·ly** *adv.* — **back′ward·ness** *n.*
ıck·wash (bak′wosh′, -wôsh′) *n.* **1.** Water moved back-'ard, as by a boat. **2.** A backward current or flow.
ıck·wa·ter (bak′wô′tər, -wot′ər) *n.* **1.** Water turned or eld back, as by a dam, a current, etc. **2.** Any place or con-ition regarded as stagnant, backward, etc.
ıck·woods (bak′wŏŏdz′) *U.S. n.pl.* Wild, heavily wooded, r sparsely settled districts. — *adj.* In, from, or like the ackwoods: also **back′wood′.** — **back′woods′man** (-mən) *n.*
·con (bā′kən) *n.* The salted and dried or smoked back and des of the hog. — **to bring home the bacon** *U.S. Informal* . To provide food, etc. **2.** To succeed. [< OF < OHG *acho, bahho* ham, side of bacon]
ı·co·ni·an (bā·kō′nē·ən) *adj.* Of or pertaining to Francis acon, his philosophy, or his literary style. — *n.* A believer ı the Baconian theory.
ıconian theory The theory that Francis Bacon wrote the 'ays attributed to Shakespeare.
c·te·ri·a (bak·tir′ē·ə) Plural of BACTERIUM.
c·te·ri·cide (bak·tir′ə·sīd) *n.* An agent destructive of bac-·ria. — **bac·te′ri·ci′dal** *adj.*
cterio- *combining form* Of or pertaining to bacteria. lso, before vowels, **bacter-.** Also **bacteri-, bactero-.** [< k. *baktron* rod, staff]
c·te·ri·ol·o·gy (bak·tir′ē·ol′ə·jē) *n.* The branch of biolo-/ and medicine that deals with bacteria. — **bac·te·ri·o·log-** :**al** (bak·tir′ē·ə·loj′i·kəl) *adj.* — **bac·te′ri·o·log′i·cal·ly** *adv.* · **bac·te′ri·ol′o·gist** *n.*
c·te·ri·o·phage (bak·tir′ē·ə·fāj′) *n. Bacteriol.* An ultra-icroscopic filter-passing agent that has the power of de-roying bacteria in a living organism.
c·te·ri·um (bak·tir′ē·əm) *n. pl.* **·te·ri·a** (-tir′ē·ə) Any of ımerous widely distributed unicellular microorganisms :hibiting both plant and animal characteristics, and rang-g from the harmless and beneficial to those that cause sease. — **Syn.** See MICROBE. [< NL < Gk. *baktron* aff, stick] — **bac·te′ri·al** *adj.* — **bac·te′ri·al·ly** *adv.*
d (bad) *adj.* **worse, worst 1.** Not good in any manner or ·gree. **2.** Evil; wicked; immoral. **3.** Defective; worthless: *:d* wiring. **4.** Faulty or incorrect: *bad* grammar. **5.** Not ılid or sound. **6.** Not sufficient; inadequate. **7.** Lacking ill or proficiency: a *bad* poet. **8.** Distressing; unfavorable: *d* news. **9.** Offensive; disagreeable: a *bad* taste. **10.** Harm-l; noxious: *bad* for the eyes. **11.** Rotted; spoiled. **12.** Se-·re: a *bad* storm. **13.** Sick; in ill health. **14.** Sorry; regret-l: He felt *bad* about it. — **in bad** *Informal* **1.** In difficulty. In disfavor. — **not bad** Rather good: also **not half bad,** **ıt so bad.** — *n.* **1.** That which is bad. **2.** Those who are ıd: with *the.* **3.** A bad state or condition; wickedness. — *v. Informal* Badly. [ME *bad, baddle,* ? < OE *bæddel* 'eminate man] — **bad′ness** *n.*
de (bad) Past tense of BID.
dge (baj) *n.* **1.** Any device worn to indicate rank, office, embership in an organization, an award or prize, etc. **2.** ıy distinguishing mark, token, or insignia. — *v.t.* **badged,** **ıdg·ing** To decorate or provide with a badge. [ME *bage*]
dg·er (baj′ər) *n.* **1.** A small, burrowing, nocturnal, car-vorous mammal, with a broad body, ort legs, and long-clawed toes. **2.** The r of a badger, or a brush made of its hair. · *v.t.* To harass; nag at. [Origin unknown]
dger State Nickname of WISCON-N.

AMERICAN BADGER (About 30 inches long; tail 6 inches)

d·i·nage (bad′ə·näzh′, bad′ə·nij) *n.* ayful raillery; banter. — *v.t.* **·naged,** **ag·ing** To subject to or tease with dinage. [< F *badin* silly, jesting]
d·lands (bad′landz′) *n.pl.* A barren ea characterized by numerous ridges, peaks, and mesas t by erosion.
d Lands An arid, eroded plateau in South Dakota and ebraska. Also **Bad′lands.**
d·ly (bad′lē) *adv.* **1.** In a bad manner; improperly, im-rfectly, or grievously. **2.** *Informal* Very much; greatly.
d·min·ton (bad′min·tən) *n.* A game played by batting shuttlecock back and forth over a high, narrow net with a ht racket. [after *Badminton,* an estate in England]
d-tem·pered (bad′tem′pərd) *adj.* Cross; irritable.
e·de·ker (bā′di·kər) *n.* **1.** Any of a series of travelers' uidebooks. **2.** Loosely, any guidebook. [after Karl *ıedeker,* 1801–59, German publisher who issued them]
f·fle (baf′əl) *v.* **·fled, ·fling** *v.t.* **1.** To confuse mentally; rplex: The problem *baffled* him. **2.** To foil or frustrate; hinder. — *v.i.* **3.** To struggle to no avail. — *n.* **1.** A partition or wall used to control and direct sound effects in radio or motion pictures. **2.** A partition or grating used to alter the flow of gases or liquids: also **baf·fle·plate** (baf′əl-plāt′). [Origin uncertain] — **baf′fle·ment** *n.* — **baf′fler** *n.* — **baf′fling** *adj.* — **baf′fling·ly** *adv.*
bag (bag) *n.* **1.** A sack or pouch, usu. of paper, cloth, or leather, used as a receptacle. **2.** The amount a bag will hold. **3.** A woman's purse. **4.** A suitcase or satchel. **5.** The quan-tity of game caught or killed in hunting. **6.** A bulging or baggy part, as of a sail. **7.** A sac or similar part in various animals, as the udder of a cow. **8.** In baseball slang, a base. **9.** *U.S. Slang* A slovenly woman. — **in the bag** *U.S. Slang* Assured; certain. — **to be left holding the bag** *U.S. Informal* To be left to assume full responsibility or blame. — *v.* **bagged, bag·ging** *v.t.* **1.** To put into a bag. **2.** To cause to fill out or bulge like a bag. **3.** To capture or kill, as game. — *v.i.* **4.** To bulge or swell like a bag. **5.** To hang loosely. [? < ON *baggi* pack, bundle]
bag and baggage *Informal* **1.** With all one's possessions: He cleared out *bag and baggage.* **2.** Entirely; completely.
ba·gasse (bə·gas′) *n.* The dry refuse of sugar cane after the juice has been expressed, used in making paper and fiber-board. Also **ba·gass′.** [< F < Sp. *bagazo* refuse of grapes, olives, etc., after pressing]
bag·a·telle (bag′ə·təl′) *n.* **1.** A trifle. **2.** A game similar to billiards. [< F < Ital. *bagatella,* dim of *baga* sack]
ba·gel (bā′gəl) *n.* A doughnut-shaped roll of yeast dough simmered in water and baked. [< Yiddish < *beigen* to twist]
bag·gage (bag′ij) *n.* **1.** *Chiefly U.S.* The trunks, packages, etc., of a traveler. **2.** An army's movable equipment. **3.** A lively or impudent woman. [< MF < Med.L *baga* sack]
bag·ging (bag′ing) *n.* A coarse cloth for making bags.
bag·gy (bag′ē) *adj.* **bag·gi·er, bag·gi·est** Like a bag; loose; bulging. — **bag′gi·ly** *adv.* — **bag′gi·ness** *n.*
bagn·io (ban′yō, bän′-) *n.* **1.** A brothel. **2.** In the Orient, a prison. [< Ital. < L < Gk. *balaneion* bath]
bag·pipe (bag′pīp′) *n. Often pl.* A reed musical instrument having several pipes, the air being forced through them from an inflated leather bag. — **bag′pip′er** *n.*
ba·guette (ba·get′) *n.* A gem or crystal cut in long, narrow, rectangular form. Also **ba·guet′.** [< F < Ital. < L *baculum* staff, stick]
bah (bä, ba) *interj.* An exclamation of contempt or dismissal.
bail[1] (bāl) *n.* A scoop or bucket for dipping out fluids, as from a boat. — *v.t. & v.i.* **1.** To dip (water) from a boat with a bail. **2.** To clear (a boat) of water by dipping out. — **to bail out** To jump with parachute from an aircraft. [< OF < LL *baca, bacca* tub] — **bail′er** *n.*
bail[2] (bāl) *n.* In cricket, one of the crosspieces of the wicket. [< OF *bailler* to enclose]
bail[3] (bāl) *Law n.* **1.** One who becomes surety for the debt or default of another, esp. of a person under arrest. **2.** The security or guaranty given or agreed upon. **3.** Release, or the privilege of release, on bail. — **to go bail for** *U.S. Slang* To provide bail for. — *v.t.* To obtain the release of (an arrested person) by giving bail: often with *out.* [< OF < L *bajulare* to carry] — **bail′a·ble** *adj.* — **bail′ment** *n.*
bail[4] (bāl) *n.* **1.** The semicircular handle of a pail, kettle, etc. **2.** An arch-shaped support, as for a canopy. — *v.t.* To provide with a bail or handle. [< ON *beygla* hook, ring]
bai·liff (bā′lif) *n.* **1.** A court officer having custody of pris-oners under arraignment. **2.** A sheriff's deputy for serving processes and warrants of arrest. **3.** One who oversees an estate for the owner; a steward. **4.** *Brit.* A subordinate mag-istrate with jurisdiction limited to a certain district or to certain functions. [< OF < L *bajalus* porter, manager]
bai·li·wick (bā′lə·wik) *n.* **1.** The office, jurisdiction, or dis-trict of a bailiff. **2.** *U.S.* A person's own area of authority or competence. [ME *bailie* bailiff + *wick* village]
bails·man (bālz′mən) *n. pl.* **·men** (-mən) One who pro-vides bail for another.
bairn (bârn) *n. Scot.* A young child; a son or daughter.
bait (bāt) *n.* **1.** Food or other enticement placed as a lure in a trap, on a hook, etc. **2.** Any allurement or enticement. **3.** A halt for food or refreshment during a journey. — *v.t.* **1.** To put food or some other lure on or in: to *bait* a trap. **2.** To set dogs upon for sport: to *bait* a bear. **3.** To harass; tor-ment. **4.** To lure; entice. [< ON *beita* food] — **bait′er** *n.*
baize (bāz) *n.* A plain woolen fabric, usu. dyed green and napped to imitate felt, used for pool table covers, etc. [< OF *baies,* fem. pl. of *bai* chestnut brown]
bake (bāk) *v.* **baked, bak·ing** *v.t.* **1.** To cook (bread, pastry, etc.) by dry heat, as in an oven. **2.** To harden or vitrify by heat, as bricks or pottery. — *v.i.* **3.** To bake bread, pastry, etc. **4.** To become baked or hardened by heat, as soil. — *n.* A baking, or the amount baked. [OE *bacan*]

bake·house (bāk′hous′) *n.* A bakery.
Ba·ke·lite (bā′kə·līt) *n.* Any of a group of thermosetting plastics having many uses: a trade name. Also **ba′ke·lite.** [after Leo Hendrik *Baekeland*, 1863–1944, U.S. chemist]
bak·er (bā′kər) *n.* **1.** One who bakes and sells bread, cake, etc. **2.** A portable oven.
baker's dozen Thirteen.
bak·er·y (bā′kər·ē, bāk′rē) *n. pl.* **·er·ies 1.** A place for baking bread, cake, etc. **2.** A shop where bread, cake, etc., are sold: also **bake′shop′.**
bak·ing (bā′king) *n.* **1.** The act of one who or that which bakes. **2.** The quantity baked.
baking powder A finely powdered mixture of baking soda and an acid salt, giving off carbon dioxide when moist, used as a leavening agent in baking.
baking soda Sodium bicarbonate.
bak·sheesh (bak′shēsh) *n.* In India, Turkey, etc., a gratuity or a gift of alms. — *v.t. & v.i.* To give a tip or alms (to). Also **bak′shish.** [< Persian *bakhshīdan* to give]
Ba·laam (bā′ləm) In the Bible, a prophet hired to curse the Israelites but who blessed them by God's command after his donkey spoke to him. *Num.* xxii.
bal·a·lai·ka (bal′ə·lī′kə) *n.* A Russian stringed instrument of the guitar family. [< Russian]
bal·ance (bal′əns) *n.* **1.** *Sometimes pl.* An instrument for weighing; esp., a bar that pivots on a central point as weights are placed in the pans suspended from each end. **2.** Figuratively, the scale by which deeds and principles are weighed and destinies determined. **3.** The power or authority to decide and determine. **4.** A state of equilibrium or equal relationship; equipoise. **5.** Bodily poise. **6.** Mental or emotional stability. **7.** Harmonious proportion, as in the design or arrangement of parts in a whole. **8.** Something used to produce an equilibrium; counterpoise. **9.** The act of balancing or weighing. **10.** In bookkeeping: **a** Equality between the debit and credit totals of an account. **b** A difference between such totals; the excess on either side. **11.** *U.S.* Whatever is left over; remainder. **12.** A balance wheel. **13.** A movement in dancing. — **to strike a balance** To find or take an intermediate position; compromise. — *v.* **·anced, ·anc·ing** *v.t.* **1.** To bring into or keep in equilibrium; poise. **2.** To weigh in a balance. **3.** To compare or weigh in the mind, as alternative courses of action. **4.** To offset or counteract. **5.** To place or keep in proportion. **6.** To be equal or in proportion to. **7.** In bookkeeping: **a** To compute the difference between the debit and credit sides of (an account). **b** To reconcile, as by making certain entries, the debit and credit sides of (an account). **c** To adjust (an account) by paying what is owed. — *v.i.* **8.** To be or come into equilibrium. **9.** To be equal. **10.** To hesitate; tilt. [< F < L *bis* two + *lanx, lancis* dish, plate] — **bal′ance·a·ble** *adj.* — **bal′an·cer** *n.*
Bal·ance (bal′əns) *n.* The constellation and sign of the zodiac Libra.
balance of power A distribution of forces among nations such that none may acquire a degree of power dangerous to the others.
balance of trade The difference in value between exports and imports of a country.
balance sheet A statement in tabular form to show assets and liabilities, profit and loss, etc., of a business.
balance wheel The oscillating wheel of a watch or chronometer, that determines its rate of motion.
bal·a·ta (bal′ə·tə) *n.* The juice of one of several tropical American trees, used as an elastic gum for making golf balls, insulating wires, etc. [< Sp. < Tupi]
bal·bo·a (bal·bō′ə) *n.* A silver monetary unit of Panama, in 1960 worth $1.00. [after Vasco de *Balboa*]
bal·brig·gan (bal·brig′ən) *n.* **1.** A fine, unbleached, knitted cotton fabric. **2.** *pl.* Underwear and hose made of this fabric. [after *Balbriggan*, a town in Ireland]
bal·co·ny (bal′kə·nē) *n. pl.* **·nies 1.** A balustraded platform projecting from a wall of a building. **2.** A projecting gallery in a theater or public building. [< Ital. < OHG *balcho* beam] — **bal′co·nied** *adj.*

BALCONY (With balusters and balustrade)

bald (bôld) *adj.* **1.** Without hair on the head. **2.** Without natural covering or growth. **3.** Unadorned. **4.** Without disguise; forthright. **5.** *Zool.* Having white feathers or fur on the head. [? < Welsh *bāl* white] — **bald′ly** *adv.* — **bald′·ness** *n.*
Bal·der (bôl′dər) In Norse mythology, god of sunlight, spring, and joy; son of Odin. Also **Bal′dr.**
bal·der·dash (bôl′dər·dash) *n.* A meaningless flow of words; nonsense. [Origin uncertain]
bald·head (bôld′hed′) *n.* One whose head is bald. — **bald′head′ed** *adj.*
bald·pate (bôld′pāt′) *n.* **1.** A baldheaded person. **2.** See under WIDGEON. — **bald′pat′ed** *adj.*

bal·dric (bôl′drik) *n.* A belt worn over one shoulder a across the breast, to support a sword, bugle, etc. A **bal′drick.** [Cf. OF *baldrei*, ult. < L *balteus* belt]
bale (bāl) *n.* A large package of bulky goods corded or oth wise prepared for transportation. — *v.t.* **baled, bal·i** To make into a bale or bales. [< OF *bale* round packa — **bal′er** *n.*
ba·leen (bə·lēn′) *n.* Whalebone. [< F < L < Gk. *phala* whale]
bale·ful (bāl′fəl) *adj.* **1.** Hurtful; malignant. **2.** Omino *baleful* predictions of his political future. [OE *bealu* evil -FUL] — **bale′ful·ly** *adv.* — **bale′ful·ness** *n.*
Ba·li·nese (bä′lə·nēz′, -nēs′) *adj.* Of or pertaining to B its people, or their language. — *n. pl.* **·nese 1.** A native inhabitant of Bali. **2.** The Indonesian language of Bali.
balk (bôk) *v.i.* **1.** To stop short and refuse to proceed take action. — *v.t.* **2.** To render unsuccessful; thwa frustrate. — *n.* **1.** A hindrance or check; defeat; dis pointment. **2.** An error or slip; blunder. **3.** In baseb an illegal motion made by the pitcher when one or m runners are on base. **4.** A ridge between furrows. **5** squared beam. Also spelled *baulk.* [OE *balca* bank, ridg
Bal·kan (bôl′kən) *adj.* **1.** Of or pertaining to the Ball Peninsula, its people, or their customs. **2.** Of or pertain to the Balkan Mountains.
balk·y (bô′kē) *adj.* **balk·i·er, balk·i·est** Given to balk
ball[1] (bôl) *n.* **1.** A spherical or nearly spherical body. Such a body, of any size and made of various substan used in a number of games. **3.** A game played with a b esp. baseball. **4.** In sports, a ball moving, thrown, or str in a specified manner. **5.** In baseball, a pitch in which ball fails to pass over the home plate between the batt armpits and knees and is not struck at by him. **6** roundish protuberance or part of something. **7.** *Usu. Slang* A testicle. — **to be on the ball** *U.S. Slang* To be a or competent. — **to have something on the ball** *U.S. Sl* To have ability. — **to play ball 1.** To begin or resu playing a ball game or some other activity. **2.** *U.S. formal* To cooperate. — *v.t. & v.i.* To form, gather, or w into a ball. — **to ball up** *Slang* To confuse. [< ON *bö*
ball[2] (bôl) *n.* A formal social dance. [< F *bal*]
bal·lad (bal′əd) *n.* **1.** A narrative poem or song of pop origin in short stanzas, often with a refrain. **2.** A sentim tal song of several stanzas, in which the melody is usually peated for each stanza. [Var. of BALLADE]
bal·lade (bə·läd′, ba-) *n.* **1.** A verse form having three st zas of eight or ten lines each and an envoy of four or five li The last line of each stanza and of the envoy is the sa **2.** A musical composition of romantic or dramatic nat usually for piano or orchestra. [< OF *balade* dancing so
bal·lad·ry (bal′əd·rē) *n.* **1.** Ballad poetry. **2.** The ar making or singing ballads.
ball-and-sock·et joint (bôl′ən·sok′it) **1.** *Mech.* A j composed of a sphere in a bearing, permitting a degre free turning in any direction. **2.** *Anat.* An enarthrosis.
bal·last (bal′əst) *n.* **1.** Any heavy substance, as sa stone, etc., laid in the hold of a vessel or in the car of a loon to steady it. **2.** Gravel or broken stone laid down stabilizer for a rail bed. **3.** That which gives stability character, morality, etc. — *v.t.* **1.** To provide or fill ballast. **2.** To steady with ballast; stabilize. [< OD *bar* bare, mere + *last* load]
ball bearing *Mech.* **1.** A bearing in which a shaft bear small metal balls that turn freely as it revolves. **2.** A m ball in such a bearing.
bal·le·ri·na (bal′ə·rē′nə) *n.* A female ballet dancer. Ital., fem. of *ballerino* dancer]
bal·let (bal′ā, ba·lā′) *n.* **1.** An elaborate dramatic gr dance using conventionalized movements, often for na tive effects. **2.** The performers or troupe of such danc [< F, dim. of *bal* dance]
bal·lis·tic (bə·lis′tik) *adj.* Of or pertaining to projec or to ballistics.
ballistic missile A missile controlled to the apex of trajectory, falling free thereafter.
bal·lis·tics (bə·lis′tiks) *n.pl.* (*construed as sing.*) **1.** science that deals with the motion of projectiles, either w they are still in the bore (**interior ballistics**) or after t leave the muzzle (**exterior ballistics**). **2.** The study of flight of all missiles. — **bal·lis·ti·cian** (bal′ə·stish′ən) *n.*
bal·loon (bə·lo͞on′) *n.* **1.** A large, impermeable bag, infla with gas lighter than air, and designed to rise and float in atmosphere; esp., such a bag having a car or basket tached, for carrying passengers, instruments, etc. **2** small, inflatable rubber bag, used as a toy. — *v.i.* **1.** To crease quickly in scope or magnitude; expand: The ru threatened to *balloon* into a full-fledged scandal. **2.** To s out like a balloon, as a sail. **3.** To ascend or travel balloon. — *v.t.* **4.** To inflate or distend with air. — Like a balloon. [< Ital. *balla* ball, sphere < Gmc.] — **loon′ist** *n.*

l·lot (bal′ət) *n.* **1.** A written or printed slip or ticket used ı casting a secret vote. **2.** The total number of votes cast ı an election. **3.** The act or system of voting secretly by allots or by voting machines. **4.** A list of candidates for of-ce; ticket. — *v.* **·lot·ed, ·lot·ing** *v.i.* **1.** To cast a ballot in oting. — *v.t.* **2.** To vote for or decide on by ballot. [< tal. *ballotta*, dim. of *balla* ball]
ll·play·er (bôl′plā′ər) *n. U.S.* A baseball player.
ll-point pen (bôl′point′) A fountain pen having for a oint a ball bearing that rolls to ink itself from a cartridge.
ll·room (bôl′ro͞om′, -ro͝om′) *n.* A large room for dancing.
llroom dancing Social dancing for two people.
ll valve *Mech.* A valve controlled by a ball that is free to se when the upward pressure exceeds gravity.
l·ly·hoo (bal′ē·ho͞o′) *n. U.S. Informal* **1.** Blatant or sen-itional advertising; noisy propaganda. **2.** Clamor; uproar. - *v.t. & v.i.* **·hooed, ·hoo·ing** To advocate or promote by allyhoo. [Origin unknown]
lm (bäm) *n.* **1.** An aromatic, resinous exudation from va-ous trees or shrubs, used as medicine; balsam. **2.** Any ly, fragrant, resinous substance. **3.** A tree or shrub yield-g such a substance. **4.** Any of various aromatic plants sembling mint. **5.** A pleasing fragrance. **6.** Anything ıat soothes. [< OF < L < Gk. *balsamon* balsam tree]
lm of Gilead **1.** The resinous, fragrant juice obtained om a small evergreen tree growing on the shores of the ed Sea. **2.** The balsam fir.
lm·y (bä′mē) *adj.* **balm·i·er, balm·i·est** **1.** Mild and othing; soft. **2.** Having the fragrance of balm; aromatic. . *Brit. Slang* Crazy. — **balm′i·ly** *adv.* — **balm′i·ness** *n.*
·lo·ney (bə·lō′nē) *n.* **1.** *Slang* Nonsense. **2.** Bologna ıusage. Also spelled *boloney*. [def. 1 < BOLOGNA SAUSAGE]
l·sa (bôl′sə, bäl′-) *n.* **1.** A tree of tropical America and e West Indies. **2.** The very light wood of this tree. **3.** A ft made of light logs. [< Sp. *balza*]
l·sam (bôl′səm) *n.* **1.** Any of a group of fragrant oleores-s obtained chiefly from the exudations of various trees. . Any tree yielding such a resinous substance, as the ılsam fir. **3.** Any fragrant ointment, esp. one used me-cinally. — *v.t.* To anoint with balsam. [< L < Gk. *bal-mon* balsam] — **bal·sam·ic** (bôl·sam′ik) *adj.*
lsam fir A tree of the pine family, growing in the U.S. ıd Canada and yielding Canada balsam: also *balm of Gilead.*
l·tic (bôl′tik) *adj.* Of or pertaining to the Baltic Sea or e Baltic States.
ltimore oriole An American oriole of which the male ıs orange and black plumage. [after the colors of the ıat of arms of Lord *Baltimore*]
l·us·ter (bal′əs·tər) *n.* One of a set of small pillars sup-ırting a handrail. For illus. see BALCONY. [< MF < Ital. *laustra* pomegranate flower]
l·us·trade (bal′ə·strād′, bal′ə·strād) *n.* A handrail sup-ırted by balusters. For illus. see BALCONY. See BALUSTER.
m·bi·no (bam·bē′nō) *n. pl.* **·ni** (-nē) or **·nos** **1.** A little ıild; a baby. **2.** A figure of the child Jesus. [< Ital., dim. *bambo* simple, childish]
m·boo (bam·bo͞o′) *n.* **1.** A tall, treelike or shrubby grass tropical and semitropical regions. **2.** Its tough, hollow, inted stem, used for furniture, etc. [< Malay *bambu*]
m·boo·zle (bam·bo͞o′zəl) *v.* **·zled, ·zling** *Informal v.t.* **1.** ɔ mislead; cheat. **2.** To perplex. — *v.i.* **3.** To practice ickery or deception. [Origin unknown] — **bam·boo′zle·ent** *n.* — **bam·boo′zler** *n.*
n (ban) *v.t.* **banned, ban·ning** **1.** To proscribe or pro-bit; forbid. **2.** To place under a ban; anathematize; inter-ct. — *n.* **1.** An official proclamation, especially of pro-bition. **2.** *Eccl.* An edict of excommunication or interdic-ɔn. **3.** A sentence of outlawry. [< OE *bannan* to pro-aim and ON *banna* to curse, prohibit]
nal (bā′nəl, bə·nal′, ban′əl) *adj.* Hackneyed; trite. [< < OF *ban* feudal summons hence, ordinary, common] — **·nal·i·ty** (bə·nal′ə·tē) *n.* — **ba′nal·ly** *adv.*
nan·a (bə·nan′ə) *n.* **1.** The elongated, edible, pulpy ıit of a herbaceous plant of tropical regions, having an sily removed rind and growing in drooping clusters. **2.** he plant bearing this fruit. [< Sp. < native African name]
nd[1] (band) *n.* **1.** A flat flexible strip of any material, ten used for binding or securing. **2.** A strip of fabric used finish, strengthen, or trim an article of dress: often in mbination: *hatband.* **3.** Any broad stripe of contrasting lor, material, or surface. **4.** *pl.* Geneva bands (which see). A high collar worn in the 16th and 17th centuries. **6.** *elecom.* A range of frequencies or wavelengths between two ated limits. — *v.t.* **1.** To unite or tie with a band; en-cle. **2.** To mark by attaching a band to. [< F *bande.*]
nd[2] (band) *n.* **1.** A company of persons associated for a mmon purpose; a group, troop, or gang. **2.** A company of rsons organized to play musical instruments. **3.** *Cana-dian* A group of reservation Indians having elective chiefs. — *v.t. & v.i.* To unite in a band. [< MF *bande*]
band·age (ban′dij) *n.* A strip of soft cloth or other mate-rial used in dressing wounds, etc. — *v.t.* **·aged, ag·ing** To bind or cover with a bandage. [< F < *bande* band]
Band-Aid (band′ād′) *n.* An adhesive strip with a gauze patch for covering minor wounds: a trade name. Also **band′-aid′.**
ban·dan·na (ban·dan′ə) *n.* A large, brightly colored hand-kerchief decorated with spots or figures. Also **ban·dan′a.** [< Hind. *bāndhnū*, a method of dyeing]
band·box (band′boks′) *n.* A light round or oval box, orig-inally used to hold collars, and now used for carrying hats.
ban·deau (ban·dō′, ban′dō) *n. pl.* **·deaux** (-dōz′, -dōz) **1.** A narrow band, esp. one worn about the hair. **2.** A narrow brassiere. [< F < OF *bande* band]
ban·di·coot (ban′di·ko͞ot) *n.* **1.** A large rat of India and Ceylon. **2.** A small marsupial of Australia, Tasmania, etc. [Alter. of Telugu *pandikokku* pig-rat]
ban·dit (ban′dit) *n. pl.* **ban·dits** or **ban·dit·ti** (ban·dit′ē) **1.** A robber. **2.** An outlaw; brigand. [< Ital. *bandire* to proscribe, outlaw] — **ban′dit·ry** *n.*
band·mas·ter (band′mas′tər, -mäs′tər) *n.* The conductor of a musical band.
ban·do·leer (ban′də·lir′) *n.* A broad belt fitted with loops or cases for holding cartridges, and worn over the shoulder. Also **ban′do·lier′.** [< MF < Ital. *banda* band]
band saw *Mech.* A saw consisting of a toothed endless belt mounted on pulleys.
band shell A bandstand having a concave hemispherical rear wall.
band·stand (band′stand′) *n.* A platform for a band of musicians, often roofed when outdoors.
band·wag·on (band′wag′ən) *n.* A high, decorated wagon used to carry a band in a parade. — **to climb (hop, get,** etc.) **on the bandwagon** *U.S. Informal* To give one's support to a principle or candidate apparently assured of success.
ban·dy (ban′dē) *v.t.* **·died, ·dy·ing** **1.** To give and take; ex-change, as blows or words. **2.** To pass along; circulate: to *bandy* stories. **3.** To pass, throw, or knock back and forth, as a ball. — *n.pl.* **·dies** A game resembling hockey; also, a crooked stick used in this game. [Origin uncertain]
ban·dy-leg·ged (ban′dē·leg′id, -legd′) *adj.* Bowlegged.
bane (bān) *n.* **1.** Anything destructive or ruinous. **2.** Poi-son: now only in combination: *henbane.* [OE *bana* killer]
bane·ful (bān′fəl) *adj.* Poisonous; destructive. — **Syn.** See PERNICIOUS. — **bane′ful·ly** *adv.* — **bane′ful·ness** *n.*
bang[1] (bang) *n.* **1.** A heavy, noisy blow or thump. **2.** A sudden, loud noise or explosion. **3.** *Informal* A sudden spurt of activity: To start with a *bang.* **4.** *U.S. Slang* Thrill; en-joyment. — *v.t.* **1.** To beat or strike heavily and noisily. — *v.i.* **2.** To make a loud sound. **3.** To strike noisily; crash. — *adv.* Abruptly and loudly. [< ON *banga* to hammer]
bang[2] (bang) *n. Usu. pl.* A fringe of hair cut straight across the forehead. — *v.t.* To cut short and straight across. [< BANG[1], adv.; from the hair being cut off abruptly]
bang[3] (bang) See BHANG.
ban·gle (bang′gəl) *n.* A decorative bracelet or anklet. [< Hind. *bangrī* glass bracelet]
bang-up (bang′up′) *adj. Slang* Excellent.
ban·ish (ban′ish) *v.t.* **1.** To compel to leave a country by political decree; exile. **2.** To expel, as from any customary or desired place; drive away; dismiss. [< OF < LL *bannire* to banish] — **ban′ish·er** *n.* — **ban′ish·ment** *n.*
ban·is·ter (ban′is·tər) *n.* **1.** *Often pl.* A balustrade. **2.** Loosely, a baluster. Also *bannister.* [BALUSTER]
ban·jo (ban′jō) *n. pl.* **·jos** or **·joes** A long-necked, four- or five-stringed musical instrument having a hoop-shaped body covered on top with stretched skin and played by plucking the strings with the fingers or a plectrum. [< a West African language; cf. Mandingo *bania*] — **ban′jo·ist** *n.*
bank[1] (bangk) *n.* **1.** Any moundlike forma-tion or mass; ridge. **2.** A steep slope; rising ground. **3.** *Often pl.* The slope of land at the edge of a watercourse or of any cut or channel. — **Syn.** See SHORE. **4.** A raised portion of the ocean floor, a river bed, etc.; a shoal; shal-low: the Newfoundland *banks.* **5.** Aeron. The controlled sidewise tilt of an airplane in a turn, used to prevent skidding. — *v.t.* **1.** To enclose, cover, or protect by a bank, dike, or border; embank. **2.** To heap up into a bank or mound. **3.** To give an upward lateral slope to, as the curve of a road. **4.** To tilt (an airplane) laterally in flight. **5.** In billiards and pool: To cause (a ball) to rebound at an angle from a cushion. — *v.i.* **6.** To form or lie in banks. **7.** To tilt an airplane laterally in flight. [ME *banke*]

BANJO

ɴUNCIATION KEY: add, āce, câre, pälm; end, ēven; it, īce; odd, ōpen, ôrder; to͝ok, po͞ol; up, bûrn; ə = a in *above*, e in *sicken*, i in *flex-*, o in *melon*, u in *focus*; yo͞o = u in *fuse*; oil; pout; check; go; ring; thin; this; zh, vision.

bank[2] (bangk) *n.* **1.** An institution for lending, borrowing, exchanging, issuing, or safeguarding money. **2.** An office or building used for such purposes. **3.** The funds of a gambling house or the fund held by the dealer or banker in some gambling games. **4.** A store or reserve supply of anything needed for future use: a blood *bank.* — *v.t.* **1.** To deposit in a bank. — *v.i.* **2.** To do business as or with a bank or banker. **3.** In gambling, to keep the bank in a game. — **to bank on** *Informal* To rely on; be sure about. [< F < Ital. *banca* money-changer's table, ult. < Gmc.]

bank[3] (bangk) *n.* **1.** A set of like articles arranged in a row. **2.** *Naut.* A rowers' bench or tier of oars in a galley. **3.** A rank of keys in a piano or organ. **4.** In journalism, lines under a headline; deck. — *v.t.* To arrange in a bank. [< OF < LL *bancus* bench, ult. < Gmc.]

bank account Money deposited in a bank to the credit of, and subject to withdrawal by, the depositor.

bank bill **1.** A bank note. **2.** A draft drawn on one bank by another: also **banker's bill.**

bank·book (bangk′bo͝ok′) *n.* A book kept by a depositor in which his accounts are entered: also called *passbook.*

bank·er[1] (bangk′ər) *n.* **1.** An employee or officer of a bank. **2.** One who keeps the bank in certain gambling games.

bank·er[2] (bangk′ər) *n.* *U.S. & Canadian* A vessel or person engaged in cod fishing on the Newfoundland banks.

bank·ing (bangk′ing) *n.* The business of a bank or banker.

bank note A promissory note issued by a bank, payable on demand and serving as currency. Abbr. *B.N.*

bank·rupt (bangk′rupt) *n.* **1.** *Law* One who is judicially declared insolvent, his property being administered for and distributed among his creditors, under a bankruptcy law. **2.** Any person unable to pay his debts, or without resources. **3.** One ruined and unproductive in some way: a spiritual *bankrupt.* — *adj.* **1.** Subject to the conditions of a bankruptcy law; insolvent. **2.** Destitute; lacking: with *in.* — *v.t.* To make bankrupt. [< F < Ital. < L *rumpere* to break]

bank·rupt·cy (bangk′rupt·sē, -rəp·sē) *n.* *pl.* **·cies** The state of being bankrupt.

ban·ner (ban′ər) *n.* **1.** A flag or standard bearing a motto or device. **2.** In journalism, a headline extending across a newspaper page. — *adj.* Leading; foremost; outstanding. [< OF < LL *bandum* banner]

ban·nis·ter (ban′is·tər) See BANISTER.

banns (banz) *n.pl.* *Eccl.* A public announcement in church of a proposed marriage, usu. made on three successive Sundays. Also **bans.** [< BAN]

ban·quet (bang′kwit) *n.* **1.** A sumptuous feast. **2.** A formal or ceremonial dinner, often followed by speeches. — *v.t. & v.i.* To entertain at a banquet; feast sumptuously or formally. [< MF, dim. of *banc* table] — **ban′quet·er** *n.*

ban·quette (bang·ket′) *n.* **1.** *Mil.* A platform or bank behind a parapet, on which soldiers may stand and fire. **2.** An upholstered bench, as along a wall. **3.** A sidewalk. [< F < Ital. *banchetta,* dim. of *banca* bench]

ban·shee (ban′shē, ban·shē′) *n.* In Gaelic folklore, a spirit whose wailing was supposed to foretell a death. Also **ban′shie.** [< Irish *bean* woman + *sīdhe* fairy]

ban·tam (ban′təm) *n.* **1.** *Often cap.* Any of various breeds of very small domestic fowl, characterized by combativeness. **2.** A small, pugnacious person. — *adj.* Like a bantam; small and combative. [after *Bantam,* Java]

ban·tam·weight (ban′təm·wāt′) *n.* A boxer or wrestler who weighs between 113 and 118 pounds.

ban·ter (ban′tər) *n.* Good-humored ridicule; raillery. — *v.t.* **1.** To tease good-naturedly. — *v.i.* **2.** To exchange good-natured repartee. [Origin unknown] — **ban′ter·er** *n.* — **ban′ter·ing·ly** *adv.*

Ban·tu (ban′to͞o) *n.* *pl.* **·tu** or **·tus** (-to͞oz) **1.** A member of any of numerous Negro tribes of central and southern Africa, including the Kaffirs, Zulus, Bechuanas, and Damaras. **2.** A family of languages spoken by these tribes. — *adj.* Of or pertaining to the Bantu tribes or their languages.

ban·yan (ban′yən) *n.* An East Indian fig-bearing tree whose branches send down roots that develop into new trunks. [< *banian,* Hindu merchant, from the use of the ground under the tree as a market place]

ban·zai (bän·zī) *Japanese* (May you live) ten thousand years: used as a cheer, battle cry, etc.

ba·o·bab (bā′ō·bab, bä′ō-) *n.* An African tree with a thick trunk, bearing edible fruit. [< native African name]

bap·tism (bap′tiz·əm) *n.* **1.** The act of baptizing or of being baptized; esp., the Christian sacrament of initiation into the Church. **2.** Any initiatory or purifying experience. [< OF < LL < Gk. *baptismos* immersion] — **bap·tis·mal** (bap·tiz′məl) *adj.* — **bap·tis′mal·ly** *adv.*

Bap·tist (bap′tist) *n.* **1.** A member of any of various Protestant denominations holding that baptism (generally by immersion) should be given only to professed believers. **2.** One who baptizes. — **the Baptist** John the Baptist.

bap·tis·ter·y (bap′tis·tər·ē, -tis·trē) *n.* *pl.* **·ter·ies** A part of a church set apart for baptism. Also **bap′tis·try** (-trē).

bap·tize (bap·tīz′, bap′tīz) *v.* **·tized, ·tiz·ing** *v.t.* **1.** To i merse in water or sprinkle water on in Christian baptis **2.** To christen. **3.** To cleanse or initiate. — *v.i.* **4.** administer baptism. Also *Brit.* **bap·tise′.** [< OF < < Gk. *baptizein* to immerse, wash] — **bap·tiz′er** *n.*

bar (bär) *n.* **1.** A piece of wood, metal, etc., evenly sha and long in proportion to its width and thickness, used a fastening, lever, etc. **2.** An oblong block of solid mater as of soap or a precious metal. **3.** Any barrier or obsta **4.** A bank, as of sand, at the entrance to a harbor or riv **5.** The railing about the place in a court occupied by judge and lawyers, or where prisoners are brought to tr **6.** A court of law. **7.** Lawyers collectively; also, the le profession. **8.** Any tribunal or place of judgment. *Music* **a** The vertical line that divides a staff into measu **b** A measure. **10** A counter or establishment serving dri and food, esp. alcoholic drinks. **11.** A stripe, as of co **12.** The metal mouthpiece of a horse's bridle. — *v.t.* **barr bar·ring** **1.** To fasten or secure with a bar. **2.** To prev or prohibit. **3.** To obstruct or hinder. **4.** To exclu **5.** To mark with stripes. — *prep.* Excepting: *bar* no [< OF < LL *barra* bar]

Ba·rab·bas (bə·rab′əs) A thief released in place of Jesus the demand of the multitude. *Matt.* xxvii 16–21.

barb[1] (bärb) *n.* **1.** A point projecting backward on a sh weapon, as on an arrow, fishhook, or spear, intended to p vent easy extraction. **2.** Any similar sharp point, as barbed wire. **3.** Pointedness; sting, as of wit; also, a sti ing remark. **4.** *Ornithol.* One of the lateral processes o bird's feather. — *v.t.* To provide with a barb or barbs: *barb* an arrow. [< F < L *barba* beard]

barb[2] (bärb) *n.* A horse of the breed introduced by Moors from Barbary into Spain. [< F < Arabic *Bar* native of North Africa]

bar·bar·i·an (bär·bâr′ē·ən) *n.* **1.** One who belongs t people, group, or tribe characterized by a primitive civil tion. **2.** A rude, coarse, or brutal person. **3.** Formerl foreigner; esp., in ancient Greece, one who was non-Helle — *adj.* **1.** Of or resembling a barbarian; uncivilized. Foreign. — **bar·bar′i·an·ism** *n.*

bar·bar·ic (bär·bar′ik) *adj.* **1.** Of or befitting barbari uncivilized. **2.** Coarse; unrestrained.

bar·ba·rism (bär′bə·riz′əm) *n.* **1.** The use of word forms not approved or standard in a language. **2.** Suc word or form. **3.** A primitive stage of civilization. **4** trait, condition, act, etc., characteristic of such a stage.

bar·bar·i·ty (bär·bar′ə·tē) *n.* *pl.* **·ties** **1.** Barbaric cond **2.** A barbaric act. **3.** Crudity in style or taste.

bar·ba·rize (bär′bə·rīz) *v.t. & v.i.* **·rized, ·riz·ing** To m or become barbarous or corrupt, as a language.

bar·ba·rous (bär′bər·əs) *adj.* **1.** Uncivilized; primit **2.** Lacking in refinement; coarse. **3.** Cruel; brutal. **4.** R or harsh in sound: *barbarous* music. **5.** Of language, abou ing in barbarisms; also, not classical. **6.** Formerly, fore esp. in ancient Greece, non-Hellenic. [< L < Gk. *barb* non-Hellenic, foreign, rude] — **bar′ba·rous·ly** *adv.* — **b ba·rous·ness** *n.*

Bar·ba·ry (bär′bər·ē) North Africa west of Egypt, inc ing the former Barbary States.

Barbary ape An easily trained, tailless ape of N Africa and southern Spain.

bar·bate (bär′bāt) *adj.* **1.** Bearded. **2.** *Bot.* Tufted long hairs. [< L *barba* beard]

bar·be·cue (bär′bə·kyo͞o) *n.* **1.** *U.S.* A social gather usu. outdoors, at which animals are roasted whole over open fire. **2.** A whole animal carcass or other meat roas over an open fire. **3.** A grill, framework, or pit for roast meat in this fashion. — *v.t.* **·cued, ·cu·ing** To roast (beef or pork) in large pieces or whole over an open fir in a trench, often using a highly seasoned sauce. [< *barbacoa* < Taino *barbacoa* framework of sticks]

barbed (bärbd) *adj.* **1.** Having a barb or barbs. **2.** Poin piercing, or wounding: a *barbed* remark.

barbed wire Fence wire having barbs at short interva

bar·bel (bär′bəl) *n.* **1.** One of the soft threadlike ap dages to the jaws, chin, or nostrils of certain fishes, funct ing as an organ of touch. **2.** A carplike, Old World f [< OF < LL < L *barba* beard]

bar·ber (bär′bər) *n.* One who cuts hair, shaves beards, e as a business. ◆ Collateral adjective: *tonsorial.* — *v.t.* cut or dress the hair of; shave or trim the beard of. [< ult. < L *barba* beard]

bar·ber·ry (bär′ber′ē, -bər·ē) *n.* **·ries** **1.** A shrub bea yellow flowers and bright red, oblong berries. **2.** Its berry. [< Med.L *berberis, barbaris*]

bar·ber·shop (bär′bər·shop′) *n.* The place of business barber. — *adj.* *Informal* Characterized by close harm and sentimentality of theme: said of a singing group.

bar·bi·can (bär′bi·kən) *n.* An outer fortification; outw [< OF *barbaquenne*; ult. origin uncertain]

bar·bi·tal (bär′bə·tôl, -tal) *n.* *Chem.* A white, odor rystalline powder, $C_8H_{12}O_3N_2$, with a bitter taste, used as a edative and hypnotic. Also *Brit.* **bar′bi·tone** (-tōn).

ır·bit·u·rate (bär·bich′ər·it, bär′bə·to͝or′it, -tyo͝or′it) *n.* *Chem.* A salt or ester of barbituric acid, esp. one used as a edative or sleeping pill.

ır·bi·tu·ric acid (bär′bə·to͝or′ik, -tyo͝or′-) *Chem.* A crysalline powder, $C_4H_4O_3N_2$, from which several sedative and ypnotic drugs are derived. [< NL (*Usnea*) *barbata* bearded lichen) + -URIC]

ır·bule (bär′byo͞ol) *n.* **1.** A small barb or beard. **2.** *Orithol.* A process fringing the barb of a feather. [< L *barula*, dim. of *barba* beard]

ır·ca·role (bär′kə·rōl) *n.* **1.** A Venetian gondolier's song. **2.** A melody in imitation of this. Also **bar′ca·rolle.** [< F < Ital. *barcaruola* boatman's song]

ırd (bärd) *n.* **1.** A Celtic poet and minstrel. **2.** A poet. < Celtic] — **bard′ic** *adj.*

ıre[1] (bâr) *adj.* **1.** Without clothing or covering; naked. **2.** Open to view; exposed. **3.** Without the usual furnishings r equipment; empty. **4.** Unadorned; plain; bald. **5.** Just ufficient; mere. **6.** Threadbare. — *v.t.* **bared, bar·ing** To make or lay bare; reveal; expose. [OE *bær*]

ıre[2] (bâr) Archaic past tense of BEAR[1].

ıre·back (bâr′bak′) *adj.* Riding a horse without a saddle. — *adv.* Without a saddle. — **bare′backed′** *adj.*

ıre·faced (bâr′fāst′) *adj.* **1.** Having the face bare. **2.** Unconcealed; open. **3.** Impudent; audacious. — **bare·fac·ed·ly** (bâr′fā′sid·lē, -fāst′lē) *adv.* — **bare′fac′ed·ness** *n.*

ıre·foot (bâr′fo͝ot′) *adj. & adv.* With the feet bare.

ıre·foot·ed (bâr′fo͝ot′id) *adj.* Having the feet bare.

ıre·hand·ed (bâr′han′did) *adj. & adv.* **1.** With the hands ncovered. **2.** Without a weapon, tool, etc.

ıre·head·ed (bâr′hed′id) *adj. & adv.* With the head bare. Also **bare′head′.**

ıre·leg·ged (bâr′leg′id, -legd′) *adj. & adv.* With the legs bare.

ıre·ly (bâr′lē) *adv.* **1.** Only just; scarcely. **2.** Openly; boldly; plainly. **3.** Nakedly.

ır·gain (bär′gən) *n.* **1.** A mutual agreement between persons, especially an agreement to buy or sell goods. **2.** That which is agreed upon or the terms of the agreement. **3.** The agreement as it affects one of the parties: He made a bad *bargain*. **4.** An article bought or offered at a low price. — **into the bargain** In addition to what was agreed; besides. — **to strike a bargain** To come to an agreement on terms. — *v.i.* **1.** To discuss terms for selling or buying. **2.** To make a bargain; reach an agreement. **3.** To negotiate. — *v.t.* **4.** To trade or arrange by bargaining. — **to bargain for** To expect; count on: more than I *bargained for*. [< OF *bargaine*] — **bar′gain·er,** *Law* **bar′gain·or** *n.*

ırge (bärj) *n.* **1.** A flat-bottomed freight boat or lighter for harbors and inland waters. **2.** A large boat, for pleasure, pageants, or for state occasions. **3.** *Naval* A ship's boat for the use of a flag officer. — *v.* **barged, barg·ing** *v.t.* **1.** To transport by barge. — *v.i.* **2.** To move clumsily and slowly. **3.** *Informal* To collide: with *into*. **4.** *Informal* To enter or intrude rudely or awkwardly. [< OF < LL *barga*]

ırge·man (bärj′mən) *n.* *pl.* **·men** (-mən) One in charge of or employed on a barge. Also *Brit.* **bar·gee** (bär·jē′).

ır·ite (bâr′īt) *n.* A heavy, vitreous, usu. white, orthorhombic barium sulfate, $BaSO_4$: also called *heavy spar.*

ır·i·tone (bar′ə·tōn) *n.* **1.** A male voice of a register higher than bass and lower than tenor. **2.** One having such a voice. **3.** A brass instrument having a similar range. — *adj.* **1.** Of or pertaining to a baritone. **2.** Having the range of a baritone. [< Ital. < Gk. < *barys* deep + *tonos* tone]

ır·i·um (bâr′ē·əm) *n.* A silver white to yellow, malleable, metallic element (symbol Ba) occurring in combination and forming salts, of which the soluble ones and the carbonate are poisonous. See ELEMENT. [< NL < Gk. *barys* heavy] — **bar·ic** (bar′ik) *adj.*

ırium sulfate An insoluble compound, $BaSO_4$, used to facilitate X-ray pictures of the stomach and intestines.

ırk[1] (bärk) *n.* **1.** The short, abrupt, explosive cry of a dog. **2.** Any sound like this. — *v.i.* **1.** To utter a bark, as a dog, or to make a sound like a bark. **2.** *Informal* To cough. **3.** To speak loudly and sharply. **4.** *U.S. Slang* To solicit customers at the entrance to a show by proclaiming its attractions. — *v.t.* **5.** To say roughly and curtly: He *barked* an order. — **to bark up the wrong tree** *U.S. Informal* To be mistaken as to one's object or as to the means of attaining it. [OE *beorcan*]

ırk[2] (bärk) *n.* The rind or covering of the stems, branches, and roots of a tree or other plant. — *v.t* **1.** To remove the bark from; scrape; girdle. **2.** To rub off the skin of. **3.** To tan or treat with an infusion of bark. [< Scand.]

ırk[3] (bärk) *n.* A sailing vessel of three or more masts, square-rigged on all but the mizzenmast, which is fore-and-aft-rigged. [< MF < LL *barca* bark]

bar·keep·er (bär′kē·pər) *n.* **1.** One who owns or manages a bar where alcoholic liquors are served. **2.** A bartender. Also **bar′keep′.**

bar·ken·tine (bär′kən·tēn) *n.* A sailing vessel of three or more masts, square-rigged on the foremast and fore-and-aft-rigged on the other masts: also spelled *barquentine.* [< BARK[3], on analogy with *brigantine*]

BARK

bark·er (bär′kər) *n.* *U.S. Informal* One who advertises a show, etc., at its entrance.

bar·ley (bär′lē) *n.* **1.** A hardy cereal grass of temperate regions. **2.** The grain borne by this grass. [OE *bærlīc*]

bar·ley·corn (bär′lē·kôrn) *n.* Barley, or a grain of barley.

Bar·ley·corn (bär′lē·kôrn), **John** A humorous personification of malt liquor, or of intoxicating liquors in general.

barm (bärm) *n.* The froth or foam rising on fermented malt liquors. [OE *beorma*]

bar·maid (bär′mād) *n.* A female bartender.

bar·man (bär′mən) *n.* *pl* **·men** (mən) A bartender.

bar mitz·vah (bär mits′və) In Judaism, a boy commencing his thirteenth year, the age of religious duty; also, the ceremony celebrating this. [< Hebrew, son of the commandment]

barm·y (bär′mē) *adj.* **barm·i·er, barm·i·est 1.** Full of barm; frothy. **2.** *Brit. Slang* Silly; flighty. Also *Scot.* **barm′ie.**

barn (bärn) *n.* **1.** A building for storing hay, stabling livestock, etc. **2.** *Brit.* A building for storing grain. [OE *bern*]

bar·na·cle (bär′nə·kəl) *n.* **1.** A marine shellfish that attaches itself to rocks, ship bottoms, etc. **2.** A European wild goose of northern seas: also **barnacle goose. 3.** One who or that which clings tenaciously. [< ME *bernacle*; origin uncertain] — **bar′na·cled** *adj.*

barn dance A social dance held in a barn and usu. consisting of square dances with appropriate music and calls.

barn owl An owl of nearly world-wide distribution, often found in barns, where it preys on mice.

barn·storm (bärn′stôrm′) *v.i.* *U.S Informal* To tour rural districts, giving shows, political speeches, exhibitions of stunt flying, etc. — **barn′storm′er** *n.* — **barn′storm′ing** *adj. & n.*

barn·yard (bärn′yärd′) *n.* A yard adjoining a barn. — *adj.* Of or fit for a barnyard; broad; smutty.

baro- *combining form* Weight; atmospheric pressure: *barometer.* [< Gk. *baros* weight]

bar·o·gram (bar′ə·gram) *n.* The record of a barograph.

bar·o·graph (bar′ə·graf, -gräf) *n.* An automatically recording barometer. — **bar′o·graph′ic** *adj.*

ba·rom·e·ter (bə·rom′ə·tər) *n.* **1.** An instrument for measuring atmospheric pressure, used in forecasting weather, measuring elevations, etc. **2.** Anything that indicates changes. — **bar·o·met·ric** (bar′ə·met′rik) or **·ri·cal** *adj.* — **bar′o·met′ri·cal·ly** *adv.* — **ba·rom′e·try** *n.*

bar·on (bar′ən) *n.* **1.** A member of the lowest order of hereditary nobility in several European countries. **2.** *U.S.* One who has great power in a commercial field. [< OF < LL *baro, -onis* man < Gmc.] — **ba·ro·ni·al** (bə·rō′nē·əl) *adj.*

bar·on·age (bar′ən·ij) *n.* **1.** Barons collectively. **2.** The dignity or rank of a baron.

bar·o·ness (bar′ən·is) *n.* **1.** The wife or widow of a baron. **2.** A woman holding a barony in her own right.

bar·on·et (bar′ən·it, -ə·net) *n.* **1.** An inheritable English title, below that of baron and not part of the nobility. **2.** The bearer of the title. — **bar′on·et·age, bar′on·et·cy** *n.*

bar·o·ny (bar′ə·nē) *n.* *pl.* **·nies** The rank, dignity, or domain of a baron.

ba·roque (bə·rōk′) *adj.* **1.** Of or characteristic of a style of art and architecture developed in Europe in the late 16th and 17th centuries, characterized by extravagantly contorted classical forms and curvilinear ornament. **2.** Fantastic in style; elaborately ornamented. **3.** Loosely, rococo. **4.** Irregular in shape: said of pearls. — *n.* **1.** The baroque style in art. **2.** An object, ornament, design, or composition in this style. [< F < Pg. *barroco* rough or imperfect pearl]

BAROQUE ARCHITECTURE (Church of Santa Maria della Salute, Venice, 1631–56)

ba·rouche (bə·ro͞osh′) *n.* A four-wheeled carriage with folding top, four inside seats, and an outside seat for the driver. [< G < Ital. < L *bis* twice + *rota* wheel]

barque (bärk), **bar·quen·tine** (bär′·kən·tēn) See BARK[3], BARKENTINE.

bar·racks (bar′əks) *n.pl.* (*construed as sing. or pl.*) **1.** A building or group of buildings for the housing of soldiers. **2.** Any large, plain building used for temporary housing. Also **bar′rack.** [< F *baraque* < Ital. *baracca* soldier's tent; ult. origin uncertain]

barracks bag A soldier's cloth bag with a draw cord, for holding clothing and equipment. Also **barrack bag.**

bar·ra·cu·da (bar′ə·kōō′də) *n. pl.* **·da** or **·das** A voracious pikelike fish of tropical seas. [< Sp.]

bar·rage (bə·räzh′) *n.* **1.** *Mil.* A curtain of fire designed to protect troops by impeding enemy movements across defensive lines or areas. **2.** Any overwhelming attack, as of words or blows. **—***v.t.* & *v.i.* **·raged, ·rag·ing** To lay down or subject to a barrage. [< F (*tir de*) *barrage* barrage (fire)]

bar·ran·ca (bə·rang′kə) *n. SW U.S.* A deep ravine. [< Sp.]

bar·ra·try (bar′ə·trē) *n. pl.* **·tries** *Law* **1.** Any willful and unlawful act by the master or crew of a ship, whereby the owners sustain injury. **2.** The offense of exciting lawsuits, stirring up quarrels, etc. Also **bar′re·try.** [< OF < *barat* fraud] **—bar′ra·tor** *n.* **—bar′ra·trous** *adj.*

barred (bärd) *adj.* **1.** Having or secured with bars. **2.** Prohibited. **3.** Marked with bars or stripes.

bar·rel (bar′əl) *n.* **1.** A large, approximately cylindrical vessel usu. of wood, flat at the base and top and bulging slightly in the middle. **2.** As much as a barrel will hold, as the standard U.S. barrel containing 3.28 bushels dry measure, or 31.5 liquid measure. **3.** Something resembling or having the form of a barrel, as the tube of a gun, the drum of a windlass, the cylindrical box containing the mainspring of a watch, etc. **—***v.* **bar·reled** or **·relled, bar·rel·ing** or **·rel·ling** *v.t.* **1.** To put or pack in a barrel. **—***v.i.* **2.** *U.S Slang* To move fast. [< OF *baril*]

bar·rel·house (bar′əl·hous′) *n. U.S. Slang* **1.** A cheap drinking house. **2.** *Music* An early style of jazz.

barrel organ A hand organ.

barrel roll *Aeron.* A maneuver in which an airplane rolls on its own axis as it spirals about its original path.

bar·ren (bar′ən) *adj.* **1.** Not producing or incapable of producing offspring; sterile. **2.** Not productive; unfruitful. **3.** Unprofitable, as an enterprise. **4.** Lacking in interest or attractiveness; dull. **5.** Empty; devoid. **—***n. Usu. pl.* A tract of level, scrubby land. [< OF *baraigne*] **—bar′ren·ly** *adv.* **—bar′ren·ness** *n.*

bar·rette (bə·ret′) *n.* A small bar with a clasp used for keeping a woman's hair in place. [< F, dim. of *barre* bar]

bar·ri·cade (bar′ə·kād′, bar′ə·kād) *n.* **1.** A barrier hastily built for obstruction or defense. **2.** Any barrier or obstruction blocking passage. **—***v.t.* **·cad·ed, ·cad·ing** To enclose, obstruct, or defend with a barricade or barricades. [< F < Sp. *barricada* barrier < *barrica* barrel; the first barricades were barrels filled with earth, stones, etc.] **—bar′ri·cad′er** *n.*

bar·ri·er (bar′ē·ər) *n.* **1.** A fence, wall, gate, etc., erected to bar passage. **2.** Any obstacle or obstruction, natural or otherwise. **3.** Something that separates or keeps apart: a *barrier* of suspicion. [< OF < *barre* bar]

barrier reef A long, narrow ridge of rock or coral parallel to the coast and close to or above the surface of the sea.

bar·ring (bär′ing) *prep.* Excepting; apart from.

bar·ris·ter (bar′is·tər) *n.* In England, a member of the legal profession who argues cases in the courts.

bar·room (bär′rōōm′, -rŏŏm′) *n.* A room where alcoholic liquors are served across a counter or bar.

bar·row[1] (bar′ō) *n.* **1.** A frame or tray with handles at either end by which it is carried, used for transporting loads. **2.** A wheelbarrow. **3.** The load carried on a barrow. **4.** *Brit.* A pushcart. [OE *bearwe* < *beran* to bear]

bar·row[2] (bar′ō) *n.* **1.** *Anthropol.* A mound of earth or stones built over a grave. **2.** A hill. [OE *beorg*]

bar sinister Erroneously, a bend sinister.

bar·tend·er (bär′ten′dər) *n.* A man who mixes and serves alcoholic drinks over a bar.

bar·ter (bär′tər) *v.i.* **1.** To trade by exchange of goods or services without use of money. **—***v.t.* **2.** To trade (goods or services) for something of equal value. **—***n.* **1.** The act of bartering; exchange of goods. **2.** Anything bartered. [< OF *barater* to exchange] **—bar′ter·er** *n.*

Bart·lett (bärt′lit) *n.* A variety of pear introduced by Enoch Bartlett of Massachusetts. Also **Bartlett pear.**

Bar·uch (bâr′ək) A book in the Old Testament Apocrypha.

bar·y·tes (bə·rī′tēz) *n.* Barite.

ba·sal (bā′səl) *adj.* **1.** Of, at, or forming the base. **2.** Basic; fundamental. **—ba′sal·ly** *adv.*

basal metabolism *Physiol.* The minimum energy required by the body at rest in maintaining essential vital activities, measured by the rate (**basal metabolic rate**) of oxygen intake and heat discharge.

ba·salt (bə·sôlt′, bas′ôlt) *n.* A dense, dark volcanic rock, haviog a columnar structure. [< L *basaltes* dark marble] **—ba·sal′tic** *adj.*

bas·cule (bas′kyōōl) *n.* A mechanical apparatus of which each end counterbalances the other, used in a kind of drawbridge (**bascule bridge**) operated by a counterpoise. [< F, seesaw]

base[1] (bās) *n.* **1.** The lowest or supporting pa of anything; bottom. **2.** An underlying principle or foundation. **3.** The essential or preponderant element; chief or fundamental ingredient. **4.** Any point, line, or quantity from which an inference, measurement, or reckoning is made. **5.** *Archit.* The lowest member of a structure, as the basement of a building. **6.** *Geom.* The side of a polygon or so figure on which it appears to rest. **7.** *Math.* A numb on which a numerical system depends: The *base* of the de mal system is 10. **8.** *Mil.* A locality or installation fr which operations are projected or supported. **9.** *Chem.* compound that is capable of so uniting with an acid as neutralize it and form a salt. **10.** *Biol.* The point of atta ment of an organ. **11.** In baseball, any of the four points the diamond, or the bag or plate marking one of these. 1 A base line. **13.** *Ling.* A form to which prefixes, suffixes, infixes are added; root or stem. **—off base 1.** In baseb not in contact with the base occupied: said of base runne **2.** *U.S. Slang* Thinking, speaking, etc., erroneously. **—** **based, bas·ing 1.** To place on a foundation or basis; grou establish: with *on* or *upon.* **2.** To form a base for. **—** **1.** Serving as a base: a *base* line. **2.** Situated at or near base: a *base* angle. [< OF < L < Gk. < *bainein* to go]

BASCULE BRIDGE
(Tower Bridge, London)

base[2] (bās) *adj.* **1.** Morally low; mean; vile; contempti **2.** Like or befitting an inferior person or thing; menial; grading: *base* flattery. **3.** Comparatively low in value: s of metals. **4.** Debased, as money; counterfeit: *base* co **5.** Not classical; corrupted: said of languages. [< OF < *bassus* low] **—base′ly** *adv.* **—base′ness** *n.*

base·ball (bās′bôl′) *n.* **1.** A game played with a wood bat and a hard ball by two teams of nine players each, team being at bat and the other in the field, alternately, object of the game being to make as many runs as possi within nine innings of play. **2.** The ball used in this ga

base·board (bās′bôrd′, -bōrd′) *n.* **1.** A board skirting interior wall of a room, next to the floor. **2.** Any bo forming a base.

base·born (bās′bôrn′) *adj.* **1.** Of humble birth; plebei **2.** Born out of wedlock. **3.** Mean; vile.

base burn·er (bās′bûr′nər) *n.* A coal stove or furnace which the fuel is fed from above into a central fuel chamb

base hit In baseball, a batted ball that enables the batter reach a base unaided by a defensive error, an attempt to out a preceding base runner, or a force play: also called

base·less (bās′lis) *adj.* Without foundation in fact; founded; groundless. **—base′less·ness** *n.*

base line 1. In baseball, a path of definite width connecti successive bases. **2.** A line, value, etc., taken as a base measurement or comparison.

base·ment (bās′mənt) *n.* **1.** The lowest story of a buildi usu. wholly or partly underground and just beneath main floor. **2.** The basal portion of any building.

base runner In baseball, a member of the team at bat w has reached a base.

bas·es[1] (bā′siz) Plural of BASE[1].

ba·ses[2] (bā′sēz) Plural of BASIS.

bash (bash) *Informal v.t.* To strike heavily; smash in. **—** A smashing blow. [? Akin to Dan. *baske* thwack]

bash·ful (bash′fəl) *adj.* **1.** Shrinking from notice; shy; ti id; diffident. **2.** Characterized by or indicating sensiti ness and timid modesty: a *bashful* glance. [< *bash*, var. ABASH + -FUL] **—bash′ful·ly** *adv.* **—bash′ful·ness** *n.*

ba·sic (bā′sik) *adj.* **1.** Pertaining to, forming, or like a b or basis; essential; fundamental. **2.** *Chem.* Of, pertaining or producing a base. **—ba′si·cal·ly** *adv.*

Basic English A simplified form of English, devised for as an international language and in the teaching of Engli It contains 850 words of general vocabulary, supplemen by an additional 150 for scientific purposes. Also **Basic.**

bas·il (baz′əl) *n.* An aromatic plant of the mint fam sometimes used in cooking. [< OF < L < Gk. *basili* (*phyton*) royal (plant), basil]

bas·i·lar (bas′ə·lər) *adj.* Pertaining to or situated at base, esp. of the skull; basal. Also **bas·i·lar·y** (bas′ə·ler′

ba·sil·i·ca (bə·sil′i·kə) *n.* **1.** In ancient Rome, a rectangu building divided by columns into a nave and two side ais used as a place of assembly. **2.** A building of this type u as a Christian church. [< L < Gk. *basilikē* (*stoa*) ro (hall), fem. of *basilikos*] **—ba·sil′i·can** *adj.*

bas·i·lisk (bas′ə·lisk) *n.* **1.** A fabled reptile whose bre and look were said to be fatal. **2.** A tropical American liz

having an erectile crest on the head. [< L < Gk. *basiliskos*, dim. of *basileus* king]
ba·sin (bā′sən) *n.* **1.** A round, wide, shallow vessel, often with sloping sides, used for holding liquids. **2.** A vessel resembling this, as the scale or pan of a balance. **3.** The amount that a basin will hold. **4.** A sink or washbowl. **5.** *Geog.* **a** Any large depression in the earth's surface, as the bed of a lake or ocean. **b** The region drained by a river. **6.** An enclosed place or hollow containing water, as a cistern, pond, etc. [< OF < LL < *bacca* bowl] **— ba′sined** *adj.*
ba·sis (bā′sis) *n. pl.* **ba·ses** (bā′sēz) **1.** That on which anything rests; support; foundation; base. **2.** Fundamental principle; groundwork. **3.** The chief component or ingredient of a thing. [< L < Gk., base, pedestal]
bask (bask, bäsk) *v.i.* **1.** To lie in and enjoy a pleasant warmth, as of the sun or a fire. **2.** To enjoy or benefit from a similar warmth, as of regard: to *bask* in royal favor. **—** *v.t.* **3.** To expose to warmth. [< ON *badhask* to bathe oneself]
bas·ket (bas′kit, bäs′-) *n.* **1.** A container made of interwoven splints, rushes, strips of wood, etc. **2.** Something like a basket in form or use. **3.** The amount a basket will hold. **4.** In basketball: **a** One of the goals, consisting of a metal ring with a cord net suspended from it. **b** The point or points made by throwing the ball through the basket. [ME]
bas·ket·ball (bas′kit·bôl′, bäs′-) *n.* **1.** A game played by two teams of five men each, in which the object is to throw the ball through an elevated goal (basket) at the opponent's end of an oblong court. **2.** The ball used in this game.
bas·ket·ry (bas′kit·rē, bäs′-) *n.* **1.** Baskets collectively; basketwork. **2.** The art or craft of making baskets.
basket weave A weave with two or more warp and filling threads woven side by side to resemble a plaited basket.
bas·ket·work (bas′kit·wûrk′, bäs′-) *n.* Work made of or resembling interlaced osiers, twigs, etc.; wickerwork.
ba·so·phile (bā′sə·fīl, -fil) *n. Biol.* A tissue or cell having a special affinity for basic staining dyes. Also **ba′si·phile.** **— ba·so·phil·ic** (bā′sə·fil′ik), **ba·soph·i·lous** (bā·sof′ə·ləs) *adj.*
basque (bask) *n.* A woman's closely fitting bodice, separate from the dress skirt.
Basque (bask) *n.* **1.** One of a people of unknown origin living in the western Pyrenees in Spain and France. **2.** The language of the Basque people. **—** *adj.* Of the Basques.
bas-re·lief (bä′ri·lēf′, bas′-) *n.* That type of sculpture in which the figures project only slightly from the background: also called *low relief.* [< F < Ital. *basso* low + *rilievo* relief]
bass[1] (bas) *n. pl.* **bass** or **bass·es** Any of various spiny-finned, marine and fresh-water food fishes. [OE *bærs*]
bass[2] (bās) *n. Music* **1.** The lowest-pitched male singing voice. **2.** The notes in the lowest register of the piano, pipe organ, etc. **3.** The lowest part in vocal or instrumental music; also, these parts collectively. **4.** One who sings or an instrument that plays such a part, esp., a bass viol. **—** *adj.* **1.** Low in pitch; having a low musical range. **2.** Of or for a bass or basses. [< OF *bas* low]
bass[3] (bas) *n.* **1.** The basswood or linden. **2.** Bast. [Alter. of BAST]
bass drum (bās) The largest of the drums, beaten on both heads and having a deep sound.
bas·set (bas′it) *n.* A hound characterized by a long, low body, long head and nose, and short, heavy, crooked forelegs. Also **basset hound.** [< OF *basset,* dim. of *bas* low]
bas·si·net (bas′ə·net′) *n.* A basket used as a baby's cradle, usu. with a hood over one end. [< F]
bas·so (bas′ō, bäs′ō; *Ital.* bäs′sō) *n. pl.* **bas·sos** (bas′ōz, bäs′ōz), *Ital.* **bas·si** (bäs′sē) **1.** A bass singer. **2.** The bass part. [< Ital., low]
bas·soon (ba·sōōn′, bə-) *n. Music* A large, low-pitched, double-reed woodwind instrument. [< F < It. *basso* low]
bass viol (bās) *Music* The double bass.
bass·wood (bas′wŏŏd′) *n.* The American linden. See under LINDEN. Also called *bass.*
bast (bast) *n. Bot.* The fibrous inner bark of trees, originally of the linden, used in making cordage: also called *bass.* [OE *bæst*]
bas·tard (bas′tərd) *n.* **1.** An illegitimate child. **2.** Any irregular, inferior, or counterfeit thing. **3.** *U.S. Slang* A worthless or cruel man. **4.** *Brit. Informal* A fellow; chap: a somewhat disparaging term. **—** *adj.* **1.** Born out of wedlock. **2.** False; spurious. **3.** Resembling but not typical of the genuine thing. **4.** Abnormal or irregular in size, shape, or proportion. [< OF < *fils de bast* packsaddle child] **— bas′tard·ly** *adj.* **— bas′tard·y** *n.*
bas·tard·ize (bas′tər·dīz) *v.* **·ized, ·iz·ing** *v.t.* **1.** To prove to be or proclaim to be a bastard. **2.** To make degenerate; debase. **—** *v.i* **3.** To become debased. **— bas′tard·i·za′tion** *n.*
baste[1] (bāst) *v.t.* **bast·ed, bast·ing** To sew loosely together, as with long, temporary stitches. [< OF < OHG *bestan* to sew with bast]
baste[2] (bāst) *v.t.* **bast·ed, bast·ing** To moisten (meat or fish) with drippings, butter, etc., while cooking. [? < OF *basser* to soak, moisten]
baste[3] (bāst) *v.t.* **bast·ed, bast·ing** *Informal* **1.** To beat; thrash. **2.** To attack verbally; abuse. [Prob. < Scand.]
bas·tille (bas·tēl′) *n.* A prison, esp. one operated tyrannically. Also **bas·tile′.** [< OF < LL < *bastire* to build]
Bas·tille (bas·tēl′, *Fr.* bȧs·tē′y′) A fortress in Paris, stormed and destroyed in the French Revolution on July 14, 1789.
bas·ti·na·do (bas′tə·nā′dō) *n. pl.* **·does** **1.** A beating with a stick, usu. on the soles of the feet. **2.** A stick or cudgel. Also **bas′ti·nade′** (-nād′). [< Sp. < *baston* cudgel]
bast·ing (bās′ting) *n.* **1.** The act of sewing loosely together. **2.** The thread used for this purpose. **3.** *pl.* Long, loose, temporary stitches.
bas·tion (bas′chən, -tē·ən) *n.* **1.** In fortifications, a projecting part of a rampart. **2.** Any fortified position. [< MF < Ital. < *bastire* to build] **— bas′tioned** *adj.*
bat[1] (bat) *n.* **1.** In baseball, cricket, and similar games: **a** A stick or club for striking the ball. **b** The act of batting. **c** A turn at bat. **2.** In cricket, the batsman. **3.** In tennis, badminton, etc., a racket. **4.** Any heavy cudgel or club. **5.** *Informal* A blow, as with a stick. **6.** *Slang* A drunken spree. **— to go to bat for** *Informal* To defend or advocate the cause of. **—** *v.* **bat·ted, bat·ting** *v.i.* **1.** In baseball, cricket, and other games, to use a bat or take a turn at bat. **—** *v.t.* **2.** To strike with or as with a bat. **3.** To have a batting average of: to *bat* .400. **— to bat around** *Slang* **1.** To travel about. **2.** To discuss. [OE *batt* cudgel]
bat[2] (bat) *n.* A nocturnal flying mammal having elongated forelimbs and digits that support a thin wing membrane. **— blind as a bat** Altogether blind. **— to have bats in the belfry** *U.S. Slang* To be crazy. [ME *bakke,* ? < Scand.]
bat[3] (bat) *v.t.* **bat·ted, bat·ting** *Informal* To wink. **— not bat an eye** or **eyelash** *Informal* Not show surprise.
batch (bach) *n.* **1.** A quantity or number taken together. **2.** The amount of bread produced at one time. **3.** The quantity of material required for one operation. **4.** Any set of things made, done, etc., at one time. [ME *bacche*]
bate (bāt) *v.t. & v.i.* **bat·ed, bat·ing** To restrain; decrease. **— with bated breath** In a state of fear, suspense, expectation, etc. [Var. of ABATE]
ba·teau (ba·tō′) *n. pl.* **·teaux** (-tōz′) **1.** *U.S. & Canadian* A light, flat-bottomed boat. **2.** A pontoon for a floating bridge. [< F < OF *batel,* ult. < Gmc.]
bat·fish (bat′fish′) *n.* **1.** A North American marine fish having a batlike appearance. **2.** A sting ray.
bath (bath, bäth) *n. pl.* **baths** (bat͟hz, bät͟hz; baths, bäths) **1.** A washing or immersing of something, esp. the body, in water or other liquid. **2.** The liquid used for this. **3.** The container for such a liquid; a bathtub. **4.** A bathroom. **5.** *Often pl.* A set of rooms or a building equipped for bathing. **6.** *Often pl.* An establishment or resort where bathing is part of a medical treatment. **—** *v.t. Brit.* To place or wash in a bath; immerse. [OE *bæth*]
bathe (bāt͟h) *v.* **bathed, bath·ing** *v.t.* **1.** To place in liquid; immerse. **2.** To wash; wet. **3.** To apply liquid to for comfort or healing. **4.** To cover or suffuse as with liquid. **—** *v.i.* **5.** To wash oneself; take a bath. **6.** To be covered or suffused as if with liquid: to *bathe* in sunshine. **—** *n. Brit.* A swim. [OE *bathian*] **— bathe′a·ble** *adj.* **— bath′er** *n.*
bath·house (bath′hous′, bäth′-) *n.* **1.** A building with facilities for bathing. **2.** A small structure at a bathing resort used as a dressing room.
bath·ing suit (bāt͟h′ing) A garment, sometimes consisting of two pieces, worn for swimming.
batho- *combining form* Depth. [< Gk. *bathos* depth]
bath·o·lith (bath′ə·lith) *n. Geol.* A large, irregular mass of igneous rock, often forming the core of mountain ranges. Also **bath′o·lite** (-līt). [< BATHO- + -LITH] **— bath′o·lith′ic** or **bath′o·lit′ic** (-lit′ik) *adj.*
ba·thos (bā′thos) *n.* **1.** A descent from the lofty to the commonplace in discourse; anticlimax. **2.** Insincere pathos; sentimentality. [< Gk. < *bathys* deep]
bath·robe (bath′rōb′, bäth′-) *n.* A long, loose garment for wear before and after bathing.
bath·room (bath′rōōm′, -rŏŏm′, bäth′-) *n.* **1.** A room in which to bathe. **2.** A toilet.
Bath·she·ba (bath·shē′bə, bath′shi·bə) In the Bible, the wife of Uriah and later of David; mother of Solomon. II *Sam.*
bath·tub (bath′tub′, bäth′-) *n.* A vessel in which to bathe, esp. one installed as a permanent fixture in a bathroom.
bathy- *combining form* Deep; of the sea or ocean depths: *bathysphere.* [< Gk. *bathys* deep]
bath·y·scaph (bath′ə·skaf) *n.* A free bathysphere with ballast and a gasoline-filled float to control depth, capable of ocean depths over 35,000 feet. Also **bath′y·scaphe** (-skāf). [< BATHY- + Gk. *skaphē* bowl]

bath·y·sphere (bath′ə·sfir) *n.* A spherical diving bell equipped with windows for deep-sea observations.

ba·tik (bə·tēk′, bat′ik) *n.* **1.** A process for coloring fabrics, in which the parts not to be dyed are covered with wax. **2.** The fabric so colored. Also spelled *battik.* [< Malay]

ba·tiste (bə·tēst′) *n.* A fine cotton fabric in plain weave. [< F; after Jean *Baptiste,* 13th c. French linen weaver]

ba·ton (ba·ton′, bat′n; *Fr.* bà·tôn′) *n.* **1.** A short staff or truncheon borne as an emblem of authority or privilege. **2.** *Music* A slender stick or rod used by a conductor. [< F < OF *baston* < LL *bastum* stick]

ba·tra·chi·an (bə·trā′kē·ən) *adj.* Of or pertaining to a former class of amphibians, esp. to frogs and toads; amphibian. — *n.* A frog or toad. [< NL < Gk. *batrachos* frog]

bats (bats) *adj. Slang* Batty.

bats·man (bats′mən) *n. pl.* **·men** (-mən) In baseball or cricket, the batter.

bat·tal·ion (bə·tal′yən) *n.* **1.** *Mil.* **a** A unit consisting of a headquarters and two or more companies, batteries, or comparable units. **b** A body of troops. **2.** *Usu. pl.* A large group or number. [< MF < Ital. < *battaglia* battle]

bat·ten[1] (bat′n) *v.i.* **1.** To grow fat; thrive. — *v.t.* **2.** To make fat, as cattle. [< ON *batna* to grow better, improve]

bat·ten[2] (bat′n) *n.* **1.** A light strip of wood, as for covering a joint between boards. **2.** A strip of sawed timber, used for flooring, scantling, etc. **3.** *Naut.* A thin strip of wood placed in a sail to keep it flat or for fastening a tarpaulin over a hatch. — *v.t.* To fasten with battens: with *up* or *down.*

bat·ter[1] (bat′ər) *v.t.* **1.** To strike with repeated, violent blows. **2.** To damage or injure with such blows or with hard usage. — *v.i.* **3.** To pound or beat with blow after blow; hammer. [Partly < OF < L *battuere* to beat]

bat·ter[2] (bat′ər) *n.* In baseball and cricket, the player whose turn it is to bat.

bat·ter[3] (bat′ər) *n.* A mixture, as of eggs, flour, and milk, beaten for use in cookery. [? < OF < *battre* to beat]

bat·ter·ing-ram (bat′ər·ing·ram′) *n.* A long, stout beam, used in ancient warfare for battering down walls.

bat·ter·y (bat′ər·ē, ba′trē) *n. pl.* **·ter·ies** **1.** Any unit, apparatus, or grouping in which a series or set of parts or components is assembled to serve a common end. **2.** *Electr.* One or more cells operating together as a single source of direct current. **3.** *Mil.* **a** An artillery unit equivalent to an infantry company. **b** A group of guns, rockets, or related equipment forming an artillery unit. **4.** *Naval* The guns of a warship, or a specific group of them. **5.** *Law* The illegal beating or touching of another person. [< OF < *battre* to beat]

bat·tik (bə·tēk′, bat′ik) See BATIK.

bat·ting (bat′ing) *n.* Wadded cotton or wool prepared in sheets or rolls, used for interlining, stuffing mattresses, etc.

bat·tle (bat′l) *n.* **1.** A combat between hostile armies or fleets. **2.** Any fighting, conflict, or struggle. — *v.* **·tled, ·tling** *v.i.* **1.** To contend in or as in battle; struggle; strive. — *v.t.* **2.** *U.S.* To fight. [< OF < LL < L *battuere* to beat] — **bat′tler** *n.*

— **Syn.** (noun) **1.** A *battle* is a more or less continuous fight and may last for many days, while a *skirmish* is brief and involves small groups of combatants. An *action* is one of the events in a *battle,* as by a part of the forces engaged. *Engagement* refers to a period of active combat, but may also be a complete *battle* or war.

bat·tle-ax (bat′l·aks′) *n.* **1.** A large ax formerly used in battle; a broadax. **2.** *U.S. Slang* A formidable, disagreeable woman. Also **bat′tle-axe′.**

battle cruiser *Naval* A war vessel having cruiser speed, but less heavily armored than a battleship.

battle cry **1.** A shout uttered by troops in battle. **2.** A slogan or distinctive phrase used in any conflict or contest.

bat·tle·dore (bat′l·dôr, -dōr) *n.* **1.** A flat paddle or bat used to strike a shuttlecock. **2.** A game in which a shuttlecock is battered back and forth: also **battledore and shuttlecock.** — *v.t. & v.i.* **·dored, ·dor·ing** To volley or hurl back and forth. [? < Provençal *batedor,* an implement for beating laundry]

battle fatigue *Psychiatry* Combat fatigue.

bat·tle·field (bat′l·fēld′) *n.* The terrain on which a battle is fought. Also **bat′tle·ground′.**

bat·tle·ment (bat′l·mənt) *n.* A parapet indented along its upper line. [< OF < *ba(s)tillier* to fortify]

battle royal **1.** A fight involving numerous combatants. **2.** A protracted, vehement altercation.

bat·tle·ship (bat′l·ship′) *n. Naval* A warship of great size, belonging to the class with heaviest armor and armament.

bat·ty (bat′ē) *adj.* **·ti·er, ·ti·est** *Slang* Crazy; odd.

bau·ble (bô′bəl) *n.* A worthless, showy trinket; gewgaw; toy. [< OF *baubel* toy, ? < L *bellus* pretty]

baulk (bôk), **baulk·y** (bô′kē) See BALK, BALKY.

baux·ite (bôk′sīt, bō′zīt) *n.* A white to red claylike substance containing aluminum oxide or hydroxide, the principal ore of aluminum. [after Les *Baux,* France]

Ba·var·i·an (bə·vâr′ē·ən) *adj.* Of or pertaining to Bavaria, its people, or their dialect. — *n.* **1.** A native or inhabitant of Bavaria. **2.** The High German dialect spoken in Bavaria.

bawd (bôd) *n.* The keeper of a brothel. [ME *bawde*]

bawd·y (bô′dē) *adj.* **bawd·i·er, bawd·i·est** Obscene; inde cent. — **bawd′i·ly** *adv.* — **bawd′i·ness** *n.*

bawd·y·house (bô′dē·hous′) *n.* A brothel.

bawl (bôl) *v.t.* **1.** To call out noisily; bellow. **2.** To cry f sale. — *v.i.* **3.** To cry or sob noisily. — **to bawl out** *U. Slang* To berate; scold. — *n.* A loud outcry. [Cf. Med *baulare* to bark and ON *baula* to low, moo] — **bawl′er** *n.*

bay[1] (bā) *n.* A body of water partly enclosed by land; inlet of the sea. [< OF *baie* < LL *baia*]

bay[2] (bā) *n.* **1.** *Archit.* **a** A bay window. **b** A principal pa or division of a structure. **c** An extension or wing of a bui ing. **2.** Any opening or recess in a wall. **3.** *Aeron.* A co partment in an aircraft. [< OF < L *badare* to gape]

bay[3] (bā) *adj.* Reddish brown: said esp. of horses. — *n.* A reddish brown color. **2.** A horse (or other animal) of t color. [< F *bai* < L *badius*]

bay[4] (bā) *n.* **1.** A deep bark or cry, as of dogs in hunting. The position of or as of a hunted animal forced to turn a fight. **3.** The condition of being kept off by or as by on quarry. — **at bay** **1.** Unable to escape; cornered. **2.** Ke off, as by one's quarry. — *v.i.* **1.** To utter a deep-throat prolonged bark, as a hound. — *v.t.* **2.** To utter with or with such a bark. **3.** To pursue or beset with barking. To bring to bay. [< OF < L *badare* to gape]

bay[5] (bā) *n.* **1.** A laurel wreath, bestowed as a garland honor, esp. on a poet. **2.** *pl.* Fame; renown. **3.** The bayber **4.** Any of several plants resembling the laurels. [< F *bai* L *bacca* berry]

bay·ber·ry (bā′ber′ē, -bər·ē) *n. pl.* **·ries** **1.** A tree or shr having aromatic berries, as the wax myrtle or laurel; also, fruit. **2.** A tropical tree yielding an oil used in bay rum.

bay leaf The leaf of the laurel, used as a cooking herb.

bay·o·net (bā′ə·nit, -net, bā′ə·net′) *n.* A daggerlike wea attachable to the muzzle of a firearm, used in close fighti — *v.t.* **·net·ed, ·net·ing** To stab or pierce with a bayon [< F after *Bayonne,* France, where first made]

bay·ou (bī′ōō) *n. U.S.* A marshy inlet or outlet of a la river, etc. [< dial. F < Choctaw *bayuk* small stream]

Bayou State Nickname of Mississippi.

bay rum An aromatic liquid used in medicines and cosm ics, originally distilled from the leaves of the bayberry, now also made from alcohol, water, and essential oils.

Bay State Nickname of Massachusetts.

bay window **1.** A window structure projecting from wall of a building and forming a recess within. **2.** *Slan* protruding belly, as of a fat person.

ba·zaar (bə·zär′) *n.* **1.** An Oriental market or street shops. **2.** A shop or store for the sale of miscellaneous wa **3.** A sale of miscellaneous articles, as for charity. A **ba·zar′.** [Ult. < Persian *bāzār* market]

ba·zoo·ka (bə·zōō′kə) *n. Mil.* A tubular, portable wea that fires an explosive rocket, used against tanks and fortifi tions. [from *bazooka,* a comical musical instrument]

be (bē, *unstressed* bi) *v.i.* **been, be·ing** Present indicati I **am,** he, she, it **is,** we, you, they **are;** past indicative: I, she, it **was,** we, you, they **were;** present subjunctive: past subjunctive: **were;** archaic forms: thou **art** (prese thou **wast** or **wert** (past) **1.** As the substantive verb, b used to mean: **a** To have existence, truth, or actuality: *is;* There *are* bears in the zoo. **b** To take place; happen: party *is* today. **c** To stay or continue: She *was* here for week. **d** To belong; befall: a subjunctive use, often wit or *unto*: Joy *be* unto you. **2.** As a copulative verb *be* form link between the subject and predicate nominative or qu fying word or phrase in sentences, and also forms infinit and participial phrases: George *is* my friend; He *is* sick; pleasure of *being* here. **3.** As an auxiliary verb *be* is use With the present participle of other verbs to express conti ous or progressive action: I *am* working. **b** With the p participle of transitive verbs to form the passive voice: *was* injured. **c** With the past participle of intransitive ve to form the perfect tense: Christ *is* come; I *am* finishe With the infinitive or present participle to express purp duty, possibility, futurity, etc.: We *are* to start on Mond

be- *prefix* Used to form words from nouns, adjectives, verbs with the following meanings: **1.** (*from verbs*) Arou all over; throughout; as in: **bedrape; befinger.** **2.** (*f verbs*) Completely; thoroughly; as in: **bedrench; bemud** **3.** (*from verbs*) Off; away from; as in: **behead.** **4.** (*f intransitive verbs*) About; at; on; over; against; for; as **becrawl; bethunder.** **5.** (*from adjectives and nouns*) make; cause to be; as in: **becripple; bedirty.** **6.** (*from nou* To provide with; affect by; cover with; as in: **becarpet; jewel.** **7.** (*from nouns,* in the form of participial adjectiv Furnished with; as in: **bechained; beflowered.** [OE *be-,* var. of *bī* near, by]

beach (bēch) *n.* The sloping shore of a body of wa strand; esp., a sandy shore used for swimming. — **Syn.** SHORE[1]. — *v.t. & v.i.* To drive or haul up (a boat or ship) a beach; strand. [Origin unknown]

ɜach·comb·er (bēch′kō′mər) *n.* **1.** A vagrant living on ·vhat he can find or beg around the wharves and beaches of ·orts. **2.** A long wave rolling upon the beach.

ɜach·head (bēch′hed′) *n. Mil.* An area on a hostile shore ·stablished by an advance force for the landing of troops and ·upplies and the launching of subsequent operations.

ɜa·con (bē′kən) *n.* **1.** A signal; esp., a signal fire or light on ı hill, building, etc., intended as a warning or guide. **2.** A ight, buoy, etc., set on a shore, shoal, or similar place to ·uide or warn mariners. **3.** A lighthouse. **4.** Anything that ·varns or signals. **5.** *Aeron.* A mark, light, or radio trans·nitter used to plot flight courses. **—** *v.t.* **1.** To furnish with ·r guide by a beacon. **—** *v.i.* **2.** To shine as a beacon. [OE *ēacn* sign, signal. Akin to BECKON.]

ɜad (bēd) *n.* **1.** A small, usually round, piece of glass, wood, ·tone, etc., pierced for stringing on thread or attaching to ·abric as decoration. **2.** *pl.* A string of beads; necklace. **·.** *pl.* A rosary. **4.** Any small body resembling a bead, as a ·ubble or a drop of liquid. **5.** Froth; foam. **6.** A small ·nob used as the front sight of a gun. **7.** *Archit.* A molding ·omposed of a row of half-oval ornaments resembling a ·tring of beads. **— to draw a bead on** To take careful aim ·t. **— to tell (count,** or **say) one's beads** To recite prayers ·vith a rosary. **—** *v.t.* **1.** To decorate with beads or beading. **—** *v.i.* **2.** To collect in beads or drops. [OE *gebed* prayer]

ɜad·ing (bē′ding) *n.* **1.** Ornamentation with beads. **2.** ·laterial consisting of or ornamented with beads. **3.** *Archit.* ı bead, or beads collectively.

ɜa·dle (bēd′l) *n.* In the Church of England, a lay officer ·vho ushers or keeps order. [< OF *bedel* messenger]

ɜads·man (bēdz′mən) *n. pl.* **·men** (-mən) One who prays ·or another. **— beads′wom′an** *n.fem.*

ɜad·work (bēd′wûrk′) *n.* **1.** Decorative work made with ·r of beads. **2.** *Archit.* A bead.

ɜad·y (bē′dē) *adj.* **bead·i·er, bead·i·est** **1.** Small and ·littering: *beady* eyes. **2.** Covered with beads. **3.** Foamy.

·a·gle (bē′gəl) *n.* A small, short-coated hound with short ·egs and drooping ears. [ME *begle*]

BEAGLE
(About 15 inches high at shoulder)

ɜak (bēk) *n.* **1.** The horny, projecting mouth parts of birds. **2.** A beaklike ·art or organ, as the horny jaws of tur·les. **3.** Something resembling a bird's ·eak, as the spout of a pitcher. **4.** *Slang* ı person's nose. [< F *bec* < LL *beccus*] **— beaked** *adj.* **— beak′less** *adj.* **— ·eak′like′** *adj.*

ɜak·er (bē′kər) *n.* **1.** A large, wide-·nouthed drinking cup or goblet. **2.** A ·ylindrical, flat-bottomed vessel of glass, ·luminum, etc., with a lip for pouring, used in chemical ·nalysis, etc. **3.** The contents or capacity of a beaker. [< ·N *bikarr*; spelling infl. by *beak*]

ɜam (bēm) *n.* **1.** A long, heavy piece of wood, metal, or ·tone, shaped for use. **2.** A horizontal piece forming part of ·he frame of a building or other structure. **3.** *Naut.* **a** One ·f the heavy pieces of timber or iron set across a vessel to ·upport the decks and stay the sides. **b** The greatest width ·f a vessel. **c** The shank of an anchor. **4.** The bar of a balance; ·lso, the balance. **5.** A ray of light, or a group of nearly ·arallel rays. **6.** *Aeron.* A radio beam. **7.** The area of ·naximum sound clarity in front of a microphone. **8.** The ·orizontal piece in a plow to which the share and handles ·re attached. **9.** The widest part of anything. **10.** *Slang* ·he hips: broad in the *beam.* **— off the beam 1.** *Aeron.* Not ·ollowing the radio beam. **2.** *Informal* On the wrong track; ·vrong. **— on the beam 1.** *Naut.* In a direction at right ·ngles with the keel; abeam. **2.** *Aeron.* Following the radio ·eam. **3.** *Informal* In the right direction; just right; cor·ect. **—** *v.t.* **1.** To send out in beams or rays. **2.** *Telecom.* ·o aim or transmit (a signal) in a specific direction. **3.** ·eron. To guide (an airplane) by radio beams. **—** *v.i.* **4.** To ·mit light. **5.** To smile or grin radiantly. [OE *bēam* tree] **— beam′less** *adj.* **— beam′like′** *adj.*

ɜam-ends (bēm′endz′) *n.pl. Naut.* The ends of a ship's ·eams. **— on her beam-ends** Of a ship, tipped over so far ·s to be in danger of capsizing.

eam·ing (bē′ming) *adj.* Radiant; bright; smiling; cheer·ul. **— beam′ing·ly** *adv.*

eam·y (bē′mē) *adj.* **beam·i·er, beam·i·est** **1.** Sending out ·eams of light; radiant. **2.** Like a beam; massive.

ɜan (bēn) *n.* **1.** The oval, edible seed of any of various ·eguminous plants. **2.** A plant that bears beans. **3.** Any of ·everal beanlike seeds or plants. **4.** *Slang* The head. **5.** *·rit. Slang* Person; chap. **—** *v.t. U.S. Slang* To hit on the ·ead. [OE *bēan*]

ean·ie (bē′nē) *n.* A small, brimless cap.

ean·pole (bēn′pōl′) *n.* **1.** A tall pole for a bean plant to ·limb on. **2.** *Slang* A tall, thin person.

bear[1] (bâr) *v.* **bore** (*Archaic* **bare**), **borne, bear·ing** *v.t.* **1.** To support; hold up. **2.** To carry; convey. **3.** To show visibly; carry. **4.** To conduct or guide. **5.** To spread; disseminate. **6.** To hold in the mind; maintain or entertain. **7.** To suffer or endure; undergo. **8.** To accept or acknowledge; assume, as responsibility or expense. **9.** To produce; give birth to. ◆ In this sense, the participial form in the passive is **born,** except when followed by *by.* **10.** To conduct or comport (oneself). **11.** To manage or carry (oneself or a part of oneself). **12.** To move by pressing against; drive. **13.** To render; give: to *bear* witness. **14.** To be able to withstand; allow. **15.** To have or stand in (comparison or relation): with *to*: What relation does his story *bear* to yours? **16.** To possess as a right or power: to *bear* title. **—** *v.i.* **17.** To rest heavily; lean; press. **18.** To endure patiently; suffer. **19.** To produce fruit or young. **20.** To carry burdens. **21.** To move or lie in a certain direction; be pointed or aimed. **22.** To be relevant; have reference. **— to bear down 1.** To force down; overpower or overcome. **2.** To exert oneself; make an effort. **— to bear down on** (or **upon**) **1.** To put pressure on; press hard on. **2.** To make a great effort. **3.** To approach, especially another vessel from windward. **— to bear out** To support; confirm; justify. **— to bear up** To keep up strength and spirits. [OE *beran* to carry, wear]

bear[2] (bâr) *n.* **1.** A large mammal having a massive, thickly furred body and a very short tail, as the grizzly bear, polar bear, etc. ◆ Collateral adjective: *ursine.* **2.** Any of various other animals resembling or likened to the bear: ant *bear.* **3.** A gruff, ill-mannered, or clumsy person. **4.** A speculator, esp. one in the stock exchange, who seeks to depress prices or who sells in the belief that a decline in prices is likely: opposed to *bull.* **— the Bear** Russia. **—** *adj.* Of, pertaining to, or caused by stock-market bears, or a decline in prices. **—** *v.t.* To endeavor to depress the price of (stocks etc.) by selling or offering to sell. [OE *bera*]

bear·a·ble (bâr′ə·bəl) *adj.* Capable of being borne; endurable. **— bear′a·ble·ness** *n.* **— bear′a·bly** *adv.*

bear·cat (bâr′kat′) *n.* The panda (def. 1).

beard (bird) *n.* **1.** The hair on a man's face, esp. on the chin, usu. excluding the mustache. **2.** Any similar growth or appendage, as the long hair on the chin of some animals. **3.** *Bot.* An awn. For illus. see WHEAT. **—** *v.t.* **1.** To take by the beard; pull the beard of. **2.** To defy courageously. **3.** To furnish with a beard. [OE] **— beard′ed** *adj.* **— beard′less** *adj.* **— beard′less·ness** *n.* **— beard′like′** *adj.*

bear·er (bâr′ər) *n.* **1.** One who or that which bears, carries, or upholds. **2.** A person who bears or presents for payment a check, money order, etc. **3.** A tree or vine producing fruit. **4.** A carrier or porter. **5.** A pallbearer.

bear·ing (bâr′ing) *n.* **1.** Manner of conducting or carrying oneself; deportment. **2.** The act, capacity, or period of producing. **3.** That which is produced; crops; yield. **4.** Endurance. **5.** *Mech.* A part on which something rests, or in which a pin, journal, etc., turns. **6.** The position or direction of an object or point. **7.** *Often pl.* The situation of an object relative to that of another, or of other points or places: to lose one's *bearings.* **8.** Reference or relation.

bear·ish (bâr′ish) *adj.* **1.** Like a bear; rough; surly. **2.** Tending toward, counting on, or causing a depression in the price of stocks. **— bear′ish·ly** *adv.* **— bear′ish·ness** *n.*

bear·skin (bâr′skin′) *n.* The skin of a bear, or a coat or robe made of it.

beast (bēst) *n.* **1.** Any animal except man; esp., any large, quadruped. **2.** Animal characteristics or animal nature. **3.** A cruel, rude, or filthy person. [< OF < LL < L *bestia* beast] **— beast′like′** *adj.*

beast·ly (bēst′lē) *adj.* **·li·er, ·li·est** **1.** Resembling a beast; bestial. **2.** *Informal* Disagreeable or unpleasant; nasty. **—** *adv. Brit. Slang* Very. **— beast′li·ness** *n.*

beat (bēt) *v.* **beat, beat·en** or **beat, beat·ing** *v.t.* **1.** To strike repeatedly; pound. **2.** To punish by repeated blows; thrash; whip. **3.** To dash or strike against. **4.** To shape or break by blows. **5.** To make flat by tramping or treading. **6.** To make, as one's way, by or as by blows. **7.** To flap; flutter, as wings. **8.** To stir or mix rapidly so as to make lighter or frothier: to *beat* eggs. **9.** To mark or measure as with a baton: to *beat* time. **10.** To sound (a signal), as on a drum. **11.** To hunt over; search. **12.** To subdue or defeat; master. **13.** To surpass; be superior to. **14.** *Informal* To baffle; perplex: it *beats* me. **15.** *U.S. Slang* To defraud; swindle. **—** *v.i.* **16.** To strike repeated blows. **17.** To strike or smite as if with blows: The sound *beat* on my ears. **18.** To throb; pulsate. **19.** To give forth sound, as when tapped or struck. **20.** To sound a signal, as on a drum. **21.** *Physics* To alternate in intensity so as to pulsate. **22.** To be adaptable to beating. **23.** To hunt through underbrush, etc., as for game. **24.** To win a victory or contest. **— to beat about** To search by one means and then another. **— to beat**

about the bush To approach a subject in a roundabout way. **— to beat a retreat** 1. To give a signal for retreat, as by the beat of drums. 2. To turn back; flee. **— to beat down** To force or persuade (a seller) to accept a lower price. **— to beat it** *Slang* To depart hastily. **— to beat off** To repel; drive away. **— to beat up** *Informal* To thrash thoroughly. — *n.* 1. A stroke or blow. 2. A regular stroke, or its sound; pulsation; throb. 3. *Physics* A regularly recurring pulsation or throb heard when two tones not quite in unison are sounded together, and caused by the interference of sound waves. 4. *Music* **a** A regular pulsation; the basic unit of musical time. **b** The gesture or symbol designating this. 5. The measured sound of verse; rhythm. 6. A round, line, or district regularly traversed, as by a sentry, policeman, or reporter. 7. *U.S.* A subdivision of a county, esp. in the South. 8. In newspaper slang, a scoop. 9. *U.S. Slang* A deadbeat. 10. A beatnik. **— on the beat** *Music* In tempo. — *adj.* 1. *U.S. Informal* Fatigued; worn out. 2. *Informal* Of or pertaining to beatniks. [OE *bēatan*] **— beat′er** *n.*

beat·en (bēt′n) Past participle of BEAT. — *adj.* 1. Shaped or made thin by beating. 2. Mixed by beating. 3. Worn by use; customary. 4. Defeated; baffled. 5. Exhausted.

be·a·tif·ic (bē′ə·tif′ik) *adj.* Imparting or expressing bliss or blessedness. **— be′a·tif′i·cal·ly** *adv.*

be·at·i·fi·ca·tion (bē·at′ə·fi·kā′shən) *n.* 1. The act of beatifying, or the state of being beatified. 2. In the Roman Catholic Church, an act of the pope declaring a deceased person beatified, usually the last step toward canonization.

be·at·i·fy (bē·at′ə·fī) *v.t.* **·fied, ·fy·ing** 1. To make supremely happy. 2. In the Roman Catholic Church, to declare as blessed and worthy of public honor, by an act of the pope. 3. To exalt above others. [< F < LL < L *beatus* happy + *facere* to make]

beat·ing (bē′ting) *n.* 1. The act of one who or that which beats. 2. Punishment by blows; flogging. 3. Pulsation; throbbing, as of the heart. 4. A defeat.

be·at·i·tude (bē·at′ə·tōōd, -tyōōd) *n.* Supreme blessedness or felicity. **— the Beatitudes** Eight declarations made by Jesus in the Sermon on the Mount. *Matt.* v 3–11. [< MF < L *beatitudo* blessedness]

beat·nik (bēt′nik) *n.* *Informal* One who acts and dresses in a manner calculated to be unconventional.

beau (bō) *n.* *pl.* **beaus** or **beaux** (bōz) 1. A sweetheart or lover of a girl or woman. 2. A dandy. [< OF, var. of *bel* < L *bellus* fine, pretty] **— beau′ish** *adj.*

Beau Brum·mell (brum′əl) A dandy or fop. [after George "*Beau*" *Brummell*, 1778–1840, English dandy]

Beau·fort scale (bō′fərt) *Meteorol.* A scale of wind velocities, ranging from 0 (calm) to 12 (hurricane). [after Sir Francis *Beaufort*, 1774–1857, British admiral]

beau monde (bō mônd′) *French* The fashionable world.

beau·te·ous (byōō′tē·əs) *adj.* Beautiful. **— beau′te·ous·ly** *adv.* **— beau′te·ous·ness** *n.*

beau·ti·cian (byōō·tish′ən) *n.* One who works in or operates a beauty parlor.

beau·ti·ful (byōō′tə·fəl) *adj.* Possessing the qualities or presenting an appearance of beauty, as in form or grace. **— beau′ti·ful·ly** *adv.* **— beau′ti·ful·ness** *n.*

beau·ti·fy (byōō′tə·fī) *v.t. & v.i.* **·fied, ·fy·ing** To make or grow beautiful. **— beau′ti·fi·ca′tion** *n.* **— beau′ti·fied** *adj.* **— beau′ti·fi′er** *n.*

beau·ty (byōō′tē) *n.* *pl.* **·ties** 1. The quality of objects, sounds, ideas, etc., that pleases and gratifies, as by their harmony, pattern, excellence, or truth. 2. One who or that which is beautiful, esp. a woman. 3. A special grace or charm. [< OF *beaute*, ult. < L *bellus* handsome, fine]

beauty parlor An establishment where women may go for hairdressing, complexion care, or other cosmetic treatment. Also **beauty salon, beauty shop.**

beauty spot 1. A small patch or mark put on the face to set off the whiteness of the skin. 2. A mole or other natural mark resembling this. Also **beauty mark.**

beaux (bōz) Plural of BEAU.

beaux-arts (bō·zàr′) *n.pl.* *French* The fine arts.

bea·ver[1] (bē′vər) *n.* 1. An amphibious rodent with a scaly, flat, oval tail and webbed hind feet, valued for its fur, and noted for its skill in damming shallow streams. 2. The fur of the beaver. 3. A high silk hat. [OE *beofor*]

bea·ver[2] (bē′vər) *n.* 1. A movable piece of medieval armor covering the lower face. 2. The visor of a helmet. 3. *Slang* A beard. [< OF *bavé* saliva]

bea·ver·board (bē′vər·bôrd′, -bōrd′) *n.* A light, stiff building material made of compressed or laminated wood pulp, used chiefly for walls and partitions.

Beaver State Nickname of Oregon..

be·calm (bi·käm′) *v.t.* 1. *Naut.* To make (a sailing vessel) motionless for lack of wind. 2. To make calm; quiet.

be·came (bi·kām′) Past tense of BECOME.

be·cause (bi·kôz′) *conj.* For the reason that; on account of the fact that; since. **— because of** By reason of; on account of. [ME *bi cause* by cause]

be·chance (bi·chans′, -chäns′) *v.t. & v.i.* **·chanced, ·char ing** To befall; happen by chance.

beck (bek) *n.* A nod or other gesture of summons. **— one's beck and call** Subject to one's slightest wish. — *ı & v.i.* To beckon. [Short for BECKON]

beck·on (bek′ən) *v.t. & v.i.* 1. To signal, direct, or summ by sign or gesture. 2. To entice or lure. — *n.* A summo ing gesture; beck. [OE *bīecnan, bēacnian* to make signs t

be·cloud (bē·kloud′) *v.t.* 1. To obscure with clouds; dar en. 2. To confuse, as an issue: to *becloud* his senses.

be·come (bi·kum′) *v.* **·came, ·come, ·com·ing** *v.i.* 1. come to be; grow to be. — *v.t.* 2. To be appropriate to; b fit. 3. To be suitable to; show to advantage. **— to becor of** To be the condition or fate of: What *became of* him? [C *becuman* to happen, come about]

be·com·ing (bi·kum′ing) *adj.* 1. Appropriate; suitable. Pleasing; attractive. — *n.* A coming to be. **— be·com′ir ly** *adv.* **— be·com′ing·ness** *n.*

bed (bed) *n.* 1. An article of furniture to rest or sleep c consisting of a bedstead, mattress, spring, and bedcloth 2. Any place or thing used for resting or sleeping. 3. lodging, esp. for the night. 4. A heap or mass resembl a bed. 5. A plot of ground prepared for planting; also t plants themselves. 6. The ground at the bottom of a bo of water. 7. A part or surface that serves as a foundati or support. 8. *Geol.* Any layer in a mass of stratified ro a seam. **— to get up on the wrong side of the bed** To irritable, grouchy, or cross. **— to put** (or **go**) **to bed** *U Slang* To go to press; be printed. — *v.* **bed·ded, bed·di** *v.t.* 1. To furnish with a bed. 2. To put to bed. 3. make a bed for; provide with litter: often with *down*: to *l* down cattle. 4. To set out or plant in a bed of earth. 5. lay flat or arrange in layers: to *bed* oysters. 6. To pl firmly; embed. — *v.i.* 7. To go to bed. 8. To form a clo ly packed layer; stratify. [OE] **— bed′der** *n.*

bed and board Lodging and meals.

be·daub (bi·dôb′) *v.t.* 1. To smear or daub; besmirch; s 2. To ornament vulgarly or excessively.

be·daz·zle (bi·daz′əl) *v.t.* **·zled, ·zling** To confuse or bl by dazzling.

bed·bug (bed′bug) *n.* A bloodsucking insect of redd brown color, infesting houses and esp. beds.

bed·cham·ber (bed′chām′bər) *n.* A bedroom.

bed·clothes (bed′klōz′, -klōthz′) *n.pl.* Covering for a b as sheets, blankets, quilts, etc.

bed·ding (bed′ing) *n.* 1. Mattress and bedclothes. Straw or other litter for animals to sleep on. 3. That wh forms a bed or foundation. 4. *Geol.* Stratification of roc

be·deck (bi·dek′) *v.t.* To adorn.

be·dev·il (bi·dev′əl) *v.t.* **·iled** or **·illed, ·il·ing** or **·il·ling** 1. treat diabolically; harass or torment. 2. To worry or c fuse; bewilder. 3. To possess with or as with a devil; witch. 4. To spoil; corrupt. **— be·dev′il·ment** *n.*

be·dew (bi·dōō′, -dyōō′) *v.t.* To moisten with dew.

bed·fel·low (bed′fel′ō) *n.* 1. One who shares a bed with a other. 2. A companion; associate.

be·dim (bi·dim′) *v.t.* **·dimmed, ·dim·ming** To make dim.

bed·lam (bed′ləm) *n.* 1. A place or scene of noisy con sion. 2. An incoherent uproar. 3. A lunatic asylum. [af *Bedlam*, an old London hospital for the insane]

bed linen Sheets, pillowcases, etc., for beds.

Bed·ou·in (bed′ōō·in) *n.* 1. One of the nomadic Arabs Syria, Arabia, etc. 2. Any nomad or vagabond. — *a* 1. Of or pertaining to the Bedouins. 2. Roving; nomad Also spelled *Beduin.* [< F < Arabic *badāwīn* desert dwell

bed·pan (bed′pan′) *n.* 1. A shallow vessel to be used a toilet by one confined to bed. 2. A warming pan.

be·drag·gle (bi·drag′əl) *v.t.* **·gled, ·gling** To make w soiled, or untidy, as by dragging through mire.

bed·rid·den (bed′rid′n) *adj.* Confined to bed. Also **be rid′.** [Earlier *bedrid* < OE *bedrida* < *bed* bed + *rida* rid

bed·rock (bed′rok′) *n.* 1. *Geol.* The solid rock underly the looser materials of the earth's surface. 2. The low level; bottom. 3. Fundamental principles; foundation.

bed·roll (bed′rōl′) *n.* Bedding rolled to facilitate carryi

bed·room (bed′rōōm′, -rŏŏm′) *n.* A room for sleeping.

bed·side (bed′sīd′) *n.* The space beside a bed, especially a sick person; the side of a bed. — *adj.* Placed beside a b

bed·sore (bed′sôr′, -sōr′) *n.* A sore caused by prolong pressure against a bed, occurring among bedridden perso

bed·spread (bed′spred′) *n.* A cloth covering for a bed, u ally for ornament.

bed·spring (bed′spring′) *n.* The framework of springs s porting the mattress of a bed; also, any of such springs.

bed·stead (bed′sted′) *n.* A framework for supporting springs and mattress of a bed.

bed·time (bed′tīm′) *n.* The time for retiring to bed.

Bed·u·in (bed′ōō·in) See BEDOUIN.

bed-wet·ting (bed′wet′ing) *n.* Urination in bed.

bee (bē) *n.* 1. A four-winged insect feeding largely u nectar and pollen, esp. the honey bee. 2. *U.S.* A so

ıthering for work, competition, entertainment, etc.: a ıilting *bee*. **— to have a bee in one's bonnet** To be excessively concerned about or obsessed with one idea. [OE *bēo*]
e·bread (bē′bred′) *n.* A mixture of pollen and certain :oteins stored by bees for food.
ech (bēch) *n.* **1.** A tree of temperate regions with smooth, sh-gray bark, and bearing an edible nut. **2.** The wood of ıe beech. **3.** A tree similar to the beech, as the hornbeam.)E *bēce*] **— beech′en** *adj.*
ech mast Beechnuts.
ech·nut (bēch′nut′) *n.* The edible nut of the beech.
ef (bēf) *n. pl.* **beeves** (bēvz) or **beefs** *for def. 2*; **beefs** *for f. 4* **1.** The flesh of a slaughtered adult bovine animal. **2.** ny adult bovine animal, as an ox, cow, steer, bull, etc., fatned for the table. **3.** *Informal* Muscle; brawn. **4.** *U.S. ang* A complaint. **— *v.i.*** *U.S. Slang* To complain. [< F < L *bos, bovis* ox]
ef·eat·er (bēf′ē′tər) *n* **1.** A yeoman of the guard, or ıe of the similarly uniformed warders of the Tower of Lon)n. **2.** *Slang* An Englishman.
ef·steak (bēf′stāk′) *n.* A slice of beef suitable for broiling.
ef tea A beverage made by boiling lean beef or made from beef extract.
ef·y (bē′fē) *adj.* **beef·i·er, beef·i·est** **1.** Muscular and ıavy. **2.** Beeflike. **3.** Stolid. **— beef′i·ness** *n.*
e·hive (bē′hīv′) *n.* **1.** A hive for a colony of honeybees. A place full of activity.
ehive State Nickname of UTAH.
e·keep·er (bē′kē′pər) *n.* One who keeps bees; an apiarist.
e·line (bē′līn′) *n.* The shortest course from one place to ıother: chiefly in the phrase **to make a beeline for.**
·el·ze·bub (bē·el′zə·bub) **1.** The prince of the demons; e devil. **2.** Any devil. [< Hebrew *ba'alzebūb* lord of flies]
en (bin, *Brit.* bēn) Past participle of BE.
ep (bēp) *n.* A short, piercing sound used as a signal or ırning. **— *v.i.*** **1.** To make such a sound. **— *v.t.*** **2.** To und (a horn). **3.** To transmit (a message) by beeps. [Imit.]
er (bir) *n.* **1.** An alcoholic fermented beverage made from alt and hops. **2.** A beverage made from the roots, etc., of ırious plants: ginger *beer* [OE *bēor*]
er·she·ba (bir·shē′bə, bir′shi·ba) An ancient city in uthwest Palestine.
er·y (bir′ē) *adj.* **beer·i·er, beer·i·est** **1.** Of or like beer. Influenced by beer; tipsy. **— beer′i·ness** *n.*
est·ings (bēs′tings) *n.pl. & sing.* The first milk from a w after calving; the colostrum: also *biestings.* [OE *bēost*]
es·wax (bēz′waks′) *n.* A yellow fatty solid secreted by neybees for honeycombs, used in medicine and the arts.
et (bēt) *n.* **1.** The fleshy succulent root of a biennial herb the goosefoot family, esp. the common or red beet, and the gar beet. **2.** The plant itself. [OE < L *beta*]
e·tle[1] (bēt′l) *n.* **1.** An insect having biting mouth parts d hard, horny front wings that serve as a cover for the sterior wings when at rest. **2.** Loosely, any insect renbling a beetle. **— *adj.*** Jutting; overhanging: a *beetle* ow: also **bee′tling.** **— *v.i.* ·tled, ·tling** To jut out; overng. [OE *bītan* to bite]
e·tle[2] (bē′tl) *n.* **1.** A heavy instrument, usu. with a)oden head, for ramming paving stones, driving wedges, c. **2.** A pestle or mallet for pounding, etc. **— *v.t.* ·tled, ing** To beat or stamp with a beetle. [OE *bīetel* mallet]
e·tle-browed (bēt′l·broud′) *adj.* **1.** Having prominent, erhanging eyebrows. **2.** Scowling; frowning.
et sugar Sucrose obtained from the sugar beet.
eves (bēvz) Alternative plural of BEEF.
fall (bi·fôl′) *v.* **·fell, ·fall·en, ·fall·ing** *v.i.* **1.** To come out; happen; occur. **— *v.t*** **2.** To happen to. [OE *be*)*allan* to fall]
fit (bi·fit′) *v.t* **·fit·ted, ·fit·ting** To be suited to; be appropriate for. **— be·fit′ting** *adj.* **— be·fit′ting·ly** *adv.*
fit·ting (bi·fit′ing) *adj.* Becoming; proper; suitable. **— ·fit·ting·ly** *adv.*
fog (bi·fôg′, -fog′) *v.t* **·fogged, ·fog·ging** **1.** To envelop fog. **2.** To confuse; obscure.
fore (bi·fôr′, -fōr′) *adv.* **1.** In front; ahead. **2.** Preceding in time; previously. **3.** Earlier; sooner. **— *prep.*** **1.** In ont of; ahead of. **2.** Earlier or sooner than. **3.** In adınce of in development, rank, etc. **4.** In preference to; ther than. **5.** In the presence of; face to face with. **6.** nder the consideration or cognizance of: the issue *before* ıu. **7.** Ahead of; awaiting. **— *conj.*** **1.** Previous to the ne when. **2.** Rather than. [OE *beforan* in front of]
fore·hand (bi·fôr′hand′, -fōr′-) *adv. & adj.* In anticipa)n or advance; ahead of time.
foul (bi·foul′) *v.t* To make foul or dirty; sully.
friend (bi·friend′) *v.t.* To act as a friend to; help.
fud·dle (bi·fud′l) *v.t.* **·dled, ·dling** To confuse, as with uor or glib arguments.

beg (beg) *v.* **begged, beg·ging** *v.t.* **1.** To ask for in charity: to *beg* alms. **2.** To ask for or of earnestly; beseech: to *beg* forgiveness. **— *v.i.*** **3.** To ask alms or charity; be a beggar. **4.** To ask humbly or earnestly. **— to beg off** To ask to be excused or released (from an engagement, obligation, etc.). **— to beg the question** **1.** To take for granted the very matter in dispute. **2.** Loosely, to avoid answering directly. **— to go begging** To fail of acceptance, adoption, or use. [? < AF < OF *begard* mendicant friar]
be·gan (bi·gan′) Past tense of BEGIN.
be·get (bi·get′) *v.t.* **·got** (*Archaic* **·gat**), **·got·ten** or **·got, ·get·ting** **1.** To procreate; be the father of. **2.** To cause to be; occasion. [OE *begitan*] **— be·get′ter** *n.*
beg·gar (beg′ər) *n.* **1.** One who asks alms, or lives by begging. **2.** A poor person; pauper. **3.** A rogue; rascal. **— *v.t.*** **1.** To reduce to want; impoverish. **2.** To exhaust the resources of: It *beggars* analysis. [< OF *begard* mendicant friar] **— beg′gar·dom, beg′gar·hood** *n.*
beg·gar·ly (beg′ər·lē) *adj.* Appropriate for a beggar; miserably poor; mean; sordid. **— beg′gar·li·ness** *n.*
be·gin (bi·gin′) *v.* **·gan, ·gun, ·gin·ning** *v.i.* **1.** To start to do something; take the first step; commence. **2.** To come into being; arise. **— *v.t.*** **3.** To do the first act or part of; start to do. **4.** To give origin to; start; originate. [OE *beginnan*]
be·gin·ner (bi·gin′ər) *n.* **1.** One beginning to learn a trade, study a subject, etc.; a novice; tyro. **— Syn.** See NOVICE. **2.** One who begins or originates; a founder.
be·gin·ning (bi·gin′ing) *n.* **1.** The act of starting; commencement. **2.** The point in time at which a thing begins. **3.** Source or first cause; origin. **4.** The first part. **5.** *Usually pl.* The first or rudimentary stage. **— *adj.*** **1.** First; opening: the *beginning* chapter. **2.** Elementary; introductory: a *beginning* course in physics.
be·gird (bi·gûrd′) *v.t.* **·girt** or **·gird·ed, ·gird·ing** To gird; encircle. [OE *begyrdan*]
be·gon·ia (bi·gōn′yə) *n.* A plant having brilliantly colored leaves and showy flowers. [after Michel *Bégon*, 1638–1710, French colonial administrator]
be·got (bi·got′) Past tense and past participle of BEGET.
be·got·ten (bi·got′n) Alternative past participle of BEGET.
be·grime (bi·grīm′) *v.t.* **·grimed, ·grim·ing** To soil.
be·grudge (bi·gruj′) *v.t.* **·grudged, ·grudg·ing** **1.** To envy one the possession or enjoyment of (something). **2.** To give or grant reluctantly. **— be·grudg′ing·ly** *adv.*
be·guile (bi·gīl′) *v.t.* **·guiled, ·guil·ing** 1. To deceive; mislead by guile. **2.** To cheat; defraud: with *of* or *out of.* **3.** To while away pleasantly, as time. **4.** To charm; divert. **— be·guile′ment** *n.* **— be·guil′er** *n*
be·gum (bē′gəm) *n.* A Moslem princess, or woman of rank in India. [< Hind. < Turkish *bigim* princess]
be·gun (bi·gun′) Past participle of BEGIN.
be·half (bi·haf′, -häf′) *n.* The interest, part, or defense: usu. preceded by *in* or *on* and followed by *of.* **— Syn.** See SAKE. [OE *be healfe* by the side (of)]
be·have (bi·hāv′) *v.* **·haved, ·hav·ing** *v.i* **1.** To act; conduct oneself or itself. **2.** To comport oneself properly. **3.** To react to stimuli or environment. **— *v.t.*** **4.** To conduct (oneself), esp. in a proper or suitable manner. [ME *be-* thoroughly + *have* to hold oneself, act]
be·hav·ior (bi·hāv′yər) *n.* **1.** Manner of conducting oneself; demeanor; deportment. **2.** The way a person, substance, machine, etc., acts under given circumstances. Also *Brit.* **be·hav′iour.**
be·hav·ior·ism (bi·hāv′yər·iz′əm) *n.* *Psychol.* The theory that the behavior of animals and man is determined by measurable external and internal stimuli acting independently. **— be·hav′ior·ist** *n.* **— be·hav′ior·is′tic** *adj.*
be·head (bi·hed′) *v.t.* To decapitate. [OE *behēafdian*]
be·held (bi·held′) Past tense and past participle of BEHOLD.
be·he·moth (bi·hē′məth, bē′ə-) *n.* **1.** In the Bible, a huge beast. **2.** Anything large. [< Hebrew *bĕhēmāh* beast]
be·hest (bi·hest′) *n.* An authoritative request; command. [OE *behǣs* promise, vow]
be·hind (bi·hīnd′) *adv.* **1.** In, at, or toward the rear. **2.** In a place, condition, or time previously passed or departed from. **3.** In arrears; late. **4.** Slow, as a watch. **— *prep.*** **1.** At the back or rear of. **2.** Toward the rear of; backward from. **3.** In a place, condition, or time left by (one): Leave your problems *behind* you. **4.** After (a set time). **5.** Not so well advanced as; inferior to. **6.** Hidden by: What is *behind* your actions? **7.** Backing up; supporting: to be *behind* a venture. **— *adj.*** **1.** Following: the man *behind* **2.** In arrears. **— *n.*** *Informal* The buttocks. [OE *behindan*]
be·hind·hand (bi·hīnd′hand′) *adv. & adj.* **1.** Behind time; late. **2.** In arrears. **3.** Behind in development; backward.
be·hold (bi·hōld′) *v.t.* **·held, ·hold·ing** To look at or upon; observe. **— *interj.*** Look! See! [OE *beh(e)aldan* to hold] **— be·hold′er** *n.*

be·hold·en (bi·hōl′dən) *adj.* Indebted; obligated.
be·hoof (bi·hōōf′) *n.* That which benefits; advantage; use. [OE *behōf* advantage]
be·hoove (bi·hōōv′) *v.* **·hooved, ·hoov·ing** *v.t.* To be incumbent upon; be needful or right for: It *behooves* me to leave. Also *Brit.* **be·hove** (bi·hōv′). [OE *behōfian*]
beige (bāzh, bāj) *n.* The color of natural, undyed, unbleached wool; grayish tan. — *adj.* Of the color beige. [< F]
be·ing (bē′ing) Present participle of BE. — *n.* **1.** Existence, as opposed to nonexistence. **2.** Essential nature; substance: His whole *being* is musical. **3.** A living thing. **4.** A human individual; person. **5.** *Philos.* **a** Perfect or unqualified subsistence; essence. **b** That which has reality in time, space, or idea; anything that exists actually or potentially.
Be·ing (bē′ing) *n.* The Supreme Being; God.
bel (bel) *n. Physics* A unit expressing the logarithmic ratio of the values of two amounts of power: a measure of sound intensity. Compare DECIBEL. [after A. G. *Bell*]
be·la·bor (bi·lā′bər) *v.t.* **1.** To beat soundly; assail with blows; drub. **2.** To assail verbally. Also *Brit.* **be·la′bour.**
be·lat·ed (bi·lā′tid) *adj.* Late or too late. — **be·lat′ed·ly** *adv.* — **be·lat′ed·ness** *n.*
be·lay (bi·lā′) *v.t. & v.i.* **·layed, ·lay·ing** **1.** *Naut.* To make fast (a rope) by winding on a cleat or pin (**belaying pin**). **2.** *Informal* To stop or hold: *Belay* there! [OE *belecgan*]
belch (belch) *v.i.* **1.** To eject wind noisily from the stomach through the mouth; eructate. **2.** To issue spasmodically from within; gush. **3.** To expel its contents violently, as a volcano. — *v.t.* **4.** To eject or throw forth violently; give vent to. — *n.* A belching. [OE *bealcian*] — **belch′er** *n.*
be·lea·guer (bi·lē′gər) *v.t.* **1.** To surround or shut in with an armed force. **2.** To surround; beset. [< Du. < *be-* about + *leger* camp] — **be·lea′guered** *adj.*
bel·fry (bel′frē) *n. pl.* **·fries** **1.** A tower in which a bell is hung. **2.** The part of a tower or steeple containing the bell. [< OF *berfrei* tower, infl. by BELL[1]] — **bel′fried** *adj.*
Bel·gian (bel′jən, -jē·ən) *adj.* Of or pertaining to Belgium. — *n.* A native or citizen of Belgium.
Be·li·al (bē′lē·əl, bēl′yəl) In the Bible, the devil.
be·lie (bi·lī′) *v.t.* **·lied, ·ly·ing** **1.** To misrepresent; disguise: His clothes *belie* his station. **2.** To prove false; contradict: Her actions *belied* her words. **3.** To fail to fulfill: to *belie* hopes. **4.** To slander. [OE *belēogan*] — **be·li′er** *n.*
be·lief (bi·lēf′) *n.* **1.** Acceptance of the truth or actuality of anything without certain proof. **2.** Something held to be true or actual. **3.** Trust in another person; confidence. **4.** A doctrine; creed. [ME < *bi-* complete + *leafe* belief]
— **Syn. 1.** *Belief* denotes acceptance with or without proof or strong emotional feelings. *Faith* is always the acceptance of something not susceptible of proof, while *conviction* is strong *belief* arising from a deep feeling of certainty.
be·lieve (bi·lēv′) *v.* **·lieved, ·liev·ing** *v.t.* **1.** To accept as true or real. **2.** To credit (a person) with veracity. **3.** To think; assume: with a clause as object. — *v.i.* **4.** To accept the truth, existence, worth, etc., of something: with *in*: to *believe* in freedom. **5.** To have confidence; place one's trust: with *in*. **6.** To have religious faith. **7.** To think: I cannot *believe* badly of you. [ME *beleven* < OE *gelēfan* to believe] — **be·liev′a·ble** *adj.* — **be·liev′er** *n.*
be·lit·tle (bi·lit′l) *v.t.* **·tled, ·tling** To cause to seem small or less; disparage; minimize.
bell[1] (bel) *n.* **1.** A hollow metallic instrument, usu. cup-shaped, which gives forth a ringing sound when struck. **2.** Anything in the shape of or suggesting a bell. **3.** The lower termination of a tubular musical instrument. **4.** A bell-shaped flower or corolla. **5.** *Naut.* A stroke on a bell every half hour to mark the periods of the watch; also, each of these periods. — *v.t.* **1.** To put a bell on. **2.** To shape like a bell. — *v.i.* **3.** To take the shape of a bell. [OE *belle*]
bell[2] (bel) *v.i.* To cry, as a hound, rutting stag, etc. — *n.* The cry of a deer, bittern, etc. [OE *bellan* to bellow]
bel·la·don·na (bel′ə·don′ə) *n.* **1.** A perennial herb with purple-red flowers and black berries: also called *deadly nightshade.* **2.** A poisonous alkaloid, as atropine, used in medicine. [< Ital. *bella donna*, lit., beautiful lady]
bell·boy (bel′boi′) *n. U.S.* A boy or man employed by a hotel to answer calls for service, carry suitcases, etc.
belle (bel) *n.* A beautiful and attractive woman or girl; a reigning social beauty. [< F, fem. of *beau* beautiful]
belles-let·tres (bel′let′rə) *n.pl.* Literature having esthetic appeal, rather than didactic or informational value; poetry, drama, fiction, etc. [< F, fine letters] — **bel·let·rist** (bel′let′rist) *n.* — **bel·le·tris·tic** (bel′le·tris′tik) *adj.*
bell·flow·er (bel′flou′ər) *n.* The campanula.
bell·hop (bel′hop′) *n. U.S. Informal* A bellboy.
bel·li·cose (bel′ə·kōs) *adj.* Pugnacious. [< L *bellum* war] — **bel′li·cose′ly** *adv.* — **bel′li·cos′i·ty** (-kos′ə·tē) *n.*
bel·lig·er·ence (bə·lij′ər·əns) *n.* **1.** The state or quality of being warlike. **2.** Belligerency.
bel·lig·er·en·cy (bə·lij′ər·ən·sē) *n.* The status of a belligerent; condition of being at war.
bel·lig·er·ent (bə·lij′ər·ənt) *adj.* **1.** Warlike; bellicose. **2** Engaged in or pertaining to warfare. — *n.* A person or n tion engaged in warfare or fighting. [< F < L *belligerare* wage war] — **bel·lig′er·ent·ly** *adv.*
bell·man (bel′mən) *n. pl.* **·men** (-mən) A town crier.
bel·low (bel′ō) *v.i.* **1.** To utter a loud, hollow cry, as a bu **2.** To roar; shout: to *bellow* with anger. — *v.t.* **3.** To utt with a loud, roaring voice. — *n.* A loud, hollow cry or roa [ME *belwen*, ? < OE *bylgian*] — **bel′low·er** *n.*
bel·lows (bel′ōz, *earlier* bel′əs) *n.pl.* (*construed as sing. pl.*) **1.** An instrument with an air chamber and flexib sides, for drawing in air and expelling it under strong pre sure through a nozzle or tube, used for blowing fires, filli the pipes of an organ, etc. **2.** The expansible portion of camera. **3.** The lungs. [OE *belg, belig* bag]
bell·weth·er (bel′weth′ər) *n.* **1.** A ram with a bell abo its neck, that leads a flock of sheep. **2.** One who leads group, esp. a thoughtless, sheeplike group.
bel·ly (bel′ē) *n. pl.* **·lies** **1.** The abdomen in vertebrat or the underpart of other animals. **2.** The stomach. The protuberance of a bulging muscle. **4.** Any curved protrusive line or surface: the *belly* of a sail. **5.** The front underpart of anything. **6.** A deep, interior cavity: the *be* of a ship. **7.** The curved front piece, containing the sou holes, of a violin, viola, etc. — *v.t. & v.i.* **·lied, ·ly·ing** swell out or fill, as a sail. [OE *belg, belig* bag]
bel·ly·ache (bel′ē·āk′) *n.* A pain in the stomach or bowe — *v.i.* **·ached, ·ach·ing** *Slang* To complain sullenly.
bel·ly·band (bel′ē·band′) *n.* A strap passing around t belly, as of a draft animal, to hold the shafts.
bel·ly·but·ton (bel′ē·but′n) *n. Informal* The navel.
bel·ly·ful (bel′ē·fōōl′) *n.* **1.** All that the stomach will ho **2.** *Slang* All that one wants, or can endure.
be·long (bi·lông′, -long′) *v.i.* **1.** To be the property of son one: with *to*. **2.** To be a part of or an appurtenance to son thing: with *to*. **3.** To have a proper place; be suitable. To have relation or be a member. [ME < *be-* completely *longen* to go along with]
be·long·ing (bi·lông′ing, -long′-) *n.* **1.** That which belon to a person or thing. **2.** *pl.* Possessions; effects.
be·lov·ed (bi·luv′id, -luvd′) *adj.* Greatly loved. — *n.* O greatly loved. [Orig. pp. of obs. *belove* love dearly]
be·low (bi·lō′) *adv.* **1.** In or to a lower place. **2.** On or t lower floor or deck. **3.** Farther down on a page or farther in a list, book, etc. **4.** On earth, as distinguished from hea en. **5.** In or to hell or Hades. **6.** In a lower rank or auth ity. — *prep.* **1.** Lower than in place, grade, degree, e **2.** Unworthy of. [ME < *bi-* near + *loogh* low]
Bel·shaz·zar (bel·shaz′ər) In the Old Testament, the l ruler of Babylon.
belt (belt) *n.* **1.** A strap or band of leather or other flexi material worn about the waist to support clothing, too weapons, etc. **2.** Any band or strip resembling a belt. *Mech.* An endless band of flexible material for transmitti power from one wheel or shaft to another. **4.** A region zone exhibiting some specific quality or condition: a sto *belt.* **5.** *Slang* A blow, as with the fist. — **below the b** In violation of the rules; unfair. — **to tighten one's belt** practice thrift. — *v.t.* **1.** To gird with or as with a belt. To fasten with a belt. **3.** To mark with belts or bands. To strike with a belt. **5.** *Informal* To give a blow to; stri [OE < L *balteus* girdle]
be·lu·ga (bə·lōō′gə) *n.* A dolphin of Arctic and sub-Arc seas: also called *white whale.* [< Russian *byelukha*]
bel·ve·dere (bel′və·dir′) *n. Archit.* A building, or an up story of a building, that commands a view.
be·mire (bi·mīr′) *v.t.* **·mired, ·mir·ing** **1.** To soil with m or mire. **2.** To sink or stall in mud.
be·moan (bi·mōn′) *v.t.* **1.** To lament, as a loss. **2.** To press sympathy or pity for. — *v.i.* **3.** To mourn or lame [OE *bemænan*] — **be·moan′a·ble** *adj.*
be·muse (bi·myōōz′) *v.t.* **·mused, ·mus·ing** To stupefy preoccupy. — **be·mused′** *adj.*
bench (bench) *n.* **1.** A long seat of wood, marble, etc., wi or without a back. **2.** A table for mechanical work. **3.** seat or thwart in a boat. **4.** The seat for judges in a cou **5.** The judge, or the judges collectively. **6.** The office dignity of a judge. **7.** A seat for persons sitting in an offic capacity. **8.** Level, elevated ground along a shore or coa or on a slope. — **on the bench** In sports, not participati — *v.t.* **1.** To furnish with benches. **2.** To seat on a ben **3.** In sports, to remove (a player) from a game. [OE *ben*
bench mark A permanent mark, of known position a elevation, for use as a reference point in surveys, etc.
bench warrant *Law* A warrant issued by a judge, dire ing that an offender be brought into court.
bend[1] (bend) *v.* **bent** (*Archaic* **bend·ed**), **bend·ing** *v.t.* **1.** cause to take the form of a curve; crook; bow. **2.** To dir or turn, as one's course, in a certain direction; deflect. **3.** subdue or cause to yield. **4.** To apply closely; concentra **5.** *Naut.* To make fast, as a rope or sail. — *v.i.* **6.** To

ume the form of a curve. **7.** To take a certain direction. **.** To bow in submission or respect. **9.** To apply one's nergies: with *to.* —*n.* **1.** An act of bending, or the state f being bent. **2.** Something curved or bent; a curve or rook. **3.** *Naut.* A knot by which a rope is fastened to somehing else. [OE *bendan*]
nd[2] (bend) *n. Heraldry* A diagonal band across a shield om the upper left to the lower right. [OE *bend* strap]
nd·er (ben′dər) *n.* **1.** One who or that which bends. **2.** *J.S. Slang* A drinking spree. **3.** *Brit. Slang* A sixpence.
nds (bendz) *n.pl. Informal* Caisson disease.
nd sinister *Heraldry* A band drawn diagonally from he upper right to the lower left, used to indicate bastardy.
·neath (bi·nēth′) *adv.* **1.** In a lower place; below. **2.** nderneath; directly below. —*prep.* **1.** Under; undereath; below. **2.** On the underside of; covered by. **3.** Uner the power or sway of; subdued by. **4.** Lower in rank or ation. **5.** Unworthy of; unbefitting. [OE *beneothan*]
n·e·dic·i·te (ben′ə·dis′ə·tē) *n.* A blessing; grace or thanksiving, esp. at table. —*interj.* Bless you!
n·e·dic·tine (ben′ə·dik′tin, -tēn; *for n. def. 3,* -tēn) *adj.* ertaining to St. Benedict or his order. —*n.* **1.** A monk of he order established by St. Benedict at Subiaco, in Italy, bout 530. **2.** A nun following the Benedictine rule. **3.** A randy liqueur formerly made by French Benedictines.
n·e·dic·tion (ben′ə·dik′shən) *n.* **1.** The act of blessing. **.** The invocation of divine favor upon a person. [< LL < *enedicere* to bless] —**ben′e·dic′tive, ben·e·dic·to·ry** (ben′ə·ik′tər·ē) *adj.*
n·e·dic·tus (ben′ə·dik′təs) *n.* **1.** Either of two canticles *uke* i 68–71, and *Matt.* xxi 9: so called from their first word n Latin. **2.** A musical setting of either canticle.
n·e·fac·tion (ben′ə·fak′shən) *n.* **1.** The act of giving elp or conferring a benefit. **2.** A charitable deed; generous ct. [< LL < *benefacere* to do well]
n·e·fac·tor (ben′ə·fak′tər, ben′ə·fak′-) *n.* One who gives elp or confers a benefit. —**ben′e·fac′tress** *n. fem.*
n·e·fice (ben′ə·fis) *n. Brit. Eccl.* **1.** A church office enowed with funds or property; a living. **2.** The revenue of ich an office. —*v.t.* **·ficed, ·fic·ing** To invest with a beneice. [< OF < L *beneficium* favor] —**ben′e·ficed** *adj.*
·nef·i·cence (bə·nef′ə·səns) *n.* **1.** The quality of being eneficent. **2.** A beneficent act or gift.
·nef·i·cent (bə·nef′ə·sənt) *adj.* **1.** Bringing about or doig good. **2.** Resulting in benefit. —**be·nef′i·cent·ly** *adv.*
n·e·fi·cial (ben′ə·fish′əl) *adj.* Producing benefit; advanageous; helpful. [< F *bénéficial* < LL < L *beneficium* ivor] —**ben′e·fi′cial·ly** *adv.* —**ben′e·fi′cial·ness** *n.*
n·e·fi·ci·ar·y (ben′ə·fish′ē·er′ē, -fish′ər·ē) *n. pl.* **·ar·ies** **.** One who receives benefits or advantages. **2.** *Eccl.* The older of a benefice. **3.** *Law* One entitled to the proceeds f property held in trust, or to whom an insurance policy or nnuity is payable. [< L < *beneficium* favor]
n·e·fit (ben′ə·fit) *n.* **1.** That which is helpful; advantage; rofit. **2.** An act of kindness; charitable deed. **3.** A thetrical or musical performance given to raise funds for a orthy cause. **4.** *Often pl.* Payments made by an insurance ompany, etc —*v.* **·fit·ed, ·fit·ing** *v.t.* **1.** To be helpful or seful to. —*v.i.* **2.** To profit; gain advantage. [<OF < *benefacere* to do well]
nefit of clergy. **1.** Churchly approval or sanction. **2.** ormerly, the privilege accorded to the clergy of demanding rial by an ecclesiastical rather than a secular court.
en·e·lux (ben′ə·luks) *n.* The economic union of Belgium, he Netherlands, and Luxembourg. [< BE(LGIUM) + E(THERLANDS) + LUX(EMBOURG)]
·nev·o·lence (bə·nev′ə·ləns) *n.* **1.** Disposition to do good; indliness. **2.** Any act of kindness.
·nev·o·lent (bə·nev′ə·lənt) *adj.* Disposed to do good; indly. [< OF < L < *bene* well + *volens,* ppr. of *velle* to ish] —**be·nev′o·lent·ly** *adv.*
en·ga·li (ben·gô′lē, beng-) *adj.* Of or pertaining to Benal. —*n.* **1.** A native of Bengal. **2.** The modern vernaclar Indic language of Bengal.
n·ga·line (beng′gə·lēn, beng′gə·lēn′) *n.* A corded silk, ool, or rayon fabric of fine weave. [< BENGAL]
·night·ed (bi·nī′tid) *adj.* **1.** Ignorant; unenlightened. **2.**)vertaken by night. —**be·night′ed·ness** *n.*
·nign (bi·nīn′) *adj.* **1.** Of a kind disposition; kindly. **.** Gentle; mild. **3.** Favorable. **4.** *Med.* Favorable for reovery. [< OF < L *benignus* kindly] —**be·nign′ly** *adv.*
·nig·nant (bi·nig′nənt) *adj.* **1.** Kind; gracious, esp.to nferiors. **2.** Favorable; benign. —**be·nig′nant·ly** *adv.*
·nig·ni·ty (bi·nig′nə·tē) *n. pl.* **·ties** **1.** The quality of eing benign. Also **be·nig·nan·cy** (bi·nig′nən·sē). **2.** A racious action or influence.
n·i·son (ben′ə·zən, -sən) *n.* A benediction; blessing. [<)F < LL *benedictio, -onis* benediction]

Ben·ja·min (ben′jə·mən) In the Old Testament, the youngest son of Jacob and Rachel. *Gen* xxxv 18. —*n.* The tribe of Israel descended from him.
ben·ne (ben′ē) *n.* The sesame. [< Malay *bijen* seed]
bent[1] (bent) Past tense and past participle of BEND[1]. —*adj.* **1.** Not straight; crooked. **2.** Set in a course; resolved. —*n.* **1.** State of being bent or turned. **2.** A personal inclination or penchant. **3.** Limit of endurance or capacity: usually in the phrase **to the top of (one's) bent.**
bent[2] (bent) *n.* **1.** A stiff, wiry grass. Also **bent grass.** **2.** The stiff flower stalk of various grasses. [OE *beonet*]
Ben·tham·ism (ben′thəm·iz′əm, -təm-) *n.* The philosophy of Jeremy Bentham, maintaining that the happiness of the greatest number is the supreme goal of society. —**Ben′·tham·ite** (-īt) *n.*
be·numb (bi·num′) *v.t.* **1.** To make numb; deaden. **2.** To stupefy. [OE *benumen* pp. of *beniman* to deprive.] —**be·numbed** (bi·numd′) *adj.* —**be·numb′ment** *n.*
Ben·ze·drine (ben′zə·drēn, -drin) *n.* Proprietary name of a brand of amphetamine. Also **ben′ze·drine.**
ben·zene (ben′zēn, ben·zēn′) *n. Chem.* A colorless, volatile, flammable, liquid hydrocarbon, C_6H_6, obtained chiefly from coal tar, used as a solvent and in organic synthesis.
ben·zine (ben′zēn, ben·zēn′) *n.* A colorless, flammable liquid derived from crude petroleum and consisting of various hydrocarbons, used as a solvent, cleaner, and motor fuel. Also **ben′zin** (-zin), **ben·zo·line** (ben′zə·lēn).
ben·zo·ate (ben′zō·it, -āt) *n. Chem.* A salt of benzoic acid.
ben·zo·ic (ben·zō′ik) *adj.* **1.** Pertaining to or derived from benzoin. **2.** Pertaining to benzoic acid.
benzoic acid *Chem.* An aromatic compound, $C_7H_6O_2$, used as a food preservative and in medicine.
ben·zo·in (ben′zō·in, -zoin) *n.* **1.** A gum resin from various East Indian plants, used in medicine and as a perfume. [< F < Pg. or Ital. < Arabic *lubān jāwī* incense of Java]
ben·zol (ben′zōl, -zol) *n.* A grade of crude benzene.
Be·o·wulf (bā′ə·wŏŏlf) The princely hero of an Anglo-Saxon epic poem of the eighth century; also, the poem.
be·queath (bi·kwēth′, -kwēth′) *v.t.* **1.** *Law* To give (property) by will. **2.** To hand down. [OE *becwethan*]
be·quest (bi·kwest′) *n.* The act of bequeathing, or that which is bequeathed. [ME *biqueste*]
be·rate (bi·rāt′) *v.t.* **·rat·ed, ·rat·ing** To scold severely.
Ber·ber (bûr′bər) *n.* **1.** One who belongs to a group of Moslem tribes, esp. the Kabyles, inhabiting northern Africa. **2.** The Hamitic language of the Berbers. —*adj.* Of or pertaining to the Berbers or their language.
ber·ceuse (ber·sœz′) *n. pl.* **·ceuses** (-sœz′) A lullaby. [< F]
be·reave (bi·rēv′) *v.t.* **·reaved** or **·reft** (-reft′), **·reav·ing** **1.** To deprive, as of hope or happiness. **2.** To leave saddened through death. [OE *berēafian*] —**be·reave′ment** *n.*
be·reft (bi·reft′) Alternative past tense and past participle of BEREAVE. —*adj.* Deprived: *bereft* of all hope.
be·ret (bə·rā′, ber′ā) *n.* A soft, flat cap, usu. of wool, originating in the Basque regions of France and Spain. [< F]
berg (bûrg) *n.* An iceberg.
ber·ga·mot[1] (bûr′gə·mot) *n.* **1.** A small tree whose fruit furnishes a fragrant essential oil. **2.** The oil itself. **3.** Any of several plants of the mint family. [? after *Bergamo,* Italy]
ber·ga·mot[2] (bûr′gə·mot) *n.* A minor variety of pear. [< F < Ital. < Turkish *beg-armūdi* prince's pear]
Berg·son·ism (berg′sən·iz′əm) *n.* The philosophy of Henri Bergson. —**Berg·so·ni·an** (berg·sō′nē·ən) *adv. & n.*
be·rhyme (bi·rīm′) *v.t.* **·rhymed, ·rhym·ing** **1.** To celebrate in rhyme. **2.** To compose in rhyme. Also **be·rime′.**
ber·i·ber·i (ber′ē·ber′ē) *n. Pathol.* A disease of the peripheral nerves resulting from the absence of B vitamins in the diet. [< Singhalese *beri* weakness] —**ber′i·ber′ic** *adj.*
berke·li·um (bûrk′lē·əm) *n.* The unstable radioactive element of atomic number 97 (symbol Bk), obtained by bombarding americium with alpha particles. [after *Berkeley,* California, location of the University of California]
Berk·shire (bûrk′shir, -shər) *n.* One of a breed of black and white swine originating in Berkshire, England.
berm (bûrm) *n.* A narrow ledge, shelf, or shoulder, as on a slope or at the side of a road: also **berme.** [< F *berme*]
Ber·mu·da shorts (bər·myōō′də) Knee-length shorts.
ber·ret·ta (bə·ret′ə) *n.* A biretta.
ber·ry (ber′ē) *n. pl.* **·ries** **1.** Any small, succulent fruit: often used in combination: *strawberry.* **2.** *Bot.* A simple fruit with the seeds in a juicy pulp, as the grape. **3.** The dry kernel of various grains, or the fruit of certain plants, as a coffee bean, etc. —*v.i.* **·ried, ·ry·ing** **1.** To form or bear berries. **2.** To gather berries. [OE *berie*]
ber·serk (bər·sûrk′, bûr′sûrk) *adj.* Violently or frenetically destructive. —**to go** (or **run**) **berserk** To have a fit of destructive rage. —*n.* A berserker. [< ON *berserkr*]

ber·serk·er (bûr′sûr′kər) *n.* In Norse legend, a warrior who fought with frenzied fury.

berth (bûrth) *n.* **1.** A bunk or bed in a vessel, sleeping car, etc. **2.** *Naut.* Any place in which a vessel may lie at anchor or at a dock. **3.** Situation or employment on a vessel. **4.** Office or employment in general. **— to give a wide berth to** To avoid; keep out of the way of. **—** *v.t.* **1.** *Naut.* To bring to a berth. **2.** To provide with a berth. **—** *v.i.* **3.** *Naut.* To come to a berth. [Origin uncertain.]

ber·tha (bûr′thə) *n.* A deep collar worn by women, falling over the shoulders from a low neckline. [< F *berthe*]

Ber·til·lon system (bûr′tə·lon, *Fr.* ber·tē·yôṅ′) A system of coded physical measurements, used as a means of identification, esp. of criminals. [after Alphonse *Bertillon*, 1853–1914, French anthropologist]

ber·yl (ber′əl) *n.* A vitreous, green, light blue, yellow, pink, or white silicate of aluminum and beryllium, of which the aquamarine and emerald are varieties used as gems. [< OF < L < Gk. *bēryllos* beryl] **— ber·yl·line** (ber′ə·lin, -līn) *adj.*

be·ryl·li·um (bə·ril′ē·əm) *n.* A hard, grayish black, noncorrosive metallic element (symbol Be), used in copper and aluminum alloys and for windows of X-ray tubes. See ELEMENT. [< NL < L *beryllus* beryl]

be·seech (bi·sēch′) *v.t.* **·sought, ·seech·ing 1.** To entreat earnestly; implore. **2.** To beg for earnestly; crave. [ME < *bi-* greatly + *sēcan* to seek] **— be·seech′er** *n.*

be·seem (bi·sēm′) *v.i.* To be fitting or appropriate: It ill *beseems* you to speak thus. **— be·seem′ing** *adj.*

be·set (bi·set′) *v.t.* **·set, ·set·ting 1.** To attack on all sides; harass. **2.** To hem in; encircle. **3.** To set or stud, as with gems. [OE *besettan*] **— be·set′ment** *n.*

be·set·ting (bi·set′ing) *adj.* Constantly attacking or troubling.

be·side (bi·sīd′) *prep.* **1.** At the side of; in proximity to. **2.** In comparison with. **3.** Away or apart from: This discussion is *beside* the point. **4.** Other than; over and above. **— beside oneself** Out of one's senses, as from anger, fear, etc. **—** *adv.* In addition; besides. [OE *be sīdan* by the side (of)]

be·sides (bi·sīdz′) *adv.* **1.** In addition; as well. **2.** Moreover; furthermore. **3.** Apart from that mentioned; otherwise; else. **—** *prep.* **1.** In addition to; other than. **2.** Beyond; apart from: I care for nothing *besides* this.

be·siege (bi·sēj′) *v.t.* **·sieged, ·sieg·ing 1.** To lay siege to, as a castle. **2.** To crowd around. **3.** To overwhelm, as with gifts. **— be·siege′ment** *n.* **— be·sieg′er** *n.*

be·smear (bi·smir′) *v.t.* To smear over; sully.

be·smirch (bi·smûrch′) *v.t.* **1.** To soil; stain. **2.** To sully; dim the luster of. **— be·smirch′er** *n.* **— be·smirch′ment** *n.*

be·som (bē′zəm) *n.* **1.** A bundle of twigs used as a broom. **2.** Broom (def. 2). [OE *besma* broom]

be·sot (bi·sot′) *v.t.* **·sot·ted, ·sot·ting 1.** To stupefy, as with drink. **2.** To make foolish or stupid. **3.** To infatuate.

be·sought (bi·sôt′) Past tense and past participle of BESEECH.

be·span·gle (bi·spang′gəl) *v.t.* **·gled, ·gling** To decorate with or as with spangles.

be·spat·ter (bi·spat′ər) *v.t.* **1.** To cover or soil by spattering, as with mud. **2.** To sully; slander.

be·speak (bi·spēk′) *v.t.* **·spoke** (*Archaic* **·spake**), **·spo·ken** or **·spoke, ·speak·ing 1.** To ask or arrange for in advance. **2.** To give evidence of. **3.** To foretell. [OE *bisprecan*]

be·spec·ta·cled (bi·spek′tə·kəld) *adj.* Wearing spectacles.

be·spoke (bi·spōk′) Past tense and alternative past participle of BESPEAK.

be·spread (bi·spred′) *v.t.* **·spread, ·spread·ing** To cover or spread over thickly.

Bes·se·mer converter (bes′ə·mər) *Metall.* A large, pear-shaped vessel for containing the molten iron to be converted into steel by the Bessemer process.

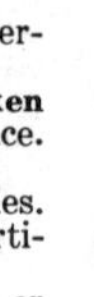

BESSEMER CONVERTER
a, b Exhaust gases. *c* Silica refractory lining. *d* Flames. *e* Steel shell. *f* Compressed air. *g* Molten iron.

Bessemer process *Metall.* A process for eliminating impurities from pig iron by forcing a blast of air through the molten metal before its conversion into steel or ingot iron.

best (best) Superlative of GOOD, WELL². **—** *adj.* **1.** Excelling all others; of the highest quality. **2.** Most advantageous, desirable, or serviceable. **3.** Most; largest: the *best* part of an hour. **—** *adv.* **1.** In the most excellent way; most advantageously. **2.** To the utmost degree; most thoroughly. **—** *n.* **1.** The best thing, part, etc. **2.** Best condition or quality; utmost: Be at your *best;* Do your *best.* **3.** One's best clothes. **— at best** Under the most favorable circumstances. **— to get** (or **have**) **the best of** To defeat or outwit. **— to make the best of** To adapt oneself to the disadvantages of. **—** *v.t.* To defeat; surpass. [OE *betst*]

be·stead (bi·sted′) *v.t.* To be of service to; help; avail.

bes·tial (bes′chəl, best′yəl) *adj.* **1.** Of or pertaining t beasts. **2.** Brutish; depraved. [< OF < L < *bestia* beast] **— bes·ti·al·i·ty** (bes′chē·al′ə·tē, -tē·al′-) *n.* **— bes′tial·l** *adv.*

bes·tial·ize (bes′chəl·īz, best′yəl-) *v.t.* **·ized, ·iz·ing** To bru talize.

be·stir (bi·stûr′) *v.t.* **·stirred, ·stir·ring** To rouse to activit

best man The chief attendant of a bridegroom at a weddin

be·stow (bi·stō′) *v.t.* **1.** To present as a gift; with *on* or *upo* **2.** To apply; expend, as time. **3.** To give in marriage. – **be·stow′a·ble** *adj.* **— be·stow′al, be·stow′ment** *n.*

be·strad·dle (bi·strad′l) *v.t.* **·dled, ·dling** To bestride.

be·strew (bi·strōō′) *v.t.* **·strewed, ·strewed** or **·strew** **·strew·ing 1.** To cover or strew (a surface). **2.** To scatt about. **3.** To lie scattered over. Also **be·strow** (bi·strō′

be·stride (bi·strīd′) *v.t.* **·strode, ·strid·den, ·strid·ing 1.** T mount; sit or stand astride of; straddle. **2.** To stride acros

best seller A book, phonograph record, etc., that sells (has sold in large numbers.

bet (bet) *n.* **1.** An agreement to risk something of one's ow in return for the chance of winning something belonging t another or others. **2.** That which is risked in a bet, as a su of money; a stake. **3.** The subject or event about which bet is made. Also called *wager.* **—** *v.* **bet** or (less commonl **bet·ted, bet·ting** *v.t.* **1.** To stake or pledge (money, etc.) a bet. **2.** To declare as in a bet: I *bet* he doesn't come. – *v.i.* **3.** To place a bet. Also *wager.* **— you bet** *U.S. Sla* Certainly. [Origin uncertain]

be·ta (bā′tə, bē′-) *n.* **1.** The second letter of the Greek a phabet (Β, β), corresponding to English *b.* See ALPHABET. The second object in any series, etc. [< Gk.]

be·take (bi·tāk′) *v.t.* **·took, ·tak·en, ·tak·ing 1.** To unde take: used reflexively: She *betook* herself to prayer. **2.** T go; take (oneself): He *betook* himself to an inn. [ME *bitake*

beta particle An electron.

beta rays *Physics* A stream of electrons projected by radi active substances.

be·ta·tron (bā′tə·tron) *n.* *Physics* An accelerator that us a magnetic field to increase the velocity of electrons.

be·tel (bēt′l) *n.* A climbing plant of Asia, the leaves which are chewed by the natives of Malaya and other Asia countries. [< Pg. < Malay *vettila*]

Be·tel·geuse (bēt′l·jōōz, bet′l·jœz) *n.* A giant red star, or of the 20 brightest, 1.2 magnitude; Alpha in the constellatio Orion. Also **Be′tel·geux.** [< F *Bételgeuse* < Arabic *bat a jauza,* ? shoulder of the giant]

be·tel·nut (bēt′l·nut′) *n.* The astringent seed of an Ea Indian palm, the **betel palm** (*Areca catechu*), used for chev ing with betel leaves and lime.

bête noire (bāt′nwär′, *Fr.* bet nwȧr′) Anything that is a object of hate or dread; a bugaboo. [< F, black beast]

Beth·a·ny (beth′ə·nē) In the New Testament, a village ne Jerusalem: the home of Lazarus, Martha, and Mary.

beth·el (beth′əl) *n.* **1.** A hallowed place. *Gen.* xxviii 19. A seamen's church. [< Hebrew *bēth-el* house of God]

be·think (bi·thingk′) *v.* **·thought, ·think·ing** *v.t.* To bear i mind; consider: generally used reflexively.

be·thought (bi·thot′) Past tense and past participle of BE THINK.

be·tide (be·tīd′) *v.t.* & *v.i.* **·tid·ed, ·tid·ing** To happen (to) (befall. [ME *bitiden*]

be·times (bi·tīmz′) *adv.* In good time; early; also, soo [ME *betymes* in time, seasonably]

be·to·ken (bi·tō′kən) *v.t.* **1.** To be a sign of; presage. **2.** T give evidence of. [ME *bitacnien*] **— be·to′ken·er** *n.*

be·took (bi·tŏŏk′) Past tense of BETAKE.

be·tray (bi·trā′) *v.t.* **1.** To aid an enemy of; be a traitor t **2.** To prove faithless to. **3.** To disclose, as secret informa tion. **4.** To reveal unwittingly. **5.** To seduce and deser **6.** To indicate; show: The smoke *betrays* a fire. [ME *b traien*] **— be·tray′al, be·tray′ment** *n.* **— be·tray′er** *n.*

be·troth (bi·trōth′, -trôth′) *v.t.* To engage to marry; aff ance. [ME < *bi-* to + *treuthe* truth]

be·troth·al (bi·trō′thəl, -trôth′əl) *n.* The act of betrothing engagement or contract to marry. Also **be·troth′ment.**

be·trothed (bi·trōthd′, -trôtht′) *adj.* Engaged to be ma ried; affianced. **—** *n.* A person engaged to be married.

bet·ter¹ (bet′ər) Comparative of GOOD, WELL². **—** *adj.* **1** Superior in quality. **2.** More advantageous, desirable, c serviceable. **3.** Larger; greater: the *better* part of the cak **4.** Improved in health; convalescent. **—** *adv.* **1.** More ad vantageously. **2.** To a larger degree; more thoroughly. **3** More: *better* than a week. **— better off** In a better conditio or improved circumstances. **—** *v.t.* **1.** To make better; im prove. **2.** To surpass; excel. **—** *v.i.* **3.** To become bette **—** *n.* **1.** That which is better. **2.** *Usu. pl.* One's superior as in ability, rank, etc. **3.** Advantage. [OE *betera*]

bet·ter² (bet′ər) *n.* One who lays bets. Also **bet′tor.**

bet·ter·ment (bet′ər·mənt) *n.* **1.** Improvement. **2.** *La* An improvement adding to the value of real property.

be·tween (bi·twēn′) *prep.* **1.** In the space that separate

;wo places or objects). **2.** Intermediate in relation to, as mes, qualities, etc. **3.** From one to another of; connecting. . Involving reciprocal action among. **5.** By the joint acon of: *Between* them, they killed three deer. **6.** In the joint ossession of: not a cent *between* them. **7.** Being one alernative over another: to judge *between* right and wrong. **- between you and me** Confidentially. **—** *adv.* In interening time, space, position, or relation: few and far *between.* **- in between** In an intermediate position or state; undeided. [Fusion of OE *bitwēonum* and *bitwēon* < *bi-* by + *weonum* and *-tweon,* both < *twā* two]

·twixt (bi·twikst′) *adv. & prep. Archaic* Between. **— etwixt and between** In an intermediate or indecisive state. OE *betweons* twofold < *be-* by + *-tweons* < *twā* two]

·v·el (bev′əl) *n.* **1.** Any inclination of two surfaces other han 90°, as at the edge of a timber, etc. **2.** An adjustable strument for measuring angles: also **bevel square.** **—** *adj.* blique; slanting. **—** *v.* **bev·eled** or **·elled, bev·el·ing** or **·el·ng** *v.t.* **1.** To cut or bring to a bevel. **—** *v.i.* **2.** To slant. ? < OF. Cf. F *beveau* bevel (n. def. 2).]

vel gear *Mech.* A gear having beveled teeth, as for transitting rotary motion at an angle. For illus. see GEAR.

·v·er·age (bev′rij, bev′ər·ij) *n.* That which is drunk; any rink. [< OF < L *bibere* to drink]

·v·y (bev′ē) *n. pl.* **bev·ies** **1.** A group, esp. of girls or omen. **2.** A flock, esp. of quail, grouse, or larks. **— Syn.** ee FLOCK. [ME *bevey;* origin uncertain]

·wail (bi·wāl′) *v.t. & v.i.* To lament. **— Syn.** See MOURN.

·ware (bi·wâr′) *v.t. & v.i.* **·wared, ·war·ing** To look out or); be cautious or wary (of). [OE *wær* cautious]

·wil·der (bi·wil′dər) *v.t.* To confuse utterly; perplex. **— e·wil′dered** *adj.* **— be·wil′dered·ly** *adv.* **— be·wil′der·ent** *n.*

·witch (bi·wich′) *v.t.* **1.** To gain power over by charms or cantations. **2.** To attract irresistibly; charm; fascinate. ME < *bi-* completely + *wicchen* to enchant] **— be·witch′·r** *n.* **— be·witch′ment, be·witch′er·y** *n.*

·witch·ing (bi·wich′ing) *adj.* Charming; captivating. **— e·witch′ing·ly** *adv.*

·y (bā) *n.* **1.** The governor of a minor Turkish province or istrict. **2.** A Turkish title of respect. [< Turkish *beg* lord]

·yond (bi·yond′) *prep.* **1.** On or to the far side of; farther n than. **2.** Later than. **3.** Outside the reach or scope of: *eyond* help. **4.** Surpassing; superior to: lovely *beyond* decription. **5.** More than; over and above. **—** *adv.* Farther n or away; at a distance. **— the (great) beyond** Whatever omes after death. [OE < *be-* near + *geondan* yonder]

·z·el (bez′əl) *n.* **1.** A bevel on the edge of a cutting tool. **.** The upper part of a cut gem, including the table and suriunding facets. [? < OF. Cf. F *biseau* bias.]

·zique (bə·zēk′) *n.* A game of cards resembling pinochle, layed with a deck of 64 cards. [Alter. of F *bésigue*]

ıang (bang) *n.* **1.** Hemp (def. 1). **2.** Hashish. Also spelled *ang.* [< Hind. < Skt. *bhangā* hemp]

ıu·tan·ese (bo͞o′tən·ēz′, -ēs′) *n. pl.* **·ese** **1.** A native of hutan. **2.** The Sino-Tibetan language of Bhutan. **—** *adj.*)f or pertaining to Bhutan, its people, or their language.

- *prefix* **1.** Twice; doubly; two; especially, occurring twice r having two: *biangular.* **2.** *Chem.* **a** Indicating the doubing of a radical, etc., in an organic compound. **b** Having ouble the proportion of the substance named: *bicarbonate.* lso: *bin-* before a vowel, as in *binaural; bis-* before *c, s,* as n *bissextile.* [< L *bi-* < *bis* twice]

·an·gu·lar (bī·ang′gyə·lər) *adj.* Having two angles.

·an·nu·al (bī·an′yo͞o·əl) *adj.* Occurring twice a year; seminnual. Compare BIENNIAL. **— bi·an′nu·al·ly** *adv.*

·as (bī′əs) *n. pl.* **bi·as·es** **1.** A line running obliquely cross a fabric: to cut on the *bias.* **2.** A mental tendency, reference, or prejudice. **— Syn.** See PREJUDICE. **—** *adj.* :ut, running, set, or folded diagonally; slanting. **—** *adv.* lantingly; diagonally. **—** *v.t.* **bi·ased** or **·assed, bi·as·ing** or **as·sing** To influence or affect unduly or unfairly. [< MF *iais* oblique]

·ax·i·al (bī·ak′sē·əl) *adj.* Having two axes, as a crystal. lso **bi·ax·al** (bī·ak′səl). **— bi·ax′i·al·ly** *adv.*

b (bib) *n.* **1.** A cloth worn under a child's chin at meals to rotect the clothing. **2.** The upper front part of an apron or f overalls. [? < L *bibere* to drink]

b and tucker *Informal* Clothes.

b·ber (bib′ər) *n.* A habitual drinker; tippler.

b·cock (bib′kok′) *n.* A faucet having the nozzle bent ownward.

be·lot (bib′lō, *Fr.* bēb·lō′) *n.* A small, decorative and ften rare object or trinket. [< F]

i·ble (bī′bəl) *n.* **1.** In Christianity, the Old Testament nd the New Testament. **2.** In Judaism, the Old Testanent. **3.** The sacred book or writings of any religion. [<)F < L < Gk., pl. of *biblion* book]

Bib·li·cal (bib′li·kəl) *adj.* **1.** Of or in the Bible. **2.** In harmony with the Bible. Also **bib′li·cal.** **— Bib′li·cal·ly** *adv.*

Bib·li·cist (bib′lə·sist) *n.* **1.** One versed in the Bible. **2.** One who adheres to the letter of the Bible.

biblio- *combining form* Pertaining to books, or to the Bible: *bibliophile.* [< Gk. *biblion* book]

bib·li·og·ra·phy (bib′lē·og′rə·fē) *n. pl.* **·phies** **1.** A list of the works of an author, or of the literature bearing on a subject. **2.** A list of books or other sources mentioned or consulted by an author, usu. appended to the end of his text. **3.** The description and history of books, including details of authorship, editions, dates, etc. **— bib′li·og′ra·pher** *n.* **— bib·li·o·graph·ic** (bib′lē·ə·graf′ik) or **·i·cal** *adj.*

bib·li·o·ma·ni·a (bib′lē·ō·mā′nē·ə) *n.* A passion for collecting books. **— bib′li·o·ma′ni·ac** (-ak) *n. & adj.*

bib·li·o·phile (bib′lē·ə·fīl′, -fil′) *n.* One who loves books. Also **bib′li·o·phil′** (-fil′), **bib·li·oph·i·list** (bib′lē·of′ə·list). **— bib′li·oph′i·lism** *n.* **— bib′li·oph′i·lis′tic** *adj.*

bib·u·lous (bib′yə·ləs) *adj.* **1.** Given to drink; fond of drinking. **2.** Absorbent. [< L *bibere* to drink]

bi·cam·er·al (bī·kam′ər·əl) *adj.* Consisting of two chambers, houses, or branches. [< BI- + L *camera* chamber]

bi·car·bo·nate (bī·kär′bə·nit, -nāt) *n. Chem.* A salt of carbonic acid in which one of the hydrogen atoms of the acid is replaced by a metal: sodium *bicarbonate.*

bicarbonate of soda Sodium bicarbonate.

bi·cen·ten·ni·al (bī′sen·ten′ē·əl) *adj.* **1.** Occurring once in 200 years. **2.** Lasting or consisting of 200 years. **—** *n.* A 200th anniversary. Also **bi·cen·te·nar·y** (bī·sen′tə·ner′ē, bī′·sen·ten′ər·ē).

bi·ceps (bī′seps) *n. pl.* **bi·ceps** *Anat.* **1.** The large front muscle of the upper arm. **2.** The large flexor muscle at the back of the thigh. [< L < *bis* twofold + *caput* head]

bi·chlo·ride (bī·klôr′īd, -id, -klō′rīd, -rid) *n. Chem.* **1.** A salt having two atoms of chlorine. **2.** Bichloride of mercury.

bi·chro·mate (bī·krō′māt, -mit) *n. Chem.* Dichromate.

bick·er (bik′ər) *v.i.* **1.** To dispute petulantly; wrangle. **2.** To flicker, as a flame; twinkle. **—** *n.* A petty altercation. **— Syn.** See QUARREL[1]. [ME *bikeren*] **— bick′er·er** *n.*

bi·col·or (bī′kul′ər) *adj.* Two-colored. Also **bi′col′ored.**

bi·con·cave (bī·kon′kāv, -kong′-, bī′kon·kāv′) *adj.* Concave on both sides, as a lens.

bi·con·vex (bī·kon′veks, bī′kon·veks′) *adj.* Convex on both sides, as a lens.

bi·cus·pid (bī·kus′pid) *adj.* Having two cusps or points. Also **bi·cus′pi·dal** (-dəl), **bi·cus′pi·date** (-dāt). **—** *n.* A premolar tooth. For illus. see TOOTH. [< BI- + L *cuspis,* point]

bi·cy·cle (bī′sik·əl) *n.* A vehicle consisting of a metal frame mounted on two wheels, one in back of the other, having a saddle, handlebars, and pedals. **—** *v.i.* **·cled, ·cling** To ride a bicycle. [< F < *bi-* two + Gk. *kyklos* wheel] **— bi′cy·cler, bi′cy·clist** *n.*

bid (bid) *n.* **1.** An offer to pay a price; also, the amount offered. **2.** In card games, the number of tricks or points that a player engages to make; also, a player's turn to bid. **3.** An effort to acquire, win, or attain: a *bid* for the governorship. **4.** *Informal* An invitation. **—** *v.* **bade** *for defs. 3, 4, 6,* or **bid** *for defs. 1, 2, 5, 7,* **bid·den** or **bid, bid·ding** *v.t.* **1.** To make an offer of (a price). **2.** In card games, to declare (the number of tricks or points one will engage to make). **3.** To command; order. **4.** To say to, as a greeting or farewell. **—** *v.i.* **5.** To make a bid. **— to bid fair** To seem probable. **— to bid in** At an auction, to outbid a prospective purchaser on behalf of the owner, when the price offered is too low. **— to bid up** To increase the price by offering higher bids. [Fusion of OE *biddan* to ask, demand and *bēodan* to proclaim] **— bid′da·ble** *adj.* **— bid′der** *n.*

bid·ding (bid′ing) *n.* **1.** A command. **2.** An invitation or summons. **3.** Bids, or the making of a bid or bids.

bid·dy (bid′ē) *n. pl.* **·dies** A hen. [Origin uncertain]

bide (bīd) *v.* **bid·ed** (*Archaic* **bode**), **bid·ing** *v.t* **1.** To endure; withstand. **2.** *Archaic* To tolerate; submit to. **—** *v.i.* **3.** To dwell; abide; stay. **— to bide one's time** To await the best opportunity. [OE *bīdan*]

bi·en·ni·al (bī·en′ē·əl) *adj.* **1.** Occurring every second year. **2.** Lasting or living for two years. **—** *n.* **1.** *Bot.* A plant that produces flowers and fruit in its second year, then dies. **2.** An event occurring once in two years. [< L < *bis* twofold + *annus* year] **— bi·en′ni·al·ly** *adv.*

bien·ve·nue (byaṅ·və·nü′) *n. French* A welcome.

bier (bir) *n.* A framework for carrying a corpse to the grave; also, a coffin. [OE *bær*]

biest·ings (bēs′tingz) See BEESTINGS.

biff (bif) *U.S Slang v.t.* To strike; hit. **—** *n.* A blow. [Imit.]

bi·fid (bī′fid) *adj.* Cleft; forked. [< L < *bis* twofold + *findere* to split] **— bi·fid′i·ty** *n.* **— bi′fid·ly** *adv.*

bi·fo·cal (bī·fō′kəl) *adj. Optics* Having two foci: said of a lens ground for both near and far vision.

ɪONUNCIATION KEY: **add, āce, câre, pälm; end, ēven; it, īce; odd, ōpen, ôrder; to͝ok, po͞ol; up, bûrn; ə** = a in *above,* e in *sicken,* i in *flex-'e,* o in *melon,* u in *focus;* **yo͞o** = u in *fuse;* **oil; pout; check; go; ring; thin; this; zh,** vision.

bi·fo·cals (bī·fō′kəlz, bī′fō·kəlz) *n.pl.* Eyeglasses with bifocal lenses.

bi·fur·cate (bī′fər·kāt, bī·fûr′kāt; *adj. also* bī·fûr′kit) *v.t. & v.i.* **·cat·ed, ·cat·ing** To divide into two branches or stems; fork. — *adj.* Forked: also **bi′fur·cat′ed** (-kā′tid), **bi·fur·cous** (bī·fûr′kəs). [< L *bi-* two + *furca* fork] — **bi·fur·cate·ly** (bī′fər·kit·lē, bī·fûr′kit·lē) *adv.* — **bi′fur·ca′tion** *n.*

big (big) *adj.* **big·ger, big·gest** **1.** Of great size, extent, etc. **2.** Pregnant: usu. with *with.* **3.** Grown. **4.** Pompous; pretentious. **5.** Important; prominent. **6.** Loud. **7.** Generous; magnanimous. — *adv. Informal* Pompously; extravagantly: to talk *big.* [ME; origin uncertain] — **big′gish** *adj.* — **big′ly** *adv.* — **big′ness** *n.*

big·a·my (big′ə·mē) *n. Law* The criminal offense of marrying any other person while having a legal spouse living. [< OF < LL < L *bis* twice + Gk. *gamos* wedding] — **big′a·mist** *n.* — **big′a·mous** *adj.* — **big′a·mous·ly** *adv.*

Big Ben **1.** A bell in the Westminster clock in the tower of the House of Parliament, London. **2.** The clock itself.

Big Dipper The constellation Ursa Major.

big-heart·ed (big′här′tid) *adj.* Generous; charitable.

big·horn (big′hôrn) *n. pl.* **·horns** or **·horn** The Rocky Mountain sheep, remarkable for its large curved horns.

big house *U.S. Slang* A penitentiary.

bight (bīt) *n.* **1.** The loop, or middle part, of a rope. **2.** A bend or curve in a shoreline, a river, etc. **3.** A bay bounded by such a bend. — *v.t.* To secure with a bight. [OE *byht*]

big·no·ni·a (big·nō′nē·ə) *n.* A climbing plant having clusters of large, trumpet-shaped flowers. [after Abbé *Bignon,* 1711–1772, librarian to Louis XV]

big·ot (big′ət) *n.* One whose attitude or behavior expresses intolerance, as because of race, religion, politics, etc. [< F; ult. origin unknown] — **big′ot·ed** *adj.* — **big′ot·ed·ly** *adv.*

big·ot·ry (big′ə·trē) *n. pl.* **·ries** Attitudes, beliefs, or actions characteristic of a bigot; intolerance.

big shot *Slang* Someone of importance. Also **big wheel.**

big top *U.S. Informal* The main tent of a circus.

big·wig (big′wig′) *n. Informal* Someone of importance.

bi·jou (bē′zhōō, bē·zhōō′) *n. pl.* **bi·joux** (bē′zhōōz, bē·zhōōz′) A jewel, or a finely wrought trinket. [< MF]

bi·ju·gate (bī′jōō·gāt, bī·jōō′git) *adj. Bot.* Two-paired, as leaves. Also **bi·ju·gous** (bī′jōō·gəs).

bike (bīk) *n. Informal* A bicycle. [Alter. of BICYCLE]

bi·ki·ni (bi·kē′nē) *n.* A type of very scanty bathing suit.

bi·la·bi·al (bī·lā′bē·əl) *adj.* **1.** *Phonet.* Articulated with both lips, as certain consonants. **2.** Having two lips. — *n. Phonet.* A bilabial speech sound, as (b), (p), (m), and (w).

bi·la·bi·ate (bī·lā′bē·āt, -it) *adj. Bot.* Two-lipped: said of a corolla.

bi·lat·er·al (bī·lat′ər·əl) *adj.* **1.** Pertaining to or having two sides; two-sided. **2.** On two sides. **3.** Mutually binding. — **bi·lat′er·al·ly** *adv.* — **bi·lat′er·al·ness** *n.*

bil·ber·ry (bil′ber′ē, -bər·ē) *n. pl.* **·ries** The whortleberry.

bil·bo (bil′bō) *n. pl.* **·boes** *pl.* A fetter consisting of two sliding shackles attached to an iron bar. [after *Bilbao*]

bile (bīl) *n.* **1.** *Physiol.* A bitter yellow or greenish liquid secreted by the liver and serving to promote digestion. **2.** Anger; peevishness. [< F < L *bilis* bile, anger]

bile ducts *Physiol.* The excretory ducts of the gall bladder.

bilge (bilj) *n.* **1.** *Naut.* The rounded part of a ship's bottom. **2.** The bulge of a barrel. **3.** Bilge water. **4.** *Slang* Stupid or trivial talk or writing. — *v.t. & v.i.* **bilged, bilg·ing** **1.** To break open in the bilge: said of a ship. **2.** To bulge. [Var. of BULGE] — **bilg′y** *adj.*

bilge water Foul water that collects in the bilge of a ship.

bil·i·ar·y (bil′ē·er′ē) *adj.* Pertaining to or conveying bile. [< F *biliare*]

bi·lin·gual (bī·ling′gwəl) *adj.* **1.** Written or expressed in or using two languages. **2.** Able to speak two languages, often with equal skill. — *n.* A bilingual person. [< L *bilinguis*] — **bi·lin′gual·ism** *n.* — **bi·lin′gual·ly** *adv.*

bil·ious (bil′yəs) *adj.* **1.** Affected or caused by an excess of bile. **2.** Of or containing bile. **3.** Ill-tempered. **4.** Of a sickly color. [< F < L *biliosus*] — **bil′ious·ly** *adv.* — **bil′ious·ness** *n.*

-bility *suffix* Forming nouns from adjectives ending in *-ble: probability* from *probable.* [< F < L *-bilitas, -tatis*]

bilk (bilk) *v.t.* **1.** To cheat; deceive. **2.** To evade payment of. **3.** To balk. — *n.* **1.** A swindler; cheat. **2.** A hoax. [Origin unknown] — **bilk′er** *n.*

bill[1] (bil) *n.* **1.** A statement listing charges for goods delivered or services rendered. **2.** A statement of particulars; itemized list. **3.** *U.S.* A piece of paper money; a bank note. **4.** A bill of exchange; also, loosely, a promissory note. **5.** A draft of a proposed law. **6.** A handbill or advertising poster. **7.** The program of a theatrical performance. **8.** *Law* A formal statement of a case, a complaint, a petition for relief, etc. — *v.t.* **1.** To enter in a bill or list. **2.** To present a bill to. **3.** To advertise by bills or placards. [< LL *billa,* var of L *bulla* edict, document] — **bill′a·ble** *adj.*

bill[2] (bil) *n.* A beak, as of a bird. — *v.i.* To join bills, as doves; caress. — **to bill and coo** To caress lovingly an speak in soft, murmuring tones. [OE *bile*]

bill[3] (bil) *n.* **1.** A hook-shaped instrument used in prunin etc.: also **bill′hook′.** **2.** An ancient weapon with a hoo shaped blade; a halberd. [OE]

bil·la·bong (bil′ə·bong) *n. Austral.* A stagnant backwate [< native Australian < *billa* water + *bong* dead]

bill·board (bil′bôrd′, -bōrd′) *n.* A panel, usu. outdoors, f notices or advertisements.

bil·let[1] (bil′it) *n.* **1.** Lodging for troops in private or no military buildings. **2.** An order for such lodging. **3.** A pla assigned, as for a sailor to sling his hammock; quarters. A job; berth. — *v.t.* To lodge (soldiers, etc.) in a priva house by billet. [< OF < L *bulla* seal, document]

bil·let[2] (bil′it) *n.* **1.** A short, thick stick, as of firewood. *Metall.* A mass of iron or steel drawn into a small bar. [OF *billete,* dim. of *bille* log]

bil·let-doux (bil′ā·dōō′, *Fr.* bē·yā·dōō′) *n. pl.* **bil·lets-dou** (bil′ā·dōōz′, *Fr.* bē·yā·dōō′) A love letter. [<F]

bill·fold (bil′fōld′) *n.* A wallet.

bill·head (bil′hed′) *n.* A heading on paper used for maki out bills; also, a blank with such a heading.

bil·liard (bil′yərd) *n. U.S. Informal* A carom. — *adj.* or pertaining to billiards: *billiard* player.

bil·liards (bil′yərdz) *n.pl.* (*construed as sing.*) Any of vario games played with hard balls (**billiard balls**) hit by cues an oblong, cloth-covered table (**billiard table**) having cus ioned edges. [< F < OF *billart* cue] — **bil′liard·ist** *n.*

bill·ing (bil′ing) *n.* The relative eminence given to an act or an act on a theater marquee, playbill, etc.

bil·lings·gate (bil′ingz·gāt) *n.* Vulgar or abusive languag [after *Billingsgate* fish market, London]

bil·lion (bil′yən) *n.* **1.** *U.S.* A thousand millions, written 1,000,000,000: called a *milliard* in Great Britain. **2.** *Brit.* million millions, written as 1,000,000,000,000: called a *tr lion* in the U.S. [< F < *bi-* two + (*mi*)*llion* million] **bil′lionth** *n. & adj.*

bil·lion·aire (bil′yən·âr′) *n.* One who owns a billion money. [< BILLION, on analogy with *millionaire*]

bill of exchange A written order for the payment of given sum to a designated person.

bill of fare A list of the dishes provided at a meal; menu

bill of health An official certificate of the crew's health i sued to a ship's master on departure from a port. — **a clea bill of health** *Informal* A good record; favorable report.

bill of lading A written acknowledgment of goods receiv for transportation.

bill of rights **1.** A formal summary and declaration of t fundamental principles and rights of individuals. **2.** *Oft cap.* The first ten amendments to the U.S. Constitution.

bill of sale An instrument attesting the transfer of propert

bil·low (bil′ō) *n.* **1.** A great wave or swell of the sea. Any wave or surge, as of sound. — **Syn.** See WAVE. — *v* To rise or roll in billows; surge; swell. [< ON *bylgja*]

bil·low·y (bil′ō·ē) *adj.* **·low·i·er, ·low·i·est** Of, full of, or r sembling billows; surging; swelling. — **bil′low·i·ness** *n.*

bill·post·er (bil′pōs′tər) *n.* A person who posts bills, n tices, or advertisements on walls, fences, etc. Also **bil stick′er.** — **bill′post′ing** *n.*

bil·ly (bil′ē) *n. pl.* **·lies** A short bludgeon, as a policema club. [< *Billy,* a nickname for William]

billy goat *Informal* A male goat.

bi·lo·bate (bī·lō′bāt) *adj* Divided into or having two lobe Also **bi·lo′bat·ed.**

Bi·lox·i (bi·lok′sē) *n.* One of a tribe of North America Indians of Siouan stock.

bi·man·u·al (bī·man′yōō·əl) *adj.* Employing or involvi both hands. — **bi·man′u·al·ly** *adv.*

bi·met·al·ism (bī·met′l·iz′əm) *n.* The concurrent use both gold and silver as the standard of currency and valu Also **bi·met′al·lism.** — **bi·met′al·ist** or **bi·met′al·list** *n.*

bi·me·tal·lic (bī′mə·tal′ik) *adj.* **1.** Consisting of or relati to two metals. **2.** Of or using bimetalism.

bi·month·ly (bī·munth′lē) *adj.* **1.** Occurring once eve two months. **2.** Occurring twice a month; semimonthl — *n.* A bimonthly publication. — *adv.* **1.** Once in tw months. **2.** Twice a month.

bin (bin) *n.* An enclosed place or large receptacle for holdi meal, coal, etc. — *v.t.* **binned, bin·ning** To store or depos in a bin. [OE *binn* basket, crib < Celtic]

bin- Var. of BI-.

bi·na·ry (bī′nər·ē) *adj.* Pertaining to, characterized by, made up of two; double; paired. — *n. pl.* **·ries** **1.** A co bination of two things. **2.** *Astron.* A binary star. [< *binarius* < *bini* two, double]

binary star *Astron.* A pair of stars revolving about a co mon center of gravity.

bi·nate (bī′nāt) *adj. Bot.* Being or growing in pairs, leaves. [< NL < L *bini* double, two] — **bi′nate·ly** *adv.*

bin·au·ral (bin·ôr′əl) *adj.* **1.** Hearing with both ears. **2** *Electronics* Stereophonic.

nd (bīnd) *v.* **bound, bind·ing** *v.t.* **1.** To tie or fasten with band, cord, etc. **2.** To fasten around; encircle; gird. **3.** To andage; swathe: often with *up.* **4.** To constrain or obliate, as by moral authority. **5.** *Law* To subject to a definite gal obligation. **6.** To enclose between covers, as a book. . To provide with a border for reinforcement or decoration. . To cause to cohere; cement. **9.** To constipate. **10.** To ake irrevocable; seal, as a bargain. **11.** To apprentice or identure: often with *out* or *over.* — *v.i.* **12.** To tie up anyning. **13.** To cohere; stick together. **14.** To have binding orce; be obligatory. **15.** To become stiff or hard, as cement; am, as gears. — **to bind over** *Law* To hold on bail or under ond for future appearance in court. — *n.* That which inds. [OE *bindan*]

nd·er (bīn′dər) *n.* **1.** One who binds; esp., a bookbinder. . Anything used to bind or tie, as a cord or band, or to ause cohesion, as tar, glue, etc. **3.** A cover in which sheets paper may be fastened. **4.** *Law* A written statement inding parties to an agreement pending preparation of a ontract. **5.** *Agric.* A machine that cuts and ties grain.

nd·er·y (bīn′dər·ē) *n. pl.* **·er·ies** A place where books are ound.

nd·ing (bīn′ding) *n.* **1.** The act of one who binds. **2.** nything that binds; binder. **3.** The cover holding together nd enclosing the leaves of a book. **4.** A strip sewed over an dge for protection. — *adj.* **1.** Tying; restraining. **2.** Obgatory. — **bind′ing·ly** *adv.* — **bind′ing·ness** *n.*

nd·weed (bīnd′wēd′) *n.* Any strongly twining plant.

ne (bīn) *n.* **1.** A flexible shoot or climbing stem, as of the op. **2.** The bindweed. **3.** The woodbine. [Var. of BIND]

nge (binj) *n. Slang* A drunken carousal; spree. [? < ial. E *binge* to soak]

n·go (bing′gō) *n.* A gambling game resembling lotto, usu. layed in large groups. [Origin unknown]

n·na·cle (bin′ə·kəl) *n. Naut.* A stand or case for a ship's ompass, usu. placed before the steering wheel. [Earlier *ittacle* < Pg. < L *habitaculum* little house]

n·oc·u·lar (bə·nok′yə·lər, bī-) *adj.* Pertaining to, using, r intended for both eyes at once. — *n. Often pl.* A telescope, pera glass, etc., adapted for use by both eyes. [< L *bini* wo, double + *ocularis* of the eyes < *oculus* eye]

·no·mi·al (bī·nō′mē·əl) *adj.* Consisting of two names or erms. — *n. Math.* An algebraic expression consisting of wo terms joined by a plus or minus sign. [< LL *binominus* aving two names] — **bi·no′mi·al·ly** *adv.*

o- *combining form* Life: *biology.* [< Gk. *bios* life]

·o·chem·is·try (bī′ō·kem′is·trē) *n.* The branch of chemstry relating to the processes and physical properties of living organisms. — **bi′o·chem′i·cal** or **bi′o·chem′ic** *adj.* — **bi′·chem′i·cal·ly** *adv.* — **bi′o·chem′ist** *n.*

·o·gen·e·sis (bī′ō·jen′ə·sis) *n.* The doctrine that life is enerated from living organisms only. Also **bi·og·e·ny** (bī·j′ə·nē). — **bi·o·ge·net·ic** (bī′ō·jə·net′ik) or **·i·cal** *adj.* — **i′o·ge·net′i·cal·ly** *adv.*

·og·ra·pher (bī·og′rə·fər, bē-) *n.* A writer of biography.

·o·graph·i·cal (bī·ə·graf′i·kəl) *adj.* **1.** Of or concerning a erson's life. **2.** Pertaining to biography. Also **bi′o·graph′·c.** — **bi′o·graph′i·cal·ly** *adv.*

·og·ra·phy (bī·og′rə·fē, bē-) *n. pl.* **·phies** An account of a erson's life; also, such accounts as a form of literature. [< Gk. < Gk. *bios* life + *graphein* to write]

·o·log·i·cal (bī′ə·loj′i·kəl) *adj.* **1.** Of or pertaining to biology. **2.** Used for or produced by biological research or ractice. Also **bi′o·log′ic.** — **bi′o·log′i·cal·ly** *adv.*

ological warfare Warfare that employs bacteria, viruses, nd other biological agents noxious to or destructive of life.

·ol·o·gy (bī·ol′ə·jē) *n.* The science of life in all its manifestations, and of the origin, structure, reproduction, growth, nd development of living organisms collectively. Its two nain divisions are botany and zoology. — **bi·ol′o·gist** *n.*

·om·e·try (bī·om′ə·trē) *n.* **1.** A measuring or calculating f the probable duration of human life. **2.** Biology from a tatistical point of view, esp. with reference to problems of ariation: also **bi·o·met·rics** (bī′ə·met′riks). — **bi·o·met′ric** r **·ri·cal** *adj.* — **bi′o·met′ri·cal·ly** *adv.*

·o·phys·ics (bī′ō·fiz′iks) *n.pl.* (*construed as sing.*) The tudy of biological function, structure, and organization in elation to and using the methods of physics. — **bi′o·phys′i·al** *adj.* — **bi′o·phys′i·cist** *n.*

·op·sy (bī′op·sē) *n. pl.* **·sies** *Med.* The examination of issue from a living subject. — **bi·op·sic** (bī·op′sik) *adj.*

·os·co·py (bī·os′kə·pē) *n. Med.* An examination to ascerain whether life exists. — **bi·o·scop·ic** (bī′ə·skop′ik) *adj.*

biosis *combining form* Manner of living: *symbiosis.* [< Gk. *biōsis* < *bios* life]

·o·tin (bī′ə·tin) *n. Biochem.* A crystalline acid, $C_{10}H_{16}O_3N_2S$, forming part of the vitamin B complex. [< Gk. *biotos* ife + -IN]

bi·par·ti·san (bī·pär′tə·zən) *adj.* Advocated by or consisting of members of two parties, esp. the Democratic and Republican parties. — **bi·par′ti·san·ship′** *n.*

bi·par·tite (bī·pär′tīt) *adj.* **1.** Consisting of two parts, esp. two corresponding parts. **2.** *Bot.* Divided into two parts almost to the base, as certain leaves. Also **bi·part′ed.** [< L *bipartire* to divide] — **bi·par′tite·ly** *adv.* — **bi·par·ti·tion** (bī′pär·tish′ən) *n.*

bi·ped (bī′ped) *n.* An animal having two feet. — *adj.* Twofooted: also **bi·pe·dal** (bī′pə·dəl, bip′ə-). [< L *bipes, bipedis*]

bi·pin·nate (bī·pin′āt) *adj. Bot.* Twice or doubly pinnate, as a leaf. Also **bi·pin′nat·ed.** — **bi·pin′nate·ly** *adv.*

bi·plane (bī′plān′) *n.* A type of airplane having two wings, one above the other.

bi·po·lar (bī·pō′lər) *adj.* **1.** Relating to or possessing two poles. **2.** Denoting or belonging to both polar regions. **3.** Containing two contradictory qualities, opinions, etc. — **bi·po·lar·i·ty** (bī′pō·lar′ə·tē) *n.*

birch (bûrch) *n.* **1.** A tree or shrub having the outer bark separable in thin layers; esp. the **canoe** or **paper birch** of North America: also called *white birch.* **2.** A rod from this tree, used as a whip. **3.** The tough, close-grained hardwood of the birch. — *v.t.* To whip with a birch rod. [OE *birce*] — **birch·en** (bûr′chən) *adj.*

bird (bûrd) *n.* **1.** A warm-blooded, feathered, egg-laying vertebrate having the forelimbs modified as wings. ◆ Collateral adjective: *avian.* **2.** A game bird. **3.** A shuttlecock. **4.** A clay pigeon. **5.** *Slang* A person, esp. one who is peculiar or remarkable. **6.** *Slang* A hiss or jeer. [OE *bridd*]

bird·call (bûrd′kôl′) *n.* **1.** A bird's note in calling. **2.** A sound imitating this, or an instrument for producing it.

bird dog A dog used in hunting game birds.

bird·ie (bûr′dē) *n.* **1.** *Informal* A small bird. **2.** In golf, one stroke less than par on a given hole.

bird·lime (bûrd′līm′) *n.* A sticky substance made from holly or mistletoe and smeared on twigs to catch small birds.

bird·man (bûrd′man′, -mən) *n. pl.* **·men** (-men′, -mən) **1.** *Informal* An aviator. **2.** A fowler. **3.** An ornithologist.

bird of paradise A tropical bird noted for the beauty of the plumage in the male.

bird of passage A migratory bird.

bird of prey A predatory bird, as an eagle, hawk, etc.

bird's-eye (bûrdz′ī′) *adj.* **1.** Marked with spots resembling birds' eyes: *bird's-eye* maple. **2.** Seen from above or from afar: a *bird's-eye* view. — *n.* **1.** A pattern woven with small, eyelike indentations. **2.** Any of various fabrics having such a pattern. Also **birds′eye′.**

bird watcher One who observes or identifies wild birds in their natural habitats as a pastime. — **bird watching**

bi·ret·ta (bi·ret′ə) *n.* A stiff, square cap with three or four upright projections on the crown, worn by clerics of the Roman Catholic church: also called *berretta.* [< Ital.]

birl (bûrl) *v.t. & v.i.* **1.** To rotate (a floating log). **2.** To whirl. — *n.* A droning noise.

birl·ing (bûr′ling) *n.* A sport in which two contestants balance on a floating log and try to dislodge one another.

birth (bûrth) *n.* **1.** The fact or act of being born. **2.** The bringing forth of offspring. **3.** Beginning; origin. **4.** Ancestry or descent. **5.** Noble lineage; good family. **6.** Natural or inherited tendency.

birth control The regulation of conception by preventive methods or devices.

birth·day (bûrth′dā) *n.* The day of one's birth or its anniversary.

birth·mark (bûrth′märk′) *n.* A mark or stain existing on the body from birth; nevus.

birth·place (bûrth′plās′) *n.* **1.** Place of birth. Abbr. *bp.* **2.** Place where something originates.

birth rate The number of births per a given number of individuals (usually 1,000), in a specified district and in a specified period of time.

birth·right (bûrth′rīt′) *n.* A privilege or possession into which one is born.

birth·stone (bûrth′stōn′) *n.* A jewel identified with the month of one's birth.

bis (bis) *adv.* Twice: used to denote repetition. [< L]

bis- Var. of BI-.

bis·cuit (bis′kit) *n.* **1.** *U.S.* A kind of shortened bread baked in small cakes, raised with baking powder or soda. **2.** *Brit.* A thin, crisp wafer. **3.** A light brown color. **4.** In ceramics, pottery baked once but not glazed. [< OF < L < *bis* twice + *coctus,* pp. of *coquere* to cook]

bi·sect (bī·sekt′) *v.t.* **1.** To cut into two parts; halve. **2.** *Geom.* To divide into two parts of equal size. — *v.i.* **3.** To fork, as a road. [< BI- + L *sectus,* pp. of *secare* to cut] — **bi·sec′tion** *n.* — **bi·sec′tion·al** *adj.* — **bi·sec′tion·al·ly** *adv.*

bi·sec·tor (bī·sek′tər) *n.* **1.** That which bisects. **2.** *Geom.* A line or plane that bisects an angle or another line.

bi·sex·u·al (bī·sek′sho͞o·əl) *adj.* **1.** Of both sexes. **2.** Having the organs of both sexes; hermaphrodite. **3.** Sexually attracted to both sexes. — *n.* **1.** A hermaphrodite. **2.** A bisexual person. — **bi·sex′u·al·ism, bi·sex·u·al·i·ty** (bī·sek′·sho͞o·al′ə·tē) *n.* — **bi·sex′u·al·ly** *adv.*
bish·op (bish′əp) *n.* **1.** A prelate in the Christian church; esp., the head of a diocese. **2.** A miter-shaped chess piece that may be moved only diagonally. [OE *biscop*]
bish·op·ric (bish′əp·rik) *n.* The office or the diocese of a bishop.
bis·muth (biz′məth) *n.* A lustrous, reddish white metallic element (symbol Bi) occurring native as well as in combination, used in medicine, in the manufacture of cosmetics, etc. See ELEMENT. [< G] — **bis·muth·al** (biz′məth·əl) *adj.*
bi·son (bī′sən, -zən) *n. pl.* **bi·son** A bovine ruminant, closely related to the true ox; esp., the North American buffalo. [< L *bison* wild ox, ult. < Gmc.]

NORTH AMERICAN BISON (5 to 6 feet high at shoulder)

bisque (bisk) *n.* **1.** A thick, rich soup made from meat or fish, esp. shellfish. **2.** Any thickened, creamy soup. **3.** A kind of ice cream containing crushed macaroons or nuts. [< F]
bis·ter (bis′tər) *n.* **1.** A yellowish brown pigment made from soot, used chiefly as a watercolor wash. **2.** A dark brown color. Also **bis′tre.** [< F *bistre* dark brown] — **bis′tered** *adj.*
bis·tro (bis′tro, *Fr.* bē·strō′) *n. Informal* A small bar, tavern or night club. [< F]
bi·sul·fate (bī·sul′fāt) *n. Chem.* An acid sulfate containing the radical HSO_4; also called *disulfate.* Also **bi·sul′phate.**
bi·sul·fide (bī·sul′fīd) *n. Chem.* A disulfide. Also **bi·sul′·phide.**
bit[1] (bit) *n.* **1.** A small piece, portion, or quantity. **2.** A short time. **3.** A small part, as in a play or movie. **4.** *U.S.* The Spanish real, worth 12½ cents: now used chiefly in the expression *two bits.* — **to do one's bit** To make one's contribution; do one's share. — *adj.* Small; insignificant; minor. [OE *bita* < *bītan* to bite]
bit[2] (bit) *n.* **1.** A sharp-edged tool for boring or drilling, having a shank for attachment to a brace, drill press, etc. **2.** The sharp or cutting part of a tool. **3.** The metallic mouthpiece of a bridle. **4.** Anything that controls or restrains. **5.** The part of a key that turns a lock. — *v.t.* **bit·ted, bit·ting** **1.** To put a bit in the mouth of (a horse). **2.** To curb; restrain. [OE *bite* a biting < *bītan* to bite]

BITS AND BRACE *a* Brace (or bitstock). Bits: *b* Screwdriver, *c* Drill, *d* Ship auger, *e* Auger, *f* Expanding, *g* Chuck (cross-section).

bit[3] (bit) Past tense and alternative past participle of BITE.
bit[4] (bit) *n.* A unit of information, expressed as a choice between two equally probable alternative messages or symbols, as a "yes" and a "no" or a dot and a dash. [< *b(inary) (dig)it*]
bitch (bich) *n.* **1.** The female of the dog or other canine animal **2.** *Slang* A malicious or promiscuous woman: an abusive term. — *v.i. Slang* to complain. — **to bitch up** *Slang* To botch. [< OE *bicce*] — **bitch′y** *adj.*
bite (bīt) *v.* **bit, bit·ten** or **bit, bit·ing** *v.t.* **1.** To seize, tear, or wound with the teeth. **2.** To cut or tear off with or as with the teeth: usually with *off.* **3.** To puncture the skin of with a sting or fangs. **4.** To cut or pierce. **5.** To cause to sting or smart. **6.** To eat into; corrode. **7.** To grip; take hold of. **8.** To cheat; deceive: usually passive. — *v.i.* **9.** To seize or cut into something with the teeth. **10.** To have the effect of biting, as mustard; sting. **11.** To take firm hold; grip. **12.** To take as bait, as fish. **13.** To be tricked. — **to bite off more than one can chew** To attempt something beyond one's capabilities. — *n.* **1.** The act of biting. **2.** A wound inflicted by biting. **3.** A painful sensation; smart; sting. **4.** A morsel of food; mouthful. **5.** *Informal* A light meal; snack. **6.** The grip or hold taken by a tool, etc. [OE *bītan*] — **bit′a·ble** or **bite′a·ble** *adj.* — **bit′er** *n.*
bit·ing (bī′ting) *adj.* **1.** Sharp; stinging. **2.** Sarcastic; caustic. — **bit′ing·ly** *adv.* — **bit′ing·ness** *n.*
bit·stock (bit′stok′) *n.* A brace for a bit. For illus. see BIT[2].
bitt (bit) *Naut. n.* A post or vertical timber on a ship's deck, to which cables, etc., are made fast, usually in pairs. — *v t.* To wind (a cable) around a bitt. [? < ON *biti* beam]
bit·ten (bit′n) Past participle of BITE.
bit·ter (bit′ər) *adj.* **1.** Having an acrid, disagreeable taste. **2.** Unpleasant to accept; distasteful. **3.** Painful to body or mind; harsh. **4.** Feeling or showing intense animosity. **5.** Stinging; sharp. — **Syn.** See SOUR. — *n.* That which

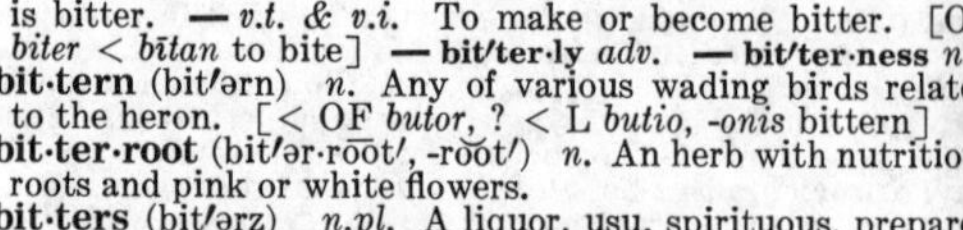

is bitter. — *v.t. & v.i.* To make or become bitter. [O *biter* < *bītan* to bite] — **bit′ter·ly** *adv.* — **bit′ter·ness** *n*
bit·tern (bit′ərn) *n.* Any of various wading birds relat to the heron. [< OF *butor,* ? < L *butio, -onis* bittern]
bit·ter·root (bit′ər·ro͞ot′, -ro͝ot′) *n.* An herb with nutritio roots and pink or white flowers.
bit·ters (bit′ərz) *n.pl.* A liquor, usu. spirituous, prepar with an infusion of bitter herbs, etc.
bitter·sweet (bit′ər·swēt′) *n.* A shrubby or climbing pla having green flowers succeeded by orange pods. — *ac* **1.** Bitter and sweet. **2.** Pleasant and unpleasant.
bi·tu·men (bi·to͞o′mən, -tyo͞o′-, bich′o͝o·mən) *n.* **1.** A natural mixture of solid and semisolid hydrocarbons, asphalt. **2.** A brown paint made by mixing asphalt with drying oil. [< L] — **bi·tu·mi·noid** (bi·to͞o′mə·noid) *adj.*
bi·tu·mi·nize (bi·to͞o′mə·nīz, -tyo͞o′-) *v.t.* **·nized, ·niz·i** To render bituminous. — **bi·tu′mi·ni·za′tion** *n.*
bi·tu·mi·nous (bi·to͞o′mə·nəs, -tyo͞o′-, bī-) *adj.* **1.** Of, pe taining to, or containing bitumen. **2.** Containing ma volatile hydrocarbons, as shale. [< F *bitumineux*]
bituminous coal A mineral coal low in carbon and burni with a yellow, smoky flame: also called *soft coal.*
bi·va·lent (bī·vā′lənt, biv′ə-) *adj. Chem.* **a** Having valence of two. **b** Having two valences. Also *divalent.* — **bi·va·lence** (bī·vā′ləns, biv′ə-), **bi·va′len·cy** (-vā′′ən·sē) *n.*
bi·valve (bī′valv′) *n. Zool.* A mollusk having a shell two lateral valves hinged together, as the oyster or cla — *adj.* Having two valves or parts: also **bi′valved′, bi·va vous** (bī·val′vəs), **bi·val·vu·lar** (bī·val′vye·lər).
biv·ou·ac (biv′o͞o·ak, biv′wak) *n.* A temporary encam ment, esp. for soldiers in the field. — *v.i.* **·acked, ·ack·i** To encamp in a bivouac. [< F < G *beiwacht* guard]
bi·week·ly (bī·wēk′lē) *adj.* **1.** Occurring once every tw weeks. **2.** Occurring twice a week; semiweekly. — *n.* biweekly publication. — *adv.* **1.** Once in two weeks. Twice a week.
bi·year·ly (bī·yir′lē) *adj. & adv.* **1.** Occurring twice yearl **2.** Biennial. — *adv.* Twice a year.
bi·zarre (bi·zär′) *adj.* Singular or eccentric in style, ma ner, etc.; odd; fantastic; grotesque. [< F, ? ult. < Basqu — **bi·zarre′ly** *adv.* — **bi·zarre′ness** *n.*
blab (blab) *v.t. & v.i.* **blabbed, blab·bing** **1.** To disclo indiscreetly. **2.** To prattle. — *n.* **1.** One who blabs. Idle chatter. Also **blab′ber.** [ME *blabbe* idle talker]
blab·ber·mouth (blab′ər·mouth′) *n.* One who talks t much and can't be trusted to keep secrets.
black (blak) *adj.* **1.** Having no brightness or color; reflec ing no light. **2.** Destitute of light. **3.** Gloomy; disma forbidding. **4.** Belonging to a racial group characterize by dark skin; esp., Negroid. **5.** Of, pertaining to, or co trolled by black men: *black* power. **6.** Soiled; staine **7.** Indicating disgrace or censure. **8.** Angry; threatenin **9.** Evil; wicked; malignant. **10.** Wearing black garment **11.** Of coffee, without cream. — *n.* **1.** The absence of ligh the darkest of all colors. **2.** Something black, as soot. **3.** Negro. — *v.t.* **1.** To make black; blacken. **2.** To put blac ing on and polish (shoes). — *v.i.* **3.** To become black. — **black out** **1.** To delete by scoring through. **2.** To suff a temporary loss of vision or consciousness. **3.** To extinguis or screen all lights. [OE *blæc* dark] — **black′ness** *n.*
black Africa Those states or parts of Africa whose i habitants are mainly dark-skinned and belong to the N groid ethnic division of mankind. — **black African**
black-and-blue (blak′ən·blo͞o′) *adj.* Discolored: said skin that has been bruised.
black and white **1.** Writing or print. **2.** A sketch or pi ture in various shades of black and white.
black art Necromancy; magic.
black·ball (blak′bôl′) *n.* A negative vote. — *v.t.* **1.** T vote against. **2.** To ostracize; exclude. — **black′ball′er**
black bass A fresh-water game fish of the eastern U. and Canada.
black bear The common North American bear, having f that varies from glossy black to cinnamon brown.
black·ber·ry (blak′ber′ē, -bər·ē) *n. pl.* **·ries.** **1.** The blac edible fruit of certain shrubs of the rose family. **2.** Any the plants producing it.
black·bird (blak′bûrd′) *n.* A common European thrus the male of which is black with a yellow bill.
black·board (blak′bôrd′, -bōrd′) *n.* A blackened surfac often of slate, for drawing and writing upon with chalk.
Black Death An exceptionally virulent plague, epidemic i Asia and Europe during the 14th century: also called *plagu*
black·en (blak′ən) *v.* **·ened, ·en·ing** **1.** To make blac or dark. **2.** To slander; defame. — *v.i.* **3.** To becom black; darken. [ME *blaknen* < *blak* black] — **black′en·er** *n*
black eye **1.** An eye with a black iris. **2.** An eye having th adjacent surface discolored by a blow or bruise. **3.** *Informa* A cause of discredit; blot. — **black′-eyed′** *adj.*
black-eyed Susan One of the coneflowers, with black centered yellow flowers: also called *yellow daisy.*

ıck·face (blak′fās′) *n.* **1.** An entertainer with exagger-ed Negro make-up, esp. a minstrel comedian. **2.** The ake-up worn by such an entertainer.
ıck flag The Jolly Roger.
ack·foot (blak′fŏŏt′) *n. pl.* **·feet** (-fēt′) A member of ıy of the tribes of Algonquian North American Indians liv-g in Alberta and Montana. — *adj.* Of the Blackfeet.
ıck·guard (blag′ərd, -ärd) *n.* An unprincipled scoundrel; rogue. — *v.t.* **1.** To revile; vilify. — *v.i.* **2.** To act like blackguard. — *adj.* Of or like a blackguard; base; vile: so **black′guard·ly.** [< *black guard*] — **black′guard·ism** *n.*
ıck·head (blak′hed′) *n.* **1.** A bird having a black head, the American scaup duck. **2.** *Vet.* A disease of turkeys. . A plug of dried, fatty matter in a pore of the skin.
ıck-heart·ed (blak′här′tid) *adj.* Evil; wicked.
ıck·ing (blak′ing) *n.* A preparation used to give black-ɔss or luster to shoes, stoves, etc.
ıck·jack (blak′jak′) *n.* **1.** A small bludgeon with a flex-le handle. **2.** A pirate's flag. **3.** A small oak of the SE .S. having black bark. **4.** Twenty-one, a card game. **5.** large drinking cup. — *v.t.* **1.** To strike with a blackjack. . To coerce by threat.
ıck lead Graphite.
ıck letter *Printing* A type face characterized by heavy ack letters resem-ing those of early ·inted works: also ılled *gothic, Old English.* — **black·let·ter** (blak′let′ər) *adj.*

This line is in black letter.

ıck·list (blak′list′) *n.* A list of persons or organizations ıder suspicion or censure, or refused approval or employ-ent for any cause. — *v.t.* To place on a blacklist.
ıck·ly (blak′lē) *adv.* Darkly, gloomily, or threateningly.
ıck magic Witchcraft.
ıck·mail (blak′māl′) *n.* Extortion by threats of public ːcusation or of exposure; also, that which is so extorted, as oney. — *v.t.* To levy blackmail upon. **2.** To force (to) something), as by threats: with *into.* [< BLACK + AIL[3]] — **black′mail′er** *n.*
ıck man **1.** A person belonging to a racial group char-ːterized by dark skin; esp., in the U.S., an Afro-American. . A male member of the so-called black race.
ack Ma·ri·a (mə·rī′ə) *Informal* A patrol wagon.
ıck mark A mark of censure, failure, etc.
ıck market A market where goods are sold in violation ' official prices, quotas, etc.
ack Muslim A member of a sect (the **Nation of Islam**) of 'egroes in the U.S., which follows the practices of Islam ıd rejects integration with the white race.
ack·out (blak′out′) *n.* **1.** The extinguishing or screening ' all lights, esp. as a precaution against air raids. **2.** *hysiol.* Partial or complete loss of vision and sometimes of ɔnsciousness, as experienced by airplane pilots during ıpid changes in velocity. **3.** In the theater, the extinguish-ıg of the lights on a stage. **4.** A ban, as on news.
ack race The Negroid ethnic division of mankind.
ack sheep One regarded as a disgrace by his family.
ack·smith (blak′smith′) *n.* **1.** One who shoes horses. . One who works iron on an anvil and uses a forge.
ack·snake (blak′snāk′) *n.* **1.** Any of various agile, non-enomous snakes of the eastern U.S., having smooth, black ːales. **2.** *U.S.* A heavy, pliant whip of braided leather.
ack·thorn (blak′thôrn′) *n.* **1.** A thorny European shrub ' the rose family. **2.** Its small, plumlike, astringent fruit. lso called *sloe.* **3.** A cane made from its wood.
ack tie **1.** A black bow tie. **2.** A tuxedo and its correct ccessories.
ack widow The venomous female of a North American ɔider: so called from its color and its eating of its mate.
ad·der (blad′ər) *n.* **1.** *Anat.* A distensible membranous ıc in the anterior part of the pelvic cavity, for the tempo-ary retention of urine. ◆ Collateral adjective: *vesical.* '. An inflatable object resembling a bladder: the *bladder* of a asketball. [OE *blǣdre*] — **blad′der·y** *adj.*
ad·der·wort (blad′ər·wûrt′) *n.* An aquatic herb having ttle bladders on the leaves in which minute organisms are rapped for nutriment.
ade (blād) *n.* **1.** The flat, cutting part of any edged tool r weapon. **2.** The thin, flat part of an oar, plow, etc. **3.** 'he leaf of grasses of other plants. **4.** A sword. **5.** A ashing or reckless young man. **6.** *Phonet.* The upper sur-ace of the tongue behind the tip. **7.** *Bot.* The broad, flat art of a leaf, petal, etc. [OE *blæd*] — **blad′ed** *adj.*
ah (blä) *n.* *U.S. Slang* Nonsense.
ain (blān) *n.* *Pathol.* A pustule; blister. [OE *blegen*]
am·a·ble (blā′mə·bəl) *adj.* Derserving blame; culpable. lso **blame′a·ble.** — **blam′a·ble·ness** *n.* — **blam′a·bly** *adv.*
ame (blām) *v.t.* **blamed, blam·ing** **1.** To hold respon-ible; accuse. **2.** To find fault with; reproach. **3.** To place the responsibility for (an action or error). — **to be to blame** To be at fault. — *n.* **1.** Expression of censure; reproof. **2.** Responsibility for something wrong; culpability. [< OF < LL *blasphemare* to revile, reproach] — **blame′ful** *adj.* — **blame′ful·ly** *adv.* — **blame′ful·ness** *n.* — **blame′·less** *adj.* — **blame′less·ly** *adv.* — **blame′less·ness** *n.*
blame·wor·thy (blām′wûr′thē) *adj.* Deserving of blame. — **blame′wor′thi·ness** *n.*
blanch (blanch, blänch) *v.t.* **1.** To remove the color from; bleach. **2.** To cause to turn pale. **3.** To remove the skin of or whiten. — *v.i.* **4.** To turn or become white or pale. — **Syn.** See WHITEN. [< F *blanc* white] — **blanch′er** *n.*
blanc·mange (blə·mänzh′) *n.* A whitish, jellylike prepara-tion of milk, eggs, sugar, cornstarch, flavoring, etc., used chiefly for desserts. [< OF *blanc-manger*, lit., white food]
bland (bland) *adj.* **1.** Gentle and soothing; suave. **2.** Not stimulating or irritating; mild, [< L *blandus* mild] — **bland′ly** *adv.* — **bland′ness** *n.*
blan·dish (blan′dish) *v.t.* To wheedle; flatter. [< OF < L *blandus* mild] — **blan′dish·er** *n.* — **blan′dish·ment** *n.*
blank (blangk) *adj.* **1.** Free from writing or print. **2.** Not completed or filled out, as a check. **3.** Showing no expres-sion or interest; vacant. **4.** Lacking variety or interest. **5.** Disconcerted; bewildered. **6.** Utter; complete: *blank* dismay. **7.** Empty or void; also, fruitless. — *n.* **1.** An empty space; void. **2.** A blank space in a printed document, to be filled in. **3.** A paper or document with such spaces. **4.** A lottery ticket that has drawn no prize. **5.** A partially prepared piece, as of metal, ready for forming into a finished object, as a key. **6.** A cartridge filled with powder but having no bullets: also **blank cartridge.** — *v.t.* **1.** To delete; invalidate: often with *out.* **2.** In games, to prevent (an opponent) from scoring. [< OF *blanc* white] — **blank′·ly** *adv.* — **blank′ness** *n.*
blank check *Informal* **1.** A check bearing a signature but no specified amount. **2.** Unlimited authority or freedom.
blan·ket (blang′kit) *n.* **1.** A large piece of woolen or other soft, warm fabric, used as a covering in bed, as a robe, etc. **2.** Anything that covers, conceals, or protects: a *blanket* of fog. — *adj.* Covering a wide range of conditions, items, or the like: a *blanket* indictment. — *v.t.* **1.** To cover with or as with a blanket. **2.** To cover or apply to uniformly. **3.** To obscure or suppress; interfere with. [< OF *blankete*, dim. of *blanc* white; orig. a white or undyed woolen cloth]
blank verse Verse without rhyme; esp., iambic pentam-eter verse, used in English epic and dramatic poetry.
blare (blâr) *v.t. & v.i.* **blared, blar·ing** **1.** To sound loudly, as a trumpet. **2.** To exclaim noisily. — *n.* **1.** A loud bra-zen sound. **2.** Brightness or glare, as of color. [Prob. imit.]
blar·ney (blär′nē) *n.* Wheedling flattery; cajolery. — *v.t. & v.i.* To flatter, cajole, or wheedle. [< BLARNEY STONE]
Blarney Stone A stone in a castle in Blarney, Ireland, that reputedly endows one who kisses it with skill in flattery.
bla·sé (blä·zā′, blä′zā) *adj.* Wearied or bored, as from over-indulgence in pleasure. [< F *blaser* to satiate]
blas·pheme (blas·fēm′) *v.* **·phemed, ·phem·ing** *v.t.* **1.** To speak in an impious manner of (God or sacred things). **2.** To speak ill of; malign. — *v.i.* **3.** To utter blasphemy. [< OF < LL < Gk. *blasphēmos* evil-speaking]
blas·phe·mous (blas′fə·məs) *adj.* Expressing blasphemy. — **blas′phe·mous·ly** *adv.* — **blas′phe·mous·ness** *n.*
blas·phe·my (blas′fə·mē) *n. pl.* **·mies** Impious or profane speaking of God, or of sacred persons or things. — **Syn.** See PROFANITY. [< OF < LL < Gk. *blasphēmia*]
blast (blast, bläst) *v.t.* **1.** To rend in pieces by or as by ex-plosion. **2.** To cause to wither or shrivel; destroy. — **to blast off** *Aerospace* To begin an ascent by means of rocket or jet propulsion. — *n.* **1.** A strong wind; gust. **2.** A loud, sudden sound, as of a trumpet. **3.** A rush of air, as from the mouth. **4.** A strong, artificial current of air, steam, etc. **5.** An explosion of dynamite, etc.; also, the charge set off. **6.** A blight. — **at full blast** At capacity operation or maxi-mum speed.. [OE *blǣst*] — **blast′er** *n.*
blast·ed (blas′tid, bläs′-) *adj.* **1.** Withered or destroyed; blighted. **2.** Damned: a euphemism.
blast furnace *Metall.* A smelting furnace in which the fire is intensified by an air blast.
blasto- *combining form Biol.* Growth; sprout. Also, before vowels, **blast-.** [< Gk. *blastos* sprout]
blast·off (blast′ôf′, -of′, bläst′-) *n.* *Aerospace* The series of events immediately before and after a rocket leaves its launching pad; also the moment of leaving.
blas·tu·la (blas′chŏŏ·lə) *n. pl.* **·lae** (-lē) *Biol.* The stage of the embryo just preceding the formation of the gastrula; a hollow sphere of one layer of cells. [< NL < Gk. *blastos* sprout] — **blas′tu·lar** *adj.*
blat (blat) *v.* **blat·ted, blat·ting** *v.t.* **1.** *Informal* To blurt out. — *v.i.* **2.** To bleat, as a sheep. [Var. of BLEAT]

ʀONUNCIATION KEY: **add, āce, câre, pälm; end, ēven; it, īce; odd, ōpen, ôrder; tŏŏk, pōōl; up, bûrn; ə** = a in *above*, e in *sicken*, i in *flex-'e*, o in *melon*, u in *focus*; **yōō** = u in *fuse*; **oil; pout; check; go; ring; thin; this; zh,** vision.

bla·tant (blā′tənt) *adj.* **1.** Offensively loud or noisy; clamorous. **2.** Obvious; obtrusive: *blatant* stupidity. [Coined by Edmund Spenser] **— bla′tan·cy** *n.* **— bla′tant·ly** *adv.*

blath·er (blath′ər) *v.t. & v.i.* To speak or utter foolishly; babble. **—** *n.* Foolish talk. [< ON *blathr* nonsense]

blath·er·skite (blath′ər·skīt) *n.* **1.** A blustering, talkative person. **2.** Foolish talk.

blaze[1] (blāz) *v.* **blazed, blaz·ing** *v.i.* **1.** To burn brightly. **2.** To burn as with emotion. **3.** To shine; be resplendent. **—** *n.* **1.** A vivid glowing flame; fire. **2.** Brilliance; glow. **3.** Sudden activity; outburst, as of anger. [OE *blæse*]

blaze[2] (blāz) *v.t.* **blazed, blaz·ing** **1.** To mark (a tree) by chipping off a piece of bark. **2.** To indicate (a trail) by marking trees in this way. **—** *n.* **1.** A white spot on the face of a horse, etc. **2.** A mark chipped on a tree to indicate a trail. [Akin to ON *blesi* white spot on a horse's face]

blaz·er (blā′zər) *n.* A lightweight, often striped, jacket for informal wear. [< BLAZE[1]]

bla·zon (blā′zən) *v.t.* **1.** To inscribe or adorn, as with names or symbols. **2.** To describe or depict (coats of arms) in technical detail. **3.** To proclaim; publish. **—** *n.* **1.** A coat of arms. **2.** A technical description of armorial bearings. **3.** Ostentatious display. [< OF *blason* coat of arms, shield] **— bla′zon·er** *n.* **— bla′zon·ment** *n.* **— bla′zon·ry** *n.*

-ble See -ABLE.

bleach (blēch) *v.t. & v.i.* To make or become colorless or white; whiten. **— Syn.** See WHITEN. **—** *n.* **1.** The act of bleaching. **2.** The degree of bleaching obtained. **3.** A fluid or powder used as a bleaching agent. [OE *blǣcean*]

bleach·er (blē′chər) *n.* **1.** One who or that which bleaches. **2.** *pl. U.S.* Unroofed outdoor seats for spectators.

bleak (blēk) *adj.* **1.** Exposed to wind and weather; bare; barren. **2.** Cold; cutting. **3.** Cheerless; dreary. [? < ON *bleikr* pale] **— bleak′ly** *adv.* **— bleak′ness** *n.*

blear (blir) *v.t.* **1.** To dim (the eyes) with or as with tears. **2.** To blur or make dim. **—** *adj.* Bleary. [ME *blere*]

blear-eyed (blir′īd′) *adj.* **1.** Having eyes bleared by tears, old age, etc. **2.** Dull of perception.

blear·y (blir′ē) *adj.* **·i·er, ·i·est** **1.** Made dim, as by tears. **2.** Blurred; dim. **— blear′i·ly** *adv.* **— blear′i·ness** *n.*

bleat (blēt) *v.i.* **1.** To utter the cry of a sheep, goat, or calf. **2.** To speak or complain with a similar sound. **—** *v.t.* **3.** To utter with a bleat. **4.** To babble; prate. **—** *n.* The act or sound of bleating. [OE *blǣtan*] **— bleat′er** *n.*

bleed (blēd) *v.* **bled, bleed·ing** *v.i.* **1.** To lose or shed blood. **2.** To suffer wounds or die. **3.** To feel grief, sympathy, or anguish. **4.** To exude sap or other fluid. **5.** *Printing* To extend to or beyond the edge of a page, as an illustration. **—** *v.t.* **6.** To draw blood from; leech. **7.** To exude, as sap, blood, etc. **8.** *Printing* To print (an illustration, etc.) so that it will bleed. [OE *blēdan*]

bleed·er (blē′dər) *n.* **1.** One who bleeds profusely, even from a slight wound. **2.** A hemophiliac.

bleeding heart A plant having racemes of pink, drooping flowers.

BLEEDING HEART (1 to 3 feet high)

blem·ish (blem′ish) *v.t.* To mar the perfection of; sully. **—** *n.* **1.** A disfiguring defect, esp. of the skin. **2.** A moral fault or stain. [< OF *blemir* to make livid] **— blem′ish·er** *n.*

blench[1] (blench) *v.i.* To shrink back; flinch. [OE *blencan* to deceive] **— blench′er** *n.*

blench[2] (blench) *v.t. & v.i.* To make or become pale; blanch. [Var. of BLANCH[1]]

blend (blend) *v.* **blend·ed** or (less commonly) **blent, blend·ing** *v.t.* **1.** To mingle and combine so as to obscure or harmonize the varying components. **2.** To mix so as to obtain a uniform product: to *blend* paints. **—** *v.i.* **3.** To mix; intermingle. **4.** To pass or shade imperceptibly into each other, as colors. **5.** To harmonize. **—** *n.* The act or result of mixing. [Prob. < ON *blanda* to mix] **— blend′er** *n.*

blende (blend) *n. Mineral.* One of a number of rather bright minerals combining sulfur with a metallic element. [< G *blendendes erz* deceptive ore]

blended whisky *U.S.* Whisky that has been blended with other whisky or neutral spirits.

blen·ny (blen′ē) *n. pl.* **·nies** A small marine fish having an elongated body. [< L < Gk. *blennos* slime]

bless (bles) *v.t.* **blessed** or **blest, bless·ing** **1.** To consecrate; make holy by religious rite. **2.** To honor and exalt; glorify. **3.** To make the sign of the cross over, as for sanctification or protection. **4.** To invoke God's favor upon (a person or thing). **5.** To bestow prosperity upon; make happy. **6.** To endow, as with a gift: She was *blessed* with a beautiful face. **7.** To guard; protect: *Bless* me! [OE *blēdsian* to consecrate (with blood) < *blōd* blood] **— bless′er** *n.*

bless·ed (bles′id, blest) *adj.* **1.** Made holy by a religious rite; consecrated. **2.** Enjoying the happiness of heaven; beatified. **3.** Blissful; happy. **4.** Causing happiness. Also spelled *blest.* **— bless′ed·ly** *adv.* **— bless′ed·ness** *n.*

bless·ed event (bles′id) *Informal* The birth of a baby.

Blessed Virgin The Virgin Mary.

bless·ing (bles′ing) *n.* **1.** An invocation or benedictic grace. **2.** The bestowal of divine favor. **3.** That whi makes happy or prosperous. **4.** Grateful adoration.

blest (blest) Alternative past participle of BLESS. **—** *a* Blessed.

blew (bloo͞) Past tense of BLOW.

blight (blīt) *n.* **1.** Any of a number of destructive pla diseases, as mildew, rust, smut, etc. **2.** Anything causi such a disease. **3.** Anything that withers hopes, destro prospects, or impairs growth. **4.** The state of being blight **—** *v.t.* **1.** To cause to decay; blast. **2.** To ruin; frustra **—** *v.i.* **3.** To suffer blight. [Origin unknown]

blimp (blimp) *n. Informal* A nonrigid dirigible. [< Ty *B-Limp,* a kind of British dirigible]

blind (blīnd) *adj.* **1.** Unable to see. **2.** Lacking in perce tion or judgment. **3.** Acting or done without intellige control; random. **4.** Unreasoning; heedless: *blind* prejudi **5.** Concealed: a *blind* ditch. **6.** Closed at one end: a *bli* alley. **7.** Having no opening or outlet: a *blind* wall. **8.** sensible. **9.** Done without the aid of visual reference: *bli* flying. **10.** Of or for blind persons. **—** *n.* **1.** Somethi that obstructs vision or shuts off light; esp., a wind shade. **2.** A hiding place, as for a hunter; ambush. Something intended to deceive. **—** *adv.* **1.** Blindly. Without the aid of visual reference: to fly *blind.* **—** **1.** To make blind. **2.** To dazzle. **3.** To deprive of juc ment or discernment. **4.** To darken; obscure. **5.** eclipse. [OE] **— blind′ing** *adj.* **— blind′ing·ly** *a* **— blind′ly** *adv.* **— blind′ness** *n.*

blind alley **1.** An alley, road, etc., open at one end on **2.** Any search, pursuit, etc., in which progress is blocked

blind date *Informal* A date with a person of the oppos sex whom one has not previously met.

blind·er (blīn′dər) *n.* **1.** One who or that which blin **2.** *U.S.* A flap on the side of a horse's bridle, serving obstruct sideways vision, also called *blinker.*

blind·fold (blīnd′fōld′) *v.t.* **1.** To cover or bandage t eyes of. **2.** To hoodwink; mislead. **—** *n.* A bandage ov the eyes. **—** *adj.* **1.** Having the eyes bandaged. **2.** Rec less; rash. [ME < *blind* blind + *fellen* to strike]

blind·man's buff (blīnd′manz′) A game in which one play is blindfolded and must catch and identify another playe

blind spot **1.** *Anat.* A small area on the retina of the e that is insensible to light because of the entrance of t optic nerve. **2.** A subject about which one is ignorant, incapable of objective thought.

blink (blingk) *v.i.* **1.** To wink rapidly. **2.** To squi as in sunlight. **3.** To twinkle; also, to flash on and o **4.** To look indifferently or evasively: with *at.* **—** *v.t.* **5.** cause to wink. **6.** To shut the eyes to; evade. **—** *n.* **1.** blinking; wink. **2.** A gleam. **3.** A glance or glimpse. [Du. *blinken*; ult. origin uncertain]

blink·er (blingk′ər) *n.* **1.** A light that blinks, as in warni or for sending messages. **2.** *pl.* Goggles. **3.** Blinder (def. 2

blint·ze (blint′sə) *n.* A thin pancake folded about a filli of cottage cheese, potato, fruit, etc., and usu. eaten wi sour cream or jam. Also **blintz.** [< Yiddish]

blip (blip) *n. Telecom.* One of the luminous signals record on a radarscope. [? Var. of *flip*]

bliss (blis) *n.* **1.** Gladness; joy. **2.** A cause of delight happiness. [OE *blīthe* joyous] **— bliss′ful** *adj.* **— blis ful·ly** *adv.* **— bliss′ful·ness** *n.*

blis·ter (blis′tər) *n.* **1.** A thin vesicle, esp. on the ski containing watery matter, as from rubbing, a burn, e **2.** A similar swelling on various other surfaces. **—** *v* **1.** To produce a blister or blisters upon. **2.** To rebu severely. **—** *v.i.* **3.** To become blistered. [< OF < O *blāstr* swelling] **— blis′ter·y** *adj.*

blister beetle The Spanish fly.

blithe (blīth, blīth) *adj.* **1.** Cheerful; gay. **2.** Casual airy in manner. [OE] **— blithe′ly** *adv.* **— blithe′ness** *n*

blithe·some (blīth′səm, blīth′-) *adj.* Showing or impartir gladness. **— blithe′some·ly** *adv.* **— blithe′some·ness** *n.*

blitz (blits) *Informal n.* A sudden attack; blitzkrieg. **—** *v* To subject to a blitzkrieg.

blitz·krieg (blits′krēg) *n.* **1.** *Mil.* A swift, sudden attac by tanks, aircraft, etc.; also, warfare so waged. **2.** Any su den attack or assault. [< G < *blitz* lightning + *krieg* wa

bliz·zard (bliz′ərd) *n.* A severe snowstorm, often wit high, cold winds. [< dial. E *blizzer* sudden blow]

bloat (blōt) *v.t.* **1.** To cause to swell, as with fluid. **2.** T puff up; make proud or vain. **—** *v.i.* **3.** To swell; becor puffed up. [ME, ? < ON *blautr* soft, soaked]

bloat·er (blō′tər) *n.* **1.** A smoked herring. **2.** A whitefis of the Great Lakes of North America.

blob (blob) *n.* **1.** A soft, globular mass; a drop, as of viscou liquid. **2.** A daub or spot, as of color. **—** *v.t.* **blobbed, blo bing** To mark with ink or color; blot. [Origin unknown]

bloc (blok) *n.* A group, as of politicians, nations, etc., con bined to foster special interests. **— Syn.** See FACTION. [< F

ɔck[1] (blok) *n.* **1.** A solid piece of wood, metal, etc., usu. ith one or more flat ırfaces. **2.** Such a ece on which cutng or chopping is ɔne. **3.** A support · form on which ɔmething is shaped · displayed: a hat ɔck. **4.** A stand om which articles e sold at auction. . A small cube used y children for building. **6.** A set or section, as of tickets, etc., handled as a unit. . A section of railroad controlled by signals. **8.** *U.S.* An ea bounded, usu. on four sides, by streets; also, one side of ıch an area. **9.** *U.S. & Canadian* An office building. **0.** *Canadian* A group of townships in the midst of unırveyed land. **11.** A pulley, or set of pulleys, in a frame ith a hook or the like at one end. **12.** A piece of wood preared for engraving. —*v.t.* **1.** To shape into blocks. . To shape, with a block, as a hat. **3.** To secure or rengthen with blocks. —**to block out** To plan broadly ithout details. [< F *bloc*, ult. < Gmc.] —**block′er** *n.*

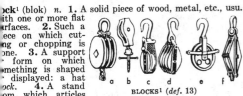

a b c d e f

BLOCKS[1] (*def.* 13)
a Tackle. *b* Dock, with attaching screw. *c* Snatch. *d* Triple-sheave steel. *e* Gin. *f* Square-cheeked.

ɔck[2] (blok) *n.* **1.** An obstacle or hindrance. **2.** The act of ɔstructing, or the state of being obstructed. **3.** In sports, ıterference with an opponent's actions. **4.** *Med. & Pathol.* An obstruction, as of a nerve or blood vessel. **b** Anesthesia f a specific region: saddle *block*. **5.** *Psychol.* The inability think or act in certain situations. —*v.t.* **1.** To obstruct. . In sports, to hinder the movements of (an opposing ayer); also, to stop (a ball), as with the body. **3.** *Med. & athol.* To stop (a nerve) from functioning, as with an anesıetic. —*v.i.* **4.** To obstruct an opponent's actions. — **block out** To obscure from view. —**to block up** To fill ın area or space) so as to prevent movement into or through. < MF *bloquer* to obstruct] —**block′age** *n.* —**block′er** *n.*

ɔck·ade (blo·kād′) *n.* **1.** The closing by hostile ships or ırces of a coast, city, etc., to traffic or communication. **2.** he ships or forces used for this. **3.** An obstruction to acɔn or passage. —**to run the blockade** To elude a blockde. —*v.t.* **·ad·ed, ·ad·ing** To subject to a blockade; obruct. —**block·ad′er** *n.*

ɔck and tackle A set of pulley blocks and ropes for pullıg or hoisting.

ɔck·bust·er (blok′bus′tər) *n. Informal* An aerial bomb, ıpable of demolishing a large area.

ɔck·head (blok′hed′) *n.* A stupid person; dolt.

ɔck·house (blok′hous′) *n.* **1.** A fortification, formerly of ıgs and heavy timbers, having loopholes from which to fire. . *U.S.* A house made of hewn logs set square.

ɔck·ish (blok′ish) *adj.* Like a block; stupid; dull. Also **lock′like′.** —**block′ish·ly** *adv.* —**block′ish·ness** *n.*

ɔck letter **1.** Printing type cut from wood. **2.** A style of tters without serifs. —**block-let·ter** (blok′let′ər) *adj.*

ɔck·y (blok′ē) *adj.* **block·i·er, block·i·est** **1.** Unequally ıaded, as if printed in blocks. **2.** Short and stout; stocky.

oke (blōk) *n. Brit. Slang* A fellow; guy.

ond (blond) *adj.* **1.** Having fair hair with light eyes and kin. **2.** Flaxen or golden, as hair. —*n.* A blond person. < F < Med.L *blondus*, prob. < Gmc.]

onde (blond) *adj.* Blond: feminine form. —*n.* A blonde oman or girl.

ood (blud) *n.* **1.** *Physiol.* The typically red fluid that ırculates through the heart, arteries, and veins of animals nd delivers oxygen and nutrients to the cells and tissues f the body. ◆ Collateral adjective: *hemal.* **2.** A liquid r juice resembling this in some way, as the sap of plants. . The shedding of blood; slaughter; murder. **4.** Disposiion of mind; temperament: hot *blood.* **5.** The principle f life; vitality; lifeblood. **6.** Descent from a common ncestor; kinship. **7.** Noble descent. **8.** Racial or national xtraction. **9.** A dashing young man; also, a rake. —**in old blood** **1.** Deliberately; without passion. **2.** Cruelly; vithout mercy. —**to make one's blood boil** (or **run cold**) To make one angry (or frightened). [OE *blōd*]

ood bank A place where blood is stored, either in liquid orm or as dried plasma, for use in transfusion.

ood bath Wanton killing; a massacre.

ood count *Med.* A measure of the number and proportion f red and white cells in a given sample of blood.

ood·cur·dling (blud′kûrd′ling) *adj.* Terrifying.

ood·ed (blud′id) *adj.* **1.** Having blood or temper of a pecified character: *cold-blooded.* **2.** Thoroughbred.

ood group *Physiol.* One of the classes into which blood nay be divided on the basis of specific differences in its omposition: also called *blood type.*

blood·hound (blud′hound′) *n.* **1.** A large, smooth-coated hound remarkable for its keen sense of smell, and often used to track fugitives. **2.** *Informal* Any persistent pursuer.

blood·less (blud′lis) *adj.* **1.** Devoid of blood; pale. **2.** Without bloodshed. **3.** Lacking vigor; listless. **4.** Coldhearted. —**blood′less·ly** *adv.* —**blood′less·ness** *n.*

blood·let·ting (blud′let′ing) *n.* **1.** Bleeding for a therapeutic purpose. **2.** Bloodshed.

blood money **1.** *Informal* Money obtained at the cost of another's life, welfare, etc. **2.** Money paid to a hired murderer. **3.** Compensation paid to the kin of a murdered man.

blood plasma *Physiol.* The liquid part of the blood, without its cellular components.

blood platelet *Physiol.* One of the minute bodies found in the blood of higher vertebrates, essential to coagulation.

blood poisoning *Pathol.* Deterioration of the blood caused by bacterial substances: also called *toxemia.*

blood pressure *Physiol.* The pressure of the blood on the walls of the arteries, varying with the force of the heart action, with age, general condition, etc.

blood relation One who is related by birth; kinsman.

blood·root (blud′ro͞ot′, -ro͝ot′) *n.* A perennial North American herb having a fleshy rootstalk with deep red sap.

blood·shed (blud′shed′) *n.* The shedding of blood; slaughter; carnage. Also **blood′shed′ding.** —**blood′shed′der** *n.*

blood·shot (blud′shot′) *adj.* Suffused or shot with blood; red and inflamed or irritated: said of the eye.

blood·stain (blud′stān′) *n.* A spot produced by blood. —*v.t.* To stain with blood. —**blood′stained′** *adj.*

blood·stone (blud′stōn′) *n.* A stone of green chalcedony flecked with particles of red jasper: also called *heliotrope.*

blood stream The blood coursing through a living body.

blood·suck·er (blud′suk′ər) *n.* **1.** An animal that sucks blood, as a leech. **2.** *Informal* One who extorts or sponges.

blood·thirst·y (blud′thûrs′tē) *adj.* Thirsting for blood; cruel. —**blood′thirst′i·ly** *adv.* —**blood′thirst′i·ness** *n.*

blood transfusion *Med.* The transfer of blood from one person or animal into another.

blood type Blood group.

blood vessel Any tubular canal, as an artery, vein, or capillary, through which the blood circulates.

blood·y (blud′ē) *adj.* **blood·i·er, blood·i·est** **1.** Stained with blood. **2.** Of, like, or containing blood. **3.** Involving bloodshed. **4.** Bloodthirsty. **5.** Deep red. **6.** *Brit. Slang* Damned: a vulgarism. —*v.t.* **blood·ied, blood·y·ing** To stain with blood. —*adv. Brit. Slang* Very: a vulgarism. [OE *blōdig*] —**blood′i·ly** *adv.* —**blood′i·ness** *n.*

bloom (blo͞om) *n.* **1.** The flower of a plant; blossom. **2.** The state of being in flower. **3.** A growing or flourishing condition; freshness. **4.** The rosy tint of the cheeks or skin; glow. **5.** *Bot.* The powdery, waxy substance on certain fruits and leaves. **6.** Any of various earthy minerals found as a powdery incrustation on certain ores. —*v.i.* **1.** To bear flowers; blossom. **2.** To glow with health; flourish. **3.** To glow with a warm color. —*v.t.* **4.** To bring into bloom; cause to flourish. **5.** To give a bloom to. [< ON *blōm* blossom] —**bloom′y** *adj.*

bloom·ers (blo͞o′mərz) *n.pl.* **1.** Loose, wide trousers gathered at the knee, worn by women as a gymnasium costume. **2.** A woman's undergarment resembling these.

bloom·ing (blo͞o′ming) *adj.* **1.** In flower; blossoming. **2.** Flourishing. —**bloom′ing·ly** *adv.* —**bloom′ing·ness** *n.*

blos·som (blos′əm) *n.* **1.** A flower, esp. one of a plant yielding edible fruit. **2.** The state or period of flowering; bloom. —*v.i.* **1.** To come into blossom. **2.** To prosper; thrive. [OE *blōstm*] —**blos′som·less** *adj.* —**blos′som·y** *adj.*

blot (blot) *n.* **1.** A spot or stain, as of ink. **2.** A stain on reputation or character; blemish. **3.** A detraction from beauty, excellence, etc. **4.** An erasure. —*v.* **blot·ted, blot·ting** *v.t.* **1.** To spot, as with ink; stain. **2.** To disgrace; sully. **3.** To mark over or obliterate, as writing: often with *out.* **4.** To obscure: usually with *out.* **5.** To dry, as with blotting paper. **6.** To paint roughly; daub. —*v.i.* **7.** To spread in a blot or blots, as ink. **8.** To become blotted; stain. **9.** To absorb. [ME *blotte*]

blotch (bloch) *n.* **1.** A spot or blot. **2.** An eruption on the skin. —*v.t.* **1.** To mark or cover with blotches. —*v.i.* **2.** To become blotched. [Blend of BLOT and BOTCH] —**blotch′i·ness** *n.* —**blotch′y** *adj.*

blot·ter (blot′ər) *n.* **1.** A sheet or pad of blotting paper. **2.** The daily record of arrests in a police station.

blotting paper Unsized paper for absorbing excess ink.

blouse (blous, blouz) *n.* **1.** A woman's garment extending from the neck to the waist or just below. **2.** A loose, kneelength smock, usu. belted at the waist, worn chiefly by European workmen. **3.** The service coat of the U.S. Army uniform. —*v.t. & v.i.* **bloused** (bloust, blouzd), **blous·ing** To drape loosely or fully. [< F] —**blouse′like′** *adj.*

blow[1] (blō) *v.* **blew, blown, blow·ing** *v.i.* **1.** To be in motion: said of wind or air. **2.** To move in a current of air. **3.** To emit a current or jet of air, steam, etc., as from the mouth. **4.** To produce sound by blowing or being blown, as a trumpet. **5.** To pant; gasp for breath. **6.** To spout air and water before breathing, as a whale. **7.** To fail or become useless, as a fuse, tire, etc.: often with *out.* **8.** *Informal* To brag. **9.** *U.S. Slang* To depart; go. **—** *v.t.* **10.** To drive or impel by a current of air. **11.** To direct a current of air upon, as from the mouth. **12.** To sound by blowing into, as a bugle. **13.** To sound (a signal): to *blow* taps. **14.** To emit, as air or smoke, from the mouth. **15.** To clear by forcing air into or through. **16.** To put out of breath, as a horse. **17.** To form by inflating a material: to *blow* bubbles. **18.** To break, shatter, or destroy by explosion: usu. with *up, down,* etc. **19.** *Informal* To melt (a fuse). **20.** *U.S. Slang* To spend (money) lavishly; also, to treat or entertain. **21.** *U.S. Slang* To depart from; leave. **— to blow hot and cold** *Informal* To vacillate; be uncertain. **— to blow off** **1.** To let off, as steam from a boiler. **2.** *Slang* To speak in anger. **— to blow out** **1.** To extinguish by blowing. **2.** To burst, as a tire. **3.** To melt, as a fuse. **— to blow over** **1.** To pass, as a storm; subside. **2.** To pass without bad result. **— to blow up** **1.** To inflate. **2.** To make an enlargement of (a photograph). **3.** To explode. **4.** *Informal* To lose one's temper. **5.** To arise; become intense, as a storm. **—** *n.* **1.** A blowing, as of wind. **2.** A storm or gale. [OE *blāwan*]

blow[2] (blō) *n.* **1.** A sudden stroke dealt with the fist, a weapon, etc. **2.** A sudden disaster. **3.** A hostile act; assault. **— Syn.** See MISFORTUNE. **— to come to blows** To start fighting. [ME *blaw*]

blow[3] (blō) *Archaic & Poetic* *v.* **blew, blown, blow·ing** *v.i.* **1.** To bloom; blossom. **—** *v.t.* **2.** To cause to bloom. **—** *n.* A display, as of blossoms. [OE *blōwan* to blossom]

blow·er (blō′ər) *n.* **1.** One who or that which blows. **2.** A device for forcing air through a building, furnace, etc.

blow·fly (blō′flī′) *n. pl.* **·flies** A blue or green fly whose larvae live in carrion or in living flesh: also called *bluebottle.*

blow·gun (blō′gun′) *n.* A long tube through which a missile, as a dart, may be blown by the breath.

blow·hole (blō′hōl′) *n.* **1.** *Zool.* The nasal openings in the heads of certain whales or other cetaceans. **2.** A vent for gas and bad air, as in mines. **3.** A hole in the ice to which seals, etc., come to breathe.

blown (blōn) Past participle of BLOW[1]. **—** *adj.* **1.** Out of breath, as from overexertion. **2.** Inflated; swollen, esp. with gas. **3.** Made with a blowtube, blowpipe, etc.

blow·out (blō′out′) *n.* **1.** A bursting, as of a tire, or the hole so made. **2.** The melting of a fuse. **3.** *Slang* An elaborate meal or party. **4.** A flameout.

blow·pipe (blō′pīp′) *n.* **1.** A tube for blowing air or gas through a flame to direct and intensify its heat. **2.** A blowgun.

blow·torch (blō′tôrch′) *n.* An apparatus for vaporizing a combustible fluid under pressure and expelling it from a nozzle as a long, intensely hot flame, used for soldering, etc.

blow·up (blō′up′) *n.* **1.** An explosion. **2.** *Informal* A loss of self-control; outburst; also, a fight; quarrel. **3.** An enlargement, as of a photograph.

blow·y (blō′ē) *adj.* **blow·i·er, blow·i·est** Windy.

blowz·y (blou′zē) *adj.* **blowz·i·er, blowz·i·est** **1.** Disheveled; slovenly. **2.** Fat and red-faced. Also **blowzed** (blouzd). [< earlier *blowse* a fat, ruddy woman; origin uncertain]

blub·ber (blub′ər) *v.i.* **1.** To weep and sob noisily. **—** *v.t.* **2.** To utter with sobs. **—** *n.* **1.** *Zool.* The layer of fat beneath the skin of a whale or other cetacean, used as a source of oil. **2.** The act of blubbering; weeping. **—** *adj.* Swollen; protruding. [ME *blubren*; imit.] **— blub′ber·er** *n.* **— blub′ber·ing·ly** *adv.* **— blub′ber·y** *adj.*

blu·cher (blo͞o′chər, -kər) *n.* A shoe in which there is no front seam, the upper meeting above in two projecting flaps. [after G. L. *Blücher*, 1742–1819, Prussian field marshal]

bludg·eon (bluj′ən) *n.* A short club, commonly loaded at one end, used as a weapon. **—** *v.t.* **1.** To strike with or as with a bludgeon. **2.** To coerce; bully. [Origin unknown]

blue (blo͞o) *adj.* **blu·er, blu·est** **1.** Having the color of the clear sky seen in daylight. **2.** Livid, as the skin from bruising or cold. **3.** Depressed in spirits; melancholy. **4.** Dismal; dreary. **5.** Puritanical; strict. **— once in a blue moon** Very seldom. **—** *n.* **1.** The color of the clear sky; azure. **2.** Any pigment or dye used to impart a blue color. **3.** Bluing. **4.** *Sometimes cap.* One who wears a blue uniform. **— out of the blue** From an unsuspected source. **— the blue** **1.** The sky. **2.** The sea. **—** *v.t.* **blued, blu·ing** **1.** To make blue. **2.** To treat with bluing. [< OF *bleu*, ult. < Gmc.] **— blue′ly** *adv.* **— blue′ness** *n.*

blue baby An infant born with cyanosis resulting from a congenital heart lesion or from defective lungs.

Blue·beard (blo͞o′bird′) In folklore, a man who married and then murdered six women in succession.

blue·bell (blo͞o′bel′) *n.* Any one of various plants that be blue, bell-shaped flowers.

blue·ber·ry (blo͞o′ber′ē, -bər·ē) *n. pl.* **·ries** **1.** An edib blue or black American berry. **2.** The plant that bears i

blue·bird (blo͞o′bûrd′) *n.* A small American passerine bi with predominantly blue plumage.

blue blood **1.** Aristocratic blood or descent. **2.** One aristocratic family: also **blue·blood** (blo͞o′blud′). **— blu blood′ed** *adj.* **— blue′blood′ed·ness** *n.*

blue·bon·net (blo͞o′bon′it) *n.* **1.** The cornflower. **2.** A annual leguminous herb with blue flowers.

blue book **1.** A register of persons employed by the U government. **2.** A register of socially prominent peop Also **blue·book** (blo͞o′bo͝ok′).

blue·bot·tle (blo͞o′bot′l) *n.* **1.** A blowfly. **2.** Any of va ous flowers with tubular, usu. blue florets.

blue cheese A type of cheese resembling Roquefort.

blue chip **1.** In finance, the stock of a well-known compa with a good sustained record of dividends, earnings, e **2.** A gambling chip of the highest value.

blue·coat (blo͞o′kōt′) *n.* A policeman.

blue devils **1.** Despondency. **2.** Delirium tremens.

blue·fish (blo͞o′fish′) *n. pl.* **·fish** or **·fish·es** A voracious fo fish common along the Atlantic coast of the U.S.

blue fox A small fox of arctic regions whose pelt acquire bluish color in summer; also, its fur.

blue·grass (blo͞o′gras′, -gräs′) *n.* One of various grass esp., the **Kentucky bluegrass.**

Bluegrass State Nickname of Kentucky.

blue·gum (blo͞o′gum′) *n.* Any of several eucalyptus tre

blue·ing (blo͞o′ing), **blue·ish** (blo͞o′ish) See BLUING, etc

blue·jack·et (blo͞o′jak′it) *n.* An enlisted man in the Unit States or British navy.

blue jay A crested, corvine bird of North America. A **blue·jay** (blo͞o′jā′).

blue law *Often pl. U.S.* A puritanical law, esp. one pr hibiting entertainment on Sunday.

blue·nose (blo͞o′nōz′) *n.* *Informal* A puritanical person

blue-pen·cil (blo͞o′pen′səl) *v.t.* **·ciled** or **·cilled, ·cil·ing ·cil·ing** To edit or cancel with or as with a blue pencil.

blue point An oyster found off the shore of Long Island.

blue·print (blo͞o′print′) *n.* **1.** A plan or drawing made b printing on sensitized paper, the drawing showing in whi lines on a blue ground. **2.** Any detailed plan. **—** *v* To make a blueprint of.

blue ribbon The highest award or distinction; first pri

blues (blo͞oz) *n.pl.* **1.** Depression of spirits; melancho **2.** *Music* A style using deliberately mistuned scale degre (**blue notes**), often in 4/4 meter with 12-measure phras also, the often mournful songs sung to this music.

blue·stock·ing (blo͞o′stok′ing) *n.* A learned, pedantic, literary woman. [from the informal blue stockings wo by a leading literary figure in 18th-century London]

blu·et (blo͞o′it) *n.* **1.** One of various plants having bl flowers. **2.** A delicate meadow flower of the madder famil

bluff[1] (bluf) *v.t. & v.i.* **1.** To deceive by putting on a bo front. **2.** To frighten with empty threats. **— to bluff one way** To obtain an object by bluffing. **—** *n.* **1.** The act bluffing. **2.** One who bluffs. [? < Du. *bluffen* to deceiv mislead] **— bluff′er** *n.*

bluff[2] (bluf) *n.* **1.** A steep headland or bank. **2.** *Canadi* A clump of trees on a prairie. **—** *adj.* **1.** Rough and hear in manner. **2.** Having a broad, steep appearance. [? Du. *blaf* flat] **— bluff′ly** *adv.* **— bluff′ness** *n.*

blu·ing (blo͞o′ing) *n.* A blue coloring matter used in laund work to counteract yellowing in linen: also spelled *blueing*

blu·ish (blo͞o′ish) *adj.* Somewhat blue: also spelled *blueis* **— blu′ish·ness** *n.*

blun·der (blun′dər) *n.* A stupid mistake; error. **—** *v.i.* To act or move awkwardly; stumble. **2.** To make a stup mistake. **—** *v.t.* **3.** To utter stupidly or confusedly: oft with *out.* **4.** To bungle. [ME *blondren* to mix up, confus **— blun′der·er** *n.* **— blun′der·ing·ly** *adv.*

blun·der·buss (blun′dər·bus) *n.* **1.** An old-fashioned, sho gun with large bore and flaring mouth, used for scattering shot at close range. **2.** A stupid, blustering person. [Blend of BLUNDER and Du. *donderbus* thunder box]

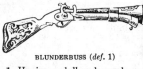

BLUNDERBUSS (*def.* 1)

blunt (blunt) *adj.* **1.** Having a dull end or edge. **2** Abrupt in manner; brusque. **3.** Slow of wit; dull. **—** *v. & v.i.* To make or become dull or less hurtful. [ME; origi unknown] **— blunt′ly** *adv.* **— blunt′ness** *n.*

— Syn. (adj.) **1.** dull, round, smooth. **2.** *Blunt* suggests a unpleasant frankness and *abrupt* a disconcerting directness: *blunt* opinion, an *abrupt* departure. *Brusque* implies ungraciou ness, while *curt* connotes undue brevity, and often intention rudeness: a *brusque* handshake, a *curt* rejoinder.

r (blûr) *v.t. & v.i.* **blurred, blur·ring** 1. To make or come vague and indistinct in outline. 2. To dim. 3. smear; smudge. — *n.* 1. A smear; smudge. 2. Something indistinct. — **blur′ry** *adj.*
rb (blûrb) *n.* A brief and highly commendatory description or advertisement, esp. one on a book jacket. [Coined Gelett Burgess, 1866–1951, U.S. humorist]
rt (blûrt) *v.t.* To utter abruptly or impulsively: often th *out.* [? Blend of BLOW and SPURT]
sh (blush) *v.i.* 1. To become red in the face from modesty or confusion; flush. 2. To become red or rosy, as wers. 3. To feel shame or regret: usually with *at* or *for.* *v.t.* 4. To make red. — *n.* 1. A reddening of the face m modesty, etc. 2. A red or rosy tint. 3. A glance; mpse: now only in the phrase **at** or **on first blush** — *adj.* ddish. [OE *blyscan* to redden] — **blush′er** *n.* — ish′ful *adj.* — **blush′ing·ly** *adv.*
s·ter (blus′tər) *v.i.* 1. To blow gustily and with violence d noise, as the wind. 2. To utter threats. — *v.t.* 3. To ter noisily and boisterously. 4. To force or bully by istering. — *n.* 1. Boisterous talk or swagger. 2. Fit- and noisy blowing of the wind; blast. — **blus′ter·er** *n.* **blus′ter·ing·ly** *adv.* — **blus′ter·y, blus′ter·ous** *adj.*
a (bō′ə) *n. pl.* **bo·as** 1. Any of several nonvenomous pents notable for the crushing power of their coils, as the aconda and python; esp. the **boa constrictor** of South America. 2. A long feather or fur scarf for women. [< L]
r (bôr, bōr) *n. pl.* **boars** or **boar.** 1. An uncastrated le swine. 2. The wild boar. [OE *bār*]
rd (bôrd, bōrd) *n.* 1. A flat, thin slab of sawed wood ich longer than it is wide. 2. A thin slab of wood or the e for a specific purpose: an ironing *board.* 2. One of the steboard covers of a book. 4. A table set for serving food. Food or meals; esp., meals furnished for pay, and sometimes including lodging. 6. An organized official body. 7. table at which meetings are held. — **across the board** *formal* 1. Designating a racing bet whereby equal sums wagered on a single horse, etc., to win, place, and show. Affecting all members or categories in the same degree: d of changes in salary, taxes, etc. — **by the board** Overard. — **on board** On or in a vessel or other conveyance. **the boards** The stage. — **to go by the board** To fall o ruin, disuse, etc. — *v.t.* 1. To cover or enclose with ards: often with *up.* 2. To furnish with meals, or meals d lodging, for pay. 3. To place (someone) where meals provided, as in a boarding school. 4. To enter, as a ship train. 5. *Naut.* To come alongside or go on board of (a p), as to attack. — *v.i.* 6. To take meals, or meals and lging. [OE *bord* board, side of a ship, table]
rd·er (bôr′dər, bōr′-) *n.* 1. One who receives regular als, or meals and lodging, for pay. 2. One who is detailed board an enemy's ship.
rd foot *pl.* **board feet** The contents of a board 1 foot uare and 1 inch thick; the common unit of measure for s and lumber in the U.S., equal to 144 cubic inches or 59.8 cubic centimeters. Abbr. *bd. ft.*
rding house A house where meals, or meals and lodg-, can be had regularly for pay. Also **board·ing·house** ôr′ding·hous′, bōr′-).
rding school A school in which pupils are boarded.
rd measure A cubic measure applied to boards, the it of which is the board foot. Abbr. *b.m.*
rd·walk (bôrd′wôk′, bōrd′-) *n.* 1. A promenade along beach, usually of boards. 2. A walk made of planks.
st (bōst) *v.i.* 1. To talk in a vain or bragging manner. To speak or possess with pride: used with *of.* — *v.t.* 3. brag about; extol. 4. To be proud to possess; take pride — *n.* 1. A boastful speech. 2. That which is boasted out. [ME *bosten*] — **boast′er** *n.* — **boast′ing·ly** *adv.*
st·ful (bōst′fəl) *adj.* Characterized by or addicted to asting. — **boast′ful·ly** *adv.* — **boast′ful·ness** *n.*
t (bōt) *n.* 1. A small, open watercraft propelled by oars, ils, or an engine. 2. *Informal* Any watercraft of any size, m a rowboat to an ocean liner. 3. A boat-shaped object, a dish. — **in the same boat** In the same situation or contion; equally involved. — *v.i.* 1. To travel by boat. 2. go boating for pleasure. — *v.t.* 3. To transport or place a boat: to *boat* oars. [OE *bāt*]
t·house (bōt′hous′) *n.* A building for storing boats.
t·ing (bō′ting) *n.* The act or sport of one who boats.
t·load (bōt′lōd′) *n.* 1. The amount that a boat can ld. 2. The load carried by a boat.
t·man (bōt′mən) *n. pl.* **·men** (-mən) 1. A man who als in or works on boats. 2. An aquatic insect.
t·swain (bō′sən, *rarely* bōt′swān′) *n.* A warrant officer a naval ship, or a subordinate officer of a merchantman o is in charge of the rigging, anchors, etc. Also spelled *sun, bo's'n.* [OE *bātswegen*]

bob[1] (bob) *v.* **bobbed, bob·bing** *v.i.* 1. To move up and down with an irregular motion. 2. To curtsy. — *v.t.* 3. To move up and down. — **to bob up** To appear or emerge suddenly. — *n.* 1. A short, jerky movement: a *bob* of the head. 2. A quick bow or curtsy. 3. In fishing, a float or cork. [ME; origin uncertain] — **bob′ber** *n.*
bob[2] (bob) *n.* 1. A short haircut for a woman or child. 2. The docked tail of a horse. 3. A small, pendant object, as the weight on a plumb line. For illus. see PLUMB BOB. 4. In fishing, a large, ball-shaped bait made of worms, rags, etc. — *v.* **bobbed, bob·bing** *v.t.* 1. To cut short, as hair. — *v.i.* 2. To fish with a bob. [ME *bobbe*] — **bob′ber** *n.*
bob[3] (bob) *n. pl.* **bob** *Brit. Informal* A shilling. [< *Bob,* a nickname for *Robert,* a personal name]
bob·bin (bob′in) *n.* A spool or reel holding thread for spinning, weaving, or machine sewing. [< F *bobine*]
bob·by (bob′ē) *n. pl.* **·bies** *Brit. Informal* A policeman. [after Sir Robert Peel, 1788–1850, who introduced police reforms]
bobby pin A metal hairpin shaped so as to clasp and hold the hair tightly. Also **bob′bie pin.**
bobby socks *Informal* Short socks worn by girls.
bob·by·sox·er (bob′ē·sok′sər) *U.S. Informal* A young girl who follows fads and fashions current among adolescents.
bob·cat (bob′kat′) *n.* The American lynx.
bob·o·link (bob′ə·lingk) *n.* A thrushlike singing bird of North America. [Imit.; from its call]
bob·sled (bob′sled′) *n.* 1. A racing sled steered by a steering wheel controlling the front runners. 2. Either of two short sleds connected in tandem; also, the vehicle so formed. — *v.i.* **·sled·ded, ·sled·ding** To go coasting on a bobsled. Also **bob′sleigh′** (-slā′). [Origin unknown]
bob·tail (bob′tāl′) *n.* 1. A short tail or a tail cut short. 2. An animal with such a tail. — *adj.* 1. Having the tail docked. 2. Cut short; incomplete. — *v.t.* 1. To cut the tail of; dock. 2. To cut short. — **bob′tailed′** *adj.*
bob·white (bob′hwīt′) *n.* A quail of North America having brownish, mottled plumage. [Imit.; from its call]
bock beer (bok) A dark, strong beer brewed in the winter and served in early spring. Also **bock.** [< G *bockbier*]
bode[1] (bōd) Archaic past tense and past participle of BIDE.
bode[2] (bōd) *v.* **bod·ed, bod·ing** *v.t.* 1. To be a foretoken of; presage. — *v.i.* 2. To presage good or ill. [OE *bodian* to announce] — **bode′ment** *n.*
bod·ice (bod′is) *n.* 1. The upper portion of a woman's dress. 2. A woman's ornamental vest. [Var. of *bodies*]
bod·ied (bod′ēd) *adj.* 1. Having a body. 2. Having a (specified kind of) body: used in combination: *full-bodied.*
bod·i·less (bod′i·lis) *adj.* Having no body; incorporeal.
bod·i·ly (bod′ə·lē) *adj.* 1. Of or pertaining to the body. 2. Physical, as opposed to mental: *bodily* illness. — *adv.* 1. In the flesh; in person. 2. All together; completely.
bod·kin (bod′kin) *n.* 1. A pointed instrument for piercing holes in cloth, etc. 2. A blunt needle for drawing tape through a hem. 3. A long pin for fastening the hair. [ME *boydekin* dagger; origin unknown]
bod·y (bod′ē) *n. pl.* **bod·ies** 1. The entire physical part of a human being, animal, or plant. 2. A corpse; carcass. 3. The torso of a human being or animal; the trunk. 4. The principal part or mass of anything. 5. A collection of persons or things taken as a whole. 6. A distinct mass or portion of matter: a *body* of clear water. 7. Density or consistency; substance: a wine with *body.* 8. That part of a garment that covers the body or the upper body. 9. *Informal* A person. — *v.t.* **bod·ied, bod·y·ing** 1. To furnish with or as with a body. 2. To exhibit in bodily form; represent: usually with *forth.* [OE *bodig*]
bod·y·guard (bod′ē·gärd′) *n.* 1. A guard responsible for the physical safety of an individual. 2. A retinue; escort.
body politic The state or nation as an organized political entity; the people collectively.
body snatcher One who steals bodies from graves.
Boe·o·tia (bē·ō′shə, -shē·o) A state of ancient Greece; capital Thebes.
Boe·o·tian (bē·ō′shən) *adj.* 1. Of or pertaining to Boeotia. 2. Dull; clownish. — *n.* 1. A native of Boeotia. 2. A stupid, doltish person.
Boer (bōr, bôr, bo͝or) *n.* A Dutch colonist, or person of Dutch descent, in South Africa. — *adj.* Of or pertaining to the Boers. [< Du., farmer]
bog (bog, bôg) *n.* Wet and spongy ground; marsh; morass. — *v.t. & v.i.* **bogged, bog·ging** To sink or be impeded in or as in a bog: often with *down.* [< Irish < *bog* soft] — **bog′gish** *adj.* — **bog′gish·ness** *n.*
bo·gey[1] (bō′gē) *n. pl.* **·geys** In golf: **a** An estimated standard score. **b** One stroke over par on a hole. Also **bo′gie.** [after Col *Bogey,* an imaginary faultless golfer]
bo·gey[2] (bō′gē) See BOGY.

bog·gle (bog′əl) *v.* **·gled, ·gling** *v.i.* **1.** To hesitate, as from doubt or scruples; shrink back: often with *at.* **2.** To start with fright, as a horse. **3.** To equivocate; dissemble. **4.** To work clumsily; fumble. — *v.t.* **5.** To make a botch of; bungle. — *n.* **1.** The act of boggling. **2.** A scruple; objection. **3.** *Informal* A botch. [< Scot. *bogle* a hobgoblin]

bog·gy (bog′ē, bôg′ē) *adj.* **·gi·er, ·gi·est** Swampy; miry.

bo·gie (bō′gē) See BOGY.

bo·gus (bō′gəs) *adj. U.S.* Counterfeit; spurious; fake.

bo·gy (bō′gē) *n. pl.* **·gies** A goblin; bugbear: also spelled *bogey, bogie.* [? Akin to BUG[2]] — **bo′gy·ism** *n.*

Bo·he·mi·an (bō·hē′mē·ən) *adj.* **1.** Of or pertaining to Bohemia. **2.** Leading the life of a Bohemian; unconventional. — *n.* **1.** An inhabitant of Bohemia. **2.** A gypsy. **3.** A person, usu. of artistic or literary tastes, who lives in an unconventional manner. Also (for *adj.* def. 2, *n.* def. 3) **bo·he′mi·an.** **4.** A former name for the Czech dialect of Czechoslovakian. — **Bo·he′mi·an·ism** *n.*

boil[1] (boil) *v.i.* **1.** To be agitated by escaping gaseous bubbles, usu. from the effect of heat: said of liquids. **2.** To reach the boiling point. **3.** To undergo the action of a boiling liquid. **4.** To be agitated like boiling water; seethe. **5.** To be stirred by rage or passion. — *v.t.* **6.** To bring to the boiling point. **7.** To cook or cleanse by boiling. **8.** To separate by means of evaporation caused by boiling. — **to boil away** To evaporate in boiling. — **to boil down** **1.** To reduce in bulk by boiling. **2.** To condense; summarize. — **to boil over** **1.** To overflow while boiling. **2.** To give vent to one's rage or passion. — *n.* The act or state of boiling. [< OF < L *bullire* to boil]

boil[2] (boil) *n. Pathol.* A painful purulent nodule of bacterial origin beneath the skin: also called *furuncle.* [OE *byl*]

boil·er (boi′lər) *n.* **1.** A closed vessel containing a system of tubes, used for generating steam, as for heating or power. **2.** A container in which something is boiled. **3.** A tank for hot water.

boiling point The temperature at which a liquid boils; at normal atmospheric pressure the boiling point of water is 212° F. or 100° C.

bois·ter·ous (bois′ter·əs, -trəs) *adj.* **1.** Noisy and unrestrained; uproarious. **2.** Stormy; violent, as the weather. [ME *boistous*] — **bois′ter·ous·ly** *adv.* — **bois′ter·ous·ness** *n.*

bo·la (bō′lə) *n.* A throwing weapon, consisting of balls fastened to cords. Also **bo·las** (bō′ləs) [< Sp., a ball]

bold (bōld) *adj.* **1.** Having courage; fearless. **2.** Showing or requiring courage; daring. **3.** Presuming unduly; brazen; forward. **4.** Vigorous in conception or expression; unconventional. **5.** Abrupt; steep, as a cliff. — **to make bold** To venture. [OE *bald*] — **bold′ly** *adv.* — **bold′ness** *n.*

bold·face (bōld′fās′) *n. Printing* A type in which the lines have been thickened to give a very black impression.

bole (bōl) *n.* The trunk of a tree. [< ON *bolr*]

bo·le·ro (bō·lâr′ō) *n. pl.* **·ros** **1.** A short jacket open at the front. **2.** A Spanish dance, usu. accompanied by castanets. **3.** The music for this dance. [< Sp.]

bol·i·var (bol′ə·vər, -vär; *Sp.* bō·lē′vär) *n. pl.* **bol·i·vars,** *Sp.* **bo·li·va·res** (bō′lē·vä′rās) The monetary unit of Venezuela. [after Simón *Bolivar*]

bo·li·via·no (bō·lē′vyä′nō) *n. pl.* **·nos** (-nōs) The monetary unit of Bolivia.

boll (bōl) *n.* A round pod or seed capsule, as of flax or cotton. — *v.i.* To form pods.

bol·lix (bol′iks) *v.t.* **·lixed, ·lix·ing** *Slang* To bungle; botch: often with *up.* [Alter. of *ballocks* testicles]

boll weevil A beetle that destroys cotton bolls.

boll·worm (bōl′wûrm′) *n.* The very destructive larva of a pale brown moth that feeds on cotton bolls.

bo·lo (bō′lō) *n. pl.* **·los** (-lōz) A large, single-edged knife used by natives of the Philippines. [< Sp. < Visayan]

Bo·lo·gna sausage (bə·lō′nə, -lōn′yə, -lō′nē) A highly seasoned sausage of mixed meats: also *baloney, boloney.*

bo·lo·ney (bə·lō′nē) See BALONEY.

Bol·she·vik (bōl′shə·vik, bol′-) *n. pl.* **Bol·she·viks** or **Bol·she·vi·ki** (bōl′shə·vē′kē, bol′-) **1.** A member of the dominant branch of the Russian Social Democratic Party or, since 1918, of the Russian Communist Party. **2.** A member of any Communist party. **3.** Loosely, any radical. Also **bol′she·vik.** [< Russian *bolshe* the majority]

Bol·she·vism (bōl′shə·viz′əm, bol′-) *n.* The Marxian doctrines and policies of the Bolsheviks; also, any practice, government, etc., based on them. Also **bol′she·vism.**

Bol·she·vist (bōl′shə·vist, bol′-) *n.* A Bolshevik. Also **bol′she·vist.** — **Bol′she·vis′tic** *adj.*

bol·ster (bōl′stər) *n.* **1.** A narrow pillow as long as a bed's width. **2.** A pad used as a support or for protection. **3.** Anything shaped like a bolster or used as a support. — *v.t.* To prop or reinforce, as something ready to fall: with *up.* [OE] — **bol′ster·er** *n.*

bolt[1] (bōlt) *n.* **1.** A sliding bar or piece for fastening a door, etc. **2.** A pin or rod for holding something in place, usu. having a head at one end, and threaded at the other. **3.** The part of a lock that is shot or withdrawn by turning the k **4.** A sliding mechanism that closes the breech of some sm firearms. **5.** An arrow, esp. for a crossbow. **6.** A stroke lightning; thunderbolt. **7.** Anything that comes sudde or unexpectedly: a *bolt* of bad luck. **8.** A sudden start spring: He made a *bolt* for the door. **9.** *U.S.* A desertion one's party, its candidate, etc. **10.** A roll of cloth, wa paper, etc. — **a bolt from the blue** **1.** A thunderbolt o clear day. **2.** A sudden and wholly unexpected event. — **shoot one's bolt** To do one's utmost. — *v.i.* **1.** To mo go, or spring suddenly: He *bolted* from the room. **2.** *U* To break away, as from a political party; refuse to supp party policy. — *v.t.* **3.** To fasten or lock with or as wit bolt or bolts. **4.** *U.S.* To break away from, as a politi party. **5.** To gulp, as food. **6.** To arrange into bolts, cloth. **7.** To blurt out. — *adv.* Like an arrow; sudden — **bolt upright** Stiffly erect. [OE, arrow for a crossbow]

bolt[2] (bōlt) *v.t.* **1.** To sift. **2.** To examine as by sifti [< OF *bulter* to sift] — **bolt′er** *n.*

bo·lus (bō′ləs) *n. pl.* **·lus·es** **1.** A large pill. **2.** Any roun lump or mass. [< Med.L < Gk. *bōlos* a lump]

bomb (bom) *n.* **1.** *Mil.* A hollow projectile containing plosive, incendiary, or chemical material to be discharged concussion or by a time fuse. **2.** Any sudden or unexpec event. — *v.t. & v.i.* To attack or destroy with or as w bombs. [< F < Sp. < L < Gk. *bombos* hollow noise]

bom·bard (*v.* bom·bärd′; *n.* bom′bärd) *v.t.* **1.** To att with bombs or shells. **2.** To attack as with bombs. — The earliest form of cannon, originally hurling stones. MF < OF < L < Gk. *bombos* hollow noise] — **bom·bard** *n.* — **bom·bard′ment** *n.*

bom·bar·dier (bom′bər·dir′) *n.* **1.** *Mil.* The member of crew of a bomber who operates the bombsight and relea bombs. **2.** *Brit. & Canadian* An artillery corporal. [< F

bom·bast (bom′bast) *n.* Grandiloquent or pompous l guage. [< OF < LL *bombax, -acis* cotton]

bom·bas·tic (bom·bas′tik) *adj.* High-flown; grandiloque Also **bom·bas′ti·cal.** — **bom·bas′ti·cal·ly** *adv.*

bom·ba·zine (bom′bə·zēn′, bom′bə·zēn) *n.* A twilled fab usu. with silk warp and worsted filling. Also **bom′ba·sin** [< F < LL *bombax* cotton]

bomb bay A compartment in military aircraft in wh bombs are carried and from which they are dropped.

bomb·er (bom′ər) *n.* **1.** An airplane designed to carry a drop bombs. **2.** One who bombs.

bomb·shell (bom′shel′) *n.* **1.** A bomb. **2.** A compl surprise.

bomb·sight (bom′sīt′) *n. Mil.* An instrument on an a craft that enables the bombardier to aim accurately.

bo·na fide (bō′nə·fīd′, -fī′dē) *adj.* Being, acting, or carr out in good faith; authentic; genuine. [< L]

bo·nan·za (bə·nan′zə) *n. U.S.* **1.** A rich mine or find of c **2.** A source of great wealth. [< Sp. < L *bonus* good]

bon·bon (bon′bon′, *Fr.* bôn·bôn′) *n.* A sugared candy. F < *bon* good]

bond (bond) *n.* **1.** That which binds or holds together band; tie. **2.** A uniting force or influence. **3.** A volunta obligation. **4.** A substance that cements or unites; also, t union itself. **5.** *Law* An obligation in writing under seal. In finance, an interest-bearing certificate of debt, usu. issu by a government or corporation, obligating the issuer to p the principal at a specified time. **7.** In insurance, a pol covering losses suffered through the acts of an employee. In commerce, the condition of goods stored in a bond warehouse until duties are paid. **9.** A bondsman; also, ba surety. **10.** *Chem.* A unit of combining power between t atoms of a molecule. — **Syn.** See SECURITY. — **bottled bond** *U.S.* Bottled under government supervision and stor in a warehouse for a stated period, as certain whiskies. *v.t.* **1.** To put a certified debt upon; mortgage. **2.** To f nish bond for; be surety for (someone). **3.** To place, goods or an employee, under bond. **4.** To unite, as wi glue, etc. **5.** To lay (bricks, etc.) in interlocking patte for strength. — *v.i.* **6.** To interlock or cohere. — *adj.* bondage; enslaved. [Var. of BAND[1]] — **bond′er** *n.*

bond·age (bon′dij) *n.* **1.** Involuntary servitude; slave serfdom. **2.** Subjection to any influence or dominati [< Med.L < OE < ON *bōnde* peasant]

bond·ed (bon′did) *adj.* **1.** Secured or pledged by a bond bonds. **2.** Stored in a warehouse; placed in bond.

bond·hold·er (bond′hōl′dər) *n.* One owning or holdi bonds. — **bond′hold′ing** *adj. & n.*

bond·man (bond′mən) *n. pl.* **·men** (-mən) **1.** A slave serf. **2.** A man bound to serve without wages. — **bon maid, bond′wom′an, bonds′wom′an** *n. fem.*

bond paper A strong grade of paper, used for documents

bond·ser·vant (bond′sûr′vənt) *n.* **1.** A person bound serve without wages. **2.** A slave; serf: also **bond′slave′.**

bonds·man (bondz′mən) *n. pl.* **·men** (-mən) **1.** One w provides bond for another. **2.** A bondman.

bone (bōn) *n.* **1.** *Anat.* **a** A hard, dense porous materi

rming the skeleton of vertebrate animals. **b** A piece of this aterial. ◆ Collateral adjectives: *osseous, osteal.* **2.** *pl.* ıe skeleton as a whole. **3.** A substance resembling bone. Something made of bone or similar material. **5.** *pl. Inrmal* Dice. **6.** A strip of whalebone. **— to feel in (one's) ınes** To be sure of; have an intuition of. **— to have a bone pick** To have grounds for complaint or dispute. **— to ake no bones about** To be direct or straightforward about with. **—** *v.* **boned, bon·ing** *v.t.* **1.** To remove the bones om. **2.** To stiffen with whalebone. **—** *v.i.* **3.** *Slang* To ıdy intensely and quickly: often with *up.* [OE *bān*]
ıe·black (bōn′blak′) *n.* A black pigment made by calıing bones in airtight containers. Also **bone black.**
ıe·head (bōn′hed′) *n. Informal* A stupid person.
ıe meal Pulverized bone, used as feed and fertilizer.
ıe of contention A cause or subject of disagreement.
ı·er (bō′nər) *n. Slang* An error; blunder.
ıe·set (bōn′set′) *n.* A composite herb, formerly used in edicine as a tonic.
ı·fire (bon′fīr′) *n.* **1.** A large fire built in the open air. Formerly, a fire for burning corpses. [< BONE + FIRE]
ı·go drums (bong′gō) A pair of connected drums played th the hands, originally from Africa. Also **bon′gos.**
ı·ho·mie (bon′ə·mē′, *Fr.* bô·nô·mē′) *n.* Good nature; nial disposition. Also **bon′hom·mie′.** [< F]
ni·to (bə·nē′tō) *n. pl.* **·to** or **·toes** A large mackerellike arine food fish: also called *skipjack.* [< Sp.]
ı jour (bôṅ zho͞or′) *French* Good day; good morning.
ı mot (bôṅ mō′) *pl.* **bons mots** (bôṅ mōz′, *Fr.* mō′) A ever saying; terse witticism. [< F]
ı·net (bon′it) *n.* **1.** An outdoor headdress for women or ildren, typically held in place by ribbons tied under the ıin. **2.** *Chiefly Scot.* A cap for men and boys. **3.** An merican Indian headdress of feathers. **—** *v.t.* To cover ith a bonnet. [< OF < Med.L *bonetus*]
ı·ny (bon′ē) *adj.* **·ni·er, ·ni·est 1.** Having beauty; come-. **2.** Fine; good. **3.** Robust; healthy. Also **bon′nie.** [< *bon* good] **— bon′ni·ly** *adv.* **— bon′ni·ness** *n.*
ı·sai (bon′sī′, bōn′) *n. pl.* **·sai 1.** A dwarfed tree or rub trained, as by pruning, into a pleasing design. **2.** The t of creating such trees or shrubs. [< Japanese]
ı soir (bôṅ swȧr′) *French* Good evening; good night.
nus (bō′nəs) *n. pl.* **bo·nus·es** Something paid or given addition to a usual or stipulated amount. [< L, good]
ı vi·vant (bôṅ vē·väṅ′) *pl.* **bons vi·vants** (bôṅ vē·väṅ′) *ench* One who enjoys luxurious living; an epicure.
ı vo·yage (bôṅ vwȧ·yȧzh′) *French* Pleasant trip.
ı·y (bō′nē) *adj.* **bon·i·er, bon·i·est 1.** Of, like, pertaining or consisting of bone or bones. **2.** Having prominent ınes; thin; gaunt. **— bon′i·ness** *n.*
o (bo͞o) *n. & interj.* A vocal sound made to indicate conmpt or to frighten. **—** *v.* **booed, boo·ing** *v.i.* **1.** To utter ɔoo." **—** *v.t.* **2.** To shout "boo" at. [Imit.]
ob (bo͞ob) *n. Slang* A simpleton; booby.
o·boo (bo͞o′bo͞o′) *n. pl.* **·boos** *Slang* An embarrassg error; blunder. Also **boo′-boo′.** [Origin uncertain]
o·by (bo͞o′bē) *n. pl.* **·bies 1.** A stupid person; dunce. **2.** some games, the person who makes the poorest score. **3.** ny of several gannets of tropical America. [< Sp. *bobo* fool]
oby hatch 1. *Naut.* A raised hood over a small hatchway. *U.S. Slang* A hospital for the mentally ill.
oby prize A mock award for a worst score or performance.
oby trap 1. A concealed bomb, mine, etc., placed so as to detonated by casual or careless movements of the victim. Any device for taking someone unawares.
o·dle (bo͞od′l) *U.S. Slang n.* **1.** Bribery money; graft. Loot; plunder. **3.** A mob. **—** *v.i.* **·dled, ·dling** To reive money corruptly. [Cf. Du. *boedel* property]
og·ie-woog·ie (bo͝og′ē-wo͝og′ē) *n.* A style of jazz piano aying marked by repetition of bass rhythms and melodic ariations in the treble. [Origin uncertain]
o·hoo (bo͞o′ho͞o′) *v.i.* **·hooed, ·hoo·ing** To weep loudly. *n. pl.* **·hoos** Noisy sobbing. [Imit.]
ok (bo͝ok) *n.* **1.** A bound set of printed sheets of paper, ıually between covers. **2.** A literary composition of some ngth, written or printed. **3.** A ledger, register, etc. **4.** A ain division of a literary composition: a *book* of the Bible. A libretto. **6.** The script of a play. **7.** A booklike packet, s of matches. **8.** Something regarded as a source of inruction: the *book* of experience. **9.** A record of bets, espeially on a horse race. **10.** A specific number of tricks or ards won. **— by the book** According to rule. **— like a ook** Thoroughly. **— on the books 1.** Recorded. **2.** Enolled. **— to make book** *U.S. Slang* To bet or accept bets. *v.t.* **1.** To enter or list in a book. **2.** To arrange for eforehand, as accommodations or seats. **3.** To engage, s actors or a play, for performance. **4.** To make a record f charges against (someone) on a police blotter. [OE]

book·bind·er (bo͝ok′bīn′dər) *n.* One whose trade is the binding of books. **— book′bind′er·y** *n.* **— book′bind′ing** *n.*
book·case (bo͝ok′kās′) *n.* A case with shelves for books.
book club 1. An organization that sells books at reduced rates to members who agree to buy a certain number. **2.** A club given over to the reading and discussion of books.
book end A support or prop used to hold books upright.
book·ie (bo͝ok′ē) *n. Informal* A bookmaker (def. 2).
book·ing (bo͝ok′ing) *n.* An engagement to perform, etc.
book·ish (bo͝ok′ish) *adj.* **1.** Fond of books; studious. **2.** Knowing only what has been read in books; pedantic. **3.** Of books. **— book′ish·ly** *adv.* **— book′ish·ness** *n.*
book jacket A dust jacket.
book·keep·ing (bo͝ok′kē′ping) *n.* The practice of recording business transactions systematically. **— book′keep′er** *n.*
book learning Knowledge obtained from books rather than from experience. **— book-learn·ed** (bo͝ok′lûr′nid) *adj.*
book·let (bo͝ok′lit) *n.* A small book or pamphlet.
book·mak·er (bo͝ok′mā′kər) *n.* **1.** One who compiles, prints, or binds books. **2.** One who makes a business of accepting bets, as in horse racing.
book·mark (bo͝ok′märk′) *n.* **1.** Any object, as a ribbon, inserted in a book to mark a place. **2.** A bookplate.
book·mo·bile (bo͝ok′mə·bēl) *n.* A motor truck equipped to serve as a traveling library.
Book of Common Prayer The book of ritual used in the Anglican church.
book·rack (bo͝ok′rak′) *n.* **1.** A frame to hold an open book. Also **book′rest′.** **2.** A rack to hold books.
book review An article or essay discussing or critically examining a book, esp. a recently published book.
book·sell·er (bo͝ok′sel′ər) *n.* One who sells books.
book·stack (bo͝ok′stak′) *n.* A tall rack containing shelves for books, as in a library.
book·stall (bo͝ok′stôl′) *n.* **1.** A stall or stand where books are sold. **2.** *Brit.* A newsstand.
book·store (bo͝ok′stôr′, -stōr′) *n.* A store where books are sold. Also **book′shop′.**
book·worm (bo͝ok′wûrm′) *n.* **1.** One excessively devoted to books and study. **2.** Any insect destructive to books.
boom[1] (bo͞om) *v.i.* **1.** To emit a deep, resonant sound. **2.** *U.S.* To grow rapidly; flourish. **—** *v.t.* **3.** To utter or sound in a deep resonant tone: often with *out.* **4.** *U.S.* To praise or advertise vigorously. **5.** *U.S.* To cause to flourish. **—** *n.* **1.** A deep, reverberating sound, as of a supersonic aircraft, of waves, etc. **2.** *U.S.* A sudden increase, as in growth; spurt. **—** *adj. U.S.* Caused or maintained by a boom: *boom* prices. [Imit.]
boom[2] (bo͞om) *n.* **1.** *Naut.* A long spar or pole used to hold or extend the bottom of certain sails. **2.** A long pole or beam extending upward at an angle from the foot of the mast of a derrick, and from which are suspended the objects to be lifted. **3.** *U.S.* A floating chain of connected logs used to enclose other floating logs, to retard the advance of a vessel, etc. **—** *v.t.* **1.** To extend (a sail) by means of a boom: with *out.* **2.** To shove off or away, as a vessel from a wharf: with *off.* [< Du. *boom* tree, beam]

BOOM[2] (*def.* 2)

boom·e·rang (bo͞o′mə·rang) *n.* **1.** A curved, wooden missile originated in Australia, one form of which will return to the thrower. **2.** A plan, statement, etc., that recoils upon the originator. **—** *v.i.* To react harmfully on the originator. [< native Australian name]
boom town A town showing sudden development or prosperity, as from a discovery of gold.
boon[1] (bo͞on) *n.* **1.** A good thing bestowed; blessing. **2.** *Archaic* A request. [< ON *bōn* petition]
boon[2] (bo͞on) *adj.* Convivial; merry: now only in the phrase **boon companion.** [< F < L *bonus* good]
boon·docks (bo͞on′doks′) *n.pl. U.S. Slang* An uncivilized or backwoods area: with *the.* [< Tagalog *bundok* mountain]
boon·dog·gle (bo͞on′dôg′əl, -dog′əl) *U.S. Informal v.i.* **·gled, ·gling** To work on wasteful or unnecessary projects. **—** *n.* Unnecessary work. [Origin uncertain] **— boon′dog′gler** *n.*
boor (bo͝or) *n.* An awkward, rude, or ill-mannered person. [< Du. *boer* farmer, rustic] **— boor′ish** *adj.* **— boor′ish·ly** *adv.* **— boor′ish·ness** *n.*
boost (bo͞ost) *U.S. v.t.* **1.** To raise by pushing from beneath or behind. **2.** To increase: to *boost* prices. **3.** To advance by speaking well of; promote or extol vigorously. **—** *n.* **1.** A lift; help. **2.** An increase. [Origin uncertain]
boost·er (bo͞os′tər) *U.S. n.* **1.** Any device or substance for increasing power. **2.** *Informal* One who gives enthusiastic support to a person, cause, etc.
boot[1] (bo͞ot) *n.* **1.** A covering, usu. of leather, for the foot and part or most of the leg. **2.** A flap on an open vehicle for shielding the driver against rain or mud. **3.** A thick patch

for the inside of a tire casing. **4.** A kick. **5.** In U.S. Navy and Marine Corps slang, a recent recruit. **— too big for one's boots** *U.S.* Proud; conceited. **— the boot** *Slang* Dismissal; discharge. **— to die with one's boots on** To die fighting or working. **—** *v.t.* **1.** To put boots on. **2.** To kick or to punt. **3.** *Slang* To dismiss; fire. [< OF *bote*]

boot[2] (bo͞ot) *Obs. n.* Advantage. **— to boot** In addition; over and above. [ME < OE *bōt* profit]

boot·black (bo͞ot′blak′) *n.* One whose business is shining boots and shoes.

boo·tee (bo͞o·tē′, bo͞o′tē) *n.* **1.** A baby's knitted woolen boot. **2.** A light half boot for women. Also **boo·tie** (bo͞o′tē).

Bo·ö·tes (bō·ō′tēz) *n.* A constellation, the Bear Keeper: also called *Herdsman.* [< L < Gk. *boōtēs* plowman]

booth (bo͞oth, bo͞oth) *n.* **1.** A small compartment or cubicle for privacy or for keeping out sound, etc. **2.** A seating compartment, as in a restaurant. **3.** A small stall for the display or sale of goods. [ME *bothe* < Scand.]

boot·jack (bo͞ot′jak′) *n.* A forked device for holding a boot while the foot is withdrawn.

boot·leg (bo͞ot′leg′) *U.S. v.t. & v.i.* **·legged, ·leg·ging** To make, sell, or carry for sale (liquor, etc.) illegally; smuggle. **—** *adj.* Unlawful: *bootleg* whisky. **—** *n.* **1.** The part of a boot above the instep. **2.** Bootleg liquor or other merchandise. [With ref. to the smuggling of liquor in bootlegs] **— boot′leg′ger** *n.* **— boot′leg′ging** *n.*

boot·less (bo͞ot′lis) *adj.* Profitless; useless; unavailing. **— boot′less·ly** *adv.* **— boot′less·ness** *n.*

boot·lick (bo͞ot′lik′) *U.S. Slang v.t. & v.i.* To flatter servilely; toady. **— boot′lick′er** *n.* **— boot′lick′ing** *n. & adj.*

boo·ty (bo͞o′tē) *n. pl.* **·ties** **1.** The spoil of war; plunder. **2.** Goods taken by violence. **3.** Any prize or gain. [< F *butin* < MLG; infl. by obs. *boot* advantage]

booze (bo͞oz) *Informal n.* **1.** Alcoholic drink. **2.** A drunken spree. **—** *v.i.* **boozed, booz·ing** To drink to excess; tipple. [< MDu. *busen* to drink, tipple] **— booz′er** *n.*

booz·y (bo͞o′zē) *adj. Informal* Drunken; alcoholic. **— booz′i·ly** *adv.* **— booz′i·ness** *n.*

bop[1] (bop) *v.t.* **bopped, bop·ping** *Slang* To hit. [Imit.]

bop[2] (bop) *n.* A variety of jazz.

bo·rac·ic (bə·ras′ik) *adj. Chem.* Boric.

bor·age (bûr′ij, bôr′-, bor′-) *n.* A European herb having blue flowers and hairy leaves, used medicinally and in salads. [< Med.L *borra, burra* rough hair]

bo·rate (bôr′āt, bō′rāt) *n. Chem.* A salt of boric acid. **— bo′rat·ed** *adj.*

bo·rax (bôr′aks, bō′raks) *n.* A white crystalline compound, $Na_2B_4O_7 \cdot 10H_2O$, found native and used in medicine, industry, etc. [< OF < Med.L < Arabic < Persian *būrah*]

bo·ra·zon (bôr′ə·zon, bō′rə-) *n. Chem.* A crystalline compound of boron and nitrogen, BN, equaling the diamond in hardness but with a much higher melting point.

Bor·deaux (bôr·dō′) *n.* A white or red wine produced in the vicinity of Bordeaux, France. Red Bordeaux is called *claret.*

bor·der (bôr′dər) *n.* **1.** A margin or edge. **2.** The frontier line or district of a country or state; boundary. **3.** A design or stripe in the margins of a page of a book, etc. **4.** A decorative edging or margin. **—** *adj.* Of, on, or forming the border. **—** *v.t.* **1.** To put a border or edging on. **2.** To lie along the border of; bound. **— to border on** (or **upon**) **1.** To lie adjacent to. **2.** To approach; verge on: That act *borders on* piracy. [< OF < *bord* edge] **— bor′der·er** *n.*

bor·der·land (bôr′dər·land′) *n.* **1.** Land on or near the border of two adjoining countries. **2.** Debatable or indeterminate ground: the *borderland* between love and hate.

bor·der·line (bôr′dər·līn′) *n.* A line of demarcation. Also **border line.** **—** *adj.* Difficult to classify; doubtful.

bore[1] (bôr, bōr) *v.* **bored, bor·ing** *v.t.* **1.** To make a hole in or through, as with a drill. **2.** To make (a tunnel, etc.) by or as by drilling. **3.** To force (one's way). **4.** To weary by being dull, long-winded, etc.; tire. **—** *v.i.* **5.** To make a hole, etc., by or as by drilling. **6.** To force one's way. **—** *n.* **1.** A hole made by or as if by boring. **2.** The interior diameter of a firearm or cylinder; caliber. **3.** One who or that which is tiresome. [OE *bor* auger]

bore[2] (bôr, bōr) *n.* A high, crested wave caused by the rush of a flood tide, as in the Amazon. [< ON *bāra* billow]

bore[3] (bôr, bōr) Past tense of BEAR[1].

bo·re·al (bôr′ē·əl, bō′rē-) *adj.* Of the north or the north wind. [< LL < L *Boreas,* the north wind]

Bo·re·as (bôr′ē·əs, bō′rē-) In Greek mythology, the god of the north wind. [< L < Gk.]

bore·dom (bôr′dəm, bōr′-) *n.* The condition of being bored.

bor·er (bôr′ər, bō′rər) *n.* **1.** A tool used for boring. **2.** A beetle, moth, or worm that burrows in plants, wood, etc.

bo·ric (bôr′ik, bō′rik) *adj. Chem.* Of, pertaining to, or derived from boron: also *boracic.*

boric acid *Chem.* A white crystalline compound, H_3BO_3, used as a preservative and as a mild antiseptic.

born (bôrn) *adj.* **1.** Brought forth, as offspring. **2.** Natural; by birth: a *born* musician. [OE *beran* to bear]

borne (bôrn, bōrn) Past participle of BEAR[1].

bo·ron (bôr′on, bō′ron) *n.* A nonmetallic element (symb B) found only in combination. See ELEMENT.

bor·ough (bûr′ō, -ə) *n.* **1.** An incorporated village or tow **2.** One of the five administrative divisions of New Yo N.Y. **3.** *Brit.* **a** A town with a municipal corporation a certain privileges granted by royal charter: also **munici borough. b** A town entitled to representation in Parliame also **parliamentary borough.** [OE *burg, burh* fort, town

bor·row (bôr′ō, bor′ō) *v.t.* **1.** To take or obtain (son thing) with the promise or understanding that one will turn it. **2.** To adopt for one's own use, as ideas. **3.** In ari metical subtraction, to withdraw (a unit of ten) from a figure of the minuend in order to add it to the next lower nomination. **—** *v.i.* **4.** To borrow something. [OE *b* pledge] **— bor′row·er** *n.*

borscht (bôrsht) *n.* A Russian beet soup, eaten hot or co Also **borsch** (bôrsh). [< Russian *borshch*]

bort (bôrt) *n.* An impure diamond, used only for cutti and polishing. Also **bortz** (bôrts). [? < OF *bort* bastar

bor·zoi (bôr′zoi) *n.* A breed of Russian hounds, resembli the greyhound but larger, and having a long, silky coat: a called *Russian wolfhound.* [< Russian, swift]

bosh (bosh) *n. Informal* Empty words; nonsense. Turkish, empty, worthless]

bo's'n (bō′sən) See BOATSWAIN.

Bos·ni·an (boz′nē·ən) *adj.* Of or pertaining to Bosnia. A **Bos·ni·ac** (boz′nē·ak). **—** *n.* **1.** A native or inhabitant Bosnia. **2.** The Serbo-Croatian language of the Bosnia

bos·om (bo͝oz′əm, bo͞o′zəm) *n.* **1.** The breast of a hum being, esp. of a woman. **2.** The breast as the seat of thoug and emotion. **3.** Something suggesting the human brea **4.** Inner circle; midst: in the *bosom* of the church. **—** *adj.* Close; intimate: a *bosom* friend. **2.** Of or pertaining to t bosom. **—** *v.t.* **1.** To have or cherish in the bosom; e brace. **2.** To hide; conceal. [OE *bōsm*]

boss[1] (bôs, bos) *U.S. Informal n.* **1.** A superintendent employer of workmen. **2.** A professional politician who co trols a political organization. **—** *v.t.* **1.** To supervise; dire **2.** To order in a highhanded manner. **—** *v.i.* **3.** To act boss. **—** *adj.* Head; chief. [< Du. *baas* master]

boss[2] (bôs, bos) *n.* **1.** A circular prominence; a knob or p jecting ornament. **2.** *Mech.* An enlarged part of a sha coupling with a wheel or another shaft. **—** *v.t.* **1.** To orn ment with bosses. **2.** To emboss. [< OF *boce* bump, kno

boss·ism (bôs′iz·əm, bos′-) *n. U.S.* Control by politi bosses.

boss·y[1] (bôs′ē, bos′ē) *adj.* **boss·i·er, boss·i·est** *U.S. Inf mal* Tending to boss; domineering.

boss·y[2] (bos′ē, bôs′ē) *n. U.S. Informal* A cow or a calf

Boston terrier A small terrier having a short, smoo brindled coat with white markings. Also **Boston bull.**

bo·sun (bō′sən) See BOATSWAIN.

bot (bot) *n.* The larva of a botfly: also spelled *bott.* [Orig unknown]

bo·tan·i·cal (bə·tan′i·kəl) *adj.* Of or pertaining to bota or to plants. Also **bo·tan′ic.** **—** *n.* A drug derived from t leaves, roots, stems, etc., of a plant. [< F < Gk. *bota* plant, pasture] **— bo·tan′i·cal·ly** *adv.* **— bot′a·nist** *n.*

bot·a·nize (bot′ə·nīz) *v.* **·nized, ·niz·ing** *v.i.* **1.** To stu botanical specimens. **2.** To gather plants for study. **—** **3.** To search for botanical specimens. **— bot′a·niz′er** *n.*

bot·a·ny (bot′ə·nē) *n.* **1.** The division of biology that trea of plants, their structure, functions, classification, etc. The total plant life of a region, country, etc. **3.** The ch acteristics of a group of plants treated collectively.

botch (boch) *v.t.* **1.** To bungle. **2.** To patch or mend clu sily. **—** *n.* **1.** A bungled piece of work. **2.** A clumsy patc [ME *bocchen;* origin unknown] **— botch′er** *n.* **— botc er·y** *n.* **— botch′i·ly** *adv.* **— botch′y** *adj.*

bot·fly (bot′flī′) *n.* A fly of which the larvae are parasitic vertebrates; esp., the **horse botfly.**

both (bōth) *adj. & pron.* The two together: *Both* gi laughed. **—** *conj. & adv.* Equally; alike; as well: with *an* [< ON *bādhar*]

both·er (both′ər) *v.t.* **1.** To pester; give trouble to. **2.** confuse; fluster. **—** *v.i.* **3.** To trouble or concern onese **—** *n.* **1.** A source or state of annoyance; vexation; troubl **2.** One who or that which bothers. [? dial. E (Irish)]

both·er·some (both′ər·səm) *adj.* Causing bother.

bott (bot) See BOT.

bot·tle (bot′l) *n.* **1.** A vessel, usu. of glass, for holding li uids, having a neck and a narrow mouth that can be stoppe **2.** As much as a bottle will hold: also **bot′tle·ful′.** **— to the bottle** *U.S. Slang* To drink liquor to excess. **—** *v.t.* **·tle ·tling** **1.** To put into a bottle or bottles. **2.** To restrai often with *up* or *in.* [< LL *buticula* flask] **— bot′tler** *n*

bottle green A dark, dull green.

bot·tle·neck (bot′l·nek′) *n.* **1.** A narrow or congested pa sageway. **2.** Anything that retards progress; hindrance.

bot·tle·nose (bot′l·nōz′) *n.* A variety of dolphin.

t·tom (bot′əm) *n.* **1.** The lowest part of anything. **2.** he underside or undersurface. **3.** The ground beneath a ody of water. **4.** Source or foundation. **5.** *Often pl.* Bot- om land. **6.** *Naut.* The part of a vessel below the water ne. **7.** *Informal* The buttocks. **8.** The seat of a chair. **9.** taying power; stamina. — **at bottom** Fundamentally. — **ottoms up!** *Informal* Empty your glass! — *adj.* Lowest; ındamental; basal. — *v.t.* **1.** To provide with a bottom. . To base or found: with *on* or *upon.* **3.** To fathom; com- rehend. — *v.i.* **4.** To be founded; rest. **5.** To touch or st on the bottom. [OE]

ttom land Lowland along a river.

t·tom·less (bot′əm·lis) *adj.* **1.** Having no bottom. **2.** nfathomable; limitless; endless. — **the bottomless pit** Hell.

t·tom·ry (bot′əm·rē) *n.* A contract whereby the owner of vessel borrows money, pledging the vessel as security.

t·u·lism (boch′ŏŏ·liz′əm) *n.* Poisoning caused by a toxin roduced by a bacillus sometimes present in improperly pre- rved food. [< G < L *botulus* sausage]

u·clé (bōō·klā′) *n.* A woven or knitted fabric with a looped knotted surface; also, the yarn from which this is made. < F, pp. of *boucler* to buckle, curl]

u·doir (bōō′dwär, bōō·dwär′) *n.* A lady's private sitting om or bedroom. [< F, lit., pouting room] ut, sulk] — **bou·doir·esque** (bōō′dwär·esk′) *adj.*

uf·fant (bōō·fänt′) *adj.* Puffed-out; flaring, as a skirt. < F, ppr. of *bouffer* to swell]

ugh (bou) *n.* A large branch of a tree. [OE *bōg* shoulder.]

ught (bôt) Past tense and past participle of BUY.

uil·la·baisse (bōōl′yə·bās′, *Fr.* bōō·yȧ·bes′) *n.* A chow- er made of several varieties of fish. [< F < Provençal *boui* boil + *abaisso* to settle, go down]

uil·lon (bŏŏl′yon, -yən; *Fr.* bōō·yôṅ′) *n.* Clear soup om beef or other meats. [< F < *bouillir* to boil]

ul·der (bōl′dər) *n.* A large, rounded rock that has been tached: also spelled *bowlder.* [ME *bulderston*]

ul·e·vard (bŏŏl′ə·värd, bōō′lə-) *n.* **1.** A broad avenue, ten lined with trees. **2.** *Chiefly Canadian* The grass be- veen sidewalk and street; also, the center strip of a divided ghway. Abbr. *blvd.* [< F < G *bollwerk* fortification]

unce (bouns) *v.* **bounced, bounc·ing** *v.i.* **1.** To move with bound or bounds, as a ball; rebound. **2.** To move sudden- and violently; spring. **3.** *U.S. Slang* To be returned by a ınk as worthless: said of a check. — *v.t.* **4.** To cause to ounce. **5.** *Slang* To eject (a person) forcibly; also, to dis- arge from employment. — *n.* **1.** A bound or rebound. . A sudden spring or leap. **3.** Ability or capacity to bounce spring. **4.** *Informal* Vivacity; verve; spirit. [ME *bunsen* thump < MLG] — **bounc′y** *adj.*

unc·er (boun′sər) *n.* *U.S. Slang* One employed in a bar, ght club, etc., to eject disorderly persons.

unc·ing (boun′sing) *adj.* Strong and active; strapping.

und[1] (bound) *v.i.* **1.** To strike and spring back from a ırface, as a ball. **2.** To leap; move by a series of leaps. — *t.* **3.** To cause to bound. — *n.* A leap or spring; also, a bound. [< MF *bondir* to resound, rebound]

und[2] (bound) *n.* **1.** *Usu. pl.* A boundary; limit: out of *unds.* **2.** *pl.* The area near or within a boundary. — *v.t.* . To set limits to; restrict. **2.** To form the boundary of. . To name the boundaries of. — *v.i.* **4.** To adjoin; abut. < OF < LL *bodina* limit.]

und[3] (bound) Past tense and past participle of BIND. — *dj.* **1.** Made fast; tied with bonds. **2.** Having a cover or inding. **3.** Morally or legally obligated. **4.** Certain; sure: *s bound* to rain. **5.** *U.S. Informal* Determined; resolved. - **bound up in** (or **with**) **1.** Inseparably connected with. . Devotedly attached to.

und[4] (bound) *adj.* Having one's course directed; on the ay: *bound* for home. [< ON < *būa* to prepare]

und·a·ry (boun′də·rē, -drē) *n.* *pl.* **·ries** Anything indi- ating a limit or confine.

und·en (boun′dən) *adj.* **1.** Obligatory: our *bounden* duty. . Under obligations; obliged.

und·er (boun′dər) *n.* *Chiefly Brit. Informal* An offen- ve, ill-mannered person; a cad.

und·less (bound′lis) *adj.* Having no limit; vast. — **ound′less·ly** *adv.* — **bound′less·ness** *n.*

un·te·ous (boun′tē·əs) *adj.* **1.** Generous; beneficent. **2.** Iarked by abundance; plentiful. [ME < OF < *bonté* good- ess] — **boun′te·ous·ly** *adv.* — **boun′te·ous·ness** *n.*

un·ti·ful (boun′tə·fəl) *adj.* **1.** Free and generous in be- owing gifts. **2.** Showing abundance; plentiful. — **boun′ti- ıl·ly** *adv.* — **boun′ti·ful·ness** *n.*

un·ty (boun′tē) *n.* *pl.* **·ties** **1.** Liberality in giving. **2.** ifts or favors generously bestowed. **3.** A reward from a overnment, as for the killing of predatory animals, etc. [< F < L *bonitas, -tatis* goodness]

u·quet (bō·kā′, bōō·kā′ *for def. 1*; bōō·kā′ *for def. 2*) *n.* **1.** A bunch of flowers. **2.** Delicate odor; esp. the distinctive aroma of a wine. [< F < OF *boschet*]

bour·bon (bûr′bən) *n.* A whiskey distilled from a fermented mash containing at least 51 per cent corn. Also **bourbon whiskey.** [after *Bourbon* County, Ky., where first made]

Bour·bon (bŏŏr′bən) *n.* **1.** A dynasty that reigned over France, 1589–1792, 1815–48, or a related branch that ruled Spain, 1700–1931. **2.** One who is stubbornly conservative in politics. — **Bour′bon·ism** *n.* — **Bour′bon·ist** *n.*

bour·geois[1] (bŏŏr′zhwä, bŏŏr·zhwä′) *n.* *pl.* **·geois** **1.** A member of the middle class; a tradesman. **2.** *pl.* The middle class. **3.** In Marxism, a member of the class in conflict with the working class. — *adj.* Of or characteristic of the middle class: often used disparagingly. [< F < OF < LL < *burgus* town] — **bour·geoise** (bŏŏr·zhwäz′) *n.* & *adj. fem.*

bour·geois[2] (bər·jois′) *n.* A size of type, about 9-point. [? after a French printer]

bour·geoi·sie (bŏŏr′zhwä·zē′) *n.* **1.** The middle class of so- ciety, esp. in France. **2.** In Marxism, that social class op- posed in the class struggle to the proletariat or working class.

bour·geon (bûr′jən) See BURGEON.

Bourse (bŏŏrs) *n.* An exchange or money market; esp., the Paris stock exchange. [< F, purse < LL *bursa* bag)

bout (bout) *n.* **1.** A contest; trial. **2.** A fit or spell, as of drinking or illness. [Var. of ME *bought* bending, turn]

bou·tique (bōō·tēk′) *n.* *French* A small retail shop.

bou·ton·niere (bōō′tən·yâr′) *n.* A bouquet or flower worn in the buttonhole. Also **bou′ton·nière′.** [< F]

bo·vine (bō′vīn, -vin) *adj.* **1.** Of or pertaining to oxen, cows, etc. **2.** Stolid; null. — *n.* A bovine animal. [< LL < L *bos, bovis* ox]

bow[1] (bou) *n.* **1.** *Naut.* The forward part of a ship, boat, etc. **2.** The forward oarsman of a boat. — *adj.* Of or at the bow. [< LG or Scand.]

bow[2] (bou) *v.* **bowed, bow·ing** *v.i.* **1.** To bend the body or head, as in salutation, worship, or assent. **2.** To bend or in- cline downward. **3.** To submit; yield. — *v.t.* **4.** To bend (the body, head, etc.) in reverence, courtesy, or submission. **5.** To express by bowing. **6.** To escort with bows. **7.** To cause to yield; subdue. **8.** To cause to bend or stoop. — **to bow out** To withdraw; resign. — *n.* An inclination of the body or head. [OE *būgan* to bend]

bow[3] (bō) *n.* **1.** A weapon made from a strip of elastic wood or other pliable material, bent by a string and used to project an arrow. **2.** An archer. **3.** Something bent or curved; a bend. **4.** A knot with a loop or loops, as of ribbon, etc. **5.** *Music* **a** A rod with hairs stretched between raised ends, used for playing a violin or related stringed instrument. **b** A stroke with a bow. — *adj.* Bent; curved; bowed. — *v.t.* & *v.i.* **bowed, bow·ing** **1.** To bend into the shape of a bow. **2.** *Music* To play (a stringed instrument) with a bow. — **Syn.** See BEND[1]. [OE *boga*]

bowd·ler·ize (boud′lər·īz) *v.t.* **·ized, ·iz·ing** To expurgate or edit prudishly. [after Dr. Thomas *Bowdler's* "family" edi- tion of Shakespeare (1818)] — **bowd′ler·ism** *n.* — **bowd′- ler·i·za′tion** *n.*

bow·el (bou′əl, boul) *n.* **1.** An intestine. **2.** *pl.* The inner part of anything: the *bowels* of the earth. — *v.t.* **bow·eled** or **·elled, bow·el·ing** or **·el·ling** To disembowel. [< OF < L *botellus,* dim. of *botulus* sausage]

bow·er (bou′ər) *n.* A shaded recess. — *v.t.* To enclose in or as in a bower. [OE *būr* chamber] — **bow′er·y** *adj.*

Bow·er·y (bou′ər·ē) A street in New York City noted for its saloons, shabby hotels, etc.: often preceded by *the.*

bow·ie knife (bō′ē, bōō′ē) A strong, single-edged hunting knife. [after James *Bowie,* 1799–1836, its reputed inventor]

BOWIE KNIFE

bow·knot (bō′not′) *n.* An ornamental slipknot made with one or more loops. For illus. see KNOT.

bowl[1] (bōl) *n.* **1.** A deep, round dish. **2.** The amount a bowl will hold. **3.** A large goblet. **4.** Convivial drinking. **5.** An amphitheater. **6.** Something shaped like a bowl: the *bowl* of a pipe. [OE *bolla*]

bowl[2] (bōl) *n.* **1.** A large ball for bowls or tenpins. **2.** A throw of the ball in bowling. — *v.i.* **1.** To play at bowls, tenpins, etc. **2.** To roll a ball or rounded object. **3.** To move smoothly and swiftly: usually with *along.* — *v.t.* **4.** To roll or throw, as a ball. **5.** To carry or transport on or as on wheels. — **to bowl over** **1.** To cause to be confused or helpless. **2.** To knock down. [< F *boule* ball] — **bowl′er** *n.*

bowl·der (bōl′dər) See BOULDER.

bow·leg (bō′leg′) *n.* A leg with an outward curvature at or below the knee. — **bow·leg·ged** (bō′leg′id, -legd′) *adj.*

bowl·er (bō′lər) *n.* *Brit.* A derby. [< BOWL[2]]

bow·line (bō′lin, -līn′) *n.* **1.** A knot tied so as to form a loop. Also **bowline knot.** **2.** *Naut.* A rope to keep a sail taut when sailing close-hauled.

bowl·ing (bō′ling) *n.* The game of bowls or of tenpins.
bowling alley A long, narrow space for playing tenpins, or the building containing it.
bowling green A smooth lawn for playing at bowls.
bowls (bōlz) *n.pl.* **1.** *Brit.* An outdoor game played by rolling slightly flattened or weighted balls at a stationary ball. **2.** Tenpins, ninepins, or skittles.
bow·man (bō′mən) *n. pl.* **·men** (-mən) An archer.
bow·shot (bō′shot′) *n.* The distance to which an arrow may be sent from the bow.
bow·sprit (bou′sprit′, bō′-) *n. Naut.* A spar projecting forward from the bow of a vessel. [? < M.Du. < *boeg* bow of a ship + *spriet* spear]
bow·string (bō′string′) *n.* The string of a bow, which projects the arrow.
bow tie A necktie worn in a bowknot.
bow window (bō) A projecting, usually curved window built up from the ground level.
box[1] (boks) *n.* **1.** A receptacle or case of wood, metal, etc., in many sizes and shapes and usu. having a lid. **2.** The quantity contained in a box. **3.** Something resembling a box in form or use. **4.** A small booth for a sentry, watchman, etc. **5.** The raised driver's seat of a coach. **6.** A space partitioned off for seating, as in a theater, courtroom, stadium, etc. **7.** In baseball, any of several designated spaces, as for the pitcher, batter, coach, etc. **8.** *Mech.* An axle bearing, casing, or other enclosed cavity. **9.** An enclosed space on a page of a newspaper, magazine, etc. **—*v.t.*** **1.** To place in a box. **2.** To furnish with a bushing or box. **— to box in 1.** In racing, to block (another contestant) so that he is unable to get ahead. **2.** To box up. **— to box the compass 1.** To recite in order the 32 points of the compass. **2.** To make a complete revolution or turn. **— to box up** To confine in, or as in, a small space. [OE < Med.L < Gk. *pyxos* boxwood] **— box′er** *n.*
box[2] (boks) *v.t.* **1.** To strike or buffet with the hand; cuff. **2.** To fight (another) in a boxing match. **—*v.i.*** **3.** To fight with one's fists; be a boxer. **—*n.*** A blow on the ear or cheek; cuff. [ME]
box[3] (boks) *n.* **1.** Any of a small family of evergreen herbs, shrubs, and trees, used as borders and hedges. **2.** The hard wood of these plants. [OE < L < Gk. *pyxos* boxwood]
box·car (boks′kär′) *n.* A roofed, enclosed freight car.
box elder A North American tree of the maple family, having compound leaflets: also called *Manitoba maple.*
box·er[1] (bok′sər) *n.* One who fights with his fists; pugilist.
box·er[2] (bok′sər) *n.* A breed of dog, related to the bulldog, having a sturdy body, smooth fawn coat, and a black mask.
Box·er (bok′sər) *n.* A member of a Chinese secret society, active in 1900, that aimed to rid China of foreigners by force.
box·ing (bok′sing) *n.* The art or practice of fighting with the fists, esp. when gloved; pugilism.
boxing glove A padded mitten used for prizefighting.
box office 1. The ticket office of a theater, etc. **2.** *Informal* Receipts at the box office, as a measure of success.
box seat A seat in a box of a theater, stadium, etc.
box spring A mattress foundation consisting of an upholstered frame set with coil springs to provide resiliency.
box·wood (boks′wŏŏd′) *n.* **1.** The hard, close-grained, durable wood of box. **2.** The shrub.
boy (boi) *n.* **1.** A male child; lad; youth. **2.** A man; fellow: a familiar use. **3.** A male servant. [ME *boi*] **— boy′ish** *adj.* **— boy′ish·ly** *adv.* **— boy′ish·ness** *n.*
boy·cott (boi′kot) *v.t.* **1.** To combine together in refusing to deal or associate with, so as to punish or coerce. **2.** To refuse to use or buy. **—*n.*** The act or practice of boycotting. [after Capt. C. *Boycott,* 1832–97, Irish landlord's agent, who was the first victim] **— boy′cot·ter** *n.*
boy friend 1. *Informal* A preferred male companion or intimate friend of a girl or woman. **2.** A male friend.
boy·hood (boi′hŏŏd) *n.* **1.** The state or period of being a boy. **2.** Boys collectively.
boy scout A member of the **Boy Scouts,** an organization for boys, stressing self-reliance and good citizenship.
boy·sen·ber·ry (boi′zən·ber′ē) *n. pl.* **·ries** The edible fruit obtained by crossing the blackberry, raspberry, and loganberry. [after Rudolph *Boysen,* 20th c. U.S. horticulturist]
bra (brä) *n. U.S. Informal* A brassiere.
brace (brās) *v.* **braced, brac·ing** *v.t.* **1.** To make firm or steady; strengthen by or as by braces. **2.** To make ready to withstand pressure, impact, assault, etc. **3.** To increase the tension of; strain. **4.** To tie or fasten firmly, as with straps. **5.** To stimulate; enliven. **—*v.i.*** **6.** To strain against pressure. **— to brace up** *Informal* To rouse one's courage or resolution. **—*n.*** **1.** A support, as of wood or metal, used to strengthen something or hold it in place. **2.** A clasp or clamp for fastening, connecting, etc. **3.** A cranklike handle for holding and turning a bit or other boring tool. **4.** A pair; couple. **5.** *Printing* A doubly curved line, { or }, used to connect words, lines, staves of music, etc. **6.** *pl. Brit.* Suspenders. **7.** *Often pl. Dent.* A wire or wires fastened on irregular teeth and gradually tightened to align them. *Med.* Any of various devices for supporting a joint, limb, other part. [< OF < L *brachia,* pl. of *brachium* arm]
brace·let (brās′lit) *n.* **1.** An ornamental band worn arou the wrist or arm. **2.** *Informal* A handcuff. [< OF, dim. *bracel* < L *brachiale* bracelet]
brac·er (brā′sər) *n.* **1.** One who or that which braces steadies. **2.** *U.S. Informal* A stimulating drink.
bra·chi·al (brā′kē·əl, brak′ē-) *adj.* Of or pertaining to arm or to armlike appendages. [< L < *brachium* arm]
brachio- *combining form* Arm; of the arm: *brachiop* Also, before vowels, **brachi-.** [< Gk. *brachiōn* arm]
bra·chi·o·pod (brā′kē·ə·pod′, brak′ē-) *n. Zool.* One o phylum or class of marine animals having a bivalve shell a a pair of armlike parts on the sides of the mouth. [< N
bra·chi·um (brā′kē·əm, brak′ē-) *n. pl.* **bra·chi·a** (brā′kē brak′ē-) **1.** *Anat.* The arm, esp. that part above the elb **2.** Any armlike process or appendage. [< L]
brachy- *combining form* Short. [< Gk. *brachys* short
brach·y·ce·phal·ic (brak′i·sə·fal′ik) *adj.* Having a sh broad skull; short-headed. Also **brach·y·ceph·a·lous** (bra i·sef′ə·ləs). [< NL < Gk. < *brachys* short + *kephalē* he **— brach′y·ceph′a·lism, brach′y·ceph′a·ly** *n.*
brac·ing (brā′sing) *adj.* Strengthening; invigorating. *n.* A brace or system of braces, as in bridge building.
brack·en (brak′en) *n.* **1.** A coarse, hardy fern with v large fronds: also called *brake.* **2.** A clump of such fer [ME *braken* < Scand.]
brack·et (brak′it) *n.* **1.** A piece of wood, metal, stone, e projecting from a wall, used to support a shelf or other weig **2.** A brace used to strengthen an angle. **3.** A project wall fixture for a gaslight, electric lamp, etc. **4.** A classifi tion according to income for tax purposes: the high-inco *bracket.* **5.** *Printing* One of two marks [ ] used to enclose a part of a text. **—*v.t.*** **1.** To provide or support wit bracket or brackets. **2.** To enclose within brackets. **3.** group or categorize together. [< Sp. < L *bracae,* breeches]
brack·ish (brak′ish) *adj.* **1.** Somewhat saline; briny. Distasteful. [< Du. *brak* salty] **— brack′ish·ness** *n.*
bract (brakt) *n. Bot.* A modified leaf situated at the base a flower. [< L *bractea* thin metal plate] **— brac·te·al** (brak′tē·əl) *adj.* **— brac·te·ate** (brak′tē·it, -āt) *adj.*
brad (brad) *n.* A small, slender nail with a small head. [< ON *broddr* spike]
brad·awl (brad′ôl′) *n.* A short awl for making holes in wood, as for brads or screws.
brady- *combining form* Slow. [< Gk. *bradys* slow]

BRACT (Aroun compos flower

brae (brā) *n. Scot.* A bank; hillside; slope.
brag (brag) *v.* **bragged, brag·ging** *v.i.* **1.** To boast about oneself or one's deeds or abilities. **—*v.t.*** **2.** declare or assert boastfully; boast of. **—*n.*** **1.** Boast language; boasting. **2.** A boast. **3.** One who brags. [C gin uncertain] **— brag′ger** *n.*
brag·ga·do·ci·o (brag′ə·dō′shē·ō) *n. pl.* **·ci·os 1.** Pret tious boasting. **2.** One who boasts; a swaggerer. [af *Braggadochio,* a boastful character in Spenser's *Faerie Quee*
brag·gart (brag′ərt) *n.* A bragger. **—*adj.*** Boastful. MF < *braguer* to brag] **— brag′gart·ism** *n.*
brah·ma (brä′mə, brā′-) *n. Often cap.* A large breed of mestic fowl developed in Asia. [after *Brahmaputra*]
Brah·ma (brä′mə) *n.* **1.** In Hindu religion, the supre soul of the universe. **2.** God, comprising the Hindu trin Brahma, Vishnu, and Siva; esp. the first of the trinity supreme creator. [< Skt. *Brahmā*]
Brah·man (brä′mən) *n. pl.* **·mans 1.** A member of highest Hindu caste, the sacerdotal caste: also spel *Brahmin.* **2.** A breed of cattle originating in India. Skt. *brāhmana* < *brahman* praise, worship] **— Brah·ma** (brä′mən·ē) *n.fem.* **— Brah·man·ic** (brä·man′ik) *adj.*
Brah·man·ism (brä′mən·iz′əm) *n.* The religious and cial system of the Brahmans: also **Brah′min·ism** (brä′mir
Brah·min (brä′min) *n.* **1.** A Brahman. **2.** A highly c tured or aristocratic person, esp. an ultraconservative snobbish one.
braid (brād) *v.t.* **1.** To weave or intertwine several stran of hair, etc. **2.** To bind or ornament (the hair) with ribbo etc. **3.** To form by braiding. **4.** To ornament (garmen with braid. **—*n.*** **1.** A narrow, flat tape or strip for bind or ornamenting fabrics. **2.** Any thing braided or plait **3.** A string or band used in arranging the hair. [OE *brega* to brandish, weave, braid] **— braid′er** *n.* **— braid′ing**
Braille (brāl) *n.* A system of printing or writing for t blind in which the characters consist of raised dots to be re by the fingers; also, the characters themselves. Also **brail** [after Louis *Braille,* 1809–52, French educator, the invent
brain (brān) *n.* **1.** *Anat.* The enlarged and greatly modif part of the central nervous system contained in the crani of vertebrates. **2.** *Often pl.* Mind; intellect. **— to have**

e brain To be obsessed by. — *v.t.* **1.** To dash out the ·ains of. **2.** *Slang* To hit on the head. [OE *brægen*]
ain child *Informal* That which one has created or originated, as an idea, technique, device, etc.
ain·less (brān′lis) *adj.* Lacking intelligence; senseless; upid. — **brain′less·ly** *adv.* — **brain′less·ness** *n.*
ain·pan (brān′pan′) *n.* The cranium; skull.
ain·sick (brān′sik′) *adj.* Affected with mental disorder.
ain·storm (brān′stôrm′) *n. Informal* A sudden inspiraon. Also **brain storm.**
ain trust A group of experts who act as consultants on atters of policy, etc. — **brain truster**
ain·wash (brān′wosh′, -wôsh′) *v.t.* To alter the convicons, beliefs, etc., of by means of intensive, coercive indocination. — **brain′wash′ing** *n.*
ain wave *Physiol.* A rhythmical fluctuation of electrical otential in the brain.
ain·y (brā′nē) *adj.* **brain·i·er, brain·i·est** *Informal* Intelgent; smart. — **brain′i·ly** *adv.* — **brain′i·ness** *n.*
aise (brāz) *v.t.* **braised, brais·ing** To cook (meat) by aring till brown and then simmering in a covered pan. [< < *braise* charcoal]
ake[1] (brāk) *n.* **1.** A device for slowing or stopping a vehie or wheel, esp. by friction. **2.** An instrument for separatg the fiber of flax, hemp, etc., by bruising or crushing. — **braked, brak·ing** *v.t.* **1.** To apply a brake to. **2.** To ·uise and crush, as flax. — *v.i.* **3.** To operate a brake or ·akes. [< MDu. *braeke* brake for flax] — **brake′age** *n.*
ake[2] (brāk) *n.* Bracken, a kind of fern. [ME]
ake[3] (brāk) *n.* An area covered with brushwood, briers, ne, etc.; thicket.
ake·man (brāk′mən) *n. pl.* **·men** (-mən) One who tends ·akes on a railroad car or assists in operating a train.
ake shoe A rigid metal casting shaped to press against a heel or brake when braking action is applied.
am·ble (bram′bəl) *n.* **1.** A plant of the rose family, esp. e blackberry of Europe. **2.** Any prickly plant. Also **am′ble·bush′** (-bŏŏsh′). [OE *bræmble*] — **bram′bly** *adj.*
an (bran) *n.* **1.** The coarse, outer coat of cereals, as sepated from the flour by sifting or bolting. **2.** Grain by-prodts used as feed. [< OF *bran, bren*] — **bran′ny** *adj.*
anch (branch, bränch) *n.* **1.** A woody outgrowth from e trunk of a tree or other large plant; limb. **2.** A part alogous to a branch; an offshoot, as of a deer's antlers. **3.** ny separate part or division of a system, subject, etc.; deirtment. **4.** A subordinate or local store, office, etc. **5.** A vision of a family, tribe, nation, etc., having or thought to ive a common ancestor. **6.** A tributary stream of a river. Any small stream or brook. — *v.i.* **1.** To put forth ·anches. **2.** To separate into branches or subdivisions. — *t.* **3.** To divide into branches. — **to branch off** **1.** To sep·ate into branches; fork, as a road. **2.** To diverge; go off on tangent. — **to branch out** To extend or expand, as one's usiness. [< OF < LL *branca* paw]
an·chi·ae (brang′ki·ē) *n. pl. of* **bran·chi·a** (brang′kē·ə) *ool.* Gills, the respiratory organs of fish. [< L < Gk. *anchia*, pl., gills] — **bran′chi·al** *adj.*
an·chi·ate (brang′kē·it, -āt) *adj.* Having gills.
and (brand) *n.* **1.** A distinctive name or trademark idenfying the product of a manufacturer. **2.** The kind or make a product: a good *brand* of coffee. **3.** A mark made with a ot iron, as on cattle, to indicate ownership. **4.** Formerly, mark burned on criminals. **5.** Any mark of disgrace; stiga. **6.** A branding iron. **7.** A burning piece of wood; also, torch. — *v.t.* **1.** To mark with a brand. **2.** To stigmaze. [OE, torch, sword.] — **brand′er** *n.*
an·died (bran′dēd) *adj.* Mixed, flavored with, or prerved in brandy: *brandied* cherries.
anding iron An iron for burning in a brand.
an·dish (bran′dish) *v.t.* To wave or flourish triumphant-, menacingly, or defiantly. — *n.* A flourish, as with a eapon. [< OF *brandir*] — **bran′dish·er** *n.*
and-new (brand′nōō′, -nyōō′, bran′-) *adj.* Very new; esh and bright. Also **bran′-new′** (bran′-).
an·dy (bran′dē) *n. pl.* **·dies** An alcoholic liquor distilled om wine or other fermented fruit juices. — *v.t.* **·died, ·dy·ng** To mix, flavor, strengthen, or preserve with brandy. [< Du. *brandewijn*, lit., distilled (burned) wine]
ant (brant) *n. pl.* **brants** or **brant** A small, black-necked ild goose of Europe and North America. Also **brant goose.**
ash[1] (brash) *adj. U.S.* **1.** Acting hastily; rash; impetuus. **2.** Impudent; saucy; pert. [Cf. G *barsch* harsh and w. *barsk* impetuous] — **brash′ly** *adv.* — **brash′ness** *n.*
ash[2] (brash) *n. Brit.* A shower of rain. [? Blend of *break* nd *crash, dash,* etc.] — **brash′i·ness** *n.* — **brash′y** *adj.*
a·sier (brā′zhər) See BRAZIER.
ass (bras, bräs) *n.* **1.** An alloy essentially of copper and inc, harder than copper, and both ductile and malleable. **2.** Formerly, any alloy of copper, esp. one with tin. **3.** *Usu. pl.* Ornaments or utensils of brass. **4.** *Sometimes pl. Music* The brass instruments of an orchestra or band collectively: also *Rare* **brass winds.** **5.** *Informal* Effrontery. **6.** *U.S. Informal* High-ranking military officers; any high officials. — *adj.* Made of brass; brazen. [OE *bræs*]
bras·sard (bras′ärd, brə·särd′) *n.* **1.** A band worn on the upper arm as a badge or insignia. **2.** A piece of armor for the arm. Also **bras·sart** (bras′ərt). [< F < *bras* arm]
brass band *Music* A band using mostly brass instruments.
brass hat *Informal* A high-ranking military officer.
brass·ie (bras′ē, bräs′ē) *n.* A wooden golf club with a brass plate on the sole. Also **brass′y.**
bras·siere (brə·zir′) *n.* A woman's undergarment to support or shape the breasts. Also **bras·sière′.** [< F]
brass knuckles A metal device that fits over the knuckles of a closed fist, used in rough fighting: also called *knuckle-dusters.* Also **brass knucks** (nuks).
brass tacks *Informal* Basic facts; essentials: usu. in the phrase **to get** (or **come**) **down to brass tacks.**
brass·y (bras′ē, bräs′ē) *adj.* **brass·i·er, brass·i·est** **1.** Of or ornamented with brass. **2.** Like brass, as in sound or color. **3.** Cheap and showy. **4.** *Informal* Insolent; brazen. — — **brass′i·ly** *adv.* — **brass′i·ness** *n.*
brat (brat) *n.* A nasty child.
bra·va·do (brə·vä′dō) *n. pl.* **·does** or **·dos** Boastful defiance; affectation of bravery. [< Sp. < *bravo* brave]
brave (brāv) *adj.* **brav·er, brav·est** **1.** Having or showing courage; intrepid. **2.** Making a fine display; elegant. — *v.* **braved, brav·ing** *v.t.* **1.** To meet with courage and fortitude. **2.** To defy; challenge. — *n.* **1.** A man of courage. **2.** A North American Indian warrior. [< F < Ital. *bravo*] — **brave′ly** *adv.* — **brave′ness** *n.*
brav·er·y (brā′vər·ē) *n. pl.* **·er·ies** **1.** The quality of being brave; valor; heroism. **2.** Elegance of attire; show; splendor.
bra·vo (brä′vō) *interj.* Good! well done! — *n. pl.* **·vos** A shout of "bravo!" [< Ital.]
bra·vu·ra (brə·vyŏŏr′ə, *Ital.* brä·vōō′rä) *n.* **1.** *Music* A passage requiring dashing and brilliant execution; also, a brilliant style of execution. **2.** Any brilliant or daring performance. [< Ital., dash, daring < *bravo.*]
brawl (brôl) *n.* **1.** A noisy quarrel; fight. **2.** *U.S. Slang* An uproarious party. — *v.i.* **1.** To quarrel noisily; fight. **2.** To move noisily, as water. [ME *braulen*, ? < LG] — **brawl′er** *n.* — **brawl′ing·ly** *adv.*
brawn (brôn) *n.* **1.** Firm or well-developed muscles. **2.** Muscular power. [< OF *braon* slice of flesh, ult. < Gmc.]
brawn·y (brô′nē) *adj.* **brawn·i·er, brawn·i·est** Muscular; strong. — **brawn′i·ness** *n.*
bray (brā) *v.i.* **1.** To utter a loud, harsh cry, as an ass. **2.** To sound harshly, as a trumpet. — *v.t.* **3.** To utter loudly and harshly. — *n.* **1.** The cry of an ass, mule, etc. **2.** Any loud, harsh sound. [< OF *braire* to cry out] — **bray′er** *n.*
braze[1] (brāz) *v.t.* **brazed, braz·ing** **1.** To make of brass. **2.** To make like brass in hardness or appearance. **3.** To ornament with or as with brass. [OE < *bræs* brass]
braze[2] (brāz) *v.t.* **brazed, braz·ing** *Metall.* To join the surfaces of (similar or dissimilar metals) with a layer of a soldering alloy applied under very high temperature. [< F *braser* solder < OF, burn, ult. < Gmc.] — **braz′er** *n.*
bra·zen (brā′zən) *adj.* **1.** Made of brass. **2.** Resembling brass in hardness, color, etc. **3.** Impudent; shameless. — *v.t.* **1.** To face with effrontery or impudence: with *out.* **2.** To make bold or reckless. [OE < *bræs* brass] — **bra′zen·ly** *adv.* — **bra′zen·ness** *n.*
bra·zen·face (brā′zən·fās′) *n.* An impudent, shameless person. — **bra′zen·faced′** *adj.*
bra zier[1] (brā′zhər) *n.* A worker in brass. [ME *brasiere*]
bra·zier[2] (brā′zhər) *n.* An open pan for holding live coals: also spelled *brasier.* [< F < *braise* hot coals]
Bra·zil·ian (brə·zil′yən) *adj* Of or pertaining to Brazil or its people. — *n.* A citizen or native of Brazil.
Brazil nut The edible seed of a South American tree.
breach (brēch) *n.* **1.** The act of breaking, or the state of being broken; infraction. **2.** Violation of a legal obligation, promise, etc. **3.** A gap or break in a dike, wall, etc. **4.** A breaking up of friendly relations; estrangement. — *v.t.* To break through. [OE *bryce*]
bread (bred) *n.* **1.** A food made with flour or meal, commonly leavened with yeast and baked. **2.** Food in general. **3.** The necessities of life. — *v.t.* To roll in bread crumbs before cooking. [OE *brēad* bit, crumb] — **bread′ed** *adj.*
bread-and-but·ter (bred′n-but′ər) *adj.* Expressing gratitude for hospitality: a *bread-and-butter* letter.
bread and butter *Informal* Subsistence; livelihood.
bread·bas·ket (bred′bas′kit, -bäs′-) *n. Slang* The stomach.
bread·fruit (bred′frōōt′) *n.* **1.** The fruit of a tree native to the South Sea Islands. **2.** The tree.

bread line A line of persons waiting to be given bread or other food as charity.
bread·stuff (bred′stuf′) *n.* **1.** Material for bread; grain, meal, or flour. **2.** Bread.
breadth (bredth, bretth) *n.* **1.** Measure or distance from side to side, as distinguished from length and thickness; width. **2.** Freedom from narrowness; liberality. **3.** That which is measured by its width, or which has a definite width: a *breadth* of cloth. [OE < *brād* broad]
breadth·wise (bredth′wīz′, bretth′-) *adv.* In the direction of the breadth. Also **breadth′ways′** (-wāz′).
bread·win·ner (bred′win′ər) *n.* One who supports himself and others by his earnings.
break (brāk) *v.* **broke** (*Archaic* **brake**), **bro·ken** (*Archaic* **broke**), **break·ing** *v.t.* **1.** To separate into pieces or fragments, as by a blow; shatter. **2.** To crack. **3.** To part the surface of; pierce: to *break* ground. **4.** To burst or cause to discharge, as an abscess. **5.** To disable; render useless. **6.** To destroy the order, continuity, or completeness of: to *break* ranks. **7.** To diminish the force or effect of: to *break* a fall. **8.** To overcome by opposing; end: to *break* a strike. **9.** To interrupt the course of, as a journey. **10.** To violate: to *break* one's promise. **11.** To reduce in spirit or health, as by toil. **12.** To tame, as a horse. **13.** To demote. **14.** To give or obtain smaller units for: to *break* a dollar. **15.** To make bankrupt or short of money. **16.** To force (a way), as through a barrier. **17.** To escape from. **18.** To surpass; excel: to *break* a record. **19.** To make known; tell, as news. **20.** To cause to discontinue a habit. **21.** *Law* To invalidate (a will) by court action. — *v.i.* **22.** To become separated into pieces or fragments. **23.** To give way; become unusable: His pencil *broke.* **24.** To dissolve and disperse: The clouds *broke.* **25.** To come into being or evidence: The storm *broke* suddenly. **26.** To appear above the surface. **27.** To start or move suddenly: He *broke* from the crowd. **28.** To become overwhelmed with grief: His heart *broke.* **29.** To fall off abruptly: The fever *broke.* **30.** To change tone, as a boy's voice. **31.** In baseball, to curve at or near the plate: said of a pitch. — **to break bread** To take or share a meal. — **to break down 1.** To undergo mechanical failure. **2.** To suffer physical or mental collapse. **3.** To yield, especially to grief or strong feelings. **4.** To cause to yield. **5.** To analyze or be analyzed. **6.** To decompose. — **to break in** To cause to obey; train; adapt. — **to break into** (or **in**) **1.** To interrupt or intervene. **2.** To enter by force. — **to break in on** (or **upon**) To interrupt. — **to break off 1.** To stop or cease, as from speaking. **2.** To sever (relations); discontinue. **3.** To become separate or detached. — **to break out 1.** To start unexpectedly or suddenly, as a fire or plague. **2.** To have an eruption or rash, as the skin. **3.** To escape, as from prison. — **to break out into** (or **forth in, into,** etc.) To begin to do or perform: The birds *broke out into song.* — **to break up 1.** To disperse; scatter: The meeting *broke up.* **2.** To dismantle. **3.** To put an end to. **4.** *Informal* To distress: The loss *broke up* the old man. **5.** *Informal* To sever relations. — **to break with** To sever relations with. — *n.* **1.** The act or result of breaking; fracture; rupture. **2.** A starting or opening: the *break* of day. **3.** *U.S.* A dash or run; especially, an attempt to escape: to make a *break* for the door. **4.** A breach of continuity, as a pause from work or an interruption in a discourse. **5.** *U.S. Informal* A chance or opportunity. **6.** *Electr.* The opening of a circuit; interruption of current. **7.** A rupture in friendship; quarrel. **8.** In prosody, a caesura. **9.** A sudden decline, as in prices, temperature, etc. **10.** *Music* **a** The point where one register or quality of a voice changes to another in singing. **b** In jazz, a syncopated cadenza bridging two phrases or choruses. **11.** In baseball or cricket, the swerving of a ball from a straight course when thrown. — **break′a·ble** *adj.* — **break′a·ble·ness** *n.*
break·age (brā′kij) *n.* **1.** A breaking, or being broken. **2.** Articles broken. **3.** Compensation for articles broken.
break·down (brāk′doun′) *n.* **1.** A collapse or failure, as of a machine, one's health, etc. **2.** An analysis or summary.
break·er (brā′kər) *n.* **1.** One who or that which breaks. **2.** A wave of the sea that breaks on rocks, a reef, etc.
break·fast (brek′fəst) *n.* The morning meal. — *v.t.* **1.** To furnish with a breakfast. — *v.i.* **2.** To eat breakfast.
break·neck (brāk′nek′) *adj.* Likely to break the neck; dangrous: *breakneck* speed.
break·through (brāk′thrōō′) *n.* **1.** *Mil.* An attack that penetrates through an enemy's defenses into the rear area. **2.** Any sudden, important success, as in scientific research.
break·up (brāk′up′) *n.* **1.** A breaking up or separation; dissolution; disruption. **2.** An ending.
break·wa·ter (brāk′wô′tər, -wot′ər) *n.* A barrier for protecting a harbor or beach from the force of waves.
bream (brēm) *n. pl.* **breams** or **bream 1.** Any of several fresh-water fishes with deep, compressed bodies. **2.** Any of various fresh-water sunfishes. [OF *bresme*]
breast (brest) *n.* **1.** *Anat.* The front of the chest from the neck to the abdomen. **2.** One of the mammary glands. That part of a garment that covers the breast. **4.** T breast as the seat of the emotions. **5.** Anything likened the human or animal breast. — **to make a clean breas** To confess. — *v.t.* To meet boldly. [OE *brēost*]
breast·bone (brest′bōn′) *n. Anat.* The sternum.
breast-feed (brest′fēd′) *v.t. & v.i.* **-fed, -feed·ing** To suc
breast·pin (brest′pin′) *n.* A pin worn at the breast.
breast·plate (brest′plāt′) *n.* Plate armor for the breast.
breast stroke In swimming, a stroke made by thrusting arms forward simultaneously from the breast.
breast·work (brest′wûrk′) *n.* A low, temporary defens work, usu. breast-high.
breath (breth) *n.* **1.** Air inhaled and exhaled in respirati **2.** Power or ability to breathe. **3.** The act of breathi also, life; existence: while *breath* remains. **4.** A single re ration. **5.** The time of a single respiration; instant. **6** slight delay. **7.** A slight movement of air. **8.** Anyth slight; trifle. **9.** A murmur; whisper. **10.** Moisture fr exhaled air, when visible in cold air. **11.** *Phonet.* An exh tion of air without vibration of the vocal cords, as in the p duction of (p) and (f). — **in the same breath** At the sa moment; without a pause or break. — **out of breath** Brea less; gasping. — **to take one's breath away** To awe produce sudden emotion in. — **under one's breath** I whisper or mutter. [OE *brǣth* vapor, odor]
breathe (brēth) *v.* **breathed** (brēthd), **breath·ing** *v.i.* To inhale and exhale air. **2.** To be alive; live. **3.** To pa for breath; rest. **4.** To murmur; whisper. **5.** To m gently, as breezes. **6.** To be exhaled, as fragrance. — **7.** To inhale and expel from the lungs, as air; respire. **8.** inject or infuse: to *breathe* life into a statue. **9.** To expr manifest: to *breathe* confidence. **10.** To exhale. **11.** To low a rest to, as for breath. **12.** *Phonet.* To utter with breath only. [ME *breth* breath] — **breath′a·ble** *adj.*
breath·er (brē′thər) *n. Informal* A brief rest period.
breath·ing (brē′thing) *adj.* Respiring; living. — *n.* **1.** T act of respiration; also, a single breath. **2.** A gentle bre **3.** Words spoken; utterance. **4.** Aspiration; longing. Time to breathe. **6.** *Phonet.* An aspiration; aspirate.
breath·less (breth′lis) *adj.* **1.** Out of breath. **2.** Hold the breath from fear, excitement, etc. **3.** That takes breath away: *breathless* speed. **4.** Devoid of breath; de **5.** Motionless. — **breath′less·ly** *adv.* — **breath′less·nes**
breath·tak·ing (breth′tā′king) *adj.* Thrilling; overawi
breath·y (breth′ē) *adj.* Characterized by audible breathi
brec·ci·a (brech′ē·ə, bresh′-) *n. Geol.* A rock made up angular fragments. [< Ital., grave] — **brec·ci·at** (brech′ē·ā′tid, bresh′-) *adj.*
bred (bred) Past tense and past participle of BREED.
breech (brēch; *for v. def. 1, also* brich) *n.* **1.** The poster and lower part of the body; the buttocks. **2.** The part gun, cannon, etc., that is behind the bore or barrel. **3.** T lower part of something, as of a pulley. — *v.t.* **1.** To clo with breeches. **2.** To provide with a breech. [OE *brēc*]
breech·cloth (brēch′klôth′, -kloth′) *n.* A loincloth. A **breech′clout′** (-klout′).
breech·es (brich′iz) *n.pl.* **1.** A man's garment covering hips and thighs. **2.** Trousers. [OE *brēc*]
breeches buoy *Naut.* A lifesaving apparatus consisting canvas breeches attached to a life buoy and run on a rope from one vessel to another or to the shore.

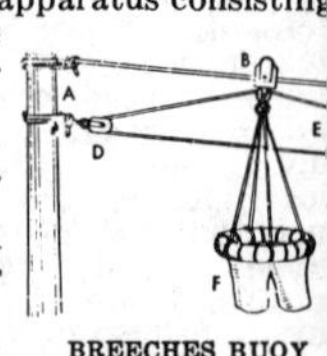

BREECHES BUOY
A Mast. *B* Traveli block. *C* Hawser. *I* Fixed block. *E* Ha ing line. *F* Breeche buoy.

breech·ing (brich′ing, brē′ching) *n.* A harness strap passing behind a horse's haunches.
breech·load·er (brēch′lō′dər) *n.* A firearm loaded at the breech. — **breech′load′ing** *adj.*
breed (brēd) *v.* **bred, breed·ing** *v.t.* **1.** To produce (offspring). **2.** To cause: Familarity *breeds* contempt. **3.** To raise: to *breed* horses. **4.** To bring up; train. — *v.i.* **5.** To procreate. **6.** To originate or be caused: Militarism *breeds* in armies. — *n.* **1.** A race or strain of animals. **2.** A sort or kind. [OE *b* brood] — **breed′er** *n.*
breed·ing (brē′ding) *n.* **1.** The act of bearing young. The rearing of the young. **3.** Good manners. **4.** The sci tific production of improved varieties of plants, animals, e
breeze (brēz) *n.* **1.** *Meteorol.* A moderate current of air gentle wind. **2.** *Brit. Informal* A flutter of excitement. **in a breeze** *Slang* Without difficulty; easily. — *v.i.* **breez breez·ing** *Slang* To go quickly and blithely. [< Sp. and *brisa, briza* northeast wind]
breeze·way (brēz′wā′) *n.* A roofed, open passageway tween two structures, as a house and garage.
breez·y (brē′zē) *adj.* **breez·i·er, breez·i·est 1.** Hav breezes; windy. **2.** Brisk or carefree; sprightly. — **breez i·ly** *adv.* — **breez′i·ness** *n.*

eth·ren (breth′rən) *n.pl.* **1.** Brothers. **2.** Members of a ·otherhood. [ME]

·et·on (bret′n) *adj.* Of or pertaining to Brittany, its in-ıbitants, or their language. **—** *n.* **1.** A native of Brittany. . The Celtic language of the Bretons.

eve (brev, brēv) *n.* **1.** A mark (˘) placed over a vowel to dicate that it has a short sound, as *a* in *hat.* **2.** In prosody, similar mark (⌣) indicating a short or unstressed syllable. . *Music* A note equivalent to two whole notes, or the sym-ɔl for it. [< Ital. < L *brevis* short]

ə·vet (brə·vet′, *esp. Brit.* brev′it) *n. Mil.* A commission łvancing an officer in honorary rank without advance in ıy or in command. **—** *v.t.* **bre·vet·ted** (brə·vet′id) or **brev·-ed** (brev′it·id), **bre·vet·ting** (brə·vet′ing) or **brev·et·ing** ·rev′it·ing) To raise in rank by brevet. **—** *adj.* Held or ·nferred by brevet. [< OF *bref* letter, document] **— bre·ət·cy** (brə·vet′sē) *n.*

evi- *combining form* Short. [< L *brevis* short]

ə·vi·ar·y (brē′vē·er′ē, brev′ē-) *n. pl.* **·ar·ies** *Eccl.* In the oman Catholic and Eastern Orthodox churches, a book of ıily prayers for the canonical hours. [< L *brevis* short]

ə·vier (brə·vir′) *n. Printing* A size of type, about 8-point. ′ < G, breviary; because once used in breviaries]

ev·i·ty (brev′ə·tē) *n.* **1.** Shortness of time. **2.** Condensa-on of language; conciseness. [< L *brevis* short]

ew (brōō) *v.t.* **1.** To make, as beer or ale, by steeping, ɔiling, and fermenting malt, hops, etc. **2.** To prepare (any ɘverage) as by boiling or mixing. **3.** To plot; devise. **—** *i.* **4.** To make ale, beer, or the like. **5.** To commence to rm, as a storm. **—** *n.* **1.** Something brewed. **2.** The nount brewed. [OE *brēowan*] **— brew′er** *n.*

ew·er·y (brōō′ər·ē) *n. pl.* **·er·ies** An establishment for ·ewing; also, the apparatus used in brewing.

əw·ing (brōō′ing) *n.* **1.** The process of making a brew. . The amount brewed at one time.

i·ar (brī′ər) See BRIER.

i·ar·root (brī′ər·rōōt′, -rŏŏt′) See BRIERROOT.

i·ar·wood (brī′ər·wŏŏd′) *n.* Brierroot.

ibe (brīb) *n.* **1.** Any gift or emolument used corruptly to fluence a person. **2.** Anything that seduces or allures. **— bribed, brib·ing** *v.t.* **1.** To offer or give a bribe to. **2.** To ıin or influence by means of bribery. **—** *v.i.* **3.** To give ·ibes. [< OF, piece of bread given a beggar] **— brib′a·e** *adj.* **— brib′er** *n.*

ib·er·y (brī′bər·ē) *n. pl.* **·er·ies** The giving, offering, or ɛcepting of a bribe.

ic-a-brac (brik′ə·brak) *n.* Small objects of curiosity or ɘcoration; antiques; knickknacks. [< F]

ick (brik) *n.* **1.** A molded block of clay, baked in various ıapes and sizes, used for building, etc. **2.** Bricks collective-. **3.** Any object shaped like a brick. **4.** *Informal* An ad-irable fellow. **—** *v.t.* **1.** To build or line with bricks. **2.** o cover with bricks: with *up* or *in.* **—** *adj.* **1.** Of brick. . Brick-red. [< MF *brique* fragment]

ick·bat (brik′bat′) *n.* **1.** A piece of a brick, esp. when ʒed as a missile. **2.** *Informal* An insulting remark.

ick·kiln (brik′kil′, -kiln′) *n.* A structure in which bricks ·e burned or baked.

ick·lay·er (brik′lā′ər) *n.* One who builds with bricks. **— rick′lay′ing** *n.*

ick red. Dull yellowish or brownish red.

ick·work (brik′wûrk′) *n.* Construction of or with bricks.

ick·yard (brik′yärd′) *n.* A place where bricks are made.

i·dal (brīd′l) *adj.* Pertaining to a bride or a wedding; ɪptial. **—** *n.* A wedding. [OE *brȳdealo* wedding feast]

idal wreath A flowering shrub of the rose family, with nall white flowers.

ide (brīd), *n.* A newly married woman, or a woman about be married. [OE *brȳd*]

ide·groom (brīd′grōōm′, -grŏŏm′) *n.* A man newly mar-ed or about to be married. [OE < *brȳd* bride + *guma* man]

ides·maid (brīdz′mād′) *n.* A young, usu. unmarried oman who attends a bride at her wedding.

idge[1] (brij) *n.* **1.** A structure erected across a waterway, .vine, road, etc., to afford passage. **2.** An observation atform built athwart the forward part of a ship for the ficers, pilot, etc. **3.** The upper bony ridge of the nose. **4.** he central part of a pair of spectacles that rests on the nose. . In some string instruments, a thin piece of wood that .ises the strings above the soundboard. For illus. see VIO-ɪN. **6.** *Music* A transitional passage connecting two sec-ons of a composition. **7.** *Dent.* A mounting for false teeth, ɪtached on each side to a natural tooth. **— to burn one's ridges (behind one)** To cut off all means of retreat. **—** *v.t.* **ridged, bridg·ing 1.** To construct a bridge or bridges over. . To make a passage over. [OE *brycg*] **— bridge′a·ble** *adj.*

idge[2] (brij) *n.* A card game, derived from whist, in which ıe trump suit (or the fact that there will be no trumps) is determined by the side proposing to take the higher number of tricks. See AUCTION BRIDGE, CONTRACT BRIDGE.

bridge·head (brij′hed′) *n. Mil.* A position on the hostile side of a river or defile, established by advance troops.

bridge·work (brij′wûrk′) *n.* **1.** *Dent.* A dental bridge. **2.** The construction of bridges.

bri·dle (brīd′l) *n.* **1.** The head harness, including bit and reins, used to guide or restrain a horse. **2.** Anything that restrains or limits. **—** *v.* **·dled, ·dling** *v.t.* **1.** To put a bridle on. **2.** To check or control with or as with a bridle. **—** *v.i.* **3.** To raise the head and draw in the chin through resentment, pride, etc. [OE *brīdel*] **— bri′dler** *n.*

bridle path A path for saddle horses or pack animals only.

brief (brēf) *adj.* **1.** Short in time or extent; quickly ending. **2.** Of few words; concise. **3.** Curt or abrupt. **—** *n.* **1.** A short or abridged statement; summary. **2.** *Law* A memorandum of the material facts, points of law, precedents, etc., of a case. **3.** *pl.* Short underpants. **— in brief** In short; briefly. **— to hold a brief for** To be on the side of. **—** *v.t.* **1.** To make a summary of; epitomize. **2.** To give a briefing to. **3.** *Brit.* To inform by a legal brief. **4.** *Brit.* To retain as counsel. [< OF < L *brevis* short] **— brief′ly** *adv.* **— brief′ness** *n.*

brief·case (brēf′kās′) *n.* A flexible, rectangular case, usually of leather, for carrying documents, papers, books, etc.

brief·ing (brē′fing) *n.* A short lecture setting forth the details of an operation or procedure.

bri·er[1] (brī′ər) *n.* **1.** A prickly bush or shrub, esp. one of the rose family, as the sweetbrier. **2.** A growth of such prickly bushes. **3.** A thorny or prickly twig. Also spelled *briar.* [OE *brǣr, brēr*] **— bri′er·y** *adj.*

bri·er[2] (brī′ər) *n.* **1.** The tree heath of southern Europe. **2.** A pipe made of brierroot. [< F *bruyère* heath]

bri·er·root (brī′ər·rōōt′, -rŏŏt′) *n.* **1.** The root of the brier or tree heath, used in making tobacco pipes. **2.** A pipe made from this wood. Also **bri·er·wood** (brī′ər·wŏŏd′).

brig[1] (brig) *n. Naut.* A two-masted ship, square-rigged on both masts. [Short for BRIGANTINE]

brig[2] (brig) *n.* A place of confinement on shipboard. [Origin unknown]

bri·gade (bri·gād′) *n.* **1.** *Mil.* A unit of two or more groups or regiments. **2.** Any considerable body of persons more or less organized: a fire *brigade.* **—** *v.t.* **·gad·ed, ·gad·ing 1.** To form into a brigade. **2.** To classify or combine. [< MF < Ital. *brigare* to brawl, fight]

BRIG

brig·a·dier (brig′ə·dir′) *n.* **1.** *Mil.* A brigadier general. **2.** In the British, Canadian, and other Commonwealth armies, an office ranking next below a major general. See table at GRADE.

brigadier general *Mil.* An officer ranking next above a colonel and next below a major general. See table at GRADE.

brig·and (brig′ənd) *n.* A robber, esp. in a band of outlaws. [< MF < Ital. *brigare* to brawl, fight] **— brig′and·ish** *adj.*

brig·an·tine (brig′ən·tēn, -tīn) *n. Naut.* A two-masted vessel, square-rigged on the foremast, and fore-and-aft rigged on the mainmast: also called *hermaphrodite brig.* [< MF < Ital. *brigare* to fight]

bright (brīt) *adj.* **1.** Emitting or reflecting much light; full of light; shining. **2.** Of brilliant color; vivid. **3.** Glorious; illustrious. **4.** Having or showing high intelligence; quick-witted. **5.** Lively; vivacious. **6.** Hopeful; auspicious. **—** *adv.* In a bright manner; brightly. [OE *beorht, bryht*] **— bright·ly** *adv.* **— bright′ness** *n.*

bright·en (brīt′n) *v.t. & v.i.* To make or become bright or brighter. **— bright′en·er** *n.*

Bright's disease (brīts) A disease marked by degeneration of the kidneys and imperfect elimination of uric acid. [after Richard *Bright,* 1789–1858, English physician]

bril·liance (bril′yəns) *n.* **1.** Intense brightness or luster. **2.** Great talent or intellect. **3.** Excellence; preeminence. **4.** *Music* Clarity of sound; vivid tone. Also **bril′lian·cy.**

bril·liant (bril′yənt) *adj.* **1.** Sparkling or glowing with light; very bright. **2.** Splendid; illustrious. **3.** Having great intellect or talent. **4.** *Music* Clear; vivid; intense. **—** *n.* **1.** A diamond of the finest cut, having as many as 58 facets above and below the girdle. **2.** *Printing* A very small size of type, about 3½-point. [< F *briller* to sparkle] **— bril′liant·ly** *adv.* **— bril′liant·ness** *n.*

bril·lian·tine (bril′yən·tēn) *n.* An oily hairdressing. [< F]

brim (brim) *n.* **1.** The rim or upper edge of a cup, bowl, etc. **2.** A projecting rim, as of a hat. **3.** An edge or margin. **—** *v.t. & v.i.* **brimmed, brim·ming** To fill or be full to the brim. **— to brim over** To overflow. [OE *brim* seashore]

brim·ful (brim′fŏŏl′, brim′fŏŏl′) *adj.* Full to the brim.

ONUNCIATION KEY: **add, āce, câre, pälm; end, ēven; it, īce; odd, ōpen, ôrder; tŏŏk, pōōl; up, bûrn; ə** = a in *above,* e in *sicken,* i in *flex-*, o in *melon,* u in *focus;* **yōō** = u in *fuse;* **oil; pout; check; go; ring; thin; this; zh,** vision.

brim·stone (brim′stōn′) *n.* Sulfur. [OE *bryn-* burning + *stān* stone] —**brim′ston′y** *adj.*
brin·dle (brin′dəl) *adj.* Brindled. —*n.* A brindled color, or a brindled animal.
brin·dled (brin′dəld) *adj.* Tawny or grayish with irregular streaks or spots; barred; streaked.
brine (brīn) *n.* **1.** Water saturated with salt. **2.** The water of the sea; the ocean. —*v.t.* **brined, brin·ing** To treat with or steep in brine. [OE *brȳne*] —**brin′ish** *adj.*
bring (bring) *v.t.* **brought, bring·ing 1.** To convey or cause (a person or thing) to come with oneself to or toward a place. **2.** To cause to come about; involve as a consequence: War *brings* destruction. **3.** To introduce into the mind. **4.** To cause (a person or oneself) to adopt or admit, as a course of action. **5.** To sell for: The house *brought* a good price. **6.** *Law* **a** To prefer, as a charge. **b** To institute: to *bring* suit. **c** To set forth, as evidence or an argument. —**to bring about 1.** To accomplish; cause to happen. **2.** *Naut.* To reverse; turn, as a ship. —**to bring around** (or **round**) **1.** To cause to adopt or admit, as an opinion. **2.** To revive; restore to consciousness. —**to bring down the house** To evoke wild applause. —**to bring forth 1.** To give birth or produce. **2.** To give rise to. —**to bring forward 1.** To adduce, as an argument. **2.** In bookkeeping, to carry, as a sum, from one page or column to another. —**to bring in 1.** To import. **2.** To render or submit (a verdict). **3.** To yield or produce, as profits. —**to bring off** To do successfully. —**to bring on 1.** To cause; lead to. **2.** To produce; cause to appear: *Bring on* the actors. —**to bring out 1.** To reveal; cause to be evident. **2.** To publish or produce. **3.** To introduce, as a young girl to society. —**to bring to 1.** To revive; restore to consciousness. **2.** *Naut.* To cause (a ship) to come up into the wind and lie to. —**to bring up 1.** To rear; educate. **2.** To suggest or call attention to, as a subject. **3.** To cough or vomit up. [OE *bringan*]
bring·ing-up (bring′ing·up′) *n.* Care, training, and education of a person in childhood; upbringing.
brink (bringk) *n.* **1.** The edge or verge, as of a steep place. **2.** The shore of a river, etc. [ME < Scand.]
brink·man·ship (bringk′mən·ship) *n.* The willingness to take major risks in order to achieve some end. [< BRINK + *manship,* on analogy with *showmanship,* etc.]
brin·y (brī′nē) *adj.* **brin·i·er, brin·i·est** Of the nature of or like brine. —**the briny** *Slang* The sea. —**brin′i·ness** *n.*
bri·oche (brē′ōsh, -osh; *Fr.* brē·ôsh′) *n.* A soft roll. [< F]
bri·quette (bri·ket′) *n.* A block of compressed coal dust, used for fuel. Also **bri·quet′.** [< F *brique* brick]
brisk (brisk) *adj.* **1.** Moving, acting, or taking place quickly; lively; energetic. **2.** Sharp or stimulating. [Cf. F *brusque* abrupt, sudden] —**brisk′ly** *adv.* —**brisk′ness** *n.*
bris·ket (bris′kit) *n.* The breast of an animal, esp. of one used as food. [< OF *bruschet*]
bris·tle (bris′əl) *n.* **1.** One of the coarse, stiff hairs of swine, used in making brushes. **2.** Any similar hair. —*v.* **·tled, ·tling** *v.i.* **1.** To erect the bristles in anger or excitement. **2.** To show anger or irritation. **3.** To stand or become erect, like bristles. **4.** To be thickly set as if with bristles. —*v.t.* **5.** To erect as or like bristles. **6.** To ruffle or agitate. [ME < OE *byrst*] —**bris′tly** *adj.*
Bri·tan·ni·a (bri·tan′ē·ə, -tan′yə) **1.** The ancient Roman name for Great Britain. **2.** The British Empire.
Bri·tan·nic (bri·tan′ik) *adj.* British. [< L *Britannicus*]
Brit·i·cism (brit′ə·siz′əm) *n.* An idiom or turn of phrase peculiar to the British.
Brit·ish (brit′ish) *adj.* Pertaining to Great Britain or the United Kingdom. —*n.* **1.** The people of Great Britain or of the British Empire: preceded by *the.* **2.** British English. [OE *Bretisc* < *Bret* a Briton]
British America 1. Canada. **2.** British possessions in or adjacent to North America. Also **British North America.**
British Commonwealth of Nations A political association comprising the United Kingdom, Canada, Australia, New Zealand, Ghana, India, Pakistan, Ceylon, Malayasia, Nigeria, Nyasaland, Cyprus, Sierra Leone, Tanganyika, Trinidad, and Tobago, Jamaica, Uganda, Western Samoa, Kenya, and Zanzibar, and including the dependencies of member nations: officially *The Commonwealth.* Also *Commonwealth of Nations.*
British Empire The sovereign states under the British Crown, comprising those in the British Commonwealth of Nations with their dependencies.
Brit·ish·er (brit′ish·ər) *n.* A native or subject of Great Britain, esp. an Englishman.
British Isles Great Britain, Ireland, the Isle of Man, and the Channel Islands.
British thermal unit *Physics* The quantity of heat required to raise the temperature of one pound of water one degree Fahrenheit.
Brit·on (brit′n) *n.* **1.** A member of a Celtic people inhabiting ancient Britain, conquered by the Romans. **2.** A Britisher. [< OF < L *Britto* < Celtic]

brit·tle (brit′l) *adj.* Liable to break or snap; fragile. **Syn.** See FRAGILE. [ME *britil*] **brit′tle·ness** *n.*
broach (brōch) *v.t.* **1.** To mention or suggest for the f time; introduce. **2.** To pierce so as to withdraw a liqu —*n.* **1.** *Mech.* A pointed, tapering tool for boring; a rean **2.** A spit for roasting. [< OF < Med.L *brocca* spike, sp —**broach′er** *n.*
broad (brôd) *adj.* **1.** Extended from side to side; wide. Of great extent; vast or spacious. **3.** Fully diffused; o and clear: *broad* daylight. **4.** Of wide scope or applicati extensive. **5.** Liberal in spirit; tolerant. **6.** Not detail general. **7.** Obvious; clear: a *broad* hint. **8.** Vulgar and delicate; unrefined. **9.** Outspoken or unrestrained. Strongly dialectal: a *broad* pronunciation. **11.** *Pho* Formed with the oral passage open wide and the tongue and flat, as the *a* in *calm.* —*n.* **1.** The broad part of a thing. **2.** *Slang* A woman or girl. —*adv.* Complete fully. [OE *brād*] —**broad′ly** *adv.* —**broad′ness** *n.*
broad·ax (brôd′aks′) *n.* An ax with a broad edge and a sh handle. Also **broad′axe′.**
broad·cast (brôd′kast′, -käst′) *v.* **·cast** or (*esp. for defs. 1* **·cast·ed, ·cast·ing** *v.t.* **1.** To send or transmit (music, ne casts, etc.) by radio or television. **2.** To scatter, as se over a wide area. **3.** To disseminate; make public. — **4.** To make a radio or television broadcast. —*n.* **1.** ' act of broadcasting. **2.** A radio or television program. *adj.* **1.** By or for radio or television transmission. **2.** S tered far and wide. —*adv.* So as to be scattered over a w area. —**broad′cast′er** *n.*
broad·cloth (brôd′klôth′, -kloth′) *n.* **1.** A fine woolen cl used for suits, skirts, etc. **2.** A closely woven fabric of s cotton, etc., used for shirts, dresses, etc.
broad·en (brôd′n) *v.t.* & *v.i.* To make or become broac
broad-gauge (brôd′gāj′) *adj.* Having a width of railr track greater than the standard gauge of 56½ inches. *A* **broad′gage′, broad′-gaged′, broad-gauged′.**
broad jump A jump or jumping contest for distance.
broad·loom (brôd′lōōm′) *n.* Carpet woven in widths from 6 to 18 feet. Also **broadloom carpet.**
broad-mind·ed (brôd′mīn′did) *adj.* Liberal and toler free from bigotry and prejudice. —**broad′-mind′ed·ly** —**broad′-mind′ed·ness** *n.*
broad·side (brôd′sīd′) *n.* **1.** All the guns on one side man-of-war, or their simultaneous discharge. **2.** A volle abuse or denunciation. **3.** *Naut.* A vessel's side above water line. **4.** A large sheet of paper, printed on one s also **broad′sheet′.** —*adv.* With the broadside exposed.
broad·sword (brôd′sôrd′, -sōrd′) *n.* A sword with a br cutting blade.
broad·tail (brôd′tāl′) *n.* The lustrous black fur obtai from lambs of the karakul sheep.
Broad·way (brôd′wā) A street in New York City, nc for its theatres and entertainment district.
bro·cade (brō·kād′) *n.* A rich fabric interwoven with a rai design, as in silken or gold or silver threads. —*v.t.* **·cad ·cad·ing** To weave (a cloth) with a raised design or fig [< Sp. < Med.L *broccare* to embroider]
broc·co·li (brok′ə·lē) *n.* A variety of cauliflower. [< It pl. of *broccolo* cabbage sprout]
bro·chure (brō·shŏŏr′) *n.* A pamphlet or similar publ tion. [< F, lit., a stitched book < *brocher* to stitch]
bro·gan (brō′gən) *n.* A coarse, heavy shoe. [< Irish *gan,* dim. of *brōg* shoe]
brogue[1] (brōg) *n.* An Irish accent in the pronunciatio English. [< Irish *barrōg* defect of speech]
brogue[2] (brōg) *n.* **1.** A heavy oxford shoe, decorated w perforations. **2.** A shoe of untanned hide worn formerl Ireland and the Scottish Highlands. [< Irish *brōg* a sh
broil[1] (broil) *v.t.* **1.** To cook, as meat, by subjecting to di heat. **2.** To expose to great heat; scorch. —*v.i.* **3.** T exposed to great heat; cook. —*n.* **1.** Something broi **2.** A broiling heat. [< OF *bruller, bruillir* to burn]
broil[2] (broil) *n.* A turmoil; noisy quarrel; brawl. —*v.i.* engage in a broil; brawl. [< F *brouiller* to confuse]
broil·er (broi′lər) *n.* **1.** A device for broiling. **2.** A you tender chicken suitable for broiling.
broke (brōk) Past tense and archaic past participle of BRE —*adj. Informal* Having no money; bankrupt.
bro·ken (brō′kən) Past participle of BREAK. —*adj.* **1.** F cibly separated into pieces; fractured. **2.** Violated; tra gressed: *broken* vows. **3.** Interrupted; disturbed. **4.** complete; fragmentary. **5.** Rough; uneven, as terrain. In disorder; scattered, as troops. **7.** Humbled; crushed. Weakened or infirm. **9.** Bankrupt. **10.** Trained in p cedure; adapted: often with *in.* **11.** Imperfectly spok disjointed. —**bro′ken·ly** *adv.* —**bro′ken·ness** *n.*
bro·ken-down (brō′kən·doun′) *adj.* **1.** Incapable of fu tioning; out of repair. **2.** Ruined; decayed.
bro·ken·heart·ed (brō′kən·här′tid) *adj.* Overwhelmed crushed in spirit, as by grief.
bro·ker (brō′kər) *n.* One who buys and sells for anot

ranges contracts, etc; esp., a stockbroker. [< AF < OF *ochier* to tap, broach (a wine cask)]
o·ker·age (brō′kər·ij) *n.* The business or commission of broker. Also **bro′kage.**
o·mide[1] (brō′mīd, -mid) *n. Chem.* A compound of bromine ith an element or an organic radical. Also **bro′mid** (-mid).
o·mide[2] (brō′mīd, -mid) *n. Informal* A platitude.
o·mid·ic (brō·mid′ik) *adj. Informal* Commonplace; trite.
o·mine (brō′mēn, -min) *n.* A dark reddish brown, nonetallic, fuming liquid element (symbol Br) with a suffocatg odor. Also **bro′min** (-min). See ELEMENT. [< F *brome* < Gk. *brōmos* stench) + -INE[2]]
omo- *combining form* Used to indicate bromine in chemil compounds. Also, before vowels, **brom-.**
on·chi (brong′kī) Plural of BRONCHUS.
on·chi·a (brong′kē·ə) *n.pl. Anat.* The bronchial tubes. < LL < Gk. *bronchia*]
on·chi·al (brong′kē·əl) *adj. Anat.* Of or pertaining to the ief air passages of the lungs.
onchial tube *Anat.* Any of the subdivisions of the traea conveying air into the lungs.
on·chi·tis (brong·kī′tis) *n. Pathol.* Inflammation of the onchial tubes. — **bron·chit·ic** (brong·kit′ik) *adj.*
oncho- *combining form* Windpipe. Also, before vowels, **onch-.** [< Gk. *bronchos*]
on·cho·scope (brong′kə·skōp) *n. Med.* An instrument for specting or treating the interior of the bronchi.
on·chus (brong′kəs) *n. pl.* **·chi** (-kī) *Anat.* One of the vo forked branches of the trachea. For illus. see LUNG. [< L < Gk. *bronchos* windpipe]
onco· (brong′kō) *n. pl.* **·cos** **1.** *U.S.* A small, wild or artly broken horse of the West. **2.** *Canadian* An Englishan. Also **bronc, bron′cho.** [< Sp. *bronco* rough]
on·co·bust·er (brong′kō·bus′tər) *n. U.S. Informal* One ho breaks a bronco to the saddle. Also **bron′cho·bust′er.**
on·to·sau·rus (bron′tə·sôr′əs) *n. pl.* **·rus·es** *Paleontol.* huge, herbivorous nosaur of the Jussic period. Also **on′to·saur.** [< Gk. *ontē* thunder + *saus* lizard]

BRONTOSAURUS
(To 70 feet long; about 20 tons)

onx cheer *U.S. ang* A noisy flutterg of the lips to show ntempt or derision: so called *raspberry, zzberry.*
onze (bronz) *n.* **1.** *Metall.* **a** A reddish brown alloy esntially of copper and tin. **b** A similar alloy of copper and me other metal, as aluminum. **2.** A pigment of the color bronze. **3.** A reddish brown color similar to bronze. **4.** A atue, bust, etc., done in bronze. — *v.* **bronzed, bronz·ing** *t.* **1.** To color like bronze. — *v.i.* **2.** To become brown or n. [< MF < Ital. *bronzo, bronzino*] — **bronz′y** *adj.*
onze Age *Archeol.* A stage of prehistory following the one Age and preceding the Iron Age, during which weapons id implements were made of bronze.
onze Star A U.S. military decoration, awarded for herom or exemplary conduct in ground combat.
ooch (brōch, broo͞ch) *n.* An ornamental pin with a clasp r wearing on the breast or shoulder. [Var. of BROACH]
ood (brood) *n.* **1.** The young of animals, esp. of birds, oduced at one time. **2.** All the young of the same mother. . Kind or species. — *v.i.* **1.** To meditate moodily and eply: usu. with *on* or *over.* **2.** To sit on eggs. — *v.t.* **3.** o sit upon or incubate (eggs). **4.** To protect (young) by vering with the wings. [OE *brōd*]
ood·er (broo͞′dər) *n.* **1.** A warmed structure for artificial· rearing young fowl. **2.** One who or that which broods.
ood·y (broo͞′dē) *adj.* **brood·i·er, brood·i·est 1.** Meditative; oody. **2.** Inclined to sit on eggs: said of hens.
ook[1] (bro͝ok) *n.* A natural stream, smaller than a river or eek; a rivulet. [OE *brōc*]
ook[2] (bro͝ok) *v.t.* To put up with; tolerate: usu. with the egative: I cannot *brook* such conduct. [OE *brūcan* to use]
ook·let (bro͝ok′lit) *n.* A little brook.
ook trout The speckled trout of eastern North America.
oom (bro͞om, bro͝om) *n.* **1.** A brush attached to a long andle for sweeping, formerly made from twigs of broom. . Any of various shrubs with yellow flowers and stiff green anches: also called *besom.* — *v.t.* To sweep. [OE *brōm*]
oom·corn (bro͞om′kôrn′, bro͝om′-) *n.* A canelike grass which brooms are made.
oom·stick (bro͞om′stik′, bro͝om′-) *n.* The handle of a oom.
oth (brôth, broth) *n.* A soup made by boiling meat, vegeables, etc., in water; a thin or strained soup. [OE]

broth·el (broth′əl, brot͟h′-, brôth′əl, brôt͟h′-) *n.* A house of prostitution. [ME, a worthless person]
broth·er (brut͟h′ər) *n. pl.* **broth·ers** (*Archaic* **breth·ren**) **1.** A male individual having the same parents as another or others of either sex. **2.** A kinsman, or one of the same tribe, etc. **3.** A fellow member, as of an organization. **4.** A comrade. **5.** One of a male religious order who is not a priest. — *v.t.* To treat or address as a brother. [OE *brōthor*]
broth·er·hood (brut͟h′ər·ho͝od) *n.* **1.** The relationship of or state of being brothers, esp. by blood. **2.** A society, fraternity, guild, etc. **3.** All the persons engaged in an enterprise, profession, etc.
broth·er-in-law (brut͟h′ər·in·lô′) *n. pl.* **broth·ers-in-law** **1.** A brother of one's husband or wife. **2.** The husband of one's sister. **3.** The husband of one's spouse's sister.
broth·er·ly (brut͟h′ər·lē) *adj.* Pertaining to or characteristic of a brother; fraternal; affectionate. — *adv.* As a brother; kindly. — **broth′er·li·ness** *n.*
brougham (bro͞om, bro͞o′əm, brō′əm) *n.* **1.** A closed, fourwheeled carriage having a high, uncovered driver's seat. **2.** A limousine with the driver's seat outside. [after Lord Henry *Brougham,* 1778–1868, British statesman]
brought (brôt) Past tense and past participle of BRING.
brow (brou) *n.* **1.** The front upper part of the head; forehead. **2.** The eyebrow. **3.** The countenance in general. **4.** The upper edge of a steep place: the *brow* of a hill. [OE *brū*]
brow·beat (brou′bēt′) *v.t.* **·beat, ·beat·en, ·beat·ing** To intimidate; bully.
brown (broun) *adj.* **1.** Of a dark color combining red, yellow, and black. **2.** Dark-complexioned; tanned. — **to do up brown** *Informal* To do thoroughly. — *n.* **1.** A brown color. **2.** A brown pigment or dye. — *v.t. & v.i.* To make or become brown. [OE *brūn*] — **brown′ness** *n.*
brown bear **1.** The black bear. **2.** One of several very large bears of North America and Europe, with fur varying from yellowish to dark brown.
brown Bet·ty (bet′ē) Baked pudding made of bread crumbs, apples, sugar, and spices. Also **brown bet′ty.**
brown bread Any bread made of a dark-colored flour.
Brown·i·an movement (brou′nē·ən) *Physics* The rapid oscillatory movement of small particles when suspended in fluids. Also **Brownian motion.** [after Robert *Brown,* 1773–1858, Scottish botanist, who discovered it]
brown·ie (brou′nē) *n.* **1.** In folklore, a goblin or sprite, supposed to do useful work at night. **2.** *U.S.* A small, flat chocolate cake with nuts. [< BROWN; from its color]
Brown·ie (brou′nē) *n.* A junior girl scout of the age group seven through nine.
brown·out (broun′out′) *n.* A partial diminishing of lights either as a defensive measure or to save fuel.
brown rice Unpolished rice grains.
Brown Shirt **1.** A storm trooper. **2.** A Nazi.
brown·stone (broun′stōn′) *n.* A brownish red sandstone used for building; also, a house with a front of brownstone.
brown study A state of absent-mindedness; reverie.
brown sugar Sugar that is unrefined or partly refined.
browse (brouz) *v.* **browsed, brows·ing** *v.i.* **1.** To feed on leaves, shoots, etc. **2.** To glance through a book or books or look over merchandise casually. — *v.t.* **3.** To nibble at; crop; also, to graze on. — *n.* Growing shoots or twigs used as fodder. [< MF *broust* bud, sprout] — **brows′er** *n.*
bru·cel·lo·sis (bro͞o′sə·lō′sis) *n. Pathol.* Undulant fever. [after Sir David *Bruce,* 1855–1931, English physician]
bru·in (bro͞o′in) *n.* A bear; esp., a brown bear. [< MDu.]
bruise (bro͞oz) *v.* **bruised, bruis·ing** *v.t.* **1.** To injure, as by a blow, without breaking the surface of the skin; contuse. **2.** To dent or mar the surface of. **3.** To hurt or offend slightly, as feelings. **4.** To crush; pound small, as in a mortar. — *v.i.* **5.** To become discolored as from a blow. — *n.* An injury caused by bruising; contusion. [Fusion of OE *brȳsan* to crush and OF *bruisier* to break, shatter]
bruis·er (bro͞o′zər) *n.* **1.** A professional boxer. **2.** *Informal* A bully.
bruit (bro͞ot) *v.t.* To noise abroad; talk about: usu. in the passive. [< F < *bruire* to roar, ? < L *rugire*] — **bruit′er** *n.*
brunch (brunch) *n. U.S. Informal* A late morning meal combining breakfast and lunch. [< BR(EAKFAST) + (L)UNCH]
bru·net (bro͞o·net′) *adj.* Dark-hued; having dark complexion, hair, and eyes. — *n.* A brunet man or boy. [< F]
bru·nette (bro͞o·net′) *adj.* Brunet: feminine form. — *n.* A brunette woman or girl. [< F]
Brun·hild (bro͞on′hild, *Ger.* bro͞on′hilt) In the *Nibelungenlied,* a queen of Iceland. Compare BRÜNNHILDE.
Brünn·hil·de (brün·hil′də) In Wagner's *Ring of the Nibelung,* a Valkyrie put in a trance and encircled by flames, but eventually released by Siegfried.
brunt (brunt) *n.* The main force or strain of a blow, attack, etc. [? < ON *bruna* to advance quickly, as a fire]

brush[1] (brush) *n.* **1.** An implement having bristles, wires, or other flexible fibrous material, fixed in a handle or a back, and used for sweeping, painting, smoothing the hair, etc. **2.** The act of brushing. **3.** A light, grazing touch. **4.** A brief encounter, esp. a skirmish. **5.** Brushwork. **6.** *Electr.* A conductor, resting on the commutator cylinder of a dynamo, for carrying off the current or for an external current through a motor. **—*v.t.* 1.** To use a brush on; sweep, paint, etc., with a brush. **2.** To remove with or as with a brush. **3.** To touch lightly in passing. **—*v.i.* 4.** To move lightly and quickly. **—to brush aside** To deny consideration to. **—to brush off** *U.S. Slang* To dismiss or refuse abruptly. **—to brush up 1.** To refresh one's knowledge of. **2.** To renovate. [< OF *brosse,* ? < Gmc.]

brush[2] (brush) *n.* **1.** A growth of small trees and shrubs. **2.** Wooded country sparsely settled; backwoods. **3.** Brushwood. [< OF *broche, brosse,* ? < Gmc.] **—brush′y** *adj.*

brush·off (brush′ôf′, -of′) *n. U.S. Slang* An abrupt refusal or dismissal.

brush·wood (brush′wo͝od′) *n.* **1.** Bushes or branches cut or broken off. **2.** A thicket of small trees or shrubs.

brusque (brusk, *esp. Brit.* bro͝osk) *adj.* Rude or curt; blunt. Also **brusk. —Syn.** See BLUNT. [< MF < Ital. *brusco* rude, rough] **—brusque′ly** *adv.* **—brusque′ness** *n.*

Brussels sprouts 1. A variety of cabbage having stems covered with heads like little cabbages. **2.** The small, edible heads of this plant.

brut (brüt, bro͞ot) *adj.* Dry: said of wines, esp. champagne. [< F, lit., rough < L *brutus*]

bru·tal (bro͞ot′l) *adj.* **1.** Characteristic of or like a brute; cruel; savage. **2.** Unfeeling; rude; coarse. [< L *brutus* stupid, rough] **—bru′tal·ly** *adv.*

bru·tal·i·ty (bro͞o·tal′ə·tē) *n. pl.* **·ties 1.** The state or quality of being brutal; cruelty. **2.** A brutal act.

bru·tal·ize (bro͞ot′l·īz) *v.t. & v.i.* **·ized, ·iz·ing** To make or become brutal. **—bru′tal·i·za′tion** *n.*

brute (bro͞ot) *n.* **1.** Any animal other than man. **2.** A brutal person. **—*adj.* 1.** Incapable of reasoning; merely animal. **2.** Like a brute or animal; unintelligent. **3.** Dominated by appetite; gross; sensual. [< F < L *brutus* stupid]

bru·ti·fy (bro͞o′tə·fī) *v.t. & v.i.* **·fied, ·fy·ing** To brutalize.

brut·ish (bro͞o′tish) *adj.* Of, relating to, or charactistic of a brute or brutes; stupid; gross; sensual. **—brut′ish·ly** *adv.* **—brut′ish·ness, brut′ism** *n.*

Bryn·hild (brün′hilt) In the *Volsunga Saga,* a Valkyrie awakened by Sigurd from an enchanted sleep. Compare BRUNHILD, BRÜNNHILDE.

bry·ol·o·gy (brī·ol′ə·jē) *n.* The branch of botany that treats of mosses. [< Gk. *bryon* moss + -LOGY] **—bry·o·log·i·cal** (brī′ə·loj′i·kəl) *adj.* **—bry·ol′o·gist** *n.*

bry·o·ny (brī′ə·nē) *n.* A common English herb of the gourd family, with white or yellowish flowers. [< L < Gk. *bryōnia*]

bry·o·phyte (brī′ə·fīt) *n. Bot.* Any moss or liverwort. [< Gk. *bryon* moss + -PHYTE] **—bry′o·phyt′ic** (-fit′ik) *adj.*

Bry·thon·ic (bri·thon′ik) *n.* The branch of the Celtic languages that includes Welsh, Breton, and the extinct Cornish; Cymric: distinguished from *Goidelic.*

bub·ble (bub′əl) *n.* **1.** A liquid globule filled with air or other gas. **2.** A globule of air or other gas confined in a liquid or solid substance. **3.** Anything unsubstantial; a delusion; fraud. **4.** The process or sound of bubbling. **5.** A glass or plastic dome. **—*v.* ·bled, ·bling *v.i.* 1.** To form or emit bubbles; rise in bubbles. **2.** To move or flow with a gurgling sound. **3.** To express joy, delight, exultation, etc., in an irrepressible manner. **—*v.t.* 4.** To cause to bubble. [ME *buble*] **—bub′bly** *adj.*

bu·bo (byo͞o′bō) *n. pl.* **bu·boes** *Pathol.* An inflammatory swelling of a lymph gland in the groin or armpit. [< LL < Gk. *boubōn* groin] **—bu·bon·ic** (byo͞o·bon′ik) *adj.*

bubonic plague *Pathol.* A contagious, epidemic disease, usually fatal, characterized by fever and buboes and transmitted to man by fleas from infected rats.

buc·cal (buk′əl) *adj. Anat.* **1.** Of or pertaining to the cheek. **2.** Pertaining to the mouth. [< L *bucca* cheek]

buc·ca·neer (buk′ə·nir′) *n.* A pirate or freebooter, esp. one who preyed along the Spanish coasts of America. [< F < Tupi *boucan* a frame for smoking and curing meat]

buck[1] (buk) *n.* **1.** The male of certain animals, as of antelopes, deer, goats, rabbits, and rats. **2.** A dandy; fop. **3.** *Informal* A young man. **—*v.i.* 1.** To leap upward suddenly, as a horse or pack animal, in an attempt to dislodge rider or burden. **2.** *U.S. Informal* To resist stubbornly; object. **3.** *U.S. Informal* To move with jerks and jolts. **—*v.t.* 4.** To throw by bucking. **5.** *U.S. Dial.* To butt with the head. **6.** *U.S. Informal* To resist stubbornly; oppose. **7.** In football, to charge into (the opponent's line) with the ball. **—to buck for** *U.S. Slang* To try hard to obtain (a promotion, raise, etc.). **—to buck up** *Informal* To encourage or take courage. [OE *bucca* he-goat]

buck[2] (buk) *n.* **1.** A sawhorse. **2.** A padded frame like a sawhorse, used for vaulting, etc. [< Du. *zaagbok* sawbuck]

buck[3] (buk) *n.* In poker, a marker put into a jackp indicating that he who receives it must order another ja pot when it is his deal. **—to pass the buck** *U.S. Infor* To shift responsibility, blame, etc., to someone else.

buck and wing An intricate, fast tap dance.

buck·a·roo (buk′ə·ro͞o, buk′ə·ro͞o′) *n. U.S.* A cowb Also **buck·ay·ro** (buk·ā′rō). [Alter. of Sp. *vaquero* cowb

buck·board (buk′bôrd′, -bōrd′) *n.* A light, four-whee open carriage having a long, flexible board in place of b and springs.

buck·et (buk′it) *n.* **1.** A deep cylindrical vessel, wit rounded handle, used for carrying water, coal, etc.; a p **2.** As much as a bucket will hold: also **buck′et·ful′. —** *& v.i.* To draw or carry in a bucket. [? < OF *buket* t

buck·eye (buk′ī′) *n. Chiefly U.S.* **1.** The horse chestn **2.** The glossy brown seed or nut of this tree.

Buck·eye (buk′ī′) *n.* A native or inhabitant of Ohio.

Buckeye State Nickname of Ohio.

Buck·ing·ham Palace (buk′ing·əm) The official Lon residence of the British sovereign.

buck·le[1] (buk′əl) *n.* **1.** A device for fastening together loose ends, as of a strap. **2.** An ornament for shoes, e resembling a buckle. **—*v.* ·led, ·ling *v.t.* 1.** To fasten or tach with or as with a buckle. **—*v.i.* 2.** To be fastenec joined by a buckle. **—to buckle down** To apply one vigorously. [< F *boucle* cheekstrap, boss of a shield]

buck·le[2] (buk′əl) *v.t. & v.i.* **·led, ·ling** To bend under p sure; warp, curl, or crumple. **—*n.*** A bend, bulge, kink twist. [< F *boucler* to bulge]

buck·ler (buk′lər) *n.* **1.** A small, round shield. **2.** A me of defense. [< OF *boucler* having a boss]

buck·o (buk′ō) *n. pl.* **buck·oes** A bully.

buck private *U.S. Slang* A private in the U.S. Army.

buck·ram (buk′rəm) *n.* A coarse cotton fabric si with glue, used for stiffening garments, in bookbinding, **—*v.t.*** To stiffen with or as with buckram. [OF *boquer* coarse cloth < *Bokhara,* Persia, where first made]

buck·saw (buk′sô′) *n.* A wood-cutting saw set in an justable H-shaped frame.

buck·shot (buk′shot′) *n.* Shot of a large size, used in hu ing deer and other large game.

buck·skin (buk′skin′) *n.* **1.** The skin of a buck. **2** soft, strong, grayish yellow leather, formerly made fr deerskins, now chiefly from sheepskins. **3.** *pl.* Breeches clothing made of such skin.

buck·thorn (buk′thôrn′) *n.* A shrub or small tree hav veined leaves and axillary flowers.

buck·tooth (buk′to͞oth′) *n. pl.* **·teeth** A projecting to **—buck′toothed′** *adj.*

buck·wheat (buk′hwēt′) *n.* **1.** A plant yielding triangu seeds used as fodder and for flour. **2.** Its seeds. **3.** flour. [OE *bōc* beech + WHEAT]

bu·col·ic (byo͞o·kol′ik) *adj.* Pertaining to or characteri of shepherds or herdsmen; pastoral; rustic. **—Syn.** RURAL. **—*n.* 1.** A pastoral poem. **2.** A rustic; farn [< L < Gk. < *boukolos* herdsmen] **—bu·col′i·cal·ly** *ac*

bud (bud) *n.* **1.** *Bot.* **a** An undeveloped stem, branch, shoot of a plant, with rudimentary leaves or unexpan flowers. **b** The act or stage of budding. **2.** *Zool.* A budl projection or part, as in some lower animals. **3.** Any mature person or thing. **—to nip in the bud** To stop in initial stage. **—*v.* bud·ded, bud·ding *v.i.* 1.** To put fo buds. **2.** To begin to grow or develop. **—*v.t.* 3.** cause to bud. **4.** To graft to another type of tree or pla [ME *budde;* origin uncertain] **—bud′der** *n.*

Bud·dhism (bo͞od′iz·əm, bo͞o′diz-) *n.* A mystical and cetic religious faith of eastern Asia, founded in northern dia by Buddha in the sixth century B.C., and teaching t the ideal state of nirvana is reached by right living and lieving, and peace of mind through meditation. **—Bu dhist** *adj. & n.* **—Bud·dhis′tic** or **·ti·cal** *adj.*

bud·ding (bud′ing) *adj.* Just beginning; incipient.

bud·dy (bud′ē) *n. pl.* **·dies** *U.S. Informal* Pal; chum.

budge (buj) *v.t. & v.i.* **budged, budg·ing** To move or slightly. [< F *bouger* to stir, move]

budg·et (buj′it) *n.* **1.** A plan for adjusting expenditures income. **2.** A collection or stock. **—*v.t.* 1.** To determ in advance the expenditure of (time, money, etc.). **2.** provide for or plan according to a budget. [< F < L *bu* leather bag] **—budg·et·ar·y** (buj′ə·ter′ē) *adj.*

buff[1] (buf) *n.* **1.** A thick, soft, flexible leather made fr the skins of buffalo, elk, oxen, etc. **2.** Its color, a li brownish yellow. **3.** A military coat made of buff leath **4.** *Informal* The bare skin; the nude. **5.** A stick or wh covered with leather, velvet, etc., and used for polishi **—*adj.* 1.** Made of buff. **2.** Light, brownish yellow. **—** To clean or polish with or as with a buff. [< F *bu* buffalo] **—buff′y** *adj.*

buff[2] (buf) *v.t.* To deaden the shock of. **—*n.*** A blow; b fet: now only in *blindman's buff.* [< OF *buffe* blow]

buff[3] (buf) *n.* An enthusiast or devotee. [Origin uncerta

f·fa·lo (buf′ə·lō) *n. pl.* **·loes** or **·los** 1. Any of various rge Old World oxen, as the **Cape buffalo** Africa, and the water buffalo. 2. The orth American bison. —*v.t.* **·loed, ·lo·g** *U.S. Slang* To overawe; intimidate; odwink. [< Ital. < LL < Gk. *boubalos* iffalo]

CAPE BUFFALO (About 5 feet high at shoulder)

ffalo grass A low, creeping grass coverg prairies east of the Rocky Mountains.

ff·er[1] (buf′ər) *n.* One who or that which iffs or polishes. [< BUFF[1], v.]

ff·er[2] (buf′ər) *n.* 1. A shock absorber. One who or that which diminishes shock any kind.

ffer state A small country situated tween two larger rival powers and garded as lessening the danger of conct between them.

f·fet[1] (bo͞o·fā′, *Brit.* buf′it) *n.* 1. A sideboard for china, assware, etc. 2. A counter for serving meals or refreshents, or a restaurant with such a counter. 3. A light meal which the guests serve themselves. [< F]

f·fet[2] (buf′it) *v.t.* 1. To strike or cuff, as with the hand. To strike repeatedly; knock about. —*v.i.* 3. To fight; ruggle. —*n.* A blow or cuff, as with the hand. [< OF *ffet*, dim. of *buffe* a blow, slap] —**buf′fet·er** *n.*

f·foon (bu·fo͞on′) *n.* 1. A clown. 2. One given to jokes, arse pranks, etc. [< F < Ital. clown < *buffa* jest] —**f·foon′er·y** *n.* —**buf·foon′ish** *adj.*

g (bug) *n.* 1. Any crawling insect with sucking mouth rts, wingless or with two pairs of wings. 2. Loosely, any sect or small arthropod. 3. *Brit.* A bedbug. 4. *Informal* microorganism; germ. 5. *Slang* An enthusiast; monoaniac. 6. *U.S. Slang* A minor defect, as in a machine. *U.S. Slang* A miniature electronic microphone, used in retapping, etc. —*v.* **bugged, bug·ging** *v.i.* 1. To stare; ck out: said of eyes. —*v.t. U.S. Slang* 2. To annoy; ster. 3. To fit (a room, telephone circuit, etc.) with a ncealed listening device.

g·bear (bug′bâr′) *n.* 1. A real or imaginary object of ead. 2. A hobgoblin. Also **bug·a·boo** (bug′ə·bo͞o).

g-eyed (bug′īd′) *adj. Slang* With the eyes bulging.

g·gy[1] (bug′ē) *n. pl.* **·gies** 1. A light, four-wheeled carge. 2. A baby carriage. [Origin uncertain]

g·gy[2] (bug′ē) *adj.* **·gi·er, ·gi·est** 1. Infested with bugs. *U.S. Slang* Crazy. —**bug′gi·ness** *n.*

gle[1] (byo͞o′gəl) *n.* 1. A brass wind instrument resemng a trumpet, usu. without keys or valves. 2. A huntsan's horn. —*v.* **·gled, ·gling** *v.t.* 1. To summon with a gle. —*v.i.* 2. To sound a bugle. [< OF < L *buculus*, n. of *bos* ox] —**bu′gler** *n.*

gle[2] (byo͞o′gəl) *n.* A tube-shaped glass bead used for namenting garments. —**bu′gled** *adj.*

hl (bo͞ol) *n.* Decoration of furniture with inlaid tortoise ell, ivory, etc.; also a piece so decorated. Also **buhl′work′**. fter A. C. Boulle, 1642–1732, French cabinetmaker]

ild (bild) *v.* **built** (*Archaic* **build·ed**), **build·ing** *v.t.* 1. To nstruct, erect, or make by assembling separate parts or aterials. 2. To establish and increase. 3. To found; ake a basis for. —*v.i.* 4. To construct or erect a house, c. 5. To base or develop an idea, theory, etc.: with *on upon*. —**to build up** 1. To create or build by degrees. To renew or strengthen; also, to increase. —*n.* The anner or style in which anything is constructed; form; ure. [OE *byldan* < *bold* house] —**build′er** *n.*

ild·ing (bil′ding) *n.* 1. That which is built; a structure; ifice, as a house or barn. 2. The occupation, act, or art constructing.

ild·up (bild′up′) *n.* 1. The act of increasing or strengthing. 2. *Informal* Extravagant publicity or praise.

ilt-in (bilt′in′) *adj.* Built as a part of the structure.

lb (bulb) *n.* 1. *Bot.* A leaf bud comprising a cluster of ickened, scalelike leaves growing usu. underground and nding forth roots, as the onion or lily. 2. Any plant growg from a bulb. 3. A rounded protuberance, as at the d of a tube. 4. An incandescent lamp. [< L < Gk. *lbos* bulbous root] —**bul·bar** (bul′bər) *adj.*

l·bous (bul′bəs) *adj.* 1. Of, producing, or growing from ilbs. Also **bul·ba·ceous** (bul·bā′shəs). 2. Shaped like a ilb; swollen.

l·gar·i·an (bul·gâr′ē·ən, bo͝ol-) *adj.* Of Bulgaria, the ilgarians, or their language. —*n.* 1. A native or citizen Bulgaria. 2. The Slavic language of the Bulgarians.

lge (bulj, bo͝olj) *n.* A protuberant, rounded part. —*. & v.i.* **bulged, bulg·ing** To swell out. [< OF < L *bulga*] **bulg′i·ness** *n.* —**bulg′y** *adj.*

lk (bulk, bo͝olk) *n.* 1. Magnitude, volume, or size. 2. he greater or principal part; main body. 3. A large body or mass. —**in bulk** 1. Not packaged; loose. 2. In large quantities. —*v.i.* 1. To appear large or important; loom. 2. To increase in magnitude; grow: with *up*. —*v.t.* 3. To cause to expand or grow large: with *out*. [Cf. ON *bulki* heap, cargo, and Dan. *bulk* rump]

bulk·head (bulk′hed′) *n.* 1. *Naut.* An upright partition in a vessel, separating compartments. 2. A partition or wall to keep back earth, gas, etc. 3. A small structure built on a roof to cover an elevator shaft.

bulk·y (bul′kē, bo͝ol′kē) *adj.* **bulk·i·er, bulk·i·est** Of great size; massive; also, large and unwieldy. —**bulk′i·ly** *adv.* —**bulk′i·ness** *n.*

bull[1] (bo͝ol) *n.* 1. The uncastrated male of a bovine animal, esp. of the domesticated types. ◆ Collateral adjective: *taurine*. 2. The male of some other animals, as of the elephant, whale, etc. 3. One likened to a bull, as in strength or manner. 4. A speculator who buys so as to profit from a rise in prices he anticipates or hopes to cause: opposed to *bear*[2]. 5. *U.S. Slang* A policeman or detective. 6. *U.S. Slang* Empty talk; nonsense, —*v.t.* 1. To speculate for a rise in price of or in. 2. To push or force (a way). —*v.i.* 3. To go up in price. 4. To go or push ahead. —*adj.* 1. Male; masculine. 2. Like a bull; large. 3. Marked by rising prices: a *bull* market. [ME *bule*]

bull[2] (bo͝ol) *n.* An official and authoritative document issued by the Pope. [< L *bulla* edict, seal]

bull·dog (bo͝ol′dôg′, -dog′) *n.* A medium-sized, shorthaired, powerful dog, with strong jaws. —*adj.* Resembling a bulldog; courageous; tenacious. —*v.t.* **·dogged, ·dog·ging** *U.S. Informal* To throw (a steer) by gripping its horns and twisting its neck.

bull·doze (bo͝ol′dōz′) *v.t.* **·dozed, ·doz·ing** 1. *U.S. Slang* To intimidate; bully. 2. To clear, dig, scrape, etc., with a bulldozer. [? < BULL[1], adj. + DOSE, with ref. to the violent or excessive treatment given to the victim]

bull·doz·er (bo͝ol′dō′zər) *n.* 1. A tractor equipped with a heavy steel blade, used for moving earth, clearing wooded areas, etc. 2. *U.S. Slang* One who intimidates.

bul·let (bo͝ol′it) *n.* 1. A small projectile for a firearm. 2. Any small ball. [< F *boulette*, dim. of *boule* ball]

bul·le·tin (bo͝ol′ə·tən, -tin) *n.* 1. A brief account of news, as in a newspaper or on radio. 2. A periodical publication, as of the proceedings of a society. —*v.t.* To make public by bulletin. [< F < Ital. *bulletino* < L]

bulletin board A board on which bulletins, etc., are posted.

bul·let·proof (bo͝ol′it·pro͞of′) *adj.* Not penetrable by bullets.

bull·fight (bo͝ol′fīt′) *n.* A combat in an arena between men and a bull or bulls, popular among the Spanish and Spanish Americans. —**bull′fight′er** *n.* —**bull′fight′ing** *n.*

bull·finch (bo͝ol′finch′) *n.* A European songbird having a short bill and red breast.

bull·frog (bo͝ol′frog′, -frôg′) *n.* A large frog with a deep bass croak. [< BULL[1], adj. + FROG]

bull·head (bo͝ol′hed′) *n.* A fresh-water catfish.

bull·head·ed (bo͝ol′hed′id) *adj.* Stubborn; headstrong.

bull·horn (bo͝ol′hôrn′) *n.* An electrical, hand-held voice amplifier resembling a megaphone.

bul·lion (bo͝ol′yən) *n.* Gold or silver uncoined or in mass, as in bars, plates, etc. [< AF, OF < *bouillir* to boil]

bull·ish (bo͝ol′ish) *adj.* 1. Bull-like. 2. Tending to cause prices to rise; also, marked by rising prices. 3. Bullheaded. —**bull′ish·ly** *adv.* —**bull′ish·ness** *n.*

bul·lock (bo͝ol′ək) *n.* A gelded bull; a steer or ox. [OE *bulluc*]

bull·pen (bo͝ol′pen′) *n. U.S.* 1. An enclosure for bulls. 2. *Informal* A place for temporary detention of prisoners. 3. In baseball, a place where pitchers practice during a game.

bull·ring (bo͝ol′ring′) *n.* A circular enclosure for bullfights.

bull session *U.S. Informal* An informal discussion.

bull's-eye (bo͝olz′ī) *n.* 1. The central colored disk on a target; also, a shot that hits this disk. 2. A thick disk of glass set in a pavement, deck, etc., to admit light. 3. A convex lens. 4. A lantern with such a lens.

bull terrier A white terrier having a long head and stiff coat, originally bred from a bulldog and a white terrier.

bull·whip (bo͝ol′hwip′) *n.* A long, heavy whip. —*v.t.* **·whipped, ·whip·ping** To strike with a bullwhip.

bul·ly[1] (bo͝ol′ē) *n. pl.* **·lies** A swaggering, quarrelsome, usu. cowardly person who terrorizes weaker people. —*v.* **·lied, ·ly·ing** *v.t.* 1. To intimidate or coerce by threats. —*v.i.* 2. To act the bully. —*adj.* 1. *U.S. Informal* Excellent; admirable. 2. Jolly; dashing; gallant. —*interj. U.S. Informal* Well done! [Cf. Du. *boel* friend, lover]

bul·ly[2] (bo͝ol′ē) *n.* Canned or pickled beef. Also **bully beef.** [Prob. < F *bouillir* to boil]

bul·ly·rag (bo͝ol′ē·rag′) *v.t.* **·ragged, ·rag·ging** To bully; intimidate. [? < BULLY, v. + RAG[1]]

bul·rush (bo͝ol′rush′) *n.* 1. A tall, rushlike plant growing in water or damp ground. **2.** In the Bible, papyrus. *Ex.* ii 3. [< BULL[1], adj. + RUSH[2]]

bul·wark (bo͝ol·wərk) *n.* **1.** A defensive wall or rampart; fortification. **2.** Any safeguard or defense. **3.** *Usu. pl. Naut.* The raised side of a ship, above the upper deck. **—** *v.t.* To surround and fortify with a bulwark. [< MHG *bolwerc*]

bum (bum) *U.S. Slang* *n.* A worthless or dissolute loafer; tramp. **— on the bum. 1.** Out of order; broken. **2.** Living as a vagrant. **— the bum's rush** Forcible ejection. **—** *adj.* Bad; inferior. **—** *v.* **bummed, bum·ming** *v.i.* **1.** To live by sponging on others. **2.** To live idly and in dissipation. **—** *v.t.* **3.** To get by begging: to *bum* a ride. [Short for *bummer*, alter. of G *bummler* loafer, dawdler] **— bum′mer** *n.*

bum·ble (bum′bəl) *v.t. & v.i.* **·bled, ·bling** To bungle, esp. in an officious manner. [? Imit.] **— bum′bling** *adj. & n.*

bum·ble·bee (bum′bəl·bē′) *n.* Any of various large, hairy, bees. [< dial. E *bumble* to hum + BEE[1]]

bump (bump) *v.t.* **1.** To come into contact with; knock into. **2.** To cause to knock into or against. **3.** *U.S. Slang* To displace, as from a position or seat. **—** *v.i.* **4.** To strike heavily or with force: often with *into* or *against.* **5.** To move with jerks and jolts. **— to bump off** *Slang* To kill, esp. with a gun. **—** *n.* **1.** An impact or collision; a blow; jolt. **2.** A protuberance or uneven place. [Imit.]

bump·er[1] (bum′pər) *n.* The horizontal bar at the front or rear of an automobile to absorb the shock of collision.

bump·er[2] (bum′pər) *n.* A cup or glass filled to the brim. **—** *adj.* Unusually full or large: a *bumper* crop. [? Alter. of F *bombarde* large cup; infl. in form by *bump*]

bump·kin (bump′kin) *n.* An awkward rustic; a lout. [? < Du. *boomkin* little tree, block]

bump·tious (bump′shəs) *adj.* Aggressively self-assertive. [Appar. < BUMP] **— bump′tious·ly** *adv.* **— bump′tious·ness** *n.*

bump·y (bum′pē) *adj.* **bump·i·er, bump·i·est 1.** Having bumps. **2.** Jolting. **— bump′i·ly** *adv.* **— bump′i·ness** *n.*

bun (bun) *n.* **1.** A small bread roll, sometimes sweetened or spiced. **2.** A roll of hair shaped like a bun. [ME *bunne*]

bu·na (bo͞o′nə, byo͞o′-) *n. Chem.* A synthetic rubber made by the polymerization of butadiene with certain other substances. [< BU(TADIENE) + NA(TRIUM)]

bunch (bunch) *n.* **1.** A number of things of the same kind growing, occurring, or fastened together; a cluster. **2.** *Informal* A group: a *bunch* of boys. **3.** *Rare* A hump; protuberance. **—** *v.t. & v.i.* **1.** To form bunches or groups. **2.** To gather, as in folds. [ME *bunche*] **— bunch′y** *adj.*

bun·co (bung′kō) *U.S. Informal n.* A swindle; confidence game. **—** *v.t.* **·coed, ·co·ing** To swindle or rob. Also spelled *bunko.* [Prob. < Sp. *banco*, a card game]

bun·combe (bung′kəm) *n.* *U.S. Informal* **1.** Empty speechmaking for political effect or to please constituents. **2.** Empty talk; humbug. Also spelled *bunkum.* [from *Buncombe* County, N.C., whose congressman (1919–21) insisted on making unimportant speeches "for Buncombe"]

bund (bo͝ond, *Ger.* bo͝ont) *n.* A league; society. [< G]

bun·dle (bun′dəl) *n.* **1.** A number of things or a quantity of anything bound together. **2.** Anything folded or wrapped and tied up; a package. **3.** A group; collection. ◆ Collateral adjective: *fascicular.* **—** *v.* **·dled, ·dling** *v.t.* **1.** To tie, roll, or otherwise secure in a bundle. **2.** To send or put hastily and unceremoniously: with *away, off, out,* or *into.* **—** *v.i* **3.** To go hastily; hustle. **4.** To lie or sleep in the same bed without undressing, formerly a courting custom in Wales and New England. **— to bundle up** To dress warmly. [< MDu. *bond* group] **— bun′dler** *n.*

bung (bung) *n.* **1.** A stopper for the hole through which a cask is filled. **2.** Bunghole. **—** *v.t.* **1.** To close with or as with a bung: often with *up* or *down.* **2.** *Slang* To damage; maul: usually with *up.* [< MDu. *bonghe*]

bun·ga·low (bung′gə·lō) *n.* A small house or cottage, usually with one or one and a half stories. [< Hind. *banglā*, lit., Bengalese (house) < *Banga* Bengal]

bung·hole (bung′hōl′) *n.* A hole in a keg or barrel from which liquid is tapped. [< BUNG + HOLE]

bun·gle (bung′gəl) *v.t. & v.i.* **·gled, ·gling** To work, make, or do (something) clumsily. **—** *n.* A clumsy job or performance; botch. **— bun′gler** *n.* **— bun′gling·ly** *adv.*

bun·ion (bun′yən) *n.* A painful swelling of the foot, usually at the base of the great toe. [< OF *bugne* swelling]

bunk[1] (bungk) *n.* **1.** A narrow, built-in bed or shelf for sleeping; a berth. **2.** *Informal* A bed. **—** *v.i. Informal* **1.** To sleep in a bunk. **2.** To go to bed. [Cf. MDu. *banc* bench]

bunk[2] (bungk) *n. U.S. Slang* Empty talk; buncombe.

bun·ker (bung′kər) *n.* **1.** A large bin, as for coal on a ship. **2.** In golf, a mound of earth serving as an obstacle. **3.** *Mil.* A steel and concrete fortification. [Cf. OSw. *bunke* hold of a ship and BANK[3] rowers' bench]

bun·ko (bung′kō) See BUNCO.

bun·kum (bung′kəm) See BUNCOMBE.

bun·ny (bun′ē) *n. pl* **·nies** A rabbit: a pet name. [Dim. of dial. E *bun* a rabbit; ult. origin unknown]

Bun·sen burner (bun′sən) A type of gas burner in whic mixture of gas and air is burned at the top of a short me tube, producing a very hot flame. [after R. W. *Buns* 1811–1899, German chemist]

bunt (bunt) *v.t. & v.i.* **1.** To strike or push as with hor butt. **2.** In baseball, to bat (the ball) lightly into the field, without swinging the bat. **—** *n.* **1.** A push or sho a butt. **2.** In baseball: **a** The act of bunting. **b** A ball th has been bunted. [Nasalized var. of BUTT[1]]

bunt·ing[1] (bun′ting) *n.* **1.** A light woolen stuff or cott fabric used for flags, etc. **2.** Flags, banners, etc., collective **3.** A type of sleeping bag for infants. [? ME *bonten* to si

bunt·ing[2] (bun′ting) *n.* One of various birds related to t finches and sparrows. [ME *bountyng*; origin unknown]

bunt·line (bunt′lin, -līn′) *n.* *Naut.* A rope used in hauli a square sail up to the yard for furling.

Bun·yan (bun′yən), **Paul** See PAUL BUNYAN.

buoy (boi, bo͞o′ē) *n.* **1.** *Naut.* A warning float moored o dangerous rock or shoal or at the ends of a channel. **2.** device for keeping a person afloat; a life buoy. **—** **1.** To keep from sinking in a liquid; keep afloat. **2.** sustain the courage or heart of; encourage: usu. with **3.** *Naut.* To mark with buoys. [< MDu. or OF < L *b* fetter; because it is chained to one spot]

buoy·an·cy (boi′ən·sē, bo͞o′yən·sē) *n.* **1.** The tendency ability to keep afloat. **2.** The power of a fluid to keep object afloat. **3.** Cheerfulness. Also **buoy′ance.**

buoy·ant (boi′ənt, bo͞o′yənt) *adj.* Having buoyan [Prob. < Sp. < *boyar* to float] **— buoy′ant·ly** *adv.*

bur[1] (bûr) *n.* **1.** *Bot.* A rough or prickly flower head or se case. **2.** A plant that bears burs. **3.** A person or thi that clings like a bur. **—** *v.t.* **burred, bur·ring** To rem burs from. Also spelled *burr.* [< Scand.]

bur[2] (bûr) See BURR[2].

bur·ble (bûr′bəl) *v.i.* **·bled, ·bling 1.** To bubble; gurgle. To talk excitedly and confusedly. [ME; imit.]

bur·bot (bûr′bət) *n. pl.* **·bot** A fresh-water fish with barb on the chin. [< F, ult., < L *barbata* bearded]

bur·den[1] (bûr′dən) *n.* **1.** Something carried; a load. Something that weighs heavily, as responsibility or anxie **3.** *Naut.* **a** The carrying capacity of a vessel. **b** The wei of the cargo. **4.** The carrying of loads: beasts of *burden.* *v.t.* To load or overload. [OE *byrthen* load]

bur·den[2] (bûr′dən) *n.* **1.** Something often repeated or dw upon; the prevailing idea. **2.** A refrain of a song. [< < LL *burdo* drone]

burden of proof The obligation to prove a point.

bur·den·some (bûr′dən·səm) *adj.* Hard or heavy to be oppressive. **— bur′den·some·ly** *adv.* **— bur′den·some·ness**

bur·dock (bûr′dok) *n.* A coarse weed of the compos family having prickly burs. [< BUR[1] + DOCK[4]]

bu·reau (byo͝or′ō) *n. pl.* **bu·reaus** or **bu·reaux** (byo͝or′ **1.** *U.S.* A chest of drawers for clothing, etc., usu. wit mirror. **2.** A government department, or a division there **3.** An office for transacting business. **4.** *Brit.* A writ desk or table with drawers. [< F, a desk]

bu·reauc·ra·cy (byo͞o·rok′rə·sē) *n. pl.* **·cies 1.** Governm by bureaus; also, the group of officials so governing. **2.** undue extension of bureaus in the departments of a gove ment. **3.** Rigid adherence to administrative routine. [< < *bureau* office, bureau + Gk. *kratia* power, rule]

bu·reau·crat (byo͝or′ə·krat) *n.* **1.** A member of a burea racy. **2.** An official who narrowly adheres to a rigid routi **— bu′reau·crat′ic** or **·i·cal** *adj.* **— bu′reau·crat′i·cal·ly** *a*

bu·rette (byo͞o·ret′) *n. Chem.* A finely graduated glass tu with a stopcock at the bottom. Also **bu·ret′.** [< F, dim. *buire* a vase, vial]

burg (bûrg) *n.* *U.S. Informal* A town; esp., a rural to [OE *burg*]

bur·geon (bûr′jən) *v.i.* **1.** To flourish; grow. **2.** To bu sprout. **—** *v.t.* **3.** To put forth (buds, etc.). **—** *n.* A bu sprout. Also spelled *bourgeon.* [< OF *burjon*]

bur·gess (bûr′jis) *n.* **1.** A citizen or officer of a borou **2.** In colonial times, a member of the lower house (**House Burgesses**) of the legislature of Virginia. [< OF *burge*

burgh (bûrg, *Scot.* bûr′ō, -ə) *n.* In Scottish law, a charte town. [Var. of BOROUGH] **— burgh·al** (bûr′gəl) *adj.*

burgh·er (bûr′gər) *n.* A citizen of a burgh, town, or ci

bur·glar (bûr′glər) *n.* One who commits burglary. [Med.L < OF < *bourg* dwelling + *laire* robbery]

bur·glar·ize (bûr′glə·rīz) *v.t.* **·ized, ·iz·ing** To comr burglary upon.

bur·gla·ry (bûr′glər·ē) *n. pl.* **·ries** *Law* The breaking a entering of a dwelling at night, with intent to commit crime. **— Syn.** See THEFT.

bur·gle (bûr′gəl) *v.t. & v.i.* **·gled, ·gling** *Informal* To co mit burglary (upon).

bur·go·mas·ter (bûr′gə·mas′tər, -mäs′-) *n.* A Dut Flemish, or German mayor. [< Du. *burgemeester*]

Bur·gun·dy (bûr′gən·dē) *n. pl.* **·dies** A kind of red or wh wine originally made in Burgundy.

ɪr·i·al (ber′ē·əl) *n.* The burying of a dead body; inter-ıent. —*adj.* Of or pertaining to burial. [ME *buryel*, *riel* < *biriels* (mistaken as plural) < OE *brygels* tomb]

·rin (byōōr′in) *n.* A steel tool with a lozenge-shaped oint for engraving or carving.

rl (bûrl) *n.* **1.** A knot or lump in wool, cloth, or thread. . A large wartlike excrescence formed on the trunks of ees. —*v.t.* To dress (cloth) by removing burls. [< OF LL *burra* shaggy hair] —**burled** *adj.* —**burl′er** *n.*

r·lap (bûr′lap) *n.* A coarse fabric made of jute or hemp, ısed for wrapping, bagging, etc. [Origin uncertain]

r·lesque (bər·lesk′) *n.* **1.** A satire or ludicrous imita-on, usually of a serious, dignified subject; parody. **2.** *U.S.* theatrical entertainment marked by low comedy, strip-ıase, etc. —*adj.* **1.** Marked by ridiculous incongruity or road caricature. **2.** *U.S.* Of or pertaining to theatrical urlesque. —*v.* **·lesqued, ·les·quing** *v.t.* **1.** To represent ughably; satirize. —*v.i.* **2.** To use broad caricature. [< < Ital. < *burla* joke]

r·ley (bûr′lē) *n.* A fine, light tobacco grown principally Kentucky. Also **Bur′ley.** [? after *Burley*, a grower]

r·ly (bûr′lē) *adj.* **·li·er, ·li·est** Large of body; bulky; stout; ısty. [ME *borlich*] —**bur′li·ly** *adv.* —**bur′li·ness** *n.*

ɪr·mese (bər·mēz′, -mēs′) *adj.* Of or pertaining to Burma, s inhabitants, or their language. Also **Bur′man** (-mən). -*n.* *pl.* **·mese** **1.** A native or inhabitant of Burma. **2.** he Sino-Tibetan language of Burma.

rn (bûrn) *v.* **burned** or **burnt, burn·ing** *v.t.* **1.** To de-roy or consume by fire. **2.** To set afire; ignite. **3.** To in-ıre or kill by fire; execute by fire. **4.** To injure or damage y friction, heat, steam, etc.; scale; wither. **5.** To produce y fire. **6.** To brand; also, to cauterize. **7.** To finish or arden by intense heat; fire. **8.** To use or employ, so as to ve off light, heat, etc. **9.** To cause a feeling of heat in. **0.** To sunburn. **11.** *Chem.* To cause to undergo com-ıstion. **12.** *U.S. Slang* To electrocute. —*v.i.* **13.** To on fire; blaze. **14.** To be destroyed or scorched by fire. **5.** To give off light, heat, etc.; shine. **16.** To die by fire. **7.** To appear or feel hot: He *burns* with fever. **18.** To be ıger, excited, or inflamed. **19.** *Chem.* To oxidize; undergo ombustion. **20.** *U.S. Slang* To be electrocuted. —**to urn down** To raze or be razed by fire. —**to burn out 1.** To ecome extinguished through lack of fuel. **2.** To destroy or ear out by heat, friction, etc. **3.** To burn up the house, ore, or property of. **4.** To drive out by heat. —**to burn p 1.** To consume by fire. **2.** *Slang* To make or become ritated or enraged. —*n.* **1.** A burned place. **2.** *Pathol.* lesion caused by heat, extreme cold, corrosive chemicals, ases, electricity, radiation, etc. [Fusion of OE *beornan* to e on fire, and OE *bærnan* to set afire]

ɪrn·er (bûr′nər) *n.* **1.** One who or that which burns. **2.** hat part of a stove, lamp, etc., from which the flame comes.

ɪrn·ing (bûr′ning) *adj.* **1.** Consuming or being consumed y or as if by fire. **2.** Causing intense feeling; urgent.

ɪrning glass A convex lens for concentrating the sun's ıys upon an object so as to heat or ignite it.

r·nish (bûr′nish) *v.t.* & *v.i.* To polish by friction; make become shiny. —*n.* Polish; luster. [< OF *burnir* to olish] —**bur′nish·er** *n.* —**bur′nish·ment** *n.*

ɪr·noose (bər·nōōs′, bûr′nōōs) *n.* An Arab hooded cloak. lso **bur·nous′.** [< F < Arabic *burnus*]

ɪrn·out (bûrn′out′) *n.* **1.** A destruction or failure due to urning or to excessive heat. **2.** *Aerospace* The cessation of urning in a jet or rocket engine, esp. when caused by stop-age or exhaustion of fuel.

ɪrn·sides (bûrn′sīdz) *n.pl.* Side whiskers and mustache: lso called *sideburns.* [after A. E. *Burnside*, 1824–81, Union eneral in the Civil War]

ɪrnt (bûrnt) Alternative past tense and past participle of URN.

ɪrnt ocher A permanent, brick red pigment.

ɪrnt offering An animal, food, etc., burned upon an altar s a sacrifice or offering to a god.

ɪrnt sienna A dark brown pigment.

ɪrnt umber A reddish brown pigment.

ɪrp (bûrp) *U.S. Informal n.* A belch. —*v.i.* To belch. —.*t.* To cause to belch: to *burp* a baby. [Imit.]

ɪrr[1] (bûr) *n.* **1.** A roughness or rough edge, esp. one left n metal in casting or cutting. **2.** Any of several tools for utting, reaming, etc. **3.** A dentist's drill with a rough ead. **4.** A protuberant knot on a tree. —*v.t.* **1.** To orm a rough edge on. **2.** To remove a rough edge from. lso spelled *bur.* [Var. of BUR[1]] —**bur′ry** *adj.*

ɪrr[2] (bûr) *n.* **1.** A rough guttural sound of *r* produced by ibration of the uvula against the back of the tongue. **2.** ny rough, dialectal pronunciation: the Scottish *burr.* **3.** A uzz. —*v.t.* **1.** To pronounce with a rough or guttural rticulation. —*v.i.* **2.** To speak with a burr. [Imit.]

bur·ro (bûr′ō, bōōr′ō) *n.* *pl.* **·ros** A small donkey. [< Sp.]

bur·row (bûr′ō) *n.* **1.** A hole made in the ground, as by a rabbit. **2.** Any similar place of refuge. —*v.i.* **1.** To live or hide in a burrow. **2.** To dig a burrow or burrows. **3.** To dig into, under, or through something. —*v.t.* **4.** To dig a burrow or burrows in. **5.** To make by burrowing. **6.** To hide (oneself) in a burrow. [ME *borow*] —**bur′row·er** *n.*

bur·sa (bûr′sə) *n.* *pl.* **·sae** (-sē) or **·sas** *Anat.* A pouch or saclike cavity; esp. one containing synovia and located at points of friction in the bodies of vertebrates. [< Med.L, sac, pouch] —**bur′sal** *adj.*

bur·sar (bûr′sər, -sär) *n.* A treasurer, as of a college. [< Med.L *bursa* bag, purse] —**bur·sar·i·al** (bər·sâr′ē·əl) *adj.*

bur·sa·ry (bûr′sər·ē) *n.* *pl.* **·ries** The treasury of a public institution or a religious order.

bur·si·tis (bər·sī′tis) *n.* *Pathol.* Inflammation of a bursa.

burst (bûrst) *n.* **burst, burst·ing** *v.i.* **1.** To break open or apart suddenly and violently. **2.** To be full to the point of breaking open; bulge. **3.** To appear or enter suddenly or violently. **4.** To become audible or evident. **5.** To give sudden expression to passion, grief, etc. —*v.t.* **6.** To cause to break open suddenly or violently; force open; punc-ture. **7.** To cause to swell to the point of breaking open. —*n.* **1.** A sudden exploding or breaking forth. **2.** A sudden effort or spurt; rush. **3.** A crack or break. [OE *berstan*] —**burst′er** *n.*

bur·y (ber′ē) *v.t.* **bur·ied, bur·y·ing** **1.** To put (a dead body) in a grave, tomb, or the sea; perform burial rites for; inter. **2.** To put underground; to conceal, as by covering. **3.** To embed; sink: to *bury* a nail in a wall. **4.** To end; put out of mind: to *bury* a friendship. **5.** To occupy deeply; engross: He *buried* himself in study. [OE *byrgan*]

burying ground A cemetery.

bus (bus) *n.* *pl.* **bus·es** or **bus·ses** **1.** A large passenger ve-hicle usu. following a prescribed route. **2.** *Informal* An automobile. —*v.t.* **bused** or **bussed, bus·ing** or **bus·sing** **1.** To transport by bus. —*v.i.* **2.** To go by bus. **3.** *In-formal* To work as a bus boy. [Short form of OMNIBUS]

bus boy An employee in a restaurant who clears tables of soiled dishes, assists the waiters, etc.

bus·by (buz′bē) *n.* *pl.* **·bies** A tall fur cap worn by British hussars, artillerymen, and engineers. [Origin uncertain]

BUSBY

bush[1] (bōōsh) *n.* **1.** A low, treelike or thickly branching shrub. **2.** A clump of shrubs; thick-et; undergrowth. **3.** Wild, uncleared land cov-ered with scrub; also, any rural or unsettled area. **4.** A fox's tail. **5.** *Canadian* Wood lot. —*v.i.* **1.** To grow or branch like a bush. **2.** To be or become bushy. —*v.t.* **3.** To decorate or support with bushes. [< ON *buskr*]

bush[2] (bōōsh) *v.t.* To put a bushing in, as a bearing. —*n.* A bushing. [< MDu. *busse* box]

bushed (bōōsht) *adj.* *Informal* **1.** *U.S.* & *Canadian* Ex-hausted. **2.** Odd from living in isolation. [< BUSH[1]]

bush·el[1] (bōōsh′əl) *n.* **1.** A unit of dry measure. **2.** A container holding this amount. See table front of book. [< OF *boissiel*, dim. of *boisse* box]

bush·el[2] (bōōsh′əl) *v.t.* & *v.i.* **bush·eled** or **·elled, bush·el·ing** or **·el·ling** *U.S.* To repair and restore (a garment). [Cf. G *bosseln* to do small jobs] —**bush′el·er** or **bush′el·ler** *n.*

bu·shi·do (bōō′shē·dō) *n.* The chivalric code of the feudal Samurai. Also **Bu′shi·do.** [< Japanese, way of the warrior]

bush·ing (bōōsh′ing) *n.* **1.** *Mech.* A metallic lining for a hole, as in the hub of a wheel, designed to insulate or to pre-vent abrasion between parts. **2.** *Electr.* A lining inserted in a socket to insulate an electric current. [< BUSH[2]]

bush league In baseball slang, an obscure minor league.

bush leaguer **1.** In baseball slang, a player in a bush league. **2.** *U.S. Slang* A mediocre person.

bush·man (bōōsh′mən) *n.* *pl.* **·men** (-mən) *Austral.* A dweller or farmer in the bush.

Bush·man (bōōsh′mən) *n.* *pl.* **·men** (-mən) **1.** One of a nomadic people of South Africa. **2.** The language of the Bushmen. [Trans. of Du. *boschjesman*]

bush·mas·ter (bōōsh′mas′tər, -mäs′) *n.* A venomous pit viper of Central and South America.

bush·whack (bōōsh′hwak′) *U.S.* *v.t.* **1.** To attack or fire upon from hiding; ambush. —*v.i.* **2.** To fight as a guer-rilla. [< Du. *boschwachter* forest keeper; infl. by *whack*] —**bush′whack′er** *n.* —**bush′whack′ing** *n.*

bush·y (bōōsh′ē) *adj.* **bush·i·er, bush·i·est** **1.** Covered with bushes. **2.** Shaggy. —**bush′i·ly** *adv.* —**bush′i·ness** *n.*

bus·ied (biz′ēd) Past tense and past participle of BUSY.

bus·i·ly (biz′ə·lē) *adv.* In a busy manner; industriously.

busi·ness (biz′nis) *n.* **1.** An occupation, trade, or profes-sion. **2.** Any of the various operations or details of trade or industry. **3.** A commercial enterprise or establishment;

a firm, factory, store, etc. 4. The amount or volume of trade. 5. A proper interest or concern; responsibility; duty. 6. A matter or affair. 7. In the theater, the movements, facial expressions, etc., apart from dialogue, by which actors interpret a part. — **Syn.** See OCCUPATION. — **to give (someone) the business** *Slang* 1. To deal with harshly or summarily. 2. To beat severely or kill. 3. To cheat or defraud. — **to have no business** To have no right (to do something). — **to mean business** *Informal* To have a serious intention. [OE *bysignis*]

business college A school that gives training in clerical and secretarial skills for positions in commerce and industry.

busi·ness·like (biz′nis·līk′) *adj.* Methodical; systematic.

busi·ness·man (biz′nis·man′) *n. pl.* **·men** (-men′) One engaged in commercial or industrial activity. — **busi′ness·wom′an** (-wŏŏm′ən) *n.fem.*

bus·kin (bus′kin) *n.* 1. A boot reaching halfway to the knee, and strapped or laced to the ankle. 2. A laced half boot, worn by Greek and Roman tragic actors. 3. Tragedy. [Origin uncertain] — **bus′kined** *adj.*

bus·man (bus′mən) *n. pl.* **men** (-mən) A bus driver.

busman's holiday A holiday spent by choice in activity similar to one's regular work.

buss (bus) *Archaic & Dial. n.* A kiss; smack. — *v.t. & v.i.* To kiss heartily. [Imit.]

bus·ses (bus′iz) Alternative plural of BUS.

bust[1] (bust) *n.* 1. The human breast, esp. the bosom of a woman. 2. A piece of statuary representing the human head, shoulders, and breast. [< F < Ital. *busto*]

bust[2] (bust) *Slang v.t.* 1. To burst. 2. To tame; train, as a horse. 3. To make bankrupt or short of funds. 4. To reduce in rank; demote. 5. To hit; strike. — *v.i.* 6. To burst. 7. To become bankrupt or short of funds. — *n.* 1. Failure; bankruptcy. 2. A spree. 3. A blow. [Alter. of BURST]

bus·tard (bus′tərd) *n.* A large Old World game bird related to the plovers and cranes. [< OF *bistarde, oustarde* < L *avis tarda*, lit., slow bird]

bust·er (bus′tər) *n. U.S. Slang* One who breaks or breaks up: trust *buster*.

bus·tle[1] (bus′əl) *n.* Excited activity; noisy stir; fuss. — *v.* **·tled, ·tling** *v.i.* 1. To move noisily or energetically; hurry. — *v.t.* 2. To cause to hurry. [? Akin to BUSK[2]]

bus·tle[2] (bus′əl) *n.* A frame or pad formerly worn by women on the back of the body below the waist to distend the skirt. [? < BUSTLE[1]]

bus·tling (bus′ling) *adj.* Active; busy. — **bus′tling·ly** *adv.*

bus·y (biz′ē) *adj.* **bus·i·er, bus·i·est** 1. Actively engaged in something; occupied. 2. Filled with activity; never still. 3. Officiously active; meddling; prying. 4. Temporarily engaged, as a telephone line. — *v.t.* **bus·ied, bus·y·ing** To make busy. [OE *bysig* active] — **bus′y·ness** *n.*

bus·y·bod·y (biz′ē·bod′ē) *n. pl.* **·bodies** One who officiously meddles in the affairs of others.

busy signal In a dial telephone, a recurrent buzzing tone indicating that the number called is already connected.

but (but, *unstressed* bət) *conj.* 1. On the other hand; yet. 2. Without the result that: It never rains *but* it pours. 3. Other than; otherwise than. 4. Except: anything *but* that. 5. With the exception that: often with *that*: Nothing will do *but* I must leave. 6. That: We don't doubt *but* he is there. 7. That . . . not: He is not so ill *but* exercise will benefit him. 8. Who . . . not; which . . . not: Few sought his advice *but* were helped by it. — *prep.* With the exception of; save: owning nothing *but* his clothes. — *adv.* Only; just: She is *but* a child. — **all but** Almost; nearly. — **but for** Were it not for. — *n.* An objection or condition; exception: no ifs or *buts*. [OE < *be* by + *ūtan* outside]

— **Syn.** (conj.) 1. *But* ranges in meaning from faintest contrast to absolute negation. *However* suggests a moderate concession or a second point to be considered. *Nevertheless* emphasizes direct opposition, and *yet* serves to introduce a mildly inconsequential outcome.

bu·ta·di·ene (byōō′tə·dī′ēn, -dī·ēn′) *n. Chem.* A hydrocarbon, C_4H_6, similar to isoprene, used in the manufacture of synthetic rubber. [< BUTA(NE) + DI-[2] (def. 2) + -ENE]

bu·tane (byōō′tān, byōō·tān′) *n. Chem.* A colorless, flammable, gaseous hydrocarbon, C_4H_{10}, of the methane series. [< L *but(yrum)* butter + -ANE[2]]

butch·er (bŏŏch′ər) *n.* 1. One who slaughters or dresses animals for market; also, a dealer in meats. 2. One guilty of needless bloodshed. 3. *U.S.* A vendor of candy, etc., on trains. 4. A botcher. — *v.t.* 1. To slaughter or dress for market. 2. To kill cruelly or indiscriminately. 3. To botch. [< OF *bouchier* slaughterer of bucks] — **butch′er·er** *n.*

butch·er·bird (bŏŏch′ər·bûrd′) *n.* The shrike, a bird.

butch·er's-broom (bŏŏch′ərz·brōōm′, -brŏŏm′) *n.* A low, evergreen shrub with leathery, leaflike branches bearing scarlet berries. Also **butch′er·broom′**.

butch·er·y (bŏŏch′ər·ē) *n. pl.* **·er·ies** 1. Wanton slaughter. 2. A slaughterhouse. 3. The butcher's trade.

but·ler (but′lər) *n.* A manservant in charge of the dining room, wine, etc., usu. the head servant in a househol [< AF, OF < Med.L < *buticula* bottle] — **but′ler·ship** *n*

butler's pantry A room between the kitchen and the di ing room, suitable for storage, serving, etc.

butt[1] (but) *v.t.* 1. To strike with the head or horns; ram. To drive, push, or bump as with the head. — *v.i.* 3. strike or attempt to strike something with the head or horr 4. To move or drive head foremost. 5. To project; jut. **to butt in** *Informal* To interrupt; intrude. — *n.* 1. A blo or push with the head. 2. A thrust in fencing. [< OF *bu* to strike, push, project] — **but′ter** *n.*

butt[2] (but) *n.* 1. A person or thing subjected to jokes, ri cule, criticism, etc. 2. A target, as on a rifle range. 3. A target range. 4. An embankment or wall behind target to stop the shot. [< OF *but* end, goal]

butt[3] (but) *n.* 1. The larger or thicker end of anythi 2. An end or extremity. 3. An unused end, as of a cigar cigarette; stub; stump. 4. The thick part of a tanned hid 5. *U.S. Informal* The buttocks. [Akin to Dan. *but* blun

butt[4] (but) *n.* 1. A large cask. 2. A measure of wine, 1 U.S. gallons. [< OF *boute*]

butte (byōōt) *n. U.S. & Canadian* A conspicuous hill, es one with steep sides and a flattened top. [< F]

but·ter (but′ər) *n.* 1. The fatty constituent of milk churn and prepared for cooking and table use. 2. A substan having the consistency or some of the qualities of butt 3. Any of several food preparations of semisolid consistenc apple *butter*. 4. *Informal* Flattery. — *v.t.* 1. To p butter on. 2. *Informal* To flatter: usu. with *up*. — **know which side one's bread is buttered on** To be awa of the true sources of one's fortune or security. [OE < < Gk. < *bous* cow + *tyros* cheese]

butter bean 1. The wax bean. 2. In the southern U. the lima bean.

but·ter·cup (but′ər·kup′) *n.* A plant of the crowfo family, with yellow, cup-shaped flowers.

but·ter·fat (but′ər·fat′) *n.* The fatty substance of mi from which butter is made.

but·ter·fin·gers (but′ər·fing′gərz) *n. Informal* One w drops things easily or often. — **but′ter·fin′gered** *adj.*

but·ter·fish (but′ər·fish′) *n. pl.* **·fish** or **·fishes** A silver laterally compressed fish common along the Atlantic coast.

but·ter·fly (but′ər·flī′) *n. pl.* **·flies** 1. An insect with larg often brightly colored wings, club-shaped antennae, a slender body. 2. A frivolous person. [OE *buttorflēoge*]

butter knife A small, blunt-edged knife for cutting spreading butter.

but·ter·milk (but′ər·milk′) *n.* The sour liquid left aft the butterfat has been separated from milk or cream.

but·ter·nut (but′ər·nut′) *n.* 1. The oily, edible nut of walnut of North America. 2. The tree or its cathartic inn bark. 3. A yellowish brown.

but·ter·scotch (but′ər·skoch′) *n.* 1. Hard, sticky can made with brown sugar, butter, and flavoring. 2. A syr or flavoring consisting of similar ingredients. — *adj.* Ma of or flavored with butterscotch.

but·ter·y[1] (but′ər·ē) *adj.* 1. Containing, like, or smear with butter. 2. *Informal* Grossly flattering; adulatory.

but·ter·y[2] (but′ər·ē, but′rē) *n. pl.* **·ter·ies** *Chiefly Brit.* pantry or wine cellar. [< OF < LL *butta* bottle]

but·tock (but′ək) *n.* 1. *Anat.* Either of the two flesl prominences that form the rump. 2. *pl.* The rump. [Di of BUTT[3]]

but·ton (but′n) *n.* 1. A knob or disk sewn to a garme etc., serving as a fastening or for ornamentation. 2. An thing resembling a button, as the knob for operating electric bell or an electric lamp. 3. *Slang* The point of t chin. — **on the button** *Informal* Exactly; precisely. — *v* 1. To fasten or provide with a button or buttons. — *v.* 2. To be capable of being fastened with or as with button [< OF *boton* button, bud] — **but′ton·er** *n.*

but·ton·hole (but′n·hōl′) *n.* A slit or loop to receive ar hold a button. — *v.t.* **·holed, ·hol·ing** 1. To work butto holes in. 2. To seize as by the buttonhole so as to detain.

but·tons (but′nz) *n.pl.* (*construed as sing.*) *Brit. Inform* A bellboy; page.

but·ton·wood (but′n·wŏŏd′) *n.* 1. A plane tree of Nort America, yielding a wood used for furniture, etc. Al **but·ton·ball** (-bôl′). 2. The wood of this tree.

but·ton·y (but′n·ē) *adj.* Of, having, or like a button.

but·tress (but′tris) *n.* 1. *Archit.* A structure built again a wall to strengthen it. 2. Any support or prop. 3. Som thing suggesting a buttress, as a projecting rock or hillsid — *v.t.* 1. To support with a buttress. 2. To prop u sustain. [< OF *bouter, buter* to push, thrust]

bu·tyl (byōō′til) *n. Chem.* A univalent hydrocarbon radica C_4H_9, from butane. [< BUT(YRIC) + -YL]

butyl alcohols *Chem.* A group of three isomeric alcoho having the formula C_4H_9OH.

bu·ty·lene (byōō′tə·lēn) *n. Chem.* A gaseous hydrocarbo C_4H_8, an ingredient of synthetic rubber.

·tyr·ic (byōō·tir′ik) *adj.* Of or derived from butter.
x·om (buk′səm) *adj.* Characterized by health and vigor; ump; comely: said of women. [ME *buhsum* pliant] — ux′om·ly *adv.* — bux′om·ness *n.*
y (bī) *v.* **bought, buying** *v.t.* **1.** To acquire with money; urchase. **2.** To obtain by some exchange or sacrifice: to *y* wisdom with experience. **3.** To bribe; corrupt: He was *ught* cheap. — *v.i.* **4.** To make purchases; be a purchaser. **- to buy in** **1.** To buy back for the owner, as at an auction hen the bids are too low. **2.** To buy stock in a company. *Slang* To pay money as a price for joining. **— to buy off** o bribe. **— to buy out** To purchase the stock, interests, c., of. **— to buy over** To win over to one's interest by a ibe. **— to buy up** To purchase the entire supply of. — *n.* *formal* **1.** Anything bought or about to be bought. **2.** bargain. [OE *bycgan*] — **buy′a·ble** *adj.*
y·er (bī′ər) *n.* **1.** One who makes purchases. **2.** A purasing agent, as for a department store.
zz (buz) *v.i.* **1.** To make the humming, vibrating sound the bee. **2.** To talk or gossip excitedly. **3.** To go busily hastily. — *v.t.* **4.** To cause to buzz. **5.** To spread by uzzing. **6.** To signal with a buzz. **7.** *Informal* To fly airplane low over. **8.** *Informal* To call by telephone. - *n.* **1.** A vibrating hum. **2.** A low murmur, as of many oices. **3.** *Informal* A phone call. [Imit.]
z·zard (buz′ərd) *n.* **1.** One of several large, slow-flying awks. **2.** A turkey buzzard. [< OF *busart*]
zz bomb A robot bomb.
zz·er (buz′ər) *n.* An electric signal making a buzzing und, as on a telephone switchboard.
zz saw A circular saw, so called from the sound it emits.
(bī) *prep.* **1.** Next to; near: the house *by* the river. **2.** ast and beyond: The train roared *by* us. **3.** Through the gency of or by means of: to hang *by* a rope; to travel *by* ane. **4.** By way of: Come *by* the nearest road. **5.** On the art of: a loss felt *by* all. **6.** According to: *by* law. **7.** In e course of; during: to travel *by* night. **8.** Not later than: e here *by* noon. **9.** After: day *by* day. **10.** According to a standard: to work *by* the day. **11.** To the extent or nount of: insects *by* the thousands. **12.** In multiplication measurement with: Multiply 6 *by* 8. **13.** With reference : to do well *by* one's friends. **14.** In the name of: *by* l that's holy. **— by the way** (or **by the by, bye the bye**) cidentally. — *adv.* **1.** At hand; near. **2.** Up to and yond something; past: The years go *by.* **3.** Apart; aside: lay something *by.* **— by and by** After a time; before ng. **— by and large** On the whole; generally. — *adj.* *n.* See BYE. [OE *bī* near, about]
- *combining form* **1.** Secondary; incidental: *by-product.* Near; close: *bystander.* **3.** Aside; out of the way: *byway.*
-and-by (bī′ən·bī′) *n.* Future time; hereafter.
e (bī) *n.* **1.** Something of minor or secondary importance. The position of one who, assigned no opponent, autoatically advances to the next round, as in a tennis tournaent. **3.** In golf, any hole remaining unplayed when the atch ends. — *adj.* Secondary. Also spelled *by.* [< BY]

bye-bye (bī′bī′) *interj.* Good-by.
by-e·lec·tion (bī′i·lek′shən) *n. Brit.* A parliamentary election between general elections, held to fill a vacancy.
Bye·lo·rus·sian (bye′lə·rush′ən) *adj.* Of or pertaining to the Byelorussian S.S.R., its people, or their language. — *n.* **1.** A native or inhabitant of the Byelorussian S.S.R. **2.** The language of the Byelorussians. Also *White Russian.*
by·gone (bī′gôn′, -gon′) *adj.* Gone by; past. — *n. Often pl.* Something past. **— to let bygones be bygones** To let disagreements and difficulties in the past be overlooked.
by·law (bī′lô′) *n.* **1.** A law adopted by a corporation, etc., and subordinate to a constitution or charter. **2.** A secondary law. [ME < *by, bi* village + *lawe* law]
by-line (bī′līn′) *n.* The line at the head of an article in a newspaper, etc., giving the name of the writer.
by-pass (bī′pas′, -päs′) *n.* **1.** Any road, path, or route connecting two points in a course other than that normally used; a detour. **2.** *Electr.* A shunt. — *v.t.* **1.** To go around or avoid (an obstacle). **2.** To provide with a by-pass.
by-path (bī′path′, -päth′) *n.* A secluded or indirect path.
by-play (bī′plā′) *n.* Action or speech apart from the main action, especially in a play.
by-prod·uct (bī′prod′əkt) *n.* A secondary product or result.
by·road (bī′rōd′) *n.* A back or side road.
By·ron·ic (bī·ron′ik) *adj.* **1.** Of or pertaining to Lord Byron. **2.** Like Byron; melancholy, romantic, passionate, etc.
by·stand·er (bī′stan′dər) *n.* One present but not taking part; an onlooker.
by·way (bī′wā′) *n.* A branch or side road.
by·word (bī′wûrd′) *n.* **1.** A proverbial saying; also, a pet phrase. **2.** A person, institution, etc., that proverbially represents a type, usually an object of scorn.
Byz·an·tine (biz′ən·tēn, -tīn, bi·zan′tin) *adj.* **1.** Of or pertaining to Byzantium or its civilization. **2.** Pertaining to the style of architecture developed in Byzantium during the fifth and sixth centuries, using rounded arches, centralized plans surmounted by large domes, and lavishness of mosaic and other decoration. — *n.* A native or inhabitant of Byzantium. Also **By·zan·ti·an** (bi·zan′shē·ən, -shən). [< L *Byzantinus* < *Byzantium*]

BYZANTINE ARCHITECTURE
(Santa Sophia, Constantinople, A.D. 538)

Byzantine Empire The eastern part of the later Roman Empire (395–1453); capital, Constantinople: also, *Byzantium, Eastern Roman Empire.*
By·zan·ti·um (bi·zan′shē·əm, -tē·əm) **1.** An ancient city on the Bosporus, later Constantinople. **2.** The Byzantine Empire.

C

C (sē) *n. pl.* **c's** or **cs, C's** or **Cs, cees** (sēz) **1.** The third tter of the English alphabet. **2.** Any sound represented by e letter *c.* — *symbol* **1.** The Roman numeral for 100. **2.** *hem.* Carbon (symbol C). **3.** *Music* **a** The tonic note of e natural scale; do. **b** A written note representing it. **c** The ale built upon C. **4.** The third in sequence or class.
a·ba (kä′bə, kä′ə·bə) See KAABA.
b (kab) *n.* **1.** A taxicab. **2.** A one-horse carriage for hire. A covered compartment of a locomotive, motor truck, c., for the operator. [Short form of CABRIOLET]
·bal (kə·bal′) *n.* **1.** A number of persons secretly united r some private purpose. **2.** An intrigue; plot. — *v.i.* **alled, ·bal·ling** To form a cabal; plot. [< MF *cabale*]
b·a·la (kab′ə·lə, kə·bä′lə) *n.* **1.** *Often cap.* An occult sysm originating in a mystical interpretation of the Scripres among certain Jewish rabbis. **2.** Any secret, occult, mystic system. Also spelled *kabala, kabbala.* [< Hebrew *ibal* to receive] — **cab′a·lism** *n.* — **cab′a·list** *n. & adj.*

cab·a·lis·tic (kab′ə·lis′tik) *adj.* **1.** Pertaining to the cabala. **2.** Having a mystic meaning; mysterious. Also **ca·bal·ic** (kə·bal′ik), **cab′a·lis′ti·cal.** — **cab′a·lis′ti·cal·ly** *adv.*
cab·al·le·ro (kab′əl·yâr′ō) *n. pl.* **·ros.** **1.** A Spanish cavalier. **2.** *SW U.S.* A horseman. [< Sp. < L *caballus* horse]
ca·ban·a (kə·ban′ə, -bä′nə) *n.* **1.** A small cabin. **2.** A beach bathhouse. Also **ca·ba·ña** (kə·bän′yə, -ban′-). [< Sp.]
cab·a·ret (kab′ə·rā′) *n.* **1.** A restaurant that provides singing, dancing, etc. **2.** Entertainment of this type. [< F]
cab·bage (kab′ij) *n.* The close-leaved edible head of a plant of the mustard family. — *v.i.* **·baged, ·bag·ing** To form a head, as cabbage. [< OF, ult. < L *caput* head]
cabbage palm A palm with a terminal leaf bud used as a vegetable.
cab·by (kab′ē) *n. pl.* **·bies** *Informal* The driver of a cab.
cab·in (kab′in) *n.* **1.** A small, rude house; a hut. **2.** In the U.S. Navy, the quarters of the captain. **3.** *Naut.* On passenger vessels, the living quarters for passengers and officers.

4. *Aeron.* The enclosed space in an aircraft for the crew, passengers, or cargo. — *v.t. & v.i.* To confine or dwell in or as in a cabin. [< F < LL *capanna* cabin]

cabin boy A boy who waits on the officers and passengers of a ship.

cabin class A class of accommodations for steamship passengers, higher than tourist class, lower than first class.

cabin cruiser A cruiser (def. 3).

cab·i·net (kab′ə·nit) *n.* **1.** A piece of furniture fitted with shelves and drawers; a cupboard. **2.** A council, or the chamber in which it meets. **3.** *Often cap.* The body of official advisers and executive chiefs serving a head of state. — *adj.* **1.** Of or suitable for a cabinet. **2.** Secret; confidential. [< F < Ital. *gabinetto* closet, chest of drawers]

cab·i·net·mak·er (kab′ə·nit·mā′kər) *n.* One who does fine woodworking, as for cabinets, furniture, etc.

cab·i·net·work (kab′ə·nit·wûrk′) *n.* Expert woodwork.

ca·ble (kā′bəl) *n.* **1.** A heavy rope, now usu. of steel wire. **2.** A cable's length. **3.** *Electr.* **a** An insulated electrical conductor or group of conductors. **b** An underwater telegraph line. **4.** A cablegram. — *v.* **·bled, ·bling** *v.t.* **1.** To make fast by a cable. **2.** To signal by underwater telegraph. — *v.i.* **3.** To send a message by underwater telegraph. [< LL < L *capere* to take, grasp]

cable car A car pulled by a moving cable.

ca·ble·gram (kā′bəl·gram) *n.* A telegraphic message sent by underwater cable.

cable's length A unit of nautical measure, in the United States 720 feet, in England 608 feet.

cab·man (kab′mən) *n. pl.* **·men** (-mən) A cab driver.

ca·boo·dle (kə·bo͞od′l) *n. Informal* Collection; lot: usu. in the phrase **the whole (kit and) caboodle.**

ca·boose (kə·bo͞os′) *n.* **1.** *U.S.* A car, usu. at the rear of a freight or work train, for use by the train crew. **2.** *Brit.* The galley of a ship. [< MDu. *cabuse* galley]

cab·ri·o·let (kab′rē·ə·lā′, -let′) *n.* **1.** A light, one-horse carriage with two seats and a folding top. **2.** An automobile of the coupé type. [< MF *cabriole* leap, caper]

ca·ca·o (kə·kā′ō, -kä′ō) *n. pl.* **·ca·os 1.** A small, evergreen tree of tropical America. **2.** The large, nutritive seeds of this tree, used in making cocoa and chocolate. [< Sp. < Nahuatl *cacauatl* cacao seed]

cacao butter Cocoa butter.

cach·a·lot (kash′ə·lot, -lō) *n.* The sperm whale. [< F]

cache (kash) *v.t.* **cached, cach·ing** To conceal or store, as in the earth. — *n.* A place for hiding or storing things; also, the things stored or hidden. [< F *cacher* to hide]

ca·chet (ka·shā′, kash′ā) *n.* **1.** A seal, as for a letter. **2.** A distinctive mark; stamp of individuality. **3.** A mark, slogan, etc., printed on mail. [< F *cacher* to hide]

cach·in·nate (kak′ə·nāt) *v.i.* **·nat·ed, ·nat·ing** To laugh immoderately or noisily. [< L *cachinnare* to laugh loudly]

ca·cique (kə·sēk′) *n.* A chief among the Indians of the West Indies, Mexico, etc. [< Sp. < native Haitian word]

cack·le (kak′əl) *v.* **·led, ·ling** *v.i.* **1.** To make a shrill, broken cry, as a hen that has laid an egg. **2.** To laugh or talk with a similar sound. — *v.t.* **3.** To utter in a cackling manner. — *n.* **1.** The shrill, broken cry of a hen or goose. **2.** Idle talk; chatter. **3.** A short, shrill laugh. [Imit.] — **cack′ler** *n.*

caco- *combining form* Bad; vile. [< Gk. *kakos* bad, evil]

ca·cog·ra·phy (kə·kog′rə·fē) *n.* Bad handwriting or spelling. — **ca·cog′ra·pher** *n.* — **cac·o·graph·ic** (kak′ə·graf′ik) or **·i·cal** *adj.*

ca·coph·o·nous (kə·kof′ə·nəs) *adj.* Having a harsh, disagreeable sound; discordant. Also **cac·o·phon·ic** (kak′ə·fon′ik) or **·i·cal.** — **ca·coph′o·nous·ly, cac′o·phon′i·cal·ly** *adv.*

ca·coph·o·ny (kə·kof′ə·nē) *n.* Disagreeable or discordant sound. [< F < Gk. < *kakos* bad + *phōneein* to sound]

cac·tus (kak′təs) *n. pl.* **·tus·es** or **·ti** (-tī) Any of various green, fleshy, mostly leafless and spiny plants, often having showy flowers, and native in arid regions of America. [< L < Gk. *kaktos,* prickly plant]

cad (kad) *n.* An ungentlemanly or despicable fellow. — **cad′dish** *adj.* — **cad′dish·ly** *adv.* — **cad′dish·ness** *n.*

ca·dav·er (kə·dav′ər, -dā′vər) *n.* A dead body; esp., a human body for dissection; a corpse. [< L]

ca·dav·er·ous (kə·dav′ər·əs) *adj.* Resembling or characteristic of a corpse; pale; ghastly; gaunt. Also **ca·dav′er·ic.** — **ca·dav′er·ous·ly** *adv.* — **ca·dav′er·ous·ness** *n.*

cad·die (kad′ē) *n.* One paid to carry clubs for golf players. — *v.i.* **·died, ·dy·ing** To act as a caddie. Also spelled *caddy.*

cad·dis fly (kad′is) Any of certain four-winged insects whose aquatic larvae (**caddis worms**) construct cylindrical cases covered with sand, gravel, etc. [Origin uncertain]

cad·dy[1] (kad′ē) *n. pl.* **·dies** A small box or case, as for tea. [< Malay *kaātī,* a measure of weight]

cad·dy[2] (kad′ē) *n. pl.* **·dies** A caddie.

ca·dence (kād′ns) *n.* **1.** Rhythmic or measured flow, as of poetry. **2.** The measure or beat of music, marching, etc. **3.** Modulation, as of the voice; intonation. **4.** *Music* A melodic, harmonic, or rhythmic formula ending a phrase, movement, etc. Also **ca′den·cy.** [< F < Ital. < LL < *cadere* to fall] — **ca′denced** *adj.*

ca·dent (kād′nt) *adj.* Having cadence or rhythm.

ca·den·za (kə·den′zə, *Ital.* kä·dent′sä) *n. Music* A flouri or thematic ornamentation, often improvised, for displayi the virtuosity of a solo performer, usu. introduced just befo the end of a composition or movement. [< Ital.]

ca·det (kə·det′) *n.* **1.** A student at a military or nav school, esp. one in training for commissioning as an offic **2.** A younger son or brother. [< F, ult. < L *caput* hea chief] — **ca·det′ship** *n.*

cadge (kaj) *v.* **cadged, cadg·ing** *v.t.* **1.** *Informal* To get b begging. — *v.i.* **2.** *Dial.* To go begging. — **cadg′er** *n.*

cad·mi·um (kad′mē·əm) *n.* A bluish white metallic e ment (symbol Cd), occurring in small quantities in zinc or and used in the manufacture of fusible alloys, in electropl ing, and in the control of atomic fission. See ELEMENT. [NL < L < Gk. *kadmeia* (*gē*) calamine]

Cad·mus (kad′məs) In Greek mythology, a Phoenici prince who killed a dragon and sowed its teeth, from whi sprang armed men who fought one another.

cad·re (kad′rē, *Fr.* kä′dr′) *n.* **1.** *Mil.* The nucleus of offic and men needed to train a new military unit. **2.** A fram work; nucleus; core. [< F, frame of a picture]

ca·du·ce·us (kə·do͞o′sē·əs, -dyo͞o′-) *n. pl.* **·ce·i** (-sē·ī) In ancient Greece and Rome, a herald's wand or staff; esp., the staff of Mercury. **2.** A similar staff used as the emblem of a medical corps or of the medical profession. [< L < Gk. (Doric) *karykion* herald's staff] — **ca·du′ce·an** *adj.*

CADUCEUS

cae- For those words not entered below, see under CE-.

cae·cum (sē′kəm) See CECUM.

Cae·sar (sē′zər) *n.* **1.** The title of the Roman emperors from Augustus to Hadrian. **2.** Any despot

cae·sar·e·an (si·zâr′ē·ən), **cae·sar·i·an,** See CESAREAN, e

Cae·sar·e·an (si·zâr′ē·ən) *adj.* Pertaining to Caesar. — Loosely, a cesarean section. Also **Cae·sar′i·an.**

cae·si·um (sē′zē·əm) See CESIUM.

caes·tus (ses′təs) See CESTUS.

cae·su·ra (si·zho͝or′ə, -zyo͝or′ə) *n. pl.* **·su·ras** or **·su·r** (-zho͝or′ē, -zyo͝or′ē) **1.** In Greek and Latin prosody, a bre occurring when a word ends within a foot. **2.** In mode prosody, a pause usu. near the middle of a line. Caesura indicated by two vertical lines (‖). **3.** *Music* A pause in cating a rhythmic division point. Also spelled *cesura.* [< *caedere* to cut] — **cae·su′ral** *adj.*

ca·fé (ka·fā′, kə-) *n.* **1.** A coffee house; restaurant. **2.** barroom. **3.** Coffee. Also *esp. U.S.* **ca·fe′.** [< F]

ca·fé au lait (kȧ·fā′ ō lā′) *French* **1.** Coffee with scald milk. **2.** A light brown.

ca·fé noir (kȧ·fā′ nwȧr′) *French* Black coffee.

caf·e·te·ri·a (kaf′ə·tir′ē·ə) *n.* A restaurant where the patro wait upon themselves. [< Am. Sp., coffee store],

caf·feine (kaf′ēn, *in technical usage* kaf′ē·in) *n. Chem.* slightly bitter alkaloid, $C_8H_{10}O_2N_4$, obtained from t leaves and berries of coffee, used as a stimulant and diuret Also **caf′fein.** [< F *café* coffee]

caf·tan (kaf′tən, käf·tän′) *n.* An undercoat having lo sleeves and a sash, worn in eastern Mediterranean countri also spelled *kaftan.* [< F < Turkish *qaftān*]

cage (kāj) *n.* **1.** A boxlike structure with openwork of wi or bars, for confining birds or beasts. **2.** Any cagelike stru ture or framework. **3.** In baseball, a movable backst for batting practice. **4.** In hockey, the frame and net us as the goal. **5.** In basketball, the basket. — *v.t.* **cage cag·ing** To shut up in a cage; confine; imprison. [< O ult. < L *cavus* empty, hollow]

cage·ling (kāj′ling) *n.* A caged bird.

cage·y (kā′jē) *adj.* **cag·i·er, cag·i·est** *Informal* Wary of b ing duped; shrewd and careful. Also **cag′y.** [Origin unc tain] — **cag′i·ly** *adv.* — **cag′i·ness** *n.*

ca·hier (kä·yā′) *n.* **1.** A number of sheets, as of print matter, loosely bound together. **2.** A report, as of procee ings, etc. [< F < OF, ult. < L *quaterni* a set of four]

ca·hoots (kə·ho͞ots′) *n.pl. U.S. Slang* Affiliation; partn ship, as in the phrase **in cahoots.** [? < F *cahute* cabin]

cai·man (kā′mən) See CAYMAN.

Cain (kān) The eldest son of Adam, who slew his broth Abel. *Gen.* iv. — *n.* A murderer. — **to raise Cain** *U. Slang* To cause a disturbance.

ca·ique (kä·ēk′) *n.* A long, narrow skiff used on the B porus. [< F < Ital. < Turkish *kāyik*]

cairn (kârn) *n.* A mound or heap of stones set up as a m morial or a marker. [< Scottish Gaelic *carn* heap of stone

cais·son (kā′sən, -son) *n.* **1.** A large watertight chamb within which work is done under water, as on a bridge pi **2.** *Naut.* A watertight device used to raise sunken ships. A two-wheeled vehicle carrying a chest of ammunition serve a gun. [< F, aug. of *caisse* box, chest]

sson disease *Pathol.* A painful, paralyzing, sometimes tal disease caused by too rapid a transition from the comessed air of caissons, diving bells, etc., while the system ill contains an excess of nitrogen.
jole (kə·jōl′) *v.t. & v.i.* **·joled, ·jol·ing** To coax with flatry or false promises; wheedle. [< F *cajoler*] **— ca·jole′·ent** *n.* **— ca·jol′er** *n.* **— ca·jol′ing·ly** *adv.*
jol·er·y (kə·jō′lər·ē) *n. pl.* **·er·ies** The act or practice of joling or wheedling; artful persuasion; coaxing.
·jun (kā′jən) *n.* A reputed descendant of the Acadian ·ench in Louisiana. [Alter. of ACADIAN]
ke (kāk) *n.* **1.** A mixture of flour, milk, sugar, etc., ked in various forms and generally sweeter and richer than ead. **2.** A small, usu. thin mass of dough, or other food, ked or fried: fish *cake.* **3.** A mass of matter compressed hardened into a compact form: a *cake* of soap. **— to take e cake** *Informal* To take or deserve a prize; excel: often ed sarcastically. **—** *v.t. & v.i.* **caked, cak·ing** To form to a hardened mass. [< ON *kaka*]
kes and ale Pleasures of life; easy living.
ke·walk (kāk′wôk′) *n.* Formerly, a dance which Amer-an Negroes performed, a cake being awarded for the most iginal steps. **—** *v.i.* To do a cakewalk strut.
·a·bash (kal′ə·bash) *n.* **1.** The calabash tree. **2.** A urd from this tree, used for making pipes, bowls, etc. [< < Sp. *calabaza* pumpkin]
labash tree **1.** A tropical American tree of the gourd mily, bearing a hard-shelled fruit. **2.** A tropical American ee of the bignonia family, with a gourdlike fruit.
·a·boose (kal′ə·bo͞os) *n. U.S. Informal* A jail; lockup. < Sp. *calabozo*]
la·di·um (kə·lā′dē·əm) *n.* A tuberous tropical American rb of the arum family. [< NL < Malay *kelādy*]
·a·mine (kal′ə·mīn, -min) *n.* A vitreous zinc carbonate, CO_3, used in the form of a lotion or ointment for the treatent of skin ailments. **—** *v.t.* **·mined, ·min·ing** To apply lamine to. [< F < LL < L < Gk. *kadmeia* calamine]
lam·i·tous (kə·lam′ə·təs) *adj.* Causing or resulting in a lamity; disastrous. **— ca·lam′i·tous·ly** *adv.*
lam·i·ty (kə·lam′ə·tē) *n. pl.* **·ties** **1.** A disaster. **2.** state of great distress. [< F < L *calamitas, -tatis*]
·a·mus (kal′ə·məs) *n. pl.* **·mi** (-mī) **1.** The sweet flag, plant. **2.** The quill of a feather. [< Gk. *kalamos* reed]
lash (kə·lash′) *n.* **1.** A low-wheeled light carriage with lding top. **2.** A folding carriage top; also **calash top.** **3.** folding bonnet of the 18th century. [< F *calèche*]
·ca·ne·us (kal·kā′nē·əs) *n. pl.* **·ne·i** (-nē·ī) *Anat.* The rge bone at the back of the foot: also called *heel bone.* Also **l·ca′ne·um.** [< L (*os*) *calcaneum* heel bone < *calx* heel]
·car·e·ous (kal·kâr′ē·əs) *adj.* **1.** Composed of, conining, or like limestone or calcium carbonate. **2.** Containg calcium. [< L *calcarius* of lime < *calx, calcis* lime]
·ced·o·ny (kal·sed′ə·nē) See CHALCEDONY.
·ces (kal′sēz) Alternative plural of CALX.
ci- *combining form* Lime. [< L *calx, calcis* lime]
·cif·er·ol (kal·sif′ər·ōl, -ol) *n. Biochem.* The antirauitic vitamin D_2, a white, crystalline compound, $C_{28}H_{44}O$. < CALCIFER(OUS) + (ERGOSTER)OL]
·cif·er·ous (kal·sif′ər·əs) *adj.* Yielding or containing lcium carbonate, as rocks.
·ci·fy (kal′sə·fī) *v.t. & v.i.* **·fied, ·fy·ing** To make or beme stony by the deposit of lime salts. **— cal·ci·fi·ca·tion** al′sə·fi·kā′shən) *n.*
l·ci·mine (kal′sə·mīn, -min) *n.* A white or tinted wash r ceilings, walls, etc. **—** *v.t.* **·mined, ·min·ing** To apply lcimine to. Also, *Brit., distemper:* also spelled *kalsomine.* < L *calx, calcis* lime; orig. a trade name]
l·cin·a·to·ry (kal·sin′ə·tôr′ē, -tō′rē) *adj.* For calcining. - *n. pl.* **·ries** An apparatus for calcining, as a furnace.
·cine (kal′sīn, -sin) *v.* **·cined, ·cin·ing** *v.t.* **1.** To render substance) friable by the expulsion of its volatile content rough heat. **2.** To reduce to a calx by subjecting to heat. - *v.i.* **3.** To become changed by dry heat into a friable owder. Also **cal′cin·ize.** [< F < Med.L *calcinare* < L *calx* me] **— cal·ci·na·tion** (kal′sə·nā′shən) *n.*
l·cite (kal′sīt) *n.* A widely distributed calcium caronate mineral, white or variously tinted, including chalk, mestone, marble, etc. **— cal·cit·ic** (kal·sit′ik) *adj.*
l·ci·um (kal′sē·əm) *n.* A silver-white, malleable, metalc element (symbol Ca), widely distributed in combination, s in chalk, gypsum, and limestone. See ELEMENT. [< NL L *calx, calcis* lime]
lcium carbide *Chem.* A compound, CaC_2, made from uicklime and carbon and used to make acetylene.
lcium carbonate *Chem.* A compound, $CaCO_3$, forming the principal constituent of certain rocks and minerals, s limestone, aragonite, and calcite, and used in the preparaon of lime and as the basis of dentifrices.

calcium chloride *Chem.* A white salt, $CaCl_2$, used as a drying agent, preservative, refrigerant, and dust preventer.
calcium hydroxide *Chem.* Slaked lime, $Ca(OH)_2$: when used in solution called *limewater.*
calc·spar (kalk′spär′) *n.* Crystallized carbonate of lime.
cal·cu·la·ble (kal′kyə·lə·bəl) *adj.* **1.** Capable of being calculated. **2.** Reliable; dependable. **— cal′cu·la·bly** *adv.*
cal·cu·late (kal′kyə·lāt) *v.* **·lat·ed, ·lat·ing** *v.t.* **1.** To determine by computation; arrive at by arithmetical means. **2.** To ascertain beforehand; form an estimate of. **3.** To plan or design: used chiefly in the passive: *calculated* to carry two tons. **4.** *U.S. Dial.* To think; expect. **—** *v.i.* **5.** To compute. **— to calculate on** To depend or rely on. [< L < *calculus* pebble; with ref. to the use of pebbles in counting]
cal·cu·lat·ing (kal′kyə·lā′ting) *adj.* Inclined to reckon or estimate, esp. for one's own interests; scheming.
cal·cu·la·tion (kal′kyə·lā′shən) *n.* **1.** The act, process, or result of computing. **2.** An estimate; forecast. **3.** Forethought; prudence. **— cal′cu·la′tive** *adj.*
cal·cu·la·tor (kal′kyə·lā′tər) *n.* **1.** One who calculates. **2.** A keyboard machine that adds, subtracts, multiplies, and divides: also **calculating machine.**
cal·cu·lous (kal′kyə·ləs) *adj. Pathol.* Pertaining to or affected with a calculus or calculi. [< L *calculosus* pebbly]
cal·cu·lus (kal′kyə·ləs) *n. pl.* **·li** (-lī) or **·lus·es** **1.** *Pathol.* A stonelike mass, as in the bladder. **2.** *Math.* A method of calculating by the use of a highly specialized system of algebraic symbols. **— differential calculus** The branch of analysis that investigates the infinitesimal changes of constantly varying quantities when the relations between the quantities are given. **— integral calculus** The branch of analysis that, from the relations among the infinitesimal changes or variations of quantities, deduces relations among the quantities themselves. [< L, a pebble (used in counting)]
cal·dron (kôl′drən) See CAULDRON.
ca·lèche (kȧ·lesh′) *n.* A calash.
Cal·e·do·ni·a (kal′ə·dō′nē·ə, -dōn′yə) *Poetic* Scotland. [< L] **— Cal′e·do′ni·an** *adj. & n.*
cal·e·fa·cient (kal′ə·fā′shənt) *adj.* Causing heat or warmth. **—** *n. Med.* A remedy that produces heat. [< L < *calere* to be warm + *facere* to make, cause]
cal·en·dar (kal′ən·dər) *n.* **1.** Any of various systems of fixing the order, length, and subdivisions of the years and months. **2.** A table showing the days, weeks, and months of a year. **3.** A schedule or list, esp. one arranged in chronological order: a court *calendar.* **—** *v.t.* To place in a calendar; schedule. [< L < *calendae* calends]
— Gregorian calendar The calendar now in general use in most parts of the world; first prescribed in 1582 by Pope Gregory XIII to correct the Julian year to the astronomical year, the first being the **Old Style** (*O.S.*) date and the second being the **New Style** (*N.S.*).
— Hebrew (or **Jewish**) **calendar** A calendar used by the Jews, based on the lunar month and reckoning the year of creation as 3761 B.C. Since the Hebrew months are mostly shorter, they do not coincide in any systematic manner with those of the Gregorian calendar except by approximation.

	Months	*Number of days*	*Approximate month in Gregorian calendar*
1	Tishri	30	October
2	Heshwan	29 or 30	November
3	Kislew	29 or 30	December
4	Tebet	29	January
5	Shebat	30	February
6	Adar	29 or 30	March
–	Veadar[1]	29	—
7	Nisan	30	April
8	Iyyar	29	May
9	Sivan	30	June
10	Tammuz	29	July
11	Ab	30	August
12	Elul	29	September

[1]The additional intercalary month.

— Julian calendar The calendar prescribed by Julius Caesar, in which the ordinary year had 365 days and every fourth year 366 (leap year). It is now replaced by the Gregorian calendar.
— Moslem (or **Mohammedan**) **calendar** The calendar generally used in all Moslem countries, reckoning time from July 16 A.D. 622, the day following Mohammed's flight from Mecca to Medina, and consisting of 12 lunar months.
— Republican (or **Revolutionary**) **calendar** The calendar instituted on Oct. 5, 1793, by the first French republic, and abolished Dec. 31, 1805. It divided the year into 12 months of 30 days each, with five (in leap years six) supplementary days (*sansculottides*) at the end of the last month.
— Roman calendar A lunar calendar, attributed to Numa.

The day of the new moon was the *calends*, and the day of the full moon the *ides* (the 13th or 15th of the month).

calendar year The 365, or, in leap year, 366 days from midnight of December 31 to the same hour twelve months thereafter.

cal·en·der (kal′ən·dər) *n.* A machine for giving a gloss to cloth, paper, etc., by pressing between rollers. —*v.t.* To press in a calender. [< F < L < Gk. *kylindros* roller]

cal·ends (kal′əndz) *n.pl.* The first day of the Roman month: also spelled *kalends.* [< L *calendae*]

ca·len·du·la (kə·len′jo͞o·lə) *n.* An annual or perennial herb of the composite family, having bright orange or yellow flowers. [< NL, dim. of L *calendae* calends]

ca·les·cence (kə·les′əns) *n.* The condition of growing warm. [< L *calescere* to grow warm] —**ca·les′cent** *adj.*

calf[1] (kaf, käf) *n.* *pl.* **calves** (kavz, kävz) **1.** The young of the cow or various other bovine animals. **2.** The young of various mammals, as the elephant, whale, etc. **3.** Calfskin. **4.** *Informal* A gawky, witless young man. [OE *cealf*]

calf[2] (kaf, käf) *n.* *pl.* **calves** (kavz, kävz) The muscular rear part of the human leg below the knee. [< ON *kālfi*]

calf love *Informal* Adolescent infatuation; puppy love.

calf·skin (kaf′skin′, käf′-) *n.* **1.** The skin or hide of a calf. **2.** Leather made from this.

Cal·i·ban (kal′ə·ban) In Shakespeare's *Tempest*, a deformed, savage slave of Prospero.

cal·i·ber (kal′ə·bər) *n.* **1.** The internal diameter of a tube. **2.** *Mil.* **a** The internal diameter of the barrel of a gun, cannon, etc. **b** The diameter of a bullet, shell, etc. **3.** Degree of personal excellence. Also *Brit.* **cal′i·bre.** [< F *calibre*]

cal·i·brate (kal′ə·brāt) *v.t.* **·brat·ed, ·brat·ing 1.** To graduate, correct, or adjust the scale of (a measuring instrument) into appropriate units. **2.** To determine the reading of (such an instrument). **3.** To ascertain the caliber of. [Cf. F *calibrer*] —**cal′i·bra′tion** *n.* —**cal′i·bra′tor** *n.*

cal·i·ces (kal′ə·sēz) Plural of CALIX.

cal·i·co (kal′i·kō) *n.* *pl.* **·coes** or **·cos** Cheap cotton cloth printed in a figured pattern of bright colors. —*adj.* **1.** Made of calico. **2.** Resembling printed calico; dappled or streaked: a *calico* cat. [after *Calicut*, where first obtained]

California poppy A plant of the poppy family having showy yellow flowers: the State flower of California.

cal·i·for·ni·um (kal′ə·fôr′nē·əm) *n.* An unstable radioactive element (symbol Cf), artificially produced by bombardment of curium with alpha particles. See ELEMENT. [after the University of *California* where first produced]

ca·lig·ra·phy (kə·lig′rə·fē) See CALLIGRAPHY.

cal·i·per (kal′ə·pər) *n.* *Usu. pl.* An instrument resembling a pair of compasses, usu. with curved legs, used for measuring diameters. Also **caliper compass.** —*v.t.* & *v.i.* To measure by using calipers. Also *calliper.* [< CALIBER]

ca·liph (kā′lif, kal′if) *n.* The spiritual and civil head of a Moslem state: also spelled *calif, kalif, kaliph, khalif.* [< F < Arabic *khalīfah* successor (to Mohammed)]

cal·i·phate (kal′ə·fāt, -fit) *n.* The office, dominion, or reign of a caliph.

cal·is·then·ics (kal′is·then′iks) *n.pl.* (*construed as sing. def.* 2) **1.** Light gymnastics to promote grace and health. **2.** The science of such exercises. [<Gk. *kalli-* beautiful + *sthenos* strength] —**cal′is·then′ic** or **·i·cal** *adj.*

calk[1] (kôk) See CAULK.

calk[2] (kôk) *n.* **1.** A spur on a horse's shoe to prevent slipping. **2.** *U.S.* A plate with sharp points worn on the sole of a boot or shoe to prevent slipping. Also **calk′er.** —*v.t.* To furnish with calks. [Prob. < L *calx* heel]

call (kôl) *v.t.* **1.** To say in a loud voice; shout; proclaim. **2.** To summon. **3.** To convoke; convene: to *call* a meeting. **4.** To invoke solemnly. **5.** To summon to a specific work: to *call* someone to the ministry. **6.** To arouse, as from sleep. **7.** To telephone to. **8.** To summon or lure (birds or animals) by imitating their cry, whistling, etc. **9.** To name. **10.** To designate or characterize in any way. **11.** To estimate loosely; consider: I *call* it 10 pounds. **12.** To bring to action or consideration: to *call* a case to court. **13.** To insist upon payment of, as by written notice. **14.** In baseball: **a** To stop or suspend (a game). **b** To designate a pitch as (a ball or strike). **c** To declare (a player) out, safe, etc. **15.** In poker, to demand a show of hands by a bet equal to that of (another). **16.** In pool, etc., to predict (a shot) before making the play. —*v.i.* **17.** To raise one's voice; speak loudly. **18.** To make a brief visit, stop, or stay: with *at, on,* or *upon.* **19.** To communicate by telephone. **20.** In poker, to demand a show of hands. **21.** In some card games, to make a demand or signal, as for trumps. —**to call back 1.** To summon back; recall. **2.** To call in return, as by telephone. —**to call down 1.** To invoke from heaven. **2.** *Informal* To rebuke; reprimand. —**to call for 1.** To stop so as to obtain. **2.** To require; need. —**to call forth** To summon into action; draw out. —**to call in 1.** To collect, as debts. **2.** To retire, as currency, from circulation. **3.** To summon, as for consultation. —**to call off 1.** To summon away. **2.** To say or read aloud. **3.** To cancel. —**to c[all] out** To shout. —**to call up 1.** To recollect. **2.** To su[m]mon. **3.** To telephone. —*n.* **1.** A shout or cry. **2.** [A] summons or invitation. **3.** A signal, as on a bell or ho[rn]. **4.** A demand; claim: the *call* of duty. **5.** A communicati[on] by telephone. **6.** A roll call. **7.** An inward urge to a [re]ligious vocation. **8.** A brief, often formal, visit. **9.** The [cry] of an animal, esp. of a bird. **10.** A whistle, etc., with whi[ch] to imitate such a cry. **11.** A need; occasion: You've no c[all] to do that. **12.** A request for payment. —**on call 1.** Pa[y]able on demand. **2.** Available when sent for. [< ON *kal*[*la*]]

cal·la (kal′ə) *n.* **1.** A plant of the arum family having [a] large white leaf that resembles a flower. Also **calla lily.** [2.] A marsh plant bearing red berries in dense clusters. [<

call·board (kôl′bôrd′, -bōrd′) *n.* A theater bulletin boa[rd] for posting notices of rehearsals, instructions, etc.

call·boy (kôl′boi′) *n.* **1.** A boy who calls actors to go [on] stage. **2.** A bellboy.

call·er (kô′lər) *n.* **1.** One who or that which calls. **2.** O[ne] making a brief visit.

calli- For words not found here, see under CALI-.

cal·lig·ra·phy (kə·lig′rə·fē) *n.* **1.** Beautiful penmansh[ip]. **2.** Handwriting in general. Also spelled *caligraphy.* [Gk. < *kalos* beautiful + *graphein* to write] —**cal·lig′r[a]pher, cal·lig′ra·phist** *n.* —**cal·li·graph′ic** *adj.*

call·ing (kô′ling) *n.* **1.** A speaking or crying aloud. **2.** [A] convocation or summons. **3.** A vocation or profession.

calling card A small card, printed or engraved with on[e's] name, used to announce a visit or call: also *visiting card.*

cal·li·o·pe (kə·lī′ə·pē, kal′ē·ōp) *n.* A musical instrum[ent] consisting of a series of steam whistles played by means o[f a] keyboard: also called *steam organ.* [after *Calliope*]

Cal·li·o·pe (kə·lī′ə·pē) The Muse of eloquence and epic [po]etry. [< L < Gk. < *kalos* beautiful + *ops* voice]

cal·lis·then·ics (kal′is·then′iks) See CALISTHENICS.

call letters The code letters identifying a radio or tele[vi]sion transmitting station. Also **call sign.**

call loan A loan of money to be repaid on demand.

call money Money borrowed as a call loan.

call number A classifying number employed by libraries [to] indicate the subject of a book and its place on the shelv[es].

cal·los·i·ty (kə·los′ə·tē) *n.* *pl.* **·ties 1.** *Physiol.* A call[us]. **2.** Callousness of feelings; insensibility.

cal·lous (kal′əs) *adj.* **1.** Thickened and hardened, as a c[al]lus. **2.** Hardened in feelings; insensible. —*v.t.* & *v.i.* [To] make or become callous. [< L < *callus* hard skin] —**ca[l]lous·ly** *adv.* —**cal′lous·ness** *n.*

cal·low (kal′ō) *adj.* **1.** Inexperienced; immature. **2.** U[n]fledged, as a bird. [OE *calu* bare, bald]

cal·lus (kal′əs) *n.* *pl.* **·lus·es 1.** *Physiol.* A thickened, har[d]ened part of the skin: also called *callosity.* **2.** *Anat.* The n[ew] bony tissue between and around the fractured ends of [a] broken bone in the process of reuniting. **3.** *Bot.* The tiss[ue] that forms over a cut on a stem and protects the expos[ed] wood. —*v.i.* To form a callus. [< L, hard skin]

calm (käm) *adj.* **1.** Free from agitation; still or nearly st[ill]. **2.** Not excited by passion or emotion; peaceful. —*n.* [1.] Lack of wind or motion; stillness. **2.** Serenity. —*v.t.* & *v.i.* To make or become quiet or calm: often with *down.* [< M[F] < Ital. < LL < Gk. *kauma* heat; with ref. to the midd[ay] siesta] —**calm′ly** *adv.* —**calm′ness** *n.*

—**Syn.** (adj.) *Calm* describes a state that may be transie[nt]; *tranquil* suggests a more enduring condition: a *calm* sea, a *tranq*[*uil*] life. A *placid* person is regarded as temperamentally stolid; [a] *placid* lake is always peaceful. Things elevated above earthly t[ur]moil are *serene*: a *serene* sky, a *serene* smile. *Quiet* and *still* im[ply] absence of noise as well as of bustle.

cal·o·mel (kal′ə·mel, -məl) *n.* *Med.* Mercurous chlori[de], HgCl, a heavy, white, tasteless compound, used as a purg[a]tive, etc. [< F < Gk. *kalos* beautiful + *melas* black]

ca·lor·ic (kə·lôr′ik, -lor′-) *adj.* Of or pertaining to heat. [—]*n.* Heat. [< F < L *calor* heat] —**cal·o·ric·i·ty** (kal′ə·ri[s′]ə·tē) *n.*

cal·o·rie (kal′ə·rē) *n.* **1.** One of two recognized units [of] heat. The **large** or **great calorie** is the amount of heat r[e]quired to raise the temperature of one kilogram of wat[er] 1° C. The **small calorie** is the amount of heat required [to] raise one gram of water 1° C. **2.** *Physiol.* The large calorie [as a] measure of the energy value of foods or the heat output [of] organisms. Also **cal′o·ry.** [< F < L *calor* heat]

cal·o·rif·ic (kal′ə·rif′ik) *adj.* Pertaining to or produci[ng] heat. [< F < L *calorificus*]

cal·o·rim·e·ter (kal′ə·rim′ə·tər) *n.* Any apparatus f[or] measuring the quantity of heat generated by friction, com[]bustion, or chemical change.

cal·o·rim·e·try (kal′ə·rim′ə·trē) *n.* The measurement [of] heat. —**ca·lor·i·met·ric** (kə·lôr′ə·met′rik, -lor′-) or **·met·i·cal** *adj.*

ca·lotte (kə·lot′) *n.* A skullcap. [< F]

cal·u·met (kal′yə·met, kal′yə·met′) *n.* A tobacco pipe wi[th] a long, ornamented stem, used by American Indians in cer[emonies]

onies, to ratify treaties, etc.: also called *peace pipe*. [< al. F, pipe stem < L *calamus* reed]
·lum·ni·ate (kə·lum′nē·āt) *v.t. & v.i.* **·at·ed, ·at·ing** To :cuse falsely; defame; slander. [< L *calumnia* slander] — **·lum′ni·a′tion** *n.* — **ca·lum′ni·a′tor** *n.*
·lum·ni·ous (kə·lum′nē·əs) *adj.* Slanderous. Also **·lum′ni·a·to′ry** (-tôr′ē, -tōr′ē). — **ca·lum′ni·ous·ly** *adv.*
·um·ny (kal′əm·nē) *n. pl.* **·nies 1.** A false and malicious :cusation or report, made to injure another. **2.** Defama-on; slander. [< MF < L *calumnia* slander]
·l·va·ry (kal′və·rē) The place, near the site of ancient :rusalem, where Christ was crucified; Golgotha. *Luke* xxiii 3. [< L *calvaria* skull, trans. of Aramaic *golgothā*]
lve (kav, käv) *v.t. & v.i.* **calved, calv·ing** To bring forth calf). [OE *cealfian* < *cealf* calf]
lves (kavz, kävz) Plural of CALF.
·l·vin·ism (kal′vin·iz′əm) *n. Theol.* The system or doc-ines of John Calvin, emphasizing the depravity and help-ssness of man, the sovereignty of God, and predestination, nd characterized by an austere moral code. — **Cal′vin·ist** — **Cal′vin·is′tic** or **·ti·cal** *adj.* — **Cal′vin·is′ti·cal·ly** *adv.*
lx (kalks) *n. pl.* **calx·es** or **cal·ces** (kal′sēz) The residue om the calcination of minerals. [< L]
l·y·ces (kal′ə·sēz, kā′lə-) Alternative plural of CALYX.
·lyp·so (kə·lip′sō) *n.* An improvised song, originally Trin-adian, dealing with news, love, etc. [Origin uncertain]
·lyp·so (kə·lip′sō) In the *Odyssey*, a nymph who kept dysseus for seven years on her island.
·lyx (kā′liks, kal′iks) *n. pl.* **ca·lyx·es** or **cal·y·ces** (kal′ə-sēz, kā′lə-) *Bot.* The outermost series of leaflike parts of a ower; the sepals. [< L < Gk. *kalyx*, husk, pod]
m (kam) *n. Mech.* An irregularly shaped piece or projec-on, as on a wheel or rotating shaft, that imparts recipro-ating or variable motion to another piece bearing on it. [< u., tooth, cog of a wheel.]
·ma·ra·de·rie (kä′mə·rä′dər·ē) *n.* Comradeship. [< F]
m·a·ril·la (kam′ə·ril′ə, *Sp.* kä·mä·rē′lyä) *n.* A clique; abal. [< Sp., dim. of *camara* chamber]
m·ass (kam′əs) *n.* An herb of the lily family having an dible bulb. Also **cam′as.** [< Chinook jargon]
m·ber (kam′bər) *v.t.* **1.** To cut or bend to a slight up-ard convex form. — *v.i.* **2.** To have or assume a slight up-ard curve, as a ship's deck. — *n.* A slight upward bend, s of a timber. [< ME < L < *camera* curved roof, vault]
m·bi·um (kam′bē·əm) *n. Bot.* A layer of tissue in ex-genous plants, from which new wood and bark are formed. < LL, exchange]
m·bri·a (kam′brē·ə) Medieval Latin name for WALES.
m·bri·an (kam′brē·ən) *adj.* **1.** Of or pertaining to Cam-ria; Welsh. **2.** *Geol.* Denoting or of the earliest of the peri-ds of the Paleozoic era. See chart under GEOLOGY. — *n.* The Cambrian strata or period. **2.** A Welshman.
m·bric (kām′brik) *n.* A fine white linen, or a similar fab-c of cotton. [< Flemish *Kameryk* Cambrai]
mbric tea A drink made of sweetened hot water and ilk, sometimes flavored with a little tea.
me (kām) Past tense of COME.
m·el (kam′əl) *n.* A large Asian r African ruminant with a humped ack, used in the desert as a beast of urden. The **Arabian camel**, or drom-dary, has one hump, and the **Bactrian amel** has two. [OE < L < Gk. *amēlos* < Semitic]
m·el·hair (kam′əl·hâr′) *n.* Cam-'s hair.
·mel·lia (kə·mēl′yə, -mel′ē·ə) *n.* tropical Asian tree or shrub with lossy leaves and white, pink, red, or ariegated flowers: also called *japoni-a.* [< NL, after G. J. *Kamel*, 1661–706, Jesuit traveler]

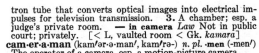

CAMELS
A Arabian (to 7 feet high at shoulder) *B* Bactrian (about 6 feet)

m·e·lot (kam′ə·lot) In Arthurian gend, the seat of King Arthur's court.
mel's hair 1. The hair of the camel. **2.** A soft, warm, sually tan cloth made of camel's hair, sometimes mixed with ool or other fibers. — **cam·el's-hair** (kam′əlz·hâr′) *adj.*
m·em·bert (kam′əm·bâr, *Fr.* kȧ·mäṅ·bâr′) *n.* A rich, reamy, soft cheese. [after *Camembert*, town in NW France]
m·e·o (kam′ē·ō) *n. pl.* **·os 1.** A gem of differently col-red layers, having a design carved in relief on one with the ther layer or layers serving as background. **2.** Carving one in this manner. [< Ital. *cammeo*; ult. origin unknown]
m·er·a (kam′ər·ə, kam′rə) *n. pl.* **·er·as** *for defs. 1 and 2,* **er·ae** (-ə·rē) *for def. 3* **1.** A lightproof chamber or box or taking photographs and consisting of a sensitized plate or lm on which light rays are projected through a lens. **2.** *'elecom.* An enclosed unit containing the light-sensitive elec-tron tube that converts optical images into electrical im-pulses for television transmission. **3.** A chamber; esp. a judge's private room. — **in camera** *Law* Not in public court; privately. [< L, vaulted room < Gk. *kamara*]
cam·er·a·man (kam′ər·ə·man′, kam′rə-) *n. pl.* **·men** (-men′) The operator of a camera, esp. a motion-picture camera.
cam·i·sole (kam′ə·sōl) *n.* **1.** A woman's fancy underwaist, worn with a sheer bodice. **2.** A brief negligée. **3.** A type of straitjacket. [< F < Sp. *camisola*, dim. of *camisa* shirt]
cam·o·mile (kam′ə·mīl) *n.* A strongly scented, bitter herb whose aromatic flowers and leaves are used in medicine. [< F < L < Gk. *chamai* on the ground + *mēlon* apple]
cam·ou·flage (kam′ə·fläzh, -fläj) *n.* **1.** *Mil.* Measures or material used to conceal or misrepresent the identity of in-stallations, ships, etc. **2.** Any disguise or pretense. — *v.t. & v.i.* **·flaged, ·flag·ing** To hide or obscure, as with disguises. [< F < *camoufler* to disguise] — **cam′ou·flag′er** *n.*
camp[1] (kamp) *n.* **1.** A group of tents or other temporary shelters, as for soldiers, hunters, or vacationers. Also, the ground or area so employed. **2.** The persons occupying a group of tents, etc. **3.** *U.S.* A town hastily constructed near a mine. **4.** Military life. **5.** A body of persons sup-porting a policy, theory, or doctrine; also, the position so up-held. — *v.i.* **1.** To set up or live in a camp; encamp. **2.** To hold stubbornly to a position. — *v.t.* **3.** To shelter or sta-tion in a camp. — **to camp out** To sleep in a tent; live in the open. [< MF < Ital. < L *campus* level plain]
camp[2] (kamp) *n.* A comical style or quality perceived in theatrical or flamboyant gestures, literary works, etc. [? < dial. E *camp* or *kemp* bold, impetuous fellow]
cam·paign (kam·pān′) *n.* **1.** A series of connected military operations conducted for a common objective, in a particular area, etc. **2.** An organized series of activities designed to obtain a definite result. — *v.i.* To serve in, conduct, or go on a campaign. [< F < Ital. *campagna*] — **cam·paign′er** *n.*
cam·pa·ni·le (kam′pə·nē′lē, *Ital.* käm′pä·nē′lā) *n. pl.* **·les** or **·li** (-lē) A bell tower. [< Ital. < LL *campana* bell]
cam·pan·u·la (kam·pan′yə·lə) *n.* A plant having bell-shaped flowers. [< NL, dim. of LL *campana* bell]
camp chair A light, folding chair.
camp·er (kamp′ər) *n.* **1.** One who camps out or is a member of a camp, as a children's summer camp. **2.** A vehicle afford-ing shelter and usu. sleeping facilities: also **camper wagon.**
cam·pes·tral (kam·pes′trəl) *adj.* Growing in or pertaining to fields or open country. [< L *campus* field]
camp·fire (kamp′fīr′) *n.* **1.** A fire in an outdoor camp, for cooking, warmth, etc. **2.** A gathering around a campfire.
campfire girl A girl between seven and eighteen years of age, belonging to the **Camp Fire Girls of America.**
camp·ground (kamp′ground′) *n.* An area used for a camp or a camp meeting.
cam·phor (kam′fər) *n.* A white, volatile, translucent crys-talline compound, $C_{10}H_{16}O$, with a penetrating odor, ob-tained from the camphor tree, used in medicine, etc. [< Malay *kāpūr*] — **cam·phor·ic** (kam·fôr′ik, -for′-) *adj.*
cam·phor·ate (kam′fə·rāt) *v.t.* **·at·ed, ·at·ing** To treat or saturate with camphor.
camphor ball A moth ball.
camphor ice A mixture of camphor, white wax, spermaceti, and castor oil, used for chapped skin, etc.
camphor tree A large evergreen tree of eastern Asia yield-ing the camphor of commerce.
camp·ing (kamp′ing) *n.* The act or practice of living out-doors, as in tents or without shelter, esp. for recreation.
cam·pi·on (kam′pē·ən) *n.* One of various herbs of the pink family, as the rose campion.
camp meeting A series of religious meetings held in a grove or field, usu. in a tent; also, one such meeting.
camp·stool (kamp′stōōl′) *n.* A light, folding stool.
cam·pus (kam′pəs) *n. U.S.* The grounds of a school or col-lege, or the court enclosed by the buildings. [< L, field]
cam·shaft (kam′shaft′, -shäft′) *n.* A shaft having one or more cams on it.
can[1] (kan, *unstressed* kən) *v.* Present *3rd person sing.* **can;** past **could** A defective verb now used only in the present and past tenses as an auxiliary and having the following senses: **1.** To be able to. **2.** To know how to. **3.** To have the right to. **4.** *Informal* To be permitted to; may. [OE *cunnan*]
◆ **can, may** In informal speech and writing, *can* is now ac-ceptable in the sense of *may*, to express permission, esp. in questions or negative statements: *Can* I leave now? You *cannot.* At the formal level, the distinction between *can* and *may* is still observed: *can*, to express ability to perform, either mentally or physically; *may*, to denote permission.
can[2] (kan) *n.* **1.** A vessel, usu. of tinned iron, for holding or carrying liquids, garbage, etc. **2.** *U.S.* A container in which fruits, tobacco, etc., are hermetically sealed. **3.** *U.S.* The contents of a sealed tin container. **4.** *U.S. Slang* **a** Jail. **b** A

toilet. **c** The buttocks. — *v.t.* **canned, can·ning** **1.** To put up in cans, jars, etc.; preserve. **2.** *Slang* To record for sound or film reproduction. **3.** *U.S. Slang* **a** To dismiss. **b** To cease: *Can* it! [OE *canne* cup] — **can′ner** *n.*

Ca·naan (kā′nən) The Promised Land of the Israelites.

Ca·naan·ite (kā′nən·īt) *n.* A dweller in Canaan prior to the Israelite conquest.

Canada balsam A yellowish turpentine derived from the balsam fir, used as a mounting cement in microscopy.

Canada goose The common wild goose of North America, brownish gray with black neck and head.

Canada jay A sooty gray bird of the crow family, native in Canada and the NE United States.

Canada sparrow A tree sparrow.

Ca·na·di·an (kə·nā′dē·ən) *adj.* Of or pertaining to Canada or its people. — *n.* A native or inhabitant of Canada.

CANADA GOOSE (To 43 inches long)

Canadian English The English language as spoken and written in Canada.

Canadian French The French language as spoken and written in Canada.

Ca·na·di·an·ism (kə·nā′dē·ən·iz′əm) *n.* **1.** A trait, custom, or tradition characteristic of the people of Canada or some of them. **2.** A word, phrase, etc. characteristic of Canadian English or French.

ca·naille (kə·nāl′, *Fr.* kȧ·nä′y′) *n.* The rabble; mob. [< F < Ital. *canaglia* pack of dogs < L *canis* dog]

ca·nal (kə·nal′) *n.* **1.** An artificial waterway for inland navigation, irrigation, etc. **2.** *Anat.* A passage or duct; tube: the auditory *canal.* **3.** *Astron.* One of the faint, linear markings visible on Mars. — *v.t.* **ca·nalled** or **·naled, ca·nal·ling** or **·nal·ing** To dig a canal through, or provide with canals. [< MF < L *canalis* groove]

canal boat A long barge, used on canals.

can·a·lic·u·late (kan′ə·lik′yə·lit, -lāt) *adj.* Channeled or grooved. Also **can′a·lic′u·lar** (-lər), **can′a·lic′u·lat′ed.**

can·a·lic·u·lus (kan′ə·lik′yə·ləs) *n.* *pl.* **·li** (-lī) *Anat.* A small tube or canal, as in a bone. [< L *canalis* groove]

ca·nal·i·za·tion (kə·nal′ə·zā′shən, kan′əl·ə-) *n.* **1.** The act of making canals. **2.** A system of canals.

ca·nal·ize (kə·nal′īz, kan′əl·īz) *v.t.* **·ized, ·iz·ing** **1.** To convert into a canal. **2.** To furnish with a canal, or a system of canals. **3.** To furnish with an outlet.

can·a·pé (kan′ə·pē, -pā, *Fr.* kȧ·nȧ·pā′) *n.* A thin piece of toast or a cracker spread with cheese, caviar, etc. [< F]

ca·nard (kə·närd′, *Fr.* kȧ·när′) *n.* A false or absurd story or rumor; a hoax. [< F, duck]

ca·nar·y (kə·nâr′ē) *n.* *pl.* **·nar·ies** **1.** A small finch having generally yellow plumage, popular as a cage bird. **2.** A bright yellow color. Also **canary yellow.** **3.** A sweet, white wine from the Canary Islands. [< F < Sp. < L *Canaria* (*Insula*) Dog (Island)]

ca·nas·ta (kə·nas′tə) *n.* A card game for two to six players, based on rummy. [< Sp., basket]

can·can (kan′kan′, *Fr.* käṅ·käṅ′) *n.* A fast dance with much high kicking and wild movements. [< MF, noise]

can·cel (kan′səl) *v.* **can·celed** or **·celled, can·cel·ing** or **·cel·ling** *v.t.* **1.** To mark out or off, as by drawing lines through. **2.** To render null and void; annul. **3.** To delete or withdraw; call off. **4.** To mark or otherwise deface, as a postage stamp. **5.** To make up for; neutralize. **6.** *Math.* To eliminate (a common factor) from the numerator and denominator of a fraction, or from both sides of an equation. — *v.i.* **7.** To cancel one another: with *out.* — **Syn.** See ANNUL. — *n.* A cancellation. [< MF < L *cancellare* to cross out] — **can′cel·a·ble** or **can′cel·la·ble** *adj.* — **can′cel·er** or **can′cel·ler** *n.*

can·cel·la·tion (kan′sə·lā′shən) *n.* **1.** The act of canceling or rendering void. **2.** The marks used in canceling. **3.** That which is canceled. Also **can′ce·la′tion.**

can·cer (kan′sər) *n.* **1.** Any of a group of often fatal diseases characterized by abnormal cellular growth and by malignancy. **2.** A malignant tumor. **3.** Any dangerous and spreading evil. [< L, crab] — **can′cer·ous** *adj.*

Can·cer (kan′sər) *n.* A constellation, the Crab; also, the fourth sign of the zodiac. See ZODIAC.

can·de·la·brum (kan′də·lä′brəm, -lā′-) *n.* *pl.* **·bra** (-brə) or **·brums** A large, branched candlestick. Also **can′de·la′bra** (-brə) *pl.* **·bras.** [< L < *candela* candle]

can·des·cence (kan·des′əns) *n.* Incandescence. [< L *candere* to gleam] — **can·des′cent** *adj.* — **can·des′cent·ly** *adv.*

can·did (kan′did) *adj.* **1.** Honest and open; sincere; frank. **2.** Impartial; fair. [< MF < L *candere* to gleam] — **can′·did·ly** *adv.* — **can′did·ness** *n.*

can·di·da·cy (kan′də·də·sē) *n.* *pl.* **·cies** The state or position of being a candidate. Also **can·di·da·ture** (kan′də·də·chŏŏr, -dā′chər), **can′di·date·ship′** (-dit·ship′).

can·di·date (kan′də·dāt, -dit) *n.* One who seeks, or is nominated for, an office, honor, or privilege. [< L *candidus* white; because office seekers in Rome wore white togas]

candid camera A small camera with a fast lens, used taking informal, unposed pictures.

can·died (kan′dēd) *adj.* **1.** Cooked with or in sugar. Crystallized or granulated. **3.** Flattering; honeyed.

can·dle (kan′dəl) *n.* **1.** A cylinder of tallow, wax, or ot solid fat, containing a wick, that gives light when burni **2.** Anything like a candle in shape or purpose. **3.** *Physic* unit of luminous intensity now equal to that of 1/60 squ centimeter of a black body operating at the temperatur solidification of platinum: also called *standard candle.* — **hold a candle to** To compare with favorably: usually use the negative. — *v.t.* **·dled, ·dling** To test, as eggs, by h ing between the eye and a light. [OE < L *candere* to glea

can·dle·ber·ry (kan′dəl·ber′ē) *n.* *pl.* **·ries** **1.** The myrtle. **2.** Its fruit.

can·dle·light (kan′dəl·līt′) *n.* Light given by a candle; tificial light. **2.** Twilight.

Can·dle·mas (kan′dəl·məs) *n.* February 2, the feast of Purification, or of the Presentation of Christ in the tem

can·dle·pow·er (kan′dəl·pou′ər) *n.* The illuminating po of a standard candle, used as a measure.

can·dle·stick (kan′dəl·stik′) *n.* A holder with sockets spikes for a candle or candles.

can·dle·wick (kan′dəl·wik′) *n.* The wick of a candle.

can·dor (kan′dər) *n.* **1.** Openness; frankness. **2.** Imp tiality; fairness. Also *Brit.* **can′dour.** [< L, sincerity]

can·dy (kan′dē) *n.* *pl.* **·dies** Any of numerous confecti consisting chiefly of sugar or syrup, usu. with chocol nuts, fruits, etc., added; also, such confections collectiv usu. called *sweets* in Great Britain. — *v.* **·died, ·dy·ing** **1.** To cause to form into crystals of sugar. **2.** To prese by boiling or coating with sugar. **3.** To render pleas sweeten. — *v.i.* **4.** To become covered with sugar. Arabic *qandī* made of sugar < *qand* sugar, ult. < Skt.]

cane (kān) *n.* **1.** A walking stick. **2.** The jointed, wo stem of the bamboo, rattan, and certain palm trees, used weaving material in chairs, etc. **3.** Sugar cane. **4.** The st of a raspberry or allied plant. **5.** Any rod, especially used for flogging. — *v.t.* **caned, can·ing** **1.** To strike or b with a cane. **2.** To make or repair with cane, as a ch [< OF < L < Gk. *kanna* reed] — **can′er** *n.*

cane·brake (kān′brāk′) *n.* A thick growth of cane.

cane sugar Sucrose obtained from the sugar cane.

ca·nine (kā′nīn) *adj.* **1.** Of or like a dog. **2.** *Zool.* Of dog family. **3.** Of or pertaining to a canine tooth. — *n.* A dog or other canine animal. **2.** *Anat.* One of the f pointed teeth situated one on either side of the upper lower incisors. For illus. see TOOTH. [< L *canis* dog]

Ca·nis Ma·jor (kā′nis mā′jər) A constellation contain the bright star Sirius. [< L, greater dog]

Canis Mi·nor (mī′nər) A constellation containing bright star Procyon. [< L, lesser dog]

can·is·ter (kan′is·tər) *n.* **1.** A container, usu. metal, tea, spices, etc. **2.** Formerly, fragments in a metallic cy der, to be fired from a cannon: also **canister shot.** [< *canistrum* basket]

can·ker (kang′kər) *n.* **1.** *Pathol.* An ulceration, chiefly the mouth and lips. **2.** Anything that causes corrupti evil, decay, etc. **3.** A disease of trees, causing decay of bark and wood. — *v.t.* **1.** To affect with canker. **2.** To away like a canker. — *v.i.* **3.** To become infected w canker. [< AF < L *cancer* crab] — **can′ker·ous** *adj.*

can·ker·worm (kang′kər·wûrm′) *n.* Any of several ins larvae that destroy fruit and shade trees.

can·na (kan′ə) *n.* An erect, mostly tropical American pl with red or yellow irregular flowers. [< L < Gk. *ka* reed] — **can·na·ceous** (kə·nā′shəs) *adj.*

canned (kand) *adj.* **1.** Preserved in a can or jar. **2.** *Sl* Recorded: *canned* music.

can·nel (kan′əl) *n.* A bituminous coal with low heat power. Also **cannel coal.**

can·ner·y (kan′ər·ē) *n.* *pl.* **·ner·ies** A place where foods canned.

can·ni·bal (kan′ə·bəl) *n.* **1.** One who eats human flesh. An animal that devours its own species. — *adj.* Of or cannibals. [< Sp. *Canibales,* var. of *Caribes* Caribs]

can·ni·bal·ism (kan′ə·bəl·iz′əm) *n.* **1.** The act or pract of eating the flesh of one's own kind. **2.** Inhuman cruel — **can′ni·bal·is′tic** *adj.* — **can′ni·bal·is′ti·cal·ly** *adv.*

can·ni·bal·ize (kan′ə·bəl·īz′) *v.t.* **·ized, ·iz·ing** *Mil.* To ta parts from (damaged tanks, etc.) in order to repair others.

can·ni·kin (kan′ə·kin) *n.* **1.** A small can. **2.** A woo pail.

can·ning (kan′ing) *n.* The act, process, or business of p serving foods in hermetically sealed tin cans, glass jars,

can·non (kan′ən) *n.* *pl.* **·nons** or **·non** **1.** *Mil.* A large tu lar weapon, usu. mounted on a fixed or mobile carriage, t discharges a projectile by the use of an explosive. **2.** large bone between the fetlock and knee or hock of the ho and allied animals. Also **cannon bone.** **3.** *Brit.* A carc — *v.i.* **1.** To fire cannon. **2.** *Brit.* To carom. — *v.t.* **3.**

ıttack with cannon shot. **4.** *Brit.* To cause to carom. [<)F < Ital. *canna* tube, pipe]
ın·non·ade (kan′ən·ād′) *v.* **·ad·ed, ·ad·ing** *v.t.* **1.** To at- ;ack with cannon shot. —*v.i.* **2.** To fire cannon repeatedly. —*n.* A continued discharge of or attack with cannon.
ınnon ball A spherical solid shot fired from a cannon.
ın·non·eer (kan′ən·ir′) *n.* An artillery gunner.
ınnon fodder Soldiers considered as that which is con- ›umed by war.
ın·not (kan′ot, ka·not′) The negative of the auxiliary verb :AN: written *can not* for emphasis. —**cannot but** Have no ılternative except to.
ın·ny (kan′ē) *adj.* *Originally Scot.* **·ni·er, ·ni·est** **1.** Cau- ;iously shrewd. **2.** Frugal; thrifty. **3.** Skillful. —*adv.* In canny manner. —**can′ni·ly** *adv.* —**can′ni·ness** *n.*
ı·noe (kə·no͞o′) *n.* A small, long, narrow boat, pointed at ɔoth ends, and propelled by paddles. —*v.* **·noed, ·noe·ing** *ı.t.* **1.** To convey by canoe. —*v.i.* **2.** To paddle, sail, or :ravel in a canoe. [< Sp. *canoa*] —**ca·noe′ist** *n.*
ın·on[1] (kan′ən) *n.* **1.** A rule or law; esp., a rule or body of ·ules of faith and practice enacted by a church council. **2.** An established rule; principle. **3.** A standard for judgment; :riterion. **4.** The books of the Bible. **5.** The sacred books of any sect or religion. **6.** A list, as of the recognized works of an author. **7.** The list of canonized saints. **8.** *Often cap.* *Eccl.* The portion of the Mass between the Sanctus and the Lord's Prayer. **9.** *Music* A composition or passage in which one or more voices follow and imitate the melody of the first voice. [OE < L < Gk. *kanōn* rule, straight rod]
ın·on[2] (kan′ən) *n.* A member of the chapter of a cathedral or collegiate church. [See CANON[1].]
a·ñon (kan′yən, *Sp.* kän·yōn′) See CANYON.
an·on·ess (kan′ən·is) *n.* A member of a religious commu- nity of women living under a rule but not under vows.
a·non·i·cal (kə·non′i·kəl) *adj.* **1.** Relating or conforming to or prescribed by, a canon or canons. **2.** Of or contained in the canon of Scripture. **3.** Authoritative; recognized. Also **ca·non′ic.** —**ca·non′i·cal·ly** *adv.*
anonical hours *Eccl.* The seven daily periods, fixed by canon, for prayer and devotion: also called *Divine Office.*
a·non·i·cals (kə·non′i·kəlz) *n.pl.* The habits or robes pre- scribed by canon to be worn by the clergy when officiating.
an·on·ist (kan′ən·ist) *n.* One skilled in canon law. —**can′on·is′tic** or **·ti·cal** *adj.*
an·on·ize (kan′ən·īz) *v.t.* **·ized, ·iz·ing** **1.** To declare (a de- ceased person) to be a saint. **2.** To recognize as part of the canon of Scripture. **3.** To sanction as being conformable to church canons. **4.** To glorify. —**can′on·i·za′tion** *n.*
anon law The ecclesiastical laws of a Christian church.
an·on·ry (kan′ən·rē) *n.* *pl.* **·ries** **1.** The office, dignity, or benefice of a canon. **2.** Canons collectively. Also **can′on·ship.**
a·no·pus (kə·nō′pəs) *n.* One of the 20 brightest stars, 0.86 magnitude; Alpha in the constellation Carina. [< L]
an·o·py (kan′ə·pē) *n.* *pl.* **·pies** **1.** A covering suspended over a throne, bed, shrine, etc., or held over a person. **2.** Any covering overhead, as the sky. **3.** *Archit.* An ornamen- tal covering over a niche, altar, or tomb. **4.** *Aeron.* The main lifting surface of a parachute. —*v.t.* **·pied, ·py·ing** To cover with or as with a canopy. [< MF < L < Gk. *kōnō- peion* bed with mosquito net]
anst (kanst) Archaic second person singular, present tense of CAN[1]: used with *thou.*
ant[1] (kant) *n.* **1.** An inclination from the vertical or hori- zontal; a slope or tilt. **2.** A sudden motion that tilts or over- turns. **3.** An outer corner or angle. **4.** A slant surface, as one produced by cutting off a corner or edge. —*v.t.* **1.** To set slantingly; tilt. **2.** To give a bevel to. **3.** To throw out or off; jerk; toss. —*v.i.* **4.** To tilt; slant. —*adj.* **1.** Ob- lique; slanting. **2.** Having canted sides or corners. [Prob. < OF < Med.L *cantus* corner, side]
ant[2] (kant) *n.* **1.** Insincere religious or moralistic talk. **2.** Phraseology used merely for effect; stock phrases. **3.** Words or phraseology peculiar to a sect, class, or calling: legal *cant.* **4.** The secret jargon of thieves, gypsies, etc.; argot. **5.** Whining speech, esp. of beggars. —*v.i.* To use cant. —*adj.* Having the character of cant; hypocritical. [< AF < L < *canere* to sing] —**cant′er** *n.*
an't (kant, känt) Cannot.
an·ta·bi·le (kän·tä′bē·lā) *Music adj.* Melodious; flowing. —*n.* Music characterized by flowing melody. [< Ital.]
an·ta·brig·i·an (kan′tə·brij′ē·ən) *adj.* Of or pertaining to Cambridge, England, or Cambridge University. —*n.* A resident of Cambridge, England; also, a student or graduate of Cambridge University. [< LL *Cantabrigia* Cambridge]
an·ta·loupe (kan′tə·lōp) *n.* A muskmelon having a ribbed, warty rind and sweet, orange flesh. Also **can′ta·loup.** [< F, after *Cantalupo,* Italian castle where first grown]
an·tank·er·ous (kan·tang′kər·əs) *adj.* Quarrelsome; ill natured; perverse. [Prob. akin to ME *contak* strife] —**can·tank′er·ous·ly** *adv.* —**can·tank′er·ous·ness** *n.*
can·ta·ta (kən·tä′tə) *n.* *Music* A vocal composition in the style of a drama, to be sung but not acted. [< Ital.]
can·teen (kan·tēn′) *n.* **1.** A small, usu. metal flask for car- rying water or other liquids. **2.** A shop at a military camp where soldiers can buy provisions, refreshments, etc. **3.** A place for refreshments. [< F < Ital. *cantina* cellar]
can·ter (kan′tər) *n.* A moderate, easy gallop. —*v.t. & v.i.* To ride or go at a canter. [Short for *Canterbury gallop;* with ref. to the pace of pilgrims riding to Canterbury]
Canterbury bell One of various cultivated bellflowers.
Canterbury Tales An uncompleted work (1387–1400) by Chaucer, consisting of a series of tales, largely in verse, told by a group of pilgrims on their way to Canterbury.
cant hook A lever equipped with an adjustable hook for handling logs. Also **cant·dog** (kant′dôg′, -dog′).
can·thus (kan′thəs) *n.* *pl.* **·thi** (-thī) *Anat.* The angle at the junction of the eyelids. [< Gk. *kanthos*]
can·ti·cle (kan′ti·kəl) *n.* A nonmetrical hymn, said or chanted in church. [< L *canticum* song]
Canticle of Can·ti·cles (kan′ti·kəlz) In the Bible, the Song of Solomon.
can·ti·lev·er (kan′tə·lev′ər, -lē′vər) *n.* **1.** *Engin.* A long struc- tural member, as a truss, beam, or slab, ly- ing across a support with the projecting arms in balance. **2.** *Archit.* Any structural part projecting hori- zontally and anchored at one end only. —*v.t. & v.i.* To project (a building member) outward and in bal- ance beyond the base. [Origin uncertain]

CANTILEVER BRIDGE
(Section of Queensboro Bridge, New York City)

cantilever bridge A bridge formed by the meeting of two freely projecting beams, trusses, etc.
can·tle (kan′təl) *n.* The hind part of a saddle, projecting upward. [< AF < Med.L *cantus* corner]
can·to (kan′tō) *n.* *pl.* **·tos** A division of an extended poem. [< Ital. < L *cantus* song]
can·ton (kan′tən, -ton, kan·ton′; *for v. def. 2* kan·ton′, -tōn′, -to͞on′) *n.* A district; esp., one of the states of Switzerland, or a subdivision of an arondissement in France. —*v.t.* **1.** To divide into cantons or districts. **2.** To assign quarters to, as troops. [< OF] —**can·ton·al** (kan′tən·əl) *adj.*
Can·ton·ese (kan′tən·ēz′, -ēs′) *n.* *pl.* **·ese** **1.** A native of Canton, China. **2.** The Chinese language spoken in parts of southern China.
Canton flannel (kan′tən) A heavy cotton flannel.
can·ton·ment (kan·ton′mənt, -tōn′-, -to͞on′-, kan′tən·mənt) *n.* The assignment of troops to temporary quarters; also, such quarters. [< F *cantonner* to quarter]
can·tor (kan′tər, -tôr) *n.* **1.** The chief liturgical singer in a synagogue. **2.** A precentor, or chief singer. [< L]
can·vas (kan′vəs) *n.* **1.** A heavy, closely woven cloth of hemp, flax, or cotton, used for sails, tents, etc. **2.** A piece of such material on which to paint, esp. in oils. **3.** A painting on canvas. **4.** Sailcloth. **5.** Sails collectively. **6.** A tent, esp. a circus tent. —**under canvas** **1.** With sails set. **2.** In tents. [< AF, ult. < L *cannabis* hemp]
can·vas·back (kan′vəs·bak′) *n.* A sea duck of North Amer- ica, having a grayish white back.
can·vass (kan′vəs) *v.t.* **1.** To go about (a region) or among (persons) to solicit votes, opinions, etc. **2.** To scrutinize. —*v.i.* **3.** To go about seeking votes, opinions, etc. —*n.* **1.** A solicitation of votes, orders, etc., often to determine the public's attitude toward a candidate, a product, etc. **2.** A detailed examination or discussion. [< CANVAS; with ref. to its early use for sifting] —**can′vass·er** *n.*
can·yon (kan′yən) *n.* A deep gorge or ravine, with steep sides: also spelled *cañon.* [< Sp. *cañón*]
caout·chouc (ko͞o′cho͝ok, kou·cho͞ok′) *n.* Rubber; esp., crude rubber. [< F < Tupi *cahuchu*]
cap (kap) *n.* **1.** A covering for the head, usu. snug, brim- less, and of soft material. **2.** Any headgear designed to de- note rank, function, membership, etc. **3.** Something sug- gesting a cap in form, function, or position. **4.** A primer, as of a cartridge. —**to set one's cap for** To try to win as a suitor or husband. —*v.t.* **capped, cap·ping** **1.** To put a cap on; cover. **2.** To serve as a cap or cover to; lie on top of. **3.** To add the final touch to. **4.** To excel. —**to cap the climax** To surpass the climax. [OE < LL, prob. < L *caput* head]
ca·pa·bil·i·ty (kā′pə·bil′ə·tē) *n.* *pl.* **·ties** **1.** The quality of being capable; capacity or ability. **2.** *Usu. pl.* Qualities that may be used or developed; potentialities.

ca·pa·ble (kā′pə·bəl) *adj.* Having ability; competent. — **capable of** **1.** Having the capacity or qualities needed for. **2.** Susceptible to. [< F < LL < L *capere* to take] — **ca′·pa·ble·ness** *n.* — **ca′pa·bly** *adv.*

ca·pa·cious (kə·pā′shəs) *adj.* Able to contain much; roomy. [< L < *capere* to take] — **ca·pa′cious·ly** *adv.* — **ca·pa′·cious·ness** *n.*

ca·pac·i·tance (kə·pas′ə·təns) *n. Electr.* The property of a circuit or body that permits it to store an electrical charge. — **ca·pac′i·tive** (-tiv) *adj.*

ca·pac·i·tate (kə·pas′ə·tāt) *v.t.* **·tat·ed, ·tat·ing** **1.** To render capable. **2.** To qualify according to law.

ca·pac·i·tor (kə·pas′ə·tər) *n. Electr.* A device consisting of conductors isolated in a dielectric medium, with each of them attached to only one side of a circuit, used to increase the capacitance to a desired value: also called *condenser*.

ca·pac·i·ty (kə·pas′ə·tē) *n. pl.* **·ties** **1.** Ability to receive, contain, or absorb. **2.** Maximum ability to hold, contain, etc. **3.** Adequate mental power to receive, understand, etc. **4.** The ability or aptitude to do something: with *for*, *of*, or the infinitive. **5.** Specific position or office. **6.** Legal qualification. **7.** Maximum output or production. **8.** *Electr.* Capacitance. [< MF < L < *capax* able to hold]

cap and bells A jester's cap ornamented with little bells.

cap and gown Ceremonial academic garb consisting of a cap or mortarboard and a characteristic robe or gown.

cap-a-pie (kap′ə·pē′) *adv.* From head to foot. Also **cap′-à-pie′.** [< OF]

ca·par·i·son (kə·par′ə·sən) *n.* **1.** An ornamental covering for a horse. **2.** Rich apparel or trappings. — *v.t.* To clothe richly. [< OF < Sp., ult. < LL *cappa* cape]

cape[1] (kāp) *n.* A point of land extending into the sea or a lake. [< F *cap*, ult. < L *caput* head]

cape[2] (kāp) *n.* A sleeveless garment fastened at the neck and hanging loosely from the shoulders. [< F < LL *cappa*]

cap·e·lin (kap′ə·lin) *n. pl.* **·lin** or **·lins** *U.S. & Canadian* A small, edible fish of northern seas, much used as bait. Also **cap′e·lan.** [< dial. F (Canadian) *capelan* < F]

Ca·pel·la (kə·pel′ə) *n.* One of the 20 brightest stars, 0.21 magnitude, in the constellation Auriga. [< L, she-goat]

ca·per[1] (kā′pər) *n.* **1.** A playful leap; a skip. **2.** A wild prank; antic. — **to cut a caper** (or **capers**) To caper; frolic. — *v.i.* To leap playfully. [Short for CAPRIOLE] — **ca′·per·er** *n.*

ca·per[2] (kā′pər) *n.* **1.** The flower bud of a low shrub of Mediterranean countries, pickled and used as a condiment. **2.** The shrub itself. [< L < Gk. *kapparis*]

cap·er·cail·lie (kap′ər·kāl′yē) *n.* A large, black European grouse. Also **cap′er·cail′zie** (-yē, -zē). [Alter. of Gaelic *capullcoille*, lit., horse of the wood]

Ca·pe·tian (kə·pē′shən) *adj.* Of or belonging to the dynasty (987–1328) founded in France by Hugh Capet.

ca·pi·as (kā′pē·əs, kap′ē·əs) *n. pl.* **·as·es** *Law* A judicial writ commanding an officer to take and hold in custody the person named therein. [< L, you may take]

cap·il·lar·i·ty (kap′ə·lar′ə·tē) *n. pl.* **·ties** **1.** The state of being capillary. **2.** *Physics* A form of surface tension between the molecules of a liquid and those of a solid. When the adhesive force is stronger (**capillary attraction**) the liquid will tend to rise in a capillary tube; when cohesion dominates (**capillary repulsion**), the liquid tends to fall. [< F]

cap·il·lar·y (kap′ə·ler′ē) *adj.* **1.** Of, pertaining to, or like hair; fine. **2.** Having a hairlike bore, as a tube or vessel. — *n. pl.* **·lar·ies** **1.** *Anat.* A minute vessel, as those connecting the arteries and veins. **2.** Any tube with a fine bore. [< L *capillus* hair]

cap·i·ta (kap′ə·tə) Plural of CAPUT.

cap·i·tal[1] (kap′ə·təl) *n.* **1.** The city or town that is the seat of government of a country, state, etc. **2.** A capital letter. **3.** The total amount of money or property owned or used by an individual or corporation. **4.** Wealth in any form employed in or available for the production of more wealth. **5.** In accounting, the net worth of a business after the deduction of all liabilities. **6.** Possessors of wealth as a class. — **to make capital of** To turn to advantage. — *adj.* **1.** Chief, as comprising the seat of government. **2.** Standing at the head; principal. **3.** Of or pertaining to funds or capital. **4.** Of the first quality. **5.** Punishable by or involving the death penalty. **6.** Very injurious; grave. [< OF < L < *caput* head]

cap·i·tal[2] (kap′ə·təl) *n. Archit.* The upper member of a column or pillar. [< L *caput* head]

capital expenditure Expenditure for permanent additions or improvements to property.

capital gain Profit from the sale of capital investments, such as stocks, real estate, etc.

cap·i·tal·ism (kap′ə·təl·iz′əm) *n.* **1.** An economic system in which the means of production and distribution are mostly privately owned and operated for private profit. **2.** The possession of private capital and its resulting power.

cap·i·tal·ist (kap′ə·təl·ist) *n.* **1.** An owner of capital; esp. one who has large means employed in productive enterpri **2.** Loosely, any person of wealth. **3.** A supporter of capit ism. — **cap′i·tal·is′tic** *adj.* — **cap′i·tal·is′ti·cal·ly** *adv.*

cap·i·tal·i·za·tion (kap′ə·təl·ə·zā′shən, -ī·zā′-) *n.* **1.** T act or process of capitalizing. **2.** A sum arrived at by ca talizing. **3.** The total capital employed in a business.

cap·i·tal·ize (kap′ə·təl·īz′) *v.* **·ized, ·iz·ing** *v.t.* **1.** To beg with capital letters, or print or write in capital letters. **2.** convert into capital. **3.** To provide capital for; organize a basis of capital. **4.** To estimate the worth of (a business stock) from earnings or potential earnings. **5.** In accou ing, to record (expenses) as assets. — *v.i.* **6.** To acquire advantage; profit: with *on* or *by*. **7.** To accumulate capit

capital letter The form of a letter used at the beginning a sentence, with proper names, etc., as the A in Africa.

cap·i·tal·ly (kap′ə·təl·ē) *adv.* In a capital or excellent wa

capital punishment The death penalty for a crime.

capital ship A warship of large size, as a battleship or a craft carrier, carrying guns of over 8-inch caliber.

capital stock **1.** The amount of stock a corporation is a thorized to issue. **2.** The total face value of such stock.

cap·i·ta·tion (kap′ə·tā′shən) *n.* An assessment on each pe son (or head); poll tax. [< LL < L *caput* head]

cap·i·tol (kap′ə·təl) *n.* The building in which a State leg lature convenes; a statehouse.

Cap·i·tol (kap′ə·təl) **1.** The official building of the U.S. Co gress in Washington, D.C. **2.** The temple of Jupiter Ca tolinus in ancient Rome. [< L *Capitolium* the Capitolin

ca·pit·u·lar (kə·pich′o͞o·lər) *adj.* Of or pertaining to an e clesiastical chapter. [< Med.L *capitulum* chapter]

ca·pit·u·late (kə·pich′o͞o·lāt) *v.i.* **·lat·ed, ·lat·ing** **1.** To su render on stipulated terms. **2.** To surrender. [< L *capi lare* to draw up in chapters] — **ca·pit′u·la′tor** *n.*

ca·pit·u·la·tion (kə·pich′o͞o·lā′shən) *n.* **1.** The act of su rendering conditionally; also, the instrument containing t terms of surrender. **2.** A surrender or giving up; yieldi **3.** A summary of a subject. — **ca·pit·u·la·to·ry** (kə·pich′ lə·tôr′ē, -tō′rē) *adj.*

cap·lin (kap′lin) See CAPELIN.

ca·pon (kā′pon, -pən) *n.* A rooster gelded to improve t flesh for eating. [OE < L *capo, -onis*]

ca·pote (kə·pōt′) *n.* **1.** A hooded cloak or overcoat. **2.** bonnet worn by women. [< F, dim. of *cape* hood]

ca·pric·ci·o (kə·prē′chē·ō, *Ital.* kä·prēt′chō) *n. pl.* **·ci·os** *Ital.* **ca·pric·ci** (kä·prēt′chē) **1.** *Music* A composition of live and spirited mood, fancifully irregular in form. **2.** A pran also, a caprice. [< Ital., whim < *capro* goat < L *caper*]

ca·price (kə·prēs′) *n.* **1.** A sudden change of mind or acti without adequate motive; a whim. **2.** A tendency to ma such changes; capriciousness. **3.** *Music* A capriccio. [< < Ital. *capriccio* whim]

ca·pri·cious (kə·prish′əs) *adj.* Characterized by or resu ing from caprice; fickle; whimsical. — **ca·pri′cious·ly** *a* — **ca·pri′cious·ness** *n.*

Cap·ri·corn (kap′rə·kôrn) *n.* A constellation, the Goat; so, the tenth sign of the zodiac. See ZODIAC. Also **Cap′ cor′nus** (-kôr′nəs). [< L < *caper* goat + *cornu* horn]

cap·ri·ole (kap′rē·ōl) *n.* **1.** A leap made by a trained hors with all feet off the ground and no forward motion. **2.** leap. — *v.i.* **·oled, ·ol·ing** To perform a capriole. [< F, lea

caps or **caps.** *Printing* Capital letters.

cap·si·cum (kap′si·kəm) *n.* **1.** An herb or shrub of t nightshade family, producing pods prepared as condimen or gastric stimulants. **2.** The fruit of these plants; red pe per. [< L *capsa* box (from the shape of the fruit)]

cap·size (kap·sīz′, kap′sīz) *v.t. & v.i.* **·sized, ·siz·ing** To u set or overturn. [? < Sp. *capuzar* to sink a ship by the hea

cap·stan (kap′stən) *n. Naut.* A drumlike apparatus, turn by bars or levers, for hoisting anchors by exerting tracti upon a cable. [< F *cabestan*, ult. < L *capere* to hold]

capstan bar A lever used in turning a capstan.

cap·stone (kap′stōn′) *n.* Copestone.

cap·su·late (kap′sə·lāt, -syo͞o-) *adj.* In or formed into capsule. Also **cap′su·lat′ed.** — **cap′su·la′tion** *n.*

cap·sule (kap′səl, -syo͞ol) *n.* **1.** A small container, us made of gelatin, for a dose of medicine. **2.** A detachab part of an airplane, rocket, etc., containing the pilot, instr ments, etc. **3.** A thin covering or seal, as over the cork of bottle. **4.** *Bot.* **a** A dry seed vessel made up of more th one carpel. **b** The spore case of a cryptogam. **5.** *Anat.* A brous or membranous structure that envelops some part the body. — *adj.* In concise form; condensed. [< F < *capsula*, dim. of *capsa* box] — **cap′su·lar** *adj.*

cap·tain (kap′tən, -tin) *n.* **1.** One at the head or in co mand; a chief; leader. **2.** The master or commander of vessel. **3.** *Mil.* A commissioned officer ranking below a m jor. See tables at GRADE. **4.** *Naval* A commissioned offic ranking below a commodore or rear admiral. See tables GRADE. **5.** A member of a team designated as its leade — *v.t.* To act as captain to; command; lead. [< OF < L < L *caput* head] — **cap′tain·cy, cap′tain·ship** *n.*

ıptain's walk A widow's walk.

ıp·tion (kap′shən) *n.* **1.** A heading, as of a chapter, docu-nent, or newspaper article. **2.** The title and descriptive natter for an illustration. **3.** A subtitle in a motion picture. — *v.t.* To provide a caption for. [< L *capere* to take]

ıp·tious (kap′shəs) *adj.* **1.** Apt to find fault; disposed to riticize. **2.** Designed to ensnare or perplex: a *captious* ques-ion. [< L *captiosus* fallacious] — **cap′tious·ly** *adv.* — **ap′tious·ness** *n.*

ıp·ti·vate (kap′tə·vāt) *v.t.* **·vat·ed, ·vat·ing** To enthrall; ascinate; charm. [< LL *captivare* to capture] — **cap′ti-a′tion** *n.* — **cap′ti·va′tor** *n.*

ıp·tive (kap′tiv) *n.* **1.** One who or that which is captured ınd held in confinement; a prisoner. **2.** One enthralled by eauty, passion, etc. — *adj.* **1.** Taken or held prisoner, as n war. **2.** Held in restraint; confined: a *captive* balloon. **3.** Captivated. **4.** Of or pertaining to a captive or captivity. < F < L *capere* to take]

ıptive audience *U.S.* A group of people forced by cir-umstances to listen to something.

ıp·tiv·i·ty (kap·tiv′ə·tē) *n.* *pl.* **·ties** The state of being eld captive; thralldom.

ıp·tor (kap′tər) *n.* One who takes or holds captive.

ıp·ture (kap′chər) *v.t* **·tured, ·tur·ing** **1.** To take by force, tratagem, etc., as in war. **2.** To gain or win, as in competi-ion. — *n.* **1.** The act of capturing; seizure. **2.** The person r thing captured. [< MF < L *capere* to take]

ıp·u·chin (kap′yŏŏ·chin, -shin) *n.* **1.** A woman's hooded loak. **2.** A long-tailed South American monkey whose head s covered with a cowl-like growth of hair. [< MF < Ital. *appa* head]

ap·u·chin (kap′yŏŏ·chin, -shin) *n.* A member of a branch f the Franciscan order.

ı·put (kā′pət, kap′ət) *n.* *pl.* **cap·i·ta** (kap′ə·tə) A head or eadlike part. [< L]

ır (kär) *n.* **1.** An automobile. **2.** A vehicle for use on ails. **3.** *Brit.* Any of various wheeled vehicles. **4.** *Poetic* A hariot. **5.** *U.S.* The enclosed platform of an elevator. [< AF < LL < L *carrus* wagon]

ı·ra·ba·o (kä′rə·bä′ō) *n.* *pl.* **·ba·os** or **·ba·o** In the Philip-ines, the water buffalo. [< Sp. < Malay *karbau*]

ır·a·bin (kar′ə·bin), **car·a·bine** (-bīn) See CARBINE.

ır·a·bin·eer (kar′ə·bin·ir′), **car·a·bin·ier** See CARBINEER.

ı·ra·ca·ra (kä′rə·kä′rə) A large, vulturelike hawk found n South America and southern U.S. [< Sp. *caracará*]

ır·ack (kar′ək) See CARRACK.

ır·a·cole (kar′ə·kōl) *n.* A half turn to the right or left nade by a horseman's mount in riding. — *v.i.* **·coled, ·col-ng** To perform caracoles; wheel. Also **car′a·col** (-kol). [< F < Ital. < Sp. *caracol* snail shell]

ır·a·cul (kar′ə·kəl) See KARAKUL.

ı·rafe (kə·raf′, -räf′) *n.* A glass water bottle. [< F]

ır·a·mel (kar′ə·məl, -mel, kär′məl) *n.* **1.** A chewy con-ection composed of sugar, butter, milk, etc. **2.** Burnt sugar, ısed to flavor foods. [< OF < Med.L *canna mellis* sugar cane]

ır·a·mel·ize (kar′ə·məl·īz′, kär′məl-) *v.t. & v.i.* **·ized, ·iz-ng** To convert into caramel. — **car′a·mel·i·za′tion** *n.*

ır·a·pace (kar′ə·pās) *n.* *Zool.* A hard, bony, or chitinous uter case or covering, as of a turtle or lobster. Also **car′a-ax** (-paks). [< F < Sp. *carapacho*]

ır·at (kar′ət) *n.* **1.** A unit of weight for gems, one metric arat being 200 milligrams, or 3.086 grains. **2.** Loosely, a karat. [< F < Ital. < Arabic < Gk. *keration* seed]

ır·a·van (kar′ə·van) *n.* **1.** A company of traders, pil-rims, or the like, traveling together, esp. across deserts. **2.** A number of vehicles traveling together. **3.** A large, cov-red vehicle; a van. [< F < Persian *kārwān* caravan]

ar·a·van·sa·ry (kar′ə·van′sə·rē) *n.* *pl.* **·ries** **1.** In Orien-al countries, an inn enclosing a court for sheltering cara-vans. **2.** Any hostelry or inn. Also **car′a·van′se·rai** (-rī, -rā). [< F < Persian *kārwān* caravan + *sarāī* inn]

ar·a·vel (kar′ə·vel) *n.* A small ship of the 15th and 16th enturies, used esp. by the Portuguese and Spanish. Also **car′a·velle.** [< MF < Sp. *caraba* boat]

ar·a·way (kar′ə·wā) *n.* An herb of the parsley family hav-ng small, spicy seeds (**caraway seeds**), used for flavoring. < Sp. < Arabic *karwiyā* caraway]

ar·bide (kär′bīd, -bid) *n.* *Chem.* A compound of carbon with a more electropositive element.

ar·bine (kär′bīn, -bēn) *n.* **1.** A light, short-barreled rifle originally devised for mounted troops: also *carabin, carabine.* **2.** *U.S. Mil.* A semi-automatic and now automatic, gas-operated, .30-caliber rifle. [Earlier *carabine* < F]

ar·bi·neer (kär′bə·nir′) *n.* A soldier armed with a carbine: also *carabineer, carabinier.*

arbo- *combining form* Carbon: *carbohydrate.* Also, before vowels, **carb-.** [< L *carbo* coal]

ar·bo·hy·drate (kär′bō·hī′drāt) *n.* *Biochem.* Any of a group of compounds containing carbon combined with hydrogen and oxygen, and including sugars, starches, and cellulose.

car·bo·lat·ed (kär′bə·lā′tid) *adj.* Containing carbolic acid.

carbolic acid (kär·bol′ik) *Chem.* Phenol.

car·bo·lize (kär′bə·līz) *v.t.* **·lized, ·liz·ing** *Chem.* To treat or impregnate with carbolic acid.

car·bon (kär′bən) *n.* **1.** A nonmetallic element (symbol C) found in all organic substances and in some inorganic sub-stances, as diamonds, graphite, coal, charcoal, lampblack, etc. See ELEMENT. **2.** *Electr.* **a** A rod of carbon, used as an electrode in an arc light. **b** The negative electrode of a pri-mary cell. **3.** A piece of carbon paper. **4.** A carbon copy. — *adj.* **1.** Of, pertaining to, or like carbon. **2.** Treated with carbon. [< F < L *carbo, -onis* coal]

carbon 14 *Physics* Radiocarbon.

car·bo·na·ceous (kär′bə·nā′shəs) *adj.* Of, pertaining to, or yielding carbon.

car·bon·ate (kär′bə·nāt; *for n., also* kär′bə·nit) *Chem.* *v.t.* **·at·ed, ·at·ing** **1.** To impregnate or charge with carbon di-oxide. **2.** To carbonize. — *n.* A salt or ester of carbonic acid. [< F] — **car′bon·a′tion** *n.*

carbon copy **1.** A copy of a letter, etc., made by means of carbon paper. **2.** An exact or close replica; duplicate.

carbon dioxide *Chem.* A heavy, odorless, incombustible gas, CO_2, taken from the atmosphere in the photosynthesis of plants and returned to it by the respiration of both plants and animals.

carboni- *combining form* Carbon; coal. [< L *carbo, -onis* coal]

car·bon·ic (kär·bon′ik) *adj.* Of, pertaining to, or obtained from carbon.

carbonic acid *Chem.* A weak, unstable acid, H_2CO_3, exist-ing only in solution.

car·bon·if·er·ous (kär′bə·nif′ər·əs) *adj.* Of, pertaining to, containing, or yielding carbon or coal.

Car·bon·if·er·ous (kär′bə·nif′ər·əs) *adj.* *Geol.* Of or per-taining to a period of the Paleozoic era characterized by the formation of extensive coal beds. — *n.* The Carboniferous period or system of rocks. See chart under GEOLOGY.

car·bon·ize (kär′bən·īz) *v.t.* **·ized, ·iz·ing** **1.** To reduce to carbon. **2.** To coat with carbon, as paper. **3.** To charge with carbon. — **car′bon·i·za′tion** *n.* — **car′bon·iz′er** *n.*

carbon monoxide *Chem.* A colorless, odorless gas, CO, formed by the incomplete oxidation of carbon, burning with a blue flame and highly poisonous when inhaled.

carbon paper Thin paper coated with carbon or the like, placed between two sheets of paper to reproduce on the bot-tom sheet what is written or typed on the upper sheet.

carbon tetrachloride *Chem.* A colorless, nonflammable liquid, CCl_4, used as a solvent, cleaning fluid, etc.

Car·bo·run·dum (kär′bə·run′dəm) *n.* An abrasive of sili-con carbide: a trade name. Also **car′bo·run′dum.**

car·box·yl (kär·bok′sil) *n.* *Chem.* A univalent acid radical, COOH, the characteristic group of most organic acids.

car·boy (kär′boi) *n.* A large glass bottle enclosed in a box or in wickerwork, used as a container for corrosive acids, etc. [Alter. of Persian *qarābah* demijohn]

car·bun·cle (kär′bung·kəl) *n.* **1.** *Pathol.* An inflammation of the subcutaneous tissue, resembling a boil but larger. **2.** A red garnet cut without facets. [< AF < L *carbo, -onis* coal] — **car·bun·cu·lar** (kär·bung′kyə·lər) *adj.*

car·bu·ret (kär′bə·rāt, -byə·ret) *v.t.* **·ret·ed** or **·ret·ted, ·ret·ing** or **·ret·ting** To combine chemically with carbon; esp. to charge (air or gas) with carbon compounds. — **car·bu·re·tion** (kär′bə·rā′shən, -byə·resh′ən) *n.*

car·bu·re·tor (kär′bə·rā′tər, -byə·ret′ər) *n.* An apparatus used to charge air or gas with volatile hydrocarbons to give it illuminative or explosive power. Also *Brit.* **car·bu·ret·tor** (kär′byə·ret′ər) or **car′bu·ret′ter.**

car·bu·rize (kär′bə·rīz, -byə-) *v.t.* **·rized, ·riz·ing** **1.** To carburet. **2.** *Metall.* To impregnate the surface layer of (low-carbon steel) with carbon, a stage in casehardening.

car·ca·jou (kär′kə·jōō, -zhōō) *n.* *Canadian* The wolverine. [< dial. F (Canadian) < native Algonquian name]

car·cass (kär′kəs) *n.* **1.** The dead body of an animal. **2.** The human body, living or dead: a contemptuous or humor-ous use. **3.** Something from which the life or essence is gone; shell. **4.** A framework or skeleton. Also **car′case.** [< AF < Med.L *carcasium*]

car·cin·o·gen (kär·sin′ə·jən) *n.* *Pathol.* A substance that causes cancer. — **car·ci·no·gen·ic** (kär·sə·nō·jen′ik) *adj.*

car·ci·no·ma (kär′sə·nō′mə) *n.* *pl.* **·mas** or **·ma·ta** (-mə·tə) *Pathol.* A malignant epithelial tumor; cancer. Also **car·ci·nus** (kär′sə·nəs). [< L < Gk. *karkinos* cancer] — **car·ci·nom·a·tous** (kär′sə·nom′ə·təs, -nō′mə-) *adj.*

card[1] (kärd) *n.* **1.** A small, usu. rectangular piece of thin pasteboard or stiff paper, used for a variety of purposes. **2.**

One of a pack of such pieces with figures, numbers, or other symbols, used for various games. **3.** *pl.* Games played with playing cards. **4.** A greeting card. **5.** A card certifying the identity of its owner or bearer: library *card.* **6.** A program or form of events, as at the races. **7.** *Naut.* The dial of a compass. **8.** An advertisement or public announcement printed on a card. **9.** *Informal* A person manifesting some peculiarity: a queer *card.* **10.** *Informal* A witty person. **— in the cards** Likely to happen; possible. **— to put one's cards on the table** To reveal one's intentions with complete frankness. — *v.t.* **1.** To fasten or write upon a card or cards. **2.** To provide with a card. [< MF < Ital. < L < Gk. *chartēs* leaf of paper]

card[2] (kärd) *n.* **1.** A wire-toothed brush for combing and cleansing wool, etc. **2.** A similar instrument for raising a nap. — *v.t. & v.i.* To comb, dress, or cleanse with a card. [< MF < Ital. < Med.L < L *carduus* thistle] **— card′er** *n.*

car·da·mom (kär′də·məm) *n.* **1.** The aromatic seeds of either of two Asian plants of the ginger family. **2.** One of the plants yielding these seeds. Also **car′da·mon** (-mən), **car′da·mum.** [< L < Gk. *kardamon* cress + *amōmon* spice]

card·board (kärd′bôrd′, -bōrd′) *n.* A thin, stiff pasteboard used for making cards, boxes, etc.

card catalogue A catalogue made out on cards, esp. one showing the books in a library.

cardi- Var. of CARDIO-.

car·di·ac (kär′dē·ak) *Med. adj.* **1.** Pertaining to, situated near, or affecting the heart. **2.** Of or pertaining to the upper orifice of the stomach. Also **car·di·a·cal** (kär·dī′ə·kəl). — *n.* **1.** One suffering from a heart disease. **2.** A cardiac remedy or stimulant. [< F < L < Gk. *kardia* heart]

car·di·gan (kär′də·gən) *n.* A jacket or sweater opening down the front. Also **cardigan jacket, cardigan sweater.** [after the seventh Earl of *Cardigan,* 1797–1868]

car·di·nal (kär′də·nəl, kärd′nəl) *adj.* **1.** Of prime importance; chief; principal. **2.** Of a deep scarlet color. **3.** Of or relating to a cardinal or cardinals. — *n.* **1.** In the Roman Catholic Church, a member of the College of Cardinals, or Sacred College. **2.** A bright red, crested finch of the eastern United States: also called *redbird*: also **cardinal bird, cardinal grosbeak. 3.** A deep scarlet. **4.** A cardinal number. [< F < L *cardo, cardinis* hinge, that on which something turns or depends] **— car′di·nal·ly** *adv.*

car·di·nal·ate (kär′də·nəl·āt, kärd′nəl·āt) *n.* The rank, dignity, or term of office of a cardinal. Also **car′di·nal·ship′.**

cardinal flower An herb of North America having large red flowers.

cardinal number *Math.* Any number that expresses the number of objects or units under consideration, as 1, 2, 3, etc.: distinguished from *ordinal number.*

cardinal point Any of the four main points of the compass.

cardinal sins The seven deadly sins.

cardinal virtues Justice, prudence, temperance, and fortitude, classified by Plato as the four types of moral excellence.

card·ing (kär′ding) *n.* **1.** The cleansing and combing of wool, flax, etc., before spinning. **2.** Carded fibers.

cardio- *combining form* Heart: *cardiogram.* Also, before vowels, *cardi-.* [< Gk. *kardia* heart]

car·di·o·gram (kär′dē·ə·gram′) *n.* The graphic record of heart movements produced by the cardiograph.

car·di·o·graph (kär′dē·ə·graf′, -gräf′) *n.* An instrument for tracing and recording the force and character of the heart movements. **— car′di·o·graph′ic** *adj.* **— car·di·og·ra·phy** (kär′dē·og′rə·fē) *n.*

car·di·tis (kär·dī′tis) *n. Pathol.* Inflammation of the heart.

cards (kärdz) *n.pl.* (*construed as sing.*) **1.** Any game played with playing cards. **2.** The playing of card games.

card·sharp (kärd′shärp′) *n.* One who cheats at cards, esp. as a livelihood. Also **card′sharp′er.**

care (kâr) *n.* **1.** A feeling of anxiety or concern; worry. **2.** A cause of worry or anxiety. **3.** Watchful regard or attention; heed. **4.** Charge or guardianship; custody; supervision. **5.** An object of solicitude or attention. — *v.i.* **cared, car·ing 1.** To have or show regard, interest, or concern. **2.** To be inclined; desire: with *to.* **3.** To mind or be concerned: I don't *care* if it rains. **— to care for 1.** To look after or provide for. **2.** To feel interest concerning; also, to have a fondness for; like. **3.** To want; desire. [OE *caru, cearu*]

ca·reen (kə·rēn′) *v.i.* **1.** *U.S.* To lurch or twist from side to side while moving. **2.** To lean sideways. **3.** To clean a ship when it is on one side. — *v.t.* **4.** To turn (a ship, etc.) on one side; tip. **5.** To clean, repair, or caulk (a careened ship). — *n.* **1.** The act of careening a vessel. **2.** The position of a ship careened or heeled over. [< F < L *carina* keel of a ship] **— ca·reen′er** *n.*

ca·reer (kə·rir′) *n.* **1.** The course or progress of a person's life: a remarkable *career.* **2.** One's lifework; profession. **3.** Successful pursuit of an occupation. **4.** Speed; full speed. — *adj. U.S.* Making one's profession a lifework: *career* diplomat. — *v.i.* To move with a swift, free motion. [< F < LL < L *carrus* wagon] **— ca·reer′er** *n.*

ca·reer·ist (kə·rir′ist) *n.* A person chiefly concerned wi advancing himself professionally. **— ca·reer′ism** *n.*

care·free (kâr′frē′) *adj.* Free of troubles or anxiety.

care·ful (kâr′fəl) *adj.* **1.** Exercising care in one's wo painstaking. **2.** Done with care: a *careful* job. **3.** Wat ful; cautious. **— care′ful·ly** *adv.* **— care′ful·ness** *n.*

care·less (kâr′lis) *adj.* **1.** Not attentive; reckless: a *ca less* worker. **2.** Not done with care; neglectful. **3.** Witho care or concern; indifferent: with *about, in,* or *of.* **4.** Artle unstudied: *careless* elegance. **5.** Carefree: a *careless* life. **care′less·ly** *adv.* **— care′less·ness** *n.*

ca·ress (kə·res′) *n.* An affectionate touch or gesture, as embrace, pat, etc. — *v.t.* To touch or treat lovingly; fond [< MF < Ital. < L *carus* dear] **— ca·ress′er** *n.* **—** ress′ing·ly *adv.* **— ca·res′sive** *adj.* **— ca·res′sive·ly** *a*

car·et (kar′ət) *n.* A sign (∧) placed below a line to indic where something should be inserted. [< L, it is missi

care·tak·er (kâr′tā′kər) *n.* One who takes care of a pla thing, or person; a custodian.

care·worn (kâr′wôrn′, -wōrn′) *adj.* Showing the effects care and anxiety; haggard; weary.

car·fare (kär′fâr′) *n.* The fare for a ride on a bus, etc.

car·go (kär′gō) *n. pl.* **·goes** or **·gos** Goods and merchand carried by a vessel, aircraft, etc.; freight; load. [< Sp. LL < L *carrus* wagon]

car·hop (kär′hop′) *n. U.S. Informal* A waiter or waitr at a drive-in restaurant.

Car·ib (kar′ib) *n.* **1.** One of a tribe of Indians now surv ing on the coasts of Guiana, Venezuela, Dominica, H duras, Guatemala, and Nicaragua. **2.** The family of la guages spoken by these Indians. [< Sp. < Cariban *car* brave] **— Car′ib·an** *adj. & n.*

Car·ib·be·an (kar′ə·bē′ən, kə·rib′ē·ən) *n.* **1.** The Car bean Sea. **2.** A Carib. — *adj.* **1.** Of or pertaining to t Caribbean Sea. **2.** Of or pertaining to the Caribs, th language, or their culture.

car·i·bou (kar′ə·bōō) *n. pl.* **·bou** or **·bous** A North American reindeer found from Maine to the Arctic. [< dial. F (Canadian) < Alonquian *khalibu* pawer]

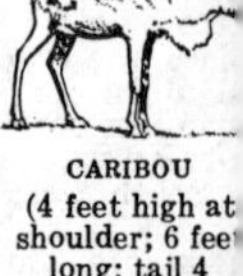

CARIBOU
(4 feet high at shoulder; 6 fee long; tail 4 inches)

car·i·ca·ture (kar′i·kə·chŏŏr, -chər) *n.* **1.** A picture or description in which features are exaggerated or distorted so as to produce an absurd effect. **2.** The act or art of caricaturing. **3.** A poor imitation. — *v.t.* **·tured, ·tur·ing** To represent so as to make ridiculous; burlesque. [< F < Ital. *caricare* to load, exaggerate] **— car′i·ca·tur′al** *adj.* **— car′i·ca·tur′ist** *n.*

car·ies (kâr′ēz, -i·ēz) *n. Pathol.* Decay of a bone or o tooth. [< L]

car·il·lon (kar′ə·lon, kə·ril′yən) *n.* **1.** A set of stationa bells rung by hammers operated from a keyboard or by mechanism. **2.** A melody rung on a carillon. **3.** An org stop imitating bells. — *v.i.* **·lonned, ·lon·ning** To play carillon. [< F < Med.L *quadrilio, -onis* set of four bell

car·il·lon·neur (kar′ə·lə·nûr′) *n.* One who plays a carill

car·i·o·ca (kar′ē·ō′kə) *n.* A type of South American dan or the music for it. [after Sierra de *Carioca,* a mounta range near Rio de Janeiro]

car·i·ole (kar′ē·ōl) *n.* **1.** A small, open carriage. **2.** A lig cart. **3.** *Canadian* A dog sled for one person lying dow Also spelled *carriole.* [< F < Ital. *carra* cart, wagon]

car·i·ous (kâr′ē·əs) *adj.* Affected with caries; decayed. A **car·ied** (kâr′ēd) **— car′i·os′i·ty** (-os′ə·tē,) **car′i·ous·ness**

carl (kärl) *n.* **1.** *Archaic* A countryman; peasant. **2.** *Sc* A churl. Also **carle.** [< ON *karl* man, freeman]

car·load (kär′lōd′) *n.* The load carried in a car. **2.** T minimum load required to ship at the **carload rate,** a ra lower than that for smaller loads.

carload lot A freight shipment meeting the official mi mum weight for a carload rate.

car·ma·gnole (kär′mən·yōl′, *Fr.* kȧr·mȧ·nyôl′) *n.* **1.** wild dance and song of the French revolutionists of 1789. The costume of the French revolutionists. [< F, after *C magnola,* a town in Piedmont]

car·man (kär′mən) *n. pl.* **·men** (-mən) **1.** The driver, one of the crew, of a streetcar, etc. **2.** One who drives a ca

Car·mel·ite (kär′məl·īt) *n.* A monk or nun of the order Our Lady of Mt. Carmel. — *adj.* Of or relating to t Carmelites.

car·min·a·tive (kär·min′ə·tiv, kär′mə·nā′tiv) *Med. a* Tending to, or used to, relieve flatulence. — *n.* A reme for flatulence. [< L *carminare* to cleanse]

car·mine (kär′min, -mīn) *n.* **1.** A deep red or purplish r color. **2.** A crimson pigment obtained from cochineal; roug — *adj.* Deep red or purplish red. [< F < Med.L < O S *carmesin* crimson]

car·nage (kär′nij) *n.* Extensive and bloody slaughter, as war; massacre. **— Syn.** See MASSACRE. [< MF < Ital. LL < L *caro, carnis* flesh, meat]

.r·nal (kär′nəl) *adj.* **1.** Relating to bodily appetites; sen-ual. **2.** Sexual. **3.** Not spiritual; worldly. [< LL < L *aro, carnis* flesh] **—car′nal·ist** *n.* **—car·nal·i·ty** (kär·nal′-·tē) *n.* **—car′nal·ly** *adv.*

.r·na·tion (kär·nā′shən) *n.* **1.** The perennial, herbaceous, ragrant flower of any of the many varieties of the pink family. **:.** A light pink, bright rose, or scarlet color. [< F < L *caro, arnis* flesh]

.r·nel·ian (kär·nēl′yən) *n.* A clear red chalcedony, used s a gem: also *cornelian.* [< L *carnis* flesh]

.r·ni·fy (kär′nə·fī) *v.t. & v.i.* **·fied, ·fy·ing** To form into esh or a fleshlike consistency. [< L < *carnis* flesh + *acere* to make] **—car′ni·fi·ca′tion** *n.*

.r·ni·val (kär′nə·vəl) *n.* **1.** An amusement show with nerry-go-round, Ferris wheel, side shows, etc. **2.** Any gay estival, wild revel, or merrymaking. **3.** A period of festiv-ty immediately preceding Lent. [< Ital. < Med.L < L < *arnis* flesh + *levare* to remove]

.r·ni·vore (kär′nə·vôr, -vōr) *n.* A flesh-eating mammal, s a cat, dog, etc.

.r·niv·o·rous (kär·niv′ə·rəs) *adj.* **1.** Eating or living on esh. **2.** Of or pertaining to carnivores. [< L < *carnis* esh + *vorare* to eat, devour] **—car·niv′o·rous·ly** *adv.* **—ar·niv′o·rous·ness** *n.*

.r·ol (kar′əl) *n.* A song of joy or praise; esp., a Christmas ong. **—***v.* **car·oled** or **·olled, car·ol·ing** or **·ol·ling** *v.i.* **1.** 'o sing, esp. in a joyous strain. **—***v.t.* **2.** To utter or praise n song. [< OF < L < Gk. < *choros* a dance + *auleein* to lay the flute] **—car′ol·er** or **car′ol·ler** *n.*

ar·o·li·nas (kar′ə·lī′nəz), **the** North and South Carolina.

ar·o·lin·gi·an (kar′ə·lin′jē·ən) *adj.* Of or pertaining to the ynasty of Charlemagne.

ar·o·lin·i·an (kar′ə·lin′ē·ən) *adj.* **1.** Of or pertaining to Jorth or South Carolina. **2.** Carolingian. **—***n.* A native or nhabitant of North or South Carolina.

.r·om (kar′əm) *n.* **1.** In billiards, a shot in which the cue all strikes against two other balls in succession: in England, alled a *cannon.* Also called *billiard.* **2.** Any impact fol-owed by a rebound. **—***v.i.* **1.** To hit and rebound. **—***v.t.* **:.** To cause to make a carom. [Earlier *carambole* < F]

.r·o·tene (kar′ə·tēn) *n. Biochem.* A deep yellow or red rystalline hydrocarbon, $C_{40}H_{56}$, found in carrots, etc., and hanged in the body to vitamin A. Also **car′o·tin** (-tin). < L *carota* carrot + -ENE]

.·rot·e·noid (kə·rot′ə·noid) *n. Biochem.* One of a large variety of pigments found in plant and animal tissues. **—** *dj.* Of carotene or carotenoids. Also **ca·rot′i·noid.**

.·rot·id (kə·rot′id) *adj. Anat.* Of, pertaining to, or near ne of the two major arteries on each side of the neck. Also **a·rot′i·dal.** [< Gk. *karos* stupor]

.·rou·sal (kə·rou′zəl) *n.* A feast or banquet.

.·rouse (kə·rouz′) *v.i.* **·roused, ·rous·ing** To drink freely nd boisterously. **—***n.* A carousal. [< G *gar aus* (*trinken*) (to drink) all out] **—ca·rous′er** *n.*

ar·ou·sel (kar′ə·sel′, -zel′) *n.* **1.** A merry-go-round (def. 1). **:.** A tournament in which horsemen perform. Also spelled *arrousel.* [< F < Ital. *carosello* tournament]

arp[1] (kärp) *v.i.* To find fault unreasonably; complain; cavil. < ON *karpa* to boast] **—carp′er** *n.*

arp[2] (kärp) *n. pl.* **carp** or **carps 1.** A fresh-water food fish widely distributed in Europe and America. **2.** Any of vari-ous related fishes, as goldfish. [< OF < LL *carpa*]

:arp *combining form* Fruit; fruit (or seed) vessel: *pericarp.* [< Gk. *karpos* fruit]

ar·pal (kär′pəl) *Anat. adj.* Of, pertaining to, or near the wrist. **—***n.* A carpale. [< NL < L < Gk. *karpos* wrist]

ar·pa·le (kär·pā′lē) *n. pl.* **·li·a** (-lē·ə) *Anat.* A bone of the carpus or wrist. [See CARPAL.]

ar·pe di·em (kär′pē dī′em) *Latin* Enjoy the present; seize today's opportunities; literally, seize the day.

ar·pel (kär′pəl) *n. Bot.* A simple pistil or seed vessel. [< NL < Gk. *karpos* fruit] **—car·pel·lar·y** (kär′pə·ler′ē) *adj.*

ar·pen·ter (kär′pən·tər) *n.* A workman who builds and re-pairs wooden structures, as houses, ships, etc. **—***v.i.* **1.** To work as a carpenter. **—***v.t.* **2.** To make or build as a car-penter. [< AF < LL < L *carpentum* two-wheeled carriage] **—car′pen·ter·ing** *n.* **—car′pen·try** *n.*

ar·pet (kär′pit) *n.* **1.** A heavy covering for floors; also, the fabric used for it. **2.** A surface or covering suggesting this. **—on the carpet 1.** Subjected to reproof or repri-mand. **2.** Under consideration or discussion. **—***v.t.* To cover with or as with a carpet. [< OF < ML < L *carpere* to pluck, card wool]

:ar·pet·bag (kär′pit·bag′) *n.* An old type of traveling bag, made of carpeting.

:ar·pet·bag·ger (kär′pit·bag′ər) *n. U.S.* One of the Northern adventurers who sought to gain advantages in the South from the unsettled conditions after the Civil War.

carpet beetle A beetle whose larvae feed on carpets, fur, etc. Also **carpet bug.**

car·pet·ing (kär′pit·ing) *n.* Carpets or carpet fabric.

carpet sweeper A hand-operated apparatus for sweeping carpets, combining a revolving brush and closed dustpan.

carp·ing (kär′ping) *adj. & n.* Faultfinding. **—carp′ing·ly** *adv.*

carpo- *combining form* Fruit. [< Gk. *karpos* fruit]

car·port (kär′pôrt′, -pōrt′) *n. U.S.* A shelter for an auto-mobile, usu. a roof projecting from the side of a building.

-carpous *combining form* Having a certain kind or number of fruits. Also **-carpic.** [< Gk. *karpos* fruit]

car·pus (kär′pəs) *n. pl.* **·pi** (-pī) *Anat.* The wrist, or the wrist bones collectively. [< NL < Gk. *karpos* wrist]

car·rack (kar′ək) *n.* A galleon: also spelled *carack.* [< OF < Med.L, ? < Arabic *qorqūr* merchant ship]

car·ra·geen (kar′ə·gēn) *n.* An edible seaweed known com-mercially as Irish moss and used in medicine. Also **car′ra·gheen.** [after *Carragheen,* Ireland, where it grows]

car·rel (kar′əl) *n.* A small space, as among the stacks in a library, for solitary study. Also **car′rell.** [Var. of CAROL]

car·riage (kar′ij; *for def. 7, also* kar′ē·ij) *n.* **1.** A wheeled, usu. horse-drawn vehicle for carrying persons. **2.** *Brit.* A railroad passenger car. **3.** Manner of carrying the head and limbs; bearing. **4.** A moving portion of a machine carrying another part: the *carriage* of a lathe. **5.** A wheeled frame for carrying something heavy. **6.** The act of carrying; transportation. **7.** The cost of transportation.

carriage trade The wealthy patrons of a restaurant, thea-ter, etc., so called because they came in private carriages.

car·ried (kar′ēd) Past tense and past participle of CARRY.

car·ri·er (kar′ē·ər) *n.* **1.** One who or that which carries. **2.** A person or company that carries persons or goods for hire. **3.** *Med.* A person who is immune to a disease but transmits it to others.

carrier pigeon A homing pigeon.

carrier wave *Telecom.* The radio-frequency wave that is varied in some respect in order to transmit intelligence.

car·ri·ole (kar′ē·ōl) See CARIOLE.

car·ri·on (kar′ē·ən) *n.* Dead and putrefying flesh. **—***adj.* **1.** Feeding on carrion. **2.** Like or pertaining to carrion; pu-trefying. [< AF < L *caro, carnis* flesh]

carrion crow The common crow of Europe.

car·rom (kar′əm) See CAROM.

car·rot (kar′ət) *n.* **1.** The long, reddish yellow, edible root of an umbelliferous plant. **2.** The plant itself. [< F < L < Gk. *karōton* carrot]

car·rot·y (kar′ət·ē) *adj.* **1.** Like a carrot, esp. in color. **2.** Having red hair.

car·rou·sel (kar′ə·sel′, -zel′) See CAROUSEL.

car·ry (kar′ē) *v.* **·ried, ·ry·ing** *v.t.* **1.** To bear from one place to another; transport; convey. **2.** To serve as a medium of conveyance for; transmit. **3.** To have or bear upon or about one's person. **4.** To bear the weight, burden, or responsi-bility of. **5.** To give support to; confirm. **6.** To bear as a mark or attribute: Her words *carried* conviction. **7.** To be pregnant with. **8.** To bear (the body, or a part of it) in a specified manner. **9.** To conduct or comport (oneself). **10.** To take by force or effort; capture; win. **11.** To win the support or interest of. **12.** To gain victory or acceptance for; also, to achieve success in. **13.** To cause to go or come; urge. **14.** To extend; continue. **15.** To have or keep for sale. **16.** To transfer, as a number or figure, to another column. **17.** To maintain on one's account books for a future settlement. **18.** *U.S.* To sing or play (a part or melody). **19.** *Southern U.S.* To escort. **—***v.i.* **20.** To act as bearer or carrier. **21.** To have or exert propelling or pro-jecting power: The rifle *carries* well. **22.** To hold the neck and head in a particular manner. **23.** To gain victory or acceptance: The motion *carried.* **—to carry all before one** To meet with uniform success. **—to carry arms 1.** To be-long to the army. **2.** To bear weapons. **3.** To hold a weap-on in a prescribed position against the shoulder. **—to carry away** To move the feelings greatly; enchant. **—to carry forward 1.** To progress or proceed with. **2.** In bookkeep-ing, to transfer (an item, etc.) to the next column or page. **—to carry off 1.** To cause to die. **2.** To win, as a prize or honor. **3.** To face consequences boldly; brazen out. **4.** To abduct. **—to carry on 1.** To keep up; keep going; con-tinue. **2.** To behave in a wild, excited, or foolish manner. **3.** To engage in. **—to carry out** To accomplish; bring to completion. **—to carry over 1.** In bookkeeping, to repeat (an item, etc.) on another page or in another column. **2.** To postpone; put off. **—to carry through 1.** To carry to com-pletion or success. **2.** To sustain or support to the end. **—** *n. pl.* **·ries 1.** Range, as of a gun; also, the distance covered by a projectile, golf ball, etc. **2.** *U.S.* A portage, as between streams. **3.** The act of carrying. [< L *carrus* cart]

car·ry·all[1] (kar′ē·ôl′) *n.* A light, four-wheeled covered vehicle having room for several people.

car·ry·all[2] (kar′ē·ôl′) *n.* A large basket or bag.

carrying charge In installment buying, the interest charged on the unpaid balance.

carrying place *Canadian* A portage (def. 2).

car·ry-o·ver (kar′ē·ō′vər) *n.* **1.** Something left over or kept until later. **2.** In bookkeeping, a sum carried forward.

car·sick (kär′sik′) *adj.* Nauseated from riding in a car.

cart (kärt) *n.* **1.** A two-wheeled vehicle, for carrying loads. **2.** A light, two-wheeled vehicle with springs, used for business or pleasure. — *v.t.* **1.** To carry in or as in a cart. — *v.i.* **2.** To drive or use a cart. [ON *kartr*] — **cart′er** *n.*

cart·age (kär′tij) *n.* The act of or charge for carting.

carte blanche (kärt′ blänsh′, *Fr.* kȧrt bläṅsh′) *pl.* **cartes blanches** (kärts′ blänsh′, *Fr.* kȧrt bläṅsh′) **1.** A signed paper granting its possessor the freedom to write his own conditions. **2.** Unrestricted authority. [< F, white card]

car·tel (kär·tel′, kär′təl) *n.* **1.** An international trust that aims at monopolistic control of a particular market. **2.** An official agreement between governments, esp. for the exchange of prisoners. **3.** A challenge to single combat. [< F < Ital. *carta* paper]

Car·te·sian·ism (kär·tē′zhən·iz′əm) *n.* The philosophy of Descartes who defended complete dualism between thought (or mind) and extension (the subject matter of physical science). [< NL *Cartesius*, Latinized form of *Descartes*] — **Car·te′sian** *n. & adj.*

Car·thage (kär′thij) An ancient city state in North Africa; destroyed by the Romans in 146 B.C. Ancient **Car·tha·go** (kär·thā′gō). — **Car·tha·gin·i·an** (kär′thə·jin′ē·ən) *adj. & n.*

Car·thu·sian (kär·thōō′zhən) *n.* A monk or nun of a contemplative order founded at Chartreuse in the French Alps by St. Bruno in 1084. — *adj.* Of or pertaining to the Carthusians. [< Med.L *Carturissium* Chartreuse]

car·ti·lage (kär′tə·lij) *n. Zool.* **1.** A tough, elastic form of connective tissue in man and animals; gristle. **2.** A part consisting of cartilage. [< MF < L *cartilago* gristle]

car·ti·lag·i·nous (kär′tə·laj′ə·nəs) *adj.* **1.** Of or like cartilage; gristly. **2.** Having a gristly skeleton, as sharks.

cart·load (kärt′lōd′) *n.* As much as a cart can hold.

car·tog·ra·phy (kär·tog′rə·fē) *n.* The art of making maps or charts. [< L *carta* map + -GRAPHY] — **car·tog′ra·pher** *n.* — **car·to·graph·ic** (kär′tə·graf′ik) or **·i·cal** *adj.*

car·ton (kär′tən) *n.* **1.** A cardboard box. **2.** A paper or plastic container for liquids. [< F, pasteboard]

car·toon (kär·tōōn′) *n.* **1.** A drawing or caricature depicting a humorous or satirical person or situation. **2.** A comic strip. **3.** A motion-picture film (**animated cartoon**) produced by photographing a series of action drawings. **4.** A full-size sketch for a fresco, mosaic, etc. — *v.t.* **1.** To make a caricature or cartoon of. — *v.i.* **2.** To make cartoons. [< F < Ital. < L *charta* paper] — **car·toon′ist** *n.*

car·tridge (kär′trij) *n.* **1.** A casing of metal, pasteboard, or the like, containing a charge of powder for a firearm and, usu., the projectile or shot and the primer. **2.** Any small similar container, as the removable case in a tone arm of a record player. **3.** *Photog.* A roll of protected sensitized film. [< F < Ital. *cartoccio* < L *charta* paper]

cartridge clip A metal container holding cartridges for a rapid-fire gun, as an automatic rifle.

cart·wheel (kärt′hwēl′) *n.* **1.** A sideways handspring. **2.** *U.S. Informal* A large coin, esp. a silver dollar.

carve (kärv) *v.* **carved, carv·ing** *v.t.* **1.** To make by cutting, or as if by cutting. **2.** To create, design, or fashion by cutting. **3.** To cut up, as cooked meat; divide. — *v.i.* **4.** To make carved work. **5.** To cut up meat. — *n.* A cut or stroke in carving. [OE *ceorfan*] — **carv′er** *n.*

carv·en (kär′vən) *adj. Poetic* or *Archaic* Carved.

carv·ing (kär′ving) *n.* **1.** The act of one who carves. **2.** Carved work; a carved figure or design.

car·y·at·id (kar′ē·at′id) *n. pl.* **·at·ids** or **·at·i·des** (-at′ə·dēz) *Archit.* A supporting column in the form of a sculptured female figure. [< L < Gk. *Karyatis* a Greek priestess]

caryo- See KARYO-.

car·y·o·tin (kar′ē·ō′tin) See KARYOTIN.

ca·sa·ba (kə·sä′bə) *n.* A winter variety of muskmelon with sweet white flesh and yellow rind: also spelled *cassaba.* Also **casaba melon.** [after *Kasaba*, a town in western Turkey]

ca·sa·va (kə·sä′və) See CASSAVA.

Cas·bah (käz′bä) The native quarter of Algiers or of other cities with a large Arab population: also *Kasbah.*

cas·cade (kas·kād′) *n.* **1.** A fall of water over steep rocks, or one of a series of such falls. **2.** Anything resembling a waterfall. — *v.i.* **·cad·ed, ·cad·ing** To fall in the form of a waterfall. [< F < Ital. < L *cadere* to fall]

cas·car·a (kas·kâr′ə) *n.* A buckthorn of the NW United States, yielding cascara sagrada. Also **cascara buckthorn.** [< Sp. *cáscara* bark]

cascara sa·gra·da (sə·grā′də) A laxative obtained from the bark of the cascara.

case[1] (kās) *n.* **1.** A particular instance or occurrence: a c of mistaken identity. **2.** The actual circumstance or st of affairs: Such is not the *case.* **3.** An instance of disease injury; also, a patient. **4.** A set of arguments, reasons, e the *case* for capital punishment. **5.** A question or proble a *case* of conscience. **6.** *Law* **a** An action or suit at law The set of facts offered in support of a claim. **7.** Condit or situation; plight. **8.** *Informal* A peculiar or exceptio person. **9.** *Gram.* The syntactical relationship of a no pronoun, or adjective to other words in a sentence. — **any case** No matter what; regardless. — **in case** In event that; if. — **in case of** In the event of: *in case of* f — *v.t.* **cased, cas·ing** *U.S. Slang* To look over carefully, pecially with intent to rob. [< OF < L *casus* event]

case[2] (kās) *n.* **1.** A box, sheath, bag, etc., for contain something. **2.** A box and its contents. **3.** A set or pair. *Printing* A tray with compartments for holding type, cal *upper case* for capital letters, and *lower case* for small lette **5.** The covers and spine in which a book, when sewed, bound. **6.** An outer or protective part, as of a watch. **7** frame or casing, as for a door. — *v.t.* **cased, cas·ing** To p into or cover with a case; incase. [< AF < L *capsa* b

ca·se·fy (kā′sə·fī) *v.t. & v.i.* **·fied, ·fy·ing** To make or come like cheese. [< L *caseus* cheese + -FY]

case·hard·en (kās′här′dən) *v.t.* **1.** *Metall.* To harden surface of (low-carbon steel). **2.** To make callous, esp. feelings.

case history A record of an individual or a family unit, which salient facts are collected for use in medical, psyc atric, sociological, or similar studies. Also **case study.**

ca·se·in (kā′sē·in, -sēn) *n. Biochem.* A protein found esp. milk and constituting the principal ingredient in cheese. L *caseus* cheese] — **ca·se·ic** (kā′sē·ik) *adj.*

case knife **1.** A knife kept in a sheath. **2.** A table kn

case law Law based on judicial decisions, as distinguish from that based on statute or other sources of law.

case·mate (kās′māt) *n.* A bombproof shelter in a fortifi tion, or an armored compartment on a warship, for a g and crew. [< MF < Ital. *casamatta*] — **case′mat′ed** *ad*

case·ment (kās′mənt) *n.* **1.** The sash of a window t opens on hinges at the side, or a window having such sash **2.** A case; covering. — **case′ment·ed** *adj.*

ca·se·ous (kā′sē·əs) *adj.* Of or like cheese; cheesy.

ca·sern (kə·zûrn′) *n.* A barrack for soldiers. Also **ca·sern** [< F < Sp. *caserna* small hut < L *quaterna* four each]

case·work (kās′wûrk′) *n.* The investigation and guida by a social worker of maladjusted individuals and famili — **case′work′er** *n.*

cash[1] (kash) *n.* **1.** Current money in hand or readily av able. **2.** Money paid down; immediate payment. — *v.t.* convert into ready money, as a check. — **to cash in 1.** gambling, to turn in one's chips and receive cash. **2.** *U Slang* To die. — **to cash in on** *U.S. Informal* **1.** To mak profit from. **2.** To turn to advantage. [< F < Ital. < *capsa* box] — **cash′a·ble** *adj.*

cash[2] (kash) *n. pl.* **cash** Coins of low value of the E Indies and China. [< Pg. < Tamil *kāsu* small coin]

cash-and-car·ry (kash′ən·kar′ē) *adj.* Operated on a s tem of cash purchase and no delivery.

cash·book (kash′bŏŏk′) *n.* A book in which a record is ke of money taken in and paid out.

cash discount A discount from the purchase price allow the buyer if he pays within a stipulated period.

cash·ew (kash′ōō, kə·shōō′) *n.* **1.** A tropical American tr of the sumac family that yields a gum. **2.** Its small, edi fruit: also **cashew nut.** [< F < Pg. < Tupi *acajoba*]

cash·ier[1] (ka·shir′) *n.* **1.** One employed to collect ca payments, as in a restaurant. **2.** A bank officer responsi for the bank's assets. [< F < Ital. < L *capsa* box]

cash·ier[2] (ka·shir′) *v.t.* **1.** To dismiss in disgrace, as a mi tary officer. **2.** To discard. [< Du. < F < LL *cassare* annul and L *quassare* to destroy]

cash·mere (kash′mir, kazh′-) *n.* **1.** A fine wool obtain from Kashmir goats. **2.** A soft fabric made from this. Something made of cashmere. [after *Kashmir*, India]

cash register A device usu. with a money drawer, th records, adds, and displays the amount of cash received.

cas·ing (kā′sing) *n.* **1.** A protective case or covering. **2.** framework, as about a door. **3.** *U.S.* The shoe of a tire.

ca·si·no (kə·sē′nō) *n. pl.* **·nos** **1.** A place for dancin gambling, etc. **2.** Cassino. [< Ital., dim. of *casa* house]

cask (kask, käsk) *n.* **1.** A barrel-shaped wooden vess made of staves, hoops, and flat heads. **2.** The quantity cask will hold. [< Sp. *casco* skull, potsherd, cask]

cas·ket (kas′kit, käs′-) *n.* **1.** *U.S.* A coffin. **2.** A small b or chest. — *v.t.* To enclose in a casket. [Orig. uncertai

casque (kask) *n.* A helmet. [< F, ult. < L *quassare.* R lated to CASK.] — **casqued** (kaskt) *adj.*

cas·sa·ba (kə·sä′bə) See CASABA.

Cas·san·dra (kə·san′drə) In Greek mythology, a daught of Priam whose prophecies were fated by Apollo to be tr ut never believed. — *n.* Anyone who utters unheeded rophecies of disaster.

s·sa·va (kə·sä′və) *n.* **1.** A tropical American shrub or erb, cultivated for the edible roots. **2.** A starch made from hese roots, the source of tapioca. [< F < Taino *casavi*]

s·se·role (kas′ə·rōl) *n.* **1.** An earthenware or glass dish ı which food is baked and served. **2.** Any food so prepared nd served. **3.** *Brit.* A saucepan. [< F]

.s·sette (kə·set′) *n.* **1.** *Photog.* A lightproof magazine for lm. **2.** *Electronics* A cartridge containing magnetic tape, sed in tape recorders. [< F, lit., small box]

.s·sia (kash′ə, kas′ē·ə) *n.* **1.** A variety of cinnamon obained from the bark (**cassia bark**) of a tree native in China. **:.** The tree itself. **3.** Any shrub, herb, or tree of tropical egions whose dried pods (**cassia pods**) yield a mild laxative. < L < Gk. < Hebrew *qātsa'* to strip off bark]

.s·si·no (kə·sē′nō) *n.* A card game for two to four players.

.s·si·o·ber·ry (kas′ē·ō·ber′ē) *n. pl.* **·ries** The shining black dible drupe of a North American shrub. [< N. Am. Ind.]

ıs·si·o·pe·ia (kas′ē·ə·pē′ə) In Greek mythology, the ıother of Andromeda. — *n.* A constellation: also **Cassio·eia's Chair.**

ıs·sock (kas′ək) *n. Eccl.* A close-fitting vestment, usu. ılack, reaching to the feet, and worn by clergymen, choir ingers, etc. [< MF < Ital. *casacca* greatcoat]

ıs·so·war·y (kas′ə·wer′ē) *n. pl.* **·war·ies** A large, threeoed, flightless bird of Australia and New Guinea, related to he emu. [< Malay *kasuāri*]

ıst (kast, käst) *v.* **cast, cast·ing** *v.t.* **1.** To throw or hurl vith force; fling. **2.** To put with violence or force. **3.** To hrow down. **4.** To cause to fall upon or over or in a paricular direction: to *cast* a shadow. **5.** To direct, as a glance ıf the eyes. **6.** To let down; drop: to *cast* anchor. **7.** To hrow forth or out. **8.** To throw off; lose; also, to shed; ıolt. **9.** To throw aside; reject or dismiss. **10.** To give ırth to, esp. prematurely. **11.** To deposit; give: He *cast* ıis vote. **12.** To throw, as dice. **13.** In the theater, moves, etc., to assign the parts of (a play) or a part in a play to an actor). **14.** To throw up, as with a shovel: to *cast* a ıound of earth. **15.** To calculate; add. **16.** To compute ıstrologically: to *cast* a horoscope. **17.** To arrange by some ystem. **18.** To contrive; devise. **19.** *Metall.* To shape in mold. **20.** *Printing* To stereotype or electroplate. **21.** 'o twist; warp. **22.** *Naut.* To turn (a ship); tack. — *v.i.* **:3.** To make a throw, as with dice, a fishing line, etc. **24.** 'o deliberate mentally; also, to scheme. **25.** To conjecture; orecast. **26.** To make arithmetical calculations; add. **27.** *Metall.* To take shape in a mold. **28.** To warp, as timber. **:9.** *Naut.* To veer; fall off; also, to tack. — **to cast about** 'o consider ways and means; scheme. — **to cast away 1.** 'o discard. **2.** To shipwreck or maroon. — **to cast down** . To overthrow; destroy. **2.** To discourage; depress. — **o cast off 1.** To reject or discard. **2.** To let go, as a ship rom a dock. **3.** *Printing* To estimate the number of pages, olumns, etc., a manuscript will yield. — **to cast up 1.** To ject; vomit. **2.** To compute; add. **3.** To drive ashore. **4.** 'o direct upward. — *n.* **1.** The act of casting or throwing. **:.** The distance to which a thing may be thrown. **3.** The hrowing of a line or fishing net into the water. **4.** A throw ıf dice; also, the number thrown. **5.** Anything thrown out, ıff, or away. **6.** *Pathol.* A plastic substance formed in and ıften taking the shape of diseased cavities and organs: a enal *cast.* **7.** *Surg.* A rigid dressing or bandage, usu. made ıf plaster of Paris, for preventing movement of fractured ıones. **8.** The actors who portray the characters in a play, novie, etc. **9.** The act of casting or founding. **10.** An imıression made of anything; a mold. **11.** Something shaped ır formed in a mold; a casting. **12.** The material poured nto molds at one operation. **13.** Kind; sort; type. **14.** 'he appearance or form of something. **15.** A tinge; shade. **16.** A twist to one side; squint. **17.** A glance; look. **18.** A warp. **19.** A stroke of fortune. [< ON *kasta* to throw]

as·ta·net (kas′tə·net′) *n.* One of a pair of small concave lisks of wood or ivory, clapped together with he fingers, as a rhythmical accompaniment to ong or dance. [< Sp. < L *castanea* chestnut]

ast·a·way (kast′ə·wā′, käst′-) *adj.* **1.** Adrift; hipwrecked. **2.** Thrown away. — *n.* **1.** One who is shipwrecked. **2.** An outcast.

aste (kast, käst) *n.* **1.** In India, one of the ıereditary social classes into which Hindus are livided. **2.** Any rigid social class. **3.** The ystem or principles of such class divisions. **4.** 'he position conferred by such a system. [< 'g. < L *castus* pure]

as·tel·lat·ed (kas′tə·lā′tid) *adj.* Having battlements and turrets. [< Med.L < L *castellum* castle] — **cas′tel·la′tion** *n.*

CASTANETS
a Outer and inner sides.
b Position in use.

cast·er (kas′tər, käs′-) *n.* **1.** One who or that which casts. **2.** One of a set of small, swiveling wheels or rollers, fastened under articles of furniture, or the like, to allow them to be moved about. **3.** A cruet for condiments; also, a stand for such cruets. Also (for defs. 2 and 3) *castor.*

cas·ti·gate (kas′tə·gāt) *v.t.* **·gat·ed, ·gat·ing** To rebuke or chastise severely; criticize. — **Syn.** See CHASTEN. [< L *castigare* to chasten] — **cas′ti·ga′tion** *n.* — **cas′ti·ga′tor** *n.*

Cas·tile soap (kas′tēl, kas·tēl′) A hard, white, odorless soap made with olive oil and soda. Also **cas′tile soap.** [after *Castile,* where first made]

Cas·til·ian (kas·til′yən) *n.* **1.** A native or citizen of Castile. **2.** The standard form of Spanish as spoken in Spain, originally the dialect of Castile. — *adj.* Of or pertaining to Castile, its people, language, or culture.

cast·ing (kas′ting, käs′-) *n.* **1.** The act of one who or that which casts. **2.** That which is cast or formed in a mold.

casting vote A deciding vote, given by the chairman of an assembly in cases where the votes of the members tie.

cast-i·ron (kast′ī′ərn, käst′-) *adj.* **1.** Made of cast iron. **2.** Like cast iron; rigid or strong; unyielding.

cast iron Iron having a high carbon content, and usu. hard, brittle, and not malleable.

cas·tle (kas′əl, käs′-) *n.* **1.** In feudal times, the fortified dwelling of a prince or noble. **2.** Any large, imposing house. **3.** A place of refuge; stronghold. **4.** In chess, a rook. — *v.* **·tled, ·tling** *v.t.* & *v.i.* In chess, to move (the king) two squares to the right or left and place the rook from that side on the square over which the king has passed. [Ult. < L *castrum* camp, fort]

castle in the air A fanciful, impractical scheme; daydream.

cast·off (kast′ôf′, -of′, käst′-) *adj.* Thrown or laid aside. — *n.* One who or that which is no longer wanted or used.

cas·tor[1] (kas′tər, käs′-) *n.* **1.** An oily, odorous secretion of beavers, used in medicine and perfumery: also **cas·to·re·um** (kas·tôr′ē·əm, -tō′rē·əm) **2.** A hat of beaver or other fur. [< L < Gk. *kastōr* beaver]

cas·tor[2] (kas′tər, käs′-) See CASTER (defs. 2 and 3).

Cas·tor and Pol·lux (kas′tər, käs′-; pol′əks) **1.** In Greek mythology, twin brothers set by Zeus among the stars. **2.** *Astron.* The two brightest stars in the constellation Gemini.

castor bean The seed of the castor-oil plant.

castor oil A viscid oil extracted from castor beans and used as a cathartic and lubricant.

cas·tor-oil plant (kas′tər·oil′, käs′-) A plant native in India, yielding the castor bean.

cas·trate (kas′trāt) *v.t.* **·trat·ed, ·trat·ing 1.** To remove the testicles from; emasculate; geld. **2.** To remove the ovaries from; spay. [< L *castrare*] — **cas·tra′tion** *n.*

cas·u·al (kazh′o͞o·əl) *adj.* **1.** Occurring by chance; accidental. **2.** Irregular; occasional: *casual* visits. **3.** Without intention or plan; offhand: a *casual* question. **4.** Negligent; nonchalant: a *casual* manner. **5.** Designed for informal wear: *casual* clothes. **6.** *Med.* Pertaining to accidental injuries. — *n.* **1.** One who is employed at irregular intervals. **2.** An occasional visitor. **3.** *Mil.* A soldier temporarily attached to a unit. [< MF < L *casus* accident < *cadere* to fall] — **cas′u·al·ly** *adv.* — **cas′u·al·ness** *n.*

cas·u·al·ty (kazh′o͞o·əl·tē) *n. pl.* **·ties 1.** One who or that which is destroyed, injured, or otherwise made ineffective by an accident. **2.** *Mil.* A soldier who is killed, wounded, captured, or otherwise lost to his command through combat action. **3.** An accident, esp. a fatal or serious one.

cas·u·ist (kazh′o͞o·ist) *n.* One who studies or resolves ethical problems: often used for one who rationalizes about such matters. [< F < L *casus* event, case] — **cas′u·is′tic** or **·ti·cal** *adj.* — **cas′u·is′ti·cal·ly** *adv.*

cas·u·ist·ry (kazh′o͞o·is·trē) *n. pl.* **·ries 1.** The science that treats of or solves ambiguous cases of conscience or questions of right and wrong. **2.** Sophistical or equivocal reasoning, esp. in cases of conscience.

ca·sus bel·li (kā′səs bel′ī) *Latin* A cause justifying war.

cat (kat) *n.* **1.** A domesticated carnivorous mammal having retractile claws, and valued because it kills mice and rats. **2.** Any other animal of the cat family, as a lion, tiger, lynx, ocelot, etc. ◆ Collateral adjective: *feline.* **3.** A gossiping or backbiting woman. **4.** *Naut.* A tackle for hoisting an anchor to the cathead. **5.** A catboat. **6.** A cat-o'-nine-tails. **7.** A catfish. **8.** *U.S. Slang* A man; guy. **9.** *U.S. & Canadian* A catepillar tractor. — **to let the cat out of the bag** To divulge a secret. — *v.t.* **cat·ted, cat·ting 1.** To hoist and fasten at the cathead. **2.** To flog. [OE *cat, catte*]

cata- *prefix* **1.** Down; against; upon. **2.** Back; over. Also, before vowels, **cat-**: also *cath-.* Also spelled *kata-.* [< Gk. *kata* down, against, back]

ca·tab·o·lism (kə·tab′ə·liz′əm) *n. Biol.* The process by which living tissue breaks down into simpler and more stable substances; destructive metabolism: opposed to *anab-*

olism. [< Gk. < *kata-* down + *ballein* to throw] **—cat·a·bol·ic** (kat′ə·bol′ik) *adj.* **—cat′a·bol′i·cal·ly** *adv.*

cat·a·clysm (kat′ə·kliz′əm) *n.* **1.** Any violent upheaval or change, as a war, revolution, etc. **2.** Any violent disturbance. **3.** A deluge. [< MF < Gk. < *kata-* down + *klyzein* to wash] **—cat′a·clys′mic, cat′a·clys′mal** (-məl) *adj.*

cat·a·comb (kat′ə·kōm) *n. Usu. pl.* An underground place of burial, consisting of passages and small rooms with excavations in their sides for tombs. [< F < LL *catacumbas*]

cat·a·falque (kat′ə·falk) *n.* A structure supporting a coffin during a funeral. Also **cat′a·fal′co.** [< F < Ital. *catafalco*]

Cat·a·lan (kat′ə·lan, -lən) *adj.* Of or pertaining to Catalonia, its people, or their language. **—***n.* **1.** A native or citizen of Catalonia. **2.** The Romance language of Catalonia and Valencia, closely related to Provençal.

cat·a·lep·sy (kat′ə·lep′sē) *n. Psychiatry* An abnormal maintenance of physical postures, accompanied by intense muscular rigidity. [< Med.L < Gk. < *kata-* upon + *lēpsis* seizure] **—cat′a·lep′tic** (-lep′tik) *adj. & n.*

cat·a·log (kat′ə·lôg, -log) *n., v.t., & v.i.* **·loged, ·log·ing** Catalogue. **—cat′a·log′er, cat′a·log′ist** *n.*

cat·a·logue (kat′ə·lôg, -log) *n.* **1.** A list or enumeration of names, objects, etc., usu. in alphabetical order. **2.** A publication containing such a list, as of articles for sale. **3.** A card catalogue (which see). Abbr. *cat.* **—***v.t. & v.i.* **·logued, ·logu·ing** To make a catalogue (of); enter (items) in a catalogue. [< F < LL < Gk. < *kata-* down + *legein* to select, choose] **—cat′a·logu′er, cat′a·logu′ist** *n.*

ca·tal·pa (kə·tal′pə) *n.* A tree of China, Japan, and North America, having large, ovate leaves, fragrant flowers, and long, slender pods. [< N. Am. Ind.]

ca·tal·y·sis (kə·tal′ə·sis) *n. pl.* **·ses** (-sēz) *Chem.* An increase in the rate of a chemical reaction, caused by the addition of a substance that is not permanently altered by the reaction: also spelled *katalysis.* [< Gk. < *kata-* wholly, completely + *lyein* to loosen] **—cat·a·lyt·ic** (kat′ə·lit′ik) *adj. & n.* **—cat′a·lyt′i·cal·ly** *adv.*

cat·a·lyst (kat′ə·list) *n. Chem.* Any substance that causes catalysis. Also **cat′a·lyz′er.**

cat·a·lyze (kat′ə·līz) *v.t.* **·lyzed, ·lyz·ing** To submit to or decompose by catalysis.

cat·a·ma·ran (kat′ə·mə·ran′) *n. Naut.* **1.** A long, narrow raft of logs, often with an outrigger. **2.** A boat having twin hulls. **3.** *Canadian* In Newfoundland, a heavy-duty wooden sled. [< Tamil *kattamaran* tied wood]

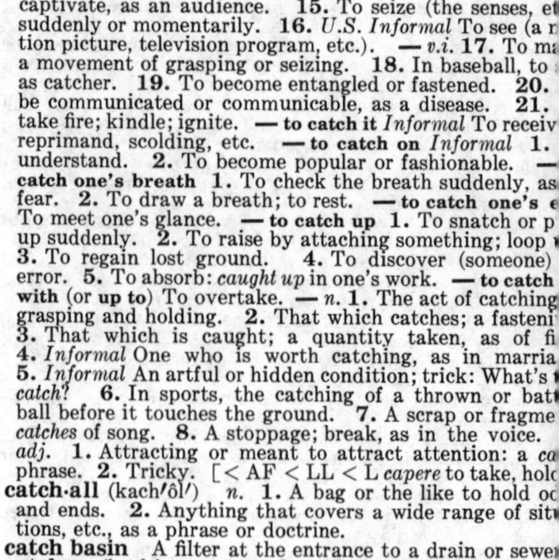

CATAMARAN (*def.* 2) (Tahitian war canoe)

cat·a·mount (kat′ə·mount) *n. U.S.* The puma; also, the lynx. [Short form of *cat of the mountain*]

cat·a·pult (kat′ə·pult) *n.* **1.** An ancient military device for throwing stones, arrows, etc. **2.** *Aeron.* A device for launching an airplane at flight speed, as from the deck of a ship. **3.** A slingshot. **—***v.t.* **1.** To hurl from or as from a catapult. **—***v.i.* **2.** To hurtle through the air. [< L < Gk. < *kata-* down + *pallein* to brandish, hurl]

cat·a·ract (kat′ə·rakt) *n.* **1.** A waterfall. **2.** A downpour. **3.** *Pathol.* **a** Opacity of the lens of the eye, causing partial or total blindness. **b** The opaque area. [< MF *cataracte* < L < Gk. < *kata-* down + *arassein* to fall headlong]

ca·tarrh (kə·tär′) *n. Pathol.* Inflammation of the mucous membrane of the air passages in the throat and head, with excessive secretion of mucus. [< MF < L < Gk. < *kata-* down + *rheein* to flow] **—ca·tarrh′al, ca·tarrh′ous** *adj.*

ca·tas·tro·phe (kə·tas′trə·fē) *n.* **1.** A great and sudden disaster; calamity. **2.** A sudden, violent change or upheaval. **3.** In a drama, the conclusion of the plot; dénouement. [< Gk. < *kata-* over, down + *strephein* to turn] **—cat′a·stroph′ic** *adj.* **—cat′a·stroph′i·cal·ly** *adv.*

Ca·taw·ba (kə·tô′bə) *n.* An American red grape; also, a dry white wine made from it.

cat·bird (kat′bûrd′) *n.* A small, slate-colored North American songbird, having a catlike cry.

cat·boat (kat′bōt′) *n. Naut.* A small sailboat, having its mast well forward and carrying a single fore-and-aft sail.

cat·call (kat′kôl′) *n.* A shrill, discordant call or whistle expressing impatience or derision. **—***v.t.* **1.** To deride or show contempt for with catcalls. **—***v.i.* **2.** To utter catcalls.

catch (kach) *v.* **caught, catch·ing** *v.t.* **1.** To take, seize, or come upon. **2.** To take by trapping; ensnare. **3.** To surprise in the act. **4.** To take hold of suddenly so as to detain. **5.** To grip; entangle. **6.** To grasp and retain: to *catch* rain water in a barrel. **7.** To overtake: We were *caught* by the storm. **8.** To reach in time: to *catch* a train. **9.** To strike. **10.** To check (oneself) in speaking. **11.** To become affected with, as by contagion: to *catch* cold. **12.** To take; get: to *catch* fire. **13.** To apprehend or perceive; also, to reproduce accurately: The artist has not *caught* her expression. **14.** To captivate, as an audience. **15.** To seize (the senses, et suddenly or momentarily. **16.** *U.S. Informal* To see (a n tion picture, television program, etc.). **—***v.i.* **17.** To ma a movement of grasping or seizing. **18.** In baseball, to as catcher. **19.** To become entangled or fastened. **20.** be communicated or communicable, as a disease. **21.** take fire; kindle; ignite. **—to catch it** *Informal* To receiv reprimand, scolding, etc. **—to catch on** *Informal* **1.** understand. **2.** To become popular or fashionable. **—catch one's breath 1.** To check the breath suddenly, as fear. **2.** To draw a breath; to rest. **—to catch one's e** To meet one's glance. **—to catch up 1.** To snatch or p up suddenly. **2.** To raise by attaching something; loop **3.** To regain lost ground. **4.** To discover (someone) error. **5.** To absorb: *caught up* in one's work. **—to catch with** (or **up to**) To overtake. **—***n.* **1.** The act of catching grasping and holding. **2.** That which catches; a fasteni **3.** That which is caught; a quantity taken, as of fi **4.** *Informal* One who is worth catching, as in marria **5.** *Informal* An artful or hidden condition; trick: What's *catch?* **6.** In sports, the catching of a thrown or batt ball before it touches the ground. **7.** A scrap or fragme *catches* of song. **8.** A stoppage; break, as in the voice. *adj.* **1.** Attracting or meant to attract attention: a *ca* phrase. **2.** Tricky. [< AF < LL < L *capere* to take, hold

catch·all (kach′ôl′) *n.* **1.** A bag or the like to hold od and ends. **2.** Anything that covers a wide range of situ tions, etc., as a phrase or doctrine.

catch basin A filter at the entrance to a drain or sewe

catch·er (kach′ər) *n.* **1.** One who or that which catch **2.** In baseball, the player stationed behind home plate catch balls that pass the batter.

catch·ing (kach′ing) *adj.* **1.** Infectious. **2.** Attractive.

catch·pen·ny (kach′pen′ē) *adj.* Designed merely to se cheap and showy. **—***n. pl.* **·nies** A catchpenny article

catch·up (kach′əp, kech′-) See KETCHUP.

catch·word (kach′wûrd′) *n.* **1.** A word or phrase taken and often repeated, esp. as a political slogan. Also **cat phrase. 2.** A word at the head of a page or column, iden fying the first or last item on the page.

catch·y (kach′ē) *adj.* **catch·i·er, catch·i·est 1.** Attracti catching the fancy; also, easily remembered: *catchy* tun **2.** Deceptive; tricky. **3.** Fitful: *catchy* winds.

cat·e·chet·ic (kat′ə·ket′ik) *adj.* Pertaining to oral instru tion by question and answer. Also **cat′e·chet′i·cal.**

cat·e·chism (kat′ə·kiz′əm) *n.* **1.** A short manual giving, the form of questions and answers, an outline of the prin ples of a religious creed. **2.** Any similar manual giving structions. **3.** Examination by questions and answers. [Med.L < Gk. *katēchizein* to instruct]

cat·e·chist (kat′ə·kist) *n.* One who catechizes; esp., an structor of catechumens. Also **cat′e·chiz′er, cat′e·chis′e —cat′e·chis′tic** or **·ti·cal** *adj.*

cat·e·chize (kat′ə·kīz) *v.t.* **·chized, ·chiz·ing 1.** To instru esp. in the principles of Christianity, by asking questic and discussing the answers. **2.** To question searchingly a at length. Also **cat′e·chise.** [< L < Gk. *katēchizein* to struct] **—cat′e·chi·za′tion** *n.*

cat·e·chu·men (kat′ə·kyōō′mən) *n.* **1.** One who is unc instruction in the elements of Christianity. **2.** One unde going elementary instruction in any subject. **—cat′e·ch me·nal, cat·e·chu·men·i·cal** (kat′ə·kyōō·men′i·kəl) *adj.*

cat·e·gor·i·cal (kat′ə·gôr′i·kəl, -gor′-) *adj.* **1.** Witho qualification; absolute; unequivocal. **2.** Of, pertaining or included in a category. **—cat′e·gor′i·cal·ly** *adv.*

cat·e·go·rize (kat′ə·gə·rīz′) *v.t.* **·rized, ·riz·ing** To put in a category; classify.

cat·e·go·ry (kat′ə·gôr′ē, -gō′rē) *n. pl.* **·ries 1.** A division any system of classification; a class: Drama is a *category* literature. **2.** *Logic* Any of the fundamental concepts classifications into which all knowledge can be placed. [L < Gk. *katēgoreein* to allege, predicate]

cat·e·nate (kat′ə·nāt) *v.t.* **·nat·ed, ·nat·ing** To connect li the links of a chain. [< L *catena* chain] **—cat′e·na′tion**

ca·ter (kā′tər) *v.i.* **1.** To furnish food or entertainment. To provide for the gratification of any need or taste. **—** **3.** To furnish food for: to *cater* a party. [< AF < LL < L *ad-* toward + *captare* to grasp, seize]

cat·er-cor·nered (kat′ər·kôr′nərd) *adj.* Diagonal. **—a** Diagonally. Also *catty-cornered, kitty-cornered.* Also **cat′e cor′ner.** [< dial. E < F < L *quattuor* four + CORNERED

ca·ter·er (kā′tər·ər) *n.* One who caters; esp., one who p vides food and services for social functions.

cat·er·pil·lar (kat′ər·pil′ər) *n.* The larva of a butterfly moth, or of certain other insects, as the sawfly. **—***adj.* Mo ing or fitted with treads mounted on endless belts. [< A < L < *catta* cat + *pilosus* < *pilum* hair]

Cat·er·pil·lar (kat′ər·pil′ər) *n.* A tractor that moves means of two endless metal tracks running along each sic a trade name. Also **cat′er·pil′lar, caterpillar tractor.**

cat·er·waul (kat′ər·wôl) *v.i.* **1.** To utter the discorda

·y of cats at mating time. **2.** To make any discordant :reeching. — *n.* Such a sound. [ME < *cater* cat + *wawen*) wail, howl]

t·fish (kat′fish′) *n. pl.* **·fish** or **·fish·es** Any of numerous :aleless fishes having sensitive barbels around the mouth.

t·gut (kat′gut′) *n.* A very tough cord made from the in- ·stines of certain animals, as sheep, and used for stringing ıusical instruments, making surgical ligatures, etc.

th- Var. of CATA-.

·thar·sis (kə·thär′sis) *n.* **1.** *Med.* Purgation, esp. of the imentary canal. **2.** A purifying or purging of the emo- ons through the effect of art. **3.** *Psychoanal.* A method of ;ychotherapy that induces the discharge of repressed emo- ons. Also spelled *katharsis.* [< Gk. *katharos* pure]

·thar·tic (kə·thär′tik) *adj.* Purgative; purifying. Also **ı·thar′ti·cal.** — *n.* A laxative. [< Gk. *katharos* pure]

·thay (ka·thā′) *Poetic* or *Archaic* China.

t·head (kat′hed′) *n. Naut.* A beam projecting over the ow, by which the anchor is supported clear of the ship.

·the·dra (kə·thē′drə, kath′ə-) *n.* **1.** A bishop's seat or ırone in the cathedral of his diocese. **2.** The see or office ' a bishop. [< L < Gk. < *kata-* down + *hedra* seat]

·the·dral (kə·thē′drəl) *n.* **1.** The church containing the ficial chair of a bishop. **2.** Loosely, any large or important ıurch. — *adj.* **1.** Pertaining to or containing a bishop's ıair or see. **2.** Authoritative; dogmatic. **3.** Of, pertaining ı, or resembling a cathedral.

th·e·ter (kath′ə·tər) *n. Med.* A slender, flexible tube in- ·oduced into body cavities for drainage, esp. one to draw ·rine from the bladder. [< L < Gk. *kata-* down + *hienai*) send, let go]

th·e·ter·ize (kath′ə·tə·rīz′) *v.t.* **·ized, ·iz·ing** To intro- ıce a catheter into.

th·ode (kath′ōd) *n. Electr.* The negatively charged ectrode that receives cations during electrolysis. Also ɔelled *kathode.* [< Gk. < *kata-* down + *hodos* road, way] **- ca·thod·ic** (kə·thod′ik) or **·i·cal** *adj.*

thode rays *Physics* A stream of electrons that pass from cathode to the opposite wall of an evacuated electron tube ·hen it is excited by a current of electricity.

thode-ray tube *Electronics* A special type of electron ıbe in which a beam of electrons is focused by an electric or ıagnetic field and deflected so as to impinge upon a sensi- zed screen, forming an image, as on a television receiver.

th·o·lic (kath′ə·lik, kath′lik) *adj.* **1.** Broad-minded, as ı belief or tastes; liberal; comprehensive; large. **2.** Uni- ersal in reach; general. [< L < Gk. < *kata-* thoroughly + ɔlos whole] — **ca·thol·i·cal·ly** (kə·thol′ik·lē) *adv.*

th·o·lic (kath′ə·lik, kath′lik) *adj.* **1.** Since the Reforma- on: **a** Of or pertaining to the Roman Catholic Church. **b**)esignating those churches that claim to have the apostolic octrine and sacraments of the ancient, undivided church, nd including the Anglican, Old Catholic, Orthodox, and ƚoman Catholic churches. **2.** Of the ancient, undivided 'hristian church. — *n.* A member of any Catholic church.

ıtholic Church The Roman Catholic Church.

ı·thol·i·cism (kə·thol′ə·siz′əm) *n.* The doctrine, system, nd practice of a Catholic church, esp. the Roman Catholic 'hurch. Also **Cath·o·lic·i·ty** (kath′ə·lis′ə·tē).

.th·o·lic·i·ty (kath′ə·lis′ə·tē) *n.* **1.** Freedom from narrow- ess; liberality. **2.** Universality.

·thol·i·cize (kə·thol′ə·sīz) *v.t. & v.i.* **·cized, ·ciz·ing** To ıake or become catholic or Catholic.

.t·i·on (kat′ī·ən) *n. Chem.* The electropositive ion of an lectrolyte, that moves toward the cathode in electrolysis: pposed to *anion*: also spelled *kation.* [< Gk. < *kata-* down ⊦ *ienai* to go] — **cat′i·on′ic** (-ī·on′ik) *adj.*

ıt·kin (kat′kin) *n. Bot.* A deciduous, scaly spike of flow- rs, as in the willow. [MDu. *katteken,* dim. of *katte* cat]

ıt nap A short, light nap; doze.

ıt·nip (kat′nip′) *n.* An aromatic herb of the mint family, f which cats are fond. Also *Brit.* **cat′mint′.** [< CAT + ial. E *nep* catnip]

ıt-o′-nine-tails (kat′ə·nīn′tālz′) *n.* A whip with nine :notted lines fastened to a handle.

ıt rig The rig of a catboat, consisting of one sail on a mast ar forward. — **cat·rigged** (kat′rigd′) *adj.*

ıt's cradle A game played with a loop of string stretched n an intricate arrangement over the fingers.

ıt's-eye (kats′ī′) *n.* **1.** A gemstone, usually chrysoberyl ·r quartz, that shows a line of light across the dome when :ut. **2.** A small metal or glass reflector.

ıt's-paw (kats′pô′) *n.* **1.** A person used as a tool or dupe. **:.** A light wind that ruffles the water. Also **cats′paw′.**

ıt·sup (kat′səp, kech′əp) See KETCHUP.

ıt·tail (kat′tāl′) *n.* A marsh plant having flowers in :ylindrical terminal spikes and long leaves used for making ıats, chair seats, etc.

cat·tle (kat′l) *n.* **1.** Domesticated bovine animals, as cows, bulls, and steers. **2.** Formerly, all livestock, as horses, sheep, etc. **3.** Human beings: a contemptuous term. [< AF < LL < L *capitale* capital, wealth]

cat·tle·man (kat′l·mən) *n. pl.* **·men** (-mən) One who raises or tends cattle.

cat·ty (kat′ē) *adj.* **·ti·er, ·ti·est** **1.** Like or pertaining to cats. **2.** Slyly malicious; spiteful. — **cat′ti·ly** *adv.* — **cat′ti·ness** *n.*

cat·ty-cor·nered (kat′ē·kôr′nərd) *adj.* Cater-cornered.

cat·walk (kat′wôk′) *n.* Any narrow walking space, as at the side of a bridge.

Cau·ca·sian (kô·kā′zhən, -shən, -kash′ən) *adj.* **1.** Of or pertaining to the Caucasus region, its people, and their lan- guages. **2.** Of or belonging to a major ethnic division of the human species loosely called the white race. Also **Cau·cas·ic** (kô·kas′ik). — *n.* **1.** A native of the Caucasus region. **2.** A member of the Caucasian division of the human race.

cau·cus (kô′kəs) *n.* A meeting of members of a political party to select candidates, plan a campaign, etc. — *v.i.* **cau·cused** or **·cussed, cau·cus·ing** or **·cus·sing** To meet in or hold a caucus. [after the 18th c. *Caucus* Club, Boston, Mass.]

cau·dal (kôd′l) *adj. Zool.* **1.** Of, pertaining to, or near the tail or posterior part of the body. **2.** Taillike. [< NL < L *cauda* tail] — **cau′dal·ly** *adv.*

cau·date (kô′dāt) *adj. Zool.* Having a tail or taillike ap- pendage. Also **cau′dat·ed.** [< L *caudatus* < *cauda* tail]

cau·dle (kôd′l) *n.* A warm drink of gruel with wine, eggs, sugar, etc., for invalids. [< AF < Med.L < L *caldus* warm]

caught (kôt, kot) Past tense and past participle of CATCH.

caul (kôl) *n.* The part of the prenatal sac that sometimes envelops the head of a child at birth. [< OF *cale* cap]

caul·dron (kôl′drən) *n.* A large kettle or boiler: also spelled *caldron.* [< AF < L *calidus* hot]

cau·li·flow·er (kô′lə·flou′ər, kol′i-) *n.* **1.** The fleshy, edible head of a variety of cabbage. **2.** The plant bearing this. [Alter. of NL *cauliflora* a flowering cabbage]

cauliflower ear An ear that has been deformed by blows.

cau·lis (kô′lis) *n. pl.* **·les** (-lēz) *Bot.* The stem of a plant. [< L < Gk. *kaulos*] — **cau·line** (kô′lin, -līn) *adj.*

caulk (kôk) *v.t.* **1.** To make tight, as a boat's seams, win- dow frame, etc., by plugging with soft material, such as oakum or tar. Also spelled *calk.* [< OF < L *calcare* to tread] — **caulk′er** *n.* — **caulk′ing** *n.*

cau·sal (kô′zəl) *adj.* Pertaining to, constituting, involving, or expressing a cause. — *n. Gram.* A form expressing cause or reason, as *therefore.* [< L *causa* cause] — **caus′al·ly** *adv.*

cau·sal·i·ty (kô·zal′ə·tē) *n. pl.* **·ties** **1.** The relation of cause and effect. **2.** Causal character or agency.

cau·sa·tion (kô·zā′shən) *n.* **1.** The act of causing. **2.** That which produces an effect; cause. **3.** The relation of cause and effect. [< Med.L < L *causa* cause]

caus·a·tive (kô′zə·tiv) *adj.* **1.** Effective as a cause. **2.** *Gram.* Expressing cause or agency: *to lay* (to cause to lie) is a *causative* verb. — *n. Gram.* A form that expresses or sug- gests causation. [< MF < L *causa* cause] — **caus′a·tive·ly** *adv.* — **caus′a·tive·ness** *n.*

cause (kôz) *n.* **1.** The agent or force producing an effect or a result. **2.** A ground for choice or action: *cause* for com- plaint. **3.** Sufficient ground; good reason: no *cause* to strike. **4.** An aim, object, or principle advocated and supported by an individual or group. **5.** *Law* A matter to be decided in court. **6.** A matter under discussion or in dispute. — *v.t.* **caused, caus·ing** To be the cause of; produce; effect. [< MF < L *causa* cause, legal case] — **caus′a·ble** *adj.* — **cause′less** *adj.* — **caus′er** *n.*

cause cé·lè·bre (kōz sā·leb′r′) *French* **1.** A famous legal case. **2.** Any well-known controversial issue.

cau·se·rie (kō′zə·rē′, *Fr.* kōz·rē′) *n.* **1.** An informal con- versation; a chat. **2.** A short, chatty piece of writing. [< F]

cause·way (kôz′wā′) *n.* **1.** A raised road or way, as over marshy ground. **2.** A paved way; a highway. — *v.t.* To make a causeway for or through, as a marshy tract. [Earlier *causeyway* < AF < LL < L *calx, calcis* heel + WAY]

caus·tic (kôs′tik) *adj.* **1.** Capable of corroding or eating away tissues; burning; corrosive. **2.** Sarcastic; biting: *caus- tic* wit. — *n.* A caustic substance. [< L < Gk. *kaiein* to burn] — **caus′ti·cal·ly** *adv.* — **caus·tic·i·ty** (kôs·tis′ə·tē) *n.*

caustic potash Potassium hydroxide.

caustic soda Sodium hydroxide.

cau·ter·ize (kô′tə·rīz) *v.t.* **·ized, ·iz·ing** To sear with a caus- tic agent or heated iron. — **cau′ter·i·za′tion** *n.*

cau·ter·y (kô′tər·ē) *n. pl.* **·ter·ies** *Med.* **1.** The destruction of tissue by the application of a caustic substance or a sear- ing iron. **2.** A cauterizing agent. [< L < Gk. *kauterion* < *kaiein* to burn]

cau·tion (kô′shən) *n.* **1.** Care to avoid injury or misfortune; prudence; wariness; discretion. **2.** An admonition or warn- ing. **3.** *Informal* One who or that which alarms, astonishes,

etc. — *v.t.* To advise to be prudent; warn. [< OF < L *cautio, -onis* < *cavere* to beware]
cau·tion·ar·y (kô′shən·er′ē) *adj.* Urging caution.
cau·tious (kô′shəs) *adj.* Using great care or prudence; wary. — **cau′tious·ly** *adv.* — **cau′tious·ness** *n.*
cav·al·cade (kav′əl·kād′, kav′əl·kād) *n.* **1.** A company of horsemen on the march or in procession. **2.** A procession; parade. [< MF < Ital. < LL < L *caballus* horse]
cav·a·lier (kav′ə·lir′) *n.* **1.** A horseman; knight. **2.** A courtly or dashing gentleman; a gallant; also, a lady's escort. — *adj.* **1.** Haughty; supercilious. **2.** Free and easy; off-hand. — *v.i.* To behave in a cavalier fashion; show arrogance. [< MF < Ital. < LL < L *caballus* horse, nag] — **cav′a·lier′ly** *adj. & adv.*
Cav·a·lier (kav′ə·lir′) *n.* A supporter of Charles I of England; a Royalist. — *adj.* Pertaining to the Cavaliers.
cav·al·ry (kav′əl·rē) *n.* *pl.* **·ries** Troops trained to maneuver and fight on horseback or, more recently, in armored motor vehicles. Abbr. *cav.* [< MF < Ital. < LL < L *caballus* horse] — **cav′al·ry·man** (-mən) *n.*
cave (kāv) *n.* A chamber beneath the earth, in a mountain or mountainside, etc. ◆ Collateral adjective: *spelean.* — *v.* **caved, cav·ing** *v.t.* **1.** To hollow out. — *v.i.* **2.** *Informal* To fall in or down; give way. — **to cave in 1.** To fall in or down, as when undermined; cause to fall in. **2.** *Informal* To yield utterly; give in. [< OF < L *cavus* hollow]
ca·ve·at (kā′vē·at) *n.* **1.** *Law* A formal notification given by an interested party to a court or officer not to do a certain act. **2.** A caution or warning, esp. to avoid misinterpretation. [< L, let him beware]
ca·ve·at emp·tor (kā′vē·at emp′tôr) *Latin* Let the buyer beware, implying that the purchase is made at his own risk.
ca·ve·a·tor (kā′vē·ā′tər) *n.* One who enters a caveat.
cave-in (kāv′in′) *n.* A collapse or falling in, as of a mine.
cave man 1. A Paleolithic man; prehistoric cave dweller; troglodyte (def. 1). **2.** *Informal* A man who is rough and brutal, esp. in his approach to women.
cav·ern (kav′ərn) *n.* A cave, esp. one that is large or extensive. — *v.t.* **1.** To shut in or as in a cavern. **2.** To hollow out. [< MF < L < *cavus* hollow]
cav·ern·ous (kav′ər·nəs) *adj.* **1.** Full of caverns. **2.** Characteristic of a cavern. **3.** Hollow. — **cav′ern·ous·ly** *adv.*
cav·i·ar (kav′ē·är, kä′vē-) *n.* The salted roe of sturgeon or other fish, used as a relish. Also **cav′i·are.** [< F < Turkish *khāvyār*]
cav·il (kav′əl) *v.* **cav·iled** or **·illed, cav·il·ing** or **·il·ling** *v.i.* **1.** To raise trivial objections; argue captiously; carp: with *at* or *about.* — *v.t.* **2.** To find fault with. — *n.* A captious objection. [< MF < L *cavilla* a jeering, a scoffing] — **cav′·il·er** or **cav′il·ler** *n.* — **cav′il·ing·ness** or **cav′il·ling·ness** *n.* — **cav′il·ing·ly** or **cav′il·ling·ly** *adv.*
cav·i·ty (kav′ə·tē) *n.* *pl.* **·ties 1.** A hollow or sunken space; hole. **2.** A natural hollow in the body. **3.** A decayed place in a tooth. [< MF < LL < L *cavus* hollow]
ca·vort (kə·vôrt′) *v.i.* *U.S.* To prance about; caper; frisk.
ca·vy (kā′vē) *n.* *pl.* **·vies** A small South American rodent with the tail absent or rudimentary, as the guinea pig. [< NL *Cavia* < Carib]
caw (kô) *v.i.* To make the high harsh sound of a crow, rook, etc. — *n.* The cry of a crow, raven, etc. [Imit.]
cay (kā, kē) *n.* A coastal reef or sandy islet, as in the Gulf of Mexico. See KEY[2]. [< Sp. *cayo* shoal]
cay·enne pepper (kī·en′, kā-) Red pepper. Also **cay·enne′.**
cay·man (kā′mən) *n.* *pl.* **·mans** A tropical American crocodilian related to the alligator. [< Sp. *caiman* < Carib]
Ca·yu·ga (kā·yōō′gə, kī-) *n.* *pl.* **·ga** or **·gas** One of a tribe of Iroquois Indians formerly living near Cayuga Lake, N.Y.
cay·use (kī·yōōs′) *n.* *U.S.* An Indian pony.
Cay·use (kī·yōōs′) *n.* A member of a tribe of North American Indians formerly inhabiting Oregon.
cease (sēs) *v.* **ceased, ceas·ing** *v.t.* **1.** To leave off or discontinue, as one's own actions. — *v.i.* **2.** To come to an end; stop; desist. — *n.* End; stopping: now only in the phrase **without cease.** [< MF < L *cedere* to withdraw, yield] — **cease′less** *adj.* — **cease′less·ly** *adv.*
cease-fire (sēs′fīr′) *n.* An armistice; truce.
ce·cro·pi·a moth (si·krō′pē·ə) A large, strikingly marked moth common in the eastern U.S.
ce·cum (sē′kəm) *n.* *pl.* **ce·ca** (sē′kə) *Anat.* A pouch, or cavity, open at one end, esp. that situated between the large and small intestine: also spelled *caecum.* For illus. see INTESTINE. [< L < *caecus* blind] — **ce′cal** *adj.*
ce·dar (sē′dər) *n.* **1.** A large tree of the pine family, having evergreen leaves and fragrant wood. **2.** The red cedar (def. 1). **3.** The wood of these and related trees. — *adj.* Pertaining to or made of cedar. [< OF < L < Gk. *kedros*]
ce·dar·bird (sē′dər·bûrd) *n.* The cedar waxwing. See under WAXWING.
cede (sēd) *v.t.* **ced·ed, ced·ing 1.** To yield or give up. **2.** To surrender title to; transfer: to *cede* land. [< MF *céder* < L *cedere* to withdraw, yield]

ce·dil·la (si·dil′ə) *n.* A mark put under the letter *c* (ç) bef *a, o,* or *u* in some French words, as in *français,* to indic that it is to be sounded as (s). [< Sp. < Gk. *zēta* letter
ceil (sēl) *v.t.* To furnish with a ceiling. [< F < L *cael* heaven, sky]
ceil·ing (sē′ling) *n.* **1.** The overhead covering or lining room. **2.** An upper limit; maximum, as one set on prices wages. **3.** *Aeron.* The maximum height to which a given craft can be flown under specified conditions.
cel·an·dine (sel′ən·dīn) *n.* **1.** A plant of the poppy fam with yellow flowers. **2.** A crowfoot having tuberous ro and yellow flowers. [< OF < L < Gk. *chelidōn* a swallo
-cele[1] *combining form* Tumor or hernia. [< Gk. *kēlē* tum
-cele[2] *combining form* Cavity; hollow space: *blastocele:* a spelled *-coele.* [< Gk. *koilos* hollow]
cel·e·brant (sel′ə·brənt) *n.* **1.** One who participates i celebration. **2.** The officiating priest at the Eucharist.
cel·e·brate (sel′ə·brāt) *v.* **·brat·ed, ·brat·ing** *v.t.* **1.** To serve, as a festival, with rejoicing. **2.** To make known famous; extol. **3.** To perform (a ceremony) publicly and ordained. — *v.i.* **4.** To observe or commemorate a day event. **5.** To perform a religious ceremony. [< L *cele* famous] — **cel′e·bra′tor** *n.*
— **Syn. 1.** *Celebrate* is used for joyous occasions: to *celebra* holiday or birthday. *Commemorate* refers to the solemnity of event, as does *solemnize,* but *commemorate* looks to the past, of with sorrow, while *solemnize* refers to a present occasion: to *c memorate* a great man's death, to *solemnize* a marriage.
cel·e·brat·ed (sel′ə·brā′tid) *adj.* Well-known; much pu cized: a *celebrated* murder trial.
cel·e·bra·tion (sel′ə·brā′shən) *n.* **1.** The act of celebrati **2.** That which is done in commemoration of any event.
ce·leb·ri·ty (sə·leb′rə·tē) *n.* *pl.* **·ties 1.** A famous or c brated person. **2.** Fame or renown. [< L *celeber* famous
ce·ler·i·ty (sə·ler′ə·tē) *n.* Quickness of motion; speed; pidity. [< F < L *celer* swift]
cel·er·y (sel′ər·ē, sel′rē) *n.* A biennial herb whose stems used as a vegetable or salad. [< F < dial. Ital. < *seli* parsley < Gk.]
ce·les·ta (sə·les′tə) *n.* A musical instrument having a k board and steel plates struck by hammers. [< F *célest*
ce·les·tial (sə·les′chəl) *adj.* **1.** Of or pertaining to the s or heavens. **2.** Of heaven; divine. **3.** *Often cap.* Chine — *n.* **1.** A heavenly being. **2.** *Often cap.* A Chinese. OF < L < *caelum* sky, heaven] — **ce·les′tial·ly** *adv.*
Celestial Empire The former Chinese Empire.
celestial equator *Astron.* The great circle in which plane of the earth's equator cuts the celestial sphere.
celestial sphere *Astron.* The imaginary spherical surf on which the heavenly bodies seem to lie, commonly c ceived as of infinite diameter and enclosing the universe.
ce·li·ac (sē′lē·ak) *adj.* Of or pertaining to the abdom Also spelled *coeliac.* [< L *coeliacus* < Gk. *koilos* hollow
cel·i·ba·cy (sel′ə·bə·sē) *n.* The state of being unmarri esp. in accordance with religious vows. [< L *caelebs* married]
cel·i·bate (sel′ə·bit, -bāt) *n.* One who remains unmarri esp. by vow. — *adj.* Unmarried, esp. by vow.
cell (sel) *n.* **1.** A small room, as for a prisoner or monk. A small compartment, receptacle, or cavity. **3.** A body persons forming a single unit in an organization of simi groups. **4.** *Biol.* The fundamental structural unit of pl and animal life, consisting of a small mass of cytoplasm a usu. enclosing a central nucleus and surrounded by a me brane (animal) or a rigid cell wall (plant). **5.** A sin

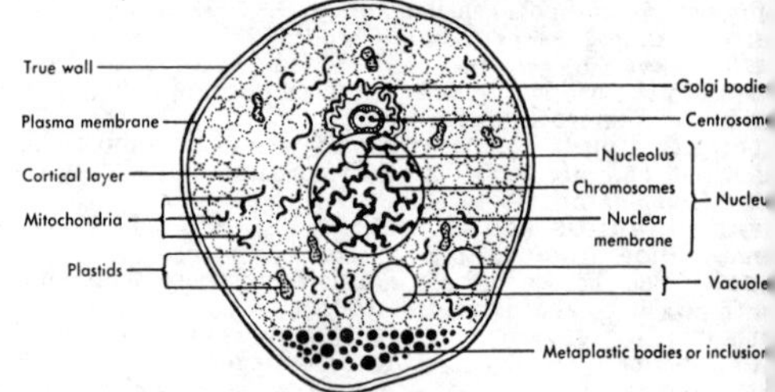

GENERALIZED CELL

compartment of a honeycomb. **6.** *Bot.* The seed-beari cavity of an ovary or pericarp. **7.** *Electr.* The unit co posing all or part of a battery, consisting of electrodes in co tact with an electrolyte and in which a current is generat by means of chemical action. — **dry cell** *Electr.* A prima cell with its electrolyte distributed in some porous su stance. [< OF < L *cella* cell, small room]
cel·lar (sel′ər) *n.* **1.** A space wholly or partly undergrou and usu. beneath a building, used for storage, etc. **2.**

ine cellar; also, a stock of wines. —*v.t.* To put or keep in a
ıllar. [< AF, OF < L *cella* cell, small room]
l·lar·age (sel′ər·ij) *n.* **1.** Space in or for a cellar. **2.** The
ıarge for storing goods in a cellar.
l·lar·er (sel′ər·ər) *n.* The keeper of a cellar, as the steward
ı a monastery.
l·lar·et (sel′ə·ret′) *n.* A case or small cabinet for wine and
quor bottles, decanters, glasses, etc. Also **cel′lar·ette′.**
ll-block (sel′blok′) *n.* In prisons, a unit of cells.
l·lo (chel′ō) *n. pl.* **·los** A bass instrument of the violin fam-
y, tuned an octave lower than the viola, and held between
ıe performer's knees: also called *violoncello.* Also **'cel′lo.**
Short for VIOLONCELLO] —**cel′list** or **'cel′list** *n.*
l·lo·phane (sel′ə·fān) *n.* A treated cellulose that has
een processed in thin, transparent strips or sheets.
l·lu·lar (sel′yə·lər) *adj.* **1.** Of or like a cell or cells. **2.**
onsisting of cells. [See CELLULE.]
l·lule (sel′yo͞ol) *n.* A small cell. [< L *cellula,* dim. of
lla cell, small room]
l·lu·loid (sel′yə·loid) *n.* A hard, elastic, flammable plas-
c, made from guncotton mixed with camphor and other
ıbstances: a trade name. Also **cel′lu·loid.**
l·lu·lose (sel′yə·lōs) *n. Biochem.* An amorphous white
ırbohydrate, insoluble in all ordinary solvents, and forming
ıe fundamental material of the structure of plants. [< L
llula. See CELLULE.]
llulose acetate *Chem.* **1.** A derivative of cellulose, used
ı making synthetic yarns and fabrics. **2.** Acetate rayon.
·lom (sē′ləm) See COELOM.
l·o·tex (sel′ə·teks) *n.* A composition board used for insu-
ıtion: a trade name. Also **cel′o·tex.**
l·si·us scale (sel′sē·əs) A temperature scale in which the
reezing point of water at normal atmospheric pressure is
° and the boiling point is 100°; the centigrade scale. [after
ınders *Celsius,* 1701–44, Swedish astronomer]
lt (selt, kelt) *n.* A person of Celtic linguistic stock, now
epresented by the Irish, Welsh, Highland Scots, and Bret-
ns, formerly by the Gauls and Britons. Also spelled *Kelt.*
lt·ic (sel′tik, kel′-) *n.* A subfamily of the Indo-European
ımily of languages, including ancient Gaulish, the Bry-
ıonic or Cymric branch (Cornish, Welsh, Breton), and the
oidelic or Gaelic branch (Irish, Scottish Gaelic, Manx). —
dj. Of or pertaining to the Celtic peoples, their languages,
r culture. Also spelled *Keltic.*
ltic cross An upright cross having a circle behind the
rossbeam.
·ment (si·ment′) *n.* **1.** A mixture, usu. of burned lime-
tone and clay, that is applied as a mortar or used for pave-
ıents and other smooth surfaces. **Portland cement** is made
y calcining limestone with chalk, mud, etc. **2.** Any ma-
erial, as glue, that, when hardened, will bind objects to-
ether. **3.** Something that unites. **4.** An adhesive material
sed in filling teeth and in other dental work. **5.** *Anat.* Ce-
ıentum. —*v.t.* **1.** To unite or join with or as with cement.
. To cover or coat with cement. —*v.i.* **3.** To become
nited by means of cement; cohere. [< OF *ciment* < L
aedere to cut] —**ce·men·ta·tion** (sē′mən·tā′shən, sem′ən-)
. —**ce·ment′er** *n.*
·men·tum (si·men′təm) *n. Anat.* The layer of bony tis-
ue developed over the roots of the teeth: also called *cement.*
'or illus. see TOOTH. [< L]
m·e·ter·y (sem′ə·ter′ē) *n. pl.* **·ter·ies** A place for bury-
ıg the dead; graveyard. [< L *coemeterium* < Gk. *koimaein*
o put to sleep]
ene *combining form Geol.* Recent; new: used in the names
f geological periods: *Pliocene.* [< Gk. *kainos* new]
no- *combining form* Common. Also spelled *coeno-*: also,
efore vowels, **cen-.** [< Gk. *koinos* common]
n·o·bite (sen′ə·bīt, sē′nə-) *n.* A member of a religious
ommunity: also spelled *coenobite.* [< LL *coenobita* < Gk.
: *koinos* common + *bios* life] —**cen′o·bit′ic** (-bit′ik) or
·cal *adj.* —**cen·o·bit·ism** (sen′ə·bīt·iz′əm, sē′nə-) *n.*
n·o·taph (sen′ə·taf, -täf) *n.* A monument erected to the
ead but not containing the remains. [< MF < L < Gk. <
enos empty + *taphos* tomb] —**cen′o·taph′ic** *adj.*
·no·zo·ic (sē′nə·zō′ik, sen′ə-) *Geol. adj.* Of or pertaining
o the fourth and latest of the eras of geologic time, following
he Mesozoic, and extending to and including the present.
ee chart for GEOLOGY. —*n.* The Cenozoic period. [<
ik. *kainos* new + *zōē* life]
n·ser (sen′sər) *n.* A vessel for burning incense: also called
urible. [< OF *censier* < Med.L *incensum* incense]
n·sor (sen′sər) *n.* **1.** An official examiner of manuscripts,
lays, etc., empowered to suppress them, wholly or in part,
: objectionable. **2.** An official who examines dispatches,
etters, etc., in time of war. **3.** Anyone who censures or ar-
aigns. **4.** In ancient Rome, one of two magistrates who
rew up the census and supervised public morals. —*v.t.*
To act as censor of. [< L < *censere* to judge] —**cen·so·ri·al** (sen·sôr′ē·əl, -sō′rē-) *adj.*
cen·so·ri·ous (sen·sôr′ē·əs, -sō′rē-) *adj.* Given to censure; judging severely; faultfinding. —**cen·so′ri·ous·ly** *adv.* —**cen·so′ri·ous·ness** *n.*
cen·sor·ship (sen′sər·ship) *n.* **1.** The action of censoring. **2.** The office or power of a censor. **3.** A system of censoring.
cen·sur·a·ble (sen′shər·ə·bəl) *adj.* Deserving censure. —**cen′sur·a·ble·ness** *n.* —**cen′sur·a·bly** *adv.*
cen·sure (sen′shər) *n.* The expression of disapproval or blame; adverse or hostile criticism; reprimand. —**Syn.** See REPROOF. —*v.* **·sured, ·sur·ing** *v.t.* **1.** To express disapproval of; condemn; blame. —*v.i.* **2.** To express disapproval. [< F < L < *censere* to judge] —**cen′sur·er** *n.*
cen·sus (sen′səs) *n. pl.* **·sus·es** **1.** An official count of the people of a country or district, with statistics as to age, sex, employment, etc. **2.** In ancient Rome, a similar enumeration to determine taxation. [< L *censere* to assess] —**cen·su·al** (sen′sho͞o·əl) *adj.*
cent (sent) *n.* **1.** The hundredth part of a dollar; also, a coin of this value: symbol ¢. **2.** A hundred: used only in *percent, per cent.* [< F < L *centum* hundred]
cen·tare (sen′târ, *Fr.* säṅ·tàr′) *n.* A measure of land area, equal to one square meter: also *centiare.* See table front of book. [< F *centi-* hundredth (< L *centum* hundred) + *are.* See ARE[2].]
cen·taur (sen′tôr) *n.* In Greek mythology, one of a race of monsters, having the head, arms, and torso of a man united to the body and legs of a horse. [< L < Gk. *Kentauros*]

CENTAUR

cen·ta·vo (sen·tä′vō) *n. pl.* **·vos** (-vōz, *Sp.* -vōs) **1.** A small coin of the Philippines and various Spanish-American countries, equal to one hundredth of the peso. **2.** A similar coin of Portugal and of Brazil. [< Sp.]
cen·te·nar·i·an (sen′tə·nâr′ē·ən) *n.* One who is 100 years old. —*adj.* **1.** Of the age of 100 years. **2.** Pertaining to a period of 100 years.
cen·te·nar·y (sen′tə·ner′ē, sen·ten′ə·rē) *adj.* **1.** Of or pertaining to 100 or 100 years. **2.** Occurring every 100 years. —*n. pl.* **·nar·ies** **1.** A period of 100 years. **2.** A centennial. [< L *centum* hundred]
cen·ten·ni·al (sen·ten′ē·əl) *adj.* **1.** Of an age or duration of 100 years. **2.** Of or marking a period of 100 years or its completion. **3.** Occurring every 100 years. —*n.* A 100th anniversary or its celebration. [< L < *centum* hundred + *annus* year] —**cen·ten′ni·al·ly** *adv.*
Centennial State Nickname of Colorado.
cen·ter (sen′tər) *n.* **1.** The point or place equally distant from the extremities or sides of anything. **2.** *Geom.* The point within a circle or sphere equidistant from every point on the circumference or surface. **3.** A point about which a thing revolves. **4.** A place or point at which activity is concentrated or toward which people seem to converge. **5.** A point from which effects, influences, etc., proceed; source. **6.** *Mil.* The part of an army occupying the front between the wings. **7.** *Often cap.* A group, party, etc., having moderate views or tendencies. **8.** In football, basketball, etc., a player who occupies a middle position, as in the forward line. —*v.t.* **1.** To place in or at the center. **2.** To direct toward one place; concentrate. **3.** To determine or mark the center of. —*v.i.* **4.** To be at the center of. —*adj.* Central; middle. Also, *Brit., centre.* [< L *centrum* < Gk. *kentron* point]
cen·ter·board (sen′tər·bôrd′, -bōrd′) *n.* A board so hung that it can be lowered below the bottom of a sailboat through a slot to prevent leeway. Also *Brit.* **cen′tre·board′.**
center of gravity *Physics* The point about which a body acted upon by gravity is in equilibrium in all positions.
cen·ter·piece (sen′tər·pēs′) *n.* A piece at the center of anything; esp., an ornament in the center of a table.
cen·tes·i·mal (sen·tes′ə·məl) *adj.* **1.** Hundredth. **2.** Pertaining to or divided into hundredths. [< L *centesimus* hundredth] —**cen·tes′i·mal·ly** *adv.*
centi- *combining form* **1.** Hundred: *centipede.* **2.** In the metric system and in technical usage, one hundredth of (a specified unit): *centiliter.* [< L *centum* hundred]
cen·ti·are (sen′tē·âr) See CENTARE.
cen·ti·grade (sen′tə·grād) *adj.* Graduated to a scale of a hundred. [< F < L *centum* hundred + *gradus* step, degree]
centigrade scale A temperature scale in which the freezing point of water at normal atmospheric pressure is 0° and the boiling point is 100°: also called *Celsius scale.*
cen·ti·gram (sen′tə·gram) *n.* In the metric system, the hundredth part of a gram. Also **cen′ti·gramme.** See table inside back cover.
cen·ti·li·ter (sen′tə·lē′tər) *n.* In the metric system, the hundredth part of a liter. Also *esp. Brit.* **cen′ti·li′tre.** See table inside back cover.

cen·time (sän′tēm, *Fr.* säṅ·tēm′) *n.* A small coin, the hundredth part of a franc. [< F < OF < L *centesimus* hundredth]
cen·ti·me·ter (sen′tə·mē′tər) *n.* In the metric system, the hundredth part of a meter. Also *esp. Brit.* **cen′ti·me′tre.** See table inside back cover.
cen·ti·me·ter-gram-sec·ond (sen′tə·mē′tər·gram′sek′ənd) *adj.* See CGS.
cen·ti·pede (sen′tə·pēd) *n.* A wormlike animal having many pairs of legs. [< F < L < *centum* hundred + *pes, pedis* foot]
cen·ti·stere (sen′tə·stir) *n.* A hundredth of a stere. See table inside back cover. [< F *centistère*]
cen·tral (sen′trəl) *adj.* **1.** At, in, or near the center. **2.** Of or constituting the center. **3.** That exercises a controlling influence; dominant. **4.** Most important; principal; chief. [< L < *centrum* center] — **cen′tral·ly** *adv.*
cen·tral·ism (sen′trəl·iz′əm) *n.* A centralizing tendency or system; concentration of control in a central authority. — **cen′tral·ist** *n. & adj.* — **cen′tral·is′tic** *adj.*
cen·tral·i·ty (sen·tral′ə·tē) *n.* **1.** The state of being central. **2.** Tendency toward or situation at a center.
cen·tral·ize (sen′trəl·īz) *v.* **·ized, ·iz·ing** *v.t.* **1.** To bring to a center; make central; especially, to bring under a central authority. — *v.i.* **2.** To come to a center; concentrate. — **cen′tral·i·za′tion** *n.* — **cen′tral·iz′er** *n.*
central nervous system *Anat.* That part of the nervous system consisting of the brain and spinal cord.
cen·tre (sen′tər) *n., adj., v.t. & v.i.* **·tred, ·tring** *Brit.* Center.
centri- *combining form* Center: used in words of Latin origin. Compare CENTRO-. [< L *centrum* center]
cen·tric (sen′trik) *adj.* At, relating to, or having a center. Also **cen′tri·cal.** [< Gk. *kentrikos* < *kentron* center] — **cen′tri·cal·ly** *adv.* — **cen·tric·i·ty** (sen·tris′ə·tē) *n.*
cen·trif·u·gal (sen·trif′yə·gəl, -trif′ə·gəl) *adj.* **1.** Directed or tending away from a center; radiating: opposed to *centripetal.* **2.** Employing centrifugal force: a *centrifugal* pump. — *n.* A centrifuge. [< NL < L *centrum* center + *fugere* to flee] — **cen·trif′u·gal·ly** *adv.*
centrifugal force *Physics* The inertial reaction by which a body tends to move away from the center of rotation.
cen·tri·fuge (sen′trə·fyōōj) *n.* A rotary machine for the separation of substances having different densities. — *v.t.* **·fuged, ·fug·ing** To subject to the action of a centrifuge. [< F] — **cen·trif·u·ga·tion** (sen·trif′yə·gā′shən, -ə·gā′-) *n.*
cen·trip·e·tal (sen·trip′ə·təl) *adj.* **1.** Directed, tending, or drawing toward a center: opposed to *centrifugal.* **2.** Acting by drawing toward a center. [< NL < L *centrum* center + *petere* to seek] — **cen·trip′e·tal·ly** *adv.*
centripetal force *Physics* A force attracting a body toward a center around which it revolves.
cen·trist (sen′trist) *n.* One who takes a moderate position in politics.
centro- *combining form* Center: used in words of Greek origin, as in *centrosphere.* Also, before vowels, **centr-.** [< Gk. *kentron* center]
cen·tro·some (sen′trə·sōm) *n. Biol.* The small area of protoplasm external to the nucleus of the cell. — **cen′tro·som′ic** (-som′ik) *adj.* For illus. see CELL.
cen·tro·sphere (sen′trə·sfir′) *n. Biol.* In living cells, the sphere that surrounds the centrosome. For illus. see CELL.
cen·tu·ple (sen′tə·pəl, sen·tōō′pəl, -tyōō′-) *v.t.* **·pled, ·pling** To increase a hundredfold. — *adj.* Increased a hundredfold. [< F < LL *centuplus* hundredfold]
cen·tu·pli·cate (*v.* sen·tōō′plə·kāt, -tyōō′-; *adj. & n.* sen·tōō′plə·kit, -tyōō′-) *v.t.* **·cat·ed, ·cat·ing** To multiply by a hundred; centuple. — *adj. & n.* Hundredfold. [< LL < L *centuplex* hundredfold] — **cen·tu·pli·ca′tion** *n.*
cen·tu·ri·on (sen·tŏŏr′ē·ən, -tyŏŏr′-) *n.* In the ancient Roman army, a captain of a century. [< L *centurio, -onis*]
cen·tu·ry (sen′chə·rē) *n. pl.* **·ries** **1.** A period of 100 years in any system of chronology, esp. in reckoning from the first year of the Christian era. **2.** In ancient Rome: **a** A body of foot soldiers, originally of 100 men. **b** One of 193 electoral divisions. **3.** A group or series of a hundred. [< L *centuria* < *centum* hundred] — **cen·tu·ri·al** (sen·tŏŏr′ē·əl) *adj.*
century plant A succulent plant of the amaryllis family, flowering in twenty to thirty years and then dying, popularly supposed to bloom once in a century.
ce·phal·ic (sə·fal′ik) *adj.* **1.** Of or pertaining to the head. **2.** At, on, in, or near the head. [< F < Gk. *kephalē* head]
-cephalic *combining form* Head; skull: *brachycephalic.*
cephalic index *Anat.* The ratio of the greatest breadth of the human head from side to side, multiplied by 100, to the greatest length.
cephalo- *combining form* Head. Also, before vowels, **cephal-.** [< Gk. *kephale* head]
ceph·a·lo·pod (sef′ə·lə·pod′) *Zool. n.* Any of a class of marine mollusks having a clearly defined head and eyes, ink sac, and tentacles or arms around the mouth, as squids and octopuses. — *adj.* Of or pertaining to cephalopods: also **ceph′a·lo·pod′ic, ceph·a·lop·o·dous** (sef′ə·lop′ə·dəs). — **ceph lop·o·dan** (sef′ə·lop′ə·dən) *n. & adj.*
ceph·a·lo·tho·rax (sef′ə·lō·thôr′aks, -thō′raks) *n.* Z The anterior portion of certain crustaceans and arachn consisting of the united head and thorax. For illus. SHRIMP. — **ceph′a·lo·tho·rac′ic** (-thə·ras′ik) *adj.*
ceph·a·lous (sef′ə·ləs) *adj.* Having a head.
-cephalous *combining form* Headed: *hydrocephalous.* Gk. *kephalē* head]
cer- Var. of CERO-.
ce·ram·ic (sə·ram′ik) *adj.* Pertaining to articles made fired and baked clay. [< Gk. *keramos* potter's clay]
ce·ram·ics (sə·ram′iks) *n.pl.* (*construed as sing in def. 1.*) The art of modeling and baking in clay. **2.** Objects mad fired and baked clay. — **ce·ram′ist** *n.*
Cer·ber·us (sûr′bər·əs) In classical mythology, the th headed dog guarding the portals of Hades. — **Cer·be·re** (sər·bir′ē·ən) *adj.*
cere[1] (sir) *v.t.* **cered, cer·ing** To wrap in cerecloth. [< < L *cera* wax]
cere[2] (sir) *n. Ornithol.* In parrots and birds of prey, a w like area about the bill. [< F < L *cera* wax]
ce·re·al (sir′ē·əl) *n.* **1.** An edible, starchy grain yielded certain plants of the grass family, as rice, wheat, rye, o etc. **2.** Any of such plants. **3.** A breakfast food made fr a cereal grain. [< L *Ceres,* goddess of grain]
cer·e·bel·lum (ser′ə·bel′əm) *n. pl.* **·bel·lums** or **·be** (-bel′ə) *Anat.* The part of the brain below and behind cerebrum serving as the coordination center of volunt movements, posture, and equilibrium. [< L, dim. of *c brum* brain] — **cer′e·bel′lar** *adj.*
cer·e·bral (ser′ə·brəl, sə·rē′-) *adj.* **1.** Of or pertaining to cerebrum or the brain. **2.** Appealing to or involving the tellect; intellectual. [< F < L *cerebrum* brain]
cerebral palsy *Pathol.* Any paralysis affecting the abi to control movement and caused by brain lesions result from prenatal defect or birth injury.
cer·e·brate (ser′ə·brāt) **·brat·ed, ·brat·ing** *v.i.* **1.** To h or manifest brain action. **2.** To think. [< L *cereb* brain] — **cer′e·bra′tion** *n.*
cerebro- *combining form* Brain: *cerebrospinal.* Also, be vowels, **cerebr-.** [< L *cerebrum* brain]
cer·e·bro·spi·nal (ser′ə·brō·spī′nəl) *adj. Anat.* Of or fecting the brain and the spinal cord.
cer·e·brum (ser′ə·brəm, sə·rē′brəm) *n. pl.* **·bra** (-brə) *A* The upper anterior part of the brain, consisting of two h ispherical masses enclosed within the cortex and constitut the seat of conscious processes. [< L] — **cer·e·bric** (se brik, sə·rē′-) *adj.*
cere·cloth (sir′klôth′, -kloth′) *n.* Cloth treated with w used to wrap the dead. [Orig. *cered cloth* < L *cera* wax
cere·ment (sir′mənt) *n. Usu. pl.* **1.** A cerecloth. **2** shroud. [< F < MF < L *cera* wax]
cer·e·mo·ni·al (ser′ə·mō′nē·əl) *adj.* Of, pertaining to characterized by ceremony; ritual; formal. — *n.* **1.** A p scribed set of ceremonies for some particular occasion; rit **2.** A rite; ceremony. — **cer′e·mo′ni·al·ism** *n.* — **ce mo′ni·al·ist** *n.* — **cer′e·mo′ni·al·ly** *adv.*
cer·e·mo·ni·ous (ser′ə·mō′nē·əs) *adj.* **1.** Studiously overly polite. **2.** Characterized by ceremony; formal. — **cer′e·mo′ni·ous·ly** *adv.* — **cer′e·mo′ni·ous·ness** *n.*
cer·e·mo·ny (ser′ə·mō′nē) *n. pl.* **·nies** **1.** A formal act ritual, or a series of them, performed in a prescribed man **2.** Formal observances collectively; ritual. **3.** An em ritual. **4.** Adherence to ritual forms; formality. **5.** An of formal courtesy. — **to stand on** (or **upon**) **ceremony** insist upon formalities. [< OF < L *caerimonia* awe]
Ce·res (sir′ēz) In Roman mythology, the goddess of gr and harvests: identified with the Greek *Demeter.*
cer·iph (ser′if) See SERIF.
ce·rise (sə·rēz′, -rēs′) *n. & adj.* Vivid red. [< F, cher
ce·ri·um (sir′ē·əm) *n.* A silver-white, ductile, highly re tive and electropositive element (symbol Ce) of the lant nide series. See ELEMENT. [after the asteroid *Ceres*]
cero- *combining form* Wax: *cerotype.* Also, before vow *cer-.* [< L *cera* or Gk. *kēros* wax]
ce·ro·plas·tic (sir′ə·plas′tik) *adj.* **1.** Pertaining to w modeling. **2.** Modeled in wax. [< Gk. < *kēros* wax *plassein* to mold]
cer·tain (sûr′tən) *adj.* **1.** Absolutely confident; convinc **2.** Sure; destined. **3.** Beyond doubt; indisputable. Sure in its workings or results; dependable; also, unerri **5.** Fixed; determined. **6.** Not explicitly stated or identifi *certain* persons. **7.** Some, or some at least: a *certain* provement. — *n.* An indefinite number or quantity: *C tain* of the students were absent. — **for certain** With doubt; surely. [< OF, ult. < L *cernere* to determine]
cer·tain·ly (sûr′tən·lē) *adv.* Without doubt: surely.
cer·tain·ty (sûr′tən·tē) *n. pl.* **·ties** **1.** The state, quali or fact of being certain. **2.** A known fact.
cer·tif·i·cate (*n.* sər·tif′ə·kit; *v.* sər·tif′ə·kāt) *n.* An offic

r sworn document stating something to be a fact. — *v.t.* **:at·ed, ·cat·ing** To furnish with or attest by a certificate. < Med.L < L < *certus* certain + *facere* to make] — **cer·if′i·ca′tor** (-kā′tər) *n.* — **cer·tif′i·ca·to′ry** *adj.*
r·ti·fi·ca·tion (sûr′tə·fi·kā′shən) *n.* **1.** The act of certifying or guaranteeing. **2.** The state of being certified. **3.** That which guarantees or vouches for. **4.** A certificate.
r·ti·fied (sûr′tə·fīd) *adj.* **1.** Vouched for in writing; endorsed. **2.** Affirmed or guaranteed by a certificate. **3.** Legally committed to a mental institution.
rtified check A check issued by a bank that guarantees that it is drawn on an account having sufficient funds.
r·ti·fy (sûr′tə·fī) *v.* **fied, ·fy·ing** *v.t.* **1.** To give certain information of; attest. **2.** To testify to in writing; vouch for. **.** To endorse as meeting set standards or requirements. **4.** 'o guarantee in writing on the face of (a check) that the account drawn on has sufficient funds for payment: said of anks. **5.** To make certain; assure. **6.** To commit to a mental institution. — *v.i.* **7.** To make attestation; vouch (*for*) r testify (*to*). [< OF < Med.L < L < *certus* certain + *facere* to make] — **cer′ti·fi′a·ble** *adj.* — **cer′ti·fi′er** *n.*
r·ti·o·ra·ri (sûr′shē·ə·râr′ē, -râr′ī) *n. Law* A writ from a uperior to an inferior court, directing that a record of a designated case be sent up for review. [< LL, to be certified]
r·ti·tude (sûr′tə·tōōd, -tyōōd) *n.* Complete confidence. < MF < LL < L < *certus* certain + *facere* to make]
·ru·le·an (sə·rōō′lē·ən, -lyən) *adj. & n.* Sky blue; vivid lue. [< L *caeruleus* dark blue]
·ru·men (sə·rōō′mən) *n.* Earwax. [< NL < L *cera* wax]
r·vi·cal (sûr′vi·kəl) *adj. Anat.* Of, pertaining to, in, or ear the neck of the cervix uteri. [< L *cervix* neck]
r·vine (sûr′vīn, -vin) *adj.* **1.** Deerlike. **2.** Of or pertaining to deer. [< L *cervinus* < *cervus* deer]
r·vix (sûr′viks) *n. pl.* **cer·vix·es** or **cer·vi·ces** (sər·vī′sēz, ûs′və·sēz) *Anat.* **1.** The neck. **2.** The cervix uteri. **3.** A ecklike part. [< L] — **cer·vi·cal** (sûr′vi·kəl) *adj.*
rvix u·ter·i (yōō′tə·rī) *Anat.* The constricted neck of the terus that distends during parturition. [< L]
·sar·e·an (si·zâr′ē·ən) *Surg. n.* A cesarean section. — *dj.* Of or pertaining to a cesarean section. Also **ce·sar′i·an.**
·sar·e·an (si·zâr′ē·ən), **Ce·sar·i·an** See CAESAREAN.
sarean section *Surg.* The birth of a child by section of he abdominal walls and the uterus. Also **cesarean operaion.** [< L *sectio caesarea* < *caedere* to cut]
·si·um (sē′zē·əm) *n.* A ductile metallic element (symbol 's) of the alkali group: also spelled *caesium.* See ELEMENT. < NL < L *caesius* bluish gray]
s·sa·tion (se·sā′shən) *n.* A ceasing; stop; pause. [< L *essatio, -onis* < *cessare* to stop]
s·sion (sesh′ən) *n.* The act of ceding; a giving up, as of erritory or rights, to another. [< L pp. of *cedere* to yield]
ss·pool (ses′pōōl′) *n.* **1.** A covered well or pit for the rainage from sinks, toilets, etc. **2.** Any repository of filth. Also **cess′pit′.** [Origin uncertain]
est la guerre (se lȧ gâr′) *French* That's war.
est la vie (se lȧ vē′) *French* That's life.
s·tus (ses′təs) *n. pl.* **·tus** A wrapping of thongs, often weighted, worn about the hands by boxers n ancient Rome: also spelled *caestus.* [< *caedere* to kill]
·su·ra (si·zhōōr′ə, -zyōōr′ə) See CAESURA.

CESTUS[1]

·ta·cean (si·tā′shən) *adj.* Of or belonging to the aquatic mammals, including he whales, dolphins, and porposes. Also **e·ta′ceous.** — *n.* A cetacean animal. < NL < L < Gk. *kētos* whale]
·tane (sē′tān) *n. Chem.* A saturated hydrocarbon of the methane series, $C_{16}H_{34}$, used as fuel for diesel engines. [< *cetus* whale + -ANE[2]]
ey·lon·ese (sēl′ən·ēz, -ēs) *adj.* Of or pertaining to Ceylon r to its people. — *n.* A native or resident of Ceylon.
gs The centimeter-gram-second system of measurement in which the unit of length is the centimeter, the unit of mass s the gram, and the unit of time is one second. Also **c.g.s., GS, C.G.S.**
ha·blis (shȧ·blē′) *n.* A dry, white, Burgundy wine made n the region of Chablis, a town in north central France.
a·conne (shȧ·kôn′) *n.* A musical form, important in the Baroque period, usu. in slow triple meter, probably derived rom a 16th century Spanish colonial dance: often called *assacaglia.* [< F < Sp. *chacona*]
aeto- *combining form* Hair. Also, before vowels, **chaet-.** < Gk. *chaitē* hair, bristle]
afe (chāf) *v.* **chafed, chaf·ing** *v.t.* **1.** To abrade or make ore by rubbing. **2.** To make warm by rubbing. **3.** To irritate; annoy. — *v.i.* **4.** To rub. **5.** To be irritated; fret; ume: to *chafe* under the abuse. — **to chafe at the bit** To be impatient and irritable because of delay. — *n.* **1.** Soreness or wear from rubbing; friction. **2.** Irritation or vexation. [< OF < L < *calere* to be warm + *facere* to make]
chaf·er (chā′fər) *n.* The cockchafer or other scarabaeid beetle. Also **chaf·fer** (chaf′ər). [OE *ceafor*]
chaff[1] (chaf, chäf) *n.* **1.** The husks of grain. **2.** Any trivial or worthless matter. [OE *ceaf*] — **chaff′y** *adj.*
chaff[2] (chaf, chäf) *v.t. & v.i.* To poke fun (at). — *n.* Good-natured raillery. [Origin uncertain] — **chaff′er** *n.*
chaf·fer (chaf′ər) *v.i.* To haggle about price; bargain. — *n.* A haggling about terms; bargaining. [ME < OE *cēap* bargain + *faru* going] — **chaf′fer·er** *n.*
chaf·finch (chaf′inch) *n.* A song finch of Europe.
chafing dish A vessel with a heating apparatus beneath it, to cook or keep food warm at the table.
cha·grin (shə·grin′) *n.* Distress or vexation caused by disappointment, failure, etc.; mortification. — *v.t.* To humiliate; mortify: used in the passive. [< F]
chain (chān) *n.* **1.** A series of connected rings or links, usu. of metal, serving to bind, drag, hold, or ornament. **2.** *pl.* Anything that confines or restrains; shackles; bonds. **3.** *pl.* Bondage. **4.** Any connected series; a succession. **5.** A series of chain stores. **6.** *Chem.* A series of atoms or radicals of the same or different kinds, linked together and acting as a unit. — *v.t.* **1.** To fasten or connect with a chain. **2.** To fetter; bind. [< OF < L *catena*] — **chain′less** *adj.*
chain gang A gang of convicts chained together while doing hard labor.
chain letter A letter intended to be sent on from one to another in a series of recipients.
chain mail Flexible armor consisting of interlinked metal chains, rings, or scales.
chain reaction **1.** *Physics* The self-sustaining fission of atomic nuclei, in which neutrons released by one fission induce fission in neighboring nuclei, as in a nuclear reactor. **2.** Any series of reactions or events, each of which develops from the preceding one.
chain stitch An ornamental stitch resembling a chain, used in sewing, crocheting, etc.
chain store *U.S.* One of a number of retail stores under the same ownership and selling similar merchandise.
chair (châr) *n.* **1.** A seat, usu. having four legs and a back, for one person. **2.** A seat of office, authority, etc., as that of a professor or bishop. **3.** The office or dignity of one who presides or is in authority. **4.** A presiding officer; chairman. **5.** The electric chair; also, execution in the electric chair. — **to take the chair** To preside at or open a meeting. — *v.t.* **1.** To seat in a chair. **2.** To install in office. **3.** To preside over (a meeting). [< OF *chaiere* < L *cathedra.*]
chair car A parlor car.
chair·man (châr′mən) *n. pl.* **·men** (-mən) One who presides over an assembly, committee, etc. — **chair·wom·an** (châr′wōōm′ən) *n.fem.*
chaise (shāz) *n.* **1.** A two-wheeled, one-horse vehicle for two persons, having a calash top. **2.** A similar carriage with four wheels. Also, *Dial., shay.* [< F, var. of *chaire* chair]
chaise longue (shāz′ lông′, *Fr.* shez lôṅg′) A couchlike chair having the seat prolonged to support the sitter's outstretched legs. [< F, lit., long chair]
cha·la·za (kə·lā′zə) *n. pl.* **·zas** or **·zae** (-zē) *Biol.* One of the two threads attached to each end of the lining membrane of an egg. [< NL < Gk., hailstone, small lump]
chal·ced·o·ny (kal·sed′ə·nē, kal′sə·dō′nē) *n. pl.* **·nies** A waxy, translucent variety of quartz, often of a pale blue or grayish color: also spelled *calcedony.* [after *Chalcedon,* an ancient Greek port]
Chal·de·a (kal·dē′ə) In Biblical times, the southernmost Tigris and Euphrates valley, sometimes including Babylonia. Also **Chal·dae′a.** — **Chal·de′an** *adj. & n.*
cha·let (sha·lā′, shal′ā) *n.* **1.** A Swiss cottage with a gently sloping, projecting roof; also, any cottage built in this style. **2.** A herdsman's hut of the Alpine regions of Europe. [< F]
chal·ice (chal′is) *n.* **1.** A drinking cup or goblet. **2.** *Eccl.* In the Eucharist, a cup in which the wine is consecrated. **3.** A cup-shaped flower. [< OF < L *calix, calicis* cup]
chalk (chôk) *n.* **1.** A soft, grayish white or yellowish compact limestone, largely composed of the shells of marine animals. **2.** A piece of limestone or similar material, frequently colored, used for marking, etc. **3.** A score, tally, or notation of credit given. — *v.t.* **1.** To mark, write, or draw with chalk. **2.** To treat or dress with chalk. **3.** To make pale. — **to chalk up** To score; credit. — *adj.* Made with chalk. [OE < L *calx* limestone] — **chalk′i·ness** *n.* — **chalk′y** *adj.*
chal·lenge (chal′ənj) *v.* **·lenged, ·leng·ing** *v.t.* **1.** To demand a contest with. **2.** To demand defiantly. **3.** To call in question; dispute. **4.** *Law* To object to. **5.** To claim as due; demand. **6.** *Mil.* To stop and demand the countersign from. **7.** *U.S.* To claim that (a person) is not qualified to

vote, or that (a vote) is invalid. — *v.i.* **8.** To make a challenge. — *n.* **1.** An invitation or dare to participate in a contest. **2.** *Mil.* A sentry's call, requiring one to halt and give the countersign. **3.** A calling in question; dispute. **4.** *U.S.* A claim that a voter is not qualified, or that a vote is not valid. **5.** *Law* A formal objection, as to a juror. **6.** *Telecom.* An electromagnetic signal requesting identification, as in radar communication. [< OF < L *calumnia* slander] — **chal′lenge·a·ble** *adj.* — **chal′leng·er** *n.*

chal·lis (shal′ē) *n.* A light fabric, usu. of printed wool, rayon, etc. Also **chal′lie.** [Origin uncertain]

cha·lyb·e·ate (kə·lib′ē·āt, -it) *adj.* **1.** Impregnated with compounds of iron, as mineral waters. **2.** Tasting of iron. — *n.* A medicine or water containing iron in solution. [< NL < L, ult. < Gk. *chalyps, chalybos* steel]

cham·ber (chām′bər) *n.* **1.** A room in a house; esp., a bedroom. **2.** *pl.* An office or suite of rooms, as of a judge. **3.** *pl. Brit.* A set of rooms for one living alone. **4.** A hall where an assembly meets; also, the assembly itself. **5.** A council; board. **6.** An enclosed space or cavity, as in a gun. — *v.t.* **1.** To provide with a chamber. **2.** To fit into or as into a chamber. [< F < L *camera* vaulted room]

chamber concert A concert of chamber music.

cham·ber·lain (chām′bər·lin) *n.* **1.** An official charged with the domestic affairs of a monarch or lord. **2.** A high officer of a royal court. **3.** A treasurer. [< OF < OHG < L *camera* vaulted room] — **cham′ber·lain·ship′** *n.*

cham·ber·maid (chām′bər·mād′) *n.* A female servant who cleans and tends bedrooms in a house, hotel, etc.

chamber music Music composed for a small group of instruments, as for a quartet.

chamber of commerce An association of merchants and businessmen for the regulation and promotion of business in a city or locality.

chamber pot A portable vessel used as a toilet.

cham·bray (sham′brā) *n.* A cotton fabric woven with colored warp and white filling. [after *Cambrai,* France]

cha·me·le·on (kə·mē′lē·ən, -mēl′yən) *n.* **1.** A lizard capable of changing color. **2.** A person of changeable disposition or habits. [< L < Gk. *chamai* on the ground + *leōn* lion]

cham·fer (cham′fər) *v.t.* **1.** To cut away the corner of. **2.** To cut a furrow in; flute. — *n.* A surface produced by chamfering. [< F < OF *chanfraindre* to cut off an edge]

cham·ois (sham′ē, *Fr.* shȧ·mwä′) *n. pl.* **·ois 1.** A mountain antelope of Europe and western Asia. **2.** A soft leather prepared from the skin of the chamois, sheep, goats, deer, etc.: also spelled *shammy, shamois*: also **cham′·my. 3.** The color of this leather, a yellowish beige. — *v.t.* To dress (leather or skin) like chamois. [< MF]

CHAMOIS
(2 feet high at shoulder; 45 inches long)

cham·o·mile (kam′ə·mīl) See CAMOMILE.

champ[1] (champ) *v.t.* **1.** To crush and chew noisily; munch. **2.** To bite upon restlessly. — *v.i.* **3.** To make a biting or chewing movement with the jaws. — *n.* The action of chewing or biting. [Prob. imit.]

champ[2] (champ) *n. Slang* Champion.

cham·pagne (sham·pān′) *n.* **1.** A sparkling white wine made in the area of Champagne, France; also, any wine made in imitation of this. **2.** A pale or greenish yellow. — *adj.* Pertaining to champagne.

cham·paign (sham·pān′) *n.* Flat and open country. — *adj.* Flat and open. [< OF < LL < L *campus* field]

cham·pi·on (cham′pē·ən) *n.* **1.** One who has defeated all opponents and is ranked first, esp. in a sport. **2.** Anything awarded first place. **3.** One who fights for another or defends a principle or cause. — *adj.* Having won first prize or rank; superior to all others. — *v.t.* To fight in behalf of; defend; support. [< OF < LL *campio, -onis* fighter]

cham·pi·on·ship (cham′pē·ən·ship′) *n.* **1.** The state of being a champion. **2.** The position or honor of a champion. **3.** The act of championing; advocacy; defense.

Champs É·ly·sées (shän zā·lē·zā′) A fashionable avenue in Paris. [< F, lit., Elysian fields]

chance (chans, chäns) *n.* **1.** The unknown or undefined cause of events; fortune; luck. **2.** An unusual and unexplained event. **3.** The probability of anything happening; possibility. **4.** An opportunity: Now is your *chance.* **5.** A risk or gamble; hazard. **6.** A ticket in a lottery. — *v.* **chanced, chanc·ing** *v.i.* **1.** To occur accidentally; happen. — *v.t.* **2.** To take the chance of; risk: I'll *chance* it. — **to chance upon** (or **on**) To find or meet unexpectedly. — *adj.* Occurring by chance. [< OF < LL *cadentia* a falling]

chan·cel (chan′səl, chän′-) *n.* The space near the altar of a church for the clergy and choir, often set apart by a screen or railing. [< OF < LL < L *cancelli,* pl., lattice, railing]

chan·cel·ler·y (chan′sə·lər·ē, -slər·ē, chän′-) *n. pl.* **·ler·ies 1.** The office or dignity of a chancellor. **2.** The building or room in which a chancellor has his office. **3.** The office of embassy or legation. Also **chan·cel·ry** (chan′səl·rē, chän′

chan·cel·lor (chan′sə·lər, -slər, chän′-) *n.* **1.** In some E ropean countries, a chief minister of state. **2.** The ch secretary of an embassy. **3.** A secretary, as of a noblem or ruler. **4.** The head of some universities. **5.** *U.S.* A jud of a court of chancery or equity. Also **chan′cel·or.** — **Lo High Chancellor** *Brit.* The highest judicial officer of t crown: also **Lord Chancellor.** [< OF < LL *cancellar* one who stands at the bar in a court] — **chan′cel·lor·ship′**

Chancellor of the Exchequer The minister of finance the British cabinet.

chance-med·ley (chans′med′lē, chäns′-) *n.* **1.** *Law* Unp meditated homicide in self-defense. **2.** Inadvertent or ra dom action. [< OF < *chance* chance + *medlee* mixed]

chan·cer·y (chan′sər·ē, chän′-) *n. pl.* **·cer·ies 1.** In t United States: **a** A court of equity. Also **court of chance b** Equity, or proceedings in equity. **2.** *Brit.* One of the f divisions of the High Court of Justice. **3.** A chancelle **4.** A court of records; archives. — **in chancery 1.** *L* Pending in a court of chancery; in litigation. **2.** In wrestli with the head caught and held under an opponent's ar **3.** In a hopeless predicament. [See CHANCELLOR.]

chan·cre (shang′kər) *n. Pathol.* A primary syphilitic lesi resembling a sore with a hard base. [< F < L *cancer* cr ulcer] — **chan·crous** (shang′krəs) *adj.*

chan·croid (shang′kroid) *n. Pathol.* A nonsyphilitic, loc ized venereal lesion.

chanc·y (chan′sē, chän′-) *adj.* **chanc·i·er, chanc·i·est** *formal* Subject to chance; risky. — **chan′ci·ly** *adv.*

chan·de·lier (shan′də·lir′) *n.* A branched support fo number of lights, suspended from a ceiling. [< F < Me < L *candela* candle]

chan·dler (chan′dlər, chän′-) *n.* **1.** A trader; dealer: sh *chandler.* **2.** One who makes or sells candles. **3.** *Brit.* shopkeeper. [< OF *chandelier* chandler, candlestick]

change (chānj) *v.* **changed, chang·ing** *v.t.* **1.** To make d ferent; alter. **2.** To exchange: to *change* places. **3.** To g or obtain the equivalent of. **4.** To put other garmen coverings, etc., on: to *change* the bed. — *v.i.* **5.** To beco different. **6.** To make a change or exchange. **7.** To tra fer from one train, etc., to another. **8.** To put on ot garments. — **to change color 1.** To blush. **2.** To tu pale. — **to change hands** To pass from one possessor another. — *n.* **1.** The act or fact of changing. **2.** A su stitution of one thing for another. **3.** Something new different; variety. **4.** A clean or different set of cloth **5.** The amount returned when a coin or bill of greater va than the sum due has been tendered. **6.** Money of lo denomination given in exchange for higher. **7.** Small coi **8.** *Usu. pl.* Any order in which a peal of bells may be stru **9.** A place for transacting business; an exchange: a **'change.** — **to ring the changes 1.** To operate a chime bells in every possible order. **2.** To repeat something wi every possible variation. [< OF < LL *cambiare* to change] — **chang′er** *n.*

change·a·ble (chān′jə·bəl) *adj.* **1.** Likely to change vary; inconstant; fickle. **2.** Capable of being chang **3.** Reflecting light so as to appear of different color fr different points of view. — **change·a·bil·i·ty** (chān′jə·bil tē,) **change′a·ble·ness** *n.* — **change′a·bly** *adv.*

change·ful (chānj′fəl) *adj.* Full of or given to change; va able. — **change′ful·ly** *adv.* — **change′ful·ness** *n.*

change·less (chānj′lis) *adj.* Free from change; endurin unchanging. — **change′less·ly** *adv.* — **change′less·ness**

change·ling (chānj′ling) *n.* A child secretly left in place another.

change of life The menopause.

change ringing The production of every possible variati in the ringing of a set of bells.

chan·nel (chan′əl) *n.* **1.** The bed of a stream. **2.** A wi strait: the English *Channel.* **3.** *Naut.* The deep part of river, harbor, etc. **4.** A tubular passage, as for liqui **5.** The course through which anything moves or pass **6.** *pl.* The official or proper routes of communication: to p a request through *channels.* **7.** *Telecom.* **a** A path for t transmission of telegraph, telephone, or radio communic tions. **b** A range of frequencies assigned for television tra mission. **8.** A groove or furrow. — *v.t.* **chan·neled ·nelled, chan·nel·ing** or **·nel·ling 1.** To cut or wear cha nels in. **2.** To direct or convey through or as through channel. [< OF < L *canalis* groove]

chan·son (shan′sən, *Fr.* shäṅ·sôṅ′) *n.* A song. [< F < *canere* to sing]

chant (chant, chänt) *n.* **1.** A simple melody in which varying number of syllables are sung or intoned on ea note. **2.** A psalm or canticle so sung or intoned. **3.** A son melody. **4.** Any monotonous singing or shouting of wor as from a mob. **5.** A singing intonation in speech. — *v.t.* **1.** To sing to a chant. **2.** To celebrate in song. **3.** recite or say in the manner of a chant. — *v.t.* **4.** To si

ıants. **5.** To make melody; sing. **6.** To talk monotoously. [< OF < L *canere* to sing] — **chant′er** *n.*
an·teuse (shäṅ·tœz′) *n. French* A woman singer.
ant·ey (shan′tē, chan′-) *n. pl.* **·eys** A rhythmical work-g song of sailors: also spelled *shantey, shanty.* Also **chan′ty.** Alter. of F *chantez,* imperative of *chanter* to sing]
an·ti·cleer (chan′tə·klir) *n.* A cock. [< OF < *chanter*) sing, crow + *cler* aloud]
an·try (chan′trē, chän′-) *n, pl.* **·tries** An endowment r the daily masses or special prayers; also, a chapel or tar so endowed. [< OF < L *canere* to sing]
a·nu·kah (khä′nōō·kə) See HANUKKAH.
a·os (kā′os) *n.* **1.** Utter disorder and confusion. **2.** The pposed unformed original state of the universe. [< L Gk., abyss]
a·ot·ic (kā·ot′ik) *adj.* Utterly disordered and confused. lso **cha·ot′i·cal.** — **cha·ot′i·cal·ly** *adv.*
ap[1] (chap) *n. Informal* A fellow; lad.
ap[2] (chap) *v.* **chapped** or **chapt, chap·ping** *v.t.* **1.** To use to split, crack, or become rough: The cold has *chapped* y hands. — *v.i.* **2.** To split, crack, or redden. — *n.* A ack or roughened place in the skin. [ME *chappen*]
ap[3] (chap, chop) *n.* **1.** A jaw. **2.** *pl.* The mouth and eeks. Also spelled *chop.* [Cf. ME *chaft* jaw]
ap·ar·ral (chap′ə·ral′) *n.* A thicket of dwarf oak, low orny shrubs, etc. [< Sp. < *chaparra* evergreen oak]
ap·book (chap′bŏŏk′) *n.* A small book containing tales, allads, etc.
a·peau (sha·pō′, *Fr.* shȧ·pō′) *n. pl.* **·peaux** (-pōz′, *Fr.* ō′) or **·peaus** (-pōz′) A hat. [< F]
ap·el (chap′əl) *n.* **1.** A place of worship smaller than a urch. **2.** A recess or enclosed part of a church, for small special services. **3.** *Brit.* A place of worship not conected with the established church. **4.** A building or room a college, school, etc., for religious services; also, the rvices. [< OF < Med.L < *cappa* cloak; orig., a sanctuary here the cloak of St. Martin was kept as a relic]
ap·er·on (shap′ə·rōn) *n.* An older person who accomanies and supervises a group of young people. — *v.t.* To t as chaperon to. Also **chap′er·one.** [< F, hood < *chape* pe] — **chap·er·on·age** (shap′ə·rōn′ij) *n.*
ap·fall·en (chap′fô′lən, chop′-) *adj.* Dejected; crestllen. Also *chopfallen.*
ap·lain (chap′lin) *n.* A clergyman who conducts reious services in a legislative assembly, for a military unit, c. [< OF < Med.L *cappa* cloak] — **chap′lain·cy, chap′·in·ship** *n.*
ap·let (chap′lit) *n.* **1.** A wreath or garland for the head. A rosary, or, more strictly, one third of a rosary. **3.** A ring of beads, or anything resembling it. [< OF < LL ppa hooded cape]
ap·man (chap′mən) *n. pl.* **·men** (-mən) *Brit.* A peddler; wker. [OE < *cēap* business + *man* man]
aps (chaps, shaps) *n.pl. U.S.* Leather overalls without a at, worn over trousers by cowboys to protect the legs.
ap·ter (chap′tər) *n.* **1.** A main division of a book or eatise, usually numbered. **2.** A branch of a society or aternity. **3.** *Eccl.* An assembly of the canons of a cathe-al or collegiate church; also, the canons collectively. A meeting of any order or society. **5.** A period of time: important *chapter* in history. — *v.t.* To divide into chaprs, as a book. [< F < OF < L *caput* head, capital]
apter house **1.** A place of assembly for a cathedral or onastery chapter. **2.** The house of a fraternity or sorority.
ar[1] (chär) *v.* **charred, char·ring** *v.t.* **1.** To burn or scorch e surface of, as timber. **2.** To convert into charcoal by complete combustion. — *v.i.* **3.** To become charred. *n.* Charcoal. [? < CHARCOAL]
ar[2] (chär) *n. pl.* **chars** or **char** Any of various fishes ied to the lake trout. [< Scottish Gaelic *ceara* blood red]
ar[3] (chär) *Brit. n.* **1.** A chore; esp., a household task: also lled *chare.* **2.** A charwoman. — *v.i.* **charred, char·ring** o work as a charwoman. [OE *cerr* turn of work]
ar·a·banc (shar′ə·bangk, -bang) *n. pl.* **·bancs** *Brit.* A ng, open vehicle with rows of seats facing forward. Also **ar′-a-banc.** [< F *char à bancs* car with benches]
ar·ac·ter (kar′ik·tər) *n.* **1.** The combination of qualis or traits that distinguishes an individual or group; pernality. **2.** Any distinguishing attribute; characteristic; operty. **3.** Moral force; integrity. **4.** A good reputation. Status; capacity: in his *character* as president. **6.** A pernage. **7.** A person in a play, novel, etc. **8.** *Informal* An centric or humorous person. **9.** A figure engraved, writn, or printed; mark; sign; letter. **10.** *Genetics* Any strucral or functional trait in a plant or animal resulting from e interaction of genes and regarded as hereditary in igin. — **in** (or **out of**) **character** In keeping (or not in eping) with the general character or role. — *v.t.* To write, print, or engrave. [< MF < L < Gk. < *charassein* to sharpen, engrave, carve, scratch] — **char′ac·ter·less** *adj.*
character actor An actor who portrays characters markedly different from himself in age, temperament, etc.
char·ac·ter·is·tic (kar′ik·tə·ris′tik) *adj.* Indicating or constituting the distinctive quality, character, or disposition; typical: a *characteristic* gesture. — *n.* **1.** A distinctive feature or trait. **2.** *Math.* The integral part of a logarithm; index. — **char′ac·ter·is′ti·cal·ly** *adv.*

— **Syn.** (noun) A *characteristic* is that by which we recognize something for what it is; a hump is one of a camel's *characteristics.* A *peculiarity* is a *characteristic* that distinguishes one individual or kind from another. We speak of the qualities of persons as *traits,* and of the qualities of objects or substances as *properties.*

char·ac·ter·ize (kar′ik·tə·rīz′) *v.t.* **·ized, ·iz·ing** **1.** To describe by qualities or peculiarities; designate. **2.** To be a mark or peculiarity of; distinguish. **3.** To give character to, as in writing or acting. — **char·ac·ter·i·za·tion** (kar′ik·tər·ə·zā′shən) *n.* — **char′ac·ter·iz′er** *n.*
cha·rades (shə·rādz′, *Brit.* shə·rädz′) *n.pl.* (*construed as sing.*) A game in which words and phrases are to be guessed, sometimes syllable by syllable, from their representation in pantomime. [< F < Provençal < *charra* to chatter, prattle]
char·coal (chär′kōl′) *n.* **1.** A black, porous substance obtained by the imperfect combustion of organic matter, as wood, used as a fuel, adsorbent, filter, etc. **2.** A drawing pencil made of charcoal dust. **3.** A drawing made with such a pencil. — *v.t.* To write, draw, mark, or blacken with charcoal. [ME *charcole;* origin unknown]
chard (chärd) *n.* A variety of edible white beet cultivated for its large leaves and leafstalks. [< F < L *carduus* thistle]
charge (chärj) *v.* **charged, charg·ing** *v.t.* **1.** To place a load upon. **2.** To place in or on (a thing) what it is intended or able to receive: to *charge* a furnace with ore. **3.** To load (a firearm). **4.** To diffuse something throughout, as water with carbon dioxide. **5.** To fill as if with electricity; make vibrant. **6.** To supply (a storage battery) with a quantity of electricity. **7.** To accuse; impute something to. **8.** To command; enjoin. **9.** To instruct, exhort: to *charge* a jury. **10.** To entrust with a duty, responsibility, etc.; burden, as with care. **11.** To set or state as a price: to *charge* a dollar. **12.** To make financially liable. **13.** To set down or record as a debt to be paid: to *charge* a purchase. **14.** To attack forcefully: to *charge* a fort. **15.** To place (a weapon) in position for use. — *v.i.* **16.** To make an onset; rush violently. **17.** To demand or fix a price. — **Syn.** See ACCUSE. — **to charge off** To regard as a loss. — *n.* **1.** A load or burden. **2.** The quantity of anything that an apparatus or receptacle can hold at one time. **3.** The amount of explosive to be detonated at one time. **4.** The quantity of static electricity present in or on an apparatus, as a storage battery. **5.** Care and custody; superintendence. **6.** A person or thing entrusted to one's care. **7.** A responsibility or duty. **8.** An accusation; allegation. **9.** An address of instruction or admonition given by a judge to a jury at the close of a trial. **10.** An order or injunction; command. **11.** The expense or cost of something; price. **12.** Any pecuniary burden; tax; lien; expense. **13.** A debt or charged purchase, or an entry recording it. **14.** An onslaught or attack; also, the signal for this. **15.** *Physics* The energy present in an atomic particle. — **in charge of** Having responsibility for or control of. [< OF < LL < L *carrus* cart]
charge·a·ble (chär′jə·bəl) *adj.* **1.** That may be or is liable to be charged. **2.** Liable to become a public charge.
charge account A retail credit account to which purchases or services may be charged for future payment.
char·gé d'af·faires (shär·zhā′ də·fâr′, *Fr.* shȧr·zhā′ dȧ·fâr′) *pl.* **char·gés d'af·faires** (shär·zhāz′ də·fâr′, *Fr.* shȧr·zhā′ dȧ·fâr′) **1.** One who temporarily heads a diplomatic mission in the absence of the ambassador or minister. **2.** A diplomatic of lower rank than an ambassador. Also **char·gé′.**
charg·er (chär′jər) *n.* **1.** One who or that which charges. **2.** A horse trained for use in battle; a war horse. **3.** An apparatus for charging storage batteries.
char·i·ly (châr′ə·lē) *adv.* In a chary manner; carefully.
char·i·ness (châr′ē·nis) *n.* The quality of being chary.
char·i·ot (char′ē·ət) *n.* An ancient two-wheeled vehicle used in war, racing, etc. — *v.t. & v.i.* To convey, ride, or drive in a chariot. [< OF < L *carrus* cart, wagon]
char·i·o·teer (char′ē·ə·tir′) *n.* One who drives a chariot.
cha·ris·ma (kə·riz′mə) *n.* **1.** *Theol.* An extraordinary spiritual grace that benefits others. **2.** Extraordinary personal power or charm. [< Gk., grace, favor]
char·is·mat·ic (kar′iz·mat′ik) *adj.* Possessing charisma.
char·i·ta·ble (char′ə·tə·bəl) *adj.* **1.** Generous in giving gifts to the poor; beneficent. **2.** Inclined to judge others leniently. **3.** Of or concerned with charity: a *charitable* enterprise. — **char′i·ta·ble·ness** *n.* — **char′i·ta·bly** *adv.*

char·i·ty (char′ə·tē) *n. pl.* **·ties** **1.** The providing of help to the poor. **2.** That which is given to help the needy; alms. **3.** An institution, organization, or fund to aid those in need. **4.** Tolerance; leniency. **5.** An act of good will. **6.** Brotherly love. [< OF < L *carus* dear]

cha·riv·a·ri (shə·riv′ə·rē′, shiv′ə·rē′, shä′rē·vä′rē) *n. pl.* **·ris** A mock serenade, as to a newly married couple, performed with tin pans, horns, etc.: also *chivaree, shivaree.* [< MF]

char·la·tan (shär′lə·tən) *n.* One who makes claim to skill and knowledge he does not possess; an impostor; quack. [< F < Ital. *ciarla* chat, idle talk] **— char′la·tan′ic** (-tan′ik) *adj.* **— char′la·tan·ism, char′la·tan·ry** *n.*

Charles's Wain The constellation Ursa Major.

Charles·ton (chärl′stən) *n.* A fast dance in 4/4 time, popular in the 1920's. [after *Charleston,* S.C.]

char·ley horse (chär′lē) *U.S. Informal* A muscular cramp in the arm or leg, caused by strain. [Origin unknown]

char·lock (chär′lək) *n.* Any of several herbs of the mustard family having yellow flowers. [OE *cerlic*]

char·lotte russe (shär′lat ro͞os) A small sponge cake with a filling of whipped cream or custard. [< F, Russian charlotte]

charm (chärm) *n.* **1.** The power to allure or delight; fascination. **2.** Any fascinating quality or feature. **3.** A small ornament worn on a necklace, bracelet, etc. **4.** Something worn to ward off evil or ensure good luck; an amulet. **5.** Any formula or action supposed to have magic power. **—** *v.t.* **1.** To attract irresistibly; delight; fascinate. **2.** To cast a spell upon or influence as if by a spell; bewitch. **3.** To protect by or as by magic power. **—** *v.i.* **4.** To be pleasing or fascinating. [< F < L *carmen* song] **— charm′er** *n.*

charm·ing (chär′ming) *adj.* **1.** Delightful; very attractive. **2.** Magically powerful. **— charm′ing·ly** *adv.*

char·nel (chär′nəl) *n.* A charnel house. **—** *adj.* Suggesting or fit for receiving the dead; sepulchral; ghastly. [< OF < LL < L *caro, carnis* flesh]

charnel house A room or vault where bones or bodies of the dead are placed.

Char·on (kâr′ən, kar′-) In Greek mythology, the ferryman who carried the dead over the river Styx to Hades. **—** *n.* A ferryman: a humorous use.

char·ry (chär′ē) *adj.* **·ri·er, ·ri·est** Like charcoal.

chart (chärt) *n.* **1.** A map, esp. one for the use of mariners. **2.** An outline map on which climatic data, military operations, etc., can be shown. **3.** A sheet showing facts graphically or in tabular form. **4.** A graph showing changes and variation of temperature, population, prices, wages, etc. **—** *v.t.* To lay out on a chart; map out. [< OF < L < Gk. *chartēs* leaf of paper] **— chart′less** *adj.*

char·ter (chär′tər) *n.* **1.** A document of incorporation of a municipality, institution, or the like, specifying its privileges and purposes. **2.** A formal document by which a sovereign or government grants special rights or privileges to a person, company, or the people. **3.** An authorization to establish a branch or chapter of some larger organization. **4.** A contract for the lease of a vessel, bus, airplane, etc. **—** *v.t.* **1.** To hire (an airplane, train, etc.). **2.** To give a charter to. [< OF < L *chartula,* dim. of *charta* paper] **— char′ter·age** *n.* **— char′ter·er** *n.*

charter member An original member of a corporation, order, or society.

char·treuse (shar·trœz′; *for def. 2,* also shär·tro͞oz′) *n.* **1.** A yellow, pale green, or white liqueur made by the Carthusian monks. **2.** A pale, yellowish green color. **—** *adj.* Of the color chartreuse. [< F < *La Grande Chartreuse,* chief Carthusian monastery in France]

char·wom·an (chär′wo͝om′ən) *n. pl.* **·wom·en** (-wim′ən) *Brit.* A woman employed to do housework, or cleaning and scrubbing, as in office buildings.

char·y (châr′ē) *adj.* **char·i·er, char·i·est** **1.** Cautious; wary. **2.** Fastidious; particular. **3.** Sparing; frugal; stingy. [OE *cearig* sorrowful, sad < *cearu* care]

Cha·ryb·dis (kə·rib′dis) In Greek mythology, a monster dwelling in a whirlpool on the Sicilian coast opposite the cave of Scylla; also, the whirlpool. See SCYLLA.

chase[1] (chās) *v.* **chased, chas·ing** *v.t.* **1.** To pursue with intent to catch or harm. **2.** To follow persistently; run after. **3.** To put to flight; drive. **—** *v.i.* **4.** To follow in pursuit. **5.** *Informal* To rush; go hurriedly. **—** *n.* **1.** The act of chasing or pursuing. **2.** The sport of hunting: preceded by *the.* **3.** That which is pursued; prey; quarry. **— to give chase** To pursue. [< OF < LL < L *capere* to take]

chase[2] (chās) *n.* **1.** *Printing* A rectangular metal frame into which pages of type are fastened for printing or platemaking. **2.** A groove or slot; hollow; trench. **—** *v.t.* **chased, chas·ing** **1.** To indent or groove. **2.** To ornament by embossing; engrave. [Fusion of F *chasse* and *chas,* both ult. < L *capsa* box; *v.* def. 2 < ENCHASE] **— chas′er** *n.*

chas·er (chā′sər) *n.* **1.** One who chases or pursues. **2.** *U.S. Informal* Water, etc. taken after strong liquor.

chasm (kaz′əm) *n.* **1.** A yawning crack in the earth's surface; a gorge. **2.** An abrupt interruption; a gap or vo **3.** Any great difference of opinion, sentiment, loyalty, e [< Gk. *chainein* to gape] **— chas·mal** (kaz′məl) *adj.*

chas·seur (sha·sûr′) *n.* **1.** One of a body of light caval or infantry trained for rapid maneuvers, as in the Fren army. **2.** A liveried servant. **3.** A huntsman. [< F, hunte

Chas·si·dim (khä·sē′dim) *n. pl. of* **Chas·sid** (khä′sid) sect of Jewish mystics: also spelled *Hasidim.* [< Hebre pious] **— Chas·si·dic** (khä·sē′dik) *adj.*

chas·sis (shas′ē, chas′ē) *n. pl.* **chas·sis** (shas′ēz, chas′ **1.** The flat, rectangular frame that supports the body o motor vehicle and includes the wheels, springs, motor, e **2.** *Aeron.* The landing gear of an aircraft. **3.** *Telecom.* T metal framework to which the tubes and other componen of a radio receiver, amplifier, etc., are attached. **4.** movable frame on which the top carriage of a gun mov backward and forward. [< F *chassis* < *chas.* See CHASE

chaste (chāst) *adj.* **1.** Not guilty of unlawful sexual int course; virtuous. **2.** Pure in character or conduct; not decent. **3.** Pure in artistic or literary style; simple. [< < L *castus* pure] **— chaste′ly** *adv.* **— chaste′ness** *n.*

chas·ten (chā′sən) *v.t.* **1.** To discipline by punishment affliction; chastise. **2.** To moderate; soften; temper. [OF < L *castigare* to correct] **— chast′en·er** *n.*

— Syn. 1. *Chasten* is a general term to cover mild or severe pu ishment, whether physical or moral. *Correct* suggests mild puni ment or sometimes mere verbal reproof. *Discipline,* like *corr* looks to future conduct, and stresses training rather than puni ment. *Chastise* and *castigate* refer to corporal punishment for p misconduct rather than as a corrective measure.

chas·tise (chas·tīz′) *v.t.* **·tised, ·tis·ing** To punish, e by beating. **— Syn.** See CHASTEN. [ME *chastisen*] **chas·tis′a·ble** *adj.* **— chas·tise·ment** (chas′tiz·mənt, ch tīz′-) *n.* **— chas·tis′er** *n.*

chas·ti·ty (chas′tə·tē) *n.* **1.** The state or quality of bei chaste. **2.** Virginity or celibacy. [< OF < L < *castus* pu

chas·u·ble (chaz′yə·bəl, chas′-) *n.* A long, sleeveless ve ment worn over the alb by a priest when celebrating t Eucharist. [< F < Med.L < L, dim. of *casa* house]

chat (chat) *v.i.* **chat·ted, chat·ting** To converse in an ea or gossipy manner; talk familiarly. **—** *n.* **1.** Easy, inform conversation. **2.** Any of several singing birds: so called fr their notes. [Short for CHATTER]

cha·teau (sha·tō′, *Fr.* shä·tō′) *n. pl.* **·teaux** (-tōz′, -tō′) **1.** A French castle. **2.** A house on a country esta Also *French* **châ·teau′.** [< F < OF < L *castrum* camp, fo

chat·e·laine (shat′ə·lān) *n.* **1.** A chain hanging from woman's belt to hold small articles, as keys; also, a clasp hold a watch or purse. **2.** The mistress of a chateau, cast or any fashionable household. [< F *châtelaine*]

chat·tel (chat′l) *n. Law* An article of personal property movable, as distinguished from real property. [< *chatel* < L *caput* head]

chattel mortgage A mortgage on personal property.

chat·ter (chat′ər) *v.i.* **1.** To click together rapidly, as t teeth in shivering. **2.** To talk rapidly and trivially. **3.** utter a rapid series of short, inarticulate sounds, as a squirr **—** *v.t.* **4.** To utter in a trivial or chattering manner. **1.** Idle or foolish talk; prattle. **2.** Jabbering, as of a m key. **3.** A rattling of the teeth. [Imit.] **— chat′ter·er**

chat·ter·box (chat′ər·boks′) *n.* An incessant talker.

chat·ty (chat′ē) *adj.* **·ti·er, ·ti·est** **1.** Given to chat; loqu cious. **2.** Easy and familiar; informal: a *chatty* style writing. **— chat′ti·ly** *adv.* **— chat′ti·ness** *n.*

Chau·ce·ri·an (chô·sir′ē·ən) *adj.* Of or like the writi of Chaucer. **—** *n.* A specialist in Chaucer's works.

chauf·feur (shō′fər, shō′fûr′) *n.* One who is employed the driver of an automobile. **—** *v.t.* To serve as driver f [< F, stoker < *chauffer* to warm]

chaul·moo·gra (chôl·mo͞o′grə) *n.* An East Indian a Malayan tree whose seeds yield **chaulmoogra oil,** forme used in treating leprosy. [< Bengali *cāulmugrā*]

chau·vin·ism (shō′vən·iz′əm) *n.* **1.** Militant and va glorious patriotism. **2.** Unreasoning attachment to on race, group, etc. [after Nicholas *Chauvin,* a soldier a overzealous supporter of Napoleon Bonaparte] **— cha vin·ist** *n.* **— chau′vin·is′tic** *adj.* **— chau′vin·is′ti·cal·ly** *a*

cheap (chēp) *adj.* **1.** Bringing a low price; inexpensi **2.** Charging low prices, as a store. **3.** Obtainable at a l price in proportion to its value. **4.** Easily obtained; costi little trouble. **5.** Being of little value; poor; inferior. Not esteemed. **7.** Vulgar; mean: a *cheap* person. **—** *a* At a low price; cheaply. [Earlier *good cheap* a bargain OE *cēap* business, trade] **— cheap′ly** *adv.* **— cheap′ness**

cheap·en (chē′pən) *v.t. & v.i.* To make or become che or cheaper. **— cheap′en·er** *n.*

cheap·skate (chēp′skāt′) *n. U.S. Slang* A miserly pers

cheat (chēt) *v.t.* **1.** To swindle or defraud. **2.** To misle or delude; trick. **3.** To elude or escape; foil. **—** *v.i.* **4.** practice fraud or act dishonestly. **5.** *U.S. Slang* To sexually unfaithful. **—** *n.* **1.** A fraud; swindle. **2.** One w eats or defrauds. [ME *chete*, short for *achete* to confiscate, prive] — **cheat′er** *n.* — **cheat′ing·ly** *adv.*

ɔck (chek) *n.* 1. A break in progress or advance; a stop-ng; rebuff; delay. 2. One who or that which stops or con-ɔls. 3. Control maintained to secure accuracy, honesty c.; supervision. 4. A test, examination, or comparison. A mark to show that something has been verified or in-stigated. 6. An order, in writing, upon a bank or banker pay a designated sum: also, *Brit. cheque.* 7. *U.S.* A tag, p, or the like, issued for identification: a baggage *check.* *U.S.* A slip listing the amount one owes, as in a restau-nt. 9. A counter used in various games; a chip. 10. A uare in a checkered surface, as on a chessboard. 11. A bric having a checkered pattern. 12. In chess, the condi-n of a king that is subject to capture on the next opposing ove. 13. A crack, as in timber or steel. — **in check** nder control or restraint. — *v.t.* 1. To bring to a stop ddenly or sharply; halt. 2. To hold back; curb; restrain. To test or verify as to accuracy, completeness, etc.; also, investigate. 4. To mark with a check, as to indicate rrectness. 5. To mark with squares or crossed lines; ecker. 6. To deposit or accept for temporary safekeep-: to *check* luggage. 7. In chess, to put (an opponent's ng) in check. 8. To cause to crack. — *v.i.* 9. To come a stop; pause. 10. *U.S.* To agree item for item; corre-ond accurately. 11. In chess, to put an opponent's king check. 12. *U.S.* To draw on a checking account. 13. crack, as paint. — **to check in** *U.S.* To register as a est at a hotel, etc. — **to check on** (or **up on**) *U.S.* To quire into; investigate. — **to check out** 1. *U.S.* To pay e's bill and leave, as from a hotel. 2. To investigate or nfirm. 3. To be true or as expected, upon investigation. *Slang* To die. — *interj.* In chess, an exclamation pro-iming that an opponent's king is in check. — *adj.* 1. *iefly Brit.* Formed or marked in a pattern of checks. Serving to verify or check. [< OF *eschec* defeat, check] **check′a·ble** *adj.*

ɔck·book (chek′bŏŏk′) *n.* A book of blank bank checks.

ɔcked (chekt) *adj.* 1. Marked with squares: *checked* ngham. 2. Kept in check; restrained. 3. Stopped.

ɔck·er (chek′ər) *n.* 1. A piece used in the game of eckers, usually a small disk. 2. One of the squares in a eckered surface; also, a pattern of such squares. 3. One o checks; esp., one who inspects, counts, or supervises e disposal of merchandise. — *v.t.* 1. To mark with squares crossed lines. 2. To fill with variations or vicissitudes. so, *Brit., chequer.* [< ME < OF *eschec* defeat, check]

ɔck·er·board (chek′ər·bôrd′, -bōrd′) *n.* A board divided to 64 squares, used in playing checkers or chess.

ɔck·ered (chek′ərd) *adj.* 1. Divided into squares. 2. arked by light and dark patches. 2. Marked by alterna-ns; eventful: a *checkered* career.

ɔck·ers (chek′ərz) *n.pl.* (*construed as sing.*) A game ayed by two persons on a checkerboard, each player start- with twelve pieces: in England usu. called *draughts.*

ɔck·ing account (check′ing) A bank account against hich a depositor may draw checks.

ɔck list A list of items to be checked.

ɔck·mate (chek′māt) *v.t.* **·mat·ed, ·mat·ing** 1. In chess, put (an opponent's king) in check from which no escape is ssible, thus winning the game. 2. To defeat by a skillful aneuver. — *n.* 1. In chess: **a** The move that check-ates a king. **b** The condition of a king when checkmated. Utter defeat. Also *mate.* [< OF < Arabic *shāh māt* the ng is dead < Persian]

ɔck-off (chek′ôf′, -of′) *n.* The collection of trade-union es by deduction from the pay of each employee.

ɔck-out (chek′out′) *n.* 1. The procedure or time of ecking out of a hotel. 2. The itemization of goods and yment for purchases, as at a supermarket: often used tributively: a *check-out* counter. Also **check′out′.**

ɔck·rein (chek′rān′) *n.* A rein from the bit to the saddle a harness to keep a horse's head up.

ɔck·room (chek′rōōm′, -rŏŏm′) *n.* A room in which ckages, coats, etc., may be left temporarily.

ɔck·up (chek′up′) *n.* An examining or searching.

ed·dar (ched′ər) *n.* Any of several types of white to llow, hard, smooth cheese. Also **ched′dar, Cheddar cheese.** fter *Cheddar*, Somerset, England, where originally made]

ɔek (chēk) *n.* 1. Either side of the face below the eye and ove the mouth. ◆ Collateral adjective: *buccal.* 2. A le or part analogous to the side of the face. 3. *Informal* npudent self-assurance. [OE *cēce, cēace*]

ɔek·bone (bhēk′bōn′) *n.* Either of two bony prominences the cheek below the eye socket.

ɔek by jowl Side by side; in close intimacy.

ɔek·y (chē′kē) *adj.* **cheek·i·er, cheek·i·est** *Informal* Im-dent; brazen. — **cheek′i·ly** *adv.* — **cheek′i·ness** *n.*

cheep (chēp) *v.t. & v.i.* To make, or utter with, a faint, shrill sound, as a young bird. — *n.* A weak chirp or squeak. [Imit.] — **cheep′er** *n.*

cheer (chir) *n.* 1. A shout of acclamation or encourage-ment. 2. Gladness or gaiety. 3. State of mind; mood. 4. That which promotes happiness or joy; encouragement. — *v.t.* 1. To make cheerful; gladden: often with *up.* 2. To acclaim with cheers. 3. To urge; incite: often with *on.* — *v.i.* 4. To become cheerful or glad: often with *up.* 5. To utter cries of encouragement, approval, etc. [< OF *chiere, chere* face] — **cheer′er** *n.* — **cheer′ing·ly** *adv.*

cheer·ful (chir′fəl) *adj.* 1. In good spirits; joyous; lively. 2. Pleasant: a *cheerful* color. 3. Willing; ungrudging: a *cheerful* giver. — **cheer′ful·ly** *adv.* — **cheer′ful·ness** *n.*

cheer·i·o (chir′ē·ō) *interj. & n. pl.* **cheer·i·os** *Brit. Informal* 1. Hello. 2. Good-by. Also **cheer′o.**

cheer·lead·er (chir′lē′dər) *n.* A person who leads organized cheering at an athletic event. Also **cheer leader.**

cheer·less (chir′lis) *adj.* Destitute of cheer; gloomy. — **cheer′less·ly** *adv.* — **cheer′less·ness** *n.*

cheer·y (chir′ē) *adj.* **cheer·i·er, cheer·i·est** Abounding in cheerfulness; gay. — **cheer′i·ly** *adv.* — **cheer′i·ness** *n.*

cheese[1] (chēz) *n.* 1. The pressed curd of milk, variously prepared and flavored. 2. Any of various substances like cheese in consistency or shape. [OE *cēse* < L *caseus* cheese]

cheese[2] (chēz) *v.t.* **cheesed, chees·ing** *Slang* To stop: esp. in the phrase **cheese it!** Look out! Run! [< CEASE]

cheese[3] (chēz) *n.* *Slang* Personage: a big *cheese.* [? < Urdu *chīz* thing]

cheese·cake (chēz′kāk′) *n.* 1. A cake containing sweet-ened curds, eggs, milk, etc.: also **cheese cake.** 2. *Slang* A photograph featuring a pretty girl's legs and figure.

cheese·cloth (chēz′klôth′, -kloth′) *n.* A thin, loosely wo-ven cotton fabric, originally used for wrapping cheese.

chees·y (chē′zē) *adj.* **chees·i·er, chees·i·est** 1. Of or like cheese. 2. *U.S. Slang* Inferior. — **chees′i·ness** *n.*

chee·tah (chē′tə) *n.* An animal of the cat family, resem-bling the leopard, native to SW Asia and northern Africa. [< Hind. *chītā* leopard < Skt. *chitraka* speckled]

chef (shef) *n.* A head cook; also, any cook. [< F *chef* (*de cuisine*) head (of the kitchen) < OF]

cheg·oe (cheg′ō) *n.* The chigoe (def. 1).

cheilo- See CHILO-.

cheiro- See CHIRO-.

che·la (kē′lə) *n. pl.* **·lae** (-lē) *Zool.* A pincerlike claw in crustaceans and arachnids. [< NL < Gk. *chēlē* claw] — **che·late** (kē′lāt) *adj.*

chem·i·cal (kem′i·kəl) *adj.* Of or pertaining to chemistry or its phenomena, laws, operations, or results. — *n.* A substance obtained by or used in a chemical process. [< F < Med.L *alchimicus* of alchemy] — **chem′i·cal·ly** *adv.*

chemical warfare The technique of using smoke screens, gases, incendiary materials, etc., in warfare.

che·mise (shə·mēz′) *n.* 1. A woman's loose undergarment resembling a short slip. 2. A dress hanging straight from the shoulders. [< OF < LL *camisia* shirt]

chem·ist (kem′ist) *n.* 1. One versed in chemistry. 2. *Brit.* A druggist. [< ALCHEMIST]

chem·is·try (kem′is·trē) *n. pl.* **·tries** 1. The science that treats of the structure, composition, and properties of sub-stances and of their transformations. 2. Chemical com-position or processes.

chemo- *combining form* Chemical; of or with chemicals or chemical reactions. Also **chemi-.** Also, before vowels, **chem-.**

chem·o·ther·a·py (kem′ō·ther′ə·pē, kē′mō-) *n. Med.* The treatment of infections by the use of chemically synthe-sized drugs. Also **chem′o·ther′a·peu′tics.** — **chem′o·ther′a·peu′tic** *adj.* — **chem′o·ther′a·pist** *n.*

chem·ur·gy (kem′ər·jē) *n.* The chemical exploitation of organic raw materials, esp. agricultural products, in the industrial development of new products. — **chem·ur·gic** (kem·ûr′jik) or **·gi·cal** *adj.*

che·nille (shə·nēl′) *n.* 1. A soft, fuzzy cord, used for embroidery, fringes, etc. 2. A fabric made with filling of this cord, used for rugs, bedspreads, or the like. [< F < L *canicula*, dim. of *canis* dog]

cheque (chek) *n. Brit.* A check (def. 6).

cheq·uer (chek′ər) *n. Brit.* A checker.

cher·ish (cher′ish) *v.t.* 1. To hold dear; treat with tender-ness; foster. 2. To entertain fondly, as a hope or an idea to. [< OF *cheriss-*, stem of *cherir* to hold dear < L *carus*] — **cher′ish·er** *n.* — **cher′ish·ing·ly** *adv.*

Cher·o·kee (cher′ə·kē, cher′ə·kē′) *n. pl.* **·kee** or **·kees** 1. One of a great tribe of Iroquoian Indians formerly occupying northern Georgia and North Carolina, now dwelling in Okla-homa. 2. The Iroquoian language of this tribe.

Cherokee rose A trailing rose having large, solitary white flowers: the State flower of Georgia.

che·root (shə·rōōt′) *n.* A cigar cut square at both ends: also spelled *sheroot.* [< F < Tamil *shuruttu* roll, cigar]
cher·ry (cher′ē) *n. pl.* **·ries 1.** Any of various trees of the rose family, related to the plum and the peach and bearing small, round or heart-shaped drupes enclosing a smooth pit. **2.** The wood or fruit of a cherry tree. **3.** A bright red color resembling that of certain cherries: also **cherry red.** — *adj.* **1.** Bright red. **2.** Made of or with cherries. **3.** Made of cherry wood. [ME *chery* < L *cerasus* cherry tree]
cher·ub (cher′əb) *n. pl.* **cher·ubs** or **cher·u·bim** (cher′ə·bim, -yə·bim) *for def. 1,* **cherubs** *for def. 2,* **cherubim** *for def. 3* **1.** A representation of a beautiful winged child, the accepted type of the angelic cherub. **2.** A beautiful child; also, a chubby, innocent-looking adult. **3.** In Scripture, a celestial being. [< LL < Hebrew *kerūb,* an angelic being] — **che·ru·bic** (chə·rōō′bik) *adj.* — **che·ru′bi·cal·ly** *adv.*
cher·vil (chûr′vəl) *n.* A garden herb of the parsley family, the young leaves of which are used for soups, salads, etc. [OE < L < Gk. *chairephyllon*]
cher·vo·nets (cher·vô′nets) *n. pl.* **·vont·si** (-vônt′sē) A former gold monetary unit of the U.S.S.R. [< Russian]
Chesh·ire cat (chesh′ər, -ir) In Lewis Carroll's *Alice's Adventures in Wonderland,* a grinning cat that gradually faded away until only its grin remained.
chess (ches) *n.* A game of skill played on a chessboard by two persons, with 16 pieces on each side. The aim of each player is to checkmate his opponent's king. [< OF *esches,* pl. of *eschec* < Arabic *shāh* king < Persian]
chess·board (ches′bôrd′, -bōrd′) *n.* A board divided into 64 alternately colored squares, used in playing chess.
chess·man (ches′man′, -mən) *n. pl.* **·men** (men′, -mən) Any of the pieces used in playing chess.
chest (chest) *n.* **1.** The part of the body enclosed by the ribs; thorax. ◆ Collateral adjective: *pectoral.* **2.** A box, usu. with a hinged lid, for storing or protecting articles, as tools, jewelry, etc. **3.** The treasury of a public institution; also, the funds contained there. **4.** A chest of drawers. [< OE < L < Gk. *kistē* basket, box]
ches·ter·field (ches′tər·fēld) *n.* **1.** A single-breasted topcoat, generally with concealed buttons. **2.** *Chiefly Canadian* A sofa. [after a 19th c. Earl of *Chesterfield*]
Ches·ter·field·i·an (ches′tər·fēl′dē·ən) *adj.* **1.** Of or pertaining to Lord Chesterfield. **2.** Suave; polished; elegant.
chest·nut (ches′nut′, -nət) *n.* **1.** The edible nut of various trees of the beech family, growing in a prickly bur; also, a tree that bears this nut. **2.** One of certain similar trees, or their fruit, as the horse chestnut. **3.** A reddish brown color. **4.** A horse of this color. **5.** *Informal* **a** A stale joke. **b** Anything trite, as a story, song, etc. — *adj.* Reddish brown. [ME < OF < L < Gk. *kastanea* + NUT]
chest of drawers A piece of furniture containing a set of drawers for storing linens, clothing, etc.
chest·y (ches′tē) *adj.* **chest·i·er, chest·i·est** *Informal* **1.** Self-assertive; proud. **2.** Large in the chest.
che·val-de-frise (shə·val′də·frēz′) *n. pl.* **che·vaux-de-frise** (shə·vō′-) A protecting line, as of broken glass or spikes, on top of a wall. [< F, lit., horse of Friesland]
che·val glass (shə·val′) A long mirror mounted on horizontal pivots in a frame.
chev·a·lier (shev′ə·lir′) *n.* **1.** A member of certain orders of knighthood or honor, as of the French Legion of Honor. **2.** A knight or cavalier. **3.** A chivalrous man; a gallant. [< OF *chevalier* < LL < L *caballus* horse]
chev·i·ot (shev′ē·ət) *n.* A rough cloth of twill weave, used for suits, overcoats, etc., originally made from Cheviot wool.
Chev·i·ot (chev′ē·ət, chē′vē-) *n.* One of a breed of large sheep, originating in the Cheviot Hills, esteemed for their wool (**Cheviot wool**).
chev·ron (shev′rən) *n.* An emblem or insignia usu. consisting of stripes meeting at an angle, worn on a uniform sleeve to indicate rank, length of service, etc., used by military, naval, and police forces. [< OF, chevron, rafter]
chev·y (chev′ē) *n. pl.* **chev·ies** *Brit.* A hunt, or a shout in hunting. — *v.* **chev·ied, chev·y·ing** *v.t.* **1.** To chase about; hunt. **2.** To harass; worry. — *v.i.* **3.** To race; scamper. Also *chivy, chivvy.* [Prob. < *Chevy* Chase]
chew (chōō) *v.t. & v.i.* **1.** To crush or grind with the teeth; masticate. **2.** To meditate upon; consider carefully. — **to chew out** *U.S. Slang* To reprimand severely; berate. — *n.* **1.** The act of chewing. **2.** That which is chewed; a quid; cut. [OE *cēowan*] — **chew′er** *n.*
chew·ing gum (chōō′ing) A preparation of some natural gum, usu. chicle, flavored for chewing.
che·wink (chi·wingk′) *n.* The towhee, a bird. [Imit.]
chew·y (chōō′ē) *adj.* **chew·i·er, chew·i·est** Relatively soft and requiring chewing: Caramels are *chewy.*
Chey·enne (shī·en′) *n. pl.* **·enne** or **·ennes** One of a tribe of North American Indians now inhabiting Montana and Oklahoma.
chi (kī) *n.* The twenty-second letter in the Greek alphabet (Χ, χ), transliterated as *ch.* See ALPHABET. [< Gk.]

chi·an·ti (kē·an′tē, *Ital.* kyän′tē) *n.* A dry, red, Ital wine; also, any similar wine. [after Monti *Chianti,* region in Italy]
chi·a·ro·scu·ro (kē·är′ə·skyŏŏr′ō) *n. pl.* **·ros 1.** The (tribution and treatment of light and shade in a picture. A kind of painting or drawing using only light and shade. An artist's treatment of light and shade. Also **chi·a·o·scu·ro** (kē·är′ə·ō·skyŏŏr′ō). [< Ital. < L < *clarus* cl + *obscurus* dark] — **chi·a′ro·scu′rist** *n.*
chic (shēk, shik) *adj.* Smart; stylish; elegant. — *n.* Or nality, elegance, and taste, esp. in dress. [< F]
chi·cane (shi·kān′) *v.* **·caned, ·can·ing** *v.t.* **1.** To deceive chicanery; trick. **2.** To quibble about. — *v.i.* **3.** To res to chicanery; use tricks. — *n.* **1.** Chicanery. **2.** A bri or whist hand containing no trumps. [< F *chicaner*]
chi·can·er·y (shi·kā′nər·ē) *n. pl.* **·er·ies 1.** Trickery a subterfuge; sophistry; quibbling. **2.** A trick; quibble.
chic·co·ry (chik′ər·ē) See CHICORY.
chi·chi (shē′shē) *adj.* *Informal* Ostentatiously stylish elegant. [< F, frill]
chick (chik) *n.* **1.** A young chicken. **2.** Any young bi **3.** A child. **4.** *U.S. Slang* A girl. [Short for CHICKEN]
chick·a·dee (chik′ə·dē) *n.* An American titmouse w the top of the head and the throat black or dark colored. [Imit. of its cry]
chick·a·ree (chik′ə·rē) *n.* The red squirrel. See under SQUIRREL. [Imit. of its cry]
Chick·a·saw (chik′ə·sô) *n. pl.* **·saw** or **·saws** One of a tribe of Muskhogean North American Indians now living in Oklahoma.
chick·en (chik′ən) *n.* **1.** The young of domestic fowl. **2.** A cock or hen of any age. **3.** The flesh of the chicken, used as food. **4.** *Informal* A child or a young person: now chiefly in the phrase **no chicken,** one no longer young. — *adj.* *U.S. Slang* Afraid, cowardly. — *v.i.* *U.S. Slang* To lose one's nerve: often with *out.* [OE *cicen*]

CHICKADEE (5¾ inches long; tail 2¾ inches; wing spread 8½ inches)

chicken feed *Slang* **1.** Small change, as pennies, nickels, dimes, etc. **2.** Food for chickens.
chicken hawk Any of various hawks that prey on poult
chick·en-heart·ed (chik′ən·här′tid) *adj.* Cowardly.
chicken pox *Pathol.* A contagious disease, principally children, characterized by skin eruptions and a slight fev
chick·pea (chik′pē′) *n.* **1.** A plant of Mediterrane regions and central Asia. **2.** Its seed, widely used as a fo [ME *chichpease*]
chick·weed (chik′wēd) *n.* Any of various weeds havi seeds and leaves that birds eat.
chic·le (chik′əl) *n.* The milky juice or latex of the sapodi used as the basic principle of chewing gum. Also **chicle gu** [< Sp. < Nahuatl *chictli*]
chic·o·ry (chik′ər·ē) *n. pl.* **·ries 1.** A perennial herb, hav usu. blue flowers and used as a salad plant. **2.** Its dri roasted, and ground roots, used for mixing with cof or as a coffee substitute. [< MF < L < Gk. *kichora*]
chide (chīd) *v.t. & v.i.* **chid·ed** or **chid** (chid), **chid·ed chid** or **chid·den** (chid′n), **chid·ing** To speak reprovin (to); scold. [OE *cīdan*] — **chid′er** *n.* — **chid′ing·ly** *a*
chief (chēf) *n.* **1.** *Often cap.* The person highest in rank authority, as the leader or head of a tribe, band, police for government bureau, etc. **2.** *Usu. cap.* A ship's chief eng eer; also, a chief petty officer. **3.** *Slang* A boss. — **in ch** Having the highest authority: commander *in chief.* — *a* **1.** Highest in rank or authority. **2.** Most important eminent; leading. [< OF *chef, chief* < L *caput* head]
chief justice The presiding judge of a court composed several justices.
chief·ly (chēf′lē) *adv.* **1.** Most of all; above all; especia **2.** Principally; mainly. — *adj.* Of or like a chief.
chief of staff *U.S.* The principal staff officer of a divis or a higher level.
Chief of Staff *U.S.* The ranking officer in the Army or Force, responsible to the Secretary of his department.
chief·tain (chēf′tən) *n.* **1.** The head of a clan or tribe. Any chief; leader. [< OF < LL < L *caput* head] **chief′tain·cy, chief′tain·ship** *n.*
chif·fon (shi·fon′, shif′on) *n.* **1.** A sheer silk or rayon f ric. **2.** *pl.* Ornamental adjuncts of feminine attire, as r bons or lace. — *adj.* **1.** Of or pertaining to chiffon. **2.** cooking, having a fluffy texture. [< F, dim. of *chiffe* ra
chif·fo·nier (shif′ə·nir′) *n.* A high chest of drawers, of with a mirror at the top. Also **chif′fon·nier′.** [< F < *chiff*
chig·ger (chig′ər) *n.* **1.** The larva of various mites of southern U.S., that attaches itself to the skin, causing tense itching. **2.** The chigoe (def. 1). [Alter. of CHIGOE
chi·gnon (shēn′yon, *Fr.* shē·nyôn′) *n.* A knot or roll of h worn at the back of the head by women. [< F]
chig·oe (chig′ō) *n.* **1.** A flea of the West Indies and Sou America. **2.** A chigger (def. 1) [< Carib]

i·hua·hua (chi·wä′wä) *n.* One of an ancient breed of :y small, smooth-coated dogs with large, pointed ears, ginally native to Mexico. [after *Chihuahua*, Mexico]
l- Var. of CHILO-.
l·blain (chil′blān) *n. Pathol.* An inflammation of the nds or feet caused by exposure to cold.
ld (chīld) *n. pl.* **chil·dren** 1. An offspring of human par- ts. 2. A boy or girl, most commonly one between infancy d youth. 3. A descendant. 4. A childish person. 5. A oduct of a specified condition, quality, etc.: a *child* of /. — **with child** Pregnant. [OE *cild*] — **child′less** *adj.*
ld·bear·ing (chīld′bâr′ing) *n.* The bringing forth of ildren.
ld·bed (chīld′bed′) *n.* The state of a woman giving birth a child.
ld·birth (chīld′bûrth′) *n.* Parturition.
ld·hood (chīld′hŏŏd) *n.* The state or time of being a ld. [OE *cildhād*]
ld·ish (chīl′dish) *adj.* 1. Of, like, or proper to a child. Unduly like a child; immature; puerile; weak. [OE *cil- c*] — **child′ish·ly** *adv.* — **child′ish·ness** *n.*
ld·like (chīld′līk′) *adj.* Like, characteristic of, or appro- ate to a child; artless, docile, etc. — **child′like′ness** *n.*
·dren (chil′drən) Plural of CHILD.
ld's play Something easy to do.
·i (chil′ē) *n. pl.* **chil·ies** 1. The acrid pod or fruit of the pepper, used as a seasoning. 2. Chile con carne. Also **l′e, chil′li.** [< Sp. < Nahuatl *chilli*]
le con car·ne (kon kär′nē) A highly seasoned dish made :h meat, chili, and often beans. [< Sp., chili with meat]
li sauce A spiced tomato sauce made with chili.
ll (chil) *n.* 1. A sensation of cold, often with shivering. A moderate degree of coldness. 3. A check to enthusi- n, joy, etc. 4. A numbing sensation of dread or anxiety. *v.t.* 1. To reduce to a low temperature. 2. To affect :h cold; seize with a chill. 3. To check, as ardor; dispirit. To harden the surface of (metal) by sudden cooling. *v.i.* 5. To become cold. 6. To be stricken with a chill. To become hard by sudden cooling, as metal. — *adj.* Moderately or unpleasantly cold. 2. Affected by or vering with cold. 3. Cold in manner; distant. 4. Dis- raging. [OE *ciele*] — **chill′ing·ly** *adv.* — **chill′ness** *n.*
l·er (chil′ər) *n.* 1. That which chills. 2. A horror ry or movie.
l·y (chil′ē) *adj.* **chill·i·er, chill·i·est** 1. Causing chill; d or chilling. 2. Feeling cold; affected by chill. 3. Dis- rtening; unfriendly. — **chill′i·ly** *adv.* — **chill′i·ness** *n.*
o- *combining form* Lip. Also spelled *cheilo-*: also, before wels, *chil-*. [< Gk. *cheilos* lip]
ne[1] (chīm) *n.* 1. *Often pl.* A set of bells, as in a bell ver, tuned to a scale. 2. A single bell: the *chime* of a clock. *Often pl.* The sounds or music produced by a chime. 4. reement; accord. — *v.* **chimed, chim·ing** *v.t.* 1. To se to sound musically by striking; ring. 2. To announce e hour) by the sound of bells. 3. To summon, welcome, send by chimes. 4. To say rhythmically; prate. — *v.i.* To sound musically. 6. To ring chimes. 7. To har- nize; agree: with *with.* — **to chime in** 1. To join in moniously. 2. To join, and so interrupt, a conversation. E < L *cymbalum* cymbal] — **chim′er** *n.*
ne[2] (chīm) *n.* The rim of a cask, barrel, etc. Also **chimb** im). [OE *cimb-* edge, as in *cimbing* joint]
me·ra (kə·mir′ə, kī-) *n.* 1. An absurd creation of the agination. 2. In painting, sculpture, etc., an imaginary, tesque monster. [< L < Gk. *chimaira* she-goat]
mer·i·cal (kə·mer′i·kəl, kī-) *adj.* 1. Of the nature of a mera; fantastic; imaginary. 2. Given to fanciful dreams; ionary. Also **chi·mer′ic.** — **chi·mer′i·cal·ly** *adv.*
n·ney (chim′nē) *n.* 1. A flue to conduct gases and oke from a fire to the outer air. 2. A structure containing h a flue, usually vertical and rising above the roof of a lding. 3. A smokestack; funnel. 4. A tube, usually of ss, for enclosing the flame of a lamp. 5. A vent of a cano. [< OF *cheminee* < LL < L < Gk. *kaminos*]
nney corner 1. The space between the jamb or side of rge fireplace and the fire. 2. The fireside.
nney piece A mantel.
nney pot A pipe placed on the top of a chimney to im- ve the draft and prevent smoking.
nney sweep One whose occupation is the cleaning of t from inside chimneys. Also **chimney sweeper.**
n·pan·zee (chim′pan·zē′, chim·pan′zē) *n.* An arboreal hropoid ape of equatorial Africa, having large ears and k brown hair, and smaller and more intelligent than the illa. [< native West African name]
ı (chin) *n.* 1. The lower part of the face, between the uth and the neck. 2. *Anat.* The central and anterior t of the lower jaw. — *v.* **chinned, chin·ning** *v.t.* 1. To lift (oneself) while grasping an overhead bar until the chin is level with the hands. — *v.i.* 2. *U.S. Informal* To talk idly. 3. To chin oneself. [OE *cin*]
chi·na (chī′nə) *n.* 1. Fine porcelain or ceramic ware, origi- nally made in China. 2. Any crockery. Also **chi′na·ware′.**
chi·na·ber·ry (chī′nə·ber′ē) *n. pl.* **·ries** 1. Either of two trees of the soapberry family, found in Mexico and the SW U.S. Also **China tree.** 2. Its berrylike fruit.
Chi·na·man (chī′nə·mən) *n. pl.* **·men** (mən) A Chinese: an offensive term.
Chi·na·town (chī′nə·toun′) The Chinese quarter of any city outside China.
chin·ca·pin (ching′kə·pin) See CHINQUAPIN.
chinch (chinch) *n.* 1. A small, brown and black hemipterous insect destructive to grain. Also **chinch bug.** 2. The bedbug. [< Sp. *chinche* < L *cimex* bug]
chin·chil·la (chin·chil′ə) *n.* 1. A small rodent native in the Andes. 2. The soft, valuable, pearl gray fur of the chinchilla. 3. A closely woven, twilled fabric having a tufted surface. [< Sp., ? alter. of Quechua *sinchi* strong]
chine[1] (chīn) *n.* 1. The spine, backbone, or back. 2. A piece of meat including all or part of the backbone. [< OF *eschine* backbone < Gmc.]
chine[2] (chīn) *n.* Chime[2].
Chi·nese (chī·nēz′, nēs) *adj.* Of or pertaining to China, its people, or their languages. — *n. pl.* **·nese** 1. A native of China, or a person of Chinese ancestry. 2. The standard language of China.
Chinese lantern A collapsible lantern made of thin paper.
Chinese puzzle 1. An intricate puzzle originally made by the Chinese. 2. Any problem difficult to solve.
chink[1] (chingk) *n.* A small, narrow cleft; crevice. — *v.t.* 1. To make cracks or fissures in. 2. To fill the cracks of, as a wall; plug up. [ME *chynke*] — **chink′y** *adj.*
chink[2] (chingk) *n.* 1. A short, sharp, metallic sound. 2. *Slang* Coin; cash. — *v.t. & v.i.* To make or cause to make a sharp, clinking sound. [Imit.]
chi·no (chē′nō) *n.* 1. A strong cotton fabric with a twilled weave. 2. *pl.* Boys' or men's trousers of this material. [< Sp., toasted; with ref. to the original tan color]
Chino- *combining form* Connected with China.
chi·nook (chi·nŏŏk′, -nŏŏk′) *n. U.S. & Canadian* 1. A warm wind of the Oregon and Washington coasts. 2. A warm, dry wind that blows off the eastern slopes of the Rocky Mountains in the NW U.S. and western Canada. [after *Chinook*]
Chi·nook (chi·nŏŏk′, -nŏŏk′) *n. pl.* **·nook** or **·nooks** 1. One of a tribe of North American Indians formerly occupying the region of the Columbia River, Oregon. 2. The language of this tribe. — **Chi·nook′an** *adj. & n.*
Chinook jargon A pidgin language comprising words from Chinook, mixed with English, French, etc.
Chinook salmon A salmon of North Pacific coastal waters.
chin·qua·pin (ching′kə·pin) *n.* 1. Any of several trees of North America. 2. A related tree of the Pacific coast. 3. The edible nut of these trees. Also **chin′ka·pin.** [< N. Am. Ind.]
chintz (chints) *n.* A cotton fabric usu. glazed and printed in bright colors. Also **chints.** [< Skt. *chitra* variegated]
chip (chip) *n.* 1. A small piece cut or broken off. 2. A small disk or counter used in certain games, as in poker. 3. A crack or imperfection caused by chipping. 4. A thinly sliced morsel: potato *chips.* 5. *pl. Brit.* French fried pota- toes. 6. *Usu. pl.* Dried animal droppings used as fuel. 7. Anything of little or no value. 8. Wood, palm leaves, etc., cut into strips for weaving. — **a chip off** (or **of**) **the old block** One who resembles either of his parents in behavior, appearance, etc. — **a chip on one's shoulder** A willingness to take offense; belligerent manner. — **in the chips** *Slang* Possessing money; affluent. — *v.* **chipped, chip·ping** *v.t.* 1. To break off small pieces of, as china. — *v.i.* 2. To become chipped. — **to chip in** *Informal* To contribute, as to a fund. [ME *chippe*] — **chip′per** *n.*
Chip·e·wy·an (chip·ə·wī′ən) *n.* 1. One of a tribe of Indians living in NW Canada. 2. The language of this tribe.
chip·munk (chip′mungk) *n.* Any of various striped North American rodents of the squirrel family: also called *ground squirrel.* Also **chip·muck** (chip′muk). [< N. Am. Ind.]
chipped beef (chipt) Beef smoked and sliced thin.
Chip·pen·dale (chip′ən·dāl) *adj.* Des- ignating or in the style of a graceful, ro- coco type of furniture made in 18th- century England. [after Thomas *Chip- pendale,* 1718–79, English cabinetmaker.]
chip·per (chip′ər) *adj. U.S. Informal* 1. Brisk; cheerful. 2. Smartly dressed; spruce. [< Brit. Dial. *kipper* frisky]

CHIPMUNK
(About 6½ inches long; tail 4½ inches)

Chip·pe·wa (chip′ə·wä, -wā, -wə) *n. pl.* **·wa** or **·was** Ojibwa. Also **Chip·pe·way** (chip′ə·wā).

chip·py (chip′ē) *n. pl.* **·pies** **1.** A chipmunk. **2.** *Slang* A young woman of easy morals; also, a prostitute.

chip shot In golf, a short, lofted shot made in approaching the green.

chiro- *combining form* Hand; of or with the hand: *chirography.* Also spelled *cheiro-*. Also, before vowels, **chir-**. [< Gk. *cheir, cheiros* hand]

chi·rog·ra·phy (kī·rog′rə·fē) *n.* The art, style, or character of handwriting. — **chi·rog′ra·pher** *n.* — **chi·ro·graph·ic** (kī′rə·graf′ik) or **·i·cal** *adj.*

chi·ro·man·cy (kī′rə·man′sē) *n.* Palmistry. [< F < Gk. < *cheir* hand + *manteia* divination] — **chi′ro·man′cer** *n.*

chi·rop·o·dy (kə·rop′ə·dē, kī-) *n.* The branch of medicine that deals with ailments of the foot: also called *pedicure, podiatry.* [< CHIRO- + Gk. *podos* foot] — **chi·rop′o·dist** *n.*

chi·ro·prac·tic (kī′rə·prak′tik) *n.* A medical therapy based on the manipulation of bodily structures, esp. the spinal column. [< CHIRO- + Gk. *praktikos* effective] — **chi·ro·prac·tor** (kī′rə·prak′tər) *n.*

chirp (chûrp) *v.i.* **1.** To give a short, acute cry, as a sparrow or locust; cheep, as a young bird. **2.** To talk in a quick and shrill manner. — *v.t.* **3.** To utter with a quick, sharp sound. — *n.* The sound of chirping. [Var. of CHIRK] — **chirp′er** *n.*

chirr (chûr) *v.i.* To make a sharp trilling sound, as that of the grasshopper, cicada, and some birds. — *n.* The trilling sound of crickets, locusts, etc. Also **chirre.** [Imit.]

chir·rup (chir′əp) *v.i.* **1.** To chirp continuously or repeatedly, as a bird. **2.** To chirp with the lips, as in urging a horse. — *v.t.* **3.** To utter with chirps. — *n.* A sound of chirruping. [< CHIRP] — **chir′rup·y** *adj.*

chis·el (chiz′əl) *n.* A cutting tool with a beveled edge, used for cutting, engraving, or mortising metal, stone, or wood. — *v.t. & v.i.* **chis·eled** or **·elled, chis·el·ing** or **·el·ling** **1.** To cut, engrave, or carve with or as with a chisel. **2.** *Slang* To cheat; swindle; also, to obtain by dishonest methods. [< AF < L *caedere* to cut] — **chis′el·er** or **chis′el·ler** *n.*

chit[1] (chit) *n.* **1.** A voucher of a sum owed, as for food. **2.** *Brit.* A memorandum: also **chit′ty.** [< Hind. *chitthī* note]

chit[2] (chit) *n.* A pert girl. [ME *chitt*]

chit·chat (chit′chat′) *n.* **1.** Small talk. **2.** Gossip.

chi·tin (kī′tin) *n. Biochem.* A horny substance forming the hard outer covering of insects and crustaceans. [< F < Gk. *chitōn* tunic]. — **chi′tin·ous** *adj.*

chit·ter·lings (chit′ər·lingz) *n.pl.* The small intestines of pigs, esp. as used for food; also **chit′lin** (chit′lin), **chit′·ling.** [Cf. G. *kutteln* entrails]

chiv·al·ric (shiv′əl·rik, shi·val′rik) *adj.* Chivalrous.

chiv·al·rous (shiv′əl·rəs) *adj.* **1.** Having the qualities of the ideal knight; gallant, courteous, generous, etc. **2.** Pertaining to chivalry. [< OF < chevalier knight] — **chiv′·al·rous·ly** *adv.* — **chiv′al·rous·ness** *n.*

chiv·al·ry (shiv′əl·rē) *n.* **1.** The feudal system of knighthood. **2.** The spirit or principles of this system; knight-errantry. **3.** The ideal qualities of knighthood, as courtesy, valor, skill in arms, etc. **4.** A body of knights, gallant gentlemen, etc. [< OF < LL *caballarius* cavalier]

chiv·a·ree (shiv′ə·rē′) See CHARIVARI.

chive (chīv) *n.* A perennial herb allied to the leek and onion, used as a flavoring in cooking. [< AF < L *cepa* onion]

chiv·y (chiv′ē), **chiv·vy** See CHEVY (def. 1).

chlor- Var. of CHLORO-.

chlo·ral (klôr′əl, klō′rəl) *n. Chem.* **1.** A colorless, oily, liquid compound, $CCl_3 \cdot CHO$, with a penetrating odor. **2.** A white, crystalline, pungent compound, $CCl_3CHO \cdot H_2O$, used medicinally as a hypnotic: also **chloral hydrate.** [< CHLOR(INE) + AL(COHOL)]

chlo·ram·phen·i·col (klôr′am·fen′i·kōl, -kol, klō′ram-) *n. Chem.* A crystalline nitrogenous compound, $C_{11}H_{12}Cl_2O_5N_2$, used as an antibiotic.

chlo·rate (klôr′āt, klō′rāt) *n. Chem.* A salt of chloric acid.

chlor·dane (klôr′dān, klōr′-) *n. Chem.* A toxic compound of chlorine, $C_{10}H_6Cl_8$ used as a fumigant and insecticide.

chlo·ric (klôr′ik, klō′rik) *adj. Chem.* Of, pertaining to, or combined with chlorine in its higher valence.

chlo·ride (klôr′īd, klō′rīd, -rid) *n. Chem.* A compound of chlorine with a more positive element or radical. Also **chlo·rid** (klôr′id, klō′rid). — **chlo·rid·ic** (klə·rid′ik) *adj.*

chloride of lime *Chem.* A disinfecting and bleaching agent made by the action of chlorine on slaked lime.

chlo·rin·ate (klôr′ə·nāt, klō′rə-) *v.t.* **·at·ed, ·at·ing** *Chem.* To treat or cause to combine with chlorine, as in purifying water, whitening fabrics, etc. — **chlo′rin·a′tion** *n.*

chlo·rine (klôr′ēn, -in, klō′rēn, -rin) *n.* A greenish yellow, poisonous, gaseous element (symbol Cl), with a suffocating odor, widely used as a bleach and disinfectant. Also **chlo·rin** (klôr′in, klō′rin). See ELEMENT. [< Gk. *chlōros* green]

chloro- *combining form* **1.** Light green: *chlorophyll.* **2.** Chlorine. Also, before vowels, *chlor-*. [< Gk. *chlōros* green]

chlo·ro·form (klôr′ə·fôrm, klō′rə-) *n. Chem.* A colorl volatile, sweetish liquid compound, $CHCl_3$, used as an an thetic and solvent. — *v.t.* **1.** To administer chloroform **2.** To anesthetize or kill with chloroform.

Chlo·ro·my·ce·tin (klôr′ə·mī·sē′tən, klō′rə-) *n.* Prop tary name for a brand of chloramphenicol, used as an a biotic: also **chlo′ro·my·ce′tin.**

chlo·ro·phyll (klôr′ə·fil, klō′rə-) *n. Biochem.* The green trogenous coloring matter contained in the chloroplasts plants, essential to the production of carbohydrates by p tosynthesis. Also **chlo′ro·phyl.** [< CHLORO- + Gk. *pl lon* leaf] — **chlo·ro·phyl·la·ceous** (klôr′ə·fi·lā′shəs, klō′r **chlo′ro·phyl′lose** (-fil′ōs), **chlo′ro·phyl′lous** (-fil′əs) *adj.*

chlo·ro·plast (klôr′ə·plast, klō′rə-) *n. Bot.* One of the f tened bodies containing chlorophyll. Also **chlo′ro·plas′ti**

chlor·pro·ma·zine (klôr·prō′mə·zēn, -zin, klōr-) *n.* A s thetic tranquilizing drug used to control severe excitem in certain mental disorders.

chock (chok) *n.* **1.** A block or wedge, so placed as to p vent or limit motion. **2.** *Naut.* **a** A heavy piece of meta wood fastened to a deck, etc., and having jaws thro which a rope or cable may pass. **b** A block or support which to rest a boat, etc. — *v.t.* **1.** To make fast or with a chock or chocks. **2.** To place on chocks, as a b — *adv.* As far or as close as possible. [< AF *choque* log

chock-a-block (chok′ə·blok′) *adj.* **1.** Drawn to the li with blocks touching: said of a tackle. **2.** Close togeth jammed. — *adv.* Close; very near.

chock-full (chok′fŏŏl′) *adj.* Completely full; stuffed: *choke-full, chuck-full.* [ME *chokke-fulle*]

choc·o·late (chôk′lit, chôk′ə·lit, chok′-) *n.* **1.** A prepa tion of cacao nuts roasted and ground and usu. sweeten **2.** A beverage or confection made from this. **3.** A d brown color. — *adj.* Flavored with or made with chocol [< Sp. < Nahuatl *chocolatl*] — **choc′o·lat·y** *adj.*

Choc·taw (chok′tô) *n. pl.* **·taw** or **·taws** **1.** A member tribe of North American Indians of Muskhogean stock, living in Oklahoma. **2.** The language of this tribe.

choice (chois) *n.* **1.** The act of choosing; selection. **2.** right or privilege of choosing; option. **3.** The person thing chosen. **4.** A number or variety from which to cho a great *choice* of dishes. **5.** A well-selected supply. **6.** alternative: He had no *choice.* **7.** The best or preferred p of anything. **8.** Excellence: wine of *choice.* — *adj.* **choic choic·est** **1.** Select; excellent. **2.** Chosen with care. [< < *choisir* to choose] — **choice′ly** *adv.* — **choice′ness** *n*

choir (kwīr) *n.* **1.** An organized body of singers, esp. church. **2.** The part of a church occupied by such sing chancel. — *v.i.* **1.** To sing, as in a choir. — *v.t.* **2.** sing or utter in chorus. [< OF *cuer* < L *chorus*]

choke (chōk) *v.* **choked, chok·ing** *v.t.* **1.** To stop the brea ing of by obstructing the windpipe; strangle. **2.** To k back; suppress. **3.** To obstruct or close up by filling; c **4.** To retard the progress, growth, or action of. **5.** lessen the air intake of the carburetor in order to enrich fuel mixture of (a gasoline engine). — *v.i.* **6.** To bec suffocated or stifled. **7.** To become clogged, fouled, obstructed. — **to choke up** **1.** To be overcome by emot tears, etc. **2.** To perform poorly because of tension, ag tion, etc. — *n.* **1.** The act or sound of choking. **2.** *M* A device to control the flow of air, as to a gasoline eng [OE *acēocian*]

choke·bore (chōk′bôr′, -bōr′) *n.* In shotguns, a bore rowed at the muzzle to concentrate the shot; also, a shot with such a bore.

choke·cher·ry (chōk′cher′ē) *n. pl.* **·ries** A wild ch of North America, or its sour fruit.

choke·damp (chōk′damp′) *n.* Any condition of the at sphere resulting in choking or suffocation.

choke-full (chōk′fŏŏl′) See CHOCK-FULL.

chok·er (chō′kər) *n.* **1.** One who or that which chokes. *Informal* A neckcloth or necklace worn high around throat; also, a high, tight collar. **3.** A small fur neckpi

chok·y (chō′kē) *adj.* **chok·i·er, chok·i·est** **1.** Causing to choke. **2.** Somewhat choked. Also **chok′ey.**

chole- *combining form* Bile; gall: *cholesterol.* Also **cho** also, before vowels, **chol-**. [< Gk. *cholē* bile]

chol·er (kol′ər) *n.* Anger; hastiness of temper, form thought to be caused by an excess of bile. [< OF < < Gk. *cholē* bile] — **chol′er·ic** *adj.*

chol·er·a (kol′ər·ə) *n. Pathol.* An acute, infectious, demic disease characterized principally by serious intest disorders. In its more malignant forms, as **Asiatic choler** is usu. fatal. [< L < Gk. *cholē* bile]

cho·les·ter·ol (kə·les′tə·rōl, -rol) *n. Biochem.* A fa crystalline alcohol, $C_{27}H_{45}OH$, derived principally f bile, present in most gallstones, and very widely distribu in animal fats and tissues. Also **cho·les′ter·in** (-in). CHOLE- + Gk. *stereos* solid + -OL[2]]

chondro- *combining form* Cartilage. Also, before vow **chondr-**. [< Gk. *chondros* cartilage]

ose (chōōz) *v.* **chose, cho·sen, choos·ing** *v.t.* **1.** To select most desirable; take by preference. **2.** To desire or have preference for. **3.** To prefer (to do something): He has *osen* to remain. — *v.i.* **4.** To make a choice. — **cannot oose but** Must. [OE *cēosan*] — **choos′er** *n.*
os·y (chōō′zē) *adj.* **choos·i·er, choos·i·est** *Informal* rticular or fussy in one's choices. Also **choos′ey.**
p[1] (chop) *v.* **chopped, chop·ping** *v.t.* **1.** To cut or make strokes of a sharp tool: to *chop* a hole. **2.** To cut up in all pieces. **3.** To utter jerkily. **4.** To make a cutting, wnward stroke at (the ball), as in tennis. — *v.i.* **5.** To ke cutting strokes. **6.** To go, come, or move with sudden violent motion. — *n.* **1.** The act of chopping. **2.** A ce chopped off; esp. a cut of meat, usu. lamb, pork, or al. **3.** A sharp, downward blow or stroke, as in boxing, nis, etc. **4.** A quick, broken motion of waves. **5.** A cleft fissure. [ME *choppen*] — **chop′per** *n.*
p[2] (chop) *v.* **chopped, chop·ping** *v.i.* To veer suddenly; ft, as the wind.
p[3] (chop) *n.* **1.** *Usually pl.* A jaw; also the part of the e about the mouth or jaws. **2.** A sudden bite or snap. *v.t.* **chopped, chop·ping 1.** To utter in a quick, abrupt nner. **2.** To seize with the jaws; snap.
p[4] (chop) *n.* **1.** In India, China, etc., an official stamp or l; also, a clearance, passport, or permit. **2.** *Anglo-In-n* Quality: first *chop.* [< Hind. *chhāp* stamp]
p chop (chop′chop′) In Pidgin English, quickly!
p·fal·len (chop′fô′lən) *adj.* Chapfallen.
p·house (chop′hous′) *n.* An eating house specializing chops and steaks.
p·py[1] (chop′ē) *adj.* **·pi·er, ·pi·est 1.** Full of short, rough ves. **2.** Full of cracks or fissures. [< CHOP[1], n.]
p·py[2] (chop′ē) *adj.* **·pi·er, ·pi·est** Variable, shifting, as nd. [< CHOP[2]]
p·sticks (chop′stiks′) *n.pl.* Slender rods of ivory or od, used in pairs by the Chinese, Japanese, etc., to convey d to the mouth. [< Pidgin English *chop* quick + STICK]
p su·ey (sōō′ē) A Chinese-American dish consisting of s of meat or chicken, bean sprouts, onions, etc., served h rice. [< Chinese *tsa-sui*, lit., mixed pieces]
·ral (kôr′əl, kō′rəl) *adj.* Pertaining to, written for, or ng by a chorus or choir. — **cho′ral·ly** *adv.*
·rale (kô·ral′, kə-) *n.* A hymn marked by a simple lody, often sung in unison. Also **cho·ral′.** [< G *choral*]
rd[1] (kôrd) *n.* *Music* A combination of three or more es sounded together. [Earlier *cord*, short for ACCORD]
rd[2] (kôrd) *n.* **1.** A string of a musical instru-nt. **2.** An emotional response or reaction. *Geom.* **a** A straight line connecting the ex-mities of an arc. **b** The portion of a straight e contained by its intersections with a curve. *Engin.* One of the principal members of a dge truss. [< L < Gk. *chordē* string of a sical instrument] — **chord′al** *adj.*

CHORD (*def.* 3) Lines *cb* and *ab* are chords respectively of arcs *cab* and *ab.*

r·date (kôr′dāt) *Zool.* *n.* Any of a large ylum of the animal kingdom that includes vertebrates and whose members are charac-ized by an internal skeleton (in primitive ms a notochord) and a dorsally located tral nervous system. — *adj.* Of, pertaining or belonging to this phylum or to a chordate. NL < L < Gk. *chordē.*]
re (chôr, chōr) *n.* *U.S.* **1.** A small or minor job. **2.** An leasant or hard task. Also, *Brit.*, *char, chare.*
·re·a (kô·rē′ə, kō-) *n.* *Pathol.* An acute nervous disease racterized by involuntary and uncontrollable muscular tching: also called *St. Vitus' dance.* [< NL < Gk. *choreia* nce] — **cho·re′al, cho·re′ic** *adj.*
reo- *combining form* Dance. Also **choro-.** [< Gk. *reia* dance]
·re·og·ra·pher (kôr′ē·og′rə·fər, kō′rē-) *n.* One who de-es ballet and other dance compositions.
·re·og·ra·phy (kôr′ē·og′rə·fē, kō′rē-) *n.* **1.** The devising ballets and incidental dances, esp. for the stage. **2.** The tten representation of figures and steps of dancing. **3.** e art of dancing; ballet. Also **cho·reg·ra·phy** (kə·reg′-ē). — **cho·re·o·graph·ic** (kôr′ē·ə·graf′ik, kō′rē-) *adj.*
·ric (kôr′ik, kō′rik) *adj.* Of or like a chorus (defs. 7–9).
r·is·ter (kôr′is·tər, kor′-) *n.* **1.** A member of a choir; ., a choirboy. **2.** A leader of a choir. [< AF < L *chorus*]
·roid (kôr′oid, kō′roid) *Anat. adj.* Pertaining to or ignating a highly vascular membrane. — *n.* The vascu-tunic of the eyeball, between the sclera and the retina. illus. see EYE. Also **cho·ri·oid** (kôr′ē·oid, kō′rē-).
r·tle (chôr′təl) *v.t. & v.i.* **·tled, ·tling** To utter or utter h chuckles of glee. — *n.* A chuckle; joyful vocal sound. lend of CHUCKLE and SNORT; coined by Lewis Carroll]
·rus (kôr′əs, kō′rəs) *n.* **1.** A musical composition, usu. in parts, to be sung by a large group. **2.** A group of singers who perform such works. **3.** A body of singers and dancers who perform together in opera, musical comedy, etc. **4.** A group of persons singing or speaking something simul-taneously. **5.** A simultaneous utterance of words, cries, etc., by many individuals. **6.** A refrain, as of a song. **7.** In ancient Greece, a ceremonial dance, usu. religious, accom-panied by the singing of odes. **8.** In Greek drama, a body of actors who comment upon and sometimes take part in the main action of a play. **9.** The part of a drama performed by a chorus. — *v.t. & v.i.* **cho·rused** or **·russed, cho·rus·ing** or **·rus·sing** To sing or speak all together in unison. [< L < Gk. *choros* dance]
chorus girl A woman in the chorus of a musical comedy, etc. — **chorus boy** *masc.*
chose (chōz) Past tense of CHOOSE.
cho·sen (chō′zən) Past participle of CHOOSE. — *adj.* **1.** Made an object of choice; selected. **2.** *Theol.* Elect.
chow (chou) *n.* **1.** A medium-sized dog having a thick, brown or black coat: also *chow-chow.* **2.** *Slang* Food.
chow-chow (chou′chou′) *n.* **1.** A relish of chopped mixed vegetables pickled in mustard. **2.** Chow[1] (def. 1). [< Pidgin English]
chow·der (chou′dər) *n.* A dish usu. made of clams or fish stewed with vegetables, often in milk. [< F *chaudière* kettle < *calidus* hot]
chow·mein (chou′mān′) A Chinese-American dish made of shredded meat, onions, celery, etc., stewed and served with fried noodles. [< Chinese *ch'ao* to fry + *mein* flour]
chrism (kriz′əm) *n.* *Eccl.* **1.** Consecrated oil used for anointing at baptism, confirmation, unction, etc. **2.** Any sacramental anointing. [OE < LL < Gk. *chriein* to anoint]
Christ (krīst) *n.* **1.** The Anointed; the Messiah: the deliv-erer of Israel foretold by the Hebrew prophets. **2.** Jesus of Nazareth, regarded as fulfilling this prophecy: at first a title (*Jesus the Christ*), later a proper name (*Jesus Christ*). [OE < L < Gk. *Christos* (< *chriein* to anoint); trans. of Hebrew *māshīah* anointed] — **Christ′li·ness** *n.* — **Christ′ly** *adv.*
chris·ten (kris′ən) *v.t.* **1.** To name in baptism. **2.** To ad-minister Christian baptism to. **3.** To give a name to. **4.** *In-formal* To use for the first time. [See CHRIST.]
Chris·ten·dom (kris′ən·dəm) *n.* **1.** Christian lands. **2.** Christians collectively.
chris·ten·ing (kris′ən·ing) *n.* A Christian baptismal cere-mony, esp. the baptizing of an infant.
Chris·tian (kris′chən) *adj.* **1.** Professing or following the religion of Christ; esp., affirming the divinity of Christ. **2.** Relating to or derived from Christ or his doctrine. **3.** Characteristic of Christianity or Christendom. **4.** *Informal* Human; civilized; decent. — *n.* **1.** One who believes in or professes belief in Jesus as the Christ; a member of any of the Christian churches. **2.** *Informal* A civilized, decent, or respectable person. — **Chris′tian·ly** *adv.*
Christian era The era beginning at the approximate date of Christ's birth, but now considered four to six years too late. Dates in this era are denoted A.D., those before it, B.C.
Chris·ti·an·i·ty (kris′chē·an′ə·tē) *n.* **1.** The Christian re-ligion. **2.** Christians collectively. **2.** The state of being a Christian.
Chris·tian·ize (kris′chən·īz) *v.* **·ized, ·iz·ing** *v.t.* **1.** To con-vert to Christianity. **2.** To imbue with Christian prin-ciples, etc. — **Chris′tian·i·za′tion** *n.* — **Chris′tian·iz′er** *n.*
Christian name A baptismal name.
Christian Science A religion and system of healing, founded in 1866 by Mary Baker Eddy: officially called the **Church of Christ, Scientist.** — **Christian Scientist**
Christ·like (krīst′līk′) *adj.* Resembling Christ; having the spirit of Christ. — **Christ′like′ness** *n.*
Christ·mas (kris′məs) *n.* December 25, held as the an-niversary of the birth of Jesus Christ and widely observed as a holy day or a holiday. Also **Christmas Day.**
Christmas Eve The evening before Christmas Day.
Christ·mas·tide (kris′mas·tīd′) *n.* The season of Christ-mas extending from Christmas Eve to Epiphany (Jan. 6).
Christmas tree An evergreen tree decorated with orna-ments and lights at Christmas.
chrom- Var. of CHROMO-.
chro·mate (krō′māt) *n.* *Chem.* A salt of chromic acid.
chro·mat·ic (krō·mat′ik) *adj.* **1.** Pertaining to color or colors. **2.** *Music* Of or pertaining to a chromatic scale, or to an instrument that can play such a scale. — **chro·mat′i·cal·ly** *adv.*
chro·mat·ics (krō·mat′iks) *n.pl.* (*construed as sing.*) The science of colors.
chromatic scale *Music* A scale proceeding by semitones.
chro·ma·tin (krō′mə·tin) *n.* *Biol.* The readily stainable substance in the protoplasm of the cell nucleus, developing into chromosomes during mitosis. For illus. see CELL.

chromato- *combining form* Color; coloring or pigmentation. Also, before vowels, **chromat-**. [< Gk. *chrōma, -atos* color]

chro·ma·tog·ra·phy (krō′mə·tog′rə·fē) *n. Chem.* A method for the analysis of mixtures, in which a solution is passed through a column of powder that selectively adsorbs the constituents in one or more sharply defined, often colored bands. — **chro·mat·o·graph·ic** (krō·mat′ə·graf′ik) *adj.*

chrome (krōm) *n.* **1.** Chrome yellow. **2.** Chromium. — *v.t.* **chromed, chrom·ing** To plate with chromium. [< F < Gk. *chrōma* color]

-chrome *combining form* **1.** Color; colored. **2.** *Chem.* Chromium. [< Gk. *chrōma* color]

chrome steel *Metall.* A very hard steel alloyed with chromium. Also **chromium steel.**

chro·mic (krō′mik) *adj. Chem.* **1.** Of, from, or pertaining to chromium. **2.** Pertaining to compounds of chromium in its higher valence.

chromic acid *Chem.* An acid, H_2CrO_4, existing only in solution and forming chromates.

chro·mi·um (krō′mē·əm) *n.* A grayish white, very hard metallic element (symbol Cr), used in making alloys and pigments. See ELEMENT. [< NL < F < Gk. *chrōma* color; so called from its many brightly colored, poisonous compounds]

chro·mo (krō′mō) *n. pl.* **·mos** A chromolithograph.

chromo- *combining form* **1.** Color; in or with color. **2.** *Chem.* Chromium. Also, before vowels, *chrom-*. [< G *chrōma* color]

chro·mo·li·thog·ra·phy (krō′mō·li·thog′rə·fē) *n.* The process of reproducing a color print by lithography. — **chro′mo·lith′o·graph** *n.* — **chro′mo·li·thog′ra·pher** *n.* — **chro·mo·lith·o·graph·ic** (krō′mō·lith′ə·graf′ik) *adj.*

chro·mo·some (krō′mə·sōm) *n. Biol.* One of the deeply staining, rod- or loop-shaped bodies into which the chromatin of the cell nucleus divides during cell division, and in which the genes are located.

chro·mo·sphere (krō′mə·sfir′) *n. Astron.* **1.** An incandescent, gaseous envelope, consisting mostly of hydrogen and helium, that surrounds the sun beyond the photosphere. **2.** A similar envelope surrounding a star. — **chro′mo·spher′ic** (-sfir′ik, -sfer′-) *adj.*

chro·mous (krō′məs) *adj. Chem.* Of or pertaining to chromium in its lower valence.

chron·ic (kron′ik) *adj.* **1.** Continuing for a long period; constant. **2.** Prolonged; lingering; also, recurrent: said of a disease: opposed to *acute.* **3.** Long affected by a disease, or given to a habit; confirmed. [< F < L < Gk. *chronos* time] — **chron′i·cal·ly** *adv.*

chron·i·cle (kron′i·kəl) *n.* A register of events in the order in which they occurred. — *v.t.* **·cled, ·cling** To record in, or in the manner of, a chronicle. [< AF < L < Gk. *chronos* time] — **chron′i·cler** *n.*

Chron·i·cles (kron′i·kəlz) *n.pl.* Either of two historical books, I and II Chronicles, of the Old Testament: also, in the Douai Bible, called *I* and *II Paralipomenon.*

chrono- *combining form* Time: *chronometer.* Also, before vowels, **chron-**. [< Gk. *chronos* time]

chron·o·log·i·cal (kron′ə·loj′i·kəl) *adj.* **1.** Arranged according to sequence in time. **2.** Pertaining to chronology. Also **chron′o·log′ic.** — **chron′o·log′i·cal·ly** *adv.*

chro·nol·o·gy (krə·nol′ə·jē) *n. pl.* **·gies 1.** The science of determining the proper sequence of historical events. **2.** Arrangement or relationship according to order of occurrence. **3.** A chronological list or table. [< NL < Gk. *chronos* time + *-logia* study] — **chro·nol′o·ger, chro·nol′o·gist** *n.*

chro·nom·e·ter (krə·nom′ə·tər) *n.* A timekeeping instrument of high precision. — **chron·o·met·ric** (kron′ə·met′rik) or **·ri·cal** *adj.* — **chron′o·met′ri·cal·ly** *adv.*

chro·nom·e·try (krə·nom′ə·trē) *n.* The science or method of measuring time or periods of time.

-chroous *combining form* Having (a certain) color. [< Gk. *chrōs, chroos* color]

chrys·a·lid (kris′ə·lid) *Entomol. n.* A chrysalis. — *adj.* Of or like a chrysalis: also **chry·sal·i·dal** (kri·sal′ə·dəl).

chrys·a·lis (kris′ə·lis) *n. pl.* **chrys·a·lis·es** or **chry·sal·i·des** (kri·sal′ə·dēz) **1.** *Entomol.* The capsule-enclosed pupa from which the butterfly or moth develops. **2.** Anything in an undeveloped stage. [< L < Gk. *chrysos* gold]

chrys·an·the·mum (kri·san′thə·məm) *n.* **1.** Any of a number of cultivated varieties of plants of the genus *Chrysanthemum,* with large heads of showy flowers. **2.** The flower. [< L < Gk. *chrysanthemon* golden flower]

chryso- *combining form* Gold; of a golden color. Also, before vowels, **chrys-**. [< Gk. *chrysos* gold]

chrys·o·lite (kris′ə·līt) *n.* A variety of olivine. [< OF < Med.L < L < Gk. < *chrysos* gold + *lithos* stone]

chrys·o·prase (kris′ə·prāz) *n.* A semiprecious, apple-green variety of chalcedony, used as a gem. [< OF < L < Gk. < *chrysos* gold + *prason* leek]

chub (chub) *n. pl.* **chubs** or **chub 1.** A carplike fish common in European rivers. **2.** Any of various other unrelated fishes. [ME *chubbe*]

chub·by (chub′ē) *adj.* **·bi·er, ·bi·est** Plump; rounded. **chub′bi·ness** *n.*

chuck[1] (chuk) *v.t.* **1.** To pat or tap affectionately, e under the chin. **2.** To throw or pitch. **3.** *Informal* throw away; discard. **4.** *Informal* To eject forcibly: w *out.* **5.** *Slang* To quit. — *n.* **1.** A playful pat under chin. **2.** A throw; toss. [Cf. F *choquer* shake, jolt]

chuck[2] (chuk) *n.* **1.** The cut of beef extending from neck to the shoulder blade. **2.** *Mech.* A clamp, chock, wedge used to hold a tool or work in a machine, as in a lat

chuck-full (chuk′fo͝ol′) *adj.* Chockfull.

chuck·le (chuk′əl) *v.i.* **·led, ·ling 1.** To laugh quietly with satisfaction. **2.** To cluck, as a hen. — *n.* A low, m ly amused laugh. [Freq. of CLUCK] — **chuck′ler** *n.*

chuck·le·head (chuk′əl·hed′) *n. Informal* A stupid fell blockhead. — **chuck′le·head′ed** *adj.*

chuck wagon *U.S.* A wagon fitted with cooking equ ment and provisions for cowboys, harvest hands, etc.

chug (chug) *n.* A dull, explosive sound, as of the exhaus an engine. — *v.i.* **chugged, chug·ging** To move or oper with a series of such sounds. [Imit.]

chuk·ker (chuk′ər) *n.* In polo, one of the eight period continuous play, lasting 7½ minutes. Also **chuk′kar.** Hind. < Skt. *chakra* wheel]

chum (chum) *n.* **1.** An intimate companion. **2.** Origi ly, a roommate. — *v.i.* **chummed, chum·ming 1.** To as ciate very closely with another. **2.** To share the sa room. [? Short for *chamber fellow*]

chum·my (chum′ē) *adj.* **·mi·er, ·mi·est** *Informal* Frien intimate. — **chum′mi·ly** *adv.*

chump[1] (chump) *n.* **1.** *Informal* A stupid or foolish pers **2.** A chunk of wood. **3.** The thick end of anything, as loin of mutton. **4.** *Slang* The head. [? Var. of CHUNK

chump[2] (chump) *v.t.* & *v.i.* To chew; munch. [< CHA

chunk (chungk) *n.* **1.** A thick mass or piece of anything of wood. **2.** A considerable quantity of something. **3.** *Informal* A strong, stocky person or animal. [Var. of CHU

chunk·y (chung′kē) *adj.* **chunk·i·er, chunk·i·est 1.** S and thickset; stocky. **2.** In chunks. — **chunk′i·ness** n

church (chûrch) *n.* **1.** A building for Christian worship. Regular religious services; public worship. **3.** A congre tion of Christians. **4.** *Usu. cap.* A distinct body of Ch tians having a common faith and discipline; a denominat Abbr. *c., C., ch., Ch.* **5.** All Christian believers collectiv **6.** Ecclesiastical organization and authority: the separa of *church* and state. **7.** The clerical profession. — *v.t.* To subject to church discipline. **2.** To conduct a religi service for (a person, esp. a woman after childbirth). [*circe,* ult. < Gk. *kyrios* Lord]

church·go·er (chûrch′gō′ər) *n.* One who goes regularl church. — **church′go′ing** *adj.* & *n.*

church·ly (chûrch′lē) *adj.* Of, pertaining to, or suitabl a church. — **church′li·ness** *n.*

church·man (chûrch′mən) *n. pl.* **·men** (-mən) member of a church. **2.** A clergyman. — **church′ma** *adj.* — **church′man·ship** *n.* — **church′wom′an** *n.fem.*

church mouse A mouse that lives in a church: usuall the phrase **poor as a church mouse,** very poor.

Church of Christ, Scientist See CHRISTIAN SCIENCE

Church of England The national church of England, tablished by law in the 16th century, claiming to be an in pendent branch of the ancient Catholic church, and rep ating papal authority: also called *Anglican Church.*

Church of Jesus Christ of Latter-day Saints Mormon Church: its official name.

church·war·den (chûrch′wôr′dən) *n.* **1.** In the Churc England, an elected lay officer who assists in the adminis tion of a parish. **2.** In the Protestant Episcopal Chu one of two elected lay officers of a vestry. **3.** A long-stem clay pipe. Also **church warden.**

church·yard (chûrch′yärd′) *n.* The ground surroundin adjoining a church, often used as a cemetery.

churl (chûrl) *n.* **1.** A rude or surly person. **2.** A st person. **3.** A rustic; countryman. [OE *ceorl*] — **churl** *adj.* — **churl′ish·ly** *adv.* — **churl′ish·ness** *n.*

churn (chûrn) *n.* **1.** A vessel in which milk or cream is tated to separate the oily globules and gather them as bu **2.** A state of unrest or agitation. — *v.t.* **1.** To stir or tate (cream or milk), as in a churn. **2.** To make in a ch as butter. **3.** To agitate violently: The oars *churned* water. — *v.i.* **4.** To work a churn. **5.** To move with lent agitation; seethe. [OE *cyrin*] — **churn′er** *n.*

chute (sho͞ot) *n.* **1.** An inclined trough or vertical pass down which water, coal, etc., may pass. **2.** A steep, nar watercourse; a rapid; shoot. **3.** A narrow pen for bran or controlling cattle. **4.** A slide, as for toboggans. **5.** *Infor* A parachute. [Fusion of F *chute* a fall and SHOOT, n.]

chut·ney (chut′nē) *n.* A piquant relish of fruit, spices, Also **chut′nee.** [< Hind. *chatnī*]

chutz·pah (ho͞ots′pə, kho͞ots′-) *n. U.S. Slang* Brazen frontery; gall. [< Yiddish < Hebrew]

·yle (kīl) *n. Physiol.* The milky emulsion of lymph and t taken up from the small intestine during digestion and ssed from the thoracic duct into the veins. [< F < L < k. *chylos* juice] — **chy·la·ceous** (kī·lā′shəs), **chy·lous** (kī′·) *adj.*

·yme (kīm) *n. Physiol.* The partly digested food in semi-uid form as it passes from the stomach into the small intes-ne. [< L < Gk. *chymos* juice] — **chy·mous** (kī′məs) *adj.*

·o·ri·um (si·bôr′ē·əm, -bō′rē-) *n. pl.* **·bo·ri·a** (-bôr′ē·ə, ō′rē·ə) **1.** An arched canopy over an altar, esp. a perma-nt one. **2.** A covered receptacle for the consecrated bread the Eucharist. [< Med.L < Gk. *kibōrion* cup]

·a·da (si·kā′də, -kä′-) *n. pl.* **·das** or **·dae** lē) A large winged insect, the male of nich is equipped with vibrating membranes at produce a loud, shrill sound: often called *ust.* [< L]

CICADA (1 to 1½ inches long)

·a·trix (sik′ə·triks) *n. pl.* **cic·a·tri·ces** k′ə·trī′sēz) **1.** *Med.* A scar or seam of w tissue remaining after the healing of wounded or ulcer-s parts. **2.** *Biol.* A scar left by the healing of a wound, e fall of a leaf, etc. Also **cic·a·trice** (sik′ə·tris). [< L] — **·a·tri·cial** (sik′ə·trish′əl), **ci·cat·ri·cose** (si·kat′ri·kōs) *adj.*

·a·trize (sik′ə·trīz) *v.t. & v.i.* **·trized, ·triz·ing** To heal by e formation of a scar. — **cic′a·tri·za′tion** *n.*

·e·ro·ne (sis′ə·rō′nē, *Ital.* chē′chā·rô′nā) *n. pl.* **·nes,** *Ital.* (-nē) A guide for tourists. [< Ital., Cicero]

·e·ro·ni·an (sis′ə·rō′nē·ən) *adj.* Of or pertaining to Cic-o, or to his rhetorical style; eloquent.

·dal *combining form* Killing; able to kill: *homicidal.* [< *caedere* to kill]

·de *combining form* **1.** Killer or destroyer of: *regicide.* **2.** urder or killing of: *parricide.* [def. 1 < L *-cida* killer < *edere* to kill; def. 2 < L *-cidium* slaughter < *caedere*]

·der (sī′dər) *n.* The expressed juice of apples used to make negar, and as a beverage before fermentation (**sweet cider**), after fermentation (**hard cider**). [< OF < LL < Hebrew *ēkār* strong drink]

·gar (si·gär′) *n.* A small roll of tobacco leaves prepared d shaped for smoking. [< Sp. *cigarro*]

·a·rette (sig′ə·ret′, sig′ə·ret) *n.* A small roll of finely cut bacco for smoking, usu. enclosed in thin paper. Also *U.S.* **·′a·ret′.** [< F, dim. of *cigare* cigar]

·i·a (sil′ē·ə) Plural of CILIUM.

·i·ar·y (sil′ē·er′ē) *adj. Biol.* Of, pertaining to, or like cilia. L *cilium* eyelid]

·i·ate (sil′ē·it, -āt) *adj. Biol.* Having cilia. Also **cil′i·at′·**

·i·um (sil′ē·əm) *n. pl.* **cil·i·a** (sil′ē·ə) **1.** *Biol.* A vibra-e, microscopic, hairlike process on the surface of a cell, gan, plant, etc. **2.** An eyelash. [< L, eyelid]

·m·me·ri·an (si·mir′ē·ən) *adj.* **1.** Of or pertaining to the mmerians, a mythical people mentioned by Homer as liv-g in perpetual darkness. **2.** Densely dark; gloomy.

·ch (sinch) *n. U.S.* **1.** A pack or saddle girth. **2.** *In-mal* A tight grip. **3.** *Slang* Something easy or sure. — **1.** To fasten a saddle girth around. **2.** *Slang* To get a ht hold upon. **3.** *Slang* To make sure of. — *v.i.* **4.** To hten a saddle girth. [< Sp. < L *cingere* to bind]

·cho·na (sin·kō′nə) *n.* **1.** A tropical tree or shrub of the adder family, widely cultivated as a source of quinine and ated alkaloids. **2.** The bark of any of these trees: also lled *Peruvian bark.* [after the Countess of *Chinchón,* 76–1639] — **cin·chon·ic** (sin·kon′ik) *adj.*

·cho·nize (sin′kə·nīz) *v.t.* **·nized, ·niz·ing** To treat with nchona or quinine. — **cin′cho·ni·za′tion** *n.*

·c·ture (singk′chər) *n.* **1.** A belt, cord, etc., put around e waist. **2.** The act of girding or surrounding. — *v.t.* **·red, ·tur·ing** To encircle with or as with a cincture. [< L *ngere* to bind, gird]

·der (sin′dər) *n.* **1.** Any partly burned substance, not luced to ashes; esp. a tiny particle of such a substance. **2.** bit of wood, coal, etc., that can burn but without flame. *pl.* Ashes. — *v.t.* To burn or reduce to a cinder. [OE *nder*] — **cin′der·y** *adj.*

·der·el·la (sin′də·rel′ə) *n.* **1.** The heroine of a popular ry tale, who is treated as a drudge, but eventually marries prince. **2.** Any girl who achieves happiness or success er a period of neglect.

·e- *combining form* Cinema. [< CINEMA]

·e·ma (sin′ə·mə) *n.* **1.** A motion picture (def. 2). **2.** A otion-picture theater. — **the cinema** Motion pictures col-tively; also, the art or business of making motion pictures. hort for CINEMATOGRAPH] — **cin·e·mat·ic** (sin′ə·mat′ik) *j.* — **cin′e·mat′i·cal·ly** *adv.*

·e·mat·o·graph (sin′ə·mat′ə·graf, -gräf) *n.* A motion-ture camera or projector. — *v.t. & v.i.* To take photo-aphs (of) with a motion-picture camera: also **cin·e·ma·tize** (sin′ə·mə·tīz′). Also *kinematograph.* [< Gk. *kinēma, -atos* movement + -GRAPH]

cin·e·ma·tog·ra·phy (sin′ə·mə·tog′rə·fē) *n.* The art and process of making motion pictures. — **cin′e·ma·tog′ra·pher** *n.* — **cin·e·mat·o·graph·ic** (sin′ə·mat′ə·graf′ik) *adj.* — **cin′·e·mat′o·graph′i·cal·ly** *adv.*

cin·e·rar·i·a (sin′ə·râr′ē·ə) *n.* A cultivated plant having heart-shaped leaves and white, red, or purple flowers. [< NL < L, fem. of *cinerarius* ashy]

cin·e·rar·i·um (sin′ə·râr′ē·əm) *n. pl.* **·rar·i·a** (-râr′ē·ə) A place for keeping the ashes of a cremated body. [< L] — **cin·er·ar·y** (sin′ə·rer′ē) *adj.*

cin·er·a·tor (sin′ə·rā′tər) *n.* A furnace for cremating dead bodies; crematory. [Short for INCINERATOR]

cin·na·bar (sin′ə·bär) *n.* **1.** A heavy, crystallized red mer-curic sulfide, HgS, the chief ore of mercury. **2.** Vermilion. [< L < Gk. < Persian *zanjifrah*]

cin·na·mon (sin′ə·mən) *n.* **1.** The aromatic inner bark of any of several tropical trees of the laurel family, used as a spice. **2.** Any tree that yields this bark. **3.** A shade of light reddish brown. [< L < Gk. < Hebrew *quinnāmōn*]

cinque·foil (singk′foil) *n.* **1.** *Archit.* A five-cusped orna-ment or window. **2.** Any of several plants of the rose family, with five-lobed leaves: also called *five-fingers.* [< F < L < *quinque* five + *folium* leaf]

CINQUE-FOIL (*def.* 1)

ci·on (sī′ən) *n.* A twig or shoot cut from a plant or tree, esp. for grafting: also spelled *scion.* [Var. of SCION]

-cion Var. of -TION.

Ci·pan·go (si·pang′gō) *Poetic* Japan.

ci·pher (sī′fər) *n.* **1.** The figure 0, the symbol of the absence of quantity; zero. **2.** A person or thing of no value or importance. **3.** Any system of secret writing that uses a prearranged scheme or key. **4.** A message in cipher; also, its key. **5.** A monogram. **6.** Any Arabic number. — *v.t.* **1.** To calculate arithmetically. **2.** To write in charac-ters of hidden meaning. — *v.i.* **3.** To work out arithmetical examples. **4.** To sound continuously, as an organ pipe. Also spelled *cypher.* [< OF < Arabic *sifr* nothing]

cir·ca (sûr′kə) *prep. Latin* About; around; used before ap-proximate date or figures.

Cir·cas·sian (sər·kash′ən, -kash′ē·ən) *n.* **1.** A member of a group of tribes of the Caucasus region. **2.** The language of these tribes. — *adj.* Of or pertaining to Circassia, its peo-ple, or their language: also **Cir·cas·sic** (sər·kas′ik).

Cir·ce (sûr′sē) In the *Odyssey,* an enchantress who changed Odysseus's companions into swine by a magic drink.

Cir·ce·an (sər·sē′ən) *adj.* **1.** Of, pertaining to, or charac-teristic of Circe. **2.** Bewitching and degrading.

cir·cle (sûr′kəl) *n.* **1.** A plane figure bounded by a curved line every point of which is equally distant from the center. **2.** The circumference of such a figure. **3.** Something like a circle, as a crown, halo, or ring. **4.** A round or spherical body; an orb. **5.** A group of persons united by some com-mon interest or pursuit; a set; coterie. **6.** The domain or scope of a special influence or action. **7.** A gallery or tier of seats in a theater: the family *circle.* **8.** A series or process that finishes at its starting point or that repeats itself with-out end: the *circle* of the seasons. **9.** *Astron.* The orbit of a heavenly body. — *v.* **·cled, ·cling** *v.t.* **1.** To enclose in a circle; encompass. **2.** To move around, as in a circle. — *v.i.* **3.** To move in a circle. [< L *circus* ring] — **cir′cler** *n.*

cir·clet (sûr′klit) *n.* A small ring or ring-shaped object, es-pecially one worn as an ornament. [< F *cercle* ring]

cir·cuit (sûr′kit) *n.* **1.** A moving or traveling round; a cir-cular route or course. **2.** A periodic journey from place to place, as by a judge or minister. **3.** The route traversed, or the district visited, in such a journey. **4.** A group of asso-ciated theaters presenting plays, films, etc., in turn. **5.** The line or distance around an area; circumference; also, the area enclosed. **6.** *Electr.* The entire course traversed by an elec-tric current. **7.** *Telecom.* A transmission and reception sys-tem. — *v.t. & v.i.* To go or move (about) in a circuit. [< F < L < *circum-* around + *ire* to go]

circuit breaker *Electr.* A switch or relay for breaking a cir-cuit under specified or abnormal conditions of current flow.

circuit court A court of law that sits in various counties or districts over which its jurisdiction extends.

circuit judge A judge of a circuit court.

cir·cu·i·tous (sər·kyōō′ə·təs) *adj.* Roundabout; indirect. — **cir·cu′i·tous·ly** *adv.* — **cir·cu′i·tous·ness** *n.*

circuit rider A minister who preaches at churches on a cir-cuit or district route.

cir·cuit·ry (sur′kit·rē) *n. Electr.* The design and arrange-ment of circuits in any device, instrument, or system.

cir·cu·i·ty (sər·kyōō′ə·tē) *n. pl.* **·ties** Roundabout proce-dure or speech; indirectness.

cir·cu·lar (sûr′kyə·lər) *adj.* **1.** Shaped like a circle; round. **2.** Moving in a circle. **3.** Of or referring to a circle. **4.** Roundabout; indirect; devious. **5.** Addressed to several persons, or intended for general circulation. — *n.* A statement, notice, or advertisement printed for general distribution. [See CIRCLE.] — **cir·cu·lar·i·ty** (sûr′kyə·lar′ə·tē), **cir′·cu·lar·ness** *n.* — **cir′cu·lar·ly** *adv.*

cir·cu·lar·ize (sûr′kyə·lə·rīz′) *v.t.* **·ized, ·iz·ing 1.** To make circular. **2.** To make into a circular. **3.** To distribute circulars to. — **cir′cu·lar·i·za′tion** *n.* — **cir′cu·lar·iz′er** *n.*

circular saw A disk-shaped saw having a toothed edge, rotated at high speed by a motor.

cir·cu·late (sûr′kyə·lāt) *v.* **·lat·ed, ·lat·ing** *v.i.* **1.** To move by a circuitous course back to the starting point, as the blood. **2.** To pass from place to place or person to person: Rumors *circulate* quickly. **3.** To be in free motion, as air. — *v.t.* **4.** To cause to circulate. [See CIRCLE.] — **cir·cu·la·tive** (sûr′·kyə·lā′tiv) *adj.* — **cir′cu·la′tor** *n.*

circulating library A library from which books may be borrowed or rented: also called *lending library.*

cir·cu·la·tion (sûr′kyə·lā′shən) *n.* **1.** A moving around or through something back to the starting point. **2.** The motion of the blood from and to the heart through the arteries and veins. **3.** A transmission or spreading from one person or place to another; dissemination. **4.** The extent or amount of distribution of a periodical; also, the number of copies distributed. **5.** A current medium of exchange, as coin.

cir·cu·la·to·ry (sûr′kyə·lə·tôr′ē, -tō′rē) *adj.* Of, pertaining to or affecting circulation: a *circulatory* disorder.

circum- *prefix* **1.** About; around; on all sides; surrounding. **2.** Revolving around. [< L *circum-* around, about]

cir·cum·am·bi·ent (sûr′kəm·am′bē·ənt) *adj.* Encompassing; surrounding. — **cir′cum·am′bi·ence, cir′cum·am′bi·en·cy** *n.*

cir·cum·cise (sûr′kəm·sīz) *v.t.* **·cised, ·cis·ing** To cut off all or part of the prepuce (of a male) or the clitoris (of a female). [< OF < L < *circum-* around + *caedere* to cut] — **cir′cum·cis′er** *n.* — **cir·cum·ci·sion** (sûr′kəm·sizh′ən) *n.*

cir·cum·fer·ence (sər·kum′fər·əns) *n.* **1.** The boundary line of any area; esp., the boundary of a circle. **2.** The length of such a line. [< L < *circum-* around + *ferre* to bear] — **cir·cum·fer·en·tial** (sər·kum′fə·ren′shəl) *adj.* — **cir·cum′fer·en′tial·ly** *adv.*

cir·cum·flex (sûr′kəm·fleks) *n.* A mark (ˆ, ˜, ˘) written over certain letters in ancient Greek, and later, in other languages, to mark a long vowel, contraction, etc., or used as a diacritical mark in phonetic transcription. — *adj.* **1.** Pronounced or marked with the circumflex accent. **2.** *Physiol.* Bent or curving around, as certain nerves. — *v.t.* **1.** To pronounce or mark with a circumflex. **2.** To wind around. [< L < *circum-* around + *flectere* to bend] — **cir·cum·flex·ion** (sûr′kəm·flek′shən) *n.*

cir·cum·flu·ous (sər·kum′floo͞·əs) *adj.* Flowing around; surrounding. Also **cir·cum·flu·ent** (sər·kum′floo͞·ənt). [< L < *circum-* around + *fluere* to flow]

cir·cum·fuse (sûr′kəm·fyo͞oz′) *v.t.* **·fused, ·fus·ing 1.** To pour, scatter, or spread about. **2.** To surround, as with a liquid. [< L < *circum-* around + *fundere* to pour] — **cir·cum·fu·sion** (sûr′kəm·fyo͞o′zhən) *n.*

cir·cum·lo·cu·tion (sûr′kəm·lō·kyo͞o′shən) *n.* An indirect lengthy way of expressing something; also, an example of this. [< L < *circum-* around + *loqui* to speak] — **cir·cum·loc·u·to·ry** (sûr′kəm·lok′yə·tôr′ē, -tō′rē) *adj.*

cir·cum·nav·i·gate (sûr′kəm·nav′ə·gāt) *v.t.* **·gat·ed, ·gat·ing** To sail around. [< L < *circum-* around + *navigare* to sail] — **cir·cum·nav·i·ga·ble** (sûr′kəm·nav′ə·gə·bəl) *adj.* — **cir′cum·nav′i·ga′tion** *n.* — **cir′cum·nav′i·ga′tor** *n.*

cir·cum·scribe (sûr′kəm·skrīb′) *v.t.* **·scribed, ·scrib·ing 1.** To mark out the limits of; define. **2.** To draw a line or figure around. **3.** *Geom.* **a** To draw (a figure) about another figure so that it touches at every possible point without intersecting. **b** To surround (another figure) in this way. [< L < *circum-* around + *scribere* to write] — **cir′cum·scrib′a·ble** *adj.* — **cir′cum·scrib′er** *n.*

cir·cum·scrip·tion (sûr′kəm·skrip′shən) *n.* **1.** The act of circumscribing, or the state of being circumscribed. **2.** Anything that limits or encloses. **3.** The periphery of an object. **4.** A space marked out or bounded. **5.** An inscription around a coin, medallion, etc. — **cir′cum·scrip′tive** *adj.*

cir·cum·spect (sûr′kəm·spekt) *adj.* Attentive to everything; watchful; cautious; wary. Also **cir′cum·spec′tive** *adj.* [< L < *circum-* around + *specere* to look] — **cir′cum·spec′·tion, cir′cum·spect′ness** *n.* — **cir′cum·spect′ly** *adv.*

cir cum·stance (sûr′kəm·stans) *n.* **1.** A factor connected with an act, event, or condition, either as an accessory or as a determining element. **2.** *Often pl.* The conditions, influences, etc., affecting persons or actions. **3.** *pl.* Financial condition in life: in poor *circumstances.* **4.** An occurrence: a happy *circumstance.* **5.** Detail, especially superfluous detail, as in narrative. **6.** Formal display: pomp and *circumstance.* — **under no circumstances** Never; under no conditions. — **under the circumstances** Since such is (or was) the case. *v.t.* **·stanced, ·stanc·ing** To place in or under limiting circu stances or conditions. [< OF < L < *circum-* around *stare* to stand] — **cir′cum·stanced** *adj.*

cir·cum·stan·tial (sûr′kəm·stan′shəl) *adj.* **1.** Pertain to or dependent on circumstances. **2.** Incidental; not ess tial. **3.** Full of details. — **cir′cum·stan′tial·ly** *adv.*

circumstantial evidence *Law* Evidence that furnis reasonable ground for inferring the existence of a fact.

cir·cum·stan·ti·al·i·ty (sûr′kəm·stan′shē·al′ə·tē) *n.* **·ties 1.** The quality of being particular, detailed, or min **2.** A particular matter; detail.

cir·cum·stan·ti·ate (sûr′kəm·stan′shē·āt) *v.t.* **·at·ed, ·ing** To set forth or establish by circumstances or in det — **cir′cum·stan′ti·a′tion** *n.*

cir·cum·val·late (sûr′kəm·val′āt) *v.t.* **·lat·ed, ·lat·ing** surround with a rampart or a trench. — *adj.* Enclosed b as by a wall. [< L < *circum-* around + *vallare* to fort — **cir′cum·val·la′tion** *n.*

cir·cum·vent (sûr′kəm·vent′) *v.t.* **1.** To surround or trap, as an enemy, by stratagem. **2.** To gain an advant over; outwit. **3.** To go around or avoid. [< L < *circ* around + *venire* to come] — **cir′cum·vent′er** or **cir′c vent′or** *n.* — **cir′cum·ven′tive** *adj.* — **cir′cum·ven′tio**

cir·cus (sûr′kəs) *n.* **1.** A traveling show of acrobats, clo etc.; also, a performance of such a show. **2.** A circular, tented area used for such shows. **3.** In ancient Rome, oblong enclosure with tiers of seats around three sides, for races, games, etc. **4.** *Brit.* An open, usu. circular junc of several streets. **5.** *U.S. Informal* Something or some uproariously entertaining. [< L, a ring, racecourse]

cir·rho·sis (si·rō′sis) *n.* *Pathol.* A disease of the liver, c acterized by an abnormal formation of connective ti with progressive cellular breakdown. [< NL < Gk. *kir* tawny; with ref. to the color of the cirrhotic liver] — **rhot·ic** (si·rot′ik) *adj.*

cir·ri (sir′ī) Plural of CIRRUS.

cirro- *combining form* Cirrus. Also **cirri-.** [< L *ci* curl]

cir·ro·cu·mu·lus (sir′ō·kyo͞om′yə·ləs) *n.* *Meteorol.* A n of fleecy, globular cloudlets (Symbol Cc) in contact with another; mackerel sky.

cir·ro·stra·tus (sir′ō·strā′təs) *n.* *Meteorol.* A fine, whi veil of cloud (Symbol Cs).

cir·rous (sir′əs) *adj.* **1.** Having or like cirri. **2.** Of or taining to a cirrus cloud. Also **cir·rose** (sir′ōs).

cir·rus (sir′əs) *n.* *pl.* **cir·ri** (sir′ī) **1.** *Meteorol.* A typ white, wispy cloud (Symbol Ci), usually consisting of crystals and seen in tufts or feathery bands across the **2.** *Bot.* A tendril. **3.** *Zool.* A threadlike appendage ser as an organ of touch. [< L, ringlet, curl]

cis- *prefix* **1.** On this side of. **2.** Since; following: *cis-El bethan.* [< L *cis* on this side]

cis·al·pine (sis·al′pīn, -pin) *adj.* On the Roman side of Alps. [< L < *cis* on this side + *Alpes* the Alps]

cis·co (sis′kō) *n.* *pl.* **·coes** or **·cos** *U.S. & Canadian* whitefish of North America. [? < N. Am. Ind.]

Cis·ter·cian (sis·tûr′shən) *n.* A monk of a very strict templative order founded in 1098 at Cistercium (mo *Cîteaux*), France, as an offshoot of the Benedictines. — Of or pertaining to this order.

cis·tern (sis′tərn) *n.* **1.** An artificial reservoir, as a tank, holding water or other liquids. **2.** *Anat.* A large lymph sp a sac. [< OF < L *cista* chest]

cit·a·del (sit′ə·dəl, -del) *n.* **1.** A fortress commandi city. **2.** Any fortress or stronghold. **3.** The heavily pl casemate in a war vessel. [< MF < Ital. *città* city]

ci·ta·tion (sī·tā′shən) *n.* **1.** A citing or quoting; als passage or authority so cited. **2.** A public commenda for outstanding achievement. **3.** A summons, as to ap in court. [See CITE.] — **ci·ta·to·ry** (sī′tə·tôr′ē, -tō′rē)

cite (sīt) *v.t.* **cit·ed, cit·ing 1.** To quote as authority or il tration. **2.** To bring forward or refer to as proof or supp **3.** *Mil.* To mention in a report, esp. for bravery. **4.** mention or enumerate. **5.** To summon to appear in co **6.** To summon to action; rouse. [< F < L *citare* < *cie* set in motion] — **cit′a·ble** or **cite′a·ble** *adj.*

cith·a·ra (sith′ə·rə) *n.* An ancient Greek stringed ins ment resembling a lyre. [< L < Gk. *kithara*]

cith·er (sith′ər) *n.* **1.** A zither. **2.** A cittern. Also **cith·** (sith′ərn). **3.** A cithara.

cit·i·fied (sit′i·fīd) *adj.* Having the ways, habits, fashi etc., of city life.

cit·i·zen (sit′ə·zən) *n.* **1.** A native or naturalized pe owing allegiance to, and entitled to protection from, a g ernment. **2.** A resident of a city or town. **3.** A civilia distinguished from a public officer, soldier, etc. [< AF *civis* citizen] — **cit′i·zen·ess** *n.fem.*

cit·i·zen·ry (sit′ə·zən·rē) *n.* *pl.* **·ries** Citizens collecti

cit·i·zen·ship (sit′ə·zən·ship′) *n.* The status of a citi with its rights, privileges, and duties.

a- *prefix* On this side; cis-. [< L]
rate (sit′rāt, -rit, sī′trāt) *n. Chem.* A salt of citric acid.
ric (sit′rik) *adj.* Of or derived from citrus fruits.
ic acid *Chem.* A white, crystalline, sharply sour com-und, $C_6H_8O_7$, contained in various fruits, and also made ıthetically.
rine (sit′rin) *adj.* Lemon yellow. — *n.* **1.** Citrine color. A light yellow variety of quartz. [< F *citrin*]
ron (sit′rən) *n.* **1.** A fruit like a lemon, but larger and s acid. **2.** The tree producing this fruit. **3.** A water-lon with a small, hard-fleshed fruit. Also **citron melon.** The rind of either of these fruits, preserved and used in ıfections. [< MF < Ital. < L *citrus* citrus tree]
ron·el·la (sit′rə·nel′ə) *n.* A grass cultivated in Ceylon, lding **citronella oil,** used in perfumery, in cooking, and as otection against mosquitoes. Also **citronella grass.** [< ⅃ < CITRON; so called from its odor]
rus (sit′rəs) *adj.* Of or pertaining to trees bearing anges, lemons, etc. Also **cit′rous.** [< L, citron tree]
tern (sit′ərn) *n.* Any of a group of old stringed instru-nts resembling a lute or guitar. [< L < Gk. *kithara*]
y (sit′ē) *n. pl.* **cit·ies** **1.** A place inhabited by a large, rmanent community. **2.** In the United States, a munici-ality of the first class with definite boundaries and various al powers. **3.** In Canada, a municipality of high rank. In Great Britain, a large incorporated town. **5.** The ople of a city, collectively. [< OF < L *civis* citizen]
y-bred (sit′ē·bred′) *adj.* Brought up in a city.
desk A department in a newspaper office where local ws is received, rewritten, and edited.
father One who directs the public affairs of a city.
manager An administrator not publicly elected but pointed by a city council to manage the city.
planning Public control of the physical development a city, as by regulation of the size and use of buildings, etc.
y-state (sit′ē·stāt′) *n.* A state consisting of a city and contiguous territories, as ancient Athens.
et (siv′it) *n.* **1.** A substance of musklike odor, secreted the genital glands of the civet cat, used in perfumery. **2.** e civet cat or its fur. [< MF *civette*]
et cat A feline carnivore of Africa.
ic (siv′ik) *adj.* Of or pertaining to a city, a citizen, or izenship; civil. [< L < *civis* citizen]
ics (siv′iks) *n.pl.* (*construed as sing.*) The division of po-cal science dealing with citizenship and civic affairs.
il (siv′əl) *adj.* **1.** Of or pertaining to community life her than military or ecclesiastical affairs. **2.** Of or per-ning to citizens and their government: *civil* affairs. **3.** curring within the state; domestic: *civil* war. **4.** Of, oper to, or befitting a citizen. **5.** Civilized. **6.** Proper; lite. **7.** *Law* Related to the rights of citizens and to legal oceedings involving such rights. — **Syn.** See POLITE. [< F < L *civis* citizen] — **civ′il·ly** *adv.*
il defense A civilian program for the maintenance of ential services in wartime.
il disobedience A refusal to comply with certain civil vs, usually done by means of passive resistance.
il engineer A professional engineer trained to design, ild, and maintain public works, as roads, bridges, etc.
il·ian (sə·vil′yən) *n.* One who is not in the military or val service. — *adj.* Of or pertaining to a civilian.
il·i·ty (sə·vil′ə·tē) *n. pl.* **·ties** **1.** The quality of being il; courtesy; politeness. **2.** A polite act or speech.
i·li·za·tion (siv′ə·lə·zā′shən, -lī·zā′-) *n.* **1.** A state of man society characterized by a high level of intellectual, ial, and cultural development. **2.** The countries and peo-s considered to have reached this stage. **3.** The cultural velopment of a specific people, country, or region. **4.** The of civilizing, or the process of becoming civilized.
i·lize (siv′ə·līz) *v.t.* **·lized, ·liz·ing** To bring into a state civilization; bring out of savagery; refine; enlighten. Also *it.* **civ′i·lise.** [< MF < Med.L < L *civis* citizen] — **civ′·z′a·ble** *adj.* — **civ′i·liz′er** *n.*
il law The body of laws having to do with the rights and vileges of private citizens.
il liberty A liberty guaranteed to the individual by the vs of a government.
il marriage A marriage solemnized by a civil or govern-nt official rather than by a clergyman.
il rights Private, nonpolitical privileges; esp., exemp-n from involuntary servitude, as established by the 13th d 14th amendments to the U.S. Constitution.
il service **1.** The branches of governmental service that not military, naval, legislative, or judicial. **2.** The per-ns employed in these branches. — **civil servant**
il war War between parties or sections of the same ıntry.
il War See table for WAR.

civ·vies (siv′ēz) *n.pl. Informal* Civilian clothes, as distin-guished from military dress; mufti.
clab·ber (klab′ər) *n.* Milk curdled by souring. — *v.t. & v.i.* To curdle, as milk. [< Irish *bainne clabair*]
clack (klak) *v.i.* **1.** To make a sharp, dry sound. **2.** To chatter heedlessly. **3.** To cluck, as a hen. — *v.t.* **4.** To cause to clack. **5.** To babble. — *n.* **1.** A short, sharp sound. **2.** Something that makes a clack. **3.** Chatter. [Imit.] — **clack′er** *n.*
clad (klad) Alternative past tense and past participle of CLOTHE.
claim (klām) *v.t.* **1.** To demand as one's right or due; as-sert ownership or title to. **2.** To hold to be true; assert. **3.** To require or deserve: The problem *claims* our attention. — *n.* **1.** A demand or an assertion of a right. **2.** An asser-tion of something as true. **3.** A ground for claiming some-thing. **4.** That which is claimed, as a piece of land. [< OF < L *clamere* to declare] — **claim′a·ble** *adj.* — **claim′er** *n.*
claim·ant (klā′mənt) *n.* One who makes a claim.
clair·voy·ance (klâr·voi′əns) *n.* **1.** The alleged ability to perceive distant or hidden objects. **2.** Knowledge of things beyond the area of normal perception. [< MF]
clair·voy·ant (klâr·voi′ənt) *adj.* Having clairvoyance or second sight. — *n.* A clairvoyant person.
clam[1] (klam) *n.* **1.** Any of various bivalve mollusks, as the quahog. **2.** *Informal* A close-mouthed person. — *v.i.* **clammed, clam·ming** To hunt for or dig clams. — **to clam up** *U.S. Slang* To become or keep silent. [< obs. *clam* a clamp]
clam·bake (klam′bāk′) *n. U.S.* **1.** A picnic where clams and other foods are baked. **2.** Any noisy gathering.
clam·ber (klam′bər, -ər) *v.t. & v.i.* To climb by using the hands and feet; mount or descend with difficulty. — *n.* The act of clambering. [Akin to CLIMB] — **clam′ber·er** *n.*
clam·my (klam′ē) *adj.* **·mi·er, ·mi·est** Stickily soft and damp, and usually cold. [< Du. *klam* sticky] — **clam′mi·ly** *adv.* — **clam′mi·ness** *n.*
clam·or (klam′ər) *n.* **1.** A loud, repeated outcry. **2.** A ve-hement protest or demand. **3.** Any loud and continuous noise; din. — *v.i.* **1.** To make loud outcries, demands, or complaints. — *v.t.* **2.** To utter with clamor. **3.** To move or drive by clamor. Also *Brit.* **clam′our.** [< OF < L *cla-mare* to cry out] — **clam′or·er** *n.*
clam·or·ous (klam′ər·əs) *adj.* Making, or made with, a clamor; noisy. — **clam′or·ous·ly** *adv.* — **clam′or·ous·ness** *n.*
clamp (klamp) *n.* Any of a number of devices for holding objects together, securing a piece in position, etc.; esp. one having two opposite parts that can be brought together by a screw or spring action. — *v.t.* To hold or bind with or as with a clamp. — **to clamp down** *U.S. Informal* To become more strict. [Cf. OE *clamm,* M.Du *klampe*]
clan (klan) *n.* **1.** A united group of relatives, or families, claiming a common ancestor and having the same surname. **2.** A clique; fraternity; club. [< Scottish Gaelic *clann*]
clan·des·tine (klan·des′tin) *adj.* Kept secret for a purpose, usually for something evil or illicit; surreptitious; furtive; — **Syn.** See STEALTHY. [< F < L *clandestinus* < *clam* in secret] — **clan·des′tine·ly** *adv.* — **clan·des′tine·ness** *n.*
clang (klang) *v.t. & v.i.* To make or cause to make a loud, ringing, metallic sound; ring loudly. — *n.* A ringing sound.
clan·gor (klang′gər, klang′ər) *n.* Repeated clanging; clam-or; din. — *v.i.* To ring noisily; clang. Also *Brit.* **clan′gour.** [< L < *clangere* to clang] — **clan′gor·ous** *adj.* — **clan′·gor·ous·ly** *adv.*
clank (klangk) *n.* A short, harsh, metallic sound. — *v.t. & v.i.* To emit, or cause to emit, a clank. [Imit.]
clan·nish (klan′ish) *adj.* **1.** Of or characteristic of a clan. **2.** Disposed to cling together, or bound by family prejudices, traditions, etc. — **clan′nish·ly** *adv.* — **clan′nish·ness** *n.*
clans·man (klanz′mən) *n. pl.* **·men** (-mən) A member of a clan. — **clans′wom′an** *n.fem.*
clap (klap) *v.* **clapped, clap·ping** *v.i.* **1.** To strike the hands together, as in applauding. **2.** To make a sound, as of two boards striking together. — *v.t.* **3.** To bring (the hands) to-gether sharply and with an explosive sound. **4.** To strike with the open hand, as in greeting. **5.** To applaud (someone or something) by clapping. **6.** To put, place, or fling quickly or suddenly: They *clapped* him into jail. **7.** To flap, as the wings. — *n.* **1.** The act or sound of clapping the hands. **2.** A loud, explosive sound, esp. of thunder. **3.** A blow with the open hand. [OE *clæppan*]
clap·board (klab′ərd, klap′bôrd′, -bōrd′) *n.* A narrow board having one edge thinner than the other, nailed over-lapping as siding on frame buildings: sometimes called *weatherboard.* — *v.t.* To cover with clapboards. [Partial trans. of M.Du. *klapholt* barrel stave]
clap·per (klap′ər) *n.* **1.** The tongue of a bell. **2.** One who or that which claps.

clap·trap (klap′trap) *n.* Pretentious language; cheap, sensational artifice. [< CLAP[1], n. + TRAP[1], n.]

claque (klak) *n.* **1.** A group of hired applauders in a theater. **2.** Any set of persons who praise or applaud from interested motives. [< F < *claquer* to clap]

clar·et (klar′ət) *n.* **1.** Any dry red wine, esp. red Bordeaux. **2.** Ruby to deep purplish red. [< OF < L *clarus* bright]

clar·i·fy (klar′ə·fī) *v.t. & v.i.* **·fied, ·fy·ing 1.** To make or become clear or free from impurities. **2.** To make or become understandable; explain. [< OF < LL < L *clarus* clear + *facere* to make] **—clar′i·fi·ca′tion** *n.* **—clar′i·fi′er** *n.*

clar·i·net (klar′ə·net′) *n.* A cylindrical woodwind instrument having a single-reed mouthpiece, finger holes, and keys. Also *Rare* **clar·i·o·net** (klar′ē·ə·net′). [< F < Ital. *clarinetto*] **—clar′i·net′ist** or **clar′i·net′tist** *n.*

clar·i·on (klar′ē·ən) *n.* **1.** An obsolete kind of trumpet having a shrill tone. **2.** The sound of a clarion. **—***v.t. & v.i.* To proclaim as with a clarion. **—***adj.* Clear and resounding. [< OF < L *clarus* clear]

clar·i·ty (klar′ə·tē) *n.* Clearness; lucidity.

clash (klash) *v.t.* **1.** To strike or dash together with a harsh, metallic sound. **—***v.i.* **2.** To collide with loud and confused noise. **3.** To conflict; be in opposition. **—***n.* **1.** A resounding, metallic noise. **2.** A conflict or opposition. [Imit.]

clasp (klasp, kläsp) *n.* **1.** A fastening, as a hook, by which things or parts are held together. **2.** A firm grasp of the hand or embrace. **—***v.t.* **1.** To embrace. **2.** To fasten with or as with a clasp. **3.** To grasp firmly in or with the hand. [ME *claspe*] **—clasp′er** *n.*

class (klas, kläs) *n.* **1.** A body of persons considered to have certain social or other characteristics in common. **2.** The division of society by relative standing; social rank, caste. **3.** A category of objects, persons, etc., based on quality or rank: of the first *class.* **4.** A number of things grouped together as having common properties; a category. **5.** A group of students under one teacher, or pursuing a study together; also, a meeting of such a group. **6.** *U.S.* A group of students in a school or college graduating together. **7.** *Biol.* A group of plants or animals standing below a phylum and above an order. **8.** *Slang* Superiority; elegance. **—***v.t.* **1.** To assign to a class; classify. **—***v.i.* **2.** *Rare* To be placed or ranked, as in a class. [< MF < L *classis* class]

class consciousness Awareness of the nature, interest, and unity of one's social group. **—class′-con′scious** *adj.*

clas·sic (klas′ik) *adj.* **1.** Belonging to the first class or highest rank; approved as a model. **2.** Of or characteristic of ancient Greece and Rome, their literature or art. **3.** In the style of ancient Greek and Roman authors and artists; balanced; formal; austere. **—***n.* **1.** An author, artist, or work generally recognized as a standard of excellence. **2.** *Informal* Any well-known event thought of as being typical or traditional. **—the classics** Ancient Greek and Roman literature. [< L *classis* order, class]

clas·si·cal (klas′i·kəl) *adj.* **1.** Classic. **2.** Generally accepted as being standard and authoritative; not new or experimental: *classical* economic theory. **3.** Of ancient Greece and Rome: *classical* civilization. **4.** Versed in the Greek and Roman classics: a *classical* scholar. **5.** Consisting of or pertaining to studies based on Greek and Roman language, literature, and thought: a *classical* curriculum. **6.** *Music* Loosely, of a serious nature, as distinguished from jazz or popular music. **—clas′si·cal·ly** *adv.* **—clas′si·cal′i·ty** *n.*

clas·si·cal·ism (klas′i·kəl·iz′əm) *n.* Classicism. **—clas′·si·cal·ist** *n.*

clas·si·cism (klas′ə·siz′əm) *n.* **1.** A group of esthetic principles (simplicity, restraint, balance, dignity, etc.) as manifested in ancient Greek and Roman art and literature: distinguished from *romanticism.* **2.** Adherence to these principles. **3.** The style of ancient Greek and Roman literature, architecture, etc. **4.** Classical scholarship. **5.** A Greek or Latin idiom or form.

clas·si·cist (klas′ə·sist) *n.* **1.** One versed in the classics. **2.** An adherent or imitator of classic style. **3.** One who actively supports the study of the classics.

clas·si·fi·ca·tion (klas′ə·fə·kā′shən) *n.* The act, process, or result of classifying. **—clas·si·fi·ca·to·ry** (klas′ə·fə·kā′·tər·ē, klə·sif′ə·kə·tôr′ē, -tō′rē) *adj.*

classified advertisement An advertisement under any of various subject headings. Also **classified ad.**

clas·si·fy (klas′ə·fī) *v.t.* **·fied, ·fy·ing 1.** To arrange or put in a class or classes on the basis of resemblances or differences. **2.** To designate as of aid to an enemy and restrict as to circulation or use, as a government document. [< L *classis* class + -FY] **—clas′si·fi′a·ble** *adj.* **—clas′si·fi′er** *n.*

class·mate (klas′māt, kläs′-) *n.* A member of the same class in school or college.

class·room (klas′rōōm′, -rŏŏm′, kläs′-) *n.* A room in a school or college in which classes are held.

class struggle 1. The conflict between classes in society. **2.** In Marxist theory, the economic and political struggle for power between the dominant class and the rising class.

class·y (klas′ē) *adj.* **class·i·er, class·i·est** *Slang* Eleg

clat·ter (klat′ər) *v.i.* **1.** To make a rattling noise; give short, sharp noises rapidly or repeatedly. **2.** To move wi rattling noise. **3.** To talk noisily; chatter. **—***v.t.* **4.** cause to clatter. **—***n.* **1.** A rattling or clattering so **2.** A disturbance or commotion. **3.** Noisy talk; cha [OE *clatrunge* a clattering noise] **—clat′ter·er** *n.*

clause (klôz) *n.* **1.** A distinct part of a composition, a article in a statute, will, treaty, etc. **2.** *Gram.* A grou words containing a subject and a predicate: distingui from *phrase.* Abbr. *cl.* **—dependent clause** A clause functions as a subject or complement (noun clause) or modifier (adjective or adverb clause) within a sentence: called *subordinate clause.* **—independent clause** A cl that can stand alone as a simple sentence, or combine other clauses to form compound or complex sentences: called *main clause, principal clause.* [< OF < Med.L *clausus,* pp. of *claudere* to close] **—claus′al** *adj.*

claus·tro·pho·bi·a (klôs′trə·fō′bē·ə) *n.* *Psychiatry* M bid fear of enclosed or confined places. [< L *claustru* closed place + -PHOBIA] **—claus′tro·pho′bic** *adj.*

cla·vate (klā′vāt) *adj.* Club-shaped. [< L *clava* a cl

clave (klāv) Archaic past tense of CLEAVE[1] and CLEAV

clav·i·chord (klav′ə·kôrd) *n.* A keyboard musical ins ment that is a forerunner of the piano. [< Med.L < *clavis* key + *chorda* string]

clav·i·cle (klav′ə·kəl) *n.* *Anat.* The bone connecting shoulder blade and breastbone: also called *collarbone.* illus. see SKELETON. [< L *clavis* key] **—cla·vic·u·lar** vik′yə·lər) *adj.*

clav·i·er (klə·vir′; for defs. 1 and 3, also klav′ē·ər) *n.* keyboard. **2.** Any keyboard stringed instrument, as a h sichord, piano, etc. **3.** A dummy keyboard for silent p ticing. [< F, keyboard < L *clavis* key]

claw (klô) *n.* **1.** A sharp, usu. curved, horny nail on the of a bird, mammal, or reptile. **2.** A chela or pincer of tain insects and crustaceans. **3.** Anything sharp and hoo as the cleft part of a hammerhead. **—***v.t. & v.i.* To scratch, dig, pull, etc., with or as with claws. [OE *claw*

claw hammer A hammer with one end of its head fo and curved like a claw for drawing nails.

clay (klā) *n.* **1.** A fine-grained, variously colored ea plastic when wet, used in the making of bricks, tiles, pott etc. **2.** Earth. **3.** The human body. **—***v.t.* To mix or t with clay. [OE *clǣg*] **—clay′ey** *adj.* **—clay′ish** *adj.*

clay·more (klā′môr, -mōr) *n.* A double-edged broadsv formerly used by the Scottish Highlanders. [< Scot Gaelic *claidheamh* sword + *mor* great]

clay pigeon In trapshooting, a saucer-shaped disk, a baked clay, projected from a trap as a flying target.

-cle *suffix of nouns* Small; minute; *particle, corpuscle.* [< L *-culus,* dim. suffix]

clean (klēn) *adj.* **1.** Free from dirt or stain; unsoiled. Morally pure; wholesome. **3.** Without obstructions, cumbrances, or restrictions: a *clean* title to land. **4.** T ough; complete: a *clean* getaway. **5.** Clever; dexterou *clean* jump. **6.** Well-proportioned; trim; shapely. **7.** N in habits. **8.** Producing an explosion relatively free of ra active fallout: said of an atomic or thermonuclear bomb. *v.t.* **1.** To render free of dirt or other impurities. **2.** To pare (fowl, game, etc.) for cooking. **—***v.i.* **3.** To underg perform the act of cleaning. **—to clean out 1.** To clea trash or rubbish. **2.** To empty (a place) of contents or cupants. **3.** *Informal* To leave without money: The pression *cleaned* him *out.* **—to clean up 1.** To clean c pletely and thoroughly. **2.** *Slang* To make a large pr **3.** *Informal* To finish: to *clean up* one's work. **—***adv.* **1** a clean manner; cleanly. **2.** Wholly; completely. [*clǣne* clear, pure] **—clean′a·ble** *adj.* **—clean′ness** *n.*

clean-cut (klēn′kut′) *adj.* **1.** Cut with smooth edg surface; well-made. **2.** Sharply defined; clear. **3.** Plea in appearance; wholesome; neat: a *clean-cut* young man

clean·er (klē′nər) *n.* **1.** A person whose work is clean esp. clothing. **2.** Any substance or device that cleans.

clean·ly (*adj.* klen′lē; *adv.* klēn′lē) *adj.* Habitually carefully clean; neat; tidy. **—***adv.* In a clean manner. **clean·li·ly** (klen′lə·lē) *adv.* **—clean·li·ness** (klen′lē·nis)

cleanse (klenz) *v.t.* **cleansed, cleans·ing** To free from or defilement; clean; purge. [OE *clǣnsian* < *clǣne* clea

cleans·er (klenz′ər) *n.* One who or that which clean esp., a soap, detergent, etc., used for cleansing.

clean·up (klēn′up′) *n.* **1.** A complete cleaning. **2.** *Slan* large profit; gain.

clear (klir) *adj.* **1.** Bright; unclouded. **2.** Without im ity or blemish. **3.** Of great transparency. **4.** Free f obstructions: a *clear* road. **5.** Understandable; plain to mind. **6.** Plain to the eye, ear, etc. **7.** Able to disc keen: a *clear* mind. **8.** Free from uncertainty; sure: Are *clear* on that point? **9.** Free from guilt or blame. **10.** in contact: usu. with *of:* to stand *clear* of a fire. **11.** E tied of cargo. **12.** Without deductions; net: a *clear* $5,(

- *adv.* **1.** In a clear manner. **2.** *Informal* All the way: *ear* through the day. — *v.t.* **1.** To make clear; brighten. . To free from foreign matter, impurities, or obstructions. . To remove (obstacles, etc.) in making something clear. . To free from blame or guilt. **5.** To make plain. **6.** To ıss or get under or over without touching: to *clear* a fence. . To free from debt by payment. **8.** To settle (a debt). . To obtain or give clearance for. **10.** To gain over and ɔove expenses. **11.** To pass (a check) through a clearing-ɔuse. — *v.i.* **12.** To become free from fog, rain, etc.; be-ɔme fair. **13.** To pass away, as mist or clouds. **14.** To ttle accounts by exchange of bills and checks, as in a clear-g-house. **15.** To obtain clearance. — **to clear away** (or **f**) **1.** To remove out of the way. **2.** To go away; disap-ɔar. — **to clear out 1.** *Informal* To go away. **2.** To npty of contents. — **to clear the air** To dispel tensions; ttle differences. — **to clear up 1.** To make clear. **2.** To ɔow fair, as the weather. **3.** To free from confusion or ystery. **4.** To put in order; tidy. — *n.* **1.** An unob-ructed space. **2.** Clearance. — **in the clear 1.** Free from nitations or obstructions. **2.** *Informal* Free from guilt or ame. [< OF < L *clarus* clear, bright] — **clear′a·ble** *j.* — **clear′ly** *adv.* — **clear′ness** *n.*

— **Syn.** (adj.) **1, 3.** A thing is *clear* when it presents no obstruc-ɔns to the sight. We see objects clearly through something *trans-rent*; that which is *translucent* allows the passage of light, but ay obscure form and color.

ar·ance (klir′əns) *n.* **1.** The act or instance of clearing. A space cleared. **3.** The space by which a moving object ɔars something. **4.** Permission for a ship, airplane, truck, c., to proceed, as after a check of its load. **5.** The passage checks, bank drafts, etc. through a clearing-house.

ar-cut (klir′kut′) *adj.* **1.** Distinctly and sharply out-ɔed. **2.** Plain; evident; obvious.

ar-head·ed (klir′hed′id) *adj.* Not mentally confused; ɔar in thought; sensible. — **clear′-head′ed·ness** *n.*

ar·ing (klir′ing) *n.* **1.** A making or becoming clear. **2.** ıat which is clear or cleared, as a tract of land. **3.** In ınking, clearance.

ar·ing-house (klir′ing·hous′) *n.* An office where bank-s exchange drafts and checks and adjust balances. Also **ɔar′ing·house′.**

ar-sight·ed (klir′sī′tid) *adj.* **1.** Having accurate per-ption and good judgment; discerning. **2.** Having keen vi-n. — **clear′-sight′ed·ly** *adv.* — **clear′-sight′ed·ness** *n.*

ar·sto·ry (klir′stôr′ē, -stō′rē) See CLERESTORY.

at (klēt) *n.* **1.** A strip of wood or iron fastened across a rface to strengthen or support. **2.** A piece of metal or ɔod with arms on which to wind or secure a rope. — *v.t.* To furnish or strengthen with a cleat or cleats. **2.** *Naut.*) fasten (rope, etc.) to or with a cleat. [ME *clete*]

av·age (klē′vij) *n.* **1.** A cleaving or being cleft. **2.** A ɩit or cleft. **3.** *Mineral.* A tendency in certain rocks or ystals to split in certain directions.

ave[1] (klēv) *v.* **cleft** or **cleaved** or **clove** (*Archaic* **clave**), ɔft or **cleaved** or **clo·ven, cleav·ing** *v.t.* **1.** To split or sun-r, as with an ax or wedge. **2.** To make or achieve by cut-ɔg: to *cleave* a path. **3.** To pass through; penetrate: to *ave* the air. — *v.i.* **4.** To part or divide along natural lines separation. **5.** To make one's way; pass: with *through.* **E** *clēofan*] — **cleav′a·ble** *adj.*

ave[2] (klēv) *v.i.* **cleaved** (*Archaic* **clave, clove**), **cleaved, ɔav·ing 1.** To stick fast; adhere: with *to.* **2.** To be faith-ɩ: with *to.* [Fusion of OE *clifan* and *clifian*]

av·er (klē′vər) *n.* **1.** One who or that which cleaves. A butcher's heavy, axlike knife. [< CLEAVE[1]]

f (klef) *n.* *Music* A symbol placed on the staff to show e pitch of the notes. [< MF < L *clavis* key]

ft (kleft) Past tense and past participle of CLEAVE[1]. — *j.* Divided partially or completely. — *n.* A fissure; crev-ɔ; rift. [ME *clift*]

ft palate A congenital longitudinal fissure in the roof of e mouth.

m·a·tis (klem′ə·tis) *n.* A perennial shrub or vine of the ɔwfoot family. [< Gk. *klēmatis*]

m·en·cy (klem′ən·sē) *n.* *pl.* **·cies 1.** Leniency; mercy. An act of mercy or leniency. **3.** Mildness of weather, ɔ. — **Syn.** See MERCY. [< L *clemens* mild]

m·ent (klem′ənt) *adj.* **1.** Lenient or merciful in tempera-ɔnt; compassionate. **2.** Mild: said of weather. [< L *clem-s, -entis* mild, merciful] — **clem′ent·ly** *adv.*

nch (klench) *v.t.* **1.** To grasp or grip firmly. **2.** To close htly or lock, as the fist or teeth. **3.** To clinch, as a nail. *n.* **1.** A tight grip. **2.** A device that clenches or grips. **E** *-clenc(e)an* in *beclencan* to hold fast]

re·sto·ry (klir′stôr′ē, -stō′rē) *n.* *pl.* **·ries 1.** *Archit.* The ɔhest story of the nave and choir of a church, with windows ening above the aisle roofs, etc. **2.** A similar part in other structures. Also spelled *clearstory.* Also **clere′sto′rey.** [< earlier *clere* clear + STORY]

cler·gy (klûr′jē) *n.* *pl.* **·gies** The whole body of men set apart by ordination for religious service. [< OF < LL < Gk. *klēros* lot, portion]

cler·gy·man (klûr′jē·mən) *n.* *pl.* **·men** (-mən) One of the clergy; an ordained minister. Abbr. *cl.*

cler·ic (kler′ik) *adj.* Clerical. — *n.* A member of the clergy.

cler·i·cal (kler′i·kəl) *adj.* **1.** Of or related to clerks or office workers or their work. **2.** Belonging to or characteristic of the clergy. **3.** Advocating great political influence for the clergy. — *n.* **1.** A clergyman. **2.** *pl.* The distinctive dress of a clergyman. — **cler′i·cal·ly** *adv.*

cler·i·cal·ism (kler′i·kəl·iz′əm) *n.* Excessive clerical influence in politics. — **cler′i·cal·ist** *n.*

clerk (klûrk, *Brit.* klärk) *n.* **1.** A worker in an office who keeps records or accounts, attends to correspondence, etc. **2.** An official or employee of a court, legislative body, or the like, charged with the care of records, etc. **3.** *U.S.* A salesperson in a store. — *v.i.* To work or act as clerk. [OE < LL < Gk. *klēros* lot, portion] — **clerk′ship** *n.*

clerk·ly (klûrk′lē, *Brit.* klärk′-) *adj.* **clerk·li·er, clerk·li·est** Of a clerk: *clerkly* duties. — *adv.* In the manner of a clerk. — **clerk′li·ness** *n.*

clev·er (klev′ər) *adj.* **1.** Mentally keen; intelligent; quick-witted. **2.** Physically adroit, esp. with the hands; dexterous. **3.** Ingeniously made, said, done, etc. [Cf. ME *cliver* adroit] — **clev′er·ly** *adv.* — **clev′er·ness** *n.*

clev·is (klev′is) *n.* A U-shaped metal fastening pierced for a bolt, used to attach chains, cables, etc. [Akin to CLEAVE[1]]

clew (klōō) *n.* **1.** In legends, a ball of thread that guides through a maze. **2.** Something that serves as a guide in solving a problem or mystery: usu. spelled *clue.* **3.** *Naut.* A lower corner of a square sail or the lower aft corner of a fore-and-aft sail; also, a loop at the corner. — *v.t.* **1.** To coil into a ball. **2.** To guide or track by or as by a clew. **3.** *Naut.* To raise the clews of (a square sail): with *up.* [OE *cliwen*]

cli·ché (klē·shā′) *n.* A trite or hackneyed expression, action, etc. [< F, pp. of *clicher* to stereotype]

click (klik) *n.* **1.** A short, sharp, nonresonant metallic sound, as that made by a latch. **2.** *Phonet.* A speech sound made by clicking the tongue, characteristic of certain African languages: also called *suction stop.* — *v.t.* **1.** To cause to make a click or clicks. — *v.i.* **2.** To produce a click or clicks. **3.** *Slang* To succeed. [Imit.] — **click′er** *n.*

cli·ent (klī′ənt) *n.* **1.** One in whose interest a lawyer acts. **2.** One who engages the services of any professional adviser. **3.** A customer. [< L *cliens, -entis* follower] — **cli·en·tal** (klī·en′təl, klī′ən·təl) *adj.*

cli·en·tele (klī′ən·tel′) *n.* A body of clients, patients, customers, etc. Also **cli·ent·age** (klī′ən·tij). [< F]

cliff (klif) *n.* A high steep face of rock; a precipice. [OE]

cliff swallow A North American swallow that builds mud nests under eaves or against cliffs.

cliff·y (klif′ē) *adj.* Abounding in or resembling cliffs.

cli·mac·ter·ic (klī·mak′tər·ik, klī′mak·ter′ik) *n.* **1.** An age or period of life characterized by marked physiological change, as the menopause. **2.** Any critical year or period. — *adj.* Pertaining to a critical year or period: also **cli·mac·ter·i·cal** (klī·mak·ter′i·kəl). [< L < Gk. *klimaktēr* rung of a ladder]

cli·mac·tic (klī·mak′tik) *adj.* Pertaining to or constituting a climax. Also **cli·mac′ti·cal.**

cli·mate (klī′mit) *n.* **1.** The temperature, precipitation, winds, etc., characteristic of a region. **2.** A region in reference to its characteristic weather. **3.** A prevailing trend or condition in human affairs: the *climate* of opinion. [< OF < LL < Gk. *klima, -atos* region, zone] — **cli·mat·ic** (klī·mat′ik) or **·i·cal** *adj.* — **cli·mat′i·cal·ly** *adv.*

climato- *combining form* Climate; pertaining to climate or climatic conditions: *climatology.* Also, before vowels, **climat-.** [< Gk. *klima, -atos* region]

cli·ma·tol·o·gy (klī′mə·tol′ə·jē) *n.* The branch of science dealing with the phenomena of climate. — **cli·ma·to·log·ic** (klī′mə·tə·loj′ik) or **·i·cal** *adj.* — **cli′ma·tol′o·gist** *n.*

cli·max (klī′maks) *n.* **1.** The point of greatest intensity or fullest development; culmination; acme. **2.** In drama, fiction, etc., the scene or moment of action that determines the dénouement. — *v.t.* & *v.i.* To reach or bring to a climax. [< L < Gk. *klimax* ladder]

climb (klīm) *v.* **climbed, climb·ing** *v.t.* **1.** To ascend or mount (something), by means of the hands and feet. — *v.i.* **2.** To rise or advance in status, rank, etc. **3.** To incline or slope upward. **4.** To rise during growth, as certain vines, by entwining a support. — **to climb down** To descend, esp. by using the hands and feet. — *n.* **1.** The act or process of climbing; ascent. **2.** A place ascended by climbing. [OE *climban*] — **climb′a·ble** *adj.* — **climb′er** *n.*

clinch (klinch) *v.t.* **1.** To secure, as a driven nail or staple, by bending down the protruding point. **2.** To fasten together by this means. **3.** To make sure; settle. —*v.i.* **4.** To grapple, as combatants. **5.** *Slang* To embrace, as lovers. —*n.* **1.** The act of clinching. **2.** That which clinches; a clamp. **3.** A grip or struggle at close quarters, as in boxing. **4.** *Slang* A close embrace. [Var. of CLENCH]

clinch·er (klin′chər) *n.* **1.** One who or that which clinches. **2.** A nail made for clinching. **3.** *Informal* A deciding statement, point, etc.

cling (kling) *v.i.* **clung, cling·ing 1.** To hold fast, as by grasping, sticking, or winding round. **2.** To resist separation: with *together*. [OE *clingan*] —**cling′er** *n.* —**cling′·ing·ly** *adv.* —**cling′y** *adj.*

clinging vine *Informal* A woman who displays extreme dependence on a man.

cling·stone (kling′stōn′) *n.* A variety of peach in which the pulp adheres to the stone.

clin·ic (klin′ik) *n.* **1.** An infirmary, usu. connected with a hospital or medical school, for the treatment of nonresident patients. **2.** The teaching of medicine by treating patients in the presence of a class; also, a class receiving such instruction. **3.** A place where patients are studied and treated by specialists. **4.** An organization that offers advice on specific problems. [< F < Gk. *klinein* to recline]

clin·i·cal (klin′i·kəl) *adj.* **1.** Of or pertaining to a clinic. **2.** Concerned with the observation and treatment of patients in clinics, as distinguished from laboratory experimentation. **3.** Coldly scientific or detached. —**clin′i·cal·ly** *adv.*

clinical thermometer An accurately calibrated thermometer used for determining body temperature.

cli·ni·cian (kli·nish′ən) *n.* A physician trained in clinical methods, or one who gives instruction in clinics.

clink[1] (klingk) *v.t.* & *v.i.* To make or cause to make a short, slight, ringing sound. —*n.* A slight tinkling sound. [Imit.]

clink[2] (klingk) *n. Slang* A prison. [? after *Clink* prison in London]

clink·er (kling′kər) *n.* **1.** The fused residue left by coal, etc., in burning. **2.** A very hard brick. —*v.i.* To form clinkers, as coal in burning. [< Du. *klinckaerd* brick]

clino- *combining form* Bend; slope; incline: *clinometer*. [< Gk. *klinein* to bend]

cli·nom·e·ter (klī·nom′ə·tər, kli-) *n.* An instrument for determining angular inclination, as of guns, slopes, etc. —**cli·no·met·ric** (klī′nə·met′rik) or **·ri·cal** *adj.*

Cli·o (klī·ō) The Muse of history.

clip[1] (klip) *n.* A device that clasps, grips, or holds articles together, as letters or papers. —*v.t.* **clipped, clip·ping** To fasten with or as with a clip. [OE *clyppan* to clasp]

clip[2] (klip) *v.* **clipped, clip·ping** *v.t.* **1.** To cut with shears or scissors, as hair or fleece; trim. **2.** To cut short; curtail: to *clip* the ends of words. **3.** *Informal* To strike with a sharp blow. **4.** *U.S. Slang* To cheat or defraud. —*v.i.* **5.** To cut or trim. **6.** *Informal* To run or move swiftly. —**to clip the wings of** To check the aspirations or ambitions of. —*n.* **1.** The act of clipping, or that which is clipped off. **2.** The wool yielded at one shearing or during one season. **3.** A sharp blow; punch. **4.** *Informal* A quick pace. [< ON *klippa*]

clip·board (klip′bôrd′, -bōrd′) *n.* A board providing a writing surface, with a spring clip for holding paper.

clipped form A shortened form of a polysyllabic word, as *bus* for *omnibus*. Also **clipped word.**

clip·per (klip′ər) *n.* **1.** *pl.* An instrument or tool for clipping or cutting. **2.** A sailing vessel of the mid-19th century, built for speed: also **clipper ship. 3.** One who clips.

clip·ping (klip′ing) *n.* **1.** The act of one who or that which clips. **2.** *Chiefly U.S.* That which is cut off or out by clipping: a newspaper *clipping*. —*adj.* That cuts or clips.

clique (klēk, klik) *n.* An exclusive or clannish group of people. —*v.i.* **cliqued, cli·quing** To unite in a clique; act clannishly. [< MF < *cliquer* to click, clap]

cli·quish (klē′kish, klik′ish) *adj.* Inclined to form cliques; exclusive. Also **cli′quey, cli′quy.** —**cli′quish·ly** *adv.* —**cli′·quish·ness** *n.*

cli·to·ris (klī′tə·ris, klit′ə-) *n. Anat.* A small erectile organ at the upper part of the vulva, homologous to the penis. [< NL < Gk. *kleitoris*] —**clit′o·ral** (-rəl) *adj.*

clo·a·ca (klō·ā′kə) *n. pl.* **·cae** (-sē) **1.** *Zool.* The common cavity into which the various ducts of the body open in certain fishes, reptiles, birds, and some mammals. **2.** A sewer or a privy. [< L, a drain] —**clo·a′cal** *adj.*

cloak (klōk) *n.* **1.** A loose outer garment, usu. without sleeves. **2.** Something that covers or hides. —*v.t.* **1.** To cover with a cloak. **2.** To conceal; disguise. [< OF < Med.L *cloca* bell, cape; so called from its bell-like shape]

cloak·room (klōk′rōōm′, -rŏŏm′) *n.* A room where hats, coats, luggage, etc., are left temporarily, as in a theater.

clob·ber (klob′ər) *v.t. U.S. Slang* **1.** To beat severely; trounce; maul. **2.** To defeat utterly. [? Freq. of CLUB[1], v.]

cloche (klōsh, *Fr.* klôsh) *n.* A woman's close-fitting, bell-shaped hat. [< F, bell]

clock[1] (klok) *n.* An instrument for measuring time; esp sizable mechanism having pointers that move over a marked off in hours. —*v.t.* To ascertain the speed or time of with a stopwatch. [< MDu. < OF < Med.L *cloc*

clock[2] (klok) *n.* An embroidered or woven ornament on side of a stocking or sock at the ankle. [Origin uncertai

clock·wise (klok′wīz′) *adj.* & *adv.* Going in the direct traveled by the hands of a clock.

clock·work (klok′wûrk′) *n.* The machinery of a clock any similar mechanism, usu. driven by a spring. — **clockwork** With regularity and precision.

clod (klod) *n.* **1.** A lump of earth, clay, etc. **2.** Earth. A dull, stupid person. [Var. of CLOT] —**clod′dish** *adj.* **clod′dish·ness** *n.* —**clod′dy** *adj.*

clod·hop·per (klod′hop′ər) *n.* **1.** *Informal* A rustic; h lout. **2.** *pl.* Large, heavy shoes.

clog (klog) *n.* **1.** Anything that impedes motion; an struction; hindrance. **2.** A block or weight attached, as horse, to hinder movement. **3.** A wooden-soled shoe. 4 clog dance. —*v.* **clogged, clog·ging** *v.t.* **1.** To choke u obstruct. **2.** To impede; hinder. **3.** To fasten a clog hobble. —*v.i.* **4.** To become clogged or choked. **5.** To here in a mass; coagulate. **6.** To perform a clog dance. [*clogge* block of wood] —**clog′gi·ness** *n.* —**clog′gy** *ad*

cloi·son·né (kloi′zə·nā′) *n.* **1.** Enamel work made by lay out the pattern with metal strips and filling the interst with enamel. **2.** The ware so produced. —*adj.* Of, taining to, or made by this method. [< F, partitioned

clois·ter (klois′tər) *n.* **1.** A covered walk along the in walls of buildings in a quadrangle, as in a monastery or lege. **2.** A monastery; convent. **3.** Any place of quiet clusion. **4.** Monastic life. —*v.t.* To seclude; confine, a a cloister. [OF < L *claustrum* enclosed place] —**cl tered** *adj.* —**clois′tral** *adj.*

—**Syn.** (noun) **2.** *Cloister* refers to a retreat for either sex, stresses loneliness. *Convent* was originally a general term, bu now usually restricted to a retreat for women, replacing the for *nunnery*. *Monasteries* are *cloisters* for men.

clo·nus (klō′nəs) *n. Pathol.* A succession of muscle spas [< NL < Gk. *klonos* motion, turmoil] —**clon·ic** (klon *adj.* —**clo·nic·i·ty** (klō·nis′ə·tē) *n.* —**clo′nism** *n.*

close (*adj., adv., n. defs. 4 and 5* klōs; *v., n. def. 2* klōz) **clos·er, clos·est 1.** Near or near together in space, time, **2.** Dense; compact: a *close* weave. **3.** Near to the surf short: a *close* haircut. **4.** Near to the mark: a *close* shot. Nearly even or equal: said of contests. **6.** Fitting tigh **7.** Conforming to an original: a *close* resemblance. Logically exact: *close* reasoning. **9.** Thorough; rigor *close* attention. **10.** Bound by strong affection, loya etc.: a *close* friend. **11.** Shut in or about; not open. Confined in space; cramped: *close* quarters. **13.** Open o to a few; restricted. **14.** Strictly guarded: a *close* sec **15.** Concealing one's thoughts or feelings; reticent. Hidden; secluded. **17.** Close-fisted; stingy. **18.** Diffi to obtain: said of money or credit. **19.** Stifling and hu stuffy. **20.** *Phonet.* Of vowels, pronounced with a par the tongue relatively close to the palate, as (ē): oppose *open*. —*v.* **closed, clos·ing** *v.t.* **1.** To shut. **2.** To obstr as an opening or passage. **3.** To bring to an end; termin —*v.i.* **4.** To become shut or closed. **5.** To come to an e **6.** To grapple; come to close quarters. **7.** To come to agreement. **8.** To be worth at the end of a business d stocks *closed* three points higher. —**to close down** To ce operations, as a factory. —**to close in** To advance from sides so as to prevent escape. —**to close out** *U.S.* To all of, usu. at reduced prices. —**to close up 1.** To c completely. **2.** To come nearer together, as troops. — **1.** The end; conclusion. **2.** An enclosed place, esp. abo cathedral or building. —*adv.* In a close manner; nea closely. [< OF < L *claudere* to close] —**close·ly** (klōs *adv.* —**close·ness** (klōs′nis) *n.* —**clos·er** (klō′zər) *n.*

close call (klōs) *U.S. Informal* A narrow escape.

closed circuit (klōzd) *Telecom.* A form of television in w broadcasts are transmitted by cable to a restricted num of receivers.

closed shop An establishment where only union mem are hired, by agreement with the union.

close-fist·ed (klōs′fis′tid) *adj.* Stingy; miserly. —**clo fist′ed·ness** *n.*

close-fit·ting (klōs′fit′ing) *adj.* Fitting snugly.

close-hauled (klōs′hôld′) *adj.* & *adv. Naut.* With sails for sailing as close to the wind as possible.

close-mouthed (klōs′mouthd′, -moutht′) *adj.* Not gi to speaking; taciturn; uncommunicative.

close quarters (klōs) **1.** In fighting, an encounter at c range or hand-to-hand. **2.** A small, confined space.

close shave (klōs) *U.S. Informal* A narrow escape.

clos·et (kloz′it) *n.* **1.** *Chiefly U.S.* A small room or re for storing clothes, linen, etc. **2.** A small, private room. A ruler's council chamber. —*v.t.* To shut up or conce or as in a closet: usu. reflexive. —*adj.* **1.** Private; confid

l. **2.** Based on theory rather than practice: *closet* strategy.
: OF, dim. of *clos* < L *claudere* to close]
se-up (klōs′up′) *n.* **1.** A picture taken at close range, or
:h a telescopic lens. **2.** A close look or view.
sure (klō′zhər) *n.* **1.** A closing or shutting up. **2.** That
ich closes or shuts. **3.** An end; conclusion. **4.** Cloture.
v.t. & v.i. **·sured, ·sur·ing** To cloture. [< OF < L *clau-*
e to close]
; (klot) *n.* A thick, viscid, or coagulated mass, as of
od. — *v.t. & v.i.* **clot·ted, clot·ting** To form into clots; co-
ılate. [OE *clott* lump, mass] — **clot′ty** *adj.*
:h (klôth, kloth) *n.* *pl.* **cloths** (klôthz, klothz, klôths,
ths) **1.** A woven, knitted, or felted fabric of wool, cotton,
on, etc.; also, a piece of such fabric. **2.** A piece of cloth
a special use, as a tablecloth. **3.** Professional attire, esp.
the clergy. — **the cloth** The clergy. [OE *clāth*]
:**he** (klōth) *v.t.* **clothed** or **clad, cloth·ing 1.** To cover or
vide with clothes; dress. **2.** To cover as if with clothing;
est. [Fusion of OE *clāthian* and *clǣthan*]
:**hes** (klōz, klōthz) *n.pl.* **1.** Garments; clothing. **2.** Bed-
thes. [OE *clāthas*, pl. of *clāth* cloth]
:**hes·horse** (klōz′hôrs′, klōthz′-) *n.* **1.** A frame on
ich to hang or dry clothes. **2.** *U.S. Slang* A person re-
ded as excessively concerned with dress.
:**hes·line** (klōz′līn, klōthz′-) *n.* A cord, rope, or wire on
ich to hang clothes to dry.
:**hes·pin** (klōz′pin′, klōthz′-) *n.* A forked peg or clamp
:h which to fasten clothes on a line.
:**hes·press** (klōz′pres′, klōthz′-) *n.* A closet; wardrobe.
:**h·ier** (klōth′yər) *n.* One who makes or sells cloth or
thing.
:**h·ing** (klō′thing) *n.* **1.** Dress collectively; apparel. **2.**
covering.
·tho (klō′thō) One of the three Fates.
:**·ty** (klot′ē) *adj.* **1.** Full of clots. **2.** Tending to clot.
ture (klō′chər) *n.* A parliamentary device to stop dete in a legislative body in order to secure a vote. — *v.t.*
stop (debate) by cloture. Also *closure.* [< F *clôture*]
ıd (kloud) *n.* **1.** A mass of visible vapor or an aggrega-
n of watery or icy particles floating in the atmosphere.
Any visible collection of particles in the air, as steam,
oke, or dust. **3.** A cloudlike mass of things in motion, esp.
flight: a *cloud* of gnats. **4.** Something that darkens, ob-
res, or threatens. **5.** A dimness or milkiness, as in glass
liquids. — **in the clouds 1.** In the realm of the unreal or
ciful. **2.** Impractical. — **under a cloud 1.** Overshad-
ed by reproach or distrust. **2.** Troubled or depressed.
v.t. **1.** To cover with or as with clouds; dim; obscure. **2.**
render gloomy or troubled. **3.** To disgrace; sully, as a
utation. **4.** To mark with different colors; variegate. —
5. To become overcast: often with *up* or *over*. [OE *clūd*
ky mass, hill] — **cloud′less** *adj.*
ıd·burst (kloud′bûrst′) *n.* A sudden, heavy downpour.
ıd chamber *Physics* An enclosed receptacle containing
or gas saturated with water vapor whose sudden cooling
licates the presence of ions by the tracks of water droplets
y produce: also called *fog chamber, Wilson Cloud Chamber.*
ıd·y (klou′dē) *adj.* **cloud·i·er, cloud·i·est 1.** Overspread
h clouds. **2.** Of or like a cloud or clouds. **3.** Marked
h cloudlike spots. **4.** Not limpid or clear. **5.** Obscure;
gue; confused: *cloudy* thinking. **6.** Full of foreboding;
omy. [OE *clūdig*] — **cloud′i·ly** *adv.* — **cloud′i·ness** *n.*
ıt (klout) *n.* **1.** *Informal* A heavy blow or cuff with the
nd. **2.** In baseball slang, a long hit. **3.** In archery, the
nter of a target, or a shot that strikes it. **4.** A type of flat-
aded nail: also **clout nail.** — *v.t.* *Informal* To hit or
ike, as with the hand. [OE *clūt*]
ve (klōv) *n.* A dried flower bud of a tree of the myrtle
nily, used as a spice. [< OF < L *clavus* nail]
ve hitch *Naut.* A knot consisting of two half hitches,
h the ends of the rope going in opposite directions, used
fastening a rope around a spar. For illustration see HITCH.
·ven (klō′vən) Alternative past participle of CLEAVE[1]. —
j. Parted; split.
ven-hoofed (klō′vən·hŏŏft′, -hōōft′) *adj.* **1.** Having the
ot cleft, as cattle. **2.** Satanic. Also **clo′ven-foot′ed.**
·ver (klō′vər) *n.* Any of several plants having dense
wer heads and trifoliolate leaves; esp., the **red clover,** used
forage and adopted as the State flower of Vermont. —
clover In a prosperous condition. [OE *clāfre* trefoil]
·ver·leaf (klō′vər·lēf′) *n.* *pl.* **·leafs** A type of intersec-
n resembling a four-leaf clover, in which two highways
ossing at different levels are connected by curving ramps.
wn (kloun) *n.* **1.** A professional buffoon in a play or cir-
s, who entertains by jokes, tricks, etc.; a zany; jester. **2.**
coarse or vulgar person; boor. — *v.i.* To behave like a
own. [Earlier *cloune* < MLG] — **clown′er·y** *n.* —
wn′ish *adj.* — **clown′ish·ly** *adv.* — **clown′ish·ness** *n.*

cloy (kloi) *v.t.* **1.** To gratify beyond desire; surfeit. — *v.i.* **2.** To cause a feeling of surfeit. [< OF < LL < L *clavus* a nail] — **cloy′ing·ly** *adv.* — **cloy′ing·ness** *n.*
club[1] (klub) *n.* **1.** A stout stick or staff; a cudgel. **2.** A stick or bat used in games to strike a ball; esp., a stick with a curved head used in golf. **3.** In card games: **a** A black marking on a playing card, shaped like a three-leaf clover. **b** A card so marked. **c** *pl.* The suit so marked. — *v.* **clubbed, club·bing** *v.t.* To beat, as with a club. [< ON *klubba*]
club[2] (klub) *n.* **1.** A group of persons organized for some mutual aim or pursuit, esp. a group that meets regularly. **2.** A house or room reserved for the meetings of such an organization. — *v.* **clubbed, club·bing** *v.t.* **1.** To contribute for a common purpose: to *club* resources. — *v.i.* **2.** To combine or unite: often with *together.* [Special use of CLUB[1]]
club car A railroad passenger car furnished with easy chairs, tables, a buffet or bar, etc.
club·foot (klub′fŏŏt′) *n.* *pl.* **·feet** *Pathol.* **1.** Congenital distortion of the foot: also called *talipes.* **2.** A foot so affected. — **club′foot′ed** *adj.*
club·house (klub′hous′) *n.* **1.** The building occupied by a club. **2.** Dressing rooms for an athletic team.
club moss A perennial evergreen herb allied to the ferns.
club sandwich A sandwich consisting of three slices of toast and layers of various meats, lettuce, tomatoes, etc.
club steak A small beefsteak cut from the loin.
club topsail *Naut.* A gaff topsail, extended at its foot by a small spar. For illus. see SCHOONER.
cluck (kluk) *v.i.* **1.** To give the low, guttural cry of a hen calling her chicks. **2.** To utter any similar sound, as in urging a horse. — *v.t.* **3.** To call by clucking. **4.** To express with a like sound: to *cluck* disapproval. — *n.* The sound of clucking. [OE *cloccian*; imit.]
clue (klōō) *n.* Something that leads to the solution of a problem or mystery. — *v.t.* **clued, clu·ing 1.** To clew. **2.** *U.S. Informal* To give (someone) information. [Var. of CLEW]
clump (klump) *n.* **1.** A thick cluster: a *clump* of bushes. **2.** A heavy, dull sound, as of tramping. **3.** An irregular mass; a lump. — *v.i.* **1.** To walk clumsily and noisily. **2.** To form clumps. — *v.t.* **3.** To place or plant in a clump. [Var. of CLUB[1]] — **clump′y, clump′ish** *adj.*
clum·sy (klum′zē) *adj.* **·si·er, ·si·est 1.** Lacking dexterity, ease, or grace. **2.** Ungainly or unwieldy. **3.** Ill-contrived: a *clumsy* excuse. [< obs. *clumse* to be numb with cold] — **clum′si·ly** *adv.* — **clum′si·ness** *n.*
clung (klung) Past tense and past participle of CLING.
clus·ter (klus′tər) *n.* **1.** A collection of objects of the same kind growing or fastened together. **2.** A number of persons or things close together; group. — *v.t. & v.i.* To grow or form into a cluster or clusters. [OE *clyster*] — **clus′tered** *adj.* — **clus′ter·y** *adj.*
clutch[1] (kluch) *v.t.* **1.** To snatch, as with hands or talons. **2.** To grasp and hold firmly. — *v.i.* **3.** To attempt to seize, snatch, or reach: with *at*: He *clutched* at her hand. — *n.* **1.** A tight grip; grasp. **2.** *pl.* Power or control: in the *clutches* of the police. **3.** *Mech.* **a** Any of a number of devices for coupling two working parts, as the engine and driveshaft of an automobile. **b** A lever or pedal for operating such a device. **4.** A contrivance for gripping and holding. [ME *clucchen*]

CLUTCH
(*n. def.* 4)
a Fixed member. *b* Movable and splined member. *c* Collar. *d* Fork. *e* Lever.

clutch[2] (kluch) *n.* **1.** The number of eggs laid at one time. **2.** A brood of chickens. — *v.t.* To hatch. [< ON *klekja* hatch]
clut·ter (klut′ər) *n.* **1.** A disordered state or collection; litter. **2.** A clatter. — *v.t.* **1.** To litter, heap, or pile in a confused manner. — *v.i.* **2.** To make a clatter. [Var. of earlier *clotter*]
Clydes·dale (klīdz′dāl) *n.* A breed of draft horses originating in the valley of the Clyde, Scotland.
clyp·e·ate (klip′ē·āt) *adj.* Shield-shaped. Also **clyp·e·i·form** (klip′ē·ə·fôrm′). Also **clyp′e·at′ed.**
clys·ter (klis′tər) *n.* *Med.* An enema. [< OF < Gk. *klyster* < *klyzein* to wash out, rinse]
Cly·tem·nes·tra (klī′təm·nes′trə) The wife of Agamemnon, daughter of Leda. See ORESTES. Also **Cly′taem·nes′tra.**
co-[1] *prefix* With; together; joint or jointly; equally: used with verbs, nouns, adjectives, and adverbs. [< L *co-* var. of *com-* before *gn, h,* and vowels < *cum* with]
Following is a list of self-explanatory words containing the prefix *co-*:

coadminister	**codefendant**	**co-owner**
coadministrator	**coeditor**	**copartner**
coambassador	**coheir**	**copassionate**
coarrange	**coinvolve**	**copatron**
coauthor	**co-oblige**	**coreign**

co-[2] *prefix* **1.** *Math.* Of the complement: *cosine.* **2.** *Astron.* Complement of. [< L *complementum* complement]

coach (kōch) *n.* **1.** A large, four-wheeled closed carriage. **2.** A passenger bus. **3.** Air coach (which see). **4.** A railroad passenger car; esp., one having only seats and offering the cheapest travel. **5.** A private tutor. **6.** A trainer or director in athletics, dramatics, etc. — *v.t.* **1.** To tutor or train; act as coach to. — *v.i.* **2.** To study with or be trained by a coach. **3.** To act as coach. **4.** To ride or drive in a coach. [< MF < Hung. *kocsi* (*szeker*) (wagon) of Kocs, the village where first used]

coach-and-four (kōch′ən·fôr′, -fōr′) *n.* A coach drawn by four horses.

coach dog A Dalmatian.

coach·man (kōch′mən) *n. pl.* **·men** (-mən) One who drives a coach.

co·ad·ju·tant (kō·aj′ōō·tənt) *adj.* Cooperating. — *n.* An assistant or co-worker. [< CO-[1] + L *adjutare* to help]

co·ad·ju·tor (kō·aj′ōō·tər, kō′ə·jōō′tər) *n.* **1.** An assistant or co-worker. **2.** A bishop who assists a diocesan bishop.

co·ae·val (kō·ē′vəl) See COEVAL.

co·ag·u·la·ble (kō·ag′yə·lə·bəl) *adj.* Capable of being coagulated. — **co·ag′u·la·bil′i·ty** *n.*

co·ag·u·lant (kō·ag′yə·lənt) *n.* A coagulating agent, as rennet. [< L *coagulare* to curdle]

co·ag·u·late (kō·ag′yə·lāt) *v.t. & v.i.* **·lat·ed, ·lat·ing** To change from a liquid into a clot or jelly, as blood. [< L *coagulare* to curdle] — **co·ag′u·la′tion** *n.* — **co·ag′u·la′tive** *adj.* — **co·ag′u·la′tor** *n.*

coal (kōl) *n.* **1.** A dark brown to black, combustible mineral produced by the carbonization of prehistoric vegetation, found in beds or veins in the earth and used as fuel and a source of hydrocarbons. **2.** A piece of coal. **3.** A glowing or charred fragment of wood or other fuel; an ember. — **to carry coals to Newcastle** To provide something already in abundant supply. — **to haul** (**rake,** etc.) **over the coals** To criticize severely; reprimand. — *v.t.* **1.** To supply with coal. — *v.i.* **2.** To take on coal. [OE *col*]

Coal may appear as a combining form or as the first element in two-word phrases as in: **coalbin, coal-burning, coal dust, coal mine, coal-producing.**

co·a·lesce (kō′ə·les′) *v.i.* **·lesced, ·lesc·ing** To grow or come together into one; blend. [< L < *co-* together + *alescere* to grow up] — **co′a·les′cence** *n.* — **co′a·les′cent** *adj.*

coal gas **1.** The poisonous gas produced by the combustion of coal. **2.** A gas used for illuminating and heating, produced by the distillation of bituminous coal.

co·a·li·tion (kō·ə·lish′ən) *n.* **1.** An alliance of persons, parties, or states. **2.** A fusion into one mass. [< L < *co-* together + *alescere* to grow up] — **co′a·li′tion·ist** *n.*

coal oil **1.** Kerosene. **2.** Crude petroleum.

coal·scut·tle (kōl′skut′l) *n.* A bucketlike container in which coal may be kept or carried. Also **coal hod.**

coal tar A black, viscid liquid produced in the distillation of bituminous coal, yielding a variety of compounds used in making dyestuffs, drugs, plastics, etc. — **coal′-tar′** *adj.*

coam·ing (kō′ming) *n.* A curb about a hatchway or skylight, to keep water from entering. [Origin unknown]

coarse (kôrs, kōrs) *adj.* **1.** Lacking refinement; vulgar; low. **2.** Inferior; base; common. **3.** Composed of large parts or particles; not fine in texture. [Adjectival use of COURSE, meaning usual, ordinary] — **coarse′ly** *adv.* — **coarse′ness** *n.*

coarse-grained (kôrs′grānd′, kōrs′-) *adj.* **1.** Having a coarse grain or texture. **2.** Not delicate or refined; crude.

coars·en (kôr′sən, kōr′-) *v.t. & v.i.* To make or become coarse.

coast (kōst) *n.* **1.** The land next to the sea; the seashore. **2.** A slope suitable for sliding, as on a sled; also, a slide down it. — **Syn.** See SHORE[1]. — **the Coast** *U.S.* That part of the United States bordering on the Pacific Ocean. — **the coast is clear** There is no danger or difficulty now. — *v.i.* **1.** To slide down a slope by force of gravity alone, as on a sled. **2.** To continue moving on acquired momentum alone. **3.** To sail along a coast. — *v.t.* **4.** To sail along, as a coast; skirt. [< OF < L *costa* rib, flank] — **coast′al** *adj.*

coast·er (kōs′tər) *n.* **1.** One who or that which coasts, as a person or vessel engaged in the coasting trade. **2.** A sled or toboggan. **3.** A small disk of glass, metal, etc., set under a drinking glass to protect the surface beneath.

coaster brake A clutchlike brake on a bicycle, operated by reversing the pressure on the pedals.

coast guard Naval or military coastal patrol and police. — **United States Coast Guard** A force set up to protect life and property at sea and to enforce customs, immigration, and navigation laws, operating under the Department of the Treasury.

coast·line (kōst′līn′) *n.* The contour or boundary of a coast.

coast·ward (kōst′wərd) *adj.* Directed or facing toward the coast. — *adv.* Toward the coast: also **coast′wards.**

coast·wise (kōst′wīz′) *adj.* Following, or along the co — *adv.* Along the coast: also **coast′ways′** (-wāz′).

coat (kōt) *n.* **1.** A sleeved outer garment, as the jacket suit, or an overcoat or topcoat. **2.** A natural coverin integument, as the fur of an animal, the rind of a melon, **3.** Any layer covering a surface, as paint, ice, etc. — *v.t.* To cover with a surface layer, as of paint. **2.** To pro with a coat. [< OF *cote*] — **coat′ed** *adj.* — **coat′less**

co·a·ti (kō·ä′tē) *n. pl.* **·tis** (-tēz) A small, carnivorous, coonlike mammal of tropical America, with a mobile sn and plantigrade feet. Also **co·a′ti-mon′di** (-mun′dē), **cc ti-mun′di** (-mun′dē). [< Tupi]

coat·ing (kō′ting) *n.* **1.** A covering layer; coat. **2.** Cl for coats.

coat of arms **1.** A shield marked with the insignia of a son or family. **2.** A representation of such insignia.

coat of mail *pl.* **coats of mail** A defensive garment m of chain mail; a hauberk.

coat·tail (kōt′tāl′) *n.* The loose, back part of a coat be the waist; also, either half of this in a coat split at the b

coax (kōks) *v.t.* **1.** To persuade or seek to persuade gentleness, tact, flattery, etc.; wheedle. **2.** To obtain coaxing: to *coax* a promise from someone. — *v.i.* **3.** To persuasion or cajolery. — *n.* One who coaxes. [< ea *cokes* a fool, dupe] — **coax′er** *n.* — **coax′ing·ly** *adv.*

co·ax·i·al (kō·ak′sē·əl) *adj.* **1.** Having a common axi coincident axes. Also **co·ax·al** (kō·ak′səl). **2.** Describi cable consisting of two or more insulated conductors cap of transmitting radio or television signals or multiple graph or telephone messages.

cob (kob) *n.* **1.** A corncob. **2.** A male swan. **3.** A th set horse with short legs. **4.** A lump. [ME *cobbe*]

co·balt (kō′bôlt) *n.* A tough, lustrous, pinkish gray, me lic element (symbol Co), used as an alloy and in pigme See ELEMENT. [< G *kobalt*, var. of *kobold* goblin] — **bal′tic** *adj.* — **co·bal′tous** *adj.*

cobalt blue **1.** A permanent, deep blue pigment, m from oxides of cobalt and aluminum. **2.** An intense bl

cob·ble[1] (kob′əl) *n.* A cobblestone. — *v.t.* **·bled, ·bling** pave with cobblestones. [Akin to COB[1]]

cob·ble[2] (kob′əl) *v.t.* **·bled, ·bling** **1.** To repair, as sh **2.** To put together roughly. [Origin uncertain]

cob·bler[1] (kob′lər) *n.* One who patches boots and shoe

cob·bler[2] (kob′lər) *n.* **1.** An iced drink made of w sugar, fruit juices, etc. **2.** *U.S.* A deep-dish fruit pie v no bottom crust. [Origin unknown]

cob·ble·stone (kob′əl·stōn′) *n.* A naturally rounded st formerly used for paving.

cob coal Coal in large, round lumps.

co·bel·lig·er·ent (kō′bə·lij′ər·ənt) *n.* A country wa war in cooperation with another or others.

co·bra (kō′brə) *n.* A venomous snake of Asia and Af that when excited can dilate its neck into a broad hood; esp., the **spectacled cobra** of India, and the **king cobra.** [< Pg. < L *colubra* snake]

COBRA
a Indian or s tacled cobr
b Markings "spectacles on back of head. (To feet long)

cob·web (kob′web′) *n.* **1.** The network of fine thread spun by a spider; also, a single thread of this. **2.** Something like a cobweb in flimsiness, or in its ability to ensnare. — *v.t.* **·webbed, ·web·bing** To cover with or as with cobwebs. [ME *coppeweb* < *coppe* spider + WEB] — **cob′web′by** *adj.*

co·ca (kō′kə) *n.* **1.** The dried leaves of a South American shrub, yielding cocaine and other alkaloids. **2.** The shrub itself. [< Sp. < Quechua]

co·caine (kō·kān′, kō′kān; *in technical usage* kō′kə·ēn) *n.* A bitter, crystalline alkaloid, $C_{17}H_{21}NO_4$, contained in coca leaves, used as a local anesthetic and as a narcotic. Also **co·cain′, co′cain.** [< COCA + -INE[2]]

cocci- *combining form* Berry; berry-shaped. [< Gk. *kokkos* berry, seed]

coc·coid (kok′oid) *adj.* *Bacteriol.* Like a coccus, as cer forms of bacteria.

coc·cus (kok′əs) *n. pl.* **coc·ci** (kok′sī) *Bacteriol.* One of principal forms of bacteria, characterized by an ovoid spherical shape. [< NL < Gk. *kokkos* berry]

-coccus *combining form* Berry-shaped. [< Gk. *kok* berry, seed]

coc·cyx (kok′siks) *n. pl.* **coc·cy·ges** (kok·sī′jēz) *Anat.* small triangular bone consisting of four or five rudiment vertebrae at the caudal end of the spine. For illus. see P VIS. [< L < Gk. *kokkyx* cuckoo; from a fancied res blance to a cuckoo's bill] — **coc·cyg·e·al** (kok·sij′ē·əl)

coch·i·neal (koch′ə·nēl′, koch′ə·nēl) *n.* A brilliant sca dye prepared from the dried bodies of the female of a s insect of tropical America and Java. [< F < Sp. < L Gk. *kokkos*]

h·le·a (kok′lē·ə) *n. pl.* **·le·ae** (-li·ē) *Anat.* A spirally und tube in the internal ear, forming an essential part of mechanism of hearing. For illus. see EAR. [< L, snail] **coch′le·ar** *adj.*

h·le·ate (kok′lē·āt) *adj.* Spirally twisted like a snail ll. Also **coch′le·at′ed.**

k[1] (kok) *n.* **1.** A full-grown male of the domestic fowl; a ster. **2.** Any male bird. **3.** A leader; champion. **4.** A cet, often with the nozzle bent downward. **5.** In a fire- n, the hammer; also, the condition of readiness for firing. A significant jaunty tip or upward turn, as of a hat brim. *v.t.* **1.** To set the mechanism of (a firearm) so as to be dy for firing. **2.** To turn up or to one side alertly, jaunt- or inquiringly, as the head, eye, ears, etc. **3.** To bring a position of readiness. — *v.i.* **4.** To cock a firearm. **5.** stick up prominently. — *adj.* Male. [OE *cocc*]

k[2] (kok) *n.* A conical pile of straw or hay. — *v.t.* To ar- ge in piles or cocks, as hay. [< ON *kökkr* lump, heap]

k·ade (kok·ād′) *n.* A knot of ribbon, or the like, worn the hat as a badge. [< MF *coq* cock] — **cock·ad′ed** *adj.*

kade State Nickname of Maryland.

k·a·too (kok′ə·tōō′, kok′ə·tōō) *n. pl.* **·toos** Any of ious brightly colored, crested parrots of the East Indies Australia. [< Du. < Malay *kakatūa*]

k·a·trice (kok′ə·tris) *n.* A fabulous serpent, said to be ched from a cock's egg, deadly to those who felt its breath met its glance. [< OF *cocatris* (infl. by *coq* cock)]

k·boat (kok′bōt) *n.* A ship's small rowboat: also called **kle boat.** [< obs. *cock* (< MF *coque* small boat) + BOAT]

k·chaf·er (kok′chā′fər) *n.* A large European beetle tructive to vegetation. [< COCK[1] (def. 3) + CHAFER]

k·crow (kok′krō′) *n.* Early morning. Also **cock′crow′·**

ked hat (kokt) A hat with the brim turned up, esp. in ee places; a tricorn. — **to knock into a cocked hat** To nolish; ruin.

k·er·el (kok′ər·əl) *n.* A cock less than a year old.

k·er spaniel (kok′ər) A small, sturdy spaniel of solid or iegated coloring, used for hunting and as a house pet. o **cocker.** [? Because used in hunting woodcock]

k·eye (kok′ī) *n.* A squinting eye.

k·eyed (kok′īd′) *adj.* **1.** Cross-eyed. **2.** *Slang* Off cen- ; askew. **3.** *Slang* Absurd; ridiculous. **4.** *Slang* Drunk.

k·fight (kok′fīt′) *n.* A fight between gamecocks that are ially fitted with steel spurs. — **cock′fight′ing** *adj. & n.*

k·horse (kok′hôrs′) *n.* A rocking horse or hobbyhorse.

k·le[1] (kok′əl) *n.* **1.** A European bivalve mollusk, esp. edible species, with ridged, somewhat heart-shaped shells. Any of various similar mollusks. **3.** A cockleshell. **4.** A inkle; pucker. — **the cockles of one's heart** The depths one's heart or feelings. — *v.t. & v.i.* **·led, ·ling** To wrin- ; pucker. [< F < L < Gk. *konchē* a shell, mussel]

k·le[2] (kok′əl) *n.* A weed that grows among grain, as the nel. [OE *coccel*]

k·le·bur (kok′əl·bûr′) *n.* **1.** A coarse, branching weed ving burs about an inch long. **2.** The burdock.

k·le·shell (kok′əl·shel′) *n.* **1.** The shell of a cockle. **2.** A llop shell. **3.** A frail, light boat. [< COCKLE[1] + SHELL]

k·ney (kok′nē) *n.* **1.** *Often cap.* A resident of the East d of London. **2.** The dialect or accent of East End Lon- ners: also **cock′ney·ese′** (-ēz′, -ēs′). — *adj.* Of or like kneys or their speech. [ME *cokeney*, lit., a pampered ld, a soft person, a city man] — **cock′ney·ish** *adj.*

k·ney·ism (kok′nē·iz′əm) *n.* A mannerism, idiom, or y of speaking peculiar to cockneys.

k·pit (kok′pit′) *n.* **1.** A compartment in the fuselage of ne small airplanes, where the pilot and copilot sit. **2.** A or ring for cockfighting. **3.** *Naut.* In small vessels, a ce toward the stern lower than the rest of the deck.

k·roach (kok′rōch′) *n.* Any of a large group of swift- ning, chiefly nocturnal insects, many of which are house- d pests. [< Sp. *cucaracha*]

ks·comb (koks′kōm′) *n.* **1.** The comb of a cock. **2.** A nt with showy red or yellowish flowers. **3.** A coxcomb.

k·spur (kok′spûr′) *n.* **1.** A spur on the leg of a cock. **2.** kind of hawthorn with long thorns.

k·sure (kok′shŏŏr′) *adj.* **1.** Absolutely sure. **2.** Overly -confident; presumptuously sure. — **cock′sure′ness** *n.*

k·swain (kok′sən, -swān′) See COXSWAIN.

k·tail (kok′tāl′) *n.* **1.** Any of various chilled alcoholic nks, consisting usu. of brandy, whisky, gin, etc., mixed th other liquors, fruit juice, etc. **2.** An appetizer, as chilled ed fruits, fruit juices, or seafood seasoned with sauce. [? er. of F *coquetel*]

k·y (kok′ē) *adj.* **cock·i·er, cock·i·est** *Informal* Pertly or aggeringly self-confident; conceited. — **cock′i·ly** *adv.* — **k′i·ness** *n.*

o (kō′kō) *n. pl.* **·cos 1.** The coconut palm. **2.** The fruit of the coconut palm. — *adj.* Made of the fiber of the coconut. [< Pg., grinning face]

co·coa (kō′kō) *n.* **1.** A powder made from the roasted, husked seed kernels of the cacao; chocolate. **2.** A beverage made from this. **3.** A reddish brown color. [Alter. of CACAO]

cocoa butter A fatty substance obtained from cacoa seeds, used for making soap, cosmetics, etc.: also called *cacao butter.*

co·co·nut (kō′kə·nut′, -nət) *n.* The fruit of the coconut palm, having white meat enclosed in a hard shell, and containing a milky liquid. Also **co′coa·nut′.**

coconut milk The milky fluid within the fresh coconut.

coconut oil The oil derived from the dried meat of the coconut, used in soaps, foodstuffs, etc.

coconut palm A tropical palm tree bearing coconuts. Also **coco palm, coconut tree.**

co·coon (kə·kōōn′) *n.* The envelope spun by the larvae of certain insects, in which they are enclosed in the pupal or chrysalis state. [< F *coque* shell]

cod (kod) *n. pl.* **cod** or **cods** An important food fish of the North Atlantic. [Origin unknown]

co·da (kō′də) *n. Music* A passage at the end of a composition or movement that brings it to a formal, complete close. [< Ital. < L *cauda* tail]

cod·dle (kod′l) *v.t.* **·dled, ·dling 1.** To boil gently; simmer in water. **2.** To treat as a baby or an invalid; pamper. [? Akin to CAUDLE] — **cod′dler** *n.*

code (kōd) *n.* **1.** A systematized body of law. **2.** Any system of principles or regulations. **3.** A set of signals, characters, or symbols used in communication. **4.** A set of words, letters, or numerals, used for secrecy or brevity in transmitting messages. — *v.t.* **cod·ed, cod·ing 1.** To systematize, as laws; make a digest of. **2.** To put into the symbols of a code. [< F < L *codex* writing tablet]

co·deine (kō′dēn, kō′di·ēn) *n. Chem.* A white crystalline alkaloid, $C_{18}H_{21}NO_3$, derived from morphine and used in medicine as a mild narcotic. Also **co·de·in** (kō′dē·in, kō′dēn), **co·de·ia** (kō·dē′ə). [< Gk. *kōdeia* head of a poppy + -INE[2]]

co·dex (kō′deks) *n. pl.* **co·di·ces** (kō′də·sēz, kod′ə-) An ancient manuscript volume, as of Scripture. [< L, tablet]

codg·er (koj′ər) *n. Informal* An eccentric or testy man, esp. an old one. [Prob. var. of *cadger*]

cod·i·cil (kod′ə·səl) *n.* **1.** *Law* A supplement to a will, changing or explaining something in it. **2.** An appendix; addition. [< L *codex* writing tablet] — **cod·i·cil·la·ry** (kod′ə·sil′ər·ē) *adj.*

cod·i·fy (kod′ə·fī, kō′də-) *v.t.* **·fied, ·fy·ing** To systematize, as laws. [< F *code* system, code] — **cod′i·fi·ca′tion** *n.* — **cod′i·fi′er** *n.*

cod·ling[1] (kod′ling) *n. pl.* **·lings** (*Rare* **·ling**) **1.** A young cod. **2.** Any of certain related fishes. [Dim. of COD[1]]

cod·ling[2] (kod′ling) *n.* **1.** One of a variety of elongated tapering cooking apples. **2.** Any hard, unripe apple for stewing. Also **cod·lin** (kod′lin). [ME *querdling*]

codling moth A moth whose larvae feed on apples, pears, quinces, etc. Also **codlin moth.**

cod-liver oil (kod′liv′ər, kod′liv′ər) Oil from the livers of cod, used in medicine as a source of vitamins A and D.

co·ed (kō′ed′) *Informal n.* A woman student at a coeducational institution. — *adj.* Coeducational. Also **co′-ed′.**

co·ed·u·ca·tion (kō′ej·ōō·kā′shən) *n.* The education of both sexes in the same school. — **co′ed·u·ca′tion·al** *adj.*

co·ef·fi·cient (kō′ə·fish′ənt) *n.* **1.** *Math.* A number or letter put before an algebraic expression and multiplying it. **2.** *Physics* A number indicating the kind and amount of change in a substance, body, or process under given conditions. — *adj.* Acting together.

coe·la·canth (sē′lə·kanth) *n. Zool.* A large-bodied, hollow-spined fish, extinct except for one species. [< COEL(O)- + Gk. *akantha* spine]

COELACANTH (4 to 5½ feet long)

-coele Var. of -CELE[2].

coe·len·ter·ate (si·len′tə·rāt) *Zool. n.* Any of a phylum of invertebrate animals having a large body cavity that functions as a vascular as well as a digestive system, including sea anemones, corals, jellyfish, and hydras. — *adj.* Belonging or pertaining to this phylum. [< COEL(O)- + Gk. *enteron* intestine] — **coe·len·ter·ic** (sē′len·ter′ik) *adj.*

coe·li·ac (sē′lē·ak) See CELIAC.

coelo- *combining form* Cavity; cavity of the body, or of an organ. Also, before vowels, **coel-.** [< Gk. *koilos* hollow]

coe·lom (sē′ləm) *n. Zool.* The body cavity of a metazoan, between the viscera and the body wall: also spelled *celom.* Also **coe·lome** (sē′lōm). [< Gk. *koilōma* cavity]

coeno- See CENO-.

coe·no·bite (sen′ə·bīt, sē′nə-) See CENOBITE.

co·e·qual (kō·ē′kwəl) *adj.* Of the same value, age, size, etc. — *n.* The equal of another or others.

co·erce (kō·ûrs′) *v.t.* **·erced, ·erc·ing 1.** To compel by force, law, authority, or fear. **2.** To restrain or repress by superior force. **3.** To bring about by forcible measures: to *coerce* compliance. [< L < *co-* together + *arcere* to shut up, restrain] — **co·er′cer** *n.* — **co·er′ci·ble** *adj.*

co·er·cion (kō·ûr′shən) *n.* **1.** Forcible constraint or restraint, moral or physical. **2.** Government by force. — **co·er·cion·ar·y** (kō·ûr′shən·er′ē) *adj.* — **co·er′cion·ist** *n.*

co·er·cive (kō·ûr′siv) *adj.* Serving or tending to coerce. — **co·er′cive·ly** *adv.* — **co·er′cive·ness** *n.*

co·e·val (kō·ē′vəl) *adj.* **1.** Of or belonging to the same age, time, or duration. **2.** Contemporary. — *n.* **1.** One of the same age. **2.** A contemporary. Also spelled *coaeval.* [< L < *co-* together + *aevum* age] — **co·e′val·ly** *adv.*

co·ex·ist (kō′ig·zist′) *v.i.* To exist together, in or at the same place or time. — **co′ex·ist′ence** *n.* — **co′ex·ist′ent** *adj.*

co·ex·tend (kō′ik·stend′) *v.t. & v.i.* To extend through the same space or time. [< CO-[1] + EXTEND] — **co′ex·ten′·sion** *n.* — **co′ex·ten′sive** *adj.* — **co′ex·ten′sive·ly** *adv.*

cof·fee (kôf′ē, kof′ē) *n.* **1.** A beverage made from the roasted and ground beans of a tropical evergreen shrub. **2.** The seeds or beans of this shrub: also **coffee beans. 3.** The shrub itself, native to Asia and Africa and widely grown in Brazil. **4.** The brown color of coffee with cream. [< Ital. < Turkish < Arabic *qahwah*]

coffee break *U.S.* A short recess from work during which coffee or other refreshments are taken.

coffee cake A kind of cake to be eaten with coffee, often containing raisins or nuts and topped with sugar or icing.

coffee house A public room where coffee is the main beverage. Also **cof·fee·house** (kôf′ē·hous′, kof′ē-).

coffee shop A restaurant or public room where coffee and food are served. Also **coffee room.**

coffee table A low table, generally placed in front of a sofa, for serving refreshments, etc.

cof·fer (kôf′ər, kof′-) *n.* **1.** A chest or box, esp. one for valuables. **2.** *pl.* Financial resources; a treasury. **3.** A decorative, sunken panel in a ceiling, dome, etc. **4.** A lock in a canal. **5.** A cofferdam. — *v.t.* **1.** To place in a coffer. **2.** To adorn with coffers. [< F < L < Gk. *kophinos* basket]

cof·fer·dam (kôf′ər·dam, kof′-) *n.* **1.** A temporary enclosure built in the water and pumped dry to permit work on bridge piers and the like. **2.** A watertight structure attached to a ship's side for repairs made below the water line.

cof·fin (kôf′in, kof′-) *n.* A box or case in which a corpse is buried. — *v.t.* To put into or as into a coffin. [< OF < L < Gk. *kophinos* basket]

cog (kog) *n.* **1.** *Mech.* A tooth or one of a series of teeth projecting from the surface of a wheel or gear to impart or receive motion. **2.** One who plays a minor but necessary part in a large or complex process. **3.** A projecting part on the end of a timber, used for forming a joint; tenon. [ME *cogge* < Scand.] — **cogged** *adj.*

co·gent (kō′jənt) *adj.* Compelling belief, assent, or action; forcible; convincing. [< L < *cogere* to compel] — **co′gen·cy** *n.* — **co′gent·ly** *adv.*

cog·i·tate (koj′ə·tāt) *v.t. & v.i.* **·tat·ed, ·tat·ing** To give careful thought (to); ponder; meditate. [< L < *co-* together + *agitare* to consider] — **cog·i·ta·ble** (koj′ə·tə·bəl) *adj.* — **cog′i·ta′tor** *n.*
— **Syn.** think, deliberate, reflect, reason, cerebrate.

cog·i·ta·tion (koj′ə·tā′shən) *n.* Careful consideration; reflection; thought.

cog·i·ta·tive (koj′ə·tā′tiv) *adj.* Capable of or given to cogitation. — **cog′i·ta′tive·ly** *adv.* — **cog′i·ta′tive·ness** *n.*

co·gnac (kōn′yak, kon′-) *n.* **1.** Brandy produced in the Cognac region of western France. **2.** Any brandy. [< F]

cog·nate (kog′nāt) *adj.* **1.** Allied by blood; kindred. **2.** Allied by derivation from the same source; belonging to the same stock or root: English "cold" and Latin "gelidus" are *cognate* words. **3.** Allied in characteristics; similar. — *n.* A cognate person or thing. [< L < *co-* together + pp. of (*g*)*nasci* to be born] — **cog·na′tion** *n.*

cog·ni·tion (kog·nish′ən) *n.* **1.** The act or faculty of knowing or perceiving. **2.** A thing known; a perception. — **Syn.** See KNOWLEDGE. [< L < *co-* together + (*g*)*noscere* to know] — **cog·ni′tion·al** *adj.* — **cog′ni·tive** *adj.*

cog·ni·za·ble (kog′nə·zə·bəl, kon′ə-, kog·nī′zə·bəl) *adj.* **1.** Capable of being known. **2.** Capable of being tried or examined by a court. — **cog′ni·za·bly** *adv.*

cog·ni·zance (kog′nə·zəns, kon′ə-) *n.* **1.** Apprehension or perception of fact; knowledge; notice. **2.** *Law* **a** The hearing of a case by a court. **b** The right of a court to hear a case. **3.** Range or sphere of what can be known. — **to take cognizance of** To acknowledge; recognize; notice. [< OF < L < *co-* together + pp. of (*g*)*nasci* to be born]

cog·ni·zant (kog′nə·zənt, kon′ə-) *adj.* Having knowledge; aware: with *of.*

cog·nize (kog′nīz) *v.t.* **·nized, ·niz·ing** To know, perceive, or recognize. Also *Brit.* **cog′nise.**

cog·no·men (kog·nō′mən) *n.* *pl.* **·no·mens** or **·nom·i·na** (-nom′ə·nə) **1.** A surname. **2.** In ancient Rome, the las a citizen's three names. **3.** Loosely, any name, nicknam appelation. [< L < *co-* together + (*g*)*nomen* name] **cog·nom·i·nal** (kog·nom′ə·nəl) *adj.*

cog·wheel (kog′hwēl′) *n.* A wheel with cogs, used to tr mit or receive motion: also called *gearwheel.*

co·hab·it (kō·hab′it) *v.i.* To live together as husband wife, esp. illegally. [< LL < L < *co-* together + *hab* to live] — **co·hab′i·tant, co·hab′it·er** *n.* — **co·hab′i tion** *n.*

co·here (kō·hir′) *v.i.* **·hered, ·her·ing 1.** To stick or firmly together. **2.** To be logically connected, as the par a story. [< L < *co-* together + *haerere* to stick]

co·her·ence (kō·hir′əns) *n.* **1.** A sticking together; junction; cohesion. **2.** Logical connection or consiste congruity: the *coherence* of his thoughts. Also **co·her′en**

co·her·ent (kō·hir′ənt) *adj.* **1.** Sticking together, as p cles of the same substance. **2.** Observing logical order connection; consistent. **3.** Intelligible or articulate speech. — **co·her′ent·ly** *adv.*

co·he·sion (kō·hē′zhən) *n.* **1.** The act or state of cohe **2.** *Physics* That force by which molecules of the same or the same body are held together.

co·he·sive (kō·hē′siv) *adj.* Having or exhibiting cohes — **co·he′sive·ly** *adv.* — **co·he′sive·ness** *n.*

co·hort (kō′hôrt) *n.* **1.** The tenth of an ancient Roma gion, 300 to 600 men. **2.** A band or group, esp. of warr **3.** A companion or follower. [< L *cohors, cohortis*]

coif (koif) *n.* A close-fitting cap or hood, as that wor nuns under the veil. — *v.t.* To cover with or as with a [< OF < LL *cofea* < Gmc.]

coif·feur (kwȧ·fœr′) *n.* *French* A hairdresser.

coif·fure (kwä·fyŏŏr′, *Fr.* kwȧ·für′) *n.* **1.** A style of arr ing or dressing the hair. **2.** A headdress. — *v.t.* To d (the hair). Also **coif** (kwäf). [< F < OF *coife.* See co

coign (koin) *n.* A projecting angle or stone; a corner. **coigne.** [Var. of QUOIN]

coil (koil) *n.* **1.** A series of concentric rings or spiral that formed by winding a rope. **2.** A single ring or spir such a series. **3.** A spiral pipe, or series of pipes, formi continuous conduit, as in a radiator. **4.** *Electr.* **a** A con tor consisting of a number of turns of wire wound on an i lating coil. **b** An induction coil. **5.** *Canadian* A small s of hay. — *v.t.* **1.** To wind spirally or in rings. — *v.i* To form rings or coils. [< OF < L < *com-* together + *l* to choose] — **coil′er** *n.*

coin (koin) *n.* **1.** A piece of metal stamped by governn authority for use as money. **2.** Metal currency collecti **3.** *Archit.* A corner or angle of a building; quoin. — *v.t* To stamp (coins) from metal. **2.** To make into coins. To originate or invent, as a word or phrase. — **to money** *Informal* To make money rapidly. [< F, wedge < L *cuneus* wedge] — **coin′a·ble** *adj.* — **coin′er** *n.*

coin·age (koi′nij) *n.* **1.** The act or right of making c **2.** The coins made; metal money. **3.** The system of coi a country; currency. **4.** The act of fabricating or inven anything, esp. a word or phrase. **5.** Something fabrica as an artificially created word.

co·in·cide (kō′in·sīd′) *v.i.* **·cid·ed, ·cid·ing 1.** To have same dimensions and position in space. **2.** To occur at same time. **3.** To agree exactly; accord. [< MF < M < L *co-* together + *incidere* to happen]

co·in·ci·dence (kō·in′sə·dəns) *n.* **1.** The fact or condi of coinciding; correspondence. **2.** A remarkable con rence of events, ideas, etc., apparently by mere chance.

co·in·ci·dent (kō·in′sə·dənt) *adj.* **1.** Having the same p tion and extent. **2.** Occurring at the same time. **3.** In e agreement; consonant: with *with.* — **co·in′ci·dent·ly** *ad*

co·in·ci·den·tal (kō·in′sə·den′təl) *adj.* Characterized b involving coincidence. — **co·in′ci·den′tal·ly** *adv.*

coir (koir) *n.* Coconut-husk fiber, used in making ro matting, etc.: also called *kyar.* [< Malay *kāyar* rope]

co·i·tion (kō·ish′ən) *n.* Sexual intercourse. Also **co·i** (kō′i·təs). [< L < *co-* together + *ire* to go]

coke (kōk) *n.* A solid, carbonaceous fuel obtained by h ing coal in ovens or retorts to remove its gases. — *v.t. &* **coked, cok·ing** To change into coke. [? ME *colke.*]

col-[1] Var. of COM-.

col-[2] Var. of COLO-.

co·la (kō′lə) A small tropical tree bearing cola nuts: spelled *kolo.* [< *kola* native African name]

cola nut The seed of the cola, yielding an extract used in manufacture of soft drinks: also spelled *kola nut.*

col·an·der (kul′ən·dər, kol′-) *n.* A perforated vessel draining off liquids: also *cullender.* [< L *colare* to str

cold (kōld) *adj.* **1.** Having a relatively low temperat having little or no perceptible heat: a *cold* night. **2.** Ha a relatively low temperature as compared with a nor body temperature: *cold* hands. **3.** Feeling no or insuffic warmth; chilled. **4.** Without vital heat; dead. **5.** tached; objective: *cold* reason. **6.** Lacking in affection.

acking in sexual desire; frigid. **8.** Unfriendly. **9.** Chilling the spirit; depressing. **10.** *U.S. Informal* Unconscious, from a blow. **11.** Lacking freshness; stale; old: a *cold* ail. **12.** *Informal* Distant from the object sought: said of a eker in a game, etc. **13.** In art, bluish in tone. **— cold et** *Informal* Loss of courage; timidity. **— to throw cold ater on** To discourage by being unenthusiastic or indiffert (about something). **—** *adv. U.S. Slang* Thoroughly; ith certainty: to know it *cold.* **—** *n.* **1.** The comparative ck of heat. **2.** The sensation caused by loss or lack of heat. An acute infection of the mucous membranes of the upper spiratory tract, caused by a virus, and characterized by eezing, coughing, etc. **— out in the cold** Ignored; neected. **— to catch** (or **take**) **cold** To become affected with cold. [OE *cald*] **— cold′ly** *adv.* **— cold′ness** *n.*

ld-blood·ed (kōld′blud′id) *adj.* **1.** Unsympathetic; artless. **2.** Sensitive to cold. **3.** *Zool.* Having a blood mperature that varies with the environments, as in repes. **— cold′-blood′ed·ly** *adv.* **— cold′-blood′ed·ness** *n.*

ld chisel A chisel of tempered steel for cutting cold metal.

ld cream A cleansing and soothing ointment for the skin.

ld front *Meteorol.* The irregular, forward edge of a cold r mass advancing beneath and against a warmer mass.

ld·heart·ed (kōld′här′tid) *adj.* Without sympathy; unnd. **— cold′heart′ed·ly** *adv.* **— cold′heart′ed·ness** *n.*

ld shoulder *Informal* A deliberate slight.

ld sore An eruption about the mouth or nostrils, often acmpanying a cold or fever.

ld turkey *U.S. Slang* **1.** The abrupt and total deprivaon of a substance, as a narcotic drug, from one addicted to s use. **2.** Blunt talk, often unwelcome to the listener.

ld war An intense rivalry between nations, as in diploatic strategy, falling just short of armed conflict.

ld wave *Meteorol.* An unusual drop in temperature; a ell of cold weather, usu. moving along a specified course.

le (kōl) *n.* A plant related to the cabbage, esp. rape. Also **le′wort′** (-wûrt). [OE *cāl, cāwl* < L *caulis* cabbage]

le·op·ter·ous (kō′lē·op′tər·əs, kol′ē-) *adj.* Belonging to a rge order of insects, including the beetles and weevils, havg horny front wings that fit as cases over the hind wings. < NL < Gk. *koleos* sheath + *pteron* wing]

le·slaw (kōl′slô′) *n.* A salad of shredded raw cabbage. lso **cole slaw.** [< Du *kool sla* cabbage salad]

l·ic (kol′ik) *n.* Acute abdominal pain resulting from muslar spasms. **—** *adj.* Pertaining to, near, or affecting the lon. [< F < L < Gk. *kolon* colon] **— col′ick·y** *adj.*

line Var. of -COLOUS.

l·i·se·um (kol′ə·sē′əm) *n.* A large building or stadium for hibitions, sports events, etc.: also spelled *colosseum.*

l·i·se·um (kol′ə·sē′əm) See COLOSSEUM.

li·tis (kə·lī′tis) *n. Pathol.* Inflammation of the colon.

l·lab·o·rate (kə·lab′ə·rāt) *v.i.* **·rat·ed, ·rat·ing** **1.** To ork or cooperate with another, esp. in literary or scientific ursuits. **2.** To be a collaborationist. [< LL < L *com-* ith + *laborare* to work] **— col·la′bo·ra′tion** *n.* **— col·ab′o·ra′tive** *adj.* **— col·lab′o·rat′or** *n.*

l·lab·o·ra·tion·ist (kə·lab′ə·rā′shən·ist) *n.* A citizen of n occupied country who cooperates with the enemy.

l·lage (kə·läzh′) *n.* An artistic composition consisting of including flat materials pasted on a picture surface; so, the technique of making such compositions. Compare SSEMBLAGE (def. 4). [< F, pasting < *colle* glue]

l·lapse (kə·laps′) *v.* **·lapsed, ·laps·ing** *v.i.* **1.** To give way; ve in. **2.** To fail utterly; come to naught. **3.** To assume a ore compact form by being folded. **4.** To lose health, rength, etc., suddenly. **5.** To lose all or part of its air connt, as a lung. **—** *v.t.* **6.** To cause to collapse. **—** *n.* **1.** he act or process of collapsing. **2.** Extreme prostration. . Utter failure; ruin. [< L < *com-* together + *labi* to fall] **— col·laps′i·ble** or **col·laps′a·ble** *adj.* **— col·laps′i·bil′i·ty** *n.*

l·lar (kol′ər) *n.* **1.** The part of a garment at the neck, ten folded over. **2.** A band of leather or metal for the eck of an animal. **3.** A cushion placed around the neck of a raft animal to bear most of the strain of the pull. **4.** *Mech.* ny of various devices encircling a rod or shaft, to form connection, etc. **—** *v.t.* **1.** To provide with a collar. **2.** To rasp by the collar; capture. [< OF, AF < L *collum* neck]

l·lar·bone (kol′ər·bōn′) *n.* The clavicle.

l·lard (kol′ərd) *n. Usu. pl.* A variety of cabbage that oes not form a head. [Alter. of *colewort.* See COLE.]

l·late (kə·lāt′, kol′āt) *v.t.* **·lat·ed, ·lat·ing** **1.** To compare itically, as writings or facts. **2.** In bookbinding, to exame (the gathered sheets to be bound) in order to verify and orrect their arrangement. [< L < *com-* together + *ferre* to ear, carry] **— col·la·tor** (kə·lā′tər, kol′ā·tər) *n.*

l·lat·er·al (kə·lat′ər·əl) *adj.* **1.** Lying or running side by de; parallel. **2.** Concomitant. **3.** Tending to the same onclusion; corroborative. **4.** Subordinate; secondary. **5.** Guaranteed by stocks, bonds, property, etc.: a *collateral* loan. **6.** Descended from a common ancestor, but in a different line. **—** *n.* **1.** *U.S.* Security pledge for a loan or obligation. **2.** A collateral kinsman. [< Med.L < L *com-* together + *lateralis* lateral] **— col·lat′er·al·ly** *adv.*

collateral adjective An adjective closely related to a given noun in meaning, but not in immediate origin, as *brachial* is to *arm.*

col·la·tion (kə·lā′shən) *n.* **1.** The act or process of collating. **2.** Any light, informal meal. [See COLLATE.]

col·league (kol′ēg) *n.* A fellow member of a profession, official body, etc.; an associate. [< F < L < *com-* together + *legere* to choose] **— col′league·ship** *n.*

col·lect[1] (kə·lekt′) *v.t.* **1.** To gather together; assemble. **2.** To bring together as a hobby: to *collect* stamps. **3.** To request and obtain (payments of money). **4.** To regain control: to *collect* one's wits. **—** *v.i.* **5.** To assemble or congregate, as people. **6.** To accumulate, as sand or dust. **7.** To gather payments or donations. **—** *adj. & adv.* To be paid for by the receiver: Send it *collect*; a *collect* call. [< L *collectus,* pp. of *colligere* < *com-* together + *legere* to choose] **— col·lect′a·ble** or **col·lect′i·ble** *adj.*

col·lect[2] (kol′ekt) *n. Eccl.* A short, formal prayer used in several Western liturgies. [See COLLECT[1].]

col·lect·ed (kə·lek′tid) *adj.* Composed; self-possessed. **— col·lect′ed·ly** *adv.* **— col·lect′ed·ness** *n.*

col·lec·tion (kə·lek′shən) *n.* **1.** The act or process of collecting. **2.** That which is collected. **3.** That which has accumulated: a *collection* of dirt. **4.** A soliciting of money, as for church expenses; also, the money.

col·lec·tive (kə·lek′tiv) *adj.* **1.** Formed or gathered together by collecting. **2.** Of, relating to, or proceeding from a number of persons or things together. **3.** *Gram.* Denoting in the singular number a collection or aggregate of individuals: a *collective* noun. **—** *n.* **1.** A collective enterprise or body, as a farm. **2.** The individuals comprising such a body or enterprise. **— col·lec′tive·ly** *adv.* **— col·lec′tive·ness, col·lec·tiv·i·ty** (kol′ek·tiv′ə·tē) *n.*

collective bargaining Negotiation between organized workers and employers on wages, hours, etc.

collective noun *Gram.* A singular noun naming a collection or group. It takes either a singular or a plural verb, depending upon whether it refers to the objects composing it as one aggregate or as separate individuals: The audience *was* large; The audience *were* divided in opinion.

col·lec·tiv·ism (kə·lek′tiv·iz′əm) *n.* A system in which the people as a whole, or the state, own and control the material and means of production and distribution. **— col·lec′tiv·ist** *adj. & n.* **— col·lec′tiv·is′tic** *adj.*

col·lec·tiv·ize (kə·lek′tiv·īz) *v.t.* **·ized, ·iz·ing** To organize (an agricultural settlement, industry, economy, etc.) on a collectivist basis. **— col·lec′tiv·i·za′tion** *n.*

col·lec·tor (kə·lek′tər) *n.* **1.** One who or that which collects. **2.** One who collects taxes, duties, debts, etc.

col·leen (kol′ēn, kə·lēn′) *n. Irish* A girl. [< Irish *cailīn*]

col·lege (kol′ij) *n.* **1.** A school of higher learning that grants a bachelor's degree at the completion of a course of study. **2.** Any of the undergraduate divisions or schools of a university. **3.** A school for instruction in a special field or a profession. **4.** A building or buildings used by a college or university. **5.** A body of associates engaged in a common task and having certain rights: the electoral *college.* [< OF < L *collegium* body of associates]

College of Cardinals In the Roman Catholic Church, the body of cardinals who elect and advise the Pope, and, in his absence, administer the Holy See: also called *Sacred College.*

col·le·gian (kə·lē′jən, -jē·ən) *n.* A college student.

col·le·giate (kə·lē′jit, -jē·it) *adj.* Of, like, or intended for a college or for college students.

col·lide (kə·līd′) *v.i.* **·lid·ed, ·lid·ing** **1.** To come together with violent impact; crash. **2.** To come into conflict; clash. [< L < *com-* together + *laedere* to strike]

col·lie (kol′ē) *n.* A large sheep dog of Scottish breed, characterized by a long, narrow head and full, long-haired coat. [Prob. < Scottish Gaelic *cuilean* puppy]

col·lier (kol′yər) *n.* **1.** *Chiefly Brit.* A coal miner. **2.** A vessel for carrying coal. [OE *col* coal + -IER]

col·lier·y (kol′yər·ē) *n. pl.* **·lier·ies** A coal mine.

col·li·mate (kol′ə·māt) *v.t.* **·mat·ed, ·mat·ing** **1.** To bring into line or make parallel, as refracted rays of light. **2.** To adjust the line of sight of (a telescope, etc.). [< L < *com-* together + *lineare* to align] **— col′li·ma′tion** *n.*

col·li·ma·tor (kol′ə·mā′tər) *n. Optics.* A device used to obtain parallel rays of light, as a fixed telescope or the convex lens in a spectroscope. For illus. see SPECTROSCOPE.

col·li·sion (kə·lizh′ən) *n.* **1.** The act of colliding; a violent striking together. **2.** A clash of views or interests; conflict.

col·lo·cate (kol′ō·kāt) *v.t.* **·cat·ed, ·cat·ing** To place together or in relation; arrange. [< L < *com-* together + *locare* to place] **—col′lo·ca′tion** *n.*

col·lo·di·on (kə·lō′dē·ən) *n.* A flammable solution used as a coating for wounds and formerly for photographic plates. Also **col·lo·di·um** (kə·lō′dē·əm). [< Gk. < *kolla* glue]

col·loid (kol′oid) *n.* **1.** Any gluelike or jellylike substance, as gelatin, starch, raw egg white, etc., that diffuses not at all or very slowly through vegetable and animal membranes. **2.** *Chem.* A state of matter in which finely divided particles of one substance are suspended in another in such manner that the electrical and surface properties acquire special importance. **—** *adj.* Of or pertaining to a colloid or the colloid state: also **col·loi·dal** (kə·loid′l). [< Gk. *kolla* glue + -OID] **—col·loi·dal·i·ty** (kol′oi·dal′ə·tē) *n.*

col·lo·qui·al (kə·lō′kwē·əl) *adj.* **1.** Denoting a manner of speaking or writing that is characteristic of familiar conversation; informal. **2.** Conversational. **—col·lo′qui·al·ly** *adv.* **—col·lo′qui·al·ness** *n.*

col·lo·qui·al·ism (kə·lō′kwē·əl·iz′əm) *n.* **1.** An expression or form of speech of the type used in informal conversation. **2.** Informal, conversational style.

col·lo·quy (kol′ə·kwē) *n.* *pl.* **·quies** A conversation or conference, esp. a formal one. [< L < *com-* together + *loqui* to speak] **—col′lo·quist** *n.*

col·lude (kə·lōōd′) *v.i.* **·lud·ed, ·lud·ing** To cooperate secretly; conspire; connive. [< L < *com-* together + *ludere* to play, trick] **—col·lud′er** *n.*

col·lu·sion (kə·lōō′zhən) *n.* A secret agreement for a wrongful purpose; conspiracy. [See COLLUDE.]

col·lu·sive (kə·lōō′siv) *adj.* Secretly arranged to defraud another or to circumvent the law. **—col·lu′sive·ly** *adv.* **—col·lu′sive·ness** *n.*

colo- *combining form Anat.* Colon. Also, before vowels, **col-**. [< Gk. *kolon* colon]

co·logne (kə·lōn′) *n.* A toilet water consisting of alcohol scented with aromatic oils: also called *eau de Cologne.* Also **Cologne water.** [after *Cologne*]

co·lon[1] (kō′lən) *n.* *pl.* **co·lons** A punctuation mark (:), used as a sign of apposition or equality to connect one clause with another that explains it, after a word introducing a quotation, citation, etc., after the salutation in a formal letter, in expressing clock time, and in mathematical proportions. [< L < Gk. *kōlon* member, limb, clause]

co·lon[2] (kō′lən) *n.* *pl.* **co·lons** or **co·la** (kō′lə) *Anat.* The portion of the large intestine between the cecum and the rectum. For illus. see INTESTINE. [< L < Gk. *kolon*] **—co·lon·ic** (kə·lon′ik) *adj.*

co·lon[3] (kō·lōn′) *n.* *pl.* **co·lons** (kō·lōnz′), *Sp.* **co·lo·nes** (kō·lō′nās) The monetary unit of Costa Rica and El Salvador.

colo·nel (kûr′nəl) *n.* *Mil.* A commissioned officer ranking next above a lieutenant colonel and next below a brigadier or brigadier general. See tables at GRADE. Abbr. *Col.* [< MF < Ital. *colonna* column of soldiers] **—colo′nel·cy, colo′nel·ship** *n.*

co·lo·ni·al (kə·lō′nē·əl) *adj.* **1.** Of, pertaining to, or living in a colony or colonies. **2.** Of or referring to the thirteen original colonies of the U.S. **3.** Describing a style of architecture that originated in the American colonies. **—** *n.* A citizen or inhabitant of a colony. **—co·lo′ni·al·ly** *adv.*

co·lo·ni·al·ism (kə·lō′nē·əl·iz′əm) *n.* The policy of a nation seeking to acquire, extend, or retain overseas dependencies.

col·o·nist (kol′ə·nist) *n.* **1.** A member or inhabitant of a colony. **2.** A settler or founder of a colony.

col·o·nize (kol′ə·nīz) *v.* **·nized, ·niz·ing** *v.t.* **1.** To set up a colony in; settle. **2.** To establish as colonists. **—** *v.i.* **3.** To establish or unite in a colony or colonies. Also *Brit.* **col′o·nise. —col′o·ni·za′tion** *n.* **—col′o·niz′er** *n.*

col·on·nade (kol′ə·nād′) *n.* *Archit.* A series of regularly spaced columns, usually supporting an entablature. [< F < *colonne* column] **—col′on·nad′ed** *adj.*

col·o·ny (kol′ə·nē) *n.* *pl.* **·nies** **1.** A body of emigrants living in a land apart from, but under the control of, the parent country. **2.** The region thus settled. **3.** Any territory politically controlled by a distant state. **4.** A group of individuals from the same country, of the same occupation, etc., living in a particular part of a city, state, or country: a Chinese *colony.* **5.** The region or quarter occupied by such a group. **6.** *Biol.* A group of organisms of the same species functioning in close association as certain bacteria. **7.** *Ecol.* A group of similar plants or animals living in a particular locality. **—the Colonies** The British colonies that became the original thirteen States of the United States: New Hampshire, Massachusetts, Rhode Island, Connecticut, New York, New Jersey, Pennsylvania, Delaware, Maryland, Virginia, North Carolina, South Carolina, and Georgia. [< L *colonus* farmer]

col·o·phon (kol′ə·fon, -fən) *n.* An emblematic device adopted by a publisher, usu. printed on the title page of his books. [< LL < Gk. *kolophōn* summit, finishing touch]

col·or (kul′ər) *n.* **1.** A visual attribute of bodies or substances that depends upon the spectral composition of the wavelengths stimulating the retina and its associated neu structures. Colors are classified as *achromatic* (black a white and the grays), and *chromatic* (green, blue, red, et **2.** A paint, dyestuff, or pigment. **3.** Complexion; hue the skin. **4.** Ruddy complexion; also, a blush. **5.** T complexion of those peoples not classed as Caucasians, e of Negroes. **6.** *pl.* The ensign or flag of a nation, military naval unit, etc. **7.** A color, ribbon, badge, etc., used identification: college *colors.* **8.** *pl.* The side, or the opinic arguments, etc., one upholds: Stick to your *colors.* **9.** O ward appearance; semblance; aspect: a *color* of reas **10.** A false appearance; pretext; disguise: under *color* religion. **11.** General character; sort; kind. **12.** Liv ness or vividness, esp. in literary work. **13.** In art a literature, the use of characteristic details to produc realistic effect: local *color.* **14.** In art, the total effect of colors in a painting. **15.** *Music* Timbre. **16.** *pl.* In U.S. Navy, the salute made when the national flag is hois in the morning or lowered in the evening. **—to cha color** **1.** To turn pale. **2.** To blush. **—to lose color** turn pale. **—to show one's (true) colors** To show one's n nature, beliefs, etc. **—** *v.t.* **1.** To apply or give color to by painting, staining, or dyeing. **2.** To misrepresent by tortion or exaggeration. **3.** To modify, influence, or cha in nature or character. **—** *v.t.* **4.** To take on or change co as ripening fruit. **5.** To blush. Also *Brit.* **col′our.** [< < L *color*] **—col′or·er** *n.*

col·or·a·ble (kul′ər·ə·bəl) *adj.* **1.** That may be colored. Capable of appearing true or right. **3.** Specious but app ently plausible; deceptive. Also *Brit.* **col′our·a·ble. —c or·a·bil′i·ty, col′or·a·ble·ness** *n.* **—col′or·a·bly** *adv.*

col·o·ra·do (kol′ə·rä′dō) *adj.* Having medium stren and color: said of cigars. [< Sp., colored, red]

col·or·a·tion (kul′ə·rā′shən) *n.* Arrangement of colors, in an animal or plant; coloring.

col·or·a·tu·ra (kul′ər·ə·tŏŏr′ə, -tyŏŏr′ə) *n.* **1.** In vo music, runs, trills, or other florid decoration. **2.** Music ch acterized by this. **3.** A coloratura soprano. **—** *adj.* Char terized by or suitable for coloratura. [< Ital., colorati

coloratura soprano A soprano voice or a singer able sing coloratura.

color blindness The inability to preceive chromatic co or, more commonly, to distinguish one of the three prim colors. **—col·or·blind** (kul′ər·blīnd′) *adj.*

col·or·cast (kul′ər·kast′, -käst′) *n.* A television broadc in color. **—** *v.t.* & *v.i.* In television, to broadcast in colc

col·ored (kul′ərd) *adj.* **1.** Having color. **2.** Of a race ot than the Caucasoid; especially, wholly or partially Neg **3.** Of or relating to Negroes. **4.** Influenced or distort biased; tainted. **5.** False or misleading; specious.

Col·ored (kul′ərd) *n.* *pl.* **Col·ored** In South Africa, a pers of mixed African and European or Asian parentage.

col·or·fast (kul′ər·fast′, -fäst′) *adj.* Resistant to fading running: *colorfast* fabrics.

col·or·ful (kul′ər·fəl) *adj.* **1.** Full of colors, especially c trasting colors. **2.** Full of variety; vivid; picturesque *colorful* story. **—col′or·ful·ly** *adv.* **—col′or·ful·ness** *n.*

color guard Those who conduct the colors in a ceremon

col·or·im·e·ter (kul′ə·rim′ə·tər) *n.* An apparatus for termining the hue, purity, and brightness of a color.

col·or·ing (kul′ər·ing) *n.* **1.** The act or manner of apply colors. **2.** A substance used to impart color. **3.** Appe ance of anything as to color. **4.** False appearance.

col·or·ist (kul′ər·ist) *n.* **1.** One who uses color. **2.** artist who uses colors skillfully. **—col′or·is′tic** *adj.*

col·or·less (kul′ər·lis) *adj.* **1.** Without color. **2.** Weak color; pallid. **3.** Lacking vividness or variety; dull.

color line A social, political, and economic distincti drawn between the white and other races.

co·los·sal (kə·los′əl) *adj.* **1.** Of immense size or exte enormous; huge. **2.** *Informal* Beyond belief or understar ing: *colossal* pride. [< COLOSSUS] **—co·los′sal·ly** *adv.*

col·os·se·um (kol′ə·sē′əm) See COLISEUM.

Col·os·se·um (kol′ə·sē′əm) An amphitheater in Ro built by Vespasian and Titus in A.D. 75–80: also *Coliseu*

Co·los·sian (kə·losh′ən) *n.* **1.** A native or inhabitant Colossae. **2.** *pl.* (*construed as sing.*) A book of the N Testament, Saint Paul's epistle to the Colossians.

co·los·sus (kə·los′əs) *n.* *pl.* **co·los·si** (kə·los′ī) or **co·l sus·es** **1.** A gigantic statue. **2.** Something of great size stature. [< L < Gk. *kolossos* gigantic statue]

Colossus of Rhodes A gigantic bronze statue of Apollo the entrance to the harbor of ancient Rhodes about 285 B

col·our (kul′ər) See COLOR.

-colous *combining form* Dwelling in or inhabiting. A *-coline.* [< L *colere* to dwell, inhabit]

colt (kōlt) *n.* **1.** A young horse, donkey, etc.; esp., young male horse. **2.** A young or inexperienced pers [OE] **—colt′ish** *adj.*

col·ter (kōl′tər) *n.* A blade or disk on a plow that cuts t sod: also spelled *coulter.* [OE < L *culter* knife]

·u·brine (kol′yə·brīn, -brin) *adj.* **1.** Of or like a snake. Of or pertaining to a family of snakes that includes the rter snake, blacksnake, etc. [< L *coluber* snake]

·um·bar·i·um (kol′əm·bâr′ē·əm) *n. pl.* **·bar·i·a** (-bâr′ē·ə) dovecote; also, a pigeonhole in a dovecote. Also **col·um·ır·y** (kol′əm·ber′ē). [< L < *columba* dove]

l·um·bi·a (kə·lum′bē·ə) *n. Poetic* The personification of e United States of America. [after Christopher *Columbus*] · **Co·lum′bi·an** *adj.*

·um·bine (kol′əm·bīn) *n.* A herbaceous plant with ıriously colored flowers of five petals; esp., the **Colorado lumbine,** State flower of Colorado. **—** *adj.* Dovelike. < F < L *columba* dove]

l·um·bine (kol′əm·bīn) A stock character im pantomimes, e daughter of Pantaloon and sweetheart of Harlequin.

lum·bi·um (kə·lum′bē·əm) *n.* Former name for the eleənt niobium. [< NL < *Columbia*, the United States]

lumbus Day October 12, a holiday in most of the U.S. ımmemorating the discovery of America by Columbus.

·umn (kol′əm) *n.* **1.** *Archit.* A post or pillar; esp., ıch a member consisting of base, shaft, ıd capital, serving as support or ornaent. **2.** Something suggesting a column: e spinal *column.* **3.** *Printing* A section printed matter on a page, usu. narrow ıd enclosed by a rule or blank space. An entertaining or instructive feature ticle that appears regularly in a newsıper or periodical. **5.** *Mil. & Naval* A rmation in which elements of troops, hicles, ships, or aircraft are placed one hind another. [< L *columna*] **— co·m·nar** (kə·lum′nər), **col·umned** (kol′·ad) *adj.*

a
b
c
d
e
f
g

CORINTHIAN COLUMN WITH ENTABLATURE (*a, b, c*)
a Cornice.
b Frieze.
c Architrave.
d Capital.
e Astragal.
f Shaft.
g Base.

lum·ni·a·tion (kə·lum′nē·ā′shən) *n.* *rch.* The use or grouping of columns.

l·um·nist (kol′əm·nist, -əm·ist) *n.* One ho writes or conducts a special column in newspaper or periodical.

·za (kol′zə) *n.* The summer rape whose eds produce rape oil. [< F < Du. *kool* ıbbage + *zaad* seed]

lza oil Rape oil.

n- *prefix* With; together: *combine, comıre.* Also: *co-* before *gn, h* and vowels; *l-* before *l*, as in *collide*; *con-* before *c, d, g, j, n, q, s, t, v*, as in *concur, confluence, nnect, conspire*; *cor-* before *r*, as in *rrespond.* [< L *com-* < *cum* with]

ma[1] (kō′mə) *n. pl.* **·mas** **1.** *Pathol.* condition of profound unconsciousness ıused by disease, poison, or severe physical or nervous jury. **2.** Stupor. [< NL < Gk. *kōma* deep sleep]

ma[2] (kō′mə) *n. pl.* **·mae** (-mē) **1.** *Astron.* A luminous, ıseous envelope around the nucleus of a comet. **2.** *Bot.* A ıft of silky hairs, as at the end of certain seeds. [< L, hair Gk. *komē*] **— co′mal** *adj.*

·man·che (kō·man′chē, kə-) *n. pl.* **·ches** **1.** An Indian Shoshonean stock, ranging between Kansas and northern [exico, now in Oklahoma. **2.** The language of this tribe.

ma·tose (kō′mə·tōs, kom′ə-) *adj.* **1.** Relating to or afıcted with coma or unconsciousness. **2.** Lethargic; torpid. < COMA[1]] **— co′ma·tose·ly** *adv.*

mb (kōm) *n.* **1.** A toothed strip of hard, often flexible aterial, used for smoothing, dressing, or fastening the hair. A thing resembling this, as a card for dressing wool or ıx. **3.** The fleshy crest on the head of a fowl. **4.** Honeyımb. **—** *v.t.* **1.** To dress or smooth with or as with a comb. To card, as wool or flax. **3.** To search carefully. **—** *v.i.* To crest and break: said of waves. [OE *camb*]

n·bat (*n.* kom′bat, kum′-; *v.* kəm·bat′) *n.* A battle or ght; struggle. **— close combat** Hand-to-hand fighting. **single combat** A fight between two persons. **—** *v.* **·bat·ed** **·bat·ted, ·bat·ing** or **·bat·ting** *v.t.* **1.** To fight or contend ith; oppose in battle. **2.** To resist. **—** *v.i.* **3.** To do ıttle; struggle: with *with* or *against.* [< F < L *com-* with *batuere* to fight, beat] **— com·bat·a·ble** (kəm·bat′ə·bəl, ım′bat·ə·bəl, kum′-) *adj.* **— com·bat·er** (kom′bat·ər, ım′-, kəm·bat′ər) *n.*

n·bat·ant (kəm·bat′nt, kom′bə·tənt, kum′-) *n.* One ıgaged in or prepared for combat or hostilities. **—** *adj.* Fighting; battling. **2.** Ready or disposed to fight.

nbat fatigue *Psychiatry* A psychoneurotic disorder ıaracterized by anxiety, depression, loss of control, etc., ısociated with the stresses of modern warfare: formerly ılled *shell shock*: also called *battle fatigue.*

n·bat·ive (kəm·bat′iv, kom′bə·tiv, kum′-) *adj.* Apt or ıger to fight. **— com·bat′ive·ly** *adv.* **— com·bat′ive·ness** *n.*

comb·er kō′mər) *n.* **1.** One who or that which combs wool, flax, etc. **2.** A long, crested wave.

com·bi·na·tion (kom′bə·nā′shən) *n.* **1.** The act of joining together or the state of being joined; union. **2.** That which is formed by combining. **3.** An alliance, as of persons, to further a common interest, activity, etc. **4.** The series of numbers or letters forming the key to a combination lock; also, the mechanism of such a lock. **5.** Underwear consisting of an undershirt and underpants made in one piece. **6.** *Math.* Any selection of a group of units such that the order of selection is immaterial, as 123, 321, and 213. **— com′bi·na′tion·al, com′bi·na′tive** *adj.*

combination lock A lock that can be opened only by moving a dial in a set sequence of turns.

com·bine (*v.* kəm·bīn′; *n.* kom′bīn) *v.* **·bined, ·bin·ing** *v.t.* **1.** To bring together into close union; blend; merge; unite. **2.** To possess in union. **—** *v.i.* **3.** To become one, or parts of a whole. **4.** To associate for a purpose. **5.** *Chem.* To enter into combination. **—** *n.* **1.** A combination. **2.** *U.S. Informal* A group of persons united in pursuit of selfish commercial or political ends; a trust; ring. **3.** *Agric.* A machine that reaps, threshes, and cleans grain while harvesting it. [< LL < L *com-* together + *bini* two by two] **— com·bin′a·ble** *adj.* **— com·bin′er** *n.*

combining form The stem of a word, usu. of Greek or Latin origin, as *tele-* and *-phone* in *telephone,* or an English word unchanged, as *over* in *overeat,* used in combination with other forms to create compounds.

com·bo (kom′bō′) *n. Informal* **1.** Combination. **2.** A small jazz or dance band, usually three or four musicians.

com·bus·ti·ble (kəm·bus′tə·bəl) *adj.* **1.** Capable of burning easily. **2.** Easily excited; fiery. **—** *n.* Any substance that will readily burn, as paper or wood. **— com·bus′ti·ble·ness, com·bus′ti·bil′i·ty** *n.* **— com·bus′ti·bly** *adv.*

com·bus·tion (kəm·bus′chən) *n.* **1.** The action or operation of burning. **2.** *Chem.* **a** Oxidation of a substance, accompanied by the generation of heat and sometimes light. **b** Slow oxidation, as of food in the body. **3.** Violent disturbance; tumult. [< LL < L *comburere* to burn up] **— com·bus′tive** *adj.*

come (kum) *v.i.* **came, come, com·ing** **1.** To move to or toward the speaker; approach. **2.** To arrive as the result of motion or progress. **3.** To advance or move into view. **4.** To arrive in due course or in orderly progression: when your turn *comes.* **5.** To occur in time: Labor Day *came* late that year. **6.** To reach or extend. **7.** To arrive at some state or condition: to *come* to harm. **8.** To happen; occur: *come* what may. **9.** To exist as an effect or result: This *comes* of trifling. **10.** To emanate or proceed; be derived. **11.** To become: The wheel *came* loose. **12.** To turn out or prove to be: His prediction *came* true. **13.** To be offered, obtainable, or produced: The car *comes* in many colors. **14.** To act as the speaker wishes: used in the imperative and expressing impatience, anger, protest, etc. **— to come about** **1.** To take place; happen. **2.** *Naut.* To turn to the opposite tack. **— to come across** **1.** To meet with or find by chance. **2.** *Slang* To give or do what is requested. **— to come around** (or **round**) **1.** To recover or revive. **2.** To change or turn, as in direction or opinion. **3.** *Informal* To pay a visit. **— to come at** **1.** To reach. **2.** To attain. **3.** To attack. **— to come back** **1.** To return. **2.** *Informal* To regain former status; make a comeback. **3.** *Slang* To reply sharply. **— to come by** **1.** To pass near. **2.** To acquire; get. **— to come down** **1.** To lose status, wealth, etc. **2.** To descend as by inheritance. **— to come in** **1.** To enter. **2.** To arrive. **3.** To be brought into use. **— to come in for** *Informal* **1.** To be eligible to receive. **2.** To acquire; get. **— to come into** **1.** To inherit. **2.** To enter into; join. **— to come of** **1.** To be descended from. **2.** To result from. **— to come off** **1.** To become detached. **2.** To happen; occur. **3.** To emerge from action or trial; acquit oneself. **— to come on** **1.** To meet by chance. **2.** To make progress; develop. **3.** To enter, as on stage. **— to come out** **1.** To be made public; be published. **2.** To make one's debut. **3.** To speak frankly; declare oneself. **4.** To result; end. **— to come out with** **1.** To declare openly. **2.** To offer; publish. **— to come through** **1.** To be successful (in). **2.** To survive. **3.** To wear through. **4.** *Informal* To give or do what is required. **— to come to** **1.** To recover; revive. **2.** To amount to. **3.** To result in. **4.** *Naut.* **a** To turn close to the wind. **b** To anchor. **— to come up** **1.** To arise; appear. **2.** *Naut.* **a** To come closer to the wind. **b** To slacken. **— to come upon** **1.** To chance upon. **2.** To attack. **— to come up to** **1.** To equal; rival. **2.** To reach. **— to come up with** *U.S. Informal* **1.** To propose or produce: *to come up with* an idea. **2.** To overtake. [OE *cuman*]

come·back (kum′bak′) *n.* **1.** *Informal* A return, as to health or lost position. **2.** *Slang* A smart retort.

co·me·di·an (kə·mē′dē·ən) *n.* **1.** An actor in comedies. **2.** An entertainer specializing in jokes, comic skits, and the like. **3.** One who continually tries to be funny. **4.** A person who writes comedy. [< F *comédien*]
co·me·di·enne (kə·mē′dē·en′) *n.* A female comedian. [< F]
come·down (kum′doun′) *n.* A descent to a lower condition or position; a humiliating or disappointing setback.
com·e·dy (kom′ə·dē) *n. pl.* **·dies 1.** A play, motion picture, etc., dealing with human folly in a light and humorous manner, and having a happy ending. **2.** The branch of drama treating of such themes. **3.** The art or theory of composing comedy. **4.** An incident, situation, etc., resembling comedy. [< MF < L < Gk. < *kōmos* revel + *aeidein* to sing] — **co·me·dic** (kə·mē′dik, -med′ik) *adj.* — **co·me′di·cal·ly** *adv.*
comedy of manners A satiric comedy portraying the manners, customs, and foibles of the fashionable world.
come·ly (kum′lē) *adj.* **·li·er, ·li·est 1.** Pleasing in person; handsome; graceful. **2.** Suitable; becoming. [OE *cȳmlic* < *cȳme* fine] — **come′li·ly** *adv.* — **come′li·ness** *n.*
come-on (kum′on′, -ôn′) *n. U.S. Slang* **1.** Someone or something that lures. **2.** A beckoning look or gesture.
com·er (kum′ər) *n.* **1.** One who comes or arrives. **2.** *Informal* One who or that which shows great promise.
co·mes·ti·ble (kə·mes′tə·bəl) *Rare adj.* Edible. — *n. Usu. pl.* Food. [< MF < LL < L *comedere* to eat up]
com·et (kom′it) *n. Astron.* A celestial body moving in an orbit about the sun and consisting of a nucleus of more or less condensed material, accompanied by a tenuous coma pointing away from the sun. [OE < L < Gk. *komētēs* long-haired] — **com·et·ar·y, co·met·ic** (kə·met′ik) *adj.*
come·up·pance (kum′up′əns) *n. U.S. Informal* The punishment one deserves; just deserts. Also **come′up′ance.**
com·fit (kum′fit, kom′-) *n.* A sweetmeat; confection. [< OF < L *confectus.* Related to CONFECT.]
com·fort (kum′fərt) *n.* **1.** A state of mental or physical ease. **2.** Relief from sorrow, distress, etc. **3.** One who or that which brings ease or consolation. **4.** Help or support: aid and *comfort.* **5.** *U.S.* A bed comforter. — *v.t.* **1.** To cheer in time of grief or trouble; solace; console. **2.** *Law* To aid; help. [< OF < LL < L *com-* with + *fortis* strong] — **com′fort·ing** *adj.* — **com′fort·ing·ly** *adv.*
com·fort·a·ble (kum′fər·tə·bəl, kumf′tə·bəl, -tər-) *adj.* **1.** Imparting comfort and satisfaction. **2.** Free from physical or mental distress; content; at ease. **3.** *Informal* Moderate; adequate: a *comfortable* income. — **com′fort·a·ble·ness** *n.* — **com′fort·a·bly** *adv.*
com·fort·er (kum′fər·tər) *n.* **1.** One who comforts. **2.** *U.S.* A thick, quilted bedcover: also called *comfort.*
comfort station A public toilet or rest room.
com·ic (kom′ik) *adj.* **1.** Of or pertaining to comedy. **2.** Provoking mirth; funny; ludicrous. — *n.* **1.** A comic actor or entertainer. **2.** The humorous element in art, life, etc. **3.** *pl. Informal* Comic strips or a book of comic strips. [< L < Gk. *kōmos* revelry]
com·i·cal (kom′i·kəl) *adj.* Causing merriment; funny; ludicrous. — **Syn.** See HUMOROUS. — **com·i·cal·i·ty** (kom′ə·kal′ə·tē), **com′i·cal·ness** *n.* — **com′i·cal·ly** *adv.*
comic opera An opera or operetta having a humorous plot and spoken dialogue.
comic strip A strip of cartoons printed in a newspaper, etc.
Com·in·form (kom′in·fôrm) *n.* The Communist Information Bureau, established in 1947 and dissolved in 1956. [< COM(MUNIST) INFORM(ATION)]
com·ing (kum′ing) *adj.* **1.** Approaching, esp. in time: the *coming* year. **2.** On the way to fame or distinction. — *n.* The act of approaching; arrival; advent.
com·ing-out (kum′ing·out′) *n. Informal* Debut into society.
Com·in·tern (kom′in·tûrn) *n.* An international organization formed in 1919 for extending the scope of Marxist socialism, and dissolved in 1943: also called *Third International.* [< COM(MUNIST) INTERN(ATIONAL)]
com·i·ty (kom′ə·tē) *n. pl.* **·ties** Courtesy; civility. [< L *comitas, -tatis* courtesy]
comity of nations The courteous recognition that one nation accords to the laws and usages of another.
com·ma (com′ə) *n.* **1.** A punctuation mark (,) indicating a slight separation in ideas or in grammatical construction within a sentence. **2.** Any pause or separation. [< L < Gk. *komma* short phrase]
comma bacillus *Bacteriol.* A bacillus shaped like a comma and causing Asiatic cholera.
com·mand (kə·mand′, -mänd′) *v.t.* **1.** To order, require, or enjoin with authority. **2.** To control or direct authoritatively; rule; have at one's disposal or use. **3.** To overlook, as from a height. **4.** To exact as being due or proper: to *command* respect. — *v.i.* **5.** To be in authority; rule. **6.** To overlook something from a superior position. — *n.* **1.** The act of commanding; bidding. **2.** The authority to command. **3.** That which is commanded; an order. **4.** Dominating power as achieved through superior position. **5.** Ability to control; mastery: *command* of one's emotic **6.** *Mil. & Naval* The unit or units under the command one person; also, the base of operations of such a unit. OF < LL < L *com-* thoroughly + *mandare* to order]
com·man·dant (kom′ən·dant′, -dänt′) *n.* A command officer, as of a service school, military district, etc.
com·man·deer (kom′ən·dir′) *v.t.* **1.** To force into milit service. **2.** To seize for public use, especially under milit necessity. **3.** *Informal* To take by force or constraint.
com·mand·er (kə·man′dər, -män′-) *n.* **1.** One who c mands or is in command. **2.** *Mil.* The commissioned offi in command of a force or post. **3.** *Naval* A commissio officer ranking next above a lieutenant commander next below a captain. See table at GRADE. — **com·ma er·ship** *n.*
commander in chief *pl.* **commanders in chief 1.** *O cap.* One holding supreme command of the armed forces nation: in the U.S., the President. **2.** The officer comma ing a fleet, major force, etc.
com·mand·ing (kə·man′ding, -män′-) *adj.* **1.** Exercis command. **2.** Impressive; imperious. **3.** Dominating, from a height. — **com·mand′ing·ly** *adv.*
commanding officer In the Royal, Royal Canadian, other Commonwealth navies, a commissioned officer. table at GRADE.
com·mand·ment (kə·mand′mənt, -mänd′-) *n.* **1.** An thoritative mandate; edict; order; law. **2.** *Sometimes c* One of the Ten Commandments.
com·man·do (kə·man′dō, -män′-) *n. pl.* **·dos** or **·does 1** special fighting force trained for quick, destructive raids i enemy territory. **2.** A member of such a unit. **3.** South Africa, especially in the Boer War, a force of mili also, a raid. [< Afrikaans < Pg., a group commanded
command post The field headquarters of a military ur
com·mem·o·rate (kə·mem′ə·rāt) *v.t.* **·rat·ed, ·rat·ing** celebrate the memory of. Also **com·mem′o·rize** (-ə·rīz). **Syn.** See CELEBRATE. [< L < *com-* together + *memor* to remember] — **com·mem′o·ra′tor** *n.*
com·mem·o·ra·tion (kə·mem′ə·rā′shən) *n.* **1.** The act commemorating, or that which commemorates. **2.** A co memorative observance. — **com·mem′o·ra′tion·al** *adj.*
com·mem·o·ra·tive (kə·mem′ə·rā′tiv, -rə·tiv) *adj.* Serv to commemorate. Also **com·mem·o·ra·to·ry** (kə·mem′ə tôr′ē, -tō′rē). — *n.* Anything that commemorates.
com·mence (kə·mens′) *v.t. & v.i.* **·menced, ·menc·ing** start; begin; originate. [< OF < L *com-* thoroughly *initiare* to begin] — **com·menc′er** *n.*
com·mence·ment (kə·mens′mənt) *n.* **1.** A beginni origin. **2.** The ceremony at a college or school during wh degrees are conferred; also, the day such a ceremony is he
com·mend (kə·mend′) *v.t.* **1.** To express a favorable op ion of; praise. **2.** To recommend. **3.** To present the gards of. **4.** To commit with confidence. [< L < co thoroughly + *mandare* to order] — **com·mend′a·ble** *a* — **com·mend′a·ble·ness** *n.* — **com·mend′a·bly** *adv.*
com men·da·tion (kom′ən·dā′shən) *n.* **1.** The act of co mending; approbation. **2.** Something that commends.
Commendation Ribbon A U.S. military decoration c sisting of a ribbon and medallion. See DECORATION.
com·mend·a·to·ry (kə·men′də·tôr′ē, -tō′rē) *adj.* Servi ing to commend; expressing commendation.
com·men·sal (kə·men′səl) *adj.* **1.** Eating together. *Zool.* Associated with another in close but nonparasitic lationship. [< OF < L *com-* together + *mensa* table]
com·men·su·ra·ble (kə·men′shər·ə·bəl, -sər·ə-) *adj.* **1.** pable of being measured by a common standard or unit. Fitting as to proportion; proportionate. [< LL < L *co* together + *mensurabilis* measurable] — **com·men′su·bil′i·ty** *n.* — **com·men′su·ra·bly** *adv.*
com·men·su·rate (kə·men′shə·rit, -sə·rit) *adj.* **1.** Havi the same measure or extent. **2.** In proper proportion; a quate. **3.** Commensurable. [< LL < L *com-* together *mensurare* to measure] — **com·men′su·rate·ly** *adv.* **com·men′su·rate·ness** *n.* — **com·men′su·ra′tion** *n.*
com·ment (kom′ent) *n.* **1.** A written note of explanati illustration, or criticism, as of a literary passage. **2.** A mark made in observation or criticism. **3.** Talk; conver tion. — *v.i.* **1.** To make a comment or comments. — **2.** To make comments on. [< OF < L *comminisci* to c trive] — **com′ment·er** *n.*
com·men·tar·y (kom′ən·ter′ē) *n. pl.* **·ries 1.** A series illustrative of explanatory notes. **2.** A comment. **3.** series of remarks. **4.** *Usu. pl.* A historical narrative memoir. [< L *comminisci* to contrive, devise] — **co men·tar·i·al** (kom′ən·târ′ē·əl) *adj.*
com·men·ta·tor (kom′ən·tā′tər) *n.* **1.** One who writes co mentaries. **2.** One who discusses or analyzes news event
com·merce (kom′ərs) *n.* **1.** The exchange of materia products, etc., esp. on a large scale between states or tions; extended trade. **2.** Social intercourse. **3.** Sexual tercourse. — **Department of Commerce** An executive

artment of the U.S. government headed by the Secretary ' Commerce, that supervises transportation and shipping, ·e census, and food and drug laws. [< F < L < *com-* ·gether + *merx, mercis* wares]
m·mer·cial (kə·mûr′shəl) *adj.* **1.** Of, relating to, or en- ıged in commerce; mercantile. **2.** Produced in large quan- ties. **3.** Having financial gain as an object. — *n.* In radio ıd television, an advertisement. — **com·mer·ci·al·i·ty** (kə- ıûr′shē·al′ə·tē) *n.* — **com·mer′cial·ly** *adv.*
m·mer·cial·ism (kə·mûr′shəl·iz′əm) *n.* **1.** The spirit or ıethods of commerce. **2.** Commercial practices or customs. - **com·mer′cial·ist** *n.* — **com·mer′cial·is′tic** *adj.*
m·mer·cial·ize (kə·mûr′shəl·īz) *v.t.* **·ized, ·iz·ing** To put ı a commercial basis; make a matter of business or profit. - **com·mer′cial·i·za′tion** *n.*
mmercial paper Any of various short-term negotiable apers, as drafts, bills of exchange, promissory notes, etc.
m·mie (kom′ē) *n. Often cap. Informal* A Communist.
m·min·gle (kə·ming′gəl) *v.t. & v.i.* **·gled, ·gling** To mix ›gether; mingle. [< COM- + MINGLE]
m·mi·nute (kom′ə·nōōt, -nyōōt) *v.t.* **·nut·ed, ·nut·ing** To ›duce to minute particles; pulverize. [< L < *com-* thor- ughly + *minuere* to lessen] — **com′mi·nu′tion** *n.*
m·mis·er·ate (kə·miz′ə·rāt) *v.* **·at·ed, ·at·ing** *v.t.* **1.** To ›el or express sympathy for; pity. — *v.i.* **2.** To express ympathy; condole: used with *with.* [< L < *com-* with + *iiserari* to feel pity] — **com·mis′er·a′tive** *adj.* — **com·** **is′er·a′tive·ly** *adv.* — **com·mis′er·a′tor** *n.*
m·mis·er·a·tion (kə·miz′ə·rā′shən) *n.* A feeling or ex- ression of sympathy; compassion.
m·mis·sar (kom′ə·sär, kom′ə·sär′) *n.* Formerly, an of- cial in charge of a commissariat of the Soviet government. < Russ. *komissar*]
m·mis·sar·i·at (kom′ə·sâr′ē·ət) *n.* **1.** The department f an army charged with providing food and daily necessi- ›es; also, the officers or supplies of such a department. **2.** ormerly, any major department of the Soviet government.
m·mis·sar·y (kom′ə·ser′ē) *n. pl.* **·sar·ies** **1.** A store elling food, equipment, etc., as at a camp or military post. . An authority delegated for a special duty. **3.** In the oviet Union, a commissar. [See COMMISSAR.] — **com·** **ıis·sar·i·al** (kom′ə·sâr′ē·əl) *adj.* — **com′mis·sar′y·ship** *n.*
m·mis·sion (kə·mish′ən) *n.* **1.** The act of committing › the charge of another; an entrusting. **2.** The matter or rust so committed; a charge. **3.** Authorization or command › act as specified. **4.** A written warrant conferring a par- icular authority or power. **5.** *Mil.* **a** An official document onferring rank and authority. **b** The rank or authority onferred. **6.** A body of persons acting under lawful au- hority to perform certain duties. **7.** The fee or percentage iven an agent or salesman for his services. **8.** The condi- ion of being authorized or delegated. **9.** The act of com- ıitting; also, the act itself. — **in commission** In active ervice or use; usable. — **out of commission** Not in active ervice or use; laid up for repairs, etc. — *v.t.* **1.** To give ank or authority to. **2.** *Naval* To put into active service ınder a commander, as a ship. **3.** To appoint; delegate. < OF < L *committere.* See COMMIT.]
m·mis·sion·er (kə·mish′ən·ər) *n.* **1.** One who holds a ommission. **2.** A member of a commission. **3.** A public fficial in charge of a department: fire *commissioner.* **4.** In aseball, etc., an official selected as supreme authority.
m·mit (kə·mit′) *v.t.* **·mit·ted, ·mit·ting** **1.** To do; per- ›etrate. **2.** To place in trust or charge; consign. **3.** To onsign for preservation: to *commit* a speech to memory. **.** To devote (oneself) unreservedly. **5.** To refer, as to a ommittee for consideration. [< L *committere* to join, en- rust < *com-* together + *mittere* to send] — **com·mit′ta·** **le** *adj.*
m·mit·ment (kə·mit′mənt) *n.* **1.** The act or process of ntrusting or consigning. **2.** The state of being committed. **.** An engagement or pledge to do something. **4.** A consign- nent to a prison, mental institution, etc.
m·mit·tal (kə·mit′l) *n.* Commitment (defs. 1 and 3).
m·mit·tee (kə·mit′ē) *n.* **1.** A group of people chosen to nvestigate, report, or act on a matter. **2.** *Law* One ap- ›ointed by a court to care for the person or property of an- ›ther. — **in committee** Under consideration by a commit- ee. [< AF *commettre* to entrust]
m·mit·tee·man (kə·mit′ē·mən) *n. pl.* **·men** (-mən) A nember of a committee. — **com·mit′tee·wom′an** *n.fem.*
m·mode (kə·mōd′) *n.* **1.** A low chest of drawers. **2.** A overed washstand. **3.** A woman's high headdress, worn ıbout 1700. **4.** A toilet. [< MF < L *commodus* convenient]
m·mo·di·ous (kə·mō′dē·əs) *adj.* Containing ample room; ›pacious. [See COMMODE.] — **com·mo′di·ous·ly** *adv.* — **om·mo′di·ous·ness** *n.*
m·mod·i·ty (kə·mod′ə·tē) *n. pl.* **·ties** **1.** Something bought and sold. **2.** Anything of use or profit. [< MF < L *commoditas, -tatis* convenience]
com·mo·dore (kom′ə·dôr, -dōr) *n.* **1.** In the U.S. Navy, an officer next above a captain and next below a rear admiral: a rank last used during World War II. **2.** In the Royal, Royal Canadian, and other Commonwealth navies, an officer rank- ing next below a rear-admiral. See table at GRADE. **3.** A title given to the presiding officer of a yacht club. [Earlier *commandore,* ? < Du. *kommandeur*]
com·mon (kom′ən) *adj.* **1.** Frequent or usual; unexcep- tional. **2.** Widespread; general. **3.** Shared equally by two or more, or by all. **4.** Pertaining to the entire community; public. **5.** Habitual; notorious: a *common* thief. **6.** Of low rank; ordinary. **7.** Vulgar; low; coarse. **8.** *Gram.* **a** Of gender, applied to either sex, as *parent, spouse, cat.* **b** Of a noun, applicable to any individual of a class of similar ob- jects; not proper or personal, as *dog.* **9.** *Math.* Referring to a number or quantity belonging equally to two or more quantities: a *common* denominator. — *n.* **1.** A tract of land considered as the property of the community, open to the use of all. **2.** *Sometimes cap. Eccl.* An office or service used for any of certain classes of feast. — **in common** Equal- ly with another or others; jointly. [< OF < L *communis* common] — **com′mon·ly** *adv.* — **com′mon·ness** *n.*
com·mon·al·ty (kom′ən·əl·tē) *n. pl.* **·ties** **1.** The common people, as opposed to the nobility. **2.** A body corporate, or its members. **3.** The entire mass; whole.
common carrier An individual or company that, for a fee, provides public transportation for goods or persons.
com·mon·er (kom′ən·ər) *n.* One of the common people.
common fraction *Math.* A fraction expressed by two num- bers, a denominator and a numerator.
common law A system of jurisprudence based on custom, traditional usage, and precedent, as that of England.
com·mon-law marriage (kom′ən·lô′) A marriage in which both members consent to live as man and wife without undergoing a religious or civil ceremony.
Common Market Any of several customs unions, esp. the European Economic Community.
common noun *Gram.* A noun that names any member of a class of things, as *man, boat:* distinguished from *proper noun.*
com·mon·place (kom′ən·plās′) *adj.* Not remarkable or interesting; ordinary. — *n.* **1.** A trite or obvious remark. **2.** Something common. — **com′mon·place′ness** *n.*
Common Prayer The public worship of the Anglican Church, as contained in the Book of Common Prayer.
com·mons (kom′ənz) *n.pl. Chiefly Brit.* **1.** The common people. **2.** (*construed as sing.*) Food provided for a common table, as in a college. **3.** Rations; fare. **4.** (*construed as sing.*) The dining hall of a college.
Com·mons (kom′ənz) *n.pl.* The House of Commons.
common sense Practical understanding; sound judgment. — **com′mon-sense′** *adj.*
common stock Corporation stock the ownership of which entitles the holder to dividends or a share in the profits only after other obligations have been met.
common time *Music* Meter in which there are four quar- ter notes to a measure: also **common measure.**
com·mon·weal (kom′ən·wēl′) *n.* The general welfare; common good. Also **common weal.**
com·mon·wealth (kom′ən·welth′) *n.* **1.** The whole people of a state or nation. **2.** A state or republic in which the sovereignty is vested in the people; loosely, any of the United States. — **The Commonwealth** The official name of the British Commonwealth of Nations.
Commonwealth of England The English government from 1649 to 1660.
Commonwealth of Nations See BRITISH COMMON- WEALTH OF NATIONS.
com·mo·tion (kə·mō′shən) *n.* **1.** A violent agitation; ex- citement. **2.** Popular tumult; social disorder; insurrection. [< L < *com-* thoroughly + *movere* to move]
com·mu·nal (kom′yə·nəl, kə·myōō′nəl) *adj.* **1.** Of or per- taining to a commune. **2.** Of or belonging to a community; common; public. — **com′mu·nal·ly** *adv.*
com·mu·nal·ism (kom′yə·nəl·iz′əm, kə·myōō′nəl-) *n.* A theory or system of government in which the state exists merely as a federation of virtually self-governing communes. — **com′mu·nal·ist** *n.* — **com′mu·nal·is′tic** *adj.*
com·mu·nal·ize (kom′yə·nəl·īz′, kə·myōō′nəl·īz) *v.t.* **·ized, ·iz·ing** To render communal. — **com′mu·nal·i·za′tion** *n.*
com·mune[1] (*v.* kə·myōōn′; *n.* kom′yōōn) *v.i.* **·muned, ·mun·** **ing** **1.** To converse intimately. **2.** To partake of the Eucharist. — *n.* Intimate conversation. [< OF *comuner* to share]
com·mune[2] (kom′yōōn) *n.* **1.** The smallest political divi- sion of France, Belgium, Italy, etc.; also, the people of such a district. **2.** Any community. — **the Commune** or **the**

Commune of Paris 1. The revolutionary government of Paris between 1789 and 1794. 2. The revolutionary government of Paris in 1871. [< L *communa* community]

com·mu·ni·ca·ble (kə·myōō′ni·kə·bəl) *adj.* Capable of being communicated, as a disease. — **com·mun′i·ca·bil′i·ty, com·mu′ni·ca·ble·ness** *n.* — **com·mu′ni·ca·bly** *adv.*

com·mu·ni·cant (kə·myōō′nə·kənt) *n.* **1.** One who communicates. **2.** One who partakes or has a right to partake of the Eucharist. — *adj.* Communicating.

com·mu·ni·cate (kə·myōō′nə·kāt) *v.* **·cat·ed, ·cat·ing** *v.t.* **1.** To cause another or others to partake of or share in; impart. **2.** To transmit, as a disease. — *v.i.* **3.** To transmit or exchange thought or knowledge. **4.** To be connected. **5.** To partake of the Eucharist. [< L *communicare* to share < *communis* common] — **com·mu′ni·ca′tor** *n.*

com·mu·ni·ca·tion (kə·myōō′nə·kā′shən) *n.* **1.** The act of imparting or transmitting. **2.** The transmission of ideas, information, etc., as by speech or writing. **3.** A message. **4.** A means of passage or of transmitting messages between places or persons. **5.** *pl.* The science of communicating.

com·mu·ni·ca·tive (kə·myōō′nə·kā′tiv, -kə·tiv) *adj.* **1.** Talkative. **2.** Of or pertaining to communication. — **com·mu′ni·ca′tive·ly** *adv.* — **com·mu′ni·ca′tive·ness** *n.*

com·mun·ion (kə·myōōn′yən) *n.* **1.** A having or sharing in common; mutual participation. **2.** A mutual sharing of thoughts, feelings, etc. **3.** Religious fellowship, as between members of a church; also, a religious denomination. **4.** *Usu. cap.* The Eucharist. [< OF < L *communis* common]

com·mu·ni·qué (kə·myōō′nə·kā′, kə·myōō′nə·kā) *n.* An official announcement or bulletin. [< F]

com·mu·nism (kom′yə·niz′əm) *n.* **1.** A social system characterized by the communal sharing of goods and services. **2.** A theory of social change advocating a classless society, public ownership of almost all productive property, and the sharing of the products of labor. **3.** *Often cap.* The system in force in any state based on this theory. [< F *commun* common, shared equally + -ISM]

com·mu·nist (kom′yə·nist) *n.* **1.** *Often cap.* A member of a Communist party. **2.** One who advocates communism. — *adj.* Pertaining to communism and communists.

com·mu·nis·tic (kom′yə·nis′tik) *adj.* **1.** Of, or of the nature of, communism. **2.** Tending to or in accordance with communism. — **com′mu·nis′ti·cal·ly** *adv.*

Communist Party **1.** The dominant party in Russia since 1917, previously called the Bolshevik Party. **2.** Any political party advocating communism.

com·mu·ni·ty (kə·myōō′nə·tē) *n. pl.* **·ties** **1.** A group of people living together or in one locality and subject to the same laws, having common interests, etc. **2.** The district or area in which they live. **3.** The public; society in general. **4.** Common ownership or participation. **5.** Identity or likeness: *community* of interests. **6.** *Ecol.* A group of plants or animals living under relatively similar conditions in a definite area. [< L *communitas, -tatis* fellowship]

community center A building or grounds used by a community for social and recreational activities.

community chest A welfare fund of contributions drawn upon by various charitable organizations.

com·mu·nize (kom′yə·nīz) *v.t.* **·nized, ·niz·ing** To make public property or cause to become communistic. — **com′mu·ni·za′tion** *n.*

com·mu·tate (kom′yə·tāt) *v.t.* **·tat·ed, ·tat·ing** *Electr.* To alter or reverse the direction of (a current).

com·mu·ta·tion (kom′yə·tā′shən) *n.* **1.** A substitution or interchange, as of one kind of payment for another. **2.** A payment or service substituted. **3.** *U.S.* Regular travel to and from work. **4.** *Electr.* The reversing of the direction of current. **5.** *Law* A reduction of a judicial penalty or sentence. [< L < *com-* thoroughly + *mutare* change]

commutation ticket *U.S.* A railroad or other ticket issued at a reduced rate and good for a specified number of trips, or for a specified period, over a given route.

com·mu·ta·tor (kom′yə·tā′tər) *n.* *Electr.* **1.** Any contrivance for reversing the direction of current. **2.** A part within a dynamo or generator, serving to collect and transmit the induced current.

com·mute (kə·myōōt′) *v.* **·mut·ed, ·mut·ing** *v.t.* **1.** To exchange reciprocally; interchange. **2.** To exchange for something less severe. **3.** To pay in gross at a reduced rate. — *v.i.* **4.** To serve as a substitute. **5.** *U.S.* To make regular trips of some distance to and from work. — **com·mut′a·ble** *adj.* — **com·mut′a·ble·ness, com·mut′a·bil′i·ty** *n.* — **com·mut′er** *n.*

com·pact[1] (*adj.* kəm·pakt′, kom′pakt; *v.* kəm·pakt′; *n.* kom′pakt) *adj.* **1.** Closely and firmly united; pressed together. **2.** Brief and to the point; terse. **3.** Packed into a small space. **4.** Composed; made up: with *of.* — *v.t.* To pack or press closely; compress. — *n.* A small, hinged box with a mirror, in which a woman carries face powder. [< L < *com-* together + *pangere* to fasten] — **com·pact′ly** *adv.* — **com·pact′ness** *n.*

com·pact[2] (kom′pakt) *n.* A covenant, agreement, or c[ontract]. [< L < *com-* together + *pacisci* to agree]

com·pan·ion[1] (kəm·pan′yən) *n.* **1.** A comrade; associa[te]. **2.** A person employed to live with, accompany, or ass[ist] another. **3.** One of a pair; a mate. — *v.t.* To be a co[m]panion to. [< OF < LL < L *com-* together + *panis* brea[d]

com·pan·ion[2] (kəm·pan′yən) *n.* *Naut.* A companionwa[y]; also, the hood or covering over a companionway. [< I *kampanje* quarter-deck, storeroom]

com·pan·ion·a·ble (kəm·pan′yən·ə·bəl) *adj.* Fitted [for] companionship; friendly; sociable. — **com·pan′ion·a·bi[li]ty** *n.* — **com·pan′ion·a·bly** *adv.*

com·pan·ion·ate (kəm·pan′yən·it) *adj.* **1.** Of or charact[er]istic of companions. **2.** Agreed upon; shared.

com·pan·ion·ship (kəm·pam′yən·ship) *n.* Fellowship.

com·pan·ion·way (kəm·pan′yən·wā′) *n.* *Naut.* A stairc[ase] leading below from a ship's deck; also, the space it occupi[es].

com·pa·ny (kum′pə·nē) *n. pl.* **·nies** **1.** A group of peop[le]. **2.** A gathering of persons for social purposes; society. **3.** guest or guests; visitors. **4.** Companionship; society. **5.** number of persons associated for some common purpose, in business. **6.** A partner or partners not named in t[he] title of a firm. **7.** A body of actors and actresses; trou[pe]. **8.** *Mil.* A body of men commanded by a captain, larger th[an] a platoon and smaller than a battalion. **9.** *Naut.* The ent[ire] crew of a ship, including the officers. — **to keep compa[ny]** (**with**) **1.** To associate (with). **2.** To court, as lovers; together. — **to part company** (**with**) To end friendsh[ip] or association (with). — *v.t.* & *v.i.* **·nied, ·ny·ing** *Archaic* keep or go in company (with). [See COMPANION[1].]

com·pa·ra·ble (kom′pər·ə·bəl) *adj.* **1.** Capable of co[m]parison. **2.** Worthy of comparison. — **com′pa·ra·ble·ne[ss]**, **com′pa·ra·bil′i·ty** *n.* — **com′pa·ra·bly** *adv.*

com·par·a·tive (kəm·par′ə·tiv) *adj.* **1.** Pertaining to, [re]sulting from, or making use of comparison: *comparat[ive]* anatomy. **2.** Not positive or absolute; relative. **3.** *Gra[m.]* Expressing a degree of an adjective or adverb higher th[an] the positive and lower than the superlative. — *n.* *Gra[m.]* The comparative degree, or a word or form by which it [is] expressed: "Better" is the *comparative of* "good." — **co[m]par′a·tive·ly** *adv.*

com·pare (kəm·pâr′) *v.* **·pared, ·par·ing** *v.t.* **1.** To rep[re]sent or speak of as similar or equal: with *to.* **2.** To exami[ne] so as to perceive similarity or dissimilarity: with *with.* *Gram.* To form or state the degrees of comparison of (an a[d]jective or adverb). — *v.i.* **4.** To be worthy of compariso[n]: with *with.* **5.** To vie or compete. — *n.* Comparison: usual[ly] in the phrase **beyond compare.** [< MF < L < *com-* t[o]gether + *par* equal]

com·par·i·son (kəm·par′ə·sən) *n.* **1.** A comparing or bei[ng] compared; a statement of relative likeness or unlikeness. Similarity. **3.** *Gram.* That inflection of adjectives or adver[bs] that indicates the three differences of degree, the positiv[e], comparative, and superlative, as *short, shorter, shortest.*

com·part·ment (kəm·pärt′mənt) *n.* **1.** One of the par[ts] into which an enclosed space is subdivided. **2.** Any separa[te] section. [< F < L < *com-* together + *partiri* to share]

com·pass (kum′pəs, kom′-) *n.* **1.** An instrument for dete[r]mining direction, consisting essentially of a freely suspende[d] magnetic needle that points toward the magnetic north. The reach or extent of something; area or range; scope. An enclosing line or boundary; circumference. **4.** *Som[e]times pl.* An instrument having two usually pointed le[gs] hinged at one end, used for taking measurements, describi[ng] circles, etc.: also **pair of compasses.** — *v.t.* **1.** To go roun[d]. **2.** To surround; encompass. **3.** To comprehend. **4.** T[o] attain or accomplish. **5.** To plot; devise. [< OF < L *co[m-]* together + *passus* step] — **com′pass·a·ble** *adj.*

compass card The circular card or dial resting on the piv[ot] of a mariner's compass, on which the 32 points and 360 degrees of the circle are marked.

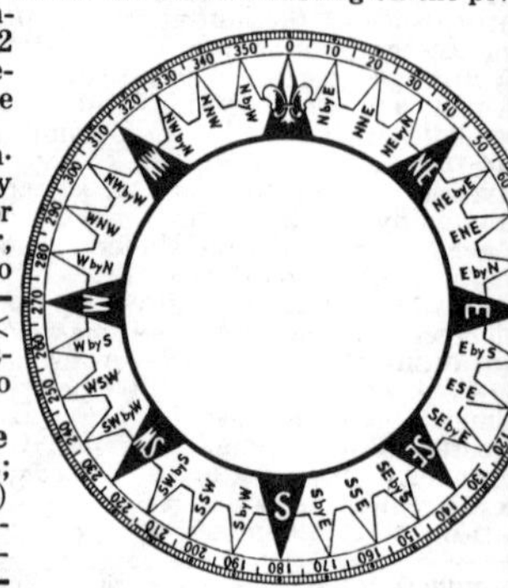

com·pas·sion (kəm·pash′ən) *n.* Pity for the suffering or distress of another, with the desire to help or spare. — **Syn.** See PITY. [< MF < LL < L *com-* together + *pati* to feel, suffer]

com·pas·sion·ate (*adj.* kəm·pash′ən·it; *v.* kəm·pash′ən·āt) *adj.* Feeling compassion or pity; merciful; sympathetic. — *v.t.* **·at·ed, ·at·ing** To ave compassion for; pity; sympathize. **—com·pas′sion·te·ly** *adv.* **—com·pas′sion·ate·ness** *n.*

m·pat·i·ble (kəm·pat′ə·bəl) *adj.* **1.** Capable of existing gether; congruous; congenial: usu. with *with.* **2.** In telesion capable of being received in black and white on sets not lapted for color reception. [< MF < Med.L < L *com-* gether + *pati* to feel, suffer] **—com·pat′i·bil′i·ty, com·at′i·ble·ness** *n.* **—com·pat′i·bly** *adv.*

m·pa·tri·ot (kəm·pā′trē·ət, -pat′rē·ət) *n.* A fellow counyman. **—***adj.* Of the same country. [< F < LL < L *m-* together + *patriota* countryman]

m·peer (kəm·pir′, kom′pir) *n.* **1.** One of equal rank; a eer. **2.** A comrade. [< OF < L < *com-* with + *par* equal]

m·pel (kəm·pel′) *v.t.* **·pelled, ·pel·ling 1.** To urge irresisbly; constrain. **2.** To obtain by force; exact. **3.** To force yield; overpower. [OF < L < *com-* together + *pellere* to rive] **—com·pel′la·ble** *adj.* **—com·pel′la·bly** *adv.* **—m·pel′ler** *n.*

m·pen·di·ous (kəm·pen′dē·əs) *adj.* Stating briefly and iccinctly the substance of something; concise. **—com·end′i·ous·ly** *adv.* **—com·pen′di·ous·ness** *n.*

m·pen·di·um (kəm·pen′dē·əm) *n. pl.* **·di·ums** or **·di·a** dē·ə) A brief, comprehensive summary; an abridgment. < L < *com-* together + *pendere* to weigh]

m·pen·sa·ble (kəm·pen′sə·bəl) *adj.* That may be comensated. **—com·pen′sa·bil′i·ty** *n.*

m·pen·sate (kom′pən·sāt) *v.* **·sat·ed, ·sat·ing** *v.t.* **1.** To iake suitable amends to or for; requite; remunerate; pay; imburse. **2.** To counterbalance or make up for; offset. *v.i.* **3.** To make returns or amends: often with *for.* [< < *com-* together + *pendere* to weigh] **—com′pen·sa′tor** **—com·pen·sa·tive** (kom′pən·sā′tiv, kəm·pen′sə·tiv) *adj.* **com·pen·sa·to·ry** (kəm·pen′sə·tôr′ē) *adj.*

m·pen·sa·tion (kom′pən·sā′shən) *n.* **1.** The act of comating, or that which compensates; payment; amends. *Biol.* The offsetting of defects of an organ or part by the evelopment of another organ. **—com′pen·sa′tion·al** *adj.*

m·pete (kəm·pēt′) *v.i.* **·pet·ed, ·pet·ing** To contend with nother or others; engage in a contest or competition; vie. < L < *com-* together + *petere* to seek]

m·pe·tence (kom′pə·təns) *n.* **1.** The state of being cometent; ability. **2.** Sufficient means for comfortable living. *Law* Legal authority, qualification, or jurisdiction. Also **om′pe·ten·cy.**

m·pe·tent (kom′pə·tənt) *adj.* **1.** Having sufficient abil-y; capable. **2.** Sufficient; adequate. **3.** *Law* Having legal ualification. [< MF < L < *com-* together + *petere* to go, eek] **—com′pe·tent·ly** *adv.* **—com′pe·tent·ness** *n.*

m·pe·ti·tion (kom′pə·tish′ən) *n.* **1.** A striving against anther or others for some object, as a prize, or for superiority. A trial of skill or ability; a contest. **3.** Business rivalry beween persons or firms striving for the same market.

m·pet·i·tive (kəm·pet′ə·tiv) *adj.* Of, pertaining to, or haracterized by competition. Also **com·pet·i·to·ry** (kəm·et′ə·tôr′ē, -tō′rē) **—com·pet′i·tive·ly** *adv.* **—com·pet′i·ive·ness** *n.*

m·pet·i·tor (kəm·pet′ə·tər) *n.* One who competes, as in ames or in business.

m·pile (kəm·pīl′) *v.t.* **·piled, ·pil·ing 1.** To put together rom materials collected from other sources. **2.** To gather various materials) into a volume. **3.** To amass; collect. < L < *com-* thoroughly + *pilare* to strip, plunder] **—om·pi·la·tion** (kom′pə·lā′shən) *n.* **—com·pil′er** *n.*

m·pla·cen·cy (kəm·plā′sən·sē) *n. pl.* **·cies** Self-satisaction; smugness. Also **com·pla′cence.**

m·pla·cent (kəm·plā′sənt) *adj.* **1.** Smug; self-satisfied. Complaisant. [< L < *com-* thoroughly + *placere* to lease] **—com·pla′cent·ly** *adv.*

m·plain (kəm·plān′) *v.i.* **1.** To express feelings of disatisfaction, resentment, pain, etc.; grumble. **2.** To describe ne's pains or ills. **3.** To make a formal accusation; present complaint. [< OF < LL < L *com-* thoroughly + *plangere* o beat (the breast in grief)] **—com·plain′er** *n.*

m·plain·ant (kəm·plā′nənt) *n.* One who enters a comlaint, as before a magistrate.

m·plaint (kəm·plānt′) *n.* **1.** An expression of pain, grief, r dissatisfaction. **2.** A cause for complaining; grievance. An ailment; disorder. **4.** *Law* A formal charge.

m·plai·sant (kəm·plā′zənt, kom′plə·zant) *adj.* Showing desire to please; yielding; compliant. [< MF < L *comlacere*] **—com·plai′sance** *n.* **—com·plai′sant·ly** *adv.*

m·ple·ment (*n.* kom′plə·mənt; *v.* kom′plə·ment) *n.* **1.** That which fills up or completes a thing. **2.** Full or complete number, allowance, or amount: The vessel has her *complement* of men. **3.** One of two parts that mutually complete each other. **4.** *Geom.* An angle that when added to another angle equals 90°. **5.** *Gram.* A word or phrase used after a verb to complete predication. A **subjective complement** describes the subject, as *happy* in *She is happy.* An **objective complement** describes or identifies the direct object, as *happy* in *It made her happy.* **—***v.t.* To make complete. [< L < *com-* thoroughly + *plere* to fill]

com·ple·men·tal (kom′plə·men′təl) *adj.* Complementary.

com·ple·men·ta·ry (kom′plə·men′tər·ē, -trē) *adj.* **1.** Serving as a complement; completing. **2.** Mutually providing each other's needs.

complementary color Either of a pair of spectrum colors that when combined give a white or nearly white light.

com·plete (kəm·plēt′) *adj.* **1.** Having all needed or normal parts; lacking nothing; entire; full. **2.** Wholly finished; ended; concluded. **3.** Perfect in quality or nature. **—***v.t.* **·plet·ed, ·plet·ing 1.** To make entire or perfect. **2.** To finish; end. [< L < *com-* thoroughly + *plere* to fill] **—com·plete′ly** *adv.* **—com·plete′ness** *n.*

com·ple·tion (kəm·plē′shən) *n.* The act of completing, or the state of being completed.

com·plex (*adj.* kəm·pleks′, kom′pleks; *n.* kom′pleks) *adj.* **1.** Consisting of various connected or interwoven parts; composite. **2.** Complicated, as in structure; involved; intricate. **—***n.* **1.** A whole made up of interwoven or connected parts. **2.** *Psychoanal.* A group of interrelated feelings, desires, memories, and ideas, that function as a unit to dominate the personality, and which, when repressed, often lead to abnormal patterns of behavior. **3.** Loosely, an excessive concern or fear; an obsession. [< L < *com-* together + *plectere* to twist] **—com·plex′ly** *adv.* **—com·plex′ness** *n.*

complex fraction *Math.* A fraction in which either the numerator or the denominator is a fraction.

com·plex·ion (kəm·plek′shən) *n.* **1.** The color and appearance of the skin, esp. of the face. **2.** General aspect or appearance; quality; character. [< F < L < *complecti* to put together] **—com·plex′ion·al** *adj.*

com·plex·ioned (kəm·plek′shənd) *adj.* Of a certain complexion: used in compounds: light-*complexioned.*

com·plex·i·ty (kəm·plek′sə·tē) *n. pl.* **·ties. 1.** The state of being complex. **2.** Something complex.

complex sentence. See under SENTENCE.

com·pli·a·ble (kəm·plī′ə·bəl) *adj.* Compliant. **—com·pli′a·ble·ness** *n.* **—com·pli′a·bly** *adv.*

com·pli·ance (kəm·plī′əns) *n.* **1.** The act of complying or yielding. **2.** A disposition to comply; complaisance. Also **com·pli′an·cy. —in compliance with** In agreement with.

com·pli·ant (kəm·plī′ənt) *adj.* Complying; yielding. **—com·pli′ant·ly** *adv.*

com·pli·cate (*v.* kom′plə·kāt; *adj.* kom′plə·kit) *v.* **·cat·ed, ·cat·ing** *v.t.* **1.** To make complex, difficult, or perplexing. **2.** To twist or wind around; intertwine. **—***v.i.* **3.** To become complex or difficult. **—***adj.* Complicated; complex. [< L < *com-* together + *plicare* to fold]

com·pli·cat·ed (kom′plə·kā′tid) *adj.* Difficult to separate, analyze, or understand; intricate; involved. **—com′pli·cat′ed·ly** *adv.* **—com′pli·cat′ed·ness** *n.*

com·pli·ca·tion (kom′plə·kā′shən) *n.* **1.** The act of complicating. **2.** An intricate or perplexing structure, condition, or relationship. **3.** Anything that complicates.

com·plic·i·ty (kəm·plis′ə·tē) *n. pl.* **·ties 1.** The state of being an accomplice, as in a wrong act. **2.** Complexity.

com·pli·ment (*n.* kom′plə·mənt; *v.* kom′plə·ment) *n.* **1.** An expression of admiration, praise, or congratulation. **2.** *Usu. pl.* A formal greeting or remembrance. **—***v.t.* **1.** To pay a compliment to. **2.** To show regard for, as by a gift. [< MF < Ital. < L *complementum*]

com·pli·men·ta·ry (kom′plə·men′tər·ē, -trē) *adj.* **1.** Conveying, using, or like a compliment. **2.** Given free: a *complimentary* copy of a book. **—com′pli·men′ta·ri·ly** *adv.*

com·plin (kom′plin) *n.* *Often cap. Eccl.* Prescribed prayers constituting the last of the seven canonical hours. Also **com·pline** (kom′plin, -plīn) [< OF < L *com-* thoroughly + *plere* to fill]

com·ply (kəm·plī′) *v.i.* **·plied, ·ply·ing 1.** To act in conformity; consent; obey: with *with.* [< Ital. *complire* < Sp. < L < *com-* thoroughly + *plere* to fill] **—com·pli′er** *n.*

com·po·nent (kəm·pō′nənt) *n.* A constituent element or part. **—***adj.* Forming a part or ingredient; constituent. [< L < *com-* together + *ponere* to pull]

com·port (kəm·pôrt′, -pōrt′) *v.t.* **1.** To conduct or behave (oneself). **—***v.i.* **2.** To be compatible; agree: with *with.* [< F < L < *com-* together + *portare* to carry] **—com·port′·ment** *n.*

com·pose (kəm·pōz′) *v.* **·posed, ·pos·ing** *v.t.* **1.** To constitute; form. **2.** To make of elements or parts; fashion. **3.** To create (a literary or musical work). **4.** To make calm or tranquil; quiet. **5.** To reconcile or settle, as differences. **6.** *Printing* To arrange (type) in lines; set. **—***v.i.* **7.** To engage in composition, as of musical works. **8.** *Printing* To set type. [< MF < *com-* together + *poser* to place]

com·posed (kəm·pōzd′) *adj.* Free from agitation; calm. — **com·pos·ed·ly** (kəm·pō′zid·lē) *adv.* — **com·pos′ed·ness** *n.*

com·pos·er (kəm·pō′zər) *n.* One who composes; esp., one who writes music.

com·pos·ite (kəm·poz′it) *adj.* **1.** Made up of separate parts or elements; combined or compounded. **2.** *Bot.* Characteristic of or pertaining to a family of plants, as the dandelion, chrysanthemum, etc., the flowers usu. occurring in dense clusters. — *n.* **1.** That which is composed or made up of parts. **2.** *Bot.* A composite plant. [< L < *com-* together + *ponere* to put] — **com·pos′ite·ly** *adv.* — **com·pos′ite·ness** *n.*

com·po·si·tion (kom′pə·zish′ən) *n.* **1.** A putting together of parts, ingredients, etc., to form a whole. **2.** That which is so formed. **3.** Constitution; make-up. **4.** The act or art of creating a literary, musical, or artistic work. **5.** The work so created, or its general structure. **6.** A short essay written as an exercise for school. **7.** An agreement or settlement, esp. by compromise. **8.** *Printing* The setting of type.

com·pos·i·tor (kəm·poz′ə·tər) *n.* One who sets type.

com·pos men·tis (kom′pəs men′tis) *Latin* Of sound mind.

com·post (kom′pōst) *n.* **1.** A fertilizing mixture of decomposed vegetable matter. **2.** A compound. [< OF, mixture]

com·po·sure (kəm·pō′zhər) *n.* Tranquillity, as of mind; calmness; serenity.

com·pote (kom′pōt, *Fr.* kôṅ·pôt′) *n.* **1.** Fruit stewed or preserved in syrup **2.** A dish for holding fruits, etc. [< F < OF *composte*]

com·pound[1] (*n.* kom′pound; *v.* kom·pound′, kəm-; *adj.* kom′pound, kom·pound′) *n.* **1.** A combination of two or more elements or parts. **2.** *Gram.* A word composed of two or more words joined with a hyphen or written in solid form, as *fly-by-night, shoestring.* **3.** *Chem.* A definite substance resulting from the combination of specific elements or radicals in fixed proportions: distinguished from *mixture.* — *v.t.* **1.** To make by combining various elements or ingredients. **2.** To mix (elements or parts). **3.** To compute (interest) on both the principal and whatever interest has accrued. **4.** To settle for less than the sum due, as a debt; compromise. — *adj.* Composed of two or more elements or parts. [< OF < L < *com-* together + *ponere* to put] — **com·pound′a·ble** *adj.* — **com·pound′er** *n.*

com·pound[2] (kom′pound) *n.* **1.** In the Orient, an enclosure containing a building, esp. one occupied by Europeans. **2.** Any similar enclosed place. [< Malay *kampong*]

compound fraction *Math.* A complex fraction.

compound interest Interest computed on the original principal together with its accrued interest.

compound leaf *Bot.* A leaf having several distinct blades on a common leafstalk.

compound number *Math.* A quantity containing more than one unit or denomination, as 6 feet 3 inches.

compound sentence See under SENTENCE.

com·pre·hend (kom′pri·hend′) *v.t.* **1.** To grasp mentally; understand fully. **2.** To take in or embrace; include. — *v.i.* **3.** To understand. — **Syn.** See APPREHEND. [< L < *com-* together + *prehendere* to grasp, seize]

com·pre·hen·si·ble (kom′pri·hen′sə·bəl) *adj.* Capable of being comprehended; understandable; intelligible. Also **com′·pre·hend′i·ble.** — **com′pre·hen·si·bil′i·ty, com′pre·hen′si·ble·ness** *n.* — **com′pre·hen′si·bly** *adv.*

com·pre·hen·sion (kom′pri·hen′shən) *n.* **1.** The mental grasping of ideas, facts, etc., or the power of so doing; understanding. **2.** An including or taking in; comprehensiveness. — **Syn.** See KNOWLEDGE.

com·pre·hen·sive (kom′pri·hen′siv) *adj.* **1.** Large in scope or content; broad. **2.** Understanding or comprehending. — **com′pre·hen′sive·ly** *adv.* — **com′pre·hen′sive·ness** *n.*

com·press (*v.* kəm·pres′; *n.* kom′pres) *v.t.* To press together or into smaller space; condense; compact. — *n.* **1.** *Med.* A cloth or pad, sometimes medicated, for applying moisture, cold, heat, or pressure to a part of the body. **2.** An apparatus for compressing bales of cotton, etc. [< OF < LL < L < *com-* together + *premere* to press] — **com·pressed′** *adj.* — **com·press′i·bil′i·ty, com·press′i·ble·ness** *n.* — **com·press′i·ble** *adj.* — **com·press′ive** *adj.*

com·pres·sion (kəm·presh′ən) *n.* **1.** The act of compressing or the state of being compressed. Also **com·pres·sure** (kəm·presh′ər). **2.** The process by which a confined gas is reduced in volume through the application of pressure, as in the cylinder of an internal-combustion engine.

com·pres·sor (kəm·pres′ər) *n.* **1.** One who or that which compresses. **2.** *Anat.* A muscle that compresses a part. **3.** *Mech.* A power-driven machine for compressing a gas in order to utilize its expansion, as for refrigeration.

com·prise (kəm·prīz′) *v.t.* **·prised, ·pris·ing** To consist of or contain; include. [< MF < L < *com-* together + *premere* to press] — **com·pris′a·ble** *adj.* — **com·pri′sal** *n.*

com·pro·mise (kom′prə·mīz) *n.* **1.** An adjustment or settlement by which each side makes concessions. **2.** The result of such concessions. **3.** Something lying midway between, or combining the qualities of, two different things. An imperiling, as of character or reputation. — *v.* **·mis·mis·ing** *v.t.* **1.** To adjust by concessions. **2.** To expose risk, suspicion, or disrepute; imperil. — *v.i.* **3.** To mak compromise. [< MF < L < *com-* together + *promittere* promise] — **com′pro·mis′er** *n.*

compte ren·du (kôṅt räṅ·dü′) *French* An official repo literally, account rendered.

Comp·tom·e·ter (komp·tom′ə·tər) *n.* A high-speed cal lating machine: a trade name. Also **comp·tom′e·ter.**

comp·trol·ler (kən·trō′lər) See CONTROLLER (def. 2).

com·pul·sion (kəm·pul′shən) *n.* **1.** The act of compelli coercion. **2.** The state of being compelled. **3.** *Psychol.* irresistible impulse or tendency to perform an act. [< M < L < *com-* together + *pellere* to drive]

com·pul·sive (kəm·pul′siv) *adj.* Compelling; compulso — **com·pul′sive·ly** *adv.* — **com·pul′sive·ness** *n.*

com·pul·so·ry (kəm·pul′sər·ē) *adj.* **1.** Employing comp sion; coercive. **2.** Required; obligatory: *compulsory edu* tion. — **com·pul′so·ri·ly** *adv.* — **com·pul′so·ri·ness** *n.*

com·punc·tion (kəm·pungk′shən) *n.* **1.** An uneasiness mind arising from wrongdoing; a sense of guilt or remor **2.** A feeling of slight regret or pity. [<OF < LL < L *co* greatly + *pungere* to prick, sting] — **com·punc′tious** *a* — **com·punc′tious·ly** *adv.*

com·pu·ta·tion (kom′pyə·tā′shən) *n.* **1.** The act or meth of computing. **2.** A computed amount or number.

com·pute (kəm·pyōōt′) *v.t. & v.i.* **·put·ed, ·put·ing** To asc tain (an amount or number) by calculation; reckon. — Computation. [< MF < L < *com-* together + *putare* reckon.] — **com·put′a·bil′i·ty** *n.* — **com·put′a·ble** *adj.*

com·put·er (kəm·pyōō′tər) *n.* **1.** One who or that whi computes. **2.** An electronic machine for the high-speed p formance of mathematical and logical operations, or for t processing of large masses of coded information.

com·rade (kom′rad, -rid, kum′-) *n.* **1.** An intimate co panion or friend. **2.** A person who shares one's own occuj tion, interests, etc. [< MF *camarade* < Sp. < L *cam* room] — **com′rade·ship** *n.*

Com·tism (kom′tiz·əm, kôn′-) *n.* The philosophy of Com positivism. — **Com·ti·an** (kom′tē·ən, kôn′-) *adj.*

con[1] (kon) *v.t.* **conned, con·ning** To study; peruse carefull commit to memory. [Var. of CAN[1]] — **con′ner** *n.*

con[2] (kon) *Naut. v.t.* **conned, con·ning** To direct the ste ing of (a vessel). — *n.* The act of conning. Also *co* [Earlier *cond* < F < L < *com-* together + *ducere* to lead

con[3] (kon) *U.S. Slang adj.* Confidence: *con* man; *con* gan — *v.t.* **conned, con·ning** To defraud; dupe; swindle. [CONFIDENCE]

con- Var. of COM-.

con·cat·e·nate (kon·kat′ə·nāt) *v.t.* **·nat·ed, ·nat·ing** ' join or link together; connect in a series. — *adj.* Connect in a series. [< L < *com-* together + *catena* chain]

con·cat·e·na·tion (kon·kat′ə·nā′shən) *n.* **1.** The act linking together. **2.** A chainlike series, as of events, etc.

con·cave (*adj.* kon·kāv′, kon′kāv, kong′-; *n.* kon′kā kong′-; *v.* kon·kāv′) *adj.* Hollow and curving inward, as t interior of a sphere or bowl: opposed to *convex.* — *n.* A co cave surface; vault. — *v.t.* **·caved, ·cav·ing** To make co cave. [< MF < L < *com-* thoroughly + *cavus* hollow] **con·cave′ly** *adv.* — **con·cave′ness** *n.*

con·cav·i·ty (kon·kav′ə·tē) *n.* *pl.* **·ties 1.** The state of b ing concave. **2.** A concave surface; a hollow.

con·ca·vo-con·cave (kon·kā′vō·kon·kāv′) *adj.* Biconca

con·ca·vo-con·vex (kon·kā′vō·kon·veks′) *adj.* Concave one side and convex on the other, as a lens.

con·ceal (kən·sēl′) *v.t.* To keep from sight, discovery, knowledge; hide; secrete. — **Syn.** See HIDE . [< OF < < *com-* thoroughly + *celare* to hide] — **con·ceal′a·ble** *a* — **con·ceal′er** *n.* — **con·ceal′ment** *n.*

con·cede (kən·sēd′) *v.* **·ced·ed, ·ced·ing** *v.t.* **1.** To acknov edge as true, correct, or proper; admit. **2.** To grant; yiel as a right or privilege. — *v.i.* **3.** To make a concessio yield. — **Syn.** See CONFESS. [< L < *com-* thoroughly *cedere* to yield, go away] — **con·ced′er** *n.*

con·ceit (kən·sēt′) *n.* **1.** Overweening self-esteem. **2.** A ingenious, fanciful thought or expression. **3.** In poetry, elaborate, extended metaphor. **4.** Imagination; fancy. **Syn.** See PRIDE. [< CONCEIVE]

con·ceit·ed (kən·sē′tid) *adj.* Having an excessively hig opinion of oneself; vain. — **con·ceit′ed·ly** *adv.* — **con·cei ed·ness** *n.*

con·ceive (kən·sēv′) *v.* **·ceived, ·ceiv·ing** *v.t.* **1.** To becon pregnant with. **2.** To form a concept or notion of; imagin to *conceive* the perfect man. **3.** To understand; grasp. To express in a particular way. — *v.i.* **5.** To form a ment image; think: with *of.* **6.** To become pregnant. [< OF L < *com-* thoroughly + *capere* to grasp, take] — **con·ceiv a·ble** *adj.* — **con·ceiv′a·bil′i·ty, con·ceiv′a·ble·ness** *n.* **con·ceiv′a·bly** *adv.* — **con·ceiv′er** *n.*

con·cen·ter (kon·sen′tər) *v.t. & v.i.* To direct or come to

ommon point or center; focus. Also *Brit.* **con·cen′tre.** [< F < L < *com-* together + *centrum* center]
n·cen·trate (kon′sən·trāt) *v.* **·trat·ed, ·trat·ing** *v.t.* **1.** To raw or direct to a common point; focus: to *concentrate* roops. **2.** To intensify or purify by removing certain contituents; condense. — *v.i.* **3.** To converge toward a center. **4.** To become compacted, intensified, or more pure. **.** To direct one's entire attention: often with *on* or *upon.* — *n.* A product of concentration, as in chemistry or metalurgy. — *adj.* Concentrated. — **con′cen·tra′tor** *n.*
n·cen·tra·tion (kon′sən·trā′shən) *n.* **1.** The act of conentrating, or the state of being concentrated. **2.** That which is concentrated, as a solution. **3.** Complete attention o some single problem, task, etc.
ncentration camp An enclosed camp for the confinenent of prisoners of war, political prisoners, aliens, etc.
n·cen·tra·tive (kon′sən·trā′tiv, kən·sen′trə·tiv) *adj.* Tending to concentrate, or characterized by concentration. — **con′cen·tra′tive·ly** *adv.* — **con′cen·tra′tive·ness** *n.*
n·cen·tric (kən·sen′trik) *adj.* Having a common center, s circles: opposed to *eccentric.* Also **con·cen′tri·cal.** — **con·en′tri·cal·ly** *adv.* — **con·cen·tric·i·ty** (kon′sen·tris′ə·tē) *n.*
n·cept (kon′sept) *n.* A mental image; esp., a generalized dea formed by combining the elements of a class into the otion of one object; also, a thought or opinion. — **Syn.** See IDEA. [< L *conceptus* a conceiving]
n·cep·tion (kən·sep′shən) *n.* **1.** A conceiving, or a being onceived, in the womb. **2.** An embryo or fetus. **3.** A beinning; commencement. **4.** The act of forming concepts or deas. **5.** A concept, idea, plan, or design. — **con·cep′tion·l** *adj.* — **con·cep′tive** *adj.*
n·cep·tu·al (kən·sep′cho͞o·əl) *adj.* Of or pertaining to onception or concepts. — **con·cep′tu·al·ly** *adv.*
n·cern (kən·sûrn′) *v.t.* **1.** To be of interest or importance o. **2.** To occupy the attention or mind of; engage; involve: ised as a reflexive or in the passive. **3.** To affect with anxity; trouble: often in the passive. — *n.* **1.** That which conerns or affects one; affair; business. **2.** Anxiety or interest; olicitous regard; care. **3.** Relation or bearing. **4.** A busiess enterprise; a firm. [< MF < Med.L < L *com-* thoroughly + *cernere* to see, discern] — **con·cerned′** *adj.*
n·cern·ing (kən·sûr′ning) *prep.* In relation to; regarding; about.
n·cern·ment (kən·sûrn′mənt) *n.* **1.** Importance. **2.** Concern; anxiety. **3.** Anything that relates to one; affair.
n·cert (*n.* kon′sûrt; *v.* kən·sûrt′) *n.* **1.** A musical perormance by singers or instrumentalists. **2.** Agreement; harmony. — **in concert** In unison; all together. — *adj.* Of or for concerts. [< MF < Ital. < *concertare* to agree]
n·cert·ed (kən·sûr′tid) *adj.* **1.** Arranged, agreed upon, or done together; combined. **2.** *Music* Arranged in parts for voices or instruments. — **con·cert′ed·ly** *adv.*
on·cer·ti·na (kon′sər·tē′nə) *n.* A small bellowslike musical instrument with buttons for keys and handles on each of the two hexagonal ends. [< CONCERT + -INA]
on·cert·mas·ter (kon′sərt·mas′tər, -mäs′-) *n.* The leader of the first violin section of an orchestra, who acts as assistant to the conductor. Also **con′cert·meis′ter** (mīs′-)
on·cer·to (kən·cher′tō) *n. pl.* **·tos,** *Ital.* **·ti** (-tē) *Music* A composition, usu. of three movements, for performance by a solo instrument or instruments accompanied by an orchestra. Abbr. *con.* [< Ital. See CONCERT.]
oncerto gros·so (grō′sō) *pl.* **concerti gros·si** (grō′sē) A concerto for a group of solo instruments and an orchestra. [< Ital., lit., big concerto]
on·ces·sion (kən·sesh′ən) *n.* **1.** The act of conceding. **2.** Anything so yielded. **3.** A right or privilege granted by a government. **4.** *U.S.* The right to operate a subsidiary business on certain premises. **5.** *Canadian* In Ontario and Quebec, a subdivision of land in township surveys. — **con·ces′sive** *adj.*
on·ces·sion·aire (kən·sesh′ən·âr′) *n.* One who holds or operates a concession. Also **con·ces′sion·er** [< F]
on·ces·sion·ar·y (kən·sesh′ən·er′ē) *adj.* Of or pertaining to a concession. — *n. pl.* **·ar·ies** A concessionaire.
oncession road *Canadian* A road following a survey line.
onch (kongk, konch) *n. pl.* **conchs** (kongks) or **conch·es** (kon′chiz) **1.** Any of various marine mollusks having large, spiral, univalve shells. **2.** Such a shell. [< L < Gk. *konchē* shell]
on·chol·o·gy (kong·kol′ə·jē) *n.* The study of shells and mollusks. [< L *concha* shell + -LOGY] — **con·cho·log·i·cal** (kong′kə·loj′i·kəl) *adj.* — **con·chol′o·gist** *n.*
on·ci·erge (kon′sē·ûrzh′, *Fr.* kôn·syârzh′) *n.* An attendant or doorkeeper of a building, esp. in France, who performs custodial services. [< F]

CONCH SHELL

con·cil·i·ate (kən·sil′ē·āt) *v.t.* **·at·ed, ·at·ing** **1.** To win over; placate; appease. **2.** To secure or attract by favorable measures; win. **3.** To make consistent. [< L < *concilium* council] — **con·cil·i·a·ble** (kən·sil′ē·ə·bəl) *adj.* — **con·cil′i·a′tion** *n.* — **con·cil′i·a′tor** *n.*
con·cil·i·a·to·ry (kən·sil′ē·ə·tôr′ē, -tō′rē) *adj.* Tending to reconcile or conciliate. Also **con·cil′i·a′tive.** — **con·cil′i·a·to′ri·ly** *adv.* — **con·cil′i·a·to′ri·ness** *n.*
con·cise (kən·sīs′) *adj.* Expressing much in brief form; compact. — **Syn.** See TERSE. [< L < *com-* thoroughly + *caedere* to cut] — **con·cise′ly** *adv.* — **con·cise′ness** *n.*
con·clave (kon′klāv, kong′-) *n.* **1.** A private or secret meeting. **2.** The private chambers in which the College of Cardinals meets to elect a pope; also, the meeting. [< F < L < *com-* together + *clavis* key] — **con′clav·ist** *n.*
con·clude (kən·klo͞od′) *v.* **·clud·ed, ·clud·ing** *v.t.* **1.** To bring to an end; terminate. **2.** To arrange or settle finally; effect. **3.** To form an opinion or judgment about; decide. **4.** To resolve (to do); determine. — *v.i.* **5.** To come to an end. **6.** To come to a decision or agreement. [< L < *com-* thoroughly + *claudere* to close, shut off] — **con·clud′er** *n.*
con·clu·sion (kən·klo͞o′zhən) *n.* **1.** The end or termination of something. **2.** A closing part, as of a speech. **3.** The result of an act or process; outcome. **4.** A judgment or opinion obtained by reasoning. **5.** A final decision; resolve. **6.** A final arranging; settlement, as of a treaty. — **in conclusion** As a final statement or summing up.
con·clu·sive (kən·klo͞o′siv) *adj.* Putting an end to a question; decisive. — **con·clu′sive·ly** *adv.* — **con·clu′sive·ness** *n.*
con·coct (kon·kokt′, kən-) *v.t.* **1.** To make by mixing ingredients, as food, a drink, etc. **2.** To make up; devise: to *concoct* a plan. [< L < *com-* together + *coquere* to cook, boil] — **con·coct′er** or **con·coc′tor** *n.* — **con·coc′tive** *adj.*
con·coc·tion (kon·kok′shən, kən-) *n.* **1.** The act of concocting. **2.** Something concocted.
con·com·i·tance (kon·kom′ə·təns, kən-) *n.* Existence or occurrence together; accompaniment. Also **con·com′i·tan·cy.**
con·com·i·tant (kon·kom′ə·tənt, kən-) *adj.* Existing or occurring together; attendant. — *n.* An attendant circumstance, state, or thing. [< L < *com-* with + *comitari* to accompany] — **con·com′i·tant·ly** *adv.*
con·cord (kon′kôrd, kong′-) *n.* **1.** Unity of feeling or interest; agreement; accord. **2.** Peace; friendly relations. **3.** A treaty establishing this. **4.** *Music* Consonance. — **Syn.** See HARMONY. [< MF < L < *com-* together + *cor, cordis* heart]
con·cor·dance (kon·kôr′dəns, kən-) *n.* **1.** Agreement; concord. **2.** An alphabetical index of the important words in a book as they occur in context: a *concordance* of the Bible.
con·cor·dant (kon·kôr′dənt, kən-) *adj.* Existing in concord; agreeing; harmonious. — **con·cor′dant·ly** *adv.*
con·cor·dat (kon·kôr′dat) *n.* **1.** An agreement between the papacy and a government on church affairs. **2.** Any official agreement or pact.
con·course (kon′kôrs, -kōrs, kong′-) *n.* **1.** A coming together; confluence. **2.** A crowd; throng. **3.** A large place for the assembling or passage of crowds. [< MF < L < *com-* together + *currere* to run]
con·crete (kon′krēt; *for adj., n., & v. def. 3,* also kon·krēt′) *adj.* **1.** Specific, as opposed to general: a *concrete* example. **2.** Physically perceptible; objectively real. **3.** *Gram.* Naming a specific thing or class of things, rather than an abstract quality or state. **4.** Constituting a composite mass or substance; solid. **5.** Made of concrete. — *n.* **1.** A building material of sand and gravel or broken rock united by cement, used for roadways, bridges, walls, etc. **2.** That which is concrete: often preceded by *the.* — *v.* **·cret·ed, ·cret·ing** *v.t.* **1.** To bring together in one mass or body; cause to coalesce. **2.** To cover with concrete. — *v.i.* **3.** To coalesce; solidify. [< L < *com-* together + *crescere* to grow] — **con·crete′ly** *adv.* — **con·crete′ness** *n.*
con·cre·tion (kon·krē′shən) *n.* **1.** The act or process of growing or coming together; a solidifying. **2.** A concrete mass. — **con·cre′tive** *adj.* — **con·cre′tive·ly** *adv.*
con·cre·tize (kon′kri·tīz) *v.t.* **·tized, ·tiz·ing** To render concrete; make specific.
con·cu·bine (kong′kyə·bīn, kon′-) *n.* **1.** A woman who cohabits with a man without being married to him. **2.** In certain polygamous societies, a secondary wife. [< F < L < *com-* with + *cumbere* to lie] — **con·cu·bi·nage** (kon·kyo͞o′·bə·nij) *n.* — **con·cu′bi·nar·y** *adj.*
con·cu·pis·cence (kon·kyo͞o′pə·səns) *n.* **1.** Sexual desire; lust. **2.** Any immoderate desire. [< L < *com-* thoroughly + *cupere* to desire] — **con·cu′pis·cent** *adj.*
con·cur (kən·kûr′) *v.i.* **·curred, ·cur·ring** **1.** To agree or approve, as in opinion or action. **2.** To cooperate or combine. **3.** To happen at the same time. **4.** To converge to a point, as lines. [< L < *com-* together + *currere* to run]

con·cur·rence (kən·kûr′əns) *n.* **1.** The act of concurring. **2.** Cooperation or combination to effect some purpose or end. **3.** Agreement in mind or opinion; assent; consent. **4.** Simultaneous occurrence; coincidence. **5.** *Geom.* The point where three or more lines meet. Also **con·cur′ren·cy.**

con·cur·rent (kən·kûr′ənt) *adj.* **1.** Occurring together at the same time. **2.** United in action or application; cooperating; coordinate. **3.** *Law* Having the same authority or jurisdiction. **4.** Meeting at or going toward the same point. **5.** In agreement or accordance. — **con·cur′rent·ly** *adv.*

con·cus·sion (kən·kush′ən) *n.* **1.** A violent shaking; jar. **2.** *Pathol.* A violent shock to some organ, esp. to the brain, by a fall, sudden blow, or blast. [< L < *com-* together + *quatere* to strike, beat] — **con·cus·sive** (kən·kus′iv) *adj.*

con·demn (kən·dem′) *v.t.* **1.** To hold to be wrong; censure. **2.** To pronounce judicial sentence against. **3.** To show the guilt of; convict. **4.** To pronounce or declare to be unfit for use, usually by official order. **5.** *U.S.* To appropriate for public use by judicial decree; declare forfeited. [< L < *com-* thoroughly + *damnare* to condemn] — **con·dem·na·ble** (kən·dem′nə·bəl) *adj.* — **con·demn·er** (kən·dem′ər) *n.*

con·dem·na·tion (kon′dem·nā′shən) *n.* **1.** The act of condemning, or the state of being condemned. **2.** A cause or occasion for condemning. — **con·dem·na·to·ry** (kən·dem′nə·tô′rē, -tō′rē) *adj.*

con·den·sa·tion (kon′den·sā′shən) *n.* **1.** The act of condensing, or the state of being condensed. **2.** Any product of condensing.

con·dense (kən·dens′) *v.* **·densed, ·dens·ing** *v.t.* **1.** To compress or make dense; consolidate. **2.** To abridge or make concise, as an essay. **3.** To change from the gaseous to the liquid state, or from the liquid to the solid state, as by cooling or compression. — *v.i.* **4.** To become condensed. [< L < *com-* together + *densus* crowded, close] — **con·den′sa·bil′i·ty** or **con·den′si·bil′i·ty** *n.* — **con·den′sa·ble** or **con·den′si·ble** *adj.*

condensed milk Cow's milk, sweetened with sugar, and thickened by evaporation of its water content.

con·dens·er (kən·den′sər) *n.* **1.** One who or that which condenses. **2.** Any device for reducing a vapor to liquid or solid form. **3.** *Electr.* A capacitor. **4.** *Optics* A combination of lenses for effectively focusing light rays.

con·de·scend (kon′di·send′) *v.i.* **1.** To lower oneself (to do something); deign. **2.** To behave in a patronizing manner. [< MF < LL < L *com-* together + *descendere* to stoop] — **con′de·scen′sion, con′de·scen′dence** *n.*

con·de·scend·ing (kon′di·sen′ding) *adj.* Showing conscious courtesy toward inferiors; esp., making a display of such courtesy; patronizing. — **con′de·scend′ing·ly** *adv.*

con·di·ment (kon′də·mənt) *n.* A sauce, relish, spice, etc., used to season food. [< L *condire* to pickle]

con·di·tion (kən·dish′ən) *n.* **1.** The state or mode of existence of a person or thing. **2.** State of health; esp., a healthful state. **3.** *Informal* An ailment: a heart *condition.* **4.** An event, fact, or circumstance necessary to the occurrence of some other; a prerequisite: Hard work is the *condition* of success. **5.** *Usu. pl.* The circumstances affecting an activity or a mode of existence: poor living *conditions.* **6.** Social status. **7.** In a will, contract, etc., a provision allowing for modification upon the occurrence of some uncertain future event. — **in** (or **out of**) **condition** Fit (or unfit) for proper performance, esp. of some physical activity. — **on condition that** Provided that; if. — *v.t.* **1.** To be a condition or prerequisite of. **2.** To specify as a condition; stipulate. **3.** To render fit or in good condition. **4.** *Psychol.* To train to a behavior pattern or conditioned response. **5.** To accustom (someone) to. — *v.i.* **6.** To bargain; stipulate. [< OF < L < *com-* together + *dicere* to say] — **con·di′tion·er** *n.*

con·di·tion·al (kən·dish′ən·əl) *adj.* **1.** Not absolute; tentative. **2.** *Gram.* Expressing or implying a condition. — *n.* *Gram.* A conditional word, tense, clause, or mood. — **con·di′tion·al′i·ty** (-al′ə·tē) *n.* — **con·di′tion·al·ly** *adv.*

con·di·tioned response (kən·dish′ənd) *Psychol.* A learned response to a previously neutral stimulus, made directly effective by its repeated association with a stimulus normally evoking the response. Also **conditioned reflex.**

con·dole (kən·dōl′) *v.* **·doled, ·dol·ing** *v.i.* To grieve or express sympathy with one in affliction: with *with.* [< LL < L *com-* together + *dolere* to grieve] — **con·do·la·to·ry** (kən·dō′lə·tôr′ē, -tō′rē) *adj.* — **con·dol′er** *n.*

con·do·lence (kən·dō′ləns, *occasionally* kon′də·ləns) *n.* Expression of sympathy with a person in pain or sorrow. Also **con·dole·ment** (kən·dōl′mənt).

con·dom (kon′dəm, kun′-) *n.* A sheath for the penis, usu. made of rubber and having an antivenereal or contraceptive function. [? Alter. of *Conton*, 18th c. English physician]

con·do·min·i·um (kon′də·min′ē·əm) *n.* **1.** Joint sovereignty or ownership. **2.** *U.S.* An apartment house in which the units are owned separately; also, an apartment in such a house. [< NL < L *com-* together + *dominium* rule]

con·done (kən·dōn′) *v.t.* **·doned, ·don·ing** To treat (an offense) as overlooked or as if it had not been committed. [< L < *com-* thoroughly + *donare* to give] — **con′do·na′ti** *n.* — **con·don′er** *n.*

con·dor (kon′dôr, -dər) *n.* A vulture of the high Andes, o of the largest flying birds, having a bare head and a whi downy neck. [< Sp. < Quechua *cuntur*]

con·duce (kən·dōōs′, -dyōōs′) *v.i.* **·duced, ·duc·ing** To he or tend toward a result; contribute: with *to.* [< L *conduc* to bring together]

con·du·cive (kən·dōō′siv, -dyōō′-) *adj.* Contributive promotive; leading; helping: with *to.* Also **con·du·cent** (kə dōō′sənt, -dyōō′-). — **con·du′cive·ness** *n.*

con·duct (*v.* kən·dukt′; *n.* kon′dukt) *v.t.* **1.** To accompa and show the way; guide; escort. **2.** To manage or contr **3.** To direct and lead the performance of, as an orchestr opera, etc. **4.** To serve as a medium of transmission fo convey; transmit. **5.** To act or behave: use reflexively. *v.i.* **6.** To serve as a conductor. **7.** To direct or lead. *n.* **1.** The way a person acts; behavior. **2.** Managemen control. **3.** The act of guiding or leading. [< L < *com-* t gether + *ducere* to lead] — **con·duct′i·bil′i·ty** *n.* — **co duct′i·ble** *adj.* — **con·duc·tive** (kən·duk′tiv) *adj.*

con·duc·tance (kən·duk′təns) *n.* *Electr.* The ability of body to pass a current: the reciprocal of *resistance.*

con·duc·tion (kən·duk′shən) *n.* **1.** *Physics* The transmi sion of heat, sound, or electricity through matter witho motion of the conducting body as a whole. **2.** *Physiol.* T transference of a stimulus along nerve fibers.

con·duc·tiv·i·ty (kon′duk·tiv′ə·tē) *n.* *Physics* The capaci to transmit sound, heat, or electricity.

con·duc·tor (kən·duk′tər) *n.* **1.** One who conducts or lead **2.** *Chiefly U.S.* One who has charge of a railroad car, bu etc. **3.** The director of an orchestra or chorus. **4.** Any su stance, material, or medium that conducts electricity, hea etc. — **con·duc′tor·ship** *n.* — **con·duc′tress** *n.fem.*

con·duit (kon′dit, -dōō·it) *n.* **1.** A channel or pipe for co veying water or other liquid; a canal; aqueduct. **2.** A co ered passage or tube for electric wires. [< MF < L < *co* together + *ducere* to lead]

cone (kōn) *n.* **1.** *Geom.* **a** A surface generated by a straig line passing through all the points of a fixed closed curve ar a fixed point (the vertex) outside the plane of the curve. **b** solid bounded by such a surface. **2.** A thing that tapers un formly from a circular part to a point, as a machine part the pastry shell used to hold ice cream. **3.** *Bot.* A dry mult ple fruit, as of the pine, composed of scales arranged sy metrically around an axis and enclosing seeds. — *v.t.* **cone con·ing** To shape conically. [< L < Gk. *kōnos*]

con·el·rad (kon′əl·rad) *n.* A technique for controlling rad signals from stations so as to prevent enemy aircraft from u ing the signals for navigation or information. [< CON(TRO OF) EL(ECTROMAGNETIC) RAD(IATION)]

Con·es·to·ga wagon (kon′is·tō′gə) *U.S.* A type of covered wagon with broad wheels, used by American pioneers for westward travel over the prairies. [after *Conestoga*, Pa., where first made]

CONESTOGA WAGON

co·ney (kō′nē, kun′ē) See CONY.

con·fab (kon′fab) *Informal v.i.* **·fabbed, ·fab·bing** To converse. — *n.* A conversation. [Short for CONFABULATION]

con·fab·u·late (kən·fab′yə·lāt) *v.i.* **·lat·ed, ·lat·ing** To chat; gossip; converse. [< L < *com-* t gether + *fabulari* to chat] — **con·fab′u·la′tion** *n.* — **co fab·u·la·to·ry** (kən·fab′yə·lə·tôr′ē, -tō′rē) *adj.*

con·fec·tion (kən·fek′shən) *n.* **1.** The act or process mixing or compounding. **2.** Any of various sweet prepar tions, as candy or preserves. — **con·fec′tion·ar·y** *adj.* &

con·fec·tion·er (kən·fek′shən·ər) *n.* One who makes deals in confectionery.

confectioner's sugar A finely ground powdered suga used in icings, confections, etc.

con·fec·tion·er·y (kən·fek′shən·er′ē) *n.* *pl.* **·er·ies** 1 Sweetmeats collectively. **2.** A confectioner's shop, or th business of a confectioner.

con·fed·er·a·cy (kən·fed′ər·ə·sē) *n.* *pl.* **·cies** **1.** A union states or persons for mutual support or action; a league; all ance. **2.** An unlawful combination; conspiracy. — **th Confederacy** The Confederate States of America: als **Southern Confederacy.**

con·fed·er·ate (*n., adj.* kən·fed′ər·it; *v.* kən·fed′ə·rāt) One who takes part in a league or plot; an associate; accom plice. — *adj.* Associated in a confederacy. — *v.t.* & *v.* **·at·ed, ·at·ing** To form or join in a confederacy. [< LL < *com-* together + *fœdus* league] — **con·fed′er·a′tive** *adj.*

Con·fed·er·ate (kən·fed′ər·it) *adj.* Pertaining to the Con federate States of America. — *n.* An adherent of the Con federate States of America. Abbr. *Confed.*

Confederate States of America A league of eleve southern States that seceded from the United States durin the period from December, 1860 to May, 1861.

n·fed·er·a·tion (kən·fed′ə·rā′shən) *n.* **1.** The act of con-
derating, or the state of being confederated. **2.** An asso-
ation of states usu. less permanent than a federation.
n·fed·er·a·tion (kən·fed′ə·rā′shən) *n.* **1.** The federa-
on formed by Ontario, Quebec, Nova Scotia, and New
runswick in 1867, now including ten provinces. **2.** The
nion of the American colonies, 1781–89, under the Articles
Confederation.
n·fer (kən·fûr′) *v.* **·ferred, ·fer·ring** *v.t.* **1.** To grant as a
ift or benefit; bestow. Abbr. *cf.* — *v.i.* **2.** To hold a con-
rence; consult together; take counsel. [< L < *com-* tother + *ferre* to bring, carry] — **con·fer′ment** *n.* — **con·**
r′ra·ble *adj.* — **con·fer′rer** *n.*
n·fer·ee (kon′fə·rē′) *n.* One who takes part in conference
a conference. Also **con′fer·ree′.**
n·fer·ence (kon′fər·əns, -frəns) *n.* **1.** A discussion or con-
ltation on some important matter; also, a formal meeting
r this. **2.** A league or association, as of athletic teams,
hools, churches, etc. — **con′fer·en′tial** (-fə·ren′shəl) *adj.*
n·fess (kən·fes′) *v.t.* **1.** To acknowledge or admit, as a
ult, guilt, or sin. **2.** To concede or admit to be true. **3.**
o acknowledge belief or faith in. **4.** *Eccl.* **a** To admit or
ake known (one's sins), esp. to a priest, in order to obtain
osolution. **b** To hear the confession of: said of a priest. —
i. **5.** To make acknowledgment, as of fault or crime: with
. **6.** To make confession to a priest. [< MF < L < *com-*
oroughly + *fateri* to own, declare] — **con·fess′ed·ly** *adv.*
— **Syn. 1.** *Confess* is now generally restricted to the sense of
aking known to others one's own error or wrongdoing: to *confess*
robbery. We *acknowledge* that for which we are responsible, often
ith no bad implication: to *acknowledge* one's signature. *Admit*
d *concede* indicate a yielding to the assertion or wish of another;
e *admit* the truth of an allegation; we *concede* a demand, claim,
posing view, etc. — **Ant.** deny, disavow, repudiate.
n·fes·sion (kən·fesh′ən) *n.* **1.** The act of confessing; ac-
nowledgment; admission, esp. of guilt. **2.** That which is
nfessed. **3.** A statement, esp. a formal document, in
hich something is confessed. **4.** *Eccl.* The contrite ac-
nowledgment of one's sins to a priest in order to obtain ab-
lution. **5.** A body of doctrine put forth as the belief of a
iurch: also **confession of faith.** **6.** A church holding a par-
cular confession of faith.
n·fes·sion·al (kən·fesh′ən·əl) *adj.* Of, pertaining to, or
ke confession. — *n.* A small enclosure or stall where a
iest hears confessions. Also *Rare* **con·fes′sion·ar′y** (-er′ē).
n·fes·sor (kən·fes′ər) *n.* **1.** A priest who hears confes-
ons. **2.** One who confesses. Also **con·fess′er.** Abbr. *conf.*
n·fet·ti (kən·fet′ē) *n.pl.* **1.** (*construed as sing.*) Small
ieces of colored paper thrown at carnivals, weddings, etc.
. Bonbons. [< Ital., pl. of *confetto* confection]
n·fi·dant (kon′fə·dant′, -dänt′, kon′fə·dant, -dänt) *n.*
person to whom secrets are confided. — **con′fi·dante′**
fem.
n·fide (kən·fīd′) *v.* **·fid·ed, ·fid·ing** *v.t.* **1.** To reveal in
ust or confidence. **2.** To put into another's trust or keep-
g. — *v.i.* **3.** To have trust; impart secrets trustingly:
ith *in.* [< L < *com-* thoroughly + *fidere* to trust] —
n·fid′er *n.*
n·fi·dence (kon′fə·dəns) *n.* **1.** A feeling of trust in a per-
n or thing; reliance; faith. **2.** A relationship of trustful in-
macy. **3.** Self-assurance; also, fearlessness. **4.** Excessive
lf-assurance. **5.** A feeling of certainty. **6.** A secret. — **to**
ke into one's confidence To trust with one's secrets.
nfidence game A swindle in which the victim is de-
auded after his confidence has been won: also, *U.S. Slang,*
n game. Also **confidence trick.**
nfidence man A swindler in a confidence game.
n·fi·dent (kon′fə·dənt) *adj.* **1.** Having confidence; as-
ured: *confident* of success. **2.** Self-assured; also, bold; pre
umptuous. — *n.* A confidant. — **con′fi·dent·ly** *adv.*
n·fi·den·tial (kon′fə·den′shəl) *adj.* **1.** Secret: *confiden-*
al information. **2.** Enjoying another's confidence; trusted.
. Denoting the confiding of secrets: a *confidential* manner.
— **con·fi·den·ti·al·i·ty** (kon′fə·den′shē·al′ə·tē), **con′fi·den′·**
al·ness *n.* — **con′fi·den′tial·ly** *adv.*
n·fid·ing (kən·fī′ding) *adj.* That trusts or confides; un-
uspicious. — **con·fid′ing·ly** *adv.* — **con·fid′ing·ness** *n.*
n·fig·u·ra·tion (kən·fig′yə·rā′shən) *n.* **1.** The arrange-
ent of the parts of a thing, or the form resulting therefrom;
onformation; contour. **2.** *Psychol.* A gestalt. [< LL < L
om- together + *figurare* to shape, fashion] — **con·fig′u·ra′·**
ion·al, con·fig·u·ra·tive (kən·fig′yər·ə·tiv, -yə·rā′tiv) *adj.*
n·fine (*v.* kən·fīn′; *n.* kon′fīn) *v.* **·fined, ·fin·ing** *v.t.* **1.** To
hut within an enclosure; imprison. **2.** To restrain or oblige
o stay within doors. **3.** To hold within limits; restrict: to
onfine remarks. — *n. Usu. pl.* A boundary or border. [<
MF < Ital. < L < *com-* together + *finis* border] — **con·**
in′a·ble or **con·fine′a·ble** *adj.* — **con·fin′er** *n.*

con·fine·ment (kən·fīn′mənt) *n.* **1.** The act of confining, or the state of being confined. **2.** Childbirth.
con·firm (kən·fûrm′) *v.t.* **1.** To assure the validity of; verify. **2.** To add firmness to; strengthen. **3.** To render valid and binding by formal approval. **4.** To receive into the church by confirmation. [< OF < L < *com-* thoroughly + *firmus* strong] — **con·firm′a·ble** *adj.* — **con·firm′er,** *Law* **con·firm·or** (kon′fər·môr′, kən·fûr′mər) *n.*
con·fir·ma·tion (kon′fər·mā′shən) *n.* **1.** The act of confirming. **2.** That which confirms; proof. **3.** A religious rite in which a person is admitted to all the privileges of a church.
con·firm·a·to·ry (kən·fûr′mə·tôr′ē, -tō′rē) *adj.* Confirming.
con·firmed (kən·fûrmd′) *adj.* **1.** Firmly established; ratified. **2.** Inveterate; chronic; habitual: a *confirmed* skeptic. **3.** Having received the rites of religious confirmation.
con·fis·cate (kon′fis·kāt) *v.t.* **·cat·ed, ·cat·ing** **1.** To seize or appropriate for the public use or treasury, usu. as a penalty. **2.** To appropriate by or as by authority. — *adj.* **1.** Appropriated or forfeited. **2.** Deprived of property through confiscation. [< L < *com-* together + *fiscus* chest, treasury] — **con′fis·ca′tion** *n.* — **con′fis·ca′tor** *n.* — **con·fis·ca·to·ry** (kən·fis′kə·tôr′ē, -tō′rē) *adj.*
con·fla·gra·tion (kon′flə·grā′shən) *n.* A great or extensive fire. [< L < *com-* thoroughly + *flagare* to burn]
con·flict (*n.* kon′flikt; *v.* kən·flikt′) *n.* **1.** A struggle; battle. **2.** Mutual antagonism, as of ideas, interests, etc. **3.** A clash between contradictory impulses within an individual. — *v.i.* **1.** To come into collision; be in mutual opposition; clash. **2.** To engage in battle; struggle. [< L < *com-* together + *fligere* to strike] — **con·flic′tive** *adj.*
con·flu·ence (kon′flo͞o·əns) *n.* **1.** A flowing together of streams; also, the place where they meet. **2.** The body or stream of water so formed. **3.** A flocking together; crowd. Also **con·flux** (kon′fluks). [< L < *com-* together + *fluere* to flow] — **con′flu·ent** *adj.* — **con′flu·ent·ly** *adv.*
con·form (kən·fôrm′) *v.i.* **1.** To show identity or resemblance; correspond: with *to*: to *conform* to specification. **2.** To adhere to conventional behavior. — *v.t.* **3.** To make the same or similar: with *to.* **4.** To bring (oneself) into harmony or agreement: with *to.* [< F < L < *com-* together + *formare* to shape] — **con·form′er** *n.*
con·form·a·ble (kən·fôr′mə·bəl) *adj.* **1.** In agreement; harmonious. **2.** Corresponding in form, character, or use; similar. **3.** Compliant or obedient; submissive. — **con·form′a·bil′i·ty, con·form′a·ble·ness** *n.* — **con·form′a·bly** *adv.*
con·form·ance (kən·fôr′məns) *n.* Conformity.
con·for·ma·tion (kon′fôr·mā′shən) *n.* **1.** The manner in which a thing is formed; structure or outline. **2.** The symmetrical arrangement and shaping of parts. **3.** The act of conforming, or the state of being conformed.
con·form·ist (kən·fôr′mist) *n.* One who conforms.
con·form·i·ty (kən·fôr′mə·tē) *n.* *pl.* **·ties** **1.** Correspondence in form, manner, or use; agreement; harmony; congruity. **2.** The act or habit of conforming; acquiescence.
con·found (kon·found′, kən-; *for def. 4* kon′found′) *v.t.* **1.** To confuse, amaze, or bewilder. **2.** To confuse with something else; fail to distinguish. **3.** To confuse or mingle indistinguishably. **4.** To damn: used as an oath. [< AF, OF < L < *com-* together + *fundere* to pour] — **con·found′er** *n.*
— **Syn. 1.** puzzle, perplex, dumfound, mystify.
con·found·ed (kon·foun′did, kən-) *adj.* **1.** Confused or abashed. **2.** *Informal* Damned; detestable: a *confounded* cheat. — **con·found′ed·ly** *adv.*
con·frere (kon′frâr) *n.* A fellow member; a colleague. [< MF < L *com-* with + *frater* brother]
con·front (kən·frunt′) *v.t.* **1.** To stand face to face with; face defiantly. **2.** To put face to face: to *confront* a liar with the truth. [< F < L *com-* together + *frons, frontis* face, forehead] — **con·front′ment** *n.* — **con·front′er** *n.*
con·fron·ta·tion (kon′frən·tā′shən) *n.* **1.** The act of confronting, or the state of being confronted. **2.** The provocation of conflict as a means of effecting political change; also, a crisis or conflict so caused.
Con·fu·cian·ism (kən·fyo͞o′shən·iz′əm) *n.* The ethical system taught by Confucius, emphasizing ancestor worship, devotion to family and friends, and the maintenance of justice and peace. — **Con·fu′cian·ist** *n.* — **Con·fu′cian** *n. & adj.*
con·fuse (kən·fyo͞oz′) *v.t.* **·fused, ·fus·ing** **1.** To perplex or perturb; confound; bewilder. **2.** To mix indiscriminately; jumble. **3.** To mistake one for the other. [< L < *com-* together + *fundere* to pour] — **con·fus·ed·ly** (kən·fyo͞o′zid·lē) *adv.* — **con·fus′ed·ness** *n.* — **con·fus′ing·ly** *adv.*
con·fu·sion (kən·fyo͞o′zhən) *n.* **1.** The act of confusing, or the state of being confused. **2.** Disarray; disorder. **3.** Perplexity of mind. **4.** Embarrassment. — **con·fu′sion·al** *adj.*
con·fute (kən·fyo͞ot′) *v.t.* **·fut·ed, ·fut·ing** **1.** To prove to be wrong, false, or invalid; refute successfully. **2.** To overwhelm with proofs or disproofs; prove (a person) to be in the

wrong. **3.** To bring to naught; confound. **— Syn.** See REFUTE. [< L *confutare* to check, restrain] **— con·fu·ta·tion** (kon′fyo͝o·tā′shən) *n.* **— con·fut′er** *n.*
con·ga (kong′gə) *n.* **1.** A dance of Latin American origin in which the dancers form a winding line. **2.** The music for this dance, in fast 4/4 time. [< Am. Sp.]
con game *U.S. Slang* A confidence game.
con·gé (kon′zhā, *Fr.* kôn·zhā′) *n.* **1.** A formal leave-taking. **2.** Dismissal. [< F < L < *com-* thoroughly + *ire* to go]
con·geal (kən·jēl′) *v.t. & v.i.* **1.** To change from a fluid to a solid condition, as by freezing or curdling. **2.** To clot or coagulate, as blood. [< MF < L < *com-* together + *gelare* to freeze] **— con·geal′a·ble** *adj.* **— con·geal′er** *n.* **— con·geal′ment** *n.*
con·gen·ial (kən·jēn′yəl) *adj.* **1.** Having similar character or tastes; sympathetic. **2.** Suited to one's disposition; agreeable: a *congenial* job. **— con·ge·ni·al·i·ty** (kən·jē′nē·al′ə·tē) *n.* **— con·gen′ial·ly** *adv.*
con·gen·i·tal (kən·jen′ə·təl) *adj.* **1.** Existing prior to or at birth: a *congenital* defect. **2.** Loosely, disposed as if by birth: a *congenital* liar. [< L < *com-* together + *genitus,* pp. of *gignere* to bear] **— con·gen′i·tal·ly** *adv.*
con·ger (kong′gər) *n.* A marine eel, used as a food fish. Also **conger eel.** [< OF < L < Gk. *gongros*]
con·ge·ries (kon′jə·rēz, kon·jir′ēz) *n.pl.* (*usu. construed as sing.*) A collection of things; a mass; heap. [< L < *congerere* to bring together]
con·gest (kən·jest′) *v.t.* **1.** To collect or crowd together; overcrowd. **2.** *Pathol.* To surcharge (an organ or part) with an excess of blood. **—** *v.i.* **3.** To become congested. [< L < *com-* together + *gerere* to bear, carry] **— con·ges′tion** *n.* **— con·ges′tive** *adj.*
con·glom·er·ate (*adj., n.* kən·glom′ər·it; *v.* kən·glom′ə·rāt) *adj.* **1.** Massed or clustered. **2.** *Geol.* Consisting of loosely cemented heterogeneous material: *conglomerate* clay: also **con·glom·er·at·ic** (kən·glom′ə·rat′ik), **con·glom′er·it′ic** (-ə·rit′ik). **—** *n.* **1.** A heterogeneous collection; cluster. **2.** *Geol.* A rock composed of pebbles, etc., loosely cemented together. **—** *v.t. & v.i.* **·at·ed, ·at·ing** To gather into a cohering mass. [< L < *com-* together + *glomus, glomeris* ball] **— con·glom′er·a′tion** *n.*
con·glu·ti·nate (kən·glo͞o′tə·nāt) *v.t. & v.i.* **·nat·ed, ·nat·ing** To glue or stick together; adhere. **—** *adj.* Glued together; united by adhesion. [< L < *com-* together + *glutinare* to stick] **— con·glu′ti·na′tion** *n.* **— con·glu′ti·na′tive** *adj.*
congo snake A tailed aquatic salamander of the SE U.S. Also **congo eel.**
con·grat·u·late (kən·grach′o͝o·lāt) *v.t.* **·lat·ed, ·lat·ing** To express pleasure in or otherwise acknowledge the achievement or good fortune of (another); felicitate. [< L < *com-* together + *gratulari* to rejoice] **— con·grat′u·lant** *adj. & n.* **— con·grat′u·la′tor** *n.* **— con·grat′u·la·to′ry** *adj.*
con·grat·u·la·tion (kən·grach′o͝o·lā′shən) *n.* **1.** The act of congratulating. **2.** *pl.* Expressions of pleasure and good wishes on another's fortune or success.
con·gre·gate (*v.* kong′grə·gāt; *adj.* kong′grə·git) *v.t. & v.i.* **·gat·ed, ·gat·ing** To bring or come together into a crowd; assemble. **—** *adj.* **1.** Relating to a congregation. **2.** Gathered together; collected. [< L < *com-* together + *gregare* to collect] **— con′gre·ga′tive** *adj.* **— con′gre·ga′tor** *n.*
con·gre·ga·tion (kong′grə·gā′shən) *n.* **1.** The act of congregating; a collecting into one mass, body, or assembly. **2.** An assemblage of people or things. **3.** A group of people met together for worship; also, the body of persons who worship in a local church; a parish. **— con′gre·ga′tion·al** *adj.*
con·gre·ga·tion·al·ism (kong′grə·gā′shən·əl·iz′əm) *n.* A form of church government in which each local congregation is autonomous in all church matters.
Con·gre·ga·tion·al·ism (kong′grə·gā′shən·əl·iz′əm) *n.* The type of organization and system of beliefs of an evangelical Protestant denomination (**Congregational Christian Churches**) practicing congregationalism. **— Con′gre·ga′tion·al** *adj.* **— Con′gre·ga′tion·al·ist** *n.*
con·gress (kong′gris) *n.* **1.** An assembly or conference. **2.** A coming together; meeting. **3.** The legislature of various nations, esp. of a republic. **—** *v.i.* To meet at a congress. [< L < *com-* together + *gradi* to walk]
Con·gress (kong′gris) *n.* The legislative body of the U.S., consisting of the Senate and the House of Representatives; also, this body during one of the two-year periods between elections to the House of Representatives.
con·gres·sion·al (kən·gresh′ən·əl) *adj.* *Often cap. U.S.* Pertaining to a congress, esp. to the U.S. Congress.
Congressional district *U.S.* A division of a State, entitled to one representative in Congress.
Congressional Medal of Honor See MEDAL OF HONOR.
Congressional Record *U.S.* An official publication containing the debates and proceedings of Congress.
con·gress·man (kong′gris·mən) *n.* *pl.* **·men** (-mən) *Often cap.* A member of the U.S. Congress, esp. of the House of Representatives. **— con′gress·wom′an** *n.fem.*

con·gru·ence (kong′gro͞o·əns) *n.* Conformity; agreemen
con·gru·ent (kong′gro͞o·ənt) *adj.* **1.** Agreeing or confor ing; congruous. **2.** *Geom.* Exactly coinciding when sup imposed. [< L *congruere* to agree] **— con′gru·en·cy** *n.* **— con′gru·ent·ly** *adv.*
con·gru·i·ty (kən·gro͞o′ə·tē) *n.* *pl.* **·ties 1.** The state quality of being congruous; agreement or fitness. **2.** example of agreement. **3.** *Geom.* Exact correspondence wh superimposed. **— Syn.** See HARMONY.
con·gru·ous (kong′gro͞o·əs) *adj.* **1.** Agreeing in nature qualities; harmonious. **2.** Appropriate; fit. **3.** *Geom.* C gruent. **— con′gru·ous·ly** *adv.* **— con′gru·ous·ness** *n.*
con·ic (kon′ik) *adj.* **1.** Cone-shaped. **2.** Of or formed or upon a cone. Also **con′i·cal.** **—** *n. Math.* A conic sectic [< Gk. *kōnos* cone] **— con′i·cal·ly** *adv.*
conic section *Math.* A curve formed by the intersection of a plane with a cone having a circular base, being an ellipse, parabola, or hyperbola, according to the inclination of the cutting plane to the axis.

CONIC SECTION
a Circle. *b* Parabola. *c* Hyperbola. *d* Ellipse. *e* Right-line.

co·nid·i·um (kō·nid′ē·əm) *n.* *pl.* **·nid·i·a** (-nid′ē·ə) *Bot.* An asexual propagative spore of many species of fungi. Also **co·nid·i·o·spore** (kō·nid′ē·ə·spôr′, -spōr′). [< NL < Gk. *konis* dust] **— co·nid′i·al** *adj.*
con·i·fer (kon′ə·fər, kō′nə-) *n.* Any of a large and widely distributed family of evergreen shrubs and trees, as the pines, spruces, firs, and junipers. [< L < *conus* cone + *ferre* bear] **— co·nif·er·ous** (kō·nif′ər·əs) *adj.*
con·jec·tur·al (kən·jek′chər·əl) *adj.* **1.** Involving or pendent upon conjecture. **2.** Given to conjecture. **— co jec′tur·al·ly** *adv.*
con·jec·ture (kən·jek′chər) *v.* **·tured, ·tur·ing** *v.t.* **1.** conclude from incomplete evidence; guess; infer. **—** *v.i.* To make a conjecture. **— Syn.** See SUPPOSE. **—** *n.* **1.** ference from incomplete evidence. **2.** A conclusion based this; a guess; surmise. **— Syn.** See HYPOTHESIS. [< L *com-* together + *jacere* to throw] **— con·jec′tur·a·ble** *a* **— con·jec′tur·a·bly** *adv.* **— con·jec′tur·er** *n.*
con·join (kən·join′) *v.t. &. v.i.* To join together; associa connect; unite. [< MF < L < *com-* together + *jungere* join] **— con·join′er** *n.*
con·joint (kən·joint′) *adj.* **1.** Associated; conjoined. Joint. **— con·joint′ly** *adv.*
con·ju·gal (kon′jo͝o·gəl, -jə-) *adj.* Pertaining to marriage to the relation of husband and wife; connubial. [< F < *conjungere* to join in marriage] **— con·ju·gal·i·ty** (kon′jo gal′ə·tē) *n.* **— con′ju·gal·ly** *adv.*
con·ju·gate (kon′jo͝o·gāt, -jə-; *for adj., n., also* kon′jo͝o·g -jə-) *v.* **·gat·ed, ·gat·ing** *v.t.* **1.** *Gram.* To give the infle tions of (a verb) for person, number, tense, mood, and voi **—** *v.i.* **2.** *Biol.* To unite in conjugation. **—** *adj.* **1.** Join in pairs; coupled. **2.** Kindred in origin and, usually, mea ing: said of words. **—** *n.* **1.** A conjugate word. **2.** A me ber of any conjugate pair. [< L < *com-* together + *jugo* to join] **— con′ju·ga′tive** *adj.* **— con′ju·ga′tor** *n.*
con·ju·ga·tion (kon′jo͝o·gā′shən, -jə-) *n.* **1.** A joining being joined together. **2.** *Gram.* **a** The inflection of verl **b** A schematic presentation of the entire inflection of a ver **c** A class of verbs that are inflected in the same manner. **con′ju·ga′tion·al** *adj.* **— con′ju·ga′tion·al·ly** *adv.*
con·junct (kən·jungkt′, kon′jungkt) *adj.* Joined togethe conjoined. [See CONJOIN.] **— con·junct′ly** *adv.*
con·junc·tion (kən·jungk′shən) *n.* **1.** The act of joining t gether, or the state of being so joined. **2.** A coincidence. *Astron.* **a** The position of two celestial bodies when they a in the same celestial longitude. **b** The position of a plan when it is on a direct line with the earth and the sun. *Gram.* A word used to connect words, phrases, clauses, sentences; one of the eight traditional parts of speech. **coordinate conjunction** A conjunction, as *and, but, or,* th joins words or groups of words of equal rank. **— subord nate conjunction** A conjunction, as *as, because, if, th though,* that joins clauses of minor rank to principal claus **— con·junc′tion·al** *adj.* **— con·junc′tion·al·ly** *adv.*
con·junc·ti·va (kon′jungk·tī′və, kən·jungk′tə·və) *n.* **·vas** or **·vae** (-vē) *Anat.* The mucous membrane lining t eyelids and covering the front part of the eyeball. For illu see EYE. [< NL (*membrana*) *conjunctiva* connective (mer brane)] **— con′junc·ti′val** *adj.*
con·junc·tive (kən·jungk′tiv) *adj.* **1.** Joining; connectiv **2.** Joined together. **3.** *Gram.* **a** Serving as a conjunctio **b** Of an adverb, serving to unite sentences in larger units, *furthermore, nevertheless,* etc. **—** *n. Gram.* A conjuncti word. [See CONJOIN.] **— con·junc′tive·ly** *adv.*
con·junc·ti·vi·tis (kən·jungk′tə·vī′tis) *n.* *Pathol.* Inflar mation of the conjunctiva.
con·junc·ture (kən·jungk′chər) *n.* **1.** A combination of ci cumstances or events; juncture. **2.** A critical situation; cr sis. **3.** Conjunction; union.

n·ju·ra·tion (kon′jo͞o·rā′shən) *n.* **1.** The doing of something by magic. **2.** A magic spell or expression.
n·jure (*v. def. 1* kən·jo͝or′; *v. defs. 2–5, adj.* kon′jər, kun′-) . **·jured, ·jur·ing** *v.t.* **1.** To call on or appeal to solemnly; adjure. **2.** To summon by incantation or spell, as a devil. **.** To accomplish by or as by magic. — *v.i.* **4.** To practice nagic, especially legerdemain. **5.** To summon a devil or pirit by incantation. — *adj. U.S. Dial.* Practicing magic. < OF < L < *com-* together + *jurare* to swear]
n·jur·er (kon′jər·ər, kun′- *for def. 1*; kən·jo͝or′ər *for def. 2*) . **1.** One who practices magic; a sorcerer or magician. **2.**)ne who appeals solemnly. Also **con′jur·or.**
nk (kongk) *n. Slang* **1.** *U.S.* The head. **2.** The nose. — *.t. U.S. Slang* To hit on the head. — **to conk out 1.** *Inormal* To stall or fail: said of engines. **2.** *U.S. Slang* To become suddenly weak and tired. [? < CONCH]
n man (kon) *U.S. Slang* A confidence man.
nn (kon) See CON².
n·nect (kə·nekt′) *v.t.* **1.** To join or fasten together; link. **.** To associate by some relation, as in thought or action. — *v.i.* **3.** To join or fit. **4.** To meet so that passengers can ransfer from one route to another: said of trains, buses, etc. < L < *com-* together + *nectere* to bind] — **con·nec′tor** or **on·nect′er** *n.*
nnecting rod *Mech.* A rod joining a piston with the rankshaft in an engine, pump, etc.: also called *piston rod.*
n·nec·tion (kə·nek′shən) *n.* **1.** The act of connecting, or he state of being connected. **2.** That which joins or relates; bond; link. **3.** Logical sequence of words or ideas; cohernce. **4.** Context. **5.** Family relationship. **6.** A religious ect. **7.** *Usually pl.* A group of friends or associates, often onsidered as influential in some way. **8.** *Often pl.* A transer or continuation from one route or vehicle to another. Also *Brit.* **con·nex′ion.** — **con·nec′tion·al** *adj.*
n·nec·tive (kə·nek′tiv) *adj.* Capable of connecting, or erving to connect. — *n.* **1.** That which connects. **2.** *Gram.* A connecting word or particle, as a conjunction. — **on·nec′tive·ly** *adv.* — **con·nec·tiv·i·ty** (kon′ek·tiv′ə·tē) *n.*
nnective tissue *Anat.* The fibrous tissue that serves to nite and support the various organs and tissues of the body.
nning tower 1. The armored pilothouse of a warship. **.** In submarines, an observation tower.
n·nip·tion (kə·nip′shən) *n. U.S. Informal* A fit of hyseria, rage, etc. [Cf. dial. E *canapshus* ill-tempered]
n·niv·ance (kə·nī′vəns) *n.* The act or fact of conniving; ilent assent, esp. to wrongdoing. Also **con·niv′ence.**
n·nive (kə·nīv′) *v.i.* **·nived, ·niv·ing 1.** To encourage or ssent to a wrong by silence or feigned ignorance: with *at.* **2.** To be in collusion: with *with.* [< L *conivere* to wink, shut he eyes] — **con·niv′er** *n.*
n·nois·seur (kon′ə·sûr′) *n.* One competent to judge ritically because of thorough knowledge, esp. in matters f art and taste. — **Syn.** See AMATEUR. [< F, ult. < L *ognoscere* to know, understand] — **con′nois·seur′ship** *n.*
n·no·ta·tion (kon′ə·tā′shən) *n.* **1.** The suggestive or associative significance of an expression, additional to the literal meaning. Compare DENOTATION. **2.** The act of connoting.
n·no·ta·tive (kon′ə·tā′tiv, kə·nō′tə·tiv) *adj.* Having or f the nature of connotation. — **con′no·ta′tive·ly** *adv.*
n·note (kə·nōt′) *v.t.* **·not·ed, ·not·ing** To suggest or imply along with the literal meaning. [< Med.L < L *com-* together + *notare* to mark]
n·nu·bi·al (kə·no͞o′bē·əl, -nyo͞o′-) *adj.* Pertaining to mariage or to the married state. [< L < *com-* together + *nubere* to marry] — **con·nu′bi·al′i·ty** *n.* — **con·nu′bi·al·ly** *adv.*
o·noid (kō′noid) *adj.* Cone-shaped. Also **co·noi′dal.** — *n.* Something cone-shaped. [< Gk. *kōnoeidēs* conical]
on·quer (kong′kər) *v.t.* **1.** To overcome or subdue by force, as in war; vanquish. **2.** To overcome by mental or moral force; surmount. — *v.i.* **3.** To be victorious. [< OF < *com-* thoroughly + *quaerere* to search for, procure] — **con′quer·or** *n.* — **con′quer·a·ble** *adj.*
on·quest (kon′kwest, kong′-) *n.* **1.** The act of conquering. **2.** The thing conquered. **3.** A winning of another's favor or love. **4.** One whose favor or love has been won.
on·quis·ta·dor (kon·kwis′tə·dôr, -kis′-; *Sp.* kōng·kēs′tä·thōr′) *n. pl.* **·dors,** *Sp.* **·do·res** (-thō′räs) A conqueror; esp., any of the Spanish conquerors of Mexico and Peru in the 16th century. [< Sp. < *conquistar* to conquer]
on·san·guin·e·ous (kon′sang·gwin′ē·əs) *adj.* Of the same blood or ancestry; akin. Also **con·san·guine** (kon·sang′gwin). [< L < *com-* together + *sanguis* blood] — **con′san·guin′e·ous·ly** *adv.*
on·san·guin·i·ty (kon′sang·gwin′ə·tē) *n.* **1.** Relationship resulting from common ancestry; blood relationship. **2.** Any close affinity or connection. — **Syn.** See RELATIONSHIP.
on·science (kon′shəns) *n.* **1.** The faculty by which distinctions are made between moral right and wrong. **2.** Conformity in conduct to the prescribed moral standard. — **in (all) conscience 1.** In truth; in reason and honesty. **2.** Certainly; assuredly. [< OF < L *conscire* to know inwardly] — **con′science·less** *adj.*
con·sci·en·tious (kon′shē·en′shəs, kon′sē-) *adj.* **1.** Governed by or done in accordance with conscience; scrupulous. **2.** Careful and thorough; painstaking. — **con′sci·en′tious·ly** *adv.* — **con′sci·en′tious·ness** *n.*
conscientious objector One who, on grounds of religious or moral convictions, refuses to perform military service.
con·scion·a·ble (kon′shən·ə·bəl) *adj. Rare* Conformable to conscience or right; just. — **con′scion·a·bly** *adv.*
con·scious (kon′shəs) *adj.* **1.** Aware of one's own existence or of external objects and conditions. **2.** Aware of some object or fact; *conscious* of one's shortcomings. **3.** Felt by oneself; internally known: *conscious* superiority. **4.** Overly aware of oneself; self-conscious. **5.** Deliberate; intentional. — *n.* That part of mental life of which an individual is aware. [< L *conscius* knowing inwardly < *com-* together + *scire* to know] — **con′scious·ly** *adv.*
con·scious·ness (kon′shəs·nis) *n.* **1.** The state of being conscious; awareness of oneself and one's surroundings. **2.** Awareness of some object, influence, etc. **3.** The mental and emotional awareness of an individual, or of a group.
con·script (*n., adj.* kon′skript; *v.* kən·skript′) *n.* One who is compulsorily enrolled for some service or job. — *adj.* Enlisted by compulsion; conscripted. — *v.t.* To force into military, naval, or other service. [< L < *com-* together + *scribere* to write] — **con·scrip′tion** *n.*
con·script fathers (kon′skript) **1.** The senators of ancient Rome. **2.** The members of any legislative body.
con·se·crate (kon′sə·krāt) *v.t.* **·crat·ed, ·crat·ing 1.** To set apart as sacred; dedicate to sacred uses. **2.** To dedicate; devote: He *consecrated* his life to the cause. **3.** To make revered; hallow: *consecrated* by time. [< L < *com-* thoroughly + *sacer* holy] — **con′se·cra′tion** *n.* — **con′se·cra′tor** *n.* — **con·se·cra·to·ry** (kon′sə·krə·tôr′ē, -tō′rē) *adj.*
con·sec·u·tive (kən·sek′yə·tiv) *adj.* **1.** Following in uninterrupted succession; successive. **2.** Characterized by logical sequence. — **con·sec′u·tive·ly** *adv.* — **con·sec′u·tive·ness** *n.*
con·sen·sus (kən·sen′səs) *n.* A collective opinion; general agreement. ◆ The phrase **consensus of opinion,** although redundant, is now widely used. [< L < *com-* together + *sentire* to feel, think]
con·sent (kən·sent′) *v.i.* To give assent; agree or acquiesce. — *n.* **1.** A voluntary yielding; compliance. **2.** Agreement; harmony; concord. [See CONSENSUS.] — **con·sent′er** *n.*
con·se·quence (kon′sə·kwens, -kwəns) *n.* **1.** That which naturally follows from a preceding action or condition; result. **2.** A logical conclusion. **3.** Distinction: a man of *consequence.* **4.** Importance: an event of no *consequence.*
con·se·quent (kon′sə·kwent, -kwənt) *adj.* **1.** Following as a natural result, or as a logical conclusion. **2.** Characterized by correctness of reasoning; logical. — *n.* **1.** That which follows something else, as in time. **2.** An outcome; result. [< L < *com-* together + *sequi* to follow]
con·se·quen·tial (kon′sə·kwen′shəl) *adj.* **1.** Following as an effect or conclusion. **2.** Of consequence; important. **3.** Having or showing self-importance. — **con′se·quen′ti·al′i·ty con′se·quen′tial·ness** *n.* — **con′se·quen′tial·ly** *adv.*
con·se·quent·ly (kon′sə·kwent′lē, -kwənt·lē) *adv.* As a result; therefore.
con·ser·va·tion (kon′sər·vā′shən) *n.* **1.** The act of keeping or protecting from loss or injury. **2.** The preservation of natural resources, as forests, fisheries, etc., for economic or recreational use; also, an area so preserved. [See CONSERVE] — **con′ser·va′tion·al** *adj.* — **con′ser·va′tion·ist** *n.*
conservation of energy *Physics* The principle that in any closed material system the total amount of energy remains constant, though it may assume different forms successively.
con·ser·va·tism (kən·sûr′və·tiz′əm) *n.* **1.** Devotion to the existing order of things; opposition to change. **2.** The principles of people or groups so devoted.
Con·ser·va·tism (kən·sûr′və·tiz′əm) *n.* The doctrines and policies of the Conservative Party.
con·ser·va·tive (kən·sûr′və·tiv) *adj.* **1.** Inclined to preserve the existing order of things; opposed to change. **2.** Moderate; cautious: a *conservative* estimate. **3.** Conserving; preservative. — *n.* **1.** A conservative person. **2.** A preservative. — **con·ser′va·tively** *adv.* — **con·ser′va·tive·ness** *n.*
Con·ser·va·tive (kən·sûr′və·tiv) *adj.* Of or pertaining to the Conservative Party. — *n.* **1.** A member of this party. **2.** A member of the Progressive-Conservative Party in Canada. Abbr. *C.*
Conservative Judaism That branch of Judaism that accepts as binding the Mosaic Laws, but allows some adjustments to the changed conditions of today.

Conservative Party In Great Britain, the principal right-wing party. See TORY.

con·ser·va·to·ry (kən·sûr′və·tôr′ē, -tō′rē) *n. pl.* **·ries** **1.** A small greenhouse or glass-enclosed room in which plants are grown and displayed. **2.** A school of music. Also **con·ser·va·toire** (kən·sûr′və·twär′). — *adj.* Adapted to preserve.

con·serve (kən·sûrv′; *for n., also* kon′sûrv) *v.t.* **·served, ·serv·ing** **1.** To keep from loss, decay, or depletion; maintain. **2.** To preserve with sugar. — *n. Often pl.* A kind of jam made of several fruits stewed together in sugar, often with nuts, raisins, etc. [< MF < L < *com-* thoroughly + *servare* to keep] — **con·serv′a·ble** *adj.* — **con·serv′er** *n.*

con·sid·er (kən·sid′ər) *v.t.* **1.** To think about or deliberate upon; examine mentally; weigh. **2.** To look upon or regard (as); think (to be). **3.** To hold as an opinion; believe. **4.** To take into account; have regard for: to *consider* the feelings of others. — *v.i.* **5.** To think carefully; deliberate. [< MF < L *considerare* to observe]

con·sid·er·a·ble (kən·sid′ər·ə·bəl) *adj.* **1.** Somewhat large in amount, extent, etc.; much; *considerable* trouble. **2.** Worthy of consideration. — **con·sid′er·a·bly** *adv.*

con·sid·er·ate (kən·sid′ər·it) *adj.* **1.** Thoughtful of others; kind. **2.** Deliberate; considered. — **con·sid′er·ate·ly** *adv.* — **con·sid′er·ate·ness** *n.*

con·sid·er·a·tion (kən·sid′ə·rā′shən) *n.* **1.** The act of considering; deliberation. **2.** A circumstance to be taken into account, as in forming an opinion. **3.** Thoughtful or kindly feeling or treatment; solicitude. **4.** A thought or reflection; opinion. **5.** Something given for a service; fee; recompense. **6.** Claim to be considered; importance. **7.** High regard; esteem. — **in consideration of** In view of, or in return for. — **under consideration** Being thought about or discussed.

con·sid·er·ing (kən·sid′ər·ing) *prep.* In view of; taking into account. — *adv. Informal* Taking all the facts into account.

con·sign (kən·sīn′) *v.t.* **1.** To entrust or commit to the care of another. **2.** To give up or turn over. **3.** To forward or deliver, as merchandise. **4.** To set apart or devote, as for a specific use. [< MF < L < *com-* with + *signum* a seal] — **con·sign′a·ble** *adj.* — **con·sig·na·tion** (kon′sig·nā′shən) *n.*

con·sign·ee (kon′sī·nē′) *n.* One to whom goods are consigned.

con·sign·ment (kən·sīn′mənt) *n.* **1.** A consigning of something, esp. of goods, for sale or disposal. **2.** That which is consigned. — **on consignment** Of goods, paid for by the retailer only after they have been sold.

con·sign·or (kən·sī′nər, kon′sī·nôr′) *n.* One who consigns, esp. goods for sale. Also **con·sign′er.**

con·sist (kən·sist′) *v.i.* **1.** To be made up or constituted: with *of.* **2.** To have as source or basis; exist; inhere: with *in.* **3.** To be compatible; harmonize: with *with.* [< L < *com-* together + *sistere* to stand]

con·sis·ten·cy (kən·sis′tən·sē) *n. pl.* **·cies** **1.** Agreement between things, acts, or statements; logical connection. **2.** Agreement with previous acts, statements, or decisions. **3.** Firmness, nearness, or density. **4.** Degree of firmness, thickness, or density. Also **con·sis′tence.**

con·sis·tent (kən·sis′tənt) *adj.* **1.** Not contradictory or self-contradictory; compatible; harmonious. **2.** Conforming to a single set of principles, or to previous action or belief. [See CONSIST.] — **con·sis′tent·ly** *adv.*

con·sis·to·ry (kən·sis′tər·ē) *n. pl.* **·ries** **1.** *Eccl.* The highest council of the Roman Catholic Church, composed of all the cardinals, and usually presided over by the Pope. **2.** The place where any such body meets, or the meeting itself. [< AF < Med.L *consistere* to stand still, wait] — **con·sis·to·ri·al** (kon′sis·tôr′ē·əl, -tō′rē-), **con′sis·to′ri·an** *adj.*

con·so·la·tion (kon′sə·lā′shən) *n.* **1.** A consoling or being consoled. **2.** One who or that which consoles.

con·sol·a·to·ry (kən·sol′ə·tôr′ē, -tō′rē) *adj.* Consoling.

con·sole[1] (kən·sōl′) *v.t.* **·soled, ·sol·ing** To comfort (a person) in grief or sorrow; cheer. [< MF < L < *com-* together + *solari* to solace] — **con·sol′a·ble** *adj.*

— **Syn.** We *console* a person by soothing or sustaining his fallen spirits, or *comfort* him by any act that brings relief to his mind or body. *Solace* stresses the feeling of relief that results from our actions. — **Ant.** distress, grieve, sadden.

con·sole[2] (kon′sōl) *n.* **1.** A bracket, especially one used to support a cornice or ornamental fixture. **2.** A console table. **3.** The portion of an organ containing the manuals and stops. **4.** A cabinet for a radio, phonograph, or television set, designed to rest on the floor. [< MF, a bracket]

console table A table supported by consoles.

con·sol·i·date (kən·sol′ə·dāt) *v.* **·dat·ed, ·dat·ing** *v.t.* **1.** To make solid, firm, or coherent; strengthen. **2.** To combine in one; form a union of. — *v.i.* **3.** To become united, solid, or firm. — *adj.* Consolidated. [< L < *com-* together + *solidus* solid] — **con·sol′i·da′tion** *n.* — **con·sol′i·da′tor** *n.*
— **Syn.** (verb) **1.** solidify. **2.** merge, unite. **3.** unify.

consolidated school *U.S. & Canadian* A school, usu. rural, for pupils from more than one district.

con·som·mé (kon′sə·mā′, *Fr.* kôn·sô·mā′) *n.* A clear soup made of meat and sometimes vegetables boiled in water. [F, *consommer* to complete, finish]

con·so·nance (kon′sə·nəns) *n.* **1.** Agreement; accord. Correspondence of sounds; esp. resemblance of consonan but not of vowels. **3.** *Music* A combination of tones r garded as stable and not requiring resolution: also *concor* Also **con′so·nan·cy.** — **Syn.** See HARMONY.

con·so·nant (kon′sə·nənt) *adj.* **1.** Being in agreement; co sistent. **2.** Corresponding in sound; having consonance. Consonantal. — *n.* **1.** *Phonet.* A sound produced by co tact or constriction of the speech organs resulting in co plete or partial blockage of the breath stream, as the soun of *b, f, k, s, t,* etc. **2.** A letter or written symbol representi such a sound. [< MF < L < *com-* together + *sonare* sound] — **con′so·nant·ly** *adv.*

con·so·nan·tal (kon′sə·nan′təl) *adj.* **1.** Of the nature of consonant. **2.** Having a consonant or consonants.

con·sort (*n.* kon′sôrt; *v.* kən·sôrt′) *n.* **1.** A husband wife; spouse. **2.** A companion or partner; mate. **3.** *Na* A vessel sailing with another. — *v.i.* **1.** To keep compan associate. **2.** To be in agreement; harmonize. — *v.t.* To join; associate. [< MF < L < *com-* together + *so* share, lot]

con·sor·ti·um (kən·sôr′shē·əm) *n. pl.* **·ti·a** (-shē·ə) coalition, as of banks or corporations for a venture requiri vast resources. [< L, fellowship]

con·spec·tus (kən·spek′təs) *n. pl.* **·tus·es** **1.** A gener view of a subject. **2.** A summary. [See CONSPICUOUS.]

con·spic·u·ous (kən·spik′yōō·əs) *adj.* **1.** Clearly visib easy to be seen. **2.** Readily attracting attention; strikin [< L < *com-* together + *specere* to look at] — **con·spic′ous·ly** *adv.* — **con·spic′u·ous·ness** *n.*

con·spir·a·cy (kən·spir′ə·sē) *n. pl.* **·cies** **1.** The plannin of two or more persons to do an evil act; also, the plan made. **2.** An acting together: a *conspiracy* of the elements

con·spir·a·tor (kən·spir′ə·tər) *n.* One who is involved in conspiracy. [See CONSPIRE.]

con·spir·a·to·ri·al (kən·spir′ə·tôr′ē·əl, -tō′rē-) *adj.* Of, pe taining to, or like conspiracy or conspirators.

con·spire (kən·spīr′) *v.* **·spired, ·spir·ing** *v.i.* **1.** To con bine secretly in an evil or unlawful enterprise. **2.** To act t gether: The winds *conspire* against us. — *v.t.* **3.** To pla secretly; plot. [< MF < L < *com-* together + *spirare* breathe] — **con·spir′er** *n.*

con·sta·ble (kon′stə·bəl, kun′-) *n.* A peace officer who a rests offenders, serves writs, executes warrants, etc. [< O < LL *comes stabuli* chief groom] — **con′sta·ble·ship′** *n.*

con·stab·u·lar·y (kən·stab′yə·ler′ē) *n. pl.* **·lar·ies** **1.** Th body of constables of a city, etc. **2.** The district of a co stable. **3.** A police force organized in a military fashion. *adj.* Pertaining to constables or their functions.

con·stan·cy (kon′stən·sē) *n.* **1.** Steadiness or faithfulne in purpose, action, affections, etc. **2.** Unchanging qualit

con·stant (kon′stənt) *adj.* **1.** Long-continuing, or co tinually recurring; persistent. **2.** Unchanging; invariabl **3.** Steady in purpose, action, affection, etc.; perseverin faithful. — *n.* **1.** That which is permanent or invariabl **2.** *Math.* A quantity that retains a fixed value throughout given discussion. **3.** In the sciences, any characteristic of substance, event, etc., numerically determined, that remai the same under specified conditions. [< MF < L < *co* thoroughly + *stare* to stand] — **con′stant·ly** *adv.*

con·stel·late (kon′stə·lāt) *v.t. & v.i.* **·lat·ed, ·lat·ing** T group in constellations.

con·stel·la·tion (kon′stə·lā′shən) *n.* **1.** *Astron.* Any of va ious groups of stars imagined to represent the outline of being or thing, usu. mythological, and named accordingl **2.** Any brilliant group of persons or things. **3.** In astrolog the aspect of the planets at the time of one's birth. *Psychol.* A group of associated emotions, ideas, etc., cente ing upon a dominant element. [< LL < L *com-* together *stella* star] — **con·stel·la·to·ry** (kən·stel′ə·tôr′ē, -tō′rē) *ad*

con·ster·nate (kon′stər·nāt) *v.t.* **·nat·ed, ·nat·ing** To ove whelm with terror and confusion; dismay. [< L < *co* thoroughly + *sternere* to cast down, prostrate]

con·ster·na·tion (kon′stər·nā′shən) *n.* Sudden, paralyzin fear or amazement; panic. — **Syn.** See ALARM.

con·sti·pate (kon′stə·pāt) *v.t.* **·pat·ed, ·pat·ing** To caus constipation in. [< L < *com-* together + *stipare* to pres crowd] — **con′sti·pat′ed** *adj.*

con·sti·pa·tion (kon′stə·pā′shən) *n.* A condition of th bowels characterized by suppressed or difficult evacuatio

con·stit·u·en·cy (kən·stich′ōō·ən·sē) *n. pl.* **·cies** **1.** A bod of voters who elect a representative to a legislative body also, the district represented. **2.** Any body of supporters.

con·stit·u·ent (kən·stich′ōō·ənt) *adj.* **1.** Serving to for or compose; constituting. **2.** Entitled to elect a represent tive. **3.** Having the power to frame or modify a constitutio — *n.* **1.** One represented politically or in business; a voter c client. **2.** A necessary part or element.

con·sti·tute (kon′stə·tōōt, -tyōōt) *v.t.* **·tut·ed, ·tut·ing** 1

[T]o be the substance or elements of; make up; compose. **2.** [T]o enact (a law, etc.). **3.** To found, as a school; establish, [a]s an assembly, in legal form. **4.** To empower; appoint: I [c]*onstitute* you my spokesman. **5.** To make by combining [e]lements or parts; frame. [< L < *com-* together + *statuere* [t]o place, station] — **con′sti·tut′er** or **con′sti·tu′tor** *n.*

[co]n·sti·tu·tion (kon′stə·tōō′shən, -tyōō′-) *n.* **1.** The act of [c]onstituting; a setting up or appointing. **2.** The composi[t]ion or make-up of a thing; esp., physical make-up: a weak [c]*onstitution.* **3.** The fundamental laws and principles that [n]ormally govern the operation of a state or association; also, [a] document recording such laws and principles. — **the Con[s]titution** The Constitution of the U.S., framed and adopted [i]n 1787 and put into effect March 4, 1789.

[co]n·sti·tu·tion·al (kon′stə·tōō′shən·əl, -tyōō′-) *adj.* **1.** Of [o]r inherent in the constitution of a person or thing; essential: [a] *constitutional* weakness. **2.** Consistent with or pertaining [t]o the constitution of a state; lawful. **3.** Acting under and [c]ontrolled by a constitution: a *constitutional* monarchy. **4.** [L]oyal to the constitution. **5.** Benefiting one's health. — [n]. Exercise taken for one's health. — **con·sti·tu·tion·al·i·ty** ([k]on′sti·tōō′shən·al′ə·tē) *n.* — **con′sti·tu′tion·al·ly** *adv.*

[co]nstitutional amendment A legal alteration of the [U].S. Constitution, ratified by three fourths of the States.

[co]nstitution State Nickname of CONNECTICUT.

[co]n·sti·tu·tive (kon′stə·tōō′tiv, -tyōō′-) *adj.* **1.** Forming [a]n essential element of something; basic. **2.** Having power [t]o enact, institute, or establish. — **con′sti·tu′tive·ly** *adv.*

[co]n·strain (kən·strān′) *v.t.* **1.** To compel by physical or [m]oral means; coerce. **2.** To confine, as by bonds. **3.** To re[s]train; compel to inaction. [< OF < L < *com-* together + [s]*tringere* to bind] — **con·strain′a·ble** *adj.* — **con·strain′er** *n.*

[co]n·strained (kən·strānd′) *adj.* Forced; unnatural: a *con[s]trained* smile. — **con·strain·ed·ly** (kən·strā′nid·lē) *adv.*

[co]n·straint (kən·strānt′) *n.* **1.** The use of force; coercion. [2]. Confinement; restriction. **3.** Unnaturalness of manner; [a]wkwardness. **4.** A constraining or being constrained.

[co]n·strict (kən·strikt′) *v.t.* To draw together by force; [c]ause to shrink or contract; bind; cramp. [< L < *com-* to[g]ether + *stringere* to bind]

[co]n·stric·tion (kən·strik′shən) *n.* **1.** The act of constrict[in]g, or the state of being constricted. **2.** A feeling of tight[n]ess. **3.** That which constricts or is constricted. — **con·s[t]ric′tive** *adj.*

[co]n·stric·tor (kən·strik′tər) *n.* **1.** That which constricts. [2]. *Anat.* A muscle that contracts an organ of the body. **3.** [A] serpent that coils about and crushes its prey.

[co]n·struct (*v.* kən·strukt′; *n.* kon′strukt) *v.t.* **1.** To form [b]y combining materials or parts; build; erect. **2.** To form [m]entally; devise. **3.** To form (anything) systematically. — *n.* Something constructed. [< L < *com-* together + [s]*truere* to build] — **con·struct′er** or **con·struc′tor** *n.*

[co]n·struc·tion (kən·struk′shən) *n.* **1.** The act of con[s]tructing; also, the business of building. **2.** Something con[s]tructed; a structure or building. **3.** The way in which a [t]hing is put together. **4.** Interpretation given a statement, [la]w, etc.; explanation. **5.** *Gram.* The arrangement of forms [s]yntactically, as in sentences. — **con·struc′tion·al** *adj.*

[co]n·struc·tive (kən·struk′tiv) *adj.* **1.** Tending to build, [i]mprove, or advance; resulting in positive conclusions. **2.** [P]ertaining to construction; structural. **3.** Assumed by in[t]erpretation; inferred though not expressly stated. — **con·s[t]ruc′tive·ly** *adv.* — **con·struc′tive·ness** *n.*

[co]n·strue (*v.* kən·strōō′; *n.* kon′strōō) *v.* **·strued, ·stru·ing** *[v.]t.* **1.** To analyze the grammatical structure of (a clause or [s]entence); parse. **2.** To interpret; explain; also, to deduce [b]y inference. **3.** To translate orally. **4.** *Gram.* To use syn[t]actically: The noun "aerodynamics" is *construed* as a singu[la]r. — *v.i.* **5.** To determine grammatical structure. **6.** To [i]nfer; deduce. **7.** To admit of grammatical analysis. — *n.* [A]n act of construing. [< L < *com-* together + *struere* to [b]uild up] — **con·stru′a·ble** *adj.* — **con·stru′er** *n.*

[co]n·sul (kon′səl) *n.* **1.** An officer residing in a foreign city [t]o protect his country's commercial interests and the welfare [o]f its citizens. **2.** Either of the two chief magistrates ruling [c]onjointly in the Roman republic. **3.** Any of the three chief [m]agistrates of the French republic, 1799–1804. [< L] — **[c]on′su·lar** (-sə·lər, -syə·lər) *adj.*

[co]n·su·late (kon′sə·lit, -syə-) *n.* **1.** The office or term of [o]ffice of a consul. Also **con′sul·ship.** **2.** The official place of [b]usiness of a consul. **3.** Government by consuls. — **the [C]onsulate** The government of France from 1799 to 1804. [< L *consulatus* < *consul* consul]

[co]nsul general A consular officer of the highest rank sta[t]ioned in an important foreign commercial city, who super[v]ises the other consuls in his district.

[co]n·sult (kən·sult′) *v.t.* **1.** To ask the advice of; go to for [c]ounsel; refer to. **2.** To have regard to in deciding or acting; consider: to *consult* one's best interests. — *v.i.* **3.** To ask advice. **4.** To compare views; take counsel: with *with.* **5.** To give professional advice. [< L *consultare,* freq. of *consulere* to seek advice] — **con·sult′er** or **con·sul·tor** *n.*

con·sult·ant (kən·sul′tənt) *n.* **1.** A person referred to for expert or professional advice. **2.** One who consults.

con·sul·ta·tion (kon′səl·tā′shən) *n.* **1.** The act or practice of consulting. **2.** A meeting of consultants. — **con·sult·a·tive** (kən·sul′tə·tiv), **con·sult′a·to′ry** (-tôr′ē, -tō′rē) *adj.*

con·sume (kən·sōōm′) *v.* **·sumed, ·sum·ing** *v.t.* **1.** To destroy, as by burning. **2.** To eat, drink, or use up. **3.** To squander, as money or time. **4.** To engross or absorb. — *v.i.* **5.** To be wasted or destroyed. [< L < *com-* thoroughly + *sumere* to take up, use] — **con·sum′a·ble** *adj.*

con·sum·ed·ly (kən·sōō′mid·lē) *adv.* Excessively.

con·sum·er (kən·sōō′mər) *n.* **1.** One who or that which consumes. **2.** One who uses an article or service, as distinguished from a producer; one of the buying public.

con·sum·mate (*v.* kon′sə·māt; *adj.* kən·sum′it) *v.t.* **·mat·ed, ·mat·ing** **1.** To bring to completion or perfection; achieve. **2.** To fulfill (a marriage) by sexual intercourse. — *adj.* Of the highest degree; perfect; complete. [< L < *com-* together + *summa* sum, total] — **con·sum′mate·ly** *adv.* — **con′sum·ma′tive** *adj.* — **con′sum·ma′tor** *n.*

con·sum·ma·tion (kon′sə·mā′shən) *n.* The act of consummating, or the state of being consummated; fulfillment.

con·sump·tion (kən·sump′shən) *n.* **1.** The act or process of consuming; destruction, as by burning, use, etc. **2.** The amount consumed. **3.** *Econ.* The using up of goods and services. **4.** *Pathol.* Pulmonary tuberculosis.

con·sump·tive (kən·sump′tiv) *adj. Pathol.* Pertaining to, affected with, or disposed to pulmonary tuberculosis. — *n.* A person affected with pulmonary tuberculosis. — **con·sump′tive·ly** *adv.* — **con·sump′tive·ness** *n.*

con·tact (kon′takt) *n.* **1.** A coming together or touching. **2.** A potentially helpful acquaintance: He has many *contacts.* **3.** *Electr.* The touching or joining of conductors, permitting the flow of a current; also, a conducting part for completing or breaking a circuit. **4.** *Med.* One who has been exposed to a contagious disease. — *v.t.* **1.** To bring or place in contact; touch. **2.** *Informal* To get in touch with (someone). — *v.i.* **3.** To be or come in contact; touch: with *with.* [< L < *com-* together + *tangere* to touch]

contact lens *Optics* A thin lens of glass or plastic ground to optical prescription and worn directly on the eyeball.

con·ta·gion (kən·tā′jən) *n.* **1.** The communication of disease by contact. **2.** A disease that is or may be communicated. **3.** The medium of transmission of disease. **4.** The communication of mental states, of ideas, etc., as by association. [< MF < L < *con-* togethər + *tangere* to touch]

con·ta·gious (kən·tā′jəs) *adj.* **1.** Transmissible by contact, as a disease. **2.** Spreading contagion. **3.** Exciting or tending to excite similar feelings, etc., in others; spreading; catching. — **con·ta′gious·ly** *adv.* — **con·ta′gious·ness** *n.*

con·tain (kən·tān′) *v.t.* **1.** To hold or enclose. **2.** To include or comprise. **3.** To be capable of containing; be able to hold. **4.** To keep within bounds; restrain, as oneself or one's feelings. **5.** *Math.* To be exactly divisible by. [< OF < L < *com-* together + *tenere* to hold] — **con·tain′a·ble** *adj.*

con·tain·er (kən·tā′nər) *n.* Something that contains, as a box, can, etc.

con·tain·ment (kən·tān′mənt) *n.* The prevention of territorial or ideological expansion on the part of another power.

con·tam·i·nate (kən·tam′ə·nāt) *v.t.* **·nat·ed, ·nat·ing** To make impure by contact or admixture; taint; defile; pollute. [< L < *contamen* pollution] — **con·tam′i·na·tion** *n.* — **con·tam′i·na′tive** *adj.* — **con·tam′i·na′tor** *n.*

con·temn (kən·tem′) *v.t.* To despise; scorn. [< OF < L < *com-* thoroughly + *temnere* to slight, scorn] — **con·temn·er** (kən·tem′ər, -tem′nər) or **con·tem·nor** (kən·tem′nər) *n.*

con·tem·plate (kon′təm·plāt) *v.* **·plat·ed, ·plat·ing** *v.t.* **1.** To look at attentively; gaze at. **2.** To consider thoughtfully; meditate upon. **3.** To intend or plan: to *contemplate* marriage. — *v.i.* **4.** To meditate; muse. [< L < *com-* together + *templum* temple; with ref. to divination] — **con·tem·pla·tion** (kon′təm·plā′shən) *n.* — **con′tem·pla′tor** *n.*

con·tem·pla·tive (kən·tem′plə·tiv, kon′təm·plā′tiv) *adj.* Of or given to contemplation; meditative. — *n.* A member of a religious order devoted to prayer and penance. — **con·tem′pla·tive·ly** *adv.* — **con·tem′pla·tive·ness** *n.*

con·tem·po·ra·ne·ous (kən·tem′pə·rā′nē·əs) *adj.* Living or occurring at the same time: also *cotemporaneous.* [< L < *com-* together + *tempus, -oris* time] — **con·tem·po·ra·ne·i·ty** (kən·tem′pə·rə·nē′ə·tē), **con·tem′po·ra′ne·ous·ness** *n.* — **con·tem′po·ra′ne·ous·ly** *adv.*

con·tem·po·rar·y (kən·tem′pə·rer′ē) *adj.* **1.** Belonging to the same age; living or occurring at the same time. **2.** Of the same age. **3.** Current; modern. — *n.* *pl.* **·rar·ies** A contemporary person or thing. Also *cotemporary.* [< L *com-* together + *tempus, -oris* time]

con·tempt (kən·tempt′) *n.* **1.** The feeling of one who views something as mean, vile, and worthless; disdain; scorn. **2.** The state of being despised. **3.** *Law* Willful disregard or disrepect of authority, as of a court. [< L < *com-* thoroughly + *temnere* to scorn]

con·tempt·i·ble (kən·temp′tə·bəl) *adj.* Deserving of contempt; despicable. **— con·tempt′i·bil′i·ty, con·tempt′i·ble·ness** *n.* **— con·tempt′i·bly** *adv.*

con·temp·tu·ous (kən·temp′cho͞o·əs) *adj.* Showing or feeling contempt; disdainful; scornful. **— con·temp′tu·ous·ly** *adv.* **— con·temp′tu·ous·ness** *n.*

con·tend (kən·tend′) *v.i.* **1.** To strive in competition or rivalry; vie: to *contend* for a prize. **2.** To argue; debate. **3.** To struggle; fight. **—** *v.t.* **4.** To assert; affirm. [< L < *com-* together + *tendere* to strive, strain] **— con·tend′er** *n.*

con·tent[1] (kon′tent) *n.* **1.** *Usu. pl.* That which a thing contains: the *contents* of a box. **2.** Subject matter, as of a document. **3.** Ability to contain; capacity. **4.** Extent or size. **5.** The quantity of a specified part. [See CONTAIN.]

con·tent[2] (kən·tent′) *adj.* **1.** Satisfied with what one has. **2.** Resigned; accepting. **—** *n.* Ease of mind; satisfaction. **—** *v.t.* To satisfy. [See CONTAIN.] **— con·tent′ment** *n.*

con·tent·ed (kən·ten′tid) *adj.* Satisfied with things as they are; content. **— con·tent′ed·ly** *adv.* **— con·tent′ed·ness** *n.*

con·ten·tion (kən·ten′shən) *n.* **1.** Controversy; argument. **2.** Competition; rivalry. **3.** A point asserted in argument. **— in contention** Being contended over. [See CONTEND.]

con·ten·tious (kən·ten′shəs) *adj.* **1.** Given to contention; quarrelsome. **2.** Involving or characterized by contention. **— con·ten′tious·ly** *adv.* **— con·ten′tious·ness** *n.*

con·ter·mi·nous (kən·tûr′mə·nəs) *adj.* **1.** Having a common boundary line. **2.** Contained within the same limits. Also *coterminous*: also **con·ter′mi·nal.** [< L < *com-* together + *terminus* limit] **— con·ter′mi·nous·ly** *adv.*

con·test (*n.* kon′test; *v.* kən·test′) *n.* **1.** A struggling against one another; conflict; strife. **2.** Verbal controversy; dispute. **3.** A competition, game, match, etc. **—** *v.t.* **1.** To fight for; strive to keep or win. **2.** To call in question; challenge: to *contest* a decision. **—** *v.i.* **3.** To struggle or dispute; contend: with *with* or *against.* [< F < L < *com-* together + *testari* to bear witness] **— con·test′a·ble** *adj.* **— con·tes·ta·tion** (kon′tes·tā′shən) *n.* **— con·test′er** *n.*

con·test·ant (kən·tes′tənt) *n.* **1.** One who enters a contest; a competitor. **2.** One who contests; a litigant.

con·text (kon′tekst) *n.* **1.** Any phrase, sentence, or passage so closely connected to a word or words as to affect their meaning. **2.** Something that surrounds and influences, as environment or circumstances. [< L < *com-* together + *texere* to weave] **— con·tex·tu·al** (kən·teks′cho͞o·əl) *adj.* **— con·tex′tu·al·ly** *adv.*

con·ti·gu·i·ty (kon′tə·gyo͞o′ə·tē) *n. pl.* **·ties** The state of being contiguous or in actual contact; nearness.

con·tig·u·ous (kən·tig′yo͞o·əs) *adj.* **1.** Touching at the edge or boundary. **2.** Close, but not touching; adjacent. [See CONTACT.] **— con·tig′u·ous·ly** *adv.* **— con·tig′u·ous·ness** *n.*

con·ti·nence (kon′tə·nəns) *n.* Self-restraint, esp. abstinence from sexual intercourse. Also **con′ti·nen·cy.**

con·ti·nent (kon′tə·nənt) *n.* One of the large land masses of the earth: Africa, Australia, Europe and Asia (the conventional divisions of the Eurasian land mass), North America, South America, and, usually, Antarctica. **— the Continent** Europe, as distinct from the British Isles. **—** *adj.* **1.** Self-restrained; moderate. **2.** Abstinent, esp. sexually; chaste. [See CONTAIN.] **— con′ti·nent·ly** *adv.*

con·ti·nen·tal (kon′tə·nen′təl) *adj.* **1.** Of, or of the proportions of, a continent. **2.** *Often cap.* Pertaining to the European continent; European. **—** *n.* **1.** *Usu. cap.* An inhabitant of the European continent; a European. **2.** A note of the money issued by the Continental Congress.

Con·ti·nen·tal (kon′tə·nen′təl) *adj.* Pertaining to the thirteen American colonies during and just after the Revolution. **—** *n.* A regular soldier in the Continental army.

Continental Congress The legislative and governing body of the Revolutionary American colonies, that convened in 1774, 1775–76, and 1776–81. It was de facto until 1781 when it became de jure the **Congress of the Confederation.**

con·tin·gen·cy (kən·tin′jən·sē) *n. pl.* **·cies 1.** Uncertainty of occurrence; the condition of being subject to chance or accident. **2.** An unforeseen but possible occurrence. **3.** Something incidental; an adjunct. Also **con·tin′gence.**

con·tin·gent (kən·tin′jənt) *adj.* **1.** Liable, but not certain, to happen; possible. **2.** Occurring by chance; accidental. **3.** Dependent upon an uncertain event or condition: with *on* or *upon.* **—** *n.* **1.** An accidental or possible occurrence: contingency. **2.** A proportionate share or quota of something to be furnished, as of troops. **3.** A representative group in an assemblage. [< L < *com-* together + *tangere* to touch] **— con·tin′gent·ly** *adv.*

con·tin·u·al (kən·tin′yo͞o·əl) *adj.* **1.** Renewed frequently; often repeated. **2.** Continuous (in time). [< OF < L *co[ntinuus]* hanging together] **— con·tin′u·al·ly** *adv.*

con·tin·u·ance (kən·tin′yo͞o·əns) *n.* **1.** A continuing something, as an action or condition, or a remaining in som[e] thing, as in a place or state. **2.** Continuation, as of a nov[el]. **3.** Duration: a disease of long *continuance.* **4.** *Law* A[d]journment to a future time.

con·tin·u·a·tion (kən·tin′yo͞o·ā′shən) *n.* **1.** The act of co[n]tinuing or the state of being continued. **2.** The extension a carrying to a further point: the *continuation* of a histor[y]. **3.** Addition; sequel.

con·tin·ue (kən·tin′yo͞o) *v.* **·tin·ued, ·tin·u·ing** *v.i.* **1.** [To] go on in some action or condition; persist. **2.** To resu[me] after an interruption. **3.** To remain in the same place, co[n]dition, or capacity. **4.** To last; endure. **—** *v.t.* **5.** To pers[e]vere or persist in; carry forward. **6.** To take up again aft[er] interruption. **7.** To extend or prolong in space, time, [or] development. **8.** To cause to last or endure; also, to ke[ep] on; retain, as in office. **9.** *Law* To postpone; grant a co[n]tinuance of. [< OF < L < *com-* together + *tenere* to hol[d]] **— con·tin′u·a·ble** *adj.* **— con·tin′u·er** *n.*

con·ti·nu·i·ty (kon′tə·no͞o′ə·tē, -nyo͞o′-) *n. pl.* **·ties 1.** T[he] state or quality of being continuous. **2.** An unbroken seri[es] succession. **3.** In motion pictures, television, etc., a scena[rio] outlining the sequence of scenes; also, the script.

con·tin·u·ous (kən·tin′yo͞o·əs) *adj.* Extended or prolong[ed] without break; uninterrupted. **— con·tin′u·ous·ly** *adv.* **— con·tin′u·ous·ness** *n.*

con·tin·u·um (kən·tin′yo͞o·əm) *n. pl.* **·tin·u·a** (-tin′yo͞o·[ə]) Something that is continuous, of which no separate pa[rts] are discernible. [< L, neut. of *continuus* continuous]

con·tort (kən·tôrt′) *v.t.* & *v.i.* To twist violently; wren[ch] out of shape or place. [< L < *com-* together + *torquere* [to] twist] **— con·tor′tion** *n.* **— con·tor′tive** *adj.*

con·tor·tion·ist (kən·tôr′shən·ist) *n.* A performer train[ed] to twist his limbs and body into unnatural positions.

con·tour (kon′to͝or) *n.* The outline of a figure or body, o[r] line representing it. **—** *v.t.* To draw the contour lines [of]. **—** *adj.* **1.** *Agric.* Following the contours of land in such [a] way in plowing as to minimize erosion. **2.** Shaped to fit t[he] outline or contour of something: *contour* sheets. [< F < I[tal.] < *com-* together + *tornare* to make round]

contour map A map showing topographic configuration [by] lines (**contour lines**) that connect the points of a surfa[ce] having similar elevation.

contra- *prefix* Against; opposite. [< L < *contra* against]

con·tra·band (kon′trə·band) *n.* **1.** Goods that, by law [or] treaty, may not be imported or exported. **2.** Smuggl[ed] goods. **3.** Goods that, by international law, a neutral m[ay] not furnish to a belligerent, and which are subject to seizu[re]: in full **contraband of war.** **—** *adj.* Prohibited by law fr[om] being imported or exported. [< Sp. < Ital. < *contra* again[st] + *bando* < LL *bannum* law] **— con′tra·ban′dist** *n.*

con·tra·bass (kon′trə·bās) *Music n.* The member of [a] family of instruments whose range is below the bass; es[p.] the double bass. Also **con′tra·bas′so** (-bä′sō). **—** *adj.* Pitc[h]ed lower than the normal bass: the *contrabass* clarinet. [< Ital. *contrabasso*] **— con·tra·bass·ist** (kon′trə·bā′sist) *n.*

con·tra·bas·soon (kon′trə·bə·so͞on′) *n.* The double b[as]soon.

con·tra·cep·tion (kon′trə·sep′shən) *n.* The deliberate p[re]vention of fertilization of the human ovum. [< CONTRA- (CON)CEPTION] **— con′tra·cep′tive** *n.* & *adj.*

con·tra·clock·wise (kon′trə·klok′wīz′) *adj.* & *adv.* Cou[n]terclockwise.

con·tract (*v.* kən·trakt′; *for v. def. 2, also* kon′trakt; *n.* ko[n′]trakt) *v.t.* **1.** To cause to draw together; reduce in size. [**2.**] To enter upon or settle by contract. **3.** To acquire or b[e]come affected with, as a disease or habit. **4.** *Gram.* [To] shorten, as a word, by omitting or combining medial lett[ers] or sounds. **—** *v.i.* **5.** To become smaller, shrink. **6.** [To] make a contract. **—** *n.* **1.** A formal agreement between t[wo] or more parties, esp. one that is legally binding. **2.** T[he] paper or writing containing such an agreement. **3.** The d[e]partment of law dealing with contracts. **4.** A betrothal [or] marriage. **5.** In bridge: **a** The highest and final bid of [a] hand, stating a denomination and the number of tricks to [be] made. **b** Contract bridge. Abbr. *cont., contr.* [< L < *co[m-]* together + *trahere* to pull, draw] **— con·tract′i·bil′i·ty, co[n]·tract′i·ble·ness** *n.* **— con·tract′i·ble** *adj.*

contract bridge A variety of the game of bridge in whi[ch] tricks made by the declarer in excess of the contract do n[ot] count toward game.

con·trac·tile (kən·trak′təl) *adj.* Able to contract or to i[n]duce contraction. **— con·trac·til·i·ty** (kon′trak·til′ə·tē) *n.*

con·trac·tion (kən·trak′shən) *n.* **1.** The act of contracti[ng] or the state of being contracted. **2.** *Gram.* The shorteni[ng] of a word or phrase by the omission of medial letters [or] sounds, as in *don't* for *do not*; also, the new word formed. **Syn.** See ABBREVIATION. **— con·trac′tive** *adj.*

con·trac·tor (kən·trak′tər; *for def. 1, also* kon′trak·tər) *n.*

ne who agrees to supply materals or perform services for a m, esp. for the construction of buildings. **2.** That which ntracts, as a muscle.

n·trac·tu·al (kən·trak′cho͞o·əl) *adj.* Connected with or plying a contract.

n·tra·dance (kon′trə·dans′, -däns′), **con·tra·danse** See NTREDANSE.

n·tra·dict (kon′trə·dikt′) *v.t.* **1.** To maintain or assert e opposite of (a statement). **2.** To deny a statement of (a rson). **3.** To be contrary to or inconsistent with. — *v.i.* To utter a contradiction. [< L < *contra* against + *dicere* say, speak] — **con′tra·dict′a·ble** *adj.* — **con′tra·dict′er con′tra·dic′tor** *n.*

n·tra·dic·tion (kon′trə·dik′shən) *n.* **1.** Assertion of the posite of a statement; denial. **2.** A statement that denies e validity of another. **3.** Obvious inconsistency, as be- een two statements; discrepancy.

n·tra·dic·to·ry (kon′trə·dik′tər·ē) *adj.* **1.** Involving or the nature of a contradiction; inconsistent; contrary. **2.** iven to contradicting. — *n. pl.* **·ries** *Logic* Either of two atements so related that if one is true the other must be lse. — **con′tra·dic′to·ri·ly** *adv.* — **con′tra·dic′to·ri·ness** *n.*

n·tra·dis·tinc·tion (kon′trə·dis·tingk′shən) *n.* Distinc- on by contrast or by contrasting qualities. — **con′tra·dis· nct′, con′tra·dis·tinc′tive** *adj.*

n·trail (kon′trāl) *n. Aeron.* A trail of condensed water por created by an airplane or rocket flying through super- oled air. [< (*con*)*densation trail*]

n·tra·in·di·cate (kon′trə·in′də·kāt) *v.t. Med.* To indi- te the danger or undesirability of (a given drug or treat- ent). — **con′tra·in′di·cant** *n.* — **con′tra·in′di·ca′tion** *n.*

n·tral·to (kən·tral′tō) *n. pl.* **·tos** or **·ti** (-tē) **1.** The low- t female voice, intermediate between soprano and tenor. One having such a voice. — *adj.* Of or pertaining to the ntralto or its range. Abbr. *contr.* [< Ital.]

n·trap·tion (kən·trap′shən) *n. Informal* A contrivance gadget. [? < CONTRIVE]

n·tra·pun·tal (kon′trə·pun′təl) *adj. Music* **1.** Of or per- ining to counterpoint. **2.** According with the principles counterpoint. [< Ital. *contrapunto* counterpoint] — **con′· a·pun′tal·ly** *adv.* — **con′tra·pun′tist, con′tra·pun′tal·ist** *n.*

n·tra·ri·e·ty (kon′trə·rī′ə·tē) *n. pl.* **·ties** **1.** The quality state of being contrary. **2.** An inconsistency. [< OF < L < L *contrarius* opposite]

n·trar·i·wise (kon′trer·ē·wīz′; *for def. 3, also* kən·trâr′ē· īz′) *adv.* **1.** On the contrary; on the other hand. **2.** In e reverse order; conversely. **3.** Contrarily; perversely.

n·trar·y (kon′trer·ē; *for adj. def. 4, also* kən·trâr′ē) *adj.* Opposed in essence, purpose, aim, etc. **2.** Opposite as to sition or direction. **3.** Adverse; unfavorable: *contrary* inds. **4.** Inclined to oppose and contradict; perverse. — *pl.* **·trar·ies** **1.** One of two contrary things. **2.** The oppo- te: the *contrary* is true. **3.** *Logic* A statement the truth of hich is undetermined by the falsity of another, but which nnot be true if the latter is true. — **on the contrary** On e other hand; conversely. — **to the contrary** To the op- site effect. — *adv.* In a contrary manner. [< AF < L < *ntra* against] — **con′trar·i·ly** *adv.* — **con′trar·i·ness** *n.* — **Syn.** (adj.) **1.** contradictory, opposed, opposite, antithetical.

n·trast (*v.* kən·trast′; *n.* kon′trast) *v.t.* **1.** To place in position so as to set off differences or discrepancies. **2.** o set (one another) off by opposition, difference, etc. — *i.* **3.** To reveal differences when set in opposition. — *n.* **1.** he act of contrasting, or the state of being contrasted. **2.** dissimilarity revealed by contrasting. **3.** One who or that hich shows unlikeness to another. [< OF to oppose < LL L *contra-* against + *stare* to stand] — **con·trast′able** *adj.*

n·tra·vene (kon′trə·vēn′) *v.t.* **·vened, ·ven·ing** **1.** To come to conflict with; run counter to; infringe; transgress: to *ntravene* a law. **2.** To oppose or contradict. [< F < L *ntra-* against + *venire* to come] — **con′tra·ven′er** *n.* —

n·tra·ven·tion (kon′trə·ven′shən) *n.*

ntre- *prefix* Counter; against; in opposition to. [< F L *contra.* See CONTRA-.]

n·tre·danse (kôn·trə·däns′) *n.* A country-dance: also *ntradance, contradanse.* Also **con·tre·dance** (kôn′trə·dans′, äns′). [< F, alter. of COUNTRY-DANCE]

n·tre·temps (kôn·trə·tän′) *n. pl.* **·temps** (-tänz′, *Fr.* än′) An embarrassing or awkward occurrence. [< F]

n·trib·ute (kən·trib′yo͞ot) *v.* **·ut·ed, ·ut·ing** *v.t.* **1.** To ve with others for a common purpose. **2.** To furnish (an ticle, story, etc.) to a publication. — *v.i.* **3.** To share in fecting a result: These causes *contributed* to the king's ownfall. **4.** To make a contribution. [< L < *com-* to- ether + *tribuere* to grant, allot] — **con·trib′ut·a·ble** *adj.* — **con·trib′u·tive** *adj.* — **con·trib′u·tive·ly** *adv.* — **con· ib′u·tive·ness** *n.* — **con·trib′u·tor** *n.*

n·tri·bu·tion (kon′trə·byo͞o′shən) *n.* **1.** The act of con- tributing. **2.** Something contributed. **3.** An article, story, etc., furnished to a periodical. **4.** A tax or levy.

con·trib·u·to·ry (kən·trib′yə·tôr′ē, -tō′rē) *adj.* **1.** Con- tributing, as money or aid. **2.** That forms a contribution. — *n. pl.* **·ries** One who or that which contributes.

con·trite (kən·trīt′, kon′trīt) *adj.* **1.** Deeply and humbly sorry for one's sins; penitent. **2.** Resulting from remorse. [< OF < L < *com-* together + *terere* to rub] — **con·trite′ly** *adv.* — **con·trite′ness, con·tri′tion** (-trish′ən) *n.*

con·triv·ance (kən·trī′vəns) *n.* **1.** The act or manner of contriving; also, the ability to do this. **2.** A device or me- chanical apparatus. **3.** An ingenious plan.

con·trive (kən·trīv′) *v.* **·trived, ·triv·ing** *v.t.* **1.** To plan, scheme, or plot. **2.** To improvise; invent. **3.** To manage, as by some scheme. — *v.i.* **4.** To plan, scheme, or plot. [OF < L *com-* together + *turbare* to stir up, disclose, find] — **con·triv′a·ble** *adj.* — **con·triv′er** *n.*

con·trol (kən·trōl′) *v.t.* **·trolled, ·trol·ling** **1.** To exercise authority over. **2.** To restrain; curb. **3.** To regulate or verify, as an experiment. **4.** To check, as an account, by means of a duplicate register; verify or rectify. — *n.* **1.** Power to regulate and direct. **2.** A restraining influence; check. **3.** A standard of comparison against which to check the results of a scientific experiment. **4.** *Often pl. Mech.* A device used for operating a machine, airplane, automobile, etc. [< MF < OF < Med.L < L *contra-* against + *rotulus* list] — **con·trol′la·bil′i·ty, con·trol′la·ble·ness** *n.* — **con· trol′la·ble** *adj.*

con·trol·ler (kən·trō′lər) *n.* **1.** One who controls, regulates, or directs. **2.** An officer appointed to examine and verify accounts: also spelled *comptroller.* **3.** A mechanism that reg- ulates the speed of a machine, etc. — **con·trol′ler·ship** *n.*

control tower A specially equipped structure at an air- field, from which aircraft traffic is directed.

con·tro·ver·sial (kon′trə·vûr′shəl) *adj.* **1.** Subject to or characterized by controversy. **2.** Given to controversy; disputatious. — **con′tro·ver′sial·ist** *n.* — **con′tro·ver′sial· ly** *adv.*

con·tro·ver·sy (kon′trə·vûr′sē) *n. pl.* **·sies** **1.** Dispute regarding a matter on which opinions differ. **2.** A dispute. [< L < *contra-* against + *versus,* pp. of *vertere* to turn]

con·tro·vert (kon′trə·vûrt, kon′trə·vûrt′) *v.t.* **1.** To argue against; contradict; oppose. **2.** To argue about. — **con′· tro·vert′er** *n.* — **con′tro·vert′i·ble** *adj.* — **con′tro·vert′i· bly** *adv.*

con·tu·ma·cious (kon′to͞o·mā′shəs, -tyo͞o-) *adj.* Stubbornly disobedient. — **con′tu·ma′cious·ly** *adv.* — **con′tu·ma′cious· ness** *n.*

con·tu·ma·cy (kon′to͞o·mə·sē, -tyo͞o-) *n. pl.* **·cies** Contemp- tuous disobedience of authority; insolent defiance; insubor- dination. [< L < *contumax, -acis* stubborn]

con·tu·me·ly (kon′to͞o·mə·lē, -tyo͞o-, -mē′lē; kən·to͞o′mə·lē, -tyo͞o′-) *n. pl.* **·lies** **1.** Insulting rudeness in speech or man- ner; insolence. **2.** An insult. [< OF < L *contumelia* re- proach] — **con·tu·me·li·ous** (kon′to͞o·mē′lē·əs, -tyo͞o-) *adj.* — **con′tu·me′li·ous·ly** *adv.* — **con′tu·me′li·ous·ness** *n.*

con·tuse (kən·to͞oz′, -tyo͞oz′) *v.t.* **·tused, ·tus·ing** To bruise by a blow. [< L < *com-* together + *tundere* to beat]

con·tu·sion (kən·to͞o′zhən, -tyo͞o′-) *n.* A bruise.

co·nun·drum (kə·nun′drəm) *n.* **1.** A riddle of which the answer depends on a pun. **2.** Any problem or puzzle. — **Syn.** See PUZZLE. [Origin unknown]

con·va·lesce (kon′və·les′) *v.i.* **·lesced, ·lesc·ing** To recover after illness; regain good health. [< L < *com-* thoroughly + *valescere,* inceptive of *valere* to be strong]

con·va·les·cence (kon′və·les′əns) *n.* **1.** Gradual recovery from illness. **2.** The period of such recovery. — **con′va· les′cent** *adj. & n.*

con·vec·tion (kən·vek′shən) *n.* **1.** *Physics* The transfer- ence of heat in a gas or liquid by currents resulting from un- equal temperature and the consequent unequal densities. **2.** The act of conveying. [< L < *com-* together + *vehere* to carry] — **con·vec′tion·al** *adj.* — **con·vec′tive** *adj.* — **con· vec′tive·ly** *adv.*

con·vene (kən·vēn′) *v.* **·vened, ·ven·ing** *v.t.* **1.** To cause to assemble; convoke. **2.** To summon to appear, as by judicial authority. — *v.i.* **3.** To come together; assemble. [< MF < *com-* together + *venire* to come] — **con·ven′a·ble** *adj.* — **con·ven′er** *n.*

con·ven·ience (kən·vēn′yəns) *n.* **1.** The quality of being convenient; suitability. **2.** Personal comfort; ease. **3.** Anything that increases comfort or saves work. Also *Rare* **con·ven′ien·cy.** — **at one's convenience** At a time or occa- sion suiting one's needs or preference.

con·ven·ient (kən·vēn′yənt) *adj.* **1.** Well suited to one's purpose or needs; conducive to ease or comfort. **2.** Within easy reach; handy. [See CONVENE.] — **con·ven′ient·ly** *adv.*

con·vent (kon′vent, -vənt) *n.* **1.** A religious community, esp. of nuns, living according to an established rule. **2.** The building or buildings of such a community. **— Syn.** See CLOISTER. [< AF, OF < L *conventus* meeting, assembly]

con·ven·ti·cle (kən·ven′ti·kəl) *n.* **1.** A meeting for religious worship, esp. a secret one. **2.** The meeting place of such an assembly. [See CONVENE.] **— con·ven′ti·cler** *n.*

con·ven·tion (kən·ven′shən) *n.* **1.** A formal meeting of delegates or members, as for political or professional purposes. **2.** The persons attending such a meeting. **3.** A rule or approved technique in conduct or art; a custom or usage. **4.** Conventionality. **5.** An agreement or contract.

con·ven·tion·al (kən·ven′shən·əl) *adj.* **1.** Growing out of or established by convention or custom. **2.** Following or conforming to approved or established practice. **3.** Formal; stylized. **4.** In art, simplified or abstracted. **5.** Established by general agreement or acceptance: a *conventional* symbol. **6.** Of or pertaining to a convention. **— con·ven′tion·al·ist** *n.* **— con·ven′tion·al·ly** *adv.*

con·ven·tion·al·ism (kən·ven′shən·əl·iz′əm) *n.* **1.** Regard for or adherence to custom. **2.** Anything conventional.

con·ven·tion·al·i·ty (kən·ven′shən·al′ə·tē) *n. pl.* **·ties 1.** The state or quality of being in accord with convention; adherence to established forms, customs, or usages. **2.** A conventional act, principle, custom, etc.

con·ven·tion·al·ize (kən·ven′shən·əl·īz′) *v.t.* **·ized, ·iz·ing 1.** To make conventional. **2.** To represent in a conventional manner. **— con·ven′tion·al·i·za′tion** *n.*

con·ven·tu·al (kən·ven′cho͞o·əl) *adj.* Belonging or pertaining to a convent. **—** *n.* One who belongs to a convent.

con·verge (kən·vûrj′) *v.* **·verged, ·verg·ing** *v.i.* **1.** To move toward one point; come together gradually. **—** *v.t.* **2.** To cause to tend toward one point. [< LL < L *com-* together + *vergere* to bend]

con·ver·gence (kən·ver′jəns) *n.* **1.** The act, fact, or state of converging. **2.** The degree or point of converging. Also **con·ver′gen·cy.**

con·vers·a·ble (kən·vûr′sə·bəl) *adj.* **1.** Approachable in conversation; affable. **2.** Fond of talking. **— con·vers′a·ble·ness** *n.* **— con·vers′a·bly** *adv.*

con·ver·sant (kon′vər·sənt, kən·vûr′sənt) *adj.* Well acquainted or familiar, as by study. [See CONVERSE[1].] **— con·ver·sance** (kon′vər·səns, kən·vûr′səns), **con′ver·san·cy** *n.* **— con′ver·sant·ly** *adv.*

con·ver·sa·tion (kon′vər·sā′shən) *n.* **1.** An informal talk with another or others. **2.** Intimate association or social intercourse. **3.** Sexual intercourse. [See CONVERSE[1].]

con·ver·sa·tion·al (kon′vər·sā′shən·əl) *adj.* **1.** Of or characteristic of conversation. **2.** Disposed to or adept at conversation. **— con′ver·sa′tion·al·ly** *adv.*

con·ver·sa·tion·al·ist (kon′vər·sā′shən·əl·ist) *n.* One who enjoys or excels in conversation. Also **con′ver·sa′tion·ist.**

conversation piece Something, as a piece of furniture, that arouses comment.

con·verse[1] (*v.* kən·vûrs′; *n.* kon′vûrs) *v.i.* **·versed, ·vers·ing** To speak together informally; engage in conversation. **—** *n.* **1.** Conversation. **2.** Social fellowship. [< OF *converser* to live with < L < *com-* together + *vertere* to turn] **— con·vers′er** *n.*

con·verse[2] (kon′vûrs; *for adj., also* kən·vûrs′) *adj.* Turned about so that two parts are interchanged; reversed; contrary. **—** *n.* That which exists in a converse relation; opposite. [< L < *com-* thoroughly + *vertere* to turn] **— con·verse·ly** (kən·vûrs′lē, kon′vûrs·lē) *adv.*

con·ver·sion (kən·vûr′zhən, -shən) *n.* **1.** The act of converting, or the state of being converted. **2.** A change in which one comes to adopt new opinions, esp. a spiritual turning to righteousness and faith. **— con·ver′sion·al, con·ver·sion·ar·y** (kən·vûr′zhən·er′ē, -shən-) *adj.*

con·vert (*v.* kən·vûrt′; *n.* kon′vûrt) *v.t.* **1.** To change into another state, form, or substance; transform. **2.** To apply or adapt to a new or different purpose or use. **3.** To change from one belief, religion, or course of action to another. **4.** To exchange for an equivalent value, as goods for money. **5.** To exchange for value of another form, as preferred for common stock. **6.** To change chemically. **7.** *Law* To assume possession of illegally. **—** *v.i.* **8.** To become changed in character. **9.** In football, to score an extra point after the touchdown **—** *n.* A person who has been converted, as from one religion to another. [See CONVERSE[2]]

con·vert·er (kən·vûr′tər) *n.* **1.** One who or that which converts. **2.** A Bessemer converter. **3.** *Electr.* An apparatus for converting direct into alternating current, or vice versa. Also **con·ver′tor.**

con·vert·i·ble (kən·vûr′tə·bəl) *adj.* Capable of being converted. **—** *n.* **1.** A convertible thing. **2.** An automobile with a top that folds back. **— con·vert′i·bil′i·ty, con·vert′i·ble·ness** *n.* **— con·vert′i·bly** *adv.*

con·vex (kon′veks; *for adj., also* kon·veks′) *adj.* Curving outward, as the exterior of a globe: opposed to *concave.* **—** *n.* A convex surface or body; convexity. [< L *convexus* vaulted, curved] **— con·vex′i·ty** *n.* **— con·vex′ly** *adv.*

con·vex·o-con·cave (kon·vek′sō·kon·kāv′) *adj.* Convex one side and concave on the other, as a lense.

con·vey (kən·vā′) *v.t.* **1.** To carry from one place to other; transport. **2.** To serve as a medium or path for; tra mit. **3.** To make known; impart; communicate. **4.** transfer ownership of, as real estate. [< AF < L *com-* gether + *via* road, way] **— con·vey′a·ble** *adj.*

con·vey·ance (kən·vā′əns) *n.* **1.** The act of conveying; co munication; transportation. **2.** Something used for conv ing, as a truck or bus. **3.** *Law* The transfer of title to pr erty; also, the document whereby title is transferred.

con·vey·anc·ing (kən·vā′ən·sing) *n.* *Law* The busines preparing conveyances of property. **— con·vey′anc·er**

con·vey·er (kən·vā′ər) *n.* **1.** One who or that which c veys, transports, or transfers. **2.** Any mechanical cont ance for conveying articles or materials, as an endless bel series of rollers, etc. Also (*esp. for def. 2*) **con·vey′or.**

con·vict (*v. adj.* kən·vikt′; *n.* kon′vikt) *v.t.* To prove gui find guilty after a judicial trial. **—** *n.* **1.** One serving a s tence in prison. **2.** One found guilty of a crime. [See C VINCE.]

con·vic·tion (kən·vik′shən) *n.* **1.** The state of being c vinced; firm belief. **2.** A firm belief. **3.** A convincing, a a truth. **4.** A pronouncing or being guilty. **— Syn.** BELIEF. **— con·vic′tion·al, con·vic′tive** *adj.*

con·vince (kən·vins′) *v.t.* **·vinced, ·vinc·ing** To cause believe something, as by proof; bring to belief: often with [< L < *com-* thoroughly + *vincere* to conquer] **— c vince′ment** *n.* **— con·vinc′er** *n.* **— con·vin′ci·ble** *adj.*

— Syn. 1. *Convince* and *persuade* agree in the sense of mak one's view or will prevail over another's. A man is *convinced* by gument or evidence; he is *persuaded* by appeals to his affecti We *convince* a man of a truth, but *persuade* him to act.

con·vinc·ing (kən·vin′sing) *adj.* **1.** Satisfying by eviden *convincing* testimony. **2.** Credible or believable: a *convi ing* act. **— con·vinc′ing·ly** *adv.* **— con·vinc′ing·ness** *n.*

con·viv·i·al (kən·viv′ē·əl) *adj.* **1.** Fond of feasting and g fellowship; jovial. **2.** Of or befitting a feast; festive. [< *convivium* a feast, banquet < *com-* together + *vivere* to li **— con·viv′i·al·ist** *n.* **— con·viv·i·al·i·ty** (kən·viv′ē·al′ə·tē **— con·viv′i·al·ly** *adv.*

con·vo·ca·tion (kon′vō·kā′shən) *n.* **1.** A calling togethe summoning to assemble. **2.** A meeting, esp. an ecclesiast one. **— con′vo·ca′tion·al** *adj.* **— con′vo·ca′tor** *n.*

con·voke (kən·vōk′) *v.t.* **·voked, ·vok·ing** To call togeth summon to meet. [< F < L < *com-* together + *vocare* call, summon] **— con·vok′er** *n.*

con·vo·lute (kon′və·lo͞ot) *adj.* Rolled one part over other or inward from one side. **—** *v.t. & v.i.* **·lut·ed, ·lut·** To coil up. [See CONVOLVE.] **— con′vo·lute′ly** *adv.*

con·vo·lu·tion (kon′və·lo͞o′shən) *n.* **1.** A coiled or con luted state. **2.** A fold or twist in something convoluted. *Anat.* One of the folds of the cortex of the brain.

con·volve (kən·volv′) *v.t. & v.i.* **·volved, ·volv·ing** To up, wind, or twist together. [< L < *com-* together + *vere* to spin, twist]

con·vol·vu·lus (kən·vol′vyə·ləs) *n.* A twining herb w large flowers, esp. the morning-glory. [< L, bindweed]

con·voy (kon′voi; *for v., also* kən·voi′) *n.* **1.** A protect escort, as for ships at sea. **2.** A formation of ships, milit vehicles, etc., traveling together. **3.** The act of convoyi or the state of being convoyed. **—** *v.t.* To act as convoy escort. [< MF < L *com-* together + *via* road]

con·vulse (kən·vuls′) *v.t.* **·vulsed, ·vuls·ing 1.** To effect w violent movements; agitate or shake. **2.** To throw into c vulsions. **3.** To cause to laugh violently. [< L < *com-* gether + *vellere* to pull]

con·vul·sion (kən·vul′shən) *n.* **1.** *Often pl. Pathol.* A olent and involuntary contraction or series of contractions the voluntary muscles. **2.** Any violent commotion or d turbance, as an earthquake. **3.** A violent fit of laughter. **con·vul′sion·ar′y** *adj. & n.*

con·vul·sive (kən·vul′siv) *adj.* Producing, characteri by, or of the nature of convulsions: *convulsive* anger. **— c vul′sive·ly** *adv.* **— con·vul′sive·ness** *n.*

co·ny (kō′nē, kun′ē) *n. pl.* **·nies 1.** A rabbit. **2.** Rab fur. Also spelled *coney.* [< OF < L *cuniculus* rabbit]

coo (ko͞o) *v.* **cooed, coo·ing** *v.i.* **1.** To utter the murmur note of a dove. **2.** To talk amorously in murmurs: to and *coo.* **—** *v.t.* **3.** To utter with a coo. **—** *n.* A murmur sound, as of a dove. [Imit.] **— coo′er** *n.* **— coo′ing·ly** *a*

cook (ko͝ok) *v.t.* **1.** To prepare (food) for eating by the tion of heat. **2.** *Informal* To tamper with. **3.** *Slang* ruin. **—** *v.i.* **4.** To act as a cook. **5.** To undergo cooki **— to cook up** *Informal* To invent; concoct: to *cook u* scandal. **—** *n.* One who prepares food for eating. [OE LL < L *coquus* a cook] **— cook′er** *n.*

cook·book (ko͝ok′bo͝ok′) *n.* A book containing recipes a other information about cooking.

cook·er·y (ko͝ok′ər·ē) *n. pl.* **·er·ies 1.** The art or practice cooking. **2.** A place for cooking.

ok·out (kŏŏk′out′) *n. U.S. Informal* A meal cooked out-oors.
ok·y (kŏŏk′ē) *n. pl.* **cook·ies** *U.S.* A small, thin, dry ake, usu. sweetened. Also **cook′ey, cook′ie.** [< Du. *koekje,* im. of *koek* cake]
ol (kōōl) *adj.* **1.** Moderately cold; lacking warmth. **2.** 'roducing a feeling of coolness: a *cool* suit. **3.** Calm in ac-on or thought; composed. **4.** Not cordial; chilling: a *cool* ›ception. **5.** Suggesting coolness: said of colors. **6.** *U.S.* *nformal* Not exaggerated; actual: a *cool* million. **7.** *U.S.* *lang* Excellent. — *adv. U.S. Informal* Coolly. — *v.t. & v.i.* . To make or become less warm. **2.** To make or become ss angry, ardent, or zealous. — *n.* A cool time, thing, lace, etc. [OE *cōl*] — **cool′ly** *adv.* — **cool′ness** *n.*
ol·er (kōō′lər) *n.* **1.** A vessel or apparatus that serves to ›ol something or to keep it cool. **2.** *Slang* A jail.
ol-head·ed (kōōl′hed′id) *adj.* Not readily excited; calm.
o·lie (kōō′lē) *n.* An unskilled Oriental laborer. Also **coo′·** . [Prob. < *Kuli,* an aboriginal Indian tribe]
on (kōōn) *n.* **1.** A raccoon. **2.** *Slang* A Negro: an offen ve term. [Short for RACCOON]
op (kōōp, kŏŏp) *n.* **1.** An enclosure or box, as for fowls. . *Slang* A jail. — **to fly the coop** *Slang* To escape from rison, etc. — *v.t.* To put into a coop.
·op (kō′op, kō·op′) *n. Informal* A cooperative.
op·er (kōō′pər, kŏŏp′ər) *n.* One who makes and repairs ısks, barrels, etc. — *v.t. & v.i.* To make or mend (casks, arrels, etc.). [ME < LG. Cf. MDu. *kupe* cask.]
op·er·age (kōō′pər·ij, kŏŏp′ər-) *n.* **1.** The work or work-ıop of a cooper. Also **coop′er·y.** **2.** A cooper's fee.
·op·er·ate (kō·op′ə·rāt) *v.i.* **·at·ed, ·at·ing** To work to-›ther for a common objective; act in combination. Also **·op′er·ate, co·öp′er·ate.** [< L < *co-* together + *operari* work] — **co·op′er·a′tor** *n.*
·op·er·a·tion (kō·op′ə·rā′shən) *n.* **1.** A working together ›ward a common end. **2.** The association of laborers, farm-'s, small capitalists, etc., for mutual economic benefit. Also **·op′er·a′tion, co·öp′er·a′tion.** — **co·op′er·a′tion·ist** *n.*
·op·er·a·tive (kō·op′rə·tiv, -ə·rā′tiv) *adj.* **1.** Cooperating willing to cooperate. **2.** Of or organized for economic co-›eration. — *n.* A business enterprise, association, or roperty organized or owned by a group for its common ›onomic benefit. Also **co·op′er·a·tive, co·öp′er·a·tive.** — **·op′er·a·tive·ly** *adv.* — **co·op′er·a·tive·ness** *n.*
operative Commonwealth Federation *Canadian* ormer name of the NEW DEMOCRATIC PARTY.
·opt (kō·opt′) *v.t.* **1.** To elect as a fellow member of a com-ittee, etc. **2.** To appoint. **3.** To make ineffectual as an strument for radical change by incorporating within the tablished order. [< L < *co-* together + *optare* to choose] **co′-op·ta′tion, co-op′tion** *n.* — **co-op·ta·tive** (kō′op′tə·v) *adj.*
·or·di·nate (kō·ôr′də·nāt; *for adj., n., also* kō·ôr′də·nit) *lj.* **1.** Of equal importance or rank; not subordinate. **2.** f or pertaining to coordinates or coordination. — *n.* **1.** ne who or that which is of the same order, rank, power, etc. . *Math.* Any of a set of magnitudes by means of which the ›sition of a point, line, or angle is determined with reference fixed elements. — *v.* **·nat·ed, ·nat·ing** *v.t.* **1.** To put in ıe same rank, class, or order. **2.** To bring into harmonious lation or action; adjust. — *v.i.* **3.** To become coordinate. . To act in harmonious or reciprocal relation. Also **co-or′di·ate.** [< Med.L < L *co-* together + *ordinare* to set in order] **co·or′di·nate·ly** *adv.* — **co·or′di·nate·ness** *n.* — **co·or′·na′tive** *adj.* — **co·or′di·na′tor** *n.*
·or·di·na·tion (kō·ôr′də·nā′shən) *n.* **1.** The act of coor-inating, or the state of being coordinated. **2.** Harmonious, tegrated action or interaction. Also **co-or′di·na′tion.**
ot (kōōt) *n.* **1.** A short-winged aquatic bird resembling ıe rail. **2.** *Informal* A simpleton. [ME *cote* < LG]
ot·ie (kōō′tē) *n. Slang* A louse. [? < Indonesian *kutu,* a arasitic insect; orig. nautical slang]
p (kop) *n. Informal* A policeman. — *v.t.* **copped, cop·ng** *Slang* **1.** To steal. **2.** To catch. — **to cop out** *U.S.* *lang* To back down; renege. [? Var. of *cap* to catch, take]
pa·cet·ic (kō′pə·set′ik) See COPESETIC.
·pal (kō′pəl) *n.* A hard resin of various tropical trees, ›ed in varnishes. [< Sp. < Nahuatl *copalli* incense]
pe[1] (kōp) *v.* **coped, cop·ing** *v.i.* To contend or strive, esp. ıccessfully: often with *with.* [< OF *coup* blow]
pe[2] (kōp) *n.* **1.** A semicircular mantle worn by priests on ›remonial occasions. **2.** Something that arches overhead; vault: the *cope* of heaven. — *v.t.* **coped, cop·ing** To dress cover in or as in a cope. [See CAP[1].]
·peck (kō′pek) See KOPECK.
·per·ni·can system (kô·pûr′nə·kən) *Astron.* The theory the solar system of Copernicus that the earth and other lanets revolve about the sun.

co·pe·set·ic (kō′pə·set′ik) *adj. U.S. Slang* Fine; excellent: also spelled *copacetic.* Also **co′pa·set′ic, co′pe·set′ic.** [< Creole *coupesètique* able to be coped with]
cope·stone (kōp′stōn) *n.* **1.** One of the stones of a coping. **2.** The final stroke. Also called *capstone.*
cop·i·er (kop′ē·ər) *n.* **1.** An imitator. **2.** A copyist.
co·pi·lot (kō′pī′lət) *n.* The assistant pilot of an aircraft.
cop·ing (kō′ping) *n.* The top course of a wall, roof, etc., usually sloping to shed water. [< COPE[2], v.]
coping saw A narrow-bladed saw set in a recessed frame and used for cutting curved pieces from wood.
co·pi·ous (kō′pē·əs) *adj.* **1.** Abundant; plentiful. **2.** Dif-fuse; wordy. [< L *copia* abundance] — **co′pi·ous·ly** *adv.* — **co′pi·ous·ness** *n.*
cop-out (kop′out′) *n. U.S. Slang* **1.** A way of avoiding responsibility; evasion. **2.** One who cops out.
cop·per[1] (kop′ər) *n.* **1.** A reddish, ductile, metallic element (symbol Cu) that is one of the best conductors of heat and electricity. See ELEMENT. **2.** A large pot. **3.** A coin of copper, or of bronze. **4.** A lustrous, reddish brown. — *v.t.* **1.** To cover or coat with copper. **2.** *U.S. Slang* To bet against (another bet). — *adj.* Of, or of the color of, copper. [OE < LL < L < Gk. *Kypros* Cyprus where copper abound-ed] — **cop′per·y** *adj.*
cop·per[2] (kop′ər) *n. Slang* A policeman. [< COP[1]]
cop·per·as (kop′ər·əs) *n.* A green, crystalline, astringent ferrous sulfate, $FeSO_4 \cdot 7H_2O$, used in dyeing, inkmaking, etc. [< MF < Med.L < (*aqua*) *cuprosa* copper (water)]
cop·per·head (kop′ər·hed′) *n.* A venomous North Ameri-can snake having reddish brown markings.
Cop·per·head (kop′ər·hed′) *n. U.S.* During the Civil War, a Northerner who sympathized with the South.
cop·per·plate (kop′ər·plāt′) *n.* **1.** An engraved or etched plate of copper. **2.** A print or engraving from such a plate.
cop·per·smith (kop′ər·smith′) *n.* One who works in copper.
copper sulfate A deep blue, crystalline substance, $CuSO_4 \cdot 5H_2O$, used in electric batteries, etc.
cop·pice (kop′is) *n.* A copse. [Alter. of COPSE]
cop·ra (kop′rə, kō′prə) *n.* The dried kernel of the coconut, yielding coconut oil. Also **cop·per·ah** (kop′ər·ə), **cop′rah, cop′pra.** [< Pg. < Malayalam *koppara*]
copse (kops) *n.* A thicket of bushes or small trees: also called *coppice.* [Earlier *coppice* < OF *copeiz* < *coper* to cut]
Copt (kopt) *n.* **1.** A native Egyptian of ancient Egyptian stock. **2.** A member of the Coptic Church. [< Med.L < Arabic < Coptic < Gk. *Aigyptios* Egyptian]
Cop·tic (kop′tik) *adj.* Of or pertaining to the Copts, or to their language. — *n.* The Hamitic language of the Copts.
Coptic Church The principal Christian sect of Egypt.
cop·u·la (kop′yə·lə) *n. pl.* **·las** or **·lae** (-lē) *Gram.* A link-ing verb. [< L, a link, band] — **cop′u·lar** *adj.*
cop·u·late (kop′yə·lāt) *v.i.* **·lat·ed, ·lat·ing** To unite in sex-ual intercourse. [< L *copula* a link] — **cop′u·la′tion** *n.*
cop·u·la·tive (kop′yə·lā′tiv, -lə·tiv) *adj.* **1.** Serving to join. **2.** *Gram.* **a** Serving as a copula. **b** Connecting words or clauses in a coordinate relationship. **3.** Copulatory. — *n.* *Gram.* A copulative word. — **cop′u·la′tive·ly** *adv.*
cop·y (kop′ē) *n. pl.* **cop·ies** **1.** A reproduction or imitation of an original; duplicate. **2.** A single specimen of a book, print, etc. **3.** Written matter as distinct from graphic mat-ter, as in advertising, etc. **4.** Something to be reproduced or imitated. **5.** *Printing* Manuscript or other matter to be reproduced in type. **6.** In journalism, subject matter for an article, etc.: The president is good *copy.* Abbr. *c., C.* — *v.* **cop·ied, cop·y·ing** *v.t.* **1.** To make a copy of; reproduce or transcribe. **2.** To follow as a model; imitate. — *v.i.* **3.** To make a copy. [< MF < Med.L *copia* transcript]
cop·y·book (kop′ē·bŏŏk′) *n.* A book containing copies to be imitated in penmanship. — *adj.* Ordinary; trite.
copy boy An errand boy in a newspaper office.
cop·y·cat (kop′ē·kat′) *n.* An imitator: a child's term.
copy desk A desk in a newspaper office where copy is edited and prepared for the typesetters.
cop·y·ist (kop′ē·ist) *n.* **1.** One who makes copies, esp. of documents. **2.** One who imitates or copies.
cop·y·read·er (kop′ē·rē′dər) *n.* A person who edits work intended for publication.
cop·y·right (kop′ē·rīt) *n.* The exclusive statutory right of authors, composers, playwrights, artists, publishers, and distributors to publish and dispose of their works for a speci-fied period of time. In the U.S. this period is 28 years, with the privilege of one renewal. — *v.t.* To secure copy-right for. — *adj.* Of or protected by copyright. — **cop′y·right′a·ble** *adj.* — **cop′y·right′er** *n.*
cop·y·writ·er (kop′ē·rī′tər) *n.* One who writes copy for advertisements.
co·quet (kō·ket′) *v.* **·quet·ted, ·quet·ting** *v.i.* To flirt. [< F *coq* a cock; with ref. to its strutting] — **co·quet′ry** *n.*

co·quette (kō·ket′) *n.* A woman who tries to attract men merely to gratify her vanity; a flirt. — *v.t. & v.i.* **·quet·ted, ·quet·ting** To coquet. — **co·quet′tish** *adj.* — **co·quet′tish·ly** *adv.* — **co·quet′tish·ness** *n.*
co·qui·na (kō·kē′nə) *n.* A soft, highly porous limestone used as building material. [< Sp., shell, ult. < L *concha*]
cor- Var. of COM-.
cor·a·cle (kôr′ə·kəl, kor′-) *n.* A small, rounded boat of hide or oilcloth on a wicker frame. [< Welsh *corwg* boat]
cor·al (kôr′əl, kor′-) *n.* **1.** The calcareous skeleton secreted in or by the tissues of various marine coelenterates, deposited in many forms and colors. **2.** A mass of these skeletons forming an island, reef, etc. **3.** An animal of this type. **4.** A pinkish or yellowish red. **5.** An object, as a jewel, made of coral. — *adj.* Of, relating to, or of the color of coral. [< OF < L < Gk. *korallion* red coral]

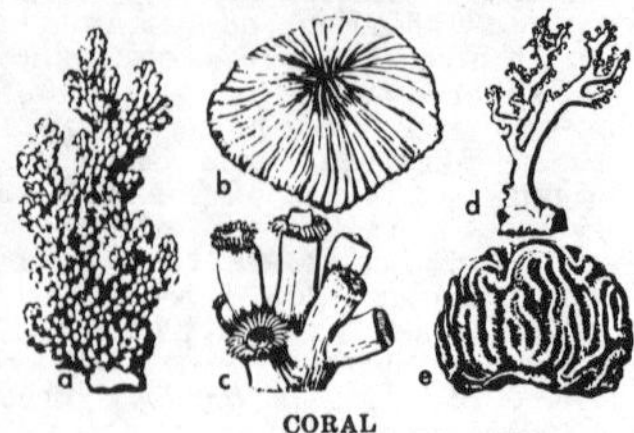

CORAL
a Reef. *b* Mushroom. *c* Bud. *d* Red. *e* Brain.

coral reef A reef, often of great extent, formed by the gradual deposit of coral skeletons.
coral snake A venomous snake of tropical America and the southern U.S., noted for its red, black, and yellow rings.
cor·bel (kôr′bəl, -bel) *n.* *Archit.* **1.** A projection from the face of a wall to support an overhanging weight. **2.** A short timber placed under a girder to increase its bearing. — *v.t.* **cor·beled** or **·belled, cor·bel·ing** or **·bel·ling** To support by or furnish with corbels. [< OF < L *corvus* crow]
cor·bel·ing (kôr′bəl·ing) *n.* *Archit.* An arrangement of stones or bricks in which each successive course projects beyond the one below it. Also **cor′bel·ling.**
cor·bie (kôr′bē) *n.* *Scot.* A crow or raven. Also **cor′by.**
cord (kôrd) *n.* **1.** A string or small rope; twine. **2.** A flexible, insulated electric wire, usu. with a plug at one end. **3.** A measure for wood, usu. for firewood, equaling a pile 4 × 4 × 8 feet, or 128 cubic feet. See table front of book. **4.** An influence that draws or restrains. **5.** A raised rib in fabric; also, fabric with such ribs. **6.** *pl.* Corduroy trousers. **7.** *Anat.* A cordlike structure: spinal *cord.* — *v.t.* **1.** To bind with cord. **2.** To furnish or ornament with cords. **3.** To pile (firewood) by the cord. [< MF < L < Gk. *chordē* string of a musical instrument] — **cord′er** *n.*
cord·age (kôr′dij) *n.* **1.** Ropes and cords collectively, especially in a ship's rigging. **2.** The amount of wood, in cords.
cor·date (kôr′dāt) *adj.* *Bot.* Heart-shaped, as a leaf. [< L *cordis* heart] — **cor′date·ly** *adv.*
cord·ed (kôr′did) *adj.* **1.** Bound or fastened with cord. **2.** Ribbed with cords: a *corded* fabric. **3.** Piled in cords.
cor·dial (kôr′jəl, *esp. Brit.* -dyəl) *adj.* **1.** Warm and hearty; sincere. **2.** Giving heart; invigorating. — *n.* **1.** A liqueur. **2.** Something that invigorates, as a medical stimulant. [< L *cor, cordis* heart] — **cor′dial·ly** *adv.* — **cor′dial·ness** *n.*
cor·dial·i·ty (kôr·jal′ə·tē, -jē·al′-, *esp. Brit.* -dē·al′-) *n.* *pl.* **·ties** Cordial quality; sincerity of feeling; warmth.
cor·dil·le·ra (kôr′dil·yâr′ə, kôr·dil′ər·ə) *n.* *Geog.* An entire system of mountain ranges continuous within a great land mass. [< Sp. < OSp. *cordilla,* dim. of *cuerda* rope] — **cor·dil·ler·an** (kôr′dil·yâr′an, kôr·dil′ər·ən) *adj.*
cord·ite (kôr′dīt) *n.* A smokeless explosive consisting of cellulose nitrate or guncotton, nitroglycerin, and a mineral jelly. [< CORD; with ref. to its appearance]
cor·don (kôr′dən) *n.* **1.** A line, as of men or ships, stationed so as to guard or enclose an area. **2.** A ribbon or cord worn as an insignia of honor. [< F < *corde* cord]
cor·do·van (kôr′də·vən) *n.* A fine leather first made at Córdoba, Spain, originally of goatskin, but now usu. of split horsehide. Also **cordovan leather.** — *adj.* Made of cordovan. [< OSp. *cordovan* of Córdoba]
cor·du·roy (kôr′də·roi, kôr′də·roi′) *n.* **1.** A durable fabric, usu. of cotton, having a ribbed pile. **2.** *pl.* Trousers made of corduroy. — *adj.* Made of corduroy. [? < *cord* (ribbed fabric) + obs. *duroy* coarse woolen cloth; prob. < F *corde du roi* king's cord]
corduroy road A road formed from logs laid transversely.
cord·wood (kôrd′wŏŏd′) *n.* Firewood or pulpwood cut for stacking in a cord or sold by the cord.
core (kôr, kōr) *n.* **1.** The central or innermost part of a thing. **2.** The fibrous central part of a fruit, containing the seeds. **3.** A cylindrical mass of rock. **4.** *Electr.* The central iron mass of an induction coil, armature, or electromagnet. — *v.t.* **cored, cor·ing** To remove the core of. [ME; origin uncertain] — **core′less** *adj.* — **cor′er** *n.*
co·re·la·tion (kō′ri·lā′shən) See CORRELATION.
co·re·lig·ion·ist (kō′ri·lij′ən·ist) *n.* An adherent of t same religion, church, or sect as another.
co·re·op·sis (kôr′ē·op′sis, kō′rē-) *n.* A plant of the co posite family, with yellow or reddish flowers. [< NL < (*koris* bug + -OPSIS; with ref. to the shape of the seed]
co·re·spon·dent (kō′ri·spon′dənt) *n.* *Law* In a suit for vorce, one charged with having committed adultery w the husband or wife. — **co′re·spon′den·cy** *n.*
co·ri·an·der (kôr′ē·an′dər, kō′rē-) *n.* **1.** A plant of t parsley family, bearing aromatic seeds used for seasoni and in medicine. **2.** The seeds of this plant. [< MF < < Gk. *koriannon*]
Cor·inth (kôr′inth, kor′-) An ancient city in Argolis, Gree
Co·rin·thi·an (kə·rin′thē·ən) *adj.* **1.** Of or pertaining ancient Corinth, noted for its luxury, licentiousness, a ornate art. **2.** Given to luxury and dissipation. **3.** *Arch* Of or pertaining to an order of Greek architecture charact ized by ornate, bell-shaped capitals decorated with sin lated acanthus leaves. — *n.* A native or inhabitant of C inth. — **Epistle to the Corinthians** Either of two lett addressed by Saint Paul to the Christians at Corinth, ea forming a book of the New Testament. Also **Corinthia**
co·ri·um (kôr′ē·əm, kō′rē-) *n.* *Anat.* The dermis. [< L
cork (kôrk) *n.* **1.** The light, porous, elastic outer bark of t cork oak, widely used in industry and the arts. **2.** Sor thing made of cork, esp. when used as a bottle stopper; al a stopper made of other material. — *v.t.* **1.** To stop wit cork. **2.** To restrain; check. **3.** *U.S.* To blacken with bu cork. [Appar. < OSp. < Arabic ? < L *quercus* oak]
cork·er (kôr′kər) *n.* **1.** One who or that which corks. *Slang* Something outstanding or astonishing. **3.** An ar ment, remark, etc., that puts an end to discussion.
cork·ing (kôr′king) *Slang adj.* Excellent; splendid.
cork oak An evergreen oak of southern Europe and No Africa, from whose bark cork is produced.
cork·screw (kôrk′skrōō′) *n.* An instrument for draw corks from bottles. — *v.t. & v.i.* To move or twist spiral — *adj.* Shaped like a corkscrew; twisted; spiral.
cork·y (kôr′kē) *adj.* **cork·i·er, cork·i·est 1.** Of or rese bling cork. **2.** Tasting of cork, as wine. — **cork′i·ness**
corm (kôrm) *n.* *Bot.* A bulblike enlargement of the und ground stem in certain plants, as the gladiolus. [<] *cormus* < Gk. *kormos* tree trunk]
cor·mo·rant (kôr′mər·ənt) *n.* **1.** A large, web-footed aqu ic bird having a hooked bill and a pouch under the beak. A greedy or voracious person. — *adj.* Greedy; rapacio [< MF < L *corvus marinus* sea crow]
corn[1] (kôrn) *n.* **1.** *U.S.* A tall, extensively cultivated real plant bearing seeds on a large ear or cob; also, the se of this plant: also called *Indian corn, maize.* **2.** *Brit.* England, wheat. **3.** In Scotland and Ireland, oats. **4** single seed of a cereal plant; kernel; grain. **5.** *U.S. Infor* Corn whisky. **6.** *U.S. Slang* Anything trite or sentiment — *v.t.* To preserve in coarse salt or in brine. [OE]
corn[2] (kôrn) *n.* A horny thickening of the skin, commo on a toe. [< OF < L *cornu*]
Corn Belt *U.S.* The chief corn-growing States, Illin Indiana, Iowa, Kansas, Missouri, Nebraska, and Ohio.
corn borer The larva of a moth that feeds on the ears a stalks of corn.
corn·bread (kôrn′bred′) *n.* Bread made from cornmeal.
corn·cob (kôrn′kob′) *n.* *U.S.* The woody spike of c around which the kernels grow.
corncob pipe A pipe whose bowl is cut from a corncob.
corn·cock·le (kôrn′kok′əl) *n.* A tall weed of the pink fa ily, with purple flowers.
cor·ne·a (kôr′nē·ə) *n.* *Anat.* The transparent part of t coat of the eyeball, continuous with the sclera. For illus. EYE. [< Med.L < L *cornu* horn] — **cor′ne·al** *adj.*
corned (kôrnd) *adj.* Preserved in salt or brine, as beef.
cor·nel (kôr′nəl) *n.* A shrub or small tree with hard wo as the dogwood. [< MF < L *cornus* cornel]
cor·nel·ian (kôr·nēl′yən) *n.* Carnelian.
cor·ne·ous (kôr′nē·əs) *adj.* Consisting of horn; of a ho like texture; horny. [< L < *cornu* horn]
cor·ner (kôr′nər) *n.* **1.** The point formed by the meeting two lines or surfaces. **2.** The place where two streets me **3.** A threatening or embarrassing position. **4.** A region place: in every *corner* of the land. **5.** A piece for formi ornamenting, or guarding a corner, as of a book. **6.** *Ec* An operation in which a commodity or security is bought by an individual or group of individuals with a view to fo ing higher prices. — **to cut corners** To economize; redu expenditures. — *v.t.* **1.** To force into a corner; place in dangerous or embarrassing position. **2.** To form a corner (a stock or commodity). **3.** To furnish with corners. **4.** place in a corner. — *v.i.* **5.** To form a corner in a stock commodity. **6.** *U.S.* To come together or be located on at a corner. — *adj.* **1.** Located on a corner. **2.** Design for a corner. [< OF < L *cornu* horn] — **cor′nered** *adj.*
cor·ner·stone (kôr′nər·stōn′) *n.* **1.** A stone uniting t

ılls at the corner of a building. **2.** Such a stone ceremonisly laid into the foundation of a building under construcn. **3.** Something of primary importance.
·ner·wise (kôr′nər·wīz′) *adv.* **1.** With the corner in ont. **2.** Diagonally. Also **cor′ner·ways′.**
·net (kôr·net′) *n.* **1.** A small wind instrument of the ımpet class, with a somewhat wider bore. **2.** A coneaped paper wrapper, as for candy, nuts, etc. [< OF < L *nu* horn] **— cor·net′tist, cor·net′ist** *n.*
n·flow·er (kôrn′flou′ər) *n.* A hardy annual plant of the mposite family, with heads of blue, purple, pink, or white wers: also called *bachelor's-button, bluebonnet, bluebottle.*
n·husk (kôrn′husk′) *n. U.S.* The leaves or husk enclos- an ear of corn: also called *corn shuck.*
n·husk·er State (kôrn′husk′ər) Nickname of Nebraska.
n·husk·ing (kôrn′hus′king) *n. U.S.* A social gathering husking corn, usu. followed by refreshments, dancing, .: also called *husking bee.* **— corn′husk′er** *n.*
·nice (kôr′nis) *n.* **1.** *Archit.* **a** The horizontal molded ɔjection at the top of a building. **b** The uppermost mem- of an entablature. **2.** A molding around the walls of a ɔm, close to the ceiling. **—** *v.t.* **·niced, ·nic·ing** To adorn th a cornice. [< Ital., ? < L < Gk. *korōnis* wreath]
·nish (kôr′nish) *adj.* Pertaining to Cornwall, England, its people. **—** *n.* The former language of Cornwall, beıging to the Brythonic branch of the Celtic languages. **— r′nish·man** (-mən) *n.*
n·meal (kôrn′mēl′) *n.* **1.** Meal made from corn: also lled *Indian meal.* **2.** *Scot.* Oatmeal. Also **corn meal.**
n pone *Southern U.S.* Bread made of cornmeal, water, d salt, usu. without milk or eggs.
n silk The soft, silky styles on an ear of corn.
n·stalk (kôrn′stôk′) *n.* A stalk of corn. Also **corn stalk.**
n·starch (kôrn′stärch′) *n.* **1.** Starch made from corn. A purified starchy cornmeal used in making puddings.
n syrup Syrup extracted from corn grains, containing ıcose mixed with dextrine and maltose.
·nu·co·pi·a (kôr′nə·kō′pē·ə) *n.* **1.** A symbol of prosper-, represented as a curved horn overflowing with fruit, getables, grains, etc. **2.** A great abundance. Also called *rn of plenty.* [< LL < L *cornu copiae* horn of plenty] **— r′nu·co′pi·an** *adj.*
n whisky Whisky distilled from corn.
n·y (kôr′nē) *adj.* **corn·i·er, corn·i·est** **1.** *Slang* Trite, bal, or sentimental. **2.** Of or producing corn.
·ol·la (kə·rol′ə) *n. Bot.* The circle of flower leaves, usu. lored, forming the inner floral envelope; the petals of a wer. [< L, dim. of *corona* crown] **— cor·ol·la·ceous** (kôr′ā′shəs, kor′-) *adj.* **— cor·ol·late** (kôr′ə·lāt, kor′-) *adj.*
·ol·lar·y (kôr′ə·ler′ē, kor′-; *Brit.* kə·rol′ər·ē) *n. pl.* **·lar· 1.** A proposition following so obviously from another ıt it requires little or no proof. **2.** An inference or deducn. **3.** A natural consequence; result. **—** *adj.* Like a corary; consequent. [< L *corolla* garland]
·o·na (kə·rō′nə) *n. pl* **·nas** or **·nae** (-nē) **1.** A crownlike ucture or part, as the top of the head, the upper part of a ɔth, etc. **2.** *Astron.* **a** A luminous circle around one of the avenly bodies, as when seen through cloud or mist. **b** The minous envelope of ionized gases visible during a total ipse of the sun. **3.** Anything resembling a corona or halo. *Bot.* A crownlike process at the top of the tube of a corolla, in jonquils. **5.** *Electr.* The luminous discharge appearing the surface or between the terminals of an electrical conctor under high voltage. [< L, crown] **— co·ro′nal** *adj.*
·o·nar·y (kôr′ə·ner′ē, kor′-) *adj.* **1.** Pertaining to or like rown. **2.** *Anat.* Designating either of two arteries rising ɔm the aorta and supplying blood to the heart muscle. For ıs. see HEART. **—** *n.* Coronary thrombosis. [< L *corona* ɔwn]
onary thrombosis *Pathol.* The formation of a thromıs, or blood clot, in one of the coronary arteries, resulting in erruption of blood supply to the heart muscle.
·o·na·tion (kôr′ə·nā′shən, kor′-) *n.* The act or ceremony crowning a monarch. [< MF, ult. < L < *corona* crown]
·o·ner (kôr′ə·nər, kor′-) *n.* A public officer whose prinɔal duty is the investigation, with the aid of a jury (**coror's jury**), of the cause of deaths not clearly due to natural uses. [< AF < L *corona*] **cor′o·ner·ship′** *n.*
·o·net (kôr′ə·net, -nit, kor′-) *n.* **1.** A small crown, deting noble rank less than sovereign. **2.** A headband ornaented with jewels, etc. [< OF < L *corona*] **— cor′o·t′ed** *adj.*
·po·ra (kôr′pər·ə) Plural of CORPUS.
·po·ral[1] (kôr′pər·əl) *adj.* **1.** Belonging or related to the dy: *corporal* punishment. **2.** Personal: *corporal* possesɔn. [< L *corpus, -oris* body] **— cor·po·ral·i·ty** (kôr′pəl′ə·tē) *n.* **— cor′po·ral·ly** *adv.*
·po·ral[2] (kôr′pər·əl, -prəl) *n. Mil.* A noncommissioned officer of the lowest rank. See tables at GRADE. [< MF < Ital. < L *caput*]
corporal punishment Physical punishment given an offender, as flogging.
cor·po·rate (kôr′pər·it) *adj.* **1.** Of or related to a corporation; incorporated. **2.** Combined as a whole; collective. [< L *corpus, -oris* body] **— cor′po·rate·ly** *adv.*
cor·po·ra·tion (kôr′pə·rā′shən) *n.* **1.** A body of persons recognized by law as an individual person or entity having its own name and identity, and with rights, privileges, and liabilities distinct from those of its members. **2.** Any group of persons acting as one body. **3.** *Informal* A bulging abdomen; paunch. **— cor′po·ra′tive** *adj.* **— cor′po·ra′tor** *n.*
cor·po·re·al (kôr·pôr′ē·əl, -pō′rē·əl) *adj.* **1.** Of, or of the nature of, the body; bodily; mortal. **2.** Of a material nature; physical. **— cor·po·re·al·i·ty** (kôr·pôr′ē·al′ə·tē, -pō′rē-) *n.* **— cor·po′re·al·ly** *adv.* **— cor·po′re·al·ness** *n.*
cor·po·re·i·ty (kôr′pə·rē′ə·tē) *n.* Bodily or material existence. [< Med.L < L *corpus, -oris* body]
corps (kôr, kōr) *n. pl.* **corps** (kôrz, kōrz) **1.** *Mil.* **a** A tactical unit, intermediate between a division and an army, consisting of two or more divisions and auxiliary arms and services. **b** A special department: the Transportation *Corps.* **2.** A number of persons acting together. [See CORPSE.]
corps de bal·let (kôr′ də ba·lā′, *Fr.* bà·le′) The ballet dancers who perform as a group and have no solo parts. [< F]
corpse (kôrps) *n.* A dead body, usu. of a human being. [ME < OF < L *corpus* body]
corps·man (kôr′mən, kōr′-) *n. pl.* **·men** (-mən) **1.** In the U.S. Navy, an enlisted man trained as a pharmacist or hospital assistant. **2.** In the U.S. Army, an enlisted man in the Medical Corps assigned to a combat area.
cor·pu·lence (kôr′pyə·ləns) *n.* An excess accumulation of fat in the body; obesity. Also **cor′pu·len·cy.** [< F < L < *corpus* body] **— cor′pu·lent** *adj.* **— cor′pu·lent·ly** *adv.*
cor·pus (kôr′pəs) *n. pl.* **·po·ra** (-pər·ə) **1.** A human or animal body. **2.** A collection of writings, generally on one subject or by one author. **3.** The main part or mass of anything. [< L]
Cor·pus Chris·ti (kôr′pəs kris′tē, -tī) In the Roman Catholic Church, a festival honoring the Eucharist on the first Thursday after Trinity Sunday. [< L, body of Christ]
cor·pus·cle (kôr′pəs·əl, -pus·əl) *n.* **1.** *Biol.* Any protoplasmic granule of distinct shape or characteristic function, esp. one of the particles forming part of the blood of vertebrates. **2.** A minute particle of matter, as a molecule, atom, or electron. Also **cor·pus·cule** (kôr·pus′kyōōl). [< L *corpus, -oris* body] **— cor·pus·cu·lar** (kôr·pus′kyə·lər) *adj.*
cor·pus de·lic·ti (kôr′pəs di·lik′tī) **1.** *Law* The essential fact of the commission of a crime, as, in a case of murder, the finding of the body of the victim. **2.** Loosely, the victim's body in a murder case. [< L, the body of the offense]
corpus ju·ris (jōōr′is) *Latin* The body of law.
cor·ral (kə·ral′) *n.* An enclosed space or pen for livestock. **—** *v.t.* **·ralled, ·ral·ling** **1.** To drive into and enclose in a corral. **2.** *U.S. Informal* To seize or capture; secure. [< Sp.]
cor·rect (kə·rekt′) *v.t.* **1.** To make free from error or mistake; set right: to *correct* false notions. **2.** To remedy or counteract; rectify. **3.** To mark the errors of: to *correct* proofs. **4.** To punish or rebuke so as to improve. **5.** To adjust, as to a standard: to *correct* a lens. **—** *adj.* **1.** Free from fault or mistake; true or exact; accurate. **2.** Conforming to custom or other standard; proper: *correct* behavior. [< L < *com-* together + *regere* to make straight] **— cor·rect′a·ble** or **cor·rect′i·ble** *adj.* **— cor·rect′ly** *adv.* **— cor·rect′·ness** *n.* **— cor·rec′tor** *n.*
cor·rec·tion (kə·rek′shən) *n.* **1.** The act of correcting. **2.** That which is offered or used as an improvement; an emendation. **3.** The act or process of disciplining or chastening; punishment. **4.** A quantity added or subtracted for correcting: chronometer *corrections.* **— cor·rec′tion·al** *adj.*
cor·rec·tive (kə·rek′tiv) *adj.* Tending or intended to set right. **—** *n.* That which corrects. **— cor·rec′tive·ly** *adv.*
cor·re·late (kôr′ə·lāt, kor′-) *v.* **·lat·ed, ·lat·ing** *v.t.* **1.** To place or put in reciprocal relation: to *correlate* literature and philosophy. **—** *v.i.* **2.** To be mutually or reciprocally related. **—** *adj.* Having a mutual or reciprocal relation. **—** *n.* Either of two things mutually related.
cor·re·la·tion (kôr′ə·lā′shən, kor′-) *n.* **1.** Mutual or reciprocal relation. **2.** The act of correlating. **— cor′re·la′tion·al** *adj.*
cor·rel·a·tive (kə·rel′ə·tiv) *adj.* **1.** Having correlation or mutual relation. **2.** Mutually related in grammatical or logical significance: *Either . . . or* are *correlative* conjunctions. **—** *n.* **1.** A correlate. **2.** A correlative term. **— cor·rel′a·tively** *adv.* **— cor·rel′a·tive·ness, cor·rel′a·tiv′i·ty** *n.*
cor·re·spond (kôr′ə·spond′, kor′-) *v.i.* **1.** To conform in fitness or appropriateness; be in agreement; suit: often with

with or *to*. **2.** To be similar in character or function: with *to*. **3.** To hold communication by means of letters. [< Med.L < L *com-* together + *respondere* to answer]

cor·re·spon·dence (kôr′ə·spon′dəns, kor′-) *n.* **1.** The act or state of corresponding; agreement; congruity; also, analogy; similarity. Also **cor′re·spon′den·cy.** **2.** Communication by letters; also, the letters written.

correspondence school A school that offers courses of study by mail.

cor·re·spon·dent (kôr′ə·spon′dənt, kor′-) *n.* **1.** One who communicates by means of letters. **2.** A person employed to report news, etc., from a distant place. **3.** A thing that corresponds; a correlative. — *adj.* Corresponding.

cor·re·spond·ing (kôr′ə·spon′ding, kor′-) *adj.* **1.** That corresponds in character or place; similar or equivalent. **2.** Handling correspondence. — **cor′re·spond′ing·ly** *adv.*

cor·ri·dor (kôr′ə·dər, -dôr, kor′-) *n.* **1.** A gallery or passageway, usu. having rooms opening upon it. **2.** A strip of land across a foreign country, as one affording a landlocked nation access to the sea. **3.** A relatively long, narrow, densely-populated region joining two or more major cities. [< MF < Ital. < L *currere* to run]

cor·ri·gen·dum (kôr′ə·jen′dəm, kor′-) *n.* *pl.* **·da** (-də) Something to be corrected, as a printer's error. [< L, gerundive of *corrigere* < *com-* together + *regere* to make straight]

cor·ri·gi·ble (kôr′ə·jə·bəl, kor′-) *adj.* **1.** Capable of being corrected or reformed **2.** Submissive to correction. [See CORRECT.] — **cor′ri·gi·bil′i·ty** *n.* — **cor′ri·gi·bly** *adv.*

cor·rob·o·rate (kə·rob′ə·rāt) *v.t.* **·rat·ed, ·rat·ing** To strengthen or support, as conviction; confirm. [< L < *com-* together + *robur, -oris* strength] — **cor·rob′o·ra′tion** *n.* — **cor·rob′o·ra′tor** *n.*

cor·rob·o·ra·tive (kə·rob′ə·rā′tiv, -ər·ə·tiv) *adj.* Tending to strengthen or confirm. Also **cor·rob·o·ra·to·ry** (kə·rob′·ər·ə·tôr′ē, -tō′rē). — **cor·rob′o·ra′tive·ly** *adv.*

cor·rode (kə·rōd′) *v.* **·rod·ed, ·rod·ing** *v.t.* **1.** To eat away or destroy gradually, as by chemical action. **2.** To destroy, consume, or impair (character, strength, etc.). — *v.i.* **3.** To be eaten away. [< L < *com-* thoroughly + *rodere* to gnaw] — **cor·rod′i·ble** or **cor·ro·si·ble** (kə·rō′sə·bəl) *adj.*

cor·ro·sion (kə·rō′zhən) *n.* **1.** An eating or wearing away. **2.** A product of corrosive action, as rust.

cor·ro·sive (kə·rō′siv) *adj.* Having the power of corroding or eating away. — *n.* A corroding substance. — **cor·ro′·sive·ly** *adv.* — **cor·ro′sive·ness** *n.*

corrosive sublimate *Chem.* Mercuric chloride.

cor·ru·gate (kôr′ə·gāt, -yə-, kor′-) *v.t. & v.i.* **·gat·ed, ·gat·ing** To contract into alternate ridges and furrows; wrinkle. — *adj.* Contracted into ridges or folds; wrinkled, furrowed: also **cor′ru·gat′ed.** [< L *com-* thoroughly + *rugare* to wrinkle] — **cor′ru·ga′tion** *n.*

cor·rupt (kə·rupt′) *adj.* **1.** Open to bribery; dishonest. **2.** Immoral or perverted. **3.** Rotting; putrid. **4.** Debased by changes or errors; altered, as a text. — *v.t. & v.i.* To make or become corrupt. [< OF < L < *com-* thoroughly + *rumpere* to break] — **cor·rupt′er** or **cor·rup′tor** *n.* — **cor·rupt′ly** *adv.* — **cor·rupt′ness** *n.*

cor·rupt·i·ble (kə·rup′tə·bəl) *adj.* Capable of being corrupted. — **cor·rupt′i·bil′i·ty, cor·rupt′i·ble·ness** *n.* — **cor·rupt′i·bly** *adv.*

cor·rup·tion (kə·rup′shən) *n.* **1.** The act of corrupting, or the state of being corrupt. **2.** Dishonesty and lack of integrity; also, bribery. **3.** Moral deterioration. **4.** Physical decay; rot. **5.** Any corrupting influence.

cor·sage (kôr·säzh′) *n.* **1.** A small bouquet of flowers for a woman to wear, as at the waist or shoulder. **2.** The bodice or waist of a woman's dress. [< OF < *cors* body]

cor·sair (kôr′sâr) *n.* **1.** A privateer. **2.** A pirate. **3.** A corsair's vessel. [< MF < Med.L < L *currere* to run]

corse·let (kôrs′lit) **1.** Body armor; also, a breastplate. Also **cors′let.** **2.** A light corset, usu. without stays. [< MF, double dim. of OF *cors* body]

cor·set (kôr′sit) *n.* **1.** A close-fitting undergarment, usu. tightened with laces and reinforced by stays, worn chiefly by women to give support or desired shape to the body. **2.** A close-fitting medieval garment. — *v.t.* To enclose or dress in a corset. [< OF, dim. of *cors* body]

cor·tege (kôr·tezh′, -tāzh′) *n.* **1.** A train of attendants. **2.** A ceremonial procession. Also *Chiefly Brit.* **cor·tège′** (-tezh′). [< F < Ital. *corteggio* < *corte* court]

cor·tex (kôr′teks) *n.* *pl.* **·ti·ces** (-tə·sēz) **1.** *Bot.* The bark of trees or the rind of fruits. **2.** *Anat.* The external layer of various organs, esp. the gray matter covering the brain. [< L, bark] — **cor′ti·cal** *adj.* — **cor′ti·cal·ly** *adv.*

cor·ti·cate (kôr′ti·kit, -kāt) *adj.* Sheathed in bark or in a cortex. Also **cor′ti·cat′ed.** [< L *cortex* bark]

cor·ti·sone (kôr′tə·sōn, -zōn) *n.* A powerful hormone extracted from the cortex of the adrenal gland and also made synthetically, used in the treatment of rheumatoid arthritis and certain other diseases. [Short for *corticosterone*]

co·run·dum (kə·run′dəm) *n.* An aluminum oxide, Al_2O_3, used as an abrasive, varieties of which include the ruby a sapphire. [< Tamil *kurundam*]

cor·us·cate (kôr′ə·skāt, kor′-) *v.i.* **·cat·ed, ·cat·ing** sparkle. [< L *coruscare* to glitter] — **cor′us·ca′tion** *n.*

cor·vette (kôr·vet′) *n.* **1.** A small, swift warship, u chiefly as an antisubmarine escort vessel. **2.** Formerl warship equipped with sails and a single tier of guns, sma than a frigate. Also **cor·vet** (kôr·vet′, kôr′vet). [< F Pg. < L *corbita* (*navis*) cargo (ship)]

cor·vine (kôr′vīn, -vin) *adj.* Of or pertaining to a cr crowlike. [< L *corvinus* < *corvus* crow]

cor·ymb (kôr′imb, -im, kor′-) *n.* *Bot.* A flat-topped or c vex open flower cluster. [< F < L < Gk. *korymbos* flo cluster] — **co·rym·bose** (kə·rim′bōs) *adj.* — **co·rym′b ly** *adv.* — **co·rym·bous** (kə·rim′bəs) *adj.*

co·ry·za (kə·rī′zə) *n.* *Pathol.* A cold in the head. [< I Gk. *koryza* catarrh]

co·se·cant (kō·sē′kənt) *n.* *Trig.* The secant of the com ment of an acute angle. [< CO-[2] + SECANT]

co·sig·na·to·ry (kō·sig′nə·tôr′ē, -tō′rē) *adj.* Signing gether or jointly. — *n.* *pl.* **·ries** One of the joint signers document: also called *cosigner*.

co·sign·er (kō′sī′nər) *n.* **1.** One who endorses the signat of another, as for a loan. **2.** A cosignatory.

co·sine (kō′sīn) *n.* *Trig.* The sine of the complement o acute angle.

cos·met·ic (koz·met′ik) *adj.* Used to beautify, esp. the c plexion. Also **cos·met′i·cal.** — *n.* A cosmetic preparati [< Gk. < *kosmos* order] — **cos·met′i·cal·ly** *adv.*

cos·mic (koz′mik) *adj.* **1.** Of or relating to the univers cosmos. **2.** Limitless; vast. Also **cos′mi·cal.** [< Gk *kosmos* order, the universe] — **cos′mi·cal·ly** *adv.*

cosmic dust Fine particles of matter collected by the ea from outer space.

cosmic rays *Physics* Radiation of intense penetrat power and high frequency, emanating from outer space consisting principally of high-energy rays formed from m types of atomic particles, positive and negative in charg

cosmo- *combining form* The universe. Also, before vow **cosm-.** [< Gk. *kosmos* the universe]

cos·mog·o·ny (koz·mog′ə·nē) *n.* *pl.* **·nies** **1.** A theory c cerning the origin of the material universe. **2.** The crea of the universe. [< Gk. < *kosmos* the universe + *-goni -gon*, stem of *gignesthai* to be born] — **cos·mo·gon·ic** (k mə·gon′ik) or **·i·cal, cos·mog′o·nal** *adj.* — **cos·mog′o·nis**

cos·mog·ra·phy (koz·mog′rə·fē) *n.* *pl.* **·phies** The scie that describes the universe, including astronomy, geol and geography. [< Gk. < *kosmos* the universe + *grap* to write] — **cos·mog′ra·pher, cos·mog′ra·phist** *n.* — **mo·graph·ic** (koz′mə·graf′ik) or **·i·cal** *adj.*

cos·mol·o·gy (koz·mol′ə·jē) *n.* *pl.* **·gies** The general losophy of the universe considered as a totality of parts phenomena subject to laws. [< NL < Gk. *kosmos* the verse + *-logia* study] — **cos·mo·log·i·cal** (koz′mə·loj′i· or **cos′mo·log′ic** *adj.* — **cos·mol′o·gist** *n.*

cos·mo·naut (koz′mə·nôt) *n.* An astronaut.

cos·mo·pol·i·tan (koz′mə·pol′ə·tən) *adj.* **1.** Common t the world; not local or limited. **2.** At home in all part the world; free from local attachments or prejudices. — A cosmopolitan person. — **cos′mo·pol′i·tan·ism, cos·mo lit·ism** (koz·mop′ə·līt·iz′əm) *n.*

cos·mop·o·lite (koz·mop′ə·līt) *n.* **1.** A cosmopolitan son. **2.** A plant or animal widely distributed over the wo [< Gk. < *kosmos* world + *politēs* citizen < *polis* city]

cos·mos (koz′məs, -mos) *n.* **1.** The world or universe c sidered as an orderly system. **2.** Any complete system. *Bot.* A plant related to the dahlia. [< Gk. *kosmos* order]

Cos·sack (kos′ak, -ək) *n.* One of a people of the south U.S.S.R., famous as cavalrymen. [< Russ. *kazak* < Tu *quzzāq* guerrilla, freebooter]

cos·set (kos′it) *v.t.* To pamper; pet. — *n.* **1.** A pet la **2.** Any pet. [? OE *cot-sǣta* dweller in a cottage]

cost (kôst) *v.* **cost** (*for def. 3, also* **cost·ed**), **cost·ing** *v.i.* To be acquirable for or have the value of a price, sum, c sideration, etc. **2.** To be gained by the expenditure c specified thing, as health, pain, effort, etc. — *v.t.* **3.** To e mate the amount spent for the production of. — *n.* **1.** price paid for anything. **2.** Loss; suffering; detriment. *pl. Law* The expenses of a lawsuit in court. — **at all c** (or **at any cost**) Regardless of cost; by all means. [< OI *com-* together + *stare* to stand]

cost accountant One who keeps track of the costs incur in production and distribution. — **cost accounting**

cos·tal (kos′təl) *adj.* Of, on, or near a rib or the ribs.

cos·ter·mon·ger (kos′tər·mung′gər, -mong′-, kôs′-) *n.* *B* A street hawker of vegetables, fruits, etc. Also **cos′ter.** *costard* a variety of apple + MONGER]

cos·tive (kos′tiv, kôs′-) *adj.* Constipated. [< OF *cost* — **cos′tive·ly** *adv.* — **cos′tive·ness** *n.*

cost·ly (kôst′lē, kost′-) *adj.* **·li·er, ·li·est** **1.** Costing v much; expensive. **2.** Sumptuous. — **cost′li·ness** *n.*

sto- *combining form* Rib: used in anatomical and surgical rms. Also, before vowels, **cost-**. [< L *costa* rib]
st of living The average cost, as to an individual or fam-, of food, clothing, shelter, etc.
·tume (*n.* kos′tōōm, -tyōōm; *v.* kos·tōōm′, -tyōōm′) *n.* **1.** ıe mode of dress, including ornaments and hair style, of a ven region, time, or class. **2.** Such dress as worn by ac-rs, dancers, etc. **3.** A set of garments for some occasion or tivity: summer *costume.* **4.** Garb; apparel, esp. that of a ɔman. — *v.t.* **·tumed, ·tum·ing** To furnish with costumes. < F < Ital. < L *consuetudo* custom]
·tum·er (kos·tōō′mər, -tyōō′-) *n.* One who makes or fur-shes costumes. Also **cos·tum·ier** (kos·tōōm′yər, -tyōōm′-; . kôs·tü·myā′).
[1] (kot) *n.* A light, narrow bed, commonly of canvas etched on a folding frame. [< Hind. *khāṭ* < Skt. *khaṭvā*]
[2] (kot) *n.* **1.** A small house; cottage. **2.** A cote. **3.** A otective covering for an injured finger. [OE]
tan·gent (kō·tan′jənt) *n. Trig.* The tangent of the com-ement of an acute angle. — **co·tan·gen·tial** (kō′tan·jen′·əl) *adj.*
e (kōt) *n.* **1.** A small shelter for sheep or birds. **2.** *Dial.* little house; hut. [OE. Akin to COT[2].]
tem·po·ra·ne·ous (kō·tem′pə·rā′nē·əs), **co·tem·po·r·y** (kō·tem′pə·rer′ē), etc. See CONTEMPORANEOUS, etc.
ten·ant (kō·ten′ənt) *n.* One of several tenants holding e same property. — **co·ten′an·cy** *n.*
te·rie (kō′tə·rē) *n.* A small, exclusive group of persons ıo share certain interests or pursuits. [< F]
er·mi·nous (kō·tûr′mə·nəs) See CONTERMINOUS.
il·lion (kō·til′yən, kə-) *n.* **1.** *U.S.* An elaborate dance ırked by frequent change of partners: also called *german.* *U.S.* A formal ball at which young ladies are presented to ciety. **3.** A lively, quick dance. **4.** The music for this nce. Also **co·til·lon** (kō·til′yən, kə-; *Fr.* kô·tē·yôn′). [< *cotillon* petticoat]
·tage (kot′ij) *n.* **1.** A small house in the suburbs or the untry. **2.** *U.S.* A temporary home at a resort. [< COT[2]]
tage cheese A soft, white cheese made of milk curds.
tage pudding Plain cake covered with a sweet sauce.
·tag·er (kot′ij·ər) *n.* **1.** One who lives in a cottage. **2.** *it.* A rural laborer. **3.** *Canadian* A summer resident.
ter pin A key, wedge, pin, etc., that is split lengthwise that the ends may be spread apart to hold parts of ma-inery together.
·ton (kot′n) *n.* **1.** The soft, fibrous, white or yellowish aterial, of high cellulose content, at-ched to the seeds of the cotton plant and dely used as a textile. **2.** The plant it-f. **3.** Cotton plants collectively. **4.** tton cloth or thread. — *adj.* Woven or mposed of cotton cloth or thread. — **to tton to** *Informal* **1.** To become friendly th. **2.** To take a liking to. — **to cotton to** *Informal* To attempt to please by endly overtures or flattery. [< F *coton* OSp. < Arabic *qutun*] — **cot′ton·y** *adj.*

COTTON
a Boll ready for picking.

ton belt *U.S.* The region of the south-ı U.S. in which cotton is the chief crop.
ton flannel A soft, warm cotton fabric, pped on one or both sides.
ton gin A machine used to separate the eds from the fiber of cotton.
·ton·mouth (kot′n·mouth′) *n.* The ter moccasin, a snake.
ton picker A machine designed to remove the ripe cot-n from standing cotton plants.
·ton·seed (kot′n·sēd′) *n.* The seed of the cotton plant.
tonseed oil A pale yellow, viscid oil pressed from cot-nseeds, used in cooking, paints, and as a lubricant.
·ton·tail (kot′n·tāl′) *n.* The American gray rabbit.
·ton·wood (kot′n·wŏŏd′) *n.* An American poplar tree ıose seeds discharge a cottony substance.
ton wool **1.** Raw cotton. **2.** *Brit.* Absorbent cotton.
·y·le·don (kot′ə·lēd′n) *n. Bot.* A seed leaf, or one of a ir of the first leaves from a sprouting seed. [< L < Gk. < *ylē* a cavity] — **cot′y·le′do·nous, cot′y·le′do·nal** *adj.*
ch (kouch) *n.* A piece of furniture, usu. upholstered and ving a back, on which several may sit or one may recline; o, a bed, or any place of repose. — *v.t.* **1.** To phrase; put o words. **2.** To cause to recline, as on a bed. **3.** To bend bring down; lower, as a spear for attack. — *v.i.* **4.** To lie wn; recline. **5.** To lie in ambush. [< OF < *coucher* to t to bed] — **couch′er** *n.*
ch·ant (kou′chənt) *adj.* Lying down. [See COUCH.]
ch grass A perennial grass multiplying injuriously in ltivated grounds by its long rootstocks: also called *quitch* ıss. [Var. of QUITCH (GRASS)]

cou·gar (kōō′gər) *n.* The puma. [< F < Tupi]
cough (kôf, kof) *v.i.* **1.** To expel air from the lungs in a noisy or spasmodic manner. — *v.t.* **2.** To expel by a cough. — **to cough up** **1.** To expel by coughing. **2.** *Slang* To surrender; hand over, as money. — *n.* **1.** A sudden, harsh expulsion of breath. **2.** An illness in which there is frequent coughing. [ME *cozen, couzen*] — **cough′er** *n.*
cough drop A medicated lozenge to relieve coughing, etc.
could (kŏŏd) Past tense of CAN[1]. [ME *coude,* OE *cuthe* knew how; *l* inserted on analogy with *should* and *would*]
could·n't (kŏŏd′nt) Could not.
cou·lee (kōō′lē) *n.* **1.** *U.S.* A deep gulch cut by rainstorms or melting snow. **2.** *Geol.* A sheet of solidified lava. Also *French* **cou·lée** (kōō·lā′). [< F *couler* to flow]
cou·lomb (kōō·lom′) *n.* The practical unit of quantity in measuring electricity; the amount conveyed by one ampere in one second. [after C. A. de *Coulomb,* 1736–1806, French physicist]
coul·ter (kōl′tər) See COLTER.
coun·cil (koun′səl) *n.* **1.** An assembly of persons convened for consultation or deliberation. **2.** A body of men elected or appointed to act in an administrative, legislative, or advisory capacity in a government. **3.** The deliberation that takes place in a council chamber. [< AF, OF < L < *com-* together + *calare* to call]
coun·cil·man (koun′səl·mən) *n. pl.* **·men** (-mən) A member of a council, esp. the governing council of a city.
coun·cil·or (koun′səl·ər, -slər) *n.* A member of a council. Also *Brit.* **coun′cil·lor.** — **coun′cil·or·ship′** *n.*
coun·sel (koun′səl) *n.* **1.** Mutual exchange of advice, opinions, etc.; consultation. **2.** Advice; guidance. **3.** A deliberate purpose; plan. **4.** A secret intent or opinion: obsolete except in **to keep one's own counsel.** **5.** A lawyer or lawyers. — *v.* **coun·seled** or **·selled, coun·sel·ing** or **·sel·ling** *v.t.* **1.** To give advice to; advise. **2.** To advise in favor of; recommend. — *v.i.* **3.** To give or take counsel. [< AF, OF < L *consulere* to deliberate]
coun·sel·or (koun′səl·ər, -slər) *n.* **1.** One who gives counsel; an adviser. **2.** An attorney at law. **3.** A supervisor at a children's camp. Also **coun′sel·lor.**
count[1] (kount) *v.t.* **1.** To list or call off one by one to ascertain the total. **2.** To list numerals in a progressive sequence up to: to *count* ten. **3.** To consider to be; judge. **4.** To take note of; include in a reckoning. — *v.i.* **5.** To list numbers in sequence. **6.** To have worth; be of importance. **7.** To be accounted or included. — **to count in** To include. — **to count on** (or **upon**) To rely on. — **to count out** **1.** In boxing, to reach a count of ten over (a downed boxer), thus declaring him defeated. **2.** To omit or exclude; disregard. — *n.* **1.** The act of counting. **2.** The number arrived at by counting; total. **3.** An accounting or reckoning. **4.** *Law* A separate and distinct charge, as in an indictment. **5.** In boxing, the ten seconds given a contestant to get up or lose the fight. [< OF < L < *com-* together + *putare* to reckon] — **count′a·ble** *adj.*
count[2] (kount) *n.* In some European countries, a nobleman having a rank corresponding to that of an earl in England. [< AF *counte,* OF *coute* < L *comes* an associate]
count·down (kount′doun′) *n.* A reverse counting of time units, reaching zero at the instant when an operation, as a rocket launching, nuclear blast, etc., is to be executed.
coun·te·nance (koun′tə·nəns) *n.* **1.** The face or features. **2.** Facial expression. **3.** An encouraging look; also, approval; support. **4.** Self-control; composure. — **out of countenance** Disconcerted; embarrassed; abashed. — *v.t.* **·nanced, ·nanc·ing** To approve; encourage. [< OF < L *continere* to hang together] — **coun′te·nanc·er** *n.*
coun·ter[1] (koun′tər) *n.* **1.** An opposite or contrary. **2.** In boxing, a blow given while receiving or parrying another. **3.** In fencing, a parry in which one foil follows another. **4.** A piece encircling the heel of a shoe. **5.** *Naut.* The curved part of a vessel's stern extending from the water line to the point of fullest outward swell. — *v.t.* **1.** To return, as a blow, by another blow. **2.** To oppose; contradict; controvert. **3.** To put a new counter on (a shoe, etc.). — *v.i.* **4.** To give a blow while receiving or parrying one. **5.** To make a countermove. — *adj.* Opposing; opposite; contrary. — *adv.* Contrary. [< F < L *contra* against]
coun·ter[2] (koun′tər) *n.* **1.** A board, table, or the like, on which to expose goods for sale, transact business, or serve refreshments or meals. **2.** A piece of wood, ivory, etc., used in counting, as in billiards. **3.** A piece in chess, checkers, etc. **4.** An imitation coin. [< AF < Med.L < L *computare* to compute]
counter- *combining form* **1.** Opposing; contrary; acting in opposition or response to the action of the main element; as in:

counteraccusation **counterblow** **countercharge**

counterdemand **counterpropaganda** **counterstatement**
counterforce **counterproposal** **countertheory**
counterinfluence **counterreform** **counterthreat**
countermeasure **counterresolution** **counterthrust**

2. Done or acting in reciprocation or exchange; as in:
counteroffer **counterquestion**

3. Complementing or corresponding; denoting the duplicate or parallel; as in:
countercheck **counterfugue** **countersecurity**

4. Opposite in direction or position; as in:
countercurrent **counterflow** **counterpressure**
counterflight **counterposition** **counterturn**

[< F < L *contra-* against]

coun·ter·act (koun′tər·akt′) *v.t.* To act in opposition to; check. — **coun′ter·ac′tion** *n.* — **coun′ter·ac′tive** *adj.*

coun·ter·at·tack (*n.* koun′tər·ə·tak′; *v.* koun′tər·ə·tak′) *n.* An attack designed to counter another attack. — *v.t. & v.i.* To make a counterattack (against).

coun·ter·bal·ance (*v.* koun′tər·bal′əns; *n.* koun′tər·bal′əns) *v.t.* **·anced, ·anc·ing** To oppose with an equal weight or force; offset. — *n.* **1.** Any power equally opposing another. **2.** A weight that balances another; counterpoise.

coun·ter·claim (*n.* koun′tər·klām′; *v.* koun′tər·klām′) *n.* A claim that opposes another claim. — *v.t. & v.i.* To make or plead (as) a counterclaim. — **coun′ter·claim′ant** *n.*

coun·ter·clock·wise (koun′tər·klok′wīz′) *adj. & adv.* Opposite to the direction taken by the hands of a clock.

coun·ter·es·pi·o·nage (koun′tər·es′pē·ə·näzh′, -nij) *n.* Measures intended to counteract enemy spying.

coun·ter·feit (koun′tər·fit) *v.t.* **1.** To make an imitation of, as money or stamps, with the intent to defraud. **2.** To copy; imitate; also, to feign; dissemble: to *counterfeit* sorrow. — *v.i.* **3.** To practice deception; feign. **4.** To make counterfeits. — *adj.* **1.** Made to resemble some genuine thing with the intent to defraud. **2.** Pretended; feigned; deceitful. — *n.* **1.** Something made fraudulently to resemble the genuine. **2.** Any imitation of copy. [< OF < L *contra-* against + *facere* to make] — **coun′ter·feit′er** *n.*

coun·ter·foil (koun′tər·foil′) *n.* The part of a check, money order, etc., kept by the issuer as a record; a stub.

coun·ter·in·tel·li·gence (koun′tər·in·tel′ə·jəns) *n.* Activities to oppose espionage, subversion, and sabotage.

coun·ter·ir·ri·tant (koun′tər·ir′ə·tənt) *n.* Anything used to excite irritation in one place so as to counteract more serious irritation elsewhere.

coun·ter·man (koun′tər·mən) *n.* A man who serves at a lunch counter.

coun·ter·mand (*v.* koun′tər·mand′, -mänd′; *n.* koun′tər·mand, -mänd) *v.t.* **1.** To revoke or reverse (a command, order, etc.). **2.** To recall or order back by a contrary command. — *n.* An order contrary to or revoking one previously issued. [< OF < L *contra-* against + *mandare* to order]

coun·ter·march (*n.* koun′tər·märch′; *v.* koun′tər·märch′) *n.* **1.** A return march. **2.** *Mil.* A reversal of direction while marching, keeping the same order. — *v.t. & v.i.* To execute or cause to execute a countermarch.

coun·ter·move (*n.* koun′tər·mōōv′; *v.* koun′tər·mōōv′) *n.* A move designed to counter another move. — *v.t. & v.i.* **·moved, ·mov·ing** To move in opposition (to).

coun·ter·of·fen·sive (koun′tər·ə·fen′siv, koun′tər·ə·fen′siv) *n.* A large-scale attack designed to stop the offensive of an enemy and to seize the initiative along an extended front.

coun·ter·pane (koun′tər·pān′) *n.* A coverlet for a bed. [< F *pan* quilt]

coun·ter·part (koun′tər·pärt′) *n.* **1.** Someone or something resembling another. **2.** One who or that which supplements or completes another.

coun·ter·plot (*n.* koun′tər·plot′; *v.* koun′tər·plot′) *n.* A plot designed to foil another plot. — *v.t. & v.i.* **·plot·ted, ·plot·ting** To oppose (a plot) by another plot.

coun·ter·point (koun′tər·point′) *n.* *Music* **1.** The technique or practice of composing two or more melodic parts to be heard simultaneously; also, the arrangement of parts so composed. **2.** Any of such parts in relation to the principal part. [< MF < Med.L < L *contra-* against + *punctus* point, note]

coun·ter·poise (*v.* koun′tər·poiz′; *n.* koun′tər·poiz′) *v.t.* **·poised, ·pois·ing** To bring to a balance by opposing with an equal weight, power, or force; counterbalance. — *n.* **1.** A counterbalancing weight, force, power, or influence. **2.** A state of equilibrium. [< OF < L *contra-* against + *pensare* to weigh]

Counter Reformation The reform movement within the Roman Catholic Church in the 16th century in reaction to the Protestant Reformation.

coun·ter·rev·o·lu·tion (koun′tər·rev′ə·lōō′shən) *n.* A revolution designed to counteract a previous revolution and to reverse its effects. — **coun′ter·rev′o·lu′tion·ar′y** *adj. & n.* — **coun′ter·rev′o·lu′tion·ist** *n.*

coun·ter·shaft (koun′tər·shaft′, -shäft′) *n.* *Mech.* An intermediate shaft driven by a main shaft.

coun·ter·sign (*v.* koun′tər·sīn′, koun′tər·sīn′; *n.* koun′tər·sīn′) *v.t.* To sign (a document already signed by anoth[er]) as in authenticating. — *n.* *Mil.* A password. [< OF *[con]tresigner*] — **coun′ter·sig′na·ture** *n.*

coun·ter·sink (*v.* koun′tər·singk′, koun′tər·singk′; *n.* ko[un′]tər·singk′) *v.t.* **·sank** or **·sunk, ·sunk** (*Obs.* **·sunk·en**), **·si[nk·]ing** **1.** To cut the edges of (a hole) so that a screw, bolthe[ad], etc., will lie flush with or below the surface. **2.** To sink, [a] bolt or screw, into such a depression. — *n.* **1.** A tool [for] countersinking. **2.** A countersunk hole.

coun·ter·ten·or (koun′tər·ten′ər) *n.* An adult male sin[ging] voice higher than the tenor. [< MF *contreteneur*]

coun·ter·vail (koun′tər·vāl′, koun′tər·vāl) *v.t.* **1.** To [op]pose with equal force or effect; counteract. **2.** To comp[en]sate or make up for; offset. — *v.i.* **3.** To be of avail: [w] *against.* [< AF < L *contra valere* to avail against]

coun·ter·weigh (koun′tər·wā′) *v.t. & v.i.* To counter[bal]ance.

coun·ter·weight (koun′tər·wāt′) *n.* Any counterbalan[cing] weight, force, or influence. — **coun′ter·weight′ed** *adj.*

counter word A word widely used without regard t[o] exact meaning, as *nice, awful, fix.*

count·ess (koun′tis) *n.* **1.** The wife or widow of a count in Great Britain, of an earl. **2.** A woman equal in rank [to a] count or earl. [See COUNT[2].]

count·ing house (koun′ting) A building or office in whi[ch a] mercantile or other firm carries on bookkeeping, correspo[nd]ence, etc. Also **count′ing·house′, counting room.**

count·less (kount′lis) *adj.* That cannot be counted; in[nu]merable. — **Syn.** See INFINITE.

coun·tri·fied (kun′tri·fīd) *adj.* Having the appeara[nce,] manner, etc., associated with the country or with cou[ntry] people; rural; rustic. Also **coun′try·fied.**

coun·try (kun′trē) *n. pl.* **·tries** **1.** A land under a part[icu]lar government, inhabited by a certain people, or wi[thin] definite geographical limits. **2.** The land of one's birt[h or] allegiance. **3.** The district outside cities and towns; r[ural] areas. **4.** A region of a specified character: sheep *cou[ntry].* **5.** The people of a nation. — **Syn.** See NATION. — [*adj.*] Rustic. [< OF < LL < L *contra* on the opposite side]

country club A club in the outskirts of a town or city, [w]a clubhouse, grounds, and facilities for outdoor sports.

coun·try-dance (kun′trē·dans′, -däns′) *n.* A folk danc[e of] English origin, in which the partners are in opposite lin[es].

country gentleman A landed proprietor who lives o[n a] country estate.

coun·try·man (kun′trē·mən) *n. pl.* **·men** (-mən) **1.** A [man] of the same country as another. **2.** A native of a partic[ular] country. **3.** A rustic. — **coun′try·wom′an** *n.fem.*

coun·try·seat (kun′trē·sēt′) *n.* A country estate.

coun·try·side (kun′trē·sīd′) *n.* A rural district, or it[s in]habitants.

coun·ty (koun′tē) *n. pl.* **·ties** **1.** An administrative divi[sion] of a state or kingdom. In the United States, it is the divi[sion] next below a State. In England a county is sometimes ca[lled] a *shire.* **2.** The people of a county. [< AF, OF < L *co[mes]* count, companion]

county seat The seat of government of a county.

coup (kōō) *n. pl.* **coups** (kōōz, *Fr.* kōō) A sudden, te[lling] blow; a masterstroke; brilliant stratagem. [< F < L < Gk. *kolaphos* a blow with the fist]

coup de grâce (kōō′ də gräs′) *French* **1.** The mortal str[oke] as delivered to a wounded enemy. **2.** Any finishing str[oke].

coup d'é·tat (kōō′dā·tä′) *French* An unexpected strok[e of] policy; esp., a sudden seizure of government.

coupe (kōōp, kōō·pā′) *n.* A closed automobile with [two] doors, seating two to six persons: also *coupé.* [< COUP[É]]

cou·pé (kōō·pā′) *n.* **1.** A low, four-wheeled, closed carr[iage] with a seat for two and an outside seat for the driver. **2.** [A] coupe. [< F, pp. of *couper* to cut]

coup·le (kup′əl) *n.* **1.** Two of a kind; a pair. **2.** Two [per]sons of opposite sex, wedded or otherwise paired, a[s in] dances, games, etc. **3.** *Informal* A few: a *couple* of hours. [4.] Something joining two things together. — *v.* **·led, ·ling** **1.** To join, as one thing to another; link. **2.** To join in w[ed]lock; marry. — *v.i.* **3.** To pair. [< OF < L *copula* bo[nd]]

coup·ler (kup′lər) *n.* **1.** One who or that which couples. [2.] A device that connects objects; esp.: **a** A contrivance [for] linking railroad cars. **b** A device enabling two or more o[rgan] keys or keyboards to play together.

coup·let (kup′lit) *n.* **1.** Two successive lines of verse, [usually] rhymed and in the same meter. **2.** A pair.

coup·ling (kup′ling) *n.* **1.** The act of one who or that wh[ich] couples. **2.** A linking device, as for joining railroad car[s].

cou·pon (kōō′pon, kyōō′-) *n.* **1.** One of a number of da[ted] certificates attached to a bond, representing interest accru[ed]. **2.** A section of a ticket, advertisement, etc., entitling [the] holder to something in exchange. [< F *couper* to cut]

cour·age (kûr′ij) *n.* That quality of mind or spirit [en]abling one to meet danger or opposition with fearlessn[ess]. [< OF *corage,* ult. < L *cor* heart]

·ra·geous (kə·rā′jəs) *adj.* Possessing or characterized courage; brave; daring: *courageous* words. — **cou·ra′·ous·ly** *adv.* — **cou·ra′geous·ness** *n.*
·ri·er (ko͝or′ē·ər, kûr′-) *n.* **1.** A messenger, esp. one aveling in haste or on official diplomatic business. **2.** One 1o arranges a journey. [< OF < L *currere* to run]
irse (kôrs, kōrs) *n.* **1.** Onward movement in a certain ·ection; progress. **2.** The path or ground passed over. **3.** rection: to take an eastward *course.* **4.** Passage or dura- n in time. **5.** Advance; progression: the *course* of evolu- n. **6.** Natural or usual development: to run its *course.* A series of actions, events, etc., constituting a unit. **8.** ne of conduct: a wise *course.* **9.** A prescribed curriculum studies leading to a degree: a liberal arts *course;* also, any it of study in a school curriculum: a history *course.* **10.** A rtion of a meal served at one time. **11.** A horizontal row layer, as of stones in a wall. — **in due course** In the oper sequence; at the right time. — **of course** **1.** As ght be expected; naturally. **2.** Certainly. — *v.* **coursed, urs·ing** *v.t.* **1.** To run through or over. **2.** To pursue. **3.** cause (hounds) to chase game. — *v.i.* **4.** To race. **5.** hunt game with hounds. [< L *currere* to run]
irs·er (kôr′sər, kōr′-) *n. Poetic* A fleet, spirited horse. : F < OF < L *currere* to run]
irt (kôrt, kōrt) *n.* **1.** A courtyard. **2.** A short street en- sed by buildings on three sides. **3.** The residence of a vereign; palace. **4.** A sovereign together with his council d retinue. **5.** A formal assembly held by a sovereign. **6.** place where justice is judicially administered; also, those dges who administer justice. **7.** The regular session of a dicial tribunal. **8.** A level space laid out for tennis, basket- ll, squash, or similar games; also, a subdivision of such a ace. **9.** Flattering attention paid another to win favor; mage. **10.** Wooing; courtship. — **out of court** **1.** With- t a trial. **2.** Without claim to a hearing. — *v.t.* **1.** To to gain the favor of. **2.** To seek the love of; woo. **3.** To tempt to gain: to *court* applause. **4.** To invite: to *cour* saster. — *v.i.* **5.** To engage in courtship. — *adj.* Of ot rtaining to a court. [< OF < L *cohors, cohortis* yard] r
irt of Common Pleas A common-law court having iginal jurisdiction over civil and criminal matters.
ır·te·ous (kûr′tē·əs) *adj.* Showing courtesy; polite. — n. See POLITE. [< OF *corteis* befitting a court] — **ur′te·ous·ly** *adv.* — **cour′te·ous·ness** *n.*
ır·te·san (kôr′tə·zən, kōr′-, kûr′-) *n.* A prostitute. Also **ır′te·zan.** [< MF < Ital. *cortigiana* court lady]
ır·te·sy (kûr′tə·sē) *n. pl.* **·sies** **1.** Habitual politeness; od manners. **2.** A courteous favor or act. **3.** Common nsent or allowance, as opposed to right: an aunt by *cour- y.* **4.** A curtsy. [< OF *corteis* courteous]
ırt·house (kôrt′hous′, kōrt′-) *n.* A public building occu- ed by judicial courts and other administrative offices.
ırt·i·er (kôr′tē·ər, -tyər, kōr′-) *n.* **1.** A member of a sov- eign's court. **2.** One who seeks favor by flattery.
ırt·ly (kôrt′lē, kōrt′-) *adj.* **·li·er, ·li·est** **1.** Pertaining to befitting a court. **2.** Elegant in manners. — *adv.* In a urtly manner. — **court′li·ness** *n.*
ırt-mar·tial (kôrt′mär′shəl, kōrt′-) *n. pl.* **courts-mar· ıl** **1.** A military court to try persons subject to military w. **2.** A trial by such a court. — *v.t.* **-mar·tialed** or **alled, -mar·tial·ing** or **·tial·ling** To try by court-martial.
ırt plaster Adhesive tape.
ırt·room (kôrt′ro͞om′, -ro͝om′, kōrt′-) *n.* A room in which dicial proceedings are held.
ırt·ship (kôrt′ship, kōrt′-) *n.* The act or period of court- g and wooing.
ırt·yard (kôrt′yärd′, kōrt′-) *n.* An enclosed yard adjoin- g a building or surrounded by buildings or walls; a court.
ıs·in (kuz′ən) *n.* **1.** One collaterally related by descent om a common ancestor, but not a brother or sister. Chil- en of brothers and sisters are **first** or **full cousins** to each her; children of first cousins are **second cousins** to each her. **2.** One of a kindred group or nation: our English *usins.* **3.** A title of address used by a sovereign to a noble a fellow sovereign. [< OF < L *consobrinus* child of a ma- rnal aunt] — **cous′in·hood, cous′in·ship** *n.* — **cous′in·ly** *j. & adv.*
ıs·in-ger·man (kuz′ən·jûr′mən) *n. pl.* **cous·ins-ger· an** A first or full cousin. [< F *cousin germain*]
ıs·in·ry (kuz′ən·rē) *n. pl.* **·ries** Cousins collectively.
ı·tu·rier (ko͞o·tü·ryā′) *n.* A male dress designer. [< F] **cou·tu·rière** (ko͞o·tü·ryâr′) *n. fem.*
va·lence (kō′vā′ləns) *n. Chem.* A bond formed by the aring of electrons between the atoms of a compound. — **′va′lent** *adj.*
ve[1] (kōv) *n.* **1.** A small bay or baylike recess in a shore- ıe. **2.** A recess among hills, in a wood, etc. **3.** *Archit.* **a** A ncave vault. For illus. see VAULT. **b** A concave molding. **c** A concave curved portion where a ceiling meets a wall. — *v.t.* **coved, cov·ing** To curve over or inward. [OE *cofa* cave]
cove[2] (kōv) *n. Brit. Slang* A boy or man; fellow. [< Romany *covo* that man]
cov·e·nant (kuv′ə·nənt) *n.* **1.** An agreement entered into by two or more persons or parties; a compact. **2.** *Theol.* The promise of God to bless those who obey him or fulfill some other condition. **3.** *Law* A written agreement, as a contract, under seal. — **Covenant of the League of Nations** The first twenty-six articles of the Treaty of Versailles. — *v.t. & v.i.* To promise by or in a covenant. [< OF, < L *convenire* to meet together, agree] — **cov·e·nant·al** (kuv′ə·nan′təl) *adj.* — **cov′e·nant′al·ly** *adv.* — **cov′e·nant·er** *n.*
cov·er (kuv′ər) *v.t.* **1.** To place something over or upon, as to protect or conceal. **2.** To provide with a cover or covering; clothe. **3.** To invest as if with a covering: *covered* with confusion. **4.** To hide; conceal: often with *up.* **5.** To provide shelter or protection for. **6.** To occupy the surface of: Snow *covered* the house. **7.** To treat of; include: His speech *covered* the tax problem. **8.** To be sufficient to pay, defray, or offset. **9.** To protect or guarantee (life, property, etc.) with insurance. **10.** To incubate or sit on, as eggs. **11.** To travel over: to *cover* 200 miles. **12.** To aim directly at, as with a firearm. **13.** *Mil.* To provide protective fire for (another person, unit, etc.). **14.** In journalism, to report the details of. **15.** In sports, to guard the activity of (an opponent); also, to protect (an area or position). **16.** To match; equal, as the wager of an opponent. **17.** In card games, to play a higher card than (the one previously played). — *v.i.* **18.** To spread over so as to overlay something. **19.** To put on a hat, cap, or the like. — *n.* **1.** That which covers or is laid over something else. **2.** Shelter; protection; concealment, as from enemy fire. **3.** Shrubbery, underbrush, etc. **4.** A pretense or pretext. **5.** In stamp collecting, an envelope or wrapper that bears a postmark. **6.** The table articles, as plate, silverware, napkin, etc., for one person. — **to break cover** To come from hiding. — **under cover** **1.** Protected. **2.** Secret or secretly. [< OF < L < *co-* thoroughly + *operire* to hide] — **cov′er·er** *n.*
cov·er·age (kuv′ər·ij) *n.* **1.** The extent to which anything is covered, included, or reported. **2.** The protection afforded by an insurance policy.
cov·er·alls (kuv′ər·ôlz) *n.pl.* A one-piece work garment with sleeves, worn to protect the clothes. Also **cov′er·all.**
cover charge A fixed charge added to the bill at cabarets, hotels, etc., for entertainment or service.
cover crop *Agric.* A crop sown to protect the ground through winter and to enrich it when plowed under in the spring.
covered wagon *U.S.* A large wagon covered with canvas stretched over hoops, used esp. by American pioneers.
cover girl A female model who poses for magazine covers.
cov·er·ing (kuv′ər·ing) *n.* That which covers, protects, etc.
cov·er·let (kuv′ər·lit) *n.* A bedspread. Also **cov′er·lid.**
cov·ert (kuv′ərt, kō′vərt) *adj.* Concealed; secret; sheltered. — *n.* **1.** A covering. **2.** A shelter or hiding place, esp. for game. **3.** *pl. Ornithol.* Small feathers overlying the bases of tail and wing quills. [See COVER.] — **cov′ert·ly** *adv.*
co·vert cloth (kō′vərt, kuv′ərt) A twilled, chiefly woolen cloth of speckled appearance, used for suits, overcoats, etc.
cov·er·ture (kuv′ər·chər) *n.* **1.** *Law* The legal status of a married woman. **2.** A covering; esp., a shelter.
cov·et (kuv′it) *v.t.* **1.** To long for, esp. for something belonging to another. — *v.i.* **2.** To feel desire. [< OF < L *cupere* to desire] — **cov′et·a·ble** *adj.* — **cov′et·er** *n.*
cov·et·ous (kuv′ə·təs) *adj.* Excessively desirous (of something); avaricious; greedy. [< OF *coveitus*] — **cov′et·ous·ly** *adv.* — **cov′et·ous·ness** *n.*
cov·ey (kuv′ē) *n. pl.* **·eys** **1.** A flock of quails or partridges. **2.** A company; set. — **Syn.** See FLOCK[1]. [< OF < L *cubare* to lie down]
cow[1] (kou) *n. pl.* **cows** (*Archaic* **kine**) **1.** The mature female of a bovine animal, esp. of the domesticated species. **2.** The mature female of some other animals, as of the whale, elephant, moose, etc. [OE *cū*]
cow[2] (kou) *v.t.* To overawe; intimidate; daunt. [< ON *kūga* to tyrannize over]
cow·ard (kou′ərd) *n.* One who yields unworthily to fear of pain or harm. — *adj.* Cowardly. [< OF < L *cauda* tail]
cow·ard·ice (kou′ər·dis) *n.* Lack of courage in the face of danger, pain, opposition, etc.; unworthy timidity.
cow·ard·ly (kou′ərd·lē) *adj.* **1.** Lacking courage; ignobly fearful. **2.** Befitting a coward: a *cowardly* lie. — *adv.* Like a coward; meanly. — **cow′ard·li·ness** *n.*
— **Syn.** (adj.) **1.** craven, pusillanimous, spineless, yellow.
cow·bell (kou′bəl) *n.* A bell hung around a cow's neck to indicate her whereabouts.
cow·ber·ry (kou′bər′ē, -bər·ē) *n. pl.* **·ries** A trailing evergreen shrub of the heath family, bearing red berries.

cow·bird (kou′bûrd′) *n.* An American blackbird, often found with cattle. Also **cow blackbird.**
cow·boy (kou′boi′) *n. U.S.* A man, usu. working on horseback, who herds and tends cattle on a ranch.
cow·catch·er (kou′kach′ər) *n.* An iron frame on the front of a locomotive or streetcar for clearing the track.
cow·er (kou′ər) *v.i.* To crouch, as in fear; tremble; quail. [ME *couren*, prob. < Scand.]
cow·fish (kou′fish) *n. pl.* **·fish** or **·fish·es 1.** Any of various small cetaceans, as the grampus, dolphin, etc. **2.** A sirenian.
cow·girl (kou′gûrl′) *n.* A girl who helps to herd and tend cattle or who dresses like a cowboy.
cow·hand (kou′hand′) *n.* A cowboy.
cow·herd (kou′hûrd′) *n.* One who herds cattle.
cow·hide (kou′hīd′) *n.* **1.** The skin of a cow, either before or after tanning. **2.** A heavy, flexible leather whip. **—** *v.t.* **·hid·ed, ·hid·ing** To whip as with a cowhide.
cow killer A large, antlike wasp of the SW U.S.
cowl (koul) *n.* **1.** A monk's hood; also, a hooded cloak. **2.** A hood-shaped top for a chimney, to increase the draft. **3.** *Aeron.* A cowling. **4.** The part of an automobile body to which the windshield, instrument board, and the rear end of the hood are attached. **—** *v.t.* To cover with or as with a cowl. [OE < LL < L *cucullus* hood]
cowled (kould) *adj.* **1.** Wearing a cowl. **2.** Like a cowl.
cow·lick (kou′lik′) *n.* A tuft of hair turned up.
cowl·ing (kou′ling) *n. Aeron.* The covering over or around the engine or any component of an aircraft. [< COWL]
cow·man (kou′mən) *n. pl.* **·men** (-mən) A rancher.
co-work·er (kō′wûr′kər) *n.* A fellow worker.
cow·pea (kou′pē′) *n.* **1.** A twining herb of the bean family, cultivated in the southern U.S. **2.** The edible pea of this herb: also called *black-eyed pea.*
cow pony *U.S.* A small horse used in herding cattle.
cow·pox (kou′poks′) *n. Vet.* An acute contagious disease of cows, forming pustules containing a virus that is used in making smallpox vaccine: also called *vaccinia.*
cow·punch·er (kou′pun′chər) *n. U.S. Informal* A cowboy. Also **cow′poke′.**
cow·ry (kou′rē) *n. pl.* **·ries** A glossy seashell of warm seas; esp. one used as money in Africa and southern Asia. Also **cow′rie.** [< Hind. *kaurī*]
cow·slip (kou′slip′) *n.* **1.** An English wildflower of the primrose family. **2.** The marsh marigold of the U.S. [OE < *cū* cow + *slyppe* dung]
cox (koks) *n. Informal* Coxswain. **—** *v.t. & v.i.* To act as coxswain to (a boat).
cox·a (kok′sə) *n. pl.* **cox·ae** (kok′sē) *Anat.* The hip or hip joint. [< L, hip] **— cox′al** *adj.*
cox·comb (koks′kōm′) *n.* **1.** A pretentious and conceited young man. **2.** A cockscomb. [Var. of *cockscomb*] **— cox·comb·i·cal** (koks·kom′i·kəl, -kō′mi-) *adj.*
cox·comb·ry (koks′kōm′rē) *n. pl.* **·ries** Vain, foppish behavior; silly conceit; also, an instance of this.
cox·swain (kok′sən, kok′swān′) *n.* One who steers or has charge of a small boat or a racing shell: also spelled *cockswain.* [< *cock* (see COCKBOAT) + SWAIN]
coy (koi) *adj.* **1.** Shy and retiring. **2.** Feigning shyness to attract attention. [< MF < OF < L *quietus* rest] **— coy′·ish** *adj.* **— coy′ly** *adv.* **— coy′ness** *n.*
coy·o·te (kī·ō′tē, kī′ōt) *n.* A small wolf of western North America: also called *prairie wolf.* [< Am. Sp. < Nahuatl]
Coyote State Nickname of South Dakota.
coy·pu (koi′po͞o) *n. pl.* **·pus** or **·pu** A South American rodent that yields a beaverlike fur known as nutria. Also **coy′·pou.** [< native name]
coz (kuz) *n. Informal* A cousin.
coz·en (kuz′ən) *v.t. & v.i.* To cheat, esp. in a petty way; deceive. [< F *cousiner* to deceive by claiming kinship < *cousin.* See COUSIN.] **— coz′en·age** *n.* **— coz′en·er** *n.*
co·zy (kō′zē) *adj.* **·zi·er, ·zi·est** Snugly comfortable. **—** *n.* A padded cover for a teapot to keep it hot: also called *tea cozy.* [< dial. E *cosie*] **— co′zi·ly** *adv.* **— co′zi·ness** *n.*
crab[1] (krab) *n.* **1.** A ten-footed crustacean having four pairs of legs, a pair of pincers, and a flattened carapace. **2.** The hermit crab. **3.** The horseshoe crab. **—** *v.* **crabbed, crab·bing** *v.t.* **1.** To take or hunt crabs. **2.** *U.S. Informal* To back out. [OE *crabba*]
crab[2] (krab) *n.* **1.** The crab apple or crab tree. **2.** An ill-tempered person. **—** *v.* **crabbed, crab·bing** *v.i.* **1.** *Informal* To find fault; complain. **—** *v.t.* **2.** *Informal* To spoil or ruin. **3.** *Informal* To criticize; disparage. [? < Scand.]
crab apple 1. A kind of small, sour apple: also called *crab.* **2.** A tree bearing crab apples.
crab·bed (krab′id) *adj.* **1.** Sour-tempered; surly. **2.** Hard to understand; abstruse. **3.** Irregular in form; cramped. [< CRAB[2]] **— crab′bed·ly** *adv.* **— crab′bed·ness** *n.*
crab·ber (krab′ər) *n.* **1.** One who fishes for crabs. **2.** A boat used for crab fishing.
crab·by (krab′ē) *adj.* **·bi·er, ·bi·est** Ill-tempered; peevish.
crab grass A low-growing grass, a lawn pest.

crack (krak) *v.i.* **1.** To break without separation of pa also, to break apart or to pieces. **2.** To make a sharp sn ping sound, as in breaking. **3.** To change tone abruptly higher register: said of the voice. **4.** *Informal* To br down; fail. **5.** *Slang* To speak flippantly; make remarks. *v.t.* **6.** To break partially or completely. **7.** To cause give forth a short, sharp sound: to *crack* a whip. **8.** *In mal* To break into; open: to *crack* a safe. **9.** *Informal* To the solution of. **10.** To cause (the voice) to crack. **11.** *formal* To strike sharply or with a sharp sound. **12.** *Sl* To tell (a joke). **13.** To break mentally; derange. **14.** reduce by distillation, as petroleum. **— to crack a b** *U.S. Slang* To open, as a textbook, and read or study. **— crack a smile** *Slang* To smile. **— to crack down** *U.S. In mal* To take severe repressive measures: with *on.* **— crack up** *Informal* **1.** To crash or be in a crash. **2.** To h a breakdown, nervous or physical. **3.** *U.S. Slang* To bec convulsed with laughter. **— to crack wise** *U.S. Slang* wisecrack. **—** *n.* **1.** A partial break, in which parts are completely separated; a fissure. **2.** A narrow space: O the door a *crack.* **3.** A sudden sharp sound, as of a rifle charging. **4.** *Informal* A resounding blow. **5.** A def flaw. **6.** A cracked tone of the voice. **7.** *Informal* A **8.** *Informal* A witty or sarcastic remark. **—** *adj. Infor* Of superior excellence: a *crack* shot. [OE *cracian*]
crack·brain (krak′brān′) *n.* A weak-minded person.
crack·brained (krak′brānd′) *adj.* Foolish; crazy.
cracked (krakt) *adj.* **1.** Having a crack or cracks. Broken to pieces. **3.** Damaged or blemished. **4.** *Infor* Mentally deranged. **5.** Uneven in tone: said of the voi
crack·er (krak′ər) *n.* **1.** *U.S.* A thin, crisp biscuit. *U.S.* A firecracker. **3.** *U.S.* A cylindrical paper roll cont ing candy, etc., and a weak explosive set off by pulling st of paper at either end: also **cracker bonbon.** **4.** An im erished white person of parts of the SE United States: a temptuous term.
crack·er-bar·rel (krak′ər·bar′əl) *adj.* Characteristic of informal, rambling discussions of those habitually gath in a country store: *cracker-barrel* philosophy.
crack·er·jack (krak′ər·jak′) *Slang adj.* Of exceptic quality; excellent. **—** *n.* A person or thing of exceptic merit or skill. Also **crack′a·jack′.**
Cracker State Nickname of Georgia.
crack·ing (krak′ing) *n. Chem.* A process by which molecular structure of petroleum is changed under pres by heat, etc., so that nonvolatile fractions are broken d to volatile fractions to produce high-octane gasoline.
crack·le (krak′əl) *v.* **·led, ·ling** *v.i.* **1.** To make a succes of light, sharp sounds. **—** *v.t.* **2.** To crush with such sou **3.** To cover, as china, with a delicate network of cracks. *n.* **1.** A sound of crackling. **2.** A network of fine cracks duced in the glaze of china, porcelain, etc. **3.** Ware ha such an appearance: also **crack′le·ware′** (-wâr′).
crack·ling (krak′ling) *n.* **1.** The giving forth of small sh sounds. **2.** The crisp browned skin of roasted pork. **3.** The crisp remains of fat after rendering.
crack·ly (krak′lē) *adj.* Likely to crackle; brittle.
crack·pot (krak′pot′) *Slang n.* A weak-minded or eccen person; a crank. **—** *adj.* Eccentric; foolish; insane.
crack·up (krak′up′) *n.* **1.** A crash, as of an airplan automobile. **2.** *Informal* A physical or mental breakdo
-cracy *combining form* Government or authority: *de racy.* [< Gk. *-krateia* power < *krateein* to rule]
cra·dle (krād′l) *n.* **1.** A small bed for an infant, usu. rockers. **2.** A place of origin. **3.** A framework for supp ing something under construction or repair. **4.** A fram protect an injured limb. **5.** The holder for the receive handset of a telephone. **6.** A frame attached to a scyth catch the cut grain; also, such a scythe. **7.** A low frame casters for a mechanic to lie on while working under an a mobile. **— to rob the cradle** *Informal* To marry or take sweetheart one much younger than oneself. **—** *v.* **·d ·dling** *v.t.* **1.** To put into or rock in or as in a cradle; soo **2.** To nurse in infancy; nurture. **3.** To cut (grain) wi cradle. **4.** To place or support in a cradle, as a ship. *Mining* To wash, as gold-bearing gravel, in a cradle. **—** **6.** To lie in or as in a cradle. **7.** To cut or reap. [OE *cra*
cra·dle·song (krād′l·sông′, -song′) *n.* A lullaby (def.
craft (kraft, kräft) *n.* **1.** Skill or proficiency, esp. in h work; loosely, art. **2.** Skill in deception. **3.** An occupat or trade, usually one calling for manual skill. **4.** The m bership of a particular trade. **5.** A vessel or an aircraft: used collectively. **— Syn.** See OCCUPATION. [OE *cr* skill, art, strength, courage]
-craft *combining form* Skill; trade; art of: *woodcraft.*
crafts·man (krafts′mən, kräfts′-) *n. pl.* **·men** (-mən) skilled in a craft or art. **— crafts′man·ship** *n.*
craft union A labor union limited to workers who perf the same type of work: also called *horizontal union.*
craft·y (kraf′tē, kräf′-) *adj.* **craft·i·er, craft·i·est** Skillfu deceiving; cunning. **— craft′i·ly** *adv.* **— craft′i·ness** *n.*

g (krag) *n.* A rough, steep, or prominently projecting
ck. [ME *cragg* < Celtic]
g·gy (krag′ē) *adj.* **·gi·er, ·gi·est** Having numerous crags.
so **crag·ged** (krag′id). **—crag′gi·ness** *n.*
ke (krāk) *n.* Any of various small, harsh-voiced birds of
e rail family. [< ON *kraka* crow]
m (kram) *v.* **crammed, cram·ming** *v.t.* **1.** To force into
inadequate space; stuff. **2.** To fill or pack tightly. **3.** To
d to excess. **4.** To force (information) into the mind, or
fill (a person or his mind) with information, as in intensive
dy. **—***v.i.* **5.** To eat greedily; stuff oneself with food.
To engage in intensive, hurried study. **—***n.* **1.** The act
process of cramming. **2.** A crowded condition; a crush.
E *crammian* to stuff] **—cram′mer** *n.*
mp[1] (kramp) *n.* **1.** An involuntary, sudden, painful
iscular contraction. **2.** A paralysis of local muscles
used by overexertion. **3.** *pl.* Acute abdominal pains. **—**
To affect with a cramp. [< OF *crampe*]
mp[2] (kramp) *n.* **1.** An iron bar bent at both ends, used
bind two stones, timbers, etc., together. **2.** An adjustable
me in which pieces may be held together; a clamp. **3.**
ything that presses or confines. **—***v.t.* **1.** To fasten with
ramp. **2.** To restrain or confine; hamper. **3.** To steer;
o, to jam (a wheel) by turning too short. **—to cramp**
e's style *Slang* To hamper one's customary skill or self-
nfidence. **—***adj.* **1.** Narrowed; contracted. **2.** Difficult
read or make out. [ME < MDu. *krampe* hook.]
mp·fish (kramp′fish′) *n.* *pl.* **·fish** or **·fish·es** The elec-
c ray.
m·pon (kram′pən) *n.* **1.** A pair of
oked pieces of iron for raising heavy
nes, etc. **2.** *Usu. pl.* An iron attach-
nt for the shoe to aid in walking on ice
in climbing. Also **cram·poon** (kram·
ōn′). [< MF *crampe* hook]

CRAMPON (*def.* 2)

n·ber·ry (kran′ber′ē, -bər·ē) *n.* *pl.*
es 1. The edible, scarlet, acid berry of
plant growing in marshy land. **2.** The
nt itself.
ne (krān) *n.* **1.** One of a family of large, long-necked,
g-legged birds, as the rare **whooping crane** of North
nerica. **2.** Loosely, any of various herons or cormorants.
A hoisting machine, usually having a projecting movable
n, by which a heavy object can be raised and moved. **4.**
y arm swinging horizontally, by which something is sus-
nded. **—***v.* **craned, cran·ing** *v.t.* & *v.i.* **1.** To stretch out
e's neck, as a crane does. **2.** To lift or move by or as if by
rane. [OE *cran*]
ne·bill (krān′bil′) *n.* Any species of geranium. Also
anes′bill′ (krānz′bil′), **crane's′-bill′.**
ne fly A fly with very long, slender legs.
nio- *combining form* Cranium; cranial. Also, before
wels, **crani-.** [< Med.L *cranium* skull]
·ni·ol·o·gy (krā′nē·ol′ə·jē) *n.* The branch of anatomy
at treats of skulls. **—cra·ni·o·log·i·cal** (krā′nē·ə·loj′i·kəl)
j. **—cra′ni·ol′o·gist** *n.*
·ni·om·e·ter (krā′nē·om′ə·tər) *n.* An instrument for
asuring skulls. **—cra′ni·o·met′ric** (-ə·met′rik) or **·ri·cal**
j. **—cra′ni·o·met′ri·cal·ly** *adv.* **—cra′ni·om′e·try** *n.*
·ni·um (krā′nē·əm) *n.* *pl.* **·ni·ums** or **·ni·a** (-nē·ə) The
ull, esp. the part enclosing the brain. [< Med.L < Gk.
mion skull] **—cra′ni·al** *adj.*
nk (krangk) *n.* **1.** A device for transmitting motion, usu.
handle attached at right angles to a shaft. **2.** *Informal*
e given to eccentric or hostile behavior. **3.** *Informal* A
ouchy person. **4.** A fantastic turn of speech; conceit. **5.**
perverse notion or action; whim. **—***v.t.* **1.** To bend into
e shape of a crank. **2.** To furnish with a crank. **3.** To
rt or operate by a crank. **—***v.i.* **4.** To turn a crank.
E *cranc*]
nk·case (krangk′kās′) *n.* *Mech.* The case enclosing an
gine crankshaft, as of an automobile.
n·kle (krang′kəl) *n.* A bend; crinkle. **—***v.t.* & *v.i.*
ed, ·kling To bend; crinkle. [Dim. of CRANK]
nk·shaft (krangk′shaft′, -shäft′) *n.* *Mech.* A shaft
iven by or driving a crank.
nk·y (krang′kē) *adj.* **crank·i·er, crank·i·est 1.** Irritable;
evish. **2.** Eccentric; queer. **3.** Loose and rickety; shaky.
Naut. Liable to heel; top-heavy: also **crank.** [< CRANK]
crank′i·ly *adv.* **—crank′i·ness** *n.*
n·ny (kran′ē) *n.* *pl.* **·nies** A narrow crevice or chink, as
a wall. [? < OF *cran, cren* notch] **—cran′nied** *adj.*
p (krap) *U.S.* *n.* **1.** The game of craps. **2.** A losing
row in craps. **3.** *Slang* Statements that lie, mislead, or ex-
gerate. **4.** *Slang* Anything worthless. [See CRAPS]
pe (krāp) See CREPE.
p·pie (krap′ē) *n.* *pl.* **·pies** or **·pie** An edible fresh-water
h of the central U.S.

craps (kraps) *n.pl.* (*construed as sing.*) *U.S.* A game of chance, played with two dice. [< F < E *crabs*, the lowest throw (two aces) in hazard]
crap·shoot·er (krap′sho͞o′tər) *n.* *U.S.* One who plays the game of craps.
crap·u·lent (krap′yo͞o·lənt) *adj.* **1.** Grossly intemperate in eating or drinking. **2.** Sick from eating or drinking too much. Also **crap′u·lous.** [< LL < L < Gk. *kraipalē* drunken headache] **—crap′u·lence** *n.*
crash[1] (krash) *v.i.* **1.** To break to pieces with a loud noise. **2.** To suffer damage or destruction, as by falling or striking something. **3.** To make a loud, sharp noise of breaking. **4.** To move with such a noise. **5.** To fail or come to ruin. **—** *v.t.* **6.** To dash violently to pieces; smash. **7.** To force or drive with a sound of crashing. **8.** To cause (an airplane, automobile, etc.) to crash. **9.** *Informal* To enter without invitation or without paying admission. **—***n.* **1.** A loud noise, as of things being violently broken. **2.** A sudden collapse, as of a business enterprise. **3.** The act of crashing, as of an airplane, automobile, etc. **—***adj.* *U.S.* *Informal* Of, pertaining to, or resembling a crash program. [Imit.]
crash[2] (krash) *n.* A course fabric woven of thick, uneven yarns, used for towels, etc. [? < Russian *krashenina*]
crash dive *Naval* The quick submergence of a submarine.
crash helmet A heavy, padded helmet.
crash landing An emergency landing of an airplane.
crash program *U.S.* *Informal* An intensive emergency undertaking in government, science, etc., having priority over all others. Also **crash project.**
crass (kras) *adj.* **1.** Grossly vulgar or stupid. **2.** Coarse or thick. [< L *crassus* thick] **—crass′ly** *adv.* **—crass′ness** *n.*
-crat *combining form* A supporter or member of a social class or of a type of government: *democrat, aristocrat.* [< F *-crate* < Gk. *-kratēs* < *krateein* to rule, govern]
crate (krāt) *n.* **1.** A protective case or framework of slats in which to pack something for shipment. **2.** *Slang* A decrepit vehicle or airplane. **—***v.t.* **crat·ed, crat·ing** To pack in a crate. [Prob. < L *cratis* wickerwork] **—crat′er** *n.*
cra·ter (krā′tər) *n.* **1.** A bowl-shaped depression at the outlet of a volcano. **2.** Any similar cavity, as one resulting from the explosion of a bomb. [< L < Gk. *kratēr* bowl]
cra·vat (krə·vat′) *n.* **1.** A necktie. **2.** A scarf. [< F *Cravate* a Croatian; with ref. to the neckcloths worn by Croatian soldiers]
crave (krāv) *v.* **craved, crav·ing** *v.t.* **1.** To long for; desire greatly. **2.** To be in need of; require. **3.** To ask for earnestly; beg. **—***v.i.* **4.** To desire or long: with *for* or *after.* [OE *crafian*] **—crav′er** *n.*
cra·ven (krā′vən) *adj.* Conspicuously lacking in courage; cowardly. **—***n.* A base coward. [? < OF < L *crepare* to creak, break] **—cra′ven·ly** *adv.* **—cra′ven·ness** *n.*
craw (krô) *n.* **1.** The crop of a bird. **2.** The stomach of any animal. **—to stick in one's craw** To be displeasing or unacceptable. [ME *crawe.* Akin to Du. *kraag* neck.]
craw·fish (krô′fish′) *n.* *pl.* **·fish** or **·fish·es** A crayfish.
crawl[1] (krôl) *v.i.* **1.** To move along slowly with the body on or close to the ground. **2.** To move slowly, feebly, or cautiously. **3.** To be covered with things that crawl. **4.** To feel as if covered with crawling things. **5.** To behave with servility. **—***n.* **1.** The act of crawling. **2.** An overarm swimming stroke performed face down, combined with a flutter kick. [Prob. < ON *krafla* to paw] **—crawl′er** *n.* **—crawl′ing·ly** *adv.*
crawl[2] (krôl) *n.* A pen in shallow water for confining fish, turtles, etc. [See KRAAL.]
crawl·y (krô′lē) *adj.* **crawl·i·er, crawl·i·est** *Informal* Creepy.
cray·fish (krā′fish′) *n.* *pl.* **·fish** or **·fish·es 1.** A fresh-water crustacean resembling the lobster. **2.** Loosely, the spiny lobster. Also *crawfish.* [Earlier *crevice* < OF < OHG *krebiz*]
cray·on (krā′ən, -on) *n.* **1.** A stick of colored wax, chalk, etc., for use in drawing. **2.** A drawing made with crayons. **—***v.t.* & *v.i.* To sketch or draw with crayons. [< F, pencil]
craze (krāz) *v.* **crazed, craz·ing** *v.t.* **1.** To render insane or demented. **2.** To make full of minute cracks, as the glaze of pottery. **—***v.i.* **3.** To become insane. **4.** To become full of minute cracks. **—***n.* **1.** A brief fashion or fad; rage. **2.** An extravagant liking or enthusiasm. **3.** Mental disorder; insanity. **4.** A minute flaw in the glaze of pottery, etc. [ME *crasen* to crack] **—crazed** *adj.*
cra·zy (krā′zē) *adj* **·zi·er, ·zi·est 1.** Disordered in mind; insane; demented; mad; maniacal. **2.** *Informal* Very enthusiastic or excited. **3.** *Informal* Unpredictable or inexplicable: a *crazy* driver. **4.** Dilapidated; rickety; unsound. **—cra′zi·ly** *adv.* **—cra′zi·ness** *n.*
crazy bone The funny bone.
crazy quilt A patchwork quilt made of pieces of various sizes, shapes, and colors.
creak (krēk) *n.* A sharp, squeaking sound, as from friction. **—***v.t.* & *v.i.* To produce or cause to produce a creak. [Imit.]

creak·y (krē′kē) *adj.* **·i·er, ·i·est 1.** Creaking. **2.** Likely to creak: a *creaky* step. **— creak′i·ly** *adv.* **— creak′i·ness** *n.*
cream (krēm) *n.* **1.** An oily, yellowish substance contained in milk. **2.** The best part. **3.** The yellowish white color of cream. **4.** A food or delicacy made with or resembling cream. **5.** Something resembling cream. **6.** A soft, oily cosmetic for cleansing or protecting the skin. **—** *v.t.* **1.** To skim cream from. **2.** To take the best part from. **3.** To add cream to, as coffee. **4.** To permit (milk) to form cream. **5.** To beat, as butter and sugar, to a creamy consistency. **6.** To cook or prepare (food) with cream or cream sauce. **7.** *U.S. Slang* To defeat decisively. **—** *v.i.* **8.** To froth or foam. **9.** To form cream. [< OF < LL *chrisma* chrism]
cream cheese Soft, white cheese made of cream or a mixture of cream and milk.
cream·er (krē′mər) *n.* **1.** A small pitcher used for serving cream. **2.** Any device in which cream is separated.
cream·er·y (krē′mər·ē) *n.* *pl.* **·er·ies 1.** A place where milk and cream are prepared for market. **2.** An establishment at which dairy products are sold.
cream of tartar Potassium bitartrate.
cream puff 1. A shell of pastry filled with whipped cream or custard. **2.** *Slang* A sissy; weakling.
cream·y (krē′mē) *adj.* **cream·i·er, cream·i·est 1.** Containing cream. **2.** Resembling cream. **— cream′i·ness** *n.*
crease[1] (krēs) *n.* A mark or line made by folding or wrinkling. **—** *v.* **creased, creas·ing** *v.t.* **1.** To make a crease, line, or fold in; wrinkle. **2.** To graze with a bullet. **—** *v.i.* **3.** To become wrinkled. [ME *creaste,* ? var. of *creste* crest, ridge] **— creas′er** *n.*
crease[2] (krēs) See KRIS.
creas·y (krē′sē) *adj.* **creas·i·er, creas·i·est** Creased.
cre·ate (krē·āt′) *v.t.* **·at·ed, ·at·ing 1.** To cause to come into existence; originate. **2.** To be the cause of; occasion: To *create* interest. **3.** To produce (a work of art, etc.). **4.** To be the first to portray, as a character or part. **5.** To invest with new office, rank, etc.; appoint. [< L *creare* to produce, create]
cre·a·tion (krē·ā′shən) *n.* **1.** The act of creating, or the fact of being created. **2.** Anything created. **3.** *Usu. cap.* God's bringing of the universe into existence. **4.** The universe; also, all living creatures. **— cre·a′tion·al** *adj.*
cre·a·tive (krē·ā′tiv) *adj.* **1.** Having the power or ability to create. **2.** Characterized by originality of thought and execution. **3.** Productive: with *of.* **— cre·a′tive·ly** *adv.* **— cre·a′tive·ness, cre·a·tiv·i·ty** (krē′ā·tiv′ə·tē, -ə·tiv′-) *n.*
cre·a·tor (krē·ā′tər) *n.* One who or that which creates. **— the Creator** God. **— cre·a′tor·ship** *n.*
crea·ture (krē′chər) *n.* **1.** A living being; especially, an animal. **2.** A person. **3.** That which has been created. **4.** One who is dependent upon, influenced by, or subordinate to something or someone; puppet; tool. **5.** *U.S.* A domestic animal. [< OF < LL < L *creare* to produce]
crèche (kresh, krāsh) *n.* **1.** A group of figures representing the scene in the stable at the Nativity. **2.** A foundling asylum. **3.** *Brit.* A public day nursery. [< F, crib, cradle]
cre·dence (krēd′ns) *n.* Belief, esp. as based upon the evidence of others. [< MF < L *credere* to believe]
cre·den·tial (kri·den′shəl) *n.* **1.** That which entitles one to authority or confidence. **2.** *Usually pl.* A certificate or letter giving evidence of one's authority or identity. [< Med.L *credentia* belief + -AL[1]]
cre·den·za (kri·den′zə) *n.* A sideboard or buffet. [< Ital. < Med.L < L *credere* to believe.]
cred·i·ble (kred′ə·bəl) *adj.* **1.** Capable of being believed. **2.** Worthy of confidence; reliable. [< L < *credere* to believe] **— cred′i·bil′i·ty, cred′i·ble·ness** *n.* **— cred′i·bly** *adv.*
cred·it (kred′it) *n.* **1.** Belief in the genuineness or truth of something; trust; faith. **2.** The quality of being trustworthy. **3.** A good reputation. **4.** A source of honor or good repute: a *credit* to one's family. **5.** Approval for some action or quality. **6.** Influence derived from the good opinion of others. **7.** *Usu. pl.* Acknowledgment of a book, motion picture, play, etc. **8.** Confidence in the ability of an individual, firm, etc., to fulfill financial obligations: to buy on *credit.* **9.** Reputation for commercial integrity. **10.** The time extended for payment of a liability. **11.** In bookkeeping: **a** The entry of any amount paid by a debtor, or the amount entered. **b** The right-hand side of an account, where values received are entered. **12.** In an account, the balance in one's favor. **13.** *U.S.* Official certification that a student has passed a course of study; also, a unit of academic study. **—** *v.t.* **1.** To accept as true. **2.** To ascribe, as intelligence or honor, to: with *with.* **3.** In bookkeeping, to give credit for or enter as credit to. **4.** *U.S.* to give educational credits to (a student). [< MF < L < *credere* to believe, trust]
cred·it·a·ble (kred′it·ə·bəl) *adj.* Deserving credit or esteem; praiseworthy. **— cred′it·a·bil′i·ty, cred′it·a·ble·ness** *n.* **— cred′it·a·bly** *adv.*
cred·i·tor (kred′i·tər) *n.* One to whom money is owed. [< AF < L < *credere* to believe, trust]
credit union A cooperative group for making loans to members at low rates of interest.
cre·do (krē′dō, krā′-) *n.* *pl.* **·dos 1.** A set of beliefs; a cre **2.** *Often cap.* The Apostles' Creed or the Nicene Creed; a a musical setting for this. [< L, I believe]
cre·du·li·ty (krə·do͞o′lə·tē, -dyo͞o′-) *n.* Readiness to beli on slight evidence; gullibility.
cred·u·lous (krej′o͞o·ləs) *adj.* **1.** Disposed to believe slight evidence. **2.** Arising from credulity. [< L < *cre* to believe] **— cred′u·lous·ly** *adv.* **— cred′u·lous·ness**
Cree (krē) *n.* *pl.* **Cree** or **Crees 1.** One of an Algonqu tribe of North American Indians formerly dwelling in M toba and Saskatchewan. **2.** The language of this tribe.
creed (krēd) *n.* **1.** A formal statement of religious belie doctrine. **2.** Any organized system or statement of beli principles, etc. **— Syn.** See DOCTRINE. **— the Creed** Apostles' Creed. [OE < L *credo* I believe.]
creek (krēk, krik) *n.* **1.** *U.S.* A stream intermediate in between a brook and a river. **2.** *Chiefly Brit.* A narrow i or cove in a shoreline. [ME *creke, crike* < Scand.]
Creek (krēk) *n.* **1.** A member of one of various tribe North American Indians, once occupying parts of Geor Alabama, and Florida. **2.** Their Muskhogean language.
creel (krēl) *n.* An angler's wicker basket for carrying [Appar. related to OF *greille* grating]
creep (krēp) *v.i.* **crept, creep·ing 1.** To move with the b close to or touching the ground; crawl. **2.** To move im ceptibly, stealthily, or timidly. **3.** To act servilely; cri **4.** To grow along a surface or support, as a vine. **5.** To h a sensation of being covered with creeping things. **6.** slip out of position. **—** *n.* **1.** The act of creeping. **2** *Informal* A feeling of apprehension. [OE *crēopan*]
creep·er (krē′pər) *n.* **1.** One who or that which creeps. *Bot.* A plant growing along or across a surface by sending short, flowering stems. **3.** *pl.* A baby's garment resemb overalls.
creep·y (krē′pē) *adj.* **creep·i·er, creep·i·est 1.** Havin producing a feeling of fear or repugnance. **2.** Character by a creeping motion. **— creep′i·ly** *adv.* **— creep′i·nes**
creese (krēs) See KRIS.
cre·mate (krē′māt, kri·māt′) *v.t.* **·mat·ed, ·mat·ing** To b (a dead body) to ashes. [< L *cremare* to burn to as **— cre·ma·tion** (kri·mā′shən) *n.* **— cre′ma·tor** *n.*
cre·ma·to·ry (krē′mə·tôr′ē, -tō′rē, krem′ə-) *adj.* Relate cremation. **—** *n.* *pl.* **·ries** A furnace or establishment cremating dead bodies: also **cre′ma·to′ri·um.**
crème (krem) *n.* *French* Cream: used in names of sa and liqueurs.
crème de ca·ca·o (də kə·kā′ō, -kä′ō) *French* A sweet, c olate-flavored liqueur.
crème de menthe (də mänt) *French* A sweet, gree white cordial with a strong flavor of mint.
Cre·mo·na (kri·mō′nə, *Ital.* krā·mō′nä) *n.* Any violin m at Cremona, Italy, from the 16th to the 18th century, by Amati family, by Antonio Stradivari, and others.
cre·nate (krē′nāt) *adj.* *Bot.* Scalloped or toothed with e rounded notches, as a leaf or margin. Also **cre′nat·ed.** NL < *crena* notch] **— cre′nate·ly** *adv.* **— cre·na′tion**
cren·el (kren′əl) *n.* **1.** One of the embrasures, or inde tions of a battlement. **2.** A crenature. **—** *v.t.* **cren·ele ·elled, cren·el·ing** or **·el·ling** To crenelate. Also **cre·n** (kri·nel′). [< OF, dim. of *cren* notch]
cren·el·ate (kren′ə·lāt) *v.t.* **·lat·ed, ·lat·ing** To provide v battlements or crenels. Also *Brit.* **cren′el·late. — cr el·a′tion, cren′el·la′tion** *n.*
Cre·ole (krē′ōl) *n.* **1.** A native of Spanish America or West Indies but of European descent. **2.** A descendan the original French settlers of the southern U.S., esp Louisiana. **3.** The French patois spoken by the Louisi Creoles. **—** *adj.* Of, relating to, or peculiar to the Crec [< F *créole* < Sp. < L *creare* to create]
Creole State Nickname of Louisiana.
cre·o·sol (krē′ə·sōl, -sol) *n.* *Chem.* A colorless, aromatic, liquid compound, $C_8H_{10}O_2$, derived from beechwood tar distillation. [< CREOS(OTE) + -OL[2]]
cre·o·sote (krē′ə·sōt) *n.* *Chem.* An oily liquid obtained the distillation of wood tar and coal tar, used as an a septic and preservative. **—** *v.t.* **·sot·ed, ·sot·ing** To trea impregnate with creosote, as shingles, etc. [< Gk. *k* flesh + *sōtēr* preserver < *sōzein* to save]
crepe (krāp) *n.* **1.** A thin fabric of silk, cotton, wool synthetic fiber, having a crinkled surface. **2.** Black cr used as a sign of mourning, as in an armband: in this se usu. *crape.* **3.** Tissue paper resembling crepe: also **cr paper.** Also spelled *crape:* also **crêpe.** [< F (*tissu*) *cr* crinkled (cloth) < L *crispus* curled]
crêpes su·zette (krep′ so͞o·zet′) Thin egg pancakes served aflame in cognac or curaçao.
crep·i·tate (krep′ə·tāt) *v.i.* **·tat·ed, ·tat·ing** To crac rattle. [< L *crepitare,* freq. of *crepare* to creak] **— cre tant** *adj.* **— crep′i·ta′tion** *n.*

ɛpt (krept) Past tense of CREEP.
ɛ·pus·cu·lar (kri·pus′kyə·lər) *adj.* **1.** Dim; obscure. **.** *Zool.* Appearing or flying in the twilight.
ɛs·cen·do (krə·shen′dō, -sen′-) *Music n. pl.* **·dos** A ·adual increase in volume: expressed by the sign ⟨ : ɔposed to *diminuendo.* — *v.i.* **·doed, ·do·ing** To produce a ·escendo. [< Ital., ppr. of *crescere* to increase < L]
ɛs·cent (kres′ənt) *n.* **1.** The visible part of the moon in s first or last quarter, having one concave edge and one ɔnvex edge. **2.** Something crescent-shaped. **3.** The de·ce on the Turkish standard. — **the Crescent** Turkish or ɩoslem power. — *adj.* **1.** Increasing: said of the moon its first quarter. **2.** Shaped like the moon in its first ɩarter. [< L *crescens, -entis,* ppr. of *crescere* to increase]
ɛ·sol (krē′sōl, -sol) *n. Chem.* A liquid or crystalline comɔund, C_7H_8O, obtained by the destructive distillation of ·al tar, used as an antiseptic. [Var. of CREOSOL]
ɛss (kres) *n.* One of various plants of the mustard family, s watercress, pungent to taste, used in salads. [OE *cresse*]
ɛs·set (kres′it) *n.* A metal holder for burning oil, wood, ·c., for illumination. [< OF *craicet, craisset*]
ɛst (krest) *n.* **1.** A comb, tuft, or projection on the head an animal, esp. of birds. **2.** The top of a wave. **3.** The ɩghest point or stage: the *crest* of a flood. **4.** The projec·on on the top of a helmet; a plume. — *v.t.* **1.** To furnish ith a crest. **2.** To reach the crest of. — *v.i.* **3.** To come a crest, as a wave. [< OF < L *crista* tuft] — **crest′ed** *ɩj.* — **crest′less** *adj.*
ɛst·fall·en (krest′fô′lən) *adj.* **1.** Depressed; dispirited; ɛjected. **2.** Having a fallen or drooping crest.
ɛ·ta·ceous (kri·tā′shəs) *adj.* Consisting of, containing, or sembling chalk. [< L < *creta* chalk]
e·ta·ceous (kri·tā′shəs) *Geol. adj.* Of or pertaining to ɩe third geologic period of the Mesozoic era. — *n.* The ʏstem of rocks deposited during this period. See chart nder GEOLOGY.
e·tin (krē′tin, krēt′n) *n.* A person afflicted with cretinm. [< F *crétin,* var. of *chrétien* Christian, human being, e., not an animal] — **cre′tin·ous** *adj.*
e·tin·ism (krē′tən·iz′əm) *n. Pathol.* A congenital condi·on associated with thyroid deficiency, marked by arrested ɦysical development, goiter, and mental retardation.
e·tonne (kri·ton′, krē′ton) *n.* A heavy, unglazed cotton, nen, or rayon fabric printed in colored patterns, used esp. ɔr draperies. [after *Creton,* a village in Normandy]
e·vasse (krə·vas′) *n.* **1.** A deep fissure or chasm, as in a lacier. **2.** *U.S.* A breach in a levee. — *v.t.* **·vassed, ·vass·ɩg** To split with crevasses. [See CREVICE]
ev·ice (krev′is) *n.* A fissure or crack on or through the ɩrface of something; cleft; chink. [< OF *crevace* < LL < L *crepare* to crack, creak] — **crev′iced** *adj.*
ew[1] (kroo) *n.* **1.** The company of men belonging to one ɩip, aircraft, etc. **2.** A body of men organized or detailed ɔr a particular job: a repair *crew.* **3.** A group trained to andle a racing shell. **4.** A company of people; crowd; ang. [< OF < L *crescere* to increase]
ew[2] (kroo) Past tense of CROW.
ew cut *U.S.* A closely cropped haircut.
ew·el (kroo′əl) *n.* A slackly twisted worsted yarn, used ɩ fancywork. [Origin uncertain] — **crew′el·work′** *n.*
ib (krib) *n.* **1.** A child's bed, with side railings. **2.** A box, in, or small building for grain, having slat or openwork ides. **3.** A rack or manger for fodder. **4.** A stall for cattle. **.** A small house, cottage, or room. **6.** A framework of ʏood or metal, used to retain or support something, as in ɩines. **7.** *Informal* A plagiarism. **8.** *Informal* A transla·on or other unauthorized aid employed by students. — *v.* **ribbed, crib·bing** *v.t.* **1.** To enclose in or as in a crib. **.** To line or bolster, as the walls of a pit, with timbers or lanking. **3.** *Informal* To plagiarize. — *v.i.* **4.** *Informal* 'o use a crib in translating. [OE *cribb*] — **crib′ber** *n.*
ib·bage (krib′ij) *n.* A game of cards for two, three, or ɔur players, the score being kept on a pegboard.
ick (krik) *n.* A painful spasm of the muscles, as of the eck; a cramp. — *v.t.* To turn or twist so as to produce a rick. [Origin uncertain]
ick·et[1] (krik′it) *n.* A leaping insect having long antennae, he male of which makes a chirping sound by friction of the orewings. [< OF < LG; orig. imit.]
ick·et[2] (krik′it) *n.* **1.** An outdoor game played with bats, ball, and wickets, between two sides of eleven each, popuar in England. **2.** *Informal* Fair play; sportsmanship. — *.i.* To play cricket. [< F] — **crick′et·er** *n.*
ick·et[3] (krik′it) *n.* A footstool. [Origin unknown]
ied (krīd) Past tense and past participle of CRY.
·i·er (krī′ər) *n.* **1.** One who cries. **2.** One who makes pubɩc announcements, as of sales, news, etc. **3.** A hawker.
ime (krīm) *n.* **1.** *Law* An act or omission in violation of public law, esp. a felony. **2.** Any grave offense against morality or social order. **3.** *Informal* Any apparent injustice; a shame. [< OF < L *crimen* accusation]
Crimean War See table for WAR.
crim·i·nal (krim′ə·nəl) *adj.* **1.** Implying or involving crime. **2.** *Law* Pertaining to the administration of penal as opposed to civil law: a *criminal* court. **3.** Guilty of crime. — *n.* One who has committed a crime. [< OF < L < *crimen* charge] — **crim′i·nal·ly** *adv.* — **crim′i·nal′i·ty** *n.*
crim·i·nol·o·gy (krim′ə·nol′ə·jē) *n.* The scientific study and investigation of crime and the behavior of criminals. [< L *crimen, criminis* crime + -LOGY] — **crim·i·no·log·i·cal** (krim′ə·nə·loj′i·kəl) *adj.* — **crim′i·nol′o·gist** *n.*
crimp[1] (krimp) *v.t.* **1.** To bend or press into ridges or folds; corrugate; flute. **2.** To curl or wave: to *crimp* the hair. — *n.* **1.** Something that has been crimped. **2.** *pl.* Waved or curled hair. — **to put a crimp in** *Informal* To hinder or obstruct. [< MDu. *crimpen* to wrinkle] — **crimp′er** *n.*
crimp[2] (krimp) *n.* One who gets sailors, soldiers, etc., to serve by decoying or entrapping them. — *v.t.* To decoy or entrap into forced military service. [Origin uncertain]
crimp·y (krim′pē) *adj.* **crimp·i·er, crimp·i·est** Having a crimped appearance; wavy; curly.
crim·son (krim′zən) *n.* A deep red color. — *adj.* **1.** Of a deep red color. **2.** Bloody. — *v.t. & v.i.* To make or become crimson. [ME < Sp. < Arabic < *qirmiz* insect]
cringe (krinj) *v.i.* **cringed, cring·ing** **1.** To shrink or crouch in fear or cowardice. **2.** To fawn. — *n.* A servile crouching. [ME *cringen, crengen*] — **cring′er** *n.*
crin·gle (kring′gəl) *n. Naut.* A small loop or grommet of rope or metal, attached to the edge of a sail. [Appar. < LG]
crin·kle (kring′kəl) *v.t. & v.i.* **·kled, ·kling** **1.** To form or cause to form wrinkles, turns, etc. **2.** To rustle or crackle. — *n.* A wrinkle or fold. [ME *crenklen* to curl up] — **crin′kly** *adj.*
cri·noid (krī′noid, krin′oid) *adj.* **1.** *Zool.* Of or pertaining to animals having jointed stems attached by stalks to the sea bottom, and radial arms. **2.** Lilylike. — *n.* A crinoid animal. [< NL < Gk. < *krinon* lily + *eidos* form]
crin·o·line (krin′ə·lin, -lēn) *n.* **1.** A stiff fabric, used in puffed sleeves, hems, interlinings, etc., originally made of horsehair and linen. **2.** A petticoat of this fabric. **3.** A hoop skirt. [< F < L *crinis* hair + *linum* linen]
crip·ple (krip′əl) *n.* A lame or disabled person or animal; one lacking the natural use of a limb or the body. — *v.t.* **·pled, ·pling** **1.** To make lame. **2.** To impair or disable. [OE *crypel*] — **crip′pler** *n.*
cri·sis (krī′sis) *n. pl.* **·ses** (-sēz) **1.** A crucial turning point in an affair or of a series of events. **2.** A critical moment. **3.** *Pathol.* Any decisive change in the course of a disease, favorable or unfavorable. [< L < Gk. < *krinein* to decide]
crisp (krisp) *adj.* **1.** Brittle; easily crumbled. **2.** Fresh and firm: *crisp* vegetables. **3.** Brisk; invigorating: a *crisp* breeze. **4.** Stimulating; lively: a *crisp* conversation. **5.** Terse or pithy; curt: a *crisp* retort. **6.** Having tight curls or waves, as hair. — *v.t. & v.i.* To make or become crisp. [OE < L *crispus* curled] — **crisp′ly** *adv.* — **crisp′ness** *n.*
crisp·y (kris′pē) *adj.* **crisp·i·er, crisp·i·est** Crisp.
criss·cross (kris′krôs′, -kros′) *v.t.* **1.** To cross with interlacing lines. — *v.i.* **2.** To move in crisscrosses. — *adj.* Marked by crossings. — *n.* **1.** The cross of one who cannot write. **2.** A group of intersecting lines. — *adv.* Crosswise. [Alter. of *Christcross*]
cri·te·ri·on (krī·tir′ē·ən) *n. pl.* **·te·ri·a** (-tir′ē·ə) or **·te·ri·ons** A standard or rule by which a judgment can be made; a model, test, or measure. [< Gk. < *krinein* to decide]
crit·ic (krit′ik) *n.* **1.** One who judges the merits of anything by some standard or criterion. **2.** A skilled judge of literary, theatrical, or other artistic creations. **3.** One who judges severely. [< L < Gk. < *kritēs* judge]
crit·i·cal (krit′i·kəl) *adj.* **1.** Given to faultfinding or severe judgments; carping. **2.** Exhibiting careful, precise judgments; analytical: a *critical* report. **3.** Of or characteristic of a critic or criticism. **4.** Of the nature of a crisis or turning point; crucial; decisive. **5.** Attended with danger; risky; perilous. **6.** Necessary for the prosecution of a war: *critical* materiel. **7.** *Physics* Indicating a decisive change in a specified condition. — **crit′i·cal·ly** *adv.* — **crit′i·cal·ness** *n.*
crit·i·cism (krit′ə·siz′əm) *n.* **1.** The act of criticizing, esp. disapprovingly. **2.** A severe or unfavorable judgment. **3.** The art of making informed and discriminating judgments. **4.** The occupation or profession of a critic. **5.** A review, article, or commentary expressing a critical judgment.
crit·i·cize (krit′ə·sīz) *v.t. & v.i.* **1.** To judge severely; censure. **2.** To pass judgment on the merits or faults of. Also *Brit.* **crit′i·cise.** — **crit′i·ciz′a·ble** *adj.* — **crit′i·ciz′er** *n.*
cri·tique (kri·tēk′) *n.* **1.** A critical review, esp. of a work of art or literature. **2.** The art of criticism. [< F]

crit·ter (krit′ər) *n. U.S. Dial.* A creature.

croak (krōk) *v.i.* **1.** To utter a hoarse, low-pitched cry, as a frog or crow. **2.** To speak in a low, hoarse voice. **3.** To talk in a doleful tone; grumble. **4.** *Slang* To die. — *v.t.* **5.** To utter with a croak. **6.** *Slang* To kill. — *n.* A hoarse vocal sound, as of a frog. [Imit.] — **croak′y** *adj.*

croak·er (krō′kər) *n.* **1.** Any of various animals that croak, as the grunt, a fish. **2.** One who speaks dolefully.

Cro·at (krō′at, -ət) *n.* **1.** A Slavic native of Croatia. **2.** The Croatian language.

Cro·a·tian (krō·ā′shən) *adj.* Pertaining to Croatia or the Croats. — *n.* **1.** A Croat. **2.** The South Slavic language of the Croats; Serbo-Croatian.

cro·chet (krō·shā′) *v.t. & v.i.* **·cheted** (-shād′), **·chet·ing** (-shā′ing) To form or ornament (a fabric) by interlacing thread with a hooked needle. — *n.* A kind of fancywork produced by crocheting. [< F, dim., of *croche* hook]

crock (krok) *n.* An earthenware pot or jar. [OE *croc*]

crocked (krokt) *adj. U.S. Slang* Drunk.

crock·er·y (krok′ər·ē) *n.* Earthen vessels collectively.

croc·o·dile (krok′ə·dīl) *n.* **1.** A large lizardlike, amphibious reptile of tropical regions, with long jaws and armored skin. **2.** A gavial. [< OF < Med.L < Gk. *krokodilos* lizard, crocodile]

CROCODILE
(To 18 feet long)

crocodile tears False weeping; hypocritical grief.

croc·o·dil·i·an (krok′·ə·dil′ē·ən) *adj.* **1.** Of or like a crocodile. **2.** Belonging to an order of reptiles that includes crocodiles, alligators, and caymans. — *n.* A crocodilian reptile. Also **croc′o·dil′e·an.**

cro·cus (krō′kəs) *n. pl.* **cro·cus·es** or **cro·ci** (krō′sī) **1.** A plant of the iris family, with long grasslike leaves and large flowers. **2.** A deep orange yellow. [< L < Gk. *krokos*]

Croe·sus (krē′səs) Sixth-century B.C. Lydian king, noted for his wealth. — *n.* Any very wealthy man.

croft (krôft, kroft) *n. Brit.* **1.** A small field near a house. **2.** A small tenant farm. [OE, field] — **croft′er** *n.*

Croix de Guerre (krwä də gâr′) A French military decoration for bravery; literally, cross of war.

Cro-Mag·non (krō·mag′non, *Fr.* krō·må·nyôn′) *Anthropol. n.* A member of a prehistoric European race considered to be a forerunner of modern man. — *adj.* Pertaining to or belonging to the Cro-Magnon race. [after the cave in France where their remains have been found]

crom·lech (krom′lek) *n.* **1.** An ancient monument of large standing stones arranged roughly in a circle. **2.** A dolmen. [< Welsh < *crom* bent + *llech* flat stone]

crone (krōn) *n.* A withered old woman. [Prob. < OF *carogne* carcass]

Cro·nus (krō′nəs) In Greek mythology, the youngest of the Titans, who deposed his father Uranus and was himself overcome by his son Zeus: identified with the Roman *Saturn*: also spelled *Kronos.*

cro·ny (krō′nē) *n. pl.* **·nies** A friend. [Orig. university slang < Gk. *chronios* contemporary]

crook (krŏŏk) *n.* **1.** A bend or curve. **2.** The curved or bent part of a thing. **3.** Something with a crook in it, as a shepherd's staff. **4.** *Informal* A thief. — *v.t.* **1.** To bend; make crooked. — *v.i.* **2.** To grow crooked. [< ON *krōkr*]

crook·ed (krŏŏk′id) *adj.* **1.** Bent; not straight. **2.** Tricky; dishonest. — **crook′ed·ly** *adv.* — **crook′ed·ness** *n.*

crook·neck (krŏŏk′nek′) *n.* Any of several varieties of squash with a long, curved neck.

croon (krōōn) *v.t. & v.i.* **1.** To sing or hum in a low tone. **2.** To sing (popular songs) in a soft and sentimental manner. — *n.* A low, mournful humming or singing. [< MDu. *kronen* to sing softly, lament] — **croon′er** *n.*

crop (krop) *n.* **1.** The cultivated produce of the land, as grain or vegetables. **2.** The product of a particular kind, place, or season. **3.** A collection or quantity of anything. **4.** A cropping, esp. of the hair. **5.** An earmark, as on cattle. **6.** An enlargement of the gullet, as in birds; the craw. **7.** The handle of a whip. **8.** A whip having a leather loop for a lash. — *v.* **cropped, crop·ping** *v.t.* **1.** To cut or eat off the stems of, as grass. **2.** To reap. **3.** To trim or clip (the hair, ears, tail, etc.) of. **4.** To raise a crop or crops on. — *v.i.* **5.** To bear or yield a crop or crops. — **to crop up** (or **out**) **1.** To appear above the surface; sprout. **2.** To develop or happen unexpectedly. [OE]

crop·per[1] (krop′ər) *n.* **1.** One who or that which crops. **2.** *U.S.* One who cultivates another's land for part of the crop.

crop·per[2] (krop′ər) *n.* A bad fall, as when one is thrown over a horse's head. — **to come a cropper** **1.** To fall headlong. **2.** To fail. [? < dial. *neck and crop* completely]

cro·quet (krō·kā′) *n.* An outdoor game played by dr ing wooden balls through a series of wire arches by means long-handled mallets. [Var. of *crochet.* See CROCHET.]

cro·quette (krō·ket′) *n.* A ball or cake of minced fo fried brown in deep fat. [< F < *croquer* to crunch]

cro·sier (krō′zhər) *n.* A staff surmounted by a crook cross, borne by or before a bishop or archbishop on occasi of ceremony. [< OF < Med.L < *crocia* bishop's crook]

cross (krôs, kros) *n.* **1.** An ancient instrument of exe tion, an upright with a horizontal piece near the top, up which the condemned persons were fastened. **2.** The e blem of Christianity, a representation of the cross up which Christ died. **3.** Any severe trial, affliction, or suff ing: to bear one's *cross.* **4.** The sign of the cross, made w the right hand as a devotional act. **5.** A monument, staff other structure in the form of a cross. **6.** The mark of who cannot write. **7.** Anything that resembles or is int mediate between two other things: a *cross* between poe and prose. **8.** A mixture of varieties or breeds of plants animals; a hybrid. — **the Cross** **1.** The cross on wh Christ was crucified. **2.** Christianity. — *v.t.* **1.** To m or pass from one side to the other side of; go across; trave **2.** To extend from side to side of; span: An overpass *cros* a highway. **3.** To pass across or intersect, as streets or lin **4.** To transport or convey across. **5.** To make the sign the cross upon or over. **6.** To draw or put a line acro to *cross* a *t.* **7.** To lay or place across or over: to *cross* legs, fingers, etc. **8.** To meet and pass: Your ship *cros* mine. **9.** To obstruct or hinder; thwart. **10.** *Biol.* crossbreed (plants or animals). — *v.i.* **11.** To pass, mo or extend from side to side. **12.** To intersect; lie athwa **13.** To meet and pass: Our paths *crossed.* **14.** *Biol.* crossbreed. — **to cross one's mind** To occur to one. **to cross up** *Informal* To betray. — *adj.* **1.** Peevish; humored. **2.** Lying across each other: *cross* streets. Embodying interchange; reciprocal. **4.** Contrary; adver at *cross* purposes. **5.** Hybrid. — *adv.* **1.** Across; cro wise; transversely. **2.** Adversely; contrarily. [< OE ON < L *crux*] — **cross′ly** *adv.* — **cross′ness** *n.*

cross-bar (krôs′bär′, kros′-) *n.* A transverse bar or line. *v.t.* **·barred, ·bar·ring** To secure or mark with crossbars

cross·beam (krôs′bēm′, kros′-) *n.* **1.** A large beam or gir going from wall to wall. **2.** Any beam that crosses anoth

cross·bill (krôs′bil′, kros′-) *n.* A finchlike bird hav points on its mandibles that cross each other.

cross·bones (krôs′bōnz′, kros′-) *n.* A representation two bones crossing each other, usu. surmounted by a sk and used as a symbol of death.

cross·bow (krôs′bō′, kros′-) *n.* A medieval weapon c sisting of a bow fixed transversely on a grooved stock alo which arrows or stones are released. — **cross′bow′man**

cross·breed (krôs′brēd′, kros′-) *v.t. & v.i.* **·bred, ·breed·i** *Biol.* To produce (a strain or animal) by interbreeding blending two varieties. — *n.* A strain or animal produ by crossbreeding; a hybrid.

cross·check (krôs′chek′) *v.t. & v.i.* To confirm or ma certain by using parallel or additional data.

cross-coun·try (krôs′kun′trē, kros′-) *adj. & adv.* Acr open country and disregarding roads, lanes, etc.

cross·cur·rent (krôs′kûr′ənt, kros′-) *n.* **1.** A current flo ing across another. **2.** A contradictory tendency.

cross·cut (krôs′kut′, kros′-) *v.t. & v.i.* **·cut, ·cut·ting** To crosswise or through. — *adj.* **1.** Used or made for purpose of crosscutting. **2.** Cut across or on the bi *crosscut* silk. — *n.* **1.** A cut across or a shortcut. **2.** *M ing* A cutting that intersects the lode or the main workin

cross-ex·am·ine (krôs′ig·zam′in, kros′-) *v.t. & v.i.* **·in ·in·ing** **1.** To question anew (a witness called by the opp ing party) for the purpose of testing the reliability of previous testimony. **2.** To question carefully. — **cros ex·am′i·na·tion** *n.* — **cross′-ex·am′in·er** *n.*

cross-eye (krôs′ī′, kros′-) *n.* Strabismus in which one both eyes are turned inward. — **cross′-eyed** *adj.*

cross-fer·ti·li·za·tion (krôs′fûr′tə·lə·zā′shən, kros′-) **1.** *Biol.* The fertilization of an organism by sexually diff entiated reproductive cells. **2.** *Bot.* The fertilization of o plant or flower by the pollen from another.

cross-fer·ti·lize (krôs′fûr′tə·līz, kros′-) *v.t.* **·lized, ·liz·i** To fertilize (a plant or animal) by cross-fertilization.

cross-grained (krôs′grānd′, kros′-) *adj.* **1.** Having t grain running transversely: a *cross-grained* board. Stubborn; perverse: a *cross-grained* man.

cross·hatch (krôs′hach′, kros′-) *v.t.* To shade, as a pictu by crossed lines. — **cross′hatch′ing** *n.*

cross-in·dex (krôs′in′deks, kros′-) *v.t. & v.i.* To ins cross-references in (an index, etc.).

cross·ing (krôs′ing, kros′-) *n.* **1.** The act of going acro hindering, etc. **2.** The place where something, as a roa may be crossed. **3.** Intersection, as of roads.

cross·patch (krôs′pach′, kros′-) *n. Informal* A crank ill-tempered person.

ss·piece (krôs′pēs′, kros′-) *n.* Any piece of material at crosses another.
ss·pol·li·nate (krôs′pol′ə·nāt, kros′-) *v.t.* **·nat·ed, ·nat·g** To cross-fertilize (a plant). **— cross′-pol′li·na′tion** *n.*
ss·pur·pose (krôs′pûr′pəs, kros′-) *n.* A purpose or m in conflict with another. **— to be at cross-purposes** To isunderstand or act counter to each other's purposes.
ss·ques·tion (krôs′kwes′chən, kros′-) *v.t.* To cross-amine. **—** *n.* A question asked in a cross-examination.
ss·re·fer (krôs′ri·fûr′, kros′-) *v.* **·ferred, ·fer·ring** *v.t.* **1.**) refer to another passage or part. **—** *v.i.* **2.** To make a oss-reference.
ss·ref·er·ence (krôs′ref′rəns, kros′-) *n.* A note or state-ent directing a reader from one part of a book, index, etc., another part.
ss·road (krôs′rōd′, kros′-) *n.* **1.** A road that intersects other. **2.** A road connecting one road to another.
ss·roads (krôs′rōdz′, kros′-) *n.pl.* (*construed as sing.*) **1.** ie place where roads meet: in rural areas, often a settle-ent. **2.** The meeting place of different cultures. **— at e crossroads** At any critical point or moment.
ss·ruff (krôs′ruf′, kros′-) *n.* In cards, a play in which ch of two partners alternately trumps the other's lead.
ss section **1.** A plane section of any object cut at right gles to its length. **2.** A sampling meant to be charac-ristic or typical of the whole: a *cross section* of opinion. **3.** cutting through anything at right angles.
ss-stitch (krôs′stich′, kros′-) *n.* **1.** A double stitch in e form of an *x*. **2.** Needlework made with this stitch. **—** . To make or mark with a cross-stitch.
ss·tie (krôs′tī′, kros′-) *n.* *Chiefly U.S.* A beam or tie id crosswise under railroad tracks to support them.
ss·town (krôs′toun′, kros′-) *adj.* Going across a town city: a *cross-town* bus. **—** *adv.* Across a town or city.
ss·tree (krôs′trē′, kros′-) *n.* *Usu. pl. Naut.* Pieces of ood or metal set crosswise at the head of a mast to sustain e top or to extend the topgallant shrouds.
ss·walk (krôs′wôk′, kros′-) *n.* A lane marked off for use pedestrians in crossing a street.
ss·way (krôs′wā′, kros′-) *n.* A crossroad.
ss·wise (krôs′wīz′, kros′-) *adv.* **1.** Across. **2.** In the rm of a cross. **3.** Contrarily. Also **cross′ways′** (-wāz′).
ss·word puzzle (krôs′wûrd′, kros′-) A puzzle worked a pattern of white and black space, of which the white aces are to be filled with letters that form words to agree ith numbered definitions or similar clues.
tch (kroch) *n.* **1.** The fork or angle formed by two di-rging parts, as by the branches of a tree. **2.** The region of e human body where the legs separate from the pelvis. **3.** forked pole, support, etc. [? < AF *croche* crook]
tched (krocht) *adj.* Having a crotch; forked.
tch·et (kroch′it) *n.* **1.** A whimsical or perverse notion whim; an eccentricity. **2.** A small hook or hooklike in-rument. **3.** *Entomol.* A hooklike process. **4.** *Music hiefly Brit.* A quarter note. [< F *croche* hook]
tch·et·y (kroch′ə·tē) *adj.* **1.** Full of eccentric or stub-orn notions; perverse; contrary. **2.** Like a crotchet. **— otch′et·i·ness** *n.*
·ton (krōt′n) *n.* **1.** A tree or shrub of the spurge family, ten used medicinally. **2.** An ornamental tropical shrub. < NL < Gk. *krotōn* a tick]
o·ton bug (krōt′n) A small, light-colored cockroach. fter *Croton* Aqueduct; the first infestation in New York ity occurred after this aqueduct was opened in 1842]
uch (krouch) *v.i.* **1.** To stoop or bend low, as an animal ady to spring. **2.** To cringe; abase oneself; cower. **—** *v.t.* . To bend low. **—** *n.* A crouching or crouching position. < OF *crochir* to be bent]
up[1] (kro͞op) *n.* *Pathol.* **1.** A disease of the throat char-cterized by hoarse coughing, laryngeal spasm, and difficult eathing. **2.** Loosely, inflammation of the larynx. [Imit.]
up[2] (kro͞op) *n.* The rump of certain animals, esp. of a orse. Also **croupe.** [< OF *crope*]
u·pi·er (kro͞o′pē·ər, *Fr.* kro͞o·pyā′) *n.* One who collects ie stakes lost and pays out those won at a gaming table. < F, lit., one who rides on the croup]
up·y (kro͞o′pē) *adj.* **1.** Of or indicating croup. **2.** Hav-g croup. Also **croup′ous.** **— crou′pi·ness** *n.*
u·ton (kro͞o′ton, kro͞o·ton′; *Fr.* kro͞o·tôn′) *n.* A small iece of toasted bread used in soups. [< F]
w[1] (krō) *n.* **1.** An omnivorous, raucous bird having lossy black plumage. **2.** Loosely, the rook or raven. ◆ ollateral adjective: *corvine*. **3.** A crowbar. **— as the crow ies** In a straight line. **— to eat crow** *Informal* To recant statement; back down; humiliate oneself. [OE *crāwe*]
ow[2] (krō) *v.i.* **crowed** or (*for def. 1*) **crew, crowed, crow·g** **1.** To utter the shrill cry of a cock. **2.** To exult; boast. . To utter sounds expressive of delight, as an infant. **—** *n.* **1.** The cry of a cock. **2.** Any shrill, inarticulate sound re-sembling this, as an infant's cry of pleasure. [OE *crāwan*]
Crow (krō) *n.* **1.** A North American Indian of a Siouan tribe formerly inhabiting the region between the Platte and Yellowstone rivers. **2.** The language of this tribe.
crow·bar (krō′bär′) *n.* A straight iron or steel bar with a flattened point often set at an angle, used as a lever.
crowd (kroud) *n.* **1.** A large number of persons gathered closely together. **2.** The populace in general; mob. **3.** *Informal* A particular set of people; a clique. **—** *v.t.* **1.** To shove or push. **2.** To fill to overflowing. **3.** To cram to-gether; force into a confined space. **4.** *Informal* To put pres-sure on, esp. for payment. **—** *v.i.* **5.** To gather in large numbers. **6.** To force one's way. **7.** To shove or push. [OE *crūdan*] **— crowd′ed** *adj.* **— crowd′er** *n.*
crow·foot (krō′fo͝ot′) *n.* *pl.* **·foots** **1.** Any of a genus of plants that includes the buttercup, columbine, etc. **2.** A plant having leaves, etc., suggestive of a bird's foot.
crown (kroun) *n.* **1.** A circlet, often of precious metal set with jewels, worn on the head as a mark of sovereign power. **2.** A decorative covering for the head. **3.** Anything shaped like a crown. **4.** A coin stamped with a crown or a crowned head, esp. the English crown, worth five shillings. **5.** The top part of the head. **6.** The head itself. **7.** The upper part of a hat. **8.** The top or summit of something. **9.** The most perfect or complete state or type. **10.** A reward or prize for achievement. **11.** *Dent.* The part of a tooth that is covered with enamel or an artificial substitute for it. **12.** *Naut.* The lowest point of junction of the two arms of an anchor. **— the Crown** **1.** The sovereign ruler; monarch. **2.** The power or the empire of a monarch. **—** *v.t.* **1.** To place a crown or garland on the head of. **2.** To make a monarch of. **3.** To endow with honor or dignity. **4.** To form the crown, ornament, or top to. **5.** To finish or make complete. **6.** *Informal* To strike on the head. **7.** In check-ers, to make (a piece) into a king by placing another piece upon it. [< AF, OF < L *corona*] **— crown′er** *n.*
crown colony A colony of Great Britain in which the Crown retains control of legislation.
crown glass Hard optical glass of low refraction.
crown prince The male heir apparent to a throne.
crown princess **1.** The wife of a crown prince. **2.** The female heir apparent to a throne.
crow's-foot (krōz′fo͝ot′) *n.* *pl.* **-feet** One of the wrinkles diverging from the outer corner of the eye.
crow's-nest (krōz′nest′) *n.* **1.** *Naut.* An observation plat-form near the top of a ship's mast. **2.** Any similar platform.
cro·zier (krō′zhər) See CROSIER.
cru·ces (kro͞o′sēz) Alternative plural of CRUX.
cruci- *combining form* Cross. [< L *crux, crucis* cross]
cru·cial (kro͞o′shəl) *adj.* **1.** Of a critical or decisive nature. **2.** Involving difficulties; severe. [< MF < L *crux, crucis* cross, torture] **— cru′cial·ly** *adv.*
cru·ci·ble (kro͞o′sə·bəl) *n.* **1.** A heat-resistant vessel for melting metals or minerals. **2.** A severely trying test or experience. [< Med.L *crucibulum* earthen pot, lamp]
cru·ci·fix (kro͞o′sə·fiks) *n.* **1.** A cross bearing an effigy of Christ crucified. **2.** The cross as a Christian emblem. [< OF < L *cruci fixus* one hanged on a cross]
cru·ci·fix·ion (kro͞o′sə·fik′shən) *n.* **1.** The act of crucifying, or the state of being crucified. **2.** A painting, etc., that represents Christ's death on the cross. **— the Crucifixion** The execution of Jesus Christ on the cross.
cru·ci·form (kro͞o′sə·fôrm) *adj.* Cross-shaped.
cru·ci·fy (kro͞o′sə·fī) *v.t.* **·fied, ·fy·ing** **1.** To put to death by nailing or fastening the hands and feet to a cross. **2.** To torture; torment. [< OF < L *cruci figere* to fasten to a cross] **— cru′ci·fi′er** *n.*
crude (kro͞od) *adj.* **crud·er, crud·est** **1.** In an unrefined or unprepared state; raw: *crude* oil. **2.** Immature; unripe. **3.** Showing a lack of skill or knowledge. **4.** Roughly made; unfinished. **5.** Lacking tact, refinement, or taste. [< L *crudus* rough] **— crude′ly** *adv.* **— crude′ness** *n.*
cru·di·ty (kro͞o′də·tē) *n.* *pl.* **·ties** **1.** The state or quality of being crude. **2.** A crude act, remark, etc.
cru·el (kro͞o′əl) *adj.* **cru·el·er** or **·el·ler, cru·el·est** or **·el·lest** **1.** Indifferent to or enjoying the suffering of others. **2.** Causing or inflicting mental or physical suffering. [< OF < L *crudelis* severe] **— cru′el·ly** *adv.* **— cru′el·ness** *n.*
cru·el·ty (kro͞o′əl·tē) *n.* *pl.* **·ties** **1.** The quality or condi-tion of being cruel; mercilessness; inhumanity. **2.** That which causes suffering; an inhuman act; brutal treatment.
cru·et (kro͞o′it) *n.* A small glass bottle for vinegar, oil, etc. [< AF, dim. of OF *crue* pot]
cruise (kro͞oz) *v.* **cruised, cruis·ing** *v.i.* **1.** To sail about with no fixed destination, as for pleasure. **2.** To travel about at a moderate speed, as a police squad car. **3.** To move at the optimum speed for sustained travel: said of

aircraft, etc. —*v.t.* **4.** To cruise over. —*n.* A cruising trip, esp. a voyage at sea. [< Du. *kruisen* to cross, traverse]

cruis·er (kro͞o′zər) *n.* **1.** One who or that which cruises. **2.** A fast, maneuverable warship, having medium tonnage and armament. **3.** A small power vessel equipped with living facilities: also called *cabin cruiser.*

crul·ler (krul′ər) *n.* A small cake of sweetened dough, fried in deep fat. [< Du. < *krullen* to curl]

crumb (krum) *n.* **1.** A tiny fragment of bread, cake, or the like. **2.** A bit or scrap of anything: *crumbs* of information. **3.** The soft inner part of bread, as distinguished from the crust. **4.** *U.S. Slang* A contemptible person. —*v.t.* **1.** To break into small pieces; crumble. **2.** In cooking, to dress or cover with bread crumbs. [OE *cruma*]

crum·ble (krum′bəl) *v.* **·bled, ·bling** *v.t.* **1.** To cause to break into tiny parts. —*v.i.* **2.** To fall to small pieces; disintegrate. [ME < OE *cruma* crumb]

crum·bly (krum′blē) *adj.* **·bli·er, ·bli·est** Apt to crumble; friable. —**crum′bli·ness** *n.*

crumb·y (krum′ē) *adj.* **crumb·i·er, crumb·i·est** **1.** Full of crumbs. **2.** Soft, like the inner part of bread.

crum·my (krum′ē) *adj.* **crum·mi·er, crum·mi·est** *U.S. Slang* Inferior; cheap; shabby.

crum·pet (krum′pit) *n.* A thin, leavened batter cake baked on a gridiron, then usu. toasted. [< ME *crompen* to curl up]

crum·ple (krum′pəl) *v.* **·pled, ·pling** *v.t.* **1.** To press into wrinkles; rumple. —*v.i.* **2.** To become wrinkled; shrivel. **3.** *Informal* To collapse. —*n.* Anything crumpled; a wrinkle. [Freq. of obs. *crump*, var. of CRIMP]

crunch (krunch) *v.t.* & *v.i.* **1.** To chew with a crushing or crackling sound. **2.** To move, press, or advance with a crushing sound. —*n.* A crunching, or its sound. [Imit.]

crup·per (krup′ər) *n.* **1.** The strap that goes under a horse's tail. **2.** The rump of a horse. [< OF *crope* croup[2]]

cru·sade (kro͞o·sād′) *n.* **1.** *Usu. cap.* Any of the military expeditions undertaken by Christians to recover the Holy Land from the Moslems. **2.** Any expedition under papal sanction against heathens or heretics. **3.** Any vigorous concerted movement or cause, esp. a reform movement. —*v.i.* **·sad·ed, ·sad·ing** To engage in a crusade. [< Sp. < Med.L *cruciare* to mark with a cross] —**cru·sad′er** *n.*

cruse (kro͞oz, kro͞os) *n.* A small bottle, flask, or jug; cruet. [? < MDu. *cruyse* jar, pot]

crush (krush) *v.t.* **1.** To press or squeeze out of shape; mash. **2.** To smash or grind into fine particles. **3.** To obtain or extract by pressure. **4.** To crowd. **5.** To subdue; conquer. —*v.i.* **6.** To become broken or misshapen by pressure. **7.** To move ahead by crushing or pressing. —*n.* **1.** The act of crushing. **2.** The state of being crushed. **3.** A crowd or throng; jam. **4.** A substance obtained by crushing: orange *crush.* **5.** *Informal* An infatuation. [< OF < MHG *krosen* to crush] —**crush′a·ble** *adj.* —**crush′er** *n.*

crust (krust) *n.* **1.** The hard outer part of bread. **2.** A piece of bread consisting mostly of crust (def. 1); also, any dry, hard piece of bread. **3.** The pastry shell of a pie, tart, etc. **4.** Any hard, crisp surface, as of snow. **5.** *Slang* Insolence; impertinence. **6.** *Geol.* The exterior shell of the earth. —*v.t.* & *v.i.* **1.** To cover with or acquire a crust. **2.** To form into a crust. [< OF < L *crusta*] —**crus′tal** *adj.*

crus·ta·cean (krus·tā′shən) *n.* One of a class of arthropods having crustlike shells, and generally aquatic, including lobsters, crabs, shrimps, etc. —*adj.* Of or pertaining to this class of arthropods. [< NL *Crustacea* < L *crusta* crust] —**crus·ta′ceous** *adj.*

crust·y (krus′tē) *adj.* **crust·i·er, crust·i·est** **1.** Like of having a crust. **2.** Harshly curt in manner or speech; surly. —**crust′i·ly** *adv.* —**crust′i·ness** *n.*

crutch (kruch) *n.* **1.** A staff used by the lame as a support in walking, esp. one having a crosspiece to fit under the armpit and a grip for the hand. **2.** Anything that gives support. **3.** Any of various devices resembling a crutch. —*v.t.* To prop up or support, as on crutches. [OE *crycc*]

crux (kruks) *n.* *pl.* **crux·es** or **cru·ces** (kro͞o′sēz) **1.** A pivotal, fundamental, or vital point. **2.** A cross. **3.** A tormenting or baffling problem. [< L, cross]

Crux (kruks) *n.* A constellation, the Southern Cross, containing the bright star Acrux.

cry (krī) *v.* **cried, cry·ing** *v.i.* **1.** To utter sobbing sounds of grief, pain, fear, etc., usu. accompanied by tears. **2.** To call out or appeal loudly; shout: often with *out.* **3.** To make characteristic calls: said of animals. —*v.t.* **4.** To utter loudly or shout out; exclaim. **5.** To affect (oneself) by weeping: to *cry* oneself to sleep. **6.** To beg for. —**to cry down** **1.** To belittle; disparage. **2.** To silence or put down by cries. —**to cry up** To praise highly. —*n.* *pl.* **cries** **1.** A loud or emotional utterance; shout; call. **2.** A fit of weeping. **3.** An appeal; entreaty. **4.** Advertisement by outcry. **5.** General report or rumor. **6.** A rallying call; battle cry. **7.** A catchword. **8.** A demand; clamor. **9.** The characteristic call of a bird or animal. **10.** A pack of hounds. —**a far cry** **1.** A long distance away. **2.** Something very unlike. —**in full cry** In full pursuit, as a p[...] of hounds. [< OF < L *quiritare* to call out]

cry·ba·by (krī′bā′bē) *n.* *pl.* **·bies** A person, esp. a ch[...] given to crying or complaining.

cry·ing (krī′ing) *adj.* **1.** That cries: a *crying* child. **2.** C[...]ing for immediate action or remedy: a *crying* shame.

cryo- *combining form* Cold; frost. [< Gk. *kryos* frost]

cry·o·gen·ics (krī′ə·jen′iks) *n.pl.* (*construed as sing.*) [...] branch of physics dealing with very low temperatures.

cry·o·lite (krī′ə·līt) *n.* A fluoride of sodium and aluminu[...] used in the production of aluminum, soda, and glass.

crypt (kript) *n.* A chamber or vault, esp. one beneat[...] church, used as a place of burial. [< L < Gk. *kryp*[...] hidden]

cryp·ta·nal·y·sis (krip′tə·nal′ə·sis) *n.* *pl.* **·ses** (-sēz) [...] scientific study of cryptograms, ciphers, codes, etc., [...] which the key is not known. —**cryp·tan·a·lyst** (krip·tan[...]list) *n.* —**cryp′tan·a·lyt′ic** *adj.*

cryp·tic (krip′tik) *adj.* **1.** Secret or hidden; occult. [...] Puzzling; mystifying. Also **cryp′ti·cal.** [< LL < [...] *kryptos* hidden]

crypto- *combining form* Hidden; secret. Also, before vow[...] **crypt-.** [< Gk. *kryptos* hidden]

cryp·to·gam (krip′tə·gam) *n.* *Bot.* Any of a former di[...]sion of plants that have no seeds or flowers, but propag[...] by spores, as algae, fungi, ferns, and mosses. [< F < [...] *kryptos* hidden + *gamos* marriage] —**cryp′to·gam**[...] **cryp·tog·a·mous** (krip·tog′ə·məs) *adj.*

cryp·to·gram (krip′tə·gram) *n.* A message written in c[...] or cipher. —**cryp′to·gram′mic** *adj.*

cryp·tog·ra·phy (krip·tog′rə·fē) *n.* **1.** The art or process[...] writing in or reconverting cipher. **2.** Any system of writ[...] in secret characters. —**cryp·tog′ra·pher, cryp·tog′ra·ph**[...] *n.* —**cryp·to·graph·ic** (krip′tə·graf′ik) *adj.*

crys·tal (kris′təl) *n.* **1.** Colorless transparent quartz, [...] rock crystal. **2.** *Physics* A homogeneous solid body, [...]hibiting a symmetrical structure, with geometrically [...]ranged planes and faces that assume any of various patte[...] associated with peculiarities of atomic structure. **3.** Fl[...] glass, or any fine clear glass; also, articles made of such gla[...] as bowls, etc. **4.** Anything transparent and colorless. [...] A glass or plastic covering over the face of a watch. **6.** A crystal detector. —*adj.* **1.** Composed of crystal. **2.** Like crystal; extremely clear; limpid. [< OF < L < Gk. *krystallos* ice, crystal]

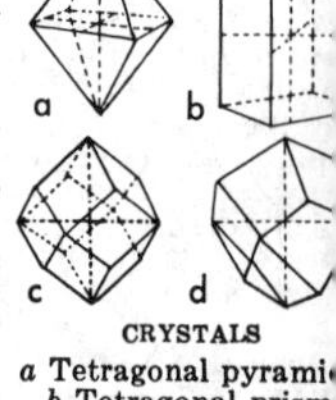

CRYSTALS
a Tetragonal pyrami[...]
b Tetragonal prism
c Dodecahedron.
d Deltahedron.

crystal ball A ball of crystal or glass used in crystal gazing.

crystal detector *Telecom.* A device consisting of metal electrodes in contact with suitable crystal materials, used to rectify incoming radio signals.

crystal gazing The act of looking into a crystal ball in order to induce a vision of distant objects or future events; also, the alleged ability to do this. —**crys·tal-gaz·er** (kris′təl·gā′zər) *n.*

crys·tal·line (kris′tə·lin, -lēn) *adj.* **1.** Of, pertaining [...] like, or made of crystal or crystals. **2.** Transparent; cle[...]

crys·tal·lize (kris′tə·līz) *v.* **·lized, ·liz·ing** *v.t.* **1.** To ca[...] to form crystals or become crystalline. **2.** To bring to de[...]nite and permanent form. **3.** To coat with sugar. —[...] **4.** To assume the form of crystals. **5.** To assume defin[...] and permanent form. Also **crys′ta·lize.** —**crys′tal·liz′a·b**[...] *adj.* —**crys′tal·li·za′tion** *n.*

crystallo- *combining form* Crystal. Also, before vowe[...] **crystall-.** [< Gk. *krystallos* crystal]

crys·tal·log·ra·phy (kris′tə·log′rə·fē) *n.* The science a[...] study of crystals. —**crys′tal·log′ra·pher** *n.*

crys·tal·loid (kris′tə·loid) *adj.* Like or having the natu[...] of a crystal or a crystalloid. Also **crys′tal·loi′dal.** —[...] *Chem.* One of a class of substances, usu. crystallizable, who[...] solutions pass easily through membranes. [< Gk. *kryst*[...] *loeidēs* like crystal]

crystal pickup A pickup that utilizes a piezoelectric cryst[...] to transform mechanical motion into sound, etc., often us[...] in electric record players.

crystal set A radio receiving set operating with a cryst[...] detector but without electron tubes.

cub (kub) *n.* **1.** The young of the bear, fox, wolf, and ce[...]tain other carnivores; a whelp. **2.** An awkward youth. [...] A beginner or learner. [Origin uncertain]

cub·by·hole (kub′ē·hōl′) *n.* A small, enclosed space. Al[...] **cub′by.** [< *cubby*, dim. of dial. E *cub* shed + HOLE]

cube (kyo͞ob) *n.* **1.** A solid bounded by six equal squar[...] and having all its angles right angles. **2.** *Math.* The thi[...] power of a quantity: the *cube* of 3 is 27, or $3^3 = 3 \times 3 \times 3 = 27$. —*v.t.* **cubed, cub·ing** **1.** To raise (a number [...] quantity) to the third power. **2.** To find the cubic capaci[...]

. 3. To form or cut into cubes or cubelike shapes; dice: to be potatoes. [< OF < L < Gk. *kybos* cube]
beb (kyōō′beb) *n.* A berry of an East Indian shrub of e pepper family, often smoked in the form of cigarettes treat catarrh. [< OF < Arabic *kabābah*]
be root The number that, taken three times as a factor, oduces a number called its cube: 4 is the *cube root* of 64.
bic (kyōō′bik) *adj.* **1.** Shaped like a cube. **2.** Having ree dimensions, or pertaining to three-dimensional content: a *cubic* foot. **3.** *Math.* Of the third power or degree.
bi·cal (kyōō′bi·kəl) *adj.* Shaped like a cube. —**cu′bi·al·ly** *adv.* —**cu′bi·cal·ness** *n.*
bi·cle (kyōō′bi·kəl) *n.* **1.** A bedroom, esp. a partially closed section in a dormitory. **2.** Any small partitioned ea, as a carrell. [< L *cubiculum* bedroom]
bic measure A unit or system of units for measuring olume, or the amount of space occupied in three dimenons. See table front of book.
bism (kyōō′biz·əm) *n.* A movement in modern art conrned with the abstract and geometric interpretation of rm, rather than with a realistic representation of nature. —**cu′bist** *adj.* & *n.* —**cu·bis′tic** *adj.*
bit (kyōō′bit) *n.* An ancient measure of length, usu. out 18 to 20 inches. [< L *cubitum* elbow]
boid (kyōō′boid) *adj.* Shaped like a cube. Also **cu·boi′·al.** —*n. Geom.* A rectangular parallelepiped.
b reporter A young, inexperienced newspaper reporter.
b scout A member of a subdivision of the Boy Scouts, mprising boys eight to ten years of age.
ck·old (kuk′əld) *n.* The husband of an unfaithful wife. —*v.t.* To make a cuckold of. [< OF *cucu* cuckoo]
ck·old·ry (kuk′əl·drē) *n.* The cuckolding of a husband.
ck·oo (kōōk′ōō; *for adj., also* kōō′kōō) *n.* **1.** A bird, as e common European cuckoo, that deposits its eggs in the ests of other birds. **2.** A simpleton; fool. **3.** A cuckoo's y. —*v.* **·ooed, ·oo·ing** *v.t.* **1.** To repeat without cessation. —*v.i.* **2.** To utter or imitate the cry of the cuckoo. —*adj. lang* Crazy; silly. [< OF *cucu, coucou*; imit.]
ckoo clock A clock in which a mechanical cuckoo announces the hours.
ckoo spit **1.** A frothy secretion exuded upon plants by rtain insect larvae. **2.** An insect that secretes such froth.
·cul·late (kyōō′kə·lāt, kyōō·kul′āt) *adj. Bot.* Shaped like hood as certain leaves. [< LL < L *cucullus* hood]
·cum·ber (kyōō′kum·bər) *n.* **1.** The cylindrical, hardnded fruit of a plant of the gourd family, cultivated as a egetable. **2.** The plant. [< OF < L *cucumis, -eris*]
d (kud) *n.* Food forced up into the mouth from the first omach of a ruminant and chewed over again. [OE *cwidu*]
d·dle (kud′l) *v.* **·dled, ·dling** *v.t.* **1.** To caress fondly within close embrace; fondle. —*v.i.* **2.** To lie close; nestle together. —*n.* An embrace or caress; a hug. [? < dial. E *outh* snug] —**cud′dle·some** (səm) *adj.* —**cud′dly** *adj.*
d·dy (kud′ē) *n. pl.* **·dies** *Naut.* A small cabin or galley.
dg·el (kuj′əl) *n.* A short, thick club. —**to take up the udgels** To enter into a contest or controversy. —*v.t.* **cudg·led** or **·elled, cudg·el·ing** or **·el·ling** To beat with a cudgel. —**to cudgel one's brains** To think hard; puzzle. [OE *cycel*] —**cudg′el·er** or **cudg′el·ler** *n.*
e[1] (kyōō) *n.* **1.** A long, tapering rod, used to strike the cue all. **2.** A queue of hair. **3.** A queue of persons. —*v.t.* **ued, cu·ing** **1.** To braid, or tie into a cue. **2.** In billiards, tc., to hit with a cue. [< F *queue* tail]
e[2] (kyōō) *n* **1.** In plays, movies, etc., any action or sound hat signals the start of another action, speech, etc. **2.** Anyhing that serves as a signal to begin. **3.** A hint or suggesion. **4.** State of mind; mood. —*v.t.* **cued, cu·ing** To call a ue to (an actor); prompt. [Earlier *Q, qu*, supposedly an bbreviation of L *quando* when]
e ball The ball struck by the cue in billiards or pool.
ff[1] (kuf) *n.* **1.** A band or fold at the lower end of a sleeve. **2.** *U.S.* The turned-up fold on the bottom of a trouser leg. **3.** A detachable band of fabric worn about the wrist. **4.** A andcuff. —**off the cuff** *U.S. Slang* Spontaneously. —**on he cuff** *U.S. Slang* On credit. [ME *cuffe, coffe*]
ff[2] (kuf) *v.t.* **1.** To strike, as with the open hand; buffet. —*v.i.* **2.** To scuffle or fight; box. —*n.* A blow, esp. with he open hand. [? < Scand.]
ff links Linked buttons or the like, used to fasten shirt cuffs.
i bo·no (kwē′ bō′nō, kī′) *Latin* For whose benefit? Also, naccurately, for what purpose?
i·rass (kwi·ras′) *n.* A piece of armor consisting of a breastplate and backplate; also, the breastplate alone. —*v.t.* To equip with a cuirass. [< MF, ult. < L < *corium* eather]
ui·ras·sier (kwi′rə·sir′) *n.* A mounted soldier wearing a cuirass.
cui·sine (kwi·zēn′) *n.* **1.** The style or quality of cooking. **2.** The food prepared. [< F < L < *coquere* to cook]
cuisse (kwis) *n.* A piece of plate armor for the thigh. Also **cuish** (kwish). [< OF < *cuisse* thigh < L *coxa* hip]
cul-de-sac (kul′də·sak′, kōōl′-; *Fr.* kü′də·sȧk′) *n. pl.* **cul-de-sacs,** *Fr.* **culs-de-sac** (kü′-) A passage open only at one end; blind alley; trap. [< F, bottom of the bag]
-cule *suffix of nouns* Small; little; *animalcule.* [< F < L *-culus*, dim. suffix]
cu·li·nar·y (kyōō′lə·ner′ē, kul′-) *adj.* Of or pertaining to cookery or the kitchen. [< L < *culina* kitchen]
cull (kul) *v.t.* **1.** To pick or sort out; select. **2.** To gather. **3.** To pick over and divide as to quality. —*n.* Something picked or sorted out, esp. something rejected as inferior. [< OF < L *colligere* to collect] —**cull′er** *n.*
culm[1] (kulm) *n. Bot.* The jointed, usu. hollow, stem or straw of grasses. —*v.i.* To form a culm. [< L *culmus* stalk] —**cul·mif·er·ous** (kul·mif′ər·əs) *adj.*
culm[2] (kulm) *n.* **1.** Coal refuse or dust. **2.** An inferior anthracite coal. [Var. of dial. *coom* soot]
cul·mi·nate (kul′min·āt) *v.i.* **·nat·ed, ·nat·ing** **1.** To reach the highest point or degree; come to a final result: with *in.* **2.** *Astron.* To reach the meridian. [< LL < L *culmen*, highest point] —**cul′mi·nant** *adj.*
cul·mi·na·tion (kul′mə·nā′shən) *n.* **1.** The act of culminating. **2.** The highest point, condition, or degree.
cu·lottes (kyōō·lots′, kōō-; *Fr.* kü·lôt′) *n.pl.* A woman's trouserlike garment cut to resemble a skirt. [< F]
cul·pa·ble (kul′pə·bəl) *adj.* Deserving of blame or censure. [< OF < L < *culpa* fault] —**cul′pa·bil′i·ty, cul′pa·ble·ness** *n.* —**cul′pa·bly** *adv.*
cul·prit (kul′prit) *n.* **1.** One guilty of some offense or crime. **2.** One charged with or arraigned for a crime. [< AF *cul prit*, short for *culpable* guilty + *prit* ready for trial]
cult (kult) *n.* **1.** A system of religious rites and observances. **2.** Zealous devotion to a person, ideal, or thing. **3.** The object of this devotion. **4.** The followers of a cult. [< F < L < *colere* to cultivate, worship]
cul·ti·va·ble (kul′tə·və·bəl) *adj.* Capable of cultivation. Also **cul′ti·vat′a·ble** (-vā′tə·bəl). —**cul′ti·va·bil′i·ty** *n.*
cul·ti·vate (kul′tə·vāt) *v.t.* **·vat·ed, ·vat·ing** **1.** To make fit for raising crops, as by plowing, fertilizing, etc.; till. **2.** To care for (plants, etc.) so as to promote growth and abundance. **3.** To raise from seeds, bulbs, etc., for later planting. **4.** To produce or improve (plants, etc.) by selective breeding or other techniques. **5.** To improve or develop by study, or training; refine: to *cultivate* one's mind. **6.** To give one's attention to in order to acquire: to *cultivate* a habit, good manners, etc. **7.** To promote the development or advancement of. **8.** To court the friendship of. [< Med.L < L *cultus*, pp. of *colere* to care for, cherish] —**cul′ti·vat·ed** *adj.*
cul·ti·va·tion (kul′tə·vā′shən) *n.* **1.** The act of cultivating the ground, plants, etc. **2.** The improvement or development of anything through study and effort. **3.** Culture; refinement. —**Syn.** See REFINEMENT.
cul·ti·va·tor (kul′tə·vā′tər) *n.* **1.** One who cultivates. **2.** *Agric.* A machine for cultivating, commonly having several blades that loosen the ground and destroy weeds
cul·tur·al (kul′chər·əl) *adj.* **1.** Of, pertaining to, or developing culture: *cultural* studies. **2.** Produced by breeding, as certain varieties of fruits or plants. —**cul′tur·al·ly** *adv.*
cul·ture (kul′chər) *n.* **1.** The cultivation of plants or animals, esp. to improve the breed. **2.** The development, and refinement of mind, morals, or taste. **3.** The condition thus produced; refinement. **4.** A specific stage in the development of a civilization. **5.** Cultivation of the soil. **6.** *Anthropol.* The sum total of the attainments and learned behavior patterns of any specific period, race, or people. **7.** *Biol.* **a** The development of microorganisms in artificial media. **b** The organisms so developed. —**Syn.** See REFINEMENT. —*v.t.* **·tured, ·tur·ing** **1.** To cultivate (plants or animals). **2.** *Biol.* **a** To develop or grow (microorganisms) in an artificial medium. **b** To inoculate with a prepared culture. [< F < L < *colere* to care for] —**cul′tur·ist** *n.*
cul·tured (kul′chərd) *adj.* **1.** Possessing or manifesting culture. **2.** Created or grown by cultivation.
cul·tus (kul′təs) *n. pl.* **·tuses** or **·ti** (-tī) A cult.
cul·ver·in (kul′vər·in) *n.* **1.** A long cannon used in the 16th and 17th centuries. **2.** An early form of musket. [< F < *couleuvre* serpent]
cul·vert (kul′vərt) *n.* An artificial, covered channel for water, as under a road. [Origin uncertain]
cum·ber (kum′bər) *v.t.* **1.** To hinder; obstruct; hamper. **2.** To weigh down; burden. —*n.* A hindrance or encumbrance. [Cf. OF *encombrer* to hinder]
cum·ber·some (kum′bər·səm) *adj.* **1.** Unwieldy; clumsy. **2.** Vexatious; burdensome. —**cum′ber·some·ly** *adv.* —**cum′ber·some·ness** *n.*

cum·brance (kum′brəns) *n.* An encumbrance.
cum·brous (kum′brəs) *adj.* Cumbersome. —**cum′brous·ly** *adv.* —**cum′brous·ness** *n.*
cum·in (kum′in) *n.* **1.** An annual of the parsley family. **2.** Its seeds, used as a condiment. Also **cum′min.** [OE < L < Gk. *kyminon* < Semitic]
cum lau·de (kum lô′dē, ko͝om lou′de) *Latin* With praise: used on diplomas to denote the special merit of the recipient's work. —**magna cum laude** With high praise. —**summa cum laude** With highest praise.
cum·mer·bund (kum′ər·bund) *n.* A broad sash worn as a waistband. [< Persian < *kamar* loin + *band* band]
cu·mu·late (kyo͞om′yə·lāt; *for adj., also* kyo͞om′yə·lit) *v.t. & v.i.* **·lat·ed, ·lat·ing** To collect into a heap; accumulate. —*adj.* Massed; accumulated. [< L < *cumulus* a heap] —**cu·mu·la′tion** *n.*
cu·mu·la·tive (kyo͞om′yə·lā′tiv, -lə·tiv) *adj.* **1.** Gathering volume, strength, or value. **2.** Gained by accumulation: *cumulative* knowledge. **3.** Increasing or accruing, as unpaid interest or dividends. —**cu′mu·la′tive·ly** *adv.*
cu·mu·lo·cir·rus (kyo͞om′yə·lō·sir′əs) *n. Meteorol.* Altocumulus.
cu·mu·lo·nim·bus (kyo͞om′yə·lō·nim′bəs) *n. Meteorol.* A massive cloud formation (Symbol Cb) in the shape of mountains, and producing thunder and showers.
cu·mu·lo·stra·tus (kyo͞om′yə·lō·strā′təs) *n. Meteorol.* Stratocumulus.
cu·mu·lus (kyo͞om′yə·ləs) *n. pl.* **·li** (-lī) **1.** A mass; pile. **2.** *Meteorol.* A dense, usu. white cloud formation (Symbol Cu) with dome-shaped upper surfaces and horizontal bases, seen in fair weather. [< L] —**cu′mu·lous** *adj.*
cu·ne·ate (kyo͞o′nē·it, -āt) *adj.* Wedge-shaped: said esp. of leaves. Also **cu′ne·at′ed, cu·ne·at·ic** (kyo͞o′nē·at′ik). [< L < *cuneus* wedge] —**cu′ne·ate·ly** *adv.*
cu·ne·i·form (kyo͞o·nē′ə·fôrm, kyo͞o′nē·ə·fôrm′) *adj.* **1.** Wedge-shaped, as the characters in some ancient Sumerian, Assyrian, Babylonian, and Persian inscriptions. **2.** *Anat.* Designating a wedge-shaped bone in the wrist, or one of three in the human foot. —*n.* Cuneiform writing. Also **cu·ni·form** (kyo͞o′nə·fôrm). [< L *cuneus* wedge + -FORM]

CUNEIFORM
a Earth. *b* Woman. *c* Man. *d* Food.

cun·ning (kun′ing) *n.* **1.** Skill in deception; craftiness. **2.** Knowledge combined with manual skill; dexterity. —*adj.* **1.** Crafty or shrewd. **2.** Executed with skill; ingenious. **3.** *U.S.* Innocently amusing; cute. [OE < *cunnan* to know, be able] —**cun′ning·ly** *adv.* —**cun′ning·ness** *n.*
cup (kup) *n.* **1.** A small, open vessel, often with a handle, used chiefly for drinking from. **2.** The contents of a cup; a cupful: as a measure, equal to 8 ounces or half a pint. **3.** The bowl of a drinking vessel that has a stem and base. **4.** In the Eucharist, the chalice, or its contents. **5.** One's lot in life: the bitter *cup* of exile. **6.** Intoxicating drink, or the habit of drinking. **7.** An alcoholic beverage, usu. chilled and served with herbs, fruits, etc. **8.** A cup-shaped object or part, as of a flower. **9.** A cup-shaped vessel given as a prize, esp. in sports. **10.** In golf, a hole, or the metal receptacle within it. —**in one's cups** Drunk. —*v.t.* **cupped, cup·ping** **1.** To shape like a cup. **2.** To place in or as in a cup. **3.** *Med.* To perform cupping on. [OE < L *cupa* tub]
cup·bear·er (kup′bâr′ər) *n.* One who serves drinks.
cup·board (kub′ərd) *n.* **1.** A closet or cabinet with shelves, as for dishes. **2.** Any small cabinet or closet.
cup·cake (kup′kāk′) *n.* A small individual cake.
cup·ful (kup′fo͝ol′) *n. pl.* **·fuls** The quantity held by a cup.
Cu·pid (kyo͞o′pid) In Roman mythology, the god of love: identified with the Greek *Eros.* —*n.* **1.** A representation of the god of love as a naked, winged boy with a bow and arrow. **2.** One who helps to arrange meetings between lovers; chiefly in the phrase **to play Cupid.** [< L < *cupido* desire]
cu·pid·i·ty (kyo͞o·pid′ə·tē) *n.* Eager desire for possession, esp. of wealth; avarice; greed. [< L *cupiditas, -tatis*]
cup of tea *Informal* A favorite object, activity, etc.
cu·po·la (kyo͞o′pə·lə) *n.* **1.** *Archit.* **a** A rounded roof; dome. **b** A small, vaulted structure, usu. hemispherical, rising above a roof. **2.** Any of various dome-shaped structures, organs, etc. —*v.t.* **·laed, ·la·ing** To provide with or shape like a cupola. [< Ital. < LL < L *cupa* tub]
cup·ping (kup′ing) *n. Med.* The process of drawing blood to the surface of the skin by creating a vacuum at that point.
cupping glass *Med.* A cup used for cupping.
cu·pre·ous (kyo͞o′prē·əs) *adj.* Of, pertaining to, containing, or resembling copper. [< LL < L *cuprum* copper]
cu·pric (kyo͞o′prik) *adj. Chem.* Of or pertaining to copper, esp. in its highest valence: *cupric* oxide, CuO.
cupro- *combining form* Copper. Also, before vowels, **cupri-.**
cu·prous (kyo͞o′prəs) *adj. Chem.* Of or pertaining to copper, esp. in its lowest valence: *cuprous* oxide, Cu_2O.
cu·prum (kyo͞o′prəm) *n.* Copper. [< L]
cur (kûr) *n.* **1.** A mongrel dog. **2.** A mean or despica person. [Short for earlier *kur-dogge*]
cur·a·ble (kyo͝or′ə·bəl) *adj.* Capable of being cured. **cur′a·bil′i·ty, cur′a·ble·ness** *n.* —**cur′a·bly** *adv.*
cu·ra·çao (kyo͝or′ə·sō′, ko͞o′rä·sou′) *n.* A liqueur made distilling spirits with the peel of the sour orange. Also **c ra·çoa′** (-sō′). [after *Curaçao*]
cu·ra·cy (kyo͝or′ə·sē) *n. pl.* **·cies** The position, duties, term of office of a curate.
cu·ra·re (kyo͞o·rä′rē) *n.* **1.** A blackish, resinous extract certain South American trees, that, when introduced i the blood stream, paralyzes the motor nerves; used as arrow poison and in general anesthesia. **2.** A plant fr which this is extracted. Also called *oorali, urare, urari, w rali*: also **cu·ra·ra** (kyo͞o·rä′rə), **cu·ra′ri.** [< Sp. < Tup
cu·rate (kyo͝or′it) *n.* A clergyman assisting a parish pri rector, or vicar. [< Med.L < L *cura* care, cure]
cur·a·tive (kyo͝or′ə·tiv) *adj.* Having the power to cure. *n.* A remedy. —**cur′a·tive·ly** *adv.* —**cur′a·tive·ness** *n*
cu·ra·tor (kyo͞o·rā′tər) *n.* A person in charge of a muse or similar institution. [< L < *cura* care] —**cu·ra·to·ri** (kyo͝or′ə·tôr′ē·əl, -tō′rē-) *adj.* —**cu·ra′tor·ship** *n.*
curb (kûrb) *n.* **1.** Anything that restrains or controls *curb* on inflation. **2.** A border of concrete or stone along edge of a street: also, *Brit.*, *kerb.* **3.** A chain or strap br ing a bit against the lower jaw of a horse, used to check horse. **4.** An enclosing or confining framework, margin, e —*v.t.* **1.** To control, as with reins and curb. **2.** To prov with a curb. **3.** To lead (a dog) off a curb for defecation the street. [< F *courbe*, orig. adj., curved < L *curvus*]
curb·ing (kûr′bing) *n.* Material forming a curb.
curb roof *Archit.* A roof consisting of two slopes of vary pitch; a mansard or gambrel roof.
curb·stone (kûrb′stōn′) *n.* A stone, row of stones, etc., the outer edge of a sidewalk. Also, *Brit.*, *kerbstone.*
cur·cu·li·o (kûr·kyo͞o′lē·ō) *n. pl.* **·os** Any of various lo snouted weevils, injurious to fruits and nuts. [< L, wee
curd (kûrd) *n. Often pl.* The coagulated portion of milk, which cheese is made, as distinct from the watery whey. *v.t. & v.i.* To form into or become curd. [Metathetic var. CRUD] —**curd′y** *adj.*
cur·dle (kûr′dəl) *v.t. & v.i.* **·dled, ·dling** To change or tu to curd; coagulate; congeal; thicken. [Freq. of CURD]
cure (kyo͝or) *n.* **1.** A restoration to a sound or healthy c dition. **2.** That which restores health or removes an evil. A special method or course of remedial or medicinal tre ment. **4.** Spiritual care, esp. of a clergyman for his cong gation: also **cure of souls.** **5.** A process of preserving food other products. —*v.* **cured, cur·ing** *v.t.* **1.** To restore t healthy or sound condition. **2.** To remedy or eradicate: *cure* a bad habit. **3.** To preserve, as by salting, smoking, aging. —*v.i.* **4.** To bring about recovery. **5.** To be become cured by a preserving process. [< OF < L *cu* care] —**cure′less** *adj.* —**cur′er** *n.*
cu·ré (kyo͞o·rā′) *n.* A parish priest, esp. in France. [<
cure-all (kyo͝or′ôl′) *n.* A cure for all ills; panacea.
cur·few (kûr′fyo͞o) *n.* **1.** A police or military regulation quiring persons to keep off the streets after a designated ho also, a similar order applying to children. **2.** A medie regulation requiring fires to be put out at the tolling of a b **3.** The bell itself. **4.** The hour of ringing such a bell, or t ringing itself. [< OF *couvrir* to cover + *feu* fire]
cu·ri·a (kyo͝or′ē·ə) *n. pl.* **cu·ri·ae** (kyo͝or′ē·ē) **1.** A court justice. **2.** *Often cap.* The collective body of officials of t papal government: also **Cu′ri·a Ro·ma·na** (rō·mä′nə). [L] —**cu′ri·al** *adj.*
cu·rie (kyo͝or′ē, kyo͞o·rē′) *n. Physics* The unit of radi activity, equal to 3.70×10^{10} nuclear disintegrations p second. [after Marie *Curie*]
cu·ri·o (kyo͝or′ē·ō) *n. pl.* **·os** A rare or curious art obje piece of bric-a-brac, etc. [Short for CURIOSITY]
cu·ri·os·i·ty (kyo͝or′ē·os′ə·tē) *n. pl.* **·ties** **1.** Eager desi for knowledge of something, esp. of something novel or u usual. **2.** Interest in the private affairs of others. **3.** Th which excites interest by its strangeness or rarity.
cu·ri·ous (kyo͝or′ē·əs) *adj.* **1.** Eager for information knowledge. **2.** Given to prying or meddling. **3.** Attracti interest because of novelty or unusualness; odd; strange. Executed with ingenuity or skill. [< OF < L *curiosus cura* care] —**cu′ri·ous·ly** *adv.* —**cu′ri·ous·ness** *n.*
cu·ri·um (kyo͝or′ē·əm) *n.* An unstable radioactive eleme (symbol Cm), produced originally by the bombardment uranium and plutonium with alpha particles. See ELEMEN [after Marie and Pierre *Curie*]
curl (kûrl) *v.t.* **1.** To twist into ringlets or curves, as t hair. **2.** To form into a curved or spiral shape. —*v.i.* To form ringlets, as the hair. **4.** To become curved; take spiral shape. **5.** To play at the game of curling. —**to cu up** **1.** To assume a position with the back curved and t legs drawn close to the body. **2.** To form into a curved spiral shape. —*n.* **1.** Something coiled or spiral, as a rin

; of hair. **2.** A curled or circular shape or mark. **3.** The t of curling, or the state of being curled. [Metathetic var. ME *crollid, crulled* curled < *crull* curly < MLG]
·l·er (kûr′lər) *n.* **1.** One who or that which curls. **2.** ıe who plays the game of curling.
·lew (kûr′lo͞o) *n.* A shore bird with a long bill and long gs. [< OF *corlieu, courlieus*; orig. imit.]
·l·i·cue (kûr′li·kyo͞o) *n.* Any fancy curl or twist, as a urish with a pen. Also **curl′y·cue.**
·l·ing (kûr′ling) *n.* A game played on ice in which the op-sing players slide heavy, smooth, circular stones (**curling ones**) toward a goal or tee at either end.
·ling iron An implement of metal, used when heated for rling or waving the hair. Also **curling irons.**
·l·y (kûr′lē) *adj.* **1.** Having curls. **2.** Tending to curl. Containing curllike marks: *curly* maple. **— curl′i·ness** *n.*
·mudg·eon (kər·muj′ən) *n.* A gruff or irritable person, o. an elderly man. [Origin unknown]
·rant (kûr′ənt) *n.* **1.** A small, round, acid berry, used making jelly. **2.** The bush producing this berry. **3.** A ıall seedless raisin of the Levant. [Back formation < F (*raisins de*) *Corauntz* (raisins from) Corinth]
·ren·cy (kûr′ən·sē) *n.* *pl.* **·cies 1.** The current medium exchange; money. **2.** General acceptance or circulation. The time during which something is current.
·rent (kûr′ənt) *adj.* **1.** Belonging to the immediate pres-t: the *current* year. **2.** Passing from person to person; culating, as money or news. **3.** Generally accepted; prev-ent. **—** *n.* **1.** A continuous onward movement, as of ater. **2.** The part of any body of water or air that has a ore or less steady flow in a definite direction: an ocean *cur-nt.* **3.** Any perceptible course or trend. **4.** *Electr.* **a** A ovement or flow of electricity passing through a conductor. The rate at which it flows. **— alternating current** *Electr.* current that periodically reverses its direction of flow, each mplete cycle having the same value. Abbr. *AC, a.c., A.C.* **direct current** *Electr.* A current flowing in one direction. bbr. *DC, d.c., D.C.* [< OF < L *currere* to run] **— cur′-nt·ly** *adv.* **— cur′rent·ness** *n.*
·ric·u·lum (kə·rik′yə·ləm) *n.* *pl.* **·lums** or **·la** (-lə) **1.** l the courses of study offered at a university or school. **2.** regular or particular course of study. [< L, a race < *cur-re* to run] **— cur·ric′u·lar** *adj.*
·ry¹ (kûr′ē) *v.t.* **·ried, ·ry·ing 1.** To rub down and clean ith a currycomb. **2.** To dress (tanned hides) by soaking, ıoothing, etc. **— to curry favor** To seek favor by flattery, c. [< OF *correier, conreder* to prepare]
·ry² (kûr′ē) *n.* *pl.* **·ries 1.** A pungent sauce of East In-an origin. **2.** A dish of meat, fish, etc., cooked with this uce. **3.** Curry powder. **—** *v.t.* **·ried, ·ry·ing** To flavor ith curry. [< Tamil *kari* sauce]
·ry·comb (kûr′ē·kōm′) *n.* A comb consisting of a series teeth or upright serrated ridges, for grooming horses, etc. *v.t.* To comb with a currycomb.
ry powder A condiment prepared from pungent spices, rmeric, etc., used in making curry and curried dishes.
rse (kûrs) *n.* **1.** An appeal for evil or injury to befall an-her, as through the intercession of God or gods. **2.** The il or injury so invoked. **3.** Any profane oath; impreca-on. **4.** A source of calamity or evil. **5.** Something cursed. *v.* **cursed** (kûrst) or **curst, curs·ing** *v.t.* **1.** To invoke evil injury upon; damn. **2.** To swear at. **3.** To cause evil or jury to; afflict. **—** *v.i.* **4.** To utter curses; swear. [OE < Irish *cursagim* to blame]
rs·ed (kûrst; *for adj., also* kûr′sid) A past tense and past articiple of CURSE. **—** *adj.* **1.** Under a curse. **2.** Deserv-g a curse; wicked. Also **curst. — curs′ed·ly** *adv.* **— ırs′ed·ness** *n.*
r·sive (kûr′siv) *adj.* Running; flowing: said of writing in hich the letters are joined. **—** *n.* **1.** A cursive character. *Printing* A typeface resembling handwriting. [< Med.L *L currere* to run] **— cur′sive·ly** *adv.*
r·so·ry (kûr′sər·ē) *adj.* Rapid and superficial. [< LL < *currere* to run] **— cur′so·ri·ly** *adv.* **— cur′so·ri·ness** *n.*
rt (kûrt) *adj.* **1.** Brief and abrupt; esp., rudely brief: a *rt* nod. **2.** Short or shortened. **— Syn.** See BLUNT. [< *curtus* shortened] **— curt′ly** *adv.* **— curt′ness** *n.*
r·tail (kər·tāl′) *v.t.* To cut off or cut short; reduce. [< bs. *curtal* cut short] **— cur·tail′er** *n.* **— cur·tail′ment** *n.*
r·tain (kûr′tən) *n.* **1.** A piece or pieces of cloth, etc. hang-g in a window or opening, usu. capable of being drawn to e sides or raised. **2.** Something that conceals or separates ke a curtain: the *curtain* of darkness. **3.** *pl. Slang* Ruin; eath. **—** *v.t.* To provide, shut off, or conceal with or as ith a curtain. [< OF < LL *cortina*]
rtain call Prolonged applause of an audience at the end f a play, scene, etc., as a call for the performers to reappear nd acknowledge it; also, their reappearance.

curtain raiser 1. A short play or sketch presented before a longer or more important play. **2.** Any introductory event.
curtain wall *Archit.* An outside wall providing enclosure but giving no structural support.
curt·sy (kûrt′sē) *n.* *pl.* **·sies** A bending of the knees and lowering of the body as a gesture of civility or respect, performed by women: sometimes spelled *courtesy.* **—** *v.i.* **·sied, ·sy·ing** To make a curtsy. Also **curt′sey.** [Var. of COURTESY]
cur·va·ceous (kûr·vā′shəs) *adj. U.S. Informal* Having voluptuous curves; shapely: said of a woman.
cur·va·ture (kûr′və·chər) *n.* **1.** The act of curving, or the state of being curved. **2.** *Physiol.* A curving, esp. when abnormal: *curvature* of the spine. [< L *curvare* to bend]
curve (kûrv) *n.* **1.** A line continuously bent, as the arc of a circle. **2.** A curving, or something curved. **3.** An instrument for drawing curves. **4.** *Math.* The locus of a point moving in such a way that its course can be defined by an equation. **5.** In baseball, a ball pitched with a spin that causes it to veer to one side. **6.** A grading system based upon a theoretical frequency distribution. **—** *v.* **curved, curv·ing** *v.t.* **1.** To cause to assume the form of or move in the path of a curve. **—** *v.i.* **2.** To assume the form of a curve. **3.** To move in a curve. **—** *adj.* Curved. [< L *curvus* bent] **— curv′ed·ly** *adv.* **— curv′ed·ness** *n.*
cur·vet (*n.* kûr′vit; *v.* kər·vet′, kûr′vit) *n.* A light, low leap of a horse, made so that all four legs are off the ground at one time. **—** *v.* **cur·vet·ted** or **·vet·ed, cur·vet·ting** or **·vet·ing** *v.i.* **1.** To make a curvet. **2.** To prance; frisk. **—** *v.t.* **3.** To cause to curvet. [< Ital. < L *curvus* bent]
curvi- *combining form* Curved. [< L *curvus* curved]
cur·vi·lin·e·ar (kûr′və·lin′ē·ər) *adj.* Formed or enclosed by curved lines. Also **cur′vi·lin′e·al.**
cush·ion (ko͝osh′ən) *n.* **1.** A flexible bag or casing filled with some soft or elastic material, as feathers, air, etc., used for lying or resting on. **2.** Anything resembling a cushion in appearance or use; esp., any device to deaden the jar or impact of parts, as padding, etc. **3.** The elastic rim of a billiard table. **4.** *Canadian* The ice of a hockey rink. **—** *v.t.* **1.** To seat or arrange on or as on a cushion. **2.** To provide with a cushion. **3.** To absorb the shock or effect of. [< F *coussin,* ult. < L *coxa* hip, thigh] **— cush′ion·y** *adj.*
Cush·it·ic (ko͝osh·it′ik) *n.* A group of Hamitic languages spoken in Ethiopia and Somaliland. **—** *adj.* Pertaining to this group of languages. Also spelled *Kushitic.*
cush·y (ko͝osh′ē) *adj. Slang* **cush·i·er, cush·i·est** Comfortable; agreeable; easy. [< CUSHION; orig. Brit. slang]
cusp (kusp) *n.* **1.** A point or pointed end. **2.** Either point of a crescent moon. **3.** *Geom.* A point at which two branches of a curve meet and end, with a common tangent. [< L *cuspis, -idis* a point] **— cus·pate** (kus′pāt), **cus′pated, cusped** (kuspt) *adj.*
cus·pid (kus′pid) *n.* A canine tooth.
cus·pi·date (kus′pə·dāt) *adj.* Having a cusp or cusps. Also **cus·pi·dal** (kus′pə·dəl), **cus′pi·dat′ed.**
cus·pi·dor (kus′pə·dôr) *n.* A spittoon. [< Pg. < L < *com-* thoroughly + *spuere* to spit]
cuss (kus) *U.S. Informal v.t. & v.i.* To curse. **—** *n.* **1.** A curse. **2.** A perverse person or animal. [Var. of CURSE] **— cuss·ed** (kus′id) *adj.* **— cuss′ed·ly** *adv.* **— cuss′ed·ness** *n.*
cus·tard (kus′tərd) *n.* A mixture of milk, eggs, sugar, and flavoring, either boiled or baked. [< F < L *crusta* crust]
cus·to·di·an (kus·tō′dē·ən) *n.* A guardian; caretaker. **— cus·to′di·an·ship′** *n.*
cus·to·dy (kus′tə·dē) *n.* *pl.* **·dies 1.** A keeping; guardianship. **2.** The state of being held in keeping or under guard. [< L < *custos* guardian] **— cus·to·di·al** (kus·tō′dē·əl) *adj.*
cus·tom (kus′təm) *n.* **1.** The habitual practice of a community or a people. **2.** An ordinary or usual manner of doing or acting; habit. **3.** *Law* An old and general usage that has obtained the force of law. **4.** Habitual patronage, as of a hotel, store, etc. **5.** *pl.* A tariff or duty upon imported or, rarely, exported goods; also, the agency of the government that collects such duties. **—** *adj.* **1.** Made to order. **2.** Specializing in made-to-order goods. [< OF < L < *com-* thoroughly + *suescere* to become used to]
cus·tom·ar·y (kus′tə·mer′ē) *adj.* **1.** Conforming to or established by custom; usual; habitual. **2.** *Law* Holding or held by custom, as a feudal estate. **—** *n.* *pl.* **·ar·ies** A written statement of laws and customs. [See CUSTOM.] **— cus·tom·ar·i·ly** (kus′tə·mer′ə·lē, kus′tə·mer′ə·lē) *adv.*
cus·tom-built (kus′təm·bilt′) *adj.* Built to order or to individual specifications: a *custom-built* boat.
cus·tom·er (kus′təm·ər) *n.* **1.** One who buys something; esp., one who deals regularly at a given establishment. **2.** *Informal* One to be dealt with: a queer *customer.*
cus·tom·house (kus′təm·hous′) *n.* The government office where duties are collected and vessels cleared for entering or leaving. Also **custom house.**

cus·tom-made (kus′təm·mād′) *adj.* Made to order.
cus·toms union (kus′təmz) An association of nations that remove tariff restrictions among themselves and have a common tariff policy toward other nations: also *common market.*
cut (kut) *v.* **cut, cut·ting** *v.t.* **1.** To open or penetrate with a sharp edge; gash; pierce. **2.** To divide with a sharp edge into parts or segments. **3.** To make or shape by cutting, as gems. **4.** To fell or hew: often with *down.* **5.** To strike sharply, as with a whip. **6.** To hurt the feelings of. **7.** *Informal* To pretend not to know; snub. **8.** *Informal* To absent oneself from: to *cut* a class. **9.** To cross or intersect. **10.** To shorten or trim, as hair, grass, etc. **11.** To shorten or edit by removing parts. **12.** To mow or reap (wheat, etc.) **13.** To reduce or lessen: to *cut* prices. **14.** To dilute or weaken, as whisky. **15.** To dissolve or break down: to *cut* grease. **16.** To have (a new tooth) grow through the gum. **17.** In certain games, to strike the ball so as to deflect it to one side. **18.** To divide (a pack of cards), as before dealing. **—** *v.i.* **19.** To make an incision. **20.** To act as a sharp edge. **21.** To penetrate like a knife. **22.** To veer sharply in one's course. **23.** To go by the shortest and most direct route: with *across, through,* etc. **24.** In certain sports and games, to deflect the ball. **25.** To grow through the gum: said of teeth. **26.** To divide a pack of cards, as before dealing. **— to cut back 1.** To shorten by removing the end. **2.** To reduce or curtail. **3.** To reverse one's direction. **— to cut down 1.** To reduce; curtail. **2.** To kill, as with a sword. **— to cut in 1.** To move into a line or queue abruptly or out of turn. **2.** To interrupt a dancing couple so as to take the place of one partner. **3.** To break in, as on a conversation; interrupt. **— to cut off 1.** To remove or detach by cutting. **2.** To put an end to; stop. **3.** To interrupt. **4.** To intercept. **5.** To disinherit. **— to cut out 1.** To remove by cutting; excise. **2.** To shape by cutting. **3.** To be suited for: He's not *cut out* for the work. **4.** To move sharply from one's course, as in traffic. **5.** To oust and supplant, as a rival. **6.** *Slang* To stop doing; cease. **— to cut up 1.** To cut in pieces. **2.** To affect deeply; distress. **3.** *Informal* To behave in an unruly manner. **—** *n.* **1.** A severing, slashing, or piercing stroke: a clean *cut.* **2.** The opening or sound made by such a stroke; gash; cleft. **3.** A part cut off; esp. the part of a meat animal. **4.** A deletion or excision of a part. **5.** A passage or channel that has been cut or dug out. **6.** A direct route: a short *cut.* **7.** Something that hurts the feelings, as an insult. **8.** *Informal* A refusal to recognize an acquaintance. **9.** The manner in which a thing is cut; fashion; style: the *cut* of a suit. **10.** A reduction in prices, wages, etc. **11.** *U.S. Slang* A share or commission. **12.** *Informal* An absence from a class at school. **13.** *Printing* An engraved block or plate; also, an impression made from this. **14.** A stroke imparting spin to a ball, as in tennis, billiards, etc. **15.** A cutting of a deck of cards. **16.** *Chem.* A fraction, as of petroleum, obtained in distillation. **— a cut above** A degree better than. **—** *adj.* **1.** That has been cut off, into, or through: a *cut* finger. **2.** Dressed or finished by a tool, as stone or glass. **3.** Reduced, as rates or prices. **4.** Diluted, as whisky. **— cut and dried 1.** Prepared or arranged beforehand. **2.** Lacking interest or suspense. [ME < Scand.]
cu·ta·ne·ous (kyōō·tā′nē·əs) *adj.* Of, pertaining to, affecting, or like skin. [< Med.L < L *cutis* skin]
cut·a·way (kut′ə·wā′) *n.* A man's formal daytime coat, having the front corners cut slopingly away from the waist down to the tails at the back: also **cutaway coat.**
cut·back (kut′bak′) *n.* **1.** A sharp reduction, as in personnel or scheduled production. **2.** A reduction.
cute (kyōōt) *adj.* **cut·er, cut·est** *U.S. Informal* Pretty, dainty, or attractive. [Var. of ACUTE] **— cute′ly** *adv.* **— cute′ness** *n.*
cut glass Glass that has been shaped or ornamented by cutting on a wheel of stone, iron, copper, etc.
cu·ti·cle (kyōō′ti·kəl) *n.* **1.** *Anat.* The epidermis. **2.** Any superficial covering. **3.** The crescent of toughened skin around the base of a fingernail or toenail. [< L *cuticula,* dim. of *cutis* skin] **— cu·tic′u·lar** *adj.*
cu·tin (kyōō′tin) *n. Bot.* A fatty or waxy protective cuticle of leaves, stems, etc., of plants. [< L *cutis* skin + -IN]
cu·tin·i·za·tion (kyōō′tən·ə·zā′shən, -ī·zā′-) *n. Bot.* The modification of cell walls by the presence of cutin, making them waterproof.
cu·tin·ize (kyōō′tən·īz) *v.t. & v.i.* **·ized, ·iz·ing** To undergo or cause to undergo cutinization.
cut·lass (kut′ləs) *n.* A short, swordlike weapon, often curved. Also **cut′las.** [< F < L *culter* knife]
cut·ler (kut′lər) *n.* One who makes repairs, or deals in cutlery. [< OF < Med.L < L *cultellus,* dim. of *culter* knife]
cut·ler·y (kut′lər·ē) *n.* **1.** Cutting instruments collectively, esp. those for use at the dinner table. **2.** The occupation of a cutler.
cut·let (kut′lit) *n.* **1.** A thin piece of meat for frying or broiling, usu. veal or mutton. **2.** A flat croquette of chopped meat, fish, etc. [< F < L *costa* rib]
cut·off (kut′ôf′, -of′) *n.* **1.** The prescribed termination limit of a process or series. **2.** *U.S.* A shorter route; sh cut. **3.** *Mech.* **a** A cutting off of the flow of something, fluid or steam. **b** The mechanism that does this.
cut·out (kut′out′) *n.* **1.** Something cut out or intended be cut out. **2.** *Electr.* A device that cuts off the curr when the flow reaches an unsafe level. **3.** A device to let exhaust gases from an internal-combustion engine pass rectly to the air without going through the muffler.
cut·o·ver (kut′ō′vər) *adj.* Cleared of timber, as land.
cut·purse (kut′pûrs′) *n.* A pickpocket; formerly, one w cut away purses that were attached to a girdle or belt.
cut-rate (kut′rāt′) *adj.* Sold or selling at reduced pri
cut·ter (kut′ər) *n.* **1.** One who cuts, esp. one who shapes, decorates, or edits by cutting. **2.** A device that cuts. *Naut.* **a** A single-masted, fast-sailing vessel of narrow be and deep draft, and normally spreading no more than f sails. **b** A small, swift, armed, and engined vessel, as used the Coast Guard for coastal patrol, etc. **c** A small to mediu sized boat either employed by or carried on a larger ve (such as a warship) and used to discharge passengers, tra port stores, etc. **4.** A small sleigh.
cut·throat (kut′thrōt′) *adj.* **1.** Bloodthirsty; murdero **2.** Ruinous; merciless. **—** *n.* A murderer.
cut·ting (kut′ing) *adj.* **1.** Adapted to cut; edged. **2.** Sha chilling. **3.** Unkind; sarcastic. **—** *n.* **1.** The act of one w or that which cuts. **2.** Something obtained or made cutting. **3.** *Brit.* A newspaper clipping.
cut·tle·bone (kut′l·bōn′) *n.* The internal calcareous pl of a cuttlefish, used as a dietary supplement for birds a when powdered, as a polishing agent.
cut·tle·fish (kut′l·fish′) *n. pl.* **·fish** or **·fish·es** A sea m lusk having lateral fins, ten sucker-bearing arms, a hard ner shell, and concealing itself by ejecting an inky fluid.
cut·up (kut′up′) *n. Informal* A person who tries to se funny, as a practical joker.
cut·wa·ter (kut′wô′tər, -wot′ər) *n.* The forward part of prow of a vessel.
cut·work (kut′wûrk′) *n.* Openwork embroidery with c out edges.
cut·worm (kut′wûrm′) *n.* Any of several nocturnal cat pillars that cut off plants at the surface of the ground.
-cy *suffix* Forming nouns: **1.** (*from adjectives*) Quality, sta or condition of: *secrecy, bankruptcy.* **2.** (*from nouns*) Ra or condition of: *chaplaincy.* [< F *-cie* < L *-cia* < Gk. *-k*
cyan- Var. of CYANO-.
cy·an·ic (sī·an′ik) *adj.* **1.** Of, pertaining to, or containi cyanogen. **2.** Blue.
cy·a·nide (sī′ə·nīd) *n. Chem.* A compound of cyanogen w a metallic element or radical. Also **cy′a·nid** (-nid). **— ·nid·ed, ·nid·ing** *Metall.* To subject to the action of cyani to extract gold by *cyaniding* the ore. **— cy′a·ni·da′tion** *n.*
cyano- *combining form* **1.** Characterized by bluish colori *cyanosis.* **2.** *Chem.* Cyanide. Also, before vowels, **cya** [< Gk. *kyanos* dark blue]
cy·an·o·gen (sī·an′ə·jən) *n. Chem.* **1.** A colorless, flamm ble, poisonous, liquefiable gas, C_2N_2, having an almondli odor. **2.** The univalent radical CN. [< F *cyanogène*]
cy·a·no·sis (sī′ə·nō′sis) *n. Pathol.* A disordered conditi due to inadequate oxygenation of the bood, causing the sk to look blue. **— cy·a·not·ic** (sī′ə·not′ik) *adj.*
cy·ber·net·ics (sī′bər·net′iks) *n.pl.* (*construed as sing.*) T science that treats of the principles of control and commu cation as they apply both to the operation of complex m chines and the functions of organisms. [< Gk. *kyberne* steersman + -ICS] **— cy′ber·net′ic** *adj.*
cy·cad (sī′kad) *n.* Any of a family of primitive, seed-be ing, mostly tropical plants of fernlike or palmlike appe ance. [< Gk. *kykas,* erroneous pl. of *koïx* a palm tree] **cyc·a·da·ceous** (sik′ə·dā′shəs) *adj.*
cyc·la·men (sik′lə·mən, -men) *n.* An Old World bulbo flowering herb of the primrose family, with white, pink, crimson flowers. [< NL < L < Gk. *kyklaminos, kyklam*
cy·cle (sī kəl) *n.* **1.** A recurring period within which certa events or phenomena occur in a definite sequence. **2.** completed round of events or phenomena in which there is final return to the original state. **3.** A pattern of regular recurring events. **4.** A vast period of time; an eon. **5.** body of poems or stories relating to the same character subject. **6.** A bicycle, tricycle, etc. **—** *v.i.* **·cled, ·cling** To pass through cycles. **2.** To ride a bicycle, tricycle, e [< OF < LL < Gk. *kyklos* circle]
cy·clic (sī′klik, sik′lik) *adj.* **1.** Pertaining to or characte ized by cycles; recurring in cycles. **2.** *Chem.* Arranged in closed chain or ring formation, as the atoms of benzen naphthalene, etc. Also **cy′cli·cal.**
cy·clist (sī′klist) *n.* One who rides a bicycle, tricycle, et
cyclo- *combining form* **1.** Circular. **2.** *Chem.* A cyclic co pound. Also, before vowels, **cycl-.** [< Gk *kyklos* circle]
cy·cloid (sī′kloid) *adj.* Resembling a circle or somewh circular. **—** *n. Geom.* The curve described by a point on t

rcumference of a circle rolling along a straight line in a ngle plane. [< Gk. *kykloeidēs* circular] —**cy·cloi′dal** *adj.*

·clom·e·ter (sī·klom′ə·tər) *n.* An instrument for record-ıg the rotations of a wheel to show speed and distance.

·clone (sī′klōn) *n.* **1.** *Meteorol.* A system of winds cir-ulating about a center of relatively low barometric pressure, nd advancing at the earth's surface with clockwise rotation ı the Southern Hemisphere, counterclockwise in the North-rn. **2.** Loosely, any violent storm. [< Gk. < *kyklos* circle] – **cy·clon·ic** (sī·klon′ik) or **·i·cal** *adj.* — **cy·clon′i·cal·ly** *adv.*

·clo·pe·an (sī′klə·pē′ən) *adj.* **1.** *Usu. cap.* Of or pertain-ıg to the Cyclopes. **2.** Gigantic: a *cyclopean* task.

·clo·pe·di·a (sī′klə·pē′dē·ə) *n.* An encyclopedia (which ee). Also **cy′clo·pae′di·a.** —**cy′clo·pe′dic** *adj.* —**cy′clo·e′di·cal·ly** *adv.* —**cy′clo·pe′dist,** or **cy′clo·pae′dist** *n.*

·clo·pro·pane (sī′klə·prō′pān) *n. Chem.* A colorless, pun-ent, inflammable gas, C_3H_6, used as an anesthetic.

·clops (sī′klops) *n. pl.* **Cy·clo·pes** (sī·klō′pēz) In Ho-neric legend, any of a race of one-eyed giants of Sicily.

·clo·ram·a (sī′klə·ram′ə, -rä′mə) *n.* **1.** A series of pic-ures on the interior of a cylindrical surface, appearing in atural perspective to a spectator standing in the center. **2.** backdrop curtain, often concave, used on theater stages. < CYCLO- + Gk. *horama* a view] —**cy′clo·ram′ic** *adj.*

·clo·tron (sī′klə·tron) *n. Physics* An accelerator that ob-ains high-energy electrified particles by whirling them at ery high speeds in a strong magnetic field.

g·net (sig′nit) *n.* A young swan. [< MF *cygne* a swan]

g·nus (cig′nəs) *n.* A constellation, the Swan, containing he bright star Deneb: also called *Northern Cross.* [< L]

l·in·der (sil′in·dər) *n* **1.** *Geom.* A solid figure generated y one side of a rectangle rotated about the opposite fixed ide, the ends of the figure being equal, parallel circles. **2.** ny object or container resembling a cylinder in form. **3.** *Mech.* In a reciprocating engine, the chamber in which the istons move. **4.** In a revolver, the rotating part that holds he cartridges. —*v.t.* To press or fit with a cylinder. [< L < Gk. < *kylindein* to roll]

·lin·dri·cal (si·lin′dri·kəl) *adj.* **1.** Of a cylinder. **2.** haped like a cylinder. Also **cy·lin′dric.** Abbr. *cyl.* —**cy·in·dri·cal·i·ty** (si·lin′dri·kal′ə·tē) *n.* —**cy·lin′dri·cal·ly** *adv.*

m·bal (sim′bəl) *n.* One of a pair of concave metal plates lashed to produce a musical ringing sound. [OE and OF < < Gk. *kymbē* cup, hollow of a vessel] —**cym′bal·ist** *n.*

me (sīm) *n. Bot* A flat-topped flower cluster in which the entral flowers bloom first. [< F < L < Gk *kyma*] —**cy·nose** (sī′mōs, sī·mōs′) *adj.*

mo- *combining form* Wave. [< Gk. *kymo-* < *kyma* wave]

ym·ric (kim′rik, sim′-) *adj.* Of or pertaining to the Cym-y; Brythonic. —*n.* **1.** The Welsh language. **2.** The Bry-honic branch of the Celtic languages.

ym·ry (kim′rē, sim′-) *n.* A collective name for the Welsh nd their Cornish and Breton kin: also *Kymry.* Also **Cym′ri.**

n·ic (sin′ik) *n.* A sneering, faultfinding person; esp., one who believes that all men are motivated by selfishness. —*dj.* Cynical. [< L < Gk < *kyōn, kynos* dog]

yn·ic (sin′ik) *n.* One of a sect of Greek philosophers of the ifth and fourth centuries B.C., who held that virtue was the oal of life. Their doctrine eventually came to represent in-olent self-righteousness. —*adj.* Pertaining to or character-stic of the Cynics: also **Cyn′i·cal.**

yn·i·cal (sin′i·kəl, -ə-) *adj.* Distrusting or contemptuous of virtue in others; sneering; sarcastic. —**cyn′i·cal·ly** *adv.*

yn·i·cism (sin′ə·siz′əm, -i-) *n.* **1.** Cynical character or at-titude; contempt for or disbelief in the virtues of others. **2.** A cynical remark, action, etc. Also **cyn′i·cal·ness.**

cy·no·sure (sī′nə·shŏŏr, sin′ə-) *n.* **1.** A person or object that attracts notice and admiration. **2.** Something that guides. [< MF < L < Gk. < *kyōn, kynos* dog + *oura* tail]

Cy·no·sure (sī′nə·shŏŏr, sin′ə-) *n.* **1.** The constellation Ursa Minor, containing the polestar. **2.** Polaris.

Cyn·thi·a (sin′thē·ə) Artemis. —*n. Poetic* The moon.

cy·pher (sī′fər) See CIPHER.

cy·press[1] (sī′prəs) *n.* **1.** An evergreen tree of the pine fam-ily, having flat, scalelike foliage. **2.** A related tree. **3.** The wood of these trees. [< OF < LL < Gk. *kyparissos*]

Cyp·ri·an (sip′rē·ən) *adj.* Of or pertaining to Cyprus. —*n.* A Cypriote.

cyp·ri·noid (sip′rə·noid, si·prī′-) *adj.* Of or pertaining to the carp family of fishes. Also **cy·pri·nid** (si·prī′nid, sip′rə·nid). [< Gk. *kyprinos* carp + -OID]

Cyp·ri·ote (sip′rē·ōt) *n.* **1.** A native or inhabitant of Cy-prus. **2.** The ancient or modern Greek dialect of Cyprus. —*adj.* Of or pertaining to Cyprus. Also **Cyp·ri·ot** (sip′rē·ət). [< F *cypriote*]

Cy·ril·lic alphabet (si·ril′ik) A Slavic alphabet based mainly on that of the Greeks, ascribed traditionally to Saint Cyril, used for Russian, Bulgarian, Serbo-Croatian, Ukrani-an, Byelorussian, and Macedonian. See ALPHABET.

cyst (sist) *n.* **1.** *Pathol.* Any abnormal sac or vesicle in which matter may collect and be retained. **2.** *Biol.* Any saclike organ in plants or animals. [< Med.L < Gk. *kyein* to con-tain] —**cys′tic, cys′toid** *adj.*

cys·ti·tis (sis·tī′tis) *n. Pathol.* Inflammation of the bladder.

cysto- *combining form* Bladder; cyst. Also, before vowels, **cyst-:** also **cysti-.** [< Gk. *kystis* bladder]

cys·to·scope (sis′tə·skōp) *n. Med.* A device for examining the interior of the urinary bladder. —**cys·to·scop·ic** (sis′tə·skop′ik) *adj.*

-cyte *combining form* Cell: *phagocyte.* [< Gk. *kytos* hollow vessel]

Cyth·e·re·a (sith′ə·rē′ə) Aphrodite. —**Cyth′e·re′an** *adj.*

cyto- *combining form* Cell. Also, before vowels, **cyt-.** [< Gk. *kytos* hollow vessel < *kyein* to contain, be pregnant with]

cy·to·ge·net·ics (sī′tō·jə·net′iks) *n.pl.* (*construed as sing.*) The study of the role of cells in heredity.

cy·tol·o·gy (sī·tol′ə·jē) *n.* The study of the structure, or-ganization, and function of cells. —**cy·to·log·ic** (sī′tə·loj′ik) or **·i·cal** *adj.* —**cy′to·log′i·cal·ly** *adv.* —**cy·tol′o·gist** *n.*

cy·to·plasm (sī′tə·plaz′əm) *n. Biol.* All the protoplasm of a cell except that in the nucleus. Also **cy′to·plast.**

czar (zär) *n.* **1.** An emperor or king; esp., one of the former emperors of Russia. **2.** An absolute ruler; despot. Also *tsar, tzar.* [< Russ. *tsar′*, ult. < L *Caesar* Caesar] —**czar′dom** *n.* —**czar′ism** *n.* —**czar′ist** *adj.* & *n.*

czar·e·vitch (zär′ə·vich) *n.* The eldest son of a czar: also *tsarevitch, tzarevitch.* [< Russ. *tsarevich*]

cza·rev·na (zä·rev′nə) *n.* **1.** The wife of the czarevitch. **2.** Formerly, the title of any daughter of the czar. Also *tsarevna, tzarevna.* [< Russ. *tsarevna*]

cza·ri·na (zä·rē′nə) *n.* The wife of a czar; an empress of Russia: also *tsarina, tzarina.* Also **cza·rit·za** (zä·rit′sə) [< G *czarin,* for Russ. *tzaritsa*]

Czech (chek) *n.* **1.** A member of the western branch of Slavs, including the peoples of Bohemia and Moravia. **2.** The West Slavic language of the Czechs, formerly called Bo-hemian. —*adj.* Relating to Czechoslovakia, the Czechs, or their language: also **Czech′ic, Czech′ish.**

Czech·o·slo·vak (chek′ə·slō′vak, -väk) *n.* A Czech or Slo-vak inhabiting Czechoslovakia. —*adj.* Of or pertaining to the Czechoslovaks. Also **Czech·o·slo·va·ki·an** (chek′ə·slō·väk′ē·ən, -vak′ē·ən).

D

, D (dē) *n. pl.* **d's** or **ds, D's** or **Ds, dees** (dēz) **1.** The fourth letter of the English alphabet. **2.** The sound repre-sented by the letter *d.* **3.** Anything shaped like the letter D. —*symbol* **1.** The Roman numeral for 500. **2.** *Music* **a** The second tone in the natural scale of C; re. **b** A written note representing it. **c** The scale built upon D. **3.** *Math.* Differ-ential. **4.** The fourth in a series or group. **5.** Pence **6.** *Chem.* Deuterium (symbol D). **7.** *Physics* Density.

dab[1] (dab) *n.* **1.** Any of various flounders. **2.** Any flatfish.

dab[2] (dab) *n.* **1.** A gentle pat. **2.** A soft, moist patch: a *dab* of paint. **3.** A little bit. —*v.t.* & *v.i.* **dabbed, dab·bing 1.** To strike softly; tap. **2.** To peck. **3.** To pat with some-thing soft and damp. **4.** To apply (paint, etc.) with light strokes. [ME *dabben*] —**dab′ber** *n.*

dab·chick (dab′chik) *n.* A small grebe of Europe, or the pied-billed grebe of North America.

PRONUNCIATION KEY: **add, āce, câre, pälm; end, ēven; it, īce; odd, ōpen, ôrder; tŏŏk, pōōl; up, bûrn; ə** = a in *above,* e in *sicken,* i in *flex-ible,* o in *melon,* u in *focus;* **yōō** = u in *fuse;* **oil; pout; check; go; ring; thin; this; zh,** vision.

dab·ble (dab′əl) *v.* **·bled, ·bling** *v.i.* **1.** To play in a liquid, as with the hands; splash gently. **2.** To engage oneself slightly or superficially: to *dabble* in art. — *v.t.* **3.** To wet slightly; bespatter. [Freq. of DAB[2], v.] — **dab′bler** *n.*

da ca·po (dä kä′pō) *Music* From the beginning: a direction to repeat the opening section of a piece.

dace (dās) *n. pl.* **dac·es** or **dace** A small fresh-water fish of the carp family. [< OF *dars*, a small fish, lit., dart]

dachs·hund (däks′hŏŏnt′, daks′hŏŏnd′, dash′-) *n.* A breed of dog native to Germany, having a long, compact body, short legs, and a short coat, usu. of red, tan, or black and tan. [< G < *dachs* badger + *hund* dog]

DACHSHUND (7 to 9 inches high at shoulder)

Da·cron (dā′kron, dak′ron) *n.* A synthetic polyester textile fiber of high tensile strength, having great resistance to stretching and wrinkling: a trade name. Also **da′cron.**

dac·tyl (dak′təl) *n.* In prosody, a metrical foot consisting of one long or accented syllable followed by two short or unaccented ones (—◡◡). [< L < Gk. *daktylos* finger, dactyl] — **dac·tyl·ic** (dak·til′ik) *adj. & n.*

dactylo- *combining form* Finger; toe. Also, before vowels, **dactyl-.** [< L < Gk. *daktylos* finger]

dad (dad) *n. Informal* Father. Also **dad·dy** (dad′ē). [Origin unknown]

da·da (dä′dä, -də) *n. Often cap.* A movement in art and literature, occurring esp. in France, Germany, and Switzerland about 1916–20, that protested against civilization and violently satirized all previous art. Also **da′da·ism.** [< F *dada*, a nonsense word] — **da′da·ist** *n.* — **da·da·ist′ic** *adj.*

dad·dle (dad′l) *v.t. & v.i.* **·dled, ·dling** Diddle[1].

dad·dy-long·legs (dad′ē·lông′legz′, -long′-) *n. pl.* **·legs** A longlegged insect resembling a spider: also called *harvestman.*

da·do (dā′dō) *n. pl.* **·does 1.** *Archit.* The part of a pedestal between the base and the cornice; the die. **2.** The lower part of an interior wall, often ornamented. [< Ital., a cube]

Daed·a·lus (ded′ə·ləs, *Brit.* dē′də-) In Greek mythology, an Athenian architect who devised the Cretan Labyrinth in which he was later imprisoned with his son Icarus, and from which they escaped by artificial wings.

daf·fo·dil (daf′ə·dil) *n.* A plant of the amaryllis family, with solitary yellow flowers. Also *Dial.* or *Poetic* **daf·fa·dil·ly** (daf′ə·dil′ē), **daf·fa·down·dil·ly** (daf′ə·doun·dil′ē), **daf·fy·down·dil·ly** (daf′ē-). [Var. of ME *affodile*]

daf·fy (daf′ē) *adj.* **daf·fi·er, daf·fi·est** *Informal* Crazy; silly; zany. [< DAFF[2]]

daft (daft, däft) *adj.* **1.** *Chiefly Brit.* Of weak mind; insane. **2.** *Chiefly Brit.* Foolish; silly. [OE *gedæfte* mild, meek] — **daft′ly** *adv.* — **daft′ness** *n.*

dag·ger (dag′ər) *n.* **1.** A short, pointed and edged weapon for stabbing. **2.** *Printing* A reference mark (†). — **double dagger** *Printing* A reference mark (‡); a diesis. — **to look daggers (at)** To glare or scowl (at). — *v.t.* **1.** To stab. **2.** *Printing* To mark with a dagger. [? ME *dag* to stab]

da·go (dā′gō) *n. pl.* **·gos** or **·goes** *U.S. Slang* An Italian, or less commonly, a Spaniard or Portuguese: an offensive term. [Alter. of Sp. *Diego*, a personal name]

da·guerre·o·type (də·ger′ə·tīp′, -ē·ə·tīp′) *n.* **1.** An early photographic process using silver-coated metallic plates that were sensitive to light. **2.** A picture made by this process. [after Louis Jacques Mandé *Daguerre*, 1789–1851, French inventor] — **da·guerre′o·typ′er, da·guerre′o·typ′ist** *n.* — **da·guerre′o·typ′y** *n.*

dahl·ia (dal′yə, däl′-, dāl′-) *n.* A tender perennial plant of the composite family, having tuberous roots and showy red, purple, yellow, or white flowers; also, the flowers. [after Anders *Dahl*, 18th c. botanist]

Dail Ei·reann (dô·əl âr′ən) The lower house of the legislature of Ireland.

dai·ly (dā′lē) *adj.* Of, occurring, or appearing every day or every weekday. — *n. pl.* **·lies** A daily publication. — *adv.* Day after day; on every day. [OE *dæg* day]

dain·ty (dān′tē) *adj.* **·ti·er, ·ti·est 1.** Delicately pretty or graceful. **2.** Of pleasing taste; delicious. **3.** Of fine sensibilities; fastidious; also, too fastidious; overnice. — *n. pl.* **·ties** Something tasty or delicious; a delicacy. [< OF < L *dignitas* worth, dignity] — **dain′ti·ly** *adv.* — **dain′ti·ness** *n.*

dai·qui·ri (dī′kər·ē, dak′ər·ē) *n.* A cocktail made of rum, lime or lemon juice, and sugar. [after *Daiquiri*, Cuba]

dair·y (dâr′ē) *n. pl.* **·ies 1.** A commercial establishment that sells milk products. **2.** A room or building on a farm where milk and cream are kept and processed. **3.** A dairy farm or dairy cattle. **4.** Dairying. [ME *deie* dairymaid]

dairy cattle Cows of a breed adapted for milk production.

dairy farm A farm for producing dairy products.

dair·y·ing (dâr′ē·ing) *n.* The business of a dairy.

dair·y·maid (dâr′ē·mād′) *n.* A female worker in a dairy.

dair·y·man (dâr′ē·mən) *n. pl.* **·men** (-mən) A man who works in or owns a dairy.

da·is (dā′is, dās) *n.* A raised platform in a room or hall which a speaker, eminent guests, etc., may sit or stand. [OF *deis* < LL *discus* table]

dai·sy (dā′zē) *n. pl.* **·sies 1.** Any of various plants of composite family; esp., the **oxeye daisy,** of the U.S., havi a yellow disk and white rays, and the **English daisy,** havi a small yellow disk and numerous white or rose rays. *Slang* Something excellent or exceptional. [OE *dægas ē* day's eye] — **dai′sied** *adj.*

Da·ko·ta (də·kō′tə) *n.* **1.** A member of the largest divisi of the Siouan stock of North American Plains Indians, n on reservations in North and South Dakota, Minnesota, a Montana. **2.** The Siouan language of the Dakotas. **3.** Sioux Indian. — **Da·ko′tan** *adj. & n.*

Da·lai La·ma (dä·lī′ lä′mə) The pontiff of the princi Buddhist faith in Tibet, and traditional chief of state.

dale (dāl) *n.* A small valley. [OE *dæl*]

dal·li·ance (dal′ē·əns) *n.* **1.** Amorous play, flirting, fondling. **2.** Idle wasting of time; trifling.

dal·ly (dal′ē) *v.* **·lied, ·ly·ing** *v.i.* **1.** To make love sportive frolic. **2.** To play; trifle. **3.** To waste time. — *v.t.* **4.** waste (time): with *away.* [< OF *dalier* to converse, ch — **dal′li·er** *n.*

Dal·ma·tian (dal·mā′shən) *n.* **1.** A large, short-haired d white with black spots: also called *coach dog.* **2.** One of t Slavic people of Dalmatia. — *adj.* Of or pertaining to D matia or its people.

dal·mat·ic (dal·mat′ik) *n. Eccl.* A wide-sleeved vestme worn by a deacon over the alb, as at High Mass. [< OF L *dalmatica* (*vestis*) Dalmatian (robe)]

dal se·gno (däl sā′nyō) *Music* From the sign: a direction repeat from the sign :S: to the end. [< Ital.]

dam[1] (dam) *n.* **1.** A barrier to obstruct or control the fl of water. **2.** The water held back by such a barrier. **3.** A obstruction. — *v.t.* **dammed, dam·ming 1.** To erect a da in; obstruct or confine by a dam. **2.** To keep back; restrai with *up* or *in.* [ME. Akin to OE *demman* to block.]

dam[2] (dam) *n.* A female parent: said of animals. [< DAM

dam·age (dam′ij) *n.* **1.** Injury to person or property. *pl. Law* Money to compensate for an injury or wrong. *Sometimes pl. Informal* Price or expense. — *v.* **·aged, ·ag·i** *v.t.* **1.** To cause damage to. — *v.i.* **2.** To be susceptible damage. [< OF < L *damnum* loss] — **dam′age·a·ble** *a*

dam·as·cene (dam′ə·sēn, dam′ə·sēn′) *v.t.* **·cened, ·cen·i** To ornament (iron, steel, etc.) with wavy patterns or by i laying or etching. Also **dam·as·keen** (dam′ə·skēn, dam·skēn′). — *adj.* Relating to damascening or to damask. *n.* Work ornamented by damascening.

Damascus steel A steel with wavy markings, former used in swords made at Damascus. Also **damask steel.**

dam·ask (dam′əsk) *n.* **1.** A rich, reversible, elaborate patterned fabric, originally made of silk. **2.** A fine, twill table linen. **3.** Damascus steel, or the wavy pattern on su steel. **4.** A deep pink or rose color. — *adj.* **1.** Of or fro Damascus. **2.** Made of Damascus steel or of damask. Deep pink or rose-colored. — *v.t.* **1.** To damascene. **2.** weave or ornament with rich patterns. [after *Damascus*

damask rose A large, fragrant, pink rose of the Near Eas

dame (dām) *n.* **1.** A mature woman; matron. **2.** *U.S. Sla* A woman. **3.** In Great Britain: **a** A title of the Order the British Empire conferred on women, equivalent to th of knight. **b** The legal title of the wife of a knight or barone [< OF < L *domina* lady]

damn (dam) *v.t.* **1.** To pronounce worthless, bad, a failur etc. **2.** To curse or swear at. **3.** *Theol.* To condemn to ete nal punishment. **4.** To pronounce guilty; bring ruin upo — *v.i.* **5.** To swear; curse. — **to damn with faint praise** T praise so reluctantly as to imply adverse criticism. — *n.* The saying of "damn" as an oath. **2.** The smallest, mo contemptible bit. — *interj.* An oath expressive of irrit tion, disappointment, etc. — *adj. & adv. Informal* Damne [< OF < L *damnare* to condemn to punishment]

dam·na·ble (dam′nə·bəl) *adj.* Meriting damnation; detes able; outrageous. [< OF < L *damnare* to condemn] — **dam′na·ble·ness** *n.* — **dam′na·bly** *adv.*

dam·na·tion (dam·nā′shən) *n.* **1.** The act of damning, the state of being damned. **2.** *Theol.* Condemnation to ete nal punishment; also, eternal punishment. — *interj.* Dam — **dam·na·to·ry** (dam′nə·tôr′ē, -tō′rē) *adj.*

damn·dest (dam′dist) *Informal adj.* **1.** Most detestable outrageous: the *damndest* lie. **2.** Most extraordinary. — The utmost: Do your *damndest.* Also **damned′est.**

damned (damd, *poetic or rhetorical* dam′nid) *adj.* **1.** Doome condemned, esp. to eternal punishment. **2.** Deserving dam nation. — *adv. Informal* Very: *damned* funny.

damn·ing (dam′ing, dam′ning) *adj.* That damns or co demns; inculpating: *damning* evidence. — **damn′ing·ly** *ad*

Dam·o·cles (dam′ə·klēz) In Greek legend, a courtier wh was forced to sit at a banquet under a sword suspended by hair that he might learn the perilous nature of a ruler's life. — **sword of Damocles** Any impending calamity.

mon and Pyth·i·as (dā′mən; pith′ē·əs) In Roman leg-
d, two devoted friends.
mp (damp) *adj.* Somewhat wet; moist. — *n.* **1.** Mois-
e or moistness; vapor; mist. **2.** Foul air or poisonous gas,
pecially in a mine. **3.** Depression of spirits. — *v.t.* **1.** To
ke damp; moisten. **2.** To discourage or dull (energy, ar-
r, etc.). **3.** To stifle, check, reduce, etc. **4.** *Physics* To
duce the amplitude of (a series of waves). [< MDu., va-
r, steam] — **damp′ly** *adv.* — **damp′ness** *n.*
mp·en (dam′pən) *v.t.* **1.** To make damp; moisten. **2.** To
eck; depress, as ardor or spirits. — *v.i.* **3.** To become
mp. — **damp′en·er** *n.*
mp·er (dam′pər) *n.* **1.** One who or that which damps,
presses, or checks. **2.** A flat plate in the flue of a stove,
nace, etc., for controlling the draft. **3.** *Music* **a** A mech-
ism for stopping the vibrations of the strings in a piano.
In brass instruments, a mute.
mp·ish (dam′pish) *adj.* Slightly damp.
n·sel (dam′zəl) *n.* A young unmarried woman; maiden.
so, *Archaic,* **dam′o·sel.** [< OF *dameisele* gentlewoman]
n·son (dam′zən, -sən) *n.* **1.** An oval purple plum. **2.**
e tree producing it. Also **damson plum.** [ME < L *Da-
scenum* from Damascus]
n (dan) In the Old Testament, a son of Jacob and Bilhah.
n. xxx 6. — *n.* The tribe of Israel descended from him.
n (dan) In the Bible, a city at the north end of Palestine.
n·a·id (dan′ē·id) *n.* One of the Danaides.
na·i·des (də·nā′ə·dēz) *n.pl.* In Greek mythology, the
ty-nine daughters of a King of Argos who murdered their
sbands on their bridal night and who were punished by hav-
to draw water in a sieve forever.
ce (dans, däns) *v.* **danced, danc·ing** *v.i.* **1.** To move the
dy and feet rhythmically, esp. to music. **2.** To move
out lightly or excitedly; leap about. **3.** To move up and
wn jerkily; bob. — *v.t.* **4.** To perform the steps of (a
ltz, tango, etc.). **5.** To cause to dance. — **to dance at-
ndance** To wait upon another constantly. — *n.* **1.** A
ies of regular rhythmic steps or movements, usually per-
rmed to music. **2.** An act or instance of dancing. **3.** A
usical composition for dancing. **4.** A gathering of people
r dancing; a ball. [< OF *danser*] — **danc′er** *n.*
n·de·li·on (dan′də·lī′ən, -dē-) *n.* A widespread plant hav-
g yellow flowers and toothed, edible leaves. [< F *dent de
n* lion's tooth; with ref. to the shape of the leaves]
n·der (dan′dər) *n.* *U.S. Informal* Ruffled temper; anger.
to get one's dander up To become angry. [? Var. of
ottish *dunder* to ferment]
n·di·fy (dan′də·fī) *v.t.* **·fied, ·fy·ing** To cause to resemble
dandy or fop. — **dan′di·fi·ca′tion** *n.*
n·dle (dan′dəl) *v.t.* **·dled, ·dling** **1.** To move up and down
htly on the knees or in the arms, as an infant or child. **2.**
o fondle; caress. [< Ital. *dandolare*] — **dan′dler** *n.*
n·druff (dan′drəf) *n.* A fine scurf that forms on the scalp
d comes off in small scales. [Origin unknown]
n·dy (dan′dē) *n.* *pl.* **·dies** **1.** A man who is excessively
terested in fine clothes and elegant appearance; a fop. **2.**
formal A particularly fine specimen of its kind. — *adj.* **1.**
ke a dandy; foppish. **2.** *U.S. Informal* Excellent; very
ne. [Alter. of *Andy,* a personal name] — **dan′dy·ish** *adj.*
ne (dān) *n.* A native or inhabitant of Denmark, or a per-
n of Danish descent. [< ON *Danir* the Danes]
ne·law (dān′lô′) *n.* A ninth-century code of laws estab-
shed by Danish settlers in NE England; also, the region of
ngland under these laws. Also **Dane′lagh′** (-lô′). [OE]
n·ger (dān′jər) *n.* **1.** Exposure to evil, injury, or loss;
eril; risk. **2.** A cause or instance of peril or risk. [< OF,
ower to harm]
n·ger·ous (dān′jər·əs) *adj.* Attended with danger; peril-
us; unsafe. — **dan′ger·ous·ly** *adv.* — **dan′ger·ous·ness** *n.*
n·gle (dang′gəl) *v.* **·gled, ·gling** *v.i.* **1.** To hang loosely;
wing to and fro. **2.** To follow or hover near someone as a
itor or hanger-on. — *v.t.* **3.** To hold so as to swing loosely.
– *n.* **1.** Manner or act of dangling. **2.** Something that
angles. [< Scand. Cf. Dan. *dangle.*] — **dan′gler** *n.*
an·iel (dan′y l) In the Bible, a young Hebrew prophet,
aptive in Babylon. *Dan.* i 3–6. — *n.* A book of the Old
estament, containing the story and prophecies of Daniel.
an·ish (dā′nish) *adj.* Of or pertaining to Denmark, the
Danes, or their language. — *n.* The North Germanic lan-
uage of the Danes. Abbr. *Dan.* [OE *Denisc*]
nk (dangk) *adj.* Unpleasantly damp; cold and wet. [ME
anke] — **dank′ly** *adv.* — **dank′ness** *n.*
an·seuse (dän·sœz′) *n.* *pl.* **·seus·es** (-sœ′ziz, *Fr.* -sœz′) A
emale ballet dancer. [< F, fem. of *danseur*]
an·tesque (dan·tesk′) *adj.* Pertaining to or in the style of
Dante Alighieri. Also **Dan·te·an** (dan′tē·ən, dan·tē′ən).
aph·ne (daf′nē) In Greek mythology, a nymph changed
nto a laurel tree to escape the pursuit of Apollo.

dap·per (dap′ər) *adj.* **1.** Smartly dressed; trim; natty. **2.** Small and active. [< MDu., strong]
dap·ple (dap′əl) *v.t.* **·pled, ·pling** To make spotted or variegated in color. — *adj.* Spotted; variegated: also **dap′pled.** — *n.* **1.** A spot or dot, as on the skin of a horse. **2.** An animal marked with spots. [Origin uncertain]
dap·ple-gray (dap′əl·grā′) *adj.* Gray with a pattern of variegated rounded markings: usu. said of horses.
dare (dâr) *v.* **dared, dar·ing** *v.t.* **1.** To have the courage or boldness to undertake; venture on. **2.** To challenge (someone) to attempt something as proof of courage, etc. **3.** To oppose and challenge; defy. — *v.i.* **4.** To have the courage or boldness to do or attempt something; venture. — **I dare say** I believe (it): also **I dare·say** (dâr′sā). — *n.* A challenge; taunt. [OE *durran*] — **dar′er** *n.*
dare·dev·il (dâr′dev′əl) *n.* One who is recklessly bold. — *adj.* Rash; reckless. — **dare′dev′il·ry, dare′dev′il·try** *n.*
dar·ing (dâr′ing) *adj.* **1.** Brave and adventurous; bold; fearless. **2.** Audacious; presuming. — *n.* Adventurous courage; bravery. — **dar′ing·ly** *adv.* — **dar′ing·ness** *n.*
dark (därk) *adj.* **1.** Having little or no light; dim: a *dark* cave. **2.** Giving off or reflecting little light; gloomy: a *dark* day. **3.** Of a deep shade; black, or almost black: a *dark* color. **4.** Brunet in complexion. **5.** Cheerless or disheartening. **6.** Sullen in disposition or appearance; frowning; dour. **7.** Unenlightened in mind or spirit; ignorant. **8.** Evil or sinister; wicked; atrocious: a *dark* deed. **9.** Not understandable; mysterious: a *dark* saying. **10.** Not known; secret. — *n.* **1.** Lack of light. **2.** A place or condition of little or no light. **3.** Night. **4.** Obscurity; secrecy. **5.** Ignorance. **6.** A dark shadow or color. — **in the dark** **1.** In secret. **2.** Ignorant; uninformed. [OE *deorc*] — **dark′ness** *n.*
Dark Ages The period in European history between the fall of the Western Roman Empire (A.D. 476) and the Italian Renaissance; the Middle Ages, esp. the early part.
Dark Continent Africa: so called because little was known about it until the 19th century.
dark·en (där′kən) *v.t.* **1.** To make dark or darker; deprive of light. **2.** To make dark in color; make black. **3.** To fill with gloom; sadden. **4.** To obscure; confuse. **5.** To blind. — *v.i.* **6.** To grow dark or darker; become obscure. **7.** To grow clouded or flushed. **8.** To become blind. — **dark′·en·er** *n.*
dark horse One who unexpectedly wins a race, contest, nomination, etc.
dark lantern A lantern having a case with one transparent side that can be covered by a shield to hide the light.
dark·ling (därk′ling) *Poetic adj.* Occurring or being in the dark; dim. — *adv.* In the dark. [< DARK + -LING[2]]
dark·ly (därk′lē) *adv.* **1.** Obscurely. **2.** Mysteriously.
dark·room (därk′rōōm′, -rŏŏm′) *n.* *Photog.* A room equipped to exclude actinic rays, for treating plates, films, etc.
dark star *Astron.* An invisible or dimly shining star, known only through spectrum analysis, gravitational effect, etc.
dar·ling (där′ling) *n.* **1.** A person tenderly loved: often a term of address. **2.** A person in great favor. — *adj.* Beloved; very dear. [OE *dēorling,* dim. of *dēor* dear]
darn[1] (därn) *v.t.* & *v.i.* To repair (a garment or a hole) by filling the gap with interlacing stitches. — *n.* **1.** A place mended by darning. **2.** The act of darning. [? OE *dernan* to conceal < *derne* hidden] — **darn′er** *n.*
darn[2] (därn) *v.t., adj., n.,* & *interj.* *U.S. Informal* Damn: a euphemism. [Alter. of DAMN]
dar·nel (där′nəl) *n.* An annual grass often found in grain fields: also called *cockle, ryegrass.* [< dial. F *darnelle*]
darn·ing needle (därn′ing) **1.** A large-eyed needle used in darning. **2.** A dragonfly.
dart (därt) *n.* **1.** A thin, pointed weapon to be thrown or shot. **2.** Anything like a dart in appearance. **3.** A sudden, rapid motion. **4.** The stinger of an insect. **5.** A tapering tuck made in a garment to make it fit. — *v.i.* **1.** To move suddenly like a dart; rush. — *v.t.* **2.** To throw or emit suddenly or swiftly. [< OF < Gmc.]
dart·er (där′tər) *n.* **1.** One who or that which darts. **2.** A small American percoid fish.
dar·tle (där′təl) *v.t.* & *v.i.* **·tled, ·tling** To dart or shoot out repeatedly.
darts (därts) *n.pl.* (*construed as sing.*) A game of skill in which small darts are thrown at a bull's-eye target.
Dar·win·i·an (där·win′ē·ən) *adj.* Pertaining to Charles Darwin, or to Darwinism. — *n.* An advocate of Darwinism: also **Dar′win·ite** (-īt).
Dar·win·ism (där′win·iz′əm) *n.* The biological doctrine of the origin of species through descent by natural selection with variation, advocated by Charles Darwin. — **Dar′win·ist** *n.* & *adj.* — **Dar′win·is′tic** *adj.*
dash (dash) *v.t.* **1.** To strike with violence, esp. so as to break or shatter. **2.** To throw, thrust, or knock suddenly

and violently: usually with *away, out, down,* etc. **3.** To bespatter. **4.** To do, write, etc., hastily: with *off* or *down.* **5.** To frustrate; confound: to *dash* hopes. **6.** To daunt or discourage. **7.** To put to shame; abash. **8.** To adulterate; mix: with *with*: to *dash* with salt. — *v.i.* **9.** To strike; hit: The waves *dashed* against the shore. **10.** To rush or move impetuously. — *n.* **1.** A collision; impact. **2.** The splashing of water or other liquid against an object. **3.** A small addition of some other ingredient: a *dash* of bitters. **4.** A hasty stroke, as with a pen or brush. **5.** A check or hindrance. **6.** A sudden advance or onset; a short rush. **7.** A short race run at full speed: the 100-yard *dash.* **8.** Spirited action. **9.** Vigor of style; verve. **10.** A horizontal line (—) used as a mark of punctuation to set off words or phrases in a sentence, to indicate an abrupt breaking off, to mark omissions of words or letters, etc. **11.** *Telecom.* The long sound in the Morse or similar code, used in combination with the dot to represent letters or numbers. [ME *daschen* < Scand.]

dash·board (dash′bôrd′, -bōrd′) *n.* **1.** The instrument panel of an automobile. **2.** An upright screen on the front of a vehicle to intercept mud, spray, etc.

dash·er (dash′ər) *n.* **1.** One who or that which dashes. **2.** A lively or showy person. **3.** The plunger of a churn.

dash·ing (dash′ing) *adj.* **1.** Spirited; bold; impetuous. **2.** Ostentatiously showy or gay. — **dash′ing·ly** *adv.*

dash·y (dash′ē) *adj.* **dash·i·er, dash·i·est** Stylish; showy.

das·tard (das′tərd) *n.* A base coward; a sneak. — *adj.* Dastardly. [? ME *dased, dast,* pp. of *dasen* to daze + -ARD]

das·tard·ly (das′tərd·lē) *adj.* Base; cowardly. — **das′·tard·li·ness** *n.*

da·ta (dā′tə, dat′ə, dä′tə) *n. orig. pl. of* **datum** Facts or figures from which conclusions may be drawn. ◆ Those who continue to regard *data* as a Latin plural use it with a plural verb (These data *are* new), but its use with a singular verb (This data *is* new) is widespread. [< L, neut. pl. of *datus,* pp. of *dare* to give]

data processing The operations involved in handling and storing information, using computers and other machines.

date¹ (dāt) *n.* **1.** A particular point of time; esp., the time of the occurrence of an event. **2.** The part of a writing, coin, statue, etc., that tells when, or where and when, it was written or made. **3.** The age or period to which a thing belongs: a town of ancient *date.* **4.** The term or duration of a thing. **5.** The day of the month. **6.** *Informal* A social appointment or engagement for a specified time. **7.** *Informal* A person of the opposite sex with whom such an appointment is made. — **to date** Up to and including the present day; till now. — *v.* **dat·ed, dat·ing** *v.t.* **1.** To furnish or mark with a date. **2.** To ascertain the time or era of; assign a date to. **3.** *U.S. Informal* To make an appointment with (a member of the opposite sex). — *v.i.* **4.** To have origin in an era or time: usually with *from*: This coin *dates* from the Renaissance. **5.** To reckon time. **6.** *Informal* To have appointments with members of the opposite sex. [< F < L *data,* fem. pp. of *dare* to give] — **dat′a·ble** *adj.* — **dat′er** *n.*

date² (dāt) *n.* **1.** The sweet fruit of a palm, enclosing a single hard seed. **2.** A palm bearing this fruit: also **date palm.** [< OF < L < Gk. *daktylos* finger]

dat·ed (dā′tid) *adj.* **1.** Marked with a date. **2.** Antiquated; old-fashioned.

date·less (dāt′lis) *adj.* **1.** Bearing no date. **2.** Without end or limit. **3.** Immemorial. **4.** Of permanent interest.

date line **1.** The line containing the date of publication of a periodical or of any contribution printed in it. **2.** An imaginary line roughly corresponding to 180° longitude from Greenwich, internationally agreed upon as determining those points on the earth's surface where a day is dropped on crossing it from west to east and added crossing east to west.

da·tive (dā′tiv) *n. Gram.* **1.** In inflected Indo-European languages, the case of a noun, pronoun, or adjective denoting the indirect object. It is expressed in English by *to* or *for* with the objective or by word order, as in *I told the story to him, I told him the story.* **2.** A word in this case. — *adj. Gram.* Pertaining to or designating the dative case or a word in this case: also **da·ti·val** (dā·tī′vəl). [< L *dativus,* trans. of Gk. (*ptōsis*) *dotikē* (the case of) giving] — **da′tive·ly** *adv.*

da·tum (dā′təm, dat′əm, dä′təm) Singular of DATA.

daub (dôb) *v.t. & v.i.* **1.** To smear or coat (something), as with plaster, grease, etc. **2.** To paint without skill. — *n.* **1.** Any sticky application, as of mud, plaster, clay, etc. **2.** A smear or spot. **3.** A poor painting. **4.** An instance or act of daubing. [< OF < L *dealbare* to whitewash] — **daub′er** *n.* — **daub′y** *adj.*

daugh·ter (dô′tər) *n.* **1.** A female child, considered in relationship to either or both of her parents. **2.** A female descendant. **3.** A woman or girl considered to be in a relationship like that of a daughter: a *daughter* of nobility. **4.** Anything regarded as a female descendant. [OE *dohtor*] — **daugh′ter·ly** *adj.* — **daugh′ter·li·ness** *n.*

daugh·ter-in-law (dô′tər·in·lô′) *n. pl.* **daugh·ters-in-law** The wife of one's son.

daunt (dônt, dänt) *v.t.* To dishearten or intimidate; c [< OF < L *domare* to tame]

daunt·less (dônt′lis, dänt′-) *adj.* Fearless; intrepid. **daunt′less·ly** *adv.* — **daunt′less·ness** *n.*

dau·phin (dô′fin, *Fr.* dō·faṅ′) *n.* The eldest son of a kin France, a title used from 1349 to 1830. [< F, a dolphi

dav·en·port (dav′ən·pôrt, -pōrt) *n. U.S.* A large, up stered sofa, often usable as a bed. [Prob. from the nam the first manufacturer]

Da·vid (dā′vid), 1040?–970? B.C., second king of Judah Israel 1010?–970? B.C., succeeded Solomon. — **Da·vi** (də·vid′ik) *adj.*

dav·it (dav′it, dā′vit) *n. Naut.* One of a pair of small cra on a ship's side for hoisting its boats, stores, etc. [Appar. from *David,* proper name]

DAVIT
a Position on deck
b Position when low ering lifeboat.

da·vy (dā′vē) *n. pl.* **·vies** A safety lamp (def. 1). [after Sir Humphry *Davy,* who invented it] Also **Davy lamp.**

Da·vy Jones (dā′vē jōnz′) The spirit of the sea.

Davy Jones's locker The bottom of the ocean, esp. as the grave of the drowned.

daw·dle (dôd′l) *v.t. & v.i.* **·dled, ·dling** To waste (time) in slow trifling; loiter: often with *away.* [? Var. of DADDLE] — **daw′dler** *n.*

dawn (dôn) *n.* **1.** Daybreak. ◆ Collateral adjective: *roral.* **2.** A beginning or unfolding. — *v.i.* **1.** To begin grow light in the morning. **2.** To begin to be understo with *on* or *upon.* **3.** To begin to expand or develop. [M *dawenyng* daybreak < Scand.]

day (dā) *n.* **1.** The period of light from dawn to dark; d light. **2.** The interval represented by one rotation of earth upon its axis; twenty-four hours. ◆ Collateral adj tive: *diurnal.* **3.** A portion of a day spent in a particu way or place: a shopping *day*; a *day* outdoors. **4.** The ho of a day devoted to work: a seven-hour *day.* **5.** A time period; age; epoch: in Caesar's *day.* **6.** *Usu. cap.* A parti lar day: Labor *Day.* **7.** *Often pl.* A lifetime: in my *day.* A period of success, influence, accomplishment, etc.: Y *day* will come. **9.** The contest or battle of the day: to the *day.* — **day after day** Every day. — **day by day** E day. — **day in, day out** Every day. — **(from) day to d** From one day to the next. [OE *dæg*]

day bed A lounge or couch that can be converted into a b

day·book (dā′bo͝ok′) *n.* **1.** In bookkeeping, the book which transactions are recorded in the order of their occ rence. **2.** A diary or journal.

day·break (dā′brāk′) *n.* The time each morning when d light replaces darkness.

day camp A camp where children spend the day in sup vised activities, returning home each evening.

day coach A railroad car without special accommodatio as distinguished from a sleeping car, dining car, etc.

day·dream (dā′drēm′) *n.* A dreamlike thought, as of a ture or desired event, situation, etc.; reverie. — *v.i.* To ha daydreams. — **day′dream′er** *n.*

day·fly (dā′flī′) *n.* A May fly.

day laborer One who works for pay by the day, esp. unskilled manual tasks.

day letter A long telegram, slower and cheaper than a re lar telegram, sent during the day.

day·light (dā′līt′) *n.* **1.** The light received from the su the light of day. **2.** Insight into or understanding of son thing formerly puzzling. **3.** Exposure to view; publicity. The period of light during the day.

day·light-sav·ing time (dā′līt′sā′ving) Time in whi more daylight is obtained at the end of each working day setting clocks one or more hours ahead of standard time, e during the summer months.

day·long (dā′lông′, -long′) *adj.* Lasting all day. — *a* Through the entire day.

day nursery A place for the care of small children, e those of working mothers, during the day.

Day of Atonement Yom Kippur.

Day of Judgment *Theol.* Judgment Day.

day school **1.** A school that holds classes only during t daytime. **2.** A private school for pupils who live at home.

day·time (dā′tīm′) *n.* The time of daylight.

daze (dāz) *v.t.* **dazed, daz·ing** To stupefy or bewilder; stu — *n.* The state of being dazed. [ME *dasen*] — **daz·ed** (dā′zid·lē) *adv.*

daz·zle (daz′əl) *v.* **·zled, ·zling** *v.t.* **1.** To blind or dim t vision of by excess of light. **2.** To bewilder or charm, as wi brilliant display. — *v.i.* **3.** To be blinded by lights or gla **4.** To excite admiration. — *n.* **1.** The act of dazzling; da zled condition. **2.** Something that dazzles; brightne [Freq. of DAZE] — **daz′zling·ly** *adv.*

D-day (dē′dā′) *n.* In military operations, the unspecified date of the launching of an attack; especially, June 6, 1944, the day on which the Allies invaded France in World War II.
DDT A powerful insecticide effective on contact. [< D(I-CHLORO)D(IPHENYL)T(RICHLOROETHANE)]
de- *prefix* **1.** Away; off: *deflect, decapitate.* **2.** Down: *decline, descend.* **3.** Completely; utterly: *derelict, denude.* **4.** The undoing, reversing, or ridding of (the action, condition or substance expressed by the main element: *decode, decentralization, decarbonization.* [< L *de* from, away, down; also < F *dé-* < L *de-*, or < OF *des-* < L *dis-* (see DIS-[1])]
dea·con (dē′kən) *n.* **1.** A lay church officer or subordinate minister. **2.** In the Anglican, Eastern Orthodox, and Roman Catholic churches, a clergyman ranking next below a priest. [OE < L < Gk. *diakonos* servant, minister] — **dea·con·ry** (dē′kən·rē), **dea′con·ship** *n.*
dea·con·ess (dē′kən·is) *n.* A woman appointed or chosen as a lay church worker or officer.
de·ac·ti·vate (dē·ak′tə·vāt) *v.t.* **·vat·ed, ·vat·ing 1.** To render inactive or ineffective, as an explosive, chemical, etc. **2.** *Mil.* To release (a military unit, ship, etc.) from active duty; demobilize. **— de·ac′ti·va′tion** *n.*
dead (ded) *adj.* **1.** Having ceased to live; lifeless. **2.** Deathlike: a *dead* faint. **3.** Inanimate. **4.** Insensible: with *to:* dead to pity. **5.** Lacking sensation; numb. **6.** Extinct: a *dead* language. **7.** No longer in force: a *dead* law. **8.** Not productively used: *dead* capital. **9.** *Informal* Very tired. **10.** Lacking activity, excitement, etc.: a *dead* town. **11.** Extinguished: a *dead* fire. **12.** Dull: said of colors. **13.** Muffled: said of sounds. **14.** Without elasticity. **15.** Complete; utter: *dead* silence. **16.** Having no outlet or opening: a *dead* end. **17.** Perfect; exact: a *dead* center. **18.** Unerring; sure: a *dead* shot. **19.** In certain games, out of play: said of the ball. **—** *n.* **1.** A dead person, or dead persons collectively: preceded by *the.* **2.** The coldest, darkest, or most intense part: the *dead* of winter. **—** *adv.* **1.** Completely: to stop *dead.* **2.** Directly: *dead* ahead. [OE *dēad*] **— dead′ness** *n.*
dead·beat (ded′bēt′) *n. U.S. Slang* **1.** One who avoids paying his bills. **2.** A sponger.
dead center *Mech.* One of two points in the motion of a crank and connecting rod when they are in alignment and the connecting rod has no power to turn the crank.
dead·en (ded′n) *v.t.* **1.** To diminish the sensitivity, force, or intensity of. **2.** To impede the velocity of; retard. **3.** To render soundproof. **4.** To make dull or less brilliant in color. **—** *v.i.* **5.** To become dead. **— dead′en·er** *n.*
dead end 1. A passage, street, etc., having no outlet. **2.** A point from which no progress can be made.
dead·eye (ded′ī′) *n. Naut.* A wooden disk pierced by holes through which lanyards are passed, and having a grooved circumference, used to set up shrouds, stays, etc.
dead·fall (ded′fôl′) *n.* A trap operated by a weight that falls upon and kills or holds an animal.
dead·head (ded′hed′) *Informal n.* **1.** One who is admitted, entertained, or accommodated free of charge. **2.** A dull, stupid person. **—** *v.t. & v.i.* To treat or go as a deadhead. **—** *adj.* Traveling without passengers or freight.
dead heat A race in which two or more competitors tie.
dead letter 1. A letter that is unclaimed, or cannot be delivered because of a faulty address. **2.** A law, issue, etc., no longer valid or enforced, though still formally in effect.
dead·line (ded′līn′) *n.* **1.** A time limit, as for the completion of newspaper copy, payment of debts, etc. **2.** Originally, a boundary line that prisoners might not cross.
dead·lock (ded′lok′) *n.* A standstill or stoppage of activity resulting from the unrelenting opposition of equally powerful forces. **—** *v.t. & v.i.* To cause or come to a deadlock.
dead·ly (ded′lē) *adj.* **·li·er, ·li·est 1.** Likely or certain to cause death. **2.** Implacable; mortal: a *deadly* enemy. **3.** Resembling death: *deadly* pallor. **4.** *Theol.* Causing spiritual death: a *deadly* sin. **5.** Excessive. **—** *adv.* **1.** As in death; deathly. **2.** *Informal* Very. **— dead′li·ness** *n.*
deadly nightshade Belladonna.
dead pan *U.S. Slang* A completely expressionless face. — **dead·pan** (ded′pan′) *adj. & adv.*
dead reckoning *Naut.* The computation of a vessel's position by log and compass without astronomical observations.
Dead Sea Scrolls A number of scrolls of parchment, leather, or copper, dating from about 100 B.C. to A.D. 100, containing Hebrew and Aramaic texts of Biblical works, found in 1947 and after in caves near the Dead Sea.
dead weight 1. A heavy weight or load, as of something inert. **2.** In transportation, the weight of a vehicle as distinguished from its load.
dead·wood (ded′wŏŏd′) *n.* **1.** Wood dead on the tree. **2.** *U.S.* Worthless material; a useless person or thing.
deaf (def) *adj.* **1.** Partly or completely lacking the power to hear. **2.** Determined not to hear; unwilling to listen. [OE *dēaf*] **— deaf′ly** *adv.* **— deaf′ness** *n.*
deaf-and-dumb alphabet (def′ən·dum′) Manual alphabet (which see).
deaf·en (def′ən) *v.t.* **1.** To make deaf. **2.** To confuse, stupefy, or overwhelm, as with noise. **3.** To drown (a sound) by a louder sound. **4.** To make soundproof.
deaf-mute (def′myōōt′) *n.* A deaf person who cannot speak, usu. because of deafness from early life. Also **deaf mute.**
deal[1] (dēl) *v.* **dealt** (delt); **deal·ing** *v.t.* **1.** To distribute or portion out, as playing cards. **2.** To apportion to (one person) as his or her share. **3.** To deliver or inflict, as a blow. **—** *v.i.* **4.** To conduct oneself; behave toward: with *with.* **5.** To be concerned or occupied: with *in* or *with:* to *deal* in facts. **6.** To consider, discuss, or take action: with *with.* **7.** To do business: with *in, with,* or *at.* **8.** In card games, to act as dealer. **—** *n.* **1.** The act of dealing. **2.** In card games: **a** The distribution of the cards to the players. **b** The right or turn to distribute the cards. **c** The cards distributed to a player; a hand. **d** A single round of play. **3.** An indefinite amount, degree, extent, etc.: a great *deal* of time. **4.** *Informal* A business transaction. **5.** *Informal* A secret arrangement, as in politics. **6.** *Informal* A plan, agreement, or treatment: a rough *deal.* [OE *dǣlan.*]
deal[2] (dēl) *n.* **1.** A fir or pine plank. **2.** Such planks collectively. **—** *adj.* Made of deal. [< MDu. *dele* plank]
deal·er (dē′lər) *n.* **1.** One engaged in a specified business; a trader. **2.** In card games, one who distributes the cards.
deal·ing (dē′ling) *n.* **1.** The act of distributing. **2.** *Usu. pl.* Transactions or relations with others. **3.** Method or manner of treatment: honest *dealing.*
dealt (delt) Past tense and past participle of DEAL.
dean (dēn) *n.* **1.** An officer of a college or university, having jurisdiction over a particular group of students, area of study, or acting as head of a faculty. **2.** The senior member, in length of service, of a group of men. **3.** The chief ecclesiastical officer of a cathedral or of a collegiate church. [< OF < LL < L *decem* ten] **— dean′ship** *n.*
dean·er·y (dē′nər·ē) *n. pl.* **·er·ies** The office, revenue, jurisdiction, or place of residence of a dean.
dear (dir) *adj.* **1.** Beloved; precious. **2.** Highly esteemed: used in letter salutations. **3.** Expensive; costly. **4.** Characterized by high prices. **5.** Intense; earnest: our *dearest* wish. **—** *n.* One who is much beloved; a darling. **—** *adv.* Dearly. **—** *interj.* An exclamation of regret, surprise, etc. [OE *dēore*] **— dear′ly** *adv.* **— dear′ness** *n.*
dearth (dûrth) *n.* Scarcity; lack; famine. [ME *derthe*]
dear·y (dir′ē) *n. pl.* **dear·ies** *Informal* Darling; dear. Also **dear′ie.**
death (deth) *n.* **1.** The permanent cessation of all vital functions in an animal or plant. **2.** The condition of being dead. **3.** *Usu. cap.* A personification of death, usu. a skeleton holding a scythe. **4.** The extinction of anything; destruction. **5.** The cause of dying. **6.** The time or manner of dying: to meet a tyrant's *death.* **7.** Something considered as terrible as death. ◆ Collateral adjectives: *lethal, mortal.* **— to death** Very much: He frightened me *to death.* **— to put to death** To kill; execute. [OE *dēath*]
death·bed (deth′bed′) *n.* **1.** The bed on which a person dies or died. **2.** The last hours of life.
death·blow (deth′blō′) *n.* That which causes the death or the end of a person or thing.
death·cup (deth′kup′) *n.* A poisonous mushroom having a usu. white, olive, or umber cap.
death house That part of a prison, as a block of cells, in which prisoners condemned to death are confined.
death·less (deth′lis) *adj.* Not liable to die; perpetual; immortal. **— death′less·ly** *adv.* **— death′less·ness** *n.*
death·ly (deth′lē) *adj.* **1.** Resembling or suggesting death. Also **death′like.** **2.** Causing death; fatal. **—** *adv.* **1.** In a deathlike manner. **2.** Extremely: *deathly* ill.
death mask A cast of the face taken just after death.
death rate The number of persons per thousand of population who die within a given time.
death rattle The rattling sound caused by the breath passing through mucus in the throat of one dying.
death's-head (deths′hed′) *n.* A human skull, or a representation of it, as a symbol of death.
death trap (deth′trap′) *n.* **1.** An unsafe building or structure. **2.** Any very dangerous situation.
death warrant 1. *Law* An official order for the execution of a person. **2.** Anything that destroys hope, happiness, etc.
death·watch (deth′woch′, -wôch′) *n.* **1.** A vigil kept at the side of one who is dying or has recently died. **2.** A guard set over a condemned man before his execution.
de·ba·cle (dā·bäk′əl, -bak′əl, di-) *n.* **1.** A sudden and disastrous breakdown or collapse. **2.** The breaking up of ice in a river. **3.** A violent flood. [< F < *débâcler* to unbar]

de·bar (di·bär′) *v.t.* **·barred, ·bar·ring** **1.** To bar or shut out: usu. with *from.* **2.** To hinder. [< F < *dé-* away + *barrer* to bar] — **de·bar′ment** *n.*

de·bark (di·bärk′) *v.t. & v.i.* To put or go ashore from a ship. [< F < *dé-* away + *barque* ship] — **de·bar·ka·tion** (dē′bär·kā′shən) *n.*

de·base (di·bās′) *v.t.* **·based, ·bas·ing** To lower in character or worth; degrade. [< DE- + obs. *base*] — **de·base′ment** *n.* — **de·bas′er** *n.*

de·bate (di·bāt′) *n.* **1.** A discussion of any question; argument; dispute. **2.** A formal contest in argumentation conducted between persons taking opposite sides of a question. — *v.* **·bat·ed, ·bat·ing** *v.t.* **1.** To argue about; discuss, as in a public meeting. **2.** To deliberate upon; consider, as alternatives. **3.** To discuss in formal debate. — *v.i.* **4.** To engage in argument; discuss a question. **5.** To take part in a formal debate. **6.** To deliberate; ponder. [< OF < *de-* down + *batre* to strike] — **de·bat′a·ble** *adj.* — **de·bat′er** *n.*

de·bauch (di·bôch′) *v.t.* **1.** To corrupt in morals; seduce; deprave. — *v.i.* **2.** To indulge in debauchery; dissipate. — *n.* **1.** An act or period of debauchery. **2.** Debauchery. [< F < OF *desbaucher* to lure from work] — **de·bauch·ed·ly** (di·bô′chid·lē) *adv.* — **de·bauch′er** *n.* — **de·bauch′ment** *n.*

deb·au·chee (deb′ô·chē′, -shē′) *n.* One habitually profligate, drunken, or lewd; a libertine.

de·bauch·er·y (di·bô′chər·ē) *n. pl.* **·er·ies** Gross indulgence of one's sensual appetites.

de·ben·ture (di·ben′chər) *n.* **1.** A certificate given as acknowledgment of debt. **2.** A bond, usu. without security, issued by a corporation and often convertible into common stock. Also **debenture bond.** [< L *debere* to owe]

de·bil·i·tate (di·bil′ə·tāt) *v.t.* **·tat·ed, ·tat·ing** To make feeble or languid; weaken. [< L *debilitare* < *debilis* weak] — **de·bil′i·ta′tion** *n.* — **de·bil′i·ta′tive** *adj.*

de·bil·i·ty (di·bil′ə·tē) *n. pl.* **·ties** Abnormal weakness; languor; feebleness. [< F < L < *debilis* weak]

deb·it (deb′it) *n.* **1.** An item of debt recorded in an account. **2.** An entry of debt in an account, or the sum of such entries. **3.** The left-hand side of an account, where debts are recorded. — *v.t.* **1.** To enter (a debt) in an account. **2.** To charge (someone) with a debt. [< L *debere* to owe]

deb·o·nair (deb′ə·nâr′) *adj.* **1.** Urbane; nonchalant. **2.** Pleasantly gracious. **3.** Cheerful; lively; gay. Also **deb′o·naire′, deb′on·naire′.** [< OF *de bon aire* of good mien] — **deb′o·nair′ly** *adv.* — **deb′o·nair′ness** *n.*

de·bouch (di·bōōsh′) *v.i.* **1.** *Mil.* To march from a narrow passage, wood, etc., into the open. **2.** To come forth; emerge; issue. — *v.t.* **3.** To cause to emerge. [< F < *dé-* from + *bouche* a mouth] — **de·bouch′ment** *n.*

de·bris (də·brē′, dā′brē; *Brit.* deb′rē) *n.* **1.** Fragments, or scattered remains, as of something destroyed; ruins; rubble. **2.** *Geol.* An accumulation of detached fragments of rocks. Also **dé·bris′.** [< F < OF *debrisier* to break away]

debt (det) *n.* **1.** That which one owes, as money, goods, or services. **2.** The obligation to pay or render something to another. **3.** The condition of owing something. **4.** *Theol.* A sin. [< OF < L *debere* to owe]

debt of honor A gambling debt.

debt·or (det′ər) *n.* One who owes a debt.

de·bunk (di·bungk′) *v.t. Informal* To expose or deride the sham, false pretensions, etc., of. [< BUNK[2]]

de·but (di·byōō′, dā-, dā′byōō) *n.* **1.** A first public appearance. **2.** A formal introduction to society. **3.** The beginning, as of a career. — *v.i.* To make a debut. Also **dé·but′.** [< F < *débuter* to begin]

deb·u·tante (deb′yōō·tänt, -yə-, *Fr.* deb′yōō·tänt′) *n.fem.* A young woman making a debut in society. Also **dé′bu·tante′.**

deca- *combining form* **1.** Ten. **2.** In the metric system, deka-. Also, before vowels, **dec-.**

dec·ade (dek′ād, de·kād′) *n.* **1.** A period of ten years. **2.** A group or set of ten. [< MF < L < Gk. < *deka* ten]

de·ca·dence (di·kād′ns, dek′ə·dəns) *n.* **1.** A process of deterioration; decay. **2.** A condition or period of decline, as in morals. [< F < Med.L < L < *de-* down + *cadere* to fall]

de·ca·dent (dek′ə·dənt, di·kād′nt) *adj.* Falling into, or characteristic of, decay and decline. — *n.* A decadent person, esp. an artist or writer. — **de·ca′dent·ly** *adv.*

dec·a·gon (dek′ə·gon) *n. Geom.* A polygon with ten sides and ten angles. [< Gk. < *deka* ten + *gōnia* angle] — **de·cag·o·nal** (di·kag′ə·nəl) *adj.* — **de·cag′o·nal·ly** *adv.*

dec·a·gram (dek′ə·gram) See DEKAGRAM.

dec·a·he·dron (dek′ə·hē′drən) *n. pl.* **·drons** or **·dra** (-drə) *Geom.* A polyhedron bounded by ten plane faces. [< DECA- + Gk. *hedra* seat] — **dec′a·he′dral** *adj.*

DECAHEDRON

de·cal (dē′kal, di·kal′) *n.* A decalcomania.

de·cal·ci·fy (dē·kal′sə·fī) *v.t.* **·fied, ·fy·ing** To remove lime or calcareous matter from (bones, teeth, etc.). — **de·cal′ci·fi·ca′tion** *n.*

de·cal·co·ma·ni·a (di·kal′kə·mā′nē·ə, -mān′yə) *n.* **1.** A process of transferring prints, designs, etc., from specially prepared paper to glass, porcelain, other material. **2.** The design or print to be transferred. [< F < *décalquer* to transfer a tracing + *-manie* -mania]

dec·a·li·ter (dek′ə·lē′tər) See DEKALITER.

Dec·a·logue (dek′ə·lôg, -log) *n.* The Ten Commandmen Also **Dec′a·log.** [< Gk. < *deka* ten + *logos* word]

dec·a·me·ter (dek′ə·mē′tər) See DEKAMETER.

de·camp (di·kamp′) *v.i.* **1.** To break camp. **2.** To lea suddenly or secretly; run away. — **de·camp′ment** *n.*

de·cant (di·kant′) *v.t.* **1.** To pour off (a liquid) without d turbing its sediment. **2.** To pour from one container in another. [< F < Med.L < *de-* from + *canthus* lip of a j — **de·can·ta·tion** (dē′kan·tā′shən) *n.*

de·cant·er (di·kan′tər) *n.* A vessel for decanting; esp decorative, stoppered bottle for serving wine, etc.

de·cap·i·tate (di·kap′ə·tāt) *v.t.* **·tat·ed, ·tat·ing** To cut the head of; behead. [< Med.L < L *de-* off + *caput* hea — **de·cap′i·ta′tion** *n.* — **de·cap′i·ta′tor** *n.*

dec·a·pod (dek′ə·pod) *adj.* Ten-footed or ten-armed. — *Zool.* **1.** A crustacean having five pairs of legs, including crabs, lobsters, shrimps, etc. **2.** Any ten-armed cephalop as a cuttlefish or squid. [< Gk. < *deka* ten + *pous* foot] **de·cap·o·dal** (di·kap′ə·dəl), **de·cap′o·dous** *adj.*

de·car·bon·ate (dē·kär′bə·nāt) *v.t.* **·at·ed, ·at·ing** To f from carbon dioxide. — **de·car′bon·a′tor** *n.*

de·car·bon·ize (dē·kär′bən·īz) *v.t.* **·ized, ·iz·ing** To dec burize. — **de·car′bon·i·za′tion** *n.* — **de·car′bon·iz′er** *n.*

de·car·bu·rize (dē·kär′byə·rīz) *v.t.* **·rized, ·riz·ing** To move carbon from (molten steel or the cylinders of an nal-combustion engine). — **de·car′bu·ri·za′tion** *n.*

dec·are (dek′âr, dek·âr′) See DEKARE.

dec·a·stere (dek′ə·stir) See DEKASTERE.

dec·a·syl·la·ble (dek′ə·sil′ə·bəl) *n.* A line of verse havi ten syllables. — **dec·a·syl·lab·ic** (dek′ə·si·lab′ik) *adj.*

de·cath·lon (di·kath′lon) *n.* An athletic contest consisti of ten different track and field events in all of which each co testant participates. [< DEC(A)- + Gk. *athlon* a contest

de·cay (di·kā′) *v.i.* **1.** To fail slowly in health, beauty, qu ity, or any form of excellence. **2.** To decompose; rot. — **3.** To cause to decay. — *n.* **1.** A falling into a ruined or r duced condition. **2.** Decomposition, as of a dead organis **3.** Rottenness. [< OF < L < *de-* down + *cadere* to fall

— **Syn.** (verb) **2.** Dead organic matter *decays* by the action bacteria; also, a great mind may *decay* with age. *Putrefy* is us only of animal matter, as is also the strong, direct *rot. Spoil* su gests mild decay or taint; food *spoils* if not refrigerated.

de·cease (di·sēs′) *v.i.* **·ceased, ·ceas·ing** To die. — Death. [< OF < L < *de-* away + *cedere* to go]

de·ceased (di·sēst′) *adj.* Dead. — **the deceased** The de person or persons.

de·ce·dent (di·sēd′nt) *n. Law* A person deceased.

de·ceit (di·sēt′) *n.* **1.** The act of deceiving. **2.** An instan of deception or a device that deceives; a trick. **3.** The qu ity of being deceptive; falseness. [See DECEIVE.]

de·ceit·ful (di·sēt′fəl) *adj.* **1.** Given to deceiving; lying treacherous. **2.** Tending to deceive; false. — **Syn.** See D CEPTIVE. — **de·ceit′ful·ly** *adv.* — **de·ceit′ful·ness** *n.*

de·ceive (di·sēv′) *v.* **·ceived, ·ceiv·ing** *v.t.* **1.** To mislead falsehood; lead into error; delude. — *v.i.* **2.** To practice d ceit. [< OF < L < *de-* away, down + *capere* to take] **de·ceiv′er** *n.* — **de·ceiv′ing·ly** *adv.*

de·cel·er·ate (dē·sel′ə·rāt) *v.t. & v.i.* **·at·ed, ·at·ing** To d minish in velocity. [< DE- + L *celarere* to hasten] — **d cel′er·a′tion** *n.* — **de·cel′er·a′tor** *n.*

De·cem·ber (di·sem′bər) *n.* The twelfth month of the yea having 31 days. [< L < *decem* ten; December was the ten month in the old Roman calendar]

de·cem·vir (di·sem′vər) *n. pl.* **·virs** or **·vi·ri** (-və·rī) A mer ber of any body of ten magistrates; esp. one in ancient Rom [< L < *decem* ten + *vir* man] — **de·cem′vi·ral** *adj.*

de·cem·vi·rate (di·sem′və·rit, -rāt) *n.* **1.** A body of te men in authority. **2.** The government of such a body.

de·cen·cy (dē′sən·sē) *n. pl.* **·cies** **1.** The quality or state being decent; propriety in conduct, speech, or dress. *Usu. pl.* Those things that are proper or decent. **3.** *pl.* Th requirements for a proper manner of life.

de·cen·ni·al (di·sen′ē·əl) *adj.* **1.** Of or continuing for te years. **2.** Occurring every ten years. — *n.* An anniversa observed every ten years. — **de·cen′ni·al·ly** *adv.*

de·cent (dē′sənt) *adj.* **1.** Characterized by propriety of co duct, speech, or dress; proper; respectable. **2.** Free of coars ness or indelicacy; modest; chaste. **3.** Adequate; satisfa tory. **4.** Generous; kind. **5.** *Informal* Adequately or pro erly clothed. [< L *decere* to be fitting, proper] — **de′cen ly** *adv.* — **de′cent·ness** *n.*

de·cen·tral·ize (dē·sen′trəl·īz) *v.t.* **·ized, ·iz·ing** To und the centralization of; reorganize into smaller and more di persed parts. — **de·cen′tral·i·za′tion** *n.*

de·cep·tion (di·sep′shən) *n.* **1.** The act of deceiving; decei **2.** The state of being deceived. **3.** Anything that deceiv or is meant to deceive; a delusion. [See DECEIVE.]

cep·tive (di·sep′tiv) *adj.* Having power or tendency to ceive. **— de·cep′tive·ly** *adv.* **— de·cep′tive·ness** *n.*
i- *combining form* In the metric system, one tenth of (a ecified unit): *decimeter.* [< L *decimus* tenth < *decem* ten]
·i·are (des′ē·âr) *n.* In the metric system, one tenth of an e. Abbr. *da.* [< F *déciare*]
·i·bel (des′ə·bəl) *n. Physics* One tenth of a bel: a meas- e of sound intensity.
cide (di·sīd′) *v.* **·cid·ed, cid·ing** *v.t.* **1.** To determine; set- , as a controversy, contest, etc. **2.** To determine the issue conclusion of: The charge *decided* the battle. **3.** To bring omeone) to a decision. **—** *v.i.* **4.** To give a decision or ver- ct. **5.** To make a decision. [< MF < L < *de-* down, ay + *caedere* to cut] **— de·cid′a·ble** *adj.*
cid·ed (di·sī′did) *adj.* **1.** Free from uncertainty; definite. Exhibiting determination; resolute; emphatic. **— de· i′ed·ly** *adv.* **— de·cid′ed·ness** *n.*
cid·u·ous (di·sij′ōō·əs) *adj.* **1.** *Biol.* Falling off or shed at aturity or at specific seasons, as petals, fruit, leaves, ant- s, etc. **2.** Characterized by such a falling off: distin- ished from *evergreen.* [< L < *de-* down, away + *cadere* to ll] **— de·cid′u·ous·ly** *adv.* **— de·cid′u·ous·ness** *n.*
·i·gram (des′ə·gram) *n.* In the metric system, the tenth rt of a gram. Also **dec′i·gramme.** See table front of ok.
·i·li·ter (des′ə·lē′tər) *n.* In the metric system, the tenth rt of a liter. Also *esp. Brit.* **dec′i·li′tre.** Abbr. *dl, dl.* See ble front of book.
cil·lion (di·sil′yən) *n.* **1.** *U.S.* A thousand nonillions, ritten as 1 followed by thirty-three zeros: a cardinal num- r. **2.** *Brit.* A million nonillions (def. 2), written as 1 fol- wed by sixty zeros: a cardinal number. **—** *adj.* Being a cillion. [< DEC(A)- + (M)ILLION] **— de·cil′lionth** *adj.*
c·i·mal (des′ə·məl) *adj.* **1.** Pertaining to or founded on e number 10. **2.** Proceeding by tens. **—** *n.* A decimal action or one of its digits. [< Med.L < L *decem* ten]
cimal fraction *Math.* A fraction whose denominator is y power of 10 and which may be expressed in decimal rm, as 7/10 (0.7), 3/100 (0.03), etc.
cimal point A dot used before a decimal fraction.
cimal system A system of reckoning by tens or tenths.
c·i·mate (des′ə·māt) *v.t.* **·mat·ed, ·mat·ing 1.** To destroy kill a large proportion of. **2.** To select by lot and kill one it of every ten of. [< L *decimare* to take a tenth part from] **— dec′i·ma′tion** *n.* **— dec′i·ma′tor** *n.*
c·i·me·ter (des′ə·mē′tər) *n.* In the metric system, the nth part of a meter. Also *esp. Brit.* **dec′i·me′tre.** Abbr. *c., decim., dm, dm.* See table front of book.
·ci·pher (di·sī′fər) *v.t.* **1.** To determine the meaning of omething obscure, illegible, etc.) **2.** To translate from pher or code into plain text; decode. **— de·ci′pher·a·ble** *lj.* **— de·ci′pher·er** *n.* **— de·ci′pher·ment** *n.*
·ci·sion (di·sizh′ən) *n.* **1.** The act of deciding (an issue, uestion, etc.). **2.** A conclusion or judgment reached by de- ding. **3.** The making up of one's mind. **4.** Firmness in dgment, action, or character. **5.** In boxing, a victory de- ded when there has not been a knockout. [See DECIDE.]
·ci·sive (di·sī′siv) *adj.* **1.** Ending uncertainty or dispute; onclusive. **2.** Characterized by decision and firmness; de- rmined. **3.** Unquestionable; unmistakable. **— deci′· ve·ly** *adv.* **— de·ci′sive·ness** *n.*
c·i·stere (des′ə·stir) *n.* In the metric system, a cubic ecimeter, or the tenth part of a stere. Abbr. *ds.*
ck (dek) *n.* **1.** *Naut.* **a** A platform covering or extending orizontally across a vessel, and serving as both floor and oof. **b** The space between two such platforms. **2.** Any milar flat surface. **3.** *U.S.* A pack of playing cards. **— to it the deck** *Slang* **1.** To rise from bed; get up. **2.** To pre- are for action. **— on deck** *Slang* Present and ready for ction. **—** *v.t.* **1.** To dress or decorate elegantly; adorn. **2.** *aut.* To furnish with a deck. [< MDu. *dek* roof, covering]
ck·er (dek′ər) *n.* Something with one or more decks, ayers, levels, etc.: usu. in combination: a *double-decker.*
ck hand A common sailor employed on deck.
ck·le (dek′əl) *n.* **1.** In making paper by hand, a frame hat limits the size of the sheet. **2.** The ragged edge of hand- ade paper: also **deckle edge.** Also **deck′el.** [< G *decke* over] **— deck′le-edged′** *adj.*
·claim (di·klām′) *v.i.* **1.** To speak loudly and rhetoric- lly. **2.** To give a formal, set speech. **3.** To attack verbally nd vehemently: with *against.* **—** *v.t.* **4.** To utter rhetori- ally. [< L < *de-* completely + *clamare* to shout] **— de· laim′er** *n.* **— dec·la·ma·tion** (dek′lə·mā′shən) *n.*
·clam·a·to·ry (di·klam′ə·tôr′ē, -tō′rē) *adj.* Of, like, or ertaining to declamation. **— de·clam′a·to′ri·ly** *adv.*
c·la·ra·tion (dek′lə·rā′shən) *n.* **1.** The act of declaring r proclaiming. **2.** That which is declared. **3.** A statement f goods liable to taxation. **4.** In bridge, a contract.
Declaration of Independence The manifesto that formally declared the political independence of the American colonies from Britain. It was written by Thomas Jefferson and adopted July 4, 1776.
de·clar·a·tive (di·klar′ə·tiv) *adj.* Making a declaration or statement. Also **de·clar·a·to·ry** (di·klar′ə·tôr′ē, -tō′rē).
de·clare (di·klâr′) *v.* **·clared, ·clar·ing** *v.t.* **1.** To make known or clear; esp. to announce formally; proclaim. **2.** To say emphatically; assert; avow. **3.** To reveal; prove. **4.** To make full statement of, as goods liable to duty. **5.** In bridge, to make a final bid designating (a trump suit or no-trump). **—** *v.i.* **6.** To make a declaration. **7.** To proclaim a choice or opinion: with *for* or *against.* [< L < *de-* completely + *clarare* to make clear] **— de·clar′er** *n.*
dé·clas·sé (dā·klȧ·sā′) *adj. French* Fallen or lowered in social status, class, rank, etc.
de·clen·sion (di·klen′shən) *n.* **1.** *Gram.* **a** The inflection of nouns, pronouns, and adjectives according to case, number, and gender. **b** A class of words similarly inflected. **2.** A sloping downward; descent. **3.** A decline. **4.** Deviation, as from a belief. [See DECLINE.] **— de·clen′sion·al** *adj.*
dec·li·na·tion (dek′lə·nā′shən) *n.* **1.** The act of inclining or bending downward. **2.** Deviation, as in direction or conduct. **3.** The angle formed between the direction of a compass needle and true north. **4.** *Astron.* The angular distance of a heavenly body north or south from the celestial equator. **5.** A polite refusal.
de·cline (di·klīn′) *v.* **·clined, ·clin·ing** *v.i.* **1.** To refuse politely to accept, comply with, or do something. **2.** To lessen or fail gradually, as in health. **3.** To draw to an end. **4.** To lower oneself, as to a mean action. **5.** To bend or incline downward or aside. **—** *v.t.* **6.** To refuse politely to accept, comply with, or do. **7.** To cause to bend or incline downward or aside. **8.** *Gram.* To give the inflected forms of (a noun, pronoun, or adjective). **—** *n.* **1.** The act or result of declining; deterioration. **2.** A period of declining. **3.** A condition in which one's mental or physical faculties weaken or deteriorate. **4.** A downward slope. [< OF < L *declinare* to lean down] **— de·clin′a·ble** *adj.* **— de·clin′er** *n.*
de·cliv·i·ty (di·kliv′ə·tē) *n. pl.* **·ties** A downward slope or surface: opposed to *acclivity.* [< L < *de-* down + *clivus* hill, slope] **— de·cliv′i·tous, de·cli′vous** (-klī′vəs) *adj.*
de·coct (di·kokt′) *v.t.* To extract by boiling; condense. [< L < *de-* down + *coquere* to cook] **— de·coc′tion** *n.*
de·code (dē·kōd′) *v.t.* **·cod·ed, ·cod·ing** To convert from code into plain language. **— de·cod′er** *n.*
dé·colle·té (dā′kol·tā′, *Fr.* dā·kôl·tā′) *adj.* **1.** Cut low in the neck, as a gown. **2.** Wearing a low-necked gown. [< F]
de·com·mis·sion (dē′kə·mish′ən) *v.t.* To take out of active service, as a ship; retire from use.
de·com·pose (dē′kəm·pōz′) *v.t. & v.i.* **·posed, ·pos·ing 1.** To separate into constituent parts. **2.** To decay. **— de′· com·pos′a·ble** *adj.* **— de′com·pos′er** *n.*
de·com·po·si·tion (dē′kom·pə·zish′ən) *n.* The act, process, or result of decomposing.
de·com·press (dē′kəm·pres′) *v.t.* **1.** To free of pressure. **2.** To remove the pressure on (divers, caisson workers, etc.). **— de′com·pres′sion** *n.*
decompression sickness Caisson disease.
de·con·tam·i·nate (dē′kən·tam′ə·nāt) *v.t.* **·nat·ed, ·nat·ing** To make (a contaminated object or area) safe by destroying or neutralizing poisonous chemicals, radioactivity, etc.
de·con·trol (dē′kən·trōl′) *v.t.* **·trolled, ·trol·ling** To remove from control. **—** *n.* The removal of controls.
dé·cor (dā′kôr, dā·kôr′) *n.* **1.** The scheme or style of decoration in a room, home, club, etc. **2.** In the theater, the scenery. Also **de′cor.** [< F < *décorer* to decorate]
dec·o·rate (dek′ə·rāt) *v.t.* **·rat·ed, ·rat·ing 1.** To embellish or furnish with things beautiful; adorn. **2.** To confer a decoration or medal upon. [< L *decus, decoris* grace, embellishment] **— dec′o·ra′tor** *n.*
dec·o·ra·tion (dek′ə·rā′shən) *n.* **1.** The act, process, or art of decorating. **2.** A thing or group of things that decorate; ornamentation. **3.** A badge or emblem; medal. ◆ The U.S. military decorations in order of precedence are: Medal of Honor, Distinguished Service Cross or Navy Cross (Navy and Marine Corps), Distinguished Service Medal, Silver Star, Legion of Merit, Distinguished Flying Cross, Soldier's Medal, Bronze Star, Air Medal, Commendation Ribbon, and Purple Heart.
Decoration Day Memorial Day.
dec·o·ra·tive (dek′ər·ə·tiv, dek′rə·tiv, dek′ə·rā′tiv) *adj.* Of, pertaining to, or suitable for decoration; ornamental. **— dec′o·ra·tive·ly** *adv.* **— dec′o·ra·tive·ness** *n.*
dec·o·rous (dek′ər·əs, di·kôr′əs, -kō′rəs) *adj.* Marked by decorum; seemly; proper. [< L *decus, decoris* grace] **— dec′o·rous·ly** *adv.* **— dec′o·rous·ness** *n.*
de·co·rum (di·kôr′əm, -kō′rəm) *n.* **1.** Conformity to the re-

quirements of good taste or social convention; propriety in behavior, dress, etc.; seemliness. **2.** *Usu. pl.* The proprieties. [See DECOROUS.]

de·coy (*n.* di·koi′, dē′koi; *v.* di·koi′) *n.* **1.** A person or thing that lures into danger, deception, etc. **2.** A bird or animal, or the likeness of one, used to lure game. **3.** An enclosed place into which game may be lured. — *v.t. & v.i.* To lure or be lured into danger or a trap. [Earlier *coy* < Du. *kooi* a cage] — **de·coy′er** *n.*

DECOY (*def.* 2)

de·crease (*v.* di·krēs′; *n.* dē′krēs, di·krēs′) *v.t. & v.i.* **·creased, ·creas·ing** To grow, or cause to grow, gradually less or smaller; diminish. — *n.* **1.** The act, process, or state of decreasing. **2.** The amount or degree of decreasing. [< OF < L < *de-* down + *crescere* to grow] — **de·creas′ing·ly** *adv.*

— **Syn.** *Decrease* is applied to amount, *lessen* to number, *dwindle* to size, and *abate* to force. To *diminish* is to grow smaller by the removal of a part. *Reduce* is used in all the foregoing senses, but is usually transitive: to *reduce* the temperature of a room.

de·cree (di·krē′) *n.* **1.** A formal and authoritative order or decision. **2.** A foreordained and eternal purpose. — *v.* **·creed, ·cree·ing** *v.t.* **1.** To order, adjudge, ordain, or appoint by law or edict. — *v.i.* **2.** To issue an edict or decree. [< Of < L < *de-* down + *cernere* to decide]

dec·re·ment (dek′rə·mənt) *n.* **1.** The act or process of decreasing. **2.** The amount lost by decrease.

de·crep·it (di·krep′it) *adj.* Enfeebled or worn out by old age or excessive use. [< L < *de-* completely + *crepare* to creak] — **de·crep′it·ly** *adv.*

de·crep·i·tude (di·krep′ə·to͞od, -tyo͞od) *n.* A decrepit or enfeebled condition, as from infirmity or old age.

de·cre·tal (di·krēt′l) *n.* A decree; esp. a papal decree.

de·cry (di·krī′) *v.t.* **·cried, ·cry·ing** **1.** To condemn or disparage openly. **2.** To depreciate, as foreign coins. [< F < *dé-* down + *crier* to cry] — **de·cri′al** *n.* — **de·cri′er** *n.*

de·cum·bent (di·kum′bənt) *adj.* **1.** Lying down. **2.** *Bot.* Prostrate: said of stems, shoots, etc., growing along the ground. [< L < *de-* down + *cumbere* to lie, recline] — **de·cum′bence, de·cum′ben·cy** *n.*

de·cus·sate (di·kus′āt, -it) *adj.* *Bot.* Having each pair of leaves at right angles with the pair below or above. [< L *decussare* to mark with an X] — **de·cus′sate·ly** *adv.* — **de·cus·sa·tion** (dē′kə·sā′shən, dek′ə-) *n.*

ded·i·cate (ded′ə·kāt, -i-) *v.t.* **·cat·ed, ·cat·ing** **1.** To set apart for sacred uses. **2.** To set apart for any special use, duty, or purpose. **3.** To inscribe (a work of literature, etc.) to someone. **4.** To commit (oneself) to a certain course of action or thought. **5.** To open or unveil (a bridge, statue, etc.) to the public. [< L < *de-* down + *dicare* to proclaim]

ded·i·ca·tion (ded′ə·kā′shən, -i-) *n.* **1.** The act of dedicating or the state of being dedicated. **2.** An inscription dedicating a literary work, etc. to someone or something.

ded·i·ca·tive (ded′ə·kā′tiv, -i-) *adj.* That dedicates.

ded·i·ca·to·ry (ded′ə·kə·tôr′ē, -tō′rē, -i-) *adj.* Constituting, containing, or serving as a dedication: a *dedicatory* preface.

de·duce (di·do͞os′, -dyo͞os′) *v.t.* **·duced, ·duc·ing** **1.** To derive as a conclusion by reasoning. **2.** To trace, as origin. [< L < *de-* down + *ducere* to lead] — **de·duc′i·ble** *adj.*

de·duct (di·dukt′) *v.t.* To take away or subtract. [See DEDUCE.] — **de·duct′i·ble** *adj.*

de·duc·tion (di·duk′shən) *n.* **1.** The act of deducing. **2.** *Logic* Reasoning from the general to the particular; also, reasoning from stated premises to logical conclusions. **3.** The act of deducting; also, the amount deducted. — **de·duc′tive** *adj.* — **de·duc′tive·ly** *adv.*

deed (dēd) *n.* **1.** Anything done; an act. **2.** A notable achievement; feat. **3.** Action in general, as opposed to words. **4.** *Law* Any written, sealed instrument of bond, contract, transfer, etc., especially of real estate conveyance. — **Syn.** See ACT. — **in deed** In fact; in truth; actually. — *v.t.* To transfer by deed. [OE *dǣd*] — **deed′less** *adj.*

deem (dēm) *v.t. & v.i.* To judge; think; believe. [OE *dēman* to judge]

deep (dēp) *adj.* **1.** Extending or situated far below a surface. **2.** Extending far inward or backward, or to either side. **3.** Having a (specified) depth or dimension: six feet *deep*. **4.** Rising to the level of: used in combination: *knee-deep*. **5.** Coming from or penetrating to a depth: a *deep* sigh. **6.** Difficult to understand. **7.** Learned and penetrating; wise. **8.** Of great intensity; extreme: *deep* sorrow. **9.** Of intense or dark hue. **10.** Of low, sonorous tone. **11.** Absorbed: *deep* in thought. **12.** Artful; cunning. — **to go off the deep end** *Informal* To become excited or hysterical. — *n.* **1.** A place or thing of great depth; an abyss. **2.** The most intense or profound part. **3.** *Naut.* The interval between two successive marked fathoms. — **the deep** *Poetic* The sea or ocean. — *adv.* **1.** Deeply. **2.** Far along in time. [OE *dēop*] — **deep′ly** *adv.* — **deep′ness** *n.*

deep-dyed (dēp′dīd′) *adj.* Thoroughgoing; absolute.

deep·en (dē′pən) *v.t. & v.i.* To make or become deep[er or] deeper.

deep·freeze (dēp′frēz′) *n.* **1.** A refrigerator for free[zing] and storing foods for long periods of time at temperat[ures] approximating 0° F. **2.** Storage, esp. of long duration. *v.t.* **·froze** or **·freezed, ·fro·zen** or **·freezed, ·freez·ing** place or store in or as in a deepfreeze.

deep-fry (dēp′frī) *v.t.* **-fried, -fry·ing** To fry in deep f[at]

deep-root·ed (dēp′ro͞o′tid, -ro͝ot′id) *adj.* **1.** Having r[oots] far below the surface. **2.** Firmly held: said of beliefs, e[tc.]

deep -seat·ed (dēp′sē′tid) *adj.* Established far within; [dif]ficult to remove, as a fear or disease.

deep-set (dēp′set′) *adj.* Deeply placed, as eyes.

deer (dir) *n. pl.* **deer** A ruminant animal having decidu[ous] antlers, usu. in the male only, as the moose, elk, and r[ed] deer. ◆ Collateral adjective: *cervine.* [OE *dēor* beast]

deer·hound (dir′hound′) *n.* A breed of hunting dog, h[av]ing a shaggy, dark gray or brindle coat: also called *staghou[nd]*

deer·skin (dir′skin′) *n.* A deer's hide, or leather m[ade] from it.

de-es·ca·late (dē·es′kə·lāt) *v.t. & v.i.* **·lat·ed, ·lat·ing** [To] decrease or be decreased gradually, as in scope, effect, [or] intensity: to *de-escalate* a war. — **de-es′ca·la′tion** *n.*

de·face (di·fās′) *v.t.* **·faced, ·fac·ing** To mar the surfac[e or] appearance of; disfigure. [< F < OF < *des-* down, av[ay] + *face* face] — **de·fac′a·ble** *adj.* — **de·face′ment** *n.*

de fac·to (dē fak′tō) Actually or really existing. [< I[L]

de·fal·cate (di·fal′kāt) *v.i.* **·cat·ed, ·cat·ing** To embez[zle] [< Med.L < L *de-* down, away + *falx* scythe] — **de·[fal]ca·tion** (dē′fal·kā′shən) *n.* — **de·fal′ca·tor** *n.*

de·fam·a·to·ry (di·fam′ə·tôr′ē, -tō′rē) *adj.* Slanderous

de·fame (di·fām′) *v.t.* **·famed, ·fam·ing** To attack the g[ood] name or reputation of; slander; libel. [< L < *dis-* aw[ay] from + *fama* a report, reputation] — **def·a·ma·tion** (d[ef′]ə·mā′shən) *n.* — **de·fam er** *n.*

de·fault (di·fôlt′) *n.* A failure or neglect to fulfill an obli[ga]tion or requirement, as to pay money due, to appear in co[urt] or to appear for or finish a contest. — **in default of** Ow[ing] to lack or failure of. — *v.i.* **1.** To fail to do or fulfill so[me]thing required. **2.** To fail to meet financial obligatio[ns]. **3.** *Law* To fail to appear in court. **4.** In sports, to fail [to] compete or to complete a game, etc. — *v.t.* **5.** To fail [to] perform or pay. **6.** In sports, to fail to compete in, a[s a] game; also, to forfeit by default. [< OF < L *de-* down [+] *fallere* to deceive] — **de·fault′er** *n.*

de·feat (di·fēt′) *v.t.* **1.** To overcome in any conflict or co[m]petition; vanquish. **2.** To prevent the successful outco[me] of; baffle; frustrate. **3.** *Law* To make void; annul. — [*n.*] **1.** The act or result of defeating; an overthrow; failu[re]. **2.** Frustration; bafflement. **3.** *Law* An annulment. [< OF < *des-* not + *faire* to do]

de·feat·ism (di·fē′tiz·əm) *n.* The practice of those who [ac]cept defeat as inevitable. — **de·feat′ist** *n. & adj.*

def·e·cate (def′ə·kāt) *v.* **·cat·ed, ·cat·ing** *v.i.* **1.** To d[is]charge excrement. **2.** To become free of dregs. — *v.t.* To refine; purify. [< L < *de-* down, away + *faex* dre[gs]] — **def′e·ca′tion** *n.* — **def′e·ca′tor** *n.*

de·fect (*n.* di·fekt′, dē′fekt; *v.* di·fekt′) *n.* **1.** Lack of som[e]thing necessary for perfection or completeness. **2.** A ble[m]ish; failing; fault. — *v.i.* To desert. [< L < *de-* not [+] *facere* to do] — **de·fec′tion** *n.*

de·fec·tive (di·fek′tiv) *adj.* **1.** Having a defect; imperfe[ct]; faulty. **2.** *Gram.* Lacking one or more of the inflected for[ms] normal for its class: *Can* is a *defective* verb. **3.** *Psychol.* Ha[v]ing less than normal intelligence. — *n.* One who or th[at] which is imperfect; esp., a mentally defective person. **de·fec′tive·ly** *adv.* — **de·fec′tive·ness** *n.*

de·fec·tor (di·fek′tər) *n.* One who deserts.

de·fend (di·fend′) *v.t.* **1.** To shield from danger, attack, injury; protect. **2.** To justify or vindicate; support. [**3.**] *Law* **a** To act in behalf of (an accused). **b** To contest [a] claim, charge, or suit). — *v.i.* **4.** To make a defense. [< L] < *de-* down, away + *fendere* to strike] — **de·fend′a·b[le]** *adj.* — **de·fend′er** *n.*

de·fen·dant (di·fen′dənt) *n.* *Law* One against whom [an] action is brought: opposed to *plaintiff.* — *adj.* Defending

de·fense (di·fens′) *n.* **1.** The act of defending against da[n]ger or attack. **2.** Anything that defends or serves to defen[d]. **3.** A plea or argument in justification or support of som[e]thing. **4.** *Law* **a** The defendant's denial of the truth of [a] complaint; also, whatever is alleged in such denial. **b** [The] defendant and his legal counsel, collectively. **5.** The act [or] science of protecting oneself or a goal, as in sports. Als[o] *Brit.*, **defence.** — **Department of Defense** An executi[ve] department of the U.S. government (established 1949) headed by the Secretary of Defense, that supervises milita[ry] and civil defense operations. [See DEFEND.] — **de·fens[e]less** *adj.* — **de·fense′less·ly** *adv.* — **de·fense′less·ness** *n.*

defense mechanism *Psychoanal.* An unconscious adjus[t]ment of behavior or mental attitude directed toward shu[t]ting out painful emotions and unacceptable impulses.

'en·si·ble (di·fen′sə·bəl) *adj.* Capable of being defended, ıintained, or justified. **— de·fen′si′bil′i·ty, de·fen′si·ble·ss** *n.* **— de·fen′si·bly** *adv.*
'en·sive (di·fen′siv) *adj.* **1.** Intended or suitable for de-ıse. **2.** Carried on for the purpose of defense: distin-ıished from *offensive.* **3.** Having an attitude of defense. *n.* **1.** An attitude or position of defense. **2.** A means of 'ense. **— de·fen′sive·ly** *adv.* **— de·fen′sive·ness** *n.*
fer[1] (di·fûr′) *v.t. & v.i.* **·ferred, ·fer·ring** To delay or put to some other time; postpone. [See DIFFER.] **— de·fer′·ble** *adj.* **— de·fer′ment, de·fer′ral** *n.*
'er[2] (di·fûr′) *v.i.* **·ferred, ·fer·ring** To yield to the opin-ıs or decisions of another: with *to.* [< MF < L < *de-* wn + *ferre* to bear, carry] **— de·fer′rer** *n.*
·er·ence (def′ər·əns) *n.* **1.** Submission or yielding to the ll, opinions, etc., of another. **2.** Respectful regard.
·er·ent (def′ər·ənt) *adj.* Deferential; respectful.
·er·en·tial (def′ə·ren′shəl) *adj.* Marked by deference; spectful; courteous. **— def′er·en′tial·ly** *adv.*
ferred (di·fûrd′) *adj.* **1.** Postponed. **2.** With benefits or yments held back for a specific time: *deferred* stock. **3.** ımporarily exempted from military draft.
fi·ance (di·fī′əns) *n.* **1.** Bold opposition; disposition to pose or resist. **2.** A challenge to meet in combat. **— ·fi′ant** *adj.* **— de·fi′ant·ly** *adv.*
fi·cien·cy (di·fish′ən·sē) *n. pl.* **·cies 1.** The state of be-ɾ deficient. **2.** A lack; insufficiency.
fi·cient (di·fish′ənt) *adj.* **1.** Lacking an adequate or oper supply. **2.** Lacking some essential; incomplete. ee DEFECT.] **— de·fi′cient·ly** *adv.*
'·i·cit (def′ə·sit) *n.* The amount by which an expected or quired sum of money falls short. [< L, it is lacking]
fi·er (di·fī′ər) *n.* One who defies.
file[1] (di·fīl′) *v.t.* **·filed, ·fil·ing 1.** To make foul or dirty. To tarnish the brightness of; corrupt the purity of. **3.**) sully or profane (a name, reputation, etc.). **4.** To vio-:e the chastity of. [< OF < *de-* down + *fouler* to trample] **de·file′ment** *n.* **— de·fil′er** *n.*
file[2] (di·fīl′, dē′fīl) *v.i.* **·filed, ·fil·ing** To march in a line. *n.* **1.** A long, narrow pass, as between mountains. **2.** A arching in file. [< MF < *de-* down + *file* row]
fine (di·fīn′) *v.t.* **·fined, ·fin·ing 1.** To state precisely the eaning of (a word, etc.). **2.** To describe the nature or operties of; explain. **3.** To determine the boundary or tent of. **4.** To bring out the outline of; show clearly. **5.**) fix with precision; specify, as the limits of power. **—** *v.i.* To make definitions. [< OF < L *de-* down + *finire* to ıish] **— de·fin′a·ble** *adj.* **— de·fin′er** *n.*
'·i·nite (def′ə·nit) *adj.* **1.** Having precise limits, quan-:y, etc.: a *definite* sum. **2.** Known for certain; positive: It *definite* that he won. **3.** Clearly defined; explicit; precise. *Gram.* Limiting; particularizing. [< L. See DEFINE.] **· def′i·nite·ly** *adv.* **— def′i·nite·ness** *n.*
finite article *Gram.* In English, the article *the,* which nits or particularizes the noun before which it stands.
'·i·ni·tion (def′ə·nish′ən) *n.* **1.** The act of stating what a ord, phrase, set of terms, etc., means or signifies. **2.** A atement of the meaning of a word, phrase, etc. **3.** The de-rmining of the outline or limits of anything. **4.** The state being clearly outlined or determined. **5.** *Optics* The)wer of a lens to give a distinct image. **6.** *Telecom.* The arity of detail in a televised image, or of sounds received a radio set. **— Syn.** See EXPLANATION.
·fin·i·tive (di·fin′ə·tiv) *adj.* **1.** Sharply defining or limit-g; explicit. **2.** Conclusive and unalterable; final. **3.** lost nearly accurate and complete: a *definitive* edition of haucer. **—** *n. Gram.* A word that defines or limits, as the ɜfinite article. **— de·fin′i·tive·ly** *adv.* **— de·fin′i·tive·ness** *n.*
·flate (di·flāt′) *v.* **·flat·ed, ·flat·ing** *v.t.* **1.** To cause to col-ıpse by removing air or gas. **2.** To take the conceit or lf-esteem out of. **3.** *Econ.* To reduce or restrict (money spending) so that prices decline. **—** *v.i.* **4.** To become eflated. [< L < *de-* down + *flare* to blow] **— de·fla′tor** *n.*
·fla·tion (di·flā′shən) *n.* **1.** The act of deflating, or the ;ate of being deflated. **2.** *Econ.* A decline in prices caused y a decrease in money supply or spending. **— de·fla′tion·r′y** (-er′ē) *adj.* **— de·fla′tion·ist** *n. & adj.*
·flect (di·flekt′) *v.t. & v.i.* To turn aside; swerve or cause) swerve from a course. [< L *de-* down + *flectere* to bend] **- de·flec′tive** *adj.* **— de·flec′tor** *n.*
·flec·tion (di·flek′shən) *n.* **1.** The act of deflecting, or the ;ate of being deflected. **2.** The amount of deviation. Also *Brit.* **de·flex′ion.**
·flow·er (di·flou′ər) *v.t.* **1.** To despoil of flowers. **2.** To eprive (a woman) of virginity. **3.** To violate; rob of beauty, harm, etc. Also **de·flo·rate** (di·flôr′āte, -flō′rāte). [< OF < LL < L *de-* down, away + *flos, floris* flower; infl. in form y *flower*] **— def·lo·ra·tion** (def′lə·rā′shən) *n.*

de·for·est (dē·fôr′ist, -for′-) *v.t.* To clear of forests or trees. **— de·for′es·ta′tion** *n.* **— de·for′est·er** *n.*
de·form (di·fôrm′) *v.t.* **1.** To distort the form of; render misshapen. **2.** To mar the beauty or excellence of. **—** *v.i.* **3.** To become deformed. [< L < *de-* away, down + *forma* form] **— de·form′a·bil′i·ty** *n.* **— de·form′a·ble** *adj.* **— de·form′er** *n.*
de·form·a·tion (dē′fôr·mā′shən, def′ər-) *n.* **1.** The act of deforming, or the state of being deformed. **2.** A change in form or condition for the worse. **3.** An altered form.
de·formed (di·fôrmd′) *adj.* **1.** Marred in form; misshapen. **2.** Morally distorted; perverted; warped. **— de·form·ed·ly** (di·fôr′mid·lē) *adv.* **— de·form′ed·ness** *n.*
de·form·i·ty (di·fôr′mə·tē) *n. pl.* **·ties 1.** A deformed condition. **2.** An abnormally shaped part, as of the body. **3.** A deformed person or thing. **4.** Moral defect; also, depravity. [< OF < L < *de-* away, down + *forma* figure, form]
de·fraud (di·frôd′) *v.t.* To take or withhold from by fraud; cheat; swindle. [< OF < L < *de-* completely + *fraus, fraudis* cheat] **— de·fraud·a·tion** (dē′frô·dā′shən), **de·fraud′·ment** *n.* **— de·fraud′er** *n.*
de·fray (di·frā′) *v.t.* To pay (the costs, expenses, etc.). [< F < OF < *de-* away + *fraier* to spend] **— de·fray′a·ble** *adj.* **— de·fray′al, de·fray′ment** *n.* **— de·fray′er** *n.*
de·frock (dē·frok′) *v.t.* To unfrock.
de·frost (dē·frôst′, -frost′) *v.t.* To remove ice or frost from.
de·frost·er (dē·frôs′tər, -fros′-) *n.* A device for removing ice or frost, or for preventing their formation.
deft (deft) *adj.* Neat and skillful in action; adroit. [OE *gedæfte* meek, gentle] **— deft′ly** *adv.* **— deft′ness** *n.*
de·funct (di·fungkt′) *adj.* Dead; deceased. **— the defunct** The dead person. [< L < *de-* not + *fungi* to perform]
de·fy (*v.* di·fī′; *n.* dē′fī) *v.t.* **·fied, ·fy·ing 1.** To resist or confront openly and boldly. **2.** To resist or withstand successfully. **3.** To challenge (someone) to do something; dare. **—** *n. pl.* **·fies** *U.S.* A challenge; defiance. [< OF < Med.L < L *di-* not + *fidare* to be faithful]
de·gen·er·a·cy (di·jen′ər·ə·sē) *n.* **1.** The process of degenerating; deterioration. **2.** The state of being degenerate.
de·gen·er·ate (*v.* di·jen′ə·rat; *adj., n.* di·jen′ər·it) *v.i.* **·at·ed, ·at·ing 1.** To become worse, or more debased. **2.** *Biol.* To revert to a lower type; deteriorate. **— Syn.** See RETROGRESS. **—** *adj.* Having become worse; degraded. **—** *n.* **1.** A deteriorated or degraded animal or human. **2.** A morally degraded person. [< L < *de-* down + *generare* to create] **— de·gen′er·ate·ly** *adv.* **— de·gen′er·ate·ness** *n.* **— de·gen·er·a·tive** (di·jen′ə·rā′tiv, -ər·ə·tiv) *adj.*
de·gen·er·a·tion (di·jen′ə·rā′shən) *n.* **1.** The process of degenerating. **2.** A degenerate condition. **3.** *Biol.* The reversion of a group of organisms into a less complex type. **4.** *Pathol.* Progressive deterioration of an organ or part.
deg·ra·da·tion (deg′rə·dā′shən) *n.* **1.** The act of degrading. **2.** The state of being reduced in rank, honor, quality, etc.
de·grade (di·grād′) *v.t.* **·grad·ed, ·grad·ing 1.** To debase or lower in character, morals, etc. **2.** To bring into contempt; dishonor. **3.** To reduce in rank; remove from office, dignity, etc. **4.** To reduce in quality, intensity, etc. **5.** *Geol.* To reduce the height of by erosion. [< OF < LL < L *de-* down + *gradi* to step] **— de·grad′ed** *adj.* **— de·grad′ed·ly** *adv.* **— de·grad′ed·ness** *n.*
de·grad·ing (di·grā′ding) *adj.* Debasing; humiliating. **— de·grad′ing·ly** *adv.* **— de·grad′ing·ness** *n.*
de·gree (di·grē′) *n.* **1.** One of a succession of steps or stages. **2.** Relative extent, amount, or intensity. **3.** Relative dignity or rank, or position. **4.** Relative condition, manner, or respect. **5.** An academic title conferred by an institution of learning upon the completion of a course of study, or as an honorary distinction. **6.** A division or unit of a scale, as of a thermometer. **7.** A step in a line of genealogical descent. **8.** *Law* Measure of culpability: murder in the first *degree.* **9.** *Geom.* One 360th of the circumference of a circle. **10.** *Math* **a** The sum of the exponents of the unknowns of an algebraic term: x^3 and xy^2 are both of the third *degree.* **b** The exponent of the highest degree term in a polynomial or equation: $x^4 + 2x^2$ is of the fourth *degree.* **11.** *Geog.* A line or point of the earth's surface defined by its angular distance east or west of a standard meridian, or north or south of the equator. **12.** *Gram.* One of the forms of comparison (positive, comparative, or superlative) of an adjective or adverb. **13.** *Music* **a** The interval between consecutive tones of a scale. **b** A line or space in a staff. **— by degrees** Little by little; gradually. **— to a degree 1.** Somewhat. **2.** Greatly. [< OF < *de-* down + *gre* < L *gradus* a step]
de·hisce (di·his′) *v.i.* **·hisced, ·hisc·ing** To split open, as the capsule of a plant. [< L < *de-* down + *hiscere,* inceptive of *hiare* to gape] **— de·his′cence** *n.* **— de·his′cent** *adj.*
de·horn (dē·hôrn′) *v.t.* To remove the horns of (cattle).
de·hu·man·ize (dē·hyōō′mən·īz) *v.t.* **·ized, ·iz·ing 1.** To

deprive of human qualities or attributes. **2.** To make mechanical, abstract, or artificial. **— de·hu′man·i·za′tion** *n.*

de·hu·mid·i·fi·er (dē′hyōō·mid′ə·fī′ər) *n.* An apparatus by which moisture is removed from the air.

de·hu·mid·i·fy (dē′hyōō·mid′ə·fī) *v.t.* **·fied, ·fy·ing** To render less humid. **— de′hu·mid′i·fi·ca′tion** *n.*

de·hy·drate (dē·hī′drāt) *v.* **·drat·ed, ·drat·ing** *v.t.* **1.** To deprive of water, as a chemical compound, vegetables, etc. **—** *v.i.* **2.** To suffer loss of water. **— de′hy·dra′tion** *n.*

de·ice (dē·īs′) *v.t.* **·iced, ·ic·ing** To free from ice.

de·ic·er (dē·ī′sər) *n.* A mechanical or thermal device that breaks up formations of ice, as on an airplane wing.

de·if·ic (dē·if′ik) *adj.* **1.** Making, or tending to make, divine. **2.** Divine. Also **de·if′i·cal.**

de·i·fy (dē′ə·fī) *v.t.* **·fied, ·fy·ing 1.** To make a god of. **2.** To regard or worship as a god. **3.** To glorify or idealize. [< F < LL < L *deus* god + *facere* to make] **— de′i·fi·ca′tion** *n.* **— de′i·fi′er** *n.*

deign (dān) *v.i.* **1.** To think it befitting oneself (to do something); condescend. **—** *v.t.* **2.** To condescend to grant or allow: He *deigned* no reply. [< OF < L *dignus* worthy]

De·i gra·ti·a (dē′ī grā′shē·ə, dā′ē grä′tē·ä) *Latin* By the grace of God. Abbr. *D.G.*

de·ism (dē′iz·əm) *n.* **1.** Belief in the existence of a personal God, based solely on the testimony of reason. **2.** Belief that God created the world subject to natural laws, but takes no interest in it. [< L *deus* a god + -ISM] **— de′ist** *n.* **— de·is′tic** or **·ti·cal** *adj.* **— de·is′ti·cal·ly** *adv.*

de·i·ty (dē′ə·tē) *n. pl.* **·ties 1.** A god, goddess, or divine person. **2.** Divine nature or status; godhead; divinity. **— the Deity** God. [< F < LL < L *deus* a god]

de·ject (di·jekt′) *v.t.* To depress in spirit; dishearten. [< L < *de-* down + *jacere* to throw]

de·ject·ed (di·jek′tid) *adj.* Depressed in spirits; disheartened. **— de·ject′ed·ly** *adv.* **— de·ject′ed·ness** *n.*

de·jec·tion (di·jek′shən) *n.* A state or condition of being dejected; lowness of spirits; depression; melancholy.

dé·jeu·ner (dā·zhœ·nā′) *n.* **1.** A late breakfast. **2.** Luncheon. [< F < *dé-* away + *jeun* fasting < L *jejunus* empty]

de ju·re (dē jōōr′ē) *Latin* By right; rightfully or legally: distinguished from *de facto.*

deka- *combining form* In the metric system, ten times (a specified unit). Also, before vowels, **dek-.** [< Gk. *deka* ten]

dek·a·gram (dek′ə·gram) *n.* In the metric system, a measure of weight equal to 10 grams: also spelled *decagram.* Also **dek′a·gramme.** See table front of book.

dek·a·li·ter (dek′ə·lē′tər) *n.* In the metric system, a measure of capacity equal to 10 liters: also spelled *decaliter.* Also *esp. Brit.* **dek′a·li′tre.** See table front of book.

dek·a·me·ter (dek′ə·mē′tər) *n.* In the metric system, a measure of length equal to 10 meters: also spelled *decameter.* Also *esp. Brit.* **dek′a·me′tre.** See table front of book.

dek·are (dek′âr) *n.* In the metric system, a thousand square meters or 10 ares: also spelled *decare.*

dek·a·stere (dek′ə·stir) *n.* In the metric system, a measure of volume equal to 10 steres: also spelled *decastere.*

Del·a·ware (del′ə·wâr) *n.* **1.** A confederacy of Algonquian tribes of North American Indians, formerly occupying the whole Delaware River valley. **2.** The language of these people. Also called *Lenape, Leni-Lenape, Lenni-Lenape.*

de·lay (di·lā′) *v.t.* **1.** To put off to a future time; postpone; defer. **2.** To cause to be late; detain. **—** *v.i.* **3.** To linger; procrastinate. **—** *n.* **1.** The act of delaying. **2.** The fact or condition of being delayed. [< OF *delaier*] **— de·lay′er** *n.*

de·le (dē′lē) *v.t.* **·led, ·le·ing** *Printing* To take out; delete: usu. an imperative represented by a sign (ϑ). Compare STET. [< L, imperative of *delere* to erase]

de·lec·ta·ble (di·lek′tə·bəl) *adj.* Giving great pleasure; delightful. [< OF < L *delectare.* See DELIGHT.] **— de·lec′ta·ble·ness, de·lec′ta·bil′i·ty** *n.* **— de·lec′ta·bly** *adv.*

de·lec·ta·tion (dē′lek·tā′shən) *n.* Delight, enjoyment.

del·e·ga·cy (del′ə·gə·sē) *n. pl.* **·cies 1.** The act of delegating, or the state of being delegated. **2.** The office or authority given a delegate. **3.** A body of delegates.

del·e·gate (*n.* del′ə·gāt, -git; *v.* del′ə·gāt) *n.* **1.** A person sent with authority to represent or act for another or others. **2.** *U.S.* **a** A person elected or appointed to represent a Territory in the House of Representatives, where he may speak but not vote. **b** A member of the lower house (**House of Delegates**) of the legislature in Maryland, Virginia, and West Virginia. **—** *v.t.* **·gat·ed, ·gat·ing 1.** To send as a representative, with authority to act. **2.** To commit or entrust (powers, authority, etc.) to another as an agent. **3.** To assign (a debtor of one's own) to one's creditor to satisfy a claim. [< L < *de-* down + *legare* to send]

del·e·ga·tion (del′ə·gā′shən) *n.* **1.** The act of delegating, or the state of being delegated; deputation. **2.** A person or persons appointed to represent others; delegates collectively.

de·lete (di·lēt′) *v.t.* **·let·ed, ·let·ing** To take out (written or printed matter); cancel. [< L *deletus,* pp. of *delere* to erase, destroy] **— de·le′tion** *n.*

del·e·te·ri·ous (del′ə·tir′ē·əs) *adj.* Causing moral or p[hys]ical injury. **— Syn.** See PERNICIOUS. [< NL < Gk. [dē]*tērios* harmful] **— del′e·te′ri·ous·ly** *adv.* **— del′e·t[e′ri]·ous·ness** *n.*

Del·fi (del′fī) See DELPHI.

delft (delft) *n.* **1.** A glazed earthenware, usu. white or b[lue], first made at Delft, Holland, about 1310. **2.** Any tablew[are] resembling this. Also **delf** (delf), **delft′ware′.**

de·lib·er·ate (*v.* di·lib′ə·rāt; *adj.* di·lib′ər·it) *v.* **·at·ed, ·[at·]ing** *v.i.* **1.** To consider carefully and at length. **2.** To [take] counsel together so as to reach a decision. **—** *v.t.* **3.** [To] think about or consider carefully; weigh. **—** *adj.* **1.** C[are]fully thought out; intentional. **2.** Slow and cautious in [de]termining or deciding. **3.** Leisurely in movement or m[an]ner. [< L *de-* completely + *librare* to weigh] **— de·lib[′er]·ate·ly** *adv.* **— de·lib′er·ate·ness** *n.*

de·lib·er·a·tion (di·lib′ə·rā′shən) *n.* **1.** Careful and [pro]longed consideration. **1.** *Often pl.* Examination and dis[cus]sion of the arguments for and against a measure. **3.** S[low]ness and care in decision or action.

de·lib·er·a·tive (di·lib′ə·rā′tiv, -rə·tiv) *adj.* Involve[d in] or characterized by deliberation: a *deliberative* body.

del·i·ca·cy (del′ə·kə·sē) *n. pl.* **·cies 1.** The quality [of] being delicate. **2.** Frailty or weakness of body or hea[lth]. **3.** Refinement of feeling, appreciation, etc. **4.** Consid[era]tion for the feelings of others. **5.** Nicety of touch or [exe]cution. **6.** Sensitivity in reaction, as of instruments. [**7.**] Need of cautious, tactful treatment: a subject of great [deli]*cacy.* **8.** Something choice and dainty, as an item of f[ood].

del·i·cate (del′ə·kit) *adj.* **1.** Exquisite and fine in w[ork]manship, texture, etc. **2.** Daintily pleasing, as in ta[ste], aroma, or color. **3.** Easily injured or destroyed; frail. [**4.**] Requiring tactful treatment. **5.** Gentle and skilled: a [deli]*cate* touch. **6.** Sensitive and subtle in feeling, perception[, or] expression: a *delicate* eye for color. **7.** Showing a fine ap[pre]ciation for what is proper and becoming. **8.** Conside[rate] of the feelings of others. **9.** Sensitively accurate: a *deli[cate]* thermometer. **10.** Subtle: a *delicate* distinction. [< *delicatus* pleasing] **— del′i·cate·ly** *adv.* **— del′i·cate·nes[s]**

del·i·ca·tes·sen (del′ə·kə·tes′ən) *n.pl.* **1.** (*often constr[ued] as sing.*) Cooked or preserved foods, as cooked meats, chee[ses,] pickles, etc. **2.** (*construed as sing.*) A store that sells s[uch] foods. [< G, pl. of *delicatesse* delicacy]

de·li·cious (di·lish′əs) *adj.* Extremely pleasant or en[joy]able, esp. to the taste. [< OF < LL < L *delicia* delig[ht]] **— de·li′cious·ly** *adv.* **— de·li′cious·ness** *n.*

De·li·cious (di·lish′əs) *n.* A variety of sweet, red apple

de·light (di·līt′) *n.* **1.** Great pleasure; gratification; [joy.] **2.** That which gives extreme pleasure. **3.** *Poetic* The qua[lity] of delighting; charm. **—** *v.i.* **1.** To take great pleasure; [re]joice: with *in* or the infinitive. **2.** To give great enjoyme[nt.] **—** *v.t.* **3.** To please or gratify highly. [< OF < L *delect[are],* freq. of *delicere* < *de-* away + *lacere* to entice] **— de·lig[ht′]ed** *adj.* **— de·light′ed·ly** *adv.*

de·light·ful (di·līt′fəl) *adj.* Affording delight; extrem[ely] pleasing. **— de·light′ful·ly** *adv.* **— de·light′ful·ness** *n.*

De·li·lah (di·lī′lə) A Philistine woman, the mistress of S[am]son, who betrayed him to the Philistines by cutting off [his] hair, thus depriving him of his strength. *Judg.* xvi 4– **—** *n.* A voluptuous but treacherous woman.

de·lim·it (di·lim′it) *v.t.* To prescribe the limits of. A[lso] **de·lim′i·tate.** [< F < L < *de-* completely + *limitare* [to] bound] **— de·lim′i·ta′tion** *n.* **— de·lim′i·ta·tive** *adj.*

de·lin·e·ate (di·lin′ē·āt) *v.t.* **·at·ed, ·at·ing 1.** To draw [in] outline. **2.** To represent by a drawing. **3.** To port[ray] verbally; describe. [< L < *de-* completely + *lineare* [to] draw a line] **— de·lin′e·a′tion** *n.* **— de·lin′e·a′tive** *a[dj.]* **— de·lin′e·a′tor** *n.*

de·lin·quen·cy (di·ling′kwən·sē) *n. pl.* **·cies 1.** Negl[ect] of duty. **2.** A fault; offense. **3.** Juvenile delinquency.

de·lin·quent (di·ling′kwənt) *adj.* **1.** Neglectful of or f[ail]ing in duty or obligation; guilty of an offense. **2.** Due a[nd] unpaid, as taxes. **—** *n.* **1.** One who fails to perform a d[uty] or commits a fault. **2.** A juvenile delinquent. [< L < *de-* down, away + *linquere* to leave] **— de·lin′quent·ly** *a[dv.]*

del·i·quesce (del′ə·kwes′) *v.i.* **·quesced, ·quesc·ing 1.** [To] melt or pass away gradually. **2.** To become liquid by [ab]sorption of moisture from the air, as certain salts. [< [L] < *de-* completely + *liquescere* to melt] **— del′i·ques′cen[ce]** *n.* **— del′i·ques′cent** *adj.*

de·lir·i·ous (di·lir′ē·əs) *adj.* **1.** Suffering from deliriu[m.] **2.** Characteristic of delirium: *delirious* dreams. **3.** Wil[dly] excited. **— de·lir′i·ous·ly** *adv.* **— de·lir′i·ous·ness** *n.*

de·lir·i·um (di·lir′ē·əm) *n.* **1.** A sporadic or tempora[ry] mental disturbance associated with fever, intoxicati[on,] etc., and marked by excitement, hallucinations, and gene[ral] incoherence. **2.** Wild emotion or excitement. [< L < [*de-*] down, away + *lira* furrow, track]

delirium tre·mens (trē′mənz) A violent delirium caus[ed] esp. by excessive use of alcoholic liquors.

de·liv·er (di·liv′ər) *v.t.* **1.** To hand over; surrender. **2.**

·ry and distribute: to *deliver* newspapers. **3.** To give forth; ıd forth: to *deliver* a blow. **4.** To give forth in words; utter. To throw or pitch, as a ball. **6.** To free from restraint, ıl, danger, etc. **7.** To assist in the birth of (offspring). **to be delivered of** To give birth. **— to deliver oneself of** put into words; express. [< OF < LL < L *de-* down, ay + *liberare* to set free] **— de·liv′er·a·ble** *adj.* **— de·** **′er·er** *n.*

iv·er·ance (di·liv′ər·əns) *n.* **1.** The act of delivering, the state of being delivered. **2.** An expression of opinion.

iv·er·y (di·liv′ər·ē) *n. pl.* **·er·ies 1.** The act of deliver- ; or distributing something. **2.** That which is distributed, mail. **3.** The act of liberating; release. **4.** A transferring handing over. **5.** The bringing forth of offspring. **6.** ınner of utterance, as in public speaking. **7.** The act or ınner of giving forth or discharging a ball, a blow, etc.

l (del) *n.* A small, secluded, usu. wooded valley. [ME]

louse (dē·lous′) *v.t.* **·loused, ·lous·ing** To remove lice or ıer insect vermin from.

·phi (del′fī) An ancient city in Phocis, Greece; famous its oracle: also *Delfi.* **— Del·phi·an** (del′fē·ən) *adj. & n.*

·phic (del′fik) *adj.* **1.** Relating to Delphi or to Apollo's ıcle there. **2.** Oracular.

·phin·i·um (del·fin′ē·əm) *n.* Any of a genus of perennial ınts of the crowfoot family, having large, spurred flowers, ı. blue; the larkspur. [< NL < Gk. *delphis* dolphin; so led from the shape of the nectary]

·ta (del′tə) *n.* **1.** The fourth letter in the Greek alpha- ; (Δ, δ), corresponding to English *d.* See ALPHABET. **2.** *ɔg.* An alluvial, typically triangular-shaped, silt deposit at in the mouth of a river. **3.** Anything triangular. [< Gk.]

·ta·he·dron (del′tə·hē′drən) *n. pl.* **·dra** (-drə) *Crystall.* :rystal form having twelve equal, trapezoidal faces. Also **′to·he′dron.** For illus. see CRYSTAL.

·toid (del′toid) *n. Anat.* A triangular muscle covering shoulder joint. **—** *adj.* Shaped like a delta; triangular. Gk. < *delta* the letter Δ + *eidos* form]

lude (di·lōōd′) *v.t.* **·lud·ed, ·lud·ing** To mislead the mind judgment of; deceive. [< L < *de-* from, away + *ludere* play] **— de·lud′er** *n.* **— de·lud′ing·ly** *adv.*

·uge (del′yōōj) *v.t.* **·uged, ·ug·ing 1.** To flood with water. To overwhelm; destroy. **—** *n.* **1.** A great flood or inun- tion. **2.** Something that overwhelms or engulfs: a *deluge* tears. **— the Deluge** The flood in the time of Noah. *Gen.* . [< OF < L < *dis-* away + *luere* to wash]

lu·sion (di·lōō′zhən) *n.* **1.** The act of deluding. **2.** The te of being deluded. **3.** A false, fixed belief, held in spite evidence to the contrary. **— de·lu′sion·al** *adj.*

lu·sive (di·lōō′siv) *adj.* Tending to delude; misleading. so **de·lu·so·ry** (di·lōō′sər·ē). **— de·lu′sive·ly** *adv.* **— de·** **sive·ness** *n.*

luxe (di lo͝oks′, di luks′; *Fr.* də lüks′) Elegant and expen- e; of superfine quality. [< F, lit., of luxury]

ve (delv) *v.* **delved, delv·ing** *v.i.* To make careful inves- ation; search for information. [OE *delfan*] **— delv′er** *n.*

mag·net·ize (dē·mag′nə·tīz) *v.t.* **·ized, ·iz·ing** To deprive substance) of magnetism. **— de·mag′net·i·za′tion** *n.* **—** **·mag′net·iz′er** *n.*

n·a·gog·ic (dem′ə·goj′ik, -gog′ik) *adj.* Of or like a dema- gue. Also **dem′a·gog′i·cal. — dem′a·gog′i·cal·ly** *adv.*

n·a·gogue (dem′ə·gôg, -gog) *n.* One who leads the popu- e by appealing to prejudices and emotions. Also **dem′a·** **g.** [< Gk < *dēmos* people + *agein* to lead]

n·a·gogu·er·y (dem′ə·gôg′ər·ē, -gog′ər·ē) *n.* The spirit, thod, or conduct of a demagogue. Also **dem′a·gog′ism.**

n·a·go·gy (dem′ə·gō′jē, -gôg′ē, -gog′ē) *n.* **1.** Dema- guery. **2.** The rule of a demagogue. **3.** Demagogues lectively.

mand (di·mand′, -mänd′) *v.t.* **1.** To ask for boldly or eemptorily. **2.** To claim as due. **3.** To inquire formally. To have need for; require. **5.** *Law* **a** To summon to urt. **b** To make formal claim to (property). **—** *v.i.* **6.** make a demand. **—** *n.* **1.** The act of demanding. **2.** at which is demanded. **3.** A claim or requirement: the *mands* on one's time. **4.** An inquiry. **5.** *Law* A request claim. **6.** *Econ.* **a** The desire to possess combined with e ability to purchase. **b** The potential amount of certain ods that will be purchased at a given time for a given ice. **— in demand** Desired; sought after. **— on demand** ı presentation: a note payable *on demand.* [< F < L < down, away + *mandare* to command, order] **— de·** **ınd′a·ble** *adj.* **— de·mand′er** *n.*

mar·cate (di·mär′kāt, dē′mär·kāt) *v.t.* **·cat·ed, ·cat·ing** To mark the limits of. **2.** To differentiate; separate.

mar·ca·tion (dē′mär·kā′shən) *n.* **1.** The fixing or mark- ; of boundaries or limits. **2.** The limits or boundaries ed. **3.** A limiting or separating. [< Sp. < *de-* down (< *de-*) + *marcar* to mark a boundary]

dé·marche (dā·mȧrsh′) *n. French* **1.** A mode of procedure. **2.** In diplomacy, a change in policy.

de·mean[1] (di·mēn′) *v.t.* To behave or conduct (oneself) in a particular way. [< OF < *de-* down (< L *de-*) + *mener* to lead < LL *minare* to threaten, drive]

de·mean[2] (di·mēn′) *v.t.* To lower in dignity or reputation; debase; degrade. **— Syn.** See ABASE.

de·mean·or (di·mē′nər) *n.* The manner in which one behaves or bears oneself. Also, *Brit.*, **de·mean′our.**

de·ment (di·ment′) *v.t.* To make insane.

de·ment·ed (di·men′tid) *adj.* Mentally ill; insane. **— de·ment′ed·ly** *adv.* **— de·ment′ed·ness** *n.*

de·men·tia (di·men′shə, -shē·ə) *n.* Loss or serious impairment of mental powers. [< L, madness]

dementia pre·cox (prē′koks) *Psychiatry* Schizophrenia: a former name. Also **de·men′tia prae′cox.**

de·mer·it (di·mer′it) *n.* **1.** A defect; fault. **2.** In schools, etc., a mark for failure or misconduct. [< Med.L < L < *de-* down, away + *merere* to deserve]

de·mesne (di·mān′, -mēn′) *n.* **1.** In law, lands held in one's own power. **2.** A manor house and the adjoining lands. **3.** A region; domain. [< OF *demeine, demaine*]

De·me·ter (di·mē′tər) The Greek goddess of agriculture, marriage, and fertility: identified with *Ceres.*

demi- *prefix* **1.** Half; intermediate. **2.** Inferior or less in size, quality, etc.; partial. [< F < L < *dis-* from, apart + *medius* middle]

dem·i·god (dem′ē·god′) *n.* **1.** An inferior diety. **2.** A man with the attributes of a god. **— dem′i·god′dess** *n.fem.*

dem·i·john (dem′ē·jon′) *n.* A narrow-necked jug, often enclosed in wickerwork. [< F *dame-jeanne,* lit., Lady Jane]

de·mil·i·ta·rize (dē·mil′ə·tə·rīz′) *v.t.* **·rized, ·riz·ing** To remove military characteristics from; free from militarism.

dem·i·mon·daine (dem′ē·mon·dān′) *n.* A woman of the demimonde. Also **dem·i·rep** (dem′ē·rep′). [< F]

dem·i·monde (dem′ē·mond, dem′ē·mond′) *n.* The class of women who have lost social position because of their scandalous behavior. [< F < *demi-* half, partial + *monde* world]

de·mise (di·mīz′) *n.* **1.** Death. **2.** *Law* A transfer of rights or an estate. **—** *v.* **·mised, ·mis·ing** *v.t.* **1.** To bestow (royal power) by death or abdication. **2.** *Law* To lease or transfer (an estate). **—** *v.i.* **3.** To pass by will or inheritance. [< OF < L < *de-* down, away + *mittere* to send]

dem·i·sem·i·qua·ver (dem′ē·sem′ē·kwā′vər) *n. Music Chiefly Brit.* A thirty-second note.

dem·i·tasse (dem′ē·tas′, -täs′) *n.* **1.** A small cup in which after-dinner coffee is served. **2.** Coffee served in such a cup. [< F, a half cup]

demo- *combining form* People. [< Gk. *dēmos* people]

de·mo·bi·lize (dē·mō′bə·līz) *v.t.* **·lized, ·liz·ing** To disband (an army or troops). **— de·mo′bi·li·za′tion** *n.*

de·moc·ra·cy (di·mok′rə·sē) *n. pl.* **·cies 1.** A form of government in which political power resides in all the people and is exercised by them directly or is given to elected representatives. **2.** A state so governed. **3.** The spirit or practice of political, legal, or social equality. [< F < Med.L < Gk. < *dēmos* people + *krateein* to rule]

De·moc·ra·cy (di·mok′rə·sē) *n.* The principles of the Democratic Party; also, the party, or its members collectively.

dem·o·crat (dem′ə·krat) *n.* **1.** One who favors a democracy. **2.** One who believes in political and social equality.

Dem·o·crat (dem′ə·krat) *n.* A member of the Democratic Party in the United States. Abbr. *D., Dem.*

dem·o·crat·ic (dem′ə·krat′ik) *adj.* **1.** Of, pertaining to, or characterized by the principles of democracy. **2.** Existing or provided for the benefit or enjoyment of all. **3.** Practicing social equality. **— dem′o·crat′i·cal·ly** *adv.*

Dem·o·crat·ic (dem′ə·krat′ik) *adj.* Of, pertaining to, or characteristic of the Democratic Party.

Democratic Party One of the two major political parties in the United States, dating from 1828.

de·moc·ra·tize (di·mok′rə·tīz) *v.t. & v.i.* **·tized, ·tiz·ing** To make or become democratic. **— de·moc′ra·ti·za′tion** *n.*

de·mol·ish (di·mol′ish) *v.t.* **1.** To tear down, as a building. **2.** To destroy utterly; ruin. [< F < L < *de-* down + *moliri* to build] **— de·mol′ish·er** *n.* **— de·mol′ish·ment** *n.*

— Syn. A building is *demolished* if smashed to fragments, and *razed* if leveled to the ground. It is *ruined* if made unfit for habitation or use, though much of its structure may remain. *Destroy* is a very general term, covering all these senses.

dem·o·li·tion (dem′ə·lish′ən) *n.* The act or result of demolishing; destruction. **— dem′o·li′tion·ist** *n.*

de·mon (dē′mən) *n.* **1.** An evil spirit; devil. **2.** A very wicked or cruel person. **3.** *Informal* A person of great skill or zeal: a *demon* with a gun. [< L < Gk. *daimōn*]

de·mon·e·tize (dē·mon′ə·tīz) *v.t.* **·tized, ·tiz·ing 1.** To deprive (currency) of standard value. **2.** To withdraw from use, as currency. **— de·mon′e·ti·za′tion** *n.*

de·mo·ni·ac (di·mō′nē·ak) *adj.* **1.** Of, like, or befitting a demon. **2.** Influenced or possessed by or as by demons; frenzied. Also **de·mo·ni·a·cal** (dē′mə·nī′ə·kəl). — *n.* One supposedly possessed of a demon. — **de′mo·ni′a·cal·ly** *adv.*

de·mon·ic (di·mon′ik) *adj.* **1.** Of or like a demon. Also **de·mo·ni·an** (di·mō′nē·ən). **2.** Inspired, as by a demon.

de·mon·ism (dē′mən·iz′əm) *n.* **1.** Belief in demons. **2.** Demonolatry. **3.** Demonology. — **de′mon·ist** *n.*

demono- *combining form* Demon. Also, before vowels, **demon-**. [< Gk. *daimōn* spirit, god]

de·mon·ol·a·try (dē′mən·ol′ə·trē) *n.* The worship of demons. [< DEMONO- + Gk. *latreia* worship] — **de′mon·ol′·a·ter** *n.*

de·mon·ol·o·gy (dē′mən·ol′ə·jē) *n.* The study of demons or of belief in demons. — **de′mon·ol′o·gist** *n.*

de·mon·stra·ble (di·mon′strə·bəl, dem′ən-) *adj.* Capable of being demonstrated or proved. — **de·mon′stra·bil′i·ty, de·mon′stra·ble·ness** *n.* — **de·mon′stra·bly** *adv.*

dem·on·strate (dem′ən·strāt) *v.* **·strat·ed, ·strat·ing** *v.t.* **1.** To explain or describe by use of experiments, examples, etc. **2.** To prove or show by reasoning; make evident. **3.** To show feelings clearly. — *v.i.* **4.** To take part in a public demonstration. **5.** To make a show of military force. [< L < *de-* completely + *monstrare* to show, point out]

dem·on·stra·tion (dem′ən·strā′shən) *n.* **1.** The act of making known or evident. **2.** Undeniable proof or evidence. **3.** An explanation or showing of how something works, as a product. **4.** A show or expression: a *demonstration* of love. **5.** A display of public feeling, as a mass meeting or parade. **6.** A show of military force or readiness.

de·mon·stra·tive (di·mon′strə·tiv) *adj.* **1.** Serving to demonstrate or point out. **2.** Able to prove beyond doubt; convincing and conclusive. **3.** Inclined to strong expression. **4.** *Gram.* Indicating the person or object referred to. — *n.* *Gram.* A demonstrative pronoun. — **de·mon′stra·tive·ly** *adv.* — **de·mon′stra·tive·ness** *n.*

demonstrative pronoun *Gram.* A pronoun that directly points out its antecedents, as *this, those.*

dem·on·stra·tor (dem′ən·strā′tər) *n.* One who or that which demonstrates.

de·mor·al·ize (di·môr′əl·īz, -mor′-) *v.t.* **·ized, ·iz·ing** **1.** To corrupt or deprave. **2.** To lower the morale of. **3.** To throw into disorder. — **de·mor′al·i·za′tion** *n.* — **de·mor′·al·iz′er** *n.*

de·mote (di·mōt′) *v.t.* **·mot·ed, ·mot·ing** To reduce to a lower grade or rank. — **de·mo′tion** *n.*

de·mul·cent (di·mul′sənt) *adj.* Soothing. — *n.* *Med.* A soothing substance. [< L < *de-* down + *mulcere* to soothe]

de·mur (di·mûr′) *v.i.* **·murred, ·mur·ring** **1.** To offer objections; take exception. **2.** To delay; hesitate. **3.** *Law* To interpose a demurrer. — *n.* **1.** The act of demurring. **2.** An objection, as to proposed action. **3.** A delay. [< OF < L < *de-* completely + *morari* to delay]

de·mure (di·myŏŏr′) *adj.* **·mur·er, ·mur·est** **1.** Grave; reserved. **2.** Prim; coy. [ME < OF < L *maturus* mature, discreet] — **de·mure′ly** *adv.* — **de·mure′ness** *n.*

de·mur·rage (di·mûr′ij) *n.* **1.** The detention of a vessel, railway freight car, or other commercial conveyance, beyond the specified time for departure, as a result of loading, unloading, etc. **2.** Compensation for such delay.

de·mur·rer (di·mûr′ər) *n.* **1.** *Law* A pleading that allows the truth of the facts stated by the opposite party, but denies that they are sufficient to constitute a good cause of action or defense in law. **2.** Any objection or exception taken. **3.** One who demurs. [< AF]

den (den) *n.* **1.** The cave or retreat of a wild animal; a lair. **2.** A site or dwelling: used pejoratively: a *den* of thieves. **3.** A small, private room for relaxation or study. — *v.i.* **denned, den·ning** To dwell in or as in a den. [OE *denn*]

de·nar·i·us (di·nâr′ē·əs) *n.* *pl.* **·nar·i·i** (-nâr′ē·ī) **1.** A silver coin of ancient Rome; the penny of the New Testament. **2.** A gold coin of ancient Rome. [< L < *decem* ten]

de·na·tion·al·ize (dē·nash′ən·əl·īz′) *v.t.* **·ized, ·iz·ing** To deprive of national character, status, or rights. Also *Brit.* **de·na′tion·al·ise′**. — **de·na′tion·al·i·za′tion** *n.*

de·nat·u·ral·ize (dē·nach′ər·əl·īz′) *v.t.* **·ized, ·iz·ing** **1.** To render unnatural. **2.** To deprive of citizenship. Also *Brit.* **de·nat′u·ral·ise′**. — **de·nat′u·ral·i·za′tion** *n.*

de·na·ture (dē·nā′chər) *v.t.* **·tured, ·tur·ing** **1.** To change the nature of. **2.** To adulterate (alcohol, fat, etc.) so as to make unfit for drinking or eating without destroying other useful properties. Also **de·na′tur·ize**. — **de·na′tur·ant** *n.*

den·drite (den′drīt) *n.* *Physiol.* A threadlike, branching process of a nerve cell that conducts impulses toward the cell body. [< Gk. < *dendron* tree] — **den·drit′ic** (-drit′ik) or **·i·cal** *adj.* — **den·drit′i·cal·ly** *adv.*

dendro- *combining form* Tree. Also **dendr-** (before vowels), **dendri-**. [< Gk. *dendron* tree]

-dendron *combining form* Tree. [< Gk. *dendron* tree]

Den·eb (den′eb) *n.* One of the 20 brightest stars, 1.33 magnitude; Alpha in the constellation Cygnus.

den·gue (deng′gē, -gā) *n.* *Pathol.* An acute, tropical, v disease transmitted by the bite of a mosquito and cha terized by fever, eruptions, and severe pains in the joi [< Sp., ult. < Swahili]

de·ni·a·ble (di·nī′ə·bəl) *adj.* That can be denied. — **ni′a·bly** *adv.*

de·ni·al (di·nī′əl) *n.* **1.** A contradiction, as of a statem **2.** Refusal to believe a doctrine, etc. **3.** A disowning or avowal. **4.** Refusal to grant, give, or allow.

de·nic·o·tin·ize (dē·nik′ə·tin·īz′) *v.t.* **·ized, ·iz·ing** Tc move nicotine from (tobacco). Also **de·nic′o·tine.**

de·ni·er[1] (di·nī′ər) *n.* One who makes denial.

den·ier[2] (den′yər, də·nir′) *n.* A unit of weight for de ing the coarseness or fineness of rayon, nylon, or silk ya [See DENARIUS.]

den·im (den′əm) *n.* **1.** A strong, twilled cotton used overalls, uniforms, etc.; also, a finer grade of this fabric for hangings, upholstery, etc. **2.** *pl.* Garments made of material. [< F (*serge*) *de Nîmes* (serge) of Nîmes]

den·i·zen (den′ə·zən) *n.* **1.** An inhabitant. **2.** A pe animal, or thing at home or naturalized in a region or dition not native to it. — *v.t.* To make (someone or sc thing) a denizen. [< AF < *deinz* inside < *de intus* f within] — **den′i·zen·a′tion** *n.*

de·nom·i·nate (*v.* di·nom′ə·nāt; *adj.* di·nom′ə·nit) *v.t.* **ed, ·nat·ing** To give a name to; call. — *adj.* Havin specific name. [< L < *de-* down + *nomen* name]

de·nom·i·na·tion (di·nom′ə·nā′shən) *n.* **1.** The act of n ing or calling by name. **2.** A name. **3.** Any specific named class or group of things or people: There were m *denominations* of criminals. **4.** A religious group; a sec

de·nom·i·na·tion·al (di·nom′ə·nā′shən·əl) *adj.* Of, taining to, or supported by a religious denomination or s sectarian. — **de·nom′i·na′tion·al·ly** *adv.*

de·nom·i·na·tion·al·ism (di·nom′ə·nā′shən·əl·iz′əm) *n* A disposition to divide into or form denominations. **2.** R adherence or devotion to a denomination or sect; sectar ism. — **de·nom′i·na′tion·al·ist** *n.* & *adj.*

de·nom·i·na·tive (di·nom′ə·nā′tiv, -nə·tiv) *adj.* **1.** gives or constitutes a name; appellative. **2.** *Gram.* Der from a noun or adjective, as the verb *to garden.* — *n.* *G* A denominative word. — **de·nom′i·na′tive·ly** *adv.*

de·nom·i·na·tor (di·nom′ə·nā′tər) *n.* *Math.* The ter a fraction below the line indicating the number of e parts into which the unit is divided.

de·no·ta·tion (dē′nō·tā′shən) *n.* **1.** The specific mea of, or the object or objects designated by, a word. **2.** act of denoting. **3.** That which indicates, as a sign.

de·note (di·nōt′) *v.t.* **·not·ed ·not·ing** **1.** To point ou make known; mark. **2.** To signify; indicate. **3.** To de nate; mean: said of words, symbols, etc. [< L < *de-* d + *notare* to mark] — **de·not′a·ble** *adj.* — **de·no·ta·** (di·nō′tə·tiv, dē′nō·tā′tiv) *adj.*

dé·noue·ment (dā·nōō·mäṅ′) *n.* **1.** The final solutio the plot of a play, novel, etc. **2.** Any final outcome. OF < *des-* away (< L *dis-*) + *nouer* to knot]

de·nounce (di·nouns′) *v.t.* **·nounced, ·nounc·ing** **1.** To tack or condemn openly and vehemently; inveigh agai **2.** To inform against; accuse. **3.** To announce as a th **4.** To give formal notice of the termination of (a tre etc.). [< OF < L < *de-* down + *nuntiare* to announce] **de·nounce′ment** *n.* — **de·nounc′er** *n.*

dense (dens) *adj.* **dens·er, dens·est** **1.** Compact; th close. **2.** Hard to penetrate. **3.** Stupid. [< L *den* — **dense′ly** *adv.* — **dense′ness** *n.*

den·si·ty (den′sə·tē) *n.* *pl.* **·ties** **1.** The state or qualit being dense; closeness of parts; compactness. **2.** Stupic **3.** *Physics* The mass of a substance per unit of its volu **4.** *Sociol.* The number of specified units, as persons, fami or dwellings, per unit of area. [< MF < L < *densus* th

dent (dent) *n.* A small depression made by striking or pı ing. — *v.t.* **1.** To make a dent in. — *v.i.* **2.** To bec dented. [Var. of DINT]

den·tal (den′təl) *adj.* **1.** Of or pertaining to the teeth. Of or pertaining to dentistry. **3.** *Phonet.* Produced the tip of the tongue against or near the upper front te — *n.* *Phonet.* A dental consonant. [< NL < L *dens,* to

dental plate A denture.

den·tate (den′tāt) *adj.* Having teeth or toothlike proces toothed; notched. [< L *dentatus* having teeth] — **d tate·ly** *adv.* — **dent′a·tion** *n.*

denti- *combining form* Tooth. Also, before vowels, **de**

den·ti·frice (den′tə·fris) *n.* A preparation, as a powde paste, for cleaning the teeth. [< MF < L < *dens, de* tooth + *fricare* to rub]

den·tine (den′tēn, -tin) *n.* *Anat.* The hard, calcified s stance forming the body of a tooth, situated just beneath enamel and cementum. Also **den′tin** (-tin). For illus. TOOTH. — **den′tin·al** *adj.*

den·tist (den′tist) *n.* One who practices dentistry. [< *dentiste* < *dent* a tooth]

ı·tist·ry (den′tis·trē) *n.* **1.** The branch of medicine con-rned with the diagnosis, prevention, and treatment of dis-ses affecting the teeth. **2.** The work of a dentist.
ı·ti·tion (den·tish′ən) *n.* **1.** The process or period of cut-ıg teeth; teething. **2.** The kind, number, and arrange-ent of teeth in man and other animals.
ı·ture (den′chər) *n.* **1.** A set of teeth. **2.** A set of tificial teeth, either partial or full: also called *dental plate.* < F < *dent* tooth] **— den′tur·al** *adj.*
nu·date (di·no͞o′dāt, -nyo͞o′-, den′yo͞o·dāt) *adj.* Stripped foliage or other covering; naked. **—** *v.t.* **·dat·ed, ·dat·ing** ɔ denude. [< L *denudatus*, pp. of *denudare*. See DENUDE.]
nude (di·no͞od′, -nyo͞od′) *v.t.* **·nud·ed, ·nud·ing 1.** To rip the covering from; make naked. **2.** *Geol.* To expose to ew by erosion. [< L < *de-* down, completely + *nudare* strip] **— den·u·da·tion** (den′yo͞o·dā′shən, dē′no͞o-, yo͞o-) *n.*
nun·ci·ate (di·nun′sē·āt, -shē-) *v.t. & v.i.* **·at·ed, ·at·ing** ɔ denounce. [< L < *de-* down + *nuntiare* to announce]
nun·ci·a·tion (di·nun′sē·ā′shən, -shē-) *n.* **1.** Open dis-proval or condemnation of a person or action. **2.** An cusation. **3.** A threat or warning. **4.** Formal notice that treaty is to be terminated.
nun·ci·a·to·ry (di·nun′sē·ə·tôr′ē, -tō′rē, -shē-) *adj.* Of e nature of or containing denunciation; accusing.
ny (di·nī′) *v.t.* **·nied, ·ny·ing 1.** To declare to be untrue; ntradict. **2.** To refuse to believe; declare to be false or in-lid, as a doctrine. **3.** To refuse to give; withhold. **4.** To fuse (someone) a request. **5.** To refuse to acknowledge; sown; repudiate. **6.** To refuse access to. **— to deny one-lf** To refuse oneself something desired; practice self-denial. < OF < L < *de-* completely + *negare* to say no, refuse]
o·dar (dē′ə·där) *n.* The East Indian cedar, prized for its ırable, light red wood. [< Skt. < *deva* god + *dāru* wood]
o·dor·ant (dē·ō′dər·ənt) *adj.* Destroying, absorbing, or sguising bad odors. **—** *n.* A deodorant substance.
o·dor·ize (dē·ō′dər·īz) *v.t.* **·ized, ·iz·ing** To modify, de-roy, or disguise the odor of. **— de·o′dor·i·za′tion** *n.* **— ·o′dor·iz′er** *n.*
ox·i·dize (dē·ok′sə·dīz) *v.t.* **·dized, ·diz·ing 1.** To remove ygen from. **2.** To reduce from the state of an oxide. **— ·ox′i·di·za′tion** *n.* **— de·ox′i·diz′er** *n.*
·ox·y- *combining form* Containing less oxygen than. Also *soxy-.*
ox·y·ri·bo·nu·cle·ic acid (dē·ok′sē·rī′bō·no͞o·klē′ik, yo͞o-) *Biochem.* A nucleic acid forming a principal con-ituent of the genes and known to play an important role the genetic action of the chromosomes. Abbr. *DNA.*
part (di·pärt′) *v.i.* **1.** To go away; leave. **2.** To deviate; ffer; vary: with *from*: to *depart* from tradition. **3.** To die. **·** *v.t.* **4.** To leave: now archaic except in the phrase **to de-ırt this life.** [< OF < *de-* away + *partir* to divide]
·part·ed (di·pär′tid) *adj.* **1.** Gone; past. **2.** Dead. **— e departed** The dead person, or the dead collectively.
·part·ment (di·pärt′mənt) *n.* **1.** A distinct part or divi-ɔn of something, as of a business or college: the English *partment.* **2.** *Usu. cap. U.S.* An executive division of the vernment, headed by a cabinet officer. **3.** In France, an ministrative district. [See DEPART.] **— de·part·men·tal** ē′pärt·men′təl) *adj.* **— de′part·men′tal·ly** *adv.*
·part·men·tal·ize (dē′pärt·men′təl·īz) *v.t. & v.i.* **·ized, ·ing** To divide into departments.
partment store A large retail establishment selling vari-ıs types of merchandise and service.
·par·ture (di·pär′chər) *n.* **1.** The act of going away or ıking leave. **2.** Deviation from an accepted or ordinary ethod, course, etc. **3.** *Archaic* Death.
·pend (di·pend′) *v.i.* **1.** To rely; trust: with *on* or *upon.* **.** To be conditioned or determined; be contingent: with *ı* or *upon.* **3.** To rely for maintenance, etc.: with *on* or *oon.* **4.** To hang down: with *from.* [< OF < L < *de-* ɔwn + *pendere* to hang]
·pend·a·ble (di·pen′də·bəl) *adj.* That can be depended ɔon; trustworthy. **— de·pend′a·bil′i·ty, de·pend′a·ble·ess** *n.* **— de·pend′a·bly** *adv.*
·pen·dence (di·pen′dəns) *n.* **1.** The state of relying on mething or someone. **2.** Reliance or trust. **3.** The state being contingent on or determined by something else. **.** Subjection to the control or guidance of another. **5.** The ɔject of one's reliance. Also **de·pen′dance.**
·pen·den·cy (di·pen′dən·sē) *n. pl.* **·cies 1.** The state of eing dependent; dependence. **2.** That which is dependent subordinate. **3.** A territory or state separate from but ıbject to another state or country. Also **de·pen′dan·cy.**
·pen·dent (di·pen′dənt) *adj.* **1.** Conditioned by or con-ngent upon something else. **2.** Subordinate. **3.** Relying ı someone or something for support. **4.** Hanging down. **—** *n.* One who depends on another. Also **de·pen′dant.**

dependent clause *Gram.* See under CLAUSE.
de·pict (di·pikt′) *v.t.* **1.** To portray or represent by or as by drawing, etc. **2.** To portray in words. [< L < *de-* down + *pingere* to paint] **— de·pic′tion** *n.*
dep·i·late (dep′ə·lāt) *v.t.* **·lat·ed, ·lat·ing** To remove hair from. [< L < *de-* away + *pilus* hair] **— dep′i·la′tion** *n.* **dep′i·la′tor** *n.*
de·pil·a·to·ry (di·pil′ə·tôr′ē, -tō′rē) *adj.* Having the power to remove hair. **—** *n. pl.* **·ries** A depilatory agent.
de·plane (dē·plān′) *v.i.* **·planed, ·plan·ing** To alight from an airplane: to *deplane* in Boston.
de·plete (di·plēt′) *v.t.* **·plet·ed, ·plet·ing 1.** To reduce or lessen, as by use, exhaustion, or waste. **2.** To empty com-pletely or partially. [< L < *de-* not + *plere* to fill] **— de·ple′tion** *n.* **— de·ple′tive** *adj. & n.*
de·plor·a·ble (di·plôr′ə·bəl, -plō′rə-) *adj.* **1.** To be deplored; lamentable. **2.** Wretched; sad. **— de·plor′a·ble·ness, de·plor′a·bil′i·ty** *n.* **— de·plor′a·bly** *adv.*
de·plore (di·plôr′, -plōr′) *v.t.* **·plored, ·plor·ing** To have or show regret or sadness over; lament. **— Syn.** See MOURN. [< L < *de-* completely + *plorare* to bewail]
de·ploy (di·ploi′) *v.t. & v.i.* To place or position (forces, people, etc.) according to a plan. [< F < OF < LL < L *dis-* from + *plicare* to fold] **— de·ploy′ment** *n.*
de·po·nent (di·pō′nənt) *adj.* In Latin and Greek grammar, denoting a verb that has the form of the passive but is active in meaning. **—** *n.* **1.** A deponent verb. **2.** *Law* One who gives sworn testimony, especially in writing.
de·pop·u·late (dē·pop′yə·lāt) *v.t.* **·lat·ed, ·lat·ing** To re-move the inhabitants from, as by massacre, famine, eviction, etc. [< L < *de-* down + *populari* to lay waste] **— de·pop′·u·la′tion** *n.* **— de·pop′u·la′tor** *n.*
de·port (di·pôrt′, -pōrt′) *v.t.* **1.** To expel from a country. **2.** To behave or conduct (oneself). [< OF < L < *de-* away + *portare* to carry] **— de′por·ta′tion** *n.*
de·port·ment (di·pôrt′mənt, -pōrt′-) *n.* Conduct or be-havior; demeanor; bearing.
de·pose (di·pōz′) *v.* **·posed, ·pos·ing** *v.t.* **1.** To deprive of rank or office; oust. **2.** *Law* To declare under oath. **—** *v.i.* **3.** *Law* To give testimony under oath. [< OF < *de-* down + *poser* to put down] **— de·pos′a·ble** *adj.* **— de·pos′al** *n.*
de·pos·it (di·poz′it) *v.t.* **1.** To set down; place; put. **2.** To put down in the form of a layer, as silt. **3.** To entrust (money, valuables, etc.) for safekeeping, as in a bank. **4.** To give as partial payment or security. **—** *v.i.* **5.** To be collected or precipitated: Sediments *deposit* in layers. **—** *n.* **1.** Something entrusted for safekeeping, especially money placed in a bank. **2.** The state of being placed for safe-keeping: chiefly in the phrase **on deposit.** **3.** Anything given as partial payment or security. **4.** That which is or has been deposited, as sediment. **5.** *Geol.* A mass of iron, coal, oil, etc. [< L < *de-* down + *ponere* to place]
de·pos·i·tar·y (di·poz′ə·ter′ē) *n. pl.* **·tar·ies 1.** One en-trusted with anything for safekeeping. **2.** A depository.
dep·o·si·tion (dep′ə·zish′ən, dē′pə-) *n.* **1.** The act of de-posing, as from an office. **2.** The act of depositing; also, that which is deposited. **3.** *Law* The written testimony of a witness who is under oath. **— Syn.** See TESTIMONY.
de·pos·i·tor (di·poz′ə·tər) *n.* One who makes a deposit.
de·pos·i·to·ry (di·poz′ə·tôr′ē, -tō′rē) *n. pl.* **·ries 1.** A place where anything is deposited. **2.** A depositary.
de·pot (dē′pō, *Mil. & Brit.* dep′ō) *n.* **1.** A warehouse or storehouse. **2.** *U.S.* A railroad station. **3.** *Mil.* **a** An in-stallation that manufactures, procures, stores, or repairs military materiel. **b** An installation for assembling and processing personnel. **— Syn.** See STATION. [See DEPOSIT.]
de·prave (di·prāv′) *v.t.* **·praved, ·prav·ing** To render bad or worse, especially in morals; corrupt; pervert. [< L < *de-* completely + *pravus* corrupt, wicked] **— dep·ra·va·tion** (dep′rə·vā′shən) *n.* **— de·prav′er** *n.*
de·prav·i·ty (di·prav′ə·tē) *n. pl.* **·ties 1.** The state of being depraved; wickedness. **2.** A depraved act or habit.
dep·re·cate (dep′rə·kāt) *v.t.* **·cat·ed, ·cat·ing 1.** To express disapproval of or regret for. **2.** To disparage or belittle. [< L < *de-* away + *precari* to pray] **— dep′re·cat′ing·ly** *adv.* **— dep′re·ca′tion** *n.* **— dep′re·ca′tor** *n.*
dep·re·ca·to·ry (dep′rə·kə·tôr′ē, -tō′rē) *adj.* Expressing deprecation. Also **dep′re·ca′tive.**
de·pre·ci·ate (di·prē′shē·āt) *v.* **·at·ed, ·at·ing** *v.t.* **1.** To les-sen the value of; lower the price or rate of. **2.** To disparage; belittle. **—** *v.i.* **3.** To become less in value, etc. [< L < *de-* down + *pretium* price] **— de·pre′ci·a′tor** *n.* **— de·pre′ci·a′tive, de·pre′ci·a·to′ry** *adj.*
de·pre·ci·a·tion (di·prē′shē·ā′shən) *n.* **1.** A loss in value or efficiency resulting from usage, age, etc. **2.** A decline in the purchasing value of money. **3.** A disparagement.
dep·re·date (dep′rə·dāt) *v.t. & v.i.* **·dat·ed, ·dat·ing** To prey upon; pillage; plunder. [< LL < L *de-* completely +

praeda booty, prey] — **dep·re·da·tion** (dep′rə·dā′shən) *n.* — **dep′re·da′tor** *n.* — **dep·re·da·to·ry** (dep′rə·dā′tər·ē, di·pred′ə·tôr′ē, -tō′rē) *adj.*

de·press (di·pres′) *v.t.* **1.** To lower the spirits of; make gloomy; sadden. **2.** To lessen in vigor, force, or energy. **3.** To lower in price or value. **4.** To press or push down. [< OF < L < *de-* down + *primere* to press]

de·pres·sant (di·pres′ənt) *Med. adj.* Tending to lessen nervous or functional activity. — *n.* A sedative.

de·pressed (di·prest′) *adj.* **1.** Sad; dejected. **2.** Pressed down; flattened. **3.** Lowered or sunk even with or below the surface. **4.** Reduced in power, amount, value, etc.

depressed area A region characterized by unemployment.

de·pres·sion (di·presh′ən) *n.* **1.** The act of depressing, or the state of being depressed. **2.** Low spirits or vitality. **3.** A low or depressed place or surface. **4.** A severe decline in business, accompanied by increasing unemployment, falling prices, etc. **5.** *Psychiatry* Deep dejection characterized by withdrawal, lack of response to stimulation, etc. — **de·pres′sive** *adj.* — **de·pres′sive·ly** *adv.*

de·pres·sor (di·pres′ər) *n.* **1.** One who or that which depresses. **2.** *Physiol.* An afferent nerve connected with the heart, controlling heart rate and blood pressure.

dep·ri·va·tion (dep′rə·vā′shən) *n.* The act of depriving, or the state of being deprived. Also **de·priv·al** (di·prī′vəl).

de·prive (di·prīv′) *v.t.* **·prived, ·priv·ing 1.** To take something away from; divest. **2.** To keep from acquiring, using, or enjoying something. [< OF < L *de-* completely + *privare* to strip, remove] — **de·priv′a·ble** *adj.*

depth (depth) *n.* **1.** The state or degree of being deep; deepness. **2.** Extent or distance downward, inward, or backward. **3.** Profundity of thought or feeling. **4.** *Usu. pl.* An extremely remote, deep, or distant part. **5.** *Usu. pl.* An intense state of being or feeling. **6.** The most intense part or stage: the *depth* of night. **7.** Richness or intensity of color, sound, etc. **8.** Lowness of pitch. [ME *depthe*]

depth charge A drum-shaped bomb that explodes under water at a desired depth. Also **depth bomb.**

dep·u·ta·tion (dep′yə·tā′shən) *n.* **1.** A person or persons acting for another or others; a delegation. **2.** The act of deputing, or the state of being deputed.

de·pute (di·pyōōt′) *v.t.* **·put·ed, ·put·ing 1.** To appoint as an agent, deputy, etc. **2.** To transfer (authority, etc.) to another. [< OF < LL < L *de-* away + *putare* to think]

dep·u·tize (dep′yə·tīz) *v.* **·tized, ·tiz·ing** *v.t.* **1.** To appoint as a deputy. — *v.i.* **2.** To act as a deputy.

dep·u·ty (dep′yə·tē) *n. pl.* **·ties 1.** One appointed to act for another: a sheriff's *deputy.* **2.** A member of a legislative assembly in certain countries. — *adj.* Acting as deputy.

de·rail (dē·rāl′) *v.t.* **1.** To cause (a train, etc.) to run off the rails. — *v.i.* **2.** To run off the rails. [< F < *dé-* from + *rail* rail] — **de·rail′ment** *n.*

de·range (di·rānj′) *v.t.* **·ranged, ·rang·ing 1.** To disturb the arrangement, working, or order of. **2.** To unbalance the reason of; render insane. [< F < *dé-* away + *ranger* to set in line] — **de·ranged′** *adj.* — **de·range′ment** *n.*

der·by (dûr′bē) *n. pl.* **·bies** A stiff felt hat with a curved, narrow brim and round crown: also, *Brit., bowler.* [< DERBY]

Der·by (dûr′bē, *Brit.* där′bē) *n.* **1.** An annual horse race for three-year-olds run at Epsom Downs in Surrey, England, since 1780. **2.** Any similar horse race, as the Kentucky Derby. [after the 12th Earl of *Derby*, the founder]

der·e·lict (der′ə·likt) *adj.* **1.** Neglectful of obligation; remiss. **2.** Deserted or abandoned. — *n.* **1.** That which is deserted or abandoned, as a ship at sea. **2.** A social outcast, etc. [< L < *de-* completely + *relinquere* to abandon]

der·e·lic·tion (der′ə·lik′shən) *n.* **1.** Neglect of or failure in duty. **2.** Voluntary abandonment of something. **3.** The state or fact of being abandoned.

de·ride (di·rīd′) *v.t.* **·rid·ed, ·rid·ing** To treat with scornful mirth; ridicule. [< L < *de-* completely + *ridere* to laugh, mock] — **de·rid′er** *n.* — **de·rid′ing·ly** *adv.*

de ri·gueur (də rē·gœr′) *French* Necessary according to etiquette; required by good form.

de·ri·sion (di·rizh′ən) *n.* **1.** The act of deriding; ridicule; mockery. **2.** An object of ridicule or scorn.

de·ri·sive (di·rī′siv) *adj.* Expressive of or characterized by derision; mocking. Also **de·ri·so·ry** (di·rī′sər·ē). — **de·ri′sive·ly** *adv.* — **de·ri′sive·ness** *n.*

der·i·va·tion (der′ə·vā′shən) *n.* **1.** The act of deriving, or the condition of being derived. **2.** That which is derived; a derivative. **3.** Origin or descent. **4.** The tracing of a word from its original form and meaning; also, a statement of this; an etymology. — **der′i·va′tion·al** *adj.*

de·riv·a·tive (di·riv′ə·tiv) *adj.* **1.** Resulting from or characterized by derivation. **2.** Not original or primary; based on other sources. — *n.* **1.** That which is derived. **2.** *Gram.* A word developed from another, as by the addition of affixes. **3.** *Chem.* A compound formed or regarded as being formed from a specified substance, usu. by partial substitution: a benzene *derivative.* — **de·riv′a·tive·ly** *adv.*

de·rive (di·rīv′) *v.* **·rived, ·riv·ing** *v.t.* **1.** To draw or rece as from a source or principle. **2.** To deduce, as from a pr ise. **3.** To trace the source of (a word, etc.). **4.** *Chem.* obtain (a compound) from another, as by partial subst tion. — *v.i.* **5.** To originate; proceed. [< L < *de-* f + *rivus* stream] — **de·riv′a·ble** *adj.* — **de·riv′er** *n.*

derm- Var. of DERMO-.

-derm *suffix* Skin. [< Gk. *derma* skin]

der·ma (dûr′mə) *n. Anat.* The dermis. [< Gk., sl — **der′mal** *adj.*

dermato- *combining form* Skin. Also, before vowels, **mat-.** [< Gk. *derma, dermatos* skin]

der·ma·tol·o·gy (dûr′mə·tol′ə·jē) *n.* The branch of med science that relates to the skin and its diseases. — **der· to·log·i·cal** (dûr′mə·tə·loj′i·kəl) *adj.* — **der′ma·tol′o·gis**

der·mis (dûr′mis) *n. Anat.* **1.** The sensitive, vasc portion of the skin below the epidermis: also called *cori derma.* **2.** The skin. [< LL < Gk. *derma* skin]

dermo- *combining form* Skin. Also, before vowels, **der**

der·o·gate (der′ə·gāt) **·gat·ed, ·gat·ing** *v.t. & v.i.* **1.** take or cause to take away; detract: with *from.* **2.** To come or cause to become inferior: with *from.* [< L < away + *rogare* to ask] — **der′o·ga′tion** *n.*

de·rog·a·tive (di·rog′ə·tiv) *adj.* Tending to derogate or tract; derogatory. — **de·rog′a·tive·ly** *adv.*

de·rog·a·to·ry (di·rog′ə·tôr′ē, -tō′rē) *adj.* Having the ef of lessening or detracting; belittling; disparaging. — **de·rog′a·to′ri·ly** *adv.* — **de·rog′a·to′ri·ness** *n.*

DERRICKS
a Hoisting.
b Oil-well.

der·rick (der′ik) *n.* **1.** An apparatus for hoisting and swinging heavy weights, usu. consisting of a tackle at the end of a boom or mast. **2.** The framework over the mouth of an oil well. [after *Derrick*, 17th c. London hangman]

der·ring-do (der′ing·dōō′) *n.* Courageous or daring action. [ME *dorrying don* daring to do]

der·rin·ger (der′in·jər) *n.* A pistol having a short barrel and a large bore. [after Henry *Deringer*, 19th c. U.S. gunsmith]

der·vish (dûr′vish) *n.* A member of any of various Mos orders, some of whom express their devotion in whirli howling, etc. [< Turkish < Persian *darvēsh*]

de·salt (dē·sôlt′) *v.t.* To remove the salt from, as sea wa to make potable. — **de·salt′er** *n.* — **de·salt′ing** *n.*

des·cant (*n.* des′kant; *v.* des·kant′, dis-) *n.* **1.** A discuss or a series of remarks. **2.** *Music* **a** A varied melody or sc **b** A counterpoint above the basic melody. **c** The upper p in part music. — *v.i.* **1.** To discourse at length: with *o upon.* **2.** *Music* **a** To make or perform a descant. **b** To si [< AF < Med.L < L *dis-* away + *cantus* a song]

de·scend (di·send′) *v.i.* **1.** To move from a higher to a lo point. **2.** To slope downward, as a path. **3.** To lower o self; stoop: to *descend* to begging. **4.** To come by inh tance; be inherited. **5.** *Biol.* To be derived by heredity. To pass from the general to the specific. **7.** To arrive come in great numbers. **8.** *Astron.* To move toward horizon. — *v.t.* **9.** To move from an upper to a lower p of; go down, as stairs. [< OF < L < *de-* down + *scand* to climb] — **de·scend′er** *n.*

de·scen·dant (di·sen′dənt) *n.* One who is descended li ally from another; offspring.

de·scen·dent (di·sen′dənt) *adj.* Proceeding downward.

de·scent (di·sent′) *n.* **1.** The act of descending. **2.** A cline or deterioration. **3.** A declivity; slope. **4.** Ancest derivation; lineage. **5.** In genealogy, a generation. **6.** *L* The succession of property or title by inheritance.

de·scribe (di·skrīb′) *v.t* **·scribed, ·scrib·ing 1.** To pres in spoken or written words. **2.** To give a picture or idea of means of words; depict. **3.** To draw the figure of; tra outline. [< L < *de-* down + *scribere* to write] — **scrib′a·ble** *adj.* — **de·scrib′er** *n.*

de·scrip·tion (di·skrip′shən) *n.* **1.** The act or technique describing. **2.** An account that describes. **3.** A drawing tracing, as of an arc. **4.** Sort, kind, or variety: birds of ev *description.* — **Syn.** See EXPLANATION.

de·scrip·tive (di·skrip′tiv) *adj.* Characterized by or c taining description; serving to describe. — **de·scrip′tive** *adv.* — **de·scrip′tive·ness** *n.*

de·scry (di·skrī′) *v.t.* **·scried, ·scry·ing 1.** To discover w the eye, as something distant. **2.** To discover by obser tion. [< OF < *des-* away + *crier* to cry]

des·e·crate (des′ə·krāt) *v.t.* **·crat·ed, ·crat·ing** To div from a sacred to a common use; treat sacrilegiously; profa [< DE- + L *sacrare* to make holy] — **des′e·crat′er** or **des cra′tor** *n.* — **des′e·cra′tion** *n.*

de·seg·re·gate (dē·seg′rə·gāt) *v.t.* **·gat·ed, ·gat·ing** To eli inate racial segregation in. — **de′seg·re·ga′tion** *n.*

sen·si·tize (dē·sen′sə·tīz) *v.t.* **·tized, ·tiz·ing** To make s sensitive, esp. in medicine, to lessen or eliminate the sen- iveness of (an individual, organ, tissue, etc.), as to an al- gen. **— de·sen′si·ti·za′tion** *n.* **— de·sen′si·tiz′er** *n.*

·ert[1] (dez′ərt) *n.* **1.** A region greatly lacking in rainfall, isture, and vegetation. **2.** Any region that is unculti- ted and desolate. **—** *adj.* Of or like a desert; uninhabited. OF < LL < L *deserere* < *de-* away + *serere* to join]

sert[2] (di·zûrt′) *v.t.* **1.** To forsake or abandon. **2.** To for- ke in violation of one's oath or orders, as a service, post, . **—** *v.i.* **3.** To abandon one's post, duty, etc. **4.** *Mil.* To absent without leave with the intention of not returning.

sert[3] (di·zûrt′) *n.* **1.** *Often pl.* That which is deserved or rited: to get one's just *deserts.* **2.** The state of deserving ward or punishment. [See DESERVE.]

sert·er (di·zûr′tər) *n.* One who forsakes a duty, friends, .; esp., one who deserts from a military service.

ser·tion (di·zûr′shən) *n.* **1.** The act of deserting. **2.** e state of being deserted; desolation. **3.** *Law* The willful andonment of one's spouse or children, or both.

serve (di·zûrv′) *v.* **·served, ·serv·ing** *v.t.* **1.** To be en- led to or worthy of. **—** *v.i.* **2.** To be worthy. [< OF < L *de-* completely + *servire* to serve] **— de·serv′er** *n.*

served (di·zûrvd′) *adj.* Earned or merited. **— de·serv′· ·ly** (di·zûr′vid·lē) *adv.* **— de·serv′ed·ness** *n.*

serv·ing (di·zûr′ving) *adj.* Worthy; meritorious: *deserv- g* of praise. **— de·serv′ing·ly** *adv.* **— de·serv′ing·ness** *n.*

·ha·bille (dez′ə·bēl′) *n.* Dishabille.

·ic·cant (des′ə·kənt) *adj.* Producing dryness; desiccat- , as a medicine. **—** *n.* A drying agent or substance.

·ic·cate (des′ə·kāt) *v.* **·cat·ed, ·cat·ing** *v.t* **1.** To dry oroughly. **2.** To preserve (foods) by drying. **—** *v.i.* **3.** become dry. [< L < *de-* completely + *siccare* to dry t] **— des′ic·ca′tion** *n.* **— des′ic·ca′tive** *adj. & n.*

sid·er·a·tum (di·sid′ə·rā′təm) *n.* *pl.* **·ta** (-tə) Some- ing needed or regarded as desirable. [< L]

sign (di·zīn′) *v.t* **1.** To draw or prepare preliminary ans or sketches of. **2.** To plan and make with skill, as a rk of art. **3.** To form or make (plans, schemes, etc.) in e mind; conceive; invent. **4.** To intend; purpose. **—** *v.i.* To be a designer. **6.** To plan; conceive. **—** *n.* **1.** A pre- inary sketch or outline; pattern. **2.** The arrangement d coordination of the parts or details of any object: the *sign* of a jet airplane. **3.** A piece of artistic or decorative rk. **4.** The art of making designs. **5.** A visual pattern or mposition. **6.** A plan or project. **7.** An object or pur- se. **8.** *Often pl.* A sinister scheme or plot. **9.** Intelligent, rposeful, or discoverable pattern, as opposed to chaos. ee DESIGNATE.] **— de·sig′na·ble** *adj.*

·ig·nate (*v.* dez′ig·nāt; *for adj., also* dez′ig·nit) *v.t.* **·nat· , ·nat·ing** **1.** To indicate or specify. **2.** To name or en- le; characterize. **3.** To select or appoint for a specific rpose, duty, etc. **—** *adj.* Designated; selected. [< L < - completely + *signare* to mark] **— des′ig·na′tive** (-nā′·) *adj.* **— des′ig·na′tor** *n.*

·ig·na·tion (dez′ig·nā′shən) *n.* **1.** A distinctive mark or le. **2.** The act of pointing out something. **3.** Appoint- ent or nomination.

sign·ed·ly (di·zī′nid·lē) *adv.* By design; intentionally.

·ig·nee (dez′ig·nē′) *n.* A person designated.

sign·er (di·zī′nər) *n.* **1.** One who creates designs, as for esses, machinery, etc. **2.** A schemer; contriver.

sign·ing (di·zī′ning) *n.* **1.** The act or art of making de- ns. **2.** The act of plotting or scheming. **—** *adj.* **1.** heming. **2.** Exercising foresight. **— de·sign′ing·ly** *adv.*

sir·a·ble (di·zīr′ə·bəl) *adj.* Worthy of or exciting desire. **de·sir′a·bil′i·ty, de·sir′a·ble·ness** *n.* **— de·sir′a·bly** *adv.*

sire (di·zīr′) *v.t.* **·sired, ·sir·ing** **1.** To wish or long for; ave. **2.** To ask for; request. **—** *n,* **1.** A longing or crav- . **2.** A request or wish. **3.** An object desired. **4.** Sexual petite; passion; lust. [< OF < L < *de-* from + *sidus, leris* star; with ref. to astrology] **— de·sir′er** *n.*

sir·ous (di·zīr′əs) *adj.* Having a desire or craving.

sist (di·zist′) *v.i.* To cease, as from an action. [< L < - from + *sistere* to stop] **— de·sis′tance,** or **de·sis′tence** *n.*

·k (desk) *n.* **1.** A table or case adapted for writing or idying, usu. having compartments or drawers. **2.** A table stand to hold reading matter; also, a pulpit. **3.** A divi- n or post in an organization: the service *desk.* **4.** *U.S.* A partment in a newspaper office: the copy *desk.* **5.** *Music* orchestral music stand. [< Med.L < LL *discus* table]

·o·late (*adj.* des′ə·lit; *v.* des′ə·lāt) *adj.* **1.** Destitute of habitants or dwellings; deserted. **2.** Made unfit for habi- tion. **3.** Gloomy; dreary. **4.** Without friends; forlorn. *v.t.* **·lat·ed, ·lat·ing** **1.** To deprive of inhabitants. **2.** To y waste; devastate. **3.** To make sorrowful or forlorn. **4.** forsake; abandon. [< L < *de-* completely + *solus* alone] **des′o·late·ly** *adv.* **— des′o·late·ness** *n.*

des·o·la·tion (des′ə·lā′shən) *n.* **1.** The act of making deso- late; a laying waste. **2.** The condition of being ruined or de- serted. **3.** Loneliness. **4.** A desolate region; waste.

des·ox·y- Var. of DEOXY-.

de·spair (di·spâr′) *v.i.* To lose or abandon hope; be or become hopeless: with *of.* **—** *n.* **1.** Utter hopelessness and discouragement. **2.** That which causes despair. [< OF < L < *de-* away + *sperare* to hope] **— de·spair′ing** *adj.* **— de·spair′ing·ly** *adv.*

— Syn. (noun) **1.** *Despair* is the utter abandonment of hope that leaves the mind apathetic or numb. *Desperation* is energized *despair,* vigorous in action and reckless of consequences. *Despond- ency* is paralyzing *despair* coupled with deep sorrow. The mere absence of hope is *hopelessness* and is often used to characterize circumstances. **— Ant.** hope, expectation, confidence.

des·per·a·do (des′pə·rä′dō, -rā′dō) *n.* *pl.* **·does** or **·dos** A desperate or violent criminal. [< OSp. See DESPAIR.]

des·per·ate (des′pər·it) *adj.* **1.** Without care for danger; reckless, as from despair. **2.** Resorted to in desperation. **3.** Regarded as almost hopeless; critical. **4.** Extreme; very great. **— des′per·ate·ly** *adv.* **— des′per·ate·ness** *n.*

des·per·a·tion (des′pə·rā′shən) *n.* The state of being des- perate; also, the recklessness growing out of despair.

des·pi·ca·ble (des′pi·kə·bəl, di·spik′ə·bəl) *adj.* That is to be despised; contemptible; vile. [See DESPISE.] **— des′pi·ca· bil′i·ty, des′pi·ca·ble·ness** *n.* **— des′pi·ca·bly** *adv.*

de·spise (di·spīz′) *v.t.* **·spised, ·spis·ing** To regard as con- temptible or worthless; disdain; scorn. [< OF < L < *de-* down + *specere* to look at] **— de·spis′er** *n.*

de·spite (di·spīt′) *prep.* In spite of; notwithstanding. **—** *n.* **1.** Contemptuous defiance. **2.** An act of defiance, malice, or injury. **— in despite of** In spite of. [See DESPISE.]

de·spoil (di·spoil′) *v.t.* To deprive of possessions; rob. [< OF < L < *de-* completely + *spoliare* to rob] **— de·spoil′er** *n.* **— de·spoil′ment, de·spo·li·a·tion** (di·spō′lē·ā′shən) *n.*

de·spond (di·spond′) *v.i.* To lose spirit, courage, or hope. **—** *n. Archaic* Despondency. [< L < *de-* away + *spondere* to promise] **— de·spond′ing·ly** *adv.*

de·spon·den·cy (di·spon′dən·sē) *n.* Dejection of spirits from loss of hope or courage. Also **de·spon′dence.**

de·spon·dent (di·spon′dənt) *adj.* Dejected in spirit; dis- heartened. **— de·spon′dent·ly** *adv.*

des·pot (des′pət, -pot) *n.* **1.** An absolute monarch; auto- crat. **2.** A tyrant. [< OF < Gk. *despotēs* master]

des·pot·ic (di·spot′ik) *adj.* Of or like a despot; tyrannical; autocratic. **— des·pot′i·cal·ly** *adv.*

des·pot·ism (des′pə·tiz′əm) *n.* **1.** Unlimited authority; ab- solute power. **2.** A state ruled by a despot.

des·sert (di·zûrt′) *n.* **1.** *U.S.* A serving of pastry, ice cream, etc., as the last course of a meal. **2.** *Brit.* Fruits, nuts, etc., served after a dinner. [< F < *desservir* to clear a table]

des·ti·na·tion (des′tə·nā′shən) *n.* **1.** The point or place set for a journey's end, or to which something is directed. **2.** The purpose or end for which anything is created or in- tended. **3.** The act of designating or appointing.

des·tine (des′tin) *v.t.* **·tined, ·tin·ing** **1.** To design for or appoint to a distinct purpose. **2.** To determine the future of, as by destiny. [< OF < L *destinare* to make fast, ult. < *de-* completely + *stare* to stand] **— des′tined** *adj.*

des·ti·ny (des′tə·nē) *n.* *pl.* **·nies** **1.** The fate to which a person or thing is destined. **2.** The preordained or prede- termined ordering of events. **3.** The power that is thought to predetermine the course of events. [See DESTINE.]

des·ti·tute (des′tə·to͞ot, -tyo͞ot) *adj.* **1.** Not having; entire- ly lacking: with *of.* **2.** Extremely poor. [< L < *de-* down + *statuere* to set]

des·ti·tu·tion (des′tə·to͞o′shən, -tyo͞o′-) *n.* **1.** Extreme pov- erty. **2.** Deficiency; lack.

de·stroy (di·stroi′) *v.t.* **1.** To ruin utterly; consume. **2.** To tear down; demolish. **3.** To put an end to. **4.** To kill. **5.** To make ineffective or useless. **— Syn.** See DEMOLISH. [< OF, ult. < L < *de-* down + *struere* to construct]

de·stroy·er (di·stroi′ər) *n.* **1.** One who or that which de- stroys. **2.** A speedy war vessel, smaller than a cruiser.

de·struct (di·strukt′) *n.* *Aerospace* The act of destroying a defective or dangerous missile or rocket after launch.

de·struc·ti·ble (di·struk′tə·bəl) *adj.* Capable of being de- stroyed. **— de·struc′ti·bil′i·ty, de·struc′ti·ble·ness** *n.*

de·struc·tion (di·struk′shən) *n.* **1.** The act of destroying, or the state of being destroyed; demolition; ruin. **2.** That which destroys, or is a means of destroying.

de·struc·tive (di·struk′tiv) *adj.* **1.** Causing destruction; tending to destroy; ruinous: with *of* or *to.* **2.** Tending to tear down or discredit. **— de·struc′tive·ly** *adv.* **— de·struc′tive· ness, de·struc·tiv·i·ty** (dē′struk·tiv′ə·tē) *n.*

destructive distillation *Chem.* The distillation of organic substances, as wood and coal, in such a way as to decompose them chemically: also called *dry distillation.*

des·ue·tude (des′wə·to͞od, -tyo͞od) *n.* A condition of disuse. [< MF < L < *de-* away + *suescere* to be used to]

de·sul·fur·ize (dē·sul′fə·rīz) *v.t.* **·ized, ·iz·ing** To remove sulfur from. Also **de·sul′fur, de·sul′fur·ate, de·sul′phur·ize.** — **de·sul′fur·i·za′tion** *n.* — **de·sul′fur·iz′er** *n.*

des·ul·to·ry (des′əl·tôr′ē, -tō′rē) *adj.* **1.** Passing abruptly from one thing to another; unmethodical. **2.** Occurring by chance. [< L < *de-* down + *sultus*, pp. of *salire* to leap] — **des′ul·to′ri·ly** *adv.* — **des′ul·to′ri·ness** *n.*

de·tach (di·tach′) *v.t.* **1.** To unfasten and separate; disconnect. **2.** To send off for special duty, as a regiment or a ship. [< F < *de-* away + OF *tache* nail] — **de·tach′a·bil′i·ty** *n.* — **de·tach′a·ble** *adj.* — **de·tach′er** *n.*

de·tached (di·tacht′) *adj.* **1.** Separated from others; disconnected. **2.** Unconcerned; impartial.

detached retina *Pathol.* A disconnection of the inner layers of the retina from the pigment layer.

de·tach·ment (di·tach′mənt) *n.* **1.** The act of detaching or separating. **2.** The state of being detached. **3.** Dissociation from surroundings or worldly affairs. **4.** Absence of prejudice or partiality. **5.** *Mil.* **a** A part of a unit separated from its parent organization for duty. **b** A permanent unit organized for a specific purpose.

de·tail (*n.* di·tāl′, dē′tāl; *v.* di·tāl′; *Mil.* dē′tāl) *n.* **1.** A separately considered part or item; particular. **2.** A dealing with particulars: to go into *detail.* **3.** A narrative account giving particulars. **4.** In art, architecture, etc., a minor or secondary part. **5.** *Mil.* A small detachment designated for a particular task. — **in detail** Item by item. — *v.t.* **1.** To report or narrate minutely. **2.** *Mil.* To select and send off for a special service, duty, etc. [< F < *dé-* completely + *tailler* to cut up]

de·tain (di·tān′) *v.t.* **1.** To keep from proceeding; stop; delay. **2.** To withhold (what belongs to another). **3.** To hold in custody; confine. [< OF < L < *de-* away + *tenere* to hold] — **de·tain′ment** *n.*

de·tect (di·tekt′) *v.t.* **1.** To perceive or find, as something obscure: to *detect* an error in spelling. **2.** To expose or uncover, as a crime. **3.** *Telecom.* To recover the (signal, audio component, etc.) from a modulated carrier wave. [< L < *de-* away, off + *tegere* to cover] — **de·tect′a·ble** or **de·tect′i·ble** *adj.* — **de·tect′er** *n.*

de·tec·tion (di·tek′shən) *n.* **1.** The act of detecting, or the fact of being detected. **2.** *Telecom.* Any method of operating on a modulated signal wave so as to obtain the signal imparted to it; demodulation of incoming electrical signals.

de·tec·tive (di·tek′tiv) *n.* A person, often a policeman, whose work is to investigate crimes, discover evidence, capture criminals, etc. — *adj.* **1.** Belonging or pertaining to detectives or their work. **2.** Fitted for or used in detection.

de·tec·tor (di·tek′tər) *n.* **1.** One who or that which detects. **2.** *Telecom.* A device for obtaining the signal from a modulated carrier.

dé·tente (dā·tänt′) *n.* An easing, as of discord between nations. [< F]

de·ten·tion (di·ten′shən) *n.* **1.** The act of detaining; a restraining. **2.** The state of being detained. [See DETAIN.]

de·ter (di·tûr′) *v.t.* **·terred, ·ter·ring** To prevent or discourage (someone) from acting by arousing fear, uncertainty, etc. [< L < *de-* away + *terrere* to frighten] — **de·ter′ment** *n.*

de·terge (di·tûrj′) *v.t.* **·terged, ·terg·ing 1.** To cleanse, as a wound. **2.** To wipe off. [< L < *de-* away + *tergere* to wipe]

de·ter·gent (di·tûr′jənt) *adj.* Having cleansing or purging qualities. — *n.* A cleansing agent. — **de·ter′gen·cy, de·ter′gence** *n.*

de·te·ri·o·rate (di·tir′ē·ə·rāt′) *v.t.* & *v.i.* **·rat·ed, ·rat·ing** To make or become worse; depreciate. [< L < *deterior* worse] — **de·te′ri·o·ra′tion** *n.* — **de·te′·ri·o·ra′tive** *adj.*

de·ter·mi·na·ble (di·tûr′mi·nə·bəl) *adj.* **1.** That may be found out, settled, or decided. **2.** *Law* Liable to be ended.

de·ter·mi·nant (di·tûr′mə·nənt) *adj.* Determinative. — *n.* That which influences or determines.

de·ter·mi·nate (di·tûr′mə·nit) *adj.* **1.** Definitely limited or fixed; specific; distinct. **2.** Settled and conclusive; decided; final. **3.** Fixed in purpose; resolute. **4.** *Bot.* Terminating in a flower or bud, as each axis of an inflorescence. — **de·ter′mi·nate·ly** *adv.* — **de·ter′mi·nate·ness** *n.*

de·ter·mi·na·tion (di·tûr′mə·nā′shən) *n.* **1.** The act of reaching a decision; also, the decision reached. **2.** The quality of being firm in purpose or action; resoluteness. **3.** The determining or fixing of the quality, degree, etc., of anything; also, the result of this. **4.** A decisive tendency or movement toward some object or end.

de·ter·mi·na·tive (di·tûr′mə·nā′tiv, -mə·nə·tiv) *adj.* Tending or having power to determine. — *n.* That which determines. — **de·ter′mi·na′tive·ly** *adv.*

de·ter·mine (di·tûr′min) *v.* **·mined, ·min·ing** *v.t.* **1.** To settle or decide, as an argument, question, or debate. **2.** To ascertain or fix. **3.** To cause to reach a decision. **4.** To fix or give definite form to; influence. **5.** To give purpose or direction to. **6.** To set bounds to; limit. **7.** *Law* To li terminate: to *determine* a contract. — *v.i.* **8.** To come decision; resolve. **9.** *Law* To come to an end. [< OF < *de-* completely + *terminare* to end] — **de·ter′min·e**

de·ter·mined (di·tûr′mind) *adj.* Having or showing fi purpose; resolute; firm. — **de·ter·mined·ly** (di·tûr′min -min·id·lē) *adv.* — **de·ter′mined·ness** *n.*

de·ter·min·ism (di·tûr′mə·niz′əm) *n.* *Philos.* The trine that every event is the inevitable result of antece conditions, and that human beings do not have free wi

de·ter·rent (di·tûr′ənt) *adj.* Tending or serving to de — *n.* Something that deters. — **de·ter′rence** *n.*

de·test (di·test′) *v.t.* To dislike with intensity; hate; ab [< MF < L *detestari* to denounce < *de-* away + *testis* a ness] — **de·test′er** *n.*

de·test·a·ble (di·tes′tə·bəl) *adj.* Deserving to be detes extremely hateful; abominable. — **de·test′a·bil′i·ty, test′a·ble·ness** *n.* — **de·test′a·bly** *adv.*

de·tes·ta·tion (dē′tes·tā′shən) *n.* **1.** Extreme dis hatred; abhorrence. **2.** One who or that which is dete

de·throne (dē·thrōn′) *v.t.* **·throned, ·thron·ing** To rem from the throne. — **de·throne′ment** *n.* — **de·thron′e**

det·o·nate (det′ə·nāt, dē′tə-) *v.* **·nat·ed, ·nat·ing** *v.t.* **1** cause to explode suddenly and with violence. — *v.i.* **2** explode suddenly with a loud report. [< L < *de-* dow *tonare* to thunder] — **det′o·na′tion** *n.* — **det′o·na′to**

de·tour (dē′to͝or, di·to͝or′) *n.* A deviation from a di route or course of action; esp., a byroad used when a r road is impassable. — *v.t.* & *v.i.* To go or cause to go roundabout way. [< F < *dé-* away + *tourner* to turn]

de·tract (di·trakt′) *v.i.* **1.** To take away a part; dimir with *from.* — *v.t.* **2.** To take away (a part). **3.** To tract; divert. [< L < *de-* away + *trahere* to pull] — **trac′tion** *n.* — **de·trac′tive** *adj.* — **de·trac′tor** *n.*

de·train (dē·trān′) *v.t.* & *v.i.* *Chiefly Brit.* To leave or c to leave a railroad train. — **de·train′ment** *n.*

det·ri·ment (det′rə·mənt) *n.* **1.** Damage or loss. **2.** So thing that impairs, injures, or causes loss. [< L < *de-* a + *terere* to rub]

det·ri·men·tal (det′rə·men′təl) *adj.* Causing damag loss. — **Syn.** See PERNICIOUS. — **det′ri·men′tal·ly** *ad*

de·tri·tus (di·trī′təs) *n.* **1.** Loose fragments or part separated from masses of rock by erosion, glacial actio other forces. **2.** Debris. [See DETRIMENT.]

de trop (də trō′) *French* Too much; superfluous.

deuce[1] (do͞os, dyo͞os) *n.* **1.** Two; esp., a card or side of having two spots. **2.** In tennis, a score tied at 40 or at or more games each, requiring either side to win two suc sive points for the game or two successive games for the [< F < OF < L *duos*, accusative of *duo* two]

deuce[2] (do͞os, dyo͞os) *n.* *Informal* The devil; bad luc mild oath. [< LG *de duus* the deuce (throw at dice)]

deu·ced (do͞o′sid, dyo͞o′-, do͞ost, dyo͞ost) *Informal adj.* founded; excessive. — *adv.* Devilishly. — **deu′ced·ly** *a*

De·us (dē′əs, dā′o͞os) *n.* *Latin* God.

deu·te·ri·um (do͞o·tir′ē·əm, dyo͞o-) *n.* The isotope of drogen having the atomic weight 2.01 (symbol, D or also called *heavy hydrogen.* [< NL < Gk. *deuteros* sec

deuterium oxide Heavy water.

deutero- *combining form* Second; secondary. Also, **deu** (before vowels), **deuto-**. [< Gk. *deuteros* second]

deu·ter·on (do͞o′tə·ron, dyo͞o′-) *n.* *Physics* The nucleus deuterium atom. [< NL < Gk. *deuteros* second]

Deu·ter·on·o·my (do͞o′tə·ron′ə·mē, dyo͞o′-) The fifth b of the Old Testament, containing a second statement of Mosaic law. [< Gk. < *deuteros* second + *nomos* law]

deut·sche·mark (doi′chə·märk′) *n.* **1.** The standard n etary unit of West Germany, equivalent to 100 pfenn in 1960 worth about 24 U.S. cents. **2.** The standard m tary unit of East Germany. Also **deutsche mark.**

de·val·u·ate (dē·val′yo͞o·āt) *v.t.* **·at·ed, ·at·ing** To red the value or worth of. Also **de·val′ue.** — **de·val′u·a′tio**

dev·as·tate (dev′ə·stāt) *v.t.* **·tat·ed, ·tat·ing 1.** To waste, as by war, fire, etc. **2.** *Informal* To confound; cr [< L < *de-* completely + *vastare* to lay waste] — **dev tat′ing·ly** *adv.* — **dev′as·ta′tion** *n.* — **dev′as·ta′tor** *n.*

de·vel·op (di·vel′əp) *v.t.* **1.** To expand or bring out the tentialities, capabilities, etc., of. **2.** To work out in de enlarge upon: to *develop* an idea. **3.** To reveal or un gradually: to *develop* a plot. **4.** To bring into active e tence: to *develop* patience. **5.** *Photog.* **a** To make visible hidden image) upon a sensitized plate that has been expo to the action of light. **b** To subject (a plate or film) to a veloper. **6.** *Music* To elaborate on (a theme). — *v.i.* To increase in capabilities, maturity, etc. **8.** To adva from a lower to a higher stage; evolve. **9.** To be disclos as events, a plot, etc. **10.** To come into existence: So tastes *develop* slowly. [< F < *dé-* away + OF *voluper* fold, wrap up] — **de·vel′op·a·ble** *adj.*

de·vel·op·er (di·vel′əp·ər) *n.* **1.** One who or that which velops. **2.** *Photog.* A solution for developing photograp

ʼel·op·ment (di·velʹəp·mənt) *n.* **1.** The act of develop-. **2.** The state or condition of that which has been de-oped. **3.** A result or product of developing. **4.** An event occurrence: a political *development*.
ʼel·op·men·tal (di·velʹəp·menʹtəl) *adj.* Of or pertaining levelopment; evolutionary. **— de·velʹop·menʹtal·ly** *adv.*
ʼi·ate (*n.* dēʹvē·it; *v.* dēʹvē·āt) **—** *n.* One whose actions beliefs differ considerably from the standards of his so-y. Also **de·vi·ant** (dēʹvē·ənt). **—** *v.* **·at·ed, ·at·ing** *v.i.* **1.** turn aside from a straight or appointed way or course. To differ, as in belief. **—** *v.t.* **3.** To cause to turn aside. LL < L *de-* from + *via* road] **— deʹvi·aʹtor** *n.*
ʼi·a·tion (dēʹvē·āʹshən) *n.* **1.** The act of deviating, or result. **2.** *Stat.* The difference between one value in a es of observations and the arithmetic mean of the series.
ʼice (di·visʹ) *n.* **1.** Something devised or constructed for ecific purpose. **2.** A scheme or plan, esp. a crafty or evil . **3.** An ornamental design, as in embroidery. **4.** An em-m in a coat of arms; also, any emblem or motto. **— to ve (someone) to his own devices** To allow (someone) to as he wishes. [< OF < L *dividere* to divide]
·il (devʹəl) *n.* **1.** *Sometimes cap.* In Jewish and Christian ology, the prince and ruler of the kingdom of evil; Satan. Any subordinate evil sprit; a demon. **3.** A wicked or licious person. **4.** A wretched fellow: poor *devil.* **5.** A son of great energy or daring. **6.** A machine for any of ious purposes, as for cutting or tearing up rags. **7.** A nter's apprentice: also called *printer's devil.* **— between devil and the deep blue sea** Between equally bad alter-ives. **— the devil** An exclamation of anger, surprise, etc. **the devil to pay** Trouble to be expected as a consequence. **to give the devil his due** To acknowledge the ability or cess of even a disliked person, antagonist, etc. **—** *v.t.* **dev·l** or **·illed, ·dev·il·ing** or **·il·ling 1.** To prepare for eating seasoning highly. **2.** To cut up (cloth, etc.) in a devil. To annoy or harass. [OE < LL < Gk. *diabolos* slanderer]
·il·fish (devʹəl·fishʹ) *n. pl.* **·fish** or **·fish·es 1.** The manta. Any of various large cephalopods, as the octopus.
·il·ish (devʹəl·ish, devʹlish) *adj.* **1.** Having the qualities he devil; diabolical. **2.** *Informal* Excessive. **—** *adv. In-mal* Excessively. **— devʹil·ish·ly** *adv.* **— devʹil·ish·ness** *n.*
·il-may-care (devʹəl·mā·kârʹ) *adj.* Careless; reckless.
·il·ment (devʹəl·mənt) *n.* Impish conduct; mischief.
il's advocate (devʹəlz) **1.** In the Roman Catholic urch, an official appointed to argue against a candidate canonization. **2.** One who argues perversely.
·il's-food cake (devʹəlz·fo͞odʹ) A chocolate cake.
·il·try (devʹəl·trē) *n. pl.* **·tries 1.** Wanton or malicious schief. **2.** Wickedness or cruelty. Also *Brit.* **devʹil·ry.**
ʼi·ous (dēʹvē·əs) *adj.* **1.** Winding or leading away from regular, straight, or direct course; rambling; swerving. Straying from the proper way; erring. [< L < *de-* from *via* way] **— deʹvi·ous·ly** *adv.* **— deʹvi·ous·ness** *n.*
ʼi·sal (di·vīʹzəl) *n.* A contriving or bequeathing.
ʼise (di·vīzʹ) *v.* **·vised, ·vis·ing** *v.t.* **1.** To form in the nd; invent; contrive; plan. **2.** *Law* To transmit (real ate) by will. **—** *v.i.* **3.** To form a plan. **—** *n. Law* **1.** The of bequeathing lands. **2.** A gift of lands by will. **3.** A l, or clause in a will, conveying real estate. [< OF < L *idere* to separate] **— de·visʹa·ble** *adj.* **— de·visʹer** *n.*
ʼi·see (di·vīʹzēʹ, devʹə·zēʹ) *n. Law* The person to whom levise is made.
ʼi·sor (di·vīʹzər, -zôr) *n. Law* One who devises property.
ʼi·tal·ize (dē·vītʹl·īz) *v.t.* **·ized, ·iz·ing** To destroy the ality of; make weak. **— de·viʹtal·i·zaʹtion** *n.*
ʼoid (di·voidʹ) *adj.* Not possessing; destitute; empty: th *of.* [ME *devoided*, pp. of obs. *devoid* to empty out]
ʼoir (də·vwärʹ, devʹwär) *n.* **1.** *Usu. pl.* Courteous atten-ns; respects. **2.** Duty. [< OF < L *debere* to owe]
ʼ·o·lu·tion (devʹə·lo͞oʹshən) *n.* **1.** A passing down from e stage to another. **2.** The passing of authority, property, ., to a successor. [See DEVOLVE.]
ʼolve (di·volvʹ) *v.* **·volved, ·volv·ing** *v.t.* **1.** To cause uthority, duty, etc.) to pass to a successor. **—** *v.i.* **2.** To ss to a successor or substitute: with *on, upon,* or *to.* [< L *de-* down + *volvere* to roll] **— devolveʹment** *n.*
·vo·ni·an (di·vōʹnē·ən) *adj.* **1.** Of or pertaining to Devon England. **2.** *Geol.* Of or pertaining to the period in the leozoic era following the Silurian. See chart for GEOLOGY. *n. Geol.* The Devonian period or its rock system. [after *von*, England; with ref. to rocks found there]
vote (di·vōtʹ) *v.t.* **·vot·ed, ·vot·ing 1.** To apply (atten-n, time, or oneself) completely to some activity, purpose, c. **2.** To dedicate. [< OF < L < *de-* completely + *vo-re* to vow] **— de·voteʹment** *n.*
vot·ed (di·vōʹtid) *adj.* **1.** Feeling or showing devotion; vout. **2.** Set apart, as by a vow; consecrated. **— de·tʹed·ly** *adv.* **— de·votʹed·ness** *n.*
dev·o·tee (devʹə·tēʹ) *n.* **1.** One who is deeply devoted to anything. **2.** One who is marked by religious ardor.
de·vo·tion (di·vōʹshən) *n.* **1.** Strong attachment or affection, as to a person or cause. **2.** Ardor or zeal in the performance of religious acts or duties. **3.** *Usu. pl.* An act of worship or prayer. **4.** The act of devoting, or the state of being devoted. **— de·voʹtion·al** *adj.* **— de·voʹtion·al·ly** *adv.*
de·vour (di·vourʹ) *v.t.* **1.** To eat up greedily. **2.** To destroy; waste. **3.** To take in greedily with the senses or the intellect. **4.** To engross the attention of. **5.** To engulf; absorb. [< OF < L < *de-* down + *vorare* to gulp, swallow] **— de·vourʹer** *n.* **— de·vourʹing·ly** *adv.*
de·vout (di·voutʹ) *adj.* **1.** Earnestly religious; pious. **2.** Heartfelt; sincere. **3.** Containing or expressing devotion. [See DEVOTE.] **— de·voutʹly** *adv.* **— de·voutʹness** *n.*
dew (do͞o, dyo͞o) *n.* **1.** Moisture condensed from the atmosphere in small drops upon cool surfaces. **2.** Anything moist, pure, or refreshing as dew. **3.** Moisture generally, esp. that which appears in minute drops, as perspiration, tears, etc. **—** *v.t.* To wet with or as with dew. [OE *dēaw*]
dew·ber·ry (do͞oʹberʹē, -bər·ē, dyo͞oʹ-) *n. pl.* **·ries** The fruit of several species of trailing blackberry; also, the plant.
dew·claw (do͞oʹklôʹ, dyo͞oʹ-) *n.* **1.** A rudimentary toe in some dogs and other mammals. **2.** The false hoof above the true hoof of hogs, deer, etc. **— dewʹclawedʹ** *adj.*
dew·drop (do͞oʹdropʹ, dyo͞oʹ-) *n.* A drop of dew.
dew·lap (do͞oʹlapʹ, dyo͞oʹ-) *n.* The pendulous skin under the throat of cattle, certain dogs, etc. [ME < *dew*, origin uncertain + *lappe* pendulous piece, lobe] **— dewʹlappedʹ** *adj.*
DEW line A chain of radar stations in North America, maintained by the United States in cooperation with Canada. [< *D(istant) E(arly) W(arning)*]
dew point The temperature at which dew forms or condensation of vapor occurs.
dew·y (do͞oʹē, dyo͞oʹē) *adj.* **dew·i·er, dew·i·est 1.** Moist. **2.** Of, resembling, or forming dew. **— dewʹi·ness** *n.*
dex·ter (dekʹstər) *adj.* **1.** Of or situated on the right side. **2.** *Heraldry* Being on the wearer's right, and thus on the observer's left: opposed to *sinister.* [< L, right]
dex·ter·i·ty (dek·sterʹə·tē) *n.* **1.** Skill in using the hands or body. **2.** Mental adroitness. [< L *dexter* on the right]
— Syn. Both *dexterity* and *adroitness* are, literally, "right-handedness," or proficiency in manual tasks. In extended use, *dexterity* is applied to technical proficiency in the use of tools, methods, etc.: the *dexterity* of a magician. *Adroitness* has become cleverness in dealing with people or in handling situations. *Handiness* applies chiefly to manual work; *skill* is acquired, at least in part and sometimes wholly, by mental training.
dex·ter·ous (dekʹstrəs, -stər·əs) *adj.* **1.** Possessing dexterity; adroit. **2.** Done with dexterity. Also **dex·trous** (dekʹ·strəs) **— dexʹter·ous·ly** *adv.* **— dexʹter·ous·ness** *n.*
dex·tral (dekʹstral) *adj.* **1.** Of or pertaining to, or turned toward the right side; right-hand. **2.** Right-handed. **— dex·tral·i·ty** (dek·stralʹə·tē) *n.* **— dexʹtral·ly** *adv.*
dex·trin (dekʹstrin) *n. Biochem.* A gummy, water-soluble substance formed from starch, and used as a substitute for gum arabic. Also **dex·trine** (dekʹstrin, -strēn).
dextro- *combining form* Turned or turning to the right, or clockwise; used esp. in chemistry and physics. Also, before vowels, **dextr-**. [< L *dexter* right]
dex·trorse (dekʹstrôrs, dek·strôrsʹ) *adj. Bot.* Twining spirally toward the right, as certain climbing plants: opposed to *sinistrorse.* Also **dex·trorʹsal.** [< L < *dexter* right + *vertere* to turn] **— dexʹtrorse·ly** *adv.*
dex·trose (dekʹstrōs) *n. Biochem.* A sugar occurring in plants. Also **dex·tro·glu·cose** (dekʹ·strō·glo͞oʹkōs).
di-[1] Var. of DIS-[1].
di-[2] *prefix* **1.** Twice; double. **2.** *Chem.* Containing two atoms, molecules, radicals, etc. Also, before *s, dis-.* [< Gk. *di-* < *dis* twice]
di-[3] Var. of DIA-.
dia- *prefix* **1.** Through; across; between; apart. **2.** Thoroughly. Also, before vowels, *di-.* [< Gk. *dia-* through]
di·a·be·tes (dīʹə·bēʹtis, -tēz) *n. Pathol.* A disease, **diabetes mel·li·tus** (mə·līʹtəs), associated with deficient insulin secretion, leading to excess sugar in the blood and urine, extreme hunger and thirst, and metabolic failure. [< NL < Gk. < *dia-* through + *bainein* to go]
di·a·bet·ic (dīʹə·betʹik, -bēʹtik) *Med. adj.* Of, pertaining to, or affected with diabetes. **—** *n.* One who has diabetes.
di·a·bol·ic (dīʹə·bolʹik) *adj.* **1.** Of, belonging to, or proceeding from the devil; satanic, infernal. **2.** Atrociously wicked or inhuman. Also **diʹa·bolʹi·cal.** [< OF < LL < Gk. < *diabolos*] **— diʹa·bolʹi·cal·ly** *adv.* **— diʹa·bolʹi·cal·ness** *n.*
di·ac·o·nal (dī·akʹə·nəl) *adj.* Of, pertaining to, or befitting a deacon or the diaconate. [< LL *diaconus* deacon]
di·ac·o·nate (dī·akʹə·nit, -nāt) *n.* **1.** The office or rank of a deacon. **2.** Deacons collectively.

di·a·crit·ic (dī′ə·krit′ik) *n.* A diacritical mark. — *adj.* Diacritical. [< Gk. < *dia-* between + *krinein* to distinguish]

di·a·crit·i·cal (dī′ə·krit′i·kəl) *adj.* Serving to mark a distinction, as between phonetic values assigned to a letter; distinguishing. — **di′a·crit′i·cal·ly** *adv.*

diacritical mark A mark, point, or sign attached to a letter to indicate its phonetic value, or to distinguish it from another letter: also called *diacritic.*

di·a·dem (dī′ə·dem) *n.* **1.** A crown or headband worn as a symbol of royalty or honor. **2.** Regal power. — *v.t.* To crown. [< OF < L < Gk. < *dia-* across + *deein* to bind]

di·aer·e·sis (dī·er′ə·sis) See DIERESIS.

di·ag·nose (dī′əg·nōs′, -nōz′) *v.t.* & *v.i.* **·nosed, ·nos·ing** To make a diagnosis.

di·ag·no·sis (dī′əg·nō′sis) *n. pl.* **·ses** (-sēz) **1.** *Med.* **a** The act or process of recognizing diseases by their characteristic symptoms. **b** The conclusion arrived at. **2.** Any similar examination, summary, and conclusion. [< NL < Gk. < *dia-* between + *gignōskein* to know] — **di·ag·nos·tic** (dī′əg·nos′·tik) *adj.* — **di′ag·nos′ti·cal·ly** *adv.*

di·ag·nos·ti·cian (dī′əg·nos·tish′ən) *n.* One who is versed in diagnosis.

di·ag·o·nal (dī·ag′ə·nəl) *adj.* **1.** Having an oblique direction from corner to corner or from side to side. **2.** Marked by oblique lines, ridges, etc. — *n.* **1.** *Geom.* A diagonal line or plane. **2.** Anything running diagonally. [< L < Gk. < *dia-* across + *gōnia* angle] — **di·ag′o·nal·ly** *adv.*

di·a·gram (dī′ə·gram) *n.* **1.** An outline figure or scheme of lines, spaces, points, etc., intended to demonstrate a geometrical proposition, represent an object or area, show the relation between parts or places, etc. **2.** A graph or chart. — *v.t.* **di·a·gramed** or **·grammed, di·a·gram·ing** or **·gram·ming** To represent or illustrate by a diagram. [< Gk. < *dia-* across + *graphein* to write] — **di·a·gram·mat·ic** (dī′ə·grə·mat′ik) or **·i·cal** *adj.* — **di′a·gram·mat′i·cal·ly** *adv.*

di·al (dī′əl, dīl) *n.* **1.** Any graduated circular plate or face upon which pressure, temperature, etc., is indicated by means of a pointer or needle. **2.** The face of a watch or clock; also, a sundial. **3.** A knob or disk on a radio or television set, used to tune in stations. **4.** A rotating disk, used to make connections in an automatic telephone system. — *v.* **di·aled** or **·alled, di·al·ing** or **·al·ling** *v.t.* **1.** To measure with a dial. **2.** To turn to or indicate by means of a dial. **3.** To call by means of a dial telephone. **4.** To adjust a radio or television set to (a station, program, etc.). — *v.i.* **5.** To use a dial, as in telephoning. [< Med.L *dialis* daily < L *dies* day] — **di′al·er** or **di′al·ler** *n.*

di·a·lect (dī′ə·lekt) *n.* **1.** A variety of speech distinguished from the standard language by variations of idiom, vocabulary, pronunciation, etc.: the Yorkshire *dialect* of England. **2.** Any of the regional forms of the standard language: the Southern *dialect* of American English. **3.** A manner of speech characteristic of the members of a particular class, trade, or profession. **4.** A language developed from an earlier language; a linguistic branch. [< MF < L < Gk. < *dia-* across + *legein* to speak]

di·a·lec·tal (dī′ə·lek′təl) *adj.* Of or characteristic of a dialect. — **di′a·lec′tal·ly** *adv.*

di·a·lec·tic (dī′ə·lek′tik) *n.* **1.** *Often pl.* The art or practice of examining statements logically, as by question and answer, to establish validity. **2.** A specific logical mode of argument: Hegel's *dialectic.* **3.** Formerly, logic. — *adj.* **1.** Pertaining to or using dialectic. **2.** Dialectal. [< OF < L < Gk. < *dia-* across + *legein* to speak]

di·a·lec·ti·cal (dī′ə·lek′ti·kəl) *adj.* Dialectic. — **di′a·lec′·ti·cal·ly** *adv.*

dialectical materialism *Philos.* The doctrine of Karl Marx and Friedrich Engels.

di·a·lec·ti·cian (dī′ə·lek·tish′ən) *n.* **1.** A logician. **2.** One who specializes in the study of dialects.

di·a·logue (dī′ə·lôg, -log) *n.* **1.** A conversation in which two or more take part. **2.** The conversation in a play, novel, etc. **3.** A literary work in which two or more characters are represented as conversing: a Platonic *dialogue.* **4.** An exchange of opinions or ideas; discussion. — *v.* **·logued, ·logu·ing** *v.t.* **1.** To express in dialogue form. — *v.i.* **2.** To carry on a dialogue. Also **di′a·log.** [< F < L < Gk. < *dialegesthai* to converse] — **di′a·log′uer** or **di′a·log′er** *n.*

di·al·y·sis (dī·al′ə·sis) *n. pl.* **·ses** (-sēz) **1.** Separation of parts previously or normally joined together. **2.** *Chem.* The separating of solutions of unequal diffusibility by means of moist membranes; esp., the separation of a colloid from a crystalloid. [< Gk. < *dia-* completely + *lyein* to loosen] — **di·a·lyt·ic** (dī′ə·lit′ik) *adj.* — **di′a·lyt′i·cal·ly** *adv.*

di·a·mag·net·ic (dī′ə·mag·net′ik) *Physics adj.* Pertaining to or designating the property of substances that tend to lie at right angles to the poles of a magnet. — **di′a·mag·net′i·cal·ly** *adv.* — **di′a·mag′net·ism** *n.*

di·am·e·ter (dī·am′ə·tər) *n. Math.* **1.** A straight line passing through the center of a circle or sphere and terminating at the circumference or surface. **2.** The length of such a line. **3.** *Optics* A unit used to measure the magnifying pow[er of] binoculars, microscopes, etc. [< OF < L < Gk. < [*dia-*] through + *metron* measure]

di·a·met·ri·cal (dī′ə·met′ri·kəl) *adj.* **1.** Of, pertaining t[o or] coinciding with a diameter. Also **di·am·e·tral** (dī·am′ə·t[rəl]). **2.** Directly opposite; as far removed as possible: *diamet[rical]* motives. Also **di′a·met′ric.** — **di′a·met′ri·cal·ly** *adv.*

di·am·ine (dī·am′ēn, -in, dī′ə·mēn, -min) *n. Chem.* A[ny of] a group of compounds containing two amino (NH_2) radi[cals]; a double amine. Also **di·am·in** (dī·am′in, dī′ə·min).

dia·mond (dī′mənd, dī′ə-) *n.* **1.** A mineral of great hard[ness] and refractive power, consisting of carbon crystallized u[nder] great pressure and temperature; also, this mineral when [used] as a gem. **2.** The uncut face of this stone, used in cu[tting] glass, etc. **3.** A figure bounded by four equal straight l[ines], having two of the angles acute and two obtuse; a loze[nge]. **4.** In card games: **a** A red, lozenge-shaped spot on a pla[ying] card. **b** A card with such a mark. **c** *pl.* A suit of car[ds so] marked. **5.** In baseball, the infield of a baseball field; [also] the entire field. **6.** *Printing* A size of type next above [bril]liant, 4- or 4½-point. — *adj.* Made of or like diamonds. [—] *v.t.* To adorn with or as with diamonds. [< OF < LL < Gk. *adamas* adamantine] — **dia′mond·ed** *adj.*

diamond anniversary A 60th or 75th anniversary.

dia·mond·back (dī′mənd·bak′, dī′ə-) *n.* **1.** An edible t[urtle] of the southern U.S., having diamond-shaped markings on the shell. Also **diamondback terrapin.** **2.** A large rattlesnake of the SE U.S., having diamond-shaped markings on the back: also **dia′mond-rat′tler** (-rat′lər).

DIAMONDBACK TERRAPIN (Upper shell 5 7½ inches long)

Diamond State Nickname of Delaware.

Di·an·a (dī·an′ə) In Roman mythology, goddess of the hunt, virginity, and the moon.

di·a·pa·son (dī′ə·pā′sən, -zən) *n.* **1.** In a pipe organ, e[ither] of two principal stops (the **open diapason** and the **sto[pped] diapason**) that extend throughout the entire compass o[f the] instrument and produce its fundamental tone. **2.** Th[e en]tire compass of an instrument or voice. [< L < Gk. *di[a pa]sōn* (*chordōn*) through all (the notes)]

di·a·per (dī′ə·pər; *for n. def. 1, v. def. 1, also* dī′pər) [*n.*] **1.** A folded piece of soft fabric used as a baby's breechc[loth]. **2.** A decorative pattern consisting of a system of repe[ated] figures or designs. — *v.t.* **1.** To put a diaper on (a ba[by]). **2.** To decorate with a repeated figure or similar figures. [< OF < Med.Gk. < *dia-* completely + *aspros* white]

di·aph·a·nous (dī·af′ə·nəs) *adj.* Showing light throug[h its] substance; transparent; translucent. [< Med.L < G[k. <] *dia-* through + *phainein* to show] — **di·aph′a·nous·ly** [*adv.*] — **di·aph′a·nous·ness** *n.*

di·a·pho·re·sis (dī′ə·fə·rē′sis) *n. Med.* Copious pers[pira]tion, esp. when produced artificially. [< LL < Gk. < [*dia-*] across + *phoreein* to carry] — **di′a·pho·ret′ic** *adj.* & *n.*

di·a·phragm (dī′ə·fram) *n.* **1.** *Anat.* A muscular wall s[epa]rating the thoracic and abdominal cavities in mammals. [**2.**] Any membrane or partition that separates. **3.** Any de[vice] resembling a diaphragm in appearance or elasticity, as [the] thin vibrating disk of a telephone. **4.** *Optics* A disk wit[h an] adjustable aperture that can control the amount of [light] passing through the lens of a camera, telescope, etc. — [*v.t.*] To act upon or furnish with a diaphragm. [< LL < G[k. <] *dia-* across + *phragma* fence]

di·a·phrag·mat·ic (dī′ə·frag·mat′ik) *adj.* Of, pertainin[g to,] or like a diaphragm. — **di′a·phrag·mat′i·cal·ly** *adv.*

di·ar·rhe·a (dī′ə·rē′ə) *n. Pathol.* A disorder of the inte[stines] marked by abnormally frequent and fluid evacuation o[f the] bowels. Also **di′ar·rhoe′a.** [< L < Gk. < *dia-* thr[ough] + *rheein* to flow] — **di′ar·rhe′al** or **·rhoe′al, di′ar·rhe′[ic]** or **·rhoe′ic, di′ar·rhet′ic** or **·rhoet′ic** (-ret′ik) *adj.*

di·a·ry (dī′ə·rē, dī′rē) *n. pl.* **·ries.** **1.** A record of d[aily] events; esp., a personal record of one's activities, ex[peri]ences, or observations; journal. **2.** A book for keeping [such] a record. [< L < *dies* day] — **di′a·rist** *n.*

Di·as·po·ra (dī·as′pər·ə) *n.* The dispersion of the [Jews] among the Gentiles after the Babylonian captivity. [< [Gk.] dispersion < *dia-* completely + *speirein* to sow, scatte[r]]

di·a·stase (dī′ə·stās) *n. Biochem.* An enzyme that conv[erts] starch and glycogen into dextrin and maltose. [< F < [Gk.] < *dia-* apart + *histanai* to set, cause to stand] — **di′a·[sta]sic, di′a·stat′ic** (-stat′ik) *adj.*

di·as·to·le (dī·as′tə·lē) *n.* **1.** *Physiol.* The usual rhyth[mic] dilatation of the heart, esp. of the ventricles, after each [con]traction. Compare SYSTOLE. **2.** In classical prosody, [the] lengthening of a syllable. [< LL < Gk. < *dia-* apar[t +] *stellein* to send, put] — **di·as·tol·ic** (dī′ə·stol′ik) *adj.*

di·as·tro·phism (dī·as′trə·fiz′əm) *n. Geol.* **1.** Any of [the] processes through which the earth's crust is deformed, [pro]ducing continents, mountains, etc. **2.** Any deformatio[n re]sulting from this. [< Gk. < *dia-* apart + *strephein* to t[urn]] — **di·a·stroph·ic** (dī′ə·strof′ik) *adj.*

a·ther·my (dī′ə·thûr′mē) *n. pl.* **·mies** *Med.* **1.** The gen-
ation of heat in the body tissues through their resistance to
ıe passage of high-frequency electric currents. **2.** The ap-
aratus used. Also **di·a·ther·mi·a** (dī′ə·thûr′mē·ə). [< NL
Gk. *dia-* through + *thermē* heat]
a·tom (dī′ə·tom, -təm) *n.* Any of various marine and
esh-water plankton, unicellular or colonial whose walls
ntain silica. [< NL < Gk. *dia-* through + *temnein* to cut]
a·ton·ic (dī′ə·ton′ik) *adj. Music* Pertaining to the order
intervals in a major or minor scale of eight tones without
ıe chromatic intervals. [< MF < LL < Gk. < *dia-*
rough, at the interval of + *tenein* to stretch] **— di′a·ton′-
:al·ly** *adv.* **— di·a·ton·i·cism** (dī′ə·ton′i·siz′əm) *n.*
a·tribe (dī′ə·trīb) *n.* A bitter or malicious denunciation.
< MF < L < Gk. < *dia-* thoroughly + *tribein* to rub]
ba·sic (dī·bā′sik) *adj. Chem.* **1.** Of an acid, containing
vo atoms of hydrogen replaceable by a base or basic radi-
l, as sulfuric acid. **2.** Of or derived from such an acid:
id of salts. Also *bibasic.* **— di·ba·sic·i·ty** (dī′bā·sis′ə·tē) *n.*
·ble (dib′əl) *n.* A gardener's pointed tool for planting
eds, setting slips, etc. Also **dib·ber** (dib′ər). **—** *v.t.* **·bled,
ling** To make holes for seeds or plants in (soil) with a dib-
e. [ME, ? < *dib,* var. of DAB[3]] **— dib′bler** *n.*
e (dīs) *n. pl. of* **die** **1.** Small cubes of bone, ivory, etc.,
ving the sides marked with spots from one to six. **2.** A
me of chance played with such cubes. **—** *v.* **diced, dic·ing**
1. To cut into small cubes. **2.** To gamble away or win
ith dice. **—** *v.i.* **3.** To play at dice. [See DIE[2]] **— dic′er** *n.*
:hlo·ro·di·phen·yl·tri·chlor·o·eth·ane (dī·klôr′ō·dī-
n′əl·trī·klôr′ō·eth′ān, -klō′rō-) *n.* DDT.
ho- *combining form* In two; in pairs. Also, before vow-
, **dich-.** [< Gk. *dicha* in two < *dis* twice]
chot·o·my (dī·kot′ə·mē) *n. pl.* **·mies** **1.** Division into
vo parts or by pairs; a cutting in two. **2.** *Logic* The divi-
n of a class into two mutually exclusive subclasses, as
inerals into gold and not-gold. **3.** *Bot.* A system of branch-
in which each successive axis forks into two equally de-
loped branches. [< Gk. < *dicho-* in two + *temnein* to cut]
di·chot′o·mous *adj.* **— di·chot′o·mous·ly** *adv.*
:hro·mat·ic (dī′krō·mat′ik) *adj.* **1.** Having two colors.
Zool. Having two color phases within the species apart
m changes due to age or sex. **3.** *Pathol.* Able to see only
o of the three primary colors. Also *dichromic.*
:hro·ma·tism (dī·krō′mə·tiz′əm) *n.* The state of being
chromatic, esp. with reference to color blindness.
chro·mic (dī·krō′mik) *adj.* **1.** Containing two atoms of
romium or their equivalents. **2.** Dichromatic.
k·er (dik′ər) *U.S. v.i.* **1.** To make a petty trade; haggle.
In politics, to work toward a deal; bargain. **—** *v.t.* **3.** To
rter; exchange. **—** *n.* The act of dickering; also, a petty
ade; a bargain. [ME *dyker* lot of ten, esp. skins or hides]
k·ey (dik′ē) *n. pl.* **·eys** **1.** A blouse front worn by
men under a jacket or low-necked dress. **2.** A detachable
irt front for a man. **3.** Any small bird. Also **dick′ey·
rd′, dick′y·bird′** (-bûrd′) **4.** A driver's outside seat on a
rriage; also, a seat for servants in the rear. Also **dick′y.**
< *Dicky,* double dim. of *Richard,* a personal name]
ot·y·le·don (dī′kot·ə·lēd′n, dī·kot′-) *n. Bot.* A plant
ving two seed leaves. **— di′cot·y·le′do·nous** *adj.*
·ta (dik′tə) Plural of DICTUM.
:·ta·phone (dik′tə·fōn) *n.* A type of phonographic in-
ument that records and reproduces speech, as for dicta-
n to a stenographer: a trade name. Also **dic′ta·phone.**
·tate (dik′tāt; *for v., also* dik·tāt′) *v.* **·tat·ed, ·tat·ing** *v.t.*
To utter or read aloud (something) to be recorded by an-
ner. **2.** To prescribe authoritatively, as commands, terms,
es, etc. **—** *v.i.* **3.** To utter aloud something to be re-
rded by another. **4.** To give orders. **—** *n.* An authorita-
e suggestion, rule, or command: the *dictates* of reason. [<
pp. of *dictare,* freq. of *dicere* to say, speak]
·ta·tion (dik·tā′shən) *n.* **1.** The act of dictating material
a copyist. **2.** That which is dictated. **3.** Authoritative
ection. **— dic·ta′tion·al** *adj.*
·ta·tor (dik′tā·tər, dik·tā′tər) *n.* **1.** A person having ab-
lute powers of government, esp. one considered to be an
pressor. **2.** A person who rules, prescribes, or suggests
thoritatively: a *dictator* of fashion. **3.** One who dictates
rds to be written down.
·ta·to·ri·al (dik′tə·tôr′ē·əl, -tō′rē-) *adj.* **1.** Given to dic-
ting: overbearing. **2.** Of or pertaining to a dictator; auto-
atic. **— dic′ta·to′ri·al·ly** *adv.* **— dic′ta·to′ri·al·ness** *n.*
·ta·tor·ship (dik′tā·tər·ship′, dik·tā′tər·ship′) *n.* **1.** The
ice or term of office of a dictator. **2.** A state under the
e of a dictator. **3.** Supreme or despotic control.
·tion (dik′shən) *n.* **1.** The use, choice, and arrangement
words in writing and speaking. **2.** The manner of utter-
speech sounds; enunciation. [< L < *dicere* to say, speak]
·tion·ar·y (dik′shən·er′ē) *n. pl.* **·ar·ies** **1.** A reference
work containing alphabetically arranged words together with their definitions, pronunciations, etymologies, etc.; a lexicon. **2.** A lexicon whose words are given in one language together with their equivalents in another. **3.** A reference work containing information relating to a special branch of knowledge and arranged alphabetically. [< Med.L *dictionarium* a collection of words and phrases < L *dicere* to speak.]

Dic·to·graph (dik′tə·graf, -gräf) *n.* A telephonic device capable of reproducing or recording sounds made at a considerable distance from the transmitter, used to transmit or overhear conversations: a trade name. Also **dic′to·graph.**

dic·tum (dik′təm) *n. pl.* **·ta** (-tə) **1.** An authoritative, dogmatic, or positive utterance; pronouncement. **2.** A popular saying; maxim. [< L < *dicere* to say]

did (did) Past tense of DO[1].

di·dac·tic (dī·dak′tik, di-) *adj.* **1.** Intended to instruct. **2.** Morally instructive; preceptive. **3.** Overly inclined to teach or moralize; pedantic. Also **di·dac′ti·cal.** [< Gk. < *didaskein* to teach] **— di·dac′ti·cal·ly** *adv.* **— di·dac′ti·cism** (-siz·əm) *n.*

di·dac·tics (dī·dak′tiks, di-) *n.pl.* (*construed as sing.*) The science or art of instruction or education.

did·dle[1] (did′l) *v.* **·dled, ·dling** *Informal v.t.* **1.** To cheat. **—** *v.i.* **2.** To dawdle; pass time idly. Also *daddle.* [? < DIDDLE[2]] **— did′dler** *n.*

did·dle[2] (did′l) *v.t. & v.i.* **·dled, ·dling** To jerk up and down or back and forth; jiggle. [? Var. of dial. *didder,* ME *diddiren* to quiver, shake, tremble]

did·n't (did′nt) Did not.

di·do (dī′dō) *n. pl.* **·dos** or **·does** *Informal* A caper; antic. [Origin unknown]

Di·do (dī′dō) In the *Aeneid,* the queen of Carthage in love with Aeneas.

didst (didst) Archaic second person singular past tense of DO[1]: used with *thou.*

di·dym·i·um (dī·dim′ē·əm, di-) *n.* A mixture of the elements neodymium and praseodymium, formerly regarded as one of the elements. [< NL < Gk. *didymos* double]

die[1] (dī) *v.i.* **died, dy·ing** **1.** To suffer death; expire. **2.** To suffer the pains of death: The coward *dies* many times. **3.** To pass gradually: with *away, down,* or *out.* **4.** To cease to exist; fade away: The smile *died* on his lips. **5.** To become extinct: often with *out* or *of.* **6.** *Informal* To desire exceedingly. **7.** To stop functioning, as an engine. **8.** To faint. **9.** *Theol.* To suffer spiritual death. **— to die hard** To resist death or defeat to the end. **— to die off** To be removed one after another by death. [< ON *deyja*]

die[2] (dī) *n. pl.* **dies** *for def. 1;* **dice** *for defs. 2 and 3.* **1.** *Mech.* Any of various hard metal devices for stamping, shaping, or cutting out some object. **2.** A small marked cube. See DICE. **3.** A cast, as in playing dice; stake; hazard. **— the die is cast** The choice or course of action is irrevocable. **—** *v.t.* **died, die·ing** To cut, stamp, or shape with or as with a die. [< OF *de* < L *datum* something given]

die casting *Metall.* **1.** The process of giving a metal or alloy a desired shape by forcing the molten material into a mold under pressure. **2.** A metal object so made.

di·e·cious (dī·ē′shəs), etc. See DIOECIOUS, etc.

die-hard (dī′härd′) *n.* One who obstinately refuses to abandon or modify his views; esp., a political conservative. **—** *adj.* Characterized by obstinate resistance. Also **die′hard′.**

di·e·lec·tric (dī′ə·lek′trik) *Electr. adj.* **1.** Nonconducting. **2.** Capable of sustaining an electric field, as by induction. Also **di′e·lec′tri·cal.** **—** *n.* A dielectric substance, medium, or material. **— di′e·lec′tri·cal·ly** *adv.*

di·en·ceph·a·lon (dī′en·sef′ə·lon) *n. Anat.* That part of the brain forming the posterior part of the forebrain. [< NL < Gk. *di(a)-* between + *enkephalos* brain]

-diene *suffix Chem.* Denoting an open-chain unsaturated hydrocarbon compound having two double bonds: *butadiene.*

di·er·e·sis (dī·er′ə·sis) *n. pl.* **·ses** (-sēz) Two dots (¨) placed over the second of two adjacent letters to indicate that two separate vowel sounds are to be pronounced, as in *Noël.* Also spelled *diaeresis.* [< LL < Gk. < *dia-* apart + *haireein* to take, seize] **— di·e·ret·ic** (dī′ə·ret′ik) *adj.*

die·sel engine (dē′zəl) An internal-combustion engine in which fuel oil is sprayed directly into the cylinder, where it is ignited by the high temperature of the air held within the cylinder at a constant pressure. Also **Diesel engine.** [after Rudolf *Diesel,* 1858–1913, German inventor]

die·sink·er (dī′singk′ər) *n.* One who engraves metal dies.

Di·es I·rae (dī′ēz ī′rē) The name of a medieval Latin hymn on the Day of Judgment, used in masses for the dead: so called from its opening words. [< L, day of wrath]

di·e·sis (dī′ə·sis) *n. pl.* **·ses** (-sēz) *Printing* The double dagger (‡). [< L < Gk. < *dia-* through + *hienai* to send]

die·stock (dī′stok′) *n. Mech.* A device for holding dies that are used to cut threads on screws, bolts, etc.

di·et[1] (dī′ət) *n.* **1.** A regulated course of eating and drinking, esp. one followed for medical or hygienic reasons. **2.** The daily fare. **3.** Food, as regards its nutritive value. — *v.t.* **1.** To regulate the food and drink of. — *v.i.* **2.** To take food and drink according to a regimen. [< OF < L < Gk. *diaita* way of living] — **di′et·er** *n.*

di·et[2] (dī′ət) *n.* A legislative assembly. [< Med.L < L *dies* a day]

Di·et (dī′ət) *n.* **1.** The legislature of certain countries, as Japan. **2.** The semiannual meeting of the estates of the Holy Roman Empire.

di·e·tar·y (dī′ə·ter′ē) *adj.* Pertaining to diet. — *n. pl.* **·tar·ies 1.** A system or regimen of dieting. **2.** A standard or regulated allowance of food.

di·e·tet·ic (dī′ə·tet′ik) *adj.* Relating to diet or the regulation of diet. Also **di′e·tet′i·cal.** — **di′e·tet′i·cal·ly** *adv.*

di·e·tet·ics (dī′ə·tet′iks) *n.pl.* (*construed as sing.*) The branch of hygiene that treats of diet and dieting.

di·e·ti·tian (dī′ə·tish′ən) *n.* One skilled in the principles of dietetics. Also **di·e·tet·ist** (dī′ə·tet′ist), **di′e·ti′cian.**

dif- Assimilated var. of DIS-.

dif·fer (dif′ər) *v.i.* **1.** To be unlike in quality, degree, etc.: often with *from.* **2.** To disagree: often with *with.* **3.** To quarrel. [< OF < L < *dis-* apart + *ferre* to carry]

dif·fer·ence (dif′ər·əns, dif′rəns) *n.* **1.** The state, quality, or degree of being unlike or different. **2.** A specific instance of such unlikeness. **3.** A distinguishing characteristic or peculiarity. **4.** A disagreement or controversy; dispute. **5.** A discrimination: She makes no *difference* between truth and falsehood. **6.** *Math.* The amount by which one quantity differs from another. — **to make a difference 1.** To affect or change the case or situation. **2.** To distinguish between. — *v.t.* **·enced, ·enc·ing** To make or mark as different.

dif·fer·ent (dif′ər·ənt, dif′rənt) *adj.* **1.** Marked by a difference; unlike. **2.** Not the same; separate; other: There is a *different* clerk there now. **3.** Differing from the ordinary; unusual. — **dif′fer·ent·ly** *adv.* — **dif′fer·ent·ness** *n.*

◆ **different from, than** In American usage, *from* is established as the idiomatic preposition to follow *different*; when, however, a clause follows the connective, *than* is gaining increasing acceptance.

dif·fer·en·ti·a (dif′ə·ren′shē·ə) *n. pl.* **·ti·ae** (shi·ē) *Logic* A specific difference; a characteristic attribute distinguishing a species from others of the same genus. [< L]

dif·fer·en·tial (dif′ə·ren′shəl) *adj.* **1.** Relating to, indicating, or exhibiting a difference or differences. **2.** Constituting or creating a difference. **3.** Based on a difference or distinction. **4.** *Math.* Pertaining to or involving differentials or differentiation. **5.** *Mech.* Of or having a construction in which a movement is obtained by the difference in two motions in the same direction. — *n.* **1.** *Math.* An infinitesimal increment of a quantity: symbol *d.* **2.** *Mech.* A differential gear. **3.** *Electr.* One of two resistance coils, the current of which flows in a direction opposite to that of the other. **4.** In commerce, a difference in rates charged. — **dif′fer·en′tial·ly** *adv.*

differential gear or **gearing** *Mech.* A coupling consisting of a train of gears used to connect two or more shafts so that the wheels can move at different speeds on curves.

DIFFERENTIAL GEAR
a Drive shaft. *b* Drive-shaft gear. *c* Axles. *d* Ring gear. *e* Epicyclic train of gears.

differential windlass *Mech.* A windlass having two drums of different diameters on the same axis, the power being increased in inverse proportion to the difference between the diameters.

dif·fer·en·ti·ate (dif′ə·ren′shē·āt) *v.* **·at·ed, ·at·ing** *v.t.* **1.** To constitute the difference between. **2.** To perceive and indicate the differences in or between. **3.** *Biol.* To develop differences in, as a species. **4.** *Math.* To find the derivative of (a function): opposed to *integrate.* — *v.i.* **5.** To acquire a distinct character; become specialized. **6.** To discriminate. **7.** *Biol.* Of cells during embryological growth, to diversify and develop into specialized organs and tissues. — **dif′fer·en′ti·a′tion** *n.*

dif·fi·cult (dif′ə·kult, -kəlt) *adj.* **1.** Hard to do, accomplish, or deal with; demanding effort or great care. **2.** Not easy to understand; perplexing. **3.** Hard to please: a *difficult* customer. **4.** Hard to persuade; stubborn. — **dif′fi·cult·ly** *adv.*

dif·fi·cul·ty (dif′ə·kul′tē, -kəl-) *n. pl.* **·ties 1.** The state, fact, or quality of being difficult. **2.** That which is difficult to do, overcome, or understand. **3.** *Usu. pl.* A troublesome state of affairs, especially financial embarrassment. **4.** A dispute. **5.** Reluctance or objection. **6.** A trouble; worry. [< L < *dis-* away, not + *facilis* easy < *facere* to do, make]

dif·fi·dent (dif′ə·dənt) *adj.* Lacking confidence in oneself; timid. [< L *diffidens, -entis,* ppr. of *diffidere* < *dis-* away + *fidere* to trust] — **dif′fi·dence** *n.* — **dif′fi·dent·ly** *adv.*

dif·fract (di·frakt′) *v.t.* **1.** To separate into parts. **2.** subject to diffraction. [< L < *dis-* away + *frangere* break] — **dif·frac′tive** *adj.* — **dif·frac′tive·ly** *adv.* — frac′tive·ness *n.*

dif·frac·tion (di·frak′shən) *n. Physics* **1.** A modificatior light rays when partially cut off by any obstacle or pass near the edges of an opening, or through a minute hole, g erally accompanied by light and dark, or colored, bands to interference. **2.** An analogous modification of other ki of wave motion, as of sound, electricity, X-rays, etc.

dif·fuse (*v.* di·fyōōz′; *adj.* di·fyōōs′) *v.t. & v.i.* **·fused, ·f ing 1.** To pour or send out so as to spread in all directic permeate. **2.** To subject to or spread by diffusion. — **1.** Characterized by the excessive use of words. **2.** Wid spread out; dispersed. [< L < *dis-* from + *fundere* to po — **dif·fuse·ly** (di·fyōōs′lē) *adv.* — **dif·fuse·ness** (di·fyō nis) *n.* — **dif·fus′er** or **dif·fus′or** *n.*

dif·fus·i·ble (di·fyōō′zə·bəl) *adj.* Capable of being diffus — **dif·fus′i·bil′i·ty, dif·fus′i·ble·ness** *n.*

dif·fu·sion (di·fyōō′zhən) *n.* **1.** The act or process of dif ing, or the state of being diffused. **2.** Imprecision of ve expression; verbosity. **3.** *Physics* **a** The intermingling thermal agitation of the molecules of two fluids, as of ga **b** The scattering and crisscrossing of light rays, produc general illumination rather than direct radiation.

dif·fu·sive (di·fyōō′siv) *adj.* Tending to diffuse; marked diffusion. — **dif·fu′sive·ly** *adv.* — **dif·fu′sive·ness** *n.*

dig (dig) *v.* **dug, dig·ging** *v.t.* **1.** To break up, turn up, or move (earth, etc.), as with a spade, claws, or the hands. To make or form by or as by digging. **3.** To take out or tain by digging: to *dig* clams. **4.** To thrust or force int against, as a heel. **5.** To discover or bring out by car effort or study: often with *up* or *out.* **6.** *U.S. Slang* understand or like. — *v.i.* **7.** To break or turn up ea etc. **8.** To force or make a way by or as by digging. **9.** *Informal* To study hard; plod. — **to dig in 1.** To dig trer es. **2.** *U.S. Informal* To entrench (oneself). **3.** *U.S. formal* To begin to work intensively. — *n. Informal* **1** thrust; poke. **2.** A sarcastic remark; slur. [< MF *digue*

di·gest (*v.* di·jest′, dī-; *n.* dī′jest) *v.t.* **1.** *Physiol.* To cha (food) chemically in the alimentary canal into material s able for assimilation by the body. **2.** To take in or assi late mentally. **3.** To arrange in systematic form, usu. condensing. **4.** To tolerate patiently; endure. **5.** *Chen* To soften or decompose with heat or moisture. **b** To trea wood, with chemical agents under pressure so as to obta desired result. — *v.i.* **6.** To be assimilated, as food. **7.** assimilate food. **8.** To be subjected to heat, moisture, ch ical agents, or pressure. — *n.* A systematically arran collection or summary of literary, scientific, legal, or o material; a synopsis. — **Syn.** See ABRIDGEMENT. [< *dis-* away + *gerere* to carry] — **di·gest′er** *n.*

di·ges·tant (di·jes′tənt, dī-) *n. Med.* Any agent that as digestion. — *adj.* Digestive.

di·gest·i·ble (di·jes′tə·bəl, dī-) *adj.* Capable of being gested. — **di·gest′i·bil′i·ty, di·gest′i·ble·ness** *n.* — **di·g i·bly** *adv.*

di·ges·tion (di·jes′chən, dī-) *n.* **1.** *Physiol.* The act, proc or function of digesting; also, the resulting condition or s of this process. **2.** Mental reception and assimilation.

di·ges·tive (di·jes′tiv, dī-) *adj.* Pertaining to or promo digestion: *digestive* tract. — *n.* A medicine to aid digest

dig·ger (dig′ər) *n.* **1.** One who digs. **2.** Any implemen part of a machine for digging.

dig·gings (dig′ingz) *n.pl.* **1.** A place of excavation; es mining region. **2.** The materials dug out of such a reg **3.** *Informal* One's lodgings.

dig·it (dij′it) *n.* **1.** A finger or toe. **2.** Any one of the Arabic numeral symbols, 0 to 9. **3.** *Electronics* One of a of characters by which, a digital computer provides requ information. [< L *digitus* finger]

dig·i·tal (dij′ə·təl) *adj.* **1.** Of, pertaining to, or like the gers or digits. **2.** Having digits. **3.** Digitate. — *n.* A on a piano, organ, etc. — **dig′i·tal·ly** *adv.*

digital computer A computing machine that rece problems and processes the answers in digital form. Comp ANALOG COMPUTER.

dig·i·tal·is (dij′ə·tal′is, -tā′lis) *n.* **1.** Any of a genus of h of the figwort family, as the foxglove. **2.** The dried leave foxglove, containing several substances, that are used heart stimulant. [< NL < L *digitus* finger]

dig·i·tate (dij′ə·tāt) *adj. Bot.* Having parts, as leaflets, ranged like the fingers of a hand. Also **dig′i·tat′ed.** [< *digitus* finger] — **dig′i·tate·ly** *adv.*

digiti- *combining form* Finger; toe. [< L *digitus* finger,

dig·i·ti·grade (dij′ə·tə·grād′) *Zool. adj.* Walking on toes, without resting on the whole sole of the foot. PLANTIGRADE. [< DIGITI- + L *gradus* a step, going]

dig·ni·fied (dig′nə·fīd) *adj.* Characterized by or inves with dignity; stately. — **dig′ni·fied·ly** *adv.*

dig·ni·fy (dig′nə·fī) *v.t.* **fied, ·fy·ing 1.** To impart or

:nity to. **2.** To give a high-sounding name to. [< OF < ɘd.L < L *dignus* worthy + *facere* to make]
ni·tar·y (dig′nə·ter′ē) *n. pl.* **·tar·ies** One having high cial position, as in the government or church.
ni·ty (dig′nə·tē) *n. pl.* **·ties 1.** Stateliness and nobility manner; gravity. **2.** The state or quality of being excelt, worthy, or honorable. **3.** Relative importance or posin. **4.** A high rank, title, or office, esp. in the church. **5.** lignitary. **6.** Persons of high rank or position collectively: ceded by *the*. [< OF < L *dignus* worthy]
raph (dī′graf, -gräf) *n.* A combination of two characs representing a single sound, as *oa* in *boat*, *sh* in *she*.
ress (di·gres′, dī-) *v.i.* **1.** To turn aside from the main ject. **2.** To ramble; wander. [< L < *di-* away, apart + *di* to go, step] — **di·gres′sion** *n.* — **di·gres′sion·al** *adj.*
res·sive (di·gres′iv, dī-) *adj.* Given to or marked by dission. — **di·gres′sive·ly** *adv.* — **di·gres′sive·ness** *n.*
e·dral (dī·hē′drəl) *adj.* **1.** Two-sided; formed by or ving two plane faces. **2.** Pertaining to or having a dihel angle. — *n. Aeron.* The upward or downward inclinan of an airplane's supporting surfaces. [< DI-[2] + Gk. *ra* base, face of a regular solid]
ədral angle *Geom.* The angle formed by two intersectplanes.
dik (dik′dik′) *n.* A NE African antelope about a foot . [< native East African name]
e (dīk) *n.* **1.** An embankment to protect low land from ng flooded. **2.** A bank formed by earth thrown up during excavation of a ditch. **3.** A ditch. **4.** A causeway. **5.** arrier or obstruction. **6.** *Geol.* A mass of igneous rock inded into a fissure in other rocks. — *v.t.* **diked, dik·ing** To surround or furnish with a dike. **2.** To drain by ditch. Also, *Chiefly Brit.*, *dyke*. [OE *dīc*] — **dik′er** *n.*
ɐp·i·date (di·lap′ə·dāt) *v.t. & v.i.* **·dat·ed, ·dat·ing** To or cause to fall into partial ruin or decay. [< L < *dis-* ay + *lapidare* to throw stones] — **di·lap′i·da′tion** *n.*
ı·tate (dī·lā′tāt, dī′lə·tāt) *adj.* Dilated.
ı·ta·tion (dil′ə·tā′shən, dī′lə-) *n.* **1.** The process of ding, or the state of being dilated. **2.** That which is diɘd. **3.** *Pathol.* An excessive enlargement of an organ, etc.
ate (dī·lāt′, di-) *v.* **·lat·ed, ·lat·ing** *v.t.* **1.** To make wider arger; cause to expand. — *v.i.* **2.** To become larger or er. **3.** To speak or write diffusely; enlarge; expatiate: *h on* or *upon*. [< F < L < *dis-* apart + *latus* wide] — **at′a·ble** *adj.* — **di·lat′a·bil′i·ty, di·lat′a·ble·ness** *n.* — **at′a·bly** *adv.* — **di·la′tive** *adj.*
ı·tion (dī·lā′shən, di-) *n.* **1.** Dilatation. **2.** *Med.* The anding of an abnormally small canal or orifice.
ı·tor (dī·lā′tər, di-) *n.* **1.** One who or that which dilates. *Med.* An instrument for expanding a wound, aperture, or ity. Also **di·la·ta·tor** (dī′lə·tā′tər, dil′ə-), **di·lat′er.**
ı·to·ry (dil′ə·tôr′ē, -tō′rē) *adj.* **1.** Given to or characzed by delay; tardy; slow. **2.** Tending to cause delay. LL < L *dilatus*, pp. of *differe* to delay] — **dil′a·to′ri·ly** . — **dil′a·to′ri·ness** *n.*
ɘm·ma (di·lem′ə) *n.* **1.** A situation requiring a choice ween equally undesirable alternatives. **2.** *Logic* An ument that presents an antagonist with alternatives that equally conclusive against him. — **the horns of a dilem-** The equal and usu. undesirable alternatives between ich a choice must be made. [< LL < Gk. < *di-* two + *ma* a premise] — **dil·em·mat·ic** (dil′ə·mat′ik) *adj.*
ɘt·tan·te (dil′ə·tan′tē, dil′ə·tänt′) *n. pl.* **·ti** (-tē) or **·tes** One who interests himself in a subject superficially or ely for amusement; a dabbler. **2.** One who loves the fine s. — **Syn.** See AMATEUR. — *adj.* Pertaining to or like a ettante. [< Ital., ppr. of *dilettare* to delight < L < *de-* ay + *lacio* to allure] — **dil′et·tan′tish** or **dil′et·tan′te·ish** . — **dil′et·tan′tism** or **dil′et·tan′te·ism** *n.*
·gence[1] (dil′ə·jəns) *n.* **1.** Persistent application to one's rk or duty; persevering effort. **2.** Proper heed; care.
·gence[2] (dil′ə·jəns, *Fr.* dē·lē·zhäns′) *n.* A public stagech used in the 18th century in Europe, esp. France. Also **ly** (dil′ē). [< F (*carrosse de*) *diligence* fast coach]
·gent (dil′ə·jənt) *adj.* **1.** Showing perseverance and apɘation in whatever is undertaken; industrious. **2.** Purd with painstaking effort: a *diligent* search. [< OF < L *gere* to care for] — **dil′i·gent·ly** *adv.*
(dil) *n.* **1.** An Old World annual of the parsley family, h aromatic seeds, used medicinally and for flavoring. **2.** e seeds or leaves of this plant. [OE *dile*]
pickle A pickle flavored with dill.
ly·dal·ly (dil′ē·dal′ē) *v.i.* **-dal·lied, -dal·ly·ing** To waste e, esp. in indecision. [Varied reduplication of DALLY]
ı·ent (dil′yōō·ənt) *adj.* Serving to dilute. — *n.* A dilu agent.
ute (di·lōōt′, dī-; *for adj., also* dī′lōōt) *v.t.* **·lut·ed, ·lut·ing** To make weaker or more fluid by adding a liquid, as water. **2.** To weaken or reduce the intensity, strength, or purity of. — *adj.* Weak; diluted. [< L *dilutus*, pp. of *diluere* < *dis-* away + *luere* to wash] — **di·lu′tion** *n.*
di·lu·vi·al (di·lōō′vē·əl) *adj.* **1.** Of or pertaining to a flood, esp. the Deluge. **2.** *Geol.* **a** Produced by a deluge or by floods. **b** Made of or related to diluvium. Also **di·lu′vi·an.**
di·lu·vi·um (di·lōō′vē·əm) *n. Geol.* Coarse rock deposited by glaciers; glacial drift. [< NL < L, a flood]
dim (dim) *adj.* **dim·mer, dim·mest 1.** Obscured or darkened from faintness of light. **2.** Not clearly seen or recognized; indistinct: a *dim* figure. **3.** Not clear to the understanding or memory; vague. **4.** Not perceiving clearly; obtuse. **5.** Not seeing clearly: said of the eye. **6.** Lacking luster or brilliance. **7.** Faint: a *dim* sound. **8.** Discouraging; pessimistic. — *v.t. & v.i.* **dimmed, dim·ming** To render or grow dim. [OE *dimm, dim*] — **dim′·ly** *adv.* — **dim′ness** *n.*
dime (dīm) *n.* A silver coin of the United States and Canada, equal to ten cents or one tenth of a dollar. [< OF < L *decima*, fem. of *decimus* a tenth part]
dime novel *Chiefly U.S.* **1.** A cheap, sensational novel, originally costing a dime. **2.** Any trashy novel.
di·men·sion (di·men′shən) *n.* **1.** Any measurable extent, as length, breadth, or thickness. **2.** *Usu. pl.* Extent or magnitude: the *dimensions* of the case. [< MF < L *-onis* < *dis-* apart + *metiri* to measure] — **di·men′sion·al** *adj.*
dime store A five-and-ten-cent store.
di·min·ish (di·min′ish) *v.t.* **1.** To make smaller or less; decrease, as in size, amount, or degree. **2.** To reduce in rank, power, or authority. — *v.i.* **3.** To dwindle; decrease. — **Syn.** See DECREASE. [Fusion of ME *diminuen* to lessen and OF *menusier* to make small] — **di·min′ish·a·ble** *adj.*
di·min·ished (di·min′isht) *adj. Music* **1.** One semitone smaller than the corresponding minor or perfect interval. **2.** Denoting a theme that has been subjected to diminution.
di·min·u·en·do (di·min′yōō·en′dō) *Music n. pl.* **·dos** A gradual lessening in volume: expressed by the sign ⟩ : opposed to *crescendo*. — *v.i.* **·doed, ·do·ing** To produce a diminuendo. [< Ital., ppr. of *diminuire* to lessen]
dim·i·nu·tion (dim′ə·nōō′shən, -nyōō′-) *n.* The act of diminishing or the condition of being diminished; decrease.
di·min·u·tive (di·min′yə·tiv) *adj.* **1.** Of relatively small size. **2.** Diminishing or tending to diminish. **3.** *Gram.* Expressing diminished size: said of certain suffixes. — *n.* **1.** *Gram.* A word formed from another to express diminished size, familiarity, affection, etc. **2.** Anything very small. — **dim·in′u·tive·ly** *adv.*
dim·i·ty (dim′ə·tē) *n. pl.* **·ties** A sheer cotton fabric woven with stripes, cords, or checks, used for dresses, curtains, etc. [< Ital. < ML < Gk. < *di-* two + *mitos* thread]
dim·mer (dim′ər) *n.* A rheostat used for varying the intensity of illumination, as in a theater lighting system.
di·mor·phism (dī·môr′fiz·əm) *n.* The existence of two distinct forms of the same organ or substance. [< Gk. < *di-* two + *morphē* form] — **di·mor′phic, di·mor′phous** *adj.*
dim-out (dim′out′) *n.* A form of modified lighting in a city, etc., used as a precautionary measure against aerial attack.
dim·ple (dim′pəl) *n.* **1.** A slight depression in the surface of the human body, esp. one made visible in the cheek by smiling. **2.** A similar depression in any smooth surface. — *v.t. & v.i.* **·pled, ·pling** To mark with or form dimples. [ME *dympull*] — **dim′ply** *adj.*
dim·wit (dim′wit′) *n. Slang* A stupid or simple-minded person. — **dim′wit′ted** *adj.* — **dim′wit′ted·ly** *adv.*
din (din) *n.* A loud, continuous noise or clamor; a rattling or clattering sound. — *v.* **dinned, din·ning** *v.t.* **1.** To assail with confusing noise. **2.** To urge or press with repetition or insistence. — *v.i.* **3.** To make a din. [OE *dyne*]
dine (dīn) *v.* **dined, din·ing** *v.i.* **1.** To eat dinner. **2.** To eat; feed: with *on* or *upon*. — *v.t.* **3.** To entertain at dinner. [< F < OF, prob. < L *dis-* away + *jejunus* fast]
din·er (dī′nər) *n.* **1.** One who dines. **2.** A dining car. **3.** A restaurant resembling a railroad car.
di·nette (dī·net′) *n.* An alcove or small room used as a dining room.
ding (ding) *v.t.* **1.** To sound, as a bell; ring. **2.** *Informal* To instill by constant repetition; din. — *v.i.* **3.** To ring or sound. **4.** *Informal* To speak with constant repetition. — *n.* The sound of a bell, or a sound resembling this. [Imit.]
ding-dong (ding′dông′, -dong′) *n.* **1.** The peal of a bell. **2.** Any monotonous repetition. — *adj. Informal* Energetically and closely contested, as a fight. [Imit.]
din·ghy (ding′gē, ding′ē) *n. pl.* **·ghies** Any of various kinds of small rowing boats. Also **din′gey, din′gy.** [< Hind. *dīngī*]
din·go (ding′gō) *n. pl.* **·goes** The native wild dog of Australia. [< native name]
ding·us (ding′əs) *n. Informal* A thing or device of which the name is unknown or forgotten; a gadget or thingamabob. [< Afrikaans < Du. *ding* thing]

din·gy (din′jē) *adj.* **·gi·er, ·gi·est** Darkened or discolored, as if soiled; dull; grimy; shabby. [Origin unknown] — **din′gi·ly** *adv.* — **din′gi·ness** *n.*
dining car A railway car in which meals are served en route.
dining room A room in which meals are served, esp. dinner.
dink·y (ding′kē) *adj.* **dink·i·er, dink·i·est** *Informal* **1.** *U.S.* Small; insignificant. **2.** *Brit.* Little; cute; neat. — *n. pl.* **din·kies** A dinkey. [< Scot. *dink* neat, tidy]
din·ner (din′ər) *n.* **1.** The principal meal of the day, taken usu. at some hour between noon and nine P.M. **2.** A banquet in honor of a person or event. [< F *dîner* to dine]
dinner coat or **jacket** A tuxedo jacket.
din·ner·ware (din′ər·wâr′) *n.* Dishes, etc., used for meals.
di·no·saur (dī′nə·sôr) *n. Paleontol.* One of a group of extinct reptiles, widely distributed during the Mesozoic period and including the largest known land animals. [< DINO- + Gk. *sauros* lizard] — **di′no·sau′ri·an** *adj. & n.*
dint (dint) *n.* **1.** Active agency; means; force: to win by *dint* of effort. **2.** A dent. — *v.t.* **1.** To make a dent in. **2.** To drive in forcibly. [OE *dynt* a blow]
di·oc·e·san (dī·os′ə·sən, dī′ə·sē′sən) *adj.* Of or pertaining to a diocese. — *n.* A bishop in charge of a diocese.
di·o·cese (dī′ə·sēs, -sis) *n.* The territory or the churches under a bishop's jurisdiction. [< OF < Med.L < L < Gk. < *dia-* completely + *oikeein* to dwell, manage]
di·ode (dī′ōd) *n. Electronics* An electron tube that permits electrons to pass in one direction only, used as a rectifier.
di·oe·cious (dī·ē′shəs) *adj. Bot.* Having the male and female organs borne by different plants; unisexual: also spelled *diecious.* [< DI-[2] + Gk. *oikia* house, dwelling]
Di·o·nys·ian (dī′ə·nish′ən, -nis′ē·ən) *adj.* Of or characteristic of Dionysius. Also **Di·o·nys·i·ac** (dī′ə·nis′ē·ak).
Di·o·ny·sus (dī′ə·nī′səs) In Greek mythology, the god of wine, fertility, etc., worshiped with orgiastic rites: identified with the Roman *Bacchus.* Also **Di′o·ny′sos.**
di·op·ter (dī·op′tər) *n. Optics* The unit for measuring the refractive power of a lens, expressed as the reciprocal of its focal length in meters. Also **di·op′tre.** [< MF < L < Gk., optical instrument]
di·op·tric (dī·op′trik) *adj. Optics* **1.** Aiding the vision by refraction, as a lens. **2.** Of or pertaining to dioptrics. **3.** Of or pertaining to a diopter. Also **di·op′tri·cal.**
di·op·trics (dī·op′triks) *n.pl.* (*construed as sing.*) The branch of optics treating of light refraction by transparent media.
di·o·ra·ma (dī′ə·rä′mə, -ram′ə) *n.* **1.** An exhibit consisting of modeled figures, etc., set in a naturalistic foreground. **2.** A picture that changes by means of cloth transparencies, etc. [< Gk. *dia-* through + *horama* a sight] — **di·o·ram·ic** (dī′ə·ram′ik) *adj.*
di·ox·ide (dī·ok′sīd, -sid) *n. Chem.* An oxide containing two atoms of oxygen to the molecule. Also **di·ox·id** (dī·ok′sid).
dip (dip) *v.* **dipped, dip·ping** *v.t.* **1.** To put or let down into a liquid momentarily. **2.** To obtain or lift up and out by scooping, bailing, etc. **3.** To lower and then raise, as a flag in salute. **4.** To baptize by immersion. **5.** To plunge (animals) into a disinfectant. **6.** To dye by immersion. **7.** To make (candles) by repeatedly immersing wicks in wax or tallow. — *v.i.* **8.** To plunge into and quickly come out of water or other liquid. **9.** To plunge one's hand or a receptacle into water, etc., or into a container, especially so as to take something out. **10.** To sink or go down suddenly. **11.** To incline downward; go down; decline. **12.** *Geol.* To lie at an angle to the horizon, as rock strata. **13.** *Aeron.* To drop rapidly and then climb. **14.** To engage in or read something slightly or superficially. — *n.* **1.** An act of dipping; a brief immersion or plunge. **2.** A liquid sauce, etc., into which something is to be dipped. **3.** The quantity of something taken up at a dipping; also, the object used for dipping. **4.** A candle made by dipping. **5.** A sloping downward; also, the degree of such a sloping. **6.** A hollow or depression. **7.** The angle that a magnetic needle makes with the horizon. **8.** *Aeron.* A rapid drop of an airplane followed by a climb. **9.** *Slang* A pickpocket. [OE *dyppan*]
diph·the·ri·a (dif·thir′ē·ə, dip-) *n. Pathol.* An acute contagious disease, caused by a bacillus and characterized by the formation of a false membrane in the air passages, fever, and weakness. [< F < Gk. *diphthera* leather, membrane]
diph·the·ri·al (dif·thir′ē·əl, dip-) *adj.* Of, pertaining to, or having diphtheria. Also **diph·the′ri·an, diph·the·ric** (dif·thir′ik, dip-), **diph·the·rit·ic** (dif′thə·rit′ik, dip′-).
diph·thong (dif′thông, -thong, dip′-) *n. Phonet.* A blend of two vowel sounds in one syllable, as *oi* in *coil,* or as *i* in *fine.* [< F < LL < Gk. < *di-* two + *phthongos* sound] — **diph·thon′gal** *adj.*
diph·thong·ize (dif′thông·īz, -thong-, dip′-) *v.* **·ized, ·iz·ing** *v.t.* **1.** To make a diphthong of; pronounce as a diphthong. — *v.i.* **2.** To become a diphthong. — **diph′thong·i·za·tion** *n.*
diplo- *combining form* Double. Also, before vowels, **dipl-.** [< Gk. *diploos* double]
dip·loid (dip′loid) *adj. Biol.* Having two sets of chromosomes.
di·plo·ma (di·plō′mə) *n.* **1.** A certificate given by a sch college, or university testifying that a student has earn degree or completed a course of study. **2.** A certificate ferring some honor or privilege. [< L < Gk. *dip* paper folded double, a letter]
di·plo·ma·cy (di·plō′mə·sē) *n. pl.* **·cies** **1.** The art, scie or practice of conducting negotiations between nations. Skill or tact in dealing with others, etc.
dip·lo·mat (dip′lə·mat) *n.* **1.** One engaged in diplom **2.** Any individual possessing skill or tact in dealing others. [See DIPLOMA.]
dip·lo·mat·ic (dip′lə·mat′ik) *adj.* **1.** Of or pertainin diplomacy. **2.** Tactful and skillful in dealing with pe Also **dip′lo·mat′i·cal.** — **dip′lo·mat′i·cal·ly** *adv.*
diplomatic corps The corps of officials, as ambassa and envoys, who are assigned to represent their count another country. Also **diplomatic body.**
diplomatic immunity Exemption of the members of a lomatic corps from the ordinary processes of local law.
di·plo·ma·tist (di·plō′mə·tist) *n. Brit.* A diplomat.
dip·per (dip′ər) *n.* **1.** One who dips. **2.** A long-han cup used to dip liquids. **3.** Any of several American b that are quick divers; esp. the water ouzel.
Dip·per (dip′ər) *n.* Either of two northern constellat the Big Dipper or the Little Dipper.
dip·so·ma·ni·a (dip′sə·mā′nē·ə) *n.* Uncontrollable cra for alcoholic drink. [< Gk. *dipsa* thirst + -MANIA]
dip·so·ma·ni·ac (dip′sə·mā′nē·ak) *n.* A person affe with dipsomania. — *adj.* Pertaining to or affected with somania: also **dip·so·ma·ni·a·cal** (dip′sə·mə·nī′ə·kəl).
dip·ter·ous (dip′tər·əs) *adj.* **1.** *Entomol.* Of or pertaini insects having a single pair of wings, including the gnats, mosquitoes, etc. **2.** Two-winged, as a seed or [< Gk. < *di-* twice + *pteron* wing]
dip·tych (dip′tik) *n.* **1.** An ancient Greek or Roman hi double writing tablet. **2.** A double picture or carving, of a religious subject. [< LL < Gk., pair of tablets]
dire (dīr) *adj.* **dir·er, dir·est** Calamitous; dreadful; terr [< L *dirus* awful] — **dire′ly** *adv.* — **dire′ness** *n.*
di·rect (di·rekt′, dī-) *v.t.* **1.** To control or conduct th fairs of; manage. **2.** To order or instruct with autho command. **3.** *Music* To lead as a conductor. **4.** To (someone) the way. **5.** To cause to move or face in sired direction: to *direct* one's gaze. **6.** To indicate the d nation of, as a letter. **7.** To intend, as remarks or insult be heard by a person; address. **8.** To guide or supervise performance of a play, film, etc.). — *v.i.* **9.** To give mands or guidance. **10.** To guide the production or i pretation of a play, film, etc. — *adj.* **1.** Having or b the straightest course; shortest; nearest. **2.** Free fro tervening agencies or conditions. **3.** Straightforward; did; plain. **4.** Complete; absolute: the *direct* antithesis In a continuous line of descent; lineal. **6.** In the e words of the speaker or writer: a *direct* quote. **7.** *Govt* the efforts of the people through referendum, etc., wit the intervention of delegates or representatives. **8.** *E* Continuous as opposed to alternating, as a current. — In a direct line or manner; directly. [< L < *dis-* apa *regere* to guide, conduct] — **di·rect′ness** *n.*
di·rec·tion (di·rek′shən, dī-) *n.* **1.** The act of direc **2.** The course or position of an object or point in relati another object or point: in the *direction* of Chicago. **3.** *pl.* Instructions about how to do or use something. **4** order, command, or regulation. **5.** Management, contr administration. **6.** Supervision and organization of a film, etc. **7.** Tendency or movement. **8.** The address letter, parcel, etc., that indicates the intended recipient.
di·rec·tion·al (di·rek′shən·əl, dī-) *adj.* **1.** Pertainin direction in space. **2.** *Telecom.* **a** Adapted for indica from which of several directions signals are received. **b** scribing an antenna that radiates or receives radio w more effectively in or from some directions than from ot
direction finder *Telecom.* A receiving device with w the direction of incoming radio signals may be determi
di·rec·tive (di·rek′tiv, dī-) *n.* An order or regulation; e governmental or military pronouncement. — *adj.* directs or points out, rules, or governs.
di·rect·ly (di·rekt′lē, dī-) *adv.* **1.** In a direct line or ma **2.** Without medium, agent, or go-between. **3.** As so possible; immediately. **4.** Exactly; precisely. — *conj.* As soon as.
di·rec·tor (di·rek′tər, dī-) *n.* **1.** One who directs, as head member of a corporation, the conductor of an orche etc. **2.** *Mil.* An apparatus that computes firing data fo against moving targets. — **di·rec′tress** *n.fem.*
di·rec·tor·ate (di·rek′tər·it, dī-) *n.* **1.** A body of direc **2.** The office or power of a director: also **di·rec′tor·ship**
di·rec·to·ri·al (di·rek′tôr′ē·əl, -tō′rē, dī-) *adj.* **1.** directs; directive. **2.** Pertaining to a director or directo
di·rec·to·ry (di·rek′tər·ē, dī-) *n. pl.* **·ries** **1.** An alpha cal or classified list, as of the names and addresses of th

ıbitants or businesses of a city. **2.** A collection of rules. A directorate. — *adj.* Serving to direct.

ect primary *Govt.* A preliminary election in which a ırty chooses its candidates for public office by direct vote.

ect tax A tax charged directly to the taxpayer.

e·ful (dīr′fŏŏl, -fəl) *adj.* Dreadful; terrible; dire. — **re′ful·ly** *adv.* — **dire′ful·ness** *n.*

ge (dûrj) *n.* **1.** A song or melody expressing mourning. A funeral hymn. [< L *dirige* (imperative of *dirigere* to rect), the first word of the antiphon (*Ps.* v 8) of matins]

·i·gi·ble (dir′ə·jə·bəl) *n.* A lighter-than-air aircraft that ay be steered by means of its own motive power. — *adj.* ıat can be steered. [< L *dirigere* to direct]

k (dûrk) *n.* A dagger. [Origin uncertain]

n·dl (dûrn′dəl) *n.* **1.** A woman's dress with a full skirt thered to a tight bodice. **2.** The skirt of such a dress: so **dirndl skirt.** [< G *dirndl*, dim. of *dirne* girl]

t (dûrt) *n.* **1.** Any foul or filthy substance, as mud, dust, crement, etc. **2.** Loose earth or soil; loam. **3.** Something ntemptible, mean, or of small worth. **4.** Obscene speech, ctures, or writing. **5.** Rude language. **6.** Gossip. **7.** *ining* Washed-down earth, broken ore or rock, etc., conıining precious metal. — *adj.* Made of earth: a *dirt* road. 1E *drit* < ON, dirt, bird droppings]

t-cheap (dûrt′chēp′) *adj.* Very inexpensive. — *adv.* At very low price.

t farmer *U.S. Informal* A farmer who does his own ırk.

t·y (dûr′tē) *adj.* **dirt·i·er, dirt·i·est** **1.** Soiled with or as th dirt; unclean; filthy. **2.** Imparting dirt; making filthy. Indecent; obscene. **4.** Despicable; mean. **5.** Lacking ightness or clarity: said of colors. **6.** Stormy: *dirty* ather. **7.** Having excessive radioactive fallout: a *dirty* omic bomb. — *v.t. & v.i.* **dirt·ied, dirt·y·ing** To make or beme dirty. — **dirt′i·ly** *adv.* — **dirt′i·ness** *n.*

-[1] *prefix* **1.** Away from; apart: *disembody.* **2.** The reverse or the undoing of (what is expressed in the rest of the ord): *disconnect.* **3.** Deprivation of some quality, power, nk, etc.: *disable.* **4.** Not: *disloyal.* **5.** Completely; thorghly (with an already negative word): *disannul.* Also: *di-* fore *b, d, l, m, n, r, s, v*, and usu. before *g*, as in *digress*, *ect*, *diverge*; *dif-* before *f*, as in *differ.* The living English efix is always in the form *dis-*. [< L *dis-*, sometimes reıcing OF *des-* (see DE-), ult. < *duo* two]

-[2] *prefix* Var. of DI-[2]. [< MF, ult. < Gk. *dis* twice]

s (dis) In Roman mythology: **a** God of the lower world: ntified with *Pluto.* **b** The kingdom of the dead.

·a·bil·i·ty (dis′ə·bil′ə·tē) *n. pl.* **·ties** **1.** That which disles. **2.** Lack of ability. **3.** Legal incapacity to act.

·a·ble (dis·ā′bəl) *v.t.* **·bled, ·bling** **1.** To render incapable; ipple. **2.** To render legally incapable. — **dis·a′ble·ment** *n.*

·a buse (dis′ə·byōōz′) *v.t.* **·bused, ·bus·ing** To free from se or mistaken ideas; undeceive.

·ad·van·tage (dis′əd·van′tij, -vän′-) *n.* **1.** An unfavorle condition or situation. **2.** That which produces an unvorable condition or situation; drawback; handicap. **3.** ss, injury, or detriment. — **at a disadvantage** In an unvorable condition or situation. — *v.t.* **·taged, ·tag·ing** To bject to a disadvantage.

·ad·van·taged (dis′əd·van′tijd, -vän′-) *adj.* Having less oney, social status, etc., than is needed for decent living.

·ad·van·ta·geous (dis·ad′vən·tā′jəs) *adj.* Attended with sadvantage; detrimental; inconvenient. — **dis·ad′van·geous·ly** *adv.* — **dis·ad′van·ta′geous·ness** *n.*

·af·fect (dis′ə·fekt′) *v.t.* To destroy or weaken the affecn or loyalty of; alienate; estrange. — **dis′af·fec′tion** *n.*

·af·fect·ed (dis′ə·fek′tid) *adj.* Alienated in feeling or yalty; estranged; unfriendly. — **dis′af·fect′ed·ly** *adv.*

·a·gree (dis′ə·grē′) *v.i.* **·greed, ·gree·ing** **1.** To vary in inion; differ; dissent. **2.** To quarrel; argue. **3.** To fail to ree or harmonize, as facts. **4.** To be unacceptable or unvorable: with *with*: Heat *disagreed* with him.

·a·gree·a·ble (dis′ə·grē′ə·bəl) *adj.* **1.** Repugnant or ofısive; not agreeable; unpleasant. **2.** Of unpleasant dispoion; quarrelsome; bad-tempered. — **dis′a·gree′a·bil′i·ty, s′a·gree′a·ble·ness** *n.* — **dis′a·gree′a·bly** *adv.*

·a·gree·ment (dis′ə·grē′mənt) *n.* **1.** Failure to agree. Dissimilarity; inconsistency; discrepancy. **3.** Difference views; dissent. **4.** A quarrel; dispute.

·al·low (dis′ə·lou′) *v.t.* **1.** To refuse to allow. **2.** To ret as untrue or invalid. — **dis′al·low′ance** *n.*

·ap·pear (dis′ə·pir′) *v.i.* **1.** To pass from sight; fade ay; vanish. **2.** To cease to exist. — **dis′ap·pear′ance** *n.*

·ap·point (dis′ə·point′) *v.t.* **1.** To fail to fulfill the expecion, hope, or desire of (a person). **2.** To prevent the fulment of (a hope or plan). — **dis′ap·point′ing·ly** *adv.*

·ap·point·ed (dis′ə·poin′tid) *adj.* Frustrated in one's exctations or hopes.

dis·ap·point·ment (dis′ə·point′mənt) *n.* **1.** The act of disappointing. **2.** The feeling of being disappointed. **3.** One who or that which disappoints.

dis·ap·pro·ba·tion (dis′ap·rə·bā′shən) *n.* Disapproval.

dis·ap·pro·val (dis′ə·prōō′vəl) *n.* The act of disapproving; the withholding of approval; censure.

dis·ap·prove (dis′ə·prōōv′) *v.* **·proved, ·prov·ing** *v.t.* **1.** To regard with disfavor or censure; condemn. **2.** To refuse to approve. — *v.i.* **3.** To have or express an unfavorable opinion: often with *of.* — **dis′ap·rov′ing·ly** *adv.*

dis·arm (dis·ärm′) *v.t.* **1.** To deprive of weapons or of any means of attack or defense. **2.** To overcome the suspicion, antagonism, etc., of. **3.** To allay or reduce (suspicion, antagonism, etc.). — *v.i.* **4.** To lay down arms. **5.** To reduce or eliminate one's military forces, equipment, etc.

dis·ar·ma·ment (dis·är′mə·mənt) *n.* The act of disarming; esp., the elimination, reduction, or limitation of armed forces, military equipment, or weapons of war.

dis·arm·ing (dis·är′ming) *adj.* Tending to overcome suspicion, etc.: a *disarming* smile. — **dis·arm′ing·ly** *adv.*

dis·ar·range (dis′ə·rānj′) *v.t.* **·ranged, ·rang·ing** To disturb the arrangement of; disorder. — **dis′ar·range′ment** *n.*

dis·ar·ray (dis′ə·rā′) *n.* **1.** Disorder; confusion. **2.** Disorder of clothing. — *v.t.* To throw into disarray.

dis·as·sem·ble (dis′ə·sem′bəl) *v.t.* **·bled, ·bling** To take apart. — **dis′as·sem′bly** *n.*

dis·as·so·ci·ate (dis′ə·sō′shē·āt) *v.t.* **·at·ed, ·at·ing** To dissociate. — **dis′as·so′ci·a′tion** *n.*

dis·as·ter (di·zas′tər, -zäs′-) *n.* An event causing great distress or ruin; sudden and crushing misfortune. [< MF < *des-* away + *astre* a star]

dis·as·trous (di·zas′trəs, -zäs′-) *adj.* Causing or accompanied by disaster; calamitous. — **dis·as′trous·ly** *adv.* — **dis·as′trous·ness** *n.*

dis·a·vow (dis′ə·vou′) *v.t.* To disclaim responsibility for or approval of; refuse to acknowledge. — **dis′a·vow′al** *n.*

dis·band (dis·band′) *v.t.* **1.** To break up the organization of; dissolve; especially, to break up (an army or similar unit) by dismissing the members. — *v.i.* **2.** To become disbanded. — **dis·band′ment** *n.*

dis·bar (dis·bär′) *v.t.* **·barred, ·bar·ring** To expel officially from the legal profession. — **dis·bar′ment** *n.*

dis·be·lief (dis′bi·lēf′) *n.* Lack of belief.

dis·be·lieve (dis′bi·lēv′) *v.t. & v.i.* **·lieved, ·liev·ing** To withhold belief (from); reject. — **dis′be·liev′er** *n.*

dis·bur·den (dis·bûr′dən) *v.t.* **1.** To relieve of a burden. **2.** To get rid of (a burden). — *v.i.* **3.** To put off a burden.

dis·burse (dis·bûrs′) *v.t.* **·bursed, ·burs·ing** To pay out; expend. [< OF < *des-* away + *bourse* a purse] — **dis·burs′·a·ble** *adj.* — **dis·burse′ment** *n.* — **dis·burs′er** *n.*

disc (disk) *n.* **1.** See DISK. **2.** *Anat.* Any approximately flat, circular outgowth, organ, or structure, as of cartilage between the joints of certain bones. [Var. of DISK]

dis·calced (dis·kalst′) *adj.* Barefooted, as certain orders of monks [< L < *dis-* not + *calceatus* a shoe]

dis·cant (dis′kant, dis·kant′) *n. & v.i.* Descant.

dis·card (*v.* dis·kärd′; *n.* dis′kärd) *v.t.* **1.** To cast aside as useless or undesirable; reject; dismiss. **2.** In card games, to throw out (a card or cards) from one's hand; also, to play (a card, other than a trump, not of the suit led). — *v.i.* **3.** In card games, to throw out a card or cards. — *n.* **1.** The act of discarding, or the state of being discarded. **2.** A card or cards discarded. **3.** One who or that which is discarded.

dis·cern (di·sûrn′, di·zûrn′) *v.t.* **1.** To perceive, as with sight or mind. **2.** To recognize as separate and different. — *v.i.* **3.** To distinguish or discriminate something. [< OF < L < *dis-* apart + *cernere* to separate] — **dis·cern′er** *n.* — **dis·cern′i·ble** *adj.* — **dis·cern′i·bly** *adv.*

dis·cern·ing (di·sûr′ning, -zûr′-) *adj.* Quick to discern; discriminating; penetrating. — **dis·cern′ing·ly** *adv.*

dis·cern·ment (di·sûrn′mənt, -zûrn′-) *n.* **1.** The act or process of discerning. **2.** Keenness of judgment; insight.

dis·charge (dis·chärj′; *n. also* dis′chärj) *v.* **·charged, ·charg·ing** *v.t.* **1.** To remove the contents of; unload. **2.** To remove by unloading. **3.** To emit (fluid). **4.** To shoot or fire, as a gun. **5.** To dismiss from office or employment. **6.** To set at liberty, as a prisoner. **7.** To relieve of duty or obligation. **8.** To perform the duties of (a trust, office, etc.). **9.** To pay (a debt) or meet and satisfy (an obligation or duty). **10.** To set aside legally; annul. **11.** *Electr.* To free of an electrical charge. — *v.i.* **12.** To get rid of a load, burden, etc. **13.** To go off, as a cannon. **14.** To give or send forth contents. **15.** *Electr.* To lose a charge of electricity. — *n.* **1.** The act of discharging or the state of being discharged. **2.** The firing of a weapon or missile. **3.** An issuing forth; emission. **4.** That which is discharged, as pus. **5.** Release or dismissal from service, employment, or custody. **6.** Something that discharges, as a certificate separating one from military service. 7. *Electr.* The flow of electricity between the terminals of a condenser when placed in very near contact. [< OF *deschargier* < *des-* away (< L *dis-*) + *chargier* to carry] — **dis·charge′a·ble** *adj.* — **dis·charg′er** *n.*

dis·ci·ple (di·sī′pəl) *n.* 1. One who accepts and follows a teacher or a doctrine. 2. One of the twelve chosen companions and apostles of Jesus Christ. — **Syn.** See ADHERENT. [OE < L *discere* to learn] — **dis·ci′ple·ship** *n.*

dis·ci·pli·nar·i·an (dis′ə·plə·nâr′ē·ən) *n.* One who administers or advocates discipline. — *adj.* Disciplinary.

dis·ci·pli·nar·y (dis′ə·plə·ner′ē) *adj.* Of, relating to, or of the nature of discipline; used for discipline.

dis·ci·pline (dis′ə·plin) *n.* 1. Training of the mental, moral, and physical powers by instruction, control, and exercise. 2. The state or condition resulting from such training. 3. Subjection to rule and authority. 4. Punishment or disciplinary action for the sake of training. 5. A system of rules, or method of practice, as of a church. 6. A branch of knowledge or instruction. 7. A penitential instrument; a scourge. — *v.t.* **·plined, ·plin·ing** 1. To train to obedience or subjection. 2. To drill; educate. 3. To punish. — **Syn.** See CHASTEN, TEACH. [< OF < L *disciplina* instruction] — **dis′ci·plin′a·ble** *adj.* — **dis′ci·plin·er** *n.*

disc jockey See DISK JOCKEY.

dis·claim (dis·klām′) *v.t.* 1. To disavow any claim to, or responsibility for. 2. To reject or deny the authority of. — *v.i.* 3. *Law* To renounce a legal claim. — **dis·cla·ma·tion** (dis′klə·mā′shən) *n.*

dis·claim·er (dis·klā′mər) *n.* 1. One who disclaims. 2. A disclaiming act, notice, or instrument.

dis·close (dis·klōz′) *v.t.* **·closed, ·clos·ing** 1. To expose to view; uncover. 2. To make known. — **dis·clos′er** *n.*

dis·clo·sure (dis·klō′zhər) *n.* 1. The act or process of disclosing. 2. That which is disclosed.

dis·coid (dis′koid) *adj.* Having the form of a disk. Also **dis·coi′dal.** — *n.* A disk or disklike object. [< L < Gk. *diskos* discus < *eidos* form]

dis·col·or (dis·kul′ər) *v.t.* 1. To change or destroy the color of; stain. — *v.i.* 2. To become discolored. Also *Brit.* **dis·col′our.** — **dis·col′or·a′tion, dis·col′or·ment** *n.*

dis·com·bob·u·late (dis′kəm·bob′yə·lāt) *v.t.* **·lat·ed, ·lat·ing** *U.S. Slang* To throw into confusion. [Origin uncertain]

dis·com·fit (dis·kum′fit) *v.t.* 1. To defeat the plans or purposes of; frustrate. 2. To throw into confusion. 3. To vanquish. [< OF < *des-* away + *confire* to prepare]

dis·com·fi·ture (dis·kum′fi·chər) *n.* The act of discomfiting, or the state of being discomfited; defeat; frustration.

dis·com·fort (dis·kum′fərt) *n.* 1. Lack of ease or comfort; disquietude. 2. That which interferes with comfort. — *v.t.* To make uneasy; distress.

dis·com·mode (dis′kə·mōd′) *v.t.* **·mod·ed, ·mod·ing** To cause inconvenience to; trouble; disturb. [< DIS-[1] + L *commodus* fit, suitable, convenient]

dis·com·pose (dis′kəm·pōz′) *v.t.* **·posed, ·pos·ing** 1. To disturb the calm of; make uneasy. 2. To disorder or disarrange. — **dis′com·pos′ed·ly** *adv.* — **dis′com·pos′ing·ly** *adv.*

dis·com·po·sure (dis′kəm·pō′zhər) *n.* The state of being discomposed; agitation; perturbation.

dis·con·cert (dis′kən·sûrt′) *v.t.* 1. To disturb the composure of; confuse; upset. 2. To frustrate, as a plan. [< MF < *dis-* apart + *concerter* to agree] — **dis′con·cert′ed** *adj.* — **dis′·con·cert′ed·ly** *adv.* — **dis′con·cert·ed′ness** *n.* — **dis′·con·cert′ing·ly** *adv.* — **dis′con·cer′tion** *n.*

dis·con·form·i·ty (dis′kən·fôr′mə·tē) *n. pl.* **·ties** Lack of conformity; nonconformity.

dis·con·nect (dis′kə·nekt′) *v.t.* To break the connection of or between. — **dis′con·nec′tion** *n.*

dis·con·nect·ed (dis′kə·nek′tid) *adj.* 1. Not connected; disjointed. 2. Incoherent; rambling. — **dis′con·nect′ed·ly** *adv.* — **dis′con·nect′ed·ness** *n.*

dis·con·so·late (dis·kon′sə·lit) *adj.* 1. Not to be consoled; inconsolable; dejected. 2. Producing or marked by gloominess; cheerless. [< Med.L < L *dis-* not + *consolari* to cheer, console] — **dis·con′so·late·ly** *adv.* — **dis·con′so·late·ness, dis·con′so·la′tion** *n.*

dis·con·tent (dis′kən·tent′) *adj.* Discontented. — *n.* Lack of contentment; dissatisfaction; uneasiness: also **dis′con·tent′ment.** — *v.t.* To make discontent.

dis·con·tent·ed (dis′kən·ten′tid) *adj.* Restless; uneasy in mind, as through frustration; dissatisfied. — **dis′con·tent′·ed·ly** *adv.* — **dis′con·tent′ed·ness** *n.*

dis·con·tin·ue (dis′kən·tin′yōō) *v.* **·tin·ued, ·tin·u·ing** *v.t.* 1. To break off or cease from; stop. 2. To cease using, receiving, etc. — *v.i.* 3. To come to an end; cease. — **dis′con·tin′u·ance, dis′con·tin′u·a′tion** *n.* — **dis′con·tin′u·er** *n.*

dis·con·ti·nu·i·ty (dis′kon·tə·nōō′ə·tē, -nyōō′-) *n. pl.* **·ties** 1. Lack of continuity. 2. A gap or break.

dis·con·tin·u·ous (dis′kən·tin′yōō·əs) *adj.* Not continuous; characterized by interruptions or breaks. — **dis′con·tin′u·ous·ly** *adv.* — **dis′con·tin′u·ous·ness** *n.*

dis·cord (*n.* dis′kôrd; *v.* dis·kôrd′) *n.* 1. Lack of agreement or concord; contention; conflict; strife. 2. A harsh or ·agreeable mingling of noises; din. 3. *Music* Dissonance. *v.i.* To be out of accord or harmony; clash. [< OF < I *dis-* apart + *cor, cordis* heart]

dis·cor·dant (dis·kôr′dənt) *adj.* 1. Characterized by l of agreement or concord; differing; clashing. 2. Dissona harsh, or disagreeable in sound. [See DISCORD.] — · **cor′dance, dis·cor′dan·cy** *n.* — **dis·cor′dant·ly** *adv.*

dis·co·thèque (dis·kə·tek′) *n.* A night club offering corded music for dancing instead of music played by a b of live musicians. [< F, lit., record library]

dis·count (*v.* dis′kount, dis·kount′; *n.* dis′kount) *v.t.* 1. deduct (an indicated sum or percent) from the full amo that would otherwise be charged or owed. 2. To buy or (a bill, note, or other negotiable paper), less the amoun interest to be accumulated before maturity. 3. To l money on (negotiable notes, etc., not immediately payal deducting the interest. 4. To reduce the cost or value of *discount* merchandise. 5. To take little or no account of; regard: *Discount* what she says. 6. To allow for exagg tion, prejudice, etc., in; accept with reservation: to *disc* stories of great heroism. 7. To take into account in adva and so lessen the full intensity or effect of. — *v.i.* 8. lend money, deducting the interest beforehand. — *n.* 1 deduction of a particular sum or percent, as one made for mediate cash payment. 2. The interest deducted bef hand in buying, selling, or lending money on negoti notes, etc. 3. The rate of interest so deducted: also **disco rate.** 4. The act of discounting. — **at a discount** 1. low the amount regularly charged; at less than face va 2. In little demand and of little value. [< MF < O Med.L < L *dis-* away + *computare.* See COMPUTE.] **dis′count·a·ble** *adj.* — **dis′count·er** *n.*

dis·coun·te·nance (dis·koun′tə·nəns) *v.t.* **·nanced, ·n ing** 1. To disapprove of. 2. To abash; disconcert.

dis·cour·age (dis·kûr′ij) *v.t.* **·aged, ·ag·ing** 1. To wea the courage or lessen the confidence of; dishearten. 2. deter or dissuade: with *from.* 3. To obstruct; hinder. 4. attempt to repress or prevent by disapproval. [< O *des-* away + *corage* courage] — **dis·cour′ag·er** *n.* — **cour′ag·ing·ly** *adv.* — **dis·cour′age·ment** *n.*

dis·course (*n.* dis′kôrs, -kōrs, dis·kôrs′, -kōrs′; *v.* dis·k -kōrs′) *n.* 1. Communication, as in conversation or writ 2. A formal, extensive, oral or written treatment of a ject. — *v.* **·coursed, ·cours·ing** *v.i.* 1. To set forth o ideas concerning a subject: with *on* or *upon.* 2. To conve confer. [< F < L < *dis-* apart + *cursus* a running, p *currere* to run] — **dis·cours′er** *n.*

dis·cour·te·ous (dis·kûr′tē·əs) *adj.* Not courteous; ir lite. — **dis·cour′te·ous·ly** *adv.* — **dis·cour′te·ous·ness**

dis·cour·te·sy (dis·kûr′tə·sē) *n. pl.* **·sies** 1. Lack of c tesy; rudeness. 2. A discourteous act.

dis·cov·er (dis·kuv′ər) *v.t.* To find out, get knowledge o come upon, esp. for the first time. [< OF < *des-* awa *covrir* to cover] — **dis·cov′er·a·ble** *adj.* — **dis·cov′er·e**

dis·cov·er·y (dis·kuv′ər·ē) *n. pl.* **·er·ies** 1. The act of covering. 2. Something discovered.

dis·cred·it (dis·kred′it) *v.t.* 1. To harm the credit or re tation of; bring into disrepute. 2. To cause to be doub disbelieved, or distrusted. 3. To refuse to believe (so thing asserted). — *n.* 1. The state of being discredited a Lack or loss of credit, reputation, or general esteem Doubt; disbelief; distrust. 2. Something that discre — **dis·cred′it·a·ble** *adj.* — **dis·cred′it·a·bly** *adv.*

dis·creet (dis·krēt′) *adj.* Tactful and judicious, esp. in d ing with others. [< OF < LL *discretus,* orig. pp. of L *cernere* to discern] — **dis·creet′ly** *adv.* — **dis·creet′nes**

dis·crep·an·cy (dis·krep′ən·sē) *n. pl.* **·cies** 1. Lac agreement or consistency; contradiction. 2. An instanc this. Also **dis·crep′ance.** [< OF < L *dis-* apart + *cre* to creak] — **dis·crep′ant** *adj.* — **dis·crep′ant·ly** *adv.*

dis·crete (dis·krēt′) *adj.* 1. Distinct or separate. 2. M up of distinct parts. [Var. of DISCREET] — **dis·cret** *adv.* — **dis·crete′ness** *n.*

dis·cre·tion (dis·kresh′ən) *n.* 1. The quality of being creet; tactfulness; prudence. 2. Freedom or power to m one's own judgments. — **at one's discretion** Accordin one's own judgment. [< OF < L < *discernere* to disc

dis·cre·tion·ar·y (dis·kresh′ən·er′ē) *adj.* Left to or de mined by one's discretion. Also **dis·cre′tion·al.**

dis·crim·i·nate (*v.* dis·krim′ə·nāt; *adj.* dis·krim′ə·nit) **·nat·ed, ·nat·ing** *v.i.* 1. To act toward someone or somet with partiality or prejudice: to *discriminate* against a mi ity. 2. To draw a clear distinction; distinguish: to *discri nate* between good and evil. — *v.t.* 3. To draw or consti a clear distinction between: differentiate: to *discrimi* good and evil. 4. To recognize as being different. — Discriminating. [< L < *dis-* apart + *crimen* judgment] **dis·crim′i·nate·ly** *adv.* — **dis·crim′i·nat·ing** *adj.* — **crim′i·nat′ing·ly** *adv.* — **dis·crim′i·na′tion** *n.* — **dis·cr i·na′tor** *n.*

·crim·i·na·to·ry (dis·krim′ə·nə·tôr′ē, -tō′rē) *adj.* Show-g prejudice or bias: *discriminatory* practices.

·cur·sive (dis·kûr′siv) *adj.* Passing quickly or disjoint-ly from one subject to another digressive. [See DIS-URSE.] **— dis·cur′sive·ly** *adv.* **— dis·cur′sive·ness** *n.*

·cus (dis′kəs) *n. pl.* **dis·cus·es** or **dis·ci** (dis′ī) **1.** A flat, avy disk, as of metal or stone, hurled for distance in ath-ic contests. **2.** Such a contest. [< L < Gk. *diskos*]

·cuss (dis·kus′) *v.t.* To have as the subject of conversa-n or writing; treat or consider formally. [< L, pp. of *dis-tere* to discuss < *dis-* apart + *quatere* to shake] **— dis·ss′er** *n.* **— dis·cuss′i·ble** *adj.*

·cus·sion (dis·kush′ən) *n.* The act of discussing; exami-tion or consideration of a subject in speech or writing.

·dain (dis·dān′) *v.t.* **1.** To consider unworthy of one's gard or notice: to *disdain* a coward. **2.** To refuse scorn-ly: to *disdain* to beg for food. **—** *n.* A feeling or attitude superiority and dislike. [< OF < L < *dis-* away + *gnare* to deign] **— dis·dain′ful** *adj.* **— dis·dain′ful·ly** *v.* **— dis·dain′ful·ness** *n.*

·ease (di·zēz′) *n.* **1.** A condition of ill health or malfunc-ning in a living organism, esp. one having particular mptoms. **2.** Any disordered or unwholesome condition. *v.t.* **·eased, ·eas·ing** To cause disease in; make unhealthy; rrupt. [< AF *desaise*. See EASE.] **— dis·eased′** *adj.*

·em·bark (dis′em·bärk′) *v.t. & v.i.* To put or go ashore m a ship; land; unload. **— dis·em′bar·ka′tion** *n.*

·em·bar·rass (dis′em·bar′əs) *v.t.* To free from embar-ssment, entanglement, etc. **— dis′em·bar′rass·ment** *n.*

·em·bod·y (dis′em·bod′ē) *v.t.* **·bod·ied, ·bod·y·ing** To e from the body or from physical existence: a *disembodied* irit. **— dis′em·bod′i·ment** *n.*

·em·bow·el (dis′em·bou′əl, -boul′) *v.t.* **·bow·eled** or **led, ·bow·el·ing** or **·el·ling** To take out the bowels or en-ils of; eviscerate. **— dis′em·bow′el·ment** *n.*

·en·chant (dis′en·chant′, -chänt′) *v.t.* To free from en-antment; disillusion. **— dis′en·chant′er** *n.* **— dis′en·ant′ment** *n.*

·en·cum·ber (dis′en·kum′bər) *v.t.* To free from encum-ance.

·en·fran·chise (dis′en·fran′chīz) *v.t.* **·chised, ·chis·ing** disfranchise. **— dis′en·fran′chise·ment** (-chiz·mənt, īz-) *n.*

·en·gage (dis′en·gāj′) *v.* **·gaged, ·gag·ing** *v.t.* **1.** To free m entanglement, obligation, occupation, etc.; set free. **—** . **2.** To free oneself; get loose. **— dis′en·gage′ment** *n.*

·en·tan·gle (dis′en·tang′gəl) *v.* **·gled, ·gling** *v.t.* **1.** To e or relieve of entanglement, confusion, etc. **—** *v.i.* **2.** become disentangled. **— dis′en·tan′gle·ment** *n.*

·en·twine (dis′en·twīn′) *v.t. & v.i.* **·twined, ·twin·ing** To twine; disentangle.

·es·tab·lish (dis′es·tab′lish) *v.t.* **1.** To deprive of fixed or ablished status or character. **2.** To take away government pport from (a state church). **— dis′es·tab′lish·ment** *n.*

·es·teem (dis′es·tēm′) *v.t.* To regard with little esteem; ve a low opinion of. **—** *n.* Lack of esteem.

seuse (dē·zœz′) *n. French* A woman entertainer who rforms dramatic impersonations, monologues, etc.

·fa·vor (dis·fā′vər) *n.* **1.** Lack of favor; disapproval; slike. **2.** The state of being frowned upon or disliked. **—** . To treat or regard disapprovingly. Also *Brit.* **dis·fa′vour.**

·fig·ure (dis·fig′yər) *v.t.* **·ured, ·ur·ing** To mar or destroy e appearance or form of; make unsightly; deform. **— dis·ur·er** *n.* **— dis·fig′ure·ment** *n.*

·fran·chise (dis·fran′chīz) *v.t.* **·chised, ·chis·ing** **1.** To prive (a citizen) of a right or privilege, esp. of the ballot. To deprive of a franchise, privilege, or right, as a corpora-n. Also *disenfranchise.* **— dis·fran′chise·ment** (-chiz·ənt, -chīz-) *n.* **— dis·fran′chis·er** *n.*

·gorge (dis·gôrj′) *v.t.* **·gorged, ·gorg·ing** **1.** To throw t, as from the throat or stomach; eject; vomit. **2.** To give unwillingly. **—** *v.i.* **3.** To disgorge something. [< OF *des-* from + *gorge* throat]

·grace (dis·grās′) *n.* **1.** A condition of shame, dishonor, infamy; ignominy. **2.** Anything that brings about dis-nor or shame. **3.** A state of being out of favor: in *disgrace* court. **—** *v.t.* **·graced, ·grac·ing** **1.** To bring reproach or ame upon. **2.** To treat with dishonor. [< MF < Ital. < s- away + *grazia* favor] **— dis·grac′er** *n.*

·grace·ful (dis·grās′fəl) *adj.* Characterized by or caus-g disgrace; shameful; disreputable. **— dis·grace′ful·ly** *v.* **— dis·grace′ful·ness** *n.*

·grun·tle (dis·grun′təl) *v.t.* **·tled, ·tling** To make dis-tisfied or sulky; put out of humor.

·guise (dis·gīz′) *v.t.* **·guised, ·guis·ing** **1.** To alter the ap-arance of so as to make unrecognizable. **2.** To conceal the tual nature of: to *disguise* the facts. **—** *n.* **1.** The act of sguising or the state of being disguised. **2.** Something that disguises, as a mask or costume. [< OF < *des-* down + *guise*. See GUISE.] **— dis·guis′er** *n.*

dis·gust (dis·gust′) *v.t.* **1.** To affect with nausea or loath-ing. **2.** To offend the sensibilities, moral values, or good taste of; sicken. **—** *n.* Strong aversion aroused by some-thing offensive. [< MF < *des-* not + *gouster* to taste] **— dis·gust′ed** *adj.* **— dis·gust′ed·ly** *adv.*

dis·gust·ing (dis·gus′ting) *adj.* Provoking disgust; repug-nant; revolting; offensive. **— dis·gust′ing·ly** *adv.*

dish (dish) *n.* **1.** An open, concave, usu. shallow container, as of china or glass, typically used for holding or serving food. **2.** A particular kind or preparation of food: a delicious *dish.* **3.** A dishful. **4.** A hollow or depression like that in a dish. **—** *v.t.* **1.** To put (food, etc.) into a dish; serve: usu. with *up* or *out.* **2.** To hollow out (a surface). **— to dish it out** *Slang* **1.** To administer severe punishment or reproof. **2.** To talk glibly. [OE < L *discus* disk] **— dish′like′** *adj.*

dis·ha·bille (dis′ə·bēl′) *n.* **1.** A state of being partially or negligently dressed. **2.** The garments worn in this state. Also *deshabille.* [< F < *des-* away + *habiller* to dress]

dis·har·mo·ny (dis·här′mə·nē) *n. pl.* **·nies** Lack of har-mony or agreement; discord. **— dis′har·mo′ni·ous** *adj.* **— dis′har·mo′ni·ous·ly** *adv.*

dish·cloth (dish′klôth′, -kloth′) *n.* A cloth used in washing dishes: also called *dishrag.*

dis·heart·en (dis·här′tən) *v.t.* To discourage. **— dis·heart′·en·ing·ly** *adv.* **— dis·heart′en·ment** *n.*

di·shev·el (di·shev′əl) *v.t.* **di·shev·eled** or **·elled, di·shev·el·ing** or **·el·ling** **1.** To muss up, disarrange, or rumple (the hair or clothing). **2.** To disorder the hair or clothing of. [< MF < *des-* away + *chevel* hair] **— di·shev′el·ment** *n.*

di·shev·eled (di·shev′əld) *adj.* **1.** Tousled or rumpled. **2.** Untidy; unkempt. Also **di·shev′elled.**

dish·ful (dish′fo͝ol′) *n.* As much as a dish holds.

dis·hon·est (dis·on′ist) *adj.* **1.** Not honest; not trust-worthy. **2.** Marked by a lack of honesty. [< OF < LL *dis-* away + *honestus* honest] **— dis·hon′est·ly** *adv.*

dis·hon·es·ty (dis·on′is·tē) *n. pl.* **·ties** **1.** Lack of honesty or integrity. **2.** A dishonest act or statement.

dis·hon·or (dis·on′ər) *v.t.* **1.** To deprive of honor; disgrace; insult. **2.** To decline or fail to pay, as a note. **—** *n.* **1.** Lack or loss of honor or of honorable character. **2.** An insult, in-dignity, taint, etc. **3.** Refusal or failure to pay a note, etc., when due. Also *Brit.* **dis·hon′our.** **— dis·hon′or·er** *n.*

dis·hon·or·a·ble (dis·on′ər·ə·bəl) *adj.* **1.** Characterized by or bringing dishonor; discreditable: a *dishonorable* act. **2.** Lacking honor or honorableness: a *dishonorable* lawyer. **— dis·hon′or·a·ble·ness** *n.* **— dis·hon′or·a·bly** *adv.*

dish·rag (dish′rag′) *n.* A dishcloth.

dis·il·lu·sion (dis′i·lo͞o′zhən) *v.t.* To free from illusion; dis-enchant. **—** *n.* The state or process of being disillusioned; also **dis′il·lu′sion·ment.**

dis·in·cli·na·tion (dis·in′klə·nā′shən) *n.* Distaste; aver-sion; unwillingness.

dis·in·cline (dis′in·klīn′) *v.t. & v.i.* **·clined, ·clin·ing** To make or be unwilling or averse.

dis·in·fect (dis′in·fekt′) *v.t.* To cleanse of disease germs; sterilize. **— dis′in·fec′tion** *n.* **— dis′in·fec′tor** *n.*

dis·in·fec·tant (dis′in·fek′tənt) *n.* A substance or agent used to disinfect. **—** *adj.* Capable of disinfecting.

dis·in·gen·u·ous (dis′in·jen′yo͞o·əs) *adj.* Lacking simpli-city, frankness, or sincerity; not straightforward; crafty. **— dis′in·gen′u·ous·ly** *adv.* **— dis′in·gen′u·ous·ness** *n.*

dis·in·her·it (dis′in·her′it) *v.t.* To deprive of an inheritance. **— dis′in·her′i·tance** *n.*

dis·in·te·grate (dis·in′tə·grāt) *v.* **·grat·ed, ·grat·ing** *v.t.* **1.** To break or reduce into component parts or particles; de-stroy the wholeness of. **—** *v.i.* **2.** To become reduced to fragments or particles; crumble. **— dis·in′te·gra·ble** (-grə·bəl) *adj.* **— dis·in′te·gra′tion** *n.* **— dis·in′te·gra′tor** *n.*

dis·in·ter (dis′in·tûr′) *v.t.* **·terred, ·ter·ring** **1.** To dig up, as from a grave; exhume. **2.** To bring to light or life as if from a grave. **— dis′in·ter′ment** *n.*

dis·in·ter·est (dis·in′tər·ist, -trist) *n.* **1.** Freedom from self-seeking and personal bias; impartiality. **2.** Loosely, lack of interest; indifference. **— dis·in′ter·est·ed** *adj.* **— dis·in′ter·est·ed·ly** *adv.* **— dis·in′ter·est·ed·ness** *n.*

dis·join (dis·join′) *v.t.* **1.** To undo or prevent the joining of; separate. **—** *v.i.* **2.** To become divided or separated.

dis·joint (dis·joint′) *v.t.* **1.** To take apart at the joints; dis-member. **2.** To put out of joint; dislocate. **3.** To separate forcibly; disunite. **4.** To upset or destroy the coherence, connection, or sequence of. **—** *v.i.* **5.** To come apart at the joints; fall apart. **6.** To get out of joint. **— dis·joint′ed** *adj.* **— dis·joint′ed·ly** *adv.* **— dis·joint′ed·ness** *n.*

dis·junct (dis·jungkt′) *adj.* Not connected; detached. [< L < *dis-* not + *jungere* to join] **— dis·junc′tion** *n.*

dis·junc·tive (dis·jungk′tiv) *adj.* **1.** Serving to disconnect or separate; dividing. **2.** *Gram.* Indicating alternation or opposition, as *either* or *or* in *either you or I.* **3.** *Logic* Involving choice between two or more predicates in a proposition. — *n.* **1.** *Gram.* A disjunctive conjunction. **2.** *Logic* A disjunctive proposition. — **dis·junc′tive·ly** *adv.*

disk (disk) *n.* **1.** A fairly flat, circular plate. **2.** *Biol.* A disc. **3.** A phonograph record. **4.** A discus. — *v.t. & v.i.* To break up or plow (land) with a disk harrow. Also, *esp. Brit.*, *disc.* [< L *discus* < Gk. *diskos* disk, platter]

disk harrow A harrow consisting of a series of rolling saucer-shaped disks set on edge and at an angle along one or more axles, used for pulverizing the soil, covering seeds, etc.

DISK HARROW

disk jockey *U.S. Informal* An announcer and commentator on a radio program presenting recorded music.

dis·like (dis·līk′) *v.t.* **·liked, ·lik·ing** To regard with aversion; feel repugnance for; consider disagreeable. — *n.* A feeling of repugnance or distaste. — **dis·lik′a·ble** *adj.*

dis·lo·cate (dis′lō·kāt, dis·lō′kāt) *v.t.* **·cat·ed, ·cat·ing** **1.** To put out of proper place or order. **2.** *Med.* To displace an organ or part, esp. a bone from a joint. — **dis′lo·ca′tion** *n.*

dis·lodge (dis·loj′) *v.* **·lodged, ·lodg·ing** *v.t.* **1.** To remove or drive out, as from an abode, hiding place, or firm position. — *v.i.* **2.** To leave a place of abode; move. — **dis·lodg′·ment,** or **dis·lodge′ment** *n.*

dis·loy·al (dis·loi′əl) *adj.* Not loyal; false to one's allegiance or obligations; faithless. — **dis·loy′al·ly** *adv.*

dis·loy·al·ty (dis·loi′əl·tē) *n. pl.* **·ties** **1.** The quality of being disloyal; unfaithfulness. **2.** A disloyal action.

dis·mal (diz′məl) *adj.* **1.** Cheerless and depressing; dark and gloomy: a *dismal* day. **2.** Devoid of joy; bleak: to feel *dismal.* [ult. < L *dies mali* evil or unpropitious days] — **dis′mal·ly** *adv.* — **dis′mal·ness** *n.*

dis·man·tle (dis·man′təl) *v.t.* **·tled, ·tling** **1.** To strip of furniture or equipment. **2.** To raze. **3.** To take apart. [< MF < *des-* away + *manteller* to cover with a cloak] — **dis·man′tle·ment** *n.*

dis·may (dis·mā′) *v.t.* To fill with consernation or apprehension; dishearten and depress. — *n.* An onrush of consternation or downheartedness. [ME *dismayen*]

dis·mem·ber (dis·mem′bər) *v.t.* **1.** To cut off or pull off the limbs or members of; tear asunder. **2.** To divide forcibly into pieces; mangle. [< OF < L *dis-* apart + *membrum* limb, member] — **dis·mem′ber·ment** *n.*

dis·miss (dis·mis′) *v.t.* **1.** To discharge, as from a job. **2.** To tell or allow to go or disperse. **3.** To get rid of: to *dismiss* all fear. **4.** To have done with quickly: He *dismissed* the matter in a few words. **5.** *Law* To put out of court without further hearing. [< LL < L *dimissus*, pp. of *dimittere* to send away] — **dis·miss′al** *n.* — **dis·miss′i·ble** *adj.*

dis·mount (dis·mount′) *v.i.* **1.** To get off, as from a horse; alight. — *v.t.* **2.** To remove from a setting, support, etc. **3.** To disassemble. **4.** To knock off or throw down, as from a horse; unseat. — **dis·mount′a·ble** *adj.*

dis·o·be·di·ence (dis′ə·bē′dē·əns) *n.* Refusal or failure to obey; lack of obedience; insubordination. — **dis′o·be′di·ent** *adj.* — **dis′o·be′di·ent·ly** *adv.*

dis·o·bey (dis′ə·bā′) *v.t. & v.i.* To refuse or fail to obey. — **dis′o·bey′er** *n.*

dis·o·blige (dis′ə·blīj′) *v.t.* **·bliged, ·blig·ing** **1.** To act contrary to the wishes of. **2.** To slight; affront. — **dis′o·blig′·ing** *adj.* — **dis′o·blig′ing·ly** *adv.*

dis·or·der (dis·ôr′dər) *n.* **1.** Lack of good order; disarrangement or confusion. **2.** Disturbance of proper civic order; tumult; riot. **3.** A sickness; ailment. **4.** An act, occurrence, or condition marked by disorder. — *v.t.* **1.** To put out of order; throw into disorder; disarrange. **2.** To disturb or upset the normal health or functions of. — **dis·or′dered** *adj.*

dis·or·der·ly (dis·ôr′dər·lē) *adj.* **1.** Devoid of good order or arrangement; full of disorder. **2.** Devoid of method; unsystematic. **3.** Undisciplined and unruly; tumultuous: a *disorderly* mob. **4.** Violating public order or decency. — *adv.* In a disorderly manner. — **dis·or′der·li·ness** *n.*

dis·or·gan·ize (dis·ôr′gən·īz) *v.t.* **·ized, ·iz·ing** **1.** To destroy the organization of; break up the systematic arrangement or unity of. **2.** To throw into confusion; disorder. — **dis·or′·gan·i·za′tion** *n.* — **dis·or′gan·i′zer** *n.*

dis·o·ri·ent (dis·ôr′ē·ent′, -ō′rē-) *v.t.* To mix up; confuse; esp., to cause to lose one's sense of direction, perspective, or time. — **dis·o′ri·en·ta′tion** *n.*

dis·own (dis·ōn′) *v.t.* To refuse to acknowledge or to admit responsibility for or connection with; deny; repudiate.

dis·par·age (dis·par′ij) *v.t.* **·aged, ·ag·ing** **1.** To treat or speak of with disrespect or contempt; belittle. **2.** To bring discredit upon; cause to have less esteem. [< OF < *des-* down, away + *parage* equality of rank] — **dis·par′age·ment** *n.* — **dis·par′ag·er** *n.* — **dis·par′ag·ing·ly** *adv.*

dis·pa·rate (dis′pər·it) *adj.* Essentially different; altogether dissimilar. [< L < *dis-* apart + *parare* to make ready] — **dis′pa·rate·ly** *adv.* — **dis′pa·rate·ness** *n.*

dis·par·i·ty (dis·par′ə·tē) *n. pl.* **·ties** **1.** Lack of equality in age or rank. **2.** Dissimilarity. **3.** An instance of ineq ity. [< MF < L *dis-* apart + *paritas* equality]

dis·pas·sion (dis·pash′ən) *n.* Freedom from passion or b

dis·pas·sion·ate (dis·pash′ən·it) *adj.* Free from passior bias. — **dis·pas′sion·ate·ly** *adv.* — **dis·pas′sion·ate·nes**

dis·patch (dis·pach′) *v.t.* **1.** To send off, as a messen telegram, or vehicle, to a particular destination. **2.** To pose of quickly, as a business matter. **3.** To kill summa — *n.* **1.** The act of dispatching. **2.** Efficient quickn promptness: to finish a job with *dispatch.* **3.** A mess usu. in writing, sent with speed; esp., an official commun tion, as a military report. **4.** A news story sent to a ne paper. [< Ital. *dispacciare* or Sp. *despachar*]

dis·patch·er (dis·pach′ər) *n.* **1.** One who dispatches. One who sends out trains, buses, etc., on schedule.

dis·pel (dis·pel′) *v.t.* **·pelled, ·pel·ling** To drive away b as by scattering; disperse: to *dispel* fear, rumors, etc. [< *dis-* away, apart + *pellere* to drive]

dis·pen·sa·ble (dis·pen′sə·bəl) *adj.* **1.** That can be re quished or dispensed with. **2.** That can be removed dispensation. — **dis·pen′sa·bil′i·ty, dis·pen′sa·ble·ness**

dis·pen·sa·ry (dis·pen′sər·ē) *n. pl.* **·ries** A place w medicines and medical advice are given out.

dis·pen·sa·tion (dis′pən·sā′shən) *n.* **1.** The act of disp ing; a dealing out; distribution. **2.** That which is dispe or distributed. **3.** A specific plan, order, or system of pensing or administering. **4.** A special exemption f something, as from a law or obligation; esp., an exemp by ecclesiastical authority from an obligation or f church law. **5.** *Theol.* **a** The arrangement or orderin events, as by a divine Providence. **b** A religious or m system: the Mosaic *dispensation.* — **dis′pen·sa′tion·al**

dis·pen·sa·to·ry (dis·pen′sə·tôr′ē, -tō′rē) *adj.* Of or taining to dispensation. — *n. pl.* **·ries** A book in w medicinal substances are described; a pharmacopoeia.

dis·pense (dis·pens′) *v.* **·pensed, ·pens·ing** *v.t.* **1.** To or deal out in portions: to *dispense* patronage. **2.** To c pound and give out (medicines). **3.** To administer, as l **4.** To excuse or exempt, as from an obligation, esp., a ligious obligation. — *v.i.* **5.** To grant dispensation. — **dispense with** **1.** To get along without. **2.** To dispos [< OF < L < *dis-* away + *pendere* to weigh]

dis·pens·er (dis·pen′sər) *n.* One who or that which penses, manages, or administers: a soap *dispenser.*

dis·perse (dis·pûrs′) *v.* **·persed, ·pers·ing** *v.t.* **1.** To c to scatter in various directions. **2.** To drive away; dis The sun *dispersed* the mists. **3.** To spread abroad; diff **4.** To separate (light) into a spectrum. — *v.i.* **5.** To sca in various directions. [< MF < L < *dis-* away + *spar* to scatter] — **dis·per′sal** *n.* — **dis·pers′ed·ly** *adv.* — **dis·pers′er** *n.* — **dis·pers′i·ble** *adj.*

dis·per·sion (dis·pûr′zhən, -shən) *n.* **1.** The act of disp ing, or the state of being dispersed. **2.** *Mil.* The patter hits made, as by bombs. **3.** *Physics* The separation of w or complex light into different colors by passing it throu prism. **4.** *Stat.* The arrangement of a series of values aro the median or mean of a distribution.

dis·per·sive (dis·pûr′siv) *adj.* Tending to disperse.

dis·pir·it (dis·pir′it) *v.t.* To make downhearted or depres — **dis·pir′it·ed** *adj.* — **dis·pir′it·ed·ly** *adv.*

dis·place (dis·plās′) *v.t.* **·placed, ·plac·ing** **1.** To remov shift from the usual or proper place. **2.** To take the place supplant. **3.** To remove from a position or office; discha [< OF < *des-* away (< L *dis-*) + *placer* to place]

displaced person A person made homeless by war forced to live in a foreign country.

dis·place·ment (dis·plās′mənt) *n.* **1.** The act of displac or the state of being displaced. **2.** *Astron.* An appa change of position, as of a star. **3.** *Physics* The weight fluid displaced by a floating body, being equal to the wei of the body.

dis·play (dis·plā′) *v.t.* **1.** To make evident or noticeable veal: to *display* ignorance. **2.** To expose to the sight; ex it. **3.** To make a prominent or ostentatious show of. *Printing* To make (printed matter) stand out prominen as by the use of large type or wide spacing. — *n.* **1.** act of displaying; exhibition. **2.** That which is display **3.** Ostentatious show. **4.** *Printing* A style or arrangem of type designed to make printed matter stand out pron ently. [< OF < LL < *dis-* apart + *plicare* to fold, ad

dis·please (dis·plēz′) *v.* **·pleased, ·pleas·ing** *v.t.* **1.** cause displeasure in or annoyance to; vex; offend. — **2.** To cause displeasure or annoyance. [< OF, ult. < *dis-* not + *placere* to please] — **dis′pleas′ing·ly** *adv.*

dis·pleas·ure (dis·plezh′ər) *n.* The state of being displeas

dis·port (dis·pôrt′, -pōrt′) *v.t.* **1.** To divert or amuse (c self). — *v.i.* **2.** To frisk about playfully. — *n.* Diversi sport. [< OF < L *dis-* away + *portare* to carry]

·pos·a·ble (dis·pō′zə·bəl) *adj.* **1.** Capable of being dis- sed of; esp., designed to be discarded after use. **2.** Free to used as occasion may require: *disposable* funds.

po·sal (dis·pō′zəl) *n.* **1.** A particular ordering or ar- ıgement; disposition. **2.** A particular way of attending or settling something, as business affairs. **3.** Transfer, as gift or sale. **4.** A getting rid of something. **5.** Liberty to al with or dispose of in any way.

·pose (dis·pōz′) *v.* **·posed, ·pos·ing** *v.t.* **1.** To put into a ·eptive frame of mind for. **2.** To condition toward some- ng; esp., to make susceptible. **3.** To put or set in a par- ·ular arrangement or position. **4.** To put into proper, finitive, or final shape; settle. — *v.i.* **5.** To control the ırse of events. — **to dispose of 1.** To attend to; deal th. **2.** To finish up with; settle. **3.** To transfer to an- ·er, as by gift or sale. **4.** To throw away. [< OF < *dis-* art + *poser* to place] — **dis·pos′er** *n.*

posed (dis·pōzd′) *adj.* Having a particular inclination, me of mind, or mood: *disposed* to take offense.

po·si·tion (dis′pə·zish′ən) *n.* **1.** One's usual frame of nd; temperament. **2.** Acquired tendency or inclination, ·. when habitual: a *disposition* to drink. **3.** Natural or- ıic tendency or inclination. **4.** A particular ordering, ar- ·gement, or distribution, as of troops. **5.** Management, of business affairs. **6.** Transfer, as by gift or sale. **7.** A ting rid of something, as by throwing away. **8.** Liberty deal with or dispose of in any way.

pos·sess (dis′pə·zes′) *v.t.* To deprive of possession of nething, as a house or land; oust. — **dis′pos·ses′sion** esh′ən) *n.* — **dis′pos·ses′sor** *n.*

praise (dis·prāz′) *v.t.* **·praised, ·prais·ing** To express approval of; disparage. — *n.* Disparagement; censure. **dis·prais′er** *n.* — **dis·prais′ing·ly** *adv.*

proof (dis·pro͞of′) *n.* **1.** The act of disproving. **2.** nething that disproves, as evidence.

pro·por·tion (dis′prə·pôr′shən, -pōr′-) *n.* **1.** Lack of ›portion or symmetry; disparity. **2.** An instance of this. *v.t.* To make disproportionate. — **dis′pro·por′tion·al** ·. — **dis′pro·por′tion·al·ly** *adv.*

pro·por·tion·ate (dis′prə·pôr′shən·it, -pōr′-) *adj.* Out proportion, as in size, form, or value. — **dis′pro·por′tion· ·ly** *adv.* — **dis′pro·por′tion·ate·ness** *n.*

prove (dis·pro͞ov′) *v.t.* **·proved, ·proved** or **·prov·en, ·ov·ing** To prove to be false, invalid, or erroneous. — **Syn.** ᵉ REFUTE. [< OF < *des-* not + *prouver* to prove] — **dis· ›v′a·ble** *adj.* — **dis·prov′al** *n.*

put·a·ble (dis·pyo͞o′tə·bəl, dis′pyo͝o·tə·bəl) *adj.* Open being disputed or called into question; arguable; debat- le. — **dis·put′a·bil′i·ty** *n.* — **dis·put′a·bly** *adv.*

pu·tant (dis′pyo͝o·tənt, dis·pyo͞o′tənt) *adj.* Engaged in ıtroversy; disputing. — *n.* One who disputes; a debater.

pu·ta·tion (dis′pyo͝o·tā′shən) *n.* **1.** The act of disput- ; argumentation; controversy. **2.** A formal debate; esp., mal argumentation in philosophy or theology.

pu·ta·tious (dis′pyo͝o·tā′shəs) *adj.* Given to disputing; umentative. Also **dis·pu·ta·tive** (dis·pyo͞o′ta·tiv). — **′pu·ta′tious·ly** *adv.* — **dis′pu·ta′tious·ness** *n.*

pute (dis·pyo͞ot′) *v.* **·put·ed, ·put·ing** *v.t.* **1.** To argue ›ut. **2.** To question the validity, genuineness, etc., of. To strive or contest for, as a prize. **4.** To resist; oppose. *v.i.* **5.** To argue. **6.** To quarrel. — *n.* **1.** A discussion; ›ate. **2.** A quarrel. [< OF < L < *dis-* away + *putare* think] — **dis·put′er** *n.*

qual·i·fy (dis·kwol′ə·fī) *v.t.* **·fied, ·fy·ing** **1.** To make qualified or unfit; incapacitate. **2.** To pronounce unqual- d or ineligible. **3.** In sports, to bar from competition be- ıse of rule infractions, etc. — **dis·qual′i·fi·ca′tion** *n.*

qui·et (dis·kwī′ət) *n.* An unsettled or disturbed condi- n. — *v.t.* To make anxious or uneasy. — **dis·qui′et·ly** *adv.*

qui·e·tude (dis·kwī′ə·to͞od, -tyo͞od) *n.* Uneasiness.

qui·si·tion (dis′kwi·zish′ən) *n.* A formal treatise or dis- ırse. [< L < *dis-* thoroughly + *quaerere* to seek]

re·gard (dis′ri·gärd′) *v.t.* **1.** To pay no attention to; ig- re. **2.** To treat as undeserving of consideration. — *n.* ck of notice or due regard, esp. when deliberate. — **dis′· gard′er** *n.* — **dis′re·gard′ful** *adj.*

re·pair (dis′ri·pâr′) *n.* The state of being out of repair.

rep·u·ta·ble (dis·rep′yə·tə·bəl) *adj.* **1.** Not in good re- te; not esteemed. **2.** Not respectable: a *disreputable* tav- ı. — **dis·rep′u·ta·ble·ness** *n.* — **dis·rep′u·ta·bly** *adv.*

re·spect (dis′ri·spekt′) *n.* Lack of courtesy or respect. *v.t.* To treat without respect. — **dis′re·spect′ful** *adj.* — **′re·spect′ful·ly** *adv.* — **dis′re·spect′ful·ness** *n.*

robe (dis·rōb′) *v.t.* & *v.i.* **·robed, ·rob·ing** To undress.

rupt (dis·rupt′) *v.t.* **1.** To throw into disorder; upset. To halt or impede the movement of, procedure of, etc. **3.** › break or burst apart. — *v.i.* **4.** To break; burst. [< L *dis-* apart + *rumpere* to burst] — **dis·rupt′er** or **dis·rup′·tor** *n.* — **dis·rup′tion** *n.* — **dis·rup′tive** *adj.* — **dis·rup′·tive·ly** *adv.*

dis·sat·is·fac·tion (dis′sat·is·fak′shən) *n.* **1.** A dissatisfied state or feeling; discontent. **2.** That which dissatisfies.

dis·sat·is·fac·to·ry (dis′sat·is·fak′tər·ē) *adj.* Causing dissatisfaction; unsatisfactory.

dis·sat·is·fy (dis·sat′is·fī) *v.t.* **·fied, ·fy·ing** To fail to satisfy; disappoint; displease. — **dis·sat′is·fied** *adj.*

dis·sect (di·sekt′, dī-) *v.t.* **1.** To cut apart or divide, as an animal body or a plant, in order to examine the structure; anatomize. **2.** To analyze in detail. [< L < *dis-* apart + *secare* to cut] — **dis·sec′tion** *n.* — **dis·sec′tor** *n.*

dis·sect·ed (di·sek′tid, dī-) *adj.* **1.** Cut in pieces; separated at the joints. **2.** *Geol.* Cut into ridges, as a plateau. **3.** *Bot.* Deeply cut into lobes or segments, as a leaf.

dis·sem·blance (di·sem′bləns) *n.* **1.** The act of dissembling; dissimulation. **2.** Lack of resemblance; dissimilarity.

dis·sem·ble (di·sem′bəl) *v.* **·bled, ·bling** *v.t.* **1.** To conceal or disguise the actual nature of (intentions, feelings, etc.). **2.** To make a false show of; feign. — *v.i.* **3.** To conceal one's true nature, intentions, etc.; act hypocritically. [Var. of earlier *dissimule* < OF < L < *dis-* not, away + *similis* alike] — **dis·sem′bler** *n.* — **dis·sem′bling·ly** *adv.*

dis·sem·i·nate (di·sem′ə·nāt) *v.t.* **·nat·ed, ·nat·ing** To scatter, as if sowing: to *disseminate* knowledge. [< L < *dis-* away + *seminare* to sow] — **dis·sem′i·na′tion** *n.* — **dis·sem′i·na′tive** *adj.* — **dis·sem′i·na′tor** *n.*

dis·sen·sion (di·sen′shən) *n.* **1.** Difference of opinion, esp. arising from dissatisfaction or anger; discord; strife. **2.** A heated quarrel or disagreement.

dis·sent (di·sent′) *v.i.* **1.** To differ in thought or opinion: with *from.* **2.** To withhold approval or consent. **3.** To refuse adherence to an established church. — *n.* **1.** Difference of opinion. **2.** Refusal to conform to an established church. [< L < *dis-* apart + *sentire* to think, feel]

dis·sent·er (di·sen′tər) *n.* One who dissents or disagrees.

dis·sen·tient (di·sen′shənt) *adj.* Dissenting. — *n.* A dissenter. — **dis·sen′tience** *n.*

dis·sent·ing (di·sen′ting) *adj.* Expressing disagreement: a *dissenting* opinion. — **dis·sent′ing·ly** *adv.*

dis·sen·tious (di·sen′shəs) *adj.* Quarrelsome; disputatious.

dis·ser·ta·tion (dis′ər·tā′shən) *n.* An extended formal treatise or discourse; esp., a written treatise required of a doctoral candidate. [< L < *dis-* apart + *serere* to join]

dis·serve (dis·sûrv′) *v.t.* **·served, ·serv·ing** To serve poorly or treat badly; do an ill turn to.

dis·ser·vice (dis·sûr′vis) *n.* Ill service; an ill turn; injury.

dis·sev·er (di·sev′ər) *v.t.* **1.** To divide; separate. **2.** To separate into parts. — *v.i.* **3.** To become separated. — **dis·sev′er·ance, dis·sev′er·ment** *n.*

dis·si·dent (dis′ə·dənt) *adj.* Dissenting; differing. — *n.* A dissenter. [< L < *dis-* apart + *sedere* to sit] — **dis′si·dence** *n.*

dis·sim·i·lar (di·sim′ə·lər) *adj.* Not similar; unlike; different: sometimes with *to.* — **dis·sim′i·lar·ly** *adv.*

dis·sim·i·lar·i·ty (di·sim′ə·lar′ə·tē) *n.* *pl.* **·ties** **1.** Lack of similarity; unlikeness; difference. **2.** An example of this.

dis·sim·i·late (di·sim′ə·lāt) *v.t.* & *v.i.* **·lat·ed, ·lat·ing** **1.** To make or become unlike. **2.** *Phonet.* To undergo or cause to undergo dissimilation. [< DIS-[1] + L *similis* alike]

dis·sim·i·la·tion (di·sim′ə·lā′shən) *n.* **1.** The act or process of making or becoming dissimilar. **2.** *Phonet.* The process whereby one of two or more similar sounds in a word is omitted, as in the pronunciation (lī′ber′ē) for *library,* or replaced by another sound, as *turtle* from Latin *turtur.*

dis·si·mil·i·tude (dis′si·mil′ə·to͞od, tyo͞od) *n.* **1.** Lack of resemblance; unlikeness. **2.** An instance of this.

dis·sim·u·late (di·sim′yə·lāt) *v.t.* & *v.i.* **·lat·ed, ·lat·ing** To conceal (intentions, feelings, etc.) by pretense. — **dis·sim′u·la′tion** *n.* — **dis·sim′u·la′tive** *adj.* — **dis·sim′u·la′tor** *n.*

dis·si·pate (dis′ə·pāt) *v.* **·pat·ed, ·pat·ing** *v.t.* **1.** To disperse or drive away; dispel. **2.** To squander. — *v.i.* **3.** To become dispersed. **4.** To engage in excessive or dissolute pleasures. [< L < *dis-* away + *supare* to scatter] — **dis′si·pat′er** or **dis′si·pa′tor** *n.* — **dis′si·pa′tive** *adj.*

dis·si·pat·ed (dis′ə·pā′tid) *adj.* **1.** Wasted; scattered. **2.** Pursuing pleasure to excess; dissolute. — **dis′si·pat′ed·ly** *adv.* — **dis′si·pat′ed·ness** *n.*

dis·si·pa·tion (dis′ə·pā′shən) *n.* **1.** The act of dissipating, or the state of being dissipated; dispersion; scattering. **2.** Excessive indulgence, esp. in dissolute pleasures. **3.** Distraction or diversion, as of the mind.

dis·so·ci·ate (di·sō′shē·āt, -sē-) *v.* **·at·ed, ·at·ing** *v.t.* **1.** To break the association of; disconnect; separate. **2.** To regard as separate in concept or nature. **3.** To subject to dissociation. — *v.i.* **4.** To break an association. **5.** To undergo dissociation. Also *disassociate.* [< L < *dis-* apart + *sociare* to join together] — **dis·so′ci·a′tive** *adj.*

dis·so·ci·a·tion (di·sō′sē·ā′shən, -shē·ā′-) *n.* **1.** The act of dissociating, or the state of being dissociated. **2.** *Chem.* **a** The resolution of a compound into simpler constituents by a change in physical state, as by heat or pressure.

dis·sol·u·ble (di·sol′yə·bəl) *adj.* Capable of being dissolved or decomposed. **— dis′sol·u·bil′i·ty, dis·sol′u·ble·ness** *n.*

dis·so·lute (dis′ə·lōōt) *adj.* Not governed by moral restraints. **— dis′so·lute·ly** *adv.* **— dis′so·lute·ness** *n.*

dis·so·lu·tion (dis′ə·lōō′shən) *n.* **1.** Separation into parts; disintegration. **2.** Change from a solid to a fluid form; liquefaction. **3.** The breaking up or liquidation of a formal or legal union, bond, or tie. **4.** Dismissal of a meeting or assembly. **5.** Termination or destruction. **6.** Separation of soul and body; death. **— dis′so·lu′tive** *adj.*

dis·solve (di·zolv′) *v.* **·solved, ·solv·ing** *v.t.* **1.** To cause to pass into solution. **2.** To overcome, as by emotion. **3.** To disintegrate. **4.** To put an end to: to *dissolve* a partnership. **5.** To dismiss (a meeting or assembly). **—** *v.i.* **6.** To pass into solution. **7.** To be overcome: to *dissolve* in tears. **8.** To come to an end; break up. **9.** To dwindle or fade away. **10.** In motion pictures and television, to change gradually from one scene to another by overlapping two shots. **—** *n.* A lap dissolve. [< L < *dis-* apart + *solvere* to loosen] **— dis·solv′a·ble** *adj.* **— dis·solv′er** *n.*

dis·so·nance (dis′ə·nəns) *n.* **1.** A discordant mingling of sounds; discord. **2.** Harsh disagreement; incongruity. **3.** *Music* A simultaneous combination of tones that seem to clash and require resolution. Also **dis′so·nan·cy.**

dis·so·nant (dis′ə·nənt) *adj.* **1.** Harsh in sound; inharmonious. **2.** Naturally hostile; incongruous. **3.** *Music* Consisting of or containing a dissonance. [< L < *dis-* away + *sonare* to sound] **— dis′so·nant·ly** *adv.*

dis·suade (di·swād′) *v.t.* **·suad·ed, ·suad·ing** To alter the plans or intentions of (someone) by persuasion or advice: with *from.* [< L < *dis-* away + *suadere* to persuade] **— dis·suad′er** *n.* **— dis·sua′sion** *n.* **— dis·sua′sive** *adj.*

dis·syl·la·ble (di·sil′ə·bəl, dis′sil′ə·bəl) *n.* A word of two syllables: also spelled *disyllable.* [< F < L < Gk. < *di-* two + *syllabē* syllable] **— dis′syl·lab′ic** *adj.*

dis·taff (dis′taf, -täf) *n. pl.* **·taffs** or *Rare* **·taves** (-tāvz) **1.** A rotating vertical staff that holds a bunch of flax or wool for spinning by hand. **2.** Women in general. **3.** Woman's work or domain. [OE < *dis* bundle of flax + *stæf* staff]

distaff side The maternal branch or female line of a family.

dis·tal (dis′təl) *adj. Anat.* Relatively remote from the center of the body or point of attachment. **— dis′tal·ly** *adv.*

dis·tance (dis′təns) *n.* **1.** The extent of spatial separation between things, places, or locations. **2.** The extent of separation between points of time; interval. **3.** The state or fact of being separated from something else, esp. to a notable extent, in space, time, or condition. **4.** A gap, as in relationship or rank, between persons or things. **5.** Remoteness; esp., reserve or aloofness: to keep one's *distance.* **6.** A point or location removed from another, esp. to a notable extent. **7.** *Music* The interval between two tones. **—** *v.t.* **·tanced, ·tanc·ing 1.** To leave behind; outdo. **2.** To cause to appear distant. **3.** To hold off or place at some distance.

dis·tant (dis′tənt) *adj.* **1.** Separated or apart by a specified amount of space or time; away: often with *from.* **2.** Remote in time or space. **3.** At, from, or to a distance: a *distant* journey. **4.** Not closely related; remote, as to similarity, kinship, etc. **5.** Reserved or unapproachable. [< F < L < *dis-* apart + *stare* to stand] **— dis′tant·ly** *adv.*

dis·taste (dis·tāst′) *n.* Dislike; aversion: a *distaste* for work.

dis·taste·ful (dis·tāst′fəl) *adj.* Causing dislike; offensive; disagreeable. **— dis·taste′ful·ly** *adv.* **— dis·taste′ful·ness** *n.*

dis·tem·per[1] (dis·tem′pər) *n.* **1.** *Vet.* Any of several infectious diseases of animals; esp., a catarrhal disease of puppies. **2.** A disorder of the mind or body; illness. **3.** Political or civil disturbance. **—** *v.t.* **1.** To derange the faculties or functions of. **2.** To ruffle; disturb. [< Med.L < L *dis-* away + *temperare* to regulate, mix]

dis·tem·per[2] (dis·tem′pər) *n.* **1.** Tempera. **2.** A painting medium in which size is the only agent used to bind the pigments. **3.** The art or method of using this medium. **4.** A painting done in distemper. **5.** *Brit.* Calcimine. **—** *v.t.* **1.** To mix (colors or pigments) with a binding medium, such as casein. **2.** To paint in distemper. [< OF < Med.L < L *dis-* apart + *temperare* to mix, soak]

dis·tend (dis·tend′) *v.t. & v.i.* **1.** To expand by or as by pressure from within. **2.** To stretch out; swell. [< L < *dis-* apart + *tendere* to stretch] **— dis·ten′si·ble** *adj.* **— dis·ten′tion, dis·ten′sion** *n.*

dis·tich (dis′tik) *n.* In prosody, a couplet. [< L < Gk. < *di-* two + *stichos* a row, line]

dis·till (dis·til′) *v.* **·tilled, ·till·ing** *v.t.* **1.** To subject to distillation so as to purify or produce, concentrate, or refine. **2.** To extract by distillation. **3.** To give forth or send down in drops. **—** *v.i.* **4.** To undergo distillation. **5.** To exude in drops. Also *Brit.* **dis·til′.** [< L < *de-* down + *stillare* to drop, trickle] **— dis·till′a·ble** *adj.*

dis·til·late (dis′tə·lit, -lāt) *n.* The condensed product se rated by distillation: also called *distillation.*

dis·til·la·tion (dis′tə·lā′shən) *n.* **1.** The act or proces separating the more volatile parts of a substance from th less volatile by heating in a retort or still and then conde ing the vapor thus produced by cooling. **2.** The purifi tion or rectification of a substance by this process. **3** distillate. **4.** The essential or abstract quality of anythi Also **dis·till·ment** (dis·til′mənt), *Brit.* **dis·til′ment.**

dis·til·ler (dis·til′ər) *n.* **1.** One who distills; esp., a ma of distilled liquors. **2.** A condenser for distilling.

dis·til·ler·y (dis·til′ər·ē) *n. pl.* **·ler·ies** An establishm for distilling, esp. alcoholic liquors.

dis·tinct (dis·tingkt′) *adj.* **1.** Recognizably not the sa clearly different. **2.** Differentiated by individualizing tures. **3.** Sharp and clear to the senses or mind; defir **4.** Undeniably such: a *distinct* step forward. [< L *disting* to separate] **— dis·tinct′ly** *adv.* **— dis·tinct′ness** *n.*

dis·tinc·tion (dis·tingk′shən) *n.* **1.** The act of distingu ing; discrimination. **2.** A difference that may be dis guished: the *distinction* between thrift and avarice. **3.** state of being different or distinguishable. **4.** A charac istic difference or distinctive quality. **5.** A mark of ho **6.** A distinguishing superiority or preeminence.

dis·tinc·tive (dis·tingk′tiv) *adj.* Serving to distingu characteristic. **— dis′tinc′tive·ly** *adv.* **— dis·tinc′tive·nes**

dis·tin·gué (dis′tang·gā′, *Fr.* dēs·taṅ·gā′) *adj.* Emine well-bred and dignified. [< F] **— dis′tin·guée′** *adj.fe*

dis·tin·guish (dis·ting′gwish) *v.t.* **1.** To indicate the ferences of or between. **2.** To be an outstanding or i vidualizing characteristic of: Honesty *distinguished* career. **3.** To classify. **4.** To bring fame or credit u **5.** To perceive with the senses. **—** *v.i.* **6.** To make or cern differences; discriminate: often with *among* or *betw* [< MF < L *distinguere* to separate] **— dis·tin′guish·a** *adj.* **— dis·tin′guish·a·bly** *adv.* **— dis·tin′guish·er** *n.*

dis·tin·guished (dis·ting′gwisht) *adj.* **1.** Conspicuous qualities of excellence; celebrated; eminent; famous. Having an air of distinction; distingué.

Distinguished Flying Cross A U.S. military decora awarded for heroism or exceptional achievement in ae flight. See DECORATION.

Distinguished Service Cross A U.S. military decora awarded for heroism in combat. See DECORATION.

Distinguished Service Medal A U.S. military dec tion awarded for meritorious service in a duty of g responsibility. See DECORATION.

dis·tort (dis·tôrt′) *v.t.* **1.** To twist or bend out of sh make misshapen. **2.** To twist the meaning of; misrepres pervert. [< L < *dis-* apart + *torquere* to twist] **— tort′ed** *adj.* **— dis·tort′ed·ly** *adv.* **— dis·tort′ed·ness** **— dis·tort′er** *n.*

dis·tor·tion (dis·tôr′shən) *n.* **1.** The act of distorting. The condition of being distorted; deformity. **3.** That wh is distorted, as a misleading statement. **4.** *Telecom* change in the wave form of a signal caused by nonunif transmission at different frequencies. **— dis·tor′tion·al**

dis·tract (dis·trakt′) *v.t.* **1.** To draw or divert (the mi etc.) from something claiming attention. **2.** To bewil confuse. **3.** To make frantic; craze. [< L < *dis-* away *trahere* to draw] **— dis·tract′er** *n.* **— dis·trac′tion** *n.*

dis·tract·ed (dis·trak′tid) *adj.* **1.** Bewildered or haras **2.** Mentally deranged; mad. **— dis·tract′ed·ly** *adv.*

dis·sract·ing (dis·trak′ting) *adj.* Serving or tending to tract. Also **dis·trac′tive.** **— dis·tract′ing·ly** *adv.*

dis·train (dis·trān′) *Law v.t. & v.i.* To seize and detain (sonal property) as security for a debt, claim, etc. [< < L *distringere* to detain, hinder] **— dis·train′a·ble** **— dis·train′or** or **dis·train′er** *n.* **— dis·traint′** *n.*

dis·trait (dis·trā′, Fr. dēs·tre′) *adj.* Absent-minded. F. See DISTRACT.]

dis·traught (dis·trôt′) *adj.* **1.** Deeply agitated in mi worried, tense, and bewildered. **2.** Driven insane; cra [Var. of earlier *distract*, pp. of DISTRACT]

dis·tress (dis·tres′) *v.t.* To inflict suffering upon; ca agony or worry to; afflict; harass. **—** *n.* **1.** Acute or treme suffering or its cause; pain; trouble. **2.** A state extreme need: a ship in *distress.* **3.** *Law* **a** The act of training. **b** The goods distrained. **— Syn.** See SUFFERI [< OF < LL < L *distringere* to detain, hinder] **— tress′ful** *adj.* **— dis·tress′ful·ly** *adv.* **— dis·tress′ful·n** *n.* **— dis·tress′ing** *adj.* **— dis·tress′ing·ly** *adv.*

dis·trib·u·tar·y (dis′trib′yōō·ter′ē) *n. pl.* **·tar·ies** A ri branch flowing away from the main branch.

dis·trib·ute (dis·trib′yōōt) *v.t.* **·ut·ed, ·ut·ing 1.** To div and deal out in shares; apportion; allot. **2.** To divide classify; arrange. **3.** To scatter or spread out, as ove surface. [< L < *dis-* away, apart + *tribuere* to give, al **— dis·trib′ut·a·ble** *adj.*

dis·tri·bu·tion (dis′trə·byōō′shən) *n.* **1.** The act of distr uting or the state of being distributed. **2.** The manne

hich something is distributed: random *distribution.* **3.** hat which is distributed. **4.** In commerce, the system of stributing goods among consumers. **5.** *Stat.* Frequency: mbolized by *t.* — **dis'tri·bu'tion·al** *adj.*
·trib·u·tive (dis·trib'yə·tiv) *adj.* **1.** Pertaining to or used by distribution. **2.** Serving or tending to distribute. *Gram.* Singling out the separate individuals of a group: *ach* and *every* are *distributive* adjectives. — *n. Gram.* A stributive word or expression. — **dis·trib'u·tive·ly** *adv.* **dis·trib'u·tive·ness** *n.*
·trib·u·tor (dis·trib'yə·tər, -tôr) *n.* **1.** One who or that hich distributes or sells merchandise. **2.** In a gasoline gine, a device that directs the electrical current to the ark plugs. Also **dis·trib'ut·er** (-yə·tər).
·trict (dis'trikt) *n.* A particular region or locality; esp., area, as within a city or state, set off for administrative judicial purposes. — *v.t.* To divide into districts. [< F < Med.L *districtus* jurisdiction]
trict attorney The prosecuting officer of a Federal or ate judicial district.
·trust (dis·trust') *v.t.* To doubt; suspect. — *n.* Doubt; spicion. — **dis·trust'ful** *adj.* — **dis·trust'ful·ly** *adv.*
·turb (dis·tûrb') *v.t.* **1.** To destroy the repose, tranillity, or peace of. **2.** To agitate the mind of; trouble. To upset the order, system, or progression of. **4.** To terrupt; break in on. **5.** To inconvenience. [< OF < L *dis-* completely + *turbare* to disorder] — **dis·turb'er** *n.*
·tur·bance (dis·tûr'bəns) *n.* **1.** The act of disturbing, or e state of being disturbed. **2.** Something that disturbs. **3.** tumult or commotion; especially, a public disorder.
·turbed (dis·tûrbd') *adj.* **1.** Characterized by disturnce. **2.** Troubled emotionally or mentally; neurotic.
sul·fate (dī·sul'fāt) *n. Chem.* A bisulfate. Also **di·sul'·ıate.**
sul·fide (dī·sul'fīd) *n. Chem.* A sulfide containing two oms of sulfur to the molecule: also called *bisulfide.* Also **di·l'fid** (-fid), **di·sul'phide.**
·un·ion (dis·yōōn'yən) *n.* **1.** The state of being disited; severance; rupture. **2.** A condition of disagreement.
·u·nite (dis'yōō·nīt') *v.* **·nit·ed, ·nit·ing** *v.t.* **1.** To break e union of; separate; part. **2.** To alienate; estrange. — *i.* **3.** To come apart. — **dis·u'ni·ty** *n.*
·use (*n.* dis·yōōs'; *v.* dis·yōōz') *n.* The state of not beg used; out of use. — *v.t.* **·used, ·us·ing** To stop using.
ch (dich) *n.* A long, narrow trench or channel dug in the ound, typically used for irrigation or drainage. — *v.t.* **1.** o make a ditch in. **2.** To surround with a ditch. **3.** To row into or as into a ditch. **4.** *U.S. Slang* To get rid of. *v.i.* **5.** To make a ditch. [OE *dīc*] — **ditch'er** *n.*
h·er (dith'ər) *n.* A state of nervous excitement or anxty, or of trembling agitation. — *v.i.* To be in a dither. Var. of earlier *didder* to tremble, shake; origin uncertain]
h·y·ramb (dith'ə·ram, -ramb) *n.* **1.** In ancient Greece, wild, passionate choric hymn in honor of Dionysus. **2.** A ghly emotional speech or piece of writing. [< L < Gk. *thyrambos*] — **dith'y·ram'bic** *adj.* & *n.*
·to (dit'ō) *n. pl.* **·tos** **1.** The same thing (as something ritten above or mentioned or done before), usually symbozed by ditto marks. **2.** A duplicate or copy of something. Ditto marks. — *adv.* As written above or as mentioned efore. — *interj. Informal* I agree. — *v.t.* **·toed, ·to·ing** To repeat. **2.** To duplicate. [< Ital. < L *dicere* to say]
to marks Two small marks (") placed beneath an item indicate that it is to be repeated. Also **ditto mark.**
·ty (dit'ē) *n. pl.* **·ties** A short, simple song. [< OF *dittie, tie* < L *distatum* a thing said]
ty bag A sailor's bag for needles, thread, personal bengings, etc. Also **ditty box.** [Origin uncertain]
u·ret·ic (dī'yōō·ret'ik) *adj.* Increasing the secretion of ine. — *n.* A diuretic medicine.
ur·nal (dī·ûr'nəl) *adj.* **1.** Of, belonging to, or occurring ch day; daily. **2.** Of or occurring during the daytime; not octurnal. [< L *diurnus* daily] — **di·ur'nal·ly** *adv.*
va (dē'və) *n. pl.* **·vas** or **·ve** (-vā) A celebrated female eratic singer; a prima donna. [< Ital., fem. of *divo* divine]
va·gate (dī'və·gāt) *v.i.* **·gat·ed, ·gat·ing** **1.** To wander or ray aimlessly. **2.** To digress. [< L < *dis-* about + *gari* to wander] — **di'va·ga'tion** *n.*
va·lent (dī·vā'lənt, div'ə-) *adj. Chem.* Bivalent.
van (di·van', dī'van) *n.* **1.** A sofa or couch, usu. without m rests or back. **2.** A room for smoking or drinking. < Turkish *divan* < Persian *dēvān* council, chamber]
ve (dīv) *v.* **dived** or **dove, dived, div·ing** *v.i.* **1.** To plunge, p. headfirst, as into water. **2.** To go underwater or to the ottom; submerge. **3.** To plunge downward at a sharp ngle. **4.** To dart away or leap into something. **5.** To rush to and become deeply engrossed in something. **6.** To ach into something eagerly. — *v.t.* **7.** To cause to plunge; especially, to cause (an airplane) to move swiftly downward at a sharp angle. — *n.* **1.** A plunge, as into water. **2.** A sharp, swift descent, as of an airplane. **3.** *Informal* A cheap, disreputable place, as a saloon, etc. — **to take a dive** *U.S. Slang* In boxing, to allow an opponent to win by prearrangement. [Blend of OE *dūfan* to dive and *dȳfan* to immerse]
dive bomber An airplane designed to bomb a target while in a steep dive.
div·er (dī'vər) *n.* **1.** One who dives, esp. one who dives to salvage sunken cargo, etc. **2.** A bird that dives, as a loon.
di·verge (di·vûrj', dī-) *v.* **·verged, ·verg·ing** *v.i.* **1.** To move or extend in different directions from a common point or from each other. **2.** To deviate. **3.** To differ. — *v.t.* **4.** To cause to diverge. [< NL < L *dis-* apart + *vergere* to incline]
di·ver·gence (di·vûr'jəns, dī-) *n.* **1.** The act of diverging, or the state of being divergent. **2.** Deviation or difference, as of opinion. Also **di·ver'gen·cy.** — **di·ver'gent** *adj.* — **di·ver'gent·ly** *adv.*
di·vers (dī'vərz) *adj.* **1.** Several. **2.** Various. [< OF < L *diversus* different]
di·verse (di·vûrs', dī-, dī'vûrs) *adj.* **1.** Marked by distinct differences; not alike. **2.** Varied in kind or form; diversified. [See DIVERS.] — **di·verse'ly** *adv.* — **di·verse'ness** *n.*
di·ver·si·fy (di·vûr'sə·fī, dī-) *v.t.* **·fied, ·fy·ing** **1.** To make diverse; give variety to; vary. **2.** To make or distribute (investments) among different types of securities so as to minimize risk. — **di·ver·si·fi·ca·tion** (di·vûr'sə·fə·kā'shən, dī-) *n.*
di·ver·sion (di·vûr'zhən, -shən, dī-) *n.* **1.** The act of diverting or turning aside, as from a course. **2.** A drawing away of the attention from something. **3.** An amusement.
di·ver·sion·ar·y (di·vûr'zhən·er'ē, -shən, dī-) *adj.* Designed to distract the enemy from the point of operation.
di·ver·si·ty (di·vûr'sə·tē, dī-) *n. pl.* **·ties** **1.** Unlikeness; difference. **2.** Variety; multiplicity.
di·vert (di·vûrt', dī-) *v.t.* **1.** To turn aside, as from a set course; deflect. **2.** To distract the attention of. **3.** To amuse; entertain. [< L < *dis-* apart + *vertere* to turn] — **di·vert'ing** *adj.* — **di·vert'ing·ly** *adv.*
di·ver·ti·men·to (di·ver'ti·men'tō) *n. pl.* **·ti** (-tē) *Music* A light instrumental composition in several movements. [< Ital., diversion]
di·ver·tisse·ment (də·vûr'təs·mənt, dē·ver·tēs·mäṅ') *n.* **1.** A diversion; amusement. **2.** *Music* A divertimento. **3.** A short ballet, etc. performed during or between the parts of an opera or play. [< MF]
di·vest (di·vest', dī-) *v.t.* **1.** To strip, as of clothes. **2.** To deprive, as of rights or possessions. [See DEVEST.]
di·vest·i·ture (di·ves'tə·chər, dī-) *n.* The act of divesting, or the state of being divested. Also **di·vest'ment, di·ves'ture.**
di·vide (di·vīd') *v.* **·vid·ed, ·vid·ing** *v.t.* **1.** To separate into pieces or portions, as by cutting. **2.** To distribute the pieces or portions of. **3.** To separate into sections. **4.** To separate into groups; classify. **5.** To split up into opposed sides; cause dissent in. **6.** To cause to be apart. **7.** *Math.* **a** To subject to the process of division. **b** To be an exact divisor of. **8.** *Mech.* To graduate; calibrate. — *v.i.* **9.** To become separated into parts; diverge. **10.** To be at variance. **11.** *Brit.* In Parliament and other legislative bodies, to separate into two groups in order to vote. **12.** To share. **13.** To perform mathematical division. — *n.* A mountain range separating one drainage system from another; watershed. [< L *dividere* to separate, divide] — **di·vid'a·ble** *adj.*
di·vid·ed (di·vī'did) *adj.* **1.** Separated into parts; parted. **2.** Disunited. **3.** *Bot.* Having incisions or indentations.
div·i·dend (div'ə·dend) *n.* **1.** *Math.* A quantity divided into equal parts. **2.** A sum of money to be distributed to stockholders, etc. **3.** The portion of such a sum given to each individual. [< L *dividendum* thing to be divided]
di·vid·er (di·vī'dər) *n.* **1.** One who or that which divides, separates, or apportions. **2.** *pl.* A pair of compasses typically used for measuring or marking off short intervals.
div·i·na·tion (div'ə·nā'shən) *n.* **1.** The act or art of knowing the future or that which is hidden or unknown. **2.** A prophecy. **3.** A clever guess. — **di·vin·a·to·ry** (div·in'ə·tôr'ē, -tō'rē) *adj.*
di·vine (di·vīn') *adj.* **1.** Of or pertaining to God or a god. **2.** Given by or derived from God or a god. **3.** Directed or devoted to God or a god; sacred. **4.** Like a god. **5.** Extraordinarily perfect. **6.** *Informal* Altogether delightful. — *n.* **1.** A clergyman. **2.** A theologian. — *v.* **·vined, ·vin·ing** *v.t.* **1.** To foretell or find out by occult means. **2.** To locate (water, etc.) by means of a divining rod. **3.** To conjecture or surmise by instinct. — *v.i.* **4.** To practice divination. **5.** To guess. [< OF < L *deus* god] — **di·vine'ly** *adv.* — **di·vine'ness** *n.* — **di·vin'er** *n.*
Divine Comedy A narrative poem by Dante Alighieri.
Divine Office The canonical hours.

diving bell A large, hollow, inverted vessel supplied with air under pressure, in which men may work under water.

diving board A flexible board upon which divers jump to gain impetus for the dive: also called *springboard.*

diving suit A waterproof garment with detachable helmet that is supplied with air through a hose, worn by divers.

divining rod A forked branch popularly asserted to indicate underground water or metal: also called *dowsing rod.*

di·vin·i·ty (di·vin′ə·tē) *n. pl.* **·ties** **1.** The state or quality of being divine. **2.** A godlike character or attribute. **3.** A deity. **4.** Theology. **5.** A soft, creamy candy. **— the Divinity** God. [< OF < L *divinitas* godhead, deity]

di·vis·i·ble (di·viz′ə·bəl) *adj.* **1.** Capable of being divided. **2.** *Math.* That can be divided and leave no remainder. **— di·vis′i·bil′i·ty, di·vis′i·ble·ness** *n.* **— di·vis′i·bly** *adv.*

di·vi·sion (di·vizh′ən) *n.* **1.** The act of dividing; separation. **2.** The state of being divided. **3.** One of the parts into which a thing is divided. **4.** A part or section of a country, government, etc., that has been divided for administrative, political, or other reasons. **5.** Something that divides or separates. **6.** Disagreement; discord. **7.** *Math.* The operation of finding how many times a number or quantity (the *divisor*) is contained in another number or quantity (the *dividend*), the number or quantity found being called the *quotient.* **8.** A voting of a legislative body. **9.** *Mil.* A major administrative and tactical unit that is larger than a regiment and smaller than a corps. **10.** In the U.S. Navy, a number of ships grouped for operational command. **11.** In the U.S. Air Force, an air combat organization with appropriate service units. [< OF < L *dividere* to divide] **— di·vi′sion·al** *adj.*

division sign *Math.* The symbol (÷) that denotes a first number is to be divided by a second, as 6 ÷ 2 = 3.

di·vi·sive (di·vī′siv) *adj.* **1.** Causing or expressing division or distribution. **2.** Creating division, dissension, or strife.

di·vi·sor (di·vī′zər) *n. Math.* **1.** A number by which another number is divided. **2.** A common divisor.

di·vorce (di·vôrs′, -vōrs′) *n.* **1.** Dissolution of a marriage bond by legal process or by accepted custom. **2.** Any radical or complete separation. Also **di·vorce′ment.** **—** *v.* **·vorced, ·vorc·ing** *v.t.* **1.** To dissolve the marriage of. **2.** To free oneself from (one's husband or wife) by divorce. **3.** To separate; cut off; disunite. **—** *v.i.* **4.** To get a divorce. [< MF < L *divertere* to divert]

di·vor·cé (di·vôr′sā′, -vōr′-, di·vôr′sā, -vōr′-) *n.* A divorced man. [< F, pp. of *divorcer* to divorce] **— di·vor′cée′** *n.fem.*

di·vor·cee (di·vôr′sē′, -vōr′-) *n.* A divorced person.

div·ot (div′ət) *n.* A piece of turf torn by a golf club.

di·vulge (di·vulj′) *v.t.* **·vulged, ·vulg·ing** To tell, as a secret; disclose; reveal. [< L < *dis-* away + *vulgare* to make public] **— di·vulge′ment, di·vul′gence** *n.* **— di·vulg′er** *n.*

div·vy (div′ē) *Slang n. pl.* **·vies** A share; portion. **—** *v.t.* **·vied, ·vy·ing** To divide: often with *up.* [Short for DIVIDE]

Dix·ie (dik′sē) **1.** Traditionally, those States that comprised the Confederacy during the Civil War. Also **Dixie Land.** **2.** A Confederate marching song.

Dix·ie·land (dik′sē·land′) *n.* A style of jazz in two-beat or four-beat rhythm, originally played in New Orleans.

diz·en (diz′ən, dī′zən) *v.t.* To dress in finery; deck out. [< M.Du. *disen* to put flax on a distaff] **— diz′en·ment** *n.*

diz·zy (diz′ē) *adj.* **·zi·er, ·zi·est** **1.** Having a feeling of whirling or unsteadiness. **2.** Causing giddiness. **3.** *Informal* Silly; stupid. **—** *v.t* **·zied, ·zy·ing** To make giddy; confuse. [OE *dysig* foolish, stupid] **— diz′zi·ly** *adv.* **— diz′zi·ness** *n.*

djin·ni (ji·nē′) See JINNI.

DNA *Biochem.* Deoxyribonucleic acid.

do[1] (dōō) *v.* **did, done, do·ing** Present: *sing.* **do, do** (*Archaic* **thou do·est** or **dost**), **does** (*Archaic* **do·eth** or **doth**), *pl.* **do**; past: **did** (*Archaic* **thou didst**); pp. **done**; ppr. **do·ing** *v.t.* **1.** To perform, as an action; produce, as a piece of work. **2.** To fulfill; complete; accomplish. **3.** To cause; bring about: to *do* no wrong. **4.** To put forth: He *did* his best. **5.** To render: to *do* homage. **6.** To work at. **7.** To work out; solve. **8.** To translate. **9.** To present (a play, reading, etc.). **10.** To enact the part of. **11.** To cover (a distance); travel. **12.** *Informal* To make a tour of; visit. **13.** To be sufficient for. **14.** *Informal* To serve, as a term in prison. **15.** *Informal* To cheat; swindle. **—** *v.i.* **16.** To exert oneself; be active: to *do* or die. **17.** To conduct oneself. **18.** To fare; get along. **19.** To serve the purpose; suffice. **— to do away with** **1.** To throw away. **2.** To kill; destroy. **— to do by** To act toward. **— to do for** **1.** To provide for; care for. **2.** *Informal* To ruin; kill. **— to do in** *Slang* To kill. **— to do over** *Informal* To redecorate. **— to do up** **1.** To wrap or tie up. **2.** To roll up or arrange. **3.** To clean; repair. **4.** To tire out. **— to do without** To get along without. **— to have to do with** To be involved with. **— to make do** To get along with (whatever is available). **—** *auxiliary* As an auxiliary, *do* is used: **1.** Without specific meaning in negative, interrogative, and inverted constructions: I *do* not want it; *Do* you want to leave? **2.** To add force to imperatives: *Do* hurry. **3.** To express emphasis: I *do* believe y **4.** As a substitute for another verb to avoid repetiti I will not affirm, as some *do.* **—** *n. pl.* **do's** or **dos** **1.** *formal* A trick; cheat. **2.** Deed; duty: chiefly in the phr **to do one's do.** **3.** *Informal* Festivity; celebration. **4.** That which ought to be done: used chiefly in the express **do's and don'ts.** [OE *dōn*]

do[2] (dō) *n. Music* The keynote syllable of a major sc also, the tone C. [< Ital.]

do·a·ble (dōō′ə·bəl) *adj.* Capable of being done.

do-all (dōō′ôl′) *n.* A general helper; factotum.

dob·bin (dob′in) *n.* A horse, esp. a plodding one. [a *Dobbin,* var. of *Robin* < *Robert,* a personal name]

Do·ber·man pinscher (dō′bər·mən) A breed of la short-haired dogs originally developed in Germany. [a Ludwig *Dobermann,* its first breeder]

doc·ile (dos′əl, *Brit.* dō′sīl) *adj.* **1.** Amenable to traini easy to manage; tractable. **2.** Easily worked or handl [< MF < L *docilis* able to be taught] **— doc′ile·ly** *a* **— do·cil·i·ty** (do·sil′ə·tē, dō-) *n.*

dock[1] (dok) *n.* **1.** The water space between two adjoin piers or wharves where ships can remain for loading, unlo ing, or repair. **2.** A wharf or pier. **3.** *Often pl.* A group wharves or piers. **4.** A shipping or loading platform, as trucks, trains, etc. **— Syn.** See WHARF. **—** *v.t.* **1.** bring (a vessel, truck, etc.) into or next to a dock. **—** *v.i.* To come into a dock. [< MDu. *docke*]

dock[2] (dok) *n.* **1.** The fleshy part of an animal's tail. The stump of a tail that remains after clipping. **—** *v.t.* To cut off the end of (a tail, etc.), or clip short the tail of. To take a part from (wages, etc.). **3.** To take from wages, etc. of. [Cf. ME *docken* to cut short] **— dock′er**

dock[3] (dok) *n.* An enclosed space for the defendant i criminal court. [< Flemish *dok* cage]

dock[4] (dok) *n.* Any of various plants of the buckwh family, as the **sour dock.** [OE *docce*]

dock·age[1] (dok′ij) *n.* **1.** A charge for docking (a ship, et **2.** Facilities for docking a vessel. **3.** The act of docking

dock·age[2] (dok′ij) *n.* **1.** Curtailment, as of wages; ded tion. **2.** Waste matter in grain, easily separated by cleani

dock·et (dok′it) *n.* **1.** A written summary or abstr **2.** *Law* **a** A record of court judgments. **b** The book in wh such a record is kept. **c** A court calendar of the cases s pending. **3.** Any calendar of things to be done. **4.** A or label attached to a parcel, listing contents, directio etc. **—** *v.t.* **1.** To enter in a docket. **2.** To put a tag or la on (a parcel, etc.). [ME; origin uncertain]

dock·yard (dok′yärd′) *n.* **1.** An area of docks, etc., wh ships are built, repaired, etc. **2.** *Brit.* A navy yard.

doc·tor (dok′tər) *n.* **1.** A licensed practitioner of medic surgery, or any of certain other healing arts, as a dent veterinarian, etc. **2.** A person who has received a diplo of the highest degree, as in law, literature, etc. **3.** A me cine man. **4.** *Informal* One who or that which remo defects, mends broken parts, etc. **—** *v.t. Informal* **1.** prescribe for or treat medically. **2.** To repair. **3.** falsify or alter, as evidence. **—** *v.i. Informal* **4.** To pract medicine. **5.** To undergo medical treatment. [< L *do* to teach] **— doc′tor·al** *adj.*

doc·tor·ate (dok′tər·it) *n.* The degree or status of a doc

doc·tri·naire (dok′trə·nâr′) *adj.* Theoretical; visionary. *n.* One whose views are derived from theories rather th from facts; an impractical theorist. **— doc′tri·nair′ism** *n*

doc·trine (dok′trin) *n.* **1.** That which is presented for ceptance or belief; teachings, as of a religious group. **2.** particular principle or tenet that is taught. [< OF < *docere* to teach] **— doc′tri·nal** *adj.* **— doc′tri·nal·ly** *adv*

— Syn. *Doctrine* primarily signifies a principle that is taug A *theory* is a proposition regarded as susceptible of verificati and thus is usually scientific. A *dogma* rests on authority, such the decision of a church council. Any *doctrine* is a *belief* on the p of those who accept it, but *belief* more often suggests matters faith rather than of reason. A *creed* is the list of *doctrines* or *dogn* of a religion or church; any single item of such a list is a *tenet.*

doc·u·ment (*n.* dok′yə·mənt; *v.* dok′yə·ment) *n.* Son thing written or printed that furnishes conclusive inforn tion or evidence, as an official paper or record. **—** *v.t.* **1.** furnish with documents. **2.** To support by conclus information or evidence. **3.** To supply (a book, etc.) wi citations that prove what is stated. [< OF < L *docere* teach] **— doc′u·men·ta′tion** *n.*

doc·u·men·ta·ry (dok′yə·men′tər·ē) *adj.* **1.** Pertaining consisting of, or based upon documents. **2.** That prese factual material objectively without fictionalizing. A **doc′u·men′tal.** **—** *n. pl.* **·ries** A motion picture deali with events, circumstances, etc., in a factual way.

dod·der (dod′ər) *v.i.* To tremble or totter, as from a [Cf. ME *didder* to tremble] **— dod′der·ing** *adj.*

dodeca- *combining form* Twelve; of or having twelve. A before vowels, **dodec-.** [< Gk. *dōdeka* twelve]

do·dec·a·gon (dō·dek′ə·gon) *n. Geom.* A polygon havi

elve sides and twelve angles. [< Gk. *dōdekagōnon*] — **de·cag·o·nal** (dō'de·kag'ə·nəl) *adj.*
lec·a·he·dron (dō'dek·ə·hē'drən) *n. pl.* **·drons** or **·dra** 'rə) *Geom.* A polyhedron bounded by twelve plane faces. r illus. see CRYSTAL. — **do'dec·a·he'dral** *adj.*
ge (doj) *v.* **dodged, dodg·ing** *v.t.* **1.** To avoid, as a blow, a sudden turn or twist. **2.** To evade, as a duty or issue. *v.i.* **3.** To move suddenly, as to avoid a blow. **4.** To ıctice trickery. — *n.* **1.** An act of dodging. **2.** A trick deceive or cheat. [Origin unknown]
g·er (doj'ər) *n.* **1.** One who dodges; a tricky fellow. **2.** S. A small handbill. **3.** *U.S.* A cake of Indian meal.
lo (dō'dō) *n. pl.* **·does** or **·dos** **1.** An extinct bird about size of a turkey, with rudimentary, functionless wings. *Informal* One who is slow or dull. [< Pg. *doudo*]
(dō) *n.* **1.** The female of the deer, antelope, rabbit, kan-·oo, and certain other animals. **2.** Loosely, the female of moose or elk (properly called *cow*). [OE *dā*]
r (dōō'ər) *n.* One who acts, does, or performs; an agent.
s (duz) Present tense, third person singular, of DO[1].
·skin (dō'skin') *n.* **1.** The skin of the female deer. **2.** ıther made from this, used especially for gloves. **3.** A ıvy, short-napped, woolen or cotton fabric.
s·n't (duz'ənt) Does not. ◆ See note at DON'T.
(dof, dôf) *v.t.* **1.** To take off, as a hat or clothing. **2.** discard. [Contraction of *do off*] — **doff'er** *n.*
(dôg, dog) *n.* **1.** A domesticated, carnivorous mammal many varieties. ◆ Collateral adjective: *canine.* **2.** Any various other species of this family, as wolves, foxes, etc. The male of any of these species. **4.** One of various ani-ls having an appearance suggestive of a dog, as a prairie g. **5.** A despicable person. **6.** *Informal* A man or boy; ow. **7.** An andiron. **8.** *Mech.* One of several devices for pping or holding logs, etc. **9.** *pl. U.S. Slang* The feet. **to go to the dogs** *Informal* To go to ruin. — **to put on dog.** *U.S. Informal* To make a pretentious display. — . Very; utterly: used in combination: *dog-tired.* — *v.t.* **gged, dog·ging** **1.** To pursue persistently; hound. **2.** *ch.* To grip or fasten (a log, etc.) with a dog. [OE *docga*]
g (dôg, dog) *n.* Either of two constellations, Canis Major e Greater Dog) or Canis Minor (the Little Dog).
·bane (dôg'bān', dog'-) *n.* A smooth, reddish-stemmed b having a milky juice.
biscuit A hard biscuit made with meat scraps, ground ıes, etc., for feeding dogs.
·cart (dôg'kärt', dog'-) *n.* **1.** A one-horse vehicle, usu. o-wheeled, with two seats set back to back. **2.** A cart ılled by one or more dogs.
·catch·er (dôg'kach'ər, dog'-) *n. U.S.* A person em-yed or elected to pick up and impound stray dogs.
days The hot, sultry days of July and early August.
e (dōj) *n.* The elective chief magistrate in the former re-olics of Venice and Genoa. [< Ital. < L *dux., ducis* chief]
·ear (dôg'ir', dog'-) *n.* A turned-down corner of a book ge. — *v.t.* To turn down the corner of (a page). Also *'s-ear.* — **dog'-eared'** *adj.*
·face (dôg'fās', dog'-) *n. U.S. Slang* A soldier in the S. Army; esp., an infantryman.
·fight (dôg'fīt', dog'-) *n.* **1.** A fight between or as be-een dogs. **2.** *Mil.* An aerial battle between planes.
·fish (dôg'fish', dôg'-) *n. pl.* **·fish** or **·fish·es** One of va-us small, littoral sharks of North American waters.
·ged (dôg'id, dog'-) *adj.* Stubborn; obdurate. — **dog'·d·ly** *adv.* — **dog'ged·ness** *n.*
·ger·el (dôg'ər·əl, dog'-) *n.* Trivial, awkwardly written ·se, usu. comic or burlesque. — *adj.* Of or composed of ·h verse. Also **dog'grel.** [ME; origin unknown]
·gish (dôg'ish, dog'-) *adj.* **1.** Relating to or suggestive a dog. **2.** Bad-tempered; snappish. **3.** *U.S. Informal* etentiously stylish. — **dog'gish·ly** *adv.* — **dog'gish·ness** *n.*
·gone (dôg'gôn', dog'gon') *Informal interj.* Damn!; **rn!** — *v.t.* **·goned, ·gon·ing** To damn.
·gy (dôg'ē, dog'ē) *n. pl.* **·gies** A dog; esp., a small dog. so **dog'gie.** — *adj.* **dog·gi·er, dog·gi·est** **1.** Of or like a g: *doggy* odor. **2.** *U.S. Informal* Showily fashionable.
·house (dôg'hous', dog'-) *n.* A small house for a dog. **in the doghouse** *U.S. Informal* In disfavor with someone.
gie (dō'gē) *n.* In the western U.S., a stray or motherless f: also spelled *dogy.* [Origin unknown]
·ma (dôg'mə, dog'-) *n. pl.* **·mas** or **·ma·ta** (-mə·tə) **1.** *eol.* A doctrine or system of doctrine maintained by a re-ious body as true and necessary of belief. **2.** A belief, inciple, or tenet. **3.** A system of such beliefs or principles. **Syn.** See DOCTRINE. [< L < Gk. *dogma* opinion]
·mat·ic (dôg·mat'ik, dog-) *adj.* **1.** Of, like, or pertain-to dogma. **2.** Marked by authoritative, often arrogant, sertion of opinions or beliefs. Also **dog·mat'i·cal.** — **dog·ıt'i·cal·ly** *adv.*

dog·ma·tism (dôg'mə·tiz'əm, dog'-) *n.* Positive or arrogant assertion, as of opinions or beliefs. — **dog'ma·tist** *n.*
dog·ma·tize (dôg'mə·tīz, dog'-) *v.* **·tized, ·tiz·ing** *v.i.* **1.** To express oneself dogmatically. — *v.t.* **2.** To declare or assert as a dogma. — **dog'ma·ti·za'tion** *n.* — **dog'ma·tiz'er** *n.*
do-good·er (dōō'gŏŏd'ər) *n. Informal* An idealistic philanthropist or reformer: a derisive term.
dog rose The wild brier of European hedges and thickets, bearing single pink flowers.
dog's-ear (dôgz'ir', dogz'-) *n.* Dog-ear.
dog sled A sled drawn by one or more dogs. Also **dog sledge.**
Dog Star **1.** The star Sirius. **2.** Procyon.
dog tag **1.** A small metal plate on the collar of a dog, usu. indicating ownership. **2.** *U.S. Informal* A soldier's identification tag, worn on a chain around the neck.
dog·tooth (dôg'tōōth', dog'-) *n.* A canine tooth.
dogtooth violet **1.** A European herb of the lily family: also called *adder's tongue.* **2.** One of various American plants, bearing yellow or pinkish flowers. Also **dog's-tooth violet.**
dog·trot (dôg'trot', dog'-) *n.* A regular and easy trot.
dog·watch (dôg'woch', dog'-) *n. Naut.* Either of two short watches aboard ship, from 4 to 6 or 6 to 8 P.M.
dog·wood (dôg'wŏŏd', dog'-) *n.* Any of certain trees or shrubs, esp. the **flowering dogwood** or **Virginia dogwood** of the U.S., with white or pink flowers. Also called *cornel.*
do·gy (dō'gē) See DOGIE.
doi·ly (doi'lē) *n. pl.* **·lies** A small, ornamental piece of lace, etc., used to protect surfaces. Also spelled *doyley, doyly.* [after *Doily* or *Doyley*, 17th c. English draper]
do·ings (dōō'ingz) *n.pl.* **1.** Activities or proceedings. **2.** Behavior; conduct.
do-it-your·self (dōō'it·yŏŏr·self') *adj. U.S. Informal* Designed to be used or done without special or hired help.
dol (dol) *n. Psychol.* A unit of pain intensity based on the sensation of heat rays on the skin. [< L *dolor* pain]
dol·drums (dol'drəmz, dōl'-) *n.pl.* **1.** Those parts of the ocean near the equator where calms or baffling winds prevail. **2.** A becalmed state. **3.** A dull, depressed, or bored condition of mind; the dumps. [Cf. OE *dol* dull, stupid]
dole (dōl) *n.* **1.** That which, as food or money, is distributed, esp. in charity. **2.** A giving out of something. **3.** A sum of money paid to an unemployed person. — **on the dole** Receiving relief payments from the government. — *v.t.* **doled, dol·ing** To dispense in small quantities; distribute: usually with *out.* [OE *dāl*]
dole·ful (dōl'fəl) *adj.* Melancholy. [< OF < LL < *dolere* to feel pain] — **dole'ful·ly** *adv.* — **dole'ful·ness** *n.*
dol·i·cho·ce·phal·ic (dol'i·kō·sə·fal'ik) *adj.* Having a long skull; longheaded. Also **dol'i·cho·ceph'a·lous** (-sef'ə·ləs). [< Gk. *dolichos* long + *kephalē* head] — **dol'i·cho·ceph'a·lism, dol'i·cho·ceph'a·ly** *n.*
doll (dol) *n.* **1.** A child's toy made to resemble the human figure. **2.** A pretty but superficial woman. **3.** A pretty or lovable child. **4.** *Slang* An attractive or charming person of either sex. — *v.t. & v.i. Informal* To adorn or dress smartly: with *up.* [from *Doll*, nickname for *Dorothy*]
dol·lar (dol'ər) *n.* **1.** The standard monetary unit of the United States, equivalent to 100 cents. **2.** The standard monetary unit of Canada, China, various British colonies, etc. **3.** A coin or a piece of paper currently worth one dollar. **4.** Loosely, a Mexican peso. **5.** Any of various coins or currency originally issued for trade. Symbol $ or $. [< earlier *daler* < LG < G *taler, thaler*, short for *Joachimstaler*, a coin of *Joachimstal*, a village in Bohemia]
dol·lar-a-year (dol'ər·ə·yir') *adj. U.S.* Designating a government employee, job, etc., having only token pay.
dollar diplomacy A practice or policy whereby a government uses public or private funds to advance its own interests abroad.
dol·lop (dol'əp) *n. Informal* A portion, serving, etc., of indefinite form or amount, as of a soft substance or liquid.
dol·ly (dol'ē) *n. pl.* **·lies** **1.** A doll: a child's term. **2.** A low, flat frame set on small wheels or rollers, used for moving heavy loads, cameras, etc. **3.** A wooden instrument for beating or stirring clothes, etc. — *v.i.* **·lied, ·ly·ing** To move a motion-picture or television camera toward or away from the action.
dol·man (dol'mən) *n.* A woman's coat with dolman sleeves or capelike arm pieces. [< F < Turkish *dōlāmān* long robe]
dolman sleeve A sleeve tapering from a wide opening at the armhole to a narrow one at the wrist.
dol·men (dol'mən) *n.* A prehistoric monument made of a huge stone set on upright stones. [< F]
dol·o·mite (dol'ə·mīt) *n.* A marblelike rock consisting principally of a brittle calcium and magnesium carbonate. [after D. de *Dolomieu*, 1750–1801, French geologist]
do·lor (dō'lər) *n. Poetic* Sorrow; anguish. Also *Brit.* **do'·lour.** [< OF < L, pain]

do·lor·ous (dō′lər·əs, dol′ər-) *adj.* **1.** Sad; mournful. **2.** Painful. — **do′lor·ous·ly** *adv.* — **do′lor·ous·ness** *n.*

dol·phin (dol′fin) *n.* **1.** Any of various cetaceans with beaklike snouts; esp. the **common dolphin** of the Mediterranean and Atlantic. **2.** *Naut.* A buoy or post to which a boat can be moored. [< OF *daulphin* < L *delphinus* < Gk. *delphis, -inos*]

DOLPHIN (*def.* 1)
(To 8 feet long)

dolt (dōlt) *n.* A stupid person. [ME *dold* stupid] — **dolt′ish** *adj.* — **dolt′ish·ly** *adv.* — **dolt′ish·ness** *n.*

-dom *suffix of nouns* **1.** State or condition of being: *freedom.* **2.** Domain of: *kingdom.* **3.** Rank of: *earldom.* **4.** The totality of those having a certain rank, state, or condition: *Christendom.* [OE *-dōm* < *dōm* state, condition]

do·main (dō·mān′) *n.* **1.** A territory under a sovereign or one government. **2.** A sphere or field of action, knowledge, etc. **3.** A landed estate. [< MF < OF < L *dominus* lord]

dome (dōm) *n.* **1.** A roof resembling an inverted cup or hemisphere. **2.** Something shaped like this. **3.** *Slang* The head. — *v.* **domed, dom·ing** *v.t.* **1.** To furnish or cover with a dome. **2.** To shape like a dome. — *v.i.* **3.** To rise or swell upward like a dome. [< MF < Ital. < L *domus* house]

domes·day (do͞omz′dā′) *n.* See DOOMSDAY.

do·mes·tic (də·mes′tik) *adj.* **1.** Of or pertaining to the home or family. **2.** Given to or fond of things concerning the home or family. **3.** Tame; domesticated: *domestic* animals. **4.** Of, produced, or pertaining to one's own country. — *n.* **1.** A household servant. **2.** *pl.* Native products. [< MF < L *domus* house] — **do·mes′ti·cal·ly** *adv.*

do·mes·ti·cate (də·mes′tə·kāt) *v.* **·cat·ed, ·cat·ing** *v.t.* **1.** To tame. **2.** To civilize. **3.** To cause to feel at ease or at home. — *v.i.* **4.** To become domestic. Also **do·mes′ti·cize.** [< Med.L < L *domus* house] — **do·mes′ti·ca′tion** *n.*

do·mes·tic·i·ty (dō′mes·tis′ə·tē) *n. pl.* **·ties** **1.** Life at home or with one's family. **2.** Devotion to home and family. **3.** *pl.* Domestic matters.

domestic science Home economics.

dom·i·cile (dom′ə·səl, -sīl) *n.* **1.** A home, house, or dwelling. **2.** The place of one's legal abode. — *v.* **·ciled, ·cil·ing** *v.t.* **1.** To establish in a place of abode. — *v.i.* **2.** To dwell. [< MF < L *domus* house] — **dom·i·cil·i·ar·y** (dom′ə·sil′ē·er′ē) *adj.*

dom·i·nance (dom′ə·nəns) *n.* The state or fact of being dominant; control; ascendancy. Also **dom′i·nan·cy.**

dom·i·nant (dom′ə·nənt) *adj.* **1.** Dominating; ruling; governing. **2.** Conspicuously prominent, as in position. **3.** *Genetics* Designating one of a pair of hereditary characters that, appearing in hybrid offspring, masks a contrasting character: opposed to *recessive.* **4.** *Music* Of or based upon the dominant. — *n.* **1.** *Genetics* A dominant character. **2.** *Music* The fifth tone of a diatonic scale, a perfect fifth above the tonic. [See DOMINATE.] — **dom′i·nant·ly** *adv.*

dom·i·nate (dom′ə·nāt) *v.* **·nat·ed, ·nat·ing** *v.t.* **1.** To exercise control over; govern. **2.** To tower above; loom over. — *v.i.* **3.** To be dominant, as in power. [< L *dominari* to rule, dominate] — **dom′i·na′tive** *adj.* — **dom′i·na′tor** *n.*

dom·i·na·tion (dom′ə·nā′shən) *n.* **1.** The act of dominating, or the state of being dominated. **2.** Control; authority.

dom·i·neer (dom′ə·nir′) *v.t.* & *v.i.* To rule arrogantly or insolently. [< Du. < F < L *dominus* lord] — **dom′i·neer′ing** *adj.* — **dom′i·neer′ing·ly** *adv.*

Do·min·i·can (də·min′i·kən) *adj.* **1.** Of or pertaining to St. Dominic or to his monastic order. **2.** Of the Dominican Republic. — *n.* **1.** A member of the monastic order founded by St. Dominic. **2.** A native of the Dominican Republic.

do·min·ion (də·min′yən) *n.* **1.** Sovereign or supreme authority. **2.** A country under a particular government. **3.** A self-governing member of the British Commonwealth of Nations. [< F < L < *dominus* lord]

Dominion Day In Canada, July 1, the anniversary of Canada's federation into a dominion, 1867: a legal holiday.

dom·i·no[1] (dom′ə·nō) *n. pl.* **·noes** or **·nos** **1.** A small mask for the eyes. For illus. see MASK[1]. **2.** A loose robe, hood, and mask worn at masquerades. **3.** A person wearing this. [< MF, hood worn by clerics]

dom·i·no[2] (dom′ə·nō) *n. pl.* **·noes** or **·nos** **1.** A small, oblong piece of wood, plastic, etc., with the upper side marked with dots. **2.** *pl.* (*construed as sing.*) A game usu. played with a set of 28 of these pieces. [? < DOMINO[1]]

don[1] (don) *n.* **1.** A Spanish gentleman or nobleman. **2.** An important personage. **3.** *Brit. Informal* A head, fellow, or tutor of a college. [< Sp. < L *dominus* lord]

don[2] (don) *v.t.* **donned, don·ning** To put on, as a garment. [Contraction of *do on*]

Don (don) *n.* Sir: a title of respect or address, used with the given name in Spanish-speaking countries.

Do·ña (dō′nyä) *n.* Lady; Madam: a title of respect or address used with the given name in Spanish-speaking countr

do·nate (dō′nāt, dō·nāt′) *v.t.* **·nat·ed, ·nat·ing** *Chiefly U* To give, as to a charitable organization; contribute. [B formation < DONATION] — **do′na·tor** *n.*

do·na·tion (dō·nā′shən) *n.* **1.** The act of giving. **2.** A [< F < L *donare* to give]

done (dun) Past participle of DO[1]. — *adj.* **1.** Comple finished; ended; agreed. **2.** Cooked sufficiently.

do·nee (dō·nē′) *n.* One who receives a gift.

done for *U.S. Informal* **1.** Ruined; finished; exhaus **2.** Dead or about to die.

done in *U.S. Informal* **1.** Utterly exhausted; worn out fatigue. Also **done up.** **2.** Killed; destroyed.

don·jon (dun′jən, don′-) *n.* The main tower or keep castle. [< OF, the lord's tower]

Don Juan (don wän′) **1.** A legendary Spanish nobler and seducer of women. **2.** Any rake or seducer.

don·key (dong′kē, dung′-) *n.* **1.** The ass. **2.** A stupi stubborn person. [? after *Duncan,* a personal name]

Don·na (don′ə, *Ital.* dôn′nä) *n.* Lady; Madam, a title o spect or address in Italian-speaking countries.

don·nish (don′ish) *adj.* **1.** Of or suggestive of a unive don. **2.** Formal; pedantic. — **don′nish·ness** *n.*

don·ny·brook (don′ē·bro͝ok′) *n.* A brawl marked by ro ness and abusive lamguage; free-for-all. [after *Donnyb Fair,* an event known for its brawls, held in Ireland]

do·nor (dō′nər) *n.* **1.** One who gives. **2.** *Med.* One furnishes blood, skin, etc. [< AF < L *donare* to give]

Don Quix·ote (don kwik′sət, kē·hō′tē; *Sp.* dôn kē·hō′tā) A satirical novel by Cervantes. **2.** The hero of this no a naive, dreamy, befuddled idealist.

don't (dōnt) **1.** Do not. **2.** Does not: now nonstandar general American speech.

doo·dad (do͞o′dad) *n. Informal* **1.** A small ornament; ble. **2.** A doohickey. [Humorous coinage; extension of

doo·dle (do͞od′l) *Informal v.t.* & *v.i.* **·dled, ·dling** To d or scribble in an aimless, preoccupied way. — *n.* A de so made. [Cf. dial. E *doodle* to be idle, trifle]

doo·dle·bug (do͞od′l·bug′) *n.* **1.** *U.S. Dial.* The larv several insects. **2.** Loosely, the tumblebug. [? < dia *doodle* idler, fool + BUG]

doo·hick·ey (do͞o′hik′ē) *n. pl.* **·eys** *U.S. Informal* A s object whose exact name is not known or remembe [Humorous coinage; extension of DO]

doom (do͞om) *v.t.* **1.** To pronounce judgment or sente upon; condemn. **2.** To destine to an unhappy fate. — **1.** An unhappy fate. **2.** An adverse judicial sentence. Death or ruin. **4.** The Last Judgment. [OE *dōm*]

dooms·day (do͞omz′dā′) *n.* **1.** The day of the Last Ju ment; the end of the world. **2.** Any day of final judgm Also spelled *domesday.* [OE *dōm* doom + *dæg* day]

door (dôr, dōr) *n.* **1.** A hinged, sliding, folding, or rota structure, as of wood, used for closing or opening an trance to a house, vehicle, etc. **2.** A doorway, often re senting an entire building or room: to live six *doors* av **3.** Any means of entrance or exit. — **Syn.** See ENTRAN [Fusion of OE *duru* pair of doors and *dor* gate]

door·bell (dôr′bel′, dōr′-) *n.* A bell at a doorway.

door·jamb (dôr′jam′, dōr′-) *n.* A vertical piece at the of a doorway supporting the lintel.

door·keep·er (dôr′kē′pər, dōr′-) *n.* A guardian or keepe a doorway.

door·knob (dôr′nob′, dōr′-) *n.* A handle to open a do

door·man (dôr′man′, -mən, dōr′-) *n. pl.* **·men** (-m -mən) An attendant at the door of a hotel, apartment ho etc., who assists persons entering and leaving the build

door mat A mat placed at an entrance for wiping the sh

door·nail (dôr′nāl′, dōr′-) *n.* A large-headed nail, form used in the construction and ornamentation of doors. **dead as a doornail** Unquestionably dead.

door·plate (dôr′plāt′, dōr′-) *n.* A metal plate on a d with the occupant's name, street number, etc.

door·post (dôr′pōst′, dōr′-) *n.* A doorjamb.

door·sill (dôr′sil′, dōr′-) *n.* The sill or threshold of a d

door·step (dôr′step′, dōr′-) *n.* A step or one of a serie steps leading to a door.

door·stop (dôr′stop′, dōr′-) *n.* A device to keep a door op

door·way (dôr′wā′, dōr′-) *n.* The passage for entrance a exit into and out of a building, room, etc. — **Syn.** See TRANCE[1].

door·yard (dôr′yärd′, dōr′-) *n.* A yard around, or esp front of, a house.

dope (dōp) *n.* **1.** A viscid substance or unusually thick uid used as a lubricant. **2.** A filler, varnish, or sim preparation used for protecting and making taut the fal of airplane wings, etc. **3.** *Photog.* A developer. **4.** *Sl* A drug or narcotic. **5.** *Slang* A dull-witted or incapa individual. **6.** *Slang* Inside information. — *v.t.* **doped, d ing** **1.** To apply dope to. **2.** To adulterate or treat (a s stance) with another. **3.** *Slang* To give drugs to; dr 'ten with *up*. **4.** *Slang* To plan or solve: usu. with *out*.)rig. U.S., prob. < Du. *doop* a dipping, sauce]

·pey (dō′pē) *adj.* **·pi·er, ·pi·est** *Slang* **1.** Lethargic from · as from narcotics. **2.** Stupid. Also **do′py.**

ppler effect *Physics* The change in the frequency of a ound, light, or other wave caused by movement of its source elative to the observer. Also **Doppler shift.** [after C. J. oppler, 1803–53, German physicist and mathematician]

r·ic (dôr′ik, dor′-) *adj. Archit.* Of or pertaining to the mplest of the three orders of Greek architecture charac- rized by heavy, fluted columns and unadorned capitals.

rm (dôrm) *n. Informal* A dormitory.

r·mant (dôr′mənt) *adj.* **1.** Asleep or as if asleep; mo- onless through sleep or torpidity. **2.** Not active; inopera- ve. **3.** *Biol.* Marked by partial suspension of vital proc- ses, as many animals and plants in winter. [< OF < L *rmire* to sleep] **— dor′man·cy** *n.*

r·mer (dôr′mər) *n.* **1.** A vertical window t in a small gable that projects from a sloping of. Also **dormer window.** **2.** The roofed ojection or gable itself. [< OF *dormeor* < L *dormire* to sleep]

DORMER WINDOW

r·mi·to·ry (dôr′mə·tôr′ē, -tō′rē) *n. pl.* **·ries** . A large room with sleeping accommodations r many persons. **2.** A building providing eeping and living accommodations, esp. a school, college, or resort. [< L < *dormire* to sleep]

r·mouse (dôr′mous′) *n. pl.* **·mice** A small, arboreal uropean rodent. [ME ? dial. E *dorm* to doze + MOUSE]

r·sal (dôr′səl) *adj. Anat.* Of, pertaining to, on or near e back. [< L *dorsum* back] **— dor′sal·ly** *adv.*

rsi- *combining form* **1.** On, to, or of the back. **2.** Dorso-. < L *dorsum* back]

rso- *combining form* Dorsal. [< L *dorsum* back]

·ry (dôr′ē, dō′rē) *n. pl.* **·ries** A deep, flat-bottomed row- oat with a sharp prow, used esp. by North Atlantic fisher- en. [< native Honduran name]

s·age (dō′sij) *n.* **1.** The administering of medicine in pre- ribed quantity. **2.** The amount of medicine to be given.

se (dōs) *n.* **1.** A particular quantity of medicine given prescribed to be given at one time. **2.** *Informal* A partic- lar amount of something usually disagreeable or painful. **— *v.* dosed, dos·ing** *v.t.* **1.** To give medicine, etc., to in oses. **2.** To give, as medicine or drugs, in doses. **— *v.i.* 3.** o take medicines. [< MF < Med.L < Gk. *dosis* gift]

·sim·e·ter (dō·sim′ə·tər) *n. Med.* An instrument for easuring the total amount of radiation absorbed in a given me. [< Gk. *dosis* dose + -METER]

·s·si·er (dos′ē·ā, dos′ē·ər; *Fr.* dô·syā′) *n.* A collection of apers, documents, etc., relating to a particular matter or erson. [< F, bundle of papers]

st (dust) Do: archaic or poetic second person singular, resent tense of DO[1]: used with *thou.*

t[1] (dot) *n.* **1.** A tiny, usu. round, mark; a speck, spot, or oint. **2.** A small amount. **3.** In writing and printing, a oint used as a part of a letter, in punctuation, etc. **4.** *lusic* **a** A point written after a note or rest that increases s time value by half. **b** A point placed over a note to indicate taccato treatment. **5.** A signal in Morse code that is of horter duration than the dash. **— on the dot** At exactly e specified time. **— *v.* dot·ted, dot·ting** *v.t.* **1.** To mark ith a dot or dots. **2.** To make by means of dots; stud. . To be scattered thickly over or about. **— *v.i.* 4.** To make dot or dots. **— to dot one's i's and cross one's t's** To e exact or correct. [OE *dott* head of a boil] **— dot′ter** *n.*

t[2] (dot, *Fr.* dō) *n.* A woman's marriage portion; dowry. < F < L *dos, dotis*] **— do·tal** (dōt′l) *adj.*

·tage (dō′tij) *n.* **1.** Feebleness of mind as a result of old ge; senility. **2.** Foolish and excessive affection.

·tard (dō′tərd) *n.* A foolish old person.

te (dōt) *v.i.* **dot·ed, dot·ing** **1.** To lavish extreme fond- ess: with *on* or *upon.* **2.** To be feeble-minded as a result of ld age. [ME *doten*] **— dot′er** *n.*

th (duth) Does: archaic or poetic third person singular, resent tense of DO[1].

t·ing (dō′ting) *adj.* **1.** Extravagantly or foolishly fond. . Feeble-minded; senile. **— dot′ing·ly** *adv.*

t·ter·el (dot′ər·əl) *n.* A migratory plover of northern urope and Asia. Also **dot′trel** (-rəl). [ME *dotrelle*]

t·tle (dot′l) *n.* The plug of tobacco ash left in a pipe after moking. Also **dot′tel.** [? Dim. of DOT[1]]

t·ty (dot′ē) *adj.* **·ti·er, ·ti·est** **1.** Consisting of or marked ith dots. **2.** *Informal* Of unsteady or feeble gait. **3.** *In- ormal* Slightly demented; mentally weak.

ouai Bible An English translation of the Vulgate Bible made by Roman Catholic scholars at Reims and Douai and ompleted in 1610. A revision of the New Testament was ublished in 1941. Also **Douay Bible** or **Version.**

doub·le (dub′əl) *adj.* **1.** Combined with another usu. iden- tical one: a *double* consonant. **2.** Two together: *double* lines. **3.** Twofold; duple. **4.** More than one; not single; dual: a *double* role. **5.** Consisting of two layers. **6.** Made for two: a *double* bed. **7.** Twice as great, as large, as many, etc.: *double* fare. **8.** Extra heavy, large, wide, etc.: a *double* blan- ket. **9.** Marked by duplicity; two-faced: a *double* life. **10.** *Music* Producing tones one octave lower than the notes indi- cated on a score: said of an instrument. **11.** *Bot.* Having the petals increased in number. **— *n.* 1.** Something that is twice as much. **2.** A duplicate. **3.** A player or singer who can substitute for another; understudy. **4.** A sharp or back- ward turn, as of a hunted fox. **5.** A trick or stratagem. **6.** A fold or pleat. **7.** *pl.* In tennis, etc., a game having two players on each side. **8.** In baseball, a fair hit that enables the batter to reach second base. **9.** In bridge, the act of challenging an opponent's bid by increasing its value and thus the penalty if the contract is not fulfilled; also, a hand warranting such an act. **— on** (or **at**) **the double** **1.** In double time. **2.** *Informal* Quickly. **— *v.* ·led, ·ling** *v.t.* **1.** To make twice as great in number, size, value, force, etc. **2.** To be twice the quantity or number of. **3.** To fold or bend one part of upon another: usu. with *over, up, back.* **4.** To clench (the fist): often with *up.* **5.** *Naut.* To sail around: to *double* a cape. **6.** *Music* To duplicate a voice or part in uni- son or in another octave. **7.** In baseball, to advance (a base runner) by making a two-base hit: He *doubled* him home. **8.** In bridge, to challenge (an opponent) by announcing a double. **— *v.i.* 9.** To become double; increase by an equal amount. **10.** To turn and go back on a course: often with *back.* **11.** To act or perform in two capacities. **12.** To serve as a double: to *double* for an actress. **13.** In baseball, to make a two-base hit. **14.** In bridge, to announce a doub- le. **— to double in brass** *U.S. Slang* **1.** To be useful or adept in another capacity apart from one's (or its) specialty. **2.** Originally, of musicians, to play a second instrument in addition to the regular one. **— to double back** **1.** To fold back. **2.** To turn and go back on the same or a parallel course. **— to double up** **1.** To bend over or cause to bend over, as from pain or laughter. **2.** *U.S. Informal* To share one's quarters, bed, etc., with another. **— *adv.*** In pairs; two- fold; doubly. [< OF < L *duplus* double]

doub·le-bar·reled (dub′əl·bar′əld) *adj.* **1.** Having two barrels, as a shotgun. **2.** Ambiguous, as a remark.

double bass **1.** The largest and deepest-toned of the stringed instruments played with a bow: also called **bass viol.** **2.** The contrabass.

double bassoon A double-reed instrument pitched an oc- tave below the ordinary bassoon: also called *contrabassoon.*

double bed A bed wide enough for two people.

double boiler A cooking utensil consisting of two pots, one fitting into the other. Food in the upper pot is cooked by the heat from water boiling in the lower pot.

dou·ble-breast·ed (dub′əl·bres′tid) *adj.* Having two rows of buttons and fastening so as to provide a double thickness of cloth across the breast: said of a coat or vest.

double chin A fat, fleshy fold under the chin.

doub·le-cross (*v.* dub′əl·krôs′, -kros′; *n.* dub′əl·krôs′, -kros′) *Slang v.t.* To betray by failing to act as promised. **— *n.*** A betrayal; a treacherous act. **— doub′le-cross′er** *n.*

doub·le-date (dub′əl·dāt′) *v.i.* **-dat·ed, -dat·ing** *U.S. In- formal* To make or go out on a social engagement of two couples. **— double date**

doub·le-deal·ing (dub′əl·dē′ling) *adj.* Treacherous; deceit- ful. **— *n.*** Treachery; duplicity. **— doub′le-deal′er** *n.*

doub·le-deck·er (dub′əl·dek′ər) *n.* **1.** A ship, vehicle, etc., having two levels. **2.** *U.S. Informal* A sandwich made with three slices of bread and two layers of filling.

doub·le-edged (dub′əl·ejd′) *adj.* **1.** Having two cutting edges. **2.** Applicable both ways, as an argument.

dou·ble-en·ten·dre (dōō·blän·tän′dr) *n.* A word or phrase of double meaning. [Alter. of F *double entente*]

double entry A method of bookkeeping in which every transaction is made to appear as both a debit and a credit.

double exposure *Photog.* The act of exposing the same film or plate twice, as in making a composite photograph; also, a print developed from a film or plate so exposed.

doub·le-faced (dub′əl·fāst′) *adj.* **1.** Having two faces. **2.** Deceitful; hypocritical; two-faced.

double feature A program of two motion pictures.

doub·le-head·er (dub′əl·hed′ər) *n.* **1.** In baseball, two games played in succession on the same day by the same two teams. **2.** A train pulled by two locomotives.

double indemnity A clause in a life insurance policy by which a payment of double the face value of the policy is made in the event of accidental death.

double jeopardy The peril under which a defendant is placed when he is tried more than once for the same offense.

doub·le-joint·ed (dub′əl·join′tid) *adj.* Having very flexible joints that allow limbs, fingers, etc., to be bent at unusual angles.
doub·le·ness (dub′əl·nis) *n.* **1.** The state or quality of being double. **2.** Duplicity; deceitfulness.
doub·le-park (dub′əl·pärk′) *v.t. & v.i.* To park (a motor vehicle) alongside another already parked at the curb.
double play In baseball, a play in which two base runners are put out during one continuous play of the ball.
double pneumonia Pneumonia affecting both lungs.
dou·ble-reed (dub′əl·rēd′) *adj. Music* Designating a group of wind instruments having two reeds united at the lower end and separated at the upper, as the oboe and bassoon.
double standard A moral standard that permits men greater freedom than women, esp. in sexual behavior.
doub·let (dub′lit) *n.* **1.** A short, close-fitting outer garment, with or without sleeves, worn by men during the Renaissance. **2.** A pair of like things; a couple. **3.** *Ling.* One of a pair of words derived from the same original but entering a language through different routes, as *regal* and *royal.* [< OF, something folded, orig. dim. of *double*]
double take Delayed reaction to a joke or unusual situation, characterized by blank acceptance initially and then sudden, startled realization of the actual significance.
double talk **1.** A rapid flow of actual words mixed with meaningless syllables, made to sound like talk. **2.** Ambiguous talk meant to deceive.
double time **1.** In the U.S. Army, a fast marching step at the rate of 180 three-foot steps per minute. **2.** A wage rate that is twice one's normal pay.
doub·le·tree (dub′el·trē′) *n. U.S.* A crossbar on a wagon, carriage or plow.
doub·loon (du·blōōn′) *n.* A former Spanish gold coin, originally worth about 16 dollars. [< Sp. *doble* double]
doub·ly (dub′lē) *adv.* **1.** In twofold degree; twice. **2.** In pairs. **3.** In twice the quantity.
doubt (dout) *v.t.* **1.** To hold the truth, validity, or reliability of as uncertain; hesitate to believe or accept. —*v.i.* **2.** To be unconvinced or mistrustful. —*n.* **1.** Lack of certainty about the truth or fact of something. **2.** A condition or state of affairs giving rise to uncertainty: Their fate was in *doubt.* **3.** An unresolved point or matter. —**beyond doubt** Unquestionably; certainly. —**no doubt 1.** Certainly. **2.** Most likely; probably. —**without doubt** Certainly. [< OF < L *dubitare*] —**doubt′er** *n.*
doubt·ful (dout′fəl) *adj.* **1.** Subject to or causing doubt; uncertain; unsettled. **2.** Having or experiencing doubt; undecided. **3.** Indistinct or obscure in appearance, meaning, etc.; vague; ambiguous. **4.** Of questionable character: a *doubtful* reputation. —**doubt′ful·ly** *adv.* —**doubt′ful·ness** *n.*
doubt·less (dout′lis) *adv.* **1.** Unquestionably. **2.** Probably. Also **doubt′less·ly.** —*adj.* Free from uncertainty.
douche (dōōsh) *n.* **1.** A jet of water, etc., directed into or onto some part of the body. **2.** A cleansing or medicinal treatment of this kind. **3.** A syringe or other device for administering a douche. —*v.* **douched, douch·ing** *v.t.* **1.** To cleanse or treat medicinally with a douche. —*v.i.* **2.** To administer a douche. [< F < Ital. < L *ducere* to lead]
dough (dō) *n.* **1.** A soft mass of moistened flour or meal and other ingredients, mixed for making bread, pastry, etc. **2.** Any soft, pasty mass. **3.** *Slang* Money. [OE *dāh*]
dough·nut (dō′nut′) *n.* A small cake of usu. leavened and sweetened dough, cooked by frying in deep fat.
dough·ty (dou′tē) *adj.* **·ti·er, ·ti·est** Valiant; brave: chiefly humorous. [OE *dyhtig, dohtig*] —**dough′ti·ly** *adv.* —**dough′ti·ness** *n.*
dough·y (dō′ē) *adj.* **dough·i·er, dough·i·est** Resembling dough in consistency or appearance; soft, pasty, pale, etc.
Douglas fir A large timber tree of the pine family, growing on the Pacific coast of the U.S.: often called *red fir, Nootka fir.* Also **Douglas hemlock, Douglas pine, Douglas spruce.** [after David *Douglas,* 1798–1834, Scottish botanist]
dour (dōōr, dour) *adj.* Forbidding and surly; morosely stern; ill-tempered. [< OF < L *durus* hard] —**dour′ly** *adv.* —**dour′ness** *n.*
dou·ra (dōōr′ə) See DURRA.
douse[1] (dous) *v.* **doused, dous·ing** *v.t.* **1.** To plunge into water or other liquid; dip suddenly; duck. **2.** To drench with liquid. —*v.i.* **3.** To become drenched or immersed. —*n.* A ducking or drenching. [Origin unknown]
douse[2] (dous) *v.t.* **doused, dous·ing 1.** *Informal* To put out; extinguish. **2.** *Informal* To take off, as clothes. **3.** *Naut.* To take in or haul down quickly, esp. a sail. [Cf. MDu. *dossen* to beat, strike]
dove[1] (duv) *n.* **1.** Any bird of the pigeon family, esp. the mourning dove, turtle dove, etc. **2.** *Usu. cap.* A symbol of the Holy Ghost. **3.** A symbol of peace. **4.** A gentle, innocent, tender person. [ME *duve*]
dove[2] (dōv) *Informal* Alternative past tense of DIVE.
dove·cote (duv′kōt′, -kot′) *n.* A box set on a pole or on a building, used for breeding pigeons. Also **dove′cot′** (-kot′).
dove·tail (duv′tāl′) *n.* **1.** A tenon shaped like a wedge and designed to interlock with a mortise of similar shape. **2.** A joint thus formed. —*v.t. & v.i.* **1.** To join by dovetails. **2.** To fit together closely or harmoniously.

DOVETAIL JOINT
a Before joining.
b Joined.

dow·a·ger (dou′ə·jər) *n.* **1.** In English law, a widow holding property or title derived from her deceased husband. **2.** *Informal* An elderly woman of dignified bearing. [< OF *douagiere,* ult. < L *dotare* to give]
dow·dy (dou′dē) *adj.* **·di·er, ·di·est** Notably devoid of smartness in dress; frumpish. —*n. pl.* **·dies** A dowdy woman. [ME *doude* slut] —**dow′di·ly** *adv.* —**dow′di·ness** *n.*
dow·el (dou′əl) *n.* A pin or peg fitted tightly into adjacent holes of two pieces so as to hold them together. Also **dowel pin.** —*v.t.* **dow·eled** or **·elled, dow·el·ing** or **·el·ling** To furnish or fasten with dowels. [ME, ? < MLG *dovel* plug]

DOWELS

dow·er (dou′ər) *n.* **1.** The part of a deceased man's estate that is assigned by law to his widow for life. **2.** A natural talent or endowment. **3.** A dowry. —*v.t.* **1.** To provide with a dower. **2.** To endow, as with a talent or quality. [< OF < LL < L *dos, dotis* dowry]
dow·er·y (dou′ər·ē) See DOWRY.
down[1] (doun) *adv.* **1.** From a higher to a lower place. In or on a lower place, level, etc. **3.** On or to the groun **4.** To or toward the south. **5.** To or in a place regarded distant or outlying: *down* on the farm. **6.** Below the surfa or horizon. **7.** From an upright to a prone or prostrate po tion: to knock a man *down.* **8.** To lesser bulk, heavier co sistency, etc.: The mixture boiled *down.* **9.** To less activi intensity, etc.: Things quieted *down.* **10.** To a low amount, rate, etc.: Prices have gone *down.* **11.** In or in subjection or control: to put the rebels *down.* **12.** In or in a depressed or prostrate physical or mental state. **13.** Co pletely; fully: loaded *down* with honors. **14.** From an earl time or individual. **15.** In cash as partial payment: fi dollars *down.* **16.** In writing: Take *down* his name. **down with** (Let us) do away with or overthrow. —*adj.* Directed downward: a *down* curve. **2.** *Informal* Downca depressed. **3.** Given in cash as a partial amount: a *do* payment. **4.** In games, behind an opponent by a specifi number of points, strokes, etc. **5.** In football, not in pla said of the ball. —**down and out** In a completely misera state, as of poverty or desolation. —**down on** *Informal* A noyed with or hostile to. —*prep.* **1.** In a descending dire tion along, upon, or in. **2.** During the course of: *down* t years. —*v.t.* **1.** To knock, throw, or put down. **2.** *Inf mal* To swallow quickly; gulp. —*n.* **1.** A downward mov ment; descent. **2.** A reverse of fortune: chiefly in the phra **ups and downs.** **3.** In football, any of the four consecuti plays during which a team must advance the ball at least t yards to keep possession of it; also, the declaring of the b as out of play, or the play immediately preceding this de laration. [OE *dūne* < *of dūne* from the hill]
down[2] (doun) *n.* **1.** The fine, soft plumage of birds und the feathers, esp. that on the breast of water birds. **2.** A feathery, fluffy substance. [< ON *dūnn*]
down[3] (doun) *n.* **1.** *pl.* Turf-covered, undulating tracts upland, esp. in southern and SE England. **2.** A hill, esp. sand; dune. [OE *dūn.* Akin to DUNE.]
down·cast (doun′kast′, -käst′) *adj.* **1.** Directed downwar *downcast* eyes. **2.** Low in spirits; dejected; depressed. — **1.** The act of casting down. **2.** An air shaft, as in a min
Down East *Informal* New England, esp. Maine. —**dow east** (doun′ēst′) *adj.* —**down′east′er** *n.*
down·fall (doun′fôl′) *n.* **1.** A sudden descent, as in reput tion or fortune; collapse; ruin. **2.** A sudden, heavy fall rain, etc. **3.** A deadfall (def. 1). —**down′fall·en** *adj.*
down·grade (doun′grād′) *n.* A descending slope, as of a h or road. —**on the downgrade** Declining in health, reput tion, status, etc. —*adj.* Downhill. —*v.t.* **·grad·ed, ·gra ing** To reduce in status, salary, etc.
down·heart·ed (doun′här′tid) *adj.* Dejected; discourage —**down′heart′ed·ly** *adv.* —**down′heart′ed·ness** *n.*
down·hill (*adv.* doun′hil′; *adj.* doun′hil′) *adv.* In a dow ward direction; toward the bottom of a hill. —**to go dow hill** To decline, as in success or health. —*adj.* Descendin
Downing Street (dou′ning) **1.** A street in London; si of many British government offices. **2.** *Informal* The Britis government.
down payment An initial payment on a purchase.
down·pour (doun′pôr′, -pōr′) *n.* A heavy fall of rain.
down·right (doun′rīt′) *adj.* **1.** Thorough; utter: *downrig* nonsense. **2.** Straightforward. —*adv.* Thoroughly; utterl
down·stairs (*adv.* doun′stârz′; *adj. & n.* doun′stârz′) *ad* **1.** Down the stairs. **2.** On or to a lower floor. —*adj.* Sit ated on a lower floor: also **down′stair′.** —*n.* The dow stairs part of a house or other building.

-n·stream (*adv.* doun′strēm′; *adj.* doun′strēm′) *adv.* -wn the stream. — *adj.* In the direction of the current.

-n·town (*adv.* doun′toun′; *adj.* doun′toun′) *adv.* To, -ward, or in the geographically lower section of a town or -y. — *adj.* Located in the geographically lower section of -own or city, usu. the chief business section.

-n·trod·den (doun′trod′n) *adj.* **1.** Trampled under foot. Subjugated; oppressed. Also **down′trod′.**

-n·ward (doun′wərd) *adv.* **1.** From a higher to a lower -el, position, etc. **2.** From an earlier or more remote time, -ce, etc. Also **down′wards,** occasionally **down′ward·ly.** -*adj.* **1.** Descending from a higher to a lower level. **2.** -scending in course from that which is more remote.

-n·y (dou′nē) *adj.* **down·i·er, down·i·est 1.** Of, like, or -ered with down. **2.** Soft; quiet. — **down′i·ness** *n.*

-·ry (dou′rē) *n. pl.* **·ries 1.** The money or property a -e brings to her husband at marriage: also called *portion.* A natural talent or endowment. [See DOWER]

-se[1] (dous) See DOUSE[1].

-se[2] (douz) *v.i.* **dowsed, dows·ing** To search for with a -ining rod. [Origin uncertain] — **dows′er** *n.*

-s·ing rod (douz′ing) A divining rod.

-ol·o·gy (dok·sol′ə·jē) *n. pl.* **·gies** A hymn or verse of -ise to God. — **greater doxology** The Gloria in excelsis -o. — **lesser doxology** The Gloria Patri. [< Med.L < . < *doxa* praise + *legein* to speak] — **dox·o·log·i·cal** -k′sə·loj′i·kəl) *adj.* — **dox′o·log′i·cal·ly** *adv.*

-ley, doy·ly (doi′lē) See DOILY.

-e (dōz) *v.* **dozed, doz·ing** *v.i.* **1.** To sleep lightly or be -wsy for brief periods of time; nap. — *v.t.* **2.** To spend -ne) in napping or in being half asleep. — **to doze off** To into a light, brief sleep. — *n.* A light, brief sleep; nap. Scand., ? ult. < ON *dūsa* to doze]

-en (duz′ən) *n. pl.* **doz·ens;** *when preceded by a number,* -·**en** A group or set of twelve things. Abbr. *doz, doz., dz.* OF < L < *duo* two + *decem* ten]

-y (dō′zē) *adj.* **·zi·er, ·zi·est** Drowsy. — **do′zi·ly** *adv.* — **zi·ness** *n.*

-b[1] (drab) *adj.* **drab·ber, drab·best 1.** Lacking bright-ss; dull and monotonous. **2.** Having a dull, yellowish -own color. **3.** Made of a thick, woolen, yellowish brown -th. — *n.* **1.** A dull, yellowish brown color. **2.** A thick, -olen, yellowish brown cloth. [< F *drap* cloth < LL *drap*-s, ? < Celtic] — **drab′ly** *adv.* — **drab′ness** *n.*

-b[2] (drab) *n.* **1.** A slipshod, untidy woman. **2.** A prosti-e; slut. — *v.i.* **drabbed, drab·bing 1.** To associate with -stitutes. **2.** To be a prostitute. [? < Celtic]

-chm (dram) *n.* **1.** A dram. **2.** A drachma.

-ch·ma (drak′mə) *n. pl.* **·mas** or **·mae** (-mē) **1.** An an-nt Greek silver coin. **2.** The standard monetary unit of -eece: in 1960 worth about 3 U.S. cents. **3.** An ancient -eek unit of weight. **4.** Any of several modern weights, as -e dram. [< L < Gk. *drachmē* a handful]

-ft (draft, dräft) *n.* **1.** The act or process of selecting an -lividual or individuals for some special duty or purpose; -., the selection of men for compulsory military service; -nscription. **2.** The condition of being selected for some -ecial duty or purpose; also, those selected. **3.** A current -air. **4.** A device for controlling the airflow, as in a furnace. A written order, as of an individual or bank, directing the -yment of money. **6.** A sketch, plan, or design of some-ng to be made. **7.** A preliminary or rough version of a -iting. **8.** A quantity of liquid for drinking: a *draft* of ale. The act of drinking; also, the liquid taken at one drink. -. The drawing of liquid from its container. **11.** The act drawing in a fishnet; also, the amount of fish taken with -e drawing of a net. **12.** The act of drawing air, smoke, -., into the lungs; also, the air, etc., taken in. **13.** The -lling of something, as a loaded wagon; also, the load -lled. **14.** A heavy demand or drain on something. **15.** Draughts. **16.** *Naut.* The depth of water required for a -ip to float, esp. when loaded. — **on draft** Ready to be -awn, as beer, from a cask, etc. — *v.t.* **1.** To draw up in -eliminary form, esp. in writing. **2.** To select and draw -, as for military service. **3.** To draw off or away. **4.** To -t a draft on (a stone). — *adj.* **1.** Suitable to be used for -lling heavy loads: a *draft* animal. **2.** Not bottled, as beer. -so *Brit.* **draught.** [ME < OE *dragan* to draw]

-ft board An official board of civilians that selects men -r compulsory service in the U.S. armed forces.

-ft dodger One who avoids or attempts to avoid con-ription into military service.

-ft·ee (draf·tē′, dräf-) *n.* A person drafted for service in -e armed forces.

-fts·man (drafts′mən, dräfts′-) *n. pl.* **·men** (-mən) **1.** -ne who draws or prepares designs or plans of buildings, -achinery, etc. **2.** One who draws up documents, as deeds. -An artist esp. skilled in drawing.

draft·y (draf′tē, dräf′-) *adj.* **draft·i·er, draft·i·est** Having or exposed to drafts of air: a *drafty* room. Also spelled *draughty.* — **draft′i·ly** *adv.* — **draft′i·ness** *n.*

drag (drag) *v.* **dragged, drag·ging** *v.t.* **1.** To pull along by main force; haul. **2.** To sweep or search the bottom of, as with a net or grapnel; dredge. **3.** To catch or recover, as with a grapnel or net. **4.** To draw along heavily and weari-ly. **5.** To harrow (land). **6.** To continue tediously: often with *on* or *out.* **7.** To introduce (an irrelevant subject or matter) into a discussion, argument, etc.: usu. with *in.* — *v.i.* **8.** To be pulled or hauled along. **9.** To move heavily or slowly. **10.** To lag behind. **11.** To pass slowly. **12.** To use a grapnel, drag, or dredge. — **to drag one's feet** *U.S. Informal* To act with deliberate slowness. — *n.* **1.** The act of dragging. **2.** The resistance encountered in dragging: a heavy *drag* on the left wheel. **3.** A slow, heavy, usu. im-peded motion or movement. **4.** Something that slows down movement, as a clog on a wheel. **5.** Something heavy that is dragged. **6.** A contrivance for dragging through water to find or bring up something. **7.** Anything that hinders. **8.** A stagecoach, with seats inside and on the top. **9.** *U.S. Slang* Influence that brings special favors; pull. **10.** *Slang* A puff on a cigarette, etc. **11.** *U.S. Slang* One who or that which is tedious or colorless. [ME, prob. < OE *dragan*]

drag·gle (drag′əl) *v.* **·gled, ·gling** *v.t.* **1.** To make soiled or wet by dragging in mud or water. — *v.i.* **2.** To become wet or soiled. **3.** To follow slowly; lag. [Freq. of DRAG]

drag·net (drag′net′) *n.* **1.** A net to be drawn along the bot-tom of the water or along the ground, to find or capture something. **2.** Any device or plan for catching a criminal.

drag·o·man (drag′ə·mən) *n. pl.* **·mans** (-mənz) or **·men** (-mən) An interpreter or guide for travelers in the Near East. [< F < LGk. < Arabic *tarjumān* translator]

drag·on (drag′ən) *n.* **1.** A mythical, serpentlike, winged monster. **2.** A fierce, violent person. **3.** An overbearing, watchful woman. [< OF < L < Gk. *drakōn* serpent]

drag·on·fly (drag′ən·flī′) *n. pl.* **·flies** A predatory insect having a slender body, four wings, and strong jaws.

dra·goon (drə·gōōn′) *n.* In some European armies, a cav-alryman. — *v.t.* **1.** To harass by dragoons. **2.** To coerce; browbeat. [< F *dragon,* a type of 17th c. firearm]

drain (drān) *v.t.* **1.** To draw off (water, etc.) gradually. **2.** To draw water, etc., from: to *drain* a swamp. **3.** To empty (a glass, cup, etc.) by drinking. **4.** To use up gradually; ex-haust. **5.** To filter. — *v.i.* **6.** To flow off gradually. **7.** To become dry by the flowing off or away of liquid. **8.** To dis-charge waters contained: said of an area: The region *drains* into the lake. — *n.* **1.** A trench, or similar device for drain-ing. **2.** *Surg.* A substance, or appliance inserted into a wound or cavity to afford a channel for discharge. **3.** A con-tinuous outflow, expenditure, or depletion. **4.** The act of draining. [OE *drēahnian*] — **drain′er** *n.*

drain·age (drā′nij) *n.* **1.** The act or method of draining. **2.** A system of drains. **3.** That which is drained off. **4.** A drainage basin.

drainage basin A large surface area whose waters are drained off into a principal river system.

drain·pipe (drān′pīp′) *n.* A pipe used for draining.

drake (drāk) *n.* A male duck. [ME]

dram (dram) *n.* **1.** An apothecaries' weight equal to 60 grains, 3.89 grams, or one eighth of an ounce. Abbr. *dr.* **2.** An avoirdupois measure equal to 27.34 grains, 1.77 grams, or one sixteenth of an ounce. See table front of book. **3.** A fluid dram. **4.** A drink of alcoholic liquor. **5.** A drachma. **6.** A small portion. Also spelled *drachm.* — *v.* **drammed, dram·ming** *v.t.* **1.** To ply with liquor. — *v.i.* **2.** To use intoxicants freely. [< OF < L < Gk. *drachmē* a handful]

dra·ma (drä′mə, dram′ə) *n.* **1.** A literary composition writ-ten to be performed upon a stage, telling a story, usu. of hu-man conflicts and emotions; a play. **2.** Stage plays as a branch of literature: the classical *drama.* **3.** The art or pro-fession of writing, acting, or producing plays. **4.** A series of dramatic events. **5.** The quality of being dramatic. [< LL < Gk., action < *draein* to act, do]

Dram·a·mine (dram′ə·mēn) *n.* Proprietary name of a drug for relieving motion sickness. Also **dram′a·mine.**

dra·mat·ic (drə·mat′ik) *adj.* **1.** Of, connected with, or like the drama. **2.** Characterized by the action or spirit of the drama; theatrical. — **dra·mat′i·cal·ly** *adv.*

dra·mat·ics (drə·mat′iks) *n.pl.* (*usu. construed as sing. in def. 2*) **1.** Dramatic performance, esp. by amateurs. **2.** The art of staging or acting plays.

dram·a·tis per·so·nae (dram′ə·tis pər·sō′nē) *Latin* The characters of a play; also, a list of these.

dram·a·tist (dram′ə·tist) *n.* One who writes plays.

dram·a·tize (dram′ə·tīz) *v.* **·tized, ·tiz·ing** *v.t.* **1.** To pre-sent in dramatic form; adapt for performance, as a play. **2.** To represent or interpret (events, oneself, etc.) in a theatrical manner. —*v.i.* **3.** To be suitable for dramatizing. Also *Brit.* **dram′a·tise.** —**dram′a·ti·za′tion** *n.*

dram·a·turge (dram′ə·tûrj) *n.* A dramatist. Also **dram′a·tur′gist.** [< F < Gk. < *drama* play + *ergein* to work]

dram·a·tur·gy (dram′ə·tûr′jē) *n.* The art of writing or producing plays, or of acting in them; dramatics. —**dram·a·tur·gic** (dram′ə·tûr′jik) or **·gi·cal** *adj.*

drank (drangk) Past tense of DRINK.

drape (drāp) *v.* **draped, drap·ing** *v.t.* **1.** To cover or adorn in a graceful fashion, as with drapery or clothing. **2.** To arrange in graceful folds. **3.** *Informal* To dispose in a leisurely or sloppy manner. —*v.i.* **4.** To hang in folds. —*n.* **1.** *U.S. & Canadian Usu. pl.* Drapery. **2.** The way in which cloth hangs, as in clothing. [< F *draper* to weave]

drap·er (drā′pər) *n.* *Brit.* A dealer in cloth or dry goods.

dra·per·y (drā′pər·ē) *n.* *pl.* **·er·ies 1.** Loosely hanging attire, esp. on figures in painting, sculpture, etc. **2.** *Often pl.* Hangings or curtains arranged in loose folds. **3.** Cloth.

dras·tic (dras′tik) *adj.* Acting vigorously; extreme. [< Gk. *drastikos* effective < *draein* to act] —**dras′ti·cal·ly** *adv.*

draught (draft, dräft) See DRAFT.

draughts (drafts, dräfts) *n.pl.* (*construed as sing.*) *Brit.* The game of checkers: also spelled *drafts.* [See DRAFT.]

draughts·man (drafts′mən, dräfts′-) *n.* *pl.* **·men** (-mən) See DRAFTSMAN.

draught·y (draf′tē, dräf′-) See DRAFTY.

Dra·vid·i·an (drə·vid′ē·ən) *n.* **1.** A member of an ancient people of southern India. **2.** A family of languages spoken in southern India and northern Ceylon. —*adj.* Of the Dravidians or their languages: also **Dra·vid′ic.**

draw (drô) *v.* **drew, drawn, draw·ing** *v.t.* **1.** To cause to move toward or to follow behind an agent exerting physical force; pull. **2.** To obtain, as from a receptacle: to *draw* water. **3.** To extract, as a tooth, cork, etc. **4.** To cause to flow forth, as blood. **5.** To bring forth; elicit: to *draw* praise. **6.** To take or pull off, on, or out, as a sword, gloves, etc. **7.** To portray with lines or words; sketch; delineate: to *draw* a portrait. **8.** To deduce or extract by a mental process: to *draw* a conclusion. **9.** To attract; entice: Honey *draws* flies. **10.** To pull tight, as a rope. **11.** To make or manufacture by stretching or hammering, as wire or dies. **12.** To take in, as air or a liquid, by inhaling or sucking. **13.** To close or shut as curtans. **14.** To disembowel. **15.** To cause (an abscess, etc.) to soften and drain by applying a poultice. **16.** To shrink or wrinkle. **17.** To extract (essence) by infusion, distillation, etc.: to *draw* tea. **18.** To select or obtain, as by chance; also, to win (a prize) in a lottery. **19.** To receive; earn, as a salary or interest. **20.** To withdraw, as money from a bank. **21.** To write out; draft (a check). **22.** *Naut.* Of a vessel, to sink to (a specified depth) in floating. **23.** To leave undecided, as a game or contest. —*v.i.* **24.** To practice the art of drawing; sketch. **25.** To exert a pulling or drawing force. **26.** To approach or retreat: to *draw* near or away. **27.** To exert an attracting influence. **28.** To pull out or unsheathe a weapon for action: usu. with *on.* **29.** To shrink or become contracted, as a wound. **30.** To cause redness or irritation of the skin, as a poultice or blister. **31.** To obtain by making an application to some source; with *on* or *upon*: to *draw* on one's credit; to *draw* on one's experience. **32.** To produce a current of air: This chimney *draws* well. **33.** To end a contest without a decision; tie. —**to draw a blank** To be unsuccessful. —**to draw on** To approach: Evening is *drawing on.* —**to draw oneself up** To straighten up or stiffen, as in anger or indignation. —**to draw out 1.** To prolong. **2.** To cause (someone) to talk freely. —**to draw the line** To fix a limit and refuse to go further. —**to draw up 1.** To write out in proper form: to *draw up* a deed. **2.** To bring or come to a standstill, as horses. **3.** To come alongside. —*n.* **1.** The act of drawing. **2.** The act of drawing out a weapon for action. **3.** Something drawn, as a ticket in a lottery. **4.** Something that attracts a large audience. **5.** A stalemate; tie. **6.** *U.S.* A gully or ravine into which water drains. [OE *dragan*]

draw·back (drô′bak′) *n.* **1.** Anything that hinders progress, success, etc. **2.** A refund on money paid, esp. on duties for reexported goods or on excess payment for freight.

draw·bridge (drô′brij′) *n.* A bridge of which the whole or a part may be raised, let down, or drawn aside.

DRAWBRIDGE

draw·ee (drô′ē′) *n.* One on whom an order for the payment of money is drawn.

draw·er (drô′ər *for def. 1*; drôr *for def. 2*) *n.* **1.** One who draws; as: **a** A draftsman. **b** One who draws a check or money order. **c** One who draws beer, etc. **2.** A sliding receptacle, as in a desk, that can be drawn out.

draw·ers (drôrz) *n.pl.* An undergarment covering the lo part of the body, including all or part of each leg.

draw·ing (drô′ing) *n.* **1.** The act of one who or that w draws. **2.** That which is drawn. **3.** The art of represen something, usu. by pen, pencil, or crayon. **4.** The pict sketch, or design produced by this art. **5.** A lottery.

drawing board A smooth, flat board to which paper, is attached for making drawings.

drawing card Something that attracts a large audien

drawing room **1.** A room in which visitors are rece and entertained. **2.** *Chiefly Brit.* A formal reception drawing room. **3.** *U.S.* A private compartment in a slee car on a train. [Short for WITHDRAWING ROOM]

draw·knife (drô′nīf′) *n.* *pl.* **·knives** (-nīvz′) A knife w handle at each end, used for shaving over a surface wi drawing motion. Also **drawing knife.**

drawl (drôl) *v.t. & v.i.* To speak or pronounce slowly, with a drawing out of the vowels. —*n.* The act of draw [? Freq. of DRAW] —**drawl′er** *n.* —**drawl′ing·ly** *adv.* **drawl·y** *adj.*

drawn (drôn) Past participle of DRAW.

drawn butter *U.S.* A sauce of melted butter.

drawn work Ornamental openwork made by pulling threads of fabric and forming various patterns.

dray (drā) *n.* A low, strong cart with removable sides carrying heavy articles. —*v.t.* To transport by dray. < *dragan* to draw] —**dray′man** *n.*

dray·age (drā′ij) *n.* **1.** The act of conveying in a dray. The charge for draying.

dread (dred) *v.t.* To anticipate with great fear or anxi —*adj.* **1.** Causing great fear; terrible. **2.** Exciting awe. *n.* **1.** A terrifying anticipation, as of evil or danger. **2.** mixed with deep respect; awe. **3.** A person or thing inspi fear or awe. [ME < OE *ondrǣdan*]

dread·ful (dred′fəl) *adj.* **1.** Inspiring dread; terrible. *Informal* Disgusting; shocking; very bad; awful. —**dre ful·ly** *adv.* —**dread′ful·ness** *n.*

dread·nought (dred′nôt′) *n.* Any battleship of great carrying large-caliber guns. Also **dread′naught′.**

dream (drēm) *n.* **1.** A series of thoughts or images pas through the mind in sleep; also, the mental state in w this occurs. **2.** A daydream; reverie. **3.** A cherishe vain hope or ambition. **4.** Anything of dreamlike qua esp. of unreal beauty or charm. —*v.* **dreamed** or **dre** (dremt), **dream·ing** *v.t.* **1.** To see or imagine in a dream. To imagine, as in a dream. **3.** To spend (time) in idle erie: with *away.* —*v.i.* **4.** To have a dream or dreams. To indulge in daydreams. **6.** To consider something as sible: with *of*: I would not *dream* of staying. —**to drean** *Informal* To concoct or create, as by ingenuity or clevern [ME < OE *drēam* joy] —**dream′er** *n.* —**dream′ful** —**dream′ful·ly** *adv.* —**dream′ing·ly** *adv.* —**dream** *adj.* —**dream′less·ly** *adv.* —**dream′like′** *adj.*

dream·y (drē′mē) *adj.* **dream·i·er, dream·i·est 1.** Of, taining to, or causing dreams. **2.** Appropriate to dreams. Given to dreams; visionary. **4.** Soothing. **5.** *Infor* Wonderful. —**dream′i·ly** *adv.* —**dream′i·ness** *n.*

drear (drir) *adj.* *Poetic* Dreary.

drear·y (drir′ē) *adj.* **drear·i·er, drear·i·est 1.** Causin manifesting sadness or gloom. **2.** Dull or monotonous. < *drēor* gore] —**drear′i·ly** *adv.* —**drear′i·ness** *n.*

dredge[1] (drej) *n.* **1.** A large, powerful scoop or suction paratus for removing mud or gravel from the bottoms channels, harbors, etc. Also **dredging machine.** **2.** A smaller device for bringing up something from under wa —*v.* **dredged, dredg·ing** *v.t.* **1.** To clear or widen by me of a dredge. **2.** To remove, catch, or gather with a dred —*v.i.* **3.** To use a dredge. [ME *dreg*] —**dredg′er** *n.*

dredge[2] (drej) *v.t.* **dredged, dredg·ing** To sprinkle or c with a powdered substance, esp. flour. [ME < OF < *tragemata* spices < Gk.]

dregs (dregz) *n.pl.* **1.** The sediment of liquids, esp. of b erages; lees. **2.** Coarse, worthless residue: the *dregs* of ciety. **3.** (*construed as sing.*) A small amount left ov [ME < ON *dregg*] —**dreg′gy** *adj.* —**dreg′gi·ness** *n.*

drench (drench) *v.t.* **1.** To wet thoroughly; soak. **2.** To administer a potion to by force. —*n.* **1.** *Vet.* A liq medicine administered by force. **2.** A large quantity fluid. **3.** A water solution for drenching. **4.** The act drenching. [OE *drencan* to cause to drink] —**drench′er**

Dres·den (drez′dən) *n.* A china made in Dresden, Germa

dress (dres) *v.* **dressed** or **drest, dress·ing** *v.t.* **1.** To p clothes on; clothe. **2.** To supply with clothing. **3.** To tr or decorate, as a store window. **4.** To treat medicinally, a wound. **5.** To comb and arrange (hair). **6.** To curry horse). **7.** To prepare (stone, timber, etc.) for use or sa **8.** To clean (fowl, game, etc.) for cooking. **9.** To till, tri or prune. **10.** To put in proper alignment, as troops. — **11.** To put on or wear clothing, esp. formal clothing. **1** To come into proper alignment. —**to dress down** *Inform* To rebuke severely; scold. —**to dress up** To put on or we rmal attire. — *n.* **1.** An outer garment for a woman or ild, consisting of a skirt and waist, usu. in one piece. **2.** lothing collectively. **3.** Formal or fashionable clothing. . External adornment or appearance. — *adj.* **1.** Of, perining to, or suitable for a dress. **2.** To be worn on formal casions: a *dress* suit. [< OF *dresser* to arrange, ult. < L *dis-* apart + *regere* to guide]

ess circle A section of seats in a theater or concert hall, su. the first gallery behind and above the orchestra.

ess·er[1] (dres′ər) *n.* **1.** One who dresses something. **2.** ne who assists another in dressing. **3.** One who dresses ell or in a particular way: a fancy *dresser.* **4.** A tool used dressing stone, leather, etc. **5.** *Brit.* A surgical assistant.

ess·er[2] (dres′ər) *n.* **1.** A chest of drawers for articles of othing, usu. with a mirror. **2.** A piece of furniture for olding dishes, silverware, etc. [< OF *dresser* to dress]

ess·ing (dres′ing) *n.* **1.** The act of one who or that which esses. **2.** That with which something is dressed, as meditted bandages for a wound, manure for the soil, etc. **3.** A uffing for poultry or roasts. **4.** A sauce for salads, etc.

ess·ing-down (dres′ing·doun′) *n. U.S. Informal* **1.** A vere scolding. **2.** A beating.

essing gown A loose gown worn while lounging at home.

essing room A room for dressing, as in a theater.

essing table A small table or stand with a mirror, used hile putting on make-up, grooming the hair, etc.

ess·mak·er (dres′mā′kər) *n.* One who makes women's esses or other articles of clothing. — *adj.* Not severely ilored; having soft, feminine lines. — **dress′mak′ing** *n.*

ess parade A formal military parade in dress uniform.

ess rehearsal A final rehearsal of a play, done with the stumes, lighting, etc., to be used in the public performance.

ess suit A man's suit for formal evening wear.

ess·y (dres′ē) *adj.* **dress·i·er, dress·i·est** *Informal* **1.** aving or giving an appearance of smart elegance; stylish; nic. **2.** Fond of dressing up. — **dress′i·ness** *n.*

ew (drōō) Past tense of DRAW.

ib (drib) *n. Dial.* Driblet. — **dribs and drabs** Small uantities. [Var. of DRIP]

ib·ble (drib′əl) *v.t. & v.i.* **·bled, ·bling** **1.** To fall or let fall drops. **2.** To drool. **3.** In basketball, to propel (the ball) y bouncing. **4.** In soccer, to propel (the ball) by successive cks. — *n.* **1.** A small quantity of a liquid falling in drops. . The act of dribbling. — **drib′bler** *n.*

ib·let (drib′lit) *n.* **1.** A small drop of water or other liqid. **2.** A tiny quantity of something. Also **drib′blet.**

ied (drīd) Past tense and past participle of DRY.

·er (drī′ər) Comparative of DRY. — *n.* **1.** One who or hat which dries. **2.** A substance added to paint, etc., to ake it dry more quickly. **3.** A mechanical device for dryg, as for drying clothes. Also spelled *dryer.*

i·est (drī′ist) Superlative of DRY: also spelled *dryest.*

ift (drift) *n.* **1.** The act of moving along, or the fact of eing carried along, in or as in a current of water, air, etc. . A force or influence that drives something along. **3.** The ourse along which something is directed; tendency or innt: the *drift* of a conversation. **4.** A usu. slow, broad curnt of water, as in some parts of an ocean. **5.** The rate at hich a current of water moves. **6.** The direction of a curnt of water. **7.** Something driven along or heaped up by ir or water currents: a snow *drift.* **8.** Material carried long from one place to another. **9.** The act of driving somehing along. **10.** The distance a ship, aircraft, missile, etc., driven from its direct or intended course by wind, sea, tc. **11.** *Mining* A horizontal passage in a mine. — *v.i* . To move along in or as in a current. **2.** To become eaped up by air currents or water currents. **3.** To move long aimlessly. — *v.t.* **4.** To cause to drift. [ME < OE *rīfan* to drive] — **drift′er** *n.* — **drift′y** *adj.*

ift·age (drif′tij) *n.* **1.** The act or process of drifting. **2.** Deviation caused by drifting. **3.** Something carried along r deposited by air currents or water currents.

ift·wood (drift′wŏŏd′) *n.* Wood floated or drifted by vater; esp., wood washed up on a seashore.

ill[1] (dril) *n.* **1.** A tool used for boring holes in metal, tone, wood, or other hard substances. **2.** A mollusk that ills oysters by drilling holes in their shells. **3.** A process of raining marked by fixed procedures and much repetition, as n gymnastics, in arithmetic, etc. **4.** The act of teaching hrough such training; also, a particular exercise. — **Syn.** See PRACTICE. — *v.t.* **1.** To pierce with or as with a drill. **2.** To make (a hole) with a drill. **3.** To train in military proedures, etc. **4.** To teach by drill. — *v.i.* **5.** To make a hole with or as with a drill. **6.** To take part in a drill. **7.** To rain someone by drill. [< Du. *drillen* to bore] — **drill′er** *n.*

rill[2] (dril) *Agric. n.* **1.** A machine for planting seeds in rows. **2.** A furrow in which seeds are sown. **3.** A row of seeds so planted. — *v.t. & v.i.* To sow or plant in rows.

drill[3] (dril) *n.* Heavy, twilled linen or cotton cloth. Also **drill′ing.** [< G *drillich* cloth with three threads]

drill[4] (dril) *n.* A baboon of West Africa, similar to the mandrill. [? < native name]

drill·mas·ter (dril′mas′tər, -mäs′-) *n.* One who teaches or trains by drilling; esp., a trainer in military exercises.

drill press A machine tool used in drilling holes.

dri·ly (drī′lē) See DRYLY.

drink (dringk) *v.* **drank** (*Archaic* **drunk**), **drunk** (*Archaic* **drunk·en** or **drank**), **drink·ing** *v.t.* **1.** To take into the mouth and swallow (a liquid). **2.** To soak up or absorb (liquid or moisture). **3.** To receive eagerly through the senses or the mind. **4.** To swallow the contents of (a glass, etc.). — *v.i.* **5.** To swallow a liquid. **6.** To drink alcoholic liquors, especially to excess. **7.** To drink a toast: with *to.* — **to drink the health of** To offer homage or good wishes to by a toast. — *n.* **1.** A drinkable liquid; beverage. **2.** A portion of liquid swallowed. **3.** Alcoholic liquor. **4.** The practice of drinking alcoholic liquor to excess. **5.** *Slang* A body of water. [OE *drincan*] — **drink′a·ble** *adj.* — **drink′er** *n.*

drip (drip) *n.* **1.** The falling of liquids in drops. **2.** Liquid falling in drops; also, the sound so made. **3.** Melted fat exuded from meat being roasted or fried. Also **drip′pings.** **4.** *Archit.* A projecting molding for shedding rain. **5.** *U.S. Slang* A disagreeable, insipid, or inept individual. — *v.t. & v.i.* **dripped** or **dript, drip·ping** To fall or cause to fall in drops. [OE *dryppan*] — **drip′py** *adj.*

drip-dry (drip′drī′) *adj.* Designating or pertaining to a garment or fabric treated to dry quickly and retain its proper shape after being hung while dripping wet. — *v.i.* **-dried, -dry·ing** To dry in such a manner.

drive (drīv) *v.* **drove, driv·en, driv·ing** *v.t.* **1.** To push or propel onward with force. **2.** To force to work or activity. **3.** To goad by force or compulsion: Failure *drove* him to despair. **4.** To cause to penetrate by force. **5.** To produce by penetration: to *drive* a well. **6.** To cause to go rapidly by striking or throwing. **7.** To control the operation of (a vehicle). **8.** To transport in a vehicle. **9.** To provide the motive power for. **10.** To carry through without letup: to *drive* a hard bargain. — *v.i.* **11.** To move along rapidly. **12.** To strike, throw, or impel a ball, etc., with force. **13.** To drive a vehicle. **14.** To be transported in a vehicle. **15.** To work toward a particular objective or meaning: with *at.* — **to drive home** **1.** To force in all the way, as a nail. **2.** To make evident with force or emphasis: to *drive home* one's meaning. — **to let drive** To aim or release (a blow, shot, etc.). — *n.* **1.** The act of driving. **2.** A road for driving. **3.** A journey in a vehicle. **4.** Urgent pressure, as of business. **5.** The gathering together of cattle, logs, etc.; also, the cattle, logs, etc., being driven. **6.** An organized campaign: a *drive* for money. **7.** *U.S. Informal* Energy; aggressiveness. **8.** *Psychol.* A strong, motivating power or stimulus: the sex *drive.* **9.** *Mil.* A large-scale, sustained attack. **10.** *Mech.* A means of transmitting power, as from the motor of an automobile to the wheels. **11.** In certain games, as golf, the act of driving the ball. [OE *drīfan*]

drive-in (drīv′in′) *n.* **1.** An outdoor motion-picture theater designed for viewing from parked cars. **2.** A restaurant, shop, etc., serving patrons in their cars.

driv·el (driv′əl) *v.* **driv·eled** or **·elled, driv·el·ing** or **·el·ling** *v.i.* **1.** To let saliva flow from the mouth. **2.** To flow like saliva. **3.** To talk foolishly. — *v.t.* **4.** To let flow from the mouth. **5.** To say in a foolish manner. — *n.* **1.** A flow of saliva from the mouth. **2.** Senseless talk; twaddle. [OE *dreflian*] — **driv′el·er** or **driv′el·ler** *n.*

driv·en (driv′ən) Past participle of DRIVE.

driv·er (drī′vər) *n.* **1.** One who drives a vehicle, animals, logs, etc. **2.** Something used for driving. **3.** In golf, a wooden-headed club with full-length shaft, for driving from the tee. **4.** *Mech.* A part that transmits motion.

drive·way (drīv′wā′) *n.* **1.** A private road providing access to a garage, house, or other building. **2.** A road for driving.

driz·zle (driz′əl) *v.t. & v.i.* **·zled, ·zling** To rain steadily in fine drops. — *n.* A light rain. [? Freq. of ME *dresen,* OE *drēosan* to fall] — **drizz′ly** *adj.*

droll (drōl) *adj.* Humorously odd; comical; funny. — **Syn.** See HUMOROUS. — *n.* A prankster; clown. — *v.i.* To clown. [< MF < MDu. *drol* a jolly man] — **drol′ly** *adv.*

droll·er·y (drō′lər·ē) *n. pl.* **·er·ies** **1.** The quality of being droll; humor. **2.** An amusing way of acting or talking. **3.** Something droll, as a funny remark.

-drome *combining form* Place for running; racecourse. [< Gk. < *dramein* to run]

drom·e·dar·y (drom′ə·der′ē, drum′-) *n. pl.* **·dar·ies** The swift, one-humped Arabian camel trained for riding. [< OF < LL < L *dromas* a running]

drone[1] (drōn) *v.* **droned, dron·ing** *v.i.* **1.** To make a dull, humming sound. **2.** To speak monotonously. — *v.t.* **3.** To utter in a monotonous tone. —*n.* **1.** A dull humming sound, as of a bee. **2.** One of the single-note pipes of the bagpipe; also, a bagpipe. [ME *drone* male bee]

drone[2] (drōn) *n.* **1.** The male of the bee, esp. of the honeybee, having no sting and gathering no honey. **2.** A loafer who lives by the labor of others. **3.** *Aeron.* An unmanned airplane piloted by remote control. —*v.i.* **droned, dron·ing** To live in idleness. [OE *drān*]

drool (drōōl) *v.t. & v.i.* To drivel; slaver. —*n.* **1.** Spittle. **2.** *Informal* Foolish talk; twaddle. [Contraction of DRIVEL]

droop (drōōp) *v.i.* **1.** To sink down; hang downward. **2.** To lose vigor or spirit; languish. —*v.t.* **3.** To let hang or sink down. —*n.* A drooping. [< ON *drūpa*]

droop·y (drōō′pē) *adj.* **droop·i·er, droop·i·est** Tending to droop. —**droop′i·ly** *adv.* —**droop′i·ness** *n.*

drop (drop) *n.* **1.** A small quantity of liquid, shaped like a tiny ball. **2.** A very small amount of anything. **3.** *pl.* A liquid medicine given in drops. **4.** Something resembling a drop in shape, size, etc. **5.** Something designed to fall, slide, or hang down, as a curtain. **6.** A slot or other aperture, as in a mailbox. **7.** A sudden or quick downward movement. **8.** A sudden or quick decrease, as in prices. **9.** The vertical distance from a higher to a lower level. **10.** A falling off or away: a sheer *drop*. **11.** A parachuting of men or supplies. —**at the drop of a hat** With little or no hesitation or provocation; at once. —**to have** (or **get**) **the drop on** To have (or get) the advantage over. —*v.* **dropped** or **dropt, drop·ping** *v.i.* **1.** To fall in drops, as a liquid. **2.** To fall or descend rapidly. **3.** To fall down exhausted, injured, or dead. **4.** To decline or decrease, as in amount. **5.** To crouch, as a hunting dog at the sight of game. **6.** To fall into some state or condition. **7.** To come to an end: to let the matter *drop*. —*v.t.* **8.** To let fall by letting go of. **9.** To let fall in drops. **10.** To give birth to: said of animals. **11.** To utter (a hint, etc.) in a casual way. **12.** To write and send (a note, etc.). **13.** To cause to fall, as by striking, etc. **14.** To have no more to do with. **15.** To let out or deposit at a particular place. **16.** To parachute (soldiers, supplies, etc.). **17.** To omit, as a word, line, or stitch. **18.** *U.S.* To discharge (an employee). **19.** To move down; lower. **20.** *Slang* To lose (money, etc.), as in gambling. **21.** In football, to drop-kick (the ball); also, to score (a goal) by drop-kicking. —**to drop behind** (or **back**) To fall behind or lag behind purposely or by necessity. —**to drop in** To make a casual visit. —**to drop off 1.** To decline or decrease. **2.** To go to sleep. —**to drop out** To withdraw, as from membership. [OE *dropa*]

drop·forge (drop′fôrj′) *v.t.* **·forged, ·forg·ing** To forge (metal) between dies with a drop hammer.

drop hammer A machine for forging, stamping, etc., in which a heavy weight sliding between vertical guides hammers the metal beneath it. Also **drop press.**

drop-kick (drop′kik′) *v.t. & v.i.* To give a drop kick (to).

drop kick In football, a kick given the ball just as it is rebounding after being dropped by the kicker.

drop·let (drop′lit) *n.* A tiny drop.

drop·out (drop′out′) *n.* *U.S. & Canadian* A child who leaves school as soon as attendance is not compulsory.

drop·sy (drop′sē) *n.* *Pathol.* An abnormal accumulation of serous fluid in body cavities. [< OF < L < Gk. *hydrōps* dropsy] —**drop′si·cal** (-si·kəl), **drop′sied** (-sēd) *adj.*

drosh·ky (drosh′kē, drôsh′-) *n. pl.* **·kies** A light, open, four-wheeled Russian carriage or any similar carriage.

dro·soph·i·la (drō·sof′ə·lə, drə-) *n. pl.* **·lae** (-lē) The fruit fly (def. 2). [< NL < Gk. *drosos* dew + *phileein* to love]

dross (drôs, dros) *n.* **1.** *Metall.* Refuse or impurity in melted metal; slag; cinders. **2.** Waste matter; refuse. [OE *drōs*] —**dross′i·ness** *n.* —**dross′y** *adj.*

drought (drout) *n.* **1.** Long-continued dry weather; lack of rain. **2.** Scarcity; dearth. **3.** *Dial.* Thirst. Also **drouth** (drouth). [OE *drūgath*] —**drought′y** *adj.*

drove[1] (drōv) Past tense of DRIVE.

drove[2] (drōv) *n.* **1.** A number of animals driven or herded for driving. **2.** A moving crowd of human beings. **3.** A stonemason's broad-edged chisel. Also **drove chisel.** —**Syn.** See FLOCK. —*v.t.* **droved, drov·ing 1.** To drive (cows, etc.) for some distance. **2.** To dress (stone) with a drove. [OE *drāf*. Akin to DRIVE.] —**drov′er** *n.*

drown (droun) *v.i.* **1.** To die by suffocation with a liquid. —*v.t.* **2.** To kill by suffocation with a liquid. **3.** To cover with or as with a flood; inundate. **4.** To lessen the sound of; muffle. **5.** To lessen or extinguish. [ME *drounen*]

drowse (drouz) *v.* **drowsed, drows·ing** *v.i.* **1.** To be only half awake; doze. —*v.t.* **2.** To make sleepy, dull, or lethargic. **3.** To pass (time) in drowsing. —*n.* The state of being half asleep; doze. [OE *drūsian* to become sluggish]

drow·sy (drou′zē) *adj.* **·si·er, ·si·est 1.** Heavy with sleepiness; dull. **2.** Produced by sleepiness or lethargy. **3.** Making sleepy; soporific. —**drow′si·ly** *adv.* —**drow′si·ness** *n.*

drub (drub) *v.t.* **drubbed, drub·bing 1.** To beat, as with a stick. **2.** To vanquish; overcome. —*n.* A blow; thump. [? < Arabic *darb* a beating] —**drub′ber** *n.*

drudge (druj) *v.i.* **drudged, drudg·ing** To work hard wearisome or menial tasks. —*n.* One who drudges. [(*drēogan* work, labor] —**drudg′er** *n.* —**drudg′ing·ly** *a*

drudg·er·y (druj′ər·ē) *n. pl.* **·er·ies** Dull, wearisome, menial work. —**Syn.** See TOIL[1].

drug (drug) *n.* **1.** Any chemical or biological substan other than food, intended for use in the treatment, prev tion, or diagnosis of disease. **2.** A narcotic. **3.** A commo ty that is overabundant: a *drug* on the market. — **drugged, drug·ging 1.** To mix drugs with (food, dri etc.). **2.** To administer drugs to. **3.** To stupefy or pois with or as with drugs. [ME *drogge*]

drug addict One who uses narcotics habitually.

drug·gist (drug′ist) *n.* **1.** One who compounds prescr tions and sells drugs; a pharmacist. **2.** A dealer in drug

drug·store (drug′stôr′, -stōr′) *n.* *U.S.* A place where p scriptions are compounded, and drugs and miscellane merchandise are sold; pharmacy. Also **drug store.**

dru·id (drōō′id) *n.* One of an order of priests or teachers an ancient Celtic religion. [< MF < L *druides* < Celt —**dru·id·ic** (drōō·id′ik) or **·i·cal** *adj.* —**dru′id·ism** *n.*

drum (drum) *n.* **1.** A hollow percussion instrument, ty cally shaped like a cylinder or hemisphere, having a me brane stretched tightly over one or both ends, and played beating the membrane with sticks, the hands, etc. **2.** sound produced by or as by a drum. **3.** Something rese bling a drum in shape; as: **a** A metal cylinder around wh cable, wire, etc., is wound. **b** A cylindrical metal contai as for oil. **4.** *Anat.* The middle ear, or the tympanic me brane. —*v.* **drummed, drum·ming** *v.i.* **1.** To beat a dru **2.** To tap or thump continuously, as with the fingers. *v.t.* **3.** To perform on or as on a drum. **4.** To summon beating a drum. **5.** To force upon by constant repetiti **6.** To work up (business or trade) by advertising, canv sing, etc.: usually with *up*. **7.** To expel in disgrace: usua with *out*. [Prob. < MDu. *tromme*] —**drum′mer** *n.*

drum·head (drum′hed′) *n.* **1.** The membrane stretch over the end of a drum. **2.** *Naut.* The circular top of a ca stan. **3.** *Anat.* The tympanic membrane.

drum major One who instructs or leads a band or dr corps. —**drum ma·jor·ette** (mā′jə·ret′) *fem.*

drum·stick (drum′stik′) *n.* **1.** A stick for beating a dru **2.** The lower joint of the leg of a cooked fowl.

drunk (drungk) Past participle and archaic past tense DRINK. —*adj.* **1.** Affected with alcoholic drink; into cated; inebriated. **2.** Overwhelmed by some powerful en tion. —*n.* *Informal* **1.** One who is drunk. **2.** A drunka **3.** A bout of drinking; binge.

drunk·ard (drungk′ərd) *n.* One who habitually drinks coholic beverages to excess.

drunk·en (drungk′ən) Archaic past participle of DRIN —*adj.* **1.** Habitually drunk. **2.** Relating to or caused b drunken state. —**drunk′en·ness** *n.* —**drunk′en·ly** *ad*

drupe (drōōp) *n.* *Bot.* A soft, fleshy fruit, as a peach cherry, enclosing a hard-shelled stone or seed. [< NL < *drupa* (*oliva*) an overripe (olive)] —**dru·pa′ceous** *adj.*

dry (drī) *adj.* **dri·er** or, occasionally, **dry·er, dri·est** or, oc sionally, **dry·est. 1.** Devoid of moisture; not wet or dam **2.** Marked by little or no rainfall. **3.** Not lying under wat *dry* land. **4.** Parched. **5.** Having all or nearly all the wat drained away, exhausted or evaporated: a *dry* stream. No longer giving milk. **7.** Devoid of tears. **8.** Thirsty. Eaten or served without butter, jam, etc.: *dry* toast. **1** Unaccompanied by the discharge of phlegm, etc. **11.** Co sisting of or pertaining to commodities, etc., that are n liquids: *dry* provisions. **12.** Lacking sweetness: said wines. **13.** Plain; unadorned; bare: the *dry* facts. **14.** Du boring: a *dry* lecture. **15.** Devoid of warmth, color, or em tion: a *dry* welcome. **16.** Crisp; quietly shrewd: *dry* hum **17.** *U.S. Informal* Opposing or prohibiting the sale of or i dulgence in alcoholic beverages: a *dry* State. —*v.* **drie dry·ing** *v.t.* **1.** To make dry. **2.** To preserve (meat, fis etc.) by removing moisture. —*v.i.* **3.** To become dry. **to dry up 1.** To become thoroughly dry. **2.** To becon unproductive. **3.** *Slang* To stop talking. [OE *drȳge*]

dry·ad (drī′əd, -ad) *n.* In classical mythology, a nym dwelling in or presiding over woods and trees. [< L < G < *drys, dryos* tree] —**dry·ad′ic** *adj.*

dry cell *Electr.* A primary cell containing an electrolyte liquid and powder combined to form a paste.

dry-clean (drī′klēn′) *v.t.* To clean (clothing, etc.) with so vents other than water, such as carbon tetrachloride. Al **dry′-cleanse′.** —**dry cleaner** —**dry cleaning**

dry distillation *Chem.* Destructive distillation.

dry-dock (drī′dok′) *v.t.* **1.** To put into dry dock. —*v.* **2.** To go into dry dock.

dry dock A floating or stationary structure from whic water can be removed, used for repairing and cleaning ship

dry·er (drī′ər) Alternative comparative of DRY. —*n.* drier.

dry·est (drī′ist) Alternative superlative of DRY.

-eyed (drī′īd′) *adj.* Not weeping; tearless.
farming In an arid country, the raising of crops with- t irrigation, mainly by saving the moisture of the soil and raising drought-resisting crops. **— dry farmer**
goods Textile fabrics, as distinguished from groceries, :dware, etc.
ice Solid carbon dioxide, having a temperature of about 110° F., and passing directly to the gaseous state, widely d as a refrigerant: also called *carbon dioxide snow.*
law *U.S.* A law banning the sale of alcoholic beverages.
-ly (drī′lē) *adv.* In a dry manner: also spelled *drily.*
measure A unit or system of units for measuring the ume of dry commodities, as fruits or grains. See table nt of book.
-ness (drī′nis) *n.* The state or quality of being dry.
nurse A nurse who rears a child without suckling it.
point **1.** A fine, hard etching needle used to incise fine es on copperplate without the use of acid. **2.** An engrav- made by this method.
rot **1.** A fungous disease of timber, causing it to crumble. A disease of potato tubers and other vegetables.
run **1.** *Mil.* A practice exercise in combat skills without ng live ammunition. **2.** Any rehearsal or trial run.
al (dōō′əl, dyōō′-) *adj.* **1.** Denoting or relating to two. Composed of two; twofold; double; binary. **3.** *Gram.* In ne languages, as Sanskrit and Greek, of or designating a rd form that denotes two: distinguished from *singular, ral.* **—** *n. Gram.* The dual number, or a word form hav- this number. [< L *duo* two]
al·ism (dōō′əl·iz′əm, dyōō′-) *n.* **1.** The state of being ofold; duality. **2.** *Philos.* The theory that the universe is nposed of two principles, as mind and matter. **— du′al·ist — du′al·is′tic** *adj.* **— du′al·is′ti·cal·ly** *adv.*
al·i·ty (dōō·al′ə·tē, dyōō-) *n. pl.* **·ties** The state, char- er, or quality of being two or composed of two.
[1] (dub) *v.t.* **dubbed, dub·bing** **1.** To confer knighthood on by tapping on the shoulder with a sword. **2.** To name style. **3.** To smooth or rub, as timber. [OE *dubbian*]
[2] (dub) *U.S. Informal n.* A clumsy, blundering person. *v.t.* **dubbed, dub·bing** To bungle. [? < DUB[1]]
[3] (dub) *v.t.* **dubbed, dub·bing** **1.** To rerecord (a record, e, etc.) in order to edit or add portions or to change vol- e, frequency, or tonal quality. **2.** To insert a new sound ck into (a film) [Short for DOUBLE]
bi·e·ty (dōō·bī′ə·tē, dyōō-) *n. pl.* **·ties** **1.** The state of ng dubious. **2.** Something doubtful. Also **du·bi·os·i·ty** ōō′bē·os′ə·tē, dyōō′-). [< LL < L *dubius* doubtful]
bi·ous (dōō′bē·əs, dyōō′-) *adj.* **1.** Unsettled in judgment opinion; doubtful. **2.** Causing doubt; equivocal. **3.** Not dictable; uncertain. **4.** Open to criticism, objection, or picion: a *dubious* reputation. [< L *dubium* doubt] **— bi·ous·ly** *adv.* **— du′bi·ous·ness** *n.*
bon·net (dōō′bə·nā′, *Fr.* dü·bô·ne′) *n.* **1.** A fortified ench wine used as an apéritif: a trade name. **2.** A red- h purple, the color of red Dubonnet. Also **du′bon·net′.**
cal (dōō′kəl, dyōō′-) *adj.* Pertaining to a duke or a chy. [< MF < LL < L *dux* leader] **— du′cal·ly** *adv.*
·at (duk′ət) *n.* **1.** Any of several gold or silver coins, merly current in Europe. **2.** *Slang* A ticket, as to a show. MF < Ital. *ducato* a coin with a picture of a duke]
h·ess (duch′is) *n.* **1.** The wife or widow of a duke. **2.** e female sovereign of a duchy [< OF < L *dux* leader]
h·y (duch′ē) *n. pl.* **duch·ies** The territory of a duke or chess; dukedom.
k[1] (duk) *n.* **1.** Any of various aquatic birds, with bbed feet and broad bills. **2.** The female of this bird. e male is called a *drake.* **3.** *Chiefly Brit. Informal* A dear; rling. **4.** *U.S. Slang* A person; fellow. [OE *dūce* diver]
k[2] (duk) *v.t* **1.** To thrust suddenly under water. **2.** To wer quickly; bob, as the head. **3.** *Informal* To dodge; ade (a blow or punishment). **4.** *Informal* To avoid (a ty, person, etc.) **—** *v.i.* **5.** To submerge suddenly under ter. **6.** *Informal* To move quickly and abruptly, as in dging. **—** *n.* The act of ducking; esp., a quick plunge der water. [ME *douken, duken* to dive, ult. < Gmc.]
k[3] (duk) *n.* **1.** A strong linen or cotton fabric similar to nvas. **2.** *pl.* Trousers made of duck. [< Du. *doek* cloth]
k·bill (duk′bil′) *n.* A platypus.
k·ling (duk′ling) *n.* A young duck.
ck·pin (duk′pin′) *n.* **1.** A small pin used in a variation of e game of tenpins. **2.** *pl.* (*construed as sing.*) The game ayed with such pins.
ck·y (duk′ē) *adj.* **duck·i·er, duck·i·est** *Slang* Delightful.
ct (dukt) *n.* **1.** Any tube, canal, or passage by which a uid, gas, etc., is conveyed. **2.** *Anat.* A tubular passage by hich a secretion is carried away. **3.** *Electr.* A tubular chan- l for carrying telegraph or telephone cables. [< L < *cere* to lead]

duc·tile (duk′təl, -til) *adj.* **1.** Capable of being hammered into thin layers, drawn out into wire, or otherwise subjected to stress without breaking, as certain metals. **2.** Easily molded or shaped; plastic. **3.** Ready to obey; easily led. [< F < L < *ducere* to lead] **— duc·til·i·ty** (duk·til′ə·tē) *n.*
duct·less gland (dukt′lis) *Physiol.* A gland that has no ex- cretory duct but releases its secretions directly into the blood or lymph, as the thyroid gland, etc.
dud (dud) *n.* **1.** *Mil.* A bomb or shell that fails to explode. **2.** *Informal* One who or that which proves a failure. [< Du. *dood* dead]
dude (dōōd, dyōōd) *n. U.S.* **1.** A man who dresses in a flashy or extremely fastidious manner; dandy; fop. **2.** *U.S. Informal* A city person; esp., an Easterner vacationing on a ranch. [Origin unknown] **— dud′ish** *adj.*
dude ranch *U.S.* A ranch operated as a resort for tourists.
dudg·eon (duj′ən) *n.* Sullen displeasure; resentment: to leave in high *dudgeon.* [Origin unknown]
duds (dudz) *n.pl. Informal* **1.** Clothing. **2.** Belongings in general. [ME *dudde* cloak]
due (dōō, dyōō) *adj.* **1.** Subject to demand for payment; esp., payable because of the arrival of a stipulated date. **2.** That should be rendered or given; proper: the honor *due.* **3.** Adequate; sufficient: *due* cause for alarm. **4.** Appointed or expected to arrive, be present, or be ready: The bus is *due.* **5.** That may be charged or attributed; ascribable: with *to*: The mistake was *due* to carelessness. **— due to** *Informal* Because of; on account of: widely used but still questioned by some. **—** *n.* **1.** That which is owed or rightfully required; a debt. **2.** *pl.* Charge or fee: club *dues.* **—** *adv.* Directly: *due* east. [< OF *deü,* pp. of *devoir* to owe < L *debere*]
du·el (dōō′əl, dyōō′-) *n.* **1.** A prearranged combat between two persons, usu. fought with deadly weapons. **2.** A strug- gle between two contending parties. **—** *v.t. & v.i.* **du·eled** or **·elled, du·el·ing** or **·el·ling** To fight, or fight with, in a duel. [< F < Ital. < L *duellum,* earliest form of *bellum* war] **— du′el·er** or **du′el·ler, du′el·ist** or **du′el·list** *n.*
du·en·na (dōō·en′ə, dyōō-) *n.* **1.** In Spain and Portugal, an elderly woman who serves as a companion and protector to a young girl. **2.** A chaperon. [< Sp. < L *domina* lady]
du·et (dōō·et′, dyōō-) *n.* A musical composition for two performers. [< Ital. < L *duo* two]
duff (duf) *n.* A thick flour pudding boiled in a cloth bag. [Var. of DOUGH]
duf·fel (duf′əl) *n.* **1.** A coarse woolen fabric napped on both sides. **2.** Equipment or supplies, esp. for camping. Also **duf′fle.** [after *Duffel,* a town near Antwerp]
duffel bag A sack, usu. of canvas or duck, used to carry clothing and personal possessions. Also **duffle bag.**
dug[1] (dug) Past tense and past participle of DIG.
dug[2] (dug) *n.* A teat or udder. [Cf. Dan. *dægge* to suckle]
du·gong (dōō′gong) *n.* A herbivorous marine mammal of warm seas, having flippers and a paddlelike tail: also called *sea cow.* [< Malay *duyong*]
dug·out (dug′out′) *n.* **1.** A canoe made by hollowing out a log. **2.** An excavated shelter or dwelling for protection against storms, bombs, etc. **3.** In baseball, a structure set back from the diamond, in which team members sit when not at bat or in the field.
duke (dōōk, dyōōk) *n.* **1.** In Great Britain and certain other European countries, a nobleman ranking immediately below a prince and above a marquis. **2.** A European prince ruling over a duchy. [< F < L *dux* leader] **— duke′dom** *n.*
dul·cet (dul′sit) *adj.* Pleasing to the ear; melodious; also, soothing; pleasant. [< OF dim. of *douz,* sweet < L *dulcis*]
dul·ci·mer (dul′sə·mər) *n.* A stringed instrument played with two padded hammers or plucked with the fingers. [< OF, ? < LL < *dulcis* sweet + *melos* a song < Gk.]
dull (dul) *adj.* **1.** Lacking in intelligence or understanding; stupid. **2.** Wanting in perception or responsiveness: a *dull* audience. **3.** Not brisk or active: Trade is *dull.* **4.** Without spirit; listless. **5.** Having a blunt edge or point. **6.** Excit- ing little or no interest: a *dull* book. **7.** Not acute or intense: a *dull* pain. **8.** Cloudy; gloomy. **9.** Not bright, clear, or vivid: a *dull* color. **10.** Unclear in sound. **—** *v.t. & v.i.* To make or become dull. [ME *dul*] **— dull′ish** *adj.* **— dull′·ness** or **dul′ness** *n.* **— dul′ly** *adv.*
dull·ard (dul′ərd) *n.* A stupid person; dolt.
dulse (duls) *n.* A reddish brown seaweed sometimes eaten as a vegetable. [< Irish *duileasg*]
du·ly (dōō′lē, dyōō′-) *adv.* **1.** In due or proper manner; fitly. **2.** At the proper time. **3.** To an adequate degree.
dumb (dum) *adj.* **1.** Having no power of speech; mute. **2.** Temporarily speechless: *dumb* with grief. **3.** Not inclined to speak; silent. **4.** *U.S. Informal* Stupid; dull-witted. **5.** Made or done without speech, as a pantomime. [OE] **— dumb′ly** *adv.* **— dumb′ness** *n.*
dumb·bell (dum′bel′) *n.* **1.** A gymnastic hand instrument

used for exercising, consisting of a wood or metal handle with a weighted ball at each end. **2.** *U.S. Slang* A stupid person.
dumb·wait·er (dum′wā′tər) *n.* **1.** *U.S.* A small elevator for conveying food, dishes, garbage, etc., between floors. **2.** *Brit.* A movable serving stand placed near a dining table.
dum·dum bullet (dum′dum′) A small-arms bullet having a soft point or a jacket cut across at the point so that it will expand on impact and tear a gaping wound. [after *Dumdum,* a town near Calcutta, India, where first made]
dum·found (dum′found′) *v.t.* To strike dumb; confuse; amaze. Also **dumb′found′.** [Blend of DUMB and CONFOUND]
dum·my (dum′ē) *n. pl.* **·mies 1.** A figure representing the human form, used for displaying clothing, for tackling in football practice, etc. **2.** An imitation object, as a false drawer. **3.** One who is dumb; a mute. **4.** *Slang* A stupid person. **5.** One who seems to be acting for his own interests while secretly representing another. **6.** *Printing* **a** A sample book or magazine, usually blank, used as a model of the final product. **b** A model page form for the printer, made up of proofs pasted into position. **7.** In certain card games, esp. bridge: **a** An exposed hand played in addition to his own by the person sitting opposite it. **b** The inactive player who has exposed such a hand. —*adj.* **1.** Sham; counterfeit. **2.** Silent; mute. **3.** Ostensibly acting for oneself, but actually for another. **4.** Played with a dummy, as in card games.
dump (dump) *v.t.* **1.** To drop or throw down heavily or abruptly. **2.** To empty out, as from a container. **3.** To empty (a container), as by overturning. **4.** To throw away, as rubbish. **5.** To put up (goods) for sale cheaply and in large quantities, esp. in a foreign market. —*v.i.* **6.** To fall or drop suddenly. **7.** To unload. **8.** To offer large quantities of goods for sale at low prices. —*n.* **1.** A dumping area, as for rubbish. **2.** That which is dumped. **3.** *Mil.* A temporary storage place for ammunition and supplies. **4.** *U.S. Slang* A shabby, poorly kept place. [ME < Scand.]
dump·ling (dump′ling) *n.* **1.** A ball of biscuit dough filled with fruit and baked or steamed. **2.** A small mass of dough dropped into boiling soup or stew.
dumps (dumps) *n.pl.* A gloomy state of mind: now only in the phrase **in the dumps.** [Cf. MDu. *domp* haze]
dump truck A truck for hauling gravel, coal, etc., that unloads by tilting back the cargo bin and opening the tailboard.
dump·y[1] (dump′ē) *adj.* **dump·i·er, dump·i·est** Sullen or discontented; sulky. [See DUMPS]
dump·y[2] (dump′ē) *adj.* **dump·i·er, dump·i·est** Short and thick; squat. —**dump′i·ly** *adv.* —**dump′i·ness** *n.*
dun[1] (dun) *v.t. & v.i.* **dunned, dun·ning** To press (a debtor) for payment; importune; pester. —*n.* **1.** One who duns. **2.** A repeated demand for payment. [Prob. var. of DIN.]
dun[2] (dun) *adj.* Of a grayish brown or reddish brown color. —*n.* **1.** Dun color. **2.** A dun-colored horse. —*v.t.* **dunned, dun·ning** To make dun-colored. [OE *dunn*]
dunce (duns) *n.* A stupid or ignorant person. [Earlier *Dunsman,* a follower of John *Duns* Scotus]
dunce cap A conical cap, formerly placed on the head of a dull student. Also **dunce's cap.**
dun·der·head (dun′dər·hed′) *n.* A blockhead; dunce. Also **dun′der·pate′** (-pāt′). [? < dial. E (Scottish) *dunder* thunder, noise + HEAD] —**dun′der·head′ed** *adj.*
dune (do͞on, dyo͞on) *n.* A hill of loose sand heaped up by the wind. [< F < MDu.]
dung (dung) *n.* **1.** Animal excrement; manure. **2.** Anything foul. —*v.t.* To cover with or as with dung. [OE]
dun·ga·ree (dung′gə·rē′) *n.* **1.** A coarse cotton cloth used for work clothes, tents, sails, etc. **2.** *pl.* Trousers or overalls made of this fabric. [< Hind. *dungrī*]
dung beetle Any of various beetles that breed in dung.
dun·geon (dun′jən) *n.* **1.** A dark confining prison or cell, esp. one underground. **2.** A donjon. [< DONJON]
dung·hill (dung′hil′) *n.* **1.** A heap of manure. **2.** A vile thing, abode, or condition.
dunk (dungk) *v.t. & v.i.* To dip (bread, doughnuts, etc.) into tea, coffee, soup, etc. [< G *tunken* to dip] —**dunk′er** *n.*
dun·lin (dun′lin) *n.* A sandpiper having in summer plumage a black belly and a reddish back. [< DUN[2] + -LING[1]]
dun·nage (dun′ij) *n.* **1.** *Naut.* Mats and battens used to protect cargo. **2.** Baggage.
du·o (do͞o′ō, dyo͞o′ō) *n. pl.* **du·os** or **du·i** (-ē) *Music* An instrumental duet. [< Ital. < L *duo* two]
duo- *combining form* Two. [< L *duo* two]
du·o·dec·i·mal (do͞o′ō·des′ə·məl, dyo͞o′-) *adj.* **1.** Pertaining to twelfth or twelfths. **2.** Reckoning by twelves. —*n.* **1.** One of the numbers used in duodecimal arithmetic; a twelfth. **2.** *pl.* A method of computing by twelves instead of by tens. [< L < *duodecim* twelve]
du·o·dec·i·mo (do͞o′ō·des′ə·mō, dyo͞o′-) *adj.* **1.** Having twelve pages to one sheet of printing paper. **2.** Measuring about 5 x 7¾ inches in size: said of a page or book. —*n. pl.* **·mos** The size of a page folded twelve to a sheet; also, a page or book of this size. Also *twelvemo.* Also written **12mo., 12°.**
du·o·de·num (do͞o′ə·dē′nəm, dyo͞o′-; do͞o·od′ə·nəm) *n. pl.* **·na** (-nə) *Anat.* The part of the small intestine exten[ding] from the stomach to the jejunum. For illus. see INTEST[INE] [< Med.L *duodenum* (*digitorum*) of twelve (fingers); w[ith] ref. to its length] —**du′o·de′nal** *adj.*
du·o·logue (do͞o′ə·lôg, -log, dyo͞o′-) *n.* **1.** A dramatic p[iece] for two performers. **2.** A dialogue. Also **du′o·log.**
dupe (do͞op, dyo͞op) *n.* One who is easily deceived or mis[led] —*v.t.* **duped, dup·ing** To make a dupe of; deceive. [< *huppe* hoopoe < L *upupa*] —**dup′er** *n.* —**dup′er·y** *n.*
du·ple (do͞o′pəl, dyo͞o′-) *adj.* Double. [< L *duplus* dou[ble]
du·plex (do͞o′pleks, dyo͞o′-) *adj.* **1.** Having two parts; t[wo]fold. **2.** *Mech.* Having two similar parts operating in[de]pendently or in conjunction within one framework. *Telecom.* Pertaining to or allowing the transmission of messages simultaneously over a single wire and in opp[osite] directions. —*n.* A duplex apartment or house. [< L *duo* two + stem of *plicare* to fold] —**du·plex′i·ty** *n.*
duplex apartment **1.** *U.S.* An apartment having room[s on] two floors. **2.** *Canadian* A two-story building having [an] apartment on each floor.
duplex house *U.S. & Canadian* A house having two [one-]family units.
du·pli·cate (*adj., n.* do͞o′plə·kit, dyo͞o′-; *v.* do͞o′plə·kāt, dyo͞[o′-]) *adj.* **1.** Made like or corresponding exactly to an origin[al]: *duplicate* key. **2.** Growing or existing in pairs. **3.** In c[ard] playing, replayed by other players with the same hand originally dealt. —*n.* **1.** An exact copy. **2.** A doubl[e;] counterpart. **3.** A duplicate game of cards. —*v.t.* **·cat[ed,] ·cat·ing 1.** To copy exactly; reproduce. **2.** To double. To do a second time. [< L < *duplex* twofold] —**du[pli]cate·ly** *adv.* —**du′pli·ca′tion** *n.* —**du′pli·ca′tive** *adj.*
du·pli·ca·tor (do͞o′plə·kā′tər, dyo͞o′-) *n.* A mechanical [de]vice for making duplicates.
du·plic·i·ty (do͞o·plis′ə·tē, dyo͞o-) *n. pl.* **·ties** Tricky dec[eit]fulness; double-dealing. [< OF < LL < L *duplex* twof[old]
du·ra (do͝or′ə) See DURRA.
du·ra·ble (do͝or′ə·bəl, dyo͝or′-) *adj.* **1.** Able to withst[and] decay or wear. **2.** Not easily changed or upset. [< OF < L *durus* hard] —**du′ra·bil′i·ty, du′ra·ble·ness** *n.*
Du·ral·u·min (do͝o·ral′yə·min, dyo͝o-) *n.* A light, strong [al]loy of aluminum and copper, with addition of magnes[ium] and manganese: a trade name. Also **du·ral′u·min.**
du·ra ma·ter (do͝or′ə mā′tər, dyo͝or′ə) *Anat.* The toug[h fi]brous membrane forming the outermost of the three co[ver]ings of the brain and spinal cord. Also **du′ra.** [< Med.L *dura* hard + *mater* mother] —**du′ral** *adj.*
du·ra·men (do͝o·rā′min, dyo͝o-) *n. Bot.* The heartwood, darker central portion, of an exogenous stem or tree tru[nk] [< L, a ligneous vine branch]
dur·ance (do͝or′əns, dyo͝or′-) *n.* Forced confinement or [im]prisonment. [< OF < L *durare* to endure]
du·ra·tion (do͝o·rā′shən, dyo͝o-) *n.* **1.** The period of t[ime] during which anything lasts. **2.** Continuance in time. [< LL < L *durare* to endure, last]
du·ress (do͝o·res′, dyo͝o-, do͝or′is, dyo͝or′-) *n.* **1.** Constr[aint] by force or fear; compulsion. **2.** *Law* **a** Coercion to d[o or] say something against one's will or judgment. **b** Impris[on]ment without full legal sanction. [< OF < L *durus* ha[rd]
dur·ing (do͝or′ing, dyo͝or′-) *prep.* **1.** Throughout the ti[me] existence, or action of. **2.** In the course of; at some period [of]. [ME. Orig. ppr. of *duren* to endure]
dur·ra (do͝or′ə) *n.* A variety of sorghum of southern A[sia] and northern Africa: also spelled *doura, dura.* Also **d[hur·ra]** (do͝or). [< Arabic *dhura*]
du·rum (do͝or′əm, dyo͝or′-) *n.* A species of wheat wid[ely] grown for macaroni products. [< L *durus* hard]
dusk (dusk) *n.* **1.** The partial darkness between day [and] night, usu. considered darker than twilight. **2.** Any deg[ree] of light or dark resembling this. —*adj.* Somewhat dark; dim; shadowy. —*v.t. & v.i.* To make grow, or app[ear] shadowy or dim; darken. [OE *dox*] —**dusk′ish** *adj.*
dusk·y (dus′kē) *adj.* **dusk·i·er, dusk·i·est 1.** Somew[hat] dark; dim; obscure. **2.** Rather dark in shade or colori[ng;] swarthy. **3.** Gloomy. —**dusk′i·ly** *adv.* —**dusk′i·ness**
dust (dust) **1.** Earthy matter reduced to particles so fine [as] to be easily borne in the air. **2.** Any substance reduced [to] fine powder. **3.** A cloud of powdered earth or other fine p[ar]ticles. **4.** Confusion; turmoil. **5.** Earth, esp. as the rec[ep]tacle of the dead. **6.** The disintegrated remains of a hum[an] body. **7.** A low or despised condition. **8.** Something wor[th]less. **9.** *Brit.* Sweepings, ashes, or other refuse. **10.** Pol[len]. **11.** Gold dust. **12.** *Slang* Money. —**to bite the dust** [To] be killed or injured. —**to lick the dust 1.** To be defeat[ed;] grovel. **2.** To be killed or wounded. —**to throw dust [in] someone's eyes** To deceive. —*v.t.* **1.** To wipe or bru[sh] dust from. **2.** To sprinkle with powder, insecticide, etc. To sprinkle (powder, etc.) over something. **4.** To soil w[ith] dust. —*v.i.* **5.** To wipe or brush dust from furniture, e[tc.] **6.** To cover oneself with dust, as a bird. **7.** To beco[me] dusty. [OE *dūst*] —**dust′less** *adj.*
dust bowl An area subject to dust storms and drought.

Dust Bowl A region in the south central U.S. where the)soil was blown away by dust storms during 1934–37.
t·er (dus′tər) *n.* **1.** One who or that which dusts. **2.** A th or brush for removing dust. **3.** A device for sprinkling)owder, insecticide, etc., over something. **4.** An outer ·ment worn to protect clothing from dust.
t jacket A removable paper cover that protects the ıding of a book: also called *book jacket.* Also **dust cover.**
t·pan (dust′pan′) *n.* An implement resembling a short-ndled shovel into which dust from a floor is swept.
t storm A windstorm of arid regions that carries clouds dust with it.
t·y (dus′tē) *adj.* **dust·i·er, dust·i·est 1.** Covered with or with dust. **2.** Like dust; powdery. **3.** Of the color of st. **4.** Having a grayish or dull cast: *dusty* pink. **— dust′·** *adv.* **— dust′i·ness** *n.*
tch (duch) *adj.* **1.** Of or relating to the Netherlands, its)ple, culture, or language. **2.** Loosely, German. **—** *n.* **1.** e people of the Netherlands: preceded by *the.* **2.** Loosely, German people: preceded by *the.* **3.** The language of the therlands. **4.** Pennsylvania Dutch. **— in Dutch** *U.S.* *formal* In trouble or disgrace. **— to beat the Dutch** *U.S.* *formal* To be most unusual or surprising. **— to go Dutch** *S. Informal* To have each participant in a meal or enter-nment pay his own expenses. [< MDu. *dutsch* Germanic]
tch door A door divided horizontally in the middle, al-ving either half to open individually.
tch·man (duch′mən) *n. pl.* **·men** (-mən) **1.** A native of Netherlands. **2.** Loosely, a German. **3.** A Dutch ship.
ch·man's-breech·es (duch′mənz·brich′iz) *n. sing. & pl.* low herb with widely spreading spurs. Also **dutch′mans·eech′es.**
tch oven **1.** A cast-iron kettle with a tight-fitting cover, ›d for meats, stews, etc. **2.** A metal box with an open e, set before a fire for cooking.
tch treat *U.S. Informal* An entertainment or meal at ıich each person pays his own bill.
tch uncle A very frank and severe critic or adviser.
te·ous (dōō′tē·əs, dyōō′-) *adj.* Obedient; dutiful. **—** **′te·ous·ly** *adv.* **— du′te·ous·ness** *n.*
ti·ful (dōō′ti·fəl, dyōō′-) *adj.* **1.** Performing one's du-s; obedient. **2.** Expressive of a sense of duty; respectful: *tiful* attentions. **— du′ti·ful·ly** *adv.* **— du′ti·ful·ness** *n.*
ty (dōō′tē, dyōō′-) *n. pl.* **·ties 1.** That which one is mor-y or legally bound to do; obligation. **2.** The impelling or ntrolling force of such obligations: *Duty* calls. **3.** Action conduct required by one's profession or position. **4.** Spe-ic obligatory service, esp. of military personnel. **5.** A tax imported or exported goods. **— off duty** Temporarily t at work. [< AF *dû.* See DUE.]
ve·tyn (dōō′və·tēn, dōō′və·tēn′) *n.* Twill-weave fabric th a napped surface, made of wool, rayon, cotton, or silk. so **du′ve·tine, du′ve·tyne.** [< F *duvet* down]
arf (dwôrf) *n.* A human being, animal, or plant that is ınted in its growth and often has abnormal physical pro-rtions. **—** *v.t.* **1.** To prevent the natural development of; ınt. **2.** To cause to appear small or less by comparison. *v.i.* **3.** To become stunted; grow smaller. **—** *adj.* Dim-ıtive; stunted. [OE *dweorh*] **— dwarf′ish** *adj.* **—** **arf′ish·ly** *adv.* **— dwarf′ish·ness** *n.*
arf chestnut The chinquapin.
ell (dwel) *v.i.* **dwelt** or **dwelled, dwell·ing 1.** To have a ed abode; reside. **2.** To linger, as on a subject: with *on* or *on.* **3.** To continue in a state or place. **— Syn.** See LIVE. E *dwellan* to go astray] **— dwell′er** *n.*
ell·ing (dwel′ing) *n.* A place of residence; abode; house.
in·dle (dwin′dəl) *v.t. & v.i.* **·dled, ·dling** To diminish or come less; make or become smaller. **— Syn.** See DE-EASE. [OE *dwinan* to waste away]

dye (dī) *v.* **dyed, dye·ing** *v.t.* **1.** To fix a color in (cloth, hair, etc.), esp. by soaking in liquid coloring matter. **—** *v.i.* **2.** To take or give color: This cloth *dyes* badly. **—** *n.* A color-ing matter used for dyeing; also, the color so produced. [OE *dēagian* to dye < *dēag* dye] **— dy′er** *n.*
dyed-in-the-wool (dīd′in·thə·wōōl′) *adj.* **1.** Dyed before being woven. **2.** Thoroughgoing; complete.
dye·ing (dī′ing) *n.* The act of fixing colors in cloth, etc.
dye·stuff (dī′stuff′) *n.* Any material used for dyeing.
dy·ing (dī′ing) *adj.* **1.** Near death; expiring. **2.** Coming to a close; destined to end: a *dying* civilization. **3.** Given, ut-tered, or manifested just before death. **—** *n.* Death.
dyke (dīk) See DIKE.
dyna- *combining form* Power. Also, before vowels, **dyn-.** [< Gk. *dynamis* power]
dy·nam·ic (dī·nam′ik) *adj.* **1.** Of or pertaining to forces not in equilibrium, or to motion as the result of force: opposed to *static.* **2.** Pertaining to dynamics. **3.** Characterized by energy or forcefulness: a *dynamic* personality. [< Gk. < *dynamis* power] **— dy·nam′i·cal·ly** *adv.*
dy·nam·ics (dī·nam′iks) *n.pl.* (*construed as sing. in defs. 1 and 2*) **1.** The branch of physics that treats of the motion of bodies and the effects of forces in producing motion, in-cluding kinetics. **2.** *Music* **a** The group of words, and sym-bols, etc., used to indicate degrees of loudness; also **dynamic marks. b** The act of producing varying degrees of loud-ness.
dy·na·mite (dī′nə·mīt) *n.* **1.** An explosive composed of nitroglycerin held in some absorbent substance. **2.** *Slang* Anything wonderful or spectacular: The news was *dynamite!* **—** *v.t.* **·mit·ed, ·mit·ing** To blow up or shatter with or as with dynamite. [< Gk. *dynamis* power] **— dy′na·mit′er** *n.*
dy·na·mo (dī′nə·mō) *n. pl.* **·mos** A generator for the con-version of mechanical energy into electrical energy.
dynamo- *combining form* Force; power. [< Gk. *dynamis* power]
dy·na·mo·e·lec·tric (dī′nə·mō·i·lek′trik) *adj.* Pertaining to the conversion of mechanical energy into electrical energy, or the reverse. Also **dy′na·mo·e·lec′tri·cal.**
dy·na·mom·e·ter (dī′nə·mom′ə·tər) *n.* An instrument for measuring force or power. **— dy·na·mo·met·ric** (dī′nə·mō·met′rik) or **·ri·cal** *adj.* **— dy′na·mom′e·try** *n.*
dy·na·mo·tor (dī′nə·mō′tər) *n.* A dynamoelectric machine having one field magnet, one armature core, and two arma-ture windings, each being insulated from the other.
dy·nast (dī′nast, -nəst; *Brit.* din′əst) *n.* A ruler, esp. a hered-itary one. [< L < Gk. < *dynasthai* to be powerful]
dy·nas·ty (dī′nəs·tē, *Brit.* din′əs·tē) *n. pl.* **·ties** A succes-sion of sovereigns in one line of descent; also, the length of time during which one family is in power. **— dy·nas·tic** (dī·nas′tik, di-) or **·ti·cal** *adj.* **— dy·nas′ti·cal·ly** *adv.*
dyne (dīn) *n. Physics* The fundamental unit of force in the cgs system that, if applied to a mass of one gram, would give it an acceleration of one centimeter per second per second. Abbr. *d., D.* [< F < Gk. *dynamis* power]
dys·en·ter·y (dis′ən·ter′ē) *n. Pathol.* A painful inflamma-tion of the large intestine, attended with bloody evacuations and some fever. [< OF < L < Gk. < *dys-* bad + *enteron* intestine] **— dys′en·ter′ic** or **·i·cal** *adj.*
dys·pep·sia (dis·pep′shə, -sē·ə) *n.* Difficult or painful diges-tion. [< L < Gk. < *dys-* hard + *peptein* to cook, digest]
dys·pep·tic (dis·pep′tik) *adj.* **1.** Relating to or suffering from dyspepsia. **2.** Gloomy; peevish. Also **dys·pep′ti·cal.** **—** *n.* A dyspeptic person. **— dys·pep′ti·cal·ly** *adv.*
dysp·ne·a (disp·nē′ə) *n. Pathol.* Labored breathing. Also **dysp·noe′a.** [< NL < L < Gk. < *dys-* hard + *pneein* to breathe] **— dysp·ne′al** or **dysp·ne′ic** *adj.*
dys·pro·si·um (dis·prō′sē·əm, -shē-) *n.* A highly magnetic element (symbol Dy) of the lanthanide series. See ELEMENT. [< NL < Gk. < *dys-* hard + *prosienai* to approach]

E

E (ē) *n. pl.* **e's, E's** or **es, Es, ees** (ēz) **1.** The fifth letter the English alphabet. **2.** Any sound represented by the tter *e.* **—** *symbol* **1.** *Music* **a** The third tone in the natural ale of C, *mi.* **b** A written note representing it. **c** The scale built upon E. **2.** *Math.* The limit of the expression $(1 + 1/n)^n$, as n increases without limit: 2.7182818284+: the base to which Napierian logarithms are calculated: written *e.*
e- Reduced var. of EX-.

each (ēch) *adj.* Being one of two or more individuals that together form an aggregate; every. — *pron.* Every one of any number or group considered individually; each one. ◆ The pronoun *each* is usu. treated as a singular, as *Each* did *his* own work. — *adv.* For or to each person, article, etc.; apiece: one dollar *each.* [OE *ǣlc* < *ā* ever + *gelīc* alike]

each other A compound reciprocal pronoun used in oblique cases: They saw *each other.* The possessive is *each other's.*

ea·ger (ē′gər) *adj.* Impatiently desirous of something. [< OF < L *acer* sharp] — **ea′ger·ly** *adv.* — **ea′ger·ness** *n.*

ea·gle (ē′gəl) *n.* **1.** A large bird of prey related to the falcon, esp. the **bald** (or **American**) **eagle,** dark brown, with the head, neck, and tail white, the national emblem of the United States; and the **imperial eagle** of Europe. ◆ Collateral adjective: *aquiline.* **2.** Any national seal or standard that bears an eagle as symbol. **3.** A former gold coin of the U.S. having a value of $10. **4.** In golf, a score of two under par on any hole. [< OF *egle, aigle,* < L *aquila*]

ea·gle-eyed (ē′gəl·īd′) *adj.* Having keen sight.

ea·glet (ē′glit) *n.* A young eagle.

ear[1] (ir) *n.* **1.** The organ of hearing in its entirety. ◆ Collateral adjective: *aural.* **2.** The fleshy or cartilaginous external part of the organ of hearing. **3.** The sense of hearing. **4.** The ability to perceive the refinements of music, poetry, or the like. **5.** Attentive consideration; heed. **6.** Something resembling the external ear in shape or position, as a projecting piece on a vase. — **to be all ears** To be eagerly attentive. — **to be up to the ears** To be submerged in work, problems, etc. — **to have an ear to the ground** To listen to or heed current public opinion. — **to lend an ear** To pay attention. [OE *ēare*] — **ear′less** *adj.*

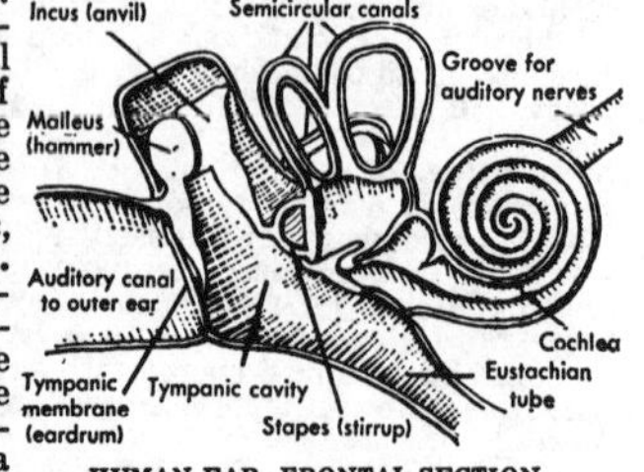

HUMAN EAR, FRONTAL SECTION
(Anatomical nomenclature)

ear[2] (ir) *n.* The fruit-bearing part of a cereal plant; the head. — **in** (or **on**) **the ear** On the cob, as corn; unhusked, as grain. — *v.i.* To form ears, as grain. [OE *ēar*]

ear·ache (ir′āk′) *n.* Pain in the middle or internal ear.

ear·drum (ir′drum′) *n.* The tympanic membrane.

eared (ird) *adj.* Having ears or earlike appendages.

earl (ûrl) *n.* A member of the British nobility next in rank above a viscount and below a marquis. [OE *eorl* nobleman] — **earl′dom** *n.*

ear·lap (ir′lap′) *n.* **1.** One of two flaps attached to a cap for protecting the ears from the cold. **2.** The ear lobes.

ear lobe The fleshy lower part of the external ear.

ear·ly (ûr′lē) *adj.* **·li·er, ·li·est 1.** Coming near the beginning of any specified period of time or of any series of related things: an *early* Shaw play. **2.** Belonging to a distant time or stage of development. **3.** Occurring ahead of the usual or arranged time: an *early* dinner. **4.** Occurring in the near future: An *early* truce is expected. — *adv.* **1.** Near the beginning of any specified period or series of things. **2.** Far back in time. **3.** Before the usual or arranged time. [OE *līce* < *ǣr* before + *-līce* -ly] — **ear′li·ness** *n.*

ear·mark (ir′märk′) *n.* **1.** A distinctive mark made on an animal's ear to denote ownership. **2.** Any mark of identification. — *v.t.* **1.** To put an earmark on. **2.** To set aside, as money, for a particular purpose.

earn (ûrn) *v.t.* **1.** To receive or deserve as recompense for labor, service, or performance. **2.** To acquire as a consequence. **3.** To produce as profit. [OE *earnian*]

ear·nest[1] (ûr′nist) *adj.* **1.** Intent and direct in purpose; zealous: an *earnest* student. **2.** Of a serious or important nature. — **in earnest** With serious intent or determination. [OE *eornoste*] — **ear′nest·ly** *adv.* — **ear′nest·ness** *n.*

ear·nest[2] (ûr′nist) *n.* **1.** *Law* Money paid in advance to bind a contract. Also **earnest money. 2.** An assurance or token of something to come. [Prob. < OF *erres* < L *arra, arrhabo* < Gk. *arrhabōn* < Hebrew *'ērābōn* pledge]

earn·ings (ûr′ningz) *n.pl.* Wages or profits.

ear·phone (ir′fōn′) *n.* A radio or telephone device held at or inserted into the ear; also, a similar part of a hearing aid.

ear·ring (ir′ring′) *n.* An ornament worn at the ear lobe.

ear·shot (ir′shot′) *n.* The distance at which sounds may be heard.

earth (ûrth) *n.* **1.** The dry land surface of the globe, as distinguished from the oceans and sky; ground. **2.** Soil; dirt. **3.** The planet on which man dwells; also, the people who inhabit it. **4.** The abode of mortal man, as opposed to heaven and hell. **5.** Worldly or temporal affairs. **6.** The mortal body. **7.** The hole or lair of a burrowing animal. — **down to earth** Realistic; practical; unaffected. — **to run to earth**
To hunt down and find, as a fox. — *v.t.* **1.** To heap
(plants, etc.) with soil for protection. **2.** To chase into
ing. — *v.i.* **3.** To burrow in the earth. [OE *eorthe*]

Earth (ûrth) *n.* The planet fifth in order of size, havin
area of about 196 million square miles and a mass of 6.57
tillion tons (6.57 × 10²¹). See PLANET. Abbr. *E.*

earth·bound (ûrth′bound′) *adj.* **1.** Having only mat
interests. **2.** Confined to the earth. Also **earth′bound′**

earth·en (ûr′thən) *adj.* Made of earth or baked clay.

earth·en·ware (ûr′thən·wâr′) *n.* Dishes, pots, and the l
made of a coarse grade of baked clay.

earth·ly (ûrth′lē) *adj.* **1.** Of or relating to the earth an
material qualities; worldly; secular. **2.** Possible; imag
ble: of no *earthly* use. — **earth′li·ness** *n.*

earth·quake (ûrth′kwāk′) *n.* A shaking of the earth's cr
caused by the splitting of a mass of rock or by volcanic
turbances. ◆ Collateral adjective: *seismic.*

earth·ward (ûrth′wərd) *adv.* Toward the earth. Also **ea
wards.** — *adj.* Moving toward the earth.

earth·work (ûrth′wûrk′) *n.* *Mil.* A fortification m
largely or wholly of earth.

earth·worm (ûrth′wûrm′) *n.* Any burrowing worm.

earth·y (ûr′thē) *adj.* **earth·i·er, earth·i·est 1.** Of or
earth. **2.** Unrefined; coarse. **3.** Natural; robust; lusty.
earth′i·ness *n.*

ear·wax (ir′waks′) *n.* A substance secreted by glands li
the passages of the external ear: also called *cerumen.*

ear·wig (ir′wig′) *n.* **1.** An insect with horny forewings
a tail pair of forceps, erroneously believed to enter the
man ear. **2.** *U.S.* A small centipede. — *v.t.* **·wigged, ·
ging** To insinuate against in secret. [OE *ēarwicga*]

ease (ēz) *n.* **1.** Freedom from physical discomfort or me
agitation. **2.** Freedom from great effort or difficulty.
Naturalness; poise. — *v.* **eased, eas·ing** *v.t.* **1.** To reli
the mental or physical pain or oppression of; comfort.
To make less painful or oppressive; alleviate. **3.** To le
the pressure, weight, tension, etc., of: to *ease* an axle. **4.**
make easier; facilitate. **5.** To move, lower, or put in p
slowly and carefully. — *v.i.* **6.** To lessen in severity,
sion, speed, etc.: often with *up* or *off.* [< OF < L *adjac
-entis* close at hand] — **ease′ful** *adj.* — **eas′er** *n.*

ea·sel (ē′zəl) *n.* A folding frame or tripod used to sup
an artist's canvas, etc. [< Du. *ezel* easel, orig. an ass]

ease·ment (ēz′mənt) *n.* **1.** Anything that gives eas
comfort. **2.** *Law* The right to use another's property.

eas·i·ly (ē′zə·lē) *adv.* **1.** In an easy manner. **2.** Bey
question. **3.** Very possibly.

eas·i·ness (ē′zi·nis) *n.* The state of being at ease, or of
ing easy to do.

east (ēst) *n.* **1.** The direction of the sun in relation to an
server on earth at sunrise. **2.** One of the four cardinal po
of the compass, directly opposite *west* and 90° clockwise f
north. See COMPASS CARD. **3.** Any direction near this po
4. *Sometimes cap.* Any region east of a specified po
— **the East** Asia and its adjacent islands; the Orient.
adj. **1.** To, toward, facing, or in the east. **2.** Coming f
the east. — *adv.* In or toward the east. [OE *ēast*]

east·bound (ēst′bound′) *adj.* Going eastward. Also **ea
bound′.**

East·er (ēs′tər) *n.* **1.** A Christian festival commemora
the resurrection of Christ. **2.** The day on which this festi
is celebrated, the Sunday immediately after the first
moon that occurs on or after March 21: also **Easter Sund**
[OE *Eastre* goddess of spring]

east·er·ly (ēs′tər·lē) *adj.* **1.** In, of, toward, or pertainin
the east. **2.** From the east, as a wind. — *adv.* Towar
from the east. — *n. pl.* **·lies** A wind or storm from the e

east·ern (ēs′tərn) *adj.* **1.** To, toward, or in the east.
Native to or inhabiting the east: an *eastern* species.
Sometimes cap. Of, or like the east or the East.

Eastern Church 1. The church of the Byzantine Emp
including the patriarchates of Constantinople, Alexand
Antioch, and Jerusalem, that separated from the West
Church in 1054: also called *Greek Church.* **2.** The East
Orthodox Church. **3.** The Uniat Church.

east·ern·er (ēs′tərn·ər) *n.* *Often cap.* One who is nativ
or lives in the east, esp. the eastern U.S.

Eastern Orthodox Church The modern churches deri
from the medieval Eastern Church, including the Greek
Russian Orthodox churches, that agree in faith and or
with the patriarch of Constantinople: also called *East
Church, Orthodox Church,* or loosely *Greek Church.*

Eastern Roman Empire The Byzantine Empire.

East·er·tide (ēs′tər·tīd′) *n.* The season of Easter, a per
extending in various churches from Easter to Ascension D
Whitsunday, or Trinity Sunday.

east·ward (ēst′wərd) *adv.* Toward the east. Also **ea
wards.** — *adj.* To, toward, facing, or in the east. — *n.*
eastward direction or point; also, an eastern part or regi

east·ward·ly (ēst′wərd·lē) *adj.* & *adv.* **1.** Toward the ea
2. Coming from the east, as a wind.

·y (ē′zē) adj. eas·i·er, eas·i·est 1. Requiring little work effort; offering few difficulties: an *easy* task. 2. Free from scomfort, trouble, or anxiety: an *easy* mind. 3. Characrized by rest or comfort: an *easy* life. 4. Not stiff or foral; relaxed: an *easy* manner. 5. Not strict; lenient; indulnt. 6. Yielding; credulous: an *easy* victim. 7. Complant; easygoing. 8. Unhurried; gentle: an *easy* trot. 9. Not rdensome; moderate: to buy on *easy* terms. 10. Well-to-; affluent: in *easy* circumstances. 11. *Econ.* In little deand: said of a commodity. — **to be on easy street** *Informal* To be well-to-do; live in comfort. — *adv. Informal* In an sy manner; easily. — **to go easy on** *Slang* 1. To use with oderation, as liquor. 2. To be lenient with. 3. To be tactl about. — **to take it easy** *Informal* 1. To relax. 2. remain calm. [< OF *aiser* to put at ease]

·y·go·ing (ē′zē·gō′ing) adj. 1. Not inclined to effort or rry. 2. Moving at an easy pace, as a horse.

(ēt) v. **ate** (āt, *Brit.* et) or *Archaic* **eat** (et, ēt), **eat·en, t·ing** v.t. 1. To take in through the mouth as nourishent; esp., to chew and swallow. 2. To consume or destroy or as by eating: usu. with *away* or *up*. 3. To wear away; ste. 4. To make (a hole, etc.) by gnawing or corroding. *v.i.* 5. To take food; have a meal. — **to eat one's words** retract what one has said. [OE *etan*] — **eat′·able** *adj.* *n.* — **eat′er** *n.*

de Co·logne (ō′ də kə·lōn′) Cologne, a toilet water.

ves (ēvz) n. (*orig. sing., now construed as pl.*) The lower ojecting edge of a sloping roof. [OE *efes* edge]

ves·drop (ēvz′drop′) v.i. **·dropped, ·drop·ping** To listen cretly, as to a private conversation. — *n.* Water that ops from the eaves. — **eaves′drop′per** *n.*

(eb) v.i. 1. To recede, as the tide: opposed to *flow*. 2. decline or weaken; fail. — *n.* 1. The flowing back of dewater to the ocean: opposed to *flood*. Also **ebb tide**. 2. A ndition or period of decline or decay. [OE *ebbian*]

on·ite (eb′ən·īt) n. Vulcanite, a rubber product.

on·y (eb′ən·ē) n. pl. **·ies** 1. A hard, heavy wood, usu. ack, used for cabinetwork, etc., furnished by various spes of tropical hardwood trees. 2. Any tree yielding this ood. — *adj.* 1. Made of ebony. 2. Like ebony; black. < L < Gk. < Egyptian *hebni*]

ul·lient (i·bul′yənt) adj. 1. Full of enthusiasm; exubert. 2. Boiling or bubbling up. [< L < *e*- out + *bullire* to il] — **e·bul′lient·ly** *adv.* — **e·bul′lience, e·bul′lien·cy** *n.*

ul·li·tion (eb′ə·lish′ən) n. 1. The bubbling of a liquid; iling. 2. Any sudden or violent agitation, as of emotions. Var. or EX-[2].

cen·tric (ek·sen′trik) adj. 1. Differing conspicuously in havior, appearance, or opinions. 2. Not situated in the nter, as an axis. 3. Deviating from a perfect circle: said iefly of an elliptical orbit. 4. *Math.* Not having the same nter: opposed to *concentric*. — *n.* An odd or erratic indidual. [< LL < Gk. < *ek*- out, away + *kentron* center] **ec·cen′tri·cal·ly** *adv.*

cen·tric·i·ty (ek′sen·tris′ə·tē) n. pl. **·ties** 1. Deviation m what is regular or expected; irregularity. 2. A peculiity. 3. The quality or degree of being eccentric.

cle·si·as·tes (i·klē′zē·as′tēz) n. A book of the Old Tesment: also, *Hebrew, Koheleth.* [< Gk. *ekklēsiastēs*, trans. Hebrew *qōhēleth* preacher]

cle·si·as·tic (i·klē′zē·as′tik) adj. Ecclesiastical. — *n.* ne officially in the service of the church; a cleric; churchan. [< Gk. < *ek*- out + *kaleein* to call]

cle·si·as·ti·cal (i·klē′zē·as′ti·kəl) adj. Of or pertaining the church, especially as an organized and governing wer. — **ec·cle′si·as′ti·cal·ly** *adv.*

cle·si·as·ti·cus (i·klē′zē·as′ti·kəs) n. One of the didac books of the Old Testament Apocrypha.

·e·lon (esh′ə·lon) n. 1. A troop, fleet, or airplane forman resembling a series of steps, in which each rank, ship, or rplane extends behind and slightly to the right or left of the eceding one. 2. *Mil.* **a** One of the different fractions of a mmand arranged from front to rear, to which a particular mbat mission is assigned: assault *echelon*; support *echelon*. One of the various subdivisions from front to rear of a miliry headquarters: forward *echelon*; rear *echelon*. **c** Level of mmand: command *echelon*. — *v.t. & v.i.* To form in echn. [< F *échelon* < *échelle* ladder < L *scala*]

hid·na (i·kid′nə) n. pl. **·nae** (-nē) An egg-laying mamal of Australia, Tasmania, and New Guinea, having strong ines intermixed with fur. [< NL < Gk., viper]

hi·no·derm (i·kī′nə·dûrm) n. A marine animal having a dial body and a hard, spiny shell, as the starfish.

·o (ek′ō) n. pl. **ech·oes** 1. The repetition of a sound by e reflection of sound waves from an opposing surface; also, e sound so produced. 2. The repetition or reproduction of e views, style, etc., of another. 3. One who imitates anher or repeats his words. 4. Prompt, sympathetic response. — *v.t.* 1. To repeat or send back (sound) by echo: The walls *echoed* the shot. 2. To repeat the words, opinions, etc., of. 3. To repeat (words, opinions, etc.) in imitation. — *v.i.* 4. To give back sound. 5. To be repeated or given back. [< L < Gk. *ēche* sound, noise] — **ech′o·er** *n.* — **e·cho′ic** *adj.*

Ech·o (ek′ō) In Greek mythology, a nymph who, because of love for Narcissus, pined away until only her voice was left.

é·clair (ā·klâr′, i·klâr′) n. A small oblong pastry shell filled with custard or whipped cream. [< F, lit., flash of lightning]

é·clat (ā·klä′, i·klä′) n. 1. Brilliance of action or effect; conspicuous success. 2. Splendor of reputation; renown; also, notoriety. 3. Acclaim. [< F < *éclater* to burst out]

ec·lec·tic (ek·lek′tik, ik-) adj. 1. Selecting what is considered best from different systems or sources. 2. Composed of elements selected from diverse sources. — *n.* One favoring no particular belief or practice, as in philosophy or art, but selecting from all schools or methods. [< Gk. < *ek*- out + *legein* to select] — **ec·lec′ti·cal·ly** *adv.* — **ec·lec′ti·cism** *n.*

e·clipse (i·klips′) n. 1. *Astron.* The apparent dimming or elimination of light from one heavenly body by another. A **lunar eclipse** is caused by the passage of the moon through the earth's shadow; a **solar eclipse** by the passage of the moon between the sun and the observer. 2. Any overshadowing or dimming, as of power or reputation. — *v.t.* **e·clipsed, e·clips·ing** 1. To cause an eclipse of; darken. 2. To obscure the beauty, fame, worth, etc., of; overshadow; surpass. [< OF < L < Gk. < *ek*- out + *leipein* to leave]

e·clip·tic (i·klip′tik, ē-) n. *Astron.* 1. The plane, passing through the center of the sun, that contains the orbit of the earth: also **plane of the ecliptic**. 2. The great circle in which this plane intersects the celestial sphere. — *adj.* Pertaining to eclipses or to the ecliptic: also **e·clip′ti·cal**. — **e·clip′ti·cal·ly** *adv.*

ec·logue (ek′lôg, -log) n. A short pastoral poem. [< F < L < Gk. < *ek*- out + *legein* to select]

e·col·o·gy (i·kol′ə·jē, ē-) n. The division of biology that treats of the relations between organisms and their environment. [< Gk. *oikos* home + -LOGY] — **ec·o·log·ic** (ek′ə·loj′ik) or **·i·cal** *adj.* — **ec′o·log′i·cal·ly** *adv.* — **e·col′o·gist** *n.*

ec·o·nom·ic (ek′ə·nom′ik, ē′kə-) adj. 1. Of or pertaining to the development and management of the material wealth of a government or community: the French *economic* policy. 2. Relating to the science of economics: *economic* theory. 3. Of or pertaining to financial matters. 4. Of practical use.

ec·o·nom·i·cal (ek′ə·nom′i·kəl, ē′kə-) adj. 1. Frugal. 2. Economic. — **ec′o·nom′i·cal·ly** *adv.*

economic determinism The theory that all human activities and institutions have economic origins.

ec·o·nom·ics (ek′ə·nom′iks, ē′kə-) n.pl. 1. (*construed as sing.*) The science that treats of the production, distribution, and consumption of wealth. 2. Economic matters.

e·con·o·mist (i·kon′ə·mist) n. 1. One who is proficient in economics. 2. One who is careful and thrifty.

e·con·o·mize (i·kon′ə·mīz) v. **·mized, ·miz·ing** v.i. 1. To be sparing in expenditure; manage thriftily. — *v.t.* 2. To use sparingly or to best advantage. Also *Brit.* **e·con′o·mise.**

e·con·o·my (i·kon′ə·mē) n. pl. **·mies** 1. Frugal management of money, materials, resources, and the like; also, an example of this. 2. The practical administration of the material resources of a country, community, or establishment: the national *economy*. 3. The orderly distribution and interplay of parts in a structure or system: the *economy* of nature. [< L < Gk. < *oikos* house + *nemein* to manage]

ec·ru (ek′rōō, ā′krōō) adj. Of the color of unbleached linen. — *n.* A light, yellowish brown. Also **é·cru.** [< F < OF < L *ex*- thoroughly + *crudus* raw]

ec·sta·sy (ek′stə·sē) n. pl. **·sies** 1. The state of being beside oneself through some overpowering emotion: in an *ecstasy* of anticipation. 2. Intense delight; rapture. 3. A trance. [< OF < LL < Gk. < *ek*- out + *histanai* to place]

ec·stat·ic (ek·stat′ik) adj. 1. Pertaining to, of the nature of, or exciting to ecstasy; rapturous. 2. In a state of ecstasy; transported. Also **ec·stat′i·cal.** — *n.* A person subject to ecstasies or trances. — **ec·stat′i·cal·ly** *adv.*

ecto- *combining form* Without; outside; external: *ectoderm.* Also, before vowels, **ect-.** [< Gk. *ekto-* < *ektos* outside]

ec·to·derm (ek′tə·dûrm) n. *Biol.* The outermost of the three primary germ layers in the embryo, developing into the skin, sense organs, and nervous system. — **ec′to·der′·mal, ec′to·der′mic** *adj.*

ec·to·mor·phic (ek′tō·môr′fik) adj. Of human body types, characterized by a lean body structure. — **ec′to·morph** *n.*

-ectomy *combining form* Removal of a part by cutting out: used in surgical terms to indicate certain kinds of operations: *appendectomy.* [< Gk. < *ek*- out + *temnein* to cut]

ec·to·plasm (ek′tə·plaz′əm) n. 1. *Biol.* The firm outer layer of the cytoplasm of a unicellular organism or of a plant cell.

2. The substance alleged to emanate from the body of a spiritualist medium during a trance. — **ec′to·plas′mic** *adj.*

ec·u·men·i·cal (ek′yo͞o·men′i·kəl) *adj.* World-wide in scope, esp. of the Christian church: an *ecumenical* council. Also **ec′u·men′ic.** [< LL < Gk. *oikeein* to inhabit]

ec·u·men·ism (ek′yo͞o·men′iz·əm) *n.* The movement for world-wide unity and cooperation among all Christian churches. Also **ec′u·men′i·cal·ism, ec′u·men′i·cism.**

ec·ze·ma (ek′sə·mə, eg′zə·mə, eg·zē′mə) *n. Pathol.* An inflammatory disease of the skin attended by itching, watery discharge, and the appearance of lesions. [< Gk. < *ek-* out + *zeein* to boil] — **ec·zem·a·tous** (eg·zem′ə·təs) *adj.*

-ed[1] *suffix* Forming the past tense of regular verbs: *walked, killed, played.* [OE *-ede, -ode, -ade*]

-ed[2] *suffix* **1.** Forming the past participle of regular verbs: *washed.* **2.** Forming adjectives from adjectives in *-ate,* with the same general meaning: *bipinnated.* [OE *-ed, -ad, -od*]

-ed[3] *suffix* Forming adjectives from nouns with the senses: **1.** Having; possessing; characterized by: *toothed, green-eyed.* **2.** Like; resembling: *bigoted.* [OE *-ede*]

ed·dy (ed′ē) *n. pl.* **·dies** A backward-circling current of water or air; whirlpool. — *v.t. & v.i.* **·died, ·dy·ing** To move, or cause to move, in or as in an eddy. [Prob. < ON *idha*]

e·del·weiss (ā′dəl·vīs) *n.* A small, perennial herb growing chiefly in the Alps, with white, woolly leaves suggesting a flower. [< G *edel* noble + *weiss* white]

EDELWEISS (To 4 inches high)

e·de·ma (i·dē′mə) *n. pl.* **·ma·ta** (-mə·tə) *Pathol.* An abnormal accumulation of serous fluid in various organs, cavities, or tissues of the body; swelling: also spelled *oedema.* [< NL < Gk. *oidein* to swell] — **e·dem·a·tous** (i·dem′ə·təs), **e·dem′a·tose** (-tōs) *adj.*

E·den (ēd′n) *n.* **1.** In the Bible, the garden that was the first home of Adam and Eve: often called *Paradise.* **2.** Any delightful place or condition. [< Hebrew *ēden* delight]

e·den·tate (ē·den′tāt, i·den′-) *adj.* **1.** Of or pertaining to an order of mammals, some of which lack teeth, including sloths, anteaters, and armadillos. **2.** Toothless. — *n.* An edentate mammal. [< L < *e-* without + *dens, dentis* tooth]

edge (ej) *n.* **1.** A bounding or dividing line; also, the part along a boundary; border; margin: the *edge* of a lawn. **2.** A verge or brink; rim: the *edge* of a cliff. **3.** The line where two surfaces of a solid meet: the *edge* of a cube. **4.** The thin, sharp, cutting side of a blade. **5.** Sharpness; keenness. **6.** *U.S. Informal* Advantage; superiority. — **on edge 1.** Keenly sensitive; tense; irritable. **2.** Eager; impatient. — *v.* **edged, edg·ing** *v.t.* **1.** To sharpen. **2.** To furnish with an edge or border. **3.** To push sidewise or by degrees. — *v.i.* **4.** To move sidewise or by degrees. [OE *ecg*]

edge·wise (ej′wīz′) *adv.* **1.** With the edge forward. **2.** On, by, with, or toward the edge. Also **edge′ways′** (-wāz′).

edg·ing (ej′ing) *n.* A trimming; border.

edg·y (ej′ē) *adj.* **edg·i·er, edg·i·est 1.** Tense, nervous, or irritable. **2.** Having an edge or edges. — **edg′i·ness** *n.*

ed·i·ble (ed′ə·bəl) *adj.* Fit to eat. — *n. Usu. pl.* Something fit to eat. [< LL < L *edere* to eat]

e·dict (ē′dikt) *n.* An official decree publicly proclaimed. [< L < *e-* out + *dicere* to say] — **e·dic·tal** (ē·dik′təl) *adj.*

ed·i·fi·ca·tion (ed′ə·fə·kā′shən) *n.* Intellectual or moral enlightenment and improvement.

ed·i·fice (ed′ə·fis) *n.* A building or other structure, esp. one that is large and imposing. [< F < L < *aedes* building + *facere* to make] — **ed·i·fi·cial** (ed′ə·fish′əl) *adj.*

ed·i·fy (ed′ə·fī) *v.t.* **·fied, ·fy·ing** To enlighten and benefit, esp. morally or spiritually. [< OF < L < *aedes* building + *facere* to make] — **ed′i·fi′er** *n.*

ed·it (ed′it) *v.t.* **1.** To correct and prepare for publication: to *edit* a manuscript. **2.** To compile, arrange, and emend for publication: to *edit* a collection of poems. **3.** To direct the preparation, publication, and editorial policies of (a newspaper, magazine, etc.). [Back formation < EDITOR]

e·di·tion (i·dish′ən) *n.* **1.** The form in which a book is published: a three-volume *edition.* **2.** The total number of copies of a publication issued at any one time; also, such a copy. [< F < L < *e-* out + *dare* to give]

ed·i·tor (ed′i·tər) *n.* **1.** One who edits. **2.** A writer of editorials. [< L] — **ed′i·tor·ship′** *n.*

ed·i·to·ri·al (ed′i·tôr′ē·əl, -tō′rē-) *n.* An article in a newspaper, magazine, or the like, published as the periodical's official expression of opinion on some issue. — *adj.* Of, pertaining to, or written by an editor. — **ed′i·to′ri·al·ly** *adv.*

ed·i·to·ri·al·ize (ed′i·tôr′ē·əl·īz′, -tō′rē-) *v.t. & v.i.* **·ized, ·iz·ing 1.** To express opinions (on a subject) editorially. **2.** To insert editorial opinions (into a news item, etc.).

editor in chief *pl.* **editors in chief** The chief editor of a publication, who establishes its policy and supervises operations.

ed·u·cate (ej′o͝o·kāt) *v.t.* **cat·ed, ·cat·ing 1.** To develop or train the mind, capabilities, or character of by instruction or study; teach. **2.** To train for some special purpose. **3.** To develop or train (taste, special ability, etc.). **4.** To pro[vide] schooling for. [< L < *e-* out + *ducere* to lead] — **e[d′u]·ca·ble** *adj.* — **ed′u·ca′tor** *n.*

ed·u·cat·ed (ej′o͝o·kā′tid) *adj.* **1.** Developed and infor[med] by education; instructed; trained. **2.** Having a cultiva[ted] mind, speech, manner, etc.

ed·u·ca·tion (ej′o͝o·kā′shən) *n.* **1.** The act of educat[ing;] systematic development or training of the mind, capabili[ties,] or character through instruction or study. **2.** Acquisitio[n of] knowledge or skills; esp., formal schooling in an institu[tion] of learning. **3.** Knowledge, skills, or cultivation acqu[ired] through instruction or study. **4.** The study of teac[hing] methods and problems, the learning process, and o[ther] matters related to the classroom; pedagogy.

ed·u·ca·tion·al (ej′o͝o·kā′shən·əl) *adj.* Of, pertaining t[o, or] imparting education: an *educational* trip. — **ed′u·ca′t[ion]·al·ly** *adv.*

ed·u·ca·tive (ej′o͝o·kā′tiv) *adj.* **1.** That educates or te[nds] to educate; educational. **2.** Of or relating to education.

e·duce (i·do͞os′, i·dyo͞os′) *v.t.* **e·duced, e·duc·ing 1.** To [draw] forth; bring out; elicit. **2.** To infer or develop from d[ata;] deduce. [< L < *e-* out + *ducere* to lead] — **e·duc′i[·ble]** *adj.* — **e·duc·tion** (i·duk′shən) *n.* — **e·duc′tive** *adj.*

-ee *suffix of nouns* **1.** One who undergoes, or benefits fr[om] some action: used esp. in legal terms, and opposed to *-er,* as in *grantor, grantee.* **2.** One who is described by the m[ain] element: *absentee.* [< AF *-é,* suffix of pp. < L *-atus*]

eel (ēl) *n. pl.* **eels** or **eel** A fish having a snakelike b[ody] usu. without scales or pelvic fins, and of both marine [and] fresh-water habitat. [OE *æl*] — **eel′y** *adj.*

e'en[1] (ēn) *adv. Poetic* Even.

e'en[2] (ēn) *n. Poetic & Dial.* Evening.

e'er (âr) *adv. Poetic* Ever.

-eer *suffix of nouns and verbs* **1.** One who is concerned w[ith,] works with, or makes something indicated: *engineer.* **2** [To be] concerned with; work at: *electioneer.* [< F *-ier* < L *-ar*[ius]]

ee·rie (ir′ē, ē′rē) *adj.* **1.** Inspiring fear; weird; ghostly. [2.] Affected by superstitious fear. Also **ee′ry.** [ME *eri* ti[mid,] var. of *erg* < OE *earg*] — **ee′ri·ly** *adv.* — **ee′ri·ness** *n.*

ef·face (i·fās′) *v.t.* **·faced, ·fac·ing 1.** To rub out, as wri[tten] characters; erase. **2.** To obliterate, as a memory. **3.** [To] make (oneself) insignificant. [< F < L *ex-* out + *facies* f[ace]] — **ef·face′ment** *n.* — **ef·fac′er** *n.*

ef·fect (i·fekt′) *n.* **1.** Something brought about by s[ome] cause or agency; result; consequence. **2.** Capacity to [pro]duce some result; efficacy. **3.** The condition or fact of b[eing] in active force: to put a law into *effect.* **4.** The state [of] being actually accomplished or realized: to carry plans [into] *effect.* **5.** The particular way in which something affect[s or] influences something else. **6.** The overall reaction or [im]pression produced by something seen, heard, or done. **7.** [A] technique used in art, literature, music, etc., to achie[ve a] certain result or produce a distinctive impression. **8.** [The] actual or basic meaning intended or conveyed; purport: [used] with *to:* She said something to that *effect.* **9.** *pl.* Mov[able] goods; belongings. — **in effect 1.** In actual fact. **2.** [For] all practical purposes; virtually. **3.** In active force or op[era]tion. — **to take effect** To begin to act upon something or become operative. — *v.t.* To bring about; cause; esp. [to] accomplish; achieve: to *effect* an escape. [< L < *ex-* ou[t +] *facere* to do, make] — **ef·fect′er** *n.* — **ef·fect′i·ble** *adj.*

ef·fec·tive (i·fek′tiv) *adj.* **1.** Producing or adapted to [pro]duce the proper result. **2.** Being in force, as a law. **3.** [Pro]ducing a striking impression, as a speaker. **4.** Ready [for] action, as an army. — *n.* **1.** One who is fit for duty. [2.] The number of men available for military service. — [ef·]**fec′tive·ly** *adv.* — **ef·fec′tive·ness** *n.*

ef·fec·tu·al (i·fek′cho͞o·əl) *adj.* **1.** Producing or having a[de]quate power to produce an intended effect. **2.** Legally v[alid] or binding. — **ef·fec′tu·al·ly** *adv.* — **ef·fec′tu·al·n[ess],** **ef·fec′tu·al′i·ty** (-al′ə·tē) *n.*

ef·fec·tu·ate (i·fek′cho͞o·āt) *v.t.* **·at·ed, ·at·ing** To br[ing] about; accomplish; effect. — **ef·fec′tu·a′tion** *n.*

ef·fem·i·nate (i·fem′ə·nit) *adj.* **1.** Having womanlike tr[aits] or qualities to a degree unbefitting a man; womanish; [un]manly. **2.** Characterized by weakness or self-indulge[nce.] [< L < *ex-* out + *femina* a woman] — **ef·fem′i·na·cy** (-[nə·]sē) *n.* — **ef·fem′i·nate·ly** *adv.* — **ef·fem′i·nate·ness** *n.*

ef·fer·ent (ef′ər·ənt) *adj. Physiol.* Carrying or carried o[ut]ward: said esp. of impulses transmitted from the cen[tral] nervous system to muscles, etc.; opposed to *afferent.* — *Physiol.* An efferent duct, vessel, or nerve. [< L < *ex-* + *ferre* to carry]

ef·fer·vesce (ef′ər·ves′) *v.i.* **·vesced, ·vesc·ing 1.** To g[ive] off bubbles of gas, as water charged with carbon dioxide. [2.] To issue out in bubbles, as a gas. **3.** To show exhilaratio[n or] lively spirits. [< L < *ex-* out + *fervescere* to boil] — [ef·]**fer·ves′cence** *n.* — **ef′fer·ves′cent** *adj.*

ef·fete (i·fēt′) *adj.* **1.** Having lost strength or virility. [2.] Incapable of further production; barren. [< L < *ex-* out [+] *fetus* a breeding] — **ef·fete′ly** *adv.* — **ef·fete′ness** *n.*

ı·ca·cious (ef′ə·kā′shəs) *adj.* Producing or capable of ɔducing an intended effect. [See EFFECT.] — **ef′fi·ca′·us·ly** *adv.* — **ef′fi·ca′cious·ness** *n.*
ı·ca·cy (ef′ə·kə·sē) *n. pl.* **·cies** Power to produce a de-ed or intended result.
ı·cien·cy (i·fish′ən·sē) *n. pl.* **·cies** **1.** The quality of be-: efficient. **2.** The ratio of work done or energy expended the energy supplied in the form of food or fuel.
ı·cient (i·fish′ənt) *adj.* **1.** Productive of results with a nimum of wasted effort. **2.** Producing an effect. [See FECT.] — **ef·fi′cient·ly** *adv.*
ı·gy (ef′ə·jē) *n. pl.* **·gies** **1.** A likeness or representation; ., a sculptured portrait. **2.** A crude image of a disliked son. [< F < L < *ex-* out + *fingere* to fashion]
lo·resce (ef′lôr·es′, -lō·res′) *v.i.* **·resced, ·resc·ing** **1.** To ssom, bloom, or flower. **2.** *Chem.* **a** To become powdery, olly or in part, and lose crystalline structure through aporation of water. **b** To become covered with a crust saline particles left by evaporation or by chemical change. L < *ex-* thoroughly + *florescere* to bloom]
lo·res·cence (ef′lôr·es′əns, -lō·res′-) *n.* **1.** The act or son of flowering. **2.** *Chem.* The act or process of efflo-cing. **3.** *Pathol.* A rash. — **ef′flo·res′cent** *adj.*
lu·ent (ef′lo͞o·ənt) *adj.* Flowing out. — *n.* An outflow, of water from a lake, industrial sewage, etc. [< L < *ex-* t + *fluere* to flow] — **ef′flu·ence** *n.*
lu·vi·um (i·flo͞o′vē·əm) *n. pl.* **·vi·a** (-vē·ə) or **·vi·ums** **1.** invisible emanation; esp., a foul-smelling exhalation, as m decaying matter. **2.** A supposed imponderable agent merly regarded as the source of electric and magnetic ces. [< L, a flowing out] — **ef·flu′vi·al** *adj.*
ux (ef′luks) *n.* **1.** A flowing out. **2.** That which flows th; emanation. [< L < *ex-* out + *fluere* to flow]
ort (ef′ərt) *n.* **1.** Expenditure of physical, mechanical, mental energy to get something done; exertion. **2.** Some-ng produced by exertion: a new theatrical *effort.* [< F OF < L *ex-* thoroughly + *fortis* strong] — **ef′fort·less** *j.* — **ef′fort·less·ly** *adv.*
ront·er·y (i·frun′tər·ē) *n. pl.* **·ies** Shameless or insolent dness; audacity. [< F < L < *ex-* out + *frontis* face]
ulge (i·fulj′) *v.t. & v.i.* **·fulged, ·fulg·ing** To shine forth; liate. [< L < *ex-* out + *fulgere* to shine]
ul·gent (i·ful′jənt) *adj.* Shining brilliantly; radiant; endid. — **ef·ful′gence** *n.* — **ef·ful′gent·ly** *adv.*
use (*adj.* i·fyo͞os′; *v.* i·fyo͞oz′) *adj.* **1.** *Bot.* Spreading t loosely or flat. **2.** *Zool.* Having the lips separated by a ɔove, as certain shells. — *v.* **·fused, ·fus·ing** *v.t.* **1.** To ur forth; shed. — *v.i.* **2.** To emanate; exude. [< L *ex-* out + *fundere* to pour] — **ef·fu′sion** *n.*
u·sive (i·fyo͞o′siv) *adj.* **1.** Overflowing with sentiment; monstrative; gushing. **2.** Pouring forth; overflowing. — **fu′sive·ly** *adv.* — **ef·fu′sive·ness** *n.*
ad (i·gad′, ē·gad′) *interj.* By God!: a mild oath.
al·i·tar·i·an (i·gal′ə·târ′ē·ən) *adj.* Of, relating to, or be-ving in political and social equality. — *n.* One who be-ves in or advocated political and social equality. Also *ualitarian.* [< F *égalitaire*] — **e·gal′i·tar′i·an·ism** *n.*
ç[1] (eg) *n.* **1.** The round or oval reproductive body pro-ced by female birds, insects, and most reptiles and fishes, nsisting of the germ and a nutritive yolk enclosed in a ell or membrane. **2.** *Biol.* The reproductive cell of female imals; ovum: also **egg cell.** **3.** The hen's egg as a food. Something oval like a hen's egg. **5.** *U.S. Slang* Person: ə's a good *egg.* — **to lay an egg** *U.S. Slang* To fail com-etely. — **to put all one's eggs in one basket** To risk all a single venture. — *v.t.* **1.** To cover with beaten egg be-re cooking. **2.** *U.S. Informal* To pelt with eggs. [< ON]
ç[2] (eg) *v.t.* To incite; urge: usu. with *on.* [< ON *eggja*]
ç·head (eg′hed′) *n.* *U.S. Slang* An intellectual; high-ow: often derisive.
ç·nog (eg′nog′) *n.* A drink made of beaten eggs and milk th sugar and nutmeg and sometimes with liquor.
ç·plant (eg′plant′, -plänt′) *n.* **1.** A widely cultivated rb with large, egg-shaped, usu. purple-skinned fruit. **2.** ıe fruit of this plant, used as a vegetable.
ç·shell (eg′shel′) *n.* The hard, brittle covering of a bird's g. — *adj.* **1.** Thin and fragile. **2.** Pale yellow or ivory.
ç white The uncooked albumen of an egg.
is (ē′jis) See AEGIS.
lan·tine (eg′lən·tīn, -tēn) *n.* Any of various fragrant ild roses. [< F < OF, ult. < L *acus* needle]
o (ē′gō, eg′ō) *n. pl.* **e·gos** **1.** The thinking, feeling, and ting self that is conscious of itself and aware of its distinc-ɔn from the objects of its thought and perceptions. **2.** *Psy-oanal.* The conscious aspect of the psyche that develops rough contact with the external world and resolves con-cts between the id and the superego. **3.** *Informal* Self-nteredness; conceit. [< L, I]
e·go·cen·tric (ē′gō·sen′trik, eg′ō-) *adj.* Regarding oneself as the object of all experience and acts. — *n.* An egocentric person. — **e′go·cen·tric′i·ty** (-sen·tris′ə·tē) *n.*
e·go·ism (ē′gō·iz′əm, eg′ō-) *n.* **1.** Inordinate concern for one's own welfare and interests. **2.** Self-conceit; egotism.
e·go·ist (ē′gō·ist, eg′ō-) *n.* **1.** One who is completely de-voted to his own interests. **2.** A conceited person; egotist. — **e′go·is′tic** or **·ti′cal** *adj.* — **e′go·is′ti·cal·ly** *adv.*
e·go·ma·ni·a (ē′gō·mā′nē·ə, -mān′yə, eg′ō-) *n.* Abnormal or excessive egotism. — **e′go·ma′ni·ac** (-ak) *n.*
e·go·tism (ē′gə·tiz′əm, eg′ə-) *n.* **1.** Excessive reference to oneself in speech or writing; self-conceit. **2.** Selfishness; egoism. — **e′go·tist** *n.* — **e′go·tis′tic** or **·ti·cal** *adj.* — **e′go·tis′ti·cal·ly** *adv.*
e·gre·gious (i·grē′jəs, -jē·əs) *adj.* Conspicuously bad; glar-ing; flagrant. [< L < *e-* out + *grex, gregis* herd] — **e·gre′·gious·ly** *adv.* — **e·gre′gious·ness** *n.*
e·gress (ē′gres) *n.* **1.** A going out, as from a building; emer-gence; also, the right of going out. Also **e·gres′sion.** **2.** A place of exit. [< L < *e-* out + *gradi* to walk]
e·gret (ē′grit, eg′rit) *n.* **1.** One of various herons character-ized in the breeding season by long and loose plumes droop-ing over the tail. **2.** Aigrette (def. 1). [Var. of AIGRETTE]
E·gyp·tian (i·jip′shən) *adj.* Of or pertaining to Egypt, its people, or their culture. — *n.* **1.** One of the people of Egypt. **2.** The ancient Hamitic language of Egypt.
E·gyp·tol·o·gy (ē′jip·tol′ə·jē) *n.* The study of the antiq-uities of Egypt. — **E′gyp·tol′o·gist** *n.*
eh (ā, e) *interj.* What: used to express uncertainty: surprise, etc.
ei·der (ī′dər) *n.* A large sea duck of northern regions. [< ON *ædhr-* in *ædhar-dūn* eiderdown]
ei·der·down (ī′dər·doun′) *n.* The down of the eider used for stuffing pillows and quilts; such also, a quilt.
eight (āt) *n.* **1.** The sum of seven and one: a cardinal num-ber. **2.** Any symbol of this number, as 8, viii, VIII. **3.** Anything consisting of eight units. — *adj.* Being one more than seven. [OE *eahta*] — **eighth** (ātth, āth) *adj. & n.*
eight·een (ā′tēn′) *n.* **1.** The sum of seventeen and one: a cardinal number. **2.** Any symbol of this number, as 18, xviii, XVIII. **3.** Anything consisting of or representing eighteen units. — *adj.* Being one more than seventeen. [OE *eahtatīene*] — **eight·eenth′** *adj. & n.*
eight·een·mo (ā′tēn′mō′) *adj. & n.* Octodecimo.
eighth note *Music* A note having one eighth the time value of a whole note: also, *Chiefly Brit., quaver.*
eight·vo (āt′vō) *adj. & n.* Octavo.
eight·y (ā′tē) *n. pl.* **·ies** **1.** The sum of seventy and ten: a cardinal number. **2.** Any symbol of this number, as 80, lxxx, LXXX. **3.** Anything consisting of or representing eighty units. — *adj.* Being ten more than seventy. [OE *eahtatig*] — **eight′i·eth** *adj. & n.*
-ein Var. of -IN.
ein·stein·i·um (īn·stī′nē·əm) *n.* A radioactive element (symbol Es), originally detected in the debris of a thermo-nuclear explosion and artificially produced by the irradiation of plutonium. See ELEMENT. [after Albert *Einstein*]
ei·ther (ē′thər, ī′thər) *adj.* **1.** One or the other of two: Use *either* foot. **2.** Each of two; one and the other: They sat on *either* side of him. — *pron.* One or the other: Choose *either.* — *conj.* In one of two or more cases, indeterminately or indifferently: a disjunctive correlative used with *or:* *Either* I shall go or he will come. — *adv.* Any more so: used after the denial of an alternative, or to emphasize a pre-ceding negative: He could not speak, and I could not *either;* I shall leave, and you can't stop me *either.* [OE *ǣgther*]
◆ **either, neither** *Either,* like *neither,* is singular and in formal writing takes a singular verb: *Either* of them *is* suit-able. In informal speech and writing, however, a plural verb is commonly used: *Are either* of you going to the party? When there are two subjects of differing number, the verb agrees with the nearer: *Neither he nor they are* ever there.
e·jac·u·late (i·jak′yə·lāt) *v.* **·lat·ed, ·lat·ing** *v.t.* **1.** To utter suddenly, as a brief exclamation. **2.** To discharge suddenly and quickly, as seminal fluid. — *v.i.* **3.** To ejaculate some-thing. — *n.* That which is ejaculated. — **Syn.** See EX-CLAIM. [< L < *e-* out + *jaculari* to throw] — **e·jac′u·la′tion** *n.* — **e·jac′u·la·tive** (-lā′tiv, -lə·tiv) *adj.* — **e·jac′·u·la·tor** *n.* — **e·jac′u·la·to′ry** *adj.*
e·ject (i·jekt′) *v.t.* **1.** To throw out with sudden force. **2.** To put forcibly outside; expel: to *eject* an intruder. **3.** *Law* To dispossess; evict. [< L < *e-* out + *jacere* to throw] — **e·jec′tion** *n.* — **e·jec′tive** *adj.* — **e·ject′ment** *n.* — **e·jec′·tor** *n.*
eke (ēk) *v.t.* **eked, ek·ing** **1.** To piece out; supplement: usually with *out.* **2.** To make a (living) with difficulty: usu-ally with *out.* [Var. of obs. *eche* to increase]
el- Assimilated var. of EN-[2].

e·lab·o·rate (*adj.* i·lab′ər·it; *v.* i·lab′ə·rāt) *adj.* Worked out with great thoroughness or exactness; developed in minute detail: *elaborate* precautions. — *v.* **·rat·ed, ·rat·ing** *v.t.* **1.** To work out in detail; develop carefully and thoroughly. **2.** To produce by labor. — *v.i.* **3.** To add details or embellishments: with *on* or *upon*: to *elaborate* on a subject. [< L < *e-* out + *laborare* to work] — **e·lab′o·rate·ly** *adv.* — **e·lab′o·rate·ness** *n.* — **e·lab′o·ra′tion** *n.* — **e·lab′o·ra·tive** *adj.* — **e·lab′o·ra′tor** *n.*

E·lam (ē′ləm) An ancient country of SW Asia between the Persian Gulf and the Caspian Sea. *Gen.* xiv 1. — **E′lam·ite** (-īt) *adj.* & *n.* — **E′lam·it′ic** (-lə·mit′ik) *adj.* & *n.*

é·lan (ā·län′) *n.* Enthusiasm; dash; vivacity. [< F]

e·land (ē′lənd) *n.* A large, oxlike African antelope with twisted horns. [< Du., elk]

e·lapse (i·laps′) *v.i.* **e·lapsed, e·laps·ing** To slip by; pass away: said of time. [< L < *e-* out, away + *labi* to glide]

e·las·mo·branch (i·las′mō·brangk, i·laz′-) *n. Zool.* One of a class or subclass of sharks, rays, etc., having cartilaginous skeletons, and lacking air bladders. [< NL < Gk. *elasmos* metal plate + *branchia* gills]

e·las·tic (i·las′tik) *adj.* **1.** Spontaneously regaining former size, shape, or bulk after compression, extension, or other distortion. **2.** Adjusting readily to fit the circumstances; flexible. **3.** Recovering quickly, as from emotional or physical distress; resilient. **4.** Marked by a springy motion. — *n.* **1.** Fabric made stretchable by interwoven threads of rubber. **2.** An article manufactured of this fabric, as a garter. **3.** A rubber band. [< NL < Gk. < *elaunein* to drive] — **e·las′ti·cal·ly** *adv.*

e·las·tic·i·ty (i·las′tis′ə·tē, ē′las-) *n. pl.* **·ties** The property or quality of being elastic; flexibility; resilience.

e·late (i·lāt′) *v.t.* **e·lat·ed, e·lat·ing** To raise the spirits of; stimulate; excite. [< L < *ex-* out + *ferre* to bear]

e·lat·ed (i·lā′tid) *adj.* Filled with joy or triumph, as over good fortune. — **e·lat′ed·ly** *adv.* — **e·lat′ed·ness** *n.*

e·la·tion (i·lā′shən) *n.* Exalted feeling, as from success.

E layer The Heaviside layer.

el·bow (el′bō) *n.* **1.** The joint at the bend of the arm between the forearm and the upper arm; esp., the projecting outer side of this joint. **2.** The joint corresponding to an elbow in the shoulder or hock of a quadruped. **3.** Something having an angle or bend like an elbow. — **at one's elbow** Within easy reach. — **out at the elbows** Shabby; impoverished. — **to rub elbows with** To associate closely with (celebrities, etc.). — **up to the elbows** (**in**) Deeply immersed (in). — *v.t.* **1.** To push or jostle with or as with the elbows. **2.** To make (one's way) by such pushing. — *v.i.* **3.** To push one's way along. [OE *elnboga*]

eld·er[1] (el′dər) *adj.* **1.** Of earlier birth; older; senior. **2.** Superior or prior in rank, office, etc. **3.** Pertaining to a previous time; earlier; former. — *n.* **1.** *Often pl.* An older person; also, a forefather or predecessor. **2.** An influential senior member of a family, community, etc. **3.** *Eccl.* A governing or counseling officer in certain Christian churches. **4.** An aged person. [OE *eldra*] — **eld′er·ship** *n.*

el·der[2] (el′dər) *n.* **1.** A shrub of the honeysuckle family, with white flowers and purple-black or red berries. **2.** Any trees or plants resembling this shrub. [OE *ellæn*]

el·der·ber·ry (el′dər·ber′ē, -bər·ē) *n. pl.* **·ber·ries** **1.** The berry of the elder, used to make wine. **2.** The elder.

eld·er·ly (el′dər·lē) *adj.* Rather advanced in age; approaching old age; quite old. — **Syn.** See OLD.

eld·est (el′dist) *adj.* Alternative superlative of OLD.

e·lect (i·lekt′) *v.t.* **1.** To choose (a person or persons) for an office by vote. **2.** To pick out; select. **3.** *Theol.* To set aside by divine will for salvation: used in the passive voice. — *v.i.* **4.** To make a choice. — *adj.* **1.** Chosen; selected. **2.** Elected to office, but not yet inducted: used in compounds: president-*elect*. — *n.* An elect person or group. [< L < *e-* out + *legere* to choose]

e·lec·tion (i·lek′shən) *n.* **1.** The formal choice of a person or persons for any position or dignity, usu. by ballot. **2.** A popular vote upon any question officially proposed. **3.** In Calvinism, the predestination of individuals to salvation.

e·lec·tion·eer (i·lek′shən·ir′) *v.i.* To work for votes for a particular candidate or political party.

e·lec·tive (i·lek′tiv) *adj.* **1.** Of or pertaining to a choice by vote. **2.** Obtained or settled by election. **3.** Having the power to elect. **4.** Subject to choice; optional. — *n. U.S.* An optional subject in a school or college curriculum.

e·lec·tor (i·lek′tər) *n.* **1.** One who elects; a person qualified to vote. **2.** *U.S.* A member of the electoral college. **3.** *Usu. cap.* One of the German princes who formerly elected the Holy Roman emperor. — **e·lec′tor·al** *adj.*

electoral college A body of electors, chosen by the voters in the States and the District of Columbia, which formally elects the president and vice president of the United States.

e·lec·tor·ate (i·lek′tər·it) *n.* **1.** The whole body of voters. **2.** A district of voters. **3.** The rank or territory of an elector.

E·lec·tra (i·lek′trə) In Greek legend, the sister of Orestes. She persuaded him to kill their mother and their moth lover to avenge their father's murder. Also *Elektra.*

e·lec·tric (i·lek′trik) *adj.* **1.** Relating to, produced by operated by electricity. **2.** Producing or carrying elec ity: an *electric* cable. **3.** Thrillingly exciting or magn an *electric* personality. — *n.* A vehicle run by electric [< NL < L < Gk. *ēlektron* amber]

e·lec·tri·cal (i·lek′tri·kəl) *adj.* **1.** Electric. **2.** Conce with the use of electricity. — **e·lec′tri·cal·ly** *adv.*

electrical transcription *Telecom.* A transcription.

electric eel An eellike, fresh-water fish of tropical Ame that is capable of delivering powerful electric shocks.

electric eye A photoelectric cell.

electric field A field of force surrounding a charged ob or a moving magnet.

e·lec·tri·cian (i·lek′trish′ən, ē′lek-) *n.* A technician designs, installs, operates, or repairs electrical apparatu

e·lec·tric·i·ty (i·lek′tris′ə·tē, ē′lek-) *n.* **1.** A fundame property of matter, associated with atomic particles w movements develop fields of force and generate kineti potential energy. **2.** A current or charge of energy generated. **3.** The science that deals with the laws, the and application of electric energy. **4.** The property of m substances to attract or repel each other when subjecte friction. **5.** A state of great tension or excitement.

electric motor A machine for transforming electric en into mechanical power: distinguished from *generator.*

electric needle A high-frequency, needle-shaped elect used in surgery for simultaneous cutting and cautery.

electric ray A fish having muscles that store and disch electricity: also called *crampfish, torpedo.*

e·lec·tri·fy (i·lek′trə·fī) *v.t.* **·fied, ·fy·ing** **1.** To charge or subject to electricity. **2.** To equip or adapt for opera by electric power, as a railroad, house, etc. **3.** To aro startle. — **e·lec′tri·fi′a·ble** *adj.* — **e·lec′tri·fi·ca′tion** *n.*

electro- *combining form* **1.** Electric; by, with, or of tricity. **2.** Electrolytic. Also, before vowels, someti **electr-**. [< Gk. *ēlektron* amber]

e·lec·tro·car·di·o·gram (i·lek′trō·kär′dē·ə·gram′) *n.* The record made by an electrocardiograph.

e·lec·tro·car·di·o·graph (i·lek′trō·kär′dē·ə·graf′, gräf′) *Med.* An instrument for recording the electric current duced by the action of the heart muscle, used in the d nosis of diseases affecting the heart.

e·lec·tro·chem·is·try (i·lek′trō·kem′is·trē) *n.* The st of electricity as active in effecting chemical change. **e·lec′tro·chem′i·cal** *adj.* — **e·lec′tro·chem′i·cal·ly** *adv.*

e·lec·tro·cute (i·lek′trə·kyōōt) *v.t.* **·cut·ed, ·cut·ing** **1.** execute in the electric chair. **2.** To kill by electricity. **e·lec′tro·cu′tion** *n.*

e·lec·trode (i·lek′trōd) *n. Electr.* **1.** Any terminal conn ing a conductor, as copper wire, with an electrolyte. Any of the elements in an electron tube, transistor, that emit, collect, or control the movement of electrons

e·lec·tro·de·pos·it (i·lek′trō·di·poz′it) *v.i.* To precipi metal from an electrolyte containing it in ionic form. That which is precipitated by electrolysis. — **e·lec dep′o·si′tion** (-dep′ə·zish′ən, -dē′pə-) *n.*

e·lec·tro·dy·nam·ics (i·lek′trō·dī·nam′iks) *n.pl.* (*const as sing.*) The branch of physics that deals with the fo of electrical attraction and repulsion and with the en transformations of magnetic fields and electric currents. **e·lec′tro·dy·nam′ic** or **·i·cal** *adj.*

e·lec·tro·en·ceph·a·lo·gram (i·lek′trō·en·sef′ə·lə·gram′) *Med.* The record made by an electroencephalograph.

e·lec·tro·en·ceph·a·lo·graph (i·lek′trō·en·sef′ə·lə·gr -gräf′) *n. Med.* An instrument for recording the stren and character of electrical impulses in the brain used in diagnosis of brain disorders. — **e·lec′tro·en·ceph′a graph′ic** *adj.*

e·lec·tro·lu·mi·nes·cence (i·lek′trō·lōō′mə·nes′əns) The emission of light from a specially coated surface s jected to the action of an alternating current.

e·lec·trol·y·sis (i·lek′trol′ə·sis) *n.* **1.** The application direct current to an electrolyte so as to attract its posi ions to the cathode and its negative ions to the anode. The removal of hair by treating the follicle with an e trically charged needle.

e·lec·tro·lyte (i·lek′trə·līt) *n.* **1.** *Chem.* A compound t when in solution or a fluid state conducts electricity by dissociation of its constituents into free ions. **2.** A solut that conducts electricity; esp., the solution used in a cel battery. — **e·lec·tro·lyt·ic** (i·lek′trə·lit′ik) or **·i·cal** — **e·lec′tro·lyt′i·cal·ly** *adv.*

e·lec·tro·lyze (i·lek′trə·līz) *v.t.* **·lyzed, ·lyz·ing** To dec pose by electric current. — **e·lec′tro·ly·za′tion** *n.*

e·lec·tro·mag·net (i·lek′trō·mag′nit) *n.* A core of soft i that temporarily becomes a magnet when an electric curr passes through a coil of wire surrounding it.

e·lec·tro·mag·net·ism (i·lek′trō·mag′nə·tiz′əm) *n.* Magnetism developed by electricity. **2.** The science t eats of the relations between electricity and magnetism and e resulting phenomena. — **e·lec′tro·mag·net′ic** (-mag·et′ik) *adj.* — **e·lec′tro·mag·net′i·cal·ly** *adv.*

ctromagnetic wave *Physics* Any of a class of waves opagated by a system of electric and magnetic fields and cluding all forms of radiant energy from radio and light aves to gamma and cosmic rays.

ec·trom·e·ter (i·lek′trom′ə·tər, ē′lek-) *n.* An instrument for measuring the voltage of an electric current.

ec·trom·e·try (i·lek′trom′ə·trē, ē′lek-) *n.* The science making electrical measurements. — **e·lec·tro·met·ric** lek′trō·met′rik) or **·ri·cal** *adj.*

ec·tro·mo·tive (i·lek′trə·mō′tiv) *adj.* Producing, or nding to produce, a flow of electric current.

ctromotive force **1.** That which tends to produce a w of electricity from one point to another. **2.** Difference electrical potential between two points in a circuit, a bat-y, etc.; voltage. Abbr. *emf., e.m.f., E.M.F.*

ec·tron (i·lek′tron) *n.* An atomic particle carrying a unit arge of negative electricity, and having a mass approxi-ately one eighteen-hundredth of that of the proton. [< k. *ēlektron* amber]

ec·tro·neg·a·tive (i·lek′trō·neg′ə·tiv) *adj.* **1.** Appear-g at the positive electrode in electrolysis. **2.** Having the operty of becoming negatively electrified by contact or emical action. **3.** Nonmetallic.

ec·tron·ic (i·lek′tron′ik, ē′lek-) *adj.* **1.** Of or pertaining electrons. **2.** Operating or produced by the movement free electrons, as in radio and radar. **3.** Pertaining to ectronics. — **e·lec′tron′i·cal·ly** *adv.*

ec·tron·ics (i·lek′tron′iks, ē′lek-) *n.pl.* (*construed as ng.*) The study of the properties and behavior of electrons der all conditions, esp. with reference to technical and dustrial applications.

ctron microscope A powerful microscope that projects greatly enlarged image of an object held in the path of a arply focused electron beam.

ctron tube A device in which a stream of electrons is nducted through a vacuum or a rarefied gas and usu. con-olled by a grid: also called *vacuum tube.*

ctron volt The energy acquired by an electron that sses through a potential difference of one volt.

ec·tro·pho·re·sis (i·lek′trō·fə·rē′sis) *n.* *Chem.* The ovement of the electrically charged colloidal particles in a id, when under the influence of an electric field.

ec·troph·o·rus (i·lek′trof′ər·əs, ē′lek-) *n.* *pl.* **·ri** (-rī) An strument for generating static electricity by induction. lso **e·lec·tro·phore** (i·lek′trə·fôr, -fōr).

ec·tro·plate (i·lek′trə·plāt′) *v.t.* **·plat·ed, ·plat·ing** To at (an object) with metal by electrodeposition. — *n.* An ectroplated article. — **e·lec′tro·plat′er** *n.*

ec·tro·pos·i·tive (i·lek′trō·poz′ə·tiv) *adj.* **1.** Appearing the negative electrode in electrolysis. **2.** Having the operty of becoming positively electrified by contact or emical action. **3.** Basic; not acid.

ec·tro·scope (i·lek′trə·skōp) *n.* An instrument for de-cting the presence of an electric charge upon a conductor the attraction or repulsion of pith balls or strips of gold af. — **e·lec′tro·scop′ic** (-skop′ik) *adj.*

ec·tro·stat·ics (i·lek′trō·stat′iks) *n.pl.* (*construed as sing.*) branch of physics that deals primarily with electric charges, lds, induction in conductors, and polarization in dielec-ics. — **e·lec′tro·stat′ic** or **·i·cal** *adj.* — **e·lec′tro·stat′i·l·ly** *adv.*

ec·tro·ther·a·peu·tics (i·lek′trō·ther′ə·pyōō′tiks) *n.pl.* *onstrued as sing.*) **1.** The treatment of disease by elec-icity. **2.** The principles of such treatment. Also **e·lec′tro·er′a·py.** — **e·lec′tro·ther′a·peu′tic** or **·ti·cal** *adj.*

ec·tro·type (i·lek′trə·tīp′) *n.* **1.** A metallic copy, made electrodeposition, of any surface, esp. of a page of type r printing. **2.** An impression from an electrotype. — *v.t.* **yped, ·typ·ing** To make an electrotype of. — **e·lec′tro·p′er, e·lec′tro·typ′ist** *n.* — **e·lec′tro·typ′ic** *adj.* — **lec′tro·typ′ing** *n.*

ec·trum (i·lek′trəm) *n.* An alloy of native gold and ver. [< L < Gk. *ēlektron* amber]

ee·mos·y·nar·y (el′ə·mos′ə·ner′ē, el′ē·ə-) *adj.* **1.** Of or rtaining to charity or alms. **2.** Aided by or dependent pon charity. **3.** Done as a charitable act. [See ALMS.]

e·gance (el′ə·gəns) *n.* **1.** The state or quality of being egant or refined; tasteful opulence. **2.** Something elegant, a fastidiously chosen word or phrase. Also **el′e·gan·cy.**

e·gant (el′ə·gənt) *adj.* **1.** Tastefully ornate in dress, rnishings, etc. **2.** Marked by grace and refinement, as in yle, manners, etc. **3.** Marked by ingenuity and simplicity. *Informal* Excellent; first-rate. [< F < L < *e-* out + *gare* to choose] — **el′e·gant·ly** *adv.*

e·gi·ac (el′ə·jī′ək, i·lē′jē·ak) *adj.* **1.** Pertaining to ele-gies. **2.** Like an elegy; sad; lamenting. — *n.* *Usu. pl.* Verse composed in elegiac form.

el·e·gize (el′ə·jīz) *v.* **·gized, ·giz·ing** *v.i.* **1.** To write ele-giac verse. — *v.t.* **2.** To lament or commemorate in elegy.

el·e·gy (el′ə·jē) *n.* *pl.* **·gies** **1.** In classical prosody, a poem written in elegiac verse. **2.** Any meditative poem of lamen-tation. **3.** *Music* A work of lamentation or mourning. [< F < L < Gk. *elegos* a song of lament] — **el′e·gist** *n.*

E·lek·tra (i·lek′trə) See ELECTRA.

el·e·ment (el′ə·mənt) *n.* **1.** A relatively simple constituent that is a basic part of a whole; an essential, principle, fact, etc.: the *elements* of poetry. **2.** A group or class of people belonging to a larger group but distinguished from it by belief, behavior, etc.: a rowdy *element* in a crowd; the conservative *element.* **3.** One of four substances (earth, air, fire, water) anciently viewed as composing the phys-ical unverse. **4.** The surrounding conditions best suited to some person or thing. **5.** *pl.* Atmospheric powers or forces: the fury of the *elements.* **6.** *Physics & Chem.* One of a limited number of substances, as gold or carbon, each of which is composed entirely of atoms having the same atomic number, and none of which may be decomposed by ordinary chemical means. See table below. **7.** *Mil.* A subdivision of an organization or formation: a command *element.* **8.** *Eccl.* The bread or wine of the Eucharist. [< L *elementum* first principle]

TABLE OF ELEMENTS

NAME	Symbol	Atomic No.	Atomic Wt.
Actinium	Ac	89	227
Aluminum	Al	13	26.9815
Americium	Am	95	243
Antimony (*stibium*)	Sb	51	121.75
Argon	Ar	18	39.948
Arsenic	As	33	74.9216
Astatine	At	85	210
Barium	Ba	56	137.34
Berkelium	Bk	97	249
Beryllium	Be	4	9.0122
Bismuth	Bi	83	208.98
Boron	B	5	10.811
Bromine	Br	35	79.909
Cadmium	Cd	48	112.40
Calcium	Ca	20	40.08
Californium	Cf	98	251
Carbon	C	6	12.01115
Cerium	Ce	58	140.12
Cesium	Cs	55	132.905
Chlorine	Cl	17	35.453
Chromium	Cr	24	51.996
Cobalt	Co	27	58.9332
Columbium See NIOBIUM	(Cb)		
Copper (*cuprum*)	Cu	29	63.54
Curium	Cm	96	247
Dysprosium	Dy	66	162.50
Einsteinium	Es	99	254
Erbium	Er	68	167.26
Europium	Eu	63	151.96
Fermium	Fm	100	253
Fluorine	F	9	18.9984
Francium	Fr	87	223
Gadolinium	Gd	64	157.25
Gallium	Ga	31	69.72
Germanium	Ge	32	72.59
Glucinum	See BERYLLIUM		
Gold (*aurum*)	Au	79	196.967
Hafnium	Hf	72	178.44
Helium	He	2	4.0026
Holmium	Ho	67	164.93
Hydrogen	H	1	1.00797
Indium	In	49	114.82
Iodine	I	53	126.9044
Iridium	Ir	77	192.2
Iron (*ferrum*)	Fe	26	55.847
Krypton	Kr	36	83.80
Lanthanum	La	57	138.91
Lawrencium	Lw	103	257?
Lead (*plumbum*)	Pb	82	207.19
Lithium	Li	3	6.939
Lutetium	Lu	71	174.97
Magnesium	Mg	12	24.312
Manganese	Mn	25	54.938
Mendelevium	Md	101	256
Mercury (*hydrargyrum*)	Hg	80	200.59
Molybdenum	Mo	42	95.94
Neodymium	Nd	60	144.24
Neon	Ne	10	20.183
Neoytterbium	See YTTERBIUM		
Neptunium	Np	93	237
Nickel	Ni	28	58.71
Niobium	Nb	41	92.906

(*continued*)

NAME	Symbol	Atomic No.	Atomic Wt.
Niton	See RADON		
Nitrogen	N	7	14.0067
Nobelium	No	102	253
Osmium	Os	76	190.2
Oxygen	O	8	15.9994
Palladium	Pd	46	106.4
Phosphorus	P	15	30.9738
Platinum	Pt	78	195.09
Plutonium	Pu	94	242
Polonium	Po	84	210
Potassium (*kalium*)	K	19	39.102
Praseodymium	Pr	59	140.90
Promethium	Pm	61	147
Proctactinium	Pa	91	231
Radium	Ra	88	226.05
Radon	Rn	86	222
Rhenium	Re	75	186.20
Rhodium	Rh	45	102.905
Rubidium	Rb	37	85.47
Ruthenium	Ru	44	101.07
Samarium	Sm	62	150.35
Scandium	Sc	21	44.956
Selenium	Se	34	78.96
Silicon	Si	14	28.086
Silver (*argentum*)	Ag	47	107.87
Sodium (*natrium*)	Na	11	22.9898
Strontium	Sr	38	87.62
Sulfur	S	16	32.064
Tantalum	Ta	73	180.948
Technetium	Tc	43	99
Tellurium	Te	52	127.60
Terbium	Tb	65	158.924
Thallium	Tl	81	204.37
Thorium	Th	90	232.038
Thulium	Tm	69	168.934
Tin (*stannum*)	Sn	50	118.69
Titanium	Ti	22	47.90
Tungsten	W	74	183.85
Uranium	U	92	238.03
Vanadium	V	23	50.942
Wolfram	See TUNGSTEN		
Xenon	Xe	54	131.30
Ytterbium	Yb	70	173.04
Yttrium	Y	39	88.90
Zinc	Zn	30	65.37
Zirconium	Zr	40	91.22

el·e·men·tal (el′ə·men′təl) *adj.* **1.** Of or relating to an element or elements. **2.** Fundamental and relatively simple; basic. **3.** Relating to first principles; rudimentary. **4.** Of or suggestive of the powerful forces at work in nature or in man. **5.** Chemically uncombined. **— el′e·men′tal·ly** *adv.*

el·e·men·ta·ry (el′ə·men′tər·ē, -men′trē) *adj.* **1.** Elemental. **2.** Fundamental; basic. **3.** Simple and rudimentary. **— el′e·men′ta·ri·ly** *adv.* **— el′e·men′ta·ri·ness** *n.*

elementary school A school giving a course of education of from six to eight years, pupils usu. entering at about six years of age: also called *grade school, grammar school.*

el·e·phant (el′ə·fənt) *n.* A massively built, almost hairless mammal of Asia and Africa, having a flexible trunk, and the upper incisors developed as tusks, which are the chief source of ivory. The **Asian elephant** has relatively small ears, and the **African elephant** has large, flapping ears. [< OF < L < Gk. *elephas, -antos* ivory]

el·e·phan·ti·a·sis (el′ə·fən·tī′ə·sis) *n. Pathol.* A disease caused by a parasitic worm, characterized by a hardening of the skin, and an enormous enlargement of the part affected. [< L < Gk. < *elephas* elephant]

el·e·phan·tine (el′ə·fən′tin, -tēn, -tīn) *adj.* **1.** Of or pertaining to an elephant. **2.** Enormous; unwieldy; ponderous.

El·eu·sin·i·an (el′yŏŏ·sin′ē·ən) **mysteries** The secret religous rites originated in ancient Greece at Eleusis.

el·e·vate (el′ə·vāt) *v.t.* **·vat·ed, ·vat·ing 1.** To lift up; raise. **2.** To raise in rank, status, etc. **3.** To raise the spirits of; cheer; elate. **4.** To raise the pitch or loudness of (the voice). **5.** To raise the moral character or intellectual level of. [< L < *e-* out + *levare* to lighten, raise]

el·e·vat·ed (el′ə·vā′tid) *adj.* **1.** Raised up; high. **2.** Lofty in character; sublime. **3.** In high spirits; elated. **—** *n. U.S. Informal* An overhead railroad.

el·e·va·tion (el′ə·vā′shən) *n.* **1.** The act of elevating, or the state of being elevated. **2.** An elevated place. **3.** Height above sea level. **4.** Loftiness of thought, feeling, station, etc. **5.** In dancing, the ability to leap. **6.** *Often cap. Eccl.* The raising of the eucharistic elements for adoration during the Mass. **7.** *Astron.* The angular distance of a celestial body above the horizon. **8.** In drafting, a side, front, or rear view of a machine or other structure.

el·e·va·tor (el′ə·vā′tər) *n.* **1.** One who or that which elevates. **2.** A mechanism for hoisting grain. **3.** *U.S.* A granary. **4.** *U.S.* A movable platform or car that carries passengers or freight up and down.

e·lev·en (i·lev′ən) *n.* **1.** The sum of ten and one: a cardi number. **2.** Any symbol of this number, as 11, xi, XI. Anything consisting of or representing eleven units. — Being one more than ten. [OE *endleofan* one left over (a ten)] **— e·lev′enth** *adj.* & *n.*

elf (elf) *n. pl.* **·elves** (elvz) **1.** In folklore, a dwarfish sp with magical powers, usu. intent upon playful misch **2.** Any mischievous creature. **3.** A tiny person. [OE **— elf′ish** *adj.* **— elf′ish·ly** *adv.* **— elf′ish·ness** *n.*

elf·in (el′fin) *adj.* Elfish. **—** *n.* An elf.

elf·lock (elf′lok′) *n.* A lock of hair tangled as if by elves.

e·lic·it (i·lis′it) *v.t.* **1.** To draw out or forth; evoke: to e a reply. **2.** To bring to light: to *elicit* the truth. [< L out + *lacere* to entice] **— e·lic′i·ta′tion** *n.* **— e·lic′i·to**

e·lide (i·līd′) *v.t.* **e·lid·ed, e·lid·ing 1.** To omit (a vowe syllable) in pronunciation. **2.** To suppress; omit; ign [< L < *e-* out + *laedere* to strike] **— e·lid′i·ble** *adj.*

el·i·gi·bil·i·ty (el′ə·jə·bil′ə·tē) *n. pl.* **·ties 1.** The qualit being eligible; suitableness. **2.** *pl.* Qualities that mak person or thing eligible.

el·i·gi·ble (el′ə·jə·bəl) *adj.* **1.** Capable of and qualified an office, position, function, etc. **2.** Fit for or worthy choice or adoption. **3.** Agreeable to have; suitable. — An eligible person. [See ELECT.] **— el′i·gi·bly** *adv.*

E·li·jah (i·lī′jə) Ninth-century B.C. Hebrew prophet: **E·li·as** (i·lī′əs). [< Hebrew, Jehovah is my God]

e·lim·i·nate (i·lim′ə·nāt) *v.t.* **·nat·ed, ·nat·ing 1.** To get of. **2.** To ignore. **3.** To remove (a contestant, team, e from further competition by defeating. **4.** *Physiol.* void; excrete. **5.** *Math.* To remove (a quantity) from a tem of algebraic equations. [< L < *e-* out + *limen* th hold] **— e·lim′i·na′tion** *n.* **— e·lim′i·na′tor** *n.* **— e·li na′tive, e·lim′i·na·to′ry** (-nə·tôr′ē, -tō′rē) *adj.*

E·li·sha (i·lī′shə) Ninth-century B.C. Hebrew prophet, s cessor of Elijah. [< Hebrew, God is Salvation]

e·li·sion (i·lizh′ən) *n.* Omission of a vowel or syllable, a "th' imperial towers." [See ELIDE.]

e·lite (ā·lēt′) **n. 1.** The choicest part, as of a social gro **2.** A size of typewriter type, equivalent to 10-point, with characters to the inch. *Also U.S.* **e·lite′**. [See ELECT.]

e·lix·ir (i·lik′sər) *n.* **1.** A sweetened alcoholic medic preparation. **2.** In ancient philosophy, a substance sou by alchemists for changing base metals into gold, or prolonging life: also **elixir vi·tae** (vī′tē). **3.** The essen principle of anything. **4.** A cure-all. [< Med.L < Ar *al-iksīr* < Gk. *zērion* medicated powder]

E·liz·a·be·than (i·liz′ə·bē′thən, -beth′ən) *adj.* Of or taining to Elizabeth I of England, or to her era. **—** *n.* Englishman living during the reign of Elizabeth I.

Elizabethan sonnet A Shakespearean sonnet.

elk (elk) *n. pl.* **elks** or **elk 1.** A large deer of northern rope and Asia. **2.** The wapiti. **3.** A pliant, tanned leat of calfskin, horsehide, etc. [ME < OE *elh*]

ell[1] (el) *n.* A measure of length now rarely used: in Engla 45 inches or 1.114 meters. [OE *eln* an arm's length]

ell[2] (el) *n.* Anything shaped like the letter L.

el·lipse (i·lips′) *n. Geom.* A plane curve such that the sum of the distances from any point of the curve to two fixed points, called *foci*, is a constant; a conic section. [< L *ellipsis*. See ELLIPSIS.]

ELLIPSE

AA′ Major axis. *B* Minor axis. *F, F′* F *P, P′* Points on cur ($FP + F'P = FP' + F'P'$)

el·lip·sis (i·lip′sis) *n. pl.* **·ses** (-sēz) **1.** *Gram.* The omission of a word or words necessary for the complete grammatical construction of a sentence, but not required for the understanding of it. **2.** Marks (. . . or * * *) indicating omission. [< L < Gk. < *en-* in + *leipsis* a leaving < *leipein* to leave]

el·lip·tic (i·lip′tik) *adj.* **1.** Of, pertaining to, or shaped like an ellipse. **2.** *Gram.* Charact ized by ellipsis; shortened. Also **el·lip′ti·cal. — el·lip′ti· ly** *adv.*

elm (elm) *n.* **1.** A shade tree of America, Europe, and A having a broad, spreading, or overarching top. **2.** wood of this tree. [OE] **— el′my** *adj.*

el·o·cu·tion (el′ə·kyōō′shən) *n.* **1.** The art of public spe ing, including vocal delivery and gesture. **2.** Manner speaking. [< L < *e-* out + *loqui* to speak] **— el′o· tion·ar′y** *adj.* **— el′o·cu′sion·ist** *n.*

E·lo·him (e·lō·him′, e·lō′him) God: Hebrew name used in Old Testament. [< Hebrew *'Elōhīm*, pl. of *'Elōah* God]

e·lon·gate (i·lông′gāt, i·long′-) *v.t.* & *v.i.* **·gat·ed, ·gat·ing** increase in length; stretch. **—** *adj.* Drawn out; lengthen [< LL < L *e-* out + *longe* far off] **— e′lon·ga′tion** *n.*

e·lope (i·lōp′) *v.i.* **e·loped, e·lop·ing 1.** To run away wit lover, usu. to get married. **2.** To abscond. [< AF *alope* **— e·lope′ment** *n.* **— e·lop′er** *n.*

el·o·quence (el′ə·kwəns) *n.* **1.** Fluent, polished, and eff

› use of language, esp. in public speaking. **2.** The quality ›eing moving, forceful, or persuasive.

›**quent** (el′ə·kwənt) *adj.* **1.** Possessed of or manifesting ›uence. **2.** Visibly expressive of emotion: *eloquent* tears. L < *e-* out + *loqui* to speak] — **el′o·quent·ly** *adv.*

(els) *adv.* **1.** In a different place, time, or way; instead: ›ere *else*? How *else*? **2.** If the case or facts were different; ›erwise: Hurry, or *else* you will be caught. — *adj.* Addi›al; different: somebody *else*. [OE *elles*. Akin to L *alius*.]

›**where** (els′hwâr′) *adv.* In or to another place or places; ›ewhere or anywhere else.

›**ci·date** (i·lo͞o′sə·dāt) *v.* **·dat·ed, ·dat·ing** *v.t.* **1.** To ›ke clear; explain. — *v.i.* **2.** To clarify something. [< < L *e-* out + *lucidus* clear] — **e·lu′ci·da′tion** *n.* — ›**′ci·da′tive** *adj.* — **e·lu′ci·da′tor** *n.*

›**de** (i·lo͞od′) *v.t.* **e·lud·ed, e·lud·ing** **1.** To avoid or escape ›n by dexterity or artifice; evade. **2.** To escape the no› or understanding of: The meaning *eludes* me. [< L < ›ut + *ludere* to play]

›**l** (e·lo͞ol′, el′o͞ol) *n.* The twelfth month of the Hebrew ›r. See (Hebrew) CALENDAR.

›**sive** (i·lo͞o′siv) *adj.* Tending to slip away; hard to grasp ›erceive: an *elusive* fragrance. Also **e·lu′so·ry** (-sər·ē). — ›**′sive·ly** *adv.* — **e·lu′sive·ness** *n.*

›**s** (elvz) Plural of ELF.

›**ish** (el′vish) *adj.* Elfish. — **elv′ish·ly** *adv.*

›**·si·um** (i·lizh′ē·əm, i·liz′-) **1.** In Greek mythology, the ›d of the blessed dead. Also **Elysian Fields.** **2.** A place ›condition of supreme delight; paradise. [< L < Gk. ›*sion* (*pedion*) the Elysian (field)] — **E·ly·sian** (i·lizh′ən, ›n) *adj.*

›(em) *n.* *Printing* The square of the body size of a type; ›, a pica em, about ⅙ of an inch, used as a standard unit ›neasurement: originally, the size of the letter M.

›1 Var. of EN-1.

›2 Var. of EN-2.

(əm, m) *pron. Informal* Them.

›**a·ci·ate** (i·mā′shē·āt) *v.t.* **·at·ed, ·at·ing** To make ab›mally lean; cause to lose flesh. [< L *macies* leanness] ›**e·ma′ci·at′ed** *adj.* — **e·ma′ci·a′tion** *n.*

›**a·nate** (em′ə·nāt) *v.i.* **·nat·ed, ·nat·ing** To flow forth ›m a source; issue. [< L < *e-* out + *manare* to flow]

›**a·na·tion** (em′ə·nā′shən) *n.* **1.** The act of emanating. ›Something that emanates; efflux; effluence. **3.** *Physics* ›gaseous product of disintegration in certain radioactive ›stances, as radon and thoron. — **em′a·na′tive** *adj.*

›**an·ci·pate** (i·man′sə·pāt) *v.t.* **·pat·ed, ·pat·ing** **1.** To ›ase from bondage, oppression, or authority; set free. **2.** ›*w* To free (a child) from paternal control. [< L < *e-* + *manus* hand + *capere* to take] — **e·man′ci·pa′tive** ›. — **e·man′ci·pa′tion** *n.* — **e·man′ci·pa·tor** *n.*

›**ancipation Proclamation** A proclamation issued by ›sident Abraham Lincoln on January 1, 1863, declaring › all Negro slaves in all States.

›**as·cu·late** (*v.* i·mas′kyə·lāt; *adj.* i·mas′kyə·lit) *v.t.* **·lat·** **·lat·ing** **1.** To deprive of procreative power; castrate; ›d. **2.** To deprive of strength and vigor; weaken. — *adj.* ›nasculated; effeminate; weakened. [< L *emasculare* < *e-* ›ay + *masculus* male] — **e·mas′cu·la′tion** *n.* — **e·mas′·** ›**la′tor** *n.* — **e·mas·cu·la·to·ry** (i·mas′kyə·lə·tôr′ē, -tō′rē), ›**as′cu·la·tive** *adj.*

›**balm** (im·bäm′) *v.t.* **1.** To preserve (a dead body) from ›ay by treatment with chemicals, etc. **2.** To preserve ›keep in memory. [< F *embaumer*] — **em·balm′er** *n.*

›**bank·ment** (im·bangk′mənt) *n.* A mound or bank ›sed to hold back water, support a roadway, etc.

›**bar·go** (im·bär′gō) *n. pl.* **·goes** **1.** An order by a gov›ment restraining merchant vessels from leaving or enter› its ports. **2.** Authoritative stoppage of foreign com›rce or of any special trade. **3.** A restraint or prohibition. ›*v.t.* **·goes, ·go·ing** To lay an embargo upon. [< Sp. < ›*bargar*, ult. < LL *barra* bar]

›**bark** (im·bärk′) *v.t.* **1.** To put or take aboard a vessel. ›To invest (money) or involve (a person) in a venture. — **3.** To go aboard a vessel for a voyage. **4.** To engage in ›venture. [< F < LL < *in-* in + *barca* boat] — **em·** ›**·ka·tion, em·bar·ca·tion** (em′bär·kā′shən) *n.* — **em·** ›**ck′ment** *n.*

›**bar·rass** (im·bar′əs) *v.t.* **1.** To make self-conscious and ›comfortable; abash; disconcert. **2.** To involve in finan›l difficulties. **3.** To hamper; impede. **4.** To render ›ficult; complicate. [< F < *em-* in + *barre* < OF] — ›**bar′rass·ing** *adj.* — **em·bar′rass·ing·ly** *adv.* — **em·** ›**′rass·ment** *n.*

›**bas·sy** (em′bə·sē) *n. pl.* **·sies** **1.** An ambassador to›her with his staff. **2.** The mission, function, or position ›an ambassador. **3.** The official residence or headquarters ›an ambassador. [< OF < Med.L < L *ambactus* servant]

em·bat·tle (em·bat′l) *v.t.* **·tled, ·tling** To form in line of battle; prepare or equip for battle. [< OF < *em*1- in + *bataille* < L *battuere* to beat]

em·bed (im·bed′) *v.t.* **·bed·ded, ·bed·ding** **1.** To set firmly in surrounding matter. **2.** To place in or as in a bed. — **em·bed′ment** *n.*

em·bel·lish (im·bel′ish) *v.t.* **1.** To beautify by adding ornamental features; decorate. **2.** To heighten the interest of (a narrative) by adding fictitious details. [< OF < *em-* in + *bel* beautiful] — **em·bel′lish·er** *n.* — **em·bel′lish·ment** *n.*

em·ber (em′bər) *n.* **1.** A live coal or unextinguished brand. **2.** *pl.* A dying fire. [OE *ǣmerge*]

em·bez·zle (im·bez′əl) *v.t.* **·zled, ·zling** To appropriate fraudulently to one's own use, as money or securities entrusted to one's care. [< AF < *em-* in + *besiler* to destroy] — **em·bez′zle·ment** *n.* — **em·bez′zler** *n.*

em·bit·ter (im·bit′ər) *v.t.* To make bitter, unhappy, or resentful. — **em·bit′ter·ment** *n.*

em·bla·zon (em·blā′zən) *v.t.* **1.** To adorn magnificently, esp. with heraldic devices. **2.** To extol; celebrate. — **em·bla′zon·er** *n.* — **em·bla′zon·ment** *n.* — **em·bla′zon·ry** *n.*

em·blem (em′bləm) *n.* **1.** An object or pictorial device that serves to represent something more or less abstract; symbol. **2.** A distinctive badge or figured object. [< L < Gk. < *em-* in + *ballein* to throw]

em·blem·at·ic (em′blə·mat′ik) *adj.* Of, pertaining to, or serving as an emblem; symbolic. Also **em′blem·at′i·cal.** — **em′blem·at′i·cal·ly** *adv.*

em·bod·i·ment (im·bod′i·mənt) *n.* **1.** The act of embodying, or the state of being embodied. **2.** That which embodies, or in which something is embodied.

em·bod·y (im·bod′ē) *v.t.* **·bod·ied, ·bod·y·ing** **1.** To invest with or as with a body; put into visible or concrete form: to *embody* ideals in action. **2.** To collect into, or make part of, an organized whole; incorporate.

em·bold·en (im·bōl′dən) *v.t.* To give courage to.

em·bo·lism (em′bə·liz′əm) *n. Pathol.* The stopping up of a vein or artery by an embolus.

em·bo·lus (em′bə·ləs) *n. pl.* **·li** (-lī) *Pathol.* A foreign body that forms an obstruction in a blood vessel, as a piece of fibrin, a blood clot, or an air bubble. [< L < Gk. < *en-* in + *ballein* to throw] — **em·bol·ic** (em·bol′ik) *adj.*

em·bos·om (em·bo͝oz′əm, -bo͞o′zəm) *v.t.* **1.** To embrace. **2.** To cherish. **3.** To enclose protectively; shelter.

em·boss (im·bôs′, -bos′) *v.t.* **1.** To cover or adorn (a surface) with raised figures, designs, etc. **2.** To raise or represent (designs, figures, etc.) from or upon a surface. **3.** To decorate sumptuously. [Origin unknown] — **em·boss′er** *n.* — **em·boss′ment** *n.*

em·bou·chure (äm·bo͞o·sho͝or′, *Fr.* äṅ·bo͞o·shür′) *n.* **1.** The mouth of a river. **2.** The opening out of a river valley into flat land. **3.** *Music* **a** The mouthpiece of a wind instrument. **b** The position or application of the lips and tongue in playing a wind instrument. [< F < *em-* in + *bouche* mouth]

em·bow·er (em·bou′ər) *v.t.* & *v.i.* To cover or shelter in or as in a bower.

em·brace (im·brās′) *v.* **·braced, ·brac·ing** *v.t.* **1.** To clasp or infold in the arms; hug. **2.** To accept willingly; adopt, as a religion or doctrine. **3.** To avail oneself of: to *embrace* an offer. **4.** To surround; encircle. **5.** To include; contain. **6.** To take in visually or mentally. **7.** To have sexual intercourse with. — *v.i.* **8.** To hug each other. — *n.* The act of embracing. [< OF *embracer*, ult. < L *in-* in + *bracchium* arm] — **em·brace′ment** *n.* — **em·brac′er** *n.*

em·bra·sure (em·brā′zhər) *n.* **1.** *Archit.* An opening in a wall, as for a window or door, sloped or beveled so as to enlarge its interior outline. **2.** An opening that enlarges inwardly or outwardly in a parapet, battlement, or wall. [< F < *embraser* (*ébraser*) to widen (an opening)]

em·broi·der (im·broi′dər) *v.t.* **1.** To ornament (cloth) with designs in needlework. **2.** To execute (a design) in needlework. **3.** To exaggerate. — *v.i.* **4.** To make embroidery. [< MF *broder* to stitch] — **em·broi′der·er** *n.*

em·broi·der·y (im·broi′dər·ē) *n. pl.* **·der·ies** **1.** Ornamental needlework. **2.** Any elaborate ornamentation.

em·broil (em·broil′) *v.t.* **1.** To involve in dissension or strife. **2.** To complicate or confuse. [< F < *em-* + *brouiller* to confuse] — **em·broil′ment** *n.*

em·bry·o (em′brē·ō) *n. pl.* **·os** **1.** *Biol.* The earliest stages in the development of an organism, before it has assumed its distinctive form, in the human species, the first eight weeks. **2.** *Bot.* The rudimentary plant within the seed. **3.** The rudimentary stage of anything. Also **em′bry·on.** — *adj.* Rudimentary. [< Gk < *en-* in + *bryein* to swell]

embryo- *combining form* Embryo; embryonic. Also, before vowels, **embry-.** [< Gk. *embryon* embryo]

em·bry·ol·o·gy (em′brē·ol′ə·jē) *n.* The science that deals with the origin, structure, and development of the embryo.

›NUNCIATION KEY: add, āce, câre, pälm; end, ēven; it, īce; odd, ōpen, ôrder; to͝ok, po͞ol; up, bûrn; ə = a in *above*, e in *sicken*, i in *flex*›o in *melon*, u in *focus*; yo͞o = u in *fuse*; oil; pout; check; go; ring; thin; this; zh, vision.

— **em·bry·o·log·i·cal** (em′brē·ə·loj′i·kəl) or **em′bry·o·log′ic** *adj.* — **em′bry·o·log′i·cal·ly** *adv.* — **em′bry·ol′o·gist** *n.*
em·bry·on·ic (em′brē·on′ik) *adj.* Of, pertaining to, or in the state of an embryo; rudimentary; immature; undeveloped.
em·cee (em′sē′) *Informal n.* Master of ceremonies. — *v.t. & v.i.* **·ceed, ·cee·ing** To act as master of ceremonies.
e·meer (ə·mir′) See EMIR.
e·mend (i·mend′) *v.t.* **1.** To make corrections or changes in (a literary work, etc.), esp. after scholarly study. **2.** To free from faults. [< L < *e-* out + *menda* fault] — **e·mend′a·ble** *adj.* — **e·mend′er** *n.*
e·men·date (ē′men·dāt) *v.t.* **·dat·ed, ·dat·ing** To emend (a text). — **e·men·da·tion** (ē′men·dā′shən, em′en-) *n.* — **e′men·da′tor** *n.* — **e·mend·a·to·ry** (i·men′də·tôr′ē) *adj.*
em·er·ald (em′ər·əld, em′rəld) *n.* **1.** A bright green variety of beryl, valued as a jewel. **2.** A rich green. — *adj.* **1.** Of, pertaining to, or like the emerald. **2.** Of a rich green color. [< OF *emeraude, esmeralde* < L < Gk. *smaragdos*]
Emerald Isle Ireland: so called from its green landscape.
e·merge (i·mûrj′) *v.i.* **e·merged, e·merg·ing** **1.** To come forth as from water, a hiding place, etc. **2.** To come to light; become apparent. [< L < *e-* out + *mergere* to dip] — **e·mer′gence** *n.* — **e·mer′gent** *adj.*
e·mer·gen·cy (i·mûr′jən·sē) *n. pl.* **·cies** A sudden and unexpected turn of events calling for immediate action.
e·mer·i·tus (i·mer′ə·təs) *adj.* Retired from active service, usu. because of age, but retained in an honorary position: professor *emeritus.* — *n. pl.* **·ti** (-tī) One who is emeritus. [< L, pp. of *emerere* < *e-* out + *merere* to earn]
e·mer·sion (ē·mûr′shən, -zhən) *n.* An emerging.
em·er·y (em′ər·ē, em′rē) *n.* A very hard, black or grayish black variety of corundum mixed with magnesite and other minerals, used as an abrasive. [F < OF < LL < Gk. *smēris* emery powder]
e·met·ic (i·met′ik) *adj.* Tending to produce vomiting. — *n.* An emetic agent. [< Gk. < *emeein* to vomit]
-emia *combining form Med.* Blood; condition of the blood: used in names of diseases: *leukemia.* Also spelled *-aemia, -haemia, -hemia.* [< Gk. *haima* blood]
em·i·grant (em′ə·grənt) *adj.* Moving from one place or country to settle in another. — *n.* A person who emigrates.
em·i·grate (em′ə·grāt) *v.i.* **·grat·ed, ·grat·ing** To move away from one country, or section of a country, to settle in another. — **Syn.** See MIGRATE. [< L < *e-* out + *migrare* to move] — **em′i·gra′tion** *n.*
é·mi·gré (em′ə·grā, *Fr.* ā·mē·grā′) An emigrant; esp. one who fled to escape the French or Russian revolution.
em·i·nence (em′ə·nəns) *n.* **1.** Superiority in rank, power, achievement, etc. **2.** A high place or elevation, as a hill. Also **em′i·nen·cy.** [< L < *e-* out + *minere* to jut out]
Em·i·nence (em′ə·nəns) *n.* A title for cardinals.
em·i·nent (em′ə·nənt) *adj.* **1.** High in station, merit, or esteem; distinguished: an *eminent* scholar. **2.** Noteworthy; conspicuous: *eminent* valor. **3.** High; lofty: an *eminent* tower. [< L *eminere* to stand out] — **em′i·nent·ly** *adv.*
eminent domain *Law* The right or power of the state to take or control private property for public use.
e·mir (ə·mir′) *n.* **1.** A Moslem prince or commander. **2.** A descendant of Mohammed. **3.** A high Turkish official. Also spelled *emeer.* [< Arabic *amīr* ruler] — **e·mir′ate** *n.*
em·is·sar·y (em′ə·ser′ē) *n. pl.* **·sar·ies** **1.** A person sent on a mission as an agent or representative of a government. **2.** A secret agent; spy. — *adj.* Of, pertaining to, or serving as an emissary. [< L *emissarius* < *emittere* to send out]
e·mis·sion (i·mish′ən) *n.* **1.** The act of emitting. **2.** That which is emitted. **3.** The issuance of currency, notes, shares, etc. [< L *emissio, -onis* < *-e* out + *mittere* to send]
e·mis·sive (i·mis′iv) *adj.* Sending or sent forth; emitting.
e·mit (i·mit′) *v.t.* **e·mit·ted, e·mit·ting** **1.** To send forth or give off (light, heat, sound, etc.); discharge. **2.** To give expression to; utter, as an opinion. **3.** To issue authoritatively, as an edict. **4.** To put into circulation, as money. [< L < *e-* out + *mittere* to send] — **e·mit′ter** *n.*
Em·man·u·el (i·man′yōō·əl) See IMMANUEL.
e·mol·lient (i·mol′yənt, -ē·ənt) *adj.* Softening or relaxing; soothing, esp. to the skin. — *n. Med.* A softening or soothing medicament. [< L < *e-* thoroughly + *mollire* to soften]
e·mol·u·ment (i·mol′yə·mənt) *n.* A salary or fee as for a service. [< L < *e-* out + *molere* to grind]
e·mote (i·mōt′) *v.i.* **e·mot·ed, e·mot·ing** *Informal* To exhibit an exaggerated emotion, as in acting. [< EMOTION]
e·mo·tion (i·mō′shən) *n.* **1.** A strong surge of feeling marked by an impulse to outward expression and often accompanied by complex bodily reactions; any strong feeling, as love, hate, or joy. **2.** The power of feeling; sensibility. [< L *emotio, -onis* < *e-* out + *movere* to move]
e·mo·tion·al (i·mō′shən·əl) *adj.* **1.** Of, pertaining to, or expressive of emotion. **2.** Easily or excessively affected by emotion. **3.** Arousing the emotions. — **e·mo′tion·al·ist** *n.* — **e·mo′tion·al′i·ty** *n.* — **e·mo′tion·al·ly** *adv.*
e·mo·tion·al·ism (i·mō′shən·əl·iz′əm) *n.* **1.** The tendency to overindulge the emotions or to be too much affecte them. **2.** A display of emotion. **3.** Appeal to the emot
e·mo·tion·al·ize (i·mō′shən·əl·īz′) *v.t.* **·ized, ·iz·ing** treat in an emotional manner. — **e·mo′tion·al·i·za′tior**
e·mo·tive (i·mō′tiv) *adj.* Characterized by, expressir tending to excite emotion: *emotive* eloquence. — **e·mo′ti** *adv.* — **e·mo′tive·ness, e·mo·tiv·i·ty** (ē′mō·tiv′ə·tē) *n.*
em·pan·el (im·pan′əl) See IMPANEL.
em·pa·thize (em′pə·thīz) *v.t. & v.i.* **·thized, ·thiz·ing** T gard with or feel empathy.
em·pa·thy (em′pə·thē) *n. Psychol.* Intellectual or ima tive apprehension of another's condition or state of r — **em·path·ic** (em·path′ik) *adj.* — **em·path′i·cal·ly** *ad*
em·per·or (em′pər·ər) *n.* The sovereign of an empire. OF < L *imperator* commander] — **em′per·or·ship′** *n.*
em·pha·sis (em′fə·sis) *n. pl.* **·ses** (-sēz) **1.** Special si cance or importance assigned to something. **2.** Stress by voice or rhetorical contrivance to a particular syl word, or phrase. **3.** Force or intensity of meaning, ac etc. [< L < Gk. < *en-* in + *phainein* to show]
em·pha·size (em′fə·sīz) *v.t.* **·sized, ·siz·ing** To give em sis to; make specially prominent or important; stress.
em·phat·ic (em·fat′ik) *adj.* **1.** Spoken or done with em sis; forcibly expressive. **2.** Characterized by forcefulne intensity. **3.** Striking; decisive. — **em·phat′i·cal·ly** *a*
em·phy·se·ma (em′fə·sē′mə) *n. Pathol.* A lung cond marked by loss of elasticity of the air sacs, causing culty in breathing. [< NL < Gk. *emphysēma* inflatio
em·pire (em′pīr) *n.* **1.** A state, or union of states, gove by an emperor; also, the historical period of such go ment. **2.** A union of dispersed states and unrelated pe under one rule. **3.** Wide and supreme dominion. [< F *imperium* rule, authority]
Empire State Nickname of New York.
em·pir·i·cal (em·pir′i·kəl) *adj.* **1.** Relating to or based direct experience or observation alone: *empirical* knowl **2.** Relying on practical experience without benefit of s tific knowledge or theory. Also **em·pir′ic.** [< L < G *en-* in + *peira* trial] — **em·pir′i·cal·ly** *adv.*
em·pir·i·cism (em·pir′ə·siz′əm) *n.* **1.** Empirical meth practice. **2.** *Philos.* The doctrine that all knowledge i rived from sensory experience. **3.** Reliance on sensor servation and experiment as the bases of knowledge. Quackery. — **em·pir′i·cist** *n.*
em·place·ment (im·plās′mənt) *n.* **1.** The position assi to guns or to a battery within a fortification; also, a gun form, the parapet, or the like. **2.** A setting in place; tion. [< F < *emplacer* to put into position]
em·ploy (im·ploi′) *v.t.* **1.** To engage the services of; **2.** To provide work and livelihood for. **3.** To make use a means or instrument: to *employ* cunning. **4.** To devo apply: to *employ* one's energies in research. — *n.* The of being employed; service. [< F *employer* < L *in-* *plicare* to fold] — **em·ploy′a·ble** *adj.* — **em·ploy′men**
em·ploy·ee (im·ploi′ē, em′ploi·ē′) *n.* One who works fo other in return for salary. Also **em·ploy′e, em·ploy′é.**
em·ploy·er (im·ploi′ər) *n.* **1.** One who employs. **2.** A son or business firm that employs persons for wages or sa
em·po·ri·um (em·pôr′ē·əm, -pō′rē-) *n. pl.* **·po·ri·um** **·po·ri·a** (-pôr′ē·ə, -pō′rē·ə) **1.** A store carrying general chandise. **2.** A trading or market center. [< L < Gk. *porion* market < *en-* in + *poros* way]
em·pow·er (im·pou′ər) *v.t.* **1.** To authorize; delegate thority to. **2.** To enable; permit.
em·press (em′pris) *n.* **1.** A woman who rules an em **2.** The wife or widow of an emperor.
emp·ty (emp′tē) *adj.* **·ti·er, ·ti·est** **1.** Containing noth void; vacant: an *empty* pitcher; an *empty* room. **2.** Wit significance; unsubstantial; hollow: *empty* promises. Carrying nothing: *empty* hands. **4.** Destitute or dev with *of*: *empty* of compassion. **5.** *Informal* Hungry. **·tied, ·ty·ing** *v.t.* **1.** To remove the contents of. **2.** To tr fer the contents of (a container): to *empty* a bucket on fire. **3.** To pour out or draw off (the contents of somethi **4.** To unburden; clear: with *of.* — *v.i.* **5.** To become em **6.** To discharge itself or its contents. — *n. pl.* **·ties** empty container, vehicle, etc. [OE *ǣmetig* < *ǣmetta* leis — **emp′ti·ly** *adv.* — **emp′ti·ness** *n.*
emp·ty-hand·ed (emp′tē·han′did) *adj.* Carrying nothi
em·pyr·e·al (em·pir′ē·əl, em′pə·rē′əl, -pī-) *adj.* **1.** O pertaining to the highest region of heaven. **2.** Of pure fiery. [< Med.L < Gk. < *en-* in + *pyr* fire]
em·py·re·an (em′pə·rē′ən, -pī-) *n.* **1.** The highest hea the abode of God and the angels, anciently conceived as gion of pure fire. **2.** The firmament. — *adj.* Empyre
e·mu (ē′myōō) *n.* A flightless, three-toed Australian related to the ostrich. [Prob. < Pg. *ema* ostrich]
em·u·late (em′yə·lāt) *v.t.* **·lat·ed, ·lat·ing** **1.** To tr equal or surpass. **2.** To rival or vie with successfully. [< *aemulus* jealous] — **em′u·la′tive** *adj.* — **em′u·la′tio** — **em′u·la′tive·ly** *adv.* — **em′u·la′tor** *n.*

u·lous (em′yə·ləs) *adj.* **1.** Eager to equal or excel an-
ıer; competitive. **2.** Pertaining to or arising from emu-
ion. — **em′u·lous·ly** *adv.* — **em′u·lous·ness** *n.*

ul·si·fy (i·mul′sə·fī) *v.t.* **·fied, ·fy·ing** To make into an
ulsion. — **e·mul′si·fi·ca′tion** *n.* — **e·mul′si·fi′er** *n.*

ul·sion (i·mul′shən) *n.* **1.** A liquid mixture in which a
ty or resinous substance is suspended in minute globules,
butter in milk. **2.** Any milky liquid. **3.** *Photog.* A light-
sitive coating for film, plates, papers, etc. [< LL < L
- out + *mulgere* to milk] — **e·mul′sive** *adj.*

en) *n.* *Printing* A space half the width of an em.

prefix Forming transitive verbs: **1.** (from nouns) To
er or surround with; place into or upon: *encircle.* **2.**
m adjectives and nouns) To make; cause to be or to re-
ble: *enable, enfeeble.* **3.** (from verbs) Often with simple
ensive force, or used to form transitive verbs from intran-
ves: *enact.* Also *em-* before *b, p,* and sometimes *m,* as in
ark. Many words in *en-* or *em-* have variant forms in
or *im-* respectively. [< OF < L *in-* < *in* in, into]

prefix In; into; on: *endemic.* Also *el-* before *l,* as in *el-*
e; em- before *b, m, p, ph,* as in *embolism, empathy; er-* be-
r, as in *errhine.* [< Gk. *en-* < *en* in, into]

suffix Forming verbs: **1.** (from adjectives) Cause to be;
ome: *deepen, harden.* **2.** (from nouns) Cause to have;
: *hearten, strengthen.* [OE *-nian*]

suffix of adjectives Made of; resembling: *woolen.* [OE]

suffix Used in the past participles of many strong verbs:
en, beaten. [OE]

suffix Used in the plurals of certain nouns: *oxen, chil-*
n. [OE *-an,* plural ending of the weak declension]

suffix Small; little: *chicken, kitten.* [OE]

·ble (in·ā′bəl) *v.t.* **·bled, ·bling** **1.** To supply with ade-
te power or opportunity; make able. **2.** To make pos-
e or practicable.

ct (in·akt′) *v.t.* **1.** To make into a law; decree. **2.** To
y out in action; perform. **3.** To represent in or as in a
; act the part of. — **en·act′a·ble** *adj.* — **en·ac′tor** *n.*

ct·ment (in·akt′mənt) *n.* **1.** The act of enacting, or
state of being enacted. **2.** That which is enacted; a law.

m·el (in·am′əl) *n.* **1.** A vitreous, usu. opaque material
lied by fusion to surfaces of metal, glass, or porcelain as a
oration or a protective surface. **2.** A piece executed in
mel. **3.** A paint, varnish, or lacquer that dries to form a
d, glossy surface. **4.** Any coating resembling enamel. **5.**
at. The hard, glossy, calcareous outer layer of the teeth.
illus. see TOOTH. — *v.t.* **en·am·eled** or **·elled, en·am·el·**
or **·el·ling** **1.** To cover or inlay with enamel. **2.** To sur-
with or as with enamel. **3.** To adorn with different
rs. [< AF < *en-* on + *amayl,* OF *esmail* enamel] —
am′el·er or **en·am′el·ler, en·am′el·ist** or **en·am′el·list** *n.*

m·el·ware (in·am′əl·wâr′) *n.* Enameled kitchenware.

m·or (in·am′ər) *v.t.* To inflame with love; also, to
rm; fascinate: chiefly in the passive, followed by *of:* He is
mored of his cousin. Also *Brit.* **en·am′our.** [< OF < *en-*
+ *amour* love] — **en·am′ored** *adj.*

amp (in·kamp′) *v.i.* **1.** To go into camp; live in a camp.
t. **2.** To place in a camp. — **en·camp′ment** *n.*

ase (in·kās′) See INCASE.

aus·tic (en·kôs′tik) *adj.* Having the pigments burned
encaustic tile. [< L < Gk. < *en-* in + *kaiein* to burn]

e *suffix of nouns* Forming nouns of action, quality, or
dition from adjectives in *-ent,* as *prominence.* Compare
CY. See note under -ANCE. [< F < L *-entia,* suffix used
orm nouns from present participles]

e·phal·ic (en′sə·fal′ik) *adj.* **1.** Of or pertaining to the
in. **2.** Situated within the cranial cavity.

eph·a·li·tis (en′sef·ə·lī′tis, en·sef′-) *n.* *Pathol.* Inflam-
tion of the brain. — **en′ceph·a·lit′ic** (-lit′ik) *adj.*

ephalitis le·thar·gi·ca (li·thär′ji·kə) *Pathol.* An acute
is form of encephalitis, affecting the central nervous sys-
and accompanied by fever, lethargy, and sensory dis-
bances: also called *sleeping sickness.*

phalo- *combining form* The brain. Also, before vow-
encephal-. [< Gk. < *en-* in + *kephalē* head]

eph·a·lon (en·sef′ə·lon) *n.* *pl.* **·la** (-lə) *Anat.* The
in. [< NL < Gk. *enkephalos*] — **en·ceph′a·lous** *adj.*

hain (in·chān′) *v.t.* **1.** To bind with or as with a chain.
To hold fast or captive, as attention. — **en·chain′ment** *n.*

hant (in·chant′, -chänt′) *v.t.* **1.** To put a spell upon;
itch. **2.** To charm completely; delight. [< F < L <
in + *cantare* to sing] — **en·chant′er** *n.* — **en·chant′-**
nt *n.* — **en·chant′ress** *n. fem.*

hant·ing (in·chan′ting, -chän′-) *adj.* Having power to
hant; charming; fascinating. — **en·chant′ing·ly** *adv.*

i·pher (en·sī′fər) *v.t.* To convert (a message, report,
) from plain text into cipher.

ir·cle (en·sûr′kəl) *v.t.* **·cled, ·cling** **1.** To form a circle
und. **2.** To go around. — **en·cir′cle·ment** *n.*

en·clave (en′klāv) *n.* **1.** A territory completely or partially enclosed by the territory of a power to which it is not politically subject, as San Marino and Vatican City in Italy. **2.** A district, as in a city, inhabited by a minority group. [< F < LL < L *in-* in + *clavis* key]

en·clit·ic (en·klit′ic) *adj.* Having no independent accent, but pronounced as part of a preceding word, as English *is* in *Tom's going,* French *je* in *ai-je.* — *n.* *Gram.* An enclitic form. [< LL < Gk. < *en-* on + *klinein* to lean]

en·close (in·klōz′) *v.t.* **·closed, ·clos·ing** **1.** To close in on all sides; surround. **2.** To transmit within the cover of a letter. **3.** To contain. Also spelled *inclose.*

en·clo·sure (in·klō′zhər) *n.* **1.** The act of enclosing, or the state of being enclosed. **2.** An enclosed object or area. **3.** That which encloses, as a wall. Also spelled *inclosure.*

en·code (en·kōd′) *v.t.* **·cod·ed, ·cod·ing** To convert (a message, document, etc.) from plain text into code.

en·co·mi·um (en·kō′mē·əm) *n.* *pl.* **·mi·ums** or **·mi·a** (-me·ə) A formal expression of praise; eulogy. [< L < Gk. *enkōmion* eulogy]

en·com·pass (in·kum′pəs) *v.t.* **1.** To form a circle around; surround. **2.** To enclose; contain. — **en·com′pass·ment** *n.*

en·core (äng′kôr, -kōr, än′-) *interj.* Again! once more! — *n.* The call by an audience, as by prolonged applause, for repetition of a performance or for an additional performance; also, that which is performed in response to this call. — *v.t.* **·cored, ·cor·ing** To call for a repetition of (a performance) or by (a performer). [< F]

en·coun·ter (in·koun′tər) *n.* **1.** A meeting with a person or thing, esp. when casual or unexpected. **2.** A hostile meeting; contest. — *v.t.* **1.** To meet, esp. casually or unexpectedly. **2.** To meet in battle. **3.** To be faced with or contend against (opposition, difficulties, etc.). — *v.i.* **4.** To meet each other unexpectedly or in conflict. [< OF < LL < L *in-* in + *contra* against]

en·cour·age (in·kûr′ij) *v.t.* **·aged, ·ag·ing** **1.** To inspire with courage, hope, or resolution. **2.** To help or foster. [< OF < *en-* in + *corage* courage] — **en·cour′age·ment** *n.*

en·cour·ag·ing (in·kûr′ij·ing) *adj.* Giving, or tending to give, courage or confidence. — **en·cour′ag·ing·ly** *adv.*

en·croach (in·krōch′) *v.i.* **1.** To intrude stealthily or gradually upon the possessions or rights of another: with *on* or *upon.* **2.** To advance beyond the proper or usual limits. [< OF < *en-* in + *croc* hook] — **en·croach′ment** *n.*

en·crust (in·krust′), etc. See INCRUST, etc.

en·cum·ber (in·kum′bər) *v.t.* **1.** To hinder in action or motion, as with a burden; impede. **2.** To block up; crowd, as with obstacles or useless additions. **3.** To weigh down, as with debts. Also spelled *incumber.* [< OF < LL < *in-* in + *combrus* obstacle]

en·cum·brance (in·kum′brəns) *n.* **1.** That which encumbers; a hindrance. **2.** A dependent, esp. a child. **3.** *Law* A lien attached to real property. Also spelled *incumbrance.*

-ency *suffix of nouns* A variant of -ENCE, as in *decency,* used to form words expressing quality or condition, the earlier form being used largely for nouns of action. [< L *-entia*]

en·cyc·li·cal (en·sik′li·kəl, -sī′kli-) *adj.* Intended for general circulation; circular: said of letters. Also **en·cyc′lic.** — *n.* A circular letter addressed by the Pope to the bishops of the world. [< LL < Gk. < *en-* in + *kyklos* circle]

en·cy·clo·pe·di·a (en·sī′klə·pē′dē·ə) *n.* **1.** A comprehensive work made up of systematically arranged articles broadly covering the whole range of knowledge or treating of one particular field. **2.** The entire circle of knowledge. Also **en·cy′clo·pae′di·a.** [< NL < Gk. < *enkyklios paideia* a general education] — **en·cy′clo·pe′dic** or **·di·cal, en·cy′clo·pae′dic** *adj.* — **en·cy′clo·pe′di·cal·ly** *adv.*

en·cy·clo·pe·dist (en·sī′klə·pē′dist) *n.* A writer for or compiler of an encyclopedia. Also **en·cy′clo·pae′dist.**

en·cyst (en·sist′) *v.t. & v.i.* *Biol.* To enclose or become enclosed in a cyst or sac. — **en·cyst′ment, en′cys·ta′tion** *n.*

end (end) *n.* **1.** The terminal point or part of anything that has length: the *end* of a street. **2.** The extreme limit of the space occupied by any extended object; boundary: the *ends* of the earth. **3.** The point in time at which something ceases. **4.** The purpose of an action. **5.** An inevitable or natural consequence. **6.** Ultimate state. **7.** The termination of existence; death. **8.** Fragment; remnant: odds and *ends.* **9.** In football, the outermost player at each side of the line of scrimmage; also, the position of this player. — **to make (both) ends meet** To live within one's income. — *v.t.* **1.** To bring to a finish or termination. **2.** To be the end of. **3.** To cause the death of. — *v.i.* **4.** To come to an end. **5.** To die. [OE *ende*]

en·da·me·ba (en′də·mē′bə) *n.* A parasitic ameba; esp. one causing dysentery and liver abscess. Also **en′da·moe′ba.**

en·dan·ger (in·dān′jər) *v.t.* To expose to danger; imperil.

en·dear (in·dir′) *v.t.* To make dear or beloved.

---

en·dear·ing (in·dir′ing) *adj.* **1.** Making dear or beloved. **2.** Manifesting affection; caressing. **— en·dear′ing·ly** *adv.*
en·dear·ment (in·dir′mənt) *n.* **1.** The act of endearing, or the state of being endeared. **2.** A loving word, act, etc.
en·deav·or (in·dev′ər) *n.* An attempt or effort to do or attain something. **—** *v.t.* **1.** To make an effort to do or effect; try: usu. with an infinitive as object. **—** *v.i.* **2.** To strive. Also *Brit.* **en·deav′our.** [ME < EN-[1] + DEVOIR]
en·dem·ic (en·dem′ik) *adj.* **1.** Peculiar to a particular country or people. **2.** *Med.* Confined to or characteristic of a given locality: said of a disease. Also **en·dem′i·cal. — Syn.** See NATIVE. [< Gk. < *en-* in + *dēmos* people]
end·ing (en′ding) *n.* **1.** The act of bringing or coming to an end. **2.** The concluding or final part; end; extremity. **3.** One or more concluding letters or syllables added to the base of a word, esp. to indicate an inflection.
en·dive (en′dīv, än′dēv) *n.* An herb whose blanched leaves are used as a salad. [< F < L *intibus* endive]
end·less (end′lis) *adj.* **1.** Enduring forever; eternal. **2.** Having no end in space; infinite. **3.** Continually recurring; incessant. **4.** Forming a closed loop or circle. **— end′less·ly** *adv.* **— end′less·ness** *n.*
end·most (end′mōst′) *adj.* Most remote; farthest.
endo- *combining form* Within; inside. Also, before vowels, **end-.** [< Gk. < *endon* within]
en·do·blast (en′dō·blast) *n. Biol.* The endoderm. **— en′·do·blas′tic** *adj.*
en·do·carp (en′dō·kärp) *n. Bot.* The inner layer of a ripened fruit, as of a cherry stone.
en·do·crine (en′dō·krin, -krēn, -krīn) *Physiol. adj.* **1.** Secreting internally. **2.** Of or pertaining to an endocrine gland or its secretion. Also **en′do·cri′nal** (-krī′nəl), **en′do·crin′ic** (-krin′ik), **en·doc·ri·nous** (en·dok′rə·nəs) *adj.* [< ENDO- + Gk. *krinein* to separate]
endocrine gland One of several ductless glands, as the thyroid, pituitary, and suprarenal glands, whose secretions, released directly into the blood or lymph, have a critical importance in many phases of physiological activity.
en·do·cri·nol·o·gy (en′dō·kri·nol′ə·jē, -krī-) *n.* The branch of medicine dealing with the endocrine glands and the various internal secretions. **— en′do·cri·nol′o·gist** *n.*
en·do·derm (en′dō·dûrm) *n. Biol.* The innermost of the three germ layers of the embryo, developing into the digestive and respiratory systems: also called *endoblast, entoblast, entoderm.* **— en′do·der′mal, en′do·der′mic** *adj.*
en·dog·a·my (en·dog′ə·mē) *n. Anthropol.* Marriage within the group, class, caste, or tribe. **— en·dog′a·mous** *adj.*
en·dog·e·nous (en·doj′ə·nəs) *adj. Biol.* Originating or growing from within, as cells within the wall of the parent cell. **— en·dog′e·nous·ly** *adv.* **— en·dog′e·ny** *n.*
en·do·mor·phic (en′dō·môr′fik) *adj.* Of human body types, characterized by a heavy body structure. **— en′do·morph** *n.* **— en′do·mor′phy** *n.*
en·do·plasm (en′dō·plaz′əm) *n. Biol.* The inner granular portion of the cytoplasm of the cell, enclosing the nucleus. Also **en·do·sarc** (en′dō·särk). **— en′do·plas′mic** *adj.*
end organ *Physiol.* Any organ adapted for the reception or delivery of nervous stimuli.
en·dorse (in·dôrs′) *v.t.* **·dorsed, ·dors·ing 1.** To write on the back of (a paper); esp., to transfer ownership or assign payment of (a check, note, etc.) by signing on the reverse side. **2.** To give sanction or support to. Also spelled *indorse.* [< OF < Med.L < L *in-* on + *dorsum* back] **— en·dors′a·ble** *adj.* **— en·dors′er** or **en·dor′sor** *n.*
en·dor·see (en′dôr·sē′, in·dôr′sē) *n.* One to whom transference by endorsement is made.
en·dorse·ment (in·dôrs′mənt) *n.* **1.** The act of endorsing. **2.** That which endorses, as a signature. **3.** Confirmation; approval. Also spelled *indorsement.*
en·do·skel·e·ton (en′dō·skel′ə·tən) *n. Anat.* The internal supporting structure of an animal, as in all vertebrates. **— en′do·skel′e·tal** *adj.*
en·do·sperm (en′dō·spûrm) *n. Bot.* The nutritive substance with the embryo sac of an ovule.
en·do·ther·mic (en′dō·thûr′mik) *adj. Chem.* Pertaining to, attended by, or produced from the absorption of heat. Also **en′do·ther′mal.** [< ENDO- + Gk. *thermē* heat]
en·dow (in·dou′) *v.t.* **1.** To bestow a permanent fund or income upon. **2.** To furnish or equip, as with talents or natural gifts: usu. with *with.* [< OF < *en-* in + L *dotare* to give]
en·dow·ment (in·dou′mənt) *n.* **1.** Money or property given for the permanent use of an institution, person, etc. **2.** Any natural gift, as talent or beauty. **3.** The act of endowing.
end table *U.S.* A small table beside a chair, sofa, etc.
en·due (in·do͞o′, -dyo͞o′) *v.t.* **·dued, ·du·ing 1.** To endow with some quality, power, etc. **2.** To put on. **3.** To clothe. [Fusion of OF *enduire* to introduce and *enduire* to clothe]
en·dur·ance (in·do͝or′əns, -dyo͝or′-) *n.* **1.** The act or capacity of bearing up, as under hardship or prolonged stress. **2.** Duration. **3.** Thatwhich is endured.
en·dure (in·do͝or′, -dyo͝or′) *v.* **·dured, ·dur·ing** *v.t.* **1.** To bear up under: to *endure* hardships. **2.** To put up w[illegible] tolerate. **—** *v.i.* **3.** To continue to be; last. **4.** To s[illegible] without yielding. [< OF < L < *in-* in + *durare* to har[illegible] **— en·dur′a·ble** *adj.* **— en·dur′a·bly** *adv.*
en·dur·ing (in·do͝or′ing, -dyo͝or′-) *adj.* **1.** Lasting; pe[illegible]nent. **2.** Long-suffering. **— en·dur′ing·ly** *adv.* **— en·[illegible]ing·ness** *n.*
end·wise (end′wīz′) *adv.* **1.** With the end foremost o[illegible] permost. **2.** On end. **3.** Lengthwise. **4.** End to end. **end′ways′** (-wāz′).
En·dym·i·on (en·dim′ē·ən) In Greek mythology, a be[illegible]ful youth loved by Selene and granted eternal youth.
-ene *suffix Chem.* **1.** Denoting a hydrocarbon comp[illegible] having one double bond: *ethylene.* **2.** Denoting a comp[illegible] of the benzene series.
en·e·ma (en′ə·mə) *n. pl.* **en·e·mas** or **e·nem·a·ta** (e·ne[illegible]tə) *Med.* **1.** A liquid injected into the rectum for clean[illegible] diagnostic, or nutritive purposes. **2.** The injection of su[illegible] liquid. [< Gk. < *en-* in + *hienai* to send]
en·e·my (en′ə·mē) *n. pl.* **·mies 1.** One who harbors h[illegible] or malicious intent toward another; also, one who or which opposes a person, cause, etc. **2.** A hostile pow[illegible] military force; also, a member of a hostile force. **—** *adj* or pertaining to a hostile army or power. [< OF < L < not + *amicus* friend]
— Syn. (noun) An *enemy* is one who manifests ill wi[illegible] broadly anyone on the opposite side in a struggle. An *opp*[illegible] may vie with one in a friendly contest, while an *antagonist* [illegible]ways hostile and unfriendly. *Adversary* is a general word and be applied to a friendly *opponent* or to the most implacable *e*[illegible]
en·er·get·ic (en′ər·jet′ik) *adj.* Having or displaying en[illegible] forceful and efficient. **— en′er·get′i·cal·ly** *adv.*
en·er·gize (en′ər·jīz) *v.* **·gized, ·giz·ing** *v.t.* **1.** To give [illegible]gy, force, or strength to; activate. **—** *v.i.* **2.** To be in o[illegible]tion; be active. **— en′er·giz′er** *n.*
en·er·gy (en′ər·jē) *n. pl.* **·gies 1.** Vigor or intensity [illegible]tion, expression, or utterance. **2.** Capacity or tendenc[illegible] vigorous action. **3.** Inherent power to produce an e[illegible] **4.** *Often pl.* Power forcefully and effectively exercised. *Physics* The capacity for doing work and for overcomin[illegible]ertia. **Potential energy** is due to the position of one [illegible] relative to another, and **kinetic energy** is manifeste[illegible] bodies in motion. [< LL < Gk. < *en-* + *ergon* work
en·er·vate (*v.* en′ər·vāt; *adj.* i·nûr′vit) *v.t.* **·vat·ed, ·va**[illegible] To sap the strength or vitality of; weaken in body or **—** *adj.* Weakened; devitalized. [< L < *e-* out + *n*[illegible] sinew] **— en′er·va′tion** *n.* **— en′er·va′tor** *n.*
en·fee·ble (en·fē′bəl) *v.t.* **·bled, ·bling** To make feeble. **en·fee′ble·ment** *n.* **— en·fee′bler** *n.*
en·fi·lade (en′fə·lād′) *Mil. v.t.* **·lad·ed, ·lad·ing** To fi[illegible] be in a position to fire down the length of, as a colum[illegible] troops. **—** *n.* **1.** Gunfire that can rake lengthwise a li[illegible] troops, etc. **2.** A position exposed to such fire. [< F < in + *fil* thread]
en·fold (in·fōld′) See INFOLD.
en·force (in·fôrs′, -fōrs′) *v.t.* **·forced, ·forc·ing 1.** To co[illegible] observance of (a law, etc.). **2.** To impose (obedience, by force. **3.** To lay stress upon; emphasize. [< OF < L *in-* in + *fortis* strong] **— en·force′a·ble** *adj.* **— [illegible]force′ment** *n.* **— en·forc′er** *n.*
en·fran·chise (in·fran′chīz) *v.t.* **·chised, ·chis·ing 1** [illegible] endow with a franchise, as with the right to vote. **2.** T[illegible] free, as from bondage or legal liabilities. [< OF < *en-* [illegible] *franc* free] **— en·fran′chise·ment** (-chiz·mənt) *n.*
en·gage (in·gāj′) *v.* **·gaged, ·gag·ing** *v.t.* **1.** To hire o[illegible]ploy (a person); also, to secure or contract for (profess[illegible] services, assistance, etc.). **2.** To reserve the use of, as [illegible]ings. **3.** To hold the interest or attention of; engross. **4** occupy; keep busy: to *engage* one's time in revelry. **5** bind by a pledge, contract, etc. **6.** To betroth: usu. i[illegible] passive. **7.** To enter into conflict with: to *engage* the en[illegible] **8.** *Mech.* To mesh or interlock with. **—** *v.i.* **9.** To oc[illegible] oneself in an undertaking. **10.** To pledge oneself; war[illegible] **11.** To enter into combat. **12.** *Mech.* To mesh. [< *en-* in + *gager* to pledge]
en·gaged (in·gājd′) *adj.* **1.** Occupied or busy. **2.** Betrot[illegible] **3.** Involved in conflict. **4.** *Mech.* Geared together. *Archit.* Partially sunk into another part of a structure.
en·gage·ment (in·gāj′mənt) *n.* **1.** The act of engagin[illegible] the state of being engaged. **2.** Something that engag[illegible] binds, as an obligation. **3.** Betrothal. **4.** A busines[illegible]pointment. **5.** A salaried position, esp. for a limited pe[illegible] **6.** A hostile encounter. **7.** *Mech.* The state of being in [illegible] **8.** *pl.* Financial obligations. **— Syn.** See BATTLE.
en·gag·ing (in·gā′jing) *adj.* Attracting interest or a[illegible]tion; winning; pleasing. **— en·gag′ing·ly** *adv.*
en garde (äṅ gärd′) *French* On guard: a fencing posi[illegible]
en·gen·der (in·jen′dər) *v.t.* **1.** To cause to exist; proc[illegible] **2.** *Rare* To beget. **—** *v.i.* **3.** To come into being. [< O[illegible] L *ingenerare* to create < *in-* in + *genus, generis* race]
en·gine (en′jən) *n.* **1.** A machine that converts heat en[illegible]

;o mechanical work. **2.** A locomotive. **3.** An apparatus mechanical contrivance for producing some effect. **4.** ·y agency, means, or instrument. [< OF < L *in-* in + ı-, root of *gignere* to beget]
gi·neer (en′jə·nir′) *n.* **1.** One versed in or practicing any ınch of engineering. **2.** One who operates an engine. **3.** *il.* A member of a corps of men engaged in constructing ·ts and bridges, clearing and building roads, etc. — *v.t.* To put through or manage by contrivance: to *engineer* a ıeme. **2.** To plan and superintend as engineer.
gi·neer·ing (en′jə·nir′ing) *n.* **1.** The art and science of signing, constructing, and operating roads, bridges, build-·s, etc. **2.** Clever planning or maneuvering.
g·lish (ing′glish) *adj.* **1.** Of, pertaining to, or derived ·m England or its people. **2.** Expressed in or belonging to ı English language. — *n.* **1.** The people of England col-tively: with *the.* **2.** The language spoken by the people the British Isles and most of the British Commonwealth, d of the United States, its territories, and possessions. — **d English** or **Anglo-Saxon** The English language from out A.D. 450 to 1050, consisting of a basically Germanic cabulary. — **Middle English** The language of England er the Norman Conquest, from about 1050 to 1475, repre-ıted by the works of Chaucer and having extensive bor-wings from Latin, French, and the Low German languages. **Modern English** The English language since 1475. **3.** *S.* In billiards, a horizontal twist or spin given to the cue ll by striking it on one side. — *v.t.* **1.** To translate into glish. **2.** To Anglicize, as a foreign word. **3.** *U.S.* In liards, to apply English to. [OE *Engle* the Angles]
glish horn A double-reed instrument having a pitch a h lower than an oboe.
g·lish·man (ing′glish·mən) *n. pl.* **·men** (-mən) **1.** A na-e or citizen of England. **2.** An English ship.
glish muffin A round, flat muffin made with little short-ng, and usu. eaten toasted.
glish sonnet The Shakespearean sonnet.
g·lish·wom·an (ing′glish·wŏŏm′ən) *n. pl.* **·wom·en** vim′in) A woman who is a native or citizen of England.
gorge (en·gôrj′) *v.t.* **·gorged, ·gorg·ing 1.** To fill with ood, as an artery. **2.** To devour or swallow greedily. [< < *en-* in + *gorge* throat] — **en·gorge′ment** *n.*
graft (en·graft′, -gräft′) *v.t.* **1.** *Bot.* To graft. **2.** To set mly; implant.
gram (en′gram) *n.* A permanently altered state in ı protoplasm of animal cells assumed to result from the nporary excitation of certain stimuli.
grave (in·grāv′) *v.t.* **·graved, ·grav·ing 1.** To carve or h figures, letters, etc., into (a surface). **2.** To impress eply on the mind. **3.** To cut (pictures, lettering, etc.) into ·tal, stone, or wood, for printing. **4.** To print from plates made. [< EN-[1] + *grave* to carve] — **en·grav′er** *n.*
grav·ing (in·grā′ving) *n.* **1.** The act or art of cutting signs, etc., into a surface. **2.** An engraved design; plate. An impression printed from an engraved plate; print.
gross (in·grōs′) *v.t.* **1.** To occupy completely; absorb. To copy legibly in a large hand, as a document. **3.** In siness, to monopolize (goods already on the market). [< ′ < LL *ingrossare* to write large] — **en·gross′ment** *n.*
gross·ing (in·grō′sing) *adj.* Holding the attention or erest completely; absorbing. — **en·gross′ing·ly** *adv.*
gulf (in·gulf′) *v.t.* To swallow up in or as in a gulf; bury overwhelm completely.
hance (in·hans′, -häns′) *v.t.* **·hanced, ·hanc·ing** To ighten or increase, as in reputation, cost, beauty, quality, :. [< AF < *en-* in, on + *haucer* to lift] — **en·hanc′er** *n.* **en·hance′ment** *n.*
har·mon·ic (en′här·mon′ik) *adj.* *Music* Of or relating tones, as C# and D♭, having different notation but the ne pitch. [< L < *en-* in + *harmonia* harmony]
ig·ma (i·nig′mə) *n.* **1.** An obscure or ambiguous saying. Anything that puzzles or baffles. — **Syn.** See PUZZLE. ; L < Gk. *ainissesthai* to speak in riddles]
ig·mat·ic (en′ig·mat′ik, ē′nig-) *adj.* Of or like an enig-; puzzling. Also **en′ig·mat′i·cal.** — **en′ig·mat′i·cal·ly** *adv.*
join (in·join′) *v.t.* **1.** To order or command (a person or oup). **2.** To impose (a condition, course of action, etc.) a person or group. **3.** To forbid or prohibit, especially by licial order. [< OF < L < *in-* on + *jungere* to join] — **·join′er** *n.* — **en·join′ment** *n.*
joy (in·joi′) *v.t.* **1.** To experience joy or pleasure in. **2.** have the use or benefit of. [< OF < *en-* in + *joir* to re-ce] — **en·joy′a·ble** *adj.* — **en·joy′a·ble·ness** *n.* — **en·′a·bly** *adv.* — **en·joy′er** *n.* — **en·joy′ment** *n.*
kin·dle (en·kin′dəl) *v.t.* **·dled, ·dling 1.** To set on fire; ıdle. **2.** To stir to action; excite. — **en·kin′dler** *n.*
large (in·lärj′) *v.* **·larged, ·larg·ing** *v.t.* **1.** To make ·ger. — *v.i.* **2.** To become larger. **3.** To express oneself in greater detail or at greater length: with *on* or *upon.* — **Syn.** See INCREASE. — **en·large′ment** *n.* — **en·larg′er** *n.*
en·light·en (in·līt′n) *v.t.* To give revealing or broadening knowledge to; cause to know. — **en·light′en·er** *n.*
en·light·en·ment (in·līt′n·mənt) *n.* The act of enlighten-ing, or the state of being enlightened. — **the Enlightenment** A philosophical movement of the 18th century, character-ized by rationalistic methods.
en·list (in·list′) *v.t.* **1.** To engage (someone) for the armed forces. **2.** To secure the active aid or participation of (a person, etc.). — *v.i.* **3.** To enter military service without being drafted. **4.** To join some venture, cause, etc.: with *in.*
en·list·ed man (in·lis′tid) Any male member of the armed forces who is not a commissioned officer or warrant officer.
en·list·ment (in·list′mənt) *n.* **1.** An enlisting or being en-listed. **2.** The term for which one enlists.
en·li·ven (in·lī′vən) *v.t.* **1.** To make lively, cheerful, or sprightly. **2.** To make active or vigorous; stimulate. — **en·li′ven·er** *n.* — **en·li′ven·ment** *n.*
en masse (en mas′, *Fr.* äṅ màs′) All together. [< F]
en·mesh (en·mesh′) *v.t.* To ensnare in or as in a net.
en·mi·ty (en′mə·tē) *n. pl.* **·ties** Deep-seated unfriendli-ness; hostility. [< OF < L < *in-* not + *amicus* friend]
en·no·ble (i·nō′bəl, en-) *v.t.* **·bled, ·bling 1.** To make honor-able or noble in nature, quality, etc.; dignify. **2.** To confer a title of nobility upon. — **en·no′ble·ment** *n.* — **en·no′bler** *n.*
en·nui (än·wē′, än′wē, *Fr.* äṅ·nwē′) *n.* A feeling of listless weariness and boredom. [< F < L *in odio* in hatred]
e·nor·mi·ty (i·nôr′mə·tē) *n. pl.* **·ties 1.** The quality of be-ing outrageous; heinousness. **2.** An outrageous offense; atrocity. [See ENORMOUS.]
e·nor·mous (i·nôr′məs) *adj.* Far exceeding the usual size, amount, degree, etc. [< L *enormis* < *e-* out + *norma* rule] — **e·nor′mous·ly** *adv.* — **e·nor′mous·ness** *n.*
e·nough (i·nuf′) *adj.* Adequate for any demand or need; suf-ficient. — *n.* An ample supply; a sufficiency. — *adv.* **1.** So as to be sufficient. **2.** Quite; very. **3.** Adequately; fairly; tolerably. — *interj.* That's enough! [OE *genōh, genōg*]
en·plane (en·plān′) *v.i.* **·planed, ·plan·ing** To board an air-plane.
en·quire (in·kwīr′), **en·quir·y** (in·kwīr′ē, in′kwər·ē) See INQUIRE, INQUIRY.
en·rage (in·rāj′) *v.t.* **·raged, ·rag·ing** To throw into a rage.
en rap·port (äṅ rà·pôr′) *French* In sympathy; in accord.
en·rapt (in·rapt′) *adj.* Rapt; enraptured.
en·rap·ture (in·rap′chər) *v.t.* **·tured, ·tur·ing** To bring into a state of rapture; delight extravagantly.
en·rich (in·rich′) *v.t.* **1.** To make rich or increase the wealth of. **2.** To make more productive, as soil. **3.** To add attrac-tive or desirable elements to; make better, more interesting, etc., by adding. **4.** To increase the food value of. — **en·rich′er** *n.* — **en·rich′ment** *n.*
en·roll (in·rōl′) *v.t.* **1.** To write or record (a name) in a roll; register; list. **2.** To enlist. **3.** To place on record; record, as a document or decree. **4.** To roll up; wrap. — *v.i.* **5.** To place one's name on a list; register oneself. Also *Brit.* **en·rol′.**
en·roll·ment (in·rōl′mənt) *n.* **1.** An enrolling or being en-rolled. **2.** A record of persons or things enrolled. **3.** The number of persons or things enrolled. Also **en·rol′ment.**
en route (än·rōōt′, en-, *Fr.* äṅ·rōōt′) On the way.
en·sconce (en·skons′) *v.t.* **·sconced, ·sconc·ing 1.** To fix securely or comfortably in some place. **2.** To shelter; hide.
en·sem·ble (än·säm′bəl, *Fr.* äṅ·säṅ′bl′) *n.* **1.** All the parts of a thing viewed as a whole. **2.** An individual's entire costume, including accessories. **3.** The over-all effect of something. **4.** The entire cast of a play, ballet, etc. **5.** *Music* **a** The degree of precision, balance, and unification achieved by a group of performers. **b** A group of players or singers performing together. [< F < L < *in-* in + *simul* at the same time]
en·shrine (in·shrīn′) *v.t.* **·shrined, ·shrin·ing 1.** To place in or as in a shrine. **2.** To cherish devoutly; hold sacred. Also spelled *inshrine.* — **en·shrine′ment** *n.*
en·shroud (in·shroud′) *v.t.* To shroud; conceal.
en·sign (en′sīn; *also, and always for def. 2,* en′sən) *n.* **1.** A flag or banner. **2.** In the U.S. Navy or Coast Guard, a com-missioned officer of the lowest grade. See table at GRADE. **3.** A badge, symbol, or distinguishing mark. [< OF < L < *in-* in + *signum* mark] — **en′sign·ship, en′sign·cy** *n.*
en·si·lage (en′sə·lij) *n.* **1.** The process of preserving green fodder in closed pits or silos. **2.** Fodder preserved in silos: also called *silage.* — *v.t.* **·laged, ·lag·ing** To store in a silo for preservation: also **en·sile** (en·sīl′). [< F]
en·slave (in·slāv′) *v.t.* **·slaved, ·slav·ing 1.** To make a slave of. **2.** To dominate; control. — **en·slave′ment** *n.*
en·snare (en·snâr′) *v.t.* **·snared, ·snar·ing** To catch in a snare; trick: also *insnare.* — **en·snare′ment** *n.*
en·sue (en·sōō′) *v.i.* **·sued, ·su·ing 1.** To follow subsequent-

ly; occur afterward. **2.** To follow as a consequence; result. [< OF < L < *in-* on, in + *sequi* to follow]

en·sure (in·sho͝or′) *v.t.* **·sured, ·sur·ing 1.** To make sure or certain: to *ensure* victory. **2.** To make safe or secure: with *from* or *against*: to *ensure* liberty against tyranny. **3.** To insure (life, etc.). [< OF < *en-* in + *seur* sure]

-ent *suffix of nouns and adjectives* **1.** Having the quality, or performing the action of (the main element); *dependent*. **2.** One who or that which performs the action of (the main element); *superintendent*. Compare -ANT. [< F *-ent* < L *-ens*, *-entis*, suffix of present participle]

ent- See ENTO-.

en·tab·la·ture (en·tab′lə·chər) *n. Archit.* **1.** The uppermost member of a classical order or columnar system, consisting of the architrave, frieze, and cornice. **2.** Any projecting frieze or cornice of several members. [< MF < Ital. < *in-* in + *tavola* base, table]

en·tail (in·tāl′) *v.t.* **1.** To impose, involve, or result in by necessity. **2.** *Law* To restrict or leave the inheritance of (real property) to an unalterable succession of heirs. — *n.* **1.** The act of entailing, or the state of being entailed. **2.** Something entailed, as an inherited estate. **3.** A restricted line of succession or inheritance. [< OF < *en-* + *taillier* to cut] — **en·tail′ment** *n.*

en·ta·me·ba (en′tə·mē′bə) *n.* Endameba.

en·tan·gle (in·tang′gəl) *v.t.* **·gled, ·gling 1.** To catch in or as in a snare; hamper. **2.** To make tangled; snarl. **3.** To involve in difficulties; perplex; embarrass. — **en·tan′gle·ment** *n.* — **en·tan′gler** *n.*

en·tente (än·tänt′, *Fr.* äṅ·täṅt′) *n.* A mutual agreement; also, the parties entering into a mutual agreement. [< F]

entente cor·diale (kôr·dyȧl′) Cordial understanding, as between governments; friendly agreement. [< F]

en·ter (en′tər) *v.t.* **1.** To come or go into. **2.** To penetrate; pierce. **3.** To set in; insert. **4.** To become a member of; join. **5.** To start out upon; embark on. **6.** To obtain admission to (a school, etc.). **7.** To cause to be admitted to; enroll in. **8.** To write down, as in a list. **9.** To file notice of (goods, a ship, etc.) at a custom house. **10.** *Law* **a** To place (a plea, evidence, etc.) on the records of a court. **b** To file a claim to (public lands). — *v.i.* **11.** To come or go into a particular place. **12.** To begin to sing, play an instrument, etc. — **to enter into 1.** To start out; embark on. **2.** To engage in. **3.** To form a part or constituent of. **4.** To consider or discuss. — **to enter on** (or **upon**) **1.** To start out on. **2.** To start to have or use. [< OF < L *intra* within]

en·ter·ic (en·ter′ik) *adj.* Intestinal. [< Gk. *enteron* intestine]

en·ter·i·tis (en′tə·rī′tis) *n. Pathol.* Inflammation of the intestines, chiefly the small intestine.

entero- *combining form* Intestine. Also, before vowels, **enter-.** [< Gk. *enteron* intestine]

en·ter·prise (en′tər·prīz) *n.* **1.** Any project, undertaking, or task, especially when difficult, demanding, or of major importance. **2.** Boldness, energy, and venturesomeness in practical affairs. **3.** Active engagement in projects. [< OF < *entre-* between + *prendre* to take]

en·ter·pris·ing (en′tər·prī′zing) *adj.* Energetic, bold, and full of initiative; venturesome. — **en′ter·pris′ing·ly** *adv.*

en·ter·tain (en′tər·tān′) *v.t.* **1.** To amuse; divert. **2.** To extend hospitality to; receive as a guest. **3.** To take into consideration, as a proposal. **4.** To keep or bear in mind: to *entertain* a grudge. — *v.i.* **5.** To receive and care for guests. [< F < *entre-* between + *tenir* to hold] — **en′ter·tain′er** *n.*

en·ter·tain·ing (en′tər·tā′ning) *adj.* That entertains; amusing; diverting. — **en′ter·tain′ing·ly** *adv.*

en·ter·tain·ment (en′tər·tān′mənt) *n.* **1.** The act of entertaining, or the state of being entertained. **2.** Something that entertains, as a play. **3.** The care of guests.

en·thrall (in·thrôl′) *v.t.* **1.** To keep spellbound; fascinate; charm. **2.** To enslave. Also **en·thral′.** — **en·thrall′ment** or **en·thral′ment** *n.*

en·throne (in·thrōn′) *v.t.* **·throned, ·thron·ing 1.** To put upon a throne. **2.** To invest with authority. **3.** To exalt; revere. — **en·throne′ment** *n.*

en·thuse (in·tho͞oz′) *v.* **·thused, ·thus·ing** *U.S. Informal v.t.* **1.** To make enthusiastic. — *v.i.* **2.** To become enthusiastic.

en·thu·si·asm (in·tho͞o′zē·az′əm) *n.* **1.** Keen, animated interest in and preoccupation with something; ardor; zeal. **2.** A cause or object of intense, lively interest. [< LL < Gk. < *entheos*, *enthous* inspired, possessed]

en·thu·si·ast (in·tho͞o′zē·ast, -ist) *n.* **1.** One given to or moved by enthusiasm. **2.** A religious fanatic.

en·thu·si·as·tic (in·tho͞o′zē·as′tik) *adj.* Full of or marked by enthusiasm; ardent. — **en·thu′si·as′ti·cal·ly** *adv.*

en·tice (in·tīs′) *v.t.* **·ticed, ·tic·ing** To lead on or attract by arousing hope of pleasure, profit, etc.; allure. [< OF *enticier* to set afire] — **en·tice′ment** *n.* — **en·tic′ing·ly** *adv.*

en·tire (in·tīr′) *adj.* **1.** Having no part missing; whole; complete. **2.** Not broken; intact. **3.** Not lessened; full; total. **4.** Consisting wholly of one piece; not divided into sections. — *n.* The whole of something; total. [< OF < *integer* whole] — **en·tire′ly** *adv.* — **en·tire′ness** *n.*

en·tire·ty (in·tī′rə·tē) *n. pl.* **·ties 1.** The state or co[ndi]tion of being entire; completeness. **2.** That which is ent[ire].

en·ti·tle (in·tīt′l) *v.t.* **·tled, ·tling 1.** To give (a perso[n or] thing) the right to receive, demand, or do something. [2.] To give a name or designation to. **3.** To give (a perso[n]) title designating rank, honor, etc.

en·ti·ty (en′tə·tē) *n. pl.* **·ties 1.** Something existing [ob]jectively or in the mind; an actual or conceivable being. [2.] Existence as opposed to nonexistence. **3.** Essence; s[ub]stance. [< L ppr. of *esse* to be]

ento- *combining form* Interior. Also, before vowels, **ent-**

en·to·blast (en′tō·blast) *n. Biol.* The endoderm. — **en[to]·blas′tic** *adj.*

en·to·derm (en′tō·dûrm) *n.* Endoderm.

en·tomb (in·to͞om′) *v.t.* **1.** To place in or as in a tomb; b[ury]. **2.** To serve as a tomb for. Also spelled *intomb*. [< O[F] *en-* in + *tombe* tomb] — **en·tomb′ment** *n.*

entomo- *combining form* Insect. Also, before vowels, **en[to]m-.** [< Gk. *entoma* insects]

en·to·mol·o·gy (en′tə·mol′ə·jē) *n.* The branch of zool[ogy] that treats of insects. — **en′to·mo·log′i·cal** or **en′to·mo·lo[g′ic]** *adj.* — **en′to·mo·log′i·cal·ly** *adv.* — **en′to·mol′o·gist** *n.*

en·tou·rage (än′to͞o·räzh′, *Fr.* äṅ·to͞o·räzh′) *n.* **1.** A gr[oup] of followers, retainers, or attendants; retinue. **2.** Envi[ron]ment. [< F < *entourer* to surround]

en·tr'acte (än·trakt′, *Fr.* äṅ·trȧkt′) *n.* **1.** The interval [be]tween the acts of a play, opera, etc. **2.** A musical interl[ude,] dance, or the like, performed between acts. [< F]

en·trails (en′trālz, -trəlz) *n.pl.* **1.** The internal parts [of] man or animal; esp., the intestines; bowels; guts. **2.** [The] internal parts of anything. [< OF < LL *intralia* intesti[nes]]

en·train (en·trān′) *v.i.* **1.** To board a train. — *v.t.* **2.** [To] put aboard a train. — **en·train′ment** *n.*

en·trance[1] (en′trəns) n. **1.** The act of entering. **2.** A [pas]sage, opening, or the like, affording a means of entering. [3.] The right or power of entering; admittance. **4.** The poin[t in] a play, ballet, etc., at which a performer is cued to ent[er].

en·trance[2] (in·trans′, -träns′) *v.t.* **·tranced, ·tranc·ing** To fill with rapture or wonder; delight; charm. **2.** To [put] into a trance. — **en·trance′ment** *n.* — **en·tranc′ing·ly** [*adv.*]

en·trance·way (en′trəns·wā′) *n.* A means of entrance.

en·trant (en′trənt) *n.* **1.** One who enters; a beginner. [2.] One who competes in a contest.

en·trap (in·trap′) *v.t.* **·trapped, ·trap·ping 1.** To catch i[n or] as in a trap. **2.** To trick into danger of difficulty; dece[ive;] ensnare. — **en·trap′ment** *n.*

en·treat (in·trēt′) *v.t.* **1.** To beseech with great intens[ity;] implore; beg. **2.** To make an earnest request of or for; p[eti]tion. — *v.i.* **3.** To ask earnestly. [< OF < *en-* in + *trai[tier]* to treat] — **en·treat′ing·ly** *adv.* — **en·treat′ment** *n.*

en·treat·y (in·trē′tē) *n. pl.* **·ies** An earnest request.

en·tre·chat (äṅ·trə·shȧ′) *n. French* In ballet, a leap [up]ward in which the dancer repeatedly crosses his feet.

en·trée (än′trā, *Fr.* äṅ·trā′) *n.* **1.** The act or privileg[e of] entering; entrance; admission. **2.** The principal course [of a] meal. **3.** In lavish or formal dinners, a dish served betw[een] the fish and meat courses or directly before the main cou[rse]. *Also U.S.* **en′tree.** [< F, orig. pp. of *entrer*. See ENTE[R]]

en·trench (in·trench′) *v.t.* **1.** To fortify or protect wit[h or] as with a trench or trenches. **2.** To establish firmly: [the] idea was *entrenched* in his mind. — *v.i.* **3.** To encroac[h;] trespass: with *on* or *upon*. — **en·trench′ment** *n.*

en·tre·pre·neur (än′trə·prə·nûr′, *Fr.* äṅ·trə·prə·nœr′) [*n.*] One who undertakes to start and conduct an enterpris[e or] business. [< F < *entreprendre*. See ENTERPRISE.]

en·tro·py (en′trə·pē) *n. Physics* **1.** A mathematical [ex]pression of the degree to which the energy of a thermo[dy]namic system is unavailable for conversion into work. [2.] The irreversible tendency of a system, including the u[ni]verse, toward increasing disorder; also, the final state [pre]dictable from this. [< Gk. < *en-* in + *trepein* to turn]

en·trust (in·trust′) *v.t.* **1.** To give over (something) [for] care, safekeeping, or performance. **2.** To place someth[ing] in the care or trust of. Also spelled *intrust*.

en·try (en′trē) *n. pl.* **·tries 1.** The act of coming in; [en]trance. **2.** A place of entrance; a small hallway or vestib[ule]. **3.** The act of entering anything in a register, list, etc.; a[lso] the item entered. **4.** The act of reporting at a customho[use] the arrival of a ship in port and the nature of her cargo. [5.] The act of assuming possession of lands or tenements [by] entering upon them. **6.** A contestant listed for a race, co[m]petition, etc. **7.** In bridge and whist, a card that will wi[n a] trick and place the lead in a specified hand: also *reentry*.

en·twine (in·twīn′) *v.t. & v.i.* **·twined, ·twin·ing** To tw[ine] around; twine or twist together: also spelled *intwine*.

e·nu·mer·ate (i·no͞o′mə·rāt, -nyo͞o′-) *v.t.* **·at·ed, ·at·ing** [1.] To name one by one; list. **2.** To ascertain the number [of.] [< L < *e-* out + *numerare* to count] — **e·nu′mer·a′tion** [*n.*] — **e·nu′mer·a′tive** *adj.* — **e·nu′mer·a′tor** *n.*

un·ci·ate (i·nun′sē·āt, -shē-) *v.* **·at·ed, ·at·ing** *v.t.* **1.** To ticulate (speech sounds), esp. in a clear and distinct manr. **2.** To state with exactness, as a theory or dogma. **3.** announce or proclaim. — *v.i.* **4.** To pronounce words, with distinct articulation. [< L < *e-* out + *nuntiare* to nounce] — **e·nun·ci·a·ble** (i·nun′sē·ə·bəl, -shē-) *adj.* — **nun′ci·a′tive, e·nun′ci·a·to′ry** (-sē·ə·tôr′ē, -tō′rē) *adj.* — **nun′ci·a′tive·ly** *adv.* — **e·nun′ci·a′tor** *n.*

un·ci·a·tion (i·nun′sē·ā′shən, -shē-) *n.* **1.** The utterance mode of utterance of speech sounds. **2.** A declaration.

u·re·sis (en′yə·rē′sis) *n. Pathol.* Involuntary urination. NL < Gk. < *en-* in + *oureein* to urinate]

vel·op (in·vel′əp) *v.t.* **·oped, ·op·ing** **1.** To wrap; enclose. To hide; conceal. **3.** To surround. [< OF < *en-* in + *uper* to wrap] — **en·vel′op·er** *n.*

ve·lope (en′və·lōp, än′-) *n.* **1.** A paper case or wrapper enclosing a letter or the like, usu. having a gummed flap sealing. **2.** Any enveloping cover or wrapper. **3.** *Aeron.* e outer fabric covering of a dirigible, balloon, etc.

vel·op·ment (in·vel′əp·mənt) *n.* **1.** The act of envelop-, or the state of being enveloped. **2.** A covering.

ven·om (en·ven′əm) *v.t.* **1.** To impregnate with venom; ison. **2.** To make vindictive; embitter.

vi·a·ble (en′vē·ə·bəl) *adj.* So admirable or desirable as arouse envy. — **en′vi·a·bly** *adv.*

vi·ous (en′vē·əs) *adj.* Full of, characterized by, or exssing envy. — **en′vi·ous·ly** *adv.* — **en′vi·ous·ness** *n.*

vi·ron (in·vī′rən) *v.t.* To extend around; encircle; surnd. [< F < *environ* around]

vi·ron·ment (in·vī′rən·mənt, -vī′ərn-) *n.* **1.** The exter- circumstances, conditions, and things that affect the stence and development of an individual, organism, or oup. **2.** The act of surrounding or being surrounded. **3.** rroundings. — **en·vi′ron·men′tal** *adj.*

vi·rons (in·vī′rəns) *n.pl.* A surrounding, outlying area, about a city; outskirts; suburbs.

vis·age (en·viz′ij) *v.t.* **·aged, ·ag·ing** **1.** To form a men- image of; visualize. **2.** To conceive of in advance; conplate. [< EN- + VISAGE] — **en·vis′age·ment** *n.*

vi·sion (en·vizh′ən) *v.t.* To see or foresee in the mind.

voy[1] (en′voi, än′-) *n.* **1.** A diplomatic representative of second class ranking next below an ambassador. **2.** A lomat on a special mission. **3.** Anyone entrusted with a ssion. [< F *envoyé* < OF < L *in-* + *via* way, road]

voy[2] (en′voi, än′-) *n.* The closing lines of a poem or ose work, often in the form of a dedication: also *l'envoie*, *woy.* Also **envoi.** [See ENVOY[1].]

vy (en′vē) *n. pl.* **·vies** **1.** A feeling of resentment or distent over another's superior attainments, endowments, possessions. **2.** A desire to possess the goods of another. Any object of envy. — *v.* **·vied, ·vy·ing** *v.t.* **1.** To regard th envy; feel envy because of: I *envy* you your calm. — **2.** To feel or show envy. [< OF < L < *in-* on + *videre* see, look] — **en′vi·er** *n.* — **en′vy·ing·ly** *adv.*

zyme (en′zīm, -zim) *n. Biochem.* A protein able to inite or accelerate specific chemical reactions in the metabon of plants and animals; an organic catalyst. Also **en′zym** im). [< L < Gk. < *en-* in + *zymē* leaven] — **en·zy·at·ic** (en′zī·mat′ik, -zi-) *adj.*

combining form Earliest; early part or early representae of. [< Gk. *ēos* dawn, daybreak]

·cene (ē′ə·sēn) *Geol. adj.* Of, pertaining to, or existing the Early Tertiary period of the Cenozoic era. — *n.* The cond epoch of the Cenozoic era. See chart for GEOLOGY. EO- + Gk. *kainos* new]

lith (ē′ə·lith) *n.* A stone tool of the earliest form; celt. EO- + Gk. *lithos* stone]

·lith·ic (ē′ə·lith′ik) *adj. Anthropol.* Of or pertaining to period of early human culture, known only by the rudest plements of bone and chipped stone.

n (ē′on, ē′ən) *n.* **1.** An incalculable period of time; an e; eternity. **2.** *Geol.* A time interval including two or more s. Also spelled *aeon.* [< L *aeon* < Gk. *aiōn* age]

s (ē′əs) In Greek mythology, the goddess of the dawn, ughter of Hyperion; identified with the Roman *Aurora.*

sin (ē′ə·sin) *n. Chem.* A reddish coloring matter, $C_{20}H_{8}Br_4O_5$, derived from coal tar, used for dyeing and as a ain in microscopy. Also **e′o·sine** (-sin, -sēn). [< Gk. *ēos* orning red, dawn + -IN] — **e′o·sin′ic** *adj.*

us *suffix* Of the nature of. [< L *-eus*]

·zo·ic (ē′ə·zō′ik) *adj. Geol.* Of or pertaining to the porn of Pre-Cambrian time immediately before the Paleozoic and showing the first signs of invertebrate life. [< EO- Gk. *zōē* life]

Var. of EPI-.

au·let (ep′ə·let) *n. Mil.* A shoulder ornament, as on litary and naval uniforms. Also **ep′au·lette.** [< F *épaule* < OF < LL < L < Gk. *spathē* blade]

é·pée (ā·pā′) *n.* A dueling sword with a sharp point and no cutting edge. [< F < OF < L] — **é·pée·ist** *n.*

eph- Var. of EPI-

e·phed·rine (i·fed′rin, ef′ə·drēn) *n. Chem.* An alkaloid, $C_{10}H_{15}ON$, used for relief of asthma, hay fever, nasal congestion, etc. Also **e·phed·rin** (i·fed′rin, ef′ə·drin). [< NL *Ephedra*, a genus of plants + -INE[2]]

e·phem·er·a (i·fem′ər·ə) *n. pl.* **·er·as** or **·er·ae** (-ə·rē) **1.** An ephemerid or May fly. **2.** Anything of very short life or duration. [< Gk. < *epi-* on + *hēmera* day]

e·phem·er·al (i·fem′ər·əl) *adj.* **1.** Lasting but a short time. **2.** Living one day only, as certain insects. — *n.* Anything lasting for a very short time. — **e·phem′er·al·ly** *adv.*

e·phem·er·id (i·fem′ər·id) *n.* A May fly.

E·phe·sian (i·fē′zhən) *adj.* Of or pertaining to Ephesus. — *n.* A citizen of Ephesus.

E·phe·sians (i·fē′zhəns) *n.pl.* (*construed as sing.*) A book of the New Testament, consisting of St. Paul's epistle to the church at Ephesus.

E·phra·im (ē′frē·əm, ē′frəm) In the Old Testament, Joseph's younger son, who obtained the birthright. *Gen.* xlvi 20. — *n.* **1.** The tribe of Israel descended from this son. *Josh.* xiv 4. **2.** The kingdom of Israel. — **E′phra·im·ite** *n.*

epi- *prefix* **1.** Upon; above; among; outside: *epidermis.* **2.** Besides; over; in addition to: *epilogue.* **3.** Near; close to; beside. Also: *ep-*, before vowels, as in *eponym*; *eph-*, before an aspirate, as in *ephemeral.* [< Gk. *epi* upon, on, besides]

ep·ic (ep′ik) *n.* **1.** A long, formal, narrative poem in elevated style, typically having as its subject heroic exploits and achievements or grandiose events. **2.** A novel, drama, etc., that in scale or subject resembles such a poem. — *adj.* **1.** Of, pertaining to, or suitable as a theme for an epic. **2.** Heroic; grandiose. Also **ep′i·cal** *adj.* [< L *epicus* < Gk. *epikos* < *epos* word, tale, song] — **ep′i·cal·ly** *adv.*

ep·i·ca·lyx (ep′ə·kā′liks, -kal′iks) *n. pl.* **·ca·lyx·es** or **·ca·ly·ces** (-kā′lə·sēz, -kal′ə-) *Bot.* An involucre resembling an accessory calyx and lying outside the true calyx of a flower.

ep·i·can·thus (ep′ə·kan′thəs) *n. pl.* **·thi** (-thī) A small fold of skin over the inner corner of the eye, typical of Mongoloid peoples. Also **epicanthic fold.** [< NL < Gk. *epi-* upon + *kanthos* corner of the eye] — **ep′i·can′thic** *adj.*

ep·i·car·di·um (ep′ə·kär′dē·əm) *n. pl.* **·di·a** (-dē·ə) *Anat.* The inner portion of the pericardium that is directly united with the substance of the heart. [< NL < Gk. *epi-* upon + *kardia* heart] — **ep′i·car′di·ac** (-ak), **ep′i·car′di·al** *adj.*

ep·i·carp (ep′ə·kärp) *n. Bot.* The outer layer of a pericarp.

ep·i·cene (ep′ə·sēn) *adj.* Belonging to or partaking of the characteristics of both sexes; hermaphrodite. — *n.* An epicene person. [< L < Gk. < *epi-* upon + *koinos* common]

ep·i·cen·ter (ep′ə·sen′tər) *n. Geol.* The point or area on the earth's surface directly above the focus of an earthquake.

ep·i·cure (ep′ə·kyŏŏr) *n.* One given to luxurious living and discriminating gratification of the senses; a sensualist; esp., a fastidious devotee of good food and drink; a gourmet. [after *Epicurus*, Greek philosopher] — **ep′i·cu·re′an** *adj.* & *n.*

Ep·i·cu·re·an·ism (ep′ə·kyŏŏ·rē′ən·iz′əm) *n.* The doctrines of Epicurus, Greek philosopher, who taught that the chief aims of life are pleasure regulated by temperance, peace of mind, and cultural pursuits. Also **Ep′i·cur·ism.** — **Ep′i·cu·re′an** *adj.* & *n.*

ep·i·cy·clic train (ep′ə·sī′klik, -sik′lik) *Mech.* A train of gear wheels in which, in addition to the motions of the wheels about their respective axes, one has a fixed axis about which the other axes revolve.

ep·i·dem·ic (ep′ə·dem′ik) *adj.* Breaking out suddenly in a particular area so as to affect many individuals at the same time: used esp. of contagious diseases. Also **ep′i·dem′i·cal.** — *n.* **1.** An epidemic disease. **2.** Anything temporarily widespread, as a fad. [< F < LL < Gk. < *epi-* among + *dēmos* people] — **ep′i·dem′i·cal·ly** *adv.*

ep·i·der·mis (ep′ə·dûr′mis) *n.* **1.** *Anat.* The outer, nonvascular covering of the skin: also called *cuticle.* **2.** Any of various other outer coverings. **3.** *Bot.* The outermost layer of cells covering the surface of a plant when there are several layers of tissue. Also **ep′i·derm.** [< NL < Gk. < *epi-* upon + *derma* skin] — **ep′i·der′mal, ep′i·der′mic** *adj.*

ep·i·der·moid (ep′ə·dûr′moid) *adj.* Of the nature of epidermis. Also **ep′i·der·moi′dal.**

ep·i·glot·tis (ep′ə·glot′is) *n. Anat.* A leaf-shaped, cartilaginous lid at the base of the tongue that covers the windpipe during the act of swallowing. [< NL < Gk. < *epi-* upon + *glōtta* tongue] — **ep′i·glot′tal** *adj.*

ep·i·gram (ep′ə·gram) *n.* **1.** A brief, clever, pointed remark or observation typically marked by antithesis. **2.** A short, pithy piece of verse with a witty, often satirical point. **3.** Epigrammatic expression. [< L < Gk. < *epi-* upon + *graphein* to write] — **ep·i·gram·mat·ic** (ep′i·grə·mat′ik) *adj.* — **ep′i·gram·mat′i·cal·ly** *adv.* — **ep′i·gram′ma·tist** *n.*

ep·i·graph (ep′ə·graf, -gräf) *n.* **1.** An inscription on a monument, tomb, etc. **2.** A quotation or motto prefixed to a book, etc. [< Gk. < *epi-* upon + *graphein* to write]

ep·i·graph·ic (ep′ə·graf′ik) *adj.* Of epigraphs or epigraphy. Also **ep′i·graph′i·cal.** — **ep′i·graph′i·cal·ly** *adv.*

e·pig·ra·phy (i·pig′rə·fē) *n.* **1.** The science that treats of the study, interpretation, etc., of inscriptions. **2.** Epigraphs collectively. — **e·pig′ra·pher, e·pig′ra·phist** *n.*

ep·i·lep·sy (ep′ə·lep′sē) *n. Pathol.* A disorder of cerebral function marked by attacks of unconsciousness with or without convulsions. See GRAND MAL, PETIT MAL. [< OF < LL < Gk. < *epi-* upon + *lambanein* to seize]

ep·i·lep·tic (ep′ə·lep′tik) *adj.* **1.** Of, relating to, or resembling epilepsy. **2.** Affected with epilepsy. — *n.* One affected with epilepsy. — **ep′i·lep′ti·cal·ly** *adv.*

ep·i·logue (ep′ə·lôg, -log) *n.* **1.** A short section appended to a novel, poem, etc., by way of commentary. **2.** A short speech appended to a play. Also **ep′i·log.** [< F < L < Gk. < *epi-* in addition + *legein* to say]

ep·i·neph·rine (ep′ə·nef′rin, -rēn) *n. Chem.* The active principle of the medullary portion of the adrenal glands, $C_9H_{13}O_3N$, used as a heart stimulant: also called *adrenalin.* Also **ep′i·neph′rin** (-rin). [< EPI- + Gk. *nephros* kidney]

E·piph·a·ny (i·pif′ə·nē) *n. Eccl.* A festival, held on January 6, commemorating the manifestation of Christ to the Gentiles as represented by the Magi: also called *Twelfth day.*

ep·i·phyte (ep′ə·fīt) *n. Bot.* A plant growing upon, but not receiving its nourishment from, another plant, as an orchid, moss, or lichen. — **ep′i·phyt′ic** (-fit′ik) or **·i·cal** *adj.*

e·pis·co·pa·cy (i·pis′kə·pə·sē) *n. pl.* **·cies 1.** Government of a church by bishops. **2.** The rank, office, or incumbency of a bishop; episcopate. **3.** Bishops, collectively. [< LL < Gk. < *epi-* over + *scopein* to look]

e·pis·co·pal (i·pis′kə·pəl) *adj.* **1.** Of, pertaining to, or governed by bishops. **2.** Advocating episcopacy. [< LL *episcopalis* < *episcopus*] — **e·pis′co·pal·ly** *adv.*

Episcopal Church The Protestant Episcopal Church.

E·pis·co·pa·li·an (i·pis′kə·pā′lē·ən, -pāl′yən) *n.* A member of the Protestant Episcopal Church. — *adj.* Belonging to the Protestant Episcopal Church, etc.; Episcopal.

e·pis·co·pate (i·pis′kə·pit, -pāt) *n.* **1.** The office, dignity, or term of office of a bishop. **2.** Bishops collectively.

ep·i·sode (ep′ə·sōd) *n.* **1.** A section of a novel, poem, etc., complete in itself. **2.** A part of a serialized story or play; installment. [< Gk. < *epi-* beside + *eisodos* entrance]

ep·i·sod·ic (ep′ə·sod′ik) *adj.* **1.** Of, relating to, or resembling an episode. **2.** Broken up into episodes; esp., disjointed. Also **ep′i·sod′i·cal.** — **ep′i·sod′i·cal·ly** *adv.*

e·pis·te·mol·o·gy (i·pis′tə·mol′ə·jē) *n. pl.* **·gies** The branch of philosophy that investigates the nature, limits, criteria, or validity of human knowledge; also, a particular theory of cognition. [< Gk. *epistēmē* knowledge + -LOGY] — **e·pis·te·mo·log·i·cal** (i·pis′tə·mə·loj′i·kəl) *adj.* — **e·pis′te·mo·log′i·cal·ly** *adv.* — **e·pis′te·mol′o·gist** *n.*

e·pis·tle (i·pis′əl) *n.* **1.** A letter, esp. when long or formal. **2.** *Usu. cap. Eccl.* **a** One of the letters written by an apostle. **b** A selection taken from one of these letters and read as part of a service. [OE < L < Gk. < *epi-* to + *stellein* to send]

e·pis·to·lar·y (i·pis′tə·ler′ē) *adj.* **1.** Of or relating to a letter or an Epistle. **2.** Included in or maintained by a letter.

ep·i·taph (ep′ə·taf, -täf) *n.* An inscription on a tomb or monument in memory of the dead. [< L < Gk. < *epi-* upon, at + *taphos* a tomb] — **ep′i·taph′ic** (-taf′ik) *adj.*

ep·i·the·li·um (ep′ə·thē′lē·əm) *n. pl.* **·li·ums** or **·li·a** (-lē·ə) *Biol.* A membranous tissue consisting of one or more layers of cells, serving to line the cavities and ducts of the body. [< NL < Gk. *epi-* upon + *thēlē* nipple] — **ep′i·the′li·al** *adj.*

ep·i·thet (ep′ə·thet) *n.* **1.** A descriptive word or phrase qualifying or used in place of the usual name of a person or thing. **2.** Loosely, any disparaging name. [< L < Gk. < *epi-* upon + *tithenai* to place] — **ep′i·thet′ic** or **·i·cal** *adj.*

e·pit·o·me (i·pit′ə·mē) *n.* **1.** A typical or extreme example; embodiment: the *epitome* of arrogance. **2.** A concise summary; abridgement. [< L < Gk. < *epi-* upon + *temnein* to cut]

e·pit·o·mize (i·pit′ə·mīz) *v.t.* **·mized, ·miz·ing** To make or be an epitome of. Also *Brit.* **e·pit′o·mise.** — **e·pit′o·miz′er** *n.*

ep·i·zo·ot·ic (ep′ə·zō·ot′ik) *adj.* Affecting many animals within a wide area: said esp. of diseases. — *n.* An epizootic disease: also **ep′i·zo′o·ty** (-zō′ə·tē).

e plu·ri·bus u·num (ē plŏŏr′ə·bəs yōō′nəm) *Latin* One out of many: motto of the U.S.

ep·och (ep′ək, *Brit.* ē′pok) *n.* **1.** A point in time marked by the beginning of a new development or state of things. **2.** An interval of time memorable for extraordinary events, important influences, unusual circumstances, etc. **3.** *Geol.* A minor subdivision of time; a time interval less than a period. See chart for GEOLOGY. **4.** *Astron.* A moment of time when a planet reaches a certain known position in relation to the sun, selected arbitrarily and thereafter used as a reference point. [< Gk. < *epi-* upon + *echein* to hold] — **ep′och·al** *adj.* — **ep′och·al·ly** *adv.*

ep·o·nym (ep′ə·nim) *n.* A real or legendary personage fr[om] whom a nation, city, epoch, theory, etc., is reputed to de[rive] its name. [< Gk. < *epi-* upon + *onyma* name] — **e·po·ny·mous** *adj.* — **e·pon′y·my** *n.*

e·pox·y (e·pok′sē) *n. Chem.* The radical -O-, esp. as bon[ded] to different atoms already joined in different ways, to f[orm] the durable, thermosetting **epoxy resins** much used for [var]nishes and adhesives. [< EP(I)- + OXY-[2]]

ep·si·lon (ep′sə·lon) *n.* The fifth letter and second vow[el of] the Greek alphabet (Ε, ε), corresponding to English sho[rt e]. See ALPHABET. [< Gk. *epsilon* < *e* e + *psilon* simple]

Epsom salts A hydrous magnesium sulfate, used as a pu[rgative] or to reduce inflammation. Also **Epsom salt.**

eq·ua·ble (ek′wə·bəl, ē′kwə-) *adj.* **1.** Not changing or v[ary]ing greatly; even. **2.** Not easily upset; tranquil. **3.** Ev[enly] proportioned; uniform. [< L *aequare* to make equal] — **eq′ua·bil′i·ty, eq′ua·ble·ness** *n.* — **eq′ua·bly** *adv.*

e·qual (ē′kwəl) *adj.* **1.** Identical in size, extent, etc. [2.] Having the same rights, rank, etc. **3.** Having the same a[bil]ities, degree of excellence, etc. **4.** Evenly proportioned; [bal]anced. **5.** Affecting or shared by all alike: *equal* rights. [6.] Having the requisite ability, power, etc.: with *to*: *equal* to [a] task. — *v.t.* **e·qualed** or **e·qualled, e·qual·ing** or **e·qual·[ling]** **1.** To be equal to; match. **2.** To do or produce someth[ing] equal to. **3.** To recompense in full. — *n.* A person or th[ing] equal to another. [< L *aequus* even] — **e′qual·ly** *ad[v.]*

e·qual·i·tar·i·an (i·kwol′ə·târ′ē·ən) *adj. & n.* Egalitar[ian]. — **e·qual′i·tar′i·an·ism** *n.*

e·qual·i·ty (i·kwol′ə·tē) *n. pl.* **·ties** The state or qualit[y of] being equal; also an instance of this.

e·qual·ize (ē′kwəl·īz) *v.t.* **·ized, ·iz·ing** To make equa[l or] uniform. — **e′qual·iz′er** *n.* — **e′qual·i·za′tion** *n.*

equal sign A sign (=) denoting numbers, quantities, [etc.] equal to one another.

e·qua·nim·i·ty (ē′kwə·nim′ə·tē, ek′wə-) *n.* Evennes[s of] mind or temper. [< L < *aequus* even + *animus* mind]

e·quate (i·kwāt′) *v.t.* **e·quat·ed, e·quat·ing 1.** To m[ake] equal; treat or consider as equivalent. **2.** To reduce [to a] common standard. **3.** *Math.* To indicate the equality [of;] express as an equation. [< L *aequus* even]

e·qua·tion (i·kwā′zhən, -shən) *n.* **1.** The process or ac[t of] making equal. **2.** The state of being equal. **3.** *Mat[h.]* [A] statement expressing (usu. by =) the equality of two qua[nti]ties. **4.** *Chem.* A symbolic representation of a chemica[l re]action, as $Na_2CO_3 + H_2SO_4 \rightarrow Na_2SO_4 + CO_2 + H_2O$

e·qua·tor (i·kwā′tər) *n.* **1.** The great circle of the eart[h, a] line lying in a plane perpendicular to the earth's polar a[xis.] **2.** Any similar circle, as of the sun. **3.** *Astron.* The cele[stial] equator. [< LL (*circulus*) *aequator* equalizer (circle)]

e·qua·to·ri·al (ē′kwə·tôr′ē·əl, -tō′rē) *adj.* **1.** Of, pertai[ning] to, or like the equator. **2.** Relating to conditions prevai[ling] at the earth's equator.

eq·uer·ry (ek′wər·ē) *n. pl.* **·ries 1.** An officer in charg[e of] the horses of a prince or nobleman. **2.** A personal attend[ant] on a member of the royal household of England. [Confus[ion] of F *écurie* stable (< OF *escuerie*) with OF *escuier* esqu[ire]]

e·ques·tri·an (i·kwes′trē·ən) *adj.* **1.** Pertaining to ho[rses] or horsemanship. **2.** Mounted on horseback; also, re[pre]senting someone as being on horseback: an *equestrian* [por]trait. — *n.* A rider on horseback, esp. when skilled. [< L *equus* horse] — **e·ques′tri·enne′** *n.fem.*

equi- *combining form* Equal; equally. [< L *aequus* eq[ual]]

e·qui·dis·tant (ē′kwə·dis′tənt) *adj.* Equally distant. — **e′qui·dis′tance** *n.* — **e′qui·dis′tant·ly** *adv.*

e·qui·lat·er·al (ē′kwə·lat′ər·əl) *n.* **1.** A side of equal len[gth] with another. **2.** A geometric figure with equal sides. [—] *adj.* Having all the sides equal. — **e′qui·lat′er·al·ly** *ad[v.]*

e·qui·li·brate (ē′kwə·lī′brāt, i·kwil′ə·brāt) *v.t. & v.i.* **·b[rat]ed, ·brat·ing 1.** To bring into or be in a state of equilibri[um.] **2.** To counterpoise. — **e′qui·li·bra′tion** *n.*

e·qui·lib·ri·um (ē′kwə·lib′rē·əm) *n.* **1.** *Physics* A stat[e of] balance between two or more forces acting within or upo[n a] body such that there is no change in the state of rest or [mo]tion of the body. **2.** Any state of balance, compromise[, or] adjustment. [< L < *aequus* equal + *libra* balance]

e·quine (ē′kwīn) *adj.* Of, pertaining to, or like a horse. [—] *n.* A horse. [< L < *equus* horse]

e·qui·noc·tial (ē′kwə·nok′shəl) *adj.* **1.** Occurring at [or] near the time of the equinox. **2.** Of or pertaining to [an] equinox. — *n. Meteorol.* A severe storm occurring usu[ally at] or near the time of the equinox.

equinoctial line *Astron.* The celestial equator.

e·qui·nox (ē′kwə·noks) *n.* One of two opposite points [at] which the sun crosses the celestial equator, when the d[ays] and nights are equal; also, the time of this crossing (ab[out] March 21, the **vernal** or **spring equinox,** and Sept. 21, [the] **autumnal equinox**). [< F < L < *aequus* equal + *nox* nig[ht]]

e·quip (i·kwip′) *v.t.* **e·quipped, e·quip·ping 1.** To furn[ish] or fit out with whatever is needed for any purpose or und[er]taking. **2.** To dress or attire. [< F < OF, prob. < O[N] *skipa* to outfit a vessel]

·ui·page (ek′wə·pij) *n.* **1.** The equipment for a camp, ·my, etc. **2.** A carriage, esp. when outfitted with horses, ;tendants, etc.

uip·ment (i·kwip′mənt) *n.* **1.** The act of equipping, or ıe state of being equipped. **2.** Material with which a per- ·n or organization is provided for some special purpose.

ui·poise (ē′kwə·poiz, ek′wə-) *n.* **1.** Equality of weight; ıual balance. **2.** A counterpoise.

·ui·ta·ble (ek′wə·tə·bəl) *adj.* **1.** Marked by equity; im- ırtially just, fair, and reasonable. **2.** *Law* Of, relating to, · valid in equity as distinguished from statute law and ımmon law. — **eq′ui·ta·ble·ness** *n.* — **eq′ui·ta·bly** *adv.*

·ui·ty (ek′wə·tē) *n. pl.* **·ties** **1.** Fairness or impartiality. . Something that is fair or equitable. **3.** *Law* **a** Justice ısed on the concepts of ethics and fairness. **b** A system of ırisprudence administered by courts of equity and designed ·imarily to mitigate the rigors of common law. **4.** In busi- ıss or property, the value remaining in excess of any liabil- y or mortgage. [< F < L *aequus* equal]

uiv·a·lent (i·kwiv′ə·lənt) *adj.* **1.** Equal in value, force, ıeaning, effect, etc. **2.** *Geom.* Equal in area, but not identi- ıl or congruent. **3.** *Chem.* Having the same valence or the ıme combining weight. — *n.* **1.** That which is equivalent. . *Chem.* The weight of an element that combines with or isplaces 1.008 grams of hydrogen. [< LL < L *aequus* equal · *valere* to be worth] — **e·quiv′a·lence, e·quiv′a·len·cy** *n.*

uiv·o·cal (i·kwiv′ə·kəl) *adj.* **1.** Having a doubtful mean- ıg; ambiguous. **2.** Of uncertain origin, character, value, c.; dubious. **3.** Questionable or suspicious: *equivocal* kind- ıss. [< LL < L *aequus* equal + *vox, vocis* voice] — **quiv′o·cal·ly** *adv.* — **e·quiv′o·cal·ness** *n.*

uiv·o·cate (i·kwiv′ə·kāt) *v.i.* **·cat·ed, ·cat·ing** To use ıbiguous language with intent to mislead or deceive. — **quiv′o·ca′tion** *n.* — **e·quiv′o·ca′tor** *n.* — **e·quiv′o·ca· ′ry** (-kə·tôr′ē, -tō′rē) *adj.*

· Assimilated var. of EN-[2].

·[1] *suffix of nouns* **1.** A person or thing that performs the ıtion of the root verb: *maker, reaper.* See -EE (def. 1). **2.** A ırson concerned with or practicing a trade or profession: *ographer, hatter.* **3.** One who lives in or comes from: *New orker, southerner.* **4.** A person, thing, or action related to · characterized by: *three-decker.* ◆ Nouns of agency are ınerally formed in English by adding *-er* to a verb, as in *ader*, but some such nouns have the suffix *-or*, as in *creditor, evator.* [OE < L *-arius, -arium*]

·[2] *suffix of nouns* A person or thing connected with: *grocer, ıiler.* [< AF, OF < L *-arius, -arium*]

·[3] *suffix* Forming the comparative degree of adjectives and lverbs: *harder, later.* [OE *-ra, -or*]

·[4] *suffix* Repeatedly: used in frequentative verbs: *stutter.*)E *-rian*]

·[5] *suffix of nouns* Denoting the action expressed by the ıot word: *rejoinder, waiver.* [< F *-er*, infinitive ending]

a (ir′ə, ē′rə) *n.* **1.** An extended period of time reckoned ıom some fixed point in the past and used as the basis of a ıronology: the Christian *era.* **2.** A period of time charac- ırized by certain events, conditions, influences, etc. **3.** The ıginning of a particular period; an epoch. **4.** *Geol.* A divi- on of geological history of highest rank. See chart for GE- LOGY. [< LL *aera* counters, orig. pl. of L *aes* brass, money]

·a·di·ate (i·rā′dē·āt) *v.t. & v.i.* **·at·ed, ·at·ing** To radiate. — **e·ra′di·a′tion** *n.*

·ad·i·cate (i·rad′ə·kāt) *v.t.* **·cat·ed, ·cat·ing** **1.** To pull up y the roots. **2.** To destroy utterly. [< L < *e-* out + *ıdix, -icis* a root] — **e·rad′i·ca·ble** (-kə·bəl) *adj.* — **e·rad′· ca′tion** *n.* — **e·rad′i·ca′tive** *adj.*

·ad·i·ca·tor (i·rad′ə·kā′tər) *n.* One who or that which ıradicates; esp., a preparation for removing ink, etc.

·ase (i·rās′) *v.t.* **e·rased, e·ras·ing** **1.** To obliterate, as by ıraping or rubbing out; efface. **2.** *U.S. Slang* To kill. [< , < *e-* out + *radere* to scrape] — **e·ras′a·ble** *adj.*

·as·er (i·rā′sər) *n.* Something used for erasing, as a piece f rubber, felt, etc.

·a·sure (i·rā′shər, -zhər) *n.* **1.** The act of erasing, or the ıate of being erased. **2.** That which is erased. **3.** A mark ıft on a surface by erasing something.

·a·to (er′ə·tō) The Muse of lyric and love poetry.

·bi·um (ûr′bē·əm) *n.* A metallic element (symbol Er) of ıe lanthanide series, found in gadolinite. See ELEMENT. [< L < (*Ytt*)*erby*, town in Sweden where first found]

e (âr) *Archaic & Poetic prep.* Prior to; before in time. — *ınj.* **1.** Before. **2.** Sooner than; rather than. [OE *ǣr*]

·e·bus (er′ə·bəs) In Greek mythology, a dark region ırough which the dead pass on their way to Hades.

·rect (i·rekt′) *v.t.* **1.** To put up (a building, etc.). **2.** To ıssemble the parts of; set up. **3.** To set upright; raise. **4.** 'o establish or found, as an empire. **5.** To work out or for- ıulate, as a theory or system. **6.** To make into; form: with *into.* — *v.i.* **7.** *Physiol.* To become rigidly upright, as through an influx of blood. — *adj.* **1.** Marked by a vertical position or posture; upright. **2.** Directed or pointed upward. [< L < *e-* out + *regere* to direct] — **e·rect′ly** *adv.* — **e·rect′ness** *n.* — **e·rec′tion** *n.*

e·rec·tile (i·rek′təl, -til) *adj.* Capable of becoming erected.

e·rec·tor (i·rek′tər) *n.* **1.** One who or that which erects. **2.** *Anat.* Any of various muscles that stiffen or hold up a part of the body. Also **e·rect′er.**

erg (ûrg) *n.* *Physics* In the cgs system, the unit of work and of energy, being the work done in moving a body one centimeter against the force of one dyne. [< Gk. *ergon* work]

er·go (ûr′gō) *conj. & adv.* *Latin* Hence; therefore. [< L]

er·got (ûr′gət) *n.* **1.** A fungus sometimes replacing the grain in rye and other cereal grasses. **2.** The disease caused by this fungus growth. **3.** The dried sclerotia of rye ergot, used in medicine to contract involuntary muscle and to check hemorrhage. [< F < OF *argot* spur of a cock]

E·rid·a·nus (i·rid′ə·nəs) *n.* A constellation, the River. [< L, the Po river]

E·rie (ir′ē) *n. pl.* **E·rie** or **E·ries** One of a tribe of North American Indians of Iroquoian stock, formerly inhabiting the southern shores of Lake Erie.

Er·in (âr′in, ir′in) *Chiefly Poetic* Ireland.

erl·king (ûrl′king′) *n.* In Germanic folklore, an evil spirit, malicious toward children. [< G *erlkönig*, wrong trans. of Dan. *ellerkonge, elverkonge* king of the elves]

er·mine (ûr′min) *n.* **1.** One of several weasels of the northern hemisphere, having brown fur that in winter turns white with a black tip on the tail. **2.** The white fur of the ermine, used in Europe for the facings of the official robes of judges, etc. **3.** The rank or functions of a judge. [< OF (*h*)*ermine*, ? < Gmc.] — **er′mined** *adj.*

ERMINE (*def.* 1) (Body 9 to 12 inches long; tail 3 to 3½ inches)

erne (ûrn) *n.* A sea eagle. Also **ern.** [OE *earn*]

e·rode (i·rōd′) *v.* **e·rod·ed, e·rod·ing** *v.t.* **1.** To wear away gradually by constant friction; wear down by scraping, rubbing, etc. **2.** To eat into; corrode. **3.** To make (a channel, gully, etc.) by wearing away or eating into. — *v.i.* **4.** To become eroded. [< L < *e-* off + *rodere* to gnaw]

Er·os (ir′os, er′os) In Greek mythology, the god of love, son of Aphrodite: identified with the Roman *Cupid.*

e·ro·sion (i·rō′zhən) *n.* **1.** The act of eroding, or the state of being eroded. **2.** *Geol.* The wearing away of the earth's surface by the action of wind, water, glaciers, etc.

e·ro·sive (i·rō′siv) *adj.* **1.** Eroding or tending to erode. **2.** Caustic or corrosive. Also **e·ro·dent** (i·rōd′nt).

e·rot·ic (i·rot′ik) *adj.* **1.** Of, pertaining to, or concerned with sexual love; amatory. **2.** Designed to arouse sexual desire. **3.** Strongly moved by sexual desire. — *n.* **1.** An erotic person. **2.** An erotic poem. [< Gk. < *erōs, -erōtos* love] — **e·rot′i·cal·ly** *adv.* — **e·rot′i·cism** *n.*

err (ûr, er) *v.i.* **erred, err·ing** **1.** To make a mistake. **2.** To go astray morally. [< OF < L *errare* to wander] — **err′ing** *adj.* — **err′ing·ly** *adv.*

er·rand (er′ənd) *n.* **1.** A trip made to carry a message or perform some task, usu. for someone else. **2.** The business or purpose of such a trip. [OE *ǣrende* message, news]

er·rant (er′ənt) *adj.* **1.** Roving or wandering, esp. in search of adventure. **2.** Straying from the proper course or standard. [< OF < L *iter* journey] — **er′rant·ly** *adv.*

er·rat·ic (i·rat′ik) *adj.* **1.** Not conforming to usual standards; eccentric. **2.** Lacking a fixed or certain course; straying. **3.** *Geol.* Transported from the original site by glaciers, currents, etc. — *n.* An erratic person or thing. [< L < *errare* to wander] — **er·rat′i·cal·ly** *adv.*

er·ra·tum (i·rä′təm, i·rā′təm) *n. pl.* **·ra·ta** (-rä′tə, -rā′tə) An error, as in writing or printing. [< L]

er·ro·ne·ous (ə·rō′nē·əs, e·rō′-) *adj.* Marked by error; incorrect. — **er·ro′ne·ous·ly** *adv.* — **er·ro′ne·ous·ness** *n.*

er·ror (er′ər) *n.* **1.** Something done, said, or believed incorrectly; a mistake **2.** The condition of deviating from what is correct or true in judgment, belief, or action. **3.** An offense against morals; sin. **4.** In baseball, a misplay by a member of the team not batting. **5.** *Math.* **a** The difference between the observed value of a magnitude and the true or mean value. **b** Any deviation from the true or mean value not due to gross blunders of observation or measurement.

er·satz (er·zäts′, er′zäts) *adj.* Substitute, and usu. inferior. — *n.* A usu. inferior substitute. [< G]

Erse (ûrs) *n.* **1.** Scottish Gaelic. **2.** Irish Gaelic. — *adj.* Of or pertaining to the Celts of Ireland or Scotland or their language. [Var. of IRISH]

erst (ûrst) *Archaic adv.* **1.** Formerly; long ago. **2.** In the beginning. — *adj.* First. [OE *ǣrest*, superl. of *ǣr* before]

erst·while (ûrst′hwīl′) *adj.* Former: an *erstwhile* colleague.
e·ruct (i·rukt′) *v.t. & v.i.* To belch. Also **e·ruc′tate.** [< L < *e-* out + *ructare* to belch] — **e·ruc′ta′tion** *n.* — **e·ruc′·ta·tive** *adj.*
er·u·dite (er′yŏŏ·dīt, er′ŏŏ-) *adj.* Very learned; scholarly. [< L < *e-* out + *rudis* untrained] — **er′u·dite·ly** *adv.* — **er′u·dite·ness** *n.*
er·u·di·tion (er′yŏŏ·dish′ən, er′ŏŏ-) *n.* Great learning.
e·rupt (i·rupt′) *v.i.* **1.** To cast forth lava, steam, etc., as a volcano or geyser. **2.** To be cast forth from a volcano, geyser, etc. **3.** To burst forth suddenly and violently. **4.** To show a rash or become covered with pimples, etc. **5.** Of new teeth, to break through the gums. — *v.t.* **6.** To make erupt. **7.** To cast forth (lava, etc.). [< L < *e-* out + *rumpere* to burst] — **e·rup′tion** *n.* — **e·rup′tive** *adj.*
-ery *suffix of nouns* **1.** A business, place of business, or place where something is done: *brewery.* **2.** A place or residence for: *nunnery.* **3.** A collection of things: *finery.* **4.** The qualities, principles, or practices of: *snobbery.* **5.** An art, trade, or profession: *cookery.* **6.** A state, or condition of being: *slavery.* Also *-ry*, as in *jewelry.* [< OF < *-ier* (< L *-arius*) + *-ie* < L *-ia*]
erythro- *combining form* Red. Also, before vowels, **erythr-.** [< Gk. *erythros* red]
e·ryth·ro·cyte (i·rith′rō·sīt) *n. Anat.* A disk-shaped red blood cell formed in bone marrow; it contains hemoglobin and transports oxygen to all tissues of the body. — **e·ryth′·ro·cyt′ic** (-sit′ik) *adj.*
es- *prefix* Out: used in words borrowed from Old French: *escape, escheat.* [< OF < L *ex* from, out of]
-es[1] An inflectional ending used to form the plural of nouns ending in a sibilant (*fuses, fishes*), an affricate (*witches*), or, in some cases, a vowel. Compare -s[1]. [OE *-as*]
-es[2] An inflectional ending used to form the third person singular present indicative of verbs ending in a sibilant, affricate, or vowel: *goes, poaches.* Compare -s[2]. [ME *-es*]
E·sau (ē′sô) The eldest son of Isaac, who sold his birthright to his brother Jacob. *Gen.* xxv 25. [< Hebrew *'ēsāw* hairy]
es·ca·drille (es′kə·dril′, *Fr.* es·kȧ·drē′y′) *n.* **1.** In France, a unit of military airplanes. **2.** A squadron of naval vessels. [< F, dim. of *escadre* squadron]
es·ca·late (es′kə·lāt) *v.t. & v.i.* **·lat·ed, ·lat·ing 1.** To increase or be increased gradually: to *escalate* a war. **2.** To ascend an escalator. [Back formation < ESCALATOR] — **es′ca·la′tion** *n.*
es·ca·la·tor (es′kə·lā′tər) *n.* A moving stairway built on the conveyor-belt principle.
es·cal·lop (e·skol′əp, e·skal′-) *n.* Scallop. — *v.t.* To scallop.
es·ca·pade (es′kə·pād) *n.* **1.** A brief piece of reckless behavior or prankish disregard of convention; fling; spree. **2.** An act of getting away from rigid restraint or confinement. [< F < Sp. < *escapar* to escape]
es·cape (ə·skāp′, e·skāp′) *v.* **·caped, ·cap·ing** *v.i.* **1.** To get free from confinement, restraint, or capture. **2.** To manage to avoid some danger or evil. **3.** To come out gradually from a container or enclosure, as by seeping, leaking, etc. **4.** To fade away and disappear; vanish. — *v.t.* **5.** To get away from (prison, captors, etc.). **6.** To succeed in avoiding (capture, harm, etc.). **7.** To get away from the notice or recollection of: No detail *escaped* him. **8.** To slip out from unintentionally: A cry *escaped* his lips. — *n.* **1.** The act of escaping, or the fact of having escaped. **2.** A means of escaping something: Drinking is an *escape* for him. **3.** A gradual leaking or seeping. — *adj.* **1.** That provides a means of getting away from reality, etc.; escapist: *escape* literature. **2.** That provides a means of lessening or avoiding liability, etc.: an *escape* clause in a contract. [< AF < L *ex-* out + *cappa* cloak] — **es·cap′a·ble** *adj.*
es·cap·ee (es′kā·pē′, ə·skā′pē, e·skā′pē) *n.* One who has escaped, as from prison.
es·cape·ment (ə·skāp′mənt, e·skāp′-) *n.* **1.** *Mech.* A device used in timepieces for securing a uniform movement, consisting of a notched escape wheel that is released one tooth at a time by a small lock. **2.** A typewriter mechanism controlling the horizontal movement of the carriage.
escape velocity *Physics* The minimum velocity a body must attain to escape a gravitational field: on the earth this velocity is approximately 7 miles per second.
escape wheel *Mech.* A notched wheel in an escapement.
es·cap·ism (ə·skā′piz·əm, e·skā′-) *n.* A desire or tendency to escape unpleasant reality by resorting to diversions, or by indulging in daydreaming.
es·cap·ist (ə·skā′pist, e·skā′-) *adj.* Catering to or providing a means of indulging in escapism: *escapist* literature. — *n.* One given to escapism.
es·ca·role (es′kə·rōl) *n.* A variety of endive whose leaves are used for salads. [< F < ML *escarius* fit for eating]
es·carp·ment (es·kärp′mənt) *n.* **1.** A precipitous artificial slope about a fortification or position. **2.** A steep slope or drop; esp., the precipitous face of a line of cliffs.
-esce *suffix of verbs* To become or grow; begin to be or do (what is indicated by the main element): *phosphore*[sce]
[< L *-escere*, suffix of inceptive verbs]
-escence *suffix of nouns* Forming nouns of state or qua[lity] corresponding to adjectives in *-escent.* [< L *-escentia*]
-escent *suffix of adjectives* Beginning to be, have, or (what is indicated by the main element): *effervescent.* [< *-escens, -escentis*, suffix of ppr. of inceptive verbs]
es·cheat (es·chēt′) *Law n.* **1.** Reversion of property to state or to the crown in default of legal heirs or other qu[ali]fied claimants. **2.** Property entering possession of state, etc., by this process. — *v.i. & v.t.* To revert or ca[use] to revert to the state, etc., by escheat. [< OF < *es-* out *cheoir* to fall] — **es·cheat′a·ble** *adj.*
es·chew (es·chōō′) *v.t.* To shun, as something unworthy injurious. [< OF *eschiver*] — **es·chew′al** *n.*
es·cort (*n.* es′kôrt; *v.* es·kôrt′) *n.* **1.** An individual or gr[oup] of individuals accompanying another so as to give prot[ec]tion or guidance. **2.** A male who takes a girl or woman t[o a] dance, party, etc. **3.** One or more planes, ships, cars, e[tc.] moving along with another so as to give protection, gu[id]ance, etc. — *v.t.* To accompany in the capacity of escort. [< F < Ital. *scorgere* to lead]
es·cri·toire (es′kri·twär′) *n.* A writing desk; secreta[ry]. [< OF < LL *scriptorium* place for writing]
es·crow (es′krō, es·krō′) *n. Law* **1.** A written deed, c[on]tract, etc., placed in the custody of a third party and ef[fec]tive upon fulfillment of a stipulated condition. **2.** [The] condition of being an escrow: a bond in *escrow.* [< *escrowe*, OF *escroe* scroll]
es·cu·do (es·kōō′dō; *Pg.* ish·kōō′thōō; *Sp.* es·kōō′thō) *n.* **·dos** (-dōz; *Pg.* -thōōs; *Sp.* -thōs) The monetary unit [of] Portugal, containing 100 centavos: in 1960 worth abou[t] U.S. cents. [< Pg. < L *scutum* shield]
es·cu·lent (es′kyə·lənt) *adj.* Edible. — *n.* Anyth[ing] edible, esp. a plant. [< L *esca* food]
es·cutch·eon (i·skuch′ən) *n. Heraldry* A usu. shield-sha[ped] surface carrying armorial bearings. Also *scutcheon.* [< < L *scutum* shield]
Es·dras (ez′drəs) The Douai Bible name for EZRA. — In the Douai Bible, either of two books of the Old Tes[ta]ment. I Esdras corresponds to the book of Ezra, and Esdras corresponds to the book of Nehemiah. [< Gk.]
-ese *suffix of nouns and adjectives* **1.** A native or inhabit[ant] of: *Milanese.* **2.** The language or dialect of: *Chin[ese].* **3.** Originating in: *Tirolese.* **4.** In the manner or style [of:] *journalese.* [< OF *-eis, -ese* < L *-ensis*]
Es·ki·mo (es′kə·mō) *n. pl.* **·mos** or **·mo 1.** One of a M[on]goloid people indigenous to the Arctic coasts of No[rth] America, Greenland, and NE Siberia. **2.** The language [of] the Eskimos. — *adj.* Of or relating to the Eskimos, th[eir] language, or their culture. Also spelled *Esquimau.* Dan. (< F *Esquimaux*) < N. Am. Ind., eaters of raw fle[sh]
Es·ki·mo·an (es′kə·mō′ən) *adj.* Eskimo. Also **Es′ki·mau′a[n]**
Eskimo dog One of a breed of large, sturdy, broad-ches[ted] dogs used by the Eskimos to draw sledges.
e·soph·a·gus (i·sof′ə·gəs) *n. pl.* **·gi** (-jī) *Anat.* The tu[be] through which food passes from the mouth to the stoma[ch;] gullet: also spelled *oesophagus.* For illus. see MOUTH, THRO[AT] [< NL < Gk. *oisophagos*] — **e·so·phag·e·al** (ē′sō·faj′ē[·əl,] i·sof′ə·jē′əl) or **e·soph′a·gal** (-ə·gəl) *adj.*
es·o·ter·ic (es′ə·ter′ik) *adj.* **1.** Understood by or mea[nt] for only a few specially instructed or initiated individua[ls:] *esoteric* doctrine. **2.** Confidential; kept secret: an *esote[ric]* motive. — **Syn.** See MYSTERIOUS. [< Gk. *esōterikos* inn[er]] — **es′o·ter′i·cal·ly** *adv.*
ESP Extrasensory perception.
es·pal·ier (es·pal′yər) *n.* **1.** A trellis or other flat fram[e]work on which small trees, shrubs, etc., are trained to gro[w]. **2.** A tree or row of plants so trained. — *v.t.* To furnish w[ith] an espalier. [< F < Ital. < L *spatula* shoulder]
es·pe·cial (es·pesh′əl) *adj.* Preeminent in place or degr[ee;] very special. [< OF < L *species* kind, type]
es·pe·cial·ly (es·pesh′əl·ē) *adv.* To a very special exte[nt] or degree; particularly: *especially* frequent; *especially* go[od].
Es·pe·ran·to (es′pə·rän′tō, -ran′tō) *n.* An artificial la[n]guage having a vocabulary based on words in the ma[jor] European languages. [after pseudonym of the inventor]
es·pi·al (es·pī′əl) *n.* **1.** The act of noticing something, the fact of being noticed. **2.** The act of spying upon. [< OF *espier* to look]
es·pi·o·nage (es′pē·ə·nij′, -näzh′; *Fr.* es·pyô·näzh′) *n.* The practice of spying. **2.** The work of spies; esp., t[he] securing of secret information. [< F *espier* to espy]
es·pla·nade (es′plə·nād′, -näd′) *n.* **1.** A level, open stret[ch] of land, as along a shore, used as a roadway or public wa[lk]. **2.** An open embankment or level area before a fortre[ss.] [< F < Sp. < L < *ex-* out + *planus* level]
es·pou·sal (es·pou′zəl) *n.* **1.** Adoption or support, as of [a] cause. **2.** A betrothal. **3.** *Often pl.* A marriage ceremon[y].
es·pouse (es·pouz′) *v.t.* **·poused, ·pous·ing 1.** To ma[ke] one's own; support, as a cause or doctrine. **2.** To take as

ouse; marry. **3.** To give in marriage. [< OF < L *ondere* to promise] **— es·pous′er** *n.*
pres·so (es·pres′ō) *n.* *pl.* **·sos** Coffee brewed from rkly roasted beans by steam pressure. [< Ital. *espresso*]
prit (es·prē′) *n.* Spirit; wit. [< F < L *spiritus*]
prit de corps (də kôr) *French* A spirit of enthusiastic votedness to and support of the common goals of a group.
py (es·pī′) *v.t.* **·pied, ·py·ing** To catch sight of (some-ing); see; descry. [< OF *espier* to look, spy]
que *suffix of adjectives* Having the manner or style of; sembling; like: *picturesque.* [< F < Ital. < L *-iscus*]
·qui·mau (es′kə·mō) *n.* *pl.* **·maux** (-mōz) See ESKIMO.
quire (es·kwīr′; *for n., also* es′kwīr) *n.* **1.** *Usu. cap.* A tle of courtesy or respect sometimes written abbreviated ter a man's surname: John Smith, *Esq.* **2.** In England, a an ranking just below a knight. **3.** A squire or young candi-te for knighthood. [< OF < LL *scutarius* shield-bearer]
s *suffix* Used to form the feminine of many nouns: *god-ss, lioness.* [< F *-esse* < LL *-issa* < Gk.]
say (*n. def. 1* es′ā; *n. defs. 2 and 3* es′ā, e·sā′; *v.* e·sā′) *n.* A short composition dealing with a single topic and pically personal in approach. **2.** An attempt; endeavor. *v.t.* **1.** To attempt to do or accomplish; try. **2.** To test e nature, etc., of. [< OF *essai* trial] **— es·say′er** *n.*
say·ist (es′ā·ist) *n.* A writer of essays.
sence (es′əns) *n.* **1.** That in which the real nature of a ing consists; intrinsic or fundamental nature. **2.** The stinctive quality of something. **3.** *Philos.* A real or true bstance. **4.** An immaterial being; spirit. **5.** An extract, of a plant or food, containing the distinctive properties of e plant; also, an alcoholic solution of such an extract. A perfume. [< F < L *esse* to be]
sen·tial (ə·sen′shəl) *adj.* **1.** Of, belonging to, or con-tuting the intrinsic nature of something. **2.** Extremely portant; vital; indispensable. **3.** Derived from the tract of a plant, etc.: an *essential* oil. **4.** Complete, total, absolute. **— *n.*** Something fundamental, indispensable, extremely important. **— es·sen′tial·ly** *adv.*
sen·ti·al·i·ty (ə·sen′shē·al′ə·tē) *n.* *pl.* **·ties** **1.** The state quality of being essential. **2.** Something essential.
sential oil Any of a group of volatile oils that give to ants their characteristic odors, flavors, etc.
t[1] *suffix* Forming the superlative degree of adjectives d adverbs: *hardest, latest.* [OE *-ast, -est, -ost*]
t[2] An archaic inflectional ending used in the second rson singular present and past indicative, with *thou*: *test, walkest.* Also, in contracted forms, *-st,* as in *hast, dst.* [OE *-est, -ast*]
tab·lish (ə·stab′lish) *v.t.* **1.** To make secure, stable, or rmanent. **2.** To set up, found, or institute: to *establish* government. **3.** To install: to *establish* oneself in a new me. **4.** To initiate and cause to last: to *establish* a prece-nt. **5.** To cause to be recognized and accepted: to *estab-h* oneself as a writer. **6.** To clear from doubt; demon-rate; prove. **8.** To cause to be the official church of a ate. [< OF < L *stabilis* stable] **— es·tab′lish·er** *n.*
ablished church A church recognized by a government d supported in part by public funds.
tab·lish·ment (ə·stab′lish·mənt) *n.* **1.** The act of tablishing, or the state or fact of being established. **2.** mething established, as a business, residence, etc. **— the stablishment** Those collectively who occupy positions of fluence and status in a society.
tate (ə·stāt′) *n.* **1.** A usu. extensive piece of landed operty or the residence built on it. **2.** One's entire prop-ty and possessions. **3.** A particular condition or state: rise to high *estate*; man's *estate.* **4.** A particular class of rsons with distinct political or social status, rights, and wers. **5.** *Law* The degree, nature, and extent of owner-ip or use of property. [< OF < L *status* a state]
teem (ə·stēm′) *v.t.* **1.** To have a high opinion of; value eatly. **2.** To think of as; rate. **— *n.*** **1.** High regard or spect. **2.** Judgment. [< F < L *aestimare* to value]
ter (es′tər) *n.* *Chem.* Any of a class of organic com-unds formed by the reaction of an acid with an alcohol. Coined by Leopold Gmelin, 1788–1853, German chemist]
·ther (es′tər) In the Old Testament, the Jewish queen, ife of King Ahasuerus (Xerxes) of Persia, who saved her eople from massacre. **— *n.*** A book of the Old Testament ntaining her story. [< Hebrew *ester,* ? < Babylonian]
·thete (es′thēt) *n.* **1.** One who is very responsive to eauty in art, nature, etc. **2.** One who cultivates an ex-avagant, usu. artificial admiration for beauty and art. lso *Brit., aesthete.* [< Gk. *aisthētēs* one who perceives]
·thet·ic (es·thet′ik) *adj.* **1.** Of or relating to esthetics. Of or relating to the beauty in art, nature, etc. **3.** Keenly sponsive to beauty in art, nature, etc. Also spelled *aes-etic*: also **es·thet′i·cal.** **— es·thet′i·cal·ly** *adv.*

es·thet·i·cism (es·thet′ə·siz′əm) *n.* **1.** A particular theory or outlook relating to the nature, forms, and importance of beauty. **2.** Keen responsiveness to and appreciation of beauty in art, etc. Also spelled *aestheticism.*
es·thet·ics (es·thet′iks) *n.pl.* (*construed as sing.*) **1.** A branch of philosophy relating to the nature and forms of beauty. **2.** Study of the mental and emotional responses to the beauty in art, etc. Also spelled *aesthetics.*
es·ti·ma·ble (es′tə·mə·bəl) *adj.* **1.** Worthy of respect or admiration. **2.** That may be estimated or calculated. **— es′ti·ma·ble·ness** *n.* **— es′ti·ma·bly** *adv.*
es·ti·mate (*v.* es′tə·māt; *n.* es′tə·mit) *v.* **·mat·ed, ·mat·ing** *v.t.* **1.** To form an approximate opinion of (size, amount, number, etc.). **2.** To form an opinion about; judge. **— *v.i.*** **3.** To make or submit an estimate. **— *n.*** **1.** A rough cal-culation based on incomplete data. **2.** A preliminary state-ment of the approximate cost for certain work. **3.** A judg-ment or opinion. [< L *aestimare* to value] **— es′ti·ma′·tive** *adj.* **— es′ti·ma′tor** *n.*
es·ti·ma·tion (es′tə·mā′shən) *n.* **1.** The act of estimating. **2.** A conclusion arrived at by estimating. **3.** Esteem; re-gard: I hold him in high *estimation.*
es·ti·val (es′tə·vəl, es·tī′-) *adj.* Of or pertaining to summer.
es·ti·vate (es′tə·vāt) *v.i.* **·vat·ed, ·vat·ing** To pass the summer in a dormant state. [< L *aestivare* to spend the summer] **— es′ti·va′tion** *n.* **— es′ti·va′tor** *n.*
Es·to·ni·an (es·tō′nē·ən) *adj.* Of or pertaining to Estonia. **— *n.*** **1.** One of a people inhabiting Estonia and part of Livonia. **2.** The Finno-Ugric language of this people.
es·trange (es·trānj′) *v.t.* **·tranged, ·trang·ing** **1.** To make (someone previously friendly or affectionate) indifferent or hostile; alienate. **2.** To remove or dissociate (oneself, etc.). [< OF < L *extraneus* foreign] **— es·trange′ment** *n.*
es·tro·gen (es′trə·jən) *n.* *Biochem.* Any of various sub-stances that influence estrus or produce changes in the sexual characteristics of female mammals: also spelled *oestrogen.* **— es′tro·gen′ic** (-jen′ik) *adj.*
es·trus (es′trəs, ēs′-) *n.* **1.** *Biol.* **a** The entire cycle of physi-ological changes in female mammals, preparing the genera-tive organs for their fertile period. **b** The peak of the sexual cycle, culminating in ovulation; heat. Also called *oestrum*: also spelled *oestrus.* Also **es′trum** (-trum). [< L *oestrus* frenzy, passion < Gk. *oistros* gadfly]
es·tu·ar·y (es′chōō·er′ē) *n.* *pl.* **·ar·ies** **1.** A wide mouth of a river where its current meets the sea and is influenced by the tides. **2.** An inlet or arm of the sea. [< L < *aestus* tide] **— es′tu·ar′i·al** (-âr′ē·əl) *adj.*
-et *suffix* Small; little: *islet*: often without appreciable force, as in *sonnet.* [< F]
e·ta (ā′tə, ē′-) *n.* The seventh letter and third vowel in the Greek alphabet (Η, η), corresponding to English long *e.* See ALPHABET. [< Gk. *ēta* < Phoenician *hēth*]
et cet·er·a (et set′ər·ə, set′rə) And other things; and the rest; and so forth. Also **et caet′er·a.** Abbr. *etc., &c.* [< L]
etch (ech) *v.t.* **1.** To engrave by means of acid or other cor-rosive fluid, esp. in making a design on a plate for printing. **2.** To outline or sketch by scratching lines with a pointed instrument. **— *v.i.*** **3.** To engage in etching. [< Du. *etsen* < G *ätzen* < OHG *ezjan* to corrode] **— etch′er** *n.*
etch·ing (ech′ing) *n.* **1.** A process of engraving in which lines are scratched with a needle on a plate covered with wax or other coating, and the parts exposed are subjected to the corrosive action of an acid. **2.** A figure or design formed by etching. **3.** An impression from an etched plate.
e·ter·nal (i·tûr′nəl) *adj.* **1.** Existing without beginning or end; forever existent. **2.** Unending: *eternal* happiness. **3.** Valid and true for and beyond all time. **4.** Seemingly end-less. **— the Eternal** God. [< OF < LL < L *aevum* age] **— e·ter′nal·ly** *adv.* **— e·ter′nal·ness** *n.*
Eternal City Rome.
e·ter·ni·ty (i·tûr′nə·tē) *n.* *pl.* **·ties** **1.** Existence without beginning or end; endless duration. **2.** An immeasurable extent of time. **3.** The endless time following death.
e·ter·nize (i·tûr′nīz) *v.t.* **·nized, ·niz·ing** **1.** To make eter-nal. **2.** To perpetuate the fame of; immortalize. Also **e·ter′·nal·ize** (-nəl·īz). **— e·ter′ni·za′tion** *n.*
eth (eth) See EDH.
-eth[1] An archaic inflectional ending used in the third person singular present indicative of some verbs: *eateth, drinketh.* Also, in contracted forms, *-th,* as in *hath, doth.* [OE *-eth, -ath*]
-eth[2] *suffix* Var. of -TH[2].
eth·ane (eth′ān) *n. Chem.* A colorless, odorless, gaseous hy-drocarbon, C_2H_6, of the methane series contained in crude petroleum and in illuminating gas. [< ETHER]
eth·a·nol (eth′ə·nōl, -nol) *n. Chem.* An alcohol, C_2H_5OH, obtained by the distillation of certain fermented sugars or starches, the intoxicant in liquors, wines, and beers: also called *ethyl alcohol, grain alcohol.* [< ETHANE + -OL[1]]

e·ther (ē′thər) *n.* **1.** Ethyl ether. **2.** *Chem.* Any of a group of organic compounds in which an oxygen atom is joined with two organic radicals. **3.** A solid or semisolid medium formerly assumed to pervade all of space: also spelled *aether.* **4.** The clear, upper regions of space: also spelled *aether.* [< L *aether* sky]

e·the·re·al (i·thir′ē·əl) *adj.* **1.** Resembling ether or air; airy. **2.** Delicate or exquisite in line, feature, etc.: an *ethereal* face. **3.** Spiritual; celestial. **4.** Of or existing in the upper regions. **5.** *Chem.* Of or pertaining to ether. — **e·the′re·al·ly** *adv.* — **e·the′re·al′i·ty** (-əl′ə·tē), **e·the′re·al·ness** *n.*

e·the·re·al·ize (i·thir′ē·əl·īz′) *v.t.* **·ized, ·iz·ing** To make ethereal; spiritualize. — **e·the′re·al·i·za′tion** *n.*

e·ther·ize (ē′thə·rīz) *v.t.* **·ized, ·iz·ing** To subject to the fumes of ether; anesthetize. — **e′ther·i·za′tion** *n.*

eth·ic (eth′ik) *n.* A philosophy or system of morals; ethics. — *adj.* Ethical; moral. [< L < Gk. *ēthos* character]

eth·i·cal (eth′i·kəl) *adj.* **1.** Pertaining to or treating of ethics and morality. **2.** Conforming to right principles of conduct as accepted by a specific profession, etc. — **eth′i·cal·ly** *adv.* — **eth′i·cal·ness, eth′i·cal′i·ty** (-kal′ə·tē) *n.*

eth·ics (eth′iks) *n.pl.* (*construed as sing. in defs. 1 and 3*) **1.** The study and philosophy of human conduct, with emphasis on the determination of right and wrong. **2.** The principles of right conduct with reference to a specific profession, mode of life, etc. **3.** A treatise on morals.

E·thi·o·pi·an (ē′thē·ō′pē·ən) *adj.* Of or pertaining to Ethiopia, its people, or their language. — *n.* A native or inhabitant of Ethiopia.

E·thi·op·ic (ē′thē·op′ik, -ō′pik) *n.* A Semitic language of ancient Ethiopia. — *adj.* Ethiopian.

eth·nic (eth′nik) *adj.* **1.** Of, belonging to, or distinctive of a particular racial, cultural, or language division of mankind. **2.** Of or belonging to a people neither Jewish nor Christian; heathen. Also **eth′ni·cal.** [< Gk. < *ethnos* nation] — **eth′ni·cal·ly** *adv.*

ethno- *combining form* Race; nation; peoples. Also, before vowels, **ethn-.**

eth·nog·ra·phy (eth·nog′rə·fē) *n.* *pl.* **·phies** **1.** The branch of anthropology concerned with the classification and description of regional, chiefly primitive human cultures. **2.** Loosely, ethnology. — **eth·nog′ra·pher** *n.* — **eth·no·graph·ic** (eth′nə·graf′ik) or **·i·cal** *adj.* — **eth′no·graph′i·cal·ly** *adv.*

eth·nol·o·gy (eth·nol′ə·jē) *n.* *pl.* **·gies** **1.** The branch of anthropology concerned with the study of racial and ethnic groups in their origins, distribution, and cultures. **2.** Loosely, ethnography. — **eth·nol′o·gist** *n.* — **eth·no·log·ic** (eth′nə·loj′ik) or **·i·cal** *adj.* — **eth′no·log′i·cal·ly** *adv.*

eth·yl (eth′əl) *n.* *Chem.* **1.** A univalent hydrocarbon radical, C_2H_5. **2.** Any gasoline treated with tetraethyl lead to reduce knock. [< ETH(ER) + -YL] — **e·thyl·ic** (i·thil′ik) *adj.*

ethyl alcohol Ethanol.

eth·y·lene (eth′ə·lēn) *n.* *Chem.* A colorless, flammable, gaseous hydrocarbon, C_2H_4, contained in coal gas, used as an anesthetic and in organic syntheses.

ethylene glycol *Chem.* A colorless, sweetish alcohol, $C_2H_4(OH)_2$, formed by decomposing certain ethylene compounds and used as an antifreeze, solvent, and lubricant.

ethyl ether *Chem.* A colorless, volatile, flammable liquid compound, $(C_2H_5)_2O$, having a characteristic odor, used as an anesthetic and solvent: also called *ether.*

e·ti·ol·o·gy (ē′tē·ol′ə·jē) *n.* *pl.* **·gies** **1.** The science of causes or reasons. **2.** *Med.* A theory of the cause of a particular disease. **3.** The giving of a cause or reason for anything; also, the reason given. Also spelled *aetiology.* [< LL < Gk. < *aitia* cause + *logos* word, study] — **e·ti·o·log·i·cal** *adj.* — **e′ti·o·log′i·cal·ly** *adv.* — **e′ti·ol′o·gist** *n.*

et·i·quette (et′ə·ket) *n.* The rules conventionally established for behavior in polite society or in official or professional life. [< F < OF *estiquette*; orig., label]

Eton College A public school for boys in Eton, England.

E·to·ni·an (i·tō′nē·ən) *n.* One who is or has been a student at Eton College. — *adj.* Of or relating to Eton College.

Eton jacket A short jacket cut off square at the hips and generally worn with a wide, overlapping, stiff collar (the **Eton collar**), originally worn at Eton College.

E·trus·can (i·trus′kən) *adj.* Of or relating to Etruria, its people, or language. Also **E·tru′ri·an.** — *n.* **1.** One of the people of Etruria. **2.** The extinct Etruscan language.

-ette *suffix of nouns* **1.** Little; small: *kitchenette.* **2.** Resembling; imitating: *leatherette.* **3.** Feminine: *farmerette.* [< F *-ette,* fem. of *-et,* dim. suffix]

é·tude (ā′to͞od, -tyo͞od; *Fr.* ā·tüd′) *n.* *Music* An exercise for solo instrument or voice, designed to perfect some phase of technique. [< F. See STUDY.]

et·y·mol·o·gize (et′ə·mol′ə·jīz) *v.* **·gized, ·giz·ing** *v.t.* **1.** To give the etymology of. — *v.i.* **2.** To give an etymology.

et·y·mol·o·gy (et′ə·mol′ə·jē) *n.* *pl.* **·gies** **1.** The history of a word as shown by breaking it down into basic elements by tracing it back to the earliest known form and indicat its changes in form and meaning; also, a statement of th **2.** The study of the derivation of words. [< F < L Gk. < *etymon* true meaning + *logos* word, study] — **e mo·log·i·cal** (et′ə·mə·loj′i·kəl) or **et′y·mo·log′ic** *adj.* **et′y·mo·log′i·cal·ly** *adv.* — **et′y·mol′o·gist** *n.*

eu- *prefix* Good; well; easy; agreeable: *euphony.* [< Gk.

eu·ca·lyp·tus (yo͞o′kə·lip′təs) *n.* *pl.* **·tus·es** or **·ti** (-tī) A of a genus of large, chiefly Australian evergreen trees, wid used as timber and yielding a volatile, pungent oil (**oil eucalyptus**) used in medicine. [< NL < Gk. *eu-* well *kalyptos* covered, from the covering of the buds]

Eu·char·ist (yo͞o′kə·rist) *n.* **1.** A Christian sacrament which bread and wine are consecrated and received in co memoration of the passion and death of Christ: also cal *Communion, Holy Communion.* **2.** The consecrated br and wine of this sacrament. [< OF < LL < Gk. < *eu-* + *charizesthai* to show favor] — **Eu′cha·ris′tic** or **·ti·cal**

eu·chre (yo͞o′kər) *n.* **1.** A card game for two to four play played with 32 cards. **2.** An instance of euchring an op nent. — *v.t.* **·chred** (-kərd), **·chring** **1.** In the game of eu er, to defeat (the trump-making side) by taking three tri **2.** *Informal* To outwit or defeat. [Origin uncertain]

Eu·clid·e·an (yo͞o·klid′ē·ən) *adj.* Of or relating to the g metric principles of Euclid. Also **Eu·clid′i·an.**

eu·gen·ic (yo͞o·jen′ik) *adj.* Of or pertaining to eugen Also **eu·gen′i·cal.** [< Gk. (< *eu-* well + *genēs* born) + — **eu·gen′i·cal·ly** *adv.*

eu·gen·i·cist (yo͞o·jen′ə·sist) *n.* A specialist in or a stud of eugenics. Also **eu·ge·nist** (yo͞o′jə·nist, yo͞o·jen′ist).

eu·gen·ics (yo͞o·jen′iks) *n.pl.* (*construed as sing.*) The ence of improving the physical and mental qualities of hun beings through control of the factors influencing heredity.

eu·lo·gist (yo͞o′lə·jist) *n.* One who eulogizes.

eu·lo·gis·tic (yo͞o′lə·jis′tik) *adj.* Relating to or having nature of eulogy; laudatory. Also **eu′lo·gis′ti·cal.** — **eu gis′ti·cal·ly** *adv.*

eu·lo·gize (yo͞o′lə·jīz) *v.t.* **·gized, ·giz·ing** To speak or w a eulogy about; praise highly; extol. — **eu′lo·giz′er** *n.*

eu·lo·gy (yo͞o′lə·jē) *n.* *pl.* **·gies** **1.** A spoken or writ piece of high praise, esp. when delivered publicly. **2.** Gr praise. [< Gk. < *eu-* well + *legein* to speak]

Eu·men·i·des (yo͞o·men′ə·dēz) *n.pl.* The Furies. [< (the kind ones: a euphemistic name]

eu·nuch (yo͞o′nək) *n.* A castrated man, esp. one emplo as a harem attendant or as an Oriental palace official. [< Gk. < *eunē* bed + *echein* to keep, guard]

eu·phe·mism (yo͞o′fə·miz′əm) *n.* **1.** Substitution of a m or roundabout word or expression for another felt to be blunt or painful. **2.** A word or expression so substituted "the departed" for "the dead." [< Gk. < *eu-* well + *mizein* < *phanai* to speak] — **eu′phe·mist** *n.* — **eu′p mis′tic** or **·ti·cal** *adj.* — **eu′phe·mis′ti·cal·ly** *adv.*

eu·phe·mize (yo͞o′fə·mīz) *v.* **·mized, ·miz·ing** *v.t. & v.i.* speak or write of (something) by using a euphemism.

eu·phon·ic (yo͞o·fon′ik) *adj.* **1.** Of or relating to eupho **2.** Agreeable in sound; euphonious. — **eu·phon′i·cal·ly**

eu·pho·ni·ous (yo͞o·fō′nē·əs) *adj.* Marked by eupho agreeable and pleasant in sound. — **eu·pho′ni·ous·ly**

eu·pho·ni·um (yo͞o·fō′nē·əm) *n.* A brass instrument hav a tone resembling that of a tuba but slightly higher in ran

eu·pho·ny (yo͞o′fə·nē) *n.* *pl.* **·nies** **1.** The quality of be pleasant and agreeable in sound, as in speech or music. Progressive change in speech sounds through assimilati allowing greater ease of pronunciation. [< Gk. < *eu-* g + *phōnē* sound]

eu·phor·bi·a (yo͞o·fôr′bē·ə) *n.* An herb having a mi juice and various medicinal properties: also called *spur* [< NL < L < Gk. *euphorbion*] — **eu·phor′bi·al** *adj.*

eu·pho·ri·a (yo͞o·fôr′ē·ə, -fō′rē-) *n.* A feeling of wellbei relaxation, and happiness. [< NL < Gk. *eu-* well + *pher* to bear] — **eu·phor′ic** *adj.*

eu·phu·ism (yo͞o′fyo͞o·iz′əm) *n.* **1.** An artificially eleg style of speech or writing, characterized by strained simi excessive use of alliteration and antithesis, etc. **2.** An pression or rhetorical device typical of such a style. [af *Euphues,* character created by John Lyly, English wri 1554?–1606 < Gk. < *eu-* well + *phyein* to grow, form] **eu′phu·ist** *n.* — **eu′phu·is·tic** *adj.* — **eu′phu·is′ti·cal·ly** *a*

Eur·a·sian (yo͞o·rā′zhən, -shən) *adj.* **1.** Pertaining to E asia. **2.** Of European and Asian descent. — *n.* A person mixed European and Asian parentage.

eu·re·ka (yo͞o·rē′kə) *interj.* I have found (it): an exclar tion of triumph or achievement. [< Gk. *heurēka*]

Eu·ro·pa (yo͞o·rō′pə) In Greek mythology, a Phoenic princess abducted by Zeus, in the guise of a bull, to Cre

Eu·ro·pe·an (yo͞or′ə·pē′ən) *adj.* Relating to or derived fr Europe or its inhabitants. — *n.* **1.** A native or inhabit of Europe. **2.** A person of European descent.

European Economic Community A customs union

ance, Italy, West Germany, and the Benelux nations: also
lled *Common Market*. Also **European Common Market.**
ro·pe·an·ize (yŏŏr′ə·pē′ən·īz) *v.t.* **·ized, ·iz·ing** To make
ıropean, as in culture. — **Eu′ro·pe′an·i·za′tion** *n.*
ropean plan At a hotel, the system of paying for room
d service separately from the charge for meals.
ro·pi·um (yŏŏ·rō′pē·əm) *n.* A steel-gray, malleable me-
llic element (symbol Eu) of the lanthanide series. See
EMENT. [< NL < L *Europa* Europe]
y- *combining form* Wide; broad. [< Gk. *eurys* wide]
ryd·i·ce (yŏŏ·rid′ə·sē) In Greek mythology, the wife of
pheus. See ORPHEUS.
ryth·mics (yŏŏ·rith′miks) *n.pl.* (*construed as sing.*) A
stem for developing grace and rhythm through bodily
vements made in response to music: also **eu·rhyth′mics.**
L < Gk. < *eu-* good + *rhythmos* symmetry] — **eu·**
th′mic or **·mi·cal** *adj.*
sta·chi·an tube (yŏŏ·stā′kē·ən, -shē·ən, -shən) *Anat.* A
ssage between the pharynx and the middle ear, serving to
ualize air pressure between the tympanic cavity and the
mosphere: also called *syrinx*. For illus. see EAR. [after
rtolomeo *Eustachio*, died 1574, Italian anatomist]
ter·pe (yŏŏ·tûr′pē) The Muse of lyric song and music.
tha·na·si·a (yŏŏ′thə·nā′zhə, -zhē·ə) *n.* **1.** Painless,
aceful death. **2.** The deliberate putting to death painless-
of a person suffering from an incurable disease: also called
rcy killing. [< Gk. < *eu-* easy + *thanatos* death]
then·ics (yŏŏ·then′iks) *n.pl.* (*construed as sing.*) The
ence of improving the physical and mental qualities of
man beings, through control of environmental factors. [<
euthēnein to thrive]
ac·u·ant (i·vak′yŏŏ·ənt) *Med. adj.* Cathartic or emetic.
n. An evacuant medicine, drug, etc.
ac·u·ate (i·vak′yŏŏ·āt) *v.* **·at·ed, ·at·ing** *v.t.* **1.** *Mil.* **a** To
ve up or abandon possession of, as a fortress or city. **b** To
ove out or withdraw (troops, inhabitants, etc.) from a
reatened area or place. **2.** To depart from and leave vant; vacate. **3.** To remove the contents of. **4.** *Physiol.*
discharge or eject, as from the bowels. — *v.i.* **5.** To
thdraw, as from a threatened area [< L < *e-* out + *vacuare*
make empty] — **e·vac′u·a′tion** *n.* — **e·vac′u·a′tor** *n.*
ac·u·ee (i·vak′yŏŏ·ē′) *n.* A person moved out or with-
awn from a destroyed or threatened area. [See EVACUATE]
ade (i·vād′) *v.* **e·vad·ed, e·vad·ing** *v.t.* **1.** To get away
om by tricks or cleverness: to *evade* pursuers. **2.** To get
t of or avoid: to *evade* a question. **3.** To baffle; elude: The
cts *evade* explanation. — *v.i.* **4.** To dodge a question, re-
onsibility, etc. [< L < *e-* out + *vadere* to go] — **e·vad′·**
ble or **e·vad′i·ble** *adj.* — **e·vad′er** *n.*
al·u·ate (i·val′yŏŏ·āt) *v.t.* **·at·ed, ·at·ing** To find or de-
rmine the amount, worth, etc., of. [< F < OF *valoir* to
worth] — **e·val′u·a′tion** *n.*
a·nesce (ev′ə·nes′) *v.i.* **·nesced, ·nesc·ing** To disappear
degrees; vanish gradually. [< L < *e-* out + *vanescere* to
nish] — **ev′a·nes′cence** *n.*
a·nes·cent (ev′ə·nes′ənt) *adj.* Passing away, or liable to
ss away, gradually or imperceptibly; fleeting. — **ev′a·**
s′cent·ly *adv.*
an·gel (i·van′jəl) *n.* **1.** The gospel. **2.** *Usu. cap.* One of
e four Gospels. **3.** Any good news or glad tidings. [< OF
LL < Gk. < *eu-* good + *angellein* to announce]
an·gel·i·cal (ē′van·jel′i·kəl, ev′ən-) *adj.* **1.** Of, relating
, or contained in the New Testament, esp. the Gospels. **2.**
, relating to, or maintaining the doctrine that the Bible is
e only rule of faith. **3.** Evangelistic. — *n.* A member of
evangelical church. Also **e′van·gel′ic.** — **e′van·gel′i·cal·**
m *n.* — **e′van·gel′i·cal·ly** *adv.*
an·gel·ism (i·van′jə·liz′əm) *n.* The zealous preaching
spreading of the gospel.
an·gel·ist (i·van′jə·list) *n.* **1.** *Usu. cap.* One of the four
riters of the New Testament Gospels: Matthew, Mark,
uke, or John. **2.** An itinerant or missionary preacher. —
van′gel·is′tic *adj.* — **e·van′gel·is′ti·cal·ly** *adv.*
an·gel·ize (i·van′jəl·īz) *v.* **·ized, ·iz·ing** *v.t.* **1.** To preach
e gospel to. **2.** To convert to Christianity. — *v.i.* **3.** To
each or act as an evangelist. — **e·van′gel·i·za′tion** *n.*
ap·o·rate (i·vap′ə·rāt) *v.* **·rat·ed, ·rat·ing** *v.t.* **1.** To con-
ert into vapor; vaporize. **2.** To remove moisture or liquid
om (milk, fruit, etc.) so as to dry or concentrate. — *v.i.* **3.**
o become vapor. **4.** To yield vapor. **5.** To vanish; dis-
ppear. [< L < *e-* out, away + *vaporare* to emit vapor] —
vap′o·ra·ble *adj.* — **e·vap′o·ra′tive** *adj.* — **e·vap′o·ra′·**
on *n.* — **e·vap′o·ra′tor** *n.*
aporated milk Unsweetened canned milk slightly thick-
ned by removal of some of the water.
a·sion (i·vā′zhən) *n.* **1.** The act of evading; esp., the act
dodging something difficult or distasteful. **2.** A piece of
ickery or shrewdness used in dodging a question, etc.

e·va·sive (i·vā′siv) *adj.* **1.** Given to or characterized by evasion; not direct and frank: an *evasive* person; *evasive* promises.
2. Elusive. — **e·va′sive·ly** *adv.* — **e·va′sive·ness** *n.*
eve (ēv) *n.* **1.** The evening before a holiday: Christmas *Eve.*
2. The time immediately preceding some event. **3.** *Poetic*
Evening. [Var. of EVEN²]
Eve (ēv) The first woman; wife of Adam and mother of the
human race. *Gen.* iii 20. [< Hebrew *hawwah* life]
e·ven¹ (ē′vən) *adj.* **1.** Flat and smooth; level: an *even* surface. **2.** Extending to the same height or depth: a tree *even*
with the housetop. **3.** Extending along; parallel to: a book-
case *even* with the wall. **4.** Equally distributed; uniform: an
even coat of paint. **5.** Calm and controlled: an *even* disposition. **6.** Equally matched: an *even* struggle. **7.** Being about
the same for any one of several alternatives: The chances for
success or failure are *even*. **8.** Being the same (score) for
each side or competitor. **9.** Having accomplished exact settlement of a debt. **10.** Identical in quantity, number, measure, etc.: *even* portions. **11.** Exactly divisible by 2: an *even*
number: opposed to *odd*. — **to break even** *Informal* To end
up with neither profit nor loss, as in a business deal. — **to**
get even To exact one's full measure of revenge. — *adv.* **1.**
To all the greater extent or degree; still: an *even* better plan.
2. During the very same moment: with *as*: *Even* as they
watched, the ship sank. **3.** In exactly the same way; precisely; just: with *as*: Do *even* as I do. **4.** In very fact; indeed; actually: to feel glad, *even* delighted. **5.** Unlikely or
inconceivable as it may seem: He was kind *even* to his enemies. **6.** All the way; as far as: faithful *even* to death. **7.**
All the same; nevertheless; notwithstanding: *Even* with that
handicap, he managed to win. **8.** Not otherwise than; right:
It is happening *even* now. **9.** *Informal* In a smooth manner;
evenly: to keep things running *even*. — **even if** Although;
notwithstanding. — *v.t.* **1.** To make even: often with *up* or
off: to *even* up accounts. — *v.i.* **2.** To become even: often
with *up* or *off*. [OE *efen*] — **e′ven·ly** *adv.* — **e′ven·ness** *n.*
e·ven² (ē′vən) *n. Archaic* Evening. [OE *ǣfen*]
e·ven·fall (ē′vən·fôl′) *n.* Early evening; twilight; dusk.
e·ven·hand·ed (ē′vən·han′did) *adj.* Treating all alike; impartial. — **e′ven·hand′ed·ly** *adv.* — **e′ven·hand′ed·ness** *n.*
eve·ning (ēv′ning) *n.* **1.** The latter part of day and the first
part of night. ◆ Collateral adjective: *vesperal*. **2.** An evening's entertainment or activity. **3.** The declining years of
life, a career, etc. [OE *ǣfnian* to approach evening]
evening dress Formal evening wear. Also **evening clothes.**
evening gown A woman's formal dress for evening wear.
evening primrose An erect American biennial herb with
conspicuous yellow flowers that open in the evening.
evening star A bright planet visible in the west just after
sunset, especially Venus. Also called *Hesperus, Vesper.*
e·vent (i·vent′) *n.* **1.** Something that takes place; a happening or an incident: the *events* of that period. **2.** An actual
or possible set of circumstances; a real or contingent situation: in the *event* of failure. **3.** Final outcome: In the *event,*
she decided not to go. **4.** One of the items forming part of a
variegated program of sports: the skating exhibition and
other *events*. — **in any event** or **at all events** Regardless of
what happens. [< OF < L < *e-* out + *venire* to come]
e·vent·ful (i·vent′fəl) *adj.* **1.** Marked by important events:
an *eventful* era. **2.** Having important consequences: an
eventful decision. — **e·vent′ful·ly** *adv.* — **e·vent′ful·ness** *n.*
e·ven·tide (ē′vən·tīd′) *n. Poetic* Evening.
e·ven·tu·al (i·ven′chŏŏ·əl) *adj.* Occurring or resulting in
due course of time. — **e·ven′tu·al·ly** *adv.*
e·ven·tu·al·i·ty (i·ven′chŏŏ·al′ə·tē) *n. pl.* **·ties** A likely or
possible occurrence; a conceivable outcome.
e·ven·tu·ate (i·ven′chŏŏ·āt) *v.i.* **·at·ed, ·at·ing** To result
ultimately: His efforts *eventuated* in success.
ev·er (ev′ər) *adv.* **1.** At any time; on any occasion: Did you
ever see it? **2.** By any possible chance: If the sun *ever* comes
out, the fog will disappear. **3.** In any possible or conceivable way: Do it as fast as *ever* you can. **4.** At all times; in-
variably: They remained *ever* on guard. **5.** Throughout the
entire course of time; always; forever: now usually followed
by *since, after,* or *afterward*. ◆ In informal speech, *ever* is
often used merely to add force. Was I *ever* glad! — **ever so**
Informal To an extremely great extent or degree: It was *ever*
so pleasant. — **ever so often** *Informal* **1.** Extremely often;
repeatedly. **2.** Now and then; every so often. — **for ever**
and ever Forever: an intensive form. [OE *ǣfre*]
ev·er·glade (ev′ər·glād) *n.* A tract of low swampy land.
Everglade State Nickname of Florida.
ev·er·green (ev′ər·grēn′) *adj.* Having foliage that remains
green until the formation of new foliage: distinguished from
deciduous. — *n.* **1.** An evergreen tree or plant. **2.** *pl.*
Evergreen branches or twigs, esp. as used for decorations.
Evergreen State Nickname of Washington.
ev·er·last·ing (ev′ər·las′ting, -läs′-) *adj.* **1.** Existing or

lasting forever; eternal: belief in an *everlasting* God. **2.** Continuing for an indefinitely long period; perpetual: *everlasting* happiness. **3.** Incessant; interminable: her *everlasting* chatter. **—** *n.* **1.** Endless duration; eternity: to love for *everlasting*. **2.** One of several plants, chiefly of the aster family, whose flowers keep their form and color when dried: also called *immortelle*. **— the Everlasting** God. [ME] **— ev′·er·last′ing·ly** *adv.* **— ev′er·last′ing·ness** *n.*

ev·er·more (ev′ər·môr′, -mōr′) *adv. Poetic* For and at all time to come; always. **— for evermore** Forever.

e·ver·sion (i·vûr′zhən) *n.* The act of everting, or the condition of being everted. **— e·ver′si·ble** (-sə·bəl) *adj.*

e·vert (i·vûrt′) *v.t.* To turn outward or inside out. [< L < *e-* out + *vertere* to turn]

eve·ry (ev′rē, ev′ər·ē) *adj.* **1.** Each without excepting any of all those that together form an aggregate. **2.** Each (member or unit singled out in some way) of a series: *every* tenth man. **3.** The utmost; all possible: Show him *every* consideration. **— every bit** *Informal* In all respects: He is *every bit* as good as you. **— every now and then** From time to time; occasionally. Also **every now and again, every once in a while. — every other** Each alternate (specified thing). **— every so often** *Informal* Every now and then. **— every which way** *Informal* In every way or direction and with little or no order. [ME < OE *ǣfre* ever + *ǣlc* each]

eve·ry·bod·y (ev′rē·bod′ē, -bud′ē) *pron.* Every person.

eve·ry·day (ev′rē·dā′, -dā′) *adj.* **1.** Happening every day; daily. **2.** Suitable for ordinary days: *everyday* clothes. **3.** Commonplace; ordinary: *everyday* folks.

eve·ry·one (ev′rē·wun′, -wən) *pron.* Everybody.

every one Each individual person or thing out of the whole number, excepting none: *Every one* of the men is ill.

eve·ry·thing (ev′rē·thing′) *pron.* **1.** Whatever exists; all things whatsoever. **2.** Whatever is relevant, needed, or important: I have *everything*. **3.** The only thing that really matters; the essential thing: Happiness is *everything*.

eve·ry·where (ev′rē·hwâr′) *adv.* At, in, or to every place.

e·vict (i·vikt′) *v.t.* **1.** To expel (a tenant) by legal process; dispossess; put out. **2.** To recover (property, etc.) by legal process or superior claim. **— Syn.** See EXPEL. [< L < *e-* out + *vincere* to conquer] **— e·vic′tion** *n.* **— e·vic′tor** *n.*

ev·i·dence (ev′ə·dəns) *n.* **1.** That which serves to prove or disprove something; support; proof. **2.** That which serves as a ground for knowing something with certainty or for believing something with conviction; corroboration. **3.** An outward indication of the existence or fact of something: Her paleness was *evidence* of her distress. **4.** *Law* That which is properly presented before a court as a means of establishing or disproving something alleged or presumed, as the statements of witnesses. **— in evidence** In the condition of being readily seen or perceived; esp., conspicuously present. **— to turn state's evidence** To testify in court against one's accomplices. **—** *v.t.* **·denced, ·denc·ing 1.** To show unmistakably. **2.** To support by oral testimony.

ev·i·dent (ev′ə·dənt) *adj.* Easily perceived or recognized; clearly perceptible; plain. [< L < *e-* out + *videre* to see]

ev·i·den·tial (ev′ə·den′shəl) *adj.* Relating to, serving as, or based on evidence. **— ev′i·den′tial·ly** *adv.*

ev·i·dent·ly (ev′ə·dənt·lē, -dent′-, ev′ə·dent′lē) *adv.* **1.** To all appearances; apparently. **2.** Quite clearly; obviously.

e·vil (ē′vəl) *adj.* **1.** Morally bad; wicked. **2.** Causing injury or any other undesirable result. **3.** Marked by or threatening misfortune or distress: an *evil* omen. **4.** Low in public esteem: an *evil* reputation. **— the Evil One** Satan. **—** *n.* **1.** That which is evil; as: **a** That which is morally bad. **b** That which is injurious. **c** That which causes suffering or misfortune. **2.** Some particular act, characteristic, etc. that is evil: one of the *evils* of that political system. **—** *adv.* In an evil manner; badly: now chiefly in combinations: an *evil-smelling* plant. [OE *yfel*] **— e′vil·ly** *adv.* **— e′vil·ness** *n.*

e·vil·do·er (ē′vəl·doo′ər) *n.* One who does evil. **— e′vil·do′ing** *n.*

evil eye A glance superstitiously supposed capable of inflicting misfortune or injury.

e·vil-mind·ed (ē′vəl·mīn′did) *adj.* Obsessed with vicious or depraved thoughts; esp., sexually indecent thoughts. **— e′vil-mind′ed·ly** *adv.* **— e′vil-mind′ed·ness** *n.*

e·vince (i·vins′) *v.t.* **e·vinced, e·vinc·ing 1.** To indicate clearly; demonstrate convincingly. **2.** To give an outward sign of having (a quality, feeling, etc.). [< L < *e-* out + *vincere* to conquer] **— e·vin′ci·ble** *adj.* **— e·vin′cive** *adj.*

e·vis·cer·ate (*v.* i·vis′ə·rāt; *adj.* i·vis′ər·it) *v.t.* **·at·ed, ·at·ing 1.** To disembowel. **2.** To remove the vital part of. **—** *adj. Surg.* Disemboweled: an *eviscerate* abdomen. [< L < *e-* out + *viscera* entrails] **— e·vis′cer·a′tion** *n.*

ev·o·ca·tion (ev′ə·kā′shən) *n.* The act of evoking; a summoning, as of memories. **— ev′o·ca′tor** *n.*

e·voc·a·tive (i·vok′ə·tiv, -vō′kə-) *adj.* Tending to evoke.

e·voke (i·vōk′) *v.t.* **e·voked, e·vok·ing 1.** To call or summon forth, as memories. **2.** To draw forth or produce (a response, reaction, etc.). **3.** To summon up (spirits) by or as by incantations. [< L < *e-* out + *vocare* to call] **— e·ca·ble** (ev′ə·kə·bəl, i·vō′kə·bəl) *adj.*

ev·o·lu·tion (ev′ə·loo′shən) *n.* **1.** The process of unfold growing, or developing, usu. by slow stages. **2.** Anyth developed by such a process. **3.** *Biol.* **a** The theory tha forms of life originated by descent from earlier forms. **b** series of changes, as by natural selection, mutation, e through which a given type of organism has acquired present characteristics. **4.** One of a series of complex mo ments. **5.** A movement or maneuver of troops, ships, **6.** The process of giving off gas, heat, sound, etc. **— e lu′tion·al, ev′o·lu′tion·ar·y** *adj.* **— ev′o·lu′tion·al·ly** *adv*

ev·o·lu·tion·ist (ev′ə·loo′shən·ist) *n.* **1.** A proponen the theory of biological evolution. **2.** One who advoca progress through gradual stages, as in political structure. *adj.* **1.** Evolutionary. **2.** Of or relating to evolutionists. **ev′o·lu′tion·ism** *n.*

e·volve (i·volv′) *v.* **e·volved, e·volv·ing** *v.t.* **1.** To work develop gradually. **2.** *Biol.* To develop, as by a differen tion of parts or functions, to a more highly organized st usu. in the passive. **3.** To give or throw off (vapor, h etc.). **4.** To unfold or expand. **—** *v.i.* **5.** To undergo process of evolution. **6.** To develop. [< L < *e-* out *volvere* to roll] **— e·volv′a·ble** *adj.* **— e·volve′ment** *n.*

ewe (yoo, *Dial.* yō) *n.* A female sheep. [OE *eowu*]

ew·er (yoo′ər) *n.* A large, wide-mouthed jug or pitcher water. [ME < AF, OF < L *aqua* water]

ex (eks) *prep.* In finance, without the right to have or p ticipate in: *ex* dividend. [< L *ex* out]

ex-[1] *prefix* **1.** Out of: *exit, exhale.* **2.** Thoroughly; *exas ate.* **3.** Not having; lacking. **4.** Being formerly: attac with a hyphen to the word it qualifies: *ex-president.* Also before consonants except *c, f, p, q, s, t*; *ef-* before *f.* [< L from, out of]

ex-[2] *prefix* Out of; from; forth: *exodus.* Also, before con nants, *ec-*, as in *eclipse.* [< Gk. *ex* out]

ex-[3] Var. of EXO-.

ex·ac·er·bate (ig·zas′ər·bāt) *v.t.* **·bat·ed, ·bat·ing 1.** make more sharp or severe; aggravate (feelings, a dise pain, etc.). **2.** To embitter or irritate (someone). [< L *ex-* very + *acerbus* bitter, harsh] **— ex·ac′er·ba′tion** *n.*

ex·act (ig·zakt′) *adj.* **1.** Perfectly clear and complete every detail; precise. **2.** Altogether accurate: to ask for *exact* answer. **3.** Being precisely (what is specified): the *ex* amount necessary. **4.** Corresponding in every detail w something taken as a model. **5.** Free from vagueness; cle *exact* thinking. **6.** Extremely careful about detail and curacy: an *exact* editor. **7.** Designed for use where the most precision is required: an *exact* scientific instrument. Rigorously demanding: an *exact* schoolmaster. **—** *v.t.* **1.** demand rigorously the full payment of: to *exact* full comp sation for an injury. **2.** To force unjustly the payment **3.** To obtain by or as if by forcing out: to *exact* a full rep **4.** To insist upon the performance or yielding of as a st right or obligation: to *exact* obedience. **5.** To require: situation *exacted* quick thinking. [< L < *ex-* out + *agere* drive] **— ex·act′ness, ex·act′i·tude** (-i·tood, -i·tyood) *n.* **ex·ac′tor** or **ex·act′er** *n.* **— ex·ac′tion** *n.*

ex·act·ing (ig·zak′ting) *adj.* **1.** Making rigorous deman severe. **2.** Involving constant hard work, attention, etc. **ex·act′ing·ly** *adv.* **— ex·act′ing·ness** *n.*

ex·act·ly (ig·zakt′lē) *adv.* **1.** In an exact manner; w great precision or accuracy. **2.** Precisely right; just so.

ex·ag·ger·ate (ig·zaj′ə·rāt) *v.* **·at·ed, ·at·ing** *v.t.* **1.** To re resent or look upon as greater than is actually the case: *exaggerate* one's troubles. **2.** To make greater in size, int sity, etc., than what would be normal or expected. **— 3.** To overstate or overemphasize something. [< L < out + *agger* heap] **— ex·ag′ger·at′ed** *adj.* **— ex·ag′ger· tion** *n.* **— ex·ag′ger·a′tive** *adj.* **— ex·ag′ger·a′tor** *n.*

ex·alt (ig·zôlt′) *v.t.* **1.** To raise in rank, character, hon etc. **2.** To glorify or praise. **3.** To fill with delight, pri etc.; elate. **4.** To increase the intensity of, as colors; heig en. [< L < *ex-* out + *altus* high] **— ex·alt′ed** *adj.* **— alt′ed·ly** *adv.* **— ex·alt′er** *n.*

ex·al·ta·tion (eg′zôl·tā′shən) *n.* **1.** The act of exalting, the state of being exalted. **2.** A state or feeling of gre often extreme, exhilaration and well-being; ecstasy.

ex·am (ig·zam′) *n. Informal* An examination.

ex·am·i·na·tion (ig·zam′ə·nā′shən) *n.* **1.** The act of exa ining, or the state of being examined. **2.** Medical scruti and testing. **3.** A formal test of knowledge or skills; al the questions or problems posed. **— ex·am′i·na′tion·al** *a*

ex·am·ine (ig·zam′in) *v.t.* **·ined, ·in·ing 1.** To inspect scrutinize with care; inquire into. **2.** To subject (a pers organ, etc.) to medical scrutiny and testing. **3.** To test questions or exercises as to qualifications, fitness, etc. **4.** question formally in order to elicit facts, etc. [< OF < < *ex-* out + *ag-*, root of *agere* to drive] **— ex·am′in·a·b** *adj.* **— ex·am′in·er** *n.*

ex·am·ple (ig·zam′pəl, -zäm′-) *n.* **1.** A particular thi t belongs to and is typical of a group of things and that is :led out as a representative specimen. **2.** Something de-ving imitation; model. **3.** An instance or object of pun-nent, reprimand, etc., designed to warn or deter others. A previous case or instance identical with or similar to ıething under consideration. **5.** A particular problem or rcise in arithmetic, algebra, etc. **— for example** By way illustration. **— to set an example** To act in such a way as rouse others to imitation. *— v.t.* **·pled, ·pling** To present example of; exemplify: now only in the passive. [< OF L < *ex-* out + *emere* to buy, take]

s·per·ate (ig·zas′pə·rāt) *v.t.* **·at·ed, ·at·ing 1.** To make y annoyed or angry; infuriate. **2.** To make (a disagree-condition, feeling, etc.) still worse; aggravate. **— Syn.** OFFEND. [< L < *ex-* out + *asper* rough] **— ex·as′per·**ər *n.* **— ex·as′per·at·ing** *adj.* **— ex·as′per·a′tion** *n.*

a·the·dra (eks kə·thē′drə, kath′i-) *Latin* With au-rity; in one's official capacity; literally, from the chair.

a·vate (eks′kə·vāt) *v.t.* **·vat·ed, ·vat·ing 1.** To make a or cavity in. **2.** To form or make (a hole, tunnel, etc.) hollowing, digging out, or scooping. **3.** To remove by ging or scooping out, as soil. **4.** To uncover by digging, uins; unearth. [< L < *ex-* out + *cavus* hollow] **— ex′·va′tion** *n.* **— ex′ca·va′tor** *n.*

eed (ik·sēd′) *v.t.* **1.** To surpass, as in quantity or qual-**2.** To go beyond the limit or extent of: to *exceed* one's ome. *— v.i.* **3.** To be superior; surpass others. [< F < < *ex-* out, beyond + *cedere* to go]

eed·ing (ik·sē′ding) *adj.* Greater than usual. *— adv.* *haic* Extremely. **— ex·ceed′ing·ly** *adv.*

el (ik·sel′) *v.* **·celled, ·cel·ling** *v.t.* **1.** To surpass, usu. in ne good quality or action; be better than; outstrip: to *el* all rivals. *— v.i.* **2.** To surpass others; be outstanding. OF < L *excellere* to rise]

el·lence (ek′sə·ləns) *n.* **1.** The state or quality of ex-ing; superiority. **2.** That in which someone or something els; a superior trait or quality. Also **ex′cel·len·cy.**

cel·len·cy (ek′sə·lən·sē) *n. pl.* **·cies** An honorary title form of address for certain dignitaries: often preceded by s, *Her, Your,* etc.

el·lent (ek′sə·lənt) *adj.* Being of the very best quality; eptionally good. **— ex′cel·lent·ly** *adv.*

el·si·or (ik·sel′sē·ər) *n. U.S.* Long, fine wood shavings d as stuffing or as packing material.

ept (ik·sept′) *prep.* With the exclusion or omission of; de from. *— conj.* **1.** Aside from the fact that. Also **cept that. 2.** Otherwise than. ◆ In this sense, *except* y also be construed as a preposition governing the follow-adverb, phrase, or clause. **— except for** If it were not *— v.t.* **1.** To exclude from consideration, enumeration, .; leave deliberately out of account. *— v.i.* **2.** To raise an jection, esp. a formal objection: now usu. with *to*: to *ex-t* to an accusation. [< F < L < *ex-* out + *capere* to take]

ept·ing (ik·sep′ting) *prep.* Barring; except.

cep·tion (ik·sep′shən) *n.* **1.** The act of excepting, or the te of being excepted. **2.** Something excluded from or not nforming to a general class, principle, rule, etc. **3.** An ob-tion or complaint; adverse criticism. **4.** *Law* A formal jection to the decision of a court during trial. **— to take ception 1.** To express disagreement. **2.** To feel resentful.

cep·tion·a·ble (ik·sep′shən·ə·bəl) *adj.* Open to excep-n or objection. **— ex·cep′tion·a·bly** *adv.*

cep·tion·al (ik·sep′shən·əl) *adj.* Being an exception; usual or extraordinary. **— ex·cep′tion·al·ly** *adv.*

cerpt (*n.* ek′sûrpt; *v.* ik·sûrpt′) *n.* An extract from a ok, speech, etc. *— v.t.* To pick out and cite (a passage m a book, etc.). [< L < *ex-* out + *carpere* to pluck]

cess (*n.* ik·ses′, ek′ses; *adj.* ek′ses, ik·ses′) *n.* **1.** The ndition or fact of going beyond what is usual, necessary, oper, etc. **2.** An overabundance. **3.** The quantity, ex-nt, or degree by which one thing is over and above another ing. **4.** Overindulgence, as in food or drink; intemper-ce. *— adj.* **1.** Being over and above what is expected or ual. **2.** Immoderate. [See EXCEED.]

ces·sive (ik·ses′iv) *adj.* Going beyond what is usual, cessary, proper, etc.; extreme. **— ex·ces′sive·ly** *adv.*

ess profits Net profits exceeding the normal average a specified period of years.

change (iks·chānj′) *v.* **·changed, ·chang·ing** *v.t.* **1.** To ve and receive reciprocally. **2.** To give up for something ken as a replacement. **3.** To return as unsatisfactory and t a replacement for. **4.** To transfer to another in return r the equivalent in goods or money; trade. *— v.i.* **5.** To change something. **6.** To be exchanged: money that *ex-anges* at face value. *— n.* **1.** The act of giving or receiving e thing as equivalent for another. **2.** A giving and receiv-g in turn: an *exchange* of compliments. **3.** The substitu-on of one thing for another. **4.** That which is given or re-ceived in trade or substitution. **5.** A place where brokers, etc., meet to buy, sell, or trade commodities or securities: stock *exchange.* **6.** A central telephone system in a part of a city or in a town. **7.** A bill of exchange; also, the system of using a bill of exchange, or the fee for it. **8.** Rate of ex-change. **9.** The mutual giving and receiving of equal sums of money, as between two countries using different curren-cies, and allowing for differences in value. **10.** *pl.* Bills, drafts, etc., presented to a clearing-house for exchange or settlement. [< AF < LL < L *ex-* out + *cambiare* to ex-change] **— ex·change′a·ble** *adj.* **— ex·change′a·bil′i·ty** *n.*

ex·cheq·uer (iks·chek′ər, eks′chek·ər) *n.* **1.** The treasury of a state, organization, etc. **2.** *Informal* One's total finan-cial resources. [ME < OF *eschaquier* chessboard, then table marked in squares for keeping of accounts]

Ex·cheq·uer (iks·chek′ər, eks′chek·ər) *n.* The department of the British government managing the public revenue.

ex·cise¹ (*n.* ek′sīz, ik·sīz′; *v.* ik·sīz′) *n.* **1.** An indirect tax on such commodities as liquor, tobacco, etc., produced, sold, used, or transported within a country. Also **excise tax. 2.** A license fee charged for various sports, trades, etc. *— v.t.* **·cised, ·cis·ing** To levy an excise upon. [< MDu. < OF < L *ad-* to + *census* tax] **— ex·cis′a·ble** *adj.*

ex·cise² (ik·sīz′) *v.t.* **·cised, ·cis·ing 1.** To cut out, as a growth. **2.** To delete (a word, passage, etc.). [< L < *ex-* out + *caedere* to cut] **— ex·ci·sion** (ik·sizh′ən) *n.*

ex·cise·man (ik·sīz′mən) *n. pl.* **·men** (-mən) *Brit.* An of-ficer who collects excise duties.

ex·cit·a·ble (ik·sī′tə·bəl) *adj.* **1.** Easily excited; high-strung. **2.** *Physiol.* Susceptible to stimuli. **— ex·cit′a·bil′·i·ty** *n.* **— ex·cit′a·ble·ness** *n.* **— ex·cit′a·bly** *adv.*

ex·ci·tant (ik·sī′tənt, ek′sə·tənt) *n.* Something that excites or stimulates. *— adj.* Tending to excite or stimulate; stimu-lating: also **ex·ci′ta·tive, ex·ci′ta·to′ry** (-tôr′ē, -tō′rē).

ex·ci·ta·tion (ek′sī·tā′shən) *n.* The act of exciting, or the state of being excited; disturbance; agitation.

ex·cite (ik·sīt′) *v.t.* **·cit·ed, ·cit·ing 1.** To arouse (a feeling, reaction, etc.) into being or activity. **2.** To arouse strong feeling in; stimulate the emotions of. **3.** To provoke action in; rouse: to *excite* someone to greater endeavor. **4.** To bring about; stir up: to *excite* a riot. [< OF < L < *ex-* out + *ciere* to arouse] **— ex·cit′ed** *adj.* **— ex·cit′ed·ly** *adv.*

ex·cite·ment (ik·sīt′mənt) *n.* **1.** The state of being excited; agitation. **2.** That which excites.

ex·cit·ing (ik·sī′ting) *adj.* Causing excitement; stirring; rousing; thrilling. **— ex·cit′ing·ly** *adv.*

ex·claim (iks·klām′) *v.t. & v.i.* To cry out abruptly; speak vehemently, as in surprise or anger. [< F < L < *ex-* out + *clamare* to cry] **— ex·claim′er** *n.*

— Syn. *Exclaim* and *ejaculate* mean to say forcefully. *Exclaim* suggests merely vehement feeling; *ejaculate* adds a note of ex-plosive utterance and incoherence.

ex·cla·ma·tion (eks′klə·mā′shən) *n.* **1.** The act of exclaim-ing. **2.** An abrupt or emphatic utterance, outcry, etc. **— ex·clam·a·to·ry** (iks·klam′ə·tôr′ē, -tō′rē) *adj.*

exclamation mark A mark (!) used in punctuation to in-dicate that the immediately preceding word, phrase, or sen-tence is an exclamation. Also **exclamation point.**

ex·clude (iks·klōōd′) *v.t.* **·clud·ed, ·clud·ing 1.** To keep from entering; bar. **2.** To refuse to notice, consider, or al-low for; leave out. **3.** To put out; eject. [< L < *ex-* out + *claudere* to close] **— ex·clud′a·ble** *adj.* **— ex·clud′er** *n.*

ex·clu·sion (iks·klōō′zhən) *n.* **1.** The act of excluding, or the state of being excluded. **2.** That which is excluded.

ex·clu·sive (iks·klōō′siv) *adj.* **1.** Intended for or possessed by a single individual or group. **2.** Belonging to or found in a single source: an *exclusive* news story. **3.** Having no du-plicate; altogether original: an *exclusive* design. **4.** Admit-ting or catering to only a very select group. **5.** Concen-trated upon only one individual, thing, or group; complete and undivided: one's *exclusive* attention. **6.** Excluding the other or others by reason of being completely opposed or un-related: mutually *exclusive* doctrines. **7.** Being the only one: the *exclusive* owner. **8.** Not including; not comprising: usu. with *of*: the expense *exclusive* of fees. **9.** Not including the items, dates, figures, etc., that are specified as the limits: from 1 to 10 *exclusive* (1 and 10 are not included). **— ex·clu′sive·ly** *adv.* **— ex·clu′sive·ness** *n.*

ex·cog·i·tate (iks·koj′ə·tāt) *v.t.* **·tat·ed, ·tat·ing** To think out carefully; think up; devise. [< L < *ex-* out + *cogitare* to think] **— ex·cog′i·ta′tion** *n.* **— ex·cog′i·ta′tive** *adj.*

ex·com·mu·ni·cate (*v.* eks′kə·myōō′nə·kāt; *adj. & n.* eks′·kə·myōō′nə·kət) *v.t.* **·cat·ed, ·cat·ing** *Eccl.* To cut off by ecclesiastical authority from sharing in the sacraments, wor-ship, privileges, or fellowship of a church. *— adj.* Excom-municated. *— n.* An excommunicated person. [< LL < *ex-* out + *communicare* to share] **— ex′com·mu′ni·ca·ble** *adj.* **— ex′com·mu′ni·ca′tion** *n.* **— ex′com·mu′ni·ca′tor** *n.*

ex·com·mu·ni·ca·tive (eks′kə·myōō′nə·kā′tiv, -kə·tiv) *adj.* Relating to, favoring, or effecting excommunication. Also **ex·com·mu·ni·ca·to·ry** (eks′kə·myōō′nə·kə·tôr′ē, -tō′rē).

ex·co·ri·ate (ik·skôr′ē·āt, -skō′rē-) *v.t.* **·at·ed, ·at·ing 1.** To tear, chafe, or burn away strips of (skin, bark, etc.). **2.** To upbraid or denounce scathingly. [< L < *ex-* out, off + *corium* skin] — **ex·co′ri·a′tion** *n.*

ex·cre·ment (eks′krə·mənt) *n.* Refuse matter expelled from the body; esp., feces. — **ex′cre·men′tal** *adj.*

ex·cres·cence (iks·kres′əns) *n.* **1.** An unnatural or disfiguring outgrowth, as a wart. **2.** Any unnatural addition or outgrowth. **3.** A natural outgrowth, as hair. [< L < *ex-* out + *crescere* to grow] — **ex·cres′cen·cy** *n.* — **ex·cres′cent** *adj.*

ex·cre·ta (iks·krē′tə) *n.pl.* Excretions, as sweat, urine, etc.

ex·crete (iks·krēt′) *v.t.* **·cret·ed, ·cret·ing** To throw off or eliminate (waste matter) by normal discharge. [< L < *ex-* out + *cernere* to separate] — **ex·cre′tion** *n.*

ex·cre·to·ry (eks′krə·tôr′ē, -tō′rē, iks·krē′tər·ē) *adj.* Relating to or adapted for excretion. Also **ex·cre·tive** (iks·krē′tiv).

ex·cru·ci·ate (iks·krōō′shē·āt) *v.t.* **·at·ed, ·at·ing** To inflict extreme pain or agony upon; rack with pain. [< L < *ex-* completely + *cruciare* to torture] — **ex·cru′ci·at′ing** *adj.* — **ex·cru′ci·at′ing·ly** *adv.* — **ex·cru′ci·a′tion** *n.*

ex·cul·pate (eks′kul·pāt, ik·skul′-) *v.t.* **·pat·ed, ·pat·ing** To free from blame or prove innocent of guilt. [< EX-[1] + L *culpare* to blame] — **ex·culp·a·ble** (ik·skul′pə·bəl) *adj.* — **ex′cul·pa′tion** *n.* — **ex·cul′pa·to′ry** *adj.*

ex·cur·sion (ik·skûr′zhən, -shən) *n.* **1.** A short trip, as for relaxation, sightseeing, etc. **2.** A short trip on a train, etc., that is available at reduced rates. **3.** A group of people making such a trip. **4.** *Physics* An oscillating movement between two points; also, half of this total distance. [< L < *ex-* + *currere* to run] — **ex·cur′·sion·ist** *n.*

ex·cur·sive (ik·skûr′siv) *adj.* Going in one direction and then another; rambling; discursive; digressive. — **ex·cur′·sive·ly** *adv.* — **ex·cur′sive·ness** *n.*

ex·cuse (*v.* ik·skyōōz′; *n.* ik·skyōōs′) *v.t.* **·cused, ·cus·ing 1.** To ask pardon or forgiveness for (oneself). **2.** To grant pardon or forgiveness to. **3.** To accept or overlook: to *excuse* a child's mistakes. **4.** To free from censure or blame; extenuate. **5.** To release or exempt, as from a duty. **6.** To allow to leave. — **to excuse onself 1.** To ask forgiveness for oneself. **2.** To ask that one be released from some duty, etc. **3.** To ask for permission to leave. — *n.* **1.** A statement made or a reason given as a ground for being excused. **2.** A cause, factor, or circumstance that frees from blame, etc. [< OF < L < *ex-* out, away + *causa* charge, accusation] — **ex·cus′a·ble** *adj.* — **ex·cus′a·bly** *adv.*

ex·e·cra·ble (ek′sə·krə·bəl) *adj.* **1.** Detestable and revolting. **2.** Extremely bad. — **ex′e·cra·bly** *adv.*

ex·e·crate (ek′sə·krāt) *v.* **·crat·ed, ·crat·ing** *v.t.* **1.** To call down evil upon; curse. **2.** To detest; abhor. — *v.i.* **3.** To utter curses. [< L < *ex-* out + *sacrare* to devote to good or evil] — **ex′e·cra′tion** *n.* — **ex′e·cra′tive, ex′e·cra·to′re** (-krə·tôr′ē, -tō′rē) *adj.* — **ex′e·cra′tor** *n.*

ex·ec·u·tant (ig·zek′yə·tənt) *n.* One who carries into effect something to be done; also, one who gives a performance.

ex·e·cute (ek′sə·kyōōt) *v.t.* **·cut·ed, ·cut·ing 1.** To follow or carry out fully. **2.** To put into force, as a law. **3.** To put to death legally. **4.** To make (a will, deed, etc.) legal or valid. **5.** To perform (something demanding skill). **6.** To produce or fashion. — **Syn.** See KILL. [< L < *ex-* throughout + *sequi* to follow] — **ex′e·cut′a·ble** *adj.* — **ex′e·cut′er** *n.*

ex·e·cu·tion (ek′sə·kyōō′shən) *n.* **1.** The act of executing, or the fact or condition of being executed. **2.** The particular way in which something is done or performed; style or technique. **3.** *Law* A judicial writ for carrying into effect a judgment or decree of a court.

ex·e·cu·tion·er (ek′sə·kyōō′shən·ər) *n.* One who executes a death sentence.

ex·ec·u·tive (ig·zek′yə·tiv) *adj.* **1.** Relating or adapted to the putting into effect of plans, projects, work programs, etc. **2.** Relating or adapted to the execution of laws and the administration of judgments, decrees, etc. — *n.* **1.** An individual or a group managing the administrative affairs of a nation, state, or other political division. **2.** An individual responsible for the management of a business, etc.

executive officer *U.S.* The principal staff officer assisting a commanding officer in units smaller than a division.

ex·ec·u·tor (ek′sə·kyōō′tər *for def. 1,* ig·zek′yə·tər *for def. 2*) *n.* **1.** One who carries plans, etc., into effect. **2.** *Law* One who is appointed by a testator to carry out the terms of the will. — **ex·ec·u·to·ri·al** (ig·zek′yə·tôr′ē·əl, -tō′rē-) *adj.*

ex·ec·u·to·ry (ig·zek′yə·tôr′ē, -tō′rē) *adj.* **1.** Executive.

ex·ec·u·trix (ig·zek′yə·triks) *n. pl* **·trix–es** or **·tri·ces** (-trī′sēz) *Law* A female executor.

ex·e·ge·sis (ek′sə·jē′sis) *n. pl.* **·ses** (-sēz) Critical explanation of the meaning of words and passages in a literary or Biblical work. [< Gk. *exēgeesthai* to explain] — **ex′e·get′·ic** (-jet′ik) *adj.* — **ex′e·get′i·cal·ly** *adv.*

ex·e·gete (ek′sə·jēt) *n.* One skilled in critical explanat as of the Bible. Also **ex·e·ge·tist** (ek′sə·jē′tist).

ex·em·plar (ig·zem′plər, -plär) *n.* **1.** A model, pattern original. **2.** A typical example or specimen. [< OF < *exemplum* a pattern]

ex·em·pla·ry (ig·zem′plər·ē) *adj.* **1.** Serving as a wor model or example. **2.** Serving as a warning: *exemplary* p ishment. — **ex·em′pla·ri·ly** *adv.* — **ex·em′pla·ri·ness** *n*

ex·em·pli·fy (ig·zem′plə·fī) *v.t.* **·fied, ·fy·ing 1.** To show example; illustrate. **2.** *Law* To make an authenticated c from. [< Med.L < L *exemplum* copy + *facere* to make] **ex·em′pli·fi·ca′tion** *n.* — **ex·em′pli·fi·ca′tive** (-fə·kā′tiv)

ex·empt (ig·zempt′) *v.t.* To free or excuse from some obl tion to which others are subject. — *adj.* Free, clear, or cused, as from some duty, etc. — *n.* A person who is empted. [< L < *ex-* out + *emere* to buy, take] — **empt′i·ble** *adj.* — **ex·emp′tion** *n.*

ex·er·cise (ek′sər·sīz) *v.* **·cised, ·cis·ing** *v.t.* **1.** To subjec drills, etc., so as to train or develop. **2.** To make use employ. **3.** To perform, as duties. **4.** To exert, as influe or authority. **5.** To occupy the mind of; especially, to m anxious or fretful. — *v.i.* **6.** To perform exercises. — *n* A putting into use: an *exercise* of patience. **2.** Activity formed for physical conditioning, etc. **3.** A lesson, probl etc., designed to train some particular function or skill. *Usu. pl.* A ceremony, etc., as at a graduation. — **Syn.** PRACTICE. [< OF < L *exercere* to practice] — **ex′er·ci** *n.* — **ex′er·cis′a·ble** *adj.*

ex·ert (ig·zûrt′) *v.t.* To put forth or into action, as f or influence. [< L *exserere* to thrust out] — **ex·er′tive**

ex·er·tion (ig·zûr′shən) *n.* **1.** The act of exerting s power, faculty, etc. **2.** Strong action or effort; labor.

ex·e·unt (ek′sē·ənt, -sē·ōōnt) They go out: a stage direct [< L]

ex·fo·li·ate (eks·fō′lē·āt) *v.t. & v.i.* **·at·ed, ·at·ing** To se rate or peel off in scales, layers, flakes, etc., as skin, b rock, etc. [< LL < L *ex-* off + *folium* leaf] — **ex·fo′l tion** *n.* — **ex·fo′li·a′tive** *adj.*

ex·ha·la·tion (eks′hə·lā′shən, eg′zə-) *n.* **1.** The act of haling. **2.** That which is exhaled, as air.

ex·hale (eks·hāl′, ig·zāl′) *v.* **·haled, ·hal·ing** *v.i.* **1.** To e air or vapor; breathe out. **2.** To pass off or rise as a vapo emanation. — *v.t.* **3.** To breathe forth or give off, as vapor, or an aroma. **4.** To draw off; cause to evaporate. F < L < *ex-* out + *halare* to breathe] — **ex·hal′a·ble**

ex·haust (ig·zôst′) *v.t.* **1.** To make extremely tired. **2.** drain of resources, strength, etc. **3.** To draw off, as steam, etc., from or as from a container. **4.** To empt container) of contents; drain. **5.** To study, treat of, or velop thoroughly. — *v.i.* **6.** To escape, as a waste steam, etc. — *n.* **1.** The escape or discharge of waste ga working fluid, etc.; also, the waste gases, etc., that esc **2.** A pipe or other engine part through which waste ga etc., escape. **3.** Creation of a partial vacuum to suck stale air, dust, etc., as from a room; also, a device to do t [< L < *ex-* out + *haurire* to draw] — **ex·haust′i·ble** — **ex·haust′i·bil′i·ty** *n.*

ex·haust·ed (ig·zôs′tid) *adj.* **1.** Entirely used up; drair spent. **2.** Extremely tired. — **ex·haust′ed·ly** *adv.*

ex·haust·ing (ig·zôs′ting) *adj.* Extremely tiring; most tiguing; wearying. — **ex·haust′ing·ly** *adv.*

ex·haus·tion (ig·zôs′chən) *n.* **1.** Extreme fatigue; u weariness. **2.** The condition of being completely used

ex·haus·tive (ig·zôs′tiv) *adj.* **1.** That exhausts or tend exhaust; exhausting. **2.** Thoroughly; comprehensive. **ex·haus′tive·ly** *adv.* — **ex·haus′tive·ness** *n.*

ex·hib·it (ig·zib′it) *v.t.* **1.** To put on view, esp. publi **2.** To make evident; reveal. **3.** *Law* To submit (evider etc.) formally or officially to a court or officer. — *v.i.* **4.** put something on display. — *n.* **1.** A putting on view; play. **2.** An object or objects displayed, as at a fair. **3.** *I* An object submitted as a piece of evidence. [< L < *ex-* + *habere* to hold, have] — **ex·hib′i·tive, ex·hib′i·to′ry** — **ex·hib′i·tor, ex·hib′it·er** *n.*

ex·hi·bi·tion (ek′sə·bish′ən) *n.* **1.** The act of exhibiti **2.** That which is exhibited. **3.** A public display of art wo

ex·hi·bi·tion·ism (ek′sə·bish′ən·iz′əm) *n.* **1.** A tende to attract attention to oneself. **2.** *Psychiatry* The tende to obtain sexual gratification by public exposure of or body or genitalia. — **ex′hi·bi′tion·ist** *n.*

ex·hil·a·rant (ig·zil′ər·ənt) *adj.* Causing exhilaration. *n.* Something that exhilarates.

ex·hil·a·rate (ig·zil′ə·rāt) *v.t.* **·rat·ed, ·rat·ing** To set ag with happiness or elation; make cheerful. [< L < *ex-* co pletely + *hilarare* to gladden] — **ex·hil′a·ra′tion** *n.* — **hil′a·ra′tor** *n.* — **ex·hil′a·ra′tive** *adj.*

ex·hort (ig·zôrt′) *v.t.* **1.** To urge by earnest appeal or ar ment; advise or recommend strongly. — *v.i.* **2.** To utte give exhortation. [< L < *ex-* completely + *hortari* to ur — **ex·hor·ta·tion** (eg′zôr·tā′shən, ek′sôr-) *n.* — **ex·hor′ tive** (-tə·tiv), **ex·hor′ta·to′ry** (-tôr′ē) *adj.* — **ex·hort′er**

ume (ig·zyōōm′, iks·hyōōm′) *v.t.* **·humed, ·hum·ing** **1.** dig up; disinter. **2.** To bring to light; reveal. [< F < L out + *humus* ground] — **ex·hu·ma·tion** (eks′hyōō·mā′·n) *n.* — **ex·hum′er** *n.*

·gen·cy (ek′sə·jən·sē) *n. pl.* **·cies** **1.** Urgency. **2.** A ıation that requires immediate attention. **3.** *Usu. pl.* A ıssing need or necessity. Also **ex′i·gence.**

·gent (ek′sə·jənt) *adj.* **1.** Urgent. **2.** Requiring or exing a great deal; unreasonably demanding. [< L < *ex-* ; + *agere* to drive] — **ex′i·gent·ly** *adv.*

g·u·ous (ig·zig′yōō·əs, ik·sig′-) *adj.* Small; scanty. [< *xiguus* scanty] — **ex·i·gu·i·ty** (ek′sə·gyōō′ə·tē) *n.*

le (eg′zīl, ek′sīl) *n.* **1.** Separation by necessity or choice m one's native country, home, etc. **2.** One who is sepaed from his native country, home, etc. — *v.t.* **·iled, ·il·ing** cause (a person) to leave and stay away from (the per's) native country, home, etc. [< OF < L *exsilium*]

st (ig·zist′) *v.i.* **1.** To have actual being or reality; be. To continue to live or be. **3.** To be present; occur. [< F L < *ex-* out + *sistere* to be located] — **ex·is′tent** *adj. & n.*

s·tence (ig·zis′təns) *n.* **1.** The state or fact of being or ıtinuing to be. **2.** Possession or continuance of animate ng; life. **3.** Way or mode of living. **4.** Presence; occurıce. **5.** Anything or all that exists. — **ex′is·ten′tial** ən′shəl) *adj.* — **ex′is·ten′tial·ly** *adv.*

s·ten·tial·ism (eg′zis·ten′shəl·iz′əm) *n.* A philosophy ıt stresses the active role of the will rather than of reason confronting problems posed by a hostile universe. — **ex′·en′tial·ist** *adj. & n.*

t (eg′zit, ek′sit) *n.* **1.** A way or passage out; egress. **2.** e departure of an actor from the stage. **3.** Any departure. *v.i.* To go out; depart. [< L < *ex-* out + *ire* to go]

i·bris (eks lī′bris, lē′-) *Latin.* **1.** From the books (of): ıd as an inscription on a book. **2.** A bookplate.

· *combining form* Out; outside; external: *exocarp.* Also, ore vowels, **ex-.** [< Gk. *exo-, ex-* < *exō* outside]

ɔ·carp (ek′sō·kärp) *n. Bot.* The epicarp.

ɔ·derm (ek′sō·dûrm) See ECTODERM.

ɔ·dus (ek′sə·dəs) *n.* A going forth. — **the Exodus** The ɔarture of the Israelites from Egypt under the guidance of ɔses, described in **Exodus,** the second book of the Old stament. [< L < Gk. < *ex-* out + *hodos* way]

of·fi·ci·o (eks ə·fish′ē·ō) *Latin.* By virtue of or because office or position.

ɔg·a·my (eks·og′ə·mē) *n.* The custom of marriage outɪe of the tribe, family, clan, etc. — **ex·og′a·mous** *adj.*

ɔ·gen (ek′sō·jen) *n. Bot.* A plant that increases in size successive concentric additions beneath the bark. [< o- + -GEN] — **ex·og·e·nous** (eks·oj′ə·nəs) *adj.*

ɔn·er·ate (ig·zon′ə·rāt) *v.t.* **·at·ed, ·at·ing** **1.** To free ɪm accusation or blame. **2.** To relieve or free from a reɔnsibility or the like. [< L < *ex-* out, away + *onus, eris* burden] — **ex·on′er·a′tion** *n.* — **ex·on′er·a′tive** *adj.*

ɔph·thal·mos (ek′sof·thal′məs) *n. Pathol.* Abnormal ɔtrusion of the eyeball. Also **ex′oph·thal′mi·a** (-mē·ə), **′oph·thal′mus.** [< NL < Gk. < *ex-* out + *ophthalmos* e] — **ex′oph·thal′mic** *adj.*

or·bi·tant (ig·zôr′bə·tənt) *adj.* Going beyond usual and ɔper limits, as in price or demand; excessive; extravagant. LL *exorbitare* to go astray] — **ex·or′bi·tance, ex·or′bi·n·cy** *n.* — **ex·or′bi·tant·ly** *adv.*

or·cise (ek′sôr·sīz) *v.t.* **·cised, ·cis·ing** **1.** To cast out (an il spirit) by prayers or incantations. **2.** To free (a person, ace, etc.) of an evil spirit. Also **ex′or·cize.** [< OF < LL Gk. < *ex-* out + *horkos* oath] — **ex′or·cis′er, ex′or·cist** — **ex·or·cism** (ek′sôr·siz′əm) *n.*

or·di·um (ig·zôr′dē·əm, ik·sôr′-) *n. pl.* **·di·ums** or **·di·a** lē·ə) The beginning or introductory part of anything, esp. a discourse, treatise, etc. [< L < *ex-* out + *ordiri* to ben] — **ex·or′di·al** *adj.*

o·sphere (ek′sō·sfir) *n. Meteorol.* The region of the rth's atmosphere beginning at about 400 miles up.

ot·ic (ig·zot′ik) *adj.* **1.** Belonging by nature or origin to ıother part of the world; not native. **2.** Strangely different ıd fascinating. — *n.* Something exotic. [< L < Gk. *ōtikos* foreign] — **ex·ot′i·cal·ly** *adv.* — **ex·ot′i·cism** *n.*

pand (ik·spand′) *v.t.* **1.** To increase the range, scope, ɔlume, size, etc., of. **2.** To spread out by unfolding; open. To develop more fully the details or form of. — *v.i.* **4.** o grow larger, wider, etc. [< L < *ex-* out + *pandere* to read] — **ex·pand′er** *n.*

·panse (ik·spans′) *n.* **1.** A wide, continuous area or retch. **2.** Expansion. [See EXPAND.]

·pan·si·ble (ik·span′sə·bəl) *adj.* Capable of being exınded. — **ex·pan′si·bil′i·ty** *n.*

·pan·sion (ik·span′shən) *n.* **1.** The act of expanding, or ıe state of being expanded. **2.** The amount of increase in ze, range, volume, etc. **3.** That which is expanded.

ex·pan·sive (ik·span′siv) *adj* **1.** Capable of expanding or tending to expand. **2.** Characterized by expansion; broad; extensive. **3.** Open and effusive; outgoing. — **ex·pan′sive·ly** *adv.* — **ex·pan′sive·ness** *n.*

ex·pa·ti·ate (ik·spā′shē·āt) *v.i.* **·at·ed, ·at·ing** To speak or write at length; elaborate: with *on.* [< L < *ex-* out + *spatiari* to walk] — **ex·pa′ti·a′tion** *n.* — **ex·pa′ti·a′tor** *n.*

ex·pa·tri·ate (*v.* eks·pā′trē·āt; *n. & adj.* eks·pā′trē·it, -āt) *v.t.* **·at·ed, ·at·ing** To exile; banish. — *n.* An expatriated person. — *adj.* Banished; expatriated. [< Med.L < L *ex-* out + *patria* native land] — **ex·pa′tri·a′tion** *n.*

ex·pect (ik·spekt′) *v.t.* **1.** To look forward to as certain or probable. **2.** To look for as right, proper, or necessary. **3.** *Informal* To presume; suppose. [< L < *ex-* out + *spectare* to look at] — **ex·pec′ta·ble** *adj.*

ex·pec·tan·cy (ik·spek′tən·sē) *n. pl.* **·cies** **1.** The action or state of expecting. **2.** An object of expectation.

ex·pec·tant (ik·spek′tənt) *adj.* **1.** Having expectations. **2.** Awaiting the birth of a child. — **ex·pec′tant·ly** *adv.*

ex·pec·ta·tion (ek′spek·tā′shən) *n.* **1.** The action of expecting, or the state of mind of one who expects; anticipation. **2.** The state of being expected: preceded by *in.* **3.** Something expected or looked forward to.

ex·pect·ing (ik·spek′ting) *adj.* Pregnant; also, due to give birth: Is she *expecting*?; She is *expecting* in July.

ex·pec·to·rant (ik·spek′tər·ənt) *adj.* Promoting expectoration. — *n.* A medicine used to promote expectoration.

ex·pec·to·rate (ik·spek′tə·rāt) *v.t. & v.i.* **·rat·ed, ·rat·ing** **1.** To discharge (phlegm, etc.) by spitting. **2.** To spit. [< L < *ex-* out + *pectus, -oris* breast] — **ex·pec′·to·ra′tion** *n.*

ex·pe·di·en·cy (ik·spē′dē·ən·sē) *n. pl.* **·cies** **1.** The state or quality of being expedient. **2.** That which is expedient. **3.** Adherence to what is opportune or politic, not for what is just or right. Also **ex·pe′di·ence.**

ex·pe·di·ent (ik·spē′dē·ənt) *adj.* 1. Serving to promote a desired end; suitable, advisable, or proper. **2.** Pertaining to or prompted by utility, interest, or advantage rather than by what is right. — *n.* **1.** Something expedient. **2.** A device; shift. [< OF < L *expedire* to free the feet from fetters]

ex·pe·dite (ek′spə·dīt) *v.t.* **·dit·ed, ·dit·ing** **1.** To speed up the process or progress of; facilitate. **2.** To do with quick efficiency. [< L *expedire* to free the feet from fetters]

ex·pe·dit·er (ek′spə·dī′tər) *n.* One who facilitates the delivery of needed material. Also **ex′pe·di·tor.**

ex·pe·di·tion (ek′spə·dish′ən) *n.* **1.** A journey or march for a definite purpose. **2.** The body of persons engaged in such a journey, together with their equipment. **3.** Speed.

ex·pe·di·tion·ar·y (ek′spə·dish′ən·er′ē) *adj.* Relating to, designed for, or constituting an expedition.

ex·pe·di·tious (ek′spə·dish′əs) *adj.* Quick; speedy. — **ex′·pe·di′tious·ly** *adv.* — **ex′pe·di′tious·ness** *n.*

ex·pel (ik·spel′) *v.t.* **·pelled, ·pel·ling** **1.** To drive out by force. **2.** To force to end attendance at a school, terminate membership, etc.: oust. [< L < *ex-* out + *pellere* to drive, thrust] — **ex·pel′la·ble** *adj.*

— **Syn.** A school *expels* an unruly pupil; water in the lungs must be promptly *expelled.* A rifle *ejects* a shell automatically; a squid *ejects* an inky fluid. To *dislodge* is to move something heavy from its place; an avalanche may *dislodge* a large boulder. A man is *evicted* from his house; an official is *ousted* from office; an employee is *dismissed* from his job.

ex·pend (ik·spend′) *v.t.* To pay out or spend; use up. [< L < *ex-* out + *pendere* to weigh, pay]

ex·pend·a·ble (ik·spen′də·bəl) *adj.* **1.** Available for spending. **2.** *Mil.* Denoting supplies or equipment that can be sacrificed. — **ex·pend′a·bil′i·ty** *n.*

ex·pen·di·ture (ik·spen′də·chər) *n.* **1.** The act of expending; outlay. **2.** That which is expended; expense.

ex·pense (ik·spens′) *n.* **1.** Outlay or consumption of money. **2.** The amount of money required to buy or do something. **3.** Something that requires or involves the spending of money. **4.** *pl.* Funds allotted or spent to cover incidental costs. **5.** Loss or injury involved in doing something: preceded by *at.* [See EXPEND.]

ex·pen·sive (ik·spen′siv) *adj.* Involving much expense; costly. — **ex·pen′sive·ly** *adv.* — **ex·pen′sive·ness** *n.*

ex·pe·ri·ence (ik·spir′ē·əns) *n.* **1.** Actual participation in or direct contact with something. **2.** A particular activity or occurrence actually participated in. **3.** Knowledge or skill derived from actual participation or training. **4.** The period of such activity. **5.** The totality of one's judgments or reactions. **6.** The accumulated variety of whatever has been actually met with or engaged in: the entire *experience* of mankind. — *v.t.* **·enced, ·enc·ing** To be personally involved in; undergo. [< OF < L < *experiri* to try out]

ex·pe·ri·enced (ik·spir′ē·ənst) *adj.* **1.** Having had considerable experience. **2.** Made skillful or proficient through actual practice, etc.

ex·pe·ri·en·tial (ik·spir′ē·en′shəl) *adj.* Pertaining to or acquired by experience; empirical. — **ex·pe′ri·en′tial·ly** *adv.*

ex·pe·ri·ment (ik·sper′ə·mənt, -ment) *n.* **1.** An act or operation designed to discover, test, or illustrate a truth, principle, or effect. **2.** The conducting of such operations. — *v.i.* To make experiments; make a test or trial. [< OF < L < *experiri* to try out] — **ex·per′i·ment′er** *n.*

ex·per·i·men·tal (ik·sper′ə·men′təl) *adj.* **1.** Pertaining to, resulting from, or known by experiment. **2.** Growing out of or based on experience; empirical. **3.** Having the nature of an experiment; provisional; tentative. — **ex·per′i·men′tal·ism** *n.* — **ex·per′i·men′tal·ist** *n.* — **ex·per′i·men′tal·ly** *adv.*

ex·per·i·men·ta·tion (ik·sper′ə·men·tā′shən) *n.* The act or practice of experimenting.

ex·pert (*n.* ek′spûrt; *for adj. also* ik·spûrt′) *n.* One who has special skill or knowledge; a specialist. — *adj.* **1.** Skillful as the result of training or experience. **2.** Characteristic of or produced by an expert. [< OF < L *expertus*, pp. of *experiri* to try out] — **ex·pert′ly** *adv.* — **ex·pert′ness** *n.*

ex·pi·ate (ek′spē·āt) *v.t.* **·at·ed, ·at·ing** To atone for; make amends for. [< L < *ex-* completely + *piare* to appease] — **ex′pi·a·ble** *adj.* — **ex′pi·a′tion** *n.* — **ex′pi·a′tor** *n.*

ex·pi·a·to·ry (eks′pē·ə·tôr′ē, -tō′rē) *adj.* Having the power or character of an expiation; offered in atonement.

ex·pi·ra·tion (ek′spə·rā′shən) *n.* **1.** The termination of anything; close. **2.** The act of breathing out air from the lungs.

ex·pire (ik·spīr′) *v.* **·pired, ·pir·ing** *v.i.* **1.** To come to an end, as a contract. **2.** To breathe out air from the lungs; exhale. **3.** To breathe one's last breath; die. **4.** To die out, as embers. — *v.t.* **5.** To breathe out from the lungs. [< F < L < *ex-* out + *spirare* to breathe] — **ex·pir′a·to′ry** *adj.*

ex·plain (ik·splān′) *v.t.* **1.** To make plain or understandable. **2.** To give the meaning of; interpret; expound. **3.** To give reasons for; account for. — *v.i.* **4.** To give an explanation. [< L < *ex-* out + *planare* to make level] — **ex·plain′a·ble** *adj.*

ex·pla·na·tion (ek′splə·nā′shən) *n.* **1.** The act or process of explaining. **2.** A statement that clarifies or accounts for something. **3.** The meaning assigned or adduced to explain something; sense; significance.

ex·plan·a·to·ry (ek·splan′ə·tôr′ē, -tō′rē) *adj.* Serving to explain. Also **ex·plan′a·tive.** — **ex·plan′a·to′ri·ly** *adv.*

ex·ple·tive (eks′plə·tiv) *n.* **1.** An exclamation, often profane. **2.** A word or syllable added solely for the completion of a syntactic pattern. — *adj.* Added merely to fill out a sentence, complete a rhythm, etc.: also **ex′ple·to′ry** (-tôr′ē, -tō′rē). [< LL < L < *ex-* completely + *plere* to fill]

ex·pli·ca·ble (eks′pli·kə·bəl, ik·splik′ə·bəl) *adj.* Capable of explanation.

ex·pli·cate (eks′plə·kāt) *v.t.* **·cat·ed, ·cat·ing** To clear from obscurity; explain. [< L < *ex-* out + *plicare* to fold] — **ex′pli·ca′tion** *n.* — **ex′pli·ca′tor** *n.*

ex·pli·ca·tive (eks′plə·kā′tiv, ik·splik′ə·tiv) *adj.* Serving to interpret or explain. Also **ex′pli·ca·to′ry** (-kə·tôr′ē).

ex·plic·it (ik·splis′it) *adj.* **1.** Plainly expressed; clear. **2.** Unreserved in expression; straightforward. [See EXPLICATE.] — **ex·plic′it·ly** *adv.* — **ex·plic′it·ness** *n.*

ex·plode (ik·splōd′) *v.* **·plod·ed, ·plod·ing** *v.t.* **1.** To cause to burst or blow up violently and with noise; detonate. **2.** To disprove utterly; refute. **3.** To cause to expand violently or pass suddenly from a solid to a gaseous state. — *v.i.* **4.** To burst into pieces or fragments; blow up. **5.** To make a noise as if bursting: to *explode* with laughter. **6.** To be exploded, as gunpowder. [< L < *ex-* out + *plaudere* to clap]

ex·ploit (*n.* eks′ploit, ik·sploit′; *v.* ik·sploit′) *n.* A deed or act, esp. one marked by heroism or daring; feat. — *v.t.* **1.** To use meanly for one's own gain or advantage: to *exploit* workers. **2.** To utilize for profitable ends: to *exploit* water power. [See EXPLICATE.] — **ex·ploit′a·ble** *adj.* — **ex′ploi·ta′tion** *n.* — **ex·ploit′a·tive** *n.* — **ex·ploi′ter** *n.*

ex·plo·ra·tion (eks′plə·rā′shən) *n.* The act of exploring; esp., the exploring of unfamiliar or unknown regions.

ex·plor·a·to·ry (ik·splôr′ə·tôr′ē, ik·splō′rə·tō′rē) *adj.* Of, for, or relating to exploration. Also **ex·plor′a·tive.**

ex·plore (ik·splôr′, -splōr′) *v.* **·plored, ·plor·ing** *v.t.* **1.** To subject to a close search or examination; scrutinize carefully. **2.** To travel through (unfamiliar territory, etc.). — *v.i.* **3.** To make an exploration. [< L < *ex-* out + *plorare* to cry out] — **ex·plor′er** *n.*

ex·plo·sion (ik·splō′zhən) *n.* **1.** The act of exploding. **2.** The sudden, loud noise produced by exploding. **3.** A sudden, violent outbreak of feeling: an *explosion* of laughter.

ex·plo·sive (ik·splō′siv) *adj.* **1.** Pertaining to or marked by explosion. **2.** Liable to explode or to cause explosion. — *n.* Any substance or mixture of substances that, on impact or by ignition, reacts by a violent expansion of gases and the liberation of relatively large amounts of thermal energy. — **ex·plo′sive·ly** *adv.* — **ex·plo′sive·ness** *n.*

ex·po·nent (ik·spō′nənt; *for def. 3, also* ek′spō·nənt) *n.* **1.** One who or that which explains or expounds. **2.** One who or that which represents or symbolizes something: an *exponent* of fair play. **3.** *Math.* A number or symbol placed superscript to the right of a quantity to indicate a powe the reciprocal or root of a power: 2 is an *exponent* in 3^2. L < *ex-* out + *ponere* to place]

ex·port (*v.* ik·spôrt′, -spōrt′, eks′pôrt, -pōrt; *n. & adj.* e pôrt, -pōrt) *v.t.* To carry or send, as merchandise or materials, to other countries for sale or trade. — *n.* **1.** act of exporting. **2.** That which is exported, as a commod — *adj.* Of or pertaining to exports or exportation. [<] *ex-* out + *portare* to carry] — **ex·port′a·ble** *adj.* — port′a·bil′i·ty *n.* — **ex′por·ta′tion** *n.* — **ex·port′er** *n.*

ex·pose (ik·spōz′) *v.t.* **·posed, ·pos·ing** **1.** To lay ope criticism, ridicule, etc.: to *expose* oneself to scorn. **2.** lay open to some force, influence, etc.: to *expose* a mix to heat. **3.** To present to view by baring: to *expose* o shoulders. **4.** To reveal (something evil, disgraceful, e to *expose* a crime. **5.** To reveal the identity of (an evild criminal, etc.); unmask. **6.** To place so as to cause death of by cold, starvation, etc. **7.** *Photog.* To admit l to (a sensitized film or plate). [< MF < *ex-* out + *p* See POSE[1].] — **ex·pos′er** *n.*

ex·po·sé (ek′spō·zā′) *n.* A making known publicly of sc thing evil or disgraceful. [< F, pp. of *exposer*]

ex·po·si·tion (eks′pə·zish′ən) *n.* **1.** The act of present explaining, or expounding facts or ideas. **2.** A deta presentation of subject matter; also, a commentary or ir pretation. **3.** A large public display or show.

ex·pos·i·tor (ik·spoz′ə·tər) *n.* One who expounds.

ex·pos·i·to·ry (ik·spoz′ə·tôr′ē, -tō′rē) *adj.* Of or pertai to exposition; explanatory. Also **ex·pos′i·tive.**

ex post fac·to (eks pōst fak′tō) *Latin* Arising or ena after some act, occurrence, etc., and having retroac effect: said esp. of a law.

ex·pos·tu·late (ik·spos′chŏŏ·lāt) *v.i.* **·lat·ed, ·lat·ing** reason earnestly with a person concerning the inadvisab of his actions, etc.; remonstrate: usu. with *with.* [< L < out + *postulare* to demand] — **ex·pos′tu·la′tion** *n.* — **pos′tu·la′tor** *n.* — **ex·pos′tu·la·to′ry** (-lə·tôr′ē, -tō′rē), **pos′tu·la′tive** *adj.*

ex·po·sure (ik·spō′zhər) *n.* **1.** The act of exposing, or state of being exposed. **2.** Situation in relation to the s elements, or points of the compass: a room with south *exposure.* **3.** *Photog.* **a** The act of subjecting a sensiti plate or film to the action of actinic rays. **b** The time quired for this. **c** A single film or plate so acted upon.

ex·pound (ik·spound′) *v.t.* **1.** To set forth in detail; st declare. **2.** To explain the meaning of; interpret. [< < L < *ex-* out + *ponere* to place] — **ex·pound′er** *n.*

ex·press (ik·spres′) *v.t.* **1.** To formulate in words; ver ize; state: to *express* an idea. **2.** To give an outward i cation of; reveal: to *express* anger by frowning. **3.** To c municate through some medium other than words or si **4.** To indicate by means of a symbol, formula, etc., a mathematics or chemistry. **5.** To squeeze out (a liq juice, etc.); press out. **6.** *U.S.* To send (goods, etc.) by s cial messenger or a system of rapid delivery. — **to expr oneself** **1.** To communicate one's thoughts. **2.** To g vent to one's feelings, desires, etc., through creative activ — *adj.* **1.** Communicated or indicated in a clear and unn takable way; explicit. **2.** Made or intended for a pre purpose. **3.** Designed for or operating at high speed: *express* highway; an *express* train. **4.** Of or relating t system of rapid delivery of goods, etc., as by railway: to s something by *express* delivery. **5.** Exact; precise. — *c* By rapid delivery: to send something *express.* — *n.* **1** system designed to convey goods, parcels, money, etc., r idly from one point to another. **2.** Goods, parcels, etc., c veyed by this system. **3.** Any means of rapid conveyar **4.** A company specializing in the rapid conveyance of goc parcels, etc. **5.** A train or other conveyance operating high speed and making few stops. **6.** A message sent w speed. [< OF < L < *ex-* out + *pressare* to press] — **press′er** *n.* — **ex·press′i·ble** *adj.*

ex·press·age (ik·spres′ij) *n.* **1.** The transportation goods by express. **2.** The charge for this.

ex·pres·sion (ik·spresh′ən) *n.* **1.** Communication thought, opinion, etc. **2.** Outward indication or manifes tion of some feeling, condition, quality, etc. **3.** A conv tional sign or set of signs used to indicate something; sy bolization. **4.** A particular cast of the features that presses a feeling, meaning, etc. **5.** The particular way which one expresses oneself. **6.** The quality of expressi oneself with understanding, insight, sensitivity, etc. **7.** particular word, phrase, etc., used in communication. **8.** T kind of language used in communication: poetic *expressi* **9.** The action of pressing or squeezing out juice, etc.

ex·pres·sion·ism (ik·spresh′ən·iz′əm) *n.* An early 20 century movement in the arts, originating in Europe, th had as its object the free expression of the inner experier of the artist rather than realistic representation. — **e pres′sion·ist** *n. & adj.* — **ex·pres′sion·is′tic** *adj.*

pres·sive (ik·spres′iv) *adj.* **1.** Of or characterized by pression. **2.** Serving to express or indicate: a manner *pressive* of contempt. **3.** Significant: an *expressive* sigh. — **ex·pres′sive·ly** *adv.* — **ex·pres′sive·ness** *n.*

press·ly (ik·spres′lē) *adv.* **1.** With definitely stated in- nt or application. **2.** Exactly and unmistakably; plainly.

press·way (ik·spres′wā′) *n.* A road for rapid travel.

pro·pri·ate (eks·prō′prē·āt) *v.t.* **·at·ed, ·at·ing 1.** To ke or transfer (property) from the owner, esp. for public use. To deprive (a person) of ownership or property. [< LL L *ex-* out + *proprium* property < *proprius* one's own] — **:·pro′pri·a′tion** *n.* — **ex·pro′pri·a′tor** *n.* — **ex·pro′pri·a· ′ry** (-ə·tôr′ē, -tō′rē) *adj.*

pul·sion (ik·spul′shən) *n.* **1.** The act of expelling. **2.** he state or fact of being expelled. — **ex·pul′sive** *adj.*

punge (ik·spunj′) *v.t.* **·punged, ·pung·ing** To erase or pe out. [< L < *ex-* out + *pungere* to prick]

pur·gate (eks′pər·gāt, ik·spûr′gāt) *v.t.* **·gat·ed, ·gat·ing** To take out obscene or otherwise objectionable material om: to *expurgate* a novel. **2.** To remove or omit (objec- nable words, lines, etc.). [< L < *ex-* out + *purgare* to eanse] — **ex′pur·ga′tion** *n.* — **ex′pur·ga′tor** *n.* — **ex· r′ga·to′ry** *adj.*

qui·site (eks′kwi·zit, ik·skwiz′it) *adj.* **1.** Marked by re and delicate beauty, craftsmanship, etc. **2.** Being of a gh degree of excellence; consummate; admirable: an *ex- isite* skill. **3.** Highly sensitive to sounds, colors, forms, c.; dscriminating: an *exquisite* eye for design. **4.** Ex- emely refined; very fastidious. **5.** Intensely keen or acute, pleasure or pain. — *n.* A person, usu. a man, who is erelegant in dress, manners, etc. [< L < *ex-* out + *qua- ere* to seek] — **ex′qui·site·ly** *adv.* — **ex′qui·site·ness** *n.*

tant (ek′stənt, ik·stant′) *adj.* Still existing; not lost nor stroyed; surviving. [< L < *ex-* out + *stare* to stand]

tem·po·ra·ne·ous (ik·stem′pə·rā′nē·əs) *adj.* **1.** Uttered, rformed, or composed with little or no advance prepara- on: an *extemporaneous* talk. **2.** Prepared with regard to ntent but not read or memorized word for word: an *ex- mporaneous* political speech. **3.** Made with anything im- ediately available; improvised to meet circumstances. [< L < L *ex-* out + *tempus, temporis* time] — **ex·tem′po· ′ne·ous·ly** *adv.* — **ex·tem′po·ra′ne·ous·ness** *n.*

tem·po·rar·y (ik·stem′pə·rer′ē) *adj.* Extemporaneous. — **ex·tem′po·rar′i·ly** *adv.* — **ex·tem′po·rar′i·ness** *n.*

tem·po·re (ik·stem′pə·rē) *adj.* Extemporaneous. — *lv.* With little or no advance preparation; extemporane- usly. [< L *ex tempore* out of the time]

tem·po·rize (ik·stem′pə·rīz) *v.t.* & *v.i.* **·rized, ·riz·ing** o do, make or perform with little or no advance prepara- on. — **ex·tem′po·ri·za′tion** *n.* — **ex·tem′po·riz′er** *n.*

tend (ik·stend′) *v.t.* **1.** To open or stretch to full length. . To make longer. **3.** To prolong; continue. **4.** To spread ıt; expand. **5.** To hold out or put forth, as the hand. **6.** o give or offer to give: to *extend* hospitality. — *v.i.* **7.** To e extended; stretch. — **Syn.** See INCREASE. [< L < *ex-* ıt + *tendere* to stretch] — **ex·tend′ed** *adj.* — **ex·tend′i· l′i·ty** *n.* — **ex·tend′i·ble** *adj.*

ten·si·ble (ik·sten′sə·bəl) *adj.* Capable of being extended. — **ex·ten′si·bil′i·ty** *n.*

ten·sion (ik·sten′shən) *n.* **1.** The act of extending, or ie state of being extended. **2.** An extended part; addition. . Range; extent. **4.** An agreement by which a creditor lows a debtor further time in which to pay a debt. **5.** *hysics* That property of matter by virtue of which it occu- ies space. — **ex·ten′sion·al** *adj.*

ten·sive (ik·sten′siv) *adj.* **1.** Large in area: an *extensive* rm. **2.** Having a wide range; broad in scope: *extensive* ex- erience. **3.** Widespread; far-reaching: *extensive* damage. — **ex·ten′sive·ly** *adv.* — **ex·ten′sive·ness** *n.*

ten·sor (ik·sten′sər, -sôr) *n.* *Anat.* A muscle that raightens out a limb.

tent (ik·stent′) *n.* **1.** The dimension, degree, or limit to hich anything is extended; compass; reach; size. **2.** Size ithin given bounds; limits; scope: the *extent* of his powers. . A vast area. [< L < *ex-* out + *tendere* to stretch]

ten·u·ate (ik·sten′yo͞o·āt) *v.t.* **·at·ed, ·at·ing 1.** To rep- esent (a fault, crime, etc.) as less blameworthy; make ex- uses for. **2.** To belittle the importance of. [< L < *ex-* out + *tenuis* thin] — **ex·ten′u·a′tion** *n.* — **ex·ten′u·a′tor** *n.*

:·ten·u·at·ing (ik·sten′yo͞o·ā′ting) *adj.* Serving to lessen he odiousness, as of a crime: *extenuating* circumstances.

:·te·ri·or (ik·stir′ē·ər) *adj.* **1.** Of, pertaining to, or situ- ted on the outside; external; outer. **2.** Coming or acting rom without: *exterior* influences. **3.** Pertaining to foreign ountries; foreign. — *n.* **1.** That which is outside, as an xternal surface. **2.** Outside appearance or demeanor. [< *exterus* outside] — **ex·te′ri·or·ly** *adv.*

cterior angle *Geom.* **1.** Any of four angles formed on the outside of two nonintersecting straight lines cut by a third line. **2.** The angle formed between any side of a polygon and the extension of an adjacent side.

ex·ter·mi·nate (ik·stûr′mə·nāt) *v.t.* **·nat·ed, ·nat·ing** To destroy (living things) entirely; annihilate. [< L < *ex-* out + *terminus* boundary] — **ex·ter′mi·na′tion** *n.* — **ex·ter′· mi·na′tive, ex·ter′mi·na·to′ry** (-nə·tôr′ē, -tō′rē) *adj.*

ex·ter·mi·na·tor (ik·stûr′mə·nā′tər) *n.* One who or that which exterminates.

ex·ter·nal (ik·stûr′nəl) *adj.* **1.** Of, pertaining to, or situ- ated on the outside; outer; exterior. **2.** Belonging to or de- rived from the outside; extrinsic: an *external* factor. **3.** Per- taining to the outer self; superficial. **4.** Pertaining to foreign countries: *external* affairs. **5.** Relating to, affecting, or meant for the outside of the body: *external* medication. — *n.* **1.** The outside; exterior. **2.** *Usu. pl.* Outward or superficial aspects, circumstances, etc. [< L *externus* outer] — **ex· ter·nal·i·ty** (ek′·stər·nal′ə·tē) *n.* — **ex·ter′nal·ly** *adv.*

ex·ter·nal·ize (ik·stûr′nəl·īz) *v.t.* **·ized, ·iz·ing 1.** To give external shape to; make external. **2.** To make outwardly real. — **ex·ter′nal·i·za′tion** *n.*

ex·tinct (ik·stingkt′) *adj.* **1.** Extinguished; inactive, as a volcano. **2.** No longer existing: an *extinct* animal. **3.** Void. [< L < *ex-* completely + *stinguere* to quench]

ex·tinc·tion (ik·stingk′shən) *n.* **1.** The act of extinguish- ing, or the state of being extinguished. **2.** The process or condition of becoming extinct; a dying out. **3.** Annihila- tion. — **ex·tinc′tive** *adj.*

ex·tin·guish (ik·sting′gwish, -wish) *v.t.* **1.** To put out or quench, as a fire. **2.** To make extinct; wipe out. **3.** To ob- scure; eclipse. [< L < *ex-* completely + *stinguere* to quench] — **ex·tin′guish·a·ble** *adj.* — **ex·tin′guish·er** *n.*

ex·tir·pate (ek′stər·pāt, ik·stûr′-) *v.t.* **·pat·ed, ·pat·ing** To root out or up; destroy wholly. [< L < *ex-* out + *stirps, stirpis* stem, root] — **ex′tir·pa′tion** *n.* — **ex′tir·pa′tive** *adj.* — **ex′tir·pa′tor** *n.*

ex·tol (ik·stōl′, -stol′) *v.t* **·tolled, ·tol·ling** To praise in the highest terms; exalt; laud. — **Syn.** See PRAISE. Also **ex· toll′.** [< L < *ex-* out, up + *tollere* to raise] — **ex·tol′ler** *n.* — **ex·tol′ment** or **ex·toll′ment** *n.*

ex·tort (ik·stôrt′) *v.t.* To obtain (money, etc.) from a per- son by threat, oppression, or abuse of authority. [< L < *ex-* out + *torquere* to twist] — **ex·tor′tive** *adj.*

ex·tor·tion (ik·stôr′shən) *n.* **1.** The act or practice of extorting. **2.** The act of exacting an exorbitant price for something. **3.** That which has been extorted. — **ex·tor′· tion·ar·y, ex·tor′tion·ate** *adj.* — **ex·tor′tion·er** *n.*

ex·tor·tion·ist (ik·stôr′shən·ist) *n.* One guilty of extortion.

ex·tra (eks′trə) *adj.* **1.** Over and above what is normal, re- quired, expected, etc.; additional. **2.** Larger or of better quality than usual. — *n.* **1.** Something beyond what is usual or required. **2.** A copy or an edition of a newspaper issued to cover news of special importance. **3.** Something for which a special charge is made: Meals are an *extra*. **4.** Something of special quality. **5.** In motion pictures, a per- son hired for a small part, as in a mob scene. — *adv.* Un- usually: *extra* good. [< L, outside, beyond]

extra- *prefix* Beyond or outside the scope, area, or limits of: used chiefly in forming adjectives and usu. written without a hypen (*extracurricular, extragovernmental, extraterritorial*) except before words beginning with *a* (*extra-atmospheric*) or with a capital letter (*extra-Scriptural*).

ex·tract (*v.* ik·strakt′; *n.* eks′trakt) *v.t.* **1.** To draw or pull out by force. **2.** To derive (happiness, instruction, etc.) from some source. **3.** To draw out or formulate (a principle, doctrine, etc.); deduce. **4.** To obtain by force or contriv- ance: to *extract* money. **5.** To obtain from a substance as by pressure, distillation, etc.: to *extract* juice. **6.** To select or copy out (a passage, word, or the like), as for quotation. **7.** *Math.* To calculate (the root of a number). — *n.* Something extracted as: **a** A concentrated form of a food, drug, etc. **b** A passage selected from a book. [< L < *ex-* out + *trahere* to draw, pull] — **ex·trac′tive** *adj.* & *n.* — **ex·trac′tor** *n.* — **ex·tract′a·ble** or **ex·tract′i·ble** *adj.*

ex·trac·tion (ik·strak′shən) *n.* **1.** The act of extracting, or the state of being extracted. **2.** That which is extracted. **3.** Lineage; descent: of European *extraction.*

ex·tra·cur·ric·u·lar (eks′trə·kə·rik′yə·lər) *adj.* Of or per- taining to those activities not a direct part of the curriculum of school or college life, as athletics, fraternities, etc.

ex·tra·dite (eks′trə·dīt) *v.t.* **·dit·ed, ·dit·ing 1.** To deliver up (an accused individual, prisoner, or fugitive) to the juris- diction of some other state, country, etc. **2.** To obtain the extradition of. — **ex′tra·dit′a·ble** *adj.*

ex·tra·di·tion (eks′trə·dish′ən) *n.* The surrender of an ac- cused individual, prisoner, or fugitive by one state, etc., to another. [< F < L < *ex-* out + *traditio* surrender]

ex·tra·mu·ral (eks′trə·myo͝or′əl) *adj.* **1.** Situated without or beyond the walls, as of a fortified city. **2.** Taking place outside of an educational institution: *extramural* games.

ex·tra·ne·ous (ik·strā′nē·əs) *adj.* **1.** Coming from without; foreign: *extraneous* rock. **2.** Unrelated to the matter at hand. [< L *extraneus* foreign, external < *extra*] **— ex·tra′ne·ous·ly** *adv.* **— ex·tra′ne·ous·ness** *n.*

ex·traor·di·nar·y (ik·strôr′də·ner′ē; *esp. for def. 3* eks′trə·ôr′də·ner′ē) *adj.* **1.** Being beyond or out of the common order, course, or method. **2.** Far exceeding the usual; exceptional; remarkable. **3.** Employed on an exceptional occasion; special: an envoy *extraordinary.* [< L < *extra* beyond + *ordo, ordinis* order] **— ex·traor′di·nar′i·ly** *adv.*

ex·trap·o·late (eks·trap′ə·lāt) *v.t. & v.i.* **·lat·ed, ·lat·ing** **1.** *Math.* To project (those values of a magnitude or function that lie beyond the range of known values) on the basis of values that have already been determined: distinguished from *interpolate.* **2.** To infer (a possibility) beyond the strict evidence of a series of facts, events, observations, etc. [< EXTRA- + (INTER)POLATE] **— ex·trap′o·la·tion** *n.* **— ex·trap′o·la′tive** *adj.*

ex·tra·sen·so·ry (eks′trə·sen′sər·ē) *adj.* Beyond the range of normal sensory perception.

ex·trav·a·gance (ik·strav′ə·gəns) *n.* **1.** Wasteful expenditure of money. **2.** Extreme lack of moderation in behavior or speech. **3.** An instance of wastefulness or excess. [< F] Also **ex·trav′a·gan·cy.**

ex·trav·a·gant (ik·strav′ə·gənt) *adj.* **1.** Overly lavish in expenditure; wasteful. **2.** Exceeding reasonable limits; immoderate; unrestrained: *extravagant* praise. **3.** Flagrantly high; exorbitant: *extravagant* prices. [< MF < L *extra* outside + *vagari* to wander] **— ex·trav′a·gant·ly** *adv.*

ex·trav·a·gan·za (ik·strav′ə·gan′zə) *n.* A lavish, spectacular theatrical production. [< Ital. *estravaganza* extravagance.]

ex·treme (ik·strēm′) *adj.* **1.** Exceedingly great or severe: *extreme* danger; *extreme* weakness. **2.** Going far beyond the bounds of moderation; exceeding what is considered reasonable; immoderate; radical: an *extreme* fashion; an *extreme* reactionary; also, very strict or drastic: *extreme* measures. **3.** Outermost: the *extreme* border of a country. **4.** Last; final: *extreme* unction. **— *n.* 1.** The highest degree; utmost point or verge: the *extreme* of cruelty. **2.** One of the two ends or farthest limits of anything: the *extremes* of joy and sorrow. **3.** *pl.* A condition of great danger or distress: He is constantly in *extremes.* **4.** *Math.* The first or last term of a proportion or series. **— in the extreme** To the greatest or highest degree. **— to go to extremes** To carry something to excess. [< OF < L *extremus,* superl. of *exterus* outside]

ex·treme·ly (ik·strēm′lē) *adv.* Exceedingly; very.

extreme unction Unction (def. 2b).

ex·trem·ist (ik·strē′mist) *n.* **1.** One who advocates extreme measures or holds extreme views. **2.** One who carries something to excess. **— *adj.*** Of or pertaining to extreme measures or views. **— ex·trem′ism** *n.*

ex·trem·i·ty (ik·strem′ə·tē) *n. pl.* **·ties** **1.** The utmost or farthest point; termination, end, or edge: the *extremity* of a line. **2.** The greatest degree: the *extremity* of grief. **3.** One's dying moments. **4.** *pl.* Extreme measures: to resort to *extremities.* **5.** A limb or appendage of the body; esp., the hands or feet.

ex·tri·ca·ble (eks′tri·kə·bəl) *adj.* That can be extricated.

ex·tri·cate (eks′trə·kāt) *v.t.* **·cat·ed, ·cat·ing** **1.** To free from entanglement, hindrance, or difficulties; disentangle. **2.** To cause to be given off; emit, as gas or moisture. [< L < *ex-* out + *tricae* trifles, troubles] **— ex′tri·ca′tion** *n.*

ex·trin·sic (ek·strin′sik) *adj.* **1.** Being outside the nature of something; not inherent: opposed to *intrinsic.* **2.** Derived or acting from without; extraneous. Also **ex·trin′si·cal.** [< F < LL < *exter* outside + *secus* besides < *sequi* to follow] **— ex·trin′si·cal·ly** *adv.* **— ex·trin′si·cal·ness** *n.*

ex·tro·ver·sion (eks′trə·vûr′zhən, -shən) *n. Psychol.* The turning of one's interest toward objects and actions outside the self rather than toward one's own thoughts or feelings. [< *extro-* outwards + L *versio, -onis* a turning]

ex·tro·vert (eks′trə·vûrt) *n. Psychol.* **1.** A person characterized by extroversion. **2.** Loosely, one who is gregarious, exuberant, etc. **— *adj.*** Characterized by extroversion.

ex·trude (ik·stro͞od′) *v.* **·trud·ed, ·trud·ing** *v.t.* **1.** To force, thrust, or push out. **2.** To shape (plastic, metal, etc.) by forcing through dies under pressure. **— *v.i.* 3.** To protrude. [< L < *ex-* out + *trudere* to thrust] **— ex·tru·sion** (ik·stro͞o′zhən) *n.* **— ex·tru′sive** *adj.*

ex·u·ber·ance (ig·zo͞o′bər·əns) *n.* **1.** The quality of being exuberant. **2.** An instance of this. Also **ex·u′ber·an·cy.**

ex·u·ber·ant (ig·zo͞o′bər·ənt) *adj.* **1.** Abounding in high spirits and vitality; full of joy and vigor. **2.** Overflowing; lavish; effusive: *exuberant* praise. **3.** Growing luxuriantly: *exuberant* foliage. [< L < *ex-* completely + *uberare* to be fruitful] **— ex·u′ber·ant·ly** *adv.*

ex·ude (ig·zo͞od′, -zyo͞od′, ik·so͞od′, -syo͞od′) *v.* **·ud·ed, ·ud·ing** *v.i.* **1.** To ooze or trickle forth, as sweat, gum, etc. **— *v.t.*** **2.** To discharge gradually in this manner. **3.** To manif[e]… display: to *exude* confidence. [< L < *ex-* out + *sudare* sweat] **— ex·u·da·tion** (eks′yo͞o·dā′shən) *n.*

ex·ult (ig·zult′) *v.i.* To rejoice greatly, as in triumph; jubilant. [< F < L < *ex-* out + *salire* to leap] **— ex·ta·tion** (eg′zul·tā′shən, ek′sul-) **— ex·ult′ing·ly** *adv.*

ex·ul·tant (ig·zul′tənt) *adj.* Jubilant; triumphant; elat… **— ex·ul′tant·ly** *adv.*

ex·u·vi·ate (ig·zo͞o′vē·āt, ik·so͞o′-) *v.t. & v.i.* **·at·ed, ·at·i…** To cast off or shed (a skin, shell, etc.). [< L *exuere* to c… off] **— ex·u′vi·a′tion** *n.*

-ey Var. of -Y¹.

eye (ī) *n.* **1.** The organ of vision in animals; in man… nearly spherical mass set in the skull and consisting of the cornea, iris, pupil, retina, and lens, and protected by the eyelids, eyelashes, and eyebrows. **2.** The area around the eye. **3.** The iris, in regard to its color. **4.** A look; gaze. **5.** Attentive observation. **6.** Sight; view: in the public *eye.* **7.** Capacity to see or discern w… discrimination. **8.** *Often pl.* Judgment; opinion. **9.** *Me…rol.* The calm central area of a hurricane or cyclone. … Anything resembling the human eye: the *eye* of a nee… **— eye of the wind** *Naut.* The direction from which … wind blows. **— to catch one's eye** To get one's attenti… **— to give (someone) the eye** *Slang* To look at (someo… admiringly or invitingly. **— to keep an eye out** (or **peel…**) To watch for something; keep alert. **— to lay** (or **set**) **e… on** To catch sight of. **— to make eyes at** To look at ar…rously or covetously. **— with an eye to** With a view … looking to. **— *v.* eyed, ey·ing** or **eye·ing** *v.t.* **1.** To look carefully. **2.** To make a hole in (a needle, etc.). [OE *ēa…*

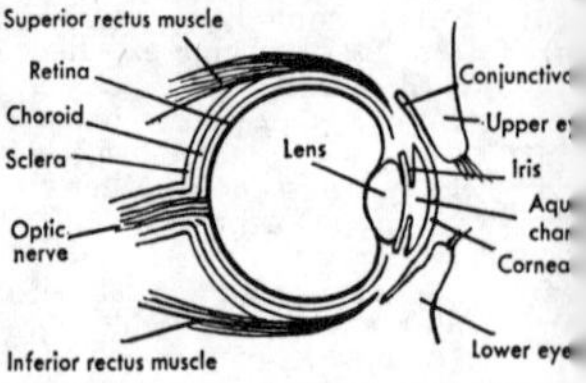

EYE (Anatomical nomenclature)

eye·ball (ī′bôl′) *n.* The globe or ball of the eye.

eye·brow (ī′brou′) *n.* **1.** The bony ridge over the eyes. … The arch of small hairs growing on this ridge.

eye·cup (ī′kup′) *n.* A small cup with a rim curved to … the eye, used in applying lotions.

eyed (īd) *adj.* Having an eye or eyes: *brown-eyed; one-ey…*

eye·ful (ī′fo͝ol′) *n.* **1.** An amount of something in the e… **2.** *Slang* A strikingly beautiful person.

eye·glass (ī′glas′, ī′gläs′) *n.* **1.** *pl.* A pair of correct… glass lenses mounted in a frame: also called *glasses, spectac…* **2.** Any lens used to assist vision. **3.** An eyepiece.

eye·hole (ī′hōl′) *n.* **1.** An opening through which to pas… pin, hook, rope, etc. **2.** A peephole. **3.** The eye's socket.

eye·lash (ī′lash′) *n.* One of the stiff, curved hairs growi… from the edge of the eyelids. ◆ Collateral adjective: *cilia…*

eye·less (ī′lis) *adj.* Lacking eyes; blind.

eye·let (ī′lit) *n.* **1.** A small hole or opening. **2.** A h… made in leather, canvas, etc., and lined with metal. **3.** … metal ring for lining such a hole. **4.** In embroidery, a sm… hole edged with ornamental stitches. **— *v.t.* ·let·ted, ·let·ti…** To make eyelets in. [< F *œillet,* dim. of *œil* eye]

eye·lid (ī′lid′) *n.* Either of the movable folds of skin … which the eyes are opened or closed.

eye opener *U.S.* **1.** That which opens the eyes or enlig… ens, as startling news, revelatory behavior, etc. **2.** *Inform…* A drink of liquor, especially one taken early in the morni…

eye·piece (ī′pēs′) *n.* The lens or combination of lenses ne… est the eye in a telescope, microscope, etc.

eye shadow A cosmetic preparation, tinted blue, gre… gray, etc., applied to the eyelids.

eye·shot (ī′shot′) *n.* The range or scope of one's sight.

eye·sight (ī′sīt′) *n.* **1.** The power or faculty of sight. … Extent or range of vision; view.

eye·sore (ī′sôr′, ī′sōr′) *n.* Something that offends the sig…

eye·strain (ī′strān′) *n.* Weariness or discomfort of the ey… caused by excessive or improper use.

eye·tooth (ī′to͞oth′) *n. pl.* **·teeth** (-tēth′) One of the upp… canine teeth.

eye·wash (ī′wosh′, ī′wôsh′) *n.* **1.** A medicinal wash for t… eye. **2.** *U.S. Slang* Nonsense; bunk; flattery.

eye·wink (ī′wingk′) *n.* **1.** A wink or glance. **2.** An instar…

eye·wit·ness (ī′wit′nis) *n.* One who has seen somethi… happen and can give testimony about it. **— *adj.*** Of or … an eyewitness: an *eyewitness* account.

ey·rie (âr′ē, ir′ē), **ey·ry** See AERIE.

E·ze·ki·el (i·zē′kē·əl, -kyəl) Sixth-century B.C. Hebre… prophet. **— *n.*** A book of the Old Testament written … him. Also, in the Douai Bible, **E·ze′chi·el.** [< Hebre… *yehez-qēl* God strengthens]

Ez·ra (ez′rə) Fifth-century B.C. Hebrew high priest. — A book of the Old Testament written in part by him. Als… in the Douai Bible, *Esdras.* [< Hebrew, help]

F

' (ef) *n.* *pl.* **f's** or **fs, F's** or **Fs, effs** (efs) **1.** The sixth let-
: of the English alphabet. **2.** The sound represented by
e letter *f.* —*symbol* **1.** *Music* **a** The fourth tone in the
ısical scale of C. **b** A note representing it. **c** The scale
ilt upon F. **d** The bass clef in musical notation. **e** Forte.
Chem. Fluorine (symbol F). **3.** *Genetics* A filial genera-
n, usu. followed by a subscript numeral, as F_1, F_2, for
ch successive filial generation offspring of a given mating.
fä) *n. Music* The fourth syllable used in solmization; the
ırth degree of a major scale; also, the tone F.
bi·an (fā′bē·ən) *adj.* Characterized by or practicing
oolicy of deliberate delay. —*n.* A member of the Fabian
ciety. [after *Fabius* Maximus, Roman general, died
3 B.C.] —**Fa′bi·an·ism** *n.* —**Fa′bi·an·ist** *n.* & *adj.*
bian Society An association formed in Great Britain in
84, aiming at the gradual achievement of socialism.
ole (fā′bəl) *n.* **1.** A brief tale embodying a moral and us-
; persons, animals, or inanimate things as characters. **2.**
legend or myth. **3.** A foolish or improbable story. —
. & *v.i.* **·bled, ·bling** To invent or tell (fables or stories).
: OF < L *fari* to say, speak] —**fa′bled** *adj.* —**fa′bler**
—**fab·u·list** (fab′yə·list) *n.*
·ric (fab′rik) *n.* **1.** A woven, felted, or knitted material,
cloth, felt, or lace. **2.** The texture or workmanship of
ch material. **3.** Structure or framework: the social *fabric.*
: F < L *faber* workman]
·ri·cate (fab′rə·kāt) *v.t.* **·cat·ed, ·cat·ing** **1.** To make or
ınufacture; build. **2.** To make by combining parts. **3.**
) make up or invent, as a lie or story. [< L *fabricare* to
nstruct] —**fab′ri·ca′tion** *n.* —**fab′ri·ca′tor** *n.*
·u·lous (fab′ye·ləs) *adj.* **1.** Passing the limits of belief;
credible; astounding. **2.** Of, like, or recorded in fable; fic-
ious; mythical. —**fab′u·lous·ly** *adv.* —**fab′u·lous·ness** *n.*
ade (fə·säd′) *n.* **1.** *Archit.* The front or principal face of
building. **2.** A front or a false appearance: a *façade* of re-
ectability. Also **fa·cade.** [< F < Ital < LL < L *facies* face]
e (fās) *n.* **1.** The front portion of the head; countenance.
The expression of the countenance. **3.** A grimacing
pression. **4.** External aspect or appearance; look. **5.**
formal Effrontery; audacity. **6.** The value as written on
e printed surface of a bond, note, etc. **7.** The front,
incipal, finished, or working surface of anything: the *face*
a clock, of a fabric, a golf club, etc. **8.** The surface of a
in. **9.** The side or surface of a solid. **10.** One of the sides
any military formation. **11.** The land surface or the
ographical features of a region. **12.** *Printing* **a** The
rface of a type body or printing plate that makes the im-
ession. **b** The size or style of the letter or character on the
pe. **c** The letter or character itself: also *type face.* **13.**
ining The end of a drift or excavation. —**face to face**
In each other's immediate presence. **2.** Confronting:
llowed by *with.* —**in the face of** **1.** Confronting. **2.** In
ite of; notwithstanding. —**on the face of it** Judging by
appearances; apparently. —**to fly in the face of** To act
open defiance of. —**to lose face** To lose dignity or repu-
tion. —**to one's face** Openly; frankly. —**to save face**
o save oneself from embarrassment or disgrace; preserve
ıe's dignity or reputation. —**to show one's face** To put
an appearance. —*v.* **faced, fac·ing** *v.t.* **1.** To bear or
ırn the face toward. **2.** To cause to turn in a given direc-
on, as soldiers. **3.** To meet face to face; confront. **4.** To
alize or be aware of. **5.** To cover with a layer or surface
another material. **6.** To make smooth the surface of.
To turn face upward, as a playing card. —*v.i.* **8.** To
ırn or be turned with the face in a given direction. —
face down To disconcert or prevail over by a bold, fixed
ıze or an audacious denial or assertion. —**to face out** To
e to completion. —**to face the music** *U.S. Slang* To
cept the consequences. —**to face up to** To meet with
ourage. [< F, ult. < L *facies* face] —**face′a·ble** *adj.*
ce card In playing cards, a king, queen, or jack.
·et (fas′it) *n.* **1.** One of the small plane surfaces cut upon
gem. **2.** A phase, side, or aspect of a subject or person.
Syn. See PHASE. —*v.t.* **·fac·et·ed** or **·et·ted, fac·et·ing**
or **·et·ting** To cut or work facets upon. [< F *facette,* dim. of *face* face]

fa·ce·tious (fə·sē′shəs) *adj.* Given to or marked by levity or flippant humor. [< F < L *facetiae* jests] —**fa·ce′tious·ly** *adv.* —**fa·ce′tious·ness** *n.*

face value **1.** The value stated on the face of a bond, coin, note, etc. **2.** Apparent value: at *face value.*

fa·cial (fā′shəl) *adj.* Of, near, or for the face. —*n. Informal* A massage or other treatment for the face.

facient *suffix* Causing; making: *sorbefacient.* [< L *faciens, -entis,* ppr. of *facere* to do]

fac·ile (fas′əl, -il) *adj.* **1.** Requiring little effort; easily achieved or performed; also, superficial: a *facile* prose style. **2.** Ready or quick in performance; also, smooth; glib. **3.** Easily moved or persuaded; affable; agreeable. [< F < L *facilis* easy to do] —**fac′ile·ly** *adv.* —**fac′ile·ness** *n.*

fa·cil·i·tate (fə·sil′ə·tāt) *v.t.* **·tat·ed, ·tat·ing** To make easier or more convenient. —**fa·cil′i·ta′tion** *n.*

fa·cil·i·ty (fə·sil′ə·tē) *n.* *pl.* **·ties** **1.** Ease of performance or action. **2.** Ready skill or ability. **3.** *Usu. pl.* Something that makes an action or operation easier: *facilities* for research. **4.** Readiness to comply. [See FACILE.]

fac·ing (fā′sing) *n.* **1.** A lining or covering of a garment, often sewn on parts exposed by being turned back. **2.** A fabric used for this. **3.** Any covering, as on a building, that protects or is ornamental.

fac·sim·i·le (fak·sim′ə·lē) *n.* **1.** An exact copy. **2.** *Telecom.* A method of transmitting messages, drawings, or the like, by means of radio, telegraph, etc. —*adj.* Of or like a facsimile. [< L *fac simile* make like]

fact (fakt) *n.* **1.** Something that actually exists or has occurred. **2.** Something asserted to be true or to have happened. **3.** Reality or actuality. **4.** A criminal deed: now only in the legal phrases **before** (or **after**) **the fact, to deny the fact,** etc. —**as a matter of fact, in fact, in point of fact** In reality; actually. [< L *factum* < *facere* to do]

faction (fak′shən) *n.* **1.** A group of people operating within, and often in opposition to, a larger group. **2.** Party strife; internal dissension. [< F < L *facere* to do] —**fac′tion·al** *adj.* —**fac′tion·al·ism** *n.* —**fac′tion·ist** *n.*

—**Syn.** **1.** *Faction, wing,* and *bloc* refer to subgroups, especially within political parties. *Faction* is often applied to a disruptive subgroup: *wing* refers to either of two directly opposed groups: the liberal and conservative *wings* of the Republican party. A *bloc* is a coalition that cuts across party lines: the farm *bloc.*

fac·tious (fak′shəs) *adj.* Given to dissension.

fac·ti·tious (fak·tish′əs) *adj.* **1.** Not spontaneous; affected: *factitious* enthusiasm. **2.** Produced by artificial conditions or standards: a *factitious* demand. [< L *factitius* artificial] —**fac·ti′tious·ly** *adv.* —**fac·ti′tious·ness** *n.*

fac·tor (fak′tər) *n.* **1.** One of the elements or causes that contribute to produce a result. **2.** *Math.* One of two or more quantities that, when multiplied together, produce a given quantity. **3.** *Biol.* A gene. **4.** One who transacts business for another on a commission basis. —*v.t. Math.* To resolve into factors. [< L, maker] —**fac′tor·ship** *n.*

fac·tor·age (fak′tər·ij) *n.* **1.** A factor's commission. **2.** The business of a factor.

fac·to·ri·al (fak·tôr′ē·əl, -tō′rē-) *n. Math.* The product of a series of consecutive positive integers from 1 to a given number. The *factorial* of four (written 4!) $= 1 \times 2 \times 3 \times 4 = 24$. —*adj.* Pertaining to a factor or a factorial.

fac·tor·ize (fak′tə·rīz) *v.t.* **·ized, ·iz·ing** *Math.* To resolve into factors. —**fac′tor·i·za′tion** *n.*

fac·to·ry (fak′tər·ē) *n.* *pl.* **·ries** An establishment for the manufacture or assembly of goods. [< L *facere* to make]

fac·to·tum (fak·tō′təm) *n.* A man of all work. [< Med.L < L *fac,* sing. imperative of *facere* to do + *totum* everything]

fac·tu·al (fak′cho͞o·əl) *adj.* Pertaining to, containing, or consisting of facts; literal and exact. —**fac′tu·al·ly** *adv.*

fac·ul·ty (fak′əl·tē) *n.* *pl.* **·ties** **1.** A natural or acquired power or ability. **2.** One of the inherent powers or capabilities of the body or mind. **3.** *U.S.* The entire teaching staff at an educational institution. **4.** A department of learning at a university: the English *faculty*. **5.** The members of a learned profession collectively. **6.** Conferred power or privilege. **7.** *Eccl.* The right to perform certain ecclesiastical functions. [< OF < L < *facilis* easy to do]

fad (fad) *n.* A temporary style, amusement, fashion, etc. [Origin unknown] —**fad′dish** *adj.* —**fad′dist** *n.*

fade (fād) *v.* **·fad·ed, fad·ing** *v.i.* **1.** To lose brightness or clearness. **2.** To vanish slowly. **3.** To lose freshness, vigor, youth, etc. —*v.t.* **4.** To cause to fade. **5.** *U.S. Slang* In dice, to cover the bet of. —**to fade in** or **out** In television, motion pictures, and radio, to come into or depart from perception gradually. [< OF *fade* pale, insipid]

fae·ces (fē′sēz), **fae·cal** (fē′kəl) See FECES, FECAL.

fag[1] (fag) *v.* **fagged, fag·ging** *v.t.* **1.** To exhaust by hard work: usu. with *out*. **2.** *Brit.* To make a fag of. —*v.i.* **3.** To weary oneself by working. **4.** *Brit.* To serve as a fag. —*n.* **1.** *Brit.* In English public schools, a boy who does menial service for one in a higher class. **2.** *U.S. Slang* A homosexual: also **fag·got** (fag′ət). [Origin unknown]

fag[2] (fag) *n. Slang* A cigarette. [< FAG END]

fag end **1.** The frayed end, as of a rope. **2.** A remnant or last part, usually of slight utility. [< FAG[1]]

fag·ot (fag′ət) *n.* **1.** A bundle of sticks, twigs, or branches, used for fuel, etc. **2.** A bundle of pieces of wrought iron or steel for working into bars, etc. —*v.t.* **1.** To make a fagot of. **2.** To ornament by fagoting. Also **fag′got.** [< OF]

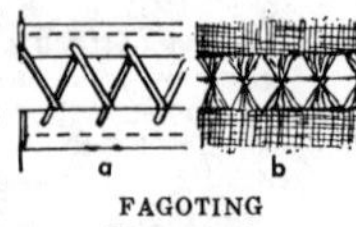

FAGOTING
a Hemstitch.
b Drawn work.

fag·ot·ing (fag′ət·ing) *n.* **1.** A mode of ornamenting textile fabrics in which a number of threads of a material are drawn out and the cross threads tied together in the middle. **2.** A kind of criss-cross hemstitch. Also **fag′got·ing.**

Fahr·en·heit scale (far′ən·hīt, *Ger.* fär′ən·hīt) A temperature scale in which the freezing point of water is 32° and the boiling point 212°, under standard atmospheric pressure. [after Gabriel Daniel *Fahrenheit*, 1686–1736, German physicist]

fail (fāl) *v.i.* **1.** To turn out to be deficient or wanting, as in ability, quality, etc. **2.** To miss doing or accomplishing something: He *failed* to make himself clear. **3.** To prove inadequate; fall short; give out. **4.** To decline in health or strength. **5.** To go bankrupt. **6.** In education, to receive a grade of failure. —*v.t.* **7.** To prove of no help to; desert: His friends *failed* him. **8.** In education: **a** To receive a grade of failure in (a course or examination). **b** To assign a grade of failure to (a student). —*n.* Failure: in the phrase **without fail.** [< OF < L *fallere* to deceive]

fail·ing (fā′ling) *n.* **1.** A minor fault; defect. **2.** The act of one who or that which fails. —**Syn.** See FOIBLE. —*prep.* In default of. —*adj.* That fails. —**fail′ing·ly** *adv.*

faille (fāl, fīl; *Fr.* fà′y′) *n.* An untwilled silk dress fabric having a light grain or cord. [< F]

fail-safe (fāl′sāf′) *adj.* Designating any of various systems designed to prevent equipment failure from causing operational failure, esp. such a system that makes the carrying out of a nuclear bombing automatically contingent upon a specific confirming order.

fail·ure (fāl′yər) *n.* **1.** A turning out to be unsuccessful, disappointing, or lacking. **2.** A breaking down in health, strength, action, efficiency, etc. **3.** Nonperformance; neglect: *failure* to obey the law. **4.** A becoming insolvent or bankrupt. **5.** One who or that which fails. **6.** In education, a failing to pass, or the grade indicating this.

fain (fān) *adv. Archaic & Poetic* Gladly; preferably: He would *fain* depart. —*adj.* **1.** *Archaic & Poetic* Glad; rejoiced. **2.** *Archaic & Poetic* Eager. [OE *fægen*]

faint (fānt) *v.i.* To lose consciousness; swoon. —*adj.* **1.** Feeble; weak. **2.** Lacking in distinctness, brightness. etc. **3.** Dizzy; weak. **4.** Lacking courage; timid. —*n.* A sudden, temporary loss of consciousness; swoon. [< OF, pp. of *faindre* to shape] —**faint′ly** *adv.* —**faint′ness** *n.*

faint·heart·ed (fānt′här′tid) *adj.* Cowardly; timorous; timid. —**faint′heart′ed·ly** *adv.* —**faint′heart′ed·ness** *n.*

fair[1] (fâr) *adj.* **1.** Light in coloring; not dark or sallow. **2.** Pleasing to the eye; beautiful. **3.** Free from blemish or imperfection: a *fair* name. **4.** Having no aspect of rain, snow, or hail. **5.** Just; upright. **6.** According to rules, principles, etc.; legitimate: a *fair* win. **7.** Properly open to attack: He is *fair* game. **8.** Moderately good or large: a *fair* crop. **9.** Likely; promising. **10.** Gracious or courteous; pleasant. **11.** In baseball, situated, falling or remaining in the area bounded by the foul lines; not foul. —*adv.* **1.** In a fair manner. **2.** Squarely; directly. —**to bid fair** To seem probable or favorable. —*n. Archaic* **1.** A fair woman. **2.** Beauty. —**for fair** For sure. [OE *fæger*]

fair[2] (fâr) *n.* **1.** A periodic and usually competitive exhibit of agricultural products, livestock, machinery, etc. **2.** A large exhibition or show of products, etc.: a world's *fair*. **3.** An exhibit and sale of fancywork. **4.** A gathering buyers and sellers. [< OF < L *feria* holiday]

fair-haired (fâr′hârd′) *adj.* **1.** Having blond hair. Favorite: the teacher's *fair-haired* boy.

fair·ing (fâr′ing) *n. Aeron.* In airplanes, an auxili structure or surface to reduce drag or resistance.

fair·ish (fâr′ish) *adj.* Moderately good, well, or large.

fair·ly (fâr′lē) *adv.* **1.** In a just manner; equitably. Moderately; somewhat. **3.** Positively; completely: crowd *fairly* roared. **4.** Clearly; distinctly.

fair-mind·ed (fâr′mīn′did) *adj.* Free from bias or bigo open to reason; unprejudiced. —**fair′-mind′ed·ness** *n.*

fair-trade (fâr′trād′) *v.t.* **-trad·ed, -trad·ing** To se price no less than the manufacturer's minimum price (a branded or trademarked product). —*adj.* Of or taining to such a price.

fair·way (fâr′wā′) *n.* **1.** That part of a golf course, tween the tees and putting greens, where the grass is short. **2.** *Naut.* The navigable or usual course throug channel or harbor.

fair-weath·er (fâr′weth′ər) *adj.* **1.** Suitable for weather, as a racetrack. **2.** Not helpful in adversity.

fair·y (fâr′ē) *n. pl.* **fair·ies** **1.** An imaginary being, o narily small and capable of working good or ill. **2.** *Sl* A male homosexual. —*adj.* **1.** Of or pertaining to fai **2.** Resembling a fairy. [< OF *faerie* fairyland]

fair·y·land (fâr′ē·land′) *n.* **1.** The fancied abode of fairies. **2.** Any delightful, enchanting place.

fairy tale **1.** A tale about fairies. **2.** An incredible highly imaginative story or statement.

fait ac·com·pli (fe·tà·kôn·plē′) *French* A thing done yond recall or opposition; literally, an accomplished fac

faith (fāth) *n.* **1.** Confidence in or dependence on a pers statement, or thing as trustworthy. **2.** Belief without n of certain proof. **3.** Belief in God or in the Scriptures other religious writings. **4.** A system of religious bel **5.** Anything given adherence or credence. **6.** Allegiar —**Syn.** See BELIEF. —**bad faith** Deceit; dishonesty. **in faith** Indeed; truly. —**in good faith** With honorable tentions. —**to break faith** **1.** To betray one's princi or beliefs. **2.** To fail to keep a promise. —**to keep fa** **1.** To adhere to one's principles or beliefs. **2.** To kee promise. —*interj.* Indeed. [< OF < L *fidere* to trust]

faith·ful (fāth′fəl) *adj.* **1.** True or trustworthy in performance of duty, the fulfillment of promises or obli tions, etc.; loyal. **2.** Worthy of belief or confidence; tru ful: a *faithful* saying. **3.** True in detail or accurate description: a *faithful* copy. —**the faithful** **1.** The lowers of a religious faith. **2.** The loyal members of a group. —**faith′ful·ly** *adv.* —**faith′ful·ness** *n.*

faith·less (fāth′lis) *adj.* **1.** Untrue to promise or obli tion; unfaithful. **2.** Not dependable or trustworthy. Devoid of faith. —**faith′less·ly** *adv.* —**faith′less·ness**

fake (fāk) *Informal n.* Any person or thing not genui —*adj.* Not genuine; spurious. —*v.* **faked, fak·ing** **1.** To make up and attempt to pass off as genuine: to *fak* pedigree. **2.** To stimulate; feign. **3.** To improvise, as music or a play. —*v.i.* **4.** To practice faking. [? Var. obs. *feague, feak* < G *fegen* to sweep] —**fak′er** *n.*

fa·kir (fə·kir′, fā′kər) *n.* **1.** A Moslem ascetic or religi mendicant. **2.** Loosely, any Hindu yogi or religious devot Also **fa·keer** (fə·kir′). [< Arabic *faqīr* poor]

fal·chion (fôl′chən, -shən) *n.* **1.** A sword of the Mid Ages. **2.** *Poetic* Any sword. [< OF, ult. < L *falx* sickl

fal·con (fal′kən, fôl-, fô′-) *n.* **1.** A bird of prey noted for powerful wings, keen vision, and swiftness of attack u its quarry. **2.** Any other birds of the same family, havi long, pointed wings, a notched bill, and strong talons. OF < LL < L *falx, falcis* sickle, because of its curved be

fal·con·ry (fôl′kən·rē, fô′-, fal′-) *n.* **1.** The art of traini falcons to hunt other birds and game. **2.** The sport hunting with falcons: also called *hawking*. —**fal′con·er**

fal·de·ral (fal′də·ral) *n.* **1.** Any foolish nonsense or fan **2.** A trifling ornament. **3.** A meaningless refrain used old songs. Also spelled *folderol*: also **fal·de·rol** (fal′də·rol

fall (fôl) *v.* **fell, fall·en, fall·ing** *v.i.* **1.** To drop from a high to a lower place or position because of removal of supp or loss of hold or attachment. **2.** To drop suddenly from erect position, striking the ground with some part of body. **3.** To collapse. **4.** To become less in number, tensity, value, etc.: Prices *fell*. **5.** To become less in ra importance, etc. **6.** To drop wounded or slain. **7.** To overthrown, as a government. **8.** To be captured: The f *fell*. **9.** To yield to temptation; sin. **10.** To hit; land: T bombs *fell* on target. **11.** To slope downward: The ro *falls* into the valley. **12.** To hang down; droop. **13.** come as though descending: Night *fell*. **14.** To pass i some specified condition: to *fall* asleep. **15.** To experie or show dejection: His face *fell*. **16.** To be cast down: eyes *fell*. **17.** To come or happen by chance or lot: to among thieves. **18.** To happen; occur at a specified ti

·lace. **19.** To pass by right or inheritance. **20.** To be ·red as if accidentally: An oath *fell* from his lips. **21.** ·be classified or divided: with *into*. **22.** To be born: said ·nimals. **—** *v.t.* **23.** *U.S.* To fell or cut down, as a tree. **·o fall away** **1.** To become lean or emaciated. **2.** To decline. **—to fall away from** To renounce allegiance **—to fall back** To recede; retreat. **—to fall back on** ·**upon**) **1.** To resort to; have recourse to. **2.** To retreat **—to fall behind** **1.** To lose ground. **2.** To be in ar- ·s. **—to fall down on** *U.S. Informal* To fail in. **—to flat** To fail to produce the intended effect or result. **—** ·**all for** *U.S. Informal* **1.** To be deceived by. **2.** To fall ·ve with. **—to fall in** *Mil.* To take proper place in a ·nation or group. **—to fall in with** **1.** To meet and ac- ·pany. **2.** To agree with. **—to fall off** **1.** To leave or ·ıdraw. **2.** To become less. **—to fall on** (or **upon**) ·o attack. **2.** To discover. **3.** To light upon: said of eyes, the glance, etc. **—to fall out** **1.** To quarrel. ·o happen; result. **3.** *Mil.* To leave ranks. **—to fall** ·**t** **1.** To fail to meet a standard, reach a particular place, : with *of*. **2.** To be or prove deficient. **—to fall through** come to nothing; fail. **—to fall to** **1.** To set about; ·n. **2.** To begin fighting. **3.** To begin eating. **4.** To ·e or drop into position. **—to fall under** **1.** To be clas- ·d as or included in. **2.** To come under (a spell, power, ·). **—** *n.* **1.** The act of falling; a descending. **2.** That ·ch falls. **3.** The amount that falls. **4.** The distance ·ugh which anything falls. **5.** A more or less sudden ·ent from a vertical or erect position. **6.** A hanging ·n. **7.** A downward direction or slope. **8.** *Usu. pl.* A ·erfall; cascade. **9.** A loss or reduction in value, price, ·ıtation, etc. **10.** A moral lapse. **11.** A surrender, as ·city or fort. **12.** *Often cap. Chiefly U.S.* Autumn. **13.** ·wrestling: **a** The throwing of an opponent to his back. ·he method used. **c** A wrestling match or part thereof. ·**he fall of man** *Theol.* The disobedience of Adam and Eve ·t resulted in original sin. [OE *feallan*]

·**la·cious** (fə·lā′shəs) *adj.* **1.** Deceptive or misleading. ·Containing or involving a fallacy. **3.** Delusive: a *fal-* ·*ous* hope. **—fal·la′cious·ly** *adv.* **—fal·la′cious·ness** *n.*

·**a·cy** (fal′ə·sē) *n. pl.* **·cies** **1.** An erroneous or mis- ·ling notion. **2.** Unsoundness or incorrectness, as of ·ef, judgment, etc. **3.** Deceptive quality. **4.** Any reason- contrary to the rules of logic. [< L *fallere* to deceive]

·**en** (fô′lən) Past participle of FALL. **—** *adj.* **1.** Having ·ne down by falling. **2.** Brought down. **3.** Overthrown; ·quished. **4.** Disgraced; ruined. **5.** Slain.

guy *U.S. Slang* One who is left to receive the blame ·enalties; a dupe; scapegoat.

·**i·ble** (fal′ə·bəl) *adj.* **1.** Liable to err. **2.** Liable to be ·led or deceived. **3.** Liable to be erroneous or false. Med.L < L *fallere* to deceive] **—fal′li·bil′i·ty, fal′li·ness** *n.* **—fal′li·bly** *adv.*

·**lo·pi·an tube** (fə·lō′pē·ən) *Anat.* One of a pair of ·g, slender ducts serving as a passage for the ovum from ovary to the uterus: also called *oviduct*. [after Gabriello ·*llopio*, 1523–62, Italian anatomist]

·**out** (fôl′out′) *n. Physics* **1.** The descent of minute ·ticles of radioactive material resulting from the explosion ·an atomic or thermonuclear bomb. **2.** The particles ·mselves. **3.** *Informal* A by-product. Also **fall′-out′**.

low[1] (fal′ō) *adj.* Left unseeded after being plowed; ·cultivated. **—to lie fallow** To remain ·ised, idle, dormant, etc. **—** *n.* **1.** Land ·t unseeded after plowing. **2.** The proc- ·of plowing or working land and leaving ·unseeded for a time. **—** *v.t. & v.i.* To ·ke, keep, or become fallow. [OE *fealg-* ·*j* fallow land] **—fal′low·ness** *n.*

low[2] (fal′ō) *adj.* Light yellowish ·own. [OE *fealu*]

·**low deer** A European deer about 3 feet ·gh at the shoulders and spotted white the summer

FALLOW DEER

·**se** (fôls) *adj.* **1.** Contrary to truth or fact. **2.** Incorrect: ·*se* reasoning. **3.** Not genuine; artificial. **4.** Deceptive misleading: a *false* impression. **5.** Given to lying. **6.** ·anting in fidelity; faithless. **7.** Supplementary; substi- ·tive. **8.** *Music* Not correct in pitch. **—** *adv.* In a false ·anner. [< OF < L *falsus*, orig. pp. of *fallere* to deceive] **·false′ly** *adv.* **—false′ness** *n.*

·**se face** A mask.

·**se-heart·ed** (fôls′här′tid) *adj.* Treacherous; deceitful.

·**se·hood** (fôls′ho͝od) *n.* **1.** Lack of accord to fact or ·uth. **2.** An intentional untruth; lie. **—Syn.** See LIE[2].

·**se ribs** *Anat.* Ribs that do not unite directly with the ·ernum. In man there are five on each side.

·**·set·to** (fôl·set′ō) *n. pl.* **·tos** **1.** The higher, less colorful register of a voice, esp. of an adult male voice: also called *head voice*. **2.** A man who sings or speaks in this register: also **fal·set′tist**. **—** *adj.* Having the quality of falsetto; shrill. **—** *adv.* In falsetto. [< Ital., dim. of *falso* false]

fal·si·fy (fôl′sə·fī) *v.* **·fied, ·fy·ing** *v.t.* **1.** To tell lies about; misrepresent. **2.** To alter or tamper with, esp. in order to deceive. **3.** To prove to be false. **—** *v.i.* **4.** To tell lies. **—Syn.** See PERVERT. [< F < LL < L < *falsus* false + *facere* to make] **—fal′si·fi·ca′tion** *n.* **—fal′si·fi′er** *n.*

fal·si·ty (fôl′sə·tē) *n. pl.* **·ties** **1.** The quality of being false. **2.** That which is false. **—Syn.** See ERROR.

Fal·staff (fôl′staf, -stäf), **Sir John** A fat, fun-loving old knight in Shakespeare's *Henry IV* and *The Merry Wives of Windsor*. **—Fal·staff′i·an** *adj.*

fal·ter (fôl′tər) *v.i.* **1.** To be hesitant or uncertain; waver. **2.** To move unsteadily. **3.** To speak haltingly. **—** *v.t.* **4.** To utter haltingly. **—Syn.** See VACILLATE. **—** *n.* **1.** An uncertainty or hesitation in voice or action. **2.** A quavering sound. [? < ON *faltrask* to be encumbered] **—fal′ter·er** *n.* **—fal′ter·ing** *adj.* **—fal′ter·ing·ly** *adv.*

fame (fām) *n.* **1.** Widespread and illustrious reputation; renown. **2.** Public reputation or estimation. **—** *v.t.* **famed, fam·ing** *Archaic* To speak of widely; celebrate. [< F < L *fama* report, reputation]

fa·mil·ial (fə·mil′yəl) *adj.* Of, pertaining to, associated with, or transmitted within the family.

fa·mil·iar (fə·mil′yər) *adj.* **1.** Having thorough knowledge of something; well-acquainted: followed by *with*. **2.** Well-known; customary. **3.** Intimate; close. **4.** Unduly intimate; forward. **5.** Informal or unconstrained. **6.** Domesticated: said of animals. **—** *n.* **1.** A friend or close associate. **2.** A spirit serving a witch, usu. in animal form. [< OF < L *familia* family] **—fa·mil′iar·ly** *adv.*

fa·mil·i·ar·i·ty (fə·mil′ē·ar′ə·tē, -mil′yar′-) *n. pl.* **·ties** **1.** Thorough knowledge of or acquaintance with something. **2.** Friendly closeness; intimacy. **3.** Offensively familiar conduct; unwarranted intimacy. **4.** *Often pl.* An action warranted only by intimate acquaintance.

fa·mil·iar·ize (fə·mil′yə·rīz) *v.t.* **·ized, ·iz·ing** **1.** To make (oneself or someone) familiar with something. **2.** To cause (something) to be familiar. **—fa·mil′iar·i·za′tion** *n.*

fam·i·ly (fam′ə·lē, fam′lē) *n. pl.* **·lies** **1.** Parents and their children. **2.** The children as distinguished from the parents. **3.** A group of persons connected by blood or marriage. **4.** A succession of persons connected by blood, name, etc.; a house; clan. **5.** Distinguished or ancient lineage or descent. **6.** A household. **7.** Any class or group of like or related things. **8.** *Biol.* A taxonomic category higher than a genus and below an order. **9.** *Ling.* A grouping of languages assumed to be descended from a common parent, as the Indo-European family. **—** *adj.* Of, belonging to, or suitable for a family. [< L < *famulus* servant]

family name A surname.

family tree **1.** A diagram showing family descent. **2.** The ancestors and descendants of a family, collectively.

fam·ine (fam′in) *n.* **1.** A widespread scarcity of food. **2.** A great scarcity of anything; dearth: a water *famine*. **3.** Starvation. [< OF < L *fames* hunger]

fam·ish (fam′ish) *v.t. & v.i.* To suffer or die, or to cause to suffer or die, from starvation. [Earlier *fame* < F *afamer* to starve] **—fam′ished** *adj* **—fam′ish·ment** *n.*

fa·mous (fā′məs) *adj.* **1.** Celebrated in history or public report; well-known; renowned. **2.** *Informal* Excellent; admirable. **—fa′mous·ly** *adv.* **—fa′mous·ness** *n.*

fan[1] (fan) *n.* **1.** A device for putting the air into motion; esp., a light, flat implement, often collapsible and opening into a wedgelike shape, a circle, etc. **2.** Anything shaped like a fan. **3.** A machine fitted with blades that revolve rapidly about a central hub, for stirring air, etc. **4.** A machine for blowing away chaff. **—** *v.* **fanned, fan·ning** *v.t.* **1.** To move or stir (air) with or as with a fan. **2.** To direct air upon; cool or refresh with or as with a fan. **3.** To move or stir to action; excite: to *fan* someone's rage. **4.** To winnow (grain or chaff). **5.** To spread like a fan. **6.** In baseball, to cause (a batter) to strike out. **—** *v.i.* **7.** To spread out like a fan. **8.** In baseball, to strike out. [OE < L *vannus* winnowing basket] **—fan′ner** *n.*

fan[2] (fan) *n. Informal* An enthusiastic devotee or admirer of a sport, diversion, celebrity, etc. [? < FANATIC]

fa·nat·ic (fə·nat′ik) *n.* A person who is moved by a frenzy of enthusiasm or zeal; esp., a religious zealot. [< L *fanum* temple] **—fa·nat′i·cal** *adj.* **—fa·nat′i·cal·ly** *adv.* **—fa·nat′i·cism** (-siz′əm) *n.*

fan·cied (fan′sēd) *adj.* Imaginary: *fancied* insults.

fan·ci·er (fan′sē·ər) *n.* **1.** One having a special taste for or interest in something. **2.** A breeder of animals.

fan·ci·ful (fan′si·fəl) *adj.* **1.** Produced by or existing only in the fancy: *fanciful* schemes. **2.** Marked by fancy in

design: a *fanciful* costume. **3.** Indulging in fancies: a *fanciful* mind. **—fan′ci·ful·ly** *adv.* **—fan′ci·ful·ness** *n.*
fan·cy (fan′sē) *n. pl.* **·cies 1.** Imagination of a capricious or whimsical sort. **2.** An extravagant, odd, or whimsical invention or image. **3.** An idea or notion not based on fact or evidence. **4.** A caprice or whim. **5.** A liking or inclination, as if resulting from caprice. **6.** Taste or judgment in art, style, etc. **—***adj.* **·ci·er, ·ci·est 1.** Adapted to please the fancy; ornamental. **2.** Coming from the fancy; imaginary. **3.** Capricious; whimsical. **4.** Of higher grade than the average: *fancy* fruits. **5.** Exorbitant: *fancy* prices. **6.** Performed with exceptional grace and skill. **7.** Selectively bred for certain points, as an animal: also **fan′cy-bred′** **—***v.t.* **·cied, ·cy·ing 1.** To imagine; picture: *Fancy* that! **2.** To take a fancy to. **3.** To believe without proof or conviction; suppose. **4.** To breed, as animals, for conventional points of symmetry or beauty. **—***interj.* An exclamation of surprise. [Contr. of FANTASY]
fan·cy-free (fan′sē·frē′) *adj.* **1.** Not in love. **2.** Carefree.
fan·cy·work (fan′sē·wûrk′) *n.* Ornamental needlework.
fan·dan·go (fan·dang′gō) *n. pl.* **·gos 1.** A Spanish dance in triple time. **2.** The music for this dance. [< Sp.]
fan·fare (fan′fâr′) *n.* **1.** A short, lively passage, as of trumpets. **2.** A noisy or showy parade. [< F]
fang (fang) *n.* **1.** A long, pointed tooth or tusk by which an animal seizes or tears at its prey. **2.** One of the long, hollow or grooved, usu. erectile teeth with which a venomous serpent injects its poison into its victim. [OE, a seizing] **—fanged** *adj.* **—fang′less** *adj.* **—fang′like′** *adj.*
fan·light (fan′līt′) *n. Archit.* **1.** A semicircular window containing a sash with bars radiating from the middle of its base: also called *fan window*. **2.** *Brit.* A transom.
fan·ny (fan′ē) *n. pl.* **·nies** *U.S. Slang* The buttocks.
fan·tail (fan′tāl′) *n.* **1.** A variety of domestic pigeon having fanlike tail feathers. **2.** Any fan-shaped end or tail.
fan-tan (fan′tan′) *n.* **1.** A Chinese gambling game. **2.** A game of cards played in sequence. [< Chinese *fan t'an*]
fan·ta·si·a (fan·tā′zhə, -zhē·ə, fan′tə·zē′ə) *n. Music* **1.** A fanciful composition observing no strict musical form. **2.** A medley of various themes, usu. with brilliant variations and embellishments. [< Ital., a fancy]
fan·ta·size (fan′tə·sīz) *v.i.* **·sized, ·siz·ing** To create mental fantasies.
fan·tas·tic (fan·tas′tik) *adj.* **1.** Odd, grotesque, or whimsical in appearance, construction, etc.: a *fantastic* room. **2.** Wildly fanciful or exaggerated. **3.** Capricious or impulsive, as moods, actions, etc. **4.** Coming from the imagination or fancy. **—***n. Archaic* One who is fantastic. [< Med.L < L < Gk. < *phantastēs* a boaster]
fan·tas·ti·cal (fan·tas′ti·kəl) *adj.* **1.** Extremely capricious, odd, or eccentric. **2.** Extravagantly fanciful, imaginative or grotesque. **—fan·tas′ti·cal′i·ty** (-kal′ə·tē), **fan·tas′ti·cal·ness** *n.* **—fan·tas′ti·cal·ly** *adv.*
fan·ta·sy (fan′tə·sē, -zē) *n. pl.* **·sies 1.** Imagination unrestrained by reality; wild fancy. **2.** An odd, unreal, or grotesque mental image. **3.** An odd or whimsical notion. **4.** A capricious mood. **5.** An ingenious or highly imaginative creation. **6.** *Psychol.* A sequence of more or less pleasant mental images, usu. fulfilling a need not gratified in the real world. **7.** *Music* A fantasia. **—***v.t.* **·sied, ·sy·ing** To envision; imagine. [< OF < L < Gk. *phainein* to show]
fan·tom (fan′təm) See PHANTOM.
fan window *Archit.* A fanlight.
far (fär) *adv.* **1.** At, to, or from a great distance. **2.** To or at a particular distance, point, or degree. **3.** To a great degree; very much: *far* wiser. **4.** Very remotely in time, degree, quality, etc.: *far* from pleasant. **—as far as** To the distance, extent, or degree that. **—by far** In a great degree; very much. **—far and away** Very much; decidedly. **—far and wide** Distantly and extensively; everywhere. Also **far and near.** **—far be it from me** I have not the audacity or desire. **—how far** To what extent, distance, or degree. **—in so far as** To the extent that. **—so far 1.** To that extent; up to that point. **2.** Up to now. **—so far as** To the extent that. **—so far so good** Up to now everything is all right. **—to go far 1.** To accomplish much; have success. **2.** To last a long time or cover a great extent. **3.** To tend strongly. **—***adj.* **far·ther** or **fur·ther, far·thest** or **fur·thest** (See note under FARTHER.) **1.** Very remote in space or time. **2.** Extending widely or at length. **3.** More distant: the *far* end of the garden. [OE *feor*]
far·ad (far′əd, -ad) *n. Electr.* The unit of capacitance; the capacitance of a condenser that retains one coulomb of charge with one volt difference of potential. [after Michael *Faraday*]
far·a·way (fär′ə·wā′) *adj.* **1.** Distant: a *faraway* town. **2.** Absent-minded; abstracted: a *faraway* look.
farce (färs) *n.* **1.** A comedy employing ludicrous or exaggerated situations. **2.** A ridiculous action or situation. **—***v.t.* **farced, farc·ing** To fill out with witticisms, jibes, etc., as a play. [< F < L *farcire* to stuff]

far·ci·cal (fär′si·kəl) *adj.* Of, belonging to, or resemb farce. **—far′ci·cal·ly** *adv.* **—far′ci·cal′i·ty, far′ci·cal·nes**
far cry A long way.
fare (fâr) *v.i.* **fared, far·ing 1.** To be in a specified st get on: He *fares* poorly. **2.** To turn out: It *fared* well v him. **3.** To be supplied with food and drink. **—***n.* **1.** fee for conveyance in a vehicle, etc. **2.** A passenger car for hire. **3.** Food and drink; diet. [OE *faran* to go, tra
Far East The countries of eastern Asia, including Ch Japan, Korea, Manchuria, and adjacent islands.
fare·well (*n.* fâr′wel′; *interj.* fâr′wel′; *adj.* fâr′wel′) *n.* parting salutation; a good-by. **2.** Leave-taking. **—***in* Good-by. **—***adj.* Parting; closing. [Earlier *fare well*]
far-fetched (fär′fecht′) *adj.* Neither natural nor obvi forced; strained: a *far-fetched* joke.
far-flung (fär′flung′) *adj.* Extending over great distan
fa·ri·na (fə·rē′nə) *n.* **1.** A meal or flour obtained ch from cereals, nuts, potatoes, or Indian corn, and used breakfast food. **2.** Starch. [< L < *far* spelt]
far·i·na·ceous (far′ə·nā′shəs) *adj.* **1.** Consisting or m of farina. **2.** Containing or yielding starch. **3.** Mealy.
far·kle·ber·ry (fär′kəl·ber′ē) *n. pl.* **·ries** A shrub or sm tree with edible black berries. [Origin unknown]
farm (färm) *n.* **1.** A tract of land forming a single prop and devoted to agriculture. **2.** A tract of water used for cultivation of marine life. **3.** In baseball, a minor-lea club used by a major-league club for training its recr **—***v.t.* **1.** To cultivate (land). **2.** To take a lease of, as use of a business or the collection of taxes, for a fixed ren retaining the profits. **3.** To let at a fixed rental, as authority to collect taxes, etc.: usu. with *out*. **4.** To let the services of (a person) for hire. **5.** To arrange for (w to be performed by persons or a firm not in the main org zation: with *out*. **6.** In baseball, to place (a player) wi minor-league team for training: often with *out*. **—** **7.** To practice farming. [< F < Med.L < L *firmare* to
farm·er (fär′mər) *n.* **1.** One who operates a farm. **2.** who pays for the privilege of collecting taxes, etc.
farm hand One who works on a farm, esp. for hire.
farm·house (färm′hous′) *n.* The homestead on a far
farm·ing (fär′ming) *n.* **1.** The business of operating a fa agriculture. **2.** The leasing of the authority to collect ta etc. **—***adj.* Engaged in, suitable for, or used for agricult
farm·stead (färm′sted) *n.* A farm and the buildings o
farm·yard (färm′yärd′) *n.* A space surrounded by f buildings, and enclosed for confining stock, etc.
far·o (fâr′ō) *n.* A game of cards in which the players against the dealer as to the order in which certain cards appear. [Alter. of *Pharaoh*]
Far·o·ese (fâr′ō·ēz′, -ēs′) *n.* **1.** *pl.* **·ese** A native or inh tant of the Faeroe Islands. **2.** The North Germanic guage spoken in these islands, closely resembling Icelan
far-off (fär′ôf′, -of′) *adj.* Distant; remote.
far·ra·go (fə·rā′gō, -rä′-) *n. pl.* **·goes** A confused mixt medley. [< L *far* spelt]
far-reach·ing (fär′rē′ching) *adj.* Having wide influe range, or effect.
far·row (far′ō) *n.* A litter of pigs. **—***v.t. & v.i.* To g birth to (young): said of swine. [OE *fearh* young pig]
far·see·ing (fär′sē′ing) *adj.* **1.** Having foresight; prud wise. **2.** Able to see distant objects clearly.
far·sight·ed (fär′sī′tid) *adj.* **1.** Able to see things at a tance more clearly than things at hand. **2.** Having f sight. **—far′sight′ed·ly** *adv.* **—far′sight′ed·ness** *n.*
far·ther (fär′thər) Comparative of FAR. **—***adv.* To or a more advanced point in space or, less often, time. **—** **1.** More distant or remote. **2.** Additional: in this se usu. *further*. [ME *ferther*; var. of FURTHER]
far·ther·most (fär′thər·mōst′) *adj.* Most distant; farth
far·thest (fär′thist) Superlative of FAR. **—***adv.* To or the greatest distance. **—***adj.* **1.** Most distant or rem **2.** Longest or most extended: the *farthest* way around.
far·thing (fär′thing) *n.* **1.** A small, bronze, English c formerly worth one fourth of a penny. **2.** Something of value; a trifle. [OE < *fēortha* a fourth]
far·thin·gale (fär′thing·gāl) *n.* A woman's hoop skirt the 16th and 17th centuries. [< OF *verdugale*, alter. of *verdugado* < *verdugo* rod, hoop]
fas·ces (fas′ēz) *n.pl.* In ancient Rome, a bundle of rods closing an ax, used as a symbol of power. [< L, pl. of *fa* bundle] **—fas·ci·al** (fash′ē·əl) *adj.*
fas·ci·a (fash′ē·ə) *n. pl.* **fas·ci·ae** (fash′i·ē) **1.** *Anat.* brous connective tissue for enclosing or connecting musc or internal organs. **2.** Something that binds together, a fillet; a band. [< L, band] **—fas′ci·al** *adj.*
fas·ci·cle (fas′i·kəl) *n.* **1.** A small bundle or cluster, as leaves, flowers, etc. **2.** One of the sections of a book tha published in installments. [< L *fascis* bundle] **—fas′ci·c** (-kəld) *adj.* **—fas·cic·u·lar** (fə·sik′yə·lər) *adj.*
fas·ci·nate (fas′ə·nāt) *v.* **·nat·ed, ·nat·ing** *v.t.* **1.** To attr irresistibly, as by beauty or other qualities; captivate.

hold spellbound, as by terror or awe. — *v.i.* **3.** To be
:inating. [< L *fascinum* spell] — **fas′ci·nat′ing** *adj.*
fas′ci·nat′ing·ly *adv.* — **fas′ci·na′tor** *n.*
ci·na·tion (fas′ə·nā′shən) *n.* **1.** The act of fascinating,
he state of being fascinated. **2.** A fascinating attraction,
uence, or quality; enchantment; charm.
cism (fash′iz·əm) *n.* A one-party system of govern-
nt in which the individual is subordinated to the state
control is maintained by military force, secret police,
d censorship, and governmental regimentation of in-
try and finance. [See FASCISTI.]
cist (fash′ist) *n.* **1.** An advocate of fascism. **2.** A
nber of a fascist party. — *adj.* Of, advocating, or prac-
ng fascism: a *fascist* state: also **fa·scis·tic** (fə·shis′tik).
·ion (fash′ən) *n.* **1.** The mode of dress, manners, living,
, prevailing in society, esp. in high society; also, good
n or style. **2.** A current practice or usage. **3.** An
ect of enthusiasm among fashionable people. **4.** Fash-
able people collectively; the élite. **5.** Manner: He walks
peculiar *fashion.* **6.** Kind; sort. — **after a fashion** To
mited extent. — *v.t.* **1.** To give shape or form to; mold.
To adapt, as to the occasion. [< AF, OF < L *factio,*
s a (special) way of making] — **fash′ion·er** *n.*
·ion·a·ble (fash′ən·ə·bəl) *adj.* **1.** Conforming to the
rent fashion. **2.** Associated with, characteristic of, or
ronized by persons of fashion. — *n.* A person of fashion.
ash′ion·a·ble·ness *n.* — **fash′ion·a·bly** *adv.*
·ioned (fash′ənd) *adj.* **1.** Made; shaped; formed. **2.**
a certain style or fashion: *old-fashioned.*
ion plate **1.** One who dresses in the latest fashion. **2.**
icture representing the prevailing fashions in dress.
[1] (fast, fäst) *adj.* **1.** Firm in place; not easily moved.
Firmly secured. **3.** Constant; steadfast: *fast* friends.
Not liable to fade: said of colors. **5.** Resistant: *acid-fast.*
Sound or deep, as sleep. **7.** Acting or moving quickly.
Performed quickly: *fast* work. **9.** Permitting or suitable
quick movement: a *fast* track. **10.** Requiring rapidity
ction or motion: a *fast* schedule. **11.** In advance of the
e time. **12.** Characterized by or given to dissipation or
ral laxity. **13.** *Photog.* Intended for short exposure, as
igh-velocity shutter or a highly sensitive film. — **to play**
t and loose To act in a tricky or untrustworthy fashion.
adv. **1.** Firmly; securely. **2.** Soundly; *fast* asleep. **3.**
ickly. **4.** Dissipatedly: to live *fast.* [OE *fæst*]
[2] (fast, fäst) *v.i.* To abstain from food; esp., to eat
ringly or abstain from certain foods, as in observance
a religious duty. — *n.* **1.** Abstinence from food or from
scribed kinds of food, particularly as a religious duty.
A period prescribed for fasting. [OE *fæstan*]
ten (fas′ən, fäs′-) *v.t.* **1.** To attach to something else;
nect. **2.** To make fast; secure. **3.** To direct (the atten-
n, eyes, etc.) steadily. **4.** To impute or attribute. — *v.i.*
To take fast hold; cling: usu. with *on.* **6.** To become firm
attached. [OE *fæstnian* fixed] — **fas′ten·er** *n.*
ten·ing (fas′ən·ing, fäs′-) *n.* **1.** The act of making fast.
That which fastens, as a bolt.
tid·i·ous (fas·tid′ē·əs, fəs-) *adj.* Hard to please in mat-
s of taste; exceedingly delicate or refined; overnice;
eamish. — **Syn.** See METICULOUS. [< L *fastidium*
gust] — **fas·tid′i·ous·ly** *adv.* — **fas·tid′i·ous·ness** *n.*
·ness (fast′nis, fäst′-) *n.* **1.** A fortress; stronghold. **2.**
e state of being firm or fixed. **3.** Swiftness.
(fat) *adj.* **fat·ter, fat·test** **1.** Having superfluous flesh or
; obese; plump. **2.** Containing much fat, oil, etc. **3.**
ch or fertile, as land. **4.** Abundant; plentiful: a *fat*
fit. **5.** Profitable: a *fat* job. **6.** Thick; broad. — **a fat**
ance *Slang* Very little chance; no chance at all. — *n.*
Biochem. Any of a large class of yellowish to white,
asy, solid or liquid substances widely distributed in
nt and animal tissues. They are compounds of various
ty acids and glycerol, and are generally odorless, taste-
s, and colorless. **2.** Animal tissue containing large
antities of such compounds. **3.** Any vegetable or animal
or oil used in cooking. **4.** Plumpness; corpulence. **5.**
e richest or most desirable part of anything. — **the fat**
in the fire The mischief is done. — **to chew the fat** *Slang*
talk. — *v.t.* & *v.i.* **fat·ted, fat·ting** To make or become
. [OE *fæt*] — **fat′ly** *adv.* — **fat′ness** *n.* — **fat′tish** *adj.*
:al (fāt′l) *adj.* **1.** Resulting in or capable of causing
ath. **2.** Bringing ruin or disaster; destructive. **3.**
ghly significant or decisive; fateful: the *fatal* hour. **4.**
ecreed or brought about by fate; destined; inevitable.
L *fatum.* See FATE.] — **fa′tal·ly** *adv.*
:al·ism (fāt′l·iz′əm) *n.* **1.** The doctrine that all events
e predetermined and thus unalterable. **2.** A disposition
accept every event or condition as inevitable. — **fa′tal·**
n. — **fa′tal·is′tic** *adj.* — **fa′tal·is′ti·cal·ly** *adv.*
:al·i·ty (fā·tal′ə·tē, fə-) *n.* *pl.* **·ties** **1.** A death brought
about through some disaster or calamity. **2.** The capability
of causing death or disaster. **3.** The state or quality of
being subject to or determined by fate. **4.** A decree of fate.
fat·back (fat′bak′) *n.* Unsmoked salt pork.
fate (fāt) *n.* **1.** A force viewed as unalterably determining
events in advance; destiny. **2.** That which inevitably happens as though determined by this force. **3.** Final result or
outcome. **4.** An evil destiny; esp., death or destruction. —
v.t. **fat·ed, fat·ing** To predestine: obsolete except in the passive. [< L *fatus,* pp. of *fari* to speak]
fat·ed (fā′tid) *adj.* **1.** Controlled by or subject to fate; destined. **2.** Condemned to ruin or destruction; doomed.
fate·ful (fāt′fəl) *adj.* **1.** Determining destiny; momentous.
2. Brought about by or as if by fate. **3.** Bringing death or
disaster; fatal. **4.** Ominously prophetic; portentous. —
fate′ful·ly *adv.* — **fate′ful·ness** *n.*
Fates (fāts) In classical mythology, the three goddesses
who control human destiny (Atropos, Clotho, and Lachesis).
fat·head (fat′hed′) *n.* A stupid person. — **fat′head′ed** *adj.*
fa·ther (fä′thər) *n.* **1.** A male parent. **2.** A male who
adopts a child or who otherwise holds a paternal relationship toward another. **3.** Any male ancestor; forefather.
4. A male who founds or establishes something. **5.** Any
elderly man: a title of respect. **6.** One of the orthodox
writers of the early Christian church. **7.** A leader or elder
of a council, assembly, etc. **8.** A member of the ancient
Roman senate. **9.** *Eccl.* **a** *Usu. cap.* A priest or other
church dignitary, as in the Roman Catholic or Anglican
church: often used as a title of respect. **b** A confessor. — *v.t.*
1. To beget. **2.** To act as a father toward. **3.** To found
or make. [OE *fæder*] — **fa′ther·less** *adj.*
fa·ther-in-law (fä′thər·in·lô′) *n.* *pl.* **fa·thers-in-law** **1.**
The father of one's husband or wife. **2.** *Rare* A stepfather.
fa·ther·land (fä′thər·land′) *n.* **1.** The land of one's birth.
2. The native country of one's forebears.
fa·ther·ly (fä′thər·lē) *adj.* **1.** Of or like a father. **2.** Showing the affection of a father. — **fa′ther·li·ness** *n.*
Father's Day The third Sunday in June.
fath·om (fath′əm) *n.* *pl.* **·oms** or **·om** A measure of length,
6 feet or 1.829 meters, used principally in marine and mining
measurements. See table front of book. — *v.t.* **1.** To
find the depth of; sound. **2.** To understand; interpret;
puzzle out. [OE *fæthm* the span of two arms outstretched]
— **fath′om·a·ble** *adj.* — **fath′om·less** *adj.*
fa·tigue (fə·tēg′) *n.* **1.** The condition of being very tired as
a result of physical or mental exertion. **2.** *Mech.* Structural
weakness or loss of resiliency in metals or other materials,
produced by excessive subjection to strain. **3.** *Mil.* **a** A
special work assignment done by soldiers in training: also
fatigue duty. **b** *pl.* Strong, durable clothes worn on fatigue
duty: also **fatigue clothes.** — *v.t.* & *v.i.* **·tigued, ·ti·guing**
1. To tire out; weary. **2.** To weaken, as metal. [< F < L
fatigare to tire] — **fat·i·ga·ble** (fat′ə·gə·bəl) *adj.*
fat·ling (fat′ling) *n.* A young animal fattened for slaughter.
fat·ten (fat′n) *v.t.* **1.** To cause to become fat. **2.** To make
(land) rich by fertilizing. **3.** To add to (a sum of money,
etc.) so as to make larger and more attractive. — *v.i.* **4.** To
grow fatter, heavier, etc. — **fat′ten·er** *n.*
fat·ten·ing (fat′n·ing) *adj.* That fattens: a *fattening* food.
fat·ty (fat′ē) *adj.* **·ti·er, ·ti·est** **1.** Containing, possessing, or
made of fat. **2.** Having the properties of fat; greasy; oily.
— **fat′ti·ly** *adv.* — **fat′ti·ness** *n.*
fatty acid *Chem.* Any of a class of organic acids derived
from hydrocarbons, and occurring in plant and animal fats.
fa·tu·i·ty (fə·tōō′ə·tē, -tyōō′-) *n.* *pl.* **·ties** **1.** Smug stupidity; asininity. **2.** An utterly stupid action, remark, etc.
fat·u·ous (fach′ōō·əs) *adj.* **1.** Foolish and silly in a self-
satisfied way; inane. **2.** Stupid: a *fatuous* grin. [< L *fatuus*
foolish] — **fat′u·ous·ly** *adv.* — **fat′u·ous·ness** *n.*
fau·ces (fô′sēz) *n.pl.* *Anat.* The passage from the back of
the mouth to the pharynx, formed by the membranous, muscular arches extending downward from each side of the soft
palate. [< L] — **fau′cal** (-kəl), **fau′cial** (-shəl) *adj.*
fau·cet (fô′sit) *n.* A fixture with an adjustable valve that
controls the flow of liquids from a pipe, vat, etc.; tap. [<
OF, prob. < *fausser* to break into, create a fault]
faugh (fô) *interj.* An exclamation of disgust, contempt, etc.
fault (fôlt) *n.* **1.** Whatever impairs excellence; a flaw. **2.**
A mistake or blunder. **3.** A slight offense;
misdeed. **4.** Responsibility for some mishap, blunder, etc.; blame. **5.** *Geol.* A
break in the continuity of rock strata or
veins of ore. **6.** In tennis, squash, etc.,
failure to serve the ball into the prescribed
area of the opponent's court; also, a ball
that is improperly served according to rule.
— **at fault** **1.** Open to blame; in the wrong;
culpable. **2.** At a loss; perplexed; astray.

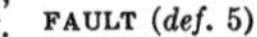
FAULT (*def.* 5)

3. Off the scent. **— to a fault** Immoderately; excessively. **— to find fault** To seek out and complain about some imperfection, error, misdeed, etc.: often with *with*. *— v.t.* **1.** *Geol.* To cause a fault in. **2.** To find fault with; blame. *— v.i.* **3.** *Geol.* To crack. [< OF, ult. < L *fallere* to deceive]

fault·find·ing (fôlt′fīn′ding) *n.* The act of one who finds fault. *— adj.* Inclined to find fault; critical; carping. **— fault′find′er** *n.*

fault·less (fôlt′lis) *adj.* Free from faults; flawless; perfect. **— fault′less·ly** *adv.* **— fault′less·ness** *n.*

fault·y (fôl′tē) *adj.* **fault·i·er, fault·i·est** Having faults; defective; imperfect. **— fault′i·ly** *adv.* **— fault′i·ness** *n.*

faun (fôn) *n.* In Roman mythology, a woodland deity typically represented as a man having the ears, horns, tail, and hind legs of a goat; satyr. [< L *Faunus*, a rural god]

fau·na (fô′nə) *n.* *pl.* **·nas** or **·nae** (-nē) The animals living within a given area or environment or during a stated period. [< NL, after L *Fauna*, a rural goddess] **— fau′nal** *adj.*

Faust (foust) In medieval legend, drama, etc., a philosopher who sells his soul to a devil, Mephistopheles, for wisdom.

faux pas (fō pä′) *pl.* **faux pas** (fō päz′, *Fr.* fō pä′) A false step; esp., a breach of etiquette. [< F, lit., false step]

fa·vor (fā′vər) *n.* **1.** A helpful or considerate act. **2.** An attitude of friendliness or approbation. **3.** The condition of being looked upon with liking or approval. **4.** Unfair discrimination; narrow partiality: to show *favor*. **5.** The condition of leading one's opponent in the score of a game. **6.** A small gift presented to each guest on some festive occasion, as at a birthday party. **7.** *pl.* Consent to sexual intimacy. **— in favor** Having approval or support: a style much *in favor*. **— in favor of 1.** On the side of. **2.** To the furtherance or advantage of. **3.** Made out to the benefit of. **— in one's favor** Of such a kind as to help one or promote one's interests. **— out of favor** Lacking approval or support; not liked. **— to find favor** To come to be looked upon with approval or liking; gain acceptance. *— v.t.* **1.** To do a favor for; oblige. **2.** To look upon with approval or liking. **3.** To show special consideration to, often in an unfair way. **4.** To increase the chances of success of. **5.** *Informal* To show a resemblance to in features. **6.** To be careful of. Also *Brit.* **fa′vour.** [< OF < L < *favere* to favor] **— fa′vor·er** *n.*

fa·vor·a·ble (fā′vər·ə·bəl) *adj.* **1.** Granting something requested or hoped for. **2.** Building up hope or confidence. **3.** Boding well; promising; approving. **4.** Well-disposed or indulgent; friendly. Also *Brit.* **fa′vour·a·ble.** **— fa′vor·a·ble·ness** *n.* **— fa′vor·a·bly** *adv.*

fa·vored (fā′vərd) *adj.* **1.** Treated with or looked upon with friendliness, liking, or approbation. **2.** Endowed with esp. good qualities. **3.** Having an (indicated) aspect or appearance: an *ill-favored* countenance. Also *Brit.* **fa′voured.**

fa·vor·ite (fā′vər·it) *adj.* Regarded with special favor; preferred. *— n.* **1.** A person or thing greatly liked or preferred. **2.** A person granted special privileges by a high official, etc. **3.** In sports, the contestant considered to have the best chance of winning. Also *Brit.* **fa′vour·ite.**

fa·vor·it·ism (fā′vər·ə·tiz′əm) *n.* **1.** Preferential treatment, esp. when unjust or narrowly discriminating. **2.** The condition of being a favorite. Also *Brit.* **fa′vour·it·ism.**

fawn[1] (fôn) *v.i.* **1.** To show cringing fondness, as a dog: often with *on* or *upon*. **2.** To show affection or seek favor by or as by cringing. [OE *fahnian*, var. of *fægnian* to rejoice] **— fawn′er** *n.* **— fawn′ing·ly** *adv.*

fawn[2] (fôn) *n.* **1.** A young deer, esp. in its first year. **2.** The light yellowish brown color of a young deer. *— adj.* Light yellowish brown. [< OF < L *fetus* offspring]

fay (fā) *n.* A fairy. [< OF < L *fatum* fate]

faze (fāz) *v.t.* **fazed, faz·ing** *U.S. Informal* To worry; disconcert. [Var. of dial. E *fease*, OE *fēsian* to frighten]

fe·al·ty (fē′əl·tē) *n.* *pl.* **·ties** **1.** The obligation of fidelity owed to a feudal lord by his vassal or tenant. **2.** Faithfulness; loyalty. [< OF < L *fidelitas*]

fear (fir) *n.* **1.** An agitated feeling aroused by awareness of actual or threatening danger, trouble, etc.; dread; terror. **2.** An uneasy feeling that something may happen contrary to one's desires. **3.** A feeling of deep, reverential awe and dread. **4.** A continuing state or attitude of fright, dread, or alarmed concern: to live in *fear*. **5.** The possibility that something dreaded or unwanted may occur: There is no *fear* that such a thing will happen. **— for fear of** So as to avoid or keep from happening. **— for fear that** (or **lest**) So that . . . not: He held her hand *for fear that* she would fall. *— v.t.* **1.** To be frightened of. **2.** To be uneasy or apprehensive over (an unwanted or unpleasant possibility). **3.** To have a deep, reverential awe of. *— v.i.* **4.** To feel dread or terror. **5.** To feel uneasy. [OE *fǣr* peril] **— fear′er** *n.*

fear·ful (fir′fəl) *adj.* **1.** Filled with dread or terror. **2.** Filled with uneasiness; apprehensive. **3.** Filled with deep, reverential awe. **4.** Causing dread or terror; terrifying; frightening. **5.** Showing fear; moved by fear: a *fearful* look. **6.** *Informal* Extremely bad. **6.** Going to extremes: a *fearful* drinker. **— fear′ful·ly** *adv.* **— fear′ful·ness** *n.*

fear·less (fir′lis) *adj.* Devoid of fear; not at all afraid. **fear′less·ly** *adv.* **— fear′less·ness** *n.*

fear·some (fir′səm) *adj.* **1.** Causing fear; alarming. Timid; frightened. **— fear′some·ly** *adv.* **— fear′some·ne**

fea·sance (fē′zəns) *n.* *Law* Fulfillment of a condition ligation, etc. [< AF < F < L *facere* to do]

fea·si·ble (fē′zə·bəl) *adj.* **1.** Capable of being put into e or accomplished; practicable: a *feasible* project. **2.** Ca of being successfully utilized; suitable. **3.** Fairly prob likely: a *feasible* explanation. [< OF < F < L *facere* **fea′si·bil′i·ty, fea′si·ble·ness** *n.* **— fea′si·bly** *adv.*

feast (fēst) *n.* **1.** A sumptuous meal. **2.** Something af ing great pleasure to the senses or intellect. **3.** An elab banquet for many persons. **4.** A day or days of celebr regularly set aside for a religious purpose or in honor of person, event, or thing; also **feast day.** *— v.t.* **1.** To g feast for; entertain lavishly. **2.** To delight; gratify. – **3.** To partake of a feast; eat heartily. **4.** To dwell deli edly, as on a painting. [< OF < L *festa*, neut. pl. of *f* joyful < *feriae* holidays] **— feast′er** *n.*

feat (fēt) *n.* A notable act, as one displaying skill or da **— Syn.** See ACT. [< OF *fait* < L *factum*. See FACT.]

feath·er (feth′ər) *n.* **1.** Any of the horny, elongated s tures that form the plumage of birds and much of the surface. **2.** *pl.* Plumage. **3.** *pl.* Dress; attire. **4.** A lo tuft of hair resembling a feather. **5.** The hairy fringe o legs and tails of some dogs. **6.** A feather or feathers fast to the shaft of an arrow to guide its flight. **7.** Somethin sembling a bird's feather, as a key, wedge, etc. **8.** Cla species; kind: birds of a *feather*. **9.** The act of featherin oar blade or propeller). **— a feather in one's ca** achievement to be proud of. **— in full feather** In full f fully equipped. **— in high, fine,** or **good feather** In spirits or health. *— v.t.* **1.** To fit with a feather, as a row. **2.** To cover, adorne, line, or fringe with feathers To join by a tongue-and-groove joint. **4.** In rowing, to (the oar blade) following each stroke so that the bla more or less horizontal as it is carried back to the pos for reentering the water. **5.** *Aeron.* To change the pit (a propeller) so that the blades are parallel with the li flight. *— v.i.* **6.** To grow feathers or become covered feathers. **7.** To move, spread, or expand like feathers. To feather an oar or propeller blade. **— to feather o nest** To grow prosperous. [OE *fether*] **— feath′ered**

feather bed A mattress stuffed with feathers or down.

feath·er·bed·ding (feth′ər·bed′ing) *n.* The practice o quiring the employment of more workers than are need as to create more jobs and prevent unemployment.

feath·er·brain (feth′ər·brān′) *n.* A flighty, stupid, or tally unbalanced individual. **— feath′er·brained** *adj.*

feath·er·edge (feth′ər·ej′) *n.* A very thin, tapering e as of a planed board. **— feath′er·edged** *adj.*

feath·er·stitch (feth′ər·stich′) *n.* An embroidery s resembling a feather, made by taking one or more s stitches alternately on either side of a straight line. – *& v.i.* To embroider with such a stitch.

feath·er·weight (feth′ər·wāt′) *n.* 1. A boxer or wre weighing between 118 pounds and 127 pounds. **2.** Any son or thing relatively light in weight or size. *— adj.* **1** or like a featherweight. **2.** Insignificant; trivial.

feath·er·y (feth′ər·ē) *adj.* **1.** Provided with or as if feathers; feathered. **2.** Suggestive of feathers in light etc. **— feath′er·i·ness** *n.*

fea·ture (fē′chər) *n.* **1.** A distinctive part of the face, as eyes, nose, or mouth. **2.** *Usu. pl.* The overall appearan structure of a face. **3.** A distinguishing mark, part, or q ity. **4.** A full-length motion picture, esp. a principal att tion. **5.** Anything given special prominence; as: **a** A sp article, department, etc., in a magazine or newspaper. **b** item publicized, as during a sale. **c** A special attraction, a a program, etc. *— v.t.* **·tured, ·tur·ing** **1.** To give sp prominence to. **2.** To be a distinctive characteristic of. *Slang* To form an idea of; imagine. [< OF < L *facere* to **— fea′ture·less** *adj.*

fea·tured (fē′chərd) *adj.* **1.** Having (specified) facial c acteristics: *hard-featured*. **2.** Presented as a special or tral attraction.

febri- *combining form* Fever. Also, before vowels, **fe** [< L *febris* fever]

fe·brif·ic (fə·brif′ik) *adj.* **1.** Causing fever. **2.** Feveri

feb·ri·fuge (feb′rə·fyōōj) *n.* A medicine efficacious in ducing or removing fever. *— adj.* Reducing or remov fever. [< F < L *febris* + *fugare* to drive away]

fe·brile (fē′brəl, feb′rəl) *adj.* Feverish.

Feb·ru·ar·y (feb′rōō·er′ē) *n.* *pl.* **·ar·ies** or **·ar·ys** The ond month of the year, having twenty-eight, or, in years, twenty-nine days. Abbr. *F.*, *Feb*, *Feb.* [< L *feb* a Roman purificatory festival celebrated on Feb. 15]

fe·ces (fē′sēz) *n.pl.* **1.** Animal excrement; ordure. **2.** foul refuse matter or sediment. Also spelled *faeces*. [< L *faex, faecis* sediment] **— fe′cal** (-kəl) *adj.*

·less (fek′lis) *adj.* **1.** Devoid of energy or effectiveness; ·le. **2.** Devoid of vitality; listless. **3.** Careless and irre- ·nsible. **— feck′less·ly** *adv.* **— feck′less·ness** *n.*
·lent (fek′yə·lənt) *adj.* Turbid or foul with impurities; ·y. [< L *faex* dregs] **— fec′u·lence, fec′u·len·cy** *n.*
·nd (fē′kənd, fek′ənd) *adj.* Fruitful; prolific. [< OF < ·cundus fruitful] **— fe·cun·di·ty** (fi·kun′də·tē) *n.*
·n·date (fē′kən·dāt, fek′ən-) *v.t.* **·dat·ed, ·dat·ing 1.** make fruitful. **2.** To fertilize. **— fe′cun·da′tion** *n.*
(fed) Past tense and past participle of FEED. **— fed up** ·ng Surfeited with something to an extreme degree.
·r·al (fed′ər·əl) *adj.* **1.** Of, relating to, or formed by an ·ement among two or more states, groups, etc., to merge a union in which control of common affairs is granted to ·ntral authority, with each member retaining jurisdiction · its own internal affairs; also, of, relating to, or support- such a union or central government. **2.** Of or pertaining confederacy (def. 1). **—** *n.* An advocate or supporter of ·deral union or federal government. [< F < L *foedus*, · compact, league] **— fed′er·al·ly** *adv.*
·er·al (fed′ər·əl) *adj.* **1.** Of, relating to, or supporting central government of a specific country, as of the U.S. ·f, relating to, or loyal to the Union cause in the Amer- · Civil War. **3.** Of, relating to, or supporting the Fed- ·ist Party. **—** *n.* **1.** One who favored the Union cause ·he Civil War. **2.** A Federalist. **— Fed′er·al·ly** *adv.*
·ral Bureau of Investigation An agency of the U.S. ·rnment that investigates violations of Federal laws.
·r·al·ism (fed′ər·əl·iz′əm) *n.* The doctrine, system, or ·ciple of federal union or federal government; also, ad- ·acy or support of this doctrine, system, or principle.
·r·al·ist (fed′ər·əl·ist) *n.* An advocate or supporter of ·ralism. **—** *adj.* Of or relating to federalism or federal- : also **fed′er·al·is′tic.**
·er·al·ist (fed′ər·əl·ist) *n.* **1.** One who supported the ·ral union of the American colonies and the adoption of Constitution of the United States. **2.** A member of the ·eralist Party. **— Fed′er·al·ism** *n.* **—** *adj.* Of or relating ·he Federalist Party or Federalists: also **Fed′er·al·is′tic.**
·ralist Party A political party (1787–1830) that advo- ·d the adoption of the U.S. Constitution and the forma- of a strong national government. Also **Federal Party.**
·r·al·ize (fed′ər·əl·īz′) *v.t.* **·ized, ·iz·ing** To unite in a ·ral union; federate. **— fed′er·al·i·za′tion** *n.*
·r·ate (*v.* fed′ə·rāt; *adj.* fed′ə·rit) *v.t. & v.i.* **·at·ed, ·at·ing** ·nite in a federal union. [See FEDERAL.]
·r·a·tion (fed′ə·rā′shən) *n.* 1. The joining together of or more states, groups, etc., into a federal union or a ·ederacy. **2.** A league or confederacy.
·ra (fə·dôr′ə, -dō′rə) *n.* A soft hat, usu. of felt, with a ·ed brim and a crown creased lengthwise. [after *Fédora*, ·ay by V. Sardou, French dramatist]
·fē) *n.* A charge, compensation, or payment for some- ·g, as: **a** A sum charged for professional services: medical **b** A sum charged for some privilege: membership *fee.* **c** A · charged for admission: an entrance *fee.* **d** A gratuity or **— to hold in fee** To have full and absolute possession **—** *v.t.* **feed, fee·ing** To pay a fee to. [< AF, var. of OF ·ief < Med.L *feudum* fief, property, money]
·le (fē′bəl) *adj.* **·bler, ·blest 1.** Lacking strength; very ·k. **2.** Lacking energy, direction, or effectiveness: *feeble* ·rts. **3.** Lacking point or substance: a *feeble* joke. **4.** In- ·inct; faint: a *feeble* light. [< OF < L *flebilis* lamentable ·ere to weep] **— fee′ble·ness** *n.* **— fee′bly** *adv.*
·le-mind·ed (fē′bəl·mīn′did) *adj.* Mentally deficient. ·ee′ble-mind′ed·ly** *adv.* **— fee′ble-mind′ed·ness** *n.*
(fēd) *v.* **fed, feed·ing** *v.t.* **1.** To supply with food: to a hungry family. **2.** To give (something) as food or ·rishment to: to *feed* carrots to rabbits. **3.** To serve as · or nourishment for; also, to produce food for: acreage · will *feed* many. **4.** To keep supplied, as with fuel: to · a fire; also, to keep supplying: to *feed* data into a com- ·ing machine. **5.** To keep or make more intense or great- ·to *feed* suspicions. **6.** To gratify; feast: to *feed* one's eyes ·eauty. **—** *v.i.* **7.** To eat: said chiefly of animals. **— to · on** (or **upon**) **1.** To consume (something) as food; use ·ood: said chiefly of animals. **2.** To draw support, en- ·ragement, etc., from: to *feed on* hope. **—** *n.* **1.** Food ·n to animals. **2.** The amount of fodder, etc., given at time. **3.** Material supplied, as to a machine. **4.** The ·plying of such material. **5.** A mechanical part, as of a ·ing machine, that keeps supplying material to be worked etc. **6.** *Informal* A meal. **— off one's feed** *Slang* Hav- little appetite. [OE *fēdan* < *fōda* food] **— feed′er** *n.*
·back (fēd′bak′) *n.* The return of part of the output of ·ystem into the input for purposes of modification and ·trol of the output, as in electronic amplifiers, automatic ·chines, certain biological and psychological processes, etc.

feel (fēl) *v.* **felt, feel·ing** *v.t.* **1.** To examine or explore with the hands, fingers, etc. **2.** To be aware of touch: to *feel* drops of sweat on one's forehead. **3.** To experience consciously (an emotion, pain, etc.): to *feel* joy. **4.** To be emotionally affected by: to *feel* disgrace deeply. **5.** To perceive or be aware of through thought: to *feel* the need for reform. **6.** To think; suppose; judge: I *feel* that you should do this. **7.** To have one's whole being respond to through understanding, etc. **8.** To experience the force or impact of: to *feel* the full weight of an attack. **—** *v.i.* **9.** To have physical sensation. **10.** To produce a sensory impression of being hard, soft, cold, hot, etc. **11.** To experience consciously the sensation or condition of being: He *feels* cold; to *feel* joyful. **12.** To produce an indicated overall condition, impression, or reaction: It *feels* good to be home. **13.** To experience compassion or pity: with *for*: I *feel* for you. **14.** To have convictions or opinions: to *feel* strongly about an issue. **15.** To search for by touching; grope: to *feel* around a darkened room. **— to feel like** *Informal* To have a desire or inclination for. **— to feel out 1.** To try to learn indirectly and cautiously the viewpoint, opinions, etc., of (a person); sound out. **2.** To explore the nature of (a situation, etc.) in a cautious way. **— to feel up to** To seem to oneself to be capable of or ready for. **—** *n.* **1.** Perception by touch or contact. **2.** The quality of something as perceived by touch. **3.** A sensation or impression. **4.** The act of feeling. [OE *fēlan*]
feel·er (fē′lər) *n.* **1.** One who or that which feels. **2.** Any action, hint, proposal, etc., intended to draw out the views or intentions of another. **3.** *Zool.* An organ of touch.
feel·ing (fē′ling) *n.* **1.** The faculty by which one perceives sensations of pain, pressure, heat, etc. **2.** Any particular sensation of this sort: a *feeling* of warmth. **3.** An emotion: a *feeling* of joy, sadness, etc. **4.** A sensation or awareness of something: a *feeling* of insecurity. **5.** A capacity to feel deeply: a woman of *feeling.* **6.** *pl.* Sensibilities; sensitivities: His *feelings* are easily hurt. **7.** A generous, sympathetic attitude; compassion. **8.** An impression produced upon a person by an object, place, etc. **9.** An opinion or sentiment; also, a foreboding. **—** *adj.* **1.** Having sensation; sentient. **2.** Having warm emotions; sympathetic: a *feeling* heart. **3.** Marked by or indicating emotion. **— feel′ing·ly** *adv.*
feet (fēt) Plural of FOOT. **— on one's** (or **its**) **feet 1.** In or into a condition of stability; well-established: to get a business *on its feet.* **2.** In or into a condition of restored health: to get a patient *on his feet.* **3.** Standing or walking.
feign (fān) *v.t.* **1.** To make a false show of; sham: to *feign madness.* **2.** To think up (a false story, a lying excuse, etc.) and give out as true; fabricate. **3.** To imitate so as to deceive. **—** *v.i.* **4.** To make pretense of something. [< OF < L *fingere* to shape] **— feigned** *adj.* **— feign′er** *n.*
feint (fānt) *n.* **1.** A deceptive appearance or movement; a ruse or pretense. **2.** An apparent or pretended blow or attack meant to divert attention. **—** *v.i.* To make a feint. [< F *feinte*, pp. of *feindre* < L *fingere* to shape]
feld·spar (feld′spär, fel′spär) *n.* Any one of a group of crystalline materials largely made up of silicates of aluminum: sometimes spelled *felspar.* Also **feld′spath** (-spath). [Partial trans. of G < *feld* field + *spat* spar] **— feld·spath′·ic, feld·spath′ose** (-ōs) *adj.*
fe·lic·i·tate (fə·lis′ə·tāt) *v.t.* **·tat·ed, ·tat·ing** To congratulate. [< L < *felix, -icis* happy] **— fe·lic′i·ta′tion** *n.*
fe·lic·i·tous (fə·lis′ə·təs) *adj.* **1.** Most appropriate; apt. **2.** Using an agreeably pertinent or effective manner or style. **— fe·lic′i·tous·ly** *adv.* **— fe·lic′i·tous·ness** *n.*
fe·lic·i·ty (fə·lis′ə·tē) *n.* *pl.* **·ties 1.** Happiness; bliss. **2.** An instance of happiness. **3.** A source of happiness. **4.** An agreeably pertinent or effective manner or style. **5.** A pleasantly appropriate remark. [< OF < L *felix* happy]
fe·line (fē′līn) *adj.* **1.** Of or relating to a cat, as the domestic cat or lions, tigers, and leopards. **2.** Resembling a cat, as in stealthiness. **—** *n.* An animal of the cat family: also **fe·lid** (fē′lid). [< L < *felis* cat] **— fe′line·ly** *adv.* **— fe′·line·ness, fe·lin·i·ty** (fə·lin′ə·tē) *n.*
fell[1] (fel) Past tense of FALL.
fell[2] (fel) *v.t.* **felled, fell·ing 1.** To strike and cause to fall down. **2.** To cut down (timber). **3.** In sewing, to finish (a seam) with a flat, smooth strip made by joining edges, folding them under, and stitching flat. **—** *n.* **1.** The timber cut down during one season. **2.** In sewing, a felled seam. [OE *fellan*, causative of *feallan* to fall] **— fell′a·ble** *adj.*
fell[3] (fel) *adj.* Cruel; vicious; inhuman. [< OF *fel* cruel]
fell[4] (fel) *n.* The skin of an animal, esp. as covered with its natural hair, wool, etc. [OE *hide*]
fel·lah (fel′ə) *n.* *pl.* **fel·lahs** or *Arabic* **fel·la·hin, fel·la·heen** (fel′ə·hēn′) In Arabic-speaking countries, a peasant or laborer. [< Arabic *fellāh*]
fell·er (fel′ər) *n.* **1.** One who or that which fells. **2.** A sewing-machine attachment for the felling of seams.

fel·low (fel′ō) *n.* **1.** A man or boy: often in informal address. **2.** *U.S. Informal* The sweetheart of a woman or girl. **3.** A person in general; anybody; one. **4.** A comrade or companion. **5.** A person viewed as being of little importance or worth. **6.** A partner or accomplice: *fellows* in crime. **7.** An individual belonging to the same kind, class, or group as oneself. **8.** Either one of a pair; mate. **9.** A member of one of several learned societies. **10.** A graduate student of a university or college who, in recognition of merit, is granted financial assistance to pursue further study. **—** *adj.* Joined through some common occupation, interests, objectives, etc.: *fellow* citizens. [OE *fēolaga* business partner]

fel·low·ship (fel′ō·ship) *n.* **1.** Companionship; association. **2.** The condition or fact of having common interests, ideals, experiences, etc. **3.** A body of individuals joined together through similar interests, beliefs, etc.; brotherhood. **4.** The status of being a fellow at a university or college; also, the financial grant made to a fellow. **—** *v* **·shiped** or **·shipped, ·ship·ing** or **·ship·ping** *Rare v.t.* **1.** To grant fellowship to. **—** *v.i.* **2.** To join in fellowship with others.

fellow traveler One who favors the ideology or program of a particular group without being a member.

fel·ly (fel′ē) *n. pl.* **·lies** A segment of or the entire rim of a wooden wheel, in which the spokes are inserted. [OE *felg*]

fel·on[1] (fel′ən) *n.* *Law* One who has committed a felony. **—** *adj. Poetic* Wicked, or cruel. [< OF *felon* base]

fel·on[2] (fel′ən) *n.* *Pathol.* An inflammation of a finger or toe in the terminal joint or at the cuticle. [? < FELON[1]]

fe·lo·ni·ous (fə·lō′nē·əs) *adj.* **1.** *Law* **a** Of, relating to, or involving a felony: *felonious* intent. **b** Constituting, resembling, or having the nature of a felony: *felonious* assault. **2.** *Poetic* Wicked. **— fe·lo′ni·ous·ly** *adv.* **— fe·lo′ni·ous·ness** *n.*

fel·o·ny (fel′ə·nē) *n. pl.* **·nies** *Law* Any of several grave crimes, as murder, rape, arson, or burglary, for which a punishment greater than that for a misdemeanor is provided.

fel·spar (fel′spär) See FELDSPAR.

felt[1] (felt) Past tense and past participle of FEEL.

felt[2] (felt) *n.* **1.** An unwoven fabric made by matting together fibers of wool, fur, or hair through pressure and the use of heat, chemicals, etc. **2.** Something made of felt, as a hat. **—** *adj.* Relating to, made of, or resembling felt. **—** *v.t.* **1.** To make into felt. **2.** To overlay with felt. **—** *v.i.* **3.** To become matted together like felt. [OE]

fe·luc·ca (fə·luk′ə, fe-) *n.* A small, swift vessel propelled by lateen sails and by oars. [< Ital. < Arabic *fulk* ship]

FELUCCA

fe·male (fē′māl) *adj.* **1.** Of or pertaining to the sex that brings forth young or produces ova. **2.** Typical of or suitable to this sex; feminine. **3.** Made up of women and girls: the *female* portion of the population. **4.** *Bot.* Designating a plant that has a pistil but no stamen and that is capable of being fertilized and of producing fruit. **5.** *Mech.* Denoting or having a bore or slot designed to receive a correlated inserted part, called *male*, as some electric plugs. **—** *n.* **1.** A human being of the female sex. **2.** A female animal or plant. [< OF < L *femina* woman]

fem·i·nine (fem′ə·nin) *adj.* **1.** Of or pertaining to the female sex; female. **2.** Of or pertaining to women and girls; typical of or appropriate to women and girls: *feminine* gentleness. **3.** Lacking manly qualities; effeminate. **4.** *Gram.* Applicable to females only or to persons or things classified, as in declension, as female. **—** *n. Gram.* **1.** The feminine gender. **2.** A word or form belonging to the feminine gender. **— fem′i·nine·ly** *adv.* **— fem′i·nine·ness** *n.*

feminine rhyme Rhyme in which the primary stress falls upon the next to the last syllable, as in *clever, never.*

fem·i·nin·i·ty (fem′ə·nin′ə·tē) *n. pl.* **·ties** **1.** The quality or state of being feminine. **2.** A feminine trait.

fem·i·nism (fem′ə·niz′əm) *n.* **1.** A doctrine advocating the granting of the same social, political, and economic rights to women as the ones granted to men; also, a movement to win these. **2.** *Med.* The existence of female characteristics in the male. **— fem′i·nist** *n. & adj.* **— fem′i·nis′tic** *adj.*

fem·i·nize (fem′ə·nīz) *v.t. & v.i.* **·nized, ·niz·ing** To make or become feminine or effeminate. **— fem′i·ni·za′tion** *n.*

femme (fâm) *n. French* Woman; wife.

femme fa·tale (fâ·tàl′) *French* A seductive woman.

fe·mur (fē′mər) *n. pl.* **fe·murs** or **fem·o·ra** (fem′ər·ə) *Anat.* The long bone extending from the pelvis to the knee. Also called *thighbone.* For illustration see PELVIS. [< L, thigh] **— fem·o·ral** (fem′ər·əl) *adj.*

fen (fen) *n.* A marsh; bog. [OE *fenn*]

fence (fens) *n.* **1.** A structure of rails, stakes, strung wire, etc., erected as an enclosure, barrier, or boundary. **2.** Fencing. **3.** Skill at making quick, effective remarks or retorts, as in a discussion or debate. **4.** A dealer in stolen goods. **— on the fence** Unwilling or unable to commit oneself one way or the other. **—** *v.* **fenced, fenc·ing** *v.t.* **1.** To enclose or as with a fence. **2.** To cause to be separated by or as fence. **—** *v.i.* **3.** To practice the art of fencing. **4.** To giving direct answers. **5.** To deal in stolen goods. [Ap var. of DEFENCE] **— fence′less** *adj.* **— fenc′er** *n.*

fenc·ing (fen′sing) *n.* **1.** The art or practice of using a sword, or similar weapon. **2.** The art or practice of ma quick, effective remarks or retorts, as in a debate. **3.** terial used in making fences; also, fences collectively.

fend (fend) *v.t.* **1.** To ward off; parry: usu. with *off.* – **2.** To offer resistance; parry. **3.** *Informal* To pro shift: with *for*: to *fend* for oneself. [Aphetic var. of DEF

fend·er (fen′dər) *n.* **1.** One who or that which fen wards off. **2.** *U.S.* A part projecting over each wheel of or other vehicle, designed to keep water, mud, dirt, etc., being thrown upwards. **3.** A metal guard set before an fire. **4.** A part projecting from the front of a locomoti streetcar, designed to push obstructions from the track

Fe·ni·an (fē′nē·ən, fēn′yən) *n.* A member of an orga tion founded in New York about 1857 to seek indepen for Ireland. **—** *adj.* Of Fenians. [< OIrish *fene* Irish

fen·nel (fen′əl) *n.* **1.** A tall herb of the parsley family produces aromatic seeds used in cookery and pharmacy The seeds of this plant. [OE < L *faeniculum* fennel]

feod (fyo͞od) See FEUD[2].

feoff (*v.* fef, fēf; *n.* fēf) *Law v.t.* **feoffed, feoff·ing** To gi grant a fief to. **—** *n.* A fief. [See FIEF.] **— feof′fer** *n* **feoff′ment** *n.*

-fer *combining form* One who or that which bears: *co* [< L < *ferre* to bear]

fe·ral (fir′əl) *adj.* **1.** Not tame nor domesticated; wild Of, relating to, or typical of a wild beast; savage. [< *feralis* < L *fera* wild beast]

fer-de-lance (fâr′də·läns′) *n.* A large, venomous sna tropical South America and Martinique. [< F, lance

fer·ment (*n.* fûr′mənt; *v.* fər·ment′) *n.* **1.** Any substan agent producing fermentation, as enzymes, yeast, ce bacteria, etc. **2.** Fermentation. **3.** Excitement or a tion. **—** *v.t.* **1.** To produce fermentation in. **2.** To e with emotion or passion; agitate. **—** *v.i.* **3.** To underg mentation; work. **4.** To be agitated, as with emo seethe. [< F < L < *fervere* to boil] **— fer·ment′a·bl** **— fer·ment′a·bil′i·ty** *n.* **— fer·ment′a·tive** *adj.*

fer·men·ta·tion (fûr′mən·tā′shən) *n.* **1.** *Chem.* The ual decomposition of organic compounds induced by th tion of various ferments; specifically, the conversion of cose into ethyl alcohol through the action of zymase. Commotion, agitation, or excitement.

fer·mi (fer′mē, fûr′-) *n.* *Physics* A unit for the mea ment of the radii of nuclear atomic particles, equal to centimeter. [after E. *Fermi*]

fer·mi·um (fer′mē·əm, fûr′-) *n.* A radioactive ele (symbol Fm), artificially produced by the bombardme einsteinium with alpha particles. See ELEMENT. [aft *Fermi*]

fern (fûrn) *n.* A plant that bears no flowers or seeds, ha roots, stems, and large, feathery fronds, and reproducin means of asexual spores. [OE *fearn*] **— fern′y** *adj.*

fern·er·y (fûr′nər·ē) *n. pl.* **·er·ies** **1.** A place in which are grown. **2.** A standing growth or bed of ferns.

fe·ro·cious (fə·rō′shəs) *adj.* **1.** Extremely savage, fi bloodthirsty, or cruel. **2.** *Informal* Very intense: *fero* heat. [< L *ferox, ferocis* fierce + -OUS] **— fe·ro′cio** *adv.* **— fe·ro′cious·ness** *n.*

fe·roc·i·ty (fə·ros′ə·tē) *n. pl.* **·ties** The state or quali being ferocious. [< F < L < *ferox* fierce]

-ferous *combining form* Bearing or producing: *conife* [< -FER + -OUS]

fer·rate (fer′āt) *n. Chem.* A salt of ferric acid. [< L *fe* iron + -ATE[3]]

fer·ret (fer′it) *n.* A small, red-eyed polecat of Europe, domesticated and used in hunting rodents and other vermin. **—** *v.t.* **1.** To search out by careful investigation: with *out.* **2.** To drive out of hiding or hunt with a ferret. **—** *v.i.* **3.** To search. **4.** To hunt by means of ferrets. [< OF < LL < L *fur* thief] **— fer′ret·er** *n.* **— fer′ret·y** *adj.*

FERRET (Body about 14 inches long; tail 5 inches)

ferri- *combining form Chem.* Containing iron in the ferric condition. [Var. of FERRO-]

fer·ric (fer′ik) *adj. Chem.* **1.** Pertaining to iron. **2.** taining to or designating compounds of iron in its hi valence. [< L *ferrum* iron + -IC]

Fer·ris wheel (fer′is) *U.S.* A giant, vertical, power-dr wheel that revolves on a stationary axle and has han seats in which passengers ride for amusement. Also **f wheel.** [after G. W. G. *Ferris*, 1859–96, U.S. engineer

fer·rite (fer′īt) *n.* **1.** *Geol.* A substance of uncertain position that is found in igneous rocks and apparently

ns iron. 2. *Chem.* One of several compounds, often magic, containing ferric oxide. 3. *Metall.* The pure metallic
stituent in iron and steel. [< L *ferrum* iron + -ITE]
o- *combining form* 1. Derived from, containing, or al-
ed with iron. 2. *Chem.* Containing iron in the ferrous
dition. [< L *ferrum* iron]
ro·con·crete (fer′ō·kon′krēt, -kon·krēt′) *n.* Reinforced
crete.
ro·mag·net·ic (fer′ō·mag·net′ik) *adj. Physics* Highly
gnetic, as is iron. — **fer′ro·mag′ne·tism** *n.*
ro·man·ga·nese (fer′ō·mang′gə·nēs, -nēz) *n.* An alloy
ron rich in manganese, used in making tough steel.
rous (fer′əs) *adj. Chem.* Of or pertaining to iron, esp.
alent iron, where its combining value is lowest: *ferrous*
oride, $FeCl_2$. [< L *ferrum* iron + -OUS]
ru·gi·nous (fə·rōō′jə·nəs) *adj.* 1. Of or like iron. 2.
st-colored. [< L < *ferrum* iron]
rule (fer′əl, -ōōl) *n.* A metal ring or cap used on or near
end of a stick, as of a cane or a tool handle, to protect
end or reinforce the stick. — *v.t.* **·ruled, ·rul·ing** To
ip with a ferrule. [< OF < L *viriae* bracelets]
rum (fer′əm) *n.* Iron. [< L]
ry (fer′ē) *n. pl.* **·ries** 1. A boat or other craft used in
veying people, cars, or merchandise across a river or other
row extent of water. 2. Delivery of a boat or other
t to a user under its own motive power. — *v.* **·ried, ·ry·**
v.t. 1. To convey across a river, etc., by a boat or other
ft. 2. To cross (a river, etc.) in a boat or other craft. 3.
deliver by ferry (def. 2). — *v.i.* 4. To cross a river, etc.,
or as by a ferry. [OE *ferian* to carry, convey]
ry·boat (fer′ē·bōt) *n.* A boat used as a ferry.
tile (fûr′təl, *esp. Brit.* -tīl) *adj.* 1. Yielding or capable of
ducing abundant crops or vegetation: *fertile* land. 2. Reducing or able to reproduce. 3. Inventive or productive:
rtile talent. [< OF < L *fertilis* < *ferre* to bear] — **fer′·
·ly** *adv.* — **fer′tile·ness** *n.*
til·i·ty (fər·til′ə·tē) *n.* The state or quality of being
ile; productiveness.
til·ize (fûr′təl·īz) *v.t.* **·ized, ·iz·ing** 1. To make fertile;
se to be productive or fruitful. 2. To cause (a female re-
ductive cell to begin development of a new individual.
To spread manure, nitrates, or other enriching material
(land). *adj.* — **fer′til·i·za′tion** (-təl·ə·zā′shən) *n.*
til·iz·er (fûr′təl·ī′zər) *n.* That which fertilizes; esp., a
terial, as manure or nitrates, used to enrich land.
ule (fer′əl, -ōōl) *n.* A flat stick or ruler sometimes used
punishing children. — *v.t.* **·uled, ·ul·ing** To punish with
rule. [< L *ferula* whip, rod]
vent (fûr′vənt) *adj.* 1. Moved by or showing great
rmth or intensity, as of emotion or enthusiasm; ardent.
Poetic Very hot; burning. [< L *fervere* to boil] — **fer′·
t·ly** *adv.* — **fer′ven·cy, fer′vent·ness** *n.*
vid (fûr′vid) *adj.* 1. Fervent, esp. to an extreme degree;
st impassioned. 2. *Poetic* Very hot; burning. [< L *fer-
e* to boil] — **fer′vid·ly** *adv.* — **fer′vid·ness** *n.*
vor (fûr′vər) *n.* 1. Great warmth or intensity, as of
otion; fervency; ardor. 2. Heat; warmth. Also *Brit.* **fer′·
r.** [< OF < L, violent heat, ardor]
cue (fes′kyōō) *n.* Any of a genus of tough grasses, used
pasturage. [< OF < L *festuca* stalk, straw]
(fes) *n. Heraldry* A horizontal band across the middle
n escutcheon. Also **fesse.** [< OF < L *fascia* band]
t *combining form Slang* Bout; session: *gabfest.* [< G.
festival]
tal (fes′təl) *adj.* Pertaining to or typical of a festival,
st, or holiday. [< OF < L *festum* feast] — **fes′tal·ly** *adv.*
ter (fes′tər) *v.i.* 1. To develop pus; ulcerate. 2. To be
become rotten and foul. 3. To be a constant source of
ation or irritation; rankle. — *v.i.* 4. To cause to fester.
n. A small, ulcerous sore. [< OF < L *fistula* ulcer]
ti·val (fes′tə·vəl) *n.* 1. A particular feast, holiday, or
ebration. 2. Any occasion for rejoicing or feasting. 3. A
cial series of performances, exhibitions, etc.: a Shake-
are *festival.* — *adj.* Festive. [See FESTIVE.]
tive (fes′tiv) *adj.* Of, relating to, or suitable for a feast
other celebration. [< L < *festum* feast < *festus* joyful]
fes′tive·ly *adv.* — **fes′tive·ness** *n.*
tiv·i·ty (fes·tiv′ə·tē) *n. pl.* **·ties** 1. A festival. 2. Glad-
ss and rejoicing. 3. *pl.* Festive merrymaking.
toon (fes·tōōn′) *n.* 1. Flowers or leaves, or colored
per, ribbon, etc., hanging in loops between two points. 2.
ornamental carving, sculpture, etc., representing this.
v.t. To decorate, fashion into, or link together by festoons.
F < Ital. *festa* feast] — **fes·toon′er·y** *n.*
al (fēt′l) *adj.* Of or typical of a fetus: also spelled *foetal.*
ch (fech) *v.t.* 1. To go after and bring back. 2. To draw
th; elicit. 3. To draw in (breath); also, to give forth (a
h, groan, etc.); heave. 4. To infer. 5. To cost or sell for.
6. *Informal* To attract or delight. 7. *Informal* To give or deal (a blow, slap, etc.). 8. *Naut.* To arrive at (a port, etc.). — *v.i.* 9. To go after something and bring it back. 10. *Naut.* To hold to a particular course; also, to swing around; veer. — *n.* 1. The act of fetching. 2. A trick; stratagem. [OE *feccan*] — **fetch′er** *n.*

fetch·ing (fech′ing) *adj. Informal* Very attractive or pleasing; charming. — **fetch′ing·ly** *adv.*

fete (fāt) *n.* 1. A festival. 2. An outdoor celebration; esp. a dinner, bazaar, etc. — *v.t.* **fet·ed, fet·ing** To honor with festivities. Also *Brit.* **fête.** [< F *fête*]

fet·id (fet′id) *adj.* Having a foul odor; stinking. [< L *fetere* to stink] — **fet′id·ly** *adv.* — **fet′id·ness** *n.*

fet·ish (fet′ish, fē′tish) *n.* 1. An object regarded as having magical powers. 2. Something to which one is devoted excessively or irrationally. 3. *Psychiatry* Some object not in itself erotic but which is sexually stimulating to certain individuals. Also **fetich.** [< F < Pg. *feitiço* charm]

fet·ish·ism (fet′ish·iz′əm, fē′tish-) *n.* 1. Superstitious belief in or worship of fetishes. 2. Excessive or irrational devotion to something. 3. *Psychiatry* Sexual stimulation produced by an object that is not in itself erotic. Also **fet′ich·ism.** — **fet′ish·ist** *n.* — **fet′ish·is′tic** *adj.*

fet·lock (fet′lok′) *n.* 1. A tuft of hair growing at the back of the leg of a horse just above the hoof. 2. The joint of the leg from which this tuft grows: also **fetlock joint.** [ME *fitlock, fetlak,* prob. < LG]

fet·ter (fet′ər) *n.* 1. A chain or other bond put about the ankles to restrain movement or prevent escape. 2. *Usu. pl.* Anything checking freedom of movement or expression. — *v.t.* 1. To put fetters upon. 2. To prevent the free movement or expression of. [OE *feter, fetor*]

fet·tle (fet′l) *v.t.* **·tled, ·tling** To put in proper order; attend to; arrange. — *n.* Proper condition of health or spirits: in fine *fettle.* [ME *fetlen* to prepare, lit., to gird up]

fe·tus (fē′təs) *n. pl.* **·tus·es** The individual unborn organism carried within the womb in the later stages of its development. Also spelled *foetus.* [< L, a bringing forth]

feud[1] (fyōōd) *n.* A state of bitter hostility existing between two or more individuals, families, etc., usu. lasting over a long period of time. — *v.i.* To take part in a feud. [ME < OF < OHG *fehida* hatred, revenge] — **feud′ist** *n.*

feud[2] (fyōōd) *n.* In feudal law, a fief: also spelled *feod.* [< Med.L *feudum* fief]

feu·dal (fyōōd′l) *adj.* 1. Of, relating to, or typical of the feudal system. 2. Of or relating to a fief. — **feu′dal·ly** *adv.*

feu·dal·ism (fyōōd′l·iz′əm) *n.* The mode of life produced by the feudal system. — **feu′dal·ist** *n.* — **feu′dal·is′tic** *adj.*

feudal system A social, political, and economic system in medieval Europe in which vassals were granted land holdings by their lords in return for military service or the performance of other duties.

feu·da·to·ry (fyōō′də·tôr′ē, -tō′rē) *n. pl.* **·ries** A vassal holding a fief; also, the fief held. — *adj.* 1. Of or typical of a feudal relationship. 2. Subject to a feudal lord.

fe·ver (fē′vər) *n.* 1. A disorder marked by unduly high body temperature, rapid pulse, often delirium, etc. 2. Any of several diseases that produce this symptom. 3. Emotional excitement or restless eagerness. ◆ Collateral adjective: *febrile.* — *v.t.* To affect with fever. [OE *fēfer* < L *febris*] — **fe′vered** *adj.*

fever blister A cold sore. Also **fever sore.**

fe·ver·few (fē′vər·fyōō′) *n.* A plant bearing white flowers.

fe·ver·ish (fē′vər·ish) *adj.* 1. Having a fever, esp. a low fever. 2. Of or resembling a fever. 3. Tending to produce fever. 4. Agitated, uneasy, or restless. Also **fe′ver·ous.** — **fe′ver·ish·ly** *adv.* — **fe′ver·ish·ness** *n.*

fe·ver·wort (fē′vər·wûrt′) *n.* 1. A perennial herb with brownish purple flowers and a root used medicinally. Also **fe′ver·root′** (-rōōt′, -rŏŏt′). 2. Boneset, an herb.

few (fyōō) *adj.* Small in number; not very many. — *pron. & n.* A small number; not very many. — **quite a few** A considerable number. — **the few** The minority. [OE *fea* little]

fey (fā) *adj.* 1. Acting as if enchanted or under a spell. 2. Suggestive of a sprite. [< F < OF *fae* fairy]

fez (fez) *n. pl.* **fez·zes** A brimless, tapering, felt cap, usu. red and having a black tassel, often worn by Egyptian men. [after *Fez,* a city in Morocco]

fi·a·cre (fē·ä′kər, *Fr.* fyȧ′kr′) *n.* A small hackney coach. [after Hotel *St. Fiacre* in Paris, where they were first hired]

fi·an·cé (fē′än·sā′, fē·än′sā; *Fr.* fē·äṅ·sā′) *n.* A man to whom a woman is engaged to be married. [< F]

fi·an·cée (fē′än·sā′, fē·än′sā; *Fr.* fē·äṅ·sā′) *n.* A woman to whom a man is engaged to be married. [< F]

fi·as·co (fē·as′kō) *n. pl.* **·coes** or **·cos** A complete or humiliating failure. [< Ital., flask]

fi·at (fī′at, -ət) *n.* 1. A positive and authoritative order or decree. 2. Authorization. [< L, let it be done]

fiat money Paper money made legal tender by decree, as of a government, and not based on gold or silver reserves.

fib (fib) *n.* A lie about something unimportant. —*v.i.* **fibbed, fib·bing** To tell a fib. [? Alter. of FABLE] —**fib′ber** *n.*

fi·ber (fī′bər) *n.* **1.** A fine, relatively long, continuous piece of something, suggestive of a thread, as a filament of asbestos, spun glass, textile or fabric. **2.** *Biol.* One of similar filaments that together form animal or plant tissue or parts: a nerve *fiber.* **3.** A material made up of fine filaments; also, collectively, the filaments themselves. **4.** The particular composition or structure of something. **5.** Character: to lack moral *fiber.* Also *Brit.* **fi′bre.** [< F < L *fibra*]

fi·ber·board (fī′bər·bôrd′, -bōrd′) *n.* **1.** A tough, pliable building material made of wood fiber or other plant fiber.

Fi·ber·glas (fī′bər·glas′, -gläs′) *n.* A flexible, nonflammable material of glass spun into filaments, used for textiles, insulation, etc.: a trade name. Also **fi′ber·glas′, fi′ber·glass′.**

fibr- See FIBRO-

fi·bril (fī′brəl) *n.* **1.** A minute fiber. **2.** *Bot.* A root hair. [< NL < L *fibra* fiber] —**fi·bril·lar** (fī′brə·lər) *adj.*

fi·bril·la (fī·bril′ə) *n. pl.* **·bril·lae** (-bril′ē) A fibril. [< NL]

fi·bril·la·tion (fī′brə·lā′shən) *n.* **1.** The formation of fibers. **2.** *Pathol.* Rapid contraction of muscle fibers of the heart.

fi·brin (fī′brin) *n. Biochem.* An insoluble protein that promotes the clotting of blood. —**fi·bri·nous** (fī′brə·nəs) *adj.*

fi·brin·o·gen (fī·brin′ə·jən) *n. Biochem.* A complex protein occurring in the formation of fibrin.

fibro- *combining form* Pertaining to or composed of fibrous tissue. Also, before vowels, **fibr-.** [< L *fibra* fiber]

fi·broid (fī′broid) *adj.* Made up of or resembling fibrous tissue.

fi·brous (fī′brəs) *adj.* Made up of, having, or resembling fiber: *fibrous* tissue.

fib·u·la (fib′yŏŏ·lə) *n. pl.* **·lae** (-lē) or **·las** **1.** *Anat.* The outer and smaller of the two bones forming the lower part of the human leg from the knee to the ankle. **2.** *Zool.* In animals, a similar bone of the hind leg. **3.** An ancient ornamental brooch. [< L, a clasp] —**fib′u·lar** *adj.*

-fic *suffix* Making, rendering, or causing: *beatific.* [< L *-ficus* < *facere* to make, render]

-fication *suffix* A causing to be (something indicated): *beatification.* [< L *facere* to make, render]

fi·chu (fish′ōō, *Fr.* fē·shü′) *n.* A capelike piece of light material worn about the neck. [< F *ficher* to put on hastily]

fick·le (fik′əl) *adj.* Inconstant in feeling or purpose; changeful; capricious. [OE *ficol* crafty] —**fick′le·ness** *n.*

fic·tile (fik′til) *adj.* Produced by molding or able to be molded. [< L *fingere* to form]

fic·tion (fik′shən) *n.* **1.** Prose works in narrative form, the characters and incidents of which are wholly or partly imaginary; also, such works collectively. **2.** Something imagined or deliberately falsified. **3.** The action of arbitrarily making up an explanation, etc. [< F < L *fictio* a making < *fingere* to form] —**fic′tion·al** *adj.* —**fic′tion·al·ly** *adv.*

fic·ti·tious (fik·tish′əs) *adj.* **1.** Not corresponding to actual fact; artificially invented. **2.** Not genuine; not real; false. **3.** Fictional. —**fic·ti′tious·ly** *adv.* —**fic–ti′tious·ness** *n.*

fic·tive (fik′tiv) *adj.* **1.** Fictitious. **2.** Relating to the creation of fiction: *fictive* ability. —**fic′tive·ly** *adv.*

fid (fid) *n. Naut.* **1.** A supporting bar or crosspiece to hold a topmast in place. **2.** A large, tapering wooden pin used for opening ropes when splicing, etc. [Origin uncertain]

-fid *combining form* **1.** Divided (into an indicated number of parts. **2.** Separated into lobes (of an indicated kind). [< L *-fidus* < *findere* to split]

fid·dle (fid′l) *n.* **1.** A violin; also, any other instrument of the violin or viol family. **2.** *Naut.* A rack used at table to prevent things from sliding off. —**fit as a fiddle** Enjoying perfect health. —**to play second fiddle** To have a position subordinate to that of another. —*v.* **·dled ·dling** *v.i.* **1.** *Informal* To play a violin. **2.** To make nervous or restless movements; fidget. —*v.t.* **3.** To spend (time) in a careless way: usu. with *away.* [OE *fithele* < ML *fidula, fidella,* dim. of L *fides* lyre] —**fid′dler** *n.*

fid·dle-de-dee (fid′l·dē′dē′) *n. & interj.* Nonsense.

fid·dle-fad·dle (fid′l·fad′l) *n. & interj.* Nonsense. —*v.i.* **·dled, ·dling** To occupy oneself with unimportant things.

fiddler crab A small burrowing crab found chiefly off the Atlantic coast of the U.S., one of whose claws is, in the male, much larger than the other.

FIDDLER CRAB
(Carapace ½ to 1 inch wide)

fid·dle·stick (fid′l·stik′) *n.* **1.** A bow used on a violin, etc. **2.** Something trifling.

fid·dle·sticks (fid′l·stiks′) *interj.* Nonsense!

fi·del·i·ty (fī·del′ə·tē, fə-) *n. pl.* **·ties** **1.** Faithfulness to duties, obligations, vows, truth, etc. **2.** Exactness of reproductive detail. **3.** *Electronics* The extent to which a phonograph, tape recorder, etc., receives and transmits input signals without distortion <F < L *fides* faith]

fidg·et (fij′it) *v.i.* **1.** To make nervous or restless moveme —*v.i.* **2.** To cause to fidget. —*n.* **1.** *Usu. pl.* The co tion of being restless or nervous. **2.** One who fidgets. [*fiken* to fidget]

fi·du·cial (fi·dōō′shəl, -dyōō′-) *adj.* **1.** Fiduciary. **2.** B on trust or faith. **3.** *Physics* Fixed as a basis of meas ment. [< L *fidere* to trust] —**fi·du′cial·ly** *adv.*

fi·du·ci·ar·y (fi·dōō′ shē·er′ē, -shər·ē, -dyōō′-) *adj.* **1.** Of, taining to, or acting as a trustee. **2.** Held in trust. **3.** (sisting of fiat money. —*n. pl.* **·ar·ies** One who holds sc thing in trust. [< L *fidere* to trust]

fie (fī) *interj.* An expression of impatience or disappro [< OF *fi, fy* < L *fi,* an expression of disgust]

fief (fēf) *n.* A landed estate held under feudal tenure. OF < Med.L *feudum*]

field (fēld) *n.* **1.** A piece of land with few or no trees, ered with grass, weeds, or similar vegetation. ◆ Colla adjective: *campestral.* **2.** A piece of land set aside for us pasture or for crops. **3.** A large expanse of open coun also, any wide expanse. **4.** An area in which a natura source is found: an oil *field.* **5.** An airport. **6.** The w extent or a particular division of knowledge, research, st etc.: the *field* of chemistry. **7.** In sports and athletics: **a** bounded area where a game is played or where athletic tests, exhibitions, etc., are held: a football *field.* **b** The m bers of a team, etc., actually engaged in active play. **c** competitors in a race or other contest. **8.** *Mil.* A regic active operations or maneuvers. **9.** In business, the away from the home office. **10.** *Physics* An extent of s within which lines of magnetic or electric force are in op tion: also called *field of force.* **11.** *Optics* The area wi which objects are seen in a telescope, etc. **12.** The part painting canvas, flag, coin, etc., used for background. — **leave the field** *U.S. Informal* To back out of a contest, st gle, dispute, etc —**to play the field** *U.S. Informal* To one's energies, interest, or attention to the entire rang something. —**to take the field** To begin a game, mili campaign, struggle, etc. —*v.t.* **1.** In baseball, cricket, **a** To catch or pick up (a ball) and return to the inner f **b** To send (a player) to a field position. —*v.i.* **2.** In b ball, cricket, etc., to play in a field position. —*adj.* **1.** pertaining to, or growing in fields. **2.** Used or designec use in fields. **3.** Played or held on an open field. [OE *fe*

field artillery Artillery so mounted as to be freely m able, and suitable for use with troops in the field.

field day **1.** A day of military maneuvers, athletic cont etc. **2.** A gala day full of pleasurable activities, etc.

field·er (fēl′dər) *n.* In baseball, etc., a player in the fielc

field events The events at an athletic meet other t races.

field glass A compact, portable, binocular telescope. **field glasses.**

field goal **1.** In football, a goal scored by a drop kick place kick, counting three points. **2.** In basketball, a scored while the ball is in active play, counting two po

field hospital A military hospital near a combat zone.

field magnet The magnet that produces the magnetic in a generator or electric motor.

field marshal In the armies of several European nati an officer just below the commander in chief.

Field-Mar·shal (fēld′mär′shəl) *n.* In the British and nadian armies, an officer of the highest rank. See tabl GRADE.

field officer *Mil.* A colonel, lieutenant colonel, or ma

field of force *Physics* Field (def. 10).

field sports Athletic events, as jumping and pole-vault held on the field, as opposed to races held on the track.

field·stone (fēld′stōn′) *n.* Loose stone found near a struction site and used in building. —*adj.* Consisting c having the appearance of fieldstone: a *fieldstone* house.

field·work (fēld′wûrk′) *n.* A temporary fortification.

field work Observations and investigations made in field, as by a scientist. —**field worker**

fiend (fēnd) *n.* **1.** An evil spirit; devil; demon. **2.** An tensely wicked or cruel person. **3.** *Informal* One wh highly skilled in a game, etc.: a bridge *fiend.* **4.** *Infor* One addicted to an injurious habit. —**the Fiend** Satan; devil. [OE *fēond* enemy, devil] —**fiend′like** *adj.*

fiend·ish (fēn′dish) *adj.* Exceedingly cruel or malicious abolical. —**fiend′ish·ly** *adv.* —**fiend′ish·ness** *n.*

fierce (firs) *adj.* **1.** Having a violent and cruel nature. Violent in action or force. **3.** Vehement; intense: *fi* anger. **4.** *Slang* Very disagreeable, bad, etc. [< OF *ferus* wild] —**fierce′ly** *adv.* —**fierce′ness** *n.*

fiery (fīr′ē, fī′ər·ē) *adj.* **fier·i·er, fier·i·est** **1.** Like, cont ing, or composed of fire. **2.** Brightly glowing; blazing. Passionate; impetuous. **4.** Inflamed, as a boil. —**fier** *adv.* —**fier′i·ness** *n.*

fi·es·ta (fē·es′tə, *Sp.* fyes′tä) *n.* **1.** A religious festival. Any holiday or celebration. [< Sp. < L *festa*]

fife (fīf) *n.* A small, shrill-toned flute used chiefly for n y music. —*v.t.* & *v.i.* **fifed, fif·ing** To play on a fife. [< < LL < L *pipare* to peep, chirp] —**fif′er** *n.*

een (fif′tēn′) *n.* **1.** The sum of fourteen and one: a car- al number. **2.** Any symbol of this number, as 15, xv, '. **3.** Anything consisting of or representing fifteen units, an organization, game token, etc. —*adj.* Being one more n fourteen. [OE *fīftēne*] —**fif′teenth** *n.* & *adj.*

ı (fifth) *adj.* **1.** Next after the fourth: the ordinal of *five.* Being one of five equal parts. —*n.* **1.** One of five equal ts. **2.** That which follows the fourth. **3.** *Music* **a** The erval between a tone and another tone five steps from it. ne of these tones, esp. the one higher in pitch. **c** The fifth ve the tonic; the dominant. **4.** One fifth of a U.S. gallon, d as a measure of liquors. —*adv.* In the fifth order, place, ank: also, in formal discourse, **fifth′ly.** [OE *fīfta*]

h Amendment An amendment to the Constitution of U.S. guaranteeing due process of law and that no person all be compelled to be a witness against himself".

ı column In wartime, the civilians within defense lines ɔ secretly assist the enemy. —**fifth columnist**

ı wheel A superfluous person or thing.

7 (fif′tē) *n. pl.* **·ties 1.** The sum of forty and ten: a car- al number. **2.** Any symbol of this number, as 50, l, L. Anything consisting of or representing fifty units, as an anization, bill, etc. —*adj.* Being ten more than forty. ; *fīftig*] —**fif′ti·eth** *n.* & *adj.*

-fifty (fif′tē·fif′tē) *Informal adj.* Sharing equally, as in efits: *fifty-fifty* partners. —*adv.* Equally.

fig) *n.* **1.** The small, edible, pear-shaped fruit of a tree, ivated in warm climates. **2.** The tree that bears this t. [< OF < L *ficus*]

t (fīt) *v.* **fought, fight·ing** *v.t.* **1.** To struggle against in tle or physical combat. **2.** To struggle against in any nner. **3.** To carry on or engage in (a duel, court action,) **4.** To make (one's way) by struggling. **5.** To manage fighting of, as boxers or gamecocks. —*v.i.* **6.** To take t in combat. **7.** To struggle in any manner. —**to fight ut** To fight until a final decision is reached. —**to fight of** To avoid meeting (an opponent or an issue) squarely; ge. —*n.* **1.** Strife or struggle; battle; conflict; combat. Power or disposition to fight; pugnacity. [OE *feohtan*]

t·er (fī′tər) *n.* **1.** One who fights. **2.** *Mil.* A fast, high- naneuverable airplane for aerial fighting: formerly called *suit plane*: also **fighter plane.**

nent (fig′mənt) *n.* A capricious product of the mind; a ion; fabrication. [< L *figmentum* anything made]

ı·ra·tion (fig′yə·rā′shən) *n.* **1.** The act of shaping some- ıg. **2.** Form, shape, or outline. **3.** The act of represent- figuratively. **4.** *Music* Ornamentation.

ır·a·tive (fig′yər·ə·tiv) *adj.* **1.** Based on, like, or con- ing a figure or figures of speech; metaphorical. **2.** Rep- nting by means of a form or figure. **3.** Pertaining to orial or sculptural representation. —**fig′ur·a·tive·ly** *adv.*

ıre (fig′yər, *Brit.* fig′ər) *n.* **1.** A character or symbol resenting a number: the *figure* 5. **2.** *pl.* The use of such racters in calculating. **3.** An amount stated in numbers, f price, etc. **4.** The visible form of anything; shape; out- . **5.** The human form or body. **6.** A personage or char- er, esp. a prominent one. **7.** The appearance or impres- that a person makes. **8.** A representation or likeness, n painting or sculpture. **9.** A pattern or design, as in a ric. **10.** A printed illustration; a cut. **11.** One who or t which represents or symbolizes something: a *figure* of dom. **12.** A figure of speech. **13.** A movement or series novements, as in a dance. **14.** *Geom.* A surface enclosed lines, as a square or a space enclosed by planes, as a cube. *Music* Any short succession of notes that produces a gle and distinct impression. —*v.* **·ured, ·ur·ing** *v.t.* **1.** compute numerically; calculate. **2.** To make an image other representation of; depict. **3.** To ornament with a ign. **4.** To picture mentally; imagine. **5.** To express by gure of speech; symbolize. **6.** *Informal* To believe; pre- . **7.** *Music* To mark with figures above or below the s notes, indicating accompanying chords. —*v.i.* **8.** To ear prominently; be conspicuous. **9.** To compute; reck- —**to figure on** (or **upon**) *U.S. Informal* **1.** To count rely on. **2.** To plan on. —**to figure out 1.** To solve; npute. **2.** To make out; understand. [< F < L *fingere* orm] —**fig′ur·er** *n.*

ıred (fig′yərd) *adj.* **1.** Adorned or marked with figures lesigns: *figured* cottons. **2.** Represented by figures.

red bass *Music* A bass part with numerals, etc., indi- ing chords: also called *thorough bass.*

re eight 1. A maneuver in ice skating that consists in cing the figure 8. **2.** A style of knot: for illus. see KNOT.

ıre·head (fig′yər·hed′) *n.* **1.** A person having nominal dership but no real power. **2.** A carved or ornamental ıre on the prow of a vessel.

figure of speech An expression that intentionally deviates from the literal meanings of words so as to create a more vivid effect, as in simile, metaphor, etc.

figure skating The art or sport of skating in prescribed dancelike patterns. —**figure skater**

fig·u·rine (fig′yə·rēn′) *n.* A small, molded or carved figure; statuette. [< F < Ital. *figurina*]

fig·wort (fig′wûrt′) *n.* A plant with small, dark flowers, formerly supposed to cure scrofula.

Fi·ji (fē′jē) *n.* **1.** One of the native people of the Fiji Islands. **2.** The Melanesian language of the Fijis.

Fi·ji·an (fē′jē·ən, fi·jē′ən) *adj.* Of Fiji, its people, or their language. —*n.* A Fiji.

fil·a·gree (fil′ə·grē) See FILIGREE.

fil·a·ment (fil′ə·mənt) *n.* **1.** A fine thread, fiber, or fibril; also, any threadlike structure or appendage. **2.** *Bot.* The stalk or support of an anther. For illus. see FLOWER. **3.** *Electr.* The slender wire of tungsten, carbon, etc., which, when heated by an electric current in a vacuum produces light. **4.** A similar wire that forms or heats the cathode of an electron tube. [< F < L *filum* thread] —**fil′a·men′ta·ry** (-men′tər·ē), **fil·a·men′tous** (-men′təs) *adj.*

fi·lar·i·a (fi·lâr′ē·ə) *n. pl.* **·lar·i·ae** (-lâr′i·ē) A worm parasitic in the blood and intestines of vertebrates. [< NL < L *filum* thread] —**fi·lar′i·al** (-əl), **fi·lar′i·an** (-ən) *adj.*

fil·bert (fil′bərt) *n.* The edible nut of the hazel or the tree it grows on: also called *hazelnut.* [after St. *Philibert,* because these nuts ripen about the time of his feast day (Aug. 22)]

filch (filch) *v.t.* To steal slyly and in small amounts; pilfer. [Origin uncertain] —**filch′er** *n.*

file[1] (fīl) *n.* **1.** Any device in which papers are systematically arranged for quick reference, as a folder, drawer, or cabinet. **2.** A collection of papers thus arranged. **3.** A line of persons, animals, or things placed one behind another. —**on file** Stored in systematic order for quick reference; in a file. —**single file** An arrangement of persons or things one behind another in a single line: also *Indian file.* —*v.* **filed, fil·ing** *v.t.* **1.** To store (papers, etc.) in systematic order. —*v.i.* **2.** To march in file, as soldiers. **3.** To make an application, as for a job. [< L *filum* thread] —**fil′er** *n.*

file[2] (fīl) *n.* A hard steel instrument with ridged cutting surfaces, used to abrade, smooth, or polish. —*v.t.* **filed, fil·ing 1.** To cut, smooth, or sharpen with or as with a file. **2.** To remove with a file. [OE *fīl*] —**fil′er** *n.*

fi·let (fi·lā′, fil′ā; *Fr.* fē·le′) *n.* **1.** Net lace having a square mesh. **2.** Fillet (def. 2). —*v.t.* **fi·leted** (fi·lād′, fil′ād); **fi·let·ing** (fi·lā′ing, fil′ā·ing) To fillet (def. 2). [< F]

fi·let mi·gnon (fi·lā′ min·yon′, *Fr.* fē·le′ mē·nyôn′) A small, choice, boneless cut of beef from the inside of the loin. [< F]

fil·i·al (fil′ē·əl, fil′yəl) *adj.* **1.** Of, pertaining to, or befitting a son or daughter: *filial* devotion. **2.** *Genetics* Pertaining to a generation following the parental. [< LL < L *filius* son] —**fil′i·al·ly** *adv.*

fil·i·bus·ter (fil′ə·bus′tər) *n.* **1.** *U.S.* In a legislative body, an instance of the use of delaying tactics, esp. the making of time-consuming speeches; also, a legislator who makes such speeches: also **fil′i·bus′ter·er.** **2.** An adventurer who takes part in an unlawful military expedition. —*v.i.* **1.** *U.S.* To obstruct legislation by long speeches and delay. **2.** To act as an adventurer. —*v.t.* **3.** *U.S.* To block passage of (legislation) by dilatory tactics. [< Sp. *filibustero* < Du. *vrijbuiter* freebooter] —**fil′i·bus′trous** *adj.*

fil·i·form (fil′ə·fôrm) *adj.* Threadlike.

fil·i·gree (fil′ə·grē) *n.* **1.** Delicate ornamental work formed of intertwisted gold or silver wire. **2.** Anything fanciful and delicate. —*adj.* Resembling, made of, or adorned with filigree; fanciful; ornate. —*v.t.* **·greed, ·gree·ing** To adorn with or work in filigree. Sometimes spelled *filagree* or *fillagree.* [< F < Ital. < L *filum* thread + *granum* grain]

fil·ings (fī′lingz) *n.pl.* Particles removed by a file.

Fil·i·pi·no (fil′ə·pē′nō) *n. pl.* **·nos** A native or inhabitant of the Philippine Islands. —*adj.* Of or pertaining to the Philippine Islands or their inhabitants.

fill (fil) *v.t.* **1.** To supply (a container, space, etc.) with as much of something as can be contained. **2.** To supply fully, as with food. **3.** To occupy or pervade the whole of. **4.** To stop up; plug: to *fill* a tooth. **5.** To put together or make up what is indicated in (an order, prescription, etc.). **6.** To satisfy or meet (a need, requirements, etc.). **7.** To occupy (an office or position). **8.** To level out (an embankment, ravine, etc.) by adding fill. —*v.i.* **9.** To become full. —**to fill away** *Naut.* To trim the yards so that the sails will catch the wind. —**to fill in 1.** To fill completely, as an excavation. **2.** To insert (something): to *fill in* one's name. **3.** To complete by inserting something; to *fill in* an application. **4.** To be a substitute. —**to fill (someone) in on** *Informal* To give (someone) additional facts or details about. —**to fill out 1.** To make or become fuller or more rounded.

2. To make complete, as an application. **—to fill the bill** *U.S. Informal* To do or be what is wanted or needed. **—to fill up** To make or become full. **—***n.* **1.** That which fills or is sufficient to fill. **2.** An embankment built up by filling in with stone, gravel, etc. [OE *fyllan* fill]

fil·la·gree (fil′ə·grē) See FILIGREE.

fill·er (fil′ər) *n.* **1.** One who fills. **2.** That which fills; as: **a** A substance added to increase bulk, weight, etc. **b** A composition for filling pores or holes in wood. **c** Tobacco used for the inside of cigars. **d** A piece of writing used to fill space.

fil·let (fil′it; *for n. def. 2 and v., also* fil′ā, fi·lā′) *n.* **1.** A narrow band or ribbon for binding the hair. **2.** A strip of boneless meat or fish. **3.** A narrow band of any material. **—***v.t.* To slice into fillets. [< F < L *filum* thread]

fill-in (fil′in′) *n.* **1.** A person or thing included to fill a gap or omission. **2.** *Informal* A summary of facts.

fill·ing (fil′ing) *n.* **1.** That which is used to fill something; esp. the material put into a prepared cavity in a tooth. **2.** The act of becoming full. **3.** In weaving, the weft.

filling station *U.S.* A retail station for supplying gasoline, oil, etc., to motor vehicles: also called *gas station.*

fil·lip (fil′əp) *n.* **1.** The snap of a finger that has been pressed down by the thumb and suddenly released. **2.** Something that serves to excite or stimulate. **—***v.t.* **1.** To strike with a fillip. **2.** To project by or as by a fillip. **3.** To stimulate; arouse. **—***v.i.* **4.** To make a fillip. [Var. of FLIP]

fil·ly (fil′ē) *n. pl.* **·lies 1.** A young mare. **2.** *Informal* A spirited young girl. [< ON *fylja* < *foli* foal]

film (film) *n.* **1.** A thin covering, layer, or membrane. **2.** A thin haze or blur. **3.** *Photog.* A sheet, roll, or strip of transparent material coated with a light-sensitive emulsion and used for making photographs. **4.** In motion pictures: **a** The film containing the pictures projected on the screen. **b** The motion picture itself. **c** *pl.* Motion pictures collectively. **—***v.t.* **1.** To cover or obscure by or as by a film. **2.** To photograph on a film. **3.** To make a motion picture of: to *film* a play. **—***v.i.* **4.** To become covered or obscured by a film. **5.** To make a motion picture. **6.** To be adaptable for filming. [OE *filmen* membrane]

film·strip (film′strip′) *n.* A length of processed film containing frames of still pictures that are projected on a screen.

film·y (fil′mē) *adj.* **film·i·er, film·i·est 1.** Composed of or like film; gauzy. **2.** Covered with or as with a film; hazy; dim. **—film′i·ly** *adv.* **—film′i·ness** *n.*

fil·ter (fil′tər) *n.* **1.** Any device, as paper, cloth, or charcoal, used as a strainer for clearing or purifying liquids, air, etc. **2.** *Physics* A device that permits the passage of waves and currents of certain frequencies and limits the flow of certain others. **3.** *Photog.* A colored screen that controls the kind and intensity of light waves in an exposure. **—***v.t.* **1.** To pass (liquids, air, etc.) through a filter; strain. **2.** To separate or remove (impurities, etc.) by or as by a filter. **3.** To act as a filter for. **—***v.i.* **4.** To pass through a filter. **5.** To leak out, as news. [< OF < Med.L *feltrum* felt (used as a filter)] **—fil′ter·er** *n.*

fil·ter·a·ble (fil′tər·ə·bəl) *adj.* **1.** Capable of being filtered. **2.** Capable of passing through a filter. Also **fil·tra·ble** (fil′·trəb·əl) **—fil′ter·a·bil′i·ty** *n.*

filterable virus Virus (def. 1).

filth (filth) *n.* **1.** Anything that is foul or dirty. **2.** A foul condition. **3.** Moral defilement; obscenity. [OE *fȳlth*]

filth·y (fil′thē) *adj.* **filth·i·er, filth·i·est 1.** Of the nature of or containing filth. **2.** Morally foul; obscene. **3.** Highly unpleasant. **—filth′i·ly** *adv.* **—filth′i·ness** *n.*

fil·trate (fil′trāt) *v.t.* **·trat·ed, ·trat·ing** To filter. **—***n.* The liquid that has been separated by filtration. [< NL < Med.L *filtrum* a filter] **—fil·tra′tion** *n.*

fin[1] (fin) *n.* **1.** A membranous extension from the body of a fish or other aquatic animal, serving to propel, balance, or steer it in the water. **2.** Any finlike or projecting part, appendage, or attachment. **3.** *Slang* The hand. **—***v.* **finned, fin·ning** *v.t.* **1.** To cut up or trim off the fins of (a fish). **—***v.i.* **2.** To beat the water with the fins, as a whale when dying. [OE *finn*] **—fin′less** *adj.*

fin[2] (fin) *n. U.S. Slang* A five-dollar bill. [< Yiddish *finf* five]

fi·na·gle (fi·nā′gəl) *v.* **·gled, ·gling** *Informal v.t.* **1.** To get (something) by trickery or deceit. **2.** To cheat or trick (someone). **—***v.i.* **3.** To use trickery or deceit; be sly. [Origin uncertain] **—fi·na′gler** *n.*

fi·nal (fī′nəl) *adj.* **1.** Pertaining to, or coming at the end; ultimate; last. **2.** Precluding further action or controversy; conclusive. **3.** Relating to or consisting in the end or purpose aimed at: a *final* cause. **—***n.* **1.** Something that is terminal or last. **2.** *Often pl.* Something decisively final, as the last match in a tournament. [< F < L *finis* end]

fi·na·le (fi·nä′lē, -nal′ē; *Ital.* fē·nä′lā) *n.* The last part, as the final scene in a play or the concluding section of a musical composition. [< Ital., final]

fi·nal·ist (fī′nəl·ist) *n.* In games, contests, etc., a contestant who takes part in the final matches.

fi·nal·i·ty (fī·nal′ə·tē) *n. pl.* **·ties 1.** The state or qu of being final or settled. **2.** A final act, offer, etc.

fi·nal·ize (fī′nəl·īz) *v.t.* **·ized, ·iz·ing** To put into fin complete form; bring to completion.

fi·nal·ly (fī′nəl·ē) *adv.* **1.** At or in the end; in conclu lastly. **2.** Completely; irrecoverably; decisively.

fi·nance (fi·nans′, fī′nans) *n.* **1.** The science of mone affairs. **2.** *pl.* Monetary affairs; funds; revenue; inc **—***v.t.* **·nanced, ·nanc·ing 1.** To supply the money **2.** To manage the finances of. [< OF, payment]

fi·nan·cial (fi·nan′shəl, fī-) *adj.* **1.** Of or pertainin finance or finances. **2.** Of or pertaining to those de with money and credit. **—fi·nan′cial·ly** *adv.*

fin·an·cier (fin′ən·sir′) *n.* One engaged or skilled in fi cial operations. **—***v.t.* To finance.

fin·back (fin′bak′) *n.* A rorqual. Also **finback whale**

finch (finch) *n.* A small, seed-eating bird, as the bun sparrow, bullfinch, goldfinch, or canary. [OE *finc*]

find (fīnd) *v.* **found, find·ing** *v.t.* **1.** To come upon u pectedly. **2.** To discover after search, experience, or e **3.** To recover (something lost). **4.** To arrive at; re **5.** To gain or recover the use of: He *found* his tongue To determine by legal inquiry and declare. **—***v.i.* **7** express a decision after legal inquiry: to *find* for the plai **—to find oneself** To discover one's special abilities or proper vocation. **—to find out 1.** To learn; disc **2.** To detect the identity or the true nature of. **—***n* The act of finding. **2.** Something found or discovered; a valuable discovery. [OE *findan*]

find·er (fīn′dər) *n.* **1.** One who or that which find *Astron.* A small telescope by the side of a large one, us locate a particular object. **3.** *Photog.* A camera attach that shows the scene as it will appear in the photograph

fin de siè·cle (fan də sye′kl′) *French* End of the cen esp. the close of the 19th century.

find·ing (fīn′ding) *n.* **1.** The act of one who finds. **2.** which is found; a discovery or conclusion.

fine[1] (fīn) *adj.* **fin·er, fin·est 1.** Superior in quality; e lent. **2.** Highly satisfactory; very good. **3.** Light or cate in texture, workmanship, structure, etc. **4.** Comp of very small particles: *fine* powder. **5.** Very thin: thread. **6.** Keen; sharp: a *fine* edge. **7.** Possessing sup ability or skill. **8.** Subtle; nice: a *fine* point. **9.** Disc nating: a *fine* ear for music. **10.** Elegant; polished; overelegant; showy; affected. **11.** Handsome; good- ing. **12.** Cloudless; clear: *fine* weather. **13.** Free impurities. **14.** Containing a given proportion of metal: gold 18 karats *fine.* **—***adv. Informal* Very we suits me *fine.* **—***v.t. & v.i.* To make or become fine or [< OF *fin* finished, perfected] **—fine′ly** *adv.* **—fine′ne**

fine[2] (fīn) *n.* A sum of money required as the pe for an offense. **—in fine** Finally; in short. **—***v.t.* **fi fin·ing** To punish by fine. [< OF *fin* settlement]

fi·ne[3] (fē′nā) *n. Music* The end; finis. [< Ital.]

fine arts The arts of painting, drawing, sculpture, architecture, and sometimes including literature, m drama, and the dance.

fine-drawn (fīn′drôn′) *adj.* Drawn out to extreme fin or subtlety: a *fine-drawn* distinction.

fin·er·y (fī′nər·ē) *n. pl.* **·er·ies** Elaborate adornm showy or fine clothes or decorations.

fine-spun (fīn′spun′) *adj.* **1.** Drawn or spun out t extreme degree of fineness. **2.** Excessively subtle.

fi·nesse (fi·nes′) *n.* **1.** Highly refined skill; subtlet style or performance. **2.** Smoothness and tact, as in dling a delicate situation; also, artful strategy; cun **3.** In bridge and other card games an attempt to ta trick with the lower of two nonsequential cards in the that the hand yet to play does not hold an intervening **—***v.* **·nessed, ·ness·ing** *v.t.* **1.** To change or bring abou finesse. **2.** In card games, to play as a finesse. **—***v.i.* To use finesse. **4.** In card games, to make a finesse. [< *fin.* See FINE[1].]

fine-toothed comb (fīn′tōōtht′) A comb with fine set very close together. Also **fine′-tooth′ comb. —t over with a fine-toothed comb** To examine minutely.

fin·ger (fing′gər) *n.* **1.** One of the terminating membe the hand, usu. excluding the thumb. **2.** That part glove made to fit the finger. **3.** Anything that resembl serves as a finger. **4.** A unit of measure based on the w of a finger (from ¾ inch to one inch); or on the length o middle finger (about 4 to 4½ inches). **—to burn o fingers** To suffer the consequences of meddling or inte ing. **—to have** (or **put**) **a finger in the pie 1.** To take pa some matter. **2.** To meddle. **—to put one's finger o** identify or indicate correctly. **—to put the finger on** *Slang* **1.** To betray as, to the police. **2.** To point out victim of a planned crime). **—to twist around one's** (li **finger** To influence or control with little or no effort. **— 1.** To touch or handle with the fingers; toy with. **2.** steal; pilfer. **3.** *Music* **a** To play (an instrument) with

gers. **b** To mark the fingering of (music). **4.** *U.S. Slang* betray, as to the police. **—** *v.i.* **5.** To touch or feel ything with the fingers. [OE] **— fin′ger·er** *n.*
er board In stringed instruments, as the violin, guitar, ., the strip of wood upon which the strings are pressed the fingers of the player. For illus. see VIOLIN.
er bowl A bowl containing water for cleansing the gers at the table after eating.
gered (fing′gərd) *adj.* **1.** Having fingers. **2.** *Music* ving the fingering marked. **3.** Marked by fingers.
ger·ing (fing′gər·ing) *n.* **1.** The act of touching or feel- with the fingers. **2.** *Music* **a** The action or technique ısing the fingers in playing an instrument. **b** The notation icating what fingers are to be used.
ger·ling (fing′gər·ling) *n.* A young, small fish.
ger·nail (fing′gər·nāl′) *n.* The horny substance along upper surface of the end of a finger.
ger·print (fing′gər·print′) *n.* An impression of the n pattern on the inner surface of a finger tip, used for poses of identification. **—** *v.t.* To take the fingerprints of.
er tip The extreme end of a finger. **— to have at one's ger tips** To have ready and available knowledge of or ac- s to.
·al (fin′ē·əl) *n.* *Archit.* An ornament at the apex of pire, pinnacle, or the like. [< L *finis* end + L]
·cal (fin′i·kəl) *adj.* Finicky. **— fin′i·cal·ly** . **— fin′i·cal·ness, fin′i·cal′i·ty** (-kal′ə·tē) *n.*
ck·ing (fin′i·king) *adj.* Finicky.
ck·y (fin′i·kē) *adj.* Excessively fastidious precise; fussy; exacting. [< FINE[1] + -ICAL]
s (fin′is, fī′nis) *n.* *pl.* **fin·is·es** The end. L]

FINIAL

sh (fin′ish) *v.t.* **1.** To complete or bring to end. **2.** To use up completely. **3.** To perfect (a person) social graces, education, etc. **4.** To give (fabric, wood, .) a particular surface quality. **5.** *Informal* To kill, stroy, or defeat. **—** *v.i.* **6.** To reach or come to an end; p. **—** *n.* **1.** The conclusion or last stage of anything. Something that finishes, completes, or perfects. **3.** Com- teness and perfection of detail. **4.** Perfection or polish in ech, manners, education, etc. **5.** The surface quality appearance of textiles, paint, etc.: a glossy *finish.* [< < L *finis* end] **— fin′ish·er** *n.*
shed (fin′isht) *adj.* **1.** Ended; completed. **2.** Per- ted to a high degree; polished. **3.** Highly accomplished.
sh·ing school (fin′ish·ing) A school that prepares girls entrance into society.
te (fī′nīt) *adj.* **1.** Having bounds, ends, or limits. **2.** at may be determined, counted, or measured. **3.** Sub- t to human or natural limitations: our *finite* minds. **—** *n.* ite things collectively, or that which is finite. [< L *itus* limited] **— fi′nite·ly** *adv.* **— fi′nite·ness** *n.*
te verb *Gram.* A verb form that is limited as to person, mber, tense, and mood, and that can serve as a predicate.
·tude (fin′ə·tōōd, -tyōōd, fī′nə-) *n.* The state of being ite.
(fingk) *n.* *U.S. Slang* **1.** A strikebreaker. **2.** An savory person. [? < FINGER, v. (def. 4)]
n (fin) *n.* **1.** A native or inhabitant of Finland. **2.** One ose native language is Finnish. [OE *Finnas* Finns]
nan had·die (fin′ən had′ē) Smoked haddock Also **fin′· n had·dock** (had′ək) [*Findhorn haddock,* after *Findhorn,* cottish fishing port where originally prepared]
ned (find) *adj.* Having fins or finlike extensions.
n·ish (fin′ish) *adj.* Of Finland, the Finns, or their lan- ge. **—** *n.* The Uralic language of the Finns.
·no-U·gric (fin′ō·ōō′grik, -yōō′grik) *n.* A subfamily the Uralic languages, including Finnish, Estonian, Lapp, gyar, etc. Also **Fin′no-U′gri·an.**
ny (fin′ē) *adj.* **1.** Having fins. **2.** Resembling a fin. **3.** or pertaining to fish. **4.** Abounding in fish.
d (fyôrd, fyōrd) *n.* A long and narrow arm of the sea nning between high, rocky cliffs or banks: also spelled *rd.* [< Norw. *fjord*]
ple (fip′əl) *n.* A plug of wood at the mouth of certain nd instruments, as recorders. [? < ON *flipi* lip of a horse]
(fûr) *n.* **1.** Any of several trees of the pine family. **2.** e wood of these trees. [OE *fyrh*] **— fir′ry** *adj.*
(fīr) *n.* **1.** The visible, active phase of combustion, nifested in light and heat. **2.** A burning mass of fuel, as a fireplace **3.** A destructive burning, as of a building. A substance or device that produces fire or a firelike dis- y: Greek *fire.* **5.** A flash or spark: to strike *fire.* **6.** A scharge of firearms: Cease *fire.* **7.** A rapid volley: a *fire* questions. **8.** Flashing brightness; brilliance: the *fire* of a mond. **9.** Intensity of spirit or feeling; ardor; passion. . Vividness of imagination. **11.** Warmth or heat, as of liquor. **12.** Fever or inflammation. **13.** An affliction or grievous trial. **— between two fires** Under attack or criti- cism from both sides. **— on fire 1.** Burning; ablaze. **2.** Ardent; zealous. **— to catch fire.** To start to burn. **— to go through fire and water** To experience great afflictions. **— to hang fire 1.** To fail to fire promptly, as a firearm. **2.** To be delayed or undecided. **— to lay a fire** To arrange fuel for igniting. **— to miss fire 1.** To fail to discharge: said of fire- arms. **2.** To be unsuccessful; fail. **— to open fire 1.** To begin to shoot. **2.** To commence. **— to play with fire** To do something rash or dangerous. **— to set fire to** or **to set on fire 1.** To make burn. **2.** To inflame or excite. **— to set the world on fire** To gain great success or fame. **— to strike fire 1.** To create a fire, as with flint. **2.** To get a re- action. **— to take fire 1.** To start to burn. **2.** To become excited, angry, or enthusiastic. **— under fire 1.** Exposed to gunshot or artillery fire. **2.** Subjected to severe criticism. **—** *v.* **fired, fir·ing** *v.t.* **1.** To set on fire. **2.** To tend the fire of. **3.** To subject to the heat of fire. **4.** To set off, as ex- plosives. **5.** To set off explosives within or near: to *fire* an oil well. **6.** To discharge, as a gun or bullet. **7.** *Informal* To hurl: to *fire* questions. **8.** *Informal* To dismiss from employment. **9.** To bake, as pottery, in a kiln. **10.** To cure by heat. **11.** To cause to glow or shine. **12.** To inspire; excite. **13.** *Vet.* To cauterize. **—** *v.i.* **14.** To take fire; become ignited. **15.** To go off, as a gun. **16.** To set off firearms, a rocket, etc. **17.** *Informal* To hurl a missile. **18.** To tend a fire. **— to fire away** To start off and proceed energetically, esp. in asking questions. [OE *fȳr*]
fire·arm (fīr′ärm′) *n.* Any weapon, usu. small, from which a missile, as a bullet, is hurled by an explosive.
fire·ball (fīr′bôl′) *n.* **1.** A luminous meteor. **2.** Ball-shaped lightning. **3.** A hot, incandescent sphere of air and vapor- ized debris, formed around the center of a nuclear explosion. **4.** *U.S. Slang* A remarkably energetic person or thing.
fire·boat (fīr′bōt′) *n.* A boat equipped for fighting fires.
fire·box (fīr′boks′) *n.* The chamber in which the fuel of a locomotive, furnace, etc., is burned.
fire·brand (fīr′brand′) *n.* **1.** A piece of burning or glowing wood. **2.** One who stirs up trouble or dissension.
fire·break (fīr′brāk′) *n.* *U.S.* A strip of land that has been plowed or cleared to prevent the spread of fire.
fire·brick (fīr′brik′) *n.* A brick made of fire clay, used for lining furnaces.
fire·bug (fīr′bug′) *n.* *U.S. Informal* One who enjoys setting fire to buildings, etc.; a pyromaniac.
fire clay A refractory material, used to make crucibles, furnace linings, and the like.
fire control *Mil.* The control of the delivery of gunfire or of guided missiles by the use of special equipment.
fire·crack·er (fīr′krak′ər) *n.* A small paper cylinder charged with an explosive, used as a noisemaker.
fire·damp (fīr′damp′) *n.* **1.** A combustible gas, chiefly methane, that enters mines from coal seams. **2.** The explo- sive mixture formed by this gas and air.
fire·dog (fīr′dôg′, -dog′) *n.* An andiron.
fire·eat·er (fīr′ē′tər) *n.* **1.** A performer who pretends to eat fire. **2.** A hot-headed person eager to fight or quarrel.
fire engine A motor truck equipped to fight fires.
fire escape A metal stairway usu. attached to the outside of a building and furnishing a means of escape in case of fire.
fire extinguisher A portable apparatus containing fire- extinguishing chemicals ejected through a short hose.
fire·fly (fīr′flī′) *n.* *pl.* **·flies** A night-flying beetle emitting a phosphorescent light from an abdominal organ.
fire·house (fīr′hous′) *n.* *U.S.* A building housing fire- fighting equipment and personnel.
fire·light (fīr′līt′) *n.* Light from a fire, as from a campfire.
fire·man (fīr′mən) *n.* *pl.* **·men** (-mən) **1.** A man employed to prevent or extinguish fires. **2.** One who tends fires.
fire opal A variety of opal having translucent orange-yellow to red colors suggesting streaks of flame.
fire·place (fīr′plās′) *n.* A recess or structure in which a fire is built; esp., the part of a chimney opening into a room.
fire·plug (fīr′plug′) *n.* A hydrant for supplying water in case of fire.
fire·pow·er (fīr′pou′ər) *n.* *Mil.* **1.** Capacity for delivering fire, as from the guns of a ship, battery, etc. **2.** The amount or effectiveness of fire delivered by a given weapon or unit.
fire·proof (fīr′pōōf′) *adj.* Resistant to fire; relatively in- combustible. **—** *v.t.* To make resistant to fire.
fire sale *U.S.* A sale of goods damaged by fire.
fire·side (fīr′sīd′) *n.* **1.** The hearth or space before the fire- place. **2.** Home or home life.
fire station A firehouse.
fire·trap (fīr′trap′) *n.* A building notoriously flammable.
fire·wa·ter (fīr′wô′tər, -wot′ər) *n.* Whiskey: term first used by the North American Indian.

fire·weed (fīr′wēd′) *n.* The willow herb.
fire·work (fīr′wûrk′) *n.* **1.** *Usu. pl.* A device containing combustibles or explosives that, when ignited, produce brilliant light or a loud noise. **2.** *pl.* A pyrotechnic display.
firing line **1.** In combat, the front line from which gunfire is delivered. **2.** The foremost position in any activity.
firing pin The part of a firearm that strikes the primer or detonator, igniting the charge of the projectile.
firing squad **1.** A military or naval detachment assigned to execute, by shooting, a person condemned to death. **2.** A similar squad to honor a deceased person with a salvo.
fir·kin (fûr′kən) *n.* **1.** A wooden vessel for butter, lard, etc. **2.** A measure of capacity, usu. equal to one fourth of a barrel. [ME < MDu. *vierde* fourth + -KIN]
firm[1] (fûrm) *adj.* **1.** Relatively solid, compact, or unyielding to touch or pressure. **2.** Difficult to move, loosen, etc. **3.** Fixedly settled and established. **4.** Constant and steadfast. **5.** Full of or indicating strength; vigorous; steady. **6.** Not fluctuating widely, as prices. — *v.t. & v.i.* To make or become firm. — *adv.* Solidly; resolutely; fixedly. [< L *firmus*] — **firm′ly** *adv.* — **firm′ness** *n.*
firm[2] (fûrm) *n.* A partnership of two or more persons for conducting business. [< Ital. < L < *firmus* firm]
fir·ma·ment (fûr′mə·mənt) *n.* The expanse of the heavens; sky. [< L *firmare* to make firm] — **fir′ma·men′tal** *adj.*
first (fûrst) *adj.* **1.** Preceding all others in the order of numbering: the ordinal of *one.* **2.** Prior to all others in time; earliest. **3.** Nearest or foremost in place. **4.** Highest or foremost in character, rank, etc.; chief. **5.** *Music* Designating one of two parts for like instruments or voices, usu. the one higher in pitch or the principal one. — **in the first place** To start with. — *n.* **1.** One who or that which is first in time, rank, order, or position. **2.** The beginning: from *first* to last. **3.** The winning position in a race or contest. **4.** *Music* One of two parts for like instruments or voices, usu. the one higher in pitch or the principal one. **5.** In English universities, the highest rank in examinations for honors; also, one winning this rank. **6.** *pl.* The best grade of certain merchandise, as of lumber, hosiery, etc. — **at first** At the beginning. — *adv.* **1.** Before all others in order, time, place, rank, etc.; also (more formally) *firstly.* **2.** For the first time. **3.** In preference to anything else: He would die *first.* [OE *fyrst*, superl. of *fore* before]
first aid Treatment given in an emergency before full medical care can be obtained. — **first-aid** (fûrst′ād′) *adj.*
First Amendment An amendment to the Constitution of the United States forbidding Congress to interfere with religion, free speech, a free press, the right to assemble peaceably, or the right to petition the government: ratified 1791.
first base In baseball, the base first reached by the runner, at the right-hand angle of the infield. — **first base′man**
first-born (fûrst′bôrn′) *adj.* First brought forth; eldest. — *n.* The first-born child.
first-class (fûrst′klas′, -kläs′) *adj.* **1.** Of highest rank or best quality. **2.** *U.S.* Of a class of sealed mail consisting wholly or partly of written matter. **3.** Of the most luxurious accommodations on a ship, plane, etc. — *adv.* By first-class mail or conveyance.
first-hand (fûrst′hand′) *adj.* Direct from the original source or producer. — *adv.* From the original source.
first lady The wife of the president of the U.S.
first lieutenant *Mil.* A commissioned officer ranking next above a second lieutenant and next below a captain.
first·ling (fûrst′ling) *n.* The first of a kind.
first·ly (fûrst′lē) *adv.* In the first place.
first mate A ship's officer ranking next below the captain.
first mortgage A mortgage having priority over all others.
first night The opening performance of a play, opera, etc. — **first-night** (fûrst′nīt′) *adj.* — **first′-night′er** *n.*
first papers Documents filed by an alien, declaring intention to be naturalized as a citizen of the U.S.
first-rate (fûrst′rāt′) *adj.* Of the finest class or quality; excellent. — *adv. Informal* Excellently.
firth (fûrth) *n. Scot.* An arm of the sea: also spelled *frith.*
fis·cal (fis′kəl) *adj.* Of or pertaining to the treasury or finances of a government; financial. [< F < L *fiscus* purse]
fiscal year Any twelve-month period at the end of which accounts are balanced.
fish (fish) *n. pl.* **·fish** or (with reference to different species) **fish·es** **1.** A vertebrate, cold-blooded aquatic animal with permanent gills, having a typically elongate, tapering body, usu. covered with scales and provided with fins for locomotion. ◆ Collateral adjective: *piscine.* **2.** Loosely, any animal habitually living in water. **3.** The flesh of fish used as food. — **like a fish out of water** Not comfortable or at ease. — *v.t.* **1.** To catch or try to catch fish in (a body of water). **2.** To catch or try to catch (fish, eels, etc.). **3.** To grope for and bring out: with *out* or *up*: to *fish* money out of one's pocket. — *v.i.* **4.** To catch or try to catch fish. **5.** To try to get something in an artful or indirect manner: with *for.* [OE *fisc*] — **fish′a·ble** *adj.* — **fish′like′** *adj.*

fish·bowl (fish′bōl′) *n.* A bowl, usu. of glass, serving small aquarium for fish.
fish cake A fried ball or cake of chopped fish, usu. codfish mixed with mashed potatoes. Also **fish ball.**
fish·er (fish′ər) *n.* **1.** A fisherman. **2.** A weasellike car ore of eastern North America; also, its fur.
fish·er·man (fish′ər·mən) *n. pl.* **·men** (-mən) **1.** One fishes as an occupation or for sport. **2.** A fishing boat.
fish·er·y (fish′ər·ē) *n. pl.* **·er·ies** **1.** The operation or b ness of catching fish or other aquatic animals. **2.** The p for such an operation; a fishing ground. **3.** A fish hatch
fish hatchery A place designed for the artificial prop tion, hatching, and nurture of fish.
fish hawk The osprey.
fish·hook (fish′hŏŏk′) *n.* A hook, usu. barbed, for fish
fishing rod A slender pole with a line and usu. a reel.
fishing tackle Equipment for fishing, as a rod, reel, etc
fish·meal (fish′mēl′) *n.* Ground dried fish, used as f lizer and feed for animals.
fish·mon·ger (fish′mung′gər, -mong′-) *n.* A dealer in
fish stick *U.S. & Canadian* A frozen fish filet in bar f
fish story *Informal* An extravagant or incredible narra
fish·tail (fish′tāl′) *adj.* Resembling the tail of a fish.
fish·wife (fish′wīf′) *n. pl.* **·wives** (-wīvz′) **1.** A wo who sells fish. **2.** A coarse, abusive woman.
fish·y (fish′ē) *adj.* **fish·i·er, fish·i·est** **1.** Of or like **2.** Abounding in fish. **3.** *Informal* Improbable. **4.** Va of expression. — **fish′i·ly** *adv.* — **fish′i·ness** *n.*
fissi- *combining form* Split; cleft. Also, before vowels, fi [< L *fissus*, pp. of *findere* to split]
fis·sile (fis′əl) *adj.* **1.** Capable of being split or separ into layers. **2.** Tending to split. [< L *fissilis* < *fin* to split] — **fis·sil·i·ty** (fi·sil′ə·tē) *n.*
fis·sion (fish′ən) *n.* **1.** The act of splitting or brea apart. **2.** *Biol.* Spontaneous division of a cell or orga into new cells or organisms, esp. as a mode of reproduc **3.** *Physics* The disintegration of the nucleus of an a leading to the formation of more stable atoms and the rel of energy. [< L *findere* to split] — **fis′sion·a·ble** *adj.*
fis·sure (fish′ər) *n.* **1.** A narrow opening, cleft or fur **2.** The act of cleaving, or the state of being cleft. **3.** A Any cleft or furrow of the body, as on the surface of brain. — *v.t. & v.i.* **·sured, ·sur·ing** To crack; split; cle [< L *fissura* < *findere* to split]
fist (fist) *n.* **1.** The hand closed tightly, as for striking; grip; clutch. **2.** *Informal* The hand. **3.** *Informal* H writing. **4.** *Printing* The index mark ☞. — *v.t.* To st with the fist. [OE *fȳst*]
fist·ful (fist′fŏŏl) *n. pl.* **·fuls** *Informal* A handful.
fist·ic (fis′tik) *adj.* Of or pertaining to boxing; pugilist
fist·i·cuff (fis′ti·kuf′) *n.* **1.** *pl.* A fight with the fists. **2** The science of boxing. **3.** A blow with the fist. — *v.t. &* To fight with the fists. — **fist′i·cuff′er** *n.*
fis·tu·la (fis′chŏŏ·lə) *n. pl.* **·las** or **·lae** (-lē) *Pathol.* A or canal formed by the imperfect closing of a wound, abs or the like, and leading either to the body surface or f one cavity or hollow organ to another. [< L, a pipe]
fis·tu·lous (fis′chŏŏ·ləs) *adj.* **1.** Of, pertaining to, or li fistula. **2.** Cylindrical and hollow like a reed. **3.** Havin consisting of cylindrical, hollow parts. Also **fis′tu·lar** (-
fit[1] (fit) *adj.* **fit·ter, fit·test** **1.** Adapted to an end, aim, or sign; suited. **2.** Proper or appropriate; becoming **3.** sessing the proper qualifications; competent. **4.** In a s of preparation; ready. **5.** In good physical condit healthy. — *v.* **fit·ted** or **fit, fit·ting** *v.t.* **1.** To be suitabl proper for. **2.** To be of the right size and shape for. **3.** prepare, make or alter to the proper size or purpose. **4.** provide with what is suitable or necessary; equip. **5.** put in place carefully or exactly. — *v.i.* **6.** To be suit or proper. **7.** To be of the proper size, shape, etc. — **t out** (or **up**) To supply with what is necessary; outfit. — **1.** Condition or manner of fitting. **2.** Something that **3.** The act of fitting. [ME *fyt*] — **fit′ness** *n.*
fit[2] (fit) *n.* **1.** A sudden onset of an organic or functional order, often attended by convulsions; spasm. **2.** A sud overmastering emotion or feeling. **3.** Impulsive and irre lar exertion or action. — **by fits** or **by fits and starts** S modically; irregularly. [OE *fitt* struggle]
fitch (fich) *n.* The polecat of Europe or its fur. Also **fitc** (-it), **fitch′ew** (-ōō) [< MDu. *vitsche* polecat]
fit·ful (fit′fəl) *adj.* Characterized by irregular acti moods; capricious. — **fit′ful·ly** *adv.* — **fit′ful·ness** *n.*
fit·ly (fit′lē) *adv.* In a fit manner, place, or time; prope
fit·ter (fit′ər) *n.* One who or that which fits.
fit·ting (fit′ing) *adj.* Fit; suitable; proper; appropri — *n.* **1.** The act of one who fits. **2.** A piece of equipm or an appliance used in an adjustment. **3.** *pl.* Furnishi fixtures, or decorations. — **fit′ting·ly** *adv.* — **fit′ting·nes**
Fitz- *prefix* Son of: formerly used in forming the surna of illegitimate children of royalty. [< OF < L *filius* son
five (fīv) *n.* **1.** The sum of four and one: a cardinal num

Any symbol of this number, as 5, v, V. **3.** Anything ving five units, as a team, playing card, etc. —*adj.* ng one more than four. [OE fīf]
-and-ten-cent store (fīv′ən·ten′sent′) **1.** Originally, tore selling miscellaneous articles priced at five and ten ts. **2.** A store selling articles priced from a few cents to dollar or more. Also called *dime store, ten-cent store.* Also **′-and-ten′, five-and-dime** (fīv′ən·dīm′).
iron In golf, an iron with a moderately sloping face, d in lofting the ball: also called *mashie.*
e Nations A confederacy of five tribes of Iroquois Ins, the Mohawks, Oneidas, Onondagas, Cayugas, and ecas, within New York State.
r (fī′vər) *n. Informal* **1.** A five-dollar bill or a fiveund note. **2.** Anything counting as five.
e-Year Plan (fīv′yir′) A plan for national economic elopment: a term first used by the Soviet Union.
(fiks) *v.t.* **1.** To make firm or secure; fasten so as to be movable. **2.** To set or place permanently. **3.** To render hangeable: to *fix* color. **4.** To hold or direct (the atten, gaze, etc.) steadily. **5.** To look at steadily or piercly. **6.** To settle or decide definitely; to determine or ablish. **7.** To place (blame or responsibility) on a person. *U.S.* To put in order; adjust. **9.** To repair or mend. *U.S.* To prepare (food or a meal). **11.** *U.S. Informal* prearrange or influence the outcome, etc., of (a race, ne, jury, etc.) as by bribery. **12.** *U.S. Informal* To chas or discipline. **13.** To prepare (specimens) for micropic study. **14.** *Chem.* To cause to form a nonvolatile or d compound. **15.** *Photog.* To bathe (a film or plate) in micals to remove light-sensitive substances and prevent ing. **16.** *Informal* To castrate or spay (a dog, cat, etc.) *v.i.* **17.** To become firm or stable. —*n.* **1.** *Informal* difficult situation; predicament. **2.** The position of a p or aircraft as determined by fixed points on shore, onomical observations, or bearings. **3.** *U.S. Slang* A ision or outcome prearranged by bribery or other corrupt ans. **4.** *U.S. Slang* An injection of heroin or other naric. [< Med.L < L *fixus,* pp. of *figere* to fasten] — **fix′a·** *adj.* — **fix′er** *n.*
·tion (fik·sā′shən) *n.* **1.** The act of fixing, or the state being fixed. **2.** *Chem.* The conversion of free nitrogen n the air into useful compounds; also, any similar process lied to an oil or a gas. **3.** *Psychoanal.* An arrested exsive attachment of the libido in a developmental stage. Loosely, a preoccupation or obsession.
·tive (fik′sə·tiv) *n.* That which serves to render pernent or fixed, as certain substances used on paintings.
d (fikst) *adj.* **1.** Placed or fastened securely; made firm position. **2.** Steadily or intently directed; set. **3.** Staary or unchanging in relative position. **4.** Definite unalterable. **5.** Permanent. **6.** *U.S. Informal* Prenged as to outcome or decision. **7.** *Chem.* **a** Formed or forming part of a compound. **b** Not volatile. **8.** *l.* Sessile. — **fix·ed·ly** (fik′sid·lē) *adv.* — **fix′ed·ness** *n.*
d charge *Econ.* A charge that cannot be changed or ided, esp. one payable at fixed intervals, as rent; taxes.
d idea *Psychiatry* An obsessional, delusional idea that uences a person's attitude or thinking: also *idée fixe.*
d star *Astron.* A star that seems to preserve the same ition with respect to the stars around it.
ngs (fik′singz) *n.pl. U.S. Informal* Trimmings.
·ty (fik′sə·tē) *n. pl.* **·ties** **1.** The state or quality of befixed; stability; permanence. **2.** That which is fixed.
ure (fiks′chər) *n.* **1.** Anything securely fixed or fased into position; esp., a permanent part or appendage a house. **2.** A person or thing regarded as fixed in a ticular place or job. **3.** *Law* **a** Any chattel or article personal property affixed to reality to become a part reof and thereafter governed by the law of real property. uch chattel of a tenant, that can be removed without ry to the premises. [< FIXURE; infl. in form by *mixture*]
(fiz) *v.i.* To make a hissing or sputtering noise. —*n.* **1.** issing sound. **2.** An effervescent beverage made with soda er, liquor, flavoring, etc.: a gin *fizz.*
le (fiz′əl) *v.i.* **·zled, ·zling** **1.** To make a hissing or ttering sound. **2.** *Informal* To fail, esp. after a good t. —*n.* **1.** Hissing. **2.** *Informal* A failure. [Freq. of *fise* to fart]
y (fiz′ē) *adj.* **fizz·i·er, fizz·i·est** Fizzing; effervescent.
l (fyôrd) See FIORD.
ber·gast (flab′ər·gast) *v.t. Informal* To astound.
by (flab′ē) *adj.* **·bi·er, ·bi·est** **1.** Lacking strength or ness; soft. **2.** Lacking vigor or force; weak, as language. **lab′bi·ly** *adv.* — **flab′bi·ness** *n.*
cid (flak′sid) *adj.* Lacking firmness or elasticity; limp; by. [< F < L *flaccus* limp] — **flac′cid·ly** *adv.* — **·cid′i·ty, flac′cid·ness** *n.*

fla·con (flȧ·kôṅ′) *n. French* A stoppered bottle or flask.
flag[1] (flag) *n.* **1.** A piece of cloth or bunting, usu. oblong, bearing devices and colors to designate a nation, state, organization, etc. **2.** The bushy part of the tail of a dog. **3.** The tail of a deer. **4.** *pl. Ornithol.* The long leg- or wing-feathers of a hawk or bird of prey. **5.** *Music* A hook. — *v.t.* **flagged, flag·ging** **1.** To mark out or adorn with flags. **2.** To signal as with a flag. **3.** To send (information) by signals. **4.** To decoy (deer, etc.), as by waving a flag. — **to flag down** To cause to stop, as a train, by signaling.
flag[2] (flag) *n.* **1.** Any of various irises having sword-shaped leaves and growing in moist places. **2.** The leaf of a flag.
flag[3] (flag) *v.i.* **flagged, flag·ging** **1.** To grow tired or weak. **2.** To become limp. [? < obs. *flack* flutter]
flag[4] (flag) *n.* A flagstone. —*v.i.* **flagged, flag·ging** To pave with flags. [< ON *flaga* slab of stone]
Flag Day June 14, the anniversary of the day in 1777 on which Congress proclaimed the Stars and Stripes the national standard of the United States.
flag·el·lant (flaj′ə·lənt, flə·jel′ənt) *n.* One who whips; esp., one who whips himself or has himself whipped from religious motives or for sexual excitement. Also **flag·el·la·tor** (flaj′ə·lā′tər). [< L *flagellum* whip] — **flag′el·la′tion** (-shən) *n.*
flag·el·late (flaj′ə·lāt) *v.t.* **·lat·ed, ·lat·ing** To whip; scourge. —*adj. Biol.* **1.** Having or producing whiplike processes or branches. **2.** Shaped like a flagellum. Also **flag′el·lat′ed.**
fla·gel·lum (flə·jel′əm) *n. pl.* **·la** (-ə) **1.** *Biol.* A lashlike appendage, as of a protozoan. **2.** A whip. [< L, whip]
flag·eo·let (flaj′ə·let′) *n.* A flutelike musical instrument blown at the end and having six finger holes. [< OF *flageol*]
flag·ging[1] (flag′ing) *adj.* Growing weak; failing; drooping.
flag·ging[2] (flag′ing) *n.* **1.** A pavement of flagstones; also, flagstones collectively. **2.** The act of paving with flagstones.
fla·gi·tious (flə·jish′əs) *adj.* Flagrantly wicked. [< L *flagitium* disgraceful act] — **fla·gi′tious·ly** *adv.*
flag·man (flag′mən) *n. pl.* **·men** (-mən) **1.** One who carries a flag. **2.** One who signals with a flag, as on a railway.
flag officer In the U.S. Navy, an officer above the rank of captain entitled to display a flag indicating his rank.
flag·on (flag′ən) *n.* A vessel with a handle, spout, and often a hinged lid, used to serve liquids. [< OF < Med.L *flasco*]
flag·pole (flag′pōl′) *n.* A pole on which a flag is displayed.
fla·grant (flā′grənt) *adj.* Openly disgraceful; notorious; heinous. [< L *flagrare* to blaze, burn] — **fla′gran·cy, fla′grance** *n.* — **fla′grant·ly** *adv.*
fla·gran·te de·lic·to (flə·gran′tē di·lik′tō) In the very act of committing a crime: literally, while the crime is blazing.
flag·ship (flag′ship′) *n.* The ship in a naval formation that carries a flag officer and displays his flag.
flag·staff (flag′staf′, -stäf′) *n. pl.* **·staffs** or **·staves** (-stāvz′) A staff on which a flag is hung or displayed.
flag·stone (flag′stōn′) *n.* A broad, flat stone for pavements.
flail (flāl) *n.* An implement for threshing grain by hand. —*v.t. & v.i.* To beat as with a flail. [OE *flygel,* prob. < L *flagellum* whip]
flair (flâr) *n.* **1.** A talent or aptitude. **2.** Instinctive perceptiveness; discernment. **3.** *Informal* A showy or dashing style. [< OF *flairer* to scent out]
flak (flak) *n.* Antiaircraft fire. [< G *fl*(*ieger*) aircraft + *a*(*bwehr*) defense + *k*(*anone*) gun]
flake (flāk) *n.* **1.** A small, thin piece peeled or split off from a surface. **2.** A small piece of light substance: a *flake* of snow. **3.** A stratum, layer, or lamina. —*v.t. & v.i.* **flaked, flak·ing** **1.** To peel off in flakes. **2.** To form into flakes. [ME < Scand.] — **flak′er** *n.*
flak·y (flā′kē) *adj.* **flak·i·er, flak·i·est** **1.** Resembling or consisting of flakes. **2.** Splitting off or easily separated into flakes. — **flak′i·ly** *adv.* — **flak′i·ness** *n.*
flam·beau (flam′bō) *n. pl.* **·beaux** (-bōz) or **·beaus** **1.** A burning torch. **2.** A large candlestick. [< F < OF *flamme*]
flam·boy·ant (flam′boi′ənt) *adj.* **1.** Extravagantly ornate; florid; showy. **2.** Brilliant in color; resplendent. **3.** *Archit.* Pertaining to a highly decorative style of architecture. [< F < OF *flambeier*] — **flam·boy′ance, flam·boy′·an·cy** *n.* — **flam·boy′ant·ly** *adv.*
flame (flām) *n.* **1.** A mass of burning vapor or gas rising from a fire in streams or darting tongues of light. **2.** A single tongue of flame. **3.** *Often pl.* A state of bright, intensely active combustion. **4.** Something resembling a flame in brilliance, shape. **5.** Intense passion or emotion; ardor. **6.** *Informal* A sweetheart. **7.** A bright, red-yellow color. — **Syn.** See FIRE. —*v.* **flamed, flam·ing** *v.i.* **1.** To give out flame; blaze; burn. **2.** To light up or glow as if on fire; flash. **3.** To become enraged or excited. —*v.t.* **4.** To subject to heat or fire. [< OF < L *flamma* flame]
fla·men·co (flə·meng′kō, -men′-, flä-) *n.* **1.** A fiery, percussive style of singing and dancing practiced esp. by the Gypsies of Andalusia. **2.** A song or dance in this style. [< Sp.]

flame·out (flām′out′) *n.* Burnout, esp. of a jet engine.
flame thrower *Mil.* A weapon that throws a stream of burning napalm or other gasoline mixture.
flam·ing (flā′ming) *adj.* **1.** In flames; blazine; fiery. **2.** Brilliant. **3.** Ardent. **4.** Flagrant. **— flam′ing·ly** *adv.*
fla·min·go (flə·ming′gō) *n. pl.* **·gos** or **·goes** A long-necked wading bird of a pink or red color, having very long legs. [< Pg. or Sp. < L *flamma* flame + -ING[3]]
flam·ma·ble (flam′ə·bəl) *adj.* Capable of catching fire easily; combustible; inflammable. **— flam′ma·bil′i·ty** *n.*
flange (flanj) *n.* **1.** A projecting rim or collar on a wheel, designed to keep it on a fixed track. **2.** A similar projecting part of a beam, pipe, etc., designed to aid attachment or to increase stiffness. **3.** A tool used to shape flanges. **—** *v.t. & v.i.* **flanged, flang·ing** To provide with or take the shape of a flange. [? < OF *flangir* to bend]
flank (flangk) *n.* **1.** The part between the ribs and the hip at either side of the body of an animal or human being; also, a cut of meat from such a part. **2.** Loosely, the outside part of the leg between the hip and the knee; thigh. **3.** The extreme right or left part of something; side. **4.** *Mil.* The right or left section of an army, fleet, fortification, etc. **—** *v.t.* **1.** To be at the side of. **2.** *Mil.* To defend, launch an attack against, or move around the flank of. **—** *v.i.* **3.** To be located at the side of something. [< F *flanc* < Gmc.] **— flank′er** *n.*
flan·nel (flan′əl) *n.* **1.** A woven fabric made of wool, or of wool and cotton. **2.** A soft fabric made chiefly of cotton, with a nap on one or both sides: also **flan·nel·ette** (flan′əl·et′), **flan′nel·et′**. **3.** *pl.* A garment or garments made of flannel. [Prob. < Welsh *gwlan* wool] **— flan′nel·ly** *adj.*
flap (flap) *v.* **flapped, flap·ping** *v.t.* **1.** To move (wings, the arms, etc.) vigorously up and down, esp. with a muffled slapping sound. **2.** To cause to move with an irregular waving or rippling motion, esp. with noise. **3.** To strike with something flat or flexible; slap. **4.** *Informal* To throw down or close up suddenly or noisily. **—** *v.i.* **5.** To flap the wings, arms, etc. **6.** To have an irregular waving motion, as a flag. **—** *n.* **1.** The part of an envelope that is folded down in closing or sealing. **2.** A loosely hanging covering over the entrance to a tent, etc. **3.** A loose cover over the opening of a pocket; also, a lapel. **4.** *Aeron.* A hinged section as on the wings of an airplane, used to increase the lift or decrease speed. **5.** *Surg.* A partially detached piece of tissue. **6.** The action or sound of flapping. **7.** A blow given with something flat or flexible; slap.
flap·jack (flap′jak′) *n. U.S.* A griddlecake.
flap·per (flap′ər) *n.* **1.** One who or that which flaps. **2.** A broad flipper, as of a seal. **3.** A young bird not yet able to fly. **4.** *U.S. Informal* A young woman trying to appear sophisticated in dress and behavior: term current in the 1920's.
flare (flâr) *v.* **flared, flar·ing** *v.i.* **1.** To blaze up or burn with a wavering light, esp. suddenly: often with *up*. **2.** To break out in sudden or violent emotion or action: often with *up* or *out*. **3.** To spread or gradually open outward, as the sides of a bell. **—** *v.t.* **4.** To cause to flare. **5.** To signal (information) with flares. **—** *n.* **1.** A bright, flickering light. **2.** An outburst, as of emotion. **3.** A spreading outward; also, that which so flares. **4.** *Photog.* Excess light striking a film. **5.** *Mil.* A signal that gives off a bright white or colored light. **— Syn.** See FIRE. [Origin unknown]
flare-up (flâr′up′) *n.* **1.** A sudden outburst of flame or light. **2.** A sudden outbreak of emotion.
flar·ing (flâr′ing) *adj.* **1.** Blazing with a bright, unsteady light. **2.** Gaudy. **3.** Spreading outward. **— flar′ing·ly** *adv.*
flash (flash) *v.i.* **1.** To burst forth suddenly or repeatedly into brilliant light or fire. **2.** To gleam brightly; glitter. **3.** To move suddenly or with lightning speed. **—** *v.t.* **4.** To cause to shine or glitter brightly. **5.** To emit bursts of (light, fire, etc.). **6.** To send or communicate with lightning speed. **7.** *Informal* To show suddenly or abruptly; also, to make an ostentatious display of. **8.** To provide (a roof, etc.) with sheet metal or flashing. **9.** In glassmaking, to cover (glass) with a thin layer of differently colored glass. **—** *n.* **1.** A quick blaze of light or fire, lasting an instant. **2.** A sudden, brilliant manifestation, as of wit or talent. **3.** Vulgar display. **4.** An extremely brief space of time; instant. **5.** *U.S.* A brief news dispatch sent by radio, etc. **6.** A volatile mixture containing metal salts, used in applying a colored glaze to glass, etc. **7.** A lock, dam, etc.; also, the sudden flow of water made available by such a device. **— flash in the pan 1.** Explosion of the powder in the pan of a flintlock musket without ignition of the charge. **2.** A person, thing, or action that shows promise for a short time and then fails. **—** *adj.* Done or occurring very quickly. [ME *flaschen*; prob. imit.] **— flash′er** *n.*
flash·back (flash′bak′) *n.* A break in the continuity of a novel, drama, motion picture, etc., to give a scene occurring earlier; also, the scene itself.
flash bulb *Photog.* Any of various electrical devices that emit an intense light of brief duration for taking photographs.
flash flood A sudden, rushing flood caused by heavy rain
flash gun *Photog.* A device that ignites a flash bulb.
flash·ing (flash′ing) *n.* Sheet metal or other protec material used to cover joints or angles, as of a roof.
flash·light (flash′līt′) *n. U.S.* A small, portable de that emits a beam of light, usu. powered by dry batteri
flash point The lowest temperature at which the vapo combustible liquids, esp. lubricating oils, will ignite.
flash·y (flash′ē) *adj.* **flash·i·er, flash·i·est 1.** Brilliant f moment; sparkling; flashing. **2.** Showy; cheap. **— fla ly** *adv.* **— flash′i·ness** *n.*
flask (flask, fläsk) *n.* Any of various small containers n of glass, metal, etc., with a narrow neck; as: **a** A flat tainer, esp. for liquor, to be carried in the pocket. rounded receptacle with a long neck, for laboratory w **c** A powder flask. [< F < Med.L *flasca*]
flat[1] (flat) *adj.* **flat·ter, flat·test 1.** Extended horizon with little or no slope. **2.** Smooth and regular with fe no hollows or projections. **3.** Stretched out level or p trate. **4.** Having the front or back in full contact wit even surface. **5.** Shallow: a *flat* dish. **6.** Absolute unqualified: a *flat* refusal. **7.** Lacking interest or zes ness; lifeless; dull. **8.** Lacking variety or contrast. Deflated: a *flat* tire. **10.** *U.S. Informal* Having little o money: broke. **11.** Fixed; uniform: at a *flat* rate. Marked by little or no commercial activity: Trade was **13.** Exact; precise: in a minute *flat*. **14.** *Music* **a** Low in pitch by a semitone. **b** Lower than the right, true p **c** Having flats in the key signature. **15.** *Phonet.* D nating the vowel sound in *man*, as opposed to the sour *calm*. **—** *adv.* **1.** In a flat state, position, or manner. Exactly. **3.** In finance, without interest. **4.** *Music* B the right, true pitch. **— to fall flat** To fail to achie desired effect. **—** *n.* **1.** The flat, plane surface or pa something. **2.** Something that has a flat surface; as: piece of stage scenery. **b** A railroad flat car. **c** A level ar land. **d** *Usu. pl.* A partially submerged plain or shal shoal. **3.** *Informal* A tire from which the air has esca **4.** *pl. Informal* Women's shoes with flat heels. **5.** *M* A sign (♭) placed before a note to indicate it is at a l semitone in pitch. **—** *v.t. & v.i.* **flat·ted, flat·ting** To n or become flat. [< ON *flatr*] **— flat′ly** *adv.*
flat[2] (flat) *n.* A suite of rooms on one floor, used as a dence; apartment. [Var. of obs. *flet* floor, OE *flet*]
flat·car (flat′kär′) *n. U.S.* A railroad car with no sid roof, used for freight.
flat·fish (flat′fish′) *n. pl.* **·fish** or **·fish·es** One of se fishes, as the halibut, flounder, or sole, having a flat bod
flat·foot (flat′fo͝ot′) *n.* **1.** *Pathol.* A condition caused flattened arch. **2.** *Slang* A policeman.
flat-foot·ed (flat′fo͝ot′id) *adj.* **1.** Having flat feet. **2.** *Informal* Direct and uncompromising; plain and resolute **flat′-foot′ed·ly** *adv.* **— flat′-foot′ed·ness** *n.*
flat·i·ron (flat′ī′ərn) *n.* An iron (def. 4).
flat·ten (flat′n) *v.t. & v.i.* To make or become fla flatter. **— flat′ten·er** *n.*
flat·ter (flat′ər) *v.t.* **1.** To praise excessively, esp. wit sincerity. **2.** To try to gain favor by praising. **3.** To upon the hopes or vanity of; beguile. **4.** To make ple as by compliments; to pamper. **5.** To show as mor tractive. **—** *v.i.* **6.** To flatter someone or something. OF *flater* to fawn] **— flat′ter·er** *n.* **— flat′ter·ing·ly** *a*
flat·ter·y (flat′ər·ē) *n. pl.* **·ter·ies 1.** The act of flatte **2.** An overly complimentary remark.
flat·top (flat′top′) *n.* A U.S. naval aircraft carrier.
flat·u·lence (flach′o͞o·ləns, flat′yo͞o-) *n.* **1.** Gas in th testines. **2.** Windy boastfulness. Also **flat′u·len·cy.** [< L *flatus* blowing] **— flat′u·lent** *adj.* **— flat′u·lent·ly**
flat·ware (flat′wâr′) *n.* **1.** Dishes that are flat, as p and saucers. **2.** Table utensils, as knives, forks, and sp
flat·work (flat′wûrk′) *n.* Sheets, tablecloths, etc., tha be ironed in a mangle and do not require hand ironing
flaunt (flônt) *v.i.* **1.** To make a brazen or gaudy dis parade impudently or boldly. **2.** To wave freely. **—** **3.** To display. **—** *n.* The act of flaunting. [ME *fla* Scand.] **— flaunt′er** *n.* **— flaunt′ing·ly** *adv.*
flaunt·y (flôn′tē) *adj.* **flaunt·i·er, flaunt·i·est** Marked b given to showy display. **— flaunt′i·ly** *adv.* **— flaunt′i·ne**
flau·tist (flô′tist) *n.* A flutist.
fla·vin (flā′vən) *n. Biochem.* One of a group of yellow ments widely distributed in plant and animal tissues an cluding riboflavin. [< L *flavus* yellow + -IN]
fla·vor (flā′vər) *n.* **1.** Taste; esp., a distinctive eleme the overall taste of something. **2.** Something adde increase or impart taste; flavoring. **3.** A special, s quality pervading something. **—** *v.t.* To give flavor to. *Brit.* **fla′vour.** [< OF < L *flare* to blow] **— fla′vor·**
fla·vor·ful (flā′vər·fəl) *adj.* Full of flavor; esp., pleasa the taste. Also **fla′vor·ous, fla′vor·some, fla′vor·y.**
fla·vor·ing (flā′vər·ing) *n.* Something, as an essence o tract, added to heighten flavor or give a distinctive tas

ʼ (flô) *n.* **1.** Something missing or faulty; defect. **2.** ıething questionable. **3.** A crack or fissure. **—** *v.t.* **1.** To ıduce a flaw in. **—** *v.i.* **2.** To become cracked or torn. : ON *flaga* slab of stone] **— flaw′less** *adj.*
ʼ (flô) *n.* A gust; also, a brief windstorm, often accomıed by precipitation; squall. [Prob. < ON *flaga* gust]
(flaks) *n.* **1.** An annual plant that yields the fiber used ıaking linen. **2.** The fiber. [OE *fleax*]
en (flak′sən) **1.** Pertaining to or made of flax. **2.** Havı light golden color like straw. Also **flax′y.**
seed (flaks′sēd′, flak′sēd′) *n.* The mucilaginous seed ıx, yielding linseed oil: also called *linseed.*
(flā) *v.t.* **1.** To remove the skin, hide, bark, etc., of; , to rip off strips of skin from, as by lashing. **2.** To ck with scathing criticism. **3.** To get the money or ls of by extortion or swindling. [OE *flēan*] **— flay′er** *n.*
ver Appleton layer.
flē) *n.* A small, wingless, parasitic insect that sucks the d of mammals and birds. [OE *flēa, flēah*]
oit·ten (flē′bit′n) *adj.* **1.** Bitten by fleas; also, covered ı fleas. **2.** *Informal* Broken-down; decrepit.
(flek) *n.* **1.** A tiny streak or spot. **2.** A bit; speck. *t.* To mark with flecks. [Cf. ON *flekkr* spot]
ion (flek′shən) *n.* The act of bending, or the state of g bent. [< L *flectere* to bend] **— flec′tion·al** *adj.*
(fled) Past tense and past participle of FLEE.
e (flej) *v.* **fledged, fledg·ing** *v.t.* **1.** To furnish with ners. **2.** To bring up (a young bird). **—** *v.i.* **3.** To v enough feathers for flight. [< OE *-flycge* ready to fly]
·ling (flej′ling) *n.* **1.** A fledged bird. **2.** A beginner. ı **fledge′ling.**
flē) *v.* **fled, flee·ing** *v.i.* **1.** To run away, as from dan- **2.** To move swiftly; leave abruptly. **—** *v.t.* **3.** To ıway from (a person, place, etc.). [OE *flēon*] **— fle′er** *n.*
e (flēs) *n.* **1.** The coat of wool covering a sheep or lar animal. **2.** The quantity of wool sheared from a p. **3.** Anything resembling fleece. **4.** A textile fabric ı a soft, silky pile, used for linings, etc.; also, the pile. *.t.* **fleeced, fleec·ing** **1.** To shear the fleece from. **2.** To ıdle; defraud. [OE *flēos*] **— fleec′er** *n.*
·y (flē′sē) *adj.* **fleec·i·er, fleec·i·est** Like, covered with, ıade of fleece. **— fleec′i·ly** *adv.* **— fleec′i·ness** *n.*
(flēt) *n.* **1.** The entire number of ships belonging to government; navy; also, a number of ships, esp. ships of operating together under one command. **2.** A group of aft, trucks, etc., organized into a unit. [OE *flēot* ship]
(flēt) *adj.* Swift; quick. **— Syn.** See SWIFT. **—** *v.i.* nove swiftly. [OE *flēotan* to float] **— fleet′ly** *adv.*
·ing (flē′ting) *adj.* Passing quickly. **— fleet′ing·ly — fleet′ing·ness** *n.*
ı·ing (flem′ing) *n.* **1.** A native of Flanders, esp. of ian Flanders. **2.** A native speaker of Flemish.
ı·ish (flem′ish) *adj.* Of or pertaining to Flanders, its le, or their language. **—** *n.* **1.** Flemings collectively. he language of the Flemings, closely related to Dutch.
(flesh) *n.* **1.** The soft substance of the body of a ıan being or animal, esp. that consisting of muscle but exclusive of fat. **2.** The edible substance of animals, uding that of fish and sometimes of birds; meat. **3.** The pulpy substance of fruits and vegetables. **4.** The ace of the body of a human being or animal. **5.** The r of the skin of a white person, usu. pink or pale orangeɔw. **6.** Plumpness; fatness; weight. **7.** The body of ı as opposed to the soul or spirit; also, the physical, ual nature. **8.** Mankind; also, living creatures. **9.** dred; kin. **—** *v.t.* **1.** To excite the hunting instinct of s, etc.) by feeding with meat. **2.** To initiate into fighting, dshed, etc. **—** *v.i.* **3.** To become fat. [OE *flǣsc*]
-col·ored (flesh′kul′ərd) *adj.* Having moderate pink ale orange-yellow color.
·ly (flesh′lē) *adj.* **·li·er, ·li·est** **1.** Pertaining to the y. **2.** Sensuous. **3.** Worldly. **— flesh′li·ness** *n.*
·pot (flesh′pot′) *n.* *Usu. pl.* Material advantages or ries; also, places for indulgence, as night clubs, etc.
·y (flesh′ē) *adj.* **flesh·i·er, flesh·i·est** **1.** Of or resemg flesh. **2.** Plump; fat. **3.** Firm and pulpy. **— flesh′·ss** *n.*
-de-lis (flœr′də·lē′, -lēs′, flo͝or′) *n. pl.* **rs-de-lis** (flœr′də·lēz′, flo͝or′-) **1.** *Heraldry* evice of three leaves or petals bound near base. **2.** The armorial bearings of the ıer royal family of France. **3.** The iris er or plant. Also **fleur-de-lys′.** [< F, er of lily]

FLEUR-DE-LIS

(flo͞o) Past tense of FLY[1].
(fleks) *v.t.* & *v.i.* **1.** To bend, as the arm. o contract, as a muscle. [< L *flexus*, pp. *ectere* to bend]

flexi- *combining form* Bent. [See FLEX.]
flex·i·ble (flek′sə·bəl) *adj.* **1.** Capable of being bent, twisted, etc.; pliant. **2.** Yielding; tractable. **3.** Able to adjust; adaptable. Also **flex·ile** (flek′sil). **— flex′i·bil′i·ty, flex′i·ble·ness** *n.* **— flex′i·bly** *adv.*
flex·or (flek′sər) *n.* *Anat.* A muscle that serves to bend a part of the body.
flex·ure (flek′shər) *n.* **1.** The act of bending, or the state of being bent. **2.** A turn; curve. [< L *flexura* a bending]
flib·ber·ti·gib·bet (flib′ər·tē·jib′it) *n.* An impulsive, flighty, or gossipy person. [Imit.]
flick (flik) *n.* **1.** A quick, light, snapping movement or blow. **2.** A slight, cracking sound made by such a blow. **3.** A slight trace of something. **—** *v.t.* **1.** To strike with a quick, light stroke, as with a whip. **2.** To cause to move or snap with a quick movement; also, to remove in such a way. **—** *v.i.* **3.** To move in a darting manner. **4.** To flutter.
flick·er[1] (flik′ər) *v.i.* **1.** To burn or shine with an unsteady or wavering light. **2.** To flash up and die away quickly, as lightning. **3.** To flutter or quiver. **—** *v.t.* **4.** To cause to flicker. **—** *n.* **1.** A wavering or unsteady light. **2.** A quivering or fluttering. **3.** A slight stirring, as of emotion. [OE *flicorian* to move the wings]
flick·er[2] (flik′ər) *n.* A woodpecker of eastern North America.
Flickertail State Nickname of North Dakota.
flied (flīd) Past tense and past participle of FLY[1] (def. 9).
fli·er (flī′ər) *n.* **1.** One who or that which flies, as an aviator. **2.** One who or that which moves very fast, as an express train. **3.** A big leap or jump. **4.** *U.S. Informal* A risky financial investment. **5.** *U.S.* A handbill. Also spelled *flyer.*
flight[1] (flīt) *n.* **1.** The act or manner of flying; also, the power of flying. **2.** Any swift movement through the air. **3.** The distance traveled or the course followed by an airplane, bird, projectile, etc. **4.** A journey by airplane; also, a scheduled trip by airplane. **5.** A group flying through the air together. **6.** In the U.S. Air Force, a tactical formation, usu. of four or more aircraft. **7.** A soaring or excursion: a *flight* of imagination. **8.** A continuous series of stairs. **—** *v.t.* To migrate, as wild fowl. [OE *flyht*]
flight[2] (flīt) *n.* The act of fleeing or escaping from danger.
flight engineer *Aeron.* The crew member of an airplane in charge of mechanical performance during flight.
flight lieutenant (lef·ten′ənt) In the Commonwealth air forces, a commissioned officer. See table at GRADE.
flight sergeant In the Commonwealth air forces, a noncommissioned officer. See table at GRADE.
flight·y (flī′tē) *adj.* **flight·i·er, flight·i·est** **1.** Moving erratically from one idea or topic to another; unable to concentrate long or well; giddy. **2.** Moved by impulse or whim; frivolous; fickle. **3.** Not quite sane or clear-headed: a *flighty* old lady. **— flight′i·ly** *adv.* **— flight′i·ness** *n.*
flim·flam (flim′flam′) *Informal* *v.t.* **·flammed, ·flam·ming** To swindle; hoax; trick. **—** *n.* **1.** Nonsense; silly talk. **2.** Petty trickery or deception. [Cf. Norw. *flim* lampoon]
flim·sy (flim′zē) *adj.* **·si·er, ·si·est** **1.** Not strong or solid in structure. **2.** Light, thin, and delicate in texture. **3.** Lacking real validity or effectiveness: a *flimsy* excuse. **—** *n. pl.* **·sies** **1.** Thin paper used for carbon copies or transfers. **2.** Copy written on this paper. [< FILM, by metathesis] **— flim′si·ly** *adv.* **— flim′si·ness** *n.*
flinch (flinch) *v.i.* To shrink back or wince, as from anything threatening or unpleasant. **—** *n.* **1.** Any act of shrinking back or wincing. **2.** A card game. [< OF *flechier* to bend] **— flinch′er** *n.* **— flinch′ing·ly** *adv.*
flin·der (flin′dər) *n.* *Usu. pl.* Small fragments; splinters; shreds. [Cf. Norw. *flindra* splinter]
fling (fling) *v.* **flung, fling·ing** *v.t.* **1.** To toss or hurl, esp. with violence. **2.** To put abruptly or violently: to *fling* someone into prison. **3.** To throw (oneself) into something completely or with energy. **4.** To send forth suddenly or rapidly: to *fling* reinforcements into battle. **5.** To move (a part of the body) with sudden vigor. **6.** To give off or diffuse. **—** *v.i.* **7.** To move, rush, or flounce, as in anger or contempt. **8.** To make abusive remarks; speak harshly: usu. with *out.* **—** *n.* **1.** The act of casting out, down, or away. **2.** A sneering or contemptuous comment. **3.** A brief period of self-indulgence, unrestraint, etc. **4.** *Informal* An attempt: to have a *fling* at painting. [ME *flingen* < Scand.]
flint (flint) *n.* **1.** A very hard, dull-colored variety of quartz that produces a spark when struck with steel. **2.** Anything very hard or cruel. **—** *v.t.* To provide with a flint. [OE]
flint glass A hard glass, used for lenses, cut glass, etc.
flint·lock (flint′lok′) *n.* **1.** A gunlock in which a flint is used to ingite the powder in the pan. **2.** An obsolete firearm that was equipped with such a gunlock.
flint·y (flin′tē) *adj.* **flint·i·er, flint·i·est** **1.** Made of, containing, or resembling flint. **2.** Hard; cruel; obdurate. **— flint′i·ly** *adv.* **— flint′i·ness** *n.*

flip (flip) *v.* **flipped, flip·ping** *v.t.* **1.** To throw or move with a jerk; flick. **2.** To propel, as a coin, by an outward snap of a finger pressed down by the thumb and suddenly released. — *v.i.* **3.** To move with a jerk. **4.** To strike lightly and quickly. **5.** *U.S. Slang* To become angry or upset. — *n.* **1.** A quick, light snapping movement, as of a lash. **2.** A drink made with liquor, as sherry, mixed with egg, sugar, and spices. — *adj. Informal* Pert; saucy; impertinent. [Imit.]

flip·pan·cy (flip′ən·sē) *n. pl.* **·cies 1.** Careless disrespect; impertinence; sauciness. **2.** An impertinent act or remark.

flip·pant (flip′ənt) *adj.* Lacking due respect or seriousness; impertinent; saucy. [< FLIP v. + -ANT] — **flip′pant·ly** *adv.* — **flip′pant·ness** *n.*

flip·per (flip′ər) *n.* **1.** A broad, flat limb adapted for swimming, as in seals, etc. **2.** A rubber, paddlelike shoe used by skin divers and other swimmers. **3.** *Slang* The hand.

flirt (flûrt) *v.i.* **1.** To act in a coquettish manner; play at love. **2.** To expose oneself to something carelessly or lightly: to *flirt* with danger. **3.** To dart; flit. — *v.t.* **4.** To move abruptly or briskly. **5.** To toss or snap quickly. — *n.* **1.** One who plays at love. **2.** A sudden movement. [Imit.]

flir·ta·tion (flûr·tā′shən) *n.* **1.** Coquettish behavior. **2.** A brief, casual love affair. — **flirt′y, flir·ta′tious** *adj.* — **flir·ta′tious·ly** *adv.*

flit (flit) *v.* **flit·ted, flit·ting** *v.i.* **1.** To move or fly rapidly and lightly; dart; skim. **2.** To pass away quickly. — *n.* A flitting movement. [< ON *flytja* to remove, move] — **flit′ter** *n.*

flitch (flich) *n.* **1.** A salted and smoked cut of meat from a pig. **2.** A piece of timber cut lengthwise. [OE *flicce*]

flit·ter (flit′ər) *v.t. & v.i. Dial.* To flutter. [Freq. of FLIT]

fliv·ver (fliv′ər) *n. U.S. Slang* **1.** An old, battered car. **2.** Formerly, the Model T Ford car. [Origin unknown]

float (flōt) *v.i.* **1.** To rest on or at the surface of a liquid. **2.** To remain suspended below the surface of a liquid. **3.** To remain suspended or be carried along in the air or some other gas. **4.** To move lightly and effortlessly. **5.** To go about from one person or thing to another in a random or unstable way. — *v.t.* **6.** To cause to float. **7.** To put (a stock, bond, etc.) on the market. **8.** To cause (a rumor, report, etc.) to circulate. **9.** To launch (a business venture, scheme, etc.). **10.** To irrigate by flooding. — *n.* **1.** An object that floats in a liquid or buoys up something in a liquid. **2.** A piece of cork or similar material attached to a fishing line. **3.** A hollow metal ball attached to a lever governing the supply of water in a tank. **4.** An anchored raft. **5.** A tableau or display carried atop a wheeled platform, truck, etc., in parades or pageants. **6.** A soda or milk shake with a ball of ice cream in it. [OE *flotian*] — **float′a·ble** *adj.*

float·age (flō′tij), **float·a·tion** (flō·tā′shən) See FLOTAGE, FLOTATION.

float·er (flō′tər) *n.* **1.** One who or that which floats. **2.** A person who drifts about from one thing to another.

float·ing (flō′ting) *adj.* **1.** That floats or is able to float. **2.** Moving about or inclined to move about from one place, job, etc., to another. **3.** *Pathol.* Abnormally movable or detached from the usual position: a *floating* kidney. **4.** *Econ.* **a** Due at various times and in various sums: said of a debt. **b** Not assigned to any particular investment: said of capital.

floating dock A type of dry dock that can be raised to leave the ship dry for repairs. Also **floating dry dock.**

floating rib A rib of either of the two lowest pairs of ribs in a human being, not attached to the other ribs or to the sternum.

floc·cu·late (flok′yə·lāt) *v.t. & v.i.* **·lat·ed, ·lat·ing** To form into small, lumpy masses, as clouds. — **floc′cu·la′tion** *n.*

floc·cu·lent (flok′yə·lənt) *adj.* **1.** Having soft, fluffy wool or hair. **2.** Marked by or producing woolly tufts. — **floc′cu·lence** *n.* — **floc′cu·lent·ly** *adv.*

flock[1] (flok) *n.* **1.** A group of animals of the same kind, esp. sheep, goats, or birds, feeding, living, or kept together. **2.** A group of members of the same church or congregation. **3.** Any group of persons under the care or supervision of someone. **4.** A large number or assemblage of persons or things. — *v.i.* To come or go in crowds. [OE *flocc*]

— **Syn.** (noun) **1.** *Flock* is applied to birds and to small mammals, now usually sheep or goats. Larger animals, as cattle and elephants, form a *herd*; when gathered together to be driven, they are a *drove*. Other terms are fairly restricted in application: a *bevy* of quail, a *covey* of partridges, a *gaggle* of geese, a *gam* of whales, a *pack* of dogs or wolves, a *pride* of lions, a *swarm* of bees.

flock[2] (flok) *n.* **1.** Refuse wool, rags, etc., used to stuff furniture. **2.** A tuft of wool, hair, etc. — *v.t.* To cover or fill with flock. [Prob. < OF < L *floccus* lock of wool]

floe (flō) *n.* A large, comparatively level field of floating ice; also, a detached section of such a field. [< ON *flō* a layer]

flog (flog, flôg) *v.t.* **flogged, flog·ging** To beat hard with a whip, rod, strap, etc. [? < L *flagellare* to whip] — **flog′ger** *n.*

flood (flud) *n.* **1.** An unusually large flow or rise of water, esp. over land not usu. covered with water; deluge. ◆ Collateral adjective: *diluvial*. **2.** The coming in of the tide; high tide: opposed to *ebb*: also **flood tide.** **3.** Any copious flow or stream: a *flood* of words. **4.** *Poetic* Any great body of water, as the ocean, a lake, etc. — **the Flood** The De — *v.t.* **1.** To cover or inundate with a flood. **2.** To overwhelm as with a flood. **3.** To supply excessivel *flood* an engine with gasoline. — *v.i.* **4.** To rise to a f overflow. **5.** To flow in a flood. [OE *flōd*]

flood control The use of dikes, dams, etc., to regulate control bodies of water that flood easily.

flood·gate (flud′gāt′) *n.* **1.** A gate or valve at the hea water channel, designed to regulate the flow or depth o water. **2.** Something restraining or checking an outbu

flood·light (flud′līt′) *n.* **1.** A lamp that throws a br broad beam of light. **2.** The light of this lamp. — **·light·ed** or **·lit, ·light·ing** To illuminate with a floodlig

floor (flôr, flōr) *n.* **1.** The surface in a room or building which one stands or walks. **2.** The area between two cent levels of a building; story. **3.** The bottom surfa any cavity: the ocean *floor*. **4.** A level structure or plat for some special purpose: a threshing *floor*. **5.** The par legislative house, stock exchange, etc., where the mem gather to conduct business. **6.** In parliamentary proce the right to speak to the assembly: to be given the *floor* The lowest or minimum price for anything. **8.** *Naut.* more or less horizontal parts of a ship's bottom on each of the keel. — *v.t.* **1.** To cover or provide with a floor To knock down, as to the floor. **3.** *Informal* To puzz vanquish completely. [OE *flōr*]

floor·ing (flôr′ing, flō′ring) *n.* **1.** Material for the maki a floor. **2.** A floor; also, floors collectively.

floor leader A party leader in either house of the U.S. gress, who directs his party's business on the floor.

floor plan An architectural plan of the rooms and spaces on one floor of a building.

floor show Entertainment consisting of dancing, sin etc., presented on the dance floor of a night club or cab

floor·walk·er (flôr′wô′kər, flōr′-) *n.* In a department s one who walks about so as to supervise the sales force, information to customers, etc.: also, *Brit.*, *shopwalker*.

flooz·y (flōō′zē) *n. pl.* **flooz·ies** *U.S. Slang* A loose wo or a prostitute. Also **floos′y.** [Cf. FLOSSY]

flop (flop) *v.* **flopped, flop·ping** *v.i.* **1.** To move, flap, or about heavily or clumsily. **2.** To fall loosely and hea **3.** *Informal* To be completely unsuccessful. — *v.t.* **4** cause to drop or fall heavily. **5.** To flap in a loose, awkv or noisy way, as wings. — *n.* **1.** The act of flopping. flopping noise. **3.** *Informal* A total failure. [Var. of F

flop·house (flop′hous′) *n.* A cheap, shabby hotel.

flop·py (flop′ē) *adj.* **·pi·er, ·pi·est** *Informal* That flo tends to flop. — **flop′pi·ly** *adv.* — **flop′pi·ness** *n.*

flo·ra (flôr′ə, flō′rə) *n. pl.* **flo·ras** or **flo·rae** (flôr′ē, fl The aggregate of plants growing in and usu. peculiar particular region or period: distinguished from *fauna*. NL, after L *Flora*, goddess of flowers]

flo·ral (flôr′əl, flō′rəl) *adj.* Of, like, or pertaining to flo

Flor·en·tine (flôr′ən·tēn, -tīn, flor′-) *adj.* Of or perta to Florence, Italy. — *n.* A native or inhabitant of Flor

flo·res·cence (flô·res′əns, flō-) *n.* **1.** The state, perio process of blossoming. **2.** A state or period of prosperi success. [< NL < L *florere* to bloom] — **flo·res′cent**

flo·ret (flôr′it, flō′rit) *n.* **1.** A little flower. **2.** *Bot.* O the small individual flowers that make up the head of a posite flower. [< OF dim. of *flor* a flower < L *flos, f*

flo·ri·bun·da (flō′rə·bun′də, flôr′ə-) *n.* A long-flow variety of rose with large blooms. [< NL, fem. of *bundus* flowering freely < *flori-* + *-bundus* adj. suffix]

flo·ri·cul·ture (flôr′ə·kul′chər, flō′rə-) *n.* The cultiv of flowers. — **flo′ri·cul′tur·al** *adj.* — **flo′ri·cul′tur·ist**

flor·id (flôr′id, flor′-) *adj.* **1.** Having a ruddy color, of the type typical of high blood pressure; flushed with ness. **2.** Ornate, esp. to an excessive degree; flowery: a style. [< L *floridus* flowery] — **flor′id·ly** *adv.*

flo·rid·i·ty (flə·rid′ə·tē) *n. pl.* **·ties 1.** Ruddiness. **2.** F eriness. Also **flor′id·ness.**

flor·in (flôr′in, flor′-) *n.* **1.** A British silver coin, equ two shillings. **2.** The guilder of the Netherlands. **3.** of several former European coins. [< OF < Ital. < L *floris* flower; from the figure of a lily stamped on it]

flo·rist (flôr′ist, flō′rist, flor′ist) *n.* A dealer in flowers.

-florous *combining form Bot.* Having (a specified nun kind, etc., of) flowers. [< L *flos, floris* a flower]

floss (flôs, flos) *n.* **1.** One of several light, silk or sil substances or fibers. **2.** Soft fibers produced by some pl as tassels of corn. **3.** The outside fibers on the cocoon silkworm. Also **floss silk.** [< OF *flosche*] — **floss′y** *ad*

flo·ta·tion (flō·tā′shən) *n.* **1.** The act or state of floa **2.** The act of financing a business undertaking, as by a sue of stocks or bonds. Also spelled *flotation*.

flo·til·la (flō·til′ə) *n.* A fleet of small vessels; also, merically small fleet. [< Sp., dim. of *flota* fleet]

flot·sam (flot′səm) *n.* Any goods from a wrecked o periled ship that are cast or swept into the sea and f floating there. [< AF < OE *flotian* to float]

sam and jetsam **1.** Parts of a wrecked ship or its cargo ting on the water or cast ashore. **2.** Worthless or trifling ngs; oddments. **3.** Transients; drifters.

nce[1] (flouns) *n.* A gathered or pleated strip of material d for trimming skirts, etc. — *v.t.* **flounced, flounc·ing** To nish with flounces. [Earlier *frounce* < OF *fronce* fold]

nce[2] (flouns) *v.i.* **flounced, flounc·ing** **1.** To move or go h exaggerated tosses of the body, as in anger or petulance. To plunge or flounder: said of animals. — *n.* The act of ncing. [< Scand.]

n·der[1] (floun′dər) *v.i.* **1.** To struggle clumsily; move kwardly as if mired. **2.** To proceed, as in speech or ac-ı, in a stumbling or confused manner. — *n.* A stumbling truggling motion. [? Blend of FLOUNCE[2] and FOUNDER[2]]

n·der[2] (floun′dər) *n.* Any of certain flatfish, valued as d. [< AF *floundre*, prob. < Scand.]

r (flour) *n.* **1.** A fine, soft, usu. white powder obtained sifting and grinding the meal of a grain, esp. wheat. **2.** y finely powdered substance. — *v.t.* **1.** To sprinkle or er with flour. **2.** To make into flour by sifting and grind- [Var. of FLOWER] — **flour′y** *adj.*

r·ish (flûr′ish) *v.i.* **1.** To grow or fare well or prosper-ly; thrive. **2.** To be at the peak of success or develop-nt. **3.** To move with sweeping motions. **4.** To write h sweeping or ornamental strokes. **5.** To use elegant, very language. **6.** *Music* **a** To play or sing a showy sage or in a showy manner. **b** To sound a fanfare. — *v.t.* To wave about or brandish, as a weapon or flag. **8.** To play ostentatiously. **9.** To embellish, as with ornamental s, notes, etc. — *n.* **1.** A brandishing, as of a sword. **2.** urved or decorative stroke in penmanship. **3.** Something e primarily for display. **4.** Ornate language. **5.** *Music* fanfare, as of trumpets. **b** A florid passage. [< OF *florere* to bloom] — **flour′ish·er** *n.*

t (flout) *v.t.* **1.** To scoff at; defy with open contempt: to *t* convention. — *v.i.* **2.** To express one's contempt. — A contemptuous act or remark. [Prob. ME *flouten* to y the flute, to deride] — **flout′er** *n.* — **flout′ing·ly** *adv.*

(flō) *v.i.* **1.** Of fluids, to move steadily and smoothly ng, as through a channel or over a surface; also, of elec-ity or other forms of energy, to pass along or be conveyed. To move along steadily and freely as a fluid. **3.** To well or pour forth. **4.** To move steadily in an agreeably rtless or rhythmic way: Conversation *flowed*. **5.** To be rked by a satisfying, harmonious continuity: The lines of statue *flow*. **6.** To hang or ripple down in rich profusion, air. **7.** To be abundant in something; also, to overflow. Of the tide, to rise: opposed to *ebb*. — *v.t.* **9.** To cover or d with some fluid. **10.** To cause to flow. — *n.* **1.** The of flowing. **2.** Something that flows, as a current or am. **3.** A continuous stream or outpouring, as of words. The amount of that which flows. **5.** The manner of flow- **6.** An overflowing. [OE *flōwan*] — **flow′ing** *adj.*

chart A schematic diagram showing a sequence of op-tions, stages, etc., as for an industrial process.

·er (flou′ər, flour) *n.* **1.** A simple or complex cluster of als, usu. brightly ored, at or near the of a seed-bearing nt or sometimes ng the stem, and losing the repro-tive parts of the nt; blossom. **2.** The reproductive ıcture of any nt. **3.** The condi-ı in which the re-ductive parts of a nt are mature, esp. en marked by ghtly colored, open als. **4.** The condi-ı of having arrived fullest growth, de-opment, or vigor; me: usu. preceded by *in*. **5.** The finest or choicest part epresentative of something: the *flower* of youth. **6.** *Usu.* A decorative feature; ornamentation. **7.** *pl. Chem.* A vdery substance usu. produced by heating a solid to a eous state and condensing the vapors: *flowers* of sulfur. *v.i.* **1.** To produce flowers; bloom. **2.** To reach fullest elopment, or vigor. — *v.t.* **3.** To decorate with flowers floral designs. [< OF < L *flos, floris* flower]

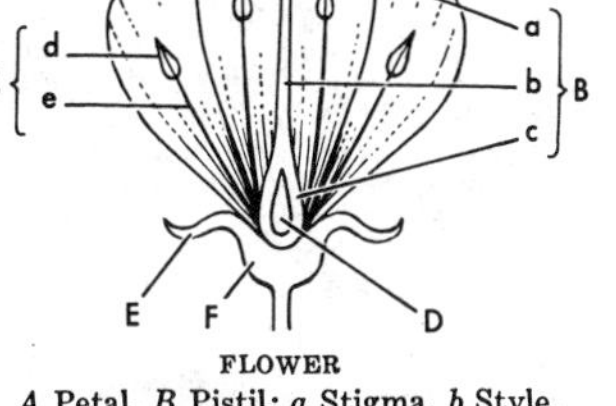

FLOWER
A Petal. *B* Pistil: *a* Stigma, *b* Style, *c* Ovary. *C* Stamen: *d* Anther, *e* Filament. *D* Ovule. *E* Sepal. *F* Receptacle.

er girl **1.** A girl or woman who sells flowers. **2.** A ıng girl who carries flowers in a procession.

er head *Bot.* A dense cluster of tiny flowers all growing ectly from the main stem of a plant.

flow·er·y (flou′ər·ē, flour′ē) *adj.* **·er·i·er, ·er·i·est** **1.** Full of or covered with flowers. **2.** Using or containing highly em-bellished language. **3.** Having a floral pattern. — **flow′er·i·ly** *adv.* — **flow′er·i·ness** *n.*

flown (flōn) Past participle of FLY[1].

flu (flo͞o) *n. Informal* Influenza.

flub (flub) *U.S. Informal v.t. & v.i.* **flubbed, flub·bing** To make a mess of (an opportunity, performance, etc.). — *n.* A botch or blunder. [Origin unknown]

fluc·tu·ate (fluk′cho͞o·āt) *v.* **·at·ed, ·at·ing** *v.i.* **1.** To change or vary often and in an irregular manner; waver. **2.** To undulate. — *v.t.* **3.** To cause to fluctuate. [< L *fluctus* wave] — **fluc′tu·ant** *adj.* — **fluc′tu·a′tion** *n.*

flue (flo͞o) *n.* **1.** A pipe or tube through which smoke, hot air, etc., is drawn off, as from a furnace or stove. **2.** A pipe or tube, as of a boiler, through which steam or hot air is car-ried so as to heat water surrounding the pipe or tube. **3.** In an organ, a flue pipe. [Origin uncertain]

flu·ent (flo͞o′ənt) *adj.* **1.** Capable of speaking or writing with effortless ease. **2.** Spoken or written with effortless ease. **3.** Marked by smoothness, grace, and expressiveness: *fluent* gestures. **4.** Running freely, as a stream of water; fluid; also, not stable; changeable. [< L *fluens, -entis*, ppr. of *fluere* to flow] — **flu′en·cy** *n.* — **flu′ent·ly** *adv.*

flue pipe An organ pipe in which the tone is produced by a stream of air passing over the lips of an opening in the side of the pipe rather than by the vibration of a reed.

fluff (fluf) *n.* **1.** A soft, light cluster, ball, or tuft of loosely gathered fibers of wool, cotton, etc. **2.** A mass of soft, fine feathers; down. **3.** *Informal* An error made in reading or speaking lines: said of actors, announcers, etc. — *v.t.* **1.** To make (pillows, blankets, etc.) soft and light by patting or shaking. **2.** *Informal* To make an error in reading or speak-ing (lines). — *v.i.* **3.** To become soft, light, or feathery. **4.** *Informal* To make an error in reading or speaking lines.

fluff·y (fluf′ē) *adj.* **fluff·i·er, fluff·i·est** Of, covered with, or resembling fluff. — **fluff′i·ly** *adv.* — **fluff′i·ness** *n.*

flu·id (flo͞o′id) *adj.* **1.** Capable of flowing; not solid. **2.** Consisting of or pertaining to liquids. **3.** Readily changing; not fixed: a *fluid* policy. — *n.* A substance capable of flow-ing; esp., a liquid or gas. [< F < L < *fluere* to flow] — **flu·id′ic** *adj.* — **flu·id′i·ty** *n.* — **flu′id·ly** *adv.*

fluid dram A measure of capacity equal to one eighth of a fluid ounce. Also **fluid drachm.** See table front of book.

fluid ounce **1.** *U.S.* One sixteenth of a pint. **2.** *Brit.* One-twentieth of a pint. See table front of book.

fluke[1] (flo͝ok) *n.* **1.** One of several parasitic trematode worms. **2.** A flatfish or flounder. [OE *flōc*]

fluke[2] (flo͝ok) *n.* **1.** A sharp projection turned backward at an angle from the principal tip or point of an arrow, harpoon, etc.; also, the entire head of an arrow, etc. **2.** The triangu-lar head at the end of either arm of an anchor. [? < FLUKE[1]]

fluke[3] (flo͝ok) *n.* **1.** A lucky stroke, as in the game of pool. **2.** Any piece of good luck. **3.** Anything that happens by chance. — *v.* **fluked, fluk·ing** *v.t.* **1.** To get, make, etc., by a fluke. — *v.i.* **2.** To make a fluke. [Origin unknown] — **fluk′ey, fluk′y** *adj.*

flume (flo͞om) *n.* **1.** *U.S.* A narrow gap in a mountain through which a torrent passes. **2.** A chute or trough for carrying water, used as a source of water power, to convey logs, etc. — *v.t.* **flumed, flum·ing** **1.** To drain away or di-vert by means of a flume, as in mining. **2.** To transport, as logs, by means of a flume. [< OF < L *flumen* river]

flum·mer·y (flum′ər·ē) *n. pl.* **·mer·ies** **1.** One of several soft, light, easily digested foods, as a custard. **2.** Vapid flattery. **3.** Utter nonsense. [< Welsh *llymru*]

flung (flung) Past tense and past participle of FLING.

flunk (flungk) *U.S. Informal v.t.* **1.** To fail in (an examina-tion, course, etc.). **2.** To give a failing grade to. — *v.i.* **3.** To fail, as in an examination. — **to flunk out** To leave or cause to leave a school or college because of failure in studies. — *n.* A failure, as in an examination. [Origin unknown]

flunk·y (flung′kē) *n. pl.* **flunk·ies** **1.** An obsequious, ser-vile fellow; toady. **2.** A manservant in livery. Also **flunk′ey.** [? Alter. of *flanker* < FLANK, *v.*] — **flunk′y·ism** *n.*

fluo- See FLUORO-.

fluor- Var. of FLUORO-.

flu·o·resce (flo͞o′ə·res′, flo͝or·es′) *v.i.* **·resced, ·resc·ing** To become fluorescent. [Back formation < FLUORESCENCE]

flu·o·res·cence (flo͞o′ə·res′əns, flo͝or·es′-) *n.* **1.** The prop-erty possessed by certain substances of absorbing radiation of a particular wavelength and emitting it as light while the stimulus is active. **2.** The light so produced. [< FLUOR-(SPAR)] — **flu′o·res′cent** *adj.*

fluorescent lamp A tubular lamp in which ultraviolet light from a low-pressure mercury arc is reradiated as visible light after impact upon a coating of phosphors.

fluor·i·date (flo͝or′ə·dāt, flo͞o′ə·ri·dāt) *v.t.* **·dat·ed, ·dat·ing**

To add sodium fluoride to (drinking water), esp. as a means of preventing tooth decay. **—fluor′i·da′tion** *n.*

flu·o·ride (flo͞o′ə·rīd, -rid; flo͝or′īd, -id) *n.* A compound of fluorine and another element. Also **flu′o·rid** (-rid).

flu·o·rine (flo͞o′ə·rēn, -rin; flo͝or′ēn, -in) *n.* A pale, greenish yellow, pungent, corrosive, and extremely reactive gaseous element (symbol F) belonging to the halogen group. See ELEMENT. Also **flu′o·rin** (-rin).

flu·o·rite (flo͞o′ə·rīt, flo͝or′īt) *n.* A cleavable, isometric, variously colored calcium fluoride, CaF_2, used as a flux in making steel and glass.

fluoro- *combining form* **1.** *Chem.* Indicating the presence of fluorine in a compound. **2.** Fluorescence. Also, before vowels, **fluor-**, also *fluo-*.

flu·o·ro·car·bon (flo͞o′ə·rō·kär′bən, flo͝or′ō-) *n. Chem.* Any of a group of very stable compounds of carbon and fluorine used as solvents, lubricants, insulators, and refrigerants.

fluor·o·scope (flo͝or′ə·skōp, flo͞o′ər·ə-) *n.* A device for observing the shadows projected upon a fluorescent screen by objects put between it and a direct beam of X-rays or other radiation. **—fluor′o·scop′ic** (-skop′ik) *adj.* **—fluor·os·co·py** (flo͝or·os′kə·pē, flo͞o′ə·ros′-) *n.*

flur·ry (flûr′ē) *v.* **·ried, ·ry·ing** *v.t.* **1.** To bewilder or confuse. **—***v.i.* **2.** To move in a flurry. **—***n. pl.* **·ries 1.** A sudden commotion or excitement. **2.** A sudden, light gust of wind. **3.** A light, brief rain or snowfall, accompanied by small gusts. **4.** In the stock exchange, a sudden, short-lived increase in trading. [Blend of FLUTTER and HURRY]

flush[1] (flush) *v.i.* **1.** To become red in the face through a rush of blood; blush. **2.** To glow or shine with a reddish brightness. **3.** To flow or rush suddenly and copiously: Blood *flushed* into his face. **4.** To become cleaned or purified through a quick gush of water, etc. **—***v.t.* **5.** To wash out, purify, etc., as a sewer, with a quick, sudden flow or gush of water. **6.** To cause to glow red or blush. **7.** To stir up or elate with the warmth of achievement, pride, etc.: usu. in the passive: to be *flushed* with success. **—***n.* **1.** A heightened, reddish color. **2.** A pervasive feeling of being hot. **3.** A pervasive, warm feeling of elation, excitement, etc. **4.** Glowing bloom or freshness. **5.** A sudden gush or flow of water, etc. [? < FLUSH[4]] **—flush′er** *n.*

flush[2] (flush) *adj.* **1.** Even or level with another surface. **2.** Of a line of print, even with the margin; not indented. **3.** Of the deck of a ship, extending on one plane from stem to stern. **4.** Having plenty of money on hand. **5.** Of a period or epoch, marked by prosperity: *flush* times. **6.** Having a heightened, reddish color: *flush* faces. **7.** Of a blow, direct: a *flush* hit. **—***adv.* **1.** In an even position with another surface; also, in alignment with a margin. **2.** In a direct manner; squarely: hit *flush* on the jaw. **—***v.t.* To make even or level, as with another surface. [? < FLUSH[1]]

flush[3] (flush) *n.* In poker, etc., a hand of cards all of one suit. **—royal flush** In poker, a hand of cards made up of the ace, king, queen, jack, and ten of one suit. **—straight flush** In poker, a hand of cards made up entirely of cards of the same suit and in sequence.

flush[4] (flush) *v.t.* **1.** To drive (an animal) from cover; esp., to startle (birds) from cover. **—***v.i.* **2.** To rush out or fly from cover. [ME *flusschen*]

flus·ter (flus′tər) *v.t.* & *v.i.* To make or become confused, agitated, or befuddled. **—***n.* Confusion or agitation of mind. [Cf. Icel. *flaustr* to hurry] **—flus·tra′tion** *n.*

flute (flo͞ot) *n.* **1.** A tubular, reedless, woodwind instrument of small diameter, equipped with holes and keys and with a mouthpiece located either along the side or at the end, and producing tones of a high pitch and clear, silvery quality. **2.** *Archit.* A groove, usu. of semicircular section, as in a column. **3.** A small groove, as in pleated cloth. **—***v.* **flut·ed, flut·ing** *v.i.* **1.** To play on a flute. **2.** To produce a flutelike sound. **—***v.t.* **3.** To sing, whistle, or utter with flutelike tones. **4.** To make flutes in (a column, dress, etc.). [< OF *flaüte*]

flut·ing (flo͞o′ting) *n.* **1.** The act of making flutes in a column, frill, etc. **2.** Flutes or grooves collectively. **3.** Ornamentation with flutes. **4.** The act of playing on a flute.

flut·ist (flo͞o′tist) *n.* A flute player: also called *flautist.*

flut·ter (flut′ər) *v.i.* **1.** To wave or flap rapidly and irregularly. **2.** To flap the wings rapidly in or as in erratic flight. **3.** To move or proceed with irregular motion. **4.** To move about lightly and quickly; flit. **5.** To be excited or nervous. **6.** To beat rapidly and sometimes unevenly, as the heart. **—***v.t.* **7.** To cause to flutter; agitate. **8.** To excite or confuse; fluster. **—***n.* **1.** A vibrating or quivering motion. **2.** Nervous agitation; dither. **3.** Excited interest; commotion. **4.** *Aeron.* A periodic oscillation set up in any part of an airplane by mechanical disturbances and maintained by inertia, structural characteristics, etc. **5.** *Telecom.* A distortion of sound caused by irregular variation in the frequency of a transmitter signal, message, or recording. **6.** *Pathol.* An abnormally rapid contraction of the atria of the heart. [OE *floterian*] **—flut′ter·er** *n.* **—flut′ter·y** *adj.*

flut·y (flo͞o′tē) *adj.* Flutelike in tone; clear and mellow.

flu·vi·al (flo͞o′vē·əl) *adj.* Pertaining to, found in, or for[...] by a river. Also **flu·vi·a·tile** (flo͞o′vē·ə·til).

flux (fluks) *n.* **1.** A flowing or discharge. **2.** Cons[...] movement or change. **3.** The flowing in of the tide. [...] *Pathol.* An abnormal discharge of fluid matter from [...] body. **5.** The act or process of melting. **6.** *Metall.* A [...] stance that promotes the fusing of metals, as borax, or [...] serves to purify metals or prevent undue oxidation of m[...] surfaces. **7.** *Physics* The rate of flow of fluids, heat, [...] tricity, light, etc. **—bloody flux** Dysentery. **—***v.t.* **1** [...] make fluid; melt. **2.** To treat, as metal, with a flux. [< L *fluere* to flow] **—flux·ion** (fluk′shən) *n.*

fly[1] (flī) *v.* **flew** or (*for def. 9*) **flied, flown** or (*for def. 9*) **f**[...] **fly·ing** *v.i.* **1.** To move through the air on wings, as a b[...] **2.** To move or travel through the air by aircraft. **3** [...] rush or be propelled through the air, as an arrow. **4** [...] wave or flutter in the air. **5.** To move swiftly or wi[...] rush. **6.** To pass swiftly: Time *flies.* **7.** To be use[...] quickly, as money. **8.** To flee; escape. **9.** In basebal[...] bat the ball high over the field. **—***v.t.* **10.** To cause t[...] or float in the air. **11.** To operate (an aircraft). **12** [...] transport by aircraft. **13.** To pass over in an aircraft. [...] To flee from. **—to fly at** To attack suddenly or violently [...] **to fly in the face of** To defy openly. **—to fly into** To e[...] suddenly into (an outburst of rage, etc.). **—to fly of**[...] leave quickly. **—to fly off the handle** To lose one's tem[...] **—to fly out** In baseball, to be retired by batting a ball [...] over the field and having it caught by an opposing pla[...] **—to fly the coop** *U.S. Slang* To sneak off; escape. **—t**[...] **fly** To utter, throw, or discharge violently, as an oat[...] stone, etc. **—***n. pl.* **flies 1.** A flap of material concea[...] the zipper or other fastening in a garment, esp. in a pa[...] trousers. **2.** The flap at the entrance to a tent. **3.** The [...] leaf of a book. **4.** The length of a flag from the staff t[...] farthest edge; also, the farthest edge. **5.** In baseball, a [...] batted high over the field. **6.** A flywheel. **7.** *pl.* [...] theater, the space above the stage and behind the pros[...] um, containing drop curtains, overhead lights, etc. **8.** [...] A light hackney coach. **—on the fly 1.** While flying. [...] *U.S. Informal* While in great haste. [OE *flēogan*]

fly[2] (flī) *n. pl.* **flies 1.** Any of various small, two-wi[...] insects; esp., the common housefly. **2.** Any of various o[...] flying insects, as the May fly. **3.** A fishhook to which [...] ored bits of material, feathers, etc., are attached to rese[...] an insect. **—fly in the ointment** Some small thing tha[...] tracts from the enjoyment of something. [OE *flӯge*]

fly·blow (flī′blō′) *n.* The egg or young larva of a blo[...] deposited on food, etc. **—***v.t.* & *v.i.* **·blew, ·blown, ·b**[...] **ing 1.** To taint (food) with flyblows. **2.** To spoil.

fly-by (flī′bī′) *n. pl.* **-bys** *Aerospace* The passage of a sp[...] craft relatively near a heavenly body.

fly-by-night (flī′bī·nīt′) *adj.* Financially unsound. [...] One who cheats a creditor by departing secretly.

fly·catch·er (flī′kach′ər) *n.* Any of a large order of passe[...] birds of limited vocal powers and migratory habits.

fly·er (flī′ər) See FLIER.

fly-fish (flī′fish′) *v.i.* To fish with artificial flies as bait

fly·ing (flī′ing) *adj.* **1.** Capable of or adapted for fligh[...] the air. **2.** Moving or passing quickly, as if in flight. [...] Waving, streaming, or floating in or through the air. [...] Hurried: a *flying* trip. **5.** Pertaining to or used in aviat[...] **6.** *Naut.* Pertaining to sails not secured on all sides by s[...] or spars. **—***n.* The act of one who or that which flies

flying buttress *Archit.* A bracing structure, usu. a ban[...] stone carried by a rampant arch from a wall to a suppor[...] abutment and receiving the outward thrust of the wall.

flying fish A fish with large pectoral fins that enable [...] glide through the air for short distances.

flying jib *Naut.* A jib set out beyond the standing jib, o[...] extended boom called the **flying-jib boom.** For illus. [...] SCHOONER.

flying officer In the Commonwealth air forces, a com[...] sioned officer. See table at GRADE.

flying saucer Any of various objects of vaguely sauce[...] shape, alleged to have been seen flying at high altitudes [...] great speeds; an unidentified flying object (UFO).

flying squirrel A squirrel having a fold of skin connec[...] its front and back limbs, enabling it to glide.

flying start 1. In racing, the passing of the starting po[...] full speed. **2.** A speedy, efficient beginning.

fly·leaf (flī′lēf′) *n. pl.* **·leaves** (-lēvz′) A blank leaf a[...] beginning or end of a book, pamphlet, etc.

fly·pa·per (flī′pā′pər) *n.* A piece of paper coated wi[...] sticky poisonous substance, placed so as to catch or kill [...]

fly·speck (flī′spek′) *n.* **1.** The dot made by the excre[...] of a fly. **2.** Any slight speck. **—***v.t.* To mark with flysp[...]

fly·trap (flī′trap′) *n.* **1.** A trap for catching flies. [...] plant, as the Venus's-flytrap, that traps insects.

fly·weight (flī′wāt′) *n.* A boxer belonging to the ligh[...] weight class, weighing 112 pounds or less.

fly·wheel (flī′hwēl′) *n.* A wheel heavy enough to resist

changes of speed, used to secure uniform motion in the
king parts of a machine.
ımber *Photog.* A number obtained by dividing the focal
;th of a lens by its effective diameter: the smaller the
nber, the shorter the exposure required.
(fōl) *n.* One of the young of an animal of the horse
ily. —*v.t.* & *v.i.* To give birth to (a foal). [OE *fola*]
ı (fōm) *n.* **1.** A frothy mass of bubbles produced on the
ace of a liquid by agitation, fermentation, etc. **2.** A
ıy mass of saliva, etc. **3.** *Chem.* A colloid system of gas
ersed in a liquid. —*v.i.* **1.** To become foam or become
ered with foam. —*v.t.* **2.** To cause to foam. [OE *fām*]
ı rubber A firm, spongy rubber produced by chemical
tment and used esp. in mattresses, cushions, etc.
ı·y (fō′mē) *adj.* **foam·i·er, foam·i·est** **1.** Pertaining to,
sisting of, or resembling foam. **2.** Producing, covered
ı, or full of foam. —**foam′i·ly** *adv.* —**foam′i·ness** *n.*
(fob) *n.* **1.** A small pocket at the front waistline of
ısers or at the front of a vest, designed to hold a watch, a
ıll amount of change, etc. **2.** *U.S.* A short chain or rib-
attached to a watch and worn dangling from such a
ket; also, a small ornament attached to the dangling end
ıch a chain or ribbon. [Cf. dial. G *fuppe* pocket]
(fob) *v.t.* **fobbed, fob·bing** **1.** To dispose of by fraud or
xery: with *off.* **2.** To put off by lies, evasion, etc.; also,
ry deceitfully to appease: with *off.* [? < FOB[1]]
.l (fō′kəl) *adj.* Of or placed at a focus. —**fo′cal·ly** *adv.*
l distance *Optics* The distance from the center of a
or curved mirror to the point where rays from a distant
ct converge. Also **focal length.**
ıl·ize (fō′kəl·īz) *v.t.* & *v.i.* **·ized, ·iz·ing** **1.** To bring to a
s or become focused. **2.** *Med.* To confine or be confined
localized area of the body. —**fo′cal·i·za′tion** *n.*
s'le (fōk′səl) See FORECASTLE.
ıs (fō′kəs) *n.* *pl.* **·cus·es** or **·ci** (-sī) **1.** *Optics* **a** The
ıt (**real focus**) at
ch a system of
rays converges
r passage through
ıs or other optical
ıngement or after
ection from a mir-
b The point (**vir-**
focus) at which
ı rays appear to
erge and where
would meet if
r direction were
ersed. **2.** The ad-

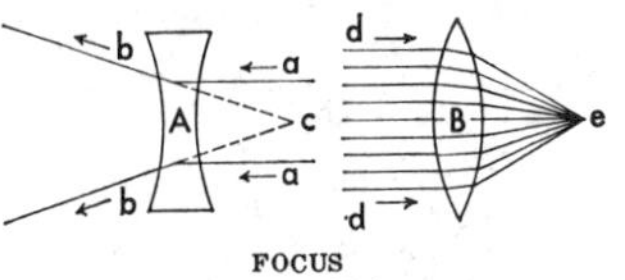

FOCUS
A Biconcave lens: light rays *a, a* refract as at *b, b* and form the virtual focus at *c.*
B Biconvex lens: light rays *d, d* converge to the real focus at *e.*

ment of the eye, a camera lens, etc., so that a clear image
roduced; also, the position of the viewed object. **3.** Focal
ance. **4.** Any central point, as of importance or interest.
Physics The meeting point of any system of rays, beams,
waves. **6.** *Geom.* **a** One of two points, the sum or differ-
of whose distances to a conic section is a constant. **b** A
ılar point in some other curve. —*v.* **·cused** or **·cussed,**
·ing or **·cus·sing** *v.t.* **1.** To adjust the focus of (the eye,
ıs, etc.) to receive a clear image. **2.** To fix; concentrate.
.i. **3.** To become focused. [< L, hearth]
ler (fod′ər) *n.* Coarse feed for horses, cattle, etc., as the
ks and leaves of field corn. —*v.t.* To feed with fodder.
fōdor]
(fō) *n.* An enemy; adversary. [Fusion of OE *fāh* hostile
gefā enemy]
nan (fō′mən) *n.* *pl.* **·men** (-mən) A foe.
al (fēt′l), **foe·tus** (fē′təs), etc. See FETAL, FETUS, etc.
(fog, fôg) *n.* **1.** A cloud of varying size formed at the
face of the earth by the condensation of atmospheric va-
and interfering to a greater or lesser extent with hori-
tal visibility. **2.** Any hazy condition of the atmosphere
sed by smoke, dust particles, etc. **3.** A state of mental
vilderment or blurred perception. **4.** *Photog.* A dark blur
ıding part or all of a developed print or plate. —*v.*
ged, fog·ging *v.t.* **1.** To surround with or as with fog. **2.**
confuse or bewilder. **3.** *Photog.* To cloud (a print or
e) with a dark blur. —*v.i.* **4.** To become enveloped by
overed with or as with fog. **5.** To become confused. **6.**
tog. Of a print or plate, to become clouded with a dark
r. [Prob. back formation < *foggy,* in the sense "marshy"]
bank A mass of fog seen at a distance, esp. at sea.
bound (fog′bound′, fôg′-) *adj.* Prevented from travel-
sailing, flying, etc., because of fog.
chamber *Physics* A cloud chamber.
gy (fog′ē, fôg′ē) *adj.* **·gi·er, ·gi·est** **1.** Full of or marked
fog. **2.** Resembling fog; cloudy. **3.** Mentally confused;
vildered. —**fog′gi·ly** *adv.* —**fog′gi·ness** *n.*
horn (fog′hôrn′, fôg′-) *n.* **1.** A horn or whistle for
nding a warning during a fog. **2.** A loud, harsh voice.

fo·gy (fō′gē) *n.* *pl.* **·gies** A person of old-fashioned or ultra-conservative notions: usu. preceded by *old.* Also **fo′gey, fo′·gie.** [? < FOGGY] —**fo′gy·ish** *adj.* —**fo′gy·ism** *n.*

foi·ble (foi′bəl) *n.* A personal weakness or failing. [< F, obs. var. of *faible* weak]

foil[1] (foil) *v.t.* **1.** To prevent the success of; thwart. **2.** In hunting, to cross and recross (a scent or trail) to confuse pursuers. —*n.* An animal's trail. [< OF *fouler, fuler* to crush < LL *fullare* to full cloth]

foil[2] (foil) *n.* **1.** A metal hammered or rolled into thin, pliant sheets. **2.** A leaf of bright metal set beneath an artificial or inferior gem to add brilliance or color. **3.** A person or thing serving by contrast to enhance the qualities of another. **4.** *Archit.* A division, space, or piece of tracery suggestive of a leaf. —*v.t.* **1.** To apply foil to; cover with foil. **2.** To intensify or set off by contrast. **3.** *Archit.* To adorn (windows, etc.) with foils. [< OF < L *folium* leaf]

foil[3] (foil) *n.* **1.** A blunted, rapierlike implement sometimes having a button on its end, used in fencing. **2.** *pl.* The art of fencing with a foil. [Origin uncertain]

foist (foist) *v.t.* **1.** To impose (someone or something) slyly or wrongfully; palm off. **2.** To insert or introduce fraudulently. [Prob. < dial. Du. *vuisten* hold in the hand]

fold[1] (fōld) *v.t.* **1.** To turn back or bend over so that one part covers or lies alongside another. **2.** To close or collapse: often with *up.* **3.** To wrap up; enclose. **4.** To place together and interlock: to *fold* one's hands; also, to bring (wings) close to the body. **5.** To embrace; enfold. **6.** To wind; coil: with *about, around,* etc. **7.** In cooking, to mix (beaten egg whites, etc.) into other ingredients by gently turning one part over the other: with *in.* —*v.i.* **8.** To become folded. **9.** *U.S. Slang* **a** To fail financially; close: The show *folded.* **b** To collapse, as from exhaustion. —*n.* **1.** One part folded over another. **2.** The space between two folded parts. **3.** The crease made by folding. **4.** The act of folding. **5.** *Anat.* A thin edge or slip of tissue folded over an organ or part. **6.** *Geol.* A bend in a layer of rock. [OE *fealdan*]

fold[2] (fōld) *n.* **1.** A pen, as for sheep. **2.** The sheep enclosed in a pen. **3.** A flock of sheep. **4.** A group of people, as the congregation of a church, having a leader, a common purpose, etc. —*v.t.* To shut up in a fold, as sheep. [OE *fald*]

-fold *suffix* **1.** Having (a specified number of) parts: a *three-fold* blessing. **2.** (A specified number of) times as great or as much: to reward *tenfold.* **3.** An amount multiplied by (a specified number): a *hundredfold.* [OE *fealdan* to fold]

fold·er (fōl′dər) *n.* **1.** One who or that which folds. **2.** A road map, timetable, etc., designed to be folded up into a small, compact form. **3.** A large binder for loose papers.

fol·de·rol (fol′də·rol) See FALDERAL.

fo·li·a·ceous (fō′lē·ā′shəs) *adj.* **1.** Of, pertaining to, or resembling the leaf of a plant: also **fo·li·ar** (fō′lē·ər). **2.** Made up of thin, laminated sheets.

fo·li·age (fō′lē·ij) *n.* **1.** The growth of leaves on a tree or other plant; also, leaves collectively. **2.** An ornamental representation of leaves, flowers, and branches. [Earlier *foillage* < F < L *folium* leaf] —**fo′li·aged** *adj.*

fo·li·ate (fō′lē·āt; *for adj.,* also fō′lē·it) *adj.* **1.** Having leaves. **2.** Foliaceous. —*v* **·at·ed, ·at·ing** *v.t.* **1.** To roll or hammer (gold, etc.) into thin plates. —*v.i.* **2.** To split into thin leaves or layers. **3.** To produce leaves, as a tree.

fo·li·a·tion (fō′lē·ā′shən′ *n.* **1.** *Bot.* **a** The act of bursting into leaf, or the state of being in leaf. **b** The arrangement or formation of leaves in a bud. **2.** *Geol.* In certain rocks, a crystalline formation into leaflike layers; also, the layers themselves. **3.** The consecutive numbering of the leaves of a book. Also **fo·li·a·ture** (fō′lē·ə·chŏŏr′).

fo·lic acid (fō′lik) *Biochem.* An orange-yellow crystalline compound, $C_{19}H_{19}N_7O_6$, included in the vitamin-B complex. It is found in green leaves, mushrooms, yeast, and some animal tissues: also *vitamin Bc.*

fo·li·o (fō′lē·ō) *n.* *pl.* **·li·os** **1.** A sheet of paper folded once to form four pages (two leaves) of a book, the height of the pages usu. ranging from 13 to 19 inches. **2.** A book, manuscript, etc., having the oversize pages made from such a sheet; also, the size of such a work. **3.** A leaf of a book, manuscript, etc., only one side of which is numbered. **4.** The page number of a book. —*adj.* Of, pertaining to, or being of the size of a folio. —*v.t.* **·li·oed, ·li·o·ing** To number in order the pages of (a book, manuscript, etc.).

fo·li·o·late (fō′lē·ə·lāt′) *adj.* *Bot.* Of, pertaining to, or composed of leaflets. [< L *foliolum,* dim. of *folium* leaf + -ATE[1]]

-folious *suffix of adjectives* Leaflike or leafy. [< L *folium* leaf]

folk (fōk) *n.* *pl.* **folk** or **folks** **1.** A people; nation. **2.** *Usu. pl.* People of a particular group or class: old *folks.* **3.** *pl. Informal* People in general. **4.** *pl. Informal* One's family, esp. one's parents —**Syn.** See PEOPLE. —*adj.* Originating among or characteristic of the common people. [OE *folc*]

folk dance 1. A dance originating among the common people of a district or country. 2. The music for such a dance.
folk etymology Popular modification of an unfamiliar word, thereby causing the word to correspond with better known forms, as *agnail* (in Middle English, a painful nail) becoming *hangnail.*
folk·lore (fōk′lôr′, -lōr′) *n.* 1. The traditions, beliefs, customs, sayings, stories, etc., preserved among the common people. 2. The study of folk cultures. **—folk′lor′ist** *n.*
folk music Music created and perpetuated by the common people.
folk singer One who sings folk songs.
folk song 1. A song, usu. of unknown authorship, originating among the common people and handed down orally. 2. A song copying the style of such a song.
folk·sy (fōk′sē) *adj.* **·si·er, ·si·est** *U.S. Informal* Friendly; sociable; unpretentious. **—folk′si·ness** *n.*
folk·ways (fōk′wāz′) *n.pl. Sociol.* The traditional habits, customs, and behavior of a group, tribe, or nation.
fol·li·cle (fol′i·kəl) *n.* 1. *Anat.* A small cavity or sac in certain parts of the body, having a protective or secretory function. 2. *Bot.* A dry seed vessel of one carpel. [< L, dim. of *follis* bag] **—fol·lic·u·lar** (fə·lik′yə·lər) *adj.*
fol·lic·u·lat·ed (fə·lik′yə·lā′tid) *adj.* 1. Having a follicle. 2. Encased in a cocoon. Also **fol·lic′u·late** (-lit).
fol·low (fol′ō) *v.t.* 1. To go or come after and in the same direction. 2. To succeed in time or order. 3. To pursue. 4. To hold to the course of: to *follow* a road. 5. To conform to: to *follow* the customs of a country. 6. To use or take as a model; imitate. 7. To watch or observe closely. 8. To have an active interest in: to *follow* sports. 9. To understand the course, sequence, or meaning of, as an explanation. 10. To come after as a consequence or result. 11. To work at as a profession or livelihood: men who *follow* the sea. 12. To be under the leadership or authority of. 13. To accompany; attend. —*v.i.* 14. To move or come after. 15. To pay attention. 16. To understand. 17. To come as a result or consequence. **—to follow out** 1. To follow to the end, as an argument. 2. To comply with, as orders or instructions. **—to follow suit** 1. In card games, to play a card of the suit led. 2. To follow another's example. **—to follow through** 1. To swing to the full extent of the stroke after having struck the ball, as in tennis or golf. 2. To perform fully. **—to follow up** 1. To pursue closely. 2. To bring to full completion. 3. To increase the effectiveness of by further action. —*n.* The act of following. [OE *folgian*]
fol·low·er (fol′ō·ər) *n.* One who or that which follows; as: **a** A pursuer. **b** A disciple or supporter. **c** A servant or attendant. **—Syn.** See ADHERENT. **—fol′low·er·ship′** *n.*
fol·low·ing (fol′ō·ing) *adj.* That comes next in time or sequence: the *following* week. —*n.* A body of adherents, attendants, or disciples.
fol·low-through (fol′ō·thrōō′) *n.* 1. In sports, the continuation and full completion of a motion; esp., in tennis and golf, the last part of the stroke after the ball has been hit. 2. Any continuing or completion.
fol·low-up (fol′ō·up′) *n.* 1. The act of following up. 2. Something, as an action, procedure, letter, etc., used in following up. —*adj.* Designed to follow up: a *follow-up* visit.
fol·ly (fol′ē) *n. pl.* **·lies** 1. The condition or state of being foolish; foolishness. 2. A foolish idea or action. 3. A foolish or ruinous undertaking. [< F < *fol* fool]
Fo·mal·haut (fô′məl·hôt) *n.* One of the 20 brightest stars, 1.29 magnitude; Alpha in the constellation Piscis Austrinus. [< F < Arabic *fom al-hūt* the whale's mouth]
fo·ment (fō·ment′) 1. To stir up or instigate (rebellion, discord, etc.). 2. To treat with warm water or medicated lotions, as in applying a poultice. [< F < LL < L *fomentum* poultice] **—fo′men·ta′tion** *n.* **—fo·ment′er** *n.*
fond (fond) *adj.* 1. Having affection (for someone or something specified): with *of.* 2. Loving or deeply affectionate. 3. Unwisely or indulgently affectionate; doting. 4. Affectionately nurtured; cherished. [ME *fonned*, pp. of *fonnen* to be foolish] **—fond′ly** *adv.*
fon·dant (fon′dənt, *Fr.* fôṅ·däṅ′) *n.* A soft, creamy confection. [< F, orig. ppr. of *fondre* to melt]
fon·dle (fon′dəl) *v.t.* **·dled, ·dling** To handle lovingly; caress. [Freq. of obs. *fond* to caress] **—fon′dler** *n.*
fond·ness (fond′nis) *n.* 1. Tender affection; liking. 2. Extravagant or foolish affection. 3. Strong preference.
fon·due (fon·dōō′, *Fr.* fôṅ·dü′) *n.* A dish made of grated cheese, cooked with eggs, butter, etc. [< F]
font[1] (font) *n.* 1. A basin, often of stone, for the water used in baptism. 2. A receptacle for holy water. 3. Source; origin. [OE < L *fons, fontis* fountain] **—font′al** *adj.*
font[2] (font) *n. Printing* A full assortment of type of a particular face and size: also, *Brit., fount.* [< F *fondre* to melt]
fon·ta·nel (fon′tə·nel′) *n. Anat.* A soft, pulsating, unossified area in the fetal and infantile skull. [< F *fontanelle*]
food (fōōd) *n.* 1. That which is eaten, drunk, or absorbed by an organism for the maintenance of life and the growth and repair of tissues. 2. Nourishment taken in more or solid form as opposed to liquid form. 3. A particular kir nourishment: breakfast *food.* 4. Anything that is used manner suggestive of food: intellectual *food.* [OE *fōda*
food poi·son·ing (poi′zən·ing) A gastrointestinal disc caused by certain bacterial toxins found in rancid or dec posed food: erroneously called *ptomaine poisoning.*
food·stuff (fōōd′stuf′) *n.* 1. Any substance suitabl food. 2. Any substance, as fat, protein, etc., that e into the composition of food.
fool (fōōl) *n.* 1. A person lacking understanding, judgm or common sense. 2. A clown formerly kept by noble for household entertainment; jester. 3. One who has duped or imposed upon. **—to be nobody's fool** *Info* To be shrewd. —*v.i.* 1. To act like a fool. 2. To speak, etc., in a playful or teasing manner. —*v.t.* 3 make a fool of; deceive. **—to fool around** or **about** *Info* 1. To waste time on trifles; putter. 2. To loiter about **—to fool with** *Informal* 1. To meddle with. 2. To or toy aimlessly with. —*adj. Informal* Stupid or silly. F < L *follis* a bellows; later, simpleton]
fool·er·y (fōō′lə·rē) *n. pl.* **·er·ies** Foolish behavior, sp etc.; also, an instance of this.
fool·har·dy (fōōl′här′dē) *adj.* **·di·er, ·di·est** Bold in a fo or reckless way. **—fool′har′di·ly** *adv.* **—fool′har′di·ne**
fool·ish (fōō′lish) *adj.* 1. Marked by or showing a la good sense; silly. 2. Resulting from folly or stupidity: *ish* consequences. 3. Utterly ridiculous; absurd. 4. *Ar* Insignificant. **—fool′ish·ly** *adv.* **—fool′ish·ness** *n.*
fool·proof (fōōl′prōōf′) *adj.* 1. So simple and strong be incapable of damage or harm even through misuse. Having no weak points; infallible: a *foolproof* plan.
fools·cap (fōōlz′kap) *n.* A writing paper measuring a 13 x 16 inches, usu. folded into a page measuring about 1 inches, so called from the watermark of a fool's cap.
fool's cap 1. A pointed cap, usu. with bells at its tip, merly worn by jesters. 2. A dunce cap.
fool's gold One of several metallic sulfides, as pyrite, re bling gold in color.
foot (fŏŏt) *n. pl.* **feet** (fēt) 1. The terminal section o limb of a vertebrate animal, upon which it stands or m ◆ Collateral adjective: *pedal.* 2. Any part, as of an inv brate animal or of a plant, piece of furniture, etc., c sponding in form or position to the foot. 3. The part boot or stocking that covers the wearer's foot. 4. The l part of anything; base; esp.: **a** The base of a hill or m tain. **b** The part of a bed, grave, etc., where the feet re The bottom of a page, ladder, etc. **d** *Naut.* The lower of a sail. 5. The last part of a series; end. 6. The inf part or section: the *foot* of the class. 7. A measure of le equivalent to 12 inches: symbol (′). See table fron book. 8. In prosody, a group of syllables having a prir stress or accent on one of the syllables and forming a n unit of poetic rhythm. 9. Foot soldiers, collectively fantry. 10. Step or manner of movement: a light *foot.* **on foot** 1. Walking or standing. 2. In progress. **—t one's best foot forward** 1. To do one's best. 2. To t look one's best. **—to put one's foot down** To act fir **—to put one's foot in it** or **in one's mouth** To make an barrassing mistake or blunder. —*v.i.* To walk or d often with indefinite *it.* —*v.t.* 3. To move on or throug foot. 4. To furnish with a foot, as a stocking. 5. *Info* To pay, as a bill. 6. To add, as a column of figures: with *up.* [OE *fōt*] **—foot′less** *adj.*
foot·age (fŏŏt′ij) *n.* The extent of something as meas in linear feet.
foot-and-mouth disease (fŏŏt′ən·mouth′) *Vet.* A tagious virus disease of cattle, swine, etc., marked by and blisters about the mouth and hoofs.
foot·ball (fŏŏt′bôl′) *n.* 1. *U.S.* A game played bet two teams of eleven men on a field with goals at each en which points are made by carrying the ball across the ponent's goal line or by kicking the ball over the oppon goal posts. 2. The ball used in this game, an infl leather-covered ball with an ellipsoidal shape. 3. *Cana* A similar game played by teams of twelve men: also c *rugby, rugby football.* 4. In Great Britain: **a** Rugby foo (def. 1); also, the ball. **b** Soccer; also, the inflated ball.
foot·board (fŏŏt′bôrd′, -bōrd′) *n.* 1. A board or small form on which to prop or rest the feet. 2. An upright at the foot of a bedstead.
foot-can·dle (fŏŏt′kan′dəl) *n.* The illumination throw one square foot of surface, all points of which are at a tance of one foot from one international candle.
foot·ed (fŏŏt′id) *adj.* 1. Having a foot or feet: a *footed* let. 2. Having or characterized by a (specified kind of) or (a specified number of) feet: *light-footed; four-footed.*
foot·er (fŏŏt′ər) *n.* One who or that which has an indic number of linear feet in height or length: a *six-footer.*
foot·fall (fŏŏt′fôl′) *n.* The sound of a footstep.
foot·hill (fŏŏt′hil′) *n.* A low hill at the base of a moun

·hold (fo͝ot′hōld′) *n.* **1.** A place on which the foot can ; securely, as in climbing. **2.** A good, firm position from ch one can begin or carry forward some course of action.
·ing (fo͝ot′ing) *n.* **1.** A place on which to stand, walk, or ıb securely. **2.** A secure support for the foot; foothold. An established or secure position or foundation. **4.** So- or professional status in relation to others; standing. **5.** act of adding a foot to something, as a shoe; also, the erial used for this. **6.** The adding up of a column of res; also, the sum obtained. **7.** *Archit.* A base or founda- wider than the structure it supports, as for a pedestal.
·lights (fo͝ot′līts′) *n.pl.* **1.** Lights in a row near the t of the stage of a theater, nearly level with the per- ners' feet. **2.** The profession of acting on the stage.
·loose (fo͝ot′lo͞os′) *adj.* Free to travel or do as one ses; unattached.
·man (fo͝ot′mən) *n. pl.* **·men** (-mən) A male servant very who answers the door, waits at table, etc.
·note (fo͝ot′nōt′) *n.* An explanatory note, reference, or ment on the text, usu. appearing at the bottom of a e. — *v.t.* **·not·ed, ·not·ing** To furnish with footnotes.
·path (fo͝ot′path′, -päth′) *n.* **1.** A path to be used only persons on foot. **2.** *Brit.* A sidewalk.
·pound (fo͝ot′pound′) *n. Mech.* A unit of energy, equal he amount of energy necessary to raise a one-pound s through one linear foot.
print (fo͝ot′print′) *n.* The outline or impression made ı foot treading on a surface.
rest (fo͝ot′rest′) *n* Something, as a small stool or plat- n, on which the feet can be propped or rested.
soldier A soldier trained and equipped to fight on foot.
sore (fo͝ot′sôr, -sōr′) *adj.* Having sore or tired feet.
·step (fo͝ot′step′) *n.* **1.** The action of taking a step with foot. **2.** The distance covered by a foot in stepping. **3.** sound made by a foot in stepping. **4.** A footprint. **5.** ep of a stairway, etc. — **to follow in someone's foot- s 1.** To repeat or duplicate the work or actions of an- r. **2.** To succeed to another's position.
stool (fo͝ot′sto͞ol′) *n.* A low stool on which the feet can ested while one is sitting.
·wear (fo͝ot′wâr′) *n.* Articles worn on the feet, as shoes.
work (fo͝ot′wûrk′) *n.* Use or control of the feet, as in ing or tennis.
·le (fo͞o′zəl) *v.t. & v.i.* **·zled, ·zling** To do awkwardly; ıble. — *n.* A misstroke or misplay, esp. in golf. [Cf. G *fuseln* to work badly] — **foo′zler** *n.*
fop) *n.* A man overly fastidious in dress or deportment; ındy. [Cf. Du. *foppen* to cheat] — **fop′pish** *adj.* — **pish·ly** *adv.* — **fop′pish·ness** *n.*
per·y (fop′ər·ē) *n. pl.* **·per·ies 1.** The conduct or ways fop. **2.** Something worn by or typical of a fop.
fôr, *unstressed* fər) *prep.* **1.** To the extent of: The ground at *for* miles. **2.** Through the duration or period of: *for* a k. **3.** To the number or amount of: a check *for* six dol- **4.** At the cost or payment of: a hat *for* ten dollars. **5.** account of: He is respected *for* his ability. **6.** In honor He is named *for* his grandfather. **7.** Appropriate to: a e *for* work. **8.** In place of: using a book *for* a desk. **9.** avor, support, or approval of. **10.** In the interest or be- of. **11.** Directed toward: an eye *for* bargains. **12.** As cting (in a particular way): good *for* your health. **13.** t, given, or assigned to. **14.** In proportion to: big *for* his **15.** As the equivalent to or requital of: blow *for* blow. In spite of. **17.** In order to reach or go toward: He left his office. **18.** In order to find or obtain: looking *for* a **19.** At (a particular time or occasion): to meet *for* the time. **20.** As being or seeming: We took him *for* an est man. **21.** In consideration of the usual character- s of: She is strong *for* a woman. **22.** With the purpose walking *for* exercise. — **O for . . . !** Would that I had! *onj.* Inasmuch as; because. [OE]
prefix **1.** Away; off (in a privative sense): *forget, forgo.* Very; extremely; *forlorn.* [OE]
See also words beginning FORE-.
ıge (fôr′ij, for′-) *n.* **1.** Food suitable for cattle or other nestic animals; fodder. **2.** A searching about for food or plies; also, a raid to find or capture provisions. — *v.* **ed, ·ag·ing** *v.i.* **1.** To search about or rummage around something, esp. for food or supplies. **2.** To make a raid s to find or capture supplies. — *v.t.* **3.** To search through food, supplies, etc. **4.** To obtain by plundering or rum- ging about. **5.** To provide with food or supplies. [< F *feurre* fodder] — **for′ag·er** *n.*
ı·men (fō·rā′mən) *n. pl.* **·ram·i·na** (-ram′ə·nə) *Biol.* mall opening or hole, usu. natural, as in a bone. [< L < *re* to bore]
ı·min·i·fer (fôr′ə·min′ə·fər, for′-) *n.* One of a large er of extremely tiny unicellular marine animals, usu. hav- ing bony shells perforated with many minute holes. [< L *foramen, -inis* hole + *-fer* having] — **fo·ram·i·nif·er·al** (fə·ram′ə·nif′ər·əl), **fo·ram′i·nif′er·ous** *adj.*

for·as·much as (fôr′əz·much′) Inasmuch as; since.

for·ay (fôr′ā, for′ā) *v.t. & v.i.* To plunder; raid. — *n.* An expedition or raid, as for plunder. [Prob. back formation < *forayer* raider < OF *feurre* fodder] — **for′ay·er** *n.*

for·bear[1] (fôr·bâr′) *v.* **·bore, ·borne, ·bear·ing** *v.t.* **1.** To refrain or abstain from (some action). **2.** To cease or desist from. — *v.i.* **3.** To abstain. **4.** To be patient. [OE] — **for·bear′er** *n.*

for·bear[2] (fôr′bâr′) See FOREBEAR.

for·bear·ance (fôr·bâr′əns) *n.* **1.** The act of forbearing. **2.** The quality of being forbearing; patience.

for·bear·ing (fôr·bâr′ing) *adj.* Disposed to forbear; patient.

for·bid (fər·bid′, fôr-) *v.t.* **·bade** (-bad′) or **·bad, ·bid·den** (*Archaic* **·bid**), **·bid·ding 1.** To command (a person) not to do something, etc.; prohibit from doing, having, etc. **2.** To prohibit the doing, use, etc., of. **3.** To have the effect of preventing; making impossible, impractical, etc. [OE *forbēodan*] — **for·bid′al, for·bid′dance** *n.*

for·bid·den (fər·bid′n, fôr-) *adj.* Not allowed; prohibited.

for·bid·ding (fər·bid′ing, fôr-) *adj.* **1.** Grim and unfriendly in appearance: a *forbidding* face. **2.** Having a threatening or ominous look: a *forbidding* swamp. — **for·bid′ding·ly** *adv.*

for·bore (fôr·bôr′, -bōr′) Past tense of FORBEAR[1].

for·borne (fôr·bôrn′, -bōrn′) Past participle of FORBEAR[1].

force (fôrs, fōrs) *n.* **1.** Power or energy; strength: the *force* of a gale. **2.** Power exerted on any resisting person or thing; also, the use of such power; coercion. **3.** The quality of anything that tends to produce an effect on the mind or will. **4.** Any moral, social, or political power or influence. **5.** A body of individuals belonging to one of a nation's military, naval, or air divisions: the armed *forces.* **6.** Any body of individuals organized for some specific work: police *force.* **7.** *Law* Binding effect; validity: the *force* of a contract. **8.** *Physics* Anything that changes or tends to change the state of rest or motion in a body. — **in (full) force 1.** Still operative or enforceable, as a law. **2.** With no one missing. — *v.t.* **forced, forc·ing 1.** To compel to do something; coerce. **2.** To get or obtain by or as by force. **3.** To bring forth or about by or as by effort: to *force* a smile. **4.** To drive or move despite resistance. **5.** To assault and capture, as a fortification. **6.** To break open, as a door or lock. **7.** To make, as a passage or way, by force. **8.** To press or impose upon someone as by force. **9.** To exert to the utmost; strain, as the voice. **10.** To rape. **11.** To stimulate the growth of artificially, as plants in a hothouse. **12.** In baseball: **a** To put out (a base runner compelled to leave one base for the next). **b** To cause (the base runner on third base) to score by walking the batter when the bases are full. **c** To allow (a run) in such a manner. **13.** In card games: **a** To compel (a player) to choose between losing a trick or playing a trump from his hand. **b** To play so as to compel (a player) to reveal the strength of a hand held. [< F < L *fortis* brave, strong] — **force′a·ble** *adj.* — **forc′er** *n.*

forced (fôrst, fōrst) *adj.* **1.** Done under force; compulsory: *forced* labor. **2.** Strained; affected: *forced* gaiety. **3.** Done in an emergency: a *forced* landing of an airplane.

force·ful (fôrs′fəl, fōrs′-) *adj.* Full of or done with force; vigorous; effective. — **force′ful·ly** *adv.* — **force′ful·ness** *n.*

force·meat (fôrs′mēt′, fōrs′-) *n.* Finely chopped, seasoned meat served separately or used as stuffing. [< *force,* alter. of FARCE, V. + MEAT]

for·ceps (fôr′səps) *n.* A pair of pincers for grasping and manipulating small or delicate objects, used by surgeons, dentists, etc. [< L < *formus* warm + *capere* to take]

for·ci·ble (fôr′sə·bəl) *adj.* **1.** Accomplished or brought about by force: a *forcible* exit. **2.** Characterized by or having force; vigorous. — **forc′i·ble·ness** *n.* — **for′ci·bly** *adv.*

ford (fôrd, fōrd) *n.* A shallow place in a stream, river, etc., that can be crossed by wading. — *v.t.* To cross (a river, stream, etc.) at a shallow place. [OE] — **ford′a·ble** *adj.*

fore (fôr, fōr) *adj.* Situated at or toward the front in relation to something else: the *fore* and hind legs of a horse. — *n.* **1.** The front part of something. **2.** *Naut.* A foremast; also, the bows of a ship. — **to the fore 1.** To or at the front part of something. **2.** In or into a prominent or conspicuous position. — *interj.* In golf, a cry made to warn anyone standing in the line of a ball. — *adv. Naut.* At or toward the bow of a ship. — *prep. & conj. Archaic* or *Dial.* Before: also **'fore.** [OE, adv. & prep.]

fore-[1] *prefix* **1.** Prior in time, place, or rank; as in:

foreacquaint	**foreanswer**	**foreconclude**

2. Situated at or near the front; as in:

forebody	**forecabin**	**forecourt**

[OE *fore-, for-* before]

fore-[2] See also words beginning FOR-.

fore-and-aft (fôr′ən·aft′, fôr′-, -äft′) *adj. Naut.* Lying or going in the direction of a ship's length: a *fore-and-aft* sail.
fore and aft *Naut.* **1.** Lengthwise of a boat. **2.** In, at, or toward both the stem and the stern of a boat.
fore·arm[1] (fôr′ärm′, fōr′-) *n.* The part of the arm between the elbow and the wrist. ◆ Collateral adjective: *cubital.*
fore·arm[2] (fôr·ärm′, fōr-) *v.t.* To arm beforehand.
fore·bear (fôr′bâr, fōr′-) *n.* An ancestor: also spelled *forbear.* [Earlier *for-be-er*]
fore·bode (fôr·bōd′, fōr-) *v.t. & v.i.* **·bod·ed, ·bod·ing 1.** To indicate in advance; portend. **2.** To have a premonition of (something evil or harmful). [< FORE-[1] + BODE[2]]
fore·brain (fôr′brān′, fōr′-) *n. Anat.* The prosencephalon.
fore·cast (fôr′kast′, -käst′, fōr′-) *v.t.* **·cast** or **·cast·ed, ·cast·ing 1.** To calculate beforehand; especially, to predict (weather conditions). **2.** To foreshadow. **3.** To arrange or plan beforehand. — *n.* **1.** A calculated prediction of weather conditions. **2.** A prediction or prophecy. — **fore′cast′er** *n.*
fore·cas·tle (fōk′səl) *n. Naut.* **1.** That part of the upper deck of a ship located forward of the mast nearest the bow. **2.** A section of a merchant ship near the bow, in which the sailors' living quarters are located. Also spelled *fo'c's'le.*
fore·close (fôr·klōz′, fōr-) *v.* **·closed, ·clos·ing** *v.t.* **1.** *Law* **a** To deprive (a mortgager in default) of the right to redeem mortgaged property. **b** To take away the power to redeem (a mortgage or pledge). **2.** To shut out; exclude. — *v.i.* **3.** To foreclose a mortgage. [< OF *forclore* to exclude]
fore·clo·sure (fôr·klō′zhər, fōr-) *n.* The act of foreclosing.
fore·deck (fôr′dek′, fōr′-) *n. Naut.* The forward part of a deck, especially of an upper deck.
fore·doom (*v.* fôr·do͞om′, fōr-; *n.* fôr′do͞om′, fōr′-) *v.t.* To doom or condemn in advance. — *n.* Preordained doom.
fore·fa·ther (fôr′fä′thər, fōr′-) *n.* An ancestor.
fore·fin·ger (fôr′fing′gər, fōr′-) *n.* The finger next to the thumb; index finger.
fore·foot (fôr′fo͝ot′, fōr′-) *n. pl.* **·feet 1.** One of the front feet of an animal, insect, etc. **2.** *Naut.* The part of a boat where the prow and keel meet.
fore·front (fôr′frunt′, fōr′) *n.* **1.** The very front of something. **2.** The position of most prominence, activity, etc.
fore·gath·er (fôr·gath′ər, fōr-) See FORGATHER.
fore·go[1] (fôr·gō′, fōr-) *v.t. & v.i.* **·went, ·gone, ·go·ing** To go before or precede in time, place, etc. [OE *foregān*]
fore·go[2] (fôr·gō′, fōr-) See FORGO.
fore·go·ing (fôr·gō′ing, fōr-; fôr′gō′ing, fōr′-) *adj.* Said, written, or done previously; preceding; antecedent.
fore·gone (fôr·gôn′, fōr·gon′; fôr′gôn′, fōr′gon′) *adj.* Already gone or finished; also, previous or past: *foregone* eras.
foregone conclusion **1.** A conclusion determined in advance of the evidence. **2.** A foreseen or inevitable result.
fore·ground (fôr′ground′, fōr′-) *n.* **1.** The part of a landscape, picture, etc., nearest or represented as nearest to the spectator. **2.** The position of most prominence or activity.
fore·hand (fôr′hand′, fōr′-) *adj.* **1.** Of or pertaining to a stroke in tennis, etc., in which the palm of the hand holding the racket faces the direction of the stroke. **2.** First or foremost; leading. — *n.* **1.** A forehand stroke, as in tennis. **2.** A position of advantage.
fore·hand·ed (fôr′han′did, fōr′-) *adj.* **1.** *U.S.* Prudent; thrifty. **2.** Done in good time. — **fore′hand′ed·ness** *n.*
fore·head (fôr′id, for′-; *occasionally* fôr′hed′) *n.* **1.** The part of the face from the eyebrows to the hair. ◆ Collateral adjective: *frontal.* **2.** The front part of anything.
for·eign (fôr′in, for′-) *adj.* **1.** Belonging to, located in, characteristic of, or concerned with another country, region, society, etc. **2.** Unfamiliar; strange: Anything mechanical is *foreign* to him. **3.** Having little or no relation; not pertinent. **4.** Occurring in a place or body in which it is not normally found. [< F *forain,* ult. < L *foras* out of doors]
foreign affairs Matters of diplomacy, commerce, etc., in the dealings of one country or nation with another.
for·eign-born (fôr′in·bôrn′, for′-) *adj.* Born in a foreign country or state; not native to a country or region.
for·eign·er (fôr′in·ər, for′-) *n.* A native or citizen of a foreign country or region; alien. — **Syn.** See ALIEN.
foreign office The department of government in charge of foreign affairs.
fore·judge (fôr·juj′, fōr-) *v.t. & v.i.* **·judged, ·judg·ing** To judge in advance.
fore·know (fôr·nō′, fōr-) *v.t.* **·knew, ·known, ·know·ing** To know beforehand. — **fore′knowl′edge** *n.*
fore·land (fôr′land′, fōr′-) *n.* A projecting point of land.
fore·leg (fôr′leg′, fōr′-) *n.* One of the front legs of an animal, insect, etc. Also **fore′limb′** (-lim′).
fore·lock (fôr′lok′, fōr′-) *n.* A lock of hair growing over the forehead.
fore·man (fôr′mən, fōr′-) *n. pl.* **·men** (-mən) **1.** The overseer of a body of workmen. **2.** The chairman and spokesman of a jury. — **fore′man·ship** *n.*
fore·mast (fôr′mast′, -mäst′, -məst, fōr′-) *n. Naut.* The mast that is closest to the bow of a ship.

fore·most (fôr′mōst, -məst, fōr′-) *adj.* First in place, rank, or order; chief. — *adv.* In the chief or principal p rank, etc. [OE *formest*]
fore·named (fôr′nāmd′, fōr′-) *adj.* Previously nam mentioned; aforesaid.
fore·noon (fôr′no͞on′, fōr′-; fôr·no͞on′, fōr-) *n.* The p of daylight preceding midday, esp. the later business h morning. — *adj.* Of or occurring in the forenoon.
fo·ren·sic (fə·ren′sik) *adj.* Relating to, characteristic used in courts of justice or public debate. [< L *f* market place, forum] — **fo·ren′si·cal·ly** *adv.*
forensic medicine Medical jurisprudence.
fore·or·dain (fôr′ôr·dān′, fōr′-) *v.t.* **1.** To decree or ap in advance. **2.** To fix the fate of in advance. — **for dain′ment, fore·or·di·na·tion** (fôr·ôr′də·nā′shən, fōr-) *n*
fore·part (fôr′pärt′, fōr′-) *n.* The first part in time, p or order. Also **fore part.**
fore·quar·ter (fôr′kwôr′tər, fōr′-) *n.* The front porti a side of beef, etc., including the leg and adjacent par
fore·reach (fôr·rēch′, fōr-) *v.t.* **1.** To catch up wi get ahead of, as a ship. — *v.i.* **2.** To catch up with or ahead of a ship, etc.: usu. with *on, upon.*
fore·run (fôr·run′, fōr-) *v.t.* **·ran, ·run, ·run·ning** foreshadow; herald. **2.** To precede. **3.** To forestall.
fore·run·ner (fôr·run′ər, fōr-, fôr′run′ər, fōr′-) *n.* **1.** who or that which precedes another; also, a forefath ancestor. **2.** One who proclaims the coming of anothe An advance indication of something; omen.
fore·sail (fôr′sāl′, -səl, fōr′-, fō′səl) *n. Naut.* **1.** The l sail on the foremast of a square-rigged vessel. **2.** The and-aft sail on a schooner's foremast, set on a boom gaff. For illus. see SCHOONER.
fore·see (fôr·sē′, fōr-) *v.t.* **·saw, ·seen, ·see·ing** To s know in advance. — **fore·see′a·ble** *adj.* — **for·se′er**
fore·shad·ow (fôr·shad′ō, fōr-) *v.t.* To give an adv indication or suggestion of; presage. — **fore·shad′ow**
fore·sheet (fôr′shēt′, fōr′-) *n. Naut.* **1.** A rope ho one of the clews of a foresail. **2.** *pl.* A boat's forward s
fore·shore (fôr′shôr′, fōr′shōr′) *n.* That part of a s uncovered at low tide.
fore·short·en (fôr·shôr′tən, fōr-) *v.t.* In drawing, to sh parts of the representation of (an object) so as to creat illusion of depth and distance.
fore·sight (fôr′sīt′, fōr′-) *n.* **1.** The act or capacity of seeing; also, a look directed toward something distant. Prudent anticipation of the future. — **fore′sight′ed** — **fore′sight′ed·ly** *adv.* — **fore′sight′ed·ness** *n.*
fore·skin (fôr′skin′, fōr′-) *n. Anat.* The prepuce.
for·est (fôr′ist, for′-) *n.* A large tract of land covered a growth of trees and underbrush; also, the trees thems — *adj.* Of, pertaining to, or inhabiting forests; sylvan. *v.t.* To plant with trees; make a forest of. [< OF < M (*silva*) *foresta* an unenclosed (wood)]
fore·stall (fôr·stôl′, fōr-) *v.t.* **1.** To hinder, preve guard against in advance. **2.** To deal with, think of, or ize beforehand; anticipate. **3.** To buy up (goods) for r ing. — **Syn.** See PREVENT. [OE *foresteall* ambush]
for·est·a·tion (fôr′is·tā′shən, for′-) *n.* **1.** The planti trees so as to make a forest. **2.** The science of forestr
fore·stay (fôr′stā′, fōr′-) *n. Naut.* A wire or rope ru from the head of the foremast to the stem and used marily to support the mast.
for·est·er (fôr′is·tər, for′-) *n.* **1.** One skilled in forest in charge of a forest. **2.** An animal dwelling in a fore
for·est·ry (fôr′is·trē, for′-) *n.* **1.** The science of pla and managing forests. **2.** Forest land.
fore·taste (*n.* fôr′tāst′, fōr′-; *v.* fôr·tāst′, fōr-) *n.* A vance experiencing or sampling of something. — *v.t.* have a foretaste of; taste in advance.
fore·tell (fôr·tel′, fōr-) *v.t. & v.i.* **·told, ·tell·ing** To tell about in advance; utter a prophecy of; predict. — See PROPHESY. — **fore·tell′er** *n.*
fore·thought (fôr′thôt′, fōr′-) *n.* **1.** Advance deliber or consideration. **2.** Prudence; foresight.
fore·top (fôr′top′, fōr′-; *Naut.* fôr′təp, fōr′-) *n. Nau* platform at the top of the lower section of a foremast.
fore·top·gal·lant (fôr′tə·gal′ənt, fōr′-) *adj. Naut.* pertaining to, or designating the mast, sail, yard, etc. mediately above the foretopmast.
fore·top·mast (fôr·top′məst, fōr-) *n. Naut.* The secti a mast above the foretop.
fore·top·sail (fôr·top′səl, fōr-) *n. Naut.* The sail set o foretopmast.
for·ev·er (fôr·ev′ər, fər-) *adv.* **1.** Throughout eternit the end of time. **2.** Incessantly; constantly.
for·ev·er·more (fôr·ev′ər·môr′, -mōr′, fər-) *adv.* For an intensive form. Also **for evermore.**
fore·warn (fôr·wôrn′, fōr-) *v.t.* To warn in advance.
fore·word (fôr′wûrd′, fōr′-) *n.* A prefatory statement ceding the text of a book.
for·feit (fôr′fit) *n.* **1.** Something taken away or give

a penalty for an offense, shortcoming, error, etc.; fine. **2.** ɩe giving up or loss of something as a penalty for an of- ɩse, etc. **—** *v.t.* To incur the deprivation of as a penalty · an offense, mistake, etc. **—** *adj.* Taken away or lost as a nalty for some offense, etc. [< OF *forfait* misdeed] **—** **·/feit·a·ble** *adj.* **— for/feit·er** *n.*

·fei·ture (fôr/fi·chər) *n.* **1.** The giving up or loss of nething by way of penalty. **2.** That which is forfeited.

·gath·er (fôr·gath/ər) *v.i.* **1.** To meet or gather to- :her; assemble. **2.** To meet by chance. **3.** To associate converse socially. Also spelled *foregather.*

·gave (fər·gāv/, fôr-) Past tense of FORGIVE.

ge[1] (fôrj, fōrj) *n.* **1.** An apparatus in which intense heat maintained, used for heating and softening metal to be ɪrked into shape. **2.** A workshop or factory in which such apparatus is used. **3.** A furnace for melting or refining ·tals, as in the production of wrought iron. **—** *v.* **forged, ·g·ing** *v.t.* **1.** To heat (metal) in a forge and work into ape; also, to produce or form as if by hammering into ape. **2.** To produce, change, or imitate so as to deceive; ecially, to counterfeit (a signature, etc.). **—** *v.i.* **3.** To ɔduce an imitation of something; esp. to counterfeit a nature, etc. **4.** To work at a forge. [< OF, ult. < L *rica* fabric] **— forg/er** *n.*

ge[2] (fôrj, fōrj) *v.i.* **forged, forg·ing** To move steadily ·ward in spite of difficulties, etc. [? Alter. of FORCE]

ger·y (fôr/jər·ē, fōr/-) *n. pl.* **·ger·ies** **1.** The act of ɩking imitations of works of art, writings, signatures, etc., · fraudulent purposes. **2.** A fraudulent imitation.

·get (fər·get/, fôr-) *v.* **·got, ·got·ten** or **·got, ·get·ting** *v.t.* To be unable to recall (something previously known). **2.** ɩ neglect (to do or take something). **3.** To lose interest in regard for. **—** *v.i.* **4.** To lose remembrance of something. **to forget oneself** **1.** To be unselfish. **2.** To lose self- ntrol and act in an unbecoming manner. **3.** To be lost in ɔught. [OE *forgietan*] **— for·get/ta·ble** *adj.*

·get·ful (fər·get/fəl, fôr-) *adj.* **1.** Inclined to forget. **2.** eglectful; inattentive. **3.** *Poetic* Producing forgetfulness. **for·get/ful·ly** *adv.* **— for·get/ful·ness** *n.*

·get-me-not (fər·get/mē·not/) *n.* A small herb having ɩe or white flowers growing in clusters.

give (fər·giv/, fôr-) *v.* **·gave, ·giv·en, ·giv·ing** *v.t.* **1.** To ant pardon for or remission of (something). **2.** To cease blame or feel resentment against. **3.** To remit, as a debt. *v.i.* **4.** To show forgiveness; grant pardon. [OE *forgie- a*] **— for·giv/a·ble** *adj.* **— for·giv/er** *n.*

·give·ness (fər·giv/nis, fôr-) *n.* **1.** The act of forgiving, the state of being forgiven. **2.** A disposition to forgive.

·giv·ing (fər·giv/ing, fôr-) *adj.* Disposed to forgive; ɛrciful. **— for·giv/ing·ly** *adv.* **— for·giv/ing·ness** *n.*

go (fôr·gō/) *v.t.* **·went, ·gone, ·go·ing** To give up or re- ɩin from; go without. Also spelled *forego.* [OE *forgān* to ss over] **— for·go/er** *n.*

·got (fər·got/, fôr-) Past tense and alternative past ɩrticiple of FORGET.

·got·ten (fər·got/n, fôr-) Past participle of FORGET.

k (fôrk) *n.* **1.** An implement consisting of a handle at e end of which are two or more prongs; as: **a** A utensil ed at table. **b** An agricultural tool used for digging, lifting, ssing, etc. **2.** The division of something into two or more parately continued parts; also, the point at which this di- sion begins, or any one of the parts. **—** *v.t.* **1.** To convey, t, toss, etc., with or as with a fork. **2.** To give the shape a fork to. **—** *v.i.* **3.** To branch into two or more separate- continued parts. [OE *forca* < L *furca*]

·ked (fôrkt, *Poetic* fôr/kid) *adj.* Having a fork or forking ɩrts; also, sharply angled; zigzag.

·lorn (fôr·lôrn/, fər·) *adj.* **1.** Left in distress; abandoned. Wretched; cheerless; desolate. **3.** Hopeless. **4.** Bereft: ith *of.* [Orig. pp. of obs. *forlese* to lose, abandon] **— for· rn/ly** *adv.* **— for·lorn/ness** *n.*

m (fôrm) *n.* **1.** The shape or contour of something as stinguished from its substance or color; external structure. The body of a living being. **3.** A mold, frame, etc., that ves shape to something. **4.** The particular state, charac- r, etc., in which something presents itself: energy in the *rm* of light. **5.** A specific type or species: a *form* of govern- ent. **6.** The style or manner of a poem, play, picture, etc.: aditional *forms.* **7.** Proper arrangement or order. **8.** The anner in which something is done: diving *form.* **9.** Fitness mind or body for performance: He is in good *form.* **10.** A ɔcument having spaces for the insertion of names, dates, :c.: an application *form.* **11.** An established method of oing something. **12.** Mere outward formality; convention. **3.** A model formula or draft, as of a letter. **14.** A pre- ribed order of words, as in religious ceremonies, etc. **15.** *'hilos.* The intrinsic nature of something; essence. **16.** *ram.* Any of the various shapes assumed by a word in a particular context, as *talk, talks, talked, talking.* **17.** *Printing* The body of type and cuts secured in a chase. **18.** *Brit.* A grade or class in school. **—** *v.t.* **1.** To give shape or form to; mold; fashion. **2.** To construct in the mind; devise: to *form* a plan. **3.** To combine or organize into: to *form* a club. **4.** To develop or acquire, as a habit. **5.** To be an element of. **—** *v.i.* **6.** To take shape; assume a specific form or arrangement. **7.** To begin to exist. [< OF < L *forma*]

-form *combining form* Like; in the shape of: *cuneiform.* [< L *-formis* -like < *forma* form]

for·mal[1] (fôr/məl) *adj.* **1.** Of, pertaining to, or based on established methods, models, or forms: *formal* procedure. **2.** Marked by and requiring more or less elaborate detail, ceremony, dress, etc.: a *formal* dinner. **3.** Appropriate for elaborate or state occasions: *formal* attire. **4.** Extremely regular and well-proportioned as to form, design, etc.: a *formal* garden. **5.** Adhering to rule, convention, or etiquette. **6.** Of or pertaining to external appearance, manner, or form: the *formal* elements of a poem. **7.** Binding and valid: a *formal* agreement. **8.** Pertaining to study in regular academic institutions or classes: a *formal* education. **9.** Pertaining to or characterized by language of a more complex and elaborate construction and vocabulary than that of informal speech or writing. **—** *n.* Something formal in character, as an evening gown. **— for/mal·ly** *adv.*

for·mal·de·hyde (fôr·mal/də·hīd) *n. Chem.* A colorless, pungent gas, CH_2O, used in solution as an antiseptic, preservative, etc. [< FORM(IC) + ALDEHYDE]

for·mal·ism (fôr/məl·iz/əm) *n.* Scrupulous observance of prescribed forms, as in religious worship, social life, art, etc. **— for/mal·ist** *n.* **— for/mal·is/tic** *adj.*

for·mal·i·ty (fôr·mal/ə·tē) *n. pl.* **·ties** **1.** The state or quality of being formal. **2.** Adherence to rules, conventions, forms, etc. **3.** Excessive devotion to outward form. **4.** A proper or customary act, method, practice, or observance.

for·mal·ize (fôr/məl·īz) *v.* **·ized, ·iz·ing** *v.t.* **1.** To make formal. **2.** To give form to. **—** *v.i.* **3.** To be formal; act formally. **— for/mal·i·za/tion** *n.* **— for/mal·iz/er** *n.*

for·mat (fôr/mat) *n.* **1.** The form, size, type face, margins, and general style of a publication. **2.** The general form or arrangement of anything. [< F < L *formare* to form]

for·ma·tion (fôr·mā/shən) *n.* **1.** The act or process of forming, or the state of being formed. **2.** That which is formed. **3.** The manner in which a thing is shaped or formed. **4.** *Mil.* The disposition of troops, as in a column, line, or square. **5.** *Aeron.* A grouping of aircraft in flight. **6.** *Geol.* Mineral deposits, or rock masses, having common characteristics.

form·a·tive (fôr/mə·tiv) *adj.* **1.** Having power to shape, form, or mold: a *formative* influence. **2.** Of or pertaining to formation or development: *formative* years. **—** *n. Gram.* **1.** An element added to the base of a word to give it a new and special grammatical form. **2.** A word so formed.

form·er[1] (fôr/mər) *n.* One who or that which forms.

for·mer[2] (fôr/mər) *adj.* **1.** Being the first of two persons or things referred to: often preceded by *the* and used absolutely: opposed to *latter.* **2.** Previous: my *former* colleague. **3.** Earlier: *former* times. [ME *formere*]

for·mer·ly (fôr/mər·lē) *adv.* Some time or a long time ago.

for·mic (fôr/mik) *adj.* **1.** Of or pertaining to ants. **2.** Designating or derived from formic acid. [< L *formica* ant]

formic acid *Chem.* A colorless, corrosive compound, HCOOH, with a penetrating odor, occurring in ants and certain other insects and in some plants.

for·mi·da·ble (fôr/mi·də·bəl) *adj.* **1.** Exciting fear or dread by reason of strength, size, etc. **2.** Extremely difficult. [< MF < L *formidare* to fear] **— for/mi·da·bil/i·ty, for/mi·da·ble·ness** *n.* **— for/mi·da·bly** *adv.*

form·less (fôrm/lis) *adj.* Lacking form or structure; shapeless. **— form/less·ly** *adv.* **— form/less·ness** *n.*

form letter One of many reproductions of a letter, etc.

For·mo·san (fôr·mō/sən) *n.* **1.** A native or inhabitant of the island of Formosa (Taiwan). **2.** The Indonesian language of the Malay aborigines of Formosa. **—** *adj.* Of or pertaining to Formosa, its people, or their language.

for·mu·la (fôr/myə·lə) *n. pl.* **·las** or **·lae** (-lē) **1.** An exact or prescribed method or form for doing something. **2.** A fixed order or form of words. **3.** A prescription or recipe; also, the mixture prepared. **4.** *Math.* A rule or combination expressed in algebraic or symbolic form. **5.** *Chem.* A symbolic representation of the composition of a chemical compound, as H_2SO_4, sulfuric acid. [< L, dim. of *forma* form]

for·mu·lar·ize (fôr/myə·lə·rīz/) *v.t.* **·ized, ·iz·ing** To formulate. **— for/mu·lar·i·za/tion** *n.*

for·mu·lar·y (fôr/myə·ler/ē) *adj.* Pertaining to, stated in, or resembling a formula. **—** *n. pl.* **·lar·ies** **1.** A compilation of formulas. **2.** A book listing pharmaceutical substances, their formulas, and preparation. **3.** A church ritual, or a book containing such rituals. **4.** A formula.

for·mu·late (fôr′myə·lāt) *v.t.* **·lat·ed, ·lat·ing 1.** To express in or as a formula. **2.** To put or state in exact and systematic form. **— for′mu·la′tion** *n.* **— for′mu·la′tor** *n.*

for·mu·lize (fôr′myə·līz) *v.t.* **·lized, ·liz·ing** To formulate.

for·ni·cate (fôr′nə·kāt) *v.i.* **·cat·ed, ·cat·ing** To commit fornication. [< L *fornix, -icis* brothel] **— for′ni·ca′tor** *n.*

for·ni·ca·tion (fôr′nə·kā′shən) *n.* Voluntary sexual intercourse between unmarried persons.

for·sake (fôr·sak′, fər-) *v.t.* **·sook, ·sak·en, ·sak·ing 1.** To renounce or relinquish (an occupation, belief, etc.). **2.** To abandon; desert. [OE *forsacan* to repudiate, deny]

for·sooth (fôr·sōōth′, fər-) *adv.* In truth; certainly. [OE]

for·swear (fôr·swâr′) *v.* **·swore, ·sworn, ·swear·ing** *v.t.* **1.** To renounce or abandon emphatically or upon oath. **2.** To deny absolutely or upon oath: to *forswear* a debt. **—** *v.i.* **3.** To swear falsely; commit perjury. **— Syn.** See RENOUNCE. [OE *forswerian* to swear falsely]

for·sworn (fôr·swôrn′, -swōrn′) *adj.* Perjured.

for·syth·i·a (fôr·sith′ē·ə, -sī′thē·ə, fər-) *n.* A shrub of the olive family, cultivated for its bright yellow flowers. [after William *Forsyth*, 1737–1804, British botanist]

fort (fôrt, fōrt) *n.* **1.** A fortified enclosure or structure capable of defense against an enemy. **2.** A permanent U.S. army post. [< F, orig. adj. strong]

forte[1] (fôrt, fōrt, fôr′tā) *n.* That which one does with excellence; strong point. [See FORT.]

for·te[2] (fôr′tā, -tē) *Music adj.* Loud; forceful. **—** *adv.* Loudly; forcefully. [< Ital.]

forth (fôrth, fōrth) *adv.* **1.** Forward in place, time, or order. **2.** Out, as from seclusion, confinement, or inaction. **3.** Away or out, as from a place of origin; abroad. **— and so forth** And the rest; and so on. [OE]

forth·com·ing (fôrth′kum′ing, fōrth′-) *adj.* **1.** Drawing near in time; approaching. **2.** Ready or about to appear, arrive, etc. **3.** Available or produced when expected or due. **—** *n.* Arrival or appearance of something due or expected.

forth·right (fôrth′rīt′, fōrth′-) *adj.* **1.** Coming straight to the point; candid; frank. **2.** Going forward in a straight line; direct. **—** *adv.* **1.** In a direct course or straightforward manner. **2.** At once; straightway. **— forth′right′ness** *n.*

forth·with (fôrth′with′, -wi*th*′, fōrth′-) *adv.* Immediately.

for·ti·fi·ca·tion (fôr′tə·fə·kā′shən) *n.* **1.** The act, art, or science of fortifying. **2.** That which fortifies, as walls, ditches, etc. **3.** A military place of defense.

for·ti·fy (fôr′tə·fī) *v.* **·fied, ·fy·ing** *v.t.* **1.** To provide with defensive works; strengthen against attack. **2.** To give physical or moral strength to. **3.** To strengthen the structure of; reinforce. **4.** To confirm. **5.** To strengthen, as wine, by adding alcohol. **6.** To enrich (food) by adding minerals, vitamins, etc. **—** *v.i.* **7.** To raise defensive works. [< F < L *fortis* strong + *facere* to make] **— for′ti·fi′a·ble** *adj.* **— for′ti·fi′er** *n.*

for·tis·si·mo (fôr·tis′ə·mō, *Ital.* fôr·tēs′sē·mō) *adj. & adv. Music* Very loud. **—** *n. pl.* **·mos** A fortissimo note, chord, or passage. [< Ital., superl. of *forte* strong]

for·ti·tude (fôr′tə·tōōd, -tyōōd) *n.* Strength of mind in the face of pain, adversity, or peril; patient courage. **— for′ti·tu′di·nous** (-də·nəs) *adj.*

fort·night (fôrt′nīt′, -nit′) *n.* A period of two weeks; fourteen days. [OE *fēowertēne* fourteen + *niht* nights]

fort·night·ly (fôrt′nīt′lē) *adj.* Occurring, coming, or issued every fortnight. **—** *adv.* Once a fortnight.

for·tress (fôr′tris) *n.* **1.** A large military stronghold; a fort, a series of forts, or a heavily fortified town. **2.** Any place of security. **—** *v.t.* To furnish or strengthen with a fortress; fortify. [< OF < L *fortis* strong]

for·tu·i·tous (fôr·tōō′ə·təs, -tyōō′-) *adj.* Occurring by chance rather than by design; casual; accidental. **— Syn.** See ACCIDENTAL. [< L *fors* chance] **— for·tu′i·tous·ly** *adv.* **— for·tu′i·tous·ness** *n.*

for·tu·i·ty (fôr·tōō′ə·tē, -tyōō′-) *n. pl.* **·ties** Chance occurrence; also, chance.

for·tu·nate (fôr′chə·nit) *adj.* **1.** Happening by a favorable chance; lucky. **2.** Favored with good fortune. **— for′tu·nate·ly** *adv.* **— for′tu·nate·ness** *n.*

for·tune (fôr′chən) *n.* **1.** That which happens or is to happen to one, whether good or bad. **2.** A power supposed to control one's future; fate: often personified. **3.** Luck or chance, esp. when favorable. **4.** An amount of wealth or possessions. **5.** Great wealth or riches. **6.** A particular condition or state of life, usu. prosperous.

for·tune·tell·er (fôr′chən·tel′ər) *n.* One who claims to foretell events in a person's future. **— for′tune·tell′ing** *n. & adj.*

for·ty (fôr′tē) *n. pl.* **·ties 1.** The sum of thirty and ten: a cardinal number. **2.** Any symbol of this number, as 40, xl, XL. **3.** Anything consisting of or representing forty units. **—** *adj.* Being ten more than thirty. [OE *fēowertig*] **— for′ti·eth** *adj. & n.*

for·ty-nin·er (fôr′tē·nī′nər) *n. U.S.* A pioneer who went to California in 1849, the year of the gold rush.

forty winks *Informal* A short nap.

fo·rum (fôr′əm, fō′rəm) *n. pl.* **fo·rums** or **fo·ra** (fôr′ə, fō **1.** The public market place of an ancient Roman city, wh popular assemblies met, and most legal and political busi was transacted. **2.** A tribunal; court. **3.** An assembly discussion of public affairs. [< L]

for·ward (fôr′wərd) *adv.* **1.** Toward what is ahead or w is in front; onward. Also **for′wards. 2.** At or in the fr part, as of a ship. **3.** Out into a conspicuous position; to forefront. **— forward of** *U.S.* In front of. **—** *adj.* **1.** ing at or near the front. **2.** Moving or directed towa point lying ahead. **3.** Overstepping the usual bound propriety in an insolent or presumptuous way; bold. Well-developed; not backward. **5.** Developing or develo earlier than usual; also, precocious. **6.** Extremely prog sive or unconventional, as in political opinions. **7.** Re or prompt. **8.** Made or done in advance: a *forward* cont for goods. **—** *n.* **1.** In football, one of the players in front lines of attack or defense. **2.** In basketball, hoc etc., a player who leads the offensive play. **—** *v.t.* **1** help onward or ahead. **2.** To send onward; esp., to s (mail) on to a new address. [OE *foreweard*] **— for′w er** *n.* **— for′ward·ly** *adv.* **— for′ward·ness** *n.*

forward pass In football, the throwing or passing of ball toward the opponent's goal.

fos·sa (fos′ə) *n. pl.* **fos·sae** (fos′ē) *Anat.* A shallow pression or cavity in the body. [< L. See FOSSE.]

fos·sil (fos′əl) *n. Paleontol.* **1.** The remains of plant animals, preserved in the rocks of the earth's crust. Some petrified trace of the existence of an early organ as a petrified footprint. **3.** *Informal* One who or that w is out of date. **—** *adj.* **1.** Of or like a fossil. **2.** Belon to the past; out-of-date. [< F < L *fodire* to dig]

fos·sil·ize (fos′əl·īz) *v.* **·ized, ·iz·ing** *v.t.* **1.** To change in fossil; petrify. **2.** To make antiquated or out of date. *v.i.* **3.** To become a fossil. **— fos′sil·i·za′tion** *n.*

fos·ter (fôs′tər, fos′-) *v.t.* **1.** To bring up (a child); rear. To promote the growth or development of: to *foster* gen **3.** To keep alive (feelings, hopes, etc.) within oneself; c ish. [OE *fōstrian* nourish] **— fos′ter·age** *n.*

foster child A child reared by a foster parent or pare

foster parent A man or woman rearing a child not hi her own.

fought (fôt) Past tense and past participle of FIGHT.

foul (foul) *adj.* **1.** Offensive or revolting to the senses; gusting: a *foul* odor. **2.** Full of dirt or impure matter; fil **3.** Clogged or packed with dirt, etc. **4.** Spoiled or rotter food. **5.** Unfavorable; adverse: *foul* weather. **6.** Obsc vulgar. **7.** Morally offensive; wicked. **8.** Not accordin rule or justice; unfair. **9.** Impeded or entangled: a anchor. **10.** In baseball, etc., of or pertaining to a foul or the foul lines. **11.** *Informal* Very bad; unsatisfact **—** *n.* **1.** An act of fouling, colliding, or becoming entang **2.** Something foul, as: **a** A foul ball. **b** A breach of rul various sports. **c** An entanglement or collision, as of ro boats, etc. **—** *v.t.* **1.** To make foul or dirty. **2.** To honor; disgrace. **3.** To clog or choke, as a drain. **4.** entangle or snarl, as a rope. **5.** To cover or encumbe ship's bottom) with barnacles, seaweed, etc. **6.** To co with. **7.** In sports, to commit a foul against. **8.** In basel to bat (the ball) outside of the foul lines. **—** *v.i.* **9.** To come foul or dirty. **10.** To become clogged or encumbe **11.** To become entangled. **12.** To collide. **13.** In spo to violate a rule. **14.** In baseball, to bat a foul ball. **— foul up** *Slang* **1.** To throw into disorder or confusion. To blunder. [OE *fūl*] **— foul′ly** *adv.* **— foul′ness** *n.*

fou·lard (fōō·lärd′) *n.* **1.** A lightweight, satiny fabri silk, rayon, cotton, etc., usu. with a printed design. **2** scarf, necktie, or other article made of this fabric. [< l Swiss F < OF < LL *fullare* to full cloth]

foul ball In baseball: **a** A batted ball that first hits ground outside the foul lines. **b** A batted ball hitting ground within the foul lines but passing outside the lines fore reaching first or third base.

foul line 1. In baseball, either of the two lines extend from home plate past first and third base to the limits of field. **2.** In basketball, the free-throw line. **3.** In bowli etc., any line limiting the area of play or action.

foul·mouthed (foul′mou*th*d′, -moutht′) *adj.* Using a sive, profane, or obscene language.

foul play 1. Unfairness; in games and sports, a violatio rule. **2.** Any unfair or treacherous action, often murder

found[1] (found) *v.t.* **1.** To give origin to; set up; establi **2.** To lay the foundation of; establish on a foundation basis. **—** *v.i.* **3.** To be established or based: with *on, up* [< OF < L *fundus* base, bottom]

found[2] (found) *v.t.* **1.** To cast, as iron, by melting and po ing into a mold. **2.** To make by casting molten metal. F < L *fundere* to pour]

found[3] (found) Past tense and past participle of FIND. *adj.* Provided with food, lodging, equipment, etc.

foun·da·tion (foun·dā′shən) *n.* **1.** The act of founding

ablishing. **2.** The state of being founded or established. That on which anything is founded; basis: Equality is the *ndation* of democracy. **4.** A base on which something :s: a machine's *foundation*. **5.** That part of a building or l, wholly or partly below the surface of the ground, that stitutes a base. **6.** A fund for the maintenance of an :itution; an endowment. **7.** An endowed institution, one that grants funds for research projects, charities, etc. A foundation garment. **— foun·da′tion·al** *adj.*
ıdation garment *U.S.* A girdle or corset.
ıd·er¹ (foun′dər) *n.* One who establishes.
ıd·er² (foun′dər) *n.* One who makes metal castings.
ı·der³ (foun′dər) *v.i.* **1.** To sink after filling with water, boat or ship. **2.** To fall or cave in, as land or buildings. To fail completely; collapse. **4.** To stumble and become e, as a horse. **—** *v.t.* **5.** To cause to sink. **—** *n.* The act oundering. [< OF < L *fundus* bottom]
ıd·ling (found′ling) *n.* A deserted infant of unknown entage. [ME *funde*, pp. of *find* + -LING¹]
ı·dry (foun′drē) *n.* *pl.* **·dries 1.** An establishment in ch metal, etc., is cast; also, an article made by casting. The act or operation of founding metal, etc.
ıt¹ (fount) *n.* **1.** A fountain. **2.** Any source. [< F < ons, *fontis* fountain]
ıt² (fount) British spelling of FONT².
ı·tain (foun′tən) *n.* **1.** A spring or jet of water issuing n the earth; esp., the source of a stream. **2.** The origin ource of anything. **3.** A jet or spray of water forced up-d artificially, as to provide water for drinking. **4.** A inlike structure for such a jet to rise and fall in. [< OF LL *fontana*, orig. fem. singular of L *fontanus* of a spring]
ı·tain·head (foun′tən·hed′) *n.* **1.** A spring from which tream takes its source. **2.** Any source or origin.
ıtain pen A pen having a supply of ink automatically to the writing end from a reservoir or cartridge.
· (fôr, fōr) *n.* **1.** The sum of three and one: a cardinal nber. **2.** Any symbol of this number, as 4, iv, IV. **3.** ything consisting of or representing four units. **— on all rs 1.** On hands and knees. **2.** On all four feet. **—** *adj.* ng one more than three; quaternary. [OE *fēower*] **—** **rth** (fôrth, fōrth) *adj. & n.*
·-flush (fôr′flush′, fōr′-) *v.i.* **1.** To bet on a poker hand ding one card to a flush. **2.** *Slang* To bluff.
·-flush·er (fôr′flush′ər, fōr′-) *n.* *Slang* A fake or cheat.
·-foot·ed (fôr′fŏŏt′id, fōr′-) *adj.* Having four feet.
·-hand·ed (fôr′han′did, fōr′-) *adj.* **1.** Designed for four yers, as certain games. **2.** Designed for performance by persons on a keyboard instrument, as a piano duet.
· hundred *U.S.* The most exclusive social group of a ce.
·-in-hand (fôr′in·hand′, fōr′-) *n.* **1.** A four-horse team ven by one person. **2.** A vehicle drawn by such a team. A necktie tied in a slip knot with the ends hanging.
·-leaf clover (fôr′lēf′, fōr′-) A clover plant having r leaflets, supposed to bring good luck.
·-pence (fôr′pəns, fōr′-) *n.* The sum of four English nies; also, a silver piece worth that sum.
·-post·er (fôr′pōs′tər, fōr′-) *n.* A bedstead with four tall ts at the corners and typically with a canopy or curtains.
·-some (fôr′səm, fōr′-) *n.* **1.** A game, esp. of golf, in ich four players take part, two on each side; also, the yers in such a game. **2.** Any group of four.
·-square (fôr′skwâr′, fōr′-) *adj.* **1.** Having four equal es; square. **2.** Firm; solid. **3.** Forthright; direct. **—** *n.* square. **—** *adv.* Squarely; bluntly.
·-teen (fôr′tēn′, fōr′-) *n.* **1.** The sum of thirteen and : a cardinal number. **2.** Any symbol of this number, as xiv, XIV. **3.** Anything consisting of or representing rteen units. **—** *adj.* Being one more than thirteen. [OE *wertēne*] **— four′teenth** *adj. & n*
rth dimension A hypothetical dimension in addition to ght, width, and thickness; esp., in the theory of relativity. **fourth′-di·men′sion·al** *adj.*
rth estate The public press; journalism.
rth·ly (fôrth′lē, fōrth′-) *adv.* In the fourth place.
rth of July Independence Day.
l (foul) *n.* *pl.* **fowl** or **fowls 1.** The common domestic n or cock; a chicken. **2.** Any related bird, as the duck, ose, etc. **3.** The flesh of fowl. **4.** Birds collectively. **—** *v.i.* catch or hunt wild fowl. [OE *fugol*] **— fowl′er** *n.*
l·ing (fou′ling) *n.* The hunting of birds for sport.
ling piece A light gun used for shooting birds.
(foks) *n.* **1.** Any of several small, wild mammals of the g family, having long, pointed muzzles, bushy tails, and ct ears, esp. the **red fox** of North America, having a ldish brown fur. ◆ Collateral adjective: *vulpine*. **2.** e fur of the fox. **3.** A sly, crafty person. **—** *v.t.* **1.** trick; outwit. **2.** To intoxicate. **3.** To stain, as paper or timber, with a reddish color. **4.** To make sour, as beer, in fermenting. **5.** To repair (shoes) with new uppers. **—** *v.i.* **6.** To act slyly and cunningly. **7.** To become sour. **8.** To become stained with red. [OE]

NORTH AMERICAN RED FOX (Body about 2 feet long; tail 16 inches)

fox·glove (foks′gluv′) *n.* A plant of the figwort family, having flowers in long one-sided racemes.
fox·hole (foks′hōl′) *n.* A shallow pit dug by a combatant as cover against enemy fire.
fox·hound (foks′hound′) *n.* One of a breed of large, strong, very swift dogs trained for fox hunting.
fox·tail (foks′tāl′) *n.* **1.** The tail of a fox. **2.** Any of various species of grass bearing a spike of flowers like a fox's tail.
fox terrier A small, white terrier with dark markings, formerly used to bring foxes out of their burrows.
fox-trot (foks′trot′) *v.i.* **·trot·ted, ·trot·ting** To do a fox trot.
fox trot A ballroom dance in 2/4 or 4/4 time, consisting of a variety of rhythmic steps.
fox·y (fok′sē) *adj.* **fox·i·er, fox·i·est 1.** Sly; crafty; sharp. **2.** Reddish brown. **3.** Discolored or stained, as from decay. **4.** Improperly fermented: said of beer, etc. **5.** Defective, esp. from age and damp. **— fox′i·ly** *adv.* **— fox′i·ness** *n.*
foy·er (foi′ər, foi′ā; *Fr.* fwȧ·yā′) *n.* **1.** A public lobby in a hotel, theater, etc. **2.** An entrance room or hall in a house or apartment. [< F < LL < L *focus* hearth]
fra·cas (frā′kəs), *Brit.* frak′ä) *n.* A noisy disturbance, fight, or dispute; brawl; row. [< F < Ital. *fracassare* to shatter]
frac·tion (frak′shən) *n.* **1.** A disconnected part of anything; small portion; fragment. **2.** *Math.* A quantity less than a whole number, expressed as a decimal (0.3) or with numerator and denominator (3/10). **3.** *Chem.* One of the components separated from a substance by distilling, etc. **— Syn.** See PORTION. **—** *v.t.* To set or separate into fractions. [< OF < L *fractus*, pp. of *frangere* to break]
frac·tion·al (frak′shən·əl) *adj.* **1.** Pertaining to or constituting a fraction. **2.** Small in size or importance. Also **frac′tion·ar′y** (-er′ē). **— frac′tion·al·ly** *adv.*
frac·tious (frak′shəs) *adj.* **1.** Apt to be unruly or rebellious. **2.** Easily annoyed or angered. [< FRACTION, in obs. sense of discord] **— frac′tious·ly** *adv.* **— frac′tious·ness** *n.*
frac·ture (frak′chər) *n.* **1.** The act of breaking, or the state of being broken. **2.** A break; crack; rupture. **3.** *Med.* The breaking or cracking of a bone; also, sometimes, the tearing of a cartilage. **4.** *Mineral.* The characteristic appearance of the freshly broken surface of a mineral. **— compound** (or **open**) **fracture** *Med.* A fracture in which the broken ends of the bone protrude through the skin. **— simple** (or **closed**) **fracture** *Med.* A bone fracture in which the skin remains unbroken. **—** *v.t. & v.i.* **·tured, ·tur·ing** To break or be broken; crack. [< F < L *fractura* a breaking] **— frac′tur·al** *adj.*
frag·ile (fraj′əl) *adj.* Easily broken or damaged; frail; delicate. [< L *frangere* to break] **— frag′ile·ly** *adv.* **— fra·gil·i·ty** (frə·jil′ə·tē), **frag′ile·ness** *n.*
— Syn. That which cannot withstand even mild shocks or jars is *fragile* or, if constructed of parts poorly connected, *frail*: a *fragile* teacup, a *frail* scaffold. *Brittle* is used to describe things that are hard but so rigid or inelastic that they crack under stress.
frag·ment (*n.* frag′mənt; *v.* frag·ment′) *n.* **1.** A part broken off; a small detached portion. **2.** A part or portion of something that has been left unfinished: a *fragment* of a novel. **3.** A separate or isolated bit: He heard *fragments* of their conversation. **—** *v.t. & v.i.* To break into fragments. [< F < L *fragmentum*] **— frag′ment·ed** *adj.*
frag·men·tar·y (frag′mən·ter′ē) *adj.* Composed of fragments; broken; incomplete. Also **frag·men′tal.** **— frag′·men·tar′i·ly** *adv.* **— frag′men·tar′i·ness** *n.*
frag·men·ta·tion (frag′mən·tā′shən) *n.* **1.** A breaking up into fragments. **2.** *Mil.* The scattering in all directions of the fragments of an exploding grenade, shell, or bomb.
frag·ment·ize (frag′mən·tīz) *v.t. & v.i.* **·ized, ·iz·ing** To fragment.
fra·grance (frā′grəns) *n.* **1.** The state or quality of being fragrant. **2.** A pleasant scent; sweet odor. Also *Rare* **fra′·gran·cy.** **— Syn.** See SMELL.
fra·grant (frā′grənt) *adj.* Having an agreeable or sweet smell. [< L *fragrare* to smell sweet] **— fra′grant·ly** *adv.*
frail (frāl) *adj.* **1.** Delicately constituted; weak. **2.** Fragile. **3.** Deficient in moral strength. **— Syn.** See FRAGILE. **—** *n.* *U.S. Slang* A young woman or girl. [< OF < L *fragilis*] **— frail′ly** *adv.* **— frail′ness** *n.*
frail·ty (frāl′tē) *n.* *pl.* **·ties 1.** The state or quality of being frail; weakness. **2.** A fault or moral weakness.
frame (frām) *n.* **1.** A case or border made to enclose something, as a picture. **2.** A supporting structure surrounding something, as around a window or door. **3.** A framework; skeleton: the *frame* of a building, ship, etc. **4.** The general

arrangement, structure, or constitution of a thing. **5.** A system or order, as of a government. **6.** Bodily structure or build, esp. of the human body. **7.** A machine built in the form of or utilizing a framework: a silk *frame*. **8.** In pool or billiards: **a** The triangular form for grouping the balls. **b** The balls placed in this form. **c** The time required to pocket all the balls. **9.** In bowling, one of the ten divisions of the game. **10.** *Informal* In baseball, an inning. **11.** One of the individual exposures on a roll of motion-picture film. **12.** *Slang* A frame-up. **— frame of mind** Mental state; mood. — *v.* **framed, fram·ing** *v.t.* **1.** To surround with or put into a frame, as a picture. **2.** To put together: to *frame* a shelter. **3.** To put into words; utter. **4.** To conceive or create (a theory, idea, etc.). **5.** To draw up; devise: to *frame* a law. **6.** To shape or adapt to a purpose: Traffic rules are *framed* for safety. **7.** *Slang* To incriminate falsely. **8.** *Slang* To plan or set up dishonestly in advance, as a race, contest, etc. [OE *framian* to be of service to, provide for] **— fram′er** *n.*

frame house A house built on a wooden framework covered on the outside by shingles, boards, stucco, etc.

frame-up (frām′up′) *n.* *Slang* **1.** A prearranged plan to bring about a fraudulent outcome, as in a contest. **2.** A conspiracy to convict a person on a false charge.

frame·work (frām′wûrk′) *n.* **1.** A skeleton structure for supporting or enclosing something; also, frames, collectively. **2.** The arrangement of the basic or component parts of something: the *framework* of society.

fram·ing (frā′ming) *n.* **1.** A frame or framework. **2.** The act of erecting or fitting with frames or frameworks.

franc (frangk) *n.* **1.** The standard monetary unit of various countries, equivalent to 100 centimes; esp.: **a** The French franc, in 1960 worth about 20 U.S. cents. **b** The Belgian franc, in 1960 worth about 2 U.S. cents. **c** The Swiss franc, in 1960 worth about 23 U.S. cents. **2.** A coin of this denomination. [< Med.L *Franc*(*orum rex*) (king of the) Franks, the motto on the earliest of these coins]

fran·chise (fran′chīz) *n.* **1.** The right to vote; suffrage. **2.** A right or privilege granted by a government or sovereign. **3.** A special privilege bestowed upon an individual or a corporate group of individuals by government grant: a *franchise* to operate a bus line. **4.** The territory over which any of the preceding special privileges or dispensations extend. [< OF < *franc, franche* free] **— fran′chised** *adj.*

Fran·cis·can (fran·sis′kən) *n.* A member of the mendicant order, the Gray Friars, founded in 1209 by St. Francis of Assisi. — *adj.* **1.** Of or pertaining to St. Francis. **2.** Belonging to a religious order following his rule.

fran·ci·um (fran′sē·əm) *n.* A radioactive element (symbol Fr), isolated from actinium, and replacing the hypothetical element known as *virginium*. See ELEMENT. [after *France*]

Franco- *combining form* French [< L *Francus* a Frank]

Fran·co·phile (frang′kə·fīl) *n.* An admirer of France or of French customs, etc. — *adj.* Kindly disposed toward France.

Fran·co·phobe (frang′kə·fōb) *n.* A person who fears or dislikes France or French things. — *adj.* Fearful of France.

Fran·co-Prus·sian War (frang′kō·prush′ən) See table for WAR.

fran·gi·ble (fran′jə·bəl) *adj.* Easily broken; brittle. [< L *frangere* to break] **— fran′gi·bil′i·ty, fran′gi·ble·ness** *n.*

fran·gi·pan·i (fran′ji·pan′ē, -pä′nē) *n.* **1.** A perfume derived from or resembling that of the West Indian red jasmine. **2.** The West Indian plant. Also **fran′gi·pane** (-pān). [after Marquis *Frangipani*, the inventor]

frank[1] (frangk) *adj.* **1.** Completely honest and unreserved in speech; candid. **2.** Marked by no effort at concealment or disguise: *frank* hostility. — *v.t.* To mark (a letter, package, etc.) in indication that no charge is to be made for delivery; also, to send (a letter, etc.) without charge by marking in this way. — *n.* **1.** The right to send mail, etc., without charge; also, the mark used to indicate this right. **2.** Mail sent without charge. [< OF *franc* frank, free] **— frank′ly** *adv.* **— frank′ness** *n.*

frank[2] (frangk) *n.* *Informal* A frankfurter.

Frank (frangk) *n.* **1.** A member of one of the Germanic tribes living on the Rhine early in the Christian era who gave their name to France. **2.** In the Near East, any European. [< L *Francus* a Frank < Gmc., a spear]

Frank·en·stein (frangk′ən·stīn) The hero of Mary Shelley's *Frankenstein*, a medical student who fashions a manlike monster that slays its maker. — *n.* **1.** Loosely, Frankenstein's monster. **2.** Anything that destroys its own creator.

frank·furt·er (frangk′fər·tər) *n.* A smoked, often highly seasoned sausage made of beef or of beef and pork. Also **frank′fort·er** (-fər·tər), **frank′furt, frank′fort** (-fərt) [after *Frankfurt*, Germany]

frank·in·cense (frangk′in·sens) *n.* An aromatic gum or resin from various trees of East Africa, used as an incense and in medicine. [< OF *franc* pure + *encens* incense]

Frank·ish (frang′kish) *adj.* Of or pertaining to the Franks, or, in the Near East, to Europeans in general. — *n.* The West Germanic language of the Franks.

fran·tic (fran′tik) *adj.* **1.** Nearly driven out of one's m as with grief, fear, or rage. **2.** Madly excited. [< OF < < Gk. *phrenitis* delirium] **— fran′ti·cal·ly, fran′tic·ly**

frap·pé (fra·pā′) *U.S. adj.* Iced; chilled. — *n.* **1.** A juice or other beverage frozen to a soft, mushy consist **2.** A liqueur or other beverage poured over shaved ice. F, pp. of *frapper* to chill]

frat (frat) *n.* *U.S. Informal* A college fraternity.

fra·ter·nal (frə·tûr′nəl) *adj.* **1.** Pertaining to or befitt brother; brotherly. **2.** Of or pertaining to a fraternal or society. **3.** *Genetics* Designating either of a pair of t that develop from separately fertilized ova: distingui from *identical*. [< L *frater* brother] **— fra·ter′nal·is — fra·ter′nal·ly** *adv.*

fraternal order A brotherhood of men organized to fu their mutual benefit or to attain a common goal.

fra·ter·ni·ty (frə·tûr′nə·tē) *n.* *pl.* **·ties** **1.** The state c ing brothers; also, the spirit of fraternal regard or affec **2.** In U.S. schools, a society of male students, usu. hav Greek letter name, and represented by chapters in man stitutions. **3.** A fraternal order. **4.** A body of people ing the same interests, profession, etc.

frat·er·nize (frat′ər·nīz) *v.* **·nized, ·niz·ing** *v.i.* **1.** To ciate closely with someone in a comradely way. **2** mingle intimately with the people of an enemy or conqu country. **— frat′er·ni·za′tion** *n.* **— frat′er·niz′er** *n.*

frat·ri·cide (frat′rə·sīd) *n.* **1.** The killing of one's bro **2.** One who has killed his brother. [< L < *frater* broth *caedere* to kill] **— frat′ri·ci′dal** *adj.*

Frau (frou) *n.* *pl.* **Frau·en** (-ən) *German* A ma woman; wife: as a title, the equivalent of *Mrs.*

fraud (frôd) *n.* **1.** Willful deceit; trickery. **2.** An a instance of this. **3.** *U.S. Informal* One who acts deceitf impostor. **4.** A deceptive or spurious thing. [< OF *fraus, fraudis* deceit]

fraud·u·lent (frô′jə·lənt) *adj.* **1.** Practicing or give fraud; dishonest or deceitful. **2.** Proceeding from, obta by, or characterized by fraud. **— fraud′u·lence, fra len·cy** *n.* **— fraud′u·lent·ly** *adv.*

fraught (frôt) *adj.* Filled; laden: with *with*: a jou *fraught* with danger. [< MDu. *vrachten* freight]

Fräu·lein (froi′līn) *n.* *German* An unmarried woman: title, the equivalent of *Miss.*

fray[1] (frā) *n.* Conflict; fight; also a noisy, quarrelsom roar or disturbance. [Aphetic var. of AFFRAY]

fray[2] (frā) *v.t.* **1.** To cause (cloth, rope, etc.) to be worn by friction. **2.** To wear holes in (cloth, etc. rubbing or chafing. — *v.i.* **3.** To become frayed. — frayed place, as of a sleeve. [< F *frayer* < L *fricare* to

fraz·zle (fraz′əl) *Informal* *v.t. & v.i.* **·zled, ·zling** **1** fray or become frayed; make or become tattered. **2** tire out; weary. — *n.* The state of being frazzled. **— to a frazzle** **1.** Worn to shreds. **2.** Tired out; exhau [? Blend of FRAY[2] + obs. *fasel* to ravel]

freak (frēk) *n.* **1.** A deformed human being, anima plant; monstrosity. **2.** Anything unusual or bizarre. A sudden whim; caprice. [Cf. OE *frician* to dance] **freak′ish** *adj.* **— freak′ish·ly** *adv.* **— freak′ish·ness**

freck·le (frek′əl) *n.* A small brownish or dark-colored on the skin. — *v.t. & v.i.* **·led, ·ling** To mark or bec marked with freckles. [< ON *freknur* freckles] **— fr led, freck′ly** *adj.*

free (frē) *adj.* **fre·er, fre·est** **1.** Having personal lib **2.** Having civil, political, or religious liberty. **3.** Not trolled by a foreign power; autonomous. **4.** Not boun restrictions or regulations: *free* trade. **5.** Released f legal charge of crime or misdeed; acquitted. **6.** Exe from certain regulations or impositions, as some taxes. Cleared or devoid of something: with *from, of*: *free* scandal. **8.** Allowed or permitted to do something: *fr* go. **9.** Not controlled, restricted, or hampered by exte agents or influences. **10.** Released from or not hindere burdens, debts, discomforts, etc.: with *from, of*: *free* care. **11.** Not occupied; not busy. **12.** Available to open: a *free* port. **13.** Not attached, bound, fixed, or h loose: the *free* end of a rope. **14.** Not obstructed; eas pass through or over: The road is now *free*; also, unimpe profuse: a *free* flow of water. **15.** Given or provided wit charge or cost: *free* seats. **16.** Easy and unconstraine *free* stride. **17.** Not adhering to strict form or rule: verse. **18.** Not closely or literally following the origin *free* translation. **19.** Informal; unconventional. **20.** Fr and honest; candid. **21.** Unrestrained by propriety, nity, or decency. **22.** Generous in giving; liberal: *free* advice. **23.** *Chem.* Uncombined: *free* hydrogen. **24.** *Ph* Available for work: *free* energy. **— free and clear** Pertaining to real property held without a mortgage or o encumbrance. **— to set free** To release, as from pri slavery, or other restraint; disengage. — *adv.* **1.** In a manner; easily. **2.** Without cost; gratuitously. **— to m free with** **1.** To use freely. **2.** To treat with undue fa

ity. —*v.t.* **freed, free·ing** **1.** To release from confine-
ɪnt, worry, etc. **2.** To clear or rid of obstruction or hind-
ɪce. [OE *frēo*] —**free′ly** *adv.* —**free′ness** *n.*

e association *Psychoanal.* A method of uncovering un-
ɪscious conflicts by encouraging spontaneous verbal asso-
.tion of memories, ideas, impressions, etc.

e·board (frē′bôrd′, -bōrd′) *n. Naut.* The side of a vessel
tween the water line and the main deck or gunwale.

e·boot·er (frē′bo͞o′tər) *n.* A pirate or buccaneer. [<
Du. < *vrij* free + *buit* booty]

e·dom (frē′dəm) *n.* **1.** The state or condition of being
e; esp., the condition of enjoying civil liberty. **2.** Politi-
l autonomy, as of a nation or people. **3.** Liberty from
ndage or slavery. **4.** Liberation, as from prison or other
nfinement. **5.** Liberty to move or act without outside
erference, coercion, or restriction. **6.** Liberty of personal
oice, action, or thought. **7.** Release or immunity from
y stated thing or condition: with *from*: *freedom* from pain.
Exemption or release from obligations, ties, etc. **9.**
.cility or ease, as in moving or acting. **10.** Boldness of
ncept or execution. **11.** Openness or frankness. **12.** Ex-
ssive familiarity or candor. [OE *frēodōm*]

edom of the seas The doctrine that any waters not
bject to the territorial jurisdiction of any one country
nation are open to unhampered navigation by any ships
in war, by the ships of any neutral country or nation.

e enterprise An economic system based upon private
vnership and operation of business with little or no govern-
ental control: also called *private enterprise.*

e-for-all (frē′fər·ôl′) *n.* A noisy, generalized fight.

e·hand (frē′hand′) *adj.* Drawn or sketched by hand
thout the help of rulers, drafting instruments, etc.

e hand Full liberty to act as one sees fit.

e·hand·ed (frē′han′did) *adj.* **1.** Having the hands free.
Openhanded; generous. —**free′hand′ed·ness** *n.*

e·hold (frē′hōld′) *n. Law* **1.** Tenure of an estate, or
metimes of an office or dignity, for life or as something
.pable of being transferred to another. **2.** The estate,
ice, or dignity held by such tenure. —**free′hold′er** *n.*

e-lance (frē′lans′, -läns′) *v.i.* **-lanced, -lanc·ing** To
ork as a free lance. —*adj.* Working as a free lance.

e lance A writer, artist, etc., whose services are not sold
clusively to any one buyer.

e·man (frē′mən) *n. pl.* **·men,** (-mən) **1.** A person not
bondage of any kind. **2.** One having full political rights.

ee·ma·son (frē′mā′sən) *n.* A member of an extensive
cret order or fraternity, the members denoting themselves
ree and Accepted Masons: also called *Mason.* —**Free·
a·son·ic** (frē′mə·son′ik) *adj.* —**Free′ma′son·ry** *n.*

e on board Delivered, without charge to the buyer,
r shipment by a common carrier. Abbr. *f.o.b., F.O.B.*

e·si·a (frē′zhē·ə, -sē·ə, -zhə) *n.* A South African plant
ving bell-shaped, variously colored, fragrant flowers. [<
L. after E. M. *Fries*, 1794–1878, Swedish botanist]

e silver The free and unlimited coinage of silver, par-
cularly at a fixed ratio to gold.

e-spo·ken (frē′spō′kən) *adj.* Unreserved or frank in
eech. —**free-spo′ken·ness** *n.*

ee State **1.** Before the Civil War, any State where
avery was forbidden. **2.** The Irish Free State.

e·stone (frē′stōn′) *adj.* Having a pit from which the
ulp easily separates, as a peach. —*n.* **1.** Any stone, as
ndstone or limestone, that can be cut in any direction
ithout breaking. **2.** A fruit easily freed from its pit.

ee·style (frē′stīl′) *adj.* In swimming, using or permit-
ng any stroke the swimmer desires. —*n.* The use of
eestyle swimming techniques.

e·think·er (frē′thing′kər) *n.* One who forms his own
ligious beliefs without regard to church authority. —**Syn.**
ee SKEPTIC. —**free′think′ing** *adj.* & *n.*

ee-throw line (frē′thrō′) In basketball, the line from
hich a free throw is made: also called *foul line.*

ee trade **1.** International commerce free from govern-
ient regulations and from import and export duties. **2.** A
ade system where duties are levied only for revenue and
ot to protect home industries.

ee verse Verse marked by an absence or irregularity of
hyme: also, *French, vers libre.*

ee·way (frē′wā′) *n.* A wide highway skirting populated
reas and passing over or around intersections.

ee will **1.** The power of personal self-determination. **2.**
he doctrine that one's ability to choose between courses of
ction is not completely determined by circumstances.

ee·will (frē′wil′) *adj.* Of one's own free choice; voluntary.

eeze (frēz) *v.* **froze, fro·zen, freez·ing** *v.i.* **1.** To become
e or a similar hard solid through loss of heat. **2.** To be-
ome sheeted or filled with ice, as water pipes. **3.** To be-
ome stiff or hard with cold, as wet clothes. **4.** To adhere to
something by the formation of ice. **5.** To be extremely cold.
6. To be damaged or killed by great cold. **7.** To become
suddenly motionless, inactive, or rigid, as through fear,
shock, etc. **8.** To become icily aloof: often with *up.* —*v.t.*
9. To cause to become ice or a similar hard solid through
loss of heat. **10.** To cause ice to form on or in. **11.** To
make stiff or hard by freezing the moisture of. **12.** To make
adhere by the formation of ice. **13.** To make extremely
cold. **14.** To damage or kill by great cold. **15.** To make
motionless or rigid, as through fear; paralyze. **16.** To make
icily aloof, unfriendly, etc.; alienate. **17.** To check abruptly
the ardor, enthusiasm, etc., of. **18.** To fix or stabilize
(prices, wages, etc.) at a particular level. **19.** To prohibit
the continued making, use, or selling of (a raw material).
20. To make the liquidation, collection, or use of (funds or
other assets) contrary to law or edict. —**to freeze one's
blood** To fill one with terror. —**to freeze onto** (or **to**) To
hold tightly to. —*n.* **1.** The act of freezing, or the state of
being frozen. **2.** Freezing weather. [OE *frēosan*]

freez·er (frē′zər) *n.* **1.** One who or that which freezes. **2.**
A refrigerator designed to freeze and preserve food.

freezing point *Physics* The temperature at which a liquid
freezes under given pressure. For water at sea level it is 32°
F. or 0° C.

freight (frāt) *n.* **1.** In the United States and Canada: **a**
The service of transporting commodities by land, air, or
water; esp., ordinary transportation as opposed to express.
b The commodities so transported. **2.** The price paid for
the transportation of commodities. **3.** *U.S. & Canadian* A
freight train. —*v.t.* **1.** To load with commodities for transportation. **2.** To load; burden. **3.** To send or transport as
or by freight. [< MDu. *vrecht*, var. of *vracht* a load]

freight·age (frā′tij) *n.* **1.** A cargo; freight. **2.** The price
charged or paid for carrying goods. **3.** The transportation
of merchandise.

freight car A railway car for carrying freight.

freight·er (frā′tər) *n.* A ship used primarily for transporting cargo.

freight train *U.S.* A railroad train of freight cars.

French (french) *adj.* Of, pertaining to, or characteristic
of France, its people, or their language; also, in Canada, per-
taining to Canadian French persons, their speech, etc.
—*n.* **1.** The people of France collectively: preceded by
the; also, in Canada, the French-speaking Canadians. **2.**
The Romance language of France. —**Old French** The
French language from about 850 to 1400, descended from
Vulgar Latin as it developed in Gaul. —**Middle French**
The French language from about 1400 to 1600. —**Modern
French** The language of France after 1600. [OE *Frencisc*]

French and Indian War See table for WAR.

French-Ca·na·di·an (french′kə·nā′dē·ən) *n.* A French
settler in Canada or a descendant of French settlers. Also
French Canadian. —*adj.* Of or pertaining to the language,
culture, etc., of French-speaking people in Canada.

French cuff A cuff of a sleeve turned back and secured with
a link.

French doors A pair of doors, usu. with glass panes, attached to opposite doorjambs and opening in the middle.

French dressing A salad dressing consisting of oil,
vinegar, and spices.

French fried Cooked by frying crisp in deep fat.

French horn A valved, brass instrument with a long,
coiled tube, flaring widely at the end and
producing a mellow tone.

French·i·fy (fren′chə·fī) *v.t.* & *v.i.* **·fied,
·fy·ing** To make or become French in form
or characteristics.

French leave An informal, secret, or hurried departure.

French·man (french′mən) *n. pl.* **·men**
(-mən) A native or citizen of France. —
French′wom′an (-wo͝om′ən) *n.fem.*

FRENCH HORN

French pastry A rich, fancy pastry often having a filling of
whipped cream, custard, or preserved fruits.

French toast Bread dipped in a batter of beaten eggs and
milk and fried in shallow fat.

French window A casement window with adjoining sashes
attached to opposite jambs and opening in the middle.

fre·net·ic (frə·net′ik) *adj.* Feverishly excited; frenzied;
frantic. Also **fre·net′i·cal.** —*n.* A frenetic person. —**fre·
net′i·cal·ly** *adv.*

fren·zy (fren′zē) *n. pl.* **·zies** A state of extreme excitement or agitation suggestive of or bordering on delirium or
insanity. —*v.t.* **·zied, ·zy·ing** To make frantic. [< OF <
LL < Gk. *phrenitis* delirium] —**fren′zied** *adj.*

fre·quence (frē′kwəns) *n. Rare* Frequency (defs. 1, 2).

fre·quen·cy (frē′kwən·sē) *n. pl.* **·cies** **1.** The state or fact
of being frequent; repeated occurrence. **2.** The number of

times something occurs within a particular extent of time, a particular group, etc. **3.** *Stat.* The number of times a given case, value, or event occurs in relation to the total number of classified cases, values, or events; distribution. **4.** *Physics* The number of occurrences of a periodic phenomenon, as oscillation, per unit time, usu. expressed in cycles per second.

frequency modulation *Telecom.* A type of modulation in which the carrier wave of a transmitter is varied in frequency rather than in amplitude. Abbr. *FM, f-m, f.m., F.M.*

fre·quent (*adj.* frē′kwənt; *v.* fri·kwent′, frē′kwənt) *adj.* **1.** Happening time after time; occurring again and again: *frequent* relapses. **2.** Showing up often; appearing repeatedly: *frequent* visitors. — *v.t.* To go to repeatedly; be in or at often: to *frequent* bars. [< L *frequens, -entis* crowded] — **fre·quen·ta′tion** *n.* — **fre·quent′er** *n.* — **fre′quent·ly** *adv.*

fre·quen·ta·tive (fri·kwen′tə·tiv) *Gram. adj.* Denoting repeated or habitual action. — *n.* A frequentative verb.

frère (frâr) *n.* *pl.* **frères** (frâr) *French* **1.** Brother. **2.** Friar; monk.

fres·co (fres′kō) *n.* *pl.* **·coes** or **·cos** **1.** The art of painting on plaster that is still moist. **2.** A picture so painted. — *v.t.* **·coed, ·co·ing** To paint in fresco. [< Ital., fresh]

fresh[1] (fresh) *adj.* **1.** Newly made, obtained, received, etc.: *fresh* coffee; *fresh* footprints. **2.** New; novel: a *fresh* approach. **3.** Recent; latest: *fresh* news. **4.** Additional; further: *fresh* supplies. **5.** Not smoked, frozen, or otherwise preserved: *fresh* vegetables. **6.** Not spoiled, stale, musty, etc. **7.** Retaining original vividness; not faded or worn, as colors or memories. **8.** Not salt: *fresh* water. **9.** Pure and clear: *fresh* air. **10.** Appearing healthy or youthful. **11.** Not fatigued; energetic. **12.** Vivid; colorful; stimulating. **13.** Inexperienced; untrained: *fresh* recruits. **14.** *Meteorol.* Moderately rapid and strong: esp. designating a breeze or a gale on the Beaufort scale. **15.** Having a renewed supply of milk: said of a cow that has recently calved. [OE *fersc,* infl. by OF *freis,* both ult. < Gmc.] — **fresh′ly** *adv.* — **fresh′ness** *n.*

fresh[2] (fresh) *adj.* *U.S. Informal* Saucy; impudent; disrespectful. [< G *frech* impudent]

fresh·en (fresh′ən) *v.t.* & *v.i.* To make or become fresh. — **fresh′en·er** *n.*

fresh·et (fresh′it) *n.* **1.** A sudden rise or overflow of a stream. **2.** A fresh-water stream emptying into the sea.

fresh·man (fresh′mən) *n.* *pl.* **·men** (-mən) **1.** A student during the first year of studies in a high school, college, or university. **2.** A beginner; novice.

fresh-wa·ter (fresh′wô′tər, -wot′ər) *adj.* **1.** Pertaining to or living in fresh water: a *fresh-water* fish. **2.** Not situated on or near the seacoast; inland. **3.** Lacking skill or experience. **4.** *U.S.* Not well known; small: a *fresh-water* college.

fret[1] (fret) *v.* **fret·ted, fret·ting** *v.i.* **1.** To be vexed, annoyed, or troubled. **2.** To become worn, chafed, or corroded. **3.** To bite away bit after bit of something with or as with the teeth; gnaw: with *on, upon, into.* **4.** To eat through something by or as if by corrosion. **5.** To rankle; fester. **6.** To become rough or agitated, as water. — *v.t.* **7.** To vex, annoy, or trouble. **8.** To wear away or eat away by or as if by chafing, gnawing, or corrosion; also, to produce (a hole, frayed ends, etc.) in this way. **9.** To roughen or agitate (the surface of water). — *n.* **1.** Vexation. **2.** The act of chafing or gnawing. **3.** A worn spot. [OE *fretan* to devour]

fret[2] (fret) *n.* One of a series of ridges, as of metal, fixed across the fingerboard of a guitar, ukulele, etc., to guide the fingers in stopping the strings. — *v.t.* **fret·ted, fret·ting** To provide (a guitar, etc.) with frets. [Cf. OF *frete* ring]

FRETS[3]

fret[3] (fret) *n.* An ornamental band or border consisting of angular or sometimes curved lines symmetrically arranged. — *v.t.* **fret·ted, fret·ting** To adorn with a fret. [Prob. < OF *frette* lattice, trellis]

fret·ful (fret′fəl) *adj.* Inclined to fret; peevish or restless. — **fret′ful·ly** *adv.* — **fret′ful·ness** *n.*

— **Syn.** complaining, impatient, pettish, petulant, restive.

fret·work (fret′wûrk′) *n.* **1.** Ornamental openwork, usu. composed of frets or interlaced parts. **2.** A pattern, as of light and shade, resembling such openwork.

Freu·di·an (froi′dē·ən) *adj.* Of, pertaining to, or conforming to the teachings of Sigmund Freud. — *n.* An adherent of the theories of Freud. — **Freu′di·an·ism** *n.*

fri·a·ble (frī′ə·bəl) *adj.* Easily crumbled or pulverized. [< F < L < *friare* to crumble] — **fri′a·bil′i·ty, fri′a·ble·ness** *n.*

fri·ar (frī′ər) *n.* A man who is a member of one of several religious orders, esp. the mendicant orders, as the Dominicans or Franciscans. [< OF *frere* < L *frater* brother]

fri·ar·y (frī′ər·ē) *n.* *pl.* **·ar·ies** **1.** A monastery, especially of a mendicant order. **2.** A community of friars.

fric·as·see (frik′ə·sē′) *n.* A dish of meat cut small, stewed, and served with gravy. — *v.t.* **·seed, ·see·ing** To make into a fricassee. [< F *fricassé,* orig. pp. of *fricasser* to sauté]

fric·a·tive (frik′ə·tiv) *Phonet. adj.* Of consonants, produ by the passage of breath through a narrow aperture with sultant audible friction, as (f), (v), (th). — *n.* A consor so produced. [< NL < L *fricare* to rub]

fric·tion (frik′shən) *n.* **1.** The rubbing of one object aga another. **2.** Conflict of opinions, differences in temperam etc. [< F < L *fricare* to rub] — **fric′tion·al** *adj.* — **f tion·al·ly** *adv.*

friction tape Cotton tape impregnated with an adhes moisture-resisting compound, used in electrical work.

Fri·day (frī′dē, -dā) *n.* The sixth day of the week. [*Frīgedæg* Frigg's day]

Fri·day (frī′dē, -dā) In Defoe's *Robinson Crusoe,* Crus native servant and companion. — *n.* Any devote faithful attendant or helper: man *Friday;* girl *Friday.*

fried (frīd) Past tense and past participle of FRY. — *Slang* Intoxicated.

fried cake A small cake or doughnut fried in deep fat.

friend (frend) *n.* **1.** One who is personally well know oneself and for whom one has warm regard or affection; mate. **2.** One with whom one is on speaking terms; an a ciate or acquaintance. **3.** One who belongs to the same tion, party, etc., as oneself; also, one with whom one is un in some purpose, cause, etc. **4.** A patron or suppo [OE *frēond*] — **friend′less** *adj.* — **friend′less·ness** *n.*

Friend (frend) *n.* A member of the Society of Frie Quaker.

friend·ly (frend′lē) *adj.* **·li·er, ·li·est** **1.** Of, pertaining t typical of a friend. **2.** Well-disposed; not antagonistic. Acting as a friend; showing friendship. **4.** Helpful; fa able: a *friendly* wind. — *adv.* In a friendly manner: **friend′li·ly.** — **friend′li·ness** *n.*

friend·ship (frend′ship) *n.* **1.** The state or fact of b friends. **2.** Mutual liking and esteem.

fri·er (frī′ər) See FRYER.

frieze[1] (frēz) *n.* **1.** The horizontal strip running betwe cornice and architrave, either plain or decorated with sc ture, scrolls, etc. **2.** Any decorative horizontal strip along the top of a wall in a room. [< F < Med.L *frisi*

frieze[2] (frēz) *n.* A coarse, woolen cloth with a shaggy r [< MF < *friser* to curl]

frig·ate (frig′it) *n.* A sailing war vessel of medium s in use from about the 17th to the 19th centuries. [< I Ital. *fregata*]

frigate bird Either of two large, rapacious, web-footed rine birds having hooked beaks and very long wings: called *man-of-war bird.*

Frigg (frig) In Norse mythology, the wife of Odin and goddess of marriage. Also **Frig·ga** (frig′ə).

fright (frīt) *n.* **1.** Sudden, violent alarm or fear. **2.** *formal* One who or that which is ugly, etc. [OE *fryhto*

fright·en (frīt′n) *v.t.* **1.** To make suddenly alarmed, f ful, or terrified; scare. **2.** To drive, force, etc., (away, into, etc.) by scaring. — *v.i.* **3.** To become afraid. **fright′en·ing** *adj.* — **fright′en·ing·ly** *adv.*

fright·ful (frīt′fəl) *adj.* **1.** Repulsive, shocking, or temptible. **2.** *Informal* Most distressing; very bad: a *fri ful* headache. **3.** *Informal* Excessively great: a *frigh* number of losses. **4.** Such as fills with fright; alarmin terrifying. — **fright′ful·ly** *adv.* — **fright′ful·ness** *n.*

frig·id (frij′id) *adj.* **1.** Bitterly cold. **2.** Lacking warmt feeling; formal. **3.** Habitually lacking sexual feeling or sponse: said of women. [< L *frigere* to be cold] — **frig ly** *adv.* — **fri·gid·i·ty** (fri·jid′ə·tē), **frig′id·ness** *n.*

fri·jol (frē′hōl) *n.* *pl.* **fri·joles** (frē′hōlz, *Sp.* frē·hō′lās) bean used as food, esp. by Latin-Americans. Also **fri·j** (frē′hōl, *Sp.* frē·hō′lā). [< Sp.]

frill (fril) *n.* **1.** An ornamental strip of lace, etc., gathe together and attached along one edge and left free along other; ruffle. **2.** *U.S. Informal* Any showy or superflu detail of dress, manner, etc. **3.** *Zool.* A ruff of feath about the neck of some birds or of hair about the neck some animals. — *v.t.* **1.** To make into a frill. **2.** To frills on. [Origin uncertain] — **frill′y** *adv.*

frill·ing (fril′ing) *n.* **1.** Frills collectively. **2.** A materia trimming suitable for use in a frill or frills.

fringe (frinj) *n.* **1.** An ornamental border of hanging cor threads, etc. **2.** Something suggestive of such a border trimming: a *fringe* of grass along a sidewalk. **3.** The a along the edge of something: the *fringes* of a city. — **fringed, fring·ing** **1.** To provide with or as with a fringe. To constitute a fringe on or along. — *adj.* Outer; margin a *fringe* area. [< OF < L *fimbria* fringe] — **fring′y** *a*

fringe benefit Anything of value given an employee in a dition to his salary or wages, as insurance, pension, etc.

frin·gil·line (frin·jil′īn, -in) *adj.* Of, pertaining to, or sembling a family of small birds including the finches a sparrows. [< L *fringilla* small bird + -INE[1]]

frip·per·y (frip′ər·ē) *n.* *pl.* **·per·ies** **1.** Cheap, flashy dr or ornamentation. **2.** Showiness or affectation in speec manner, etc. [< F < OF *frepe* rag]

s·co (fris′kō) *Informal* San Francisco, California.
sé (fri·zā′) *n.* An upholstery or rug fabric faced with a ck pile of uncut loops or of cut and uncut loops in design. F, orig. pp. of *friser* to curl]
s·ian (frizh′ən, frizh′ē·ən) *adj.* Of or pertaining to the itch province of Friesland, its people, or their language. *n.* **1.** A native or inhabitant of Friesland. **2.** The Ger-nic language of the Frisians. Also spelled *Friesian.*
k (frisk) *v.i.* **1.** To move or leap about playfully; frolic. *v.t.* **2.** To move with quick jerks: a lamb *frisking* its tail. *U.S. Slang* To search (someone) for a concealed weapon, ., by quickly feeling the pockets and clothing. **4.** *Slang* rob of valuables in this way. **—** *n.* **1.** A playful skipping out. **2.** *U.S. Slang* A search of someone for a weapon, etc. obs. *frisk* lively < F *frisque*] **— frisk′er** *n.*
k·y (fris′kē) *adj.* **frisk·i·er, frisk·i·est** Lively or playful. **frisk·i·ly** *adv.* **— frisk·i·ness** *n.*
(frit) *n.* The material formed by the partial fusion of d and fluxes in the process of making glass. **—** *v.t.* To ke (a mixture of sand, alkalis, etc.) into frit. Also **fritt.** F < Ital. *fritta,* pp. of *friggere* to fry]
·ter¹ (frit′ər) *v.t.* To waste or squander little by little, as ney, time, etc.: usu. with *away.* [< L *frangere* to break]
·ter² (frit′ər) *n.* A small cake made of plain batter or of n, meat, fruit, etc., covered with batter and fried in deep . [< F < L *frigere* to fry]
·o·lous (friv′ə·ləs) *adj.* **1.** Lacking importance or sig-icance; petty. **2.** Inclined to levity; not serious; silly; kle. [< L *frivolous* silly] **— fri·vol·i·ty** (fri·vol′ə·tē) *n.* **friv′o·lous·ly** *adv.* **— friv′o·lous·ness** *n.*
z (friz) *v.t. & v.i.* **1.** To form into tight, crisp curls, the hair. **2.** To make or form into small, tight tufts or ots, as the nap of cloth. **—** *n.* **1.** That which is frizzed, hair. **2.** The condition of being frizzed. Also **friz.** F *friser* to curl] **— friz′zer** or **friz′er** *n.*
·zle¹ (friz′əl) *v.t. & v.i.* **·zled, ·zling 1.** To fry or cook th a sizzling noise. **2.** To make or become curled or crisp, by frying. [Blend of FRY and SIZZLE; ? infl. by FRIZZLE²]
·zle² (friz′əl) *v.t. & v.i.* **·zled, ·zling** To form into tight rls, as the hair; frizz. **—** *n.* A crisp curl; frizz. [? Freq. obs. *frieze* produce a nap on < MF *friser* to curl]
·zly (friz′lē) *adj.* Having tight, crisp curls.
z·y (friz′ē) *adj.* **frizz·i·er, frizz·i·est** Frizzly. **— friz′·y** *adv.* **— friz′zi·ness** *n.*
(frō) *adv.* Away from; back: used in the phrase *to and fro.* *prep. Scot.* From. [< ON *frā* from]
ck (frok) *n.* **1.** A long, loose-fitting robe with wide sleeves rn by monks; also, the clerical or priestly state. **2.** Any several types of garments; as: **a** A dress. **b** A workers' ock. **c** A frock coat. **—** *v.t.* **1.** To furnish with or clothe a frock. **2.** To invest with ecclesiastic office. [< OF *froc*]
ck coat A man's dress overcoat, worn esp. in the 19th ntury, having knee-length skirts and a tight-fitting, double-easted upper part.
g (frog, frôg) *n.* One of a genus small, tailless, web-oted animals with ort front legs and rge, strong hind legs apted to leaping. One of several sim-r amphibians, as a ee frog. **3.** A slight ritation, accumula-on of phlegm, etc., oducing difficulty hoarseness in eaking: also **frog the** (or **one's**) **roat. 4.** A trian-lar prominence in e sole of a horse's ot. **5.** A section of tersecting railroad acks designed to permit wheels to pass over the junction ithout difficulty. **6.** An ornamental braid or cord, as on a cket, often looped, so as to permit passage of a button. **—** *v.i.* **frogged, frog·ging** To hunt frogs. [OE *frogga*]

STAGES IN THE DEVELOPMENT OF THE FROG
a Eggs. *b* Embryo. *c-h* Development of the tadpole. *i* Young frog. *j* Adult frog.

og·man (frog′mən, -man′, frôg′-) *n.* *pl.* **·men** (-mən, men′) An underwater reconnaissance and demolition ex-ert, able to swim and operate under water using a scuba.
ol·ic (frol′ik) *n.* **1.** Merriness. **2.** A gay occasion or di-ersion. **3.** A playful antic. **—** *v.i.* **·icked, ·ick·ing 1.** To ove about or behave in a frisky way. **2.** To be prankish. < Du. < MDu. *vro* glad] **— frol′ick·er** *n.*
ol·ic·some (frol′ik·səm) *adj.* Gay and lighthearted. Also **ol′ick·y.** **— frol′ic·some·ly** *adv.* **— frol′ic·some·ness** *n.*

from (frum, from; *unstressed* frəm) *prep.* **1.** Starting at (a particular place or time): the plane *from* New York. **2.** With (a particular person, place or thing) as the origin or instrument: a letter *from* your mother. **3.** Out of (a holder, container, etc.). **4.** Out of the control of: He escaped *from* his captors. **5.** Out of the totality of: to subtract 3 *from* 8. **6.** At a distance in relation to: far *from* the city. **7.** Beyond the possibility of: He kept her *from* falling. **8.** By reason of; because of. **9.** As being other or another than: He couldn't tell me *from* my brother. [OE *fram, from*]
frond (frond) *n. Bot.* **1.** A leaflike expansion in which the functions of stem and leaf are not fully differentiated, as in ferns and seaweeds. **2.** A large leaf of tropical plants and trees, as of the palm tree. [< L *frons, frondis* leaf]
front (frunt) *n.* **1.** The part or side of an object or body that faces forward or is viewed as facing forward. **2.** An area or position located directly ahead or before: He stood in *front* of her. **3.** An area or position of principal or most important activity. **4.** *Mil.* **a** The lateral space from flank to flank occupied by a unit. **b** The line of contact of two opposing forces. **5.** The outer side of a building, usu. the side where the main entrance is. **6.** An extent of land lying directly along a lake, road, etc. **7.** A group or movement uniting various individuals with a common aim. **8.** One chosen to head a group, movement, etc., to give it prestige, often lacking real authority. **9.** An apparently respectable person, business, etc., used for cloaking objectionable or illegal activities. **10.** One's bearing or attitude in facing a particular situation, problem, etc.: to put on a bold *front.* **11.** *Informal* An outward air of pretense of wealth, social importance, etc. **12.** A detachable, starched part of a man's formal dress shirt covering the chest. **13.** In hotels, the bellhop first in line. **14.** *Meteorol.* The fore part of a mass of warm or cold air; also, the line of separation between a mass of warm and cold air. **15.** *Phonet.* The part of the tongue immediately behind the blade and directly below the hard palate. **—** *adj.* **1.** Of, pertaining to, or directed toward the front. **2.** Located on, in, or at the front. **—** *v.t.* **1.** To face toward. **2.** To meet face to face. **3.** To provide with a front. **4.** To serve as a front for. **—** *v.i.* **5.** To face toward something. [< OF < L *frons, frontis* forehead]
front·age (frun′tij) *n.* **1.** The front part of a lot or building; also, the linear extent of this. **2.** The direction in which something faces; exposure. **3.** Land adjacent to a street, body of water, etc.
fron·tal (frun′təl) *adj.* **1.** Of or pertaining to the front. **2.** Of or pertaining to the forehead or to the bone forming the anterior part of the skull. **— fron′tal·ly** *adv.*
fron·tier (frun·tir′) *n.* **1.** The part of a nation's territory lying along the border of another country. **2.** The part of a settled region lying along the border of an unsettled region. **3.** A new or unexplored area of thought or knowledge. **—** *adj.* Of or pertaining to a frontier. [< OF *front* front]
fron·tiers·man (frun·tirz′mən) *n.* *pl.* **·men** (-mən) One who lives on the frontier.
fron·tis·piece (frun′tis·pēs′, fron′-) *n.* **1.** A picture or drawing on the page facing the title page of a book; also, formerly, the title page itself. **2.** *Archit.* **a** A façade; also, a highly decorated section of a façade. **b** A pediment. [< F < Med.L < L *frons, frontis* forehead + *specere* to look at]
front matter *Printing* The pages preceding the actual text of a book or pamphlet.
front-page (frunt′pāj′) *adj.* Appearing on or important enough to appear on the first page of a newspaper.
frosh (frosh) *n.* *pl.* **frosh** *U.S. Slang* A college freshman.
frost (frôst, frost) *n.* **1.** A feathery deposit of ice formed on the ground or on the surface of exposed objects by dew or water vapor that has frozen. **2.** Rime. **3.** Frozen moisture within a porous substance, as in the ground. **4.** Temperature cold enough to freeze. **5.** The act of freezing. **6.** Coldness of manner. **7.** *Slang* A cold reception by the public. **—** *v.t.* **1.** To cover with frost. **2.** To damage or kill by frost. **3.** To produce a frostlike surface or effect on (glass, etc.). **4.** To apply frosting to. [OE] **— frost′less** *adj.*
frost·bite (frôst′bīt′, frost′-) *n.* The condition of having some part of the body partially frozen, often resulting in gangrene. **—** *v.t.* **·bit, ·bit·ten, ·bit·ing** To injure, as a part of the body, by partial freezing. **— frost′bit′ten** (-bit′n) *adj.*
frost·ed (frôs′tid, fros′-) *adj.* **1.** Covered with frost. **2.** Covered with frosting, as a cake. **3.** Presenting a surface resembling frost, as translucent glass. **4.** Frostbitten.
frost·ing (frôs′ting, fros′-) *n.* **1.** A mixture of sugar, egg white, butter, etc., cooked or beaten together, and used to cover cakes. **2.** The rough or lusterless surface produced on metal, glass, etc., in imitation of frost. **3.** Coarsely powdered glass, etc., used for decorative work.
frost·y (frôs′tē, fros′-) *adj.* **frost·i·er, frost·i·est 1.** Attended with frost; freezing: *frosty* weather. **2.** Composed of

or covered with frost. **3.** Lacking warmth of manner. **4.** Having white hair; hoary. — **frost′i·ly** *adv.* — **frost′i·ness** *n.*

froth (frôth, froth) *n.* **1.** A mass of bubbles resulting from fermentation or agitation. **2.** Any foamy excretion or exudation, as of saliva. **3.** Any unsubstantial or trivial thing, as a foolish conversation. — *v.t.* **1.** To cause to foam. **2.** To cover with froth. **3.** To give forth in the form of foam. — *v.i.* **4.** To form or give off froth. [< ON *frodha*]

froth·y (frô′thē, froth′ē) *adj.* **froth·i·er, froth·i·est** **1.** Consisting of, covered with, or full of froth; foamy. **2.** Unsubstantial or trivial. — **froth′i·ly** *adv.* — **froth′i·ness** *n.*

frou·frou (fro͞o′fro͞o′) *n.* **1.** A rustling, as of silk; swish. **2.** *Informal* Affected elegance; fanciness. [< F]

fro·ward (frō′ərd, -wərd) *adj.* Disobedient; intractable. — **fro′ward·ly** *adv.* — **fro′ward·ness** *n.*

frown (froun) *v.i.* **1.** To contract the brow, as in displeasure or concentration; scowl. **2.** To look with distaste: with *on* or *upon.* — *v.t.* **3.** To make known (one's displeasure, disgust, etc.) by contracting one's brow. **4.** To silence, rebuke, etc., by or as by a frown. — *n.* **1.** A wrinkling of the brow, as in displeasure; scowl. **2.** Any showing of displeasure. [< OF *froignier,* prob. < Gmc.] — **frown′ing·ly** *adv.*

frow·zy (frou′zē) *adj.* **·zi·er, ·zi·est** **1.** Slovenly in appearance; unkempt. **2.** Having a disagreeable smell; musty. Also **frou′zy, frow′sy.** [Origin uncertain]

froze (frōz) Past tense of FREEZE.

fro·zen (frō′zən) Past participle of FREEZE. — *adj.* **1.** Changed into or covered or clogged with ice, as a river. **2.** Killed or damaged by cold. **3.** Extremely cold, as a climate. **4.** Cold and unfeeling in manner. **5.** Made rigid or immobile: *frozen* with fear. **6.** *Econ.* **a** Arbitrarily maintained at a given level: said of prices, wages, etc. **b** Not readily convertible into cash: *frozen* assets. **7.** Made solid by cold.

fruc·ti·fy (fruk′tə·fī, fro͝ok′-) *v.* **·fied, ·fy·ing** *v.t.* **1.** To make fruitful; fertilize. — *v.i.* **2.** To bear fruit. [< F < L < *fructus* fruit + *facere* to do, make] — **fruc′ti·fi·ca′tion** *n.*

fruc·tose (fruk′tōs, fro͝ok′-) *n.* *Biochem.* A very sweet sugar, $C_6H_{12}O_6$, occurring in fruits: also called *fruit sugar, levulose.* [< L *fructus* + -OSE[2]]

fru·gal (fro͞o′gəl) *adj.* **1.** Exercising economy; saving. **2.** Costing little money: a *frugal* meal. [< L < *frugi* temperate, orig. dative singular of *frux* food] — **fru·gal′i·ty** (-gal′ə·tē) *n.* — **fru′gal·ly** *adv.* — **fru′gal·ness** *n.*

fru·giv·o·rous (fro͞o·jiv′ər·əs) *adj.* Fruit-eating. [< L *frux, frugis* fruit + -VOROUS]

fruit (fro͞ot) *n.* **1.** *Bot.* **a** The pulpy, usu. edible mass covering the seeds of various plants and trees. **b** In flowering plants, the mature seed vessel and its contents. **c** In spore plants, the spores with their enveloping or accessory organs. **2.** Any useful plant product, as cotton or flax. **3.** The outcome, consequence, or result of some action, effort, etc.: the *fruit* of labor. — *v.i.* & *v.t.* To produce or cause to produce fruit. [< OF < L *fructus* < *frui* to enjoy]

fruit·age (fro͞o′tij) *n.* **1.** Fruit collectively. **2.** The state, process, or time of producing fruit. **3.** Any result or effect.

fruit·cake (fro͞ot′kāk′) *n.* A rich, spiced cake containing nuts, raisins, citron, and other dried fruits.

fruit·er (fro͞o′tər) *n.* **1.** A ship that carries fruit; also, a fruit dealer or grower. **2.** A fruit-bearing tree or plant.

fruit fly **1.** Any of various flies whose larvae attack fruit. **2.** A fly whose larvae feed on fruit and which is used in research in genetics: also called *drosophila.*

fruit·ful (fro͞ot′fəl) *adj.* **1.** Bearing fruit or offspring abundantly. **2.** Producing results: a *fruitful* discussion. — **fruit′ful·ly** *adv.* — **fruit′ful·ness** *n.*

fru·i·tion (fro͞o·ish′ən) *n.* **1.** The accomplishment or realization of things worked for or hoped for; fulfillment. **2.** The enjoyment of this. **3.** The bearing of fruit. [< OF < LL < L *frui* to enjoy]

fruit·less (fro͞ot′lis) *adj.* **1.** Yielding no fruit; barren. **2.** Ineffectual; useless; unproductive. — **Syn.** See FUTILE. — **fruit′less·ly** *adv.* — **fruit′less·ness** *n.*

fruit sugar Fructose.

frump (frump) *n.* A dowdy, sometimes ill-tempered woman. [? < MDu. *frompelen,* var. of *verrompelen* to wrinkle]

frump·ish (frum′pish) *adj.* **1.** Dowdy or old-fashioned in dress. **2.** Ill-tempered; peevish. Also **frump′y.** — **frump′ish·ly** *adv.* — **frump′ish·ness** *n.*

frus·trate (frus′trāt) *v.t.* **·trat·ed, ·trat·ing** **1.** To keep (someone) from doing or achieving something; baffle the efforts, hopes, or desires of. **2.** To keep, as plans or schemes, from being fulfilled. [< L *frustrari* to disappoint]

frus·tra·tion (frus·trā′shən) *n.* **1.** The state of being frustrated or thwarted. **2.** Something that frustrates.

frus·tum (frus′təm) *n.* *pl.* **·tums** or **·ta** (-tə) *Geom.* **1.** That which is left of a cone or pyramid after cutting off the upper part along a plane parallel to the base. **2.** That part of a solid included between any two, usu. parallel planes. [< L, fragment]

FRUSTUM OF A PYRAMID

fry[1] (frī) *v.t.* & *v.i.* **fried, fry·ing** To cook in hot fat, over direct heat. — *n.* *pl.* **fries** **1.** A dish of anyt fried. **2.** A social occasion, at which foods are fried eaten. [< F *frier* < L *frigere*]

fry[2] (frī) *n.* *pl.* **fry** **1.** Very young fish; also, small adult when together in large numbers. **2.** The young of cer animals, as of frogs, when produced in very large quanti **3.** Young children, etc. See SMALL FRY. [< ON *friō* s

fry·er (frī′ər) *n.* **1.** One who or that which fries. young chicken suitable for frying. Also spelled *frier.*

fuch·sia (fyo͞o′shə, -shē·ə) *n.* **1.** Any of various plant the evening-primrose family, with red, pink, white, or ple, drooping, four-petaled flowers. **2.** A bright bluish the typical color of the fuchsia. [after Leonhard *Fu* 1501–66, German botanist]

fuch·sin (fo͞ok′sin) *n.* *Chem.* One of two deep red or vi dye compounds obtained from aniline, used as a bact stain, dye, etc.: also called *magenta.* Also **fuch·sine** (-sēn). [< FUCHSIA + -IN]

fud·dle (fud′l) *v.* **·dled, ·dling** *v.t.* **1.** To confuse or m stupid with or as with liquor. — *v.i.* **2.** To tipple. dial. G *fuddeln* to swindle]

fud·dy-dud·dy (fud′ē·dud′ē) *n.* *pl.* **-dud·dies** *Informa* An old-fashioned person. **2.** A faultfinding, fussy per [Varied reduplication, ? < dial. E *fud* the buttocks]

fudge (fuj) *n.* **1.** A soft, cooked confection made of bu sugar, chocolate, etc. **2.** Humbug; nonsense. — *v.t.* **fud fudg·ing** To make, adjust, or fit together in a clumsy or honest manner. [Origin uncertain]

Fuehr·er (fyo͝or′ər, *Ger.* fü′rər) See FÜHRER.

fu·el (fyo͞o′əl) *n.* **1.** Combustible matter used as a sour heat energy or to feed a fire. **2.** Whatever sustain heightens emotion, etc. — *v.t.* & *v.i.* **fu·eled** or **·elled, f ing** or **·el·ling** To supply with or take in fuel. [< OF *fou* < LL < L *focus* hearth] — **fu′el·er** or **fu′el·ler** *n.*

fu·gal (fyo͞o′gəl) *adj.* *Music* Of or pertaining to a fu

fu·gi·tive (fyo͞o′jə·tiv) *adj.* **1.** Fleeing or having fled from pursuit, arrest, etc. **2.** Not fixed or lasting; transi fleeting. **3.** Treating of subjects of passing interest; o sional. **4.** Wandering about; shifting. — *n.* One flees, as from pursuit, danger, etc.; runaway. [< F < *fugere* to flee] — **fu′gi·tive·ly** *adv.* — **fu′gi·tive·ness** *n.*

fugue (fyo͞og) *n.* *Music* A contrapuntal compositio which a theme is introduced by one part, repeated by o parts, and subjected to complex development. [< F < I *fuga* < L, flight]

Füh·rer (fyo͝or′ər, *Ger.* fü′rər) *n.* *German* Leader: a title plied to Adolf Hitler by his adherents: also spelled *Fueh*

-ful *suffix* **1.** Full of; characterized by: *joyful.* **2.** Able tending to: *helpful.* **3.** Having the character of: *manful.* The quantity or number that will fill: *cupful.* ◆ Nouns e ing in *-ful* form the plural by adding *-s,* as in *cupfuls, sp fuls.* [OE *-full, -ful* < *full* full]

ful·crum (fo͝ol′krəm) *n.* *pl.* **·crums** or **·cra** (-krə) **1.** support on which a lever rests or about which it turns w raising a weight. For illus. see LEVER. **2.** Any prop or s port. [< L, bedpost < *fulcire* to prop up]

ful·fill (fo͝ol·fil′) *v.t.* **·filled, ·fill·ing** **1.** To bring about accomplishment of (something promised, hoped for, ant pated, etc.); make an actuality of. **2.** To execute or perf (something commanded or requested). **3.** To come up t satisfy (something stipulated). **4.** To get through to end of (a period of time, a task, etc.); finish up. Also *B* **ful·fil′.** [OE *fullfyllan*] — **ful·fill′ment** or **ful·fil′ment** *n.*

full[1] (fo͝ol) *adj.* **1.** Filled up with as much or as many a possible. **2.** Containing an abundant or sufficient sup **3.** Complete or sufficient in number, quantity, etc.; not ficient: a *full* dozen; also, whole or entire: to pay the price. **4.** Maximum in size, extent, degree, etc.: a *full* lo *full* speed. **5.** Of the tide, risen to its highest level. **6.** the moon, having the face wholly illuminated. **7.** Hav had ample food or drink. **8.** Of the face, figure, etc., rounded out; plump. **9.** Engrossed or preoccupied: w *of*: *full* of plans for the future. **10.** Charged with emoti a *full* heart. **11.** Having satisfying resonance and volu *full* tones. **12.** Of garments, cut in ample folds; flowing long, *full* cape. — **in full cry** In close pursuit: said esp. dogs. — **in full view** In a position allowing complete v bility. — *n.* The maximum size, extent, degree, etc. — **in full** **1.** To the entire amount: paid *in full.* **2.** With abridgement, condensation, or abbreviation: to reprint text *in full.* — **to the full** To the most complete extent: enjoy something *to the full.* — *adv.* **1.** To a complete deg or extent: now chiefly in compounds: *full-fledged.* **2.** rectly; straight; right: I looked him *full* in the face. — **1.** To gather or pleat (the fabric of a garment). — *v.i.* To become full: said of the moon. [OE *ful*]

full[2] (fo͝ol) *v.t.* **1.** To make (cloth, yarn, etc.) thicker a more compact, as by moistening and beating or pressing. *v.i.* **2.** Of cloth, etc., to become thicker and more comp through special treatment. [Back formation < FULLE

ll·back (fŏŏl′bak′) *n.* In football, a player stationed be-ind the line of scrimmage, usu. just behind the quarterback nd the halfbacks; also, this position.
ll-blood·ed (fŏŏl′blud′id) *adj.* Unmixed in race or breed; so, related to another through descent from the same arents: also **full-blood** (fŏŏl′blud′).
ll-blown (fŏŏl′blōn′) *adj.* **1.** Blooming fully: a *full-own* rose. **2.** Fully developed: a *full-blown* genius.
ll-bod·ied (fŏŏl′bod′ēd) *adj.* Of beverages, having a sat-fying richness and strength.
ll-dress (fŏŏl′dres′) *adj.* **1.** Characterized by or requir-g full dress; formal: a *full-dress* dinner. **2.** Undertaken or ngaged in to the fullest possible extent: a *full-dress* debate.
ll dress Formal or ceremonial attire.
ll·er (fŏŏl′ər) *n.* One who fulls cloth, etc. [OE *fullere*]
ll·er's earth (fŏŏl′ərz) A soft, absorbent material resem-ing clay, used in removing grease from material to be lled, and also as a catalyst, and in talcs, poultices, etc.
ll-fledged (fŏŏl′flejd′) *adj.* **1.** Having the feathers fully rown. **2.** Completely developed or trained.
ll gainer A dive in which one springs forward off the oard and makes a complete back somersault.
ll-grown (fŏŏl′grōn′) *adj.* Having reached full growth.
ll house In poker, a hand made up of three cards of one nd plus two cards of another kind. Also **full hand.**
ll-length (fŏŏl′lengkth′) *adj.* **1.** Showing the entire ngth of an object or figure: a *full-length* portrait. **2.** Being f the original or usual length; not abridged.
ll moon **1.** The moon when the whole of its face is illu-inated. **2.** The time of month when this occurs.
ll·ness (fŏŏl′nis) *n.* The state or quality of being full. lso **ful′ness.**
ll-scale (fŏŏl′skāl′) *adj.* **1.** Scaled to actual size; not re-uced: a *full-scale* drawing. **2.** Engaged in or undertaken to ne fullest possible extent; all-out: a *full-scale* attack.
ll swing **1.** The height of activity: a party in *full swing.* . Freedom of activity: to be given *full swing.*
l·ly (fŏŏl′ē) *adv.* **1.** To the fullest extent or degree; en-rely: *fully* convinced. **2.** Adequately; sufficiently: *fully* ed. **3.** At the lowest estimate: *fully* three hundred.
l·mi·nate (ful′mə·nāt) *v.* **·nat·ed, ·nat·ing** *v.i.* **1.** To nake loud or violent denunciations; make scathing verbal ttacks; inveigh: to *fulminate* against taxes. **2.** To explode uddenly and violently, as a chemical. — *v.t.* **3.** To issue decrees, censures, etc.) in scathing rebuke or condemnation. . To cause, as a chemical, to explode with sudden violence. — *n. Chem.* Any explosive compound. [< L *fulmen, ful-inis* lightning] — **ful′mi·na′tion** *n.* — **ful·mi·na·to·ry** ful′mə·nə·tôr′ē, -tō′rē) *adj.* — **ful′mi·na′tor** *n.*
l·some (fŏŏl′səm, ful′-) *adj.* Distastefully excessive in n insincere way: a *fulsome* compliment. [< FULL, adj. + SOME; infl. by FOUL] — **ful′some·ly** *adv.* — **ful′some·ness** *n.*
m·ble (fum′bəl) *v.* **·bled, ·bling** *v.i.* **1.** To try to locate omething by groping blindly or clumsily: with *for, after.* **2.** To try awkwardly to do something: with *at.* **3.** In football, tc., to get hold of the ball and then let it slip awkwardly rom one's grasp. — *v.t.* **4.** To handle awkwardly or inef-ectually; botch. **5.** To drop awkwardly (a ball in one's rasp). — *n.* The act of fumbling. [Prob. < Scand. *famla* o grope] — **fum′bler** *n.*
me (fyōōm) *n.* **1.** A gaseous exhalation or smoke, esp. vhen acrid or otherwise disagreeable. **2.** A sharply pene-rating odor. **3.** Something with no more substance than moke. **4.** A state of rage: in a *fume.* — *v.* **fumed, fum·ing** .*i.* **1.** To give off fumes. **2.** To pass off in a mist or vapor. **.** To be filled with or show rage, irritation, etc. — *v.t.* **.** To subject to fumes. [< OF < L *fumus* smoke]
ı·mi·gate (fyōō′mə·gāt) *v.t.* **·gat·ed, ·gat·ing** To subject o smoke or fumes, as for disinfection or to kill vermin. < L < *fumus* smoke + *agere* to drive] — **fu′mi·ga′tion** *n.* — **fu′mi·ga′tor** *n.*
n (fun) *n.* **1.** Pleasant diversion or amusement. **2.** Light-earted playfulness: full of *fun.* — *adj. Informal* Full of un: a *fun* game. — **for** (or **in**) **fun** In jest. — **like fun** *In-ormal* Absolutely not; by no means. — **to make fun of** To ridicule. — *v.i.* **funned, fun·ning** *Informal* To behave or speak in jest. [< obs. *fonnen* to befool]
nc·tion (fungk′shən) *n.* **1.** The specific, natural, or proper action or activity of anything. **2.** The special duties or ac-ion required of anyone in an occupation, office, or role. **3.** Any more or less formal or elaborate social gathering or ceremony. **4.** Any fact, quality, or thing depending upon or varying with another. **5.** *Math.* A quantity whose value s dependent on the value of some other quantity. — *v.i.* **1.** To perform as expected or required. **2.** To perform the role of something else. [< OF < L *fungi* to perform]
unc·tion·al (fungk′shən·əl) *adj.* **1.** Of or pertaining to a function or functions. **2.** Designed for or suited to a partic-ular operation or use. **3.** Affecting the functions of an organ or part: *functional* disease: distinguished from *organic.* — **func′tion·al·ly** *adv.*
func·tion·al·ism (fungk′shən·əl·iz′əm) *n.* The doctrine that the function or use of an object should determine the form, structure, or material of the object.
func·tion·ar·y (funk′shən·er′ē) *n. pl.* **·ar·ies** One who serves in a specific capacity; esp., an official.
fund (fund) *n.* **1.** A sum of money, or its equivalent, accu-mulated or reserved for a specific purpose. **2.** *pl.* Money readily available. **3.** A ready supply: a *fund* of humor. **4.** *pl. Brit.* The government debt; also, government securi-ties: with *the.* — *v.t.* **1.** In finance: **a** To convert into a long-term debt. **b** To accumulate or furnish a fund for. **2.** To gather up a supply of.
fun·da·ment (fun′də·mənt) *n.* The buttocks; also, the anus. [< L *fundus* bottom]
fun·da·men·tal (fun′də·men′təl) *adj.* **1.** Pertaining to or constituting a foundation; basic. **2.** *Music* Of or pertaining to a root. **3.** *Physics* Designating the component of a wave form or other periodic oscillation on which all harmonic frequencies are based. — *n.* **1.** Anything that serves as the basis of a system, as a truth, law, etc. **2.** *Music* A root. **3.** *Physics* That frequency on which a harmonic or group of harmonics is based. — **fun′da·men′tal·ly** *adv.*
fun·da·men·tal·ism (fun′də·men′təl·iz′əm) *n.* **1.** The be-lief that all statements in the Bible are to be taken literally. **2.** In the U.S., a movement among Protestants holding such a belief. — **fun′da·men′tal·ist** *n. & adj.*
fu·ner·al (fyōō′nər·əl) *n.* **1.** The burial, cremation, or other final disposal of the body of a dead person, together with accompanying services. **2.** A procession held for the final disposal of the body of a dead person. — *adj.* Of, pertaining to, or suitable for a funeral. [< OF < Med.L < L *funus, funeri* burial rite] — **fu·ner·ar·y** (fyōō′nə·rer′ē) *adj.*
fu·ne·re·al (fyōō·nir′ē·əl) *adj.* **1.** Depressingly sad or gloomy; doleful: a *funereal* countenance. **2.** Pertaining to or suitable for a funeral. — **fu·ne′re·al·ly** *adv.*
fungi- *combining form* Fungus. Also, before vowels, **fung-.** [< L *fungus* mushroom]
fun·gi·cide (fun′jə·sīd, -gə-) *n.* Something, as a chemical compound, used in destroying fungi. — **fun′gi·ci′dal** *adj.*
fun·goid (fung′goid) *adj.* Resembling or typical of fungi. — *n. Pathol.* A fungus-like growth.
fun·gous (fung′gəs) *adj.* Of, pertaining to, or having the nature of a fungus.
fun·gus (fung′gəs) *n. pl.* **fun·gus·es** or **fun·gi** (fun′jī, -gī, -gē) **1.** Any nonflowering plants that have no chlorophyll, usu. reproduce asexually, and grow on dead organic matter or live parasitically, including mushrooms, molds, and mil-dews. **2.** Something that appears or spreads rapidly in a manner suggestive of a mushroom, etc. **3.** *Pathol.* A soft, spongy, granular growth of tissue. — *adj.* Fungous. [< L, mushroom.] — **fun′gal** *adj. & n.*
fu·nic·u·lar (fyōō·nik′yə·lər) *adj.* Moved by the pull of a cable, as a streetcar in a hilly section. — *n.* A railway along which cable cars are drawn: also **funicular railway.**
funk (fungk) *Chiefly Brit. Informal n.* **1.** A state of fear or panic: esp. in the phrase **to be in a blue funk.** **2.** One who quails with fear. — *v.t.* **1.** To shrink back from (something difficult, etc.). **2.** To cause to quail. — *v.i.* **3.** To be in a funk. [Cf. Flemish *fonck* fear]
fun·nel (fun′əl) *n.* **1.** A utensil, usu. conical, with a wide mouth tapering to a small outlet or narrow tube, through which liquids, or other free-running substances are poured into bottles, etc., having narrow necks. **2.** One of the smokestacks of a large ship, locomotive, etc. **3.** Any chimney, flue, or similar shaft or tube. — *v.t. & v.i.* **fun·neled** or **·nelled, fun·nel·ing** or **·nel·ling** **1.** To pass through or as through a funnel. **2.** To converge to a particular point, area, etc. [Earlier *fonel,* ult. < L < *in-* into + *fundere* to pour]
fun·nies (fun′ēz) *n.pl. U.S. Informal* Comic strips, or the section of a newspaper containing them.
fun·ny (fun′ē) *adj.* **·ni·er, ·ni·est** **1.** Causing one to laugh or be amused; comical. **2.** *Informal* Peculiar; strange; odd. — **fun′ni·ly** *adv.* — **fun′ni·ness** *n.*
funny bone The part of the elbow where the ulnar nerve joins the humerus very close to the surface and which, when struck, produces an unpleasant, tingling sensation in the arm and hand: also called *crazy bone.*
fur (fûr) *n.* **1.** The soft, fine, hairy coat covering the skin of foxes, bears, squirrels, cats, and many other mammals. **2.** An animal skin or a part of an animal skin covered with such a coat, esp. when prepared for use in garments, rugs, etc.; also, such skins collectively. **3.** A layer of foul matter, as on the tongue when the digestive tract is upset. — **to make the fur fly** *U.S. Informal* To stir up a furor, as by making accusations, revealing faults, etc. — *adj.* Made of

or lined or trimmed with fur. — *v.t.* **furred, fur·ring** **1.** To cover, line, trim, or clothe with fur. **2.** To cover, as the tongue, with a layer of foul matter. **3.** To apply furring. [< OF *forrer* to line with fur < Gmc.]

fur·be·low (fûr′bə·lō) *n.* **1.** A ruffle, frill, or similar piece of ornamentation. **2.** Any showy bit of decoration. — *v.t.* To provide with furbelows. [Var. of obs. *falbala* < F]

fur·bish (fûr′bish) *v.t.* **1.** To make bright by rubbing; burnish. **2.** To restore to brightness or beauty; renovate: often with *up*. [< OF < OHG *furban* to clean] — **fur′bish·er** *n.*

fur·cate (fûr′kāt; *for adj., also* -kit) *v.i.* **·cat·ed, ·cat·ing** To divide into branches. — *adj.* Forked: also **fur′cat·ed** (-kāt·id). [< Med.L < L *furca* fork] — **fur·ca′tion** *n.*

Fu·ries (fyŏŏr′ēz) *n.pl.* In classical mythology, the three goddesses who avenge unpunished crimes: also called *Eumenides.*

fu·ri·ous (fyŏŏr′ē·əs) *adj.* **1.** Extremely angry; raging. **2.** Extremely violent or intense; fierce. **3.** Pushed to the limit; extremely great: a *furious* rate of speed. [< L *furere* to rage] — **fu′ri·ous·ly** *adv.* — **fu′ri·ous·ness** *n.*

furl (fûrl) *v.t.* **1.** To roll up (a sail, flag, etc.) and make secure, as to a mast or staff. — *v.i.* **2.** To become furled. — *n.* **1.** The act of furling, or the state of being furled. **2.** A rolled-up section of a sail, flag, etc. [< F *ferler* < OF < L *firmum* firm + *ligare* to tie]

fur·long (fûr′lông, -long) *n.* A measure of length, equal to ⅛ mile, 220 yards, or 201.168 meters. See table front of book. [OE *furlang* < *furh* furrow + *lang* long]

fur·lough (fûr′lō) *n.* Permission to be absent from duty, esp. in the armed services: now called *leave* or *leave of absence.* — *v.t.* To grant a furlough to. [< Du. *verlof*]

fur·nace (fûr′nis) *n.* **1.** A large apparatus with an enclosed chamber designed to produce intense heat for warming a building, melting metal, creating steam power, etc. **2.** Any intensely hot place. [< OF < L < *furnus* oven]

fur·nish (fûr′nish) *v.t.* **1.** To equip, or fit out, as with fittings or furniture. **2.** To supply; provide. [< OF *furnir* < OHG *frumjan* to provide] — **fur′nish·er** *n.*

fur·nish·ings (fûr′nish·ingz) *n.pl.* **1.** Articles of clothing, including accessories. **2.** Articles of furniture and other fixtures for a home, office, etc.

fur·ni·ture (fûr′nə·chər) *n.* **1.** The movable articles used in a home, office, etc., as sofas, chairs, tables, or mirrors. **2.** Any necessary equipment, as for a factory or ship. [< F *fourniture* < OF *furnir* < OHG *frumjan* to provide]

fu·ror (fyŏŏr′ôr) *n.* **1.** A great stir; commotion; rumpus. **2.** A state of intense excitement or enthusiasm. [< L *furor* < *furere* to rage]

furred (fûrd) *adj.* **1.** Having or clad in fur. **2.** Made of or trimmed with fur, as garments. **3.** Coated, as the tongue.

fur·ri·er (fûr′ē·ər, -yər) *n.* **1.** One who deals in, repairs, or stores furs. **2.** One who processes furs for garments, etc.

fur·ring (fûr′ing) *n.* **1.** A trimming or lining of fur. **2.** Furs collectively. **3.** An animal's coat of fur. **4.** A coating of foreign matter, as on the tongue. **5.** Strips of wood, metal, etc., fixed to a wall, floor, etc., so as to make a level surface or create air spaces.

fur·row (fûr′ō) *n.* **1.** A narrow channel made in the ground by or as if by a plow. **2.** Any long, narrow, deep depression, as a groove, rut, or deep wrinkle. — *v.t.* **1.** To make furrows or deep wrinkles in. **2.** To plow. — *v.i.* **3.** To become furrowed or wrinkled. [OE *furh*]

fur·ry (fûr′ē) *adj.* **fur·ri·er, fur·ri·est** **1.** Of, pertaining to, or resembling fur. **2.** Covered or provided with fur. **3.** Coated, as the tongue. — **fur′ri·ness** *n.*

fur·ther (fûr′thər) Comparative of FAR. — *adv.* **1.** At or to a more distant or remote point in time or space. **2.** To a greater degree; more. **3.** In addition; besides; moreover. — *adj.* **1.** More distant or advanced in time or degree. **2.** More distant in space; farther. **3.** Additional. — *v.t.* To help forward; promote. [OE *furthra*] — **fur′ther·er** *n.*

fur·ther·ance (fûr′thər·əns) *n.* **1.** The act of furthering; advancement. **2.** That which furthers.

fur·ther·more (fûr′thər·môr′, -mōr′) *adv.* In addition; moreover.

fur·ther·most (fûr′thər·mōst′) *adj.* Furthest.

fur·thest (fûr′thist) Superlative of FAR. — *adv.* **1.** At or to the most remote or distant point in space of time. **2.** To the greatest degree. — *adj.* **1.** Most distant, remote, or advanced in time or degree. **2.** Most distant in space.

fur·tive (fûr′tiv) *adj.* **1.** Done in secret; surreptitious; stealthy. **2.** Evasive; shifty. — **Syn.** See STEALTHY. [< F < L < *fur* thief] — **fur′tive·ly** *adv.* — **fur′tive·ness** *n.*

fu·ry (fyŏŏr′ē) *n.* *pl.* **·ries** **1.** Vehement and uncontrolled anger; ungovernable rage. **2.** A fit of such anger or rage. **3.** Violent action or agitation; fierceness: the storm's *fury.* **4.** A person of violent temper, esp. a woman. [< L *furia* < *furere* to rave]

furze (fûrz) *n.* A spiny evergreen shrub of the bean family, having many branches and yellow flowers: also called *gorse, whin.* [OE *fyrs*] — **furz′y** *adj.*

fuse[1] (fyōōz) *n.* **1.** A length of combustible material passi into the charge of an explosive, designed to be lit so as ignite the charge. **2.** *Mil.* Any mechanical or electronic vice designed to detonate a bomb, projectile, etc. **3.** *Ele* A device consisting of a small strip of metal mounted i casing and completing a circuit when put into position, metal melting and breaking the circuit if the current comes excessive. — *v.t.* To attach a fuse to (a rocket, bom etc.). Also spelled *fuze.* [< Ital. < L *fusus* spindle]

fuse[2] (fyōōz) *v.t. & v.i.* **fused, fus·ing** **1.** To liquefy by he melt. **2.** To join by or as if by melting together. [< *fusus*, pp. of *fundere* to pour]

fu·see (fyōō·zē′) *n.* **1.** A friction match with a large he capable of burning in the wind. **2.** A flare used as a railrc signal. Also spelled *fuzee.* [< F < Med.L < L *fusus* spind

fu·se·lage (fyōō′sə·lij, -läzh, -zə-) *n.* *Aeron.* The body of airplane, containing the cockpit, cabin, etc. [< F]

fu·sel oil (fyōō′zəl, -səl) A volatile, poisonous, oily liqu obtained from rectified corn, potato, or grape spirits a used as a solvent in various chemical processes. Also **fu′s** [< G *fusel* inferior spirits]

fu·si·ble (fyōō′zə·bəl) *adj.* Capable of being fused. — **fu bil′i·ty** *n.* — **fu′si·ble·ness** *n.* — **fu′si·bly** *adv.*

fu·si·form (fyōō′zə·fôrm) *adj.* Shaped like a spindle.

fu·sil (fyōō′zəl) *n.* A flintlock musket. [< F < OF *fo* a steel for striking sparks, ult. < L *focus* hearth]

fu·si·lier (fyōō′zə·lir′) *n.* **1.** A soldier armed with a fli lock musket. **2.** *pl.* Soldiers of certain regiments of British army: used in titles of the regiments. Also **fu′si·lee**

fu·sil·lade (fyōō′zə·lād′) *n.* **1.** A simultaneous or quic repeated discharge of firearms. **2.** Anything resembli this: a *fusillade* of hail. — *v.t.* **·lad·ed, ·lad·ing** To attack bring down with a fusillade. Also **fu′si·lade′.** [< F < *fus ler* to shoot < *fusil* musket]

fu·sion (fyōō′zhən) *n.* **1.** A melting or blending togeth **2.** Something formed by fusing. **3.** In politics, the union two parties or two factions within a party. **4.** *Physics* thermonuclear reaction in which the nuclei of a light eleme undergo transformation into those of a heavier eleme with the release of great energy: also called *nuclear fusic* [< L *fusio, -onis,* < *fundere* to pour]

fuss (fus) *n.* **1.** Nervous activity; bustle; commotion; a **2.** One excessively concerned with trifles: also **fuss′er.** *v.i.* **1.** To be too much concerned with trifles. — *v.t.* **2.** bother with trifles. [Origin unknown]

fuss·y (fus′ē) *adj.* **fuss·i·er, fuss·i·est** **1.** Too much co cerned with trifles; finicky. **2.** Fidgety; fretful. **3.** Requ ing meticulous attention. **4.** Having elaborate and sho trimmings, as clothing. — **fuss′i·ly** *adv.* — **fuss′i·ness**

fus·tian (fus′chən) *n.* **1.** Formerly, a kind of stout clo made of cotton and flax; now, a coarse, twilled cotton fabr as corduroy. **2.** Pretentious verbiage; bombast. — *adj.* Made of fustian. **2.** Pompous; bombastic. [< OF < Med < L *fustis* cudgel]

fust·y (fus′tē) *adj.* **fust·i·er, fust·i·est** **1.** Musty; mold rank. **2.** Old-fashioned; fogeyish. [< obs. *fust* moldy od <OF, wine cask] — **fust′i·ly** *adv.* — **fust′i·ness** *n.*

fu·tile (fyōō′təl, -til; *esp. Brit.* -tīl) *adj.* **1.** Being of no ava done in vain; useless. **2.** Frivolous; trivial: *futile* chatt [< F < L *futilis* pouring out easily, useless] — **fu′tile** *adv.* — **fu′tile·ness** *n.* — **fu·til·i·ty** (fyōō·til′ə·tē) *n.*

— **Syn.** **1.** vain, fruitless, abortive.

fu·ture (fyōō′chər) *n.* **1.** The time yet to come. **2.** Wh will be in time to come. **3.** A condition, usu. of success prosperity, in time to come: a man with a *future.* **4.** *Usu.* Any commodity or security sold or bought upon agreeme of future delivery. **5.** *Gram.* **a** A verb tense denoting acti that will take place at some time to come. **b** A verb in th tense. — *adj.* **1.** Such as will be in time to come. **2.** Pe taining to or expressing time to come. [< OF < L *futuru* future participle of *esse* to be] — **fu′ture·less** *adj.*

future perfect *Gram.* **1.** The verb tense expressing a futu action or state completed before a specified future tim He *will have finished* by tomorrow. **2.** A verb in this tens

fu·tur·ism (fyōō′chə·riz′əm) *n.* A movement in art, musi and literature during World War I that rejected tradition forms in an effort to portray more vividly the intensity an speed of contemporary life. — **fu′tur·ist** *adj. & n.*

fu·tu·ri·ty (fyōō·tŏŏr′ə·tē, -tyŏŏr′-) *n.* *pl.* **·ties** **1.** Time t come; the future. **2.** The state or quality of being futur **3.** A future event or possibility.

fuze (fyōōz) See FUSE[1].

fu·zee (fyōō·zē′) See FUSEE.

fuzz (fuz) *n.* **1.** Fine, loose particles, fibers, or hairs. **2.** fluffy mass of these. — *v.t. & v.i.* To become or cause to be come fuzzy. [Origin unknown]

fuzz·y (fuz′ē) *adj.* **fuzz·i·er, fuzz·i·est** **1.** Having fuzz. Resembling fuzz. **3.** Lacking sharp distinctness or clarity blurred. — **fuzz′i·ly** *adv.* — **fuzz′i·ness** *n.*

-fy *suffix of verbs* **1.** Cause to be or become: *deify.* **2.** Be come: *liquefy.* [< OF < L *facere* to do, to make]

G

G (jē) *n. pl.* **g's** or **gs, G's** or **Gs, gees** (jēz) **1.** The sev-
th letter of the English alphabet. Also *gee.* **2.** Any sound
presented by the letter *g.* **3.** *Usu. cap. U.S. Slang* One
ousand dollars; a grand. — *symbol* **1.** *Music* **a** The fifth
ne in the scale of C major or the seventh in the natural
ale of A minor. **b** A written note representing this tone.
A scale built upon the tone of G. **d** The treble clef. **2.**
ysics The acceleration of a body due to the earth's grav-
, about 32 feet per second per second; also, a unit of accel-
ation equal to that due to the earth's gravity (symbol g).
b (gab) *Informal v.i.* **gabbed, gab·bing** To talk, esp.
oly or excessively; chatter; prate. — *n.* Glib or excessive
eech. [Prob. < ON *gabba* to mock] — **gab′ber** *n.*
b·ar·dine (gab′ər·dēn, gab′ər·dēn′) *n.* **1.** A firm, twilled,
orsted fabric, having a diagonal raised weave, used for
ats, suits, etc. **2.** A similar, softer fabric of mercerized
tton. **3.** A gaberdine. [Var. of GABERDINE]
b·ble (gab′əl) *v.* **·bled, ·bling** *v.i.* **1.** To talk quickly or in-
herently. **2.** To utter rapid, cackling sounds, as geese. —
. **3.** To utter rapidly or incoherently. — *n.* **1.** Glib, inherent, or foolish talk. **2.** Cackling sounds, as of geese.
req. of GAB] — **gab′bler** *n.*
b·er·dine (gab′ər·dēn, gab′ər·dēn′) *n.* **1.** A loose, coarse
at or frock. **2.** A long, loose, coarse cloak worn by Jews in
edieval times. **3.** Gabardine. [< Sp. *garbardina*]
bi·on (gā′bē·ən) *n.* **1.** *Mil.* A cylindrical wicker basket
ed with earth, stones, etc., used as a defense. **2.** An open
linder, usu. of metal, filled with stones, etc., and used in
e preliminary construction of dams, etc. [< F < Ital.
bbione, aug. of *gabbia* cage < L *cavea* cage]
ble (gā′bəl) *n. Archit.* **1.** The outside, usu. triangular
ction of a wall extending upward from
e level of the eaves of a sloped roof to the
dge pole. **2.** The end wall of a building
hose upper part is a gable. **3.** Any
blelike feature, as above a door. — *v.t.*
To cause to form a gable: a *gabled* roof.
v.i. **2.** To form a gable. [< OF, prob.
ON *gafl* gable]

GABLES

ble roof A roof that forms a gable.
bri·el (gā′brē·əl) In the Bible, one of
e archangels, chosen as a special messenger of God.
d[1] (gad) *v.i* **gad·ded, gad·ding** To roam about restlessly
capriciously; ramble. — *n.* The act of gadding. [? < obs.
dling vagabond] — **gad′der** *n.*
d[2] (gad) *n.* **1.** In mining, a pointed tool. **2.** A goad. —
. **gad·ded, gad·ding** To break up (ore) with a gad. [<
N *gaddr* goad]
d·a·bout (gad′ə·bout′) *Informal n.* One who goes about
mlessly, frivolously, etc. — *adj.* Fond of gadding.
d·fly (gad′flī′) *n. pl.* **1.** One of various large flies, as a
orsefly, that bite cattle, horses, etc. **2.** An irritating,
othersome individual. [< GAD[2] + FLY]
dg·et (gaj′it) *n. Informal* **1.** Any small device or con-
ivance. **2.** Some little thing whose exact name is unknown.
d·o·lin·i·um (gad′ə·lin′ē·əm) *n.* A metallic element
ymbol Gd) of the lanthanide series. See ELEMENT. [after
hn *Gadolin,* 1760–1852, Finnish chemist]
d·wall (gad′wôl) *n. pl.* **·walls** or **·wall** A large fresh-
ater duck found in the northern hemisphere.
e·a (jē′ə) In Greek mythology, the goddess of earth
d mother and wife of Uranus. [< Gk. *Gaia* Earth]
el (gāl) *n.* One of the Celts of Ireland or the Scottish
ighlands. [< Scottish Gaelic *Gaidheal*]
el·ic (gā′lik) *adj.* Belonging or relating to the Gaels or
eir languages. — *n.* **1.** The languages of the Gaels. **2.**
he Goidelic branch of the Celtic languages.
ff (gaf) *n.* **1.** A sharp iron hook at the end of a pole, for
nding a large fish; also, the pole. **2.** *Naut.* A spar for
tending the upper edge of a fore-and-aft sail. **3.** *Slang*
oud or annoying talk. — *v.t.* To strike or land with a gaff.
to stand the gaff *U.S. Informal* To endure hardship,
c., patiently. [< OF *gaffe,* prob. < Celtic]
f·fer (gaf′ər) *n.* An old man. [Alter. of GODFATHER]

gag (gag) *n.* **1.** Something, as a wadded cloth, forced into or over the mouth to prevent a person from speaking or crying out. **2.** Any restraint or suppression of free speech, as by censorship. **3.** A device to keep the jaws open, as in dentistry. **4.** *Slang* A joke or hoax. **5.** *Slang* Something interpolated by an actor into a role, as a topical comment. — **to pull a gag** *U.S. Slang* To perform or perpetrate a practical joke, deception, etc. — *v.* **gagged, gag·ging** *v.t.* **1.** To keep from speaking out by means of a gag. **2.** To keep from speaking or discussing freely, as by force or authority. **3.** To cause nausea in; cause to retch. **4.** To keep (the mouth) open with a gag. — *v.i.* **5.** To heave with nausea; also, to choke on something. [ME *gaggen*] — **gag′ger** *n.*
ga·ga (gä′gä′) *adj. Slang* Foolish; crazy. [< F (slang), a foolish old man]
gage[1] (gāj) See GAUGE.
gage[2] (gāj) *n.* **1.** Something given as security for an action to be performed; pledge. **2.** Anything, as a glove, proffered as a challenge. **3.** Any challenge. [< OF *gage* pledge]
gag·gle (gag′əl) *v.i.* **·gled, ·gling** To cackle; gabble. — *n.* **1.** A flock of geese. **2.** A chattering group of women.
gai·e·ty (gā′ə·tē) *n. pl.* **·ties** **1.** The state of being gay; cheerfulness. **2.** Bright colorfulness or showiness, as of dress. **3.** Fun; merrymaking. Also *gayety.* [< F *gai*]
gail·lar·di·a (gā·lär′dē·ə) *n.* A western American herb with showy yellow or reddish flowers.
gai·ly (gā′lē) *adv.* In a gay manner: also spelled *gayly.*
gain (gān) *v.t.* **1.** To obtain; acquire; get: to *gain* an advantage. **2.** To succeed in winning (a victory, etc.). **3.** To develop an increase of: to *gain* momentum. **4.** To put on (weight). **5.** To earn (a living, etc.). **6.** To arrive at; reach: to *gain* port. — *v.i.* **7.** To grow better: to *gain* in health. **8.** To draw nearer; also, to increase one's lead: usu. with *on* or *upon.* — *n.* **1.** *Often pl.* Something obtained by way of profit, winnings, etc.: small *gains.* **2.** An advantage or lead. **3.** An increase, as in size, amount, etc. **4.** The act of gaining. [< F < OF *gaaignier* < Gmc.]
— **Syn.** (verb) **1.** See GET. **2.** attain, achieve. **7.** prosper, flourish.
gain·er (gā′nər) *n.* **1.** One who or that which gains. **2.** A full gainer. **3.** A half gainer.
gain·ful (gān′fəl) *adj.* Yielding profit; lucrative. — **gain′·ful·ly** *adv.* — **gain′ful·ness** *n.*
gain·say (gān′sā′) *v.t.* **·said, ·say·ing** **1.** To deny. **2.** To contradict. **3.** To act against; oppose. [OE *gegn-* against + SAY[2]] — **gain′say′er** *n.*
'gainst (genst, *esp. Brit.* gānst) *prep.* Against.
gait (gāt) *n.* **1.** One's manner of moving along on foot. **2.** One of the ways in which a horse steps or runs. — *v.t.* To train (a horse) to take a gait. [< ON *gata* way]
gai·ter (gā′tər) *n.* **1.** A covering, as of leather or canvas, worn over the leg, as a puttee. **2.** A similar covering for the ankle and instep; a spat. **3.** An old-fashioned shoe with a high top. [< F *guêtre*]
gal (gal) *n. Slang* **1.** A girl. **2.** A girl friend.
ga·la (gā′lə, gal′ə, gä′lə) *adj.* Appropriate to a festive occasion; festive. — *n.* An occasion marked by joyous festivity. [< F < Ital., holiday dress]
galacto- *combining form* Milk; milky. Also, before vowels, **galact-**. [< Gk. *galaktos* milk]
Gal·a·had (gal′ə·had) **1.** In Arthurian legend, the noblest knight of the Round Table, son of Lancelot, who accomplished the quest for the Holy Grail. **2.** Any pure man.
Gal·a·te·a (gal′ə·tē′ə) In Greek mythology, a statue of a maiden brought to life by Aphrodite after its sculptor, Pygmalion, had fallen in love with it.
Ga·la·tia (gə·lā′shə, -shē·ə) An ancient country of Asia Minor, so called from the Gauls who conquered it.
Ga·la·tian (gə·lā′shən) *adj.* Of ancient Galatia. — *n.* A native of Galatia. — **Epistle to the Galatians** A book of the New Testament, a letter written by the apostle Paul.
gal·ax·y (gal′ək·sē) *n. pl.* **·ax·ies** **1.** *Astron.* Any very large system of stars, nebulae, or other celestial bodies. **2.** *Usu. cap.* The Milky Way. **3.** A brilliant group, as of persons. [< F < L < Gk. < *gala* milk]

ONUNCIATION KEY: **add, āce, câre, pälm; end, ēven; it, īce; odd, ōpen, ôrder; to͝ok, po͞ol; up, bûrn; ə** = a in *above,* e in *sicken,* i in *flex-*
, o in *melon,* u in *focus;* **yo͞o** = u in *fuse;* **oil; pout; check; go; ring; thin; this; zh,** vision.

gale (gāl) *n.* **1.** *Meteorol.* A wind stronger than a stiff breeze. **2.** An outburst, as of hilarity. [Origin uncertain]

ga·le·na (gə·lē′nə) *n.* A metallic, dull gray, cleavable, isometric lead sulfide, PbS, one of the principal ores of lead. Also **ga·le·nite** (gə·lē′nīt). [< L, lead ore]

Ga·li·cian (gə·lish′ən) *adj.* **1.** Of Spanish Galicia, its people, or their language. **2.** Of Polish Galicia or its people. — *n.* **1.** A native of Spanish Galicia. **2.** The Portuguese dialect spoken there. **3.** A native of Polish Galicia.

Gal·i·le·an (gal′ə·lē′ən) *adj.* Of Galilee, in ancient northern Palestine. — *n.* **1.** An inhabitant of Galilee. **2.** A Christian. — **the Galilean** Jesus Christ. Also **Gal′i·lae′an.**

Gal·i·le·an (gal′ə·lē′ən) *adj.* Of or pertaining to Galileo.

gall[1] (gôl) *n.* **1.** *Physiol.* The bitter fluid secreted by the liver; bile. **2.** Bitter feeling; rancor. **3.** Something bitter. **4.** *U.S. Slang* Impudence. [OE *gealla*]

gall[2] (gôl) *n.* **1.** An abrasion or sore produced by friction. **2.** Something that irritates or vexes. **3.** Exasperation. — *v.t.* **1.** To injure (the skin) by friction; chafe. **2.** To vex or irritate. — *v.i.* **3.** To become or be chafed. [Prob. < GALL[1]]

gall[3] (gôl) *n.* An abnormal plant growth that on certain oaks yields tannin. [< F < L *galla* gallnut]

gal·lant (gal′ənt *for adj. defs. 1, 4, 5;* gə·lant′, gal′ənt *for adj. defs. 2 & 3; n.* gal′ənt, gə·lant′; *v.* gə·lant′) *adj.* **1.** Possessing spirit and courage; brave: *gallant* soldiers. **2.** Chivalrously attentive to women; also, dashingly amorous. **3.** Stately; imposing. **4.** Showy: *gallant* attire. — *n.* **1.** A brave, spirited man. **2.** A man chivalrously attentive to women or amorous in a courtly way; a paramour. — *v.t.* **1.** To be chivalrously attentive to (a woman). **2.** To escort. — *v.i.* **3.** To be a suitor. [< OF *galer* to rejoice] — **gal′lant·ly** *adv.*

gal·lant·ry (gal′ən·trē) *n. pl.* **·ries 1.** Nobility and bravery. **2.** Chivalrous or amorous behavior. **3.** An instance of gallant speech or behavior.

gall bladder *Anat.* A small, pear-shaped muscular pouch situated beneath the liver in man and serving as a reservoir for bile conducted through the **gall duct.**

gal·le·on (gal′ē·ən) *n.* A large sailing vessel of the 15th to 17th centuries. [< Sp. < Med.L]

gal·ler·y (gal′ər·ē) *n. pl.* **·ler·ies 1.** A roofed promenade, esp. an open-sided one extending along an inner or outer wall of a building. **2.** Any similar long, usu. narrow enclosed area, as a hall. **3.** *Southern U.S.* A veranda. **4.** An elevated rear floor section for seating in a theater or other large building, over the back of the main floor. **5.** A group of spectators, as of those in a grandstand. **6.** A part of the general public viewed as shallow, undiscriminating, etc. **7.** A room or building in which statues, paintings, etc., are displayed. **8.** A room or building in which articles are sold to the highest bidder. **9.** An enclosed place, as at a fair, where one shoots at targets for amusement. **10.** A tunnel or underground passage, as in a mine. — **to play to the gallery** To play or cater to the common crowd. — *v.t.* **·ler·ied, ·ler·y·ing** To provide with a gallery. [< F < Med.L *galeria*]

gal·ley (gal′ē) *n. pl.* **·leys 1.** A long, low vessel used in ancient times, propelled by oars and sails. **2.** A large rowboat. **3.** The kitchen of a ship. **4.** *Printing* **a** A long tray for holding composed type. **b** A galley proof. [< OF < Med.L < LGk. *galaia*]

galley proof *Printing* **1.** A proof taken from type composed in a galley and used for making corrections before page composition. **2.** Two or more such proofs collectively.

galley slave 1. A slave or convict condemned to row a galley. **2.** One who does monotonous work; drudge.

gall·fly (gôl′flī′) *n. pl.* **·flies** A small insect that deposits eggs in plant tissue, with consequent production of galls.

gal·lic (gal′ik) *adj. Chem.* **1.** Of, pertaining to, or derived from gallium. **2.** Relating to or derived from gallnuts.

gallic acid *Chem.* A white, odorless, crystalline organic compound, $C_7H_6O_5 \cdot H_2O$, found in many plants and used in the making of inks, dyestuffs, paper, etc.

Gal·lic (gal′ik) *adj.* Of or pertaining to ancient Gaul or modern France; French. [< L *Gallus* inhabitant of Gaul]

Gal·li·cism (gal′ə·siz′əm) *n.* An idiom or turn of phrase peculiar to French.

Gal·li·cize (gal′ə·sīz) *v.t. & v.i.* **·cized, ·ciz·ing** To make French in character, language, etc.; Frenchify.

gal·li·na·ceous (gal′ə·nā′shəs) *adj.* Of or pertaining to an order of birds including the common hen, turkeys, partridges, etc. [< L < *gallina* hen] — **gal′li·na′cean** *n.*

gall·ing (gô′ling) *adj.* Very annoying or exasperating.

gal·li·nule (gal′ə·nyōōl, -nōōl) *n.* Any of several cootlike wading birds of the rail family. [< L *gallina* hen]

gal·li·pot (gal′i·pot) *n.* A small earthen jar, as for ointments, used esp. by druggists. [? < GALLEY + POT]

gal·li·um (gal′ē·əm) *n.* A rare, bluish white, metallic element in the aluminum group, having a low melting point (86° F.). See ELEMENT. [< NL < L *gallus* cock, trans. of *Lecoq* de Boisbaudran, 1838–1912, its discoverer]

gal·li·vant (gal′ə·vant, gal′ə·vant′) *v.i.* To roam about [...]priciously; gad. [? Alter. of GALLANT]

gall·nut (gôl′nut′) *n.* A gall produced on certain oak[s or] other plants.

Gallo- *combining form* Gaulish or French. [< L *Gallus*

gal·lon (gal′ən) *n.* **1.** A liquid measure of capacity tha[t] the U.S. standard contains 231 cubic inches or 4 quarts by the British standard (**imperial gallon**) 277.3 cubic in[ches] or 4 imperial quarts. **2.** A dry measure equivalent ⅛ bushel. **3.** A container with a capacity of 1 gallon. [...]table front of book. [< AF *galon,* ? < Celtic]

gal·lop (gal′əp) *n.* **1.** The fastest gait of a horse, characterized by regular leaps during which all four are off the ground at once. **2.** A ride at a gallop. **3.** A rapid pace. — *v.i.* **1.** To ride at a gallop. **2.** To go v[ery] fast. — *v.t.* **3.** To cause to gallop. [< OF < *galope*[r] Gmc.] — **gal′lop·er** *n.*

gal·lows (gal′ōz) *n. pl.* **·lows·es** or **·lows 1.** A framew[ork] of two or more upright beams supporting a crossbeam, u[sed] for execution by hanging. Also **gallows tree. 2.** A similar structure, as a set of crossbars. [OE *galga*]

gallows bird *Informal* One who merits hanging.

gall·stone (gôl′stōn′) *n. Pathol.* A small, stony mass so[me]times formed in the gall bladder or bile passages.

gal·op (gal′əp) *n.* **1.** A lively round dance. **2.** Music [for] this dance, written in duple meter. [< F, gallop]

ga·lore (gə·lôr′, -lōr′) *adv.* In great numbers or abunda[nce] to offer bargains *galore.* [< Irish *go leōr* enough]

ga·losh (gə·losh′) *n. Usu. pl.* An overshoe reaching ab[ove] the ankle and worn in bad weather. [< F *galoche*]

ga·lumph (gə·lumf′) *v.i.* To clump along pompously. [< GAL(LOP) + (TRI)UMPH; coined by Lewis Carroll]

gal·van·ic (gal·van′ik) *adj.* **1.** Of or caused by electri[city] as produced by chemical action. **2.** Pertaining to a reac[tion] to an electric shock; convulsive. Also **gal·van′i·cal.**

gal·va·nism (gal′və·niz′əm) *n.* **1.** Electricity as produ[ced] by chemical action: also called *voltaism.* **2.** *Med.* The th[era]peutic application of a continuous electric current from [vol]taic cells. [after Luigi *Galvani* + -ISM]

gal·va·nize (gal′və·nīz) *v.t.* **·nized, ·niz·ing 1.** To stimu[late] to muscular action by electricity. **2.** To rouse to acti[on;] excite. **3.** To provide steel, etc. with a protective coa[t] of zinc. — **gal′va·ni·za′tion** *n.* — **gal′va·niz′er** *n.*

galvanized iron Iron coated with zinc, as for protect[ion] against rust.

galvano- *combining form* Galvanic; galvanism.

gal·va·nom·e·ter (gal′və·nom′ə·tər) *n. Electr.* An appa[ra]tus for indicating the presence and determining the stren[gth] and direction of an electric current. — **gal·va·no·met**[**ric**] (gal′və·nō·met′rik, gal·van′ō-) or **·ri·cal** *adj.*

gal·va·no·scope (gal′və·nō·skōp′, gal·van′ə-) *n.* An inst[ru]ment for detecting an electric current and showing its di[rec]tion. — **gal·va·no·scop·ic** (gal′və·nō·skop′ik, gal·van[...]) *adj.* — **gal′va·nos′co·py** (-nos′kə·pē) *n.*

gam (gam) *n. Slang* A leg, esp. of a woman. Also **ga**[...]

gam·bit (gam′bit) *n.* **1.** In chess, an opening in whic[h a] player risks or sacrifices a piece to gain a favorable positi[on]. **2.** Any opening move, as one to promote discussion. [< OF *gambet,* a tripping up, ult. < LL *gamba* leg]

gam·ble (gam′bəl) *v.* **·bled, ·bling** *v.i.* **1.** To risk or [stake] something of value on the outcome of a game of chance, [etc.] **2.** To take a risk to obtain a result. — *v.t.* **3.** To wage[r or] bet (something of value). **4.** To lose by taking risks: u[sually] with *away.* — *n. Informal* **1.** Any risky venture. **2** [A] gambling transaction. [Cf. OE *gamenian* to sport, pl[ay]] — **gam·bler** (gam′blər) *n.*

gam·boge (gam·bōj′, -bōōzh′) *n.* **1.** A gum resin obtai[ned] from a tropical tree, used as a pigment and cathartic. **2** [A] bright yellow or orange-yellow color.

gam·bol (gam′bəl) *v.i.* **gam·boled** or **·bolled, gam·bol**[**·ing**] or **·bol·ling** To skip or leap about in play; frolic. — *n.* [A] skipping about in sport. [< F < Ital. *gamba* leg]

gam·brel (gam′brəl) *n.* **1.** The hock of a horse, etc. **2** [A] gambrel roof. [< OF < LL *gamba*]

gambrel roof *Archit.* A ridged roof with the slope broken on each side.

GAMBREL ROOF

game[1] (gām) *n.* **1.** A contest governed by set rules, entered into for amusement, as a test of prowess, or for money or other stakes. **2.** *pl.* Athletic competitions. **3.** A single contest forming part of a fixed series. **4.** The number of points for winning, as in tennis or cards. **5.** The score during a contest: The *game* was 6–6. **6.** The equ[ip]ment used in playing games, as chess boards and piec[es]. **7.** The style or prowess in a contest: His *game* of golf is [not] good. **8.** A form of playful activity: Love is a *game.* [**9.**] *Informal* Any profession, business, etc.: the teaching *ga*[*me*]. **10.** A plan designed to attain an objective. **11.** Anima[ls,] fish, etc., that are hunted or taken; also, the flesh of su[ch] animals, etc. **12.** Anything hunted; quarry. **13.** A target for ridicule, criticism, etc.: They were fair *game.*

make game of To subject to ridicule, etc. —to play the ame 1. To act with honor, consideration, etc. 2. To act accordance with what is expected. —v. gamed, gam·ing . 1. To gamble at cards, etc., for money or other stakes. v.t. 2. To lose by gambling: with away. —adj. 1. Of nted animals, etc., or their flesh. 2. Having a fighting irit; plucky. 3. Informal Ready; willing. [OE gamen]
me[2] (gām) adj. Informal Lame: a game leg.
me·cock (gām′kok′) n. A rooster bred and trained for ckfighting.
me·keep·er (gām′kē′pər) n. A person having the care game, as on an estate.
ne·ly (gām′lē) adv. In a game manner; pluckily.
ne·ness (gām′nis) n. Pluck; bravery; endurance.
me·ster (gām′stər) n. One who gambles.
m·ete (gam′ēt, gə·mēt′) n. Biol. Either of two mature productive cells, an ovum or sperm, that in uniting proce a zygote. [< NL < Gk. gametē wife, or gametēs husnd] —ga·met·ic (gə·met′ik) adj.
neto- combining form Gamete. [< Gk. < gamos arriage]
me·to·phyte (gə·mē′tə·fīt) n. Bot. The phase or generan that produces the sexual organs of a plant.
m·in (gam′in, Fr. gà·maṅ′) n. A homeless youngster 10 wanders about the streets of a city or town. [< F]
m·ma (gam′ə) n. The third letter in the Greek alphabet , γ), corresponding to g (as in go). See ALPHABET.
nma globulin Biochem. A globulin present in blood asma and containing antibodies effective against certain thogenic microorganisms.
nma rays Physics A type of electromagnetic radiation great penetrating power.
m·mer (gam′ər) n. An old woman: now humorous or ntemptuous. Compare GAFFER. [Alter. of GODMOTHER]
m·mon (gam′ən) n. In backgammon, a double victory, which one player removes all his pieces before the other ayer removes any. —v.t. To obtain a gammon over. [? E gamen game]
mo- combining form 1. Biol. Sexually joined. 2. Bot. used; united. [< Gk. gamos marriage]
mous combining form Pertaining to marriage or union r reproduction: used in adjectives corresponding to nouns -gamy: polygamous. [< Gk. gamos marriage + -OUS]
m·ut (gam′ət) n. 1. The whole range of anything: the mut of emotions. 2. Music a The entire range or compass tones used in modern music. b The major diatonic scale. < Med.L gamma ut < gamma, the first note of the early usical scale + ut (later, do). The names of the notes of the ale were taken from a medieval Latin hymn: Ut queant xis Resonare fibris, Mira gestorum Famuli tuorum, Solve lluti Labii reatum, Sancte Iohannes.]
m·y (gā′mē) adj. gam·i·er, gam·i·est 1. Having the flar or odor of game, esp. game that has been kept raw until mewhat tainted. 2. Full of pluck; disposed to fight.
my combining form Marriage or union for reproduction: lygamy. [< Gk. gamos marriage]
n·der (gan′dər) n. 1. A male goose. 2. U.S. Slang A ok or glance: to take a gander. [OE gandra]
ng[1] (gang) n. 1. A group of persons organized or associed together for disreputable or illegal purposes. 2. A ew of persons who work together. 3. Informal A group of ersons associated together for some purpose. 4. A set of milar tools or other devices designed to operate as a unit. -v.t. 1. To unite into or as into a gang. 2. Informal To tack as a group. —v.i. 3. To form a gang. [OE gangan go]
ng[2] (gang) v.i. Scot. To go or walk.
n·gli·at·ed (gang′glē·ā′tid) adj. Possessing ganglia. Also an′gli·ate (-it, -āt), gan·gli·on·at·ed (gang′glē·ən·ā′tid).
n·gling (gang′gling) adj. Awkwardly tall and lanky. lso gan′gly. [Cf. dial. E gangrel a lanky person]
nglio- combining form Ganglion. Also, before vowels, angli- or ganglion-.
n·gli·on (gang′glē·ən) n. pl. ·gli·ons or ·gli·a (glē·ə) 1. hysiol. A collection of nerve cells, outside of the central ervous system. 2. Any center of energy, activity, or rength. [< LL < Gk. ganglion tumor] —gan·gli·on·ic ang′glē·on′ik) adj.
ng plank (gang′plangk′) n. A temporary bridge for pasngers between a vessel and a wharf.
n·grene (gang′grēn, gang·grēn′) n. Pathol. The rotting f tissue in the body, caused by a failure in the circulation f the blood, as from infection, etc. —v.t. & v.i. ·grened gren·ing To cause gangrene in or become affected by ganrene. [< L < Gk. gangraina] —gan′gre·nous (-grəəs] adj.
ng·ster (gang′stər) n. A member of a criminal gang.
ng·way (n. gang′wā, interj. gang′wā′) n. 1. A passageway through, into, or out of any enclosure. 2. Naut. a A passage on a ship's upper deck. b An opening in a ship's side to give entrance to passengers or freight. c A gangplank. —interj. Get out of the way! [OE gangweg]
gan·net (gan′it) n. Any of several large sea birds related to the pelicans and herons. [OE ganot]
gan·oid (gan′oid) adj. 1. Pertaining to a large division of fishes, including sturgeons, bowfins, etc. 2. Having an enamellike appearance, as the scales of such fishes. —n. A ganoid fish. [< Gk. ganos brightness + -OID]
gant·let[1] (gônt′lit, gant′-) See GAUNTLET[1].
gant·let[2] (gônt′lit, gant′-) n. 1. A former military punishment in which the offender ran between two lines of men armed with clubs, whips, etc., who struck him as he passed. 2. An onslaught of difficulties or criticism from all sides. —to run the gantlet 1. To be punished by the gantlet. 2. To be subjected to a fierce onslaught, as of criticism, difficulties, etc. Also spelled gauntlet. [Earlier gantlope, alter. of Sw. gatlopp a running down a lane]
gan·try (gan′trē) n. pl. ·tries 1. A bridgelike framework for holding the rails of a traveling crane or for supporting railway signals. 2. A gantry scaffold. 3. A frame to support a barrel in a horizontal position. Also spelled gauntry. [< OF < L canterius beast of burden, framework]
gantry scaffold Aerospace A large mobile scaffolding used to assemble and service a large rocket on its launching pad.
gaol (jāl) n. Brit. Jail. [Var. of JAIL] —gaol′er n.
gap (gap) n. 1. An opening or wide crack, as in a wall. 2. A deep notch or ravine in a mountain ridge. 3. A break in continuity; interruption. 4. A difference, as in character, opinions, etc. —v.t. gapped, gap·ping To make or adjust a breach or opening in. [< ON gap gap, abyss]
gape (gāp, gap) v.i. gaped, gap·ing 1. To stare with or as with the mouth wide open. 2. To open the mouth wide, as in yawning. 3. To be or become open wide. —n. 1. The act of gaping. 2. A wide opening; gap. 3. Zool. The width of the fully opened mouth, as of birds, fishes, etc. [< ON gapa] —gap′er n.
gap·py (gap′ē) adj. ·pi·er, ·pi·est Having gaps.
gar (gär) n. 1. Any of several fresh-water fishes having a spearlike snout and elongate body. [Short for GARFISH]
ga·rage (gə·räzh, -räj′; Brit. gar′ij) n. A building in which motor vehicles are stored, serviced, or repaired. —v.t. ·raged, ·rag·ing To put or keep in a garage. [< F < garer to protect]
Gar·and rifle (gar′ənd, gə·rand′) U.S. Mil. The M-1 rifle. [after J. C. Garand, born 1888, U.S. inventor]
garb (gärb) n. 1. Clothes; esp., apparel characteristic of some office, rank, etc. 2. External appearance, form, or expression. —v.t. To clothe; dress. [< MF garbe gracefulness]
gar·bage (gär′bij) n. 1. Refuse from a kitchen, etc., consisting of unwanted or unusable pieces of meat, vegetable matter, eggshells, etc. 2. Anything worthless or offensive. [Prob. < AF. Cf. OF garbe sheaf of grain, animal fodder.]
gar·ble (gär′bəl) v.t. ·bled, ·bling 1. To mix up or confuse (a story, facts, etc.) unintentionally. 2. To change or distort the meaning of (facts, texts, etc.) with intent to mislead or misrepresent. —n. 1. The act of garbling. 2. That which is garbled. [< Ital. < Arabic gharbala to sift]
gar·çon (gàr·sôṅ′) n. pl. ·çons (-sôṅ′) French 1. A boy or youth. 2. A waiter. 3. A male servant.
gar·den (gär′dən) n. 1. A place for the cultivation of flowers, vegetables, or small plants. 2. Any territory remarkable for the beauty of its vegetation. 3. Often pl. A piece of ground, commonly used as a place of public resort. —adj. 1. Grown or capable of being grown in a garden. 2. Ordinary; common. —v.t. 1. To cultivate as a garden. —v.i. 2. To till or work in a garden. [< AF gardin] —gar′den·er n. —gar′den·ing n.
gar·de·ni·a (gär·dē′nē·ə, -dēn′yə) n. Any of mainly tropical shrubs or trees with large, fragrant, yellow or white flowers. [after Alexander Garden, 1730–91, U.S. botanist]
Garden State Nickname of New Jersey.
gar·fish (gär′fish′) n. pl. ·fish or ·fish·es A gar. Also gar′·pike. [OE gar spear + FISH]
Gar·gan·tu·a (gär·gan′chōō·ə) The peace-loving giant of Rabelais' satirical romance Gargantua (1534), noted for his enormous appetite. —Gar·gan′tu·an adj.
gar·gle (gär′gəl) v. ·gled, ·gling v.i. 1. To rinse the throat with a liquid kept agitated by slowly expelling air through the liquid. —v.t. 2. To rinse (the throat and mouth) by gargling. 3. To utter throatily as if gargling. —n. A liquid used for gargling. [< OF gargouille throat]
gar·goyle (gär′goil) n. A waterspout, usu. made in the form of a grotesque human or animal figure, projecting from the gutter of a building. [< OF gargouille throat]
gar·ish (gâr′ish) adj. Vulgarly showy or gaudy: Her new

dress is very *garish*. [Cf. obs. *gaure* to stare] — **gar′ish·ly** *adv.* — **gar′ish·ness** *n.*

gar·land (gär′lənd) *n.* **1.** A wreath or rope of flowers, leaves, vines, etc. **2.** Anything resembling a garland. **3.** A collection of poems, bits of prose, etc. **4.** *Naut.* A ring of rope, wire, etc., lashed to a spar to aid in hoisting it. — *v.t.* To decorate with or make into a garland. [< OF *garlande*]

gar·lic (gär′lik) *n.* **1.** A hardy bulbous perennial with a compound bulb. **2.** One of the cloves of this perennial, used in cooking and medicine. [OE *gār* spear + *lēac* leek] — **gar′lick·y** *adj.*

gar·ment (gär′mənt) *n.* **1.** An article of clothing, esp. of outer clothing. **2.** *pl.* Clothes. **3.** Outer covering. — *v.t.* To clothe. [< OF *garnir* to garnish]

gar·ner (gär′nər) *v.t.* To gather or store as in a granary; accumulate. — *n.* **1.** A granary. **2.** Any storage place. [< OF < L *granum* grain]

gar·net (gär′nit) *n.* **1.** Any of a group of vitreous silicate minerals varying in color; esp., any of the deep red varieties, used as gems. **2.** A deep red color. [< OF < Med.L *granatum* < L, pomegranate]

gar·nish (gär′nish) *v.t.* **1.** To add something to by way of decoration; embellish. **2.** In cookery, to decorate (a dish) with flavorsome or colorful trimmings. **3.** *Law* To garnishee. — *n.* **1.** Something that garnishes food. **2.** An added decoration; embellishment. [< OF *garnir* to prepare]

gar·nish·ee (gär′nish·ē′) *Law v.t.* **·nish·eed, ·nish·ee·ing 1.** To attach (any debt or property in the hands of a third person that is due or belongs to a defendant) with notice that no return or disposal is to be made until a court judgment is issued. **2.** To issue a garnishment to. — *n.* A person who has been garnisheed.

gar·nish·ment (gär′nish·mənt) *n.* **1.** The act of garnishing. **2.** That which garnishes; embellishment. **3.** *Law* **a** A summons to appear in court, issued to one who is not a litigant in the case. **b** A notice to a person holding money or effects belonging to a defendant not to return or dispose of the money or effects pending court judgment.

gar·ni·ture (gär′ni·chər) *n.* Anything used to garnish.

gar·ret (gar′it) *n.* A room or set of rooms in an attic. [< OF *garir* to watch, defend]

gar·ri·son (gar′ə·sən) *n.* **1.** The military force stationed in a fort, town, etc. **2.** The place where such a force is stationed. — *v.t.* **1.** To place troops in, as a fort or town, for defense. **2.** To station (troops) in a fort, town, etc. **3.** To occupy as a garrison. [< OF *garir* to defend]

gar·rote (gə·rot′, -rōt′) *n.* **1.** A former Spanish method of execution with a cord or metal collar tightened by a screwlike device; also, the cord or collar used. **2.** Any similar method of strangulation. — *v.t.* **·rot·ed, ·rot·ing 1.** To execute with a garrote. **2.** To throttle in order to rob, silence, etc. Also **ga·rote′, ga·rotte′.** [< Sp. *garrote*]

gar·ru·lous (gar′ə·ləs, -yə-) *adj.* **1.** Given to continual or glib talking. **2.** Rambling and wordy. [< L *garrulus* talkative] — **gar′ru·lous·ly** *adv.* — **gar·ru·li·ty** (ga·rōō′lə·tē), **gar′ru·lous·ness** *n.*

gar·ter (gär′tər) *n.* A band worn around the leg or a tab attached to an undergarment to hold a stocking in place. — *v.t.* To support or fasten with a garter. [< AF < OF *garet* bend of the knee < Celtic]

Gar·ter (gär′tər) *n.* **1.** The distinctive badge of the **Order of the Garter,** the highest order of knighthood in Great Britain. **2.** The order itself.

garter snake Any of various small, harmless, viviparous, brightly striped snakes.

gas (gas) *n. pl.* **gas·es** or **gas·ses 1.** A form of matter having extreme molecular mobility and capable of diffusing and expanding rapidly in all directions. **2.** A combustible mixture used for lighting or heating. **3.** A mixture used to produce anesthesia; laughing *gas.* **4.** A chemical or mixture of chemicals designed to stupefy. **5.** An explosive mixture of air and methane, etc., sometimes accumulated in coal mines. **6.** A noxious exhalation given off by improperly digested food in the stomach or intestines. **7.** *U.S. Informal* Gasoline. **8.** *Slang* Long-winded talking. **9.** *Slang* Something very exciting, satisfying, etc. — *v.* **gassed, gas·sing;** he, she, it **gas·ses** or **gas·es** — *v.t.* **1.** To subject to or affect with gas. **2.** To fill or supply with gas. **3.** *U.S. Slang* To evoke a strong reaction, as of amusement or excitement, from: His remark *gassed* them. — *v.i.* **4.** To give off gas. **5.** *Slang* To talk excessively. [Coined by J. B. van Helmont, 1577–1644, Belgian chemist, either < Du. *geest* spirit or < L < Gk. *chaos* formless mass]

Gas·con (gas′kən) *adj.* Of or pertaining to Gascony or sit assertedly boastful people. — *n.* A native of Gascony.

gas·e·ous (gas′ē·əs, -yəs) *adj.* **1.** Of, pertaining to, or resembling gas. **2.** Light and unsubstantial; superficial.

gas fitter One who fits and puts up gas fixtures.

gash (gash) *v.t.* To make a long, deep cut in. — *n.* A long, deep cut or flesh wound. [< OF *garser* to scratch]

gas·ket (gas′kit) *n.* **1.** *Mech.* A ring, disk or plate of pa ing to make a joint or closure watertight or gastight. *Naut.* A rope or cord used to confine furled sails to the y or boom. [Cf. Ital. *gaschetta* end of rope]

gas·light (gas′līt′) *n.* Light produced by the burning illuminating gas. Also **gas light.**

gas·man (gas′man′) *n. pl.* **·men** (-men′) A man emplo to read gas meters and note the amount of gas used.

gas mantle A fabric tube that gives light when heated gas.

gas mask A protective mask with an air filter worn to p vent poisoning or irritation by noxious gases.

gas meter An apparatus for measuring the quantity of that passes through it.

gas·o·line (gas′ə·lēn, gas′ə·lēn′) *n. U.S.* A colorless, v tile, flammable liquid hydrocarbon, made by the distillat of crude petroleum and used chiefly as a fuel and as a solv for fats. Also **gas′o·lene.**

gas·om·e·ter (gas·om′ə·tər) *n.* **1.** An apparatus for m uring gases. **2.** A reservoir for gas. — **gas·om′e·try** *n.*

gasp (gasp, gäsp) *v.i.* **1.** To take in the breath suddenly sharply, as from fear. **2.** To have great longing or des with *for* or *after.* — *v.t.* **3.** To say or utter while gaspi — *n.* **1.** An act of gasping. **2.** An utterance made w gasping. [< ON *geispa* yawn]

gas station *U.S.* A filling station.

gas·sy (gas′ē) *adj.* **·si·er, ·si·est 1.** Filled with, contain or causing the formation of gas. **2.** Resembling or s gestive of gas. **3.** *Informal* Very talkative.

gas·tric (gas′trik) *adj.* Of or pertaining to the stomac

gastric juice *Biochem.* A fluid secreted by stomach glar essential to digestion and containing several enzymes.

gastric ulcer *Pathol.* An ulcer formed on the stomach ing, often by excess secretion of gastric juice.

gas·tri·tis (gas·trī′tis) *n. Pathol.* Inflammation of the ing of the stomach. — **gas·trit·ic** (gas·trit′ik) *adj.*

gastro- *combining form* **1.** Stomach. **2.** Stomach a Also **gastero-** or, before vowels, **gastr-.** [< Gk. *ga* stomach]

gas·tro·in·tes·ti·nal (gas′trō·in·tes′tə·nəl) *adj. Anat.* or pertaining to the stomach and intestines.

gas·tro·nome (gas′trə·nōm) *n.* A gourmet. Also **gas·tr o·mer** (gas·tron′ə·mər), **gas·tron′o·mist.**

gas·tro·nom·ic (gas′trə·nom′ik) *adj.* Of or pertaining gastronomes or gastronomy. Also **gas′tro·nom′i·cal.**

gas·tron·o·my (gas·tron′ə·mē) *n.* The art of good eati epicurism. [< F < Gk. < *gastēr* stomach + *nomos* law

gas·tro·pod (gas′trə·pod) *n.* One of a large class of aqu and terrestrial mollusks, including snails, slugs, limp etc., usu. having a univalve, spiral shell and a musc creeping organ. — *adj.* Of or pertaining to this class. NL < Gk. *gastēr* stomach + *pous, podos* foot] — **gas·tr o·dan** (gas·trop′ə·dən) *adj. & n.* — **gas·trop′o·dous** *adj*

gas·tru·la (gas′trŏŏ·lə) *n. pl.* **·lae** (-lē) *Biol.* An ea embryonic form, consisting of a two-layered sac enclosin central cavity opening to the outside at one end. [< N dim. of Gk. *gastēr* stomach] — **gas′tru·lar** *adj.*

gas turbine A turbine engine in which liquid or gase fuel is burned and the gases sent through a rotor unit.

gas·works (gas′wûrks′) *n. pl.* **·works** An establishm where illuminating gas or heating gas is made.

gat (gat) *n. Slang* A pistol. [Short for GATLING GUN

gate (gāt) *n.* **1.** A movable barrier, commonly swinging hinges, that closes or opens a passage through a wall, fen etc. **2.** An opening for exit or entrance through a wall fence. **3.** The structure on either side of such an openi **4.** Anything that gives access: the *gate* to success. **5.** mountain gap or other natural passageway. **6.** A protect barrier capable of being raised or lowered, as at a railrc crossing. **7.** A structure or valvelike device for controlli the supply of water, oil, gas, etc. **8.** The total paid atte ance at a sports event, theatrical presentation, etc.; al the money collected. — **to get the gate** *Slang* To be s away or be rejected. — **to give the gate to** *Slang* To d miss, reject, or get rid of. [OE *gatu*, pl. of *geat* opening

gate·crash·er (gāt′krash′ər) *n. Informal* One who ga admittance without paying or being invited.

gate-leg table (gāt′leg′) A table with swinging legs th support drop leaves and fold against the frame when t leaves are let down. Also **gate-legged table** (-legd′).

gate·way (gāt′wā′) *n.* **1.** An entrance that is or may closed with a gate. **2.** That which is regarded as a means entry or exit: the *gateway* to the Orient.

gath·er (gath′ər) *v.t.* **1.** To bring together into one place group. **2.** To bring together from various places, sourc etc. **3.** To harvest or pick, as crops, fruit, etc. **4.** To a cumulate or gain more and more of: The storm *gather* force. **5.** To clasp or enfold. **6.** To wrinkle (the brow **7.** To draw into folds, as cloth on a thread. **8.** To becor aware of; infer. **9.** To summon up or muster, as on energies. — *v.i.* **10.** To come together or assemble. **1**

o increase by accumulation. **12.** To become wrinkled or eased, as the brow. **13.** To come to a head, as a boil. - *n. Usu. pl.* A pleat or fold in cloth, held by a thread assing through the folds. [OE *gadrian*] — **gath′er·er** *n.*
th·er·ing (gath′ər·ing) *n.* **1.** The action of one who or at which gathers. **2.** That which is gathered. **3.** An semblage of people; group. **4.** A series of gathers in cloth, c. **5.** An abscess or boil. **6.** In bookbinding, a collection printed sheets in proper order.
uche (gōsh) *adj.* Awkward; clumsy; boorish. [< F, t-handed]
uche·rie (gōsh·rē′) *n.* **1.** An awkward or tactless action, atement, etc. **2.** Clumsiness; tactlessness. [< F]
u·cho (gou′chō) *n. pl.* **·chos** A cowboy of the South merican pampas. [< Sp.]
ud·y (gô′dē) *adj.* **gaud·i·er, gaud·i·est** Tastelessly brilnt or showy; garish. — **gaud′i·ly** *adv.* — **gaud′i·ness** *n.*
uge (gāj) *v.t.* **gauged, gaug·ing 1.** To determine the diensions, amount, force, etc., of. **2.** To determine the conents or capacity of, as a cask. **3.** To estimate, appraise, or dge. **4.** To make conform to a standard measurement. · *n.* **1.** A standard measurement, dimension, or quantity. A means or standard of comparing, estimating, or judgg; criterion. **3.** Any of various instruments or devices r measuring something. **4.** The distance between rails a railway. **5.** The distance between wheel treads. **6.** ne diameter of the bore of a gun. Also spelled *gage.* [< F *gauger* to measure]
ug·er (gā′jər) *n.* **1.** One who or that which gauges: also nd *gauger.* **2.** An officer of the revenue service who meases the contents of casks, etc. **3.** A tax collector.
ul (gôl) An ancient name for the territory south and west the Rhine, west of the Alps, and north of the Pyrenees; ughly the area of modern France.
ul (gôl) *n.* **1.** A native of ancient Gaul. **2.** A Frenchan.
ul·ish (gô′lish) *adj.* Of ancient Gaul, its people, or their eltic language. — *n.* The extinct Celtic language of Gaul.
unt (gônt) *adj.* **1.** Emaciated and hollow-eyed, as from nger, illness, or age; haggard. **2.** Desolate or gloomy in pearance: a *gaunt* region. [? < OF *gent* elegant] — **unt′ly** *adv.* — **gaunt′ness** *n.*
unt·let[1] (gônt′lit, gänt′-) *n.* **1.** In medieval armor, a ove covered with metal plates to protect the hand. **2.** ny glove with a long, often flaring extension over the wrist. ometimes spelled *gantlet.* — **to take up the gauntlet** To cept a challenge. — **to throw** (or **fling**) **down the gaunt**t To challenge to combat. [< OF *gant* mitten]
unt·let[2] (gônt′lit, gänt′-) See GANTLET[2].
un·try (gôn′trē) See GANTRY.
uss (gous) *n. Physics* The electromagnetic unit of magtic induction, equal to 1 maxwell per square centimeter. fter K. F. *Gauss*]
uze (gôz) *n.* **1.** A lightweight, transparent fabric with an en weave, made of silk, cotton, etc. **2.** Any thin, openesh material: wire *gauze.* **3.** A mist or light fog. — *adj.* esembling or made of gauze. [< MF *gaze,* appar. after *za,* where originally made] — **gauz′y** *adj.* — **gauz′i·ess** *n.*
ve (gāv) Past tense of GIVE.
v·el (gav′əl) *n.* A mallet used by a presiding officer to ll for order or attention. [< OF (Norman) *keville* pin]
·vi·al (gā′vē·əl) *n.* A large crocodile of India, having long, ender jaws. [< F < Hind. *ghariyal*]
·votte (gə·vot′) *n.* **1.** A dance of French origin, popular the 17th and 18th centuries and resembling a quick-movg minuet. **2.** Music for this dance, written in duple meter. lso **ga·vot′.** [< F < Provençal *gavoto* Alpine dance]
wk (gôk) *Informal v.i.* **1.** To stare stupidly; gape. **2.** To ove about or behave awkwardly. — *n.* An ungainly, stud individual. [Cf. dial. E *gawk* lefthanded]
wk·y (gô′kē) *adj.* **gawk·i·er, gawk·i·est** Awkward or umsy; ungainly. — *n. pl.* **gawk·ies** An awkward or ngainly person. — **gawk′i·ly** *adv.* — **gawk′i·ness** *n.*
y (gā) *adj.* **1.** Happy and carefree; merry. **2.** Brightly olorful or ornamental. **3.** Jaunty; sporty. **4.** Full of or ven to lighthearted pleasure. **5.** Rakish; libertine. [< F < Gmc.] — **gay′ness** *n.*
y·e·ty (gā′ə·tē) See GAIETY.
y·ly (gā′lē) See GAILY.
ze (gāz) *v.i.* **gazed, gaz·ing** To look steadily or fixedly at omething, as in wonder or admiration; stare. — *n.* A eady or fixed look. [ME *gasen* < Scand.] — **gaz′er** *n.*
·zelle (gə·zel′) *n.* A small, delicately formed antelope of orthern Africa and Arabia, with curved horns and large yes. [< OF < Arabic *ghazāl*]
·zette (gə·zet′) *n.* **1.** A newspaper or similar periodical. . An official publication, as of a government or society; esp., one of several publications issued by the British government listing government appointments, public bankruptcies, etc. — *v.t.* **·zet·ted, ·zet·ting** To publish or announce in a gazette. [< F < Ital. < dial. Ital. (Venetian) *gazeta* coin]
gaz·et·teer (gaz′ə·tir′) *n.* **1.** A work or section of a work listing countries, cities, rivers, etc., together with their location, size, etc. **2.** A writer for or publisher of a gazette.
gear (gir) *n.* **1.** *Mech.* **a** A mechanical assembly of interacting parts that serves to transmit motion or to change the rate or direction of motion. **b** A related group of parts that work together for a special purpose: steering *gear.* **2.** *Naut.* **a** The ropes, blocks, etc., used in working a spar or sail. **b** A ship's rigging or equipment. **c** The personal baggage or effects of a sailor. **3.** Any equipment, as clothing, tools, etc., used for a special task: a plumber's *gear.* — *v.t.* **1.** *Mech.* **a** To put into gear. **b** To equip with gears. **c** To connect by means of gears. **2.** To regulate so as to match or suit something else: to *gear* production to demand. **3.** To put gear on; dress. — *v.i.* **4.** To come into or be in gear; to mesh. — **out of gear 1.** Not engaged or connected, as one gear with another or with a motor. **2.** Not in working order or not in good condition. [< ON *gervi* equipment]

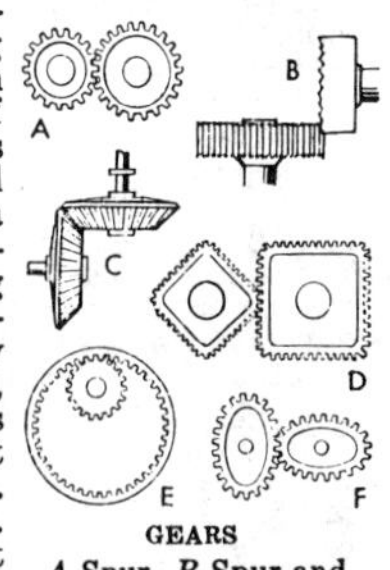

GEARS
A Spur. *B* Spur and crown. *C* Bevel. *D* Square. *E* Annular. *F* Elliptical.

gear·ing (gir′ing) *n.* **1.** *Mech.* Any system of gears or parts that transmit power or motion. **2.** *Naut.* Rope and tackle.
gear·shift (gir′shift′) *n. Mech.* A device for engaging or disengaging the gears in a power-transmission system.
gear·wheel (gir′hwēl′) *n. Mech.* A cogwheel. Also **gear wheel.**
geck·o (gek′ō) *n. pl.* **·os** or **·oes** Any of a family of small lizards having toes with adhesive disks. [< Malay *gēkoq*]
gee[1] (jē) *interj.* A cry used to guide horses, cattle, etc., to the right or (usu. with *up*) to urge them to move forward or faster. — *v.t. & v.i.* **geed, gee·ing 1.** To turn to the right. **2.** To move onward or faster: usu. with *up.* **3.** To evade. Opposed to *haw:* also spelled *jee.* [Origin uncertain]
gee[2] (jē) *interj.* An exclamation expressing mild surprise, sympathy, etc.: a euphemism for *Jesus.* Also **gee whiz.**
gee·zer (gē′zər) *n. Slang* A fellow; guy; esp., an old man. [Var. of *guiser* mummer < GUISE, v.]
Ge·hen·na (gi·hen′ə) *n.* **1.** A place of torment. **2.** In the New Testament, hell. [< LL < Gk. < Hebrew *ge hinnom* valley of Hinnom near Jerusalem where refuse was thrown]
Gei·ger counter (gī′gər) *Physics* An instrument for detecting ionizing radiation by means of a sealed tube containing a gas that when struck by ionizing particles conducts an electrical impulse between two electrodes connected to a suitable counting device. Also **Geiger-Müller counter** (mü′·lər), **geiger counter.** [after Hans *Geiger* and W. *Müller,* 20th c. German physicists]
gei·sha (gā′shə) *n. pl.* **·sha** or **·shas** A Japanese girl furnishing entertainment by singing, dancing, etc. [< Japanese]
gel (jel) *n. Chem.* A colloidal dispersion of a solid in a liquid, typically having a jellylike consistency, as gelatin, mucilage, uncooked egg white, etc. — *v.t. & v.i.* **gelled, gel·ling** To change into a gel; jellify. [Short for GELATIN]
gel·a·tin (jel′ə·tin) *n.* **1.** An almost tasteless, odorless, dried protein soluble in water and extracted by boiling the bones, tendons, skins, etc., of animals, used in food and drug preparation and in the manufacture of photographic film, plastics, etc. **2.** A jelly made from gelatin. Also **gel′a·tine** (-tin, -tēn). [< F *gélatine,* orig. a soup made from fish]
ge·lat·i·nate (ji·lat′ə·nāt) *v.t. & v.i.* **·nat·ed, ·nat·ing** To change into gelatin or jelly. — **ge·lat′i·na′tion** *n.*
ge·lat·i·nize (ji·lat′ə·nīz) *v.* **·nized, ·niz·ing** *v.t.* **1.** To gelatinate. **2.** To treat or coat with gelatin. — *v.i.* **3.** To be changed into gelatin or jelly. — **ge·lat′i·ni·za′tion** *n.*
ge·lat·i·nous (ji·lat′ə·nəs) *adj.* **1.** Having the nature of or resembling gelatin. **2.** Of or consisting of gelatin. — **ge·lat′i·nous·ly** *adv.* — **ge·lat′i·nous·ness** *n.*
geld (geld) *v.t.* **geld·ed** or **gelt, geld·ing 1.** To castrate or spay. **2.** To deprive of an essential part. [< ON *gelda*]
geld·ing (gel′ding) *n.* A castrated animal, esp. a horse.
gel·id (jel′id) *adj.* Very cold; icy; frozen. [< L *gelidus*] — **ge·lid·i·ty** (ji·lid′ə·tē) *n.* — **gel′id·ly** *adv.*
gem (jem) *n.* **1.** A cut and polished precious or semiprecious stone; jewel. **2.** One who or that which is treasured for having perfect or nearly perfect qualities. **3.** A kind of small, light cake. — *v.t.* **gemmed, gem·ming** To decorate or set with or as with gems. [OE < L *gemma* jewel]

gem·i·nate (jem′ə·nāt) *v.t. & v.i.* **·nat·ed, ·nat·ing** To double or become doubled; form into an identical pair. —*adj.* Formed into or appearing as a pair. [< L *geminus* twin]

Gem·i·ni (jem′ə·nī) *n.pl.* A constellation, the Twins; also, the third sign of the zodiac. See ZODIAC.

gem·ma (jem′ə) *n. pl.* **gem·mae** (jem′ē) *Biol.* **1.** A bud. **2.** A part of a plant or animal that grows outward, detaches, and forms a new individual. Also **gem′mule** (-yōōl). [< L]

gem·mate (jem′āt) *adj. Biol.* Bearing or reproducing by gemmae. —*v.i.* **·mat·ed, ·mat·ing** To form or reproduce by gemmae. —**gem·ma′tion** *n.*

gems·bok (gemz′bok) *n. pl.* **·bok** or **·boks** A South African antelope having long, sharp horns and a tufted tail. [< Afrikaans < G *gemse* chamois + *bock* a buck]

Gem State Nickname of Idaho.

gem·stone (jem′stōn′) *n.* A precious or semiprecious stone, esp. before it is cut and polished for use as a gem.

-gen *suffix of nouns* **1.** *Chem.* That which produces: *oxygen.* **2.** *Biol.* That which is produced: *antigen.* [< F < Gk. *gen-*, stem of *gignesthai* to be born, become]

gen·darme (zhän′därm, *Fr.* zhäṅ·dȧrm′) *n. pl.* **·darmes** (-därmz, *Fr.* -dȧrm′) **1.** One of a corps of armed police, esp. in France. **2.** Any policeman: a humorous use. [< F < *gens d'armes* men-at-arms]

gen·der (jen′dər) *n.* **1.** *Gram.* **a** One of two or more categories of words (esp. nouns and pronouns) or affixes based upon differences of sex or absence of sex or sometimes upon other distinctions (as of animateness or inanimateness), each category having distinctive forms for the words or affixes themselves or for the words modifying them. **b** Such categories collectively, or a system of such categories. **c** The distinctive form or forms used for such categories. **2.** *Informal* The quality of being of the male or female sex: a humorous use. [< OF < L *genus, -eris*]

gene (jēn) *n. Biol.* One of the complex protein molecules associated with the chromosomes of reproductive cells and acting, as a unit or in various biochemically determined combinations, in the transmission of specific hereditary characters from parents to offspring. [< Gk. *genea* breed, kind]

ge·ne·al·o·gist (jē′nē·al′ə·jist, jen′ē-, -nē·ol′-) *n.* One who traces genealogies or who is a student of genealogy.

ge·ne·al·o·gy (jē′nē·al′ə·jē, jen′ē-, -nē·ol′-) *n. pl.* **·gies** **1.** A record or table showing the descent of an individual or family from a certain ancestor. **2.** Descent in a direct line from a progenitor; pedigree. **3.** The study of pedigrees. [< Gk. *genea* race + -LOGY] —**ge·ne·a·log·i·cal** (jē′nē·ə·loj′i·kəl, jen′ē-) or **·log·ic** *adj.* —**ge′ne·a·log′i·cal·ly** *adv.*

gen·e·ra (jen′ər·ə) Plural of GENUS. [< L]

gen·er·al (jen′ər·əl) *adj.* **1.** Pertaining to, including, or affecting all or the whole; not particular. **2.** Common to or current among the majority: the *general* opinion. **3.** Not restricted in application: a *general* principle. **4.** Not limited to a special class; miscellaneous: a *general* cargo. **5.** Not detailed or precise: a *general* idea. **6.** Usual or customary. **7.** Dealing with all branches of a business or pursuit; not specialized: a *general* practitioner. **8.** Superior in rank: a second element in some titles: attorney *general.* **9.** *Med.* Relating to or affecting the entire body. —*n.* **1.** *Mil.* **a** In the U.S. Army, Air Force, or Marine Corps, a high-ranking officer. **b** In the Canadian Army, an officer ranking just below Field-Marshal. **c** An equivalent officer in other armies. Abbr. *Gen.* See tables at GRADE. **2.** A general officer: a shortened form. **3.** The head of a religious order. **4.** A general statement, fact, or principle. —**in general** **1.** Without going into detail. **2.** All things considered. **3.** Usually; commonly. [< OF < L *generalis* of a race or king < *genus, generis* kind]

gen·er·al·cy (jen′ər·əl·sē) *n. pl.* **·cies** **1.** The rank or office of a general. **2.** The time during which it is held.

general delivery *U.S.* **1.** A building or department of the post office in which an addressee's mail is kept until called for. **2.** Mail directed to this department.

general election **1.** An election in which all the people vote. **2.** An election held to make a final choice for office among candidates selected in a preliminary election.

gen·er·al·is·si·mo (jen′ər·əl·is′i·mō) *n. pl.* **·mos** **1.** In certain countries, one chosen as supreme commander of all the armed forces. **2.** The supreme commander of several armies in a particular campaign. [< Ital.]

gen·er·al·i·ty (jen′ə·ral′ə·tē) *n. pl.* **·ties** **1.** The state or quality of being general. **2.** Something lacking detail or precision, as a statement or idea: a speech filled with *generalities.* **3.** The greater number of a group; mass.

gen·er·al·i·za·tion (jen′ər·əl·ə·zā′shən, -ī·zā′-) *n.* **1.** The act of generalizing. **2.** Something, as a broad, overall statement or conclusion, arrived at by generalizing.

gen·er·al·ize (jen′ər·əl·īz′) *v.* **·lized, ·liz·ing** *v.t.* **1.** To make general; as: **a** To make broad in application. **b** To avoid making detailed. **c** To cause to be widespread. **2.** To derive a broad conclusion, principle, etc., from (particular instances, facts, etc.). —*v.i.* **3.** To write or speak without going into details, etc. Also *Brit.* **gen′er·al·ise′.**

gen·er·al·ly (jen′ər·əl·ē) *adv.* **1.** For the most part; or narily. **2.** Without going into specific details or instanc *generally* speaking. **3.** Commonly: *generally* believed.

general officer *Mil.* Any officer ranking above a colonel a general, lieutenant general, major general, etc.

General of the Air Force The highest-ranking officer the U.S. Air Force. See table at GRADE.

General of the Army The highest rank in the U.S. Arn See table at GRADE.

general paresis *Pathol.* Chronic paralysis of syphilitic gin, characterized by degeneration of body and brain tiss and progressive dementia. Also **general paralysis.**

general practitioner A physician whose practice is limited to a medical specialty.

gen·er·al·ship (jen′ər·əl·ship) *n.* **1.** A general's office rank; generalcy. **2.** A general's military skill or mana ment. **3.** Management or leadership of any sort.

general staff **1.** A body of officers who direct the milit policy and strategy of a national state. **2.** *Mil.* A grour officers who assist the commander in planning, coordinati and supervision of operations.

gen·er·ate (jen′ə·rāt) *v.t.* **·at·ed, ·at·ing** **1.** To produce cause to be; bring into being. **2.** To beget; procreate. *Geom.* To trace out by motion: A moving point *generate* line. [< L *generatus*, pp. of *generare* to generate]

gen·er·a·tion (jen′ə·rā′shən) *n.* **1.** The process of begett offspring. **2.** A successive step or degree in natural desce **3.** The average period between any two such success steps, about 30 years among human beings. **4.** Any gro of individuals born at about the same time. **5.** The act process of generating or being generated.

gen·er·a·tive (jen′ə·rā′tiv) *adj.* **1.** Of or pertaining to g eration. **2.** Having the power to produce or originate.

gen·er·a·tor (jen′ə·rā′tər) *n.* **1.** One who or that wh generates. **2.** *Chem.* An apparatus designed to generat gas. **3.** Any of a class of machines for the conversion of r chanical energy into electrical energy.

gen·er·a·trix (jen′ə·rā′triks) *n. pl.* **gen·er·a·tri·ces** (je ər·ə·trī′sēz) **1.** *Geom.* A line, point, or figure that genera another figure by its motion. **2.** A female that generate

ge·ner·ic (ji·ner′ik) *adj.* **1.** Pertaining to a genus or clas related things. **2.** Applicable to every member of a class genus. **3.** Having a wide, general application. Also **ge·n i·cal.** [< L *genus, -eris* race, kind + -IC]

gen·er·os·i·ty (jen′ə·ros′ə·tē) *n. pl.* **·ties** **1.** The quality being generous. **2.** The quality of being free of pettine magnanimity. **3.** A generous act.

gen·er·ous (jen′ər·əs) *adj.* **1.** Marked by or showing gr liberality; munificent. **2.** Having gracious or noble qualit a *generous* nature. **3.** Abundant and overflowing: a *gener* serving. **4.** Stimulating or strong, as wine. **5.** Fert *generous* soil. [< F < L *generosus* of noble birth < *ge* race] —**gen′er·ous·ly** *adv.* —**gen′er·ous·ness** *n.*

gen·e·sis (jen′ə·sis) *n. pl.* **·ses** (-sēz) **1.** The act or m of originating. **2.** Origin. [< L < Gk. *genesis* origin]

Gen·e·sis (jen′ə·sis) The first book of the Old Testame

-genesis *combining form* Genesis; evolution: *biogenesis.*

gen·et[1] (jen′it, jə·net′) *n.* A small carnivore related to civet. Also **ge·nette′.** [< F < Sp. < Arabic *jarnait* genet]

gen·et[2] (jen′it) *n.* A jennet.

ge·net·ic (jə·net′ik) *adj.* **1.** Of, pertaining to, or based on genetics. **2.** Of, or pertaining to the origin or development of something. Also **ge·net′i·cal.** [< GENESIS; formed on analogy with *synthetic*, etc.] —**ge·net′i·cal·ly** *adv.*

GENET[1]
(About 22 inches long; tail about 18 inches)

ge·net·ics (jə·net′iks) *n.pl.* **1.** (*construed as sing.*) The s ence dealing with the interaction of the genes in produc similarities and differences between individuals related descent. **2.** The inherited characteristics of an organis —**ge·net′i·cist** (-ə·sist) *n.*

Geneva Convention An international agreement signed Geneva in 1864 governing the war-time treatment of pris ers of war and of the sick and the wounded.

gen·ial (jēn′yəl, jē′nē·əl) *adj.* **1.** Kindly, pleasant, or c dial in disposition or manner. **2.** Imparting warmth, co fort, or life. [< L *genius* tutelary spirit] —**ge·ni·al·i** (jē′nē·al′ə·tē) *n.* —**gen′ial·ly** *adv.*

-genic *combining form* Related to generation or productic *biogenic.* [< -GEN + -IC]

ge·nie (jē′nē) See JINNI.

ge·ni·i (jē′nē·ī) Plural of GENIUS (def. 4).

gen·i·tal (jen′ə·təl) *adj.* Of or pertaining to the reprod tive organs or the process of reproduction. [< L *genit* pp. of *gignere* to beget]

gen·i·tals (jen′ə·təlz) *n.pl.* The external sexual organs. A **gen·i·ta·li·a** (jen′ə·tā′lē·ə, -tāl′yə).

gen·i·tive (jen′ə·tiv) *adj.* **1.** Indicating source, origin, p session, or the like. **2.** *Gram.* Pertaining to a case in Lat

eek, etc., corresponding in part to the English possessive. n. *Gram.* **1.** The genitive case. **2.** A word in this case. L *gignere* to beget] — **gen′i·ti′val** (-tī′vəl) *adj.* — **gen′i·**
al·ly *adv.*
ito- *combining form* Genital. [< L *genitus*, pp. of
nere to beget]
·i·to·u·ri·nar·y (jen′ə·tō·yŏŏr′ə·ner′ē) *adj. Anat.* Of or
taining to the genital and the urinary organs.
·ius (jēn′yəs) *n. pl.* **gen·ius·es** *for defs 1, 2, 3, & 5*; **ge·**
(jē′nē·ī) *for def. 4* **1.** Extraordinary intelligence surpass-
that of most intellectually superior individuals; also, one
o possesses such intelligence. **2.** An outstanding gift for
ne specialized activity; also, one who possesses such a
. **3.** The essential spirit or distinguishing characteristics
a particular individual, people, era, etc. **4.** In ancient
thology, a supernatural being appointed to guide a person
oughout life. **5.** A person who exerts a strong influence
er another. [< L *gen-*, stem of *gignere* to beget]
·o·cide (jen′ə·sīd) *n.* The systematic extermination or
struction of an entire people or national group. [< Gk.
os race, tribe + -CIDE] — **gen′o·ci′dal** *adj.*
·o·ese (jen′ō·ēz′, -ēs′) *adj.* Of or pertaining to Genoa.
n. pl. **·ese** A native or citizen of Genoa.
·o·type (jen′ə·tīp) *n. Biol.* **1.** The genetic constitution
an organism. **2.** A group of organisms with the same ge-
ic constitution. **3.** A type species. — **gen·o·typ·ic** (jen′·
ip′ik) or **·i·cal** *adj.* — **gen′o·typ′i·cal·ly** *adv.*
nous *suffix of adjectives* **1.** Generating; yielding. **2.**
oduced or generated by.
·re (zhän′rə, *Fr.* zhän′r′) *n.* **1.** A particular sort, kind,
category; esp., a category of art or literature character-
d by a certain form, style, or subject matter. **2.** A class
painting or other art depicting everyday life. — *adj.* Of
pertaining to genre. [< F < L *genus, -eris* race, kind]
s (jenz) *n. pl.* **gen·tes** (jen′tēz) **1.** *Anthropol.* In primi-
e society, a body of blood kindred having a common de-
nt traced through the male line. **2.** In ancient Rome, a
n descended through the male line. [< L]
t (jent) *n. Slang* A gentleman. [Short for GENTLEMAN]
·teel (jen·tēl′) *adj.* **1.** Well-bred or refined; elegant;
lite. **2.** Pertaining or appropriate to well-bred persons.
Stylish or fashionable. ◆ This word is now used chiefly
a derogatory or humorous sense. [< MF *gentil*] — **gen·**
el′ly *adv.* — **gen·teel′ness** *n.*
·tian (jen′shən) *n.* An annual or perennial herb with
owy blue, red, yellow, or white flowers. [< L *gentiana*,
par. after *Gentius*, an Illyrian king]
·tian·el·la (jen′shən·el′ə) *n.* **1.** A European alpine gen-
n having blue flowers. **2.** A bright blue color. [< NL,
n. of L *gentiana*. See GENTIAN.]
tian violet *Chem.* A purple dye used as an antiseptic.
·tile (jen′til, -tīl; *for adj. def. 2* -tīl) *adj.* **1.** Of or pertain-
to a gens, tribe, or people. **2.** Of or pertaining to Gen-
es. [< F < LL *gentilis* foreign]
n·tile (jen′tīl) *n.* **1.** Among Jews, one not a Jew. **2.**
nong Christians, a heathen or pagan. **3.** Among Mor-
ons, one not a Mormon. — *adj.* Of, pertaining to, or be-
a Gentile.
·til·i·ty (jen·til′ə·tē) *n. pl.* **·ties** **1.** The quality of being
nteel; refinement: now often used ironically. **2.** Gentle
rth; good extraction. **3.** Well-born or well-bred persons
llectively. [< OF < L *gentilis* of good birth]
·tle (jen′təl) *adj.* **·tler** (-tlər), **·tlest** (-tlist) **1.** Mild and
niable in nature or disposition. **2.** Not harsh, rough, or
ud; mild. **3.** Not steep or abrupt; gradual: a *gentle* ascent.
Easily managed; docile. **5.** Of good family and breeding.
Like or befitting one of good family; polite. **7.** *Meteorol.*
esignating a moderate breeze. — *v.t.* **·tled, ·tling** To make
sy to control; tame. — *n.* A bluebottle larva used as fish
it. [< OF < L *gentilis* of good birth < *gens, gentis* race,
an] — **gen′tly** (-tlē) *adv.* — **gen′tle·ness** *n.*
n·tle·folk (jen′təl·fōk′) *n.pl.* Persons of good family and
od breeding. Also **gen′tle·folks′.**
n·tle·man (jen′təl·mən) *n. pl.* **·men** (-mən) **1.** A man of
od birth and social position. **2.** A courteous, considerate
an. **3.** Any man: in the plural, used as a form of address.
n·tle·man-at-arms (jen′təl·mən·ət·ärmz′) *n. pl.* **·men**
mən) *n. Brit.* One of forty gentlemen who attend the sov-
eign on various state and solemn occasions.
n·tle·man-com·mon·er (jen′təl·mən·kom′ən·ər) *n. pl.*
n·tle·men-com·mon·ers (jen′təl·mən·kom′ən·ərz) *Brit.*
ormerly, a commoner at Oxford and Cambridge Universi-
es, enjoying special privileges.
n·tle·man-farm·er (jen′təl·mən·fär′mər) *n.* One who
wns a farm but hires others to work it.
ntleman in waiting A gentleman of a royal household
aff, appointed to attend the sovereign or his son.
n·tle·man·ly (jen′təl·mən·lē) *adj.* Pertaining to or befitting a gentleman; courteous. Also **gen′tle·man·like′** (-līk′).
gentleman of fortune **1.** An adventurer or gambler. **2.** Formerly, a pirate.
gentleman of the road **1.** A highwayman. **2.** *U.S.* A hobo.
gen·tle·man's agreement (jen′təl·mənz) An understanding about something to be done, arrived at by informal mutual agreement and guaranteed solely by the pledged word of the parties involved. Also **gentlemen's agreement.**
gen·tle·man's gentleman (jen′təl·mənz) A valet.
gentle sex Women collectively. Also **gentler sex.**
gen·tle·wom·an (jen′təl·wŏŏm′ən) *n. pl.* **·wom·en** (-wim′·in) **1.** A woman of good family or superior social position; lady. **2.** A gracious, well-mannered woman.
gen·try (jen′trē) *n.* **1.** People of good family or superior social background; in England, the upper ranks of the middle class. **2.** Individuals of a particular area, profession, etc.: the local *gentry*: now chiefly a patronizing or humorous term. [< OF *genterise* < *gentil* gentle]
ge·nu (jē′nōō, -nyōō) *n. pl.* **gen·u·a** (jen′yōō·ə) *Anat.* **1.** The knee. **2.** A kneelike structure or part. [< L]
gen·u·flect (jen′yə·flekt) *v.i.* To bend the knee, as in worship. [< Med.L < L *genu* knee + *flectere* to bend] — **gen′u·flec′tion** or **gen′u·flex′ion** *n.*
gen·u·ine (jen′yōō·in) *adj.* **1.** Being actually of the origin, authorship, or character claimed. **2.** Not spurious or counterfeit. **3.** Not affected or hypocritical; sincere. **4.** Being of the original or true stock: a *genuine* Indian. [< L *genuinus* innate] — **gen′u·ine·ly** *adv.* — **gen′u·ine·ness** *n.*
ge·nus (jē′nəs) *n. pl.* **gen·e·ra** (jen′ər·ə) or, less commonly, **ge·nus·es** **1.** *Biol.* A grouping or category of plants and animals ranking next above the species and next below the family or subfamily. **2.** *Logic* A class of things divisible into two or more subordinate classes or species. **3.** A particular sort, kind, or class. [< L, race, kind]
-geny *combining form* Mode of production of; generation or development of: *anthropogeny.* [< F < L < Gk. *gen-*, stem of *gignesthai* to become]
geo- *combining form* Earth; ground; soil.
ge·o·cen·tric (jē′ō·sen′trik) *adj.* **1.** Calculated or viewed with relation to the earth's center. **2.** Formulated on the assumption that the earth is the center of the universe. Also **ge′o·cen′tri·cal** *adj.* — **ge′o·cen′tri·cal·ly** *adv.*
ge·o·chem·is·try (jē′ō·kem′is·trē) *n.* A specialized branch of chemistry dealing with the chemical composition of the earth's crust. — **ge′o·chem′i·cal** *adj.* — **ge′o·chem′ist** *n.*
ge·ode (jē′ōd) *n. Geol.* **1.** A rock, usually globular, having a cavity lined with crystals. **2.** The cavity in such a rock. [< F *géode* < L *geodes*, a precious stone < Gk. *geōdēs* earthy] — **ge·od·ic** (jē·od′ik) *adj.*
ge·o·des·ic (jē′ə·des′ik) *adj.* **1.** Of or pertaining to the geometry of geodesic lines or curved surfaces. **2.** Geodetic. Also **ge′o·des′i·cal.** — *n.* A geodesic line.
geodesic dome *Archit.* A light and strong hemispherical dome made of prefabricated polyhedral or triangular lattice nodules and covered with a thin, strong material.
geodesic line *Math.* The shortest line connecting two points on a given, esp. a curved, surface.
ge·od·e·sist (jē·od′ə·sist) *n.* One who specializes in geodesy.
ge·od·e·sy (jē·od′ə·sē) *n.* The science dealing with the determination of the shape, area, and curvature of the earth, with the precise mapping of continents or other large tracts, or location of specific points. Also **ge·o·det·ics** (jē′ə·det′iks). [< F < NL < Gk. < *gē* earth + *daiein* to divide]
ge·o·det·ic (jē′ə·det′ik) *adj.* **1.** Of or pertaining to geodesy. **2.** Geodesic. Also **ge′o·det′i·cal.** — **ge′o·det′i·cal·ly** *adv.*
ge·o·dy·nam·ics (jē′ō·dī·nam′iks, -di-) *n.pl.* (*construed as sing.*) The branch of geology concerned with the forces affecting the structure of the earth.
ge·o·graph·i·cal (jē′ə·graf′i·kəl) *adj.* **1.** Of or pertaining to geography. **2.** Relating to topographical facts and influences. Also **ge′o·graph′ic.** — **ge′o·graph′i·cal·ly** *adv.*
geographic determinism *Sociol.* The theory that attributes the forms and characteristics of a given society to geographic factors.
ge·og·ra·phy (jē·og′rə·fē) *n. pl.* **·phies** **1.** The science that describes the surface of the earth and its associated physical, biological, economic, political, and demographic characteristics. **2.** The natural aspect, features, etc., of a place or area: the *geography* of the Arctic. **3.** A particular work on or system of geography. [< L < Gk. < *gē* earth + *graphein* to write, describe] — **ge·og′ra·pher** *n.*
ge·oid (jē′oid) *n.* The earth considered hypothetically as an ellipsoidal solid whose surface coincides with the mean level of the ocean. [< Gk. *geoidēs* earthlike < *gē* earth + *eidos* form]
ge·o·log·ic (jē′ə·loj′ik) *adj.* Of or pertaining to geology. Also **ge′o·log′i·cal.** — **ge′o·log′i·cal·ly** *adv.*

ge·ol·o·gy (jē·ol′ə·jē) *n.* *pl.* **·gies 1.** The science that treats of the origin and structure of the earth, including the physical forces which have shaped it and its physical and organic history, esp. as shown by rocks and rock formations. **2.** The structure of the earth in a given region. **— ge·ol′o·gist** *n.*

ge·o·met·ric (jē′ə·met′rik) *adj.* **1.** Pertaining to or according to the rules and principles of geometry. **2.** Forming, consisting of, or characterized by straight lines, bars, crosses, zigzags, etc., as in painting or sculpture. Also **ge′o·met′ri·cal. — ge′o·met′ri·cal·ly** *adv.*

ge·o·pol·i·tics (jē′ō·pol′ə·tiks) *n.pl.* (*construed as sing.*) The study of political and economic geography. **2.** A trine, of Nazi Germany, advocating aggressive expans also *German* **Ge·o·pol·i·tik** (gā′ō·pôl·ē·tēk′). **— ge′o·po i·cal** (-pə·lit′i·kəl), **ge′o·pol′i·tic** *adj.* **— ge′o·po·lit′i·ca** *adv.* **— ge′o·pol′i·ti′cian** (-pol′ə·tish′ən) *n.*

Geor·gian (jôr′jən) *adj.* **1.** Of or pertaining to the reign period of the first four Georges in England, 1714–1830, c George V, 1910–36. **2.** Of or pertaining to Georgia or G gians. **3.** Of or pertaining to the language of Georgia (

GEOLOGICAL TIME SCALE

Read from bottom to top.

ERAS	TIME PERIODS ROCK SYSTEMS	TIME EPOCHS ROCK SERIES	APPROX. DURATION MILLION YEARS	APPROX. PERCENT TOTAL AGE	LIFE FORMS
CENOZOIC	Quaternary	Recent Pleistocene	1	2	Rise and dominance of Man.
	Upper Tertiary	Pliocene Miocene	65		Modern animals and plants.
	Lower Tertiary	Oligocene Eocene Paleocene			Rapid development of modern mammals, insects, and plants.
MESOZOIC	Upper Cretaceous		75	5	Primitive mammals; last dinosaurs; last ammonites.
	Lower Cretaceous				Rise of flowering plants.
	Jurassic		45		First birds, first mammals. Diversification of reptiles; climax of ammonites; coniferous trees.
	Triassic		45		Rise of dinosaurs; cycadlike plants; bony fishes.
PALEOZOIC	Permian		45	9	Rise of reptiles. Modern insects. Last of many plant and animal groups.
	Pennsylvanian } Carboniferous		75		First reptiles. Amphibians; primitive insects; seed ferns; primitive conifers.
	Mississippian } Carboniferous				Climax of shell-crushing sharks. Primitive ammonites.
	Devonian		50		First amphibians, first land snails. Primitive land plants. Climax of brachiopods.
	Silurian		20		First traces of land life. Scorpions. First lungfishes. Widespread coral reefs.
	Ordovician		70		First fish. Climax of trilobites. First appearance of many marine invertebrates.
	Cambrian		50		First marine invertebrates, including trilobites.
PROTEROZOIC } Pre-Cambrian			About 3000	84	First signs of life. Algae.
ARCHEOZOIC } Pre-Cambrian					

Age of oldest dated rocks: about 3,500,000,000 years.

ge·om·e·tri·cian (jē·om′ə·trish′ən, jē′ə·mə-) *n.* A specialist in geometry. Also **ge·om′e·ter** (-ə·tər).

geometric progression *Math.* A sequence of terms of which each member is greater than its predecessor by a constant ratio, as 2, 4, 8, 16, 32, 64.

ge·om·e·try (jē·om′ə·trē) *n.* *pl.* **·tries** The branch of mathematics that treats of space and its relations, esp. as shown in the properties and measurement of points, lines, angles, surfaces, and solids. [< OF < L < Gk. < *gē* earth + *metreein* to measure]

ge·o·phys·ics (jē′ō·fiz′iks) *n.pl.* (*construed as sing.*) The study of the earth as the product of complex physico-chemical forces acting upon it internally and from outer space, esp. with reference to exploration of its less accessible regions. **— ge′o·phys′i·cal** *adj.* **— ge′o·phys′i·cist** *n.*

2.). **—** *n.* **1.** A native or inhabitant of Georgia. **2.** One an ancient mountain people native to the Caucasus. **3.** T Caucasian language of the Georgians of the Soviet Unio

ge·o·stat·ics (jē′ə·stat′iks) *n.pl.* (*construed as sing.*) T statics of rigid bodies in relation to balanced forces on or neath the earth's surface. **— ge′o·stat′ic** *adj.*

ge·ra·ni·um (ji·rā′nē·əm) *n.* **1.** A plant with showy pi or purple flowers: also called *cranebill*. **2.** A closely relat plant, originally from South Africa. **3.** A very deep pi almost red, color. [< L < Gk. *geranos* crane]

ger·fal·con (jûr′fal′kən, -fôl′-, -fô′-) *n.* A large falcon of t arctic regions, with feathered shanks: also spelled *gyrfalc* [< OF < OHG *gir* vulture + OF *faucon* falcon]

ger·i·at·rics (jer′ē·at′riks) *n.pl.* (*construed as sing.*) **1.** T branch of medicine that deals with the structural chang

hysiology, diseases, and hygiene of old age. **2.** Gerontol-
;y. [< Gk. *gēras* old age + -IATRICS] — **ger′i·at′ric** *adj.*
· **ger′i·a·tri′cian** (-ə·trish′ən), **ger′i·at′rist** *n.*

rm (jûrm) *n.* **1.** A microorganism that causes disease; microbe. **2.** Something in its essential though rudimen- ıry form: the *germ* of an idea. **3.** That which gives rise to ıe production or development of something: to sow the *rms* of war. **4.** *Biol.* **a** A reproductive cell. **b** An organism its embryonic form. [< F < L *germen* sprig]

r·man[1] (jûr′mən) *n.* A cotillion (def. 1). [Short for *Ger- an cotillion*]

r·man[2] (jûr′mən) *adj.* **1.** Having the same father and other as oneself: *sister-german.* **2.** Related to oneself ırough being the child of one's uncle or aunt: *cousin-ger- an.* **3.** Germane. [< OF < L *germanus* closely related]

r·man (jûr′mən) *adj.* Of, pertaining to, or characteristic Germany, its people, or their language. — *n.* **1.** A native inhabitant of Germany. **2.** The language of the Germans, ɛlonging to the West Germanic branch. — **High German** he standard literary and spoken language used throughout ermany and Austria and in parts of Switzerland and Al- ce: also called *New High German.* — **Low German** Col- ctively, the languages of the Low Countries, including utch, Flemish, and Frisian, and of the northern lowlands Germany (*Plattdeutsch*). — **Old High German** The lan- ıage of southern Germany from about 800 to 1100. — **iddle High German** The High German language from 1100 1450. — **Middle Low German** The Low German lan- ıage from 1100 to 1450. [< L *Germanus*, prob. < Celtic]

r·man·der (jər·man′dər) *n.* An herb of the mint family, ith pale purple flowers. [< OF < Med.L < LGk. < Gk. *chamai* on the ground + *drys* an oak]

r·mane (jər·mān′) *adj.* Related to what is being discussed considered; pertinent; relevant. [See GERMAN[2]]

r·man·ic (jər·man′ik) *adj.* **1.** Of or pertaining to a oup of early Indo-European tribes living in the region be- veen the Rhine, Danube, and Vistula rivers: later including ıe Germans, English, Dutch, Flemings, Danes, Scandinavi- ns, and German-Swiss. **2.** Relating to the language or istoms of any of these people. — *n.* A sub-family of the ıdo-European family of languages, divided into **East Ger- anic,** including Gothic (extinct); **North Germanic** or Scan- navian, including Norwegian, Swedish, Danish, Icelandic, ıd Faroese; and **West Germanic,** including all the High and ɔw German languages and dialects.

r·ma·ni·um (jər·mā′nē·əm) *n.* A grayish white, metallic ement (symbol Ge) of the silicon group, used in electronics ıd optics. See ELEMENT. [< NL < L *Germania* Germany]

rman measles *Pathol.* A contagious virus disease ac- ɔmpanied by fever, sore throat, and a skin rash: also called *ıbella, rubeola.*

rmano- *combining form* German.

rman shepherd A breed of dog with a large, strong ɔdy and thick, smooth coat: also called *police dog.*

rman silver A white alloy of copper, nickel, and zinc, sed in the manufacture of cutlery and as a base for plated are: also called *nickel silver.*

rm cell *Biol.* A cell specialized for reproduction.

r·mi·cide (jûr′mə·sīd) *n.* An agent used to destroy dis- ıse germs or other microorganisms. — **ger·mi·ci·dal** (jûr′- ə·sī′dəl) *adj.*

r·mi·nal (jûr′mə·nəl) *adj.* **1.** Of, relating to, or consti- ıting a germ or germ cell. **2.** Pertaining to the earliest ;age of development. [< NL < L *germen, -inis* sprig]

r·mi·nate (jûr′mə·nāt) *v.* **·nat·ed, ·nat·ing** *v.i.* **1.** To be- n to grow or develop; sprout. — *v.t.* **2.** To cause to sprout. < L *germinatus*, pp. of *germinare* to sprout] — **ger′mi·na- le** (-nə·bəl) *adj.* — **ger′mi·na′tion** *n.* — **ger′mi·na′tive** *dj.* — **ger′mi·na′tor** *n.*

rm plasm *Biol.* The part of the protoplasm of a germ ɜll that contains the chromosomes and genes.

ronto- *combining form* Old age; pertaining to old people: *ɜrontology.* Also, before vowels, **geront-.** [< Gk. *gerōn, ɜrontos* old man]

r·on·tol·o·gy (jer′on·tol′ə·jē) *n.* **1.** The scientific study the processes and phenomena of aging. **2.** Geriatrics. — **er′on·tol′o·gist** *n.*

erous *suffix* Bearing or producing. [< L *gerere* to bear + ɔus]

r·ry·man·der (jer′i·man′dər, ger′-) *v.t.* **1.** To alter (a oting area) so as to advance unfairly the interests of a po- tical party. **2.** To adapt to one's advantage; manipulate. — *n.* The act or result of gerrymandering. [after Elbridge *'erry*, 1744–1814, + (SALA)MANDER; from the shape of a istrict formed in Massachusetts while he was governor]

r·und (jer′ənd) *Gram.* *n.* **1.** A form of a verb used like a oun. **2.** In English, the *-ing* form of a verb, as *doing*, or a ompound tense of a verb made with the *-ing* form of an auxiliary, as *having done*, when used as the subject or object of a verb or as the object of a preposition. [< LL < L *gerere* to do] — **ge·run·di·al** (jə·run′dē·əl) *adj.*

ge·run·dive (jə·run′div) *Gram.* *n.* **1.** In Latin, a form of the verb constituting the future passive participle, having the stem of the gerund and expressing obligation, propriety, etc. **2.** In some other languages, a form similar to a gerun- dive in form or function. — *adj.* Of, pertaining to, or re- sembling a gerundive, or, sometimes, a gerund.

gest (jest) *n.* *Archaic* **1.** A noteworthy deed; exploit. **2.** A tale of adventure or romance; esp., a metrical romance. Also **geste.** [< OF < L *gesta* deeds < *gerere* to do]

ge·stalt (gə·shtält′, -shtôlt′) *n.* *pl.* **·stalts** or **·stalt·en** (-shtält′ən, -shtôlt′-) A synthesis of separate elements of emotion, experience, etc., that constitutes more than the mechanical sum of the parts. Also **Ge·stalt′.** [< G, form]

gestalt psychology Psychology based on the theory of the gestalt.

Ge·sta·po (gə·stä′pō, *Ger.* gə·shtä′pō) *n.* The German state secret police under the Nazi regime, noted for their brutality. [< G *Ge(heime) Sta(ats) Po(lizei)* Secret State Police]

ges·tate (jes′tāt) *v.t.* **·tat·ed, ·tat·ing** To carry in the uterus during pregnancy. [< L *gestare* to carry] — **ges·ta′tion** *n.*

ges·tic·u·late (jes·tik′yə·lāt) *v.* **·lat·ed, ·lat·ing** *v.i.* **1.** To make emphatic or expressive gestures, as in speaking. — *v.t.* **2.** To express by gestures. [< L *gesticulus*, dim. of *gestus* gesture] — **ges·tic′u·la′tive** *adj.* — **ges·tic′u·la′tor** *n.*

ges·tic·u·la·tion (jes·tik′yə·lā′shən) *n.* **1.** The act of ges- ticulating. **2.** An energetic or expressive gesture.

ges·ture (jes′chər) *n.* **1.** A bodily motion, as of the hands in speaking, used to emphasize or express some idea or emo- tion. **2.** Such motions collectively. **3.** Something said or done as a mere formality, or for effect. — *v.* **·tured, ·tur·ing** *v.i.* **1.** To make gestures. — *v.t.* **2.** To express by gestures. [< Med.L < L *gerere* to carry on, do] — **ges′tur·er** *n.*

Ge·sund·heit (gə·zo͝ont′hīt) *interj.* *German* (Your) health: said to someone who has just sneezed.

get (get) *v.* **got, got** or *U.S.* **got·ten, get·ting** *v.t.* **1.** To come into possession of; obtain. **2.** To go for and bring back. **3.** To capture; seize. **4.** To cause to come, go, etc.: to *get* baggage through customs. **5.** To carry away; take: *Get* this out of the house. **6.** To prepare: to *get* lunch. **7.** To bring to a state or condition: to *get* the work done. **8.** To per- suade: *Get* her to sign the paper. **9.** To find out or obtain by calculation, experiment, etc.: to add the totals and *get* 100. **10.** To receive (reward or punishment). **11.** To learn or master, as by study or practice: Have you *got* your history lesson? **12.** To become sick with. **13.** To establish con- tact with: I'll *get* him on the phone. **14.** To catch, as a train; board. **15.** To beget: now said chiefly of animals. **16.** *Informal* To come to an understanding of. **17.** *Infor- mal* To possess: with *have* or *has*: He has *got* quite a temper. **18.** *Informal* To obtain the advantage over: Drink will *get* him. **19.** *Informal* To square accounts with: I'll *get* you yet. **20.** *Informal* To be obliged or forced (to do something speci- fied): with *have* or *has.* **21.** *Informal* To hit: The shrapnel *got* him in the arm. **22.** *Slang* To puzzle or baffle. **23.** *Slang* To please, irritate, etc.: That music *gets* me. **24.** *Slang* To take note of. **25.** To bring to or place in some specified location. — *v.i.* **26.** To arrive: When does the train *get* there? **27.** To come, go, or move: *Get* in here. **28.** To board; enter: with *on, in*, etc. **29.** To become. — **to get about** **1.** To become known, as gossip. **2.** To move about. **3.** To be active socially. — **to get across** **1.** To make or be convincing or clear, as to an audience. **2.** To be successful, as in projecting one's personality. — **to get ahead** To at- tain success. — **to get along** **1.** To leave; go: *Get along* with you! **2.** To be successful, as in business. **3.** To be friendly or compatible. **4.** To proceed. **5.** To grow old or older. — **to get around** **1.** To become known, as gossip. **2.** To move about. **3.** To attend social or public functions, etc. **4.** To flatter, cajole, etc., so as to obtain the favor of. **5.** To dodge; circumvent. — **to get around to** To give attention to after some delay. — **to get at** **1.** To arrive at; reach. **2.** To intend; mean: I don't see what you're *getting at.* **3.** To apply oneself to: to *get at* a problem. **4.** *Informal* To prevail upon; influence. — **to get away** **1.** To escape. **2.** To leave; go. **3.** To start, as a race horse. — **to get away with** *Slang* To do (something) without discovery, criticism, or punish- ment. — **to get back** To return to a previous position or state. — **to get back at** *Slang* To revenge oneself on. — **to get by** **1.** To pass: This *got by* the censor. **2.** *Informal* To manage to survive. **3.** *Informal* To get away with. — **to get down** To descend, as from a horse or ladder. — **to get down to** (**business, facts,** etc.) To begin to act on, investi- gate, or consider. — **to get in** **1.** To arrive or enter. **2.** To slip in (a remark, etc.). **3.** To become involved or familiar with. — **to get it** *Informal* **1.** To understand. **2.** To be punished in some way. **— to get off 1.** To descend from; dismount. **2.** To depart. **3.** To be relieved or freed, as of a duty. **4.** To be released with a lesser penalty, etc., or none at all. **5.** To utter: to *get off* a joke. **— to get on 1.** To mount (a horse, vehicle, etc.). **2.** To get along. **— to get out 1.** To depart or leave. **2.** To escape. **3.** To become known, as a secret. **4.** To publish. **5.** To express or utter with difficulty. **6.** To take out. **— to get out of 1.** To obtain from. **2.** To escape or evade. **3.** To depart from. **— to get over 1.** To recover from (illness, surprise, anger, etc.). **2.** To get across. **— to get there** *Informal* To succeed. **— to get through 1.** To complete. **2.** To survive. **— to get through (to) 1.** To establish communication (with). **2.** To make clear (to). **— to get to 1.** To begin. **2.** To be able to (do something). **3.** To get through to. **— to get together 1.** To assemble. **2.** To come to an agreement. **— to get up 1.** To rise, as from sleep. **2.** To climb. **3.** To devise. **4.** To acquire, develop, or work up. **5.** *Informal* To dress up. [< ON *geta*] **— get′ta·ble** *adj.* **— get′ter** *n.*

— Syn. (verb) **1.** obtain, procure, gain, acquire.

get·a·way (get′ə·wā′) *n.* **1.** An escape, as of a criminal. **2.** The start, as of an automobile, race horse, etc.

get-to·geth·er (get′tə·geth′ər) *n. Informal* A gathering.

get-up (get′up′) *n. Informal* **1.** Overall arrangement and appearance, esp. of a book or magazine. **2.** The combination of articles of dress worn on a particular occasion. **3.** Vigorous initiative: also **get′-up′-and-go′** (-ən·gō′).

gew·gaw (gyōō′gô) *n.* Some little ornamental article of small value. **—** *adj.* Showy; gaudy. [ME *giue-goue*]

gey·ser (gī′zər, -sər) *n.* A natural hot spring from which intermittent jets of steam, hot water, or mud are ejected in a fountainlike column. [< Icel. *geysan* to gush]

ghast·ly (gast′lē, gäst′-) *adj.* **·li·er, ·li·est 1.** Horrible; terrifying. **2.** Deathlike in appearance; pale; wan. **3.** *Informal* Very bad or unpleasant. **—** *adv.* **1.** Spectral in manner or appearance. **2.** Fearfully; horribly. [ME < OE *gæstan* to terrify + *-lich* -ly[1]] **— ghast′li·ness** *n.*

ghat (gôt) *n. Anglo-Indian* **1.** A stairway leading down to the edge of a river. **2.** A mountain pass. **3.** A range or chain of mountains. Also **ghaut.** [< Hind. *ghāt*]

ghee (gē) *n. Anglo-Indian* A butterlike substance made with the butterfat of buffalo milk. [< Hind. < Skt. *ghrta*]

gher·kin (gûr′kin) *n.* **1.** A very small, prickly cucumber pickled as a relish. **2.** The plant producing it. **3.** Any small, immature cucumber used for pickling. [< Du. *agurk* cucumber < G < Slavic, ult. < LGk. *angourion*]

ghet·to (get′ō) *n. pl.* **·tos 1.** An often run-down section of a city inhabited chiefly by a minority group that cannot live elsewhere, as because of racial or social prejudice. **2.** A section of a city in certain European countries in which Jews were formerly required to live. [< Ital.]

ghost (gōst) *n.* **1.** A disembodied spirit; a wraith, specter, or phantom. **2.** The animating spirit or soul: now only in the phrase **to give up the ghost,** to die. **3.** A haunting recollection of something: *ghosts* from the past. **4.** A mere suggestion of something: the *ghost* of a smile. **5.** *Informal* A ghostwriter. **6.** *Optics & Telecom.* An unwanted false or secondary image. **—** *v.t. & v.i.* **1.** To haunt as a ghost. **2.** *Informal* To write as a ghostwriter. [OE *gāst* spirit]

ghost·ly (gōst′lē) *adj.* **·li·er, ·li·est 1.** Of or like an apparition; spectral. **2.** Of religion; spiritual. **— ghost′li·ness** *n.*

ghost town A deserted town, esp. a former boom town.

ghost·write (gōst′rīt′) *v.t. & v.i.* **·wrote, ·writ·ten, ·writ·ing** To write or act as a ghostwriter.

ghost·writ·er (gōst′rī′tər) *n.* One who writes for someone else to whom the authorship is to be attributed.

ghoul (gōōl) *n.* **1.** One who robs graves. **2.** One who takes pleasure in revolting things. **3.** In Moslem legend, an evil spirit who preys on corpses. [< Arabic *ghūl*] **— ghoul′ish** *adj.* **— ghoul′ish·ly** *adv.* **— ghoul′ish·ness** *n.*

GI (jē′ī′) *U.S. Informal n. pl.* **GIs** or **GI's** An enlisted man in the U.S. Army. **— the GIs** (or **GI's**) *Mil. Slang* Diarrhea. **—** *adj.* **1.** Of or characteristic of GIs. **2.** Furnished by the government for the use of the armed forces. **—** *v.t.* **GIed** or **GI'ed, GIing** or **GI'ing** To clean or scrub, as for military inspection. [< *G(overnment) I(ssue)*]

gi·ant (jī′ənt) *n.* **1.** In legend, a manlike being of supernatural size and strength, as in Greek mythology, one of the race who warred against the gods of Olympus. **2.** Any person or thing of great size, capability, etc. **—** *adj.* **1.** Of or typical of a giant. **2.** Huge; great. [< OF < L < Gk. *gigas, -antos*] **gi′ant·ess** *n. fem.*

gi·ant·ism (jī′ənt·iz′əm) *n.* Gigantism.

giant panda The panda (def. 2).

giaour (jour) *n.* Among Moslems, a nonbeliever; esp., a Christian. [< Turkish < Persian *gabr* infidel]

gib·ber (jib′ər, gib′-) *v.i. & v.t.* To talk rapidly and incoherently; jabber. **—** *n.* Gibberish.

gib·ber·ish (jib′ər·ish, gib′-) *n.* **1.** Rapid or unintelligible talk; gabble. **2.** Needlessly difficult or obscure language.

gib·bet (jib′it) *n.* Formerly, a gallows. **—** *v.t.* **gib·bet·ed** or **·bet·ted, gib·bet·ing** or **·bet·ting 1.** To execute by hangi[ng] **2.** To hold up to public contempt. [< OF *gibet* staff]

gib·bon (gib′ən) *n.* A slender, long-armed arboreal anth[ro]poid ape of southern Asia and the East Indies. [< F]

gib·bos·i·ty (gi·bos′ə·tē) *n. pl.* **·ties 1.** The state of be[ing] gibbous or convex. **2.** A rounded protuberance; hump.

gib·bous (gib′əs) *adj.* **1.** Irregularly rounded or convex[,] the moon when more than half full and less than full. [**2.**] Hunchbacked. Also **gib·bose** (gib′ōs, gi·bōs′). [< L *gib*[bus] hump] **— gib′bous·ly** *adv.* **— gib′bous·ness** *n.*

gibe[1] (jīb) *v.* **gibed, gib·ing** *v.i.* **1.** To utter jeers or deris[ive] remarks. **—** *v.t.* **2.** To taunt. **—** *n.* A jeer. [Cf. OF *g*[iber] to treat roughly] **— gib′er** *n.* **— gib′·ing·ly** *adv.*

gibe[2] (jīb) See JIBE[1].

gib·let (jib′lit) *n. Usu. pl.* The heart, liver, gizzard, etc. [of] a fowl. [< OF *gibelet* stew made from game]

gid·dy (gid′ē) *adj.* **·di·er, ·di·est 1.** Affected by a reeling[,] whirling sensation; dizzy. **2.** Tending to cause such a sen[sa]tion. **3.** Rotating rapidly; whirling. **4.** Frivolous; he[ed]less. **—** *v.t. & v.i.* **·died, ·dy·ing** To make or become diz[zy] [OE *gydig* insane] **— gid′di·ly** *adv.* **— gid′di·ness** *n.*

gift (gift) *n.* **1.** Something that is given; present. **2.** T[he] action or right of giving. **3.** A natural aptitude; talent. **to look a gift horse in the mouth** To find fault with a gif[t] favor. [OE < *gifan* to give]

gift·ed (gif′tid) *adj.* Endowed with talent.

gig[1] (gig) *n.* **1.** A light, two-wheeled vehicle drawn by [a] horse. **2.** A machine for raising a nap on cloth. **3.** *Nau[t.]* long ship's boat usu. for the captain; also, a speedy, li[ght] rowboat. **—** *v.* **gigged, gig·ging** *v.i.* **1.** To ride in a gig. *v.t.* **2.** To raise the nap on (cloth).

gig[2] (gig) *n.* An arrangement of fishhooks. **—** *v.t. &* **gigged, gig·ging** To spear or catch (fish) with a gig. FISHGIG]

gig[3] (gig) *Slang n.* A demerit, as in the army, school, etc. *v.t.* **gigged, gig·ging 1.** To give a demerit to. **2.** To puni[sh]

gi·ga- *combining form* A billion (10^9) times (a speci[fied] unit).

gi·gan·tic (jī·gan′tik) *adj.* **1.** Of, like, or suited to a gia[nt] **2.** Tremendous; huge. Also **gi·gan·te·an** (jī′gan·tē′ən). L *gigas, -antis* giant + -IC] **— gi·gan′ti·cal·ly** *adv.*

gi·gan·tism (jī·gan′tiz·əm) *n.* Abnormal size, esp., exc[es]sive growth of the body due to disturbances in the pituit[ary] gland: also called *giantism.*

gig·gle (gig′əl) *v.i.* **·gled, ·gling** To laugh in a high-pitch[ed,] silly, or nervous manner. **—** *n.* A titter. **— gig′gler** *n*

gig·gly (gig′lē) *adj.* **·gli·er, ·gli·est** Tending to giggle.

gig·o·lo (jig′ə·lō, *Fr.* zhē·gô·lō′) *n. pl.* **·los** (-lōz, *Fr.* -lō′) A professional male dancer who dances with women patro[ns;] also, a woman's paid escort. **2.** A man supported b[y a] woman not his wife. [< F, prob. < *gigolette* prostitute]

gig·ot (jig′ət) *n.* **1.** A leg-of-mutton sleeve. **2.** A coo[ked] haunch of lamb, veal, etc. [< F]

gigue (zhēg) *n.* **1.** A jig (def. 1). **2.** *Music* A lively da[nce] form, often the final movement of a suite.

Gi·la monster (hē′lə) A large, venomous lizard of the American desert, having an orange and black body.

gild[1] (gild) *v.t.* **gild·ed** or **gilt, gild·ing 1.** To coat with a t[hin] layer of gold. **2.** To brighten or adorn. **3.** To gloss ov[er] [OE *gyldan*] **— gil′ding** *n.*

gild[2] (gild) *n.* A guild.

gild·er[1] (gil′dər) *n.* One who or that which gilds.

gild·er[2] (gil′dər) *n.* A guilder.

Gil·e·ad (gil′ē·əd) A mountainous region of ancient Pal[es]tine east of the Jordan. *Josh.* xii 2.

gill[1] (gil) *n.* **1.** *Zool.* The organ for underwater breathing [of] fishes, amphibians, and other aquatic vertebrates. **2.** *U[su.] pl.* The wattles of a fowl. **3.** *pl. Informal* The face a[nd] throat: usu. in the phrase **green around the gills,** Sickly appearance. **—** *v.t.* **1.** To catch by the gills. **2.** To g[ut] (fish). [ME *gile*]

gill[2] (jil) *n.* A liquid measure equal to ¼ pint. See tab[le,] front of book. [< OF *gell* measure for wine]

gil·ly·flow·er (jil′ē·flou′ər) *n.* **1.** A plant of the musta[rd] family, as the wallflower. **2.** A plant of the pink family, the clove pink. Also **gil′li·flow′er.** [Alter. of ME *gilofr*[e]]

gilt (gilt) Alternative past tense and past participle of GI[LD] **—** *adj.* Gold-colored; gilded. **—** *n.* A material for gildi[ng]

gilt-edged (gilt′ejd′) *adj.* **1.** Having the edges gilded. Of the best quality: *gilt-edged* securities. Also **gilt′-edge′.**

gim·bals (jim′bəlz, gim′-) *n.pl.* A set of three metal rings pivoted one within the other that it maintains an object supported by it, as a ship's compass, on a horizontal plane. [OF < L *geminus* twin]

GIMBALS

gim·crack (jim′krak) *n.* A useless, gaudy object; knick-knack. **—** *adj.* Cheap and showy. **— gim′crack·er·y** *n.*

gim·let (gim′lit) A small, sharp tool with a bar handle and a pointed, spiral tip for boring holes. **—** *v.t.* To make a hole in with a gimlet. [< OF *guimbelet*]

let eyes Sharp eyes. **—gim′let-eyed′** *adj.*

·mick (gim′ik) *n. U.S. Slang* **1.** A novel or tricky fea-e or detail. **2.** A hidden or deceptive device, as one used a magician. **3.** Some little gadget of uncertain name. — **·/mick·ry** *n.* **—gim′mick·y** *adj.*

p[1] (gimp) *n.* A narrow piece of fabric, often stiffened h wire, used to trim curtains, etc. [Cf. OF *guimpre,* a d of trimming]

p[2] (gimp) *U.S. Slang n.* One who limps; also, a limp.

(jin) *n.* An aromatic alcoholic liquor distilled from va-ıs grains, esp. rye, and flavored with juniper berries or ıetimes with other flavoring agents. [Short for GENEVA]

(jin) *n.* **1.** A cotton gin. **2.** A tripodlike machine for ısting. **3.** A type of pulley and block. For illus. see BLOCK. A snare or trap. **—***v.t.* **ginned, gin·ning 1.** To remove seeds from (cotton) in a gin. **2.** To trap or snare. ɔhetic var. of OF *engin* ingenuity] **—gin′ner** *n.*

ger (jin′jər) *n.* **1.** The pungent, spicy rootstock of a ɔical plant, used in medicine and cookery. **2.** The plant lf. **3.** A tawny, reddish brown color. **4.** *Informal* Pep. *v.t.* **1.** To spice with ginger. **2.** *Informal* To make lively: en with *up.* [< OF < LL < Gk. *zingiberis,* ult. < Skt.]

ger ale An effervescent soft drink flavored with ginger.

ger beer An effervescent, nonalcoholic ginger drink.

ger·bread (jin′jər·bred′) *n.* **1.** A dark, ginger-flavored e or cooky. **2.** Gaudy ornamentation, as ornate carvings furniture, etc. **—***adj.* Cheap and tawdry.

ger·ly (jin′jər·lē) *adv.* In a cautious manner. **—***adj.* reful. [Cf. OF *gent* delicate] **—gin′ger·li·ness** *n.*

ger·snap (jin′jər·snap′) *n.* A brittle, ginger cooky.

ger·y (jin′jər·ē) *adj.* **1.** Having the piquantly spicy vor of ginger. **2.** Having the reddish brown color of gin-. **3.** Sharply pointed or peppery, as a remark.

g·ham (ging′əm) *n.* A cotton fabric, yarn-dyed, woven solid colors, checks, etc. [< F < Malay *ginggang* striped]

gi·vi·tis (jin′jə·vī′tis) *n. Pathol.* Inflammation of the ns. [< L *gingiva* gum]

k (gingk) *n. U.S. Slang* A man or boy; fellow; guy.

k·go (ging′kō, jing′kō) *n. pl.* **·goes** A large tree native China and cultivated in the U.S., with edible fruits and ts. Also **ging′ko.** [< Japanese]

mill *Slang* A saloon.

rummy A variety of rummy.

·seng (jin′seng) *n.* **1.** An herb native to China and rth America, having a root of aromatic and stimulant ɔperties. **2.** The root of this herb as used in a medicinal ɔparation. [< Chinese *jen shen*]

sy (jip′sē), **Gip·sy** See GYPSY, GYPSY.

affe (jə·raf′, -räf′) *n. pl.* **·raffes** or **·raffe** An African minant, the tallest of all mammals, having a very long ck and long slender legs. [< F, ult. < Arabic *zarāfah*]

d[1] (gûrd) *v.t.* **gird·ed** or **girt, gird·ing 1.** To surround or ke fast with a belt or girdle. **2.** To encircle; surround. To prepare (oneself) for action. **4.** To clothe, equip, or low, as with some quality or attribute. [OE *gyrdan*]

d[2] (gûrd) *v.t. & v.i.* To attack with sarcasm; gibe. [ME *den*; origin unknown]

d·er (gûr′dər) *n.* A long heavy beam, as of steel or wood, at supports the joists of a floor, etc.

dle (gûr·dəl) *n.* **1.** A belt or cord worn around the ist; sash. **2.** Anything that encircles like a belt. **3.** A man's flexible undergarment worn to give support and ape. **4.** An encircling cut made through the bark of a tree nk or branch. **5.** The outer edge of a cut gem. **—***v.t.* **ed, ·dling 1.** To fasten a girdle or belt around. **2.** To en-cle; encompass. **3.** To make an encircling cut through bark of (a branch or tree). [OE *gyrdle*] **—gir′dler** *n.*

l (gûrl) *n.* **1.** A female infant or child. **2.** A young, un-rried woman. **3.** A female servant. **4.** *Informal* A sweet-art. **5.** *Informal* Any woman of any age. [ME *gurle*] — **·l′ish** *adj.* **—girl′ish·ly** *adv.* **—girl′ish·ness** *n.*

l guide A member of a British and Canadian organiza-n, the **Girl Guides,** resembling the Girl Scouts.

l scout A member of an organization of girls between the es of 7 and 17, founded in the U.S. in 1912 to develop alth, character, etc.

t[1] (gûrt) Past tense and past participle of GIRD[1].

t[2] (gûrt) *v.t. & v.i.* **1.** To gird. **2.** To measure in girth. *n.* Girth. [< GIRD[1]]

th (gûrth) *n.* **1.** The circumference of anything. **2.** A nd passed under the belly of a horse or other animal to ake fast a saddle, harness, pack, etc. **3.** A girdle or band. *v.t.* **1.** To bind with a girth. **2.** To encircle; girdle. — . **3.** To measure in girth. [< ON *gjordh*]

·mo (giz′mō) *n. pl.* **·mos** *U.S. Slang* A gadget. Also elled *gizmo.*

t (jist) *n.* The main idea or substance, as of an argu-ent, question, etc. [< OF *giste* place of rest]

git·tern (git′ərn) *n.* A cittern. [< OF < L < Gk. *kithara*]

give (giv) *v.* **gave, giv·en, giv·ing** *v.t.* **1.** To transfer freely (what is one's own) to the permanent possession of another without asking anything in return. **2.** To put into the hands of another for temporary use; hand over; let have. **3.** To put into the grasp of another: *Give* me your hand. **4.** To make available; furnish. **5.** To be a source of. **6.** To grant or concede, as permission. **7.** To impart: to *give* advice. **8.** To administer (a dose of medicine, a treatment, etc.). **9.** To assign or allot. **10.** To deal, deliver, or inflict (a blow, beating, etc.). **11.** To transmit or communicate (a disease, etc.). **12.** To perform or do: to *give* a play. **13.** To issue (an order, etc.). **14.** To part with; relinquish or yield: to *give* one's life. **15.** To devote, as oneself, to a cause, etc. — *v.i.* **16.** To make donations; make free gifts. **17.** To move down, back, etc., as under pressure: The door *gave.* **18.** To be springy, flexible, etc.: The bed *gives* comfortably. **19.** To furnish a view or passage; open: with *on* or *onto.* **—to give a good account of** To conduct (oneself) creditably. — **to give and take** To exchange on equal terms. **—to give away 1.** To bestow as a gift. **2.** To hand over (the bride) to the bridegroom. **3.** *Informal* To make known, as a secret; reveal. **—to give back** To restore or return. **—to give birth** To bear offspring. **—to give birth to 1.** To bear (offspring). **2.** To create or originate, as an idea. **3.** To result in. **—to give forth** To discharge; emit. **—to give in 1.** To yield, as to something demanded. **2.** To cease opposition; acknowledge oneself vanquished. **3.** To deliver or hand in (a report, resignation, etc.). **—to give it to** To administer a scolding, beating, etc., to. **—to give off** To send forth, as odors; emit. **—to give out 1.** To send forth; emit. **2.** To hand out or distribute. **3.** To make known; publish. **4.** To become completely used up or exhausted. **—to give over 1.** To hand over, as to another's care. **2.** To cease; desist. **—to give rise to** To cause or produce; result in. **—to give up 1.** To surrender. **2.** To stop; cease. **3.** To desist from as hopeless. **4.** To lose all hope for, as a sick person. **5.** To devote wholly: to *give* oneself *up* to art. **—to give way 1.** To collapse, bend, fail, etc., as under pressure or force. **2.** To draw back. **3.** To concede or yield. **4.** To abandon oneself, as to despair. **—***n.* **1.** The quality of being resilient; elasticity. **2.** The act or process of bending or yielding. [Fusion of OE *giefan* and ON *gefa*] **—giv′er** *n.*

give-and-take (giv′ən·tāk′) *n.* The making of mutual concessions, exchanges, etc.

give·a·way (giv′ə·wā′) *Informal n.* **1.** A disclosure or betrayal, generally unintentional. **2.** Something given free or at a greatly reduced price. **—***adj.* Characterized by prizes.

giv·en (giv′ən) *adj.* **1.** Presented; bestowed. **2.** Habitually inclined; addicted: with *to.* **3.** Specified; stated: a *given* date. **4.** Issued on an indicated date: said of official documents, etc. **5.** Admitted as a fact. **—Syn.** See ADDICTED.

given name The name bestowed on a person at birth, or shortly thereafter, as distinguished from his surname.

giz·mo (giz′mō) See GISMO.

giz·zard (giz′ərd) *n.* **1.** A second stomach in birds, in which partly digested food is finely ground. **2.** *Informal* The human stomach. [< OF < L *gigeria* cooked entrails of poultry]

gla·brous (glā′brəs) *adj. Biol.* **1.** Devoid of hair or down. **2.** Having a smooth surface. [< L *glaber* smooth]

gla·cé (gla·sā′) *adj.* **1.** Sugared or candied, as preserved fruits. **2.** Having a glossy surface, as certain leathers. **3.** Iced; frozen. **—***v.t.* **·céed, ·cé·ing 1.** To cover with icing. **2.** To make smooth and glossy. [< F *glace* ice]

gla·cial (glā′shəl) *adj.* **1.** Pertaining to, caused by, or marked by the presence of glaciers. **2.** Freezingly cold. **3.** Indifferent. [< F < L *glacies* ice] **—gla′cial·ly** *adv.*

glacial epoch *Geol.* Any portion of geological time characterized by ice sheets over much of the earth's surface.

gla·ci·ate (glā′shē·āt) *v.t.* **·at·ed, ·at·ing** To cover with or subject to the action of glaciers. **—gla′ci·a′tion** *n.*

gla·cier (glā′shər) *n.* A field of ice, formed in regions of perennial frost from compacted snow, that moves slowly until it either breaks off to form icebergs or melts in warmer regions. [< F < L *glacies* ice]

glad[1] (glad) *adj.* **glad·der, glad·dest 1.** Having a feeling of joy, pleasure, or content; gratified: often with *of* or *at.* **2.** Showing joy; brightly cheerful: a *glad* face. **3.** Giving reason to rejoice; bringing joy. **4.** Very willing: He'd be *glad* to help. [OE *glæd* shining, glad]

glad[2] (glad) *n. Informal* A gladiolus.

glad·den (glad′n) *v.t.* To make glad. **—glad′den·er** *n.*

glade (glād) *n.* **1.** A clearing in a wood. **2.** *U.S.* An everglade. [Prob. akin to *glad* in obs. sense of "bright, sunny"]

glad eye *Slang* A flirtatious glance: esp. in the phrase **to get** (or **give**) **the glad eye.**

glad hand *Slang* A display, often insincere, of cordiality.

glad·i·a·tor (glad′ē·ā′tər) *n.* **1.** In ancient Rome, a slave, captive, or paid freeman who fought other men or animals as public entertainment. **2.** One who engages in any kind of struggle. [< L *gladius* sword] — **glad·i·a·to·ri·al** (glad′ē·ə·tôr′ē·əl, -tō′rē-) *adj.*

glad·i·o·lus (glad′ē·ō′ləs, glə·dī′ə·ləs) *n. pl.* **·lus·es** or **·li** (-lī) A plant of the iris family with fleshy bulbs, sword-shaped leaves, and spikes of colored flowers. Also **glad′i·o′la.**

glad·ly (glad′lē) *adv.* In a glad manner; with joy; willingly.

glad·ness (glad′nis) *n.* The state of being glad; joy.

glad·some (glad′səm) *adj.* Glad. — **glad′some·ly** *adv.* — **glad′some·ness** *n.*

Glad·stone (glad′stōn, -stən) *n.* A suitcase hinged to open flat and form two equal compartments. Also **Gladstone bag.** [after W. E. *Gladstone*, 1809–98, English statesman]

glair (glâr) *n.* **1.** Raw egg white, used in making size or glaze; also, the glaze or size. **2.** Any sticky matter. — *v.t.* To coat with glair. [< F < L *clarus* clear] — **glair′y** *adj.*

glam·or·ize (glam′ər·īz) *v.t.* **·rized, ·riz·ing** To make glamorous.

glam·or·ous (glam′ər·əs) *adj.* Full of glamour; alluring. — **glam′or·ous·ly** *adv.* — **glam′or·ous·ness** *n.*

glam·our (glam′ər) *n.* Alluring charm or fascination. Also *U.S.* **glam′or.** [< Scot *gramarye* magic power]

glance (glans, gläns) *v.* **glanced, glanc·ing** *v.i.* **1.** To take a quick look. **2.** To touch briefly on some matter. **3.** To be deflected at an angle after obliquely striking. **4.** To flash intermittently; glint. — *v.t.* **5.** To cause to strike a surface obliquely. — *n.* **1.** A quick look. **2.** A flash; glint. **3.** Oblique impact and deflection. [< OF *glacier* to slip]

gland (gland) *n. Anat.* Any of various organs by means of which certain constituents are removed from the blood, either for use in the body or for elimination from it. [< F < L *glans, glandis* acorn]

glan·ders (glan′dərz) *n. Vet.* A contagious disease of horses and other equines, characterized by nasal discharges and ulcerative lesions of the lungs and other organs. [< OF *glandre* gland] — **glan′dered, glan′der·ous** *adj.*

glan·du·lar (glan′jə·lər) *adj.* **1.** Of, pertaining to, or resembling a gland. **2.** Having glands. Also **glan′du·lous.**

glan·dule (glan′jōōl) *n.* A small gland.

glare[1] (glâr) *v.* **glared, glar·ing** *v.i.* **1.** To shine with a steady and dazzling intensity. **2.** To gaze or stare fiercely or in hostility. **3.** To be conspicuous or showy. — *v.t.* **4.** To express or send forth with a glare. — *n.* **1.** A dazzling, steady light or reflection. **2.** An intense, piercing look or gaze, usually hostile. **3.** Gaudy or showy display; vulgar brilliance. [ME *glaren* < LG]

glare[2] (glâr) *U.S. n.* A glassy, smooth surface, as of ice. — *adj.* Having a glassy, smooth surface. [? < GLARE[1], n.]

glar·ing (glâr′ing) *adj.* **1.** Looking or staring fixedly or with hostility. **2.** Emitting an excessively brilliant light. **3.** Gaudy. **4.** Plainly conspicuous. — **glar′ing·ly** *adv.*

glar·y[1] (glâr′ē) *adj.* **glar·i·er, glar·i·est** Dazzling; glaring.

glar·y[2] (glâr′ē) *adj. U.S.* Slippery, as ice.

glass (glas, gläs) *n.* **1.** A hard, amorphous, brittle, usu. transparent substance made by fusing one or more of the oxides of silicon, boron, or phosphorus with certain basic oxides, followed by rapid cooling to prevent crystallization. ◆ Collateral adjective: *vitreous*. **2.** Any substance made of or resembling glass. **3.** An article made wholly or partly of glass; as: **a** A windowpane, lens, or mirror, tumbler, etc. **b** *pl.* A pair of eyeglasses; also, binoculars. **4.** Glassware. **5.** The contents of a drinking glass; glassful. — *v.t.* **1.** To put in a glass container. **2.** To enclose in or cover with glass. **3.** To equip with glass parts. **4.** To give a glassy surface or appearance to. — *adj.* **1.** Of, pertaining to, or consisting of glass. **2.** Fitted with glass: a *glass* frame. [OE *glæs*]

glass blowing The art or process of directing a controlled stream of air through a tube into a mass of molten glass at the end of the tube so as to form the glass into various shapes.

glass·ful (glas′fōōl, gläs′-) *n. pl.* **·fuls** The amount contained in a drinking glass.

glass snake A lizard of the southern U.S., having a very brittle tail.

glass·ware (glas′wâr′, gläs′-) *n.* Articles made of glass.

glass wool Fibers of spun glass of woollike appearance, used for insulation, filters, etc.

glass·work (glas′wûrk′, gläs′-) *n.* **1.** The manufacture of glass. **2.** Glass as a material used in glassware, decoration, etc. **3.** Glassware. **4.** The fitting of panes of glass.

glass·works (glas′wûrks′, gläs′-) *n.pl.* (*usu. construed as sing.*) A factory where glass is made.

glass·wort (glas′wûrt, gläs′-) *n.* Any of several seaside herbs: also called *saltwort*

glass·y (glas′ē, gläs′ē) *adj.* **glass·i·er, glass·i·est** **1.** Resembling glass. **2.** Fixed, blank, and uncomprehending: a *glassy* stare. — **glass′i·ly** *adv.* — **glass′i·ness** *n.*

glau·co·ma (glô·kō′mə) *n. Pathol.* A disease of the eye characterized by pressure of fluids within the eyeball with gradual loss of vision. [< L < Gk. *glaukos* bluish gray] — **glau·co·ma·tous** (glô·kō′mə·təs, -kom′ə-) *adj.*

glau·cous (glô′kəs) *adj.* **1.** Yellowish green; also, green. **2.** *Bot.* Covered with a whitish bloom, as gra[pes] [< L < Gk. *glaukos* bluish gray]

glaze (glāz) *v.* **glazed, glaz·ing** *v.t.* **1.** To fit, as a win[dow] with glass panes; also, to provide (a building, etc.) with [win]dows. **2.** To cover or coat with a thin film; as: **a** To [coat] (pottery) with a glasslike surface applied by fusing. **b** [To] cover (foods) with a thin coating of eggs, syrup, etc. **c** [To] cover (paintings) with a thin, transparent coating to mo[dify] the tone. — *v.i.* **3.** To become covered with a thin coa[ting] or film. — *n.* **1.** A thin, glossy coating; also, the subst[ance] used to make such a coating. **2.** A filmy haze. **3.** *U.[S.]* thin coating of ice. [ME *glas* glass] — **glaz′er** *n.*

gla·zier (glā′zhər) *n.* **1.** One who fits windows, doors, [etc.] with panes of glass. **2.** One who applies glaze to pott[ery]

gla·zier·y (glā′zhər·ē) *n.* The work of a glazier.

glaz·ing (glā′zing) *n.* **1.** The act of setting glass, as [in a] window. **2.** The glass used. **3.** A glaze. **4.** The act o[f] of applying a glaze.

glaz·y (glā′zē) *adj.* **glaz·i·er, glaz·i·est** **1.** Covered wit[h or] as with a glaze. **2.** Resembling a glaze. — **glaz′i·nes[s]**

gleam (glēm) *n.* **1.** An intermittent or momentary ra[y or] beam of light. **2.** A soft radiance; glow; also, reflected li[ght]. **3.** A brief manifestation, as of humor; a faint trace, a[s of] hope. — *v.i.* **1.** To shine softly; emit gleams. **2.** To ap[pear] briefly as in a small burst of light. — *v.t.* **3.** To em[it] gleams. — **Syn.** See SHINE. [OE *glǣm*] — **gleam′y** *a[dj.]*

glean (glēn) *v.t.* & *v.i.* **1.** To collect (facts, etc.) by pat[ient] effort. **2.** To gather (the leavings) from a field after the [crop] has been reaped. **3.** To gather the leavings from (a f[ield,] etc.). [< OF < LL *glenare* < Celtic] — **glean′er** *n.*

glean·ing (glē′ning) *n. Usu. pl.* That which is gleane[d].

glebe (glēb) *n. Brit.* A portion of land attached to a ch[urch] benefice as part of its endowment. [< OF < L *gleba* c[lod]

glee (glē) *n.* **1.** Lively, exuberant joy. **2.** A musical c[om]position for male voices, without accompaniment. [OE *g*

glee club A group of singers organized to sing part so[ngs]

glee·ful (glē′fəl) *adj.* Feeling or exhibiting glee; mirth[ful]. Also **glee′some** (-səm). — **glee′ful·ly** *adv.* — **glee′ful·nes[s]**

glen (glen) *n.* A small, secluded valley. [< Scot. Gael. *gle*

Glen·gar·ry (glen·gar′ē) *n.* A Scottish cap having slo[ping] sides and streamers in back. [after a valley in Scotland]

glib (glib) *adj.* **glib·ber, glib·best** **1.** Speaking fluently w[ith]out much thought: a *glib* talker. **2.** More facile than [sin]cere. **3.** Characterized by smoothness, as of manner. [< MLG *glibberich* slippery] — **glib′ly** *adv.* — **glib′ness**

glide (glīd) *v.* **glid·ed, glid·ing** *v.i.* **1.** To move, slip, or [flow] smoothly or effortlessly. **2.** To pass unnoticed or imper[cep]tibly, as time: often with *by*. **3.** *Aeron.* To descend alon[g an] oblique line gradually without motor power; also, to f[ly a] glider. **4.** *Music & Phonet.* To produce a glide. — *v.t.* To cause to glide. — *n.* **1.** The act of gliding. **2.** *Phone[t.]* transitional sound made in passing from one speech so[und] to another. [OE *glīdan*] — **glid′ing·ly** *adv.*

glid·er (glī′dər) *n.* **1.** One who or that which glides. [2.] *Aeron.* An engineless airplane, constructed to soar on [air] currents. **3.** A swing gliding in a metal frame.

glim·mer (glim′ər) *v.i.* **1.** To gleam unsteadily; flicker. [2.] To appear fitfully or faintly. — *n.* **1.** A faint, unste[ady] light. **2.** A trace; inkling. [ME *glimeren* to shine] — **glim′mer·ing** *n.* & *adj.* — **glim′mer·ing·ly** *adv.*

glimpse (glimps) *n.* **1.** A momentary view or look. **2** [A] faint intimation; inkling. — *v.* **glimpsed, glimps·ing** *v.t.* **1.** To see for an instant; catch a glimpse of. — *v.i.* **2.** [To] look for an instant: with *at*. [ME *glimsen* to shine faint[ly]]

glint (glint) *v.i.* **1.** To gleam; glitter. **2.** To dart. — [*v.t.*] **3.** To reflect; shine. — *n.* **1.** A gleam. **2.** A luster, a[s of] metal. [ME *glinten* to shine < Scand.]

glis·sade (gli·säd′, -sād′) *n.* **1.** The act of skillfully slid[ing] down an icy slope. **2.** A gliding dance step. — *v.i.* **·sad·[ed,] ·sad·ing** To execute a glissade. [< F *glisser* to slip]

glis·san·do (gli·sän′dō) *Music n. pl.* **·di** (-dē) or **·dos** [1.] A passing from one tone to another by a continuous cha[nge] of pitch; also, a rapid succession of tones. **2.** A passag[e] written or performed. — *adj.* Of a glissando. — *adv.* I[n] a glissando. [< F *glissant* slipping + Ital. *-ando*]

glis·ten (glis′ən) *v.i.* To shine, as reflected light. — [*n.*] Brightness; sparkle. [OE *glisnian* to shine]

glit·ter (glit′ər) *v.i.* **1.** To sparkle brightly or brilliantly[, as] a diamond. **2.** To display striking magnificence; be b[ril]liantly showy. — *n.* Sparkling magnificence; brilliar[ce.] [< ON *glitra*] — **glit′ter·ing·ly** *adv.* — **glit′ter·y** *adj.*

gloam·ing (glō′ming) *n.* The dusk of early evening; t[wi]light. [OE *glōmung*]

gloat (glōt) *v.i.* To take an intense, often malicious delig[ht:] usu. with *over*. [Cf. ON *glotta* to grin] — **gloat′ing** *adj.*

glob (glob) *n.* **1.** A small drop or ball of something. **2** [A] rounded, often large mass of something.

glob·al (glō′bəl) *adj.* **1.** Involving the whole world: *glo[bal]* war. **2.** Spherical. — **glob′al·ly** *adv.*

globe (glōb) *n.* **1.** A perfectly round body; ball; sphe[re]

…o, anything like a sphere, as a fishbowl. **2.** The earth. **3.** …spherical model of the earth or heavens. **4.** A ball, usu. of …ld, used as an emblem of authority. — *v.t. & v.i.* **globed,** …ob·ing To form into a globe. [< F < L *globus* ball] — …o·bate (glō′bāt) *adj.*

…be·fish (glōb′fish) *n. pl.* **·fish** or **·fish·es** Any of various …iny-finned, tropical fishes that inflate their bodies into …obular form.

…be·trot·ter (glōb′trot′ər) *n.* One who travels all over …e world, esp. for sightseeing. — **globe′trot′ting** *n.*

…bin (glō′bin) *n. Biochem.* The protein constituent of …moglobin. [< L *globus* ball + -IN]

…bose (glō′bōs, glō·bōs′) *adj.* Spherical. Also **glo′bous** …əs). [< L *globus* ball] — **glo·bos·i·ty** (glō·bos′ə·tē) *n.*

…b·u·lar (glob′yə·lər) *adj.* **1.** Spherical. **2.** Formed of …bules.

…b·ule (glob′yōōl) *n.* A tiny sphere of matter or drop of …uid. [< F < L *globulus* ball]

…b·u·lin (glob′yə·lin) *n. Biochem.* Any of a group of …mple plant and animal proteins, insoluble in water but …uble in dilute saline solutions.

…b·u·lous (glob′yə·ləs) *adj.* **1.** Containing or consisting …globules. **2.** Spherical; globular. Also **glob′u·lose** (-lōs).

…ck·en·spiel (glok′ən·spēl) *n.* A portable musical in…ument with a series of chromatically tuned metal bars …yed by hammers. [< G < *glocken* bells + *spiel* play]

…m·er·ate (glom′ər·āt, -it) *adj.* Gathered or wound into …ounded mass. [< L *glomus* mass] — **glom′er·a′tion** *n.*

…om (glōōm) *n.* **1.** Partial or total darkness; heavy shad… **2.** Darkness or depression of the mind or spirits. **3.** A …k or gloomy place. — *v.i.* **1.** To look sullen or dejected. …To be dark or threatening. — *v.t.* **3.** To make dark, sad, …sullen. [ME *glom(b)en* to look sad]

…om·y (glōō′mē) *adj.* **gloom·i·er, gloom·i·est 1.** Dark; …mal. **2.** Melancholy; morose. **3.** Producing gloom or …lancholy. — **gloom′i·ly** *adv.* — **gloom′i·ness** *n.*

…ri·a (glôr′ē·ə, glō′rē·ə) *n. Eccl.* **a** The section of the …ass consisting of the recitation or singing of *Gloria in ex…sis Deo.* **b** Its musical setting. [< L, glory]

…ri·fi·ca·tion (glôr′ə·fə·kā′shən, glō′rə-) *n.* **1.** The act of …rifying or exalting. **2.** Invested with glory. **3.** *Informal* …glorified form of something.

…ri·fy (glôr′ə·fī, glō′rə-) *v.t.* **·fied, ·fy·ing 1.** To make …rious. **2.** To honor; worship. **3.** To give great praise to; …d. **4.** To make seem more splendid than is so. [< OF < *gloria* glory + *facere* to make] — **glo′ri·fi′er** *n.*

…ri·ous (glôr′ē·əs, glō′rē-) *adj.* **1.** Full of glory; illustri…s. **2.** Bringing glory or honor. **3.** Resplendent. **4.** *In…mal* Delightful. — **glo′ri·ous·ly** *adv.* — **glo′ri·ous·ness** *n.*

…ry (glôr′ē, glō′rē) *n. pl.* **·ries 1.** Distinguished honor …praise; exalted reputation. **2.** Something bringing praise. …Worshipful adoration: to give *glory* to God. **4.** Magnifi…nce; splendor: the *glory* of Rome. **5.** The bliss of heaven. …A state of extreme well-being: to be in one's *glory.* **7.** A …mbus; halo. — *v.i.* **·ried, ·ry·ing 1.** To take pride: with …**2.** To boast; brag. [< OF < L *gloria*]

…ss[1] (glôs, glos) *n.* **1.** The luster or sheen of a polished …rface. **2.** A deceptive or superficial appearance. — *v.t.* …To make lustrous, as by polishing. **2.** To hide (errors, …) by falsehood: usu. with *over.* — *v.i.* **3.** To become …ny. [< Scand. Cf. ON *glossi* blaze.] — **gloss′er** *n.*

…ss[2] (glôs, glos) *n.* **1.** An explanatory note, esp. marginal …interlinear; a commentary; a translation; a glossary. **2.** …artful or deceptive explanation to cover up a fault, etc. …*v.t.* **1.** To write glosses for (a text, etc.); annotate. **2.** …excuse by false explanations. — *v.i.* **3.** To make glosses. …OF < L < Gk. *glōssa* foreign word] — **gloss′er** *n.*

…s·sa·ry (glos′ə·rē, glôs′-) *n. pl.* **·ries** A lexicon of the …chnical, obscure, or foreign words of a work or field. [< L …*glossa*] — **glos·sar·i·al** (glo·sâr′ē·əl, glô-) *adj.* — **glos·…r′i·al·ly** *adv.* — **glos·sa·rist** (glos′ə·rist, glôs′-) *n.*

…sso- *combining form* The tongue; speech; language. Also, …fore vowels, **gloss-.** [< Gk. *glōssa* tongue]

…ss·y (glôs′ē, glos′ē) *adj.* **gloss·i·er, gloss·i·est 1.** Having …bright sheen; lustrous. **2.** Made superficially attractive. …Specious. — **gloss′i·ly** *adv.* — **gloss′i·ness** *n.*

…ot *combining form* Using or able to use (a number of) …nguages: *polyglot.* [< Gk. *glōssa* tongue, language]

…t·tal (glot′l) *adj.* Of or articulated in the glottis.

…t·tis (glot′is) *n. pl.* **glot·ti·des** (glot′ə·dēz) or **glot·tis·es** …*nat.* The cleft between the vocal cords at the upper opening …the larynx. [< NL < Gk. < *glōtta* tongue]

…tto- *combining form* Language. [< Gk. *glōtta*]

…ve (gluv) *n.* **1.** A covering for the hand, having a sep…ate sheath for each finger. **2.** In baseball, a large leather …tt for catching the ball. **3.** A boxing glove. — **to be hand …glove (with)** To be in close relationship (with). — **to …ndle with kid gloves** To use great care and tact in dealing with. — **to put on the gloves** *Informal* To box or spar. — *v.t.* **gloved, glov·ing 1.** To put gloves on. **2.** To furnish with gloves. **3.** To be a glove for. [OE *glōf*]

glov·er (gluv′ər) *n.* A maker of or dealer in gloves.

glow (glō) *v.i.* **1.** To give off light and heat, esp. without flame; be incandescent. **2.** To shine but without heat. **3.** To be red, as from heat; flush. **4.** To be animated, as with emotion, etc. **5.** To be very hot; burn. — *n.* **1.** The incandescence given off by a heated substance. **2.** Vividness. **3.** Ruddiness, as from health. **4.** Strong emotion; ardor. [OE *glōwan*] — **glow′ing** *adj.* — **glow′ing·ly** *adv.*

glow·er (glou′ər) *v.i.* To stare with an angry frown; scowl sullenly. — *n.* The act of glowering; a fierce stare. [? Obs. *glow* to stare] — **glow′er·ing·ly** *adv.*

glow·worm (glō′wûrm′) *n.* **1.** A European beetle, the larva and wingless female of which display phosphorescent light. **2.** The firefly.

glox·in·i·a (glok·sin′ē·ə) *n.* A plant with large, bell-shaped flowers. [after *Gloxin,* 18th c. Ger. doctor]

gloze (glōz) *v.* **glozed, gloz·ing** *v.t.* To explain away.

glu·cose (glōō′kōs) *n.* **1.** *Chem.* A monosaccharide carbohydrate, $C_6H_{12}O_6$, less sweet than cane sugar, found as dextrose in plants and animals and obtained by hydrolysis. **2.** The thick yellowish syrup obtained by incomplete hydrolysis of starch and used in confectionery, baking, etc. [< F < Gk. *glykys* sweet] — **glu·cos′ic** (-kos′ik) *adj.*

glu·co·side (glōō′kə·sīd) *n. Chem.* Any of a class of carbohydrate compounds that yield glucose or other sugar.

glue (glōō) *n.* **1.** An adhesive in the form of a gelatine made from animal substances, as skin, bones, etc. **2.** An adhesive or cement made of casein or other synthetics. **3.** Any sticky adhesive. — *v.t.* **glued, glu·ing** To stick or fasten with or as with glue. [< OF *glu* birdlime]

glue·y (glōō′ē) *adj.* **glu·i·er, glu·i·est 1.** Having the nature of glue; sticky; viscous. **2.** Covered or spread with glue.

glum (glum) *adj.* **glum·mer, glum·mest** Moody and silent; sullen. — **glum′ly** *adv.* — **glum′ness** *n.*

glume (glōōm) *n. Bot.* One of the two lowest bracts on the spikelet of certain grassy plants. [< L *gluma* husk]

glut (glut) *v.* **glut·ted, glut·ting** *v.t.* **1.** To feed or supply to excess; satiate. **2.** To supply (the market) with an excess of goods so that the price falls. — *v.i.* **3.** To eat to excess. — *n.* **1.** An excessive supply. **2.** The act of glutting or being glutted. [< obs. *glut* glutton < OF *gloutir* to swallow]

glu·ten (glōōt′n) *n.* A tough, sticky mixture of proteins obtained by washing out the starch from wheat flour. [< L, glue] — **glu·te·nous** (glōōt′n·əs) *adj.*

glu·te·us (glōō·tē′əs) *n. pl.* **·te·i** (-tē′ī) *Anat.* Any of three muscles of the buttocks. [< NL < Gk. *gloutos* rump] — **glu·te′al** *adj.*

glu·ti·nous (glōōt′n·əs) *adj.* Resembling glue; sticky. — **glu′ti·nous·ly** *adv.* — **glu′ti·nous·ness** *n.*

glut·ton[1] (glut′n) *n.* **1.** One who eats to excess. **2.** One who has a great appetite or capacity for something. [< OF < L *gluto, -onis* glutton]

glut·ton[2] (glut′n) *n.* A wolverine, esp. of Asia or Europe. [Trans. of G *vielfrass* great eater]

glut·ton·ous (glut′n·əs) *adj.* **1.** Given to excess in eating; voracious. **2.** Desiring excessively. — **glut′ton·ous·ly** *adv.*

glut·ton·y (glut′n·ē) *n. pl.* **·ton·ies** The act or habit of eating to excess.

glyc·er·ide (glis′ər·īd, -id) *n. Chem.* An ether or ester of glycerol with a fatty acid.

glyc·er·in (glis′ər·in) *n.* Glycerol. Also **glyc′er·ine** (-in, -ēn).

glyc·er·ol (glis′ər·ōl, -ol) *n. Chem.* A sweet, oily, colorless alcohol, $C_3H_8O_3$, formed by decomposition of natural fats with alkalis or superheated steam, used in medicine, industry, and the arts. [< Gk. *glykeros* sweet + -OL[2]]

glyc·er·yl (glis′ər·il) *n. Chem.* The trivalent glycerol radical C_3H_5.

glyco- *combining form* Sweet. [< Gk. *glykys* sweet]

gly·co·gen (glī′kə·jən) *n. Biochem.* A white, mealy, amorphous polysaccharide, $(C_6H_{11}O_5)_x$, contained principally in the liver and hydrolized into glucose.

gly·co·gen·ic (glī′kə·jen′ik) *adj.* **1.** Relating to the formation of glycogen. **2.** Caused by glycogen.

gly·col (glī′kōl, -kol) *n. Chem.* **1.** One of several alcohols containing two hydroxyl radicals, having the general formula $C_nH_{2n}(OH)_2$. **2.** Ethylene glycol.

gly·co·side (glī′kə·sīd) *n. Chem.* Any of a group of carbohydrates that when decomposed yield glucose or other sugar.

G-man (jē′man′) *n. pl.* **-men** (-men′) An agent of the Federal Bureau of Investigation. [< G(OVERNMENT) MAN]

gnarl (närl) *n.* A protuberance on a tree; a tough knot. — *v.t.* To make knotty and twisted like an old tree.

gnarled (närld) *adj.* **1.** Having snarls. **2.** Weather-beaten and rugged. **3.** Of the hands, having prominent knuckles and twisted fingers as from hard work. Also **gnarl′y.**

gnash (nash) *v.t.* **1.** To grind or snap (the teeth) together, as in rage. **2.** To bite or chew by grinding the teeth. — *v.i.* **3.** To grind the teeth. — *n.* A bite of the teeth. [< Scand.]

gnat (nat) *n.* Any of various small stinging or biting flies. — **to strain at a gnat** To fuss. [OE *gnæt*]

-gnathous *combining form* Having a jaw of an indicated kind: *prognathous.* [< Gk. *gnathos* jaw + -OUS]

gnaw (nô) *v.t.* **gnawed, gnawed** or sometimes **gnawn, gnaw·ing 1.** To bite or eat away little by little as with the teeth; to make by gnawing; also, to bite on repeatedly. **2.** To torment or oppress with fear, pain, etc. — *v.i.* **3.** To bite, chew, or corrode persistently. **4.** To cause constant worry, etc. [OE *gnagan*] — **gnaw′er** *n.* — **gnaw′ing·ly** *adv.*

gnaw·ing (nô′ing) *n.* **1.** A dull, persistent sensation of discomfort or distress. **2.** *pl.* Pangs of hunger.

gneiss (nīs) *n.* A coarse-grained, banded rock like granite but having layered components. [< G] — **gneiss′ic** *adj.*

gnome (nōm) *n.* In folklore, one of a group of dwarfish, little old men, living in caves and guarding buried treasure, etc. [< F < NL *gnomus*] — **gnom′ish** *adj.*

gno·mic (nō′mik, nom′ik) *adj.* Consisting of or resembling maxims; aphoristic. Also **gno′mi·cal.** — **gno′mi·cal·ly** *adv.*

gno·mon (nō′mon) *n.* A pointer or similar device used to indicate time by the shadow it casts, as on a sundial. For illus. see SUNDIAL. [< Gk. < *gnō-* stem of *gignōskein* to know] — **gno·mon·ic** (nō·mon′ik) or **·i·cal** *adj.*

-gnomy *combining form* Knowledge or art of judging: *physiognomy.* [< Gk. *gnōmē* judgment]

-gnosis *combining form Med.* Knowledge; recognition: *prognosis.* [< Gk. *gnōsis* knowledge]

gnos·tic (nos′tik) *adj.* Of or possessing knowledge, esp. spiritual knowledge or insight. Also **gnos′ti·cal.**

Gnos·ti·cism (nos′tə·siz′əm) *n.* A system of ancient Greek and Oriental philosophy, an attempted synthesis with Christian doctrine, denounced as heretical by the Church. — **Gnos′tic** *adj. & n.*

gnu (nōō, nyōō) *n. pl.* **gnus** or **gnu** A South African antelope having an oxlike head with curved horns, a mane, and a long tail: also called *wildebeest.* [< Xhosa *nqu*]

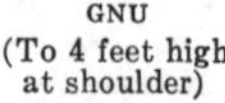

GNU
(To 4 feet high at shoulder)

go[1] (gō) *v.* **went, gone, go·ing;** *3rd person sing. present* **goes** *v.i.* **1.** To proceed or pass along; move. **2.** To move from a place; leave; depart: often used as a command or signal, as in a race: *Go!* **3.** To have a scheduled route destination: This train *goes* to Chicago daily. **4.** To be in operation; also, to work or function properly. **5.** To extend or reach: This pipe *goes* to the basement. **6.** To emit a specified sound or act in a certain way: The chain *goes* "clank." **7.** To fail, give away, or collapse; also, to disappear. **8.** To have a specific place: belong: The plates *go* on the shelf. **9.** To be awarded or given; also, to be allotted or applied: This *goes* for rent. **10.** To pass from one person to another. **11.** To pass into a condition; become: to *go* insane. **12.** To be, continue, or appear in a specified state: to *go* unpunished. **13.** To happen or end in a specific manner: The election *went* badly. **14.** To be considered or ranked: good as lunches *go.* **15.** To be suitable; harmonize; fit. **16.** To be phrased; have a certain form: How does the tune *go*? **17.** To have recourse; resort: to *go* to court. **18.** To die. **19.** To pass: said of time. **20.** To be abolished or given up; These expenses must *go.* **21.** To serve, contribute, or help; also, to make up a certain quantity: Two ounces *go* to each serving. **22.** To be sold or bid for: with *at* or *for*: These shoes will *go* at a high price. **23.** To subject oneself; put oneself: He *went* to great pains. **24.** To continue one's actions to or beyond certain limits: He *goes* too far in his criticism. **25.** To endure; last: Can he *go* two more rounds? **26.** To be about to: used in the progressive form and followed by the present infinitive: They are *going* to protest. — *v.t.* **27.** *Informal* To furnish or provide (bail). **28.** *Informal* To risk or bet; wager. **29.** *Informal* To put up with; tolerate: I cannot *go* that music. — *adj. Aerospace* Operating or proceeding as planned. — **to go** *Informal* **1.** Remaining: ten pages *to go.* **2.** Prepared for taking outside: a sandwich *to go.* — **to go about 1.** To be occupied or busy with. **2.** To circulate. **3.** *Naut.* To tack; turn. — **to go after 1.** To try to catch; chase. **2.** To follow in sequence. — **to go against** To be opposed to; act contrary to. — **to go along 1.** To continue; carry on. **2.** To be in accord; agree: often with *with.* **3.** To escort; accompany: with *with.* — **to go around 1.** To move about or circulate. **2.** To enclose; encircle. **3.** To be enough for all to have some. — **to go at** To attack; work at. — **to go back on 1.** To be disloyal to; forsake. **2.** To fail to fulfill. — **to go behind** To inquire or investigate so as to test the validity of. — **to go beyond** To surpass; exceed. — **to go by 1.** To pass. **2.** To conform to or be guided by. **3.** To be known by. — **to go down 1.** To sink or descend. **2.** To experience defeat. **3.** To attain lasting remembrance, as in history. **4.** To decrease, as prices. — **to go for 1.** To to get. **2.** To advocate. **3.** *Informal* To attack. **4.** *formal* To be attracted by. — **to go halves** (or **shares**) *formal* To share equally. — **to go hard with** To bring tr le to. — **to go in for** *Informal* **1.** To strive for; advocate. To like or participate in. — **to go into 1.** To investig **2.** To take up, as a study. **3.** To be contained in. — t **in with** To unite or join forces with. — **to go off 1.** To plode or be discharged, as a gun. **2.** To depart; leave. *Informal* To occur. — **to go on 1.** To act; behave. **2.** happen: What's *going on* here? **3.** To persevere; end **4.** In the theater, to make an entrance. — **to go (somec better** *Informal* To surpass (someone). — **to go out 1.** go to social gatherings, etc. **2.** To be extinguished, light. **3.** To become outdated, as fashions. **4.** To g strike. **5.** To sympathize. My heart *goes out* to him. – **go over 1.** To repeat; also, to rehearse. **2.** To exan carefully. **3.** *Informal* To succeed. **4.** To change side allegiance. — **to go through 1.** To search thoroughly. To undergo; suffer; endure. **3.** To run over, as a role. To spend. **5.** To be accepted or approved. — **to go thro with** To perform to the finish; complete. — **to go toge 1.** To be suitable; harmonize. **2.** To be sweethearts. – **go under 1.** To be overwhelmed. **2.** To fail, as a busir — **to go up** To increase, as prices. — **to go with 1.** To monize with. **2.** To accompany. **3.** *Informal* To be sw hearts. — **to go without** To do or be without. — t **without saying** To be taken for granted. — **to let go 1.** release one's hold; set free. **2.** To abandon. — **to let c self go** To be uninhibited. — *n.* **1.** The act of going. *Informal* The capacity for action; He has plenty of *go.* *Informal* A try: to have a *go* at something. **4.** *Inform* success: He made a *go* of it. **5.** *Informal* An agreem bargain: It's a *go.* — **no go** *Informal* Useless; hopeless. **on the go** *Informal* In constant motion; very busy. [OE g

go[2] (gō) *n.* A Japanese game resembling chess or check

goad (gōd) *n.* **1.** A stick for urging on oxen, etc. **2.** So thing that drives. — *v.t.* To drive; incite. [OE *gād*]

go-a·head (gō′ə·hed′) *n.* A signal or permission to m ahead or proceed.

goal (gōl) *n.* **1.** Something toward which effort or movem is directed; an end or objective. **2.** The terminal point journey or race. **3.** In some games, the point to which players try to bring the ball, puck, etc., to score; also, scoring; also, the score made. [ME *gol*]

goal·ie (gō′lē) *n.* *Informal* A goalkeeper.

goal·keep·er (gōl′kē′pər) *n.* In hockey, soccer, etc player whose function is to prevent the ball or puck f passing over the goal for a score. Also **goal′tend′er.**

goat (gōt) *n* **1.** A cud-chewing mammal related to sheep and having hollow horns. **2.** A lecherous man. *Slang* One who is the butt of a joke; scapegoat. — **to one's goat** *Slang* To move one to anger or annoyance. [*gāt*] — **goat′ish** *adj.* — **goat′ish·ly** *adv.* — **goat′ish·nes**

Goat (gōt) *n.* The constellation and sign of the zo Capricorn.

goat·ee (gō·tē′) *n.* A man's short, pointed beard.

goat·herd (gōt′hûrd′) *n.* One who tends goats.

goat·skin (gōt′skin′) *n.* **1.** The hide of a goat. **2.** Lea made from this hide. **3.** Something made from this leat

goat·suck·er (gōt′suk′ər) *n.* Any of numerous noctur insectivorous birds, as the whippoorwill.

gob[1] (gob) *n.* *Informal* **1.** A piece or lump, as of a soft s stance. **2.** *pl.* Great quantities. [< OF *gobe* mouthful

gob[2] (gob) *n.* *Slang* A sailor of the U.S. Navy.

gob·bet (gob′it) *n.* **1.** A piece or hunk of raw meat. *Archaic* A large lump of food. [See GOB[1].]

gob·ble[1] (gob′əl) *v* **·bled, ·bling** *v.t.* **1.** To swallow (fo greedily. **2.** *U.S. Slang* To seize in a grasping manner. *v.i.* **3.** To eat greedily. [< F *gover* to bolt, devour]

gob·ble[2] (gob′əl) *v.i.* **·bled, ·bling** To make the throaty so of a male turkey. — *n.* This sound. [Var. of GABBLE

gob·ble·dy·gook (gob′əl·dē·gŏŏk′) *n.* *Informal* Invol pedantic, repetitious, and pompous jargon. [Coined by Maverick, U.S. Congressman, about 1940]

gob·bler (gob′lər) *n.* A male turkey.

Gob·e·lin (gob′ə·lin, gō′bə-; *Fr* gō·blaṅ′) *n.* A rich tape made in Paris or Beauvais, France. [after *Gobelin,* nam its first creator]

go-be·tween (gō′bə·twēn′) *n.* One who acts as an agen mediator between other persons.

gob·let (gob′lit) *n.* **1.** A drinking vessel, typically wi base and stem. **2.** A large, festive shallow drinking cup. OF *gobel* a drinking cup]

gob·lin (gob′lin) *n.* In folklore, an ugly elf regarded as or mischievous. [< OF *gobelin*]

go·bo (gō′bō) *n. pl.* **·bos 1.** A portable shield pla around a microphone to keep out extraneous sounds. **2** screen for shielding the lens of a television camera from direct rays of light. [Origin uncertain]

go·by (gō′bē) *n. pl.* **·by** or **·bies** Any of a family of fis

…ving ventral fins and a funnel-shaped suction disk. [< L Gk. *kōbios*, a small fish]
-by (gō′bī′) *n. Informal* An intentional slight.
-cart (gō′kärt′) *n.* **1.** A small wagon for young children. . A framework with rollers, designed to support babies arning to walk. **3.** A handcart.
d (god) *n.* **1.** One of various beings, usu. male, in mythol- ;y, primitive religions, etc., conceived of as immortal, as nbodying a particular quality or having special powers 'er some phase of life. **2.** A statue, image, or symbol of ch a being. **3.** Any person or thing much loved. [OE]
d (god) *n.* In monotheism, the ruler of life and the uni- rse.
d·child (god′chīld′) *n. pl.* **·chil·dren** One whom a person onsors at baptism, circumcision, etc.
d·dam (god′dam′) *interj.* A strong oath used to express ger, annoyance, surprise, etc. Also **God damn.** — *adj. & v.* Goddamned.
d·damned (god′damd′) *adj.* Utterly detestable or out- geous. — *adv. Informal* To an extreme degree; very.
d·daugh·ter (god′dô′tər) *n.* A female godchild.
d·dess (god′is) **1.** A female deity. **2.** A woman or girl of traordinary beauty.
d·fa·ther (god′fä′thər) *n.* A man who sponsors a child at baptism. — *v.t.* To act as a godfather to.
d-fear·ing (god′fir′ing) *adj.* **1.** *Often cap.* Having rev- ence for God. **2.** Pious; devout.
d·for·sak·en (god′fər·sā′kən) *adj.* **1.** *Often cap.* Aban- ned by God. **2.** Totally wicked. **3.** Wretched; desolate.
d·head (god′hed′) *n.* Goodhood; divinity.
d·head (god′hed′) *n.* The essential nature of God.
d·hood (god′hŏŏd) *n.* The state or quality of being divine.
·di·va (gə·dī′və) A legendary lady who agreed to ride ked through Coventry if her husband would remove op- essive taxes.
d·less (god′lis) *adj.* **1.** Having or believing in no god. . Wicked. — **god′less·ly** *adv.* — **god′less·ness** *n.*
d·like (god′līk) *adj.* **1.** Befitting or like God or a god. **2.** eing of supreme excellence, beauty, etc. — **god′like′ness** *n.*
d·ly (god′lē) *adj.* **·li·er, ·li·est** Filled with love for God. **god′li·ness** *n.*
d·moth·er (god′muth′ər) *n.* A woman who sponsors a ild at its baptism. — *v.t.* To act as a godmother to.
d·par·ent (god′pâr′ənt) *n.* A godfather or godmother.
d's acre A burying ground.
d·send (god′send′) *n.* Something received or acquired nexpectedly that is just what one needed or wanted.
d·son (god′sun′) *n.* A male godchild.
d·speed (god′spēd′) *n.* Best wishes for someone's jour- y or venture. [Shortened form of *God speed you*]
d·wit (god′wit) *n.* A shore bird resembling a curlew, with ng legs and bill. [Origin uncertain]
-get·ter (gō′get′ər) *n. U.S. Informal* A hustling, ener- tic, aggressive person.
g·gle (gog′əl) *n.* **1.** *pl.* Spectacles designed to protect the es against dust, sparks, wind, etc. **2.** An erratic move- ent or bulging of the eyes. — *v.* **·gled, ·gling** *v.i.* **1.** To ll the eyes erratically. **2.** Of the eyes, to move erratically, ılge, or be fixed in a stare. — *v.t.* **3.** To cause (the eyes) goggle. — *adj.* Of the eyes, rolling erratically, staring, or ulging. [ME *gogelen* to look aside]
g·gle-eyed (gog′əl·īd′) *adj.* Having eyes that goggle.
i·del·ic (goi·del′ik) *n.* The branch of the Celtic languages cluding Irish, the Gaelic of the Scottish Highlands, and anx; Gaelic: distinguished from *Brythonic.* — *adj.* Of or ertaining to the Gaels or their languages. Also **Goi·dhel′ic.** < OIrish *Goídel* Gael]
ing (gō′ing) *n.* **1.** The act of departing or moving; leav- g. **2.** The condition of ground or roads as affecting walk- g, riding, racing, etc. **3.** *Informal* A condition influencing rogress or activity. — **goings on** *Informal* Actions or be- avior: used chiefly to express disapproval. — *adj.* **1.** That es, moves, or works. **2.** Continuing to function; moving head: a *going* concern. **3.** In existence; available.
i·ter (goi′tər) *n. Pathol.* Any abnormal enlargement of e thyroid gland, visible as a swelling in the front of the eck. Also **goi′tre.** [< F, ult. < L *guttur* throat] — **goi- ·ous** (goi′trəs) *adj.*
ld (gōld) *n.* **1.** A precious, yellow, metallic element (sym- ol Au) that is highly ductile and resistant to oxidation: also alled *aurum.* See ELEMENT. **2.** Coin made of this metal. . Wealth; riches. **4.** A bright yellow color. **5.** Something aluable, etc.: a heart of *gold.* — *adj.* **1.** Pertaining to, ade of, containing, or like gold. **2.** Based on or redeem- ble in gold. [OE]
ld·brick (gōld′brik′) *U.S. Slang n.* One who shirks work: aid esp. of soldiers. Also **gold′brick′er.** — *v.t. & v.i.* **1.** To hirk (work or duty). **2.** To cheat or swindle.

gold brick *Informal* Anything deceitfully substituted for an object of value.
gold digger **1.** One who or that which digs for gold. **2.** *U.S. Slang* A woman who uses feminine wiles to get money.
gold·en (gōl′dən) *adj.* **1.** Made of or containing gold. **2.** Bright yellow. **3.** Resembling gold. **4.** Happy, prosperous, etc. — **gold′en·ly** *adv.* — **gold′en·ness** *n.*
golden age **1.** In Greek and Roman legend, an early period marked by perfect innocence, peace, and happiness. **2.** Any period of prosperity or excellence.
golden anniversary A 50th anniversary.
golden calf **1.** A molten image worshiped by the Israelites. *Ex.* xxxii. **2.** Riches, as unduly prized.
gold·en·eye (gōl′dən·ī′) *n.* A large diving duck of America and Europe with yellow eyes.
golden glow A tall garden plant having many-rayed yellow flowers.
golden mean Moderation; avoidance of extremes.
gold·en·rod (gōl′dən·rod′) *n.* A widely distributed North American herb of the composite family, having small, usu. yellow flowers: the State flower of Alabama, Kentucky, and Nebraska.
golden rule The rule or principle of treating others as one wants to be treated. *Matt.* vii 12.
golden section In esthetics, the division of a line or figure so that the smaller length is to the larger as the larger is to the whole, roughly a ratio of 3 to 5.
Golden State Nickname of California.
golden wedding The 50th anniversary of a marriage.
gold-filled (gōld′fild′) *adj.* Filled with a base metal over which a thick covering of gold is laid.
gold·finch (gōld′finch′) *n.* **1.** A European finch having a yellow patch on each wing. **2.** An American finch of which the male, in the summer, has a yellow body with black tail.
gold·fish (gōld′fish′) *n. pl.* **·fish** or **·fish·es** A small carp, usu. golden in color, cultivated as an aquarium fish.
gold foil Thin sheets of gold, thicker than gold leaf.
gold leaf Sheets of gold hammered to extreme thinness, used in gilding, etc.
gold mine **1.** A mine producing gold ore. **2.** *Informal* Any source of great profit, riches, etc.
gold plate Vessels and utensils of gold, collectively.
gold reserve **1.** Gold held in reserve by the U.S. Treasury to protect U.S. promissory notes. **2.** The quantity of gold bullion or coin owned by the central bank of a country.
gold rush A mass movement of people to an area where gold has been discovered, as that to California in 1849.
gold·smith (gōld′smith′) *n.* One who makes or deals in articles of gold.
gold standard A monetary system based on gold of a specified weight and fineness as the unit of value.
go·lem (gō′lem, -ləm) *n.* In medieval Jewish legend, an automaton made to resemble a human being and given life by a magic incantation. [< Hebrew, embryo, monster]
golf (gôlf, golf) *n.* An outdoor game played on a large course with a small resilient ball and a set of clubs, the object being to direct the ball into a series of variously distributed holes (usually nine or eighteen) in as few strokes as possible. — *v.i.* To play golf. [Cf. dial. E (Scot.) *gowf* strike] — **golf′er** *n.*
golf club **1.** One of several slender clubs with wooden or metal heads, used in playing golf. **2.** An organization of golfers; also, the building and grounds used by them.
golf course The course over which a game of golf is played. Also **golf links.**
Gol·gi body (gôl′jē) *Biol.* A netlike structure of rod-shaped elements found in the cytoplasm of animal cells. Also **Golgi apparatus.** For illus. see CELL. [after Camillo *Golgi,* 1844–1926, Italian pathologist]
Gol·go·tha (gol′gə·thə) A place near Jerusalem where Jesus was crucified; Calvary. *Matt.* xxvii 33. [< LL < Gk. < Aramaic *gogolthā* skull]
Go·li·ath (gə·lī′əth) In the Bible, a giant Philistine slain by David with a sling. I *Sam.* xvii 4.
gol·li·wog (gol′ē·wog) *n.* **1.** A grotesque black doll. **2.** A grotesque person. Also **gol′li·wogg.** [after illustrations by Florence Upton (1895) for a series of children's books]
gol·ly (gol′ē) *interj.* An exclamation of mild surprise, impatience, etc. [Euphemistic alter. of GOD]
Go·mor·rah (gə·môr′ə, -mor′ə), **Go·mor·rha** See SODOM.
gon- Var. of GONO-.
-gon *combining form* Having (an indicated number of) angles: *pentagon.* [< Gk. *gōnia* angle]
gon·ad (gō′nad, gon′ad) *n. Anat.* A male or female sex gland, in which the reproductive cells develop; an ovary or testis. — **gon′a·dal, go·na·di·al** (gō·nā′dē·əl), **go·nad·ic** (gō·nad′ik) *adj.*
gon·do·la (gon′də·lə, gon·dō′lə) *n.* **1.** A long, narrow, flat-bottomed Venetian boat propelled by one man with an oar

at the stern. **2.** *U.S.* A large, flat-bottomed, river boat; also, a gondola car. **3.** *Aeron.* The car attached below a dirigible. [< Ital. < *gondolar* to rock]
gondola car *U.S.* A long, shallow, open freight car.
gon·do·lier (gon′də·lir′) *n.* The boatman of a gondola.
gone (gôn, gon) Past participle of GO. — *adj.* **1.** Moved away; left. **2.** Beyond hope; ruined; lost. **3.** Dead; departed. **4.** Ended; past. **5.** Marked by faintness or weakness. **6.** Consumed; spent. — **far gone 1.** Exhausted; wearied. **2.** Almost ended or dead.
gon·er (gôn′ər, gon′-) *n. Informal* A person or thing that is close to death, ruined, or beyond all hope of saving.
gon·fa·lon (gon′fə·lən) *n.* A banner or ensign, usu. cut so as to end in streamers. Also **gon·fa·non** (gon′fə·nən). [< Ital. < OHG *gundfano* war banner]
gong (gông, gong) *n.* **1.** A heavy metal disk giving a deep, resonant tone when struck. **2.** A flat, saucerlike bell struck with a small mechanical hammer. [< Malay]
gonio- *combining form* Angle; corner. [< Gk. *gōnia* angle]
-gonium *combining form* Reproductive cell; seed. [< Gk. *gonos* seed]
gono- *combining form* Procreative; sexual. Also, before vowels, **gon.-** [< Gk. *gonos* seed]
gon·o·coc·cus (gon′ə·kok′əs) *n. pl.* **·coc·ci** (-kok′sī) The bacterium that causes gonorrhea. [< NL]
gon·or·rhe·a (gon′ə·rē′ə) *n. Pathol.* A contagious venereal infection, caused by the gonococcus, in which there is a purulent inflammation of the mucous membranes of the genitourinary tract. Also **gon′or·rhoe′a.** [< LL < Gk. < *gonos* seed + *rheein* to flow] — **gon′or·rhe′al** *adj.*
-gony *combining form* Production of; generation: *cosmogony.* [< L *-gonia* < Gk. < *gonos* seed, reproduction. Cf. -GENY.]
goo (gōō) *n. U.S. Slang* Any sticky substance.
goo·ber (gōō′bər) *n. U.S.* A peanut. Also **goober pea.** [? < Bantu *nguba*]
good (good) *adj.* **bet·ter, best 1.** Morally excellent; virtuous. **2.** Honorable; worthy: a *good* reputation. **3.** Generous; loving; kind. **4.** Well-behaved; tractable. **5.** Proper; desirable: *good* manners. **6.** Favorable: a *good* opinion. **7.** Pleasant; agreeable. **8.** Having beneficial effects; helpful: *good* advice. **9.** Reliable; safe: a *good* investment. **10.** Suitable; qualified: a *good* man for the job. **11.** Skillful; expert: He is *good* at sports. **12.** Genuine; valid: a *good* excuse. **13.** Backed by sufficient funds: a *good* check. **14.** Excellent in quality or degree: *good* literature. **15.** Orthodox; conforming. **16.** Sufficient; ample: a *good* rest. **17.** Unspoiled; fresh: *good* meat. **18.** Healthy: *good* lungs. **19.** Satisfactory or appropriate: *good* weather for flying. **20.** Attractive or striking: She looks *good* in that hat. **21.** Great in amount; also, maximum; full. — **as good as** Practically; virtually: *as good as* done. — **good and** *Informal* Completely; very: *good and* hot. — **good for 1.** Capable of lasting for. **2.** *Informal* Able to pay, give, or produce. — **no good** Worthless. — *n.* **1.** That which is fitting, etc. **2.** Benefit: for the *good* of mankind. **3.** That which is morally or ethically desirable. — **for good (and all)** For the last time; forever. — **to make good 1.** To be successful. **2.** To compensate for. **3.** To fulfill. **4.** To prove; substantiate. — *interj.* An exclamation of satisfaction. — *adv. Informal* Well. ◆ *Good* is gaining acceptance in informal usage as a substitute for *well* when reference is made to the functioning of a machine or the like, as in *This watch runs good.* In other contexts it is usually nonstandard. [OE *gōd*]
good book The Bible. Also **Good Book.**
good-by (good′bī′) *adj., n. & interj. pl.* **-bys** (-bīz′) Farewell. Also **good′-bye′.** [Contraction of *God be with you*]
good-for-noth·ing (good′fər·nuth′ing) *n.* A worthless person. — *adj.* Having no use or worth.
Good Friday The Friday before Easter, a day observed by Christians as a commemoration of the crucifixion of Jesus.
good·heart·ed (good′här′tid) *adj.* Kind; charitable; generous. — **good′heart′ed·ly** *adv.* — **good′heart′ed·ness** *n.*
good-hu·mored (good′hyōō′mərd, -yōō′-) *adj.* Having a cheerful temper or mood. — **good′-hu′mored·ly** *adv.*
good·ish (good′ish) *adj.* **1.** Somewhat good. **2.** Rather big.
good-look·ing (good′look′ing) *adj.* Handsome.
good·ly (good′lē) *adj.* **·li·er, ·li·est 1.** Having a pleasing appearance. **2.** Of fine quality. **3.** Large. — **good′li·ness** *n.*
good-na·tured (good′nā′chərd) *adj.* Having a pleasant disposition; not easily provoked. Also **good-tempered** (good′·tem′pərd). — **good′-na′tured·ly** *adv.* — **good′-na′tured·ness** *n.*
good·ness (good′nis) *n.* **1.** The state or quality of being good; esp.: **a** Excellence of character, morals, etc.; virtue. **b.** Generous and kindly feelings; benevolence. **2.** The best part. **3.** God: *Goodness* knows. — **Syn.** See VIRTUE.
goods (goodz) *n.pl.* **1.** Merchandise; wares. **2.** Fabric; material. **3.** Property, esp. when personal and movable.
Good Samaritan 1. In a New Testament parable, the only passer-by to aid a man who had been injured and robbed. *Luke* x 30–37. **2.** A humane, compassionate person.
Good Shepherd A name for Jesus. *John* x 11, 12.
good will 1. A desire for the well-being of others; bene lence. **2.** Cheerful, ready consent or willingness. **3.** tangible assets in terms of prestige and friendly relati Also **good·will** (good′wil′).
good·y (good′ē) *n. pl.* **good·ies** *Informal* **1.** *Usu. pl.* So thing tasty. **2.** A prissy person: also **good′y-good′y.** *adj.* Good or pious in a weak, sentimental way: also **goo good′y.** — *interj.* A childish exclamation.
goof (gōōf) *Slang n.* **1.** A dull-witted person; dope. **2** mistake; blunder. — *v.i.* **1.** To blunder. — *v.t.* **2.** make a mess of. — **to goof off** *Slang* To loaf.
goon (gōōn) *n. U.S. Slang* **1.** A thug or hoodlum, esp. hired to break strikes. **2.** A stupid person. [after a cha ter created by E. C. Segar, 1894–1938, U.S. cartoonist]
goose (gōōs) *n. pl.* **geese** (gēs) **1.** A subfamily of w footed birds larger than ducks. **2.** The female: distinguis from *gander.* **3.** The flesh as food. **4.** A fool. — **to c one's goose** *Informal* To spoil one's chances. [OE *gos*]
goose·ber·ry (gōōs′ber′ē, -bər·ē, gōōz′-) *n. pl.* **·ries 1.** tart berry of a spiny shrub of the saxifrage family, used jams, pies, etc. **2.** The shrub itself.
goose flesh A taut, prickling sensation in the skin. A **goose bumps, goose pimples, goose skin.**
goose·foot (gōōs′foot′) *n. pl.* **·foots** A plant, having gr flowers, as beets and spinach.
goose·neck (gōōs′nek′) *n.* Any of various mechanical vices curved like a goose's neck.
goose-step (gōōs′step′) *v.i.* **-stepped, -step·ping** To ma along or mark time kicking stiffly and sharply.
goose step 1. The action of goose-stepping. **2.** The m ner of moving the legs in goose-stepping.
go·pher (gō′fər) *n. U.S. & Canadian* **1.** A burrowing A erican rodent with large cheek pouches. **2.** A North Am can ground squirrel. [< F *gaufre* honeycomb]
Gor·di·an knot (gôr′dē·ən) **1.** A legendary knot tied **Gordius,** king of Phrygia, which an oracle predicted wo be undone by a ruler of Asia. Alexander the Great cut **2.** Any difficulty solved only by drastic measures.
gore[1] (gôr, gōr) *n.* Blood that has been shed; esp., a copi amount of thickened, clotted, or dried blood. [OE *gor* di
gore[2] (gôr, gōr) *v.t.* **gored, gor·ing** To pierce with the ho or tusks. [ME *goren*]
gore[3] (gôr, gōr) *n.* A triangular or tapering section into a garment, sail, etc., for greater fullness. — *v.t.* **gor gor·ing 1.** To cut into gore-shaped pieces. **2.** To furn with gores. [OE *gāra* triangular piece of land]
gorge (gôrj) *n.* **1.** A narrow, deep ravine, esp. with a stre flowing through. **2.** The act of gorging. **3.** That whic gorged, as a greedily swallowed meal. **4.** Deep or viol disgust. **5.** A mass obstructing a passage. — *v.* **gorg gorg·ing** *v.t.* **1.** To stuff with food. **2.** To swallow glutt ously. — *v.i.* **3.** To stuff oneself with food. [< OF < *gurges* whirlpool] — **gorg′er** *n.*
gor·geous (gôr′jəs) *adj.* **1.** Dazzlingly colorful; brillia **2.** *Informal* Extremely beautiful, etc. [< OF *gorgias* gant] — **gor′geous·ly** *adv.* — **gor′geous·ness** *n.*
gor·gon (gôr′gən) *n.* A terrifyingly ugly woman.
Gor·gon (gôr′gən) In Greek mythology, one of three sist with serpents for hair, so terrifying that the sight of th turned the beholder to stone. [< L < Gk. < *gorgos* rible] — **Gor·go·ni·an** (gôr·gō′nē·ən) *adj.*
Gor·gon·zo·la (gôr′gən·zō′lə) *n.* A strongly flavored, wh Italian cheese. [after *Gorgonzola,* a town]
go·ril·la (gə·ril′ə) *n.* An African jungle ape, the larg and most powerful of the anthropoids, having a mass body, long arms, and tusklike canine teeth. [< NL < G appar. < native name]
gorse (gôrs) *n. Brit.* Furze, a plant. [OE *gors(t)*]
go·ry (gôr′ē, gō′rē) *adj.* **·ri·er, ·ri·est 1.** Covered, stai with, or resembling gore. **2.** Full of bloodshed: a *gory* bat — **gor′i·ly** *adv.* — **go′ri·ness** *n.*
gosh (gosh) *interj.* An exclamation. [Euphemism for G
gos·hawk (gos′hôk′, gôs′-) *n.* Any of various large, sh winged hawks formerly used in falconry. [OE *gōshafoc*]
Go·shen (gō′shən) **1.** The region in Egypt inhabited by Israelites. *Gen.* xlv 10. **2.** Any place of peace or plenty.
gos·ling (goz′ling) *n.* A young goose. [< ON *gæsling*
gos·pel (gos′pəl) *n.* **1.** The teachings of the Christ church as originally preached by Jesus Christ and the ap tles. **2.** A narrative of Christ's life and teachings, as in first four books of the New Testament. **3.** Any informati accepted as unquestionably true. **4.** A doctrine conside of major importance. [OE *godspell* good news]
Gos·pel (gos′pəl) *n.* Any of the first four books of the N Testament, attributed to Matthew, Mark, Luke, and Jo
gos·sa·mer (gos′ə·mər) *n.* **1.** Fine strands of spider's si esp. when floating in the air. **2.** Any flimsy, delicate s stance, as filmy, gauzelike fabric. — *adj.* Resembling g samer; flimsy; unsubstantial: also **gos′sa·mer·ry** (-mər [< ME *gossomer* Indian summer, lit., goose summer]

ı·sip (gos′əp) *n.* **1.** Idle, often malicious talk, esp. about hers. **2.** Informal talk or writing, as of personages. **3.** A ·rson, esp. a woman, who indulges in idle talk. — *v.* **·siped ·sipped, ·sip·ing** or **·sip·ping** *v.t. & v.i.* To talk idly; re·at as gossip. [OE *god* + *sibb* a relative] — **gos′sip·er** *n.*

ı·sip·y (gos′əp·ē) *adj.* **1.** Indulging in gossip. **2.** Chatty.

; (got) Past tense and past participle of GET. ◆ See note ıder GOTTEN.

th (goth, gôth) *n.* **1.** A member of a Germanic people ıat invaded the Roman Empire in the third to fifth cen·ries: including the Ostrogoths (**East Goths**) and Visigoths **Vest Goths**). **2.** A barbarian. [< LL < Gk. *Gothoi* < ›thic]

th·am (goth′əm, gō′thəm; *Brit.* got′əm) A nickname for ɘw York City. — **Goth′am·ite** (-īt) *n.*

th·ic (goth′ik) *adj.* **1.** Of or pertaining to the Goths or to ıeir language. **2.** Of ıstyle of architecture ɘd in Europe, from ›out 1200 to 1500, ıaracterized by ›inted arches, ribbed ›ulting, flying but·esses, etc. **3.** De·ting a literature ıu. medieval in set·g, and emphasiz·g the grotesque and ɘ supernatural. **4.** the Middle Ages. Barbarous. — *n.* The extinct East ɘrmanic language of ɘ Goths. **2.** Gothic chitecture or art. so (*for adj. defs.* 5) **goth′ic.** — **Goth′·al·ly** *adv.*

GOTHIC ARCHITECTURE
Westminster Abbey, London, 13th-15th century.

h·ic (goth′ik) *n.* ·*metimes cap. Print·* *g* **a** *U.S.* Sans serif. *Brit.* Black letter.

·ten (got′n) Past ›rticiple of GET. ◆ *›tten,* obsolete in ›itish, is current in ›merican English ›ng with *got.*

ıache (gwosh) *n.* A method of painting using opaque colors mixed with ›ter and gum. **2.** The opaque pigment so used. **3.** A ›inting done in this medium. [< F < Ital. *guazzo* a spray L *aqua* water]

u·da cheese (gou′də, gōō′-) A mild, yellow cheese simi· to Edam cheese. [after *Gouda,* town in the Netherlands]

ıge (gouj) *n.* **1.** A chisel having a scoop-shaped blade, ›ed for woodcarving. **2.** A groove made as by a gouge. *U.S. Informal* The action of cutting as with a gouge. *U.S. Informal* The act of cheating. — *v.t.* **gouged, goug·g** **1.** To cut or carve as with a gouge. **2.** To scoop, force, tear out. **3.** *U.S. Informal* To cheat; esp., to charge orbitant prices. [< F < LL *gulbia*] — **goug′er** *n.*

ı·lash (gōō′läsh, -lash) *n.* A stew made with beef or veal ›d vegetables, seasoned with paprika, etc.: also called *Hun·rian goulash.* [< Hung. *gulyas* (*hus*) shepherd's (meat)]

ı·ra·mi (gōō·rä′mē, gōōr′ə·mē) *n.* **1.** A large, fresh·ıter fish of SE Asia. **2.** Any of various related fishes fre·ıently kept in home aquariums, as the **dwarf gourami** and ɘ **three-spot gourami.** [< Malay *gurami*]

ırd (gôrd, gōōrd) *n.* **1.** The fruit of any of various ›ants, having hard, durable shells. **2.** The fruit of the ›labash tree. **3.** A utensil, as a ladle, made from the dried ›ell. [< F *gourde* < L *cucurbita* gourd]

ur·mand (gōōr′mənd, *Fr.* gōōr·mäṅ′) *n.* One who takes ›arty pleasure in eating. [< F, glutton]

ur·met (gōōr·mā′, *Fr.* gōōr·me′) *n.* A fastidious devotee good food and drink. [< F < OF, winetaster]

ıt (gout) *n. Pathol.* A disease arising from a defect in ›etabolism and characterized by attacks of painful inflam·ation of the joints. [< F *goutte* drop < L *gutta*]

ıt·y (gou′tē) *adj.* **gout·i·er, gout·i·est** **1.** Of, from or like ›ut. **2.** Affected with gout; swollen. — **gout′i·ly** *adv.* — **gout′i·ness** *n.*

v·ern (guv′ərn) *v.t.* **1.** To rule or direct by right or au·ıority: to *govern* a nation. **2.** To guide or control the action ; influence. **3.** To serve as a rule or deciding factor for. To keep in check. — *v.i.* **5.** To exercise authority; rule. < OF < L *gubernare* to steer < Gk.] — **gov′ern·a·ble** *adj.*

gov·ern·ance (guv′ər·nəns) *n.* Exercise of authority.

gov·ern·ess (guv′ər·nis) *n.* A woman employed in a private household to train and instruct children.

gov·ern·ment (guv′ərn·mənt, -ər-) *n.* **1.** The authoritative administration of the affairs of a nation, state, city, etc.; the jurisdiction exercised over the people; rule. **2.** The official governing body of a nation, community, etc. **3.** The system or established form by which a nation, etc., is controlled: democratic *government.* **4.** Any governed territory, district, etc. **5.** Control. — **gov·ern·ment·al** (guv′ərn·men′təl, -ər-) *adj.* — **gov′ern·men′tal·ly** *adv.*

gov·er·nor (guv′ər·nər) *n.* **1.** One who governs; as: **a** The elected chief executive of any State in the U.S. **b** An official appointed to administer a province, territory, etc. **c** *Brit.* The manager of a society, etc. **2.** *Mech.* A device for controlling speed, as of a motor. — **gov′er·nor·ship** *n.*

governor general *pl.* **governors general** **1.** *Often cap. Brit.* The chief representative of the Crown in a dominion or colony. **2.** A governor or governors under his jurisdiction. Also *Brit.* **gov′er·nor-gen′er·al.**

gown (goun) *n.* **1.** A woman's dress, esp. one for formal occasions: evening *gown.* **2.** Any long, loose garment. **3.** A long, loose outer robe worn by certain officials, scholars, clergymen, etc. — *v.t. & v.i.* To dress in a gown. [< OF < Med.L *gunna* a loose robe]

Graaf·i·an follicle (grä′fē·ən) *Anat.* One of the numerous, small, round sacs embedded in the cortex of a mammalian ovary, each of which contains a single ovum. Also **Graafian vesicle.** [after Regnier de *Graaf,* 1641–73, Dutch physician and anatomist]

grab (grab) *v.* **grabbed, grab·bing** *v.t.* **1.** To grasp or seize suddenly. **2.** To take possession of by force or by dishonest means. — *v.i.* **3.** To make a sudden grasp. — *n.* **1.** The act of grabbing. **2.** That which is grabbed. **3.** A dishonest acquisition. **4.** A mechanical apparatus used to grasp and lift. [Cf. MDu. *grabben* to grip] — **grab′ber** *n.*

grab bag *U.S.* A bag or other receptacle filled with miscellaneous unidentified articles, from which one draws an object at random.

grab·ble (grab′əl) *v.i.* **·bled, ·bling** **1.** To feel about with the hands; grope. **2.** To flounder; sprawl. [Cf. Du. *grabbelen,* freq. of *grabben* to grab]

gra·ben (grä′bən) *n. Geol.* A generally elongate depression of the land caused by the downward faulting of a portion of the earth's crust. [< G, ditch]

grace (grās) *n.* **1.** Beauty or harmony of motion, form, or manner. **2.** Any attractive quality. **3.** Service freely rendered; good will. **4.** The act of showing favor. **5.** Clemency; mercy. **6.** The perception of what is appropriate: He had the *grace* to go. **7.** An extension of time granted after a set date, as for paying a debt. **8.** A short prayer at a meal. **9.** *Theol.* **a** The love of God toward man. **b** The divine influence operating in man. **c** The state of being pleasing to God. **d** Any divinely inspired spiritual virtue or excellence. **10.** *Music* A note or notes added as an ornament. — **to be in the good** (or **bad**) **graces of** To be regarded with favor (or disfavor) by. — **with good** (or **bad**) **grace** In a willing (or grudging) manner. — *v.t.* **graced, grac·ing** **1.** To add grace and beauty to; adorn. **2.** To dignify; honor. **3.** *Music* To ornament with grace notes. [< OF < L *gratia* favor]

Grace (grās) *n.* A title or form of address for a duke, duchess, archbishop, or bishop: preceded by *Your, His, Her,* etc.

grace·ful (grās′fəl) *adj.* Characterized by grace, elegance, or beauty. — **grace′ful·ly** *adv.* — **grace′ful·ness** *n.*

grace·less (grās′lis) *adj.* **1.** Lacking grace, charm, or elegance. **2.** Having no sense of what is right or decent. — **grace′less·ly** *adv.* — **grace′less·ness** *n.*

grace note *Music* A note written smaller than those of the main text, played or sung as an embellishment.

Grac·es (grā′siz) In Greek mythology, three sister goddesses who confer grace, beauty, and joy. Also **the three Graces.**

gra·cious (grā′shəs) *adj.* **1.** Having or showing kindness, affability, etc. **2.** Condescendingly polite or indulgent. **3.** Full of compassion; merciful. **4.** Refined. — *interj.* An exclamation of mild surprise. [< OF < L *gratia* favor] — **gra′cious·ly** *adv.* — **gra′cious·ness** *n.*

grack·le (grak′əl) *n.* Any of various New World blackbirds having long tails. [< NL < L *graculus* jackdaw]

grad (grad) *n. U.S. Informal* A graduate.

gra·date (grā′dāt) *v.t. & v.i.* **·dat·ed, ·dat·ing** **1.** To pass or cause to pass imperceptibly from one shade or degree to another, as color. **2.** To arrange or be arranged in grades.

gra·da·tion (grā·dā′shən) *n.* **1.** An orderly and gradual progression or arrangement according to size, quality, rank, etc. **2.** *Usu. pl.* A step, degree, or relative position in such a progression. **3.** The act of arranging in grades. [< F < L *gradus* step] — **gra·da′tion·al** *adj.*

grade (grād) *n.* **1.** A degree or step in any scale, as of quality, merit, rank, etc. **2.** A stage or degree in an orderly progression, classification, or process. **3.** A group or category. **4.** *U.S.* In education: **a** A level of progress in school, generally constituting a year's work. **b** The pupils in such a division. **c** *pl.* Elementary school: preceded by *the.* **5.** *U.S.* A rating or mark indicating the quality of school work done. **6.** In the U.S. armed forces, rank or rating. See below. **7.** The degree of inclination of a road, track, or other surface as compared with the horizontal **8.** A rise or elevation in a road, track, etc. — **to make the grade** *Informal* To succeed in any undertaking. — **up to grade** In accordance with an established standard of quality, progress, etc. — *v.* **grad·ed, grad·ing** *v.t.* **1.** To arrange or classify by grades or degrees; sort according to size, quality, type, etc. **2.** In education, to assign a grade to. **3.** To level or reduce (a road, ground, etc.) to a desirable gradient. **4.** To gradate. — *v.i.* To be of a specific grade or rank. [< F < L *gradus* step]

-grade *combining form* **1.** Progressing or moving: *retrograde.* **2.** *Zool.* Walking in a specified manner. [< L *gradi* to walk]

grade crossing An intersection of two railroads, or a r and a railroad, at the same level: also called *level crossi*

gra·der (grā′dər) *n.* **1.** One who or that which grades. *U.S.* A pupil in a specified school grade: a third *grader.*

grade school An elementary school.

gra·di·ent (grā′dē·ənt) *n.* **1.** Degree of inclination, as slope; grade. **2.** An incline; ramp. **3.** *Physics* A rate change in certain variable factors, as pressure, temperat etc. — *adj.* Rising or descending gradually or by unif degrees. [< L *gradiens, -entis,* ppr. of *gradi* to walk]

grad·u·al (graj′o͞o·əl) *adj.* **1.** Moving, changing, slowly and by degrees. **2.** Having a slight degree of incl tion; not abrupt or steep, as a slope. [< Med.L < L *gra* a step] — **grad′u·al·ly** *adv.* — **grad′u·al·ness** *n.*

grad·u·ate (*v.* graj′o͞o·āt; *n.* & *adj.* graj′o͞o·it) *v.* **·at·ed, ·ing** *v.i.* **1.** To receive a diploma or degree upon comple of a course of study. **2.** To change gradually or by degr — *v.t.* **3.** To grant an academic diploma or degree to (so one). **4.** To arrange or sort according to size, degree, **5.** To mark (a thermometer, scale, etc.) in units or degr

TABLE OF COMPARATIVE GRADES (UNITED STATES ARMED SERVICES)

Grade	Army	Air Force	Marine Corps	Navy	Coast Guard
O–11	General of the Army	General of the Air Force	(no equivalent)	Admiral of the Fleet	(no equivalent)
O–10	General	General	General	Admiral	Admiral
O–9	Lieutenant General	Lieutenant General	Lieutenant General	Vice Admiral	Vice Admiral
O–8	Major General	Major General	Major General	Rear Admiral (upper half)	Rear Admiral (upper half)
O–7	Brigadier General	Brigadier General	Brigadier General	Rear Admiral (lower half)	Rear Admiral (lower half)
O–6	Colonel	Colonel	Colonel	Captain	Captain
O–5	Lieutenant Colonel	Lieutenant Colonel	Lieutenant Colonel	Commander	Commander
O–4	Major	Major	Major	Lieutenant Commander	Lieutenant Commande
O–3	Captain	Captain	Captain	Lieutenant	Lieutenant
O–2	1st Lieutenant	1st Lieutenant	1st Lieutenant	Lieutenant (Junior Grade)	Lieutenant (Junior Grade)
O–1	2nd Lieutenant	2nd Lieutenant	2nd Lieutenant	Ensign	Ensign
W–4	Chief Warrant Officer				
W–3	Chief Warrant Officer	SAME	SAME	SAME	SAME
W–2	Chief Warrant Officer				
W–1	Warrant Officer				
E–9	Sergeant Major Specialist 9	Chief Master Sergeant	Master Gunnery Sergeant Sergeant Major	Master Chief Petty Officer	Master Chief Petty Of
E–8	Master Sergeant First Sergeant Specialist 8	Senior Master Sergeant	Master Sergeant First Sergeant	Senior Chief Petty Officer	Senior Chief Petty Offi
E–7	Sergeant First Class Platoon Sergeant Specialist 7	Master Sergeant	Gunnery Sergeant	Chief Petty Officer	Chief Petty Officer
E–6	Staff Sergeant Specialist 6	Technical Sergeant	Staff Sergeant	Petty Officer First Class	Petty Officer First Clas
E–5	Sergeant Specialist 5	Staff Sergeant	Sergeant	Petty Officer Second Class	Petty Officer Second C
E–4	Corporal Specialist 4	Airman First Class	Corporal	Petty Officer Third Class	Petty Officer Third Cl
E–3	Private First Class	Airman Second Class	Lance Corporal	Seaman	Seaman
E–2	Private	Airman Third Class	Private First Class	Seaman Apprentice	Seaman Apprentice
E–1	Recruit	Recruit	Private	Seaman Recruit	Seaman Recruit

TABLE OF COMPARATIVE GRADES

Royal Canadian Navy	Canadian Army	Royal Canadian Air Force
Admiral of the Fleet	Field-Marshal	Marshal of the Royal Canadian Ai Force
Admiral	General	Air Chief Marshal
Vice-Admiral	Lieutenant-General	Air Marshal
Rear-Admiral	Major-General	Air Vice-Marshal
Commodore	Brigadier	Air Commodore
Captain	Colonel	Group Captain
Commander	Lieutenant-Colonel	Wing Commander
Lieutenant-Commander	Major	Squadron Leader
Lieutenant	Captain	Flight Lieutenant
Commanding Officer	—	—
Sub-Lieutenant	Lieutenant	Flying Officer
Acting Sub-Lieutenant	Second Lieutenant	Pilot Officer
Midshipman	—	—
Chief Petty Officer, First Class	Warrant Officer, First Class	Warrant Officer, First Class
Chief Petty Officer, Second Class	Warrant Officer, Second Class	Warrant Officer, Second Class
Petty Officer, First Class	Staff Sergeant	Flight Sergeant
Petty Officer, Second Class	Sergeant	Sergeant
Leading Seaman	Corporal	Corporal
Able Seaman	Private	Leading Aircraftman
Ordinary Seaman (trained)	Private (trained)	Aircraftman, First Class
Ordinary Seaman (entry)	Private (entry)	Aircraftman, Second Class
Ordinary Seaman (under 17 years)	Private (under 17 years)	Aircraftman, Second Class (under 1 years)

librate. — *n.* **1.** One who has been granted a diploma degree by an educational institution. **2.** A beaker or nilar vessel marked in units or degrees, used for measuring uids, etc. — *adj.* **1.** Denoting a graduate student. **2.** rtaining to or intended for such a student. [< Med.L < *gradus* step, degree]

aduate student A student who has received a college gree and is working toward a more advanced degree.

ad·u·a·tion (graj′o͞o·ā′shən) *n.* **1.** The act of graduating, the state of being graduated. **2.** The ceremony of grant- g diplomas or degrees. **3.** A mark or division in a gradu- ed scale; also, such divisions collectively.

ae·cism (grē′siz·əm) *n.* A Grecism.

ae·cize (grē′sīz) *v.t. & v.i.* **·cized, ·ciz·ing** To Grecize.

aeco- See GRECO-.

aft[1] (graft, gräft) *n.* **1.** A shoot (the cion) inserted into a epared slit in a tree or plant (the stock) so as to become a ing part of it. **2.** A plant, fruit, etc., obtained as a result this operation. **3.** *Surg.* A piece of viable tissue trans- anted to another part of the body or to the body of an- her individual. — *v.t.* **1.** To insert (a cion) into a tree or ant. **2.** To obtain (a plant, fruit, etc.) by grafting. **3.** *rg.* To transplant (a piece of viable tissue) as a graft. To attach or incorporate, as by grafting: to *graft* new eas on outworn concepts. — *v.i.* **5.** To insert or trans- ant grafts. **6.** To be or become grafted. [< OF < LL < *k. graphein* to write] — **graft′age** *n.* — **graft′er** *n.*

aft[2] (graft, gräft) *U.S. n.* **1.** The act of getting personal vantage or profit by dishonest or unfair means, esp. rough one's political connections. **2.** Anything thus ined. — *v.t.* **1.** To acquire by graft. — *v.i.* **2.** To prac- e graft. [Cf. dial. E *graft* work, livelihood] — **graft′er** *n.*

·ham (grā′əm) *adj.* Made of unsifted whole-wheat flour. fter Sylvester *Graham*, 1794–1851, U.S. vegetarian]

ail (grāl) *n.* In medieval legend, the cup or dish used at e Last Supper by Jesus Christ, in which some of the blood ed at the Crucifixion was caught. Also called *Holy Grail.* OF < Med.L *gradalis*]

ain (grān) *n.* **1.** A hard seed or kernel; esp., that of any the cereal plants, as wheat, oats, etc. **2.** The harvested eds of these plants. **3.** These plants collectively. **4.** Any ry small, hard mass. **5.** The smallest possible quantity of ything: a *grain* of truth. **6.** The smallest unit of weight ed in several systems in the U.S. and Great Britain. Abbr. *G., gr.* See table front of book. **7.** The direction or rangement of the fibers or fibrous particles in various kinds wood; also, the resulting markings or pattern. **8.** The de of a piece of leather from which the hair has been re- oved; also, the characteristic texture or patterned mark- gs of this side. **9.** A paint, stamp, or pattern used to imi- te the characteristic markings of leather, wood, etc. **0.** The comparative size or texture of the particles com- sing a substance, surface, or pattern: marble of fine *grain.* **.** The direction of cleavage of a mineral substance, as dia- ond, coal, etc. **12.** A state of crystallization. **13.** Nat- al disposition or temperament. — **against the grain** ontrary to one's temperament or inclinations. — *v.t.* . To form into grains; granulate. **2.** To paint or stain in iitation of the grain of wood, marble, etc. **3.** To give a ughened or granular appearance or texture to. **4.** In athermaking: **a** To scrape the hair from. **b** To soften or ise the grain or pattern of. — *v.i.* **5.** To form grains. < OF < L *granum* seed] — **grain′er** *n.* — **grain′less** *adj.*

ain alcohol Ethanol.

ain elevator *U.S.* A building designed to store grain.

ain·y (grā′nē) *adj.* **grain·i·er, grain·i·est** **1.** Full of or nsisting of grains or kernels. **2.** Having a granular tex- ire. **3.** Resembling the grain in wood. — **grain′i·ness** *n.*

am (gram) *n.* The unit of mass or weight in the metric ystem, equivalent to 15.432 grains, or one thousandth of a ilogram. Also **gramme.** Abbr. *g, g., gm., gr.* See table ront of book. [< F < LL < Gk. *gramma* small weight]

ram[1] *combining form* Something written or drawn: *tele- ram.* [< Gk. *gramma* letter, writing < *graphein* to write]

ram[2] *combining form* A gram: used in the metric system: *ilogram.* [< GRAM]

am atom *Chem.* The quantity of an element, expressed grams, that is equal to the atomic weight of that element. lso **gram′-a·tom′ic weight** (-ə·tom′ik).

am·mar (gram′ər) *n.* **1.** The scientific study and de- cription of the morphology and syntax of a language or ialect. **2.** A system of morphologic and syntactic rules r the regulation of a given language. **3.** A treatise or ook dealing with grammatical matters. **4.** Speech or riting considered with regard to current standards of cor- ectness. **5.** The elements of any science or art, or a book r treatise dealing with them. [< OF < L < Gk. *gram- matikē* (*technē*) literary (art) < *grammata* literature]

gram·mar·i·an (grə·mâr′ē·ən) *n.* A specialist in grammar.

grammar school **1.** An elementary school. **2.** *Brit.* A secondary school.

gram·mat·i·cal (grə·mat′i·kəl) *adj.* **1.** Of or pertaining to grammar. **2.** Conforming to the usage of standard speech or writing. — **gram·mat′i·cal·ly** *adv.* — **gram·mat′i·cal·ness** *n.*

gram molecule *Chem.* The quantity of a compound, expressed in grams, that is equal to the molecular weight of that compound: also called *mole.* Also **gram′-mo·lec′u·lar weight** (-mə·lek′yə·lər).

gram·o·phone (gram′ə·fōn) *n.* *Chiefly Brit.* A record player. [< *Gramophone*, a trade name]

gram·pus (gram′pəs) *n.* *pl.* **·pus·es** A large, dolphinlike cetacean of Atlantic and Pacific waters. [Alter. of obs. *grapeys* < OF < Med.L *crassus piscis* fat fish]

gran·a·ry (gran′ər·ē, grā′nər-) *n.* *pl.* **·ries** **1.** A storehouse for threshed grain. **2.** A region where grain grows in abundance. [< L *granum* grain]

grand (grand) *adj.* **1.** Impressive because of great size, extent, or splendor. **2.** In literature and the arts, lofty or sublime in subject or treatment. **3.** Majestic; stately. **4.** Worthy of respect because of age, experience, or dignity: often with *old:* the *grand* old man of politics. **5.** Of high or highest rank or official position: a *grand* duke; the *grand* jury. **6.** Principal; main: the *grand* ballroom. **7.** Characterized by pomp or luxury. **8.** Conscious of one's wealth or importance. **9.** Comprehensive; all-inclusive: the *grand* total. **10.** Having a family relationship one degree more distant than: used in combination: *grandson.* **11.** *Informal* Highly satisfactory; excellent. — *n.* **1.** A grand piano. **2.** *U.S. Slang* A thousand dollars. [< OF < L *grandis*] — **grand′ly** *adv.* — **grand′ness** *n.*

gran·dam (gran′dam, -dəm) *n.* *Archaic* A grandmother; an old woman. Also **gran′dame** (-dām, -dəm). [< AF *graund dame*]

Grand Army of the Republic An organization of Union veterans of the Civil War, founded in 1866. Abbr. *G.A.R.*

grand·aunt (grand′ant′, -änt′) *n.* A great-aunt.

Grand Canyon State Nickname of Arizona.

grand·child (grand′chīld′) *n.* *pl.* **·chil·dren** (-chil′drən) A child of one's son or daughter.

grand·dad (gran′dad′) *n.* *Informal* Grandfather. Also **grand′dad′dy.**

grand·daugh·ter (gran′dô′tər, grand′-) *n.* A daughter of one's son or daughter.

grand duchess **1.** The wife or widow of a grand duke. **2.** A woman who is sovereign of a grand duchy. **3.** Formerly, in Russia, a daughter of a czar.

grand duchy The territory under the rule of a grand duke or grand duchess.

grand duke **1.** The sovereign of a grand duchy, holding a rank just below king. **2.** Formerly, in Russia, a ruler of a principality; later, a son or grandson of a czar.

gran·dee (gran·dē′) *n.* **1.** A Spanish or Portuguese nobleman of the highest rank. **2.** Any person of high rank or great importance. [< Sp. *grande* great]

gran·deur (gran′jər, -jo͝or) *n.* **1.** The quality or condition of being grand; magnificence. **2.** Greatness of character.

grand·fa·ther (grand′fä′thər) *n.* **1.** The father of one's father or mother. **2.** An ancestor. — **grand′fa′ther·ly** *adv.*

grandfather clock A clock having a pendulum and enclosed in a tall cabinet. Also **grandfather's clock.**

gran·dil·o·quent (gran·dil′ə·kwənt) *adj.* Speaking in or characterized by a pompous or bombastic style. [< L *grandis* great + *loqui* to speak] — **gran·dil′o·quence** *n.*

gran·di·ose (gran′dē·ōs, gran′dē·ōs′) *adj.* **1.** Producing an effect of grandeur; imposing. **2.** Pretentiously grand; pompous; bombastic. [< F < Ital. < L *grandis* great] — **gran′di·ose′ly** *adv.* — **gran·di·os·i·ty** (gran′dē·os′ə·tē) *n.*

grand jury A body of persons called to hear complaints of the commission of offenses and to ascertain whether there is prima-facie evidence for an indictment.

Grand Lama The Dalai Lama.

grand·ma (grand′mä′, gran′mä′, gram′mä, gram′ə) *n.* *Informal* Grandmother. Also **grand·ma·ma** (grand′mə·mä′, -mä′mə), **grand′mam·ma′.**

grand mal (grän mal′) *Pathol.* A type of epilepsy characterized by severe convulsions and loss of consciousness: distinguished from *petit mal.* [< F, lit., great sickness]

grand·moth·er (grand′muth′ər) *n.* **1.** The mother of one's father or mother. **2.** A female ancestor.

grand·neph·ew (grand′nef′yo͞o, -nev′-, gran′-) *n.* A son of one's nephew or niece.

grand·niece (grand′nēs′, gran′-) *n.* A daughter of one's nephew or niece.

Grand Old Party In U.S. politics, the Republican Party.

grand opera A form of opera, usu. having a serious and complex plot, in which the entire text is set to music.

grand·pa (grand′pä′, gram′pä′, gram′pə) *n. Informal* Grandfather. Also **grand′pa·pa′** (-pə·pä′, -pä′pə).
grand·par·ent (grand′pâr′ənt, gran′-) *n.* A grandmother or grandfather.
grand piano A large piano having strings arranged horizontally in a curved, wooden case.
grand·sire (grand′sīr′, -sər) *n. Archaic* **1.** A grandfather. **2.** An ancestor. **3.** Any venerable old man.
grand slam In bridge, the winning, by the declarer, of all thirteen tricks in a round of play; also, a bid to do so.
grand·son (grand′sun′, gran′-) *n.* A son of one's child.
grand·stand (grand′stand′, gran′-) *n.* A raised series of seats for spectators at a racetrack, sports stadium, etc.
grand tour **1.** Formerly, an extended journey through the chief cities of continental Europe. **2.** Any extended trip.
grand·un·cle (grand′ung′kəl) *n.* A great-uncle.
grange (grānj) *n.* **1.** *Often cap. U.S.* Any subsidiary lodge or branch of the Grange. **2.** *Brit.* A farm, with its dwelling house, barns, etc.; esp., the residence of a gentleman farmer. [< AF, OF < Med.L < L *granum* grain]
Grange (grānj) *n.* The order of Patrons of Husbandry, an association of U.S. farmers founded in 1867.
grang·er (grān′jər) *n.* **1.** *Often cap. U.S.* A member of a grange. **2.** A farmer. — **grang′er·ism** *n.*
grani- *combining form* Grain. [< L *granum* grain]
gran·ite (gran′it) *n.* **1.** A hard, coarse-grained, igneous rock composed principally of quartz, feldspar, and mica, much used as a building material, in sculpture, etc. **2.** Great hardness, firmness, endurance, etc. [< Ital. < L *granum* seed] — **gra·nit·ic** (grə·nit′ik) *adj.*
Granite State Nickname of New Hampshire.
gran·ite·ware (gran′it·wâr′) *n.* **1.** A variety of ironware coated with hard enamel. **2.** A type of fine, hard pottery.
gra·niv·o·rous (grə·niv′ər·əs) *adj.* Feeding on grain.
gran·ny (gran′ē) *n. pl.* **·nies** **1.** Grandmother: used familiarly. **2.** An old woman. **3.** *Informal* A fussy, interfering person. **4.** A granny knot. Also **gran′nie.**
granny knot A knot resembling the square knot but crossed in such a way as to form an insecure fastening. For illus. see KNOT. Also **granny's knot, granny's bend.**
grant (grant, gränt) *v.t.* **1.** To confer or bestow, as a privilege, charter, etc. **2.** To allow (someone) to have; give, as permission. **3.** To accede to; yield to, as a request. **4.** To admit as true, as for the sake of argument. **5.** To transfer (property), esp. by deed. — *n.* **1.** The act of granting. **2.** That which is granted, as a piece of property, a sum of money, or a special privilege. — **to take for granted** **1.** To assume to be true. **2.** To accept as one's due. [< AF, ult. < L *credere* to believe]
gran·tee (gran·tē′, grän-) *n.* The recipient of a grant.
grant·or (gran′tər, gran·tôr′, grän-) *n.* The person by whom a grant is made.
gran·u·lar (gran′yə·lər) *adj.* **1.** Composed of, like, or containing grains or granules. **2.** Having a granulated surface. — **gran′u·lar′i·ty** (-lar′ə·tē) *n.* — **gran′u·lar·ly** *adv.*
gran·u·late (gran′yə·lāt) *v.t. & v.i.* **·lat·ed, ·lat·ing** **1.** To make or become granular; form into grains. **2.** To become or cause to become roughened, as by the formation of granules. — **gran′u·la′tion** *n.* — **gran′u·la′tive** *adj.*
gran·ule (gran′yōōl) *n.* A small grain or particle; tiny pellet. [< LL *granulum*, dim. of L *granum* grain]
grape (grāp) *n.* **1.** One of the smooth-skinned, juicy, edible berries borne in clusters by various climbing vines or small shrubs, cultivated in many species as a fruit and for making wine. **2.** Any of the vines bearing these berries. **3.** A dark, purplish blue color. **4.** Grapeshot. [< OF, bunch of grapes]
grape·fruit (grāp′frōōt′) *n.* **1.** A large, round citrus fruit having a pale yellow rind and tart, juicy pulp. **2.** The tree bearing this fruit.
grape·shot (grāp′shot′) *n.* A kind of shot consisting of a cluster of iron balls, formerly fired from cannons.
grape·stone (grāp′stōn′) *n.* A seed of a grape.
grape sugar Dextrose.
grape·vine (grāp′vīn′) *n.* **1.** Any of the climbing vines that bear grapes. **2.** *U.S.* A secret or unofficial means of relaying information, usu. from person to person.
graph (graf, gräf) *n.* A diagram representing variations in the relationship between two or more factors by means of a series of connected points, or by bars, curves, lines, etc. — *v.t.* To express or represent in the form of a graph.
-graph *combining form* **1.** That which writes or records: *seismograph.* **2.** A writing or record: *autograph.* [< F < L < Gk. *graphein* to write]
-grapher *combining form* Forming nouns of agency corresponding to words in *-graph* or *-graphy*: *photographer.*
graph·ic (graf′ik) *adj.* **1.** Describing in full detail; vivid. **2.** Of, pertaining to, or illustrated by graphs or diagrams. **3.** Pertaining to, consisting of, or expressed by writing. **4.** Of, pertaining to, or characteristic of the graphic arts. Also **graph′i·cal.** [< L < Gk. *graphē* writing] — **graph′i·cal·ly** or **graph′ic·ly** *adv.*

-graphic *combining form* Forming adjectives correspond to nouns ending in *-graph*: *photographic.* Also **-graphic**
graphic arts **1.** Those visual arts involving the use of l or strokes on a flat surface, as painting, drawing, engrav etc. **2.** In recent usage, those arts that involve impress or reproductions taken from blocks, plates, type, or the
graph·ite (graf′īt) *n.* A soft, black variety of carbon ha a metallic luster and a slippery texture, used as a lubric and in making pencils, etc. Also called *black lead.* [< Gk. *graphein* to write + -ITE[1]] **gra·phit′ic** (-fit′ik) *adj.*
grapho- *combining form* Of or pertaining to writing. A before vowels, **graph-.** [< Gk. *graphein* to write]
graph·ol·o·gy (gra·fol′ə·jē) *n.* The study of handwrit esp. as a method of estimating the writer's character. **graph·o·log·i·cal** (graf′ə·loj′i·kəl) *adj.* — **graph·ol′o·gis**
-graphy *combining form* **1.** A writing, recording, or pro of representation: *biography, photography.* **2.** A descrip science: *petrography.* [< Gk. *graphein* to write]
grap·nel (grap′nəl) *n.* **1.** A small anchor with several fl at the end of the shank. **2.** Any of various devices con ing of a hook or arrangement of hooked parts, used to s and hold objects. [ME *grapenel*, dim. of OF *grapin* ho
grap·ple (grap′əl) *v.* **·pled, ·pling** *v.t.* **1.** To seize or t hold of with or as with a grapnel. — *v.i.* **2.** To stru in close combat, as in wrestling. **3.** To struggle or conte with *with.* **4.** To use a grapnel. — *n.* **1.** A grapnel. The act of grappling. **3.** A grip or close hold, as in wrest [< OF *grappil* grapnel] — **grap′pler** *n.*
grappling iron A grapnel. Also **grappling hook.**
grasp (grasp, gräsp) *v.t.* **1.** To seize firmly with or as the hand; grip. **2.** To grab. **3.** To comprehend. **4.** To make the motion of grasping or clutching. **grasp at** **1.** To try to seize. **2.** To accept eagerly, as offer or suggestion. — *n.* **1.** The act of grasping; a grip of the hand. **2.** The power or ability to seize; re **3.** Absolute domination: the tyrant's *grasp.* **4.** Intellec comprehension or mastery. [ME *graspen*, metathetic of *grapsen* < LG] — **grasp′a·ble** *adj.* — **grasp′er** *n.*
grasp·ing (gras′ping, gräs′-) *adj.* **1.** Greedy. **2.** T grasps. — **grasp′ing·ly** *adv.* — **grasp′ing·ness** *n.*
grass (gras, gräs) *n.* **1.** Any plant of a large family ha rounded and hollow jointed stems, narrow, sheathing lea flowers borne in spikes or panicles, and hard, grainlike se **2.** Herbage generally; esp., the herbaceous plants eaten grazing animals. **3.** Any of numerous plants with grass foliage. **4.** Ground on which grass is growing. **5.** Gra ground; pasture. **6.** *pl.* Stalks or sprays of grass. — **t the grass grow under one's feet** To let opportunity go — *v.t.* **1.** To cover with grass or turf. **2.** To feed with gr **3.** To spread (cloth, etc.) on the grass, for bleaching. — **4.** To graze. **5.** To become grassy. [OE *græs*]
grass·hop·per (gras′hop′ər, gräs′-) *n.* **1.** Any of sev insects, as the locust and katydid, with powerful hind adapted for leaping, many species of which are destruc to crops and vegetation. **2.** *U.S. Slang* Any small, li airplane, used for dusting crops, military observation, e
grass·land (gras′land′, gräs′-) *n.* **1.** Land reserved for turage or mowing. **2.** Land in which grasses are the dominant vegetation, as the American prairies.
grass·roots (gras′rōōts′, -rōōts, gräs′-) *U.S. Informal* n The common people, thought of as having practical highly independent views or interests. — *adj.* **1.** Com from, pertaining to, or directed toward such people. Basic. Also **grass′-roots′.**
grass widow A woman who is divorced, separated, or li apart from her husband.
grass widower A man who is divorced, separated, or li apart from his wife.
gras·sy (gras′ē, gräs′ē) *adj.* **grass·i·er, grass·i·est** **1.** C ered with or abounding in grass. **2.** Of or containing gr **3.** Like grass. — **grass′i·ly** *adv.* — **grass′i·ness** *n.*
grate[1] (grāt) *v.* **grat·ed, grat·ing** *v.t.* **1.** To reduce to pieces or powder by rubbing against a rough or sharp s face. **2.** To rub or grind to produce a harsh sound. — **3.** To have an irritating effect: with *on* or *upon.* **4.** To p duce a harsh sound. [< OF *grater* < Gmc.] — **grat′er**
grate[2] (grāt) *n.* **1.** A framework of crossed or parallel b placed over a window, drain, etc. **2.** A metal framew to hold burning fuel in a furnace, etc. **3.** A fireplace. *v.t.* **grat·ed, grat·ing** To fit with a grate or grates. [< I < L *cratis* lattice]
grate·ful (grāt′fəl) *adj.* **1.** Thankful for benefits or ki nesses; appreciative; also, expressing gratitude. **2.** Giv pleasure; welcome; agreeable. [< L *gratus* pleasing] **grate′ful·ly** *adv.* — **grate′ful·ness** *n.*
grat·i·fi·ca·tion (grat′ə·fə·kā′shən) *n.* **1.** The act of gra fying, or the state of being gratified. **2.** That which gratifi
grat·i·fy (grat′ə·fī) *v.t.* **·fied, ·fy·ing** **1.** To give pleasure satisfaction to. **2.** To satisfy, humor, or indulge. — **Sy** See SATISFY. [< MF < L *gratus* pleasing + *facere* to mak — **grat′i·fi′er** *n.* — **grat′i·fy′ing** *adj.* — **grat′i·fy′ing·ly** *a*

ıt·ing[1] (grā′ting) *n.* **1.** An arrangement of bars or slats ›ed as a cover or screen. **2.** *Physics* A diffraction grating.
ıt·ing[2] (grā′ting) *adj.* **1.** Harsh or disagreeable in sound; ›ping. **2.** Irritating; annoying. — **grat′ing·ly** *adv.*
·tis (grā′tis, grat′is) *adv.* Without requiring payment. *adj.* Free of charge. [< L, var. of *gratiis* out of kindness]
ıt·i·tude (grat′ə·tōōd, -tyōōd) *n.* Appreciation for ›vors, kindness, etc. [< F < L *gratus* pleasing]
·tu·i·tous (grə·tōō′ə·təs, -tyōō′-) *adj.* **1.** Given or ob›ned without payment or return; free. **2.** Lacking cause justification; uncalled-for. [< L *gratuitus*] — **gra·tu′i·ıs·ly** *adv.* — **gra·tu′i·tous·ness** *n.*
·tu·i·ty (grə·tōō′ə·tē, -tyōō′-) *n. pl.* **·ties** A gift, usu. money, given in return for services rendered; tip.
·va·men (grə·vā′men) *n. pl.* **·vam·i·na** (-vam′ə·nə) **1.** *ıw* The burden or gist of a charge. **2.** A grievance. [< › < L < *gravis* heavy]
ıve[1] (grāv) *adj.* **1.** Of great importance; weighty: a *ıve* responsibility. **2.** Filled with danger; critical: a *grave* ›uation. **3.** Solemn and dignified; sober. **4.** Somber, as ›lors. **5.** *Music* Slow and solemn. **6.** *Phonet.* **a** Having › tonal quality indicated by the grave accent; also, marked ›th this accent. **b** Unaccented, as a syllable. — *n.* A mark › used in French to indicate open *e*, or to make a distinc›n, as in *ou*, *où*: also **grave accent.** [< F < L *gravis* ›avy] — **grave′ly** *adv.* — **grave′ness** *n.*
ıve[2] (grāv) *n.* **1.** A burial place for a dead body, usu. a ›le in the earth. **2.** A sepulcher; tomb. **3.** Death. **4.** ›y place or state regarded as an end or final loss. — **to** ›**ve one foot in the grave** **1.** To be very old or frail. **2.** › be dangerously ill. — **to turn (over) in one's grave** To › presumably uneasy after one's death because of the ›havior of the living. [OE *græf*] — **grave′less** *adj.*
ıve[3] (grāv) *v.t.* **graved, grav·en, grav·ing** **1.** To carve › sculpt. **2.** To engrave or incise. **3.** To impress firmly, › on the memory. [OE *grafan* to dig] — **grav′er** *n.*
ıve·dig·ger (grāv′dig′ər) *n.* One who digs graves.
ıv·el (grav′əl) *n.* **1.** A mixture of small, rounded pebbles › fragments of stone, often with sand. **2.** *Pathol.* **a** A ›posit of sandlike crystals formed in the kidneys. **b** The ›sease of which these are characteristic. — *v.t.* **grav·eled** **·elled, grav·el·ing** or **·el·ling** **1.** To cover or pave with ›avel. **2.** To confound; baffle. [< OF *gravele* beach] **grav′el·ly** *adj.*
ıve·stone (grāv′stōn′) *n.* A stone marking a grave.
ıve·yard (grāv′yärd′) *n.* A burial place; cemetery.
ıveyard shift *U.S. Informal* A work shift during the ›ght, generally beginning at midnight.
ıv·i·met·ric (grav′ə·met′rik) *adj. Chem.* **1.** Determined › weight, as the constituents of a compound. **2.** Pertain›g to measurement by weight. Also **grav′i·met′ri·cal.** — **›av′i·met′ri·cal·ly** *adv.*
·vim·e·try (grə·vim′ə·trē) *n.* The measurement of ›ight, density, or specific gravity.
ıv·i·tate (grav′ə·tāt) *v.i.* **·tat·ed, ·tat·ing** **1.** To move or ›nd to move as a result of the force of gravity. **2.** To move › though from a force or natural impulse. **3.** To sink or ›ttle to a lower level. [< NL < L *gravis* heavy] — **grav′·›at′er** *n.* — **grav′i·ta·tive** *adj.*
ıv·i·ta·tion (grav′ə·tā′shən) *n.* **1.** *Physics* The force ›hereby any two bodies attract each other. **2.** The act or ›ocess of gravitating. — **grav′i·ta′tion·al** *adj.* — **grav′i·′tion·al·ly** *adv.*
ıv·i·ty (grav′ə·tē) *n. pl.* **·ties** **1.** *Physics* Gravitation as ›anifested by the tendency of material bodies to fall to›ard the center of the earth. **2.** Gravitation in general. **3.** ›eight; heaviness. **4.** Great importance; seriousness. › Solemnity; dignified reserve. **6.** Lowness of pitch, as of ›usic. [< F < L *gravitas* heaviness]
ı·vure (grə·vyŏŏr′, grāv′yər) *n.* **1.** A process of printing › engraving by photographically prepared plates. **2.** A ›ate, usu. copper or wood, used in this process; also, a print ›ade from such a plate. [< F < *graver* to engrave]
ı·vy (grā′vē) *n. pl.* **·vies** **1.** The juice, exuded by cook›g meat; also, a sauce made from it. **2.** *U.S. Slang* Money › profit easily acquired. [ME *gravey*]
ay (grā) *adj.* **1.** Of a color produced by a mixture of black ›d white. **2.** Dark or dull, as from insufficient light; dis›al. **3.** Having gray hair. **4.** Characteristic of old age; ›d. — *n.* **1.** A color consisting of a mixture of black and ›hite. **2.** Something gray, as an animal. **3.** The state of ›ing unbleached or undyed: said of fabrics. — *v.t. & v.i.* ›o make or become gray. Also, *esp. Brit.*, *grey.* [OE *græg*] **- gray′ly** *adv.* — **gray·ness** *n.*
ay·beard (grā′bird′) *n.* An old man.
ay·ling (grā′ling) *n. pl.* **·ling** or **·lings** **1.** A troutlike fish ›ving a large, colorful dorsal fin. **2.** Any of several North ›merican butterflies having gray and brown markings.

gray matter **1.** *Anat.* The reddish gray nervous tissue of the brain and spinal cord, composed largely of nerve cells and nerve fibers. **2.** *Informal* Brains; intelligence.
graze[1] (grāz) *v.* **grazed, graz·ing** *v.i.* **1.** To feed upon growing grass or herbage. — *v.t.* **2.** To put (livestock) to feed on grass, pasturage, etc. **3.** To tend at pasture, **4.** To cause (a field, etc.) to be fed on. [OE *græs* grass] — **graz′er** *n.*
graze[2] (grāz) *v.* **grazed, graz·ing** *v.t.* **1.** To brush against lightly in passing. **2.** To scrape or abrade slightly: The bullet *grazed* his arm. — *v.i.* **3.** To move so as to scrape lightly against something. — *n.* **1.** A grazing. **2.** A scrape made by grazing. — **graz′ing·ly** *adv.*
graz·ing (grā′zing) *n.* Pasturage.
gra·zi·o·so (grä·tsyō′sō) *Music adj.* Graceful; elegant. — *adv.* Gracefully; elegantly. [Ital.]
grease (*n.* grēs; *v.* grēs, grēz) *n.* **1.** Animal fat in a soft state, as after melting or rendering. **2.** Any thick fatty or oily substance, as a lubricant. — *v.t.* **greased, greas′ing** To smear or lubricate with grease or fat. [< OF < L *crassus* fat] — **greas′er** *n.*
grease paint A waxy substance used for theater make-up.
grease·wood (grēs′wŏŏd) *n.* A stunted, prickly shrub of the SW U.S. Also **grease′bush′.**
greas·y (grē′sē, -zē) *adj.* **greas·i·er, greas·i·est** **1.** Smeared or spotted with grease. **2.** Containing grease or fat; oily. **3.** Appearing or feeling like grease; smooth; slick. — **greas′i·ly** *adv.* — **greas′i·ness** *n.*
great (grāt) *adj.* **1.** Very large in bulk, volume, expanse, etc.; immense; big. **2.** Large in quantity or number: a *great* army. **3.** Prolonged in duration or extent; a *great* distance. **4.** More than ordinary; considerable: *great* pain. **5.** Of unusual importance; momentous; also, renowned: a *great* victory. **6.** Marked by nobility of thought, action, etc.: *great* deeds. **7.** Unusual in ability or achievement; highly gifted. **8.** Impressive; remarkable. **9.** Favored; popular. **10.** Absorbed or enthusiastic; also, proficient; skillful. **11.** Being of a relationship more remote by a single generation: used in combination: *great-uncle.* — *n.* **1.** Those who are eminent, powerful, etc.: preceded by *the.* **2.** *Usu. pl. Informal* An outstanding person: one of baseball's *greats.* — *adv. Informal* Very well; splendidly. [OE *grēat*] — **great′ness** *n.*
great-aunt (grāt′ant′, -änt′) *n.* An aunt of either of one's parents; grandaunt.
Great Bear The constellation Ursa Major.
great circle *Geom.* A circle formed on the surface of a sphere by a plane that passes through the center of the sphere.
Great Dane One of a breed of large, smooth-haired dogs.
great·er (grāt′ər) Comparative of GREAT. — *adj. Usu. cap.* Comprising a (specified) city and suburbs: *Greater* London.
great-grand·child (grāt′grand′chīld′) *n.* A child of a grandchild.
great-grand·daughter (grāt′gran′dô′tər) *n.* A daughter of a grandchild.
great-grand·father (grāt′grand′fä′thər) *n.* The father of a grandparent.
great-grand·mother (grāt′grand′muth′ər) *n.* The mother of a grandparent.
great-grand·parent (grāt′grand′pâr′ənt) *n.* The father or mother of a grandparent.
great-grand·son (grāt′grand′sun′) *n.* A son of a grandchild.
great gross Twelve gross, a unit of quantity.
great·heart·ed (grāt′här′tid) *adj.* **1.** Noble or generous in spirit; magnanimous. **2.** High-spirited; courageous.
great horned owl A large owl having tufts of feathers that resemble horns, found chiefly in North America.
great·ly (grāt′lē) *adv.* **1.** To a great degree; very much. **2.** In a way characteristic of or befitting greatness.
great-neph·ew (grāt′nef′yōō, -nev′-) *n.* A grandnephew.
great-niece (grāt′nēs′) *n.* A grandniece.
Great Rebellion The Civil War in England. See table under WAR.
Great Russian *adj.* Of or pertaining to Great Russia. — *n.* **1.** A native of Great Russia. **2.** The East Slavic language of the Great Russians.
great seal *Often cap.* The chief seal of a government.
great-un·cle (grāt′ung′kəl) *n.* An uncle of either of one's parents; granduncle.
Great White Way The brightly lighted theater district of New York City near Broadway and Times Square.
grebe (grēb) *n.* Any of a family of swimming and diving birds having partially webbed feet and very short tails; esp., the **pied-billed grebe** or dabchick. [< F *grèbe*]
Gre·cian (grē′shən) *adj.* Greek. — *n.* **1.** A Greek. **2.** One learned in the language or literature of Greece.
Gre·cism (grē′siz·əm) *n.* **1.** A Greek idiom. **2.** The style or spirit of Greek art, culture, etc. Also spelled *Graecism.*
Gre·cize (grē′sīz) *v.* **·cized, ·ciz·ing** *v.t.* **1.** To make Greek

in form, character, etc.; Hellenize. **2.** To translate into Greek. **—** *v.i.* **3.** To adopt or imitate Greek customs, speech, etc. Also spelled *Graecize.* [< F < L *Graecus* a Greek]

Greco- *combining form* Greek. Also spelled *Graeco-.*

Greco-Persian Wars See table for WAR.

Gre·co-Ro·man (grē′kō·rō′mən) *adj.* Of or pertaining to Greece and Rome together: also *Graeco-Roman.*

greed (grēd) *n.* Selfish and grasping desire for possession, esp. of wealth; avarice, covetousness. [< GREEDY]

greed·y (grē′dē) *adj.* **greed·i·er, greed·i·est 1.** Excessively eager for acquisition or gain; covetous; grasping. **2.** Having an excessive appetite for food and drink; voracious; gluttonous. [OE *grædig*] **— greed′i·ly** *adv.* **— greed′i·ness** *n.*

Greek (grēk) *adj.* **1.** Of or pertaining to Greece, or its people, language, or culture. **2.** Of or pertaining to the Greek Church. **—** *n.* **1.** One of the people of ancient or modern Greece. **2.** The Indo-European language of ancient or modern Greece. **— Late Greek** The Greek language from about A.D. 200 to 600. **— Medieval Greek** The Greek language of the Byzantine period, from 600 to 1500. **—Modern Greek** The language of Greece since 1500: also called *Romaic,* especially in its spoken form. **3.** Language or information that is unintelligible. **4.** *U.S. Slang* A member of a fraternity. [< L < Gk. *Graikos* Greek]

Greek Catholic 1. A member of the Eastern Orthodox Church. **2.** A member of a Uniat Church.

Greek Church 1. The Eastern Church. **2.** Loosely, the Eastern Orthodox Church,

Greek fire An incendiary substance first used by the Byzantine Greeks in naval warfare.

Greek Orthodox Church The established church of Greece, a branch of the Eastern Orthodox Church.

green (grēn) *adj.* **1.** Of the color between blue and yellow in the spectrum, as in the foliage of growing plants. **2.** Covered with or abounding in grass, growing plants, etc. **3.** Consisting of edible green leaves or plant parts: a *green* salad. **4.** Not fully developed; immature. **5.** Not cured or ready for use. **6.** Lacking training or skill; inexperienced. **7.** Wan. **—** *n.* **1.** The color between blue and yellow in the spectrum, characteristic of the foliage of growing plants. **2.** A green pigment, dye, or substance. **3.** Green material, clothing, etc. **4.** A smooth grassy area or plot: the village *green.* **5.** In golf, the area of smooth, clipped grass surrounding the hole. **6.** *pl.* Freshly cut leaves, branches, vines, etc. **7.** *pl.* The edible leaves and stems of certain plants, as spinach, beets, etc. **—** *v.t. & v.i.* To make or become green. [OE *grēne*] **— green′ly** *adv.* **— green′ness** *n.*

green algae A class of algae in which the cells containing chlorophyll are dominant.

green·back (grēn′bak′) *n.* One of a class of U.S. notes used as legal tender.

green bean A string bean.

green·bri·er (grēn′brī′ər) A thorny vine having small, greenish flowers.

green·er·y (grē′nər·ē) *n. pl.* **·er·ies 1.** Green plants; verdure. **2.** A place where plants are grown or kept.

green-eyed (grēn′īd′) *adj.* **1.** Having green eyes. **2.** Jealous.

green·gage (grēn′gāj′) *n.* A variety of sweet plum.

green·gro·cer (grēn′grō′sər) *n. Brit.* A shopkeeper dealing in fresh vegetables, fruit, etc. **— green′gro′cer·y** (-sər·ē) *n.*

green·horn (grēn′hôrn′) *n.* **1.** An inexperienced person; beginner. **2.** One easily imposed upon or duped.

green·house (grēn′hous′) *n.* A heated shed or building constructed chiefly of glass, in which tender or exotic plants are grown or sheltered; hothouse.

green·ing (grē′ning) *n.* One of several varieties of apples having a green skin when ripe.

green·ish (grē′nish) *adj.* Somewhat green.

green light 1. A green signal light indicating that vehicles, pedestrians, etc., may proceed. **2.** *Informal* Approval or authorization to proceed.

Green Mountain State Nickname of Vermont.

green pepper 1. The unripe fruit of the sweet pepper. **2.** The unripe fruit of the red pepper, used in pickling.

green·room (grēn′ro͞om′, -ro͝om′) *n.* The waiting room in a theater used by performers when they are off-stage.

green soap A soap made from linseed oil and the hydroxides of potassium and sodium, used for skin diseases.

green·sward (grēn′swôrd′) *n.* Turf green with grass.

green tea Tea from tea leaves that have been heated, withered, and rolled without undergoing fermentation.

green thumb A special knack for making plants thrive.

green vitriol Copperas.

Greenwich mean time Time as reckoned from the meridian at Greenwich, England. Also **Greenwich time.**

green·wood (grēn′wo͝od′) *n.* A forest in leaf.

greet (grēt) *v.t.* **1.** To express friendly recognition or courteous respect to, as upon meeting. **2.** To meet or receive in a specified manner. **3.** To present itself to; be evident to: The warmth of a fire *greeted* us. **—** *v.i.* **4.** To offer a sa tation upon meeting. [OE *grētan*] **— greet′er** *n.*

greet·ing (grē′ting) *n.* **1.** The act of one who greets; sa tation; welcome. **2.** A friendly or complimentary messa

gre·gar·i·ous (gri·gâr′ē·əs) *adj.* **1.** Habitually associat with others, as in flocks, herds, or groups. **2.** Enjoying seeking others; sociable. **3.** Of or characteristic of a flo crowd, or aggregation. **4.** *Bot.* Growing in compact grou clustered. [< L *grex, gregis* flock] **— gre·gar′i·ous·ly** *a* **— gre·gar′i·ous·ness** *n.*

Gre·go·ri·an (gri·gôr′ē·ən, -gō′rē-) *adj.* Of, pertaining or associated with Pope Gregory I or Pope Gregory XII

Gregorian Chant The system of plainsong associated w the liturgical reforms made by Pope Gregory I.

grem·lin (grem′lin) *n.* A mischievous, imaginary creat jokingly said to cause mechanical trouble in airplanes; a any similar gnomelike troublemaker. [Origin uncertain

gre·nade (gri·nād′) *n.* **1.** A small explosive or incendi bomb designed either to be thrown by hand or projec from a rifle. **2.** A glass container that shatters and diffu its volatile contents when thrown. [< F, pomegranate

gren·a·dier (gren′ə·dir′) *n.* **1.** Formerly, a soldier assig to throw grenades. **2.** A member of a special corps or r ment, as the British Grenadier Guards. [See GRENADE.

gren·a·dine[1] (gren′ə·dēn′, gren′ə·dēn) *n.* A silk, wool cotton fabric of loose, open weave. [< F, ? after *Grana*

gren·a·dine[2] (gren′ə·dēn′, gren′ə·dēn) *n.* A syrup m from pomegranates or red currants, used for flavoring.

Gresh·am's law (gresh′əmz) *Econ.* The principle stat that of two forms of currency, the less valuable form tend drive the other from circulation, owing to the hoarding of preferred form. Also **Gresham's theorem.** [after Sir Tho *Gresham,* 1519–79, English merchant]

grew (gro͞o) Past tense of GROW.

grew·some (gro͞o′səm) See GRUESOME.

grey (grā) See GRAY.

grey·hound (grā′hound′) *n.* **1.** One of a breed of t slender, smooth-coated dogs noted for their speed. **2.** A fast ocean vessel. Also, *Rare, grayhound.* [OE *grīghund*]

GREYHOUN
(28 inches hi at shoulder

grid (grid) *n.* **1.** An arrangement of regularly spaced parallel or intersecting bars, wires, etc.; grating; gridiron. **2.** A system of intersecting parallel lines dividing a map, chart, etc., into squares. **3.** A network of high-tension wires transmitting electric power over a wide area. **4.** *Electr.* A perforated or grooved metal plate in a storage cell or battery. **5.** *Electronics* An electrode, betw the cathode and anode of an electron tube that controls flow of electrons. [Back formation < GRIDIRON]

grid·dle (grid′l) *n.* A flat pan used for cooking pancal etc. **—** *v.t.* **·dled, ·aling** To cook on a griddle. [< AF *gre*

grid·dle·cake (grid′l·kāk′) *n.* A pancake baked on a g dle: also, *U.S., flapjack.*

grid·i·ron (grid′ī′ərn) *n.* **1.** A football field. **2.** A me grating set in a frame, used for broiling meat, fish, e **3.** Something resembling a cooking gridiron. [ME *gred* var. of *gredile* griddle]

grief (grēf) *n.* **1.** Deep sorrow or mental distress caused loss, remorse, affliction, etc. **2.** A cause of such sorr **— to come to grief** To end badly; meet with disaster; fa

grief-strick·en (grēf′strik′ən) *adj.* Overwhelmed by gri

griev·ance (grē′vəns) *n.* **1.** A real or imaginary wrong garded as cause for complaint or resentment. **2.** A feeli of resentment arising from a sense of having been wrong

grieve (grēv) *v.* **grieved, griev·ing** *v.t.* **1.** To cause to f sorrow or grief. **—** *v.i.* **2.** To feel sorrow or grief. [< < L *gravis* heavy] **— griev′er** *n.* **— griev′ing·ly** *adv.*

griev·ous (grē′vəs) *adj.* **1.** Causing grief, sorrow, or m fortune. **2.** Meriting severe punishment or censure: *grievous* sin. **3.** Expressing grief or sorrow. **4.** Causi physical suffering. **— griev′ous·ly** *adv.* **— griev′ous·ness**

grif·fin (grif′ən) *n.* In Greek mythology, a creature w the head and wings of an eagle and the body of a lion: a spelled *gryphon.* Also **grif′fon.** [< OF < L < Gk. *gryp*

grift·er (grif′tər) *n.* *U.S. Slang* A petty swindler or co fidence man; esp., one who operates a dishonest game chance at a carnival or circus. [? < GRAFTER]

grill (gril) *v.t.* **1.** To cook on a gridiron or similar uten **2.** To subject to or torment with extreme heat. **3.** *U Informal* To question or cross-examine persistently a searchingly. **—** *v.i.* **4.** To undergo grilling. **—** *n.* **1.** gridiron or similar cooking utensil. **2.** A meal or portion grilled food. **3.** A grillroom. **4.** A grille. [< F *gril,* v of *grille* grating] **— grilled** *adj.* **— grill′er** *n.*

gril·lage (gril′ij) *n.* A framework of crossed timbers or st beams serving as a foundation, esp. on soft ground.

grille (gril) *n.* A grating, often of decorative, open met work, used as a screen, divider, etc.: also spelled *grill.* [< < OF, ult. < L *craticula,* dim. of *cratis* grating, lattice]

ll·room (gril′rōōm′, -rŏŏm′) *n.* A restaurant or eating ace where grilled foods are prepared and served.

lse (grils) *n. pl.* **grilse** (*Rare* **grils·es**) A young salmon at has returned for the first time from the sea to fresh ater. [Origin unknown]

m (grim) *adj.* **grim·mer, grim·mest** **1.** Stern or forbid-ng in appearance or character. **2.** Unyielding; relentless. Sinisterly ironic; ghastly: a *grim* joke. **4.** Savagely structive; fierce. [OE] **— grim′ly** *adv.* **— grim′ness** *n.*

·mace (gri·mās′) *n.* A distorted facial expression, usu. dicative of pain, annoyance, disgust, etc. **—** *v.i.* **·maced, ac·ing** To distort the features; make faces. [< MF < . *grimazo*, prob. < Gmc.] **— gri·mac′er** *n.*

·mal·kin (gri·mal′kin, -môl′-) *n.* **1.** A cat, particularly old female cat. **2.** A shrewish old woman.

me (grīm) *n.* Dirt, esp. soot, rubbed into or coating a rface. **—** *v.t.* **grimed, grim·ing** To make dirty; begrime. < Flemish *grijm*]

m·y (grī′mē) *adj.* **grim·i·er, grim·i·est** Full of or covered th grime; dirty. **— grim′i·ly** *adv.* **— grim′i·ness** *n.*

n (grin) *v.* **grinned, grin·ning** *v.i.* **1.** To smile broadly. To draw back the lips so as to show the teeth, as in a snarl a grimace of pain, rage, etc. **—** *v.t.* **3.** To express by inning. **—** *n.* **1.** The act of grinning. **2.** A facial expres-on produced by grinning, as a broad smile. **— Syn.** See ILE. [OE *grennian*] **— grin′ner** *n.* **— grin′ning·ly** *adv.*

nd (grīnd) *v.* **ground, grind·ing** *v.t.* **1.** To reduce to fine rticles, as by crushing; pulverize. **2.** To sharpen, lish, or wear down by friction or abrasion. **3.** To rub gether or press down with a scraping or turning motion: *grind* the teeth. **4.** To oppress; crush. **5.** To operate by as by turning a crank, as a coffee mill. **6.** To produce by as by grinding. **7.** To produce mechanically or labori-usly: followed by *out.* **8.** To teach or instill with great d constant effort: with *into.* **—** *v.i.* **9.** To perform the eration or action of grinding. **10.** To undergo grinding. **1.** To scrape; grate. **12.** *Informal* To study or work stead-y and laboriously. **—** *n.* **1.** The act of grinding. **2.** The und made by grinding. **3.** A specified state of pulveriza-on, as of coffee. **4.** *Informal* Prolonged and laborious ork or study. **5.** *U.S. Informal* A student who studies nstantly. [OE *grindan*] **— grind′ing·ly** *adv.*

nd·er (grīn′dər) *n.* **1.** One who grinds; esp., one who arpens tools, etc. **2.** A device used for grinding, as a ffee mill, etc. **3.** A molar. **4.** *pl. Informal* The teeth.

nd·stone (grīnd′stōn′) *n.* **1.** A flat, circular stone ro-ted on an axle, used for sharpening tools, abrading, polish-g, etc. **2.** A millstone. **— to keep** (or **have**) **one's nose to e grindstone** To work hard and continuously.

n·go (gring′gō) *n. pl.* **·gos** In Latin America, a foreigner, p. one from any country where English is the official nguage: an offensive term. [< Am. Sp., gibberish]

ip[1] (grip) *n.* **1.** The act of seizing and holding firmly. . The ability to seize or maintain a hold; grasping power. . Control; domination. **4.** Mental or intellectual grasp. . The manner of grasping or holding something, as a tool or nplement. **6.** A distinctive handclasp, as one used by embers of a fraternal organization in greeting one another. . The handle of an object. **8.** A device or mechanical art that seizes or holds something. **9.** The strength of the and in grasping. **10.** *U.S.* A suitcase or valise. **11.** *U.S.* . stagehand. **— to come to grips** **1.** To struggle in hand-o-hand combat. **2.** To deal decisively or energetically, as ith a problem. **—** *v.* **gripped** or **gript, grip·ping** *v.t.* **1.** o seize; grasp firmly. **2.** To capture, as the mind or imag-ation; attract and hold the interest of. **3.** To join or ttach securely with a grip or similar device. **—** *v.i.* **4.** To ake firm hold. **5.** To capture the imagination or attention. OE *gripan* to seize] **— grip′per** *n.* **— grip′ping·ly** *adv.*

ip[2] (grip) *n.* Influenza.

ipe (grīp) *v.* **griped, grip·ing** *v.t.* **1.** *U.S. Informal* To nnoy; anger. **2.** To cause sharp pain or cramps in the owels of. **—** *v.i.* **3.** *U.S. Informal* To complain; grumble. . To cause or experience sharp pains in the bowels. **—** *n.* . *U.S. Informal* A grievance. **2.** *Usu. pl.* Spasmodic pain n the bowels. [OE *grīpan*] **— grip′er** *n.*

ippe (grip) *n.* Influenza. [< F *gripper* to seize] **— rip′py** *adj.*

ip·sack (grip′sak′) *n. U.S.* A traveling bag; valise.

is·ly (griz′lē) *adj.* **·li·er, ·li·est** Inspiring horror; gruesome. OE *grislic*] **— gris′li·ness** *n.*

ist (grist) *n.* **1.** Grain that is to be ground; also, a batch f such grain. **2.** Ground grain. **— grist for one's mill** omething that can be used to one's advantage. [OE < *rindan* to grind]

is·tle (gris′əl) *n.* Cartilage, esp. in meat. [OE]

is·tly (gris′lē) *adj.* **1.** Pertaining to or resembling gristle. **.** Consisting of or containing gristle. **— gris′tli·ness** *n.*

grist·mill (grist′mil′) *n.* A mill for grinding grain.

grit (grit) *n.* **1.** Small, rough, hard particles, as of sand, stone, etc. **2.** A hard, coarse-grained sandstone. **3.** Reso-lute spirit; pluck. **—** *v.* **grit·ted, grit·ting** *v.t.* **1.** To grind or press together, as the teeth. **2.** To cover with grit. **—***v.i.* **3.** To make a grating sound. [OE *grēot*]

grits (grits) *n.pl.* **1.** Coarse meal. **2.** *U.S.* Coarsely ground hominy: also called *hominy grits.* [OE *grytte*]

grit·ty (grit′ē) *adj.* **·ti·er, ·ti·est** **1.** Like, containing, or con-sisting of grit. **2.** Courageous; plucky. **— grit′ti·ly** *adv.* **— grit′ti·ness** *n.*

griz·zle (griz′əl) *v.t.* & *v.i.* **·zled, ·zling** To become or cause to become gray. **—** *n.* **1.** The color gray, esp. when pro-duced by intermixed hairs, specks, etc., of black and white. **2.** Gray or graying hair. **—** *adj.* Gray. [< OF *gris* gray] **— griz′zled** *adj.*

griz·zly (griz′lē) *adj.* **·zli·er, ·zli·est** Grayish; grizzled. **—** *n. pl.* **·zlies** A grizzly bear.

grizzly bear A large bear of western North America.

groan (grōn) *v.i.* **1.** To utter a low, prolonged sound of or as of pain, disapproval, etc. **2.** To make a noise resembling such a sound; creak harshly. **3.** To suffer, as from cruel or unfair treatment: usu. with *under* or *beneath.* **4.** To be over-burdened. **—** *v.t.* **5.** To utter or express with or as with a groan. **—** *n.* **1.** A low moaning or murmuring sound ex-pressing pain, derision, etc. **2.** A creaking or roaring sound. [OE *grānian*] **— groan′er** *n.* **— groan′ing·ly** *adv.*

groat (grōt) *n.* **1.** A former English silver coin, worth four-pence. **2.** A tiny sum. [< MDu. *groot*, orig., large]

groats (grōts) *n.pl.* Hulled, usu. coarsely crushed grain, as barley, oats, or wheat. [OE *grotan*]

gro·cer (grō′sər) *n.* One who deals in foodstuffs and various household supplies. [< OF < Med.L < LL *grossus* gross]

gro·cer·y (grō′sər·ē, grōs′rē) *n. pl.* **·cer·ies** **1.** *U.S.* A store in which foodstuffs and household supplies are sold. **2.** *pl.* The merchandise sold by a grocer.

grog (grog) *n.* Any alcoholic liquor, esp. rum, mixed with water. [after Old *Grog*, nickname of Admiral E. Vernon, 1684–1757, who first rationed it to English sailors]

grog·gy (grog′ē) *adj.* **·gi·er, ·gi·est** *Informal* **1.** Dazed or not fully conscious, as from a blow or exhaustion. **2.** Drunk. [< GROG] **— grog′gi·ly** *adv.* **— grog′gi·ness** *n.*

grog·ram (grog′rəm) *n.* A loosely woven, sometimes stiff-ened, fabric of coarse silk, or silk mixed with mohair or wool. [< F *gros grain* coarse grain]

groin (groin) *n.* **1.** *Anat.* The fold or crease formed at the juncture of either of the thighs with the abdomen. **2.** *Archit.* The curve formed by the intersection of two vaults. For illus. see VAULT. **—** *v.t.* To build with or form into groins. [? OE *grynde* abyss, hollow]

groin rib *Archit.* A rib covering a groin.

GROIN RIBS IN GROIN VAULTING

grom·met (grom′it) *n.* **1.** A reinforcing eyelet of metal or other material, through which a rope, cord, or fastening may be passed. **2.** *Naut.* A ring of rope or metal used to secure the edge of a sail. [< F < *gourmer* to curb]

groom (grōōm, grŏŏm) *n.* **1.** A man or boy employed to tend horses; stableman. **2.** A bridegroom. **3.** One of several honorary functionaries in the British royal household. **—** *v.t.* **1.** To attend to the neatness or appear-ance of. **2.** To take care of (a horse) by cleaning, currying, etc. **3.** *U.S.* To prepare by giving special training or atten-tion to, as for a political office. [ME *grom.*]

grooms·man (grōōmz′mən, grŏŏms′-) *n. pl.* **·men** (-mən) The best man at a wedding.

groove (grōōv) *n.* **1.** A long, narrow indentation or furrow cut into a surface, esp. by a tool. **2.** Any narrow depression, channel, or rut. **3.** A fixed, settled routine or habit. **4.** *Anat.* Any of various furrows or depressions in an organ or part of the body. **— in the groove** *U.S. Slang* Operating or performing expertly or smoothly. **—** *v.t.* **grooved, groov·ing** To form a groove in. [< Du. *groeve*]

groov·y (grōō′vē) *adj.* **groov·i·er, groov·i·est** *U.S. Slang* Satisfying; delightful; great: a *groovy* feeling.

grope (grōp) *v.* **groped, grop·ing** *v.i.* **1.** To feel about with or as with the hands, as in the dark; feel one's way. **2.** To search bewilderedly or uncertainly. **—** *v.t.* **3.** To seek out or find by or as by groping. **—** *n.* The act of groping. [OE *grāpian*] **— grop′er** *n.* **— grop′ing·ly** *adv.*

gros·beak (grōs′bēk′) *n.* Any of various finchlike birds having a short, stout beak. [< F < *gros* large + *bec* beak]

gros·grain (grō′grān) *n.* A strong, horizontally corded silk or rayon fabric, usu. woven as ribbon.

gross (grōs) *adj.* **1.** Undiminished by deductions; total: distinguished from *net*: *gross* income. **2.** Conspicuously bad or wrong: *gross* errors. **3.** Excessively fat or large. **4.**

Coarse in composition, structure, or texture. **5.** Coarse or obscene in character. **6.** Insensitive; dull. **7.** Dense; thick. **8.** *Anat.* or *Pathol.* Visible without the aid of a microscope: a *gross* lesion. **—** *n. pl.* **gross** *for def. 1,* **gross·es** *for def. 2* A unit of quantity comprising twelve dozen. **2.** The entire amount; bulk. **— in the gross. 1.** In bulk; all together. **2.** Wholesale. **—** *v.t.* To earn or produce as total income or profit, before deductions for expenses. etc. [< OF < LL *grossus* thick] **— gross′ly** *adv.* **— gross′ness** *n.*

gross weight Total weight. Abbr. *gr. wt.*

grosz (grôsh) *n. pl.* **grosz·y** (grôsh′ē) A monetary denomination of Poland, the hundredth part of a zloty.

gro·tesque (grō·tesk′) *adj.* **1.** Distorted, incongruous, or fantastically ugly in appearance or style; outlandish. **2.** Characterized by fantastic combinations of human and animal figures with conventional design forms. **—** *n.* **1.** One who or that which is grotesque. **2.** Grotesque style or quality. [< F < Ital. *grotta* excavation; from art found in excavations] **— gro·tesque′ly** *adv.* **— gro·tesque′ness** *n.*

grot·to (grot′ō) *n. pl.* **·toes** or **·tos 1.** A cave. **2.** An artificial cavelike structure, as for a recreational retreat, shrine, etc. [< Ital. *grotta* < L *crypta*]

grouch (grouch) *U.S. Informal v.i.* To be surly, grumble. **—** *n.* **1.** A discontented, grumbling person. **2.** A grumbling, sulky mood. [< OF *groucher* to murmur]

grouch·y (grou′chē) *adj.* **grouch·i·er, grouch·i·est** *U.S. Informal* Ill-humored. **— grouch′i·ly** *adv.* **— grouch′i·ness** *n.*

ground[1] (ground) *n.* **1.** The layer of solid substances constituting the surface of the earth; land. **2.** Soil, sand, etc., at or near the earth's surface. **3.** *Sometimes pl.* An area or tract of land; esp., one reserved or used for a specific purpose: a burial *ground.* **4.** *pl.* Private land, as the surrounding premises of a dwelling, public institution, etc. **5.** *Usu. pl.* The fundamental cause, reason, or motive for an action, belief, etc.: *grounds* for suspicion: when plural, often construed as singular. **6.** A subject; topic. **7.** *Often pl.* A foundation or basis, as for a decision, argument, or relationship; footing: when plural, often construed as singular. **8.** *pl.* Sediment; dregs; esp., the particles remaining after a beverage has been brewed. **9.** The solid bottom of a body of water. **10.** In various arts and crafts, the background against which colors, designs, etc., are placed. **11.** *Electr.* The connection of an electrical current or circuit with the earth through a conductor. **12.** *Music* A ground bass. **— Syn.** See REASON. **— from the ground up** In every detail; thoroughly. **— on home** (or **on one's own**) **ground 1.** In accustomed circumstances or surroundings. **2.** Dealing with a thoroughly familiar subject. **— to break ground 1.** To dig into or cut through the soil, as in plowing, excavating a building site, etc. **2.** To make a start in any undertaking. **3.** *Naut.* To be raised or loosened from the bottom, as an anchor. **— to cover ground 1.** To move or travel, esp. over a considerable distance. **2.** To make progress. **— to gain ground 1.** To advance; make headway. **2.** To increase in favor, influence, etc. **— to give ground** To yield a position or advantage; retreat. **— to hold** (or **stand**) **one's ground** To refuse to yield or retreat. **— to lose ground 1.** To fail to maintain an advantage or gain. **2.** To decline in favor, influence, etc. **— to shift one's ground** To change one's point of view, as in an argument or discussion. **—** *adj.* **1.** Being on, near, or at a level with the ground. **2.** Living, growing, or active on or in the ground. **—** *v.t.* **1.** To place on the ground. **2.** To base on or as on a foundation; establish; found. **3.** To teach fundamentals to. **4.** *Aeron.* To confine (an aircraft, pilot, etc.) to the ground. **5.** *Electr.* To place in connection with the earth or a ground, as a circuit. **6.** *Naut.* To run (a vessel) aground. **7.** To supply with a ground or background. **—** *v.i.* **8.** To come or fall to the ground. **9.** In baseball, to hit a ground ball. **10.** *Naut.* To run aground. [OE *grund*]

ground[2] (ground) Past tense and past participle of GRIND.

ground alert *Mil.* A state of preparedness in which airplanes and their crews stand ready for a quick takeoff.

ground ball In baseball, etc., a batted ball that rolls or bounces along the ground. Also **ground·er** (groun′dər).

ground bass *Music* A short melodic phrase in the bass, repeated continually with varied melody and harmony.

ground crew *Aeron.* A group of workers responsible for the servicing and maintenance of aircraft on the ground.

ground floor In a building, the floor that is level or almost level with the ground. **— to get in on the ground floor** *U.S. Informal* To enter upon a project at its beginning.

ground glass 1. Glass of which the surface has been treated so that it is not fully transparent. **2.** Finely powdered glass.

ground hog The woodchuck.

ground-hog day (ground′hôg′, -hog′) February 2, on which, allegedly, if the ground hog sees his shadow, he goes underground again for six more weeks of winter.

ground·less (ground′lis) *adj.* Having no reason or cause; baseless. **— ground′less·ly** *adv.* **— ground′less·ness** *n.*

ground·ling (ground′ling) *n.* **1.** A plant or animal living, growing, or remaining on or close to the ground. **2.** A fish that keeps close to the bottom of the water. **3.** A persoı crude or undiscriminating tastes.

ground·nut (ground′nut′) A plant bearing edible tubers underground nutlike seed pods, as the peanut.

ground pine Any of various creeping, evergreen plant the club moss family.

ground plan 1. A diagrammatic plan of any floor o building. **2.** Any preliminary plan or basic outline.

ground·sel (ground′səl) *n.* A common herb of the comp ite family having numerous yellow flowers. [OE *gund welge,* lit., that swallows pus (with ref. to its use in poultice

ground·sill (ground′sil′) *n.* The lowest horizontal tim in a frame building. Also **ground′sel.**

ground squirrel One of several small, terrestrial rodent the squirrel family, as the gopher or chipmunk.

ground swell A billowing of the ocean in broad, deep wa caused by a prolonged storm, earthquake, etc.

ground water Underground water, accumulating by se age, and serving as the source of springs, wells, etc.

ground wire *Electr.* The wire connecting an electrical paratus with the ground or with a grounded object.

ground·work (ground′wûrk′) *n.* A foundation; basis.

ground zero The point on the ground vertically beneath above the point of detonation of an atomic or thermonucl bomb: also called *hypocenter.*

group (grōōp) *n.* **1.** A collection or assemblage of persons things, considered as a unit; aggregation; cluster. **2.** A nu ber of persons or things having in common certain charact istics, interests, etc. **3.** *Biol.* A number of plants or a mals considered to be related because of certain comm characteristics. **4.** In painting or sculpture, two or m figures or objects forming a harmonious unit or design. In the U.S. Air Force, a subdivision of a wing, designa for a specific purpose. **6.** *Chem.* An arrangement of ato constituting part of a molecule; a radical. **—** *v.t.* **1.** arrange or classify in a group or groups. **—** *v.i.* **2.** To fo or be part of a group. [< F < Ital. *groppo* knot, lump]

group captain In the Commonwealth air forces, a co missioned officer. See table at GRADE.

group·er (grōō′pər) *n.* A food fish related to the sea bass esp. the **red grouper.** [< Pg. *garupa,* appar. < S. Am. In

grouse[1] (grous) *n. pl.* **grouse** Any of a family of game bi characterized by rounded bodies and mottled plumage, the ruffed grouse. [Origin uncertain]

grouse[2] (grous) *Informal v.i.* **groused, grous·ing** To gru ble. **—** *n.* A complaint. [? < OF *grousser* to murmur]

grove (grōv) *n.* A small wood or group of trees, esp. wh cleared of underbrush. [OE *grāf*]

grov·el (gruv′əl, grov′-) *v.i.* **grov·eled** or **·elled, grov·el·i** or **·el·ling 1.** To lie prostrate or crawl face downward, as abjection, fear, etc. **2.** To act with abject humility. **3.** take pleasure in what is base or sensual. [Back formation GROVELING] **— grov′el·er** or **grov′el·ler** *n.*

grov·el·ing (gruv′əl·ing, grov′-) *adj.* **1.** Lying or crawli in an abject, prostrate position. **2.** Abjectly humble. Low; sordid. Also **grov′el·ling.** [ME *grovelynge,* adv. < *gruff* face down + -LING[2]] **— grov′el·ing·ly** *adv.*

grow (grō) *v.* **grew, grown, grow·ing** *v.i.* **1.** To increase size by the assimilation of nutriment; progress toward n turity. **2.** To germinate and develop to maturity, as fron seed or spore; originate, as from a basic source or cause. To flourish; thrive. **4.** To increase in size, amount, or degr **5.** To become: She *grew* angry. **6.** To become joined or tached by or as by growth. **—** *v.t.* **7.** To cause to gro cultivate. **8.** To produce by a natural process: to *grow* ha **9.** To cover with a growth: used in the passive. **— to gr on** To become increasingly acceptable, pleasing, or necessa to. **— to grow out of 1.** To outgrow. **2.** To result fro [OE *grōwan*] **— grow′er** *n.*

growl (groul) *v.i.* **1.** To utter a deep, guttural sound, that made by a hostile or agitated animal. **2.** To speak gru ly and angrily. **3.** To rumble, as distant thunder. **—** *v* **4.** To utter or express by growling. **—** *n.* **1.** A deep, su tained, guttural sound uttered by a hostile or agitated a mal. **2.** Any sound resembling this. **3.** A gruff, angry u terance. [? < OF *grouler* to mumble < Gmc.] **— growl′er**

grown (grōn) Past participle of GROW. **—** *adj.* Arrived full physical growth or stature; mature; adult.

grown-up (grōn′up′) *n.* A mature person; adult.

grown-up (grōn′up′) *adj.* **1.** Physically or mentally m ture; adult. **2.** Characteristic of or appropriate to an adu

growth (grōth) *n.* **1.** The act or process of growing. **2.** gradual increase in size, influence, etc. **3.** Something grow or in the process of growing: a *growth* of timber. **4.** Origi source. **5.** *Pathol.* An abnormal formation of tissue.

grub (grub) *v.* **grubbed, grub·bing** *v.i.* **1.** To dig in t ground. **2.** To lead a dreary or miserable existence; drudg **3.** To make careful or plodding search; rummage. **—** *v* **4.** To dig from the ground; root out: often with *up* or *ou* **5.** To clear (ground) of roots, stumps, etc. **6.** *U.S. Sla* To scrounge. **—** *n.* **1.** The wormlike larva of certain i

:ts, as of the June beetle. **2.** A drudge. **3.** *Slang* Food. 1E *grubben*] — **grub′ber** *n.*

ıb·by (grub′ē) *adj.* **·bi·er, ·bi·est 1.** Dirty; sloppy. **2.** fested with grubs. — **grub′bi·ly** *adv.* — **grub′bi·ness** *n.*

ıb·stake (grub′stāk′) *U.S. Informal n.* **1.** Money, sup- ies, or equipment provided a prospector on condition that share his finds with the donor. **2.** Money or assistance rnished to advance any venture. — *v.t.* **·staked, ·stak·ing** ɔ supply with a grubstake.

ıdge (gruj) *n.* A feeling of ill will, rancor, or enmity, har- ɔred for a remembered wrong, etc. — *v.* **grudged, grudg·g** *v.t.* **1.** To be displeased or resentful because of the pos- ssions, good fortune, etc. of (another): They *grudge* him his ealth. **2.** To give or allow unwillingly and resentfully. < OF *groucher*] — **grudg′er** *n.* — **grudg′ing·ly** *adv.*

ı·el (grōō′əl) *n.* A semiliquid food made by boiling meal water or milk. — *v.t.* **gru·eled** or **·elled, gru·el·ing** or **·el·g** To disable or exhaust by hard work, punishment, re- ıtless questioning, etc. [< OF, ult. < Med.L *grutum* ɔarse meal < Gmc.] — **gru′el·er** or **gru′el·ler** *n.*

ı·el·ing (grōō′əl·ing) *adj.* Causing strain or exhaustion. *n.* Any grueling experience. Also **gru′el·ling.**

ıe·some (grōō′səm) *adj.* Inspiring repugnance; frightful; so spelled *grewsome.* [< Scot. *grue* to shudder + -SOME[1]] **grue′some·ly** *adv.* — **grue′some·ness** *n.*

ıff (gruf) *adj.* **1.** Brusque and rough in manner or speech. Hoarse and guttural; harsh. [< Du. *grof* rough] — **uff′ly** *adv.* — **gruff′ness** *n.*

ım·ble (grum′bəl) *v.* **·bled, ·bling** *v.i.* **1.** To complain in surly manner. **2.** To utter low, throaty sounds; growl. **3.** ɔ rumble. — *v.t.* **4.** To utter or express by grumbling. — **1.** A low, muttered complaint. **2.** A rumble. [Cf. Du. *ommelen* < *grommen* to growl] — **grum′bler** *n.* — **grum′·ing·ly** *adv.* — **grum′bly** *adj.*

ımp·y (grum′pē) *adj.* **grump·i·er, grump·i·est** Ill-tem- red; cranky; surly. Also **grump′ish.** [? Blend of GRUNT d DUMP] — **grump′i·ly** *adv.* — **grump′i·ness** *n.*

ınt (grunt) *v.i.* **1.** To make the deep, guttural sound of a ɔg. **2.** To make a similar sound, as in annoyance, assent, fort, etc. — *v.t.* **3.** To utter or express by grunting. — *n.* A short, deep, guttural sound, as of a hog. **2.** A food h of warm American seas. [OE *grunnettan*] — **grunt′er** *n.*

u·yère cheese (grē·yâr′, grōō-; *Fr.* grü·yâr′) *n.* A light llow, whole-milk Swiss cheese having a firm texture and w or no holes. [after *Gruyère,* a town in Switzerland]

string (jē′string′) *n.* **1.** A narrow loincloth supported by waistband. **2.** A similar garment worn by stripteasers. On musical instruments, a string tuned to G.

a·no (gwä′nō) *n. pl.* **·nos 1.** The excrement of sea birds, ound on the Peruvian coast, and used as a fertilizer. **2.** ny similar fertilizer. [< Sp. < Quechua *huanu* dung]

ıa·ra·ni (gwä′rä·nē′) *n. pl.* **·nis** or **·ni 1.** A member of a outh American Indian tribe, formerly occupying the val- ys of the Paraná and the Uruguay. **2.** The Tupian lan- ıage of these tribes. [< Tupi, warrior]

ar·an·tee (gar′ən·tē′) *n.* **1.** A pledge or formal promise ıat something will meet stated specifications or that a speci- ed act will be performed or continued: also called *warranty.* A guaranty (def. 2). **3.** A guarantor. **4.** One who re- ives a guaranty. — *v.t.* **1.** To certify; vouch for: We *ıarantee* our work. **2.** To accept responsibility for. **3.** To ve security to (a person or thing), as against loss, damage, jury, etc. [Var. of GUARANTY]

ar·an·tor (gar′ən·tər, -tôr′) *n.* One who makes or gives a uaranty.

ıar·an·ty (gar′ən·tē) *n. pl.* **·ties 1.** A pledge or promise be responsible for the contract, debt, or duty of another erson in case of his default or miscarriage. **2.** Something iven or taken as security. **3.** A guarantor. — *v.t.* **·tied, y·ing** To guarantee. [< OF *guarant* warrant < Gmc.]

ıard (gärd) *v.t.* **1.** To watch over or care for; protect. **2.** ɔ watch over so as to prevent escape, etc. **3.** To control or revent exit or entry through. **4.** To maintain cautious con- ɔl over. **5.** To furnish (something) with a protective de- ice or shield. — *v.i.* **6.** To take precautions: followed by *ıainst.* **7.** To serve as a guard. — *n.* **1.** One who guards; **a** A warder; keeper. **b** One who has control over a point entry exit, etc. **2.** A group of persons serving as a cere- ıonial escort. **3.** The act of guarding. **4.** That which pro- ides protection. **5.** A defensive posture or stance, as in oxing or fencing. **6.** In football, one of two linemen whose osition in the front line is usually between one of the tack- s and the center. **7.** In basketball, one of two players who irect the offense and are in the front line of defense. — **off ɔne's) guard** Unprepared. — **on (one's) guard** Watchful, autious. — **to mount guard** To go on duty as a sentry. **to stand guard 1.** To maintain a protective watch. **2.** ɔ serve as a sentry. [< OF *guarder*] — **guard′er** *n.*

guard·ed (gär′did) *adj.* **1.** Cautious; prudent; reserved: *guarded* criticism. **2.** Closely defended or kept under sur- veillance by a guard. — **guard′ed·ly** *adv.* — **guard′ed·ness** *n.*

guard·house (gärd′hous′) *n.* **1.** The quarters and head- quarters for military guards. **2.** A jail confining military personnel convicted of minor offenses, etc.

guard·i·an (gär′dē·ən) *n.* **1.** One who guards or watches over something. **2.** One who is legally assigned care of the person, property, etc., esp. of an infant or minor. ◆ Col- lateral adjective: *custodial.* — *adj.* Keeping guard; pro- tecting. — **guard′i·an·ship** *n.*

guard·room (gärd′rōōm′, -rōōm′) *n.* A room for the use and accommodation of military or other guards.

guards·man (gärdz′mən) *n. pl.* **·men** (-mən) **1.** A guard. **2.** *U.S.* A member of the National Guard.

gua·va (gwä′və) *n.* **1.** A tree or shrub of the myrtle family, native to tropical America. **2.** Its small, pear-shaped edible fruit. [< Sp. *guayaba.*]

gu·ber·na·to·ri·al (gōō′bər·nə·tôr′ē·əl, -tō′rē, gyōō′-) *adj.* Of or pertaining to a governor. [< L *gubernator* governor]

guck (guk) *n. U.S. & Canadian Slang* Goo; muck.

gudg·eon (guj′ən) *n.* **1.** A small, carplike, fresh-water fish of Europe. **2.** A minnow. **3.** A bait or enticement. — *v.t.* To cheat; dupe. [< OF < L *gobio* small fish]

guer·don (gûr′dən) *Poetic n.* Reward; recompense. — *v.t.* To reward. [< OF < Med.L < OHG < *widar* in turn + *lōn* reward] — **guer′don·er** *n.*

guern·sey (gûrn′zē) *n. pl.* **·seys** A closely fitting knitted woolen shirt or sweater worn by seamen.

Guern·sey (gûrn′zē) *n. pl.* **·seys** One of a breed of dairy cattle having fawn and white coloration.

guer·ril·la (gə·ril′ə) *n.* One of a combatant band often op- erating in rear of the enemy. — *adj.* Of guerrillas or their warfare. Also **gue·ril′la.** [< Sp., dim. of *guerra* war]

guess (ges) *v.t.* **1.** To form a judgment or opinion of (some quantity, fact, etc.) on uncertain or incomplete knowledge. **2.** To conjecture correctly. **3.** *U.S.* To believe: I *guess* we'll be late. — *v.i.* **4.** To form a judgment or opinion on un- certain or incomplete knowledge: often with *at.* **5.** To con- jecture correctly: How did you *guess?* — *n.* **1.** An opinion or conclusion arrived at by guessing. **2.** The act of guessing. [ME *gessen*] — **guess′er** *n.*

guess·ti·mate (ges′tə·mit) *n. Slang* An estimate that is little better than a guess. [Blend of GUESS and ESTIMATE]

guess·work (ges′wûrk′) *n.* **1.** The process of guessing. **2.** Something based on a guess or guesses, as an opinion.

guest (gest) *n.* **1.** One who is received and entertained by another or others, as at a party or meal, or for a visit, etc. **2.** One who pays for lodging, etc., as at a hotel. — *adj.* **1.** Intended for guests. **2.** Acting on invitation. [OE *giest*]

guff (guf) *n. Slang* Empty talk; nonsense; baloney. [Imit.]

guf·faw (gə·fô′) *n.* A loud burst of boisterous laughter. — *v.i.* To utter such a laugh. [Imit.]

gui·dance (gīd′ns) *n.* **1.** The act, process, or result of guid- ing. **2.** Something that guides.

guide (gīd) *v.* **guid·ed, guid·ing** *v.t.* **1.** To lead or direct, as to a destination. **2.** To direct the motion or physical prog- ress of, as a vehicle, tool, animal, etc. **3.** To lead or direct the affairs, standards, opinions, etc., of. — *v.i.* **4.** To act as a guide. — *n.* **1.** A person who guides; esp., one who con- ducts others on trips, through museums, on sight-seeing tours, etc. **2.** One who or that which is taken as a model. **3.** A book that guides or explains; esp., a guidebook. **4.** *Mech.* Any device that regulates or controls the operation of a part. [< OF *guider*] — **guid′a·ble** *adj.* — **guid′er** *n.*

guide·book (gīd′bŏŏk′) *n.* A handbook containing direc- tions and other information for tourists, visitors, etc.

guid·ed missile (gī′did) *Mil.* An unmanned aerial missile whose course can be altered during flight by mechanisms that are preset, self-reacting, or actuated by radio signals.

guide·line (gīd′līn′) *n.* **1.** A line, as a rope, for guiding. **2.** Any suggestion, rule, etc., intended as a guide.

guide·post (gīd′pōst′) *n.* **1.** A post on which directions for travelers are given. **2.** A guideline.

gui·don (gī′don, gīd′n) *n. Mil.* A small flag for unit identi- fication. [< F < Ital. *guidone*]

guild (gild) *n.* **1.** In medieval times, an association of ar- tisans or merchants, formed for mutual aid, etc. **2.** Any similar association or fellowship. Also spelled *gild.* [Fusion of OE *gild* payment and *gegyld* association]

guil·der (gil′dər) *n.* The basic monetary unit of the Nether- lands: in 1960 worth about 27 U.S. cents. Also called *gulden:* also spelled *gilder.* [< Du. *gulden* golden]

guild·hall (gild′hôl′) *n. Brit.* **1.** The hall where a guild meets. **2.** A town hall.

guilds·man (gildz′mən) *n. pl.* **·men** (-mən) A member of a guild.

guild socialism An English theory of socialism that advocates ownership of all industry by the state with guilds of workers exercising the powers of management and control.

guile (gīl) *n.* Treacherous cunning or craft; deceit. [< OF < Gmc.]

guile·ful (gīl′fəl) *adj.* Full of guile; treacherous; deceitful. **— guile′ful·ly** *adv.* **— guile′ful·ness** *n.*

guile·less (gīl′lis) *adj.* Free from guile; sincere. **— Syn.** See INGENUOUS. **— guile′less·ly** *adv.* **— guile′less·ness** *n.*

guil·le·mot (gil′ə·mot) *n.* Any of several narrow-billed auks found in northern latitudes. [< F, dim. of *Guillaume* William]

guil·lo·tine (*n.* gil′ə·tēn, gē′ə·tēn; *v.* gil′ə·tēn′, gil′ə·tēn) *n.* **1.** The instrument of capital punishment in France, consisting of a weighted blade that slides down between two vertical guides and beheads the victim. **2.** A similar machine for cutting paper, etc. — *v.t.* **·tined, ·tin·ing** To behead with the guillotine. [< F, after J. I. *Guillotin,* 1738–1814, French physician who advocated a humane means of execution]

GUILLOTINE
b Basket for body.
r Receptacle for head.

guilt (gilt) *n.* **1.** The fact or condition of having committed a legal or moral offense. **2.** A feeling of remorse arising from a real or imagined commission of an offense. **3.** Guilty conduct. [OE *gylt*]

guilt·less (gilt′lis) *adj.* **1.** Free from guilt; innocent. **2.** Lacking knowledge or experience: with *of.* **— guilt′less·ly** *adv.* **— guilt′less·ness** *n.*

guilt·y (gil′tē) *adj.* **guilt·i·er, guilt·i·est** **1.** Deserving of blame for some offense. **2.** Convicted of some offense. **3.** Involving, pertaining to, or showing guilt. **— guilt′i·ly** *adv.* **— guilt′i·ness** *n.*

guimpe (gimp, gamp) *n.* A short blouse. [< F]

guin·ea (gin′ē) *n.* **1.** Formerly, an English gold coin. **2.** A British money of account, equal to 21 shillings. **3.** The guinea fowl. **4.** *U.S. Slang* A person of Italian descent: an offensive term.

guinea fowl A gallinaceous bird of African origin, having dark gray plumage speckled with white spots, long domesticated in Europe and America. Also **guinea, guinea hen.**

guinea pig **1.** A small, domesticated rodent, usu. white, having a short tail and widely used in biological and medical experiments. **2.** Any person used in experimentation.

Guinea worm A threadlike aquatic worm of tropical Africa and Asia, whose larvae infect the legs and lower trunk of men and animals.

Guin·e·vere (gwin′ə·vir) In Arthurian legend, Arthur's unfaithful queen and the mistress of Lancelot.

guise (gīz) *n.* **1.** External appearance or aspect; semblance. **2.** Assumed or false appearance; pretense. [< OF < Gmc.]

gui·tar (gi·tär′) *n.* A musical instrument having a fretted fingerboard, a large sound box with indented sides, and strings, usu. six, that are plucked with the fingers or plectrum. [< Sp. *guitarra*] **— gui·tar′ist** *n.*

gu·lar (go͞o′lər, gyo͞o′-) *adj.* Of or pertaining to the throat; pharyngeal. [< L *gula* throat]

gulch (gulch) *n.* *U.S.* A deep, narrow ravine cut out by a rushing stream. [? < dial. *gulch* to swallow greedily]

gul·den (go͝ol′dən) *n.* The guilder. [< Du., lit., golden]

gules (gyo͞olz) *n.* **1.** The color red. **2.** *Heraldry* The tincture red. [< OF *gueules* red-dyed ermine fur]

gulf (gulf) *n.* **1.** A large area of ocean or sea partially enclosed by an extended sweep of land. **2.** An abyss; chasm; gorge. **3.** A wide or impassable separation, as in social position, education, etc. — *v.t.* To swallow up; engulf. [< OF < Ital. < LGk. < Gk. *kolpos* bay]

Gulf Stream A warm ocean current flowing NE along the eastern coast of North America toward Europe.

gulf·weed (gulf′wēd′) *n.* Sargasso.

gull[1] (gul) *n.* A long-winged, web-footed sea bird, usu. white and gray, and having the upper mandible hooked. [ME]

gull[2] (gul) *n.* *Archaic* A person easily tricked. **— *v.t.*** *Archaic* To deceive; swindle; cheat. [? < obs. *gull* swallow]

Gul·lah (gul′ə) *n.* **1.** One of a group of Negroes dwelling on a narrow coastal strip of South Carolina, Georgia, and NE Florida, or on islands lying off this coast. **2.** The mixed (English and African) language of these people.

gul·let (gul′it) *n.* **1.** The passage from the mouth to the stomach; esophagus. **2.** The throat; pharynx; also, anything resembling a throat. [< OF < L *gula*]

gul·li·ble (gul′ə·bəl) *adj.* Easily cheated or fooled; credulous. **— gul′li·bil′i·ty** *n.* **— gul′li·bly** *adv.*

Gul·li·ver (gul′ə·vər), **Lemuel** The hero of Jonathan Swift's satire **Gulliver's Travels** (1726).

gul·ly (gul′ē) *n.* *pl.* **·lies** A channel, ravine, or ditch; esp., a ravine cut in the earth by running water. — *v.t.* **·lied, ·ly·ing** To cut or wear a gully in. [Var. of GULLET]

gulp (gulp) *v.t.* **1.** To swallow greedily or in large amounts. **2.** To choke back or stifle. — *v.i.* **3.** To swallow convulsively as a sign of surprise, etc. — *n.* **1.** The act of gulpi **2.** The amount swallowed in gulping. [< Du. *gulpen*] **gulp′er** *n.* **— gulp′ing·ly** *adv.*

gum[1] (gum) *n.* **1.** A sticky, viscid substance exuded fr various trees and plants, soluble in water and hardening exposure to air. **2.** Any similar substance, as resin. **3** preparation made from gum and used in art, industry, **4.** Chewing gum. **5.** Mucilage; glue. **6.** The gum tree. Rubber. **8.** *U.S. Dial. pl.* Rubber overshoes. — *v.* **gumm gum·ming** *v.t.* **1.** To smear, stiffen, or clog with gum. **2.** glue or stick together with gum — *v i.* **3.** To exude form gum. **4.** To become sticky or clogged with gum. **to gum up** *Slang* To bungle. [< OF < L < Gk. *komm*

gum[2] (gum) *n.* *Often pl.* The fleshy tissue that covers arches of the jaws and surrounds the necks of the tee — *v.t. & v.i.* **gummed, gum·ming** *U.S. Dial.* To chew wi out teeth. [OE *goma* inside of the mouth]

gum ammoniac Ammoniac[2].

gum arabic The gum from various species of acacia, u in medicine, candy, ink, etc.

gum·bo (gum′bō) *n.* *pl.* **·bos** **1.** The okra or its edible, sl pery pods. **2.** A thick soup or stew containing okra po **3.** *U.S. & Canadian* In the West, a type of fine, silty s Also **gumbo soil.** **4.** A patois of French spoken by Negr in Louisiana. [< Bantu (Angola)]

gum·boil (gum′boil′) *n.* A small boil or abscess on the gu

gum·drop (gum′drop′) *n.* *U.S.* A small, round piece jellylike candy, usu. colored and coated with sugar.

gum·my (gum′ē) *adj.* **·mi·er, ·mi·est** **1.** Of or like gu sticky; viscid. **2.** Covered or clogged with gum or a gu like substance. **3.** Exuding gum. **— gum′mi·ness** *n.*

gump·tion (gump′shən) *n.* *Informal* **1.** Bold, energe initiative. **2.** Shrewd common sense. [< dial. E (Scot

gum resin A mixture of gum and resin that exudes a milky juice from incisions in certain plants.

gum·shoe (gum′sho͞o′) *n.* *U.S.* **1.** A rubber shoe or ov shoe. **2.** *pl.* Sneakers. **3.** *Slang* A detective. — *v.i.* **·sho ·shoe·ing** *Slang* To go stealthily and noiselessly; sneak.

gum tree Any of various trees that produce gum.

gun (gun) *n.* **1.** A weapon or projectile device from whic missile is thrown by the force of an explosive, by compress air, by a spring, etc. **2.** Loosely, any portable firearm. *Mil.* **a** Any of various cannons with a flat trajectory, hi muzzle velocity, and a barrel of over .25 caliber: anti-ta *gun.* **b** Any of various automatic weapons: machine *gun.* Any device resembling a gun: grease *gun.* **5.** The discha ing of a firearm. **6.** *U.S. Slang* The throttle controlling engine. **7.** *U.S. Slang* A gunman. **— big gun** *Slang* A p son of influence. **— to give it** (or **her**) **the gun** *Slang* **1.** increase sharply the speed of a motor. **2.** To give add speed, efficiency, etc., to some action. **— to go great gu** *U.S. Slang* To work or perform with great skill, speed, e **— to spike (someone's) guns** To destroy or make ineffect someone's plans, ideas, etc. **— to stick to one's guns** continue in one's actions, plans, opinions, etc., in spite of c position. **— *v.* gunned, gun·ning** *v.i.* **1.** To go shooting hunting with a gun. — *v.t.* *U.S. Slang* **2.** To open t throttle of (an engine). **3.** To shoot (a person) with a gu **— to gun for** (or **after**) *U.S. Slang* **1.** To seek with inte to injure or kill. **2.** To seek out in order to win favor, e [ME *gonne, gunne*]

gun·boat (gun′bōt′) *n.* A small, armed naval vessel, us for patrolling rivers and coastal waters.

gun carriage The mechanical structure, often wheele upon which a cannon is mounted for firing or maneuverin

gun·cot·ton (gun′kot′n) *n.* A type of cellulose nitrate us as an explosive.

gun·fire (gun′fīr′) *n.* **1.** The firing of a gun or guns. **2.** *M* The use of artillery or small arms in warfare.

gung ho (gung′hō′) *U.S. Slang* Eager; enthusiastic; ze ous: *gung ho* about army life. [< Chinese]

gun·lock (gun′lok′) *n.* The mechanism in certain guns which the hammer is driven and the charge exploded.

gun·man (gun′mən) *n.* *pl.* **·men** (-mən) **1.** A man arm with a gun; esp., an armed criminal. **2.** A gunsmith.

gun-met·al (gun′met′l) *adj.* Of the color of gun metal.

gun metal **1.** A bronze made of copper, tin, and zinc. Any of various metal alloys of a dark bluish gray color, us for metal novelties. **3.** A dark bluish gray color.

gun moll *U.S. Slang* **1.** A female associate or accompli of criminals. **2.** A female thief.

gun·nel[1] (gun′əl) See GUNWALE.

gun·nel[2] (gun′əl) *n.* *pl.* **·nels** or **·nel** A fish of the blen family, found in North Atlantic waters.

gun·ner (gun′ər) *n.* **1.** One who operates a gun. **2.** In t U.S. Navy and Marine Corps, a warrant officer whose duti were traditionally connected with ordnance. **3.** In the U. Army, a noncommissioned officer who does the actual firi of a gun. **4.** *Brit. Mil.* An artilleryman.

gun·ner·y (gun′ər·ē) *n.* **1.** The science and art of construc ing and operating guns. **2.** Guns collectively.

ı·ning (gun′ing) *n.* The art or act of hunting with a gun.
ı·ny (gun′ē) *n. pl.* **·nies** **1.** A coarse, heavy material ıde of jute or hemp, used for making sacks, etc. **2.** A bag sack made from this material: also **gunny bag, gunny ck.** [< Hind. *gonī* gunny sack]
ı·pow·der (gun′pou′dər) *n.* An explosive mixture of potssium nitrate, charcoal, and sulfur, used in blasting and eworks, and still occasionally as a propellant in guns.
ı·run·ning (gun′run′ing) *n.* The smuggling of guns and ımunition into a country. **— gun′run′ner** *n.*
ı·shot (gun′shot′) *n.* **1.** The range or reach of a gun. **2.** ıe shooting of a gun; also, the noise or the shot. **—** *adj.* used by a gunshot.
ı·shy (gun′shī′) *adj.* Afraid of a gun or of its sound.
ı·smith (gun′smith′) *n.* One who makes or repairs guns.
ı·stock (gun′stok′) *n.* The wooden stock of a gun.
ı·wale (gun′əl) *n. Naut.* The upper edge of the side of ɔoat: also spelled *gunnel.* [< GUN + WALE[1] (plank)]
ɔ·py (gup′ē) *n. pl.* **·pies** A small, tropical, fresh-water h, valued as an aquarium fish because of its coloring. fter R. J. L. *Guppy,* British scientist]
·gle (gûr′gəl) *v.* **·gled, ·gling** *v.i.* **1.** To flow irregularly, th a bubbling sound, as water issuing from a bottle. **2.** To ake such a sound. **—** *v.t.* **3.** To utter with a gurgling und. **—** *n.* **1.** The act of gurgling. **2.** The sound of gurng. [Var. of GARGLE] **— gur′gling·ly** *adv.*
·nard (gûr′nərd) *n. pl.* **·nards** or **·nard** Any of various arine fishes having a spiny head. Also **gur′net** (-nit). [< F *grognard* grumbler]
ru (gōō′rōō) *n.* In the East, a spiritual teacher or guide. < Hind.]
sh (gush) *v.i.* **1.** To pour out in volume and with sudden rce. **2.** To emit a sudden flow, as of blood, tears, etc. **3.** *formal* To be overly enthusiastic. **—** *v.t.* **4.** To pour forth lood, tears, words, etc.). **—** *n.* **1.** A sudden flow or outrst. **2.** *Informal* An extravagant effusion of emotion, aise, etc. [ME *guschen*] **— gush′ing·ly** *adv.*
sh·er (gush′ər) *n.* **1.** One who gushes. **2.** An oil well at spurts oil without the need of pumps.
sh·y (gush′ē) *adj.* **gush·i·er, gush·i·est** *Informal* Overly thusiastic. **— gush′i·ness** *n.*
s·set (gus′it) *n.* **1.** A triangular piece inserted into a garent, glove, shoe, etc., for added strength or roomier fit. A bracket used to strengthen a corner or angle of a strucre. **—** *v.t.* To furnish with a gusset. [< OF *gousse* pod]
st (gust) *n.* **1.** A sudden, violent rush of wind or air. **2.** sudden burst or outpouring of fire, sound, water, etc. **3.** brief outburst of emotion. [< ON *gustr*]
s·ta·to·ry (gus′tə·tôr′ē, -tō′rē) *adj.* Of or pertaining to e sense of taste or the act of tasting.
s·to (gus′tō) *n.* **1.** Keen enjoyment or enthusiasm; relh. **2.** Individual taste or preference. **3.** In art, a characristic style or treatment. [< Ital. < L *gustus* taste]
st·y (gus′tē) *adj.* **gust·i·er, gust·i·est** **1.** Characterized fitful gusts of wind or rain; blustery. **2.** Given to sudden tbursts of feeling, etc. **— gust′i·ly** *adv.* **— gust′i·ness** *n.*
t (gut) *n.* **1.** The alimentary canal or any part of it; esp., ıe stomach or intestine. **2.** *pl.* Bowels; entrails. **3.** The ecially prepared intestines of certain animals, used as rings for musical instruments, surgical sutures, etc. **4.** *pl. lang* **a** Courage; stamina; grit. **b** Effrontery. **5.** A narrow ıssage, as a strait. **—** *v.t.* **gut·ted, gut·ting** **1.** To take out ıe intestines of. **2.** To plunder. **3.** To destroy the connts of. [OE *guttas*]
t·ta-per·cha (gut′ə·pûr′chə) *n.* A coagulated, rubberke material, formed from the juice of various Malayan ees, used in electrical insulation, in the arts, as a dental astic, etc. [< Malay *getah* gum + *percha* gum tree]
t·ter (gut′ər) *n.* **1.** A channel or ditch at the side of a reet, for carrying off surface water. **2.** A furrow or ditch rmed by running water. **3.** A trough, fixed below or along ıe eaves of a house, for carrying off rain water from the ɔof. **4.** A state or condition of life, marked by poverty, lth, etc. **5.** Any groove or channel. **—** *v.t.* **1.** To form hannels or grooves in. **2.** To furnish with gutters, as a ouse. **—** *v.i.* **3.** To flow in channels, as water. **4.** To melt apidly: said of lighted candles. [< OF < *goute* drop]
t·ter·snipe (gut′ər·snīp′) *n.* A neglected child, usu. of he slums, who spends much time in the streets.
t·tur·al (gut′ər·əl) *adj.* **1.** Pertaining to the throat. **2.** Having a harsh, or muffled, grating quality. **3.** *Phonet.* elar. **—** *n. Phonet.* A velar sound. [< NL < L *guttur* hroat] **— gut′tur·al′i·ty** *n.* **— gut′tur·al·ly** *adv.*
ıy[1] (gī) *n.* **1.** *Informal* A man or boy; fellow. **2.** *Brit.* A erson of grotesque appearance. **—** *v.t.* **guyed, guy·ing** *Informal* To ridicule. [after *Guy* Fawkes, leader of an abortive onspiracy in 1605 to assassinate King James I]
ıy[2] (gī) *n.* A rope, cable, wire, etc., used to steady, guide, or secure something. **—** *v.t.* To secure, steady, or guide with a guy. [< OF *guider* to guide]
guz·zle (guz′əl) *v.t. & v.i.* **·zled, ·zling** To drink greedily or to excess. [? < OF *gosier* throat] **— guz′zler** *n.*
gym (jim) *n. U.S. Informal* **1.** A gymnasium. **2.** A course in physical training. [Short for GYMNASIUM]
gym·na·si·um (jim·nā′zē·əm) *n. pl.* **·si·ums** or **·si·a** (-zē·ə) **1.** A building or room equipped for certain athletic activities. **2.** A place where ancient Greek youths met for physical exercise and discussion. [< L < Gk. *gymnazein* to exercise]
Gym·na·si·um (gim·nä′zē·ŏŏm) *n.* In Europe, esp. Germany, a secondary school to prepare students for the universities.
gym·nast (jim′nast) *n.* One skilled in gymnastics.
gym·nas·tic (jim·nas′tik) *adj.* Of or pertaining to gymnastics. Also **gym·nas′ti·cal.** **— gym·nas′ti·cal·ly** *adv.*
gym·nas·tics (jim·nas′tiks) *n.pl.* **1.** Any physical exercises designed to improve strength, agility, etc. **2.** (*construed as sing.*) The art or practice of such exercises.
gym·no·sperm (jim′nə·spûrm′) *n.* One of a class of plants whose ovules and seeds are not enclosed in a case, as certain evergreens. [< Gk. *gymnos* naked + *sperma* seed] **— gym′no·sper′mous** *adj.*
gyneco- *combining form* Female; pertaining to women. Also, before vowels, **gynec-.** [< Gk. *gynē, gynaikos* woman]
gy·ne·col·o·gy (gī′nə·kol′ə·jē, jī′nə-, jin′ə-) *n.* That branch of medicine dealing with the functions and diseases peculiar to women. **— gy·ne·co·log·i·cal** (gī′nə·kə·loj′i·kəl, jī′nə-, jin′ə-) *adj.* **— gy′ne·col′o·gist** *n.*
gyno- *combining form* **1.** Woman; female. **2.** *Bot. & Med.* Female reproductive organ; ovary; pistil. Also, before vowels, **gyn-.** [< Gk. *gynē* woman]
gy·noe·ci·um (jī·nē′sē·əm, ji-) *n. pl.* **·ci·a** (-sē·ə) *Bot.* The female parts of a flower collectively; the pistil or pistils taken as a unit. Also **gy·nae′ce·um, gy·nae′ci·um, gy·ne′ci·um.**
-gynous *combining form* **1.** Female; of women. **2.** *Biol.* Having or pertaining to female organs or pistils: *androgynous.* [< Gk. *gynē* woman]
gyp (jip) *U.S. Informal v.t. & v.i.* **gypped, gyp·ping** To cheat, swindle, or defraud. **—** *n.* A fraud. [? < GYPSY]
gyp·sum (jip′səm) *n.* A mineral, hydrous calcium sulfate, $CaSO_4 \cdot 2H_2O$, used in plaster of Paris, fertilizer, etc. [< L < Gk. *gypsos* chalk]
gyp·sy (jip′sē) *n. pl.* **·sies** A person who looks like, or leads the life of, a Gypsy. **—** *adj.* Of, pertaining to, or like a gypsy or the Gypsies. **—** *v.i.* **·sied, ·sy·ing** To live or wander like a gypsy or the Gypsies. Also spelled *gipsy.*
Gyp·sy (jip′sē) *n. pl.* **·sies** **1.** A member of a wandering, dark-haired, dark-skinned Caucasian people believed to have migrated to Europe from India in the 15th century, and known as fortunetellers, musicians, etc. **2.** Romany (def. 2). Also spelled *Gipsy.* [Var. of *Egypcyan* Egyptian]
gypsy moth A moth having larvae destructive to foliage.
gy·rate (jī′rāt) *v.i.* **·rat·ed, ·rat·ing** **1.** To rotate or revolve, usu. around a fixed point or axis. **2.** To turn in a spiral motion. **—** *adj.* Winding or coiled about; convolute. [< L *gyrare* to gyrate < Gk. *gyros*] **— gy·ra·tor** (jī′rā′tər, jī·rā′-) *n.* **— gy′ra·to′ry** *adj.*
gy·ra·tion (jī·rā′shən) *n.* **1.** The act of gyrating; a spiral or whirling motion. **2.** A single whorl of a spiral shell.
gyre (jīr) *n.* A spiral or round form, as a ring or vortex; also, whirling motion. [< L < Gk. *gyros* circle] **— gy′ral** *adj.*
gyr·fal·con (jûr′fal′kən, -fôl′-, -fô′-) See GERFALCON.
gy·ro (jī′rō) *n.* A gyroscope or gyrocompass.
gyro- *combining form* **1.** Rotating; gyrating. **2.** Spiral. Also, before vowels, **gyr-.** [< Gk. *gyros* circle]
gy·ro·com·pass (jī′rō·kum′pəs, -kom′-) *n.* A compass that employs a motor-driven gyroscope so mounted that its axis of rotation maintains a constant position with reference to the true or geographic north.
gyro pilot *Aeron.* An automatic pilot.
gy·ro·plane (jī′rə·plān′) *n.* An aircraft that obtains its lift from rotating airfoils, as a helicopter.
gy·ro·scope (jī′rə·skōp) *n.* Any of a class of devices consisting essentially of a heavy wheel, so mounted that when set to rotate at high speeds it resists all forces tending to change the angular position of its axis of rotation. [< F] **— gy′ro·scop′ic** (-skop′ik) *adj.*

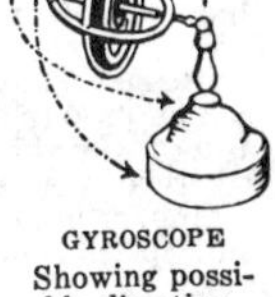

GYROSCOPE
Showing possible directional movements.

gy·ro·sta·bi·liz·er (jī′rō·stā′bə·lī′zər) *n.* A gyroscopic device designed to reduce the rolling motion of ships.
gy·ro·stat·ics (jī′rə·stat′iks) *n.pl.* (*construed as sing.*) The branch of physics that investigates the laws governing the rotation of solid bodies. **— gy′ro·stat′ic** *adj.* **— gy′ro·stat′i·cal·ly** *adv.*

H

h, H (āch) *n. pl.* **h's** or **hs, H's** or **Hs, aitch·es** (ā′chiz) **1.** The eighth letter of the English alphabet. **2.** The sound represented by the letter *h*, a voiceless, glottal fricative. In a few English words of French origin, as *heir, honor, hour*, etc., the letter *h* has no phonetic value. **3.** Anything shaped like an H. **4.** *U.S. Slang* Heroin. — *symbol* **1.** *Chem.* Hydrogen. **2.** *Physics* Strength or intensity of magnetic field (symbol H). **3.** *Electr.* Henry (symbol H).

ha (hä) *n. & interj.* An exclamation or sound expressing surprise, discovery, triumph, laughter, etc. Also spelled *hah.*

ha·ba·ne·ra (ä′bä·nā′rä) *n.* **1.** A slow, Cuban dance of African origin. **2.** Music for it. [< Sp., of Havana]

ha·be·as cor·pus (hā′bē·əs kôr′pəs) *Law* A writ commanding a person who detains another to produce the detained person before a court, esp. in order to determine the lawfulness of the detention. [< L, (you) have the body]

hab·er·dash·er (hab′ər·dash′ər) *n. U.S.* A shopkeeper who deals in men's furnishings, as shirts, hats, socks, etc. [Prob. < AF *hapertas*, kind of fabric]

hab·er·dash·er·y (hab′ər·dash′ər·ē) *n. pl.* **·er·ies** **1.** The goods sold by haberdashers. **2.** A haberdasher's shop.

ha·bil·i·ment (hə·bil′ə·mənt) *n. Usu. pl.* Clothing; attire. [< OF < L *habilis* fit, apt]

ha·bil·i·tate (hə·bil′ə·tāt) *v.t.* **·tat·ed, ·tat·ing** *U.S.* In the West, to supply (a mine) with money, equipment, etc. [< L *habilis* fit] — **ha·bil′i·ta′tion** *n.*

hab·it (hab′it) *n.* **1.** An act or practice so frequently repeated as to become almost automatic. **2.** A tendency or disposition to act consistently or to repeat. **3.** An addiction: the drug *habit.* **4.** Mental or moral disposition: the scholar's *habit* of mind. **5.** A characteristic appearance or condition of the body. **6.** The clothing associated with a particular profession, etc.: a monk's *habit.* **7.** *Biol.* A characteristic action, aspect, or mode of growth of a plant or animal. — *v.t.* To clothe; dress. [< OF < L *habitus* condition, dress]

hab·it·a·ble (hab′it·ə·bəl) *adj.* Suitable for habitation. [< L *habitare* to inhabit] — **hab′it·a·bil′i·ty, hab′it·a·ble·ness** *n.* — **hab′it·a·bly** *adv.*

hab·i·tant (hab′ə·tənt) *n.* **1.** An inhabitant. **2.** A French farmer in Canada or Louisiana. [< F < L *habitare* to dwell]

hab·i·tat (hab′ə·tat) *n.* **1.** The region or environment where a plant or animal is normally found, as salt water, desert, equatorial forest, etc. **2.** The place where a person or thing usu. resides or is found. [< NL, it dwells]

hab·i·ta·tion (hab′ə·tā′shən) *n.* **1.** A place of abode; residence. **2.** The act of dwelling or inhabiting.

ha·bit·u·al (hə·bich′o͞o·əl) *adj.* **1.** Practiced or recurring by habit; customary: *habitual* courtesy; also, occurring constantly. **2.** Given to or addicted to a practice. **3.** Expected from habit or usage: her *habitual* place. [< Med.L < L *habitus*] — **ha·bit′u·al·ly** *adv.* — **ha·bit′u·al·ness** *n.*

hab·it-form·ing (hab′it·fôr′ming) *adj.* Producing or resulting in a habitual practice or addiction.

ha·bit·u·ate (hə·bich′o͞o·āt) *v.t.* **·at·ed, ·at·ing** To accustom (oneself, an animal, etc.) to a condition by repetition. [< LL *habituare* to condition] — **ha·bit′u·a′tion** *n.*

hab·i·tude (hab′ə·to͞od, -tyo͞od) *n.* **1.** Customary or characteristic state of mind or body. **2.** A usual course of action.

ha·bit·u·é (hə·bich′o͞o·ā, hə·bich′o͞o·ā′; *Fr.* à·bē·tü·ā′) *n.* One who frequents a specific restaurant, club, etc. [< F *habituer* to accustom]

ha·chure (*n.* ha·sho͝or′, hash′o͝or) *n.* One of the short, parallel lines used in drawing and mapmaking. [< F < *hacher*]

ha·ci·en·da (hä′sē·en′də, *Sp.* ä·syen′dä) *n.* In Spanish America: **a** A landed estate; a country house. **b** A farming, mining, or manufacturing establishment in the country. [< Am. Sp. < L *facienda* things to be done]

hack[1] (hak) *v.t.* **1.** To cut or chop crudely or irregularly, as with an ax, cleaver, etc. **2.** In basketball, to strike (an opposing player) on the arm. — *v.i.* **3.** To make cuts or notches with heavy, crude blows. **4.** To emit short, dry coughs. — *n.* **1.** A gash, cut, or nick made as by a sharp instrument. **2.** An ax, hoe, or tool for hacking. **3.** A short, dry cough. [OE *haccian* to cut] — **hack′er** *n.*

hack[2] (hak) *n.* **1.** A horse for hire, as a saddle horse. **2.** An old, worn-out horse; jade. **3.** A person hired to do routine work, esp. literary work. **4.** *U.S.* A hackney coach. **5.** *U.S. Informal* A taxicab. — *v.t.* **1.** To let out for hire, a horse. **2.** To use or employ as a hack. **3.** To make stal trite by constant use; hackney. **4.** *U.S. Informal* To dr a taxicab. **5.** To ride on horseback at a jog. — *adj.* **1.** or for hack: a *hack* stand. **2.** For hire as a hack: a *h* writer. **3.** Of a routine, mercenary, or hackneyed natu

hack[3] (hak) *n.* A frame or rack on which to dry bric cheese, fish, etc. — *v.t.* To set on hacks to dry.

hack·ber·ry (hak′ber′ē, -bər·ē) *n. pl.* **·ries** **1.** An Ameri tree resembling the elm and having small, sweet, edible fr **2.** The fruit or wood. [< ON < *neggr* hedge + BERRY

hack·ie (hak′ē) *n. U.S. Slang* The driver of a taxicab.

hack·le (hak′əl) *n.* **1.** One of the long, narrow feathers the neck of a rooster, pigeon, etc.; also, such feathers col tively. **2.** In angling: A tuft of these used in a **hack′le fly.** *pl.* The hairs on the neck and back of a dog, that rise in ger, etc. — **to make (someone's) hackles rise** To m angry; infuriate. — *v.t.* **·led, ·ling** To furnish (a fly) wit hackle. [Var. of *hatchel* a comb for flax]

hack·ma·tack (hak′mə·tak) *n. U.S. & Canadian* **1.** tamarack. **2.** The wood of this tree. [< N. Am. Ind.]

hack·ney (hak′nē) *n. pl.* **·neys** **1.** A horse of medium s used for ordinary driving and riding. **2.** A carriage for hi [< OF *haquenee* horse]

hack·neyed (hak′nēd) *adj.* Made commonplace by f quent use; trite. — **Syn.** See TRITE.

hack·saw (hak′sô′) *n.* A saw with a fine-toothed, narrow blade set in a frame, used for cutting metal. Also **hack saw.**

HACKSAW

had (had) Past tense and past participle of HAVE.

had·dock (had′ək) *n. pl.* **·dock** or **·docks** A food fish of North Atlantic, allied to but smaller than the cod. [M

Ha·des (hā′dēz) **1.** In Greek mythology: **a** The brother Zeus, god of the underworld, identified with the Greek a Roman *Pluto.* **b** The underground kingdom of the dead. In the New Testament, the condition or the abode of dead. [< Gk. *a-* not + *idein* to see]

ha·des (hā′dēz) *n. Often cap. Informal* Hell: a euphemis

hadj (haj) *n.* The pilgrimage to Mecca required of eve Moslem at least once in his life. [< Turkish < Arabic *h* pilgrimage. Akin to HEGIRA.]

hadj·i (haj′ē) *n.* A Moslem who has made his hadj: us also as a title. Also **hadj′ee.**

hae (hā, ha) *v.t. Scot.* To have.

haem-, haemo- See HEMO-.

haema- See HEMA-.

haemat-, haemato- See HEMATO-.

-haemia See -EMIA.

haf·ni·um (haf′nē·əm) *n.* A metallic element (symbol H found in zirconium minerals. See ELEMENT. [< NL, fr L *Hafnia* Copenhagen]

haft (haft, häft) *n.* A handle of a knife, sword, etc. *v.t.* To fit with a haft. [OE *hæft* handle]

hag (hag) *n.* **1.** A repulsive, usu. malicious old woman. A witch; sorceress. [OE *hægtes* witch]

Ha·gar (hā′gər) Abraham's concubine. *Gen.* xvi 1.

hag·fish (hag′fish′) *n. pl.* **·fish** or **·fish·es** A primitive e like, marine fish allied to the lamprey, that bores its way in the bodies of living fishes by means of a rasping mouth.

Hag·ga·dah (hə·gä′də, *Hebrew* ha·gô′dô) *n. pl.* **·doth** (-dōt **1.** The nonlegal elements of Talmudic literature, consisti of fables, proverbs, etc. **2.** The story of the Exodus read Passover. **3.** A book containing this story. Also **Ha·ga′da Hag·ga′da.** [< Hebrew < *higgid* to tell]

Hag·ga·i (hag′ē·ī, hag′ī) Sixth-century B.C. Hebrew prophe — *n.* A book of the Old Testament written by him. Als in the Douai Bible, *Aggeus.*

hag·gard (hag′ərd) *adj.* **1.** Having a worn, gaunt, or wi look, as from fatigue, worry, hunger, etc. **2.** Wild or i tractable. [< OF *hagard* wild] — **hag′gard·ly** *adv.*

hag·gish (hag′ish) *adj.* Characteristic of a hag; haglike. — **hag′gish·ly** *adv.* — **hag′gish·ness** *n.*

hag·gle (hag′əl) *v.* **·gled, ·gling** *v.i.* **1.** To argue or barga in a petty, mean way, esp. about price or terms. — *v.t.* To cut unskillfully; hack; mangle. **3.** To tire or harass, by wrangling. — *n.* The act of haggling. — **hag′gler** *n.*

io- *combining form* Sacred: *hagiography.* Also, before vels, **hagi-.** [< Gk. *hagios* sacred]
i·og·ra·pha (hag′ē·og′rə·fə, hā′jē-) *n.pl.* The third of three ancient divisions of the Old Testament, containing those books not found in the Pentateuch or the Prophets. e Hagiographa consist of the following books (names in Douai Bible, when different, are given in parentheses): hronicles (I Parlipomenon), II Chronicles (II Paralinenon), Ruth, Ezra (I Esdras), Nehemiah (II Esdras), her, Job, Psalms, Proverbs, Ecclesiastes, Song of Solon (Canticle of Canticles), Lamentations, Daniel. [< Gk. *agios* sacred + *graphein* to write]
i·og·ra·pher (hag′ē·og′rə·fər, hā′jē-) *n.* **1.** A writer of uthority on the lives of saints. **2.** Any writer on sacred jects; esp., one of the authors of the Hagiographa.
i·og·ra·phy (hag′ē·og′rə·fē, hā′jē-) *n. pl.* **·phies 1.** study of the lives of saints. **2.** A book of such studies. **ag·i·o·graph·ic** (hag′ē·ə·graf′ik, hā′jē-) or **·i·cal** *adj.*
i·ol·o·gy (hag′ē·ol′ə·jē, hā′jē-) *n. pl.* **·gies 1.** That t of literature dealing with the lives of the saints. **2.** A k on saints' lives. **3.** A list of saints. **— hag·i·o·log·ic** g′ē·ə·loj′ik, hā′jē-) or **·i·cal** *adj.* **— hag′i·ol′o·gist** *n.*
(hä) See HA.
ha (hä′hä′, hä′hä′) *n. & interj.* A sound imitating laugh- **—** *v.i.* To laugh. Also spelled *haw-haw.* [Imit.]
ku (hī′kōō) *n. pl.* **·ku** A Japanese verse form in three rt lines. Also called *hokku.* [< Japanese]
[1] (hāl) *n.* **1.** Small lumps of ice that fall from the sky ing a storm; hailstones. **2.** A rapid or heavy showering: *ail* of blows. **—** *v.i.* **1.** To pour down hail. **2.** To fall hail. **—** *v.t.* **3.** To hurl or pour like hail. [OE *hægel*]
[2] (hāl) *v.t.* **1.** To call loudly to in greeting. **2.** To call to as to attract attention. **3.** To name as; designate. **— 4.** To call out to, esp. between ships. **— to hail from** To ne from, as a birthplace, residence, etc. **—** *n.* **1.** The act nailing. **2.** A shout, as of greeting or for attention. **3.** e distance a shout can be heard; earshot: within *hail.* E < ON < *heill* whole, hale] **— hail′er** *n.*
fellow A pleasant companion. Also **hail fellow well t.**
(hâr) *n.* **1.** One of the fine, threadlike structures that w from the skin of most mammals. ◆ Collateral adjece: *capillary.* **2.** Such structures collectively, esp. those t grow on the human head and on the skin of most mamls. **3.** *Bot.* A hairlike outgrowth of the epidermis in nts. **4.** Material woven of hair. **5.** Any exceedingly nute measure, etc. **— not to turn a hair** To show or rel no sign of embarrassment, etc. **— to a hair** With the nost exactness; in minute detail. **— to get in one's hair** *ng* To vex or annoy one. **— to let one's hair down** *U.S. ng* To discard one's reserve. **— to make one's hair stand end** To horrify one. **— to split hairs** To make trivial tinctions. **—** *adj.* **1.** Like, or made of, hair. **2.** For the r: *hair* oil. [OE *hær*] **— hair′less** *adj.*
r·ball (hâr′bôl′) *n.* A rounded mass of hair often found stomachs of animals that groom themselves by licking.
r·breadth (hâr′bredth′, -bretth′) *n.* An extremely small ce or margin. **—** *adj.* Very narrow or close: *hairbreadth* ape. Also **hair's′-breadth′** (hârz′-), **hairs′breadth′.**
r·brush (hâr′brush′) *n.* A brush for grooming the hair.
r·cloth (hâr′klôth′, -kloth′) *n.* A stiff fabric of horsehair.
r·cut (hâr′kut′) *n.* The act of cutting the hair or the le in which it is cut.
r·do (hâr′dōō′) *n. pl.* **·dos 1.** A style of dressing or arnging a woman's hair. **2.** The hair so arranged.
r·dress·er (hâr′dres′ər) *n.* One who cuts or arranges the r, esp. women's hair.
r·dres·sing (hâr′dres′ing) *n.* **1.** The act of arranging or ssing the hair. **2.** A preparation used in dressing the hair.
red (hârd) *adj.* Having or characterized by a (specified d of) hair: used in combination: *gray-haired.*
r·line (hâr′līn′) *n.* **1.** The edge of the growth of hair on head. **2.** A very thin line. **3.** *Printing* A very thin line a type face; also, a style of type.
r·pin (hâr′pin′) *n.* A thin, U-shaped piece of metal, ne, etc., used by women to hold the hair or a headdress in ce. **—** *adj.* Bending sharply in a U: a *hairpin* curve.
r-rais·er (hâr′rā′zər) *n. Informal* Something that uses excitement or fear. **— hair′-rais′ing** *adj.*
r shirt A girdle or shirt made of haircloth, worn next to e skin by religious ascetics as a penance or mortification.
r space *Printing* The thinnest of the metal spaces for parating letters or words.
r·split·ting (hâr′split′ing) *n.* Insistence upon minute trivial distinctions. **—** *adj.* Characterized by petty or erly fine distinctions. **— hair′split′ter** *n.*
r·spring (hâr′spring′) *n.* The fine spring that regulates e movement of the balance wheel in a watch or clock.

hair trigger A trigger so delicately adjusted that it discharges the firearm at the slightest pressure.
hair-trig·ger (hâr′trig′ər) *adj. Informal* Stimulated or set in operation by the slightest provocation.
hair·y (hâr′ē) *adj.* **hair·i·er, hair·i·est 1.** Covered with or having much hair. **2.** Made of hair. **— hair′i·ness** *n.*
Hai·ti·an (hā′tē·ən, -shən) *adj.* Of or pertaining to Haiti, its people, or their culture. **—** *n.* **1.** A native or inhabitant of Haiti. **2.** A French patois spoken by the Haitians: also **Haitian Creole.** Also spelled *Haytian.*
hake (hāk) *n. pl.* **hake** or **hakes 1.** A marine food fish related to the cod. **2.** The codling[1] (def. 2). [OE *haca* hook]
ha·kim (hä′kēm) *n.* In Moslem countries: **1.** A judge or governor. **2.** A physician. [< Arabic *hakīm* wise]
hal- Var. of HALO-.
hal·berd (hal′bərd; *earlier* hôl′-, hô′-) *n.* A weapon used in the 15th and 16th centuries, an ax and spear combined. [< OF < MHG *helm* handle + *barte* broadax]
hal·cy·on (hal′sē·ən) *n.* A legendary bird supposed to calm the wind and the sea at the winter solstice so as to be able to breed on the water. **—** *adj.* **1.** Calm; peaceful. **2.** Of the halcyon. [< L < Gk. *alkyōn* kingfisher]
halcyon days 1. The seven days before and the seven days after the winter solstice. **2.** Any period of peace and quiet.
hale[1] (hāl) *v.t.* **haled, hal·ing** To compel to go: to *hale* into court. [Var. of HAUL] **— hal′er** *n.*
hale[2] (hāl) *adj.* Having sound and vigorous health; robust. [OE *hāl*] **— hale′ness** *n.*
half (haf, häf) *n. pl.* **halves** (havz, hävz) **1.** Either of two equal or approximately equal parts or quantities into which a thing may be divided. **2.** In sports: **a** In basketball, football, etc., either of two periods into which a game is divided between which play is suspended. **b** *Informal* In football, a halfback. **— better half** *Informal* One's wife or husband. **—** *adj.* **1.** Being either of two equal parts of a thing, amount, value, etc. **2.** Not complete; partial; imperfect. **—** *adv.* **1.** To the extent of half or approximately half. **2.** To a considerable extent; very nearly. **3.** *Informal* To any extent; at all: used with *not*: not *half* bad. [OE *healf*]
half-and-half (haf′ənd·haf′, häf′ənd·häf′) *n.* **1.** A mixture of half one thing and half another. **2.** A mixture of two malt liquors, esp. of porter and ale. **—** *adj.* Half of one thing and half of another. **—** *adv.* In two equal parts.
half·back (haf′bak′, häf′-) *n.* **1.** In football, either of two players who with the quarterback and fullback make up the backfield; also, his position. **2.** In other sports, as field hockey and soccer, a player behind the forward line.
half-baked (haf′bākt′, häf′-) *adj.* **1.** Incompletely baked; doughy. **2.** *Informal* Stupid; half-witted. **3.** *Informal* Imperfectly planned or conceived: a *half-baked* venture.
half blood 1. The relationship between persons with one parent in common; also, a person in such a relationship. **2.** A half-breed. **3.** A half-blooded animal. Also **half-blood** (haf′blud′, häf′-). **— half′-blood′ed** *adj.*
half-breed (haf′brēd′, häf′-) *n.* One having parents of different races; esp., the offspring of a white person and an American Indian. **—** *adj.* Hybrid: also **half-bred** (-bred′).
half brother A brother related through only one parent.
half-caste (haf′kast′, häf′käst′) *n.* **1.** A person having one Asian and one European parent; Eurasian. **2.** A halfbreed. **—** *adj.* Of or pertaining to mixed racial stock.
half cock In a firearm, the position of the hammer when raised halfway and so locked. **— to go off at half cock 1.** To discharge too soon. **2.** *Informal* To act or speak too hastily. Also **to go off half-cocked** (haf′kokt′, häf′-).
half crown An English silver coin worth 2½ shillings.
half dollar A U.S. silver coin worth fifty cents.
half gainer A dive in which one springs forward off the board, twists about, and plunges into the water head first.
half-heart·ed (haf′här′tid, häf′-) *adj.* Possessing or showing little interest, enthusiasm, etc. **— half′heart′ed·ly** *adv.* **— half′heart′ed·ness** *n.*
half hitch A knot made by passing the end of a rope once around the rope, then through the loop, and then drawing the end tight. For illus. see HITCH.
half-hour (haf′our′, häf′-) *n.* **1.** Thirty minutes. **2.** Thirty minutes past the beginning of an hour. **—** *adj.* **1.** Lasting for a half-hour. **2.** Occurring at the half-hour. **— half′-hour′ly** *adj. & adv.*
half life *Physics* The period of time during which half the atoms of a radioactive element or isotope will disintegrate.
half-mast (haf′mast′, häf′mäst′) *n.* The position of a flag flown about halfway up the staff, used in public mourning. **—** *v.t.* To put (a flag, etc.) at half-mast. Also *half-staff.*
half-moon (haf′mōōn′, häf′-) *n.* **1.** The moon when only half its disk is brightly illuminated. **2.** Something similar in shape to a half-moon. **—** *adj.* Shaped like a half-moon.
half nel·son (nel′sən) A wrestling hold in which one arm

is passed under the opponent's armpit, usu. from behind, and the hand pressed against the back of his neck.

half note *Music* A note having one half the time value of a whole note. Also, *esp. Brit., minim.*

half·pen·ny (hā′pən·ē, hāp′nē) *n. pl.* **half·pence** (hā′pəns) or **half·pen·nies** (hā′pən·ēz, hāp′nēz) **1.** The sum of one half of a penny. **2.** A British bronze coin equivalent to such a sum. —*adj.* **1.** Costing a halfpenny. **2.** Of little value.

half pint **1.** A measure of capacity equal to one half of a pint. **2.** *U.S. Slang* A person of short stature.

half sister A sister related through only one parent.

half-sole (haf′sōl′, häf′-) *v.t.* **·soled, ·sol·ing** To repair (a shoe, boot, etc.) by attaching a half sole.

half sole The part of the sole of a boot or shoe extending from the shank or arch to the toe.

half step **1.** *Music* A semitone. **2.** *Mil.* A step of fifteen inches at quick time; in double time, one of eighteen inches.

half·tone (haf′tōn′, häf′-) *n.* **1.** In photoengraving: **a** A picture whose lights and shadows are composed of minute dots obtained by photographing the original through a finely lined screen. **b** The process by which such pictures are made. **2.** In art, photography, etc., any tone or shading halfway between a highlight and a deep shadow.

half tone *Music* A semitone (which see).

half-track (haf′trak′, häf′-) *n.* A vehicle propelled by caterpillar treads in the rear and wheels in front.

half·way (haf′wā′, häf′-) *adv.* **1.** At or to half the distance. **2.** Incompletely; partially. —*adj.* **1.** Midway between two points. **2.** Partial; inadequate.

half-wit (haf′wit′, häf′-) *n.* A feeble-minded person.

half-wit·ted (haf′wit′id, häf′-) *adj.* **1.** Feeble-minded. **2.** Frivolous. —**half′-wit′ted·ly** *adv.* —**half′-wit′ted·ness** *n.*

hal·i·but (hal′ə·bət, hol′-) *n. pl.* **·but** or **·buts** Either of two large flatfishes of northern seas, much esteemed as food. [ME *halybutte*, OE *halig* holy + BUT²]

hal·ide (hal′īd, -id; hā′līd, -lid) *n. Chem.* Any compound of a halogen with an element or radical. Also **hal·id** (hal′id).

hal·ite (hal′īt, hā′līt) *n.* A massive or granular, white or variously colored sodium chloride: also called *rock salt*.

hal·i·to·sis (hal′ə·tō′sis) *n.* Offensive or foul-smelling breath. [< NL < L *halitus* breath + -OSIS]

hall (hôl) *n.* **1.** A passage or corridor in a building. **2.** A vestibule; lobby. **3.** A large building or room used for public business or entertainment. **4.** In a university or college, a large building used for various purposes, as for dormitories, classrooms, etc. **5.** In British universities: **a** A college dining room; also, the dinner. **b** A building where university students reside. **6.** The main house on an estate. **7.** In medieval times, the large main room of a castle. [OE *heall*]

hal·le·lu·jah (hal′ə·lo͞o′yə) *interj.* Praise ye the Lord! —*n.* A musical composition of praise. *Also* **hal′le·lu′iah.** [< Hebrew *hallelū* praise + *yāh* Jehovah]

hal·liard (hal′yərd) See HALYARD.

hall·mark (hôl′märk′) *n.* **1.** An official mark stamped on gold and silver articles in England to guarantee their purity. **2.** Any proof of excellence. —*v.t.* To stamp with a hallmark. [< Goldsmiths' *Hall*, London, where the assaying and stamping were formerly exclusively done + MARK]

hal·loo (hə·lo͞o′) *interj.* A shout to attract attention, etc. —*n.* A cry of "halloo." —*v.i.* **1.** To shout "halloo"; cry out. —*v.t.* **2.** To incite with shouts. **3.** To shout to; hail. **4.** To shout (something). Also **hal·lo** (hə·lō′), **hal·loa** (hə·lō′), **hal·low** (hə·lō). [< OF *halloer* to pursue noisily]

hal·low (hal′ō) *v.t.* **1.** To make holy; consecrate. **2.** To look upon as holy; reverence. [OE *hālig* holy]

hal·lowed (hal′ōd, *in liturgical use* hal′ō·id) *adj.* **1.** Made holy. **2.** Honored as holy. —**hal′lowed·ness** *n.*

Hal·low·een (hal′ō·ēn′, hol′-) *n.* The evening of Oct. 31, vigil of All Saints' Day, celebrated by children with masquerading. Also **Hal′low·e'en′.** [< (ALL) HALLOW(S) E(V)EN]

hal·lu·ci·nate (hə·lo͞o′sə·nāt) *v.t.* **·nat·ed, ·nat·ing** To affect with hallucinations. [< L *hallucinari* to wander mentally]

hal·lu·ci·na·tion (hə·lo͞o′sə·nā′shən) *n.* **1.** *Psychol.* Any of numerous auditory, visual, or tactile perceptions that have no external cause or stimulus. **2.** A mistaken notion.

hal·lu·ci·na·to·ry (hə·lo͞o′sə·nə·tôr′ē, -tō′rē) *adj.* Of, characterized by, or causing hallucination.

hal·lu·ci·no·gen (hə·lo͞o′sin·ə·jən) *n.* Any drug or chemical capable of inducing hallucinations.

hal·lu·ci·no·gen·ic (hə·loo′sə·nə·jen′ik) *adj.* **1.** Causing or having to do with hallucinations or with a distortion of perception. **2.** Of or pertaining to hallucinogens.

hall·way (hôl′wā′) *n. U.S.* **1.** A hall or corridor. **2.** A passage or room leading into the main part of a building.

ha·lo (hā′lō) *n. pl.* **·los** or **·loes** **1.** In art, a disk or ring of light surrounding the head of a deity or holy person; nimbus. **2.** A splendor investing a person or thing held in reverence, etc. **3.** *Meteorol.* A luminous circle around the sun or moon. —*v.t.* **1.** To enclose with a halo. —*v.t.* **2.** To form a halo. [< L < Gk. *halōs* circular threshing floor]

halo- *combining form* **1.** Of or relating to salt. **2.** Of the sea. **3.** Related to or containing a halogen. Also, be vowels, **hal-.** [< Gk. *hals, halos* salt, the sea]

hal·o·gen (hal′ə·jən) *n. Chem.* Any of the group of metallic elements, fluorine, chlorine, bromine, iodine, astatine. [< Gk. *hals* sea, salt + -GEN]

hal·oid (hal′oid, hā′loid) *adj.* Of, like, or derived fr halogen. —*n.* A salt formed from a halogen and a m

halt¹ (hôlt) *n.* A complete but temporary stop in any ac ty or movement. —*v.t. & v.i.* To bring or come to a [< F < G *halten* to stop] —**halt′er** *n.*

halt² (hôlt) *v.i.* **1.** To be imperfect or defective in s way. **2.** To be in doubt; waver. —**the halt** Lame or pled persons. [OE *healt* lame] —**halt′er** *n.*

hal·ter¹ (hôl′tər) *n.* **1.** A strap or rope to lead or secu horse, cow, etc. **2.** A woman's upper garment designe leave the arms and back bare, and held up by a band arc the neck. **3.** A rope with a noose for hanging a person. Death by hanging. —*v.t.* **1.** To secure with a halter. To hang (someone). [OE *hælftre*]

hal·ter² (hal′tər) *n. pl.* **hal·te·res** (hal·tir′ēz) *Ento* One of a pair of appendages on each side of a winged in used to give balance in flight. [< NL < Gk. *haltēres* wei used in jumping]

ha·lutz (ḵhä·lo͞ots′) *n. pl.* **ha·lu·tzim** (ḵhä′lo͞o·tsēm′ pioneer Jewish farmer in Palestine or Israel. [< Heb

halve (hav, häv) *v.t.* **halved, halv·ing** **1.** To divide into equal parts; share equally. **2.** To lessen by half; take a half of. **3.** In golf, to play (a match or hole) in the s number of strokes as one's opponent. [< HALF]

halves (havz, hävz) Plural of HALF. —**by halves** **1.** perfectly. **2.** Half-heartedly.

hal·yard (hal′yərd) *n. Naut.* A rope for hoisting or lo ing a sail, a yard, or a flag: also spelled *halliard, haulya*

ham (ham) *n.* **1.** The thigh of an animal, as of the hog. The meat of a hog's thigh, used for food. **3.** *pl.* The bac the thigh together with the buttocks. **4.** That part of leg behind the knee joint. **5.** *Slang* An actor who over or exaggerates. **6.** *Informal* An amateur radio opera —*v.t. & v.i.* **hammed, ham·ming** *Slang* To act in an e gerated manner. [OE *hamm*] —**ham′my** *adj.*

Ha·man (hā′mən) In the Bible, a Persian minister who hanged when his plot to destroy the Jews was disclosed Esther to King Ahasuerus (*Esth.* iii-vii).

ham·burg (ham′bûrg) *n.* Hamburger.

ham·burg·er (ham′bûr′gər) *n.* **1.** Ground or chopped b Also **hamburger steak.** **2.** A sandwich consisting of s meat placed between the halves of a round roll. [a *Hamburg*, Germany]

Ham·ite (ham′īt) *n.* **1.** A descendant of Ham, one of sons of Noah. **2.** A member of an ethnic group that inclu the ancient Egyptians, inhabiting NE Africa.

Ha·mit·ic (ha·mit′ik) *adj.* **1.** Of or pertaining to Ham the Hamites. **2.** Designating a group of languages spo by the Hamites. —*n.* A North African subfamily of Hamito-Semitic family of languages, including anci Egyptian, the modern Berber dialects, etc.

ham·let (ham′lit) *n.* **1.** A little village. **2.** *Brit.* A vill without a church. [< OF < LL *hamellum* village]

Ham·let (ham′lit) In Shakespeare's play of this name, hero, a Danish prince.

ham·mer (ham′ər) *n.* **1.** A tool usu. consisting of a har with a metal head set crosswise at one end, used for driv nails, etc. **2.** Any object or machine that serves the sa function as or resembles such a tool. **3.** A mechanical p that operates by striking; as: **a** The part of a gunlock t strikes the primer or firing pin. **b** One of the levers that st the strings of a piano. **c** A piece that strikes a bell or go **4.** *Anat.* The malleus, a small bone of the middle ear. illus. see EAR. **5.** An auctioneer's mallet. **6.** A metal b attached to a flexible handle, thrown for distance in athl contests. —**to go** (or **come**) **under the hammer** To be sale at an auction. —*v.t.* **1.** To strike, beat, or drive w or as with a hammer. **2.** To produce or shape with or as w hammer blows. **3.** To join by hammering, as with nails. To force, impress, etc., by emphatic repetition. —*v.i.* To strike blows with or as with a hammer. **6.** To have sound or feeling of rapid pounding: My heart *hammers*. To work at persistently: to *hammer* away at a task. [*hamer*] —**ham′mer·er** *n.*

ham·mer·head (ham′ər·hed′) *n.* A voracious shark warm seas, having a transversely elongated head with eyes at each end.

hammer lock A wrestling hold in which an opponent's a is twisted behind his back and upward.

ham·mock (ham′ək) *n.* A hanging bed or couch of stu cloth or netting, suspended from a support at each end. Sp. *hamaca* < native West Indian name]

ham·per¹ (ham′pər) *v.t.* To interfere with the moveme of; impede. [ME *hampren*]

ham·per² (ham′pər) *n.* A large, usu. covered basket, oft used to store soiled laundry. [< OF *hanapier* a cup case

·ster (ham′stər) *n.* Any of various burrowing rodents, d as a laboratory animal. [< G < OHG *hamastro*]
·string (ham′string′) *n.* **1.** One of the tendons at the k of the human knee. **2.** The large sinew at the back of hock of a quadruped. —*v.t.* **·strung, ·string·ing 1.** To ple by cutting the hamstring of. **2.** To frustrate.
d (hand) *n.* **1.** In man and other primates, the end of the arm beyond the wrist, comprising the palm, fingers, and mb. ◆ Collateral adjective: *manual.* **2.** In other organs, a part that serves a similar function. **3.** An action formed by the hand or as by the hand: to die by one's n *hand.* **4.** The use of the hand or hands: to launder by d. **5.** A characteristic mark, or kind of work: the *hand* master. **6.** A part or role: We all had a *hand* in it **7.** istance: to give a *hand.* **8.** *Usu. pl.* Supervisory care: in d's *hands.* **9.** A pledge or promise, often of marriage. A position to the side: on the right *hand.* **11.** One of or more sides, aspects, or viewpoints: usu. with *on*: on one *hand.* **12.** A source of information, etc.: at second d. **13.** A person, considered as producing something. A person, considered with reference to his skill. **15.** A nual laborer: a stage *hand.* **16.** Style of handwriting. A person's signature. **18.** Show of approval by clapg. **19.** Something that resembles a hand in function, as pointer of a clock. **20.** A unit of measurement four hes long, used to state the height of horses. **21.** In card nes: **a** The cards held by a player in one round of a game. he player. **c** The complete playing of all the cards given at one deal. **—at hand 1.** Near by; readily available. About to occur. **—at the hand** (or **hands**) **of** By the ion of. **—clean hands** Freedom from guilt. **—from nd to hand** Into the possession of one person after aner. **—from hand to mouth** Using or spending immediy all of one's income, provisions, etc. **—hand and foot** So as to satisfy all needs or wishes. **2.** So as to be unable move the hands and feet. **—hand in** (or **and**) **glove** In se alliance or connection. **—hand in hand** Each holding hand of the other; in close association. **—hands down** th ease; effortlessly. **—Hands off!** A command not to ch or interfere. **—Hands up!** A command to raise the nds, intended to forestall resistance. **—in hand 1.** In 's immediate grasp or possession. **2.** Under control. **3.** process of execution. **—off one's hands** Out of one's e or responsibility. **—on hand 1.** In one's possession; ailable for use. **2.** *U.S.* Present. **—on one's hands** In 's care or responsibility. **—out of hand 1.** Unruly; untrollable. **2.** Immediately. **3.** Finished and done with. **to hand 1.** Within reach; readily accessible. **2.** In one's session. **—to have one's hands full** To be engaged in a at or excessive amount of work. **—to keep one's hand** To continue an activity or interest so as not to lose skill or owledge. **—to lay hands on 1.** To do physical harm to. To bless, consecrate, ordain, etc. **—to show one's hand** disclose one's involvement or intentions. **—to turn** (or t) **one's hand to** To engage in; undertake. **—to throw up e's hands** To give up in despair. **—to wash one's hands** To refuse further responsibility for. **—upper hand** The ntrolling advantage. **—with a heavy hand 1.** In a msy manner or style. **2.** In an overbearing manner. **—h a high hand** In an arrogant, tyrannical manner. —*v.t.* give, offer, assist, or transmit with the hand or hands. **— hand down 1.** To transmit to one's heirs. **2.** To deliver announce the decision or verdict of a court. **—to hand in** give to a person or persons in authority; submit. **—to nd it to** *Slang* To give deserved praise or recognition to. **— hand on** To give to the next in succession. **—to hand out** distribute. **—to hand over** To give up possession of. — j. Of or pertaining to the hand or hands; as: **a** Suitable for rying in the hand. **b** Operated by hand. **c** Executed by nd: *hand* embroidery. [OE *hand*]
nd·bag (hand′bag′) *n.* **1.** A woman's purse or other bag carrying small articles. **2.** A small suitcase.
nd·ball (hand′bôl′) *n.* A game in which the players hit ball with their hand against the wall of a court.
nd·bar·row (hand′bar′ō) *n.* A flat framework for carry loads, having handles at either end for the bearers.
nd·bill (hand′bil′) *n.* A printed advertisement or notice.
nd·book (hand′bo͝ok′) *n.* **1.** A small guidebook or book instructions. **2.** *U.S.* A place away from a racetrack here bets are made; also, the record of such bets.
nd·breadth (hand′bredth′, -bretth′) *n.* A unit of measurement, usually 2½ to 4 inches: also *hand's breadth.*
nd·car (hand′kär′) *n.* A small, open railroad car propelled by a hand pump or a motor.
nd·cart (hand′kärt′) *n.* A cart pushed or pulled by hand.
nd·clasp (hand′klasp′, -kläsp′) *n.* The act of clasping a rson's hand, as in greeting, an introduction, etc.
nd·cuff (hand′kuf′) *n.* *Usu. pl.* One of a pair of metal rings joined by a chain, designed to lock around the wrist or wrists; a manacle. —*v.t.* To fetter with handcuffs.
hand·ed (han′did) *adj.* **1.** Characterized by or designed for the use of a (specified) hand: a *left-handed* batter. **2.** Having or characterized by a (specified kind of) hand or (a specified number of) hands: *four-handed; empty-handed.*
hand·ful (hand′fo͝ol) *n. pl.* **·fuls 1.** As much or as many as a hand can hold at once. **2.** A small number or quantity. **3.** *Informal* Something or someone difficult to control.
hand·i·cap (han′dē·kap) *n.* **1.** A race or contest in which disadvantages are imposed on superior contestants or advantages given to those of inferior ability, so that each may have an equal chance of winning. **2.** One of the conditions stipulated; esp., a disadvantage. **3.** Any disadvantage. — *v.t.* **·capped, ·cap·ping 1.** To serve as a hindrance or disadvantage to. **2.** To assign handicaps in a race. [? < *hand in cap,* a lottery game] **—hand′i·cap·per** *n.*
hand·i·craft (han′dē·kraft′, -kräft′) *n.* **1.** Skill and expertness in working with the hands. **2.** An occupation requiring such skill. Also *U.S.* **hand′craft′.** [OE *handcræft*]
hand·i·ly (han′də·lē) *adv.* **1.** In a handy manner; dexterously; easily. **2.** Conveniently.
hand·i·ness (han′dē·nis) *n.* **1.** Manual skill; expertness. **2.** Convenience. **—Syn.** See DEXTERITY.
hand·i·work (han′dē·wûrk′) *n.* **1.** Work done by the hands; any article or articles made by hand. **2.** The result or product of working or action. [OE *handgeweorc*]
hand·ker·chief (hang′kər·chif) *n.* A piece of cloth, usu. square, used for wiping the nose or face.
han·dle (han′dəl) *v.* **·dled, dling** *v.t.* **1.** To touch, hold, or move with the hand or hands. **2.** To use the hands upon; manipulate: to *handle* clay. **3.** To have control over. **4.** To dispose of; deal with. **5.** To treat of or discuss. **6.** To act or behave toward. **7.** To trade or deal in as a commodity. —*v.i.* **8.** To respond to manipulation or control. —*n.* **1.** That part of an object designed to be grasped in the hand. **2.** Something that resembles or serves as a handle. **3.** That which serves as an opportunity in achieving a desired end. **4.** *Informal* A title added to a person's name. **—to fly off the handle** To become angry. [OE *hand* hand]
han·dle·bar (han′dəl·bär′) *n.* *Usu. pl.* **1.** The curved steering bar of a bicycle, etc. **2.** *U.S. Informal* A luxuriant mustache resembling handlebars: also **handlebar mustache.**
han·dler (hand′lər) *n.* **1.** One who handles. **2.** In sports, one who trains or manages animals, boxers, etc.
hand·made (hand′mād′) *adj.* Made by hand.
hand-me-down (hand′mē·doun′) *n.* *Informal* A worn or outgrown garment passed on to another person.
hand organ A large music box played by turning a hand crank; barrel organ.
hand·out (hand′out′) *n.* **1.** Any free ration of food, money, apparel, etc. **2.** A prepared, distributed statement.
hand-pick (hand′pik′) *v.t.* **1.** To gather by hand. **2.** To choose with care. **3.** To select for a particular purpose or job.
hand·rail (hand′rāl′) *n.* A railing of a height for grasping in the hand, used at a staircase, balcony, etc.
hand·saw (hand′sô′) *n.* A saw used with one hand.
hand's breadth A handbreadth.
hand·sel (hand′səl, han′-) *n.* A gift given at the start of a new year, enterprise, or situation in life. —*v.t.* **hand·seled** or **·selled, hand·sel·ing** or **·sel·ling** To give a handsel to. Also spelled *hansel.* [OE *hand* hand + *selen* gift]
hand·set (hand′set′) *n.* A telephone receiver and transmitter combined in a unit that may be held in one hand.
hand·shake (hand′shāk′) *n.* The act of clasping and shaking a person's hand, as in greeting, agreement, parting, etc.
hand·some (han′səm) *adj.* **1.** Pleasing or well-proportioned in appearance, form, feature, etc. **2.** Considerable; ample. **3.** Generous; gracious. [< HAND + -SOME "easy to handle"] **—hand′some·ly** *adv.* **—hand′some ness** *n.*
hand·spike (hand′spīk′) *n.* A bar used as a lever for moving heavy objects.
hand·spring (hand′spring′) *n.* An acrobatic turn in which the body is supported by one or both hands while the feet are quickly passed in an arc over the head.
hand-to-hand (hand′tə·hand′) *adj.* At close quarters.
hand-to-mouth (hand′tə·mouth′) *adj.* Consuming immediately what is obtained; improvident or impoverished.
hand·work (hand′wûrk′) *n.* Work done by hand.
hand·writ·ing (hand′rī′ting) *n.* **1.** Writing done by hand, as distinct from printing, typing, etc.; calligraphy. **2.** A characteristic style or form of writing. **—to see the handwriting on the wall** To sense or be aware beforehand of impending misfortune, etc.
hand·y (han′dē) *adj.* **hand·i·er, hand·i·est 1.** Ready at hand; available; nearby. **2.** Skillful. **3.** Useful.
hand·y·man (han′dē·man′) *n. pl.* **·men** (-men′) A man employed to perform odd jobs. Also **handy man.**

hang (hang) *v.* **hung** or (*esp. for defs 3, 12*) **hanged, hang·ing** *v.t.* **1.** To fasten, attach, or support from above only. **2.** To attach by means of a hinge, etc. **3.** To put to death on a gallows, cross, etc. **4.** To cause to bend downward; to *hang* one's head. **5.** To decorate or cover with things suspended; also, to fasten (wallpaper) to a wall. **6.** To suspend (pictures, etc.) in a gallery for display. **7.** *U.S.* To cause (a jury, etc.) to be unable to reach a decision. **8.** To damn: used as a mild oath. — *v.i.* **9.** To be suspended from above; dangle. **10.** To be attached so as to swing easily. **11.** To fall, drape, or fit. **12.** To be put to death or to die by hanging. **13.** To bend or project downward; droop. **14.** To keep one's hold; cling: with *on* or *onto*. **15.** To hover; float in the air. **16.** To be imminent; threaten: with *over*. **17.** To depend; be contingent: with *on* or *upon*. **18.** To be in a state of uncertainty or indecision. **19.** To pay close attention: He *hung* on her words. — **to be hung up** *U.S. Slang* To be halted or impeded, usu. temporarily. — **to hang around** (or **about**) *Informal* To loiter or linger about. — **to hang back** To be reluctant or unwilling. — **to hang in the balance** To be undecided or doubtful. — **to hang on** To be tenacious; persist. — **to hang one on** *U.S. Slang* **1.** To get very drunk. **2.** To strike (someone) with the fist. — **to hang out 1.** To lean out, as through a window. **2.** *Slang* To spend one's time. — **to hang together 1.** To remain in close association. **2.** To be coherent or consistent. — **to hang up 1.** *Chiefly U.S.* To end a telephone conversation. **2.** To delay or suspend the progress of. — *n.* **1.** The way in which a thing hangs. **2.** *Informal* A bit; a rap: I don't give a *hang*. — **to get the hang of** *U.S. Informal* **1.** To acquire the knack of. **2.** To understand the basic idea of. [Fusion of ME *hangen* and ME *henge* to cause to hang]

han·gar (hang′ər) *n.* A shelter, esp. one for aircraft. [< F]

hang·dog (hang′dôg′, -dog′) *adj.* Sneaky, furtive, or degraded in manner or appearance. — *n.* A low sneak.

hang·er (hang′ər) *n.* **1.** A device on or from which something may be hung; esp., a hooked frame of shoulder width for garments. **2.** One who hangs something.

hang·er-on (hang′ər·on′, -ôn′) *n. pl.* **hang·ers-on** (hang′·ərz-) A clinging or self-seeking follower; parasite.

hang·fire (hang′fīr′) *n.* A delay in the explosion of a propelling charge, igniter, or the like.

hang·ing (hang′ing) *adj.* **1.** Suspended from something. **2.** Leaning or inclining downward. **3.** Lying on a steep slope: a *hanging* meadow. **4.** Worthy of or involving capital punishment. **5.** Undecided: The matter was left *hanging*. — *n.* **1.** The act of suspending, or the state of being suspended. **2.** Execution by being hanged from the neck. **3.** *Usu. pl.* Something hung on a wall, window, etc.

hang·man (hang′mən) *n. pl.* **·men** (-mən) A public executioner who hangs condemned persons.

hang·nail (hang′nāl′) *n.* Skin partially torn loose at the side or root of a fingernail.

hang·out (hang′out′) *n. Slang* A habitual loitering or dwelling place of some person or group: a thieves' *hangout*.

hang·o·ver (hang′ō′vər) *n. U.S. Informal* **1.** The headache following overindulgence in alcoholic liquor. **2.** Something or someone remaining from a past era or regime.

hang-up (hang′up′) *n. Slang* **1.** A psychological difficulty, esp. an obsession. **2.** Any block or obstacle to a process.

hank (hangk) *n.* **1.** A skein of yarn or thread. **2.** A measure of yarn or thread. **3.** A loop or curl, as of hair. [ME]

han·ker (hang′kər) *v.i.* To yearn; have desire: with *after*, *for*, or an infinitive. [Cf. Flemish *hankeren* to long for.]

hank·er·ing (hang′kər·ing) *n.* A yearning; craving.

han·ky-pan·ky (hang′kē·pang′kē) *n. Slang* **1.** Deceitful or mischievous behavior. **2.** Foolish talk; blather. [? Formed on analogy with HOCUS-POCUS]

Hanse (hans) *n.* The Hanseatic League.

Han·se·at·ic League (han′sē·at′ik) A medieval league of free towns in northern Germany and neighboring countries for mutual protection and trade advantages.

han·sel (han′səl) See **HANDSEL.**

Han·sen's disease (han′sənz) Leprosy. [after Gerhart *Hansen*, 1841–1912, Norwegian physician]

han·som (han′səm) *n.* A low, two-wheeled, one-horse carriage, with the driver seated behind and above the cab: also **hansom cab.** [after J. A *Hansom*, 1803–82, English inventor]

HANSOM

Ha·nuk·kah (khä′nōō·kə, hä′-) *n.* A Jewish festival, lasting eight days from Kislev 25 (early December), in memory of the rededication of the temple at Jerusalem under the Maccabees in 164 B.C.: also *Chanukah*. Also **Ha′nu·kah.** [< Hebrew *hanukkah* dedication]

hap·haz·ard (hap′haz′ərd) *adj.* Dependent upon or happening by chance; accidental; random. — *n.* Mere chance; hazard. — *adv.* By chance; at random. — **hap′haz′ard·ly** *adv.* — **hap′haz′ard·ness** *n.*

hap·less (hap′lis) *adj.* Having no luck; unfortunate; unlucky. — **hap′less·ly** *adv.* — **hap′less·ness** *n.*

haplo- *combining form* Simple; single: also, before vo **hapl-.** [< Gk. *haploos* simple]

hap·loid (hap′loid) *adj. Biol.* Having only one set of paired chromosomes, as a germ cell, in contradistinctio the normal diploid number as found in somatic cells. **hap·loid′ic.** — *n.* A haploid organism or cell.

hap·pen (hap′ən) *v.i.* **1.** To take place or occur; com pass. **2.** To occur by chance rather than by design. **3** chance: We *happened* to hear him sing. **4.** To com chance: with *on* or *upon*. **5.** To come or go by chance: *in, along, by*, etc. — **to happen to 1.** To befall. **2.** T come of: What *happened to* your old friend? [ME *happe*

hap·pen·ing (hap′ən·ing) *n.* **1.** An event; occurrence. A staged event, usu. partly improvised and often spectac

hap·pen·stance (hap′ən·stans, -stəns) *n. U.S. Info* A chance occurrence; accident.

hap·py (hap′ē) *adj.* **·pi·er, ·pi·est 1.** Enjoying, showin characterized by pleasure; joyous; contented. **2.** Atte with good fortune; lucky. **3.** Produced or uttered with and aptness; felicitous: a *happy* phrase. [ME *happi* < an occurrence] — **hap′pi·ly** *adv.* — **hap′pi·ness** *n.*

hap·py-go-luck·y (hap′ē·gō·luk′ē) *adj.* Trusting habitu to luck; cheerful; unconcerned; easygoing.

ha·ri-ki·ri (har′ə·kir′ē; hä′rä·kē′rē) *n.* Suicide by embowelment, traditionally practiced by high-ranking J nese when disgraced: also *hari-kari*. Also **ha′ra-ka′ri** (- rē). [< Japanese *hara* belly + *kiri* cut]

ha·rangue (hə·rang′) *n.* A lengthy, loud, and vehem speech; tirade. — *v.* **·rangued, ·rangu·ing** *v.t.* **1.** To dress in a harangue. — *v.i.* **2.** To deliver a harangue. F < Med.L < OHG *hari* army, host + *hringa* ring] — **rangu′er** *n.*

har·ass (har′əs, hə·ras′) *v.t.* **1.** To trouble or pursue rel lessly with cares, annoyances, etc.; torment. **2.** *Mil.* worry (an enemy) by raids and small attacks. [< O *harer* to set dogs on] — **har′ass·er** *n.* — **har′ass·men**

har·bin·ger (här′bin·jər) *n.* One who or that which goes fore and announces the coming of something; herald. — To act as a harbinger to; presage; herald. [< OF < *berge* shelter < Gmc.]

har·bor (här′bər) *n.* **1.** A sheltered place, natural or ar cial, on the coast of a sea, lake, etc., used to provide protec and anchorage for ships; port. **2.** Any place of refug rest. — *v.t.* **1.** To give refuge to; shelter; esp., to conce be hospitable to harmful persons or things: to *harbor* thie **2.** To entertain in the mind; cherish: to *harbor* a grudge. *v.i.* **3.** To take shelter in or as in a harbor. Also *Brit.* **h bour.** [ME < OE *here* army + *beorg* refuge]

har·bor·age (här′bər·ij) *n.* **1.** A port or place of ancho for ships. **2.** Shelter; lodging; entertainment.

har·bor·mas·ter (här′bər·mas′tər, -mäs′-) *n.* An office charge of enforcing the regulations of a harbor.

hard (härd) *adj.* **1.** Resisting indentation or compress solid; firm; unyielding. **2.** Requiring vigorous menta physical effort to do, solve, understand, explain, etc.; d cult. **3.** Energetic and steady; industrious: a *hard* wor **4.** Showing little mercy or feeling; stern: a *hard* judge. Strict or exacting in terms: a *hard* bargain. **6.** Having f or intensity; severe; violent: a *hard* knock. **7.** Involvin inflicting sorrow, discomfort, pain, poverty, etc.: *hard* ti **8.** *U.S. Informal* Verified and specific: said of facts, in mation, etc. **9.** Given to shrewdness, practicality, and stinacy: a *hard* head. **10.** Too harsh, brilliant, or penet ing: a *hard* light. **11.** *U.S. Informal* Menacing, cruel disreputable in character or appearance; tough: a *hard* f **12.** Containing certain mineral salts that interfere with cleansing action of soap: said of water. **13.** *U.S.* Contai much alcohol; strong: *hard* cider. **14.** *Agric.* High in glu content: said of wheat. **15.** *Phonet.* Denoting (c) or when articulated as a stop, as in *cod* or *god*, and not a fricative or affricate. **16.** *Physics* Denoting radiant ene of great penetrating power, as gamma rays. — **hard fast** Fixed and unalterable. — **hard of hearing** Dea partially deaf. — **hard up** *Informal* **1.** Poor; broke. **2.** need of (something): with *for*. — **to be hard on** To severe, cruel, or damaging to. — *adv.* **1.** With great ene or force; vigorously: to work *hard*. **2.** Intently; earnes to look *hard* for something. **3.** With effort or difficulty breathe *hard*. **4.** With resistance; reluctantly: to die *h* **5.** Securely; tightly: to hold on *hard*. **6.** So as to bec firm or solid: to freeze *hard*. **7.** In close proximity; n with *after*, *by*, or *upon*. **8.** *Naut.* To the extreme li fully: *Hard* aport. — **to be hard put** To have great d culty. — **to go hard with** To be very painful and harsh [OE *heard*] — **hard′ness** *n.*

hard-bit·ten (härd′bit′n) *adj.* Tough; unyielding.

hard-boiled (härd′boild′) *adj.* **1.** Boiled until cool through: said of an egg. **2.** *Informal* Callous; tough.

hard cash Actual money; cash on hand.

l cider Cider that has fermented.
l coal Anthracite.
l-core (härd′kôr′, -kōr′) *adj. U.S.* Unlikely to change; exible; rigid: a *hard-core* radical.
l·en (här′dən) *v.t. & v.i.* To make or become hard in ious senses. — **hard′en·er** *n.*
l-fist·ed (härd′fis′tid) *adj.* **1.** Stingy; miserly. **2.** Hav- hard hands, as a laborer. — **hard′-fist′ed·ness** *n.*
l·head (härd′hed′) *n. pl.* **·heads** **1.** A shrewd and ctical person. **2.** An obstinate person.
l·head·ed (härd′hed′id) *adj.* **1.** Having a shrewd and ctical mind. **2.** Having a stubborn character; obstinate. **hard′head′ed·ly** *adv.* — **hard′head′ed·ness** *n.*
l·heart·ed (härd′här′tid) *adj.* Lacking pity; unfeeling. **hard′heart′ed·ly** *adv.* — **hard′heart′ed·ness** *n.*
di·hood (här′dē·ho͝od) *n.* **1.** Resolute courage; bold- s; daring. **2.** Audacity; impudence.
l labor Compulsory physical labor imposed upon im- oned criminals as part of their punishment.
d·ly (härd′lē) *adv.* **1.** Scarcely; barely; only just: I *dly* felt it. **2.** Not quite; not: That is *hardly* enough.
d-nosed (härd′nōzd′) *adj. Slang* Hard-bitten; unyielding.
l·pan (härd′pan′) *n. U.S.* **1.** A layer of very hard, n claylike matter under soft soil. **2.** Solid, unbroken und. **3.** The firm foundation of anything.
l rubber Vulcanite.
l sauce Butter, sugar, and flavorings creamed together eaten on puddings, etc.
d-shell (härd′shel′) *adj.* **1.** Having a hard shell. **2.** *S. Informal* Rigidly orthodox; inflexible.
d·ship (härd′ship) *n.* **1.** A difficult, painful condition, rom privation, suffering, etc. **2.** An instance of this.
d·tack (härd′tack′) *n.* Hard, crackerlike biscuit.
d·top (härd′top′) *n.* An automobile with the body design a convertible, but with a rigid top.
d·ware (härd′wâr′) *n.* **1.** Manufactured articles of tal, as utensils or tools. **2.** Weapons: military *hardware.* Any of the machinery that makes up a digital computer tallation: distinguished from *software.*
d·wood (härd′wo͝od′) *n.* **1.** Wood from deciduous trees, oak, maple, etc., as distinguished from the wood of conifer- trees. **2.** Any hard, compact, heavy wood. **3.** A tree lding such wood.
·dy[1] (här′dē) *adj.* **·di·er, ·di·est** **1.** Able to endure hard- p, fatigue, privation, etc.; robust; tough. **2.** Having cour- and valor. **3.** Foolhardy; rash. **4.** Able to survive the ter outdoors: said of plants. [< OF < OHG *hartjan* to ke hard] — **har′di·ly** *adv.* — **har′di·ness** *n.*
·dy[2] (här′dē) *n. pl.* **·dies** A square-shanked chisel or er for insertion in a square hole (**hardy hole**) in a black- ith's anvil.
e (hâr) *n. pl.* **hares** or **hare** **1.** A mammal allied to but ger than the rabbit, having long ears and long hind legs. Collateral adjective: *leporine.* **2.** The common American bit. [OE *hara*]
e·bell (hâr′bel′) *n.* A perennial herb with blue, bell- ped flowers. Also called *bluebell.*
e·brained (hâr′brānd′) *adj.* Foolish; flighty; giddy.
e·lip (hâr′lip′) *n.* A congenital fissure of the upper lip, embling the cleft lip of a hare. — **hare′lipped′** *adj.*
·em (hâr′əm, har′-) *n.* **1.** The apartments of a Moslem isehold reserved for females. **2.** The women occupying harem. [< Arabic < *harama* to forbid]
·i·cot (har′ə·kō) *n.* **1.** A stew of meat, esp. mutton, and getables; ragout. **2.** The kidney bean or its pods. [< F]
·i-ka·ri (har′ē·kar′ē; hä′rē·kä′rē) *n.* Hara-kiri.
k (härk) *v.i.* To listen; harken: usu. in the imperative. **to hark back** To return to some previous point; revert. *n.* A cry used to urge on or guide hounds. [ME *herkien*]
k·en (här′kən) *v.i. Poetic* To listen; give heed. Also lled *hearken.* [OE *heorcnian*]
·le·quin (här′lə·kwin, -kin) *n.* A buffoon. — *adj.* **1.** rti-colored; motley, like the dress of a Harlequin. **2.** Des- ating eyeglasses with frames slanting upward like the eyes a Harlequin's mask. [< MF < Ital. *arlecchino*, prob. akin OF *Herlequin*, a devil in medieval legend]
·le·quin (här′lə·kwin, -kin) A pantomime character ditionally dressed in parti-colored tights, with masked e, and bearing a wooden sword.
·lot (här′lət) *n.* A prostitute. [< OF, rogue]
·lot·ry (här′lət·rē) *n. pl.* **·ries** Prostitution.
m (härm) *n.* **1.** Injury; damage; hurt. **2.** Wrong; evil. *v.t.* To do harm to; damage; hurt. [OE *hearm* an insult]
m·ful (härm′fəl) *adj.* Having power to injure or do rm. — **harm′ful·ly** *adv.* — **harm′ful·ness** *n.*
m·less (härm′lis) *adj.* Inflicting no injury; not harmful; nocuous. — **harm′less·ly** *adv.* — **harm′less·ness** *n.*
·mon·ic (här·mon′ik) *adj.* **1.** Producing, characterized by, or pertaining to harmony; consonant; harmonious. **2.** *Music* **a** Pertaining to harmony in musical sounds. **b** Pertaining to a tone whose rate of vibration is an integral multiple of a given primary tone. **3.** *Physics* Designating or characterized by a harmonic. — *n.* **1.** *Music* **a** A tone on a stringed instrument produced by touching a string lightly at a point. **b** A partial tone with a vibration rate that is an integral multiple of a given primary tone. **2.** *Physics* Any component of a periodic quantity that is an integral multiple of a given fundamental frequency. [< L < Gk. < *harmonia* harmony] — **har·mon′i·cal·ly** *adv.*
har·mon·i·ca (här·mon′i·kə) *n.* **1.** A musical instrument consisting of metal reeds fixed in slots in a small oblong frame, and played by blowing and inhaling through the slots: also called *mouth organ.* **2.** An instrument composed of glass or metal strips, struck by hammers.
har·mon·ics (här·mon′iks) *n.pl.* (*construed as sing. in def. 1*) **1.** The branch of acoustics dealing with musical sounds. **2.** *Music* The overtones of a fundamental.
har·mo·ni·ous (här·mō′nē·əs) *adj.* **1.** Made up of sounds, colors, or other elements that combine agreeably: a *harmonious* pattern. **2.** Manifesting agreement and concord in views, attitudes, feelings, etc. **3.** Pleasing to the ear; euphonious. — **har·mo′ni·ous·ly** *adv.* — **har·mo′ni·ous·ness** *n.*
har·mo·ni·um (här·mō′nē·əm) *n.* A type of reed organ in which air is compressed in the bellows, then driven out through the reeds; melodeon. [< F < L *harmonia*]
har·mo·nize (här′mə·nīz) *v.t. & v.i.* **·nized, ·niz·ing** **1.** To make or become harmonious, suitable, or agreeable. **2.** To arrange or sing in musical harmony. **3.** To show the harmony or agreement of, as the Gospels. Also *Brit.* **har′mo·nise.** — **har′mo·ni·za′tion** *n.* — **har′mo·niz′er** *n.*
har·mo·ny (här′mə·nē) *n. pl.* **·nies** **1.** Accord or agreement in feeling, manner, action, etc.: to live in *harmony.* **2.** A state of order, agreement, or esthetically pleasing relationships among the elements of a whole. **3.** Pleasing sounds; music. **4.** *Music* **a** A simultaneous combination of tones or a group of melodic tones that suggest a simultaneous combination. **b** Musical structure in terms of the relations between successive harmonies. **c** The science or study of this structure. **5.** A scholarly work displaying the similarities, etc., of different books or passages: a *harmony* of the Gospels. [< OF < L < Gk. < *harmozein* to join]
— **Syn. 1, 2.** Concord, accord, consonance, congruity.
har·ness (här′nis) *n.* **1.** The combination of traces, straps, etc., forming the gear of a draft animal and used to attach it to a wheeled vehicle or plow. **2.** Any similar arrangement of straps, cords, etc.; esp., one used for attaching something, as a parachute, to the body. — **in harness** Working at one's routine job. — *v.t.* **1.** To put harness on (a horse, etc.). **2.** To make use of the power or potential of: to *harness* a waterfall. [< OF *harneis*; ult. origin unknown] — **har′ness·er** *n.*
harp (härp) *n.* **1.** A stringed musical instrument that in its present form is upright and triangular in shape, and is played by plucking with the fingers. **2.** A harplike object or device. — **to harp on** (or **upon**) To talk or write about persistently and vexatiously. [OE *hearpe*] — **harp′er** *n.*
harp·ist (här′pist) *n.* One who plays the harp.
har·poon (här·po͞on′) *n.* A barbed missile weapon, carrying a long cord, for striking whales or large fish. — *v.t.* To strike, take, or kill with or as with a harpoon. [< F < *harpe* claw] — **har·poon′er, har′poon·eer′** (ir′) *n.*
harpoon gun A gun that fires a harpoon, used in whaling.
harp·si·chord (härp′sə·kôrd) *n.* A keyboard instrument widely used from the 16th to the 18th century and revived in the 20th, having the strings plucked by quills or leather points instead of struck. [< MF *harpechorde* < Ital. < LL *harpa* harp + L *chorda* string]
har·py (här′pē) *n. pl.* **·pies** **1.** A rapacious, predatory person, esp. a woman. **2.** A large, crested, voracious tropical American eagle: also **harpy eagle.** [< HARPY]
Har·py (här′pē) *n. pl.* **·pies** In Greek mythology, one of several winged monsters with the head of a woman and the body of a bird, who carried off the souls of the dead, etc. [< F *Harpie* < L < Gk. < *harpazein* to seize]
har·que·bus (här′kwə·bəs) *n.* An early portable firearm, in its later form having a matchlock and fired from a forked rest: also *arquebus.* [< F < MLG *hakebusse* hooked gun]
har·ri·dan (har′ə·dən) *n.* A hateful old woman; vicious hag. [< OF *haridelle* jade]
har·ri·er (har′ē·ər) *n.* **1.** A small hound used for hunting hares. **2.** A cross-country runner.
har·row (har′ō) *n.* A farm implement set with spikes or disks, for leveling plowed ground, breaking clods, etc. For illus. see DISK HARROW. — *v.t.* **1.** To draw a harrow over (a field, etc.). **2.** To disturb the mind or feelings of painfully; distress. — *v.i.* **3.** To undergo harrowing. [ME *harwe*, prob. < Scand.] — **har′row·er** *n.*

NUNCIATION KEY: add, āce, câre, pälm; end, ēven; it, īce; odd, ōpen, ôrder; to͝ok, po͞ol; up, bûrn; ə = a in *above*, e in *sicken*, i in *flex-* o in *melon*, u in *focus*; yo͞o = u in *fuse*; oil; pout; check; go; ring; thin; this; zh, vision.

har·row·ing (har′ō·ing) *adj.* Lacerating or tormenting to the feelings. — **har′row·ing·ly** *adv.*
har·ry (har′ē) *v.* **·ried, ·ry·ing** *v.t.* **1.** To lay waste, as in war or invasion; pillage; sack. **2.** To harass in any way. — *v.i.* **3.** To make raids. [OE *hergian* to ravage]
harsh (härsh) *adj.* **1.** Grating, rough, or unpleasant to any of the senses: a *harsh* tone; a *harsh* light. **2.** Unpleasing to the mind or the artistic sense; ungraceful; crude. **3.** Manifesting severity; cruel: a *harsh* punishment. [ME *harsk*, prob. < Scand.] — **harsh′ly** *adv.* — **harsh′ness** *n.*
hart (härt) *n.* The male of the red deer, esp. after it has passed its fifth year. [OE *heort*]
harte·beest (härt′bēst, här′tə-) *n.* A large, grayish brown antelope of Africa. Also **hart′beest.** [< Afrikaans < Du. *hert* hart + *beest* beast]
harts·horn (härts′hôrn′) *n.* **1.** The antler of a hart, **2.** Ammonium carbonate or a preparation made from it.
har·um-scar·um (hâr′əm·skâr′əm) *adj.* Reckless and wild; harebrained; irresponsible. — *adv.* In a wild, unrestrained manner. — *n.* **1.** A reckless person. **2.** Wild and heedless behavior. [prob. < obs. *hare* to frighten + SCARE]
har·vest (här′vist) *n.* **1.** The act of gathering or collecting a ripened crop of grain, fruit, vegetables, etc. **2.** The yield of such a crop; also, the crop itself. **3.** The time of year when such crops are gathered. **4.** The products of any effort. — *v.t. & v.i.* **1.** To gather (a crop). **2.** To gather the crop of (a field, hive, etc.). **3.** To reap or suffer (consequences, etc.). [OE *harfest* autumn, harvest]
har·vest·er (här′vis·ter) *n.* **1.** One who harvests. **2.** A reaping machine.
har·vest·man (här′vist·mən) *n.* *pl.* **·men** (-mən) **1.** One who labors in the harvest. **2.** A daddy-longlegs.
harvest moon The full moon that occurs near the autumnal equinox.
has (haz) Present indicative, third person singular, of HAVE.
has-been (haz′bin′) *n.* *Informal* One who or that which is no longer popular or effective.
ha·sen·pfef·fer (hä′sən·fef′ər) *n.* A highly seasoned dish made of marinated rabbit, braised and simmered. [< G < *hase* rabbit, hare + *pfeffer* pepper]
hash (hash) *n.* **1.** A dish of chopped meat and potatoes or other vegetables, usu. sautéed, then baked or browned. **2.** A mess; jumble; mishmash. — **to make a hash of** *Informal* **1.** To bungle; spoil; mess up. **2.** To destroy or overcome (an argument, adversary, etc.). — **to settle** (or **fix**) **one's hash** *Informal* To deal with punitively; to subdue. — *v.t.* **1.** To cut or chop into small pieces; mince. **2.** *U.S. Informal* To discuss at length: often with *over.* **3.** *U.S. Informal* To make a mess of things. [< OF *hacher* to chop]
hash house *U.S. Slang* A cheap restaurant.
hash·ish (häsh′ēsh, -ish) *n.* The tops and sprouts of hemp, used as a narcotic and intoxicant. Also called *bhang.* Also **hash′eesh.** [< Arabic *hashīsh* hemp]
hash mark *Mil. Slang* A service stripe.
Has·i·dim (has′i·dim, *Hebrew* khä·sē′dim) See CHASSIDIM.
has·n't (haz′ənt) Has not.
hasp (hasp, häsp) *n.* A hinged fastening for a door, lid, etc., esp. one that passes over a staple and is secured by a padlock. — *v.t.* To shut or fasten with or as with a hasp. [OE *hæpse*]
has·sle (has′əl) *n.* *U.S. Slang* An argument; squabble; fight. Also **has′sel.** [? < HAGGLE + TUSSLE]
has·sock (has′ək) *n.* **1.** An upholstered stool or cushion, used for kneeling or as a footstool. **2.** A rank tuft of coarse or boggy grass. [OE *hassuc* coarse grass, ? < Celtic]
hast (hast) Archaic or poetic second person singular, present tense, of HAVE: used with *thou.*
haste (hāst) *n.* **1.** Swiftness of movement or action; rapidity. **2.** Undue or reckless hurry. **3.** The necessity to act quickly; urgency. — **to make haste** To hurry. — *v.t. & v.i.* **hast·ed, hast·ing** *Poetic* To hasten. [< OF < Gmc.]
has·ten (hā′sən) *v.i.* **1.** To move or act with speed; be quick; hurry. — *v.t.* **2.** To cause to hurry or move quickly; expedite. — **has′ten·er** *n.*
hast·y (hās′tē) *adj.* **hast·i·er, hast·i·est** **1.** Speedy; quick; rapid. **2.** Acting or made with excessive speed; rash. **3.** Manifesting anger: *hasty* words. **4.** Easily excited to anger. — **hast′i·ly** *adv.* — **hast′i·ness** *n.*
hasty pudding **1.** A dish made of meal, seasoning, and boiling water or milk. **2.** *U.S.* A mush made with cornmeal.
hat (hat) *n.* A covering for the head, esp. one with a crown and brim. — **to pass the hat** To solicit and collect contributions of money. — **to talk through one's hat** *Informal* To talk nonsense; also, to bluff. — **to throw** (**toss,** etc.) **one's hat into the ring** To enter a contest or competition, esp. a contest for political office. — **under one's hat** *U.S. Informal* Secret; private. — *v.t.* **hat·ted, hat·ting** To provide or cover with a hat. [OE *hæt*]
hat·band (hat′band′) *n.* A ribbon or band of cloth around a hat just above the brim.
hatch[1] (hach) *n.* **1.** An opening in a floor, deck, etc., giving access to spaces beneath: also called *hatchway.* **2.** A cover or grating over such an opening: also **hatch cover. 3.** A or gate with an opening above; also, the lower half of a that is divided into two independently swinging parts. floodgate (def. 1). — **Down the hatch!** *U.S. Slang* D up! [OE *hæcc* grating]
hatch[2] (hach) *v.t.* **1.** To bring forth (young) from the eg incubation. **2.** To bring forth young from (the egg). To devise, as a plan or plot. — *v.i.* **4.** To emerge from egg. — *n.* **1.** The act of hatching. **2.** The brood hat at one time. **3.** The result or outcome of any plan. [*hacchen*] — **hatch′er** *n.*
hatch[3] (hach) *v.t.* To mark with close parallel or crc lines in order to produce shading effects, etc. — *n.* Ar these lines. [< OF *hache* an ax < Gmc.] — **hatch′in**
hatch·er·y (hach′ər·ē) *n.* *pl.* **·er·ies** A place for hatc eggs, esp. those of poultry or fish.
hatch·et (hach′it) *n.* **1.** A small, short-handled ax, fo with one hand. **2.** A tomahawk. — **to bury the hatc** To make peace. [< F, dim. of *hache* an ax]
hatch·way (hach′wā′) *n.* Hatch[1] (def. 1).
hate (hāt) *v.* **hat·ed, hat·ing** *v.t.* **1.** To regard with extr aversion; detest. **2.** To dislike: I *hate* doing that. — **3.** To feel hatred. — *n.* **1.** An extreme feeling of dislik animosity; hatred. **2.** A person or thing detested. *hatian*] — **hat′a·ble** or **hate′a·ble** *adj.* — **hat′er** *n.*
— **Syn.** (verb) **1.** *Hate* frequently refers to a deep, pers feeling actuated by enmity or malice; Iago *hated* Othello. *L* and *abhor* both suggest aversion or disgust; *loathe* pictures which causes a nauseating repugnance, and *abhor*, that from w we turn or shrink away. *Abominate* is used of things *hate* moral reasons, and often indicates a righteous indignation.
hate·ful (hāt′fəl) *adj.* Arousing or worthy of hatred; testable. — **hate′ful·ly** *adv.* — **hate′ful·ness** *n.*
hath (hath) Archaic or poetic third person singular, pre tense, of HAVE.
ha·tred (hā′trid) *n.* Intense dislike or aversion; animo enmity. [ME < *hate* + *-red* < OE *-ræden* state]
haugh·ty (hô′tē) *adj.* **·ti·er, ·ti·est** Exhibiting great dis for others; supercilious. [< OF *haut* high] — **haugh** *adv.* — **haugh′ti·ness** *n.*
haul (hôl) *v.t.* **1.** To pull or draw strongly; drag; tug. To transport or carry, as in a truck, car, etc. **3.** *Naut* change the course of (a ship), esp. so as to sail closer to wind. — *v.i.* **4.** To pull or drag; tug. **5.** To change d tion: said of the wind. **6.** To change one's views or cour action. **7.** *Naut.* To change course; especially, to steer n er the wind. — **to haul off** To draw back the arm so a punch. — **to haul up** **1.** To compel to go: I was *haule* before the court. **2.** To come to a stop. **3.** *Naut.* To nearer the wind. — *n.* **1.** A strong pull; tug. **2.** which is caught, won, taken, etc., at one time: a good *ha* fish. **3.** The distance over which something is hauled. That which is hauled. [< OF *haler* < Gmc.] — **haul′e**
haul·age (hô′lij) *n.* **1.** The act or operation of hauling. A charge for hauling. **3.** Force expended in hauling.
haul·yard (hôl′yərd) See HALYARD.
haunch (hônch, hänch) *n.* **1.** In man and animals, upper thigh, including the hip and buttock. **2.** The leg loin of an animal, considered as meat. [< OF *hanche*]
haunch bone The innominate bone.
haunt (hônt, hänt) *v.t.* **1.** To visit or resort to (a perso place) repeatedly; esp., to do so, as a ghost or spirit. **2.** recur persistently to the mind or memory of: The t *haunts* me. **3.** To linger about; pervade. — *v.i.* **4.** appear or recur often, esp. as a ghost. — *n.* A place o visited; resort; habitat. [< OF *hanter*] — **haunt′er** *n.*
haunt·ed (hôn′tid, hän′-) *adj.* Supposedly visited by gho
haunt·ing (hôn′ting, hän′-) *adj.* Recurring to the mi difficult to forget: a *haunting* tune. — **haunt′ing·ly** *adv*
haut·boy (hō′boi, ō′-) *n.* An oboe. [< F *haut* high tone) + *bois* wood]
hau·teur (hō·tûr′, *Fr.* ō·tœr′) *n.* Haughtiness. [< F.
haut monde (ō môṅd′) *French* High society.
have (hav) *v.t.* Present indicative: I, you, we, they h (*Archaic* **thou hast**), he, she, it **has** (*Archaic* **hath**); past dicative **had** (*Archaic* **thou hadst**); present subjunctive **ha** past subjunctive **had;** *pp.* **had;** *ppr.* **hav·ing** **1.** To pos as property; own. **2.** To be connected with; be possessed to *have* a good government. **3.** To bear or possess as an tribute, quality, etc. **4.** To hold in the mind or among feelings; entertain. **5.** To receive, take, or acquire. **6.** achieve mastery of: Now I *have* it. **7.** To suffer from *have* boils. **8.** To engage in: to *have* a quarrel. **9.** To unc go or experience: to *have* a bad fright. **10.** To plan, arran and carry out: to *have* a party. **11.** To give birth to. To manifest or exercise: to *have* patience. **13.** To cause or cause to be: *Have* it cleaned. **14.** To allow; tolerate. To maintain; declare: So rumor *has* it. **16.** *Informal* catch (someone) at a disadvantage in a game, etc. **17.** *formal* To cheat; trick. **18.** *Informal* To perform the sex act with. **19.** As an auxiliary, *have* is used: **a** With p

ticiples to form perfect tenses expressing completed ac-: I *have* gone. **b** With the infinitive to express obligation ompulsion: I *have* to go. **— to have at** To attack. **— to e done** To stop; desist. **— to have it in for** *Informal* To d a grudge against. **— to have it out** To continue a fight discussion to a final settlement. **— to have on** To be ssed in. **— to let someone have it** *Informal* To attack ssault someone. **—** *n. Informal* A relatively wealthy per- or country: the *haves* and the have-nots. [OE *habban*]

'en (hā'vən) *n.* **1.** A harbor; port. **2.** A refuge; shelter. *.t.* To shelter in or as in a haven. [OE *hæfen*]

e-not (hav'not') *n. Informal* A person or country rela- ly lacking in wealth: the haves and *have-nots.*

e·n't (hav'ənt) Have not.

er·sack (hav'ər·sak) *n.* A bag for carrying rations, etc., a march or hike. [< F < G *habersack* oat sack]

oc (hav'ək) *n.* General carnage or destruction; ruin. **— ry havoc** To give the signal for pillage and destruction. **o play havoc with** To ruin; destroy; devastate. [< OF ot to plunder < Gmc.]

[1] (hô) *v.i.* To hesitate in speaking: to hem and *haw.* **—** *interj.* A hesitating sound made by a speaker.

[2] (hô) *n.* The hawthorn or its fruit. [OE *haga*]

[3] (hô) *n. & interj.* An order to turn to the left or near in driving horses: opposed to *gee.* **—** *v.t. & v.i.* To turn he left. [Origin uncertain]

wai·ian (hə·wī'yən) *adj.* Of or pertaining to Hawaii, Hawaiians, or their language. **—** *n.* **1.** A native or in- itant of Hawaii. **2.** The Polynesian language of Hawaii.

vaiian guitar A guitar played horizontally, the chords ng selected by a metal bar sliding on the strings.

-haw (hô'hô') See HA-HA.

k[1] (hôk) *n.* **1.** Any of a large and widely distributed ily of birds of prey, having broad, rounded wings, a long and powerful talons. **2.** Any of various related birds, the gerfalcon, kestrel, and osprey. **3.** A person who ys on others. **—** *v.i.* **1.** To hunt game with hawks. **2.** fly in search of prey, as a hawk. [OE *hafoc, hafuc*]

k[2] (hôk) *v.t. & v.i.* To cry (goods) for sale in the streets; dle. [Back formation < HAWKER]

k[3] (hôk) *v.t.* **1.** To cough up (phlegm). **—** *v.i.* **2.** To r the throat with a coughing sound. **—** *n.* An effort to r phlegm from the throat; also, the sound of this. [Imit.]

k·er (hô'kər) *n.* One who peddles goods in the street. MLG *hoker* peddler, huckster]

vk·eye (hôk'ī') *n.* A native or inhabitant of Iowa.

k-eyed (hôk'īd') *adj.* Having very keen eyesight.

vkeye State Nickname of Iowa.

k moth A large, stout-bodied moth that flies by twi- t and sucks nectar from flowers.

ks·bill (hôks'bil') *n.* A tropical turtle that furnishes best grade of tortoise shell used in commerce. Also **vk's'-bill', hawksbill turtle.**

k·weed (hôk'wēd') *n.* A weedy perennial herb having all red, yellow, or orange flowers.

se (hôz) *n. Naut.* **1.** The part of a ship's bow where hawseholes are located. **2.** *pl.* Hawseholes. **3.** The ce between the bow of a moored ship and her anchor. [< *hals* neck, bow of a ship]

vse·hole (hôz'hōl') *n. Naut.* A hole in the bow of a ship, ough which cables and hawsers pass.

v·ser (hô'zər) *n. Naut.* A rope or cable used for moor- , towing, etc. [< OF *haucier* to lift]

v·thorn (hô'thôrn) *n.* A shrub or tree of the rose family ving a white or pink flower and a small pome fruit called *v*: the State flower of Missouri. [OE *haguthorn*]

(hā) *n.* Grass, clover, or the like, cut and dried for fod- . **— not hay** *U.S. Slang* Not a small sum of money. **— hit the hay** *U.S. Slang* To go to bed. **— to make hay ile the sun shines** To take full advantage of an opportu- y. **—** *v.i.* **1.** To mow, cure, gather, and store hay. **— 2.** To make (grass, etc.) into hay. **3.** To feed with hay. To sow (land, etc.) with hay plants. [OE *hēg*]

·cock (hā'kok') *n.* A dome-shaped pile of hay in the field.

fever *Pathol.* An allergic reaction to pollen of certain nts, characterized by sneezing, running nose, etc.

·loft (hā'lôft', -loft') *n.* An open upper section of a barn stable, used for storing hay.

·mak·er (hā'mā'kər) *n.* **1.** One who makes hay. **2.** *ng* A powerful punch. **— hay'mak'ing** *n.*

·mow (hā'mou') *n.* **1.** A mass of hay, esp. one stored a loft or bay. **2.** A hayloft.

·rack (hā'rak') *n.* **1.** A frame or rack mounted on a gon body, in which hay is hauled; also, a wagon so uipped. **2.** A framework for holding hay to feed livestock.

·seed (hā'sēd') *n.* **1.** Grass seed that has shaken loose m hay. **2.** The chaff, seeds, etc., that fall from hay. **3.** *S.* A hick; rustic; yokel.

hay·wire (hā'wīr') *adj. U.S. Slang* **1.** Broken; broken down; dilapidated. **2.** Crazy; nutty. **— to go haywire** *Informal* To act or become crazy.

haz·ard (haz'ərd) *n.* **1.** Danger of loss, injury, etc.; peril. **2.** Chance; accident. **3.** A gambling game played with dice. **4.** An obstacle or trap on a golf course. **5.** In tennis, any of various winning openings. **—** *v.t.* **1.** To put in danger; risk. **2.** To venture (a statement, opinion, etc.). **3.** To gamble on. [< OF < Arabic *al-zahr* a die]

haz·ard·ous (haz'ər·dəs) *adj.* **1.** Exposed to or involving danger, risk, loss, etc. **2.** Dependent on chance; fortuitous. **— haz'ard·ous·ly** *adv.* **— haz'ard·ous·ness** *n.*

haze[1] (hāz) *n.* **1.** A light suspension of water vapor, smoke, dust, etc., in the air. **2.** Mental confusion. [< HAZY]

haze[2] (hāz) *v.t.* **hazed, haz·ing** *U.S.* To subject (newcomers or initiates) to pranks and humiliating horseplay. [< OF *haser* to irritate] **— haz'er** *n.* **— haz'ing** *n.*

ha·zel (hā'zəl) *n.* **1.** A bushy shrub or small tree of the birch family; also, the wood of this tree. **2.** The hazelnut. **3.** A medium yellowish brown. **—** *adj.* **1.** Of or pertaining to the hazel. **2.** Of the color hazel. [OE *hæsel*]

ha·zel·nut (hā'zəl·nut') *n.* The edible nut of the hazel.

haz·y (hā'zē) *adj.* **haz·i·er, haz·i·est** **1.** Misty. **2.** Lacking clarity; vague. **— haz'i·ly** *adv.* **— haz'i·ness** *n.*

H-bomb (āch'bom') *n.* A hydrogen bomb.

he (hē) *pron., possessive* **his,** *objective* **him;** *pl. nominative* **they,** *possessive* **their** or **theirs,** *objective* **them** **1.** The nominative singular pronoun of the third person, used of the male person. **2.** That person; anyone; one: *He* who hesitates is lost. **—** *n. pl.* **hes** A male person or animal. [OE *hē*]

he- *combining form* Male; masculine: used in hyphenated compounds: *he-goat.* [< HE]

head (hed) *n. pl.* **heads** or *for def. 15* **head** **1.** The part of a vertebrate animal situated at the top or front of the spinal column, containing the brain, eyes, ears, nose, and mouth. ◆ Collateral adjective: *cephalic.* **2.** The analogous part of other animals and organisms. **3.** A part like a head: the *head* of a pin. **4.** A representation of the head. **5.** A leader or chief person. **6.** The position or rank of a leader. **7.** The front or beginning part of something. **8.** The highest part of something. **9.** The superior part of something. **10.** The source, as of a river. **11.** The part of a bomb or other missile that contains the explosive. **12.** Mind; intelligence. **13.** Self-control; self-possession. **14.** A person: two dollars a *head.* **15.** Of animals, a single specimen. **16.** The length of a head. **17.** A newspaper headline. **18.** A subject: He had much to say on that *head.* **19.** The side of a coin on which a face is struck. **20.** The tip or point of a boil, abscess, etc. **21.** Progress; headway. **22.** A climax, culmination, or crisis. **23.** A compact cluster of leaves or leaf stalks. **24.** The foam on the surface of beer or ale. **25.** An amount of stored-up pressure. **26.** A projecting, usu. high, piece of land on a coast. **27.** The taut, sounding membrane of a drum, tambourine, etc. **28.** The part of a tape recorder that imparts magnetic patterns to the tape or removes them from it. **29.** *Naut.* A toilet. **— head and shoulders above** (or **over**) Much better than. **— head over heels** **1.** End over end. **2.** Rashly; impetuously. **2.** Entirely; totally. **— Heads up!** *U.S. Informal* Watch out! **— one's head off** *Informal* Excessively; vigorously: to yell *one's head off.* **— out of** (or **off**) **one's head** *Informal* **1.** Crazy; deluded. **2.** Delirious. **— over one's head** **1.** Too difficult to understand. **2.** Beyond one's power to cope with or manage. **3.** To a higher authority. **— to come to a head** **1.** Of boils, etc., to form a core or tip of pus. **2.** To reach a crisis. **— to give someone his head** To give someone freedom of action or unrestricted authority. **— to go to one's head** **1.** To decrease one's sobriety, etc. **2.** To make one conceited. **— to have a head** *Informal* To have a bad headache. **— to have rocks** (or **holes**) **in the head** *U.S. Slang* **1.** To be crazy. **2.** To be stupid. **— to keep one's head above water** **1.** To keep afloat. **2.** To manage to exist, keep out of debt, etc. **— to make head or tail of** To understand: usu. used in the negative. **— to take it into one's head** To do or originate something on one's own initiative. **— to turn one's head** To spoil or make vain by praising. **—** *v.t.* **1.** To be first or most prominent on: to *head* the list. **2.** To command; preside over. **3.** To direct the course of. **4.** To furnish with a head. **5.** To cut off the head or top of. **—** *v.i.* **6.** To move in a specified direction or toward a specified point. **7.** To come to or form a head. **8.** To originate: said of streams. **— to head off** To intercept the course of. **—** *adj.* **1.** Principal; chief. **2.** Situated at the front. **3.** Bearing against the front: a *head* wind. [OE *hēafod*]

head·ache (hed'āk') *n.* **1.** A pain in the head. **2.** *U.S. Informal* A difficulty or vexation. **— head'ach'y** *adj.*

head·board (hed'bôrd', -bōrd') *n.* A board at the head end of a bed, grave, etc.

head·cheese (hed′chēz′) *n. U.S.* A cooked and jellied cheeselike meat made of the head and feet of a hog or calf.
head·dress (hed′dress′) *n.* **1.** A covering or ornament for the head. **2.** The style in which the hair is arranged; coiffure.
head·ed (hed′id) *adj.* **1.** Having a head. **2.** Having or characterized by a (specified kind of) head or (a specified number of) heads: *clear-headed*; *two-headed.*
head·er (hed′ər) *n.* **1.** One who or that which makes or puts on heads, as of nails, rivets, etc. **2.** *Agric.* A harvesting machine that cuts off the ripe ends of the grain. **3.** *Informal* A fall or plunge: now only in the phrase **to take a header.**
head·first (hed′fûrst′) *adv.* **1.** With the head first. **2.** Without deliberation; recklessly. Also **head′fore′most′.**
head·gear (hed′gir′) *n.* **1.** A hat, headdress, etc. **2.** The parts of the harness placed about the horse's head.
head-hunt·ing (hed′hun′ting) *n.* Among certain savage tribes, the custom of decapitating slain enemies and preserving the heads as trophies. **—head′-hunt′er** *n.*
head·ing (hed′ing) *n.* **1.** A caption or title, as of a chapter. **2.** A section or division of a subject or discourse. **3.** Something serving as the front or top part of anything. **4.** *Naut. & Aeron.* Direction; course.
head·land (hed′lənd *for def. 1*; hed′land′ *for def. 2*) *n.* **1.** A cliff projecting into the water. **2.** A strip of unplowed land.
head·less (hed′lis) *adj.* **1.** Having no head; decapitated. **2.** Having no leader. **3.** Stupid; erratic; brainless.
head·light (hed′līt′) *n.* A powerful light, as at the front of a locomotive, motor vehicle, etc.
head·line (hed′līn′) *n.* **1.** A summarizing word or words set in bold type, as in a newspaper. **2.** A line at the head of a page, containing title, page number, etc. **—***v.t.* **head·lined, head·lin·ing 1.** To provide with a headline, as a news story. **2.** To be a headliner in (a show, etc.).
head·lin·er (hed′lī′nər) *n.* One billed as the main attraction or star of a theatrical performance.
head·long (hed′lông′, -long′) *adv.* **1.** Headfirst. **2.** Without deliberation; recklessly; rashly. **3.** With unbridled speed or force. **—***adj.* **1.** Made with the head foremost. **2.** Advancing impetuously; rash. **3.** *Rare* Steep.
head·mas·ter (hed′mas′tər, -mäs′-) *n.* The principal of a school, esp. a private school. Also **head master.**
head·mis·tress (hed′mis′tris) *n.fem.* The female principal of a school. Also **head mistress.**
head·most (hed′mōst′) *adj.* Most advanced; foremost.
head-on (hed′on′, -ôn′) *adj. & adv.* Front end to front end: a *head-on* collision; to collide *head-on.*
head·phone (hed′fōn′) *n.* An earphone, usu. attached by a band passing over the head.
head·piece (hed′pēs′) *n.* **1.** A hat, helmet, or other covering for the head. **2.** The head; intelligence. **3.** A headset.
head·quar·ters (hed′kwôr′tərz) *n.pl.* (*construed as sing. or pl.*) **1.** The place from which a chief or leader directs the operations of a military unit, police force, etc. **2.** Any center of operations; also, the persons working there.
head·set (hed′set′) *n.* A pair of headphones.
head·ship (hed′ship) *n.* The position or function of a chief authority; command.
heads·man (hedz′mən) *n. pl.* **·men** (-mən) A public executioner who carries out the death sentence by decapitation.
head·stall (hed′stôl′) *n.* The part of a bridle that fits over the horse's head.
head start An advance start; also, an advantage.
head·stock (hed′stok′) *n. Mech.* One of various machine parts that support or hold some revolving part.
head·stone (hed′stōn′) *n.* **1.** The memorial stone at the head of a grave. **2.** The cornerstone or keystone of a structure: also **head stone.**
head·strong (hed′strông′, -strong′) *adj.* **1.** Stubbornly bent on having one's own way; obstinate; determined. **2.** Proceeding from willfulness or obstinacy.
head·wait·er (hed′wā′tər) *n.* A restaurant employee who supervises waiters, seats guests, makes reservations, etc.
head·wa·ters (hed′wô′tərz, -wot′ərz) *n.pl.* The tributaries or other waters that form the source of a river.
head·way (hed′wā′) *n.* **1.** Forward motion; progress. **2.** The space or time interval between two trains, ships, etc., traveling over the same route. **3.** Overhead clearance.
head wind A wind from ahead, blowing directly opposite to the course of a ship, aircraft, etc.
head·y (hed′ē) *adj.* **head·i·er, head·i·est 1.** Tending to affect the senses; intoxicating: a *heady* fragrance. **2.** Headstrong; obstinate. **—head′i·ly** *adv.* **—head′i·ness** *n.*
heal (hēl) *v.t.* **1.** To restore to health or soundness. **2.** To bring about the remedy or cure of. **3.** To remedy or mend (a quarrel, breach, etc.). **4.** To cleanse of sin, grief, worry, etc. **—***v.i.* **5.** To become well. **6.** To perform a cure or cures. [OE *hǣlan*] **—heal′er** *n.* **—heal′a·ble** *adj.*
health (helth) *n.* **1.** Freedom from defect or disease. **2.** General condition of body or mind. **3.** A toast wishing health or happiness. **—***adj.* Of, pertaining to, connected with, or conducive to health. [OE *hǣlth* < *hāl* whole]

Health, Education and Welfare, Department of executive department of the U.S. government (establi 1953), administering Social Security and other services
health·ful (helth′fəl) *adj.* **1.** Promoting health; salubr **2.** Having or manifesting health; healthy. **—health′f** *adv.* **—health′ful·ness** *n.*
health·y (hel′thē) *adj.* **health·i·er, health·i·est 1.** Ha good health. **2.** Conducive to health. **3.** Indicati characteristic of sound condition. **—health′i·ly** *adv.* **health′i·ness** *n.*
heap (hēp) *n.* **1.** A collection of things piled up; a **2.** *Informal* A large number; lot. **—***v.t.* **1.** To pile ir heap. **2.** To fill or pile (a container) full or more than **3.** To bestow in great quantities: to *heap* insults on some **—***v.i.* **4.** To form or rise in a heap or pile. [OE *hēap* cro
hear (hir) *v.* **heard** (hûrd), **hear·ing** *v.t.* **1.** To perceiv means of the ear. **2.** To listen to; give ear to. **3.** To b formed of: to *hear* good news. **4.** To attend (an opera, cert, recitation, etc.). **5.** To listen officially or judiciall *hear* a case. **6.** To respond or accede to: to *hear* a pr **—***v.i.* **7.** To perceive sound. **8.** To be informed or aware. **—to hear of** To approve of: usu. in the nega He won't *hear of* it. [OE *hēran*] **—hear′er** *n.*
hear·ing (hir′ing) *n.* **1.** The capacity to hear. **2.** Th of perceiving sound. **3.** Reach or range within which s may be heard. **4.** An opportunity to be heard, as in a c **5.** *Law* **a** The examination of an accused person. **b** A cial trial, esp. without a jury.
heark·en (här′kən) See HARKEN.
hear·say (hir′sā′) *n.* Common talk; report; rumor.
hearse (hûrs) *n.* A vehicle for conveying a dead pers the place of burial. [< F *herse* harrow]
heart (härt) *n.* **1.** *Anat.* The primary organ of the circulatory system of animals, a hollow muscular structure that maintains the circulation of the blood by alternate contraction and dilatation. ◆ Collateral adjective: *cardiac.* **2.** The seat of emotion. **3.** Tenderness; affection; love. **4.** The capacity for kindness. **5.** Courage. **6.** One's inmost thoughts or feelings. **7.** Enthusiasm; energy. **8.** State of mind; mood. **9.** A person, esp. a dear one. **10.** The central or inner part of anything. **11.** The vital or essential part. **12.** Anything represented as or shaped like a heart. **13.** A playing card bearing red, heart-shaped spots. **14.** *pl.* The suit of such playing cards. **15.** *pl.* A game of cards. **—after one's own heart** Suiting one's taste. **—at heart** In one's deepest thoughts or feelings. **—by heart** By memory. **—from (the bottom of) one's heart** With all sincerity. **—heart and soul** With complete sincerity. **—one's heart of hearts** The deepest and most intimate part of one's being. **—to break the heart of** To cause deep disappointment and sorrow to. **—to eat one's heart out 1.** To endure great remorse or grief. To have a great longing. **—to have a heart** To be sym thetic and generous. **—to have a change of heart** change one's opinions, attitudes, etc. **—to have o heart in one's mouth** To be excessively excited or fri ened. **—to have the heart** To be callous or cruel eno usually in the negative. **—to lose heart** To become couraged. **—to lose one's heart (to)** To fall in love (wi **—to set one's heart on** To long for; crave. **—to tak heart 1.** To consider seriously. **2.** To be concerned or ious about. **—to wear one's heart on one's sleeve** show one's feelings openly. **—with all one's heart 1.** W great willingness. **2.** With great sincerity. [OE *heorte*]

HEART
a Right atri *b* Right ven cle. *c* Left ventricle. *d* Aorta. *e* P monary arte *f* Inferior ve cava. *g* Supe or vena cav *h* Anterior c onary arter *i* Posterior coronary arte

heart·ache (härt′āk′) *n.* Mental anguish; grief; sorro
heart·beat (härt′bēt′) *n. Physiol.* A pulsation of the h consisting of one full systole and diastole.
heart·break (härt′brāk′) *n.* Deep grief; overwhelming row. **—heart′break′er** *n.* **—heart′break′ing** *adj. & n.*
heart·bro·ken (härt′brō′kən) *adj.* Overwhelmingly grie **—heart′bro′ken·ly** *adv.* **—heart′bro′ken·ness** *n.*
heart·burn (härt′bûrn′) *n.* **1.** *Pathol.* A burning sensa in the esophagus due to acidity. **2.** Discontent; jealou
heart·burn·ing (härt′bûrn′ing) *n.* Gnawing discontent from envy or jealousy. **—***adj.* Deeply felt; distressful
heart·ed (här′tid) *adj.* Having or characterized by a (sp fied kind of) heart: used in combination: *lighthearted.*
heart·en (här′tən) *v.t.* To give heart or courage to.
heart·felt (härt′felt′) *adj.* Deeply felt; most sincere.
hearth (härth) *n.* **1.** The floor of a fireplace, furnace, or like. **2.** The fireside; home. **3.** In a blast furnace, the l est part, through which the melted metal flows. [OE *heo*
hearth·stone (härth′stōn′) *n.* **1.** A stone forming a hea **2.** The fireside; home.

rt·i·ly (här′tə·lē) *adv.* **1.** With sincerity or cordiality. Abundantly and with good appetite. **3.** Completely; roughly: to be *heartily* disgusted.
rt·land (härt′land′) *n.* In geopolitics, any central, itegically important area.
rt·less (härt′lis) *adj.* **1.** Having no sympathy or kind-s; pitiless. **2.** Having little courage or enthusiasm; dis-ted. — **heart′less·ly** *adv.* — **heart′less·ness** *n.*
rt-rend·ing (härt′ren′ding) *adj.* Causing great distress motional anguish; grievous.
rts·ease (härts′ēz′) *n.* Freedom from sorrow or care.) **heart's′ease′**.
rt·sick (härt′sik′) *adj.* Deeply disappointed or despon-t. Also **heart′sore′** (-sôr′, -sōr′).
rt-strick·en (härt′strik′ən) *adj.* Overwhelmed with f or fear. Also **heart′-struck′** (-struk′).
rt·strings (härt′stringz′) *n.pl.* The strongest feelings affections.
rt-to-heart (härt′tə·härt′) *adj.* Marked by frankness, macy, and sincerity.
rt·wood (härt′wo͝od′) *n. Bot.* The duramen.
rt·y (här′tē) *adj.* **heart·i·er, heart·i·est 1.** Full of affec-ate warmth or cordiality. **2.** Strongly felt; unrestrained. Iealthy and strong. **4.** Supplying or enjoying abundant rishment: a *hearty* meal; a *hearty* appetite. — *n. pl.* **rt·ies** A hearty fellow. — **heart′i·ness** *n.*
; (hēt) *n.* **1.** The state or quality of being hot; hotness; , degree of hotness. **2.** That which raises the tempera-; also, the rise itself. **3.** *Physics* A form of energy asso-ed with and proportional to the molecular motions of a stance or body. ◆ Collateral adjective: *thermal.* **4.** sensation produced by hotness. **5.** Condition, appear-e, or color indicating high temperature. **6.** Hot weather limate. **7.** Warmth supplied for a building, room, etc. *Metall.* A single heating or smelting operation, as in work-iron or steel. **9.** A single effort or trial, esp. in a race. Great intensity of feeling: the *heat* of debate. **11.** The lest point of excitement or fury: the *heat* of battle. **12.** *l.* **a** Sexual excitement. **b** The period of sexual excite-it. **13.** *U.S. Slang* **a** Any vigorous activity. **b** In the erworld, pressure applied to obtain information; also, nsive police action. — *v.t. & v.i.* **1.** To make or become or warm. **2.** To excite or become excited. [OE *hǣtu*] **ieat′ed** *adj.* — **heat′ed·ly** *adv.*
:·er (hē′tər) *n.* An apparatus for producing heat.
t exhaustion A mild form of heat stroke.
th (hēth) *n.* **1.** Any of a large genus of hardy evergreen ıbs, including the arbutus, azalea, and rhododendron. The common heather. **3.** *Brit.* An area of open land rgrown with heath or coarse herbage. [OE *hǣth*]
then (hē′thən) *n. pl.* **·thens** or **·then 1.** One who has adopted Christianity, Judaism, or Islam. **2.** In the Old tament, a non-Jew; Gentile. **3.** Any irreligious or un-ivated person. — *adj.* **1.** Unbelieving; irreligious. **2.** or pertaining to heathen peoples. [OE *hǣthen*. Akin to TH.] — **hea′then·dom** *n.* — **hea′then·ish** *adj.* — **hea′·n·ish·ly** *adv.* — **hea′then·ish·ness** *n.* — **hea′then·ism** *n.*
:h·er (heth′ər) *n.* **1.** A hardy evergreen shrub related he heath and having pinkish flowers. **2.** A dull, grayish color. [ME *hadder*] — **heath′er·y** *adj.*
th grouse A grouse found in Great Britain, the male of ch is mostly black: also called *black grouse.* Also **heath·i** (hēth′bûrd′), **heath cock.**
t lightning A fitful play of lightning without thunder, letimes seen near the horizon on hot evenings.
t prostration Heat exhaustion.
t stroke A state of exhaustion or collapse, usu. accom-ied by fever, caused by excessive heat.
t wave A period of very hot weather.
ve (hēv) *v.* **heaved** or (*esp. Naut.*) **hove, heav·ing** *v.t.* **1.** throw or hurl, esp. with great effort. **2.** To raise with rt. **3.** To cause to rise or bulge. **4.** To utter painfully. *Naut.* **a** To pull or haul on (a rope, cable, etc.). **b** To se (a ship) to move in a specified direction by or as by ling on cables or ropes. — *v.i.* **6.** To rise or swell up; ge. **7.** To rise and fall repeatedly. **8.** To vomit; retch. *Naut.* **a** To move or proceed: said of ships. **b** To haul or l, as on a rope. — **heave, ho!** *Naut.* Pull (or push) hard ether! — **to heave in** (or **into**) **sight** To appear to rise) view. — **to heave to 1.** To bring (a ship) to a stand-l by heading into the wind with the sails hauled in or rtened. **2.** To cause a ship to lie to, as in a storm. — *n.* e act or exertion of heaving. [OE *hebban* to lift] — **ıv′er** *n.*
v·en (hev′ən) *n.* **1.** *Theol.* The abode of God and his els, where virtuous souls receive eternal reward after th. **2.** In various religious systems, any supernatural ion inhabited by a deity or deities, slain heroes, etc. **3.** *Usu. pl.* The regions around and above the earth; sky. **4.** Any condition of great happiness. **5.** Any place resembling heaven. [OE *heofon*] — **heav′en·li·ness** *n.*
Heav·en (hev′ən) God or the celestial powers.
heav·en·ly (hev′ən·lē) *adj.* **1.** Of or belonging to the heaven of God. **2.** Of or pertaining to the sky. **3.** Full of the beauty and peace befitting heaven. — **heav′en·li·ness** *n.*
heav·en·ward (hev′ən·wərd) *adv.* Toward heaven. Also **heav′en·wards.** — *adj.* Directed toward heaven.
heav·i·er-than-air (hev′ē·ər·thən·âr′) *adj.* Having a weight greater than that of the air it displaces: said of airplanes, etc.
Heav·i·side layer (hev′i·sīd) The lower region of the ion-osphere, about 60 miles above the earth, that reflects radio waves of relatively low frequency back to the earth. [after O. *Heaviside*, 1850–1925, English physicist]
heav·y (hev′ē) *adj.* **heav·i·er, heav·i·est 1.** Having great weight; hard to move. **2.** Having relatively great weight in relation to size: the *heavy* metals. **3.** Having more than usual quantity, volume, etc.: a *heavy* snowfall. **4.** Practicing or indulging on a large scale: a *heavy* smoker. **5.** Having force and severity: a *heavy* blow. **6.** Exceeding the usual weight: *heavy* woolens. **7.** Having great importance; grave; serious: a *heavy* responsibility. **8.** Hard to do or accomplish: *heavy* labor. **9.** Hard to endure or bear; oppressive: *heavy* taxes. **10.** Of food, not easily digested. **11.** Of bread, pastry, etc., dense in texture; poorly leavened. **12.** Giving an impression of weight or ponderousness; thick: *heavy* lines. **13.** Despondent: a *heavy* heart. **14.** Lacking animation and grace; tedious: a *heavy* prose style. **15.** Lacking preci-sion and delicacy: a *heavy* hand. **16.** Permeating and strong: a *heavy* odor. **17.** Profound; unbroken: a *heavy* silence. **18.** Showing fatigue: *heavy* eyes. **19.** Producing massive or basic goods: *heavy* industry. **20.** Weighted down. **21.** Pregnant. **22.** In the theater, designating a serious or tragic role, or the role of a villain. **23.** *Physics* Designating an isotope having a mass greater than that of others occur-ring in the same element: *heavy* hydrogen. **24.** *Mil.* **a** Desig-nating the more massive types of weapons. **b** Formerly, designating troops or units with relatively massive equip-ment. — *adv.* Heavily. — **to hang heavy** To drag by tedi-ously, as time. — *n. pl.* **heav·ies 1.** In the theater, the role of a villainous or tragic personage; also, the actor por-traying him. **2.** *U.S. Informal* In sports, a heavyweight. [OE *hefig*] — **heav′i·ly** *adv.* — **heav′i·ness** *n.*
heav·y-du·ty (hev′ē·do͞o′tē, -dyo͞o′-) *adj.* Strongly con-structed for long strain, hard use, etc.
heav·y-hand·ed (hev′ē·han′did) *adj.* **1.** Bungling; clumsy. **2.** Oppressive; domineering; cruel. — **heav′y-hand′ed·ly** *adv.* — **heav′y-hand′ed·ness** *n.*
heav·y-heart·ed (hev′ē·här′tid) *adj.* Melancholy; sad. — **heav′y-heart′ed·ly** *adv.* — **heav′y-heart′ed·ness** *n.*
heavy hydrogen Deuterium.
heav·y-lad·en (hev′ē·lād′n) *adj.* **1.** Bearing a heavy bur-den. **2.** Troubled; oppressed.
heavy spar Barite.
heavy water Deuterium oxide, D_2O, the compound of oxy-gen and the heavy isotope of hydrogen.
heav·y·weight (hev′ē·wāt′) *n.* **1.** A person or animal of much more than average weight. **2.** A boxer or wrestler over 175 pounds in weight. — *adj.* Of more than average weight or thickness.
heb·dom·a·dal (heb·dom′ə·dəl) *adj.* Weekly. Also **heb·dom′a·dar′y** (-der′ē). — **heb·dom′a·dal·ly** *adv.*
He·be (hē′bē) In Greek mythology, the goddess of youth and spring, cupbearer to the gods.
He·bra·ic (hi·brā′ik) *adj.* Relating to or characteristic of the Hebrew people and their culture and language. Also **He·bra′i·cal.** [< LL < Gk. *Hebraios* a Hebrew] — **He·bra′i·cal·ly** *adv.*
He·bra·ism (hē′brā·iz′əm, -brə-) *n.* **1.** A Hebrew idiom. **2.** Hebrew thought, character, practice, etc. **3.** The reli-gion of the Hebrews; Judaism. — **He′bra·ist, He′brew·ist** *n.* — **He′bra·is′tic** or **·ti·cal** *adj.*
He·brew (hē′bro͞o) *n.* **1.** A member of that group of Semitic peoples claiming descent from the house of Abraham; Is-raelite; Jew. **2.** The ancient Semitic language of the Israel-ites as used in much of the Old Testament. **3.** The modern Hebrew language: official language of the republic of Israel. — **Epistle to the Hebrews** A book of the New Testament addressed to Hebrew Christians: also **Hebrews.** — *adj.* Hebraic; Jewish. [< OF < L < Gk. < Hebrew *'ibhri*, lit., one from beyond (Jordan)]
Hebrew calendar See (Hebrew) CALENDAR.
Hec·a·te (hek′ə·tē) In Greek mythology, a goddess of earth, moon, and underworld: also spelled *Hekate.*
heck (hek) *interj. Slang* Darn: a euphemism for *hell.*
heck·le (hek′əl) *v.t.* **·led, ·ling** To try to annoy with taunts, questions, etc. [ME *hechelen*] — **heck′ler** *n.*

hec·tare (hek′târ) *n.* A unit of area in the metric system: also spelled *hektare*. Abbr. *ha.* See table front of book.
hec·tic (hek′tik) *adj.* **1.** Characterized by great excitement, turmoil, haste, etc.: a *hectic* trip. **2.** Denoting a condition of body, as in wasting diseases. **3.** Designating the fever accompanying wasting diseases. Also **hec′ti·cal.** [< F < LL < Gk. *hektikos* consumptive] **— hec′ti·cal·ly** *adv.*
hecto- *combining form* In the metric system and in technical usage, a hundred times (a specified unit). Also spelled *hekto-*. Also, before vowels, **hect-.** [< F < Gk. *hekaton* hundred]
hec·to·gram (hek′tə·gram) *n.* In the metric system, a measure of weight: also spelled *hektogram.* Also **hec′to·gramme.** Abbr. *hg.* See table front of book.
hec·to·graph (hek′tə·graf, -gräf) *n.* A gelatin pad for making multiple copies of a writing or drawing. **—** *v.t.* To copy by hectograph. **— hec′to·graph′ic** *adj.*
hec·to·li·ter (hek′tə·lē′tər) *n.* In the metric system, a measure of capacity. Also *esp. Brit.* **hec′to·li′tre.** Abbr. *hl, hl.* See table front of book.
hec·to·me·ter (hek′tə·mē′tər, hek·tom′ə·tər) *n.* In the metric system, a measure of length. Also *esp. Brit.* **hec′to·me′·tre.** Abbr. *hm., hm* See table front of book.
hec·tor (hek′tər) *v.t. & v.i.* **1.** To bully; bluster; rant. **2.** To tease; torment. **—** *n.* A bully. [after *Hector*]
Hec·tor (hek′tər) In the *Iliad*, a Trojan hero, son of Priam and Hecuba: killed by Achilles.
Hec·u·ba (hek′yŏŏ·bə) In the *Iliad*, the wife of Priam and mother of Hector, Troilus, Paris, Cassandra, and others.
he'd (hēd) **1.** He had. **2.** He would.
hedge (hej) *n.* **1.** A fence or barrier formed of privet or other bushes set close together; also, any boundary or barrier. **2.** The act of hedging a bet, risk, etc.; also, that which is used to hedge. **—** *v.* **hedged, hedg·ing** *v.t.* **1.** To border or separate with a hedge. **2.** To set barriers and restrictions to, so as to hinder freedom of movement or action; hem: often with *in* or *about.* **3.** To guard against undue loss from (a bet, investment, etc.) by making compensatory bets, etc. **—** *v.i.* **4.** To make compensatory bets, etc., in order to restrict losses. **5.** To avoid forthright statement or action. [OE *hegg*] **— hedg′er** *n.* **— hedg′y** *adj.*
hedge·hog (hej′hôg′, -hog′) *n.* **1.** A small, nocturnal, insectivorous mammal of Europe, having stout spines on the back and sides. **2.** *U.S.* The porcupine. **3.** *Mil.* An obstacle made of barbed wire on frames.

EUROPEAN HEDGEHOG (About 10 inches long)

hedge·hop (hej′hop′) *v.i.* **·hopped, ·hop·ping** To fly close to the ground in an airplane. **— hedge′hop′per** *n.*
hedge·row (hej′rō′) *n.* A dense row of bushes, trees, etc., planted as a hedge.
he·don·ism (hēd′n·iz′əm) *n.* **1.** The doctrine that pleasure is the only proper goal of moral endeavor. **2.** The pursuit of pleasure. [< Gk. *hēdonē* pleasure] **— he′don·ist** *n.* **— he′don·is′tic** *adj.* **— he′don·is′ti·cal·ly** *adv.*
-hedral *combining form* Having (a specified number of) sides or faces: *octahedral.*
-hedron *combining form* A figure having (a specified number of) sides or faces: *octahedron.* [< Gk. *hedra* surface]
heed (hēd) *v.t.* **1.** To pay attention to; take more than casual notice of. **—** *v.i.* **2.** To pay attention; listen. **—** *n.* Careful attention. [OE *hēdan*] **— heed′er** *n.*
heed·ful (hēd′fəl) *adj.* Giving heed; attentive; mindful. **— heed′ful·ly** *adv.* **— heed′ful·ness** *n.*
heed·less (hēd′lis) *adj.* Not showing any heed or attention; reckless. **— heed′less·ly** *adv.* **— heed′less·ness** *n.*
hee·haw (hē′hô′) *n.* The braying sound of a donkey. **—** *v.i.* To bray. [Imit.]
heel[1] (hēl) *n.* **1.** In man, the rounded posterior part of the foot under and in back of the ankle; also, the rounded part of the palm of the hand nearest the wrist. **2.** The analogous part of the hind foot of an animal. **3.** That part of a shoe, stocking, etc., covering the heel. **4.** In a shoe or boot, the built-up portion on which the rear of the foot rests. **5.** Something analogous to the human heel, as the rounded end of a loaf of bread. **6.** *Slang* A habitually dishonorable person; contemptible chiseler. **— at heel** Close behind. **— down at the heel 1.** Having the heels of one's shoes worn down. **2.** Shabby; rundown. **— on** (or **upon**) **the heels of 1.** Right behind. **2.** Close after; quickly following. **— to cool one's heels** To be kept waiting. **— to heel 1.** To an attendant position close behind one. **2.** To submission; under control. **— to kick up one's heels 1.** To have a good time. **2.** To let oneself go. **— to take to one's heels** To run away; flee. **—** *v.t.* **1.** To supply with a heel, as a shoe. **2.** To pursue closely. **3.** *U.S. Slang* To supply with something, esp. with money or a weapon. **—** *v.i.* **4.** To move the heels. **5.** To follow at one's heels. [OE *hēla*] **— heel′less** *adj.*
heel[2] (hēl) *Naut. v.t. & v.i.* To lean or cause to lean to one side; cant, as a ship. **—** *n.* The act of heeling; a cant; list: also **heel′ing.** [Earlier *heeld*, OE *hieldan*]

heel bone The calcaneus.
heeled (hēld) *adj.* **1.** Having heels: *high-heeled.* **2.** *Slang* Supplied with money or a weapon.
heel·er (hē′lər) *n.* **1.** One who heels shoes. **2.** *U.S.* A ward heeler.
heel·tap (hēl′tap′) *n.* **1.** A thickness of leather on the of a shoe. **2.** A small quantity of liquor left in a glass
heft (heft) *Informal v.t.* **1.** To test or gauge the weig by lifting. **2.** To lift up; heave. **—** *v.i.* **3.** To weigh. **1.** Weight. **2.** *U.S.* The bulk or gist. [Akin to HEA
heft·y (hef′tē) *adj.* **heft·i·er, heft·i·est** *Informal* **1.** H weighty. **2.** Big and powerful; muscular.
He·ge·li·an·ism (hə·gā′lē·ən·iz′əm) *n.* The philoso doctrine of Hegel that dialectic reasoning, a process wh thought passes repeatedly in ascending stages from the antithesis to synthesis, can unravel the order of develop in which human consciousness and reality participate. **He·gel·ism** (hā′gəl·iz′əm). **— He·ge′lian** *n. & adj.*
he·gem·o·ny (hə·jem′ə·nē, hej′ə·mō′nē, hē′jə-) *n.* *pl.* Domination or leadership; esp., the predominant infl of one state over others. [< Gk. *hēgeesthai* to lead] **heg·e·mon·ic** (hej′ə·mon′ik) *adj.*
he·gi·ra (hi·jī′rə, hej′ə·rə) *n.* Any precipitate depar also spelled *hejira.* [< Med.L < Arabic *hijrah* depar
He·gi·ra (hi·jī′rə, hej′ə·rə) *n.* **1.** The flight of Mohan from Mecca to Medina in 622, now taken as the beginni the Moslem era. **2.** The Moslem era. Also spelled *H*
heif·er (hef′ər) *n.* A young cow that has not produ calf. [OE *heahfore*]
height (hīt) *n.* **1.** The state or quality of being high or tively high. **2.** The distance from the base to the top tude. **3.** The distance above a given level, as the s horizon. **4.** *Often pl.* A lofty or high place; eminence. The highest part of anything; summit. **6.** The highes gree: the *height* of quality. [OE *hīehtho*]
height·en (hīt′n) *v.t. & v.i.* **1.** To make or become hi higher; raise or lift. **2.** To make or become more in de amount, size, etc.; intensify. **— height′en·er** *n.*
heil (hīl) *German interj.* Hail! **—** *v.t.* To salute with "
hei·nous (hā′nəs) *adj.* Extremely wicked; atrocious; ous. [< OF *haine* hatred < *hair* to hate] **— hei′no** *adv.* **— hei′nous·ness** *n.*
heir (âr) *n.* **1.** Anyone inheriting rank or property fr deceased person; also, anyone likely to inherit upon death of an incumbent or holder. **2.** One who or that w takes over or displays the qualities of some forerunner. OF < L *heres*] **— heir′ess** *n.fem.* **— heir′less** *adj.*
heir apparent *pl.* **heirs apparent** *Law* One who mu course of law become the heir if he survives his ancest
heir·dom (âr′dəm) *n.* Heirship; inheritance.
heir·loom (âr′lōōm) *n.* **1.** Anything that has been ha down in a family for generations. **2.** *Law* Those ch and articles that descend to an heir along with the est
heir presumptive *pl.* **heirs presumptive** *Law* An whose claim to an estate may become void by the birth nearer relative.
heir·ship (âr′ship) *n.* **1.** The state or condition of bei heir. **2.** The right to inheritance.
heist (hīst) *v.t.* *U.S. Slang* To steal. [Var. of HOIST]
he·ji·ra (hi·jī′rə, hej′ə·rə) See HEGIRA.
He·ji·ra (hi·jī′rə, hej′ə·rə) See HEGIRA.
Hek·a·te (hek′ə·tē) See HECATE.
hek·tare (hek′târ), **hek·to·gram** (hek′tə·gram), etc. See TARE, etc.
hekto- See HECTO-.
held (held) Past tense of HOLD.
Helen of Troy In Greek mythology, the beautiful w Menelaus, king of Sparta. Her elopement to Troy with caused the Trojan War.
hel·i·cal (hel′i·kəl) *adj.* Pertaining to or shaped like a h
hel·i·ces (hel′ə·sēz) Alternative plural of HELIX.
helico- *combining form* Spiral; helical. Also, before vo **helic-.** [< Gk. *helix* spiral]
hel·i·coid (hel′ə·koid) *adj.* Coiled spirally, as certain valve shells. Also **hel′i·coid′al.** **—** *n.* *Geom.* A surface g ated by a straight line moving along a fixed helix in su way as to maintain a constant angle with its axis. [< *helikoeidēs* spiral-shaped] **— hel′i·coi′dal·ly** *adv.*
hel·i·con (hel′i·kon, -kən) *n.* *Music* A large, circular t [< HELICON; infl. by HELIX]
Hel·i·con (hel′i·kon, -kən) A mountain in Greece, legen home of the Muses. **— Hel·i·co·ni·an** (hel′i·kō′nē·ən)
hel·i·cop·ter (hel′ə·kop′tər, hē′lə-) *n.* *Aeron.* A type o craft whose aerodynamic support is obtained from en driven airfoil blades rotating around a vertical axis, and is capable of rising and descending vertically. [< F < *helix, -ikos* spiral + *pteron* wing]
helio- *combining form* Sun; of the sun. Also, before vo **heli-.** [< Gk. *hēlios* the sun]
he·li·o·cen·tric (hē′lē·ə·sen′trik) *adj.* Having or regar the sun as the center. Also **he′li·o·cen′tri·cal.**

i·o·graph (hē′lē·ə·graf′, -gräf′) *n.* **1.** *Astron.* An instru-
nt for taking photographs of the sun. **2.** A mirror for sig-
ing by flashes of light. Also **he′li·o** (-lē·ō). — *v.t. & v.i.*
signal with a heliograph. — **he·li·og·ra·pher** (hē′lē·og′·
ər) *n.* — **he′li·o·graph′ic** *adj.* — **he′li·og′ra·phy** *n.*
i·os (hē′lē·os) In Greek mythology, the sun god.
i·o·scope (hē′lē·ə·skōp′) *n.* *Astron.* A device within a
scope by which the eyes are protected from pain or in-
y while observing the sun.
i·o·ther·a·py (hē′lē·ō·ther′ə·pē) *n.* *Med.* Exposure to
sun for purposes of treatment.
i·o·trope (hē′lē·ə·trōp′, hēl′yə-) *n.* **1.** An herb of the
age family, with white or purplish fragrant flowers. **2.**
y plant that turns toward the sun. **3.** The bloodstone.
A soft, rosy purple. [< F < L < Gk. < *hēlios* sun +
ein to turn]
i·ot·ro·pism (hē′lē·ot′rə·piz′əm) *n.* *Biol.* The tendency
ome organisms to move or turn toward or away from the
. Also **he′li·ot′ro·py.** — **he′li·o·trop′ic** *adj.*
i·port (hel′ə·pôrt′, -pōrt′, hē′lə-) *n.* An airport for heli-
ters.
i·um (hē′lē·əm) *n.* An inert, odorless, nonflammable,
eous element (symbol He) that is found chiefly in certain
ural gas deposits, used to inflate balloons, dirigibles, etc.
ELEMENT. [< NL < Gk. *hēlios* sun]
ix (hē′liks) *n.* *pl.* **he·lix·es** or **hel·i·ces** (hel′ə·sēz) **1.** A
, thread, wire, or the like, curved as if wound in a single
er round a cylinder; a form like a screw thread. **2.** Any
ral. **3.** *Anat.* The recurved border of the external ear. **4.**
chit. A small volute. [< L, spiral < Gk.]
l (hel) *n.* **1.** *Sometimes cap.* In various religions, the
de of the dead or the place of punishment for the wicked
er death; the abode of evil spirits. **2.** Any condition of
at mental or physical suffering; also, anything causing
h suffering. — **a** (or **one**) **hell of a** *Slang* A remarkably
l, good, difficult, etc. (thing). — **like hell** *Slang* **1.** Very
ch, very fast, very bad, etc.: He ran *like hell.* **2.** Not at all;
ver. *Like hell* he will! — **to be hell on** *Slang* **1.** To be
naging or harmful to. **2.** To be unpleasant or difficult
3. To be very harsh or strict with. — **to catch** (or **get**)
U.S. Slang To be roundly scolded or punished, as for a
deed. — **to give (someone) hell** *Slang* To upbraid or
ish (someone) severely. — **to raise hell** *Slang* To cre-
a disturbance. — *interj.* An exclamation used as an im-
cation or an expression of anger or impatience. [OE *hel*]
l (hēl) He will.
las (hel′əs) Ancient or modern Greece. [< Gk.]
·bend·er (hel′ben′dər) *n.* *U.S.* A large aquatic sala-
nder common to the Ohio River Valley.
-bent (hel′bent′) *adj.* *U.S. Slang* Determined to have
do; recklessly eager: *hell-bent* for home.
·cat (hel′kat′) *n.* **1.** A shrewish woman. **2.** A witch.
le·bore (hel′ə·bôr, -bōr) *n.* **1.** A perennial herb of the
wfoot family, having serrated leaves and large flowers;
. the **black hellebore** of Europe, the root of which is a
verful cathartic. [< L < Gk. *helleboros*]
·lene (hel′ēn) *n.* A Greek. Also **Hel·le′ni·an.** [< Gk.]
·len·ic (he·len′ik, -lē′nik) *adj.* Greek; Grecian. — *n.*
roup of Indo-European languages, including Greek.
·len·ism (hel′ə·niz′əm) *n.* **1.** Ancient Greek character,
als, or civilization. **2.** An idiom or turn of phrase peculiar
Greek. **3.** Assimilation of Greek speech, ideas, and cul-
e. — **Hel′le·nist** *n.*
·le·nis·tic (hel′ə·nis′tik) *adj.* **1.** Pertaining to, resem-
ng, or characteristic of the Hellenists or Hellenism. **2.** Of
pertaining to the period that began with the conquests of
xander the Great and ended about 300 years later, char-
erized by the spread of Greek language and culture
oughout the Near East. Also **Hel′le·nis′ti·cal.**
·le·nize (hel′ə·nīz) *v.t. & v.i.* **·nized, ·niz·ing** To make or
ome Greek; adopt or imbue with Greek language or cus-
ns. — **Hel′le·ni·za′tion** *n.* — **Hel′le·niz′er** *n.*
·les·pont (hel′əs·pont) The ancient name for the DAR-
NELLES.
l·fire (hel′fīr′) *n.* The flames or the punishment of hell.
lion (hel′yən) *n.* *Informal* A person who delights in
iltry; a mischief-maker. [< HELL]
l·ish (hel′ish) *adj.* **1.** Of, like, or pertaining to hell. **2.**
ndish; horrible. — **hell′ish·ly** *adv.* — **hell′ish·ness** *n.*
lo (hə·lō′) *interj.* **1.** An exclamation of greeting, esp.
er the telephone. **2.** An exclamation used to gain atten-
n. **3.** An exclamation of surprise. — *n.* *pl.* **·loes** The
ing or calling of "hello." — *v.t. & v.i.* **·loed, ·lo·ing** To
l or say "hello" to.
m (helm) *n.* **1.** *Naut.* The steering apparatus of a vessel,
. the tiller or wheel. **2.** Any place of control or responsi-
ity; administration. — *v.t.* To manage the helm of; steer;
ect. [OE *helma* rudder]

hel·met (hel′mit) *n.* **1.** Any of a number of protective coverings for the head; as: **a** The topmost piece of a suit of medieval or ancient armor. **b** The metal headguard worn by modern soldiers. **c** The leather or plastic headgear used by football players. **d** A head protector, as worn by firemen, welders,
divers, etc. **e** A pith sun hat worn in hot countries. **2.** Something resembling a helmet in appearance or position. [< OF,
dim. of *helme* helmet < Gmc.] — **hel′met·ed** *adj.*
hel·minth (hel′minth) *n.* A worm; esp., a parasitic intestinal worm. [< Gk. *helmins, -inthos* worm]
helms·man (helmz′mən) *n.* *pl.* **·men** (-mən) A steersman;
one who guides a ship.
hel·ot (hel′ət, hē′lət) *n.* **1.** A slave; serf. **2.** *Usu. cap.* One
of a class of serfs in ancient Sparta. [< L < Gk., appar. <
Helos, a Laconian town enslaved by Sparta] — **hel′ot·ry** *n.*
help (help) *v.t.* **1.** To assist (someone) in doing something;
cooperate with. **2.** To assist (someone or something) in
some action, change, etc.: with *onto, into, out of, up, down,*
etc. **3.** To provide aid or relief to. **4.** To be, or be considered, responsible for: He can't *help* being lame. **5.** To
refrain from: I couldn't *help* laughing. **6.** To remedy;
alleviate. **7.** To contribute to. **8.** To serve; wait on, as a
salesclerk. — *v.i.* **9.** To give assistance. — **cannot help
but** Cannot avoid; be obliged to. — **to help oneself** **1.** To
serve oneself, as with food. **2.** To take without requesting
or being offered. — *n.* **1.** The act of helping. **2.** Remedy;
relief. **3.** One who or that which gives assistance. **4.** Any
hired worker or helper. [OE *helpan*] — **help′er** *n.*
help·ful (help′fəl) *adj.* Affording help; giving service; beneficial. — **help′ful·ly** *adv.* — **help′ful·ness** *n.*
help·ing (hel′ping) *n.* **1.** The act of assisting or aiding. **2.**
A single portion of food served at table.
help·less (help′lis) *adj.* **1.** Unable to help oneself; dependent; feeble. **2.** Incompetent; incapable. **3.** Without recourse to help. — **help′less·ly** *adv.* — **help′less·ness** *n.*
help·mate (help′māt′) *n.* **1.** A helper; partner. **2.** A wife.
Also **help·meet** (help′mēt′).
hel·ter·skel·ter (hel′tər·skel′tər) *adv.* In a hurried and
confused manner. — *adj.* Hurried and confused. — *n.*
Disorderly hurry; confused and hasty action. [Imit.]
helve (helv) *n.* The handle, as of an ax or hatchet. — *v.t.*
helved, helv·ing To furnish with a helve. [OE *helfe*]
Hel·ve·tia (hel·vē′shə) **1.** A country of Roman times including a large part of what is now Switzerland. **2.** The
Latin name for SWITZERLAND. — **Hel·ve′tian** *adj. & n.*
hem[1] (hem) *n.* **1.** A finished edge made on a piece of fabric
or a garment by turning the raw edge under and sewing it
down. **2.** Any similar border or edging. — *v.t.* **hemmed,
hem·ming** **1.** To provide with a hem. **2.** To shut in; enclose; restrict: usu. with *in, about,* etc. [OE] — **hem′mer** *n.*
hem[2] (hem) *interj.* A sound made as in clearing the throat
to attract attention, cover embarrassment, etc.; ahem. —
v.i. **hemmed, hem·ming** **1.** To make the sound "hem." **2.**
To hesitate in speaking. — **to hem and haw** To hesitate in
speaking so as to keep from being explicit. [Imit.]
hem- See also words beginning HAEM-.
hem- See HEMO-.
hema- *combining form* Blood. Also spelled *haema-*. [<
Gk. *haima* blood]
he·mal (hē′məl) *adj.* **1.** Pertaining to blood or the vascular
system. **2.** Pertaining to or situated on the side of the body
that contains the heart. Also spelled *haemal.*
he-man (hē′man′) *n.* *pl.* **·men** (-men′) *Informal* A virile,
muscular man.
hem·a·tite (hem′ə·tīt, hē′mə-) *n.* Red ferric oxide, Fe_2O_3,
an ore of iron, occurring in masses and crystallizing in the
hexagonal system: also called *ferric oxide.* Also spelled *hae-
matite.* [< L < Gk. < *haima* blood] — **hem·a·tit·ic** (hem′·
ə·tit′ik, hē′mə-) *adj.*
hemato- *combining form* Blood. Also, before vowels, **he-
mat-**. Also spelled *haemato-*. [< Gk. *haima, haimatos,*
blood]
he·ma·tol·o·gy (hē′mə·tol′ə·jē, hem′ə-) *n.* The branch of
biology that treats of the blood and its diseases. Also **he′·
ma·to·lo′gi·a** (-tə·lō′jē·ə). — **he′ma·tol′o·gist** *n.*
he·ma·tol·y·sis (hē′mə·tol′ə·sis, hem′ə-) *n.* Hemolysis.
he·ma·to·ma (hē′mə·tō′mə, hem′ə-) *n.* *pl.* **·to·ma·ta** (-tō′·
mə·tə) *Pathol.* A tumor or swelling formed by the effusion
of blood.
hemi- *prefix* Half: *hemisphere.* Also, before vowels, **hem-**.
[< Gk., half]
-hemia See -EMIA.
he·mic (hē′mik, hem′ik) *adj.* Of or pertaining to blood.
hem·i·dem·i·sem·i·qua·ver (hem′ē·dem′ē·sem′ē·kwā′vər)
n. *Music Chiefly Brit.* A sixty-fourth note.
hem·i·ple·gi·a (hem′i·plē′jē·ə) *n.* *Pathol.* Paralysis of one
side of the body. — **hem′i·ple′gic** (-plē′jik, -plej′ik) *adj.*
he·mip·ter·ous (hi·mip′tər·əs) *adj.* Of an order of insects

generally having sucking mouth parts and four wings, including the cicadas, crickets, etc. [< NL < Gk. *hēmi-* half + *pteron* wing] — **he·mip′ter·an** *adj.* & *n.*

hem·i·sphere (hem′ə·sfir) *n.* **1.** A half-sphere formed by a plane passing through the center of the sphere. **2.** A half of the terrestrial or celestial globe, or a map or projection of one. The world is usu. divided either at the equator into the **Northern** and **Southern Hemispheres,** or at some meridian between Europe and America into the **Eastern** and **Western Hemispheres.** [< F < L < Gk. *hēmi-* half + *sphaira* sphere] — **hem·is·pher·ic** (hem′ə·sfir′ik, -sfer-) *adj.*

hem·i·stich (hem′i·stik) *n.* Half a line of verse.

hem·line (hem′līn′) *n.* The line formed by the lower edge of a garment, as a dress or coat.

hem·lock (hem′lok) *n.* **1.** One of several North American. or Asian evergreen trees of the pine family, having coarse, nonresinous wood used for paper pulp. Also **hemlock spruce.** **2.** A large, biennial herb of the parsley family, yielding a poison: also **poison hemlock.** [OE *hymlice*]

hemo- *combining form* Blood. Also, before vowels, **hem-.** Also spelled *haemo-.* [< Gk. *haima* blood]

he·mo·glo·bin (hē′mə·glō′bin, hem′ə-) *n. Biochem.* The respiratory pigment in red blood corpuscles, composed of globin and heme, and serving as a carrier of oxygen.

he·mol·y·sis (hi·mol′ə·sis) *n.* Breakdown of red blood corpuscles with liberation of hemoglobin: also called *hematolysis.* — **he·mo·lyt·ic** (hē′mə·lit′ik, hem′ə-) *adj.*

he·mo·phil·i·a (hē′mə·fil′ē·ə, -fil′yə, hem′ə-) *n. Pathol.* A disorder characterized by immoderate bleeding even from slight injuries. [< NL < Gk. *haima* blood + *philia* fondness] — **he′mo·phil′i·ac, he′mo·phile′** (-fīl, -fil) *n.*

he·mo·phil·ic (hē′mə·fil′ik, hem′ə-) *adj.* **1.** Of hemophilia. **2.** Thriving in blood, as certain bacteria.

hem·or·rhage (h··′ər·ij, hem′rij) *n.* Copious discharge of blood from a rup··red blood vessel. — *v.i.* **·rhaged, ·rhag·ing** To bleed copiously. [< L < Gk. *haima* blood + *rhēgnynai* to burst] — **hem·or·rhag·ic** (hem′ə·raj′ik) *adj.*

hem·or·rhoid (hem′ə·roid) *n. Pathol.* A tumor or dilation of a vein in the anal region, usu. painful: also, in the plural, *piles.* [< F < L < Gk. < *haima* blood + *rheein* to flow] — **hem·or·rhoi·dal** (hem′ə·roid′l) *adj.*

he·mo·stat (hē′mə·stat, hem′ə-) *n. Med.* A device or drug for checking the flow of blood from a ruptured vessel.

he·mo·stat·ic (hē′mə·stat′ik, hem′ə-) *Med. adj.* **1.** Stopping the flow of blood. **2.** Preventive of bleeding.

hemp (hemp) *n.* **1.** A tall, annual herb of the mulberry family, native in Asia but cultivated elsewhere. **2.** The tough, strong fiber from this plant, used for cloth and cordage. **3.** A narcotic prepared from the plant. [OE *henep*]

hemp·en (hem′pən) *adj.* Made of or like hemp.

hem·stitch (hem′stich′) *n.* The ornamental finishing of a hem, made by pulling out several threads and drawing the cross threads together in groups. — *v.t.* To embroider with a hemstitch. — **hem′stitch′er** *n.*

hen (hen) *n.* **1.** The mature female of the domestic fowl and related birds. **2.** The female of the lobster. [OE *henn*]

hen·bane (hen′bān) *n.* A poisonous Old World herb of the nightshade family, with sticky, malodorous foliage.

hence (hens) *adv.* **1.** As a consequence; therefore; thus. **2.** From this time or date: a week *hence*; also, ever afterwards; henceforth. **3.** Away from this place. — *interj. Archaic & Poetic* Go! Depart! [ME < OE *heonan* from here]

hence·forth (hens′fôrth′, -fōrth′; hens′fôrth′, -fōrth′) *adv.* From this time on. Also **hence′for′ward** (-fôr′wərd).

hench·man (hench′mən) *n. pl.* **·men** (-mən) **1.** A faithful follower. **2.** *U.S.* A political supporter who works chiefly for personal gain. [ME < OE *hengst* horse + *man* groom]

hen·e·quen (hen′ə·kin) *n.* **1.** A tough fiber obtained from the leaves of a Mexican plant. **2.** The plant. Also **hen′e·quin.** [< Sp. < Taino]

hen·na (hen′ə) *n.* **1.** An ornamental Oriental shrub or small tree. **2.** A cosmetic made from its leaves, used for dyeing the hair, fingernails, etc. **3.** A color varying from reddish orange to coppery brown. — *v.* **hen·naed, hen·na·ing** *v.t.* To dye with henna. [< Arabic *henna*]

hen·ner·y (hen′ər·ē) *n. pl.* **·ner·ies** A place where hens are kept.

hen·peck (hen′pek′) *v.t.* To domineer over or harass (one's husband) by nagging, ill temper, and petty annoyances.

hen·pecked (hen′pekt′) *adj.* Dominated by one's wife.

hen·ry (hen′rē) *n. pl.* **·ries** or **·rys** *Electr.* The unit equal to the inductance of a circuit in which the variation of a current at the rate of one ampere per second induces an electromotive force of one volt. [after Joseph *Henry,* 1797–1878, U.S. physicist]

hep·a·rin (hep′ə·rin) *n. Biochem.* A substance found in liver and other tissues, having the power to prevent coagulation of blood, used in medicine. [< Gk. *hēpar* liver]

he·pat·ic (hi·pat′ik) *adj.* **1.** Of or like the liver. **2.** Acting upon the liver. **3.** Liver-colored. — *n.* A drug acting upon the liver. Also **he·pat′i·cal.** [< L < Gk. *hepar* liver]

he·pat·i·ca (hi·pat′ə·kə) *n. pl.* **·cas** or **·cae** (-sē) A s perennial herb with delicate flowers: also called *liver* [< NL < L *hepaticus* of the liver]

hepatico- *combining form* Hepato-.

hep·a·ti·tis (hep′ə·tī′tis) *n. Pathol.* Inflammation o liver.

hepato- *combining form* Pertaining to the liver. Also fore vowels, **hepat-.** [< Gk. *hēpar, hēpatos* the liver]

Hep·ple·white (hep′əl·hwīt) *adj.* Denoting an En style of furniture characterized by graceful curves and light, slender woodwork, developed in the reign of George III. [after G. *Hepplewhite,* died 1786, the designer]

HEPPLEWH CHAIR

hepta- *combining form* Seven. Also, before vowels, **hept-.** [< Gk. *hepta* seven]

hep·ta·gon (hep′tə·gon) *n.* A polygon having seven sides and seven angles. — **hep·tag·o·nal** (hep·tag′ə·nəl) *adj.*

hep·tam·e·ter (hep·tam′ə·tər) *n.* In prosody, a line of verse consisting of seven metrical feet.

hep·tane (hep′tān) *n. Chem.* A colorless flammable liquid hydrocarbon of the methane series, C_7H_{16}, used as a solvent and in the dete nation of the octane number of motor fules.

her (hûr) *pron.* The objective case of the pronoun *she* *pronominal adj.* The possessive case of *she.* [OE *hire*]

He·ra (hir′ə) In Greek mythology, the queen of the gods goddess of women and marriage, sister and wife of Z identified with the Roman *Juno.* Also spelled *Here.*

Her·a·cles (her′ə·klēz) Hercules. Also **Her′a·kles.**

her·ald (her′əld) *n.* **1.** Any bearer of important news; senger. **2.** One who or that which shows what is to fo harbinger. **3.** *Brit.* An official whose duty is to grar record arms, trace genealogies, etc. **4.** Formerly, an o who carried messages, arranged tournaments, etc. — To announce or proclaim publicly. [< OF < OHG h to call] — **he·ral·dic** (hi·ral′dik) *adj.*

her·ald·ry (her′əl·drē) *n. pl.* **·ries** **1.** The art or sci that treats of armorial bearings, genealogies, etc., as in aldic symbolism. **2.** The office or function of a herald

herb (ûrb, hûrb) *n.* **1.** A plant without woody tissue, withers and dies after flowering. **2.** Any such plant medicine, seasoning, scent, etc. [< L *herba* grass, herb

her·ba·ceous (hûr·bā′shəs) *adj.* **1.** Like herbs. **2.** Ha the semblance, color, or structure of a leaf.

herb·age (ûr′bij, hûr′-) *n.* **1.** Herbs collectively, esp. turage. **2.** The succulent parts of herbaceous plants.

herb·al (hûr′bəl, ûr′-) *adj.* Of or pertaining to herbs. - Formerly, a treatise on herbs or plants.

herb·al·ist (hûr′bəl·ist, ûr′-) *n.* A dealer in herbs.

her·bar·i·um (hûr·bâr′ē·əm) *n. pl.* **·bar·i·ums** or **·ba** (-bâr′ē·ə). **1.** A collection of dried plants scientificall ranged. **2.** A room or building containing such a collec

her·biv·o·rous (hûr·biv′ər·əs) *adj.* **1.** Feeding on vege matter; plant-eating. **2.** Belonging to a group of mam that feed mainly on herbage, as cows, horses, camels, [< L *herba* grass] — **her·biv′o·rous·ly** *adv.*

her·cu·le·an (hûr·kyōō′lē·an, hûr′kyə·lē′ən) *adj.* **1.** ing great strength. **2.** Requiring great strength.

Her·cu·le·an (hûr·kyōō′lē·ən, hûr′kyə·lē′ən). *adj.* Of or taining to Hercules (Heracles); Heraclean.

Her·cu·les (hûr′kyə·lēz) In classical mythology, the s Zeus, renowned for his great strength: also called *Her* — *n.* **1.** Any man of great strength. **2.** A constellatio

herd (hûrd) *n.* **1.** A number of cattle or other animals f ing, moving about, or kept together. **2.** A large crow people: a contemptuous term. — *v.t.* & *v.i.* To brin drive together in a herd. — **Syn.** See FLOCK. [OE *h*

-herd *combining form* Herdsman: *swineherd, cowherd,* [OE *hierde* herdsman]

herds·man (hûrdz′mən) *n. pl.* **·men** (-mən) *Brit.* One owns or tends a herd. Also **herd′er, herd′man.**

here (hir) *adv.* **1.** In, at, or about this place: oppose *there.* Also used to indicate or emphasize: George *here* is a swimmer. **2.** To this place; hither. **3.** At this poi time, in an action, etc.: *Here* you begin; *Here* are my rea **4.** In the present life: distinguished from *hereafter.* — *i* An exclamation used to answer a roll call, attract atten call an animal, etc. — **here and there** **1.** Irregularly tered. **2.** Hither and thither. — **here goes!** For bett worse, I start now! — **neither here nor there** Beside point; irrelevant. — *n.* **1.** This place. **2.** This time; life: the *here* and now. [OE *hēr*]

He·re (hir′ē) See HERA.

here·a·bout (hir′ə·bout′) *adv.* About this place; in thi cinity. Also **here′a·bouts′.**

here·af·ter (hir·af′tər, -äf′-) *adj.* **1.** At some future t **2.** From this time forth. **3.** In the state of life after de — *n.* A future state or existence. [OE *hēræfter*]

here·at (hir·at′) *adv.* **1.** At this time. **2.** Because of

·**by** (hir·bī′) *adv.* By means or by virtue of this.
ed·i·ta·ble (hə·red′i·tə·bəl) *adj.* Heritable. [< MF *ditable*] — **he·red′i·ta·bil′i·ty** *n.* — **he·red′i·ta·bly** *adv.*
e·dit·a·ment (her′ə·dit′ə·mənt) *n. Law* Every kind of perty capable of being inherited.
ed·i·tar·y (hə·red′ə·ter′ē) *adj.* **1.** Derived from ances- ; inherited. **2.** Of or pertaining to heredity or inheri- ce. **3.** *Biol.* Transmitted or transmissible directly from animal or plant to its offspring: distinguished from *con- tal.* **4.** *Law* **a** Passing by inheritance to an heir. **b** Hold- possession or title through inheritance. — **he·red′i·tar′·** *adv.* — **he·red′i·tar′i·ness** *n.*
ed·i·ty (hə·red′ə·tē) *n. pl.* **·ties** *Biol.* **1.** Transmission haracteristics from parents to offspring. **2.** The tenden- nanifested by an organism to develop in the likeness of a genitor. **3.** The sum total of an individual's inherited racteristics. [< F < L *hereditas, -tatis* inheritance]
e·ford (her′ə·fərd, *U.S.* hûr′fərd) *n.* One of a breed of cattle having a white face and a red and white coat.
·**in** (hir·in′) *adv.* **1.** In or into this place; in this. **2.** In case, circumstance, matter, etc. [OE *hērinne*]
·**in·af·ter** (hir′in·af′tər, -äf′-) *adv.* In a subsequent of this document, deed, contract, etc.
·**in·be·fore** (hir′in·bi·fôr′, -fōr′) *adv.* In a preceding of this document, deed, contract, etc.
·**in·to** (hir·in′to͞o) *adv.* **1.** Into this place. **2.** Into this , circumstance, matter, etc.
·**of** (hir·uv′, -ov) *adv.* **1.** Of this. **2.** In regard to this.
·**on** (hir·on′, -ôn′) *adv.* On this; hereupon.
·**sy** (her′ə·sē) *n. pl.* **·sies** **1.** A belief contrary to the blished doctrines of a church or religious system. **2.** Any ef contrary to established doctrine. **3.** The holding of a belief or opinion. [< OF < Gk. *hairesis* sect]
·**tic** (her′ə·tik) *n.* **1.** One who holds beliefs or opinions rary to the established doctrines of his religion. **2.** One maintains unorthodox opinions on any subject.
et·i·cal (hə·ret′i·kəl) *adj.* Of, pertaining to, or charac- ed by heresy. — **he·ret′i·cal·ly** *adv.*
·**to** (hir·to͞o′) *adv.* To this thing, matter, etc.
·**to·fore** (hir′tə·fôr′, -fōr′) *adv.* Before now; previously.
·**un·der** (hir·un′dər) *adv.* **1.** Under this heading, etc. Under the terms of this statement, etc.
·**un·to** (hir′un·to͞o′) *adv.* To this; hereto.
·**up·on** (hir′ə·pon′, -pôn′) *adv.* Immediately resulting n or following this; upon this.
·**with** (hir·with′, -wi*th*′) *adv.* **1.** Along with this. **2.** means of or through this.
·**ta·ble** (her′ə·tə·bəl) *adj.* **1.** That can be inherited. **2.** Capable of inheriting. [< OF < *heriter* to inherit] — **i·ta·bil′i·ty** *n.* — **her′i·ta·bly** *adv.*
·**tage** (her′ə·tij) *n.* **1.** That which is inherited. **2.** A ural tradition, body of knowledge, etc., handed down n past times. **3.** *Law* Property that is or can be inher- by descendants. [< OF *heriter* to inherit]
·**tor** (her′ə·tər) *n.* An inheritor. — **her′e·trix** or **her′i·** (-triks) or **her′i·tress** (-tris) *n.fem.*
maph·ro·dite (hûr·maf′rə·dīt) *n.* **1.** An individual hav- both male and female reproductive organs. **2.** *Bot.* A t having both stamens and pistils. — *adj.* Hermaphro- . [after *Hermaphroditus*, son of Hermes, who became ed with a nymph in a single body]
naphrodite brig *Naut.* A brigantine.
naph·ro·dit·ic (hûr·maf′rə·dit′ik) *adj.* Of, pertaining or characteristic of a hermaphrodite.
maph·ro·dit·ism (hûr·maf′rə·dīt·iz′əm) *n.* The state ondition of being a hermaphrodite.
mes (hûr′mēz) In Greek mythology, the messenger of gods, usually depicted with winged sandals, a hat, and a uceus: identified with the Roman *Mercury.*
met·ic (hûr·met′ik) *adj.* **1.** Made impervious to air and ids; airtight. **2.** Of or relating to alchemy; occult; magi- Also **her·met′i·cal.** [< Med.L *hermeticus*] — **her·** ′**i·cal·ly** *adv.*
mit (hûr′mit) *n.* **1.** One who abandons society and s in seclusion, often for religious reasons. **2.** A molasses ky. [< OF < LL < Gk. *erēmia* desert] — **her·mit′ic** or l *adj.* — **her·mit′i·cal·ly** *adv.*
mit·age (hûr′mə·tij) *n.* **1.** The retreat or dwelling of a nit. **2.** Any secluded dwelling place.
nit crab Any of various soft-bodied crustaceans that in the empty shells of snails, etc.
ni·a (hûr′nē·ə) *n. pl.* **·ni·as** or **·ni·ae** (ni·ē) *Pathol.* The rusion of an organ or part of an organ, as of the intestine, ugh an opening in the wall surrounding it; rupture. [< — **her′ni·al** *adj.*
nio- *combining form* Hernia.
o (hir′ō, hē′rō) *n. pl.* **·roes** **1.** A man distinguished for eptional courage, fortitude, or bold enterprise. **2.** One idealized for superior qualities or deeds of any kind. **3.** The principal male character in a drama, fictional work, etc. **4.** In classical mythology and legend, a man of great nobility or physical prowess, often the son of a god and a mortal. **5.** *U.S.* A sandwich made with a loaf of bread cut lengthwise. [< L < Gk. *hērōs*]
He·ro (hir′ō) In Greek legend, a priestess whose lover, Leander, nightly swam the Hellespont to join her. Finding him drowned one night, she cast herself into the sea.
he·ro·ic (hi·rō′ik) *adj.* **1.** Characteristic of or befitting a hero. **2.** Resembling a hero. **3.** Showing great daring or boldness; extreme in action or effect: a *heroic* attempt. **4.** Of or pertaining to the heroes of antiquity. **5.** Relating to or describing a hero or heroic deeds; epic: *heroic* poetry. **6.** Grandiose in style or language. **7.** Of sculpture, considerably larger than life size. Also **he·ro′i·cal.** — *n.* **1.** *Often pl.* Heroic verse. **2.** *pl.* Melodramatic or extravagant language, action, or ideas. — **he·ro′i·cal·ly** *adv.*
heroic couplet An English verse form consisting of two rhyming lines of iambic pentameter.
heroic verse One of several verse forms used especially in epic and dramatic poetry, as the iambic pentameter of the English heroic couplet and blank verse.
her·o·in (her′ō·in) *n.* A white, odorless, crystalline derivative of morphine, $C_{21}H_{23}O_5N$, a powerful, habit-forming narcotic. [< G]
her·o·ine (her′ō·in) *n.fem.* **1.** A girl or woman of heroic character. **2.** The principal female character of a drama, fictional work, etc. [< L < Gk. *hērōinē*]
her·o·ism (her′ō·iz′əm) *n.* **1.** The character or qualities of a hero or heroine. **2.** Heroic behavior.
her·on (her′ən) *n.* **1.** Any of several wading birds, having a long neck, a long, slender bill, and long legs. **2.** Any of various similar or related birds, as the egret or the bittern. [< OF *hairon*, ult. < Gmc.]
her·on·ry (her′ən·rē) *n. pl.* **·ries** A place where herons congregate and breed.
hero worship Enthusiastic or extravagant admiration for heroes or other persons. — **hero worshiper**
her·pes (hûr′pēz) *n. Pathol.* A virus infection of the skin and mucous membranes, characterized by the eruption of blisters. [< L < Gk. *herpein* to creep]

GREAT BLUE HERON (About 4 feet high)

herpes zos·ter (zos′tər) *Pathol.* Shingles. [< L, herpes + *zoster* (< Gk., girdle, belt)]
her·pe·tol·o·gy (hûr′pə·tol′ə·jē) *n.* The branch of zoology that treats of reptiles and amphibians. [< Gk. *herpeton* reptile + -LOGY] — **her·pe·to·log·i·cal** (hûr′pə·tə·loj′i·kəl) *adj.* — **her′pe·tol′o·gist** *n.*
Herr (her) *n. pl.* **Her·ren** (her′ən) *German* A title of address equivalent oo the English *Mister.* Abbr. *Hr.*
her·ring (her′ing) *n. pl.* **·rings** or **·ring** **1.** A small food fish frequenting the North Atlantic, the young of which are canned as sardines, and the adults smoked, pickled, or salted. **2.** Any of various fish allied to the herring, as the shad, sardine, etc. [OE *hæring*]
her·ring·bone (her′ing·bōn′) *n.* **1.** A pattern utilizing a design, often repeated, resembling the spinal structure of a herring, in which the ribs form slanting parallel lines on either side of the spine. **2.** Something made in or consisting of such a pattern. — *adj.* Having or forming the pattern of a herringbone. — *v.* **·boned, ·bon·ing** *v.t.* **1.** To ornament with or arrange in a herringbone pattern. — *v.i.* **2.** To produce a herringbone pattern. **3.** In skiing, to walk up an incline with the skis pointed outward.
hers (hûrz) *pron.* **1.** The possessive case of the pronoun *she*, used predicatively: That book is *hers.* **2.** The one or ones belonging to or relating to her. — **of hers** Belonging or relating to her. [OE *hire* + *-s* (after *his*)]
her·self (hər·self′) *pron.* A form of the third person singular feminine pronoun, used: **1.** As a reflexive or as object of a preposition in a reflexive sense: She excused *herself*; She talks to *herself.* **2.** As an emphatic or intensive form of *she*: She *herself* called the police. **3.** As a designation of a normal or usual state: After her illness, she was *herself* again. **4.** *Irish* As a pronoun meaning *she*: How is *herself*?
Hertz·i·an wave (hert′sē·ən, hûrt′-) An electromagnetic wave in the radio and radar range, artificially produced. [after H. R. *Hertz*]
he's (hēz) **1.** He is. **2.** He has.
Hesh·wan (hesh·vän′, hesh′van) *n.* The second month of the Hebrew year. Also **Hesh·van′.** See (Hebrew) CALENDAR.
hes·i·tan·cy (hez′ə·tən·sē) *n. pl.* **·cies** The act or condition of hesitating; hesitation; uncertainty. Also **hes′i·tance.**
hes·i·tant (hes′ə·tənt) *adj.* Lacking certainty or decisiveness; hesitating; irresolute. — **hes′i·tant·ly** *adv.*

hes·i·tate (hez′ə·tāt) *v.i.* **·tat·ed, ·tat·ing 1.** To be slow or doubtful in acting, making a decision, etc.; be uncertain; waver. **2.** To be reluctant. **3.** To pause or falter. **4.** To falter in speech. [< L *haesitare*, freq. of *haerere* to stick]

hes·i·ta·tion (hez′ə·tā′shən) *n.* **1.** The act of hesitating. **2.** A pause or delay caused by indecision or uncertainty. **3.** A pause or faltering in speech. **— hes′i·ta′tive** *adj.*

Hes·pe·ri·an (hes·pir′ē·ən) *adj.* **1.** *Poetic* In or of the west. **2.** Of the Hesperides. [< L < Gk. *hesperios* western]

Hes·per·i·des (hes·per′ə·dēz) *n.pl.* **1.** In Greek mythology, the daughters of Atlas who, together with a dragon, guarded the golden apples given to Hera. **2.** The garden where these apples grew. [< Gk. *hesperis* western]

Hes·pe·rus (hes′pər·əs) *n.* The evening star, esp. Venus. Also *Poetic* **Hes′per.** [< L < Gk. *Hesperos*]

Hes·sian (hesh′ən) *n.* **1.** A native of Hesse. **2.** A soldier from Hesse hired by the British to fight in the American Revolution. **—** *adj.* Of Hesse or its inhabitants.

Hessian fly A small, blackish fly, whose larvae are very destructive to wheat, barley, and rye.

het (het) *Dial.* Past tense and past participle of HEAT. **— het up** Excited; angry.

he·tae·ra (hi·tir′ə, -tī′rə) *n. pl.* **·tae·rae** (-tir′ē, -tī′rē) In ancient Greece, a professional courtesan or concubine. Also **he·tae·ra** (hi·tī′rə). [< Gk. *hetaira* companion]

hetero- *combining form* Other; different: opposed to *homo-*. Also, before vowels, **heter-.** [< Gk. *hetero-* < *heteros* other]

het·er·o·cy·clic (het′ər·ə·sī′klik, -sik′lik) *adj. Chem.* Pertaining to or designating an organic ring compound containing atoms of one or more elements other than carbon.

het·er·o·dox (het′ər·ə·doks′) *adj.* **1.** At variance with accepted or established doctrines or beliefs, esp. in religion. **2.** Holding unorthodox beliefs or opinions. [< Gk. *hetero-* other + *doxa* opinion] **— het′er·o·dox′y** *n.*

het·er·o·dyne (het′ər·ə·dīn′) *adj. Telecom.* Denoting a radio circuit, receiver, etc., in which the incoming signal is combined with a signal of fixed frequency and the signal resulting from their beats is used as the amplifier input. **—** *v.i.* **·dyned, ·dyn·ing** To modify a signal in this manner.

het·er·o·ge·ne·i·ty (het′ər·ə·jə·nē′ə·tē) *n. pl.* **·ties** The state of being heterogeneous; dissimilarity.

het·er·o·ge·ne·ous (het′ər·ə·jē′nē·əs) *adj.* **1.** Consisting of parts or elements that are dissimilar or unrelated; not homogeneous. **2.** Differing in nature or kind; unlike. [< Med.L < Gk. < *hetero-* other + *genos* kind] **— het′er·o·ge′ne·ous·ly** *adv.* **— het′er·o·ge′ne·ous·ness** *n.*

het·er·og·e·nous (het′ə·roj′ə·nəs) *adj. Biol.* Originating outside the organism.

het·er·o·nym (het′ər·ə·nim′) *n.* A word spelled like another, but having a different sound and meaning, as *bass*, a male voice, and *bass*, a fish. Compare HOMOGRAPH. [< HETER(O)- + Gk. *onyma* name; on analogy with *synonym*] **— het·er·on·y·mous** (het′ə·ron′ə·məs) *adj.*

het·er·op·ter·ous (het′ə·rop′tər·es) *adj.* Designating a suborder of hemipterous insects that includes the true bugs. [< NL < Gk. *hetero-* other + *pteron* wing]

het·er·o·sex·u·al (het′ər·ə·sek′shōō·əl) *adj.* **1.** Of, or having sexual desire for those of the opposite sex. **2.** *Biol.* Of or pertaining to the opposite sex or to both sexes. **—** *n.* A heterosexual individual. **— het′er·o·sex′u·al′i·ty** (-al′ə·tē) *n.*

het·er·o·zy·gote (het′ər·ə·zī′gōt, -zig′ōt) *n. Biol.* A hybrid that carries different alleles of the same character and that does not breed true. **— het′er·o·zy′gous** (-zī′gəs) *adj.*

heu·ris·tic (hyōō·ris′tik) *adj.* **1.** Aiding or guiding in discovery. **2.** Designating an educational method by which a pupil is stimulated to make his own investigations and discoveries. [< Gk. *heuriskein* to find out]

hew (hyōō) *v.* **hewed, hewn** or **hewed, hew·ing** *v.t.* **1.** To make or shape with or as with blows of an ax or other cutting tool. **2.** To cut or strike with an ax, sword, etc. **3.** To fell with or as with ax blows. **—** *v.i.* **4.** To make cutting and repeated blows, as with an ax or sword. **5.** To conform, as to a principle. [OE *hēawan*] **— hew′er** *n.*

hex (heks) *U.S. Dial.* or *Informal n.* **1.** An evil spell. **2.** A witch. **—** *v.t.* To bewitch. [< G *hexe* witch]

hexa- *combining form* Six. Also, before vowels, **hex-.** [< Gk. *hexa-* < *hex* six]

hex·a·gon (hek′sə·gon) *n. Geom.* A polygon having six sides and six angles. [< L < Gk. *hex* six + *gonia* angle] **— hex·ag·o·nal** (hek·sag′ə·nəl) *adj.* **— hex·ag′o·nal·ly** *adv.*

hex·a·gram (hek′sə·gram) *n.* **1.** A six-pointed star made by or as by completing the equilateral triangles based on the sides of a regular hexagon. **2.** Any of various figures formed by six intersecting lines.

HEXAGRAM

hex·am·e·ter (hek·sam′ə·tər) *n.* **1.** In prosody, a line of verse consisting of six metrical feet. **2.** The dactylic verse of Greek and Latin epics. **—** *adj.* Having six metrical feet. [< L < Gk. *hexametros*] **— hex·a·met·ric** (hek′sə·met′rik), **hex·am′e·tral** (-ə·trəl), **hex′a·met′ri·cal** *adj.*

hex·a·pod (hek′sə·pod) *n.* One of the true or six-legge sects. **—** *adj.* Having six feet. [< Gk. *hexapous*, - six-footed] **— hex·ap·o·dous** (hek·sap′ə·dəs) *adj.*

hex·ose (hek′sōs) *n. Biochem.* Any simple sugar, as gl or fructose, containing six carbon atoms to the molecu

hey (hā) *interj.* An exclamation calling for attention c pressing surprise, pleasure, inquiry, etc. [ME *hei*]

hey·day (hā′dā′) *n.* **1.** Period of greatest vigor; heig of power. **2.** Exuberance; ardor. [Prob. < HIGH DAY

H-hour (āch′our′) *n.* The hour appointed for a militar eration to begin: also called *zero hour.*

hi (hī) *interj.* **1.** *U.S.* An exclamation of greeting. **2.** A call to attract attention. [Var. of HEY]

hi·a·tus (hī·ā′təs) *n. pl.* **·tus·es** or **·tus 1.** A gap or from which something is missing, as in a manuscript; la **2.** Any break or interruption. **3.** A pause due to the co together in a word or successive words of two separately nounced vowels without an intervening consonant. [

Hi·a·wath·a (hī′ə·woth′ə, -wô′thə, hē′ə-) **1.** A Mo chief credited with organizing the Five Nations. **2** hero of Longfellow's poem *The Song of Hiawatha* (185

hi·ba·chi (hi·bä′chē) *n. pl.* **·chis** A deep container to burning coals, used for heating and cooking. [< Japa

hi·ber·nal (hī·bûr′nəl) *adj.* Of or pertaining to winter; try. [< L *hibernus* wintry]

hi·ber·nate (hī′bər·nāt) *v.i.* **·nat·ed, ·nat·ing 1.** To pa winter in a dormant state, as certain animals. **2.** To re inactive or secluded. [< L *hibernare*] **— hi′ber·na′ti**

Hi·ber·ni·a (hī·bûr′nē·ə) Latin and poetic name for Ire [< L, alter. of *Iverna*] **— Hi·ber′ni·an** *n. & adj.*

hi·bis·cus (hī·bis′kəs, hi-) *n.* A shrub or tree of the m family, having large, showy flowers: the state flower o waii. [< L < Gk. *hibiskos* mallow]

hic·cup (hik′əp) *n.* **1.** An involuntary contraction of t aphragm, causing a sudden, audible inspiration of b checked by a spasmodic closure of the glottis. **2.** *pl.* A dition characterized by repetition of such spasms. **·cuped** or **·cupped, ·cup·ing** or **·cup·ping —** *v.i.* **1.** To a sound of or as of a hiccup. **—** *v.t.* **2.** To utter wit cups. Also **hic·cough** (hik′əp). [Imit.]

hic ja·cet (hik jā′set) *Latin* Here lies: often inscrib tombstones.

hick (hik) *n. Informal* One having the clumsy, unsop cated manners, etc. supposedly typical of rural areas; b kin. **—** *adj.* Of or typical of hicks. [Alter. of *Richard*

hick·ey (hik′ē) *n. pl.* **·eys** *U.S. Informal* **1.** Any g or contrivance. **2.** A pimple or blemish. [Origin unkn

hick·o·ry (hik′ər·ē, hik′rē) *n. pl.* **·ries 1.** A North A can tree of the walnut family, having hard, durable and yielding edible nuts. **2.** The wood of such trees. switch made of this wood. [< Algonquian *pawcohicc*

hid (hid) Past tense and alternative past participle of H

hi·dal·go (hi·dal′gō, *Sp.* ē·thäl′gō) *n. pl.* **·gos** (-gōz -gōs) A Spanish nobleman of lower rank than a grandee Sp. < *hijo de algo* son of something]

hid·den (hid′n) Past participle of HIDE[1]. **—** *adj.* Not or known; concealed; obscure; mysterious.

hide[1] (hīd) *v.* **hid, hid·den** or **hid, hid·ing** *v.t.* **1.** To p keep out of sight; conceal. **2.** To keep secret; withhold knowledge. **3.** To block or obstruct the sight of. **—** *v.* To keep oneself out of sight; remain concealed. **— to out** *U.S. Informal* To remain in concealment, esp. as a tive. [OE *hӯdan*] **— hid′er** *n.*

— Syn. 1. *Hide, conceal,* and *secrete* mean to put or keep sight. We may *hide* without intention, but we *conceal* intentio An object is *hidden* or *concealed* when covered from view, disguised as something else, or when buried out of reach. *secreted* when put into some private, secret place.

hide[2] (hīd) *n.* **1.** The skin of an animal, esp. when str from the carcass or made into leather. **2.** *Informal* Th man skin. **—** *v.t.* **hid·ed, hid·ing** *Informal* To flog seve whip. [OE *hӯd* skin]

hide-and-seek (hīd′n·sēk′) *n.* A children's game in those who hide are sought by one who is "it." Also **h and-go-seek′.**

hide·a·way (hīd′ə·wā′) *n.* A place of concealment.

hide·bound (hīd′bound′) *adj.* **1.** Obstinately fixed in ion; narrow-minded; bigoted. **2.** Having the skin too ti adhering to the back and ribs: said of cattle, etc.

hid·e·ous (hid′ē·əs) *adj.* **1.** Extremely ugly: a *hideous* **2.** Morally odious or detestable; shocking. [< AF < *hisde, hide* fright] **— hid′e·ous·ly** *adv.* **— hid′e·ous·ne**

hide-out (hīd′out′) *n. Informal* A place of concealme refuge, especially from legal authority. Also **hide′out′.**

hid·ing[1] (hī′ding) *n.* **1.** The act of one who or that w hides. **2.** A state or place of concealment.

hid·ing[2] (hī′ding) *n. Informal* A flogging; whipping.

hie (hī) *v.t. & v.i.* **hied, hie·ing** or **hy·ing** To hasten; h often reflexive: I *hied* myself home. [OE *hīgian*]

hi·er·arch (hī′ə·rärk) *n.* A high priest or prelate. Med.L < Gk. *hierarchēs* sacred + *hieros* ruler]

r·ar·chi·cal (hī′ə·rär′ki·kəl) *adj.* Of, belonging to, or racteristic of a hierarchy. Also **hi′er·ar′chic, hi′er·ar′·l.** — **hi′er·ar′chi·cal·ly** *adv.*
r·ar·chy (hī′ə·rär′kē) *n. pl.* **·chies 1.** Any group of pers or things arranged in successive orders or classes, each which is subject to or dependent on the one above it. **2.** A y of ecclesiastics so arranged. **3.** Government or rule by a body of ecclesiastics. **4.** In science and logic, a series ystematic groupings in graded order.
r·at·ic (hī′ə·rat′ik) *adj.* **1.** Of or pertaining to priests or stly usage. **2.** Of or pertaining to a shortened form of oglyphic writing used by priests in ancient Egypt.
o- *combining form* Sacred; divine. Also, before vowels, **r-.** [< Gk. *hieros* sacred]
r·o·glyph·ic (hī′ər·ə·glif′ik, hī′rə·glif′ik) *n.* **1.** *Usu. pl.* icture or symbol representing an object, idea, ound, as in the writing system of the ancient yptians. **2.** *pl.* A system of writing using h pictures or symbols. **3.** Any symbol or racter having an obscure or hidden meaning. ol. Illegible writing. Also **hi·er·o·glyph** (hī′-·glif′, hī′rə·glif). — *adj.* **1.** Pertaining to, sisting of, or resembling hieroglyphics. **2.** itten in or inscribed with hieroglyphics. **3.** ficult to decipher. Also **hi′er·o·glyph′i·cal.** LL < Gk. < *hieros* sacred + *glyphein* to ve] — **hi′er·o·glyph′i·cal·ly** *adv.* — **hi·er·y·phist** (hī′ər·og′lə·fist, hī·rog′-) *n.*

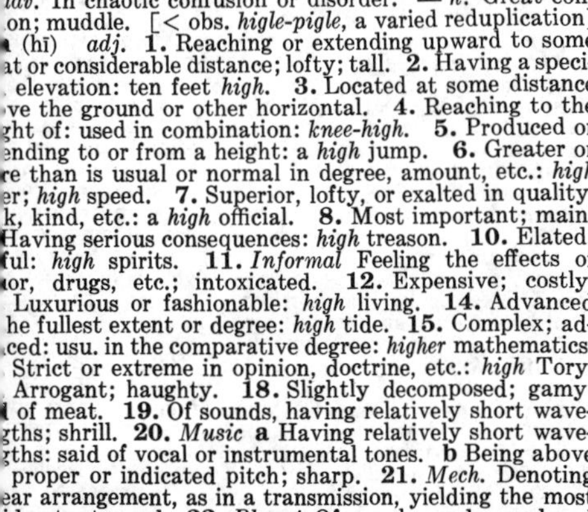
HIERO-GLYPHICS

(hī′fī′) *n.* **1.** High fidelity. **2.** Radio, phoraph, or recording equipment capable of reducing sound with high fidelity. — *adj.* Of pertaining to high fidelity.
gle (hig′əl) *v.i.* **·gled, ·gling** To argue over ns, prices, etc.; haggle. [Var. of HAGGLE] **hig′gler** *n.*
gle·dy-pig·gle·dy (hig′əl·dē·pig′əl·dē) *adj.* ordered or confused; jumbled; topsy-turvy. *adv.* In chaotic confusion or disorder. — *n.* Great conon; muddle. [< obs. *higle-pigle*, a varied reduplication]
(hī) *adj.* **1.** Reaching or extending upward to some at or considerable distance; lofty; tall. **2.** Having a specielevation: ten feet *high.* **3.** Located at some distance ve the ground or other horizontal. **4.** Reaching to the ght of: used in combination: *knee-high.* **5.** Produced or ending to or from a height: a *high* jump. **6.** Greater or e than is usual or normal in degree, amount, etc.: *high* er; *high* speed. **7.** Superior, lofty, or exalted in quality, k, kind, etc.: a *high* official. **8.** Most important; main. Having serious consequences: *high* treason. **10.** Elated; ful: *high* spirits. **11.** *Informal* Feeling the effects of or, drugs, etc.; intoxicated. **12.** Expensive; costly. Luxurious or fashionable: *high* living. **14.** Advanced he fullest extent or degree: *high* tide. **15.** Complex; adced: usu. in the comparative degree: *higher* mathematics. Strict or extreme in opinion, doctrine, etc.: *high* Tory. Arrogant; haughty. **18.** Slightly decomposed; gamy: of meat. **19.** Of sounds, having relatively short wavegths; shrill. **20.** *Music* **a** Having relatively short wavegths: said of vocal or instrumental tones. **b** Being above proper or indicated pitch; sharp. **21.** *Mech.* Denoting ear arrangement, as in a transmission, yielding the most id output speed. **22.** *Phonet.* Of vowel sounds, produced h the tongue raised close to the roof of the mouth, as in *bead*: opposed to *low.* — **high and dry 1.** Completely ve water level. **2.** Stranded; helpless. — **high and hty** *Informal* Overbearing; haughty. — *adv.* **1.** To or a high level, position, degree, price, rank, etc. **2.** In a h manner. — **high and low** Everywhere. — *n.* **1.** A h level, position, etc. **2.** *Mech.* A gear arrangement ding the most rapid output speed. **3.** *Meteorol.* An area igh barometric pressure. [OE *hēah*]
·ball[1] (hī′bôl′) *n. U.S.* A drink of whisky or other liquor ed with soda, ginger ale, etc., and served with ice in a tall ss. [Prob. < HIGH + *ball*, obs., a drink of whisky]
·ball[2] (hī′bôl′) *n.* A railroad signal to go ahead. — *v.i.* *Slang* To go at great speed. [From a large ball once d as a semaphore]
·born (hī′bôrn′) *adj.* Of noble birth or ancestry.
·boy (hī′boi′) *n.* A tall chest of drawers, usu. in two ions, the lower one mounted on legs. [Origin unknown]
·bred (hī′bred′) *adj.* **1.** Descended from fine stock; l-born. **2.** Characteristic of or indicating good breeding.
·brow (hī′brou′) *Informal n.* One who has or claims to e intellectually superior tastes: sometimes a term of derii. — *adj.* Of, pertaining to, or suitable for a highbrow: **high′browed′.** — **high′brow′ism** *n.*
·chair (hī′châr′) *n.* A baby's chair standing on tall s and equipped with an eating tray. Also **high chair.**

High-Church (hī′chûrch′) *adj.* Of or pertaining to a group (**High Church**) in the Anglican Church that stresses authority and ritual. — **High′-Church′man** *n.*
high-class (hī′klas′, -kläs′) *adj. Slang* High or superior in quality, condition, status, etc.
high comedy Comedy dealing with the world of polite society and relying chiefly on witty dialogue for its effect.
high·er-up (hī′ər·up′) *n. Informal* A person of superior rank or position.
high·fa·lu·tin (hī′fə·lōōt′n) *adj. Informal* Extravagant, pompous, or high-flown in manner, speech, etc. Also **high′·fa·lu′ting.** [? < HIGH-FLOWN]
high fidelity *Electronics* The reproduction of a signal or sound with a minimum of distortion, esp. by phonographic equipment: also called *hi-fi.*
high·fli·er (hī′flī′ər) *n.* **1.** One who or that which flies high. **2.** *Informal* One having extravagantly pretentious or unrealistic ambitions, opinions, tastes, etc. Also **high′fly′er.**
high-flown (hī′flōn′) *adj.* **1.** Extravagant or bombastic in style, language, etc. **2.** Pretentious: *high-flown* tastes.
high frequency *Telecom.* A radio frequency in the band from 3 to 30 megacycles.
High German See under GERMAN.
high-grade (hī′grād′) *adj.* Of superior quality.
high·hand·ed (hī′han′did) *adj.* Arbitrary and overbearing. — **high′hand′ed·ly** *adv.* — **high′hand′ed·ness** *n.*
high hat A top hat.
high-hat (hī′hat′) *Informal v.t.* **-hat·ted, -hat·ting** To snub. — *adj.* **1.** Snobbish. **2.** Fashionable. — *n.* A snob.
high·jack (hī′jak′) See HIJACK.
high jinks (jingks) Boisterous fun or roughhousing.
high jump In athletics, a jump for height.
high·land (hī′lənd) *n.* **1.** Elevated land, as a plateau or promontory. **2.** *Usu. pl.* A hilly or mountainous region. — *adj.* Of, pertaining to, or of the nature of a highland.
High·land·er (hī′lən·dər) *n.* **1.** A native or inhabitant of the Highlands. **2.** A soldier of a Highlands regiment.
Highland fling A lively Scottish dance.
high·light (hī′līt′) *n.* **1.** An area or point in a painting, photograph, etc., showing or representing a brightly lighted part. **2.** An event, detail, etc., of special importance. — *v.t.* **1.** *Informal* To give special emphasis to; feature. **2.** To provide or emphasize with a highlight or highlights.
high·ly (hī′lē) *adv.* **1.** In or to a high degree; extremely. **2.** With great approval or appreciation. **3.** In a high position or rank. **4.** At a high price or rate.
High Mass *Eccl.* A Mass celebrated with full ceremony, music, incense, etc.
high-mind·ed (hī′mīn′did) *adj.* Possessing or manifesting noble thoughts or sentiments. — **high′-mind′ed·ly** *adv.*
high·ness (hī′nis) *n.* The state or quality of being high.
High·ness (hī′nis) *n.* A title or form of address for persons of royal rank: often preceded by *His, Her, Your,* etc.
high-pitched (hī′picht′) *adj.* **1.** High in pitch; shrill. **2.** Of a roof, having a steep slope. **3.** Lofty or exalted.
high-pres·sure (hī′presh′ər) *adj.* **1.** Using or sustaining high steam pressure, as an engine. **2.** Having or showing high barometric pressure. **3.** *Informal* Exerting vigorously persuasive methods or tactics. — *v.t.* **·sured, ·sur·ing** *Informal* To persuade by aggressive or insistent methods.
high priest A chief priest.
high-rise (hī′rīz′) *adj.* Describing a relatively tall building or structure. — *n.* A tall building: also **high rise.**
high·road (hī′rōd′) *n.* **1.** A main road. **2.** An easy or sure method or course: the *highroad* to fame.
high school A school following elementary school or junior high school, in the U.S. typically comprising grades 9 to 12.
high seas The open waters of an ocean or sea that are beyond the territorial jurisdiction of any one nation.
high-sound·ing (hī′soun′ding) *adj.* Pretentious or imposing in sound or implication: *high-sounding* praise.
high-spir·it·ed (hī′spir′it·ed) *adj.* Having a courageous, vigorous, or fiery spirit; mettlesome.
high-ten·sion (hī′ten′shən) *adj. Electr.* Pertaining to, characterized by, or operating under very high voltage.
high-test (hī′test′) *adj.* **1.** Designating a substance or product that has passed severe tests for fitness, quality, etc. **2.** Denoting a grade of gasoline with a low boiling point.
high tide 1. The maximum level reached by the incoming tide. **2.** The time that this occurs. **3.** A culminating point.
high time 1. So late as to be almost past the proper time. **2.** *Informal* A hilarious and enjoyable time.
high-toned (hī′tōnd′) *adj.* **1.** *U.S. Informal* Stylish; modish. **2.** Characterized by a lofty character, high principles, etc.: often used ironically. **3.** High in tone or pitch.
high treason Treason against the sovereign or state.
high-up (hī′up′) *Informal adj.* Of high rank or position. — *n.* One who is in a high rank or position.

high water 1. High tide. 2. The condition of a body of water at its time of highest elevation, as during a flood.
high-wa·ter mark (hī′wô′tər, -wot′ər) 1. The highest point reached by a body of water, as during high tide, a flood, etc. 2. A mark left by such waters after receding. 3. A point of highest achievement or development.
high·way (hī′wā′) *n.* 1. A road or thoroughfare; esp., a main or principal road of some length that is open to the public. 2. A main route on land or water. 3. An ordinary, natural, or direct course of action, progress, etc.
high·way·man (hī′wā′mən) *n. pl.* **·men** (-mən) Formerly, a robber who waylaid travelers on highways.
hi·jack (hī′jak′) *v.t. U.S. Slang* 1. To seize illegally while in transit, as cargo, vehicles, etc. 2. To hold up and rob (a truck, etc.). 3. To seize or steal valuables from (a person). 4. To coerce or compel (someone). Also spelled *highjack.* [Orig. from hoboes who hailed their victim with "Hi Jack"]
hike (hīk) *v.* **hiked, hik·ing** *v.i.* 1. To walk for a considerable distance, esp. through rugged terrain, woods, etc. 2. To rise or be uneven, as part of a garment: often with *up.* — *v.t.* 3. *Informal* To raise or lift: usu. with *up.* 4. *Informal* To increase (prices, etc.): usu. with *up.* — *n.* 1. A long walk or march. 2. *Informal* An increase. [? Var. of HITCH] — **hik′er** *n.*
hi·lar·i·ous (hi·lâr′ē·əs, hī-) *adj.* Boisterously gay or cheerful. — **hi·lar′i·ous·ly** *adv.* — **hi·lar′i·ous·ness** *n.*
hi·lar·i·ty (hi·lar′ə·tē, hī-) *n. pl.* **·ties** Noisy, exuberant gaiety. [< OF < L < Gk. *hilaros* cheerful]
hill (hil) *n.* 1. A conspicuous, usu. rounded, elevation of the earth's surface, not as high as a mountain. 2. A heap or pile: often used in combination: a *molehill.* 3. A small mound of earth placed over or around certain plants and tubers. 4. A plant or group of plants thus covered. — *v.t.* 1. To surround or cover with hills, as potatoes. 2. To form a hill or heap of. [OE *hyll*] — **hill′er** *n.*
hill·bil·ly (hil′bil′ē) *n. pl.* **·lies** *U.S. Informal* A person coming from or living in the mountains or a backwoods area, esp. of the southern U.S.: originally a disparaging term.
hill·ock (hil′ək) *n.* A small hill or mound. — **hill′ock·y** *adj.*
hill·side (hil′sīd′) *n.* The side or slope of a hill.
hill·top (hil′top′) *n.* The summit of a hill.
hill·y (hil′ē) *adj.* **hill·i·er, hill·i·est** 1. Having many hills. 2. Resembling a hill; steep. — **hill′i·ness** *n.*
hilt (hilt) *n.* The handle of a sword, dagger, etc. — **to the hilt** Thoroughly; fully. — *v.t.* To provide with a hilt. [OE]
hi·lum (hī′ləm) *n. pl.* **·la** (-lə) *Bot.* The scar on a seed at the point where it was attached to the placenta. [< L, a trifle]
him (him) *pron.* The objective case of the pronoun *he.*
him·self (him·self′) *pron.* A form of the third person singular masculine pronoun, used: 1. As a reflexive or as object of a preposition in a reflexive sense: He cut *himself.* 2. As an intensive form of *he*: He *himself* will do it. 3. As a designation of a normal or usual state: He is not *himself.*
hind[1] (hīnd) *adj.* **hind·er, hind·most** or **hind·er·most** Situated at or toward the rear part; posterior. [OE *hindan*]
hind[2] (hīnd) *n.* The female of the red deer, esp. when fully grown. [OE]
hind·brain (hīnd′brān′) *n. Anat.* The rhombencephalon.
hind·er[1] (hin′dər) *v.t.* 1. To interfere with the progress of; retard. 2. To prevent from acting or occurring; deter; thwart. — *v.i.* 3. To be an impediment or obstacle. [OE *hinder* behind] — **hin′der·er** *n.*
hind·er[2] (hīn′dər) Comparative of HIND[1]. — *adj.* Pertaining to or situated at the rear or posterior end. [OE]
Hin·di (hin′dē) *n.* 1. The principal language of northern India, belonging to the Indic branch of the Indo-Iranian languages, usu. divided into **Western Hindi,** of which Hindustani is the major dialect, and **Eastern Hindi.** 2. A form of literary Hindustani used by Hindus. [< Hind. < Persian < OPersian < Skt. *sindhu* river, the Indus]
hind·most (hīnd′mōst′) Superlative of HIND[1]. Also **hind′·er·most′** (hīn′dər-).
hind·quar·ter (hīnd′kwôr′tər) *n.* 1. One of the two back quarters of a carcass of beef, lamb, etc. 2. *pl.* The rump.
hin·drance (hin′drəns) *n.* 1. The act of hindering. 2. One who or that which hinders.
hind·sight (hīnd′sīt′) *n.* 1. The understanding of an event after it has happened. 2. The rear sight of a gun, rifle, etc.
Hin·du (hin′dōō) *n.* 1. A native of India who speaks one of the Indic languages. 2. One whose religion is Hinduism. 3. Loosely, a native of Hindustan. — *adj.* Of, pertaining to, or characteristic of the Hindus or Hinduism. Also **Hin′doo.**
Hin·du·ism (hin′dōō·iz′əm) *n.* The religion of the Hindus of India, characterized by worship of Brahma.
Hin·du·sta·ni (hin′dōō·stä′nē, -stan′ē) *n.* The major dialect of Hindi, the official language and general medium of communication in India. See URDU. — *adj.* 1. Of or pertaining to Hindustan or its people. 2. Of or pertaining to Hindustani. Abbr. *Hind.*
hinge (hinj) *n.* 1. A device consisting of two parts, usu. metal plates, connected by a pin inserted into interlo[cking] grooves, and constituting a movable joint on which a [door,] gate, lid, etc., swings or turns. 2. A natural movable [joint] connecting two parts, as the shells of a bivalve. 3. Th[at on] which something turns or depends. — *v.* **hinged, hin[g·ing]** *v.t.* 1. To attach by or equip with a hinge or hinges. — 2. To hang or turn on or as on a hinge. 3. To depend [or be] contingent: with *on.* [ME, prob. < ON *hengja* to ha[ng]]
hin·ny (hin′ē) *n. pl.* **·nies** The hybrid offspring of a st[allion] and a she-ass. Compare MULE[1]. [< L < Gk. *ginnos*]
hint (hint) *n.* 1. An indirect suggestion or implicatio[n.] A slight indication or trace. — *v.t.* 1. To suggest indir[ectly;] imply. — *v.i.* 2. To show one's wishes, intentions, et[c., by] a hint or hints. 3. To give a slight indication or sugge[stion:] with *at.* [OE *hentan*]
hin·ter·land (hin′tər·land′) *n.* 1. An inland region i[mme]diately adjacent to a coastal area. 2. A region remote [from] urban areas; back country. 3. An area adjacent to an[d de]pendent upon a port or other urban center. [< G]
hip[1] (hip) *n.* 1. The part of the human body projectin[g be]low the waist on either side, formed by the edge of the [ilium] and the upper part of the femur. 2. An analogous p[art in] animals. 3. *Archit.* The angle at the juncture of adj[acent] sloping sides of a roof. — *v.t.* **hipped, hip·ping** *Arch[it.] To* build (a roof) with a hip or hips. [OE *hype*]
hip[2] (hip) *n.* The ripened fruit of a rose. [OE *hēope*]
hip[3] (hip) *adj. U.S. Slang* Aware; informed.
hip·bone (hip′bōn′) *n.* The innominate bone.
hipped[1] (hipt) *adj.* 1. Having or characterized by (a [speci]fied kind of) hips: used in combination: *slim-hipped.* [2.] *Archit.* Having a hip or hips, as a roof.
hipped[2] (hipt) *adj. U.S. Slang* Fanatically interes[ted or] concerned; obsessed: followed by *on*: *hipped* on moder[n ...]
hip·pet·y-hop (hip′ə·tē·hop′) *adv. Informal* With a [hopping] gait or motion. Also **hip·pet·y-hop·pet·y** (-hop′ə·tē).
hip·pie (hip′ē) *n.* One of a group of chiefly young p[eople] whose unconventional dress and behavior and use of [drugs] express withdrawal from middle-class life and indiffe[rence] to its values. [Var. of HIPSTER]
hip·po (hip′ō) *n. pl.* **·pos** *Informal* A hippopotamus.
hippo- *combining form* Horse. Also, before vowels, [hipp-.] [< Gk. *hippos* horse]
Hip·po·crat·ic oath (hip′ə·crat′ik) An oath, attribut[ed to] Hippocrates, incorporating a code of ethics for physi[cians] and administered to those about to receive a medical d[egree.]
hip·po·drome (hip′ə·drōm) *n.* 1. An arena or similar [struc]ture for horse shows, circuses, etc. 2. In ancient Greec[e and] Rome, a course or track for horse races and chariot [races.] [< F < L < Gk. < *hippos* horse + *dromos* running, c[ourse]]
hip·po·pot·a·mus (hip′ə·pot′ə·məs) *n. pl.* **·mus·es** [or **·mi**] (-mī) A large, chiefly aquatic, herbivorous mammal, [native] to Africa, and having short legs, a massive, thick-ski[nned] hairless body, and a very broad muzzle. [< L < G[k.] *hippos* horse + *potamos* river]
-hippus *combining form Paleontol.* Horse. [< Gk. *h[ippos*] horse]
hip roof *Archit.* A roof having sloping ends and side[s.]
hip·ster (hip′stər) *n. U.S. Slang* One who is hip; esp[., one] versed in jazz music. [< HIP[3] + -STER]
hire (hīr) *v.t.* **hired, hir·ing** 1. To obtain the services [of (a] person) for compensation. 2. To acquire the use of (a t[hing]) for a fee; rent. 3. To grant the use or services of (so[me]one or something) in return for payment: often with *out.* — **to hire out** To provide one's services in return for comp[ensa]tion. — *n.* 1. Compensation paid for labor, services[, etc.] 2. The act of hiring, or the condition of being hired. [OE] *hȳr*] — **hir′able** or **hire′a·ble** *adj.* — **hir′er** *n.*
hire·ling (hīr′ling) *n.* One who serves for hire; esp[., one] who does something unpleasant or reprehensible for [mer]cenary motives: usu. a contemptuous term.
hir·sute (hûr′sōōt, hûr·sōōt′) *adj.* Covered with hair. [<] L *hirsutus* rough] — **hir′sute·ness** *n.*
his (hiz) *pron.* 1. The possessive case of the pronou[n *he*] used predicatively: This room is *his.* 2. The one or on[es be]longing or pertaining to him: Her book is better tha[n his.] — **of his** Belonging or pertaining to him: a double posse[ssive.] — *pronominal adj.* The possessive case of the pronou[n *he*] used attributively: *his* book. [OE]
His·pa·ni·a (his·pā′nē·ə, -nyə, -pä′-) 1. The Latin na[me of] the region comprising modern Spain and Portugal. 2. *[Poetic]* Spain. — **His·pan·ic** (his·pan′ik) *adj.*
hiss (his) *v.i.* 1. To utter or produce a prolonged, sib[ilant] sound, as that of *ss*, of air or steam escaping under pres[sure,] etc. 2. To utter such a sound as an expression of d[isap]proval or derision. — *v.t.* 3. To utter with a hiss. 4[. To] express disapproval of by hissing. 5. To rout or silen[ce by] hissing: with *off, down,* etc. — *n.* The sound produce[d by] hissing. [ME *hissen,* imit.] — **hiss′er** *n.*
his·ta·mine (his′tə·mēn, -min) *n. Biochem.* A white, [crys]talline substance, $C_5H_9N_3$, found in plant and anima[l tis]sues. It reduces blood pressure, has a contracting actio[n]

uterus, and is released in allergic reactions. — **his·ta·**
ı·ic (his′tə·min′ik) *adj.*
·o- *combining form* Tissue. Also, before vowels, **hist-.**
Gk *histos* web]
tol·o·gy (his·tol′ə·jē) *n. pl.* **·gies** **1.** The branch of
logy that treats of the microscopic structure of tissues.
The tissue structure of an organism, part, etc. — **his·**
og·i·cal (his′tə·loj′i·kəl) *adj.* — **his·tol′o·gist** *n.*
to·ri·an (his·tôr′ē·ən, -tō′rē-) *n.* **1.** A writer of or au-
rity on history. **2.** A compiler of a record, esp. for a
cific group or purpose: the class *historian.*
tor·ic (his·tôr′ik, -tor′-) *adj.* **1.** Important or famous in
ory. **2.** Memorable; significant. **3.** Historical.
tor·i·cal (his·tôr′i·kəl, -tor′-) *adj.* **1.** Constituting, be-
ging to, or of the nature of history. **2.** Pertaining to,
cerned with, or treating of events of history: a *historical*
ount. **3.** Of, pertaining to, or based on known facts as
inct from legendary or fictitious accounts. **4.** Serving as
urce for knowledge of the past. **5.** Historic. — **his·**
i·cal·ly *adv.* — **his·tor′i·cal·ness** *n.*
orical present *Gram.* The present tense used to nar-
a past event.
o·ri·og·ra·pher (his·tôr′ē·og′rə·fər, -tō′rē-) *n.* A histo-
or chronicler, esp. one officially associated with a group
ublic institution. — **his·to′ri·og′ra·phy** *n.*
o·ry (his′tə·rē, his′trē) *n. pl.* **·ries** **1.** That branch of
wledge concerned with past events, esp. those involving
nan affairs. **2.** A record or account, usu. written and in
onological order, of past events, esp. those concerning a
ticular nation, people, field of knowledge or activity,
3. A connected or related series of facts, events, etc.,
those concerning a specific group or subject: the *history*
political party. **4.** Past events in general. **5.** Some-
g in the past. **6.** An unusual or noteworthy past: That
se has a *history.* **7.** A drama depicting historical events.
A long narrative or story. [< L < Gk. *histōr* knowing]
ri·on·ic (his′trē·on′ik) *adj.* **1.** Of or pertaining to ac-
or acting. **2.** Overly dramatic. Also **his′tri·on′i·cal.**
L *histrio, -onis* actor] — **his′tri·on′i·cal·ly** *adv.*
ri·on·ics (his′trē·on′iks) *n.pl.* (*construed as sing. in*
1) **1.** Theatrical art or representation; dramatics. **2.**
gned emotional display; affectation in manner, speech, etc.
hit) *v.* **hit, hit·ting** *v.t.* **1.** To give a blow to; strike for-
y. **2.** To reach or strike with or as with a missile, hurled
alling object, etc. **3.** To come forcibly in contact with;
ide with. **4.** To cause (something) to make forcible
tact: often with *on, against,* etc. **5.** To inflict (a blow,
) on: I *hit* him a tremendous blow. **6.** To set in motion
ropel by striking. **7.** To arrive at, achieve, or discover.
To accord with; suit. **9.** To affect adversely; cause to
er. **10.** To attack; beset. **11.** In baseball, to succeed
naking (a specified kind of base hit). **12.** *U.S. Informal*
begin to journey on: to *hit* the road. **13.** *U.S. Informal*
arrive in or reach (a place). — *v.i.* **14.** To deliver a
w; strike. **15.** To make forcible contact; bump: often
a *against, on,* etc. **16.** To come or light; happen: fol-
ed by *on* or *upon:* to *hit* on the right answer. — **to hit it**
To be friendly; get along well. — **to hit on** (a specified
nber of) **cylinders** To function by or as by firing the
rge in the cylinders: said originally of an internal-com-
tion engine. — *n.* **1.** A blow, stroke, shot, etc., that
hes the objective aimed at. **2.** A forceful impact;
ision. **3.** A popular or obvious success. **4.** A fortunate
nce or circumstance. **5.** An apt or telling remark,
icism, piece of sarcasm, etc. **6.** In baseball, a base hit.
< ON *hitta* to come upon] — **hit′ter** *n.*
and-run (hit′n·run′) *adj.* Designating or caused by
driver of a vehicle who illegally continues on his way
r hitting a pedestrian or another vehicle.
h (hich) *v.t.* **1.** To fasten or tie, esp. temporarily, with
notted rope, strap, etc. **2.** To
ness to a vehicle: sometimes with
3. To move, pull, raise, etc.,
h a jerk: often with *up:* He *hitched*
pants up. **4.** *Informal* To marry.
U.S. Slang To obtain (a ride) by
hhiking. — *v.i.* **6.** To move with
erk or limp: to *hitch* forward.
To become fastened, caught, or
angled. **8.** *U.S. Slang* To travel by hitchhiking. — *n.*
An obstacle; halt; delay. **2.** A sudden, jerking move-
nt; tug. **3.** A limp or hobble. **4.** A fastening or device
d to fasten. **5.** Any of various knots used for quick, tem-
ary fastening. **6.** *U.S. Informal* A period of enlistment
military service, esp. in the navy. **7.** *U.S. Slang* In
hhiking, a ride. [ME *hicchen*]

HITCHES
a Half-hitch.
b Clove-hitch.
c Rolling-hitch.

h·hike (hich′hīk′) *v.i.* **·hiked, ·hik·ing** To travel by
aling for rides in passing vehicles. — **hitch′hik′er** *n.*
hitch·ing post (hich′ing) A post to which a horse, etc., may be hitched.
hith·er (hith′ər) *adv.* To or toward this place: Come *hither.* — *adj.* Situated toward this side; nearer. [OE *hider*]
hith·er·most (hith′ər·mōst′) *adj.* Nearest to this place.
hith·er·to (hith′ər·to͞o, hith′ər·to͞o′) *adv.* Until this time.
hit or miss Without regard for the outcome; at random.
hit-or-miss (hit′ər·mis′) *adj.* Haphazard; careless.
Hit·tite (hit′īt) *n.* **1.** One of an ancient people who established a powerful empire in Asia Minor and northern Syria about 2000–1200 B.C. **2.** Their language. — *adj.* Of or relating to the Hittites or their language. [< Hebrew *Hittīm*]
hive (hīv) *n.* **1.** An artificial structure serving as a habitation for honeybees; beehive. **2.** A colony of bees inhabiting a hive; swarm. **3.** A place astir with industrious activity. **4.** A teeming multitude; throng. — *v.* **hived, hiv·ing** *v.t.* **1.** To induce (bees) to enter into or collect in a hive. **2.** To house or shelter in or as in a hive. **3.** To store (honey) in a hive. **4.** To store or hoard for future use. — *v.i.* **5.** To enter a hive. **6.** To dwell in or as in a hive. [OE *hȳf*]
hives (hīvz) *n.* Any of various skin disorders characterized by swellings, itching, etc., as urticaria. [Origin unknown]
ho (hō) *interj.* **1.** An exclamation, often repeated, expressing exultation, derision, etc. **2.** A call to attract attention.
Ho *Chem.* Holmium.
hoar (hôr, hōr) *adj.* **1.** Having white or gray hair. **2.** Ancient. **3.** White or grayish, as with frost. — *n.* Hoariness. [OE *hār* gray-haired]
hoard (hôrd, hōrd) *n.* An accumulation of something stored away for safekeeping or future use. — *v.t.* **1.** To amass and store or hide (money, valuables, etc.). — *v.i.* **2.** To amass and store. [OE *hord* treasure] — **hoard′er** *n.*
hoard·ing[1] (hôr′ding, hōr′-) *n.* **1.** The act of one who hoards. **2.** *Usu. pl.* That which is hoarded.
hoard·ing[2] (hôr′ding, hōr′-) *n. Brit.* **1.** A temporary fence. **2.** A billboard. [< OF *hourd* palisade]
hoar·frost (hôr′frôst′, -frost′, hōr′-) *n.* Frost whitening the surface on which it is formed.
hoar·hound (hôr′hound′, hōr′-) See HOREHOUND.
hoarse (hôrs, hōrs) *adj.* **1.** Deep, harsh, and grating in sound. **2.** Having a husky, gruff, or croaking voice. [OE *hā(r)s*] — **hoarse′ly** *adv.* — **hoarse′ness** *n.*
hoars·en (hôr′sən, hōr′-) *v.t. & v.i.* To make or become hoarse.
hoar·y (hôr′ē, hō′rē) *adj.* **hoar·i·er, hoar·i·est** **1.** Ancient; aged; venerable. **2.** Gray or white with age. **3.** White or whitish in color. — **hoar′i·ness** *n.*
hoax (hōks) *n.* A trick or deception, usu. on the public. — *v.t.* To deceive by a hoax. — **hoax′er** *n.*
hob[1] (hob) *n.* A projection at the interior of a fireplace, serving as a shelf on which to keep things warm.
hob[2] (hob) *n.* A hobgoblin or elf. — **to play** (or **raise**) **hob** To cause mischief or confusion. [Orig. a nickname for *Robert, Robin*]
hob·ble (hob′əl) *v.* **·bled, ·bling** *v.i.* **1.** To walk with a limp. **2.** To progress clumsily or irregularly. — *v.t.* **3.** To hamper the free movement of, as a horse, by fettering the legs. **4.** To cause to move lamely or awkwardly. — *n.* **1.** An awkward or limping gait. **2.** A rope, etc., used to hobble the legs of an animal. — **hob′bler** *n.*
hob·ble·de·hoy (hob′əl·dē·hoi′) *n.* An adolescent boy, esp. when awkward and gawky. [Origin uncertain]
hob·by (hob′ē) *n. pl.* **·bies** A pursuit of interest, undertaken for pleasure during one's leisure; avocation. [after *Robin,* a personal name]
hob·by·horse (hob′ē·hôrs′) *n.* **1.** A rocking horse. **2.** A toy consisting of a stick surmounted by a horse's head.
hob·gob·lin (hob′gob′lin) *n.* **1.** An imaginary cause of terror or dread. **2.** A mischievous imp.
hob·nail (hob′nāl′) *n.* A nail used to stud the soles of heavy shoes against wear or slipping. — **hob′nailed′** *adj.*
hob·nob (hob′nob′) *v.i.* **·nobbed, ·nob·bing** **1.** To associate in a friendly manner; be on intimate terms. **2.** To drink together. [OE *habban* to have + *nabban* to have not]
ho·bo (hō′bō) *n. pl.* **·boes** or **·bos** *U.S.* **1.** A tramp. **2.** An itinerant, usu. unskilled worker. [< *Hey, Bo,* a vagabond's greeting] — **ho′bo·ism** *n.*
Hob·son's choice (hob′sənz) A choice in which one must take what is offered or nothing. [after Thomas *Hobson,* 1544?–1631, English liveryman, who required each customer to take the horse nearest the door]
hock[1] (hok) *n.* **1.** The joint of the hind leg in the horse, ox, etc., corresponding to the ankle in man. **2.** The corresponding joint in a fowl. — *v.t.* To disable by cutting the tendons of the hock; hamstring. [OE *hōh* heel]
hock[2] (hok) *n.* Any white Rhine wine: originally **Hoch·hei·mer** (hok′hī·mər). [*Hochheim,* a German town]
hock[3] (hok) *U.S. Informal v.t.* To pawn. — *n.* The state

of being in pawn. **— in hock** *Informal* **1.** In pawn. **2.** In prison. **3.** In debt. [< Du. *hok* prison, debt]

hock·ey (hok′ē) *n.* **1.** A game played on ice (*ice hockey*), in which players, wearing skates and wielding sticks, try to drive a disk (puck) into the opponent's goal. **2.** A similar game played on a field (*field hockey*), in which a small ball is used instead of a puck. [< *hock* bent stick, var. of HOOK]

hockey stick A stick having a characteristic curve or bend at one end, used to move the ball or puck in hockey.

hock·shop (hok′shop′) *n. U.S. Informal* A pawnshop. Also **hock shop.**

ho·cus (hō′kəs) *v.t.* **·cused** or **·cussed, ·cus·ing** or **·cus·sing** **1.** To deceive by a trick; dupe; cheat. **2.** To drug, as a drink. [Abbr. of HOCUS-POCUS]

ho·cus-po·cus (hō′kəs·pō′kəs) *n.* **1.** A verbal formula used in conjuring or sleight of hand. **2.** Deceptive skill. **3.** Any trickery or deception, as misleading gestures. **—** *v.t. & v.i.* **-po·cused** or **·cussed, -po·cus·ing** or **·cus·sing** To trick; cheat. [A sham Latin phrase]

hod (hod) *n.* **1.** A trough rested on the shoulder, to carry bricks, etc. **2.** A coalscuttle. [< OF *hotte* pannier]

hodge·podge (hoj′poj′) *n.* **1.** A jumbled mixture or collection; conglomeration. **2.** A stew. Also *hotchpotch.*

Hodg·kin's disease (hoj′kinz) *Pathol.* A generally fatal disease characterized by progressive enlargement of the lymph nodes, lymphoid tissue, and spleen. [after Dr. Thomas *Hodgkin*, 1798–1866, English physician, who described it]

hoe (hō) *n.* An implement as for weeding, having a flat blade attached to a long handle. **—** *v.t. & v.i.* **hoed, hoe·ing** To dig with a hoe. [< OF < OHG *houwan* to cut]

hoe·cake (hō′kāk′) *n. Southern U.S.* A thin, flat cake made from cornmeal, originally baked on a hoe.

hoe-down (hō′doun′) *n. U.S. Informal* A lively country dance or square dance; also, its music. [Origin uncertain]

hog (hog, hôg) *n.* **1.** A pig, esp. one weighing more than 120 pounds and raised for the market. **2.** An animal related to the pig, as the peccary. **3.** *Informal* A gluttonous or filthy person. **—** *v.* **hogged, hog·ging** *v.t. Slang* To take more than one's share of; grab selfishly. [OE *hog*]

hog·back (hog′bak′, hôg′-) *n. Geol.* A sandy or rocky ridge caused by unequal erosion on the edges of tilted strata.

hog·gish (hog′ish, hôg′-) *adj.* **1.** Of or like a hog. **2.** Greedy or dirty; piggish. **— hog′gish·ly** *adv.*

hog·nose (hog′nōz′, hôg′-) *n.* Any of several American nonvenomous snakes with flat heads and prominent snouts.

hogs·head (hogz′hed′, hôgz′-) *n.* **1.** A large cask, esp. one with a capacity of 63 to 140 gallons. **2.** A liquid measure, esp. one equal to 63 gallons, or 8.42 cubic feet.

hog-tie (hog′tī′, hôg′-) *v.t.* **-tied, -ty·ing** or **-tie·ing** **1.** To tie together four feet, or the hands and feet of. **2.** *Informal* To render (a person) ineffective, as by tying. Also **hog′tie′.**

hog·wash (hog′wosh′, -wôsh′, hôg′-) *n.* **1.** Kitchen refuse, etc., fed hogs. **2.** Any nonsense; insincere talk.

hoicks (hoiks) *interj.* A cry to the hounds in hunting. Also *yoicks.*

hoi pol·loi (hoi′ pə·loi′) The common people; the masses: usu. used contemptuously. [< Gk., the many]

hoist (hoist) *v.t.* To raise, lift, or heave up, esp. by mechanical means. **—** *n.* **1.** Any machine for raising large objects; a lift. **2.** The act of hoisting. [? < Du. *hijschen*]

hoi·ty-toi·ty (hoi′tē·toi′tē) *interj.* An exclamation of disapproval. **—** *adj.* **1.** Self-important; haughty. **2.** Flighty; giddy. **3.** Easily offended. **—** *n. pl.* **-toi·ties** **1.** Arrogance. **2.** Flighty behavior. [Obs. *hoit* to romp]

ho·kum (hō′kəm) *n. U.S. Slang* **1.** The devices used by a performer, etc., to get a response. **2.** Meaningless bunk. **3.** Insincere flattery. [Alter. of HOCUS]

hold[1] (hōld) *v.* **held, held, hold·ing** *v.t.* **1.** To take and keep in the hand, arms, etc.; clasp. **2.** To sustain or keep, as in position; support: to *hold* one's head high. **3.** To contain or enclose: The barrel *holds* ten gallons. **4.** To keep under control; restrain; also, to retain possession of. **5.** To keep in reserve; designate for future use. **6.** To have the benefit or responsibilities of: to *hold* office. **7.** To regard in a specified manner: to *hold* someone dear. **8.** To bind by contract or duty: *Hold* him to his agreement. **9.** *Music* To prolong or sustain (a tone). **10.** *Law* **a** To adjudge; decide. **b** To have title to. **11.** To maintain in the mind; harbor: to *hold* a grudge. **12.** To engage in; carry on: to *hold* a conference. **—** *v.i.* **13.** To maintain a grip or grasp. **14.** To withstand strain or remain unbroken: The rope *holds.* **15.** To continue in a state: the breeze *held.* **16.** To remain true: This decision *holds.* **17.** To adhere, as to a principle or purpose; cling. **— to hold back** **1.** To keep in check; restrain. **2.** To refrain. **3.** To retain. **— to hold down** **1.** To suppress; keep under control. **2.** *Informal* To be employed at (a job). **— to hold forth** To preach or speak at great length. **— to hold in** **1.** To keep in check; curb. **2.** To conceal (one's feelings, etc.). **— to hold off** **1.** To keep at a distance, as from attacking. **2.** To refrain from doing something. **— to hold on** **1.** To maintain a grip or hold. **2.** To persist or continue. **3.** *Informal* To sto wait. **— to hold one's own** To maintain one's positior in a contest. **— to hold out** **1.** To stretch forth; c **2.** To last; endure: Our supplies *held out.* **3.** To cont resistance. **4.** *Slang* To refuse something anticipated or **— to hold over** **1.** To put off to a later time. **2.** To ren or retain beyond the expected limit, as in office. **3.** To as a means of controlling. **— to hold up** **1.** To supp prop. **2.** To exhibit to view. **3.** To delay; stop. **4.** *formal* To endure; remain firm. **5.** *Informal* To stop s to rob. **6.** *Informal* To charge too high a price. **— to water** **1.** To contain without leaking. **2.** *Informal* T credible or sound, as an argument. **— to hold with** Tc prove of. **—** *n.* **1.** The act or method of grasping, as the hands. **2.** Something grasped, held, or seized for port. **3.** A controlling force or influence. **4.** *Law* A hol or tenure: used in combination: *freehold.* **5.** *Music* **a** holding of a note or rest beyond its time value. **b** The sy (𝄐) indicating this: also called *pause.* [OE *haldan*]

hold[2] (hōld) *n. Naut.* The space below the decks of a ve where cargo is stowed. [< HOLE or < MDu. *hol*]

hold·er (hōl′dər) *n.* **1.** One who or that which holds. An object used as an aid in holding. **3.** An owner; posse chiefly in compounds: *householder.* **4.** *Law* One who h check, etc., for which he is entitled to payment.

hold·ing (hōl′ding) *n.* **1.** The act of one who or that w holds. **2.** A piece of land rented. **3.** *Often pl.* Property by legal right, esp. stocks or bonds.

holding company A company that invests in the stoc one or more other corporations, which it may thus con

hold·o·ver (hōld′ō′vər) *n. Informal* **1.** One who or which remains from a previous time or situation. **2.** A cumbent continuing in office after his term has expired

hold·up (hōld′up′) *n.* **1.** Stoppage or delay. **2.** *Inform* waylaying and robbing.

hole (hōl) *n.* **1.** A cavity in a solid mass or body; **2.** An opening in anything; aperture. **3.** An animal's row or enclosed hiding place. **4.** Any small, crow squalid place, esp. a dwelling; also, a prison cell. defect; fault. **6.** *Informal* An awkward situation. golf: **a** A small cavity into which the ball is played. division of the course, usu. one of nine or eighteen. **8.** A deep, wide place in a creek, etc.; also, a cove. **— in one** In golf, the act of sinking the ball into a hole with drive from the tee. **— in the hole** *Informal* In debt. **holed, hol·ing** *v.t.* **1.** To make a hole in; perforate. **2** drive (a ball, etc.) into a hole. **3.** To dig (a shaft, tu etc.). **—** *v.i.* **4.** To make a hole or holes. **— to hole o** golf, to hit the ball into a hole. **— to hole up** To hide a isolate oneself. [OE *hol*] **— hole′y** *adj.*

hol·i·day (hol′ə·dā) *n.* **1.** A day appointed by law suspension of business in commemoration of some e **2.** Any day of rest. **3.** A day for special religious o vance. **4.** *pl. Chiefly Brit.* A vacation. **—** *v.i. Chiefly* To spend a holiday or vacation. [OE *hālig dæg* holy d

ho·li·er-than-thou (hō′lē·ər·than·thou′) *adj. Informa* fecting an attitude of superior goodness or virtue.

ho·li·ly (hō′lə·lē) *adv.* In a holy manner; piously; sacre

ho·li·ness (hō′lē·nis) *n.* The state or quality of being h

Ho·li·ness (hō′lē·nis) *n.* A title or form of address for Pope: preceded by *His* or *Your.*

hol·land (hol′ənd) *n.* A cotton or linen fabric, often gla used for making window shades, upholstery, etc.

hol·lan·daise sauce (hol′ən·dāz′) A creamy sauce of ter, egg yolks, and lemon juice served with vegetables, [< F, fem. of *hollandais* of Holland]

Hol·land·er (hol′ən·dər) *n.* A native or citizen of the N erlands; a Dutchman.

Hol·lands (hol′əndz) *n.* Gin in which juniper is adde the mash instead of to the spirits. Also **Holland gin.**

hol·ler (hol′ər) *U.S. Informal v.t. & v.i.* To call out lou shout; yell. **—** *n.* A loud shout; yell.

hol·low (hol′ō) *adj.* **1.** Having a cavity within; enclo an empty space. **2.** Having a deep opening; concave. Sunken; fallen: *hollow* cheeks. **4.** Deep or muffled in t a *hollow* groan. **5.** Not genuine; meaningless; em **6.** Hungry. **—** *n.* **1.** A cavity or empty space in anyth depression; hole. **2.** A valley. **—** *v.t. & v.i.* To mak become hollow: usu. with *out.* **—** *adv. Informal* Comple used in the phrase **to beat (all) hollow.** [OE *holh*] **— low·ly** *adv.* **— hol′low·ness** *n.*

hol·low·ware (hol′ō·wâr′) *n.* Utensils, serving dishes, esp. of silver, that are hollow.

hol·ly (hol′ē) *n. pl.* **·lies** A tree or shrub having dark g leaves edged with spines, and scarlet berries. [OE *holen*

hol·ly·hock (hol′ē·hok) *n.* A tall, cultivated plant of mallow family, having spikes of showy flowers. [ME holy + *hoc* mallow]

hol·mi·um (hōl′mē·əm) *n.* A metallic element (syn Ho) of the lanthanide series, found in gadolinite. See MENT. [after *Holmia*, Latinized name of Stockholm, Swe

o·caust (hol′ə·kôst) *n.* **1.** Wholesale destruction and ; of life, esp. by fire. **2.** A sacrificial offering that is wholly ısumed by fire. [< F < LL < Gk. < *holos* whole + *kaustos* ·nt] — **hol′o·caus′tal, hol′o·caus′tic** *adj.*

o·graph (hol′ə·graf, -gräf) *adj.* Denoting a document, ı will, in the handwriting of the person whose signature it ,rs. — *n.* A document so written. [< F < Gk. < *holos* ire + *graphein* to write] — **hol′o·graph′ic** or **·i·cal** *adj.*

·stein (hōl′stīn, -stēn) *n.* A breed of black-and-white tle. Also **Hol′stein-Frie′sian** (-frē′zhən).

ster (hōl′stər) *n.* A leather case for a pistol, generally ·n on a belt or attached to a saddle. [< Du.]

y (hō′lē) *adj.* **·li·er, ·li·est 1.** Regarded with or charac- zed by reverence because associated with God; having a ine origin; sacred. **2.** Having spiritual and moral worth. Designated for religious worship; consecrated. **4.** Evok- or meriting reverence or awe. — *n. pl.* **·lies** A sacred or y place. [OE *hālig*]

y City A city considered sacred by the members of a ticular religion.

y Communion The Eucharist.

y·day (hō′lē·dā′) *n.* A day designated as a religious fes- ıl: sometimes called *holiday*. Also **holy day.**

y Father A title of the Pope.

y Ghost The third person of the Trinity. Also **Holy rit.**

y Grail The Grail.

y Land Palestine.

of holies 1. The innermost shrine of the Jewish taber- le and temple, in which the ark of the covenant was kept. Any very sacred place. Also called *sanctum sanctorum.*

orders *Eccl.* **1.** The rite of admission to the priest- d or ministry; ordination. **2.** The rank of the ministry.

y Roman Empire An empire in central and western :ope, 962–1806, regarded as the reestablishment of the stern Roman Empire under the Pope.

y·stone (hō′lē·stōn′) *n.* A piece of sandstone used to ır the decks of a ship. — *v.t.* **·stoned, ·ston·ing** To scrub h a stone. [Said to be used to clean decks for Sunday]

y Week The week before Easter Sunday.

y Writ The Scriptures.

·age (hom′ij, om′-) *n.* **1.** Respect or honor given or wn, esp. by action. **2.** A payment, etc., indicating alle- nce. [< OF < LL *homo* vassal, man]

·bre (om′brā, om′brē) *n.* *U.S. Slang* Man. [< Sp.]

·burg (hom′bûrg) *n.* A felt hat having a brim slightly ned up at the sides, and the crown indented lengthwise. o **hom′burg.** [after *Homburg*, Germany]

e (hōm) *n.* **1.** A house, apartment, or other dwelling ving as the abode of a person or household; residence. **2.** amily or other group dwelling together: a happy *home.* The country, region, city, etc., where one lives. **4.** One's :hplace or residence during formative years. **5.** A place ural or dear because of personal relationships or feelings comfort and security. **6.** A peaceful or restful place; ha- . **7.** The natural environment of an animal. **8.** The ce in which something originates or is found: New Or- ns is the *home* of jazz. **9.** A shelter for care of the or- ned, needy, infirm, etc. **10.** In some games, esp. base- , the goal or base that must be reached in order to win or re. — **at home 1.** In one's own residence, town, coun- , etc. **2.** At one's ease, as if in one's residence. **3.** Hav- a knowledge of; conversant: *at home* in the sciences. **4.** pared to receive callers. **5.** An informal social gathering one's home. — *adj.* **1.** Of or pertaining to one's home, ntry, etc.; domestic. **2.** Being at the base of operations place of origin: the *home* office. **3.** Going straight to the nt; effective. — *adv.* **1.** To or at one's home. **2.** To the ce or point intended; to the mark. **3.** Deeply and inti- tely; to the heart. — *v.* **homed, hom·ing** *v.t.* **1.** To cause aircraft or guided missile) to proceed toward a target by ans of radio waves, radar, or automatic timing devices. To furnish with a home. — *v.i.* **3.** To go home; return me. **4.** To be directed toward a target by automatic de- es: said of guided missiles: usu. with *in* or *in on.* **5.** To e residence. [OE *hām*] — **home′less** *adj.*

e·bod·y (hōm′bod′ē) *n. pl.* **·ies** One who prefers to y at home or whose main interest is in the home.

e·bred (hōm′bred′) *adj.* **1.** Bred at home. **2.** Uncul- ated; unsophisticated. **3.** *Canadian Slang* A home-brew.

e-brew (hōm′bro͞o′) *n.* An alcoholic beverage made at me, as for home use. — **home′-brewed′** *adj.*

e·com·ing (hōm′kum′ing) *n.* **1.** A return to one's me. **2.** *U.S.* In colleges, an annual alumni celebration.

e economics The science of home management, as of d, clothing, children, budgets, etc.

e·land (hōm′land′) *n.* The country of one's birth or giance.

home·ly (hōm′lē) *adj.* **·li·er, ·li·est 1.** Having a familiar, everyday character. **2.** Having plain or ugly features. **3.** Lacking in refinement. — **home′li·ness** *n.*

home·made (hōm′mād′) *adj.* **1.** Made at home. **2.** Simply or crudely fashioned.

home·mak·er (hōm′mā′kər) *n.* One in charge of managing her own home; housewife. — **home′mak′ing** *n.*

homeo- *combining form* Like; similar: *homeomorphism:* also spelled *homoeo-*, *homoio-*. [< Gk. *homoios* similar]

ho·me·op·a·thist (hō′mē·op′ə·thist, hom′ē-) *n.* One who practices homeopathy. Also **ho·me·o·path** (hō′mē·ə·path′).

ho·me·op·a·thy (hō′mē·op′ə·thē, hom′ē-) *n.* A system of therapy using minute doses of medicines that produce the symptoms of the disease treated. — **ho′me·o·path′ic** *adj.* — **ho′me·o·path′i·cal·ly** *adv.*

ho·me·o·sta·sis (hō′mē·ə·stā′sis, hom′ē-) *n.* *Biol.* The tendency of an organism to maintain a uniform and beneficial physiological stability within and between its parts; organic equilibrium. — **ho′me·o·stat′ic** (-stat′ik) *adj.*

home plate In baseball, the marker at which a player stands when batting, and to which he returns in scoring a run.

hom·er (hō′mər) *n.* *U.S. Informal* **1.** In baseball, a home run. **2.** A homing pigeon.

Ho·mer·ic (hō·mer′ik) *adj.* Of, pertaining to, or suggestive of Homer or his epic poetry. Also **Ho·mer′i·cal.**

home rule Self-government in local affairs within the framework of state or national laws. — **home ruler**

home run In baseball, a hit that cannot be fielded, thus permitting the batter to touch all the bases and score a run.

home·sick (hōm′sik′) *adj.* Unhappy or ill through longing for home; nostalgic. — **home′sick′ness** *n.*

home·spun (hōm′spun′) *adj.* **1.** Spun at home. **2.** Plain and simple; unsophisticated. **3.** Made of homespun. — *n.* **1.** Fabric woven at home or by hand. **2.** A rough, loosely woven fabric similar to this.

home·stead (hōm′sted) *n.* **1.** A house and its land, etc. **2.** *U.S.* A tract of land occupied under the Homestead Act. — *v.i.* **1.** *U.S.* To occupy land under the Homestead Act. — *v.t.* **2.** *U.S.* To settle on (land) under the Homestead Act. — **home′stead′er** *n.*

Homestead Act *U.S.* A Congressional enactment of 1862 that provided a settler with 160 acres of free public land for cultivation and eventual ownership.

homestead law *U.S.* A law exempting up to a certain amount a dwelling and its land from certain liabilities incurred by the owner. Also **homestead exemption law.**

home·stretch (hōm′strech′) *n.* **1.** The straight portion of a racetrack forming the final approach to the finish. **2.** The last stage of any journey or endeavor.

home·ward (hōm′wərd) *adv.* Toward home. Also **home′wards** (-wərdz). — *adj.* Directed toward home.

home·work (hōm′wûrk′) *n.* Work done at home, esp. school work.

home·y (hō′mē) *adj.* **hom·i·er, hom·i·est** Suggesting the comforts of home. — **home′y·ness** or **hom′i·ness** *n.*

hom·i·ci·dal (hom′ə·sīd′l, hō′mə-) *adj.* **1.** Of homicide. **2.** Tending to homicide; murderous. — **hom′i·ci′dal·ly** *adv.*

hom·i·cide (hom′ə·sīd, hō′mə-) *n.* **1.** The killing of any human being by another. **2.** A person who has killed another. [< F < L *homo* man + *caedere* to cut, kill]

hom·i·let·ic (hom′ə·let′ik) *adj.* **1.** Pertaining to or having the nature of a sermon or homily. **2.** Of or pertaining to homiletics. Also **hom′i·let′i·cal.** — **hom′i·let′i·cal·ly** *adv.*

hom·i·let·ics (hom′ə·let′iks) *n.pl.* (*construed as sing.*) The branch of theological study that treats of the art of writing and delivering sermons. [< Gk. *homilētikos* sociable]

hom·i·ly (hom′ə·lē) *n. pl.* **·lies 1.** A sermon, especially one based on a Biblical text. **2.** A solemn discourse or lengthy reproof, especially on morals or conduct. [< OF < LL < Gk. *homilos* assembly] — **hom′i·list** *n.*

hom·ing (hō′ming) *adj.* **1.** Returning home. **2.** Helping or causing an aircraft, missile, etc., to home.

homing pigeon A pigeon capable of making its way home from great distances: also called *carrier pigeon.*

hom·i·noid (hom′ə·noid, hō′mə-) *adj.* Like or related to man. — *n.* An animal resembling man. [< NL < L *homo, hominis* man]

hom·i·ny (hom′ə·nē) *n.* Kernels of dried, hulled white corn, prepared as a food by boiling. [< Algonquian *rockahominie* parched corn]

hominy grits Grits (def. 2).

homo- *combining form* Same; like: opposed to *hetero-*. [< Gk. *homo-* < *homos* same]

homoeo- See HOMEO-.

ho·mo·ge·ne·i·ty (hō′mə·jə·nē′ə·tē, hom′ə-) *n.* The quality or condition of being homogeneous.

ho·mo·ge·ne·ous (hō′mə·jē′nē·əs, hom′ə-) *adj.* **1.** Having the same composition, structure, or character throughout;

uniform. **2.** Similar or identical in nature or form; like. [< Med.L < Gk. < *homos* same + *genos* race] **— ho′mo·ge′ne·ous·ly** *adv.* **— ho′mo·ge′ne·ous·ness** *n.*

ho·mog·en·ize (hə·moj′ə·nīz, hō′mə·jə·nīz′) *v.t.* **·ized, ·iz·ing 1.** To make or render homogeneous. **2.** To process, as milk, so as to break up fat globules and disperse them uniformly. **— ho·mog′en·i·za′tion** *n.* **— ho·mog′en·iz′er** *n.*

hom·o·graph (hom′ə·graf, -gräf, hō′mə-) *n.* A word identical with another in spelling, but differing from it in origin and meaning and sometimes in pronunciation, as *wind*, an air current, and *wind*, to coil: also called *homonym.* [< Gk. < *homos* same + *graphein* to write] **— hom′o·graph′ic** *adj.*

homoio- See HOMEO-.

ho·mol·o·gize (hō·mol′ə·jīz) *v.* **·gized, ·giz·ing** *v.t.* **1.** To make or demonstrate to be homologous. **—** *v.i.* **2.** To be homologous; have correspondence.

ho·mol·o·gous (hō·mol′ə·gəs) *adj.* **1.** Similar or related in structure, position, proportion, value, etc.; corresponding in nature or relationship. **2.** *Biol.* Corresponding in structure or origin, as an organ or part of one animal to a similar organ or part of another: The foreleg of a horse and the wing of a bird are *homologous*: distinguished from *analagous.* [< Gk. < *homos* same + *logos* measure, proportion]

ho·mol·o·gy (hō·mol′ə·jē) *n. pl.* **·gies 1.** The state or quality of being homologous. **2.** A homologous relationship.

ho·mo·mor·phism (hō′mə·môr′fiz·əm, hom′ə-) *n. Biol.* Resemblance between unrelated parts or organisms. Also **ho′mo·mor′phy. — ho′mo·mor′phic, ho′mo·mor′phous** *adj.*

hom·o·nym (hom′ə·nim, hō′mə-) *n.* **1.** A word identical with another in pronunciation but differing from it in origin, spelling, and meaning, as *fair* and *fare, read* and *reed*: also called *homophone.* **2.** A word identical with another in spelling and pronunciation, but differing from it in origin and meaning, as *butter*, the food, and *butter*, one who butts. **3.** A homograph. [< Gk. *homos* same + *onyma* name] **— hom·o·nym·ic** (hom′ə·nim′ik, hō′mə-), **ho·mon·y·mous** (hō·mon′ə·məs) *adj.*

hom·o·phone (hom′ə·fōn, hō′mə-) *n.* A homonym (def. 1). [< Gk. *homos* same + *phōnē* sound]

hom·o·phon·ic (hom′ə·fon′ik, hō′mə-) *adj.* **1.** Of, pertaining to, or having the same sound. **2.** *Music* Having one predominant part carrying the melody, with the other parts used for harmonic effect: opposed to *polyphonic.* **— ho·moph·o·ny** (hō·mof′ə·nē) *n.*

ho·mop·ter·ous (hō·mop′tər·əs) *adj.* Of or pertaining to insects with sucking mouth parts and usu. two pairs of wings. [< NL < Gk. *homos* same + *pteron* wing] **— ho·mop′ter·an** *adj. & n.*

Homo sa·pi·ens (sā′pē·enz) The scientific name for modern man. [< NL < L *homo* man + *sapiens* wise]

ho·mo·sex·u·al (hō′mə·sek′shōō·əl, hom′ə-) *adj.* Of or having sexual desire for persons of the same sex. **—** *n.* A homosexual individual. **— ho′mo·sex′u·al′i·ty** (-al′ə·tē) *n.*

ho·mun·cu·lus (hō·mung′kyə·ləs) *n. pl.* **·li** (-lī) A midget; dwarf. [< L *homo* man] **— ho·mun′cu·lar** *adj.*

hone (hōn) *n.* A fine, compact whetstone used for sharpening edged tools, razors, etc. **—** *v.t.* **honed, hon·ing** To sharpen, as a razor, on a hone. [OE *hān* stone]

hon·est (on′ist) *adj.* **1.** Not given to lying, cheating, stealing, etc. **2.** Not characterized by falsehood or intent to mislead: an *honest* statement. **3.** Giving or having full worth or value. **4.** Performed or earned in a conscientious manner. **5.** Sincere; frank. [< OF < L *honos* honor]

hon·est·ly (on′ist·lē) *adv.* **1.** In an honest manner. **2.** Really; truly; indeed: used for emphasis: *Honestly*, I'll go.

hon·es·ty (on′is·tē) *n.* **1.** The state or quality of being honest. **2.** Truthfulness; sincerity; fairness.

hon·ey (hun′ē) *n. pl.* **hon·eys 1.** A sweet, viscous substance made by bees from nectar gathered from flowers. **2.** Anything resembling honey. **3.** Sweetness. **4.** Darling: a term of endearment. **5.** *U.S. Slang* Something regarded as a superior example of its kind: a *honey* of a car. **—** *v.* **hon·eyed** or **hon·ied, hon·ey·ing —** *v.t.* **1.** To sweeten with or as with honey. **2.** To talk in a loving or flattering manner to. **—** *adj.* Of or like honey; sweet. [OE *hunig*]

honey bag The receptable or dilatation of the esophagus in which the bee produces honey. Also **honey sac.**

hon·ey·bee (hun′ē·bē′) *n.* A bee that produces honey.

hon·ey·comb (hun′ē·kōm′) *n.* **1.** A structure consisting of series of hexagonal, wax cells, made by bees for the storage of honey, pollen, or their eggs. **2.** Anything like a honeycomb. **—** *v.t.* **1.** To fill with small holes or cavities; riddle. **2.** To penetrate or pervade so as to undermine or weaken. **—** *adj.* Like a honeycomb.

hon·ey·dew (hun′ē·dōō′, -dyōō′) *n.* **1.** A sweet fluid exuded by the leaves of various plants during warm weather. **2.** A sweetish substance secreted by certain insects.

honeydew melon A variety of melon having a smooth, white skin and sweet, greenish pulp.

hon·eyed (hun′ēd) *adj.* **1.** Full of, consisting of, or resembling honey. **2.** Sweet, soothing, or flattering.

honey locust A large, thorny North American tree bea long pods with a sweet pulp between the seeds.

hon·ey·moon (hun′ē·mōōn′) *n.* **1.** A vacation spent newly-married couple. **2.** The first, happy period of a riage. **3.** *U.S. Informal* The early and easy period of an lationship. **—** *v.i.* To spend one's honeymoon.

hon·ey·suck·le (hun′ē·suk′əl) *n.* **1.** A climbing shrub ing white, buff, or crimson flowers. **2.** Any of a numb similar fragrant plants. [OE *hunisūce*]

honk (hôngk, hongk) *n.* **1.** The sound made by a goose A sound resembling this, as that of an automobile horn. *v.i.* **1.** To make the sound of the goose. **2.** To make sound of an automobile horn. **—** *v.t.* **3.** To cause (an a mobile horn) to sound. [Imit.] **— honk′er** *n.*

hon·ky-tonk (hông′kē·tôngk′, hong′kē·tongk′) *n. Slang* A noisy, squalid barroom or tavern. [Prob. imit

hon·or (on′ər) *n.* **1.** High regard, respect, or esteem. Glory; fame; credit. **3.** *Usu. pl.* An outward token, act, etc., of regard or esteem. **4.** A strong sense of wh right. **5.** A reputation for high standards of conduct. cause or source of esteem or pride: to be an *honor* to c profession. **7.** A privilege or pleasure: May I have the *h* of this dance? **8.** *Usu. pl.* Special recognition given to a dent for superior scholarship, etc. **9.** Chastity in wo **10.** In bridge, one of the five highest cards of a suit. **11** golf, the privilege of playing first from the tee. **— t honor to 1.** To pay homage to. **2.** To bring respect or c it to. **— to do the honors 1.** To act as host or hostess. To perform any of various social courtesies, as propo toasts, etc. **—** *v.t.* **1.** To regard with honor or respect. To treat with courtesy. **3.** To confer an honor upon; nify. **4.** To accept or pay, as a check or draft. Also **hon′our.** [< OF < L] **— hon′or·er** *n.*

Hon·or (on′ər) *n.* A title or form of address for a ju mayor, etc.: preceded by *Your, His,* or *Her.*

hon·or·a·ble (on′ər·ə·bəl) *adj.* **1.** Worthy of honor o spect. **2.** Conferring honor or credit. **3.** Having emin or high rank. **4.** Possessing or according to high moral p ciples. **5.** Accompanied by marks of honor. Also *Brit.* **h our·a·ble. — hon′or·a·ble·ness** *n.* **— hon′or·a·bly** *adv.*

Hon·or·a·ble (on′ər·ə·bəl) *adj.* A formal title of cour for certain important officials, as cabinet members, jus of the Supreme Court, etc.: preceded by *The.*

hon·o·rar·i·um (on′ə·râr′ē·əm) *n. pl.* **·rar·i·ums** or **·ra** (-râr′ē·ə) A payment given, as to a professional man services rendered when law or propriety forbids a set fee. [< L *honorarium* honorary]

hon·or·ar·y (on′ə·rer′ē) *adj.* **1.** Designating an office, t etc., bestowed as an honor, without the customary pov duties, or salaries. **2.** Having such a title, office, etc. *honorary* chairman. **3.** Bringing, conferred in, or deno honor: an *honorary* membership. [< L *honorarius*]

hon·or·if·ic (on′ə·rif′ik) *adj.* **1.** Conferring or impl honor or respect. **2.** Denoting certain phrases, words word elements, as in Oriental languages, used in respe address. **—** *n.* Any honorific title, word, phrase, etc. [< *honor* honor + *facere* to make] **— hon′or·if′i·cal·ly**

honors system In some colleges, a plan for selected dents to undertake individual, specialized work.

honor system In some colleges, schools, etc., a syster government without immediate supervision.

hooch (hōōch) *n. U.S. Slang* Alcoholic liquor, esp. illeg distilled whisky. [< *hoochinoo*, alter. of *Hutanuwu*, nam Alaskan Indian tribe that made liquor]

hood[1] (hŏŏd) *n.* **1.** A covering for the head and back of neck, sometimes forming part of a garment. **2.** Anyt resmbling a hood in form or use; as: **a** *U.S.* The mov metal cover protecting the engine of an automobile. **b** A jecting cover for a hearth, ventilator, etc. **3.** In falconr cover for the head and eyes of a hawk when it is not hunt **4.** *Zool.* In certain animals, as the cobra, the folds of near the head, capable of expansion. **—** *v.t.* To cove furnish with or as with a hood. [OE *hōd*] **— hood′ed** *ad*

hood[2] (hŏŏd) *n. U.S. Slang* A hoodlum. [< HOODLU

-hood *suffix of nouns* **1.** Condition or quality of; state of ing: *babyhood, falsehood.* **2.** Class or totality of those ha a certain character: *priesthood.* [OE *hād* state, conditi

hood·lum (hōōd′ləm) *n. U.S.* **1.** A young street rowd tough. **2.** A thug or ruffian. [? < dia. G *hodalum* rowd

hoo·doo (hōō′dōō) *n.* **1.** Voodoo. **2.** *Informal* One wh that which brings bad luck; a jinx. **3.** *Informal* Bad l **—** *v.t. Informal* To bring bad luck to. [Var. of VOODO

hood·wink (hŏŏd′wingk′) *v.t.* **1.** To blindfold. **2.** trick; cheat. **3.** To conceal or hide. **— hood′wink′er**

hoo·ey (hōō′ē) *n. & interj. U.S. Slang* Nonsense.

hoof (hŏŏf, hōōf) *n. pl.* **hoofs** or **hooves** (hŏŏvz, hōōvz) The horny sheath incasing the foot in various mammals horses, cattle, swine, etc. ◆ Collateral adjective: *ungu* **2.** The entire foot of such an animal. **3.** An animal v hoofs, especially as a unit of a herd. **4.** The human foo humorous usage. **— on the hoof** Alive; not butchered:

cattle. — *v.t. & v.i.* **1.** To trample with the hoofs. **2.** *formal* To walk or dance: usually with *it.* [OE *hōf*]
f·beat (ho͝of′bēt′, ho͞of′-) *n.* The sound made by a ofed animal in walking, trotting, etc.
f·er (ho͝of′ər, ho͞o′fər) *n. U.S. Slang* A professional ncer, esp. a tap dancer.
f·print (ho͝of′print′, ho͞of′-) *n.* One of the tracks left by oofed animal.
k (ho͝ok) *n.* **1.** A curved or bent piece of metal, wood, ne, etc., having one free end that serves to hold up, fasten, drag something. **2.** A fishhook. **3.** A curved cutting l. **4.** The fixed half of a hinge from which a door, gate, ., swings. **5.** Something that ensnares; a trap. **6.** Someng resembling a hook; as: **a** A recurved organ or part of an mal or plant. **b** A curved point of land. **c** A bend in a river. A hook-shaped part of a letter. **7.** In baseball, a curve. In boxing, a short, swinging blow, with the elbow bent. In golf, a stroke that sends the ball curving to his left. **10.** *usic* One of the lines at the end of the stem of a note, used indicate the note's value. **11.** *Naut. Slang* An anchor. — **hook or by crook** In one way or another. — **hook, line, d sinker** *Informal* Entirely; unreservedly. — **off the ok** *Slang* Free from a troublesome situation, obligation, . — **on one's own hook** *Informal* By one's own efforts. *v.t.* **1.** To fasten, attach, or take hold of with or as with a ok. **2.** To catch on a hook, as fish. **3.** To make into the pe of a hook. **4.** To catch on or wound with the horns, those of a bull. **5.** To make (a rug, mat, etc.) by looping rn through a backing of canvas or burlap. **6.** In baseball, pitch (the ball) in a curve. **7.** In boxing, to strike with a ort, swinging blow. **8.** In golf, to drive (the ball) to one's . **9.** In hockey, to check illegally with the stick. **10.** *formal* To trick; dupe. **11.** *Slang* To pilfer; steal. — *v.i.* . To curve like a hook; bend. **13.** To be fastened or ght with or as with a hook or hooks. — **to hook up** **1.** fasten or attach with a hook or hooks. **2.** To put tother or connect. — **to hook up with** *Slang* **1.** To become ompanion of. **2.** To marry. [OE *hōc*] — **hook′y** *adj.*
k·ah (ho͝ok′ə) *n.* An Oriental tobacco pipe having a g, flexible tube that passes through a vessel of water, thus ling the smoke. Also **hook′a.** [< Arabic *huqqah*]
k and eye A fastening for clothes, consisting of a small ok that passes through a loop of metal or thread.
ked (ho͝okt) *adj.* **1.** Curved like a hook. **2.** Supplied h a hook or hooks. **3.** Made by means of a hook, as a rug. *Slang* Married. **5.** *Slang* Addicted to a habit or practice, ecially a harmful one. — **hook·ed·ness** (ho͝ok′id·nis) *n.*
ked rug A rug made by looping yarn or strips of cloth h a hooked tool through a backing of burlap or canvas.
k·nose (ho͝ok′nōz′) *n.* A nose with a downward curve; uiline nose. — **hook′-nosed′** (-nōzd′) *adj.*
k·up (ho͝ok′up′) *n.* **1.** *Telecom.* The arrangement of the paratus and connections used for a radio broadcast or er electrical transmission. **2.** *Informal* A relationship or nection, as between countries, persons, etc.
k·worm (ho͝ok′wûrm′) *n.* A nematode worm with oked mouth parts, parasitic in the intestines and causing cylostomiasis in man.
kworm disease Ancylostomiasis.
k·y (ho͝ok′ē) *n. U.S. Informal* Absence without leave, from school: now only in the phrase **to play hooky,** to be a ant. [< HOOK, in dial. sense of "make off"]
·li·gan (ho͞o′lə·gən) *n. Slang* A young hoodlum; petty ngster. [after *Hooligan,* name of an Irish family]
p (ho͞op, ho͝op) *n.* **1.** A circular band of metal, wood, .; esp., such a band used to confine the staves of a barrel, . **2.** A child's toy in the shape of a large ring. **3.** One of rings of flexible metal, whalebone, etc., used to make a man's skirt stand out from her body. **4.** The band of a ger ring. — *v.t.* **1.** To surround or fasten with a hoop or ops. **2.** To encircle. [OE *hōp*]
p·er (ho͞o′pər, ho͝op′ər) *n.* A cooper.
p·la (ho͞op′lä) *n. U.S. Slang* Noise and excitement.
·poe (ho͞o′po͞o) *n.* An Old World bird having a long bill d an erectile crest. Also **hoo′poo.** [< F L *upupa*]

HOOPOE
(About 12 inches long; bill 2½ inches)

p skirt **1.** A bell-shaped structure de from several hoops of graduated es, used to expand a woman's skirt. **2.** e skirt worn over this.
·ray (ho͞o·rā′, hə-, ho͞o-) See HURRAH.
se·gow (ho͞os′gou) *n. U.S. Slang* Jail prison. Also **hoos′gow.** [< Sp. *juzgado* bunal]
·sier (ho͞o′zhər) *n. U.S.* A native or ident of Indiana. [Prob. < dial. *hoosier* untaineer]
osier State A nickname of Indiana.

hoot[1] (ho͞ot) *n.* **1.** The cry of an owl. **2.** A sound similar to this, as of a train whistle. **3.** A loud, derisive outcry. — *v.i.* **1.** To make the sound of an owl. **2.** To make a sound similar to this. **3.** To jeer, as in contempt. — *v.t.* **4.** To jeer at or mock with derisive cries. **5.** To drive off with hoots. **6.** To express (disapproval, scorn, etc.) by hooting. [< Scand. Cf. Sw. *huta.*]
hoot[2] (ho͞ot) *n. U.S. Informal* An insignificant amount; bit: commonly in the expression **I don't give a hoot,** I don't care a bit. [Earlier *hooter,* ? alter. of *iota.* Cf. JOT.]
hoot·en·an·ny (ho͞ot′n·an′ē) *n. pl.* **·nies** **1.** *U.S.* A gathering of folk singers, especially for a public performance. **2.** *Informal* A gadget; thingamajig. Also **hoot·nan·ny** (ho͞ot′nan′ē). [Origin unknown]
hooves (ho͞ovz, ho͝ovz) Alternative plural of HOOF.
hop[1] (hop) *v.* **hopped, hop·ping** *v.i.* **1.** To move by making short leaps on one foot. **2.** To move in short leaps on both feet or on all four feet. **3.** To limp. **4.** *Informal* To dance. **5.** *Informal* To go, especially by airplane. — *v.t.* **6.** To jump over, as a fence. **7.** *Informal* To get on or board. — **to hop off** To leave the ground in flight, as an airplane. — *n.* **1.** The act of hopping. **2.** *Informal* A dance or dancing party. **3.** *Informal* A trip in an airplane. [OE *hoppian*]
hop[2] (hop) *n.* **1.** A perennial climbing herb with scaly fruit. **2.** *pl.* The dried cones, used medicinally, and as a flavoring in beer. [< MDu. *hoppe*]
hope (hōp) *v.* **hoped, hop·ing** *v.t.* **1.** To desire with expectation of fulfillment. **2.** To wish; want. — *v.i.* **3.** To have desire or expectation: usually with *for.* — **to hope against hope** To continue hoping even when it may be in vain. — *n.* **1.** Desire accompanied by expectation of fulfillment. **2.** Confident expectation. **3.** That which is desired. **4.** One who or that which is a cause of hopeful expectation. [OE *hopa*]
hope chest A box or chest used by young women to hold linen, clothing, etc., in anticipation of marriage.
hope·ful (hōp′fəl) *adj.* **1.** Full of or manifesting hope: a *hopeful* attitude. **2.** Affording grounds for hope; promising: a *hopeful* situation. — *n.* A young person who seems likely to succeed. — **hope′ful·ly** *adv.* — **hope′ful·ness** *n.*
hope·less (hōp′lis) *adj.* **1.** Without hope; despairing: a *hopeless* feeling. **2.** Affording no ground for hope: a *hopeless* predicament. — **hope′less·ly** *adv.* — **hope′less·ness** *n.*
Ho·pi (hō′pē) *n.* **1.** One of a group of North American Pueblo Indians of Shoshonean stock, now on a reservation in NE Arizona. **2.** Their Shoshonean language. [< Hopi *hópitu,* lit., peaceful ones]
hopped-up (hopt′up′) *adj. U.S. Slang* **1.** Stimulated by narcotics; drugged. **2.** Supercharged, as an engine.
hop·per (hop′ər) *n.* **1.** One who or that which hops. **2.** A jumping insect or larva. **3.** Any of various funnel-shaped receptacles in which coal, sand, grain, etc., may be kept until ready for discharge through the bottom.
hop·scotch (hop′skoch′) *n.* A children's game in which the player hops on one foot over the lines of a diagram, so as to recover a block or pebble.
ho·ral (hō′rəl) *adj.* Hourly. [< L *hora* hour]
Ho·ra·tian (hə·rā′shən) *adj.* Of or pertaining to Horace.
horde (hôrd, hōrd) *n.* **1.** A multitude, pack, or swarm, as of people, animals, etc. **2.** A tribe of nomadic Mongols. **3.** Any nomadic tribe. — *v.i.* **hord·ed, hord·ing** To gather in or live in a horde. [< F < G < Polish *horda*]
hore·hound (hôr′hound′, hōr′-) *n.* **1.** A whitish, bitter, perennial herb of the mint family. **2.** The juice or extract of this plant. **3.** A candy or cough remedy flavored with this extract. Also spelled *hoarhound.* [OE *hārhūne*]
ho·ri·zon (hə·rī′zən) *n.* **1.** The line of the apparent meeting of the sky with the earth or sea. **2.** The bounds or limits of one's observation, knowledge, or experience. [< OF < L < Gk. *horizein* to bound]
hor·i·zon·tal (hôr′ə·zon′təl, hor′-) *adj.* **1.** Of, pertaining to, or close to the horizon. **2.** Parallel to the horizon; level: opposed to *vertical.* **3.** Equal and uniform: a *horizontal* tariff. — *n.* A line, plane, etc., assumed to be parallel with the horizon. — **Syn.** See LEVEL. — **hor′i·zon′tal·ly** *adv.*
horizontal union A craft union.
hor·mone (hôr′mōn) *n.* **1.** *Physiol.* An internal secretion produced by one of the endocrine glands, as the pituitary, thyroid, adrenals, etc., and carried by the blood stream to other parts of the body where it has a specific effect. **2.** *Bot.* A similar substance in plants. [< Gk. *hormaein* to excite] — **hor·mo·nal** (hôr·mō′nəl), **hor·mon·ic** (hôr·mon′ik) *adj.*
horn (hôrn) *n.* **1.** A hard, bonelike, permanent growth of epidermal tissue, usu. occurring in pairs and projecting from the head in various hoofed animals, as in oxen, sheep, cattle, etc. **2.** Either of the two antlers of a deer, shed annually. **3.** Any outgrowth projecting naturally from the head of an animal. **4.** The substance of which animal horn is made. **5.** The appendage like an animal's horn attributed to demons,

deities, etc. **6.** In the Bible, a symbol of glory and power. **7.** *Usu. pl.* The imaginary projections from the forehead of a cuckold. **8.** A vessel or implement formed from or shaped like a horn: a powder *horn*. **9.** One of the extremities of the crescent moon. **10.** The pommel of a saddle. **11.** A device for sounding warning signals: an automobile *horn*. **12.** A cornucopia. **13.** Any pointed or tapering projection, as the point of an anvil. **14.** One of the two or more alternatives of a dilemma. **15.** *Music* **a** Any of the various brass instruments, formerly made from animal horns, in the shape of a long, coiled tube widening out into a bell at one end. **b** The French horn. **16.** *Informal* Any musical wind instrument. **17.** *Electronics* A hollow, tubular device terminating in a cone of varying cross section, for collecting sound waves, as in a loudspeaker. **18.** *Geog.* **a** One of the branches forming the delta of a stream or river. **b** A cape or peninsula. **— to blow one's own horn** To brag. **— to haul** (or **pull** or **draw**) **in one's horns** **1.** To check one's anger, zeal, etc. **2.** To retract or withdraw, as a previous statement. — *adj.* Of or like horn. — *v.t.* **1.** To provide with horns. **2.** To shape like a horn. **3.** To attack with the horns; gore. **— to horn in** *Slang* To intrude or enter without being invited. [OE]

horn·bill (hôrn′bil′) *n.* A tropical bird, having a large bill surmounted by a hornlike extension.

horn·blende (hôrn′blend) *n.* A common variety of amphibole, greenish black or black, containing iron and silicate of magnesium, calcium, and aluminum. — **horn′blend′ic** *adj.*

horn·book (hôrn′bo͝ok′) *n.* **1.** A leaf or page containing a printed alphabet, etc., covered with transparent horn and framed, formerly used in teaching reading to children. **2.** A primer or book of rudimentary knowledge.

horned (hôrnd, *Poetic* hôr′nid) *adj.* **1.** Having a horn or horns. **2.** Having a projection or process resembling a horn.

horned owl Any of various American owls with conspicuous ear tufts; esp. the screech owl.

horned toad A flat-bodied, spiny lizard with a short tail and toadlike appearance, common in semiarid regions of the western U.S. Also **horn toad.**

horned viper A venomous African or Indian viper with a hornlike growth over each eye.

hor·net (hôr′nit) *n.* Any of various wasps capable of inflicting a severe sting. [OE *hyrnet*]

horn of plenty A cornucopia.

horn·pipe (hôrn′pīp′) *n.* **1.** An obsolete musical instrument resembling the clarinet. **2.** A lively English dance for one or more performers. **3.** The music for such a dance.

horn·y (hôr′nē) *adj.* **horn·i·er, horn·i·est** **1.** Made of horn or a similar substance. **2.** Having horns or projections resembling horns. **3.** Hard as horn; tough. — **horn′i·ness** *n.*

hor·o·loge (hôr′ə·lōj, hor′-) *n.* A timepiece, as a watch, clock, etc. [< OF < L < Gk. < *hōra* time + *legein* to tell]

ho·rol·o·ger (hô·rol′ə·jər, hō-) *n.* One skilled in horology; also, one who makes or sells timepieces. Also **ho·rol′o·gist.**

ho·rol·o·gy (hô·rol′ə·jē, hō-) *n.* The science of the measurement of time or of the construction of timepieces. — **hor·o·log·ic** (hôr′ə·loj′ik, hor′-) or **·i·cal** *adj.*

hor·o·scope (hôr′ə·skōp, hor′-) *n.* **1.** In astrology, the aspect of the heavens, with special reference to the positions of the planets at any specific instant, esp. at a person's birth. **2.** The diagram of the twelve divisions or houses of the heavens, used in predicting the future. [< L < Gk. < *hōra* hour + *skopos* watcher] — **ho·ros·co·py** (hô·ros′kə·pē) *n.*

hor·ren·dous (hô·ren′dəs, ho-) *adj.* Horrible; frightful. [< L *horrere* to bristle] — **hor·ren′dous·ly** *adv.*

hor·ri·ble (hôr′ə·bəl, hor′-) *adj.* **1.** Exciting or tending to excite horror; shocking. **2.** *Informal* Inordinate; excessive: a *horrible* liar. **3.** *Informal* Unpleasant; ugly. [< F < L *horrere* to bristle] — **hor′ri·ble·ness** *n.* — **hor′ri·bly** *adj.*

hor·rid (hôr′id, hor′-) *adj.* **1.** Causing great aversion or horror; dreadful. **2.** *Informal* Very objectionable; offensive. — **hor′rid·ly** *adv.* — **hor′rid·ness** *n.*

hor·ri·fy (hôr′ə·fī, hor′-) *v.t.* **·fied, ·fy·ing** **1.** To affect or fill with horror. **2.** *Informal* To shock or surprise painfully; startle. — **hor′ri·fi·ca′tion** *n.*

hor·ror (hôr′ər, hor′-) *n.* **1.** A painful, strong emotion caused by extreme fear, dread, repugnance, etc. **2.** One who or that which excites such an emotion. **3.** *Often pl.* A quality that excites horror: the *horrors* of crime. **4.** Great aversion; loathing. **5.** *Informal* Something disagreeable, ugly, etc. [< L]

hors d'oeuvre (ôr dûrv′, *Fr.* ôr dœ′vr′) *Usu. pl.* An appetizer, as olives, celery, etc. [< F]

horse (hôrs) *n. pl.* **hors·es** or **horse** **1.** A large, strong, herbivorous mammal with solid hoofs and a long mane and tail, employed in the domestic state as a draft or pack animal or for riding. ◆ Collateral adjective: *equine.* **2.** The full-grown male horse as contrasted with the mare; a gelding or stallion. **3.** Mounted soldiers; cavalry. **4.** A device, generally having four legs, for holding or supporting something: often in combination: *clotheshorse.* **5.** In gymnastics, a wooden leather-covered block on four legs, used for vaulting and other exercises. **6.** *Informal* In chess, a knight. **— a ho[rse] of another** (or **a different**) **color** A completely different m[at]ter. **— out of** (or **straight from**) **the horse's mouth** F[rom] the most direct and reliable source. **— to be** (or **get**) **[on] one's high horse** *Informal* To act haughtily or scornfu[lly]. **— to hold one's horses** *Slang* To restrain one's impetuo[sity] or impatience. **— To horse!** A command for cavalry tro[ops] to mount. — *v.* **horsed, hors·ing** *v.t.* **1.** To furnish wi[th a] horse or horses. **2.** To put on horseback. **3.** *U.S. Slang* [To] subject to horseplay or ridicule. — *v.i.* **4.** To mount or [ride] on a horse. **5.** *Slang* To engage in horseplay: often w[ith] *around.* — *adj.* **1.** Of or pertaining to a horse or hor[ses]. **2.** Mounted on horses. **3.** Large for its kind. [OE *hors*]

horse·back (hôrs′bak′) *n.* **1.** A horse's back. **2.** A ri[dge] of earth or rock; hogback. — *adv.* On a horse's back.

horse·car (hôrs′kär′) **1.** A tramcar drawn by horses. A car for transporting horses.

horse chestnut **1.** A tree having digitate leaves, cluste[red] flowers, and chestnutlike fruits. **2.** The fruit of this tree

horse·flesh (hôrs′flesh′) *n.* Horses collectively.

horse·fly (hôrs′flī′) *n. pl.* **·flies** A large fly, the femal[e of] which sucks the blood of horses, cattle, etc.

horse·hair (hôrs′hâr′) *n.* **1.** The hair of horses, esp. tha[t of] their manes and tails. **2.** A fabric made of such hair; h[air]cloth. — *adj.* Covered, stuffed, or made of horsehair.

horse·hide (hôrs′hīd′) *n.* **1.** The hide of a horse. **2.** Lea[ther] made from a horse's hide.

horse latitudes *Naut.* A belt at about 35° north or so[uth] latitude, characterized by calms and light variable wi[nds] with diminishing to prevailing westerlies toward the p[oles] and trade winds toward the equator.

horse·laugh (hôrs′laf′, -läf′) *n.* A loud, scornful laug[h].

horse·man (hôrs′mən) *n. pl.* **·men** (-mən) **1.** A man [who] rides a horse. **2.** A cavalryman. — **horse′man·ship** *n.*

horse pistol A large pistol formerly carried by horsem[en].

horse·play (hôrs′plā′) *n.* Rough, boisterous play or fu[n].

horse·pow·er (hôrs′pou′ər) *n.* *Mech.* A unit of the rat[e of] work, equal to 550 pounds lifted one foot in one second.

horse·rad·ish (hôrs′rad′ish) *n.* **1.** A garden herb of [the] mustard family. **2.** A condiment made from its root.

horse sense *Informal* Innate common sense.

horse·shoe (hôr′sho͞o′, hôrs′-) *n.* **1.** A piece of metal shaped to fit the edge of a horse's hoof, to which it is na[iled] as a protective device. **2.** Something resembling a ho[rse]shoe in shape. **3.** *pl.* A game similar to quoits, in which [the] object is to throw horseshoes over or near a stake. — **·shoed, ·shoe·ing** To furnish with horseshoes.

horseshoe crab A large marine arthropod having a ho[rse]shoe-shaped carapace and a long telson: also called *king c[rab]*.

horse·tail (hôrs′tāl′) *n.* **1.** The tail of a horse. **2.** A pe[ren]nial flowerless plant of wide distribution.

horse·whip (hôrs′hwip′) *n.* A whip for managing hor[ses]. — *v.t.* **·whipped, ·whip·ping** To flog with a horsewhip.

horse·wom·an (hôrs′wo͝om′ən) *n. pl.* **·wom·en** (-wim[′ən]) **1.** A woman who rides on horseback. **2.** A woman wh[o is] skilled in riding or managing horses.

hors·y (hôr′sē) *adj.* **hors·i·er, hors·i·est** **1.** Pertaining [to or] suggestive of, or having the nature of a horse or horses. Associated with or devoted to horses, horseracing, fox h[unt]ing, etc. Also **hors′ey.** — **hors′i·ly** *adv.* — **hors′i·nes[s]**

hor·ta·to·ry (hôr′tə·tôr′ē, -tō′rē) *adj.* Of, characterized [by] or giving exhortation or encouragement. Also **hor′ta·t[ive]** [< L *hortatorius*] — **hor′ta·tive·ly** *adv.*

hor·ti·cul·ture (hôr′tə·kul′chər) *n.* **1.** The cultivation [of a] garden. **2.** The art or science of growing garden vegetab[les,] fruits, flowers, etc. [< L *hortus* garden + *cultura* cult[iva]tion] — **hor′ti·cul′tur·al** *adj.* — **hor′ti·cul′tur·ist** *n.*

ho·san·na (hō·zan′ə) *interj.* Praised be the Lord. — *n.* A cry of "hosanna." **2.** Any exultant praise. [< LL < [Gk.] < Hebrew *hōshi āhnnā* save, we pray]

hose (hōz) *n. pl.* **hose** (*Archaic* **hos·en**) *for defs. 1, 2;* **ho[ses]** *for def. 3* **1.** *pl.* Stockings or socks. **2.** *pl.* Formerly, a [gar]ment worn by men for covering the legs and lower part of [the] body like tight trousers. **3.** A flexible tube of rubber, p[las]tic, etc., for conveying water and other fluids. — *v.t.* **hos[ed],** **hos·ing** **1.** To water, drench, or douse with a hose. *Canadian Slang* To cheat or defeat. [OE *hosa*]

Ho·se·a (hō·zē′ə, -zā′ə) Eighth-century B.C. Hebrew pro[ph]et. — *n.* A book of the Old Testament bearing his na[me]; also, in the Douai Bible, *Osee.*

ho·sier·y (hō′zhər·ē) *n.* Stockings and socks of all types.

hos·pice (hos′pis) *n.* A place of rest or shelter, usu. m[ain]tained by a religious order for pilgrims, travelers, etc. [< [F] < L *hospitium* inn, hospitality]

hos·pi·ta·ble (hos′pi·tə·bəl, hos·pit′ə·bəl) *adj.* **1.** Behav[ing] in a kind and generous manner toward guests. **2.** Afford[ing] or expressing welcome and generosity toward guests. Receptive in mind. [< OF < L *hospitare* to entertain] **hos′pi·ta·ble·ness** *n.* — **hos′pi·ta·bly** *adv.*

hos·pi·tal (hos′pi·təl) *n.* An institution that provides m[edi]cal, surgical, or psychiatric treatment and nursing care

ill or injured temporarily lodged there; also, the building for this purpose. [< OF < L *hospes* guest]
)i·tal·i·ty (hos′pə·tal′ə·tē) *n. pl.* **·ties** The spirit, prac- or act of being hospitable.
)i·tal·ize (hos′pi·təl·īz′) *v.t.* **·ized, ·iz·ing** To put in a)ital for treatment and care.
)i·tal·i·za·tion (hos′pi·təl·ə·zā′shən, -ī·zā′shən) *n.* **1.** act of hospitalizing. **2.** *U.S.* A form of insurance that rantees all or partial payment of hospital expenses: also **)ital insurance.**
(hōst) *n.* **1.** A man who extends hospitality to others, to guests in his own home. **2.** *Biol.* Any living organ- from which a parasite obtains nourishment and protec- . — *v.t. Informal* To conduct or entertain in the role ost. [< OF < L *hospes* guest, host]
[2] (hōst) *n.* **1.** A large number of men or things; a multi- . **2.** An army. [< OF < L *hostis* enemy]
(hōst) *n. Eccl. Sometimes cap.* The Eucharistic bread vafer. [< OF < L *hostia* sacrificial victim]
tage (hos′tij) *n.* **1.** A person given or held as a pledge l specified conditions are met, as in war. **2.** The state of person so treated. **3.** A pledge or security. [< OF]
:el (hos′təl) *n.* One of a chain of supervised lodging ses for young people on bicycle or hiking trips.
:el·ry (hos′təl·rē) *n. pl.* **·ries** *Archaic* A lodging e; inn. — **hos′tel·er, hos′tel·ler** *n.*
·ess (hōs′tis) *n.* **1.** A woman who performs the duties host. **2.** A woman employed in a restaurant, etc., to t and serve guests. **3.** A woman paid to dance with the ons of a public dance hall. **4.** A female innkeeper.
:ile (hos′təl, *esp. Brit.* -tīl) *adj.* **1.** Having or express- enmity or opposition; unfriendly. **2.** Of, pertaining to, haracteristic of an enemy: *hostile* acts; *hostile* forces. [< L *hostilis*] — **hos′tile·ly** *adv.*
til·i·ty (hos·til′ə·tē) *n. pl.* **·ties** **1.** The state of being :ile. **2.** A hostile act. **3.** *pl.* War or acts of war.
:ler (hos′lər, os′-) *n.* A stableman; groom: also spelled r. [< OF *hostelier* innkeeper]
(hot) *adj.* **hot·ter, hot·test** **1.** Having or giving off great t; having a high temperature. **2.** Having a relatively degree of heat; very warm. **3.** Feeling or showing ab- mal bodily warmth. **4.** Giving the sensation of heat or ning to the tongue or skin: *hot* pepper. **5.** Carrying an tric current, esp. one of high voltage. **6.** Dangerously oactive. **7.** Constantly in action or use: War news kept wires *hot*. **8.** In hunting, strong or fresh, as a scent. **9.** far behind: in *hot* pursuit. **10.** Marked by or showing ng or violent emotion: *hot* words. **11.** Marked by in- e activity; raging; violent: a *hot* battle. **12.** *Slang* Lust- sexy. **13.** *Slang* Strongly disposed toward; eager: often *for*. **14.** *Informal* Controversial: a *hot* issue. **15.** *In- nal* So new as not to have lost its currency, excitement, : a *hot* item. **16.** *Slang* Excellent, skillful, etc.: He is not *ot* tonight. **17.** *U.S. Slang* Recently stolen or illegally cured. **18.** *Music Slang* **a** Designating jazz marked by a tempo, heavily accented beat, exciting improvisations, **b** Playing or performing such jazz: a *hot* trumpet. — **in water** *Informal* In trouble. — **to make it hot for** *In- nal* To make the situation extremely uncomfortable for. *dv.* In a hot manner. [OE *hāt*] — **hot′ly** *adv.*
air *Slang* Empty or pretentious talk; exaggeration.
bed (hot′bed′) *n.* **1.** A bed of rich earth, protected by s and warmed usu. by fermenting manure, used to pro- e the growth of plants in advance of their season. **2.** A e or condition favoring rapid growth or great activity.
blood·ed (hot′blud′id) *adj.* Easily moved or excited.
cake A pancake or griddlecake. — **to go** (or **sell**) **like cakes** *Informal* To be disposed of quickly.
cross bun A circular cake or bun marked with a cross rosting, eaten esp. during Lent.
dog *Informal* A cooked frankfurter, usu. grilled, served split roll, and garnished with mustard, relish, etc.
el (hō·tel′) *n.* **1.** An establishment or building provid- lodging, food, etc., to travelers and long-term residents. *Canadian* Beer parlor. [< F < OF *hostel* inn]
foot (hot′fo͝ot′) *v.i. Informal* To hurry: often with *it.*
head (hot′hed′) *n.* A hotheaded person.
head·ed (hot′hed′id) *adj.* **1.** Quick-tempered. **2.** Im- uous. — **hot′head′ed·ly** *adv.* — **hot′head′ed·ness** *n.*
house (hot′hous′) *n.* A greenhouse kept warm artifi- ly for the growth of out-of-season or delicate plants.
line A direct means of communication, esp. a telephone line emergency use between Washington, D.C. and Moscow.
plate A small portable gas or electric stove.
rod *U.S. Slang* An automobile, usu. an older model, lified for high speeds.
spring A natural spring emitting waters with a tem- ature of 98° F. or above: also called *thermal spring.*

Hot·ten·tot (hot′ən·tot) *n.* **1.** A member of a South African people believed to be related to both the Bantus and the Bushmen. **2.** The language of this people. — *adj.* Of or pertaining to the Hottentots or their language.
hou·dah (hou′də) See HOWDAH.
hound (hound) *n.* **1.** A dog of any of several breeds kept for hunting, esp. one that hunts by scent and in a pack. **2.** A dog of any breed. **3.** A mean, detestable man. — **to follow** (or **ride to**) **the hounds** To engage in hunting (a fox, etc.) on horseback and with a pack of hounds. — *v.t.* **1.** To hunt with or as with hounds. **2.** To incite to pursue. **3.** *Informal* To nag persistently; pester. [OE *hund* dog]
hour (our) *n.* **1.** A space of time equal to 1/24 of a day; sixty minutes. ◆ Collateral adjective: *horal.* **2.** Any one of the twelve points on a timepiece indicating such a space of time. **3.** A definite time of day as shown in hours and minutes by a timepiece: The *hour* is 6:15. **4.** An indefinite, but usu. short, period of time: The happiest *hour* of one's life. **5.** A particular or regularly fixed time for some activity. **6.** *pl.* A set period of time for work or other regular pursuits: school *hours.* **7.** *pl.* One's usual time of rising and of going to bed: to keep regular *hours.* **8.** The present time or current situation. **9.** Distance calculated by the time ordinarily required to cover it: an *hour* away from home. **10.** In education, a single class session or period, usu. 50 minutes long. **11.** *Eccl.* **a** The canonical hours. **b** The office or prayers recited or sung at these hours. **12.** *Astron.* An angular measure of right ascension or longitude, being 15 degrees or the 24th part of a great circle of the sphere. — **the small** (or **wee**) **hours** The early hours of the morning. [< L < Gk. *hōra* time, period]
hour·glass (our′glas′, -gläs′) *n.* An old device for measuring time, consisting of two globular glass vessels connected by a narrow neck through which a quantity of sand, mercury, or water runs from the upper vessel to the lower during a stated interval of time, usu. an hour.

HOURGLASS

hou·ri (ho͞o′rē, hour′ē) *n.* In Moslem belief, one of the beautiful virgins allotted to those who attain Paradise. [< F < Persian < Arabic *hūrīyah* black-eyed woman]
hour·ly (our′lē) *adj.* **1.** Of, happening, or performed every hour. **2.** Occurring or accomplished in the course of an hour. **3.** Frequent. — *adv.* **1.** At intervals of an hour. **2.** Hour by hour. **3.** Frequently; often.
house (*n.* hous; *v.* houz) *n. pl.* **hous·es** (hou′zəz) **1.** A building intended as a dwelling for human beings, esp. one used as the residence of a family or single tenant. **2.** A household; family. **3.** The abode of a fraternity, religious community, or other group living together as a unit. **4.** A dormitory or resident hall, esp. in a college or university. **5.** *Brit.* A college in a university. **6.** Anything providing shelter or protection to an animal, as the shell of a snail. **7.** A structure for storing or sheltering something, as goods, plants, etc. **8.** A building used for any of various purposes: a *house* of correction. **9.** A place of worship. **10.** A theater or other place of entertainment. **11.** The audience in such a place of entertainment. **12.** *Govt.* **a** A legislative or deliberative body: *House* of Representatives. **b** A quorum of such a body. **c** The chamber or building such a body occupies. **13.** *Often cap.* A line of ancestors and descendants regarded as forming a single family: the *House* of Stuart. **14.** A business firm or establishment: a publishing *house.* **15.** In astrology: **a** One of the twelve divisions of the heavens. **b** A sign of the zodiac considered as the seat of greatest influence of a particular planet. — **like a house on fire** Very quickly and vigorously. — **on the house** At the expense of the proprietor. — **to bring down the house** To receive loud and enthusiastic applause. — **to clean house** *U.S. Slang* To get rid of undesirable conditions or persons, as in an organization. — **to keep house** To manage the affairs or work of a home. — **to put** (or **set**) **one's house in order** To tidy up one's personal or business affairs. — *v.* **housed, hous·ing** *v.t.* **1.** To take or put into a house; lodge. **2.** To store in a house or building. **3.** In carpentry, to fit into a mortise, joint, etc. — *v.i.* **4.** To take shelter or lodgings; dwell. [OE *hūs*] — **house′ful** *n.* — **house′less** *adj.*
house·boat (hous′bōt′) *n.* A barge or flat-bottomed boat fitted out as a dwelling and used in quiet waters.
house·break·ing (hous′brā′king) *n.* The act of breaking into and entering another's home with intent to commit theft or some other felony. — **house′break′er** *n.*
house·bro·ken (hous′brō′kən) *adj.* Trained to urinate and defecate outdoors or in a specific place, as a dog.
house·coat (hous′kōt′) *n.* A woman's garment, usu. long with a loose skirt, for informal wear within the house.
house·dress (hous′dres′) *n.* A dress, usu. of printed cotton fabric, worn esp. during household chores.

house·fly (hous′flī′) *n. pl.* **·flies** The common fly, found in nearly all parts of the world.

house·hold (hous′hōld′) *n.* **1.** A number of persons dwelling as a unit under one roof; esp., a family living together, including servants, etc. **2.** A home or the various domestic affairs of a home. — *adj.* Of or pertaining to the home.

house·hold·er (hous′hōl′dər) *n.* **1.** One who owns or occupies a house. **2.** The head of a family.

household word A person, product, place, etc., that is known or familiar to many people. Also **household name.**

house·keep·er (hous′kē′pər) *n.* **1.** One who performs the tasks of maintaining a home, as a housewife. **2.** A paid manager of a home. — **house′keep′ing** *n.*

house·maid (hous′mād′) *n.* A girl or woman employed to do housework.

housemaid's knee *Pathol.* A chronic inflammation of the bursa in front of the knee, afflicting housemaids, etc.

house·mas·ter (hous′mas′tər, -mäs′-) *n. Chiefly Brit.* A teacher in charge of one of the houses of a boys' school.

house·moth·er (hous′muth′ər) *n.* A woman acting as a supervisor for a group of people living together.

House of Commons **1.** The lower house of the British Parliament, the members of which are elected. **2.** The lower house of the Canadian Parliament.

house of correction An institution confining those given short-term sentences for minor offenses and considered to be capable of rehabilitation.

House of Lords The upper and nonelective house of the British Parliament, made up of the peerage and the highest ranking clergy.

House of Representatives **1.** The lower, larger branch of the United States Congress, and of many State legislatures, composed of members elected on the basis of population. **2.** A similar legislative body, as in Australia, Mexico, etc.

house organ A publication regularly issued by a business organization for its employees and customers.

house party An entertainment of a group of guests for several days, usu. in a house or a college fraternity.

house physician A physician resident by appointment in a hospital, hotel, or other institution.

house·top (hous′top′) *n.* The roof of a house. — **to shout** (or **cry**) **from the housetops** To give wide publicity to.

house·wares (hous′wârz′) *n.* Kitchen utensils, dishes, glassware, and other wares used in the home.

house·warm·ing (hous′wôr′ming) *n.* A party held by or for those who have just moved into new living quarters.

house·wife (hous′wīf′ *for def. 1,* huz′if *for def. 2*) *n. pl.* **house·wives** (hous′wīvz′) *for def. 1*; **house·wifes** (huz′ifs) or **house·wives** (huz′ivz) *for def. 2* **1.** A married woman who manages her own household and does not work for a living. **2.** *Chiefly Brit.* A kit holding sewing articles. — **house′·wife′ly** *adj. & adv.*

house·wife·ry (hous′wī′fər·ē, -wīf′rē) *n.* The duties of a housewife; housekeeping.

house·work (hous′wûrk′) *n.* The chores involved in keeping house, washing, cooking, etc.

hous·ing[1] (hou′zing) *n.* **1.** The act of providing shelter or lodging; also, the shelter or lodging so provided. **2.** The providing of houses on a large scale. **3.** Houses or dwellings collectively. **4.** That which serves as a shelter, cover, etc.: a bamboo *housing* for plants. **5.** *Mech.* **a** Something that holds part of a machine in place, as a frame or set of brackets. **b** A casing or cover for a machine or part of a machine.

hous·ing[2] (hou′zing) *n.* **1.** An ornamental cover for a horse. **2.** *Usu. pl.* Trappings. [< OF *houce,* prob. < Gmc.]

hove (hōv) Past tense of HEAVE.

hov·el (huv′əl, hov′-) *n.* **1.** A small, wretched dwelling. **2.** A low, open shed for sheltering cattle, tools, etc. — *v.t.* **hov·eled** or **·elled, hov·el·ing** or **·el·ling** To shelter or lodge in a hovel. [? Dim. of OE *hof* building]

hov·er (huv′ər, hov′-) *v.i.* **1.** To remain suspended in or near one place in the air. **2.** To linger or remain nearby, as if watching: with *around, near,* etc. **3.** To remain in an uncertain or irresolute state: with *between.* — *n.* The act or state of hovering. [< obs. *hove* to float] — **hov′er·er** *n.*

Hov·er·craft (huv′ər·kraft′, hov′-, -kräft′) *n.* A vehicle designed to travel just above the surface of land or water on a cushion of air generated by powerful fans: a trade name. Also **hov′er·craft.**

how (hou) *adv.* **1.** In what way or manner. **2.** To what degree, extent, or amount. **3.** In what state, or condition. **4.** For what reason or purpose. **5.** At what price: *How* is the stock selling today? **6.** With what meaning: *How* is that remark to be taken? **7.** By what name or designation. **8.** *Informal* What: *How* about having lunch? — *n.* A manner or means of doing. [OE *hū*]

how·be·it (hou·bē′it) *adv. Archaic* Be that as it may.

how·dah (hou′də) *n.* A seat for riders on an elephant or camel, often fitted with a canopy. [< Hind. *haudah*]

how-do-you-do (hou′də·yə·dōō′) *n. Informal* An embarrassing or difficult situation: usu. preceded by *fine, pretty,* etc.

How do you do? What is the state of your health?: as a formal greeting when being introduced to a perso

how·dy (hou′dē) *interj. Informal* An expression of gre

how·ev·er (hou·ev′ər) *adv.* **1.** In whatever manne whatever means. **2.** To whatever degree or extent: S *however* much it costs. — *conj.* Nevertheless; in spi still; yet. — **Syn.** See BUT[1]. Also **how·e'er′** (-âr′).

how·it·zer (hou′it·sər) *n.* A cannon with a barrel of me length and operating at a relatively high angle of fire. Du., ult. < Czechoslovakian *houfnice* catapult]

howl (houl) *v.i.* **1.** To utter the loud, mournful wai dog, wolf, or other animal. **2.** To utter such a cry in grief, or rage. **3.** To make a sound similar to this. laugh loudly. — *v.t.* **5.** To utter or express with ho **6.** To condemn, suppress, or drive away by howling: with *down.* — *n.* **1.** The wailing cry of a wolf, dog, or animal. **2.** Any howling sound. [ME *houlen*]

howl·er (hou′lər) *n.* **1.** One who or that which howls A monkey of Central and South America, having a grasping tail and making loud howling sounds. **3.** *Inf* An absurd blunder in speaking or writing.

howl·ing (hou′ling) *adj.* **1.** Producing or uttering h **2.** Characterized by or filled with howls: the *howling* w ness. **3.** *Slang* Very great; tremendous: a *howling* su

how·so·ev·er (hou′sō·ev′ər) *adv.* **1.** In whatever ma **2.** To whatever degree or extent.

hoy·den (hoid′n) *n.* A boisterous or ill-mannered girl *adj.* Boisterous. — *v.i.* To act like a hoyden. [Origi certain] — **hoy′den·ish** *adj.* — **hoy′den·ish·ness** *n.*

Hoyle (hoil) *n.* A book of rules and instructions for i games, esp. card games. [after Sir Edmund *Hoyle,* 1769, English writer on card games]

hub (hub) *n.* **1.** The center part of a wheel into whic axle is inserted. **2.** Any center of great activity or int

hub·bub (hub′ub) *n.* **1.** A loud, confused noise, as of voices shouting or talking. **2.** Uproar. [Origin unkn

huck·le·ber·ry (huk′əl·ber′ē) *n. pl.* **·ries** **1.** The e black or dark blue berry of any of various North Ame shrubs. **2.** A shrub yielding this berry.

huck·ster (huk′stər) *n.* **1.** A peddler of wares, esp. and vegetables. **2.** A petty, greedy tradesman. **3.** *Slang* One engaged in the advertising business. — *v.* To sell; peddle. **2.** To haggle. [< MDu. *heuken* to r

hud·dle (hud′l) *v.* **·dled, ·dling** *v.i.* **1.** To crowd or together closely, as from fear or cold. **2.** To draw or h oneself together. **3.** In football, to gather in a huddle *v.t.* **4.** To bring or crowd together closely. **5.** To draw self) together: often with *up.* **6.** To make or do hurrie confusedly, as dressing. — *n.* **1.** A number of perso things crowded together. **2.** A state of confusion o order. **3.** In football, the grouping of a team before **4.** *U.S. Informal* Any small conference. [Origin uncert

hue[1] (hyōō) *n.* **1.** The attribute of a color that deter its position in the spectrum and differentiates it fro achromatic color of the same brightness. **2.** Color autumnal *hues.* **3.** A particular tint or shade of color. *hīw* appearance] — **hued** *adj.*

hue[2] (hyōō) *n.* A loud clamor; shouting. — **hue an** Any great public stir. [< OF *huer* to shout after]

huff (huf) *n.* A fit of sudden anger or irritation. — *v.* To offend; make angry. — *v.i.* **2.** To take offense. **3** puff; blow. — **huf′fish** *adj.*

huf·fy (huf′ē) *adj.* **huff·i·er, huff·i·est** **1.** Touchy. **2.** lant; sulky. — **huff′i·ly** *adv.* — **huff′i·ness** *n.*

hug (hug) *v.* **hugged, hug·ging** *v.t.* **1.** To take and affectionately within the arms; press in close embrace. To squeeze between the forepaws, as a bear. **3.** To ch or cling to, as a belief. **4.** To keep close to. — *v.i.* **5** crowd closely together; snuggle. — *n.* **1.** A close, affec ate embrace. **2.** A tight clasp with the arms, as in wrest **3.** A bear's grip. [Prob. < ON *hugga* to console]

huge (hyōōj) *adj.* Very great in size, quantity, extent, [< OF *ahuge* high] — **huge′ly** *adv.* — **huge′ness** *n.*

hug·ger·mug·ger (hug′ər·mug′ər) *n.* Disorder; fusion. — *adj.* **1.** Secret; sly. **2.** Disorderly; sloven

Hu·gue·not (hyōō′gə·not) *n.* Any French Protestant o 16th and 17th centuries. [< F < G *eidgenoss* confede

huh (hu) *interj.* An exclamation of inquiry, surprise,

hu·la (hōō′lə) *n.* A Hawaiian dance characterized by ous arm movements that tell a story in pantomime. **hu′la-hu′la.** [< Hawaiian]

hulk (hulk) *n.* **1.** The body of an old, wrecked, or dis tled ship. **2.** *Often pl.* An old ship used for a prison, etc Any bulky, unwieldy object or person. — *v.i.* **1.** To ri loom bulkily: usu. with *up.* **2.** *Dial.* To lounge or sl about. [OE, prob. < Med.L < Gk. *helkein* to drag]

hulk·ing (hul′king) *adj.* Big and unwieldy, bulky, or c sy: a great *hulking* fellow. Also **hulk′y.**

hull (hul) *n.* **1.** The outer covering of certain fruits or s **2.** The calyx of some fruits, as the strawberry. **3.** outer covering. **4.** *Naut.* The body of a ship, exclusi masts, etc. — *v.t.* **1.** To remove the hull of. **2.** To :e or pierce the hull of (a ship). [OE *hulu*]

a·ba·loo (hul′ə·bə·lo͞o′) *n.* A loud, confused noise; up-. Also **hul′la·bal·loo′.** [Imit. reduplication of HULLO]

¹ (hum) *v.* **hummed, hum·ming** *v.i.* **1.** To make a low, muring or droning sound. **2.** To sing with the lips d. **3.** To give forth an indistinct sound: The streets *med* with traffic. **4.** To mumble indistinctly, as from usion; hem. **5.** *Informal* To be very busy or active: The *hummed.* — *v.t.* **6.** To sing with closed lips without ls. **7.** To put into a state by humming: to *hum* a child eep. — *n.* The act or sound of humming. [ME *hum-* — **hum′mer** *n.*

interj. A nasal, murmuring sound made to express tal concentration, deliberation, hesitation, etc.

an (hyo͞o′mən) *adj.* **1.** Of or characteristic of man. aving the nature or attributes of a man. **3.** Consisting man or men: *human* race. — *n.* A human being. [< < L *humanus*] — **hu′man·ness** *n.*

an being A man, woman, or child; a person.

ane (hyo͞o·mān′) *adj.* **1.** Having kindness, sympathy, benevolent. **2.** Tending to refine or civilize: *humane* ing. — **hu·mane′ly** *adv.* — **hu·mane′ness** *n.*

an·ism (hyo͞o′mən·iz′əm) *n.* **1.** The character or qualf being human. **2.** A system or attitude in thought, ren, etc., in which human ideals and the perfection of perlity are made central. **3.** The study of the humanities.

an·ism (hyo͞o′mən·iz′əm) *n.* The intellectual and ary movement of the Renaissance, characterized by the y of Greek and Roman classics and by an emphasis on an interests rather than on religion.

an·ist (hyo͞o′mən·ist) *n.* **1.** One learned in or devoted e study of the humanities; esp., a classical scholar. **2.** who subscribes to humanism (def. 2). — **hu′man·is′tic** — **hu′man·is′ti·cal·ly** *adv.*

an·i·tar·i·an (hyo͞o·man′ə·târ′ē·ən) *n.* One who seeks romote the welfare of mankind; philanthropist. — *adj.* aining to humanitarians. — **hu·man′i·tar′i·an·ism** *n.*

an·i·ty (hyo͞o·man′ə·tē) *n. pl.* **·ties** **1.** The human ; mankind. **2.** The state of being human; human na-. **3.** The state of being humane; benevolence. — **the anities** **1.** The study of classical Greek and Latin litera-. **2.** Literature, philosophy, the fine arts, etc., as disuished from the sciences. [< OF < L *humanus* human]

an·ize (hyo͞o′mən·īz) *v.* **·ized, ·iz·ing** *v.t.* **1.** To make an; give human characteristics to. **2.** To make gentle, ly, etc. — *v.i.* **3.** To become human or humane. — **an·i·za′tion** (-ə·zā′shən, -ī·zā′-) *n.* — **hu′man·iz′er** *n.*

an·kind (hyo͞o′mən·kīnd′) *n.* The human race; people.

an·ly (hyo͞o′mən·lē) *adv.* **1.** In a human manner. **2.** hin human power or ability: Is this *humanly* possible? **3.** ccordance with man's experience or knowledge.

·ble (hum′bəl) *adj.* **·bler, ·blest** **1.** Free from pride or ty; modest. **2.** Lowly in station, condition, etc.; unentious. **3.** Servile; fawning. **4.** Respectful. — *v.t.* **l, ·bling** **1.** To reduce the pride of. **2.** To lower in rank ignity. [< F < L *humus* ground] — **hum′ble·ness** *n.* **um′bler** *n.* — **hum′bly** *adv.*

ble pie Formerly, a pie containing the inner and less ce parts (**humbles**) of a deer and given to the servants at ing feasts: also spelled *umble pie.* — **to eat humble pie** e forced to apologize. [< OF < LL *lumbus* loin]

·bug (hum′bug) *n.* **1.** Anything intended or used to de; fraud. **2.** One who seeks to deceive others. **3.** The ity or practice of deceiving. — *v.* **·bugged, ·bug·ging** **1.** To delude; trick. — *v.i.* **2.** To practice deception. gin unknown] — **hum′bug·ger** *n.* — **hum′bug·ger·y** *n.*

·ding·er (hum·ding′ər) *n. Slang* One who or that which markable or out of the ordinary.

·drum (hum′drum′) *adj.* Lacking interest, variety, or tement; dull. — *n.* **1.** That which is tedious or dull. **2.** resome person; bore. [Reduplication of HUM]

ıer·us (hyo͞o′mər·əs) *n. pl.* **·mer·i** (-mər·ī) *Anat.* The of the upper part of the arm, from shoulder to elbow. illus. see SKELETON. [< L, shoulder] — **hu′mer·al** *adj.*

ıid (hyo͞o′mid) *adj.* Containing vapor or water; moist; p. [< L *humere* to be moist] — **hu′mid·ly** *adv.*

ıid·i·fy (hyo͞o·mid′ə·fī) *v.t.* **·fied, ·fy·ing** To make moist umid. — **hu·mid′i·fi·ca′tion** *n.* — **hu·mid′i·fi′er** *n.*

ıid·i·ty (hyo͞o·mid′ə·tē) *n.* Moisture; dampness, esp. he atmosphere. — **relative humidity** The ratio of the unt of water vapor actually in the air to the total unt it could hold at the same temperature.

ıi·dor (hyo͞o′mə·dôr) *n.* A container in which moisture tained, used for cigars, etc.

ıil·i·ate (hyo͞o·mil′ē·āt) *v.t.* **·at·ed, ·at·ing** To lower the e or self-esteem of; mortify. [< L *humilis* lowly] — **nil′i·a·to′ry** (-ə·tôr′ē, -ə·tō′rē) *adj.* — **hu·mil′i·a′tion** *n.*

hu·mil·i·ty (hyo͞o·mil′ə·tē) *n. pl.* **·ties** The state or quality of being humble. [< L *humilitas* lowness]

hum·ming·bird (hum′ing·bûrd′) *n.* Any of a family of very small birds of the New World, having a long, slender bill for sipping nectar from flowers, and rapidly vibrating wings that produce a humming sound during flight.

hum·mock (hum′ək) *n.* **1.** A low mound of earth or rock; hillock. **2.** Wooded land above a marsh. **3.** A ridge or pile in an ice field. [Origin unknown] — **hum′mock·y** *adj.*

hu·mor (hyo͞o′mər, yo͞o′-) *n.* **1.** The quality of anything that is funny or appeals to the comic sense. **2.** The ability to appreciate or express what is amusing, comic, etc. **3.** Speech, writing, or actions that are amusing or comic. **4.** A temporary mood: to be in a good *humor.* **5.** Temperament; disposition. **6.** A sudden liking, etc.; whim; caprice. **7.** *Physiol.* **a** A liquid or semiliquid substance of the body, as blood, bile, lymph, etc. **b** The aqueous humor of the eye. **8.** In ancient physiology, one of the four principal bodily fluids (**cardinal humors**), blood, phlegm, choler (yellow bile), and melancholy (black bile), which, according to their proportions in the body, were believed to influence health and temperament. — *v.t.* **1.** To comply with the moods of; indulge. **2.** To adapt oneself to the nature of (something). Also *Brit.* **hu′mour.** [< OF < L *umere* to be moist]

hu·mor·esque (hyo͞o′mə·resk′, yo͞o′-) *n.* A playful, lively musical composition; caprice. [< G *humoreske*]

hu·mor·ist (hyo͞o′mər·ist, yo͞o′-) *n.* **1.** One who exercises a sense of humor; joker; wag. **2.** A professional writer, entertainer, etc., in humor or jokes. — **hu′mor·is′tic** *adj.*

hu·mor·ous (hyo͞o′mər·əs, yo͞o′-) *adj.* **1.** Full of or characterized by humor; laughable; funny. **2.** Displaying or using humor. — **hu′mor·ous·ly** *adv.* — **hu′mor·ous·ness** *n.* — **Syn.** Comical, droll, witty.

hump (hump) *n.* **1.** A rounded protuberance, esp. on the back, as in the camel, bison, etc., or the deformity produced in man by a curvature of the spine. **2.** A low mound; hummock. — **over the hump** Beyond the most critical point. — *v.t.* To round into a hump; hunch. [Akin to LG *hump*]

hump·back (hump′bak′) *n.* **1.** A back with a hump. **2.** A person having a back with a hump; hunchback. **3.** A large whale. — **hump′backed′** *adj.*

humph (humf) *interj.* An exclamation of dissatisfaction.

Hump·ty Dump·ty (hump′tē dump′tē) A character in a nursery rhyme and riddle personifying an egg that fell from a wall and could not be pieced together again.

hump·y (hum′pē) *adj.* **hump·i·er, hump·i·est** **1.** Covered with or full of humps. **2.** Like a hump.

hu·mus (hyo͞o′məs) *n.* The black or brown substance of the soil, formed by the decay of animal and vegetable matter, and providing nutrition for plant life. [< L, ground]

Hun (hun) *n.* **1.** One of a barbarous Asian people who invaded Europe in the fourth and fifth centuries, led by Attila. **2.** Any barbarous or destructive person. [OE < LL *Hunnus*] — **Hun′nish** *adj.* — **Hun′nish·ness** *n.*

hunch (hunch) *n.* **1.** *U.S. Informal* A premonition of some coming event. **2.** A hump. **3.** A lump or hunk. — *v.t.* **1.** To bend or draw up so as to form a hump. — *v.i.* **2.** To move or thrust forward jerkily. [Origin unknown]

hunch·back (hunch′bak′) *n.* **1.** A deformed back with a hump. **2.** A person so deformed. — **hunch′backed′** *adj.*

hun·dred (hun′drid) *n.* **1.** The sum of ninety and ten, written as 100, c, or C: a cardinal number. **2.** Anything consisting of a hundred units. — *adj.* Being ten more than ninety. [OE] — **hun·dredth** (hun′dridth) *adj.* & *n.*

hun·dred·fold (hun′drid·fōld′) *n.* An amount or number a hundred times as great as a given unit. — *adv.* So as to be a hundred times as many or as great. — *adj.* **1.** Consisting of one hundred parts. **2.** One hundred times as great.

hun·dred·weight (hun′drid·wāt′) *n.* A unit of weight commonly reckoned in the United States at 100 pounds avoirdupois, in England at 112 pounds.

Hundred Years' War See table for WAR.

hung (hung) Past tense and past participle of HANG.

Hun·gar·i·an (hung·gâr′ē·ən) *adj.* Of Hungary, its people, or their language. — *n.* **1.** A native or citizen of Hungary; esp., a Magyar. **2.** The Finno-Ugric language of the Hungarians: also called *Magyar.* [< Med.L *Hungarus*]

hun·ger (hung′gər) *n.* **1.** The state of discomfort or weakness caused by lack of food. **2.** A desire or need for food. **3.** Any strong desire or craving. — *v.i.* **1.** To be hungry. **2.** To have a desire or craving: with *for* or *after.* — *v.t.* **3.** To cause to undergo hunger; starve. [OE *hungor*]

hunger strike A self-imposed fast, as by a prisoner, political or religious leader, etc., as a means of protest.

hun·gry (hung′grē) *adj.* **·gri·er, ·gri·est** **1.** Desiring or in need of food. **2.** Eagerly craving: *hungry* for applause. **3.** Indicating hunger: a *hungry* look. **4.** Not fertile. [OE *hungor*] — **hun′gri·ly** *adv.* — **hun′gri·ness** *n.*

hunk (hungk) *n. Informal* A large piece or lump; chunk: a *hunk* of meat. [Prob. < Flemish *hunke*]

hun·ky-do·ry (hung′kē·dôr′ē, -dō′rē) *adj. U.S. Slang* Fully satisfactory; all right. Also **hunk′y.**

hunt (hunt) *v.t.* **1.** To pursue (game) for the purpose of killing or catching. **2.** To range over (an area) in search of game. **3.** To use in the chase, as hounds. **4.** To chase, drive away, or pursue with hostility, violence, etc. **5.** To search for eagerly; seek: to *hunt* the truth. **6.** To search (a place) thoroughly. — *v.i.* **7.** To seek or pursue game. **8.** To search or seek: often with *for* or *after.* — **to hunt down 1.** To pursue until caught or killed. **2.** To search for until found. — *n.* **1.** The act of hunting game; chase. **2.** A group of huntsmen. **3.** A search; pursuit. **4.** An area used for hunting. [OE *huntian*]

hunt·er (hun′tər) *n.* **1.** One who hunts. **2.** An animal used in hunting, as a dog or horse.

hunt·ing (hun′ting) *n.* The act of one who or that which hunts. — *adj.* Of or used for hunting.

hunt·ress (hun′tris) *n.* A woman who hunts.

hunts·man (hunts′mən) *n. pl.* **·men** (-mən) **1.** One who hunts game; hunter. **2.** One who directs a hunt, hounds, etc.

Hu·pa (hoo′pə) *n.* **1.** One of a tribe of North American Indians in NW California. **2.** The language of this tribe.

hur·dle (hûr′dəl) *n.* **1.** A light, portable barrier for horses or runners to leap over in races. **2.** *pl.* A race in which such barriers are used: often with *the.* **3.** An obstacle or difficulty to be surmounted. — *v.* **·dled, ·dling** *v.t.* **1.** To leap over (a barrier) in a race. **2.** To make, cover, or enclose with hurdles. **3.** To surmount or overcome (a difficulty, etc.). — *v.i.* **4.** To leap over hurdles, etc. [OE *hyrdel*] — **hur′dler** *n.*

hur·dy-gur·dy (hûr′dē·gûr′dē) *n. pl.* **·dies** Musical instruments played by turning a crank, as the barrel organ.

hurl (hûrl) *v.t.* **1.** To throw, fling, or send with force. **2.** To throw down; overthrow. **3.** To utter with vehemence. — *v.i.* **4.** To throw something. — *n.* The act of hurling; also, a forceful throw. [ME *hurlen*] — **hurl′er** *n.*

hurl·ing (hûr′ling) *n.* An Irish game resembling field hockey. Also **hur′ley.** [< HURL]

hur·ly-bur·ly (hûr′lē·bûr′lē) *n. pl.* **·lies** Tumult; confusion; turmoil. — *adj.* Full of turmoil and confusion; tumultuous. [< earlier *hurling and burling*]

Hu·ron (hyoor′ən, -on) *n.* A member of any of four tribes of North American Indians of Iroquoian stock, formerly between Lakes Huron and Ontario. [< F, ruffian]

hur·rah (hoo·rô′, hə·rä′) *n. & interj.* An exclamation expressing triumph, joy, encouragement, etc. — *v.i.* **1.** To shout a hurrah or hurrahs. — *v.t.* **2.** To cheer with hurrahs. Also spelled *hooray.* Also **hur·ray′** (-rā′). [? < G *hurra*]

hur·ri·cane (hûr′ə·kān) *n.* **1.** *Meteorol.* A tropical cyclone, esp. one originating in the West Indies and often covering a wide area, having a wind velocity exceeding 75 miles per hour. **2.** Anything suggesting a hurricane in violence or speed. [< Sp. *huracán* < Carib]

hurricane deck A light, upper deck on a passenger vessel.

hur·ried (hûr′ēd) *adj.* **1.** Urged or forced to move, act, etc., in haste. **2.** Done or carried on in great or too great haste; a *hurried* decision. — **hur′ried·ly** *adv.* — **hur′ried·ness** *n.*

hur·ry (hûr′ē) *v.* **·ried, ·ry·ing** *v.i.* **1.** To act or move rapidly or in haste; hasten. — *v.t.* **2.** To cause or urge to act or move more rapidly. **3.** To hasten the progress, etc., of, often unduly. — *n. pl.* **·ries 1.** The act of hurrying; haste. **2.** Eagerness to move, act, etc. [ME *horyen*]

hur·ry-scur·ry (hûr′ē·skûr′ē) *n. pl.* **·ries** A hasty, confused bustling about. — *v.i.* **·ried, ·ry·ing** To rush pell-mell. — *adv.* In disorderly haste. — *adj.* Hurried; confused. Also **hur′ry-skur′ry.**

hurt (hûrt) *v.* **hurt, hurt·ing** *v.t.* **1.** To cause physical harm or pain to; injure. **2.** To impair in some way: to *hurt* one's reputation. **3.** To grieve or distress; cause mental suffering to. — *v.i.* **4.** To cause discomfort, suffering, or damage. **5.** To give out a feeling of pain. — *n.* **1.** Any injury, wound, etc. **2.** Damage; impairment. **3.** An injury to the feelings; affront. [< OF *hurter* to hit] — **hurt′er** *n.*

hurt·ful (hûrt′fəl) *adj.* Causing hurt; injurious. — **hurt′·ful·ly** *adv.* — **hurt′ful·ness** *n.*

hur·tle (hûr′təl) *v.* **·tled, ·tling** *v.i.* **1.** To collide or strike violently; clash. **2.** To rush headlong or impetuously. **3.** To make a rushing or crashing sound. — *v.t.* **4.** To hurl, throw, or drive violently. [Freq. of ME *hurten* to hit, hurt]

hus·band (huz′bənd) *n.* A man joined to a woman in lawful wedlock. — *v.t.* To use or spend wisely; conserve: to *husband* one's forces. [OE *hūs* house + *bonda* freeholder]

hus·band·ry (huz′bən·drē) *n.* **1.** The occupation or business of farming. **2.** Careful management; economy; thrift. **3.** Management of household affairs, expenditures, etc.

hush (hush) *v.t.* **1.** To make silent; cause to be quiet. **2.** To keep hidden or secret: usu. with *up.* **3.** To soothe or allay, as fears. — *v.i.* **4.** To be or become quiet or still. — *n.* Deep silence; quiet. — *interj.* Be quiet! [Back formation < ME *hussht* quiet]

hush·a·by (hush′ə·bī′) *interj.* Go to sleep.

hush-hush (hush′hush′) *adj. Informal* Done in sec

hush money A bribe to secure silence or secrecy.

hush·pup·py (hush′pup′ē) *n. pl.* **·pies** *Southern U.* small fried ball of cornmeal dough.

husk (husk) *n.* **1.** The outer coating of certain fru seeds, esp. of an ear of corn. **2.** Any outer covering when comparatively worthless. — *v.t.* To remove the or outer covering of. [ME, prob. < Du. *huus* house

husk·ing bee (hus′king) *U.S.* A cornhusking.

husk·y[1] (hus′kē) *adj.* **husk·i·er, husk·i·est 1.** Roug coarse in vocal quality. **2.** Full of or made of husks. **3.** a husk. [< HUSK] — **husk′i·ly** *adv.* — **husk′i·ness**

husk·y[2] (hus′kē) *U.S. Informal adj.* **husk·i·er, husk** Physically strong; burly. — *n. pl.* **husk·ies** A stro powerful person. [HUSKY[1], with ref. to toughness of h

Hus·ky (hus′kē) *n. pl.* **Husk·ies** *U.S. & Canadian* heavily furred Eskimo dog. Also **husk′y. 2.** An Es **3.** The Eskimo language. [? Alter. of ESKIMO]

hus·sar (hoo·zär′) *n.* A member of a cavalry reg found in some European armies and usu. distinguish brilliant dress uniforms. [< Hungarian < Serbian < < Med.L *corsarius*]

hus·sy (huz′ē, hus′ē) *n. pl.* **·sies 1.** A woman of que able behavior or reputation. **2.** A pert or forward minx. [Alter. of HOUSEWIFE]

hust·ings (hus′tingz) *n.pl.* (*usu. construed as sing.*) **1** proceedings at an election. **2.** Any place where po speeches are made. [OE < ON *hūs* house + *thing* asser

hus·tle (hus′əl) *v.* **·tled, ·tling** *v.t.* **1.** To push abo crowd roughly; jostle. **2.** To force, push, or thrust hu ly. **3.** *U.S. Informal* To cause to proceed rapidly o rapidly; hurry. **4.** *U.S. Slang* To sell or solicit (somet in an aggressive or unethical manner. — *v.i.* **5.** To pu shove; elbow. **6.** *U.S. Informal* To move or work with energy. **7.** *U.S. Slang* To make money by clever or ur pulous means. — *n.* **1.** The act of hustling. **2.** *U.S formal* Energetic activity; drive; push. [< Du. *hutse* shake, toss] — **hus′tler** *n.*

hut (hut) *n.* A small, rude house or cabin; hovel. — *v.i.* **hut·ted, hut·ting** To shelter or live in a hut. [< (OHG *hutta*]

hutch (huch) *n.* **1.** A coop or pen for small animals: r *hutch.* **2.** A chest, locker, or bin in which to store, th also, a cupboard for dishes. **3.** A small hut or cabin. trough, as used by bakers for kneading dough — *v.* store up or hoard, as in a chest. [< F < LL *hutica*]

hutz·pah (hoots′pə, khoots′-) See CHUTZPAH.

huz·za (hə·zä′) *Archaic n. & interj.* An exclamation o triumph, etc. — *v.* **·zaed, za·ing** *v.i.* **1.** To shout huzza *v.t.* **2.** To cheer with huzzas. [Origin uncertain]

hwan (hwän) *n. pl.* **hwan** The monetary unit of S Korea: in 1960 worth about 3/20 of a U.S. cent.

hy·a·cinth (hī′ə·sinth) *n.* **1.** A plant of the lily family, having clusters of fragrant, bell-shaped flowers. **2.** The bulb or flower of this plant. **3.** A brownish, reddish, or orange zircon: also called *jacinth.* **4.** In ancient times, a bluish or purplish gem, probably the sapphire or amethyst. **5.** A blue or purplish blue color. [< OF < L < Gk. *hyakinthos.*] — **hy′a·cin′thine** (-thin, -thīn) *adj.*

HYAC
(*def.*

hy·ae·na (hī·ē′nə) See HYENA.

hy·a·line (hī′ə·lin, -līn) *adj.* Resembling glass; transparent. — *n.* Something transparent, like glass. L < Gk. *hyalos* glass]

hy·brid (hī′brid) *n.* **1.** An animal or plant produced male and female of different species, varieties, or breeds Anything of mixed origin. **3.** *Ling.* A word composed c ments from more than one language. — *adj.* Of, perta to, or like a hybrid. [< L *hybrida* offspring of tame sow wild boar] — **hy′brid·ism, hy·brid·i·ty** (hī·brid′ə·tē).

hy·brid·ize (hī′brid·īz) *v.t. & v.i.* **·ized, ·iz·ing** To produ cause to produce hybrids. Also *Brit.* **hy′brid·ise.** — **hy i·za·tion** (hī′brid·ə·zā′shən, -ī·zā′-) *n.* — **hy′brid·iz′er**

hydr- Var. of HYDRO-.

hy·dra (hī′drə) *n. pl.* **·dras** or **·drae** (-drē) **1.** Any of ous small, fresh-water polyps characterized by a long, sl body and tentacles. **2.** An evil that persists or reappe

Hy·dra (hī′drə) *n.* **1.** In Greek mythology, a nine-he serpent that grew two heads for each cut off. **2.** A co lation, the Hydra. [< L < Gk. *hydra* water serpent]

hy·dran·ge·a (hī·drān′jē·ə, -jə) *n.* A tree or shrub, h large clusters of white, blue, or pink flowers. [< NL < *hydōr* water + *angeion* vessel]

hy·drant (hī′drənt) *n.* A large, upright pipe connecte water main, used for firefighting; fireplug. [< Gk. water + -ANT]

hy·drar·gy·rum (hī·drär′jə·rəm) *n. Chem.* Mercury. NL < L < Gk. *hydōr* water + *argyros* silver] — **hy′ gy′ric** (-jir′ik) *adj.*

drate (hī′drāt) *Chem. n.* Any of a class of compounds sociated with water in definite proportions. — *v.t.* **·drat·** , **·drat·ing** To form a hydrate. — **hy·dra′tion** *n.*

drau·lic (hī·drô′lik) *adj.* **1.** Of or pertaining to hydrau-s. **2.** Operated by water or other liquid under pressure. Hardening under water: *hydraulic* cement. [< L < Gk. *dōr* water + *aulos* pipe] — **hy·drau′li·cal·ly** *adv.*

drau·lics (hī·drô′liks) *n.pl.* (*construed as sing.*) The sci-ce of the laws governing the motion of water and other uids and of their practical applications in engineering.

dra·zine (hī′drə·zēn, -zin) *n. Chem.* A colorless fuming uid, N_2H_4, used esp. as a rocket or jet fuel.

dric (hī′drik) *adj.* Of or containing hydrogen.

dride (hī′drīd, -drid) *n. Chem.* A compound of hydrogen th another element or radical. Also **hy′drid** (-drid).

dro (hī′drō) *Canadian adj.* Hydroelectric.

dro- *combining form* **1.** Water; of, related to, or resem-ng water. **2.** *Chem.* Denoting a compound of hydrogen. so, before vowels, *hydr-*. [< Gk. *hydōr* water]

dro·car·bon (hī′drə·kär′bən) *n. Chem.* One of a large d important group of organic compounds that contain hy-ogen and carbon only, as benzene, ethylene, methane, etc.

dro·ceph·a·lus (hī′drə·sef′ə·ləs) *n. Pathol.* A condition aracterized by the accumulation of fluid within the brain, using abnormal enlargement of the head. Also **hy·dro·ph′a·ly.** [< HYDRO- + Gk. *kephalē* head] — **hy′dro·ph′a·loid** (-loid), **hy′dro·ceph′a·lous** *adj.*

dro·chlo·ric acid (hī′drə·klôr′ik, -klō′rik) *Chem.* An ueous solution of hydrogen chloride, widely used in indus-y, medicine, and the arts: also called *muriatic acid.*

dro·chlo·ride (hī′drə·klôr′īd, -klō′rīd) *n. Chem.* A salt hydrochloric acid with an organic base.

dro·cy·an·ic acid (hī′drō·sī·an′ik) *Chem.* An aqueous ution of hydrogen cyanide, a colorless, volatile, very poi-nous liquid with a bitter odor: also called *prussic acid.*

dro·dy·nam·ic (hī′drō·dī·nam′ik) *adj.* **1.** Of or pertain-g to the force or motion of water and other fluids. **2.** Of or rtaining to hydrodynamics. Also **hy′dro·dy·nam′i·cal.**

dro·dy·nam·ics (hī′drō·dī·nam′iks) *n.pl.* (*construed as ng.*) The branch of dynamics that treats of the motions d forces of liquids, especially water.

dro·e·lec·tric (hī′drō·i·lek′trik) *adj.* Of or pertaining to ectricity generated by the energy of water. — **hy·dro·e·c·tric·i·ty** (hī′drō·i·lek′tris′ə·tē, -ē′lek-) *n.*

dro·flu·or·ic acid (hī′drə·flōō·ôr′ik, -or′-, -flŏŏr′ik) *Chem.* n aqueous solution of hydrogen fluoride, used for etching ass, treating metals, etc.

dro·foil (hī′drə·foil) *n.* **1.** A streamlined surface designed provide support in the water through which it moves, as attachment to a boat. **2.** A horizontal rudder used in sing or submerging a submarine.

dro·gen (hī′drə·jən) *n.* The lightest of the elements ymbol H), an odorless, colorless, flammable gas, occurring iefly in combination. See ELEMENT. [< F < Gk. *hydōr* ater + -GEN] — **hy·drog·e·nous** (hī·droj′ə·nəs) *adj.*

dro·gen·ate (hī′drə·jə·nāt′, hī·droj′ə·nāt) *v.t.* **·at·ed, ·at·g** *Chem.* To combine with, treat with, or expose to the emical action of hydrogen. — **hy′dro·gen·a′tion** *n.*

drogen bomb A very destructive thermonuclear bomb ving no theoretical limit in size and power, releasing en-gy by the fusion, under extremely high temperatures, of ght elements, as hydrogen isotopes: also called *H-bomb.*

drogen chloride *Chem.* A corrosive, pungent, gaseous mpound of hydrogen and chlorine, HCl.

drogen cyanide *Chem.* An unstable, colorless, intensely oisonous gas, HCN, used chiefly as an extermination agent.

drogen ion The positively charged ion (H^+) present in l acid solutions.

drogen peroxide *Chem.* An unstable, colorless, syrupy quid, H_2O_2, used for bleaching, etc.

drogen sulfide *Chem.* A colorless, gaseous, poisonous mpound, H_2S, having a characteristic odor of rotten eggs.

drog·ra·phy (hī·drog′rə·fē) *n.* The science of surveying, escribing, and mapping seas, lakes, rivers, etc. — **hy·drog′·a·pher** *n.* — **hy′dro·graph′ic** or **·i·cal** *adj.* — **hy′dro·raph′i·cal·ly** *adv.*

·droid (hī′droid) *Zool. adj.* **1.** Pertaining or belonging a group of hydrozoans. **2.** Designating a stage in the de-elopment of hydrozoans, characterized by the budding of olyps. — *n.* A hydroid coelenterate, esp. a polyp.

·dro·ki·net·ics (hī′drō·ki·net′iks) *n.pl.* (*construed as ng.*) The branch of hydrodynamics dealing with the laws overning fluids in motion. — **hy′dro·ki·net′ic** *adj.*

·drol·o·gy (hī·drol′ə·jē) *n.* The branch of physical geog-aphy that deals with the waters of the earth, their distribu-on, characteristics, and effects in relation to human activi-es. — **hy·dro·log·ic** (hī′drə·loj′ik) or **·i·cal** *adj.* — **hy′dro·g′i·cal·ly** *adv.* — **hy·drol′o·gist** *n.*

hy·drol·y·sis (hī·drol′ə·sis) *n. pl.* **·ses** (-sēz) *Chem.* **1.** Action between the ions of water (H^+ and OH^-) and those of a salt to form an acid and a base. **2.** The decomposition of a compound by water. — **hy·dro·lyt·ic** (hī′drə·lit′ik) *adj.*

hy·dro·lyte (hī′drə·līt) *n.* Any substance affected by hydrolysis.

hy·dro·lyze (hī′drə·līz) *v.t. & v.i.* **·lyzed, ·lyz·ing** To undergo or cause to undergo hydrolysis. — **hy′dro·lyz′a·ble** *adj.* — **hy·dro·ly·za·tion** (hī′drə·lə·zā′shən, -lī·zā′-) *n.*

hy·drom·e·ter (hī·drom′ə·tər) *n.* A sealed tube marked with a graduated scale and weighted at one end, that determines the specific gravity or density of a liquid. — **hy·dro·met·ric** (hī′drə·met′rik) or **·ri·cal** *adj.* — **hy·drom′e·try** *n.*

hy·drop·a·thy (hī·drop′ə·thē) *n.* A treatment that professes to cure diseases by the use of water both internally and externally: also called *water cure.* — **hy·dro·path·ic** (hī′drə·path′ik) or **·i·cal** *adj.* — **hy·drop′a·thist, hy′dro·path** *n.*

hy·dro·pho·bi·a (hī′drə·fō′bē·ə) *n.* **1.** Rabies. **2.** Any morbid fear of water. [< L < Gk., *hydōr* water + *phobos* fear] — **hy′dro·pho′bic** (hī′drə·fō′bik, -fob′ik) *adj.*

hy·dro·phyte (hī′drə·fīt) *n. Bot.* A plant growing in water or in wet ground. — **hy·dro·phyt·ic** (hī′drə·fit′ik) *adj.*

hy·dro·plane (hī′drə·plān′) *n.* **1.** A seaplane. **2.** A type of motor boat designed so that its hull is raised partially out of the water when driven at high speeds. **3.** A hydrofoil (def. 2). — *v.i.* **·planed, ·plan·ing** To move at great speed on the water.

hy·dro·pon·ics (hī′drə·pon′iks) *n.pl.* (*construed as sing.*) The science of growing plants with their roots in nutrient solutions rather than in soil: also called *tank farming.* [< HYDRO- + Gk. *ponos* labor] — **hy′dro·pon′ic** *adj.*

hy·dro·sphere (hī′drə·sfir) *n.* **1.** The total water on the surface of the earth. **2.** The moisture in the earth's atmosphere. — **hy′dro·spher′ic** (-sfir′ik, -sfer′-) *adj.*

hy·dro·stat (hī′drə·stat) *n.* **1.** A device for preventing the explosion of a steam boiler due to lack of water. **2.** An electrical device for detecting the presence of water.

hy·dro·stat·ics (hī′drə·stat′iks) *n.pl.* (*construed as sing.*) The science that deals with the pressure and equilibrium of fluids, especially of liquids. — **hy′dro·stat′ic** or **·i·cal** *adj.* — **hy′dro·stat′i·cal·ly** *adv.*

hy·dro·sul·fide (hī′drə·sul′fīd) *n. Chem.* A compound derived from hydrogen sulfide by replacing one of the hydrogen atoms with a basic radical or a base.

hy·dro·sul·fu·rous acid (hī′drō·sul·fyŏŏr′əs, hī′drə·sul′fər·əs) Hyposulfurous acid.

hy·dro·ther·a·peu·tics (hī′drō·ther′ə·pyōō′tiks) *n.pl.* (*construed as sing.*) Hydrotherapy. — **hy′dro·ther′a·peu′tic** *adj.*

hy·dro·ther·a·py (hī′drō·ther′ə·pē) *n. Med.* The scientific use of water in the treatment of various diseases.

hy·drot·ro·pism (hī·drōt′rə·piz′əm) *n. Biol.* A tropism in response to water. — **hy·dro·trop·ic** (hī′drə·trop′ik) *adj.*

hy·drous (hī′drəs) *adj.* **1.** Watery. **2.** *Chem.* Containing water of crystallization or hydration.

hy·drox·ide (hī·drok′sīd) *n. Chem.* A compound containing the **hydroxyl ion,** which consists of one atom each of oxygen and hydrogen and bears a charge of − 1.

hy·dro·zo·an (hī′drə·zō′ən) *adj. Zool.* Pertaining or belonging to a class of freshwater and marine coelenterates, including the hydra, certain jellyfishes and corals, etc. — *n.* A hydrozoan organism.

hy·e·na (hī·ē′nə) *n.* Any of a group of wolflike, carnivorous mammals of Africa and Asia, feeding chiefly on carrion, with short hind legs, a bristly mane, and strong teeth. Also *hyaena.* [< L < Gk. *hyaina* sow]

Hy·ge·ia (hī·jē′ə) In Greek mythology, the goddess of health. [< Gk. *hygieia* health]

hy·giene (hī′jēn, -ji·ēn) *n.* The science of health. [< F < Gk. *hygieinos* healthful]

hy·gi·en·ic (hī′jē·en′ik, hī·jē′nik, -jen′ik) *adj.* **1.** Of or pertaining to hygiene. **2.** Sanitary. — **hy′gi·en′i·cal·ly** *adv.*

hy·gi·en·ics (hī′jē·en′iks, hī·jē′niks) *n.pl.* (*construed as sing.*) The science of preserving or promoting health; hygiene.

hy·gi·en·ist (hī′jē·ən·ist) *n.* One who studies or is versed in the principles of hygiene. Also **hy′ge·ist** (-jē·ist), **hy′gie·ist.**

hygro- *combining form* Wet; moist. Also, before vowels, **hygr-.** [< Gk. *hygros* wet, moist]

hy·grom·e·ter (hī·grom′ə·tər) *n.* An instrument for measuring the humidity or moisture in the atmosphere. — **hy·gro·met·ric** (hī′grə·met′rik) *adj.*

hy·grom·e·try (hī·grom′ə·trē) *n.* The branch of physics that deals with the measurement of moisture in the air.

hy·gro·scope (hī′grə·skōp) *n.* A device for indicating the approximate humidity of the air.

hy·gro·scop·ic (hī′grə·skop′ik) *adj.* **1.** Pertaining to the hygroscope. **2.** Absorbing moisture from the air.

hy·la (hī′lə) *n.* Any of a genus of amphibians, esp. the tree frog. [< NL < Gk. *hylē* wood]

hy·men (hī′mən) *n. Anat.* A thin mucous membrane partially covering the external entrance of the vagina in a virgin. [< Gk. *hymēn* skin, membrane]
Hy·men (hī′mən) In Greek mythology, the god of marriage.
hy·me·ne·al (hī′mə·nē′əl) *adj.* Of or pertaining to marriage or a wedding. — *n.* A wedding song or poem.
hy·men·op·ter·on (hī′mən·op′tər·on) *n. pl.* **·ter·a** (-tər·ə) A hymenopterous insect. Also **hy′men·op′ter.**
hy·men·op·ter·ous (hī′mən·op′tər·əs) *adj. Entomol.* Of or belonging to an order of insects, typically having four wings, including bees, wasps, sawflies, etc. [< NL < Gk. *hymēn* membrane + *pteron* wing] — **hy·men·op·ter·an** (hī′mən·op′tə·rən) *adj.* & *n.*
hymn (him) *n.* A song of praise, adoration, thanksgiving, etc., esp. one sung at a religious service. — *v.t.* **1.** To praise or express with a hymn. — *v.i.* **2.** To sing hymns. [< LL < Gk. *hymnos* song, ode] — **hym′nic** (-nik) *adj.*
hym·nal (him′nəl) *n.* A book of hymns. Also *Canadian* **hym′na·ry** (-nə·rē), **hymn′book′** (-bŏŏk′). — *adj.* Of or relating to a hymn or hymns.
hym·nist (him′nist) *n.* A writer of hymns.
hym·nol·o·gy (him·nol′ə·jē) *n.* **1.** The study of hymns. **2.** The writing of hymns. **3.** Hymns collectively. — **hym·no·log·ic** (him′nə·loj′ik) or **·i·cal** *adj.* — **hym·nol′o·gist** *n.*
hy·oid (hī′oid) *n. Anat.* In man, a U-shaped bone at the base of the tongue. Also **hyoid bone.** For illus. see MOUTH. — *adj.* Pertaining to the hyoid bone. [< F *hyoïde*]
hyp·aes·the·si·a (hip′is·thē′zhə, -zhē·ə) See HYPESTHESIA.
hyper- *prefix* **1.** Over; above; excessive: *hypercritical.* **2.** *Med.* Denoting an abnormal state of excess: *hypertension*: opposed to *hypo-*. **3.** *Chem.* Denoting the highest in a series of compounds: now generally replaced by *per-*. [< Gk. *hyper* above]
hy·per·a·cid·i·ty (hī′pər·ə·sid′ə·tē) *n. Med.* An excess of acidity, as of the gastric juice.
hy·per·bar·ism (hī·per′bə·riz′əm) *n. Med.* A disturbed condition caused by atmospheric pressure greater than the pressure within the body: opposed to *hypobarism.* [< HYPER- + Gk. *baros* weight] — **hy′per·bar′ic** (-bar′ik) *adj.*
hy·per·bo·la (hī·pûr′bə·lə) *n. Math.* The curve produced by the intersection of a plane with the surface of a cone, the plane intersecting both nappes. [< NL < Gk. *hyperbolē* a throwing beyond, excess]
hy·per·bo·le (hī·pûr′bə·lē) *n.* An exaggeration or overstatement intended to produce an effect without being taken literally, as: *He was centuries old.* [< L < Gk. *hyperbolē* a throwing beyond, excess] — **hy·per′bo·lism** *n.*
hy·per·bol·ic (hī′pər·bol′ik) *adj.* **1.** Of, pertaining to, or using hyperbole. **2.** *Math.* Of or pertaining to the hyperbola. Also **hy′per·bol′i·cal.** — **hy′per·bol′i·cal·ly** *adv.*
hy·per·bo·lize (hī·pûr′bə·līz) *v.t.* & *v.i.* **·lized, ·liz·ing** To express in or use hyperbole; exaggerate.
hy·per·bo·re·an (hī′pər·bôr′ē·ən, -bō′rē-) *adj.* Of or pertaining to the far north; frigid; arctic.
Hy·per·bo·re·an (hī′pər·bôr′ē·ən, -bō′rē-) *n.* In Greek mythology, one of the people who lived in the far north in a land of everlasting peace and sunshine. [< L < Gk. *hyper-* beyond + *Boreas* north wind]
hy·per·crit·i·cal (hī′pər krit′i·kəl) *adj.* Excessively critical or carping; faultfinding. — **hy′per·crit′i·cal·ly** *adv.* — **hy′per·crit′i·cism** (-siz′əm) *n.*
hy·per·gol·ic (hī′pər·gol′ik) *adj. Aerospace* Denoting a type of rocket propellant that ignites spontaneously on contact with an oxidizer. [< HYPER- + G *gola*, a code word used in German rocketry]
Hy·pe·ri·on (hī·pir′ē·ən) In Greek mythology: **a** A Titan, the son of Uranus. **b** Helios. **c** In later use, Apollo.
hy·per·me·tro·pi·a (hī′pər·mə·trō′pē·ə) *n. Pathol.* Farsightedness. Also **hy′per·met′ro·py** (-met′rə·pē). [< NL < Gk. *hypermetros* excessive + *ōps* eye] — **hy′per·me·trop′ic** (-mə·trop′ik, -trō′pik) *adj.*
hy·per·on (hī′pər·on) *n. Physics* Any of a class of atomic particles having a mass intermediate between that of a neutron and a deuteron.
hy·per·sen·si·tive (hī′pər·sen′sə·tiv) *adj.* **1.** Excessively sensitive. **2.** Allergic. — **hy′per·sen′si·tive·ness, hy′per·sen′si·tiv′i·ty** (-sen′sə·tiv′ə·tē) *n.*
hy·per·sen·si·tize (hī′pər·sen′sə·tīz) *v.t.* **·tized, ·tiz·ing** *Photog.* To increase the sensitiveness or speed of, as a film.
hy·per·son·ic (hī′pər·son′ik) *adj.* Of, pertaining to, or characterized by supersonic speeds of mach 5 or greater.
hy·per·son·ics (hī′pər·son′iks) *n.pl.* (*construed as sing.*) The branch of dynamics concerned with the design, performance, etc., of objects moving at hypersonic speeds.
hy·per·ten·sion (hī′pər·ten′shən) *n. Pathol.* High blood pressure. — **hy′per·ten′sive** (-siv) *adj.*
hy·per·thy·roid·ism (hī′pər·thī′roid·iz′əm) *n. Pathol.* **1.** Excessive activity of the thyroid gland. **2.** Any disorder caused by this. — **hy′per·thy′roid** *adj.* & *n.*
hy·per·tro·phy (hī·pûr′trə·fē) *n. Pathol.* **1.** The excessive development of an organ or part. **2.** The enlargement resulting from such a condition. — *v.i.* & *v.t.* **·phied, ·phy**[ing] To grow or cause to grow excessively. — **hy·per·trop**[hic] (hī′pər·trof′ik, -trō′fik) or **·i·cal** *adj.*
hyp·es·the·sia (hip′is·thē′zhə, -zhē·ə) *n. Pathol.* Dim[in]ished sensitiveness; partial loss of sensation: also spelled *paesthesia.* — **hyp′es·the′sic** (-sik) or **·thet′ic** (-thet′ik) [*adj.*]
hy·pha (hī′fə) *n. pl.* **·phae** (-fē) *Bot.* One of the lo[ng] threadlike, branching bodies that constitute the myceliu[m of] a fungus. [< NL < Gk. *hyphē* web] — **hy′phal** *adj.*
hy·phen (hī′fən) *n.* A mark (‐ or - or ⸗) used to connect elements of certain compound words or to show division [of a] word at the end of a line. — *v.t.* To hyphenate. [< L[L <] Gk. *hyph′ hen* under one, together < *hypo-* under + *hen* [one]
hy·phen·ate (hī′fən·āt) *v.t.* **·at·ed, ·at·ing** **1.** To connect [with] a hyphen. **2.** To write with a hyphen. — **hy′phen·a′tio[n]**
hypno- *combining form* Sleep; of or related to sleep. A[lso] before vowels, **hypn-.** [< Gk. *hypnos* sleep]
hyp·noi·dal (hip·noid′l) *adj. Psychiatry* Resembling li[ght] hypnosis. Also **hyp·noid′.**
hyp·nol·o·gy (hip·nol′ə·jē) *n.* The science of sleep.
hyp·no·sis (hip·nō′sis) *n. pl.* **·ses** (-sēz) *Psychol.* A tra[nce]like condition that can be artificially induced, characteri[zed] by an increased responsiveness to suggestion.
hyp·no·ther·a·py (hip′nō·ther′ə·pē) *n. Med.* The us[e of] hypnotism in treating disease, esp. mental disease.
hyp·not·ic (hip·not′ik) *adj.* **1.** Pertaining to hypnosi[s or] hypnotism. **2.** Readily hypnotized. **3.** Tending to prod[uce] sleep. — *n.* **1.** A drug or other agent producing sleep. **2** [A] hypnotized person or one susceptible to hypnosis. [< [Gk.] *hypnos* sleep] — **hyp·not′i·cal·ly** *adv.*
hyp·no·tism (hip′nə·tiz′əm) *n.* **1.** The act or practic[e of] inducing hypnosis. **2.** The study of the techniques of h[yp]nosis. **3.** Hypnosis. — **hyp′no·tist** *n.*
hyp·no·tize (hip′nə·tīz) *v.t.* **·tized, ·tiz·ing** **1.** To prod[uce] hypnosis in. **2.** To fascinate; charm. Also *Brit.* **hyp′no·t**[ise.] — **hyp′no·tiz′a·ble** *adj.* — **hyp′no·ti·za′tion** (-tə·zā′sh[ən], -tī·zā′-) *n.* — **hyp′no·tiz′er** *n.*
hy·po[1] (hī′pō) *n. Photog.* Sodium thiosulfate (formerly ca[lled] *sodium hyposulfite*), used as a fixing agent.
hy·po[2] (hī′pō) *n. pl.* **·pos** *Informal* A hypodermic injecti[on.]
hy·po[3] (hī′pō) *n. pl.* **·pos** *Slang* A hypochondriac.
hypo- *prefix* **1.** Under; beneath. **2.** Less than. **3.** *M[ed.]* Denoting a lack of or deficiency in: opposed to *hyper-*. [4.] *Chem.* Indicating the lowest member in a series of compou[nds] (that is, the lowest degree of oxidation). Also, before vow[els] **hyp-.** [< Gk. < *hypo* under]
hy·po·bar·ism (hī′pə·bär′iz·əm) *n. Med.* A condit[ion] brought about when the atmospheric pressure is less t[han] that of the gases within the body: opposed to *hyperbari[sm].* [< HYPO- + Gk. *baros* weight] — **hy′po·bar′ic** *adj.*
hy·po·cen·ter (hī′pə·sen′tər) *n.* Ground zero.
hy·po·chlo·rite (hī′pə·klôr′īt, -klō′rīt) *n. Chem.* A sal[t of] hypochlorous acid.
hy·po chlo·rous acid (hī′pə·klôr′əs, -klō′rəs) *Chem.* [An] unstable acid, HClO, used in aqueous solution as an oxidi[zer] and bleach.
hy·po·chon·dri·a (hī′pə·kon′drē·ə, hip′ə-) *n.* A persist[ent] anxiety about one's health, often with imagined sympt[oms] of illness. Also **hy·po·chon·dri·a·sis** (hī′pō·kən·drī′ə·sis). [< L, abdomen (once taken to be the seat of this condition)]
hy·po·chon·dri·ac (hī′pə·kon′drē·ak, hip′ə-) *adj.* **1.** P[er]taining to or affected with hypochondria. **2.** Of, pertain[ing] to, or situated in the hypochondrium. Also **hy·po·chon·d**[**ri·**]**a·cal** (hī′pō·kən·drī′ə·kəl). — *n.* A person subject to or [af]fected with hypochondria. — **hy′po·chon·dri′a·cal·ly** *a*[*dv.*]
hy·po·chon·dri·um (hī′pə·kon′drē·əm, hip′ə-) *n. pl.* **·dr**[**i·a**] (-drē·ə) *Anat.* The region of the abdomen situated on eit[her] side of the body, under the short ribs. [< NL < Gk.]
hy·po·cot·yl (hī′pə·kot′l) *n. Bot.* The part of the axis o[f a] seedling below the seed leaves or cotyledons. — **hy′po·c**[**ot·**]**y·lous** *adj.*
hy·poc·ri·sy (hi·pok′rə·sē) *n. pl.* **·sies** The pretense of h[av]ing feelings or characteristics one does not possess; esp., t[he] deceitful assumption of virtue. [< OF < L < Gk. *hypok*[*ri*]*nesthai* to play a part, act]
hyp·o·crite (hip′ə·krit) *n.* One who practices hypocrisy. — **hyp′o·crit′i·cal** *adj.* — **hyp′o·crit′i·cal·ly** *adv.*
hy·po·derm (hī′pə·dûrm) *n. Zool.* The layer that secre[tes] the outer skin of an arthropod: also called *hypodermis.*
hy·po der·ma (hī′pə·dûr′mə) *n. Bot.* The distinct shea[th] of tissue beneath the epidermis of stems in plants. [< N[L] < Gk. *hypo-* under + *derma* skin]
hy·po·der·mic (hī′pə·dûr′mik) *adj.* **1.** Of or pertaining [to] the area under the skin. **2.** Injected under the skin. — [*n.*] A hypodermic injection or syringe.
hypodermic syringe A syringe having a sharp, holl[ow] needle for injection of substances beneath the skin.
hy·po·der·mis (hī′pə·dûr′mis) *n. Zool.* The hypoderm.
hy·po·gas·tric (hī′pə·gas′trik) *adj.* Pertaining to or sit[u]ated in the hypogastrium.
hy·po·gas·tri·um (hī′pə·gas′trē·əm) *n. pl.* **·tri·a** (-trē[·ə])

at. The region at the lower part of the abdomen on the ddle line. [< NL < Gk. *hypo-* below + *gastēr* belly]
po·sul·fite (hī′pə·sul′fīt) *n. Chem.* **1.** Sodium thiosul-e. **2.** A salt of hyposulfurous acid.
po·sul·fu·rous acid (hī′pō·sul·fyŏŏr′əs, hī′pə·sul′fər·əs) *em.* An unstable acid, $H_2S_2O_4$, of strong reducing and aching properties: also called *hydrosulfurous acid.*
pot·e·nuse (hī·pot′ə·nōōs, -nyōōs, hi-) *n. Geom.* The e of a right triangle opposite the right angle. Also **hy·th′e·nuse** (-poth′-). [< L < Gk. *hypo-* under + *teinein* stretch]
po·thal·a·mus (hī′pə·thal′ə·məs, hip′ə-) *n. pl.* **·mi** *Anat.* roup of structures forming part of the diencephalon, con-lling visceral activities, regulating body temperature and ny metabolic processes, and influencing certain emotional tes. — **hy·po·tha·lam·ic** (hī′pə·thə·lam′ik) *adj.*
poth·e·cate (hī·poth′ə·kāt, hi-) *v.t.* **·cat·ed, ·cat·ing** *Law* pledge (personal property) as security for debt without nsfer of possession. [< Med.L < LL *hypotheca* pledge] **hy·poth′e·ca′tion** *n.* — **hy·poth′e·ca′tor** *n.*
poth·e·sis (hī·poth′ə·sis, hi-) *n. pl.* **·ses** (-sēz) **1.** An proved scientific conclusion drawn from known facts. **2.** assumption or set of assumptions provisionally accepted. NL < Gk., foundation, supposition]
—**Syn.** In science, a *hypothesis* is a proposition advanced as sibly true, and consistent with known data, but requiring ther investigation; a *theory* is a *hypothesis* so well substantiated to be generally accepted. *Supposition* and *assumption* are propo-ons accepted with less assurance than a *hypothesis.* A *conjecture* a conclusion drawn from admittedly insufficient data; it differs m a guess only in not being wholly random and uninformed.
poth·e·size (hī·poth′ə·sīz, hi-) *v.* **·sized, ·siz·ing** *v.t.* **1.** To offer or assume as a hypothesis. —*v.i.* **2.** To make a hypothesis; theorize.
hy·po·thet·i·cal (hī′pə·thet′i·kəl) *adj.* **1.** Pertaining to or of the nature of a hypothesis. **2.** Based on hypothesis; theoretical. **3.** Characterized by the use of hypotheses. **4.** *Logic* Denoting a proposition based on another proposition; conditional. Also **hy′po·thet′ic.** — **hy′po·thet′i·cal·ly** *adv.*
hy·po·thy·roid·ism (hī′pō·thī′roid·iz′əm) *n. Pathol.* **1.** Deficient functioning of the thyroid gland. **2.** A disorder resulting from this, as goiter. — **hy′po·thy′roid** *adj. & n.*
hy·son (hī′sən) *n.* A green tea from China. [< Chinese]
hys·sop his′əp) *n.* **1.** A bushy, medicinal herb of the mint family, with small clusters of blue flowers. **2.** In the Bible, an unidentified plant furnishing the twigs used in the Mosaic rites, etc. [OE and OF < L < Gk. *hyssōpos*]
hys·ter·ec·to·my (his′tə·rek′tə·mē) *n. pl.* **·mies** *Surg.* Complete removal of part or all of the uterus.
hys·te·ri·a (his·tir′ē·ə, -ter′-) *n.* **1.** Abnormal excitement; wild emotionalism; frenzy. **2.** *Psychiatry* A psychoneurotic condition characterized by violent emotional paroxysms and disturbances in the sensory and motor functions. —**Syn.** See FRENZY. [< NL < Gk. *hystera* the womb]
hys·ter·ic (his·ter′ik) *adj.* Hysterical. —*n.* **1.** One who is subject to hysteria. **2.** *pl.* A fit of hysteria.
hys·ter·i·cal (his·ter′i·kəl) *adj.* **1.** Resembling hysteria; uncontrolled; violent. **2.** Characterized or caused by hysteria. **3.** Inclined to hysteria. — **hys·ter′i·cal·ly** *adv.*
hystero- *combining form* **1.** The womb; uterine. **2.** Hysteria. Also, before vowels, **hyster-.** [< Gk. *hystera* the womb]
hys·ter·ot·o·my (his′tə·rot′ə·mē) *n. pl.* **·mies** *Surg.* **1.** The operation of cutting into the womb. **2.** Cesarean section.

I

(ī) *n. pl.* **i's** or **is, I's** or **Is, eyes** (īz) **1.** The ninth letter the English alphabet. **2.** Any sound represented by the ter *i.* — *symbol* **1.** The Roman numeral for 1: written I i. **2.** *Chem.* Iodine (symbol I).
Reduced var. of IN-[1].
See Y-.
pron., possessive **my** or **mine,** *objective* **me**; *pl. nominative* , *possessive* **our** or **ours,** *objective* **us** The nominative sin-lar pronoun of the first person, used by a speaker or writer referring to himself. —*n. pl.* **I's 1.** The pronoun *I* used a noun: His talk was full of *I's.* **2.** *Philos.* The ego. [OE *ic*]
suffix of nouns Occurring in: **1.** *Geog.* Names of coun-es: *Australia.* **2.** *Pathol.* Names of diseases and related rms: *hysteria.* **3.** *Bot.* Names of genera: *Lobelia.* **4.** Words rrowed directly from Latin or Greek: *militia.* [< L and . *-ia,* suffix of fem. nouns]
suffix of nouns Occurring in: **1.** *Biol.* Names of classes: *ammalia.* **2.** Names of classical festivals: *Bacchanalia.* **3.** ords, usu. collectives, borrowed from Latin or Greek: *ɔalia.* [< L and Gk. *-ia,* plural suffix of neut. nouns]
·go (ē·ä′gō) The villain of Shakespeare's *Othello.*
suffix of adjectives Var. of -AL[1], with connective *-i-,* as in *ial, nuptial.*
mb (ī′amb) *n.* **1.** In prosody, a metrical foot consisting an unaccented syllable followed by an accented one (˘ ¯). A line of verse made up of such feet: Thĕ bīrd | wăs grēen nd gōld | ĕn īn | thĕ sūn. [< L < Gk. *iambos*]
m·bic (ī·am′bik) *adj.* Consisting of, using, or like iambs. *n.* **1.** A foot, line, or stanza consisting of an iamb or mbs. **2.** Iambic verse.
m·bus (ī·am′bəs) *n. pl.* **·bi** (-bī) or **·bus·es** An iamb.
n *suffix of adjectives and nouns* Var. of -AN, with *-i-* of the em or as a connective: *amphibian, Bostonian.*
na See -ANA.
sis *suffix Med.* Denoting a process and its results, esp. in seased conditions: *psoriasis.* [Var. of -OSIS]
trics *combining form* Medical treatment: *pediatrics.* [< . *iatrikos* pertaining to the art of healing]
ro- *combining form* Medicine and. [< Gk. *iatros* physi-an]
try *combining form* Medical or curative treatment: *psy-iatry.* [< Gk. *iatreia* healing]
I-beam (ī′bēm′) *n.* A beam or joist that in cross section has the shape of the letter I.
I·be·ri·an (ī·bir′ē·ən) *adj.* Of, pertaining to, or characteristic of the Iberian Peninsula, its people, or their culture. —*n.* **1.** One of the ancient or modern inhabitants of the Iberian Peninsula. **2.** The unclassified language of the Iberian Peninsula. [< Gk. *Iberes* Spaniards]
i·bex (ī′beks) *n. pl.* **i·bex·es** or **i·bi·ces** (ī′bə·sēz, ib′ə-) One of various wild goats of Europe and Asia, with long, recurved horns.
i·bi·dem (i·bī′dem) *adv. Latin* In the same place; in the work, chapter, etc., just mentioned. Abbr. *ib., ibid.*
i·bis (ī′bis) *n. pl.* **i·bis·es** or **i·bis** One of various wading birds related to the heron. [< Egyptian]
-ible See -ABLE.
-ic *suffix* **1.** Forming adjectives with the meanings: **a** Of, pertaining to, or connected with: *volcanic.* **b** Of the nature of; resembling: *angelic.* **c** Produced by or in the manner of: *Homeric.* **d** Consisting of; containing: *alcoholic.* **e** *Chem.* Having a higher valence than that indicated by *-ous*: said of elements in compounds: *sulfuric* acid. **2.** Forming nouns by the substantive use of adjectives in *-ic*: *classic, lunatic.* **3.** Occurring in nouns derived from Latin and Greek nouns formed from adjectives: *stoic, music.* See note under -ICS. [< F *-ique* or L *-icus* or Gk. *-ikos*]
-ical *suffix* **1.** Forming parallel adjectives from adjectives in *-ic,* often in the same sense, as *alphabetic, alphabetical,* but sometimes with extended or special senses, as *economic, economical.* **2.** Forming adjectives from nouns in *-ic* or *-ics*: *musical, mathematical.* [< LL *-icalis* < L *-icus* + *-alis*]
Ic·a·rus (ik′ə·rəs, ī′kə-) In Greek mythology, the son of Daedalus, who, by means of artificial wings, flew so high that the sun melted the wax that fastened the wings and he fell into the sea and drowned.
ice (īs) *n.* **1.** Congealed or frozen water. ◆ Collateral adjective: *glacial.* **2.** The frozen surface of a body of water. **3.** Something resembling ice. **4.** A frozen dessert made without cream. **5.** Icing for cake. **6.** *Slang* A diamond. — **to break the ice 1.** To dispel reserve or formality, esp. at a social gathering. **2.** To make a start. — **to cut no ice** *U.S. Informal* To have no influence. — **on ice** *U.S. Slang* **1.** Set aside; in reserve. **2.** Certain to be achieved or won. **3.** In-

communicado. — *v.* **iced, ic·ing** *v.t.* **1.** To cause to turn to ice; freeze. **2.** To cover or surround with ice. **3.** To chill with ice. **4.** To decorate with icing. **5.** In hockey, to put (a team) on the ice. — *v.i.* **6.** To turn to ice. [OE *īs*]
-ice *suffix of nouns* Condition, quality, or act: *cowardice, notice.* [< OF *-ice* < L *-itius, -itia, -itium*]
ice bag A flexible, waterproof container designed to hold ice, applied to parts of the body: also called *ice pack.*
ice·berg (īs′bûrg′) *n.* A thick mass of ice separated from a glacier and floating in the ocean. [Prob. < Du. *ijsberg*]
ice·boat (īs′bōt′) *n.* **1.** A framework with skatelike runners and sails for sailing over ice. **2.** An icebreaker (def. 1).
ice·bound (īs′bound′) *adj.* Surrounded or obstructed by ice.
ice·box (īs′boks′) *n. U.S.* A cabinet for holding ice, in which food or other perishables are stored.
ice·break·er (īs′brā′kər) *n.* **1.** A vessel used to break up ice in waterways and harbors. **2.** A structure for deflecting floating ice from the base of a bridge, a pier, etc.
ice·cap (īs′kap′) *n.* A covering of ice and snow permanently overlying an extensive tract of land.
ice cream A mixture of cream, butterfat, or milk, flavoring, sweetening, and often egg whites, beaten to a uniform consistency and frozen. [Orig., *iced cream*]
iced (īst) *adj.* **1.** Coated or covered with ice or sleet. **2.** Made cold with ice. **3.** Covered with icing, as a cake.
ice field A large, flat expanse of floating ice. Also **ice floe.**
ice hockey Hockey played by skaters on ice.
ice·house (īs′hous′) *n.* A building in which ice is stored.
Ice·land·er (īs′lan′dər) *n.* A native or citizen of Iceland.
Ice·land·ic (īs·lan′dik) *adj.* Of or pertaining to Iceland, its inhabitants, or their language. — *n.* The North Germanic language of Iceland. — **Old Icelandic** The language of Iceland before the 16th century: sometimes called *Old Norse.*
Iceland spar *Mineral.* A transparent variety of calcite exhibiting double refraction and polarizing light.
ice·man (īs′man′, -mən) *n. pl.* **·men** (men′, -mən) One who supplies or delivers ice to consumers.
ice pack **1.** A large expanse of floating ice cakes jammed together and frozen into a single mass. **2.** An ice bag.
ice pick An awllike tool for breaking ice into small pieces.
ich·neu·mon (ik·nōō′mən, -nyōō′-) *n.* **1.** An Egyptian species of mongoose. **2.** An ichneumon fly. [< L < Gk. *ichneumōn,* lit., tracker]
ichneumon fly A hymenopterous insect whose larvae feed upon caterpillars or other larvae.
i·chor (ī′kôr, ī′kər) *n.* **1.** In classical mythology, the ethereal fluid supposed to flow in the veins of the gods. **2.** *Pathol.* A watery, acrid fluid discharged from sores. [< Gk. *ichōr*] — **i·chor·ous** (ī′kər·əs) *adj.*
ichthyo- *combining form* Fish. Also, before vowels, **ichthy-.** [< Gk. *ichthys* fish]
ich·thy·ol·o·gy (ik′thē·ol′ə·jē) *n.* The branch of zoology that treats of fishes. — **ich·thy·o·log·ic** (ik′thē·ə·loj′ik) or **·i·cal** *adj.* — **ich′thy·ol′o·gist** *n.*
ich·thy·o·saur (ik′thē·ə·sôr′) *n. Paleontol.* Any of an order of extinct marine reptiles of the Mesozoic era, having a porpoiselike form. [< ICHTHYO- + Gk. *sauros* lizard]
ich·thy·o·sau·rus (ik′thē·ə·sôr′əs) *n. pl.* **·sau·ri** (-sôr′ī) An ichthyosaur.
-ician *suffix of nouns* One skilled in or engaged in some specified field: *musician, beautician.* [< F *-icien*]
i·ci·cle (ī′si·kel) *n.* A hanging, tapering rod of ice formed by dripping water. [OE *īsgicel*] — **i′ci·cled** *adj.*
i·ci·ly (ī′sə·lē) *adv.* In an icy manner.
i·ci·ness (ī′sē·nis) *n.* **1.** The state or quality of being frozen or extremely cold. **2.** Marked aloofness of manner.
ic·ing (ī′sing) *n.* **1.** A coating made of sugar, usu. mixed with egg whites or cream, used to cover cakes, pastry, etc. **2.** The formation of ice on the surface of an aircraft.
i·con (ī′kon) *n. pl.* **i·cons** or **i·co·nes** (ī′kə·nēz) **1.** In the Eastern Orthodox Church, a pictorial representation of Jesus Christ, the Virgin Mary, or some other sacred figure. **2.** An image; likeness; picture. Also spelled *ikon.* [< Gk. *eikōn* image] — **i·con′ic** *adj.*
icono- *combining form* Image. Also, before vowels, **icon-.** [< Gk. *eikōn* image]
i·con·o·clast (ī·kon′ə·klast) *n.* **1.** One who attacks conventional or cherished beliefs and institutions. **2.** One who opposes the ues of religious images. [< LL < G,. *eikōn* image + *-klastēs* breaker] — **i·con′o·clasm′** *n.* — **·i·con′o·clas′tik** *adj.*
i·con·o·scope (ī·kon′ə·skōp) *n. Telecom.* The part of a television camera that converts the image to be transmitted into electrical impulses.
-ics *suffix of nouns* **1.** An art or a field of study: *mathematics.* **2.** Methods, practices, or activities: *athletics.* [See -IC]
i·cy (ī′sē) *adj.* **i·ci·er, i·ci·est** **1.** Consisting of, containing, or covered with ice. **2.** Resembling or having the characteristics of ice: *icy* green. **3.** Extremely cold. **4.** Forbiddingly aloof: an *icy* greeting. [OE *īsig*]
id (id) *n. Psychoanal.* The unconscious part of the psyche, but actuated by fundamental impulses toward fulfilling instinctual needs; the reservoir of psychic energy or lib [< NL < L *id* it, trans. of G *es*]
-id[1] *suffix of nouns* **1.** Offspring of: often occurring in na from classical mythology: *Danaid, Nereid.* **2.** An epic al a specified person or subject: *Aeneid.* **3.** *Zool.* **a** A men of a family: *leporid.* **b** A member of a class: *arachnid.* *Astron.* A meteor seeming to originate in a specified con lation: *Perseid.* [< L *-is, -idis* < Gk. *-is, -idos,* suffi patronymics]
-id[2] *suffix of adjectives* Having a particular quality, or e ing in a particular state: *humid, fluid.* [< F *-ide* < L *-i* or directly < L]
-id[3] *Chem.* Var. of -IDE.
I'd (īd) **1.** I would. **2.** I should. **3.** I had.
-idae *suffix Zool.* Forming the names of families: *Can* [< NL *-idae* < L < Gk. *-idai,* plural patronymic suffix
-ide *suffix Chem.* Used in the names of compounds, binary, and attached to the electronegative element or r cal: sodium *chloride.* Also spelled *-id.* [< F *-ide.* See -
i·de·a (ī·dē′ə) *n.* **1.** That which is conceived in the min thought. **2.** An impression or notion. **3.** A convict opinion; belief. **4.** An intention; plan. **5.** Vague kn edge; inkling: I had an *idea* you might come. **6.** A pas fancy; whim. **7.** *Informal* Significance; meaning: Do get the *idea?* **8.** *Philos.* The Platonic concept of an ar type or fundamental example, of which an existing thin but a representation. [< L < Gk. < *ideein* to see]
— **Syn.** Concept, conception, thought, notion, image.
i·de·al (ī·dē′əl, ī·dēl′) *n.* **1.** A concept or standard of preme perfection. **2.** A person or thing taken as a stan of perfection. **3.** A high principle; lofty aim. **4.** That w exists only as a concept of the mind. — *adj.* **1.** Conforn to an absolute standard of excellence. **2.** Completely s factory: an *ideal* situation. **3.** Capable of existing as a n tal concept only; utopian; imaginary. **4.** Pertaining t existing in the form of an idea or ideas. **5.** *Philos.* Pertai to or existing as a Platonic idea. [< F < L *idealis*]
i·de·al·ism (ī·dē′əl·iz′əm) *n.* **1.** The envisioning of th as they should be or are wished to be rather than as they **2.** Pursuit of an ideal. **3.** That which is idealized. **4** literature and art, the imaginative treatment of subject r ter in accordance with preconceived standards of perfect opposed to *realism.* **5.** *Philos.* Any of several theories there is no reality, no world of objects or thing in itself a from a reacting mind or consciousness and therefore that ality is essentially spiritual or mental.
i·de·al·ist (ī·dē′əl·ist) *n.* **1.** One who formulates or atten to live in accordance with ideals. **2.** An impractical drea **3.** An exponent of idealism in literature, art, or philoso
i·de·al·is·tic (ī′dē·əl·is′tik, ī·dē′əl-) *adj.* Of, pertaining or characteristic of idealists or idealism. Also **i′de·al·is′ti** — **i′de·al·is′ti·cal·ly** *adv.*
i·de·al·ize (ī·dē′əl·īz) *v.* **·ized, ·iz·ing** *v.t.* **1.** To conside be ideal; hold in high esteem. **2.** To glorify. — *v.i.* **3.** form an ideal or ideals. **4.** To consider or represent th in their ideal form. Also *Brit.* **i·de′al·ise.** — **i·de′al·i·za′** *n.* — **i·de′al·iz′er** *n.*
i·de·al·ly (ī·dē′əl·ē, ī·dēl′ē) *adv.* **1.** In conformance wit ideal; perfectly. **2.** As conceived in the mind.
i·de·ate (ī·dē′āt) *v.t. & v.i.* **·at·ed, ·at·ing** To form an ide ideas of something; think.
i·de·a·tion (ī′dē·ā′shən) *n.* Thinking. — **i′de·a′tion·al**
i·dée fixe (ē·dā′ fēks′) *French* A fixed idea; obsession.
i·dem (ī′dem) *pron. & adj. Latin* The same: used as a re ence to what has been previously mentioned. Abbr. *id.*
i·den·ti·cal (ī·den′ti·kəl) *adj.* **1.** One and the same; very same. **2.** Alike in every respect. **3.** *Genetics* Desig ing human twins that develop from a single fertilized ov distinguished from *fraternal.* [< Med.L *idem* the same]
— **i·den′ti·cal·ly** *adv.* — **i·den′ti·cal·ness** *n.*
i·den·ti·fi·ca·tion (ī·den′tə·fə·kā′shən) *n.* **1.** The act identifying, or the state of being identified. **2.** Anything which identity can be established.
i·den·ti·fy (ī·den′tə·fī) *v.* **·fied, ·fy·ing** *v.t.* **1.** To estab as being a particular person or thing; recognize. **2.** To gard as the same. **3.** To serve as a means of recognizing characteristic of. **4.** To associate closely. **5.** To consi (oneself) as one with another person. **6.** *Psychol.* To im ine (oneself) to be thinking or behaving like a person w whom one has formed a strong emotional tie. — *v.i.* **7.** put oneself in the place of another. [< LL *identificare*] **i·den′ti·fi′a·ble** *adj.* — **i·den′ti·fi′er** *n.*
i·den·ti·ty (ī·den′tə·tē) *n. pl.* **·ties** **1.** The state of be identical. **2.** The state of being a specific person or th and no other. **3.** The distinctive character belonging to individual. [< F < LL < L *idem* the same]
ideo- *combining form* Idea. [< Gk. *idea* form, idea]
id·e·o·graph (id′ē·ə·graf′, -gräf′, ī′dē-) *n.* **1.** A picto symbol of an object or idea. **2.** A graphic symbol, as +, ¶, 4, $. Also **id·e·o·gram** (id′ē·ə·gram′, ī′dē-). — **id′ graph′ic** or **·i·cal** *adj.* — **id′e·o·graph′i·cal·ly** *adv.*

·ol·o·gist (ī′dē·ol′ə·jist, id′ē-) *n.* **1.** One who formulates supports an ideology. **2.** One who studies or is expert in ology or ideologies. **3.** A visionary.

·ol·o·gy (ī′dē·ol′ə·jē, id′ē-) *n. pl.* **·gies 1.** The ideas and jectives that influence a whole group or national culture, aping their political and social procedure. **2.** The science at treats of the origin, evolution, and expression of human eas. **3.** Fanciful or visionary speculation. **— i·de·o·log·ic** dē·ə·loj′ik, id′ē-) or **·i·cal** *adj.* **— i′de·o·log′i·cal·ly** *adv.*

s (īdz) *n.pl.* In the ancient Roman calendar, the 15th of arch, May, July, and October, and the 13th of the other onths. [< OF < L *idus*]

est (id est) *Latin* That is. Abbr. *i.e.*

o- *combining form* One's own; peculiar to a person or ing; individual: *idiosyncrasy.* [< Gk. *idios* own, private]

·o·cy (id′ē·ə·sē) *n. pl.* **·cies 1.** The condition of being an ot. **2.** Extreme stupidity or foolishness.

·om (id′ē·əm) *n.* **1.** An expression peculiar to a language, t readily understandable from the meaning of its parts, as *put up with* (tolerate, endure). **2.** The language or dialect a region or people. **3.** The special terminology of a class, cupational group, etc. **4.** The distinctive character of a ecific language. **5.** Typical style, form, or character, as in , literature, or music. [< F < L < Gk. *idios* one's own]

·o·mat·ic (id′ē·ə·mat′ik) *adj.* **1.** Characteristic of a speic language. **2.** Of the nature of an idiom. **3.** Employing any idioms. Also **id′i·o·mat′i·cal.** **— id′i′o·mat′i·cal·ly** *adv.*

·o·mor·phic (id′ē·ō·môr′fik) *adj.* **1.** Having its own disactive form. **2.** *Mineral.* Possessing crystal faces: said of nerals of a rock. **— id′i·o·mor′phi·cal·ly** *adv.*

·o·syn·cras·y (id′ē·ō·sing′krə·sē) *n. pl.* **·sies 1.** A habit, annerism, expression, etc., peculiar to an individual; odd-y. **2.** The distinctive physical or psychological constitun of an individual. [< Gk. *syn* together + *krasis* mixing] **· id′i′o·syn·crat′ic** (-sin·krat′ik) *adj.* **— id′i·o·syn·crat′i·l·ly** *adv.*

·ot (id′ē·ət) *n.* **1.** A person exhibiting mental deficiency its most severe form. **2.** An extremely foolish or stupid rson. [< OF < L < Gk. *idios* one's own]

— Syn. 1. The *idiot* is incapable of learning, and is completely lpless. An *imbecile* may learn to communicate, but is incapable earning his own living. A *moron* may take a normal place in ciety, but needs constant supervision.

·ot·ic (id′ē·ot′ik) *adj.* Of or characteristic of an idiot; nseless; stupid. Also **id′i·ot′i·cal.** **— id′i·ot′i·cal·ly** *adv.*

le (īd′l) *adj.* **i·dler** (īd′lər), **i·dlest** (īd′list) **1.** Not ened in work. **2.** Not being used; not operating. **3.** Unilling to work; avoiding effort; lazy. **4.** Spent in inactivy; reserved for leisure: *idle* moments. **5.** Having no efctiveness; fruitless: *idle* threats. **6.** Of little value; frivols; trifling. **7.** Having no basis; unfounded. **—** *v.* **i·dled, dling** *v.i.* **1.** To be engaged in trivial or useless activities; af. **2.** To move or progress lazily or aimlessly; linger. **3.** *'ech.* To operate without transmitting power, usu. at reuced speed: said of motors or machines. **—** *v.t.* **4.** To end (time) wastefully; fritter: often with *away.* **5.** *U.S. iformal* To cause to be idle. **6.** To cause to idle, as a mor. [OE *īdel* empty, useless] **— i′dle·ness** *n.* **— i′dly** *adv.*

ler (īd′lər) *n.* **1.** One who idles; a lazy person; loafer. **2.** n idle wheel or pulley.

ol (īd′l) *n.* **1.** An image representing a god, and woriped as divine. **2.** In the Christian and Jewish religions, a lse or nonexistent god; object of heathen worship. **3.** One ho is loved or admired to an excessive degree; object of intuation. **4.** A false or misleading idea. [< OF < L < k. *eidos* form, shape]

ol·a·ter (ī·dol′ə·tər) *n.* **1.** One who worships an idol or ols. **2.** A blindly devoted admirer. [< OF < LL < Gk. *dōlatrēs*] **— i·dol′a·tress** (-tris) *n. fem.*

ol·a·trous (ī·dol′ə·trəs) *adj.* **1.** Of or characterized by orship of idols. **2.** Blindly devoted. **— i·dol′a·trous·ly** *dv.* **— i·dol′a·trous·ness** *n.*

ol·a·try (ī·dol′ə·trē) *n. pl.* **·tries 1.** The worship of idols. . Excessive admiration or veneration; blind infatuation. < OF < LL < Gk. < *eidolon* idol + *latreia* worship]

ol·ize (īd′l·īz) *v.* **·ized, ·iz·ing** *v.t.* **1.** To love or admire lindly or to excess; adore. **2.** To worship as an idol. **—** *v.i.* . To worship idols. **— i′dol·i·za′tion** *n.* **— i′dol·iz′er** *n.*

yl (īd′l) *n.* **1.** A poem or prose piece, usu. short, depicting imple scenes of pastoral, domestic, or country life. **2.** An vent, scene, etc., suitable for an idyl. Also *Brit.* **i′dyll.** [< < Gk. *eidyllion* form]

yl·lic (ī·dil′ik) *adj.* **1.** Of or having the qualities of an dyl. **2.** Charmingly simple or picturesque. Also **i·dyl′li·cal.** **— i·dyl′li·cal·ly** *adv.*

e *suffix* Little; dear: used affectionately: *birdie.*

er *suffix of nouns* One who is concerned with or works with: *ashier.* Also, after *w*, *-yer,* as in *lawyer.* [< F]

if (if) *conj.* **1.** In the event that; in case: We shall turn back *if* it rains. **2.** On condition that; provided that. **3.** Allowing the possibility that; granting that: *If* I am wrong, I'm sorry. ◆ In the preceding senses, *if* is often used in elliptical constructions: I'll do it *if* possible; He's sixty, *if* a day. **4.** Whether: See *if* the mail has come. **5.** Even though; although: Her clothes are neat, *if* not stylish. **—** *n.* A possibility or condition. [OE *gif*]

ig·loo (ig′lo͞o) *n. pl.* **·loos** A dome-shaped hut used by Eskimos, usu. built of blocks of snow. [< Eskimo *igdlu* house]

ig·ne·ous (ig′nē·əs) *adj.* **1.** *Geol.* Formed by the action of great heat within the earth, as rocks consolidated from a molten state. **2.** Of or like fire. [< L *ignis* fire]

ig·nis fat·u·us (ig′nis fach′o͞o·əs) *pl.* **ig·nes fat·u·i** (ig′nēz fach′o͞o·ī) **1.** A flickering, phosphorescent light sometimes seen over marshes, thought to be caused by the spontaneous combustion of marsh gas: also called *will-o'-the-wisp.* **2.** A deceptive attraction. [< Med.L, foolish fire]

ig·nite (ig·nīt′) *v.* **·nit·ed, ·nit·ing** *v.t.* **1.** To set on fire; make burn. **2.** To enkindle; arouse. **3.** *Chem.* To cause to glow with intense heat; bring to combustion. **—** *v.i.* **4.** To start to burn. [< L *ignire* to burn] **— ig·nit′a·ble** or **ig·nit′i·ble** *adj.* **— ig·nit′a·bil′i·ty** or **ig·nit′i·bil′i·ty** *n.*

ig·nit·er (ig·nī′tər) *n.* **1.** One who or that which ignites. **2.** A detonator (def. 1). Also **ig·ni′tor.**

ig·ni·tion (ig·nish′ən) *n.* **1.** The act of igniting, or the state of being ignited. **2.** The process of igniting the explosive mixture of fuel and air in a cylinder of an internal-combustion engine. **3.** The device or system that fires this mixture. [< Med.L < L *ignire* to burn]

ig·no·ble (ig·nō′bəl) *adj.* **1.** Dishonorable in purpose or character; base. **2.** Not of noble rank. **3.** Of low quality; inferior. [< F < L < *in-* not + *gnobilis* known] **— ig·no·bil·i·ty** (ig′nō·bil′ə·tē), **ig·no′ble·ness** *n.* **— ig·no′bly** *adv.*

ig·no·min·i·ous (ig′nə·min′ē·əs) *adj.* **1.** Marked by or involving dishonor or disgrace; shameful. **2.** Meriting disgrace; despicable. **3.** Tending to diminish one's self-respect. **— ig′no·min′i·ous·ly** *adv.* **— ig′no·min′i·ous·ness** *n.*

ig·no·min·y (ig′nə·min′ē) *n. pl.* **·min·ies 1.** Disgrace; dishonor. **2.** That which causes disgrace; dishonorable conduct. [< L < *in-* not + *gnomen* name, reputation]

ig·no·ra·mus (ig′nə·rā′məs, -ram′əs) *n.* An ignorant person. [< L, we do not know]

ig·no·rance (ig′nər·əns) *n.* The state of being ignorant; lack of knowledge, information, or awareness. [< F < L *ignorantia*]

ig·no·rant (ig′nər·ənt) *adj.* **1.** Having no learning or education; unenlightened. **2.** Lacking awareness: with *of*: *ignorant* of the facts. **3.** Uninformed; inexperienced: with *in.* [< OF < L *ignorare.* See IGNORE.] **— ig′no·rant·ly** *adv.*

ig·nore (ig·nôr′, -nōr′) *v.t.* **·nored, ·nor·ing 1.** To refuse to notice or recognize; disregard. **2.** *Law* To reject (a bill of indictment) for insufficient evidence. [< F < L *in-* not + *gnoscere* to know] **— ig·nor′er** *n.* **— ig·nor′a·ble** (-ə·bəl) *adj.*

i·gua·na (i·gwä′nə) *n.* Any of several tropical American lizards that sometimes attain a length of 6 feet. [< Sp. < Carib]

IHS A monogram of the name Jesus, derived from the Greek IH(ΣOY)Σ, Jesus.

i·kon (ī′kon) See ICON.

il- Assimilated var. of IN-[1] and IN-[2].

-ile *suffix* Found in adjectives derived from French and Latin, and in nouns based on such adjectives: *docile, agile, juvenile.* Also, sometimes, **-il,** as in *civil, fossil.* [< F < L *-ilis,* suffix of adjectives; or directly < L]

il·e·um (il′ē·əm) *n. pl.* **il·e·a** (il′ē·ə) *Anat.* The lowest of the three divisions of the small intestine. For illus. see INTESTINE. [< LL < L *ileum* groin, small intestine] **— il·e·ac** (il′ē·ak) *adj.*

i·lex (ī′leks) *n.* Any tree or shrub of the holly family. [< L, holm oak]

Il·i·ad (il′ē·əd) An ancient Greek epic poem ascribed to Homer, describing the siege of Troy. **—** *n.* Any similar long narrative poem. [< L < Gk. *Ilion* Ilium (Troy)]

il·i·um (il′ē·əm) *n. pl.* **il·i·a** (il′ē·ə) *Anat.* The large upper portion of bones of the pelvis. For illus. see PELVIS. [< NL < L *ilia* loins, belly] **— il′i·ac** (-ak) *adj.*

Il·i·um (il′ē·əm) See TROY. Also **Il·i·on** (-ən).

ilk (ilk) *n.* Breed; sort; class: Smith and others of his *ilk.* [OE *ilca* same]

ill (il) *adj.* **worse, worst 1.** Not in good health; suffering from a disorder; sick. **2.** Destructive in effect; harmful. **3.** Hostile or malevolent; unfriendly; spiteful. **4.** Portending danger or disaster; unfavorable. **5.** Morally bad; evil. **6.** Contrary to accepted standards; improper. **— Syn.** See SICK[1]. **—** *n.* **1.** Evil; wrong. **2.** Injury; harm: I wish him no *ill.* **3.** A cause of unhappiness, misfortune, etc. **4.** Disaster; trouble: to bode *ill.* **5.** A malady; sickness. **—** *adv.*

1. Not well; badly. **2.** With difficulty; hardly. **3.** Unsuitably; poorly. [ME < ON *illr*]
Ill may be used in combination. Such combinations are hyphenated when they appear before the words they modify, as in *ill-concealed* envy, but are not hyphenated when used predicatively, as in: His envy was *ill concealed.*
I'll (īl) **1.** I will. **2.** I shall.
ill-ad·vised (il′əd·vīzd′) *adj.* Undertaken or acting in accordance with poor or insufficient advice; injudicious; rash.
ill-bred (il′bred′) *adj.* Unmannerly; impolite; rude.
ill-con·sid·ered (il′kən·sid′ərd) *adj.* Done with insufficient deliberation or forethought; thoughtless; unwise.
ill-dis·posed (il′dis·pōzd′) *adj.* **1.** Having an unpleasant disposition; unfriendly. **2.** Disinclined; averse. **—ill′-dis·pos′ed·ly** (-əd·lē) *adv.* **—ill′-dis·pos′ed·ness** (-əd·nes) *n.*
il·le·gal (i·lē′gəl) *adj.* **1.** Not legal; contrary to law. **2.** Violating official rules. **—il·le′gal·ly** *adv.*
il·le·gal·i·ty (il′ē·gal′ə·tē) *n. pl.* **·ties 1.** The state or quality of being illegal; unlawfulness. **2.** An illegal act.
il·leg·i·ble (i·lej′ə·bəl) *adj.* Not legible; incapable of being read. **—il·leg′i·bil′i·ty, il·leg′i·ble·ness** *n.* **—il·leg′i·bly** *adv.*
il·le·git·i·ma·cy (il′i·jit′ə·mə·sē) *n. pl.* **·cies** The state or quality of being illegitimate; esp., the status or condition of a person born out of wedlock.
il·le·git·i·mate (il′i·jit′ə·mit) *adj.* **1.** Born out of wedlock. **2.** Not according to law; unlawful. **3.** Contrary to good usage; incorrect. **4.** Contrary to logic; unsound. [< L < *in-* not + *legitimus* lawful] **—il′le·git′i·mate·ly** *adv.*
ill fame Bad repute. **— house of ill fame** A brothel.
ill-fa·vored (il′fā′vərd) *adj.* **1.** Unpleasant in appearance; ugly. **2.** Objectionable; disagreeable. **—ill′-fa′vored·ly** *adv.* **—ill′-fa′vored·ness** *n.*
ill-found·ed (il′foun′did) *adj.* Based on weak or incorrect evidence or premises; unsupported.
ill-got·ten (il′got′n) *adj.* Obtained illegally or evilly.
ill humor A disagreeable mood; ill temper; sullenness.
ill-hu·mored (il′hyōō′mərd) *adj.* Irritable; cross. **—ill′-hu′mored·ly** *adv.* **—ill′-hu′mored·ness** *n.*
il·lib·er·al (i·lib′ər·əl) *adj.* **1.** Not generous in giving; stingy. **2.** Narrow-minded; intolerant. **3.** Lacking breadth of culture; provincial. **—il·lib′er·al′i·ty** *n.* **—il·lib′er·al·ly** *adv.*
il·lic·it (i·lis′it) *adj.* Not permitted; unlawful; unauthorized. [< L < *in-* not + *licitus*] **—il·lic′it·ly** *adv.* **—il·lic′it·ness** *n.*
il·lim·it·a·ble (i·lim′it·ə·bəl) *adj.* Incapable of being limited; limitless; boundless. **—il·lim′it·a·bil′i·ty, il·lim′it·a·ble·ness** *n.* **—il·lim′it·a·bly** *adv.*
Il·li·nois (il′ə·noi′, -noiz′) *n. pl.* **·nois** A North American Indian of a tribe belonging to a confederacy of Algonquian tribes. [< F < N.Am.Ind.]
il·lit·er·a·cy (i·lit′ər·ə·sē) *n. pl.* **·cies 1.** The state of being illiterate; esp., inability to read and write. **2.** An error in speaking or writing indicative of lack of education.
il·lit·er·ate (i·lit′ər·it) *adj.* **1.** Lacking education; esp., unable to read and write. **2.** Of language, characteristic of the uneducated. **—** *n.* An illiterate person. [< L *in-* not + *litteratus* lettered] **—il·lit′er·ate·ly** *adv.* **—il·lit′er·ate·ness** *n.*
ill-man·nered (il′man′ərd) *adj.* Characterized by bad manners; discourteous; rude. **—ill-man′nered·ly** *adv.*
ill nature Unpleasant or spiteful disposition; surliness. **—ill′-na′tured** *adj.* **—ill′-na′tured·ly** *adv.*
ill·ness (il′nis) *n.* **1.** The state of being in poor health; sickness. **2.** An ailment; disease.
il·log·i·cal (i·loj′i·kəl) *adj.* Not logical; neglectful of reason. **—il·log′i·cal′i·ty, il·log′i·cal·ness** *n.* **—il·log′i·cal·ly** *adv.*
ill repute Evil reputation. **— house of ill repute** Brothel.
ill-spent (il′spent′) *adj.* Wasted; misspent.
ill-starred (il′stärd′) *adj.* Unlucky, as if under the influence of an evil star.
ill temper Cross disposition; irritable mood. **—ill′-tem′pered** *adj.* **—ill′-tem′pered·ly** *adv.*
ill-timed (il′tīmd′) *adj.* Occurring at an unsuitable time.
ill-treat (il′trēt′) *v.t.* To act cruelly toward; maltreat.
il·lu·mi·nant (i·lōō′mə·nənt) *n.* Something that gives light. [< L *illuminare* to give light]
il·lu·mi·nate (i·lōō′mə·nāt) *v.* **·nat·ed, ·nat·ing** *v.t.* **1.** To give light to; light up. **2.** To shed light upon; clarify. **3.** To enlighten, as the mind. **4.** To make illustrious; glorify. **5.** To decorate with lights. **6.** To decorate, as a manuscript, with ornamental borders, figures, etc., often of gold. **—** *v.i.* **7.** To shed light; become lighted. [< L < *in-* thoroughly + *luminare* to light] **—il·lu′mi·na′tor** *n.*
il·lu·mi·na·tion (i·lōō′mə·nā′shən) *n.* **1.** The act of illuminating, or the state of being illuminated. **2.** An amount or source of light. **3.** Decoration by means of lighting. **4.** Mental or spiritual enlightenment. **5.** Embellishment, as of a manuscript, by means of gold or colored decorations, letters, etc.; also, a letter, ornament, etc., so used.
il·lu·mi·na·tive (i·lōō′mə·nā′tiv) *adj.* Capable of illuminating; serving to illuminate.
il·lu·mine (i·lōō′min) *v.t. & v.i.* **·mined, ·min·ing** To illuminate or be illuminated. [< F < L *illuminare* to illuminate]
ill-use (*v.* il′yōōz′; *n.* il′yōōs′) *v.t.* **-used, -us·ing** To t cruelly or unjustly; abuse. **—** *n.* Bad or unjust treatm also **ill′-us′age** (-yōō′sij, -yōō′zij) *n.*
il·lu·sion (i·lōō′zhən) *n.* **1.** A false, misleading, or ov optimistic idea: youthful *illusions.* **2.** A general impres not consistent with fact: Red gives an *illusion* of heat. A delicate, transparent, netted fabric. [< OF < L *illu* to make sport of < *in-* toward, against + *ludere* to p **—il·lu′sion·al** (-əl), **il·lu′sion·ar·y** (-er·ē) *adj.*
il·lu·sive (i·lōō′siv) *adj.* Deceptive; unreal; illusory. **il·lu′sive·ly** *adv.* **—il·lu′sive·ness** *n.*
il·lu·so·ry (i·lōō′sər·ē) *adj.* Of the nature of illusion; de tive. **—il·lu′so·ri·ly** *adv.* **—il·lu′so·ri·ness** *n.*
il·lus·trate (il′ə·strāt, i·lus′trāt) *v.t.* **·trat·ed, ·trat·ing** To explain or make clear by means of examples, comp sons, etc. **2.** To supply or accompany (a book, etc.) v pictures, as for instruction or decoration. [< L < *in-* t oughly + *lustrare* to illuminate] **—il′lus·tra′tor** *n.*
il·lus·tra·tion (il′ə·strā′shən) *n.* **1.** An example, comp son, anecdote, etc., by which a statement is explained. 2 print, drawing, or picture in written or printed text. **3.** act or art of illustrating. [< L *illustratio*]
il·lus·tra·tive (i·lus′trə·tiv, il′ə·strā′tiv) *adj.* Serving t lustrate. **—il·lus′tra·tive·ly** *adv.*
il·lus·tri·ous (i·lus′trē·əs) *adj.* **1.** Greatly distinguish renowned. **2.** Conferring greatness or glory. [< L < in + *lustrum* light] **—il·lus′tri·ous·ly** *adv.* **—il·lus′tri· ness** *n.*
ill will Hostile feeling; malevolence.
il·ly (il′lē) *adv.* Not well; badly; ill. ◆ While *illy* is regu ly formed from the adjective *ill,* the form *ill* is preferred the adverb as well.
Il·lyr·i·a (i·lir′ē·ə) An ancient country bordering the e coast of the Adriatic. **—Il·lyr′i·an** *adj.*
im-[1] Var. of EM-[1].
im-[2] Assimilated var. of IN-[1] and IN-[2].
I'm (īm) I am.
im·age (im′ij) *n.* **1.** A representation or likeness of a rea imaginary person, creature, or object. **2.** A mental repres tation of something not perceived at the moment thro the senses; mental picture. **3.** The way in which a per or thing is popularly perceived or regarded; public imp sion: a politician's *image.* **4.** A person or thing that clos resembles another. **5.** A sculptured likeness, as a stat **6.** A representative example; embodiment. **7.** A liter device that evokes a mental picture, as a figure of spee **8.** *Optics* The counterpart of an object produced by reflecti refraction, or the passage of rays through a small apertu **9.** The optical replica of a scene reproduced by a televis camera. **—** *v.t.* **·aged, ·ag·ing 1.** To form a mental pict of. **2.** To make a visible representation of; portray. **3.** mirror; reflect. **4.** To describe effectively or vividly. **5.** symbolize. [< OF < L *imitari* to imitate]
im·age·ry (im′ij·rē) *n. pl.* **·ries 1.** Mental images coll tively. **2.** The act or process of forming mental images. The use of vivid descriptions or figures of speech in speaki or writing. **4.** Images used in art or decoration.
im·ag·i·nar·y (i·maj′ə·ner′ē) *adj.* Existing in the ima nation only; unreal. **—im·ag′i·nar′i·ly** *adv.* **—im·a nar′i·ness** *n.*
im·ag·i·na·tion (i·maj′ə·nā′shən) *n.* **1.** The process of for ing mental images of the objects of perception or thought the absence of the concrete external stimuli. **2.** The men ability to reproduce the images of memory. **3.** The men ability to create original and striking images and concep the creative faculty. **4.** A creation of the mind; men image. **5.** An absurd fancy. **—im·ag′i·na′tion·al** *adj.*
im·ag·i·na·tive (i·maj′ə·nə·tiv, -nā′tiv) *adj.* **1.** Endow with imagination. **2.** Given to flights of fancy. **3.** Of characterized by the creative imagination: *imaginative* p etry. **—im·ag′i·na·tive·ly** *adv.* **—im·ag′i·na·tive·ness**
im·ag·ine (i·maj′in) *v.* **·ined, ·in·ing 1.** To form a men picture or idea of. **2.** To suppose; guess: I *imagine* he will elected. **—** *v.i.* **3.** To use the imagination. **4.** To suppo guess. [< L *imago* image] **—im·ag′i·na·ble** *adj.*
im·a·gism (im′ə·jiz′əm) *n.* A movement in poetry chara terized by precise images and freedom in form. [< F *L Imagistes,* the title of the first anthology of imagist poetr **—im′a·gist** *n. & adj.* **—im′a·gis′tic** *adj.*
i·ma·go (i·mā′gō) *n. pl.* **i·ma·goes** or **i·mag·i·nes** (i·maj nēz) **1.** *Entomol.* An insect in its adult, sexually matu stage. **2.** *Psychoanal.* An infantile, unconscious concept a parent or other loved one persisting in the adult. [<
im·bal·ance (im·bal′əns) *n.* **1.** The state of being out balance. **2.** *Physiol.* Any defective coordination.
im·be·cile (im′bə·sil) *n.* **1.** A person exhibiting a degree mental deficiency between that of the idiot and the moro **2.** A foolish or stupid person. **— Syn.** See IDIOT. **—** *a* **1.** Mentally deficient. **2.** Stupid; senseless. [< F < *imbecillus* weak, feeble] **—im′be·cil′i·ty** *n.*
im·bibe (im·bīb′) *v.* **·bibed, ·bib·ing** *v.t.* **1.** To drink.

suck up; absorb. 3. To take in mentally: to *imbibe* rning. —*v.i.* 4. To drink. [< F < L *in-* in + *bibere* to nk] —**im·bib′er** *n.*
bri·cate (*adj.* im′brə·kit; *v.* im′brə·kāt) *adj.* 1. Arnged in a regular pattern with overlapping edges, as shins on a roof. 2. Covered or decorated with a design renbling overlapping scales, leaves, etc. Also **im′bri·ca′tive** ā′tiv). —*v.t.* & *v.i.* **·cat·ed, ·cat·ing** To overlap in a gular arrangement. [< L *imbrex* gutter tile < *imber* rain]
bro·glio (im·brōl′yō) *n.* *pl.* **·glios** 1. A confused state affairs. 2. A confused heap or tangle. [< Ital.]
brue (im·broo′) *v.t.* **·brued, ·bru·ing** To stain or drench, . with blood. [< OF < L *in-* in + *bibere* to drink]
bue (im·byoo′) *v.t.* **·bued, ·bu·ing** 1. To pervade or perate (with emotions, ideals, etc.). 2. To wet thoroughly; urate, as with color. [< L *imbuere* to wet, soak]
i·ta·ble (im′ə·tə·bəl) *adj.* Capable of being imitated.
i·tate (im′ə·tāt) *v.t.* **·tat·ed, ·tat·ing** 1. To behave or atmpt to behave in the same way as; follow the example of. To mimic or impersonate. 3. To make a copy or reproction of. 4. To have or take on the appearance of. [< L *itari* to imitate] —**im′i·ta′tor** *n.*
i·ta·tion (im′ə·tā′shən) *n.* 1. The act of imitating. 2. at which is done by or results from imitating; copy. 3. *ol.* Mimicry. —*adj.* Resembling or made to resemble mething superior; not genuine. [< L *imitatio, -onis*]
i·ta·tive (im′ə·tā′tiv) *adj.* 1. Tending to imitate; charterized by imitation. 2. Patterned after or reproducing e characteristics of an original. 3. Not genuine; spurious. *Ling.* Designating words that resemble natural sounds, *buzz, swish.* —**im′i·ta′tive·ly** *adv.* —**im′i·ta′tive·ness** *n.*
mac·u·late (i·mak′yə·lit) *adj.* 1. Without spot or stain; sullied. 2. Without sin; pure. 3. Without error or blem; faultless; flawless. [< L < *in-* not + *macula* spot] —**·mac′u·late·ly** *adv.* —**im·mac′u·late·ness** *n.*
maculate Conception *Theol.* The doctrine that the rgin Mary was conceived without original sin.
·ma·nent (im′ə·nənt) *adj.* 1. Existing or remaining thin; indwelling. 2. Of God, pervading all creation. [< < *in-* in + *manere* to stay] —**im′ma·nence, im′ma·nen·** *n.* —**im′ma·nent·ly** *adv.*
·man·u·el (i·man′yoo·əl) A name of the Messiah. *Isa.* i 14; *Matt.* i 23. Also *Emmanuel.*
·ma·te·ri·al (im′ə·tir′ē·əl) *adj.* 1. Of little or no imortance; inconsequential; irrelevant. 2. Not consisting of aterial substance. [< Med.L < *in-* not + *materia* matr] —**im′ma·te′ri·al·ly** *adv.* —**im′ma·te′ri·al·ness** *n.*
·ma·ture (im′ə·choor′, -tyoor′, -toor′) *adj.* 1. Not mare or ripe. 2. *Geog.* In an early stage of development. [< < *in-* not + *maturus* mature] —**im′ma·ture′ly** *adv.* —**′ma·ture′ness, im′ma·tur′i·ty** *n.*
·meas·ur·a·ble (i·mezh′ər·ə·bəl) *adj.* Not capable of ing measured; without limit; immense. —**im·meas′ur·a·y** *adv.* —**im·meas′ur·a·bil′i·ty, im·meas′ur·a·ble·ness** *n.*
·me·di·a·cy (i·mē′dē·ə·sē) *n.* 1. The state or quality of ing immediate; direct relationship. 2. Intuitive knowlge as distinguished from that arrived at by reasoning.
·me·di·ate (i·mē′dē·it) *adj.* 1. Done or occurring withut delay or lapse of time; instant. 2. Pertaining to the esent moment: We have no *immediate* vacancies. 3. Separted by no appreciable interval of time or space: the *imediate* future. 4. Very close in rank or relationship: the *mmediate* family. 5. Occurring or acting directly or withut an intervening agency or cause. [< Med.L < *in-* not + *ediare* to stand between] —**im·me′di·ate·ness** *n.*
·me·di·ate·ly (i·mē′dē·it·lē) *adv.* 1. Without lapse of me; instantly; at once. 2. In direct or close succession. 3. Vithout an intervening agency or cause; directly. —*conj.* s soon as; at the instant that.
·me·mo·ri·al (im′ə·môr′ē·əl, -mō′rē-) *adj.* Reaching ack beyond memory; ancient. —**im′me·mo′ri·al·ly** *adv.*
·mense (i·mens′) *adj.* 1. Of great size, degree, or extent; uge. 2. Having no limits; infinite. 3. *Slang* Excellent; dmirable. [< F < L < *in-* not + *mensus*, pp. of *metiri* to easure] —**im·mense′ly** *adv.* —**im·mense′ness** *n.*
·men·si·ty (i·men′sə·tē) *n.* *pl.* **·ties** 1. The condition or uality of being immense; vastness. 2. Boundless space.
·men·sur·a·ble (i·men′shoor·ə·bəl, -sə·rə-) *adj.* Immeasrable. [< MF < L < *in-* not + *mensurare* to measure] —**im·men′sur·a·bil′i·ty** *n.*
·merge (i·mûrj′) *v.* **·merged, ·merg·ing** *v.t.* 1. To imerse. —*v.i.* 2. To plunge or sink into a liquid. [< L < *n-* in + *mergere* to dip] —**im·mer′gence** *n.*
·merse (i·mûrs′) *v.t.* **·mersed, ·mers·ing** 1. To plunge or lip into water or other fluid so as to cover completely. 2. To involve deeply; engross. 3. To baptize by plunging the ntire body under water. [< L *immersus*, pp. of *immergere* o dip] —**im·mer′sion** *n.*

im·mi·grant (im′ə·grənt) *adj.* Coming into a country or region of which one is not a native in order to settle there. Compare EMIGRANT. —*n.* A person who immigrates.
im·mi·grate (im′ə·grāt) *v.* **·grat·ed, ·grat·ing** *v.i.* 1. To come into a country or region of which one is not a native in order to settle there. —*v.t.* 2. To bring in as immigrants. —**Syn.** See MIGRATE. [< L < *in-* in + *migrare* to migrate]
im·mi·gra·tion (im′ə·grā′shən) *n.* 1. The act of immigrating. 2. The total number of immigrants entering a country during a stated period. 3. Immigrants collectively. —**im·mi·gra·to·ry** (im′ə·grə·tôr′ē, -tō′rē) *adj.*
im·mi·nence (im′ə·nəns) *n.* 1. The state or quality of being imminent. 2. That which is imminent; esp., impending disaster. Also **im′mi·nen·cy.**
im·mi·nent (im′ə·nənt) *adj.* About to happen; impending; threatening: said esp. of danger or catastrophe. [< L < *in-* on + *-minere* so project] —**im′mi·nent·ly** *adv.*
im·mis·ci·ble (i·mis′ə·bəl) *adj.* Not capable of being mixed, as oil and water. [< L *in-* not + *miscere* to mix] —**im·mis′ci·bil′i·ty** *n.* —**im·mis′ci·bly** *adv.*
im·mo·bile (i·mō′bəl, -bēl) *adj.* 1. Incapable of being moved. 2. Not moving; motionless. [< OF < LL < L *in-* not + *movere* to move] —**im′mo·bil′i·ty** *n.*
im·mo·bil·ize (i·mō′bə·līz) *v.t.* **·lized, ·liz·ing** 1. To make immovable; fix in place. 2. To make unable to move or mobilize, as a body of troops. —**im·mo′bi·li·za·tion** *n.*
im·mod·er·ate (i·mod′ər·it) *adj.* Not moderate; exceeding reasonable or proper bounds. —**im·mod′er·ate·ly** *adv.* —**im·mod′er·ate·ness** *n.* —**im·mod′er·a′tion** *n.*
im·mod·est (i·mod′ist) *adj.* 1. Without sense of decency; improper. 2. Lacking humility; bold. —**im·mod′est·ly** *adv.* —**im·mod′es·ty** *n.*
im·mo·late (im′ə·lāt) *v.t.* **·lat·ed, ·lat·ing** To sacrifice; esp., to kill as a sacrificial victim. [< L < *in-* on + *mola* meal] —**im′mo·la′tion** *n.* —**im′mo·la′tor** *n.*
im·mor·al (i·môr′əl, i·mor′-) *adj.* 1. Violating the moral law; contrary to conscience or public morality. 2. Sexually impure; licentious. —**im·mor′al·ly** *adv.*
—**Syn. 1.** The *immoral* person violates moral principles knowingly; he is consciously wicked, dissolute, evil, etc. The *amoral* person lacks the sense of right and wrong, and thus may violate morality without evil intent. *Unmoral* and *nonmoral* mean not within the realm of morality; a baby is *unmoral.*
im·mo·ral·i·ty (im′ə·ral′ə·tē, -ôr·al′-) *n.* *pl.* **·ties** 1. The state or quality of being immoral; wickedness; dissoluteness. 2. Sexual impurity or misconduct. 3. An immoral act.
im·mor·tal (i·môr′təl) *adj.* 1. Not subject to death; living forever; deathless. 2. Having unending existence; eternal. 3. Pertaining to immortality or to beings or concepts that are immortal; divine. 4. Of enduring fame; memorable. —*n.* 1. An immortal being. 2. *pl.* The gods of classical mythology. 3. A person who has gained enduring fame. —**im·mor′tal·ly** *adv.*
im·mor·tal·i·ty (im′ôr·tal′ə·tē) *n.* 1. Unending existence; eternal life. 2. Eternal fame.
im·mor·tal·ize (i·môr′təl·īz) *v.t.* **·ized, ·iz·ing** To make immortal; endow with perpetual fame. Also *Brit.* **im·mor′tal·ise.** —**im·mor′tal·i′zer** *n.* —**im·mor′tal·i·za′tion** *n.*
im·mor·telle (im′ôr·tel′) *n.* An everlasting (def. 2). [< F]
im·mov·a·ble (i·moo′və·bəl) *adj.* 1. Incapable of being moved; stable. 2. Unable to move; stationary. 3. Firm of purpose or opinion; unyielding. 4. Not easily aroused emotionally; impassive. —*n.pl.* *Law* Real property. —**im·mov′a·bil′i·ty, im·mov′a·ble·ness** *n.* —**im·mov′a·bly** *adv.*
im·mune (i·myoon′) *adj.* 1. Protected against a disease, poison, or the like, as by inoculation. 2. Not susceptible to harmful influence. 3. Not subject to obligation, penalty, etc. —*n.* One who is immune, esp. to a disease.
im·mu·ni·ty (i·myoo′nə·tē) *n.* *pl.* **·ties** 1. Protection against or lack of susceptibility to a disease, poison, infection, or the like. 2. Resistance to harmful influence. 3. Exemption from civil obligations or jurisdiction. [< OF < L < *in-* not + *munis* serviceable]
im·mu·nize (im′yə·nīz) *v.t.* **·nized, ·niz·ing** To make immune; esp., to protect against a disease by inoculation. —**im′mu·ni·za′tion** *n.*
im·mu·nol·o·gy (im′yə·nol′ə·jē) *n.* The branch of medical science that deals with immunity to disease. —**im·mu·no·log·i·cal** (i·myoo′nə·loj′i·kəl) *adj.* —**im′mu·nol′o·gist** *n.*
im·mure (i·myoor′) *v.t.* **·mured, ·mur·ing** 1. To enclose within walls; imprison. 2. To place in seclusion; confine. 3. To entomb within a wall. [< Med.L < *in-* in + LL *murare* to wall] —**im·mure′ment** *n.*
im·mu·ta·ble (i·myoo′tə·bəl) *adj.* Not mutable; unchanging; unalterable. —**im·mu′ta·bil′i·ty, im·mu′ta·ble·ness** *n.* —**im·mu′ta·bly** *adv.*
imp (imp) *n.* 1. An evil spirit; small or minor demon. 2. A mischievous or unruly child. [OE *impian* to ingraft]

im·pact (*n.* im′pakt; *v.* im·pakt′) *n.* **1.** A striking together; collision. **2.** The forcible momentary contact of a moving body with another either moving or at rest. **3.** Strong influence; powerful effect. — *v.t.* To press or drive firmly into something. [< L *impactus*, pp. of *impingere* to impinge]

im·pact·ed (im·pak′tid) *adj. Dent.* Denoting a tooth unable to emerge through the gum.

im·pac·tion (im·pak′shən) *n.* **1.** The act of impacting, or the state of being impacted. **2.** *Dent.* An impacted tooth.

im·pair (im·pâr′) *v.t.* To cause to become less in quality, power, or value; make worse. [< OF < LL *in-* thoroughly + *pejorare* to make worse] — **im·pair′ment** *n.*

im·pale (im·pāl′) *v.t.* **·paled, ·pal·ing 1.** To fix upon a pale or sharp stake. **2.** To torture or put to death by thrusting a sharp stake through the body. **3.** To make helpless as if by fixing upon a stake. [< OF < LL < *in-* + *palus* stake] — **im·pale′ment** *n.* — **im·pal′er** *n.*

im·pal·pa·ble (im·pal′pə·bəl) *adj.* **1.** Not capable of being perceived by the sense of touch. **2.** Not capable of being distinguished by the mind. — **im·pal′pa·bil′i·ty** *n.* — **im·pal′pa·bly** *adv.*

im·pan·el (im·pan′əl) *v.t.* **·pan·eled** or **·elled, ·pan·el·ing** or **·el·ling 1.** To enroll upon a panel or list, as for jury duty. **2.** To choose (members of a jury, etc.) from such a list. Also spelled *empanel.* — **im·pan′el·ment** *n.*

im·part (im·pärt′) *v.t.* **1.** To make known; disclose. **2.** To bestow a measure or quantity of: to *impart* happiness. [< OF < L < *in-* in + *partire* to share] — **im·par·ta·tion** (im′·pär·tā′shən), **im·part′ment** *n.* — **im·part′er** *n.*

im·par·tial (im·pär′shəl) *adj.* Not favoring one above another; free from bias; disinterested. — **im·par′tial·ly** *adv.* — **im·par′tial·ness** *n.*

im·par·ti·al·i·ty (im′pär·shē·al′ə·tē, im·pär′-) *n.* Freedom from bias; fairness.

im·pass·a·ble (im·pas′ə·bəl, -päs′-) *adj.* That cannot be traveled over or through: an *impassable* jungle. — **im·pass′a·bil′i·ty, im·pass′a·ble·ness** *n.* — **im·pass′a·bly** *adv.*

im·passe (im′pas, im·pas′; *Fr.* aṅ·päs′) *n.* **1.** A situation in which no further progress is possible; deadlock. **2.** A way or passage open at one end only; blind alley. [< F]

im·pas·si·ble (im·pas′ə·bəl) *adj.* **1.** Incapable of emotion; unfeeling. **2.** Incapable of suffering pain. **3.** Invulnerable. [< OF < Med.L < *in-* not + *pati* to suffer] — **im·pas′si·bil′i·ty, im·pas′si·ble·ness** *n.* — **im·pas′si·bly** *adv.*

im·pas·sion (im·pash′ən) *v.t.* To fill with passion; inflame.

im·pas·sioned (im·pash′ənd) *adj.* Filled with passion or strong feeling; fervent. — **im·pas′sioned·ly** *adv.*

im·pas·sive (im·pas′iv) *adj.* **1.** Not feeling emotion; unmoved. **2.** Calm; serene. **3.** Unconscious. — **im·pas′sive·ly** *adv.* — **im·pas′sive·ness, im·pas·siv·i·ty** (im′pa·siv′ə·tē) *n.*

im·pa·ti·ens (im·pā′shē·enz) *n.* An herb with stems enlarged at the joints and irregular flowers, as the jewelweed: also called *touch-me-not.* [< L, impatient; because the ripe seed pods burst open at a touch.]

im·pa·tient (im·pā′shənt) *adj.* **1.** Lacking patience; easily annoyed at delay, discomfort, etc.; irritable. **2.** Unwilling to tolerate: with *of.* **3.** Restlessly eager: *impatient* for success. **4.** Exhibiting lack of patience: an *impatient* gesture. — **im·pa′tience** *n.* — **im·pa′tient·ly** *adv.*

im·peach (im·pēch′) *v.t.* **1.** To charge (a high public official) before a legally constituted tribunal with crime or misdemeanor in office. **2.** To challenge or bring discredit upon the honesty or validity of. [< OF < LL < *in-* in + *pedica* fetter] — **im·peach′a·bil′i·ty** *n.* — **im·peach′a·ble** *adj.* — **im·peach′ment** *n.*

im·pec·ca·ble (im·pek′ə·bəl) *adj.* **1.** Free from error, fault, or flaw. **2.** Incapable of doing wrong; unerring. — *n.* An impeccable person. [< LL < L *in-* not + *peccare* to sin] — **im·pec′ca·bil′i·ty** *n.* — **im·pec′ca·bly** *adv.*

im·pe·cu·ni·ous (im′pə·kyōō′nē·əs) *adj.* Having no money; penniless. Also **im·pe·cu·ni·ar·y** (im′pə·kyōō′nē·er′ē). [< F < L *in-* not + *pecunia* money] — **im′pe·cu′ni·ous·ly** *adv.* — **im′pe·cu′ni·ous·ness, im′pe·cu′ni·os′i·ty** (-os′ə·tē) *n.*

im·ped·ance (im·pēd′ns) *n. Electr.* The total opposition to an alternating current presented by a circuit.

im·pede (im·pēd′) *v.t.* **·ped·ed, ·ped·ing** To retard or hinder in progress or action; put obstacles in the way of. [< L *impedire*, lit., to shackle the feet < *in-* in + *pes, pedis* foot] — **im·ped′er** *n.* — **im·ped′ing·ly** *adv.*

im·pe·di·ent (im·pē′dē·ənt) *adj.* That impedes. — *n.* That which impedes.

im·ped·i·ment (im·ped′ə·mənt) *n.* **1.** That which hinders or obstructs; an obstacle. **2.** A physical handicap, esp. a speech defect. **3.** *Law* **a** A disability that prevents the making of a valid contract, as infancy, insanity, etc. **b** A disability that affects the validity of a marriage. — **im·ped′i·men′tal** (-men′təl), **im·ped′i·men′ta·ry** (-men′tər·ē) *adj.*

im·ped·i·men·ta (im·ped′ə·men′tə) *n.pl.* **1.** The baggage, supplies, and equipment carried by an army. **2.** Cumbersome baggage or equipment; also, any drawbacks or burdens. **3.** *Law* Impediments. [< L]

im·pel (im·pel′) *v.t.* **·pelled, ·pel·ling 1.** To force or driv[e to] an action; move by an impulse; urge on. **2.** To driv[e or] push forward. — **Syn.** See ACTUATE. [< L < *in-* o[n +] *pellere* to drive] — **im·pel′lent** *adj.* & *n.* — **im·pel′ler** [*n.*]

im·pend (im·pend′) *v.i.* **1.** To be about to occur; be im[mi]nent. **2.** To be suspended: with *over.* [< L < *in-* or[n +] *pendere* to hang] — **im·pen′dent** *adj.* — **im·pen′denc[e]**

im·pend·ing (im·pen′ding) *adj.* **1.** About to occur; im[mi]nent; threatening. **2.** Overhanging.

im·pen·e·tra·bil·i·ty (im·pen′ə·trə·bil′ə·tē) *n.* **1.** The s[tate] or quality of being impenetrable. **2.** *Physics* The prop[erty] of matter that makes impossible the occupation of the s[ame] space by two bodies at the same time.

im·pen·e·tra·ble (im·pen′ə·trə·bəl) *adj.* **1.** Incapabl[e of] being penetrated; that cannot be pierced, entered, [seen] through, etc.; impervious. **2.** Incapable of being un[der]stood. **3.** Inaccessible to intellectual or moral influen[ces.] **4.** *Physics* Possessing impenetrability. [< OF < L < not + *penetrare* to put within] — **im·pen′e·tra·bil′i·ty, im·pen′e·tra·ble·ness** *n.* — **im·pen′e·tra·bly** *adv.*

im·pen·i·tent (im·pen′ə·tənt) *adj.* Not penitent; obdur[ate.] — **im·pen′i·tence, im·pen′i·ten·cy** *n.* — **im·pen′i·ten[t·ly]** *adv.* — **im·pen′i·tent·ness** *n.*

im·per·a·tive (im·per′ə·tiv) *adj.* **1.** Urgently necess[ary;] obligatory. **2.** Having the nature of or expressing a c[om]mand. **3.** *Gram.* Designating the mood used to exp[ress] commands, requests, exhortations, etc. — *n.* **1.** T[hat] which is imperative. **2.** *Gram.* The mood used to exp[ress a] command, exhortation, etc., or a verb or verb form in [this] mood. [< LL *imperare* to command] — **im·per′a·tiv[e·ly]** *adv.* — **im·per′a·tive·ness** *n.*

im·per·cep·ti·ble (im′pər·sep′tə·bəl) *adj.* **1.** That [can] barely be perceived, as by reason of smallness, extreme d[eli]cacy, subtlety, etc. **2.** Not discernible by the mind [or] senses. — **im′per·cep′ti·ble·ness, im′per·cep′ti·bil′i·ty** *n.* — **im′per·cep′ti·bly** *adv.*

im·per·cep·tive (im′pər·sep′tiv) *adj.* Not perceptive; la[ck]ing the power of perception. — **im·per·cep·tiv·i·ty** (im′[per]·sep·tiv′ə·tē), **im′per·cep′tive·ness** *n.*

im·per·fect (im·pûr′fikt) *adj.* **1.** Falling short of per[fec]tion; faulty: an *imperfect* performance. **2.** Wanting in c[om]pleteness; deficient. **3.** Denoting a tense that indicates [ac]tion, usu. past action, as uncompleted, continuing, or s[yn]chronous with some other action. — *n. Gram.* The [im]perfect tense, or a verb or verb form in this tense, as [was] *speaking* in *He was speaking when I entered.* — **im·per′f[ect]·ly** *adv.* — **im·per′fect·ness** *n.*

im·per·fec·tion (im′pər·fek′shən) *n.* **1.** The state or qu[ali]ty of being imperfect. **2.** A defect; flaw. [< OF < LL < *imperfectus* incomplete.]

im·per·fo·rate (im·pûr′fər·it) *adj.* **1.** Without perfo[ra]tions; not perforated. **2.** Not separated by lines of perfo[ra]tions: said of stamps. Also **im·per′fo·rat′ed** (-rā′tid). — An imperforated stamp. — **im·per′fo·ra′tion** *n.*

im·pe·ri·al (im·pir′ē·əl) *adj.* **1.** Of or pertaining to an e[m]pire. **2.** Designating a nation having sovereign power o[ver] colonies or dependencies. **3.** Pertaining to or suitable to [the] rank of an emperor or supreme ruler. **4.** Possessing co[m]manding power or dignity; majestic; magnificent. **5.** Ex[er]cising the authority of or having the manner of a supre[me] ruler or commander; overbearing. **6.** Superior in size [or] quality. **7.** Designating or conforming to the legal sta[nd]ards of weights and measures of the United Kingdom. — **1.** A pointed tuft of hair on the chin. **2.** An article of m[ore] than usual size or of superior excellence. **3.** A size of pap[er,] in the U.S. 23 x 31 inches. [< OF < L < *imperium* ru[le,] power] — **im·pe′ri·al·ly** *adv.* — **im·per′i·al·ness** *n.*

im·pe·ri·al·ism (im·pir′ē·əl·iz′əm) *n.* **1.** The creati[on,] maintenance, or extension of an empire, comprising ma[ny] nations and areas, all controlled by a central governme[nt.] **2.** A system of imperial government. **3.** Imperial charact[er,] authority, or spirit. — **im·pe′ri·al·ist** *n.* & *adj.* — **im·p[e′]ri·al·is′tic** *adj.* — **im·pe′ri·al·is′ti·cal·ly** *adv.*

im·per·il (im·per′il) *v.t.* **·per·iled** or **·illed, ·per·il·ing** or [**·per·il**]**·ling** To place in peril; endanger.

im·pe·ri·ous (im·pir′ē·əs) *adj.* **1.** Characterized by an at[ti]tude of command; domineering; arrogant. **2.** Urgent; i[m]perative. [< L *imperium*] — **im·pe′ri·ous·ly** *adv.* — **i[m]·pe′ri·ous·ness** *n.*

im·per·ish·a·ble (im·per′ish·ə·bəl) *adj.* Not perishable; n[ot] subject to decay; enduring; everlasting. — **im·per′ish[·a]·bil′i·ty, im·per′ish·a·ble·ness** *n.* — **im·per′ish·a·bly** *adv.*

im·per·ma·nent (im·pûr′mə·nənt) *adj.* Not permanen[t;] fleeting. — **im·per′ma·nence, im·per′ma·nen·cy** *n.*

im·per·me·a·ble (im·pûr′mē·ə·bəl) *adj.* **1.** Not permitti[ng] passage or penetration. **2.** Impervious to moisture. — **i[m]·per′me·a·bil′i·ty, im·per′me·a·ble·ness** *n.* — **im·per′me[·a]·bly** *adv.*

im·per·mis·si·ble (im′pər·mis′ə·bəl) *adj.* Not to be pe[r]mitted. — **im′per·mis′si·bil′i·ty** *n.* — **im′per·mis′si·bly** *a[dv.]*

im·per·son·al (im·pûr′sən·əl) *adj.* **1.** Not personal; obje[ctive] ve: an *impersonal* observation. **2.** Not having the charac-ristics of a person: an *impersonal* deity. **3.** *Gram.* Of a rb, having no specific subject: in English the word *it* is u. used with such verbs. — *n. Gram.* An impersonal verb. **·im·per′son·al′i·ty** (-al′ə·tē) *n.* **—im·per′son·al·ly** *adv.*

·per·son·ate (*v.* im·pûr′sən·āt; *adj.* im·pûr′sən·it) *v.t.* **·at-**, **·at·ing 1.** To adopt or mimic the appearance, manner-ns, etc., of. **2.** To act or play the part of. **3.** *Archaic* To present in human form. — *adj.* Embodied in one person. **im·per′son·a′tion** *n.* **—im·per′son·a′tor** *n.*

·per·ti·nence (im·pûr′tə·nəns) *n.* **1.** Deliberate disre-ectfulness; rudeness. **2.** Irrelevancy. **3.** Unsuitability; appropriateness; incongruity. **4.** An impertinent remark, t, etc. Also **im·per′ti·nen·cy.**

·per·ti·nent (im·pûr′tə·nənt) *adj.* **1.** Deliberately disre-ectful or unmannerly; impudent. **2.** Not pertinent; ir-levant. **3.** Not suitable; inappropriate; incongruous. — **·per′ti·nent·ly** *adv.*

·per·turb·a·ble (im′pər·tûr′bə·bəl) *adj.* Incapable of ing disturbed or agitated; calm. **—im′per·turb′a·bil′i·ty, ′per·turb′a·ble·ness** *n.* **—im′per·turb′a·bly** *adv.*

·per·vi·ous (im·pûr′vē·əs) *adj.* **1.** Incapable of being ssed through, as by moisture or light rays; impermeable. Not open; unreceptive: a mind *impervious* to reason. Also **ı·per′vi·a·ble.** [< L < *in-* not + *per-* through + *via* way, ad] **—im·per′vi·ous·ly** *adv.* **—im·per′vi·ous·ness** *n.*

·pe·ti·go (im′pə·tī′gō) *n. Pathol.* A contagious skin dis-se marked by pustules. [< L < *impetere* to attack]

·pet·u·os·i·ty (im·pech′ōō·os′ə·tē) *n. pl.* **·ties 1.** The uality of being impetuous. **2.** An impetuous action.

·pet·u·ous im·pech′ōō·əs) *adj.* **1.** Tending to act on dden impulse and without forethought. **2.** Resulting om sudden impulse; rashly hasty. **3.** Moving with violent rce: an *impetuous* wind. [< MF < L < *impetere* to attack] **—im·pet′u·ous·ly** *adv.* **—im·pet′u·ous·ness** *n.*
— **Syn. 1.** impulsive, reckless, rash. **2.** sudden, spontaneous, ecipitate, swift, headlong. — **Ant.** deliberate.

·pe·tus (im′pə·təs) *n.* **1.** The force that sets a body in otion; also, the energy with which a body moves or is riven. **2.** Any motivating force; stimulus; incentive. [< < *in-* upon + *petere* to seek]

·pi·e·ty (im·pī′ə·tē) *n. pl.* **·ties 1.** Lack of reverence for od; ungodliness. **2.** Lack of respect for those to whom re-pect is due; undutifulness. **3.** An impious act.

·pinge (im·pinj′) *v.i.* **·pinged, ·ping·ing 1.** To strike; ll: with *on, upon,* or *against.* **2.** To encroach; infringe: ith *on* or *upon.* [< L < *in-* against + *pangere* to strike] **—im·pinge′ment** *n.* **—im·ping′er** *n.*

·pi·ous (im′pē·əs) *adj.* **1.** Lacking in reverence for God; ngodly; blasphemous. **2.** Lacking in due respect, as for ne's parents. [< L < *in-* not + *pius* reverent] **—im′pi·us·ly** *adv.* **—im′pi·ous·ness** *n.*

·p·ish (imp′ish) *adj.* Characteristic of or resembling an mp; mischievous. **—imp′ish·ly** *adv.* **—imp′ish·ness** *n.*

ı·pla·ca·ble (im·plā′kə·bəl, -plak′ə-) *adj.* That cannot be ppeased or pacified. [< F < L < *in-* not + *placere* to lease] **—im·pla′ca·bil′i·ty, im·pla′ca·ble·ness** *n.* **—im·la′ca·bly** *adv.*

ı·plant (*v.* im·plant′, -plänt′; *n.* im′plant′, -plänt′) *v.t.* **1.** 'o fix firmly, as in the ground; plant; embed. **2.** To instill n the mind: to *implant* new ideas; inculcate. **3.** *Med.* To nsert or embed in (living tissue). — *n. Med.* **1.** A tissue mplanted in the body. **2.** A small tube containing radio-ctive material, embedded in tissue for therapeutic or reme-ial purposes. [< F *implanter*] **—im′plan·ta′tion** *n.*

n·plau·si·ble (im·plô′zə·bəl) *adj.* Not plausible; lacking he appearance of truth or trustworthiness. **—im·plau′si·il′i·ty, im·plau′si·ble·ness** *n.* **—im·plau′si·bly** *adv.*

n·ple·ment (*n.* im′plə·mənt; *v.* im′plə·ment) *n.* **1.** A piece f equipment used in some form of work or activity; tool; in-trument; utensil. **2.** Any means or agent for the accom-lishment of a purpose. — *v.t.* **1.** To provide for the accom-lishment or carrying into effect of. **2.** To accomplish; ful-ill. **3.** To furnish with implements. [< L < *in-* in + *plere* o fill] **—im′ple·men′tal** *adj.* **—im′ple·men·ta′tion** *n.*

n·pli·cate (im′plə·kāt) *v.t.* **·cat·ed, ·cat·ing 1.** To show to e involved or concerned, as in a plot or crime. **2.** To indi-ate as something to be inferred; imply. **3.** To fold or twist ogether; intertwine. [< L < *in-* in + *plicare* to fold]

n·pli·ca·tion (im′plə·kā′shən) *n.* **1.** The act of involving, r the state of being involved. **2.** The act of implying, or he state of being implied. **3.** That which is implied.

n·pli·ca·tive (im′plə·kā′tiv) *adj.* Tending to implicate. Also **im·pli·ca·to·ry** (im′pli·kə·tôr′ē, -tō′rē). **—im′pli·ca′·ive·ly** *adv.*

n·plic·it (im·plis′it) *adj.* **1.** Unreserved; absolute. **2.** Im-plied or understood, but not specifically expressed: *implicit* agreement. **3.** Essentially contained, but not apparent; in-herent: with *in*: The man is *implicit* in the child. [< F < L *implicare* to involve] **—im·plic′it·ly** *adv.* **—im·plic′it·ness** *n.*

im·plied (im·plīd′) *adj.* Understood, suggested, or included without being specifically expressed. **—im·pli′ed·ly** *adv.*

im·plore (im·plôr′, -plōr′) *v.* **·plored, ·plor·ing** *v.t.* **1.** To call upon in humble or urgent entreaty; beseech. **2.** To beg for urgently. — *v.i.* **3.** To make urgent supplication. [< L < *in-* thoroughly + *plorare* to cry out] **—im·plo·ra·tion** (im′·plə·rā′shən) *n.* **—im·plor′er** *n.* **—im·plor′ing·ly** *adv.*

im·ply (im·plī′) *v.t.* **·plied, ·ply·ing 1.** To involve neces-sarily as a circumstance, condition, effect, etc.: An action *im-plies* an agent. **2.** To indicate or suggest without stating; hint at; intimate. **3.** To signify. ◆ See note at INFER. [< OF < L < *in-* in + *plicare* to fold]

im·po·lite (im′pə·līt′) *adj.* Lacking in politeness; discourte-ous; rude. **—im′po·lite′ly** *adv.* **—im′po·lite′ness** *n.*

im·pol·i·tic (im·pol′ə·tik) *adj.* Not in keeping with good policy; not prudent; inexpedient; injudicious. **—im·pol′i·tic·ly** *adv.* **—im·pol′i·tic·ness** *n.*

im·pon·der·a·ble (im·pon′dər·ə·bəl) *adj.* Incapable of be-ing estimated, calculated, or valued. — *n.* An imponder-able factor or circumstance. **—im·pon′der·a·bil′i·ty, im·pon′der·a·ble·ness** *n.* **—im·pon′der·a·bly** *adv.*

im·port[1] (*v.* im·pôrt′, -pōrt′, im′pôrt, -pōrt; *n.* im′pôrt, -pōrt) *v.t.* **1.** To bring or cause to be brought into a country from abroad for commercial purposes, as merchandise. **2.** To bring in from an outside source or another relationship; in-troduce. **3.** To have as its meaning; signify. — *n.* **1.** An imported commodity. **2.** The act of importing. **3.** That which is implied; meaning. [< F < L < *in-* + *portare* to carry] **—im·port′a·ble** *adj.* **—im·port′a·bil′i·ty** *n.*

im·port[2] (*n.* im′pôrt, -pōrt; *v.* im·pôrt′, -pōrt′) *n.* Impor-tance: a matter of no *import.* — *v.i.* To be of consequence; matter. [< F < Ital. < Med.L *importare* to be important]

im·por·tance (im·pôr′təns) *n.* **1.** The quality of being im-portant; consequence; significance. **2.** Worthiness of es-teem; standing: a man of *importance.* **3.** Pretentiousness.

im·por·tant (im·pôr′tənt) *adj.* **1.** Having much signifi-cance, value, or influence; outstanding; great. **2.** Deserving of special notice or attention; noteworthy. **3.** Having spe-cial relevance; mattering greatly: with *to.* **4.** Considering oneself worthy of high esteem or special attention; pompous. **—im·por′tant·ly** *adv.*

im·por·ta·tion (im′pôr·tā′shən, -pōr-) *n.* **1.** The act of im-porting. **2.** That which is imported.

im·port·er (im·pôr′tər, -pōr′-) *n.* One who is in the busi-ness of importing merchandise.

im·por·tu·nate (im·pôr′chə·nit) *adj.* **1.** Urgently or stub-bornly persistent in demand; insistent: an *importunate* credi-tor. **2.** Of a demand or request, repeatedly made; pressing. **—im·por′tu·nate·ly** *adv.* **—im·por′tu·nate·ness** *n.*

im·por·tune (im′pôr·tōōn′, -tyōōn′, im·pôr′chən) *v.* **·tuned, ·tun·ing** *v.t.* **1.** To harass with persistent demands or re-quests. **2.** To ask or beg for persistently or urgently. — *v.i.* **3.** To make persistent requests or demands. — *adj.* Im-portunate. [< F < L *importunus* not blowing towards port (of a wind), hence unfavorable] **—im′por·tune′ly** *adv.* **—im′por·tun′er** *n.*

im·por·tu·ni·ty (im′pôr·tōō′nə·tē, -tyōō′-) *n. pl.* **·ties 1.** Persistence in making demands or requests. **2.** *pl.* Repeated demands or requests.

im·pose (im·pōz′) *v.t.* **·posed, ·pos·ing 1.** To establish by authority as an obligation, penalty, etc.: to *impose* a fine. **2.** To inflict or enforce in an arbitrary or authoritarian man-ner. **3.** To force (oneself, one's company, etc.) upon others. **4.** To palm off as true or genuine; foist. **5.** *Eccl.* To lay on (hands), as in confirmation. **6.** *Printing* To arrange in cor-rect order in a form, as pages of type. **—to impose on** (or **upon**) **1.** To take advantage of; make unwarranted or un-fair use of. **2.** To deceive; cheat. [< F *im-* on + *poser* to put down] **—im·pos′a·ble** *adj.* **—im·pos′er** *n.*

im·pos·ing (im·pō′zing) *adj.* Impressive in appearance or manner; grand; stately. **—im·pos′ing·ly** *adv.*

im·po·si·tion (im′pə·zish′ən) *n.* **1.** The act of imposing or imposing on. **2.** That which is imposed, as a tax or an ex-cessive requirement. **3.** An act of trickery or deception. **4.** The laying on of hands, as in the religious ceremonies. [< L *impositio, -onis* < *impositus.* See IMPOST.]

im·pos·si·bil·i·ty (im·pos′ə·bil′ə·tē) *n. pl.* **·ties 1.** The quality of being impossible. **2.** Something impossible.

im·pos·si·ble (im·pos′ə·bəl) *adj.* **1.** Incapable of existing or taking place. **2.** Incapable of being done or put into prac-tice. **3.** Contrary to fact or reality; inconceivable. **4.** Not acceptable; objectionable; intolerable. [< F. See POSSIBLE.] **—im·pos′si·bly** *adv.*

im·post[1] (im′pōst) *n.* A tax or customs duty. — *v.t.* To classify (imported goods) for the purpose of determining cus-toms duties. [< OF < L < *in-* on + *ponere* to lay, place]

im·post[2] (im′pōst) *n. Archit.* The top section of a pillar or wall, serving as support for an arch. [See IMPOST.[1]]

im·pos·tor (im·pos′tər) *n.* One who deceives; esp., one who assumes the name of another. [< F < LL *impostor*]

im·pos·ture (im·pos′chər) *n.* Deception by means of false pretenses; esp., the act of posing under a false name.

im·po·tence (im′pə·təns) *n.* The condition or quality of being impotent; esp., an incapacity for sexual intercourse: said of males. Also **im′po·ten·cy.** [< OF < L *impotentia*]

im·po·tent (im′pə·tənt) *adj.* **1.** Powerless to act or to accomplish anything. **2.** Physically weak. **3.** Incapable of sexual intercourse: said of males. **—im′po·tent·ly** *adv.*

im·pound (im·pound′) *v.t.* **1.** To shut up in a pound, as a stray dog. **2.** To place in legal custody. **3.** To collect (water) for irrigation. **—im·pound′age** (-poun′dij) *n.*

im·pov·er·ish (im·pov′ər·ish) *v.t.* **1.** To reduce to poverty. **2.** To exhaust the fertility of, as soil. [< OF < L *pauperare* to impoverish] **—im·pov′er·ish·ment** *n.*

im·pow·er (im·pou′ər) See EMPOWER.

im·prac·ti·ca·ble (im·prak′ti·kə·bəl) *adj.* **1.** Incapable of being carried out or put into effect; not feasible. **2.** Incapable of being used for an intended purpose. **3.** Hard to get on with; intractable. **—im·prac′ti·ca·bil′i·ty, im·prac′ti·ca·ble·ness** *n.* **—im·prac′ti·ca·bly** *adv.*

im·prac·ti·cal (im·prak′ti·kəl) *adj.* Not practical. **—im·prac′ti·cal′i·ty** (-kal′ə·tē) *n.*

im·pre·cate (im′prə·kāt) *v.t.* **·cat·ed, ·cat·ing** To invoke or call down (some curse or calamity): to *imprecate* evil upon a person. [< L < *in-* on + *precari* to pray] **—im′pre·ca′tor** *n.* **—im′pre·ca·to′ry** (-kə·tôr′ē, -tō′rē) *adj.*

im·pre·ca·tion (im′prə·kā′shən) *n.* **1.** The act of imprecating. **2.** A malediction; curse.

im·preg·na·ble (im·preg′nə·bəl) *adj.* **1.** Incapable of being taken by force. **2.** Incapable of being overcome; unyielding. [< OF < *im-* not + *prendre* to take] **—im·preg′na·bil′i·ty** *n.* **—im·preg′na·bly** *adv.*

im·preg·nate (im·preg′nāt) *v.t.* **·nat·ed, ·nat·ing** **1.** To make pregnant. **2.** To fertilize, as an ovum. **3.** To saturate or permeate. **4.** To fill or imbue, as with ideas, etc. **—** *adj.* Made pregnant. [< LL < L *in-* in + *praegnans* pregnant] **—im′preg·na′tion** *n.* **—im·preg′na·tor** *n.*

im·pre·sa·ri·o (im′prə·sä′rē·ō) *n. pl.* **·sa·ri·os** or **·sa·ri** (-sä′rē) One who manages or sponsors performers or performances for entertainment. [< Ital. *impresa* enterprise]

im·press[1] (*v.* im·pres′; *n.* im′pres) *v.t.* **1.** To produce a marked effect upon the mind or feelings of; influence. **2.** To establish firmly in the mind, as ideas, beliefs, etc. **3.** To form or make (an imprint or mark) by pressure; stamp. **4.** To form or make an imprint or mark upon. **5.** *Electr.* To establish (a voltage) in a conductor or circuit. **—** *n.* **1.** The act or process of impressing. **2.** A mark, indentation, or design produced by pressure. **3.** Distinctive character or mark; stamp. [< L < *in-* on + *premere* to press] **—im·press′er** *n.*

im·press[2] (*v.* im·pres′; *n.* im′pres) *v.t.* **1.** To force to enter public service, esp. naval service. **2.** To seize (property) for public use. **—** *n.* The act of impressing; impressment. **—im·press′er** *n.* **—im·press′ment** *n.*

im·press·i·ble (im·pres′ə·bəl) *adj.* Capable of being impressed or of receiving an impression; susceptible. **—im·press′i·bil′i·ty, im·press′i·ble·ness** *n.* **—im·press′i·bly** *adv.*

im·pres·sion (im·presh′ən) *n.* **1.** An effect produced on the mind, the senses, or the feelings. **2.** A vague remembrance or uncertain belief. **3.** A material change produced by any agency. **4.** A mark made by pressure. **5.** The act or process of impressing. **6.** *Printing* **a** The act or result of pressing type or plates to paper. **b** The total number of copies of a publication printed at one time; also, a single copy: distinguished from *edition.* [< OF < L *impressio, -onis*]

im·pres·sion·a·ble (im·presh′ən·ə·bəl) *adj.* Highly receptive to impressions; readily influenced or molded; sensitive. [< F] **—im·pres′sion·a·bil′i·ty, im·pres′sion·a·ble·ness** *n.*

im·pres·sion·ism (im·presh′ən·iz′əm) *n.* **1.** In art, a theory of painting, developed in the 19th century, that attempted to produce, by simulating the appearance of light, etc., the impressions made by the subject on the artist. **2.** In literature, the presenting of the most arresting aspects of character, emotion, etc., with relatively little realistic detail. **3.** In music, a style of composition, developed by Debussy and Ravel, that attempted to create impressions or moods. **—im·pres′sion·ist** *n. & adj.* **—im·pres′sion·is′tic** *adj.*

im·pres·sive (im·pres′iv) *adj.* Producing or tending to produce an impression; exciting emotion or admiration. **—im·pres′sive·ly** *adv.* **—im·pres′sive·ness** *n.*

im·pri·ma·tur (im′pri·mā′tər, -mä′-) *n.* **1.** Official license or approval for publication of a literary work, esp. that granted by a censor or by the Roman Catholic Church. **2.** Authorization in general. [< L, let it be printed.]

im·print (*v.* im·print′; *n.* im′print) *v.t.* **1.** To produce (a figure, mark, etc.) by pressure. **2.** To mark or produce a mark on, as with a stamp or seal. **3.** To fix firmly in the heart, mind, etc. **—** *n.* **1.** A mark or indentation made by printing, stamping, or pressing. **2.** Characteristic eff impression; stamp. **3.** The name of the publisher, plac publication, date of issue, etc., printed in a book usu. on title page. [< OF < L < *in-* in + *premere* to press]

im·pris·on (im·priz′ən) *v.t.* **1.** To put into a prison; hol confinement. **2.** To confine or restrain forcibly, as in a sr space, tight garment etc. **—im·pris′on·ment** *n.*

im·prob·a·bil·i·ty (im′prob·ə·bil′ə·tē, im·prob′-) *n. pl.* · **1.** The quality of being improbable; unlikelihood. **2.** unlikely circumstance, event, or result.

im·prob·a·ble (im·prob′ə·bəl) *adj.* Not probable; not lik to be true or not reasonably to be expected. **—im·prob ble·ness** *n.* **—im·prob′a·bly** *adv.*

im·promp·tu (im·promp′tōō, -tyōō) *adj.* Made, done uttered on the spur of the moment. **—** *n.* Anything p duced on the impulse of the moment. **—** *adv.* With preparation. [< F < L *in promptu* in readiness]

im·prop·er (im·prop′ər) *adj.* **1.** Deviating from fact, tru or established usage. **2.** Not conforming to accepted sta ards of conduct or good taste. **3.** Unsuitable. **—im·pr er·ly** *adv.* **—im·prop′er·ness** *n.*

improper fraction *Math.* A fraction in which the nume tor exceeds the denominator.

im·pro·pri·e·ty (im′prə·prī′ə·tē) *n. pl.* **·ties** **1.** The qua of being improper. **2.** An improper action. **3.** An impro usage in speech or writing.

im·prove (im·prōōv′) *v.* **·proved, ·prov·ing** *v.t.* **1.** To ra to a higher or more desirable quality, value, or conditi make better. **2.** *U.S.* To increase the value or profit of land. **3.** To use to good advantage; utilize. **—** *v.i.* **4.** become better. **—to improve on** (or **upon**) To do or p duce something better than. [< AF < OF *en-* into + *p* profit] **—im·prov′a·bil′i·ty, im·prov′a·ble·ness** *n.* **—i prov′a·ble** *adj.* **—im·prov′a·bly** *adv.* **—im·prov′er** *n.*

im·prove·ment (im·prōōv′mənt) *n.* **1.** The act of maki better, or the state of becoming better. **2.** A modification addition by means of which a thing's excellence or value increased. **3.** A person, thing, or process that constitutes advance in excellence. **4.** Advantageous use.

im·prov·i·dent (im·prov′ə·dənt) *adj.* **1.** Lacking foresig incautious; rash. **2.** Taking no thought of future nee thriftless. **—im·prov′i·dence** *n.* **—im·prov′i·dent·ly** *a*

im·pro·vi·sa·to·ry (im′prə·vī′zə·tôr′ē, -tō′rē) *adj.* **1.** Of pertaining to an improviser. **2.** Of the nature of improvis tion. Also **im·prov·i·sa·to·ri·al** (im·prov′ə·zə·tôr′ē·əl, -tō′r

im·pro·vise (im′prə·vīz) *v.* **·vised, ·vis·ing** *v.t.* **1.** To p duce (music, verse, drama, etc.) without previous thought preparation. **2.** To contrive or construct from whate comes to hand. **—** *v.i.* **3.** To produce anything extem raneously. [< F < Ital. < L < *in-* not + *providere* to fo see] **—im·pro·vi·sa·tion** (im′prə·vī·zā′shən, im′prov·ə-) **—im·pro′vi·sa′tion·al** *adj.* **—im·pro·vis′er, im′prov·i·sa·** (im·prov′ə·zā′tər, im′prə·vī-) *n.*

im·pru·dent (im·prōōd′nt) *adj.* Not prudent; lacking d cretion; unwise. **—im·pru′dence** *n.*

im·pu·dence (im′pyə·dəns) *n.* **1.** The quality of being i pudent; offensive boldness. **2.** Impudent speech or condu Also **im′pu·den·cy.**

im·pu·dent (im′pyə·dənt) *adj.* Offensively bold; insolent assured; saucy; brazen. [< OF < L < *in-* not + *pude* modest] **—im′pu·dent·ly** *adv.*

im·pugn (im·pyōōn′) *v.t.* To attack (a statement, motiv etc.) with criticism or arguments; dispute the truth of. [OF < L *in-* against + *pugnare* to strike, fight] **—im·pug a·ble** *adj.* **—im·pug·na·tion** (im′pəg·nā′shən), **im·pug ment** *n.* **—im·pugn′er** (im·pyōō′nər) *n.*

im·pulse (im′puls) *n.* **1.** A brief exertion or communic tion of force tending to produce motion. **2.** The motion pr duced. **3.** A sudden, unreasoned inclination to action, oft induced by an emotion, etc. **4.** *Physiol.* The transference a stimulus through a nerve fiber. [See IMPEL.]

im·pul·sion (im·pul′shən) *n.* **1.** The act of impelling, or t state of being impelled. **2.** An impelling force.

im·pul·sive (im·pul′siv) *adj.* **1.** Actuated by impul rather than by reflection. **2.** Prompted by impulse; spo taneous; unpremeditated. **3.** Having the power of inciti to action. **—im·pul′sive·ly** *adv.* **—im·pul′sive·ness** *n.*

im·pu·ni·ty (im·pyōō′nə·tē) *n. pl.* **·ties** Freedom or exem tion from punishment, harm, or unpleasant consequence. [L *in-* not + *poena* punishment]

im·pure (im·pyŏŏr′) *adj.* **1.** Containing something offe sive or contaminating. **2.** Mixed with an inferior or wort less substance, adulterated. **3.** Contrary to moral purit sinful. **4.** Not for religious use. **5.** Having the characte istics of more than one style, period, color, language, et mixed. **—im·pure′ly** *adv.* **—im·pure′ness** *n.*

im·pu·ri·ty (im·pyŏŏr′ə·tē) *n. pl.* **·ties** **1.** The state quality of being impure. **2.** That which is impure.

im·put·a·ble (im·pyōō′tə·bəl) *adj.* Capable of being im puted; ascribable; chargeable. **—im·put′a·bil′i·ty, im·pu a·ble·ness** *n.* **—im·put′a·bly** *adv.*

ɔu·ta·tion (im′pyōō·tā′shən) *n.* **1.** The act of imput; accusation. **2.** That which is imputed or charged.

ɔu·ta·tive (im·pyōō′tə·tiv) *adj.* **1.** Transferred or trans:ted by imputation; imputed. **2.** Tending to impute. — **pu′ta·tive·ly** *adv.*

ɔute (im·pyōōt′) *v.t.* **·put·ed, ·put·ing** **1.** To attribute fault, crime, etc.) to a person; charge. **2.** To consider as cause or source of; ascribe: with *to.* — **Syn.** See ATTRIB:. [< OF < L < *in-* in + *putare* to reckon]

n) *prep.* **1.** Held by or within the confines of; enclosed apples *in* a bag. **2.** Surrounded by; amidst: buried *in* mud. **3.** Within the limits of: sightseeing *in* Paris. **4.** :hin the range or scope of: He said it *in* my hearing. **5.** :hin the category, class, or number of; included as a mem- of; belonging to: twelve inches *in* a foot; *in* the best so- ty. **6.** Existing as a part, characteristic, or property of: :he works of Shaw. **7.** Affecting: dust *in* one's eye. **8.** aring; covered by; decorated with: a man *in* a straw hat. Made of a specified color, style, or material. **10.** Ar- ged, disposed, or proceeding so as to form: trees *in* a row. . Engaged at; occupied by: *in* business. **12.** For the ·pose of: to run *in* pursuit. **13.** By means of: speaking *in* ispers. **14.** According to: *In* my opinion. **15.** With re- d or respect to: Students vary *in* talent. **16.** Affected ; under the influence of: to shout *in* rage. **17.** During: a cert given *in* the evening. — **Syn.** See AT. — **in that** · the reason that; because; since. — *adv.* **1.** To or toward inside from the outside: Please come *in.* **2.** In one's ne, place of business, etc.: We stayed *in* all day. **3.** In or ɔ some activity or office; to join *in.* **4.** Into some place, ıdition, or position: Tuck the baby *in.* **5.** Into some lerstood substance, object, etc.: Blend *in* the oil. — **to be or** *Informal* To be certain to experience (usu. something ɔleasant). — **to have it in for** *Informal* To hold a grudge iinst. — *adj.* **1.** That is in or remains within. **2.** That gained power or control: the *in* group. **3.** Coming or ding in: the *in* door. — *n.* **1.** A member of the group in wer or at an advantage. **2.** *Informal* A means of entrance ıccess; also, a position of favor or influence: to have an *in.* **ins and outs** The full complexities or particulars: the *ins l outs* of a business. — *v.t.* **inned, in·ning** To enclose, as d. [OE]

prefix Not; without; un-; non-. Also: *i-* before *gn,* as in *ore*; *il-* before *l,* as in *illiterate*; *im-* before *b, m, p,* as in *im- ance, immiscible, impecunious*; *ir-* before *r,* as in *irresist- ?.* ◆ See note under UN-². [< L]

prefix In; into; on; within; toward: *include, incur, in- 'e*: also used intensively, as in *inflame,* or without percep- le force. Also *il-* before *l,* as in *illuminate*; *im-* before *b, m,* as in *imbibe, immigrate, impress*; *ir-* before *r,* as in *irradi-* . [< OE *in*; sometimes < L *in-* in, prep.]

suffix Chem. Occasionally used to denote neutral com- ınds, as fats, proteins, and glycerides: *stearin, albumin, thin.* Also *-ein.* [Var. of -INE²]

.bil·i·ty (in′ə·bil′ə·tē) *n.* The state or quality of being able; lack of the necessary power or means.

ıb·sen·ti·a (in ab·sen′shē·ə, -shə) *Latin* In absence (of person concerned).

ıc·ces·si·ble (in′ak·ses′ə·bəl) *adj.* Not accessible; in- ɔable of being reached or closely approached. — **in′ac· s′si·bil′i·ty, in′ac·ces′i·ble·ness** *n.* — **in′ac·ces′si·bly** *adv.*

ıc·cu·ra·cy (in·ak′yər·ə·sē) *n. pl.* **·cies** **1.** The state or ality of being inaccurate. **2.** An error; mistake.

ıc·cu·rate (in·ak′yər·it) *adj.* Not accurate; inexact; in- ·rect. — **in·ac′cu·rate·ly** *adv.* — **in·ac′cu·rate·ness** *n.*

ıc·tion (in·ak′shən) *n.* Absence of action; idleness.

ıc·ti·vate (in·ak′tə·vāt) *v.t.* **·vat·ed, ·vat·ing** To make ıctive. — **in·ac′ti·va′tion** *n.*

ıc·tive (in·ak′tiv) *adj.* **1.** Characterized by inaction; e; inert. **2.** Marked by absence of effort or action; in- lent. **3.** *Mil.* Not mobilized. — **in·ac′tive·ly** *adv.* — **in· ·tiv·i·ty** (in′ak·tiv′ə·tē), **in·ac′tive·ness** *n.*

ıd·e·qua·cy (in·ad′ə·kwə·sē) *n. pl.* **·cies** **1.** The state quality of being inadequate; insufficiency. **2.** A defect.

ıd·e·quate (in·ad′ə·kwit) *adj.* Not adequate; not equal that which is required; insufficient. — **in·ad′e·quate·ly** *v.* — **in·ad′e·quate·ness** *n.*

ıd·mis·si·ble (in′əd·mis′ə·bəl) *adj.* Not admissible; not be considered, approved, or allowed. — **in′ad·mis′si·bil′i· n.** — **in′ad·mis′si·bly** *adv.*

ıd·ver·tence (in′əd·vûr′təns) *n.* **1.** The fact or quality being inadvertent; lack of due care or attention. **2.** A re- lt of inattention; oversight. Also **in′ad·ver′ten·cy.**

ıd·ver·tent (in′əd·vûr′tənt) *adj.* **1.** Not exercising due re or consideration; negligent. **2.** Resulting from inatten- n or oversight; unintentional. — **in′ad·ver′tent·ly** *adv.*

ıd·vis·a·ble (in′əd·vī′zə·bəl) *adj.* Not advisable; injudi- ɔus; unwise. — **in′ad·vis′a·bil′i·ty** *n.*

-inae *suffix Zool.* Used in the names of subfamilies: *Cervinae.* [< NL < L, fem. pl. of *-inus,* adj. suffix]

in·al·ien·a·ble (in·āl′yən·ə·bəl) *adj.* Not transferable; that cannot be rightfully taken away. — **in·al′ien·a·bil′i·ty** *n.* — **in·al′ien·a·bly** *adv.*

in·am·o·ra·ta (in·am′ə·rä′tə, in′am-) *n. pl.* **·tas** A woman who is loved or in love. [< Ital. < *in-* in + *amore* love]

in·ane (in·ān′) *adj.* **1.** Lacking in sense; empty-headed; silly. **2.** Empty of meaning; pointless. [< L *inanis* empty] — **in·ane′ly** *adv.*

in·an·i·mate (in·an′ə·mit) *adj.* **1.** Not living or animate. **2.** Lacking animation; torpid; spiritless. — **in·an′i·mate·ly** *adv.* — **in·an′i·mate·ness** *n.*

in·a·ni·tion (in′ə·nish′ən) *n.* **1.** Exhaustion caused by lack of nourishment or inability to assimilate food. **2.** Emptiness. [< F < LL < L *inanire* to empty]

in·an·i·ty (in·an′ə·tē) *n. pl.* **·ties** **1.** Lack of sense or meaning; silliness; foolishness. **2.** A foolish remark, action, etc. **3.** Emptiness. [< OF < L *inanis* empty]

in·ap·pli·ca·ble (in·ap′li·kə·bəl) *adj.* Not applicable; irrelevant; unsuitable. — **in·ap′pli·ca·bil′i·ty, in·ap′pli·ca·ble·ness** *n.* — **in·ap′pli·ca·bly** *adv.*

in·ap·po·site (in·ap′ə·zit) *adj.* Not pertinent or suitable. — **in·ap′po·site·ly** *adv.*

in·ap·pre·ci·a·ble (in′ə·prē′shē·ə·bəl, -shə·bəl) *adj.* Imperceptible; unnoticeable. — **in′ap·pre′ci·a·bly** *adv.*

in·ap·pro·pri·ate (in′ə·prō′prē·it) *adj.* Not appropriate; unsuitable; unfitting. — **in′ap·pro′pri·ate·ly** *adv.* — **in′ap·pro′pri·ate·ness** *n.*

in·apt (in·apt′) *adj.* **1.** Not apt or fit. **2.** Lacking skill or aptitude; inept; clumsy. — **in·apt′ly** *adv.* — **in·apt′ness** *n.*

in·ap·ti·tude (in·ap′tə·tōōd, -tyōōd) *n.* **1.** Lack of skill. **2.** Unsuitability.

in·ar·tic·u·late (in′är·tik′yə·lit) *adj.* **1.** Uttered without the distinct sounds of spoken language: *inarticulate* cries. **2.** Incapable of speech; dumb. **3.** Unable to speak coherently. **4.** Unspoken; unexpressed: *inarticulate* grief. **5.** *Zool.* Not segmented, as certain worms. — **in′ar·tic′u·late·ly** *adv.* — **in′ar·tic′u·late·ness** *n.*

in·ar·tis·tic (in′är·tis′tik) *adj.* **1.** Contrary to the principles of art; made or done without skill or taste. **2.** Lacking in artistic ability. — **in′ar·tis′ti·cal·ly** *adv.*

in·as·much as (in′əz·much′) **1.** Considering the fact that; seeing that; because. **2.** Insofar as; according as.

in·at·ten·tion (in′ə·ten′shən) *n.* Lack of attention.

in·at·ten·tive (in′ə·ten′tiv) *adj.* Not attentive; heedless. — **in′at·ten′tive·ly** *adv.* — **in′at·ten′tive·ness** *n.*

in·au·di·ble (in·ô′də·bəl) *adj.* Incapable of being heard. — **in·au′di·bil′i·ty, in·au′di·ble·ness** *n.* — **in·au′di·bly** *adv.*

in·au·gu·ral (in·ô′gyər·əl) *adj.* Of or pertaining to an inauguration. — *n.* A speech made at an inauguration.

in·au·gu·rate (in·ô′gyə·rāt) *v.t.* **·rat·ed, ·rat·ing** **1.** To begin or commence upon formally; initiate. **2.** To induct into office with formal ceremony. **3.** To celebrate the public opening of. [< L *inaugurare* to take omens, consecrate, install] — **in·au′gu·ra′tion** *n.* — **in·au′gu·ra′tor** *n.*

Inauguration Day The day (January 20th) on which the inauguration of the President of the United States takes place.

in·aus·pi·cious (in′ô·spish′əs) *adj.* Not auspicious; ill-omened; unfavorable. — **in′aus·pi′cious·ly** *adv.* — **in′aus·pi′cious·ness** *n.*

in·board (in′bôrd′, -bōrd′) *adj. & adv.* **1.** *Naut.* **a** Inside the hull. **b** Toward the center line of a vessel. **2.** *Aeron.* Inward from the tip of an airfoil; close to the fuselage.

in·born (in′bôrn′) *adj.* Implanted by nature; existing from birth; natural; inherent.

in·bound (in′bound′) *adj.* Approaching a destination.

in·bred (in′bred′; *for def. 2, also* in′bred′) *adj.* **1.** Inborn; innate. **2.** Produced by inbreeding; also, bred in-and-in.

in·breed (in′brēd′, in′brēd′) *v.t.* **·bred, ·breed·ing** To breed by continual mating of closely related stock.

In·ca (ing′kə) *n.* A member of a group of Quechuan Indian tribes dominant in Peru at the time of the Spanish conquest. [< Sp. < Quechua *ynca* royal prince]

in·cal·cu·la·ble (in·kal′kyə·lə·bəl) *adj.* **1.** Incapable of being calculated. **2.** Unpredictable. — **in·cal′cu·la·bil′i·ty** *n.* — **in·cal′cu·la·bly** *adv.*

in cam·er·a (in kam′ər·ə) In closed or secret session; privately. [< L, in a room]

In·can (ing′kən) *adj.* Of or pertaining to the Incas, their culture, or their empire. — *n.* **1.** An Inca. **2.** The language of the Incas; Quechua.

in·can·desce (in′kən·des′) *v.t. & v.i.* **·desced, ·desc·ing** To be or become, or cause to become, luminous with heat.

in·can·des·cent (in′kən·des′ənt) *adj.* **1.** Luminous or glowing with intense heat. **2.** Shining with intense brilliance. — **in′can·des′cence, in′can·des′cen·cy** *n.* — **in′can·des′cent·ly** *adv.*

incandescent lamp A lamp having a filament that is heated to incandescence by an electric current.

in·can·ta·tion (in′kan·tā′shən) *n.* **1.** The uttering or intoning of words or syllables supposed to produce magical results. **2.** The magic words or formula so uttered. [< F < L *incantare* to make an incantation]

in·ca·pa·ble (in·kā′pə·bəl) *adj.* **1.** Lacking in natural ability, power, or capacity; incompetent. **2.** *Law* Not legally qualified. **— incapable of 1.** Lacking the necessary ability or fitness for. **2.** Of such a nature or condition as not to allow or admit of: *incapable of* deceit. **—** *n.* A totally incompetent person. **— in·ca′pa·bil′i·ty, in·ca′pa·ble·ness** *n.* **— in·ca′pa·bly** *adv.*

in·ca·pac·i·tate (in′kə·pas′ə·tāt) *v.t.* **·tat·ed, ·tat·ing 1.** To disable, as for normal physical activity. **2.** *Law* To deprive of legal capacity; disqualify. **— in′ca·pac′i·ta′tion** *n.*

in·ca·pac·i·ty (in′kə·pas′ə·tē) *n. pl.* **·ties 1.** Lack of ability, power, or fitness; disability. **2.** *Law* A condition or circumstance that legally disqualifies.

in·cap·su·late (in·kap′sə·lāt, -syŏŏ-) *v.t.* **·lat·ed, ·lat·ing** To enclose as in a capsule.

in·car·cer·ate (*v.* in·kär′sə·rāt; *adj.* in·kär′sər·it, -sə·rāt) *v.t.* **·at·ed, ·at·ing 1.** To put in prison; imprison. **2.** To confine; enclose. **—** *adj.* Imprisoned. [< Med.L < L *in-* in + *carcer* jail] **— in·car′cer·a′tion** *n.* **— in·car′cer·a′tor** *n.*

in·car·na·dine (in·kär′nə·dīn, -din) *adj.* **1.** Flesh-colored; pale red; pink. **2.** Blood-red; crimson. **—** *n.* An incarnadine color. **—** *v.t.* **·dined, ·din·ing** To color deep red or flesh-color. [< F < Ital. *incarnato* flesh-colored]

in·car·nate (*adj.* in·kär′nit; *v.* in·kär′nāt) *adj.* **1.** Embodied in flesh, esp. in human form: a fiend *incarnate.* **2.** Personified; exemplified: cruelty *incarnate.* **—** *v.t.* **·nat·ed, ·nat·ing 1.** To give bodily form to. **2.** To invest with concrete shape or form. [< LL < L *in-* in + *caro, carnis* flesh]

in·car·na·tion (in′kär·nā′shən) *n.* **1.** The assumption of bodily form, esp. human form. **2.** *Often cap.* The assumption by Jesus Christ of the human form and condition. **3.** The bodily form assumed by a deity. **4.** A person, animal, or thing in which some ideal or quality is incarnated.

in·case (in·kās′) *v.t.* **·cased, ·cas·ing** To enclose in or as in a case: also spelled *encase.* **— in·case′ment** *n.*

in·cau·tion (in·kô′shən) *n.* Lack of caution; carelessness.

in·cau·tious (in·kô′shəs) *adj.* Lacking in caution; heedless; imprudent. **— in·cau′tious·ly** *adv.* **— in·cau′tious·ness** *n.*

in·cen·di·ar·y (in·sen′dē·er′ē) *adj.* **1.** Of or pertaining to the malicious burning of property. **2.** Inciting to riot, rebellion, etc.; inflammatory. **3.** Capable of generating intense heat. **—** *n. pl.* **·ar·ies 1.** One who maliciously sets fire to property. **2.** One who stirs up mob violence, etc. **3.** An incendiary bomb. [< L *incendere* to set on fire] **— in·cen′di·a·rism** (-ə·riz·əm) *n.*

incendiary bomb A bomb designed to start a fire.

in·cense[1] (in·sens′) *v.t.* **·censed, ·cens·ing** To inflame with anger; enrage. [< OF < L *incendere* to set on fire]

in·cense[2] (in′sens) *n.* **1.** An aromatic substance that gives off an agreeable odor when burned. **2.** The odor or smoke produced in burning such a substance. **3.** Any pleasant fragrance or aroma. **—** *v.* **·censed, ·cens·ing** *v.t.* **1.** To perfume with incense. **2.** To burn incense to. **—** *v.i.* **3.** To burn incense. [< OF < L *incendere* to set on fire]

in·cen·tive (in·sen′tiv) *n.* That which incites, or tends to incite, to action; motivating force. **—** *adj.* Serving to incite to action. [< L *in-* in + *canere* to sing]

in·cep·tion (in·sep′shən) *n.* Beginning, as of an undertaking; start. [< L *incipere* to begin]

in·cep·tive (in·sep′tiv) *adj.* **1.** Beginning; incipient; initial. **2.** *Gram.* Denoting the beginning of an action, as certain verbs. **—** *n. Gram.* An inceptive word or construction.

in·cer·ti·tude (in·sûr′tə·tōōd, -tyōōd) *n.* **1.** Uncertainty; doubtfulness; indecisiveness. **2.** Insecurity.

in·ces·sant (in·ses′ənt) *adj.* Continuing without interruption; never ceasing. [< LL < L *in-* not + *cessare* to cease] **— in·ces′san·cy** *n.* **— in·ces′sant·ly** *adv.*

in·cest (in′sest) *n.* Sexual intercourse between persons so closely related that marriage between them is forbidden by law or taboo. [< L < *in-* not + *castus* chaste]

in·ces·tu·ous (in·ses′chōō·əs) *adj.* **1.** Guilty of incest. **2.** Involving incest. **— in·ces′tu·ous·ly** *adv.*

inch (inch) *n.* **1.** A measure of length equal to the twelfth part of a foot: symbol ″. Abbr. *in.* See table front of book. **2.** *Meteorol.* **a** The amount of rainfall or snowfall capable of covering a level surface to the depth of one inch. **b** A unit of atmospheric pressure expressed by an inch of the mercury column of a barometer. **3.** A very small distance, quantity, or degree. **— every inch** In every way; completely. **—** *v.t. & v.i.* To move or advance by inches or small degrees. [OE < L *uncia* the twelfth part, inch, ounce]

inch·meal (inch′mēl′) *adv.* Inch by inch.

in·cho·ate (in·kō′it) *adj.* **1.** In an early or rudimentary stage. **2.** Lacking order, form, coherence, etc. [< L *incohare* to begin] **— in·cho′ate·ly** *adv.* **— in·cho′ate·ness** *n.*

in·cho·a·tive (in·kō′ə·tiv) *adj.* **1.** *Gram.* Inceptive. **2.** *Rare* Inchoate. **—** *n. Gram.* An inceptive.

inch·worm (inch′wûrm′) *n.* A measuring worm.

in·ci·dence (in′sə·dəns) *n.* **1.** The degree of occurrenc effect: a high *incidence* of illiteracy. **2.** The act or ma of falling on, impinging upon, or affecting something.

in·ci·dent (in′sə·dənt) *n.* **1.** A distinct event or piece o tion. **2.** A minor episode or event. **—** *adj.* **1.** Naturall usu. appertaining or attending: with *to*: the dangers *inci* to travel. **2.** Attached as a subsidiary. **3.** Falling or s ing: *incident* rays of light. [< F < L *in-* on + *cadere* to

in·ci·den·tal (in′sə·den′təl) *adj.* **1.** Occurring in the co of something. **2.** Naturally or usually attending: wit problems *incidental* to adolescence. **3.** Minor; second *incidental* expenses. **—** *n.* **1.** An incidental circumstan event. **2.** *pl.* Minor or casual expenses or items.

in·ci·den·tal·ly (in′sə·den′təl·ē; *for def. 2, also* in′sə·den *adv,* **1.** As a subordinate, casual, or chance occurrence a with something else: The book *incidentally* contains s valuable references. **2.** By the by; by the way.

in·cin·er·ate (in·sin′ə·rāt) *v.t.* **·at·ed, ·at·ing** To cons with fire; reduce to ashes; cremate. [< Med.L < *in-* i *cinis, cineris* ashes] **— in·cin′er·a′tion** *n.*

in·cin·er·a·tor (in·sin′ə·rā′tər) *n.* An apparatus for b ing refuse or for cremating.

in·cip·i·ent (in·sip′ē·ənt) *adj.* Coming into existence; beginning to appear. [< L *incipere* to begin] **— in·c ence, in·cip′i·en·cy** *n.* **— in·cip′i·ent·ly** *adv.*

in·cise (in·sīz′) *v.t.* **·cised, ·cis·ing 1.** To cut into, or marks upon, with a sharp instrument. **2.** To engr carve. [< OF < L *in-* in + *caedere* to cut] **— in·cised′**

in·ci·sion (in·sizh′ən) *n.* **1.** The act of incising. **2.** A gash. **3.** *Surg.* A cut made in soft tissue. **4.** Incisive c ity; acuteness. [< OF < L *incisio, -onis*]

in·ci·sive (in·sī′siv) *adj.* **1.** Sharp; keen; penetrating *incisive* mind. **2.** Cutting; biting; sarcastic. [< Med.I *cisivus*] **— in·ci′sive·ly** *adv.* **— in·ci′sive·ness** *n.*

in·ci·sor (in·sī′zər) *n.* A front tooth adapted for cuttin man, one of eight such teeth, four in each jaw. For illus TOOTH. [< NL]

in·cite (in·sīt′) *v.t.* **·cit·ed, ·cit·ing** To spur to action; on; instigate. [< OF < L < *in-* thoroughly + *cita* rouse] **— in′ci·ta′tion** *n.* **— in·cite′ment** *n.* **— in·cit′e**

in·ci·vil·i·ty (in′sə·vil′ə·tē) *n. pl.* **·ties 1.** The state or q ity of being uncivil; discourtesy. **2.** An uncivil or rude

in·clem·ent (in·klem′ənt) *adj.* **1.** Of the weather, sev stormy. **2.** Without mercy; harsh. [< L *inclemens, -e* **— in·clem′en·cy** (-ən·sē) *n.* **— in·clem′ent·ly** *adv.*

in·cli·na·tion (in′klə·nā′shən) *n.* **1.** A personal leanin bent; liking. **2.** A tendency toward a state or condit trend. **3.** An activity, state, etc., toward which one is clined. **4.** The act of inclining, or the state of being incli **5.** Deviation or degree of deviation from the vertica horizontal; slope. **6.** A sloping surface. **7.** *Geom.* The gle formed between two intersecting lines, planes, etc. **in′cli·na′tion·al, in·cli·na·to·ry** (in·klī′nə·tôr′ē) *adj.*

in·cline (*v.* in·klīn′; *n.* in′klīn, in·klīn′) *v.* **·clined, ·clin** *v.i.* **1.** To diverge from the horizontal or vertical; sl slope. **2.** To have a bent or preference; be disposed. **3.** tend in some quality or degree: purple *inclining* toward b **4.** To bend the head or body, as in courtesy; bow. **— 5.** To cause to bend, lean, or slope. **6.** To impart a te ency or leaning to (a person); dispose; influence. **7.** To or nod, as the head. **—** *n.* An inclined plane or surf gradient; slope. [< OF < L < *in-* on + *clinare* to lean] **in·clin′a·ble** *adj.* **— in·clin′er** *n.*

in·clined (in·klīnd′) *adj.* **1.** Having a tendency or incl tion; disposed. **2.** Sloping; bent. **3.** Bending or inters ing so as to form an angle with another line, plane, etc.

inclined plane A plane forming any but a right angle v a horizontal plane.

in·cli·nom·e·ter (in′klə·nom′ə·tər) *n.* An instrument measuring the attitude or tilt of an aircraft, ship, etc., v relation to the horizontal.

in·close (in·klōz′), **in·clo·sure** (in·klō′zhər) See ENCLO etc.

in·clude (in·klōōd′) *v.t.* **·clud·ed, ·clud·ing 1.** To have component part or parts; comprise; contain. **2.** To plac a general category, group, etc.; consider in a reckoning. To have or involve as a subordinate part, quality, etc.; ply. [< L < *in-* in + *claudere* to shut] **— in·clud′a·bl in·clud′i·ble** *adj.*

in·clu·sion (in·klōō′zhən) *n.* **1.** The act of including, or state of being included. **2.** That which is included.

in·clu·sive (in·klōō′siv) *adj.* **1.** Including: with *of.* **2.** cluding the limits specified: from 1959 to 1964 *inclusive.* Comprehensive: an *inclusive* report. [< Med.L *inclusiv* **— in·clu′sive·ly** *adv.* **— in·clu′sive·ness** *n.*

in·cog·ni·to (in·kog′nə·tō, in′kog·nē′tō) *adj. & adv.* Un an assumed name or identity, esp. so as to avoid recognit or attention; in disguise. **—** *n. pl.* **·tos** (-tōz) **1.** The st being incognito. **2.** The name or disguise assumed by ne who is incognito. **3.** One who takes on an assumed ame or identity. [< Ital. < L < *in-* not + *cognitus*, pp. of *gnoscere* to know] **— in·cog′ni·ta** (-tə) *n. & adj. fem.*

cog·ni·zant (in·kog′nə·zənt) *adj.* Not cognizant; unaare; with *of.* **— in·cog′ni·zance** *n.*

co·her·ence (in′kō·hir′əns) *n.* **1.** The state of being inherent. **2.** That which is incoherent. Also **in′co·her′en·cy.**

co·her·ent (in′kō·hir′ənt) *adj.* **1.** Lacking in logical conction; confused: an *incoherent* speech. **2.** Unable to think early or express oneself logically. **3.** Consisting of parts or gredients that do not stick together; loose: an *incoherent* ass. **4.** Lacking in agreement or harmony; disorganized. **- in′co·her′ent·ly** *adv.* **— in′co·her′ent·ness** *n.*

com·bus·ti·ble (in′kəm·bus′tə·bəl) *adj.* Incapable of ing burned; not flammable. **—** *n.* An incombustible subance or material. **— in′com·bus′ti·bil′i·ty, in′com·bus′ti·e·ness** *n.* **— in′com·bus′ti·bly** *adv.*

come (in′kum) *n.* Money, or sometimes its equivalent, ceived periodically by an individual, a corporation, etc., in turn for labor or services rendered, or from property, etc.

come tax A tax levied on annual income over a specified mount and with certain legally permitted deductions.

com·ing (in′kum′ing) *adj.* Coming in or about to come : *incoming* profits. **—** *n.* The act of coming in.

com·men·su·ra·ble (in′kə·men′shər·ə·bəl, -sər·ə-) *adj.* . Lacking a common measure or standard of comparison. . *Math.* Not expressible in terms of a common factor or diisor. **3.** Greatly out of proportion; not in accordance: conusions *incommensurable* with the facts. **—** *n.* That which incommensurable. **— in′com·men′su·ra·bil′i·ty, in′com·en′su·ra·ble·ness** *n.* **— in′com·men′su·ra·bly** *adv.*

com·men·su·rate (in′kə·men′shər·it) *adj.* **1.** Inadeuate; disproportionate: a salary *incommensurate* with the osition. **2.** Incommensurable. **— in′com·men′su·rate·ly** *dv.* **— in′com·men′su·rate·ness** *n.*

com·mode (in′kə·mōd′) *v.t.* **·mod·ed, ·mod·ing** To cause convenience to; disturb; bother. [< MF < L < *in-* not + *mmodus* convenient]

·com·mo·di·ous (in′kə·mō′dē·əs) *adj.* **1.** Uncomfortably mall; cramped. **2.** Causing discomfort; inconvenient. **— ′com·mo′di·ous·ly** *adv.* **— in′com·mo′di·ous·ness** *n.*

·com·mu·ni·ca·ble (in′kə·myōō′ni·kə·bəl) *adj.* Incapale of being communicated. **— in′com·mu′ni·ca·bil′i·ty** *n.*

·com·mu·ni·ca·do (in′kə·myōō′nə·kä′dō) *adj. & adv.* onfined without means of communication. [< Sp., < L *n-* not + *communicare* to share]

·com·mu·ni·ca·tive (in′kə·myōō′nə·kā′tiv, -kə·tiv) *adj.* ot communicative; taciturn; reserved. **— in′com·mu′ni·a′tive·ly** *adv.* **— in′com·mu′ni·ca′tive·ness** *n.*

·com·pa·ra·ble (in·kom′pər·ə·bəl) *adj.* **1.** Incapable of eing equaled or surpassed; matchless. **2.** Lacking in qualiies or characteristics that can be compared. **— in·com′pa·a·bil′i·ty, in·com′pa·ra·ble·ness** *n.* **— in·com′pa·ra·bly** *adv.*

·com·pat·i·ble (in′kəm·pat′ə·bəl) *adj.* **1.** Incapable of oexisting harmoniously. **2.** Disagreeing in nature; conicting. **3.** Incapable of being held or occupied by one peron at the same time, as more than one rank or office. **4.** *Med.* Having a harmful or undesirable effect when combined r used together. **—** *n.pl.* Incompatible persons, drugs, etc. **— in′com·pat′i·bil′i·ty** *n.* **— in·com·pat′i·ble·ness** *n.* **— in′·om·pat′i·bly** *adv.*

·com·pe·tent (in·kom′pə·tənt) *adj.* **1.** Lacking in ability r skill; inadequate to the task; unfit. **2.** Reflecting a lack f ability or skill. **3.** *Law* Not legally qualified. **—** *n.* One who is incompetent. [< F < L *incompentem*] **— in·com′pe·ence, in·com′pe·ten·cy** *n.* **— in·com′pe·tent·ly** *adv.*

·com·plete (in′kəm·plēt′) *adj.* **1.** Not having all essenial elements or parts; unfinished. **2.** Not fully developed; efective; imperfect: *incomplete* growth. **— in′com·plete′ly** *dv.* **— in′com·plete′ness, in′com·ple′tion** *n.*

·com·pre·hen·si·ble (in′kom·pri·hen′sə·bəl, in·kom′-) *dj.* **1.** Incapable of being understood; unintelligible. **2.** *Archaic* Boundless. **— in′com·pre·hen′si·bil′i·ty, in′com·re·hen′si·ble·ness** *n.* **— in′com·pre·hen′si·bly** *adv.*

·com·pre·hen·sion (in′kom·pri·hen′shən, in·kom′-) *n.* ack of understanding.

·com·pre·hen·sive (in′kom·pri·hen′siv, in·kom′-) *adj.* Not comprehensive; limited in scope.

·com·press·i·ble (in′kəm·pres′ə·bəl) *adj.* Incapable of eing compressed. **— in′com·press′i·bil′i·ty** *n.*

·con·ceiv·a·ble (in′kən·sē′və·bəl) *adj.* Incapable of being onceived by the mind; unbelievable. **— in′con·ceiv′a·bil′i·y, in′con·ceiv′a·ble·ness** *n.* **— in′con·ceiv′a·bly** *adv.*

·con·clu·sive (in′kən·klōō′siv) *adj.* **1.** Not leading to an ltimate conclusion; indeterminate; indecisive: *inconclusive* evidence. **2.** Not achieving a definite result; ineffective. **— n′con·clu′sive·ly** *adv.* **— in′con·clu′sive·ness** *n.*

in·con·gru·i·ty (in′kong·grōō′ə·tē, in′kən-) *n. pl.* **·ties 1.** The state or quality of being incongruous; unsuitableness; inappropriateness. **2.** That which is incongruous.

in·con·gru·ous (in·kong′grōō·əs) *adj.* **1.** Not suitable; inappropriate. **2.** Not corresponding or conforming; at odds: with *with* or *to.* **3.** Consisting of elements or qualities not properly belonging together. [< L < *in-* not + *congruus* agreeing] **— in·con′gru·ous·ly** *adv.* **— in·con′gru·ous·ness** *n.*

in·con·se·quent (in·kon′sə·kwənt) *adj.* **1.** Not following from the premises; contrary to logical inference. **2.** Not proceeding according to the usual course; irrelevant; disconnected. **3.** Illogical in thought or action; eccentric. **— in·con′se·quence** *n.* **— in·con′se·quent·ly** *adv.*

in·con·se·quen·tial (in′kon·sə·kwen′shəl, in·kon′-) *adj.* **1.** Having little or no consequence; unimportant; trivial. **2.** Inconsequent. **—** *n.* A thing of no importance. **— in·con′·se·quen′ti·al′i·ty** (-kwen′shē·al′ə·tē), **in′con·se·quen′tial·ness** *n.* **— in·con′se·quen′tial·ly** *adv.*

in·con·sid·er·a·ble (in′kən·sid′ər·ə·bəl) *adj.* **1.** Small in quantity, size, or value. **2.** Not worth considering; trivial. **— in′con·sid′er·a·ble·ness** *n.* **— in′con·sid′er·a·bly** *adv.*

in·con·sid·er·ate (in′kən·sid′ər·it) *adj.* **1.** Lacking in concern for the rights or needs of others; thoughtless. **2.** Not carefully considered or thought out. **— in′con·sid′er·ate·ly** *adv.* **— in′con·sid′er·ate·ness, in′con·sid·er·a′tion** *n.*

in·con·sis·ten·cy (in′kən·sis′tən·sē) *n. pl.* **·cies 1.** The quality of being inconsistent. **2.** Something that is inconsistent. Also **in′con·sis′tence.**

in·con·sis·tent (in′kən·sis′tənt) *adj.* **1.** Lacking in agreement or compatibility; inconsonant; at variance. **2.** Containing contradictory elements or parts. **3.** Lacking uniformity in behavior or thought; erratic; changeable. **— in′·con·sis′tent·ly** *adv.*

in·con·sol·a·ble (in′kən·sō′lə·bəl) *adj.* Not to be consoled; disconsolate; dejected. **— in′con·sol′a·bil′i·ty, in′con·sol′a·ble·ness** *n.* **— in′con·sol′a·bly** *adv.*

in·con·so·nant (in·kon′sə·nənt) *adj.* Not consonant; not in accord. **— in·con′so·nance** *n.* **— in·con′so·nant·ly** *adv.*

in·con·spic·u·ous (in′kən·spik′yōō·əs) *adj.* **1.** Not conspicuous; not prominent or striking. **2.** Not attracting attention to oneself; shrinking from or not meriting notice. **— in′con·spic′u·ous·ly** *adv.* **— in′con·spic′u·ous·ness** *n.*

in·con·stant (in·kon′stənt) *adj.* Not constant; variable; fickle. **—** *n.* One who or that which is inconstant. **— in·con′stan·cy** *n.* **— in·con′stant·ly** *adv.*

in·con·test·a·ble (in′kən·tes′tə·bəl) *adj.* Not admitting of question; unassailable: *incontestable* evidence. [< F] **— in′con·test′a·bil′i·ty, in′con·test′a·ble·ness** *n.* **— in′con·test′a·bly** *adv.*

in·con·ti·nence (in·kon′tə·nəns) *n.* **1.** The quality or condition of being incontinent. **2.** An instance of incontinence. Also **in·con′ti·nen·cy.**

in·con·ti·nent (in·kon′tə·nənt) *adj.* **1.** Exercising little control or restraint, esp. in sexual desires. **2.** Incapable of keeping back: often with *of.* **3.** Unrestrained; unchecked: an *incontinent* flow of abuse. **— in·con′ti·nent·ly** *adv.*

in·con·trol·la·ble (in′kən·trō′lə·bəl) *adj.* Incapable of being controlled; uncontrollable. **— in′con·trol′la·bly** *adv.*

in·con·tro·vert·i·ble (in′kon·trə·vûr′tə·bəl) *adj.* Not admitting of controversy; undeniable. **— in′con·tro·vert′i·bil′·i·ty, in′con·tro·vert′i·ble·ness** *n.* **— in′con·tro·vert′i·bly** *adv.*

in·con·ven·ience (in′kən·vēn′yəns) *n.* **1.** The state or quality of being inconvenient. **2.** Something that is inconvenient. **—** *v.t.* **·ienced, ·ienc·ing** To cause inconvenience to.

in·con·ven·ient (in′kən·vēn′yənt) *adj.* Causing or lending itself to discomfort and difficulty; troublesome; awkward. **— in′con·ven′ient·ly** *adv.*

in·con·ver·sant (in·kon′vər·sənt, in′kən·vûr′sənt) *adj.* Not conversant or familiar: with *in* or *with.*

in·con·vert·i·ble (in′kən·vûr′tə·bəl) *adj.* Incapable of being changed, exchanged, or converted; esp., of paper money, not exchangeable for specie. **— in′con·vert′i·bil′i·ty, in′con·vert′i·ble·ness** *n.* **— in′con·vert′i·bly** *adv.*

in·con·vin·ci·ble (in′kən·vin′sə·bəl) *adj.* Not to be convinced; not convincible. **— in′con·vin′ci·bil′i·ty, in′con·vin′ci·ble·ness** *n.* **— in′con·vin′ci·bly** *adv.*

in·co·or·di·nate (in′kō·ôr′də·nit, -nāt) *adj.* Not coordinated. Also **in′co·or′di·nat′ed** (-nā′tid).

in·cor·po·rate (*v.* in·kôr′pə·rāt; *adj.* in·kôr′pə·rit) *v.* **·rat·ed, ·rat·ing** *v.i.* **1.** To form a legal corporation or other association capable of acting as an individual. **2.** To become combined or merged as one body or whole. **—** *v.t.* **3.** To take in or include as part of a whole. **4.** To add or inject (an ingredient, certain elements, etc.). **5.** To form (persons, groups, etc.) into a legal corporation or other association. **6.** To combine or merge into a whole. **— Syn.** See ENROLL, MIX, UNITE. **—** *adj.* **1.** Joined or combined into a single unit or whole; closely blended. **2.** Legally incorporated.

[< LL < *in-* in + *corporare* to form into a body] —**in·cor′po·ra′tive** *n.* —**in·cor′po·ra′tor** *n.*

in·cor·po·rat·ed (in·kôr′pə·rā′tid) *adj.* **1.** Forming one body or whole; combined. **2.** Organized into a legal corporation. Abbr. (def. 2) *inc.*, *incor.*, *incorp.*

in·cor·po·ra·tion (in·kôr′pə·rā′shən) *n.* **1.** The act or process of incorporating. **2.** A corporation.

in·cor·po·re·al (in′kôr·pôr′ē·əl, -pō′rē-) *adj.* **1.** Not consisting of matter; insubstantial. **2.** Of or pertaining to nonmaterial things; spiritual. **3.** *Law* Having no material existence, but regarded as existing by the law: *incorporeal* rights. [< L < *in-* not + *corpus, -oris* body] —**in′cor·po′re·al′i·ty** (-al′ə·tē) *n.* —**in′cor·po′re·al·ly** *adv.*

in·cor·rect (in′kə·rekt′) *adj.* **1.** Inaccurate or untrue as to fact or usage; wrong. **2.** Not proper or fitting; unsuitable: *incorrect* behavior. **3.** Not conforming to known or accepted standards; faulty: an *incorrect* idea. [< L *incorrectus*] —**in′cor·rect′ly** *adv.* —**in′cor·rect′ness** *n.*

in·cor·ri·gi·ble (in·kôr′ə·jə·bəl, -kor′-) *adj.* **1.** Incapable of being reformed or chastened. **2.** Firmly implanted; ineradicable, as a bad habit. **3.** Incapable of being corrected or amended. —*n.* One who is incorrigible. —**in·cor′ri·gi·bil′i·ty, in·cor′ri·gi·ble·ness** *n.* —**in·cor′ri·gi·bly** *adv.*

in·cor·rupt (in′kə·rupt′) *adj.* **1.** Not morally corrupt; esp., not susceptible to bribery; honest; upright. **2.** Not marred by decay or spoilage; untainted; fresh. **3.** Free from errors or alterations, as language, a literary text, etc. Also **in′cor·rupt′ed.** —**in′cor·rupt′ly** *adv.* —**in′cor·rupt′ness** *n.*

in·cor·rupt·i·ble (in′kə·rup′tə·bəl) *adj.* **1.** Not accessible to bribery; steadfastly honest. **2.** Incapable of corruption; not subject to decay or spoilage. —**in′cor·rupt′i·bil′i·ty, in′cor·rupt′i·ble·ness** *n.* —**in′cor·rupt′i·bly** *adv.*

in·crease (*v.* in·krēs′, *n.* in′krēs) *v.* **·creased, ·creas·ing** *v.i.* **1.** To become greater, as in amount, size, degree, etc.; grow. **2.** To grow in number, esp. by reproduction; multiply. —*v.t.* **3.** To make greater, as in amount, size, degree, etc.; augment; enlarge. —*n.* **1.** A growing or becoming greater, as in size, quantity, etc. **2.** The amount of growth or augmentation; that which is added; increment. [< OF < L < *in-* in + *crescere* to grow] —**in·creas′a·ble** *adj.* —**in·creas′er** *n.* —**in·creas′ing·ly** *adv.*

—**Syn.** (verb) augment, enlarge, extend, multiply.

in·cred·i·ble (in·kred′ə·bəl) *adj.* **1.** Not credible; impossible to believe; unbelievable. —**in·cred′i·bil′i·ty, in·cred′i·ble·ness** *n.* —**in·cred′i·bly** *adv.* **2.** Amazing; wonderful.

in·cre·du·li·ty (in′krə·dōō′lə·tē, -dyōō′-) *n.* The quality or state of being incredulous; disbelief; skepticism.

in·cred·u·lous (in·krej′ə·ləs) *adj.* **1.** Not willing or not disposed to believe; skeptical. **2.** Characterized by or showing disbelief. [< L < *in-* not + *credulus* < *credere* to believe] —**in·cred′u·lous·ly** *adv.* —**in·cred′u·lous·ness** *n.*

in·cre·ment (in′krə·mənt) *n.* **1.** A quantity added to another quantity. **2.** The act of increasing; enlargement. [< L *increscere* to increase] —**in′cre·men′tal** *adj.*

in·crim·i·nate (in·krim′ə·nāt) *v.t.* **·nat·ed, ·nat·ing** **1.** To imply the wrongdoing or guilt of (a person, etc.). **2.** To charge with a crime or fault. —**Syn.** See ACCUSE. [< Med.L < *in-* in + *criminare* to accuse one of a crime] —**in·crim′i·na′tion** *n.* —**in·crim′i·na·to′ry** (-nə·tôr′ē) *adj.*

in·crust (in·krust′) *v.t.* **1.** To cover with or as with a crust or hard coating; form a crust on. **2.** To decorate lavishly, as with jewels. Also spelled *encrust.* [< OF < L < *in-* on + *crustare* to form a crust] —**in·crus·ta′tion** *n.*

in·cu·bate (in′kyə·bāt, ing′-) *v.* **·bat·ed, ·bat·ing** *v.t.* **1.** To sit upon (eggs) in order to hatch them; brood. **2.** To hatch (eggs) in this manner or by artificial heat. **3.** To maintain under conditions favoring optimum growth or development, as bacterial cultures. —*v.i.* **4.** To sit on eggs; brood. **5.** To undergo incubation. [< L < *in-* on + *cubare* to lie] —**in′cu·ba′tive** *adj.*

in·cu·ba·tion (in′kyə·bā′shən, ing′-) *n.* **1.** The act of incubating, or the state of being incubated. **2.** *Med.* The period between the time of exposure to an infectious disease and the appearance of the symptoms. [< L *incubatio, -onis*]

in·cu·ba·tor (in′kyə·bā′tər, ing′-) *n.* **1.** An apparatus kept at a uniform warmth for artificial hatching of eggs. **2.** *Bacteriol.* A device for the artificial development of microorganisms. **3.** An apparatus for keeping warm a prematurely born baby. [< L, a hatcher]

in·cu·bus (in′kyə·bəs, ing′-) *n.* *pl.* **·bus·es** or **·bi** (-bī) **1.** Anything that tends to oppress or discourage. **2.** A nightmare. **3.** In folklore, a male demon that has sexual intercourse with sleeping women. [< Med.L < LL, nightmare < L *incubare* to lie on]

in·cul·cate (in·kul′kāt, in′kul-) *v.t.* **·cat·ed, ·cat·ing** To impress upon the mind by frequent repetition or forceful admonition; instill. [< L < *in-* on + *calcare* to tread] —**in′cul·ca′tion** *n.* —**in′cul·ca′tor** *n.*

in·cul·pate (in·kul′pāt, in′kul-) *v.t.* **·pat·ed, ·pat·ing** To involve in an accusation; incriminate. [< Med.L < *in-* in + *culpa* fault] —**in′cul·pa′tion** *n.*

in·cum·ben·cy (in·kum′bən·sē) *n.* *pl.* **·cies** **1.** The st[ate] or quality of being incumbent. **2.** That which is incumbe[nt]. **3.** The holding of an office or the period in which it is held.

in·cum·bent (in·kum′bənt) *adj.* **1.** Resting upon one a[s a] moral obligation, or as necessary under the circumstanc[es]; obligatory. **2.** Resting, leaning, or weighing wholly or par[tly] upon something. —*n.* One who holds an office or perfor[ms] official duties. [< L < *in-* on + *cubare* to lie] —**in·cum′bent·ly** *adv.*

in·cum·ber (in·kum′bər), **in·cum·brance** (in·kum′brən[s]) etc. See ENCUMBER, etc.

in·cu·nab·u·la (in′kyōō·nab′yə·lə) *n.* *pl.* *of* **in·cu·nab·u·lum** (-ləm) **1.** Specimens of early European printing fr[om] movable type; esp., books printed before A.D. 1500. **2.** T[he] earliest stages of development; beginnings. [< L < *in-* + *cunabula*, dim. of *cunae* cradle] —**in′cu·nab′u·lar** *ad[j.]*

in·cur (in·kûr′) *v.t.* **·curred, ·cur·ring** To become subject [to] (unpleasant consequences); bring on oneself. [< L < *in-* + *currere* to run] —**in·cur′rence** *n.*

in·cur·a·ble (in·kyŏŏr′ə·bəl) *adj.* Not curable or remediab[le]. —*n.* One suffering from an incurable disease. —**in·cur′a·bil′i·ty, in·cur′a·ble·ness** *n.* —**in·cur′a·bly** *adv.*

in·cur·sion (in·kûr′zhən, -shən) *n.* **1.** A hostile, often su[d]den entrance into a territory; an invasion; raid. **2.** A ru[n]ning in or running against; encroachment. [< L < *in-* + *currere* to run] —**in·cur′sive** *adj.*

in·curve (*v.* in·kûrv′; *n.* in′kûrv) *v.i.* & *v.t.* To curve inwa[rd]. —*n.* In baseball, a pitch that curves toward the batter.

in·cus (ing′kəs) *n.* *pl.* **in·cu·des** (in·kyōō′dēz) *Anat.* T[he] anvil-shaped central bone of the group of three bones in t[he] middle ear of mammals: also called *anvil.* [< L, anvil]

in·debt·ed (in·det′id) *adj.* **1.** Legally obligated to pay f[or] value received; in debt. **2.** Morally obligated to ackno[wl]edge benefits or favors. [< OF < *en-* in + *dette* debt]

in·debt·ed·ness (in·det′id·nis) *n.* **1.** The state of being i[n]debted. **2.** The amount of one's debts.

in·de·cen·cy (in·dē′sən·sē) *n.* *pl.* **·cies** **1.** The quality [or] condition of being indecent. **2.** An indecent act, speech, e[tc.]

in·de·cent (in·dē′sənt) *adj.* **1.** Offensive to one's mo[ral] sense or modesty; immodest. **2.** Contrary to propriety [or] good taste; indelicate; vulgar. —**in·de′cent·ly** *adv.*

in·de·ci·pher·a·ble (in′di·sī′fər·ə·bəl) *adj.* Not decipher[a]ble; unreadable. —**in′de·ci′pher·a·bil′i·ty** *n.*

in·de·ci·sion (in′di·sizh′ən) *n.* Inability to make decision[s].

in·de·ci·sive (in′di·sī′siv) *adj.* **1.** Not bringing about [a] definite conclusion, solution, etc. **2.** Incapable of maki[ng] decisions. —**in′de·ci′sive·ly** *adv.* —**in′de·ci′sive·ness** *n.*

in·dec·o·rous (in·dek′ər·əs, in′di·kôr′əs) *adj.* Not decorou[s]; unseemly. —**in·dec′o·rous·ly** *adv.* —**in·dec′o·rous·ness**

in·de·co·rum (in′di·kôr′əm, -kō′rəm) *n.* Lack of propriet[y].

in·deed (in·dēd′) *adv.* In fact; in truth: used to emphasi[ze] an affirmation, to mark a qualifying word or clause, or to d[e]note a concession. —*interj.* Is that true?

in·de·fat·i·ga·ble (in′də·fat′ə·gə·bəl) *adj.* Not yieldi[ng] readily to fatigue; tireless; unflagging. [< MF < L < *i[n-]* not + *de-*, intens. + *fatigare* to tire out] —**in′de·fat′i·ga·bil′i·ty, in′de·fat′i·ga·ble·ness** *n.* —**in′de·fat′i·ga·bly** *ad[v.]*

in·de·fea·si·ble (in′də·fē′zə·bəl) *adj.* Incapable of bei[ng] annulled, set aside, or made void. —**in′de·feas′i·bil′i·ty** —**in′de·fea′si·bly** *adv.*

in·de·fen·si·ble (in′di·fen′sə·bəl) *adj.* **1.** Incapable of bei[ng] justified. **2.** Incapable of being defended. —**in′de·fen′si·bil′i·ty, in′de·fen′si·ble·ness** *n.* —**in′de·fen′si·bly** *adv.*

in·de·fin·a·ble (in′di·fī′nə·bəl) *adj.* Incapable of being d[e]fined or described; vague; subtle; ineffable. —**in′de·fin′a·ble·ness** *n.* —**in′de·fin′a·bly** *adv.*

in·def·i·nite (in·def′ə·nit) *adj.* **1.** Not definite or precis[e]; vague. **2.** Without a fixed number; indeterminate. [3.] *Gram.* Not definite or determining, as the *indefinite* articl[e]. —**in·def′i·nite·ly** *adv.* —**in·def′i·nite·ness** *n.*

indefinite pronoun *Gram.* A pronoun that represents [an] object indefinitely or generally, as *each, none, another.*

in·de·his·cent (in′də·his′ənt) *adj.* *Bot.* Not opening spo[n]taneously when ripe, as certain grains and fruits. —**in′de·his′cence** *n.*

in·del·i·ble (in·del′ə·bəl) *adj.* **1.** Incapable of being blott[ed] out or effaced. **2.** Leaving a mark or stain not easily erase[d]. [< L < *in-* not + *delibilis* perishable] —**in·del′i·bil′i·t[y], in·del′i·ble·ness** *n.* —**in·del′i·bly** *adv.*

in·del·i·ca·cy (in·del′ə·kə·sē) *n.* *pl.* **·cies** **1.** The quality [of] being indelicate; coarseness. **2.** An indelicate thing, act, et[c.]

in·del·i·cate (in·del′ə·kit) *adj.* **1.** Lacking or offending [a] sense of delicacy or good taste; crude. **2.** Unconcerned abo[ut] the feelings of others; tactless. —**in·del′i·cate·ly** *adv.*

in·dem·ni·fy (in·dem′nə·fī) *v.t.* **·fied, ·fy·ing** **1.** To compe[n]sate (a person, etc.) for loss or damage sustained. **2.** T[o] make good (a loss). **3.** To give security against future lo[ss] or punishment. [< L *indemnis* unhurt (< *in-* not + *da[m]num* harm) + -FY] —**in·dem′ni·fi·ca′tion** *n.*

in·dem·ni·ty (in·dem′nə·tē) *n.* *pl.* **·ties** **1.** That which [is] given as compensation for a loss or for damage. **2.** An agre[e-]

ent to remunerate another for loss or protect him against ability. 3. Exemption from penalties or liabilities.
dent[1] (in·dent′; *for n., also* in′dent) *v.t.* **1.** To set in from le margin, as the first line of a paragraph. **2.** To cut or ark the edge or border of with toothlike notches; serrate. . To indenture, as an apprentice. — *v.i.* **4.** To be notched cut; form a recess. **5.** To set a line, paragraph, etc., in om the margin. — *n.* **1.** A cut or notch on the edge of a ing. **2.** A space before the first word of a paragraph; inention. [< OF < Med.L < *in-* in + *dentis* tooth]
dent[2] (in·dent′; *for n., also* in′dent) *v.t.* **1.** To press or ish in so as to form a dent or depression; impress. **2.** To ake a dent in. — *n.* A dent or depression; indentation.
den·ta·tion (in′den·tā′shən) *n.* **1.** A notch or series of otches in an edge or border. **2.** The act of notching, or the ndition of being notched. **3.** A dent. **4.** An indention.
den·tion (in·den′shən) *n.* **1.** *Printing* **a** The setting in of line or body of type at the left side. **b** The space thus left ank. **2.** A dent; indentation.
den·ture (in·den′chər) *n.* **1.** *Law* A deed or contract ade between two or more parties. **2.** *Usu. pl.* Such a conact between master and apprentice. **3.** The act of indenting, or the state of being indented. **4.** Indentation. — *v.t.* **ured, ·tur·ing** **1.** To bind by indenture. **2.** To make an dentation in.
de·pen·dence (in′di·pen′dəns) *n.* **1.** The quality or ndition of being independent. **2.** Sufficient income for ne's needs; a competence.
dependence Day July 4, a holiday in the U.S. comemorating the adoption of the Declaration of Independence, July 4, 1776.
de·pen·den·cy (in′di·pen′dən·sē) *n.* *pl.* **·cies** **1.** Indendence. **2.** An independent state or territory.
de·pen·dent (in′di·pen′dənt) *adj.* **1.** Not subject to the thority of another; autonomous. **2.** Not dependent on or rt of some larger group, system, etc.: an *independent* nion. **3.** Not an adherent of a party or faction: an *independent* voter. **4.** Not influenced or guided by others. **5.** cting so as to manage one's own affairs; self-reliant. **6.** lf-supporting. **7.** Having a competence; also, constituting competence: *independent* means. **8.** *Gram.* Constituting or pable of constituting a complete sentence: said of clauses. *n.* One who or that which is independent, esp. one not an herent of a party or faction. — **in′de·pen′dent·ly** *adv.*
dependent clause *Gram.* A clause constituting or capae of constituting a sentence.
de·scrib·a·ble (in′di·skrī′bə·bəl) *adj.* Incapable of being scribed; esp., too complex, extreme, etc., to be described; effable. — **in′de·scrib′a·bil′i·ty, in′de·scrib′a·ble·ness** *n.* **in′de·scrib′a·bly** *adv.*
de·struc·ti·ble (in′di·struk′tə·bəl) *adj.* Incapable of beg destroyed; very tough and durable. — **in′de·struc′ti·bil′·y, in′de·struc′ti·ble·ness** *n.* — **in′de·struc′ti·bly** *adv.*
de·ter·mi·na·ble (in′di·tûr′mi·nə·bəl) *adj.* **1.** Incapable being ascertained. **2.** Incapable of being decided. — **in′·e·ter′mi·na·ble·ness** *n.* — **in′de·ter′mi·na·bly** *adv.*
de·ter·mi·na·cy (in′di·tûr′mə·nə·sē) *n.* The state or uality of being indeterminate.
de·ter·mi·nate (in′di·tûr′mə·nit) *adj.* **1.** Not definite in tent, amount, or nature. **2.** Not clear or precise; vague. . Not decided; unsettled. **4.** Not fixed; inconclusive. — **′de·ter′mi·nate·ly** *adv.* — **in′de·ter′mi·nate·ness** *n.*
de·ter·mi·na·tion (in′di·tûr′mə·nā′shən) *n.* **1.** Lack of etermination. **2.** The condition of being indeterminate.
dex (in′deks) *n.* *pl.* **·dex·es** or **·di·ces** (-də·sēz) **1.** An alnabetical list, as at the end of a book or similar publication, topics, names, etc., and the numbers of the pages where ey occur in the text. **2.** A descriptive list, as of items in a llection. **3.** Anything that serves as an indicator, as the eedle on the dial of scientific instruments. **4.** The index nger. **5.** Anything that indicates or gives evidence of; gn: Alertness is an *index* of intelligence. **6.** *Printing* A ark (☞) used to direct attention to a specific word, pasge, etc.: also called *fist, hand.* **7.** A numerical expression the ratio between one dimension or magnitude and anher: the cephalic *index.* **8.** *Math.* A subscript or superript. — *v.t.* **1.** To provide with an index, as a book. **2.** o enter in an index, as a subject. **3.** To indicate. [< L, refinger, sign] — **in′dex·er** *n.* — **in·dex′i·cal** *adj.*
dex (in′deks) *n.* A list of books the Roman Catholic Church rbids its members to read except with special permission.
dex finger The finger next to the thumb: also called *refinger.*
dex number *Stat.* A figure indicating the relative changes costs, production, etc., at a given period of time, as comared with those of a specific period in the past reprented by the number 100 and used as an arbitrary base.
dia ink **1.** A black pigment composed of lampblack mixed with a binding material and molded in sticks or cakes. **2.** A liquid ink made from this pigment.
In·di·an (in′dē·ən) *n.* **1.** A citizen of the Republic of India. **2.** A native of India or the East Indies. **3.** A member of the aboriginal races of North America, South America, and the West Indies. **4.** Loosely, any of the languages of the American Indian. — *adj.* **1.** Of or pertaining to India and the East Indies and their peoples. **2.** Of or pertaining to the aborigines of North America, South America, and the West Indies. **3.** Made by or used by Indians. [< L *India*]
Indian club A bottle-shaped wooden club used in gymnastics, usu. in pairs.
Indian corn Corn (def. 1).
Indian file Single file.
Indian giver *U.S. Informal* One who gives a present and then wants it back.
Indian hemp **1.** Hemp (def. 1). **2.** A perennial American herb of the dogbane family.
Indian meal Cornmeal.
Indian pipe An herb with one pipe-shaped white flower.
Indian pudding A pudding of cornmeal, milk, and molasses.
Indian summer A period of mild, warm weather occurring in late autumn, often after the first frost.
India paper A thin, yellowish, absorbent printing paper, used in taking the finest proofs from engraved plates.
India rubber Rubber (def. 1).
In·dic (in′dik) *adj.* Pertaining to India, its peoples, languages, and culture; Indian. — *n.* A branch of the Indo-Iranian subfamily of Indo-European languages, including Sanskrit, Hindi, etc.
in·di·cate (in′də·kāt) *v.t.* **·cat·ed, ·cat·ing** **1.** To be or give a sign of; signify. **2.** To direct attention to; point out. **3.** To express or make known. [< L < *in-* in + *dicare* to point out, proclaim]
in·di·ca·tion (in′də·kā′shən) *n.* **1.** The act of indicating. **2.** That which indicates; sign. **3.** A degree or quantity shown on a measuring instrument.
in·dic·a·tive (in·dik′ə·tiv) *adj.* **1.** Suggestive of; pointing out. **2.** *Gram.* Pertaining to or denoting a mood in which an act or condition is stated or questioned as an actual fact. — *n.* *Gram.* **a** The indicative mood. **b** A verb in this mood. — **in·dic′a·tive·ly** *adv.*
in·di·ca·tor (in′də·kā′tər) *n.* **1.** One who or that which indicates or points out. **2.** An instrument or device that measures or shows position; also, its pointer or needle.
in·di·ces (in′də·sēz) Alternative plural of INDEX.
in·dict (in·dīt′) *v.t.* **1.** *Law* To prefer an indictment against. **2.** To charge with a crime or offense. — **Syn.** See ACCUSE. [< AF *enditer* to make known, inform; later infl. in form by Med.L *dictare* to accuse] — **in·dict′a·ble** *adj.* — **in·dict·ee** (in·dī·tē′) *n.* — **in·dict′er, in·dict′or** *n.*
in·dict·ment (in·dīt′mənt) *n.* **1.** The act of indicting, or the state of being indicted. **2.** *Law* A formal written charge of crime, presented by a grand jury on oath to the court, as the basis for trial of the accused. [< AF *enditement*]
in·dif·fer·ence (in·dif′ər·əns) *n.* **1.** The state or quality of being indifferent. **2.** Unimportance; insignificance. **3.** Mediocrity. — **Syn.** See APATHY. Also **in·dif′fer·en·cy.**
in·dif·fer·ent (in·dif′ər·ənt) *adj.* **1.** Having no interest or feeling; unconcerned. **2.** Lacking in distinction; mediocre. **3.** Only average in size, amount, etc. **4.** Having little importance or significance. **5.** Showing no preference; unbiased. **6.** Not active; inert: said of chemical compounds, electrical or magnetic properties, etc. [< OF < L *indifferens*] — **in·dif′fer·ent·ly** *adv.*
in·di·gence (in′də·jəns) *n.* The state of being indigent; poverty. Also **in′di·gen·cy.**
in·dig·e·nous (in·dij′ə·nəs) *adj.* **1.** Originating or occurring naturally in the place specified; native. **2.** Innate; inherent. — **Syn.** See NATIVE. Also **in·dig′e·nal.** [< LL < L *indu-* within + *gignere* to be born] — **in·dig′e·nous·ly** *adv.*
in·di·gent (in′də·jənt) *adj.* Lacking means of subsistence; poor. [< F < L < *indu-* within + *egere* to need] — **in′di·gent·ly** *adv.*
in·di·gest·i·ble (in′də·jes′tə·bəl) *adj.* Difficult to digest; not digestible. — **in′di·gest′i·bil′i·ty, in′di·gest′i·ble·ness** *n.* — **in′di·gest′i·bly** *adv.*
in·di·ges·tion (in′də·jes′chən) *n.* Difficulty in digesting food. [< F]
in·dig·nant (in·dig′nənt) *adj.* Feeling or showing indignation. — **in·dig′nant·ly** *adv.*
in·dig·na·tion (in′dig·nā′shən) *n.* Anger aroused by injustice or baseness. [< OF < L < *in-* not + *dignus* worthy]
in·dig·ni·ty (in·dig′nə·tē) *n.* *pl.* **·ties** An act that humiliates, degrades, or injures self-respect.
in·di·go (in′də·gō) *n.* *pl.* **·gos** or **·goes** **1.** A blue coloring substance obtained from certain plants of the pea family or

made synthetically. **2.** A deep violet blue. Also **indigo blue.** **3.** A plant yielding a blue dyestuff. — *adj.* Deep violet blue. [< Sp. < L < Gk. *Indikon* (*pharmakon*) Indian (dye)]
indigo bunting A finch of North America, the male of which is a brilliant indigo. Also **indigo bird.**
in·di·rect (in′də·rekt′) *adj.* **1.** Not following a direct line or path. **2.** Not straightforward or open; underhand. **3.** Not coming as an immediate result: *indirect* benefits. **4.** Not aimed directly: an *indirect* proof. **5.** Not proceeding through a direct line of succession, as an inheritance. **6.** *Gram.* Not expressed in the exact words of the source: an *indirect* question. — **in′di·rect′ly** *adv.* — **in′di·rect′ness** *n.*
in·di·rec·tion (in′də·rek′shən) *n.* **1.** Indirect method or practice. **2.** Dishonest dealing; deceit.
indirect lighting Lighting that is reflected, as from a white ceiling, or diffused to give a minimum of glare and shadow.
indirect tax A tax, the burden of which is ultimately passed on to another, as in the form of higher market prices.
in·dis·cern·i·ble (in′di·sûr′nə·bəl, -zûr′-) *adj.* Incapable of being discerned; imperceptible. — **in′dis·cern′i·ble·ness** *n.* — **in′dis·cern′i·bly** *adv.*
in·dis·cov·er·a·ble (in′dis·kuv′ər·ə·bəl) *adj.* Incapable of being discovered. — **in′dis·cov′er·a·bil′i·ty** *n.*
in·dis·creet (in′dis·krēt′) *adj.* Lacking discretion; imprudent. — **in′dis·creet′ly** *adv.* — **in′dis·creet′ness** *n.*
in·dis·crete (in′dis·krēt′) *adj.* Not discrete; not separated; unified. — **in′dis·crete′ly** *adv.* — **in′dis·crete′ness** *n.*
in·dis·cre·tion (in′dis·kresh′ən) *n.* **1.** The state or quality of being indiscreet. **2.** An indiscreet act, speech, etc.
in·dis·crim·i·nate (in′dis·krim′ə·nit) *adj.* **1.** Showing no discrimination; not perceiving differences. **2.** Confused; chaotic. — **in′dis·crim′i·nate·ly** *adv.* — **in′dis·crim′i·nate·ness** *n.* — **in′dis·crim′i·nat′ing** *adj.* — **in′dis·crim′i·na′tion** *n.* — **in′dis·crim′i·na′tive** *adj.*
in·dis·pen·sa·ble (in′dis·pen′sə·bəl) *adj.* **1.** Not to be dispensed with; essential. **2.** Not to be ignored: an *indispensable* responsibility. — *n.* An indispensable person or thing. — **in′dis·pen′sa·bil′i·ty, in′dis·pen′sa·ble·ness** *n.* — **in′dis·pen′sa·bly** *adv.*
in·dis·pose (in′dis·pōz′) *v.t.* **·posed, ·pos·ing** **1.** To render unwilling; disincline. **2.** To render unfit. **3.** To make slightly ill or ailing. — **in′dis·po·si′tion** *n.*
in·dis·posed (in′dis·pōzd′) *adj.* **1.** Mildly ill; unwell. **2.** Disinclined; not willing. — **Syn.** See SICK[1].
in·dis·put·a·ble (in′dis·pyōō′tə·bəl, in·dis′pyŏŏ·tə·bəl) *adj.* Incapable of being disputed. — **in′dis·put′a·bil′i·ty, in′dis·put′a·ble·ness** *n.* — **in′dis·put′a·bly** *adv.*
in·dis·sol·u·ble (in′di·sol′yə·bəl, in·dis′ə·lyə·bəl) *adj.* **1.** Incapable of being dissolved, separated into its elements, or destroyed. **2.** Binding; extremely durable. — **in′dis·sol′u·bil′i·ty, in′dis·sol′u·ble·ness** *n.* — **in′dis·sol′u·bly** *adv.*
in·dis·tinct (in′dis·tingkt′) *adj.* **1.** Not clearly perceptible; blurred. **2.** Not readily distinguishable from something else; confused. **3.** Not producing clear impressions, images, etc. — **in′dis·tinct′ly** *adv.* — **in′dis·tinct′ness** *n.*
in·dis·tin·guish·a·ble (in′di·sting′gwish·ə·bəl) *adj.* Incapable of being perceived. — **in′dis·tin′guish·a·ble·ness, in′dis·tin′guish·a·bil′i·ty** *n.* — **in′dis·tin′guish·a·bly** *adv.*
in·di·um (in′dē·əm) *n.* A soft, malleable, silver-white metallic element (symbol In). See ELEMENT. [< NL < *indicum* indigo; with ref. to its spectrum color]
in·di·vid·u·al (in′də·vij′ōō·əl) *adj.* **1.** Existing as a unit; single. **2.** Separate, as distinguished from others of the same kind. **3.** Pertaining to or meant for a single person, animal, etc.: an *individual* serving. **4.** Differentiated from others by distinctive characteristics. — *n.* **1.** A single human being as distinct from others. **2.** A person. [< Med.L < L < *in-* not + *dividere* to divide] — **in′di·vid′u·al·ly** *adv.*
in·di·vid·u·al·ism (in′də·vij′ōō·əl·iz′əm) *n.* **1.** Personal independence in action, thought, etc. **2.** The state of being individual. **3.** Self-interest; egoism. **4.** The social theory that emphasizes the importance of the individual.
in·di·vid·u·al·ist (in′də·vij′ōō·əl·ist) *n.* **1.** One who is independent in character, action, thought, etc. **2.** One who advocates individualism. — **in′di·vid′u·al·is′tic** *adj.*
in·di·vid·u·al·i·ty (in′də·vij′ōō·al′ə·tē) *n. pl.* **·ties** **1.** A quality or trait that distinguishes one person or thing from others. **2.** Strikingly distinctive character or personality. **3.** The state of having separate, independent existence.
in·di·vid·u·al·ize (in′də·vij′ōō·əl·īz′) *v.t.* **·ized, ·iz·ing** **1.** To make individual; distinguish. **2.** To treat, mention, or consider individually. — **in′di·vid′u·al·i·za′tion** *n.*
in·di·vis·i·ble (in′də·viz′ə·bəl) *adj.* Not divisible; incapable of being divided. — *n.* Something that is indivisible. — **in′di·vis′i·ble·ness, in′di·vis′i·bil′i·ty** *n.* — **in′di·vis′i·bly** *adv.*
Indo- *combining form* Indian. [< Gk. *Indos* Indian]
In·do·chi·nese (in′dō·chī·nēz′, -nēs′) *adj.* Of or pertaining to Indochina, its inhabitants, or their language. — *n. pl.* **·nese** **1.** A member of one of the Mongoloid peoples of Indochina. **2.** The Sino-Tibetan family of languages.
in·doc·tri·nate (in·dok′trə·nāt) *v.t.* **·nat·ed, ·nat·ing** To instruct in doctrines; esp., to teach partisan or sectar[ian] dogmas. [< Med.L *in-* into + *doctrinare* to teach < *docere* to teach] — **in·doc′tri·na′tion** *n.*
In·do-Eu·ro·pe·an (in′dō·yŏŏr′ə·pē′ən) *n.* The larg[est] family of languages in the world, comprising most of the la[n]guages of Europe and many languages of India and SW As[ia] and including as subfamilies Hellenic, Italic, Celtic, G[er]manic, Indo-Iranian, Armenian, Albanian, and Bal[to-]Slavic. — *adj.* Of or pertaining to the Indo-Europe[an] family of languages, or to the peoples speaking them.
In·do-I·ra·ni·an (in′dō·ī·rā′nē·ən) *n.* A subfamily of [the] Indo-European family of languages, consisting of Indic a[nd] Iranian branches. — *adj.* Of or pertaining to this subfami[ly].
in·do·lent (in′də·lənt) *adj.* Averse to exertion or wo[rk]; lazy. [< LL *in-* not + *dolere* to feel pain] — **in′do·lenc[e]** — **in′do·lent·ly** *adv.*
in·dom·i·ta·ble (in·dom′i·tə·bəl) *adj.* Not easily defea[ted] or subdued. [< LL < L < *in-* not + *domitare* to tame] — **in·dom′i·ta·bly** *adv.*
In·do·ne·sian (in′dō·nē′zhən, -shən) *n.* **1.** A citizen [of] Indonesia. **2.** One of a small, light-brown-skinned peo[ple] native throughout the Malay Peninsula and Archipela[go], the Philippines, Sumatra, Java, etc. **3.** The langua[ges] spoken by these people, including Malay, Tagalog, e[tc.]: also called *Malayan.* — *adj.* Of or pertaining to Indone[sia], its peoples, or their languages.
in·door (in′dôr′, -dōr′) *adj.* **1.** Pertaining to or meant [for] the interior of a house or building. **2.** Located or perform[ed] within a house or building. [Earlier *within-door*]
in·doors (in′dôrz′, -dōrz′) *adv.* Inside or toward the ins[ide] of a building.
in·dorse (in·dôrs′), etc. See ENDORSE, etc.
in·du·bi·ta·ble (in·dōō′bə·tə·bəl, -dyōō′-) *adj.* Not to [be] doubted. — **in·du′bi·ta·ble·ness** *n.* — **in·du′bi·ta·bly** *a[dv.]*
in·duce (in·dōōs′, -dyōōs′) *v.t.* **·duced, ·duc·ing** **1.** [To] cause to act, speak, etc., by convincing or other influen[ce]; persuade. **2.** To bring on; cause. **3.** To reach, as a con[clu]sion, by inductive reasoning. [< L *in-* in + *ducere* to le[ad]] — **in·duc′er** *n.* — **in·duc′i·ble** *adj.*
in·duce·ment (in·dōōs′mənt, -dyōōs′-) *n.* **1.** That wh[ich] induces; incentive. **2.** The act of inducing.
in·duct (in·dukt′) *v.t.* **1.** *U.S.* To bring (a draftee) i[nto] military service. **2.** To install formally in an office, [etc.] **3.** To initiate in knowledge, experience, etc.: with *to.* [**4.**] *Physics* To produce by induction. [See INDUCE.]
in·duc·tance (in·duk′təns) *n.* *Electr.* The ability of a [cir]cuit to produce induction.
in·duc·tee (in′duk·tē′) *n.* One inducted or being induct[ed].
in·duc·tile (in·duk′təl, -til) *adj.* **1.** Not ductile; not ma[lle]able. **2.** Not submissive; unyielding. — **in·duc·til′i·ty** *n.*
in·duc·tion (in·duk′shən) *n.* **1.** The act of inducting, [or] state of being inducted. **2.** The act of inducing or causi[ng]. **3.** The bringing forward of separate facts as evidence [in] order to prove a general statement; also, the resulting sta[te]ment. **4.** *Electr.* The production of magnetization or e[lec]trification in a body by the mere proximity of a magne[tic] field or electric charge, or of an electric current in a cond[uc]tor by the variation of the magnetic field in its vicini[ty]. [< OF < L *inductio, -onis*] — **in·duc′tion·al** *adj.*
induction coil *Electr.* A device that changes a low stea[dy] voltage into a high intermittent alternating voltage by el[ec]tromagnetic induction.
in·duc·tive (in·duk′tiv) *adj.* **1.** Pertaining to or result[ing] from induction: *inductive* reasoning. **2.** *Electr.* Produced or causing induction or inductance. [< LL *inductivus*] — **in·duc′tive·ly** *adv.* — **in·duc′tive·ness** *n.*
in·duc·tiv·i·ty (in′duk·tiv′ə·tē) *n.* *Electr.* **1.** Specific ca[pa]bility for induction. **2.** Inductance.
in·duc·tor (in·duk′tər) *n.* **1.** One who or that which [in]ducts. **2.** *Electr.* Any part of an electrical apparatus t[hat] acts inductively upon another.
in·dulge (in·dulj′) *v.* **·dulged, ·dulg·ing** *v.t.* **1.** To yield [to] or gratify, as desires or whims. **2.** To yield to or gratify [the] desires, whims, etc., of; humor. **3.** In business, to gra[nt] more time (to someone) for payment of a bill. — *v.i.* **4.** [To] gratify one's own desire. — **Syn.** See PAMPER. [< L *ind[ul]gere* to be kind to] — **in·dulg′er** *n.*
in·dul·gence (in·dul′jəns) *n.* **1.** The act of indulging, [or] state of being indulgent. **2.** That which is indulged in. [**3.**] Something granted as a favor. **4.** In business, permission [to] defer paying a bill, etc. **5.** In the Roman Catholic Chur[ch], remission of temporal punishment due for a sin after it [has] been forgiven through sacramental absolution. Also [**in**]**·dul′gen·cy.** [< OF < L *indulgentia*]
in·dul·gent (in·dul′jənt) *adj.* Prone to indulge; lenie[nt]. — **in·dul′gent·ly** *adv.*
in·du·rate (*v.* in′dōō·rāt, -dyōō-; *adj.* in′dōō·rit, -dyōō-) *v.t.* & *v.i.* **·rat·ed, ·rat·ing** **1.** To make or become hard or u[n]feeling. **2.** To make or become hardy. — *adj.* Hard; u[n]feeling: also **in′du·rat′ed.** [< L *indurare* to make har[d]] — **in′du·ra′tion** *n.* — **in′du·ra′tive** *adj.*

us·tri·al (in·dus′trē·əl) *adj.* **1.** Of, characteristic of, or ılting from industry. **2.** Engaged in industry. **3.** Having many industries: an *industrial* area. **4.** Intended for use ndustry. **5.** Relating to, affecting, or benefiting workers ndustry. — *n. pl.* Stocks or securities of industrial erprises. [< F *industriel* and Med.L *industrialis*] — **us′tri·al·ly** *adv.*
strial arts The technical skills used in industry, esp. ubjects of study in schools.
strial design. The esthetic and practical design of intrial products; also, the study of such design.
strial engineer An engineer who supervises produc in factories, lays out machinery, etc.
us·tri·al·ism (in·dus′trē·əl·iz′əm) *n.* An economic sys based chiefly on large-scale industries and production of ds rather than on agriculture, foreign trade, etc.
us·tri·al·ist (in·dus′trē·əl·ist) *n.* A person important in ownership or management of industry.
us·tri·a·lize (in·dus′trē·əl·īz′) *v.t.* **·ized, ·iz·ing 1.** To blish large-scale industries in. **2.** To make or form into industry. — **in·dus′tri·al·i·za′tion** *n.*
strial relations The relations between management employees in industrial concerns.
strial union A labor union to which all workers in a ticular industry may belong: also called *vertical union.*
us·tri·ous (in·dus′trē·əs) *adj.* Hard-working. — **in· ·tri·ous·ly** *adv.* — **in·dus′tri·ous·ness** *n.*
us·try (in′dəs·trē) *n. pl.* **·tries 1.** Any specific branch roduction or manufacture. **2.** Manufacturing and productive interests collectively. **3.** Diligent and regular application to work or tasks. [< MF < L *industrius* diligent]
well (in′dwel′) *v.* **·dwelt, ·dwel·ling** *v.t.* **1.** To dwell in. *i.* **2.** To dwell. — **in′dwell′er** *n.* — **in′dwell′ing** *n.*
suffix Like; pertaining to; of the nature of: *marine, ine.* [< F < L *-inus,* adj. suffix]
suffix **1.** *Chem.* **a** Used in the names of halogens: *bro e.* **b** Used to indicate an alkaloid or basic substance: *phine.* **c** Var. of -IN. **2.** Used in names of commercial ducts: *brilliantine.* [Special use of -INE[1]]
suffix **1.** Used to form feminine words, names, and es: *heroine.* **2.** Used to form originally feminine abct nouns: *medicine, doctrine.* [< F < L *-ina,* suffix of . nouns < Gk. *-inē*; or directly < L or < Gk.]
suffix Like; resembling: *crystalline.* [< L < Gk. *-inos*]
bri·ate (*v.* in·ē′brē·āt; *n. & adj.* in·ē′brē·it, -āt) *v.t.* **ed, ·at·ing 1.** To make drunk; intoxicate. **2.** To exrate; excite. — *n.* A habitual drunkard. — *adj.* Intoxied. [< L < *in-* thoroughly + *ebriare* to make drunk] **n·e′bri·a′ted** *adj.* — **in·e′bri·a′tion** *n.*
d·i·ble (in·ed′ə·bəl) *adj.* Not eatable. — **in·ed′i·bil′i·ty** *n.*
f·fa·ble (in·ef′ə·bəl) *adj.* **1.** Too overpowering to be exssed in words. **2.** Too lofty or sacred to be uttered. **3.** escribable; indefinable. [< MF < L < *in-* not + *effa* s utterable] — **in·ef′fa·bil′i·ty, in·ef′fa·ble·ness** *n.* — **f′fa·bly** *adv.*
f·fec·tive (in′i·fek′tiv) *adj.* **1.** Not effective. **2.** Incompetent. — **in′ef·fec′tive·ly** *adv.* — **in′ef·fec′tive·ness** *n.*
f·fec·tu·al (in′i·fek′chōō·əl) *adj.* **1.** Not effectual. **2.** successful; fruitless. — **in′ef·fec′tu·al′i·ty, in′ef·fec′tu· ness** *n.* — **in′ef·fec′tu·al·ly** *adv.*
f·fi·ca·cious (in′ef·ə·kā′shəs) *adj.* Not producing the ect desired or intended, as a medicine. — **in′ef·fi·ca′cious·** *dv.* — **in′ef·fi·ca′cious·ness** *n.*
f·fi·ca·cy (in·ef′ə·kə·sē) *n.* The state of being inefficaus.
f·fi·cient (in′i·fish′ənt) *adj.* **1.** Not efficient; not perming a function economically; wasteful. **2.** Incompetent. **in′ef·fi′cien·cy** *n.* — **in′ef·fi′cient·ly** *adv.*
·las·tic (in′i·las′tik) *adj.* Not elastic; inflexible; unaotable. — **in·e·las·tic·i·ty** (in′i·las·tis′ə·tē) *n.*
l·e·gance (in·el′ə·gəns) *n.* **1.** The quality of being inelent. **2.** Something inelegant. — **in·el′e·gant·ly** *adv.*
l·e·gan·cy (in·el′ə·gən·sē) *n. pl.* **·cies** Inelegance.
l·e·gant (in·el′ə·gənt) *adj.* **1.** Not elegant. **2.** Coarse; de. — **in·el′e·gant·ly** *adv.*
l·i·gi·ble (in·el′ə·jə·bəl) *adj.* Not eligible; not qualified suitable. — *n.* One who is not eligible. — **in·el′i·gi· ′i·ty** *n.* — **in·el′i·gi·bly** *adv.*
·luc·ta·ble (in′i·luk′tə·bəl) *adj.* Not to be escaped from avoided; inevitable. [< L < *in-* not + *eluctabilis* retible] — **in′e·luc′ta·bil′i·ty** *n.* — **in′e·luc′ta·bly** *adv.*
pt (in·ept′) *adj.* **1.** Not suitable or appropriate. **2.** umsy; awkward. [< L < *in-* not + *aptus* fit] — **in· ′ly** *adv.* — **in·ept′ness** *n.*
p·ti·tude (in·ep′tə·tōōd, -tyōōd) *n.* **1.** The state or ality of being inept. **2.** An inept act or remark.
·qual·i·ty (in′i·kwol′ə·tē) *n. pl.* **·ties 1.** The state of ing unequal. **2.** An instance of this. **3.** Lack of evenness of proportion; variableness. **4.** Disparity of social position, opportunity, justice, etc. [< OF < L *inaequalitas*]
in·eq·ui·ta·ble (in·ek′wə·tə·bəl) *adj.* Not equitable; unfair. — **in·eq′ui·ta·bly** *adv.*
in·eq·ui·ty (in·ek′wə·tē) *n. pl.* **·ties 1.** Lack of equity; injustice. **2.** An unfair act or course of action.
in·e·rad·i·ca·ble (in′i·rad′ə·kə·bəl) *adj.* Not eradicable; impossible to remove or root out. — **in′e·rad′i·ca·bly** *adv.*
in·e·ras·a·ble (in′i·rā′sə·bəl) *adj.* Not erasable; impossible to erase or rub out. — **in′e·ras′a·bly** *adv.*
in·ert (in·ûrt′) *adj.* **1.** Lacking independent power to move or to resist applied force. **2.** Disinclined to move or act; sluggish. **3.** *Chem.* Devoid of active properties. [< L < *in-* not + *ars* art] — **in·ert′ly** *adv.* — **in·ert′ness** *n.*
in·er·tia (in·ûr′shə) *n.* **1.** The state of being inert; inactivity. **2.** *Physics* The property of matter by virtue of which any physical body persists in its state of rest or of uniform motion until acted upon by some external force. [< L, idleness] — **in·er′tial** *adj.*
in·es·cap·a·ble (in′ə·skā′pə·bəl) *adj.* Impossible to escape; unavoidable. — **in′es·cap′a·bly** *adv.*
in·es·ti·ma·ble (in·es′tə·mə·bəl) *adj.* **1.** Not to be estimated. **2.** Having great value. — **in·es′ti·ma·bly** *adv.*
in·ev·i·ta·ble (in·ev′ə·tə·bəl) *adj.* That cannot be avoided or prevented from happening. — *n.* Something inevitable. [< L < *in-* not + *evitare* to avoid] — **in·ev′i·ta·bil′i·ty, in·ev′i·ta·ble·ness** *n.* — **in·ev′i·ta·bly** *adv.*
in·ex·act (in′ig·zakt′) *adj.* Not exact; not completely accurate or true. — **in′ex·act′ly** *adv.* — **in′ex·act′ness** *n.*
in·ex·cus·a·ble (in′ik·skyōō′zə·bəl) *adj.* Not excusable; impossible to excuse or justify. — **in′ex·cus′a·bil′i·ty, in′ex· cus′a·ble·ness** *n.* — **in′ex·cus′a·bly** *adv.*
in·ex·haust·i·ble (in′ig·zôs′tə·bəl) *adj.* **1.** Incapable of being exhausted or used up. **2.** Incapable of fatigue; tireless. — **in′ex·haust′i·bil′i·ty, in′ex·haust′i·ble·ness** *n.* — **in′ex· haust′i·bly** *adv.*
in·ex·o·ra·ble (in·ek′sər·ə·bəl) *adj.* **1.** Not to be moved by entreaty or persuasion; unyielding. **2.** Unalterable; relentless. [< L *inexorabilis*] — **in·ex′o·ra·bil′i·ty, in·ex′o·ra· ble·ness** *n.* — **in·ex′o·ra·bly** *adv.*
in·ex·pe·di·ent (in′ik·spē′dē·ənt) *adj.* Not expedient; unsuited to a particular purpose; inadvisable. — **in′ex·pe′di· ence, in′ex·pe′di·en·cy** *n.* — **in′ex·pe′di·ent·ly** *adv.*
in·ex·pen·sive (in′ik·spen′siv) *adj.* Not expensive; costing little. — **in′ex·pen′sive·ly** *adv.* — **in′ex·pen′sive·ness** *n.*
in·ex·pe·ri·ence (in′ik·spir′ē·əns) *n.* Lack of experience.
in·ex·pe·ri·enced (in′ik·spir′ē·ənst) *adj.* Not experienced.
in·ex·pert (in·ek′spûrt) *adj.* Not expert; unskilled; inept. — **in·ex′pert·ly** *adv.* — **in·ex′pert·ness** *n.*
in·ex·pi·a·ble (in·ek′spē·ə·bəl) *adj.* Incapable of being expiated or atoned for; unpardonable.
in·ex·pli·ca·ble (in·eks′pli·kə·bəl, in′iks·plik′ə·bəl) *adj.* Not explicable; impossible to explain. — **in·ex′pli·ca·bil′i·ty, in·ex′pli·ca·ble·ness** *n.* — **in·ex′pli·ca·bly** *adv.*
in·ex·press·i·ble (in′ik·spres′ə·bəl) *adj.* Incapable of being expressed or put into words. — **in′ex·press′i·bil′i·ty, in′ex· press′i·ble·ness** *n.* — **in′ex·press′i·bly** *adv.*
in·ex·tin·guish·a·ble (in′ik·sting′gwish·ə·bəl) *adj.* Incapable of being extinguished; unquenchable. — **in′ex·tin′guish· a·ble·ness** *n.* — **in′ex·tin′guish·a·bly** *adv.*
in ex·tre·mis (in·iks·trē′mis) *Latin* At the point of death.
in·ex·tri·ca·ble (in·eks′tri·kə·bəl) *adj.* **1.** Impossible to extricate oneself from. **2.** Impossible to disentangle or undo. **3.** Too intricate to be solved. — **in·ex′tri·ca·bil′i·ty, in· ex′tri·ca·ble·ness** *n.* — **in·ex′tri·ca·bly** *adv.*
in·fal·li·ble (in·fal′ə·bəl) *adj.* **1.** Exempt from fallacy or error of judgment. **2.** Not liable to fail; sure: an *infallible* remedy. **3.** In Roman Catholic doctrine, incapable of error in matters of faith and morals. — *n.* One who or that which is infallible. — **in·fal′li·bil′i·ty** — **in·fal′li·bly** *adv.*
in·fa·mous (in′fə·məs) *adj.* **1.** Having a vile reputation. **2.** Deserving or producing infamy; odious. [< Med.L < L < *in-* not + *fama* fame] — **in′fa·mous·ly** *adv.* — **in′fa· mous·ness** *n.*
in·fa·my (in′fə·mē) *n. pl.* **·mies 1.** Dishonor; disgrace. **2.** The state of being infamous. **3.** An infamous act.
in·fan·cy (in′fən·sē) *n. pl.* **·cies 1.** The state or period of being an infant; babyhood. **2.** The beginnings of anything. **3.** *Law* The years before attaining the age of legal majority.
in·fant (in′fənt) *n.* **1.** A child in the earliest stages of life; baby. **2.** *Law* One who has not attained the age of legal majority, usu. 21; a minor. — *adj.* **1.** Of or typical of infancy or infants. **2.** Beginning to exist or develop. [< OF < L < *in-* not + *fari* to speak.] — **in′fant·hood** *n.*
in·fan·ta (in·fan′tə) *n.* A daughter of a Spanish or Portuguese king. [< Sp., infant (fem.)]
in·fan·te (in·fan′tā) *n.* A son, except the eldest, of a Spanish or Portuguese king. [< Sp., infant (masc.)]

NUNCIATION KEY: add, āce, câre, pälm; end, ēven; it, īce; odd, ōpen, ôrder; tŏŏk, pōōl; up, bûrn; ə = a in *above,* e in *sicken,* i in *flex-* o in *melon,* u in *focus;* **yōō** = u in *fuse;* **oil**; **pout**; **check**; **go**; **ring**; **thin**; **this**; **zh**, vision.

in·fan·ti·cide (in·fan′tə·sīd) *n.* **1.** The killing of an infant, esp. at birth. **2.** One who has killed an infant. [< F < LL < L *infans* child + *caedere* to kill]

in·fan·tile (in′fən·tīl, -til) *adj.* **1.** Of infancy or infants. **2.** Like or characteristic of infancy or infants; babyish. **3.** Being at the earliest stage of development. Also **in′fan·tine** (-tīn, -tin). [< LL *infantilis*]

infantile paralysis Poliomyelitis.

in·fan·til·ism (in·fan′tə·liz·əm) *n.* Abnormal persistence of infantile mental and physical characteristics into adult life.

in·fan·try (in′fən·trē) *n.* *pl.* **·tries** Soldiers, units, or a branch of an army trained and equipped to fight on foot. [< F < Ital. < L *infans, infantis* child]

in·fan·try·man (in′fən·trē·mən) *n.* *pl.* **·men** (-mən) A soldier of the infantry.

in·fat·u·ate (*v.* in·fach′ōō·āt; *for adj., also* in·fach′ōō·it) *v.t.* **·at·ed, ·at·ing 1.** To inspire with a foolish and unreasoning love or passion. **2.** To make foolish or fatuous. **—** *adj.* Infatuated. [< L *infatuare* to make a fool of] **— in·fat′u·a′tion** *n.*

in·fat·u·at·ed (in·fach′ōō·ā·tid) *adj.* **1.** Possessed by a foolish passion, esp. for another person. **2.** Made fatuous. **— in·fat′u·at·ed·ly** *adv.*

in·fect (in·fekt′) *v.t.* **1.** To affect or infuse with disease-producing organisms, as a wound. **2.** To cause (a person, etc.) to contract a communicable disease. **3.** To contaminate with impurities; pollute. **4.** To affect or inspire, as with attitudes or beliefs, esp. harmfully. [< L *inficere* to dip into, stain] **— in·fec′tor** or **in·fect′er** *n.*

in·fec·tion (in·fek′shən) *n.* **1.** An injurious invasion of body tissue by disease-producing organisms. **2.** A disease or other harmful condition resulting from an invasion by injurious organisms. **3.** The communication or transference of a disease, idea, mood, etc. [< OF]

in·fec·tious (in·fek′shəs) *adj.* **1.** Liable to produce infection. **2.** Denoting diseases communicable by infection. **3.** Tending to excite similar reactions: *infectious* laughter. **— in·fec′tious·ly** *adv.* **— in·fec′tious·ness** *n.*

infectious mononucleosis *Pathol.* An acute communicable disease marked by fever, sore throat, a swelling of the lymph nodes and an increase in mononuclear cells.

in·fec·tive (in·fek′tiv) *adj.* Liable to produce infection.

in·fe·lic·i·tous (in′fə·lis′ə·təs) *adj.* Not felicitous or suitable. **— in′fe·lic′i·tous·ly** *adv.* **— in′fe·lic′i·tous·ness** *n.*

in·fe·lic·i·ty (in′fə·lis′ə·tē) *n.* *pl.* **·ties 1.** The state of being infelicitous. **2.** That which is infelicitous, as an inappropriate remark, etc. [< L *infelicitas*]

in·fer (in·fûr′) *v.* **·ferred, ·fer·ring** *v.t.* **1.** To derive by reasoning; conclude or accept from evidence or premises. **2.** To involve or imply as a conclusion: said of facts, statements, etc. **—** *v.i.* **3.** To draw an inference. [< L < *in-* in + *ferre* to bring, carry] **— in·fer′a·ble** *adj.* **— in·fer′a·bly** *adv.*

◆ **infer, imply** *Infer* means to derive or conclude by reasoning: I *inferred* from the noise that you were at home. *Imply* means to suggest implicitly something that might be *inferred* by an observer: The noise *implied* that you were at home. *Infer* stresses the use of reason, whereas *imply*, the more general term, may be applied also to conclusions that are suggested or presumed.

in·fer·ence (in′fər·əns) *n.* **1.** That which is inferred; a conclusion. **2.** The act or process of inferring.

in·fer·en·tial (in′fə·ren′shəl) *adj.* Deducible by inference. **— in′fer·en′tial·ly** *adv.*

in·fer·i·or (in·fir′ē·ər) *adj.* **1.** Lower in quality, worth, or adequacy. **2.** Lower in rank or importance. **3.** Mediocre; ordinary: an *inferior* wine. **4.** *Astron.* **a** Between the earth and the sun: an *inferior* planet. **b** Below the horizon. **—** *n.* A person inferior in rank or in attainments. [< L, lower]

in·fe·ri·or·i·ty (in·fir′ē·ôr′ə·tē, -or′-) *n.* *pl.* **·ties** The state or quality of being inferior.

in·fer·nal (in·fûr′nəl) *adj.* **1.** Of or pertaining to the mythological world of the dead, or to hell. **2.** Diabolical; hellish. **3.** *Informal* Damnable; hateful. [< OF < L *infernus* situated below] **— in·fer′nal·ly** *adv.*

in·fer·no (in·fûr′nō) *n.* *pl.* **·nos 1.** The infernal regions; hell. **2.** Any place comparable to hell. [< Ital.]

in·fer·tile (in·fûr′til) *adj.* Not fertile or productive; sterile.

in·fest (in·fest′) *v.t.* To overrun or occur in large numbers so as to be annoying or dangerous. [< MF *infester* or L *infestare* to assail] **— in′fes·ta′tion** *n.* **— in·fest′er** *n.*

in·fi·del (in′fi·dəl) *n.* **1.** One who rejects all religious belief; unbeliever. **2.** Among Christians, one who is not a Christian. **3.** Among Moslems, one who is not a Moslem. **—** *adj.* **1.** Having no religious belief. **2.** Rejecting a particular faith, esp. Christianity or Islam. **3.** Of or relating to infidels or unbelief. [< MF < L < *in-* not + *fidelis* faithful]

in·fi·del·i·ty (in′fi·del′ə·tē) *n.* *pl.* **·ties 1.** Lack of fidelity. **2.** A disloyal act. **3.** Adultery. **4.** Lack of belief in a particular religion, esp. Christianity or Islam.

in·field (in′fēld′) *n.* In baseball: **a** The space within the base lines of the field, and some adjacent space beyond second and third base lines. **b** The infielders collectivel

in·field·er (in′fēld′ər) *n.* In baseball, either the first b man, second baseman, shortstop, or third baseman, or pitcher or catcher considered as a fielder.

in·fil·trate (in·fil′trāt, in′fil·trāt) *v.* **·trat·ed, ·trat·ing** *v.* To gain or seek control of (an organization, etc.) by sec occupying positions of power. **2.** To cause (a liquid or ga pass into or through pores. **3.** To filter or move throu into. **—** *v.i.* **4.** To pass into or through a substance. That which infiltrates. **— in′fil·tra′tion** *n.*

in·fin·ite (in′fə·nit) *adj.* **1.** Having no boundaries or li extending without end. **2.** Very numerous or great; **3.** All-embracing; perfect: *infinite* wisdom. **4.** *Math.* designating a quantity conceived as always exceeding other quantity in value. **—** *n.* **1.** That which is inf **2.** *Math.* An infinite quantity. **— the Infinite** God. OF < L < *in-* not + *finitus* finite] **— in′fi·nite·ly — in′fi·nite·ness** *n.*

— Syn. (adj.) **1.** *Infinite* is applied to those things whic believe to have no bounds. *Measureless, numberless, countless innumerable* often mean merely vast in dimension or nu *Eternal* means *infinite* in time, but is also used to mean conti for a very long time.

in·fin·i·tes·i·mal (in′fin·ə·tes′ə·məl) *adj.* **1.** Infinitely s **2.** So small as to be incalculable. **—** *n.* An infinites quantity. [< NL < *infinitus* infinite + *-esimus* (after *esimus* hundredth)] **— in′fin·i·tes′i·mal·ly** *adv.*

in·fin·i·tive (in·fin′ə·tiv) *Gram.* *adj.* **1.** Without limit of person or number. **2.** Of or pertaining to the infin **—** *n.* A verb form generally used either as the prin verb of a verb phrase, most often without *to*, or as a n most often with *to*. [< Med.L *infinitivus*]

in·fin·i·tude (in·fin′ə·tōōd, -tyōōd) *n.* **1.** The quality o ing infinite or boundless. **2.** An unlimited quantity.

in·fin·i·ty (in·fin′ə·tē) *n.* *pl.* **·ties 1.** The state of b infinite. **2.** Something considered infinite, as space or t **3.** A very large amount or number. [< OF < L < not + *finitus* finite]

in·firm (in·fûrm′) *adj.* **1.** Feeble or weak, as from old **2.** Lacking firmness of purpose. [< OF < L *infirm in-* not + *firmus* firm] **— in·firm′ly** *adv.* **— in·firm′ne**

in·fir·ma·ry (in·fûr′mər·ē) *n.* *pl.* **·ries** A place fo treatment of the sick, esp. in a school, etc. [< Med.L *infirmus* infirm, indisposed]

in·fir·mi·ty (in·fûr′mə·tē) *n.* *pl.* **·ties 1.** The state of b infirm. **2.** A physical or mental defect.

infix (in·fiks′) *v.t.* **1.** To set firmly or insert in. **2** implant (an idea, fact, etc.) in the mind. **3.** *Gram.* T sert (an infix) within a word. **—** *n.* *Gram.* A modif addition inserted in the body of a word. **— in·fix′ion**

in·flame (in·flām′) *v.* **·flamed, ·flam·ing** *v.t.* **1.** To se fire; kindle. **2.** To excite to violent emotion or acti **3.** To increase or make more intense, as anger, passion, **4.** To produce heat, swelling, and soreness in. **—** *v.i.* To catch fire. **6.** To become excited or aroused. **7.** T come inflamed. [< OF < L < *in-* in + *flamma* flame]

in·flam·ma·ble (in·flam′ə·bəl) *adj.* **1.** Flammable. Easily excited or aroused. **—** *n.* A flammable thing or stance. **— in·flam′ma·bil′i·ty, in·flam′ma·ble·ness — in·flam′ma·bly** *adv.*

in·flam·ma·tion (in′flə·mā′shən) *n.* **1.** The act of inf ing, or the state of being inflamed. **2.** *Pathol.* A dise condition characterized by redness, swelling, and pain.

in·flam·ma·to·ry (in·flam′ə·tôr′ē, -tō′rē) *adj.* **1.** Ten to arouse excitement, anger, etc. **2.** *Med.* Characterize or causing inflammation.

in·flat·able (in·flā′tə·bəl) *adj.* Capable of being inflat

in·flate (in·flāt′) *v.* **·flat·ed, ·flat·ing** *v.t.* **1.** To cause to pand by filling with or as with gas or air. **2.** To enl excessively; puff up: to *inflate* one's ego. **3.** *Econ.* T crease (prices, credit, etc.) in excess of usual or prior le **—** *v.i.* **4.** To become inflated. [< L < *in-* in + *fla* to blow] **— in·flat′er** or **in·flat′or** *n.*

in·fla·tion (in·flā′shən) *n.* **1.** The act of inflating, or state of being inflated. **2.** *Econ.* An unstable rise in p levels due to an increase in currency and a mounting dem for goods. **— in·fla′tion·ar′y** *adj.*

in·flect (in·flekt′) *v.t.* **1.** To vary the tone or pitch of voice) modulate. **2.** To turn from a straight or usual cou bend. **3.** *Gram.* To give the inflections of (a word) by jugating or declining. [< L < *in-* in + *flectere* to benc

in·flec·tion (in·flek′shən) *n.* **1.** The act of inflecting, or state of being inflected. **2.** An angle or bend. **3.** Mod tion of the voice. **4.** *Gram.* **a** A change in form underg by words to express grammatical and syntactical relati as of case, number, tense, etc. The inflection of nouns, nouns, and adjectives is called *declension*; that of ve *conjugation*. **b** An inflected form. **— in·flec′tion·al** *adj.*

in·flex·i·ble (in·flek′sə·bəl) *adj.* **1.** Incapable of being be rigid. **2.** Unyielding; stubborn. **3.** That cannot be alte

ed: the *inflexible* laws of nature. [< L *inflexibilis*] — **lex′i·bil′i·ty, in·flex′i·ble·ness** *n.* — **in·flex′i·bly** *adv.*
lict (in·flikt′) *v.t.* **1.** To deal; lay on: to *inflict* a blow. To impose. [< L < *in-* on + *fligere* to strike] — **in·t′er** or **in·flic′tor** *n.* — **in·flic′·tive** *adj.*
ic·tion (in·flik′shən) *n.* **1.** The act of inflicting. **2.** at which is inflicted, as pain, punishment, etc.
o·res·cence (in′flə·res′əns) *n.* **1.** A flowering; flourish-. **2.** *Bot.* **a** The mode of arrangement of flowers in rela-n to the stem or axis. **b** A cluster of flowers. **c** A single wer. [< NL < LL *inflorescere* to come into flower] — **lo·res′cent** *adj.*
ow (in′flō′) *n.* **1.** The act of flowing in. **2.** That which ws in.
u·ence (in′flōō·əns) *n.* **1.** The power of persons or ngs to produce effects on others, esp. by indirect means. Power resulting from social position, wealth, etc. **3.** e who or that which possesses the power to affect others. *v.t.* **·enced, ·en·cing** **1.** To produce an effect upon the ions or thought of. **2.** To have an effect upon. [< OF LL < L < *in-* in + *fluere* to flow] — **in′flu·enc·er** *n.*
u·en·tial (in′flōō·en′shəl) *adj.* **1.** Having or exercising uence. **2.** Wielding influence. — **in′flu·en′tial·ly** *adv.*
u·en·za (in′flōō·en′zə) *n.* *Pathol.* A contagious, in-tious virus disease characterized by respiratory inflam-tion and fever: also called *flu, grip, grippe.* [< Ital., ness due to) the influence (of the stars)]
lux (in′fluks′) *n.* **1.** A flowing in, as of a fluid. **2.** A tinuous coming, as of people. **3.** The mouth of a river. MF < LL *influere* to flow in]
old (in·fōld) *v.t.* **1.** To wrap in folds. **2.** To embrace. To turn or fold inward. Also spelled *enfold.*
orm (in·fôrm′) *v.t.* **1.** To notify. **2.** To give character with *with* or *by.* — *v.i.* **3.** To disclose information. OF < L *informare* to give form to]
or·mal (in·fôr′məl) *adj.* **1.** Not in the usual or pre-ibed form; unofficial. **2.** Without formality; relaxed; ual. **3.** Not requiring formal attire. **4.** Characteristic or suitable to the language of ordinary conversation or iliar writing. ◆ Informal language is widely used by cated people and is not to be confused with nonstandard ge or slang. — **in·for′mal·ly** *adv.*
or·mal·i·ty (in′fôr·mal′ə·tē) *n.* *pl.* **·ties** **1.** The state being informal. **2.** An informal act or proceeding.
orm·ant (in·fôr′mənt) *n.* One who gives information.
or·ma·tion (in′fər·mā′shən) *n.* **1.** Knowledge acquired derived; facts. **2.** Timely knowledge; news. **3.** The of informing, or the state of being informed. **4.** A vice or facility for providing facts: Call *information.* F < L *informatio, -onis*] — **in′for·ma′tion·al** *adj.*
orm·a·tive (in·fôr′mə·tiv) *adj.* Affording information; tructive. Also **in·form′a·to·ry** (-tôr′ē, -tō′rē).
ormed (in·fôrmd′) *adj.* Having a high degree of knowl-e, information, or education.
orm·er (in·fôr′mər) *n.* **1.** One who informs against oth-; stool pigeon; tattletale. **2.** An informant.
ra- *prefix* Below; beneath; on the lower part. [< L]
rac·tion (in·frak′shən) *n.* The act of breaking or violat- (a pledge, law, etc.); infringement. [< L *infractio, -onis*]
ran·gi·ble (in·fran′jə·bəl) *adj.* **1.** Not breakable or ca-ble of being broken into parts. **2.** Inviolable. — **in·n′gi·bil′i·ty, in·fran′gi·ble·ness** *n.* — **in·fran′gi·bly** *adv.*
ra·red (in′frə·red′) *adj.* *Physics* Having a wavelength ater than that of visible red light, and radiating heat.
re·quent (in·frē′kwənt) *adj.* Present or occurring at dely separated intervals; uncommon. — **in·fre′quence, fre′quen·cy** *n.* — **in·fre′quent·ly** *adv.*
ringe (in·frinj′) *v.t.* **fringed, fring·ing** To break or dis-ard the terms of, as a law; violate. — **to infringe on** (or **on**) To transgress or trespass on rights or privileges. [< < *in-* in + *frangere* to break] — **in·fring′er** *n.*
ringe·ment (in·frinj′mənt) *n.* **1.** The act of infringing. Any violation of a right, privilege, regulation, etc.
u·ri·ate (*v.* in·fyŏŏr′ē·āt) *v.t.* **·at·ed, ·at·ing** To make ious or very angry; enrage. [< Med.L *infuriare* to dden] — **in·fu′ri·ate·ly** *adv.* — **in·fu′ri·at′ing·ly** *adv.*
use (in·fyōōz′) *v.t.* **·fused, ·fus·ing** **1.** To instill or incul-e, as principles. **2.** To inspire; imbue: with *with.* **3.** To ur in. [< L < *in-* in + *fundere* to pour] — **in·fus′er** *n.*
us·i·ble[1] (in·fyōō′zə·bəl) *adj.* Incapable of or resisting sion or melting. — **in·fus′i·bil′i·ty, in·fus′i·ble·ness** *n.*
us·i·ble[2] (in·fyōō′zə·bəl) *adj.* Capable of being infused poured in. — **in·fus′i·bil′i·ty, in·fus′i·ble·ness** *n.*
u·sion (in·fyōō′zhən) *n.* **1.** The act of infusing. **2.** at which is infused. **3.** A liquid extract obtained by king a substance in water. [< OF or < L *infusio, -onis*]
u·sor·i·an (in′fyōō·sôr′ē·ən, -sō′rē-) *n.* One of a class one-celled animals. [< NL < L *infundere* to pour into]

-ing[1] *suffix* **1.** The act or art of doing the action expressed in the root verb: *hunting.* **2.** The product or result of an action: a *painting.* **3.** Material for: *flooring.* **4.** That which performs the action of the root verb: a *covering.* ◆ In formal writing when the *-ing* form of the verb (see *gerund*) is modified by a noun or pronoun the modifier appears in the possessive. Thus, "We objected to *his leaving*" is preferred to "We objected to *him leaving.*" [OE, *-ung, -ing*]
-ing[2] *suffix* Used in the present participle of verbs and in participial adjectives: He is *talking*; an *eating* apple. [ME < OE *-ende*]
-ing[3] *suffix of nouns* **1.** One having the quality of: *sweeting.* **2.** Descendant of: *Browning.* **3.** Small; little. [OE]
in·gen·ious (in·jēn′yəs) *adj.* **1.** Showing ingenuity; cleverly conceived. **2.** Having inventive and adaptive ability; clever. [< MF < L < *in-* in + *gignere* to beget] — **in·gen′ious·ly** *adv.* — **in·gen′ious·ness** *n.*
in·gé·nue (an′zhə·nōō′, *Fr.* aṅ·zhā·nü′) *n.* *pl.* **·nues** (-nōōz′, *Fr.* -nü′) The role of a young girl in a play, film, etc.; also, an actress who plays such roles. [< F]
in·ge·nu·i·ty (in′jə·nōō′ə·tē, -nyōō′-) *n.* *pl.* **·ties** **1.** Imaginative resources; inventiveness. **2.** Originality of design or execution. **3.** A cleverly conceived act, device, etc.
in·gen·u·ous (in·jen′yōō·əs) *adj.* **1.** Straightforward; candid; frank. **2.** Innocent and simple; naive. [< L *ingenuus* inborn, natural < *in-* in + *genus* birth, origin] — **in·gen′·u·ous·ly** *adv.* — **in·gen′u·ous·ness** *n.*
in·gest (in·jest′) *v.t.* To take or put (food, etc.) into the body by or as by swallowing. [< L *ingerere* < *in-* in + *gerere* to carry] — **in·ges′tion** *n.* — **in·ges′tive** *adj.*
in·glo·ri·ous (in·glôr′ē·əs, -glō′rē-) *adj.* Not reflecting honor or courage; disgraceful. — **in·glo′ri·ous·ly** *adv.*
in·go·ing (in′gō′ing) *adj.* Entering; going in.
in·got (ing′gət) *n.* A mass of cast metal from the crucible or mold. [? ME < OE *in-* in + *geotan* to pour]
in·grain (*v.* in·grān′) *v.t.* To impress firmly on the mind.
in·grained (in·grānd′) *adj.* **1.** Worked into the inmost texture; deep-rooted. **2.** Thorough; inveterate.
in·grate (in′grāt) *n.* An ungrateful person. [< OF < L < *in-* not + *gratus* pleasing]
in·gra·ti·ate (in·grā′shē·āt) *v.t.* **·at·ed, ·at·ing** To bring (oneself) deliberately into the favor or confidence of others. — **in·gra′ti·at′ing·ly** *adv.* — **in·gra′ti·a′tion** *n.* — **in·gra′·ti·a·to′ry** (-ə·tôr′ē, -tō′rē) *adj.* [< L *in-* into + *gratia* favor]
in·grat·i·tude (in·grat′ə·tōōd, -tyōōd) *n.* Lack of gratitude; insensibility to kindness; thanklessness.
in·gre·di·ent (in·grē′dē·ənt) *n.* **1.** Anything that enters into the composition of a mixture. **2.** A component of anything. [< F < L < *in-* in + *gradi* to walk]
in·gress (in′gres) *n.* **1.** A going in, as into a building. Also **in·gres·sion** (in·gresh′ən). **2.** A place of entrance. [< L *ingredi* to enter] — **in·gres′sive** *adj.*
in-group (in′grōōp′) *n.* *Sociol.* Any group with strong feelings of mutual cohesiveness and identification.
in·grow·ing (in′grō′ing) *adj.* **1.** Growing into the flesh: an *ingrowing* hair. **2.** Growing within or into.
in·grown (in′grōn′) *adj.* **1.** Grown into the flesh, as a toenail. **2.** Grown within; innate: *ingrown* vice.
in·gui·nal (ing′gwə·nəl) *adj.* *Anat.* Of, pertaining to, or located in the groin. [< L *inguen, -inis* groin]
inguino- *combining form* In or related to the groin. Also, before vowels, **inguin-.** [< L *inguen, -inis* groin]
in·hab·it (in·hab′it) *v.t.* To live in; occupy as a home. [< OF < L < *in-* in + *habitare* to dwell] — **in·hab′it·a·bil′i·ty** *n.* — **in·hab′it·a·ble** *adj.* — **in·hab′it·er** *n.* — **in·hab′i·ta′tion** *n.*
in·hab·i·tant (in·hab′ə·tənt) *n.* One who or that which dwells permanently, as distinguished from a visitor.
in·ha·la·tion (in′hə·lā′shən) *n.* **1.** The act of inhaling. **2.** That which is inhaled.
in·ha·la·tor in′hə·lā′tər) *n.* A device for enabling one to inhale air, medicinal vapors, anesthetics, etc.
in·hale (in·hāl′) *v.* **·haled, ·hal·ing** *v.t.* **1.** To draw into the lungs, as breath, tobacco smoke, etc.; breathe in. — *v.i.* **2.** To draw breath, tobacco smoke, etc., into the lungs. Opposed to *exhale.* [< L < *in-* in + *halare* to breathe]
in·hal·er (in·hāl′ər) *n.* **1.** One who inhales. **2.** *Med.* An inhalator. **3.** A respirator.
in·har·mo·ni·ous (in′här·mō′nē·əs) *adj.* Lacking harmony; discordant. Also **in′har·mon′ic** (-mon′ik), **in′har·mon′i·cal.** — **in′har·mo′ni·ous·ly** *adv.* — **in′har·mo′ni·ous·ness** *n.*
in·here (in·hir′) *v.i.* **·hered, ·her·ing** To be a permanent or essential part: with *in.* [< L < *in-* to + *haerere* to stick] — **in·her′ence, in·her′en·cy** *n.*
in·her·ent (in·hir′ənt, -her′-) *adj.* Forming an essential element or quality of something. — **in·her′·ent·ly** *adv.*
in·her·it (in·her′it) *v.t.* **1.** To receive (property, title, etc.) by legal succession or will. **2.** To derive (traits, qualities,

etc.) from one's parents or ancestors. **3.** To receive from one's predecessors. —*v.i.* **4.** To take possession of an inheritance. [< OF < LL *inhereditare* to appoint an heir]

in·her·it·a·ble (in·her′ə·tə·bəl) *adj.* **1.** Capable of being inherited. **2.** Entitled to inherit. —**in·her′it·a·bil′i·ty, in·her′it·a·ble·ness** *n.* —**in·her′it·a·bly** *adv.*

in·her·i·tance (in·her′ə·təns) *n.* **1.** The act of inheriting. **2.** That which is legally transmissible to an heir; legacy. **3.** Derivation of qualities from one's forebears. **4.** A property, quality, etc., derived from predecessors. **5.** Hereditary right. [< OF *enheritance*]

inheritance tax A tax imposed on an inherited estate.

in·her·i·tor (in·her′ə·tər) *n.* An heir. —**in·her′i·tress** (-tris), **in·her′i·trix** (-triks) *n.fem.*

in·hib·it (in·hib′it) *v.t.* To restrain or check (an impulse, action, etc.) [< L < *in-* in + *habere* to have, hold] —**in·hib′i·ter** or **in·hib′i·tor** *n.* —**in·hib′it·a·ble** *adj.* —**in·hib′i·tive, in·hib′i·to′ry** (-tôr′ē, -tō′rē) *adj.*

in·hi·bi·tion (in′hi·bish′ən, in′i-) *n.* **1.** A checking or re. straining; esp., a self-imposed restriction on one's behavior. **2.** *Psychol.* The blocking of one impulse or by another.

in·hos·pi·ta·ble (in·hos′pi·tə·bəl, in′hos·pit′ə·bəl) *adj.* **1.** Not hospitable. **2.** Not affording shelter, comfort, etc. —**in·hos·pi·ta·ble·ness** (in·hos′pi·tə·bəl·nis, in′hos·pit′-) *n.* —**in·hos·pi·ta·bly** (in·hos′pi·tə·blē, in′hos·pit′-) *adv.* —**in·hos′pi·tal′i·ty** (-tal′ə·tē) *n.*

in·hu·man (in·hyōō′mən) *adj.* **1.** Not befitting human nature; bestial. **2.** Not of the ordinary human type.

in·hu·mane (in′hyōō·mān′) *adj.* Not humane; cruel.

in·hu·man·i·ty (in′hyōō·man′ə·tē) *n. pl.* **·ties 1.** Lack of human or humane qualities. **2.** A cruel act, word, etc.

in·im·i·cal (in·im′i·kəl) *adj.* **1.** Characterized by harmful opposition; antagonistic. **2.** Behaving as an enemy; hostile. [< LL < L < *in-* not + *amicus* friend] —**in·im′i·cal′i·ty** (-kal′ə·tē) *n.* —**in·im′i·cal·ly** *adv.*

in·im·i·ta·ble (in·im′ə·tə·bəl) *adj.* Matchless; unique. —**in·im′i·ta·bil′i·ty, in·im′i·ta·ble·ness** *n.* —**in·im′i·ta·bly** *adv.*

in·iq·ui·tous (in·ik′wə·təs) *adj.* Characterized by iniquity; unjust. —**in·iq′ui·tous·ly** *adv.* —**in·iq′ui·tous·ness** *n.*

in·iq·ui·ty (in·ik′wə·tē) *n. pl.* **·ties 1.** Grievous violation of right or justice; wickedness. **2.** A wrongful act; sin. [< OF < L < *in-* not + *aequus* equal]

in·i·tial (in·ish′əl) *adj.* **1.** Standing at the beginning. **2.** Of or pertaining to the beginning; first. —*n.* **1.** *pl.* The first letters of one's proper name. **2.** The first letter of a word, name, etc. —*v.t.* **·tialed** or **·tialled, ·tial·ing** or **·tial·ling** To mark or sign with initials. [< L *initialis* < *initium* beginning] —**in·i′tial·ly** *adv.*

Initial Teaching Alphabet An alphabet representing the sounds of English, used in teaching children to read: also called *Augmented Roman.* Abbr. *I.T.A.*

in·i·ti·ate (in·ish′ē·āt; *for adj. & n., also* in·ish′ē·it) *v.t.* **·at·ed, ·at·ing 1.** To begin; commence; originate. **2.** To admit to membership in an organization, fraternity, cult, etc. **3.** To instruct in fundamentals. —*adj.* Initiated. —*n.* One who has been ritually admitted to an organization, cult, etc. [< L *initiare* to begin] —**in·i′ti·a·tor** *n.*

in·i·ti·a·tion (in·ish′ē·ā′shən) *n.* **1.** The act of initiating, or the state of being initiated. **2.** The rites admitting one to some position, society, knowledge, etc.

in·i·ti·a·tive (in·ish′ē·ə·tiv, -ē·ā′tiv, -ish′ə·tiv) *n.* **1.** The power or right to take the first step or the next step in some action. **2.** The action of commencing or originating. **3.** The spirit needed to originate action. **4.** In government: **a** The right or power to propose legislative measures. **b** The process by which the electorate acts to originate legislation. —**on one's own initiative** Without instruction or compulsion; freely. —*adj.* **1.** Of or pertaining to initiation. **2.** Serving to initiate. [< MF] —**in·i′ti·a·tive·ly** *adv.*

in·ject (in·jekt′) *v.t.* **1.** To drive (a fluid, drug, etc.) into a bodily cavity, blood vessel, etc. by means of a syringe, needle, etc. **2.** To introduce (some new element): with *into.* **3.** To throw in or introduce abruptly (a comment, etc.). [< L < *in-* in + *jacere* to throw] —**in·jec′·tion** *n.*

in·ju·di·cious (in′jōō·dish′əs) *adj.* Not judicious; imprudent. —**in′ju·di′cious·ly** *adv.* —**in′ju·di′cious·ness** *n.*

in·junc·tion (in·jungk′shən) *n.* **1.** The act of enjoining. **2.** An authoritative order. **3.** *Law* A judicial order requiring the party to do or refrain from some specified action. [< LL *injungere* to join to, enjoin] —**in·junc′tive** *adj.*

in·jure (in′jər) *v.t.* **·jured, ·jur·ing 1.** To harm, damage, or impair, especially physically; hurt. **2.** To wrong or offend. [Back formation < INJURY] —**in′jur·er** *n.*

in·ju·ri·ous (in·jŏŏr′ē·əs) *adj.* **1.** Causing damage or hurt; harmful. **2.** Slanderous; abusive. —**in·ju′ri·ous·ly** *adv.* —**in·ju′ri·ous·ness** *n.*

in·ju·ry (in′jər·ē) *n. pl.* **·ries 1.** Harm, damage, or grievous distress inflicted or suffered. **2.** A particular instance of such harm. [< OF < L < *in-* not + *jus, juris* right]

in·jus·tice (in·jus′tis) *n.* **1.** The fact or quality of being unjust. **2.** An unjust act; wrong. [< OF < L *injustus* unjust]

ink (ingk) *n.* **1.** Any of various colored substances in a fluid or viscous consistency for writing, drawing, printing. **2.** The dark fluid ejected by cuttlefish, etc. *v.t.* To spread ink upon; stain or color with ink. [< < LL *encaustum* purple ink] —**ink′er** *n.*

ink·horn (ingk′hôrn′) *n.* A small container for ink.

inkhorn term A bookish, pedantic word.

ink·ling (ingk′ling) *n.* **1.** A slight suggestion or hint. A vague idea or notion. [ME < OE *inca* suspicion]

ink·stand (ingk′stand′) *n.* **1.** A rack or device for hol ink, pens, etc. **2.** An inkwell.

ink·well (ingk′wel′) *n.* A container for ink.

ink·y (ing′kē) *adj.* **ink·i·er, ink·i·est 1.** Resembling in color; dark; black. **2.** Of, pertaining to, or containing **3.** Smeared or stained with ink. —**ink′i·ness** *n.*

in·laid (in′lād, in·lād′) *adj.* **1.** Decorated with wood, iv or other material embedded flush with the surface. **2.** serted to form a flush embedded pattern.

in·land (in′lənd; *for n. and adv., also* in′land′) *adj.* **1.** mote from the sea or the border. **2.** Pertaining to or loc in the interior of a country: *inland* population. **3.** foreign; domestic: *inland* trade. —*n.* The interior country. —*adv.* In or towards the interior of a land.

in·land·er (in′lən·dər, -land′ər) *n.* One who lives inla

in-law (in′lô′) *n. Informal* A close relative by marri

in·lay (*v.* in·lā′, in′lā′; *n.* in′lā′) *v.t.* **·laid, ·lay·ing 1.** T or embed (ivory, gold, etc.) flush into a surface so as to f a pattern. **2.** To decorate by inserting such designs. *n.* **1.** That which is inlaid. **2.** A pattern or design so duced. **3.** *Dent.* A filling for a tooth. —**in′lay′er** *n.*

in·let (*n.* in′let, -lit; *v.* in·let′) *n.* **1.** A relatively na channel of water; as: **a** A stream or bay leading into l **b** A passage between nearby islands, floes, etc. **c** An e from one body of water into another. **2.** An opening.

in lo·co pa·ren·tis (in lō′kō pə·ren′tis) *Latin* In the p of a parent.

in·mate (in′māt′) *n.* **1.** One who is lodged or confined prison, asylum, hospital, etc. **2.** An inhabitant. **3.** who dwells with another or others. [? < INN + MATE

in me·di·as res (in mē′dē·əs rēz) *Latin* In the mids things; in the middle of events and not at the beginnin

in me·mo·ri·am (in mə·môr′ē·əm, -mō′rē) *Latin* In m ory (of); as a memorial (to).

in·most (in′mōst′, -məst) *adj.* **1.** Located farthest from outside. **2.** Most private or intimate. [OE *innemest*]

inn (in) *n.* A hotel, etc., where travelers may obtain m or lodging. [OE *inn* room, house]

in·nards (in′ərdz) *n.pl. Dial. & Informal* The inte organs or parts of the body, a machine, etc.; insides.

in·nate (i·nāt′, in′āt) *adj.* Inherent in one's nature; born; not acquired. [< L *in-* in + *nasci* to be born] **in·nate′ly** *adv.* —**in·nate′ness** *n.*

in·ner (in′ər) *adj.* **1.** Located or occurring farther ins internal; interior. **2.** Pertaining to the mind or spirit; s jective. **3.** More obscure; hidden; esoteric. [OE *inne* compar. of *inne* in (adv.)] —**in′ner·ly** *adv.* —**in′ner·nes**

in·ner·most (in′ər·mōst′) *adj.* Inmost; farthest withi

inner tube A flexible, inflatable tube, usu. of rubber, u inside a pneumatic tire.

in·ning (in′ing) *n.* **1.** In baseball, a division of the g during which each team has a turn to bat. **2.** *pl.* In cric the period during which one side bats. **3.** *Often pl.* A cha for action. [OE *innung*, gerund of *innian* to put in]

inn·keep·er (in′kē′pər) *n.* The proprietor or host of an

in·no·cence (in′ə·səns) *n.* The quality or fact of be innocent. Also **in′no·cen·cy.**

in·no·cent (in′ə·sənt) *adj.* **1.** Not tainted with sin, evi moral wrong; pure. **2.** Free from blame or guilt, especi legally. **3.** Not tending to harm or injure: *innocent* times. **4.** Not maliciously intended: an *innocent* lie. Lacking in worldly knowledge; naive. **6.** Devoid of; tirely lacking in: with *of*: *innocent* of grammar. —*n.* One who is free from evil or sin. **2.** A simple or unsusp ing person. [< OF < L < *in-* not + *nocere* to harm] **in′no·cent·ly** *adv.*

in·noc·u·ous (i·nok′yōō·əs) *adj.* Having no harmful qu ties or effects; harmless. [< L < *in-* not + *nocuus* harm —**in·noc′u·ous·ly** *adv.* —**in·noc′u·ous·ness** *n.*

in·nom·i·nate bone (i·nom′a·nit) *Anat.* One of two la irregular bones that form the sides of the pelvis: also ca *haunch bone, hipbone.*

in·no·vate (in′ə·vāt) *v.* **·vat·ed, ·vat·ing** *v.t.* **1.** To in duce or bring in (something new). —*v.i.* **2.** To brin new ideas, methods, etc. [< L *in-* in + *novare* to make n —**in′no·va′tive** *adj.* —**in′no·va′tor** *n.*

in·no·va·tion (in′ə·vā′shən) *n.* **1.** Something newly in duced. **2.** The act of introducing something new. — **no·va′tion·al** *adj.* —**in′no·va′tion·ist** *n.*

in·nu·en·do (in′yōō·en′dō) *n. pl.* **·does** An oblique c ment, hint, or suggestion, usu. derogatory. [< L < *in* + *-nuere* to nod]

u·mer·a·ble (i·nōō′mər·ə·bəl, i·nyōō′-) *adj.* Too nu-ous to be counted; numberless. Also **in·nu′mer·ous.** **Syn.** See INFINITE. — **in·nu′mer·a·bil′i·ty, in·nu′mer·a·ness** *n.* — **in·nu′mer·a·bly** *adv.*

c·u·late (in·ok′yə·lāt) *v.* **·lat·ed, ·lat·ing** *v.t.* **1.** To com-nicate a mild form of a disease to (a person, animal, etc.) as to produce immunity; also, to implant (a disease, teria, etc.). **2.** To inject immunizing serums, vaccines, into. **3.** To implant ideas, opinions, etc., in the mind — *v.i.* **4.** To perform inoculation. [< L *inoculare* to an eye or bud into] — **in·oc′u·la′tion** *n.* — **in·oc′u·ive** (-lā′tiv) *adj.* — **in·oc′u·la′tor** (-lā′tər) *n.*

f·fen·sive (in′ə·fen′siv) *adj.* Giving no offense; in-uous. — **in′of·fen′sive·ly** *adv.* — **in′of·fen′sive·ness** *n.*

)·er·a·ble (in·op′ər·ə·bəl) *adj.* **1.** Incapable of being ed or improved by surgical operation: *inoperable* cancer. Not practicable; unworkable. — **in·op′er·a·bil′i·ty, in·er·a·ble·ness** *n.* — **in·op′er·a·bly** *adv.*

p·er·a·tive (in·op′ər·ə·tiv) *adj.* **1.** Not functioning. **2.** effectual or in effect. — **in·op′er·a·tive·ness** *n.*

o·por·tune (in·op·ər·tōōn′, -tyōōn′) *adj.* Untimely or ppropriate; unsuitable. — **in·op′por·tune′ly** *adv.*

r·di·nate (in·ôr′də·nit) *adj.* **1.** Exceeding proper limits; noderate; excessive. **2.** Unrestrained: *inordinate* pas-. — **in·or′di·na·cy** (-nə·sē), **in·or′di·nate·ness** *n.* — **r′di·nate·ly** *adv.*

r·gan·ic (in′ôr·gan′ik) *adj.* **1.** Not having the organ-structure of animal or vegetable life; not living; inan-te. **2.** Not characterized by life processes. **3.** *Chem.* Of, taining to, or designating the branch of chemistry dealing h compounds lacking carbon or containing it only in the n of carbonates, carbides, and most cyanides.

a·tient (in′pā′shənt) *n.* A patient who is lodged and fed well as medically treated in a hospital, clinic, or the like.

ut (in′pŏŏt′) *n.* **1.** The amount of energy delivered to a chine, storage battery, etc. **2.** *Electr.* The voltage, cur-t, power, etc., delivered to a circuit. **3.** *Electronics* Infor-tion placed in an electronic computer for later use.

uest (in′kwest) *n.* **1.** A legal investigation into a cial matter; esp., one undertaken before a jury or by a oner. **2.** The body of men chosen to make such an in-ry; also, its findings. [See INQUIRE.]

ui·e·tude (in·kwī′ə·tōōd, -tyōōd) *n.* **1.** A state of rest-ness; uneasiness. **2.** *pl.* Anxieties; disquieting thoughts. **n·qui′et** *adj.* — **in·qui′et·ly** *adv.*

uire (in·kwīr′) *v.* **·quired, ·quir·ing** *v.i.* **1.** To seek in-nation by asking questions; ask. **2.** To make an inves-ation: with *into.* — *v.t.* **3.** To ask information about: ey *inquired* the way. Also spelled *enquire.* — **Syn.** See . [< OF < L < *in-* into + *quaerere* to seek] — **in·r′er** *n.* — **in·quir′ing·ly** *adv.*

uir·y (in·kwīr′ē, in′kwər·ē) *n.* *pl.* **·quir·ies 1.** The act nquiring or seeking. **2.** Investigation; research. **3.** A stion; query. Also spelled *enquiry.* [ME *enquery*]

ui·si·tion (in′kwə·zish′ən) *n.* **1.** An investigation of beliefs and activities of individuals, political groups, etc., the ultimate purpose of enforcing orthodoxy. **2.** The of inquiring or searching out. **3.** An inquest. — **in′·si′tion·ist, in·quis·i·tor** (in·kwiz′ə·tər) *n.*

ui·si·tion (in′kwə·zish′ən) *n.* A former judicial system he Roman Catholic Church for the discovery, examina-n, and punishment of heretics: also called *Holy Office.*

ui·si·tion·al (in′kwə·zish′ən·əl) *adj.* **1.** Of or pertain-to an inquisition or the Inquisition. **2.** Characterized by estioning, prying, etc. — **in′qui·si′tion·al·ly** *adv.*

uis·i·tive (in·kwiz′ə·tiv) *adj.* **1.** Somewhat too curious; luly questioning; prying. **2.** Eager for knowledge or rning. [< OF < LL *inquisitivus*] — **in·quis′i·tive·ly** . — **in·quis′i·tive·ness** *n.*

uis·i·tor (in·kwiz′ə·tər) *n.* **1.** One who inquires, inves-ates, or examines. **2.** A member of the Inquisition. [< < L *inquisitor*]

uis·i·to·ri·al (in·kwiz′ə·tôr′ē·əl, -tō′rē, in′kwiz-) *adj.* Of, pertaining to, or resembling an inquisitor or inquisi-n; offensively curious. **2.** Acting as an inquisitor. — **quis′i·to′ri·al·ly** *adv.* — **in·quis′i·to′ri·al·ness** *n.*

e (in rē′) *Law* In the matter (of); concerning. [< L]

.R.I. Jesus of Nazareth, King of the Jews (L *Iesus Naza-us, Rex Iudaeorum*).

oad (in′rōd′) *n.* **1.** *Usu. pl.* A serious encroachment; mful trespass: with *on* or *upon*: *inroads* on one's happi-ss. **2.** A hostile raid or foray. [< IN-[2] + obs. *road* riding]

ush (in′rush′) *n.* A sudden rushing in; invasion.

a·lu·bri·ous (in′sə·lōō′brē·əs) *adj.* Not wholesome; not lthful. [< L *insalubris*] — **in′sa·lu′bri·ous·ly** *adv.*

ane (in·sān′) *adj.* **1.** Not sane; mentally deranged or sound. **2.** Characteristic of one who is not sane. **3.** tremely foolish; hare-brained. **4.** Set apart for demented persons: *insane* asylum. [< L *in-* not + *sanus* whole] — **in·sane′ly** *adv.* — **in·sane′ness** *n.*

in·san·i·tar·y (in·san′ə·ter·ē) *adj.* Not sanitary; dangerous to health; unhygienic. — **in·san′i·ta′tion** *n.*

in·san·i·ty (in·san′ə·tē) *n.* *pl.* **·ties 1.** The state of being insane: not a technical term in medicine or psychiatry. **2.** *Law* A defect or weakness of mind that releases a person from legal responsibility. **3.** Extreme folly.

in·sa·tia·ble (in·sā′shə·bəl, -shē·ə·bəl) *adj.* Incapable of being sated or satisfied; extremely greedy. Also **in·sa·ti·ate** (in·sā′shē·it). — **in·sa′ti·a·bil′i·ty, in·sa′tia·ble·ness** *n.* — **in·sa′tia·bly, in·sa′ti·ate·ly** *adv.* — **in·sa′ti·ate·ness** *n.*

in·scribe (in·skrīb′) *v.t.* **·scribed, ·scrib·ing 1.** To write, mark, or engrave (words, names, characters, etc.). **2.** To mark (a document, tablet, etc.) with writing or engraving. **3.** To enter (a name) on a formal or official list. **4.** To sign or dedicate (a book, photograph, etc.) for presentation. **5.** *Geom.* To draw (one figure) in another so that the latter circumscribes the former. [< L < *in-* on, in + *scribere* to write] — **in·scrib′er** *n.*

in·scrip·tion (in·skrip′shən) *n.* **1.** That which is inscribed; also, the act of inscribing. **2.** A durable marking or engraving on a solid object. **3.** An informal written dedication. — **in·scrip′tion·al, in·scrip′tive** *adj.*

in·scru·ta·ble (in·skrōō′tə·bəl) *adj.* That cannot be searched into or understood; incomprehensible. — **Syn.** See MYSTERIOUS. [< LL < *in-* not + *scrutare* to explore] — **in·scru′ta·bil′i·ty, in·scru′ta·ble·ness** *n.* — **in·scru′ta·bly** *adv.*

in·sect (in′sekt) *n.* **1.** *Zool.* Any of a large, cosmopolitan class of small to minute air-breathing invertebrate animals, usu. having six legs, a body divided into a head, thorax, and abdomen, and one or two pairs of wings or none. **2.** Loosely, any small, air-breathing invertebrate resembling an insect, as spiders, centipedes, ticks, etc. [< L (*animal*) *insectum* (animal) notched, alluding totheir segmented bodies]

in·sec·ti·cide (in·sek′tə·sīd) *n.* A substance used or prepared for killing insects.

in·sec·ti·val (in′sek·tī′vəl, in·sek′tə-) *adj.* Of, pertaining to, or resembling an insect.

in·sec·tiv·o·rous (in′sek·tiv′ər·əs) *adj.* Feeding or subsisting upon insects, as shrews, moles, hedgehogs, etc.

in·se·cure (in′sə·kyŏŏr′) *adj.* **1.** Liable to break, fail, collapse, etc.; unsafe. **2.** Troubled by anxiety and apprehensiveness; threatened. [< Med.L *insecurus*] — **in′se·cure′·ly** *adv.* — **in′se·cure′ness** *n.*

in·se·cu·ri·ty (in′sə·kyŏŏr′ə·tē) *n.* *pl.* **·ties 1.** The state or quality of being unsafe or liable to injury, failure, loss, etc. **2.** A condition of anxiety and apprehensiveness; sense of being unsafe and threatened. **3.** *Often pl.* An instance of insecurity. [< Med.L *insecuritas*]

in·sem·i·nate (in·sem′ə·nāt) *v.t.* **·nat·ed, ·nat·ing 1.** To make pregnant; inject semen into the vagina of. **2.** To sow (seed); also, to implant (ideas, etc.). **3.** To sow seed in; implant in. [< L < *in-* in + *seminare* to sow] — **in·sem′i·na′tion** *n.*

in·sen·sate (in·sen′sāt, -sit) *adj.* **1.** Showing a lack of humane feeling; unmoved; brutish. **2.** Stupid; foolish. **3.** Lacking physical sensation; inanimate. [< LL *insensatus*] — **in·sen′sate·ly** *adv.* — **in·sen′sate·ness** *n.*

in·sen·si·ble (in·sen′sə·bəl) *adj.* **1.** Deprived of consciousness; unconscious. **2.** Incapable of feeling or perceiving; indifferent: *insensible* to pain. **3.** So slight or gradual as to escape notice; imperceptible. [< LL *insensibilis*] — **in·sen′si·bil′i·ty** *n.* — **in·sen′si·bly** *adv.*

in·sen·si·tive (in·sen′sə·tiv) *adj.* **1.** Not keenly responsive in feeling or reaction. **2.** Without physical feeling or sensation. **3.** Not affected by physical agencies: *insensitive* to light. — **in·sen′si·tiv′i·ty, in·sen′si·tive·ness** *n.* — **in·sen′·si·tive·ly** *adv.*

in·sen·ti·ent (in·sen′shē·ənt, -shənt) *adj.* Lacking senses or consciousness; inanimate. — **in·sen′ti·ence** *n.*

in·sep·a·ra·ble (in·sep′ər·ə·bəl) *adj.* Incapable of being separated or parted. — *n.* *Usu. pl.* Persons or things that are always together. — **in·sep′a·ra·bil′i·ty, in·sep′a·ra·ble·ness** *n.* — **in·sep′a·ra·bly** *adv.*

in·sert (*v.* in·sûrt′; *n.* in′sûrt) *v.t.* **1.** To put in; place; set. **2.** To introduce into a body of printed matter. — *n.* **1.** That which is inserted. **2.** In bookbinding, illustrations, maps, etc., not part of the printed text, bound into the finished book: also called *inset.* **3.** *U.S.* A circular, pamphlet, etc., set within a newspaper, magazine, or book for mailing. [< L *in-* in + *serere* to sow, plant] — **in·sert′er** *n.*

in·ser·tion (in·sûr′shən) *n.* **1.** The act of inserting. **2.** That which is inserted; as: **a** A word, sentence, etc. **b** A strip of lace or embroidery sewn into plain cloth. **c** Each appearance of an advertisement, as in a newspaper.

in·set (*v.* in·set′; *n.* in′set) *v.t.* **·set, ·set·ting** To set in; insert; implant. — *n.* **1.** In bookbinding, an insert. **2.** A

small diagram, map, etc., inserted in the border of a larger one. 3. A piece of material let or set into a garment.
in·sheathe (in·shēth′) *v.t.* **·sheathed, ·sheath·ing** To place in or as in a sheath.
in·shore (in′shôr′, -shōr′) *adj.* Near or coming toward the shore. — *adv.* Toward the shore.
in·shrine (in·shrīn′) See ENSHRINE.
in·side (*n. & adj.* in′sīd′, -sīd′; *adv. & prep.* in′sīd′) *n.* **1.** The part, surface, space, etc., that lies within; interior. **2.** The internal nature or workings that are concealed. **3.** *pl. Informal* The inner parts of the body or a machine; innards. — **inside out** Reversed so that the inside is exposed. — *adj.* **1.** Situated within; inner; internal; interior. **2.** Restricted to a few; confidential. **3.** In baseball, passing too close to the batter: said of pitches. **4.** Suitable for, used, or working indoors; indoor. — *adv.* **1.** In or into the interior; within. **2.** Indoors. — *prep.* In or into the interior of. — **inside of** *Informal* **1.** Within; enclosed by. **2.** Within the time or distance specified: *inside of* a year.
in·si·der (in′sī′dər) *n.* **1.** A member of a given group, club, etc. **2.** One close to a source, as of knowledge or influence.
inside track **1.** The shortest path around a race track. **2.** *Informal* A position of special advantage.
in·sid·i·ous (in·sid′ē·əs) *adj.* **1.** Subtly cunning or deceitful; treacherous; wily. **2.** Progressing imperceptibly but harmfully: *insidious* disease. [< L *insidere* to sit in, lie in wait] — **in·sid′i·ous·ly** *adv.* — **in·sid′i·ous·ness** *n.*
in·sight (in′sīt′) *n.* Perception into the inner nature or real character of a thing. — **Syn.** See ACUMEN.
in·sig·ni·a (in·sig′nē·ə) *n.* *pl. of* **in·sig·ne** (in·sig′nē) **1.** Badges, emblems, brassards, and the like, used as marks of membership, office, or honor: the royal *insignia*. **2.** Marks betokening anything: the *insignia* of grief. [< L]
in·sig·nif·i·cance (in′sig·nif′ə·kəns) *n.* The quality or state of being insignificant; unimportance.
in·sig·nif·i·can·cy (in′sig·nif′ə·kən·sē) *n.* *pl.* **·cies** **1.** Insignificance. **2.** An insignificant person or thing.
in·sig·nif·i·cant (in′sig·nif′ə·kənt) *adj.* **1.** Having no importance; trivial; trifling. **2.** Meaningless. **3.** Lacking size or quantity. **4.** Of persons, lacking distinction, character, etc. — **in′sig·nif′i·cant·ly** *adv.*
in·sin·cere (in′sin·sir′) *adj.* Not sincere; hypocritical. — **in′sin·cere′ly** *adv.* — **in′sin·cer′i·ty** (-ser′ə·tē) *n.*
in·sin·u·ate (in·sin′yōō·āt) *v.* **·at·ed, ·at·ing** *v.t.* **1.** To suggest by innuendo; hint. **2.** To introduce subtly and gradually. — *v.i.* **3.** To give sly and indirect intimations. [< L < *in-* in + *sinuare* to curve] — **in·sin′u·at′ing·ly** *adv.* — **in·sin′u·a′tive** *adj.* — **in·sin′u·a′tor** *n.*
in·sin·u·a·tion (in·sin′yōō·ā′shən) *n.* **1.** That which is insinuated; a sly hint. **2.** The act of insinuating.
in·sip·id (in·sip′id) *adj.* **1.** Lacking spirit and vivacity; vapid; dull. **2.** Lacking flavor or savor; tasteless; flat; bland. [< L < *in-* not + *sapidus* savory] — **in·si·pid·i·ty** (in′si·pid′ə·tē), **in·sip′id·ness** *n.* — **in·sip′id·ly** *adv.*
in·sist (in·sist′) *v.i.* **1.** To demand or assert firmly and forcefully: with *on* or *upon*. **2.** To dwell on or repeatedly emphasize something: with *on* or *upon*. — *v.t.* **3.** To demand or maintain forcefully: with a noun clause as object: He *insisted* that the gate be opened. [< OF < L *insistere* to stand on, tread on] — **in·sis′tence, in·sis′ten·cy** *n.*
in·sis·tent (in·sis′tənt) *adj.* **1.** Insisting; persistent; urgent. **2.** Demanding attention. — **in·sis′tent·ly** *adv.*
in·snare (in·snâr′) See ENSNARE.
in·so·bri·e·ty (in′sə·brī′ə·tē) *n.* *pl.* **·ties** Lack of sobriety; intemperance, esp. in drinking.
in·so·far (in′sō·fär′) *adv.* To such an extent; in such measure: followed by *as*. Also **in so far.**
in·sole (in′sōl′) *n.* **1.** The fixed inner sole of a shoe or boot. **2.** A removable inner sole placed in a shoe to improve its fit or to protect against dampness.
in·so·lence (in′sə·ləns) *n.* **1.** The character or quality of being insolent. **2.** An insult.
in·so·lent (in′sə·lənt) *adj.* Overbearing or offensively impertinent in conduct or speech; insulting; disrespectful. — *n.* An insolent person. [< L *insolens, -entis* unusual, haughty] — **in′so·lent·ly** *adv.*
in·sol·u·ble (in·sol′yə·bəl) *adj.* **1.** Not soluble; incapable of being dissolved. **2.** Not solvable; incapable of being solved. — **in·sol′u·bil′i·ty, in·sol′u·ble·ness** *n.* — **in·sol′u·bly** *adv.*
in·solv·a·ble (in·sol′və·bəl) *adj.* Not solvable.
in·sol·ven·cy (in·sol′vən·sē) *n.* *pl.* **·cies** The state of being insolvent; bankruptcy.
in·sol·vent (in·sol′vənt) *adj.* *Law* **1.** Unable to meet the claims of creditors; bankrupt. **2.** Insufficient for the payment of debts. **3.** Of insolvency. — *n.* An insolvent person.
in·som·ni·a (in·som′nē·ə) *n.* Chronic inability to sleep. [< L < *in-* without + *somnus* sleep] — **in·som′ni·ac** *n.* — **in·som′ni·ous** *adj.*
in·so·much (in′sō·much′) *adv.* **1.** To such a degree: with *that* or *as*. **2.** Inasmuch: with *as*.
in·sou·ci·ant (in·sōō′sē·ənt, *Fr.* aṅ·sōō·syäṅ′) *adj.* Lighthearted; carefree; unconcerned. [< F] — **in·sou′ci·an**[ce] — **in·sou·ci·ant·ly** (in·sōō′sē·ənt·lē) *adv.*
in·spect (in·spekt′) *v.t.* **1.** To look at or examine caref[ully] esp., to examine for faults or defects. **2.** To examine o[r] view officially and with ceremony, as troops. [< L < *i*[*n-*] to + *specere* to look]
in·spec·tion (in·spek′shən) *n.* **1.** The act of inspec[ting;] careful or critical examination. **2.** An official examina[tion,] check, or review, as of troops. — **in·spec′tion·al** *adj.*
in·spec·tor (in·spek′tər) *n.* **1.** One who inspects. **2.** A[n of]ficial examiner or checker. **3.** An officer of police usu. r[ank]ing next below the superintendent. [< L] — **in·spe**[**cto**]**ral, in′spec·to′ri·al** (-tôr′ē·əl, -tō′rē·əl) *adj.* — **in·spe**[**ctor**]**ate, in·spec′tor·ship** *n.*
in·spi·ra·tion (in′spə·rā′shən) *n.* **1.** The infusion or ar[ousal] within the mind of some idea, feeling, or impulse, esp[.] that leads to creative action. **2.** The state or quality o[f be]ing inspired. **3.** One who or that which acts as an insp[iring] influence. **4.** Something that results from being insp[ired,] as an idea, etc. **5.** *Theol.* Divine influence exerted upo[n the] mind or spirit. **6.** The act of drawing in the breath; in[hala]tion. — **in′spi·ra′tion·al** *adj.* — **in′spi·ra′tion·al·ly** *ad*[*v.*]
in·spire (in·spīr′) *v.* **·spired, ·spir·ing** *v.t.* **1.** To exert a vigorative influence upon (a person); animate; stir. **2.** [To] move (a person) to a particular feeling, idea, etc.: It *ins*[*pired*] me with hope. **3.** To arouse or create (a feeling, idea, e[tc.];) generate: to *inspire* fear. **4.** To direct or guide, as by sp[ecial] divine influence. **5.** To breathe in; inhale: opposed t[o *ex*]*pire*. — *v.i.* **6.** To inhale. **7.** To give or provide ins[pira]tion. [< OF < L < *in-* into + *spirare* to breathe] — [**in·**]**spir′a·ble** *adj.* — **in·spir′er** *n.*
in·spir·it (in·spir′it) *v.t.* To fill with renewed spirit or animate; exhilarate; enliven. — **in·spir′it·ing·ly** *adv.*
in·spis·sate (in·spis′āt) *v.t. & v.i.* **·sat·ed, ·sat·ing** To t[hick]en, as by evaporation. [< L < *in-* thoroughly + *spiss*[*are* to] thicken] — **in·spis·sa·tion** (in′spi·sā′shən) *n.* — **in·**[**spis**]**sa·tor** (in′spi·sā′tər) *n.*
in·sta·bil·i·ty (in′stə·bil′ə·tē) *n.* *pl.* **·ties** **1.** Lack of [sta]bility. **2.** Unsteadiness of character; unreliability.
in·sta·ble (in·stā′bəl) *adj.* Unstable.
in·stall (in·stôl′) *v.t.* **1.** To fix in position and adjus[t for] service or use: to *install* a hot-water system. **2.** To pla[ce in] any office, rank, etc. **3.** To establish in a place or posi[tion;] settle. Also *Chiefly Brit.* **in·stal′**. [< MF < Med.L < *i*[*n-*] + *stallum* seat < OHG *stal* seat] — **in·stall′er** *n.*
in·stal·la·tion (in′stə·lā′shən) *n.* **1.** Any device or sys[tem,] esp. mechanical, set in place and readied for use. **2.** Th[e act] of installing, or the state of being installed. **3.** *Mil.* [A] large, fixed base or facility of the armed service.
in·stall·ment[1] (in·stôl′mənt) *n.* **1.** A portion of a de[bt or] sum of money made payable in specified amounts at spec[ified] intervals. **2.** One of several parts, as of a serial in a new[spa]per or magazine. Also *Brit.* **in·stal′ment.**
in·stall·ment[2] (in·stôl′mənt) *n.* Installation.
installment plan A system of paying for goods or ser[vices] by fixed, periodic amounts.
in·stance (in′stəns) *n.* **1.** A case or example. **2.** A st[age in] proceedings: in the first *instance*. — **at the instance of** the request or urging of. — **for instance** For example. — *v.t.* **·stanced, ·stanc·ing** To cite as an example. [< OF *instantia* presence, urgent pleading]
in·stant (in′stənt) *n.* **1.** A very short time; moment; t[win]kling. **2.** A specific point in time: at the same *instant*. — *adj.* **1.** Instantaneous; immediate: *instant* recognition. [**2.**] Pressing; urgent. **3.** Prepared quickly by the additio[n of] water, milk, etc.: *instant* coffee. — *adv. Poetic* Instant[ane]ously; instantly. [< OF < L < *in-* upon + *stare* to st[and]]
in·stan·ta·ne·ous (in′stən·tā′nē·əs) *adj.* **1.** Happening [with] no delay; immediate. **2.** Acting or completed within a [mo]ment. [< INSTANT, on analogy with *simultaneous*] — [**in′**]**stan·ta′ne·ous·ly** *adv.* — **in′stan·ta′ne·ous·ness** *n.*
in·stant·er (in·stan′tər) *adv.* Immediately; at once. [<
in·stant·ly (in′stənt·lē) *adv.* **1.** Without delay; at once. [**2.**] *Archaic* With urgency. — *conj.* As soon as.
in·stead (in·sted′) *adv.* **1.** In place or lieu; rather than: [with] *of*: a friend *instead* of an enemy. **2.** In the place of that mentioned: to look for silver and find gold *instead*.
in·step (in′step′) *n.* **1.** *Anat.* The arched upper part of [the] human foot, extending from the toes to the ankle. **2.** [The] part of a shoe or stocking covering this.
in·sti·gate (in′stə·gāt) *v.t.* **·gat·ed, ·gat·ing** **1.** To spu[r on] or goad to some drastic course or deed; incite. **2.** To b[ring] about by inciting; foment; provoke: to *instigate* treason. [< L < *in-* against + the root *-stig-* to prick, goad] — **in′sti**[**ga**]**tion** *n.* — **in′sti·ga′tive** *adj.* — **in′sti·ga′tor** *n.*
in·still (in·stil′) *v.t.* **1.** To introduce (a quality, feel[ing,] idea, etc.) gradually or by degrees: to *instill* courage. **2.** [To] pour in gradually by drops. Also *esp. Brit.* **in·stil′**. [< L *in-* + *stillare* to drop] — **in·stil·la·tion** (in′stə·lā′shən) *n.* — **in·still′er** *n.* — **in·still′ment** or **in·stil′ment** *n.*
in·stinct (*n.* in′stingkt; *adj.* in·stingkt′) *n.* **1.** *Biol. &*

. An innate tendency or response of a given species to act
'ays that are essential to its existence, development, and
ervation. **2.** A natural aptitude; knack. — *adj.* Ani-
ed from within; alive: usu. with *with.* [< L *instinctus,*
of *instinguere* to impel] — **in·stinc'tu·al** (-cho͞o·əl) *adj.*
inc·tive (in·stingk'tiv) *adj.* **1.** Arising from or as from
inct: an *instinctive* fear. **2.** Of or pertaining to instinct.
n·stinc'tive·ly *adv.*
i·tute (in'stə·to͞ot, -tyo͞ot) *v.t.* **·tut·ed, ·tut·ing 1.** To set
r establish; found. **2.** To set in operation; initiate; start.
Eccl. To place (a clergyman) in spiritual charge of a par-
with *in* or *into.* — *n.* **1.** A group or society devoted to
promotion of some particular field, often of a learned na-
: an art *institute;* also, the building or buildings housing
a society. **2.** In education: **a** *Usu. cap.* A college for
ialized instruction, often technical. **b** A center for post-
uate study and research. **3.** Something instituted, as an
blished principle, rule, or order. [< L < *in-* in, on +
ere to set up] — **in'sti·tut'er, in'sti·tu'tor** *n.*
i·tu·tion (in'stə·to͞o'shən, -tyo͞o'-) *n.* **1.** A principle,
om, etc., that forms part of a society or civilization: the
itution of slavery. **2.** A corporate body organized to per-
some particular function, often in education, research,
ity, etc.; also, the building or buildings housing such a
y. **3.** A mental hospital, prison, or other place of con-
nent: a euphemistic use. **4.** *Informal* A familiar and
acteristic object, custom, or person. **5.** The act of inting, establishing, or setting in operation.
i·tu·tion·al (in'stə·to͞o'shən·əl, -tyo͞o'-) *adj.* **1.** Of, per-
ing to, or characteristic of an institution. **2.** Designat-
a form of advertising intended to promote good will and
tige. — **in'sti·tu'tion·al·ly** *adv.*
i·tu·tion·al·ize (in'stə·to͞o'shən·əl·īz', -tyo͞o'-) *v.t.* **·ized,**
ng 1. To make institutional. **2.** To turn into or regard
n institution. **3.** *U.S. Informal* To put (someone) in an
tution, as for the aged. — **in'sti·tu'tion·al·i·za'tion** *n.*
ruct (in·strukt') *v.t.* **1.** To impart knowledge or skill
sp. by systematic method; educate; teach. **2.** To give
ific orders or directions to; order — **Syn.** See TEACH.
L < *in-* in + *struere* to build]
ruc·tion (in·struk'shən) *n.* **1.** The act of instructing or
hing. **2.** Knowledge or factual matter imparted; also,
em of such knowledge taught, as a rule, precept, or les-
3. *pl.* Directions; orders. — **in·struc'tion·al** *adj.*
ruc·tive (in·struk'tiv) *adj.* Serving to instruct; infor-
ive. — **in·struc'tive·ly** *adv.* — **in·struc'tive·ness** *n.*
ruc·tor (in·struk'tər) *n.* **1.** One who instructs; teacher.
J.S. A college teacher not having professorial rank. [<
— **in·struc'tor·ship** *n.* — **in·struc·tress** *n. fem.*
ru·ment (*n.* in'strə·mənt; *v.* in'strə·ment) *n.* **1.** A tool
nplement, esp. one used for exacting work: a surgical *in-*
ment. **2.** A device for producing musical sounds. **3.** An
aratus for measuring or recording; as: **a** A gauge or de-
for indicating engine performance, etc., in aircraft, re-
ies, and other complex systems. **b** A system or device
for navigation and control in aircraft, ships, rockets,
4. Anything serving to accomplish a purpose; means;
ncy. **5.** A person doing the will of another; dupe. **6.**
A formal legal document, as a contract, deed, etc. —
nstruments *Aeron.* Flying, landing, or navigating by
ns of instruments rather than by visual observation of
horizon, ground objects, etc. — **Syn.** See TOOL. — *v.t.*
provide instrumentation for (an aircraft, missile, or other
aratus). [See INSTRUCT]
ru·men·tal (in'strə·men'təl) *adj.* **1.** Serving as a means
nstrument; useful; helpful. **2.** Of or pertaining to an
rument or tool. **3.** Of, pertaining to, composed for, or
ormed on musical instruments. — **in'stru·men'tal·ly**
[< Med.L *instrumentum*]
ru·men·tal·ist (in'strə·men'təl·ist) *n.* One who plays
usical instrument.
ru·men·tal·i·ty (in'strə·men·tal'ə·tē) *n. pl.* **·ties 1.**
thing serving to accomplish a purpose; means; agency.
The condition of being instrumental.
ru·men·ta·tion (in'strə·men·tā'shən) *n.* **1.** The use of
ruments; work performed with instruments. **2.** *Music* **a**
study of the characteristics and groupings of instru-
ts. **b** Loosely, orchestration. **3.** A branch of engineering
cerned with the use of instruments in military, technical,
scientific operations; also, an assembly of instruments,
sidered as a unit. **4.** Instrumentality.
rument panel The panel holding the gauges and other
cators of performance in an automobile, airplane, engine
m, etc. Also **instrument board.**
ub·or·di·nate (in'sə·bôr'də·nit) *adj.* Not subordinate
bedient; rebellious. — *n.* An insubordinate person. —
ub·or'di·nate·ly *adv.* — **in'sub·or'di·na'tion** *n.*
ub·stan·tial (in'səb·stan'shəl) *adj.* **1.** Not real; imagi-
nary; illusive. **2.** Not substantial, solid, or firm; flimsy. — **in'sub·stan'ti·al'i·ty** (-shē·al'ə·tē) *n.*

in·suf·fer·a·ble (in·suf'ər·ə·bəl) *adj.* Not to be endured; intolerable. — **in·suf'fer·a·ble·ness** *n.* — **in·suf'fer·a·bly** *adv.*

in·suf·fi·cien·cy (in'sə·fish'ən·sē) *n. pl.* **·cies** Lack of adequate effectiveness, amount, quality, etc.; inadequacy.

in·suf·fi·cient (in'sə·fish'ənt) *adj.* Not enough; inadequate; deficient. — **in'suf·fi'cient·ly** *adv.*

in·su·lar (in'sə·lər, -syə-) *adj.* **1.** Of or like an island. **2.** Dwelling or situated on an island. **3.** Composing or forming an island. **4.** Narrow or limited in customs, opinions, etc.; provincial. — *n.* An islander. [< L *insula* island] — **in'·su·lar·ism, in·su·lar·i·ty** (in'sə·lar'ə·tē, -syə-) *n.*

in·su·late (in'sə·lāt, -syə-) *v.t.* **·lat·ed, ·lat·ing 1.** To surround or separate with nonconducting material in order to prevent or lessen the leakage of electricity, heat, sound, radiation, etc. **2.** To isolate. [< L *insula* island]

in·su·la·tion (in'sə·lā'shən, -syə-) *n.* **1.** Nonconducting material used for insulating. **2.** The act of insulating, or the state of being insulated.

in·su·la·tor (in'sə·lā'tər, -syə-) *n.* **1.** *Electr.* A device made of dielectric material, as glass, and used to insulate and support a conductor. **2.** One who or that which insulates.

in·su·lin (in'sə·lin, -syə-) *n. Biochem.* **1.** A hormone secreted by the pancreas, essential in regulating the metabolism of sugar. **2.** A preparation of this hormone, used in treating diabetes. [< L *insula* island (of Langerhans) + -IN]

in·sult (*v.* in·sult'; *n.* in'sult) *v.t.* To treat with insolence or contempt; disparage; abuse; affront. — **Syn.** See OFFEND. — *n.* An act, remark, etc., that offends or affronts. [< MF < L < *in-* on + *salire* to leap] — **in·sult'er** *n.* — **in·sult'·ing** *adj.* — **in·sult'ing·ly** *adv.*

in·su·per·a·ble (in·so͞o'pər·ə·bəl) *adj.* Not to be surmounted or overcome. [< L *insuperabilis*] — **in·su'per·a·bil'i·ty, in·su'per·a·ble·ness** *n.* — **in'su'per·a·bly** *adv.*

in·sup·port·a·ble (in'sə·pôr'tə·bəl, -pōr'-) *adj.* **1.** Not bearable; insufferable. **2.** Having no grounds; unjustifiable. — **in'sup·port'a·ble·ness** *n.* — **in'sup·port'a·bly** *adv.*

in·sur·ance (in·sho͝or'əns) *n.* **1.** Protection against risk, loss, or ruin, by a contract in which an insurer or underwriter guarantees to pay a sum of money to the insured or the beneficiary in the event of death, accident, fire, etc., in return for the payment of premiums; also, the business of providing this protection. **2.** A contract guaranteeing such protection. Also **insurance policy.** **3.** The payment made by the insured party. **4.** The amount for which anything is insured. **5.** Any safeguard against risk or harm.

in·sure (in·sho͝or') *v.* **·sured, ·sur·ing** *v.t.* **1.** To guarantee against loss of (life, property, etc.) with insurance. **2.** To ensure. — *v.i.* **3.** To issue or buy insurance. [< AF < *en-* in + *seur* sure] — **in·sur'a·bil'i·ty** *n.* — **in·sur'a·ble** *adj.*

in·sured (in·sho͝ord') *n.* The person protected by insurance.

in·sur·er (in·sho͝or'ər) *n.* A person or company that insures against specified loss or damage.

in·sur·gence (in·sûr'jəns) *n.* The act of rising in insurrection; revolt; uprising. Also **in·sur'gen·cy.**

in·sur·gent (in·sûr'jənt) *adj.* Rising in revolt against established authority; rebellious. — *n.* An insurgent person. [< L < *in-* against + *surgere* to rise]

in·sur·mount·a·ble (in'sər·moun'tə·bəl) *adj.* Incapable of being surmounted or overcome. — **in'sur·mount'a·bly** *adv.*

in·sur·rec·tion (in'sə·rek'shən) *n.* An organized resistance to established government. [< F < LL < L *insurrectus,* pp. of *insurgere* to rise up against] — **in'sur·rec'tion·al** *adj.* — **in'sur·rec'tion·ar'y** *adj. & n.* — **in'sur·rec'tion·ist** *n.*

in·sus·cep·ti·ble (in'sə·sep'tə·bəl) *adj.* Incapable of being affected or infected; immune. — **in'sus·cep'ti·bil'i·ty** *n.*

in·tact (in·takt') *adj.* Remaining whole, unchanged, and undamaged; unimpaired. [< L < *in-* not + *tactus,* pp. of *tangere* to touch] — **in·tact'ness** *n.*

in·ta·glio (in·tal'yō, *Ital.* ēn·tä'lyō) *n. pl.* **·glios** or **·gli** (-lyē) **1.** Incised carving; a sunken design. **2.** The art of making such designs. **3.** A work, esp. a gem, with incised carving. [< Ital. < *in-* in + *tagliare* to cut]

in·take (in'tāk') *n.* **1.** The act of taking in or absorbing. **2.** That which is taken in: the annual *intake.* **3.** The amount or quantity absorbed. **4.** The place where water is drawn into a pipe, channel, or conduit.

in·tan·gi·ble (in·tan'jə·bəl) *adj.* **1.** Incapable of being perceived by touch; impalpable. **2.** Indefinite or vague to the mind. — *n.* That which is intangible; esp., any incorporeal asset, as good will. [< Med.L *intangibilis*] — **in·tan'gi·bil'i·ty, in·tan'gi·ble·ness** *n.* — **in·tan'gi·bly** *adv.*

in·te·ger (in'tə·jər) *n.* **1.** Any of the numbers 1, 2, 3, etc., as distinguished from a fraction or mixed number: also called *whole number.* **2.** A whole entity. [< L, untouched < *in-* not + root *tag-,* of *tangere* to touch]

in·te·gral (in'tə·grəl) *adj.* **1.** Being an indispensable part of a whole; essential; constituent. **2.** Formed of parts that together constitute a unity: an *integral* whole. **3.** Whole; entire; complete. **4.** *Math.* **a** Pertaining to an integer. **b** Produced by integration. **—** *n.* **1.** An entire thing; a whole. **2.** *Math.* The result of integration. [< LL *integralis*] **—in′te·gral′i·ty** (-gral′ə·tē) *n.* **—in′te·gral·ly** *adv.*

in·te·grate (in′tə·grāt) *v.* **·grat·ed, ·grat·ing** *v.t.* **1.** To bring together into a whole; unify. **2.** *U.S.* To make the use or occupancy of (a school, neighborhood, etc.) available to persons of all races. **3.** To make whole or complete by the addition of necessary parts. **4.** *Math.* To determine a function from its derivatives: opposed to *differentiate.* **—** *v.i.* **5.** *U.S.* To become available to persons of all races, as a school, etc. [< *integratus,* pp. of *integrare* to make whole, renew] **—in′te·gra′tion** *n.* **—in′te·gra′tor** *n.*

in·teg·ri·ty (in·teg′rə·tē) *n. pl.* **·ties 1.** Uprightness of character; honesty. **2.** The condition or quality of being unimpaired or sound. **3.** The state of being complete or undivided: [< L *integer* untouched]

in·teg·u·ment (in·teg′yə·mənt) *n.* A covering or outer coating; esp., a natural covering or envelope, as the skin of an animal, coat of a seed, etc. [< L < *in-* thoroughly + *tegere* to cover] **—in·teg′u·men′ta·ry** *adj.*

in·tel·lect (in′tə·lekt) *n.* **1.** The power of the mind to grasp ideas and relations, and to exercise dispassionate reason and rational judgment; reason. **2.** A mind or intelligence, especially a strong or brilliant one. **3.** An intelligent person. **4.** Mental power collectively: the *intellect* of the nation. [< L *intellectus,* pp. of < *intelligere* to understand]

—Syn. 1. *Intellect* refers to the powers of knowing and thinking, as distinguished from those of feeling and willing, while *mind* is the sum of all these powers or faculties. *Reason* is the ability to think, or at its simplest the ability to elaborate sense impressions into concepts. *Intelligence* is chiefly used to mean the capacity to learn or to deal with new situations.

in·tel·lec·tu·al (in′tə·lek′cho͞o·əl) *adj.* **1.** Of or pertaining to the intellect; mental. **2.** Engaging, or requiring the use of, the intellect. **3.** Possessing or showing intellect, esp. of a high order. **—** *n.* **1.** One who pursues and enjoys matters of the intellect and of refined taste. **2.** One whose work requires primarily the use of the intellect. [<L *intellectualis*] **—in′tel·lec′tu·al′i·ty** *n.* **—in′tel·lec′tu·al·ly** *adv.*

in·tel·lec·tu·al·ism (in′tə·lek′cho͞o·əl·iz′əm) *n.* **1.** Devotion to intellectual interests. **2.** The exercise of the intellect. **—in′tel·lec′tu·al·ist** *n.* **—in′tel·lec′tu·al·is′tic** *adj.*

in·tel·lec·tu·al·ize (in′tə·lek′cho͞o·əl·īz) *v.* **·ized, ·iz·ing** *v.t.* **1.** To make intellectual; view or express intellectually. **—** *v.i.* **2.** To think; reason.

in·tel·li·gence (in·tel′ə·jəns) *n.* **1.** The faculty of perceiving and comprehending meaning; active intellect; understanding. **2.** The ability to adapt to new situations. **3.** The collection of secret information, as by police or military authorities. **4.** Information that has been so collected; also, the persons so occupied. **— Syn.** See INTELLECT.

intelligence quotient *Psychol.* A number indicating the level of a person's mental development, obtained by multiplying his mental age by 100, and dividing by his chronological age.

intelligence test *Psychol.* Any standardized test, or series of tests, designed to determine relative mental capacity.

in·tel·li·gent (in·tel′ə·jənt) *adj.* **1.** Having an active, discerning mind; acute: an *intelligent* reader. **2.** Marked or characterized by intelligence. **3.** Endowed with intellect or understanding; reasoning. [< L < *inter-* between + *legere* to choose] **—in·tel′li·gent·ly** *adv.*

in·tel·li·gent·si·a (in·tel′ə·jent′sē·ə, -gent′-) *n.pl.* Intellectual or educated people collectively, esp. those with a broad and informed point of view. [< Russian, ? < Ital. < L *intelligentia*]

in·tel·li·gi·ble (in·tel′ə·jə·bəl) *adj.* Capable of being understood. [< L *intelligibilis*] **—in·tel′li·gi·bil′i·ty** *n.* **—in·tel′li·gi·bly** *adv.*

in·tem·per·ance (in·tem′pər·əns) *n.* Lack of temperance or moderation; esp., excessive use of alcoholic drinks.

in·tem·per·ate (in·tem′pər·it) *adj.* **1.** Lacking moderation; unrestrained. **2.** Given to excessive use of alcoholic drinks. **3.** Excessive or extreme, as climate or the weather. **—in·tem′per·ate·ly** *adv.* **—in·tem′per·ate·ness** *n.*

in·tend (in·tend′) *v.t.* **1.** To have as a specific aim or purpose; plan. **2.** To make, design, or destine for a purpose, use, etc.: a dress *intended* for summer. **3.** To mean or signify; indicate. **—** *v.i.* **4.** To have a purpose or plan. [< OF < L < *in-* in, at + *tendere* to stretch]

in·ten·dan·cy (in·ten′dən·sē) *n. pl.* **·cies** The office or work of an intendant; intendants collectively.

in·ten·dant (in·ten′dənt) *n.* A superintendent; provincial administrator, as under the Bourbons in France. [< F]

in·tend·ed (in·ten′did) *adj.* **1.** Planned; proposed: the *intended* results. **2.** Prospective: one's *intended* wife. **—** *n.* *Informal* Prospective husband or wife.

in·tense (in·tens′) *adj.* **1.** Having great force; overpowering: *intense* feelings. **2.** Performed strenuously and stea[dily]: *intense* study. **3.** Expressing strong emotion: an *in*[tense] look; also, characterized by strong and earnest feeling[: an] *intense* person. **4.** Having its quality strongly concentr[ated] [< OF < L *intensus,* pp. of *intendere* to stretch out] **—in·tense′ly** *adv.* **—in·tense′ness** *n.*

in·ten·si·fy (in·ten′sə·fī) *v.* **·fied, ·fy·ing** *v.t.* **1.** To [make] more intense or acute; aggravate; also, to make intense. [**2.**] *Photog.* To increase the contrast of (a negative or print). *v.i.* **3.** To become more intense; become intense. **—in[·ten′]si·fi·ca′tion, in·ten′si·fi′er** *n.*

in·ten·si·ty (in·ten′sə·tē) *n. pl.* **·ties 1.** The state or [qual]ity of being intense; extreme force, brightness, conce[ntra]tion, etc. **2.** The strength or degree of some action, qu[ality,] feeling, etc.: pain of low *intensity.* **3.** Power and vehem[ence] of thought or feeling; also, extreme effort and concentr[ation].

in·ten·sive (in·ten′siv) *adj.* **1.** Of, pertaining to, or m[arked] by intensity. **2.** Intensifying. **3.** *Agric.* Pertaining [to a] method of farming whereby much capital and labor a[re ex]pended upon making a small area highly productive. [**4.**] *Gram.* Adding emphasis or force. **—** *n.* **1.** That which [gives] intensity or emphasis. **2.** *Gram.* An intensive particle, [word,] or phrase. [< F < Med.L *intensivus*] **—in·ten′si[ve·ly]** *adv.* **—in·ten′sive·ness** *n.*

in·tent (in·tent′) *n.* **1.** Purpose; aim; goal; design. **2.** [The] act of intending. **3.** *Law* The state of mind in which [or] purpose with which one does an act; also, the characte[r] the law imputes to an act. **—** *adj.* **1.** Firmly direct[ed;] fixed: an *intent* stare. **2.** Directing one's mind or e[ffort] steadfastly: with *on* or *upon.* [< OF < L *intendere* to st[retch] out, endeavor] **—in·tent′ly** *adv.* **—in·tent′ness** *n.*

in·ten·tion (in·ten′shən) *n.* **1.** Purpose, either ultim[ate or] immediate; aim; goal. **2.** The act of intending. **3.** *p[l.]* *formal* Purpose with regard to marriage.

in·ten·tion·al (in·ten′shən·əl) *adj.* Resulting from pur[pose;] deliberate; intended. **—in·ten′tion·al·ly** *adv.*

in·ten·tioned (in·ten′shənd) *adj.* Having or characte[rized] by (a specified kind of) intention or intentions: used in [com]bination: *well-intentioned.*

in·ter (in·tûr′) *v.t.* **·terred, ·ter·ring** To place in a g[rave;] bury. [< OF < LL < *in-* in + *terra* earth]

inter- *prefix* **1.** With each other; together: *intertwine*. [**2.**] Mutual; mutually: *intercommunicate.* **3.** Between (the [things] signified): *intercollegiate.* **4.** Occurring or situated bet[ween]: *interlinear.* [< L *inter-* < *inter* between, among]

in·ter·act (in′tər·akt′) *v.i.* To act on each other. **—i[n′ter·]ac′tion** *n.* **—in′ter·ac′tive** *adj.* **—in′ter·ac·tiv′i·ty** *n.*

in·ter·brain (in′tər·brān′) *n.* *Anat.* The diencephalo[n].

in·ter·breed (in′tər·brēd′) *v.* **·bred, ·breed·ing** *v.t.* [**1.** To] breed (different stocks) together; crossbreed. **2.** To pr[oduce] (offspring) by crossbreeding. **—** *v.i.* **3.** To breed geneti[cally] dissimilar stocks or individuals.

in·ter·ca·lar·y (in·tûr′kə·ler′ē) *adj.* **1.** Added to the c[alen]dar. **2.** Having an added day or month. **3.** Interpo[lated].

in·ter·ca·late (in·tûr′kə·lāt) *v.t.* **·lat·ed, ·lat·ing 1.** T[o in]sert or interpolate. **2.** To insert, as an additional d[ay or] month, into the calendar. [< L < *inter-* between + *c*[*alare*] to proclaim, call] **—in·ter′ca·la′tion** *n.*

in·ter·cede (in′tər·sēd′) *v.i.* **·ced·ed, ·ced·ing 1.** To [plead] or petition in behalf of another or others. **2.** To com[e be]tween parties in a dispute; mediate. [< L < *inter-* bet[ween] + *cedere* to pass, go] **—in′ter·ced′er** *n.*

in·ter·cel·lu·lar (in′tər·sel′yə·lər) *adj.* *Biol.* Situate[d be]tween or among cells.

in·ter·cept (*v.* in′tər·sept′; *n.* in′tər·sept) *v.t.* **1.** To sei[ze or] stop on the way; prevent from reaching the destination. [**2.**] To meet, as a moving person, ship, etc. **3.** To interrup[t the] course of; obstruct: to *intercept* the light. **4.** *Math.* To [cut] off or bound a line, plane, surface, or solid. **—** *n.* **1.** I[n the] U.S. Air Force, an act or instance of interception. **2.** *M*[*ath.*] **a** An intercepted part. **b** A point of interception. [< *inter-* between + *capere* to seize] **—in′ter·cep′tion** *n* **in′ter·cep′tive** *adj.*

in·ter·cep·tor (in′tər·sep′tər) *n.* **1.** One who or that w[hich] intercepts. **2.** An airplane designed for the pursuit an[d in]terception of enemy aircraft. Also **in′ter·cept′er.** [<

in·ter·ces·sion (in′tər·sesh′ən) *n.* The act of interce[ding;] entreaty or prayer in behalf of others. [< L < *interce*[*ssus*,] pp. of *intercedere* to come between] **—in′ter·ces′sion·a[l]**

in·ter·ces·sor (in′tər·ses′ər) *n.* One who intercedes; a [me]diator. [< L] **—in′ter·ces′so·ry** *adj.*

in·ter·change (in′tər·chānj′) *v.* **·changed, ·chang·in[g]** **1.** To put each of (two things) in the place of the other [**2.**] To cause to alternate. **3.** To give and receive in retur[n:] gifts. **—** *v.i.* **4.** To change places one with the other. [**—** *n.*] **1.** A reciprocal giving in exchange. **2.** An exchangi[ng of] places. **3.** Alternation. **4.** An intersection of a superh[igh]way with another highway, so designed that vehicles [may] enter or turn off without obstructing traffic. [< O[F] *entre-* between + *changier* to exchange] **—in′ter·chang[e·a·ble]**

in·ter·change·a·ble (in′tər·chān′jə·bəl) *adj.* Capab[le]

ng interchanged or substituted one for the other; per-ting transposition. — **in′ter·change′a·bil′i·ty, in′ter·nge′a·ble·ness** *n.* — **in′ter·change′a·bly** *adv.*
er·col·le·giate (in′tər·kə·lē′jit, -jē·it) *adj.* Pertaining or involving two or more colleges: *intercollegiate* sports.
er·com (in′tər·kom′) *n. Informal* A telephone or radio tem for intercommunication.
er·com·mu·ni·cate (in′tər·kə·myōō′nə·kāt) *v.i.* **·cat-, ·cat·ing** To communicate with one another; esp., by a phone system. — **in′ter·com·mu′ni·ca′tion** *n.* — **in′ter·n·mu′ni·ca′tive** *adj.* — **in′ter·com·mun′i·ca·tor** *n.*
er·con·nect (in′tər·kə·nekt′) *v.t. & v.i.* To connect or connected one with the other. — **in′ter·con·nec′tion** *n.*
er·con·ti·nen·tal (in′tər·kon′tə·nen′təl) *adj.* Reaching capable of reaching from one continent to another; also, taining to or involving two or more continents.
er·cos·tal (in′tər·kos′təl) *adj. Anat.* Situated or oc-ring between the ribs. [< NL < L *inter-* between + *a* rib] — **in′ter·cos′tal·ly** *adv.*
er·course (in′tər·kôrs, -kōrs) *n.* **1.** Mutual exchange; mmerce. **2.** The interchange of ideas. **3.** Sexual connec-n; coitus. [< OF < L < *inter-* between + *currere* to run]
er·de·nom·i·na·tion·al (in′tər·di·nom′ə·nā′shən·əl) *adj.* or pertaining to two or more religious denominations.
er·de·pen·dent (in·tər·di·pen′dənt) *adj.* Dependent on another; reciprocally dependent. — **in′ter·de·pend′·e, in′ter·de·pend′en·cy** *n.* — **in′ter·de·pend′ent·ly** *adv.*
er·dict (in′tər·dikt′) *v.t.* **1.** To prohibit or debar (some ion, right of use, etc.) authoritatively; also, to forbid (a son or persons) to have or do something. **2.** *Eccl.* To ex-de (a place or certain persons) from participation in rites l services. — *n.* In the Roman Catholic Church, a ban bidding the sacraments and solemn services to a place or certain church members, but not imposing excommunica-n. [< OF < L < *inter-* between + *dicere* to say] — **in′·dic′tion** *n.* — **in′ter·dic′tive, in′ter·dic′to·ry** (-tə·rē) *adj.* **in′ter·dic′tive·ly** *adv.* — **in′ter·dic′tor** *n.*
er·est (in′tər·ist, -trist) *n.* **1.** A feeling of curiosity or at-tiveness. **2.** The power to arouse curiosity or attentive-s; also, something that has such power: Tennis is his chief *erest.* **3.** That which is of advantage; benefit. **4.** In-vement or concern in something; also, selfish concern. **5.** yment for the use of money or credit, usu. expressed as a centage of the amount owed or used, and depending also on duration of the debt. **6.** Something added in making a urn: to give back a blow with *interest.* **7.** Legal or finan-l right, claim, or share, as in a business or estate; also, t in which one has such a right, claim, or share. **8.** *Usu.* A group of persons involved in a particular business, use, etc.: the dairy *interests.* — **in the interest** (or **inter-s**) **of** In behalf of. — *v.t.* **1.** To excite or hold the curi-ty or attention of. **2.** To cause to be concerned in; olve: with *in.* [< OF < L < *inter-* between + *esse* to be]
er·est·ed (in′tər·is·tid, -tris-, -tə·res′-) *adj.* **1.** Having or playing curiosity; having the attention involved. **2.** Hav-a concern or wish for something. **3.** Having a right or are in. **4.** Seeking personal advantage; biased. — **in′ter·t·ed·ly** *adv.* — **in′ter·est·ed·ness** *n.*
er·est·ing (in′tər·is·ting, -tris-, -tə·res′-) *adj.* Exciting erest, attention, or curiosity; attractive. — **in′ter·est·g·ly** *adv.* — **in′ter·est·ing·ness** *n.*
er·fere (in′tər·fir′) *v.i.* **·fered, ·fer·ing 1.** To get in the y; be an obstacle or obstruction; impede: often with *with.* To intervene and take part in the affairs of others; esp., to erpose oneself without invitation or warrant; meddle. **3.** sports, to obstruct the play of an opponent illegally. **4.** *ysics* To cause interference. [< OF < L *inter-* between + *ire* to strike] — **in′ter·fer′er** *n.* — **in′ter·fer′ing·ly** *adv.*
er·fer·ence (in′tər·fir′əns) *n.* **1.** The act of interfering. In sports, illegal obstruction of the play of an opponent. In football, the protection given the ball carrier from op-sing tacklers. **4.** *Physics* The effect produced by two or ore sets of waves, as of light or sound, that on meeting tend neutralize or augment each other by a combination of dis-nilar or like phases. **5.** *Telecom.* A disturbance in the re-ption of radio, etc., due to conflict with undesired signals.
ter·fold (in′tər·fōld′) *v.t. & v.i.* To fold together or one thin another.
ter·fuse (in′tər·fyōōz′) *v.* **·fused, ·fus·ing** *v.t.* **1.** To cause permeate or spread throughout, as a fluid. **2.** To spread rough or permeate with something. **3.** To intermix. — . **4.** To become intermixed. — **in′ter·fu′sion** *n.*
ter·im (in′tər·im) *n.* A time between periods or events; intervening time. — *adj.* For an intervening period of ne; temporary. [< L, meanwhile]
te·ri·or (in·tir′ē·ər) *adj.* **1.** Of or situated on the inside; ner. **2.** Remote from the coast or border; inland. **3.** Per-ining to the internal affairs of a country. **4.** Not exposed to view; private. — *n.* **1.** The internal part; the inside. **2.** The inland region of a country, continent, etc. **3.** The do-mestic affairs of a country. **4.** The inner nature of a person or thing. **5.** A representation of the inside of a building or room. — **Department of the Interior** An executive depart-ment of the U.S. government (established 1849), headed by the Secretary of the Interior, that controls Indian affairs and conservation of natural resources. [< OF < L *interior,* com-par. of *inter* within] — **in·te′ri·or′i·ty** (-ôr′ə·tē, -or′-) *n.* — **in·te′ri·or·ly** *adv.*
interior decoration The decorating and furnishing of in-teriors, as homes, offices, etc.; also, this occupation.
in·ter·ject (in′tər·jekt′) *v.t.* To throw in between other things: to *interject* a comment. [< L < *inter-* between + *jacere* to throw]
in·ter·jec·tion (in′tər·jek′shən) *n.* **1.** The act of interject-ing. **2.** That which is interjected. **3.** *Gram.* An exclama-tion lacking any grammatical connection, as *Oh!, Alas!* — **in′ter·jec′tion·al** *adj.* — **in′ter·jec′tion·al·ly** *adv.*
in·ter·lace (in′tər·lās′) *v.* **·laced, ·lac·ing** *v.t.* **1.** To join by or as by weaving together; intertwine. **2.** To blend; com-bine. **3.** To vary or relieve the sameness of. — *v.i.* **4.** To interlock or alternate with one another. [< OF *entrelacier*]
in·ter·lard (in′tər·lärd′) *v.t.* **1.** To vary by interjecting something different: to *interlard* speech with profanity. **2.** To occur frequently in. [< MF *entrelar der* to lard]
in·ter·lay (in′tər·lā′) *v.t.* **·laid, ·lay·ing 1.** To place between **2.** To decorate with something put or laid between.
in·ter·leaf (in′tər·lēf′) *n. pl.* **·leaves** (-lēvz′) An extra leaf. usu. blank, inserted between the regular leaves of a book.
in·ter·leave (in′tər·lēv′) *v.t.* **·leaved, ·leaving** To insert interleaves into (a book).
in·ter·line[1] (in′tər·līn′) *v.t.* **·lined, ·lin·ing 1.** To insert (words, phrases, etc.) between written or printed lines. **2.** To annotate between the lines. [< OF < Med.L < L *inter-* between + *linea* line] — **in′ter·lin′er** *n.*
in·ter·line[2] (in′tər·līn′) *v.t.* **·lined, ·lin·ing** To put a lining between the usual lining and the outer fabric of (a garment).
in·ter·lin·e·ar (in′tər·lin′ē·ər) *adj.* **1.** Situated or written between the lines. **2.** Having lines inserted between the lines. Also **in′ter·lin′e·al.** [< Med.L *interlinearis*]
in·ter·lin·ing (in′tər·lī′ning) *n.* **1.** An intermediate lining placed between the usual lining and the outer fabric of a gar-ment. **2.** The material of which such a lining is made.
in·ter·lock (*v.* in′tər·lok′) *v.t. & v.i.* To join firmly. — **in′·ter·lock′er** *n.*
interlocking directorates *Econ.* Boards of directors that control separate corporations by overlapping membership.
in·ter·loc·u·tor (in′tər·lok′yə·tər) *n.* One who takes part in a conversation. [< L *interloqui* to speak between, con-verse] — **in′ter·loc′u·tress** (-tris) *n.fem.*
in·ter·loc·u·to·ry (in′tər·lok′yə·tôr′ē, -tō′rē) *adj.* **1.** Per-taining to or having the nature of dialogue. **2.** Interposed, as in a conversation. **3.** *Law* Pronounced while a suit is pending; provisional.
in·ter·lope (in′tər·lōp′) *v.i.* To intrude in the affairs of others; meddle. [< INTER- + *lope* < Du. *loopen* to run] — **in′ter·lo′per** *n.*
in·ter·lude (in′tər·lōōd) *n.* **1.** A period that occurs in and divides some longer process. **2.** In English drama, a sepa-rate episode, usu. light or humorous, introduced between the acts or parts of a longer performance. **3.** A short passage of instrumental music played between the stanzas of a hymn, etc. [< Med.L < L *inter-* between + *ludus* game, play]
in·ter·lu·nar (in′tər·lōō′nər) *adj. Astron.* Pertaining to the period between old and new moon, during which the moon is invisible. Also **in′ter·lu′na·ry.**
in·ter·mar·ry (in′tər·mar′ē) *v.i.* **·ried, ·ry·ing 1.** To marry someone not a member of one's own religion, race, class, etc. **2.** To become connected through the marriage of members: said of different families, etc. — **in′ter·mar′riage** *n.*
in·ter·me·di·ar·y (in′tər·mē′dē·er′ē) *adj.* **1.** Situated, act-ing, or coming between; intermediate. **2.** Acting as a medi-ator. — *n. pl.* **·ar·ies 1.** One who acts as a mediator;go-be-tween. **2.** An intermediate form, stage, or product.
in·ter·me·di·ate[1] (in′tər·mē′dē·it) *adj.* Situated or occur-ring between two points, places, levels, etc. — *n.* Something intermediate. [< L < *inter-* between + *medius* middle] — **in′ter·me′di·ate·ly** *adv.* — **in′ter·me′di·ateness** *n.*
in·ter·me·di·ate[2] (in′tər·mē′dē·āt) *v.i.* **·at·ed, ·at·ing** To act as an intermediary; mediate. — **in′ter·me′di·a′tion** *n.* — **in′ter·me′di·a′tor** *n.*
in·ter·ment (in·tûr′mənt) *n.* The act of interring; burial.
in·ter·mez·zo (in′tər·met′sō, -med′zō) *n. pl.* **·zos** or **·zi** (-sē, -zē) **1.** A short musical offering given between the acts of a play or opera. **2.** *Music* A short movement connecting the main divisions of a large musical composition. [< Ital. < L *intermedius* intermediate]

in·ter·mi·na·ble (in·tûr′mə·nə·bəl) *adj.* Having no apparent end or limit; continuing for a very long time; endless. [< OF] — **in·ter′mi·na·bly** *adv.*

in·ter·min·gle (in′tər·ming′gəl) *v.t. & v.i.* **·gled, ·gling** To mingle together; mix.

in·ter·mis·sion (in′tər·mish′ən) *n.* **1.** An interval of time between events or activities; recess. **2.** The act of intermitting, or the state of being intermitted. **3.** *U.S.* The time between acts of a play, opera, etc. — **in′ter·mis′sive** *adj.*

in·ter·mit (in′tər·mit′) *v.t. & v.i.* **·mit·ted, ·mit·ting** To stop temporarily or at intervals; pause. [< L < *inter-* between + *mittere* to send, put] — **in′ter·mit′tence** *n.*

in·ter·mit·tent (in′tər·mit′ənt) *adj.* Ceasing from time to time; coming at intervals. — **in′ter·mit′tent·ly** *adv.*

in·ter·mix (in′tər·miks′) *v.t. & v.i.* To mix together. **in′·ter·mix′ture** *n.*

in·tern (*n.* in′tûrn; *v.* in·tûrn′) *n.* **1.** A medical graduate serving in and living at a hospital for clinical training before being licensed to practice medicine. **2.** One who is interned; internee. Also spelled *interne.* — *v.t.* **1.** To confine or detain during wartime. — *v.i.* **2.** To serve as an intern. [< F < L *internus* internal] — **in·tern′ment** *n.*

in·ter·nal (in·tûr′nəl) *adj.* **1.** Of or situated on the inside; inner. **2.** Belonging to or derived from the inside: *internal* evidence. **3.** Pertaining to the inner self or the mind. **4.** Pertaining to the domestic affairs of a country: *internal* revenue. **5.** Relating to or affecting the inside of the body. **6.** Intended to be taken or applied inwardly, as medication. **7.** *Anat.* Situated relatively nearer to the axis of the body. [< LL *internus*] — **in·ter′nal·ly** *adv.*

in·ter·nal-com·bus·tion (in·tûr′nəl·kəm·bus′chən) *adj.* Designating a heat engine in which the fuel burns inside the engine itself, most often in a cylinder.

internal medicine The branch of medicine that is concerned with the diseases of the internal organs.

internal revenue Revenue (def. 1).

in·ter·na·tion·al (in′tər·nash′ən·əl) *adj.* **1.** Existing or conducted among nations. **2.** Of or affecting various nations and their peoples. — *n.* A person having ties with more than one nation. — **in′ter·na′tion·al·ly** *adv.*

In·ter·na·tion·al (in′tər·nash′ən·əl) *n.* Any of several international socialistic organizations of the late 19th and early 20th centuries. — **First International** A federation of trade unions founded in London in 1864 by Karl Marx and Friedrich Engels. — **Second International** An organization formed at Paris in 1889 to unite Socialist Party groups. — **Third International** The Comintern.

International Court of Justice The principal judicial organ of the United Nations. Also called *World Court.*

International Date Line See DATE LINE (def. 2).

in·ter·na·tion·al·ism (in′tər·nash′ən·əl·iz′əm) *n.* **1.** The belief that cooperation among nations will advance the common welfare. **2.** The state of being international. — **in′·ter·na′tion·al·ist** *n.* — **in′ter·na′tion·al′i·ty** *n.*

in·ter·na·tion·al·ize (in′tər·nash′ən·əl·īz′) *v.t.* **·ized, ·iz·ing** To place under international control; make international.

International Phonetic Alphabet An alphabet in which each symbol represents a specific sound defined as to place and manner of articulation.

in·terne (in′tûrn) See INTERN.

in·ter·ne·cine (in′tər·nē′sin, -sīn) *adj.* **1.** Destructive to both sides. **2.** Involving great slaughter. [< L < *inter-* among + *necare* to kill]

in·tern·ee (in′tûr·nē′) *n.* An interned person.

in·ter·nist (in·tûr′nist) *n.* A specialist in internal medicine.

in·ter·pel·late (in′tər·pel′āt, in·tûr′pə·lāt) *v.t.* **·lat·ed, ·lat·ing** To subject (a member of the government) to a demand for an explanation of an official act or policy. [< L < *inter-* between + *pellere* to drive] — **in′ter·pel·la′tion** *n.*

in·ter·pen·e·trate (in′tər·pen′ə·trāt) *v.* **·trat·ed, ·trat·ing** *v.t.* **1.** To penetrate thoroughly or mutually. — *v.i.* **2.** To penetrate each other. — **in′ter·pen′e·tra′tion** *n.* — **in′ter·pen′e·tra′tive** *adj.*

in·ter·plan·e·tar·y (in′tər·plan′ə·ter′ē) *adj.* **1.** Between or among planets. **2.** Situated or occurring in the solar system, but not within the atmosphere of the sun or any other planet.

in·ter·play (in′tər·plā′) *n.* Reciprocal action, movement, or influence. — *v.i.* To act on each other; interact.

in·ter·po·late (in·tûr′pə·lāt) *v.* **·lat·ed, ·lat·ing** *v.t.* **1.** To introduce (additions, comments, etc.) into a discourse, process, or series. **2.** To interrupt with additions. **3.** *Math.* **a** To compute intermediate values in (a series): distinguished from *extrapolate.* **b** To insert (intermediate values) into a series. — *v.i.* **4.** To make additions, insertions, interruptions, etc. [< L < *inter-* between + root of *polire* to polish] — **in·ter′po·la′ter, in·ter′po·la′tor** *n.* — **in·ter′po·la′tion** *n.*

in·ter·pose (in′tər·pōz′) *v.* **·posed, ·pos·ing** *v.t.* **1.** To put between other things, esp. as a separation or barrier. **2.** To put in or inject (a comment, etc.) in the course of speech or argument. **3.** To exercise (authority, action, etc.) in order to intervene. — *v.i.* **4.** To come between; intervene. **5.** To put in a remark. [< F *interposer* to place between] **in′ter·po′sal** *n.* — **in′ter·pos′er** *n.* — **in′ter·po·si′tion**

in·ter·pret (in·tûr′prit) *v.* **·pret·ed, ·pret·ing** *v.t.* **1.** To the meaning of; explain. **2.** To judge (persons, events, in a personal way. **3.** To convey the meaning of (an ex ence, a play, etc.) by artistic representation or performa — *v.i.* **4.** To explain or construe. **5.** To restate orall one language what is said in another. [< F < L *inter* agent, interpreter] — **in·ter′pret·a·ble** *adj.* — **in·ter′** **a·bil′i·ty, in·ter′pret·a·ble·ness** *n.*

in·ter·pre·ta·tion (in·tûr′prə·tā′shən) *n.* **1.** The proce interpreting. **2.** The sense arrived at in interpreting; th planation given. **3.** The meaning assigned to actions, in tions, works of art, etc. — **in·ter′pre·ta′tion·al** *adj.*

in·ter·pre·ta·tive (in·tûr′prə·tā′tiv) *adj.* **1.** Of or per ing to interpretation. **2.** Providing an interpretation planatory. Also **in·ter′pre·tive.** — **in·ter′pre·ta′tive·ly**

in·ter·pret·er (in·tûr′prit·ər) *n.* One who interprets; one who serves as oral translator between people spea different languages.

in·ter·ra·cial (in′tər·rā′shəl) *adj.* **1.** Of or for membe different races. **2.** Between, among, or affecting diffe races, or persons of different races.

in·ter·reg·num (in′tər·reg′nəm) *n.* **1.** An interval bet the end of a sovereign's reign and the accession of his la successor. **2.** Any suspension of the usual ruling powers state. **3.** Any break in continuity. [< L < *inter*-bet + *regnum* reign]

in·ter·re·lat·ed (in′tər·ri·lā′tid) *adj.* Reciprocally rel

in·ter·re·la·tion (in′tər·ri·lā′shən) *n.* Mutual or recipr relation. — **in′ter·re·la′tion·ship** *n.*

in·ter·ro·gate (in·ter′ə·gāt) *v.* **·gat·ed, ·gat·ing** *v.t.* **1** examine formally by questioning. — *v.i.* **2.** To ask q tions. — **Syn.** See ASK. [< L *inter-* between + *roga* ask] — **in·ter′ro·ga′tor** *n.*

in·ter·ro·ga·tion (in·ter′ə·gā′shən) *n.* **1.** The act of in rogating or questioning. **2.** A question; query.

interrogation point A question mark (?). Also **interr tion mark.**

in·ter·rog·a·tive (in′tə·rog′ə·tiv) *adj.* **1.** Asking or ha the nature of a question. **2.** *Gram.* Used to ask or indic question. — *n. Gram.* An interrogative word, phrase, [< L *interrogativus*] — **in′ter·rog′a·tive·ly** *adv.*

interrogative pronoun *Gram.* A pronoun that is use introduce a question, as *which, whose, what.*

in·ter·rog·a·to·ry (in′tə·rog′ə·tôr′ē, -tō′rē) *adj.* Of, pressing, or implying a question. — *n. pl.* **·tor·ies** A q tion. — **in′ter·rog′a·to′ri·ly** (-tôr′ə·lē, -tō′rə-) *adv.*

in·ter·rupt (in′tə·rupt′) *v.t.* **1.** To break the continuit regularity of. **2.** To hinder or stop (someone talking, w ing, etc.) by intervening. — *v.i.* **3.** To intervene abru [< L *inter-* between + *rumpere* to break] — **in′ter·rup′** *adj.* — **in′ter·rup′tive·ly** *adv.*

in·ter·rupt·ed (in′tə·rup′tid) *adj.* **1.** Lacking contin **2.** *Bot.* Exhibiting an abrupt change, as the alternatio leaflets with larger leaves. — **in′ter·rupt′ed·ly** *adv.*

in·ter·rup·tion (in′tə·rup′shən) *n.* **1.** The act of interr ing, or the state of being interrupted. **2.** That which in rupts. **3.** A temporary cessation; intermission; interva

in·ter·scho·las·tic (in′tər·skə·las′tik) *adj.* Betweer among schools, esp. elementary and secondary schools.

in·ter·sect (in′tər·sekt′) *v.t.* **1.** To divide by cuttin passing across. — *v.i.* **2.** To cross each other. [< *inter*-between + *secare* to cut]

in·ter·sec·tion (in′tər·sek′shən) *n.* **1.** A place of cross esp., a place where streets or roads cross. **2.** The act o tersecting, or the state of being intersected.

in·ter·sperse (in′tər·spûrs′) *v.t.* **·spersed, ·spers·ing 1.** scatter among other things. **2.** To diversify or adorn other things; interlard. [< L < *inter-* among + *sparge* scatter] — **in′ter·spers′ed·ly** *adv.* — **in′ter·sper′** (-spûr′zhən) *n.*

in·ter·state (in′tər·stāt) *adj.* Between, among, or invol different States of the U.S., or their citizens.

in·ter·stel·lar (in′tər·stel′ər) *adj.* Among the stars.

in·ter·stice (in·tûr′stis) *n. pl.* **·sti·ces** (-stə·sēz) A nar opening or crack. [< F < L *intersistere* to stand betwe — **in′ter·sti′tial** (-stish′əl) *adj.* — **in′ter·sti′tial·ly** *adv.*

in·ter·twine (in′tər·twīn′) *v.t. & v.i.* **·twined, ·twin·ing** unite by twisting together or interlacing; intertwist. — **ter·twine′ment** *n.* — **in′ter·twin′ing·ly** *adv.*

in·ter·ur·ban (in′tər·ûr′bən) *adj.* Between or among cit — *n.* An interurban railroad, electric trolley line, etc.

in·ter·val (in′tər·vəl) *n.* **1.** The time coming between events, points in time, etc. **2.** A space between two obj or distance between two points. **3.** A break in the conti ity or course of something. **4.** *Brit.* An intermission, as play or concert. **5.** *Music* The difference in pitch betw two tones. [< OF < L *inter-* between + *vallum* ramp

in·ter·vene (in′tər·vēn′) *v.i.* **·vened, ·ven·ing 1.** To in fere or take a decisive role, esp. to correct or settle somethi

To occur so as to modify an action, expectation, etc. **3.** be located between. **4.** To take place between other nts or times: Many years *intervened.* [< L < *inter-* be-2en + *venire* to come] **—in′ter·ven′er** *n.*

er·ven·tion (in′tər·ven′shən) *n.* **1.** The act of interven-. **2.** Interference with the acts of others. **—in′ter·ven′-ı·ist** *adj. & n.*

er·view (in′tər·vyōō) *n.* **1.** A conversation conducted, by a reporter, with a person from whom information is ght; also, the record of such a conversation. **2.** A meet-with a person applying for a job. **—***v.t.* To have an in-view with. [< MF < L *inter-* between + *videre* to see] **n′ter·view′er** *n.*

er·weave (in′tər·wēv′) *v.t. & v.i.* **·wove** or **·weaved, ·wo-ı, ·weav·ing** To weave together; blend.

es·tate (in·tes′tāt, -tit) *adj.* **1.** Not having made a will a valid will before death. **2.** Not legally disposed of by . **—***n.* One who dies intestate. [< L < *in-* not + *ari* to make a will] **—in·tes′ta·cy** (-tə·sē) *n.*

es·ti·nal (in·tes′tə·nəl) *adj.* Of, found in, or affecting intestine. **—in·tes′ti·nal·ly** *adv.*

es·tine (in·tes′tin) *n. Anat. Often pl.* The section of the nentary canal extending from the orus to the anus, consisting of the **all intestine,** including the du-num, jejunum, and ileum; and the **ge intestine,** including the cecum vermiform appendix, the colon, the rectum. **—***adj.* Domestic; l. [< L *intestinus* internal]

INTESTINES
a Duodenum. *b* Small intestine. *c* Large intestine. *d* Appendix. *e* Jejunum. *f* Ileum. *g* Cecum. *h* Rectum. *A* Ascending colon. *B* Transverse colon. *C* Descending colon.

i·ma·cy (in′tə·mə·sē) *n. pl.* **·cies** The state of being intimate. **2.** instance of this. **3.** *Usu. pl.* Sex-relations, esp. when illicit.

ı·mate[1] (in′tə·mit) *adj.* **1.** Char-erized by pronounced closeness of ndship or association. **2.** Deeply sonal; private: *intimate* thoughts. Having illicit sexual relations: h *with*: a euphemism. **4.** Result-from close study. **—***n.* A close onfidential friend. [< F < L *in-us,* superl. of *intus* within] **—i·mate·ly** *adv.* **—in′ti·mate·ness** *n.*

i·mate[2] (in′tə·māt) *v.t.* **·mat·ed, ıt·ing** To make known without direct statement; hint. L *intimus,* superl. of *intus* within]

ı·ma·tion (in′tə·mā′shən) *n.* **1.** Information given in-ectly; a hint. **2.** A declaration or notification. [< F]

im·i·date (in·tim′ə·dāt) *v.t.* **·dat·ed, ·dat·ing 1.** To make id; scare. **2.** To discourage from acting by threats or vi-nce: to *intimidate* a witness. [< Med.L < L *in-* very + *idus* afraid] **—in·tim′i·da′tion** *n.* **—in·tim′i·da′tor** *n.*

o (in′tōō) *prep.* **1.** To or toward the inside of from out-: to go *into* the forest. **2.** To a time in the midst of: on the night. **3.** To the form or condition of: to change er *into* steam. **4.** Dividing: Two *into* six is three. [OE]

ol·er·a·ble (in·tol′ər·ə·bəl) *adj.* Not tolerable; that can-be borne or endured; insufferable. **—in·tol′er·a·bil′i·ty, ol′er·a·ble·ness** *n.* **—in·tol′er·a·bly** *adv.*

ol·er·ance (in·tol′ər·əns) *n.* **1.** The state of being intol-nt. **2.** Incapacity or unwillingness to tolerate.

ol·er·ant (in·tol′ər·ənt) *adj.* **1.** Not tolerant, esp. of be-s, racial or social types, etc., different from one's own; oted. **2.** Unable or unwilling to bear or endure. **—***n.* e who is intolerant. **—in·tol′er·ant·ly** *adv.*

omb (in·tōōm′), **in·tomb·ment** (in·tōōm′mənt), etc. ENTOMB, etc.

o·na·tion (in′tō·nā′shən) *n.* **1.** Way of speaking a lan-ige or utterance; esp., the meaning and melody given to eech by changing levels of pitch. **2.** The act of intoning. *Music* **a** The production of tones of accurate pitch. **b** ch or the accuracy of pitch.

one (in·tōn′) *v.* **·toned, ·ton·ing** *v.t.* **1.** To utter or recite a musical monotone; chant. **2.** To give particular tones intonation to. **3.** To sing the opening notes of (a plain-ıg, psalm, etc.). **—***v.i.* **4.** To speak or sing in a mono-ne. **5.** To emit a slow, protracted sound. [< MF < ed.L *intonare* to intone, thunder] **—in·ton′er** *n.*

o·to (in tō′tō) *Latin* In the whole; altogether; entirely.

ox·i·cant (in·tok′sə·kənt) *n.* That which intoxicates. **—** *j.* Intoxicating.

ox·i·cate (in·tok′sə·kāt) *v.* **·cat·ed, ·cat·ing** *v.t.* **1.** To ıke drunk. **2.** To elate or excite to a degree of frenzy. **3.** *ed.* To poison. **—***v.i.* **4.** To possess intoxicating proper-s. [< Med.L < L *toxicum* poison] **—in·tox′i·ca′tion** *n.* **in·tox′i·ca′tive** *adj.* **—in·tox′i·ca′tor** *n.*

ra- *prefix* Situated or occurring within; inside of: **intra-abdominal; intracollegiate; intra-urban.** [< L *intra-* < *intra* within]

in·trac·ta·ble (in·trak′tə·bəl) *adj.* **1.** Not tractable; unruly. **2.** Difficult to manipulate, treat, or work. **—in·trac′-ta·bil′i·ty, in·trac′ta·ble·ness** *n.* **—in·trac′ta·bly** *adv.*

in·tra·dos (in·trā′dos) *n.* The interior curved surface of an arch or vault. [< F < L *intra-* within + *dorsum* back]

in·tra·mu·ral (in′trə·myōō′rəl) *adj.* **1.** Taking place within a school, college, etc.: *intramural* football. **2.** Situated or occurring within the walls or limits of a city, building, organization, etc. **—in′tra·mu′ral·ly** *adv.*

in·tra·mus·cu·lar (in′trə·mus′kyə·lər) *adj.* Situated in or affecting the inside of a muscle. **—in′tra·mus′cu·lar·ly** *adv.*

in·tran·si·gent (in·tran′sə·jənt) *adj.* Refusing to compromise or come to terms, esp. in politics; unbending. **—***n.* One who is intransigent: also **in·tran′si·gent·ist.** [< F < Sp. < L *in-* not + *transigere* to agree] **—in·tran′si·gence, in·tran′si·gen·cy** *n.* **—in·tran′si·gent·ly** *adv.*

in·tran·si·tive (in·tran′sə·tiv) *Gram. adj.* Of or pertaining to intransitive verbs. **—***n.* An intransitive verb. **—in·tran′si·tive·ly** *adv.*

intransitive verb *Gram.* A verb that has or needs no complement to complete its meaning.

in·tra·state (in′trə·stāt′) *adj.* Confined within or pertaining to a single state, esp. of the U.S.

in·tra·ve·nous (in′trə·vē′nəs) *adj.* Situated in or affecting the inside of a vein: an *intravenous* injection.

in·treat (in·trēt′) See ENTREAT.

in·trep·id (in·trep′id) *adj.* Unshaken by fear; bold. [< L < *in-* not + *trepidus* agitated] **—in·tre·pid·i·ty** (in′trə·pid′ə·tē) *n.* **—in·trep′id·ly** *adv.*

in·tri·ca·cy (in′tri·kə·sē) *n. pl.* **·cies 1.** The state or quality of being intricate. **2.** That which is intricate.

in·tri·cate (in′tri·kit) *adj.* **1.** Perplexingly entangled, complicated, or involved. **2.** Difficult to follow or understand; puzzling. [< L < *in-* in + *tricae* difficulties] **—in′tri·cate·ly** *adv.* **—in′tri·cate·ness** *n.*

in·trigue (in·trēg′; *for n., also* in′trēg) *v.* **·trigued, ·tri·guing** *v.t.* **1.** To arouse the interest or curiosity of; fascinate; beguile. **—***v.i.* **2.** To use secret or underhand means; plot; conspire. **3.** To carry on a secret or illicit love affair. **—***n.* **1.** A plotting or scheming by secret or underhand means. **2.** A plot or scheme. **3.** A secret or illicit love affair. **4.** The quality or power of arousing curiosity or interest. [< F < Ital. < L *intricare* to entangle] **—in·tri′guer** *n.*

in·trin·sic (in·trin′sik) *adj.* Belonging to or arising from the true or fundamental nature of a thing; essential; inherent. Also **in·trin′si·cal.** [< OF < Med.L < L *intrinsecus* internally] **—in·trin′si·cal·ly** *adv.* **—in·trin′si·cal·ness** *n.*

intro- *prefix* In; within: *introvert.* [< L < *intro* inwardly]

in·tro·duce (in′trə·dōōs′, -dyōōs′) *v.t.* **·duced, ·duc·ing 1.** To make (a person or persons) acquainted face to face, usu. in a formal manner: often with *to.* **2.** To bring into use or notice first; launch: to *introduce* a new technique. **3.** To broach or propose: to *introduce* an idea. **4.** To bring in as something added; establish as a new element. **5.** To present (a person, product, etc.) to a specific group or the general public. **6.** To bring (a person or persons) to first knowledge of something: with *to*: to *introduce* a class to algebra. **7.** To put in; insert. **8.** To bring forward for official notice or action. **9.** To begin; open. [< L < *intro-* within + *ducere* to lead] **—in′tro·duc′er** *n.* **—in′tro·duc′i·ble** *adj.*

in·tro·duc·tion (in′trə·duk′shən) *n.* **1.** The act of introducing. **2.** First knowledge or acquaintance; initiation. **3.** The presentation of a person to another, to a group, etc.; also, a means of acquainting persons, as a letter, etc. **4.** Something that leads up to what follows, as the first part of a book, etc. **5.** An elementary treatise in any branch of study. **6.** Something introduced.

in·tro·duc·to·ry (in′trə·duk′tər·ē) *adj.* Serving as an introduction; preliminary. Also **in′tro·duc′tive.** **—in′tro·duc′-to·ri·ly** *adv.*

in·tro·it (in·trō′it) *n. Eccl.* **1.** In the Roman Catholic Church, the opening act of worship in the Mass, consisting usu. of a part of a psalm followed by the Gloria Patri. **2.** In the Anglican Church, a hymn sung at the beginning of public worship. [< F < L < *intro-* in + *ire* to go] **—in·tro′i·tal** (-təl) *adj.*

in·tro·spect (in′trə·spekt′) *v.i.* To practice introspection or self-examination. [< L *intro-* within + *specere* to look]

in·tro·spec·tion (in·trə·spek′shən) *n.* The observation and analysis of one's own mental processes and emotional states. **—in′tro·spec′tive** *adj.* **—in′tro·spec′tive·ly** *adv.*

in·tro·ver·sion (in′trə·vûr′zhən, -shən) *n.* **1.** The act of introverting, or the state of being introverted. **2.** *Psychol.* The turning of one's interest inward upon the self rather than toward external objects. **—in·tro·ver′sive** (-vûr′siv) *adj.*

in·tro·vert (in′trə·vûrt) *n.* **1.** *Psychol.* A person whose interest is directed primarily toward the self. **2.** One who is sober, reserved, and withdrawn. — *v.t.* **1.** To turn inward; cause to bend in an inward direction. **2.** To turn (the mind or thoughts) toward the self. — *adj.* Characterized by or tending to introversion. [< INTRO- + L *vertere* to turn]

in·trude (in·trōōd′) *v.* **·trud·ed, ·trud·ing** *v.t.* **1.** To thrust or force in. **2.** *Geol.* To cause to enter by intrusion. — *v.i.* **3.** To come in without leave or invitation: often with *upon.* [< L < *in-* in + *trudere* to thrust] — **in·trud′er** *n.*

in·tru·sion (in·trōō′zhən) *n.* **1.** The act or condition of intruding; encroachment. **2.** That which intrudes. **3.** *Geol.* **a** The movement of molten rock into an earlier solid rock formation. **b** An intrusive rock.

in·tru·sive (in·trōō′siv) *adj.* **1.** Coming or thrusting in without warrant; obtrusive. **2.** Prone to intrude. **3.** *Geol.* Formed by intrusion. **4.** *Phonet.* Denoting speech sounds that result from the adjustment of the vocal organs to the sounds preceding and following and have no etymological basis, as the (d) in *spindle* (Old English *spinel*). [See INTRUDE.] — **in·tru′sive·ly** *adv.* — **in·tru′sive·ness** *n.*

in·trust (in·trust′) See ENTRUST.

in·tu·it (in·tyōō′it, -tōō′-) *v.t. & v.i.* **·tu·it·ed, ·tu·it·ing** To know or discover by intuition.

in·tu·i·tion (in′tōō·ish′ən, -tyōō-) *n.* **1.** A direct knowledge or awareness of something without conscious attention or reasoning. **2.** Anything perceived or learned without conscious attention, reasoning, concentration, etc. **3.** The ability or quality of perceiving without conscious attention or reasoning. [< Med.L < *in-* on + *tueri* to look] — **in′tu·i′tion·al** *adj.* — **in′tu·i′tion·al·ly** *adv.*

in·tu·i·tive (in·tōō′ə·tiv, -tyōō′-) *adj.* **1.** Perceived or learned by intuition; proceeding from intuition. **2.** Characterized by, or knowing through intuition. — **in·tu′i·tive·ly** *adv.* — **in·tu′i·tive·ness** *n.*

in·turn (in′turn′) *n.* A turning inward, as of the toes.

in·twine (in·twīn′) See ENTWINE.

in·un·dant (in·un′dənt) *adj.* Inundating; overflowing.

in·un·date (in′un·dāt) *v.t.* **·dat·ed, ·dat·ing** **1.** To cover by overflowing; flood. **2.** To overwhelm with abundance or excess. [< L < *in-* in, on + *undare* to overflow] — **in′un·da′tion** *n.* — **in′un·da′tor** *n.* — **in·un·da·to·ry** (in·un′də·tôr′ē, -tō′rē) *adj.*

in·ure (in·yōōr′) *v.* **·ured, ·ur·ing** *v.t.* **1.** To cause to accept or tolerate by use or exercise; accustom; habituate. — *v.i.* **2.** *Rare* To have or take effect. [< IN-[2] + obs. *ure* work < OF < L *opera* work] — **in·ure′ment** *n.*

in va·cu·o (in vak′yōō·ō) *Latin* In a vacuum.

in·vade (in·vād′) *v.* **·vad·ed, ·vad·ing** *v.t.* **1.** To enter by force with the intent of conquering or plundering. **2.** To rush or swarm into as if to occupy or overrun. **3.** To trespass upon; intrude upon: to *invade* privacy. **4.** To penetrate and spread through injuriously. — *v.i.* **5.** To make an invasion. [< L < *in-* in + *vadere* to go] — **in·vad′er** *n.*

in·vag·i·nate (in·vaj′ə·nāt) *v.* **·nat·ed, ·nat·ing** *v.t.* **1.** To put into or as into a sheath; ensheathe. **2.** To infold so as to form a depression or pouch. — *v.i.* **3.** To undergo invagination. [< L *in-* in + *vagina* sheath + -ATE[2]] — **in·vag′i·na·ble** (-nə·bəl) *adj.* — **in·vag′i·na′tion** *n.*

in·va·lid[1] (in′və·lid) *n.* A sickly or bedridden person; one disabled by injury or chronic disease. — *adj.* **1.** Enfeebled by ill health. **2.** Of or pertaining to disabled persons. — *v.t.* **1.** To cause to become an invalid; disable. **2.** *Chiefly Brit.* To release or classify (a soldier, sailor, etc.) as unfit for duty because of ill health. — *v.i.* **3.** To become an invalid. [< F < L *invalidus* not strong] — **in′va·lid·ism** *n.*

in·va·lid[2] (in·val′id) *adj.* Not valid; having no force, weight, or cogency; null; void. [< L *invalidus*] — **in·val′id·ly** *adv.*

in·val·i·date (in·val′ə·dāt) *v.t.* **·dat·ed, ·dat·ing** To weaken or destroy the validity of; render invalid; annul. — **in·val′i·da′tion** *n.* — **in·val′i·da′tor** *n.*

in·va·li·di·ty (in′və·lid′ə·tē) *n.* Lack of validity.

in·val·u·a·ble (in·val′yōō·ə·bəl, -yŏŏ·bəl) *adj.* Having a value beyond estimation; priceless. — **in·val′u·a·bly** *adv.*

in·var·i·a·ble (in·vâr′ē·ə·bəl) *adj.* Not variable; not subject to alteration; unchangeable; constant. — **in·var′i·a·bil′i·ty, in·var′i·a·ble·ness** *n.* — **in·var′i·a·bly** *adv.*

in·var·i·ant (in·vâr′ē·ənt) *adj.* Not subject to change or variation; constant. — *n.* *Math.* A quantity that remains unchanged; constant. — **in·var′i·ance, in·var′i·an·cy** *n.*

in·va·sion (in·vā′zhən) *n.* **1.** The act of invading with hostile armed forces; a military inroad. **2.** Any attack or onset of something injurious or disagreeable, as a disease. **3.** Encroachment by intrusion or trespass. **4.** Entrance with intent to overrun or occupy. — **in·va′sive** *adj.*

in·vec·tive (in·vek′tiv) *n.* Violent accusation or denunciation; abuse. — *adj.* Using or characterized by vituperation or abuse. [< OF < LL < L *invectus*, pp. of *invehere* to carry into] — **in·vec′tive·ly** *adv.* — **in·vec′tive·ness** *n.*

in·veigh (in·vā′) *v.i.* To utter vehement censure or invective: with *against.* [< L < *in-* into + *vehere* to carry] — **in·veigh′er** *n.*

in·vei·gle (in·vē′gəl, -vā-) *v.t.* **·gled, ·gling** To entice o duce by guile or flattery; draw; cajole: often with *into.* [*aveugle* blind, ult. < L *ab-* without + *oculus* eye] – **vei′gle·ment** *n.* — **in·vei′gler** *n.*

in·vent (in·vent′) *v.t.* **1.** To devise or create by origina fort; esp., to conceive or make originally (some mechan electrical, or other device). **2.** To make up, as somet untrue or contrary to fact: to *invent* an excuse. [< L < on + *venire* to come] — **in·vent′i·ble** *adj.*

in·ven·tion (in·ven′shən) *n.* **1.** The act or process of in ting. **2.** A device or useful contrivance conceived or m by original effort. **3.** The skill or ingenuity needed fo venting or contriving; inventive powers. **4.** A mental f cation or concoction. — **in·ven′tion·al** *adj.*

in·ven·tive (in·ven′tiv) *adj.* **1.** Skillful at invention or trivance; ingenious. **2.** Characterized by or created b vention. **3.** Pertaining to invention. — **in·ven′tive·ly** — **in·ven′tive·ness** *n.*

in·ven·tor (in·ven′tər) *n.* One who invents; esp., one has originated some method, process, etc. Also **in·vent′**

in·ven·to·ry (in′vən·tôr′ē, -tō′rē) *n. pl.* **·ries** **1.** A li articles, with the description and quantity of each. **2.** A of all finished goods in stock, goods in the process of m facture, and the raw materials used, made annually business concern. **3.** The process of making such a list The value of the goods or stock of a business. — *v.t.* · **·ry·ing** **1.** To make an inventory of. **2.** To insert in a ventory. [< Med.L < L *inventorium*] — **in′ven·to′** (-tôr′ē·əl, -tō′rē) *adj.* — **in′ven·to′ri·al·ly** *adv.*

in·ver·ness (in′vər·nes′) *n.* *Often cap.* **1.** A type of c coat having a detachable cape. **2.** The cape itself: called **Inverness cape.** [after *Inverness*, Scotland]

in·verse (in·vûrs′, in′vûrs) *adj.* **1.** Reversed or opposi order, effect, etc. **2.** Turned upside down; inverted. · That which is in direct contrast or opposition; the reve opposite. — **in·verse′ly** *adv.*

in·ver·sion (in·vûr′zhən, -shən) *n.* **1.** The act of invert or the state of being inverted. **2.** That which is inve **3.** In grammar and rhetoric, a reversing of the usual order in a phrase, clause, or sentence. — **in·ver′sive** *a*

in·vert (*v.* in·vûrt′; *adj.* & *n.* in′vûrt) *v.t.* **1.** To turn side down; turn completely over. **2.** To reverse the o effect, or operation of. **3.** To alter by inversion, as in c istry, music, etc. — *v.i.* **4.** To undergo inversion. — *Chem.* Inverted. — *n.* **1.** One who or that which is inve **2.** *Psychiatry* A homosexual. [< L < *in-* in + *verte* turn] — **in·ver′ter** *n.* — **in·vert′i·ble** *adj.*

in·ver·te·brate (in·vûr′tə·brit, -brāt) *adj.* **1.** *Zool.* vertebrate; lacking a backbone or spinal column. **2.** L ing firmness or character; irresolute. Also **in·ver′te** (-brəl). — *n.* **1.** An invertebrate animal. **2.** One lacks firmness of character.

in·vest (in·vest′) *v.t.* **1.** To commit or use (money, cap etc.) for the purchase of property, securities, a business, with the expectation of profit. **2.** To spend or use (mo time, effort, etc.) for: often with *in.* **3.** To place in c formally; install. **4.** To give power, authority, or ran **5.** To cover or surround as if with a garment; shroud. **6** provide or endow with qualities or traits: to *invest* a with glory. **7.** *Mil.* To surround or hem in; besiege. — **8.** To make an investment or investments. [< L < *in* + *vestire* to clothe] — **in·ves′tor** *n.*

in·ves·ti·gate (in·ves′tə·gāt) *v.* **·gat·ed, ·gat·ing** *v.t.* **1** search or inquire into; make a formal or official examina of. — *v.i.* **2.** To make an investigation. [< L < *in-* i *vestigare* to trace] — **in·ves′ti·ga·ble** (-gə·bəl) *adj.* — **in·ves·ti·ga′tive** *adj.* — **in·ves′ti·ga·to′ry** (-gə·tôr′ē, -tō′rē) *a*

in·ves·ti·ga·tion (in·ves′tə·gā′shən) *n.* **1.** A formal or cial examination or study, as by the police or a governr tal body. **2.** The act of investigating. [< F]

in·ves·ti·ga·tor (in·ves′tə·gā′tər) *n.* **1.** A detective, es private detective. **2.** One who investigates. — **in·ves′ti to′ri·al** (-tôr′ē·əl, -tō′rē·əl) *adj.*

in·ves·ti·tive (in·ves′tə·tiv) *adj.* **1.** Of or pertaining t vestiture. **2.** Having the function of investing.

in·ves·ti·ture (in·ves′tə·chər) *n.* **1.** The act or ceremor investing with an office, authority, or right. **2.** An inves or clothing, as with a quality, garment, etc.

in·vest·ment (in·vest′mənt) *n.* **1.** The investing of mo or capital to gain interest or income. **2.** Money or cap so invested. **3.** The form of property in which one inve **4.** The act of investing, or the state of being invested. Investiture. **6.** *Biol.* An outer covering of an animal, pl organ, or part. **7.** *Mil.* The surrounding of a fort or tow create a state of siege; blockade.

in·vet·er·ate (in·vet′ər·it) *adj.* **1.** Firmly established long continuance; deep-rooted. **2.** Confirmed or harde in a particular character, habit, or opinion: an *invete* bigot. [< L < *in-* very + *vetus* old] — **in·vet′er·a·c** — **in·vet′er·ate·ly** *adv.* — **in·vet′er·ate·ness** *n.*

in·vid·i·ous (in·vid′ē·əs) *adj.* **1.** Exciting or creating ill dislike; offensive: *invidious* remarks. **2.** Provoking anger resentment by unjust discrimination. [< L < *invidia* vy.] **— in·vid′i·ous·ly** *adv.* **— in·vid′i·ous·ness** *n.*

ig·or·ate (in·vig′ər·āt) *v.t.* **·at·ed, ·at·ing** To give vigor d energy to; animate. [< L *in-* in + *vigor* vigor + -ATE[2]] **in·vig′or·at′ing·ly** *adv.* **— in·vig′or·a′tion** *n.* **— in·vig′·a′tive** *adj.* **— in·vig′or·a′tive·ly** *adv.* **— in·vig′or·a′tor** *n.*

in·ci·ble (in·vin′sə·bəl) *adj.* Not to be overcome; un-nquerable. [< F < L *invincibilis*] **— in·vin′ci·bil′i·ty, vin′ci·ble·ness** *n.* **— in·vin′ci·bly** *adv.*

i·o·la·ble (in·vī′ə·lə·bəl) *adj.* **1.** Not to be profaned, de-d, etc.; sacrosanct. **2.** Not to be violated or broken. **— vi′o·la·bil′i·ty, in·vi′o·la·ble·ness** *n.* **— in·vi′o·la·bly** *adv.*

i·o·late (in·vī′ə·lit) *adj.* **1.** Not violated; not profaned broken; intact. **2.** Inviolable. **— in·vi′o·la·cy** *n.* **— in·o·late·ly** *adv.* **— in·vi′o·late·ness** *n.*

is·i·ble (in·viz′ə·bəl) *adj.* **1.** Not visible; not capable of ng seen. **2.** Not in sight; concealed. **3.** Not publicly or enly acknowledged. **4.** *Econ.* Not appearing in regular ocesses or financial statements: *invisible* assets. **—** *n.* One o or that which is invisible. [< OF] **— in·vis′i·bil′i·ty, vis′i·ble·ness** *n.* **— in·vis′i·bly** *adv.*

i·ta·tion (in′və·tā′shən) *n.* **1.** The act of inviting. **2.** e means or words by which one invites or is invited: a itten *invitation.* **3.** The act of alluring or inducing; en-ement. **— in′vi·ta′tion·al** *adj.*

ite (*v.* in·vīt′; *n.* in′vīt) *v.* **·vit·ed, ·vit·ing** *v.t.* **1.** To ask meone) courteously to be present in some place, to attend ne event, or to perform some action. **2.** To make formal polite request for: to *invite* suggestions. **3.** To present op-rtunity or inducement for; attract: his opinions *invite* ticism. **4.** To tempt; entice. **—** *v.i.* **5.** To give invita-n; entice. **—** *n. Slang* An invitation. [< F < L *invi-e* to entertain] **— in·vit′er** *n.*

vit·ing (in·vī′ting) *adj.* That invites or allures; attrac-e. **— in·vit′ing·ly** *adv.* **— in·vit′ing·ness** *n.*

vo·ca·tion (in′və·kā′shən, -vō-) *n.* **1.** The act of invok-g or appealing to a deity, or other agent for help, inspira-n, witness, etc. **2.** A prayer, as at the opening of a cere-ony. **3.** An appeal for assistance to the Muses or some di-ne being at the beginning of an epic or other poem. **4.** The t of conjuring an evil spirit. **— in·voc·a·tive** (in·vok′ə·tiv), **·voc·a·to·ry** (in·vok′ə·tôr′ē, -tō′rē) *adj.*

voice (in′vois) *n.* **1.** A descriptive list of merchandise nt or services rendered to a purchaser, including quanti-s, prices, shipping and other costs, etc. **2.** The merchan-se or services so itemized. **—** *v.t.* **·voiced, ·voic·ing** To ake an invoice of; list on an invoice. [< F *envoyer* to send.]

voke (in·vōk′) *v.t.* **·voked, ·vok·ing** **1.** To call upon for d, protection, witness, etc. **2.** To declare relevant and op-ative, as a law, power, right, etc.: to *invoke* the Fifth Amend-ent. **3.** To appeal to for confirmation; quote as an author-. **4.** To summon or conjure by incantation. **5.** To call or tition for: to *invoke* a blessing. [< F < L < *in-* on + *vo-re* to call] **— in·vok′er** *n.*

vo·lu·cre (in′və·lōō′kər) *n. Bot.* A ring of bracts at the se of a compound flower. [< F < L < *involvere* to roll up] **· in′vo·lu′cral** (-krəl) *adj.*

vol·un·tar·y (in′vol′ən·ter′ē) *adj.* **1.** Done or occurring thout one's consent or choice; unintentional. **2.** *Physiol.* unctioning without conscious control: *involuntary* muscles. **· in·vol′un·tar′i·ly** *adv.* **— in·vol′un·tar′i·ness** *n.*

vo·lute (in′və·lōōt) *adj.* **1.** Having complications and in-icacies; involved. **2.** *Bot.* Having the edges rolled inward, a leaf. **3.** *Zool.* Having the whorls nearly or entirely con-aling the axis, as a shell. Also **in′vo·lut′ed.** [< L *involutus,* o. of *involvere* to involve]

vo·lu·tion (in′və·lōō′shən) **1.** A complicating or inter-vining; entanglement. **2.** Something involved or compli-ted. **3.** *Biol.* Arrest and reversal of development; degen-ation. **4.** In rhetoric, complicated or cumbrous arrange-ent of words, clauses, or phrases. **— in′vo·lu′tion·al** *adj.*

volve (in·volv′) *v.t.* **·volved, ·volv·ing** **1.** To include as a levant or necessary aspect. **2.** To have effect on; affect y drawing in or spreading. **3.** To implicate; associate sig-ficantly: usu. with *in* or *with:* He is *involved* in the scandal. . To absorb or engross: usu. with *in.* **5.** To make intricate tangled. **6.** To envelop: to *involve* an issue in obscurity. < L < *in-* in + *volvere* to roll] **— in·volve′ment** *n.*

·volved (in·volvd′) *adj.* Complicated; intricate. **— in·olv·ed·ness** (in·vol′vid·nis) *n.*

·vul·ner·a·ble (in·vul′nər·ə·bəl) *adj.* **1.** Not capable of eing wounded or physically injured. **2.** Not to be over-ome or damaged by attack; unconquerable. **— in·vul′ner·bil′i·ty, in·vul′ner·a·ble·ness** *n.* **— in·vul′ner·a·bly** *adv.*

·ward (in′wərd) *adv.* **1.** Toward the inside, center, or in-erior. **2.** In or into the mind or thoughts. Also *inwards.* **— dj.** **1.** Situated within, esp. with reference to the body; internal. **2.** Pertaining to the mind or spirit. **3.** Proceeding toward the inside: an *inward* thrust. **4.** Inland. **5.** Inherent; intrinsic. **—** *n.* The inner part. [OE *inweard*]

in·ward·ly (in′wərd·lē) *adv.* **1.** Within the mind or heart; secretly: *inwardly* anxious. **2.** On the inside; within. **3.** Toward the center or interior. **4.** Essentially; intrinsically.

in·ward·ness (in′wərd·nis) *n.* **1.** The state of being inward; existence within. **2.** Inner quality or meaning; essence. **3.** Intensity of feeling. **4.** Unworldliness.

in·wards (in′wərdz; *for n., also* in′ərdz) *adv.* Inward. **—** *n.pl.* The entrails.

in·weave (in·wēv′) *v.t.* **·wove** or **·weaved, ·wo·ven** or *less frequently* **·wove, ·weav·ing** To weave in or together.

in·wrap (in·rap′) See ENWRAP.

in·wrought (in·rôt′) *adj.* **1.** Worked into a fabric, metal, etc., as a pattern. **2.** Decorated with such a pattern or design. **3.** Closely combined with something; blended in.

i·o·dide (ī′ə·dīd) *n. Chem.* A compound of iodine and one other element. Also **i′o·did** (-did).

i·o·dine (ī′ə·dīn, -din; *in technical usage* ī′ə·dēn) *n.* **1.** A grayish black non-metallic element (symbol I), yielding, when heated, corrosive fumes of a rich violet color, used in medicine as an antiseptic and also in photography and organic synthesis. See ELEMENT. **2.** *Informal* A solution of iodine used as an antiseptic. Also **i·o·din** (ī′ə·din). [< F < Gk. *iōdēs* violetlike (< *ion* a violet + *eidos* form) + -INE[2]]

i·o·dize (ī′ə·dīz) *v.t.* **·dized, ·diz·ing** To treat with, combine with, or expose to the vapor of iodine. **— i′o·diz′er** *n.*

i·o·do·form (ī·ō′də·fôrm) *n. Chem.* A light yellow crystalline compound, CHI_3, used in medicine as an antiseptic.

i·on (ī′ən, ī′on) *n. Physics* An electrically charged atom, radical, or molecule, resulting from the action of an electrolyte, electric fields, high temperatures, various forms of radiation, etc., in adding or removing electrons. [< Gk. *ion,* neut. of *iōn,* ppr. of *ienai* to go] **— i·on′ic** *adj.*

-ion *suffix of nouns* **1.** Action, state, quality, or process of: *communion.* **2.** State or result of being: *union.* Also *-ation, -tion.* [< F < L *-io, -ionis*]

ion exchange *Chem.* A process whereby ions may be reversibly interchanged at the boundary of a liquid and solid in contact, the composition of the solid not being altered.

I·o·ni·a (ī·ō′nē·ə) The ancient coastal region of western Asia Minor, colonized by the Greeks in the 11th century B.C. **— I·o′ni·an** *adj. & n.*

I·on·ic (ī·on′ik) *adj.* **1.** Ionian. **2.** *Archit.* Of or pertaining to an order of Greek architecture characterized by a capital having typical scroll-like ornaments. **—** *n.* A dialect of ancient Greek. [< L < Gk. *Iōnikos*]

i·o·ni·um (ī·ō′nē·əm) *n.* A radioactive isotope of thorium, of mass 230 and a half life of about 80,000 years. [< ION + (URAN)IUM; from its ionizing action]

i·on·ize (ē′ən·īz) *v.t. & v.i.* **·ized, ·iz·ing** To convert or become converted, totally or in part, into ions. **— i′on·i·za′·tion** *n.* **— i′on·iz′er** *n.*

i·on·o·sphere (ī·on′ə·sfir) *n.* A region of the earth's atmosphere above the mesosphere, consisting of several layers subject to ionization, with seasonal variations. **— i·on′o·spher′·ic** (-sfir′ik, -sfer′-) *adj.*

i·o·ta (ī·ō′tə) *n.* **1.** The ninth letter in the Greek alphabet (Ι, ι), corresponding to English *i.* See ALPHABET. **2.** A very small or insignificant amount. [< L < Gk. *iōta.*]

IOU A written acknowledgment of indebtedness having on it these letters (meaning *I owe you*). Also **I.O.U.**

-ious *suffix of adjectives* Characterized by; full of: occurring esp. in adjectives formed from nouns ending in *-ion: suspicious, cautious.* [< L *-iosus* full of]

ip·e·cac (ip′ə·kak) *n.* **1.** Either of two plants of the madder family, yielding a medicinal alkaloid. **2.** The dried root of either of these plants. **3.** An extract of this root, used as an emetic or cathartic. Also **ip·e·cac·u·an·ha** (ip′ə·kak′yōō·ä′·nə). [< Pg. < Tupi < *ipe* little + *kaa* tree, herb]

Iph·i·ge·ni·a (if′ə·jə·nī′ə) In Greek legend, a daughter of Agamemnon and Clytemnestra who was offered as a sacrifice to Artemis so that the Greek fleet might sail on to Troy.

ip·se dix·it (ip′sē dik′sit) *Latin* **1.** Literally, he himself said (it). **2.** An improved or dogmatic assertion.

ip·so fac·to (ip′sō fak′tō) *Latin* By the fact itself; by that very fact or act: outlawed *ipso facto.*

ir- Assimilated var. of IN-[1] and IN-[2].

I·ra·ni·an (ī·rā′nē·ən) *adj.* Of or pertaining to Iran, its people, or their language. **—** *n.* **1.** A native or inhabitant of Iran; a Persian. **2.** A branch of the Indo-Iranian subfamily of Indo-European languages, including Modern Persian, Kurdish, and Pashto, and such ancient languages as Old Persian and Scythian. **3.** Modern Persian.

I·ra·qi (ē·rä′kē) *adj.* Of or pertaining to Iraq, its people, or their language. **—** *n.* **1.** A native or inhabitant of Iraq. **2.** The dialect of Arabic spoken in Iraq.

i·ras·ci·ble (i·ras′ə·bəl, ī·ras′-) *adj.* **1.** Easily provoked to anger; quick-tempered. **2.** Resulting from or characterized by anger or irritability. [< OF < LL *irasci* to be angry] — **i·ras′ci·bil′i·ty, i·ras′ci·ble·ness** *n.* — **i·ras′ci·bly** *adv.*
i·rate (ī′rāt, ī·rāt′) *adj.* Angry; enraged. [< L *iratus*, pp. of *irasci* to be angry] — **i′rate·ly** *adv.*
IRBM The intermediate range ballistic missile, having a range between 200 and 1500 miles.
ire (īr) *n.* Wrath; anger. [< OF < L *ira* anger]
ire·ful (īr′fəl) *adj.* Full of ire; wrathful; angry. — **ire′ful·ly** *adv.* — **ire′ful·ness** *n.*
ir·i·des·cent (ir′ə·des′ənt) *adj.* Displaying the colors of the rainbow in shifting hues and patterns, as soap bubbles, mother-of-pearl, etc. [< Gk. *iris, iridos* rainbow] — **ir′i·des′cence** *adj.* — **ir′i·des′cent·ly** *adv.*
i·rid·i·um (i·rid′ē·əm, ī·rid′-) *n.* A hard, brittle, silver-gray metallic element (symbol Ir) of the platinum group, used in certain alloys for making penpoints, jewelry, etc. See ELEMENT. [< NL < L < Gk. *iris* rainbow + -IUM]
irido- *combining form* The iris of the eye. Also, before vowels, **irid-**. [< Gk. *iris, iridos* iris]
ir·i·dos·mine (ir′ə·doz′min, -dos′-, ī′rə-) *n.* Osmiridium. Also **ir′i·dos′mi·um** (-mē·əm). [< IRID(IUM) + OSMIUM]
i·ris (ī′ris) *n.* *pl.* **i·ris·es** or **ir·i·des** (ir′ə·dēz, ī′rə-) **1.** *Anat.* The colored, circular, contractile membrane between the cornea and the lens of the eye, having the pupil as its central aperture. For illus. see EYE. **2.** *Bot.* A plant with sword-shaped leaves and large handsome flowers, as the crocus, gladiolus, etc. [< L < Gk. *iris*]
I·ris (ī′ris) In Greek mythology, the goddess of the rainbow and a messenger of the gods.
I·rish (ī′rish) *adj.* Of or pertaining to Ireland, its people, or their language. — *n.* **1.** The people of Ireland or of Irish ancestry: preceded by *the*. **2.** The ancient or modern language of Ireland, belonging to the Goidelic branch of the Celtic languages: also called *Irish Gaelic*: sometimes called *Erse*. **3.** The dialect of English spoken in Ireland: also called *Irish English*. [ME *Irisc* < OE *Ir-* + *-isc*]

IRIS
a Bearded.
b Japanese.
c Siberian.

Irish English Irish (def. 3).
Irish Gaelic Irish (def. 2).
I·rish·man (ī′rish·mən) *n.* *pl.* **·men** (-mən) A man of Irish birth or ancestry.
Irish moss Carrageen, a seaweed.
Irish potato The common or white potato.
Irish setter A reddish brown variety of setter.
Irish terrier A small terrier having a wiry, reddish coat.
Irish wolfhound A large, powerful hunting dog of an ancient breed, characterized by a hard, rough coat.
irk (ûrk) *v.t.* To annoy or weary; vex. [ME *irken*]
irk·some (ûrk′səm) *adj.* Troublesome; tiresome; tedious. — **irk′some·ly** *adv.* — **irk′some·ness** *n.*
i·ron (ī′ərn) *n.* **1.** A tough, abundant, malleable, easily oxidized and strongly magnetic metallic element (symbol Fe): also called *Ferrum*. See ELEMENT. **2.** That which is firm, harsh, unyielding, or indestructible. **3.** An implement or tool made of iron. **4.** A metal implement or appliance having a smooth, flat undersurface and a handle, heated either by direct contact with fire or by electric current, and used to press or smooth cloth, etc. **5.** *pl.* Chains used to confine a prisoner; shackles. **6.** A golf club having a metal head with an angled face. **7.** *Slang* A pistol or similar firearm: also called *shooting iron*. **8.** *Med.* A preparation containing iron. — **to have irons in the fire** To be engaged in various enterprises. — **to strike while the iron is hot** To act at the right moment. — *adj.* **1.** Made of or consisting of iron. **2.** Resembling iron. **3.** Inexorable; unyielding; firm. **4.** Grim; pitiless. — *v.t.* **1.** To smooth or press, as with a heated flatiron. **2.** To add or apply iron to. **3.** To put in chains; shackle. — *v.i.* To press clothes, etc., with an iron. — **to iron out** To remove, as difficulties. [OE *īrenīsen, īsern*]
Iron Age The most recent and advanced of three early stages of human progress, following the Stone Age and the Bronze Age.
i·ron·bound (ī′ərn·bound′) *adj.* **1.** Bound with iron. **2.** Surrounded with rocks, as a seacoast. **3.** Unyielding.
i·ron·clad (ī′ərn·klad′) *adj.* **1.** Covered by or in armor. **2.** Strict; unbreakable, as a rule, etc. — *n.* Formerly, a warship sheathed with armor.
iron curtain An impenetrable barrier of censorship and secrecy imposed by the Soviet Union between its sphere of influence and the rest of the world.
i·ron·er (ī′ərn·ər) *n.* One who or that which irons.
i·ron·hand·ed (ī′ərn·han′did) *adj.* Exerting strict discipline or rigorous control; despotic.
i·ron·ic (ī·ron′ik) *adj.* **1.** Of the nature of or characterized by irony. **2.** Given to the use of irony. Also **i·ron′ic·al.** **i·ron′i·cal·ly** *adv.* — **i·ron′i·cal·ness** *n.*
i·ron·ing board (ī′ərn·ing) A board or folding table, padded, on which articles of clothing, etc., are ironed.
iron lung A cabinetlike enclosure in which the respira of a patient is artificially maintained.
i·ron·mon·ger (ī′ərn·mung′gər, -mong′-) *n.* *Brit.* One sells iron articles; a hardware dealer. — **i′ron·mon′ger·**
iron pyrites Pyrite.
I·ron·sides (ī′ərn·sīdz′) Nickname of Oliver Cromwell. *n.pl.* Any of Cromwell's soldiers.
i·ronstone (ī′ərn·stōn′) *n.* Glazed, usu. white pottery
i·ron·ware (ī′ərn·wâr′) *n.* Articles made of iron; hardw
i·ron·weed (ī′ərn·wēd′) *n.* An herb or shrub having mo purple or reddish flowers.
i·ron·wood (ī′ərn·wo͝od′) *n.* Any of various trees hav unusually hard wood; also, the wood.
i·ron·work (ī′ərn·wûrk′) *n.* **1.** Parts or objects mad iron, as parts of a building. **2.** The act of working in i — **i′ron·work′er** *n.*
i·ron·works (ī′ərn·wûrks′) *n.pl.* (*often construed as si* An establishment where iron or ironwork is made.
i·ro·ny (ī′rə·nē) *n.* *pl.* **·nies** **1.** A sarcastic or humor manner of discourse in which what is said is meant to press its opposite, as when "That's very good" me "That's very bad". **2.** A result, ending, etc., the revers what was expected. **3.** A situation, event, pairing, etc. which main elements are rationally or emotionally inc patible because of contrast, conflict, or surprise. **4.** The of irony in literature, art, etc. **5.** The feigning of ignora as a tehnique in argument; Socratic irony. — **Syn.** SARCASM. [< L < Gk. *eirōn* dissembler]
Ir·o·quoi·an (ir′ə·kwoi′ən) *n.* **1.** A family of North Am can Indian languages, including Cayuga, Cherokee, Cor toga, Erie, Mohawk, Oneida, Seneca and other langua **2.** A member of a tribe speaking these languages. — *adj.* the Iroquois Indians or their languages.
Ir·o·quois (ir′ə·kwoi, -kwoiz) *n.* *pl.* **·quois** **1.** A membe any of the North American Indian tribes known as the F Nations; also, these tribes collectively. See FIVE NATIC **2.** A member of a tribe speaking an Iroquoian language. *adj.* Of or pertaining to the Iroquois. [< F < Algonqu *Irinakoiw*, lit., real adders]
ir·ra·di·ant (i·rā′dē·ənt) *adj.* Sending forth light; shini — **ir·ra′di·ance, ir·ra′di·an·cy** *n.*
ir·ra·di·ate (*v.* i·rā′dē·āt; *adj.* i·rā′dē·it, -āt) *v.* **·at·ed, ·at·** *v.t.* **1.** To light up; illuminate. **2.** To make clear or unc standable. **3.** To send forth in or as in rays of light. **4.** subject to X-rays, ultraviolet light, or similar rays. **5.** expose to radiant energy. — *v.i.* **6.** To be radiant; shi — *adj.* Made bright; illuminated. [< L *in-* thoroughly *radiare* to shine] — **ir·ra′di·a′tion** *n.* — **ir·ra′di·a′tive** *(*
ir·ra·tion·al (i·rash′ən·əl) *adj.* **1.** Incapable of exercis the power of reason. **2.** Contrary to reason; absurd. *Math.* Denoting a number that cannot be expressed as integer or a quotient of integers. [< L *irrationalis*] — **ra′tion·al·ism** *n.* — **ir·ra′tion·al·ly** *adv.* — **ir·ra′tion ness** *n.*
ir·ra·tion·al·i·ty (i·rash′ən·al′ə·tē) *n.* *pl.* **·ties** **1.** T state of being irrational. **2.** That which is irrational.
ir·re·claim·a·ble (ir′i·klā′mə·bəl) *adj.* Incapable of be reclaimed. — **ir·re·claim′a·bil′i·ty, ir′re·claim′a·ble·ness** — **ir′re·claim′a·bly** *adv.*
ir·rec·on·cil·a·ble (i·rek′ən·sī′lə·bəl, i·rek′ən·sī′lə·bəl) *a* Not able or willing to be reconciled or brought into acco — *n.* **1.** One who refuses to yield or compromise. **2.** *pl.* compatible ideas. — **ir·rec′on·cil′a·bil′i·ty, ir·rec′on·ci ble·ness** *n.* — **ir·rec′on·cil′a·bly** *adv.*
ir·re·cov·er·a·ble (ir′i·kuv′ər·ə·bəl) *adj.* **1.** Incapable being recovered. **2.** Incapable of being remedied. — **ir′ cov′er·a·ble·ness** *n.* — **ir′re·cov′er·a·bly** *adv.*
ir·re·deem·a·ble (ir′i·dē′mə·bəl) *adj.* **1.** Incapable of be recovered, bought back, or paid off. **2.** Not to be convert into coin: said of some types of paper money. **3.** Beyo redemption or change; incorrigible. — **ir′re·deem′a·bly** *a*
ir·re·den·tist (ir′i·den′tist) *n.* *Usu. cap.* A member o party formed in Italy about 1878, that had as its aim t acquisition of certain regions subject to other governme but having an Italian-speaking population. — *adj.* Of pertaining to the irredentists or their policies. [< Ital. < *in-* not + *redemptus* redeemed] — **ir·re′den′tism** (-tiz·əm)
ir·re·duc·i·ble (ir′i·do͞o′sə·bəl, -dyo͞o′-) *adj.* **1.** Incapable being decreased or diminished. **2.** Incapable of being cc verted to a simpler or more basic form. — **ir′re·duc′i·bil′i** *n.* — **ir′re·duc′i·bly** *adv.*
ir·ref·ra·ga·ble (i·ref′rə·gə·bəl) *adj.* That cannot be refut or disproved. [< LL < L *in-* not + *refragari* to oppose] **ir·ref′ra·ga·bil′i·ty** *n.* — **ir·ref′ra·ga·bly** *adv.*
ir·ref·u·ta·ble (i·ref′yə·tə·bəl, ir′i·fyo͞o′tə·bəl) *adj.* Incapal of being disproved. — **ir·ref·u·ta·bil·i·ty** (i·ref′yə·tə·bil′ə· ir′i·fyo͞o′-) *n.* — **ir·ref·u·ta·bly** (i·ref′yə·tə·blē, ir′i·fyo͞o′-) *a*

e·gard·less (ir′i·gärd′lis) *adv.* Regardless: a nonstand- or humorous usage.

eg·u·lar (i·reg′yə·lər) *adj.* **1.** Lacking symmetry or uni- mity. **2.** Occurring at unequal intervals: an *irregular* ise. **3.** Not according to established rules or procedure. Not conforming to accepted standards of conduct. **5.** *am.* Not conforming to the usual pattern of inflection or ıjugation. **6.** *Mil.* Of troops, not belonging to a regularly ganized military force. — *n.* One who or that which is ir- ular. [< OF < Med.L *irregularis*] — **ir·reg′u·lar·ly** *adv.*

eg·u·lar·i·ty (i·reg′yə·lar′ə·tē) *n. pl.* **·ties** **1.** The state quality of being irregular. **2.** That which is irregular.

el·a·tive (i·rel′ə·tiv) *adj.* Irrelevant. — **ir·rel′a·tive·ly** . — **ir·rel′a·tive·ness** *n.*

el·e·vant (i·rel′ə·vənt) *adj.* Not relevant; not pertinent; pplicable. — **ir·rel′e·vance, ir·rel′e·van·cy** *n.* — **ir- ′e·vant·ly** *adv.*

e·lig·ion (ir′i·lij′ən) *n.* **1.** Lack of religious faith. **2.** In- ference or hostility toward religion. — **ir′re·lig′ion·ist** *n.*

e·lig·ious (ir′i·lij′əs) *adj.* **1.** Lacking in religious faith or ty. **2.** Profane. — **ir′re·lig′ious·ly** *adv.*

e·me·di·a·ble (ir′i·mē′dē·ə·bəl) *adj.* Incapable of being nedied; incurable; irreparable. [< L *irremediabilis*] — **re·me′di·a·ble·ness** *n.* — **ir′re·me′di·a·bly** *adv.*

e·mis·si·ble (ir′i·mis′ə·bəl) *adj.* Not remissible; un- rdonable, as a sin. — **ir′re·mis′si·bil′i·ty, ir′re·mis′si·ble- ss** *n.* — **ir′re·mis′si·bly** *adv.*

e·mov·a·ble (ir′i·mōō′və·bəl) *adj.* Not removable.

ep·a·ra·ble (i·rep′ər·ə·bəl) *adj.* Incapable of being re- ired, rectified, remedied, or made good. — **ir·rep′a·ra- ′i·ty, ir·rep′a·ra·ble·ness** *n.* — **ir·rep′a·ra·bly** *adv.*

e·place·a·ble (ir′i·plā′sə·bəl) *adj.* Not replaceable.

e·pres·si·ble (ir′i·pres′ə·bəl) *adj.* Not repressible; in- pable of being controlled or restrained. — **ir′re·pres′si- ′i·ty, ir′re·pres′si·ble·ness** *n.* — **ir′re·pres′si·bly** *adv.*

e·proach·a·ble (ir′i·prō′chə·bəl) *adj.* Not meriting re- oach; blameless. [< F *irréprochable*] — **ir′re·proach′a- e·ness** *n.* — **ir′re·proach′a·bly** *adv.*

e·sis·ti·ble (ir′i·zis′tə·bəl) *adj.* **1.** Not resistible. **2.** ompletely fascinating or enchanting. — **ir′re·sis′ti·bil′i·ty, re·sis′ti·ble·ness** *n.* — **ir′re·sis′ti·bly** *adv.*

es·o·lute (i·rez′ə·lōōt) *adj.* Not resolute or resolved; cking firmness of purpose; wavering; hesitating. — **ir·res′- lute′ly** *adv.* — **ir·res′o·lute′ness, ir·res′o·lu′tion** *n.*

e·spec·tive (ir′i·spek′tiv) *adj.* Existing without rela- onship to something else: now chiefly in the phrase **irre- ective of,** regardless of. — **ir′re·spec′tive·ly** *adv.*

e·spon·si·ble (ir′i·spon′sə·bəl) *adj.* **1.** Lacking in re- onsibility; unreliable. **2.** Free from or incapable of re- onsibility. — *n.* One who is irresponsible. — **ir′re·spon′- bil′i·ty, ir′re·spon′si·ble·ness** *n.* — **ir′re·spon′si·bly** *adv.*

e·spon·sive (ir′i·spon′siv) *adj.* Not responsive. — **ir′- ·spon′sive·ness** *n.*

e·trace·a·ble (ir′i·trā′sə·bəl) *adj.* Incapable of being re- aced, as a path, footsteps, etc.

e·triev·a·ble (ir′i·trē′və·bəl) *adj.* Not retrievable; irre- verable; irreparable. — **ir′re·triev′a·bil′i·ty, ir′re·triev′a- e·ness** *n.* — **ir′re·triev′a·bly** *adv.*

rev·er·ence (i·rev′ər·əns) *n.* **1.** Lack of awe, veneration, respect. **2.** Behavior or utterance indicative of this.

rev·er·ent (i·rev′ər·ənt) *adj.* Characterized by or show- g irreverence. — **ir·rev′er·ent·ly** *adv.*

re·vers·i·ble (ir′i·vûr′sə·bəl) *adj.* **1.** Incapable of being ırned in the opposite direction. **2.** Incapable of being an- ulled, repealed, or undone. — **ir′re·vers′i·bil′i·ty, ir′re- ers′i·ble·ness** *n.* — **ir′re·vers′i·bly** *adv.*

rev·o·ca·ble (i·rev′ə·kə·bəl) *adj.* **1.** Incapable of being voked. **2.** Incapable of being brought back. — **ir·rev′o- a·bil′i·ty, ir·rev′o·ca·ble·ness** *n.* — **ir·rev′o·ca·bly** *adv.*

ri·ga·ble (ir′ə·gə·bəl) *adj.* Capable of being irrigated.

ri·gate (ir′ə·gāt) *v.t.* **·gat·ed, ·gat·ing** **1.** To supply (land) ith water, as by means of ditches. **2.** To revitalize or re- esh by or as if by watering. **3.** *Med.* To moisten or wash ut with water. [< L < *in-* to + *rigare* to water] — **ir′- ·ga′tion** *n.* — **ir′ri·ga′tion·al** *adj.* — **ir′ri·ga′tor** *n.*

ri·ta·bil·i·ty (ir′ə·tə·bil′ə·tē) *n. pl.* **·ties** The state or uality of being irritable.

ri·ta·ble (ir′ə·tə·bəl) *adj.* **1.** Easily annoyed or angered. . *Biol.* Responding to stimuli. **3.** *Pathol.* Influenced ab- ormally by the action of stimulants. — **ir′ri·ta·ble·ness** *n.* — **ir′ri·ta·bly** *adv.*

ri·tant (ir′ə·tənt) *n.* That which irritates or causes irrita- ion. — *adj.* Causing irritation. — **ir′ri·tan·cy** *n.*

ri·tate (ir′ə·tāt) *v.t.* **·tat·ed, ·tat·ing** **1.** To excite annoy- nce, impatience, or ill temper in; vex. **2.** To make sore or nflamed. **3.** *Biol.* To stimulate (a cell, tissue, or organ) to a haracteristic function or action. [< L *irritare* to irritate] — **ir′ri·ta′tive** *adj.* — **ir′ri·ta′tor** *n.*

ir·ri·tat·ing (ir′ə·tā′ting) *adj.* Causing irritation. — **ir′ri·tat′ing·ly** *adv.*

ir·ri·ta·tion (ir′ə·tā′shən) *n.* **1.** The act of irritating, or the state of being irritated; annoyance. **2.** *Pathol.* A condition of abnormal excitability or sensitivity in an organ or part.

ir·rup·tion (i·rup′shən) *n.* **1.** A breaking or rushing in. **2.** A violent, sudden invasion. [< L < *in-* in + *rumpere* to break] — **ir·rup′tive** *adj.*

is (iz) Present indicative, third person singular of BE. [OE]

is- Var. of ISO-.

I·saac (ī′zək) A Hebrew patriarch, son of Abraham and Sarah. *Gen.* xxi 3. [< Hebrew *ṣaḥaq* to laugh]

i·sa·go·ge (ī′sə·gō′jē) *n.* An introduction, as to a field of study. [< L < Gk. *eisagōgē* < *eisagein* to introduce < *eis-* into + *agein* to lead] — **i′sa·gog′ic** (-goj′ik) *adj.*

I·sa·iah (ī·zā′ə, ī·zī′ə) Eighth-century B.C. Hebrew prophet. — *n.* A book of the Old Testament attributed to him. Also, in the Douai Bible, **I·sai′as** (-əs). [< Hebrew *yesha'yāhu* Salvation of God]

Is·car·i·ot (is·kar′ē·ət) See JUDAS ISCARIOT.

is·che·mi·a (is·kē′mē·ə) *n. Pathol.* A localized anemia, due to a contracted blood vessel. Also **is·chae′mi·a.** [< NL < Gk. *ischein* to hold + *haima* blood] — **is·che′mic** *adj.*

is·chi·at·ic (is′kē·at′ik) *adj.* Of or pertaining to the ischium. Also **is′chi·ad′ic** (-ad′ik), **is·chi·al** (is′kē·əl).

is·chi·um (is′kē·əm) *n. pl.* **·chi·a** (-kē·ə) *Anat.* The lowest of the three sections composing the hipbone. For illus. see PELVIS. [< L < Gk. *ischion* hip, hip joint]

-ise Var. of -IZE.

I·seult (i·sōōlt′) In medieval romance Iseult the Beautiful of Ireland, married to King Mark and beloved of Tristan. See TRISTAN. Also called *Isolde, Isolt, Yseult.*

-ish[1] *suffix of adjectives* **1.** Of or belonging to (a specified national group): *Danish.* **2.** Of the nature of; like: *boyish.* **3.** Having the bad qualities of: *selfish.* **4.** Tending toward; inclined to: *bookish.* **5.** Somewhat: *tallish.* **6.** *Informal* Approximately: *fortyish.* [OE *-isc,* adjectival suffix]

-ish[2] *suffix of verbs* Appearing chiefly in verbs of French origin: *brandish, establish.* [< OF *-iss-,* stem ending of *-ir* verbs]

Ish·ma·el (ish′mē·əl) In the Bible, the son of Abraham and Hagar, banished with his mother. *Gen.* xxi 9–21. — *n.* An outcast. [< Hebrew *Yishmā'ēl* God heareth]

Ish·ma·el·ite (ish′mē·əl·īt′) *n.* **1.** A descendant of Ishmael. **2.** A wanderer. — **Ish′ma·el·it′ish** (-ī′tish) *adj.*

i·sin·glass (ī′zing·glas′, -gläs′, ī′zən-) *n.* **1.** A preparation of nearly pure gelatin made from the swim bladders of certain fishes. **2.** Mica, chiefly in the form of thin sheets. [Prob. < MDu. *huysenblas* sturgeon bladder]

I·sis (ī′sis) In Egyptian mythology, the goddess of fertility.

Is·lam (is·läm′, is′ləm, iz′-) *n.* **1.** The religion of the Muslims, that maintains that there is but one God, Allah, and that Mohammed is his prophet: also called *Mohammedanism, Muslimism.* Also **Is·lam·ism** (is′ləm·iz′əm, iz′ləm-). **2.** Muslims collectively. **3.** The areas of the world where Islam is the main religion. [< Arabic *islām* submission]

Is·lam·ic (is·lam′ik, -läm′-, iz-) *adj.* Muslim. Also **Is′lam·it′ic** (-it′ik).

Is·lam·ite (is′ləm·īt, iz′-) *n.* A Muslim.

Is·lam·ize (is′ləm·īz, iz′-) *v.t. & v.i.* **·ized, ·i·zing** To convert or adapt to Islam.

is·land (ī′lənd) *n.* **1.** A tract of land entirely surrounded by water. The major continental land masses are not usually considered islands. **2.** Something resembling an island and set apart from its surroundings. **3.** *Anat.* Any of various isolated cells of the body differentiated from those of the surrounding tissues. — *v.t.* To cause to become or resemble an island; isolate. [OE < *īg, īeg* island + *land*]

is·land·er (ī′lən·dər) *n.* A native or inhabitant of an island.

isle (īl) *n.* An island, esp. one of comparatively small size: used in place names, as the British *Isles,* or poetically. — *v.* **isled, isl·ing** *v.t.* **1.** To island. — *v.i.* **2.** To live on an isle or island. [< OF < L *insula*]

is·let (ī′lit) *n.* A small island. [< OF *islette,* dim. of *isle*]

ism (iz′əm) *n.* A distinctive theory, doctrine, or system: usually used disparagingly. [< -ISM]

-ism *suffix of nouns* **1.** The act, process, or result of: *ostracism.* **2.** The condition of being: *skepticism.* **3.** The characteristic action or behavior of: *heroism.* **4.** The beliefs, teachings, or system of: *Calvinism.* **5.** Devotion to; adherence to the teachings of: *nationalism.* **6.** A characteristic or peculiarity of: said especially of a language or idiom: *Americanism.* **7.** *Med.* An abnormal condition resulting from an excess of: *alcoholism.* [< L *-ismus* < Gk. *-ismos*]

is·n't (iz′ənt) Is not.

iso- *combining form* **1.** Equal; the same; identical. **2.** *Chem.* Isomeric with, or an isomer of. Also, before vowels, *is-.* [< Gk. *isos* equal]

i·so·bar (ī′sə·bär) *n.* **1.** *Meteorol.* A line drawn on a weather map connecting all points having the same barometric pressure for a given time or period. **2.** *Physics* Any of two or more atoms having the same mass number but different atomic numbers. [< Gk. *isos* equal + *baros* weight] — **i·so·bar·ic** (ī′sə·bar′ik) *adj.*

i·so·cline (ī′sə·klīn) *n. Geol.* An anticline or syncline in which the strata are so closely folded that they have the same dip. [< ISO- + Gk. *klinein* to bend] — **i′so·cli′nal, i′so·clin′ic** (-klin′ik) *adj.*

i·so·gon·ic (ī′sə·gon′ik) *adj.* **1.** Having equal angles. **2.** Denoting a line on the earth's surface such that all points on it have equal magnetic declination. Also **i·sog·o·nal** (ī·sog′ə·nəl). — *n.* An isogonic line. [< Gk. *isogōnios* equiangular]

i·so·gram (ī′sə·gram) *n.* A line on a map, chart, diagram, etc., such that all points on it have equal value with respect to a given geographical feature, physical condition, etc.

i·so·late (ī′sə·lāt, is′ə-) *v.t.* **·lat·ed, ·lat·ing 1.** To set apart, as from a mass, group, or situation; cause to be alone. **2.** *Chem.* To obtain (an element or substance) in a free or uncombined state. [< Ital. *isolare* to isolate] — **i′so·la·ble** *adj.* — **i′so·la′tor** *n.*

i·so·la·tion (ī′sə·lā′shən, is′ə-) *n.* **1.** The act of isolating. **2.** The state of being isolated; aloneness; solitude.

i·so·la·tion·ism (ī′sə·lā′shən·iz′əm, is′ə-) *n.* A national policy advocating freedom from foreign political and economic alliances. — **i′so·la′tion·ist** *adj. & n.*

I·solde (i·sōld′, *Ger.* i·zôl′də) See ISEULT.

i·sol·o·gous (ī·sol′ə·gəs) *adj. Chem.* Having similar molecular structure but different atoms of the same valence.

i·so·mer (ī′sə·mər) *n.* **1.** *Chem.* One of two or more compounds identical in composition, but having different structural arrangements and different properties. **2.** *Physics* One of two or more nuclides having the same mass and atomic number but differing in energy characteristics. [< Gk. < *isos* equal + *meros* part] — **i·so·mer′ic** (-mer′ik) *adj.*

i·som·er·ism (ī·som′ə·riz′əm) *n. Chem.* The condition of being isomeric.

i·som·er·ous (ī·som′ər·əs) *adj.* **1.** Having an equal number of parts, organs, markings, etc. **2.** *Bot.* Equal in number, as the members of successive whorls of flowers.

i·so·met·ric (ī′sə·met′rik) *adj.* **1.** Pertaining to or characterized by equality in dimensions or measurements. **2.** Based upon contraction of muscles against resistance without shortening muscle fibers: *isometric* exercises. — **i′so·met′ri·cal·ly** *adv.*

i·so·mor·phic (ī′sə·môr′fik) *adj.* Having similar form or appearance but of different ancestry, genetic constitution, or chemical composition.

i·so·mor·phism (ī′sə·môr′fiz·əm) *n.* A similarity in form shown by substances of different composition, or by organisms belonging to different groups. — **i′so·morph** *n.*

i·so·oc·tane (ī′sō·ok′tān) *n. Chem.* Trimethylpentane.

i·so·prene (ī′sə·prēn) *n. Chem.* A volatile liquid hydrocarbon, C_5H_8, of the terpene group, obtained when crude rubber is subjected to pyrolysis. [Appar. an arbitrary coinage]

i·sos·ce·les (ī·sos′ə·lēz) *adj. Geom.* Of a triangle, having two sides of equal length. [< LL < Gk. *isos* equal + *skelos* leg]

B

A C

ISOSCELES TRIANGLE
$AB = CB$

i·sos·ta·sy (ī·sos′tə·sē) *n.* **1.** *Geol.* The equilibrium that the earth's crust tends to assume as a result of the action of terrestrial gravitation upon rock masses. **2.** Equilibrium resulting from equal pressure on all sides. [< ISO- + Gk. *stasis* standing] — **i·so·stat·ic** (ī′sə·stat′ik) *adj.*

i·so·therm (ī′sə·thûrm) *n. Meteorol.* A line drawn on a weather map connecting all points having the same mean temperature. [< ISO- + Gk. *thermē* heat] — **i′so·ther′mal** *adj. & n.*

i·so·ton·ic (ī′sə·ton′ik) *adj. Physiol.* Having the same osmotic pressure on opposite sides of a membrane: said of solutions, esp. blood or plasma. [< Gk. < *isos* equal + *tonos* accent]

i·so·tope (ī′sə·tōp) *n. Physics* Any of two or more forms of an element having the same atomic number and similar chemical properties but differing in mass number and radioactive behavior. [< ISO- + Gk. *topos* place] — **i·so·top·ic** (ī′sə·top′ik) *adj.* — **i·sot·o·py** (ī·sot′ə·pē) *n.*

i·so·trop·ic (ī′sə·trop′ik, -trō′pik) *adj. Physics* Exhibiting the same physical properties in every direction. Also **i·sot·ro·pous** (ī·sot′rə·pəs).

Is·ra·el (iz′rē·əl) The patriarch Jacob. *Gen.* xxxii 28. — *n.* The Jewish people, regarded as descended from Jacob. [< Hebrew *Yisrā'ēl* God persevereth]

Is·rae·li (iz·rā′lē) *adj.* Of modern Israel, its people, or their culture. — *n. pl.* **·lis** A native or inhabitant of Israel.

Is·ra·el·ite (iz′rē·əl·īt′) *n.* Any of the people of Israel or their descendants; a Hebrew; a Jew. — *adj.* Of or pertaining to the Hebrews; Jewish: also **Is′ra·el·it′ish** (-ī′tish), **Is′·ra·el·it′ic** (-it′ik).

Is·sei (ēs·sā) *n. pl.* **·sei** or **·seis** A Japanese who emigrated to the U.S. after 1907, and was not legally eligible to bec an American citizen. [< Japanese *is* first + *sei* generati

is·su·ance (ish′ōō·əns, -yōō-) *n.* The act or procedur issuing; promulgation. — **is′su·ant** *adj.*

is·sue (ish′ōō, -yōō) *n.* **1.** The act of giving out or publ ing, esp. from an official source. **2.** An item or set of ite as stamps, magazines, etc., published at a single time. result; consequence; outcome. **4.** A matter of importa to be resolved. **5.** An outflow; discharge. **6.** A poin egress; outlet; exit. **7.** Offspring; progeny. **8.** Profits; ceeds, as from property. **9.** *Med.* A discharge, as of b or pus. — **at issue** In question; in controversy. — **to issue** To enter into a controversy. — **to take issue** To agree. — *v.* **·sued, ·su·ing** *v.i.* **1.** To come forth; flow emerge. **2.** To be derived or descended; originate. **3.** come as a consequence; result. **4.** To terminate: often lowed by *in*. **5.** To be circulated or published; appear. To be produced as profit. — *v.t.* **7.** To publish; annou **8.** To give out; distribute, as supplies. [< OF < L < out of + *ire* to go] — **is′su·a·ble** *adj.* — **is′su·er** *n.*

-ist *suffix of nouns* **1.** One who or that which does or ha do with: *catechist*. **2.** One whose profession is: *pharma* **3.** A student or devotee of: *genealogist*. **4.** One who ad cates or adheres to: *socialist*. [< F < L < Gk. *-istēs*]

isth·mus (is′məs, isth′-) *n. pl.* **·mus·es** or **·mi** (-mī) narrow piece of land extending into a body of water and c necting two larger land masses. [< L < Gk. *isthmos* nar passage] — **isth′mi·an** *adj. & n.*

-istic *suffix of adjectives* Having the qualities of: forr from nouns ending in *-ist* or *-ism*: *communistic*.

is·tle (is′lē, ist′lē) *n.* A fiber derived from an agave pl used for carpets, etc.

it (it) *pron., possessive* **its**; *pl. nominative* **they,** *possessive* **th** or **theirs,** *objective* **them** The nominative and objective sin lar neuter pronoun of the third person, used: **1.** As a sub tute for a specific noun or name when referring to things places or to infants or animals of unspecified sex. **2.** represent some implied idea, condition, action, or situati How was *it*? **3.** As the subject or predicate nominative verb whose logical subject is anticipated: Who is *it*? **4.** the subject of an impersonal verb: *It* rained yesterday. **5.** the indefinite subject of a verb introducing a clause o phrase: *It* seems that he knew. **6.** As the indefinite object a certain verbs in idiomatic expressions: to brazen *it* out. — In certain children's games, the player required to perfo some specified act. [OE *hit*]

I.T.A. Initial Teaching Alphabet.

I·tal·ian (i·tal′yən) *adj.* Of Italy, its people, or their l guage. — *n.* **1.** A native or naturalized inhabitant of Ita **2.** The Romance language of Italy.

i·tal·ic (i·tal′ik) *n. Usu. pl.* A style of type in which letters slant, often used to denote emphasis: *These words printed in italics*. — *adj.* Designating or printed in ital

I·tal·ic (i·tal′ik) *adj.* Relating to any of the peoples of cient Italy. — *n.* A subfamily of the Indo-European l guages, comprising three branches, and including Latin a the Romance languages.

i·tal·i·cize (i·tal′ə·sīz) *v.* **·cized, ·ciz·ing** *v.t.* **1.** To print italics. **2.** To underscore to indicate italics. — *v.i.* **3.** use or indicate the use of italics. — **i·tal′i·ci·za′tion** *n.*

itch (ich) *v.i.* **1.** To experience or produce an irritation t causes a desire to scratch or rub the affected area. **2.** have a restless or unsatisfied desire to do something; hank — *n.* **1.** An itching sensation or irritation. **2.** Any of va ous usu. contagious skin diseases accompanied by itchi **3.** A restless desire or yearning. [ME < OE *giccan*]

itch·y (ich′ē) *adj.* **itch·i·er, itch·i·est** Having or produc an itching sensation. — **itch′i·ness** *n.*

-ite[1] *suffix of nouns* **1.** A native or inhabitant of: *suburb ite*. **2.** A follower of or sympathizer with: *Pre-Raphael* **3.** A descendant of: *Israelite*. **4.** Resembling or related *dynamite*. **5.** *Mineral.* A rock or mineral: *graphite*. **6.** *Pa ontol.* A fossil: *trilobite*. **7.** *Zool.* A part of the body or of organ: *dendrite*. [< F < L < Gk. *-itēs*]

-ite[2] *suffix Chem.* A salt or ester of an acid having a na that ends in *-ous*: *sulfite*. [< F *-ite*]

-ite[3] *suffix* Derived from the past participial form of cert Latin verbs and occurring in: **1.** Adjectives: *infinite, poli* **2.** Verbs: *unite*. **3.** Nouns: *appetite*. [< L *-itus*]

i·tem (ī′təm) *n.* **1.** A single unit or article included in category, series, or enumeration. **2.** An entry in an accou **3.** A brief article of news, etc., as in a newspaper. — *v.t.* record or take note of as an item. — *adv.* Likewise; als used to introduce an entry in a list or series. [< L, thus]

i·tem·ize (ī′təm·īz) *v.t.* **·ized, ·iz·ing** To set down or speci by items. — **i′tem·i·za′tion** *n.* — **i′tem·iz′er** *n.*

it·er·ate (it′ə·rāt) *v.t.* **·at·ed, ·at·ing** To state or utter aga or repeatedly. [< L *iterum* again] — **it′er·a′tion** *n.* — **i er·a·tive** *adj.*

i·tin·er·an·cy (ī·tin′ər·ən·sē, i·tin′-) *n.* The act or state being itinerant. Also **i·tin′er·a·cy** (-ə·sē).

·er·ant (ī·tin′ər·ənt, i·tin′-) *adj.* **1.** Going from place to ce; wandering. **2.** Traveling to a series of places in order fulfill official duties. — *n.* One who travels from place to ce. [< LL *itineris* journey, route] — **i·tin′er·ant·ly** *adv.*
·er·ar·y (ī·tin′ə·rer′ē, i·tin′-) *n. pl.* **·ar·ies** **1.** A route owed in traveling. **2.** A plan for or graphic representa- n of a journey. **3.** A detailed account or record of a jour- y. **4.** A guidebook for travelers. — *adj.* Pertaining to vel or routes of travel. [< LL *iter, itineris* journey, route]
on *suffix of nouns* **1.** Condition or quality: *ambition.* **2.** t or process, or the result of an act or process: *audition.* L *-itio, -onis*]
ous *suffix of adjectives* Characterized by; having the ality of: *ambitious.* [< L *-icius, -itius*]
suffix Pathol. Inflammation of: *peritonitis.* [< Gk.]
(it′l) **1.** It will. **2.** It shall.
suffix Chem. Denoting a class of alcohols containing o or more hydroxyl radicals.
(its) *pronominal adjective* The possessive case of the pro- un *it*, used attributively: *its* leaves. [< IT + 's, posses- e case ending; written *it's* until the 19th century]
(its) **1.** It is. **2.** It has.
elf (it·self′) *pron.* A form of the third person singular ter pronoun, used: **a** As a reflexive or as object of a prep- tion in a reflexive sense: The motor started by *itself.* **b** As intensifier or to give emphasis: simplicity *itself.* **c** As a signation for a normal or usual state: The house isn't *itself* h the children gone.
suffix of nouns State or quality [< F < L *-itas*]
m *suffix Chem.* Denoting certain elements or com- unds: *titanium.* [< L]
e (īv) I have.
suffix of adjectives **1.** Having a tendency or predisposi- tion to: *disruptive.* **2.** Having the nature, character, or qual- ity of: *massive.* Also *-ative.* [< F < L *-ivus*]
i·vied (ī′vēd) *adj.* Covered or overgrown with ivy.
i·vo·ry (ī′vər·ē) *n. pl.* **·ries** **1.** A hard, white, smooth- textured dentine, the chief substance of the tusks of ele- phants, walruses, etc. **2.** Any substance resembling ivory. **3.** The creamy white color of ivory. **4.** *Usu. pl.* Articles made of ivory. **5.** Any form of dentine. **6.** A tusk, esp. of an elephant. **7.** *pl. Slang* **a** The teeth. **b** The keys of a piano. **c** Dice. — *adj.* **1.** Made of or resembling ivory. **2.** Of the color ivory. [< OF < L *ebur, -oris* ivory]
ivory tower A condition or attitude of withdrawal from the world and reality.
i·vy (ī′vē) *n. pl.* **i·vies** A climbing plant, having glossy, evergreen leaves: also **English ivy.** [OE *īfig*]
Ivy League An association of colleges in the NE U.S. (Brown, Columbia, Cornell, Dartmouth, Harvard, Prince- ton, the University of Pennsylvania, and Yale).
Iy·yar (ē·yär′, ē′yär) *n.* The eighth month of the Hebrew year. Also **I·yar′.** See (Hebrew) CALENDAR.
-ization *suffix* Used to form nouns from verbs in *-ize*, and denoting a condition, act, process, or result: *civilization.*
-ize *suffix of verbs* **1.** To cause to become or resemble: *Christianize.* **2.** To subject to the action of: *oxidize.* **3.** To change into: *mineralize.* **4.** To act in the manner of: *sym- pathize.* Also *-ise.* [< F < LL < Gk. *-izein*]
◆ The spelling of this suffix varies in British and American usage; *-ize* is the preferred spelling in the United States, while *-ise* is preferred in England. However, certain words, as *advise*, are always spelled with *-ise*, whereas others, as *baptize*, are always spelled with *-ize.*
iz·zard (iz′ərd) *n. Archaic* The letter Z. — **from A to iz- zard** From beginning to end. [< earlier *ezed*, var. of ZED]

J

J (jā) *n. pl.* **j's** or **js, J's** or **Js, jays** (jāz) **1.** The tenth tter of the English alphabet. **2.** The sound represented by e letter *j.*
(jab) *v.t. & v.i.* **jabbed, jab·bing** **1.** To poke or thrust arply. **2.** To punch or strike with short blows. — *n.* **1.** sharp thrust. **2.** A rapid punch.
·ber (jab′ər) *v.t. & v.i.* To speak rapidly or without mak- g sense. — *n.* Rapid or unintelligible talk; chatter. — **b′ber·er** *n.*
bot (zhā·bō′, *Fr.* zhȧ·bō′) *n. pl.* **·bots** (-bōz′, *Fr.* -bō′) A uffle or similar decoration falling from the neckline or at the ont of a blouse, shirt, or bodice. [< F, lit., gizzard]
cinth (jā′sinth, jas′inth) *n.* Hyacinth. [< OF < L *hya- inthus*]
ck (jak) *n.* **1.** *Sometimes cap.* A man or boy; fellow; esp.: A manual laborer: usu. in combination: *jack-of-all-trades*; *umberjack.* **b** A sailor. **2.** Any of various devices that per- orm an operation formerly done by a man or boy: often used n combinations: *bootjack.* **3.** Any of various devices used or raising heavy weights through short distances, usu. by neans of a lever. **4.** In names or designations of animals: **a** male: sometimes used in combination: *jackass.* **b** Any of arious kinds of animals, birds, or fish: often in combination: *ackdaw; jack* rabbit. **5.** A playing card showing the picture f a young man; the knave. **6.** A flag, flown at the bow of a hip as a signal or as an indication of nationality when in ort. **7.** *U.S. Slang* Money. **8.** A jackstone. **9.** *Electr.* A netallic connecting device with spring clips to which the vires of a circuit may be attached. — *v.t.* **1.** To raise or lift vith or as with a jack: usu. with *up.* **2.** *Informal* To in- crease, as a price or charge: with *up.* [after *Jack*, a nick- name for John]
ck·al (jak′əl, -ôl) *n.* **1.** Any of various African or Asian doglike carnivorous mammals. **2.** One who does menial work to serve another. [< Turkish < Persian *shaghal*]
ck·a·napes (jak′ə·nāps) *n.* An impertinent fellow; an upstart. [< *Jack Napes*, nickname of William de la Pole, 15th c. Duke of Suffolk]
ck·ass (jak′as′) *n.* **1.** A male ass. **2.** A stupid person.
ck·boot (jak′bo͞ot′) *n.* A heavy topboot reaching above the knee.
jack·daw (jak′dô′) *n.* A glossy, black, crowlike bird of Europe, sometimes tamed as a pet.
jack·et (jak′it) *n.* **1.** A short coat, usu. not extending be- low the hips. **2.** An outer covering or case, as the removable paper cover for a bound book, the skin of a cooked potato, etc. — *v.t.* To cover or surround with or as with a jacket. [< OF *jaque* short jacket]
Jack Frost A personification of frost or winter weather.
jack-in-the-box (jak′in·thə·boks′) *n.* A toy consisting of a box containing a grotesque figure that springs up when the lid is unfastened: also **jack′-in-a-box′.**
jack-in-the-pul·pit (jak′in·thə·po͝ol′pit) *n.* A common American herb of the arum family, growing from a turnip-shaped bulb.
jack·knife (jak′nīf′) *n. pl.* **·knives** (-nīvz′) **1.** A large pocketknife. **2.** A dive in which the body is doubled forward with the knees unbent and the hands touching the ankles, and then straightened before entering the water. — *v.t. & v.i.* **·knifed, ·knif·ing** To double up in the manner of a jackknife.
jack-of-all-trades (jak′əv·ôl′trādz′) *n.* One who is able to do many kinds of work.
jack-o'-lan·tern (jak′ə·lan′tərn) *n.* **1.** A lan- tern made of a pumpkin hollowed and carved into a grotesque face. **2.** A will-o'-the-wisp.

JACK-IN-THE-PULPIT
a Flower. *b* Fruit.

jack·pot (jak′pot′) *n.* **1.** In poker, a pot that accumulates until a player is dealt a pair of jacks or better with which he may open the betting. **2.** Any pot, pool, or prize in which the amount won is cumulative. — **to hit the jackpot** *U.S. Informal* **1.** To win the biggest possible prize. **2.** To achieve a major success.
jack rabbit A large American hare with long hind legs and long ears.
jacks (jaks) *n.pl.* (*construed as sing.*) The game of jack- stones.
jack·stone (jak′stōn′) *n.* **1.** A stone or knobbed metal piece used in a children's game in which the pieces are tossed and picked up in a variety of ways: also called *jack.* **2.** *pl.* (*con- strued as sing.*) The game itself. [Var. of earlier *checkstone*]
jack·straw (jak′strô′) *n.* **1.** One of a set of thin strips of

wood, bone, etc., used in a game in which the players attempt to pick up each strip without moving any of the others. **2.** *pl.* (*construed as sing.*) The game itself.

Ja·cob (jā′kəb) The second son of Isaac and father of the founders of the twelve Hebrew tribes. Also *Israel.* [< Hebrew *Ya'aqob* he grasps the heel. Cf. *Gen.* xxv 26.]

Jac·o·be·an (jak′ə·bē′ən) *adj.* Of or pertaining to James I of England or the period in which he reigned. — *n.* A notable person of the Jacobean era. [< LL < *Jacobus* James]

Jac·o·bin (jak′ə·bin) *n.* During the French Revolution, a member of a French political society that inaugurated the Reign of Terror. [< OF *Jacobin* of St. James; with ref. to the church of St. James, in Paris, where the society first met]

Jac·o·bite (jak′ə·bīt) *n.* An adherent of James II of England after his abdication in 1688. — *adj.* Of the Jacobites: also **Jac·o·bit·ic** (jak′ə·bit′ik) or **·i·cal.** [< L *Jacobus* James]

Jacob's ladder **1.** A ladder from earth to heaven that Jacob saw in a dream. *Gen.* xxviii 12. **2.** *Naut.* A rope ladder, often with wooden rungs.

jade[1] (jād) *n.* **1.** A hard, translucent mineral, usu. green, used as a gemstone. **2.** A green color characteristic of jade. [< F < Sp. (*piedra de*) *ijada* (stone of) the side; because supposed to cure pain in the side]

jade[2] (jād) *n.* **1.** An old, worthless, or unmanageable horse. **2.** A disreputable, ill-tempered, or perverse woman; hussy. — *v.t.* & *v.i.* **jad·ed, jad·ing** To weary or become weary through hard work or overuse; tire. [Origin uncertain]

jad·ed (jā′did) *adj.* **1.** Worn-out; exhausted. **2.** Dulled, as from overindulgence. — **jad′ed·ly** *adv.* — **jad′ed·ness** *n.*

jae·ger (yā′gər, jā′-) *n.* Any of a group of sea birds that pursue and harass gulls and terns until they drop or disgorge their prey. Also **jä′ger.** [< G, hunter]

jag[1] (jag) *n.* A sharp, projecting point; notch; tooth. — *v.t.* **1.** To cut notches or jags in. **2.** To cut unevenly or with slashing strokes. Also **jagg.** [ME *jagge*]

jag[2] (jag) *n.* *Slang* **1.** A period of unrestrained activity: a crying *jag.* **2.** A drunken spree.

jag·ged (jag′id) *adj.* Having jags or notches; serrate. — **Syn.** See ROUGH. — **jag′ged·ly** *adv.* — **jag′ged·ness** *n.*

jag·uar (jag′wär, jag′yōō·är) *n.* A large, spotted feline of Central and South America. [< Pg. < Tupi *jaguara*]

jai a·lai (hī ə·lī′) A game popular in Latin America, similar to handball but played with a long, curved, wicker basket strapped to the arm. [< Sp. < Basque, jolly festival]

jail (jāl) *n.* **1.** A place of confinement for those guilty of minor offenses or those awaiting trial. **2.** Loosely, any prison. — *v.t.* To put or hold in jail; imprison. Also, *Brit.*, *gaol.* [< OF *jaiole*, ult. < L *cavea* cave]

jail·bird (jāl′bûrd′) *n.* *Informal* A prisoner or ex-prisoner.

jail·er (jā′lər) *n.* The officer in charge of a jail: also, *Brit.*, *gaoler.* Also **jail′or.**

Jain·ism (jī′niz·əm) *n.* A religion of India, founded about 500 B.C., having elements of Brahmanism and Buddhism.

jal·ap (jal′əp) *n.* **1.** The dried root of any of several Mexican plants used as a purgative. **2.** Any allied plant yielding a similar drug. [< Sp. (*purga de*) *Jalapa* (medicine from) Jalapa] — **ja·lap·ic** (jə·lap′ik) *adj.*

ja·lop·y (jə·lop′ē) *n.* *pl.* **·lop·ies** *U.S. Informal* A decrepit automobile. Also **ja·lop′py.** [Origin uncertain]

ja·lou·sie (jal′ōō·sē, zhal′ōō·zē′) *n.* A window blind or shutter of overlapping horizontal slats or strips that may be tilted to keep out sun and rain while admitting air and some light. [< F, lit., jealousy]

jam[1] (jam) *v.* **jammed, jam·ming** *v.t.* **1.** To force or ram into or against something. **2.** To pack and block up by crowding. **3.** To cause (a machine, door, etc.) to become wedged or stuck. **4.** To interfere electronically with (a radio broadcast, etc.). **5.** To bruise or crush. — *v.i.* **6.** To become wedged; stick fast. **7.** To cease operation, as a machine, gun, etc., because parts have stuck or wedged together. **8.** To take part in a jam session. — *n.* **1.** A crowding together, as of people, cars, etc. **2.** The act of jamming. **3.** *Informal* An embarrassing or dangerous predicament. [Akin to CHAMP[1]]

jam[2] (jam) *n.* A pulpy, sweet conserve of whole fruit boiled with sugar. [? < JAM[1], v.]

Ja·mai·can (jə·mā′kən) *adj.* Of or pertaining to Jamaica and its people. — *n.* A native or inhabitant of Jamaica.

jamb (jam) *n.* A side post or side of a doorway, window, etc. [< OF < LL *gamba* hoof, leg]

jam·bo·ree (jam′bə·rē′) *n.* **1.** *Informal* A boisterous frolic. **2.** A large, esp. international, assembly of Boy Scouts.

James (jāmz) One of the brothers of Jesus: called **Saint James.** — *n.* A book of the New Testament consisting of the epistle attributed to him.

jam session An informal gathering of jazz musicians performing improvisations on various themes.

jan·gle (jang′gəl) *v.* **·gled, ·gling** *v.i.* **1.** To make harsh, unmusical sounds. **2.** To wrangle; bicker. — *v.t.* **3.** To cause to sound discordantly. — *n.* **1.** A discordant sound. **2.** A quarrel; wrangling. [< OF *jangler*] — **jan′gler** *n.*

jan·i·tor (jan′i·tər) *n.* **1.** One who is employed to care f building, etc. **2.** A doorkeeper; porter. [< L *janua* d — **jan′i·to′ri·al** (-tôr′ē·əl) *adj.* — **jan′i·tress** *n.fem.*

jan·i·zar·y (jan′ə·zer′ē) *n.* *pl.* **·zar·ies** *Often cap.* **1.** A dier in the Turkish sultan's army before 1826. **2.** Turkish soldier. Also **jan′i·sar·y, jan′is·sar·y** (-ser′ē). F < Turkish *yenicheri* new army]

Jan·u·ar·y (jan′yōō·er′ē) *n.* *pl.* **·ar·ies** or **·ar·ys** The month of the year, containing 31 days. [< L *Januariu* *Janus* Janus]

Ja·nus (jā′nəs) In Roman mythology, the god of po and of beginnings and endings, usu. depicted as having faces looking in opposite directions.

Ja·nus-faced (jā′nəs·fāst′) *adj.* Two-faced; deceitful.

Jap (jap) *adj.* & *n.* *Slang* Japanese: an offensive tern

ja·pan (jə·pan′) *n.* **1.** Any of various glossy black lacq or varnishes, used for coating objects. **2.** A glossy, b vitreous enamel baked onto machine parts, etc. **3.** O mental objects decorated or lacquered in the Japanese n ner. — *adj.* Pertaining to, enameled with, or lacqu with japan. — *v.t.* **·panned, ·pan·ning** To enamel or lacc with or as with japan. [< JAPAN]

Jap·a·nese (jap′ə·nēz′, -nēs′) *adj.* Of or pertaining to pan, its people, or their language. — *n.* *pl.* **·nese** **1.** A tive of Japan, or a person of Japanese ancestry. **2.** The guage of Japan.

Japanese beetle A destructive beetle introduced to U.S. from Japan. The adults eat the leaves and fruits of v ous plants, and the larvae feed on grass roots.

jape (jāp) *Archaic* *v.* **japed, jap·ing** *v.i.* **1.** To joke; m jests. — *v.t.* **2.** To mock; jibe at. — *n.* A jest; jibe. [*jappen*] — **jap′er** *n.* — **jap′er·y** *n.*

Ja·pheth (jā′fith) Third and youngest son of Noah. *Ge* 32. Also **Ja′phet** (-fit). [< Hebrew *Yepheth*, lit., extens

ja·pon·i·ca (jə·pon′i·kə) *n.* **1.** An Asian shrub with flowers. **2.** The camellia. [< NL, Japanese]

jar[1] (jär) *n.* **1.** A wide-mouthed vessel of glass or eart ware, usu. deep and cylindrical. **2.** The quantity a jar c tains: also **jar′ful′** (-fōōl′). [< F < Arabic *jarrah*]

jar[2] (jär) *v.* **jarred, jar·ring** *v.t.* **1.** To strike against or bu so as to cause shaking, movement, etc.; jolt. **2.** To af (one's nerves, feelings, etc.) unpleasantly or painfully. — **3.** To have an unpleasant or painful effect: with *on* or *up* **4.** To disagree or conflict; clash. **5.** To bump or jolt: w *against.* **6.** To make or have a disagreeable sound. — **1.** A shaking, shock, or jolt. **2.** A disagreeable sound jumble of sounds; discord. **3.** A painful or irritating sh to the feelings. [Imit.]

jar·di·nière (jär′də·nir′, *Fr.* zhàr·dē·nyâr′) *n.* An ornam tal pot or stand for flowers or plants. [< F, fem. of *jardin* gardener]

jar·gon (jär′gən) *n.* **1.** Confused, unintelligible spee gibberish. **2.** A language, dialect, or form of speech regar as meaningless or confusing. **3.** The technical or speciali vocabulary or phraseology used among themselves by members of a particular profession, sect, or similarly stricted group: legal *jargon.* **4.** A mixture of two or m dissimilar languages, often serving as a lingua franca; pidg — *v.i.* To speak in jargon. [< OF, a chattering]

jar·gon·ize (jär′gən·īz) *v.* **·ized, ·iz·ing** *v.t.* **1.** To transl into jargon. — *v.i.* **2.** To express oneself in jargon.

jas·mine (jas′min, jaz′-) *n.* **1.** An ornamental plant of olive family, with fragrant, generally white flowers. **2.** A of various other similar plants. Also called *jessamine.* [< < Persian *yāsmin*]

Ja·son (jā′sən) In Greek legend, a prince who led the Ar nauts in search of the Golden Fleece, and who marr Medea. [< Gk., healer]

jas·per (jas′pər) *n.* **1.** An opaque, usu. red, brown, or y low variety of quartz, admitting of a high polish: also **ja per·ite.** **2.** In the Bible, one of the twelve stones in t breastplate of the high priest. *Ex.* xxviii 20. [< MF *jaspis* < Gk. < Semitic] — **jas·pid′e·an** (-pid′ē·ən), **ja pid′e·ous** (-pid′ē·əs) *adj.*

jaun·dice (jôn′dis, jän′-) *n.* **1.** *Pathol.* A diseased conditi of the liver due to the presence of bile pigments in the blo and characterized by yellowness of the skin and eyeballs. A state of mind, feeling, perception, etc., that distorts t judgment. — *v.t.* **·diced, ·dic·ing** **1.** To affect with jau dice. **2.** To alter or influence (the mind, feelings, etc.) so to affect the judgment. [< OF *jaune* < L *galbus* yellow

jaunt (jônt, jänt) *n.* A short journey, esp. for pleasure. *v.i.* To make such a journey. [Origin unknown]

jaunt·y (jôn′tē, jän′-) *adj.* **jaunt·i·er, jaunt·i·est** **1.** Havi a lively and self-confident air or manner; cheerfully brisk. Trim; dashing; a *jaunty* hat. [< F *gentil* genteel] — **jaun i·ly** *adv.* — **jaunt′i·ness** *n.*

ja·va (jav′ə, jä′və) *n.* *Sometimes cap.* *U.S. Slang* Coffe

Ja·va (jav′ə, jä′və) *n.* A type of coffee. [after *Java*]

Java man Pithecanthropus.

Jav·a·nese (jav′ə·nēz′, -nēs′) *adj.* Of or pertaining to Jav language, or its people. — *n.* *pl.* **·nese** **1.** A native or ·turalized inhabitant of Java. **2.** The Indonesian language ·central Java, closely related to Malay.

·e·lin (jav′lin, jav′ə·lin) *n.* **1.** A light spear thrown as a ·apon. **2.** A long spear with a wooden shaft, thrown for ·tance in an athletic contest. [< F, prob. < Celtic]

· (jô) *n.* **1.** *Anat.* **a** Either of the two bony structures ·ming the framework of the mouth and holding the teeth, ·nsisting of the **upper jaw** or maxilla, and the **lower jaw** or ·ndible. **b** *pl.* The mouth and its associated parts. **2.** One ·a pair of gripping parts capable of opening and closing, ·of a tool. **3.** Anything suggesting the action of the jaws: ·*jaws* of death. **4.** *pl.* The narrow entrance of a gorge, ·nyon, etc. **5.** *Informal* A talk; chat. **6.** *Informal* Impu·nt talk. — *v.i.* **1.** *Informal* To talk; jabber. — *v.t.* **2.** ·*formal* To scold or abuse. [ME < F *joue* cheek]

·bone (jô′bōn′) *n.* One of the bones of the jaw, esp. that ·the lower jaw.

·break·er (jô′brā′kər) *n.* **1.** *U.S. Informal* A type of ·ry hard candy. **2.** A machine that crushes ore: also **jaw′·** ·**ush′er** (-krush′ər). **3.** *Informal* A word hard to pronounce.

· (jā) *n.* Any of various corvine birds, usu. of brilliant ·loring, as the blue jay. [< OF < Med.L *gaius*]

·hawk·er (jā′hô′kər) *n.* **1.** A guerrilla raider of the ·vil War period in Kansas; also, any freebooting guerrilla. ·*Usu. cap.* A Kansan. [Origin uncertain]

·walk (jā′wôk′) *v.i.* *Informal* To cross a street reckless·, violating traffic regulations or signals. — **jay′walk′er** *n.*

·z (jaz) *n.* **1.** A kind of music, chiefly extemporaneous ·t sometimes arranged, characterized by melodic, har·onic, and rhythmic variation, syncopation, flatted thirds ·d sevenths, and a melody played against various chord ·tterns. **2.** Loosely, any contemporary popular dance ·usic. **3.** *U.S. Slang* Lying and exaggerated talk; also, idle ·d foolish talk. **4.** *U.S. Slang* Liveliness and animation. ·*adj.* Of or pertaining to jazz. — *v.t.* **1.** *U.S. Slang* To ·icken the tempo of; speed up. **2.** To play or arrange ·usic) as jazz. — **to jazz up** *U.S. Slang* To make more ·citing. [< Creole *jass* coition; from its origin in the ·othels of New Orleans] — **jazz′y** *adj.* — **jazz′i·ly** *adv.*

·l·ous (jel′əs) *adj.* **1.** Fearful or suspicious of being dis·aced by a rival in affection or favors. **2.** Vindictive toward ·other because of supposed or actual rivalry. **3.** Vigilant ·guarding: to be *jealous* of a privilege. **4.** Resulting or ·ising from jealousy: *jealous* fears. **5.** Demanding exclu·ve worship and love: a *jealous* God. [< OF < Med.L < ·L < Gk. *zēlos* zeal] — **jeal′ous·ly** *adv.* — **jeal′ous·ness** *n.*

·l·ous·y (jel′əs·ē) *n.* *pl.* **·ous·sies** **1.** The state or quality ·being jealous. **2.** The fact of being jealous.

·n (jēn, jān) *n.* **1.** A sturdy, twilled cotton cloth used in ·orkclothes. **2.** *pl.* Trousers or overalls made of this ma·rial. [after F *Gênes* Genoa, where it was made]

· (jē) See GEE.

·p (jēp) *n.* A small, military and civilian motorcar ·uipped with four-wheel drive. [< G(ENERAL) P(URPOSE) ·VEHICLE)]

·r (jir) *v.i.* **1.** To speak or shout in a derisive, mocking ·anner; scoff. — *v.t.* **2.** To treat with derision or mockery; ·off at. — *n.* A derisive and flouting word or remark. [Ori·n unknown] — **jeer′er** *n.* — **jeer′ing·ly** *adv.*

·f·fer·so·ni·an (jef′ər·sō′nē·ən) *adj.* Of, pertaining to, or ·haracteristic of Thomas Jefferson or his political ideas and ·eliefs. — *n.* An adherent of Jefferson or his school of ·hought. — **Jef′fer·so′ni·an·ism** *n.*

·hosh·a·phat (ji·hosh′ə·fat, -hos′-) Ninth-century B.C. ·ing of Judah. I *Kings* xxii 41.

·ho·vah (ji·hō′və) In the Old Testament, God; the Lord. ·ee YAHWEH. [< Hebrew *JHVH* Yahweh, either Creator or ·ternal] **Je·ho′vi·an, Je·ho′vic** *adj.*

·hovah's Witnesses A Christian sect opposed to war and ·he authority of the government in matters of conscience.

·june (jə·jōōn′) *adj.* **1.** Lacking in substance or nourish·ment; barren. **2.** Lacking interest; insipid; dry. [< L ·*jejunus* hungry] — **je·june′ly** *adv.* — **je·june′ness** *n.*

·ju·num (jə·jōō′nəm) *n.* *pl.* **·na** (-nə) *Anat.* That por·ion of the small intestine that extends from the duodenum ·o the ileum. [< NL < L *jejunus* hungry]

·ll (jel) *v.t.* & *v.i.* *U.S. Informal* **1.** To jelly; congeal. **2.** To ·ssume or cause to assume definite form. [< JELLY]

·l·lied (jel′ēd) *adj.* **1.** Made gelatinous, as by chilling: *jel·ied* consommé. **2.** Covered with or prepared in jelly.

·l·li·fy (jel′ə·fī) *v.t.* & *v.i.* **·fied, ·fy·ing** To make into or be·ome a jelly. — **jel′li·fi·ca′tion** *n.*

·l·lo (jel′ō) *n.* A fruit-flavored gelatin dessert. [< *Jell-O*, ·trade name]

·l·ly (jel′ē) *n.* *pl.* **·lies** **1.** Any food preparation made with ·elatin or pectin, and having a consistency such that it quiv·rs when shaken; esp., such a food made of boiled and sweet·ened fruit juice and used as a spread or filler. **2.** Any gelatinous substance. — *v.* **·lied, ·ly·ing** *v.t.* **1.** To make into a jelly. **2.** To cover or fill with jelly. — *v.i.* **3.** To become jelly. [< OF < L *gelata*, pp. of *gelare* to freeze]

jel·ly·bean (jel′ē·bēn′) *n.* *U.S.* A bean-shaped candy having a hard, colored coating over a gelatinous center.

jel·ly·fish (jel′ē·fish′) *n.* *pl.* **·fish** or **·fish·es** **1.** Any of a number of marine animals of jellylike substance, often having umbrella-shaped bodies with trailing tentacles. **2.** *Informal* One lacking determination or stamina; weakling.

je ne sais quoi (zhən se kwå′) *French* An indefinable something; literally, I know not what.

jen·net (jen′it) *n.* A breed of small Spanish horses. Also spelled *genet*. [< OF < Sp. *jinete* a light horseman.]

jen·ny (jen′ē) *n.* *pl.* **·nies** **1.** A spinning jenny. **2.** The female of some birds and animals: *jenny* wren; *jenny* ass. [after *Jenny*, a personal name]

jeop·ard·ize (jep′ər·dīz) *v.t.* **·ized, ·iz·ing** To put in jeopardy; expose to loss or injury; imperil. Also **jeop′ard.**

jeop·ar·dy (jep′ər·dē) *n.* **1.** Danger of death, loss, or injury; peril. **2.** *Law* The peril in which a defendant is put when placed on trial for a crime. [< OF < L *jocus partitus* divided play]

jer·bo·a (jər·bō′ə) *n.* Any of various nocturnal rodents of Asia and North Africa, with very long hind legs adapted for leaping. [< NL < Arabic *yarbu'*]

jer·e·mi·ad (jer′ə·mī′əd) *n.* A lament or tale of woe; complaint. [< F *Jérémie* Jeremiah]

Jer·e·mi·ah (jer′ə·mī′ə) Seventh-century B.C. Hebrew prophet. — *n.* The Old Testament book containing his prophecies. Also, in the Douai Bible, **Jer′e·mi′as** (-əs). [< Hebrew *Yirmĕyāhū*, lit., God looseneth (from the womb)]

jerk[1] (jûrk) *v.t.* **1.** To give a sharp, sudden pull or twist to. **2.** To throw, move, or thrust with a sharp, suddenly arrested motion. **3.** To utter in a gasping or broken manner: with *out*. — *v.i.* **4.** To give a jerk or jerks. **5.** To move with sharp, sudden motions; twitch. — *n.* **1.** A sudden sharp pull, twist, or thrust. **2.** *Physiol.* An involuntary contraction of a muscle caused by reflex action. **3.** *Slang* A stupid man. [? Var. of archaic *yerk*] — **jerk′y** *adv.* — **jerk′i·ly** *adv.* — **jerk′i·ness** *n.*

jerk[2] (jûrk) *v.t.* To cure (meat) by cutting into strips and drying. — *n.* Jerked meat, esp. beef. [< Sp. *charqui* < Quechua *echarqui* dried beef]

jer·kin (jûr′kin) *n.* **1.** A close-fitting jacket or vest, usu. sleeveless. **2.** Formerly, such a garment, often of leather, worn in the 16th and 17th centuries. [Origin unknown]

jerk·wa·ter (jûrk′wô′tər, -wot′ər) *U.S. Informal* *adj.* **1.** Not on the main line: a *jerkwater* town. **2.** Insignificant; small. — *n.* A train serving a branch line.

jer·ry·build (jer′ē·bild′) *v.t.* **·built, ·build·ing** To build flimsily and with inferior materials. [Origin unknown]

jer·sey (jûr′zē) *n.* *pl.* **·seys** **1.** A ribbed elastic fabric of wool, cotton, etc., used for clothing. Also **jersey cloth.** **2.** A close-fitting knit upper garment.

Jer·sey (jûr′zē) *n.* *pl.* **·seys** One of a breed of small cattle, usu. fawn-colored, originating in the island of Jersey and noted for milk rich in butterfat.

jes·sa·mine (jes′ə·min) *n.* Jasmine, a plant.

jest (jest) *n.* **1.** Something said or done to provoke laughter; joke. **2.** Playfulness; fun: to speak in *jest*. **3.** An object of laughter; laughingstock. — *v.i.* **1.** To make amusing remarks; tell jokes; quip. **2.** To speak or act in a playful way; trifle. [< OF < L *gesta* deeds]

jest·er (jes′tər) *n.* One who jests; esp., a court fool.

jest·ing (jes′ting) *n.* The action of one who jokes. — *adj.* Of the nature of a jest; prone to jest. — **jest′ing·ly** *adv.*

Jes·u·it (jezh′ōō·it, jez′yōō-) *n.* **1.** A member of the Society of Jesus, a religious order founded in 1534 by Ignatius Loyola to combat the Reformation and propagate the faith among the heathen. **2.** A crafty or scheming person; an equivocator: a derogatory term. [< NL < L *Jesus* Jesus] — **Jes′u·it′ic** or **·i·cal** *adj.* — **Jes′u·it′i·cal·ly** *adv.*

Jes·u·it·ize (jezh′ōō·it·īz′, jez′yōō-) *v.t.* & *v.i.* **·ized, ·iz·ing** To be or make Jesuitic.

Je·sus (jē′zəs) Founder of Christianity, 6? B.C.–29? A.D., son of Mary; regarded in the Christian faith as Christ, the Messiah. Also **Jesus Christ, Jesus of Nazareth.**

jet[1] (jet) *n.* **1.** A hard black lignite, taking a high polish, used for jewelry, buttons, etc. **2.** A deep, glossy black. — *adj.* **1.** Made of or resembling jet. **2.** Black as jet; jet-black. [< OF < L < Gk. *gagatēs*, after *Gagai*, a Lycian town where it was mined]

jet[2] (jet) *n.* **1.** A sudden spurt or gush of liquid or gas emitted from a narrow orifice. **2.** Liquid or gas that spurts from an orifice. **3.** A spout or nozzle. **4.** A jet-propelled aircraft. — *v.t.* & *v.i.* **jet·ted, jet·ting** To spurt forth or emit in a stream. [< F, ult. < L *jactare*, freq. of *jacere* to throw]

Jet, meaning operating by, of, or relating to jet propulsion, may appear as a combining form or as the first element in two-word phrases; as in:

jet aircraft	**jet bomber**	**jet pilot**
jet airplane	**jet fighter**	**jet plane**
jet aviation	**jetliner**	**jet-propelled**

jet-black (jet′black′) *adj. & n.* Deep black, like jet.
jet engine A reaction and heat engine that takes in outside air to oxidize fuel that it converts into the energy of a powerful jet of heated gas expelled to the rear under high pressure.
jet propulsion **1.** Propulsion by means of a jet of gas or other fluid. **2.** *Aeron.* Propulsion by means of jet engines.
jet·sam (jet′səm) *n.* **1.** Goods thrown into the sea to lighten an imperiled vessel. **2.** Such goods washed ashore. [Earlier *jetson*, short for JETTISON]
jet stream **1.** The strong flow of gas or other fluid expelled from a jet engine, rocket motor, and the like. **2.** *Meteorol.* A high-velocity wind circulating, usu. from west to east, near the base of the stratosphere.
jet·ti·son (jet′ə·sən) *v.t.* **1.** To throw overboard (goods or cargo). **2.** To discard (something that hampers). — *n.* **1.** The act of jettisoning. **2.** Jetsam. [< AF < L < *jactare* to throw]
jet·ty (jet′ē) *n. pl.* **·ties** **1.** A structure of piling, rocks, etc., extending out into a body of water to protect a harbor, etc. **2.** A wharf or pier. [< OF *jeter* to throw]
jeu d'es·prit (zhœ des·prē′) *pl.* **jeux d'esprit** (zhœ) A witticism. [< F]
Jew (jo͞o) *n.* **1.** A member or descendant of the Hebrew people. **2.** Any person professing Judaism. **3.** Originally, a member of the tribe or the kingdom of Judah. — *adj.* Jewish: an offensive usage. [< OF < L < Gk. < Hebrew *y'hudi* descendant of Judah] — **Jew′ess** *n.fem.*
jew·el (jo͞o′əl) *n.* **1.** A precious stone; gem. **2.** An article for personal adornment, esp. one made of cut gems and precious metal. **3.** A person or thing of rare excellence or value. **4.** A bit of gem, crystal, glass, etc., used to form a durable bearing, as in a watch. — *v.t.* **jew·eled** or **·elled, jew·el·ing** or **·el·ling** To adorn with jewels; set jewels in. [< OF ult. < L *jocus* a joke, sport]
jew·el·er (jo͞o′əl·ər) *n.* A dealer in or maker of jewelry. Also **jew′el·ler.**
jew·el·ry (jo͞o′əl·rē) *n.* Jewels, collectively. Also *Brit.* **jew′el·ler·y.**
jew·el·weed (jo͞o′əl·wēd′) *n.* A species of touch-me-not having deep yellow flowers.
Jew·ish (jo͞o′ish) *adj.* Of, pertaining to, or resembling the Jews, their customs, religion, etc. — *n.* Loosely, Yiddish.
Jewish holidays See HANUKKAH, PASSOVER, ROSH HASHANA, SUKKOTH, and YOM KIPPUR.
Jew·ry (jo͞o′rē) *n.* The Jewish people.
jew's-harp (jo͞oz′härp′) *n.* A small musical instrument that is held between the teeth when played and consists of a lyre-shaped frame with a flexible steel tongue that is plucked with the finger. Also **jews'-harp.**
Jez·e·bel (jez′ə·bəl) The wife of Ahab, notorious for her evil actions. I *Kings* xvi 31. — *n.* A bold, vicious woman.
jib[1] (jib) *n.* **1.** *Naut.* A triangular sail, set on a stay and extending from the foretopmast head to the jib boom or the bowsprit. For illus. see SCHOONER. **2.** The boom of a crane or derrick. — *v.t. & v.i.* **jibbed, jib·bing** *Naut.* To jibe. [? Short for GIBBET]
jib[2] (jib) *v.i.* **jibbed, jib·bing** **1.** To move restively sidewise or backward, as a horse. **2.** To balk. — *n.* A horse that jibs: also **jib′ber.** [Cf. OF *giber* kick]
jib boom *Naut.* A spar forming a continuation of the bowsprit and holding a jib.
jibe[1] (jīb) *v.* **jibed, jib·ing** *v.i.* **1.** *Naut.* To swing from one side of a vessel to the other: said of a fore-and-aft sail or its boom. **2.** To change course so that the sails shift in this manner. — *v.t.* **3.** To cause to swing from one side of a vessel to the other. Also spelled *gibe, jib.* [< Du. *gijben*]
jibe[2] (jīb) See GIBE[1].
jibe[3] (jīb) *v.i.* **jibed, jib·ing** *U.S. Informal* To agree; be in accordance. [Origin uncertain]
jif·fy (jif′ē) *n. pl.* **·fies** *Informal* An instant; moment. Also **jiff.** [Origin unknown]
jig (jig) *n.* **1.** A fast, lively dance; also, the music for such a dance. **2.** *Mech.* A device for holding the material being worked or for guiding a tool. **3.** In fishing, any of various combinations of hooks, spoons, etc., that are agitated in the water to attract and catch fish. **4.** *Mining* A wire sieve or other device for separating or cleaning coal by jolting and shaking in water. — **the jig is up** *Slang* All hope of success is gone. — *v.* **jigged, jig·ging** *v.i.* **1.** To dance or play a jig. **2.** To move jerkily, esp. up and down; bob. **3.** To use or operate a jig in working. **4.** To fish with a jig. — *v.t.* **5.** To jerk up and down or to and fro; jiggle. **6.** To hold, form, process, etc., with a jig. **7.** To catch (fish) with a jig. [Cf. OF *gigue* a fiddle]
jig·ger (jig′ər) *n.* **1.** One who or that which jigs. **2.** A small glass or cup for measuring liquor, holding about and one half ounces; also, the amount of liquor so measu **3.** A jig used in catching fish. **4.** *Mech.* A jig. **5.** An various types of jolting mechanisms, as an apparatus separating ores, a potter's wheel, etc. **6.** *Naut.* **a** A s sail set in the stern of a sailing craft, as a yawl. **b** A tackle used on board ship. **c** A jigger mast. **7.** *Informal* small device or thing one is unable to name definitely.
jigger mast *Naut.* The aftermost mast of a four- or masted vessel.
jig·gle (jig′əl) *v.t. & v.i.* **·gled, ·gling** To move unsteadil and down or backwards and forwards with slight, q jerks. — *n.* A jerky, unsteady movement. [Freq. of JIG,
jig·saw (jig′sô′) *n.* A saw having a slim blade set vertic in a frame and operated with a reciprocating motion, for cutting curved or irregular lines.
jigsaw puzzle A puzzle consisting of a picture mounte wood or cardboard and then cut or stamped into irreg interlocking pieces for reassembly.
jilt (jilt) *v.t.* To cast off or discard (a previously fav lover or sweetheart). — *n.* A woman or girl who discar lover. [Cf. dial. E (Scottish) *jillet* giddy girl] — **jilt′e**
jim-crow (jim′krō′) *U.S. Slang adj.* Serving to segre Negroes: *jim-crow* laws. — *v.t.* To subject (Negroes) to regation or discrimination. Also **Jim′-Crow′.**
Jim Crow *U.S. Slang* **1.** A Negro: an offensive term. The segregation of Negroes. — **Jim-Crow′ism** *n.*
jim·my (jim′ē) *n. pl.* **·mies** A burglar's crowbar. — **·mied, ·my·ing** To break or pry open with or as with a my. [after *Jimmy*, dim. of *James*, a personal name]
jim·son·weed (jim′sən·wēd′) *n.* A tall, coarse, evil-sm ing, poisonous annual weed of the nightshade family, yiel atropine and scopolamine: also called *stramonium.* **Jimson weed.** [Alter. of *Jamestown weed* Jamestown,
jin·gle (jing′gəl) *v.* **·gled, ·gling** *v.i.* **1.** To make light r ing or tinkling sounds. **2.** To have an intrusive rhym rhythm: said of writing or music, often in deprecation. *v.t.* **3.** To cause to make ringing or tinkling sounds. — **1.** A tinkling, clinking, or rapidly ringing sound. **2** catchy short song or poem, esp. one used for advertis **3.** Rapid repetition in rhyme, rhythm, alliteration, [Imit.] — **jin′gly** *adj.*
jin·go (jing′gō) *n. pl.* **·goes** One who boasts of his patr ism and favors an aggressive foreign policy. — *adj.* pertaining to, or characteristic of the jingoes. [Origin a magician's nonsense word] — **jin′go·ish** *adj.* — **jin′ ism** *n.* — **jing·o′ist** *n.* — **jin′go·is′tic** *adj.*
jin·ni (jin′ē, ji·nē′) *n. pl.* **jinn** (jin) In Moslem mytholo one of the supernatural beings able to assume human or mal form and often at the service of men: sometimes spel *djinni, genie.* Also **jin·nee′.** [< Arabic *jinnī*]
jin·rik·sha (jin·rik′shə, -shô) *n.* A small oriental t wheeled carriage drawn by one or two men: also called *r shaw, ricksha.* Also **jin·rick′sha, jin·rik′i·sha.** [< Japan *jin* man + *riki* power + *sha* carriage]
jinx (jingks) *Slang n.* A person or thing supposed to br bad luck. — *v.t.* To bring bad luck to. [< earlier *jynx* Gk. *iynx* the wryneck (a bird anciently used in witchcraf
jit·ney (jit′nē) *n. U.S.* **1.** A motor vehicle that car passengers for a small fare. **2.** *Obs. Slang* A small coin.
jit·ter (jit′ər) *v.i. U.S. Slang* To be nervous. — **the ters** *Slang* Intense nervousness. — **jit′ter·y** *adj.*
jit·ter·bug (jit′ər·bug′) *U.S. Slang n.* One who dan rapidly and spasmodically to jazz. — *v.i.* **·bugged, ·b ging** To dance to jazz in a fast, violent way.
jiu·jit·su (jo͞o·jit′so͞o), **jiu·jut·su** (jo͞o·jit′so͞o, -jo͝ot′so͞o) JUJITSU.
jive (jīv) *n. Slang* **1.** The jargon of jazz music and mu cians. **2.** Jazz music. [Origin unknown]
job (job) *n.* **1.** Anything that is to be done, esp. a defin single piece of work done for a set fee; also, the thing work on. **2.** A position or situation of employment. **3.** Son thing done ostensibly for the public good, but actually private profit. **4.** *Informal* An affair; circumstance. *Slang* A robbery or other criminal act. — **odd job** A pie of occasional or miscellaneous work. — **on the job** *Inform* **1.** During working hours. **2.** Attending strictly to t matter at hand. — **to lie** (or **lay**) **down on the job** *Inform* To evade work or responsibility. — *v.* **jobbed, job·bing** *v* **1.** To work by the job or piece. **2.** To be a jobber middleman. **3.** To use a position of public trust for priva advantage. — *v.t.* **4.** To buy in bulk and resell in lo to dealers. **5.** To sublet (work) among separate contracto [Origin uncertain] — **job′less** *adj.* — **job′less·ness** *n.*
Job (jōb) In the Bible, the chief character in the Book Job, who, despite great suffering and adversity, kept h faith in God. — *n.* The book itself.
job·ber (job′ər) *n.* **1.** One who buys goods in bulk from th manufacturer or importer and sells to the retailer; whol saler. **2.** One who works by the job, or on small jobs; piec worker.

ɔer·y (job′ər·ē) *n. pl.* **·ber·ies** Corrupt use of a public ɔe or trust for private or partisan gain.

hold·er (job′hōl′dər) *n.* One who has a steady job.

lot 1. A collection of miscellaneous goods sold to a re-er. **2.** Any collection of things inferior in quality.

as·ta (jō·kas′tə) In Greek legend, the queen who un-tingly marries her own son Oedipus.

·ey (jok′ē) *n. p.* **·eys** One employed to ride horses in es. — *v.t. & v.i.* **1.** To maneuver for an advantageous ition. **2.** To ride (a horse) in a race. **3.** To cheat; k. [Dim. of JOCK] — **jock′ey·ing** *n.* — **jock′ey·ism** *n.*

ɔse (jō·kōs′) *adj.* Humorous; playful; joking. [< L *us* joke] — **jo·cose′ly** *adv.* — **jo·cose′ness, jo′cos·i·ty** ɔs′ə·tē) *n.*

ı·lar (jok′yə·lər) *adj.* Given to joking; also, like a joke. o **joc′u·la·to′ry** (-tôr′ē, -tō′rē). [< L *jocus* joke] — **u·lar′i·ty** (-lâr′ə·tē) *n.* — **joc′u·lar·ly** *adv.*

ınd (jok′ənd, jō′kənd) *adj.* Cheerful; gay; jovial. [< < LL *juvare* to delight] — **jo·cun·di·ty** (jō·kun′də·tē) — **joc′und·ly** *adv.* — **joc′und·ness** *n.*

·purs (jod′pərz) *n.pl.* Wide riding breeches, close-ing from knee to ankle. [after *Jodhpur*, India]

l (jō′əl) A Hebrew prophet. — *n.* A book of the Old stament by this prophet. [< Hebrew, the Lord is God]

(jog) *v.* **jogged, jog·ging** *v.i.* **1.** To proceed slowly or notonously: with *on* or *along.* — *v.t.* **2.** To push or ch lightly; esp. to nudge (someone). **3.** To stimulate: *jog* the memory. — *n.* **1.** The act of jogging. **2.** A dge. **3.** A slow, jolting motion or pace. **4.** *U.S.* An gle or projection in a surface, as in a wall; jag. **5.** *U.S.* sudden temporary turning or veering in a road, course, . [Prob. imit. Akin to SHOG.] — **jog′ger** *n.*

gle (jog′əl) *v.* **·gled, ·gling** *v.t.* **1.** To shake slightly; . **2.** To fasten or join together by a joggle or joggles. — **3.** To move with an irregular or jolting motion; shake. *n.* **1.** The act of joggling. **2.** A projection formed on a ce, as of stone, timber, etc., that serves to fit it firmly an adjoining piece having a corresponding notch. **3.** A wel. [Freq. of JOG, v.]

trot 1. A slow, easy trot, as of a horse. **2.** A slow, hum-um habit of living or doing the daily tasks.

n (jon) *n. Slang* A toilet.

ın (jon) One of the twelve apostles, son of Zebedee and other of James: called **Saint John the Evangelist, Saint hn the Divine.** — *n.* **1.** The fourth Gospel of the New stament, attributed to him. **2.** One of the three New stament epistles that bear his name.

ın Bull 1. The English people. **2.** A typical English-ın. Also **Johnny Bull.** [after a character in a satire (1712) Dr. John Arbuthnot] — **John-Bul·lism** (jon′bŏŏl′iz·əm).

hn Doe (dō) A name to designate a fictitious or real per-nage in any legal transaction or proceeding.

ın Han·cock (han′kok) *U.S. Informal* A person's auto-aph. [after *John Hancock*]

n·ny·cake (jon′ē·kāk′) *n. U.S.* A flat cake of cornmeal, ked on a griddle. [? < obs. *jonikin*, a type of bread]

n·ny-jump-up (jon′ē·jump′up′) *n.* **1.** Any of various merican spring violets. **2.** The wild pansy.

hn·son·ese (jon′sən·ēz′, -ēs′) *n.* A ponderous and elabo-te literary style similar to that of Samuel Johnson.

hn·so·ni·an (jon·sō′nē·ən) *adj.* Pertaining to or resem-ing Samuel Johnson or his work. — *n.* An admirer of Dr. ɔhnson, esp. a student of his life and work.

hn the Baptist, 6? B.C.–A.D. 30?, forerunner and bap-zer of Jesus; beheaded by Herod Antipas.

e de vi·vre (zhwȧ də vēv′r′) *French* Joy of living.

n (join) *v.t.* **1.** To become a member of, as a club, party, aff, etc. **2.** To come to as a companion or participant. . To unite in act or purpose. **4.** To come to a junction ith. **5.** To connect. **6.** To unite in marriage. **7.** To take place with, in, or among. **8.** *Informal* To adjoin. — *v.i.* . To enter into association or agreement: often with *with.* **0.** To take part: usually with *in.* **11.** To come together; ɔnnect; unite. — **to join battle** To engage in a battle or onflict. — **to join up** *Informal* To enlist. — *n.* A joint r seam. [< OF < L *jungere* to join]

in·der (join′dər) *n.* **1.** The act of joining. **2.** *Law* **a** A ɔining of causes of action or defense. **b** A joining of parties n an action. **c** The acceptance of an issue tendered.

in·er (joi′nər) *n.* **1.** One who or that which joins. **2.** *U.S. Informal* One who joins many clubs, lodges, etc.

in·e·ry (joi′nər·ē) *n.* **1.** The art or skill of a joiner. **2.** The rticles constructed by a joiner.

int (joint) *n.* **1.** A place or point at which two or more ɔarts of the same thing are joined together. **2.** *Anat.* A place of union between two separate bones, usu. permitting movement; articulation. **3.** *Bot.* The portion of the stem of a plant from which branches grow; a node. **4.** A large cut of meat from a shoulder or leg containing the bone, used for roasting. **5.** *Slang* **a** A place of low repute, as for drinking, gambling, etc. **b** Any place of dwelling or gathering. — **out of joint 1.** Dislocated. **2.** Disordered; disorganized. — *adj.* **1.** Belonging to or used by two or more: *joint* bank account. **2.** Sharing with another: *joint* owner. **3.** Produced by combined action: a *joint* literary effort. — *v.t.* **1.** To fasten by means of a joint or joints. **2.** To form or shape with a joint or joints, as a board. **3.** To cut at the joints, as meat. [< OF < L *jungere* to join]

joint account A bank account in the name of two or more persons, each of whom may deposit and withdraw funds.

Joint Chiefs of Staff *U.S.* A body within the Department of Defense, consisting of a military chairman, the Chief of Staff of the Army, the Chief of Naval Operations, and the Chief of Staff of the Air Force.

joint·ed (join′tid) *adj.* **1.** Having a joint or joints. **2.** Having a (specified kind of) joint: *short-jointed.*

joint·ly (joint′lē) *adv.* In a joint manner; unitedly.

joint resolution *U.S.* A resolution passed by both houses of Congress, becoming a law if signed by the President.

joint-stock company (joint′stok′) An unincorporated business association of many persons, each of whom owns shares of stock which he may sell or transfer at will.

join·ture (join′chər) *n. Law* A settlement of property made to a woman by her husband after his death; also, the property. — *v.t.* **·tured, ·tur·ing** To settle a jointure on. [< F < L *jungere* to join]

joist (joist) *n.* Any of the parallel beams placed horizontally from wall to wall, to which the boards of a floor or the laths of a ceiling are fastened. — *v.t.* To furnish with joists. [< OF < L *jacere* to lie]

joke (jōk) *n.* **1.** Something said or done to amuse; esp., a funny story. **2.** Something said or done in fun rather than in earnest. **3.** One who or that which excites mirth. **4.** A trifling matter. — *v.* **joked, jok·ing** *v.i.* **1.** To tell or make jokes; jest. **2.** To say something in fun and not in earnest. [< L *jocus*] — **jok′ing·ly** *adv.*

jok·er (jō′kər) *n.* **1.** One who jokes. **2.** In a deck of cards, an extra card used in certain games. **3.** *U.S.* An unobtrusive clause in a legislative bill, etc., that undermines or nullifies its original purpose. **4.** Any hidden difficulty.

jol·li·fy (jol′ə·fī) *v.t. & v.i.* **·fied, ·fy·ing** *Informal* To be or cause to be merry or jolly. — **jol′li·fi·ca′tion** *n.*

jol·li·ty (jol′ə·tē) *n. pl.* **·ties 1.** The state or quality of being jolly; gaiety. **2.** *Brit.* A festive occasion or gathering.

jol·ly (jol′ē) *adj.* **·li·er, ·li·est 1.** Full of good humor and high spirits. **2.** Festive; merry. **3.** *Brit. Informal* Extraordinary: a *jolly* bore. — *v.t.* **·lied, ·ly·ing** *Informal* **1.** To attempt to put or keep in good humor: often with *along* or *up.* **2.** To make fun of. — *n. pl.* **·lies 1.** *Brit. Informal* A merry or festive gathering. **2.** *Brit. Slang* A sailor. — *adv. Brit. Informal* Extremely; very: *jolly* ugly. [< OF *joli*] — **jol′li·ly** *adv.* — **jol′li·ness** *n.*

jolly boat A small boat belonging to a ship. [< Dan. *jolle* yawl + BOAT]

Jolly Roger The pirate flag bearing the skull and cross-bones.

jolt (jōlt) *v.t.* **1.** To strike or knock against; jar; jostle. **2.** To shake up or about with a blow or bump. — *v.i.* **3.** To move with a series of irregular bumps or jars, as over a rough road. — *n.* **1.** A sudden bump or jar as from a blow. **2.** An unexpected surprise or emotional shock. [ME *jot* bump and *joll* bump] — **jolt′er** *n.* — **jolt′y** *adj.*

Jo·nah (jō′nə) Eighth- or ninth-century B.C. Hebrew prophet, who, cast overboard during a storm, was swallowed by a great fish and then cast up on the shore alive three days later. — *n.* **1.** A book of the Old Testament containing his story: also, in the Douai Bible, **Jo′nas** (-nəs). **2.** Any person bringing bad luck. [< Hebrew *Yōnāh*, lit., dove]

jon·gleur (jong′glər, *Fr.* zhôn·glœr′) *n.* A wandering minstrel of medieval England and France. [< OF < L *joculator.* See JUGGLER.]

jon·quil (jon′kwil, jong′-) *n.* **1.** A species of narcissus related to the daffodil, having fragrant, white or yellow flowers. **2.** The flower. [< F < L *juncus* a rush]

Jordan almond A large Spanish almond, frequently sugar-coated as a confection. [ME *jardyne almaunde*]

Jo·seph (jō′zəf) In the Old Testament, a son of Jacob and Rachel, sold into slavery in Egypt by his brothers. *Gen.* xxx 24. [< Hebrew *Yōsēph*, lit., He will add]

Joseph Husband of Mary, the mother of Jesus. *Matt.* i 18.

Joseph of Ar·i·ma·the·a (ar′ə·mə·thē′ə) A wealthy disciple of Christ who provided a tomb for his burial. *Matt.* xxvii 57–60.

josh (josh) *U.S. Slang v.t. & v.i.* To make good-humored fun of (someone); tease; banter. — *n.* A good-natured joke. [Blend of JOKE and BOSH] — **josh′er** *n.*

Josh·u·a (josh′ōō·ə) Israelite leader and successor of Moses. —*n.* The book of the Old Testament bearing his name. [< Hebrew *Yehōshua'* God is salvation]
joss (jos) *n.* A Chinese god. [Pidgin English < Pg. *deos* God]
joss house A Chinese temple or place for religious images.
joss paper Paper burnt by the Chinese at funerals, etc.
joss stick A stick of perfumed paste burnt by the Chinese.
jos·tle (jos′əl) *v.t. & v.i.* **·tled, ·tling** To push or crowd roughly so as to shake up; elbow; shove. —*n.* A shoving or colliding against; jostling. [Freq. of JOUST] —**jos′tler** *n.*
jot (jot) *v.t.* **jot·ted, jot·ting** To make a hasty and brief note of: usually with *down.* —*n.* The least bit; iota. [< IOTA]
jot·ting (jot′ing) *n.* That which is jotted down; short note.
joule (joul, jōōl) *n. Physics* A unit of work equal to 10,000,000 ergs or 0.737324 foot-pounds. [after J. P. *Joule,* 1818–1889, English physicist]
jounce (jouns) *v.t. & v.i.* **jounced, jounc·ing** To bounce; jolt. —*n.* A shake; a bump. [Origin unknown]
jour·nal (jûr′nəl) *n.* **1.** A diary or record of daily occurrences; esp. a ship's log. **2.** A newspaper, esp. one published daily. **3.** Any periodical or magazine. **4.** An official record of the daily proceedings of a legislature. **5.** In bookkeeping: **a** A daybook. **b** In double entry, a book in which daily transactions are entered to facilitate later posting in the ledger. **6.** *Mech.* The part of a shaft or axle that rotates in or against a bearing. [< OF < L *diurnalis* daily]
journal box *Mech.* The box or bearing for a journal.
jour·nal·ese (jûr′nəl·ēz′, -ēs′) *n.* The style of writing supposedly characteristic of newspapers, magazines, etc.: a derogatory term.
jour·nal·ism (jûr′nəl·iz′əm) *n.* The occupation, practice, and academic field concerned with writing, editing, and publishing newspapers and other periodicals.
jour·nal·ist (jûr′nəl·ist) *n.* One whose occupation is writing, editing, and publishing newspapers, etc. —**jour·nal·is·tic** (jûr′nəl·is′tik) *adj.* —**jour′nal·is′ti·cal·ly** *adv.*
jour·nal·ize (jûr′nəl·īz) *v.* **·ized, ·iz·ing** *v.t.* **1.** To enter in a journal or diary. —*v.i.* **2.** To keep a journal or diary.
jour·ney (jûr′nē) *n.* **1.** Travel from one place to another. **2.** The distance traveled. —*v.i.* To make a trip; travel. [< OF *journee* a day's travel] —**jour′ney·er** *n.*
jour·ney·man (jûr′nē·mən) *n. pl.* **·men** (-mən) A worker who has completed his apprenticeship in a skilled trade.
joust (just, joust, jōōst) *n.* **1.** A formal combat between two mounted knights armed with lances; tilt. **2.** *pl.* Tournament. —*v.i.* To engage in a joust. Also spelled *just.* [< OF < LL *juxtare* to approach] —**joust′er** *n.*
Jove (jōv) Jupiter. —**by Jove!** A mild oath expressing surprise, emphasis, etc. —**Jo′vi·an** *adj.*
jo·vi·al (jō′vē·əl) *adj.* Good-natured; convivial; jolly. [< F < LL *Jovialis* born under the influence of Jupiter] —**jo′vi·al·ly** *adv.* —**jo′vi·al·ness** *n.*
jo·vi·al·i·ty (jō′vē·al′ə·tē) *n.* The quality or state of being jovial; conviviality; merriment. Also **jo·vi·al·ty** (jō′vē·əl·tē).
jowl[1] (joul, jōl) *n.* The fleshy part under the lower jaw, esp. when fat; double chin. [ME *cholle* < OE *ceolu* throat]
jowl[2] (joul, jōl) *n.* **1.** The jaw, esp. the lower jaw. **2.** The cheek. [ME *chavel* < OE *ceafl*]
joy (joi) *n.* **1.** A strong feeling of happiness; gladness; delight. **2.** A state of contentment or satisfaction. **3.** Anything that causes delight or gladness. —*v.i.* To be glad; rejoice. [< OF < L *gaudere* to rejoice]
joy·ful (joi′fəl) *adj.* **1.** Full of joy. **2.** Showing or causing joy. —**joy′ful·ly** *adv.* —**joy′ful·ness** *n.*
joy·less (joi′lis) *adj.* Completely lacking in joy; causing no joy; dreary; sad. —**joy′less·ly** *adv.* —**joy′less·ness** *n.*
joy·ous (joi′əs) *adj.* Joyful. —**joy′ous·ly** *adv.* —**joy′ous·ness** *n.*
joy ride *Informal* **1.** A ride taken for pleasure. **2.** A reckless ride in a stolen vehicle. —**joy rider** —**joy riding**
joy stick *Informal* The control stick of an airplane.
ju·bi·lant (jōō′bə·lənt) *adj.* Exultingly joyful or triumphant. [< L *jubilare* to exult] —**ju′bi·lance, ju′bi·lan·cy** *n.* —**ju′bi·lant·ly** *adv.*
ju·bi·late (jōō′bə·lāt) *v.t. & v.i.* **·lat·ed, ·lat·ing** To rejoice.
ju·bi·la·tion (jōō′bə·lā′shən) *n.* Rejoicing; exultation.
ju·bi·lee (jōō′bə·lē) *n.* **1.** In Jewish history, a celebration (*Lev.* xxv 8–17) observed every fiftieth year, at which time slaves were freed, alienated lands returned, and the fields left uncultivated. **2.** In the Roman Catholic Church, a year of special indulgence occurring usu. every twenty-fifth year. **3.** A special anniversary of an event. **4.** Any time of rejoicing. Also **ju′bi·le.** [< OF < LL < Gk. < Hebrew *yōbēl* ram's horn, trumpet]
Judaeo- See JUDEO-.
Judah (jōō′də) In the Old Testament, a son of Jacob and Leah. *Gen.* xxix 35. —*n.* The tribe of Israel descended from him. [< Hebrew *Yehūdhāh* praised]
Ju·da·ic (jōō·dā′ik) *adj.* Of or pertaining to the Jews. Also **Ju·da′i·cal.** [< L *Judaicus*] —**Ju·da′i·cal·ly** *adv.*
Ju·da·ism (jōō′dē·iz′əm) *n.* **1.** The religious beliefs or practices of the Jews. **2.** The observance of Jewish rit practices. See CONSERVATIVE JUDAISM, ORTHODOX J ISM, REFORM JUDAISM. —**Ju′da·ist** *n.* —**Ju′da·is′tic**
Ju·da·ize (jōō′dē·īz) *v.* **·ized, ·iz·ing** *v.t.* **1.** To bring conformity with Judaism. —*v.i.* **2.** To accept Judais
Ju·das (jōō′dəs) **1.** The disciple of Jesus who betrayed with a kiss: also **Judas Is·car·i·ot** (is·kar′ē·ət). **2.** Jude *n.* One who betrays another under the guise of friendsh
Judas tree A tree with reddish purple flowers. [fr tradition that Judas hanged himself upon a tree of this k
Jude (jōōd) **1.** One of the twelve apostles: called *Judas* Iscariot). *Luke* vi 16, *Acts* i 13, *John* xiv 22. **2.** The au of a book of the New Testament, possibly the broth James and Jesus: called *Judas.* *Matt.* xiii 55, *Mark* —*n.* A book of the New Testament by this author.
Ju·de·a (jōō·dē′ə) The southern part of ancient Pale under Persian, Greek, and Roman dominion: also **Ju·da** —**Ju·de′an, Ju·dae′an** *n. & adj.*
Judeo- *combining form* Jewish. Also spelled *Judaeo-.* L *Judaeus*]
judge (juj) *n.* **1.** A public officer invested with the pow administer justice by hearing cases in a court of law. One appointed to make decisions. **3.** One considered c petent to make critical evaluations: a *judge* of music. 4 Jewish history, one of the rulers of Israel before the ki —*v.* **judged, judg·ing** *v.t.* **1.** To hear and decide the m of (a case) or the guilt of (a person). **2.** To decide autho tively, as a contest. **3.** To hold as judgment or opinion. To form an opinion or judgment concerning. **5.** To gov said of the ancient Hebrew judges. —*v.i.* **6.** To act judge. **7.** To make a judgment or decision. [< OF *judex, -icis* < *ius* right + *dicere* to speak]
judge advocate *Mil.* **1.** A commissioned officer in the Army belonging to the Judge Advocate General's Corps. The legal staff officer for a commander.
Judge Advocate General A major general in the Army or the U.S. Air Force, serving as head of the Ju Advocate General's Department and supervising milit justice and other legal matters.
Judg·es (juj′iz) *n.pl.* (*construed as sing.*) A book of the Testament, containing a history of the Jewish people.
judg·ment (juj′mənt) *n.* **1.** The act of judging. **2.** decision or opinion reached through judging. **3.** The abi to judge wisely. **4.** *Law* **a** The sentence or decision. debt resulting from such a decision. **c** The record of suc decision. **5.** A disaster or misfortune regarded as inflic by God. **judge′ment.**
Judgment Day *Theol.* The day or time of the Last Ju ment: also *Day of Judgment.*
ju·di·ca·tor (jōō′də·kā·tər) *n.* One who acts as judge.
ju·di·ca·to·ry (jōō′də·kə·tôr′ē, -tō′rē) *adj.* Pertaining the administration of justice. —*n. pl.* **·ries** **1.** Any tri nal. **2.** The judicial process.
ju·di·ca·ture (jōō′də·kə·chŏŏr) *n.* **1.** The action or fu tion of administering justice, as in courts of law. **2.** right, power, or authority of administering justice; juris tion. **3.** A court of law; also, judges collectively.
ju·di·cial (jōō·dish′əl) *adj.* **1.** Of or pertaining to the ministering of justice, to courts of law or to judges. **2.** creed or enforced by a court of law. **3.** Of or befittin judge. **4.** Inclined to make judgments; discriminati critical. [< L *judex, -icis* judge] —**ju·di′cial·ly** *adv.*
ju·di·ci·ar·y (jōō·dish′ē·er′ē, -dish′ə·rē) *adj.* Of or perta ing to courts, judges, or judgments. —*n. pl.* **·ar·ies** The department of government that administers the la **2.** The system of courts set up to carry out this function. The judges collectively.
ju·di·cious (jōō·dish′əs) *adj.* Having, showing, or exercisi good judgment; prudent. [< F < L *judicium* judgmen —**ju·di′cious·ly** *adv.* —**ju·di′cious·ness** *n.*
Ju·dith (jōō′dith) **1.** A book in the Old Testament Apoc pha and the Douai Bible. **2.** A Jewish woman, heroine this book, who rescued her countrymen by slaying the A syrian general, Holofernes. [< Hebrew *Jehūdhīth*]
ju·do (jōō′dō) *n.* A system of physical conditioning devis in Japan in 1882, based on jujitsu. [< Japanese *ju* gent pliant + *do* way of life]
jug[1] (jug) *n.* **1.** A pitcher or similar vessel for holding li uids. **2.** *Slang* A prison or jail. —*v.t.* **jugged, jug·ging** To put into a jug. **2.** *Slang* To imprison; jail. [after *Jug* nickname for *Joan*]
jug[2] (jug) *n.* The sound of a nightingale's note. —*v* **jugged, jug·ging** To make the sound of the nightingale.
ju·gate (jōō′git, -gāt) *adj.* **1.** *Biol.* Occurring in pairs. *Bot.* Having paired leaflets. [< L *jugare* to bind togethe
jug·ger·naut (jug′ər·nôt) *n.* Any slow and irresistible d structive force.
Jug·ger·naut (jug′ər·nôt) The eighth avatar of Vishn whose idol at Puri, India, is annually drawn on a heavy c under the wheels of which devotees are said to have throw themselves. [< Skt. *jagannātha* lord of the universe]

·gle (jug′əl) *v.* **·gled, ·gling** *v.t.* **1.** To keep (two or more ·lls or other objects) continuously moving from the hand ·o the air. **2.** To manipulate dishonestly. —*v.i.* **3.** To ·rform as a juggler. **4.** To practice deception or fraud. — **1.** An act of juggling. **2.** A trick or deception. [< OF L *joculari* to jest] —**jug′gler** *n.*

·gler·y (jug′lər·ē) *n. pl.* **·gler·ies** **1.** The juggler's art; ·erdemain. **2.** Deception; fraud.

·u·lar (jug′yə·lər, jōō′gyə-) *adj. Anat.* Of or pertaining the throat or the jugular vein. —*n. Anat.* A jugular ·in. [< NL < L *jugulum* collar bone]

·ular vein *Anat.* One of the large veins on either side of ·e neck that returns blood from the brain, face, and neck.

·ce (jōōs) *n.* **1.** The liquid part of a vegetable, fruit, or ·imal. **2.** *Usually pl.* The fluids of the body. **3.** *U.S.* ·*ang* Electricity. **4.** *U.S. Slang* Gasoline. **5.** *U.S. Slang* ·tal force; strength. [< OF *jus* < L]

·c·er (jōō′sər) *n.* A device for extracting juice.

·c·y (jōō′sē) *adj.* **juic·i·er, juic·i·est** **1.** Abounding with ·ice; moist. **2.** Full of interest; colorful; spicy. —**juic′i·ly** ·*v.* —**juic′i·ness** *n.*

·it·su (jōō·jit′sōō) *n.* A Japanese system of hand-to-hand ·hting in which surprise and a knowledge of anatomy and ·verage are used: also spelled *jiujitsu, jiujutsu.* Also **ju·jut·** · (jōō·jit′sōō, -jōōt′sōō). Compare JUDO. [< Japanese *ju* ·iant + *jutsu* art]

·ube (jōō′jōōb; *for def. 1, also* jōō′jōō·bē) *n.* **1.** A gelati·us candy lozenge. **2.** An Old World tree or shrub of the ·ckthorn family. [< F or < Med.L *jujuba*]

·e box (jōōk) A large automatic phonograph, usu. coin·erated and permitting selection of the records to be played.

·e joint *U.S. Slang* A roadhouse or barroom for drinking ·d dancing. [< Gullah *jook* disorderly, wicked]

·lep (jōō′lip) *n.* **1.** A mint julep. **2.** A sweetened, syrupy ·ink. [< OF < Persian < *gul* rose + *āb* water]

·l·ian (jōōl′yən) *adj.* Of, pertaining to, or named after ·lius Caesar.

·li·enne (jōō′lē·en′, *Fr.* zhü·lyen′) *n.* A clear meat soup ·ntaining vegetables chopped or cut into thin strips. — ·*dj.* Cut into thin strips: *julienne* potatoes. [< F]

·li·et (jōō′lē·et, jōōl′yit) The heroine of Shakespeare's ·*omeo and Juliet.*

·ly (jōō·lī′, jōō-) *pl.* **·lys** The seventh month of the calen·ar year, having 31 days. [< AF < L (*mensis*) *Julius* ·nonth) of Julius Caesar]

·m·ble (jum′bəl) *v.* **·bled, ·bling** *v.t.* **1.** To mix in a con·ised mass; put or throw together without order. **2.** To mix ·p in the mind; muddle. —*v.i.* **3.** To meet or unite con·isedly. —*n.* **1.** A confused mixture or collection; hodge·odge: also **jum′ble·ment.** **2.** A thin sweet cake. **3.** Any of ·arious hairless bees. [Imit.]

·m·bo (jum′bō) *n. pl.* **·bos** A very large person, animal, or ·hing. —*adj.* Very large. [after *Jumbo,* an unusually large ·lephant exhibited by P. T. Barnum < ? W African]

·mp (jump) *v.i.* **1.** To spring from the ground, floor, etc., ·y using the foot and leg muscles; leap; bound. **2.** To move ·r be moved jerkily; bob; bounce. **3.** To rise abruptly: ·rices *jumped.* **4.** To pass suddenly, as if by leaping: to ·*ump* to a conclusion. **5.** To start in astonishment. **6.** To ·pring down from or out of a window, ladder, airplane, etc. ·**7.** In checkers, to capture a piece by passing another over it ·o a vacant square beyond. **8.** In bridge, to bid so as to ex·eed the preceding bid by more than the minimum. —*v.t.* ·**9.** To leap over or across. **10.** To cause to leap over or ·across: to *jump* a horse. **11.** To increase (prices, demands, ·etc.). **12.** To pass over; skip; omit. **13.** In bridge, to ·ause (a bid) to exceed the preceding bid by more than the ·minimum. **14.** *U.S.* To leave or quit abruptly: to *jump* ·town. **15.** *Informal* To get onto; board: to *jump* a train. **16.** *Informal* To attack suddenly or by surprise. —**to jump a claim** To take possession of another's mining or land claim by force and fraud. —**to jump at** To accept hastily. —**to jump bail** *U.S.* To forfeit one's bail bond by failing to appear when legally summoned. —**to jump off** *Mil.* To begin an attack. —**to jump on** (or **all over**) *Informal* To assail with abuse; scold. —**to jump ship** *Naut.* To end one's service in a ship's crew by desertion. —**to jump the gun** *Slang* **1.** To begin before the starting signal is given. **2.** To start prematurely. —**to jump the track** Of a train, etc., to leave the rails. —*n.* **1.** The act of jumping; a leap; spring; bound. **2.** An abrupt movement upward or outward; a jerk. **3.** A sudden rise or transition. **4.** The length or height of a leap. **5.** Something that is jumped over or across, as a hurdle, obstacle, or fence. **6.** A leap by parachute from an airplane. **7.** In sports, a competition in jumping: broad *jump.* —**on the jump** *Informal* Working or moving about at top speed; very busy. —**to get** (or **have**) **the jump on** *U.S. Slang* To get or have a head start on or an advantage over. —*adj.* **1.** *Mil.* Of or pertaining to paratroops. **2.** *U.S. Slang* Of popular music, having a fast, excited tempo. [Cf. Scand. *gumpa* to jump]

jump·er[1] (jum′pər) *n.* **1.** One who or that which jumps. **2.** A piece of mechanism having a jumping motion. **3.** *Electr.* A short wire used to bypass or join parts of a circuit.

jum·per[2] (jum′pər) *n.* **1.** A sleeveless dress, usu. worn over a blouse or sweater. **2.** A loose jacket or smock worn over other clothes. [Prob. alter. of OF *juppe* jacket]

jump·ing bean (jump′ing) The seed of certain Mexican shrubs of the spurge family, that jumps about owing to the movements of a small larva inside.

jumping jack A toy figure of a man, whose jointed limbs are moved by strings.

jump·y (jum′pē) *adj.* **jump·i·er, jump·i·est** **1.** Subject to sudden changes; fluctuating. **2.** Given to startled movements; nervous; apprehensive. —**jump′i·ness** *n.*

jun·co (jung′kō) *n. pl.* **·cos** Any of various small birds of North America, commonly seen in flocks during winter: also called *snowbird.* [< Sp. < L *juncus* rush]

junc·tion (jungk′shən) *n.* **1.** The act of joining, or the state of being joined. **2.** The place where lines or routes, as roads, railways, streams, etc., come together or cross.

junc·ture (jungk′chər) *n.* **1.** The act of joining, or the state of being joined; junction. **2.** A point or line of junction; a joint or seam. **3.** A point in time. **4.** A crisis; emergency. [< L *junctura* < *jungere* to join]

June (jōōn) The sixth month of the calendar year, having 30 days. [OE < L, or ME < OF *Juin* < L (*mensis*) *Junius* (month) of the Junii, a Roman family]

June bug A large, brightly colored beetle that flies in June. Also **June beetle.**

jun·gle (jung′gəl) *n.* **1.** A dense tropical thicket of high grass, reeds, vines, brush, or trees, usu. inhabited by wild animals. **2.** Any similar tangled growth. **3.** *U.S. Slang* A camp for hoboes. [< Hind. *jangal* forest] —**jun′gly** *adj.*

jun·ior (jōōn′yər) *adj.* **1.** Younger in years or lower in rank. **2.** Denoting the younger of two. **3.** Belonging to youth or earlier life. **4.** Later in effect or tenure. **5.** Pertaining to the third year of a high-school or collegiate course of four years. —*n.* **1.** The younger of two. **2.** One later or lower in service or standing. **3.** A student in the third or junior year. Abbr. *jr., Jr.* [< L *junior,* compar. of *juvenis* young]

junior college A school giving college courses up to and including the sophomore year.

junior high school A school intermediate between grammar school and high school, in the U.S. typically comprising grades 7 and 8, and sometimes grade 9.

Junior League A local branch of the Association of the Junior Leagues of America, Inc., composed of young society women engaged in volunteer welfare work.

ju·ni·per (jōō′nə·pər) *n.* **1.** An evergreen pinaceous shrub of Europe and America. **2.** The dark blue berry of this shrub, used in making gin and as a diuretic. [< L *juniperus*]

junk[1] (jungk) *n.* **1.** Castoff material, as scrap iron, old bottles, or paper. **2.** *Informal* Worthless matter; rubbish; trash. **3.** *Slang* Narcotics; dope. **4.** *Naut.* Old cable or cordage used for making gaskets, oakum, etc. —*v.t. Informal* To discard as trash; scrap. [ME *jonke*]

junk[2] (jungk) *n.* A large Chinese vessel with high poop, prominent stem, and battened lugsails. [< Sp. and Pg. *junco* < Malay *djong* ship]

CHINESE JUNK

Jun·ker (yōōng′kər) *n.* One of the landed aristocracy of Prussia. [< G *jung* young + *herr* master] —**Jun′·ker·dom** *n.* —**Jun′ker·ism** *n.*

jun·ket (jung′kit) *n.* **1.** A feast, banquet, picnic, or pleasure trip. **2.** *U.S.* A trip taken by a public official with all expenses paid from public funds. **3.** A delicacy made of curds or of sweetened milk and rennet. —*v.i.* **1.** To have a feast; banquet. **2.** *U.S.* To go on a trip, esp. at public expense. — *v.t.* **3.** To entertain by feasting; regale. [< It. < L *juncus* rush] —**jun′ket·er** *n.*

junk·ie (jung′kē) *n. Slang* A dope addict. Also **junk′y.**

junk·man (jungk′man′) *n. pl.* **·men** (-men′) One who purchases, collects, and sells junk. Also **junk′deal′er** (-dē′lər).

Ju·no (jōō′nō) In Roman mythology, the wife of Jupiter, queen of the gods and goddess of marriage: identified with the Greek *Hera.* —*n.* A woman of queenly beauty.

Ju·no·esque (jōō′nō·esk′) *adj.* Stately and beautiful.

jun·ta (jun′tə, *Sp.* hōōn′tä) *n.* **1.** A Central or South American legislative council. **2.** A body of men engaged in secret, usu. political intrigue: also **jun′to** (-tō). [< Sp. < L *jungere* to join]

Ju·pi·ter (jōō′pə·tər) In Roman mythology, the god ruling over all other gods and all men: identified with the Greek *Zeus*: also called *Jove*. — *n.* The largest planet of the solar system, fifth in order from the sun. See PLANET.

Ju·ras·sic (jo͝o·ras′ik) *Geol. adj.* Of or pertaining to a period of the Mesozoic era succeeding the Triassic and followed by the Cretaceous. See chart for GEOLOGY. — *n.* The Jurassic period or rock system. [< F *jurassique*, after *Jura*]

ju·rid·i·cal (jo͝o·rid′i·kəl) *adj.* Pertaining to the law and to the administration of justice. Also **ju·rid′ic.** [< L *juris* law + *dicere* to say, speak] —**ju·rid′i·cal·ly** *adv.*

ju·ris·dic·tion (jo͝or′is·dik′shən) *n.* **1.** Lawful right to exercise authority, whether executive, legislative, or judicial. **2.** Those things over which such authority may be exercised. **3.** Power in general; authority. [< OF < L *juris* law + *dicere* to say, speak] —**ju′ris·dic′tion·al** *adj.*

ju·ris·pru·dence (jo͝or′is·pro͞od′ns) *n.* **1.** The philosophy or science of law. **2.** A system of laws. [< L *juris* law + *prudentia* knowledge] —**ju′ris·pru·den′tial** (-pro͞o·den′·shəl) *adj.*

ju·ris·pru·dent (jo͝or′is·pro͞od′nt) *adj.* Skilled in the law. — *n.* One skilled in the law.

ju·rist (jo͝or′ist) *n.* One versed in the law.

ju·ris·tic (jo͝o·ris′tik) *adj.* Of or pertaining to a jurist or the profession of law. Also **ju·ris′ti·cal.** —**ju·ris′ti·cal·ly** *adv.*

ju·ror (jo͝or′ər) *n.* **1.** One who serves on a jury. **2.** One who takes an oath. [< AF < L *jurare* to swear]

ju·ry[1] (jo͝or′ē) *n. pl.* **·ries 1.** A body of legally qualified persons summoned to serve on a judicial tribunal and give a verdict according to the evidence. See GRAND JURY, PETIT JURY. **2.** A committee of award in a competition. [< AF < L *jurare* to swear]

ju·ry[2] (jo͝or′ē) *adj. Naut.* Rigged up temporarily: a *jury* mast. [Prob. < OF *ajurie* aid < L *adjutare* to help]

ju·ry·man (jo͝or′ē·mən) *n. pl.* **·men** (-mən) A juror.

just[1] (just) *adj.* **1.** Fair and impartial in acting or judging. **2.** Upright; honest. **3.** Legally valid; legitimate. **4.** Merited; deserved. **5.** True; correct; accurate. **6.** Fitting; proper. **7.** *Archaic* Righteous in the sight of God. — *adv.* **1.** To the exact point; precisely: *just* right. **2.** Exactly now: He is *just* leaving. **3.** A moment ago: He *just* left. **4.** By very little; barely: It *just* missed. **5.** Only; merely: *just* a layman. **6.** *Informal* Simply; really; very: It's *just* lovely. [< OF < L *jus* law] —**just′ly** *adv.* —**just′ness** *n.*

just[2] (just) See JOUST.

jus·tice (jus′tis) *n.* **1.** The quality of being just. **2.** The rendering of what is due or merited; also, that which is due or merited. **3.** Conformity to the law. **4.** The administration of law. **5.** A judge. **6.** *Theol.* An attribute of God, and of his laws and judgments. **7.** The abstract principle by which right and wrong are defined. — **Department of Justice** An executive department of the U.S. government, headed by the Attorney General, that represents the governm in legal matters, enforces antitrust laws, civil rights la etc., and supervises internal security and immigration. — **to bring to justice** To arrest and try (a wrongdoer). — **do justice to** To show appreciation of. [See JUST[1].]

justice of the peace A local magistrate of limited juris tion with authority to fine and imprison in minor cases, c mit to a higher court, perform marriages, etc.

jus·ti·fi·a·ble (jus′tə·fī′ə·bəl) *adj.* Capable of being ju fied; defensible. —**jus′ti·fi′a·bil′i·ty, jus′ti·fi′a·ble·ness** —**jus′ti·fi′a·bly** *adv.*

jus·ti·fi·ca·tion (jus′tə·fə·kā′shən) *n.* **1.** The act of ju fying, or the state of being justified. **2.** The ground of ju fying, or that which justifies. —**jus′ti·fi·ca′tive** *adj.*

jus·ti·fi·er (jus′tə·fī′ər) *n.* One who justifies.

jus·ti·fy (jus′tə·fī) *v.* **·fied, ·fy·ing** *v.t.* **1.** To show t just, right, or reasonable; vindicate. **2.** To declare g less; absolve. **3.** To provide adequate grounds for; warr **4.** *Printing* To adjust (lines) to the proper length by spac — *v.i.* **5.** *Printing* To be properly spaced; fit. [< OF < L *justus* just + *facere* to make]

jus·tle (jus′əl) See JOSTLE.

jut (jut) *v.i.* **jut·ted, jut·ting** To extend beyond the main p tion; protrude; project: often with *out*. — *n.* Anything t juts; a projection. [Var. of JET[2]]

jute (jo͞ot) *n.* **1.** A tall annual Asian herb of the linden f ily. **2.** The tough fiber obtained from the inner bark of t plant, used for bags, cordage, etc. [< Bengali < Skt. *j* braid of hair]

Jute (jo͞ot) *n.* A member of a Germanic tribe, some of wh invaded Britain in the fifth century. [< LL *Jutae* the Jut — **Jut·ish** (jo͞o′tish) *adj.*

ju·ve·nes·cent (jo͞o′və·nes′ənt) *adj.* **1.** Becoming you growing young again. **2.** Making young; rejuvenating. L *juvenescere* to grow younger] —**ju′ve·nes′cence** *n.*

ju·ve·nile (jo͞o′və·nəl, -nīl) *adj.* **1.** Young; youthful; a immature. **2.** Designed for young persons: *juvenile* boo — *n.* **1.** A young person. **2.** An actor of youthful roles. A book for young persons. [< L *juvenis* young person] **ju′ve·nile·ly** *adv.* —**ju′ve·nile·ness, ju′ve·nil′i·ty** *n.*

juvenile court A court that has jurisdiction in cases volving dependent, neglected, and delinquent children.

juvenile delinquent One who is guilty of antisocial havior or of violations of the law, but is too young to be pu ished as an adult criminal. —**juvenile delinquency**

ju·ve·nil·i·a (jo͞o′və·nil′ē·ə, -nil′yə) *n.pl.* Works produ in youth, esp. writings or paintings.

juxta- *prefix* Near; next to. [< L *juxta* near]

jux·ta·pose (juks′tə·pōz′) *v.t.* **·posed, ·pos·ing** To pla together; put side by side. [< F < L *juxta* near + *po* to put down] —**jux·ta·po·si·tion** (juks′tə·pə·zish′ən) *n.*

K

k, K (kā) *n. pl.* **k's** or **ks, K's** or **Ks, kays** (kāz) **1.** The eleventh letter of the English alphabet. **2.** The sound represented by the letter. It normally has no phonetic value when initial before *n*, as in *knee, knight, know*, etc. — *symbol Chem.* Potassium (K for *kalium*).

Ka·a·ba (kä′ə·bə, kä′bə) *n.* The Moslem shrine at Mecca enclosing a sacred black stone, supposedly given to Abraham by the angel Gabriel, toward which worshipers face when praying: also spelled *Caaba*. [< Arabic *ka'b* cube]

kab·a·la (kab′ə·lə, kə·bä′lə), **kab·ba·la** See CABALA.

ka·bu·ki (kä·bo͞o′kē) *n.* A form of Japanese play on popular or comic themes, employing elaborate costume, stylized gesture, music, and dancing. [< Japanese]

Kad·dish (kä′dish) *n.* In Judaism, a prayer recited by mourners and part of the daily service. [< Aramaic, holy]

kaf·fee·klatsch (kôf′ē·kläch′, *Ger.* käf′ā·kläch′) *n. Sometimes cap.* An informal conversational gathering where coffee is drunk. [< G < *kaffee* coffee + *klatsch* chitchat]

kaf·fir (kaf′ər) *n.* A variety of sorghum grown in dry regions as a grain and forage plant. Also **kaffir corn.** [after *Kaffir*]

Kaf·fir (kaf′ər) *n.* **1.** A member of a powerful group of South African Bantu tribes. **2.** Xhosa, the language of these tribes. Also **Kaf′ir.** [< Arabic *kāfir* unbeliever]

kaf·tan (kaf′tən, käf·tän′) See CAFTAN.

kai·ak (kī′ak) See KAYAK.

kai·ser (kī′zər) *n.* Emperor. [< G < L *Caesar* Caesar]

Kai·ser (kī′zər) Title of the emperors of the Holy Roma Empire, 962–1806; the Austrian emperors, 1804–1918; ar the German emperors, 1871–1918.

kale (kāl) *n.* **1.** A variety of headless cabbage. **2.** *U. Slang* Money. [Var. of COLE]

ka·lei·do·scope (kə·lī′də·skōp) *n.* **1.** A tube-shaped optic toy that shows constantly changing symmetrical patter as loose bits of colored glass are moved about under a set mirrors. **2.** A swiftly changing scene, pattern, etc. [< G *kalos* beautiful + *eidos* form + -SCOPE]

ka·lei·do·scop·ic (kə·lī′də·skop′ik) *adj.* **1.** Of or pertainin to a kaleidoscope. **2.** Rapidly changing and intricate. Al **ka·lei′do·scop′i·cal.** —**ka·lei′do·scop′i·cal·ly** *adv.*

kal·ends (kal′əndz) See CALENDS.

ka·lif (kā′lif, kal′if), **ka·liph** See CALIPH.

Kal·muck (kal′muk) *n.* **1.** A member of one of the Bu dhistic Mongol tribes inhabiting a region extending fro western China to the Volga river. **2.** The Mongolian lar guage of these tribes. Also **Kal′muk, Kal·myk** (kal′mik).

kal·so·mine (kal′sə·mīn) See CALCIMINE.

kan·ga·roo (kang′gə·ro͞o′) *n. pl.* **·roos** A herbivorous ma supial of Australia and Tasmania, having short, weak fore limbs, stout tails, and powerful hind limbs adapted fo leaping. [< Australian]

kangaroo court *U.S.* An unauthorized court in whic the law is disregarded or willfully misinterpreted.

garoo rat A pouched rodent of the SW U.S. and xico having elongated hind limbs and tail.
t·i·an (kan′tē·ən) *adj.* Of or pertaining to Kant or his losophy. — *n.* A follower of Kantianism.
t·i·an·ism (kan′tē·ən·iz′əm) *n.* The philosophy of Imnuel Kant, stating that man experiences the material ld through sense perception, but its reality is determined mental forms and categories. Also **Kant′ism.**
·lin (kā′ə·lin) *n.* A claylike hydrous aluminum silicate d in making porcelain. Also **ka′o·line** (-lin). [< F < nese *Kao-ling* mountain where first mined]
ok (kā′pok) *n.* A cottony or silky fiber covering the ds of the kapok tree, used for mattresses, life preservers, ılation material, etc. [< Malay *kāpoq*]
ok tree A tropical tree having seeds covered with silky r. Also called *silk-cotton tree.*
·pa (kap′ə) *n.* The tenth letter in the Greek alphabet κ), corresponding to the English *k.* See ALPHABET.
ut (kä·pŏŏt′) *adj. Slang* Ruined; done for. [< G]
a·kul (kar′ə·kəl) *n.* **1.** A breed of sheep raised in the iet Union, Iran, Iraq, etc. **2.** The black or gray, loosely led fur made from the pelt of the karakul lamb. Also lled *caracul.* [after *Kara Kul,* a lake in Bukhara]
·at (kar′ət) *n.* **1.** The twenty-fourth part by weight of d in an article: 18-*karat* gold has 18/24 or 3/4 gold by weight. Loosely, a carat. [Var. of CARAT]
ra·te (kä·rä′tā, -tē) *n.* An Oriental method of hand-to-ıd combat utilizing a variety of sudden, forceful blows, as h the side of the hand or the fingertips. [< Japanese]
·roo (kə·rōō′, ka-) *n. pl.* **·roos** A dry plateau or tabled of South Africa. Also **ka·roo′.** [< Hottentot]
yo- *combining form Biol.* Nucleus: also spelled *caryo-.* so, before vowels, **kary-.** [< Gk. *karyon* nut]
·y·o·tin (kar′ē·ō′tin) *n. Biol.* Chromatin.
s·bah (käz′bä) See CASBAH.
sh·mi·ri (kash·mir′ē) *n.* The Indic language of the shmirians.
sh·mi·ri·an (kash·mir′ē·ən) *adj.* Of or pertaining to ıshmir or its people. — *n.* A native of Kashmir.
a See CATA-.
al·y·sis (kə·tal′ə·sis) See CATALYSIS.
thar·sis (kə·thär′sis) See CATHARSIS.
h·ode (kath′ōd) See CATHODE.
·i·on (kat′ī′ən) See CATION.
ty·did (kā′tē·did) *n.* A green, arboreal insect allied to e grasshoppers and crickets. [Imit., from sound produced the males]
ı·ri (kou′rē) *n.* **1.** A large timber tree of New Zealand. Its wood. **3.** Kauri gum. Also **kau′ry.** [< Maori]
uri gum A resinous exudation of the kauri tree, used in rnishes, for linoleum, etc. Also **kauri copal, kauri resin.**
y·ak (kī′ak) *n. U.S. & Canadian* The hunting canoe of ctic America, made of seal skins stretched over a frame, th a hole amidships where the user sits. [< Eskimo]
y·o (kā′ō) *Slang v.t.* **kay·oed, kay·o·ing** In boxing, to ıock out. — *n.* In boxing, a knockout. Also **K.O., KO, o.** [< *k*(*nock*) *o*(*ut*)]
dge (kej) *Naut. n.* A light anchor used in warping, freeg a vessel from shoals, etc.: also **kedge anchor.** — *v.* **edged, kedg·ing** *v.i.* **1.** To move a vessel by hauling up to kedge that has been dropped at a distance. **2.** Of a vessel, be moved in this way. — *v.t.* **3.** To move (a vessel) in is way. [Origin uncertain]
el (kēl) *n.* **1.** *Naut.* The main structural member of a essel, running fore and aft along the bottom, to which all e crosswise members are solidly fixed; the backbone of a ip. **2.** A ship. **3.** Any part or object resembling a keel in ape or function. **4.** *Aeron.* **a** A vertical fin extending ngitudinally at the bottom of an airship. **b** The center botm of an airplane fuselage. **5.** *Biol.* A longitudinal ridge or rocess, as of the breastbone of a fowl. — **on an even keel** n equilibrium; steady. — *v.t. & v.i.* To turn over with the eel uppermost; capsize. — **to keel over 1.** To turn botm up; capsize. **2.** To fall over or be felled, as from an inry. [< ON *kjölr* or OHG *kiol*]
el·haul (kēl′hôl′) *v.t.* **1.** *Naut.* To haul (a man) under he keel of a ship as punishment. **2.** To reprove severely; astigate. Also **keel·hale** (kēl′hāl′). [< Du. *kielhalen*]
el·son (kēl′sən) *n. Naut.* A beam running above the eel of a ship: also spelled *kelson.* [Akin to KEEL]
en[1] (kēn) *adj.* **1.** Able to cut or penetrate readily; very harp. **2.** Having mental acuteness, refined perception, etc. . Manifesting intense absorption or eagerness: a *keen* inerest. **4.** Of senses or sense organs, having great acuity and ensitivity. **5.** Having a piercing, intense quality or impact. . Eager; enthusiastic: with *about, for, on,* or an infinitive. . *U.S. Slang* Fine; excellent. [ME < OE *cēne*] — **keen′ly** dv. — **keen′ness** *n.*

keen[2] (kēn) *n.* A wailing lamentation for the dead. — *v.i.* To wail loudly over the dead. [< Irish *caoinim* I wail] — **keen′er** *n.*
keep (kēp) *v.* **kept, keep·ing** *v.t.* **1.** To retain possession or control of; avoid releasing or giving away: to *keep* one's earnings; to *keep* a secret. **2.** To hold or continue to hold in some specified state, relation, place, etc.: *Keep* your hands off; *Keep* the car in repair. **3.** To store, hold, or confine in a regular place. **4.** To maintain: to *keep* the peace. **5.** To be faithful to or abide by (a promise, vow, etc.). **6.** To do the required work of; manage: to *keep* house. **7.** To defend from harm. **8.** To care for; tend: to *keep* the flocks. **9.** To detain. **10.** To prevent: with *from.* **11.** To observe, as with rites or ceremony: to *keep* the Sabbath. **12.** To be the support of; maintain in food, clothing, etc. **13.** To write down and preserve in good order: to *keep* a diary. **14.** To stay in or on: *Keep* your seat. **15.** To have regularly for sale. **16.** To maintain for use or employ for service: to *keep* a butler. **17.** To preserve in good condition, as foods. — *v.i.* **18.** To persist in; continue: often with *on:* to *keep* on working. **19.** To remain; stay: *Keep* away; *Keep* indoors. **20.** To stay in good condition. **21.** To remain good for a later time: The news will *keep.* — **to keep back 1.** To restrain. **2.** To withhold. — **to keep in with** *Informal* To remain in the good graces of. — **to keep to oneself 1.** To remain solitary. **2.** To avoid revealing. — **to keep track of** (or **tabs on**) To continue to be informed about. — **to keep up 1.** To hold the pace. **2.** To maintain in good condition. **3.** To cause to continue: *Keep up* the good work. **4.** To cause to stay awake or out of bed. — **to keep up with** To stay abreast of (someone or something). — *n.* **1.** Means of subsistence: to earn one's *keep.* **2.** Guard or custody: They are in my *keep.* **3.** The donjon or strongest building of a castle; also, a castle or fortress. — **for keeps 1.** Very seriously; not for mere amusement. **2.** Permanently. [OE *cēpan* to observe]
keep·er (kē′pər) *n.* **1.** One who keeps or guards; as: **a** A guardian or protector. **b** The overseer of a prison. **c** The caretaker of a wild animal. **2.** One in charge of (a specified place, thing, etc.): used in combination: *gatekeeper.*
keep·ing (kē′ping) *n.* **1.** The act of one who keeps. **2.** Custody, charge, or possession. **3.** Maintenance; support. — **in keeping** (**with**) In right relation or proportion (to).
keep·sake (kēp′sāk′) *n.* Anything kept, or given to be kept, for the sake of the giver; a memento.
keg (keg) *n.* A small, strong barrel, usu. holding 5 to 10 gallons. [ME *cag,* prob. < ON *kaggi*]
keg·ler (keg′lər) *n. Informal* A bowler. [< G *kegel* ninepin]
kelp (kelp) *n.* **1.** Any of various large, coarse, brown algae; esp., the **giant kelp,** found mainly on the Pacific coast. **2.** The ashes of such algae, a source of iodine. [ME *culp*]
kel·pie (kel′pē) *n. Scot.* A water sprite in the form of a horse, supposed to be an omen of drowning. Also **kel′py.**
kel·son (kel′sən) See KEELSON.
Kelt (kelt), **Kelt·ic** (kel′tik) See CELT, CELTIC.
Kelvin scale (kel′vin) *Physics* The absolute scale of temperature, in which zero is equal to −273° Celsius or −459.4° Fahrenheit. [after William Thompson, 1824–1907, Lord *Kelvin,* English physicist]
ken (ken) *v.* **kenned** or **kent, ken·ning** *v.t.* **1.** *Scot.* To know. **2.** *Archaic* To see. — *v.i.* **3.** *Scot. & Brit. Dial.* To have knowledge or understanding. — *n.* Range of sight or knowledge. [OE *cennan,* infl. by ON *kenna*]
ken·nel (ken′əl) *n.* **1.** A house for a dog or for a pack of hounds. **2.** *Often pl.* An establishment where dogs are bred for sale, boarded, trained, etc. **3.** A pack of hounds. **4.** The hole or lair of a fox or like beast. **5.** A vile lodging. — *v.* **ken·neled** or **·nelled, ken·nel·ing** or **·nel·ling** — *v.t.* **1.** To keep or confine in or as in a kennel. — *v.i.* **2.** To lodge or take shelter in a kennel. [< MF < L *canis* dog]
Ken·nel·ly-Heav·i·side layer (ken′əl·ē·hev′ē·sīd) The Heaviside layer.
ken·o·tron (ken′ə·tron) *n. Electronics* A two-electrode electron tube used as a rectifier. [< Gk. *kenōsis* an emptying + (ELEC)TRON]
kept (kept) Past tense and past participle of KEEP.
ker·a·tin (ker′ə·tin) *n. Biochem.* An albuminous compound that forms the essential ingredient of horny tissue, as of horns, claws, and nails. — **ke·rat·i·nous** (kə·rat′ə·nəs) *adj.* [< Gk. *keras, -atos* horn + -IN]
ker·a·ti·tis (ker′ə·tī′tis) *n. Pathol.* Inflammation of the cornea.
kerb (kûrb) *n. Brit.* Curb (def. 2).
ker·chief (kûr′chif) *n.* A square of fabric used to cover the head or neck, or as a handkerchief. [ME < OF < *covrir* to cover + *chef* head]
ker·mes (kûr′mēz) *n.* The dried bodies of the females of a scale insect, used as a red dyestuff. [< Arabic *qirmiz*]
ker·mis (kûr′mis) *n.* **1.** In Flanders, etc., a periodical out-

door festival. **2.** An indoor or outdoor festival imitative of this. [< Du < *kerk* church + *miss* mass]

kern (kûrn) *Printing n.* The part of the face of a type that projects beyond the shaft or shank. — *v.t.* To form (type) with a kern. [< F < L *cardo, -inis* hinge]

ker·nel (kûr′nəl) *n.* **1.** The entire contents of a seed or grain within its coating. **2.** The edible part of a nut. **3.** The central part of anything; nucleus; gist. — *v.i.* **ker·neled** or **·nelled, ker·nel·ing** or **·nel·ling** To envelop as a kernel. [OE *cyrnel*, dim. of *corn* seed]

ker·o·sene (ker′ə·sēn, ker′ə·sēn′) *n.* A mixture of hydrocarbons distilled from crude petroleum and used for burning in lamps, stoves, and some engines: also called *coal oil.* Also **ker·o·sine** (ker′ə·sēn, ker′ə·sēn′). [< Gk. *kēros* wax + -ENE]

ker·sey (kûr′zē) *n.* A coarse, ribbed, closely napped woolen cloth. [after *Kersey*, village in Suffolk, England]

kes·trel (kes′trəl) *n.* A European falcon resembling the American sparrow hawk. [ME < OF *cresserelle*]

ketch (kech) *n.* A fore-and-aft rigged, two-masted vessel similar to a yawl but having the mizzen or jiggermast forward of the rudder post. [ME *cache*, prob. < CATCH, v., because used as a pursuit vessel]

ketch·up (kech′əp) *n.* A spicy sauce or condiment for meat, fish, etc., of which the base is tomatoes, or sometimes mushrooms or walnuts: also spelled *catchup, catsup.* [< Malay *kĕchap*, ? ult. < Chinese *ke-tsiap* brine of pickled fish]

ke·tone (kē′tōn) *n. Chem.* One of a class of organic compounds in which the carbonyl radical unites with two hydrocarbon radicals. The simplest member is acetone. [< G, var. of F *acétone* acetone] — **ke·ton·ic** (ki·ton′ik) *adj.*

ket·tle (ket′l) *n.* **1.** A metallic vessel for boiling or stewing. **2.** A teakettle. **3.** A kettle-shaped cavity, as in rock or glacial drift: also **kettle hole. 4.** A kettledrum. — **kettle of fish** A trying or difficult situation. [OE < L *catillus*, dim. of *catinus* a deep vessel]

ket·tle·drum (ket′l·drum′) *n.* A large drum having a brass hemispherical shell and a parchment head that can be tuned through a small range of definite pitches; timpano.

Kew·pie (kyōō′pē) *n.* A chubby, cherubic doll, made of plastic, etc.: a trade name. Also **kew′pie doll.**

key[1] (kē) *n. pl.* **keys 1.** An instrument for moving the bolt or tumblers of a lock in order to lock or unlock. **2.** An instrument for holding and turning a screw, nut, valve, or the like, as for winding a clock. **3.** Anything serving to disclose, open, or solve something. **4.** Something that opens or prepares a way: the *key* to the situation. **5.** A gloss, table, or group of notes interpreting certain symbols, ciphers, problems, etc. **6.** Any one of the finger levers in typewriters, computers, etc. **7.** *Telecom.* A circuit breaker or opener operated by the fingers, as in a telegraph or radiotelegraph sending apparatus. **8.** *Music* **a** In musical instruments, a lever to be pressed by the finger or thumb. **b** A system of tones in which a piece of music is written or performed, where all the tones bear a definite relationship to some specific tone (the keynote or tonic): the *key* of C. **9.** The tone or pitch of the voice. **10.** Level of intensity of expression, feeling, or artistic execution: He writes in a high *key.* **11.** *Mech.* **a** A wedge, cotter, bolt, or pin used to secure various parts. **b** One of various instruments for fixing a collar to a shaft. **12.** *Archit.* A keystone. **13.** *Bot.* A key fruit. — *v.t.* **keyed, key·ing 1.** To fasten with or as with a key. **2.** To wedge tightly or support firmly with a key, wedge, etc. **3.** To complete (an arch) by adding the keystone. **4.** To provide with a key or keys. **5.** To provide with a cross-reference or a system of cross-references. **6.** To provide with a solution. **7.** *Music* To regulate the pitch or tone of. — **to key up** To cause excitement, expectancy, etc., in. — *adj.* Of chief and decisive importance: a *key* figure. [OE *cǣg*]

key[2] (kē) *n. pl.* **keys** A low island, esp. one of coral, along a coast; cay. [< Sp. < Taino, islet]

key·board (kē′bôrd′, -bōrd′) *n.* A row or rows of keys as in a piano or typewriter.

key·hole (kē′hōl′) *n.* A hole for a key, as in a door or lock.

key·note (kē′nōt′) *n.* **1.** The basic idea or principle of a philosophy, political platform, literary work, etc. **2.** *Music* The tonic of a key, from which it is named: also **key tone.** — *v.t.* **·not·ed, ·not·ing** To sound the keynote of.

keynote address *U.S.* An opening address, esp. at a political convention, presenting the basic issues and partisan principles. Also **keynote speech.**

key plug The part of a cylinder lock that receives the key. For illus. see LOCK.

key signature *Music* The sharps or flats following the clef sign at the beginning of each staff, placed so as to apply to specific tones whenever they occur.

key·stone (kē′stōn′) *n.* **1.** *Archit.* The uppermost and last-set stone of an arch, that completes it and locks its members together. **2.** The fundamental element, as of a science.

Keystone State Nickname of Pennsylvania.

khak·i (kak′ē, kä′kē; *in Canada, often* kär′kē) *n. pl.* **khak·is 1.** A color ranging from light sand to medium brown. **2.** A stout cotton cloth of this color used for uniforms. 3 A uniform made of khaki. — *adj.* Of the color khaki. Hind. < Persian *khāk* dust]

kha·lif (kā′lif, kal′if) See CALIPH.

khan (kän, kan) *n.* **1.** The title of the imperial succe to the Mongol conqueror Genghis Khan. **2.** A title for ers, officials, or dignitaries in Central Asia, Iran, etc. Turkic *khān* lord, prince] — **khan′ate** (-āt) *n.*

kib·butz (ki·bŏŏts′) *n. pl.* **·but·zim** (-bŏŏt·sēm′) A coop tive or collective farm in Israel. [< Hebrew, gathering]

kib·itz (kib′its) *v.i. Informal* To act as a kibitzer. [formation < KIBITZER]

kib·itz·er (kib′it·sər) *n. Informal* One who meddles in affairs of others; esp., a spectator who gives gratuitous vice to card players. [< Yiddish < G *kiebitzen* to look

kick (kik) *v.i.* **1.** To strike out with the foot or feet, swimming, propelling a ball, etc. **2.** To strike out habitu with the foot, hooves, etc. **3.** Of firearms, to recoil. **4** football, to punt, try for an extra point or field goal by k ing, etc. **5.** *U.S. Informal* To object or complain. — **6.** To strike with the foot. **7.** To drive or impel by stri with the foot. **8.** In football, to score (an extra point field goal) by kicking the ball. **9.** Of firearms, to strik recoiling. — **to kick around** *U.S. Informal* **1.** To ab neglect. **2.** To roam from place to place. **3.** To thought to; discuss. — **to kick back 1.** To recoil viole or unexpectedly, as a gun. **2.** *U.S. Slang* To pay back (of a salary, fee, etc.) to someone in a position to grant fav usu. as a bribe. — **to kick in** *U.S. Informal* To contrib or participate by contributing. — **to kick off 1.** In footb to put the ball in play by kicking it toward the oppo team. **2.** *U.S. Slang* To die. — **to kick out** *U.S. Infor* To exclude or eject violently or suddenly, as with a kick. **to kick the bucket** *Slang* To die. — **to kick up** *U.S. Sl* To make or stir up (trouble, confusion, etc.). — *n.* **1** blow or thrust with the foot. **2.** *U.S. Informal* An objec or complaint. **3.** *U.S. Slang* Power to stimulate, excite intoxicate: whisky with a *kick.* **4.** *U.S. Slang* A pleas and exciting sensation; thrill. **5.** *U.S. Slang* Energy; p **6.** The recoil of a firearm. **7.** In football, a kicking of the b esp., a punt. [ME *kike*] — **kick′er** *n.*

kick·back (kik′bak′) *n.* **1.** *Informal* A strong reaction; coil; repercussion. **2.** *U.S. Slang* A paying back of part salary, fee, etc., also, the money so paid.

kick·off (kik′ôf′, -of′) *n.* **1.** In football, the kick with wh play is begun. **2.** Any beginning: the *kickoff* of a politi campaign.

kid (kid) *n.* **1.** A young goat. **2.** Leather made from skin of a kid. **3.** *pl.* Gloves or shoes made of kidskin. The meat of a young goat. **5.** *Informal* A child; youngs — *adj. Informal* Younger: my *kid* brother. — *v.t.* & **kid·ded, kid·ding 1.** *Slang* To make fun of (someone); tease. **2.** *Slang* To deceive or try to deceive (someone); f **3.** Of a goat, to give birth. [ME < ON *kith*] — **kid′de**

kid·dy (kid′ē) *n. pl.* **·dies** *Slang* A small child. Also **kid′**

kid glove A glove made of kidskin or similar material. **to handle with kid gloves** To treat tactfully or gingerly.

kid·nap (kid′nap) *v.t.* **kid·naped** or **·napped, kid·nap·ing ·nap·ping 1.** To seize and carry off (someone) by force fraud, usu. so as to demand a ransom. **2.** To steal (a chil [< KID (def. 5) + *nap*, dial. var. of NAB] — **kid′nap·er kid′nap·per** *n.*

kid·ney (kid′nē) *n. pl.* **·neys 1.** *Anat.* Either of two gl dular organs situated at the back of the abdominal cavity close to the spinal column in vertebrates, serving to separate waste products from the blood and to excrete them as urine. ◆ Collateral adjective: *renal.* **2.** The meat of the kidney of certain animals, used as food. **3.** Temperament, nature, or type: a man of my own *kidney.* [Origin unknown]

HUMAN KIDNE
a Pyramid. *b* Papillae. *c* Cortex. *d* Ur ter. *e* Pelvis.

kidney bean 1. A kidney-shaped bean. **2.** The bean of the scarlet runner.

kidney stone *Pathol.* A hard mineral concretion formed in the kidney; renal calculus.

kid·skin (kid′skin′) *n.* Leather tanned from the skin of a young goat, used for gloves, shoes, etc.

kill[1] (kil) *v.t.* **1.** To cause the death of. **2.** To slaughter for food; butcher. **3.** To bring to an end; d stroy. **4.** *U.S. Slang* To make a strong emotional impressi upon, as of amusement. **5.** To destroy the active qualiti of; neutralize. **6.** To cancel by contrast, as a color. **7.** printing, to delete. **8.** To turn off or stop (a motor, live c cuit, etc.). **9.** To pass (time) aimlessly. **10.** To veto quash (legislation). — *v.i.* **11.** To cause death. **12.** murder; slay. **13.** To undergo death; die. — *n.* **1.** T act of killing, esp. in hunting. **2.** An animal or anima killed as prey. [ME *cullen, killen*]

-Syn. (verb) 1. *Kill* is the general term applicable to all or-isms, and frequently extended to inanimate things: frost *killed* buds, to *kill* a story. *Murder, assassinate,* and *execute* are said of persons. *Murder* refers to a deliberate, often premeditated, ng; *assassinate* is often applied to political killings. *Execute* rs to the carrying out of a legal sentence of death.
(kil) *n.* A creek, stream, or channel: an element in geo-phical names: *Schuylkill.* [< Du. < MDu. *kille*]
deer (kil′dir) *n. pl.* **·deers** or **·deer** A North American ing bird of the plover family, having a loud cry. Also **′dee** (-dē). [Imit., from its cry]
er (kil′ər) *n.* One who or that which kills.
r whale A voracious whale related to the dolphins.
ing (kil′ing) *n.* **1.** Homicide. **2.** The act of one who hat which kills. **—to make a killing** To get or win a e amount of money. **—***adj.* **1.** Used to kill. **2.** Likely ill. **3.** Resulting in death; fatal.
joy (kil′joi′) *n.* One who spoils pleasure for others.
(kil, kiln) *n.* An oven or furnace for baking, burning, or ing bricks, pottery, etc. [OE < L *culina* kitchen]
(kil′ō, kē′lō) *n. pl.* **kil·os** **1.** A kilogram. **2.** A kilo-er.
- *prefix* In the metric system, a thousand times (a speci-unit): *kilogram.* [< F < Gk. *chilioi* a thousand]
·cy·cle (kil′ə·sī′kəl) *n.* **1.** *Telecom.* A unit of electro-gnetic wave frequency of 1,000 cycles per second. **2.** thousand cycles. Abbr. *kc, kc.*
·gram (kil′ə·gram) *n.* In the metric system, a thou-d grams. Also **kil′o·gramme.** [< F *kilogramme*] Abbr. *K., kg, kg., kilo.* See table front of book.
·gram-me·ter (kil′ə·gram·mē′tər) *n.* A unit of work, equivalent of the force expended in raising a mass of one gram one meter against gravity, about 7.2 foot-pounds.
o·li·ter (kil′ə·lē′tər) *n.* In the metric system, a thousand rs. Abbr. *kl, kl.* See table front of book.
o·me·ter (kil′ə·mē′tər, ki·lom′ə·tər) *n.* In the metric tem, a thousand meters. Abbr. *km, km., kilo.* See table nt of book. **— kil′o·met·ric** or **·ri·cal** *adj.*
o·ton (kil′ə·tun′) *n.* **1.** A weight of 1,000 tons. **2.** A unit uivalent to the explosive power of 1,000 tons of TNT.
o·watt (kil′ə·wät) *n.* *Electr.* A unit of power equal to 00 watts. Abbr. *kw, kw.*
o·watt-hour (kil′ə·wät·our′) *n.* The work done or the rgy resulting from one kilowatt acting for one hour, equal approximately 1.34 horsepower-hours.
(kilt) *n.* A short pleated skirt worn by ottish Highland men and Irishmen. **—***v.t.* make broad, vertical pleats in; pleat. [ME; ob. < Scand.] **— kilt′ing** *n.*

KILT
a Tartan.
b Kilt.
c Sporran.
d Brooch.

ter (kil′tər) *n.* *Informal* Proper or working der: now only in the phrase **out of kilter,** out order. [Origin uncertain]
no·no (kə·mō′nə, ki·mō′nō) *n. pl.* **·nos** **1.** loose robe fastened with a wide sash, worn in pan as an outer garment. **2.** A woman's neg-ee. [< Japanese]
(kin) *n.* One's relatives by blood, collec-ely; one's family. **— next of kin** In law, one's arest relative or relatives. **—***adj.* **1.** Related by blood. Similar; kindred; alike. [OE *cyn*]
n *suffix* Little; small: *lambkin.* [< MDu. *-kijn, -ken*]
d[1] (kīnd) *adj.* **1.** Gentle and considerate; goodhearted. Proceeding from goodheartedness. [OE *gecynde*]
d[2] (kīnd) *n.* **1.** A class or grouping; type. **2.** The dis-nguishing character of something: They differ in *kind.* **— kind** **1.** With a thing of the same sort: to return an insult *kind.* **2.** In produce instead of money: to pay taxes *in nd.* **— kind of** *Informal* In a way; somewhat. **— of a nd** Inferior in quality. [OE *gecynd*]
·der·gar·ten (kin′dər·gär′tən) *n.* A school or class for ung children, usu. from the ages of four to six. [< G]
nd·heart·ed (kīnd′här′tid) *adj.* Having or showing a kind ature. **— kind′heart′ed·ly** *adv.* **— kind′heart′ed·ness** *n.*
·dle (kin′dəl) *v.* **·dled, ·dling** *v.t.* **1.** To cause to burn; nite. **2.** To excite, as the feelings. **3.** To make bright or owing as if with flame. **—***v.i.* **4.** To take fire. **5.** To be-me excited or inflamed. **6.** To become bright or glowing. ME < ON *kynda*] **— kin·dler** *n.*
n·dling (kind′ling) *n.* **1.** Sticks, wood chips, etc., with hich a fire is started. **2.** The act of one who kindles.
nd·ly (kīnd′lē) *adj.* **·i·er, ·li·est** **1.** Having or showing indness; sympathetic. **2.** Having a favorable effect. **—** *dv.* **1.** In a kind manner; good-naturedly. **2.** Enthusiasti-ally; heartily. **— to take kindly to** **1.** To accept with lik-g. **2.** To be naturally attracted to. **— kind′li·ness** *n.*
nd·ness (kīnd′nis) *n.* **1.** The quality of being kind. **2.** kind act or service; a favor. **3.** A kindly feeling.
n·dred (kin′drid) *adj.* **1.** Related by blood; akin. **2.** Having a like nature; similar. **—***n.* One's relatives by blood. [ME < OE *cynn* kin + *rǣden* condition]
kine (kīn) *n.* *Archaic* Cattle: plural of cow[1].
kin·e·mat·ics (kin′ə·mat′iks) *n.pl.* (*construed as sing.*) The branch of physics treating of motion without reference to particular forces or bodies. [< Gk. < *kineein* to move] **— kin′e·mat′ic** or **·i·cal** *adj.* **— kin′e·mat′i·cal·ly** *adv.*
kin·e·mat·o·graph (kin′ə·mat′ə·graf, -gräf) *See* CINEMATOGRAPH.
kin·e·scope (kin′ə·skōp) *n.* **1.** The cathode-ray tube of a television set, which reproduces by the action of an electron beam upon a fluorescent screen, the image impinging upon a similar tube in the television camera: also called *picture tube.* **2.** A filmed record of a television program: also **kin·e** (kin′ē).
kinesi- *combining form* A movement. [< Gk. *kinēsis* motion]
-kinesis *combining form* A movement; motion. [< Gk. *kinēsis* motion]
kin·es·the·si·a (kin′is·thē′zhə, -zhē·ə) *n.* *Physiol.* The perception of muscular movement, tension, etc., derived from the functioning of afferent nerves connected with muscle tissue, skin, joints, and tendons. Also **kin′es·the′sis** (-thē′sis). [< NL < Gk. *kineein* to move + *aisthēsis* perception] **— kin′es·thet′ic** (-thet′ik) *adj.*
ki·net·ic (ki·net′ik) *adj.* **1.** Of or pertaining to motion. **2.** Producing or caused by motion: *kinetic* energy. [< Gk. < *kineein* to move]
ki·ne·tics (ki·net′iks) *n.pl.* (*construed as sing.*) The branch of physics dealing with the effect of forces in the production or modification of motion in bodies.
kin·folk (kin′fōk′) *n.pl.* *Informal* Kinsfolk. Also **kin′·folks′.**
king (king) *n.* **1.** The sovereign male ruler of a kingdom; monarch. ◆ Collateral adjective: *regal.* **2.** One who is preeminent: a cattle *king.* **3.** A playing card bearing the likeness of a king. **4.** In chess, the principal piece, for whose defense all the moves of the other pieces are made. **5.** In checkers, a piece that, having reached the opponent's last rank of squares, is then crowned and may move in any direction. Abbr. *k., K.* [OE *cyng, cyning*]
King Arthur See ARTHUR.
king·bird (king′bûrd′) *n.* Any of various North American flycatchers.
king·bolt (king′bōlt′) *n.* A vertical central bolt usu. attaching the body of a wagon or similar vehicle to the fore axle, and serving as a pivot in turning: also called *kingpin.*
king crab **1.** The horseshoe crab. **2.** Any of a genus of usu. large crablike crustaceans common in the north Pacific, with a small, triangular body and very long legs.
king·dom (king′dəm) *n.* **1.** The territory, people, state, or realm ruled by a king or a queen; monarchy. **2.** Any place or area thought of as a sovereign domain. **3.** Any of the three primary divisions of natural objects known as the *animal, vegetable,* and *mineral kingdoms.* **4.** The spiritual dominion of God. [OE *cyningdom*]
king·fish (king′fish′) *n. pl.* **·fish** or **·fish·es** Any of various American food fishes.
king·fish·er (king′fish′ər) *n.* Any of several nonpasserine birds of world-wide distribution, that feed on fish.
King James Bible An English translation of the Bible from Hebrew and Greek, proposed by James I and completed in 1611. Also **Authorized Version.** Complete revisions were published in England in 1885 (**Revised Version**) and in the U.S. in 1901 (**American Standard Version**) and in 1952 (**Revised Standard Version**).
king·let (king′lit) *n.* **1.** A young or insignificant king. **2.** Any of several small birds, resembling the warblers.
king·ly (king′lē) *adj.* **·li·er, ·li·est** Of or worthy of a king; regal. **—***adv.* In a kingly way. **— king′li·ness** *n.*
king·pin (king′pin′) *n.* **1.** In bowling or tenpins, the foremost pin of a set arranged in order for playing. **2.** In ninepins, the center pin. **3.** A kingbolt. **4.** *Informal* The person of central importance in a group, etc.
king post In carpentry, a single vertical strut supporting the apex of a triangular truss and resting on a crossbeam. For illustration see ROOF. Also **king·post** (king′pōst′)
Kings (kingz) *n.pl.* (*construed as sing.*) **1.** Either of two books, I Kings, and II Kings, of the Old Testament, recounting the histories of the Hebrew kings after David. **2.** In the Douai version of the Old Testament, a group of four books, comprising I Samuel, II Samuel, I Kings, and II Kings.
king's English Standard English considered as set by official authority: also called *queen's English.*
king·ship (king′ship) *n.* **1.** The state, power, office, or dignity of a king. **2.** The monarchical type of government. **3.** As a title, the person of a king: his royal *kingship.*
king-size (king′sīz′) *adj.* *Informal* Greater in length or size than is usual. Also **king′sized′.**

king snake A large, harmless snake of the southern U.S. that feeds on rats and mice.
kink (kingk) *n.* **1.** An abrupt bend, curl, loop, or tangle in a line, wire, hair, etc. **2.** A mental quirk. **3.** A sharp, painful muscular spasm; crick. — *v.i. & v.t.* To form or cause to form a kink or kinks. [< Du., twist, curl]
kink·a·jou (king′kə·jōō) *n.* An arboreal, carnivorous mammal of Central and South America, having large eyes, soft woolly fur, and a long tail. [< F *quincajou* < Tupi]
kink·y (kingk′ē) *adj.* **kink·i·er, kink·i·est** Kinked; frizzy. — **kink′i·ness** *n.*
kins·folk (kinz′fōk′) *n.pl.* One's relatives or family; kin: also, *Informal, kinfolk.*
kin·ship (kin′ship) *n.* Relationship, esp. by blood. — **Syn.** See RELATIONSHIP.
kins·man (kinz′mən) *n.* *pl.* **·men** (-mən) A male blood relation. — **kins′wom′an** (-wŏŏm′ən) *n.fem.*
ki·osk (kē·osk′, kē′osk, kī′-) *n.* **1.** In Turkey, a lightly constructed, open summerhouse or pavilion. **2.** A similar structure, used as a booth, newsstand, etc. [< F < Turkish < Persian *kūskh* palace]
kip[1] (kip) *n.* **1.** The untanned skin of a calf, a lamb, or an adult of any small breed of cattle. **2.** A collection of such skins. Also **kip′skin′** (-skin′). [ME < Du.]
kip[2] (kip) *n.* *pl.* **kip** The monetary unit of Laos: in 1960 worth about one U.S. cent.
kip·per (kip′ər) *n.* **1.** A salmon or herring cured by kippering. **2.** The male salmon during the spawning season. — *v.t.* To cure (fish) by splitting, salting, and drying or smoking. [? OE *cypera* spawning salmon]
kirk (kûrk) *n.* *Scot & Brit. Dial.* A church.
kir·mess (kûr′mis) See KERMIS.
kir·tle (kûrt′l) *n.* *Archaic* **1.** A woman's skirt. **2.** A man's outer garment. [OE < L *curtus* short] — **kir′tled** *adj.*
Kis·lew (kis·lef′, kis′lef) *n.* The third month of the Hebrew year. Also **Kish′lev, Kis′lev.** See (Hebrew) CALENDAR.
kis·met (kiz′met, kis′-) *n.* Appointed lot; fate. [< Turkish < Arabic *qasama* to divide]
kiss (kis) *v.t. & v.i.* **1.** To touch or caress with the lips as a sign of greeting, love, etc. **2.** To meet or touch lightly. — *n.* **1.** A touch or caress with the lips. **2.** A light meeting or touching. **3.** A small candy. [OE *cyssan*]
kiss·er (kis′ər) *n.* **1.** One who kisses. **2.** *Slang* The mouth or the face.
kit (kit) *n.* **1.** A collection of articles, tools, etc., for a special purpose. **2.** A set of parts, etc., from which something is to be made. **3.** One's effects or outfit, esp. for traveling. **4.** A box, bag, knapsack, etc. **5.** *Informal* A collection of persons or things. [ME < MDu. *kitte* jug, vessel]
kitch·en (kich′ən) *n.* **1.** A room set apart and equipped for cooking food. **2.** A culinary department; cuisine. [OE < L *coquere* to cook]
kitch·en·ette (kich′ən·et′) *n.* A small, compactly arranged kitchen. Also **kitch′en·et′.**
kitchen police *Mil.* Enlisted men detailed to perform routine kitchen chores; also, such duty.
kitch·en·ware (kich′ən·wâr′) *n.* Kitchen utensils.
kite (kīt) *n.* **1.** A lightweight structure of wood and paper, flown in the wind at the end of a long string. **2.** A predatory bird of the hawk family (*Falconidae*) with long, pointed wings. **3.** *Naut.* One of several light sails to use in a light wind. **4.** In commerce, any negotiable paper not representing a genuine transaction, employed to obtain money, sustain credit, etc. — *v.* **kit·ed, kit·ing** *v.i.* **1.** To soar or fly like a kite. **2.** To obtain money, etc., by the use of kites. — *v.t.* **3.** In commerce, to issue, as a kite. [OE *cȳta*]
kith (kith) *n.* *Archaic* One's friends, acquaintances, or associates: now only in **kith and kin.** [OE *cūth* known]
kit·ten (kit′ən) *n.* A young cat. [ME < OF *chaton* kitten]
kit·ten·ish (kit′ən·ish) *adj.* Playfully coy. — **kit′ten·ish·ly** *adv.* — **kit′ten·ish·ness** *n.*
kit·ti·wake (kit′ē·wāk) *n.* A gull of northern seas, having a rudimentary hind toe. [Imit.]
kit·ty[1] (kit′ē) *n.* *pl.* **·ties** **1.** Money pooled, as by card players, for any specific purpose. **2.** In certain card games, a hand or part of a hand left over after a deal; a widow. [Origin uncertain]
kit·ty[2] (kit′ē) *n.* *pl.* **·ties** **1.** A kitten or cat. **2.** A pet name for a cat.
kit·ty-cor·nered (kit′ē·kôr′nərd) *adj.* Cater-cornered.
Ki·wa·nis (kə·wä′nis, -wô′-) An international chain of men's clubs to promote higher business standards and to provide service to the community. [< N. Am. Ind. *keewanis* to make oneself known] — **Ki·wa′ni·an** *adj. & n.*
ki·wi (kē′wē) *n.* A flightless bird of New Zealand, the apteryx. [< Maori]
Klan (klan) The Ku Klux Klan. — **Klans′man** *n.*
klep·to·ma·ni·a (klep′tə·mā′nē·ə) *n.* An obsessive impulse to steal. [< Gk. *kleptēs* thief + -MANIA] — **klep′to·ma′·ni·ac** (-mā′nē·ak) *n.*
klieg light (klēg) A powerful arc floodlight, used in making motion pictures. [after the *Kliegl* brothers, lighting engineers born in Germany]
knack (nak) *n.* **1.** The ability to do something readily and well. **2.** Cleverness; adroitness. [ME *knak, knekke*]
knap·sack (nap′sak′) *n.* A case or bag worn strapped across the shoulders, for carrying equipment or supplies; rucksack. [< Du < *knappen* to bite, eat + *zak* sack]
knave (nāv) *n.* **1.** A dishonest person; rogue. **2.** A playing card, the jack. [OE *cnafa* youth]
knav·er·y (nā′vər·ē) *n.* *pl.* **·er·ies** **1.** Deceitfulness; trickery; rascality. **2.** An act of trickery or deceit.
knav·ish (nā′vish) *adj.* Of, pertaining to, or characteristic of a knave. — **knav′ish·ly** *adv.* — **knav′ish·ness** *n.*
knead (nēd) *v.t.* **1.** To mix and work (dough, clay, etc.) into a uniform mass, usu. by pressing and pulling with the hands. **2.** To work upon by squeezes of the hands; massage. **3.** To make by kneading. [OE *cnedan*] — **knead′er** *n.*
knee (nē) *n.* **1.** *Anat.* The joint of the human leg that articulates the femur with the tibia and fibula and includes the patella. **2.** *Zool.* A part homologous to the human knee, as the stifle joint in horses, dogs, etc. **3.** Something like a bent knee, as a bent piece of metal or wood used in construction, etc. **4.** The part of a garment covering the knee. — *v.t.* To touch or strike with the knee. [OE *cnēow*]
knee·cap (nē′kap′) *n.* The patella. Also **knee′pan′.**
knee-deep (nē′dēp′) *adj.* Rising or sunk to the knee.
knee·hole (nē′hōl′) *n.* A space for the knees, as in a desk.
kneel (nēl) *v.i.* **knelt** or **kneeled, kneel·ing** To fall or rest on the bent knee or knees. [OE *cnēowlian*] — **kneel′er** *n.*
knell (nel) *n.* **1.** The tolling of a bell, esp. one announcing a death. **2.** Any sad or doleful sound. — *v.i.* **1.** To sound a knell. **2.** To toll mournfully. — *v.t.* **3.** To proclaim by or as by a knell. [OE *cynllan* to knock]
knelt (nelt) Past tense and past participle of KNEEL.
knew (nōō, nyōō) Past tense of KNOW.
Knick·er·bock·er (nik′ər·bok′ər) *n.* **1.** A descendant of one of the early Dutch settlers in New York State. **2.** A New Yorker. [after Diedrich *Knickerbocker*, fictitious Dutch author of Washington Irving's *History of New York*]
knick·er·bock·ers (nik′ər·bok′erz) *n.pl.* Wide short breeches gathered below the knee: also **knick·ers** (nik′ərz).
knick·knack (nik′nak) *n.* A trifling article; trinket; trifle: also spelled *nicknack.* [Reduplication of KNACK]
knife (nīf) *n.* *pl.* **knives** (nīvz) **1.** An instrument for cutting, piercing, or spreading, with one or more sharp-edged, often pointed, blades, commonly set in a handle. **2.** A blade forming a part of an implement or machine. **3.** A weapon, such as a dagger. — *v.t.* **knifed, knif·ing** **1.** To stab or cut with a knife. **2.** *U.S. Slang* To discredit or betray behind one's back. [OE *cnīf*]
knight (nīt) *n.* **1.** In medieval times: **a** A feudal tenant serving his superior as a mounted soldier. **b** A gentleman, usu. of the nobility, trained for mounted combat and raised to the order of chivalry. **2.** In Great Britain, the holder of a nonhereditary dignity below the rank of baronet, conferred by the sovereign as a reward for personal merit or for service to the country. The holder is entitled to use *Sir* before his given name. **3.** In chess, a piece bearing a horse's head. — *v.t.* To make (a man) a knight. [OE *cniht* boy, military attendant] — **knight′ly** *adv.*
knight errant *pl.* **knights errant** A wandering knight who went forth to redress wrongs or seek adventures.
knight-er·rant·ry (nīt′er′ən·trē) *n.* *pl.* **·ries** **1.** The customs and practices of the knights errant; chivalry. **2.** Quixotic behavior or action.
knight·hood (nīt′hŏŏd) *n.* **1.** The character, rank, or vocation of a knight. **2.** Knights collectively.
Knights of Columbus A fraternal society of American Roman Catholic men, founded 1882.
Knight Templar *pl.* **Knights Templars** *for def. 1,* **Knights Templar** *for def. 2.* **1.** A member of a military and religious order founded in 1119 by the Crusaders for the protection of pilgrims. **2.** A Freemason of an order claiming descent from the medieval order of Knights Templars.
knit (nit) *v.* **knit** or **knit·ted, knit·ting** *v.t.* **1.** To form (a fabric or garment) by interlocking loops of a single yarn or thread by means of needles. **2.** To fasten or unite closely and firmly. **3.** To draw (the brows) together into wrinkles. — *v.i.* **4.** To make a fabric by interlocking loops of yarn or thread. **5.** To grow together, as broken bones. **6.** To come together in wrinkles; contract. — *n.* The fabric made by knitting. [OE *cnyttan*] — **knit′ter** *n.*
knit·ting (nit′ing) *n.* **1.** The act of one who or that which knits. **2.** The fabric produced by knitting.
knitting needle A slender, pointed rod, used in knitting.
knives (nīvz) Plural of KNIFE.
knob (nob) *n.* **1.** A rounded protuberance, bunch, or lump. **2.** A rounded handle, as of a door. **3.** A rounded mountain; knoll. [ME < MLG *knobbe*]
knob·by (nob′ē) *adj.* **·bi·er, ·bi·est** **1.** Full of knobs. **2.** Resembling a knob.

k (nok) *v.t.* **1.** To deal a blow to; hit. **2.** To strike to-er. **3.** To drive or move by hitting. **4.** To make by :ing or pounding: to *knock* a hole in the wall. **5.** To :e or push so as to make fall: with *down, over, off*, etc. **6.** *Slang* To find fault with; disparage. **—** *v.i.* **7.** To strike ɔw or blows; rap: to *knock* at a door. **8.** To come into sion; bump. **9.** To make a pounding or clanking noise, n engine. **— to knock around** (or **about**) **1.** *Informal* wander from place to place. **2.** To treat roughly; abuse. **ɔ knock down 1.** To take apart for shipping or storing. t auctions, to sell to the highest bidder. **— to knock** . *Informal* To stop or leave off (work, talking, etc.) **2.** leduct. **3.** *Informal* To do or make quickly or easily. *J.S. Slang* To kill; also, to overwhelm or defeat. **— to ck (oneself) out** *U.S. Slang* **1.** To make a great effort; k very hard. **2.** To become exhausted. **— to knock out** n boxing, to defeat (an opponent) by knocking to the vas for a count of ten. **2.** To make unconscious. **3.** *Slang* To tire greatly. **— to knock together** To build nake roughly or hurriedly. **—** *n.* **1.** A sharp blow; rap. noise made by an engine in faulty condition. **3.** A ortune, setback, or reversal. **4.** *U.S. Slang* Hostile crit-n; disparagement. [OE *cnocian*]

:k·a·bout (nok′ə·bout′) *n. Naut.* A small sailboat rigged a sloop. **—** *adj.* **1.** Marked by roughness. **2.** Suitable rough or casual occasions.

:k·down (nok′doun′) *adj.* **1.** Powerful enough to upset verthrow. **2.** Made so as to be easily taken apart or put ɔther: a *knockdown* chair. **—** *n.* **1.** A felling or upsetting, by a blow. **2.** An article made for easy assembly.

:k·er (nok′ər) *n.* **1.** One who or that which knocks. **2.** inged metal hammer fastened to a door for knocking.

:k-knee (nok′nē′) *n.* **1.** An inward curvature of the that causes the knees to knock or rub together in walk-**2.** *pl.* Legs so curved.

ck-kneed (nok′nēd′) *adj.* Having knock-knees.

ck·out (nok′out′) *adj.* Forcible enough and so placed o render unconscious. **—** *n.* **1.** A knocking unconscious knocking out of action. **2.** In boxing, a flooring of one ter for a count of ten; a kayo. **3.** *Slang* A remarkably ressive person or thing.

ll (nōl) *n.* A small round hill; a mound. [OE *cnoll* hill]

t (not) *n.* **1.** An intertwining of rope, string, etc., one end being passed ough a loop and wn tight; also, the ıp thus made. **2.** ornamental bow silk, lace, braid, . **3.** A hard, rled portion of the nk of a tree, or the nd mark on sawed nber left by this. A cluster or group persons or things. A bond or union. **6.** An enlargement in a muscle, of a nd, etc. resembling a knot. **7.** Something not easily ved; problem. **8.** *Naut.* **a** A speed of a nautical mile in hour, equivalent to 1.1516 statute miles per hour. **b** A utical mile. **—** *v.* **knot·ted, knot·ting** *v.t.* **1.** To tie in a ot. **2.** To secure or fasten by a knot. **3.** To form knobs, sses, etc., in. **—** *v.i.* **4.** To form a knot or knots. **5.** To come knotted or tangled. [OE *cnotta*]

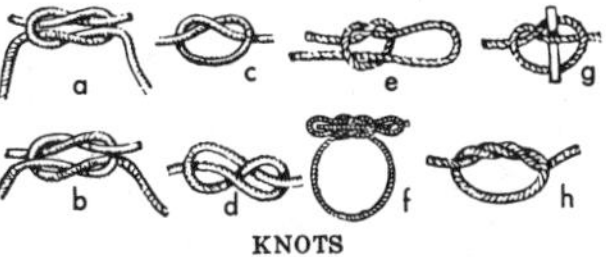

KNOTS
a Square or reef. *b* Granny. *c* Overhand. *d* Figure-eight. *e* Slipknot. *f* Double bowknot. *g* Boat. *h* Surgeon's.

ɔt·grass (not′gras′, -gräs′) *n.* A widely distributed herb th jointed stems.

ɔt·hole (not′hōl′) *n.* A hole in a plank or board left by e falling out of a knot.

ɔt·ty (not′ē) *adj.* **·ti·er, ·ti·est 1.** Full of or tied in knots. Difficult or intricate; puzzling. **— knot′ti·ness** *n.*

out (nout) *n.* A whip or scourge formerly used for flog-ng in Russia. **—** *v.t.* To flog with the knout. [< Russian ON *knūtr, knūta* knot]

ow (nō) *v.* **knew, known, know·ing** *v.t.* **1.** To be cog-zant of; have a concept of in the mind. **2.** To be certain ; apprehend as true. **3.** To be acquainted or familiar ith. **4.** To be sure about the identity of; recognize. **5.** To ve a practical grasp of through instruction, study, etc.: *know* French. **6.** To be able: with *how*: to *know* how to vim. **7.** To distinguish between: to *know* good from bad. To have memorized: The actor *knows* his lines. **9.** To have xperienced: We *know* poverty. **—** *v.i.* **10.** To have aware-ess; apprehend. **11.** To have understanding or certainty; e sure. **— to know better** To be aware of something truer more correct than what one says or does. **—** *n. Informal* he fact of knowing: now only in the phrase **to be in the now,** to have inside or secret information. [OE *cnāwan*] **— know′a·ble** *adj.* **— know′er** *n.*

know-how (nō′hou′) *n. Informal* Mastery of a complicated operation or procedure; technical skill.

know·ing (nō′ing) *adj.* **1.** Perceptive; astute; also, hinting at having sly or secret knowledge concerning something. **2.** Conscious; intentional. **3.** Having knowledge or information. **— know′ing·ly** *adv.* **— know′ing·ness** *n.*

knowl·edge (nol′ij) *n.* **1.** A result or product of knowing; information or understanding acquired through experience; practical ability, or skill. **2.** Deep and extensive learning; erudition. **3.** The cumulative culture of the human race. **4.** A sure conviction; certainty. **5.** The act, process, or state of knowing; cognition. **6.** Any object of knowing or mental apprehension; that which is or may be known. **7.** Specific information; notice. **8.** *Archaic* Sexual intercourse: often preceded by *carnal*. [ME < OE *cnāwlǣc* acknowledgement] **— Syn. 5.** Cognition, apprehension, comprehension.

knowl·edge·a·ble (nol′ij·ə·bəl) *adj.* Having knowledge; well-informed; intelligent.

known (nōn) Past participle of KNOW. **—** *adj.* Recognized by all as the truth; understood; axiomatic: *known* facts.

know-noth·ing (nō′nuth′ing) *n.* An ignoramus.

knuck·le (nuk′əl) *n.* **1.** One of the joints of the fingers, or the region about it; esp., one of the joints connecting the fingers to the hand. **2.** The protuberance formed by one of these joints when the finger is bent. **3.** The carpal joint of the pig, calf, etc., the flesh of which is used as food. **4.** *pl.* Brass knuckles. **—** *v.* **knuck·led, knuck·ling** *v.t.* **1.** To rub, press, or hit with the knuckles. **—** *v.i.* **2.** To hold the knuckles on the ground in shooting a marble. **— to knuckle down** To apply oneself seriously and assiduously. **— to knuckle under** To yield; submit; give in. [ME *knokel*]

knuck·le·bone (nuk′əl·bōn′) *n.* **1.** In man, one of the bones forming a knuckle. **2.** In certain animals, as sheep, a leg bone with a knob at the end; also, this knob.

knuck·le-dus·ters (nuk′əl·dus′tərz) *n.pl.* Brass knuckles.

knurl (nûrl) *n.* **1.** A protuberance; lump. **2.** One of a series of small ridges on the edge of a metal object, as a coin, thumbscrew, etc. **—** *v.t.* To ridge or mill, as the edge of a coin. [? Dim. of KNUR] **— knurl′y** *adj.*

KO or **K.O.** or **k.o.** Knockout (boxing).

ko·a·la (ko·ä′lə) An arboreal marsupial having gray, woolly fur and no tail, and feeding on the leaves of the eucalyptus. [< native Australian name]

KOALAS
(28 to 32 inches long)

Ko·dak (kō′dak) *n.* A small portable camera carrying a roll of sensitized film: a trade name. Also **ko′dak.**

Ko·di·ak bear (kō′dē·ak) A very large brown bear found on Kodiak Island and adjacent islands off the Alaskan coast.

Koh·i·noor (kō′i·nŏŏr′) *n.* A famous Indian diamond weighing when cut about 106 carats, a British crown jewel since 1849. Also **Koh′i·nor′, Koh′i·nur′.** [< Persian *kōhinūr*, lit., mountain of light]

kohl·ra·bi (kōl′rä·bē, kōl·rä′-) *n. pl.* **·bies** A variety of cabbage with an edible turnip-shaped stem. [< G < Ital. < L *caulis* cabbage + *rapa* turnip]

ko·la (kō′lə), **kola nut tree** See COLA.

kola nut See COLA NUT.

ko·lin·sky (kə·lin′skē, kō-) *n. pl.* **·skies 1.** Any of several minks of Asia and Russia. **2.** The fur of any of these animals, often dyed to resemble sable. Also called *Tartar mink.* [< Russian *kolinski* of Kola]

kol·khoz (kol·khôz′) *n.* A collective farm in the Soviet Union. Also **kol·hoz′, kol·khos′.** [< Russian *kol(lektivnoe)* collective + *khoz(yaĭstvo)* farm, household]

ko·peck (kō′pek) *n.* A Russian bronze coin, the hundredth part of a ruble: also spelled *copeck.* Also **ko′pek.** Abbr. *k., K., kop.* [< Russian *kopye* lance]

Ko·ran (kō·rän′, -ran′) *n.* The sacred book of the Moslems, recording in Arabic the revelations of Allah (God) to Mohammed: also *Alcoran, Alkoran.* [< Arabic *Qur'ān*, lit., recitation < *qar'ā* to read]

Ko·re·an (kô·rē′ən, kō-) *adj.* Of or pertaining to Korea, its inhabitants, or their language. **—** *n.* **1.** A native of Korea, or a person of Korean ancestry. **2.** The language of Korea.

Korean War See table for WAR.

ko·ru·na (kô′rŏŏ·nä) *n. pl.* **ko·ru·ny** (kô′rŏŏ·nē) or **ko·run** (kô′rŏŏn) The monetary unit of Czechoslovakia: in 1960 worth about 14 U.S. cents. Also called *crown.* [< Czechoslovakian < L *corona* crown]

ko·sher (*adj., n.* kō′shər; *v.* kosh′ər) *adj.* **1.** Permitted by or conforming to Jewish (ceremonial) law: most often said of food. **2.** *Slang* Legitimate; proper. **—** *n.* Kosher food. **—** *v.t.* To make kosher. [< Hebrew *kāshēr* fit, proper]

kou·miss (kōō′mis), **kou·mys** See KUMISS.

kow·tow (kou′tou, kō′-) *v.i.* **1.** To behave in an obsequious,

servile manner. **2.** To strike the forehead on the ground as a sign of reverence, etc. — *n.* The act of kowtowing. [< Chinese *k'o-t'ou,* lit., to knock the head] — **kow'tow'er** *n.*
kraal (kräl) *n.* **1.** In South Africa, a village or group of native huts, usu. surrounded by a stockade. **2.** A fenced enclosure for cattle or sheep, esp. in South or central Africa. [< Afrikaans < Pg. *curral* pen for cattle]
krait (krīt) *n.* Any of several venomous snakes of Asia, esp. India. [< Hind. *karait*]
K ration A highly condensed, packaged emergency ration provided for soldiers of the U.S. Army in World War II.
Krem·lin (krem'lin) **1.** The walled citadel of Moscow containing the government offices of the Soviet Union. **2.** The government of the Soviet Union. [< Russian *kreml'* citadel]
kris (krēs) *n.* A Malay dagger or short sword with a wavy-edged blade: also spelled *crease, creese.* [< Malay]
Krish·na (krish'nə) A widely worshiped Hindu god, the eighth avatar of Vishnu. — **Krish'na·ism** *n.*
Kriss Krin·gle (kris kring'gəl) St. Nicholas; Santa Claus. [< G *Christkindl,* dim. of *Christkind* Christ child]
krō·na[1] (krō'nə) *n. pl.* **·nur** (-nər) The monetary unit of Iceland: also called *crown.* [< Icel.]
kro·na[2] (krō'nə, *Sw.* kroo'nə) *n. pl.* **·nor** (-nôr) The monetary unit of Sweden; also, a Swedish silver coin of this value. Also called *crown.* [< Sw.]
kro·ne (krō'ne) *n. pl.* **·ner** (-ner) **1.** The monetary unit of Denmark. **2.** The monetary unit of Norway. **3.** A Danish or Norwegian silver coin of this denomination. [< Dan.]
kryp·ton (krip'ton) *n.* A colorless, gaseous element (symbol Kr), present in minute amounts in the atmosphere, used as a filler in incandescent and fluorescent electric lamps ELEMENT. [< Gk., neut. of *kryptos* hidden]
ku·chen (koo'khən) *n.* A yeast-dough coffee cake usu. taining fruits and nuts, and covered with sugar. [<
ku·dos (kyoo'dos, koo-) *n.* Glory; credit; praise: used in the singular. [< Gk. *kydos* glory]
Ku Klux Klan (koo' kluks' klan', kyoo') **1.** A secret ety formed in the South after the Civil War to prevent gro equality. **2.** An anti-Negro, anti-Catholic, and Jewish secret society founded in Georgia in 1915 and active during the 1920's. — **Ku' Klux' Klan'ner**
ku·lak (koo·läk') *n.* In Russia, a wealthy peasant whc ployed labor, and opposed the Soviet collectivizatic farms. [< Russian, lit., fist, tight-fisted man]
ku·miss (koo'mis) *n.* Fermented mare's or camel's used as a beverage by the nomads of central Asia. **ku'mys** [< Russian < Tatar *kumiz*]
küm·mel (kim'əl, *Ger.* kü'məl) *n.* A liqueur flavored aniseed, cumin, or caraway. [< G, caraway seed]
kum·quat (kum'kwot) *n.* **1.** A small, round orange with a sour pulp and edible rind, used in making prese or confections. **2.** The tree bearing this fruit. [Cantc alter. of Pekinese *chin-chü,* lit., golden orange]
Kuo·min·tang (kwō'min'tang') *n.* The nationalist p of China. [< Chinese *kuo* nationalist + *min* people' *tang* party]
Kurd (kûrd, kŏŏrd) *n.* A member of a nomadic Moslem ple dwelling chiefly in Kurdistan. — **Kurd'ish** *adj.*
kvass (kväs, kvas) *n.* A Russian fermented drink resemb sour beer, made from rye, barley, etc. [< Russian *kva*

L

l, L (el) *n. pl.* **l's** or **ls, L's** or **Ls, ells** (elz) **1.** The twelfth letter of the English alphabet. **2.** The sound represented by the letter *l.* **3.** Anything shaped like the letter L. — *symbol* The Roman numeral 50.
la[1] (lä) *n. Music* The sixth syllable used in solmization; the sixth degree of a major scale; also, the tone A.
la[2] (lä, lô) *interj.* An exclamation expressing surprise, emphasis, etc.: also spelled *law.* [OE *lā*]
lab (lab) *n. U.S. Informal* Laboratory.
la·bel (lā'bəl) *n.* **1.** A slip of paper, printed legend, etc., on a container or article showing its nature, producer, destination, etc. **2.** A term or phrase used to classify or describe persons, schools of thought, etc. — *v.t.* **la·beled** or **·belled, la·bel·ing** or **·bel·ling 1.** To mark with a label. **2.** To classify. [< OF, ribbon] — **la'bel·er** or **la'bel·ler** *n.*
la·bi·a (lā'bē·ə) Plural of LABIUM.
la·bi·al (lā'bē·əl) *adj.* **1.** Of or pertaining to a labium or the lips. **2.** *Phonet.* Articulated or modified by the lips, as are (p), (b), (m), (w), or the rounded vowels (ō) and (oo). — *n.* A labial sound. [< Med.L < L *labium* lip]
la·bi·ate (lā'bē·āt, -it) *adj.* Having lips or liplike parts. Also **la'bi·at'ed.** [< NL < L *labium* lip]
la·bile (lā'bil) *adj.* Liable to lapse or change; unstable. [< L < *labi* to slip, fall] — **la·bil'i·ty** *n.*
labio- *combining form* Related to, or formed by the lips and (another organ): *labiodental.* [< L *labium* lip]
la·bi·o·den·tal (lā'bē·ō·den'təl) *Phonet. adj.* Formed with the lower lip and the upper front teeth, as (f) and (v) in English. — *n.* A sound so formed.
la·bi·um (lā'bē·əm) *n. pl.* **·bi·a** (-bē·ə) *Anat.* **1.** A lip or liplike part. **2.** One of the four folds of the vulva, comprising the two outer folds of skin (**labia majora**) and the two inner folds of mucous membrane (**labia minora**). [< L, lip]
la·bor (lā'bər) *n.* **1.** Physical or manual work done for hire in economic production. **2.** Arduous physical or mental exertion; toil. **3.** The working class collectively, esp. as organized into labor unions. **4.** A piece of work; task. **5.** *Med.* The pain and stress of childbirth; esp., the uterine contractions prior to giving birth. — **Department of Labor** An executive department of the U.S. government (established 1913), headed by the Secretary of Labor, that carries out policies regarding wages, unemployment, etc. — *v.i.* **1.** To work hard physically or mentally. **2.** To progress with great effort or painful exertion. **3.** To suffer the pangs of childbirth. **4.** To be oppressed or hampered. — *v.t.* **5.** To work out laboriously; overwork: to *labor* an argument. Also *Brit.* **la'bour.** [< OF < L *labor* toil, distress]
lab·o·ra·to·ry (lab'rə·tôr'ē, -tō'rē; *Brit.* lə·bor'ə·trē) *n.* **·ries 1.** A building or room equipped for conducting sc tific experiments, analyses, etc. **2.** A department, as factory, for research, testing, etc. Also, *Informal, lab.* Med.L < L *labor* toil]
Labor Day In most States of the United States and Canada, a legal holiday, usu. the first Monday in Septem
la·bored (lā'bərd) *adj.* **1.** Performed laboriously; diffic *labored* breathing. **2.** Overelaborate: *labored* prose.
la·bor·er (lā'bər·ər) *n.* One who performs physical or m ual labor, esp. unskilled labor.
la·bo·ri·ous (lə·bôr'ē·əs, -bō'rē-) *adj.* **1.** Requiring m labor; toilsome. **2.** Diligent; industrious. — **la·bo'ri·ou** *adv.* — **la·bo'ri·ous·ness** *n.* [< OF < L *labor* labor, t
la·bor·ite (lā'bər·īt) *n.* One who supports labor intere esp. in politics. Also *Brit.* **la'bour·ite.**
la·bor·sav·ing (lā'bər·sā'ving) *adv.* Doing away with diminishing the need for, manual work: *laborsaving* devi
labor union An association of workers organized to impr and advance mutual interests: also called *trade union.*
La·bour·ite (lā'bər·īt) *n.* A member of a Labour party Great Britain or in one of the Commonwealth nations.
Labour Party 1. In Great Britain, a political party dr ing its chief support from labor and trade unions and cc mitted to socialist reforms. **2.** A similar party in ot members of the British Commonwealth of Nations.
la·bur·num (lə·bûr'nəm) *n.* Any of a group of legumin Old World trees yielding a poisonous alkaloid, with pen lous yellow flowers and hard, dark wood. [< NL < L
lab·y·rinth (lab'ə·rinth) *n.* **1.** A system of winding, in cate passages or paths designed to confuse whoever tries go through and find the exit; maze. **2.** Anything resembl a labyrinth, as a confusing network of streets. **3.** Any tricate or perplexing set of difficulties. **4.** *Anat.* The wi ing passages of the inner ear.
Lab·y·rinth (lab'ə·rinth) In Greek mythology, the m used to confine the Minotaur, constructed by Daedalus Minos of Crete. [< L < Gk.]
lab·y·rin·thine (lab'ə·rin'thin, -thēn) *adj.* Of, pertaini to, or like a labyrinth. Also **lab'y·rin'thi·an, lab'y·rin'th**
lac (lak) *n.* A resinous deposit left on certain trees by lac insect and used in making varnishes, paints, etc. Hind. < Prakrit < Skt. *lākshā*]
lace (lās) *n.* **1.** A cord or string passed through eyelets over hooks for fastening together the edges of a shoe, g ment, etc. **2.** A delicate openwork fabric or network, ma by hand or on a machine, of linen, silk, cotton, etc. **3.**

r or gold braid used to decorate uniforms, hats, etc. — **ced, lac·ing** *v.t.* **1.** To fasten or draw together by tying lace or laces of. **2.** To pass (a cord or string) through ets or over hooks as a lace. **3.** To trim with or as with **4.** To compress the waist of (a person) by tightening of a corset. **5.** To intertwine or interlace. **6.** To k with lines or colors. — *v.i.* **7.** To be fastened by ns of laces. — **to lace into** *Informal* **1.** To strike or at- . **2.** To scold; berate. [< OF < L *laqueus* noose, trap]

r·ate (las′ər·āt) *v.t.* **·at·ed, ·at·ing** **1.** To tear raggedly; to wound the flesh by tearing. **2.** To injure: to *lacerate* s feelings. — *adj.* **1.** Jagged; torn. **2.** Harrowed; dis- ed. **3.** *Biol.* Having the edges jagged or irregularly . [< L *lacer* mangled] — **lac′er·a·ble** *adj.*

r·a·tion (las′ər·ā′shən) *n.* **1.** The act of lacerating. he wound or jagged tear resulting from lacerating.

wing (lās′wing′) *n.* An insect with four lacy wings.

work (lās′wûrk′) *n.* **1.** Lace. **2.** Any decorative work resembling lace.

es (lach′iz) *n.* *Law* Unreasonable delay in asserting a , so that the court is warranted in refusing relief. [< OF < L *laxus* lax]

·e·sis (lak′ə·sis) One of the three Fates.

·ry·mal (lak′rə·məl) *adj.* Of, pertaining to, or produc- ears. — *n.* *pl.* The organs secreting tears: also **lach- al glands.** [< Med.L < L *lacrima* tear]

·ry·ma·to·ry (lak′rə·mə·tôr′ē, -tō′rē) *n.* *pl.* **·ries** A l bottle found in ancient tombs, formerly supposed to e held the tears of mourners. — *adj.* Of or producing s. [< Med.L < L *lacrima* tear]

·ry·mose (lak′rə·mōs) *adj.* **1.** Tearful. **2.** Provoking s; sad. — **lach′ry·mose′ly** *adv.*

ng (lā′sing) *n.* **1.** The act of one who or that which s. **2.** A cord or string for holding together opposite parts shoe, etc.; lace. **3.** A fastening made with lacing. **4.** *rmal* A thrashing; beating. **5.** An ornamental braid.

nsect Any of a family of insects, esp. an Indian species, females of which exude lac.

(lak) *n.* **1.** Deficiency or complete absence of some- g. **2.** That which is absent or deficient; need. — *v.t.* o be without. **2.** To be short by. — *v.i.* **3.** To be ting or deficient. [ME, prob. < MLG *lak* deficiency]

·a·dai·si·cal (lak′ə·dā′zi·kəl) *adj.* Affectedly pensive melancholy; listless. — **lack′a·dai′si·cal·ly** *adv.*

·ey (lak′ē) *n.* *pl.* **·eys** **1.** A male servant of low status, in livery; footman. **2.** Any servile follower. — *v.t.* & To attend or act as a lackey. [< OF < Sp. *lacayo*]

·lus·ter (lak′lus′tər) *adj.* **1.** Lacking sheen and bright- s; dull. **2.** Lacking spirit; mediocre: a *lackluster* per- mance. — *n.* A lack of brightness. Also **lack′lus′tre.**

n·ic (lə·kon′ik) *adj.* Brief and concise in expression. **la·con′i·cal.** [< L < Gk. *Lakōn* a Spartan; with ref. to terseness of Spartan speech] — **la·con′i·cal·ly** *adv.*

uer (lak′ər) *n.* **1.** A transparent varnish made from ous resins, dissolved in volatile solvent. **2.** A resinous nish obtained from the lacquer tree of China and Japan, used to impart a high polish to wood. **3.** Decorative odwork or articles of wood painted with this lacquer: **lac′quer·work′** (-wûrk′). — *v.t.* To coat with or as h lacquer. [< MF *lacre* a kind of sealing wax < Pg. a gum lac] — **lac′quer·er** *n.*

rosse (lə·krôs′, -kros′) *n.* *U.S. & Canadian* A ball ne of American Indian origin, played with long, racket- implements by two teams of ten men each, the object g to advance the ball into the opponents' goal. [< dial. Canadian) *la crosse*, lit., the crozier, hooked stick]

- Var. of LACTO-.

tate (lak′tāt) *v.i.* **·tat·ed, ·tat·ing** **1.** To form or secrete k. **2.** To suckle young. — *n.* A salt or ester of lactic d. [< L *lactare* to suckle]

ta·tion (lak·tā′shən) *n.* **1.** The mammalian formation secretion of milk. **2.** The period during which milk is duced. **3.** The act of suckling young.

te·al (lak′tē·əl) *adj.* **1.** Of, pertaining to, or resembling k; milky. **2.** Carrying chyle. Also **lac′te·an, lac′te·ous.** *n.* *Anat.* Any of the lymphatic vessels that carry chyle m the small intestine to the blood. [< L *lac, lactis* milk]

tic (lak′tik) *adj.* Of, pertaining to, or derived from milk.

ic acid *Chem.* A limpid, syrupy acid, $C_3H_6O_3$, with a ter taste, present in sour milk.

o- *combining form* Milk. Also, before vowels, *lact-.* [< *ac, lactis* milk]

to·fla·vin (lak′tō·flā′vin) *n.* Riboflavin.

tose (lak′tōs) *n.* *Biochem.* A white, odorless, crystalline ar, $C_{12}H_{22}O_{11}$, present in milk.

u·na (lə·kyōō′nə) *n.* *pl.* **·nas** or **·nae** (-nē) **1.** A space m which something is missing or has been omitted, esp. a manuscript; hiatus. **2.** *Anat.* Any of the minute cavi- ties in bone containing bone cells. Also **la·cune′** (-kyōōn′). [< L *lacus* basin, pond] — **la·cu′nal, la·cu′nar, lac·u·nar·y** (lak′yōō·ner′ē) *adj.*

lac·y (lā′sē) *adj.* **lac·i·er, lac·i·est** Made of or resembling lace. — **lac′i·ly** *adv.* — **lac′i·ness** *n.*

lad (lad) *n.* **1.** A boy or youth; stripling. **2.** Familiarly, any male. [< ME *ladde*, ? ult. < ON]

lad·der (lad′ər) *n.* A device of wood, metal, rope, etc., for climbing and descending, usu. consisting of two parallel side pieces connected by a series of rungs, or rounds, placed at regular intervals to serve as footholds. [OE *hlǣd(d)er*]

lad·die (lad′ē) *n.* A lad.

lade (lād) *v.* **lad·ed, lad·ed** or **lad·en, lad·ing** *v.t.* **1.** To load with a cargo or burden; also, to load as a cargo. **2.** To dip or lift (a liquid) in or out, as with a ladle. — *v.i.* **3.** To receive cargo. **4.** To dip or lift a liquid. [OE *hladan* to load]

lad·en[1] (lād′n) Alternative past participle of LADE. — *adj.* **1.** Burdened; oppressed. **2.** Weighed down; loaded.

lad·en[2] (lād′n) *v.t. & v.i.* **lad·ened, lad·en·ing** To lade.

lad·ing (lā′ding) *n.* **1.** The act of one who or that which lades. **2.** A load or cargo.

la·dle (lād′l) *n.* A cup-shaped vessel with a long handle, for dipping or conveying liquids. — *v.t.* **·dled, ·dling** To dip up or carry in a ladle. [OE *hladan* to lade] — **la′dler** *n.*

la·dy (lā′dē) *n.* *pl.* **·dies** **1.** A woman showing refinement, gentility, and tact. **2.** A woman of superior position in society. **3.** A term of reference or address for any woman. **4.** A woman at the head of a domestic establishment: now only in the phrase **the lady of the house.** **5.** The woman a man loves. **6.** A wife. — *adj.* **1.** Of or pertaining to a lady; ladylike. **2.** Denoting a female: a *lady* doctor. ◆ *Woman* doctor is preferable here. [OE *hlǣfdīge*, lit., bread-kneader < *hlāf* bread, loaf + *-dige*, a stem akin to *dah* dough]

La·dy (lā′dē) **1.** In Great Britain a title given to women of various ranks. **2.** The Virgin Mary: usu. with *Our.*

la·dy·bird (lā′dē·bûrd′) *n.* Any of a family of brightly colored beetles, usu. red spotted with black, that feeds on aphids and other insects. Also **lady beetle, la′dy·bug′.**

Lady Day **1.** March 25, the church festival of the Annunciation. **2.** Formerly, a day honoring the Virgin Mary.

la·dy·fin·ger (lā′dē·fing′gər) *n.* A small sponge cake of about the size and shape of a finger. Also **la′dys·fin′ger** (lā′dēz-).

lady in waiting *pl.* **ladies in waiting** A lady appointed to attend upon a queen or princess.

la·dy-kill·er (lā′dē·kil′ər) *n.* *Slang* A man supposed to be unusually fascinating to women. — **la′dy-kill′ing** *adj. & n.*

la·dy·like (lā′dē·līk′) *adj.* **1.** Like or suitable to a lady; gentle; delicate. **2.** Effeminate.

la·dy·love (lā′dē·luv′) *n.* A woman beloved; sweetheart.

la·dy·ship (lā′dē·ship) *n.* The rank or condition of a lady: used as a title, with *Her* or *Your.*

lady's man A man attentive to and fond of the company of women. Also **ladies' man.**

lady's-slipper (lā′dēz·slip′ər) *n.* An orchid having a flower that suggests a slipper in shape. Also **la′dy·slip′per** (lā′dē-).

laevo- See LEVO-.

lag (lag) *v.i.* **lagged, lag·ging** **1.** To move slowly; stay or fall behind; straggle: sometimes followed by *behind.* **2.** In marbles, to throw one's taw as near as possible to a line on the ground to decide the order of play. — *n.* **1.** The condition or act of retardation or falling behind. **2.** The amount or period of retardation. **3.** In marbles, an act of lagging. [? < Scand.] — **lag′ger** *n.*

lag·an (lag′ən) *n.* In maritime law, goods cast from a vessel in peril, but to which a buoy or float is attached as evidence of ownership: also called *ligan.* [< AF < Gmc.]

la·ger (lä′gər) *n.* A beer stored for sedimentation before use. Also **lager beer.** [< G < *lager* storehouse + *bier* beer]

lag·gard (lag′ərd) *n.* One who lags; straggler. — *adj.* Falling behind; loitering; slow. — **lag′gard·ly** *adv.*

la·gniappe (lan·yap′, lan′yap) *n.* **1.** *Southern U.S.* A small present given to the purchaser of an article by a merchant or storekeeper. **2.** *Informal* Anything given beyond strict obligation; an extra. Also **la·gnappe′.** [< dial. F (Creole) < F *la* the + Sp. *ñapa* lagniappe < Quechua *yapa*]

la·goon (lə·gōōn′) *n.* A body of shallow water, as a bay, inlet, pond, or lake, usu. connecting with a river, larger lake, or the sea; esp., the water within a coral atoll. Also **la·gune′.** [< F < Ital. < L *lacuna* pool]

la·ic (lā′ik) *adj.* Lay[2]. — *n.* A layman. [< LL < Gk. *laikos* < *laos* the people] — **la′i·cal·ly** *adv.*

la·i·cize (lā′ə·sīz) *v.t.* **·cized, ·ciz·ing** To remove from ecclesiastical control; secularize. — **la′i·ci·za′tion** *n.*

laid (lād) Past tense and past participle of LAY[1].

lain (lān) Past participle of LIE[1].

lair (lâr) *n.* A resting place or den, esp. that of a wild animal. — *v.i.* **1.** To live or rest in a lair. — *v.t.* **2.** To place in a lair. **3.** To serve as a lair for. [OE *leger* bed]

laird (lârd) *n. Scot.* The proprietor of a landed estate. [Northern ME *laverd, lard*] — **laird′ly** *adj.* — **laird′ship** *n.*
lais·sez faire (les′ā·fâr′) **1.** In economics, the theory that the state should exercise as little control as possible in trade and industrial affairs. **2.** Noninterference or indifference. Also **lais′ser faire′.** [< F, lit., let do < *laisser* to let + *faire* to do, make]
la·i·ty (lā′ə·tē) *n. pl.* **·ties 1.** The people collectively; laymen: distinguished from *clergy.* **2.** All of those outside a specific profession or occupation.
La·i·us (lā′yəs) In Greek legend, a king of Thebes, husband of Jocasta, who was unwittingly killed by his son Oedipus.
lake[1] (lāk) *n.* **1.** A sizable inland body of either salt or fresh water. **2.** A large pool of any liquid: a *lake* of pitch. [Fusion of OE *lacu* stream, pool and OF *lac* basin, lake]
lake[2] (lāk) *n.* **1.** A deep red pigment made by combining cochineal with a metallic oxide. **2.** The color of this pigment. **3.** Any metallic compound yielding pigments by the interaction of mordant and dye. [Var. of LAC]
lake dwelling A habitation built on piles over the surface of a lake, esp. in prehistoric times. — **lake dweller**
lake herring A whitefish of the Great Lakes.
lake trout A salmonoid fish of the Great Lakes region of North America, somewhat resembling the brook trout.
la·la·pa·loo·za (lol′ə·pə·lōō′zə) See LOLLAPALOOZA. Also **lal′la·pa·loo′za.**
lam (lam) *Slang v.* **lammed, lam·ming** *v.i.* **1.** To run away, esp. to avoid arrest; flee. — *v.t.* **2.** To beat; thrash. — *n.* Sudden flight or escape. — **on the lam** In flight; fleeing. [? < ON *lemja* to thrash]
la·ma (lä′mə) *n.* A priest or monk of Lamaism. See DALAI LAMA. [< Tibetan *blama*]
La·ma·ism (lä′mə·iz′əm) *n.* The form of Buddhism practiced in Tibet and Mongolia, characterized by a complex hierarchy and Shamanistic beliefs and practices. — **La′ma·ist** *n.* — **La′ma·is′tic** *adj.*
La·marck·ism (lə·märk′iz·əm) *n. Biol.* The theory of organic evolution holding that species have developed through the inheritance of acquired characteristics. [after Chevalier de *Lamarck,* 1744–1829, French naturalist]
la·ma·ser·y (lä′mə·ser′ē) *n. pl.* **·ser·ies** A Lamaist monastery. [< F]
lamb (lam) *n.* **1.** A young sheep. **2.** The meat of a lamb used as food. **3.** Lambskin. **4.** Any gentle or innocent person, esp. a child. **5.** A gullible person. — **the Lamb** Christ. — *v.i.* To give birth: said of a ewe. [OE]
lam·baste (lam·bāst′) *v.t.* **·bast·ed, ·bast·ing** *Slang* **1.** To beat or thrash. **2.** To scold; castigate. — **lam·bast′ing** *n.*
lamb·da (lam′də) *n.* The eleventh letter in the Greek alphabet (Λ, λ), corresponding to the English *l.* See ALPHABET. [< Gk. < Phoenician *lamed*]
lam·bent (lam′bənt) *adj.* **1.** Playing over a surface with a soft, undulatory movement; flickering; licking: a *lambent* flame. **2.** Softly radiant. **3.** Lightly and playfully brilliant: *lambent* wit. [< L *lambens, -entis,* ppr. of *lambere* to lick] — **lam′ben·cy** *n.* — **lam′bent·ly** *adv.*
lamb·kin (lam′kin) *n.* **1.** A little lamb. **2.** A small child: a term of affection. Also **lamb′ie.** [Dim. of LAMB]
Lamb of God Christ, as the Paschal Lamb. *John* i 29.
lam·bre·quin (lam′bər·kin, -brə-) *n.* **1.** *U.S.* A draped strip of cloth, leather, etc., hanging from the casing above a window or doorway, and covering the upper half of the opening. **2.** In medieval times, a covering of heavy fabric for a helmet. [< F < Du. *lamperkin,* dim. of *lamper* veil]
lamb·skin (lam′skin) *n.* **1.** The dressed hide and wool of a lamb. **2.** Dressed leather made from a lamb's hide.
lame (lām) *adj.* **lam·er, lam·est 1.** Crippled or disabled, esp. in the legs or feet. **2.** Sore; painful: a *lame* back. **3.** Weak; ineffective: a *lame* effort. — *v.t.* **lamed, lam·ing** To make lame. [OE *lama*] — **lame′ly** *adv.* — **lame′ness** *n.*
la·mé (la·mā′) *n.* A fabric woven of flat gold or silver thread, sometimes mixed with silk or other fiber. [< F]
lame duck *Informal* **1.** *U.S.* An officeholder whose term continues for a time after his defeat for reelection. **2.** On the stock exchange, one who cannot fulfill his contracts. **3.** An ineffectual or disabled person.
la·mel·la (lə·mel′ə) *n. pl.* **·mel·lae** (-mel′ē) A thin plate, scale, or layer, as in bone or the gills of bivalves. [< NL < L, dim. of *lamina* plate, leaf] — **lam·el·lar** (lə·mel′ər, lam′·ə·lər), **lam′el·late** *adj.*
la·mel·li·branch (lə·mel′i·brangk) *n. Zool.* One of a class of bivalve mollusks including clams, mussels, and oysters. [< NL < L *lamella* plate + Gk. *branchia* gills] — **la·mel′li·bran′chi·ate** (-brank′kē·āt, -it) *adj.* & *n.*
la·ment (lə·ment′) *v.t.* To feel remorse or regret over. — *v.i.* To feel or express sorrow, grief, or regret. — *n.* **1.** An expression of grief; lamentation. **2.** An elegiac melody or writing. [< L *lamentum* wailing, weeping] — **la·ment′er** *n.*
lam·en·ta·ble (lam′ən·tə·bəl, lə·ment′ə-) *adj.* **1.** That warrants lamenting; deplorable: a *lamentable* failure. **2.** *Archaic* Expressing grief; mournful. — **lam′en·ta·bly** *adv.*
lam·en·ta·tion (lam′ən·tā′shən) *n.* **1.** The act of la ing or bewailing. **2.** A lament; wail; moan.
Lam·en·ta·tions (lam′ən·tā′shənz) *n.pl.* (*construed as* A lyrical poetic book of the Old Testament, attribut Jeremiah the prophet.
lam·en·ted (lə·men′təd) *adj.* Mourned for; grieved usu. said of one who has died.
lam·i·na (lam′ə·nə) *n. pl.* **·nae** (-nē) or **·nas 1.** A scale or sheet. **2.** A layer or coat lying over another, bone, minerals, armor, etc. **3.** *Bot.* The blade or fl panded portion of a leaf, or the blade of a petal. [<
lam·i·nate (lam′ə·nāt) *v.* **·nat·ed, ·nat·ing** *v.t.* **1.** To roll, or press (metal) into thin sheets. **2.** To separate into thin sheets. **3.** To make of layers united by the of heat and pressure. **4.** To cover with thin sheets or nae. — *v.i.* **5.** To separate into sheets. — *adj.* Lamir [< NL < L *lamina* leaf] — **lam′i·na′tion** *n.*
lam·i·nat·ed (lam′ə·nā′təd) *adj.* Made up of or arran thin sheets; laminate.
lam·i·nose (lam′ə·nōs) *adj.* Laminate.
lamp (lamp) *n.* **1.** A device for holding one or more el light bulbs and directing their light; also, an electric bulb. **2.** Any of various devices for producing ligl combustion, incandescence, electric arc, or fluores **3.** A vessel in which oil or alcohol is burned through a to produce light or heat. **4.** Any of several devic producing therapeutic heat or rays: sun *lamp.* [< OF < Gk. *lampein* to shine]
lamp·black (lamp′blak′) *n.* A black pigment consist fine carbon deposited from the smoke of burning oil o
lamp·light (lamp′līt′) *n.* Light from lamps; artificial
lamp·light·er (lamp′lī′tər) *n.* **1.** One whose work is ing lamps, esp. street lamps. **2.** Anything by which a is lighted, as a torch, electric device, etc.
lam·poon (lam·pōōn′) *n.* A scurrilous, but often humo attack in prose or verse directed against a person. To satirize in a lampoon. [< MF *lampons* let's dri song refrain)] — **lam·poon′er, lam·poon′ist** *n.* — **poon′er·y** *n.*
lamp·post (lamp′pōst′) *n.* A post supporting a lam
lam·prey (lam′prē) *n. pl.* **·preys** An eellike, carniv aquatic animal having a circular suctorial mouth sharp rasping teeth on its inner surface. Also **lam·pe** (lam′pər). [< OF < Med.L *lampreda lampetra*]
Lan·cas·ter (lang′kəs·tər), **House of** A royal house of land, reigning from 1399 to 1461. — **Lan·cas′tri·an** & *n.*
lance (lans, läns) *n.* **1.** A spearlike weapon used by mo soldiers or knights. **2.** One who is armed with a l lancer. **3.** Any of various long, slender weapons resem a lance, as a whaler's spear, etc. **4.** A lancet. **lanced, lanc·ing 1.** To pierce with a lance. **2.** To c open with a lancet. [ME < OF < L *lancea* light spear
lance corporal 1. *Mil.* In the U.S. Marine Corps, a listed man. See table at GRADE. **2.** *Brit. Mil.* A pr acting as a corporal, usu. without increased pay.
lance·let (lans′lit, läns′-) *n.* A small, fishlike animal ing primitive vertebrate characteristics, and living i sand: also called *amphioxus.* [Dim. of LANCE]
Lan·ce·lot of the Lake (lan′sə·lot, län′-) In Arth romance, the bravest and ablest of the knights of the R Table. Also **Lancelot du Lac** (dü lák). [< F, servant
lan·ce·o·late (lan′sē·ə·lit, -lāt) *adj.* **1.** Shaped lik head of a lance. **2.** *Bot.* Narrowing to a point; tape as certain leaves. [< LL < *lanceola* small lance]
lanc·er (lan′sər, län′-) *n.* A calvaryman armed with a l
lance sergeant *Brit. Mil.* A corporal acting tempo as a sergeant without additional pay.
lan·cet (lan′sit, län′-) *n.* A small, two-edged, usu. po surgical knife, used to open abscesses, boils, etc. [< F *cette,* dim. of *lance* < OF < L *lancea* light spear]
lancet arch *Archit.* A narrow, acutely pointed arch.
lancet window A narrow, acutely pointed window.
lance·wood (lans′wŏŏd′, läns′-) *n.* **1.** A tough, el wood used for carriage shafts, fishing rods, billiard cues. **2.** Any of various tropical American trees yielding this w
land (land) *n.* **1.** The solid, exposed surface of the ear distinguished from the waters of the seas. **2.** A count region, esp. considered as a place of human habita **3.** The people of such a country or region. **4.** Ground sidered with reference to its uses, location, character, pasture *land.* **5.** *Law* **a** Any tract of ground whatever may be owned as goods together with all its appurtena as water, forests, buildings, etc. **b** A share or intere such land. **6.** Rural places as distinguished from citi towns. **7.** *Econ.* Natural resources as used in produc — *v.t.* **1.** To transfer from a vessel to the shore; put as **2.** To bring (something in flight) down to rest. **3.** To b to some point, condition, or state: His words *landed* hi trouble. **4.** To pull (a fish) out of the water; catch. **5.** *formal* To obtain; win: to *land* a job. **6.** *Informal* To

: (a blow) —*v.i.* **7.** To go or come ashore from a ship oat. **8.** To touch at a port; come to land. **9.** To de- d and come to rest after a flight or jump. **10.** To come ome place or state; end up: to *land* in jail. [OE]
d *combining form* **1.** A region of a certain kind: *wood- l.* **2.** The country of: *Scotland.* [< LAND]
dau (lan′dô, -dou) *n.* **1.** A former type of closed sedan ing a back seat with a collapsible top. **2.** A four-wheeled iage with a collapsible top. [after *Landau*, a Bavarian where it was first made]
l bank *U.S.* A bank making mortgage loans on land or er real property.
l·ed (lan′did) *adj.* **1.** Having an estate in land: *landed* try. **2.** Consisting in land: *landed* property.
d·er *combining form* From or of a land. [< LAND]
l·fall (land′fôl′) *n.* A sighting of or coming to land; , the land so sighted or reached.
l grant Government land granted to a railroad, educa- al institution, etc.
l-grant (land′grant) *adj.* Denoting a State college or versity that received grants of land from the Federal ernment under the Morrill Act of 1862.
l·grave (land′grāv′) *n.* **1.** In medieval and Renaissance many, a count having jurisdiction over a specified terri- . **2.** Later, the title of any of various German princes. MHG < *lant, land* land + *grave, graf* count]
l·hold·er (land′hōl′dər) *n.* An owner or occupant of l.
l·ing (lan′ding) *n.* **1.** The act of going or placing ashore n any kind of craft or vessel. **2.** The place where a craft vessel lands; wharf; pier. **3.** The act of descending and ling on the ground after a flight, leap, etc. **4.** *Archit.* e platform or floor at the top of a flight of stairs, between hts of stairs, or interrupting a flight of stairs.
ling field A tract of ground selected or prepared for the ding and takeoff of aircraft.
l·la·dy (land′lā′dē) *n. pl.* **·dies 1.** A woman who owns l rents out real estate. **2.** The wife of a landlord. **3.** A man who keeps an inn.
l·ler (lent′lər) *n.* **1.** A slow Austrian country dance. Music for or in the manner of this dance, in triple meter. G < dial. G *Landl* upper Austria]
d·less (land′lis) *adj.* Owning no land.
l·locked (land′lokt′) *adj.* **1.** Surrounded by land; hav- no seacoast. **2.** Living in landlocked water: said esp. normally anadromous fish: *landlocked* salmon.
d·lord (land′lôrd′) *n.* **1.** A man who owns and rents real estate. **2.** An innkeeper. **3.** *Brit.* The lord of a nor. [OE < *land* land + *hlaford* lord]
d·lub·ber (land′lub′ər) *n.* An awkward or inexperi- ed person on board a ship.
l·mark (land′märk′) *n.* **1.** A fixed object serving as a indary mark to a tract of land, as a guide to travelers, etc. A prominent object in the landscape. **3.** A distinguishing t, event, etc. [OE *land* land + *mearc* boundary]
d mine *Mil.* An explosive bomb placed in the ground.
d office A government office for the transaction of busi- s pertaining to the public lands.
d-of·fice business (land′ô′fis, -of′is) *U.S. Informal* siness conducted at a rapid pace.
id of Enchantment Nickname of New Mexico.
id of Opportunity Nickname of Arkansas.
id of Promise See PROMISED LAND.
id of the Midnight Sun Norway.
id of the Rising Sun Japan.
d·own·er (land′ō′nər) *n.* One who owns real estate. — **d′own′er·ship** *n.* —**land′own·ing** *n. & adj.*
d·scape (land′skāp) *n.* **1.** A stretch of inland natural nery as seen from a single point. **2.** A picture represent- such scenery. **3.** The branch of painting, photography, ., that deals with inland natural scenery. —*v.* **·scaped, ap·ing** *v.t.* **1.** To improve or change the features or pearance of a park, garden, etc. —*v.i.* **2.** To be a land- pe gardener. [< Du. < *land* land + *-schap* -ship]
dscape architect One whose profession is to plan the corative arrangement of outdoor features.
dscape gardener One who plans and carries out the angement of plants, trees, etc. —**landscape gardening**
d·scap·ist (land′skā·pist) *n.* A painter of landscapes.
d·slide (land′slīd′) *n.* **1.** The slipping down of a mass of l, rock, and debris on a mountain side or other steep slope. The mass of soil, rock, etc., slipping down. Also *Chiefly it.*, **land′slip′** (-slip′). **3.** An overwhelming plurality of tes for one political party or candidate in an election.
ds·man (landz′mən) *n. pl.* **·men** (-mən) One who lives d works on land: distinguished from *seaman.*
d·ward (land′wərd) *adj. & adv.* Being, facing, or going ward the land. Also **land′wards** (-wərdz).

lane (lān) *n.* **1.** A narrow rural path or way, confined between fences, walls, hedges, or similar boundaries; also, a narrow city street. **2.** Any narrow way, passage, or similar course. **3.** A prescribed route for transoceanic shipping or for aircraft. **4.** A marked division of a highway or road for traffic moving in the same direction. **5.** In sports, any of a set of parallel courses for contestants in races. [OE *lanu*]
Lang·er·hans (läng′ər·häns), **islands of** See ISLANDS OF LANGERHANS.
lang·lauf (läng′louf) *n.* A cross-country ski run. [< G < *lang* long + *lauf* course] —**lang′läuf·er** (-loi·fər) *n.*
lang·syne (lang′sīn′, -zīn′) *adv. Scot.* Long since; long ago.
lan·guage (lang′gwij) *n.* **1.** The expression and communication of emotions or ideas between human beings by means of speech and hearing. **2.** Transmission of emotions or ideas between any living creatures by any means. **3.** The words used in communication among members of a single nation or group at a given period. **4.** The impulses, capacities, and powers that induce and make possible the creation and use of language. **5.** The vocabulary used in a specific business, science, etc. **6.** One's characteristic manner of expression or use of speech. [< OF < L *lingua* tongue, language]
language arts Reading, spelling, literature, and composition, considered as basic language skills.
lan·guid (lang′gwid) *adj.* **1.** Indisposed toward physical exertion; affected by weakness or fatigue. **2.** Feeling little interest in or inclination toward anything; listless. **3.** Lacking in activity or quickness of movement. [< L *languere* to languish] —**lan′guid·ly** *adv.* —**lan′guid·ness** *n.*
lan·guish (lang′gwish) *v.i.* **1.** To become weak or feeble; fail in health or vitality; grow listless. **2.** To droop gradually from restless longing; pine. **3.** To pass through a period of external discomfort and mental anguish: to *languish* in prison. **4.** To adopt a look of sentimental longing or melancholy. [< OF < L *languescere*, inceptive of *languere* to be weary, languish] —**lan′guish·er** *n.* —**lan′guish·ment** *n.*
lan·guish·ing (lang′gwish·ing) *adj.* **1.** Lacking alertness or force. **2.** Sentimentally pensive or melancholy. **3.** Becoming weak or listless. —**lan′guish·ing·ly** *adv.*
lan·guor (lang′gər) *n.* **1.** Lassitude of body; weakness; fatigue. **2.** A lack of energy or enthusiasm. **3.** A mood of tenderness or sentimental dreaminess. **4.** The absence of activity; stagnation. **5.** Oppressiveness; stillness.
lan·guor·ous (lang′gər·əs) *adj.* **1.** Languid. **2.** Producing languor. —**lan′guor·ous·ly** *adv.* —**lan′guor·ous·ness** *n.*
lan·gur (lung·gŏŏr′) *n.* A slender, long-tailed Asian monkey. [< Hind. < Skt. *lāngūlin*, lit., having a tail]
lan·iard (lan′yərd) See LANYARD.
lank (langk) *adj.* **1.** Lean; shrunken. **2.** Long, flat, and straight; not curly: *lank* hair. [OE *hlanc* flexible] —**lank′·ly** *adv.* —**lank′ness** *n.*
lank·y (lang′kē) *adj.* **lank·i·er, lank·i·est** Ungracefully tall and thin; loose-jointed. —**lank′i·ly** *adv.* —**lank′i·ness** *n.*
lan·o·lin (lan′ə·lin) *n.* A fatty substance obtained from the wool of sheep and used in ointments, cosmetics, soaps, etc.; also called *wool fat.* Also **lan′o·line** (-lin, -lēn). [< L *lan(a)* wool + *ol(eum)* oil + -IN]
lan·tern (lan′tərn) *n.* **1.** A protective, usu. portable, case with transparent or translucent sides for enclosing a light. **2.** *Archit.* An open structure built on top of a building to admit light and air. **3.** A lighthouse, esp. the top that protects the light. **4.** *Archaic* A slide projector. [< F < L < Gk. *lampein* to shine]
lantern jaws Long, sunken jaws that make the face appear thin. —**lan·tern-jawed** (lan′tərn·jôd′) *adj.*
lan·tha·nide series (lan′thə·nīd) *Physics* The rare-earth elements beginning with lanthanum (according to some authorities, with cerium) and ending with lutetium. [< LANTHAN(UM) + *-ide*, var. of -ID[2]]
lan·tha·num (lan′thə·nəm) *n.* A dark lead gray metallic element (symbol La) chemically related to aluminum. See ELEMENT. [< NL < Gk. *lanthanein* to lie concealed]
lan·yard (lan′yərd) *n.* **1.** *Naut.* A small, usu. four-stranded hemp rope used on a ship for fastening riggings, etc. **2.** A cord used in firing certain types of cannon. **3.** A cord worn around the neck, used by sailors for attaching a knife. Also spelled *laniard.* [Alter. of obs. *lanyer* < OF *lasniere* thong]
La·o (lä′ō) *n. pl.* **La·o 1.** A Buddhistic people living in Laos and parts of Thailand. **2.** Their Thai language.
La·oc·o·on (lā·ok′ə·won, -ō·won) In Greek legend, a Trojan priest who warned against the wooden horse and was destroyed with his two sons by two serpents.
La·o·tian (lou′shən, lā·ō′shən, lä·ō′shən) *adj.* Of or pertaining to Laos. —*n.* A native or inhabitant of Laos.
lap[1] (lap) *n.* **1.** The chairlike place formed by the lower torso and thighs of a person seated; also, the clothing that covers this part. **2.** The front part of a skirt when lifted up. **3.** A place of nurture or fostering: fortune's *lap.* **4.** Control,

care, or custody: in the *lap* of the gods. **—to throw into someone's lap** To give over the responsibility or control of something to someone else. [OE *laeppa*]
lap[2] (lap) *n.* **1.** The state of overlapping. **2.** A rotating disk used for grinding and polishing gems, etc. **3.** One circuit of a race course. **4.** The part of one thing that lies over another. **—*v.t.*** **1.** To fold or wrap about something. **2.** To lay (one thing) partly over or beyond another. **3.** To extend over or beyond; overlap. **4.** To grind or polish with a lap. **5.** To surround with love, etc.: now only in the passive: to be *lapped* in maternal tenderness. **—*v.i.*** **6.** To be folded. **7.** To overlap. **8.** To project beyond or into something else. [ME *lappen* to fold]
lap[3] (lap) *v.t. & v.i.* **lapped, lap·ping** **1.** To drink (a liquid) by taking it up with the tongue, as an animal does. **2.** To wash against (the shore, etc.) with a sound resembling that of lapping. **—*n.*** **1.** The act of one who or that which laps. **2.** The sound of lapping. **—to lap up** **1.** To drink by lapping. **2.** *Informal* To eat or drink gluttonously. **3.** To listen to eagerly. [OE *lapian* to lap] **—lap′per** *n.*
lap dog A dog small enough to be held on the lap.
la·pel (lə·pel′) *n.* The front of a coat, jacket, etc., that is folded back to form an extension of the collar. [< LAP[1]]
lap·ful (lap′fŏŏl′) *n.* As much as the lap can hold.
lap·i·dar·y (lap′ə·der′ē) *n. pl.* **·dar·ies** One whose work is to cut, engrave, or polish precious stones. **—*adj.*** Pertaining to the art of cutting or engraving precious stones. [< L *lapidarius* of stone]
lap·in (lap′in, *Fr.* là·pàn′) *n.* **1.** A rabbit. **2.** Rabbit fur, usu. dyed to resemble more expensive furs. [< F]
lap·is laz·u·li (lap′is laz′yŏŏ·lī) **1.** A bluish violet variety of lazurite valued as a gemstone. **2.** The color of lapis lazuli. Also **lap′is.** [< NL < L *lapis* stone + Med.L *lazulus* azure]
lap joint A joint in which a layer of material laps over another, as in shingling. **—lap-joint·ed** (lap′join′tid) *adj.*
Lapp (lap) *n.* **1.** A member of a formerly nomadic Mongoloid people of Lapland, now settled largely in Sweden and Norway. Also **Lap·land·er** (lap′lan·dər). **2.** The Finno-Ugric language of the Lapps: also **Lap′pish.** [< Sw.]
lap·pet (lap′it) *n.* **1.** A flap or fold on a headdress or garment. **2.** A loose or pendent flap of flesh, as the lobe of the ear, the wattle of a bird, etc. [Dim. of LAP[1]]
lapse (laps) *n.* **1.** A gradual passing away, as of time. **2.** A pronounced fall into ruin, decay, or disuse. **3.** A slip or mistake, usually trivial. **4.** A fault or negligence: a *lapse* of justice. **5.** *Law* A forfeiture brought about by the failure to perform some necessary act. **—*v.i.*** **lapsed, laps·ing** **1.** To sink slowly; slip: to *lapse* into a coma. **2.** To fall into ruin or a state of neglect. **3.** To deviate from one's principles or beliefs. **4.** To become void, usually by failure to meet obligations. **5.** *Law* To pass or be forfeited to another because of negligence, failure, or death of the holder. **6.** To pass away, as time. [< L *labi* to glide, slip] **—laps′a·ble, laps′i·ble** *adj.* **—laps′er** *n.*
lap·wing (lap′wing′) *n.* A ploverlike bird of the Old World, noted for its flopping flight and shrill cry. [OE *hleapan* to leap + *wince*, prob. < *wancol* unsteady]
lar·board (lär′bərd, -bôrd′, -bōrd′) *Naut. adj.* Being on or toward the left side of the ship as one faces the bow. **—*n.*** The left-hand side of a ship: now replaced by *port.* [ME *laddebord*, lit., prob., lading side]
lar·ce·ny (lär′sə·nē) *n. pl.* **·nies** *Law* The unlawful removal of the personal goods of another with intent to defraud the owner; theft. The distinction between **grand larceny** and **petty** (or **petit**) **larceny** is based on the value of the stolen property. **—Syn.** See THEFT. [< OF < L *latrocinari* to rob] **—lar′ce·ner, lar′cen·ist** *n.* **—lar′ce·nous** *adj.* **—lar′ce·nous·ly** *adv.*
larch (lärch) *n.* Any of several coniferous, deciduous trees of the pine family; also, the wood. [< G < L *larix, laricis*]
lard (lärd) *n.* The semisolid fat of a hog after rendering. **—*v.t.*** **1.** To cover or smear with lard. **2.** To prepare (lean meat or poultry) by inserting strips of fat before cooking. **3.** To intersperse (speech or writing) with embellishments, quotations, etc. [< OF, < L *lardum* lard] **—lard′y** *adj.*
lar·der (lär′dər) *n.* **1.** A room or cupboard where articles of food are stored. **2.** The provisions of a household. [< AF < Med.L *lardum* lard]
lar·es (lâr′ēz, lā′rēz) *n.pl. of* **lar** (lär) In ancient Rome, tutelary dieties, esp. those presiding over the household.
lares and pe·na·tes (pə·nā′tēz) **1.** The household gods. **2.** The cherished belongings of one's household.
large (lärj) *adj.* **larg·er, larg·est** **1.** Having considerable size, quantity, capacity, extent, etc.; big. **2.** Bigger than another. **3.** Sympathetic and broad in scope: to take a *large* view. **—*adv.*** In a size greater than usual: Print *large.* **—at large** **1.** Free; at liberty: The maniac is *at large.* **2.** In general: the people *at large.* **3.** Elected from the whole State. **4.** Exhaustively; fully. [< OF < L *larga*, fem. of *largus* abundant] **—large′ness** *n.*
large·heart·ed (lärj′här′tid) *adj.* Generous; openha[rted]. **—large′heart′ed·ness** *n.*
large·ly (lärj′lē) *adv.* **1.** To a great extent; mainly; ch[iefly]. **2.** On a big scale; extensively; abundantly.
large-scale (lärj′skāl′) *adj.* **1.** Of large size or scope. [2.] Made according to a large scale: said of maps.
lar·gess (lär·jes′; lär′jis, -jes) *n.* Liberal giving; something liberally given. Also **lar′gesse.** [< F *larg[e]*
lar·ghet·to (lär·get′ō) *Music adj.* Moderately slow. **—** In a moderately slow tempo. **—*n.*** *pl.* **·tos** A moder[ately] slow movement. [< Ital., dim. of *largo.* See LARGO.]
lar·go (lär′gō) *Music adj.* Slow; broad. **—*adv.*** In a [slow] tempo. **—*n.*** *pl.* **·gos** A slow movement or passage. [< Ital., slow, large]
lar·i·at (lar′ē·ət) *n.* **1.** A rope for tethering animals. [2.] lasso. **—*v.t.*** To fasten or catch with a lariat. [< S[p.] *reata* < *la* the + *reata* rope]
lark[1] (lärk) *n.* **1.** Any of numerous small singing bir[ds,] the skylark. **2.** Any similar bird, as the meadow[lark.] [ME < OE *lāferce, læwerce*]
lark[2] (lärk) *n.* *Informal* A hilarious time. **—*v.t.*** [1. To] jump (a fence) on horseback. **—*v.i.*** **2.** To play pr[anks.] [Origin uncertain] **—lark′er** *n.* **—lark′some** *adj.*
lark·spur (lärk′spûr) *n.* Any of several showy her[bs of] the crowfoot family with clusters of white, pink, blu[e, or] red flowers.
lar·ri·gan (lar′ə·gən) *n.* *Canadian* A high moccasin, [worn] by lumbermen, trappers, etc. [Origin unknown]
lar·rup (lar′əp) *Informal v.t.* To beat; thrash. **—*n.*** A [blow.] [< dial. E, ? < Du. *larpen* to thrash]
lar·va (lär′və) *n. pl.* **·vae** (-vē) **1.** *Entomol.* The first s[tage] of an insect after leaving the egg, as the maggot. **2.** The immature form of any animal that must undergo m[eta]morphosis. [< L, ghost, mask] **—lar′val** *adj.*
la·ryn·ge·al (lə·rin′jē·əl, -jəl) *adj.* Of, pertaining t[o, or] near the larynx. Also **la·ryn·gal** (lə·ring′gəl). [< N[L <] Gk. *larynx, laryngos* larynx]
lar·yn·gi·tis (lar′ən·jī′tis) *n.* *Pathol.* Inflammation o[f the] larynx. **—lar′yn·git′ic** (-jit′ik) *adj.*
laryngo- *combining form* The larynx; pertaining t[o the] larynx. Also, before vowels, **laryng-.** [< Gk. *lar[yngos]* *laryngos* larynx]
la·ryn·go·scope (lə·ring′gə·skōp) *n.* An instrumen[t for] examining the larynx. **—la·ryn′go·scop′ic** (-skop′ik) **—lar′yn·gos′co·py** (-gos′kə·pē) *n.*
lar·ynx (lar′ingks) *n. pl.* **la·ryn·ges** (lə·rin′jēz) or **lar·yn[xes]** *Anat.* An organ of the respiratory tract situated at the u[pper] part of the trachea, and consisting of a cartilaginous [box] containing the valvelike vocal cords. See illus. at L[...] [< NL < Gk. *larynx* larynx]
la·sa·gna (lə·zän′yə) *n.* Broad, flat noodles, often se[rved] baked in a meat and tomato sauce. Also **la·sa′gne.** [< I[tal.]
las·civ·i·ous (lə·siv′ē·əs) *adj.* Having, manifesting[, or] arousing sensual desires; lustful. [< LL < L *lasc[ivus]* lustful] **—las·civ′i·ous·ly** *adv.* **—las·civ′i·ous·ness** *n.*
la·ser (lā′zər) *n.* *Physics* A maser that can generat[e or] amplify light waves: also called *optical maser.* [< *l(ight)* *a(mplification by) s(timulated) e(mission of) r(adiation)*]
lash[1] (lash) *n.* **1.** A whip or scourge. **2.** A single [whip] stroke. **3.** Anything that wounds the feelings. **4.** An [eye]lash. **—*v.t.*** **1.** To strike, punish, or command with [or as] with a whip; flog. **2.** To switch spasmodically: The [cat] *lashes* his tail. **3.** To beat or dash against violently. [4.] To assail sharply in speech or writing. **5.** To incite. **—*v.i.*** [6.] To deliver a whip stroke or strokes. **7.** To switch or wri[the] rapidly. **—to lash out** **1.** To hit out suddenly and [vio]lently. **2.** To break into angry verbal abuse. [< P[rob.] fusion of MLG *lasch* flap and OF *laz* cord] **—lash′er**
lash[2] (lash) *v.t.* To bind or tie with rope or cord. [< O[F <] L *laqueus* noose] **—lash′er** *n.*
lash·ing[1] (lash′ing) *n.* **1.** The act of one who or that w[hich] lashes. **2.** A flogging; whipping. **3.** A berating; scold[ing.]
lash·ing[2] (lash′ing) *n.* The act of lashing with a rope, e[tc.;] also, the rope.
lass (las) *n.* **1.** A young woman; girl. **2.** A sweethe[art.] **3.** *Scot.* A servant girl; maid. [< Scand.]
las·sie (las′ē) *n.* A little girl; lass. [Dim. of LASS]
las·si·tude (las′ə·tōōd, -tyōōd) *n.* A state of wearines[s or] fatigue; languor. [< F < L *lassus* faint]
las·so (las′ō) *n. pl.* **·sos** or **·soes** A long rope with a runn[ing] noose, used for catching horses, etc. **—*v.t.*** To catch wi[th a] lasso. [< Sp. < L *laqueus* snare] **—las′so·er** *n.*
last[1] (last, läst) *adj.* **1.** Coming after all others; final in [or]der, sequence, or time: the *last* page. **2.** Being the only [one] remaining: his *last* dime. **3.** Most recent: *last* year. [4.] Least probable or suitable: the *last* man for the job. [5.] Newest; most fashionable. **6.** Conclusive; final: the [last] word. **7.** *Rare* Least: the *last* of nations. **8.** *Rare* Ultima[te;] utmost: to the *last* degree. **—*adv.*** **1.** After all others [in] time or order. **2.** At a time next preceding the prese[nt:] He was *last* seen going west. **3.** In conclusion; finally. **—**

'he end; final part or portion. **2.** The final appearance, erience, or mention: We'll never hear the *last* of this. **t last** At length; finally. [OE *latost*, superl. of *læt* slow] (last, läst) *v.i.* **1.** To remain in existence; continue to endure. **2.** To continue unimpaired or unaltered. 'o hold out: Will our supplies *last*? [OE *lǣstan*, to w a track, continue, accomplish] **—last′er** *n.*
(last, läst) *n.* A shaped form, usu. of wood, on which ake a shoe or boot. **—** *v.t.* To fit to or form on a last. **stick to one's last** To attend to one's own business. *lǣste*, *lāst* footstep, track] **—last′er** *n.*
tex (las′teks) *n.* Rubber manufactured in fine strands wound with rayon, cotton, silk, or wool: a trade name. **las′tex.** [< (E)LAS(TIC) + TEX(TILE)]
ing (las′ting, läs′-) *adj.* Continuing; durable; perma-. **—** *n.* Endurance; continuance. [< LAST[2]] **—** **ing·ly** *adv.* **—last′ing·ness** *n.*
Judgment *Theol.* **a** The final trial and sentencing by of all mankind. **b** The time of this.
ly (last′lē, läst′-) *adv.* In the last place; in conclusion.
rites *Eccl.* Sacraments administered to persons in peril eath.
Supper The last meal of Jesus Christ and his disciples re the Crucifixion: also called *Lord's Supper*.
word **1.** The final and most authoritative utterance. *nformal* The most fashionable thing.
1 (lach) *n.* **1.** A fastening for a door or gate, usu. a able bar that falls or slides into a notch. **2.** Any similar ening. **— Syn.** See LOCK[1]. **—** *v.t.* & *v.i.* To fasten by ns of a latch; close. **—to latch on to** *U.S. Slang* To in, esp. something desirable. [OE *laeccean* to seize]
·key (lach′kē′) *n.* A key for releasing a latch.
1·string (lach′string′) *n.* A string on the outside of a , used for lifting the latch.
(lāt) *adj.* **lat·er** or **lat·ter, lat·est** or **last** **1.** Appearing oming after the expected time; tardy. **2.** Occurring at nusually advanced time: a *late* hour. **3.** Beginning at ontinuing to an advanced hour. **4.** Recent or com- tively recent: the *late* war. **5.** Deceased: the *late* king. *dv.* **1.** After the expected time; tardily. **2.** At or until dvanced time of the day, month, year, etc. **3.** *Archaic* ently. **—of late** Recently. [OE *læt*] **—late′ness** *n.*
en (la·tēn′) *adj.* *Naut.* Designating a rig common in Mediterranean, having a triangular sail (**lateen sail**) ended from a long yard set obliquely to the mast. [< F *e) latine* Latin (sail)]
nt (lā′tənt) *adj.* Not visible or apparent, but capable eveloping or being expressed; dormant. [< L *latere* to idden] **—la′ten·cy** *n.* **—la′tent·ly** *adv.*
r (lā′tər) *adv.* At a subsequent time; after some time.
r·al (lat′ər·əl) *adj.* Pertaining to the side or sides; ated at, occurring, or coming from the side. **—** *n.* **1.** ething occurring at or on the side. **2.** In football, a ral pass. [< L *latus, lateris* side] **—lat′er·al·ly** *adv.*
ral pass In football, a pass that travels across the field oward the passer's goal line, rather than forward.
er·an (lat′ər·ən) **1.** The basilica of St. John Lateran, cathedral church of the pope as bishop of Rome. **2.** The oining palace. [< name of a Roman family]
s·cent (lə·tes′ənt) *adj.* Becoming obscure, latent, or den. [< L *latere* to be hidden] **—la·tes′cence** *n.*
x (lā′teks) *n.* *pl.* **lat·i·ces** (lat′ə·sēz) or **la·tex·es** The ky emulsion secreted by certain plants, as the rubber , milkweed, etc., that coagulates on exposure to air is the basis of natural rubber. [< L, liquid]
(lath, läth) *n.* **1.** Any of a number of thin strips of d, etc., nailed to studs or joists to support a coat of ter, or on rafters to support shingles or slates. **2.** Other lar materials used to support plaster, tiles, etc. **3.** hs collectively: also **lath′work′** (-wûrk′). **—** *v.t.* To er or line with laths. [Prob. fusion of OE *laett* and OE *hth* (assumed)] **—lath′er** *n.*
e (lāth) *n.* A machine that holds and spins pieces of od, metal, plastic, etc., so that they are cut and shaped en the operator holds cutting tools against them. **—** *v.t.* **hed, lath·ing** To form on a lathe. [< MDu. *lade*]
·er (lath′ər) *n.* **1.** The suds or foam formed by soap or ergents and water. **2.** The foam of profuse sweating, as a horse. **—in a lather** *U.S. Slang* In a state of intense itement or agitation. **—** *v.t.* **1.** To cover with lather. *Informal* To flog; thrash. **—** *v.i.* **3.** To form lather. To become covered with lather, as a horse. [OE *lēathor* shing soda, soap] **—lath′er·er** *n.* **—lath′er·y** *adj.*
·ing (lath′ing, läth′-) *n.* **1.** The act or process of cover- with laths. **2.** Laths collectively.
i·ces (lat′ə·sēz) Plural of LATEX.
·in (lat′n) *adj.* **1.** Pertaining to ancient Latium, its in- bitants, culture, or language. **2.** Pertaining to or denot- ing the peoples or countries of France, Italy, and Spain. **3.** Of or belonging to the Western or Roman Catholic Church. **—** *n.* **1.** The Indo-European, Italic language of ancient Latium and Rome, extensively used in western Europe until modern times as the language of learning, and still the official language of the Roman Catholic Church. **2.** A member of one of the modern Latin peoples. **3.** A member of the Western or Roman Catholic Church. **4.** One of the people of ancient Latium. **—Old Latin** The language before the first century B.C., as preserved in inscriptions and the comedies of Plautus. **—Classical Latin** The liter- ary and rhetorical language of the period 80 B.C. to A.D. 200. **—Late Latin** The language from 200–600. **—Low Latin** The language of any period after the classical, such as Medi- eval Latin. **—Medieval Latin** The language used by the writers of the Middle Ages, from 600–1500: also called *Mid- dle Latin*. **—New** (or **Neo-**) **Latin** A form of the language based on Latin and Greek elements, now used chiefly for sci- entific and taxonomic terms. **—Vulgar Latin** The popular speech of the Romans from about A.D. 200 through the medieval period. [< L *Latinus* Latin]
Latin America The countries of the western hemisphere south of the Rio Grande, in which the official languages are derived from Latin. See SPANISH AMERICA. **—Lat·in- A·mer·i·can** (lat′n·ə·mer′ə·kən) *adj.* **—Latin American**
Lat·in·ate (lat′ən·āt) *adj.* Of, like, or from Latin.
Latin Church The Roman Catholic Church.
Latin cross A cross in which the upright is longer than the beam that crosses it near the top.
Lat·in·ism (lat′ən·iz′əm) *n.* An idiom in another language taken from or imitating Latin.
Lat·in·ist (lat′ən·ist) *n.* One versed or learned in Latin.
Lat·in·ize (lat′ən·īz) *v.* **·ized, ·iz·ing** *v.t.* **1.** To translate into Latin. **2.** To make Latin in customs, thought, etc. **—** *v.i.* **3.** To use Latin words, forms, etc. **—Lat′in·i·za′·tion** *n.* **—Lat′in·iz′er** *n.*
Latin Quarter A section of Paris on the south bank of the Seine, known for its many artists and students.
lat·i·tude (lat′ə·tōōd, -tyōōd) *n.* **1.** *Geog.* Angular distance on the earth's surface northward or southward of the equa- tor, measured in degrees along a meridian. **2.** *Often pl.* A region or place considered with reference to its distance from the equator. **3.** Freedom from narrow restrictions. **4.** *Astron.* The angular distance of a heavenly body from the ecliptic (**celestial latitude**). [< L *latitudo* breadth]
lat·i·tu·din·al (lat′ə·tōō′də·nəl, -tyōō′-) *adj.* Of or pertain- ing to latitude. **—lat′i·tu′di·nal·ly** *adv.*
lat·i·tu·di·nar·i·an (lat′ə·tōō′də·nâr′ē·ən, -tyōō′-) *adj.* Characterized by or tolerant of liberal or unorthodox atti- tudes, beliefs, etc., esp. in matters of religion. **—** *n.* One who is latitudinarian. **—lat′i·tu′di·nar′i·an·ism** *n.*
La·ti·um (lā′shē·əm) An ancient country in central Italy.
la·trine (lə·trēn′) *n.* A public toilet, as in a camp, barracks, etc. [< F < L *latrina* bath, privy]
-latry *combining form* Worship of; excessive devotion to. [< Gk. *latreia* worship]
lat·ter (lat′ər) *adj.* **1.** Being the second of two persons or things referred to: often preceded by *the*: The *latter* state- ment is truer than the former. **2.** Later or nearer to the end: His *latter* years were happy. [OE *lætra*, compar. of *læt* late]
lat·ter-day (lat′ər·dā′) *adj.* Modern: a *latter-day* martyr.
Latter-day Saint A Mormon.
lat·ter·ly (lat′ər·lē) *adv.* **1.** Recently; lately. **2.** At a later time; toward the end.
lat·tice (lat′is) *n.* **1.** A structure consisting of strips of metal, wood, etc., crossed or interlaced to form regularly spaced openings. **2.** A win- dow, screen, gate, etc., made from or consisting of such a structure. **—** *v.t.* **·ticed, ·tic·ing** **1.** To furnish or enclose with a lattice. **2.** To form into or arrange like a lattice. [< OF *latte* lath]

LATTICE

lat·tice·work (lat′is·wûrk′) *n.* Openwork made from or resembling a lattice. Also **lat′·tic·ing.**
Lat·vi·an (lat′vē·ən) *adj.* Of or pertaining to Latvia, its people, or their language; Lettish. **—** *n.* **1.** A native or in- habitant of Latvia; a Lett. **2.** The Lettish language.
laud (lôd) *v.t.* To praise highly; extol. **— Syn.** See PRAISE. **—** *n.* *pl.* *Eccl.* The prescribed prayers immediately follow- ing matins, the two offices together constituting the first of the seven canonical hours. [< OF < L *laus, laudis* praise]
laud·a·ble (lô′də·bəl) *adj.* Deserving approbation. **—laud′·a·bil′i·ty, laud′a·ble·ness** *n.* **—laud′a·bly** *adv.*
lau·da·num (lô′də·nəm) *n.* **1.** Tincture of opium. **2.** For- merly, any opium preparation. [< NL < L *ladanum*]
laud·a·tion (lô·dā′shən) *n.* The act of lauding; praise.
laud·a·to·ry (lô′də·tôr′ē, -tō′rē) *adj.* Expressing or con- taining praise; complimentary. Also **laud′a·tive.**

laugh (laf, läf) *v.i.* **1.** To produce the characteristic physical manifestations expressive of merriment, elation, etc. **2.** To express or experience amusement, satisfaction, etc. —*v.t.* **3.** To express or utter with laughter. **4.** To induce, persuade, or bring about by or as by laughing: I *laughed* myself sick. —**to laugh at** **1.** To express amusement at. **2.** To ridicule; mock. **3.** To make light of. —**to laugh away** To dispel or minimize with laughter. —**to laugh off** To rid one's self of or dismiss laughingly. —**to laugh up** (or **in**) **one's sleeve** To be covertly amused or exultant. —*n.* **1.** An act or sound of laughing. **2.** *Informal* A cause for or provocation to laughter. —**to have the last laugh** To triumph or succeed after seeming at a disadvantage. [OE *hliehhan, hlæhhan*] —**laugh′er** *n.*

laugh·a·ble (laf′ə·bəl, läf′-) *adj.* Provoking laughter; amusing. —**laugh′a·ble·ness** *n.* —**laugh′a·bly** *adv.*

laugh·ing (laf′ing, läf′-) *adj.* **1.** Like or expressing laughter. **2.** Causing laughter. —*n.* Laughter. —**laugh′ing·ly** *adv.*

laughing gas Nitrous oxide.

laugh·ing·stock (laf′ing·stok′, läf′-) *n.* One who or that which provokes ridicule; a butt.

laugh·ter (laf′tər, läf′-) *n.* **1.** The sound, expression, or action of laughing. **2.** A cause of laughing.

Laun·ce·lot (lôn′sə·lot, län′-) See LANCELOT.

launch[1] (lônch, länch) *v.t.* **1.** To move or push (a vessel, etc.) into the water, esp. for the first time. **2.** To set in flight or motion, as a rocket, missile, etc. **3.** To start (a person, etc.) on a career or course of action. **4.** To initiate; open: to *launch* a campaign. **5.** To hurl; fling. —*v.i.* **6.** To make a beginning; start: usu. with *out* or *forth.* **7.** To begin (an action, speech, etc.) vehemently or impetuously: usu. with *into.* —*n.* The action of launching a vessel, missile, etc. [< AF *lancher* to launch] —**launch′er** *n.*

launch[2] (lônch, länch) *n.* **1.** An open or half-decked motor boat. **2.** Formerly, the largest of the boats carried by a ship. [< Sp. < Malay *lanca* three-masted boat]

launching pad *Aerospace* The platform from which a rocket or guided missile is fired. Also **launch pad.**

laun·der (lôn′dər, län′-) *v.t.* **1.** To wash (clothing, linens, etc.). **2.** To wash and prepare for use by or as by ironing. —*v.i.* **3.** To do the work of washing and ironing. **4.** To undergo washing: Nylon *launders* easily. [< OF < LL < L *lavare* to wash] —**laun′der·er** *n.*

laun·dress (lôn′dris, län′-) *n.* A woman paid or employed to do laundry; washerwoman.

laun·dro·mat (lôn′drə·mat, län′-) *n. U.S.* A place where laundry is washed and dried in coin-operated automatic machines. [< *Laundromat,* a trade name]

laun·dry (lôn′drē, län′-) *n. pl.* **·dries** **1.** A room, commercial establishment, etc., where laundering is done. **2.** Articles to be laundered. **3.** The work of laundering.

laun·dry·man (lôn′drē·mən, län′-) *n. pl.* **·men** (-mən) **1.** A man who works in or manages a commercial laundry. **2.** A man who calls for and delivers laundry.

laun·dry·wom·an (lôn′drē·wo͝om′ən, län′-) *n. pl.* **·wom·en,** (-wim′ən) A laundress.

lau·re·ate (lô′rē·it; *v.* -āt) *adj.* **1.** Singled out for special honor. **2.** Crowned or decked with laurel as a mark of honor. —*n.* **1.** A person honored with a prize or award. **2.** A poet laureate (which see). —*v.t.* **·at·ed, ·at·ing** **1.** To crown with or as with laurel. **2.** To confer the title of poet laureate upon. [< L *laureatus* crowned with laurel]

lau·rel (lôr′əl, lor′-) *n.* **1.** An evergreen tree or shrub typifying a family that includes cinnamon, sassafras, etc. **2.** Any of various similar trees and shrubs. **3.** *Often pl.* A crown or wreath of laurel leaves, conferred as a symbol of honor, achievement, etc. **4.** *pl.* Honor or distinction gained by outstanding achievement. —**to look to one's laurels** To be on guard against losing a position of eminence, honor, etc. —**to rest on one's laurels** To be content with what one has already achieved. —*v.t.* **lau·reled** or **·relled, lau·rel·ing** or **·rel·ling** **1.** To honor by or as by crowning with laurel. **2.** To adorn with laurel. [< OF < L *laurus*]

la·va (lä′və, lav′ə) *n.* **1.** Molten rock that issues from an active volcano or through a fissure in the earth's crust. **2.** Rock formed by the solidifying of this substance. [< Ital., orig., a stream formed by rain < *lavare* to wash]

lav·a·liere (lav′ə·lir′) *n.* An ornamental pendant worn on a thin chain around the neck. Also **lav′a·lier′,** *French* **la·val·lière** (là·và·lyâr′). [< F *la vallière* a type of necktie, ? after Louise de *La Vallière,* 1644–1710, mistress of Louis XIV]

lav·a·to·ry (lav′ə·tôr′ē, -tō′rē) *n. pl.* **·ries** **1.** A room equipped with washing and usu. toilet facilities. **2.** A basin, sink, etc., used for washing. [< LL < L *lavare* to wash]

lav·en·der (lav′ən·dər) *n.* **1.** An Old World plant of the mint family, having spikes of fragrant, pale violet flowers; esp., the **true lavender,** of which the dried flowers and aromatic oil (**oil of lavender**) are much used in perfumery. **2.** The dried flowers and foliage of this plant, used to scent linen, clothing, etc. **3.** A pale, reddish violet color. —*adj.* Pale reddish violet. —*v.t.* To perfume with lave[…] [< AF < Med.L, ? < L *lividus* blue]

la·ver (lā′vər) *n.* In the ancient Jewish Temple, a ceremonial vessel for washing. [< OF < LL *lavatori*[…]

lav·ish (lav′ish) *adj.* **1.** Generous and unrestrained i[…] ing, spending, etc.; prodigal. **2.** Provided or expend[…] great abundance. —*v.t.* To give or bestow gener[…] [< OF *lavasse, lavacho* downpour of rain] —**lav′ish**[…] —**lav′ish·ly** *adv.* —**lav′ish·ness** *n.*

law (lô) *n.* **1.** A rule of conduct, recognized by cust[…] decreed by formal enactment, considered as binding o[…] members of a community, nation, etc. **2.** A system or of such rules. **3.** The condition of society when such are observed: to establish *law* and order. **4.** The bo[…] authoritatively established rules relating to a spe[…] subject or activity: criminal *law.* **5.** Remedial justi[…] administered by legal authorities: to resort to the *la*[…] The branch of knowledge concerned with jurisprudenc[…] The vocation of an attorney, etc.; the legal profe[…] **8.** The rules and principles of common law and statut[…] as distinguished from equity. **9.** An authoritative r[…] command: His will is *law.* **10.** *Often cap.* Divine will, [...]mand, or precept; also, a body of rules having such [...] origin. **11.** Any generally accepted rule, procedur[…] principle governing a specified area of conduct, bo[…] knowledge, etc. **12.** In science and philosophy, a f[…] statement of the manner or order in which a set of na[…] phenomena occur under certain conditions. **13.** *Ma*[…] rule or formula governing a function or operation. –[…] **law.** **1.** The legal authorities; the police. **2.** *Inform*[…] policeman. —**the Law** **1.** The Mosaic Law. **2.** Th[…] rah. —**to go to law** To engage in litigation. —**t**[…] **down the law** To utter one's wishes, instructions, etc., authoritative manner. [OE < ON *lag* something la[…] fixed, in pl., law]

law-a·bid·ing (lô′ə·bī′ding) *adj.* Obedient to the la[…]

law·break·er (lô′brā′kər) *n.* One who violates the la[…] **law′break′ing** *n.* & *adj.*

law·ful (lô′fəl) *adj.* **1.** Permitted by law. **2.** Recog[…] by the law: *lawful* debts. **3.** Valid, authentic, etc., ac[…]ing to law: *lawful* marriage. —**law′ful·ly** *adv.* —[…] **ful·ness** *n.*

law·giv·er (lô′giv′ər) *n.* One who originates or institu[…] law or system of laws. —**law′giv′ing** *n.* & *adj.*

law·less (lô′lis) *adj.* **1.** Not controlled by law, auth[…] discipline, etc. **2.** Contrary to law. —**law′less·ly** —**law′less·ness** *n.*

law·mak·er (lô′mā′kər) *n.* One who enacts or helps t[…] act laws; a legislator. —**law′mak′ing** *n.* & *adj.*

lawn[1] (lôn) *n.* A stretch of grassy land; esp., an ar[…] closely mown grass near a house, in a park, etc. [[…] *laund* < OF *launde* heath] —**lawn′y** *adj.*

lawn[2] (lôn) *n.* A fine, thin linen or cotton fabric. [[…] *Laon,* France, where it was formerly made] —**lawn′y**[…]

lawn mower A machine operated by a motor or prop[…] by hand, used to cut the grass of lawns.

Law of Moses The Mosaic Law.

law·ren·ci·um (lô·ren′sē·əm) *n.* A very short-lived r[…] active element (symbol Lw), originally produced by [...]barding californium with the nuclei of a boron isotope ELEMENT. [after E. O. *Lawrence,* 1901–58, U.S. physici[…]

law·suit (lô′so͞ot′) *n.* A case, action, or proceeding bro[…] to a court of law for settlement.

law·yer (lô′yər) *n.* A member of any branch of the profession; esp., one who advises and acts for clien[…] pleads in court.

lax (laks) *adj.* **1.** Lacking strictness or disciplinary co[…] **2.** Lacking precision; vague. **3.** Lacking firmness or [...]ity. [< L *laxus* loose] —**lax′ly** *adv.* —**lax′ness** *n.*

lax·a·tive (lak′sə·tiv) *n.* A medicine taken to produce e[…]uation of the bowels. —*adj.* **1.** Loosening or produ[…] evacuation of the bowels. **2.** Characterized by or ha[…] loose bowel movements. [< F, fem. of *laxatif*]

lax·i·ty (lak′sə·tē) *n.* The state or quality of being lax.

lay[1] (lā) *v.* **laid, lay·ing** **1.** To cause to lie; deposit; to place in a horizontal, reclining, or low position. **2** put or place; esp., to cause to be in a specified plac[…] condition. **3.** To construct or establish as a basis or port: to *lay* the groundwork. **4.** To place or arrang[…] proper position: to *lay* bricks. **5.** To produce internally deposit (an egg or eggs). **6.** To think out; devise: to plans. **7.** To attribute or ascribe: to *lay* the blame. **8.** impose as a penalty, obligation, etc.: to *lay* a fine. **9.** T[…] forth; present: to *lay* one's claim before a court. **10** cause to fall; knock down. **11.** To cause to settle, subs[…] or lie level: to *lay* the dust. **12.** To render ineffective; q[…] as a rumor. **13.** To bury, as in a grave; inter. **14.** apply in or as in a layer; spread, as paint. **15.** To se[…] prepare (a trap, etc.). **16.** To prepare (a table, etc.) for by setting out the necessary equipment. **17.** To se[…] locate (a scene, action, etc.). **18.** To strike or inflict b[…]

th. **19.** To offer or stake as a bet. **20.** To twist strands
as to produce (rope, cable, etc.). **—** *v.i.* **21.** To produce
d deposit eggs. **22.** To make a bet or bets. **23.** *Naut.*
move to a specified place or position: to *lay* aloft. **— to**
r **away** **1.** To store up; save. **2.** To bury in or as in a
ve. **— to lay down** **1.** To place or put aside, in a low
sition. etc. **2.** To give up; sacrifice: to *lay down* one's
. **3.** To state authoritatively or dogmatically: to *lay*
vn the rules. **4.** To bet. **— to lay for** *U.S. Informal* To
ait an opportunity to attack or harm (someone). **— to**
in To procure and store. **— to lay into** To attack vigor-
sly. **— to lay it on** *Informal* To be extravagant, lavish,
exorbitant, esp. in praise or flattery. **— to lay low** **1.**
strike down; prostrate. **2.** *U.S. Slang* To go into hiding.
to lay off **1.** To mark out; plan. **2.** *U.S.* To dismiss
m a job, usu. temporarily. **3.** *U.S. Informal* To stop
rking; take a rest. **4.** *U.S. Slang* To stop or cease. **—**
lay out **1.** To arrange or display for use, inspection, etc.
To arrange according to a plan; map. **3.** To spend or
ply (a sum of money). **4.** To prepare (a corpse) for
rial. **5.** *Informal* To strike down; prostrate. **— to lay**
er **1.** To overlay. **2.** *U.S. Informal* To stop for a time in
course of a journey. **— to lay to** **1.** To work vigorously
2. *Naut.* To maintain a vessel facing into the wind in a
tionary or nearly stationary position. **— to lay up** **1.**
make a store of. **2.** To incapacitate or confine, as by ill-
s, injury, etc. **—** *n.* The manner in which something
or is placed. [OE pt. of *licyan* to lie, recline]
◆ **lay, lie** Formal writing demands a distinction between
se two words. *Lay* takes an object: We *lay* the papers
his desk every morning. *Lie,* meaning recline or be situ-
d, does not take an object: The papers *lie* on the desk.
e past tenses of these verbs are particularly liable to mis-
and should be handled carefully: We *laid* the papers
his desk, and they *lay* there until he arrived.
[2] (lā) *adj.* **1.** Of or belonging to the laity; secular. **2.**
t belonging to or endorsed by a learned profession: a *lay*
nion. [< OF < Med.L < Gk. *laos* the people]
[3] (lā) Past tense of LIE[1].
[4] (lā) *n.* **1.** A song, ballad, or narrative poem. **2.** A mel-
y. [< OF *lai*]
·er (lā′ər) *n.* **1.** A single thickness, coating, covering,
. **2.** One who or that which lays; esp., a hen considered
an egg producer. **3.** A shoot or twig constituting part
a growing plant, of which a part is placed in the ground
rooting. **—** *v.t. & v.i.* **1.** To form a layer or layers.
To propagate (a plant) by means of a layer or layers.
er cake A cake, usu. frosted, made in layers having a
eetened filling between them.
·ette (lā′et′) *n.* The supply of clothing, bedding, etc.,
ovided for a newborn infant. [< F, dim. of *laie* packing
x, drawer < Flemish < MDu. *lade* chest, trunk]
·man (lā′mən) *n. pl.* **·men** (mən) **1.** One without train-
; or skill in a profession or branch of knowledge. **2.** A man
onging to the laity, as distinguished from the clergy.
·off (lā′ôf′, -of′) *n. U.S.* **1.** The temporary dismissal of
ployees. **2.** A period of enforced unemployment.
·out (lā′out′) *n.* **1.** A planned arrangement, as: **a** The
ative positions of streets, rooms, etc. **b** Written matter,
istrations, etc., arranged for printing. **2.** That which is
d out or provided, as equipment.
·o·ver (lā′ō′vər) *n.* A break in a journey; a stopover.
zar (lā′zər, laz′ər) *n. Archaic* A beggar or pauper af-
cted with a loathsome disease; esp., a leper. [< Med.L
arus, after *Lazarus* (*Luke* xvi 20)]
·a·ret·to (laz′ə·ret′ō) *n. pl.* **·tos** **1.** A hospital for the
atment of contagious diseases, as leprosy. Also **lazar**
use. **2.** A ship or building used as a place of quarantine.
Naut. A storage space between decks in the stern of a
ssel: also **laz′a·ret′, laz′a·rette′** (-ret′). [< Ital. dial.
enetian) *lazareto, nazareto* (Santa Madonna di) *Nazaret,*
netian church formerly used as a hospital]
z·a·rus (laz′ə·rəs) In the New Testament: **a** A brother of
artha and Mary, raised from the dead by Christ. *John*
1. **b** A sick beggar in the parable of the rich and the poor
an. *Luke* xvi 20.
e (lāz) *v.* **lazed, laz·ing** *v.i.* **1.** To be lazy; loaf; idle. **—**
. **2.** To pass (time) in idleness. [< LAZY]
·u·rite (laz′yōō·rīt) *n.* A deep blue silicate of sodium and
uminum containing sulfur, the principal constituent of
ois lazuli. [< Med.L *lazur* azure]
zy (lā′zē) *adj.* **·zi·er, ·zi·est** **1.** Unwilling to work or en-
ge in energetic activity; slothful. **2.** Moving or acting
owly or heavily. **3.** Characterized by idleness or languor.
′rob. < MLG *lasich* loose, feeble] **— la′zi·ly** *adv.* **—**
′zi·ness *n.*
zy·bones (lā′zē·bōnz′) *n. pl.* **·bones** *Informal* A lazy
rson.

Lazy Susan A revolving tray, often divided into compartments, used to hold condiments, etc. Also **lazy Susan.**

lea (lē) *n. Chiefly Poetic* A grassy field or tract; meadow. [OE *lēah,* orig., open ground in a wood]

leach (lēch) *v.t.* **1.** To cause (a liquid) to percolate or filter through something. **2.** To subject to the filtering action of a liquid. **3.** To remove or dissolve by or as by filtering. **—** *v.i.* **4.** To be removed or dissolved by percolation or filtration. **—** *n.* **1.** The process of leaching. **2.** A solution obtained from leaching. [OE *leccan* to wet, irrigate] **— leach′er** *n.*

lead[1] (lēd) *v.* **led, lead·ing** *v.t.* **1.** To go with or ahead of so as to show the way; guide. **2.** To cause to progress by or as by pulling or holding: to *lead* a child by the hand. **3.** To serve as or indicate a route for: The path *led* him to the hut. **4.** To control the actions or affairs of; direct. **5.** To influence the ideas, conduct, or actions of. **6.** To be first among. **7.** To be the principal participant in: to *lead* a discussion. **8.** To conduct the performance of (musicians or music). **9.** To experience or live; also, to cause to experience or go through: to *lead* a merry life; They *led* him a wild chase. **10.** To direct or effect the course of (water, conduits, cable, etc.). **11.** In card games, to begin a round by playing (a specified card). **—** *v.i.* **12.** To act as guide; conduct. **13.** To be led; yield readily to being pulled or guided. **14.** To afford a way or passage: The road *leads* through a swamp. **15.** To be conducive; tend: followed by *to*: Delinquency *leads* to crime. **16.** To have control or command. **17.** To be first or in advance. **18.** In card games, to make the first play. **— to lead off** **1.** To make a start; begin. **2.** In baseball, to be the first batter in a line-up or inning. **— to lead on** **1.** To entice or tempt, esp. to wrongdoing. **2.** To go first or in advance. **—** *n.* **1.** Position in advance or at the head. **2.** The distance or interval by which someone or something leads. **3.** Position of primary importance, responsibility, etc. **4.** Guidance; leadership; example: Follow his *lead.* **5.** Indication; clue: Give me a *lead.* **6.** In dramatic presentations: **a** A starring role. **b** A performer having such a role. **7.** In journalism, the introductory portion or paragraph of a news story. **8.** In card games: **a** The right or obligation to play first in a game or round. **b** The card, suit, etc., thus played. **9.** In baseball, a position taken by a runner part of the way between the base he has attained and the next base. **10.** *Electr.* A short wire or conductor, used as a connection to a source of current. **11.** A cord, leash etc., for leading an animal. [OE *lǣden* to cause to go]

lead[2] (led) *n.* **1.** A soft, heavy, malleable, dull gray metallic element (symbol Pb), occurring most commonly in the sulfide mineral galena. See ELEMENT. **2.** Any of various objects made of lead or similar metal; esp., a weight suspended from a line, used in sounding, etc. **3.** Graphite, esp. in the form of thin rods, used as the writing material in pencils. **4.** Bullets, shot, etc. **5.** White lead. **6.** *Printing* A thin strip of type metal used to provide space between printed lines. **—** *v.t.* **1.** To cover, weight, fasten, treat, or fill with lead. **2.** *Printing* To separate or space (lines of type) with leads. [OE *lēad*]

lead·en (led′n) *adj.* **1.** Dull gray, as lead. **2.** Made of lead. **3.** Weighty; inert: a *leaden* mass. **4.** Heavy or labored in movement, etc., sluggish. **5.** Oppressive; gloomy. **— lead′·en·ly** *adv.* **— lead′en·ness** *n.*

lead·er (lē′dər) *n.* **1.** One who or that which goes ahead or in advance. **2.** One who acts as a guiding force, commander, etc. **3.** An article of merchandise offered at a special low price to attract customers. **4.** A pipe for draining a liquid, as rainwater. **5.** In fishing, a length of gut, etc., used for attaching a hook or lure to the line. **6.** *pl. Printing* Dots or hyphens in a horizontal row, serving to guide the eye across a page, column, etc.

lead·er·ship (lē′dər·ship) *n.* **1.** The office, position, or capacity of a leader; guidance. **2.** Ability to lead, exert authority, etc. **3.** A group of leaders.

lead-in (lēd′in′) *n. Telecom.* A wire connecting a radio receiving set with its antenna.

lead·ing[1] (lē′ding) *adj.* **1.** Having the capacity or effect of controlling, influencing, guiding, etc. **2.** Most important; chief. **3.** Situated or going at the head; first. **—** *n.* The act of one who or that which leads; guidance.

lead·ing[2] (led′ing) *n.* **1.** The act or process of filling, covering, or separating with lead. **2.** A border of lead. **3.** *Printing* Spacing between lines.

leading question (lē′ding) A question having the intention or effect of eliciting the reply desired by the questioner.

lead·off (lēd′ôf′, -of′) *n.* **1.** A beginning action, move, etc., as the opening play in a competitive game. **2.** A player or participant who begins the action in a game or competition.

lead pencil (led) A pencil having a thin stick of graphite as its writing material.

lead poisoning (led) *Pathol.* Poisoning caused by the absorption of lead by the tissues.
leaf (lēf) *n. pl.* **leaves** (lēvz) **1.** One of the outgrowths from the stem of a plant, commonly flat, thin, and green in color, and functioning as the principal area of photosynthesis. **2.** Foliage collectively; leafage. **3.** Loosely, a petal. **4.** A product, as tobacco, tea, etc., in the form of gathered leaves. **5.** One of the sheets of paper in a book, etc., each side being a single page. **6.** A flat piece, hinged or otherwise movable, constituting part of a table, gate, etc. **7.** Metal in a very thin sheet or plate: gold *leaf.* —**to turn over a new leaf** To begin anew, esp. with the intention of improving one's ways. —*v.i.* To put forth or produce leaves. [OE *lēaf*]
leaf·age (lē′fij) *n.* Leaves collectively; foliage.
leaf·less (lēf′lis) *adj.* Having or bearing no leaves. —**leaf′·less·ness** *n.*
leaf·let (lēf′lit) *n.* **1.** One of the divisions of a compound leaf. **2.** A small printed sheet or circular, often folded. **3.** A little leaf or leaflike part.
leaf·stalk (lēf′stôk) *n.* A petiole (def. 1).
leaf·y (lē′fē) *adj.* **leaf·i·er, leaf·i·est** **1.** Bearing, covered with, or characterized by a profusion of leaves. **2.** Consisting of or resembling leaves. —**leaf′i·ness** *n.*
league[1] (lēg) *n.* A measure of distance varying from about 2.42 to 4.6 statute miles, but usu. reckoned as approximately 3 miles. [< OF < LL *leuga, leuca* Gaulish mile]
league[2] (lēg) *n.* **1.** An association or confederation of persons, organizations, or states. **2.** A compact or covenant binding such a union. **3.** An association of athletic teams. —**in league** In close alliance. —*v.t. & v.i.* **leagued, lea·guing** To unite in a league. [< OF < Ital. *legare* to bind]
League of Nations An international organization established in 1920, primarily for the preservation of world peace, and formally dissolved in 1946.
Le·ah (lē′ə) In the Old Testament, Rachel's elder sister, who became the first wife of Jacob. *Gen.* xxix 16.
leak (lēk) *n.* **1.** An opening, as a crack, permitting an undesirable escape or entrance of fluid, light, etc. **2.** Any condition or agency by which something is let through or escapes: a *leak* in the security system. **3.** An act or instance of leaking; leakage. —*v.i.* **1.** To let a fluid, etc., pass or escape through a hole, crack, or similar opening. **2.** To pass, flow, or escape through a hole, crack, etc. **3.** To be divulged despite secrecy: The plans *leaked* out. —*v.t.* **4.** To let (a liquid, etc.) escape. **5.** To disclose (information, etc.) without authorization. [< ON *leka* to drip]
leak·age (lē′kij) *n.* **1.** The act or circumstance of leaking. **2.** That which escapes or passes through by leaking.
leak·y (lē′kē) *adj.* **leak·i·er, leak·i·est** Having a leak; permitting leakage. —**leak′i·ness** *n.*
lean[1] (lēn) *v.* **leaned** or **leant** (lent), **lean·ing** *v.i.* **1.** To rest or incline for support: usu. with *against* or *on.* **2.** To bend or slant from an erect position. **3.** To have a tendency, preference, etc.: to *lean* toward conservatism. **4.** To depend for support, etc.; rely. —*v.t.* **5.** To cause to incline. **6.** To place or rest (something) so as to be supported by something else: usu. with *against, on,* or *upon.* —*n.* The act or condition of leaning; slant. [OE *hleonian, hlinian*]
lean[2] (lēn) *adj.* **1.** Not fat or plump; thin; spare. **2.** Not containing fat: *lean* meat. **3.** Not rich, plentiful, or satisfying; meager. —*n.* Meat or flesh having little or no fat. [OE *hlǣne* thin] —**lean′ly** *adv.* —**lean′ness** *n.*
Le·an·der (lē·an′dər) In Greek legend, the lover of Hero.
lean·ing (lē′ning) *n.* **1.** An inclination; tendency; predisposition. **2.** The act of one who or that which leans.
lean-to (lēn′to͞o′) *n. pl.* **-tos** (-to͞oz′) **1.** A crude hut of branches, etc., sloping to the ground from a raised support. **2.** A shed or extension of a building having a sloping roof and supported by an adjoining wall or structure.
leap (lēp) *v.* **leaped** or **leapt** (lept, lēpt), **leap·ing** *v.i.* **1.** To rise or project oneself by a sudden thrust from the ground; jump; spring. **2.** To move, react, etc., suddenly or impulsively. **3.** To make an abrupt transition: to *leap* to a conclusion. —*v.t.* **4.** To traverse by a jump. **5.** To cause to jump. —*n.* **1.** The act of leaping. **2.** The space traversed by leaping. **3.** A place from which a leap may be made. **4.** An abrupt transition. [OE *hlēapan*] —**leap′er** *n.*
leap·frog (lēp′frog′, -frôg′) *n.* A game in which each player puts his hands on the back of another, who is bending over, and leaps over him in a straddling position.
leap year A year of 366 days, in which a 29th day is added to February. Every year divisible by 4 (as 1964) is a leap year, except those completing a century, which must be divisible by 400 (as 2000).
Lear (lir) Hero of Shakespeare's tragedy *King Lear.*
learn (lûrn) *v.* **learned** or **learnt, learn·ing** *v.t.* **1.** To acquire knowledge of or skill in by study, practice, etc. **2.** To find out; become aware of. **3.** To commit to memory; memorize. **4.** To acquire by experience or example. —*v.i.* **5.** To gain knowledge or acquire skill. **6.** To become informed; know: with *of* or *about.* [OE *leornian*] —**learn′er** *n.*

learn·ed (lûr′nid) *adj.* **1.** Having profound or exte knowledge. **2.** Characterized by or devoted to scholar
learn·ing (lûr′ning) *n.* **1.** Knowledge obtained by st erudition. **2.** The act of acquiring knowledge or skill.
lease (lēs) *n.* **1.** A contract for the temporary occupati use of premises, property, etc., in exchange for payme rent. **2.** The period of such occupation or use. —*v.* To grant use of under a lease. **2.** To hold under a lease. AF, OF < L *laxus* loose] —**leas′a·ble** *adj.*
leash (lēsh) *n.* **1.** A thong, cord, etc., by which a d other animal is led or restrained. **2.** Restraint; control *v.t.* To hold or secure by a leash. [< OF < L *laxus* l
least (lēst) Alternative superlative of LITTLE. — Smallest in degree, value, size, etc.; most insignificant; sl est. —*n.* That which is smallest, slightest, or most ins icant. —**at least** **1.** By the lowest possible estimate. At any rate. —**in the least** In the slightest degree; a —*adv.* In the lowest or smallest degree. [OE *lǣssa* l
least·wise (lēst′wīz′) *adv. Informal* At least; at any Also *Dial.* **least′ways′** (-wāz′).
leath·er (leth′ər) *n.* **1.** Animal skin, usu. with the ha moved, prepared for use by tanning. **2.** An article ma leather. —*v.t.* To cover or equip with leather. [OE *le*
leath·ern (leth′ərn) *adj. Archaic* **1.** Made of leather Resembling leather; leathery. [OE *lether* leather]
leath·er·neck (leth′ər·nek′) *n. U.S. Slang* A marin
leath·er·y (leth′ər·ē) *adj.* Resembling leather in textu appearance; tough. —**leath′er·i·ness** *n.*
leave[1] (lēv) *v.* **left, leav·ing** *v.t.* **1.** To go or depart f **2.** To allow to remain behind or in a specified place, c tion, etc. **3.** To have or cause as an aftermath: Oil *l* stains. **4.** To cause to be made available in one's abs *Leave* your name at the desk. **5.** To commit for action, entrust: *Leave* it to me. **6.** To terminate one's connecti association with. **7.** To abandon; forsake. **8.** To hav maining after one's death. **9.** To transmit as a legacy queath. **10.** To have as a remainder as the result c arithmetic operation. —*v.i.* **11.** To go away; set out. **to leave alone** **1.** To refrain from interfering with, etc. To allow to remain solitary. —**to leave off** To stop; c —**to leave out** **1.** To omit. **2.** To exclude. [OE *l* lit., to let remain] —**leav′er** *n.*
◆ **leave, let** *Leave* means to depart or to permit to re (*He left the room; He left the book on the table*), as distingui from *let,* which means simply to permit (*Let him stay*) can be followed by the infinitive without *to; leave* car *Leave it to him to decide* and *Let him decide* are standard *Leave him decide* is nonstandard.
leave[2] (lēv) *n.* **1.** Permission to do something. **2.** Per sion to be absent; esp., **a** Official permission to be ab from duty. **b** The period covered by such permission: **leave of absence.** **3.** Formal farewell: usu. in the phra **take (one's) leave.** —**on leave** Absent from work or with permission. [OE *lēaf* permission]
leave[3] (lēv) *v.i.* **leaved, leav·ing** To put forth leaves;
leaved (lēvd) *adj.* **1.** Having a leaf or leaves. **2.** Havir characterized by (a specified kind or number of) leaves
leav·en (lev′ən) *n.* **1.** An agent of fermentation, as y added to dough or batter to produce a light texture. portion of fermented dough used for this purpose. **3.** pervasive influence that produces a significant change. **leav′en·ing.** —*v.t.* **1.** To cause fermentation in. **2.** T fect in character; temper. [< OF < L *levare* to raise]
leaves (lēvz) Plural of LEAF.
leave-tak·ing (lēv′tā′king) *n.* An act of departure.
leav·ings (lē′vingz) *n.pl.* Unused portion; remnants.
Leb·a·nese (leb′ə·nēz′, -nēs′) *adj.* Of or pertaining to anon or its people. —*n.* A native or citizen of Leban
Le·bens·raum (lā′bəns·roum′) *n. German* Terri claimed by a nation as necessary for its economic indep ence or growth; literally, space for living.
lech·er (lech′ər) *n.* A lewd and prurient man. [< O OHG *leccōn* to lick]
lech·er·ous (lech′ər·əs) *adj.* Given to lewdness or inci to lust. —**lech′er·ous·ly** *adv.* —**lech′er·ous·ness** *n.*
lech·er·y (lech′ər·ē) *n. pl.* **·ries** Unconstrained sexua dulgence.
lec·tern (lek′tərn) *n.* **1.** A stand on which a speaker, structor, etc., may place books or papers. **2.** In s churches, a reading desk from which certain parts of service are read. [< OF < LL < L *legere* to read]
lec·ture (lek′chər) *n.* **1.** A discourse on a specific subj delivered to an audience for instruction or information. A formal reproof or lengthy reprimand. —*v.* **·tured, · ing** *v.i.* **1.** To deliver a lecture or lectures. —*v.t.* **2.** To liver a lecture to. **3.** To rebuke sternly or at length. [*legere* to read] —**lec′tur·er** *n.*
led (led) Past tense and past participle of LEAD[1].
Le·da (lē′də) In Greek mythology, the mother of Clyt nestra, Castor, Pollux, and Helen, of which the latter th were fathered by Zeus in the form of a swan.

e (lej) *n.* **1.** A narrow, shelflike projection along the of a rocky formation. **2.** A shelf or sill projecting from ɔrming the top of a wall, etc. **3.** An underwater or coast-idge. **4.** *Mining* A metal-bearing rock stratum; vein. E *legge*] — **ledg′y** *adj.*
ger (lej′ər) *n.* An account book in which all final entries usiness transactions are recorded. [ME *legger*]
er line *Music* A short line added above or below the : also spelled *leger line.*
ē) *n.* **1.** Shelter or protection, esp. from the wind. **2.** *fly Naut.* **a** The side sheltered from the wind. **b** The di-ion opposite that from which the wind is blowing. — *Chiefly Naut.* Pertaining to or being on the lee: opposed *eather.* [OE *hlēo* shelter]
[1] (lēch) *n.* **1.** Any of a class of carnivorous or blood-ing, chiefly aquatic annelid worms; esp. the **medicinal h,** formerly used for bloodletting. **2.** One who clings to her for gain; a parasite. **3.** *Archaic* A physician. — *v.t. haic* To treat with leeches. [OE *lǣce*, orig., physician]
[2] (lēch) *n. Naut.* **1.** Either of the side edges of a square **2.** The after edge of a fore-and-aft sail. [ME *leche*]
(lēk) *n.* **1.** A culinary herb of the lily family, closely d to the onion but having a narrow bulb and broader, green leaves: the national emblem of Wales. **2.** Any of ous related plants. [OE *lēac*]
(lir) *n.* A sly look or sidewise glance expressing sala-s desire, malicious intent, knowing complicity, etc. — To look with a leer. [OE *hlēor* cheek, face]
y (lir′ē) *adj. Informal* **1.** Suspicious; wary. **2.** Sly.
(lēz) *n.pl.* Sediment, esp. in wine or liquor; dregs. [Pl. bs. *lee* < OF *lie*]
ward (lē′wərd, *Naut.* lo͞o′ərd) *adj.* **1.** Of or pertaining he direction toward which the wind is blowing. **2.** Being r toward the side sheltered from the wind. — *n.* The or direction toward which the wind is blowing. — *adv.* ard the lee. Opposed to *windward.*
way (lē′wā′) *n.* **1.** Additional space, time, range, etc., viding greater freedom of action. **2.** *Naut.* The lateral of a vessel or an aircraft in motion.
(left) Past tense and past participle of LEAVE[1].
(left) *adj.* **1.** Pertaining to, designating, or being on the of the body that is toward the north when one faces east, usu. having the weaker and less dominant hand, etc. **2.** taining to or situated on the corresponding side of any-g. **3.** Nearest to or tending in the direction of the left **4.** Worn on a left hand, foot, etc. **5.** *Sometimes cap.* ignating a person, party, faction, etc., having liberal, nocratic, socialistic, or laborite views and policies. — *n.* Any part, area, etc., on or toward the left side. **2.** *Often* A group, party, etc., whose views and policies are left . def. 5); esp., in Europe, such parties whose members o the presiding officer's left in a deliberative assembly. n boxing: **a** A blow with the left hand. **b** The left hand. *adv.* On, to, or toward the left. [ME (Kentish) var. of umed OE *lyft* weak]
face In military drill, a 90-degree pivot to the left. using ball of the right foot and the heel of the left.
hand (left′hand′) *adj.* **1.** Of, for, pertaining to, or ated on the left side or the left hand. **2.** Turning, open-or swinging to the left.
-hand·ed (left′han′did) *adj.* **1.** Using the left hand ha-ually and more easily than the right. **2.** Done with the hand. **3.** Adapted or intended for use by the left hand. Turning or moving from right to left, or counterclock-e. **5.** Ironical or insincere in intent or effect: a *left-handed* npliment. **6.** Clumsy. — *adv.* With the left hand. — **′-hand′ed·ly** *adv.* — **left′-hand′ed·ness** *n.*
ist (lef′tist) *n.* One whose views and policies are left . def. 5). — *adj.* Left (*adj.* def. 5). — **left′ism** *n.*
o·ver (left′ō′vər) *n. Usu. pl.* An unused part or rem-t, esp. of prepared food. — *adj.* Left as a remnant.
wing **1.** *Sometimes cap.* A party, group, faction, etc., ing leftist policies. **2.** The wing, part, etc., on the left le. — **left-wing** (left′wing′) *adj.* — **left′-wing′er** *n.*
(leg) *n.* **1.** One of the limbs or appendages serving as a ans of support and locomotion in animals and man. **2.** *at.* **a** A lower limb of the human body, extending from the to the ankle. **b** The part of the lower limb between the e and the ankle. **3.** A support resembling a leg in shape, ition, or function. **4.** The portion of an article of cloth-, as hose, trousers, etc., that covers a leg. **5.** A division or tion of a course or journey. **6.** One of the divisions of an led or forked object, as a pair of compasses. **7.** *Geom.* her of the sides of a triangle adjacent to the base or the potenuse. **8.** *Naut.* The distance traveled by a vessel in a gle direction while tacking. — **on one's last legs** On the ge of collapse or death. — **to have not a leg to stand on** have no sound or logical basis, as for argument, justification, etc. — **to pull one's leg** *Informal* To make fun of; fool. — **to shake a leg** *Slang* **1.** To hurry. **2.** To dance. — *v.i.* **legged, leg·ging** *Informal* To walk or run: usu. followed by *it.* [< ON *leggr*]
leg·a·cy (leg′ə·sē) *n. pl.* **·cies** **1.** Personal property, money, etc., bequeathed by will; a bequest. **2.** Anything received from or passed on by an ancestor, predecessor, or earlier era. [< OF < Med.L *legatia* the district of a legate]
le·gal (lē′gəl) *adj.* **1.** Of, pertaining to, or concerned with law: *legal* documents. **2.** Established or authorized by law. **3.** Conforming with or permitted by law. **4.** According to, determined by, or coming under the jurisdiction of statute law, rather than equity. **5.** Characteristic of or appropriate to those who practice law. — **Syn.** See LAWFUL. [< OF < L *lex, legis* law] — **le′gal·ly** *adv.*
legal age Age (*n.* def. 3).
legal holiday *U.S.* A day on which banks are closed and official business is suspended or limited by law.
le·gal·ism (lē′gəl·iz′əm) *n.* Strict conformity to law; esp., the stressing of the letter and forms of the law rather than the spirit of justice. — **le′gal·ist** *n.* — **le′gal·is′tic** *adj.*
le·gal·i·ty (li·gal′ə·tē) *n. pl.* **·ties** **1.** The condition or quality of being legal; lawfulness. **2.** Adherence to law.
le·gal·ize (lē′gəl·īz) *v.t.* **·ized, ·iz·ing** To make legal. Also *Brit.* **le′gal·ise.** — **le′gal·i·za′tion** (-ə·zā′shən, -ī·zā′-) *n.*
legal medicine Medical jurisprudence.
legal tender Coin or other money that may be legally offered in payment of a debt, and that a creditor must accept.
leg·ate (leg′it) *n.* **1.** An ecclesiastic appointed as an official representative of the Pope. **2.** An official envoy, usu. acting as a diplomatic representative of a government. — **Syn.** See AMBASSADOR. [< OF < L *legare* to send as a deputy] — **leg·a·tine** (leg′ə·tin, -tīn) *adj.* — **leg′ate·ship** *n.*
leg·a·tee (leg′ə·tē′) *n.* One to whom a legacy is bequeathed.
le·ga·tion (li·gā′shən) *n.* **1.** The official residence or business premises of a diplomatic minister or envoy of lower rank than an ambassador. **2.** The official staff of a foreign envoy or diplomatic mission. **3.** The position or rank of a legate.
le·ga·to (li·gä′tō) *Music adj.* Smooth and flowing, with unbroken transition between successive notes. — *adv.* In a legato manner. — *n. pl.* **·tos** A smooth, connected style, performance, or passage. [< Ital., lit., bound]
le·ga·tor (li·gā′tər, leg′ə·tôr′) *n.* One who makes a will.
leg·end (lej′ənd) *n.* **1.** An unauthenticated story from earlier times, preserved by tradition and popularly thought to be historical. **2.** A body of such stories, as those connected with a people or culture. **3.** An inscription or motto, as on a coin, banner, etc. **4.** A caption or explanatory description accompanying an illustration, chart, etc. [< OF < Med.L < L *legere* to read]
leg·en·dar·y (lej′ən·der′ē) *adj.* **1.** Of, presented in, or of the nature of a legend. **2.** Famous; celebrated.
leg·end·ry (lej′ən·drē) *n.* Legends collectively; legend.
le·ger line (lej′ər) See LEDGER LINE.
leg·er·de·main (lej′ər·də·mān′) *n.* **1.** Sleight of hand. **2.** Any artful trickery or deception. [ME < MF *léger de main*, lit., light of hand] — **leg′er·de·main′ist** *n.*
le·ges (lē′jēz) Plural of LEX.
leg·ged (leg′id, legd) *adj.* Having or characterized by (a specified kind or number of) legs: *bow-legged; two-legged.*
leg·ging (leg′ing) *n.* A gaiter or similar covering for the leg, usu. extending from the knee to the instep.
leg·gy (leg′ē) *adj.* **·gi·er, ·gi·est** **1.** Having disproportionately long legs. **2.** *Informal* Having or displaying attractive, shapely legs. — **leg′gi·ness** *n.*
leg·horn (leg′hôrn, -ərn) *n.* **1.** Finely plaited wheat straw. **2.** A hat made from this straw. **3.** *Usu. cap.* One of a breed of small, hardy domestic fowl. [after *Leghorn*]
leg·i·ble (lej′ə·bəl) *adj.* **1.** Capable of being read or deciphered; easy to read. **2.** Readily perceived or discovered from apparent signs or evidence. [< LL < L *legere* to read] — **leg′i·bil′i·ty, leg′i·ble·ness** *n.* — **leg′i·bly** *adv.*
le·gion (lē′jən) *n.* **1.** In ancient Rome, a major military unit consisting primarily of infantry troops with an auxiliary force of cavalry, altogether comprising between 4,200 and 6,000 men. **2.** *Usu. pl.* Any large military force; army. **3.** A great number; multitude. ◆ Sometimes used predicatively with the adjectival sense *innumerable*, as in Their members are *legion.* **4.** *Usu. cap.* Any of various military or honorary organizations, usu. national in character. [< OF < L *legere* to choose, levy troops]
le·gion·ar·y (lē′jən·er′ē) *adj.* Of, or pertaining to a legion. — *n. pl.* **·ar·ies** A soldier or member of a legion.
le·gion·naire (lē′jən·âr′) *n. Often cap.* A member of a legion (def. 4). [< F *légionnaire*]
Legion of Merit *U.S.* A military decoration awarded for exceptionally meritorious conduct in the performance of outstanding services. See DECORATION.

leg·is·late (lej′is·lāt) *v.* **·lat·ed, ·lat·ing** *v.i.* **1.** To make a law or laws. — *v.t.* **2.** To cause to be in a specified state by legislation: often with *into* or *out of.* [Back formation < LEGISLATOR]

leg·is·la·tion (lej′is·lā′shən) *n.* **1.** The act or procedures of enacting laws. **2.** An officially enacted law or laws.

leg·is·la·tive (lej′is·lā′tiv) *adj.* **1.** Of, pertaining to, or involved in legislation. **2.** Having the power to legislate: the *legislative* branch of the government: distinguished from *executive, judicial.* **3.** Of or pertaining to a legislature. **4.** Enacted by or resulting from legislation. — *n.* The legislative branch of a government. — **leg′is·la′tive·ly** *adv.*

leg·is·la·tor (lej′is·lā′tər) *n.* **1.** One active in the formation and enactment of laws; a lawmaker. **2.** A member of a legislature. [< L < *lex, legis* law + *lator* bearer, proposer] — **leg′is·la′tress** (-tris), **leg′is·la′trix** (-triks) *n. fem.*

leg·is·la·ture (lej′is·lā′chər) *n.* A body of persons officially constituted and empowered to make and enact the laws of a nation or state; esp., in the U.S., the lawmaking body of a State, Territory, etc., as distinguished from Congress.

le·git (lə·jit′) *Slang n.* Legitimate drama, theatrical productions, etc. — *adj.* Legitimate.

le·git·i·ma·cy (lə·jit′ə·mə·sē) *n.* The state or condition of being legitimate.

le·git·i·mate (*adj.* lə·jit′ə·mit; *v.* lə·jit′ə·māt) *adj.* **1.** In accordance with law; lawful. **2.** Based on or resulting from orderly, rational deduction or inference. **3.** Authentic; valid. **4.** Born in wedlock. **5.** According to or based on strict hereditary right. **6.** In the theater, denoting drama performed by living actors before an audience as distinguished from motion pictures, television, etc. — *v.t.* **·mat·ed, ·mat·ing 1.** To make or establish as legitimate. **2.** To show reason or authorization for. [< Med.L < L *legitimus* lawful < *lex, legis* law] — **le·git′i·mate·ly** *adv.* — **le·git′i·mate·ness** *n.* — **le·git′i·ma′tion** (-mā′shən) *n.*

le·git·i·mist (lə·jit′ə·mist) *n.* An advocate of rule or authority based on hereditary right; esp., of claims to a monarchy. — **le·git′i·mism** *n.* — **le·git′i·mis′tic** *adj.*

le·git·i·mize (lə·jit′ə·mīz) *v.t.* **·mized, ·miz·ing** To legitimate. Also **le·git′i·ma·tize** (-mə·tīz). — **le·git′i·mi·za′tion** *n.*

leg·less (leg′lis) *adj.* Having no legs.

leg-of-mut·ton (leg′ə·mut′n) *adj.* Having the characteristically triangular or tapering shape of a haunch of mutton.

leg-of-mutton sleeve A sleeve puffed on the upper arm and fitting closely on the forearm: also called *gigot.*

leg·ume (leg′yōōm, lə·gyōōm′) *n.* **1.** The fruit or seed of any leguminous plant, esp. when used as food or fodder. **2.** Any leguminous plant. **3.** *Bot.* The characteristic, sutured seed vessel of such a plant; a pod. [< F < L *legumen,* lit., something gathered < *legere* to gather]

le·gu·mi·nous (lə·gyōō′mə·nəs) *adj.* Of or belonging to a large family of plants including peas, beans, etc.

leg·work (leg′wûrk′) *n. Informal* Chores, errands, etc., accomplished by or as by going about on foot.

lei (lā, lā′ē) *n. pl.* **leis** A festival garland of blossoms, feathers, etc., as worn in Hawaii. [< Hawaiian]

lei·sure (lē′zhər, lezh′ər) *n.* **1.** Freedom from the demands of work or duty. **2.** Time available for recreation or relaxation. — **at leisure 1.** Free from pressing necessity or obligation; having time to spare. **2.** Unoccupied; not employed. **3.** When one has time or opportunity: also **at one's leisure.** — *adj.* **1.** Not spent in work or necessary activity: *leisure* time. **2.** Having considerable leisure: the *leisure* classes. [< OF < L *licere* to be permitted]

lei·sure·ly (lē′zhər·lē, lezh′ər-) *adj.* Free from exertion or pressure; relaxed and unhurried. Also **lei′sured** (-zhərd). — *adv.* In a leisurely manner. — **lei′sure·li·ness** *n.*

leit·mo·tif (līt′mō·tēf′) *n. Music* A theme used for a certain person, event, or idea throughout an opera, etc. Also **leit′mo·tiv′** (-tēf′). [< G < *leiten* to lead + *motiv* motive]

lem·ming (lem′ing) *n.* Any of several small arctic rodents, having a short tail and furry feet; esp., a European species, noted for recurrent mass migrations often terminated by drowning in the ocean. [< Norw.]

LEMMING (To 6 inches long)

lem·on (lem′ən) *n.* **1.** The oval, citrus fruit of an evergreen tree, having juicy, acid pulp and a yellow rind yielding an essential oil (**lemon oil**) used as a flavoring and perfuming agent. **2.** The tree. **3.** A bright, clear yellow. **4.** *Slang* Something or someone disappointing or unattractive. — *adj.* Bright, clear yellow. [< OF < Sp. < Arabic < Persian *limūn*]

lem·on·ade (lem′ən·ād′) *n.* A drink made of lemon juice, water, and sugar.

le·mur (lē′mər) *n.* Any of various small, arboreal, mostly nocturnal mammals related to the monkeys; esp., one having a foxlike face and soft fur, found chiefly in Madagascar. [< NL < L *lemures* ghosts]

Len·a·pe (len′ə·pē) *n.* The generic name of the Delawares, an Algonquian people; also, their language: also called *Leni-Lenape, Lenni-Lenape.* [Short for Algonquian (Len*Leni-lenape,* lit., real man < *leni* real + *lenape* man]

lend (lend) *v.* **lent, lend·ing** *v.t.* **1.** To grant the use or session of with the understanding that the thing or its e alent will be returned. **2.** To grant the use of (money) stipulated rate of interest. **3.** To impart, as an abs quality. **4.** To make available, as for aid or support. adapt or suit (itself or oneself) to a specific purpose. **6.** To make a loan or loans. [OE *lǣn* a loan] — **lend′**

lending library A circulating library.

length (lengkth, length) *n.* **1.** Linear extent from e end; usu., the longest dimension of a thing, as distingu from its width and thickness. **2.** Extent from beginni end, as of a period of time, series, book, word, etc. **3.** state or quality of being long or prolonged, either in tir space. **4.** Duration or continuance, esp. in respect to **5.** The measurement along, extent of, or distance equiv to something specified: arm's *length.* **6.** A piece or star unit of something, measured longitudinally. **7.** *Ofte* The limit of one's efforts, ability, etc.: to go to great *le* **8.** In racing, the extent from front to back of a comp horse, boat, etc., used as a unit of estimating position. **length 1.** Finally. **2.** In full. [OE *lengthu* < *lang* lo

length·en (lengk′thən, leng′-) *v.t.* & *v.i.* To make o come longer.

length·wise (lengkth′wīz′, length′-) *adv.* In the dire or dimension of length; longitudinally. Also **length′w** (-wāz′). — *adj.* According to length; longitudinal.

length·y (lengk′thē, leng′-) *adj.* **length·i·er, length·i·es** usually or unduly long. — **length′i·ly** *adv.* — **length′i·ne**

le·ni·en·cy (lē′nē·ən·sē, lēn′yən·sē) *n.* The state or qu of being lenient. Also **le′ni·ence.** — **Syn.** See MERCY.

le·ni·ent (lē′nē·ənt, lēn′yənt) *adj.* Gentle or mercif disposition, effect, etc.; mild. [< L *leniens, -entis,* pp *lenire* to soothe] — **le′ni·ent·ly** *adv.*

Len·i-Len·a·pe (len′ē·len′ə·pē) *n.* Lenape. Also **Le Len′a·pe.**

Len·in·ism (len′in·iz′əm) A modification of Marxism stituting the doctrine and practice of the Bolsheviks an Communist Party in the Soviet Union under Lenin. **Len′in·ist, Len′in·ite** *n.* & *adj.*

len·i·tive (len′ə·tiv) *adj.* Having the power or tenden allay pain or distress; soothing. — *n.* That which sooth mitigates. [< Med.L < L *lenitus,* pp. of *lenire* to soo

len·i·ty (len′ə·tē) *n.* The state or quality of being len [< OF < L *lenitas, -tatis* softness]

lens (lenz) *n.* **1.** *Optics* A piece of glass or other transp substance, bounded by two curved surfaces or by one cu and one plane surface, by which rays of light are ma converge or diverge. See illus. for FOCUS. **2.** Two or such pieces in combination. **3.** Any device that co trates or disperses radiation, etc., other than light by a similar to that of an optical lens. **4.** *Anat.* A transparen convex body situated behind the iris of the eye and servi focus an image on the retina. For illus. see EYE. [< L *lentis* lentil; so called from the form]

lent (lent) Past tense and past participle of LEND.

Lent (lent) *n. Eccl.* The period of forty days, exclu Sundays, from Ash Wednesday to Easter, observed ann as a season of fasting, penitence, and self-denial. [Shor *Lenten* < OE *lencten, lengten* the spring]

Len·ten (len′tən) *adj.* Of, pertaining to, suitable fo characteristic of Lent. Also **len′ten.**

len·til (len′təl) *n.* **1.** A leguminous plant, having b pods containing flattish, edible seeds. **2.** The seed of plant. [< F < L *lenticula,* dim. of *lens, lentis* lentil]

len·to (len′tō) *Music adj.* Slow. — *adv.* Slowly: a d tion to the performer. — *n. pl.* **·tos** A slow moveme passage. [< Ital. < L *lentus*]

l'en·voi (len′voi, *Fr.* läṅ·vwȧ′) See ENVOY[2]. Also **l'en′**

Le·o (lē′ō) *n.* A constellation, the Lion; also, the fifth of the zodiac. See ZODIAC. [< NL < L]

Le·o Mi·nor (lē′ō mī′nər) A constellation, the Lesser L

Le·o·nid (lē′ə·nid) *n. pl.* **Le·o·nids** or **Le·o·ni·des** (lē· dēz) *Astron.* One of the meteors of a meteor shower ha its radiant point in the constellation Leo, and appearing nually about November 14.

le·o·nine (lē′ə·nīn, -nin) *adj.* Pertaining to, resemblin characteristic of a lion. [< L *leo, leonis* lion]

leop·ard (lep′ərd) *n.* **1.** A large member of the cat fam native to Asia and Africa, having a tawny coat with brown or black spots grouped in rounded clusters: also ca *panther.* **2.** Any of various similar felines, as the chee jaguar, or snow leopard. **3.** The fur of a leopard. [< LL < Gk. < *leōn* lion + *pardos* panther]

le·o·tard (lē′ə·tärd) *n. Often pl.* A close-fitting, stretch garment worn by dancers, acrobats, etc. [after Jules *tard,* 19th c. French aerialist]

lep·er (lep′ər) *n.* One afflicted with leprosy. [< obs. *l* leprosy < OF < L < Gk., orig. fem. of *lepros* scaly]

lep·i·dop·ter·ous (lep′ə·dop′tər·əs) *adj.* Belonging or

ıng to an order of insects comprising the butterflies and ns, characterized by four wings covered with minute s. [< NL < Gk. *lepis, -idos* scale + *pteron* wing] Also **dop′ter·al.** — **lep′i·dop′ter·an** *n. & adj.*
rine (lep′ə·rīn, -rin) *adj.* Pertaining to or character- of hares. [< L *lepus, leporis* hare]
e·chaun (lep′rə·kôn) *n.* In Irish folklore, a tiny elfin ıler supposed to own hidden treasure. [< Irish < OIrish little + *corpān*, dim. of *corp* body < L *corpus, -oris*]
o·sy (lep′rə·sē) *n. Pathol.* A chronic, communicable se caused by a microorganism and characterized by lar skin lesions, nerve paralysis, and physical mutila- also called *Hansen's disease.* [See LEPER.]
ous (lep′rəs) *adj.* **1.** Affected with leprosy. **2.** Of or nbling leprosy. — **lep′rous·ly** *adv.*
y *combining form* Seizure; attack: *catalepsy.* Also **-lep-** [< Gk. *lepsis* seizure]
on (lep′ton) *n. pl.* **·tons** *Physics* An atomic particle of small mass, as the electron, positron, or neutrino. [< neut. of *leptos* fine]
i·an (lez′bē·ən) *Sometimes cap. n.* A homosexual wom- — *adj.* Pertaining to or characteristic of homosexual en. [< LESBIAN] — **les′bi·an·ism** *n.*
i·an (lez′bē·ən) *n.* **1.** A native or inhabitant of Les- **2.** Sappho or one of her followers, alleged to have been osexuals. — *adj.* **1.** Of or pertaining to Lesbos or its bitants. **2.** Of or pertaining to Sappho or her poetry. < Gk. *Lesbos* Lesbos, the home of Sappho]
ma·jes·ty (lēz′ maj′is·tē) An offense against sovereign ority or a sovereign; treason. Also *Fr.* **lèse-ma·jes·té** mȧ·zhes·tā′). [< F < L < *laesa*, fem. of *laesus*, pp. of *re* to injure + *majestas* majesty]
n (lē′zhən) *n.* **1.** *Pathol.* Any abnormal or harmful ge in the structure of an organ or tissue. **2.** An injury; age. [< F < L < *laesus*, pp. of *laedere* to injure]
(les) Alternative comparative of LITTLE. — *adj.* **1.** as great in quantity or degree; not as much. **2.** Inferior egree; smaller; lower: with *than.* — *adv.* To a smaller ee or extent; not as: followed by an adjective or adverb. . A smaller amount or part. — *prep.* With the subtrac- **tion** of; minus. [OE *læs*]
suffix of adjectives **1.** Devoid of; without: *blameless,* *ıless.* **2.** Deprived of; lacking: *motherless, stemless.* **3.** able to (do something): *restless;* not susceptible of (some on): *countless.* [OE *leas* free from]
ee (les·ē′) *n.* One to whom a lease is granted. [< AF e, OF *lesse*, pp. of *lesser, laissier* to let, leave]
en (les′ən) *v.t.* **1.** To decrease. **2.** To make little of; arage. — *v.i.* **3.** To become less. — **Syn.** See DE- ASE.
er (les′ər) *adj.* Not as large or important; minor.
er Bear The constellation Ursa Minor.
er panda The panda (def. 1).
on (les′ən) *n.* **1.** An instance or experience from which ul knowledge may be gained. **2.** A division or portion of urse of study. **3.** An assignment to be studied or learned, y a student. **4.** A reprimand; reproof. **5.** A portion of Bible read or designated to be read at a religious service. *t. Rare* **1.** To give a lesson or lessons to; instruct. **2.** admonish; rebuke. [< OF < L *lectio, -ionis* a reading]
or (les′ôr, les·ôr′) *n.* One who grants a lease; a land- letting property under a lease. [See LESSEE]
(lest) *conj.* **1.** In order to prevent the chance that nething might happen); for fear that. **2.** That: after ex- ssions denoting anxiety: We worried *lest* the money uld not last. [OE (*thȳ*) *læs the* (by the) less that]
(let) *v.* **let, let·ting** *v.t.* **1.** To allow; permit. **2.** To per- to pass, come, go, etc.: followed by a proposition: *Let* by. **3.** To cause; make: with *know* or *hear*: *Let* me know n you arrive. **4.** To grant or assign, as a contract for k to be performed. **5.** An auxiliary verb, usu. in the im- ative, signifying: **a** An exhortation or command: *Let's* **b** Acquiescence; inability to prevent the inevitable: *Let* ain. **c** An assumption or suggestion: *Let* x equal the sum two numbers. **6.** *Chiefly Brit.* To rent (a house, room,) to a tenant. **7.** To cause to flow, as blood. — *v.i.* **8.** *efly Brit.* To be rented: rooms to *let.* — **let alone** *Informal* d surely not; not to say: He can't even float, *let alone* m. — **to let down** **1.** To cause to fall or descend; loosen, hair. **2.** To disappoint. — **to let in** To insert into the stance, material, or body of something. — **to let loose** To free; release. — **to let off** **1.** To emit; release, as from ssure or tension. **2.** To discharge, dismiss, or excuse, as m work or obligation. **3.** To allow to escape a punish- nt or penalty. — **to let on** *Informal* **1.** To make it own; reveal. **2.** To pretend. — **to let out** **1.** To give vent emit. **2.** To release or unfasten in order to make a gar- nt, etc., wider or longer. — **to let up** **1.** To grow less; abate. **2.** To reduce tension. — **to let up on** *Informal* To cease to subject to force or severe treatment. ◆ See note under LEAVE[1]. [OE *lǣtan*]
let[2] (let) *n.* In tennis or similar games, a service, point, etc., that must be repeated because of some interruption or hindrance of playing conditions. — *v.t.* **let** or **let·ted, let·ting** *Archaic* To hinder; impede. [OE *lettan*, lit., to make late]
-let *suffix of nouns* **1.** Small; little: *booklet.* **2.** A band or ornament for (a specified part of the body): *anklet.* [< OF *-let, -lette* < *-el* + *-et*, dim. suffixes]
let·down (let′doun′) *n.* **1.** A decrease; slackening, as of speed, force, or energy. **2.** *Informal* Disappointment.
le·thal (lē′thəl) *adj.* **1.** Causing death; deadly; fatal. **2.** Pertaining to or characteristic of death. [< L < *lethum, letum* death] — **le·thal·i·ty** (lē·thal′ə·tē) *n.*
le·thar·gic (li·thär′jik) *adj.* **1.** Affected with or characterized by lethargy; drowsy; apathetic. **2.** Pertaining to or causing lethargy. Also **le·thar′gi·cal.** — **le·thar′gi·cal·ly** *adv.*
leth·ar·gize (leth′ər·jīz) *v.t.* **·gized, ·giz·ing** To make lethargic.
leth·ar·gy (leth′ər·jē) *n. pl.* **·gies** **1.** A state of indifference; apathy. **2.** *Pathol.* Excessive drowsiness or abnormally deep sleep. [< OF < LL < Gk. *lēthargos* forgetful]
Le·the (lē′thē) *n.* **1.** In Greek mythology, a river in Hades, a drink from which produced oblivion. **2.** Oblivion. [< Gk. *lēthē* oblivion] — **Le·the·an** (lē·thē′ən) *adj.*
Lett (let) *n.* **1.** A Latvian. **2.** The Latvian language.
let·ter (let′ər) *n.* **1.** A standardized sign or character used in writing or printing to represent a speech sound. **2.** A written or printed message directed to a specified person or group of persons. **3.** An official document granting certain rights or privileges to a specified person: a *letter* of credit. **4.** Literal meaning: the *letter* of the law. **5.** *pl.* Literature in general; literary profession: a man of *letters.* **6.** *U.S.* An emblem in the form of the initial letter of a college, school, etc., conferred as an award for outstanding performance in athletics. — **to the letter** In accordance with the exact words or literal meaning. — *v.t.* **1.** To inscribe letters on; mark with letters. **2.** To print or inscribe by means of letters. — *v.i.* **3.** To form letters, as by hand. [< OF < L *littera* letter of the alphabet, in pl., epistle] — **let′ter·er** *n.*
let·tered (let′ərd) *adj.* **1.** Versed in letters; learned; literary; educated. **2.** Inscribed or marked with letters.
let·ter·head (let′ər·hed′) *n.* A printed heading, as a name and address, on a sheet of writing paper; also, a sheet of paper bearing such a heading.
let·ter·ing (let′ər·ing) *n.* **1.** The act or art of forming letters; process of marking or stamping with letters. **2.** Letters collectively, esp. a single example.
letter of credit A letter issued by a bank and authorizing the bearer to draw a specified amount of money from other banks, etc.
let·ter-per·fect (let′ər·pûr′fikt) *adj.* **1.** Perfect in memorization, as an actor. **2.** Correct in all details, as a piece of writing. — *adv.* Perfectly: said of memorizing or writing.
let·ter·press (let′ər·pres′) *n. Printing* **1.** Any printed matter, as distinguished from illustrations, etc. **2.** Printing produced from type or similar raised surfaces.
letters patent *Law* The instrument granting a patent.
Let·tish (let′ish) *adj. & n.* Latvian.
let·tuce (let′is) *n.* A cultivated herb having crisp, edible leaves; also, the leaves. [< OF < L *lac, lactis* milk]
let·up (let′up′) *n. Informal* **1.** A lessening or relaxation, as of force or intensity; lull. **2.** A respite; pause; interlude.
leuco- *combining form* White; lacking color: also, before vowels, **leuc-.** Also *leuko-, leuk-.* [< Gk. *leukos* white]
leu·co·cyte (lo͞o′kə·sīt) *n. Physiol.* A white or colorless blood corpuscle, constituting an important agent in protection against infectious diseases. Also spelled *leukocyte.*
leu·co·cyt·ic (lo͞o′kə·sit′ik) *adj.* **1.** Of or pertaining to leucocytes. **2.** Characterized by an excess of leucocytes.
leuk- Var. of LEUCO-.
leu·ke·mi·a (lo͞o·kē′mē·ə) *n. Pathol.* A generally fatal disease of the blood and bloodmaking tissues, characterized by a marked increase in the number of leucocytes, accompanied by anemia, exhaustion, etc. Also **leu·kae′mi·a.** [< LEUK- + Gk. *haima* blood]
leuko- See LEUCO-.
leu·ko·cyte (lo͞o′kə·sīt) See LEUCOCYTE.
le·vant (lə·vant′) *n.* A kind of morocco leather having an irregularly grained surface. Also **Levant morocco.**
Levant (lə·vant′) *n.* The regions bordering the eastern Mediterranean, between western Greece and western Egypt: usu. preceded by *the.* [< F < L *levare* to raise] — **Le·van·tine** (lə·van′tin, lev′ən·tīn, -tēn) *adj. & n.*
le·va·tor (lə·vā′tər) *n. pl.* **le·va·to·res** (lev′ə·tôr′ēz, -tō′rēz) or **le·va·tors** *Anat.* A muscle that raises an organ or part. [< LL < L *levare* to raise]

lev·ee[1] (lev′ē) *n. U.S.* **1.** An embankment along the shore of a river, built for protection against floods. **2.** A landing place; wharf. [< F *lever* to raise < L *levare*]

lev·ee[2] (lev′ē, lə·vē′) *n.* A reception or formal gathering of visitors, usu. held early in the day by a person of rank or distinction. [< F *levé* an arising]

lev·el (lev′əl) *n.* **1.** Relative place, degree, or stage: a high *level* of development. **2.** Position in the vertical dimension: the *level* of the lower branches. **3.** A horizontal line or surface: sea *level*. **4.** A flat expanse, as of land. **5.** Any of various devices used to find the conformity of a line or surface with the horizontal plane. **— on the level** *Informal* Without deception; fair and square. **— to find one's** (or **its**) **level** To come to the appropriate place on a vertical scale of distances, values, etc. **—** *adj.* **1.** Having a surface with no irregularities in height; even; flat. **2.** Conforming to a horizontal plane. **3.** Being in the same plane with or at the same height as something else. **4.** Measured so as to have a surface even with the edge of the container. **5.** Equal to something or someone else, as in importance, development, etc. **6.** Even, as in quality or tone. **— a level head** A calm and sensible mind. **— one's level best** *Informal* The best one can possibly do. **—** *v.* **lev·eled** or **·elled, lev·el·ing** or **·el·ling** *v.t.* **1.** To give an even or horizontal surface to. **2.** To destroy by or as by smashing to the ground. **3.** To knock down. **4.** To bring to a common state or condition. **5.** To aim or point as a weapon. **6.** To aim or direct (something) with force of emphasis: to *level* an accusation. **—** *v.i.* **7.** To bring persons or things to a common state or condition. **8.** To take measurements with a level. **9.** To aim a weapon at a target. **10.** *U.S. Slang* To be honest. **—** *adv.* In an even line or plane. [< OF < L *libra* a balance] **— lev′el·er** or **·el·ler** *n.* **— lev′el·ly** *adv.* **— lev′el·ness** *n.*

level crossing A grade crossing.

lev·el·head·ed (lev′əl·hed′id) *adj.* Characterized by common sense and cool judgment. **— lev′el·head′ed·ness** *n.*

level of usage *Ling.* A distinguishable variety of vocabulary, grammar, pronunciation, etc., considered appropriate for a class within the speech community.

lev·er (lev′ər, lē′vər) *n.* **1.** *Mech.* A device consisting of a rigid structure, often a straight bar, pivoting on a fixed support (the fulcrum), and serving to impart pressure or motion from a force or effort applied at one point to a resisting force at another point. **2.** Any of various tools, devices or parts operating on the above principle, as a crowbar. **3.** Any means of exerting effective power. **—** *v.t. & v.i.* To move or pry with or as with a lever. [< OF < L *levare* to raise]

lev·er·age (lev′ər·ij, lē′vər-) *n.* **1.** The use of a lever. **2.** The mechanical advantage gained by use of a lever.

lev·er·et (lev′ər·it) *n.* A young hare less than a year old. [< AF, OF *levre* hare]

Le·vi (lē′vī) In the Old Testament, a son of Jacob and Leah. *Gen.* xxix 34. **—** *n.* The tribe of Israel descended from him.

LEVERS
A First class.
B Second class.
C Third class.
f Fulcrum.
p Force.
w Weight.

le·vi·a·than (lə·vī′ə·thən) *n.* **1.** A gigantic water beast mentioned in the Bible. **2.** Any enormous creature or thing.

Le·vis (lē′vīz) *n.pl.* Close-fitting, heavy denim trousers having rivets to reinforce points of greatest strain: a registered trade mark. [after *Levi* Strauss, U.S. manufacturer]

lev·i·tate (lev′ə·tāt) *v.* **·tat·ed, ·tat·ing** *v.i.* **1.** To rise and float in the air, as through buoyancy or supposed supernatural power. **—** *v.t.* **2.** To cause to rise and float in the air. [< L *levis* light, on analogy with *gravitate*] **— lev′i·ta′tor** *n.*

lev·i·ta·tion (lev′ə·tā′shən) *n.* **1.** The act of levitating, or the state of being levitated. **2.** The illusion of suspending a heavy object or the human body in the air without support.

Le·vite (lē′vīt) *n.* In Jewish history, one of the tribe of Levi, from whom were chosen those who assisted the priests.

Le·vit·i·cal (lə·vit′i·kəl) *adj.* **1.** Of or pertaining to the Levites. **2.** Of or pertaining to the book of Leviticus.

Le·vit·i·cus (lə·vit′i·kəs) The third book of the Old Testament, consisting chiefly of a compilation of ceremonial laws.

lev·i·ty (lev′ə·tē) *n. pl.* **·ties** **1.** Lack of seriousness; inappropriate gaiety; frivolity. **2.** Fickleness; inconstancy. **3.** Lightness. [< L *levis* light]

levo- *combining form* Turned or turning to the left: used in chemistry and physics. Also spelled *laevo-*. [< L *laevus* left]

le·vo·ro·ta·to·ry (lē′vō·rō′tə·tôr′ē, -tō′rē) *adj. Optics* Causing the plane of polarization of light to rotate to the left, or counterclockwise: said of certain crystals: opposed to *dextrorotatory*.

lev·u·lose (lev′yə·lōs) *n. Biochem.* Fructose. [< L *laevus* left + -UL(E) + -OSE[2]]

lev·y (lev′ē) *v.* **lev·ied, lev·y·ing** *v.t.* **1.** To impose and collect by authority or force, as a tax, fine, etc. **2.** To enlist or call up (troops, etc.) for military service. **3.** To prepa begin, or wage (war). **—** *v.i.* **4.** To make a levy. **5** To seize property by judicial writ in order to fulfill a ment: usu. with *on*. **—** *n. pl.* **lev·ies** **1.** The act of le **2.** That which is levied, as money or troops. [< OF *levare* to raise] **— lev′i·er** *n.*

lewd (lōōd) *adj.* **1.** Characterized by or inciting to l debauchery. **2.** Obscene; ribald; bawdy. [OE *lǣwed* unlearned] **— lewd′ly** *adv.* **— lewd′ness** *n.*

lew·is·ite (lōō′is·īt) *n. Chem.* An oily liquid, C_2H_2 used in chemical warfare as a blistering agent. [after *Lewis*, 1878–1943, U.S. chemist]

lex (leks) *n. pl.* **le·ges** (lē′jēz) *Latin* Law.

lex·i·cog·ra·pher (lek′sə·kog′rə·fər) *n.* One who wo writing or compiling a dictionary.

lex·i·cog·ra·phy (lek′sə·kog′rə·fē) *n.* The practice o fession of compiling dictionaries. [< NL < Gk. < *l* lexicon + *graphein* to write] **— lex′i·co·graph′ic** (-kō ik) or **·i·cal** *adj.* **— lex′i·co·graph′i·cal·ly** *adv.*

lex·i·con (lek′sə·kon) *n.* **1.** A dictionary; esp., a dicti of Latin, Greek, or Hebrew. **2.** A vocabulary or list of relating to a particular subject, occupation, or activity Gk. *lexikos* pertaining to words]

Leyden jar *Electr.* A device for accumulating a cha static electricity, consisting principally of a glass jar c with tinfoil inside and out. [after *Leyden*, earlier na Leiden, where it was invented]

li·a·bil·i·ty (lī′ə·bil′ə·tē) *n. pl.* **·ties** **1.** The state or tion of being liable. **2.** That for which one is liable, a nancial obligation or debt. **3.** *pl.* In accounting, the e on a balance sheet showing the debts or obligations of a ness: opposed to *assets*. **4.** Any obstacle or hindrance

li·a·ble (lī′ə·bəl) *adj.* **1.** Justly or legally responsible, damages; answerable. **2.** Subject or susceptible, as jury, illness, etc. **3.** Officially obligated to be availabl *U.S. Informal* Likely. [< F < L *ligare* to bind]

li·ai·son (lē′ā·zon′, lē·ā′zon, lē′ə·zon; *Fr.* lē·e·zôn′) *n.* means or agency for maintaining or furthering comm tion or unity, as between parts of an armed force or d ments of a government. **2.** An illicit love affair. **3.** I ken French and in many other languages, the carrying of a final consonant to the initial vowel of a succeeding as in *il est arrivé* (ē le tȧ·rē·vā′). [< F < L *ligare* to

li·ar (lī′ər) *n.* One who lies or utters falsehoods. [OE *lēo*

li·ba·tion (lī·bā′shən) *n.* **1.** A liquid ceremonially p out, as in honor of a deity; also, the act of pouring s liquid. **2.** Humorously, a drink. [< F < L *libare* to out (as an offering)]

li·bel (lī′bəl) *n.* **1.** *Law* **a** A written statement or gr representation, esp. in published form, that damages a son's reputation. **b** The act or crime of publishing s statement. **2.** Any defamatory or grossly unflattering ment. **—** *v.t.* **·beled** or **·belled, ·bel·ing** or **·bel·ling** publish or perpetrate a libel against. **2.** To defame c credit, as by false or malicious statements. [< OF < *bellus*, dim. of *liber* book] **— li′bel·er, li′bel·ler** *n.*

li·bel·ous (lī′bəl·əs) *adj.* Constituting, containing, or libel. Also, *esp. Brit.*, **li′bel·lous.** **— li′bel·ous·ly** *adv.*

lib·er·al (lib′ər·əl, lib′rəl) *adj.* **1.** Characterized by clining toward opinions or policies favoring progress form, as in politics or religion. **2.** Not intolerant or p diced; broad-minded. **3.** Characterized by generosi lavishness in giving. **4.** Given or yielded freely or in quantity; ample. **5.** Not literal or strict: a *liberal* inte tation of the law. **6.** Suitable for persons of broad cu interests: *liberal* arts. **—** *n.* One having liberal opinio convictions, esp. in politics or religion. [< OF < L *lib* pertaining to a freeman] **— lib′er·al·ly** *adv.*

Lib·er·al (lib′ər·əl, lib′rəl) *adj.* Designating or belongi one of various political parties, as the Liberal Party of ada or Great Britain. **—** *n.* A member of such a part

liberal arts A group of subjects or college courses incl literature, philosophy, languages, history, etc., and d guished from scientific, technical, or purely practical jects; the arts, as in Bachelor of *Arts*; the humanities.

lib·er·al·ism (lib′ər·əl·iz′əm) *n.* **1.** Liberal beliefs or cies, esp. in regard to politics, social changes, religion, et *Sometimes cap.* The policies of the Liberal Party.

lib·er·al·i·ty (lib′ə·ral′ə·tē) *n. pl.* **·ties** **1.** The quali being liberal in giving; generosity. **2.** Broad-mindednes

lib·er·al·ize (lib′ər·əl·īz′) *v.t. & v.i.* **·ized, ·iz·ing** To r or become liberal. **— lib′er·al·i·za′tion** (lib′ər·əl·ə·zā′s -ī·zā′-, lib′rəl-) *n.* **— lib′er·al·iz′er** *n.*

Liberal Party **1.** One of the principal political parti Canada. **2.** In Great Britain, a Whiggish political p formed in the 1830's and the major opponent of the servative Party until after World War I.

lib·er·ate (lib′ə·rāt) *v.t.* **·at·ed, ·at·ing** **1.** To set fre from bondage or confinement. **2.** To extricate, as fron tanglement. **3.** To release from chemical combination, gas. [< L *liberatus*, pp. of *liberare* to free] **— lib′er·a′ti**

ər·a·tor (lib′ər·ā′tər) *n.* One who liberates; esp., one o emancipates a nation, people, etc.
ər·tine (lib′ər·tēn) *n.* One completely lacking in moral traint; a profligate. — *adj.* Characteristic of a libertine. L *libertus* freedman] — **lib′er·tin·ism** *n.*
ər·ty (lib′ər·tē) *n. pl.* **·ties 1.** Freedom from oppres- ı, tyranny, or the domination of a government not freely sen. **2.** The state of being free, as from confinement or very. **3.** Freedom of thought or action, or exemption n forms of compulsion or indignity, regarded as a human nt. **4.** An overly free, familiar, or disrespectful act or nner. **5.** Permission to be present in and make free use specified place: followed by *of.* **6.** In the U.S. Navy and er maritime services, official permission to be absent from 's ship or place of duty, usu. for less than 48 hours. — **at rty 1.** Free; authorized or permitted (to do something). Not engaged in an activity or occupation; unemployed. Able to move about freely. [< F < L < *liber* free]
erty Bell The bell in Independence Hall, Philadelphia, g July 4, 1776, to celebrate the adoption of the Declara- ı of Independence, and cracked in 1835.
erty Ship A type of U.S. cargo ship built in large num- s during World War II.
d·i·nous (li·bid′ə·nəs) *adj.* Characterized by or inclin- toward excesses of sexual desire; lustful. — **li·bid′i·nous·** *dv.* — **li·bid′i·nous·ness** *n.*
·do (li·bē′dō, -bī-′) *n.* **1.** Sexual desire or impulse. **2.** *choanal.* The instinctual craving or drive behind all hu- n activities. [< L, lust] — **li·bid′i·nal** (-bid′ə·nəl) *adj.*
ra (lī′brə, lē′-) *n.* A constellation, the Balance or Scales;), the seventh sign of the zodiac. See ZODIAC. [< L]
ar·i·an (lī·brâr′ē·ən) *n.* **1.** One who has charge of a li- ry. **2.** A person qualified by training for library service.
rar·y (lī′brer·ē, -brə·rē) *n. pl.* **·brar·ies 1.** A collection books, pamphlets, etc.; esp., such a collection arranged to ilitate reference. **2.** A building, room, etc., housing such collection. **3.** A commercial establishment that rents oks. [< OF < L *liber, libri* book]
rary of Congress The national library of the U.S. in shington, D.C., established in 1800.
rate (lī′brāt) *v.i.* **·brat·ed, ·brat·ing 1.** To move back l forth; oscillate. **2.** To be poised; hover. [< L < *libra* ance] — **li·bra′tion** *n.* — **li′bra·to·ry** *adj.*
ret·tist (li·bret′ist) *n.* The writer of a libretto.
ret·to (li·bret′ō) *n. pl.* **·tos** or **·ti** (-tē) **1.** The verbal t of an opera or other large-scale vocal work. **2.** A book taining such a text. [< Ital., little book, dim. of *libro*]
·y·an (lib′ē·ən) *adj.* Of or pertaining to Libya, its in- bitants, or their language. — *n.* **1.** A native or inhabi- t of Libya. **2.** The Hamitic language of ancient Libya.
(līs) Plural of LOUSE.
ense (lī′sens) *n.* **1.** An official document giving permis- n to engage in a specified activity, perform a specified act, . **2.** Unrestrained liberty of action. **3.** Abuse of free- m or privilege; laxity. **4.** Deviation from or relaxation of ablished rules or standards, esp. for artistic effect: poetic *ense.* — *v.t.* **·censed, ·cens·ing** To grant a license to or ; authorize. Also, *esp. Brit.,* **li′cence.** [< OF < L *licens, tis,* ppr. of *licere* to be permitted] — **li′cens·a·ble** *adj.* **li′cen·ser** or **li′cenc·er** or *Law* **li′cen·sor** *n.*
en·see (lī′sən·sē′) *n.* One to whom a license has been nted. Also **li′cen·cee′.**
en·ti·ate (lī·sen′shē·it, -āt) *n.* **1.** A person licensed to ctice a certain profession: a *licentiate* in dental surgery. In some Continental universities, a person holding a de- e intermediate between bachelor and doctor.
en·tious (lī·sen′shəs) *adj.* Lacking in moral restraint; vd. [< F < L *licentiosus*] — **li·cen′tious·ly** *adv.* — **li· n′tious·ness** *n.*
hee (lē′chē) *n.* **1.** The edible fruit of a tree native to ina, having a hard seed and sweet pulp enclosed within a n, brittle shell: also **lichee nut.** **2.** The tree itself. [< inese *li-chih*]
hen (lī′kən) *n.* Any of various flowerless plants com- sed of fungi and algae, commonly growing in flat patches rocks, trees, etc. [< L < Gk., prob. < *leichein* to lick] **li′chen·ous, li′chen·ose** (-ōs) *adj.*
it (lis′it) *adj.* Lawful. [< F ult. < L *licere* to be allowed] **lic′it·ly** *adv.* — **lic′it·ness** *n.*
k (lik) *v.t.* **1.** To pass the tongue over the surface of. **2.** remove or consume by taking with the tongue: often fol- wed by *up, off,* etc. **3.** To move or pass lightly over or out: The flames *licked* the coals. **4.** *Informal* To defeat. *Informal* To thrash; beat. — *v.i.* **6.** To move quickly or htly; flicker. — **to lick into shape** To put in proper form condition. — **to lick one's chops** To show pleased antici- ation. — *n.* **1.** A stroke of the tongue in licking. **2.** A nall amount. **3.** *U.S.* A salt lick. **4.** *Informal* A blow; whack. **5.** *Often pl. Informal* An opportunity to do some- thing; a turn. **6.** *Informal* A stroke; spell, as of work. — **a lick and a promise** *Informal* Hasty washing or cleaning. [OE *liccian*]
lick·e·ty-split (lik′ə·tē·split′) *adv. U.S. Informal* At full speed.
lick·ing (lik′ing) *n.* **1.** The act of one who or that which licks. **2.** *Informal* A whipping; beating.
lic·o·rice (lik′ə·ris, -rish) *n.* **1.** A perennial leguminous herb of Europe. **2.** The dried root of this plant, or an extract made from it, used in medicine and confections. **3.** A con- fection flavored with this extract. Also, *esp. Brit., liquorice.* [< AF, OF < LL < Gk. < *glykys* sweet + *rhiza* root]
lic·tor (lik′tər) *n.* In ancient Rome, one of the officers or guards who attended the chief magistrates, and who bore the fasces as a symbol of office. [< L, prob. < *ligare* to tie]
lid (lid) *n.* **1.** A hinged or removable cover placed at the top of a receptacle or over an opening. **2.** An eyelid. **3.** *Bot.* A top, as of a pyxis, separating at a transverse dividing line; an operculum. [OE *hlid*] — **lid′·ded** *adj.* — **lid′less** *adj.*
lie[1] (lī) *v.i.* **lay, lain, ly·ing 1.** To be in a recumbent or pros- trate position. **2.** To place oneself in a recumbent position; rest at full length: often with *down.* **3.** To be placed upon or rest against a surface, esp. in a horizontal position. **4.** To be buried, as in a grave or tomb. **5.** To be or remain in a specified condition or state: to *lie* dormant. **6.** To exist; be inherent: often followed by *in* or *within.* **7.** To occupy a lo- cation; be situated. **8.** To continue or extend: The future *lies* before us. ◆ See note under LAY[1]. — **to lie in wait (for)** To wait in concealment so as to attack by surprise. — **to lie low** *Informal* To remain in concealment; conceal one's in- tentions. — **to lie with** To rest with; be up to: The choice *lies with* him. — *n.* **1.** The position, manner, or situation in which something lies; aspect. **2.** The resting place or haunt of an animal, bird, or fish. [OE *licgan*]
lie[2] (lī) *n.* **1.** An untrue statement made with the intent of deceiving; a falsehood. **2.** That which creates or is intended to produce a false impression. — **to give the lie (to) 1.** To accuse (someone) of lying. **2.** To expose as false. — **white lie** A false statement made with the intent of being polite or kind. — *v.* **lied, ly·ing** *v.i.* **1.** To make an untrue state- ment or statements, esp. with intent to deceive. **2.** To give an erroneous or misleading impression: Figures don't *lie.* — *v.t.* **3.** To put or promote (oneself or someone) into a speci- fied situation by telling lies. [OE *lyge*]
— **Syn.** (noun) **1.** A *lie* is a statement, known to be untrue, and made with the intent to deceive. *Falsehood* leaves open the ques- tion of intent to deceive, and *untruth* often implies error rather than malice; both *falsehood* and *untruth* are also used euphemisti- cally for *lie. Fib* and *story* are almost exclusively used of *falsehoods* told by young children, and both are generally regarded as trivial.
lied (lēd, *Ger.* lēt) *n. pl.* **lied·er** (lē′dər) A German song; esp., a ballad or lyric poem set to music. [< G]
Lie·der·kranz (lē′dər·kränts) *n.* A soft cheese similar to but milder than Limburger: a trade name. Also **lie′der· kranz.** [< G, lit., garland of songs]
lie detector A polygraph (def. 3) used to establish the truth or falsity of an accused person's statements.
lief (lēf) *adv.* Willingly; readily: used chiefly in the phrase **would as lief.** — *adj. Archaic* **1.** Dear; beloved. **2.** Will- ing; inclined. [OE *lēof* dear]
liege (lēj) *n.* **1.** A lord or sovereign to whom allegiance or feudal service is due. **2.** A vassal or subject owing allegiance to a lord or sovereign. — *adj.* **1.** Entitled to feudal alle- giance, as of a vassal: now used chiefly in the phrase **liege lord.** **2.** Bound in vassalage or owing allegiance to a lord or sovereign. [< OF < Med.L < *laeticus* free < OHG *ledig*]
lien (lēn, lē′ən) *n.* A legal right to claim or dispose of prop- erty in payment of or as security for a debt or charge. [< F < L *ligare* to tie]
lieu (lōō) *n.* Place; stead: now only in the phrase **in lieu of.** [ME *live* < OF < L *locus* place]
lieu·ten·an·cy (lōō·ten′ən·sē, *Brit.* lef·ten′ən·sē, or *Brit. Na- val* lə·ten′-) *n.* The office, rank, or authority of a lieutenant.
lieu·ten·ant (lōō·ten′ənt, *Brit.* lef·ten′ənt, or *Brit. Naval* lə· ten′-) *n.* **1.** *Mil.* A commissioned officer holding either of two ranks, **first** or **second lieutenant,** the former ranking next below a captain. See tables at GRADE. **2.** *Naval* **a** *U.S.* A commissioned officer holding either of two ranks, **lieu- tenant** or **lieutenant (junior grade),** the former ranking next below a lieutenant commander and the latter next above an ensign. **b** *Brit. & Canadian* A commissioned officer ranking next below a lieutenant-commander. See tables at GRADE. **3.** One deputized to perform the duties of a superior. [< F < *lieu* place + *tenant,* ppr. of *tenir* to hold]
lieutenant colonel *Mil.* An officer ranking next above a major. Also *Brit. & Canadian* **lieu·ten·ant-col·on·el** (lef· ten′ənt·ker′nəl). See tables at GRADE.

lieutenant commander *Naval* An officer ranking next above a lieutenant and next below a commander. Also *Brit. & Canadian* **lieu·ten·ant-com·man·der** (lə·ten′ənt·kə·man′dər). See tables at GRADE.
lieutenant general *Mil.* An officer ranking next above a major general. Also *Brit. & Canadian* **lieu·ten·ant-gen·er·al** (lef·ten′ənt·gen′ər·əl). See tables at GRADE.
lieutenant governor 1. *U.S.* An elected official who performs the duties of the governor of a State during his absence or disability or who replaces him in case of death or resignation. 2. In the British Empire, a deputy governor of a territory under the jurisdiction of a governor general.
life (līf) *n. pl.* **lives** (līvz) 1. The form of existence that distinguishes animals and plants from inorganic substances and dead organisms, characterized by metabolism, growth, reproduction, irritability, etc. 2. The characteristic state of an organism that has not died. 3. Existence regarded as a desirable condition: *life*, liberty, and the pursuit of happiness. 4. A spiritual state regarded as a continuation or perfection of animate existence after death: eternal *life*. 5. Living organisms collectively. 6. A living being; person: to save a *life*. 7. The period of an individual's existence between birth and death; also, a specified portion of this period. 8. A biography. 9. The period during which something continues to be effective, useful, etc.: the *life* of an engine. 10. Human affairs or relationships: daily *life*. 11. Manner of existence; characteristic activities, as of a specified group, locality, etc.: city *life*. 12. Energetic force; animation: full of *life*. 13. A source of liveliness; animating spirit: the *life* of the party. 14. A living model; also, a representation of such a model. **— for dear life** With urgent effort, speed, etc. **— for life** For the remainder of one's existence. **— for the life of me (him,** etc.) Under any circumstances; at all: usu. with the negative. **— to bring to life** 1. To make vital; animate. 2. To recall vividly to the mind or senses. **— to come to life** 1. To regain consciousness. 2. To become animated. 3. To seem to be real or alive. **— to take life** To kill. [OE *līf*]
life belt A life preserver in the form of a belt.
life·blood (līf′blud′) *n.* 1. The blood necessary to life. 2. Anything indispensable to existence; vital force.
life·boat (līf′bōt′) *n.* A boat constructed and equipped for saving lives at sea in the event of shipwreck, storm, etc.; esp., such a boat carried on board a larger vessel.
life buoy A life preserver, often in the form of a ring.
life expectancy The probable length of life of an individual, esp. as predicted statistically.
life·guard (līf′gärd′) *n. U.S.* An expert swimmer employed at a beach, etc., to protect the safety of bathers.
life insurance Insurance on the life of an individual, providing payment to the beneficiary or beneficiaries upon the death of the insured or to the insured upon reaching a certain age. Also *Brit.* **life assurance.**
life jacket A life preserver in the form of a jacket or vest.
life·less (līf′lis) *adj.* 1. Not possessing the characteristics of living organisms. 2. Deprived of life; dead. 3. Not inhabited by or incapable of sustaining living organisms: a *lifeless* desert. 4. Lacking animation or vitality. 5. Exhibiting no signs of life. **— life′less·ly** *adv.* **— life′less·ness** *n.*
life·like (līf′līk′) *adj.* 1. Resembling actual life. 2. Accurately representing a person or thing. **— life′like′ness** *n.*
life line 1. A rope affording support to those in precarious situations. 2. Any route used for transporting vital supplies.
life·long (līf′lông′, -long′) *adj.* Lasting through life.
life net A strong net designed to rescue those who jump or fall from great heights, used by firemen, etc.
life preserver A buoyant device, either inflatable or filled with cork, kapok, etc., and made as a belt, jacket, or ring, used to keep afloat those in danger of drowning.

LIFE PRESERVERS
A Solid block cork.
B Cork ring buoy.
C Collar-type jacket.

lif·er (lī′fər) *n. Slang* One sentenced to prison for life.
life raft A raftlike structure used as a rescue craft; esp., an inflatable rubber boat equipped with oars.
life·sav·er (līf′sā′vər) *n.* 1. One who saves another's life. 2. A person trained to rescue those in danger of drowning. 3. *Informal* One who or that which provides aid, relief, etc., in time of need. **— life′sav′ing** *n. & adj.*
life-size (līf′sīz′) *adj.* Having the same size as the thing or person portrayed. Also **life′-sized′.**
life span The extreme length of life regarded as biologically possible in an organism or the group to which it belongs.
life·time (līf′tīm′) *n.* The period of animate existence; also, the period of effective functioning: the *lifetime* of the car.
life·work (līf′wûrk′) *n.* The work of a productive lifetime.
lift (lift) *v.t.* 1. To take hold of and raise to a higher place or position; hoist. 2. To move, direct, or cause to rise to a higher position or level. 3. To hold up. 4. To bring to a higher or more desirable degree or condition; exalt. 5. [To] emit in loud or clearly audible tones, as the voice: to l[ift a] cry. 6. To subject (the face) to surgery in order to rem[ove] signs of age. 7. *Informal* To take surreptitiously; s[teal;] also, to plagiarize. **—** *v.i.* 8. To exert effort in attemp[ting] to raise something. 9. To yield to upward pressure; 10. To become dispersed or move away by or as by ris[ing:] the fog *lifted.* **—** *n.* 1. The act of lifting or raising. 2. [The] power or ability to lift or impart upward motion. 3. [The] height, distance, or degree to which something rises [or is] raised. 4. Assistance given by or as by raising. 5. A [ride] given to a traveler to or in the direction of his destina[tion.] 6. A feeling of exaltation, exhilaration, or well-being. [7.] Elevated or erect position, bearing, etc.: the *lift* of her c[hin.] 8. A machine or device used in lifting or hoisting. 9. [The] amount lifted or capable of being lifted. 10. *Brit.* An el[eva]tor. 11. Any of the layers of leather, etc., constituting [the] heel of a shoe. 12. *Aeron.* The component of aerodyn[amic] forces acting on an aircraft, exerted perpendicular to [the] relative wind and generally opposing the pull of gra[vity.] [ME < ON *lypta* to raise in the air.] **— lift′er** *n.*
lift-off (lift′ôf′, -of′) *n. Aerospace* The vertical ascent [of a] rocket or spacecraft from its launching pad.
lig·a·ment (lig′ə·mənt) *n.* 1. *Anat.* A band of firm, fib[rous] tissue forming a connection between bones, or suppo[rting] an organ. 2. A bond or connecting tie. [< L *ligare* to b[ind]] **— lig′a·men′tal, lig′a·men′ta·ry, lig′a·men′tous** *adj.*
li·gan (lī′gən) *n.* Lagan.
li·gate (lī′gāt) *v.t.* **·gat·ed, ·gat·ing** To bind or cons[trict] with a ligature. [< L *ligatus*, pp. of *ligare*, to bind, tie]
lig·a·ture (lig′ə·choor, -chər) *n.* 1. The act of tying u[p or] constricting by binding. Also **li·ga·tion** (lī·gā′shən). [2. A] band, strip, etc., used to tie, bind, or constrict. 3. In pr[int]ing, a character consisting of two or more connected let[ters,] as *æ, fi, ffi.* 4. *Music* A slur indicating a group of notes s[ung] or played as a connected phrase; also, the group of n[otes] thus indicated. **—** *v.t.* To ligate.
light[1] (līt) *n.* 1. *Physics* **a** The form of radiant energy [that] stimulates the organs of sight, having for normal huma[n vi]sion wavelengths ranging from about 3900 to 7700 angstr[oms] and traveling at a speed of about 186,300 miles a secon[d. **b**] A closely related form of radiant energy not stimulating [hu]man vision; ultraviolet or infrared light. 2. The condi[tion] or medium that makes vision possible; illumination. 3. [The] sensation produced by stimulation of the organs of vi[sion] and visual centers of the brain. 4. Any source of brightn[ess,] as a lamp, the sun, etc. 5. An emission of brightness, from a particular source or direction. 6. The daily ill[umi]nation shed on the earth by the sun; daylight; also the pe[riod] of daylight. 7. Mental or spiritual understanding or insi[ght.] 8. The state of being unhidden and observable: to com[e to] *light.* 9. Way of being regarded; aspect: to see things [in a] new *light.* 10. *pl.* Ability and understanding: to live [ac]cording to one's own *lights.* 11. A lively or intense exp[res]sion on the face, esp. in the eyes. 12. An instance of [kin]dling; ignition. 13. An opening admitting illumination, [a] window. 14. In graphic arts: **a** The representation of l[ight] or atmosphere. **b** A part of a picture showing an illumin[ated] area. 15. A person of authority or eminence; luminar[y:] lesser *light.* **— in the light of** In view of; considering. **—** [to] **see the light** 1. To come into being. 2. To be presente[d to] public notice. 3. To become enlightened. **— to strik[e a] light** To ignite something, as a match, by friction. **—** [*adj.*] 1. Full of light; bright. 2. Diluted or combined with wh[ite,] as a color; pale. **—** *v.* **light·ed** or **lit, light·ing** *v.t.* 1. To [ig]nite; kindle. 2. To illuminate or cause to illuminate. 3. [To] make bright, cheerful, animated, etc. 4. To guide or c[on]duct with light. **—** *v.i.* 5. To become ignited. 6. To [be]come luminous, radiant, or bright: often with *up.* [OE *lē*[oht]]
light[2] (līt) *adj.* 1. Having little weight; not heavy. 2. H[av]ing little weight in proportion to bulk or size; low in spe[cific] gravity. 3. Having less than standard or correct wei[ght.] 4. Not burdensome or oppressive. 5. Not difficult or a[rdu]ous. 6. Having comparatively little effect; not inte[nse,] severe, etc. 7. Not great in degree or concentration; thi[n:] *light* fog. 8. Exerting little force or pressure; gentle: a *l*[*ight*] tap. 9. Characterized by buoyancy or ease in motion. [10.] Moving or working swiftly and skillfully; deft. 11. [Not] clumsy, coarse, or massive in form or appearance; delic[ate.] 12. Intended or enjoyed as entertainment; not lofty or [he]roic: *light* verse. 13. Slight in importance or conseque[nce.] 14. Frivolous; trivial. 15. Easily distracted or divert[ed;] flighty. 16. Morally unrestrained; wanton. 17. Sligh[tly] faint or delirious; giddy. 18. Easily eaten or digested. [19.] Comparatively low in alcoholic content: *light* wines. [20.] Well-leavened; spongy or airy in texture: *light* biscuits. 2[1.] Crumbly in texture; porous: *light* soil. 22. Relatively sw[ift] and maneuverable: a *light* cruiser. 23. *Mil.* **a** Designat[ing] the less massive types of weapons or equipment. **b** Forme[rly,] designating troops or units with relatively less mass[ive] equipment: *light* cavalry. 24. *Meteorol.* Designating

ze moving at 4 to 7 miles per hour. **25.** In phonetics, ody, etc., designating an unaccented or unstressed syl- e or vowel. **—to make light of** To treat or consider as ng. **—*v.i.* light·ed** or **lit, light·ing 1.** To descend and e down after flight, as a bird. **2.** To happen or come, y chance: with *on* or *upon.* **3.** To get down, as from a e or carriage. **4.** To fall; strike, as a blow. **—to light** *U.S. Informal* To attack; assail. **—to light out** *U.S.* *rmal* To depart in haste. **—*adv.* 1.** Lightly. **2.** With- encumbrance or excess equipment. [OE *lēoht, līht*]

t·en[1] (līt′n) *v.t.* **1.** To make light or bright; illuminate. *i.* **2.** To become light; grow brighter. **3.** To glow with t; gleam. **4.** To emit or display lightning.

t·en[2] (līt′n) *v.t.* **1.** To reduce the weight or load of; e less heavy. **2.** To make less oppressive, troublesome, ; diminish the severity of. **3.** To relieve, as of distress, asiness, etc. **—*v.i.* 4.** To become less heavy.

t·er[1] (lī′tər) *n.* One who or that which lights; esp., a ice used to light cigarettes, cigars, etc.

t·er[2] (lī′tər) *Naut. n.* A bargelike vessel used in loading nloading ships, or in transporting loads for short dis- es. **—*v.t. & v.i.*** To transport (goods) by lighter. [< *lichten* to make light, unload]

t·er·age (lī′tər·ij) *n.* **1.** The removal or conveying of o by lighter. **2.** A price charged for this service.

t·er-than-air (lī′tər·thən·âr′) *adj. Aeron.* Designating raft, as balloons, dirigibles, etc., that depend for flight on ecific gravity less than that of air.

t·face (līt′fās′) *n. Printing* Type having characters ned of light, thin lines.

t-fin·gered (līt′fing′gərd) *adj.* Expert at picking pock- etc. **—light′-fin′gered·ness** *n.*

t-foot·ed (līt′fo͝ot′id) *adj.* **1.** Stepping with buoyancy grace. **2.** Running lightly and swiftly. Also *Poetic* **t′foot′. —light′-foot′ed·ly** *adv.* **—light′-foot′ed·ness** *n.*

t·head·ed (līt′hed′id) *adj.* **1.** Frivolous; giddy. **2.** zy. **—light′head′ed·ly** *adv.* **—light′·head′ed·ness** *n.*

t·heart·ed (līt′här′tid) *adj.* Free from care; blithe; gay. **ight′heart′ed·ly** *adv.* **—light′heart′ed·ness** *n.*

t·house (līt′hous′) *n.* A tower or similar structure ipped with a powerful beacon, erected at or near a dan- ous place to serve as a warning or guide for ships.

t·ing (lī′ting) *n.* **1.** The providing of light or the state eing lighted. **2.** A system or apparatus supplying illu- ation, as in a public building, theater, etc. **3.** The ar- gement or effect of lighted areas in a painting, etc.

t·ly (līt′lē) *adv.* **1.** With little weight or pressure; tly. **2.** To a slight degree; moderately. **3.** With a t, buoyant step or motion. **4.** In a carefree manner or it. **5.** With insufficient seriousness or concern; frivo- sly; irresponsibly: often with the negative. **6.** With le esteem or appreciation; slightingly. **7.** *Archaic* Easily.

t-mind·ed (līt′mīn′did) *adj.* Thoughtless; frivolous. **ight′-mind′ed·ly** *adv.* **—light′-mind′ed·ness** *n.*

t·ness[1] (līt′nis) *n.* **1.** The state or quality of being il- inated or bright. **2.** Paleness of color.

t·ness[2] (līt′nis) *n.* **1.** The quality of having relatively le weight, force, etc. **2.** Buoyancy or ease of motion. **3.** edom from sorrow or care. **4.** Lack of seriousness.

t·ning (līt′ning) *n.* **1.** A sudden flash of light caused by discharge of atmospheric electricity between electrified ions of cloud, or between a cloud and the earth. **2.** The charge itself. [ME *lighten* to flash]

tning bug *U.S.* A firefly.

tning rod A pointed metal rod that protects buildings m lightning by grounding it harmlessly through a cable.

t opera Operetta.

t quantum *Physics* A photon.

ts (līts) *n.pl.* The lungs, esp. of animals used as food. E *lihtes*; so called from their light weight]

t·ship (līt′ship′) *n.* A vessel equipped with warning nts, signals, etc., and moored in dangerous waters as a de to ships.

t·some (līt′səm) *adj.* **1.** Untroubled by care; cheerful; y. **2.** Buoyant, airy, or graceful. **3.** Frivolous; flighty. **light′some·ly** *adv.* **—light′some·ness** *n.*

t·weight (līt′wāt′) *n.* **1.** A person or animal of much s than average weight. **2.** A boxer or wrestler weighing ween 127 and 135 pounds. **3.** *U.S. Informal* An unim- tant, incompetent, or inadequate person. **—*adj.*** Of less n average or required weight.

t-year (līt′yir′) *n. Astron.* A unit of interstellar space asurement equal to the distance traversed by light in one ar, approximately six trillion miles.

ne·ous (lig′nē·əs) *adj.* Having the composition, texture, appearance of wood. [< L < *lignum* wood]

i- *combining form* Wood. Also, before vowels, **lign-.** so **ligno-.** [< L *lignum* wood]

lig·nite (lig′nīt) *n.* A compact, carbonized, brownish vege- table substance often retaining a woodlike structure, form- ing a fuel intermediate between peat and bituminous coal. [< F] **—lig·nit′ic** (-nit′ik) *adj.*

lig·num vi·tae (lig′nəm vī′tē) **1.** A tree of tropical America, having hard, greenish brown wood. **2.** The wood of this tree. **3.** Any of various related or similar trees. [< NL < L, wood of life]

lik·a·ble (lī′kə·bəl) *adj.* Of a nature to be liked; attractive; pleasing. Also **like′a·ble. —lik′a·ble·ness** *n.*

like[1] (līk) *v.* **liked, lik·ing** *v.t.* **1.** To take pleasure in; enjoy. **2.** To feel affectionately toward; be fond of. **3.** To desire; prefer: I *like* that one. **—*v.i.* 4.** To feel disposed; choose: Do as you *like.* **—*n. Usu. pl.*** Preference; inclination: chiefly in the phrase **likes and dislikes.** [OE *lician*]

like[2] (līk) *prep.* **1.** Having a close resemblance to; similar to. **2.** With the characteristics or qualities of: to smell *like* a rose. **3.** Characteristic or typical of: How *like* him to be- have that way! **4.** Indicative of; likely to result in: It looks *like* rain. **5.** As though having the need for: with *feel*: to feel *like* resting. **6.** Such as: cities *like* London, Rome, New York. **7.** In the manner of: He used the board *like* a ham- mer. **—like anything** (or **blazes, mad, hell,** etc.) *Informal* With great intensity, force, effort, etc. **—*adj.* 1.** Having the same or similar characteristics; related. **2.** Equal or nearly equal; equivalent. **3.** Similar to what is portrayed or represented, as a portrait. **—like . . . , like . . .** As (the one is), so (is the other): *Like* father, *like* son. **—*adv.* 1.** *Dial.* or *Informal* Probably: *Like* enough he'll go. **2.** *Dial.* or *Illit.* To a certain degree; somewhat: I'm hungry *like.* **3.** *U.S. Slang* or *Illit.* A meaningless interpolation, as be- fore adjectives, etc.: It's *like* cool. **—*n.* 1.** Anything similar or in the same category: preceded by *the*: physics, chemistry, and the *like.* **2.** One of equal value, standing, etc.: We will not see his *like* again. **—*conj.* 1.** *Informal* or *Illit.* As; in the manner that: It turned out *like* you said. **2.** *Informal* As if: It looks *like* it's going to rain. [OE *gelīc*]

-like *suffix of adjectives* **1.** Resembling or similar to: *wave- like.* **2.** Having the characteristics of: *childlike.* [< LIKE[2]]

◆ Compounds in *-like* are usu. solid, but are hyphenated when three *l's* occur together, as in *shell-like.*

like·li·hood (līk′lē·ho͝od) *n.* **1.** The state or quality of be- ing probable; probability. **2.** Something probable.

like·ly (līk′lē) *adj.* **·li·er, ·li·est 1.** Having or showing an apparent tendency or possibility: He is *likely* to go. **2.** Seemingly about to happen; imminent; probable: His pro- motion is *likely.* **3.** Apparently true; plausible; believable. **4.** Suitable; appropriate: a *likely* spot. **5.** Capable; prom- ising: a *likely* lad. **—*adv.*** Probably.

like-mind·ed (līk′mīn′did) *adj.* Having similar opinions, purposes, tastes, etc.

lik·en (lī′kən) *v.t.* To represent as similar; compare.

like·ness (līk′nis) *n.* **1.** The state or quality of being like; resemblance. **2.** A pictorial representation; portrait; image. **3.** Imitative form; guise: to take on the *likeness* of someone.

like·wise (līk′wīz′) *adv.* **1.** Moreover; also; too. **2.** In like manner; similarly.

lik·ing (lī′king) *n.* **1.** Feeling of attraction or affection; fondness. **2.** Preference; taste.

li·lac (lī′lak, -lək, -lok) *n.* **1.** A flowering shrub of the olive family, having fragrant purplish or white flowers. **2.** A light pinkish purple color. **—*adj.*** Having a purplish color. [< F < Sp. < Arabic < Persian *līlak* bluish]

lil·i·a·ceous (lil′ē·ā′shəs) *adj.* Belonging to or characteris- tic of the lily family. [< LL < L *lilium* lily]

Lil·li·put (lil′ə·put, -pət) In Swift's *Gulliver's Travels* (1726), a country inhabited by a race of tiny people. **—Lil′li·pu′·tian** *adj., n.*

lilt (lilt) *n.* **1.** A lively quality of speech, voice, song, etc., with pronounced variations of pitch. **2.** A light, buoyant motion or manner. **—*v.i. & v.t.*** To speak, sing, move, etc., in a cheerful rhythmic manner. [ME *lulte*]

lil·y (lil′ē) *n. pl.* **·ies 1.** Any of numerous wild or cultivated plants, having bulbous rootstocks and showy, usu. funnel- shaped flowers. **2.** Any of various other plants resembling a lily, as the calla or the water lily. **—*adj.*** Resembling a lily in whiteness, delicacy, beauty, etc. [OE < L *lilium*]

lil·y-liv·ered (lil′ē·liv′ərd) *adj.* Cowardly; fainthearted.

lil·y-of-the-val·ley (lil′ē·əv·thə·val′ē) *n. pl.* **lil·ies-of-the- valley** A perennial herb having small, fragrant white flowers. Also **lily of the valley.**

lily pad One of the large, floating leaves of the water lily.

li·ma bean (lī′mə) **1.** A species of the common bean, hav- ing large, flat, edible seeds. **2.** The seed of this plant, eaten as a vegetable. Also **Lima bean.** [after *Lima*, Peru]

limb[1] (lim) *n.* **1.** A part of the animal or human body at- tached to but distinct from the torso, as an arm, leg, or wing. **2.** One of the major divisions of a tree trunk; a large branch.

3. An extended or branching part, division, etc. 4. A person or thing regarded as a part of a larger body, group, etc. —**out on a limb** *U.S. Informal* In a risky, vulnerable, or questionable position. [OE *lim*] —**limb′less** *adj.*

limb[2] (lim) *n. Astron.* The edge of the disk of the sun, moon, or other heavenly body. [< F < L *limbus* edge, border]

limbed (limd) *adj.* 1. Having limbs. 2. Having or characterized by a (specified kind of) limb or (a specified number of) limbs: used in combination: *strong-limbed; four-limbed.*

lim·ber[1] (lim′bər) *adj.* 1. Pliant; flexible. 2. Able to bend or move easily; lithe. —*v.t.* 1. To make pliant. —*v.i.* 2. To exercise so as to become limber: with *up*. [Origin uncertain] —**lim′ber·ly** *adv.* —**lim′ber·ness** *n.*

lim·ber[2] (lim′bər) *n. Mil.* A two-wheeled, detachable vehicle at the forepart of a gun carriage. —*v.t. & v.i.* To attach a limber to (a gun). [Origin uncertain]

lim·bo[1] (lim′bō) *n. pl.* **·bos** 1. *Theol.* A region on the edge of hell for the souls of the righteous who died before the coming of Christ, and those of infants who die before baptism. 2. A place or condition for the relegation of unwanted or forgotten persons, things, etc. [< L *limbus* border]

lim·bo[2] (lim′bō) *n. pl.* **·bos** A dance popular in the West Indies, in which dancers pass under a bar placed at successively lower levels. [Origin uncertain]

Lim·burg·er cheese (lim′bûr·gər) A soft, white cheese having a strong odor and flavor. Also **Lim′burg cheese, Lim′burg·er.** Also **lim′burg·er.** [after *Limburg*, Belgium]

lime[1] (līm) *n.* A white, earthy substance, calcium oxide, CaO, prepared by calcining limestone or other forms of calcium carbonate, and used in mortars and cements. When dry it is called **quicklime** or **unslaked lime,** becoming **slaked lime** upon the addition of water. —*v.t.* **limed, lim·ing** To treat, mix, or spread with lime. [OE *līm*]

lime[2] (līm) *n.* 1. A small, green, lemonlike citrus fruit whose juice is used for flavoring, in beverages, etc. 2. The tropical tree yielding this fruit. [< F < Sp. *lima* < Arabic *līmah*]

lime[3] (līm) *n.* The European linden tree. [OE *lind* linden]

lime·kiln (līm′kil′, -kiln′) *n.* A kiln in which limestone, seashells, etc., are burned to produce lime.

lime·light (līm′līt′) *n.* 1. Public attention or notice. 2. A bright light used to illuminate a performer, stage area, etc., and originally produced by heating lime to incandescence.

lim·er·ick (lim′rik, -ə·rik) *n.* A humorous verse of five anapestic lines. Also **Lim′er·ick.** [? from the line "Will you come up to *Limerick,*"]

lime·stone (līm′stōn′) *n.* A sedimentary rock composed wholly or in part of calcium carbonate.

lime·wa·ter (līm′wô′tər, -wot′ər) *n.* An aqueous solution of calcium hydroxide, used in medicine.

lime·y (lī′mē) *n. pl.* **lime·ys** *U.S. Slang* 1. A British sailor. 2. Any Englishman. [from the former British maritime practice of drinking *lime* juice to prevent scurvy]

lim·it (lim′it) *n.* 1. The furthest or utmost extent, range, degree, etc., beyond which an activity, power, or function cannot or may not proceed: one's *limit* of endurance. 2. *Usu. pl.* The boundaries or extent of a specified area. 3. An amount or quantity established as the greatest permissible: Four fish are the *limit.* 4. *Math.* A definite quantity or value that a series is conceived or proved to approach but never reach. —**off limits** Forbidden to military personnel except on official business. —**the limit** *Informal* 1. One who or that which tries one's patience, credulity, etc., to the utmost. 2. To the utmost extent: usu. with *go.* —*v.t.* To set a bound or bounds to; confine; restrict. [< L *limes, limites*] —**lim′it·a·ble** *adj.* —**lim·i·ta·tive** (lim′ə·tā′tiv) *adj.* —**lim′it·er** *n.*

lim·i·ta·tion (lim′ə·tā′shən) *n.* 1. That which limits; restriction; shortcoming. 2. The act of limiting, or the state of being limited. 3. *Law* **a** A restrictive condition. **b** A legally fixed period within which certain acts must be performed. [< L *limitatio, -onis*]

lim·it·ed (lim′it·id) *adj.* 1. Confined within or defined by a limit or limits; restricted. 2. Falling short of fullness or impressiveness: a *limited* success. 3. Having powers restricted by constitutional law or authority, as a government. 4. Of a train, bus, etc., making few stops. 5. *Chiefly Brit. & Canadian* Restricted in liability to the amount invested by shareholders in its stock: a *limited* company. —*n.* A limited train, bus, etc. —**lim′i·ted·ly** *adv.* —**lim′i·ted·ness** *n.*

lim·it·ing (lim′it·ing) *adj. Gram.* Denoting adjectives that indicate the number or quantity of nouns rather than describe them, as *these* words, *seven* swans.

lim·it·less (lim′it·lis) *adj.* Having no limit; boundless.

limn (lim) *v.t.* To draw or paint; also, to describe in words. [ME < OF < L *illuminare*] —**lim·ner** (lim′nər) *n.*

Li·moges (lē·mōzh′, *Fr.* lē·môzh′) *n.* A type of fine porcelain manufactured at Limoges, France. Also **Limoges ware.**

lim·ou·sine (lim′ə·zēn′, lim′ə·zēn) *n.* 1. A large automobile, originally having a closed compartment for passengers and an open driver's seat under a projecting roof. 2. Any large, luxurious automobile. [< F]

limp[1] (limp) *v.i.* 1. To walk with a halting or irregular as with an injured leg or foot. 2. To progress in an irre or labored manner. —*n.* The manner of walking of who is lame. [OE *lempheal*t lame] —**limp′er** *n.*

limp[2] (limp) *adj.* 1. Lacking stiffness or firmness; fl 2. Lacking force or vigor; weak. [Origin uncertain **limp′ly** *adv.* —**limp′ness** *n.*

lim·pet (lim′pit) *n.* Any of various small marine an having conical shells and noted for their ability to cli rocks. [OE < LL *lampreda* limpet, lamprey]

lim·pid (lim′pid) *adj.* 1. Characterized by crystalline ness; transparent. 2. Characterized by clarity, lucidi purity, as of style. —**Syn.** See CLEAR. [< L *lim* clear] —**lim·pid′i·ty, lim′pid·ness** *n.* —**lim′pid·ly** *a*

lim·y (lī′mē) *adj.* **lim·i·er, lim·i·est** Containing or resem lime.

lin·age (lī′nij) *n.* 1. The number of lines in a piece of ten or printed matter. 2. Alignment. Also *lineage.*

linch·pin (linch′pin′) *n.* A pin placed through the end axle in order to keep a wheel from sliding off. [OE

lin·den (lin′dən) *n.* Any of various shade trees having white wood, heart-shaped leaves, and fragrant, crea ored flowers: also called *basswood.* [OE *lind* linden]

line[1] (līn) *n.* 1. A slender, continuous mark or indent as that drawn by a pen, pencil, or pointed tool. 2. Any row band or strip resembling such a mark. 3. A wrin crease in the skin. 4. Contour or profile, as of the edge area. 5. A division or boundary between adjoining a border. 6. A demarcation or limit separating contr concepts, kinds of behavior, etc. 7. A row of perso things. 8. A chronological succession of persons: the *line.* 9. A row of written or printed words. 10. A letter; note. 11. A single row of words forming a ver of a stanza. 12. Course of movement or progress; r *line* of march. 13. Course of action, thought, or per ance: a *line* of thought. 14. *Often pl.* General plan or cept, as of form, content, etc.: a work on heroic *lines.* Alignment; agreement; accord: to bring into *line.* 16. S or field of activity, ability, etc.: that work is not in my 17. Kind of work; occupation. 18. Merchandise of a ticular sort. 19. *pl.* The words of an actor's or perfor part. 20. *pl. Brit.* A certificate of marriage. 21. *pl.* L life; luck: hard *lines.* 23. *U.S. Slang* A glib mann speech intended to ingratiate or persuade. 24. A pipe, duit, or system of channels to convey liquids, gas, electr etc. 25. In telephonic communication, etc.: **a** A wi cable carrying power signals. **b** A system of such co tions. **c** A connection or channel of communication: to a *line* open. 26. Any system of public transportation an established route or routes. 27. The roadbed, trac system of tracks of a railroad. 28. A rope, string, cor the like, as used in fishing, measuring, etc. 29. *Math.* theoretical trace or course of a moving point, conceived having length, but no other dimension. 30. In the ar The representation of form by the use of strokes, rather by shading or coloring. **b** The distinctive form or contou any artistic creation. 31. *Mil.* **a** A trench or rampart. system of fortifications presenting an extended front. **c** *pl.* The disposition of troops: the front *lines.* **d** The com ant forces, as distinguished from the supporting services the staff. 32. In the naval services, those officers in ch of combat operations. 33. In bridge, a horizontal div of the score, separating points counting toward game, ten below it, and bonus points, written above it. —**in** 1. So as to form a line or row. 2. In accordance with ac ed standards or limitations. —**in line for** Next in c for. —**on a line** At the same level; evenly aligned. — **the line** Paid directly and promptly. —**out of line** 1. in conformity with accepted standards or practices. 2. subordinate; unruly. —**to get a line on** *U.S. Informa* acquire information about. —**to hold the line** 1. To m tain a defense or opposition. 2. To wait while mainta an open telephone connection. 3. In football, to pre the opposing team from gaining ground. —*v.* **lined, li** *v.t.* 1. To mark with lines. 2. To place in a line. 3. form a row or line along; border. 4. To indicate by or a lines; sketch. 5. In baseball, to bat (a ball, hit, etc.) i approximately horizontal trajectory. —*v.i.* 6. To for line; assume positions in a line: usually with *up.* —**to out** In baseball, to be retired by hitting a line drive th caught. —**to line up** 1. To form a line. 2. To bring alignment. 3. To take a stand, as in support of someth 4. To gather; marshal. 5. To compare. [OE *līne* cord

line[2] (līn) *v.t.* **lined, lin·ing** 1. To put a covering or facin the inner surface of. 2. To constitute a covering or sur for: Tapestries *lined* the room. 3. To fill or stuff, as money, food, etc. [OE *līn* flax]

lin·e·age[1] (lin′ē·ij) *n.* 1. Line of descent from a progen 2. Ancestry; family; stock. [< OF < L *linea* line]

line·age[2] (lī′nij) See LINAGE.

lin·e·al (lin′ē·əl) *adj.* 1. Being or occurring in the di

of descent. **2.** Pertaining to or based upon direct des- . **3.** Consisting of lines; linear. — **lin′e·al·ly** *adv.*

a·ment (lin′ē·ə·mənt) *n.* **1.** A facial contour or fea- . **2.** A distinguishing characteristic.

ar (lin′ē·ər) *adj.* **1.** Of or pertaining to a line or lines. nvolving or pertaining to length. **3.** Composed of lines. esembling a line. — **lin′e·ar·ly** *adv.*

ar A, Linear B See under MINOAN.

r measure **1.** Measurement by length. **2.** A unit or em of units for measuring length. See table front of

lrive In baseball, a batted ball that travels in an ap- imately horizontal trajectory: also called *liner.*

man (līn′mən) *n. pl.* **·men** (-mən) **1.** A man who in- s or repairs telephone or electric power lines: also *lines-* . **2.** A man who inspects a railroad track. **3.** In foot- a center, guard, tackle, or end. **4.** In surveying, a man holds the line, tape, or chain.

n (lin′ən) *n.* **1.** A fabric woven from the fibers of flax. rticles or garments made of linen, or now often of cot- bed *linen.* — *adj.* **1.** Made of the textile fiber of flax. Iade of linen. [OE *līnen* made of flax]

of force *Physics* A hypothetical line in a field of force, ciding at every point with the direction of the field.

r[1] (lī′nər) *n.* **1.** A ship or airplane operated by a trans- ation line. **2.** In baseball, a line drive. **3.** One who or which marks or produces lines.

r[2] (lī′nər) *n.* **1.** One who makes or fits linings. **2.** Some- g used as a lining.

·man (līnz′mən) *n. pl.* **·men** (-mən) **1.** In certain es, as tennis, an official making decisions on play at the of the court. **2.** In football, the official marking the ances gained or lost in each play. **3.** A lineman (def. 1).

up (līn′up′) *n.* **1.** An arrangement of persons or things line. **2.** In sports: **a** The formation of players drawn up ction. **b** The players. **c** A list of the team members play- at the start of a game. **3.** In police work, a row of possi- riminal suspects. Also **line′up′.**

y (lī′nē) See LINY.

(ling) *n. pl.* **ling** or **lings** A codlike food fish of the th Atlantic. [? < Du. *leng*]

[1] *suffix of nouns* **1.** Little; young: *duckling.* **2.** Minor; y: often used contemptuously: *princeling.* **3.** A person ing related to or characterized by: *worldling.* [OE]

[2] *suffix* Forming adverbs and adjectives: **1.** (from ns) Toward: *sideling.* **2.** (from adjectives) Being; be- ing: *darkling.* Also **-lings.** [OE *-ling, -linga*]

er (ling′gər) *v.i.* **1.** To stay on as if reluctant to leave. 'o proceed in a slow manner; dawdle. **3.** To continue to or exist; endure. **4.** To pause or dwell with interest, sure, etc.: usually with *over.* — *v.t.* **5.** To spend or te (time, one's life, etc.) idly or wearisomely: with *away* ut. [Northern ME *lenger* to delay] — **lin′ger·er** *n.*

e·rie (län′zhə·rē, län′zhə·rā′, *Fr.* lan·zhrē′) *n.* Wom- light undergarments, nightgowns, etc. [< F]

er·ing (ling′gər·ing) *adj.* **1.** Protracted; drawn out. ong-lasting; enduring. **3.** Slow. — **lin′ger·ing·ly** *adv.*

o (ling′gō) *n. pl.* **·goes** **1.** Language: used contemp- usly or humorously of a tongue one does not understand. The specialized vocabulary and idiom of a profession, s, etc.: medical *lingo.* [< Pg. < L *lingua* tongue]

ua fran·ca (ling′gwə frang′kə) **1.** Any jargon or pidgin l as a commercial or trade language, as pidgin English. A mixture of French, Spanish, Italian, Greek, and Arabic, ken in Mediterranean ports. [< Ital., lit., language of Franks]

ual (ling′gwəl) *adj.* Of or pertaining to the tongue or a guelike part. [< Med.L < L *lingua* tongue]

ui·form (ling′gwi·fôrm) *adj.* Tongue-shaped.

uist (ling′gwist) *n.* **1.** One who is fluent in several guages. **2.** A student of or specialist in linguistics.

uis·tic (ling·gwis′tik) *adj.* Of or pertaining to language inguistics. Also **lin·guis′ti·cal.** — **lin·guis′ti·cal·ly** *adv.*

uis·tics (ling·gwis′tiks) *n.pl.* (*construed as sing.*) The ntific study of language.

uistic stock A family of languages, including a parent guage together with all the languages derived from it.

·ment (lin′ə·mənt) *n.* A liquid rubbed on the skin to eve pain and stiffness. [< L *linire* to anoint]

ng (lī′ning) *n.* An inner surface or facing inserted in a ment, container, etc., as for protection, reinforcement, ; also, the material used.

(lingk) *n.* **1.** One of the loops, rings, or interlocking ts constituting a chain. **2.** A single element in a series, uence, or set: a weak *link* in his argument. **3.** That which s or connects separate parts, concepts, etc. **4.** A single ssage. **5.** In surveying, etc., the hundredth part of a in, equal to 7.92 inches. — *v.t. & v.i.* To join or connect by or as by links; interlock; couple; unite. — **Syn.** See UNITE. [ME *linke* < Scand.]

link·age (ling′kij) *n.* **1.** The act of linking, or the state of being linked. **2.** A system of links.

link·ing verb (ling′king) *Gram.* A verb that merely connects the subject and predicate of a sentence without asserting action, esp. the verbs *be, appear, become, feel, look, seem, smell, sound,* and *taste:* also called *copula.*

links (lingks) *n.pl.* A golf course. [OE *hlinc* slope]

Lin·ne·an (li·nē′ən) *adj.* Pertaining to Linnaeus or his system of classifying plants and animals. Also **Lin·nae′an.**

lin·net (lin′it) *n.* A common songbird of Europe. [< OF < L *linum* flax; from its feeding on flax seeds]

li·no·le·um (li·nō′lē·əm) *n.* A material used as a floor covering, etc., made from oxidized linseed oil and cork pressed upon canvas or burlap. [< L *linum* flax + *oleum* oil]

Li·no·type (lī′nə·tīp) *n.* A typesetting machine operated by a keyboard, and casting a complete line of type on a single metal piece: a trade name. Also **li′no·type.**

li·no·typ·er (lī′nə·tīp′ər) *n.* One who operates a Linotype. Also **li′no·typ·ist.**

lin·seed (lin′sēd′) *n.* Flaxseed. [OE *līnsǣd*]

linseed oil A yellowish oil made from flaxseed and used as a drying agent in the preparation of oil paints, linoleum, etc.

lin·sey-wool·sey (lin′zē·wŏŏl′zē) *n. pl.* **-wool·seys** A coarse cloth woven of linen and wool or cotton and wool threads. [ME *lin* linen + *saye* cloth + WOOL]

lint (lint) *n.* **1.** Bits of thread, fluff, etc. **2.** A downy substance used as a surgical dressing. **3.** *U.S.* The fibers of seeds of unginned cotton. [ME *linnet* lint] — **lin′ty** *adj.*

lin·tel (lin′təl) *n.* A horizontal part above the opening of a door or window, supporting the structure above it. [< OF < LL *lintellus, limitellus,* dim. of *limes, limites* limit]

lint·ers (lin′tərz) *n.pl.* *U.S.* The short fibers adhering to cotton seeds after ginning.

lin·y (lī′nē) *adj.* **lin·i·er, lin·i·est** **1.** Resembling a line; narrow. **2.** Marked with lines or streaks. Also *liney.*

li·on (lī′ən) *n.* **1.** A large, tawny or brownish gray carnivorous mammal of the cat family, native to Africa and SW Asia, the adult male having a shaggy mane. ◆ Collateral adjective: *leonine.* **2.** Any of various animals related or similar to the lion, as the mountain lion. **3.** One of noble courage, great strength, etc. **4.** A celebrity. — **the lion's share** The largest portion; an unduly large part. [< F < L *leo* < Gk. *leōn*] — **li′on·ess** (-is) *n.fem.*

Li·on (lī′ən) *n.* The constellation and sign of the zodiac Leo.

li·on·heart·ed (lī′ən·härt′id) *adj.* Admirably brave.

li·on·ize (lī′ə·nīz) *v.t.* **·ized, ·iz·ing** To treat or regard as a celebrity. — **li′on·iz·a′tion** *n.* — **li′on·iz′er** *n.*

lip (lip) *n.* **1.** One of the two folds of flesh that bound the mouth and serve as organs of speech. ◆ Collateral adjective: *labial.* **2.** A marginal part or structure resembling this. **3.** The rim or edge of any opening or cavity. **4.** The flared edge of a pitcher, bell, etc. **5.** *Slang* Brash and impudent talk; sass. **6.** *Music* The shaping and control of the mouth in playing a wind instrument. **7.** *Anat.* A labium. **8.** *Bot.* Either of the two divisions, upper or lower, of a corolla or calyx. — **to button one's lip** *Slang* To stop talking; shut up. — **to hang on (someone's) lips** To listen to with rapt attention. — **to keep a stiff upper lip** To maintain one's fortitude. — **to smack one's lips** To express anticipatory or remembered gusto; gloat. — *v.t.* **lipped, lip·ping** **1.** To touch with the lips; apply the lips to. **2.** *Music* In playing a wind instrument, to produce the correct pitch of (a tone) by adjusting the position of the lips. — *adj.* **1.** Of, pertaining to, or applied to the lips. **2.** Made or formed by the lips or a lip; labial. **3.** Insincere; hypocritical. [OE *lippa*]

lip·oid (lip′oid) *adj.* Resembling fat. — *n. Biochem.* A fatlike substance. [< Gk. *lipos* fat]

lipped (lipt) *adj.* Having a lip or lips.

lip·py (lip′ē) *adj.* **·pi·er, ·pi·est** *Slang* Sassy.

lip-read (lip′rēd′) *v.t. & v.i.* **-read** (red), **-read·ing** (rēd′ing) To interpret (speech) by watching the movements of lips.

lip reading The interpretation of speech by watching the movement of the lips, as by the deaf. — **lip reader**

lip·stick (lip′stik′) *n.* A pastelike cosmetic, usu. in the form of a small cylinder, used to color the lips.

liq·ue·fac·tion (lik′wə·fak′shən) *n.* The process of liquefying, or the state of being liquid.

liq·ue·fi·er (lik′wə·fī′ər) *n.* **1.** One who or that which liquefies. **2.** An apparatus in which a gas is liquefied.

liq·ue·fy (lik′wə·fī) *v.t. & v.i.* **·fied, ·fy·ing** To convert into or become liquid. [< L *liquere* to be liquid + *facere* to make] — **liq′ue·fi′a·ble** *adj.*

li·ques·cent (li·kwes′ənt) *adj.* Becoming or likely to become liquid; melting. [< L *liquere* to become liquid] — **li·ques′cence, li·ques′cen·cy** *n.*

li·queur (li·kûr′) *n.* An alcoholic beverage usu. made by

adding sugar syrup and flavoring to brandy: also called *cordial.* [< F < OF *licur*]
liq·uid (lik′wid) *adj.* **1.** Capable of flowing or of being poured. **2.** Clear and flowing, as sounds. **3.** Clear and bright; limpid. **4.** Free and facile, as movement; fluent. **5.** Consisting of or readily converted into cash. **6.** *Physics* Not gaseous or solid. **7.** *Phonet.* Of consonants, produced without friction; vowellike, as (l) and (r). — *n.* **1.** A substance in that state in which the molecules move freely among themselves but remain in one mass; a fluid that is not a gas. **2.** *Phonet.* The sound (l) or (r), or sometimes other sonorants. [< F < L < *liquere* to be liquid] — **li·quid·i·ty** (li·kwid′ə·tē), **liq′uid·ness** *n.* — **liq′uid·ly** *adv.*
liquid air An extremely cold, liquid mixture of nitrogen and oxygen, used chiefly as a refrigerant.
liq·ui·date (lik′wə·dāt) *v.* **·dat·ed, ·dat·ing** *v.t.* **1.** To pay off or settle, as an obligation or debt. **2.** To wind up the affairs of (a business firm, etc.) by using the assets to settle debts or obligations. **3.** To convert into cash, as securities. **4.** To do away with. **5.** *Slang* To kill or murder. — *v.i.* **6.** To settle one's debts. [< Med.L *liquidare* to make liquid]
liq·ui·da·tion (lik′wə·dā′shən) *n.* The act or procedure of liquidating, or the state of being liquidated. — **to go into liquidation** Of a business firm, to cease transacting business and to settle debts or discharge obligations.
liquid measure A unit or system of units for measuring liquids. See table front of book.
liquid oxygen Oxygen liquefied by a reduction of temperature and an increase of pressure, used extensively to oxidize other components of rocket fuels: also called *lox.*
liq·uor (lik′ər) *n.* **1.** Any alcoholic beverage; esp., distilled spirits, as whisky, brandy, etc. **2.** A liquid such as broth, juice, etc. — *v.t.* **1.** *Slang* To ply with alcoholic drink: usu. with *up.* — *v.i.* **2.** To drink liquor, esp. in large amounts: usu. with *up.* [< OF < L *liquor*]
liq·uo·rice (lik′ə·ris, -rish) See LICORICE.
li·ra (lir′ə, *Ital.* lē′rä) *n. pl.* **li·re** (lir′ə, *Ital.* lē′rā) or **li·ras** (lir′əz) The monetary unit of Italy equivalent to 100 centesimi: in 1960 worth about 4/25 of a U.S. cent; also a coin of this value. [< Ital. < L *libra* pound]
lisle (līl) *n.* **1.** A fine twisted cotton thread used in knitting hosiery, etc. Also **lisle thread.** **2.** A fabric, usu. knitted, made from such thread. [after *Lisle,* now Lille, France]
lisp (lisp) *n.* **1.** A speech defect or affectation in which the sibilants (s) and (z) are articulated like (th) in *thank* and (th) in *this.* **2.** The act or habit of speaking with a lisp. **3.** A sound resembling a lisp. — *v.t. & v.i.* **1.** To pronounce with a lisp. **2.** To speak in a childlike manner. [OE *āwlyspian*]
lis·some (lis′əm) *adj.* **1.** Flexible; pliant. **2.** Agile; lithe. Also **lis′som.** — **lis′some·ly** *adv.* — **lis′some·ness** *n.*
list[1] (list) *n.* **1.** An itemized series of names, words, etc., usu. recorded in a set order. **2.** A classification of persons or things belonging in the same category: usu. with *on.* — *v.t.* **1.** To place on or in a list. **2.** To include in a register, catalogue, etc. [< OF < OHG *līsta*] — **list′a·ble** *adj.*
list[2] (list) *n.* **1.** A strip, edging, or selvage, as of cloth. **2.** Fabric consisting of or woven like a selvage. — *v.t.* To edge with list. [OE *līste*]
list[3] (list) *v.t. & v.i. Naut.* Of a vessel, to lean or tilt to one side. — *n.* A leaning or inclination to one side.
list[4] (list) *Poetic v.t.* **1.** To listen to; hear. — *v.i.* **2.** To listen. [OE *hlyst* hearing]
lis·ten (lis′ən) *v.i.* **1.** To make conscious use of the sense of hearing; be attentive in order to hear. **2.** To pay attention; give heed. **3.** To be influenced or persuaded. — **to listen in** **1.** To participate in hearing (a broadcast, etc.). **2.** To eavesdrop. [OE *hlysnan*] — **lis′ten·er** *n.*
list·er (lis′tər) *n. U.S.* A plow with a double moldboard that produces a ridged furrow.
list·ing (lis′ting) *n.* **1.** The act of one who or that which lists. **2.** An entry in a list. **3.** A list.
list·less (list′lis) *adj.* Languidly indifferent; apathetic; lackadaisical. — **list′less·ly** *adv.* — **list′less·ness** *n.*
list price The retail price of merchandise, from which a discount is sometimes made.
lists (lists) *n.pl.* **1.** The barriers enclosing the jousting field of a medieval tournament. **2.** The field thus enclosed. **3.** Any arena or scene of conflict. — **to enter the lists** To engage in a contest or controversy. [OE *liste* border]
lit (lit) Alternative past tense and past participle of LIGHT[1] and LIGHT[2].
lit·a·ny (lit′ə·nē) *n. pl.* **·nies** *Eccl.* A liturgical form of prayer consisting of a series of supplications said by the clergy, to which the congregation repeat a fixed response. [OE < LL < Gk. *litaneuein* to pray]
-lite *combining form Mineral.* Stone; stonelike. [< F < Gk. *lithos* stone]
li·ter (lē′tər) *n.* In the metric system, a measure of capacity equal to the volume of one kilogram of water at 4° C. and normal atmospheric pressure, or to 1.0567 liquid quarts. Also, *esp. Brit., litre.* See table front of book.

lit·er·a·cy (lit′ər·ə·sē) *n.* The state of being literate.
lit·er·al (lit′ər·əl) *adj.* **1.** Restricted to the exact, s meaning; not figurative: the *literal* sense of the Script **2.** Following the exact words and order of an original: *eral* translation. **3.** Tending to recognize or accept s meanings only; matter-of-fact. **4.** Free from figurative guage, etc., as a literary style; factual. [< OF < L *littera* letter] — **lit·er·al·i·ty** (lit′ər·al′ə·tē), **lit′er·al·ne**
lit·er·al·ly (lit′ər·ə·lē) *adv.* **1.** In a literal manner; i strictest sense. **2.** Actually; really. **3.** In effect; virtu
lit·er·ar·y (lit′ə·rer′ē) *adj.* **1.** Of, pertaining to, or tre of literature. **2.** Characteristic of or appropriate to l ture. **3.** Versed in or devoted to literature. **4.** Profes ally engaged in the field of literature. [< L *litterarius*
lit·er·ate (lit′ər·it) *adj.* **1.** Able to read and write. **2.** cated; cultured. **3.** Literary. — *n.* **1.** One able to rea write. **2.** An educated person. [< L < *littera* letter]
lit·e·ra·ti (lit′ə·rä′tē, -rā′tī) *n.pl.* **1.** Men of letters; s ars. **2.** Literate or educated persons collectively. [<
lit·e·ra·tim (lit′ə·rā′tim, -rä′-) *adv.* Letter for letter; ally. [< L]
lit·er·a·ture (lit′ər·ə·cho͝or, -chər, lit′rə·chər) *n.* **1.** W works collectively, esp. those of enduring importance, e iting creative imagination and artistic skill. **2.** Poetr tion, essays, etc., as distinguished from factual writing The writings of a particular period, language, etc.: Eli than *literature.* **4.** The writings pertaining to a parti subject. **5.** The occupation of a professional writer. **6** *formal* Any printed matter used or distributed for adv ing. [< L *littera* letter]
lith- Var. of LITHO-.
-lith *combining form* Stone; rock. [< Gk. *lithos* ston
lith·arge (lith′ärj, li·thärj′) *n.* A yellowish monoxi lead, PbO, made by heating lead in air, and used in making, as a pigment, etc. [< F *litarge* < L *lithargyr* Gk. *lithargyros* silver scum < *lithos* stone + *argyros* si
lithe (līth) *adj.* Bending easily or gracefully; supple; p limber. [OE, soft] — **lithe′ly** *adv.* — **lithe′ness** *n.*
lithe·some (līth′səm) *adj.* Lithe.
lith·i·a (lith′ē·ə) *n.* Lithium oxide, Li_2O, a white, ca compound. [< NL < Gk. *lithos* stone]
-lithic *combining form* Pertaining to a (specified) an pological stage in the use of stone implements: *Neolith*
lith·i·um (lith′ē·əm) *n.* A soft, silver-white element bol Li), the lightest of the metals, found only in com tion. See ELEMENT. [< NL < Gk. *lithos* stone]
litho- *combining form* Stone. Also, before vowels, [< Gk. *lithos* stone]
lith·o·graph (lith′ə·graf, -gräf) *n.* A print produced b process of lithography. — *v.t.* To produce or reprodu lithography. — **li·thog·ra·pher** (li·thog′rə·fər) *n.* — **li graph′ic** or **·i·cal** *adj.* — **lith′o·graph′i·cal·ly** *adv.*
li·thog·ra·phy (li·thog′rə·fē) *n.* The art or process of ducing printed matter from a flat stone or zinc or alumi plate on which a drawing or design has been made in a gr or water-repellent material.
lith·o·sphere (lith′ə·sfir) *n.* The solid crust of the eart distinguished from the atmosphere and the hydrosphe
Lith·u·a·ni·an (lith′o͞o·ā′nē·ən) *adj.* Of or pertainin Lithuania, its people, or their language. — *n.* **1.** A n or inhabitant of Lithuania. **2.** The Balto-Slavic langua the Lithuanians.
lit·i·ga·ble (lit′ə·gə·bəl) *adj.* Subject to legal dispute.
lit·i·gant (lit′ə·gənt) *n.* A participant in a lawsuit. — Engaged in litigation. [< F < L < *litigare* to litigate]
lit·i·gate (lit′ə·gāt) *v.* **·gat·ed, ·gat·ing** *v.t.* **1.** To brin dispute, claim, etc.) before a court of law for decision; test at law. — *v.i.* **2.** To engage in a lawsuit. [< L < *litis* lawsuit + *agere* to do, act] — **lit′i·ga′tor** *n.*
lit·i·ga·tion (lit′ə·gā′shən) *n.* **1.** The act or process o gaging in legal action. **2.** A judicial contest; lawsuit.
li·tig·ious (li·tij′əs) *adj.* **1.** Inclined to litigation; qua some. **2.** Subject to litigation. **3.** Of or pertaining to gation. — **li·tig′ious·ly** *adv.* — **li·tig′ious·ness** *n.*
lit·mus (lit′məs) *n.* A blue dyestuff made from certa chens. It is turned red by acids and remains blue when t ed with an alkali. [< AF < ON < *litr* color + *mosi* m
litmus paper Paper dyed with litmus, used to test aci
li·tre (lē′tər) See LITER.
lit·ter (lit′ər) *n.* **1.** Waste materials, scraps, or objects c lessly strewn about. **2.** Untidy or chaotic condition; m **3.** The young brought forth at one birth by any mam normally having several offspring at one time. **4.** A stret for carrying sick or wounded persons. **5.** A couch car between shafts by men or beasts of burden. **6.** Straw, etc., spread in animal pens, or over plants as protection. *v.t.* **1.** To make untidy or unsightly by carelessly discar trash, etc. **2.** To drop or scatter carelessly. **3.** To pro with litter, as for bedding. **4.** To give birth to (pups, tens, etc.) — *v.i.* **5.** To give birth to a litter of young. To drop or scatter refuse. [< OF < Med.L < L *lectus* be

er·bug (lit′ər·bug′) *n. U.S. Slang* One who litters pub- places, roads, etc., with trash.
le (lit′l) *adj.* **lit·tler** or (for defs. 2 and 3) **less, lit·tlest** or · defs. 2 and 3) **least 1.** Small, or smaller compared to ers, in physical size: a *little* house. **2.** Not long; short; ef: a *little* time; a *little* distance away. **3.** Small or relaely small in quantity or degree: *little* wealth; *little* probaty. **4.** Having small force or effectiveness; weak: a *little* ort. **5.** Not having great influence, power, or significance; nor; trivial. **6.** Narrow or limited in viewpoint; petty: *le* minds. — *adv.* **less, least 1.** Only slightly; not much: sleeps *little.* **2.** Not at all: used before a verb: She *little* pects. — *n.* **1.** A small amount: Give me a *little.* **2.** An gnificant amount: *Little* can be done about it. **3.** A short ile or distance. — **little by little** By small degrees; gradly. — **to make little of** To treat or regard as inconseential. [OE < *lȳt* small] — **lit′tle·ness** *n.*
le theater An amateur or community theater group.
o·ral (lit′ər·əl) *adj.* Of a shore or coastal region. — *n.* shore and its adjacent areas. [< L < *lit(t)us, -oris* seare]
ur·gi·cal (li·tûr′ji·kəl) *adj.* Of or associated with public rship, ritual, etc. Also **li·tur′gic.** — **li·tur′gi·cal·ly** *adv.*
ur·gy (lit′ər·jē) *n. pl.* **·gies 1.** In various religions, the escribed form for public worship; religious ritual. **2.** The e of the Eucharist. [< Med.L < Gk. *leitourgia* public ty, ult. < *laos* people + *ergon* work]
a·ble (liv′ə·bəl) *adj.* **1.** Suitable or agreeable for living **2.** Worth living; tolerable. **3.** Agreeable, as for comnionship. Also **live′a·ble.**
e[1] (liv) *v.* **lived, liv·ing** *v.i.* **1.** To function as an animate ganism; be alive. **2.** To remain alive: as long as you *live.* To remain or persist, as in the mind. **4.** To remain valid operative; endure. **5.** To have as one's home; reside: th *in* or *at.* **6.** To use as one's sole or customary nourishent: with *on*: to *live* on air. **7.** To maintain or support eself: with *on* or *by*: to *live* on one's income. **8.** To pass e in a specified manner: to *live* in peace. **9.** To regulate e's life, as in accordance with principles, etc.: to *live* by a ict code. **10.** To enjoy a varied or satisfying life. — *v.t.* . To spend or pass (life, time, etc.). **12.** To put into actice: to *live* one's religion. — **to live down** To live or have so as to expiate the memory of (an error, crime, etc.). **to live in** To reside, as a domestic servant, at one's place employment. — **to live through** To survive or withstand n experience). — **to live up to 1.** To satisfy (an ideal, exctations, etc.). **2.** To fulfill (a bargain, obligation, etc.). E *libban, lifian*]
— **Syn. 5.** Dwell, reside, abide.
e[2] (līv) *adj.* **1.** Functioning as an animate organism; alive. Pertaining to, characteristic of, or abounding in life. **3.** present interest and importance: a *live* issue. **4.** Forceful d energetic; dynamic. **5.** Burning or glowing: a *live* coal. Vivid or brilliant, as color. **7.** Charged with electricity: *live* wire. **8.** Capable of being detonated, as a bomb. **9.** television, radio, etc., consisting of or performed by perns present at the time of transmission. **10.** In mechanical e, having motion or the power to impart motion or force. **1.** In printing, publishing, etc., ready or retained for use: *ve* copy. **12.** In sports, being in play, as a ball.
e·bear·er (līv′bâr′ər) *n.* An ovoviviparous fish, as a gupy. — **live′bear′ing** *adj.*
ed (līvd) *adj.* Having a (specified kind of) life or life span: ed in combination: *long-lived.*
e·li·hood (līv′lē·hŏŏd) *n.* Means of supporting or mainining one's existence. [ME < OE < *līf* life + *lād* way]
e·long (liv′lông′, -long′) *adj.* Long or seemingly long in assing; entire: the *livelong* day. [ME *lefe longe,* lit., lief ng; *lief,* here orig. intens., was later confused with *live*]
e·ly (līv′lē) *adj.* **·li·er, ·li·est 1.** Full of vigor or motion; nergetic. **2.** Arousing activity or excitement: a *lively* tune. . Vivid; keen: a *lively* imagination. **4.** Striking and forcel to the mind: a *lively* impression. **5.** Filled with activity: *lively* day. **6.** Invigorating; brisk: a *lively* breeze. **7.** ouncing readily, as a ball; resilient. — *adv.* In a lively anner; briskly: now usu. in the expression **to step lively,** hurry up. [OE *līflīce*] — **live′li·ly** *adv.* — **live′li·ness** *n.*
ven (lī′vən) *v.t. & v.i.* To make or become lively or cheerl: often with *up.* — **liv′en·er** *n.*
e oak Any of several evergreen trees having hard, wood.
·er[1] (liv′ər) *n.* **1.** *Anat.* The largest glandular organ of ertebrates, secreting bile and active in metabolism, in man ituated just under the diaphragm and on the right side. ◆ Collateral adjective: *hepatic.* **2.** A similar digestive gland in nvertebrates. **3.** Food consisting of or prepared from the ver of certain animals. [OE *lifer*]
·er[2] (liv′ər) *n.* **1.** One who lives in a specified manner: a uxurious *liver.* **2.** A dweller.

liv·er·ied (liv′ər·ēd) *adj.* Dressed in livery, as a servant.
liv·er·ish (liv′ər·ish) *adj. Informal* Feeling or exhibiting supposed symptoms of disordered liver; bilious; irritable.
liv·er·wort (liv′ər·wûrt′) *n.* **1.** Any mosslike cryptogam forming mats in damp, shady places. **2.** A hepatica.
liv·er·wurst (liv′ər·wûrst′) *n.* A sausage made of or containing ground liver. [< G *leberwurst*]
liv·er·y (liv′ər·ē) *n. pl.* **·er·ies 1.** The distinctive clothing or uniform worn by male household servants. **2.** The distinguishing dress of an organization or group. **3.** Characteristic garb or outward appearance. **4.** The stabling and care of horses for pay. **5.** *U.S.* A livery stable. [< OF *livree* gift of clothes by a master to a servant < L *liber* free]
liv·er·y·man (liv′ər·ē·mən) *n. pl.* **·men** (-mən) A man who keeps or works in a livery stable.
livery stable A stable where horses and vehicles are cared for or kept for hire.
lives (līvz) Plural of LIFE.
live·stock (līv′stok′) *n.* Domestic farm animals, as cattle, horses, and sheep, esp. when raised for profit.
live wire 1. A wire carrying an electric current or potential. **2.** *Informal* An energetic, enterprising person; a go-getter.
liv·id (liv′id) *adj.* **1.** Having the skin abnormally discolored, as: **a** Flushed, purplish, etc., as from intense emotion. **b** Black-and-blue, as from contusion. **2.** Having a leaden pallor; bluish gray. **3.** *Informal* Furious; enraged. [< F < L *livere* to be livid] — **liv′id·ly** *adv.* — **liv′id·ness, li·vid·i·ty** (li·vid′ə·tē) *n.*
liv·ing (liv′ing) *adj.* **1.** Alive; animate; not dead. **2.** Of or characteristic of everyday life: *living* conditions. **3.** Used or intended for maintaining existence: a *living* wage. **4.** Having contemporary value, force, or application: *living* languages. **5.** Of or pertaining to those who are alive. **6.** Lifelike; real: the *living* image of his father. — *n.* **1.** The state of one who or that which lives. **2.** Those that are alive: preceded by *the.* **3.** Manner or conduct of life: virtuous *living.* **4.** Means of supporting existence; livelihood.
living death A prolonged painful experience.
living room A room designed and furnished for the general use, social activities, etc., of a household; sitting room.
liz·ard (liz′ərd) *n.* **1.** Any of various reptiles typically having elongate, scaly bodies, long tails, and four legs, as the chameleon, iguana, skink, etc. **2.** Loosely, any similar reptile or amphibian. **3.** Leather made from the skin of a lizard. [< OF < L *lacerta*]
-'ll Contracted form of SHALL or WILL (*v.*) or of TILL (*prep*).
lla·ma (lä′mə) *n.* A camellike, humpless ruminant of South America, having thick, woolly hair, and frequently used as a beast of burden. [< Sp. < Quechua]

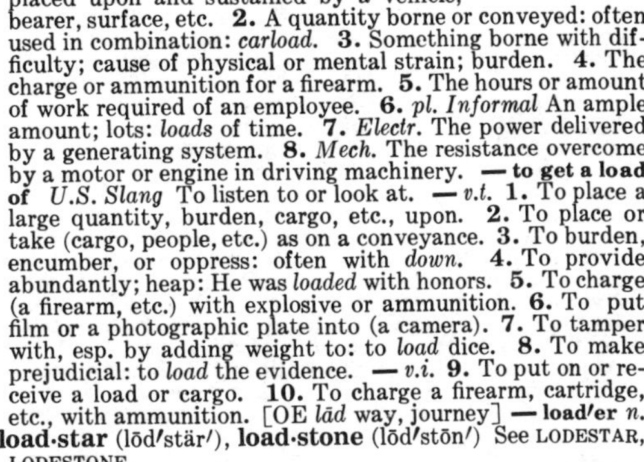

LLAMA (3½ to 4 feet high at shoulder)

lla·no (lä′nō, *Sp.* lyä′nō) *n. pl.* **·nos** (-nōz, *Sp.* -nōs) A flat, treeless plain, as those of the SW U.S. and northern Latin America. [< Sp., plain, flat < L *planus*]
lo (lō) *interj.* See! observe!: *Lo* and behold! [OE *lā*]
loach (lōch) *n.* Any of various fresh-water fishes related to the carp and minnow. [< F *loche*]
load (lōd) *n.* **1.** The weight or quantity placed upon and sustained by a vehicle, bearer, surface, etc. **2.** A quantity borne or conveyed: often used in combination: *carload.* **3.** Something borne with difficulty; cause of physical or mental strain; burden. **4.** The charge or ammunition for a firearm. **5.** The hours or amount of work required of an employee. **6.** *pl. Informal* An ample amount; lots: *loads* of time. **7.** *Electr.* The power delivered by a generating system. **8.** *Mech.* The resistance overcome by a motor or engine in driving machinery. — **to get a load of** *U.S. Slang* To listen to or look at. — *v.t.* **1.** To place a large quantity, burden, cargo, etc., upon. **2.** To place or take (cargo, people, etc.) as on a conveyance. **3.** To burden, encumber, or oppress: often with *down.* **4.** To provide abundantly; heap: He was *loaded* with honors. **5.** To charge (a firearm, etc.) with explosive or ammunition. **6.** To put film or a photographic plate into (a camera). **7.** To tamper with, esp. by adding weight to: to *load* dice. **8.** To make prejudicial: to *load* the evidence. — *v.i.* **9.** To put on or receive a load or cargo. **10.** To charge a firearm, cartridge, etc., with ammunition. [OE *lād* way, journey] — **load′er** *n.*
load·star (lōd′stär′), **load·stone** (lōd′stōn′) See LODESTAR, LODESTONE.
loaf[1] (lōf) *v.i.* **1.** To loiter lazily or aimlessly. **2.** To shirk or dawdle over one's work. — *v.t.* **3.** To spend (time) idly: with *away.* [Back formation < LOAFER]
loaf[2] (lōf) *n. pl.* **loaves** (lōvz) **1.** A rounded or elongated mass of bread baked in a single piece. **2.** Any shaped mass of food, as of cake, chopped meat, etc. [OE *hlāf* bread]

loaf·er (lō′fər) *n.* **1.** One who loafs; an idler or slacker. **2.** A casual shoe resembling a moccasin.
loam (lōm) *n.* **1.** Loose-textured soil consisting of a mixture of sand and clay containing organic matter. **2.** A moistened mixture of clay, sand, and straw, used in plastering. — *v.t.* To coat or fill with loam. [OE *lām*] — **loam′y** *adj.*
loan (lōn) *n.* **1.** Something lent; esp., a sum of money lent at interest. **2.** The act of lending: the *loan* of a knife. — *v.t.* & *v.i.* To lend. [ME < ON *lān*]
loan shark *U.S. Informal* One who lends money at an excessively high or illegal rate of interest.
loan-word (lōn′wûrd′) *n.* A word adopted from another language and partly or completely naturalized, as the English word *chauffeur*, taken from the French. Also **loan word, loan′word′.** [< G *lehnwort*]
loath (lōth) *adj.* Strongly disinclined; reluctant; unwilling: often followed by *to.* Also spelled *loth.* [OE *lāth* hateful]
loathe (lōth) *v.t.* **loathed, loath·ing** To feel great hatred or disgust for; abhor; detest. — **Syn.** See HATE. [OE *lāthian* to be hateful] — **loath′er** *n.*
loath·ing (lō′thing) *n.* Extreme dislike; abhorrence. — **loath′ing·ly** *adv.*
loath·some (lōth′səm) *adj.* Causing revulsion or disgust; repulsive. — **loath′some·ly** *adv.* — **loath′some·ness** *n.*
loaves (lōvz) Plural of LOAF.
lob (lob) *v.* **lobbed, lob·bing** *v.t.* **1.** To pitch, or strike (a ball, etc.) in a high, arching curve. — *v.i.* **2.** To move clumsily or heavily. **3.** To lob a ball. — *n.* In tennis, a stroke that sends the ball high into the air. [ME]
lo·bar (lō′bər, -bär) *adj.* **1.** Of or pertaining to a lobe. **2.** Affecting one or more lobes of the lungs. [< NL *lobaris*]
lo·bate (lō′bāt) *adj.* **1.** Having or consisting of lobes. **2.** Resembling a lobe. Also **lo′bat·ed.** [< NL *lobatus*]
lo·ba·tion (lō·bā′shən) *n.* **1.** The condition of having or forming lobes. **2.** A lobe or lobelike part.
lob·by (lob′ē) *n.* *pl.* **·bies 1.** An entrance hall, vestibule, or public lounge in an apartment house, hotel, theater, etc. **2.** *U.S.* A group representing persons or organizations with a common interest, who attempt to influence the votes of legislators. — *v.* **·bied, ·by·ing** *U.S. v.i.* **1.** To attempt to influence legislators in favor of some interest. — *v.t.* **2.** To attempt to influence (legislators, etc.). **3.** To exert influence for the passage of: often with *through.* [< Med.L *lobia*]
lob·by·ism (lob′ē·iz′əm) *n.* *U.S.* The practice of lobbying. — **lob′by·ist** *n.*
lobe (lōb) *n.* **1.** A rounded division, protuberance, or part, as of a leaf. **2.** The soft lower part of the human ear. **3.** *Anat.* Any of several well-defined, often symmetrical portions of an organ or part of the body, as of the brain, lungs, liver, etc. [< F < L < Gk. *lobos*] — **lobed** *adj.*
lo·be·li·a (lō·bē′lē·ə, -bēl′yə) *n.* Any of a genus of herbaceous plants having flowers usu. borne in racemes. [< NL, after Matthias de *Lobel*, 1538–1616, Flemish botanist]
lob·lol·ly (lob′lol·ē) *n.* *pl.* **·lies 1.** *U.S.* A pine of the southern U.S., having scaly bark and wood valuable as lumber. **2.** The wood of this tree. Also **loblolly pine.** [< dial. E *lob* bubble + *lolly* broth]
lo·bo (lō′bō) *n.* *pl.* **·bos** The timber wolf of the western U.S. [< Sp., wolf < L *lupus*]
lo·bot·o·my (lō·bot′ə·mē) *n.* *pl.* **·mies** *Surg.* The operation of cutting into or across a lobe of the brain, esp. in order to modify or eliminate some function associated with a mental disorder. [< Gk. *lobos* lobe + -TOMY]
lob·ster (lob′stər) *n.* **1.** Any of various ten-legged marine crustaceans having the first pair of legs modified as claws, and compound eyes on flexible stalks. **2.** Any of various similar crustaceans. **3.** The flesh of any of these crustaceans eaten as food. [OE < L *locusta* lobster, locust]
lob·ule (lob′yōōl) *n.* **1.** A small lobe. **2.** A subdivision of a lobe. [< NL < *lobus* lobe] — **lob′u·lar, lob′u·lose** *adj.*
lo·cal (lō′kəl) *adj.* **1.** Pertaining to, characteristic of, or confined to a relatively small area. **2.** Restricted, as by environmental influences, etc. **3.** Of or pertaining to a particular place or position in space: *local* time. **4.** Stopping at all stations along its run, as a train. **5.** *Med.* Relating to or affecting a specific part of the body. — *n.* **1.** A branch or chapter of an organization, as a trade union. **2.** A bus, train, etc., that stops at all stations. **3.** A news item of local interest. [< F < L < *locus* place] — **lo′cal·ly** *adv.*
local color The characteristic appearance, mannerisms, etc., of a place or period, esp. as presented in literature.
lo·cale (lō·kal′) *n.* **1.** A place or locality, esp. with reference to some event or circumstance. **2.** The setting of a literary, dramatic, or artistic work; scene. [< F]
lo·cal·ism (lō′kəl·iz′əm) *n.* **1.** A local custom or idiom. **2.** A word, meaning of a word, pronunciation, etc., peculiar to a locality. **3.** Narrowness; provincialism.
lo·cal·i·ty (lō·kal′ə·tē) *n.* *pl.* **·ties 1.** A place, region, etc. **2.** Position, esp. in relation to surroundings, etc. **3.** The state of being local. [< F < LL *localitas*]
lo·cal·ize (lō′kəl·īz) *v.t.* **·ized, ·iz·ing 1.** To make local; confine or assign to a specific area. **2.** To determine the p of origin of. — **lo′cal·iz′a·ble** *adj.* — **lo′cal·i·za′tion** *n.*
local option The right of a county or town, etc., to rest or prohibit certain activities, as the sale of liquor.
lo·cate (lō′kāt, lō·kāt′) *v.* **·cat·ed, ·cat·ing** *v.t.* **1.** To cover the position of; find. **2.** To establish or place at a ticular site: The store is *located* on the corner. **3.** To p hypothetically as to setting, a relative position, etc. **4.** To survey and fix the site or boundaries of (property, a ing claim, etc.). — *v.i.* **5.** *U.S. Informal* To settle. [< *locus* place] — **lo·cat′a·ble** *adj.* — **lo′ca·ter** *n.*
lo·ca·tion (lō·kā′shən) *n.* **1.** The act of locating, or state of being located. **2.** A site or situation, esp. consid in regard to its surroundings. **3.** Exact position or p occupied. **4.** A motion picture or television locale a from the studio on location. **5.** *U.S.* A tract of land ha established boundaries. [< L *locatio*]
loc·a·tive (lok′ə·tiv) *adj.* *Gram.* In certain inflected guages, as Latin, Greek, and Sanskrit, designating a n case denoting place where or at which. — *n.* *Gram.* **1.** locative case. **2.** A word in this case. [< L *locatus*]
loch (lokh, lok) *n.* *Scot.* **1.** A lake. **2.** An arm of the
lo·ci (lō′sī) Plural of LOCUS.

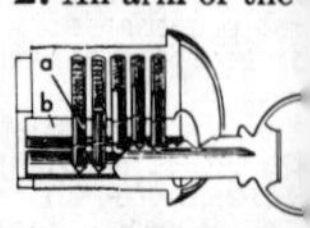

LOCK
Insertion of key raises tumblers (a thus releasing key plug (b) and permi ting key to turn.

lock[1] (lok) *n.* **1.** A mechanical fastening device having a bolt or combination of bolts secured or released by a key, dial, etc., and used to prevent unauthorized entry, access, or operation. **2.** Any part or device that fastens, secures, or holds something firmly in place. **3.** A section of a canal, etc., enclosed by gates, within which the water depth may be varied to raise or lower boats from level to level. **4.** The mechanism that explodes the charge of a gun. **5.** An interlocking, tening, or jamming together of parts. **6.** A wrestling gri hold. — **lock, stock, and barrel** Altogether; complet — *v.t.* **1.** To fasten, or secure by means of a lock. **2.** keep, confine, etc., in or as in a locked enclosure: with *in*, or *away.* **3.** To fit together securely; interlock. **4.** To cl or grip in or as in a firm hold. **5.** To make immovable b as by jamming or fastening together. **6.** To move (a ves through a waterway by means of locks. — *v.i.* **7.** To come locked. **8.** To become firmly joined or interlock — **to lock out 1.** To prevent (employees) from working closing a factory, shop, etc. **2.** To keep out by lock [OE *loc* fastening, enclosure] — **lock′a·ble** *adj.*
lock[2] (lok) *n.* **1.** Strands of hair forming a curl. **2.** *pl.* hair of the head. **3.** A tuft of wool, etc. [OE *locc*]
lock·er (lok′ər) *n.* **1.** A closet, cabinet, storage space, e fastened with a lock; as: **a** One of a series of metal cabin as in a school or gymnasium, in which clothes, equipme etc., are kept. **b** A cabinet in which frozen foods are k **2.** A chest, etc., as on a ship, in which equipment or p sonal belongings are kept. **3.** One who or that which loc
locker room A room having lockers for clothing, etc.
lock·et (lok′it) *n.* A small ornamental case for enclosin picture or keepsake, usu. worn on a chain, ribbon, e around the neck. [< OF < *loc* latch < Gmc.]
lock·jaw (lok′jô′) *n.* *Pathol.* A form of tetanus causing ri closure of the jaws: also called *trismus.*
lock·out (lok′out′) *n.* The closing of a place of business an employer in order to make employees agree to terms.
lock·smith (lok′smith′) *n.* A maker or repairer of lock
lock step A marching style in which each marcher follo as closely as possible the one in front of him.
lock·up (lok′up′) *n.* A jail or prison cell.
lo·co (lō′kō) *adj.* *U.S. Informal* Crazy; insane. — *n.* **·cos** Locoweed. — *v.t.* **·coed, ·co·ing 1.** To poison with lo weed. **2.** *U.S. Slang* To make insane. [< Sp., insane]
lo·co·mo·tion (lō′kə·mō′shən) *n.* The act or power of mo ing from one place to another. [< L *loco* from a place *motio, -onis* movement]
lo·co·mo·tive (lō′kə·mō′tiv) *n.* An engine that moves its own power, used to pull passenger or freight trains on railroad. — *adj.* **1.** Of, pertaining to, or used in locomotio **2.** Moving or able to move from one place to another. Capable of moving by its own power, as an engine.
lo·co·weed (lō′kō·wēd′) *n.* Any of several leguminous plan of the SW U.S., often poisonous to livestock.
lo·cus (lō′kəs) *n.* *pl.* **·ci** (-sī) **1.** A place; locality; area. *Math.* **a** A surface or curve regarded as traced by a line point moving under specified conditions. **b** Any figure ma up wholly of points or lines that satisfy given conditions.
lo·cust[1] (lō′kəst) *n.* **1.** Any of a family of widely distribut winged insects resembling grasshoppers but having short a tennae, including those of migratory habits that destr vegetation. **2.** A cicada. [< OF < L *locusta*]
lo·cust[2] (lō′kəst) *n.* **1.** A leguminous tree of North Americ having compound leaves and clusters of fragrant wh

ers. **2.** The wood of this tree. **3.** Any of various similar , as the acacia and honey locust. [< L *locusta*]

·tion (lō·kyōō′shən) *n.* **1.** A verbal expression or se. **2.** Manner of speech or expression; phraseology. *locutio, -onis* a speaking < *loqui* to speak]

(lōd) *n. Mining* **1.** A deposit of metallic ore filling a re or series of fissures in native rock. **2.** Any deposit of ocated between definite boundaries of associated rock. called *vein.* [OE *lād* way, journey]

star (lōd′stär′) *n.* **1.** A star used as a guide in naviga- or travel; esp., the polestar. **2.** A guiding principle, Also spelled *loadstar.* [ME *lode* course + STAR]

stone (lōd′stōn′) *n.* **1.** A variety of magnetite exhib- magnetism. **2.** Something that attracts by or as by netism. [ME *lode* course + STONE]

e (log) *n.* **1.** A local branch of a secret or fraternal so- ; also, the meeting place of such a society. **2.** A small cabin, etc., esp. one used as a base for outdoor activity. small house on the grounds of an estate, etc., usu. serv- s quarters for an employee. **4.** A North American In- tepee or wigwam, etc.; also, a group living in such a lling. **5.** The characteristic den of certain animals, as vers. **— *v.* lodged, lodg·ing *v.t.*** **1.** To furnish with porary quarters; house. **2.** To rent a room or rooms to. o serve as a shelter or dwelling for. **4.** To place or im- t firmly, as by thrusting or inserting. **5.** To deposit for keeping or storage. **6.** To submit or enter (a complaint, formally. **7.** To confer or invest (power, etc.): usu. *in* or *with.* **— *v.i.*** **8.** To take temporary quarters. **9.** ive in a rented room or rooms. **10.** To become fixed mbedded. [< OF < Med.L < OHG *loub* foliage]

·er (loj′ər) *n.* **1.** One who lives in a rented room or ns in another's residence. **2.** Something fixed in place.

·ing (loj′ing) *n.* **1.** A temporary dwelling place. **2.** *pl.* ng quarters consisting of a rented room or rooms in an- r's house. **3.** Accommodation for living and sleeping.

·ment (loj′mənt) *n.* The act of lodging, or the state eing lodged. Also **lodge′ment.**

s (lō′is, lœs) *n. Geol.* A pale, yellowish silt or clay ning finely powdered, usu. wind-borne deposits. [< G < *n* to pour, dissolve] **— loes′si·al** *adj.*

(lôft, loft) *n.* **1.** A floored space directly under a roof; c. **2.** *U.S.* A large, open workroom or storeroom on an er story of a commercial building. **3.** A hayloft. **4.** An er section or gallery, as in a church: the choir *loft.* **5.** In **a** The slope of the club face away from the vertical line he shaft, intended to make a struck ball rise sharply in air. **b** A stroke that causes the ball to rise sharply when ck. **c** The upward travel of a struck ball. **— *v.t.*** **1.** In ts, to strike (a ball) so that it travels in a high arc. o keep or store in a loft. **— *v.i.*** **3.** In golf, to strike a so that it rises in a high arc. [Late OE < ON, air, sky]

y (lôf′tē, lof′-) *adj.* **loft·i·er, loft·i·est** **1.** Having great mposing height. **2.** Elevated in character, quality, style, ; noble. **3.** Exalted in rank or position; eminent. **4.** ogant; haughty. **— loft′i·ly** *adv.* **— loft′i·ness** *n.*

(log, lôg) *n.* **1.** A full length or cut section of a felled trunk, limb, etc., stripped of branches. **2.** Something omeone inert, stupefied, etc. **3.** *Naut.* **a** A record of the y progress of a vessel and of the events of a voyage. **b** y of various devices for measuring the speed and mileage a vessel. **4.** A record of operation or progress, as of an raft in flight. **— *v.* logged, log·ging *v.t.*** **1.** To cut down trees of (a forest, etc.) for timber. **2.** To convert (tim- into logs. **3.** *Naut. & Aeron.* **a** To enter in a logbook. o travel (a specified distance, etc.). **c** To travel at (a cified speed). **— *v.i.*** **4.** To engage in the operation of ting and transporting timber. [ME *logge*]

(log, lôg) A logarithm.

Var. of LOGO-.

(log) Var. of -LOGUE.

an·ber·ry (lō′gən·ber′ē) *n. pl.* **·ries** **1.** A hybrid plant, ained by crossing the red raspberry with the blackberry. The edible fruit of this plant. [after J. H. *Logan,* 1841– 8, U.S. horticulturist]

a·rithm (log′ə·rith′əm, lôg′-) *n. Math.* The power to ich a fixed number, called the base, must be raised in er to produce a given number, the antilogarithm. [< < Gk. *logos* word, ratio + *arithmos* number] **— log′a· ′mic** or **·mi·cal** *adj.* **— log′a·rith′mi·cal·ly** *adv.*

book (log′bo͝ok′, lôg′-) *n.* The book in which the offi- l record of a ship, aircraft, etc., is entered. Also **log book.**

chip *Naut.* A quadrant-shaped board weighted on the ved edge and suspended in the water from a moving ssel in order to measure its speed.

e (lōzh) *n.* A box in a theater. [< F < OF]

·ger (log′ər, lôg′-) *n.* **1.** A person engaged in logging; nberjack. **2.** A machine for hauling and loading logs.

log·ger·head (log′ər·hed, lôg′-) *n.* A large marine turtle of tropical Atlantic waters. Also **loggerhead turtle.** **— at loggerheads** Engaged in a quarrel; unable to agree. [< dial. E *logger* log tied to a horse's leg + HEAD]

log·gi·a (loj′ē·ə, lô′jə; *Ital.* lôd′jä) *n.* A roofed gallery or portico that is open and supported by columns on one or more sides. [< Ital. < OF *loge*]

LOGGIA

log·ging (log′ing, log′-) *n.* The occupation of felling timber and transporting logs to a mill or market.

log·ic (loj′ik) *n.* **1.** The science concerned with the principles of valid reasoning and correct inference, either deductive or inductive. **2.** Method of reasoning, inference, etc.; esp., correct or sound reasoning. **3.** Effective force, influence, etc. **4.** The apparently inevitable chain of events involved in an outcome, etc. **5.** A system of or treatise on logic. [< F < L < Gk. < *logos* word, speech, thought]

log·i·cal (loj′i·kəl) *adj.* **1.** Relating to or of the nature of logic. **2.** Conforming to the laws of logic. **3.** Capable of or characterized by clear reasoning. **— log′i·cal′i·ty** (-kal′ə·tē), **log′i·cal·ness** *n.* **— log′i·cal·ly** *adv.*

-logical *combining form* Of or related to a (specified) science or study: *biological, geological.* Also **-logic.**

lo·gi·cian (lō·jish′ən) *n.* One versed in logic.

lo·gis·tics (lō·jis′tiks) *n.pl.* (*construed as sing.*) The branch of military science dealing with supplying, equipping, and moving troops. [< F *loger* to quarter] **— lo·gis′tic** *adj.*

logo- *combining form* Word; speech. Also, before vowels, *log-.* [< Gk. *logos* word, speech]

Log·os (log′os, lôg′-, lō′gōs) *n. Theol.* In the Christian religion, God, the second person of the Trinity, incarnate as Jesus Christ. *John* i 1–14.

log·roll (log′rōl′, lôg′-) *U.S. v.t.* To obtain passage of (a bill) by logrolling. **— *v.i.*** To engage in logrolling. Also **log′-roll′.** [Back formation < LOGROLLING]

log·roll·ing (log′rō′ling, lôg′-) *n. U.S.* **1.** The trading of votes and influence between politicians; also, any such trading of help or approval for one's own benefit. **2.** Birling. Also **log′-roll′ing.** **— log′roll′er** *n.*

-logue *combining form* Discourse; recitation: *monologue, prologue.* Also *-log.* [< OF < L < Gk. *logos* word, speech]

log·wood (log′wo͝od′, lôg′-) *n.* **1.** The reddish wood of a Central American tree, used as a dyestuff. **2.** The tree itself.

lo·gy (lō′gē) *adj.* **·gi·er, ·gi·est** *U.S. Informal* Dull; heavy; lethargic. [Prob. < Du. *log* dull, heavy]

-logy *combining form* **1.** The science or study of. **2.** Speech; discourse. [< Gk. *logos* word, study]

Lo·hen·grin (lō′ən·grin) In medieval German legend, a knight of the Holy Grail and son of Parsifal.

loin (loin) *n. Usu. pl.* **1.** The part of the back and flanks between the lower ribs and the hipbone. ◆ Collateral adjective: *lumbar.* **2.** *pl. Chiefly Poetic* The lower back, thighs, and groin regarded as a zone to be clothed. **3.** The forepart of the hindquarters of beef, lamb, veal, etc., with the flank removed. **— to gird (up) one's loins** To prepare for action. [< OF *loigne, logne* < L *lumbus*]

loin·cloth (loin′klôth′, -kloth′) *n.* A garment consisting of a piece or strip of cloth worn about the loins and hips.

loi·ter (loi′tər) *v.i.* **1.** To linger idly or aimlessly; loaf. **2.** To dawdle. **— *v.t.*** **3.** To pass (time) idly: with *away.* [ME *lotere*] **— loi′ter·er** *n.*

Lo·ki (lō′kē) In Norse mythology, a god who created disorder and mischief. [< ON]

loll (lol) *v.i.* **1.** To lie or lean in a relaxed or languid manner; lounge. **2.** To hang loosely; droop. **— *v.t.*** **3.** To permit to droop or hang, as the tongue. **— *n.*** The act of lolling. [Cf. ME *lull,* MDu. *lollen* to sleep] **— loll′er** *n.*

lol·la·pa·loo·za (lol′ə·pə·lo͞o′zə) *n. U.S. Slang* Something extraordinary. Also **lol′la·pa·loo′sa.** [Origin unknown]

Lol·lard (lol′ərd) *n.* A follower of John Wycliffe, 14th-century English religious reformer. Also **Lol′ler.** [< MDu. *lollaerd* mumbler (of prayers)]

lol·li·pop (lol′ē·pop′) *n.* A lump or piece of candy on the end of a stick: also called *sucker.* Also **lol′ly·pop′.** [Prob. < dial. E *lolly* tongue + POP[1]]

Lom·bard (lom′bərd, -bärd, lum′-) *n.* **1.** One of a Germanic tribe that established a kingdom in northern Italy in the sixth century. **2.** A native or inhabitant of Lombardy. **— Lom·bar′dic** *adj.*

London broil Broiled flank steak sliced thin.

lone (lōn) *adj.* **1.** Being without companions; solitary. **2.** Isolated. **3.** Unfrequented; deserted. [< ALONE]

lone·ly (lōn′lē) *adj.* **·li·er, ·li·est** **1.** Unfrequented by human beings; deserted; desolate. **2.** Sad from lack of companionship or sympathy; lonesome. **3.** Characterized by or inducing loneliness. **— lone′li·ly** *adv.* **— lone′li·ness** *n.*

lone·some (lōn′səm) *adj.* **1.** Depressed or uneasy because of being alone; lonely; forlorn. **2.** Inducing a feeling of loneliness. **3.** Unfrequented; secluded: a *lonesome* retreat. **— lone′some·ly** *adv.* **— lone·some·ness** *n.*

Lone Star State Nickname of Texas.

lone wolf *U.S. Informal* One who prefers to work, live, etc., by himself: also **lon·er** (lō′nər).

long[1] (lông, long) *adj.* **1.** Characterized by extent or measurement relatively great in proportion to breadth or width; not short. **2.** Having relatively great duration in time; prolonged. **3.** Having relatively great extension from beginning to end: a *long* tunnel. **4.** Being of a specified measurement in extent or duration: ten miles *long*; three hours *long*. **5.** Having more than the standard or usual quantity, extent, or duration: a *long* ton, a *long* play. **6.** Consisting of many items or entries, as a list. **7.** Slow; tedious. **8.** Extending far into time or space; having considerable range. **9.** Well supplied: *long* on excuses. **10.** In gambling: **a** Denoting odds indicating little likelihood of winning. **b** Denoting a bet, chance, guess, etc., characterized by such odds. **11.** In finance, holding considerable amounts of a stock, commodity, etc., in anticipation of a rise in its price. **12.** *Phonet.* Denoting the vowel sounds of *Dane, dean, dine, dome, dune* as contrasted with those of *Dan, den, din, don, duck*. **13.** In prosody, stressed, as in English verse. **— in the long run** As the ultimate result of inevitable consequences; eventually. **—** *adv.* **1.** For or during an extensive period of time: Will he stay *long*? **2.** For a time or period (to be specified): How *long* will he stay? **3.** For the whole extent or duration (of a specified period): It rained all day *long*. **4.** At a considerably distant time: *long* after midnight. **— as** (or **so**) **long as 1.** For or during the time that. **2.** Inasmuch as; since. **—** *n.* **1.** Something relatively long. **2.** A long syllable or sound, as in phonetics, prosody, etc. **— before long** Soon. **— the long and the short** The entire sum and substance; the whole. [OE *long, lang*]

long[2] (lông, long) *v.i.* To have a strong or eager desire; wish earnestly; yearn. [OE *langian* to grow long]

long·boat (lông′bōt′, long′-) *n. Naut.* The largest boat carried by a sailing vessel.

long·bow (lông′bō′, long′-) *n.* A large bow drawn by hand and projecting long, feathered arrows.

long·cloth (lông′klôth′, long′kloth′) *n.* A fine, soft, cotton cloth used for making children's garments.

long-dis·tance (lông′dis′təns, long′-) *adj.* Connecting or covering relatively long distances or places. **—** *adv.* **1.** By long-distance telephone. **2.** At a distance.

long distance The telephone exchange, operator, or service that handles calls outside the immediate locality.

long division Arithmetical division, usu. with large numbers in which all the steps of the process are shown.

long-drawn (lông′drôn′, long′-) *adj.* Prolonged; protracted. Also **long′-drawn′-out′** (-out′).

lon·gev·i·ty (lon·jev′ə·tē) *n.* **1.** Great age or length of life. **2.** The tendency to live long. [< L < *longus* long + *aevum* age] **— lon·ge·vous** (lon·jē′vəs) *adj.*

long·hair (lông′hâr′, long′-) *U.S. Slang adj.* **1.** Of or pertaining to intellectuals or their tastes. **2.** Of or pertaining to serious rather than popular music. **—** *n.* **1.** A longhair person; intellectual. **2.** Longhair music. Also **long′-hair′**.

long·hand (lông′hand′, long′-) *n.* Ordinary handwriting with the words spelled in full.

long·head·ed (lông′hed′id, long′-) *adj.* **1.** Dolichocephalic. **2.** Characterized by shrewdness, foresight, etc. Also **long′-head′ed.** **— long′head′ed·ly** *adv.* **— long′head′ed·ness** *n.*

long·horn (lông′hôrn′, long′-) *n.* One of a breed of domestic cattle with long horns. Also **Texas longhorn.**

long house Among North American Indians, esp. the Iroquois, a council house or community dwelling.

longi- *combining form* Long. [< L *longus* long]

long·ing (lông′ing, long′-) *n.* A strong, earnest, persistent craving; desire. **—** *adj.* Having or showing such a craving. **— Syn.** See APPETITE. **— long′ing·ly** *adv.*

lon·gi·tude (lon′jə·tōōd, -tyōōd, long′gə-) *n.* **1.** *Geog.* Distance east or west on the earth's surface, usu. measured by the angle that the meridian through a particular place makes with the prime meridian that runs through Greenwich, England. Longitude may be expressed either in hours and minutes (**longitude in time**) or in degrees (**longitude in arc**). **2.** *Astron.* The angular distance eastward from the vernal equinox to the intersection with the ecliptic of the perpendicular from a heavenly body (**celestial longitude**). [< F < L *longus* long]

lon·gi·tu·di·nal (lon′jə·tōō′də·nəl, -tyōō′-, long′gə-) *adj.* **1.** Of or pertaining to longitude or length. **2.** Running lengthwise. **— lon′gi·tu′di·nal·ly** *adv.*

long-lived (lông′līvd′, -livd′, long′-) *adj.* Having a long life or period of existence. **— long′-lived′ness** *n.*

long measure Linear measure.

long-play·ing (lông′plā′ing, long′-) *adj.* LP.

long-range (lông′rānj′, long′-) *adj.* **1.** Designed to shoot or move over distances. **2.** Taking account of, or exter over, a long span of future time: *long-range* plans.

long·shore·man (lông′shôr′mən, -shōr′-, long′-) *n.* ·**men** (-mən) A man employed on the waterfront to loac unload vessels; stevedore. [< *alongshore* + MAN]

long shot *Informal* **1.** In betting, a race horse or gambling choice, backed at great odds and having chance of winning. **2.** Any similar venture, scheme, etc **not by a long shot** *Informal* Decidedly not; not at al

long-sight·ed (lông′sī′tid, long′-) *adj.* **1.** Far-sighted Characterized by or having foresight; sagacious. **— lo sight′ed·ly** *adv.* **— long′-sight′ed·ness** *n.*

long-stand·ing (lông′stan′ding, long′-) *adj.* Having e ed over a long period: a *long-standing* debt.

long-sta·ple (lông′stā′pəl, long′-) *adj.* Having a long said of fabrics, esp. cotton.

long-suf·fer·ing (lông′suf′ər·ing, long′-) *adj.* Patient during injuries, misfortune, etc., for a long time. **— n** tient endurance of injuries, etc.: also **long′-suf′fer·anc**

long-term (lông′tûrm′, long′-) *adj.* Involving or exter over a relatively long period of time: a *long-term* contr

long-time (lông′tīm′, long′-) *adj.* Being such for a cons able period of time: a *long-time* friend.

long-wind·ed (lông′win′did, long′-) *adj.* **1.** Continuin a long time in speaking or writing: a *long-winded* lecturer Capable of vigorous activity without becoming sho breath. **— long′-wind′ed·ly** *adv.* **— long′-wind′ed·ne**

long·wise (lông′wīz′, long′-) *adv.* Lengthwise. Also **l ways′** (-wāz′).

loo (lōō) *n. pl.* **loos** A game of cards in which each p deposits a forfeit in a pool. [< F *lanturelu*]

look (lo͝ok) *v.i.* **1.** To use one's sense of sight. **2.** To the eyes in a specified direction. **3.** To gaze so as to co a specific feeling or meaning. **4.** To use one's eyes in to examine, repair, etc.: Let's *look* at the engine. **5.** To sider: *Look* at his fine record. **6.** To seem: He *looks* reli **7.** To face in a specified direction. **8.** To expect: wit infinitive: I *look* to hear from you soon. **—** *v.t.* **9.** T press or influence by a glance or gaze: to *look* one's a **— it looks like 1.** It promises or suggests the coming of *Informal* It seems as if: *It looks like* I'll have to move. **look after 1.** To take care of. **2.** To watch or follow the eye. **— to look alive** *Informal* To be alert or atten **— to look back** To reflect on the past; recall. **— to down on** (or **upon**) To regard with condescension or tempt. Also **to look down one's nose on** (or **upon**). **look for 1.** To search for. **2.** To anticipate; expect. **look forward to** To anticipate. **— to look in** (or **in on**) make a short visit to. **— to look into 1.** To examine clo **2.** To make inquiries about. **— to look on. 1.** To spectator. **2.** To consider; regard. **— to look oneself** appear to be in a normal, usual, or healthy condition, **— to look out for 1.** To protect: to *look out for* one's interests. **2.** To be watchful; be on guard. **— to look** To examine; scrutinize. **— to look the other way** To ig or avoid an unpleasant or unfavorable situation, sight, **— to look to 1.** To attend to. **2.** To turn to, as for advice, etc. **3.** To anticipate; expect. **— to look up** *U.S.* To search for and find, as in a file, book, etc. **2.** *formal* To discover the whereabouts of. **3.** *Informal* To prove; become better. **— to look up and down 1.** T spect critically or appraisingly. **2.** To search everywh **— to look up to** To have respect for. **—** *n.* **1.** The a looking. **2.** A search, examination, etc., by or as by m of one's eyes. **3.** Aspect or expression: a saintly *look*. *Often pl. Informal* General appearance: I like the *looks* of place. **5.** *pl. Informal* Personal appearance: the *looks* model. **—** *interj.* **1.** See! **2.** Listen! [OE *lōcian*]

look·er (lo͝ok′ər) *n.* **1.** One who looks or watches. **2.** *Slang* A handsome or good-looking person.

look·er-on (lo͝ok′ər·on′, -ôn′) *n. pl.* **look·ers-on** A s tator; onlooker.

look·ing glass (lo͝ok′ing) A glass mirror.

look·out (lo͝ok′out′) *n.* **1.** The act of watching for some or something. **2.** A place where such a watch is kept. The person or persons watching. **4.** *Naut.* A crow's-nest. *Informal* Concern; worry: It's your *lookout*.

look-see (lo͝ok′sē′) *n. Slang* A brief inspection or sur

loom[1] (lōōm) *v.i.* **1.** To appear or come into view indisti ly, as through a mist. **2.** To appear to the mind as larg threatening. [Origin uncertain]

loom[2] (lōōm) *n.* Any of various machines on which threa yarn is woven into fabric. [OE *gelōma* tool]

loon[1] (lōōn) *n.* Any of various diving, fish-eating waterfo having a weird, laughing cry. [Ult. < ON *lomr*]

loon[2] (lōōn) *n.* **1.** A stupid or crazy person. **2.** A worth person; idler. [Cf. Du. *loen* stupid fellow]

loon·y (lōō′nē) *Informal adj.* **loon·i·er, loon·i·est 1.** Luna or demented. **2.** Foolish; erratic; silly. **—** *n* *pl.* ·**ies** A mented or insane person. [< LUNATIC]

loop (lōōp) *n.* **1.** A folding or doubling over of one end o

…e of thread, rope, wire, etc., so as to form an oval opening. …A ring or bent piece of metal, wood, thread, etc., serving …a fastener, staple, or the like. 3. Something having or …gesting the shape of a loop. 4. *Electr.* A complete mag-…c or electrical circuit. 5. *Aeron.* A complete circular …n made by an aircraft flying in a vertical plane. — *v.t.* …To form a loop in or of. 2. To fasten, connect, or encircle …means of a loop. 3. *Aeron.* To fly (an aircraft) in a loop …oops. — *v.i.* 4. To make a loop or loops. 5. To move …ward by forming loops. — **to loop the loop** To make a …ical circular turn in the air, esp. in an aircraft. [ME …e] — **loop′y** *adj.*

…**hole** (loop′hōl′) *n.* 1. A narrow slit in a wall, esp. one …fortification. 2. An opportunity for escaping or evading …ething. — *v.t.* **·holed, ·hol·ing** To furnish with loopholes.

…**e** (lōōs) *adj.* **loos·er, loos·est** 1. Not fastened or con-…d; unattached. 2. Not taut; slack: a *loose* rein. 3. …ed from bonds or restraint. 4. Not firmly fitted or em-…ded. 5. Not closely fitted, as clothing. 6. Not bound …astened together. 7. Not compact, firm, or dense: *loose* … 8. Not packaged: *loose* butter. 9. Not constricted; …n: said of lax bowels or a cough. 10. Not properly con-…lled: a *loose* tongue. 11. Dissolute; unchaste. 12. Lack-…in exactness or precision: a *loose* translation. 13. *In-…nal* Not set aside for a specific use: *loose* funds. — **on the …se** 1. Not confined; at large. 2. *Informal* Behaving in a …, uninhibited, and usu. dissolute manner. — *adv.* 1. In …ose manner; loosely. 2. So as to be or become loose: to …ak *loose*. — **to cut loose** *Informal* To behave in a free, …nhibited manner. — *v.* **loosed, loos·ing** *v.t.* 1. To set …, as from bondage, penalty, etc. 2. To untie or undo. 3. …loosen. 4. To make less strict; relax. 5. To let fly; …ot, as an arrow. — *v.i.* 6. To become loose. 7. To loose …nething. [< ON *lauss*] — **loose′ly** *adv.* — **loose′ness** *n.*

…**se end** Something left undecided or undone, as a task, de-…ion, etc. — **at loose ends** 1. In an unsettled state. 2. …thout a job.

…**se-joint·ed** (lōōs′join′tid) *adj.* 1. Having joints not …htly articulated. 2. Limber or flexible in movement.

…**se-leaf** (lōōs′lēf′) *adj.* Designed for or having pages that …easily inserted or removed: a *loose-leaf* notebook.

…**s·en** (lōō′sən) *v.t.* 1. To untie or undo, as bonds. 2. To …free; release. 3. To make less tight, firm, or compact. …*v.i.* 4. To become loose or looser. — **to loosen up** *In-…mal* 1. To relax. 2. To talk with ease; talk freely. 3. …give more generously, as money. — **loos′en·er** *n.*

…**se·strife** (lōōs′strīf′) *n.* 1. Any of various plants of the …mrose family. 2. Any of several related plants. [< …OSE + STRIFE; direct trans. of L *lysimachia*]

…**t** (lōōt) *n.* 1. Goods taken as booty by a victorious army …m a sacked city, enemy forces, etc. 2. Anything unlaw-…ly taken. 3. *U.S. Slang* Money. — *v.t.* 1. To plunder-…lage. — *v.i.* 2. To engage in plundering. [< Hind. *lūt* …Skt. *lunt*] — **loot′er** *n.*

…[1] (lop) *v.t.* **lopped, lop·ping** 1. To cut or trim the branches, …igs, etc., from. 2. To cut off, as branches, twigs, etc. — *n.* …part lopped off. [Origin unknown]

…[2] (lop) *v.* **lopped, lop·ping** *v.i.* 1. To droop or hang down …osely. 2. To move about in an awkward manner. — *v.t.* …To permit to droop or hang down loosely. — *adj.* Pendu-…us; drooping. [Origin unknown]

…**e** (lōp) *v.t.* & *v.i.* **loped, lop·ing** To run or cause to run …th a steady, swinging stride or gallop. — *n.* A slow, easy …ride or gallop. [< ON *hlaupa* to leap, run]

…**-eared** (lop′ird′) *adj.* Having drooping ears.

…**·py** (lop′ē) *adj.* **·pi·er, ·pi·est** Pendulous; limp.

…**·sid·ed** (lop′sī′did) *adj.* Heavier, larger, or sagging on …e side. — **lop′sid′ed·ly** *adv.* — **lop′sid′ed·ness** *n.*

…**qua·cious** (lō·kwā′shəs) *adj.* Characterized by continu-…s talking. [< L *loqui* to speak] — **lo·qua′cious·ly** *adv.* …**lo·qua′cious·ness** *n.*

…**quac·i·ty** (lō·kwas′ə·tē) *n.* *pl.* **·ties** Talkativeness.

…**ran** (lôr′an, lō′ran) *n.* A system in which the position of …ship or aircraft is determined by comparing the time inter-…als between radio signals from a network of synchronized …round stations. [< LO(NG) RA(NGE) N(AVIGATION)]

…**d** (lôrd) *n.* 1. One possessing great power and authority. … In Great Britain: **a** Any one of the noblemen or peers …**ords temporal**) having the title of marquis, earl, viscount, … baron and having seats in the House of Lords. **b** Any of …e higher churchmen (**lords spiritual**) who are members of …e House of Lords. 3. In feudal law, the owner of a manor. …*v.t.* To invest with the title of lord. — **to lord it (over)** To …ct in a domineering or arrogant manner (toward). [OE …*lāford, hlāfweard*, lit., bread keeper]

…**rd** (lôrd) 1. God: preceded by *the* except in direct address. … Jesus Christ: also *Our Lord*. 3. In Great Britain, a title …f honor or nobility.

lord·ly (lôrd′lē) *adj.* **·li·er, ·li·est** 1. Befitting the rank and position of a lord. 2. Noble; dignified. 3. Arrogant; haughty. — *adv.* In a lordly manner. — **lord′li·ness** *n.*

lor·do·sis (lôr·dō′sis) *n.* *Pathol.* Inward curvature of the spine resulting in a hollow back. [< NL < Gk. *lordos* bent backward] — **lor·dot′ic** (-dot′ik) *adj.*

Lord's Day Sunday; the Sabbath.

lord·ship (lôrd′ship) *n.* 1. The dominion, power, or authority of a lord. 2. Sovereignty in general; supremacy. 3. *Often cap.* In Great Britain, the title by which noblemen (excluding dukes), bishops, and judges are addressed or spoken of: preceded by *Your* or *His*. [OE *hlafordscipe*. See LORD.]

Lord's Prayer The prayer beginning *Our Father*, taught by Christ to his disciples. *Matt.* vi 9–13.

Lord's Supper, the 1. The Last Supper. 2. The Eucharist; Holy Communion.

lore (lôr, lōr) *n.* 1. The body of traditional, popular, often anecdotal knowledge about a particular subject: the *lore* of the woods. 2. Learning or erudition. [OE *lār*]

Lo·re·lei (lôr′ə·lī, *Ger.* lō′rə·lī) In German romantic literature, a siren on a rock in the Rhine who lured boatmen to shipwreck by her singing. [< G]

lor·gnette (lôr·nyet′) *n.* 1. A pair of eyeglasses with an ornamental handle. 2. An opera glass with a long handle. [< F < *lorgner* to spy, peer]

lo·ris (lôr′is, lō′ris) *n.* *pl.* **·ris** or **·ris·es** A small, arboreal and nocturnal Asian lemur. [< F < Du. *loeres* booby]

lorn (lôrn) *adj.* *Archaic & Poetic* Abandoned; lonely; wretched; forlorn. [OE *loren*, pp. of *lēosan* to lose]

lor·ry (lôr′ē, lor′ē) *n.* *pl.* **·ries** 1. A low, four-wheeled wagon without sides. 2. A motor truck. [Prob. dial. E *lurry* to pull]

lo·ry (lō′rē, lôr′ē) *n.* *pl.* **·ries** Any of a number of small parrots of Australia and the neighboring islands. [< Malay *lūrī*]

lose (lōōz) *v.* **lost, los·ing** *v.t.* 1. To be unable to find; mislay. 2. To fail to keep, control, or maintain: to *lose* one's footing. 3. To be deprived of; suffer the loss of: to *lose* a leg. 4. To fail to win. 5. To fail to take advantage of; miss. 6. To fail to see or hear. 7. To fail to keep in sight, memory, etc. 8. To occupy or absorb wholly; engross: usually in the passive. 9. To cease to have: to *lose* one's courage. 10. To squander; waste. 11. To cause (someone or something) to be or become lost. 12. To disappear: used reflexively: The river *loses* itself in the swamp. 13. To outdistance or elude. 14. To cause the loss of: His rashness *lost* him the election. 15. To bring to destruction or death; ruin: usu. in the passive. — *v.i.* 16. To suffer loss. 17. To be defeated, as in battle or a contest. — **to lose oneself** 1. To lose one's way. 2. To disappear or hide. 3. To become engrossed or absorbed. — **to lose out** *Informal* To fail or be defeated. — **to lose out on** *Informal* To fail to secure; miss. [From OE *losian* to be lost and *lēosan* to lose] — **los′er** *n.*

los·ing (lōō′zing) *n.* 1. The act of one who or that which loses. 2. *pl.* Money lost, esp. in gambling. — *adj.* 1. Incurring loss: a *losing* business. 2. Not winning.

loss (lôs, los) *n.* 1. The act of losing or the state of being lost. 2. One who or that which is lost. 3. The harm, inconvenience, deprivation, etc., caused by losing something or someone. 4. *pl.* *Mil.* **a** Casualties. **b** The number of casualties. 5. In insurance: **a** Death, injury, property damage, etc., sustained by an insured. **b** The sum payable by the insurer on that account. — **at a loss** Perplexed. [ME]

loss leader An article that a retail store sells below or near cost to promote sales of other merchandise.

lost (lôst, lost) *adj.* 1. Not to be found or recovered. 2. No longer possessed, seen, or known: *lost* friends. 3. Not won, gained, or secured. 4. Having gone astray. 5. Bewildered; perplexed. 6. Helpless. 7. Not used or taken advantage of; wasted. 8. Destroyed; ruined. 9. No longer known or practiced: a *lost* art. — **to be lost in** To be absorbed or engrossed in. — **to be lost to** 1. To no longer belong to. 2. To be impervious or insensible to. 3. To be no longer available to. — **to be lost upon** (or **on**) To have no effect upon.

lot (lot) *n.* 1. That which is used in determining something by chance, as objects drawn at random from a container. 2. The process of deciding something by this method. 3. The decisions arrived at by such means. 4. The share or portion that comes to one as a result of drawing lots. 5. One's portion in life as ascribed to chance, fate, custom, etc. 6. A number of things or persons considered as a single group. 7. A job lot. 8. A plot or quantity of land: a parking *lot*. 9. *Informal* A (specified) type of person: He's a bad *lot*. 10. In motion pictures, a studio and the adjacent area. 11. *Often pl.* *Informal* A great deal: a *lot* of money; *lots* of trouble. — **Syn.** See DESTINY. — **a lot** (or **lots**) *Informal* Very much: He is *a lot* better; *lots* better. — **the lot** The whole of a certain number or quantity: He bought *the lot*. — **to cast** (or

draw) lots To come to a decision or solution by the use of lots. **—to cast** (or **throw**) **in one's lot with** To join with and share the fortunes of. **—***v.* **lot·ted, lot·ting** *v.t.* **1.** To apportion by lots; allot. **2.** To draw lots for. **3.** To divide, as land, into lots. **—***v.i.* **4.** To cast lots. [OE *hlot*]

Lot (lot) In the Old Testament, a nephew of Abraham, whose wife was turned into a pillar of salt when she looked back upon the destruction of Sodom. *Gen.* xi 27, xix.

loth (lōth) See LOATH.

lo·tion (lō′shən) *n.* A liquid preparation used for external cleansing of the skin, eyes, etc. [< L < *lavare* to wash]

lot·ter·y (lot′ər·ē) *n. pl.* **·ter·ies** A method of distributing prizes in which numbered tickets are sold, the winning tickets being selected by lot. [< Ital. *lotto* lottery, lot]

lot·to (lot′ō) *n.* A game of chance played by drawing numbers from a container and covering with counters the corresponding numbers on cards, the winner being the first to cover a row of numbers. [< Ital.]

lo·tus (lō′təs) *n.* **1.** Any of various tropical water lilies noted for their large floating leaves and showy flowers; esp., the **white lotus** and the **blue lotus** of Egypt and the **sacred lotus** of India. **2.** A representation of any of these plants in art, architecture, sculpture, etc. **3.** Any of a genus of herbs of the bean family. Also **lo′tos.** [< L < Gk. *lōtos*]

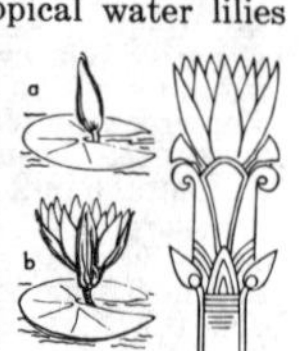

LOTUS
a Bud and leaf. *b* Flower and leaf. *c* Stylized lotus in Egyptian architecture.

lo·tus-eat·er (lō′təs·ē′tər) *n.* **1.** In the *Odyssey*, one of a people who lived a life of indolence induced by eating the fruit of the lotus tree. **2.** Anyone considered to be living an indolent, irresponsible existence.

lotus tree Any of a genus of Old World trees of the buckthorn family.

loud (loud) *adj.* **1.** Having great volume or intensity of sound: *loud* thunder. **2.** Making or uttering a great noise or sound: a *loud* trumpet. **3.** Emphatic or urgent; insistent: *loud* demands. **4.** *Informal* Crude; vulgar, as manners, persons, etc. **5.** *Informal* Excessively showy: a *loud* shirt. **—***adv.* In a loud manner. [OE *hlūd*] **—loud′ly** *adv.* **—loud′ness** *n.*

loud·mouthed (loud′mouthd′, -moutht′) *adj.* Having a loud voice; offensively clamorous or talkative.

loud-speaker (loud′·spē′kər) *n.* Any of various devices for converting an electric current into sound, as in a public-address system, radio, etc.: also called *speaker.*

lou·is d'or (lōō′ē dôr) *pl.* **lou·is d'or 1.** A former French gold coin worth twenty francs. **2.** An old French coin, fluctuating in value, first minted in 1640. Also **lou′is.**

lounge (lounj) *v.* **lounged, loung·ing** *v.i.* **1.** To recline, walk, etc., in a relaxed, lazy manner. **2.** To pass time in doing nothing. **—***v.t.* **3.** To spend or pass in idleness, as time. **—***n.* **1.** A couch or sofa, esp. one with little or no back and a headrest at one end. **2.** A room in a hotel, club, train, etc., suitable for lounging and often having facilities for drinking. **3.** A lounging pace or gait. **4.** The act of lounging; also, a period of lounging. [Origin unknown] **—loung′er** *n.*

loupe (lōōp) *n.* A small magnifying glass, esp. one adapted as an eyepiece for jewelers or watchmakers. [< F]

louse (lous) *n. pl.* **lice** (līs) **1.** A small, flat-bodied, wingless insect living as an external parasite on man and some animals. **2.** Any of various other parasitic insects. **3.** *Slang* A contemptible person. **—***v.t. & v.i.* **loused, lous·ing** *Slang* To ruin; bungle: with *up.* [OE *lūs*]

lous·y (lou′zē) *adj.* **lous·i·er, lous·i·est 1.** Infested with lice. **2.** *Slang* Contemptible; mean. **3.** *Slang* Worthless; inferior. **4.** *Slang* Having plenty (of): with *with*: *lousy* with money.

lout (lout) *n.* An awkward fellow; clown; boor. [? < ON *lutr* bent, stooped] **—lout′ish** *adj.*

lou·ver (lōō′vər) *n.* **1.** A window or opening, as in a gable, provided with louver boards; also, a louver board. **2.** One of several narrow openings serving as an outlet for heated air. [OF *lover*]

LOUVER
a Construction. *b* Set in gable.

louver board One of a series of horizontal, overlapping slats in a window or opening, sloped downward to shed rain while admitting light and air. Also **louver boarding.**

Lou·vre (lōō′vr′) A royal palace in Paris, begun in 1554 and made into an art museum in the late 18th century.

lov·a·ble (luv′ə·bəl) *adj.* Worthy of love; amiable; also, evoking love. Also **love′a·ble. —lov′a·bil′i·ty, lov′a·ble·ness** *n.* **—lov′a·bly** *adv.*

love (luv) *n.* **1.** A deep devotion or affection for another person or persons: *love* for one's children. **2.** A strong sexual passion for another person. **3.** Sexual passion in general or the gratification of it. **4.** One who is beloved. **5.** A very great interest in, or enjoyment of, something; also, the thing so enjoyed. **6.** In tennis, a score of nothing. **—in love**

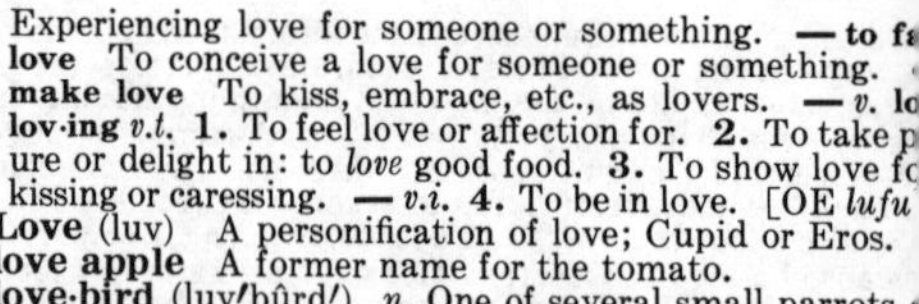

Experiencing love for someone or something. **—to f**
love To conceive a love for someone or something.
make love To kiss, embrace, etc., as lovers. **—***v.* **lo**
lov·ing *v.t.* **1.** To feel love or affection for. **2.** To take p
ure or delight in: to *love* good food. **3.** To show love f
kissing or caressing. **—***v.i.* **4.** To be in love. [OE *lufu*

Love (luv) A personification of love; Cupid or Eros.

love apple A former name for the tomato.

love·bird (luv′bûrd′) *n.* One of several small parrots
kept as cage birds: so called from the affection they sh

love knot A knot tied in pledge of love and constancy;
a representation of it, as in jewelry.

love·less (luv′lis) *adj.* **1.** Having no love. **2.** Recei
no love. **—love′less·ly** *adv.* **—love′less·ness** *n.*

love-lies-bleed·ing (luv′līz′blē′ding) *n.* A species of
ranth having crimson flowers.

love·lorn (luv′lôrn) *adj.* Pining for one's lover.

love·ly (luv′lē) *adj.* **·li·er, ·li·est 1.** Possessing qualities
inspire admiration or love. **2.** Beautiful: a *lovely* rose.
Informal Delightful; pleasing. **—love′li·ness** *n.*

love potion A magic draft or drink designed to arouse
toward a certain person in the one who drinks.

lov·er (luv′ər) *n.* **1.** One who loves: a *lover* of humanity
One in love with or making love to a person of the opp
sex: in the singular now used only of the man. **3.** One
especially enjoys diversion, pursuit, etc.: a *lover* of golf.
lov′er·ly *adj. & adv.*

love seat A double chair or small sofa for two person

love·sick (luv′sik′) *adj.* **1.** Languishing with love. **2**
dicating such a state: a *lovesick* serenade. **—love′sick′ne**

lov·ing (luv′ing) *adj.* **1.** Affectionate; devoted; kind.
Indicative of love. **—lov′ing·ly** *adv.* **—lov′ing·ness**

loving cup A wine cup, usu. with two or more handles,
merly passed around a circle of friends at a banquet.

lov·ing-kind·ness (luv′ing·kīnd′nis) *n.* Kindness
comes from or indicates personal affection or regard.

low[1] (lō) *adj.* **1.** Having relatively little upward extens
not high or tall. **2.** Located or placed below the norma
usual level: a *low* marsh. **3.** Near the horizon: a *low* m
4. Pertaining to latitudes nearest the equator. **5.** Relat
ly small in depth, height, amount, degree, etc. **6.** Of or
ducing sounds of relatively long wavelengths: a *low* pi
7. Not loud; faint: a *low* rustle. **8.** Extending far do
ward; deep: a *low* bow. **9.** Exposing part of the wea
shoulders, back, or chest: a *low* blouse. **10.** Melanchol
sad; depressed: *low* spirits. **11.** Lacking vigor; feeble.
Not adequately provided with; short of: to be *low* on gro
ies. **13.** *Informal* Having little or no ready cash. **14.** I
pensive: a *low* price. **15.** Poor, unfavorable, or disparag
to have a *low* estimate of one's abilities. **16.** Humble o
ferior, as in origin, rank, position, etc. **17.** Inferior in q
ity: a *low* grade of tobacco. **18.** Lacking in refinement;
gar: *low* companions. **19.** Morally base or mean. **20.**
atively recent, as a date. **21.** Relatively simple in struct
function, or organization: a *low* form of animal life. **22.**
the Anglican Church, of or pertaining to the Low Chu
23. *Mech.* Denoting a gear arrangement, as in trans
sions, yielding a slow or the slowest output speed. **24.** *P*
net. Of vowel sounds, produced with the tongue depre
and flat, as (ä) in *large*: opposed to *high.* **—***adv.* **1.** In o
a low level, position, degree, etc. **2.** In a low manner.
Softly; quietly. **4.** With a low pitch. **5.** At a low pr
cheaply. **6.** In or to a humble, poor, or degraded condit
—*n.* **1.** A low level, position, degree, etc. **2.** *Meteorol.*
area of low barometric pressure. **3.** *Mech.* An arrangem
of gears that yields a slow or the slowest output spe
[Early ME *lah* < ON *lagr*] **—low′ness** *n.*

low[2] (lō) *v.i.* **1.** To make the hollow, bellowing sound of c
tle; moo. **—***v.t.* **2.** To utter by lowing. **—***n.* The vo
sound made by cattle: also **low′ing.** [OE *hlōwan*]

low·born (lō′bôrn′) *adj.* Of humble birth.

low·boy (lō′boi) *n.* A short-legged chest of drawers of ab
table height, similar to the lower part of a highboy.

low·bred (lō′bred′) *adj.* **1.** Of humble or inferior origin
birth. **2.** Vulgar; coarse.

low·brow (lō′brou′) *n.* *Informal* A person of uncultiva
or vulgar tastes. **—***adj.* Of or suitable for such a pers
also **low′browed′. —low′brow′ism** *n.*

Low-Church (lō′chûrch′) *adj.* Of or belonging to a gro
(**Low Church**) in the Anglican Church that stresses ev
gelical doctrine and is, in general, opposed to extreme ritu
ism. **—Low′-Church′man** (-mən) *n.*

low comedy Comedy that is characterized by slapstick a
lively physical action rather than by witty dialogue.

low·down[1] (lō′doun′) *n.* *Slang* The truth.

low-down[2] (lō′doun′) *adj.* *Informal* **1.** Unethical or me
2. In jazz, slow, sad, or sensuous, as the blues.

low·er (lou′ər) *v.i.* **1.** To look sullen; scowl. **2.** To app
dark and threatening, as the weather. **—***n.* **1.** A sull
look; a scowl. **2.** A dark, threatening look, as of the wea
er. [Cf. G *lauern* to lurk]

er[2] (lō′ər) Comparative of LOW. — *adj.* **1.** Inferior in k, value, etc. **2.** Situated below something else. **3.** *n cap. Geol.* Older; designating strata normally beneath newer (and upper) rock formations. — *n.* That which eneath something else; esp., a lower berth. — *v.t.* **1.** To g to a lower position or level; let down, as a window. **2.** reduce in degree, quality, amount, etc.: to *lower* prices. To undermine or weaken. **4.** To bring down in estima-, rank, etc. **5.** To change (a sound) to a lower pitch or me. — *v.i.* **6.** To become less; decrease; sink.
er-case (lō′ər·kās′) *Printing adj.* Of, in, or indicating ll letters, as distinguished from capitals. — *v.t.* **-cased, -ing** To set as or change to lower-case letters.
er case *Printing* **1.** In type cases, the lower tray, con-ing the small letters of the alphabet. See CASE[2]. **2.** The ll letters of the alphabet.
er class The socially or economically inferior group in iety. — **low·er-class** (lō′ər·klas′, -kläs′) *adj.*
er·class·man (lō′ər·klas′mən, -kläs′-) *n. pl.* **·men** ən) A student in either of the first two years of a four-r course; a freshman or sophomore.
er House The larger and more widely representative nch of a bicameral legislative body, as the House of Rep-entatives in the U.S. Also **Lower Chamber.**
er·most (lō′ər·mōst′) *adj.* Lowest.
er Paleolithic See under PALEOLITHIC.
er world **1.** The abode of the dead; hell; Hades; Sheol. o **lower regions.** **2.** The earth.
frequency *Telecom.* Radio waves having a frequency rom 30 to 300 kilocycles.
German See under GERMAN.
·land (lō′lənd, -land′) *n. Usu. pl.* Land lying lower n the adjacent country. — *adj.* Of, pertaining to, or racteristic of a low or level country.
·land (lō′lənd, -land′) *n.* The speech or dialect of the ttish Lowlands. — *adj.* Pertaining or belonging to the ttish Lowlands.
Latin See under LATIN.
·ly (lō′lē) *adj.* **·li·er, ·li·est** **1.** Humble or low in rank, gin, nature, etc. **2.** Full of humility; meek. **3.** Situated lying low. — *adv.* **1.** In a low condition, manner, posi-n, etc. **2.** Modestly; humbly. — **low′li·ness** *n.*
Mass A form of Mass celebrated without music and by e priest usu. assisted by a server or altar boy.
-mind·ed (lō′mīn′did) *adj.* Having low, vulgar, or mean oughts, sentiments, or motives. — **low′-mind′ed·ly** *adv.* **low′-mind′ed·ness** *n.*
-necked (lō′nekt′) *adj.* Having a low neckline.
-pitched (lō′picht′) *adj.* **1.** Low in tone or range of ne. **2.** Having little slope, as a roof. **3.** *Music* Built for a ch lower than standard pitch: said of instruments.
-pres·sure (lō′presh′ər) *adj.* **1.** Having or operating der a low degree of pressure. **2.** *Meteorol.* Designating at-ospheric pressure below that normal at sea level.
relief Bas-relief.
-spir·it·ed (lō′spir′it·id) *adj.* Despondent; melancholy. **low′-spir′it·ed·ly** *adv.* — **low′-spir′it·ed·ness** *n.*
tide **1.** The ebb tide at its lowest stage. **2.** The time is lowest stage occurs. **3.** The lowest point or level reached.
water A very low level of water in a stream, etc.
[1] (loks) *n.* A salty, smoked salmon, often eaten with eam cheese, bagels, etc. [< Yiddish < G *lachs* salmon]
[2] (loks) *n.* Liquid oxygen.
·al (loi′əl) *adj.* **1.** Bearing true allegiance to a constituted thority, as to one's sovereign, government, etc. **2.** Con-ant and faithful in any relation or obligation implying ust, confidence, etc. **3.** Indicating or professing loyalty. OF < L *legalis*] — **loy′al·ism** *n.* — **loy′al·ly** *adv.*
·al·ist (loi′əl·ist) *n.* One who supports and defends his overnment, esp. in times of crisis or war.
y·al·ist (loi′əl·ist) *n.* **1.** In the American Revolution, a lonist who remained loyal to the British crown. **2.** In the panish Civil War, one who supported the government of e Republic against the uprising of Franco.
·al·ty (loi′əl·tē) *n. pl.* **·ties** The state, quality, or fact of eing loyal; fidelity; allegiance.
z·enge (loz′inj) *n.* **1.** A small sweetened tablet or candy, ow usu. medicated. **2.** *Math.* A diamond-shaped figure. < OF < L *lapis, -idis* stone]
P (el′pē′) *adj.* Designating a phonograph record pressed ith microgrooves and played at a speed of 33⅓ revolutions er minute: also *long-playing.* — *n.* An LP record: a trade ark. [< l(ong)-p(laying)]
SD (el′es′dē′) *n.* A drug that produces states similar to hose of schizophrenia, used in medicine and illicitly as a allucinogen. See LYSERGIC ACID. Also **LSD-25.** [< *l(y)s ergic acid) d(iethylamide)*]
·au (lōō·ou′) *n.* A Hawaiian feast with entertainment.

lub·ber (lub′ər) *n.* **1.** An awkward, ungainly fellow. **2.** A landlubber. [Origin uncertain] — **lub′ber·ly** *adj. & adv.*
lu·bri·cant (lōō′brə·kənt) *n.* A substance, as oil, grease, graphite, etc., used to coat moving parts in order to reduce friction and wear. — *adj.* Lubricating.
lu·bri·cate (lōō′brə·kāt) *v.t.* **·cat·ed, ·cat·ing** **1.** To apply a lubricant to. **2.** To make slippery or smooth. [< L < *lubricus* slippery] — **lu′bri·ca′tion** *n.* — **lu′bri·ca′tive** *adj.* — **lu′bri·ca′tor** *n.*
lu·bric·i·ty (lōō·bris′ə·tē) *n. pl.* **·ties** **1.** Lewdness; lasciviousness. **2.** Shiftiness; elusiveness. **3.** Slipperiness. [< F < L < *lubricus* slippery]
lu·cent (lōō′sənt) *adj.* **1.** Showing or giving off radiance. **2.** Transparent or semitransparent. [< L *lucens, -entis,* ppr. of *lucere* to shine] — **lu′cen·cy** *n.* — **lu′cent·ly** *adv.*
lu·cerne (lōō·sûrn′) *Brit.* Alfalfa. [< F]
lu·ces (lōō′sēz) Plural of LUX.
lu·cid (lōō′sid) *adj.* **1.** Easily understood; clear: a *lucid* explanation. **2.** Mentally sound, clear, or rational: a *lucid* interval. **3.** Shining; bright. [< L *lucere* to shine] — **lu·cid·i·ty** (lōō·sid′ə·tē), **lu′cid·ness** *n.* — **lu′cid·ly** *adv.*
Lu·ci·fer (lōō′sə·fər) *n.* **1.** The archangel who led the revolt of the angels and fell from Heaven: identified with *Satan.* **2.** The planet Venus when it appears as the morning star. [< L, light-bearer < *lux, lucis* light + *ferre* to bear]
Lu·cite (lōō′sīt) *n.* A transparent acrylic resin, easily machined into various shapes.
luck (luk) *n.* **1.** That which happens by chance; fortune; lot. **2.** Good fortune; success. **3.** Any object regarded as bringing good fortune. — **to be down on one's luck** To suffer failure, poverty, etc. — **to be in luck** To meet with success or good fortune. — **to be out of luck** To be unlucky. — **to try one's luck** To attempt to do something without any certainty of success. [Prob. < MDu. *luk, geluk*]
luck·less (luk′lis) *adj.* Having bad luck; unlucky. — **luck′less·ly** *adv.* — **luck′less·ness** *n.*
luck·y (luk′ē) *adj.* **luck·i·er, luck·i·est** **1.** Accompanied by or having good fortune. **2.** Bringing or resulting in good fortune. **3.** Believed to bring good fortune. — **luck′i·ly** *adv.* — **luck′i·ness** *n.*
lu·cra·tive (lōō′krə·tiv) *adj.* Producing or yielding gain, profit, or wealth; profitable. [< L < *lucratus,* pp. of *lucrari* to gain] — **lu′cra·tive·ly** *adv.* — **lu′cra·tive·ness** *n.*
lu·cre (lōō′kər) *n.* Money or riches: now chiefly in the humorous phrase: **filthy lucre.** [< F < L *lucrum* gain]
lu·cu·brate (lōō′kyōō·brāt) *v.i.* **·brat·ed, ·brat·ing** **1.** To study or write laboriously, esp. at night. **2.** To write in a learned manner. [< L *lucubrare* to work by candlelight]
lu·cu·bra·tion (lōō′kyōō·brā′shən) *n.* **1.** Earnest and labored study. **2.** The product of such study, esp. a pedantic literary composition. **3.** *pl.* Any literary effort. — **lu′cu·bra′tor** *n.* — **lu′cu·bra·to′ry** (-brə·tôr′ē, -tō′rē) *adj.*
lu·di·crous (lōō′də·krəs) *adj.* Exciting laughter or ridicule; ridiculous; absurd. [< L < *ludere* to play] — **lu′di·crous·ly** *adv.* — **lu′di·crous·ness** *n.*
luff (luf) *Naut. n.* **1.** The sailing of a ship close to the wind. **2.** The rounded and fullest part of a vessel's bow. **3.** The foremost edge of a fore-and-aft sail. — *v.i.* **1.** To bring the head of a vessel nearer the wind. **2.** To bring the head of a vessel into the wind, with the sails shaking. Also *loof.* [ME *lof, loven*]
Luft·waf·fe (lŏŏft′väf′ə) *n. German* The German air force during World War II.
lug[1] (lug) *n.* **1.** An earlike projection for holding or supporting something. **2.** *Mech.* A nut, closed at one end. **3.** *Slang* A fellow, esp. a clumsy one. [Origin uncertain]
lug[2] (lug) *v.* **lugged, lug·ging** *v.t.* **1.** To carry or pull with effort. — *v.i.* **2.** To pull or drag with effort; tug. — *n.* **1.** The act or exertion of lugging; also, that which is lugged. **2.** *Naut.* A lugsail. [Prob. Scand.]
lug[3] (lug) *n.* A lugworm. [Origin uncertain]
lug·gage (lug′ij) *n.* Suitcases, trunks, etc., used for traveling; baggage. [< LUG[2]]
lug·ger (lug′ər) *n. Naut.* A one-, two-, or three-masted vessel having lugsails only. [< LUG(SAIL) + -ER[2]]
lug·sail (lug′səl, -sāl′) *n. Naut.* A four-cornered sail having no boom and bent to a yard that hangs obliquely on the mast: also called *lug.*
lu·gu·bri·ous (lōō·gōō′brē·əs, -gyōō′-) *adj.* Very sad, or mournful, esp. in a ludicrous manner. [< L < *lugere* to mourn] — **lu·gu′bri·ous·ly** *adv.* — **lu·gu′bri·ous·ness** *n.*
lug·worm (lug′wûrm′) *n.* An annelid worm with two rows of tufted gills on the back, living in the sand of seashores.
Luke (lŏŏk) Physician and companion of St. Paul; traditionally thought to be the author of the third Gospel: called **Saint Luke.** — *n.* The third Gospel of the New Testament.
luke·warm (lŏŏk′wôrm′) *adj.* **1.** Moderately warm; tepid. **2.** Lacking in ardor, enthusiasm, or conviction; indifferent:

a *lukewarm* greeting. [Prob. OE *hlēow* warm.] — **luke′warm′ly** *adv.* — **luke′warm′ness** *n.*

lull (lul) *v.t.* **1.** To quiet or put to sleep by soothing sounds or motions. **2.** To calm or allay, esp. by deception: to *lull* someone's suspicions. — *v.i.* **3.** To become calm or quiet. — *n.* **1.** A brief interval of calm or quiet during noise or confusion. **2.** A period of diminished activity, prosperity, etc.: a *lull* in business. [Prob. imit.]

lull·a·by (lul′ə·bī) *n. pl.* **·bies 1.** A song to lull a child to sleep; a cradlesong. **2.** A piece of instrumental music in the manner of a lullaby. — *v.t.* **·bied, ·by·ing** *Rare* To soothe with a lullaby.

lum·ba·go (lum·bā′gō) *n.* Pain in the lumbar region of the back; backache, esp. in the small of the back.

lum·bar (lum′bər, -bär) *adj.* Pertaining to or situated near the loins. — *n.* A lumbar vertebra, nerve, artery, etc. [< NL < L *lumbus* loin]

lum·ber[1] (lum′bər) *n.* **1.** *U.S. & Canadian* Timber sawed into boards, planks, etc., of specified lengths. **2.** *Chiefly Brit.* Household articles no longer used and usu. stored away. — *adj.* Made of, pertaining to, or dealing in lumber. — *v.t.* **1.** *U.S. & Canadian* To cut down (timber); also, to cut down the timber of (an area). **2.** *Chiefly Brit.* To fill or obstruct with useless articles. — *v.i.* **3.** *U.S. & Canadian* To cut down or saw timber for marketing. [Var. of *Lombard* in obs. sense of "money-lender, pawnshop," hence, stored articles] — **lum′ber·er** *n.* — **lum′ber·ing** *n.*

lum·ber[2] (lum′bər) *v.i.* **1.** To move or proceed in a heavy or awkward manner. **2.** To move with a rumbling noise. — *n.* A rumbling noise. [ME *lomerer*] — **lum′ber·ing** *adj.* — **lum′ber·ing·ly** *adv.*

lum·ber·jack (lum′bər·jak) *n. U.S. & Canadian* A person who fells or transports timber; a logger. [< LUMBER[1] + *jack* man, boy]

lum·ber·man (lum′bər·mən) *n. pl.* **·men** (mən) *U.S. & Canadian* **1.** A lumberjack. **2.** One who is engaged in the business of lumbering.

lum·ber·yard (lum′bər·yärd′) *n. U.S. & Canadian* A yard for the storage or sale of lumber.

lu·men (lo͞o′mən) *n. pl.* **·mens** or **·mi·na** (-mə·nə) **1.** *Anat.* The inner passage of a tubular organ, as a blood vessel. **2.** *Physics* A unit for measuring the flow of light, equal to the flow of one international candle. [< L, light]

lu·mi·nar·y (lo͞o′mə·ner′ē) *n. pl.* **·nar·ies 1.** Any body that gives light, esp. the sun or the moon. **2.** One who has achieved great eminence. [< OF < LL < *lumen* light]

lu·mi·nesce (lo͞o′mə·nes′) *v.i.* **·nesced, ·nesc·ing** To be or become luminescent.

lu·mi·nes·cence (lo͞o′mə·nes′əns) *n.* An emission of light, such as fluorescence and phosphorescence, not directly attributable to the heat that produces incandescence. [< L *lumen* light + -ESCENT] — **lu′mi·nes′cent** *adj.*

lumini- *combining form* Light; luminescence. Also **lumin-** (before vowels), **lumino-**. [< L *lumen, luminis* light]

lu·mi·nif·er·ous (lo͞o′mə·nif′ər·əs) *adj.* Producing light.

lu·mi·nous (lo͞o′mə·nəs) *adj.* **1.** Full of light. **2.** Giving off light; shining. **3.** Easily understood; clear. **4.** Brilliantly intelligent. [< L < *lumen* light] — **lu′mi·nous·ly** *adv.* — **lu′mi·nous·ness, lu′mi·nos′i·ty** *n.*

lum·mox (lum′əks) *n. U.S. Informal* A stupid, clumsy person.

lump[1] (lump) *n.* **1.** A shapeless mass, esp. a small mass. **2.** A swelling. **3.** A mass of things thrown together; aggregate. **4.** A heavy, ungainly, and usu. stupid person. — **a lump in one's throat** A feeling of tightness in the throat, as from emotion. — **in a** (or **the**) **lump** All together. — *adj.* Formed in a lump or lumps: *lump* sugar. — *v.t.* **1.** To put together in one mass, group, etc. **2.** To consider or treat as one mass, group, etc. **3.** To make lumps in or on. — *v.i.* **4.** To become lumpy. [< ME]

lump[2] (lump) *v.t. Informal* To put up with; endure: You can like it or *lump* it.

lump·ish (lum′pish) *adj.* **1.** Like a lump. **2.** Stupid; clumsy. — **lump′ish·ly** *adv.* — **lump′ish·ness** *n.*

lump sum A full or single sum of money paid at one time.

lump·y (lum′pē) *adj.* **lump·i·er, lump·i·est 1.** Full of lumps. **2.** Covered with lumps. **3.** Lumpish. **4.** Running in rough waves. — **lump′i·ly** *adv.* — **lump′i·ness** *n.*

Lu·na (lo͞o′nə) In Roman mythology, the goddess of the moon: identified with the Greek *Selene.* [< L]

lu·na·cy (lo͞o′nə·sē) *n. pl.* **·cies 1.** Irresponsible or senseless conduct. **2.** *Law* Insanity.

Luna moth A large North American moth having light green wings with long tails and lunate spots.

lu·nar (lo͞o′nər) *adj.* **1.** Of the moon. **2.** Round or crescent-shaped like the moon. **3.** Measured by the revolutions of the moon: a *lunar* month. [< L < *luna* moon]

lunar month See under MONTH.

lunar year A period of twelve lunar months, one month being added at intervals to make the mean length of the astronomical year, as in the Hebrew calendar.

lu·nate (lo͞o′nāt) *adj.* Crescent-shaped. Also **lu′nat·e**

lu·na·tic (lo͞o′nə·tik) *adj.* **1.** Insane. **2.** Wildly foolis irrational. **3.** Of or for the insane. Also **lu·nat·i·cal** nat′i·kəl). — *n.* An insane person. [< LL < L *luna* m

lunatic fringe Those followers or devotees of a moven idea, etc., who are extreme or fanatical in their enthusi

lunch (lunch) *n.* **1.** A light meal, esp. the noonday mea Food for a lunch. — *v.i.* To eat lunch. — **lunch′er** *n.*

lunch·eon (lun′chən) *n.* A noonday meal, esp. a formal

lunch·eon·ette (lun′chən·et′) *n.* A restaurant where lunches and other meals may be obtained.

lunch·room (lunch′ro͞om′, -ro͝om′) *n.* A restaurant ing light lunches; luncheonette. Also **lunch room.**

lung (lung) *n. Anat.* **1.** Either of two saclike organ respiration in the thorax of man and other airbreathing vertebrates. ◆ Collateral adjective: *pulmonary.* **2.** An analogous organ in certain invertebrates. [OE *lungen*]

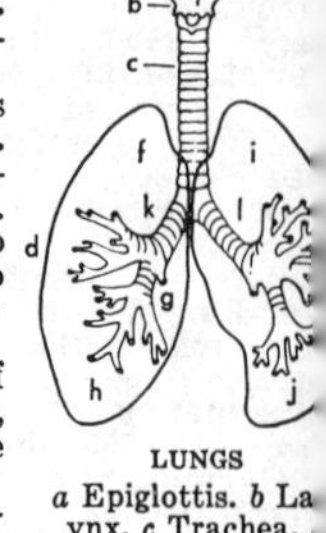

LUNGS
a Epiglottis. *b* Larynx. *c* Trachea. Right lung. *e* Le lung. *f, i* Upper lobes. *g* Middle lobe. *h, j* Lower lobes. *k, l* Bronch

lunge (lunj) *n.* **1.** A sudden pass or thrust, as with a sword, etc. **2.** A quick movement or plunge forward. — *v.* **lunged, lung·ing** — *v.i.* **1.** To make a lunge; thrust. **2.** To move with a lunge. — *v.t.* **3.** To cause to lunge. [< F < L *ad* to + *longus* long]

lung·wort (lung′wûrt′) *n.* Any of various plants of the borage family, esp., a European herb having white blotches on its leaves.

luni- *combining form* Of or pertaining to the moon; lunar. [< L *luna* moon]

lu·pine[1] (lo͞o′pīn) *adj.* **1.** Of, like, or related to a wolf or wolves. **2.** Fierce; ravenous. [< L < *lupus* wolf]

lu·pine[2] (lo͞o′pin) *n.* **1.** Any of various plants of the family, bearing mostly blue, white, or purple flowers, as **white lupine** of Europe, whose seeds are edible. **2.** seeds of the white lupine. [< F < L *lupinus* wolflike]

lu·pus (lo͞o′pəs) *n. Pathol.* Any of various forms of a tu culous disease of the skin, characterized by brownish nod or scaly red patches. [< L, wolf]

lurch[1] (lûrch) *v.i.* **1.** To roll suddenly to one side. **2.** stagger. — *n.* **1.** A sudden swaying. **2.** A reeling.

lurch[2] (lûrch) *n.* **1.** An embarrassing or difficult positi predicament: now only in the phrase **to leave (someone) the lurch.** **2.** In cribbage, the state of a player who made 30 points or less while his opponent has won with [< F *lourche* deceived < Gmc.]

lure (lo͝or, lyo͝or) *n.* **1.** Anything that attracts or entic **2.** In angling, an artificial bait. **3.** In falconry, a dev consisting of a bunch of feathers and a bait, fastened t long cord and used to recall a hawk. — *v.t.* **lured, lur·ing** To attract or entice; allure. **2.** To recall (a hawk) wit lure. [< OF < MHG *luoder* to bait] — **lur′er** *n.*

lu·rid (lo͝or′id, lyo͝or-) *adj.* **1.** Shocking or sensational. Pale and sickly in color. **3.** Lighted up with a yellowish glare or glow esp. in smoke or darkness. [< L *luridus* s low] — **lu′rid·ly** *adv.* — **lu′rid·ness** *n.*

lurk (lûrk) *v.i.* **1.** To lie hidden, as in ambush. **2.** To e unnoticed or unsuspected. **3.** To move secretly or furtive slink. [ME *lurken*] — **lurk′ing·ly** *adv.*

lus·cious (lush′əs) *adj.* **1.** Very pleasurable to the sense taste or smell. **2.** Pleasing to any sense. **3.** Excessiv sweet; cloying. — **lus′cious·ly** *adv.* — **lus′cious·ness** *n.*

lush[1] (lush) *adj.* **1.** Abounding in vigorous growth: a *l countryside.* **2.** Delicious and succulent. **3.** Elaborate effects, etc. [< OF < L *laxus* loose] — **lush′ness** *n.*

lush[2] (lush) *Slang n.* A heavy drinker; drunkard.

lust (lust) *n.* **1.** Sexual appetite. **2.** Excessive sexual ap tite, esp. that seeking immediate or ruthless satisfaction. An overwhelming desire: a *lust* for power. — *v.i.* To ha passionate or inordinate desire, esp. sexual desire: often w *after* or *for.* [OE, pleasure]

lus·ter (lus′tər) *n.* **1.** Sheen; gloss. **2.** Brilliance of ligh radiance. **3.** Splendor, glory, or distinction. **4.** A source center of light, esp. a chandelier. **5.** Any of various su stances used to give a polish to a surface. **6.** In ceramics, glossy, metallic, and often iridescent finish given to the su face of an object. **7.** A fabric of mixed wool and cotton a having a glossy finish. **8.** *Mineral.* The surface appearan of a mineral as determined by the intensity or quality of t light it reflects. — *v.* **lus·tered** or *Brit.* **·tred, lus·ter·ing** *Brit.* **·tring** *v.t.* **1.** To give a luster or gloss to. — *v.i.* **2.** be or become lustrous. Also *Brit.* **lus′tre.** [< F < Ital. < < *lustrum* purification]

lus·ter·ware (lus′tər·wâr′) *n.* Pottery having a lustro and often iridescent sheen.

:·ful (lust′fəl) *adj.* Characterized or driven by lust. — **t′ful·ly** *adv.* — **lust′ful·ness** *n.*
trate (lus′trāt) *v.t.* **·trat·ed, ·trat·ing** To purify by an ering or ceremony. [< L *lustrum* purification] — **lus·′tion** *n.* — **lus·tra·tive** (lus′trə·tiv) *adj.*
trous (lus′trəs) *adj.* **1.** Having a luster; glossy. **2.** illiant; shining. — **lus′trous·ly** *adv.* — **lus′trous·ness** *n.*
trum (lus′trəm) *n.* **1.** A period of five years. **2.** In cient Rome, the solemn ceremony of purification of the tire people made every five years.
t·y (lus′tē) *adj.* **lust·i·er, lust·i·est 1.** Full of vigor; ro- st. **2.** Powerful. — **lust′i·ly** *adv.* — **lust′i·ness** *n.*
a·nist (lo͞o′tə·nist, lyo͞o′-) *n.* One who plays the lute. so **lu′te·nist.**
e[1] (lo͞ot, lyo͞ot) *n.* An old musical trument having strings that are icked by the fingers, a large body aped like half of a pear, and a long, itted neck usu. bent at a sharp an- just below the peg box. [< OF Pg. < Arabic *al′ūd* the piece of od]
e[2] (lo͞ot, lyo͞ot) *n.* A composition finely powdered clay, used as a aling agent for joints of pipes, etc. so **lut′ing.** — *v.t.* **lut·ed, lut·ing** seal with lute. [< OF < L *lutum* ud]

LUTE

te·ous (lo͞o′tē·əs) *adj.* Light or oderate greenish yellow in color. [< *luteus* < *lutum* weed used by dyers]
te·ti·um (lo͞o·tē′shē·əm, -tē′shəm) *n.* A metallic element ymbol Lu) of the lanthanide series, isolated from ytter- um. Also **lu·te′ci·um.** See ELEMENT.
·ther·an (lo͞o′thər·ən) *adj.* Of or pertaining to Martin uther, his doctrines, or to the Lutheran Church. — *n.* A ember of the Lutheran Church. — **Lu′ther·an·ism** *n.*
tist (lo͞o′tist) *n.* One who makes or plays lutes.
x (luks) *n. pl.* **lux·es** or **lu·ces** (lo͞o′sēz) *Physics* The unit illumination in the metric system, equivalent to .0929 ot-candle, or 1 lumen per square meter. [< L, light]
x·u·ri·ance (lug·zho͝or′ē·əns, luk·sho͝or′-) *n.* The state or uality of being luxuriant. Also **lux·u′ri·an·cy.**
x·u·ri·ant (lug·zho͝or′ē·ənt, luk·sho͝or′-) *adj.* **1.** Growing shly and profusely, as vegetation. **2.** Abundant, exuber- it, or ornate, as in design, etc. — **lux·u′ri·ant·ly** *adv.*
x·u·ri·ate (lug·zho͝or′ē·āt, luk·sho͝or′-) *v.i.* **·at·ed, ·at·ing** . To take great pleasure; indulge oneself fully: with *in.* **2.** o live sumptuously. **3.** To grow profusely. [See LUXURY.] — **lux·u′ri·a′tion** *n.*
x·u·ri·ous (lug·zho͝or′ē·əs, luk·sho͝or′-) *adj.* **1.** Character- ed by or conducive to luxury or extreme comfort; opulent; imptuous. **2.** Indulging in or given to luxury. — **lux·′ri·ous·ly** *adv.* — **lux·u′ri·ous·ness** *n.*
x·u·ry (luk′shər·ē, *occasionally* lug′zhər·ē) *n. pl.* **·ries 1.** nything, usu. expensive or rare, that ministers to comfort r pleasure but is not a necessity to life, health, etc. **2.** Free idulgence in that which is expensive, rare, or extremely ratifying. [< OF < L *luxus* extravagance]
y[1] *suffix of adjectives* **1.** Like; characteristic of; pertaining o: *manly, godly.* **2.** Occurring every (specified interval): *eekly, daily.* Compare -LIKE. [OE *-līc*]
y[2] *suffix of adverbs* **1.** In a (specified) manner: used to form dverbs from adjectives, or (rarely) from nouns: *brightly, usily.* **2.** At every (specified interval): *hourly, yearly.* [OE *lice* < *-lic* -ly[1]]
·cée (lē·sā′) *n. French* In France, a secondary school fi- anced by the government. [See LYCEUM.]
·ce·um (lī·sē′əm, lī′-) *n. pl.* **·ce·ums** or **·ce·a** (-sē′ə) **1.** *U.S.*. An organization providing popular instruction by lec- ures, concerts, etc.; also, its building. **2.** A lycée.
y·ce·um (lī·sē′əm, lī′-) A grove near Athens in which Aris- otle taught. [< L < Gk. *lykeios,* epithet of Apollo]
d·dite (lid′īt) *n.* A high explosive, composed chiefly of icric acid, used in shells. [after *Lydd,* a town in England]
yd·i·a (lid′ē·ə) An ancient country in western Asia Minor, amous for its wealth and luxury. — **Lyd′i·an** *adj.* & *n.*
e (lī) *n.* **1.** A solution leached from ashes, or derived from substance containing alkali, used in making soap. **2.** Any olution obtained by leaching. [OE *lēah*]
·ing[1] (lī′ing) *n.* The act of telling lies; untruthfulness. — *dj.* Deceitful or false; untrue: a *lying* tongue.
·ing[2] (lī′ing) Present participle of LIE[1].
·ing-in (lī′ing·in′) *n.* The confinement of women during childbirth. — *adj.* Of or pertaining to childbirth.
mph (limf) *n. Physiol.* A yellowish alkaline fluid derived from the body tissues, consisting of lymphcytes and a plasma similar to that of blood. [< L *limpa* water]

lym·phat·ic (lim·fat′ik) *adj.* **1.** Containing, conveying, or pertaining to lymph. **2.** Caused by or affecting the lymph nodes. **3.** Sluggish; indifferent. — *n.* A vessel that con- veys lymph into the veins.
lymphato- *combining form* Lymphatic. Also, before vowels, **lymphat-.**
lymph node *Anat.* Any of numerous glandlike bodies found in the course of the lymphatic vessels and producing lympho- cytes and monocytes. Also **lymph gland.**
lympho- *combining form* Lymph; of the lymph or the lym- phatics. Also, before vowels, **lymph-.** [See LYMPH]
lym·pho·cyte (lim′fə·sīt) *n. Physiol.* A variety of nucleated, colorless leucocyte formed in the tissue of the lymph nodes and resembling white blood corpuscles. Also **lymph cell.**
lym·phoid (lim′foid) *adj.* Of, pertaining to, or resembling lymph or the tissues of a lymph node.
lynch (linch) *v.t.* To kill (a person accused of a crime) by mob action, as by hanging, without due process of law. [< LYNCH LAW] — **lynch′er** *n.* — **lynch′ing** *n.*
lynch law The practice of administering punishment by lynching. [? after Charles *Lynch,* 1736–96, or William *Lynch,* 1742–1820, Virginia magistrates]
lynx (lingks) *n. pl.* **lynx·es** or **lynx** A wildcat of Europe and North America having a short tail, tufted ears, and relatively long limbs. Also called *bobcat.* [< L < Gk. *lynx*]
lynx-eyed (lingks′īd′) *adj.* Having sharp sight.
ly·on·naise (lī′ə·nāz′, *Fr.* lē·ô·nez′) *adj.* Made with finely sliced onions; esp. designating a method of preparing pota- toes with fried onions. [< F, fem. of *lyonnais* of Lyon]
ly·o·phil·ic (lī′ə·fil′ik) *adj. Chem.* Designating a colloidal system in which the solid particles attract and hold molecules of the dispersion medium. [< LYO- + Gk. *philos* loving]
ly·o·pho·bic (lī′ə·fō′bik) *adj. Chem.* Designating a coloidal system in which the solid particles are easily precipitated out of the dispersion medium. [< LYO- + Gk. *phobos* fear]
Ly·ra (lī′rə) *n.* A constellation, the Harp or the Lyre, con- taining the star Vega. [< L < Gk.]
ly·rate (lī′rāt) *adj.* Shaped like a lyre. Also **ly′rat·ed.** [< NL *lyratus*] — **ly′rate·ly** *adv.*
lyre (līr) *n.* An ancient harplike stringed instrument, used by the Greeks to accompany poetry and song. [< OF < L *lyra* < Gk.]
Lyre (līr) *n.* The constellation Lyra.
lyre·bird (līr′bûrd′) *n.* Either of two species of Australian birds, the male of which spreads its tail feathers into the shape of a lyre.
lyr·ic (lir′ik) *adj.* **1.** Of poetry, expressing the poet's per- sonal or inner feelings; also, pertaining to the method, per- sonality, etc., of a writer of such verse. **2.** Meant to be sung. **3.** *Music* Having a singing voice of a light, flexible quality: a *lyric* soprano. **4.** Pertaining to a lyre. Also **lyr′i·cal.** — *n.* **1.** *Usu. pl.* The words of a song. **2.** A lyric poem. [< L < Gk. *lyra* a lyre] — **lyr′i·cal·ly** *adv.*
lyr·i·cism (lir′ə·siz′əm) *n.* The quality of emotional self- expression in the arts.
lyr·i·cist (lir′ə·sist) *n.* **1.** One who writes the words of a song or the lyrics for a musical play. **2.** A lyric poet.
ly·ri·form (lī′rə·fôrm) *adj.* Shaped like a lyre.
lyse (līs) *v.t.* & *v.i.* **lysed, lys·ing** To undergo or cause to un- dergo lysis. [< Gk. *lysis* loosening]
ly·ser·gic acid (lī·sûr′jik) *n. Biochem.* A crystalline alka- loid derived from ergot and forming the base of **lysergic acid di·eth·yl·am·ide-25** (d′eth·əl·am′īd), or LSD. [< LYS- + *erg*(*ot*) + -IC]
lysi- *combining form* A loosening; dissolving: *lysergic acid, lysine.* Also, before vowels, **lys-.** [< Gk. *lysis* a loosen- ing]
ly·sine (lī′sēn, -sin) *n. Biochem.* An amino acid $C_6H_{14}O_2N_2$, necessary to animal growth, produced by the hydrolysis of various proteins. Also **ly′sin.** [< LYS- + -INE[2]]
ly·sis (lī′sis) *n.* **1.** *Med.* The gradual disappearing of the symptoms of a disease. **2.** *Biochem.* The process of disinte- gration or destruction of cells, bacteria, etc. [< NL < Gk., < *lyein* to loosen]
-lysis *combining form* A loosing, dissolving, etc.: *hydrolysis, paralysis.* [< Gk., *loosening*]
Ly·sol (lī′sôl, -sōl, -sol) *n.* Proprietary name for a liquid dis- infectant containing soap and cresol. Also **ly′sol.**
-lyte *combining form* A substance decomposed by a (speci- fied) process: *electrolyte.* [< Gk. *lytos* loosened, dissolved]
ly·tic (lit′ik) *adj.* Of, relating to, or effecting lysis, esp., of cells. [See -LYTIC.]
-lytic *combining form* Loosing; dissolving: used in adjectives corresponding to nouns in *-lysis*: *hydrolytic, paralytic.* [< Gk. *lytikos* loosing < *lysis* a loosening]
-lyze *suffix of verbs* To perform, cause, or undergo: formed from nouns in *-lysis*: *electrolyze, paralyze.* Also *esp. Brit.* **-lyse.** [< -LYSIS]

M

m, M (em) *n. pl.* **m's** or **ms, M's** or **Ms** or **ems** (emz) **1.** The thirteenth letter of the English alphabet. **2.** The sound represented by the letter *m*, usually a bilabial nasal. — *symbol* **1.** The Roman numeral 1,000. **2.** *Printing* An em.

M-1 (em′wun′) **carbine** *U.S. Mil.* The carbine.

M-1 rifle *U.S. Mil.* A semiautomatic .30 caliber rifle adopted by the U.S. Army in World War II: also *Garand rifle.*

ma (mä, mô) *n. Informal & Dial.* Mama.

ma'am (mam, mäm, *unstressed* məm) *n.* **1.** A term of respectful address used to women; madam. **2.** *Brit.* A term of respectful address used to the queen or to a royal princess.

Mac- *prefix* In Scottish and Irish names, son of: *MacDougal*, son of Dougal: abbr. *Mc*, *M*ᶜ, or *M'*. See also Mc-. Compare FITZ-, O'. [< Scottish Gaelic and Irish, son]

ma·ca·bre (mə·kä′brə, -bər) *adj.* Suggesting death and decay; gruesome; ghastly. Also **ma·ca′ber.** [< F < OF (*danse*) *macabre* (dance) of death]

mac·ad·am (mə·kad′əm) *n.* **1.** A macadamized pavement or road. **2.** Broken stone used in macadamizing a road. [after John L. *McAdam*, 1756–1836, Scottish engineer]

mac·ad·am·ize (mə·kad′ə·mīz) *v.t.* **·ized, ·iz·ing** To pave by spreading and compacting small stones, often with tar or asphalt. — **mac·ad′am·i·za′tion** *n.* — **mac·ad′am·iz′er** *n.*

mac·a·ro·ni (mak′ə·rō′nē) *n.* **1.** A dried paste of wheat flour made into short tubes and prepared as a food by boiling. **2.** An 18th-century English dandy. Also **mac′ca·ro′ni.** [< Ital. *maccaroni* pl. of *macherone* groats]

mac·a·roon (mak′ə·rōōn′) *n.* A small cooky made of ground almonds or sometimes coconut, egg, and sugar. [< MF *macaron*]

ma·caw (mə·kô′) *n.* Any of various large tropical American parrots with a long tail, harsh voice, and brilliant plumage. [< Pg. *macao*, prob. < Tupi]

Mac·beth (mək·beth′), died 1057?, king of Scotland 1040–1057?; hero of Shakespeare's *Macbeth.*

Mac·ca·bees (mak′ə·bēz) The family of Jewish patriots who led a revolt against Syrian religious oppression. — *n.pl.* Four books in the Old Testament Apocrypha treating of oppression against the Jews from 222 to 135 B.C. [< LL < Gk. < Aramaic *maqqābā* a hammer] — **Mac′ca·be′an** *adj.*

mace[1] (mās) *n.* **1.** A heavy medieval war club,, usu. with a spiked metal head for use against armor. **2.** A club-shaped staff symbolic of office or authority. [< OF *masse, mace*]

mace[2] (mās) *n.* An aromatic spice ground from the covering between the husk and the seed of the nutmeg. [< OF < L < Gk. *maker* a spicy bark from India]

Mace (mās) *n.* A chemical solution similar to tear gas that temporarily blinds or incapacitates one when sprayed in the face, used as a weapon. — *v.t.* **Maced, Mac·ing** To spray with Mace. [< Chemical *Mace*, a trade name]

Mac·e·do·ni·a (mas′ə·dō′nē·ə) The ancient kingdom of **Mac·e·don** (mas′ə·don) that became a leading world power under Alexander the Great. — **Mac′e·do′ni·an** *adj. & n.*

mac·er·ate (mas′ə·rāt) *v.* **·at·ed, ·at·ing** *v.t.* **1.** To reduce (a solid substance) to a soft mass by soaking in liquid. **2.** To break down the structure of (food) in digestion. **3.** To cause to grow thin; emaciate. — *v.i.* **4.** To become macerated. [< L < *macerare* to make soft, knead] — **mac′er·a′ter** or **mac′er·a′tor** *n.* — **mac′er·a′tion** *n.*

mach (mäk) *n. Often cap.* A mach number.

ma·chet·e (mə·shet′ē, mə·shet′; *Sp.* mä·chā′tā) *n.* A heavy knife or cutlass used as an implement and a weapon in tropical America. [< Sp., dim. of *macho* an ax, hammer]

Mach·i·a·vel·li·an (mak′ē·ə·vel′ē·ən) *adj.* Pertaining to, resembling, or based upon the amoral principles for getting and keeping political power prescribed in Niccolò Machiavelli's *The Prince.* — *n.* A follower of Machiavelli's principles. Also **Mach′i·a·vel′i·an.** — **Mach′i·a·vel′li·an·ism, Mach′i·a·vel′lism** *n.* — **Mach′i·a·vel′list** *adj. & n.*

ma·chic·o·late (mə·chik′ə·lāt) *v.t.* **·lat·ed, ·lat·ing** *Archit.* To furnish with machicolations. [< Med.L < OF *macher* to crush + *couler* to flow]

ma·chic·o·la·tion (mə·chik′ə·lā′shən) *n.* **1.** *Archit.* An opening between the corbels of a projecting parapet, through which missiles or boiling liquids may be dropped. **2.** The act of dropping missiles through such openings.

mach·i·nate (mak′ə·nāt) *v.t. & v.i.* **·nat·ed, ·nat·ing** To scheme or contrive. [< L *machinari* to contrive] — **ma i·na′tor** *n.*

mach·i·na·tion (mak′ə·nā′shən) *n. Usu. pl.* A conce working and scheming for some devious purpose.

ma·chine (mə·shēn′) *n.* **1.** Any combination of interrela parts for using or applying energy to do work. **2.** The pa organization of a city, county, or state: a derogatory te **3.** The organization and operating principles of a comp structure: the human *machine.* **4.** An automobile. **5** person who behaves with machinelike precision, regular etc. **6.** In the ancient theater, a windlass used for spectacular entrance and exit of gods, etc. — *adj.* **1.** O pertaining to a machine or machines. **2.** Produced machine. **3.** Characterized by the use of machines: *mach* age. — *v.t.* **·chined, ·chin·ing** To shape, mill, make, etc., machine. [< F < L < Gk. *mēchos* a contrivance] — **chin′a·ble, ma·chin′al** *adj.* — **ma·chin′a·bil′i·ty** *n.*

ma·chine-gun (mə·shēn′gun′) *v.t.* **-gunned, -gun·ning** fire at or shoot with a machine gun.

machine gun A rapid-firing automatic gun, usually mou ed, that fires small-arms ammunition. — **machine gunn**

ma·chin·er·y (mə·shē′nər·ē, -shēn′rē) *n.* **1.** A collection machines or machine parts. **2.** The mechanism or operat parts and principles of a complex structure: the *machinery* the law. **3.** In literary works, plot devices.

machine shop A shop where metal and other materials cut, shaped, milled, finished, etc., with machine tools.

machine tool A power-driven tool, partly or wholly au matic in action, for cutting, shaping, boring, milling, etc

ma·chin·ist (mə·shē′nist) *n.* **1.** One who is skilled in operation or repair of machines or machine tools. **2.** the U.S. Navy and Coast Guard, a warrant officer who is sistant to the engineer officer.

mach number A number representing the ratio betwe the speed of an object moving through a fluid medium, as a and the speed of sound in the same medium. Also **Ma number.** [after Ernst *Mach*, 1838–1916, Austrian physici

ma·chree (mə·krē′) *n.* My heart; my love: an Anglo-Ir term of endearment. [< Irish < *mo* my + *croidhe* hear

-machy *combining form* A fight between, or by means [< Gk. *-machia* < *machē* a battle]

mac·in·tosh (mak′ən·tosh) See MACKINTOSH.

mack·er·el (mak′ər·əl) *n.* **1.** A food fish of the Atlant steel blue with blackish bars above, and silvery beneath. Any of various fishes resembling it. [< OF *makerel*]

mackerel sky Cirrocumulus.

mack·i·naw (mak′ə·nô) A Mackinaw blanket, boat, coat. [< dial. F (Canadian) *Mackinac* Mackinac Island

Mackinaw blanket A thick, heavy blanket formerly us by Indians and traders of the western United States.

Mackinaw coat A thick, short, double-breasted wool coat, commonly with a plaid pattern.

mack·in·tosh (mak′ən·tosh) *n. Chiefly Brit.* **1.** A wat proof overgarment or cloak; raincoat. **2.** Thin, rubbe coated cloth. Also *macintosh.* [after Charles *Macintos* 1766–1843, Scottish chemist, inventor of the cloth]

macro- *combining form* **1.** *Pathol.* Enlarged or overdev oped. **2.** Large or long in size or duration: *macrocosm.* Als before vowels, **macr-.** [< Gk. *makros* large]

mac·ro·ceph·a·ly (mak′rō·sef′ə·lē) *n.* Abnormal largene of the head. [< MACRO- + Gk. *kephalē* head] — **mac′r ce·phal′ic** (-sə·fal′ik) *adj. & n.* — **mac′ro·ceph′a·lous** (-lə *adj.*

mac·ro·cosm (mak′rə·koz′əm) *n.* The whole universe, es when regarded in contrast to man. [< OF < Med.L < G *makros* long, great + *kosmos* world] — **mac′ro·cos′mic** *ad*

ma·cron (mā′krən, -kron) *n.* A straight line (—) over a vow letter to show that it represents a long sound, as *ā* in *mad* [< Gk. *makron*, neut. of *makros* long]

mac·u·la (mak′yə·lə) *n. pl.* **·lae** (-lē) A spot, as on the ski the sun, etc. [< L, a spot]

mad (mad) *adj.* **mad·der, mad·dest** **1.** Suffering from c manifesting severe mental disorder; insane; psychotic. **2** *Chiefly U.S. Informal* Feeling or showing anger; angry. **3** Wildly foolish; rash: a *mad* project. **4.** Subject to an ove powering emotion: *mad* with grief. **5.** Turbulent and con fused: a *mad* jumble. **6.** Of animals, suffering from hydro ɔia; rabid. **7.** *Informal* Showing a passionate infatua- with or desire for: with *about, for,* or *over.* **8.** *Infor-* Flamboyant; daring. **— like mad** *Informal* As if in- ; frantically. **— mad as a hatter** (or **March hare**) To- ' insane; crazy. **— mad money** *Slang* Money to be used girl to pay her way home from a date in case she quar- with her escort. **—** *n.* *U.S.* *Informal* A fit of temper: only in the phrase **to have a mad on,** to be angry. **—** *& v.i.* **mad·ded, mad·ding** *Rare* To make or become mad. *gemād* insane] **— mad′ly** *adv.* **— mad′ness** *n.*

·am (mad′əm) *n.* *pl.* **mes·dames** (mā·dăm′, *Fr.* mā· ′) *for def. 1;* **mad·ams** *for def. 2.* **1.** My lady; mistress: a of courtesy. See MA'AM. **2.** A woman who manages a hel. [< OF *ma dame* < *ma* my + *dame* lady]

·ame (mad′əm, *Fr.* mȧ·dȧm′) *n.* *pl.* **mes·dames** (mā· ′, *Fr.* mā·dȧm′) The French title of courtesy for a mar- woman, equivalent to the English *Mrs.* Abbr. *Mme.,* *e, Mdme.* [< F < OF *ma dame*]

·cap (mad′kap′) *adj.* Wild; rattlebrained. **—** *n.* One acts wildly or rashly.

·den (mad′n) *v.t. & v.i.* To make or become mad or in- ; inflame; infuriate. **— mad′den·ing·ly** *adv.*

·der[1] (mad′ər) Comparative of MAD.

·der[2] (mad′ər) *n.* **1.** Any of various perennial herbs, an Old World species, the root of which yields a bril- ; red extract. **2.** The red coloring matter. **3.** A brilliant **—** *v.t.* To dye with madder. [OE *mædere, mæddre*]

·ding (mad′ing) *adj.* Being or growing mad; delirious; ng. **— mad′ding·ly** *adv.*

e (mād) Past tense and past participle of MAKE. **—** *adj.* 'roduced by fabrication, invention, or skill; not occur- naturally. **2.** Assured of success or fortune. **— to have ade** *U.S. Slang* To be sure of success.

lei·ra (mə·dir′ə, *Pg.* mə·thā′rə) *n.* A fortified dessert ə made in the Madeira islands.

·e·moi·selle (mad′ə·mə·zel′, *Fr.* mȧd·mwȧ·zel′) *n.* *pl.* **·e·moi·selles,** *Fr.* **mes·de·moi·selles** (mād·mwȧ·zel′) **1.** French title of courtesy for unmarried women, equiva- to the English *Miss.* **2.** A French nurse. [< F < *ma* + *demoiselle* (< OF *dameisele* gentlewoman)]

e-to-order (mād′to͞o·ôr′dər) *adj.* **1.** Made according pecific instructions. **2.** Perfectly adapted or useful.

e-up (mād′up′) *adj.* **1.** Devised by fabrication or in- tion; fictitious. **2.** Adorned or altered by cosmetics. Complete; finished: a *made-up* sample. **4.** Compensated or provided: said of work, money, etc.

·house (mad′hous′) *n.* **1.** A hospital for the mentally nsane asylum. **2.** A place of confusion or uproar; bedlam.

·man (mad′man′) *n.* *pl.* **·men** (-men′) A maniac.

lon·na (mə·don′ə) *n.* **1.** The Virgin Mary. **2.** A ting or statue of the Virgin Mary. [< Ital. < *ma* my *onna* lady]

lras (mə·dras′, -dräs′, mad′rəs) *n.* **1.** A cotton cloth thick strands at intervals, giving either a striped, led, or checked effect. **2.** A silk cloth, usually striped. er *Madras,* India, because originally made there]

·re·pore (mad′rə·pôr, -pōr) *n.* *Zool.* Any of various y corals that form reefs in tropical seas. [< NL < . *madrepora,* lit., mother stone] **— mad′re·por′al** ôr′əl, -pō′rəl), **mad′re·po′ric** (-pôr′ik, -por′ik) *adj.*

·ri·gal (mad′rə·gəl) *n.* **1.** *Music* An unaccompanied t song, often in counterpoint, usu. for four to six voices, ular during the 16th and 17th centuries. **2.** A short c poem. **3.** Any song, esp. a part song. [< Ital. < *matricale* original, chief] **— mad′ri·gal·ist** *n.*

·wom·an (mad′wo͝om′ən) *n.* *pl.* **·wom·en** (-wim′in) insane woman; lunatic.

·ce·nas (mi·sē′nəs) *n.* A patron, esp. of the arts. [after *ecenas,* died 8 B.C., Roman patron of Horace and Vergil]

l·strom (māl′strəm) *n.* **1.** Any dangerous and irre- ible force, or a place where it prevails. **2.** A whirlpool. Du. < *malen* to whirl around + *stroom* stream]

l·strom (māl′strəm) A famous whirlpool in the Arctic an off the NW coast of Norway.

e·nad (mē′nad) *n.* **1.** A female votary or priestess of onysius, a bacchante. **2.** Any woman beside herself with nzy. Also spelled *menad.* [< L < Gk. < *mainesthai* to e] **— mae·nad′ic** *adj.* **— mae·nad′i·cal·ly** *adv.*

es·to·so (mä′es·tō′sō) *Music* *adj.* Majestic; stately. *adv.* In a stately manner. [< Ital., majestic]

es·tro (mä·es′trō, mīs′trō) *n.* *pl.* **·tros** A master in any , esp., an eminent conductor, composer, or performer of sic. [< Ital., master]

·fi·a (mä′fē·ä, maf′ē·ə) *n.* A secret criminal organiza- n of Sicilians and Italians believed to exist in many coun- es, including the U.S. Also **Maf′fi·a.** [< Ital.]

g·a·zine (mag′ə·zēn′, mag′ə·zēn) *n.* **1.** A periodical blication, usu. with a paper cover, containing articles, stories, etc., by various writers. **2.** A warehouse or depot, esp. for military supplies. **3.** A building or storeroom for explosives and ammunition. **4.** A receptacle or part of a gun holding ammunition ready for chambering. **5.** A sup- ply chamber in a battery, camera, etc. [< MF < OF < Arabic *makhāzin* storehouses]

mag·da·len (mag′də·lin) *n.* A reformed prostitute. Also **mag′da·lene** (-lēn). [after Mary *Magdalene*]

Mag·da·le·ni·an (mag′də·lē′nē·ən) *adj.* *Anthropol.* Of or pertaining to the most advanced culture stage of the Paleo- lithic period in Europe. [< F, after *La Madeleine* in west central France, where artifacts were found]

Mag·el·lan·ic cloud (maj′ə·lan′ik) *Astron.* Either of two aggregations of star clusters and nebulae near the south ce- lestial pole.

ma·gen·ta (mə·jen′tə) *n.* **1.** Fuchsin, a dye. **2.** The pur- plish red color produced by fuchsin. [after *Magenta,* Italy]

mag·got (mag′ət) *n.* The legless larva of an insect, as the housefly, esp. one found in decaying matter. [Prob. alter. of ME < ON *mathkr* worm] **— mag′got·y** *adj.*

Ma·gi (mā′jī) *n.* *pl.* *of* **Ma·gus** (mā′gəs) **1.** The three "wise men from the east" who came to Bethlehem to pay homage to the infant Jesus. *Matt.* ii 1–12. **2.** The priestly caste of the Medes and Persians: also **ma′gi.** [< L < Gk. < Persian *magu* priest, magician] **— Ma·gi·an** (mā′jē·ən) *adj. & n.*

mag·ic (maj′ik) *n.* **1.** Seeming control over or foresight of natural events, forces, etc., through supernatural agencies. **2.** An overpowering influence: the *magic* of his voice. **3.** Sleight of hand; legerdemain. **—** *adj.* **1.** Of or used in magic. **2.** Producing the effects of magic. **3.** Mysteriously impressive; beautiful. [< OF < LL *magica* (*ars*) magic (art) < Gk. < *magikos* of the Magi]

mag·i·cal (maj′i·kəl) *adj.* Of, pertaining to, or produced by or as by magic. **— mag′i·cal·ly** *adv.*

ma·gi·cian (mə·jish′ən) *n.* One who performs magic; esp., an entertainer who uses illusion and legerdemain.

magic lantern *Archaic* A slide projector.

mag·is·te·ri·al (maj′is·tir′ē·əl) *adj.* **1.** Of or like a master. **2.** Dictatorial; domineering. **3.** Of or pertaining to a magis- trate. **— mag′is·te′ri·al·ly** *adv.*

mag·is·tra·cy (maj′is·trə·sē) *n.* *pl.* **·cies** **1.** The office, function, or term of a magistrate. **2.** Magistrates collec- tively. **3.** The district under a magistrate's jurisdiction.

mag·is·trate (maj′is·trāt, -trit) *n.* **1.** A public official with the power to enforce the law. **2.** A minor judicial officer, as a justice of the peace. [< L < *magister* master]

mag·ma (mag′mə) *n.* *pl.* **·ma·ta** (-mə·tə) *Geol.* The molten, plastic mass of rock material from which igneous rocks are formed. [< L < Gk. < *massein* to knead]

Mag·na Car·ta (mag′nə kär′tə) **1.** The Great Charter of English liberties, delivered June 19, 1215, by King John on the demand of the English barons. **2.** Any document that secures liberty and rights. Also **Mag′na Char′ta.** [< Med.L, lit., Great Charter]

mag·na·nim·i·ty (mag′nə·nim′ə·tē) *n.* *pl.* **·ties** **1.** The quality of being magnanimous. **2.** A magnanimous act.

mag·nan·i·mous (mag·nan′ə·məs) *adj.* **1.** Manifesting generosity in forgiving insults or injuries. **2.** Characterized by magnanimity. [< L < *magnus* great + *animus* mind, soul] **— mag·nan′i·mous·ly** *adv.* **— mag·nan′i·mous·ness** *n.*

mag·nate (mag′nāt) *n.* One notable or powerful, esp. in industry: a railroad *magnate.* [< LL *magnus* great]

mag·ne·sia (mag·nē′zhə, -shə, -zē·ə) *n.* *Chem.* Magnesium oxide, MgO, a light, white powder used in medicine as an antacid and laxative, and in the manufacture of firebrick. [< Med.L < Gk. *Magnēsia* (*lithos*) (stone) of Magnesia]

mag·ne·si·um (mag·nē′zē·əm, -zhē-, -shē-) *n.* A light, silver-white, malleable and ductile metallic element (symbol Mg), that burns with a very hot, bright flame and is used in lightweight alloys. See ELEMENT. [< NL < *magnesia*]

mag·net (mag′nit) *n.* **1.** A body that has a magnetic field and therefore attracts iron and other magnetic material. **2.** A lodestone. **3.** One who or that which exercises a strong attraction. [< OF < L < Gk. *Magnēs* (*lithos*) Magnesian (stone), i.e., a magnet]

mag·net·ic (mag·net′ik) *adj.* **1.** Pertaining to magnetism or a magnet. **2.** Capable of setting up a magnetic field. **3.** Capable of being attracted by a magnet or a lodestone. **4.** Possessing personal magnetism. Also **mag·net′i·cal. — mag·net′i·cal·ly** *adv.*

magnetic field That region in the neighborhood of a magnet or current-carrying body in which magnetic forces are observable.

magnetic needle A freely movable magnetized needle that tends to point to the magnetic poles of the earth.

magnetic north The direction, usu. differing from true north, toward which the needle of a compass points.

magnetic pickup A phonograph pickup that employs a

magnet and coils to transform vibrations into electrical impulses.

magnetic pole 1. Either of the poles of a magnet. 2. Either of two points (**north magnetic pole** and **south magnetic pole**) on the surface of the earth where the lines of magnetic force converge and are vertical. These poles attract the compass needle, slowly change position, and do not coincide with the geographical poles.

magnetic tape *Electronics* A thin ribbon coated with magnetic particles that form patterns corresponding to the electromagnetic impulses generated by a tape recorder.

mag·net·ism (mag′nə·tiz′əm) *n.* 1. The specific properties of a magnet. 2. The science that treats of the laws and conditions of magnetic phenomena. Also **mag·net·ics** (mag·net′iks). 3. The amount of magnetic moment in a magnetized body. 4. A personal quality that attracts.

mag·net·ite (mag′nə·tīt) *n.* A massive black iron oxide, Fe_3O_4, that is strongly magnetic and is called *lodestone* when it has polarity. — **mag′net·it′ic** (-tit′ik) *adj.*

mag·net·ize (mag′nə·tīz) *v.t.* **·ized, ·iz·ing** 1. To communicate magnetic properties to. 2. To attract by personal influence. — **mag′net·i·za′tion** *n.* — **mag′net·iz′er** *n.*

mag·ne·to (mag·nē′tō) *n. pl.* **·tos** Any of various devices in which the rotation of a coil of wire between the poles of a permanent magnet induces an electric current in the coil; esp., such a device used to produce the ignition spark in some internal-combustion engines. Also **mag·ne·to·dy·na·mo** (mag·nē′tō·dī′nə·mō), **mag·ne·to·gen·er·a·tor** (mag·nē′tō·jen′ə·rā′tər). [Short for *magnetoelectric machine*]

magneto- *combining form* Magnetic; magnetism.

mag·ne·to·e·lec·tric·i·ty (mag·nē′tō·i·lek·tris′ə·tē) *n.* 1. Electricity generated by the inductive action of a magnet. 2. The science that treats of such electricity. — **mag·ne′to·e·lec′tric, mag·ne′to·e·lec′tri·cal** *adj.*

mag·ne·to·hy·dro·dy·nam·ics (mag·nē′tō·hī′drō·dī·nam′·iks) *n.pl.* (*construed as sing.*) The branch of physics that treats of the interaction of electromagnetic, thermal, and hydrodynamic forces. — **mag·ne′to·hy′dro·dy·nam′ic** *adj.*

mag·ne·tom·e·ter (mag′nə·tom′ə·tər) *n.* An instrument for measuring the intensity and direction of magnetic forces.

mag·ne·to·sphere (mag·nē′tə·sfir, -net′ə-) *n. Physics* A region of the upper atmosphere forming a continuous band of ionized particles trapped by the earth's magnetic field.

magni- *combining form* Great; large; long. [< L *magnus* great]

mag·nif·ic (mag·nif′ik) *adj. Archaic* 1. Magnificent; sumptuous. 2. Pompous. Also **mag·nif′i·cal.** [< F < L < *magnus* great + *facere* to make] — **mag·nif′i·cal·ly** *adv.*

Mag·nif·i·cat (mag·nif′ə·kat) *n.* 1. The canticle of the Virgin Mary. *Luke* i 46–55. 2. A musical setting for this. [< L, it magnifies]

mag·ni·fi·ca·tion (mag′nə·fə·kā′shən) *n.* 1. The act, process, or degree of magnifying. 2. The state of being magnified. 3. The magnifying power of a lens or other optical device. 4. A magnified representation of an object, as in a drawing, photograph, etc. [< L < *magnificus* great]

mag·nif·i·cence (mag·nif′ə·səns) *n.* The state or quality of being magnificent; splendor; impressiveness.

mag·nif·i·cent (mag·nif′ə·sənt) *adj.* 1. Presenting an extraordinarily imposing appearance; splendid; beautiful. 2. Exceptionally pleasing; superb. 3. Exalted or sublime in expression or concept. — **mag·nif′i·cent·ly** *adv.*

mag·nif·i·co (mag·nif′ə·kō) *n. pl.* **·coes** Any lordly personage. [< Ital.]

mag·ni·fy (mag′nə·fī) *v.* **·fied, ·fy·ing** *v.t.* 1. To increase the perceived size of, as by a lens. 2. To increase the size of; enlarge. 3. To cause to seem greater or more important; exaggerate. 4. *Archaic* To extol; exalt. — *v.i.* 5. To increase or have the power to increase the apparent size of an object, as a lens. [< OF < L < *magnificus* great] — **mag′ni·fi′a·ble** *adj.* — **mag′ni·fi′er** *n.*

mag·nil·o·quent (mag·nil′ə·kwənt) *adj.* Speaking or spoken in a grandiose style; grandiloquent. [< L *magnus* great + *loquens, -entis,* ppr. of *loqui* to speak] — **mag·nil′o·quence** *n.* — **mag·nil′o·quent·ly** *adv.*

mag·ni·tude (mag′nə·tōōd, -tyōōd) *n.* 1. Size or extent. 2. Greatness or importance: the *magnitude* of the achievement. 3. *Astron.* The relative brightness of a star, ranging from one for the brightest to six for those just visible to the naked eye. [< L *magnus* large]

mag·no·li·a (mag·nō′lē·ə, -nōl′yə) *n.* 1. An ornamental flowering shrub or tree with large fragrant flowers. 2. The fragrant white flower of the **evergreen magnolia,** the State flower of Louisiana and Mississippi. [< NL, genus name, after Pierre *Magnol,* 1638–1715, French botanist]

Magnolia State Nickname of Mississippi.

mag·num (mag′nəm) *n.* A wine bottle holding about two quarts; also, the quantity such a bottle will hold. [< L, neut. of *magnus* great]

magnum o·pus (ō′pəs) A great work; masterpiece; esp., the greatest single work of a writer, artist, etc. [< L]

mag·pie (mag′pī) *n.* 1. Any of various large, noisy co birds having a long tapering tail and black and white mage: sometimes called *pie.* 2. A chatterbox. [< diminutive of MARGARET + PIE[2])

mag·uey (mag′wā, *Sp.* mä·gā′ē) *n.* 1. Any of the aga Mexico with fleshy leaves, esp. the species yielding pu and the century plant. 2. The tough fibers taken from plants and used in rope, etc. [< Sp., prob. < Taino]

Ma·gus (mā′gəs) Singular of MAGI.

Mag·yar (mag′yär, mäg′-; *Hungarian* mud′yär) *n.* member of the dominant group of the population of gary. 2. Hungarian, a Finno-Ugric language. — *adj.* pertaining to the Magyars or their language.

ma·ha·ra·ja (mä′hə·rä′jə, *Hind.* mə·hä′rä′jə) *n.* A ti certain princes of India, particularly one ruling an I state. Also **ma′ha·ra′jah.** [< Hind. < Skt. < *maha* + *rājā* king]

ma·ha·ra·ni (mä′hə·rä′nē, *Hind.* mə·hä′rä′nē) *n.* 1 wife of a maharaja. 2. A sovereign princess of India. **ma′ha·ra′nee.** [< Hind. < *maha* great + *rānī* queen

ma·hat·ma (mə·hat′mə, -hät′-) *n.* In theosophy and Asian religions, one of a group of holy men possessed o cial occult knowledge: often a title of respect. [< Sk *maha* great + *ātman* soul] — **ma·hat′ma·ism** *n.*

Ma·hi·can (mə·hē′kən) *n.* One of a tribe of North Ame Indians of Algonquian stock formerly occupying the tory from the Hudson River to Lake Champlain: also c *Mohican.* [< Algonquian, lit., wolf]

mah·jong (mä′zhong′, -zhông′) *n.* A game of Ch origin, usu. played with 144 pieces or tiles. Also **mah′-j mah′jongg′.** [< dial. Chinese < Chinese *ma ch'iao* l sparrow; from the design on one of the tiles]

ma·hog·a·ny (mə·hog′ə·nē) *n. pl.* **·nies** 1. Any of va tropical trees yielding fine-grained reddish hardwood used for furniture and cabinet work. 2. The wood 3. Any of various trees yielding a similar wood. 4. of the various shades of brownish red of the finished w — *adj.* Having a mahogany color. [< obs. Sp. *mahog*

Ma·hom·et (mə·hom′it) Mohammed.

Ma·hom·e·tan (mə·hom′ə·tən) *adj.* & *n.* Mohamme

ma·hout (mə·hout′) *n.* In India and the East Indies keeper and driver of an elephant. [< Hind. < Skt. *m mātra,* lit., great in measure]

Mah·rat·i (mə·rat′ē) See MARATHI.

Mah·rat·ta (mə·rat′ə) *n.* One of a Hindu people of SW central India: also *Maratha.* [< Hind. < Marathi < *Mahārāstra,* lit., great country]

Mai·a (mā′yə, mī′ə) In Greek mythology, the elde the Pleiades, mother by Zeus of Hermes.

maid (mād) *n.* 1. A young unmarried woman or maiden. 2. A female servant. [Short for MAIDEN]

maid·en (mād′n) *n.* 1. An unmarried woman, es young. 2. A virgin. — *adj.* 1. Of, pertaining to, o fitting a maiden. 2. Unmarried: said of women. 3. (pertaining to the first use, trial, or experience: *maiden* e 4. Untried. [OE *mægden,* prob. dim. of *mægeth* virgin]

maid·en·hair (mād′n·hâr′) *n.* A very delicate and gra fern with an erect black stem, common in damp, r woods. Also **maidenhair fern.**

maid·en·head (mād′n·hed′) *n.* The hymen.

maid·en·hood (mād′n·hŏŏd) *n.* The state or time of b a maiden.

maid·en·ly (mād′n·lē) *adj.* Of, pertaining to, or befitti maiden or young girl. — **maid′en·li·ness** *n.*

maiden name A woman's surname before marriage.

maid of honor 1. The chief unmarried attendant of a b at a wedding. 2. An unmarried woman, usu. of noble b attendant upon an empress, queen, or princess.

maid·ser·vant (mād′sûr′vənt) *n.* A female servant.

mail[1] (māl) *n.* 1. Letters, printed matter, parcels, etc., or received through a governmental postal system. 2. postal system itself. 3. Postal matter collected or deliv at a specified time: the morning *mail.* 4. A conveyance, train, plane, etc., for carrying postal matter. — *adj.* taining to or used for the handling or conveyance of m — *v.t. U.S.* To send by mail, as letters; post. [< O OHG *malha* wallet] — **mail′a·ble** *adj.* — **mail′er** *n.*

mail[2] (māl) *n.* 1. Flexible armor made of interlinked r or overlapping scales. 2. Loosely, any defensive arr 3. A defensive covering, as a turtle's shell. — *v.t.* To c with or as with mail. [< OF < L *macula* spot, mesh of a

mail·bag (māl′bag′) *n.* A bag in which mail is carrie shipped. Also **mail′pouch′** (-pouch′).

mail·box (māl′boks′) *n. U.S.* 1. A box in which lett etc., are deposited for collection: also called *post box.* 2 box into which private mail is delivered. Also **mail box**

mail·man (māl′man′, -mən) *n. pl.* **·men** (-men′, -m One who carries and delivers letters: also called *postma*

mail order An order for merchandise to be sent by ma

mail-or·der house (māl′ôr′dər) A business enterprise t sells its merchandise wholly or in part by mail order.

·m (mām) *v.t.* **1.** To deprive of the use of a bodily part; ·tilate; disable. **2.** To render imperfect; make defective. OF *mahaignier, mayner*] — **maim'er** *n.*
·n[1] (mān) *adj.* **1.** First or chief in size, importance, etc.; ·ing: *main* event. **2.** Fully exerted; sheer: by *main* ·e. **3.** Of or pertaining to a broad expanse of land, sea, — *n.* **1.** A principal conduit or pipe in a system con·ing gas, water, etc. **2.** Utmost effort; force: now chiefly ·he phrase **with might and main.** **3.** The chief or most ·ortant point or part. **4.** *Naut.* The mainmast. — **in for) the main** For the most part; chiefly. [OE *mægen*]
·n[2] (mān) *n.* In cockfighting, a match of several battles.
·n clause *Gram.* An independent clause. See under ·USE.
·n deck *Naut.* The chief deck of a vessel.
·n·land (mān'land, -lənd) *n.* The main part of a conti·t, as distinguished from an island or peninsula.
·n line The principal line of a railroad or highway.
·n·ly (mān'lē) *adv.* Chiefly; principally.
·n·mast (mān'məst, -mast', -mäst') *n.* *Naut.* **1.** The ·ond mast from the bow in a schooner, brig, etc. **2.** The ·st nearer the bow in a two-masted vessel.
·n·sail (mān'səl, -sāl') *Naut.* **1.** A sail bent to the main ·d of a square-rigged vessel: also **main course.** **2.** The ·ncipal sail on a mainmast.
·in·sheet (mān'shēt') *n.* *Naut.* The sheet by which the ·insail is trimmed and set.
·n·spring (mān'spring') *n.* **1.** The principal spring of a ·chanism, as of a watch. **2.** The principal or most com·ling cause or agency.
·in·stay (mān'stā') *n.* **1.** *Naut.* The rope from the main·st head forward, used to steady the mast in that direction. A chief support: the *mainstay* of my old age.
·in·stream (mān'strēm') *n.* The main or middle course.
·in Street **1.** The principal business street of a town. The typical manners, customs, etc., of a small town.
·in·tain (mān·tān') *v.t.* **1.** To carry on or continue; keep ·existence. **2.** To preserve or keep. **3.** To keep in proper ·ndition. **4.** To supply with a livelihood; support. **5.** To ·im to be true; uphold. **6.** To hold or defend (a position, ·ce, etc.) against attack. [< OF < L < *manu*, albative *manus* hand + *tenere* to hold]
·in·te·nance (mān'tə·nəns) *n.* **1.** The act of maintain·, or the state of being maintained. **2.** Means of support subsistence; livelihood. **3.** The work of keeping roads, ·chines, buildings, etc., in good condition.
·in·top (mān'top') *n.* *Naut.* A platform at the head of ·e lower section of the mainmast.
·in·top·mast (mān'top'məst) *n.* *Naut.* **1.** On a square·ged vessel, the section of the mast above the maintop·llantmast. **2.** On a fore-and-aft-rigged ship, the section the mast next above the mainmast.
·in·top·sail (mān'top'səl) *n.* *Naut.* The sail set on the ·aintopmast.
·in yard *Naut.* The lower yard on the mainmast.
·ître d'hô·tel (me'tr' dō·tel') **1.** A headwaiter or stew·d. Also *U.S. Informal* **mai·tre d'** (mā'trə dē'). **2.** The ·oprietor or manager of a hotel. **3.** Having a sauce of ·elted butter, parsley, and lemon juice or vinegar. [< F]
·ize (māz) *n.* **1.** Corn (def. 1). **2.** The deep shade of ·llow of ripe corn. [< Sp. < Taino *mahiz*]
·jes·tic (mə·jes'tik) *adj.* Having or exhibiting majesty; ·ately; royal. Also **ma·jes'ti·cal.** — **ma·jes'ti·cal·ly** *adv.*
·j·es·ty (maj'is·tē) *n.* *pl.* **·ties** **1.** Exalted dignity; state·ess; grandeur. **2.** Sovereign authority: the *majesty* of ·e law. [< OF < L *majestas, -tatis*]
·j·es·ty (maj'is·tē) *n.* *pl.* **·ties** A title or form of address ·r a sovereign: preceded by *His, Her, Your*, etc. Abbr. *M.*
·jol·i·ca (mə·jol'i·kə, -yol'-) *n.* A kind of glazed and ·lorfully decorated Italian pottery. [< Ital., prob. < *Ma·rca*, where formerly made]
·jor (mā'jər) *adj.* **1.** Greater in quantity, number, or ·tent. **2.** Having primary or greater importance, excel·nce, rank, etc.: a *major* writer. **3.** Of, relating to, or mak·g up a majority. **4.** *Music* **a** Denoting the larger of two ·milarly named intervals: *major* third. **b** Denoting a triad ·which the third above the fundamental is major. **c** De·oting a type of diatonic scale, or a key based on this scale. ·ompare MINOR. **5.** *Logic* Having a greater degree of ·enerality: *major* premise. **6.** *U.S.* In education, pertaining ·the principal area of specialized study of a degree candi·ate in a college or university. **7.** Having attained the age ·one's majority. — *n.* **1.** *Mil.* An officer ranking next ·bove a captain. See tables at GRADE. **2.** *Music* A major ·terval, triad, or scale. **3.** *U.S.* The principal area of ·pecialized study of a degree candidate in a college or uni·ersity. **4.** One who has reached his majority or full legal ·ge. **5.** One of superior status within a given group. **6.** *pl.* *U.S.* The major leagues. — *v.i.* *U.S.* In education, to study as a major: with *in.* [< L, compar. of *magnus* great]
ma·jor-do·mo (mā'jər·dō'mō) *n.* *pl.* **·mos** The chief steward or butler, esp. of a royal or noble household. [< Sp. < Med.L < *major* an elder + *domus* house]
ma·jor·ette (mā'jər·et') *n.* *U.S. Informal* A girl who marches and twirls a baton with a band, as in a parade.
major general *Mil.* An officer ranking next above a brigadier or brigadier general. Also *Brit. & Canadian* **ma·jor-gen·er·al** (mā'jər·jen'ər·əl). See tables at GRADE.
ma·jor·i·ty (mə·jôr'ə·tē, -jor'-) *n.* *pl.* **·ties** **1.** More than half of a given number or group; the greater part. **2.** The number of jurors, voters, etc., in accord who compose more than half of the total group. **3.** The number of votes cast for a particular candidate, bill, etc., over and above the total number of remaining votes. Distinguished from *plurality.* **4.** The party or group having the most power. **5.** The age when full civil and personal rights may be legally exercised. **6.** The rank, commission, or office of a major. [< MF < L *majoritas, -tatis*]
major key A key based on a major scale. See SCALE[2].
major league In baseball, either of the two main groups of professional teams in the U.S., the **National League** or the **American League.**
major mode An arrangement of tones found in or characteristic of a major key or scale. See SCALE[2].
major premise *Logic* The more general premise in a syllogism. See SYLLOGISM.
major scale See under SCALE[2].
major suit In bridge, either spades or hearts.
major term *Logic* The predicate of both the major premise and the conclusion of a syllogism. See SYLLOGISM.
ma·jus·cule (mə·jus'kyōōl) *adj.* **1.** Large, as either capital or uncial letters. **2.** Written in such letters. — *n.* A majuscule letter. [< F < L *majuscula* (*littera*), fem. of *majusculus*, dim. of *major* major] — **ma·jus'cu·lar** *adj.*
make (māk) *v.* **made, mak·ing** *v.t.* **1.** To bring about the existence of by shaping or combining of materials; produce; construct; fashion. **2.** To cause: Don't *make* trouble. **3.** To bring to some state: The wind *makes* him cold. **4.** To put into a specified rank or position: They *made* him president. **5.** To form or create in the mind, as a plan, conclusion, or judgment. **6.** To compose (a poem). **7.** To entertain mentally, as doubts, scruples, etc.: *Make* no mistake about it. **8.** To understand the meaning or significance; interpret: with *of.* **9.** To utter or express, as an announcement. **10.** To represent as being or appearing: That hat *makes* you look old. **11.** To put forward or proffer: to *make* friendly overtures. **12.** To engage in: to *make* war. **13.** To earn or acquire: to *make* a fortune. **14.** To act in such a way as to win or gain. **15.** To amount to; add up to. **16.** To bring the total to. **17.** To draw up, enact, or frame, as laws, treaties, etc. **18.** To effect or form, as an agreement or arrangement. **19.** To estimate to be; reckon. **20.** To prepare or arrange for use: to *make* a bed. **21.** To induce or force; compel. **22.** To be the essential element or determinant of: Nourishing food *makes* strong bodies. **23.** To afford or provide: Venison *makes* good eating. **24.** To become through development: He will *make* a good soldier. **25.** To cause the success of: His last book *made* him. **26.** To perform (a specific physical movement). **27.** To cover (distance) by traveling. **28.** To travel at the rate of. **29.** To arrive at; reach: to *make* Boston. **30.** To arrive in time for. **31.** In games and sports, to achieve as a score. **32.** *Electr.* To complete (a circuit). **33.** *U.S. Informal* To win a place or position, as on a team; also, to achieve the rank or status of: to *make* colonel. — *v.i.* **34.** To cause something to assume a specified condition: to *make* sure. **35.** To act or behave in a certain manner: to *make* merry. **36.** To start, or appear to start, to do something: They *made* to go. **37.** To be made: It *makes* easily. — **to make after** To pursue; follow. — **to make away with** **1.** To carry off; steal. **2.** To kill. **3.** To get rid of; destroy. — **to make believe** To pretend; feign. — **to make do** To get along with what is available, esp. with an inferior substitute. — **to make for** **1.** To go toward, esp. rapidly. **2.** To rush at in order to attack. — **to make it** *Informal* To succeed in doing something. — **to make off** To leave suddenly; run away. — **to make off with** To steal. — **to make or break** To bring about the success or failure of. — **to make out** **1.** To see; discern. **2.** To comprehend. **3.** To establish by evidence. **4.** To fill out or draw up, as a document, bank check, etc. **5.** To succeed. **6.** To do well enough; get by. — **to make over** **1.** To renovate; refashion. **2.** To transfer title or possession of. — **to make up** **1.** To compose; compound, as a prescription. **2.** To be the parts of; constitute. **3.** To settle differences and become friendly again. **4.** To devise; fabricate. **5.** To supply what is lacking in. **6.** To

compensate; atone. **7.** To settle; decide: to *make up* one's mind. **8.** *Printing* To arrange lines of type, illustrations, etc., for (a book, etc.). **9.** To put cosmetics on (the face). **10.** In education: **a** To repeat (an examination or course one has failed). **b** To take (an examination one has missed). — *n.* **1.** Style or type: a good *make* of car. **2.** The manner in which something is made. **3.** The quantity produced. **4.** The act of making. **5.** The closing of an electric circuit. — **on the make** *Informal* **1.** Greedy for profit or advancement. **2.** Eager for amorous conquest. [OE *macian*]

make-be·lieve (māk′bi·lēv′) *n.* **1.** Pretense; sham. **2.** One who pretends or feigns. — *adj.* Pretended; unreal.

mak·er (mā′kər) *n.* **1.** One who or that which makes. **2.** *Law* One who signs a promissory note.

Ma·ker (mā′kər) *n.* God, the creator.

make·shift (māk′shift′) *n.* A temporary means devised for an emergency; stopgap. — *adj.* Having the nature of or used as a temporary substitute: also **make′shift′y.**

make-up (māk′up′) *n.* **1.** The arrangement or combination of parts or qualities of which anything is composed. **2.** The cosmetics, etc., used by an actor in a specific role; also, the art of applying or assuming them. **3.** Cosmetics used by women. **4.** Physical or mental constitution. **5.** *Printing* The arranging of composed type and cuts into pages, columns, or forms. Also **make′up′.**

mak·ing (mā′king) *n.* **1.** The act of one who or that which makes, fashions, or constructs. **2.** That which contributes to improvement or success: Discipline is the *making* of a soldier. **3.** *Usu. pl.* The materials or qualities from which something can be made. **4.** A quantity made at one time; batch. **5.** *pl.* Paper and tobacco for cigarettes. — **in the making** In the process of being made.

mal- *prefix* **1.** Bad; ill; wrong: maladjustment. **2.** Defective; imperfect: malformation. [< F < L *malus* bad]

Ma·lac·ca (mə·lak′ə) *n.* The stem of a rattan palm, used for walking sticks, umbrella handles, etc. Also **Malacca cane.** [after *Malacca*, Malaya]

Mal·a·chi (mal′ə·kī) Fifth-century B.C. Hebrew prophet. — *n.* A book of the Old Testament containing his prophecies. Also, in the Douai Bible, **Ma·la·chi·as** (mal·ə·kī′əs).

mal·a·chite (mal′ə·kīt) *n.* A green basic copper carbonate, $Cu_2CO_3(OH)_2$, a common ore of copper. [< OF, ult. < L < Gk. *malachē* mallow; so called because of its color]

mal·ad·just·ed (mal′ə·jus′tid) *adj.* **1.** Poorly adjusted. **2.** *Psychol.* Poorly adapted to one's environment through conflict between personal desires and external circumstances.

mal·ad·just·ment (mal′ə·just′mənt) *n.* Poor adjustment.

mal·a·droit (mal′ə·droit′) *adj.* Lacking skill; clumsy; blundering. [< F < *mal-* mal- + *adroit* clever] — **mal′a·droit′ly** *adv.* — **mal′a·droit′ness** *n.*

mal·a·dy (mal′ə·dē) *n. pl.* **·dies** **1.** A disease, esp. when chronic or deep-seated. **2.** Any disordered or disturbed condition. [< OF < LL < L *male* ill + *habere* to have]

Mal·a·ga (mal′ə·gə) *n.* **1.** A rich, sweet white wine made in Málaga, Spain. **2.** A white, sweet grape of the muscat variety, grown in Spain and California.

mal·aise (mal·āz′, *Fr.* mȧ·lez′) *n.* A feeling of vague discomfort or lassitude, sometimes indicating the beginning of an illness. [< F < *mal* ill + *aise* ease]

ma·la·mute (mä′lə·myoot, mal′ə-) *n. U.S. & Canadian* A large Alaskan sled dog with a thick, long coat: also spelled *malemute, malemiut.* [Orig. name of an Innuit tribe, alter. of Eskimo *Mahlemut* < *Mahle*, the tribe's name + *mut* village]

Mal·a·prop (mal′ə·prop), **Mrs.** A character in Sheridan's play *The Rivals* (1775), who uses words in an absurdly inappropriate manner. [< MALAPROPOS]

mal·a·prop·ism (mal′ə·prop·iz′əm) *n.* **1.** The absurd misuse of words. **2.** An instance of this.

mal·ap·ro·pos (mal′ap·rə·pō′) *adj.* Not appropriate. — *adv.* Inappropriately. [< F *mal à propos* not to the point]

ma·lar·i·a (mə·lâr′ē·ə) *n.* **1.** *Pathol.* Any of several forms of a disease caused by certain parasitic protozoans introduced into the blood by the bite of the infected female anopheles mosquito and characterized by periodic attacks of chills, fever, and profuse sweating. **2.** Foul or noxious vapors; miasma. [< Ital. *mal' aria, mala aria*, lit., bad air] — **ma·lar′i·al, ma·lar′i·ous** *adj.*

ma·lar·key (mə·lär′kē) *n. U.S. Slang* Insincere or senseless talk; bunk. Also **ma·lar′ky.** [Origin unknown]

Ma·lay (mā′lā, mə·lā′) *n.* **1.** A member of a people dominant in Malaysia; a Malayan. **2.** The language spoken on the Malay Peninsula and now adopted as the official language of Indonesia. **3.** A variety of domestic fowl. —*adj.* Of or pertaining to the Malays; Malayan.

Mal·a·ya·lam (mal′ə·yä′ləm) *n.* The Dravidian language of the Malabar coast, India, related to Tamil.

Ma·lay·an (mə·lā′ən) *adj.* **1.** Malay. **2.** Indonesian. — *n.* **1.** A Malay (def. 1). **2.** An Indonesian. **3.** The Indonesian subfamily of Austronesian languages.

Ma·lay·o-Pol·y·ne·sian (mə·lā′ō·pol′ə·nē′zhən, -shən) *adj.* & *n.* Austronesian.

mal·con·tent (mal′kən·tent) *adj.* Discontented or satisfied, esp. with a government or economic system. One who is malcontent.

mal de mer (mȧl′ də mâr′) *French* Seasickness.

male (māl) *adj.* **1.** Of or belonging to the sex that be young or produces sperm. **2.** Of, characteristic of, or s ble for members of this sex; masculine. **3.** Made up of or boys. **4.** *Bot.* **a** Designating a plant having stamens no pistil. **b** Adapted to fertilize, but not to produce f as stamens **5.** *Mech.* Denoting a part, as in some ele plugs, etc., designed to be inserted into a correlated sl bore known as *female.* — *n.* **1.** A male person or ani **2.** *Bot.* A plant with only staminate flowers. [< OF *masculus*] — **male′ness** *n.*

mal·e·dic·tion (mal′ə·dik′shən) *n.* **1.** The pronounci a curse against someone. **2.** Slander; calumny. [< L < ill + *dicere* to speak] — **mal′e·dic′·to·ry** (-tər·ē) *adj.*

mal·e·fac·tor (mal′ə·fak′tər) *n.* **1.** One who comm crime; criminal. **2.** An evildoer. [< L < *male* ill + *f* to do] — **mal′e·fac′tion** *n.* — **mal′e·fac′tress** (-tris) *n.*

ma·lef·i·cent (mə·lef′ə·sənt) *adj.* Causing or doing ev mischief; harmful: opposed to *beneficent.*

ma·le·mute (mä′lə·myōōt, mal′ə-) See MALAMUTE. **ma′le·miut.**

ma·lev·o·lent (mə·lev′ə·lənt) *adj.* Wishing evil tov others; malicious. [< OF < L < *male* ill + *volens*, -*e* ppr. of *velle* to wish] — **ma·lev′o·lence** *n.* — **ma·lev′o·ly** *adv.*

mal·fea·sance (mal·fē′zəns) *n. Law* The performanc some act that is wrongful or that one has specifically tracted not to perform: said usu. of official miscond [< AF < OF < L *malus* bad + *facere* to do] — **mal·f sant** *adj.* & *n.*

mal·for·ma·tion (mal′fôr·mā′shən) *n.* Defective st ture, esp. in an organism.

mal·formed (mal·fôrmd′) *adj.* Badly formed; deform

mal·func·tion (mal′fungk′shən) *n.* **1.** Failure to funct **2.** Defective functioning. — *v.i.* **1.** To fail to function. To function improperly.

mal·ic (mal′ik, mā′lik) *adj.* Of, pertaining to, or made f apples. [< F < L *malum* apple]

mal·ice (mal′is) *n.* **1.** An intention or desire to in another; specific ill will; spite. **2.** *Law* A willfully forr design to do another an injury: also, **malice aforethou malice prepense.** [< OF < L < *malus* evil]

ma·li·cious (mə·lish′əs) *adj.* **1.** Revealing or character by malice; spiteful. **2.** *Law* Resulting from or prompted malice. — **ma·li′cious·ly** *adv.* — **ma·li′cious·ness** *n.*

ma·lign (mə·līn′) *v.t.* To speak slander of; defame. *adj.* **1.** Having an evil disposition toward others; m volent. **2.** Tending to injure; pernicious. [< OF < LL *malignus* ill-disposed] — **ma·lign′ly** *adv.* — **ma·lign′er**

ma·lig·nan·cy (mə·lig′nən·sē) *n. pl.* **·cies** **1.** The stat being malignant. **2.** A malignant tumor. Also **ma·lig′nan**

ma·lig·nant (mə·lig′nənt) *adj.* **1.** *Pathol.* **a** Of tumors, r idly growing and liable to metastasize: opposed to *benig* Becoming progressively worse; virulent. **2.** Tending to great harm. **3.** Having an evil disposition toward oth malign. — *n.* A malcontent. [< LL < L *malignus* disposed] — **ma·lig′nant·ly** *adv.*

ma·lig·ni·ty (mə·lig′nə·tē) *n. pl.* **·ties** **1.** The state or ch acter of being malign; intense ill will. **2.** A harmful t dency; virulence. **3.** *Often pl.* Something evil.

ma·lines (mə·lēn′, *Fr.* mȧ·lēn′) *n.* A gauzelike veiling trimming hats, etc.: also **ma·line′.** [< F, after *Mali* Mechlin]

ma·lin·ger (mə·ling′gər) *v.i.* To pretend sickness so as avoid work or duty. [< F *malingre* sickly, ? < *mal* ill OF *heingre* lean] — **ma·lin′ger·er** *n.*

mall[1] (môl, mal) See MAUL.

mall[2] (môl, mal, mel) *n.* **1.** A promenade or walk, u public and often shaded. **2.** *U.S. & Canadian* A street shops closed off to vehicles and enhanced with trees, bench etc. [Short for *Pall-Mall*, a street in London]

mal·lard (mal′ərd) *n. pl.* **·lards** or **·lard** **1.** A comm wild duck, the ancestor of the domestic breeds, havi brownish plumage, and, in the male, a bright green he **2.** The male or drake of this duck. [< OF < *masle* ma

mal·le·a·ble (mal′ē·ə·bəl) *adj.* **1.** Capable of being ha mered or rolled out without breaking: said esp. of meta **2.** Capable of being shaped or molded; flexible; pliab [< OF < L *malleare* to hammer] — **mal′le·a·bil′i· mal′le·a·ble·ness** *n.* — **mal′le·a·bly** *adv.*

mal·let (mal′it) *n.* **1.** A hammer having a head of woo rubber, etc. **2.** A long-handled wooden hammer used in t game of croquet. **3.** A wooden-headed flexible stick us in the game of polo. [< OF < L *malleus* hammer]

mal·le·us (mal′ē·əs) *n. pl.* **·le·i** (-lē·ī) *Anat.* The clu shaped bone of the middle ear, articulating with the incu also called *hammer.* For illus. see EAR. [< L, hammer]

mal·low (mal′ō) *n.* **1.** Any of various herbs having rou n leaves, pale pink flowers, and disklike fruit. **2.** Any ilar plant, as the hibiscus. [OE < L *malva*]

m·sey (mäm′zē) *n. pl.* **·seys** A rich, sweet wine made he Canary Islands, Madeira, etc.; also, the grape used for s wine. [< Med.L < Gk. *Monembasia* Monemvasia, eece, a town formerly exporting wine]

·nu·tri·tion (mal′nōō·trish′ən, -nyōō-) *n.* Faulty or in-quate nutrition; undernourishment.

·o·dor·ous (mal·ō′dər·əs) *adj.* Having a disagreeable ell. — **mal·o′dor·ous·ly** *adv.* — **mal·o′dor·ous·ness** *n.*

·prac·tice (mal·prak′tis) *n.* **1.** In medicine or surgery, improper, injurious, or negligent treatment of a patient. Improper or immoral conduct in a professional or public ition. — **mal·prac·ti·tion·er** (mal′prak·tish′ən·ər) *n.*

t (môlt) *n.* **1.** Grain, usu. barley, germinated by soak-and then kiln-dried. **2.** Liquor made with malt, as beer, etc. — *v.t.* **1.** To cause (grain) to become malt. **2.** To it or combine with malt or malt extract. — *v.i.* **3.** To ome malt. **4.** To change grain into malt. [OE *mealt*] **malt·y** (môl′tē) *adj.*

·ted milk (môl′tid) **1.** A beverage made of milk, a pow-of malted cereals and dried milk, and usu. ice cream: **malt′ed.** **2.** The powder used in this beverage.

·tese (môl·tēz′, -tēs′) *adj.* Of or pertaining to Malta, inhabitants, or their language. — *n. pl.* **·tese** **1.** A ive or inhabitant of Malta. **2.** The language of Malta. A Maltese cat or dog.

tese cat A cat with long, silky, bluish gray hair.

tese cross An eight-pointed cross formed by four ar-heads joining at their points.

t extract Wort (def. 2).

·thu·si·an (mal·thōō′zē·ən, môl′-, -zhən) *adj.* Of or taining to the theory of T. R. Malthus that population ds to outrun its means of support, and will be checked by aster unless restricted by sexual restraint. — *n.* A be-er in the theories of Malthus. — **Mal·thu′si·an·ism** *n.*

t·ose (môl′tōs) *n. Biochem.* A white, crystalline sugar, $_{2}H_{22}O_{11}H_2O$, formed by the action of diastase on starch. o **malt sugar.**

·treat (mal·trēt′) *v.t.* To treat badly, roughly or un-dly; abuse. [< F *maltraiter*] — **mal·treat′ment** *n.*

t·ster (môlt′stər) *n.* A maker of or dealer in malt.

ma (mä′mə, mə·mä′) *n.* Mother: used familiarly. epetition of infantile syllable *ma*]

m·bo (mäm′bō) *n. pl.* **·bos** A dance resembling the nba; also the syncopated four-beat music for this dance. *v.i.* To dance the mambo. [< Haitian Creole]

m·ma (mam′ə) *n. pl.* **·mae** (-mē) In mammals, the or-n that secretes milk; a breast; udder. [< L, breast]

m·mal (mam′əl) *n.* Any of a class of vertebrates whose nales have mammae to nourish their young, including n, all warm-blooded quadrupeds, seals, etc. [< NL < < L *mamma* breast] — **mam·ma·li·an** (ma·mā′lē·ən, āl′yən) *adj. & n.*

m·ma·ry (mam′ər·ē) *adj.* Of, pertaining to, or of the ture of a mamma or breast, or the mammae.

m·mon (mam′ən) *n.* **1.** Riches regarded as an evil in-ence and ignoble goal. **2.** Worldliness; avarice. [< LL Gk. < Aramaic *māmōnā* riches] — **mam′mon·ish** *adj.*

m·mon (mam′ən) The personification of riches, avarice, d worldly gain.

m·moth (mam′əth) *n. Paleontol.* large, once very abundant, now ex-ct elephant having a thick hairy at and long curved tusks. — *adj.* ge; gigantic. [< Russian *mam-t, mamant*]

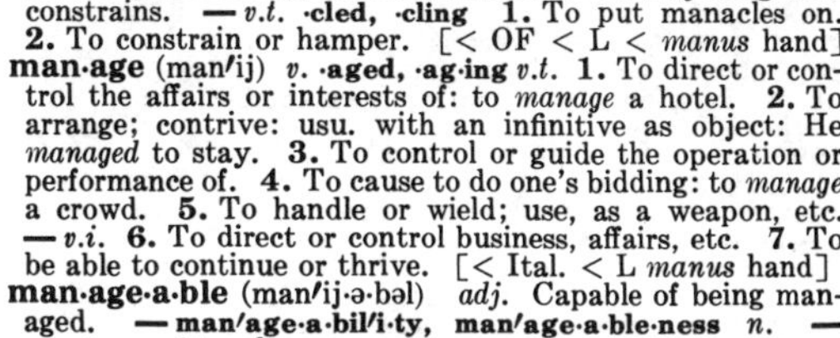

WOOLLY MAMMOTH (9 to 12 feet high at shoulder)

m·my (mam′ē) *n. pl.* **·mies** **1.** other: used familiarly. **2.** *Southern S.* A Negro nurse or foster mother white children. Also spelled *ammie.* [Dim. of MAMA]

n (man) *n. pl.* **men** (men) **1.** An ult male human being. **2.** Human ings collectively; the human race; ankind. **3.** A person or individual. **4.** One having pro-unced masculine traits and virtues; a genuine male. An adult male subordinate or employee; as: **a** A worker a factory, office, etc. **b** A servant, esp. a valet. **6.** A hus-nd. **7.** A piece or counter used in certain games, as chess, eckers, etc. — **as one man** Unanimously. — **to a man** nanimously. — **to be one's own man** To be independent. *interj. Slang* An exclamation of surprise, pleasure, etc. *adj.* Male. — *v.t.* **manned, man·ning** **1.** To supply with en, as for work, defense, etc.: to *man* the fort. **2.** To take ations on, at, or in for work, defense, etc.: *Man* the pumps! E *monn, mann*]

n·a·cle (man′ə·kəl) *n.* **1.** *Usually pl.* A device for re-straining the hands; shackle; handcuff. **2.** Anything that constrains. — *v.t.* **·cled, ·cling** **1.** To put manacles on. **2.** To constrain or hamper. [< OF < L < *manus* hand]

man·age (man′ij) *v.* **·aged, ·ag·ing** *v.t.* **1.** To direct or con-trol the affairs or interests of: to *manage* a hotel. **2.** To arrange; contrive: usu. with an infinitive as object: He *managed* to stay. **3.** To control or guide the operation or performance of. **4.** To cause to do one's bidding: to *manage* a crowd. **5.** To handle or wield; use, as a weapon, etc. — *v.i.* **6.** To direct or control business, affairs, etc. **7.** To be able to continue or thrive. [< Ital. < L *manus* hand]

man·age·a·ble (man′ij·ə·bəl) *adj.* Capable of being man-aged. — **man′age·a·bil′i·ty, man′age·a·ble·ness** *n.* — **man′age·a·bly** *adv.*

managed currency (man′ijd) A monetary system in which the amount in circulation is regulated in an attempt to control prices, credit, etc.

man·age·ment (man′ij·mənt) *n.* **1.** The act, art, or prac-tice of managing. **2.** The person or persons who manage a business, etc.. **3.** Managers collectively, esp. in their rela-tions with labor unions. **4.** The skillful use of means.

man·ag·er (man′ij·ər) *n.* **1.** One who manages; esp., one who directs an enterprise, business, etc. **2.** One skilled in managing, esp. business affairs. — **man′ag·er·ship** *n.*

man·a·ge·ri·al (man′ə·jir′ē·əl) *adj.* Of or pertaining to a manager or management. — **man′a·ge′ri·al·ly** *adv.*

ma·ña·na (mä·nyä′nä) *n. & adv. Spanish* Tomorrow; some other time.

Ma·nas·seh (mə·nas′ə) In the Old Testament, a son of Joseph. *Gen.* xli 51. — *n.* The tribe of Israel descended from Manasseh. Also **Ma·nas·ses** (mə·nas′is).

man-at-arms (man′ət·ärmz′) *n. pl.* **men-at-arms** (men′-) A soldier; esp., an armed medieval mounted soldier.

man·a·tee (man′ə·tē′) *n.* A sluggish aquatic mammal of the coastal waters of Florida, the Gulf of Mexico, and the West Indies: also called *sea cow.* [< Sp. < Carib *manattoui*]

Man·chu (man·chōō′, man′chōō) *n.* **1.** One of a Mongoloid people that conquered China in 1643 and established the dy-nasty overthrown in 1912. **2.** The language of this people. — *adj.* Of or pertaining to Manchuria, its people, or its language. Also **Man·choo′.** [< Manchu, lit., pure]

-mancy *combining form* Divining or foretelling by means of: *necromancy.* [< OF < LL < Gk. *manteia* power of divination]

man·da·mus (man·dā′məs) *n. Law* A writ issued by a higher court to subordinate courts, corporations, etc., com-manding them to do something. [< L, we command]

man·da·rin (man′də·rin) *n.* **1.** A member of any of the nine grades of well-educated officials of the Chinese Empire. **2.** A powerful person; esp., an intellectual arbiter. **3.** A tangerine: also **mandarin orange.** **4.** An orange or reddish yellow dye. [< Pg. < Malay < Skt. *mantra* counsel]

Man·da·rin (man′də·rin) *n.* The Chinese language of north and west China, including the Peking dialect upon which the official language of the country is based.

man·da·tar·y (man′də·ter′ē) *n. pl.* **·tar·ies** One having or receiving a mandate.

man·date (man′dāt; *for n., also* -dit) *n.* **1.** In politics, an instruction from an electorate to its representative, ex-pressed by the result of an election. **2.** Formerly, a charge to a nation from the League of Nations authorizing the administration of a territory, colony, etc.; also, the territory given in charge. **3.** An authoritative command; order. **4.** *Law* A judicial command issued by a higher court or official to a lower one. — *v.t.* **·dat·ed, ·dat·ing** To assign (a territory, etc.) to a specific nation under a mandate. [< L < *manus* hand + *dare* to give] — **man·da′tor** (-dā′tər) *n.*

man·da·to·ry (man′də·tôr′ē, -tō′rē) *adj.* **1.** Required by or as if by mandate or command; obligatory. **2.** Of or pertain-ing to a mandate. **3.** Holding a mandate. — *n. pl.* **·ries** A mandatary. — **man′da·to′ri·ly** *adv.*

man·di·ble (man′də·bəl) *n. Biol.* **1.** The lower jaw bone. **2.** Either part of the beak of a bird **3.** Either the upper or outer pair of jaws in an insect or other arthropod. [< L *mandere* to chew] — **man·dib·u·lar** (man·dib′yə·lər) *adj.*

man·do·lin (man′də·lin, man′də·lin′) *n.* A musical instru-ment with a fretted neck, a pear-shaped body, and eight metal strings. [< F < Ital. < L < Gk. *pandoura* lute]

man·drake (man′drāk) *n.* **1.** A short-stemmed Old World plant of the nightshade family with narcotic properties and fleshy forked roots sometimes resembling the human form. **2.** The May apple. Also **man·drag·o·ra** (man·drag′ə·rə). [< OE < LL < L < Gk. *mandragoras*]

man·drel (man′drəl) *n. Mech.* **1.** A shaft or spindle on which material may be fixed for working on a machine. **2.** A metal bar used as a core about which wire, glass, metal, etc., may be bent, forged, or shaped. Also **man′dril.** [Prob. alter. of F *mandrin* lathe]

man·drill (man′dril) *n.* A large, ferocious West African baboon.

MANDRILL (About 2½ feet high at shoulder; 3 to 4 feet long)

mane (mān) *n.* The long hair growing on and about the neck of some animals, as the horse, lion, etc. [OE *manu*] —**maned** *adj.*

man-eat·er (man′ē′tər) *n.* **1.** A cannibal. **2.** An animal, as a tiger, shark, etc., that devours or is said to devour human flesh. —**man′-eat′ing** *adj.*

ma·nège (ma·nezh′) *n.* **1.** The art of training and riding horses; also, a school for horsemanship. **2.** The movements of a trained horse. Also **man·ege′**. [< F < Ital. *maneggiare* to handle, train horses]

ma·nes (mā′nāz) *n.pl. Often cap.* In ancient Roman religion, the spirits of the dead, esp. of ancestors. [< L]

ma·neu·ver (mə·nōō′vər, -nyōō′-) *n.* **1.** *Mil.* **a** A planned movement or shift, as of troops, warships, etc. **b** *pl.* Large-scale tactical exercises simulating war. **2.** Any skillful move or stroke. —*v.t.* **1.** To manage or conduct skillfully. **2.** To put (troops, vessels, etc.) through a maneuver or maneuvers. —*v.i.* **3.** To perform a maneuver or maneuvers. **4.** To use artful moves or strokes. Also, *esp. Brit., manoeuver, manoeuvre.* [< F < OF < LL < L *manu operari* to work with the hand] —**ma·neu′ver·a·bil′i·ty** or **·vra·bil′i·ty** *n.* —**ma·neu′ver·a·ble** or **·vra·ble** *adj.* —**ma·neu′ver·er** *n.*

man Friday A person devoted or subservient to another, like Robinson Crusoe's servant of that name; a factotum.

man·ful (man′fəl) *adj.* Having a manly spirit; sturdy. —**man′ful·ly** *adv.* —**man′ful·ness** *n.*

man·ga·nese (mang′gə·nēs, -nēz) *n. Chem.* A hard, brittle, grayish white metallic element (symbol Mn), oxidizing readily and forming an important component of certain alloys. See ELEMENT. [< F < Ital., alter. of Med.L *magnesia*]

mange (mānj) *n. Vet.* An itching skin disease of dogs and other domestic animals, caused by parasitic mites. [< OF *manjue* an itch, eating]

man·ger (mān′jər) *n.* A trough or box for feeding horses or cattle. [< OF < L *manducare* to chew]

man·gle[1] (mang′gəl) *v.t.* **·gled, ·gling 1.** To disfigure or mutilate by cutting, bruising, crushing, etc. **2.** To mar or ruin; spoil. [< AF, appar. freq. of OF *mahaignier*] —**man′gler** *n.*

man·gle[2] (mang′gəl) *n.* A machine for smoothing and pressing fabrics by passing them between rollers. —*v.t.* **·gled, ·gling** To smooth with a mangle. [< Du. < MDu. < Ital. < LL < Gk. *manganon* a pulley, a war machine]

man·go (mang′gō) *n. pl.* **·goes** or **·gos 1.** An edible tropical fruit having a slightly acid taste. **2.** The tree producing this fruit. [< Pg. < Malay < Tamil < *mān* mango tree + *kāy* a fruit]

man·grove (mang′gōv, man′-) *n.* A tropical evergreen shrub or tree, sometimes having aerial roots, growing in marshy and coastal areas. [< Sp. *mangle* < Taino]

man·gy (mān′jē) *adj.* **·gi·er, ·gi·est 1.** Affected with or resembling mange. **2.** Squalid; shabby. —**man′gi·ly** *adv.* —**man′gi·ness** *n.*

man·han·dle (man′han′dəl) *v.t.* **·dled, ·dling 1.** To handle with rough force. **2.** To handle by manpower alone.

Man·hat·tan District (Man·hat′an, man-) In World War II, the project that developed the atomic bomb.

man·hole (man′hōl′) *n.* A usu. circular and covered opening by which a man may enter a sewer, boiler, etc.

man·hood (man′hŏŏd) *n.* **1.** The state of being an adult male human being. **2.** The masculine qualities collectively. **3.** Men collectively. **4.** The state of being human.

man-hour (man′our′) *n.* The amount of work a man can do in an hour.

ma·ni·a (mā′nē·ə, mān′yə) *n.* **1.** An extraordinary enthusiasm, craving, etc. **2.** *Psychiatry* An exaggerated sense of well-being with excessive but disordered mental and physical activity, often alternating with melancholia, as in manic-depressive psychosis. [< L < Gk., madness]

-mania *combining form* An exaggerated or irrational craving for or infatuation with. [< Gk. *mania* madness]

In the following list each entry denotes a mania for what is indicated:

- **acromania** high places
- **agoramania** open places
- **ailuromania** cats
- **anthomania** flowers
- **chionomania** snow
- **choreomania** dancing
- **chrematomania** money
- **cynomania** dogs
- **entomomania** insects
- **gymnomania** nakedness
- **gynemania** women
- **heliomania** exposure to sun
- **hippomania** horses
- **hodomania** travel
- **hylomania** woods
- **hypnomania** sleep
- **ichthyomania** fish
- **necromania** death or the dead
- **noctimania** night
- **ophidiomania** reptiles
- **ornithomania** birds
- **pedomania** children
- **phonomania** noise
- **thalassomania** ocean or sea
- **xenomania** strangers
- **zoomania** animals

ma·ni·ac (mā′nē·ak) *n.* A violently insane person; man. —*adj.* Insane; mad. —**ma·ni·a·cal** (mə·nī′ *adj.* —**ma·ni′a·cal·ly** *adv.*

-maniac *combining form* Used to form nouns and adjec from nouns ending in *-mania*: *kleptomaniac.*

man·ic (man′ik, mā′nik) *adj.* **1.** Extraordinarily anim or excited. **2.** *Psychiatry* Of or affected by mania.

man·ic-de·pres·sive (man′ik·di·pres′iv) *adj. Psych* Denoting or characteristic of a mental disorder in w periods of depression alternate with periods of exciter —*n.* One who suffers from this disorder.

man·i·cure (man′ə·kyŏŏr) *n.* The care of the hands fingernails. —*v.t. & v.i.* **·cured, ·cur·ing** To treat (the etc.). [< F < L *manus* hand + *cura* care]

man·i·cur·ist (man′ə·kyŏŏr′ist) *n.* One whose work care for the hands and fingernails.

man·i·fest (man′ə·fest) *adj.* Plainly apparent; obv —*v.t.* **1.** To reveal; show; display. **2.** To prove; be dence of. **3.** To record in a manifest. —*n.* In transp tion, an itemized account or list, as of passengers, cargo, [< L *manifestus* evident, lit., struck by the hand] —**m i·fes′ta·ble** *adj.* —**man′i·fest′ly** *adv.*

—**Syn.** (adj.) patent, visible, palpable, plain, evident.

man·i·fes·ta·tion (man′ə·fes·tā′shən) *n.* **1.** The a manifesting, or the state of being manifested. **2.** A indication.

man·i·fes·to (man′ə·fes′tō) *n. pl.* **·toes** or **·tos** A p and formal declaration or explanation of principles, ir tions, etc., usually by a political faction or similar grou

man·i·fold (man′ə·fōld) *adj.* **1.** Having many and va forms, types, instances, etc.: *manifold* sorrows. **2.** Ha an assortment of features, etc. —**Syn.** See COMPLEX. **1.** *Mech.* A pipe or chest having several or many openi as for exhaust gas. **2.** A copy made by manifolding. Something that is manifold. —*v.t.* **1.** To make more one copy of. **2.** To multiply. —*adv.* By many or by m to increase *manifold.* [OE *manigfeald* varied, numerous] **man′i·fold·ly** *adv.* —**man′i·fold·ness** *n.*

man·i·kin (man′ə·kin) *n.* **1.** A little man; dwarf. **2.** MANNEQUIN. [< Du. *manneken,* dim. of *man* man]

ma·nil·a (mə·nil′ə) *n. Often cap.* The fiber of the aba banana plant, used for making rope, etc. Also **ma·nil′a he**

Manila paper A heavy, light brown paper, originally m of Manila hemp, now made of various fibers.

Manila rope Rope made of Manila hemp.

man in the street The common or ordinary person.

man·i·oc (man′ē·ok, mā′nē-) *n.* Cassava (def. 1). [< Tupi *mandioca* manioc root]

ma·nip·u·late (mə·nip′yə·lāt) *v.* **·lat·ed, ·lat·ing** *v.t.* **1.** manage (persons, figures, stocks, etc.) shrewdly and d ously for one's own profit. **2.** To control, move, treat, with or as with the hands; esp., to handle skillfully. — **3.** To perform manipulation. [Back formation < MAN LATION] —**ma·nip′u·la·ble** *adj.* —**ma·nip′u·la′tive,** **nip′u·la·to′ry** *adj.* —**ma·nip′u·la′tor** *n.*

ma·nip·u·la·tion (mə·nip′yə·lā′shən) *n.* **1.** The act of nipulating, or the state of being manipulated. **2.** *Sur* manual procedure, esp. in orthopedics or obstetrics. [< ult. < L < *manus* hand + *plere* to fill]

man·kind (man′kīnd; *for def. 1, also* man′kīnd′) **1.** whole human species. **2.** Men collectively, as distinguis from women.

man·ly (man′lē) *adj.* **·li·er, ·li·est 1.** Pertaining to or propriate for a man; virile: *manly* charm. **2.** Having qualities and virtues of a man, as courage, determinat strength, etc. —**the manly art** Boxing. —*adv. Arc* Manfully. —**man′li·ly** *adv.* —**man′li·ness** *n.*

man·na (man′ə) *n.* **1.** The food miraculously given to Israelites in the wilderness as they fled from Egypt (*Ex.* 14–36); also, any nourishment, help, etc., received as by vine bounty. **2.** A sweetish substance obtained from v ous plants, esp. from the flowering ash, and used as a mild ative. [< LL < Gk. < Aramaic < Hebrew *mān* What is

man·ne·quin (man′ə·kin) *n.* **1.** A full-sized model human figure used for cutting, fitting, or displaying ments. **2.** A woman who models clothing; model. spelled *manikin.* [< F < Du. *manneken.* See MANIKIN

man·ner (man′ər) *n.* **1.** A way of doing or a way in wh something happens or is done. **2.** A style of speech and tion: a grave *manner.* **3.** *pl.* Social conduct; etiquette; e polite and civil social behavior: to learn *manners* from Em Post. **4.** *pl.* The modes of social behavior prevailing group, nation, period, etc. **5.** Typical or customary pr tice; esp., a characteristic style in literature, music, art, —**in a manner of speaking** Approximately; more or l —**to the manner born** Familiar or fitted from or as fr birth. [< AF, OF, ult. < L *manuarius* of the hand]

man·nered (man′ərd) *adj.* **1.** Having (a specific kind manner or manners: used in combination: *mild-manne* **2.** Having mannerisms in writing, speaking, etc.

man·ner·ism (man′ər·iz′əm) *n.* **1.** Marked use of a

:ive style, as in writing. **2.** A distinctive trait; idiosyn-y. — **man′ner·ist** *n.* — **man′ner·is′tic** or **·ti·cal** *adj.*
·ner·ly (man′ər·lē) *adj.* Well-behaved; polite. — *adv.* ı good manners; politely. — **man′ner·li·ness** *n.*
·ni·kin (man′ə·kin) See MANIKIN.
·nish (man′ish) *adj.* Resembling a man; masculine; of women. — **man′nish·ly** *adv.* — **man′nish·ness** *n.*
ıoeu·ver (mə·no͞o′vər, -nyo͞o′-), **ma·noeu·vre** See MA-VER.
of the world A worldly-wise and sophisticated man.
-of-war (man′əv·wôr′, -ə·wôr′) *n. pl.* **men-of-war** n′-) *Chiefly Archaic* An armed ship; warship.
-of-war bird A frigate bird (which see). Also **man-of-hawk.**
ıom·e·ter (mə·nom′ə·tər) *n.* Any of various instru-ts used to measure pressure, as of gases, liquids, vapors, [< F < Gk. *manos* thin, rare + *-mètre* -meter] — **ı·o·met·ric** (man′ə·met′rik) or **·ric·al** *adj.*
. on horseback A military leader whose popularity is a at to the civil government.
·or (man′ər) *n.* **1.** In England: **a** Formerly, a feudal ain. **b** A landed estate. **2.** A manor house. **3.** A man-. **4.** In colonial America, a landed estate with heredi-feudal rights. [< OF < L *manere* to dwell] — **ma·i·al** (mə·nôr′ē·əl, -nō′rē-) *adj.*
ıor house The residence of the lord of a manor.
ı·pow·er (man′pou′ər) *n.* **1.** The force of human physi-strength. **2.** The number of men whose strength and are available to a nation, army, project, etc.; personnel.
ı·qué (mäṅ·kā′) *adj. French* Lacking fulfillment; in ı but not in fact: a writer *manqué.*
ı·sard (man′särd) *n. Archit.* A curb roof having the er slope almost vertical and the upper almost horizontal, ı the same profile on all four sides of the building. [after *Mansard,* 1598–1666, French architect who revived it]
ıse (mans) *n.* **1.** A clergyman's house. **2.** *Archaic* A ıor house. [< Med.L *mansa,* pp. of L *manere* to dwell]
ı·ser·vant (man′sûr′vənt) *n.* An adult male servant.
ı·sion (man′shən) *n.* A large and impressive house, ically that of a wealthy person or family. [< OF < L *ısio, -onis* a dwelling]
ı·slaugh·ter (man′slô′tər) *n.* **1.** *Law* The unlawful ing of a human being without malice. **2.** Slaying of men.
ı·ta (man′tə) *n.* **1.** Any of several y large rays common in tropical Amer-ı waters: also called *devilfish.* Also **nta ray.** **2.** A woman's shawl made of oarse fabric. [< Sp., blanket < LL *ıtum* cloak]

MANTA (To 20 feet long)

ı·teau (man′tō, *Fr.* mäṅ·tō′) *n. pl.* **ıus** (-tōz) or **·teaux** (*Fr.* -tō′) A cloak mantle. [< F. See MANTLE.]
ı·tel (man′təl) *n.* **1.** The shelf above replace. **2.** A facing of wood, brick, stone, etc., around a place: also called *chimney piece.* Also **man′tel·piece′** ēs′). [< F *manteau* mantelpiece]
ıntic *combining form* Used to form adjectives from ıns ending in *-mancy.* [< Gk. *mantikos* prophetic]
n·til·la (man·til′ə) *n.* A light scarf often of black lace rn over the head and shoulders of women in Spain and anish America. [< Sp. dim. of *manta.* See MANTA.]
n·tis (man′tis) *n. pl.* **·tis·es** or **·tes** (-tēz) A carnivorous, g-bodied insect with large eyes and swiveling head, that nds with its forelegs folded as if in prayer: also called *ıying mantis.* [< NL < Gk., a prophet]
n·tle (man′təl) *n.* **1.** A loose and usu. sleeveless garment rn over other garments. **2.** Anything that clothes, en-lops, or conceals. **3.** *Zool.* The variously modified flap or ds of the membranous covering of a mollusk. **4.** A man-. **5.** A gas mantle. — *v.* **·tled, ·tling** *v.t.* **1.** To cover with as with a mantle; conceal. — *v.i.* **2.** To overspread or rer the surface of something. **3.** To be or become covered suffused, as a blush, etc. [OE < OF < L *mantellum*]
n·tu·a (man′cho͞o·ə, -to͞o·ə) *n.* A woman's cloak, worn out 1700. [Alter. of F *manteau;* infl. in form by *Mantua*]
n·u·al (man′yo͞o·əl) *adj.* Involving, used, or operated by hands. — *n.* **1.** A small book of instructions. **2.** An or-n keyboard. **3.** A prescribed drill in manipulating a rifle, g, etc. [< OF < L *manus* hand] — **man′u·al·ly** *adv.*
nual alphabet A series of manual signs or gestures used the deaf and deaf-mutes as a substitute for vocal speech: metimes called *deaf-and-dumb alphabet.*
.nual training In U.S. schools, practical training in rpentry, woodworking, etc.
.n·u·fac·ture (man′yə·fak′chər) *v.* **·tured, ·tur·ing** *v.t.* To make or process a product, esp. on a large scale and th machinery. **2.** To fabricate or invent (a lie, alibi, :.). **3.** To produce (poetry, art, etc.) mechanically. — *v.i.* **4.** To make or process something. — *n.* **1.** The act or process of manufacturing. **2.** Something that is manu-factured. [< MF < L *manus* hand + *factura* a making] — **man′u·fac′tur·a·ble** *adj.* — **man′u·fac′tur·er** *n.*
man·u·mit (man′yə·mit′) *v.t.* **·mit·ted, ·mit·ting** To free from bondage, as a slave. [< L *manumittere,* lit., to send forth from one's hand] — **man′u·mis′sion** (-mish′ən) *n.*
ma·nure (mə·no͝or′, -nyo͝or′) *n.* Dung, compost, etc., used to fertilize soil. — *v.t.* **·nured, ·nur·ing** To apply manure or other fertilizer to, as soil. [< AF *maynoverer* to work with the hands] — **ma·nur′er** *n.*
man·u·script (man′yə·skript) *n.* **1.** A usu. typewritten copy of a book, article, document, etc., prepared or submit-ted for publication. **2.** Something written by hand. — *adj.* Written by hand. [< Med.L < LL < L *manus* hand + *scriptus,* pp. of *scribere* to write]
Manx (mangks) *adj.* Of or pertaining to the Isle of Man, its people, or their language. — *n.* **1.** The people of the Isle of Man. **2.** The Gaelic language of the Manx, nearly extinct. [< Scand. ult. < Celtic *Man* Isle of Man]
Manx cat A type of domestic cat having no tail.
Manx·man (mangks′mən) *n. pl.* **·men** (-mən) A native of the Isle of Man.
man·y (men′ē) *adj.* **more, most** Adding up to a large num-ber; numerous. — *n.* **1.** A large number. **2.** The masses: with *the.* — **a great many** Many: with plural verb. — **many a** (or **an** or **another**) Many: with singular noun. — *pron.* A large number of persons or things. [OE *manig*]
Mao·ism (mou′iz′əm) *n.* The communist doctrines or prac-tices of Mao Tse-tung. — **Mao′ist** *n., adj.*
Ma·o·ri (mä′ō·rē, mou′rē) *n.* **1.** One of an aboriginal, light brown people of New Zealand, chiefly Polynesian mixed with Melanesian. **2.** The Polynesian language of these people. — *adj.* Of or pertaining to the Maoris or their language.
map (map) *n.* **1.** A representation on a plane surface of any region, as of the earth's surface; a chart. **2.** Anything resembling a map. **3.** *Slang* The face. — **off the map** Out of existence. — *v.t.* **mapped, map·ping** **1.** To make a map of. **2.** To plan in detail: often with *out.* [< OF < Med.L *mappa* (*mundi*) map (of the world)]
ma·ple (mā·pəl) *n.* **1.** Any of numerous deciduous trees of the north temperate zone, with opposite leaves and a fruit of two joined samaras, as the sugar maple, etc. **2.** The wood of these trees. **3.** The amber-yellow color of the finished wood. **4.** The flavor of the sap of the sugar maple. [OE *mapul* (*trēow*) maple (tree)]
maple sugar Sugar made from the sap of the sugar maple.
maple syrup The refined sap of the sugar maple.
ma·quis (mȧ·kē′) *n.* A zone of shrubby, mostly evergreen plants in the Mediterranean region, known as cover for game, bandits, etc. [< F < Ital. *macchia* thicket]
Ma·quis (mȧ·kē′) *n. pl.* **·quis** **1.** The French resistance movement against the Germans during World War II. **2.** A member of this group. [< MAQUIS]
mar (mär) *v.t.* **marred, mar·ring** **1.** To do harm to; dam-age. **2.** To injure so as to deface. — *n.* A disfiguring mark; blemish. [OE *mierran* to hinder] — **mar′rer** *n.*
mar·a·bou (mar′ə·bo͞o) *n.* **1.** A stork of Africa, whose soft, white, lower tail and wing feathers are used in millinery. **2.** A plume from the marabou. **3.** The adjutant (def. 2). Also **mar′a·bout** (-bo͞ot). [< F *marabou, marabout* hermit]
ma·ra·ca (mə·rä′kə, *Pg.* mä·rä·kä′) *n.* A percussion in-strument made of a gourd or gourd-shaped rattle with beans or beads inside it. [< Pg *maracá,* ? < Tupi]
mar·a·schi·no (mar′ə·skē′nō) *n.* A cordial distilled from the fermented juice of a small wild cherry and flavored with the cracked pits. [< Ital. < *marasca.* See MARASCA.]
maraschino cherries Cherries preserved in a syrup usu. flavored with imitation maraschino.
mar·a·thon (mar′ə·thon) *n.* **1.** A footrace of 26 miles, 385 yards: so called from a messenger's run from Marathon to Athens to announce the Athenian victory over the Persians, 490 B.C. **2.** Any endurance contest.
Mar·a·thon (mar′ə·thon) A plain in Attica, Greece, scene of decisive victory of the Athenians over the Persians, 490 B.C.
ma·raud (mə·rôd′) *v.i.* **1.** To rove in search of plunder. — *v.t.* **2.** To invade for plunder. — *n.* A foray. [< F < *ma-raud* rogue] — **ma·raud′er** *n.*
mar·ble (mär′bəl) *n.* **1.** A compact, granular, partly crys-tallized limestone occurring in many colors, used for build-ing, sculpture, etc. **2.** A piece, block, statue, etc., of this stone. **3.** A small ball of this stone, or of glass, porcelain, etc. **4.** *pl.* A boys' game played with balls of glass, etc. — *v.* **·bled, ·bling** *v.t.* **1.** To color or vein in imitation of marble, as book edges. — *v.i.* **2.** To be flecked with fat: said of meat. — *adj.* **1.** Made of or consisting of marble. **2.** Re-sembling marble as to chilliness, lack of feeling, etc. [< OF < L < Gk. *marmaros,* lit., sparkling stone] — **mar′bly** *adj.*

marble cake A cake made of light and dark batter mixed to give a marblelike appearance.
mar·ble·ize (mär′bəl·īz) *v.t. & v.i.* **·ized, ·iz·ing** *U.S.* To marble.
mar·ca·site (mär′kə·sīt) *n.* **1.** A pale, bronze-yellow, iron disulfide, FeS_2: also called *white iron pyrites.* **2.** An ornament made of crystallized marcasite or of polished steel. [< Med.L *marcasita*]
mar·cel (mär·sel′) *v.t.* **·celled, ·cel·ling** To dress (the hair) in even, continuous waves by means of special irons. [after M. *Marcel,* 19th c. French hairdresser] **— mar·cel′ler** *n.*
march[1] (märch) *v.i.* **1.** To walk or proceed with measured, regular steps, as a soldier or body of troops. **2.** To walk in a solemn or dignified manner. **3.** To advance steadily. **—** *v.t.* **4.** To cause to march. **—** *n.* **1.** The act of marching. **2.** A regular, measured step, as of a body of troops. **3.** The distance passed over in marching: a full day's *march.* **4.** Onward progress: the *march* of events. **5.** A musical composition for marching. [< MF *marcher* to walk, orig., to trample] **— mar′cher** *n.*
march[2] (märch) *n.* A region or district lying along a boundary line; frontier. Also **march′land′** (-land′). [< OF < OHG *marka* mark]
March (märch) The third month of the year, containing 31 days. [< AF, OF < L *Martius* (*mensis*) (month) of Mars < *Mars* Roman god of war]
mar·che·se (mär·kā′zā) *n. pl.* **·che·si** (-kā′zē) *Italian* A marquis. **— mar·che′sa** (-zä) *n.fem.*
Mar·ches·van (mär·khesh′vən) Heshwan. See (Hebrew) CALENDAR.
mar·chion·ess (mär′shən·is) *n.* **1.** The wife or widow of a marquis. **2.** A woman having in her own right the rank corresponding to that of a marquis. [< Med.L *marchionissa* < *marchio, -onis* captain of the marches]
march·pane (märch′pān) *n.* Marzipan. [< MF < Ital. *marzapane.* See MARZIPAN.]
Mar·di gras (mär′dē grä′) Shrove Tuesday, the last day before Lent, often a carnival. [< F, lit., fat Tuesday]
mare[1] (mâr) *n.* The female of the horse and other equine animals. [OE *miere,* fem. of *mearh* horse]
mar·e[2] (mâr′ē) *n. pl.* **mar·i·a** (mâr′ē·ə) Any of a number of dark, seemingly flat areas of the moon's surface. [< L, sea; because of their resemblance to seas]
mare's nest **1.** A discovery that proves worthless or false. **2.** Loosely, a cluttered and confusing mess.
mare's-tail (mârz′tāl′) *n. Meteorol.* Long, fibrous, cirrus clouds, supposed to indicate rain.
mar·ga·rine (mär′jə·rin, -rēn, -gə-) *n.* **1.** A substitute for butter, made from vegetable oils and milk. **2.** Oleomargarine. Also **mar·ga·rin** (mär′jə·rin, -gə-). [< F]
mar·gin (mär′jin) *n.* **1.** The part of a page around the body of printed or written text. **2.** A bounding line or surface; border. **3.** An extra amount of something, as space, time, money, etc. **4.** A limiting or end point; limit. **5.** In commerce, the difference between the cost and selling price of a commodity. **6.** In the stock market, security deposited with a broker to protect him against loss in trading. **—** *v.t.* **1.** To furnish with a margin. **2.** To enter, place, or specify on the margin of a page, as a note. **3.** In the stock market, to deposit a margin upon. [< L *margo*]
mar·gi·nal (mär′jə·nəl) *adj.* **1.** Pertaining to or constituting a margin. **2.** Situated or written at or on a margin. Also *Archaic* **mar′gent** (-jənt). **3.** Having relatively low quality or value; meager. **4.** *Econ.* Barely profitable. [< F] **— mar′gin·al′i·ty** *n.* **mar′gin·al·ly** *adv.*
mar·gi·na·li·a (mär′jə·nā′lē·ə, -nāl′yə) *n.pl.* Marginal notes.
marginal land *Econ.* Land so poor as to remain unused until the lack of more desirable land forces its development.
mar·grave (mär′grāv) *n.* **1.** Formerly, the lord or governor of a German mark, march, or border. **2.** A hereditary title of certain princes of the Holy Roman Empire. [< MDu. *marke* march[2] + *graf* count]
mar·gra·vi·ate (mär·grā′vē·it) *n.* The territory of a margrave. Also **mar·gra·vate** (mär′grə·vāt).
mar·gue·rite (mär′gə·rēt′) *n.* Any of several flowers, esp. the oxeye daisy. [< F pearl, daisy]
Mar·i·an (mâr′ē·ən) *n.* A worshiper or devotee of the Virgin Mary. **—** *adj.* Of or pertaining to the Virgin Mary.
mar·i·gold (mar′ə·gōld) *n.* **1.** Any of several plants of the composite family with golden-yellow flowers. **2.** Any plant resembling these. [< Virgin Mary + GOLD]
mar·i·jua·na (mar′ə·wä′nə, *Sp.* mä′rē·hwä′nä) *n.* **1.** Hemp (def. 1). **2.** The dried leaves and flower tops of this plant, capable of producing disorienting or hallucinogenic effects when smoked in cigarettes or ingested. Also **ma′·ri·hua′na.** [< Am. Sp. *marihuana, mariguana*]
ma·rim·ba (mə·rim′bə) *n.* A form of xylophone having a resonator beneath each tuned bar. [< Bantu *marimba, malimba,* pl. of *limba,* kind of musical instrument]
ma·ri·na (mə·rē′nə) *n. U.S.* A docking area or basin for small vessels. [< Ital., seacoast < L *marinus.* See MARINE.]
mar·i·nade (mar′ə·nād′) *n.* **1.** A brine pickle some[...] flavored with wine, oil, spices, etc., in which meat or fi[...] soaked before cooking. **2.** Pickled meat or fish. [...] **·nad·ed, ·nad·ing** To marinate. [< F < Sp. *mari*[...] pickle in brine]
mar·i·nate (mar′ə·nāt) *v.t.* **·nat·ed, ·nat·ing** **1.** To [...] (food) in marinade. **2.** To allow, as salad, to soak in F[...] dressing before serving. [< Ital. *marinare*]
ma·rine (mə·rēn′) *adj.* **1.** Of, pertaining to, existing [...] formed by the sea. **2.** Pertaining to the navigation o[...] dling of ships on the sea; nautical. **3.** Relating to the [...] naval. **4.** Used or intended for use at sea or in navig[...] **5.** Serving aboard ship. **—** *n.* **1.** A soldier trained f[...] vice at sea and on land; a member of the Marine Corps[...] **Ma·rine′.** **2.** Shipping vessels, shipping, or the nav[...] lectively. **3.** A seascape. **4.** The department of naval a[...] in some countries. [< OF < L *mare, maris* sea]
— Syn. (adj.) Maritime, nautical, naval.
Marine Corps A branch of the U.S. Navy, made up of [...] bat troops, air forces, etc., under their own officers: offic[...] the *United States Marine Corps.*
mar·i·ner (mar′ə·nər) *n.* One who navigates or assi[...] navigating a ship; sailor; seaman. [< OF *marinier*]
mar·i·o·nette (mar′ē·ə·net′) *n.* A small jointed hum[...] animal figure of wood, cloth, etc., used in shows anc[...] mated by manipulating strings: also called *puppet.* [...] *marionnette,* dim. of *Marion,* dim. of *Marie*]
Mar·i·po·sa lily (mar′ə·pō·sə, -zə) Any of various lilia[...] Mexican and Californian plants. Also **Mariposa tulip.**
mar·i·tal (mar′ə·təl) *adj.* Of or pertaining to mar[...] [< L *maritus* husband, orig., married] **— mar′i·tal·ly**
mar·i·time (mar′ə·tīm) *adj.* **1.** Situated on or nea[...] sea. **2.** Of or pertaining to the sea, its navigation, comm[...] etc. **— Syn.** See MARINE. [< MF < L *mare, maris* s[...]
Maritime Provinces New Brunswick, Nova Scotia[...] Prince Edward Island on the Atlantic coast of Canada
Mar·i·tim·er (mar′ə·tī′mər) *n.* A resident or native o[...] Maritime Provinces.
mar·jo·ram (mär′jər·əm) *n.* Any of several perennial [...] of the mint family, one of which, **sweet marjoram,** is us[...] cookery. [< OF *majorane,* ult. origin uncertain]
mark[1] (märk) *n.* **1.** A visible trace, impression, or figu[...] something, as a line, scratch, spot, or dot. **2.** An identif[...] symbol, seal, inscription, or label; trademark. **3.** A cro[...] other sign made by one who cannot write. **4.** A letter, [...] ber, or symbol used to indicate achievement, quality, de[...] etc., as of a student's work. **5.** A symbol, written or pri[...] **6.** An object, point, sign, etc., serving to indicate, guid[...] direct. **7.** That which indicates the presence of a t[...] quality, process, etc.: a *mark* of distinction. **8.** A v[...] indication of some quality, trait, position, etc.: the *ma*[...] an outcast. **9.** That which is aimed at, or toward w[...] effort is directed. **10.** A standard or criterion of qua[...] performance, etc. **11.** *Informal* A person easily dupe[...] victimized: a *mark* for every schemer. **12.** In track sp[...] the starting line of the contest. **13.** *Naut.* A knot, t[...] rag, etc., on a lead line at intervals to indicate fathon[...] depth. **14.** Notice; attention; heed: worthy of *mark.* **beside the mark** **1.** Missing the point aimed at. **2.** Ir[...] vant. **— hit the mark** **1.** To be accurate. **2.** To ach[...] one's goal. **— to leave** (or **make**) **a mark** To leave or m[...] an impression; influence. **— to make one's mark** To [...] ceed. **— of mark** Having, or worthy of distinction, ren[...] etc. **— up to the mark** Up to standard; in good healt[...] condition, etc. **— wide of the mark** **1.** Striking far [...] the point aimed at. **2.** Irrelevant. **—** *v.t.* **1.** To ma[...] mark or marks on. **2.** To trace the boundaries of; set li[...] to: often with *out.* **3.** To indicate or show by a mark or s[...] **4.** To characterize; distinguish: a year *marked* by g[...] events. **5.** To designate, appoint, or select, as if by m[...] ing: to be *marked* for death. **6.** To pay attention to; no[...] heed. **7.** To make known or clear; manifest; display. [...] To apply or attach a price tag, identification label, etc., t[...] article. **9.** To evaluate by giving marks to. **10.** To [...] (record or score) in various games. **11.** To produce [...] drawing, writing, etc. **—** *v.i.* **12.** To take notice; pay [...] tention; consider. **13.** To make a mark or marks. **14.** [...] keep score in games. **— to mark down** **1.** To note dow[...] writing. **2.** To put a lower price on, as for sale. **— to m[...] time** **1.** To keep time by moving the feet but not advanc[...] **2.** To pause in action or progress temporarily. **— to m[...] up** **1.** To make marks on; scar. **2.** To increase the pric[...] [ME < OE *mearc,* orig., boundary] **— mark′er** *n.*
mark[2] (märk) *n.* The former standard monetary unit [...] silver coin of Germany, equivalent to 100 pfennigs, su[...] seded after World War II by the deutschemark in West [...] many and a deutschemark of different value in East Germa[...] [OE *marc* a unit of weight]
Mark (märk) The evangelist who wrote the second of [...] gospel narratives in the New Testament: called **Saint Ma[...]** **—** *n.* The second Gospel of the New Testament.

·ked (märkt) *adj.* **1.** Clearly evident; noticeable. **2.** ving a mark or marks. **— a marked man** One singled out vengeance, punishment, etc. **— mark·ed·ly** (mär′ked·lē) **— mark′ed·ness** *n.*

·ket (mär′kit) *n.* **1.** Trade and commerce in a specific vice or commodity: the boat *market*; also, trade and comrce generally: with *the.* **2.** A region where one can buy or ; also, a category of persons, institutions, etc., considered ouyers: the college *market.* **3.** The state of trade: a brisk *rket.* **4.** A place where something is offered for sale. **5.** ublic gathering, often weekly, for buying and selling. **6.** rket value (which see). **— in the market** Seeking to buy. **on the market** Up for sale. **—** *v.t.* **1.** To sell. **—** *v.i.* **2.** deal in a market. **3.** To buy household provisions. [ME AF < L < *merx, mercis* merchandise]

·ket·a·ble (mär′kit·ə·bəl) *adj.* Suitable for sale; in nand. **— mar′ket·a·bil′i·ty** *n.*

·ket·place (mär′kit·plās′) *n.* **1.** A market (def. 4). The imagined place where ideas, opinions, works, etc., tested and traded. Also **market place.**

rket value The amount that can be obtained for goods the open market. Also **market price.**

rk·ing (mär′king) *n.* **1.** A mark or an arrangement of rks. **2.** *Often pl.* The color pattern on a bird, animal, . **3.** The act of making a mark.

rk·ka (märk′kä) *n.* The standard monetary unit of land, equivalent to 100 pennia. [< Finnish < Sw. *mark*]

rks·man (märks′mən) *n. pl.* **·men** (-mən) **1.** One lled in hitting the mark, as with a rifle or other weapon. *Mil.* In the U.S. Army, the lowest of three grades for l in the use of small arms. **— marks′man·ship** *n.* **— rks′wom′an** (-wŏŏm′ən) *n.fem.*

rk·up (märk′up′) *n.* **1.** A raising of price. **2.** The ount of price increase.

rl (märl) *n.* **1.** An earthy deposit containing lime, clay, d sand, used as fertilizer. **2.** A soft, crumbly soil. **3.** *etic* Earth. **—** *v.t.* To spread with marl. [< OF < LL L *marga* marl] **— marl′y, mar·la′ceous** (-lā′shəs) *adj.*

r·lin (mär′lin) *n.* Any of various deep-sea game fishes; ., the **blue marlin** of the Atlantic, and the **striped marlin** the Pacific. [< MARLINE(SPIKE); because of its shape]

r·line (mär′lin) *n. Naut.* A small rope of two strands osely twisted together, used for winding ropes, cables, etc. Du. *marren* to tie + *lijn* a line]

r·line·spike (mär′lin·spīk′) *n. Naut.* A sharp-pointed n pin used in splicing ropes. Also **mar′lin·spike′, mar′·g·spike′** (-ling-).

r·ma·lade (mär′mə·lād) *n.* A preserve made by boiling th sugar the pulp and rind of fruits, usu. citrus fruits, to e consistency of jam. [< MF < Pg *marmelada*]

r·mo·re·al (mär·môr′ē·əl, -mō′rē-) *adj.* Pertaining to, de of, or resembling marble. Also **mar·mo′re·an** (-môr′ē-, ō′rē-). [< L *marmoreus* < *marmor.* See MARBLE.]

r·mo·set (mär′mə·zet) *n.* Any of various small Central d South American monkeys with soft, woolly hair and a g hairy tail. [< OF *marmouset* grotesque figure]

r·mot (mär′mət) *n.* Any of various rodents, as the oodchuck or ground hog. [Fusion of OF *marmotte* monkey d Romansch *murmont* marmot]

·roon[1] (mə·rōōn′) *v.t.* **1.** To put ashore and abandon on desolate island or coast. **2.** To abandon; leave helpless. *n.* One of a class of Negroes, chiefly fugitive slaves or eir descendants, living wild in the mountains of some West dies islands and of Guiana. [< Am. Sp. *cimarron* wild]

·roon[2] (mə·rōōn′) *n.* A dull, dark red color. **—** *adj.* aving a dull, dark red color. [< F *marron* chestnut]

r·quee (mär·kē′) *n.* **1.** A canopy used as a shelter over e sidewalk in front of a theater, hotel, etc. **2.** A large field nt, as one used at outdoor parties. [< *marquise* canopy]

r·quess (mär′kwis) See MARQUIS.

r·que·try (mär′kə·trē) *n.* Inlaid work of wood often terspersed with stones, ivory, etc., esp. as used in furniture. so **mar′que·te·rie.** [< MF < *marqueter* to variegate]

r·quis (mär′kwis, *Fr.* mår·kē′) *n.* The title of a noblean next in rank below a duke. Also, *Brit., marquess.* [< F < Med.L *markensis* commander of the marches]

r·quis (mär′kwis) *n.* An important variety of wheat, st developed in Canada.

r·quis·ate (mär′kwiz·it) *n.* The rank of a marquis.

r·quise (mär·kēz′) *n.* **1.** The wife or widow of a French arquis. **2.** An ornamental hood over a door; a marquee.

r·qui·sette (mär′ki·zet′, -kwi-) *n.* A lightweight, openesh fabric of cotton, silk, rayon, or nylon, or a combination these, used for curtains and women's and children's garents. [< F, dim. of *marquise* a marquise]

ar·riage (mar′ij) *n.* **1.** The state of being married; a gal contract, entered into by a man and a woman, to live gether as husband and wife; wedlock. ◆ Collateral adjectives: *hymeneal, marital.* **2.** The act of marrying; also, the accompanying rites or festivities; wedding; nuptials. **3.** Any close union. [< OF < L *maritare* to marry]

mar·riage·a·ble (mar′ij·ə·bəl) *adj.* Fitted or suitable for marriage. **— mar′riage·a·bil′i·ty, mar′riage·a·ble·ness** *n.*

mar·ried (mar′ēd) *adj.* **1.** United in matrimony; having a spouse. **2.** Of or pertaining to marriage or to persons united in marriage. **3.** Closely related or joined.

mar·ron (mar′ən, *Fr.* må·rôn′) *n. Often pl.* A large variety of chestnut, esp. when preserved in syrup, etc. [< F]

mar·row (mar′ō) *n.* **1.** A soft, vascular tissue found in the central cavities of bones. **2.** The essence of anything; pith. **3.** Vitality. [OE *mearg*] **— mar′row·y** *adj.*

mar·row·bone (mar′ō·bōn′) *n.* **1.** A bone containing edible marrow. **2.** *pl.* One's knees: used humorously.

mar·row·fat (mar′ō·fat′) *n.* A variety of green pea, having a large, succulent seed. Also **marrow pea.**

mar·ry (mar′ē) *v.* **·ried, ·ry·ing** *v.t.* **1.** To accept as husband or wife; take in marriage. **2.** To join as husband and wife in marriage. **3.** To give in marriage. **4.** To unite closely. **—** *v.i.* **5.** To take a husband or wife. **6.** To join or unite closely. [< OF < L < *maritus* husband, married]

Mars (märz) In Roman mythology, the god of war: identified with the Greek *Ares.* **—** *n.* The seventh largest planet of the solar system and fourth from the sun. See PLANET.

Mar·sa·la (mär·sä′lä) *n.* A dark-colored, sweet, heavy wine, originally made in Marsala, Sicily.

Mar·seil·laise (mär′sə·lāz′, *Fr.* mår·sā·yez′) The national anthem of France, written in 1792 by Rouget de Lisle.

mar·seille (mär·sāl′) *n.* A thick cotton fabric. Also **mar·seilles** (mär·sālz′). [after *Marseille,* France]

marsh (märsh) *n.* A tract of low, wet land; swamp. [OE *mersc, merisc*]

mar·shal (mär′shəl) *n.* **1.** In various foreign countries, a military officer of high rank, usu. just below the commander in chief: a field *marshal.* **2.** *U.S.* **a** An officer of the Federal courts, assigned to a judicial district and having duties similar to those of a sheriff. **b** In some cities, the chief of the police or fire department. **3.** An officer authorized to organize or regulate processions, ceremonies, etc. **4.** A title of certain royal court or household officials, often in charge of matters of protocol. **—** *v.t.* **mar·shaled** or **·shalled, mar·shal·ing** or **·shal·ling** **1.** To arrange or dispose in order, as facts. **2.** To array or draw up, as troops for battle. **3.** To lead; usher. [< OF < Med.L < OHG < *marah* horse + *scalh* servant] **— mar′shal·cy, mar′shal·ship** *n.* **— mar′·shal·er, mar′shal·ler** *n.*

Marshal of the Royal Canadian Air Force In the Royal Canadian Air Force, a commissioned officer of the highest rank. See table at GRADE.

marsh gas Methane.

marsh hawk A marsh-dwelling American hawk having gray or brown plumage, a white rump, and rounded wings.

marsh·mal·low (märsh′mel′ō, -mal′ō) *n.* **1.** A confection made of starch, sugar, corn syrup, and gelatin, and coated with powdered sugar. **2.** A sweetmeat formerly made from the root of the marsh mallow.

marsh mallow A plant of the mallow family growing in marshy places.

marsh marigold A showy swamp plant of the crowfoot family, having yellow flowers: also called *cowslip.*

marsh·y (mär′shē) *adj.* **marsh·i·er, marsh·i·est** **1.** Of, pertaining to, or containing a marsh. **2.** Swampy; boggy. **3.** Growing or produced in a marsh. **— marsh′i·ness** *n.*

mar·su·pi·al (mär·sōō′pē·əl) *n.* Any member of an order of mammals, as the kangaroos, opossums, wombats, etc., whose females carry their undeveloped young in a marsupium. **—** *adj.* Having a marsupium or pouch. **— mar·su′pi·a′li·an** (-ā′lē·ən), **mar·su′pi·an** *adj. & n.*

mar·su·pi·um (mär·sōō′pē·əm) *n. pl.* **·pi·a** (-pē·ə) A pouchlike receptacle on the abdomen of female marsupials, containing the teats and used for carrying the young. [< L < Gk. *marsypion,* dim. of *marsipos* bag]

mart (märt) *n.* A market. [< MDu. < L *mercatus*]

mar·ten (mär′ten) *n.* **1.** A weasellike carnivorous mammal having arboreal habits, as the **pine marten** of eastern North America. **2.** The valuable, dark brown fur of a marten. [< OF *martrine* of the marten < WGmc.]

Mar·tha (mär′thə) A sister of Lazarus and Mary, who served Jesus at Bethany. *Luke* x 38–41.

mar·tial (mär′shəl) *adj.* **1.** Of, pertaining to, or concerned with war or the military life. **2.** Suggestive of or suitable for war or military operations. **3.** Of or characteristic of a warrior. [< OF < L *martialis* pertaining to Mars] **— mar′·tial·ism** *n.* **— mar′tial·ist** *n.* **— mar′tial·ly** *adv.*

martial law Temporary jurisdiction or rule by military forces over the citizens of an area where civil law and order no longer function or exist.

Mar·tian (mär′shən) *adj. Astron.* Of or pertaining to the planet Mars. — *n.* One of the supposed inhabitants of Mars. [< L *Martius*]

mar·tin (mär′tən) *n.* **1.** Any of certain birds of the swallow family, having a tail that is less forked than that of the common swallow; esp., the **house martin** of Europe, and the **purple martin** of North America. **2.** Any of various similar birds. [< F]

mar·ti·net (mär′tə·net′) *n.* **1.** A strict military disciplinarian. **2.** One who demands rigid adherence to rules, etc. [after General Jean *Martinet*, 17th c. French drillmaster]

mar·tin·gale (mär′tən·gāl) *n.* A forked strap that prevents a horse from rearing its head, connecting the head gear with the bellyband. Also **mar′tin·gal** (-gal). [< F < Provençal *martengalo*, appar. fem. of *martengo* an inhabitant of Martigues, miserly person < Sp. *almartaga* < Arabic]

mar·ti·ni (mär·tē′nē) *n. pl.* **·nis** A cocktail made of gin and dry vermouth, usu. served with an olive or lemon peel. [after *Martini* and Rossi, a company making vermouth]

mar·tyr (mär′tər) *n.* **1.** One who submits to death rather than renounce his religion. **2.** One who dies, suffers, or sacrifices everything for a principle, cause, etc. **3.** One who suffers much, as from ill health or misfortune. — *v.t.* **1.** To make a martyr of. **2.** To torture or persecute. [OE < LL < Gk. *martyr*, Aeolic form of *martyrs, martyros* witness] — **mar′tyr·dom** (-dəm) *n.*

mar·tyr·ize (mär′tər·īz) *v.* **·ized, ·iz·ing** *v.t.* **1.** To make a martyr of. — *v.i.* **2.** To become a martyr. — **mar′tyr·i·za′tion** *n.*

mar·vel (mär′vəl) *v.* **mar·veled** or **·velled, mar·vel·ing** or **·vel·ling** *v.i.* **1.** To be filled with wonder, surprise, etc. — *v.t.* **2.** To wonder at or about: with a clause as object. — *n.* That which excites wonder; a prodigy. [< OF < L *mirabilia* neut. pl. of *mirabilis* wonderful]

mar·vel·ous (mär′vəl·əs) *adj.* **1.** Causing astonishment and wonder; amazing; extraordinary. **2.** Miraculous; incredible. **3.** *Informal* Very good; excellent; admirable. Also **mar′vel·lous.** — **mar′vel·ous·ly** *adv.* — **mar′vel·ous·ness** *n.*

Marx·ism (märk′siz·əm) *n.* The body of socialist doctrines formulated by Karl Marx and Friedrich Engels, the basic tenets of which are dialectical materialism, the theory of class struggle, and the labor theory of value. — **Marx′ist, Marx·ian** (mark′sē·ən) *n.* & *adj.*

Marx·ism-Len·in·ism (märk′siz·əm·len′in·iz·əm) *n.* The modification of Marxist philosophy or doctrines attributed to Lenin. — **Marx′ist-Len′in·ist** *n., adj.*

Mar·y (mâr′ē) The mother of Jesus: also *Virgin Mary.*

Mary The sister of Lazarus and Martha. *Luke* x 39–42.

Mary Mag·da·lene (mag′də·lēn, mag′də·lē′nē) A woman from Magdala out of whom Jesus cast seven devils, often identified with the penitent sinner whom Jesus forgave.

mar·zi·pan (märt′sə·pan, mär′zə-) *n.* A confection of grated almonds, sugar, and white of eggs, usu. made into a paste and molded into various shapes: also called *marchpane.* [< G < Ital. < Med.L *matapanus* a Venetian coin]

-mas *combining form* Mass; a (specified) festival or its celebration: *Christmas.* [< MASS²]

mas·car·a (mas·kar′ə) *n.* A cosmetic preparation used to darken or tint the eyelashes and eyebrows. [< Sp. *máscara* mask < Arabic *maskharah* buffoon]

mas·cot (mas′kot, -kət) *n.* A person, animal, or object thought to bring good luck by its presence. [< F < Provençal *mascot*, dim. of *masco* sorcerer, lit., mask]

mas·cu·line (mas′kyə·lin) *adj.* **1.** Of or pertaining to the male sex; male. **2.** Of, pertaining to, typical of, or appropriate for men or boys: *masculine* sports. **3.** Mannish: said of a female. **4.** *Gram.* Applicable to males only or to persons or things classified, as in declension, as male. — *n. Gram.* **1.** The masculine gender. **2.** A word or form belonging to the masculine gender. [< OF < L < *masculus* male] — **mas′cu·line·ly** *adv.* — **mas′cu·lin′i·ty, mas′cu·line·ness** *n.*

masculine rhyme Rhyme in which the primary stress and the rhyme fall upon the final or only syllable, as in *breaks, takes* and *alert, convert.*

ma·ser (mā′zər) *n. Physics* Any of various devices that generate or amplify electromagnetic waves of precise frequency without loss of frequency and phase, by using the excess energy of an atomic or molecular system. [< *m(icrowave) a(mplification by) s(timulated) e(mission of) r(adiation)*]

mash (mash) *n.* **1.** A soft, pulpy mixture or mass. **2.** A mixture of meal, bran, etc., and water, fed warm to horses and cattle. **3.** Crushed or ground grain or malt, steeped in hot water to produce wort for making beer. — *v.t.* **1.** To crush into a mash or pulp. **2.** To steep (malt, grain meal, etc.) in hot water to produce wort. [OE *max-, māsc* (*wyrt*) mash (wort), infused malt]

mash·er (mash′ər) *n.* **1.** One who or that which mashes. **2.** *Slang* A man who flirts or attempts familiarities, usu. with women unknown to him.

mash·ie (mash′ē) *n.* In golf, a five iron. Also **mash′·y** [? Alter. of F *massue* club < Celtic]

mask (mask, mäsk) *n.* **1.** A covering used to conceal all or part of the face; esp.: **a** A covering, often grotesque or comic, worn at a masquerade, at Halloween, etc. **b** A large, headlike covering for an actor's face, used to represent a specific character or trait, as in Greek and Roman drama. **c** A covering made of heavy wire or other material, worn to [pro]tect the face from a fencing foil, baseball, glass, etc. **d** A [death] mask. **2.** A cast of a face, usu. made of plaster. **3.** [That] which hides or conceals something from the sight or m[ind]: under the *mask* of piety. **4.** One who wears a mask. [5.] masquerade. **6.** See MASQUE. **7.** *Mil.* A screen or cove[r] concealing any military installation or operation. — *v.t* To cover (the face, head, etc.) with a mask. **2.** To disg[uise] — *v.i.* **3.** To put on a mask; assume a disguise. [< Ital. < Arabic *maskharah* buffoon] — **masked** *adj.* **mas′ker** *n.*

MASKS
a Greek tragedy. *b* Greek comed[y] *c* Tibetan ceremonial. *d* Ancient Shinto. *e* Domino.

mask·ing tape (mas′king, mäs′-) An adhesive tap[e] [to] cover those parts of a surface not to be painted, sprayed,

mas·o·chism (mas′ə·kiz′əm) *n.* **1.** *Psychol.* A conditi[on in] which sexual gratification depends largely on underg[oing] physical pain or humiliation. **2.** A tendency to de[rive] pleasure from one's own suffering. [after Leopold [von] Sacher-*Masoch*, 1835–95, Austrian novelist, who descri[bed] this condition] — **mas′o·chist** *n.* — **mas′o·chis′tic** *adj.* **mas′o·chis′ti·cal·ly** (-kə·lē, -klē) *adv.*

ma·son (mā′sən) *n.* **1.** One skilled in building with st[one,] brick, concrete, etc. **2.** A stonecutter. — *v.t.* To buil[d] or strengthen with brick, stone, etc. [< OF < Me[d.L] *matio, macio, -onis*, prob. < Gmc.]

Ma·son (mā′sən) *n.* Freemason. — **Ma′son·ry** *n.*

ma·son·ic (mə·son′ik) *adj.* **1.** *Usu. cap.* Of, pertaining [to,] or like Freemasons or Freemasonry. **2.** Of or pertai[ning] to masons or masonry.

Ma·son·ite (mā′sən·īt) *n.* A tough fiberboard made fr[om] wood fibers, used as a building and construction mate[rial:] a trade name. Also **ma′son·ite.**

Ma·son jar (mā′sən) A glass jar having a tightly fitt[ing] screw top, used for canning and preserving. [after Joh[n] *Mason*, 19th c. American inventor]

ma·son·ry (mā′sən·rē) *n. pl.* **·ries 1.** The art or work [of a] mason. **2.** That which is built by masons.

masque (mask, mäsk) *n.* **1.** An elaborately staged [dra]matic performance, popular during the 16th and 17th [cen]turies in England; also, something written for this. **2** masquerade. Also spelled *mask.* [See MASK.]

mas·quer·ade (mas′kə·rād′, mäs′-) *n.* **1.** A social gat[her]ing in which the guests are masked and dressed in fa[ncy] costumes. **2.** The costumes worn at such a gathering. [3.] A false show, disguise, or pretense. Also called *mask, mas[que]* — *v.i.* **·ad·ed, ·ad·ing 1.** To take part in a masquerade. [2.] To wear a mask or disguise. **3.** To disguise one's true ch[ar]acter; assume a false appearance. [Alter. of F *mascarad[e]* Sp. < *máscara* mask] — **mas′quer·ad′er** *n.*

mass (mas, mäs) *n.* **1.** A body of matter having no defi[nite] shape but relatively large in size. **2.** An assemblage of [in]dividual parts or objects that collectively make up a si[ngle] body. **3.** A great amount or number of anything. **4.** [The] principal or greater part of anything; majority. **5.** [The] volume or magnitude of a solid body; bulk; size. **6.** [In] painting, the solid, unified portions of color or light i[n a] composition. **7.** *Physics* The measure of the inertia o[f a] body, expressed as the quotient of the weight of the b[ody] divided by the acceleration due to gravity. — **the mass[es]** The great body or majority of ordinary people. — *adj.* [1.] Attended by, designed for, characteristic of, or affectin[g a] large mass of people. **2.** Done in a large-scale manner; p[ro]duced in large amounts. **3.** Total; all-over: the *mass* eff[ect.] — *v.t.* & *v.i.* To form into a mass; assemble. [< OF < [L] *massa*, prob. < Gk. *maza* barley cake]

Mass (mas, mäs) *n. Eccl.* **1.** In the Roman Catholic a[nd] some Anglican churches, the eucharistic liturgy, consist[ing] of various prayers and ritual ceremonies and regarded a[s a] commemoration or repetition of Christ's sacrifice on [the] Cross. **2.** A celebration of this liturgy. **3.** A musical s[et]ting for some of the fixed portions of this liturgy. [OE < LL < L *missa*, pp. fem. of *mittere* to send, dismiss < *missa est* go, you are dismissed; said by the priest]

Mas·sa·chu·set (mas′ə·chōō′sit) *n.* **1.** One of a large tr[ibe] of North American Indians of Algonquian stock, formerly [in]habiting the region around Massachusetts Bay. **2.** Th[eir] language. Also **Mas′sa·chu′sett.** [< Algonquian (Mas[sa]chuset) < *mass* big + *wadchu* hill + *es*, dim. + *et* at th[e]

sa·cre (mas′ə·kər) *n.* **1.** A savage and indiscriminate ng of human beings, as in warfare, acts of persecution, nge, etc. **2.** *U.S. Informal* A crushing defeat, as in ts. —*v.t.* **·cred** (-kərd), **·cring** **1.** To kill indiscriminately or in great numbers. **2.** *U.S. Informal* To defeat sely, as in sports. [< MF < OF, ? < *mache-col* butcher acher to smash + *col* neck] —**mas′sa·crer** *n.*

Syn. (noun) A *massacre* is the killing of those who are deless or unresisting, as in barbarous warfare. *Slaughter* may be in the same sense, but frequently is applied to any great loss e in battle, riot, etc. In a more restricted sense, *slaughter* is of the killing of animals for food. *Carnage* retains much of its nal sense of the heaped up bodies of the slain, and refers to esult rather than to the process of a *massacre* or *slaughter*.

sage (mə·säzh′) *n.* A manual or mechanical manipun of parts of the body, as by rubbing, kneading, slap- or the like, used to promote circulation, relax muscles, —*v.t.* **·saged, ·sag·ing** To treat by massage. [< F < < Gk. *massein* to knead] —**mas·sag′er, mas·sag′ist** *n.*

as·sa·geuse (mas′ə·zhœz′) *n.fem.*

seur (ma·sûr′, *Fr.* mȧ·sœr′) *n.* A man who practices ives massage. [< F] —**mas·seuse** (ma·so͞oz′, -so͞os′; mȧ·sœz′) *n.fem.*

sive (mas′iv) *adj.* **1.** Forming or constituting a large s; having great bulk and weight; ponderous. **2.** Relaly large or heavy: a *massive* head. **3.** Imposing or imsive in scale, scope, degree, etc. **4.** *Mineral.* Lacking nite or externally observable crystalline form. **5.** *Geol.* nogeneous, as certain rock formations. **6.** *Pathol.* Exing over or affecting a large area: a *massive* swelling. F *massif*] —**mas′sive·ly** *adv.* —**mas′sive·ness** *n.*

s media The various means of disseminating informa to a wide public audience, as newspapers, radio, etc.

s meeting A large public gathering for the discussion romotion of some topic or cause, usu. political.

s number *Physics* The total number of nucleons of atom; the integer nearest the observed mass of an isotope.

s production The manufacture or production, usu. by hinery, of goods or articles in great numbers or quans. —**mass-pro·duced** (mas′prə·do͞ost′, -dyo͞ost′) *adj.*

s ratio *Aerospace* The ratio of the mass of a rocket at time of liftoff to its mass after the fuel has been used up.

ss spectrograph *Physics* An instrument for deterning the relative masses of electrically charged particles passing a stream of them through a magnetic field and ing the variable deflections from a straight path.

s·y (mas′ē) *adj.* **mass·i·er, mass·i·est** Massive. —**ss′i·ness** *n.*

st[1] (mast, mäst) *n.* **1.** *Naut.* A pole or spar set upright a sailing vessel to sustain the yards, sails, etc. **2.** Any e, upright pole, as of a derrick, crane, etc. —**before the st** Serving as a common sailor. —*v.t.* To furnish with ast or masts. [OE *mæst*]

st[2] (mast, mäst) *n.* The fruit of the oak, beech, etc., en used as food for swine. [OE *mæst* mast, fodder]

st- Var. of MASTO-.

·ta·ba (mas′tə·bə) *n.* In ancient Egypt, an oblong ilding with sloping sides and a flat top, covering the uth of a burial pit and used as a chapel and place of offer-. Also **mas′ta·bah**. [< Arabic *mastabah* bench]

s·ter (mas′tər, mäs′-) *n.* **1.** One who has control, direcn, or authority over someone or something, as over a isehold, an animal, etc. **2.** One exceptionally gifted or lled in an art, science, etc.: a *master* of oratory. **3.** A ftsman or worker whose skill or experience qualifies him practice his craft on his own and to train apprentices. **4.** e who has the ability to control or dispose of something to od advantage. **5.** A teacher or leader in philosophy, reion, etc., who has followers or disciples. **6.** *Chiefly Brit.* male teacher. **7.** One who has received a Master of Arts gree. **8.** One who has charge of or presides over a place, titution, ceremony, etc.: a *master* of ceremonies. **9.** Someng considered as having the power to control or influence: ver let fear be your *master*. **10.** Something, as a matrix, ncil, etc., from which copies or impressions are made. **11.** u. *cap.* A youth or boy; also, a title prefixed to a boy's me. **12.** *Usu. cap.* A title of respect or of address, now nerally replaced by *Mister*. **13.** In the Scottish peerage, e title of the eldest son or heir apparent of a viscount or ron. **14.** A victor or conqueror. **15.** *Law* An officer of e court who assists the judge. —*v.t.* **1.** To bring under ntrol; defeat. **2.** To become expert in: to *master* Greek. To control or govern as a master. —*adj.* **1.** Of, pertaing to, or characteristic of a master. **2.** Having or exercising ntrol. **3.** Principal; main: the *master* plan. **4.** Designatg a device or mechanism that controls, operates, or acts as pattern or norm for something else: a *master* switch. [OE L *magnus* great] —**mas′ter·dom** *n.* —**mas′ter·hood** *n.*

master builder **1.** An architect. **2.** One who supervises building construction.

mas·ter·ful (mas′tər·fəl, mäs′-) *adj.* **1.** Vigorously bold or authoritative in conduct, decision, manner, etc. **2.** Domineering; imperious. **3.** Having or displaying the skill of a master. —**mas′ter·ful·ly** *adv.* —**mas′ter·ful·ness** *n.*

master key A key that will unlock two or more locks, each of which has its own key that fits no other lock.

mas·ter·ly (mas′tər·lē, mäs′-) *adj.* Characteristic of or befitting a master: a *masterly* performance. —*adv.* In a masterly manner. —**mas′ter·li·ness** *n.*

master mechanic An able, experienced mechanic.

mas·ter·mind (mas′tər·mīnd′, mäs′-) *n.* A person of great executive ability; esp., one who plans and directs at the highest levels of policy and strategy. —*v.t.* To plan and direct (a project, etc.) at the highest strategic level.

Master of Arts **1.** A degree given by a college or university to a person who has completed a prescribed course of graduate study of at least one year in the humanities, social sciences, etc. **2.** A person who has received this degree.

master of ceremonies **1.** A person presiding over an entertainment or dinner and introducing the performers or speakers. **2.** A person who supervises the ceremonies at a public or formal function. Also called *emcee*.

Master of Science **1.** A degree given by a college or university to a person who has completed a prescribed course of graduate study of at least one year in science. **2.** A person who has received this degree.

mas·ter·piece (mas′tər·pēs′, mäs′-) *n.* **1.** Something of notable excellence; an unusually brilliant achievement. **2.** Something considered the greatest achievement of its creator. Also **mas′ter·work′**. [Trans. of G *meisterstück*]

mas·ter·ship (mas′tər·ship, mäs′-) *n.* **1.** The state of being a master or ruler. **2.** The status or function of a master. **3.** The skill, experience, or authority of a master.

mas·ter·stroke (mas′tər·strōk′, mäs′-) *n.* A masterly or decisive action or achievement.

mas·ter·y (mas′tər·ē, mäs′-) *n.* *pl.* **·ter·ies** **1.** Superior knowledge or skill. **2.** Victory or superiority, as in a contest. **3.** The act of mastering a craft, technique, etc.

mast·head (mast′hed′, mäst′-) *n.* **1.** *Naut.* The top of a mast. **2.** The part of a periodical that gives the names of the editors, staff, and owners. —*v.t.* To display at the masthead.

mas·tic (mas′tik) *n.* **1.** A small Mediterranean evergreen tree of the cashew family. **2.** The resin obtained from this tree, used in varnishes and as a flavoring agent. [< F < LL < Gk. *mastichē*]

mas·ti·cate (mas′tə·kāt) *v.t.* **·cat·ed, ·cat·ing** **1.** To chew. **2.** To reduce, as rubber, to a pulp by crushing or kneading. [< LL < Gk. *mastichaein* to gnash the teeth] —**mas′ti·ca′·tion** *n.* —**mas′ti·ca′tor** *n.*

mas·ti·ca·to·ry (mas′tə·kə·tôr′ē, -tō′rē) *adj.* **1.** Of or pertaining to mastication. **2.** Adapted for chewing. —*n.* *pl.* **·ries** A substance chewed to increase salivation.

mas·tiff (mas′tif, mäs′-) *n.* A breed of large hunting dogs, having a thickset, heavy body, drooping ears, and pendulous lips. [< OF < L < pp. of *mansuescere* to tame]

mas·ti·tis (mas·tī′tis) *n.* *Pathol.* Inflammation of the breast.

masto- *combining form Med.* The breast or the mammary glands. Also, before vowels, **mast-**. [< Gk. *mastos* breast]

mas·to·don (mas′tə·don) *n.* *Paleontol.* Any of various large, extinct mammals resembling the elephant. [< NL < MAST- + Gk. *odous, odontos* tooth]

mas·toid (mas′toid) *adj.* **1.** *Anat.* Designating a nipple-shaped process of the temporal bone located behind the ear. **2.** Having the shape of a breast or nipple. —*n.* The mastoid process. [< Gk. < *mastos* breast + *eidos* form]

mas·toid·i·tis (mas′toid·ī′tis) *n.* *Pathol.* Inflammation of the mastoid process.

mas·tur·bate (mas′tər·bāt) *v.i.* **·bat·ed, ·bat·ing** To perform masturbation. [< L *masturbatus*, pp. of *masturbari*]

mas·tur·ba·tion (mas′tər·bā′shən) *n.* Stimulation of the sexual organs, usu. by oneself: also called *onanism*. —**mas′·tur·ba′tor** *n.*

ma·su·ri·um (mə·so͝or′ē·əm) *n.* A supposed metallic element whose place in the periodic table is now occupied by technetium. [after *Masuria*, where first found]

mat[1] (mat) *n.* **1.** A flat piece of material made of fiber, rushes, rubber, etc., and used primarily to cover floors; also, a smaller piece of this material, used to sit or lie on. **2.** A thickly padded piece of material placed on the floor for protection in various gymnastic sports. **3.** A small, flat piece of material, as lace, straw, or plastic, used as a table protection, ornament, etc. **4.** Any dense, twisted, or tangled mass, as of hair. —*v.* **mat·ted, mat·ting** *v.t.* **1.** To cover with or as with a mat or mats. **2.** To knot or entangle into a mat. —*v.i.* **3.** To become entangled together. [OE < LL *matta*]

mat[2] (mat) *n.* **1.** A border of cardboard or other material, serving as the frame or part of the frame of a picture. **2.** *Printing* A matrix. **3.** A lusterless, dull, or roughened surface, as on metal or glass. **—*v.t.* mat·ted, mat·ting 1.** To produce a dull surface on, as on metal or glass. **2.** To furnish (a picture) with a mat. **—*adj.*** Having a lusterless surface. [OF, defeated]

mat·a·dor (mat′ə·dôr) *n.* In bullfighting, the man who kills the bull after completing various maneuvers with a cape in order to tire the animal. [< Sp. < *matar* to slay]

match[1] (mach) *n.* **1.** One who or that which is similar to another in some quality or characteristic. **2.** One who or that which is exactly equal to another. **3.** One who or that which is able to cope with or oppose another as an equal. **4.** Either of two things that harmonize or correspond with each other. **5.** A suitable or fit pair. **6.** A game or contest. **7.** A marriage or mating; also, an agreement to marry or mate. **8.** A possible partner in marriage. **—*v.t.* 1.** To be similar to or in accord with in quality, degree, etc. **2.** To make, provide, or select as equals or as suitable for one another: to *match* pearls. **3.** To cause to correspond; adapt: *Match* your expenses to your income. **4.** To compare so as to decide superiority; test. **5.** To set (equal opponents) in opposition. **6.** To equal; oppose successfully. **7.** To flip (a coin or coins) so as to compare or bet on the faces that land upright; also, to flip coins in this manner with (another person). **8.** To place together as mates; marry. **—*v.i.* 9.** To be equal or similar. **10.** To be married; mate. [OE *gemæcca* companion] **—match′a·ble** *adj.* **—match′er** *n.*

match[2] (mach) *n.* **1.** A splinter of soft wood or a piece of waxed thread or cardboard tipped with a combustible composition that ignites by friction. **2.** A wick or cord formerly used for firing cannon. [< OF *mesche* wick]

match·box (mach′boks′) *n.* A small box for matches.

match·less (mach′lis) *adj.* Having no match or equal; peerless. **—match′less·ly** *adv.* **—match′less·ness** *n.*

match·lock (mach′lok′) *n.* **1.** An old type of musket fired by igniting the powder with a slow-burning wick or match. **2.** The gunlock on such a musket.

match·mak·er[1] (mach′mā′kər) *n.* **1.** One who tries to bring about a marriage between other persons. **2.** One who arranges an athletic match. **—match′mak′ing** *adj.* & *n.*

match·mak·er[2] (mach′mā′kər) *n.* One who makes matches for lighting. **—match′mak′ing** *adj.* & *n.*

match play In golf, a form of competitive play in which the score is computed by totaling the number of holes won or lost by each side. Compare MEDAL PLAY.

mate[1] (māt) *n.* **1.** Something matched, paired, or joined with another. **2.** A husband or wife. **3.** The male or female of two animals paired for propagation. **4.** A companion; comrade. **5.** An officer of a merchant vessel, ranking next below the captain. **6.** *Naval* A petty officer. **—*v.* mat·ed, mat·ing *v.t.* 1.** To join together; pair. **2.** To join in marriage. **3.** To unite for breeding, as animals. **—*v.i.* 4.** To marry. **5.** To pair. **6.** To consort; associate. [< MLG < *ge-* together + *mat* meat, food]

mate[2] (māt) *v.t.* **mat·ed, mat·ing** In chess, to checkmate. **—*n.*** A checkmate. **—*interj.*** Checkmate.

ma·te[3] (mä′tā, mat′ā) *n.* **1.** An infusion of the leaves of a Brazilian holly, much used as a beverage in South America. **2.** The plant itself. [< Sp. < Quechua *mati* calabash]

ma·ter (mā′tər, mä′-) *n. Brit. Informal* Mother. [< L]

ma·te·ri·al (mə·tir′ē·əl) *n.* **1.** That of which anything is or may be composed or constructed. **2.** Anything that may be used in creating, working up, or developing something. **3.** *pl.* The tools, instruments, etc., for doing something. **4.** Cloth or fabric. **—*adj.* 1.** Of, pertaining to, or composed of matter; physical. **2.** Of, related to, or affecting the body or sensual appetites: *material* well-being. **3.** Concerned with or devoted to things primarily physical rather than spiritual or intellectual. **4.** Substantial; important. **5.** Relevant; pertinent: with *to.* [< LL < L *materia* matter, stuff]

ma·te·ri·al·ism (mə·tir′ē·əl·iz′əm) *n.* **1.** *Philos.* The doctrine that everything in the universe is reducible to matter and can be explained in terms of physical laws. **2.** Undue regard for the material rather than the spiritual or intellectual aspects of life. **—ma·te′ri·al·ist** *n.* **—ma·te′ri·al·is′tic** *adj.* **—ma·te′ri·al·is′ti·cal·ly** *adv.*

ma·te·ri·al·ize (mə·tir′ē·əl·īz′) *v.* **·ized, ·iz·ing** *v.t.* **1.** To give material or actual form to. **2.** In spiritualism, to cause (a spirit, etc.) to appear in visible form. **3.** To make materialistic. **—*v.i.* 4.** To assume material or visible form; appear. **5.** To take form or shape; be realized. **—ma·te′ri·al·i·za′tion** *n.* **—ma·te′ri·al·iz′er** *n.*

ma·te·ri·al·ly (mə·tir′ē·əl·ē) *adv.* **1.** In an important manner or to a considerable degree. **2.** Physically. **3.** In respect to matter as distinguished from form.

ma·te·ri·a med·i·ca (mə·tir′ē·ə med′i·kə) *Med.* **1.** Substances, as drugs, etc., employed as remedial agents. **2.** The branch of medicine that treats of these substances. [< Med.L < *materia* matter + *medica,* fem. of *medicus* medical]

ma·te·ri·el (mə·tir′ē·el′) *n.* **1.** The equipment and su of a military force. **2.** The equipment of any organiz Also *Fr.* **ma·té·riel** (mȧ·tā·ryel′). [< F, material]

ma·ter·nal (mə·tûr′nəl) *adj.* **1.** Pertaining to a m motherly. **2.** Inherited from one's mother. **3.** C through the relationship of a mother. [< F < L < mother] **—ma·ter′nal·ly** *adv.*

ma·ter·ni·ty (mə·tûr′nə·tē) *n. pl.* **·ties 1.** The st being a mother. **2.** The qualities of a mother. **—*ad*** Fashioned for pregnant women: *maternity* clothes. **2** signed to accommodate women and babies during and childbirth: a *maternity* ward. [< F < L *maternitas*]

math (math) *n. U.S. Informal* Mathematics.

math·e·mat·i·cal (math′ə·mat′i·kəl) *adj.* **1.** Of, perta to, or like mathematics. **2.** Used in mathematics. **3.** ly exact or precise. Also **math′e·mat′ic.** [< L < G *manthanein* to learn] **—math′e·mat′i·cal·ly** *adv.*

math·e·ma·ti·cian (math′ə·mə·tish′ən) *n.* One wh cializes or is expert in mathematics.

math·e·mat·ics (math′ə·mat′iks) *n.pl.* (*construed as* The study of quantity, form, arrangement, and magni esp., the methods and processes for disclosing the prop and relations of quantities and magnitudes.

mat·in (mat′in) *n.* **1.** *pl. Eccl.* **a** The prescribed pr that, with lauds, constitute the first of the seven can hours. **b** In the Anglican Church, the order for public ship in the morning. **2.** *Poetic* Any morning song. **—** Of matins or the morning: also **mat′in·al.** Also spelled *m* [< OF < L *matutinus* (*tempus*) (time) of the morning

mat·i·nee (mat′ə·nā′) *n.* A performance or entertain as a play, concert, etc., held in the daytime, usu. in the a noon. Also **mat′i·née′.** [< F *matin* morning]

mat·ing (mā′ting) *n.* The act of pairing or matching.

matri- *combining form* Mother. [< L *mater* mothe

ma·tri·arch (mā′trē·ärk) *n.* A woman holding the pos corresponding to that of a patriarch in her family or t **—ma′tri·ar′chal, ma′tri·ar′chic** *adj.*

ma·tri·ar·chy (mā′trē·ar′kē) *n. pl.* **·chies** A socia ganization having the mother as the head of the famil which descent is traced through the mother.

mat·ri·cide (mat′rə·sīd) *n.* **1.** The killing of one's mo **2.** One who kills his mother. [< L < *mater* moth *caedere* to kill] **—mat′ri·ci′dal** *adj.*

ma·tric·u·late (mə·trik′yə·lāt) *v.t.* & *v.i.* **·lat·ed, ·la** To register or enroll in a college or university as a cand for a degree. **—*n.*** One who is so enrolled. [< Med *matriculare* to enroll < *matrix* womb] **—ma·tric′u·la** **—ma·tric′u·la′tion** *n.* **—ma·tric′u·la′tor** *n.*

mat·ri·mo·ny (mat′rə·mō′nē) *n. pl.* **·nies 1.** The sta condition of being married. **2.** The act, ceremony, or rament of marriage. [< L < *mater* mother] **—mat′ri·ni·al** *adj.* **—mat′ri·mo′ni·al·ly** *adv.*

ma·trix (mā′triks) *n. pl.* **ma·trix·es** or **ma·tri·ces** (mā sēz, mat′rə-) **1.** That in which anything originates, velops, takes shape, or is contained. **2.** The womb. mold in or from which anything is cast or shaped. **4.** *P ing* **a** A mold in which the face of a type is cast. **b** In st typing, a papier-mâché or other impression of a form which a plate for printing may be made. [< L, womb]

ma·tron (mā′trən) *n.* **1.** A married woman or widow is usu. a mother. **2.** A female attendant or guard, as woman's prison, rest room, etc. **3.** A female superinten of an institution, etc. [< OF < L < *mater* mother] **—** **tron·li·ness** *n.* **—ma′tron·ly** *adj.* & *adv.*

matron of honor A married woman acting as chief att ant to a bride at a wedding.

mat·ted (mat′id) *adj.* **1.** Covered with or made from n or matting. **2.** Tangled or twisted in a mass. **3.** Cov with a dense or twisted growth.

mat·ter (mat′ər) *n.* **1.** That which makes up the subst of anything; constituent material. **2.** That which is mat and physical, occupies space, and is perceived by the se **3.** A specific kind of substance: organic *matter.* **4.** A ject, event, or situation that is an object of discussion, cern, etc.: a *matter* of faith. **5.** Cause, occasion, or rea usu. with *of* or *for*: a *matter* of great concern. **6.** Importa consequence: It's of no *matter* what happens. **7.** Somet of importance or consequence. **8.** A usu. unpleasant co tion or circumstance: with *the*: What's the *matter* with y **9.** The content or meaning of a book, etc., as distinguis from the style or form. **10.** An indefinite amount, quant etc.: a *matter* of a few dollars. **11.** Pus. **12.** That whic written, printed, etc.: *matter* for reading. **13.** Anything by mail: third-class *matter.* **14.** *Printing* **a** Type set u composed. **b** Material to be set up; copy. **—*v.i.* 1.** To b concern; signify: It *matters* little. **2.** To form or disch pus. [< OF < L *materia* stuff]

mat·ter-of-course (mat′ər·əv·kôrs′, -kōrs′) *adj.* **1.** T expected. **2.** Accepting things as a matter of course.

matter of course Something expected to follow as a nat or logical result.

MATHEMATICAL SYMBOLS

Symbol	Meaning	Symbol	Meaning
	Plus; positive; sign of addition	Σ	Summation of
	Minus; negative; sign of subtraction	$\sum_{1}^{n}$	Summation of n terms, one for each positive integer from 1 to n
	Plus or minus		
	Minus or plus	Π	Product of
	Multiplied by	$\prod_{1}^{n}$	Product of n terms, one for each positive integer from 1 to n
	Divided by	$\int$	Integral of
	Equals	$\int_{b}^{a}$	Definite integral between limits a and b
	Approximately equal; congruent	$\doteq, \rightarrow$	Approaches as a limit
	Greater than	$f(x), F(x), \phi(x)$	Function of x
	Less than	Δ	Increment of, as Δy
	Is not; does not: drawn through another symbol, as $a \neq b$, a is not equal to b	d	Differential, as dx
	Greater than or equal to	$\frac{dy}{dx}, f'(x)$	Derivative of $y = f(x)$ with respect to x
	Less than or equal to		
	Similar to; equivalent	δ	Variation, as δy
	Therefore	π	Pi; the ratio of the circumference and a diameter of the same circle; 3.14159...
	Since; because	$n!, \lfloor n$	n factorial; factorial n
	Identical; identically equal to	$(\,), [\,], \{\,\}$	Indicate that the enclosed symbols are to be treated as a single number
	Directly proportional to; varies directly as	$\overline{}$	Indicates that the symbols below it are to be treated as a single number, as $\overline{PQ}^2$. See VINCULUM.
	Infinity		
	Square root of minus one		
$_2$, etc.	Particular values of a (a variable)	$\angle$	Angle
	a multiplied by itself n times	$\parallel$	Parallel to
	a divided by b	$\perp$	Perpendicular to; perpendicular
	Square root of a. See RADICAL SIGN.	$\triangle$	Triangle
	nth root of a	$\llcorner$	Right angle
	Base of natural system of logarithms; 2.718...	$'$	Minutes of arc; prime
		$''$	Seconds of arc; double prime

·ter-of-fact (mat′ər·əv·fakt′) *adj.* Closely adhering to ts; not fanciful: unimaginative; practical.
·thew (math′yōō) One of the twelve apostles and hor of the first Gospel: called **Saint Matthew.** — *n.* The t Gospel of the New Testament.
·tin (mat′in) See MATIN.
·ting[1] (mat′ing) *n.* **1.** A woven fabric of fiber, straw, other material, used as a floor covering, for packing, etc. The act of making mats. **3.** Mats collectively.
·ting[2] (mat′ing) *n.* **1.** A mat for framing a picture. **2.** dull, lusterless surface, as on metal or glass.
·tock (mat′ək) *n.* Either of two tools resembling ickax, having a blade on one end and a pick on the other, a blade on each end. [OE *mattuc*]
·tress (mat′rəs) *n.* A large pad made of a ong fabric and filled with a resilient material, cotton, rubber, hair, feathers, etc., used on or a bed. [< OF < Ital. < Arabic *matrah* place ere something is thrown]

MATTOCK

·u·rate (mach′ōō·rāt, mat′yōō-) *v.i.* **·rat·ed, ·rat·ing** To form pus; suppurate. **2.** To ripen or mature. [< L *maturus* ripe, fully developed] — **mat′u·ra′tion** *n.* — **t′u·ra′tive** *adj.*
·ture (mə·tyōōr′, -tōōr′, -chōōr′) *adj.* **1.** Completely veloped; fully ripe, as plants, fruit, animals, etc. **2.** ghly developed in intellect, outlook, etc.: a *mature* think- **3.** Thoroughly developed, perfected, etc.: a *mature* ieme. **4.** Due and payable: a *mature* bond. — *v.* **·tured, r·ing** *v.t.* **1.** To cause to ripen; bring to full development. To perfect; complete. — *v.i.* **3.** To come to full development. **4.** To become due, as a note. [< L *maturus* ripe, of l age] — **ma·ture′ly** *adv.* — **ma·ture′ness** *n.*
·tur·i·ty (mə·tyōōr′ə·tē, -tōōr′-, -chōōr′-) *n.* **1.** The ate of being mature. **2.** Full physical development. **3.** ie time at which a note, etc., becomes due.
·tu·ti·nal (mə·tōō′tə·nəl, -tyōō′-, mach·ə·tī′nəl) *adj.* Of, rtaining to, or taking place in the morning; early. [< L *matutinus* early in the morning] — **ma·tu′ti·nal·ly** *adv.*
t·zo (mät′sə) *n. pl.* **·zos** or **·zot** (-sōt) or **·zoth** (-sōth, ōt) A large, flat piece of unleavened bread, traditionally eaten during Passover. Also **mat′za, mat′zah, mat′zoh.** [< Hebrew *matstāh* unleavened bread]
maud·lin (môd′lin) *adj.* **1.** Excessively and tearfully emotional or sentimental. **2.** Overly sentimental or emotional from too much liquor. — **Syn.** See SENTIMENTAL. [< OF *Madeleine* (Mary) Magdalen, often depicted weeping]
maul (môl) *n.* A heavy mallet for driving wedges, piles, etc. — *v.t.* **1.** To beat and bruise. **2.** To handle roughly; manhandle; abuse. Also spelled *mall.* [< OF *mail* < L *malleus* hammer] — **maul′er** *n.*
Mau Mau (mou′ mou′) *pl.* **Mau Mau** or **Mau Maus** A member of a secret society of Kikuyu tribesmen in Kenya organized against European colonists. [< native name]
maun·der (môn′dər) *v.i.* **1.** To talk in a wandering or incoherent manner; drivel. **2.** To move dreamily or idly. [? Freq. of obs. *maund* to beg] — **maun′der·er** *n.*
Maun·dy Thursday (môn′dē) The day before Good Friday, commemorating the Last Supper of Christ. [< OF < L *mandatum* command]
Mau·ser (mou′zər) *n.* A magazine rifle having great range and velocity; also, a type of automatic pistol: a trade name. [after P. S. *Mauser,* 1838–1914, German inventor]
mau·so·le·um (mô′sə·lē′əm) *n. pl.* **·le·ums** or **·le·a** (-lē′ə) A large, stately tomb. [< L < Gk. *Mausōleion,* tomb of King Mausolus at Halicarnassus] — **mau′so·le′an** *adj.*
mauve (mōv) *n.* Any of various purplish rose shades. [< F, mallow]
mav·er·ick (mav′ər·ik) *n.* **1.** *U.S.* An unbranded or orphaned animal, as a calf, traditionally belonging to the first person to claim or brand it. **2.** *U.S. Informal* One who is unorthodox in his ideas, attitudes, etc. [after Samuel A. *Maverick,* 1803–70, Texas lawyer who did not brand his cattle]
ma·vour·neen (mə·vōōr′nēn, -vôr′-) *n.* My darling. Also **ma·vour′nin.** [< Irish *mo muirnin*]
maw (mô) *n.* **1.** The jaws, mouth, or gullet of a voracious mammal or fish. **2.** The craw of a bird. **3.** The stomach. [OE *maga* stomach]
mawk·ish (mô′kish) *adj.* **1.** Characterized by false or feeble sentimentality. **2.** Sickening or insipid. [< ON *mathkr* maggot] — **mawk′ish·ly** *adv.* — **mawk′ish·ness** *n.*

max·il·la (mak·sil′ə) *n. pl.* **max·il·lae** (mak·sil′ē) **1.** In vertebrates, the upper jaw or jawbone. **2.** *Zool.* In insects, crustaceans, etc., either of two pairs of jawlike appendages behind the mandibles. [< L *mala* jaw]

max·il·lar·y (mak′sə·ler′ē, mak·sil′ər·ē) *adj.* Of, pertaining to, or situated near the upper jaw or a maxilla. **—** *n. pl.* **·lar·ies** The upper jaw or a maxilla.

max·im (mak′sim) *n.* A brief statement of a general principle, truth, or rule of conduct. [< F < L *maxima (sententia, propositio)* greatest (authority, premise)]

max·i·mal (mak′sə·məl) *adj.* Of or being a maximum; greatest or highest possible. **— max′i·mal·ly** *adv.*

max·i·mize (mak′sə·mīz) *v.t.* **·mized, ·miz·ing** To make as great as possible; increase or intensify to the maximum.

max·i·mum (mak′sə·məm) *n. pl.* **·mums** or **·ma** (-mə) **1.** The greatest possible quantity, amount, or degree. **2.** The greatest quantity, degree, etc., reached or recorded. **—** *adj.* **1.** Consisting of the greatest amount or degree possible, permissible, attainable, etc. **2.** Of or pertaining to a maximum or maximums. [< L *magnus* great]

may[1] (mā) *v.* Present: *sing.* **may, may** (*Archaic* **may·est** or **mayst), may,** *pl.* **may;** past: **might** A defective verb now used only in the present and past tenses as an auxiliary followed by the infinitive without *to*, or elliptically with the infinitive understood, to express: **1.** Permission or allowance: *May* I go? **2.** Desire, prayer, or wish: *May* your tribe increase! **3.** Contingency, especially in clauses of result, concession, purpose, etc.: He died that we *might* live. **4.** Possibility: You *may* be right. **5.** *Law* Obligation or duty: the equivalent of *must* or *shall*. [OE *mæg*]

may[2] (mā) *n. Brit.* A species of hawthorn having white, rose, or crimson flowers. [< MAY, when it blooms]

May (mā) *n.* **1.** The fifth month of the year, containing 31 days. **2.** The prime of life; youth. **3.** May Day festivities. [< OF < L *(mensis) Maius* (month of) May]

Ma·ya[1] (mä′yə) *n.* In Hindu philosophy, illusion, often personified as a maiden: also **ma′ya.** [< Skt. *māyā* illusion]

Ma·ya[2] (mä′yə) *n.* **1.** One of a tribe of Central American Indians, having an early advanced civilization and still living in Yucatán, northern Guatemala, and British Honduras. **2.** The language of the Mayas. **—** *adj.* Of the Mayas, their culture, or their language. **— Ma′yan** *adj. & n.*

May apple A North American herb whose roots yield a purgative; also, its edible fruit. Also called *mandrake*.

may·be (mā′bē) *adv.* Perhaps; possibly. [< *(it) may be*]

May Day The first day of May, traditionally celebrated as a spring festival and, in recent times, celebrated in some countries by demonstrations commemorating labor.

may·est (mā′ist) May: archaic or poetic second person singular, present tense of MAY: used with *thou*. Also **mayst.**

may·flow·er (mā′flou′ər) *n.* Any of various plants that blossom in the spring; esp., in the U.S., the trailing arbutus, and in Great Britain, the hawthorn.

Mayflower The ship on which the Pilgrims came to America in 1620.

May fly Any of a large group of insects, having transparent forewings, a relatively long nymphal life, and a short-lived adult stage: also called *dayfly, ephemerid*. Also **may′fly** *n.*

may·hem (mā′hem) *n.* **1.** *Law* The offense of injuring a person's body so as to render him less able to defend himself. **2.** Any situation characterized by violence, confusion, noise, etc. [< OF *mehaing, mahaym*]

may·on·naise (mā′ə·nāz′, mī′-) *n.* **1.** A dressing, as for salads, made by beating together raw egg yolk, butter or olive oil, lemon juice or vinegar, and condiments. **2.** A dish, as of meat or fish, mixed with this dressing. [< F]

may·or (mā′ər, mâr) *n.* The chief magistrate of a city, borough, or municipal corporation. [< F < L *major* greater] **— may′or·al** *adj.*

may·or·al·ty (mā′ər·əl·tē, mâr′əl-) *n. pl.* **·ties** The office or term of service of a mayor. [< OF *mairalté*]

May·pole (mā′pōl′) *n.* A decorated pole around which dancing takes place on May Day. Also **may′pole′.**

May·time (mā′tīm′) *n.* The month of May. Also **May′·tide′** (-tīd′).

may tree *Brit.* The hawthorn.

maze (māz) *n.* **1.** An intricate network of paths or passages; a labyrinth. **2.** A state of bewilderment, uncertainty, or perplexity. [< AMAZE] **— ma′zy** *adj.* **— maz′·i·ly** *adv*

ma·zur·ka (mə·zûr′kə, -zōōr′-) *n.* **1.** A lively Polish dance in 3/4 time. **2.** The music for such a dance. Also **ma·zour′·ka.** [< Polish, woman from Mazovia, a province]

maz·zard cherry (maz′ərd) The sweet cherry, esp. the fruit of a wild sweet cherry. [Earlier *mazer* maple wood]

Mc- See also MAC-.

Mc·Car·thy·ism (mə·kär′thē·iz′əm) *n.* The practice of making public accusations of disloyalty or corruption, usu. with little evidence, ostensibly to expose pro-Communist activity. [after Joseph *McCarthy*, 1909–57, U.S. Senator]

Mc·Coy (mə·koi′), **the (real)** *U.S. Slang* The authentic person or thing.

Mc·In·tosh (mak′ən·tosh) *n. U.S. & Canadian* A red, autumn, eating apple. Also **McIntosh red.** [after *McIntosh* of Ontario, who discovered it about 1796]

M-Day (em′dā′) *n. Mil.* Mobilization day, the day th partment of Defense orders mobilization for war.

me (mē) *pron.* The objective case of the pronoun *I*. *mē*, dat. sing.]

◆ **It's me,** etc. Anyone who answers the question "V there?" by saying "It's me" is using acceptable inf idiom. Here *It is I* would seem stilted, although at th mal level of writing it is expected: They have warne that *it is I*, and not he, who will have to bear the bu

mead[1] (mēd) *n.* An alcoholic beverage of fermented h and water to which yeast and spices are added. [OE *n*

mead[2] (mēd) *n. Poetic* A meadow. [OE *mǣd*]

mead·ow (med′ō) *n.* **1.** A tract of grassland, usu. us grazing or for growing hay. **2.** A low or level piece of as near a river, used for growing grass or hay. [OE *m* oblique case of *mǣd*] **— mead′ow·y** *adj.*

mead·ow·lark (med′ō·lärk′) *n.* Any of various song of North America, marked with black on a yellow bre

mea·ger (mē′gər) *adj.* **1.** Deficient in quantity or qu scanty; inadequate. **2.** Lacking in fertility, strengt richness: *meager* soil. **3.** Thin; emaciated. Also *Brit.* **r gre.** [< OF < L *macer* lean] **— mea′ger·ly** *adv.*

meal[1] (mēl) *n.* **1.** The edible seeds of any grain, co ground and unbolted. **2.** Any powdery material. *melu*]

meal[2] (mēl) *n.* **1.** The food served or eaten regularly a tain times during the day. **2.** The time or occasion of t such food. [OE *mǣl* measure, time, meal]

meal·ie (mē′lē) *n.* In Africa: **a** An ear of corn (def. 1). Corn. [< Afrikaans *milje* < Pg. *milho* millet]

meal ticket **1.** A ticket or card bought for a specified and redeemable at a restaurant for food. **2.** *U.S. Slan* who or that which provides a livelihood for another.

meal·time (mēl′tīm′) *n.* The habitual time for a me

meal·y (mē′lē) *adj.* **meal·i·er, meal·i·est** **1.** Resem meal; dry; powdery; soft. **2.** Containing meal. **3.** Sp kled or covered with or as with meal. **4.** Anemic or p color, etc. **5.** Mealy-mouthed. **— meal′i·ness** *n.*

meal·y-mouthed (mē′lē·moutht′, -mouthd′) *adj.* Un ing to express facts or opinions plainly and frankly.

mean[1] (mēn) *v.* **meant** (ment), **mean·ing** *v.t.* **1.** To in mind as a purpose or intent. **2.** To intend or desig some purpose, destination, etc.: Was that remark *mea* me? **3.** To intend to express or convey: That's not w *meant*. **4.** To have as the particular sense or significa **—** *v.i.* **5.** To have disposition or intention: He *means* **6.** To be of specified importance or influence: Her *means* everything to her. [OE *mǣnan* to tell]

mean[2] (mēn) *adj.* **1.** Poor or inferior in grade or qua **2.** Having little worth or consequence. **3.** Ignoble in r or character. **4.** Miserly; stingy. **5.** Poor in appeara shabby. **6.** Humble in birth, rank, or station. **7.** *Info* Disagreeable; nasty; vicious. **8.** *Informal* Ashamed; hu iated. **9.** *U.S. Informal* Ill; out of sorts: to feel *mean*. *U.S. Informal* Difficult; troublesome. **11.** *U.S. Slang* E lent; expert. [OE *(ge) mǣne* ordinary]

mean[3] (mēn) *n.* **1.** *pl.* The medium, method, or instrum by which some end is or may be accomplished. **2.** *pl.* M ey; wealth. **3.** The middle point or state between two tremes. **4.** Avoidance of excess; moderation. **5.** *Mat* A number or quantity contained within the range of a se numbers or quantities and representative of each of the an average. **b** Arithmetic mean (which see). **c** Geome mean (which see). **d** The second or third term in a propor containing four terms. **— by all means** Without hesitat certainly. **— by any means** In any manner possible; at somehow. **— by means of** With the help of; through us **— by no** (or **no manner of**) **means** Most certainly not; no account whatever. **—** *adj.* **1.** Intermediate or aver in size, degree, quality, etc.; medium. **2.** Halfway betw extremes; average. [< OF < L *medius* middle]

me·an·der (mē·an′dər) *v.i.* **1.** To wind and turn in a cou **2.** To wander aimlessly. **—** *n.* **1.** *Often pl.* A tortuous winding course. **2.** Aimless wandering. [< L < Gk. *M andros*, the river Meander] **— me·an′der·er** *n.*

mean·ing (mē′ning) n. **1.** That which is intended or mea aim; purpose; end. **2.** That which is signified; sense; port. **3.** Interpretation or significance. **—** *adj.* **1.** Hav purpose or intention: usu. in combination: *well-meaning*. Significant; expressive. **— mean′ing·ly** *adv.*

mean·ing·ful (mē′ning·fəl) *adj.* Full of meaning. **— mea ing·ful·ness** *n.* **— mean′ing·ful·ly** *adv.*

mean·ing·less (mē′ning·lis) *adj.* Having no meaning, s nificance, or importance. **— mean′ing·less·ly** *adv.* **— mea ing·less·ness** *n.*

mean·ly (mēn′lē) *adv.* In a mean, poor, or ignoble mann

mean·ness (mēn′nis) *n.* **1.** The state or quality of be mean. **2.** A mean act.

mant (ment) Past tense and past participle of MEAN[1].
mean·time (mēn′tīm′) *n.* Intervening time. — *adv.* **1.** In during the intervening time. **2.** At the same time.
mean·while (mēn′hwīl′) *n. & adv.* Meantime.
mea·sles (mē′zəlz) *n.pl.* (*construed as sing. or pl.*) **1.** An acute, highly contagious virus disease affecting children and sometimes adults, characterized by an extensive eruption of small red spots: also called *rubeola*. **2.** Any similar disease, as German measles. [ME *maseles*, pl. of *masel* blister]
mea·sly (mēz′lē) *adj.* **·sli·er, ·sli·est 1.** Affected with measles. **2.** *Slang* Contemptibly stingy, scanty, or petty.
meas·ur·a·ble (mezh′ər·ə·bəl) *adj.* **1.** Capable of being measured or compared. **2.** Notable; significant. — **meas′·ur·a·bil′i·ty, meas′ur·a·ble·ness** *n.* — **meas′ur·a·bly** *adv.*
meas·ure (mezh′ər) *n.* **1.** The extent, range, dimensions, capacity, etc., of anything. **2.** A standard or unit of measurement, as a yard. **3.** Any standard of criticism or judgment. **4.** A system of measurements: liquid *measure*. **5.** An instrument for taking measurements. **6.** The act of measuring. **7.** A specific quantity: a full *measure*. **8.** A fixed or suitable limit or bound: talkative beyond all *measure*. **9.** A certain amount, extent, or degree of anything: a *measure* of freedom. **10.** *Often pl.* A specific action, step, or procedure. **11.** A legislative bill. **12.** Rhythmic movement or beat. **13.** *Music* **a** A group of beats marked off by regularly recurring primary accents. **b** The portion of music contained between two bar lines; bar. **14.** In prosody: **a** Meter (def. 1). **b** A metrical foot. — **for good measure** As something additional or extra. — **in a measure** To some degree or extent. — **to take one's measure** To estimate or form an opinion of one's character, skill, etc. — *v.* **·ured, ·ur·ing** *v.t.* **1.** To take or ascertain the dimensions, quantity, capacity, etc., of. **2.** To set apart, mark off, allot, etc., or as by measuring: often with *off* or *out*. **3.** To estimate; judge; weigh. **4.** To serve as the measure of. **5.** To bring into competition or comparison. **6.** To travel over. **7.** To adjust; regulate: *Measure* your actions to your aspirations. — *v.i.* **8.** To make or take measurements. **9.** To yield a specified measurement. **10.** To admit measurement. — **to measure one's length** To fall or lie prostrate at full length. — **to measure up to** To fulfill, or meet, as expectations. [< OF < L *mensura* < *metiri* to measure] — **meas′ur·er** *n.*
meas·ured (mezh′ərd) *adj.* **1.** Determined by some standard. **2.** Slow and stately; rhythmical. **3.** Carefully considered or weighed; deliberate. **4.** Moderate. **5.** Metrical. — **meas′ured·ly** *adv.* — **meas′ured·ness** *n.*
meas·ure·less (mezh′ər·lis) *adj.* Incapable of being measured; very great; immense. — **Syn.** See INFINITE.
meas·ure·ment (mezh′ər·mənt) *n.* **1.** The act or process of measuring anything. **2.** The amount, capacity, or extent determined by measuring. **3.** A system of measures.
measuring worm The larva of a geometrid moth, that advances its body by a succession of loops: also *inchworm*.
meat (mēt) *n.* **1.** The flesh of animals used as food, esp. the flesh of mammals as opposed to fish or fowl. **2.** The edible part of anything. **3.** Anything eaten for nourishment, as in **meat and drink. 4.** The essence, gist, or main idea of something. **5.** *Informal* Anything one particularly enjoys or does with ease. [OE *mete*] — **meat′less** *adj.*
meat packing *U.S.* The commercial slaughtering of meat-producing animals and the processing, packaging, and distribution of meat and meat products. — **meat packer**
me·a·tus (mē·ā′təs) *n. pl.* **·tus** or **·tus·es** *Anat.* A passage, duct, or canal: the auditory *meatus*. [< L, passage]
meat·y (mē′tē) *adj.* **meat·i·er, meat·i·est 1.** Of, pertaining to, or like meat. **2.** Full of meat. **3.** Full of substance; significant. — **meat′i·ness** *n.*
Mec·ca (mek′ə) *n.* **1.** A place or attraction visited by many people. **2.** The goal of one's aspirations. [after *Mecca*]
me·chan·ic (mə·kan′ik) *n.* One skilled in the making, operation, or repair of tools or machinery. — *adj.* **1.** Involving or pertaining to manual labor or skill. **2.** Mechanical. [< L < Gk. *mēchanē* machine]
me·chan·i·cal (mə·kan′i·kəl) *adj.* **1.** Of, involving, or having to do with the construction, operation, design, etc., of machinery or tools. **2.** Operated or produced by a machine. **3.** Of, pertaining to, or in accordance with the science of mechanics. **4.** Made or performed without spontaneity or by force of habit; automatic; lifeless. — **me·chan′i·cal·ly** *adv.* — **me·chan′i·cal·ness** *n.*
mechanical drawing A drawing done with the aid of compasses, squares, etc.
mech·a·ni·cian (mek′ə·nish′ən) *n.* One who builds, operates, or repairs machines or tools.
me·chan·ics (mə·kan′iks) *n.pl.* (*construed as sing. in defs. 1 and 2*) **1.** The branch of physics that treats of motion and of the action of forces on material bodies. **2.** The body of knowledge dealing with the design, operation, and maintenance of machinery. **3.** The technical aspects of anything.
mech·a·nism (mek′ə·niz′əm) *n.* **1.** The parts or arrangement of parts of a machine. **2.** Something similar to a machine. **3.** The process or technique by which something works. **4.** A theory that all natural phenomena can be explained by the laws of chemistry and physics.
mech·a·nist (mek′ə·nist) *n.* **1.** A mechanician. **2.** A believer in mechanism (def. 5). — *adj.* Mechanistic.
mech·a·nis·tic (mek′ə·nis′tik) *adj.* **1.** Of, pertaining to, or of the nature of mechanics. **2.** Pertaining to or based on mechanism (def. 4). — **mech′a·nis′ti·cal·ly** *adv.*
mech·a·nize (mek′ə·nīz) *v.t.* **·nized, ·niz·ing 1.** To make mechanical. **2.** To convert (an industry, etc.) to machine production. **3.** *Mil.* To equip with tanks, trucks, etc. — **mech′a·ni·za′tion** *n.*
med·al (med′l) *n.* A small piece of metal, bearing an image, inscription, etc., and often given as an award for some outstanding act or service. — *v.t.* **med·aled** or **·alled, med·al·ing** or **·al·ling** To confer a medal upon. [< F < Ital. < L *metallum* mine]
med·al·ist (med′l·ist) *n.* **1.** A collector or maker of medals. **2.** The recipient of a medal awarded for services or merit. **3.** In golf, the winner at medal play.
me·dal·lion (mə·dal′yən) *n.* **1.** A large medal. **2.** An ornamental subject usu. set in a circular or oval frame, and used as a decorative element. [< F *médaillon*]
Medal of Honor The highest U.S. military decoration, awarded to one who risked his life beyond the call of duty. Also called *Congressional Medal of Honor*. See DECORATION.
medal play In golf, a form of competitive play in which the score is computed by counting the strokes of each competitor in a round of play. Compare MATCH PLAY.
med·dle (med′l) *v.i.* **·dled, ·dling 1.** To participate or interfere officiously: often with *in* or *with*. **2.** To tamper. [< OF *medler* < L *miscere* to mix] — **med′dler** *n.*
med·dle·some (med′l·səm) *adj.* Inclined to meddle. — **med′dle·some·ly** *adv.* — **med′dle·some·ness** *n.*
Me·de·a (mə·dē′ə) In Greek legend, a sorceress of Colchis who helped Jason obtain the Golden Fleece.
me·di·a (mē′dē·ə) Alternative plural of MEDIUM.
me·di·ae·val (mē′dē·ē′vəl, med′ē-), **me·di·ae·val·ism,** etc. See MEDIEVAL, etc.
me·di·al (mē′dē·əl) *adj.* **1.** Of, pertaining to, or situated in the middle. **2.** Of or pertaining to a mathematical average; mean. [< LL < L *medius* middle] — **me′di·al·ly** *adv.*
me·di·an (mē′dē·ən) *adj.* **1.** Pertaining to or situated in the middle; medial. **2.** *Stat.* Designating the middle point in a series of values: 8 is the *median* of 2, 5, 8, 10, 13. — *n.* A median point, line, or number. [< L < *medius* middle] — **me′di·an·ly** *adv.*
me·di·ate (*v.* mē′dē·āt; *adj.* -it) *v.* **·at·ed, ·at·ing** *v.t.* **1.** To settle or reconcile (differences) by intervening as a peacemaker. **2.** To serve as the medium for effecting (a result) or conveying (an object, etc.). — *v.i.* **3.** To act between disputing parties to bring about a settlement, etc. **4.** To be in an intermediate position. — *adj.* **1.** Acting as an intervening agency. **2.** Occurring or effected as a result of indirect or median agency. [< LL < *mediare* to stand between] — **me′di·ate·ly** *adv.* — **me′di·a′tive** *adj.*
me·di·a·tion (mē′dē·ā′shən) *n.* The act of mediating; intercession; interposition. — **me′di·a′tor** *n.*
me·di·a·tor·y (mē′dē·a·tôr′ē, -tō′rē) *adj.* **1.** Of or pertaining to mediation. **2.** Serving to mediate. Also **me′di·a·to′·ri·al** (-tôr′ē·əl, -tō′rē·əl). — **me·di·a·to′ri·al·ly** *adv.*
med·ic[1] (med′ik) *n.* Any of several cloverlike plants, esp. alfalfa. [< L < Gk. *Mēdikē* (*poa*) Median (grass)]
med·ic[2] (med′ik) *n.* *Informal* **1.** A physician or intern. **2.** A medical student. **3.** A corpsman.
med·i·ca·ble (med′ə·kə·bəl) *adj.* Capable of being relieved by medical treatment; curable.
med·i·cal (med′i·kəl) *adj.* **1.** Of or pertaining to medicine. **2.** Having curative properties.
medical jurisprudence The application of medical principles in law: also called *forensic medicine, legal medicine*.
med·i·ca·ment (med′ə·kə·mənt, mə·dik′ə-) *n.* Any substance for the cure of disease or the alleviation of pain.
med·i·care (med′i·kâr) *n.* *U.S. & Canadian* Government medical care or health insurance.
med·i·cate (med′ə·kāt) *v.t.* **·cat·ed, ·cat·ing 1.** To treat medicinally. **2.** To tincture or impregnate with medicine. [< L < *medicare* to heal] — **med′i·ca′tion** *n.* — **med′i·ca′·tive** *adj.*
me·dic·i·nal (mə·dis′ə·nəl) *adj.* Pertaining to or having the properties of medicine; healing, curative, or alleviating.
med·i·cine (med′ə·sən, *Brit.* med′sən) *n.* **1.** Any substance used in the treatment of disease or in the relief of pain. **2.** The science of the preservation and restoration of health and of treating disease, esp., as distinguished from surgery. **3.**

The profession of medicine. **4.** Among American Indians, any magic spell or power. **— to take one's medicine** To endure punishment, etc. [< OF < L *medicus* physician]
medicine ball A large, heavy, leather-covered ball, thrown and caught for physical exercise.
medicine man Among North American Indians, one professing supernatural powers of healing, etc.; magician.
med·i·co (med′ə·kō) *n. pl.* **·cos** *Informal* A physician or a medical student. [< Ital. or Sp., physician]
medico- *combining form* Pertaining to medical science and: *medico-legal.* Also, before vowels, **medic-.** [< L *medicus* physician]
me·di·e·val (mē′dē·ē′vəl, med′ē-) *adj.* Of, like, or characteristic of the Middle Ages: also spelled *mediaeval.* [< L *medius* middle + *aevum* age] **— me′di·e′val·ly** *adv.*
me·di·e·val·ism (mē′dē·ē′vəl·iz′əm, med′ē-) *n.* **1.** The spirit, beliefs, customs, and practices of the Middle Ages. **2.** Devotion to the Middle Ages. **3.** Any custom, idea, etc., surviving from the Middle Ages. Also spelled *mediaevalism.*
me·di·e·val·ist (mē′dē·ē′vəl·ist, med′ē-) *n.* **1.** A scholar or specialist in medieval history, literature, or art. **2.** One devoted to the Middle Ages. Also spelled *mediaevalist.*
medio- *combining form* Middle. Also, before vowels, **medi-.** [< L *medius* middle]
me·di·o·cre (mē′dē·ō′kər, mē′dē·ō′kər) *adj.* Of only average quality; ordinary. [< F < L < *medius* middle]
me·di·oc·ri·ty (mē′dē·ok′rə·tē) *n. pl.* **·ties 1.** The condition or quality of being mediocre. **2.** Mediocre ability or performance. **3.** A mediocre person.
med·i·tate (med′ə·tāt) *v.* **·tat·ed, ·tat·ing** *v.i.* **1.** To engage in continuous and contemplative thought; muse; cogitate. — *v.t.* **2.** To think about doing; plan. [< L < *meditari* to muse, ponder] **— med′i·tat′er, med′i·ta′tor** *n.* **— med′i·ta′tive** *adj.* **— med′i·ta′tive·ly** *adv.*
med·i·ta·tion (med′ə·tā′shən) *n.* The act of meditating; reflection upon a subject; contemplation.
med·i·ter·ra·ne·an (med′ə·tə·rā′nē·ən) *adj.* Enclosed nearly or wholly by land. [< L *medius* middle + *terra* earth]
Med·i·ter·ra·ne·an (med′ə·tə·rā′nē·ən) *adj.* Of or pertaining to the Mediterranean Sea or its shores. — *n.* **1.** The Mediterranean Sea. **2.** One who lives in a Mediterranean country, or belongs to the Mediterranean race.
Mediterranean fever Undulant fever.
me·di·um (mē′dē·əm) *n. pl.* **·di·ums** (always for def. 5) or **·di·a** (-dē·ə) **1.** An intermediate degree or condition; mean. **2.** The surrounding or enveloping element; environment. **3.** An intervening substance in which something may act or an effect be produced. **4.** A means or agency; instrument: an advertising *medium.* **5.** One through whom the spirits of the dead are believed to communicate with the material world. **6.** An area or form of artistic expression, or the materials used. **7.** In painting, a liquid with which pigments are mixed to make them fluid enough to be applied. **8.** *Biol.* A culture medium. — *adj.* Intermediate in quantity, quality, size, etc. [< L, orig. neut. sing. of *medius* middle]
medium frequency *Telecom.* Radio waves ranging in frequency from 300 to 3000 kilocycles.
med·lar (med′lər) *n.* **1.** A small, European tree of the rose family. **2.** The fruit of this tree, eaten when it begins to decay. [< OF *mesle* fruit of the medlar]
med·ley (med′lē) *n.* **1.** A mingled and confused mass of elements; jumble. **2.** A musical composition made up of different airs or parts of songs. — *adj.* Made up of heterogeneous parts; jumbled; mixed. [< OF *medlee,* orig. fem. pp. of *medler* to meddle]
Mé·doc (mā·dôk′) *n.* A red wine made in Médoc, France.
me·dul·la (mə·dul′ə) *n. pl.* **·lae** (-lē) **1.** *Anat.* **a** The soft inner portion of an organ or part, such as the kidney. **b** The marrow of bones. **c** The medulla oblongata. **2.** *Bot.* Pith (def. 1). [< L, marrow, pith] **— med·ul·lar·y** (med′ə·ler·ē, mi·dul′ər·ē), **me·dul′lar** *adj.*
medulla ob·lon·ga·ta (ob′lông·gā′tə) *Anat.* The hindmost and lowest part of the brain, narrowing down into the spinal cord, and controlling breathing, circulation, etc.
me·du·sa (mə·do͞o′sə, -zə, -dyo͞o′-) *n. pl.* **·sas** or **·sae** (-sē, -zē) A jellyfish. [< L] **— me·du′san, me·du′soid** *adj. & n.*
Me·du·sa (mə·do͞o′sə, -zə, -dyo͞o′-) In Greek mythology, one of the Gorgons, killed by Perseus.
meek (mēk) *adj.* **1.** Having a patient, gentle disposition. **2.** Lacking spirit or backbone; submissive. [ME < ON *miukr* gentle, soft] **— meek′ly** *adv.* **— meek·ness** *n.*
meer·schaum (mir′shəm, -shôm, -shoum) *n.* **1.** A light, heat-resisting magnesium silicate, used for tobacco pipes, etc. **2.** A tobacco pipe made from this. [< G < *meer* sea + *schaum* foam]
meet[1] (mēt) *v.* **met, meet·ing** *v.t.* **1.** To come upon; encounter. **2.** To be at, or go to the place of arrival of: to *meet* him at the station. **3.** To make the acquaintance of. **4.** To come into the company of or in association with, as for a conference. **5.** To come into contact or conjunction with. **6.** To keep an appointment with. **7.** To come into the observation, perception, or recognition of (the eye, ear, e **8.** To experience; undergo: to *meet* adversity. **9.** To op in battle. **10.** To answer (a blow, move, etc.) by anoth return. **11.** To deal or cope with; handle. **12.** To co or act in accordance with: to *meet* the requirements diploma. **13.** To pay (a bill, debt, etc.). **14.** To fulfil obligation, need, etc.). — *v.i.* **15.** To come together; face to face. **16.** To come together in conjunction, or u **17.** To assemble. **18.** To make acquaintance or be i duced. **19.** To come together in conflict or opposition; tend. **— to meet with 1.** To come upon; encounter. **2** deal or confer with. **3.** To experience. — *n.* An assem for a sport or an athletic contest; also, the persons so as bled, or the place of assembly. [OE *mētan*]
meet[2] (mēt) *adj.* Suitable; proper. [OE *gemǣte*] **— m ly** *adv.*
meet·ing (mē′ting) *n.* **1.** A coming together. **2.** An as bly or gathering of persons; also, the persons present. joining or conjunction of things. **4.** An assembly of Qua for religious services; also, their meeting house.
meeting house 1. A house used for public meetings. place of worship used by the Quakers.
mega- *combining form* **1.** Great; large: *megaphone.* **2** the metric system, a million times (a specified unit): *m cycle.* Also, before vowels, **meg-.** [< Gk. *megas* large]
meg·a·cy·cle (meg′ə·sī′kəl) *n.* **1.** *Telecom.* A unit of tromagnetic wave frequency of 1,000,000 cycles per sec **2.** One million cycles.
megalo- *combining form* Big; indicating excessive or normal size. Also, before vowels, **megal-.** [< Gk. *me megalou* big]
meg·a·lo·ceph·a·ly (meg′ə·lō·sef′ə·lē) *n.* Unusual la ness of the head. Also **meg′a·lo·ce·pha′li·a** (-sə·fā′l [< MEGALO- + Gk. *kephalē* head] **— meg′a·lo·ce·ph** (-sə·fal′ik), **meg′a·lo·ceph′a·lous** *adj.*
meg·a·lo·ma·ni·a (meg′ə·lō·mā′nē·ə, -mān′yə) *n.* **1.** *chiatry* A mental disorder in which the subject thinks l self great or exalted. **2.** A tendency to magnify and e gerate. **— meg′a·lo·ma′ni·ac** *adj. & n.*
meg·a·phone (meg′ə·fōn) *n.* A funnel-shaped device amplifying or directing sound. — *v.t. & v.i.* **·phoned, ·ph ing** To speak through or as through a megaphone.
meg·a·ton (meg′ə·tun′) *n.* **1.** One million tons. **2.** A equal to the explosive power of one million tons of TN
me·grim (mē′grim) *n.* **1.** *pl.* Depression of spirits; dulln **2.** Migraine. [< F < L < Gk. *hēmi* half + *krania* sk
mei·o·sis (mī·ō′sis) *n.* *Biol.* The cell divisions leading the formation of gametes in which the number of chro somes is reduced by half. [< Gk. *meiōn* less] **— mei·o** (-ot′ik) *adj.*
Meis·ter·sing·er (mīs′tər·sing′ər, *Ger.* mīs′tər·zing′ər) *pl.* **·sing·er** *German* Any of the poets and musicians, mai artisans and tradesmen, active in the principal cities of G many between the 14th and 16th centuries.
mel·a·mine (mel′ə·mēn, -min) *n.* *Chem.* A crystalline trogen compound, $C_3N_2(NH_2)_3$, that reacts with forma hyde to produce a high-grade thermosetting resin. [< *r (am),* a chemical compound + AMINE]
melan- Var. of MELANO-.
mel·an·cho·li·a (mel′ən·kō′lē·ə) *n.* *Psychiatry* Great pression of spirits and excessive brooding without appar or sufficient cause. [< L] **— mel′an·cho′li·ac** *adj. & n*
mel·an·chol·y (mel′ən·kol′ē) *adj.* **1.** Excessively gloo sad. **2.** Suggesting or promoting sadness: a *melancholy* d **3.** Somberly thoughtful; pensive. — *n. pl.* **·chol·ies 1.** L spirits; depression. **2.** Pensive or sober reflection. [< < L < Gk. < *melas,* -*anos* black + *cholē* bile] **— mel′ chol′ic** *adj.* **— mel′an·chol′li·cal·ly** *adv.*
Mel·a·ne·sian (mel′ə·nē′zhən, -shən) *adj.* Of or pertain to Melanesia, its native inhabitants, or their languages. *n.* **1.** A member of any of the dark-skinned, kinky-hai peoples of Melanesia. **2.** Any of the languages of the A tronesian group spoken in Melanesia.
mé·lange (mā·läṅzh′) *n.* *French* A mixture or medley.
mel·a·nin (mel′ə·nin) *n.* *Biochem.* A brownish black p ment contained in animal tissues, as the skin and hair.
melano- *combining form* Black; dark-colored. Also, bef vowels, *melan-.* [< Gk. *melas, melanos* black]
Mel·ba toast (mel′bə) Thinly sliced bread toasted un brown and crisp.
meld (meld) *v.t. & v.i.* In pinochle and other card games, announce or declare (a combination of cards) for inclusion one's total score. — *n.* A group of cards to be declared, the act of declaring them. [< G *melden* to announce]
me·lee (mā′lā, mā·lā′) *n.* A confused, general hand-to-ha fight; affray. Also *Fr.* **mê·lée** (me·lā′). [< F < OF *mesl* var. of *medlee* medley]
mel·io·rate (mēl′yə·rāt) *v.t. & v.i.* **·rat·ed, ·rat·ing** To i prove, as in quality or condition; ameliorate. [< LL *melior* better] **— mel′io·ra·ble** *adj.* **— mel′io·ra′tion** *n.* **— mel′io·ra′tive** *adj.* **— mel′io·ra′tor** *n.*

lif·er·ous (mə·lif′ər·əs) *adj.* Producing or bearing ›y. Also **mel·lif′ic.** [< L < *mel* honey + *ferre* to bear]
lif·lu·ent (mə·lif′loo·ənt) *adj.* Mellifluous. — **mel·lif′** ›nce *n.* — **mel·lif′lu·ent·ly** *adv.*
lif·lu·ous (mə·lif′loo·əs) *adj.* Sweetly or smoothly ›ing: *mellifluous* speech. [< L < *mel* honey + *fluere* to] — **mel·lif′lu·ous·ly** *adv.* — **mel·lif′lu·ous·ness** *n.*
low (mel′ō) *adj.* **1.** Soft, sweet, and full-flavored by ›on of ripeness, as fruit. **2.** Well-matured, as wines. **3.** › and soft in quality, as colors or sounds. **4.** Made gen- ›nd sympathetic by maturity or experience. **5.** Made ›l or genial by liquor. **6.** Soft and friable, as soil. — ›& *v.i.* To make or become mellow; soften. [ME, ? < OE › meal] — **mel′low·ly** *adv.* — **mel′low·ness** *n.*
o·de·on (mə·lō′dē·ən) *n.* A small reed organ or har- ›ium. [A pseudo-Greek formation < MELODY]
od·ic (mə·lod′ik) *adj.* **1.** Pertaining to or containing ›ody. **2.** Melodious. — **me·lod′i·cal·ly** *adv.*
o·di·ous (mə·lō′dē·əs) *adj.* **1.** Producing or character- by melody; tuneful. **2.** Pleasant to hear. — **me·lo′di·ly** *adv.* — **me·lo′di·ous·ness** *n.*
o·dra·ma (mel′ə·drä′mə, -dram′ə) *n.* **1.** A play or ›na in which the emotions displayed are violent or extrav- ›ntly sentimental, and the plot is made up of sensational ›dents. **2.** Formerly, a romantic drama with sensational ›dents, usu. including music and songs. **3.** Sensational highly emotional behavior or language. [< F < Gk. ›s song + *drama* drama] — **mel′o·dram′a·tist** *n.*
o·dra·mat·ic (mel′ə·drə·mat′ik) *adj.* Of, pertaining to, ›ke melodrama; sensational; exaggerated. — **mel′o·dra·** **′i·cal·ly** *adv.*
o·dra·mat·ics (mel′ə·drə·mat′iks) *n.pl.* Melodramatic ›avior.
o·dy (mel′ə·dē) *n.* *pl.* **·dies** **1.** Pleasing sounds, or an ›eable succession of such sounds. **2.** *Music* **a** An organ- › succession of tones, usu. in the same voice or instrument. ›he leading part in a homophonic composition; the air. OF < LL < Gk. < *melos* song + *aoidos* singer]
on (mel′ən) *n.* **1.** The large fruit of any of various ›ts of the gourd family, as the muskmelon and the water- ›on. **2.** Any of these plants. [< F < LL *melo, melonis*]
pom·e·ne (mel·pom′ə·nē) In Greek mythology, the ›se of tragedy.
t (melt) *v.t.* & *v.i.* **melt·ed, melt·ed** (*Archaic* **mol·ten** ›l′tən), **melt·ing** **1.** To reduce or change from a solid to ›quid state by heat. **2.** To dissolve, as in water. **3.** To ›ppear or cause to disappear; dissipate: often with *away.* ›o blend by imperceptible degrees: often with *into.* **5.** make or become softened in feeling or attitude. — *n.* **1.** ›nething melted. **2.** A single operation of fusing. **3.** The ›ount of a single fusing. [OE *meltan, mieltan*] — **melt′a·** *adj.* — **melt′a·bil′i·ty** *n.* — **melt′er** *n.*
ting point The temperature at which a specified solid ›stance melts or fuses.
ting pot **1.** A vessel in which a substance is melted. **2.** ›ountry, city, or region in which immigrants of various ra- › and cultural backgrounds are assimilated.
·ton (mel′tən) *n.* A heavy woolen cloth with a short ›, used for overcoats. [after *Melton* Mowbray, England]
m·ber (mem′bər) *n.* **1.** One who belongs to a society, ›b, party, etc. **2.** *Usu. cap.* One who belongs to a legisla- ›e body. **3.** *Biol.* A part or organ of an animal body, esp. ›mb. **4.** A part or element of a structural or composite ›ole. **5.** *Math.* Either side of an algebraic equation. [< › < L *membrum* limb]
m·ber·ship (mem′bər·ship) *n.* **1.** The state or fact of ›ng a member. **2.** The members of an organization, etc., ›lectively; also, the total number of members.
m·brane (mem′brān) *n.* A thin, pliable, sheetlike layer ›animal or vegetable tissue serving to cover or line an organ part, separate adjoining cavities, or connect adjoining ›uctures. [< L *membrana,* lit., limb coating]
m·bra·nous (mem′brə·nəs) *adj.* **1.** Of, pertaining to, or ›e a membrane. **2.** Marked by the formation of a mem- ›ane. Also **mem·bra·na·ceous** (mem′brə·nā′shəs).
·men·to (mə·men′tō) *n.* *pl.* **·tos** or **·toes** Anything that ›ves as a hint or reminder of the past; souvenir. [< L, ›member, imperative of *meminisse* to remember]
mento mo·ri (môr′ī) *Latin* An emblem or reminder of ›ath, as a skull, etc.: literally, remember that you must die.
m·o (mem′ō) *n.* *pl.* **mem·os** *Informal* A memorandum.
m·oir (mem′wär) *n.* **1.** *pl.* Personal reminiscences or ›cords; esp., a narrative of events based on the writer's per- ›nal observations and experiences. **2.** A biography. **3.** *pl.* › account of the proceedings of a learned society. **4.** A ›onograph. [< F < L *memoria* memory]
m·o·ra·bil·i·a (mem′ə·rə·bil′ē·ə) *n.pl.* Things or events ›rthy of remembrance and record. [< L]

mem·o·ra·ble (mem′ər·ə·bəl) *adj.* Worthy to be remembered; noteworthy. — **mem′o·ra·bil′i·ty, mem′o·ra·ble·ness** *n.* — **mem′o·ra·bly** *adv.*
mem·o·ran·dum (mem′ə·ran′dəm) *n.* *pl.* **·dums** or **·da** (-də) **1.** A brief note of a thing or things to be remembered. **2.** A record of transactions, etc., esp. for future use. **3.** An informal letter, usu. sent between departments in an office. **4.** *Law* A brief written outline of the terms of a transaction or contract. **5.** In business, a statement of goods sent from a consignor to a consignee. [< L, a thing to be remembered]
me·mo·ri·al (mə·môr′ē·əl, -mō′rē-) *adj.* **1.** Serving to keep in memory a deceased person or an event; commemorative. **2.** Of or pertaining to memory. — *n.* **1.** Something serving to keep in remembrance a person, event, etc. **2.** A written summary or presentation of facts addressed to a legislative body, official, etc., as the grounds for or in the form of a petition. [< OF < L < *memoria*]
Memorial Day *U.S.* A day set apart to honor the dead of any American war; in most states May 30. Also called *Decoration Day.*
me·mo·ri·al·ize (mə·môr′ē·əl·īz′, -mō′rē-) *v.t.* **·ized, ·iz·ing** **1.** To commemorate. **2.** To present a memorial to; petition. Also *Brit.* **me·mo′ri·al·ise′.** — **me·mo′ri·al·i·za′tion** *n.*
mem·o·rize (mem′ə·rīz) *v.t.* **·rized, ·riz·ing** To commit to memory. — **mem′o·ri·za′tion** *n.* — **mem′o·riz′er** *n.*
mem·o·ry (mem′ər·ē) *n.* *pl.* **·ries** **1.** The mental function or capacity of recalling or recognizing previously learned behavior or past experience. **2.** The total of what is remembered. **3.** One who or that which is remembered. **4.** The period of time covered by the faculty of remembrance. **5.** The state of being remembered. **6.** Remembrance or commemoration. [< OF < L *memor* mindful]
mem·sah·ib (mem′sä·ib) *n.* *Anglo-Indian* A European lady: a name given by native servants. [< MA'AM + Hind. *sāhib* master < Arabic]
men (men) Plural of MAN.
men·ace (men′is) *v.* **·aced, ·ac·ing** *v.t.* **1.** To threaten with evil or harm. — *v.i.* **2.** To make threats; appear threatening. — *n.* **1.** A threat. **2.** *Informal* A troublesome person; pest. [< OF < L < *minax, -acis* threatening] — **men′ac·er** *n.* — **men′ac·ing·ly** *adv.*
me·nad (mē′nad), etc. See MAENAD, etc.
mé·nage (mā·näzh′, *Fr.* mā·nȧzh′) *n.* **1.** The persons of a household, collectively. **2.** Household management. Also **me·nage′.** [< F < L *mansio, -onis* house]
me·nag·er·ie (mə·naj′ər·ē) *n.* **1.** A collection of wild animals kept for exhibition. **2.** The enclosure in which they are kept. [< F]
mend (mend) *v.t.* **1.** To make sound or serviceable again by repairing. **2.** To correct errors or faults in; improve. *Mend* your ways. **3.** To correct (some defect). — *v.i.* **4.** To become better, as in health. **5.** To improve: said of conditions. — *n.* **1.** A repairing. **2.** A mended place, as on a garment. — **on the mend** Recovering health. [Var. of AMEND] — **mend′a·ble** *adj.* — **mend′er** *n.*
men·da·cious (men·dā′shəs) *adj.* **1.** Lying; deceitful. **2.** Untrue; false. [< L *mendax, -acis* lying] — **men·da′cious·ly** *adv.* — **men·da′cious·ness** *n.*
men·dac·i·ty (men·das′ə·tē) *n.* *pl.* **·ties** **1.** The quality of being mendacious. **2.** A lie; untruth.
men·de·le·vi·um (men′də·lē′vē·əm) *n.* A short-lived radioactive element (symbol Md). See ELEMENT. [after Dmitri Ivanovich *Mendeleyev*]
Mendel's laws *Genetics* Principles formulated by Gregor Mendel, stating that alternative unit characters of hybrids segregate from one another in transmission to offspring and that different pairs of such characters segregate independently of each other. — **Men·de·li·an** (men·dē′lē·ən) *adj.*
men·di·cant (men′də·kənt) *adj.* **1.** Begging; depending on alms for a living. **2.** Pertaining to or like a beggar. — *n.* **1.** A beggar. **2.** A begging friar. [< L < *mendicus* needy] — **men′di·can·cy, men·dic·i·ty** (men·dis′ə·tē) *n.*
Men·e·la·us (men′ə·lā′əs) In Greek legend, a king of Sparta and the husband of Helen of Troy.
men·ha·den (men·hād′n) *n.* A fish of North Atlantic and West Indian waters, used as a source of oil, as fertilizer, and as bait. [Alter. of Algonquian *munnawhat* fertilizer]
me·ni·al (mē′nē·əl, mēn′yəl) *adj.* **1** Pertaining to or appropriate to servants. **2.** Servile; abject. — *n.* **1.** A domestic servant. **2.** One who has a servile nature. [< AF < OF < LL < L *mansio* house] — **me′ni·al·ly** *adv.*
me·nin·ges (mə·nin′jēz) *n.* *pl.* of **me·ninx** (mē′ningks) *Anat.* The three membranes enveloping the brain and spinal cord. [< NL < Gk. *mēninx, mēningos* membrane] — **me·nin′ge·al** *adj.*
men·in·gi·tis (men′ən·jī′tis) *n.* *Pathol.* Inflammation of the meninges, esp. through infection. — **men′in·git′ic** (-jit′·ik) *adj.*

›NUNCIATION KEY: add, āce, câre, pälm; end, ēven; it, īce; odd, ōpen, ôrder; to͝ok, po͞ol; up, bûrn; ə = a in *above,* e in *sicken,* i in *flex-* › o in *melon,* u in *focus;* yo͞o = u in *fuse;* oil; pout; check; go; ring; thin; this; zh, vision.

me·nis·cus (mə·nis′kəs) *n. pl.* **·nis·cus·es** or **·nis·ci** (-nis′ī) **1.** A crescent or crescent-shaped body. **2.** *Optics* A lens concave on one side and convex on the other. **3.** *Physics* The curved upper surface of a liquid column. [< L < Gk. *mēniskos* crescent, dim. of *mēnē* moon]

Men·non·ite (men′ən·īt) *n.* A member of a Protestant Christian sect founded in the 16th century, opposing the taking of oaths, the holding of public office, and military service. [after *Menno* Simons, 1492–1559, a leader of the sect]

Me·nom·i·nee (mə·nom′ə·nē) *n. pl.* **·nee 1.** One of an Algonquian tribe of North American Indians, inhabiting central Wisconsin. **2.** The Algonquian language of this tribe. Also **Me·nom·i·ni** (-nē).

men·o·pause (men′ə·pôz) *n. Physiol.* The final cessation of menstruation, occurring normally between the ages of 45 and 50. [< Gk. *mēn* month + *pauein* to cause to cease]

Me·no·rah (mə·nôr′ə, -nō′rə) *n.* In the Jewish religion, a candelabrum having nine candles lighted in increasing numbers during Hannukah. [< Hebrew, candlestick]

men·ses (men′sēz) *n.pl. Physiol.* Menstruation. [< L, pl. of *mensis* month]

Men·she·vik (men′shə·vik) *n. pl.* **·vi·ki** (-vē′kē) or **·viks** A member of the conservative element in the Russian Social Democratic Party. Compare BOLSHEVIK. Also **Men′she·vist.** [< Russian *menshe* minority] — **Men′she·vism** *n.*

men·stru·al (men′stro͞o·əl) *adj.* **1.** *Physiol.* Of or pertaining to menstruation. Also **men′stru·ous. 2.** Monthly. [< L < *menstruus* monthly]

men·stru·ate (men′stro͞o·āt) *v.i.* **·at·ed, ·at·ing** To undergo menstruation.

men·stru·a·tion (men′stro͞o·ā′shən) *n. Physiol.* **1.** The periodical flow of bloody fluid from the uterus, occurring normally about every 28 days: also called *menses*. **2.** An occurrence of this flow: also called *period*.

men·stru·um (men′stro͞o·əm) *n. pl.* **·stru·ums** or **·stru·a** (-stro͞o·ə) The medium in which a substance is dissolved.

men·su·ra·ble (men′shər·ə·bəl) *adj.* That can be measured. [< LL < *mensurare* to measure] — **men′su·ra·bil′i·ty** *n.*

men·su·ral (men′shər·əl) *adj.* Pertaining to measure.

men·su·ra·tion (men′shə·rā′shən) *n.* **1.** The art, act, or process of measuring. **2.** The branch of mathematics having to do with determining length, area, and volume.

-ment *suffix of nouns* **1.** The product or result of: *achievement*. **2.** The instrument or means of: *atonement*. **3.** The process or action of: *government*. **4.** The quality, condition, or state of being: *astonishment*. [< F < L *-mentum*]

men·tal (men′təl) *adj.* **1.** Of or pertaining to the mind or intellect. **2.** Effected by or taking place in the mind, esp. without the aid of written symbols: *mental* calculations. **3.** Affected by mental illness: a *mental* patient. **4.** For the care of the mentally ill: *mental* hospital. [< F < LL < L *mens, mentis* mind] — **men′tal·ly** *adv.*

mental age See under AGE.

mental deficiency *Psychol.* A condition characterized by subnormal intelligence to the extent that the individual is handicapped from participating fully in ordinary life.

mental healing The alleged curing of any disorder, ailment, or disease by mental concentration and suggestion.

mental hygiene The scientific study and application of methods to preserve and promote mental health.

men·tal·i·ty (men·tal′ə·tē) *n. pl.* **·ties 1.** The mental faculties or powers; mental activity. **2.** Intellectual capacity or power: an average *mentality*. **3.** Cast or habit of mind.

men·thol (men′thôl, -thōl, -thol) *n. Chem.* A white, waxy, crystalline alcohol, $C_{10}H_{19}OH$, obtained from and having the odor of oil of peppermint, used as a flavoring agent, in perfumery, and in medicine. [< G < L *mentha* mint + -OL]

men·tho·lat·ed (men′thə·lā′tid) *adj.* Treated with, containing, or impregnated with menthol.

men·tion (men′shən) *v.t.* To refer to incidentally, briefly, or in passing. — *n.* **1.** The act of one who mentions. **2.** Slight reference; casual allusion. [< OF < L *mens, mentis* mind] — **men′tion·a·ble** *adj.* — **men′tion·er** *n.*

men·tor (men′tər, -tôr) *n.* A wise and trusted teacher or guide. [< MENTOR] — **men·to′ri·al** (-tôr′ē·əl, -tō′rē-) *adj.*

Men·tor (men′tər, -tôr) In the *Odyssey*, the sage guardian appointed by Odysseus for Telemachus.

men·u (men′yo͞o, mān′-; *Fr.* mə·nü′) *n.* A bill of fare; also, the dishes included in it. [< F < L *minutus* small, detailed]

me·ow (mē·ou′, myou) *n.* The crying sound made by a cat. — *v.t.* To make the sound of a cat. [Imit.]

Meph·is·toph·e·les (mef′is·tof′ə·lēz) **1.** In medieval legend, a devil to whom Faust sold his soul for wisdom and power. **2.** A leading character in Marlowe's *Dr. Faustus*, Goethe's *Faust*, etc. — *n.* A diabolical or crafty person. Also **Me·phis·to** (mə·fis′tō). — **Me·phis·to·phe·le·an** (mə·fis′tə·fē′lē·ən), **Me·phis′to·phe′li·an** *adj.*

me·phit·ic (mə·fit′ik) *adj.* **1.** Poisonous; foul. **2.** Offensive to the sense of smell. Also **me·phit′i·cal.**

me·pro·ba·mate (mə·prō′bə·māt, me·prō·ba′māt) *n. Chem.* A white, nearly odorless, bitter powder, $C_9H_{18}N_2O_4$, used in medicine as a tranquilizer. [< ME(THYL) + PRO(PANE + (DI-) + (CAR)BAMATE]

mer·can·tile (mûr′kən·til, -tīl) *adj.* **1.** Of, pertaining characteristic of merchants or commerce. **2.** Of or pe ing to the mercantile system. [< F < Ital. < L *mer -antis*, pp. of *mercari* to traffic]

mercantile system The theory in political economy the wealth of a country consists in its quantity of gol silver, and that the importation of precious metals, an exportation of goods should be encouraged by the state. called **mer·can·til·ism** (mûr′kən·til·iz′əm).

Mer·ca·tor projection (mər·kā′tər) A map projecti which the earth is shown as projected on a cylinder, the meridians and parallels forming a rectangular grid, with areas and distances being less truly represented the farther they are from the equator. [after Gerardus *Mercator*, 1512–94, Flemish cartographer]

MERCATOR PROJECTION

mer·ce·nar·y (mûr′sə·ner′ē) *adj.* **1.** Influenced by a desire for gain or reward. **2.** Serving for pay: now said only of soldiers hired by a foreign state. — *n. pl.* **·nar·ies** A hire esp., a hired soldier in foreign service. [< L *merces* rev hire] — **mer′ce·nar′i·ly** *adv.* — **mer′ce·nar′i·ness** *n.*

mer·cer·ize (mûr′sə·rīz) *v.t.* **·ized, ·iz·ing** To treat ton fabrics) with caustic soda so as to increase strength part a gloss, and render more receptive to dyes. [after *Mercer*, 1791–1866, English inventor. — **mer′cer·i·za′ti**

mer·chan·dise (mûr′chən·dīz, -dīs) *n.* Anything bo and sold for profit; goods; wares. — *v.t. & v.i.* **·dised, ing 1.** To buy and sell; trade. **2.** To promote the sa (goods) through advertising, etc. Also **mer′chan·dize.** MERCHANT.] — **mer′chan·dis′er** *n.*

mer·chant (mûr′chənt) *n.* **1.** One who buys and sells modities for profit. **2.** A storekeeper. — *adj.* **1.** Of or taining to merchants or trade. **2.** Of or pertaining to merchant marine. [< OF < L *mercari* to traffic, buy]

mer·chant·a·ble (mûr′chən·tə·bəl) *adj.* Marketable.

mer·chant·man (mûr′chənt·mən) *n. pl.* **·men** (-mən trading or merchant vessel.

merchant marine **1.** All the merchant or trading ve of a nation, collectively. **2.** The officers and men empl on these vessels.

mer·ci (mer·sē′) *interj. French* Thank you.

Mer·ci·a (mûr′shē·ə, -shə) An ancient Anglo-Saxon king of central England. — **Mer′ci·an** *adj. & n.*

mer·ci·ful (mûr′sə·fəl) *adj.* **1.** Full of or exercising me compassionate. **2.** Characterized by or indicating merc *merciful* death. — **mer′ci·ful·ly** *adv.* — **mer′ci·ful·ness**

mer·ci·less (mûr′sə·lis) *adj.* Having or showing no me pitiless. — **mer′ci·less·ly** *adv.* — **mer′ci·less·ness** *n.*

mer·cu·ri·al (mər·kyo͝or′ē·əl) *adj.* **1.** Lively; volatile; c er: a *mercurial* wit. **2.** Of, pertaining to, containing caused by the action of mercury, or quicksilver. **3.** *C cap.* Of or pertaining to the god Mercury or the planet M cury. — *n. Med.* A preparation containing mercury. **mer·cu′ri·al·ly** *adv.* — **mer·cu′ri·al·ness** *n.*

mer·cu·ri·al·ism (mər·kyo͝or′ē·əl·iz′əm) *n. Pathol.* soning produced by excessive amounts of mercury.

mer·cu·ri·al·ize (mər·kyo͝or′ē·əl·īz′) *v.t.* **·ized, ·iz·ing 1.** make mercurial. **2.** To treat with mercury. — **mer·cu al·i·za′tion** *n.*

mer·cu·ric (mər·kyo͝or′ik) *adj. Chem.* Of, pertaining to containing mercury in its highest valence.

mercuric chloride *Chem.* A white, crystalline, very p sonous compound, $HgCl_2$, used in industry, the arts, and a strong disinfectant: also called *bichloride of mercury*, *rosive sublimate*. Also **mercury chloride.**

mercuric sulfide Cinnabar.

mer·cu·rous (mər·kyo͝or′əs) *adj. Chem.* Of, pertaining or containing mercury in its lowest valence.

mer·cu·ry (mûr′kyə·rē) *n. pl.* **·ries 1.** A heavy, silv white metallic element (symbol Hg), liquid at ordinary te peratures: also called *hydrargyrum, quicksilver*. See E MENT. **2.** The quicksilver in a thermometer or barome as indicating temperature, etc. **3.** A messenger.

Mer·cu·ry (mûr′kyə·rē) In Roman mythology, the mess ger of the gods, god of commerce, eloquence, and skill, a patron of travelers, merchants, and thieves: identified w the Greek *Hermes*. — *n.* The smallest planet of the so system, and that nearest the sun. See PLANET.

·cy (mûr′sē) *n. pl.* **·cies 1.** Kind or compassionate ·tment of an offender, adversary, prisoner, etc., in one's ·er. **2.** A disposition to be kind, forgiving, or helpful. **3.** · power to show mercy or compassion. **4.** A thing to be ·nkful for. **— at the mercy of** Wholly in the power of. OF < L *merces, mercedis* payment, reward;

· Syn. 1. *Mercy* comes from compassion, kindness, or other en·ing sentiment. *Clemency* is a colder word, chiefly applied to ·eration in the exercise of legal power to punish. *Leniency* ·otes easygoing forbearance, sometimes with a suggestion of un· laxity or indulgence.

·cy killing Euthanasia.

·e (mir) *adj.* Being nothing more or less than: a *mere* ·e. [< L *merus* unmixed, bare]

·re *combining form Zool.* A part or division. [< Gk. ·*os* part]

·e·ly (mir′lē) *adv.* Nothing more than; solely; only.

·e·tri·cious (mer′ə·trish′əs) *adj.* Artificially and vul·ly attractive. [< L < *merere* to earn, gain] **— mer′e·cious·ly** *adv.* **— mer′e·tri′cious·ness** *n.*

·gan·ser (mər·gan′sər) *n.* Any of several fish-eating, ·ing ducks having the head usu. crested. [< NL < L < ·*gere* to plunge + *anser* goose]

·ge (mûrj) *v.t. & v.i.* **merged, merg·ing** To combine or ·combined so as to lose separate identity; blend. [< L ·*gere* to dip, immerse] **— mer′gence** *n.*

·g·er (mûr′jər) *n.* **1.** The combining of two or more ·nmercial interests into one. **2.** The act of merging.

·rid·i·an (mə·rid′ē·ən) *n.* **1.** *Geog.* **a** A great circle drawn ·m any point on the earth's surface and passing through ·h poles. **b** Half of a circle so drawn between the poles. **2.** ·*ron.* An imaginary great circle of the celestial sphere pass· through its poles and the zenith of an observer at any ·nt. **3.** The highest or culminating point; zenith. **—** *adj.* Of or pertaining to a meridian. **2.** Of or pertaining to ·dday. [< OF < L < *medius* middle + *dies* day]

·ringue (mə·rang′) *n.* **1.** The stiffly beaten white of eggs ·nded with sugar and usu. baked, used as a topping for ·stry or pies. **2.** A small cake or tart shell made of this. F < G *meringe*, lit., cake of Mehringen (in Germany)]

·ri·no (mə·rē′nō) *n. pl.* **·nos 1.** A breed of sheep having ·e, closely set, silky wool and heavy curled horns in the ·ale; also, the wool of this sheep. **2.** A fine fabric originally ·ade of merino wool. **3.** A type of fine yarn used for knitted ·derwear, hosiery, etc. **—** *adj.* Made of merino wool, yarn ·cloth. [< Sp., roving from pasture to pasture, shepherd]

·r·it (mer′it) *n.* **1.** Worth or excellence; high quality. **2.** ·at which deserves esteem, praise, or reward. **3.** *Some·es pl.* The quality or fact of being entitled to reward, ·aise, etc. **4.** *pl.* The actual rights or wrongs of a matter, ·. a legal matter. **—** *v.t.* To earn as a reward or punish·ent; deserve. [< OF < L < *merere* to deserve] **— mer′it·** *adj.*

·r·i·to·ri·ous (mer′ə·tôr′ē·əs, -tō′rē-) *adj.* Deserving of ·ward or praise. **— mer′i·to′ri·ous·ly** *adv.* **— mer′i·to′ri·s·ness** *n.*

·rit system A system adopted in the U.S. Civil Service ·hereby appointments and promotions are made on the ·sis of merit, ascertained through qualifying examinations.

·rle (mûrl) *n.* The European blackbird. Also **merl.** [< < L *merula* blackbird]

·r·lin (mûr′lin) In the Arthurian cycle and other medi·al legends, a magician and prophet. [< Med.L < Welsh ·*yrrdin*, lit., sea fortress]

·r·maid (mûr′mād′) *n.* A legendary marine creature hav·g the head and upper body of a woman and the tail of a ·sh. Also **mer′maid′en** (-mād′n). [OE *mere* sea, lake + MAID]

·ero- *combining form* Part; partial. Also, before vowels, ·*er-*. [< Gk. *meros* part, division]

·erous *suffix Zool.* Having (a specified number or kind of) ·arts. [< Gk. *meros* part, division]

·er·o·vin·gi·an (mer′ə·vin′jē·ən, -jən) *adj.* Of or pertain·g to the first Frankish dynasty founded about A.D. 500 and ·sting until 751. **—** *n.* A member of the Merovingian dy·asty. Also **Mer′o·win′gi·an.** [< L *Merovingi*, descendants · Marovaeus, a legendary Frankish king]

·er·ri·ment (mer′i·mənt) *n.* Laughter; fun.

·er·ry (mer′ē) *adj.* **·ri·er, ·ri·est 1.** Full of mirth and ·aughter; joyous; gay. **2.** Characterized by or conducive to ·nirth, cheerfulness, etc. [OE *myrige* pleasant] **— mer′ri·ly** ·*dv.* **— mer′ri·ness** *n.*

·er·ry-an·drew (mer′ē·an′drōō) *n.* A clown or buffoon.

·er·ry-go-round (mer′ē·gō·round′) *n.* **1.** A revolving ·latform fitted with wooden horses, seats, etc., on which ·eople, esp. children, ride for amusement; carousel. **2.** A ·whirl, as of business or pleasure. Also, *Brit.*, *roundabout.*

·er·ry·mak·ing (mer′ē·mā′king) *n.* The act of having fun ·nd making merry. **—** *adj.* Festive. **— mer′ry·mak′er** *n.*

mes- Var. of MESO-.

me·sa (mā′sə, *Sp.* mā′sä) *n.* A high, flat tableland descending sharply to the surrounding plain, common in the SW U.S. [< Sp. < L *mensa* table]

mé·sal·li·ance (mā·zal′ē·əns, *Fr.* mā·zȧ·lyäṅs′) *n.* A marriage with one of inferior position; misalliance. [< F]

mes·cal (mes·kal′) *n.* **1.** A spineless cactus, native to the SW U.S. and northern Mexico, whose dried tops, **mescal buttons,** are chewed by the Indians for their narcotic effect: also called *peyote.* **2.** An intoxicating liquor distilled from certain species of agave. [< Sp. < Nahuatl *mexicalli*]

mes·dames (mā·däm′, *Fr.* mā·dȧm′) Plural of MADAME.

mes·de·moi·selles (mād·mwȧ·zel′) *French* Plural of MADEMOISELLE.

me·seems (mē·sēmz′) *v. impersonal Archaic* It seems to me.

mes·en·ceph·a·lon (mes′en·sef′ə·lon′) *n. Anat.* One of the three principal divisions of the central nervous system of the embryo: also called *midbrain.* [< NL < MES- + ENCEPHALON] **— mes·en·ce·phal·ic** (mes·en′sə·fal′ik) *adj.*

mes·en·ter·y (mes′ən·ter′ē) *n. pl.* **·ter·ies** *Anat.* A membranous fold that invests an intestine and connects it with the posterior abdominal wall. Also **mes′en·te′ri·um** (-tir′ē·əm). [< Med.L < Gk. < *mesos* middle + *enteron* intestine] **— mes′en·ter′ic** *adj.*

mesh (mesh) *n.* **1.** One of the open spaces between the cords of a net or the wires of a screen. **2.** *pl.* The cords or wires bounding such a space or spaces. **3.** A net or network. **4.** *Usu. pl.* Anything that entangles or involves; a snare. **5.** *Mech.* The engagement of gear teeth. **—** *v.t. & v.i.* **1.** To make or become entangled, as in a net. **2.** To make or become engaged, as gear teeth. [< MDu. *maesche* mesh]

mesh·work (mesh′wûrk′) *n.* Meshes; network.

mes·mer·ism (mes′mə·riz′əm, mez′-) *n.* Loosely, hypnotism: also called *animal magnetism.* [after Franz Anton *Mesmer*, 1733–1815, German physician] **— mes·mer·ic** (mes·mer′ik, mez-) *adj.* **— mes′mer·ist** *n.*

mes·mer·ize (mes′mə·rīz, mez′-) *v.t.* **·ized, ·iz·ing** To hypnotize. Also *Brit.* **mes′mer·ise. — mes′mer·i·za′tion** *n.*

meso- *combining form* **1.** Situated in the middle. **2.** Intermediate in size or degree. Also, before vowels, *mes-.* [< Gk. *mesos* middle]

mes·o·blast (mes′ə·blast, mē′sə-) *n. Biol.* The mesoderm in its early stages. [< MESO- + Gk. *blastos* sprout] **— mes′·o·blas′tic** *adj.*

mes·o·carp (mes′ə·kärp, mē′sə-) *n. Bot.* The middle layer of a pericarp, as the fleshy part of certain fruits.

mes·o·derm (mes′ə·dûrm, mē′sə-) *n.* The middle of the three primary germ layers in the embryo of animals, developing into the skeletal and muscular systems.

Mes·o·lith·ic (mes′ə·lith′ik, mē′sə-) *adj. Anthropol.* Pertaining to or designating the period of human culture followed by the Neolithic and characterized by an economy transitional between food gathering and a settled agriculture.

mes·o·mor·phic (mes′ə·môr′fik, mē′sə-) *adj.* Designating a human body type characterized by a sturdy body structure. **— mes′o·morph** *n.* **— mes′o·mor′phy** *n.*

mes·on (mē′son, mes′on) *n. Physics* Any of a group of unstable nucleons having a mass intermediate between that of the electron and the proton. [< Gk. *mesos* middle]

mes·o·tho·ri·um (mes′ə·thôr′ē·əm, -thō′rē-; mē′sə-) *n.* Either of two isotopes resulting from the radioactive disintegration of thorium, intermediate between thorium and radiothorium.

Mes·o·zo·ic (mes′ə·zō′ik, mē′sə-) *Geol. adj.* Pertaining to the era between the Paleozoic and the Cenozoic. **—** *n.* This era, including the Triassic, Jurassic, and Cretaceous periods.

mes·quite (mes·kēt′, mes′kēt) *n.* A spiny, leguminous shrub or small tree, found in SW U.S. and extending southward to Peru, that yields sweet pods used for cattle fodder: also called *honey mesquite.* Also spelled *mezquit, mezquite.* Also **mes·quit** (mes·kēt′, mes′kēt). [< Sp. < Nahuatl *mizquitl*]

mess (mes) *n.* **1.** A state of disorder; esp., a condition of dirty or untidy confusion. **2.** A confusing, difficult, or embarrassing situation or condition; muddle. **3.** An unpleasant or confused mixture or collection; hodgepodge. **4.** A quantity of food sufficient for a meal or dish. **5.** A portion of soft, partly liquid food. **6.** A disagreeable or sloppy preparation of food. **7.** A number of persons who regularly take their meals together, as in the military; also, a meal taken by them. **—** *v.i.* **1.** To busy oneself; dabble: often with *around* or *about.* **2.** To make a mess; bungle: often with *up.* **3.** To interfere; meddle: often with *around.* **4.** To eat with as a member of a mess. **—** *v.t.* **5.** To make a mess of; botch: often with *up.* **6.** To make dirty: often with *up.* **7.** To provide meals for. [< OF < L *missus* course at a meal]

mes·sage (mes′ij) *n.* **1.** A communication sent by any of various means. **2.** An official or formal communication, as from a chief executive to a legislative body. **3.** A communication embodying important principles or counsel. [< OF < Med.L < *mittere* to send]

mes·sa·line (mes′ə·lēn′, mes′ə·lēn) *n.* A lightweight, lustrous, twilled silk fabric.

mes·sen·ger (mes′ən·jər) *n.* **1.** One sent with a message or on an errand; esp., one whose work is running errands. **2.** A bearer of official dispatches; courier. **3.** *Archaic* A harbinger. [ME < OF *messagier*. The *n* is nonhistoric.]

mess hall A place where a group of persons regularly take their meals, as in the army, navy, etc.

Mes·si·ah (mə·sī′ə) *n.* **1.** In Judaism, a deliverer of Israel promised by God and expected by the Jews. **2.** In Christianity, Jesus regarded as this deliverer. **3.** Any expected liberator of a country, people, etc. Also **Mes·si′as.** [< LL < Gk. < Aramaic *měshīhā*, Hebrew *māshīah* anointed] — **Mes·si′ah·ship** *n.* — **Mes·si·an·ic** (mes′ē·an′ik) *adj.*

mes·sieurs (mes′ərz, *Fr.* mā·syœ′) *n.pl.* of *Fr.* **mon·sieur** (mə·syœ′) Sirs; gentlemen: in English in the contracted form *Messrs.*, used as plural of *Mr.*

mess jacket A man's tailored jacket, usu. white and terminating at the waistline, worn on semiformal occasions.

mess kit A small, compact unit containing cooking and eating utensils, used by soldiers in the field and campers.

mess sergeant A noncommissioned officer who plans meals, issues rations, and superintends the company mess.

mes·sy (mes′ē) *adj.* Being in or causing a condition of dirt or confusion; untidy. — **mess′i·ly** *adv.* — **mess′i·ness** *n.*

mes·ti·zo (mes·tē′zō) *n. pl.* **·zos** or **·zoes** Any one of mixed blood; in Mexico and the western U.S., a person of Spanish and Indian blood: also called *Ladino*. Also **mes·te′so, mes·ti′no** (-nō). [< Sp. < LL < L *mixtus*, pp. of *miscere* to mix] — **mes·ti′za** (-zə) *n.fem.*

met (met) Past tense and past participle of MEET[1].

met- Var. of META-.

meta- *prefix* **1.** Changed in place or form; reversed; altered. **2.** *Anat. & Zool.* Behind; after; on the farther side of; later: often equivalent to *post-* or *dorso-*. **3.** With; alongside. **4.** Beyond; over; transcending: *metaphysics, metapsychology.* **5.** *Chem.* **a** A modification of. **b** A derivative of. Also, before vowels and *h*, *met-*. [< Gk. < *meta* after, beside, with]

met·a·bol·ic (met′ə·bol′ik) *adj. Biol. & Physiol.* Of, pertaining to, or having the nature of metabolism.

me·tab·o·lism (mə·tab′ə·liz′əm) *n. Biol. & Physiol.* The aggregate of all chemical processes constantly taking place in a living organism, including those that use energy to convert nutritive materials into protoplasm (anabolism) and those that release energy for vital processes in breaking down protoplasm into simpler substances (catabolism). [< Gk. < *meta-* beyond + *ballein* to throw]

me·tab·o·lize (mə·tab′ə·līz) *v.t. & v.i.* **·lized, ·liz·ing** To subject to or change by metabolism.

met·a·car·pus (met′ə·kär′pəs) *n. Anat.* The part of the forelimb between the carpus or wrist and the phalanges or bones of the finger. [< NL < Gk. < *meta-* beyond + *karpos* wrist] — **met′a·car′pal** *adj. & n.*

met·a·gal·ax·y (met′ə·gal′ək·sē) *n. pl.* **·ax·ies** *Astron.* The entire material universe, regarded esp. as a system including all the galaxies.

met·al (met′l) *n.* **1.** Any of a class of elements characterized by a distinctive luster, malleability, ductility, thermal and electrical conductivity, and capable of forming positive ions. **2.** A composition of such metallic elements; alloy. **3.** Molten glass. **4.** The constituent material of anything. — **white metal** Any one of the various white alloys, as pewter, Babbitt metal, etc., used for ornaments, castings, etc. — *v.t.* **met·aled** or **·alled, met·al·ing** or **·al·ling** To furnish or cover with metal. [< OF < L < Gk. *metallon*]

me·tal·lic (mə·tal′ik) *adj.* **1.** Of, pertaining to, or consisting of metal. **2.** Resembling or having the nature of metal: a *metallic* sound. **3.** Yielding or containing metal.

met·al·lif·er·ous (met′ə·lif′ər·əs) *adj.* Yielding or containing metal.

met·al·lur·gy (met′ə·lûr′jē) *n.* **1.** The art or science of extracting a metal or metals from ores. **2.** The art or science of working with metals and alloys for the purpose of their development, improvement, etc. [< NL < Gk. < *metallon* mine + *-ergos* working] — **met′al·lur′gic** or **·gi·cal** *adj.* — **met′al·lur′gi·cal·ly** *adv.* — **met′al·lur′gist** *n.*

met·al·work (met′l·wûrk′) *n.* **1.** Articles made of metal. **2.** The art of making such things. — **met′al·work′er** *n.* — **met′al·work′ing** *n.*

met·a·mor·phic (met′ə·môr′fik) *adj.* **1.** Of or pertaining to metamorphosis. **2.** *Geol.* Of, pertaining to, or exhibiting metamorphism. Also **met′a·mor′phous.**

met·a·mor·phism (met′ə·môr′fiz·əm) *n.* **1.** *Geol.* The changes in the composition and texture of rocks caused by force, heat, pressure, moisture, etc. **2.** Metamorphosis.

met·a·mor·phose (met′ə·môr′fōz) *v.t.* **·phosed, ·phos·ing** **1.** To change the form of. — *v.i.* **2.** To undergo metamorphosis. Also **met′a·mor′phize.** [< MF *métamorphoser*]

met·a·mor·pho·sis (met′ə·môr′fə·sis) *n. pl.* **·pho·ses** (-fə·sēz) **1.** Change from one form, shape, or substance int other by any means. **2.** Complete transformation of ch ter, purpose, circumstances, etc. **3.** One who or that w is metamorphosed. **4.** *Biol.* Any marked change in the and structure of an animal in its development from em to adult, as from tadpole to frog. [< L < Gk. < beyond + *morphē* form]

met·a·phor (met′ə·fôr, -fər) *n.* A figure of speech in w one object is likened to another by speaking of it as if it that other, as *He was a lion in battle*: distinguished *simile*. — **Syn.** See SIMILE. — **mixed metaphor** A fi tive expression in which two or more incongruous meta are used, as *He kept a tight rein on his boiling passions.* F < L < Gk. < *meta-* beyond, over + *pherein* to carry — **met′a·phor′ic** (-fôr′ik, -for′ik) or **·i·cal** *adj.* — **met′a·p**

met·a·phys·i·cal (met′ə·fiz′i·kəl) *adj.* **1.** Of, pertainin or of the nature of metaphysics. **2.** Highly abstruse stract. **3.** Of or designating certain English poets o 17th century whose poetry is characterized by comple tellectual imagery and paradox. [See METAPHYSICS.] — **met′a·phys′i·cal·ly** *adv.*

met·a·phys·ics (met′ə·fiz′iks) *n.pl.* (*construed as sing* The branch of philosophy that investigates principl reality transcending those of any particular science, t tionally including cosmology and ontology. **2.** All sp lative philosophy. [< Med.L < Med.Gk. < *ta me physika* the (works) after the *Physics* of Aristotle]

me·tas·ta·sis (mə·tas′tə·sis) *n. pl.* **·ses** (-sēz) *Pathol* The transfer of a disease from one part of the body to other, as in certain types of cancer. **2.** A site to which a transfer has been made. [< L < Gk. < *meta-* afte *histanai* to place] — **met′a·stat′ic** (-stat′ik) *adj.* — **m stat′i·cal·ly** *adv.*

me·tas·ta·size (mə·tas′tə·sīz) *v.i.* **·sized, ·siz·ing** *Pa* To shift or spread from one part of the body to another, malignant growth.

met·a·tar·sus (met′ə·tär′səs) *n. pl.* **·si** (-sī) *Anat.* **1** man, the part of the foot situated between the tarsus and bones of the toes. **2.** An analogous part in the hind or pe limb of animals or birds. — **met′a·tar′sal** *adj. & n.*

me·tath·e·sis (mə·tath′ə·sis) *n. pl.* **·ses** (-sēz) The tr position of letters, syllables, or sounds in a word: Old E lish *bridd* became *bird* by *metathesis*. [< LL < Gk. < *m* over + *tithenai* to place] — **met·a·thet·ic** (met′ə·thet or **·i·cal** *adj.*

met·a·zo·an (met′ə·zō′ən) *n. Zool.* Any of a primary sion of animals, whose bodies are made up of many c Also **met′a·zo′on.** — *adj.* Of the metazoans: also **me zo′ic.** [< META- + Gk. *zōion* animal]

mete[1] (mēt) *v.t.* **met·ed, met·ing** To allot or distribute b as by measure: usu. followed by *out*. [OE *metan* to meas

mete[2] (mēt) *n.* A boundary line; limit: now chiefly in phrase **metes and bounds.** [< OF < L *meta* goal, bounda

me·tem·psy·cho·sis (mə·temp′sə·kō′sis, met′əm·sī-) Transmigration of souls. [< LL < Gk. < *meta-* over + *psychoein* to animate]

met·en·ceph·a·lon (met′en·sef′ə·lon) *n. pl.* **·la** (-lə) *A* That part of the brain comprising the cerebellum and pons Varolii: also called *afterbrain*. — **met′en·ce·pha** (-sə·fal′ik) *adj.*

me·te·or (mē′tē·ər, -ôr) *n.* **1.** *Astron.* A meteoroid that entering the earth's atmosphere at great speed is heated luminosity and is visible as a streak of light: also ca *shooting star*. **2.** Loosely, a meteorite or meteoroid. Med.L < Gk. < *meta-* beyond + *eōra* suspension]

me·te·or·ic (mē′tē·ôr′ik, -or′ik) *adj.* **1.** Of, pertaining or consisting of meteors. **2.** Resembling a meteor; brillia rapid, and dazzling: a *meteoric* career. **3.** Of or pertaining atmospheric phenomena. — **me′te·or′i·cal·ly** *adv.*

me·te·or·ite (mē′tē·ə·rīt′) *n.* A portion of a meteor t has not been completely destroyed by combustion and fallen to earth. — **me′te·or·it′ic** (-ə·rit′ik) *adj.*

me·te·or·oid (mē′tē·ə·roid′) *n. Astron.* One of the pieces matter moving through outer space, that upon entering t earth's atmosphere form meteors.

me·te·or·ol·o·gy (mē′tē·ə·rol′ə·jē) *n.* **1.** The science t treats of atmospheric phenomena, esp. those that relate weather. **2.** The weather conditions of any particular pla [< Gk. < *meteōros* high in the air + *logos* discourse] — **m te·or′o·log′ic** (-ôr′ə·loj′ik) or **·i·cal** *adj.* — **me′te·or′o·lo cal·ly** *adv.* — **me′te·or·ol′o·gist** *n.*

meteor shower *Astron.* Any of various displays of me ors that recur at definite intervals and appear to radia from a single point or region.

me·ter[1] (mē′tər) *n.* An instrument or device used to me ure and indicate quantity or variation in amount, as of liquid or gas, electric current, light, etc.; also, a similar d vice for measuring speed, time, distance, etc. — *v.t.* measure or test by means of a meter. [< METE[1]]

me·ter[2] (mē′tər) *n.* **1.** A measured verbal rhythm constitu one of the chief characteristics of verse, and, in prosody, ning definite groups (feet) of accented and unaccented ables, usu. of a specified number for each line. **2.** *Music* combining of rhythmic pulses into successive groups ing like arrangement and duration. Also, *esp. Brit.*, *metre.* < L < Gk. *metron* a measure]

er³ (mē′tər) *n.* The basic unit of length in the metric em, equivalent to 39.37 inches. Also *metre.* See table t of book. [< F *mètre* < Gk. *metron*]

er *combining form* **1.** A device for measuring (a speci- quality, thing, etc.). **2.** Division into (a specified num- of) prosodic feet: *pentameter.* **3.** A (specified kind of) in the metric system: *kilometer*: also, *esp. Brit.*, *-metre.*

er·age (mē′tər·ij) *n.* The process or result of measuring or as by a meter.

er-kil·o·gram-sec·ond (mē′tər·kil′ə·gram′sek′ənd) See MKS.

h- *combining form Chem.* Used to indicate the presence methyl group in a compound. Also, before consonants, *ho-.* [< METHYL]

h·ane (meth′ān) *n. Chem.* A colorless, odorless, flam- ble gas, CH_4, the first member of the methane series, chief constituent of firedamp and marsh gas, and com- cially obtained from natural gas.

hane series *Chem.* A group of saturated hydrocarbons ing the general formula C_nH_{2n+2}: also called *paraffin es.*

h·a·nol (meth′ə·nōl, -nol) *n. Chem.* A colorless, flam- ble, highly toxic alcohol, CH_3OH, obtained by the de- ctive distillation of wood, and widely used in industry the arts: also called *methyl alcohol, wood alcohol.*

thinks (mē·thingks′) *v. impersonal,* **me·thought** *Ar- ic & Poetic* It seems to me. [OE *thyncan* to seem]

ho- Var. of METH-.

h·od (meth′əd) *n.* **1.** A way, means, or manner of pro- ding; esp., a regular, systematic, or orderly way of doing thing. **2.** System, order, or regularity in action or ught. **3.** The techniques used in a particular field of wledge, thought, practice, etc.: the scientific *method.* **4.** tematic and orderly arrangement, as of ideas, facts, ics, etc. **— the method** A system or style of acting in ch the actor makes a strong emotional identification h the role portrayed. [F < L < Gk. < *meta-* after + *os* way] **— meth′od·ism** *n.* **— meth′od·ist** *n.*

thod·i·cal (mə·thod′i·kəl) *adj.* **1.** Arranged in or per- med in systematic order. **2.** Characterized by orderly or tematic habits, behavior, etc.: a *methodical* man. Also **·thod′ic. — me·thod′i·cal·ly** *adv.* **— me·thod′i·cal·ness** *n.*

th·od·ist (meth′əd·ist) *n.* A member of any of the Prot- ant denominations having their origin in a religious move- nt begun in England in the first half of the 18th century John and Charles Wesley and their followers. **—** *adj.* rtaining to or characteristic of Methodism or Methodists. **Meth′od·ism** *n.* **— Meth′od·is′tic** or **·ti·cal** *adj.*

th·od·ize (meth′ə·dīz) *v.t.* **·ized, ·iz·ing** To reduce to or ange in accordance with a method. **— meth′od·i·za′tion** *n.*

th·od·ol·o·gy (meth′ə·dol′ə·jē) *n. pl.* **·gies 1.** The prin- les, practices, etc., of orderly thought or procedure ap- ed to a particular branch of learning. **2.** The branch of ic dealing with such procedures. [< Gk. *methodos* meth- + -LOGY] **— meth·od·o·log·i·cal** (meth′əd·ə·loj′i·kəl) *adj.* **meth′od·o·log′i·cal·ly** *adv.*

·thought (mē·thôt′) Past tense of METHINKS.

·thu·se·lah (mə·thōō′zə·lə) In the Old Testament, a ebrew patriarch reputed to have lived 969 years. *Gen.* v **—** *n.* A very old man.

th·yl (meth′əl) *n. Chem.* A univalent organic radical, H_3, existing chiefly in combination, as in methanol, etc. METHYLENE] **— me·thyl·ic** (mə·thil′ik) *adj.*

thyl alcohol *Chem.* Methanol.

th·yl·ate (meth′əl·āt) *Chem. n.* A compound derived om methanol by replacing the hydroxyl group with a met- **—** *v.t.* **·at·ed, ·at·ing 1.** To mix with methanol. **2.** To mbine with the methyl radical. **— meth′yl·a′tion** *n.*

thylated spirit Denatured alcohol prepared by the lmixture of methanol. Also **methylated spirits.**

e·tic·u·lous (mə·tik′yə·ləs) *adj.* Extremely or overly ecise about details, esp. in minor or trivial matters. [< F L *meticulosus* fearful] **— me·tic′u·los′i·ty** (-los′ə·tē), **me· c′u·lous·ness** *n.* **— me·tic′u·lous·ly** *adv.*
— Syn. Scrupulous, punctilious, fastidious.

é·tier (mā·tyā′) *n.* **1.** One's occupation, trade, or pro- ssion. **2.** Work or activity for which one is esp. well suited. < OF < L *ministerium* service, employment]

et·o·nym·i·cal (met′ə·nim′i·kəl) *adj.* **1.** Pertaining to or haracterized by metonymy. **2.** Used in metonymy. Also **et′o·nym′ic. — met′o·nym′i·cal·ly** *adv.*

e·ton·y·my (mə·ton′ə·mē) *n.* A figure of speech that consists in substituting an associated term for the name it- self, as in "the *crown* decrees" for "the *ruler* decrees." [< L < Gk. < *meta-* altered + *onyma* name]

metr- Var. of METRO-.

Met·ra·zol (met′rə·zōl, -zol) *n.* Proprietary name of a synthetic drug, $C_6H_{10}N_4$, used in medicine as a heart stimulant and in the shock treatment of certain mental disorders. Also **met′ra·zol.**

me·tre¹ (mē′tər) See METER².

me·tre² (mē′tər) See METER³.

-metre See -METER (def. 3).

met·ric (met′rik) *adj.* Of, pertaining to, or using the meter as a unit of measurement. [< F *métrique*]

met·ri·cal (met′ri·kəl) *adj.* **1.** Of, pertaining to, or char- acterized by meter; rhythmic. **2.** Composed in or constitut- ing a unit of poetic meter. **3.** Of, pertaining to, or involving measurement. Also **met′ric. — met′ri·cal·ly** *adv.*

metric hundredweight A unit of weight equal to 50 kilo- grams.

met·rics (met′riks) *n.pl.* (*construed as sing.*) **1.** The art or branch of learning concerned with meter in prosody. **2.** The science or theory of measurement.

metric system A decimal system of weights and measures having as fundamental units the gram, the meter, and the liter. See table front of book.

metric ton A unit of weight equal to 1,000 kilograms, or 2,204.62 pounds avoirdupois.

met·rist (met′rist) *n.* One who is skillful in using poetic meter. Also **met′ri·cist** (-rə·sist). [< Med.L *metrista*]

met·ro (met′rō) *n. Often cap. Informal* An underground railroad; subway; esp., the subway system of Paris. Also **mé·tro** (mā·trō′). [< F *métro* < (*chemin de fer*) *métro- (politain)* metro(politan railroad)]

metro-¹ *combining form* The uterus; pertaining to the uterus. Also, before vowels, *metr-.* [< Gk. *metra* uterus]

metro-² *combining form* Measure. Also, before vowels, *metr-.* [< Gk. *metron* a measure]

met·ro·nome (met′rə·nōm) *n.* An in- strument for indicating exact tempo in music, usu. producing audible clicks con- trolled by a reversed pendulum whose motion is regulated by a sliding weight. [< METRO-² + Gk. *nomos* law] **— met′· ro·nom′ic** (-nom′ik) *adj.*

METRONOME

me·tro·nym·ic (mē′trə·nim′ik, met′rə-) *adj.* Derived from the name of one's moth- er or a female ancestor. **—** *n.* A metro- nymic name or designation. [< Gk. < *mētēr* mother + *onyma* name]

me·trop·o·lis (mə·trop′ə·lis) *n. pl.* **·lis·es 1.** The capital or the largest or most im- portant city of a country, state, or area. **2.** An urban center of activity, culture, trade, etc. **3.** The see or city over which a metropolitan has authority. [< Gk. < *mētēr* mother + *polis* city]

met·ro·pol·i·tan (met′rə·pol′ə·tən) *adj.* **1.** Constituting a major urban center and its environs: the *metropolitan* area. **2.** Pertaining to or designating a bishop having authority over a metropolis (def. 3). **—** *n.* **1.** In various churches, an archbishop having authority over the bishops within his jurisdiction. **2.** One who lives in or has the viewpoint, etc., of one living in a metropolis.

-metry *combining form* The process, science, or art of meas- uring: *geometry.* [< Gk. *metria* < *metron* a measure]

met·tle (met′l) *n.* **1.** Character or temperament. **2.** Cour- age; pluck. **— on one's mettle** Aroused to one's best efforts. [Var. of METAL]

met·tle·some (met′l·səm) *adj.* Full of spirit; courageous; valiant. Also **met·tled** (met′əld).

mew¹ (myōō) *n.* **1.** A cage in which molting hawks are kept. **2.** *pl.* Stables built around a court or alley: so called from the royal stables in London. **3.** *pl.* (*construed as sing.*) *Chiefly Brit.* A narrow street or alley, often with dwellings converted from stables. **—** *v.t.* To confine in or as in a cage; often with *up.* [< OF *muer* to change, molt < L *mutare*]

mew² (myōō) *v.i.* To utter the high-pitched cry of a cat. **—** *n.* The high-pitched, plaintive cry of a cat. [Imit.]

mew³ (myōō) *n.* A gull; esp. the common gull of Europe: also called *sea mew.* [OE *mǣw*]

mewl (myōōl) *v.i.* To whimper or cry feebly, as an infant. **—** *n.* A whimper or feeble cry. [Freq. of MEW²]

Mex·i·can (mek′sə·kən) *n.* **1.** A native or inhabitant of Mexico. **2.** A language indigenous to Mexico, as Nahuatl. **—** *adj.* Of Mexico, its inhabitants, or their language.

Mexican hairless One of a breed of small dogs, hairless except for a tuft on the head and the end of the tail.

Mexican War See table for WAR.

mez·cal (mez·kal′) See MESCAL.

mez·quit (mez·kēt′, mez′kēt), **mez·quite** See MESQUITE.
mez·za·nine (mez′ə·nēn, -nin) *n.* **1.** An intermediate story, usu. not of full width, between two main floors. **2.** In a theater, the first balcony, or the front rows of the balcony. [< F < Ital. *mezzanino* < L *medianus*]
mez·zo (met′sō, med′zō, mez′ō) *adj.* Half; medium; moderate: often used in combination: *mezzo-soprano.* — *adv. Music* Moderately: *mezzo* forte. — *n. pl.* **·zos** A mezzo-soprano. [< Ital., < L *medius* middle]
mez·zo-so·pran·o (met′sō·sə·pran′ō, -prä′nō, med′zō-, mez′ō-) *n. pl.* **·pran·os** or **·pra·ni** (-nē) **1.** A female voice intermediate between a soprano and a contralto. **2.** A person having such a voice. — *adj.* Of or pertaining to such a voice. [< Ital.]
mez·zo·tint (met′sō·tint′, med′zō-, mez′ō-) *n.* **1.** A method of engraving in which the roughened surface of a copper or steel plate is scraped or burnished to produce effects of light and shade. **2.** A print produced from such a plate. — *v.t.* To engrave by or represent in mezzotint. [< Ital. < *mezzo* middle + *tinto* painted] — **mez′zo·tint′er** *n.*
mi (mē) *n. Music* The third syllable used in solmization; the third tone of a major scale; also, the tone E.
Mi·am·i (mī·am′ē, -am′ə) *n. pl.* **Mi·ami** or **Mi·am·is** A member of an Algonquian tribe of North American Indians formerly inhabiting a region in Wisconsin, Indiana, and Ohio. [< N.Am.Ind.]
mi·aou, mi·aow (mē·ou′) See MEOW.
mi·as·ma (mī·az′mə, mē-) *n. pl.* **·mas** or **·ma·ta** (-mə·tə) **1.** Noxious or unwholesome influence, etc. **2.** The poisonous effluvium once supposed to rise from swamps, etc. Also **mi′asm** (-az·əm). [< NL < Gk. < *miainein* to stain, defile] — **mi·as′mal, mi·as·mat·ic** (mī′əz·mat′ik), **mi·as′mic** *adj.*
mib (mib) *n. U.S. Dial.* **1.** A marble. **2.** *pl.* The game of marbles. [? Alter. of MARBLE]
mi·ca (mī′kə) *n.* Any of a class of silicate minerals, cleaving into tough, thin, often transparent and flexible laminae: sometimes called *isinglass.* [< L, crumb] — **mi·ca·ceous** (mī·kā′shəs) *adj.*
Mi·cah (mī′kə) Eighth-century B.C. Hebrew prophet. — *n.* A book of the Old Testament bearing his name. Also, in the Douai Bible, **Mi·che·as** (mī·kē′əs).
mice (mīs) Plural of MOUSE.
Mi·chael (mī′kəl) One of the archangels, represented as a militant protector and defender of the faithful: sometimes called *the Archangel. Dan.* x 10–12, *Rev.* xii 7–9.
Mich·ael·mas (mik′əl·məs) *n.* September 29, the church festival of the archangel Michael, in Great Britain serving as the fall quarter day. Also **Michaelmas Day.**
mick·ey (mik′ē) *n. pl.* **·eys** *U.S. Slang* A Mickey Finn.
Mick·ey Finn (mik′ē fin′) *U.S. Slang* An alcoholic drink secretly drugged so as to render the drinker unconscious. Also **mick′ey finn.** [Origin unknown]
Mic·mac (mik′mak) *n. pl.* **·mac** or **·macs** A member of an Algonquian tribe living in Nova Scotia, New Brunswick, and Newfoundland. [< N.Am.Ind., lit., allies]
mi·cra (mī′krə) Plural of MICRON.
micro- *combining form* **1.** Very small; minute. **2.** Enlarging or magnifying size or volume: *microscope.* **3.** *Pathol.* Abnormally small or underdeveloped. **4.** Of a science, depending on, using, or requiring a microscope: *microbiology.* **5.** In the metric system and in technical usage, one millionth of (a specified unit): *microwatt.* Sometimes, before vowels, **micr-.** [< Gk. *mikros* small]
mi·crobe (mī′krōb) *n.* A microscopic organism; esp., one of the bacteria that cause disease. [< F < Gk. *mikros* small + *bios* life] — **mi·cro′bi·al, mi·cro′bi·an, mi·cro′bic** *adj.*
— **Syn.** *Microbe* was originally a general term, applied at first to protozoa, and then to *bacteria; germ* originally denoted a reproductive cell. Both words are now popularly used to refer to disease-producing *bacteria. Microorganism* developed as a general term for protozoa, *bacteria,* and *viruses. Bacteria* are unicellular organisms, distinguished from protozoa because they possess both plant and animal characteristics. *Bacillus* properly denotes one class only of *bacteria.* A *virus* is a complex protein molecule capable of invading the cells and there reproducing itself.
mi·cro·bi·ol·o·gy (mī′krō·bī·ol′ə·jē) *n.* The branch of biology concerned with the study of microorganisms. — **mi′·cro·bi′o·log′i·cal** (-bī′ə·loj′i·kəl) *adj.* — **mi·cro·bi·ol′o·gist** *n.*
mi·cro·ceph·a·ly (mī′krō·sef′ə·lē) *n.* Abnormal smallness of the head and cranial capacity. [< MICRO- + Gk. *kephalē* head] — **mi′cro·ce·phal′ic** (-sə·fal′ik) *adj. & n.* — **mi′cro·ceph′a·lous** *adj.*
mi·cro·chem·is·try (mī′krō·kem′is·trē) *n.* A branch of chemistry dealing with minute quantities.
mi·cro·coc·cus (mī′krə·kok′əs) *n. pl.* **·coc·ci** (-kok′sī) Any member of a group of spherical bacteria that occur in irregular masses and are often pathogenic. [< NL]
mi·cro·cop·y (mī′krə·kop′ē) *n. pl.* **·cop·ies** A reduced photographic copy of a letter, manuscript, etc. — *v.t. & v.i.* **·cop·ied, ·cop·y·ing** To reproduce in the form of microcopy.
mi·cro·cosm (mī′krə·koz′əm) *n.* **1.** A little world; the universe in miniature. **2.** Man regraded as epitomizin[g the] universe. Also **mi′cro·cos′mos** (-koz′məs). [< LL < *mikros cosmos,* lit., little world] — **mi′cro·cos′mic** *ad[j.]*
mi·cro·film (mī′krə·film) *n.* A photographic reprodu[ction] on film of a printed page, document, or other object, h[ighly] reduced for ease in transmission and storage, and capa[ble of] reenlargement. — *v.t. & v.i.* To reproduce on microf[ilm.]
mi·cro·gram (mī′krə·gram) *n.* In the metric system[, one] millionth of a gram. Also **mi′cro·gramme.**
mi·cro·groove (mī′krə·grōōv) *n.* An extremely fine g[roove] cut in the surface of a long-playing phonograph recor[d.]
Mi·cro·groove (mī′krə·grōōv) *n.* A long-playing reco[rd:] trade name.
mi·crom·e·ter (mī·krom′ə·tər) *n.* **1.** An instrument for measuring very small distances or dimensions, as in conjunction with a microscope or telescope. **2.** A micrometer caliper.
micrometer caliper A caliper or gauge having a micrometer screw, used for precise measurements.
micrometer screw A screw with a very finely cut thread and a graduated head, used in micrometers, etc.

MICROMETER
a Frame. *b* Anv[il] *c* Movable spin[dle] *d* Sleeve. *e* Thim[ble]

mi·crom·e·try (mī·krom′ə·trē) *n.* Measurement by means of a micrometer. — **mi·cro·met·ric** (mī′krō·met′·rik) or **·ri·cal** *adj.* — **mi′cro·met′ri·cal·ly** *adv.*
mi·cro·mil·li·me·ter (mī′krō·mil′ə·mē′tər) *n.* A mi[lli]cron. Also **mi′cro·mil′li·me′tre.**
mi·cron (mī′kron) *n. pl.* **·cra** (-krə) A unit of mea[sure]ment equal to one thousandth of a millimeter. [< N[L <] Gk. *mikron,* neut. of *mikros* small]
Mi·cro·ne·sian (mī′krə·nē′zhən, -shən) *adj.* Of or per[tain]ing to Micronesia, its people, or their languages. — *n.* [**1.** A] native of Micronesia. **2.** Any of the Austronesian langu[ages] spoken in Micronesia.
mi·cro·or·gan·ism (mī′krō·ôr′gən·iz′əm) *n.* Any m[icro]scopic or ultramicroscopic organism, as a bacterium or [pro]tozoan. Also **mi′cro-or′gan·ism.** — **Syn.** See MICROBE.
mi·cro·phone (mī′krə·fōn) *n.* A device for converting s[ound] waves into electric currents, forming the principal ele[ment] of a telephone transmitter or of any sound-reproducing [sys]tem, as in broadcasting. — **mi·cro·phon′ic** (-fon′ik) *ad[j.]*
mi·cro·pho·to·graph (mī′krō·fō′tə·graf, -gräf) *n.* [**1.** A] very small or microscopic photograph, as on microfilm. [**2.**] Loosely, a photomicrograph. — **mi′cro·pho′to·graph′ic** — **mi′cro·pho·tog′ra·phy** (-fə·tog′rə·fē) *n.*
mi·cro·print (mī′krə·print) *n.* A microphotograph re[pro]duced in a print that may be examined or read by means [of a] magnifying glass. — *v.t. & v.i.* To represent or repro[duce] by means of a microprint.
mi·cro·scope (mī′krə·skōp) *n.* An optical instrument [used] for magnifying objects too small to be seen or clearly obse[rved] by ordinary vision. [< NL *microscopium*]
mi·cro·scop·ic (mī′krə·skop′ik) *adj.* **1.** So minute as t[o be] visible only under a microscope. **2.** Exceedingly small. [**3.**] Of, pertaining to, or of the nature of a microscope or mic[ros]copy. **4.** Performed with or depending on use of a mi[cro]scope. **5.** Characterized by or done with minute obse[rva]tion. Also **mi′cro·scop′i·cal.** — **mi′cro·scop′i·cal·ly** *adv.*
mi·cros·co·py (mī·kros′kə·pē, mī′krə·skō′pē) *n.* **1.** [The] process or technique of using the microscope. **2.** Investi[ga]tion by means of the microscope. — **mi·cros·co·pist** (mī·kros′kə·pist, mī′krə·skō′pist) *n.*
mi·cro·tome (mī′krə·tōm) *n.* An instrument for cutt[ing] very thin sections of organic tissue, etc., for microscopic [ob]servations. — **mi′cro·tom′ic** (-tom′ik) or **·i·cal** *adj.*
mi·cro·wave (mī′krə·wāv) *n.* An electromagnetic w[ave] having a frequency between about 1,000 and 30,000 me[ga]cycles. Compare RADIO WAVE.
mic·tu·rate (mik′chə·rāt) *v.i.* **·rat·ed, ·rat·ing** To urina[te.] [< L *micturire* to desire to urinate] — **mic′tu·ri′tion** (-ris[h′]ən) *n.*
mid[1] (mid) *adj.* Being approximately in the middle; c[en]tral. [OE *midd-*]
mid[2] (mid) *prep. Chiefly Poetic* Amid; among. Also **'m[id].**
mid- *combining form* **1.** Middle point or part of, as [in:] **midafternoon, mid-century. 2.** Being in the middle or c[en]ter, as in: **midpoint; mid-position 3.** With adjectives, [of] or pertaining to the middle part of that which is modif[ied] or implied, as in: **mid-Asian, midmonthly.**
mid·air (mid′âr′) *n.* A point or region seemingly in t[he] middle or midst of the air. Also **mid′-air′.**
Mi·das (mī′dəs) In Greek legend, a king of Phrygia who h[ad] the power of turning whatever he touched into gold.
mid·brain (mid′brān′) *n. Anat.* The mesencephalon.
mid·day (mid′dā′) *n.* The middle of the day; noon. — *a[dj.]* Of, pertaining to, or occurring in the middle of the day.
mid·den (mid′n) *n. Brit. Dial.* A dunghill or heap of refu[se.] [ME *midding* < Scand.]

-dle (mid′l) *adj.* **1.** Equally distant from the extremes, phery, etc.; central. **2.** Intermediate in position, status, **3.** Intervening between the earlier part and the latter of a sequence, period of time, etc. **4.** Moderate, as in or effect. **5.** *Usu. cap.* Designating a language in a stage ween an earlier and a recent form: *Middle* English. — *n.* The area or point equally distant from the extremes, etc. The intermediate section of anything. **3.** The middle of the body; the waist. — *v.t.* **·dled, ·dling** To place in middle. [OE *middel*]
dle age The time of life between youth and old age, . thought of as the years between 40 and 60. — **mid′dle-d′** (mid′l·ājd′) *adj.*
dle Ages The period in European history between sical antiquity and the Renaissance, usu. regarded as nding from the downfall of Rome, in 476, to about 1450.
dle Atlantic States New York, New Jersey, and nsylvania.
dle C *Music* The note written on the first ledger line ve the bass staff and the first ledger line below the treble f; also, the corresponding tone.
dle class The part of a society occupying a social or nomic position between the laboring class and the very lthy or the nobility. — **mid′dle-class** *adj.*
dle ear *Anat.* The portion of the ear between the tym-ic membrane and the opening of the Eustachian tube; , the membrane itself: also called *tympanum.*
dle East **1.** The region including Egypt and the coun-s of SW Asia west of Pakistan and India. **2.** *Brit.* This ion with the exception of Turkey and including India, kistan, Burma, Tibet, Libya, Ethiopia, and Somaliland.
dle Latin Medieval Latin. See under LATIN.
·dle·man (mid′l·man′) *n. pl.* **·men** (-men′) **1.** One o acts as an agent; go-between. **2.** One who buys in bulk m producers and sells to retailers or consumers.
·dle·most (mid′l·mōst′) *adj.* Situated exactly or most arly in the middle: also *midmost.*
dle of the road A moderate position or course.
·dle-of-the-road·er (mid′l·əv·thə·rō′dər) *n.* One who dorses a moderate course, esp. in politics.
·dle·weight (mid′l·wāt′) *n.* **1.** A person or animal of erage weight. **2.** A boxer or wrestler weighing between 7 and 160 pounds.
·dling (mid′ling) *adj.* **1.** Of middle size, quality, or con-tion; mediocre. **2.** *Informal* In fair health. — *adv. In-mal* Fairly; moderately. — *n.* **1.** *pl.* Any of various com-odities regarded as intermediate in quality, size, etc. **2.** The coarser part of ground grain. — **mid′dling** *adv.*
·dy (mid′ē) *n. pl.* **·dies** *Informal* **1.** A midshipman. A middy blouse (which see).
ddy blouse A loosely fitting blouse with a sailor collar.
dge (mij) *n.* **1.** A gnat or small fly; esp. any of various nall, dipterous insects. **2.** An extremely small person or eature. [OE *mycge*]
·get (mij′it) *n.* **1.** A person of abnormally small size but normal physical proportions. **2.** Anything very small of s kind. — *adj.* Very small; diminutive.
·i·an·ite (mid′ē·ən·īt′) *n.* One of an ancient nomadic ibe of Arabia. *Gen.* xxv 2. [< *Midian* a son of Abraham]
·i·ron (mid′ī′ərn) *n.* In golf, a five iron.
·land (mid′lənd) *n.* The central or interior part of a untry or region. — *adj.* Of, pertaining to, or situated in inland or interior region.
·land (mid′lənd) *n.* The dialects of Middle English oken in London and the Midlands; esp., **East Midland,** e direct predecessor of Modern English.
·most (mid′mōst′) *adj.* Middlemost. — *adv.* In the idst or middle. [OE *mydmest*]
·night (mid′nīt′) *n.* The middle of the night; twelve clock at night. — *adj.* **1.** Of or occurring at midnight. . Resembling midnight; very dark. — **to burn the mid-ight oil** To work or study late into the night.
idnight sun The sun visible at midnight during summer t latitudes greater than 70° north or south of the equator.
id·rib (mid′rib′) *n. Bot.* The central vein of a leaf.
id·riff (mid′rif) *n.* The part of the body between the chest nd the abdomen, in the region of the diaphragm; also, the iaphragm itself. [OE < *midd* mid + *hrif* belly]
id·ship (mid′ship′) *adj. Naut.* Of, pertaining to, or situ-ted in the middle of a ship.
id·ship·man (mid′ship′mən) *n. pl.* **·men** (-mən) **1.** In he U.S. Navy, a student training to be commissioned as an fficer, esp. at the U.S. Naval Academy at Annapolis. **2.** In he Commonwealth navies, an officer ranking between a aval cadet and the lowest commissioned officer. See table t GRADE. [< *amidshipman*; so called from being amidships when on duty]
id·ships (mid′ships′) *Naut. adv.* Amidships.

midst (midst) *n.* **1.** The condition of being surrounded, as by people or things, engaged, as in an activity, or beset, as by troubles: used chiefly in the phrase **in the midst of.** **2.** The central part; middle. — **in our (your, their) midst** Among us (you, them). — *prep.* Amid. [ME *middest*]
mid·sum·mer (mid′sum′ər) *n.* The middle of summer.
mid·term (mid′tûrm′) *n.* **1.** The middle of a term. **2.** *U.S.* An examination given in the middle of a school term.
mid-Vic·to·ri·an (mid′vik·tôr′ē·ən, -tō′rē-) *adj.* **1.** Of or pertaining to the middle period of Queen Victoria's reign, about 1850–80. **2.** Characteristic of the popular moral at-titudes, culture, etc., of this period; prudishly old-fashioned. — *n.* **1.** One who lived during this period. **2.** One having mid-Victorian tastes, standards, or ideas.
mid·way (mid′wā′; *for adj. and adv., also* mid′wā′) *adv.* In the middle of the way or distance. — *adj.* Being in the mid-dle of the way or distance. — *n. U.S.* At a fair, exposition, etc., the area or mall where amusements, side shows, or ex-hibitions are situated. [OE *midweg*]
mid·week (mid′wēk′) *n.* The middle of the week.
mid·wife (mid′wīf′) *n. pl.* **·wives** (-wīvz′) A woman who assists women in childbirth. [OE *mid* with + *wīf* woman]
mid·wife·ry (mid′wī′fər·ē, -wīf′rē) *n.* The skill or practice of assisting women in childbirth; obstetrics.
mid·win·ter (mid′win′tər) *n.* The middle of winter.
mid·year (mid′yir′) *n.* **1.** The middle of the year. **2.** *U.S.* An examination given in the middle of a school year.
mien (mēn) *n.* Manner, bearing, expression, etc. [? Aphet-ic form of DEMEAN]
miff (mif) *Informal v.t.* **1.** To cause to be offended or an-noyed. — *v.i.* **2.** To take offense. — *n.* **1.** An ill-tempered mood; huff. **2.** A minor quarrel; tiff.
mig (mig) *n. U.S. Dial.* **1.** A marble. **2.** *pl.* The game of marbles. Also **mig·gle** (mig′əl).
might[1] (mīt) Past tense of MAY[1].
might[2] (mīt) *n.* **1.** Power to dominate; force; strength. **2.** Physical strength. — **with (all one's) might and main** With all one's strength or ability. [OE *miht*]
might·y (mī′tē) *adj.* **might·i·er, might·i·est** **1.** Possessed of might; powerful. **2.** Of great size, importance, etc. — *adv. Informal* Very; exceedingly. — **might′i·ly** (mī′tə·lē) *adv.* — **might′i·ness** *n.*
mi·gnon·ette (min′yən·et′) *n.* A plant having racemes of fragrant, yellowish green flowers. Also called *reseda.* [< F]
mi·graine (mī′grān) *n.* A type of severe, recurrent head-ache, usu. in one side of the head: also called *hemicrania.* [< F < LL < Gk. < *hēmi* half + *kranion* skull]
mi·grant (mī′grənt) *adj.* Migratory. — *n.* One who or that which migrates, as a bird or animal, an itinerant worker, etc. [< L *migrare* to roam, wander]
mi·grate (mī′grāt) *v.i.* **·grat·ed, ·grat·ing** **1.** To move from one country, region, etc., to settle in another. **2.** To move seasonally from one region or climate to another, as birds or fish. [< L *migrare*] — **mi′gra·tor** *n.*
— **Syn. 1.** One may *migrate* to or from a place, whether perma-nently or transiently. *Emigrate* and *immigrate* imply a more or less permanent change. They are both applied to the same action per-formed by the same person, but *emigrate* refers to the place of de-parture and *immigrate* to the new home.
mi·gra·tion (mī·grā′shən) *n.* **1.** An act or instance of mi-grating. **2.** Those participating in a single instance of mi-grating. **3.** *Chem.* **a** The shifting of one or more atoms from one position to another. **b** The movement of ions under the influence of electromotive force toward one or the other electrode. [< L *migratio*] — **mi·gra′tion·al** *adj.*
mi·gra·to·ry (mī′grə·tôr′ē, -tō′rē) *adj.* **1.** Characterized by migration. **2.** Pertaining to or characteristic of migra-tion or those that migrate. **3.** Roving; nomadic.
mi·ka·do (mi·kä′dō) *n. pl.* **·dos** The emperor of Japan. [< Japanese *mi* august + *kado* door]
mike (mīk) *n. Informal* A microphone.
mil (mil) *n.* **1.** A unit of length or diameter, equal to one thousandth of an inch. See table front of book. **2.** *Mil.* **a** A unit of angular measure equal to 1/6400 of a circle, or about 0.0560 degree. **b** A unit of angular measure equal to 0.001 radian. [< L *mille* thousand]
mi·la·dy (mi·lā′dē) *n. pl.* **·dies** **1.** An English noblewoman or gentlewoman: a Continental term. **2.** A fashionable woman. Also **mi·la′di.** [< F < E *my lady*]
mil·age (mī′lij) See MILEAGE.
Mil·an·ese (mil′ən·ēz′, -ēs′) *adj.* Of or pertaining to Milan or its people. — *n. pl.* **·ese** A native or inhabitant of Milan.
milch (milch) *adj.* Giving milk, as a cow. [OE *-milc*]
mild (mīld) *adj.* **1.** Kind or amiable in disposition or man-ners. **2.** Gentle or moderate: *mild* words; *mild* weather. **3.** Not intense or strong: a *mild* flavor. [OE *milde*] — **mild′·ly** *adv.* — **mild′ness** *n.*
mil·dew (mil′dōō, -dyōō) *n.* **1.** A disease of plants usu.

caused by a parasitic fungus that deposits a whitish or discolored coating. **2.** Any of the fungi causing such a disease. — *v.t. & v.i.* To affect or be affected with mildew. [OE *meledēaw* honeydew] — **mil′dew·y** *adj.*

mile (mīl) *n.* **1.** A measure of distance used in the U.S. and other English-speaking countries, equal to 5,280 feet, 1,760 yards, or 1,609.35 meters: also called *statute mile.* See table front of book. **2.** Any considerable distance or amount. — **geographical, nautical,** or **air mile** One sixtieth of a degree of the earth's equator, or 6,080.2 feet. — **international nautical mile** A unit of distance by sea equal to 1,852 meters or 6,076.103 feet. [OE < LL < L *mille (passuum)* thousand (paces)]

mile·age (mī′lij) *n.* **1.** Total length or distance expressed in miles. **2.** Number of miles traveled by an automobile, etc., as estimated for each gallon of fuel used. **3.** Period of usefulness, estimated by miles used or traveled. **4.** *U.S.* A traveling allowance estimated at a fixed amount per mile. Also spelled *milage.*

mile·post (mīl′pōst′) *n.* A post or similar marker indicating distance in miles, as along a highway.

mil·er (mī′lər) *n.* A runner, racehorse, etc., trained to compete in mile races.

mile·stone (mīl′stōn′) *n.* **1.** A post or stone set up to indicate mileage from a given point. **2.** An important event or turning point.

mi·lieu (mē·lyœ′) *n.* Environment; surroundings. [< F < OF *mi* middle + *lieu* place]

mil·i·tant (mil′ə·tənt) *adj.* **1.** Combative or warlike; aggressive. **2.** Positive and forceful in action; resolute. **3.** Engaged in conflict; fighting. — *n.* One who is militant. [< L *militare* to be a soldier] — **mil′i·tan·cy** *n.* — **mil′i·tant·ly** *adv.*

mil·i·ta·rism (mil′ə·tə·riz′əm) *n.* **1.** The ideals characteristic of a military class; emphasis on martial qualities. **2.** A national policy that promotes a powerful military position. — **mil′i·ta·rist** *n.* — **mil′i·ta·ris′tic** *adj.*

mil·i·ta·rize (mil′ə·tə·rīz) *v.t.* **·rized, ·riz·ing 1.** To convert to a military system or adapt for military purposes. **2.** To prepare for warfare. — **mil′i·ta·ri·za′tion** *n.*

mil·i·tar·y (mil′ə·ter′ē) *adj.* **1.** Of or pertaining to the armed forces. **2.** Of or characteristic of warfare. **3.** Characteristic of or befitting a soldier or soldiers. — *n.* Soldiers collectively; armed forces: preceded by *the.* [< F < L < *miles, militis* soldier] — **mil′i·tar′i·ly** *adv.*

military police Soldiers who perform police duty.

mil·i·tate (mil′ə·tāt) *v.i.* **·tat·ed, ·tat·ing** To have influence or effect: with *against*, or, more rarely, *for*: The evidence *militated* against him. [< L *miles, militis* soldier]

mi·li·tia (mə·lish′ə) *n.* A body of citizens enrolled and drilled in military organizations other than the regular military forces, and called out only in emergencies. [< L, military service]

mi·li·tia·men (mə·lish′ə·mən) *n. pl.* **·men** (mən) A member of the militia.

milk (milk) *n.* **1.** The opaque, whitish liquid secreted by the mammary glands of female mammals for the nourishment of their young; esp., cow's milk. **2.** Any of various liquids resembling this, as the sap of certain plants, or the liquid contained in a coconut. — *v.t.* **1.** To draw or express milk from the mammary glands of. **2.** To draw off or drain by or as by milking. **3.** To draw or extract something from: to *milk* someone of information. **4.** To exploit; take advantage of: to *milk* a client. — *v.i.* **5.** To milk (a cow, cows, etc.). **6.** To yield milk. [OE *meolc, milc*]

milk leg A painful swelling of the leg in women shortly after childbirth, resulting from phlebitis of the femoral vein.

milk·maid (milk′mād′) *n.* A woman or girl who milks cows or works in a dairy.

milk·man (milk′man′) *n. pl.* **·men** (-men′) A man who sells or delivers milk.

milk of magnesia A white, aqueous suspension of magnesium hydroxide, $Mg(OH)_2$, used as a laxative and antacid.

milk shake A drink made of chilled, flavored milk, and sometimes ice cream, shaken, beaten, or whipped.

milk snake A nonpoisonous snake of eastern North America, feeding on rodents, frogs, etc.

milk·sop (milk′sop′) *n.* A weak, timorous fellow; sissy.

milk sugar Lactose.

milk·toast (milk′tōst′) *n.* **1.** A dish of buttered toast served in hot milk. **2.** See MILQUETOAST.

milk tooth A temporary tooth of a young mammal.

milk·weed (milk′wēd′) *n.* Any of various herbs, shrubs, and vines having milky juice.

milk·y (mil′kē) *adj.* **milk·i·er, milk·i·est 1.** Resembling or suggestive of milk. **2.** Containing or yielding milk or a milklike substance. **3.** Very mild or bland. — **milk′i·ly** *adv.* — **milk′i·ness** *n.*

Milky Way A luminous band visible across the night sky, composed of distant stars and nebulae not separately distinguishable to the naked eye: also called the *Galaxy.*

mill[1] (mil) *n.* **1.** A machine or mechanical device by m[eans] of which a solid or coarse substance is ground, crushe[d, or] reduced to a pulp. **2.** A device, machine, building, or e[stab]lishment in which grain is ground. **3.** Any of various [ma]chines that process materials used in combination: *saw[mill,] windmill.* **4.** A manufacturing or industrial establishm[ent;] factory. **5.** A steel roller for impressing a design on a p[rint]ing plate, etc. **6.** A trying experience; ordeal: used c[hiefly] in the phrase **through the mill.** — *v.t.* **1.** To grind, shape, polish, etc., in or with a mill. **2.** To raise, inde[nt, or] ridge the edge of (a coin, etc.). **3.** To cause to move [in a] circle, as cattle. — *v.i.* **4.** To move with a circular or [churn]ing motion, as cattle. [OE < LL < L *mola* millstone]

mill[2] (mil) *n.* A monetary denomination of the U.S., [one] tenth of a cent. [< L *mille* thousand]

mill·dam (mil′dam′) *n.* A dam constructed across a w[ater]course to raise its level sufficiently to turn a mill whee[l.]

mil·len·ni·um (mi·len′ē·əm) *n. pl.* **·ni·a** (-nē·ə) or **·ni[·ums]** **1.** A period of a thousand years. **2.** The thousand y[ears] during which Christ is to rule the world. *Rev.* xx 1–5. [3.] Any period of happiness, prosperity, etc. [< NL < [L *mille*] thousand + *annus* year] — **mil·len′ni·al** *adj.*

mil·le·ped (mil′ə·ped), **mil·le·pede** (mil′ə·pēd) See [MIL]LIPEDE.

mil·le·pore (mil′ə·pôr, -pōr) *n. Zool.* Any of a grou[p of] corals that form large branching structures containing [nu]merous tiny surface cavities. [< F < *mille* thousand + pore]

mill·er (mil′ər) *n.* **1.** One who operates or tends a [mill.] **2.** A milling machine. **3.** Any of various moths having [...] dusty wings.

mil·let (mil′it) *n.* **1.** A grass cultivated in the U.S. [for] forage, and in many parts of the Old World for its sm[all] edible seeds. **2.** Any of various similar grasses. **3.** [The] seed of these grasses. [< F, dim. of *mil* < L *milium*]

milli- *combining form* In the metric system and in tec[hni]cal use, one thousandth of (a specified unit), as in the [fol]lowing: **milliampere, millivolt.** [< L *mille* thousand]

mil·liard (mil′yərd) *n. Brit.* A thousand millions: ca[lled] a *billion* in the U.S. [< F < Provençal *milhar* thousa[nd]]

mil·li·gram (mil′ə·gram) *n.* A unit of weight in the m[etric] system, equal to one thousandth of a gram. Also **m[illi]gramme.** See table front of book.

mil·li·li·ter (mil′ə·lē′tər) *n.* A unit of capacity in [the] metric system, equal to one thousandth of a liter. Also **[mil]li·li′tre.** See table front of book.

mil·li·me·ter (mil′ə·mē′tər) *n.* A unit of length in the m[et]ric system, equal to one thousandth of a meter. Also **mi[lli]me′tre.** See table front of book.

mil·li·mi·cron (mil′ə·mī′kron) *n.* A unit of length eq[ual] to one thousandth of a micron: also called *micromillim[eter.]*

mil·li·ner (mil′ə·nər) *n.* One who makes or sells wom[en's] hats. [< *Milaner* an inhabitant of Milan, Italy]

mil·li·ner·y (mil′ə·ner′ē, -nər·ē) *n.* **1.** The articles m[ade] or sold by milliners. **2.** The business of a milliner.

mil·lion (mil′yən) *n.* **1.** A thousand thousands, writte[n] 1,000,000: a cardinal number. **2.** A million units of mon[ey,] as of dollars: He is worth a *million.* **3.** An indefinitely gr[eat] number. — *adj.* **1.** Being a million in number. **2.** V[ery] many. [< OF < Ital. *millione* (now *milione*), aug. of *m[ille]* thousand] — **mil′lionth** *n. & adj.*

mil·lion·aire (mil′yən·âr′) *n.* One whose wealth is val[ued] at a million or more, as of dollars, pounds, etc. Also **m[il]lion·naire′.** [< F *millionnaire*] — **mil′lion·air′ess** *n.f[em.]*

mil·li·pede (mil′ə·pēd) *n.* Any of various wormlike a[ni]mals having a rounded body divided into numerous s[eg]ments, nearly all of which bear two pairs of appendag[es:] also called *wireworm*: also spelled *milliped, millepede.* A[lso] **mil′li·ped** (-ped). [< L *mille* thousand + *pes, pedis* fo[ot]]

mill·pond (mil′pond′) *n.* A body of water dammed up [to] supply power for running a mill.

mill·race (mil′rās′) *n.* **1.** The current of water that op[er]ates a mill wheel. **2.** The channel in which it runs.

mill·stone (mil′stōn′) *n.* **1.** One of a pair of thick, hea[vy] stone disks used for grinding grain, etc. **2.** That whi[ch] crushes or bears down. **3.** A heavy or burdensome weig[ht.]

mill·stream (mil′strēm′) *n.* **1.** A stream whose curre[nt] is used to operate a mill. **2.** The water in a millrace.

mill wheel A water wheel that drives a mill.

mill·work (mil′wûrk′) *n.* Objects or material finished [or] processed in a mill; esp. woodwork ready for use.

mill·wright (mil′rīt′) *n.* One who plans, builds, or repa[irs] mills or mill machinery.

mi·lord (mi·lôrd′) *n.* An English nobleman or gentlema[n:] a Continental term. [< F < E *my lord*]

milque·toast (milk′tōst′) *n.* A timid, meek, or very apol[o]getic person: also spelled *milktoast.* [after Caspar *Milqu[e]toast*, a creation by H. T. Webster, U.S. cartoonist]

milt (milt) *n.* **1.** Fish sperm. **2.** The reproductive orga[ns] of a male fish when filled with seminal fluid. — *v.t.* To im[]pregnate (fish roe) with milt. [OE *milte*]

·ton·ic (mil·ton′ik) *adj.* Of or like the poet Milton or works; sublime. Also **Mil·to′ni·an** (-tō′nē·ən).
town (mil′toun) *n.* Proprietary name for a brand of orobamate used in pill form as a tranquilizer.
ıe (mīm) *n.* **1.** An actor, comedian, etc., who special- in pantomime. **2.** In ancient Rome or Greece, a type of matic farce in which actual persons or events were ludi- usly represented. **3.** An actor in such performances. — **mimed, mim·ing** — *v.i.* **1.** To play a part with gestures , usu., without words. — *v.t.* **2.** To portray by panto- ne. [< L < Gk. *mimos*] — **mim′er** *n.*
ı·e·o·graph (mim′ē·ə·graf′, -gräf′) *n.* **1.** A duplicating ice that reproduces copies of written matter etc., by ıns of a stencil wrapped around a drum: also **Mim′e·o·ph′**. **2.** A copy so made. — *v.t. & v.i.* To reproduce by neograph. [< *Mimeograph*, a trade name]
met·ic (mi·met′ik, mī-) *adj.* **1.** Tending to imitate or mic; imitative. **2.** Pertaining to or like mimicry. **3.** ıke-believe. [< Gk. < *mimēsis* imitation] — **mi·met′i·ly** *adv.*
ı·ic (mim′ik) *v.t.* **·icked, ·ick·ing 1.** To imitate the ech or actions of. **2.** To copy closely; ape. **3.** To have assume the color, shape, etc., of. — *n.* **1.** One who mim- or imitates. **2.** A copy; imitation. — *adj.* **1.** Of the ure of mimicry; imitative; mimetic. **2.** Make-believe; ulated; mock. [< L < Gk. < *mimos* mime] — **mim′i·** *adj.* — **mim′ick·er** *n.*
ı·ic·ry (mim′ik·rē) *n. pl.* **·ries 1.** The act, practice, art of mimicking or imitating. **2.** *Biol.* A resemblance an organism to another or to its environment, for pur- ses of concealment, etc.
mo·sa (mi·mō′sə, -zə) *n.* Any of a group of leguminous pical herbs, shrubs, or trees with feathery foliage, and all, often yellow, flowers. [< NL < L *mimus* mime]
ı·a·ret (min′ə·ret′) *n.* A high, slender tower attached a Moslem mosque and surrounded by balconies, from ich a muezzin calls the summons to prayer. [< Sp. < rkish < Arabic *manārah* lamp, lighthouse]
ı·a·to·ry (min′ə·tôr′ē, -tō′rē) *adj.* Conveying or ex- essing a threat. Also **min′a·to′ri·al.** [< OF < LL < *nari* to threaten] — **min′a·to′ri·al·ly, min′a·to′ri·ly** *adv.*
nce (mins) *v.* **minced, minc·ing** *v.t.* **1.** To cut or chop o small bits, as food. **2.** To subdivide minutely. **3.** To oderate the force or strength of (language, ideas, etc.): He ln't *mince* words with her. **4.** To say or express with af- cted primness or elegance. — *v.i.* **5.** To walk with short ps or affected daintiness. **6.** To speak or behave with fected primness. — *n.* *Chiefly Brit.* Any finely chopped od, as mincemeat. [< OF < L *minuere* to lessen, make aller] — **minc′er** *n.*
nce·meat (mins′mēt′) *n.* A mixture of chopped apples, isins, spices, etc., used as a pie filling. — **to make mince- eat of** To cut up, destroy, or annihilate utterly.
nce pie A pie filled with mincemeat.
nc·ing (min′sing) *adj.* Affectedly precise, refined, or inty, as in manner, gait, etc. — **minc′ing·ly** *adv.*
nd (mīnd) *n.* **1.** The aggregate of processes originating or associated with the brain, involving conscious and sub- nscious thought, interpretation of perceptions, insight, agination, etc. **2.** Memory: within the *mind* of man. **3.** pinion; sentiment: to change one's *mind*. **4.** Desire; in- nation: to have a *mind* to leave. **5.** Way or state of think- g or feeling: a logical *mind*. **6.** Intellectual power or ca- acity: He has the *mind* for such work. **7.** A highly intelli- ent individual. **8.** Sound mental condition; sanity. **9.** ttention: to keep one's *mind* on a subject. — **Syn.** See TELLECT. — **a piece of one's mind 1.** One's bluntly or andidly expressed opinion. **2.** A severe scolding. — **on ne's mind** In one's thoughts, esp. so as to cause concern or orry. — **out of one's mind 1.** Insane; mad. **2.** Dis- acted; frantic. — **to bear** (or **keep**) **in mind** To focus ne's thoughts or attention on; remember. — **to be of one aind** To be in accord; agree. — **to have a good** (or **great**) **aind** To feel strongly disposed (to do something). — **to ave in mind** To be thinking about. — **to make up one's aind** To decide; be determined. — *v.t.* **1.** To pay atten- ion to. **2.** To be careful concerning: *Mind* your step. **3.** o obey: *Mind* your leaders. **4.** To look after; tend. **5.** To bject to: Do you *mind* the noise? **6.** *Dial.* To notice; per- eive. **7.** *Dial.* To remember. — *v.i.* **8.** To pay attention; eed: *Mind* you now, not a word. **9.** To be obedient. **10.** To be concerned; care; object: I don't *mind*. **11.** To be areful. [OE *gemynd*] — **mind′er** *n.*
aind·ed (mīn′did) *adj.* **1.** Having or characterized by a specified kind of) mind: used in combination: *evil-minded*. **2.** Having an inclination; disposed: often with *to*.
aind·ful (mīnd′fəl) *adj.* Keeping in mind; heeding; aware. — **mind′ful·ly** *adv.* — **mind′ful·ness** *n.*

mind·less (mīnd′lis) *adj.* **1.** Devoid of intelligence; sense- less. **2.** Not giving heed or attention; careless. — **mind′·less·ly** *adv.* — **mind′less·ness** *n.*
mind reader One supposedly able to perceive the thoughts of others. — **mind reading**
mine[1] (mīn) *n.* **1.** An excavation in the earth dug to obtain coal, precious stones, etc. **2.** The site of such an excavation, together with its buildings, equipment, etc. **3.** Any deposit of ore, coal, etc. **4.** Any source or abundant store of some- thing: a *mine* of talent. **5.** *Mil.* **a** An encased explosive charge placed in the earth or water and designed to be actu- ated by contact, a time fuse, or remote control. **b** Formerly, an undergound tunnel dug beneath an enemy's fortifica- tions. — *v.* **mined, min·ing** *v.t.* **1.** To dig (coal, ores, etc.) from the earth. **2.** To dig into (the earth, etc.) for coal, ores, etc. **3.** To make by digging, as a tunnel. **4.** To obtain useful material or information from. **5.** To undermine by slow or secret means. **6.** To place an explosive mine in or under. — *v.i.* **7.** To dig in a mine for coal, ores, etc. **8.** To make a tunnel, etc., by digging. **9.** To place explosive mines. [< OF < Celtic. Cf. Irish *mein* vein of metal]
mine[2] (mīn) *pron.* **1.** The possessive case of the pronoun *I*, used predicatively: That book is *mine*. **2.** The one or ones belonging or relating to me: His work is better than *mine*. — **of mine** Belonging or relating to me; my. — *pronominal adj.* *Archaic* My: formerly used before a vowel or *h*: *mine* eyes. [OE *mīn*]
mine detector An electromagnetic device used to locate the position of explosive mines. — **mine detection**
mine·field (mīn′fēld′) *n.* An area on land or in water in which explosive mines have been systematically placed.
mine·lay·er (mīn′lā′ər) *n.* A vessel provided with special equipment for laying explosive mines.
min·er (mīn′ər) *n.* One who works in a mine.
min·er·al (min′ər·əl) *n.* **1.** A naturally ocurring inorganic substance having a characteristic set of physical properties, a definite range of chemical composition, and a molecular structure usu. expressed in crystalline form. **2.** Inorganic material, esp. as distinguished from animal or vegetable matter. — *adj.* Of, like, or containing a mineral or miner- als. [< OF < Med.L < *mineralis* of a mine]
min·er·al·ize (min′ər·əl·īz′) *v.t.* **·ized, ·iz·ing 1.** To con- vert (a metal) to a mineral. **2.** To convert to a mineral sub- stance; petrify. **3.** To impregnate with minerals. — **min′·er·al·iz′er** *n.* — **min′er·al·i·za′tion** *n.*
min·er·al·o·gy (min′ə·ral′ə·jē, -rol′-) *n. pl.* **·gies 1.** The science of minerals, embracing their origin, structure, char- acteristics, properties, and classification. **2.** A treatise on minerals. — **min′er·a·log′i·cal** (-ər·ə·loj′i·kəl) *adj.* — **min′·er·a·log′i·cal·ly** *adv.* — **min′er·al′o·gist** *n.*
mineral oil Any of various oils, esp. petroleum, derived from minerals and used as a fuel, in medicine, etc.
mineral spring A spring containing natural mineral water.
mineral water Any water naturally containing or artifi- cially impregnated with mineral salts or gases.
mineral wool A fibrous, woollike material, used as packing and as insulation: also called *rock wool, slag wool*.
Mi·ner·va (mi·nûr′və) In Roman mythology, the goddess of wisdom and invention: identified with the Greek *Athena*.
min·e·stro·ne (min′ə·strō′nē, *Ital.* mē′nā·strō′nā) *n.* *Italian* A thick vegetable soup having a meat stock.
mine·sweep·er (mīn′swē′pər) *n.* A ship equipped to de- tect, destroy, and remove marine mines.
Ming (ming) *n.* In Chinese history, the last ruling dynasty (1368–1644) of truly Chinese origin, noted for its scholarly and artistic achievements, esp. for its porcelains.
min·gle (ming′gəl) *v.* **·gled, ·gling** *v.t.* **1.** To mix or unite together; blend. **2.** To make by combining. — *v.i.* **3.** To be or become mixed, united, or closely joined. **4.** To enter into company; mix or associate, as with a crowd. [OE *men- gan*] — **min′gler** *n.*
min·i·a·ture (min′ē·ə·chər, min′ə·chər) *n.* **1.** A portrayal or representation of anything on a small scale. **2.** Reduced dimensions, form, or extent. **3.** In art: **a** A painting done on a very small scale. **b** The art of executing such paintings. — *adj.* On a very small or reduced scale. [< F < Ital. < L *miniatus* painted red; later infl. by L *minuere* to lessen]
min·i·a·tur·ize (min′ē·ə·chər·īz′, min′ə·chər·īz′) *v.t.* **·ized, ·iz·ing** To reduce the size of. — **min′i·a·tur′i·za′tion** *n.*
min·im (min′im) *n.* **1.** A small liquid measure, 1/60 of a fluid dram, or about one drop. See table front of book. **2.** *Music Chiefly Brit.* A half note. **3.** One who or that which is very small or insignificant. **4.** A small particle; jot. — *adj.* Extremely small. [< L *minimus* least, smallest]
min·i·mal (min′ə·məl) *adj.* Of a minimum amount, degree, etc.; least possible; smallest. — **min′i·mal·ly** *adv.*
min·i·mize (min′ə·mīz) *v.t.* **·mized, ·miz·ing 1.** To reduce to the smallest amount or degree. **2.** To regard or represent

as of the least possible importance, size, etc. Also *Brit.* **min′i·mise.** — **min′i·mi·za′tion** *n.* — **min′i·miz′er** *n.*

min·i·mum (min′ə·məm) *n.* *pl.* **·mums** or **·ma** (-mə) **1.** The least possible quantity, amount, or degree. **2.** The lowest quantity, degree, number, etc., reached or recorded. — *adj.* **1.** Consisting of or showing the least amount or degree possible, permissible, attainable, etc. **2.** Of or pertaining to a minimum or minimums. [< L, neut. of *minimus*]

minimum wage The smallest wage, fixed by law or by agreement, an employer may offer an employee.

min·ing (mī′ning) *n.* The act, process, or business of extracting coal, ores, etc., from mines.

min·ion (min′yən) *n.* **1.** A servile favorite or follower. **2.** *Printing* A size of type, 7-point. [< F *mignon* darling]

min·is·ter (min′is·tər) *n.* **1.** One who is authorized to administer the sacraments, preach, etc., in a church; clergyman; pastor. **2.** One appointed to head an administrative department of a government. **3.** One authorized to represent his government to another government in diplomatic matters and ranking next below an ambassador. **4.** One who or that which acts as the agent of another person or thing: a *minister* of good. — **Syn.** See AMBASSADOR. — *v.i.* **1.** To provide for the wants or needs of someone. **2.** To be helpful or useful. — *v.t.* **3.** To administer or apply (a sacrament, medicine, etc.). [< OF < L *minister* attendant]

min·is·te·ri·al (min′is·tir′ē·əl) *adj.* **1.** Of, or pertaining to a minister or to the ministry. **2.** Administrative; executive. **3.** Contributive; instrumental. — **min′is·te′ri·al·ly** *adv.*

min·is·trant (min′is·trənt) *adj.* Ministering. — *n.* One who ministers. [< L < *ministrare* to serve]

min·is·tra·tion (min′is·trā′shən) *n.* **1.** The act of serving. **2.** *Often pl.* Help or aid. — **min′is·tra′tive** *adj.*

min·is·try (min′is·trē) *n.* *pl.* **·tries** **1.** The profession, duties, length of service, etc., of a minister of religion. **2.** The clergy. **3.** *Govt.* **a** An executive or administrative department presided over by a minister; also, its building. **b** A body of ministers collectively. **c** The duties of a minister; also, his term of office. **4.** The act of ministering.

min·i·track (min′i·trak′) *n.* *Aerospace* An electronic system for tracking earth satellites by the radio signals received from the satellite. Also **Min′i·track′.**

min·i·um (min′ē·əm) *n.* A vivid, opaque, red lead oxide Pb_3O_4, used chiefly as a pigment: also called *red lead.* [< L]

min·i·ver (min′ə·vər) *n.* **1.** A white or gray and white fur, used in the Middle Ages as trimming, etc. **2.** Any white fur, as ermine. [< OF *menu vair,* lit., little spotted (fur)]

mink (mingk) *n.* **1.** A semiaquatic, slender-bodied carnivorous mammal, resembling a weasel. **2.** The valuable, soft, brown fur of this mammal. [< Scand. Cf. Sw. *menk.*]

min·ne·sing·er (min′ə·sing′ər) *n.* A lyric poet and singer of medieval Germany. [< G < *minne* love + *singer* singer]

min·now (min′ō) *n.* *pl.* **min·nows** (*Rare* **min·now**) **1.** A small European cyprinoid fish of the carp family. **2.** Any of various related fishes. **3.** Any small fish. [ME *menawe*]

Mi·no·an (mi·nō′ən) *adj.* **1.** Of or pertaining to an advanced Bronze Age civilization that flourished in Crete from about 3000 to 1100 B.C. **2.** Designating two varieties of linear script, one (**Linear A**) deciphered in 1957, the other (**Linear B**) deciphered in 1952 and found to be an Achaean dialect of Greek.

mi·nor (mī′nər) *adj.* **1.** Less in quantity, number, or extent. **2.** Of secondary or lesser importance: a *minor* poet. **3.** Under legal age. **4.** *Music* **a** Denoting an interval smaller by a half step than the corresponding major interval. **b** Denoting a triad in which the third above the fundamental is minor. **c** Denoting a type of diatonic scale, or a key based on this scale. **5.** Sad or plaintive; mournful: said of a sound or voice. **6.** *U.S.* In education, of or pertaining to an area of specialized study usu. requiring fewer class hours than a major field of study. **7.** Of or constituting a minority — *n.* **1.** One who is below full legal age. **2.** *U.S.* In education, a minor subject or area of study. **3.** *Music* A minor chord, interval, scale, key, etc. — *v.i.* *U.S.* In education, to study as a minor subject: with *in:* to *minor* in philosophy. [< L]

mi·nor·i·ty (mə·nôr′ə·tē, -nor′-, mī-) *n.* *pl.* **·ties** **1.** The smaller in number of two parts or parties: opposed to *majority.* **2.** A racial, religious, political, or national group smaller than and usu. different in some ways from the larger group of which it is a part. **3.** The state or period of being under legal age. [< F *minorité* or L *minoritas*]

minor league *U.S.* Any professional sports league not having the standing of a major league. — **mi·nor-league** (mī′nər-lēg′) *adj.*

minor suit In bridge, diamonds or clubs.

Mi·nos (mī′nəs, -nos) In Greek mythology: **a** A king of Crete who became a judge of the lower world after his death. **b** His grandson. [< Gk. *Minōs*]

Min·o·taur (min′ə·tôr) In Greek mythology, a monster with the body of a man and the head of a bull, confined in the Labyrinth until it was killed by Theseus. [< L < Gk. *Minōtauros*]

min·ster (min′stər) *n.* *Chiefly Brit.* **1.** A monastery chu **2.** A cathedral or large church. [OE *mynster*]

min·strel (min′strəl) *n.* **1.** In the Middle Ages, a wan ing musician who made his living by singing and reci poetry. **2.** A performer in a minstrel show. **3.** *Poet.* poet, musician, etc. [< OF < LL *ministerialis* servant, jes

minstrel show A comic variety show of songs, dar jokes, etc., given by a company of performers in black

min·strel·sy (min′strəl·sē) *n.* *pl.* **·sies** **1.** The art or o pation of a minstrel. **2.** Ballads or lyrics collectively, those sung by minstrels. **3.** A troupe of minstrels.

mint[1] (mint) *n.* **1.** A place where the coin of a countr lawfully manufactured. **2.** An abundant supply, esp money. **3.** A source of manufacture or inspiration. — **1.** To make (money) by stamping; to coin. **2.** To inven fabricate (a word, etc.). — *adj.* In original condition; used. [OE < L < *Moneta* epithet of Juno, whose templ Rome was used as a mint] — **mint′er** *n.*

mint[2] (mint) *n.* **1.** Any of several aromatic herbs; esp. sp mint and peppermint, used as a flavoring, garnish, etc. A mint-flavored candy. [OE < L < Gk. *mintha*]

mint·age (min′tij) *n.* **1.** The act or process of minting. The money manufactured by a mint. **3.** The fee paid coining. **4.** The authorized impression stamped upon a c

mint julep A drink made of bourbon mixed with crus ice and sugar and flavored with sprigs of fresh mint.

min·u·end (min′yōō·end) *n.* *Math.* The number from wh another is to be subtracted. [< L *minuere* to lessen]

min·u·et (min′yōō·et′) *n.* **1.** A stately dance for coup introduced in France in the 17th century. **2.** Music fo in the manner of this dance, in moderate triple meter. [< L *minutus*]

mi·nus (mī′nəs) *prep.* **1.** Lessened or reduced by; less. *Informal* Lacking; deprived of. — *adj.* **1.** Of or denot subtraction. **2.** Negative: a *minus* value. **3.** Less in qu ity or value than: a C *minus.* **4.** *Informal* Non-existe lacking: His chances were *minus.* — *n.* **1.** The minus s (−). **2.** A minus quantity. **3.** A deficit or loss. [< neut. of *minor*]

mi·nus·cule (mi·nus′kyōōl, min′ə·skyōōl) *n.* Any smal lower-case letter. — *adj.* **1.** Of, pertaining to, like, or co posed of minuscules. **2.** Very small; miniature. [< L *nusculus,* dim. of *minor* less]

minus sign A sign (−) denoting subtraction or a negat quantity.

min·ute[1] (min′it) *n.* **1.** The 60th part of an hour; 60 s onds. **2.** Any very brief period of time; moment. **3.** A s cific instant of time. **4.** A unit of angular measure equal the 60th part of a degree, indicated by the sign (′) and cal **a minute of arc.** **5.** A memorandum. **6.** *pl.* An official r ord of the business discussed and transacted at a meeti conference, etc. — **up to the minute** In accord with latest fashion, equipment, etc. — *v.t.* **·ut·ed, ·ut·ing** **1.** make a minute or brief note of; record. **2.** To time to t minute. [< F < Med.L < L *minutus* small]

mi·nute[2] (mī·nōōt′, -nyōōt′, mi-) *adj.* **1.** Exceedingly sma tiny. **2.** Having little importance or value. **3.** Demo strating or characterized by careful, precise attention small details. [< L *minutus* small] — **mi·nute′ness** *n.*

min·ute·hand (min′it) The hand that indicates the minu on a clock or similar timepiece.

min·ute·ly[1] (min′it·lē) *adj.* & *adv.* At intervals of a minu

mi·nute·ly[2] (mī·nōōt′lē, -nyōōt′-, mi-) *adv.* In a minu manner or degree; with great detail, precision, or exactne

min·ute·man (min′it·man′) *n.* *pl.* **·men** (-men′) In t American Revolution, one of the armed citizens who volu teered to be ready for combat at a minute's notice.

min·ute steak (min′it) A small, thin cut of steak that c be cooked quickly.

mi·nu·ti·ae (mi·nōō′shi·ē, -nyōō′-) *n.* *pl.* *of* **mi·nu·ti·a** (-sh ə, -shə) Small or unimportant details; trifles. [< L]

minx (mingks) *n.* A saucy, bold, or flirtatious girl. [Pro < LG *minsk* impudent woman. Akin to G *mensch* person

Mi·o·cene (mī′ə·sēn) *adj.* Pertaining to or designating th fourth geological epoch of the Tertiary period. See cha for GEOLOGY. — *n.* The Miocene epoch or series. [< G *meiōn* less + *kainos* recent]

mir·a·cle (mir′ə·kəl) *n.* **1.** An event that appears to b neither a part nor result of any known natural law or agenc and is therefore often attributed to a supernatural sourc **2.** Any wonderful or amazing thing, fact, or event. **3.** On who or that which is of surpassing merit or excellence. **4.** miracle play. [< F < L < *mirari* to wonder]

miracle play A medieval play dealing with the lives saints and with their miracles. Compare MYSTERY PLAY.

mi·rac·u·lous (mi·rak′yə·ləs) *adj.* **1.** Wonderful and amaz ing. **2.** Apparently caused by the direct intervention of a su pernatural power. **3.** Having the power to work miracles — **Syn.** See SUPERNATURAL. — **mi·rac′u·lous·ly** *adv.* — **mi·rac′u·lous·ness** *n.*

mi·rage (mi·räzh′) *n.* **1.** An optical illusion, as of a sheet o

er, upside-down ship, etc., that sometimes appears in a ert or in the air, and is caused by reflection from layers of osphere having different densities. 2. Anything that ears to be real but is not. [< F < L *mirari* to wonder at]
e (mīr) *n.* 1. An area of wet, yielding earth; swampy und. 2. Deep mud or slush. — *v.* **mired, mir·ing** *v.t.* 1. cause to sink or become stuck in mire. 2. To smear or with mud; defile. 3. To entangle or entrap. — *v.i.* 4. sink in mire; bog down. [< ON *mýrr* swampy ground] **mir′y** *adj.* — **mir′i·ness** *n.*
·i·am (mir′ē·əm) Sister of Moses and Aaron. *Ex.* xv 20.
k (mûrk), **mirk·i·ly** (mûrk′i·lē), etc. See MURK, etc.
·ror (mir′ər) *n.* 1. Any smooth reflecting surface, as of ss backed with a coating of silver, aluminum, etc. 2. atever reflects or depicts truly. — *v.t.* To reflect or show image of, as in a mirror. [< OF < LL < L *mirari* to nder at, admire]
th (mûrth) *n.* Spirited gaiety; social merriment. [OE *rig* pleasant, merry]
th·ful (mûrth′fəl) *adj.* Full of or characterized by mirth; rry. — **mirth′ful·ly** *adv.* — **mirth′ful·ness** *n.*
-[1] *prefix* Bad; amiss; badly; wrongly; unfavorably: used combination, as in *miscalculate, miscolor, miscopy,* etc. E *mis-* wrong; infl. in meaning by ME *mes-* mis-[2]]
-[2] *prefix* Bad; amiss; not: found with negative or de-ciatory force in words borrowed from Old French: *mis-enture, miscreant.* [< OF *mes-* < L *minus* less]
-[3] Var. of MISO-.
·ad·ven·ture (mis′əd·ven′chər) *n.* A disastrous event.
·ad·vise (mis′ad·vīz′) *v.t.* **·vised, ·vis·ing** To give bad vice or erroneous information or advice to.
·al·li·ance (mis′ə·lī′əns) *n.* An undesirable alliance or rriage. [< F *mésalliance*]
·al·ly (mis′ə·lī′) *v.t.* **·lied, ·ly·ing** To ally badly.
·an·thrope (mis′ən·thrōp, miz′-) *n.* One who hates or trusts his fellow men. Also **mis·an·thro·pist** (mis·an′thrə·t). [< Gk. < *misein* to hate + *anthrōpos* man]
·an·throp·ic (mis′ən·throp′ik) *adj.* Of, pertaining to, like a misanthrope. Also **mis′an·throp′i·cal.** — **mis′an·rop′i·cal·ly** *adv.*
·an·thro·py (mis·an′thrə·pē) *n.* Hatred of mankind.
·ap·ply (mis′ə·plī′) *v.t.* **·plied, ·ply·ing** To use or apply correctly or wrongfully. — **mis′ap·pli·ca′tion** *n.*
·ap·pre·hend (mis′ap·ri·hend′) *v.t.* To apprehend or in-rpret wrongly. — **mis′ap·pre·hen′sion** *n.*
·ap·pro·pri·ate (mis′ə·prō′prē·āt) *v.t.* **·at·ed, ·at·ing** To e or take improperly or dishonestly; misapply. — **mis′ap·o′pri·a′tion** *n.*
·be·come (mis′bi·kum′) *v.t.* **·came, ·come, ·com·ing** To unbecoming or not appropriate to.
·be·have (mis′bi·hāv′) *v.i.* & *v.t.* **·haved, ·hav·ing** To have badly. — **mis′be·hav′ior** *n.*
·be·lief (mis′bi·lēf′) *n.* False belief or opinion.
·be·lieve (mis′bi·lēv′) *v.* **·lieved, ·liev·ing** *v.i.* To hold false, unorthodox, or heretical belief. — **mis′be·liev′er** *n.*
·cal·cu·late (mis·kal′kyə·lāt) *v.t.* & *v.i.* **·lat·ed, ·lat·ing** o calculate wrongly. — **mis′cal·cu·la′tion** *n.*
is·call (mis·kôl′) *v.t.* To call by a wrong name.
is·car·riage (mis·kar′ij) *n.* 1. A premature delivery of a onviable fetus. 2. Failure to bring about a proper con-usion. 3. Failure to reach an intended destination.
is·car·ry (mis·kar′ē) *v.i.* **·ried, ·ry·ing** 1. To fail; go rong. 2. To bring forth a fetus prematurely. 3. To fail reach an intended destination, as freight, mail, etc.
is·cast (mis·kast′, -käst′) *v.t.* **·cast, ·cast·ing** To cast (a lay, role, or an actor) inappropriately.
is·ce·ge·na·tion (mis′i·jə·nā′shən) *n.* Interbreeding of thnic stocks or races. [< L *miscere* to mix + *genus* race] — **mis′ce·ge·net′ic** (-jə·net′ik) *adj.*
is·cel·la·ne·ous (mis′ə·lā′nē·əs) *adj.* 1. Composed of arious and diverse things or elements; mixed. 2. Posses-ing diverse qualities or capabilities. [< L *miscellus* mixed] — **mis′cel·la′ne·ous·ly** *adv.* — **mis′cel·la′ne·ous·ness** *n.*
is·cel·la·ny (mis′ə·lā′nē) *n.* *pl.* **·nies** A miscellaneous ollection, esp. of literary works.
is·chance (mis·chans′, -chäns′) *n.* Bad luck; also, an in-tance of bad luck; mishap.
is·chief (mis′chif) *n.* 1. Action, often playful, that causes ome irritation, harm, or trouble. 2. The disposition to an-oy, tease, or disturb. 3. Harm or injury: High winds can ause great *mischief.* 4. A cause or source of damage, evil, tc. [< OF < *meschever* to come to grief]
is·chief-mak·er (mis′chif·mā′kər) *n.* One who causes mischief. — **mis′chief-mak′ing** *adj.* & *n.*
is·chie·vous (mis′chi·vəs) *adj.* 1. Inclined to or full of mischief. 2. Troubling or annoying. 3. Having a playful, teasing nature or quality. 4. Causing harm or injury. — **mis′chie·vous·ly** *adv.* — **mis′chie·vous·ness** *n.*
mis·ci·ble (mis′i·bəl) *adj.* Capable of being mixed. [< L *miscere* to mix] — **mis′ci·bil′i·ty** *n.*
mis·con·ceive (mis′kən·sēv′) *v.t.* & *v.i.* **·ceived, ·ceiv·ing** To conceive wrongly; misunderstand. — **mis′con·ceiv′er** *n.* — **mis′con·cep′tion** *n.*
mis·con·duct (*n.* mis·kon′dukt; *v.* mis′kən·dukt′) *n.* 1. Improper or immoral behavior. 2. Unlawful conduct. — *v.t.* 1. To behave (oneself) improperly. 2. To mismanage.
mis·con·strue (mis′kən·strōō′) *v.t.* **·strued, ·stru·ing** 1. To interpret wrongly; misunderstand. 2. *Gram.* To construe incorrectly. — **mis′con·struc′tion** *n.*
mis·count (mis·kount′) *v.t.* & *v.i.* To count incorrectly; miscalculate. — *n.* An incorrect count or reckoning.
mis·cre·ant (mis′krē·ənt) *n.* An unscrupulous wretch; evil-doer. — *adj.* Villainous; vile. [< OF < *mes-* mis-[2]- + *croire* to believe]
mis·cue (mis·kyōō′) *n.* 1. In billiards, a stroke spoiled by a slipping of the cue. 2. *Informal* An error; slip-up. — *v.i.* **·cued, ·cu·ing** 1. To make a miscue. 2. In the theater, etc., to miss one's cue or to answer another's cue.
mis·date (mis·dāt′) *v.t.* **·dat·ed, ·dat·ing** To date incorrectly; assign a wrong date to. — *n.* An incorrect date.
mis·deal (mis·dēl′) *v.t.* & *v.i.* **·dealt** (-delt′), **·deal·ing** In card games, to deal incorrectly or improperly. — *n.* An incorrect deal. — **mis·deal′er** *n.*
mis·deed (mis·dēd′) *n.* An evil or immoral act.
mis·de·mean·or (mis′di·mē′nər) *n.* *Law* Any offense less serious than a felony, or for which the punishment is less severe.
mis·di·rect (mis′di·rekt′, -dī·rekt′) *v.t.* To direct or guide wrongly, as a letter, person, etc. — **mis′di·rec′tion** *n.*
mis·do (mis·dōō′) *v.t.* & *v.i.* **·did, ·done, ·do·ing** To do wrongly. [OE *misdōn*] — **mis·do′er** *n.* — **mis·do′ing** *n.*
mis·em·ploy (mis′im·ploi′) *v.t.* To put to a wrong or improper use. — **mis′em·ploy′ment** *n.*
mi·ser (mī′zər) *n.* One who saves or hoards avariciously, often sacrificing his own comfort. [< L, wretched]
mis·er·a·ble (miz′ər·ə·bəl, miz′rə-) *adj.* 1. Being in a state of misery, poverty, or wretched unhappiness. 2. *Informal* In poor health; not well. 3. Causing misery or extreme discomfort: a *miserable* headache. 4. Proceeding from or exhibiting misery: a *miserable* life. 5. Of inferior quality; worthless. 6. Paltry or meager; skimpy. 7. Deserving of pity: a *miserable* creature. 8. Disreputable; shameful: a *miserable* scoundrel. [< OF < L < *miserari* to pity] — **mis′er·a·ble·ness** *n.* — **mis′er·a·bly** *adv.*
Mis·e·re·re (miz′ə·râr′ē, -rir′ē) *n.* 1. The 51st Psalm (in the Vulgate and Douai versions, the 50th): from the opening word of the Latin version. 2. A musical setting of this psalm. [< L, imperative of *misereri* to have mercy]
mis·e·ri·cor·di·a (miz′ə·ri·kôr′dē·ə) *n.* *Latin* Pity; mercy.
mi·ser·ly (mī′zər·lē) *adj.* Of, like, or characteristic of a miser; grasping; avaricious. — **mi′ser·li·ness** *n.*
mis·er·y (miz′ər·ē) *n.* *pl.* **·er·ies** 1. A condition of great wretchedness or suffering, as caused by poverty, pain, etc. 2. Intense mental or emotional anguish; extreme unhappiness. 3. A cause or source of suffering or unhappiness. — **Syn.** See SUFFERING. [< OF < L < *miser* wretched]
mis·fea·sance (mis·fē′zəns) *n.* *Law* The performance of a lawful act in an unlawful or culpable manner. [< OF < *mes-* mis- + *faire* to do] — **mis·fea′sor** *n.*
mis·fire (*v.* mis·fīr′; *n.* mis′fīr) *v.i.* **·fired, ·fir·ing** 1. To fail to fire, ignite, or explode at the desired time, as a firearm, internal-combustion engine, etc. 2. To fail in achieving the proper or desired effect. — *n.* An instance of misfiring.
mis·fit (mis·fit′; *for n. def. 2,* mis′fit′) *v.t.* & *v.i.* **·fit·ted, ·fit·ting** To fail to fit or make fit. — *n.* 1. Something that fits badly. 2. One who is not well adjusted to his environment. 3. The act or condition of fitting badly.
mis·for·tune (mis·fôr′chən) *n.* 1. Adverse or ill fortune; bad luck; adversity. 2. A calamity; mishap.
mis·giv·ing (mis·giv′ing) *n.* A feeling of doubt, distrust, or apprehension.
mis·gov·ern (mis·guv′ərn) *v.t.* To govern badly; administer improperly. — **mis·gov′ern·ment** *n.*
mis·guide (mis·gīd′) *v.t.* **·guid·ed, ·guid·ing** To guide wrongly; mislead. — **mis·guid′ance** *n.* — **mis·guid′er** *n.*
mis·guid·ed (mis·gī′did) *adj.* Guided or led wrongly in thought or action. — **mis·guid′ed·ly** *adv.*
mis·han·dle (mis·han′dəl) *v.t.* **·dled, ·dling** To handle, treat, or manage badly; abuse.
mis·hap (mis′hap, mis·hap′) *n.* An unfortunate accident.
mish·mash (mish′mash′, -mosh′) *n.* A confused mixture or collection of things; hodgepodge. Also **mish′-mash.**
mis·in·form (mis′in·fôrm′) *v.t.* To give false or erroneous information to. — **mis′in·form′ant, mis′in·form′er** *n.* — **mis′in·for·ma′tion** *n.*
mis·in·ter·pret (mis′in·tûr′prit) *v.t.* To interpret or under-

stand incorrectly. — **mis′in·ter′pre·ta′tion** *n.* — **mis′in·ter′pret·er** *n.*

mis·judge (mis·juj′) *v.t. & v.i.* **·judged, ·judg·ing** To judge wrongly or unfairly. — **mis·judg′ment** or *Brit.* **mis·judge′·ment** *n.*

mis·lay (mis·lā′) *v.t.* **·laid, ·lay·ing 1.** To put or lay in a place not remembered; misplace. **2.** To place or put down incorrectly: He *mislaid* the carpet. — **mis·lay′er** *n.*

mis·lead (mis·lēd′) *v.t.* **·led** (-led′), **·lead·ing 1.** To guide or lead in the wrong direction. **2.** To lead into error, as of judgment or conduct. — **mis·lead′er** *n.* — **mis·lead′ing** *adj.* — **mis·lead′ing·ly** *adv.*

mis·man·age (mis·man′ij) *v.t. & v.i.* **·aged, ·ag·ing** To manage badly or improperly. — **mis·man′age·ment** *n.* — **mis·man′ag·er** *n.*

mis·match (mis·mach′) *v.t.* To match badly or inappropriately, as in marriage. — *n.* A bad or incongruous match.

mis·mate (mis·māt′) *v.t. & v.i.* **·mat·ed, ·mat·ing** To mate unsuitably.

mis·name (mis·nām′) *v.t.* **·named, ·nam·ing** To call by a wrong name.

mis·no·mer (mis·nō′mər) *n.* **1.** A name wrongly applied to someone or something. **2.** The act of misnaming, esp. in a legal document. [< AF < OF < *mes-* wrongly + *nomer* < L *nominare* to name]

miso- *combining form* Hating; hatred. Also, before vowels, *mis-*. [< Gk. *misein* to hate]

mis·og·a·my (mis·og′ə·mē) *n.* Hatred of marriage. — **mis·og′a·mist** *n.*

mis·og·y·ny (mis·oj′ə·nē) *n.* Hatred of women [< Gk. < *misein* to hate + *gynē* woman] — **mis·og′y·nist** *n.* — **mis·og′y·nous** *adj.*

mis·place (mis·plās′) *v.t.* **·placed, ·plac·ing 1.** To put in a wrong place. **2.** To put (confidence, faith, trust, etc.) in an unworthy or unsuitable person, thing, or idea. **3.** To mislay (def. 1). — **mis·place′ment** *n.*

mis·play (mis·plā′; *for n., also* mis′plā) *v.t. & v.i.* In games, to play badly or incorrectly. — *n.* A bad play or move.

mis·print (mis·print′; *for n., also* mis′print′) *v.t.* To print incorrectly. — *n.* An error in printing.

mis·pri·sion (mis·prizh′ən) *n. Law* **1.** Concealment of a crime, esp. of treason or felony. **2.** Misconduct of a public official. **3.** A mistake; often, a clerical error. [< OF < *mes-* mis- + *prendre* to take]

mis·prize (mis·prīz′) *v.t.* **·prized, ·priz·ing** To fail to appreciate the worth of; undervalue; despise.

mis·pro·nounce (mis′prə·nouns′) *v.t. & v.i.* **·nounced, ·nounc·ing** To pronounce incorrectly or in an unorthodox manner. — **mis·pro·nun·ci·a·tion** (mis′prə·nun′sē·ā′shən) *n.*

mis·quote (mis·kwōt′) *v.t. & v.i.* **·quot·ed, ·quot·ing** To quote incorrectly. — **mis·quo·ta·tion** (mis′kwō·tā′shən) *n.*

mis·read (mis·rēd′) *v.t.* **·read** (-red′), **·read·ing** (-rē′ding) To read incorrectly or with the wrong sense; misinterpret.

mis·rep·re·sent (mis′rep·ri·zent′) *v.t.* **1.** To give an incorrect or false representation of. **2.** To represent inadequately or poorly. — **mis′rep·re·sen·ta′tion** *n.* — **mis′rep·re·sen′·ta·tive** *adj. & n.* — **mis′rep·re·sent′er** *n.*

mis·rule (mis·rōōl′) *v.t.* **·ruled, ·rul·ing** To rule unwisely or unjustly; misgovern. — *n.* **1.** Bad or unjust rule or government. **2.** Disorder or confusion, as from lawlessness.

miss[1] (mis) *v.t.* **1.** To fail to hit, reach, or land upon (a specified object). **2.** To fail to meet or catch, as a train. **3.** To fail to obtain, accomplish, or achieve: to *miss* the presidency by a few votes. **4.** To fail to see, hear, perceive, etc. **5.** To fail to attend, keep, perform, etc. **6.** To overlook or fail to take advantage of. **7.** To discover the absence of, usu. belatedly: to *miss* one's wallet. **8.** To feel the loss or absence of. **9.** To escape; avoid. — *v.i.* **10.** To fail to hit; strike wide of the mark. **11.** To be unsuccessful; fail. — *n.* A failure to hit, find, succeed, etc. [OE *missan*]

miss[2] (mis) *n.* **1.** *Often cap.* A title used in speaking to an unmarried woman or girl: used without name. **2.** A young girl: chiefly informal or trade usage. [Contr. of MISTRESS]

Miss (mis) *n.* A title of address used before the name of a girl or unmarried woman. ◆ In referring to two or more unmarried women bearing the same name, either *the Misses Brown* or *the Miss Browns* is acceptable.

mis·sal (mis′əl) *n.* **1.** A book containing all the prayers, responses, etc., for celebrating Mass throughout the year. **2.** Loosely, any prayer book. [< Med.L *missale*, neut. of *missalis* (*liber*) mass (book)]

mis·shape (mis·shāp′) *v.t.* **·shaped, ·shaped** or **·shap·en, ·shap·ing** To shape badly; deform. — **mis·shap′en** *adj.*

mis·sile (mis′əl, *Brit.* mis′īl) *n.* **1.** An object, esp. a weapon, intended to be thrown or discharged, as a bullet, arrow, etc. **2.** A guided missile. — *adj.* **1.** Such as may be thrown or discharged. **2.** Used or adapted for throwing or discharging missiles. [< L < *missus*, pp. of *mittere* to send]

mis·sil·ry (mis′əl·rē) *n.* The science and art of designing, building, and operating missiles, esp. rockets and guided missiles. Also **mis′sile·ry.**

miss·ing (mis′ing) *adj.* **1.** Not present; absent; lacking *Mil.* Absent: said of one whose whereabouts or fate in b has not been determined: also **missing in action.**

missing link 1. A hypothetical animal intermediate i velopment between man and the anthropoid apes. **2.** S thing needed to complete a chain or series.

mis·sion (mish′ən) *n.* **1.** Any body of persons sent place in order to perform or accomplish a specific wo service; esp., such a body sent to a foreign country to duct business, negotiations, etc., on behalf of its own c try. **2.** The specific task or responsibility that a pers body of persons is assigned to do or fulfill. **3.** A bod missionaries sent by a religious organization to a fo country or region to convert, aid, or instruct the inhabit **4.** *pl.* The organized work of such missionaries. **5.** place or establishment where missionaries carry on work and often live; also, the entire district or locality they serve. **6.** A special program or series of religious vices or exercises for stimulating piety or converting u lievers. **7.** *U.S.* The permanent foreign office of an am sador or envoy; embassy. **8.** The particular work or that one is or feels destined to do or accomplish; a cal **9.** *Mil.* A definite task or field of operation assigned to a dividual or unit of the armed forces. **10.** A flight opera of a single aircraft or formation, esp. in wartime. — Pertaining or belonging to a mission. — *v.t.* **1.** To sen a mission. **2.** To establish a mission in or among. [< *missus*, pp. of *mittere* to send] — **mis′sion·er** *n.*

mis·sion·ar·y (mish′ən·er′ē) *n.* *pl.* **·ar·ies 1.** A pe sent to propagate religion or to do educational or charit work in some foreign country or region. **2.** One who a cates or spreads any new system or doctrine. — *adj.* pertaining to, or characteristic of missionaries.

mis·sis (mis′əz) *n. Informal & Dial.* **1.** A wife: often *the.* **2.** The female head of a household: with *the.* Also **m sus.** [Alter. of MISTRESS]

Mis·sis·sip·pi·an (mis′ə·sip′ē·ən) *adj.* **1.** Of or pertai to the Mississippi River or to the State. **2.** *Geol.* Rela to the earliest of the two geological periods or systems in American Carboniferous division of the Paleozoic era. chart for GEOLOGY. — *n.* **1.** One born or residing in Mis sippi. **2.** The Lower Carboniferous geological formation.

mis·sive (mis′iv) *n.* A letter, esp. one of an official nat — *adj.* Sent or designed to be sent. [< Med.L < L *mis* pp. of *mittere* to send]

Mis·sou·ri (mi·zōōr′ē, -zōōr′ə) *n.* *pl.* **·ri** One of a trib North American Indians of the Siouan family, formerly habiting northern Missouri.

mis·speak (mis·spēk′) *v.t. & v.i.* **·spoke, ·speak·ing** speak or pronounce incorrectly.

mis·spell (mis·spel′) *v.t. & v.i.* **·spelled** or **·spelt, ·spell·** To spell incorrectly.

mis·spell·ing (mis·spel′ing) *n.* An incorrect spelling.

mis·spend (mis·spend′) *v.t.* **·spent, ·spend·ing** To spe wrongfully or wastefully.

mis·state (mis·stāt′) *v.t.* **·stat·ed, ·stat·ing** To state wro ly or falsely. — **mis·state′ment** *n.*

mis·step (mis′step′) *n.* **1.** A false step; a stumble. **2.** error or blunder, as in conduct.

mist (mist) *n.* **1.** An aggregation of fine drops of water s pended in the atmosphere at or near the earth's surface. *Meteorol.* A very thin fog with a horizontal visibility ar trarily set at not more than two kilometers. **3.** Wate vapor condensed on and blurring a surface. **4.** Any cloud particles forming a haze, as of dust, smoke, etc. **5.** A fi or haze before the eyes that blurs one's vision. **6.** Anythi that clouds or obscures one's memory, perceptions, etc. *v.i.* **1.** To be or become dim or misty; blur. **2.** To rain very fine drops. — *v.t.* **3.** To make dim or misty. [OE

mis·tak·a·ble (mis·tāk′ə·bəl) *adj.* Capable of being m taken or misunderstood. — **mis·tak′a·bly** *adv.*

mis·take (mis·tāk′) *n.* An error or fault in action, jud ment, perception, understanding, etc. — *v.* **·took, ·tak·e ·tak·ing** *v.t.* **1.** To understand wrongly; acquire a wro conception of. **2.** To take (a person or thing) to be anothe — *v.i.* **3.** To make a mistake. [< ON *mistaka*]

mis·tak·en (mis·tā′kən) *adj.* **1.** Based on or arising fro error, as of judgment, understanding, perception, etc. Wrong in opinion, action, etc. — **mis·tak′en·ly** *adv.*

mis·ter (mis′tər) *n. Informal* Sir: used without the nam [Var. of MASTER]

Mis·ter (mis′tər) *n.* **1.** Master: a title of address prefixe to the name and to some official titles of a man: commonl written *Mr.* **2.** The official term of address for certain mi tary and naval persons.

mis·time (mis·tīm′) *v.t.* **·timed, ·tim·ing 1.** To time wrong ly or inappropriately. **2.** To misjudge the time of.

mis·tle·toe (mis′əl·tō) *n.* **1.** A European parasitic shrul found growing on various deciduous trees and having yellow ish green leaves, inconspicuous flowers, and glutinous whit berries, used as a Christmas decoration. **2.** A related Ame

plant used as a Christmas decoration and the State
er of Oklahoma. [OE *misteltān* mistletoe twig]
ook (mis·to͝ok′) Past tense of MISTAKE.
ral (mis′trəl, *Fr.* mēs·träl′) *n.* A cold, dry, violent
herly wind blowing down the Rhône Valley through
hern France and adjacent areas. [< F < Provençal,
master wind < L < *magister* master]
trans·late (mis′trans·lāt′, -tranz-, mis·trans′lāt,
nz′-) *v.t.* **·lat·ed, ·lat·ing** To translate incorrectly. —
trans·la′tion *n.*
treat (mis·trēt′) *v.t.* To treat badly or improperly. —
treat′ment *n.*
tress (mis′tris) *n.* **1.** A woman in a position of author-
or control; as: **a** The head of a household, institution, or
te. **b** The head of a staff of servants. **c** The owner of an
nal or slave. **2.** A woman who unlawfully cohabits with
an, usu. over an extended period of time. **3.** A woman
ing supreme control over anything. **4.** *Often cap.* Any-
g considered feminine that has actual or potential power
r something else. **5.** A woman who has mastered a skill,
t, or branch of learning. **6.** *Chiefly Brit.* A female school-
her. [< OF *maistresse*, fem. of *maistre* master]
tress (mis′tris) *n.* Formerly, a title of address applied
vomen, now supplanted by *Mrs.* and *Miss.*
tri·al (mis·trī′əl) *n. Law* **1.** A trial made void because
ome legal errors or defects. **2.** A trial terminated by the
y's inability to agree on a verdict.
trust (mis·trust′) *v.t.* **1.** To regard (someone or some-
ng) with suspicion or doubt; be skeptical of. — *v.i.* **2.**
be wary or suspicious. — *n.* Lack of trust or confidence.
mis·trust′er *n.* — **mis·trust′ing·ly** *adv.*
trust·ful (mis·trust′fəl) *adj.* Full of mistrust; suspi-
us. — **mis·trust′ful·ly** *adv.* — **mis·trust′ful·ness** *n.*
t·y (mis′tē) *adj.* **mist·i·er, mist·i·est** **1.** Consisting of,
racterized by, or like mist. **2.** Dimmed or obscured. **3.**
king clarity; vague. — **mist′i·ly** *adv.* — **mist′i·ness** *n.*
·un·der·stand (mis′un·dər·stand′, mis·un′-) *v.t.* & *v.i.*
ood, ·stand·ing To understand wrongly; misinterpret.
·un·der·stand·ing (mis′un·dər·stan′ding, mis·un′-) *n.*
A failure to understand the meaning, motive, etc., of
neone or something. **2.** A disagreement or quarrel.
·un·der·stood (mis′un·dər·sto͝od′, mis·un′-) *adj.* **1.**
ongly understood. **2.** Not valued or appreciated.
·us·age (mis·yo͞o′sij, -zij) *n.* **1.** Incorrect or improper
, as of words. **2.** Ill-treatment.
·use (*n.* mis·yo͞os′; *v.* mis·yo͞oz′) *n.* Erroneous or imper use; misapplication. — *v.t.* **·used, ·us·ing** **1.** To use
apply wrongly or improperly. **2.** To treat badly; abuse;
ltreat. — **mis·us′er** *n.*
·val·ue (mis·val′yo͞o) *v.t.* **·ued, ·u·ing** To value wrongly.
e[1] (mīt) *n.* Any of various small arachnids, many of
ich are parasitic on men, animals, and plants, and feed
on stored grain. [OE *mīte*] — **mit′y** *adj.*
e[2] (mīt) *n.* **1.** A very small particle, object, or creature.
Any very small coin or sum of money. [< Du. *mijt*]
ter (mī′tər) *n.* **1.** A tall ornamental headdress, rising in
aks at the front and back, worn by popes, bishops, and ab-
ts. **2.** The office or dignity of a bishop. **3.** In carpentry:
A miter joint. **b** The beveled edges that come together to
rm a miter joint. — *v.t.* **1.** To confer a miter upon; raise
the rank of bishop. **2.** To make or join with a miter joint.
Also, *Brit.*, *mitre.* [< OF < L *mitra* < Gk., belt, turban]
mi′ter·er *n.*
·tered (mī′tərd) *adj.* **1.** Shaped like an ecclesiastical mi-
r. **2.** Wearing or permitted to wear a miter.
ter joint A joint made of two pieces of material whose
ined ends have been beveled at equal angles, as at the
rner of a picture frame.
t·i·gate (mit′ə·gāt) *v.t.* & *v.i.* **·gat·ed, ·gat·ing** To make
become milder or less severe. [< L < *mitis* mild + *agere*
do, drive] — **mit′i·ga·ble** *adj.* — **mit′i·ga′tion** *n.* —
it′i·ga′tor *n.*
t·i·ga·tive (mit′ə·gā′tiv) *adj.* Tending to mitigate. —
Something that mitigates pain, discomfort, etc. Also
it′i·gant (-gənt), **mit′i·ga·to′ry** (-gə·tôr′ē, -tō′rē).
i·to·chon·dri·a (mī′tə·kon′drē·ə) *n.pl. Biol.* Small gran-
lar bodies found in the cytoplasm of a cell, believed to func-
on in certain phases of metabolism. For illus. see CELL.
< NL < Gk. *mitos* thread + *chondros* cartilage, granule]
i·to·sis (mī·tō′sis) *n. Biol.* The series of changes in cell
ivision by which the chromatin is modified into two sets of
hromosomes, one set going to each pole before the cell di-
ides into two mature daughter cells. [< NL < Gk. *mitos*
hread + -OSIS] — **mi·tot·ic** (mī·tot′ik) *adj.* — **mi·tot′i·
al·ly** *adv.*
i·tral (mī′trəl) *adj.* **1.** Pertaining to or resembling a mi-
er. **2.** Of or pertaining to a mitral valve.
itral valve *Anat.* A membranous valve between the left
atrium and the left ventrical of the heart, that prevents the
blood from flowing back into the atrium.
mi·tre (mī′tər), **mi·tred** (mī′tərd), etc. See MITER, etc.
mitt (mit) *n.* **1.** In baseball, a covering somewhat like a
mitten, to protect the hand catching the ball. **2.** A woman's
glove, sometimes extending to or above the elbow but without fully covering the fingers. **3.** A mitten (def. 1). **4.**
Slang Usu. pl. A hand. **5.** *Slang* A boxing glove.
mit·ten (mit′n) *n.* A covering for the hand, encasing the
four fingers together and the thumb separately. [< F *mi-
taine*]
mix (miks) *v.* **mixed** or **mixt, mix·ing** *v.t.* **1.** To combine or
put together in one mass or compound so as to render the
constituent parts wholly or partially indistinguishable from
one another. **2.** To make by combining ingredients: to *mix*
cake batter. **3.** To put or add, as an ingredient: to *mix* two
eggs into the batter. **4.** To combine or join: to *mix* age
with wisdom. **5.** To bring into contact with; cause to mingle. **6.** To crossbreed. — *v.i.* **7.** To become mixed or have
the capacity to become mixed; mingle. **8.** To associate; get
along: He does not *mix* well with others. **9.** To take part;
become involved. **10.** To crossbreed. — **to mix up 1.** To
mix or blend together. **2.** To confuse. **3.** To mistake for
another or others: He *mixed up* the meanings of those two
words. **4.** To implicate or involve. — *n.* **1.** The act or
product of mixing. **2.** A mixture of ingredients, often prepared and sold commercially: a cake *mix*. **3.** A beverage, as
water, soda, ginger ale, etc., used in making cocktails and
other mixed drinks. **4.** Confusion or bewilderment; a mess.
5. *Telecom.* The correct blending of the outputs of two or
more microphones. [Back formation < MIXED] — **mix′a·
ble** or **mix′i·ble** *adj.*
mixed (mikst) *adj.* **1.** Mingled or blended together in a
single mass or compound. **2.** Composed of different, dissimilar, or incongruous elements, qualities, classes, races,
etc.: *mixed* motives. **3.** Made up of or involving persons of
both sexes. **4.** Mentally confused: followed by *up*. Also
mixt. [< F < L *mixtus*, pp. of *miscere* to mix]
mixed marriage Marriage between persons of different religions or races.
mixed metaphor See under METAPHOR.
mixed number A number, as 3½, 5¾, that is the sum of an
integer and a fraction.
mix·er (mik′sər) *n.* **1.** One who or that which mixes. **2.**
Informal A person with ability to mix socially or get along
well in various groups. **3.** *Informal* A dance or gathering for
the purpose of getting acquainted. **4.** A mix (def. 3).
mix·ture (miks′chər) *n.* **1.** Something formed by or resulting from mixing. **2.** Anything composed of unlike or various
elements; as: **a** A cloth made of several types or colors of
yarn. **b** A blend of different kinds or qualities of tea, tobacco,
etc. **3.** *Chem.* A commingling of two or more substances in
varying proportions, in which the components retain their
individual chemical properties: distinguished from *compound*. **4.** The act of mixing, or the state of being mixed.
[< F < L *miscere* to mix]
mix-up (miks′up′) *n.* **1.** A state of confusion; also, an instance of this. **2.** *Informal* A fight.
miz·zen (miz′ən) *Naut. n.* **1.** A triangular sail set on the
mizzenmast. **2.** A mizzenmast. — *adj.* Of or pertaining to
the mizzen or mizzenmast. Also **miz′en.** [< F < Ital. *mez-
zana*, fem. of *mezzano* middle, ? < L *medianus*]
miz·zen·mast (miz′ən·məst′, -mast′, -mäst′) *n. Naut.* **1.**
In a ship with three masts, the mast nearest the stern. **2.**
In a ship having more than three masts, the third mast from
the forward end of the ship. **3.** In a ketch or yawl, the
shorter of the two masts. Also **miz′en·mast′.**
mks The meter-kilogram-second system of measurement in
which the unit of length is the meter, the unit of mass is the
kilogram, and the unit of time is one second. Also **m.k.s.,
MKS, M.K.S.**
mne·mon·ic (nē·mon′ik, ni-) *adj.* **1.** Aiding or designed to
aid the memory. **2.** Of or relating to mnemonics or memory. Also **mne·mon′i·cal.** — *n.* **1.** A device to assist memory. **2.** Mnemonics. [< Gk. < *mnasthai* to remember]
mne·mon·ics (nē·mon′iks, ni-) *n.pl.* (*construed as sing.*) A
system of principles and formulas designed to assist or improve the memory. Also **mne·mo·tech·nics** (nē′mō·tek′niks).
mo·a (mō′ə) *n.* Any of a family of extinct, flightless birds of
New Zealand, resembling the ostrich and having very powerful legs. [< Maori]
Mo·ab (mō′ab) An ancient country east of the Dead Sea.
— **Mo′ab·ite** *adj.* & *n.*
moan (mōn) *n.* **1.** A low, sustained, mournful sound, as
from grief or pain. **2.** Any similar sound. — *v.i.* **1.** To utter moans. **2.** To make a low, mournful sound, as wind. **3.**
To complain or lament. — *v.t.* **4.** To lament; bewail. **5.**
To utter with moans. [Cf. OE *mǣnan* to lament, moan]

moat (mōt) *n.* A deep, wide, and usu. water-filled trench around a castle, fortress, or town, designed to discourage attempts at invasion. —*v.t.* To surround with or as with a moat. [< OF *mote* embankment]

mob (mob) *n.* **1.** A disorderly or lawless crowd or throng; a rabble. **2.** Any large assemblage, group, or class of individuals or things: the ruling *mob.* **3.** The lower class or classes of people; the masses. **4.** *Informal* A gang of thieves, hoodlums, etc. —*v.t.* **mobbed, mob·bing 1.** To attack in a mob. **2.** To crowd around and jostle or molest, as from adulation or curiosity. **3.** To attend or crowd into (a hall, theater, etc.). [< L *mob(ile vulgus)* movable crowd] —**mob′ber** *n.* —**mob′bish** *adj.* —**mob′bish·ly** *adv.*

mo·bile (*adj.* mō′bəl, -bēl; *n.* mō′bēl; *Brit.* mō′bīl) *adj.* **1.** Characterized by freedom of movement. **2.** Flowing freely: a *mobile* liquid. **3.** Capable of changing or responding easily or quickly, as to emotions, etc. **4.** Moving easily from one thing to another; versatile: a *mobile* mind. **5.** Capable of being easily and quickly moved. **6.** Capable of moving with relative ease from one social group or status to another. **7.** Of, pertaining to, or like a mobile. —*n.* A form of freely moving sculpture consisting of parts that are suspended from rods, wires, etc. [< F < L *mobilis* movable] —**mo·bil′i·ty** *n.*

mo·bi·lize (mō′bə·līz) *v.* **·lized, ·liz·ing** *v.t.* **1.** To make ready for war, as an army, industry, men, etc. **2.** To assemble for use; organize. **3.** To put into activity, circulation, or use: to *mobilize* one's talents. —*v.i.* **4.** To undergo mobilization. Also *Brit.* **mo′bi·lise.** [< F *mobiliser*] —**mo′·bi·li·za′tion** (-lə·zā′shən, -lī·zā′-) *n.*

mob·ster (mob′stər) *n. Slang* A gangster.

moc·ca·sin (mok′ə·sin) *n.* **1.** A heelless foot covering, made of buckskin or of any soft leather and formerly worn by North American Indians. **2.** A shoe or slipper resembling a moccasin. **3.** The water moccasin. [< Algonquian *mohkisson*]

moccasin flower Any of certain lady's-slippers.

mo·cha (mō′kə) *n.* **1.** A choice, pungent coffee, originally brought from Mocha, Arabia. **2.** A flavoring made of an infusion of coffee or of coffee and chocolate. **3.** A fine sheepskin leather used for making gloves.

mock (mok) *v.t.* **1.** To treat or address scornfully or derisively. **2.** To mimic, as in sport, derision, or contempt. **3.** To deceive or disappoint; delude. **4.** To defy; make futile or meaningless. **5.** *Poetic* To imitate; counterfeit. —*v.i.* **6.** To express or show ridicule or contempt; scoff. —*adj.* Merely imitating or resembling the reality; sham. —*n.* **1.** An act of mocking or derision; a jeer. **2.** One who or that which is mocked. **3.** An imitation or counterfeit. [< OF *mocquer*] —**mock′er** *n.* —**mock′ing·ly** *adv.*

mock·er·y (mok′ər·ē) *n. pl.* **·er·ies 1.** Derision; ridicule. **2.** A contemptuous or derisive speech or action. **3.** An object of derision or ridicule. **4.** A deceitful, impudent, or contemptible imitation: His trial was a *mockery.* **5.** Something ludicrously futile, inadequate, or unsuitable.

mock-he·ro·ic (mok′hi·rō′ik) *adj.* Imitating or satirizing the heroic manner, style, attitude, or character. Also **mock′-he·ro′i·cal.**

mock·ing·bird (mok′ing·bûrd′) *n.* **1.** A bird common in the southern U.S., noted for its ability to imitate the calls of other birds. **2.** Any of various birds of the same family.

mock turtle soup A soup prepared from calf's head or other meat and seasoned to taste like green turtle soup.

mock·up (mok′up′) *n.* A model, usu. full-scale, of a proposed structure, machine, apparatus, etc.

mo·dal (mōd′l) *adj.* **1.** Of or pertaining to mode or a mode. **2.** *Gram.* **a** Of or pertaining to mood. **b** Conveying a meaning similar to those meanings conveyed by a mood. **3.** *Music* Of or pertaining to the modes. **4.** *Stat.* Typical. —**mo·dal′i·ty** (-dal′ə·tē) *n.* —**mo′dal·ly** *adv.*

mode (mōd) *n.* **1.** Manner or form of being, doing, etc.; way. **2.** Prevailing or current style or fashion, as in dress. **3.** *Gram.* Mood. **4.** *Music* Any of the arrangements of tones achieved by starting at various points in a given scale and proceeding through one octave; esp. the modes of the diatonic scale, as major mode, minor mode, etc. **5.** *Philos.* The manner or form in which a basic substance is manifested. **6.** *Stat.* The value, magnitude, or score that occurs the greatest number of times in a given series of observations: also called *norm.* [< L *modus* measure, manner]

mod·el (mod′l) *n.* **1.** An object, usu. in miniature and often built according to scale, that represents something to be made or something already existing. **2.** A pattern, example, or standard that is or may be used for imitation or comparison. **3.** A representation in clay, plaster, etc., of something later to be reproduced in more permanent material. **4.** One who or that which serves as a figure or pattern for an artist, sculptor, etc. **5.** One who is employed to display or advertise merchandise; esp. one who displays articles of clothing by wearing them. **6.** A representative style, plan, or design. **7.** In merchandise, a particular style or design. —*v.* **mod·eled** or **·elled, mod·el·ing** or **·el·ling** *v.t.* **1.** To plan or fashion after a model or pattern. **2.** To m[ake a] model of. **3.** To shape or fashion. **4.** To display by [wear]ing. —*v.i.* **5.** To make a model or models. **6.** To p[ose or] serve as a model (defs. 4 & 5). —*adj.* **1.** Serving or u[sed as] a model. **2.** Worthy or suitable to be used as a model. [< O]F < Ital. < L *modus* measure, manner] —**mod′el·[er]**, **mod′el·ler** *n.*

mod·el·ing (mod′ling, -əl·ing) *n.* **1.** The act or art of [mak]ing a model, esp. a sculptor's clay or wax model. [2. In] painting, drawing, etc., the representation of depth or t[hree-]dimensional solidity. **3.** The surfaces or planes of a [three-dimensional] form or shape. **4.** The act or occupation of being a m[odel] (defs. 4 & 5). Also **mod′el·ling.**

mod·er·ate (*adj.* & *n.* mod′ər·it; *v.* mod′ə·rāt) *adj.* **1.** K[eep]ing or kept within reasonable limits; temperate. **2.** [Hold]ing or characterized by ideas or convictions that are n[ot ex]treme or radical. **3.** Of medium or average quality, qua[ntity,] scope, extent, etc. **4.** *Meteorol.* Designating a breeze (N[o. 4]) or a gale (No. 7) on the Beaufort scale. —*n.* One h[aving] moderate views or practices, esp. in politics or religion. [—*v.* **·at·ed, ·at·ing** *v.t.* **1.** To reduce the violence, severity, [etc.,] of. **2.** To preside over. —*v.i.* **3.** To become less inten[se or] violent. **4.** To act as a moderator. [< L *moderare* to r[egu]late] —**mod′er·ate·ly** *adv.* —**mod′er·ate·ness** *n.*

mod·er·a·tion (mod′ə·rā′shən) *n.* **1.** The state or qu[ality] of being moderate. **2.** The act of moderating. —**in m[od]eration** Within reasonable limits; temperately.

mod·e·ra·to (mod′ə·rä′tō) *Music adj.* Moderate. —[*adv.*] In moderate time; moderately. —*n. pl.* **·tos** A mod[erate] passage or movement. Abbr. *mod.* [< Ital.]

mod·er·a·tor (mod′ə·rā′tər) *n.* **1.** One who or that w[hich] moderates. **2.** One who presides over a meeting, forum[, or] debate. **3.** The arbitrator of a dispute. **4.** *Physics* A [sub]stance, as graphite or beryllium, used to slow down neut[rons] in an atomic-energy reactor. —**mod′er·a′tor·ship** *n.*

mod·ern (mod′ərn) *adj.* **1.** Of or pertaining to the pre[sent] or recent time. **2.** Characteristic of or serving to express current times; up-to-date. **3.** *Usu. cap.* Of, pertaining t[o, or] characteristic of the most recent period in the developm[ent] of a language: *Modern* French. —*n.* **1.** One who live[s in] modern times. **2.** One who has opinions, habits, prejud[ices,] etc., characteristic of modern times. **3.** *Printing* A sty[le of] type face characterized by heavy stems and extremely [thin] serifs. [< LL *modernus* recent] —**mod′ern·ly** *adv.*

mod·ern·ism (mod′ərn·iz′əm) *n.* **1.** The character or q[ual]ity of thought, action, etc., that is peculiar to modern ti[mes.] **2.** Something characteristic of modern times, as an [act,] practice, idiom, attitude, etc. **3.** *Often cap.* In religio[n, a] movement to reinterpret the Bible and church teaching[s to] make them consistent with modern science and philosop[hy.]

mod·ern·ist (mod′ərn·ist) *n.* **1.** One who is sympath[etic] with or has a preference for modern things, practices, id[eas,] etc. **2.** *Often cap.* An advocate of religious modernism. [—] **mod′ern·is′tic** *adj.*

mo·der·ni·ty (mo·dûr′nə·tē) *n. pl.* **·ties 1.** The condit[ion] or quality of being modern. **2.** Something modern.

mod·ern·ize (mod′ərn·īz) *v.* **·ized, ·iz·ing** *v.t.* **1.** To m[ake] modern in method, style, character, etc.; bring up to d[ate.] —*v.i.* **2.** To accept or adopt modern ways, ideas, idio[ms,] etc. —**mod′ern·i·za′tion** *n.* —**mod′ern·iz′er** *n.*

mod·est (mod′ist) *adj.* **1.** Having or displaying a moder[ate] or unexaggerated regard for oneself or one's abilities, acc[om]plishments, etc.; humble. **2.** Not showy, gaudy, or osten[ta]tious. **3.** Not excessive or extreme; moderate. **4.** Reser[ved] in speech, manner, dress, etc. [< L *modestus* moderate] [—] **mod′est·ly** *adv.*

mod·es·ty (mod′is·tē) *n. pl.* **·ties 1.** Freedom from va[nity] or excessive pride. **2.** Freedom from showiness or osten[ta]tion. **3.** Propriety in speech, dress, etc. **4.** Moderation.

mod·i·cum (mod′i·kəm) *n. pl.* **·cums** or **·ca** (-kə) A mod[er]ate or small amount. [< L < *modus* measure]

mod·i·fi·ca·tion (mod′ə·fə·kā′shən) *n.* **1.** The act of mo[di]fying, or the state of being modified. **2.** That which resu[lts] from modifying. **3.** A small adjustment, alteration, or qu[al]ification. **4.** *Biol.* A noninheritable change in an organis[m] resulting from its own activity or its environment.

mod·i·fi·er (mod′ə·fī′ər) *n.* **1.** One who or that which mo[di]fies. **2.** *Gram.* A word, phrase, or clause that restricts [or] qualifies the meaning of another word or group of words.

mod·i·fy (mod′ə·fī) *v.* **·fied, ·fy·ing** *v.t.* **1.** To make so[me]what different in form, character, etc. **2.** To revise by ma[k]ing less extreme, severe, or uncompromising. **3.** *Gram.* [To] qualify the meaning of; limit. —*v.i.* **4.** To be or beco[me] modified. [< F < L < *modus* measure + *facere* to mak[e]] —**mod′i·fi′a·ble** *adj.*

mod·ish (mō′dish) *adj.* Conforming to the current mode [or] fashion; stylish. —**mod′ish·ly** *adv.* —**mod′ish·ness** *n.*

mo·diste (mō·dēst′) *n.* A woman who deals in fashiona[ble] women's clothing, esp. hats or dresses. [< F]

mod·u·lar (moj′o͞o·lər) *adj.* **1.** Of, like, or pertaining to a mo[d]ule or modulus. **2.** Composed of modules: *modular* homes.

u·late (moj′o͝o·lāt) *v.* **·lat·ed, ·lat·ing** *v.t.* **1.** To vary :one, inflection, pitch, or volume of. **2.** To regulate or ıst; modify. **3.** To sing or intone, as a prayer. **4.** *Tele-* To alter some characteristic of (a radio carrier wave). *i.* **5.** *Music* To change from one key to another. **6.** *:om.* To alter some characteristic of a carrier wave. [< *ɔdulatus*, pp. of *modulari* to regulate] **— mod′u·la′tor** *n.* **ıod′u·la·to′ry** (-lə·tôr′ē, -tō′rē) *adj.*

u·la·tion (moj′o͝o·lā′shən) *n.* **1.** The act of modulat- or the state of being modulated. **2.** *Music* A change ı one key to another. **3.** A melodious or rhythmical in- ion of the voice. **4.** A melodious use of language, as in e or poetry. **5.** *Telecom.* **a** The process whereby some ·acteristic of one carrier wave is varied in accordance ı another wave. **b** The result of this process.

·ule (moj′o͞ol) *n.* **1.** A standard or unit of measure- :t. **2.** *Archit.* A unit of measure used to determine the ɔortion among parts of a classical order. **3.** A standard ctural component repeatedly used, as in a building, com- ər, etc. **4.** A self-contained component or subassembly: ɔusing *module.* [< L *modulus*, dim. of *modus* measure]

lus op·er·an·di (mō′dəs op′ə·ran′dī) *Latin* A manner perating or proceeding.

us vi·ven·di (vi·ven′dī) *Latin* **1.** A manner of living. \ temporary agreement in a dispute.

gul (mō′gul, mō·gul′) *n.* **1.** One of the conquerors of ·a, who in 1526 founded a Moslem empire. **2.** Any of ır descendants. **3.** A member of the Mongoloid race. **—** Of or pertaining to the Moguls or their empire. Also lled *Mughal, Mughul:* also **Mo·ghal′, Mo·ghul′.** [< Per- ı *mugal* Mongol]

hair (mō′hâr) *n.* **1.** The hair of the Angora goat. **2.** A ssy, wiry fabric made of mohair and cotton in a plain or ıl weave. **3.** A fabric having a mohair pile, used for up- stery. [Earlier *mocayare* < Arabic *mukhayyar*]

ham·me·dan (mō·ham′ə·dən) *adj.* Of or pertaining to ·hammed or to his religion and institutions. **—** *n.* A fol- ·er of Mohammed or a believer in Islam; a Muslim. Also *·hometan, Muhammadan, Muhammedan.*

ıammedan calendar See under CALENDAR.

ham·me·dan·ism (mō·ham′ə·dən·iz′əm) *n.* Islam.

·ha·ve (mō·hä′vē) *n.* One of a tribe of North American lians of Yuman stock, formerly living along the Colorado ver: also spelled *Mojave.*

hawk (mō′hôk) *n.* **1.** One of a tribe of North American lians of Iroquoian stock, one of the original Five Nations, merly ranging from the Mohawk River to the St. Law- ıce. **2.** The language of this tribe. [< N.Am.Ind.]

·he·gan (mō·hē′gən) *n.* **1.** One of a tribe of North Amer- n Indians of Algonquian stock, formerly living along the ames River in Connecticut. **2.** Loosely, Mahican. [< gonquian *maingan* wolf]

·hi·can (mō·hē′kən) *n.* A Mahican.

·hole (mō′hōl′) *n.* A hole drilled or to be drilled through ɘ ocean floor to the level of the Mohorovicic discontinuity.

·hor·o·vic·ic discontinuity (mə·hôr′ə·vis′ik, -vich′ik) *Geol.* A rock layer forming a boundary zone beneath the ·rth's crust at depths of from about 6 to 25 miles and be- ·ved to explain certain changes in the character and veloci- of seismic waves. Also **Mo·ho** (mō′hō). [after Andrija *ohorovičić*, Yugoslavian geologist]

·hs scale (mōz) *Mineral.* A qualitative scale in which e hardness of a mineral is determined by its ability to ·ratch, or be scratched by, any one of 15 minerals arranged order of increasing hardness from talc to diamond. [after ·iedrich *Mohs*, 1773–1839, German mineralogist]

·i·e·ty (moi′ə·tē) *n. pl.* **·ties 1.** A half. **2.** Any portion, ·rt, or share. **3.** *Anthropol.* Either of two basic groups that ·gether constitute a tribe. [< F < L < *medius* half]

·il (moil) *v.i.* **1.** To work hard; toil. **2.** To move about ·aselessly. **—** *v.t.* **3.** To make wet. **—** *n.* **1.** Toil; drudg- y. **2.** Confusion; uproar. [< OF *moillier, muiller* to wet L *mollis* soft] **— moil′er** *n.* **— moil′ing·ly** *adv.*

ɔi·ré (mwä·rā′) *adj.* Having a wavelike or watered appear- ıce, as certain fabrics. **—** *n.* **1.** A ribbed fabric, usu. silk · rayon, having a wavy or watered pattern: also **moire** ıwär, mōr). **2.** A wavy pattern produced on fabrics by ıgraved cylinders. [< F < *moire* watered silk]

ɔist (moist) *adj.* **1.** Slightly wet or damp. **2.** Saturated ith or characterized by moisture or liquid. **3.** Tearful or ·arfully sentimental. [< OF, a fusion of L *musteus* dew + *·ucidus* moldy] **— moist′ly** *adv.* **— moist′ness** *n.*

ɔis·ten (mois′ən) *v.t. & v.i.* To make or become moist. **—** **ıois′ten·er** *n.*

ɔis·ture (mois′chər) *n.* **1.** Water or other liquid diffused s a vapor in the air or as a liquid through or on the surface f objects. **2.** Dampness. [< OF *moisteur*]

o·ja·ve (mō·hä′vē) See MOHAVE.

mo·lar (mō′lər) *n.* A grinding tooth, of which there are 12 in man, situated behind the canine and incisor teeth and having a broad, flattened crown. For illus. see TOOTH. **—** *adj.* **1.** Grinding or adapted for grinding. **2.** Pertaining to a molar. [< L < *mola* mill]

mo·las·ses (mə·las′iz) *n. pl.* **mo·las·ses** Any of various thick, dark-colored syrups obtained from sugar, sorghum, etc., during the refining process: also, *Brit., treacle.* [< Pg. < L *mellaceus* honeylike]

mold[1] (mōld) *n.* **1.** A form or matrix that gives a particular shape to anything in a fluid or plastic condition. **2.** A frame or model on or around which something is shaped or made: a basket *mold.* **3.** That which is shaped or made in or on a mold. **4.** The shape or pattern rendered by a mold. **5.** General shape, form, or pattern. **6.** Distinctive nature, character, or type. **7.** *Archit.* A molding or set of moldings. **—** *v.t.* **1.** To work into a particular shape or form. **2.** To shape or form in or as in a mold. **3.** To influence, determine, or direct: to *mold* public sentiment. **4.** To follow the contours of; cling to. **—** *v.i.* **5.** To assume or come to fit a particular shape or pattern. Also, *Brit., mould.* [< OF < L < *modus* measure, limit] **— mold′a·ble** *adj.* **— mold′er** *n.*

mold[2] (mōld) *n.* **1.** Any of a variety of fungous growths commonly found on the surfaces of decaying food or in warm, moist places, and usu. having a woolly or furry texture. **2.** A fungus producing one of these growths. **—** *v.i.* To become moldy. Also *Brit., mould.* [< obs. *mouled*, pp. of *moulen* to grow moldy]

mold[3] (mōld) *n.* Soft, loose earth that is esp. suitable for plants because it is rich in decaying organic matter. **—** *v.t.* To cover with mold. Also, *Brit., mould.* [OE *molde* earth]

mold·board (mōld′bôrd′, -bōrd′) *n.* The curved metal plate of a plow that digs into and turns over the soil.

mold·er (mōl′dər) *v.i.* **1.** To decay gradually and turn to dust; crumble. **2.** To atrophy from lack of use. **—** *v.t.* **3.** To cause to crumble. **4.** To waste or squander. Also, *Brit., moulder.* [Freq. of obs. *mold* to crumble]

mold·ing (mōl′ding) *n.* **1.** The act or process of one who or that which molds. **2.** That which is molded. **3.** *Archit.* **a** A cornice or other depressed or projecting member, used to decorate the surface or angle of a building, room, etc. **b** The decoratively molded surface of a cornice, jamb, etc. **4.** A strip of decoratively shaped wood or other material, used to decorate or finish walls, doors, etc. Also, *Brit., moulding.*

mold·y (mōl′dē) *adj.* **mold·i·er, mold·i·est 1.** Covered with or containing mold. **2.** Musty, as from age, lack of use, etc. Also, *Brit., mouldy.* **— mold′i·ness** *n.*

mole[1] (mōl) *n.* A small, permanent spot on the human skin, slightly protuberant and often dark and hairy. [OE *māl*]

mole[2] (mōl) *n.* Any of a number of small insectivorous mammals that live mainly underground and have soft fur, small eyes, and broad forefeet adapted for digging and burrowing: also called *taupe.* [ME *molle*]

COMMON MOLE (6 to 8 inches long; tail 1 inch)

mole[3] (mōl) *n.* **1.** A massive, usu. stone barricade in the sea, built to enclose an anchorage or harbor for which it acts as a breakwater or pier. **2.** An anchorage or harbor so enclosed. [< F < L < Gk. *mylē* millstone]

mole[4] (mōl) *Chem.* The gram molecule: also spelled *mol.*

mo·lec·u·lar (mə·lek′yə·lər) *adj.* Pertaining to, consisting of, or caused by molecules. [< NL *molecularis*]

molecular weight *Chem.* The sum of the atomic weights of all the atoms in a molecule.

mol·e·cule (mol′ə·kyo͞ol) *n.* **1.** *Chem.* One or more atoms constituting the smallest part of an element or compound that can exist separately without losing its chemical properties. **2.** Any very small particle. [< F < NL *molecula*, dim. of L *moles* mass]

mole·hill (mōl′hil′) *n.* **1.** A small heap or mound of earth raised by a burrowing mole. **2.** Something trivial or inconsequential: to make a mountain out of a *molehill.*

mole·skin (mōl′skin′) *n.* **1.** The dark gray pelt of a mole, very soft and fragile and used as a fur. **2.** A heavy, twilled cotton fabric with a thick, soft nap on one side. **3.** *Usu. pl.* Items of clothing, esp. trousers, made of this fabric.

mo·lest (mə·lest′) *v.t.* **1.** To disturb or annoy by unwarranted, excessive, or malicious interference. **2.** To interfere with improperly or illicitly, esp. with a sexual motive. [< OF < L *molestus* troublesome] **— mo·les·ta·tion** (mō′les·tā′shən, mol′es-) *n.* **— mo·lest′er** *n.*

moll (mol) *n. Slang* **1.** The girl friend of a gangster. **2.** A prostitute. [< *Moll*, dim. of *Mary*]

mol·lie (mol′ē) *n.* Any of a variety of tropical fishes often raised in aquariums. Also **mol′ly.**

mol·li·fy (mol′ə·fī) *v.t.* **·fied, ·fy·ing 1.** To make less angry, violent, or agitated; soothe. **2.** To reduce the harshness, severity, or intensity of. [< F < LL < L *mollis* soft + *facere* to make] — **mol′li·fi′a·ble** *adj.* — **mol′li·fi·ca′tion** *n.* — **mol′li·fi′er** *n.* — **mol′li·fy·ing·ly** *adv.*

mol·lus·coid (mə·lus′koid) *adj.* Of or like a mollusk. Also **mol·lus·coi·dal** (mol′əs·koid′l).

mol·lusk (mol′əsk) *n. Zool.* A large group of unsegmented, soft-bodied invertebrates, usu. protected by a calcareous shell of one or more pieces, and including snails, mussels, oysters, clams, octopi, whelks, etc. Also **mol′lusc.** [< F < L *molluscus* (*nux*) soft, thin-shelled (nut)] — **mol·lus·can** (mə·lus′kən) *adj. & n.* — **mol·lus′cous** *adj.*

mol·ly·cod·dle (mol′ē·kod′l) *n.* Any overprotected or pampered person; also, an effeminate man or boy. — *v.t.* **·dled, ·dling** To pamper; coddle. [< *Molly* a personal name + CODDLE] — **mol′ly·cod′dler** *n.*

Mo·loch (mō′lok) In the Bible, a god of the Ammonites and Phoenicians to whom parents offered their children to be burnt in sacrifice. — *n.* Anything exacting merciless sacrifices. [< LL < Gk. < Hebrew *Mōlekh* a king]

molt (mōlt) *v.t. & v.i.* To cast off or shed (feathers, horns, skin, etc.) in preparation for periodic replacement by new growth. — *n.* **1.** The act or process of molting. **2.** That which is molted. Also, *Brit.*, *moult.* [ME < OE < L *mutare* to change] — **molt′er** *n.*

mol·ten (mōl′tən) Archaic past participle of MELT. — *adj.* **1.** Made fluid by heat; melted: *molten* metal. **2.** Made by melting and casting in a mold: *molten* images.

mol·to (môl′tō) *adv. Music* Much; very. [< Ital. < L *multum* much]

mo·lyb·de·nite (mə·lib′də·nīt) *n.* A soft, lead-gray molybdenum disulfide, MoS_2, the chief ore of molybdenum.

mo·lyb·de·num (mə·lib′də·nəm, mol′ib·dē′nəm) *n.* A hard, heavy, silver-white, metallic element (symbol Mo) of the chromium group, occurring only in combination, used to harden steel. See ELEMENT. [< NL < L < Gk. < *molybdos* lead]

mom (mom) *n.* Mother: used familiarly. [< MAMA]

mo·ment (mō′mənt) *n.* **1.** A very short or relatively short period of time. **2.** A particular point in time, usu. the present time. **3.** A particular period or stage in a series of events: a great *moment* in history. **4.** Importance; consequence: matters of great *moment.* **5.** A brief period of excellence, distinction, enjoyment, etc.. **6.** *Mech.* **a** The tendency to produce motion, esp. rotatory motion. **b** A measure of such a tendency. [< F < L *momentum* movement]

mo·men·tar·i·ly (mō′mən·ter′ə·lē, mō′mən·ter′ə·lē) *adv.* **1.** For a moment: *momentarily* at a loss. **2.** In a moment; at any moment. **3.** From moment to moment; progressively.

mo·men·tar·y (mō′mən·ter′ē) *adj.* **1.** Lasting no more than a moment; fleeting. **2.** Occurring or operating at every moment. — **mo′men·tar′i·ness** *n.*

mo·ment·ly (mō′mənt·lē) *adv.* **1.** From moment to moment; at any instant. **2.** For a moment.

mo·men·tous (mō·men′təs) *adj.* Of great importance or consequence. — **mo·men′tous·ly** *adv.* — **mo·men′tous·ness** *n.*

mo·men·tum (mō·men′təm) *n. pl.* **·ta** (-tə) or **·tums** **1.** *Physics* The quantity of motion in a body as measured by the product of its mass and velocity. **2.** Impetus, as of a body in motion.

mon- *combining form* Var. of MONO-.

mon·ad (mon′ad, mō′nad) *n.* **1.** An indestructible unit; a simple and indivisible substance. **2.** *Biol.* A minute, simple, single-celled organism. **3.** *Chem.* An atom, radical, or element with a valence of one. — *adj.* Of, pertaining to, or consisting of a monad: also **mo·nad·ic** (mə·nad′ik) or **i·cal.** [< LL < Gk. *monas* unit]

mon·arch (mon′ərk) *n.* **1.** A hereditary constitutional ruler, as a king, queen, etc. **2.** Formerly, a sole ruler of a state. **3.** One who or that which surpasses others of the same kind. **4.** *Entomol.* A large, orange and brown butterfly whose larvae feed on milkweed. [< LL < Gk. < *monos* alone + *archein* to rule] — **mo·nar·chal** (mə·när′kəl) *adj.* — **mo·nar′chal·ly** *adv.*

mo·nar·chi·cal (mə·när′ki·kəl) *adj.* **1.** Of, pertaining to, or characteristic of a monarchy or monarch. **2.** Governed by or favoring a monarch or monarchy. Also **mo·nar′chi·al, mo·nar′chic.** — **mo·nar′chi·cal·ly** *adv.*

mon·arch·ism (mon′ərk·iz′əm) *n.* **1.** The principles or system of a monarchy. **2.** The advocacy of a monarchy. — **mon′arch·ist** *n.* — **mon′arch·is′tic** *adj.*

mon·ar·chy (mon′ər·kē) *n. pl.* **·chies** **1.** Government by a monarch; sovereign control. **2.** A government or territory ruled by a monarch. — **absolute monarchy** A government in which the will of the monarch is positive law; a despotism. — **constitutional** or **limited monarchy** A monarchy in which the power and prerogative of the sovereign are limited by constitutional provisions.

mon·as·ter·y (mon′əs·ter′ē) *n. pl.* **·ter·ies** **1.** A dwelling place occupied by monks living under religious vows and in seclusion. **2.** The monks living in such a place. [< LL < LGk. < Gk. < *monazein* to live alone]

mo·nas·tic (mə·nas′tik) *adj.* **1.** Of, pertaining to, or characteristic of monasteries or their inhabitants; ascetic Characteristic of a life of religious seclusion. Also **m te·ri·al** (mon′əs·tir′ē·əl), **mo·nas′ti·cal.** — *n.* A mo other religious recluse. [< F < LL < Gk. *monastiko* **mon·as′ti·cal·ly** *adv.*

mo·nas·ti·cism (mə·nas′tə·siz′əm) *n.* The monastic system.

mon·a·tom·ic (mon′ə·tom′ik) *adj. Chem.* Consistin single atom, as the molecules of certain elements.

mon·au·ral (män′ôr·əl, mōn′-) *adj.* **1.** Pertaining characterized by the perception of sound by one ear onl *Electronics* Designating a system of sound reproducti which the sound is perceived as coming from one dir only.

mon·ax·i·al (mon·ak′sē·əl) *adj.* Having but one axi

mon·a·zite (mon′ə·zīt) *n.* A resinous, brownish red or phosphate of the lanthanide metals, chiefly cerium, la num, and didymium, an important source of thorium. G < Gk. *monazein* to live alone]

Mon·day (mun′dē, -dā) *n.* The second day of the [OE *mōn(an)dæg* day of the moon]

mo·ne·cious (mə·nē′shəs, mō-) See MONOECIOUS.

Mo·nel metal (mō·nel′) A corrosion-resistant nickel containing copper, iron, and manganese, used for indu equipment machine parts, etc.: a trade name. [after brose *Monel*, d. 1921, U.S. manufacturer]

mon·e·tar·y (mon′ə·ter′ē, mun′-) *adj.* **1.** Of or perta to currency or coinage. **2.** Pertaining to or concerned money. [< L *monetarius* of a mint] — **mon′e·tar′i·ly**

mon·ey (mun′ē) *n. pl.* **mon·eys** or **mon·ies** **1.** Officia sued coins and paper currency that serve as a medium change and a measure of value and may be used as pay for goods and services and for settlement of debts. ◆ lateral adjective: *pecuniary.* **2.** Any substance or o used similarly, as checks, wampum, etc. **3.** Propert any type having monetary value. **4.** Money of acc **5.** A system of coinage. **6.** *pl.* Sums of money. **7.** Pe ary profits. — **to put money on** To place a bet on. [< L *moneta* mint]

mon·ey·bag (mun′ē·bag) *n.* **1.** A bag for holding mo **2.** *pl. Slang* A wealthy person; also, wealth.

money belt A belt with pouches for carrying money.

mon·ey·chang·er (mun′ē·chān′jər) *n.* **1.** One whose ness it is to change money at a prescribed rate. **2.** A d for holding and dispensing coins.

mon·eyed (mun′ēd) *adj.* **1.** Possessed of money; wea **2.** Consisting of, arising from, or representing mone wealth: *moneyed* interests. Also spelled *monied.*

mon·ey·lend·er (mun′ē·len′dər) *n.* One whose busine the lending of money at interest.

mon·ey·mak·ing (mun′ē·mā′king) *adj.* Likely to brin money; profitable. — *n.* The acquisition of money wealth. — **mon′ey·mak′er** *n.*

money of account A monetary denomination used in k ing accounts, usu. not represented by a coin, as the U.S.

money order An order for the payment of a specified su money; esp., such an order issued at one post office or graph office and payable at another.

mon·ger (mung′gər, mong′-) *n.* **1.** *Brit.* A dealer or tra chiefly in combination: *fishmonger.* **2.** One who engag discreditable matters: chiefly in compounds: a *scandaln ger.* [OE < L *mango* dealer]

Mon·gol (mong′gəl, -gol, -gōl) *n.* **1.** A member of any of native tribes of Mongolia; esp., one inhabiting eastern M golia or a Kalmuck. **2.** Any of the Mongolian langua **3.** A member of the Mongoloid ethnic division. — Mongolian (def. 1). [< Mongolian *mong* brave]

Mon·go·li·an (mong·gō′lē·ən, -gōl′yən, mon-) *adj.* **1.** O pertaining to Mongolia, its people, or their languages. Exhibiting Mongolism. — *n.* **1.** A native of Mongolia. A subfamily of the Altaic languages, including the langua of the Mongols. **3.** A person afflicted with Mongolism.

Mon·gol·ism (mong′gəl·iz′əm) *n.* A form of congen mental deficiency characterized by a broad flat face a skull, obliquely set, narrow eyes, etc.

Mon·go·loid (mong′gə·loid) *adj.* **1.** *Anthropol.* Of, perta ing to, or belonging to a major ethnic division of the hum species, characterized by yellowish skin, slanting ey straight head hair, high cheek bones, etc. **2.** Resembli related to, or characteristic of Mongols or Mongolians. Characterized by Mongolism. — *n.* A Mongoloid person.

mon·goose (mong′gōōs, mung′-) *n. pl.* **·goos·es** A small, ferretlike, carnivorous mammal that destroys rats and can kill venomous snakes without injury to itself. [< Marathi *mangus*]

MONGOOSE (To 18 inches long; tail 18 inches)

mon·grel (mung′grəl, mong′-) *n.* **1.** The progeny produced by crossing different breeds or varieties of plants or animals; esp. a dog of mixed breed. **2.** Any incongruous mixture.

Of mixed breed, origin, nature, etc.: often a contemptu-
:term: a *mongrel* language. [ME < obs. *mong* mixture +
dim. suffix]
igst (mungst) *prep. Poetic* Amongst.
ied (mun′ēd) See MONEYED.
i·ker (mon′ə·kər) *n. Informal* A name, signature, or
name. Also **mon′ick·er.** [Prob. blend of MONOGRAM and
KER]
ism (mon′iz·əm, mō′niz·əm) *n. Philos.* The doctrine
there is but one principle of being or ultimate substance,
aind or matter. [< NL < Gk. *monos* single] — **mon′·**
. — **mo·nis′tic** or **·ti·cal** *adj.*
i·tion (mō·nish′ən) *n.* **1.** A warning or admonition,
f impending danger. **2.** An official, legal, or formal no-
. [< OF < L *monitus*, pp. of *monere* to warn]
i·tor (mon′ə·tər) *n.* **1.** In some schools, a student seed to perform certain duties in class, as helping to keep
rds, maintain order, etc. **2.** One who advises or cau-
s, esp. in matters of conduct. **3.** Something that warns
eminds. **4.** Formerly, an ironclad warship having a low,
deck and low freeboard, and fitted with one or more re-
ing turrets carrying heavy guns. **5.** *Zool.* Any of several
e, carnivorous lizards of Africa, Asia, and Australia. **6.**
ecom. A receiver, loudspeaker, or other apparatus used to
ck radio or television broadcasts for quality of transmis-
, frequency, compliance with laws, material transmitted,
— *v.t. & v.i.* **1.** *Telecom.* To listen to or watch (a broad-
) with a monitor. **2.** To act or supervise as a monitor
. 1). [< L < *monere* to warn] — **mon′i·to′ri·al** (-tôr′·
, -tō′rē-) *adj.* — **mon′i·tor·ship′** *n.*
i·to·ry (mon′ə·tôr′ē, -tō′rē) *adj.* Conveying a warning;
nonitory. — *n.* A monitory letter. [< L *monitor*]
ık (mungk) *n.* **1.** One who has taken the religious vows
overty, chastity, and obedience, usu. a member of a mo-
tic order. **2.** Formerly, a religious hermit. [OE < LL <
k. < Gk. *monos* alone]
ı·key (mung′kē) *n.* **1.** Any of the primates, excluding
anthropoid apes, having elongate limbs, hands and feet
pted for grasping, and a highly developed nervous system;
., the marmosets, baboons, macaques, etc. **2.** One who
s in a way suggestive of a monkey, as a mischievous child.
v.i. Informal To play or trifle; meddle; fool: often with
h or *around.* [? < MLG *Moneke*, name of the son of Mar-
the Ape in *Reynard the Fox*]
ıkey business *Slang* Foolish tricks; deceitful or mis-
evous behavior.
ı·key·shine (mung′kē·shīn′) *n. Usu. pl. Slang* A mis-
evous or playful trick, prank, or joke.
ıkey wrench A wrench having an adjustable jaw for
sping nuts, bolts, etc., of various sizes. — **to throw a**
ıkey wrench into *U.S. Informal* To disrupt.
ık's cloth (mungks) A sturdy cotton fabric with a bas-
weave used for drapes, curtains, etc.
ıks·hood (mungks′ho͝od′) *n.* A plant having the upper
al arched like a hood; esp., a poisonous variety: also
led *aconite.*
no- *combining form* **1.** Single; one: *monologue.* **2.**
em. Denoting the presence in a compound of a single
om, or an equivalent of the element or radical to the name
which it is prefixed. Also, before vowels, **mon-.** [< Gk.
nos single]
n·o·ba·sic (mon′ə·bā′sik) *adj. Chem.* Possessing but a
igle hydrogen atom replaceable by a metal or positive radi-
: applied to acids.
n·o·chrome (mon′ə·krōm) *n.* A painting or drawing in a
igle color or in various shades of the same color. [< L <
k. *monos* single + *chrōma* color] — **mon′o·chro·mat′ic,**
on′o·chro′mic or **i·cal** *adj.* — **mon′o·chro′mist** *n.*
n·o·cle (mon′ə·kəl) *n.* An eyeglass for one eye. [< F <
L < Gk. *monos* single + L *oculus* eye] — **mon′o·cled** *adj.*
n·o·cli·nal (mon′ə·klī′nəl) *Geol. adj.* Having an inclina-
on in only one direction, or composed of rock strata so in-
ined. — *n.* A monocline. — **mon′o·cli′nal·ly** *adv.*
on·o·cline (mon′ə·klīn) *n. Geol.* A monoclinal rock struc-
ire. [< MONO- + Gk. *klinein* to incline]
on·o·cli·nous (mon′ə·klī′nəs) *adj. Bot.* Containing both
amens and pistils in the same flower; hermaphroditic. [<
ONO- + Gk. *klinē* bed, couch]
on·o·cot·y·le·don (mon′ə·kot′ə·lēd′n) *n. Bot.* Any seed
lant bearing one cotyledon in the embryo. Also **mon′o·cot′.**
< NL] — **mon′o·cot′y·le′do·nous** *adj.*
on·o·dy (mon′ə·dē) *n. pl.* **·dies 1.** A poem in which the
oet laments the death of another. **2.** An ode performed by
ne voice; esp., a lyric ode in a Greek tragedy; dirge. **3.**
Music A composition in which there is only one vocal part;
lso, the style of such a composition. [< LL < Gk. *monos*
lone + *aeidein* to sing] — **mo·nod·ic** (mə·nod′ik) or **·i·cal**
adj. — **mo·nod′i·cal·ly** *adv.* — **mon′o·dist** *n.*

mo·noe·cious (mə·nē′shəs) *adj.* **1.** *Biol.* Hermaphroditic.
2. *Bot.* Monoclinous. Also *monecious, monoicous.* Also **mo·**
ne′cian. [< MON- + Gk. *oikos* house]
mo·nog·a·my (mə·nog′ə·mē) *n.* The condition or practice of having only one wife or husband at a time. [< F <
LL < Gk. *monos* single + *gamos* marriage] — **mon·o·gam·**
ic (mon′ə·gam′ik) *adj.* — **mo·nog′a·mist** *n.* — **mo·nog′a·**
mous *adj.*
mon·o·gram (mon′ə·gram) *n.* Two or more letters intertwined into one; esp., the initials of one's name. — *v.t.* **mon·**
o·gramed or **·grammed, mon·o·gram·ing** or **·gram·ming** To
mark with a monogram. [< LL < Gk. *monos* single +
grammē letter] — **mon′o·gram·mat′ic** (-grə·mat′ik) *adj.*
mon·o·graph (mon′ə·graf, -gräf) *n.* A book, pamphlet, or
treatise on one subject or on a single aspect of a subject. —
mo·nog·ra·pher (mə·nog′rə·fər) *n.* — **mon′o·graph′ic** *adj.*
mon·o·lith (mon′ə·lith) *n.* A single block of stone, usu. very
large, used in architecture and sculpture. [< LL < Gk. <
mono- + *lithos* stone]
mon·o·lith·ic (mon′ə·lith′ik) *adj.* **1.** Of or resembling a
monolith. **2.** Having a massive, uniform structure that does
not permit individual variations: a *monolithic* state.
mon·o·logue (mon′ə·lôg, -log) *n.* **1.** A lengthy speech by
one person, esp. one that interferes with conversation. **2.** A
play or dramatic composition for one actor only. **3.** A soliloquy. **4.** A poem, etc., written as a soliloquy. Also **mon′o·**
log. [< F < Gk. < *monos* alone + *-logos* speech] — **mo·**
nol·o·gist (mə·nol′ə·jist) *n.*
mon·o·ma·ni·a (mon′ə·mā′nē·ə, -mān′yə) *n.* **1.** A mental
disorder in which a person, otherwise rational, is obsessed
with one idea or subject. **2.** An exaggerated fondness or irrational enthusiasm for something; craze. [< NL] — **mon′·**
o·ma′ni·ac *n.* — **mon′o·ma·ni′a·cal** (-mə·nī′ə·kəl) *adj.*
mon·o·mer (mon′ə·mər) *n. Chem.* The structural unit of a
polymer. [< MONO- + Gk. *mēros* part]
mon·o·met·al·ism (mon′ō·met′əl·iz′əm) *n.* The theory or
system of a single metallic standard in coinage. Also **mon′o·**
met′al·lism. — **mon′o·me·tal′lic** (-mə·tal′ik) *adj.*
mo·no·mi·al (mō·nō′mē·əl) *adj.* Consisting of a single word
or term. — *n.* A monomial term or expression.
mon·o·nu·cle·ar (mon′ə·no͞o′klē·ər, -nyo͞o′-) *adj.* Having
only one nucleus, as certain cells of the body.
mon·o·nu·cle·o·sis (mon′ō·no͞o′klē·ō′sis, -nyo͞o′-) *n. Pathol.*
1. The presence in the blood of an abnormal number of mononuclear leucocytes. **2.** Infectious mononucleosis.
mon·o·plane (mon′ə·plān) *n. Aeron.* An airplane with only
one wing or pair of wings.
mo·nop·o·lize (mə·nop′ə·līz) *v.t.* **·lized, ·liz·ing 1.** To obtain a monopoly of. **2.** To assume exclusive possession or
control of. — **mo·nop′o·li·za′tion** *n.* — **mo·nop′o·liz′er** *n.*
mo·nop·o·ly (mə·nop′ə·lē) *n. pl.* **·lies 1.** The exclusive
control of a commodity, service, or means of production in a
particular market, with the resulting power to fix prices. **2.**
Law An exclusive privilege, granted by a government, of
buying, selling, making, or using anything. **3.** A company
having a monopoly. **4.** The commodity, service, etc., controlled under a monopoly. **5.** Exclusive possession or control of anything. [< L < Gk. < *monos* alone + *pōlein* to
sell] — **mo·nop′o·lism** *n.* — **mo·nop′o·list** *n. & adj.* —
mo·nop′o·lis′tic *adj.*
mon·o·pro·pel·lant (mon′ō·prə·pel′ənt) *n. Aerospace* A
liquid rocket propellant consisting of fuel and oxidizer mixed
and ready for simultaneous ignition.
mon·o·rail (mon′ō·rāl′) *n.* **1.** A single rail serving as a
track for cars either suspended from it or balanced upon it.
2. A railway using such a track.
mon·o·sac·cha·ride (mon′ə·sak′ə·rīd, -rid) *n. Biochem.*
Any of a class of simple sugars that cannot be decomposed
by hydrolysis, as glucose and fructose.
mon·o·syl·la·bic (mon′ə·si·lab′ik) *adj.* **1.** Having only one
syllable. **2.** Using or speaking in monosyllables. **3.** Composed of monosyllables. — **mon′o·syl·lab′i·cal·ly** *adv.*
mon·o·syl·la·ble (mon′ə·sil′ə·bəl) *n.* A word of one syllable, as *no.*
mon·o·the·ism (mon′ə·thē·iz′əm) *n.* The doctrine or belief that there is but one God. [< MONO- + Gk. *theos* god]
— **mon′o·the′ist** *n.* — **mon′o·the·is′tic** or **·ti·cal** *adj.* —
mon′o·the·is′ti·cal·ly *adv.*
mon·o·tone (mon′ə·tōn) *n.* **1.** The utterance of a succession of words, etc., in a single tone. **2.** Sameness in expression, style, color, etc. **3.** A single musical tone unvaried in
pitch. [< LGk. < Gk. *mōnos* single + *tōnos* tone]
mo·not·o·nous (mə·not′ə·nəs) *adj.* **1.** Unvaried in tone.
2. Tiresome by reason of monotony. [< LGk. *monotonos*]
— **mo·not′o·nous·ly** *adv.* — **mo·not′o·nous·ness** *n.*
mo·not·o·ny (mə·not′ə·nē) *n.* **1.** Tiresome uniformity; irk-
some sameness. **2.** Lack of variety in cadence, pitch, or inflection. [< LGk. < Gk. *monos* single + *tonos* tone]

mon·o·treme (mon′ə·trēm) *n.* A member of the lowest order of mammals, including the egg-laying platypuses and the echidnas, that have a single opening for the excretory and reproductive functions. [< MONO- + Gk. *trēma* hole] — **mon′o·trem′a·tous** (-trem′ə·təs) *adj.*
mon·o·type (mon′ə·tīp) *n. Printing* A print from a metal plate on which a design, painting, etc., has been made.
Mon·o·type (mon′ə·tīp) *n. Printing* A machine that casts and sets type in single characters or units: a trade name.
mon·o·typ·ic (mon′ə·tip′ik) *adj. Biol.* **1.** Having only one type: a *monotypic* genus. **2.** Being a monotype.
mon·o·va·lent (mon′ə·vā′lənt) *adj. Chem.* Univalent. — **mon′o·va′lence, mon′o·va′len·cy** *n.* [< MONO- + L *valere* to be strong]
mon·ox·ide (mon·ok′sīd, mə·nok′-) *n. Chem.* An oxide containing a single atom of oxygen in each molecule.
Monroe Doctrine The doctrine, essentially formulated by President Monroe, that any attempt by European powers to interfere in the affairs of the American countries or to acquire territory on the American continents would be regarded by the U.S. as an unfriendly act.
mons (monz) *n. pl.* **mon·tes** (mon′tēz) *Anat.* The rounded fatty swelling over the pubic symphysis, covered with hair in the adult; the **mons pu·bis** (pyōō′bis) of the male, or the **mons ven·er·is** (ven′ər·is) of the female. [< L, hill]
Mon·sei·gneur (mon·sēn′yər; *Fr.* môṅ·se·nyœr′) *n. pl.* **Mes·sei·gneurs** (me·se·nyœr′) **1.** My lord: a French title given to the higher nobility, bishops, etc. **2.** One having this title. [< F *mon* my + *seigneur* lord < L *senior* older]
mon·sieur (mə·syûr′, *Fr.* mə·syœ′) *n. pl.* **mes·sieurs** (mes′ərz, *Fr.* me·syœ′) The French title of courtesy for men, equivalent to *Mr.* and *sir.* [< F *mon* + *sieur*, short for *seigneur* lord]
Mon·si·gnor (mon·sēn′yər, *Ital.* môn′sēn·nyōr′) *n. pl.* **·gnors** or *Ital.* **·gno·ri** (-nyō′rē) **1.** In the Roman Catholic Church, a title of honor of certain prelates. **2.** One having this title. [< Ital. < F *monseigneur*]
mon·soon (mon·sōōn′) *n. Meteorol.* **1.** A seasonal wind that blows along the Asian coast of the Pacific and from the Indian Ocean, in winter from the northeast, in summer from the southwest. **2.** The summer monsoon, characterized by heavy rains. [< MDu. < Pg. < Arabic *mausim* season]
mon·ster (mon′stər) *n.* **1.** One who or that which is abnormal, unnatural, or hideous in form. **2.** An animal or plant that is malformed; monstrosity. **3.** One who or that which inspires hate or horror because of cruelty, wickedness, etc. **4.** A huge person or thing. **5.** A fabulous creature, as a centaur, dragon, etc. — *adj.* Enormous; huge. [< OF < L *monstrum* divine warning < *monere* to warn]
mon·strance (mon′strəns) *n.* In Roman Catholic ritual, a vessel in which the consecrated Host is exposed for adoration. [< OF < Med.L < L *monstrare* to show]
mon·stros·i·ty (mon·stros′ə·tē) *n. pl.* **·ties** **1.** One who or that which is monstrous; also, a monster. **2.** The condition or character of being monstrous. [< L *monstrositas*]
mon·strous (mon′strəs) *adj.* **1.** Deviating greatly from the natural in form, structure, or character. **2.** Enormous; huge. **3.** Hideous; horrible; atrocious. **4.** Strikingly wrong; ridiculous; absurd. **5.** Having the appearance or nature of a fabulous monster. [< OF < LL < L *monstrum*] — **mon′strous·ly** *adv.* — **mon′strous·ness** *n.*
mon·tage (mon·täzh′) *n.* **1.** A picture made by superimposing or arranging a number of different pictorial elements; also, the art or process of making such a picture. **2.** In motion pictures or television, a rapid sequence of images used to illustrate a group of associated ideas. **3.** Similar techniques in radio and writing. [< F < *monter* to mount]
mon·te (mon′tē) *n.* A Spanish or Spanish-American gambling game of cards. Also **monte bank.** [< Sp., lit., mountain < L; in ref. to the pile of unplayed cards]
month (munth) *n.* **1.** One of the twelve parts (**calendar month**) into which the calendar year is divided. **2.** A period of thirty days or four weeks. **3.** The twelfth part (**solar month**) of the solar year. **4.** The period (**lunar month**), equivalent to 29.53 days, during which the moon makes a complete revolution. ◆ Collateral adjective *mensal.* [OE *mōnath*]
month·ly (munth′lē) *adj.* **1.** Happening, done, appearing, etc., every month. **2.** Of or pertaining to a month. **3.** Pertaining to the menses. **4.** Continuing or lasting for a month. — *adv.* Once a month. — *n. pl.* **·lies** **1.** A periodical published once a month. **2.** *pl.* Menstruation.
mon·u·ment (mon′yə·mənt) *n.* **1.** A statue, pillar, plaque, etc., erected to perpetuate the memory of a person, event, or historical period. **2.** A tombstone. **3.** Any conspicuous or fine structure surviving from the past. **4.** A work of art, scholarship, etc., regarded as having enduring value. **5.** A stone boundary marker. [< L *monere* to remind]
mon·u·men·tal (mon′yə·men′təl) *adj.* **1.** Of, pertaining to, or serving as a monument. **2.** Like a monument; enduring; imposing; massive. **3.** Having great significance: a *monumental* study. **4.** *Informal* Very large; huge. [*monumentalis*] — **mon′u·men′tal·ly** *adv.*
-mony *suffix of nouns* The condition, state, or thing re ing from: *parsimony.* [< L *-monia*]
moo (mōō) *v.i.* To make the deep, moaning sound of a to low. — *n. pl.* **moos** The sound made by a cow. [I
mooch (mōōch) *Slang v.t.* **1.** To obtain without pa beg; cadge. **2.** To steal. — *v.i.* **3.** To loiter. **4.** To s sneak. [< OF *muchier* to hide, skulk] — **mooch′er** *n*
mood[1] (mōōd) *n.* **1.** A specific state of mind or feeling a temporary one. **2.** *pl.* Fits of sullen or morose beha — **in the mood** Disposed; inclined. [OE *mōd* mind]
mood[2] (mōōd) *n. Gram.* The set of distinctive forms verb showing the attitude and understanding of the spe regarding the action or condition expressed: also *mode* IMPERATIVE, INDICATIVE, SUBJUNCTIVE. [Var. of MODE
mood·y (mōō′dē) *adj.* **mood·i·er, mood·i·est** **1.** Give sudden moods of moroseness. **2.** Expressive of such mo [OE *mōd* courage] — **mood′i·ly** *adv.* — **mood′i·ness** *n.*
moon (mōōn) *n.* **1.** A celestial body revolving aroun earth from west to east in a lunar month of 29.53 days, accompanying the earth in its yearly revolution abou sun. **2.** This celestial body at a specific time of the mo new *moon*; full *moon.* **3.** Any satellite revolving abo planet. **4.** A month; esp., a lunar month. **5.** Somet resembling a full moon or crescent. **6.** Moonlight. — **1.** *Informal* To stare or wander about abstractedly. — **2.** To pass (time) in such a way. [OE *mōna*]
moon·beam (mōōn′bēm′) *n.* A ray of moonlight.
moon·calf (mōōn′kaf′, -käf′) *n.* An imbecile; idiot.
moon·light (mōōn′līt′) *n.* The light of the moon. — Pertaining to, illuminated by, or performed by moonlig *moonlight* excursion. — **moon′lit′** (-lit′) *adj.*
moon·light·ing (mōōn′līt′ing) *n. Slang* The act of who holds a job in addition to the regular day's work. **moon′light′er** *n.*
moon·shine (mōōn′shīn′) *n.* **1.** Moonlight. **2.** Nonse **3.** *Informal* Smuggled or illicitly distilled whisky, etc.
moon·shin·er (mōōn′shī′nər) *n. U.S. Informal* One conducts an illegal trade by night, esp. distilling.
moon·stone (mōōn′stōn′) *n.* A pearly, opalescent var of orthoclase and albite, valued as a gemstone.
moon·struck (mōōn′struk′) *adj.* Lunatic; deranged. **moon′strick′en** (-strik′ən).
moon·y (mōō′nē) *adj.* **moon·i·er, moon·i·est** *Infor* Absent-minded; dreamy.
moor[1] (mŏŏr) *n. Brit.* A tract of wasteland someti covered with heath, often elevated, marshy, and abounc in peat; a heath. [OE *mōr*]
moor[2] (mŏŏr) *v.t.* **1.** To secure (a ship, etc.) in place means of cables attached to shore, anchors, etc. **2.** secure; fix. — *v.i.* **3.** To secure a ship, etc., in position. To be secured by chains or cables. [ME < MDu. *mo* to fasten] — **moor′age** (-ij) *n.*
Moor (mŏŏr) *n.* **1.** A Moslem of mixed Berber and A ancestry, esp. one of the Saracen invaders of Spain in 8th century. **2.** A native of Morocco. [< OF < L < *Mauros*, lit., dark] — **Moor′ish** *adj.*
moor cock The male of the red grouse.
moor·fowl (mŏŏr′foul′) *n.* The red grouse.
moor hen *n.* The female of the red grouse.
moor·ing (mŏŏr′ing) *n.* **1.** *Chiefly pl.* A mooring pla **2.** *Chiefly pl.* That which secures an object, as a cable.
mooring mast The tower to which a dirigible or bli may be secured when not in flight. Also **mooring tower**
moose (mōōs) *n. pl.* **moose** **1.** A large, heavily built ma mal of the deer family, found in northern U.S. and Canada, the male of which bears huge palmate antlers. **2.** The elk (def. 1). [< Algonquian *moosu* he strips off; because it eats the bark of trees]

MOOSE
(To 7 feet hi at shoulder

moot (mōōt) *adj.* Open to discussion: debatable: a *moot* point. — *v.t.* **1.** To bring up for discussion or debate. **2.** To argue (a case) in a moot court. — *n.* **1.** Discussion or argument. **2.** In early English history, a meeting of freemen to discuss local affairs. [OE *mōt* assembly, court] — **moot′er** *n.*
moot court A court for the trial of hypothetical legal cases by law students.
mop[1] (mop) *n.* **1.** A device for cleaning floors, consisting a bunch of heavy cotton yarn attached to a handle. **2.** A loosely tangled bunch, esp. of hair. — *v.t.* **mopped, mo ping** To rub or wipe with or as with a mop. — **to mop** *Informal* To finish. [ME *mappe*]
mop[2] (mop) *n.* A wry mouth. — *v.i.* To make a wry face.
mope (mōp) *v.* **moped, mop·ing** *v.i.* To be gloomy, listles or dispirited. — *n.* **1.** One who mopes. **2.** *pl.* Dejectio depression. — **mop′er** *n.* — **mop′ish** *adj.* — **mop′ish·** *adv.* — **mop′ish·ness** *n.*

pet (mop′it) *n. Informal* A child. [Dim. of MOP¹]
aine (mə·rān′, mō-) *n. Geol.* Debris in various topo-hic forms that has been carried by a glacier, either along ourse, at its edges, or at its lower terminus. [< F < *morēna*] — **mo·rain′al, mo·rain′ic** *adj.*
al (môr′əl, mor′-) *adj.* **1.** Of or related to conduct or acter from the point of view of right and wrong: *moral* ness. **2.** Of good character; right or proper in behavior. exually virtuous. **4.** Teaching standards of right and ıg. **5.** Capable of distinguishing between right and ıg: Man is a *moral* agent. **6.** Concerned with the estab-nent and application of principles of right and wrong: *ıl* theology. **7.** Arising from a sense of duty and right luct: a *moral* obligation. **8.** Acting not by physical e but by appeal to character, etc.: *moral* support. **9.** ed on probability rather than on objective evidence: *ıl* certainty. — *n.* **1.** The lesson or teaching contained r implied by a fable, poem, etc. **2.** *pl.* Conduct or be-ior with regard to right and wrong, esp. in sexual mat-. **3.** A maxim. [< OF < L *mos* custom; in the pl., *es* manners, morals] — **mor′al·ly** *adv.*
— **Syn.** (adj.) **2.** ethical, conscientious, scrupulous, upright, honest. — **Ant.** See synonyms for IMMORAL.
·ale (mə·ral′, -räl′, mô-) *n.* State of mind with rence to confidence, courage, hope, zeal, etc. [< F]
·al·ist (môr′əl·ist, mor′-) *n.* **1.** A teacher of morals. **2.** who practices morality. — **mor′al·is′tic** *adj.*
·al·i·ty (mə·ral′ə·tē, mô-) *n. pl.* **·ties** **1.** The quality of ng morally right; virtue. **2.** Conformity to standards ight conduct. **3.** Virtuous conduct, often sexual virtue. A system of the principles of right and wrong conduct; cs. **5.** A lesson in morals. **6.** A morality play.
·ality play A form of allegorical drama of the 15th and h centuries in which the characters were personified vir-s, vices, mental attributes, etc.
·al·ize (môr′əl·īz, mor′-) *v.* **·ized, ·iz·ing** *v.i.* **1.** To ke moral reflections; talk about morality. — *v.t.* **2.** To lain in a moral sense; derive a moral from. **3.** To im-ve the morals of. [< MF *moraliser*] — **mor′al·i·za′tion** — **mor′al·iz′er** *n.*
rass (mə·ras′, mô-, mō-) *n.* **1.** A tract of low-lying, soft, t ground; marsh; bog. **2.** Anything that impedes, per-xes, or traps. [< Du. < OF *maresc* < Gmc.]
·a·to·ri·um (môr′ə·tôr′ē·əm, -tō′rē, mor′-) *n. pl.* **·ri·a** ē·ə) or **·ri·ums** **1.** A legal authorization to a debtor to sus-nd payments for a given period. **2.** The period during ich such suspension is in effect. **3.** Any authorized sus-nsion or deferment of action. [< NL < LL < L *morari* delay]
·a·to·ry (môr′ə·tôr′ē, -tō′rē, mor′-) *adj.* Pertaining to intended to delay; especially, designating legislation au-orizing a moratorium. [< LL < L *morari* to delay]
·ra·vi·an (mô·rā′vē·ən, mō-) *adj.* Pertaining to Moravia, e Moravians, or the Moravian Church. — *n.* **1.** A native Moravia. **2.** A member of the Moravian Church.
·ray (môr′ā, mō·rā′) *n.* A brightly colored, voracious eel habiting tropical and subtropical waters. Also **mo′ray eel.** rigin uncertain]
·r·bid (môr′bid) *adj.* **1.** Taking or showing an excessive terest in matters of a gruesome or unwholesome nature. Grisly; gruesome: a *morbid* fantasy. **3.** Pertaining to, ising from, or affected by disease. [< L < *morbus* disease] — **mor′bid·ly** *adv.* — **mor·bid′i·ty, mor′bid·ness** *n.*
·r·dant (mor′dənt) *adj.* **1.** Biting; cutting; sarcastic: a *ordant* wit. **2.** Acting to fix colors in dyeing. — *n.* **1.** A bstance that, by combining with a dyestuff, serves to oduce a fixed color in a textile, leather, etc. **2.** In etching, corrosive used to bite into the lines traced on a metal plate. — *v.t.* To treat or imbue with a mordant. [< F, ppr. of F *modre* to bite] — **mor′dan·cy** *n.*
·r·de·cai (mor′də·kī, -kā·ī) In the Old Testament, Es-er's cousin, instrumental in saving the Jews. *Esth.* ii 5.
·r·dent (mor′dənt) *n. Music* A trill-like melodic orna-entation; also, the symbol that indicates this. [< G < al. < *mordere* to bite]
ore (môr, mōr) *adj. superlative* **most** **1.** Greater in amount, xtent, degree, or number: comparative of *much* and *many.* . Additional: *More* coffee, please. — *n.* **1.** A greater or dditional quantity, amount, etc. **2.** That which exceeds r excels something else. — *adv.* **1.** In or to a greater extent r degree: used to form the comparative of many adjectives nd adverbs of two or more syllables: *more* beautiful. **2.** n addition; further. — **more or less** **1.** In some unde-ermined degree. **2.** Approximately. [OE *māra*]
ore·o·ver (môr·ō′vər, mōr-) *adv.* Beyond what has been aid; further; besides; likewise; in addition.
o·res (môr′āz, mō′rāz, môr′ēz, mō′rēz) *n.pl. Sociol.* **1.** The established, traditional customs regarded by a social group as essential to its preservation. **2.** The accepted conventions of a group. [< L, pl. of *mos, moris* custom]
mor·ga·nat·ic (môr′gə·nat′ik) *adj.* Of or designating a form of legitimate marriage between a member of certain royal families of Europe and a person of inferior rank, in which the titles and estates are not shared by the inferior partner or their children. [< NL < LL < OHG *morgangeba* morning gift] — **mor′ga·nat′i·cal·ly** *adv.*
morgue (môrg) *n.* **1.** A place where the bodies of unknown dead persons and of those killed in accidents are kept for identification. **2.** In a newspaper editorial office, the de-partment in charge of filed items and biographical material used for obituary notices, etc. [< F]
mor·i·bund (môr′ə·bund, -bənd, mor′-) *adj.* **1.** At the point of death; dying. **2.** Approaching extinction. [< L < *mori* to die] — **mor′i·bun′di·ty** *n.* — **mor′i·bund·ly** *adv.*
mo·ri·on (môr′ē·on, mō′rē-) *n.* An open, crested, visorless helmet, worn in the 16th and 17th centuries. [< MF < Sp. < *morra* crown of the head]
Mo·ris·co (mə·ris′kō) *adj.* Moorish. — *n. pl.* **·cos** or **·coes** A Moor, especially one of Spain. [< Sp. < *moro* Moor]
Mor·mon (môr′mən) *n.* **1.** A member of the Mormon Church; a Latter-day Saint. **2.** In Mormon belief, a prophet of the fourth century who wrote, on golden tablets, a history of the early American people. — *adj.* Of or pertaining to the Mormons or their religion. — **Mor′mon·ism** *n.*
Mormon Church The Church of Jesus Christ of Latter-day Saints, founded by Joseph Smith in 1830.
Mormon State Nickname of Utah.
morn (môrn) *n. Poetic* The morning. [OE *morne*]
morn·ing (môr′ning) *n.* **1.** The early part of the day; the time from midnight to noon, or from sunrise to noon. **2.** The early part or stage of anything. — *adj.* Pertaining to or occurring in the morning. ◆ Collateral adjective: *matutinal.* [ME *morwen* + *-ing* by analogy with evening]
morn·ing-glo·ry (môr′ning·glôr′ē, -glō′rē) *n.* Any of vari-ous twining plants with colored, funnel-shaped flowers.
morning star A planet, esp. Venus, when rising in the east shortly before the sun.
Mo·ro (môr′ō, mō′rō) *n. pl.* **·ros** **1.** A member of any of the various Moslem Malay tribes of the southern Philippines. **2.** The language of the Moros. — *adj.* Of or pertaining to the Moros or their language. [< Sp., Moor]
mo·roc·co (mə·rok′ō) *n.* **1.** A fine flexible leather, made originally in Morocco from goatskin tanned with sumac. **2.** Any soft, grained leather. Also **morocco leather.**
Mo·roc·can (mə·rok′ən) A native or inhabitant of Morocco. — *adj.* Of or pertaining to Morocco.
mo·ron (môr′on, mō′ron) *n.* **1.** A person exhibiting the mildest degree of mental deficiency, permitting adequacy in simple activities. **2.** Loosely, a very stupid person. — **Syn.** See IDIOT. [< Gk. < *mōros* stupid] — **mo·ron·ic** (mô·ron′ik, mō-) *adj.* — **mo·ron′i·cal·ly** *adv.*
mo·rose (mə·rōs′) *adj.* Ill-humored; sullen; gloomy, as a person, mood, etc. [< L < *mos, moris* manner, mood] — **mo·rose′ly** *adv.* — **mo·rose·ness** *n.*
— **Syn.** glum, dour, crabbed. — **Ant.** cheerful, genial.
-morph *combining form* Having the form or shape of: *allo-morph.* [< Gk. *morphē* form]
mor·pheme (môr′fēm) *n. Ling.* The smallest meaningful unit of a language or dialect, whether a word, base, or affix. See ALLOMORPH. [< F < Gk. *morphē* form]
Mor·phe·us (môr′fē·əs, -fyo͞os) In Greek mythology, the god of dreams. [< L < Gk. *morphē* form; from the shapes he calls up in dreams] — **Mor′phe·an** *adj.*
-morphic *combining form* Having the form or shape of: *an-thropomorphic.* [< Gk.*morphē* form]
mor·phine (môr′fēn) *n. Chem.* A bitter, white crystalline compound, $C_{17}H_{19}NO_3$, the principal alkaloid of opium, used as an analgesic and narcotic. Also **mor′phin** (-fin). [< F < L *Morpheus* god of dreams]
morpho- *combining form* Form; shape. Also, before vowels, **morph-.** [< Gk. *morphē* form]
mor·phol·o·gy (môr·fol′ə·jē) *n. pl.* **·gies** **1.** *Biol.* The study of the form and structure of plants and animals con-sidered apart from function. **2.** *Ling.* **a** The arrangement and interrelationship of morphemes in words. **b** The branch of linguistics dealing with this. — **mor·pho·log·ic** (môr′fə·loj′ik) or **·i·cal** *adj.* — **mor·phol′o·gist** *n.*
-morphous *combining form* Having a (specified) form: often equivalent to *-morphic*: *anthropomorphous.*
mor·ris (môr′is, mor′-) *n.* An old English dance, performed especially on May Day. [Earlier *morys, morish* Moorish]
Morris chair A large armchair with an adjustable back. [after William *Morris*, who invented it]
mor·ro (môr′ō, mor′ō; *Sp.* môr′rō) *n. pl.* **mor·ros** (môr′ōz, mor′-; *Sp.* môr′rōs) A round hill or promontory. [< Sp.]
mor·row (môr′ō, mor′ō) *n. Archaic & Poetic* **1.** The next

succeeding day. 2. A time immediately following a specified event. 3. Formerly, morning. [See MORNING]
Morse code A system of telegraphic signals invented by S.F.B. Morse, composed of dots and dashes or short and long flashes representing the letters of the alphabet, numerals, etc., and used in transmitting messages.
mor·sel (môr′səl) *n.* 1. A small fragment or bite of food. 2. A tempting dish; tidbit. 3. A small piece or bit of something. — *v.t.* **mor·seled** or **·selled, mor·sel·ing** or **·sel·ling** To divide into small pieces. [< OF, dim. of *mors* bite]
mor·tal (môr′təl) *adj.* 1. Subject to death. 2. Of or pertaining to humanity as subject to death. 3. Of or relating to this life or world. 4. Causing or liable to cause death. 5. Relating to or accompanying death. 6. Grievous; dire: *mortal* terror. 7. Likely to remain so until death; implacable: a *mortal* enemy. 8. *Theol.* Incurring spiritual death unless repented of and forgiven: distinguished from *venial*: *mortal* sin. 9. *Informal* Possible; conceivable: There's no *mortal* reason for his action. — *n.* One who is mortal; a human being. — *adv. Informal* Very; exceedingly. [< OF < L *mors, mortis* death]
mor·tal·i·ty (môr·tal′ə·tē) *n. pl.* **·ties** 1. The condition of being mortal or subject to death. 2. Loss of life on a large scale, as caused by war, disease, etc. 3. The frequency of death; death rate. 4. Humanity; mankind.
mor·tal·ly (môr′təl·ē) *adv.* 1. Fatally. 2. After the manner of a mortal. 3. Extremely: *mortally* offended.
mor·tar[1] (môr′tər) *n.* A bowl-shaped vessel in which substances are crushed with a pestle. For illustration see PESTLE. [OE < L *mortarium* mixing trough]
mor·tar[2] (môr′tər) *n.* A building material consisting of a mixture of lime, cement, etc., with sand and water, used in bricklaying, plastering walls, etc. [< OF < L *mortarium* trough, mixture of sand and lime]
mor·tar[3] (môr′tər) *n. Mil.* A smooth-bored or rifled muzzleloading weapon, firing a relatively heavy shell, having a shorter range and higher trajectory than a howitzer. [< F *mortier*]
mor·tar·board (môr′tər·bôrd′, -bōrd′) *n.* 1. A square board with a handle, on which a mason holds mortar. 2. A type of academic cap topped by a stiff, flat, four-cornered piece, worn at graduations.
mort·gage (môr′gij) *n. Law* 1. A transfer of property pledged as security for the repayment of a loan. 2. The contract specifying such a pledge. — *v.t.* **·gaged, ·gag·ing** 1. To make over or pledge (property) by mortgage. 2. To pledge; stake. [< OF, dead pledge]
mort·ga·gee (môr′gi·jē′) *n.* The holder of a mortgage.
mort·ga·gor (môr′gi·jər) *n.* One who mortgages his property to another as security for a loan. Also **mort′gag·er.**
mor·tice (môr′tis) *n.* A mortise. — *v.t.* **·ticed, ·tic·ing** To mortise.
mor·ti·cian (môr·tish′ən) *n. U.S.* A funeral director; undertaker. [< L *mors, mortis* death + -ICIAN]
mor·ti·fi·ca·tion (môr′tə·fə·kā′shən) *n.* 1. A feeling of loss of self-esteem; humiliation; shame. 2. That which causes such humiliation. 3. The ascetic practice of subduing the appetites and strengthening the will by fasting, etc. 4. *Pathol.* The death of a part by gangrene or necrosis.
mor·ti·fy (môr′tə·fī) *v.* **·fied, ·fy·ing** *v.t.* 1. To humiliate. 2. To discipline or punish (the body, appetities, etc.) by fasting or other ascetic practices. 3. *Pathol.* To cause mortification in (part of an animal body). — *v.i.* 4. To practice ascetic self-discipline. 5. *Pathol.* To undergo mortification. [< OF < LL < L *mors, mortis* death + *facere* to make] — **mor′ti·fi′er** *n.* — **mor′ti·fy′ing·ly** *adv.*
mor·tise (môr′tis) *n.* A space hollowed out in a piece of timber, stone, etc., and shaped to fit a tenon to which it is to be joined. — *v.t.* **·tised, ·tis·ing** 1. To cut or make a mortise in. 2. To join by a tenon and mortise. Also spelled *mortice.* [< F < Arabic *murtazz* joined, fixed in]

MORTISE (*a*) AND TENON (*b*)

mort·main (môrt′mān) *n. Law* The holding of lands and buildings in perpetual ownership. [< OF < Med.L *mortua manus* dead hand]
mor·tu·ar·y (môr′chōō·er′ē) *n. pl.* **·ar·ies** A place for the temporary reception of the dead before burial. — *adj.* 1. Of the burial of the dead. 2. Relating to death. [< MF < L *mortuarius* of the dead]
mo·sa·ic (mō·zā′ik) *n.* 1. Inlaid work composed of bits of stone, glass, etc., forming a pattern or picture; also, the process of making this. 2. A design, arrangement, etc., resembling such work. — *adj.* Of, pertaining to, or resembling mosaic. — *v.t.* **·icked, ·ick·ing** 1. To make by or as if by combining in a mosaic. 2. To decorate with mosaic. [< OF < Med.L < Gk. *mouseios* of the Muses, artistic] — **mo·sa·i·cist** (mō·zā′ə·sist) *n.*
Mo·sa·ic (mō·zā′ik) *adj.* Of or pertaining to Moses or the laws attributed to him. Also **Mo·sa′i·cal.**
Mosaic Law The code of civil and religious laws contained in the Pentateuch and traditionally attributed to M[oses]; also called *Law of Moses, the Law.*
Mo·selle (mō·zel′) *n.* A light, dry wine made in the [valley] of the Moselle, chiefly in Luxembourg.
Mo·ses (mō′zis, -ziz) In the Old Testament, the leade[r who] led the Israelites out of Egypt to the Promised Land[; he] received the Ten Commandments from God. [< He[b.] *Mōsheh*, ? < Egyptian *mesu* son]
mo·sey (mō′zē) *v.i. U.S. Slang* 1. To saunter, or s[hamble;] shuffle along. 2. To go away; move off. [Origin unkn[own]]
Mos·lem (moz′ləm) *n.* A believer in Islam; Mohamm[edan.] — *adj.* Of or pertaining to Islam or the Muslims. Also [*Mus*]*lim, Muslem.* [< Arabic *muslim* one who submits]
Mos·lem·ism (moz′ləm·iz′əm) *n.* Islam.
mosque (mosk) *n.* A Moslem temple of worship. [< F] < Ital. < Arabic *masjid* < *sajada* to worship, pray]
mos·qui·to (məs·kē′tō) *n. pl.* **·toes** or **·tos** Any of va[rious] winged insects, having in the female a long proboscis ca[pable] of puncturing the skin of man and animals for extra[cting] blood, certain species of which transmit malaria, y[ellow] fever, etc. [< Sp., dim. of *mosca* fly] — **mos·qui′tal**
mosquito boat A patrol torpedo boat.
mosquito net A fine net or gauze (**mosquito netting**) p[laced] over windows, beds, etc., to keep out mosquitoes.
moss (môs, mos) *n.* 1. A delicate plant having a stem [and] distinct leaves, and growing in tufts or clusters on [the] ground, decaying wood, rocks, etc. 2. A clump or tu[ft of] such plants. 3. Any of several similar plants, as ce[rtain] lichens. 4. *Chiefly Scot.* A peat bog. [OE *mos* ma[rsh]] — **moss′y** *adj.* — **moss′i·ness** *n.*
moss agate A variety of agate containing mineral ox[ides] and showing patterns arranged in mosslike forms.
moss·back (môs′bak′, mos′-) *n.* 1. An old fish or turt[le] whose back is a growth of algae or the like. 2. *U.S. S[lang]* A very conservative or old-fashioned person; fogy.
Möss·bau·er effect (mœs′bou′ər) The absorption of g[am]ma rays emitted from a radioactive isotope by nuclei of [the] same isotope, both of which are anchored in crystals; [used] in the determination of wavelengths, and in testing var[ious] concepts of relativity and quantum theory. [after Ru[dolf] L. *Mössbauer*, born 1929, U.S. physicist born in Germa[ny]]
moss rose A cultivated variety of the rose with a m[ossy] calyx and stem.
most (mōst) *adj.* 1. Consisting of the greatest number: [su]perlative of *many.* 2. Consisting of the greatest amoun[t or] degree: superlative of *much.* 3. In the greatest numbe[r of] instances: *Most* people are honest. — **for the most p[art]** Generally; mostly. — *n.* 1. (*construed as pl.*) The grea[test] number; the largest part. 2. (*construed as pl.*) The grea[test] number of persons: too difficult for *most.* 3. The grea[test] amount, quantity or degree; utmost. — **at (the) most** [At] more than; at the extreme point or limit. — **to make most of** 1. To use to the fullest advantage. 2. To ex[ag]gerate the importance of. — *adv.* 1. In or to the grea[test] or highest degree, quantity, extent, etc.: used with ad[jec]tives and adverbs to form the superlative degree. 2. Ve[ry]. 3. *Informal* Almost; nearly. [OE *mǣst, māst*]
-most *suffix* Most: added to adjectives and adverbs to fo[rm] superlatives: *innermost; outmost.*
most·ly (mōst′lē) *adv.* For the most part; principally.
mot (mō) *n.* A witty or pithy saying: bon *mot.* [< [F,] word]
mote (mōt) *n.* A minute particle or speck, esp., of d[ust]. [OE *mot* dust]
mo·tel (mō·tel′) *n. U.S.* A roadside hotel for motori[sts,] often comprising private cabins that open on parking fac[ili]ties: also called *motor court.*
mo·tet (mō·tet′) *n. Music* A polyphonic vocal composit[ion] of a sacred nature, usu. unaccompanied. [< OF]
moth (môth, moth) *n. pl.* **moths** (môthz, môths, mot[hz,] moths) Any of a large group of insects, usu. noctur[nal,] distinguished from the butterflies by having smaller win[gs,] stouter bodies, and duller coloring. [OE *moththe*]
moth·ball (môth′bôl′, moth′-) *Mil. & Nav. adj.* Design[at]ing ships or military equipment laid up in reserve and co[v]ered with protective materials. — *v.t.* To put in storage.
moth ball A small ball of camphor or naphthalene used [to] repel moths from clothing, etc., during storage.
moth-eat·en (môth′ēt′n, moth′-) *adj.* 1. Eaten or da[m]aged by moths. 2. Worn out. 3. Old-fashioned.
moth·er[1] (muth′ər) *n.* 1. A female who has borne offsprin[g.] 2. A female who adopts a child, or who otherwise holds [a] maternal relationship toward another. 3. The chara[c]teristics regarded as belonging to a mother. 4. Anythi[ng] that creates, nurtures, or protects something else. 5. *Us[ually] cap.* A title given to certain nuns. — *adj.* 1. Nativ[e:] *mother* tongue. 2. Relating to or characteristic of a mothe[r:] *mother* love. 3. Holding a maternal relation: the *moth[er]* church. — *v.t.* 1. To bring forth as a mother; produc[e;] create. 2. To care for or protect as a mother. 3. To adm[it] or claim parentage, authorship, etc., of. [OE *mōder*]

·er² (muth′ər) *n.* A slimy film composed of bacteria yeast cells, active in the production of vinegar.
er Goose 1. The imaginary narrator of a volume of tales, compiled in French by Charles Perrault in 1697. he imaginary writer of a collection of nursery rhymes nglish folk origin, first published in London about 1790.
·er·hood (muth′ər·hood) *n.* 1. The state of being a ner. 2. The spirit or qualities of a mother. 3. Mothers ctively.
er Hub·bard (hub′ard) A woman's loose, flowing ı, unconfined at the waist: also **mother hubbard.**
er-in-law (muth′ər·in·lô′) *n. pl.* **moth·ers-in-law** mother of one's spouse.
·er·land (muth′ər·land′) *n.* 1. The land of one's ; native land. 2. The land of one's ancestors.
er lode In mining, any principal or very rich vein.
·er·ly (muth′ər·lē) *adj.* Resembling, characteristic of, ke a mother. — *adv.* In the manner of a mother. — **′er·li·ness** *n.*
·er-of-pearl (muth′ər·əv·pûrl′) *n.* The pearly, iri- ent internal layer of certain shells, as those of the pearl er and abalone, used in ornamental work, for buttons, also called *nacre.* — *adj.* Of mother-of-pearl.
·er's Day (muth′ərz) *U.S.* A memorial day in honor of hers, observed annually on the second Sunday in May.
er's helper *U.S.* A girl or woman hired to help a mother for her children and do light housekeeping chores.
er tongue 1. One's native language. 2. A parent uage.
er wit Inherent or native intelligence; common sense.
·y (môth′ē, moth′ē) *adj.* **moth·i·er, moth·i·est** 1. Moth- n. 2. Full of moths.
if (mō·tēf′) *n.* 1. The underlying theme or main ele- t in a literary or artistic work. 2. In decoration, a inct element of design. 3. *Music* The shortest intelligi- melodic or rhythmic fragment of a theme. Also *motive.* F]
ile (mō′til, -təl) *adj. Zool.* Having the power of mo- , as certain minute organisms. [< L *motus,* pp. of *ere* to move] — **mo·til′i·ty** *n.*
ion (mō′shən) *n.* 1. The act or process of changing tion; movement: also, an instance of this. 2. Change of e or position in the body or any of its parts. 3. A for- proposal or suggestion in an assembly or meeting: to nd the *motion.* 4. An impulse; inclination. — **in ion** Moving; in operation. — *v.i.* 1. To make a gesture irection or intent, as with the hand. — *v.t.* 2. To direct uide by a gesture. [< OF < L *movere* to move]
ion picture 1. A sequence of pictures of moving ob- s photographed on a strip of film, that, when projected a screen, gives the optical illusion of continuous move- ıt. 2. A specific drama, story, etc., made by means of h photographs: also called *cinema, film, movie, moving ure, photoplay, picture, screen play.*
ion sickness Nausea, dizziness, etc., caused by the cts of motion, as in travel on land, water, and in the air.
ti·vate (mō′tə·vāt) *v.t.* **·vat·ed, ·vat·ing** To provide h a motive. [< F *motiver*] — **mo′ti·va′tion** *n.* — **mo′· a′tion·al** *adj.*
tive (mō′tiv) *n.* 1. A conscious or unconscious need, ve, etc., that incites a person to some action or behavior; entive; goal. 2. A motif. — **Syn.** See REASON. — *adj.* Causing or having the power to cause motion. 2. Re- ng to or acting as a motive. — *v.t.* To motivate. [< < Med.L *movere* to move]
·ley (mot′lē) *adj.* 1. Made up of diverse elements; het- geneous. 2. Variegated in color. 3. Clothed in vari- ored garments. — *n.* 1. A heterogeneous mixture or lection. 2. A woolen cloth of mixed colors worn between 14th and 17th centuries. 3. A garment of various colors h as formerly worn by court jesters. [ME *motteley*]
tor (mō′tər) *n.* 1. An engine; esp., an internal-com- stion engine propelling an automobile, motor boat, etc. Something that imparts or produces motion. 3. *Chiefly it.* An automotive vehicle. — *adj.* 1. Causing, produc- , or imparting motion. 2. Equipped with or driven by a otor. 3. Of, pertaining to, or for automotive vehicles. *Psychol.* Transmitting impulses from nerve centers to the iscles. 5. *Psychol.* Relating to or involving the movements muscles. — *v.i.* To travel or ride in an automobile. [< L *motus,* pp. of *movere* to move]
tor·bike (mō′tər·bīk′) *n. Informal* 1. A bicycle driven a small motor. 2. A motorcycle.
·tor·boat (mō′tər·bōt′) *n.* A boat propelled by a motor: o called *power boat.*
·tor·bus (mō′tər·bus′) *n.* A passenger bus powered by motor. Also **motor bus, motor coach.**
·tor·cade (mō′tər·kād) *n.* A procession of automobiles.
mo·tor·car (mō′tər·kär′) *n.* An automobile.
motor court A motel.
mo·tor·cy·cle (mō′tər·sī′kəl) *n.* A two-wheeled vehicle, larger and heavier than a bicycle, propelled by an internal-combustion engine. — *v.i.* **·cled, ·cling** To travel or ride on a motorcycle. — **mo′tor·cy′clist** *n.*
mo·tor·ist (mō′tər·ist) *n.* One who drives or travels by automobile.
mo·tor·ize (mō′tər·īz) *v.t.* **·ized, ·iz·ing** 1. To equip with a motor. 2. To equip with motor-propelled vehicles in place of horses or horse-drawn vehicles. — **mo′tor·i·za′tion** *n.*
mo·tor·man (mō′tər·mən) *n. pl.* **·men** (-mən) 1. One who operates an electric street car or electric railway locomotive. 2. One who operates a motor.
motor scooter A two-wheeled vehicle similar to a child's scooter, having a driver's seat and powered by an internal-combustion engine.
mot·tle (mot′l) *v.t.* **·tled, ·tling** To mark with spots or streaks of different colors or shades; blotch. — *n.* 1. A spotted, blotched, or variegated appearance, as of skin or marble. 2. A spot, blotch, etc. [back formation < MOTLEY]
mot·tled (mot′ld) *adj.* Marked with spots of different color or shade; blotched; spotted.
mot·to (mot′ō) *n. pl.* **·toes** or **·tos** 1. A word or phrase expressing a rule of conduct, principle, etc.; a maxim. 2. An appropriate or indicative phrase inscribed on something, prefixed to a literary work, etc. [< Ital. < F *mot* word]
mouch (mo͞och) See MOOCH.
mou·choir (mo͞o·shwär′) *n. French* A pocket handkerchief.
moue (mo͞o) *n.* A pouting grimace, as of disdain. [< F]
mou·jik (mo͞o·zhēk′) See MUZHIK.
mould (mōld), etc. See MOLD, etc.
moult (mōlt) See MOLT, etc.
mound (mound) *n.* 1. A heap or pile of earth, debris, etc., either natural or artificial. 2. A small natural elevation; a hillock. 3. In baseball, the slightly raised ground from which the pitcher pitches. — *v.t.* 1. To fortify or enclose with a mound. 2. To heap up in a mound. [Origin unknown]
Mound Builder One of the prehistoric Indians who built the burial mounds and fortifications found in the Mississippi basin and adjoining regions.
mount¹ (mount) *v.t.* 1. To ascend or climb (a slope, stairs, etc.). 2. To get up on; climb upon. 3. To put or set on horseback. 4. To furnish with a horse. 5. To set or place in an elevated position: to *mount* a picture on a wall. 6. To set, fix, or secure in or on a support, frame, etc., as for exhibition or use: to *mount* a drawing; to *mount* a specimen on a microscope slide. 7. To furnish with scenery, costumes, etc.: to *mount* a play. 8. *Mil.* **a** To set or raise into position, as a gun. **b** To carry or be equipped with. **c** To stand or post (guard). **d** To prepare and begin: to *mount* an offensive. — *v.i.* 9. To rise or ascend; go or come up. 10. To increase in amount, number, or degree. 11. To get up on something, as on a horse. — *n.* 1. Anything on or in which an object is placed for use, preparation, display, etc., as a setting for a jewel, etc. 2. A horse or other animal used for riding. 3. The act or style of mounting. 4. The act of riding a horse. [< OF *monter* < L *mons, montis* mountain] — **mount′a·ble** *adj.* — **mount′er** *n.*
mount² (mount) *n.* A mountain or hill: used poetically or as part of a proper name. [OE < L *mons, montis* mountain]
moun·tain (moun′tən) *n.* 1. A natural elevation of the earth's surface, typically having steep sides and a narrow summit, and rising higher than a hill. 2. Any large heap or pile: a *mountain* of paper. 3. Anything of great size: a *mountain* of a man. — *adj.* 1. Of, pertaining to, or like a mountain. 2. Living, growing, or situated in or on mountains. [< OF < L < *mons, montis* mountain]
mountain ash 1. A small tree of the rose family, having white flowers and orange-red berries. 2. Any of various related trees.
mountain cat 1. The puma. 2. The lynx.
moun·tain·eer (moun′tən·ir′) *n.* 1. An inhabitant of a mountainous district. 2. One who climbs mountains. — *v.i.* To climb mountains.
mountain goat The Rocky Mountain goat.
mountain laurel A low-growing evergreen shrub of the eastern U.S., having white or pink flowers: the State flower of Connecticut and Pennsylvania.
mountain lion The puma.
moun·tain·ous (moun′tən·əs) *adj.* 1. Full of mountains. 2. Huge; gigantic. — **moun′tain·ous·ly** *adv.*
moun·te·bank (moun′tə·bangk) *n.* 1. One who sells quack medicines at fairs after drawing a crowd with jokes, tricks, etc. 2. Any charlatan. [< Ital. < *montare* to mount + *in* upon + *banco* bench]
mount·ed (moun′tid) *adj.* 1. Riding or seated on a horse.

2. Serving on or equipped with horses for transportation: *mounted* police. **3.** Set into position or fitted for use.
Moun·ty (moun′tē) *n. pl.* **·ties** *Informal* A member of the Royal Canadian Mounted Police. Also **Mount′ie.**
mourn (môrn, mōrn) *v.i.* **1.** To feel or express grief or sorrow, esp. for the dead; grieve. —*v.t.* **2.** To lament or sorrow for (someone dead). **3.** To grieve over or bemoan (misfortune, failure, etc.). [OE *murnan*] —**mourn′er** *n.*
mourners' bench *U.S.* At revival meetings, a bench near the preacher, reserved for penitents.
mourn·ful (môrn′fəl, mōrn′-) *adj.* **1.** Indicating, expressing, or exciting grief. **2.** Doleful; melancholy; sad. —**mourn′ful·ly** *adv.* —**mourn′ful·ness** *n.*
mourn·ing (môr′ning, mōr′-) *n.* **1.** The act of one who expresses grief or sorrow, esp. for the dead. **2.** The manifestations of grief, as the wearing of black dress, etc. **3.** The period during which one mourns. —*adj.* Of or expressive of mourning. —**mourn′ing·ly** *adv.*
mourning dove A dove common in North America, having a mournful cry: also called *turtledove.*
mouse (*n.* mous; *v.* mouz) *n. pl.* **mice** (mīs) **1.** One of various small rodents frequenting human habitations throughout the world. ◆ Collateral adjective: *murine.* **2.** Any of various similar animals. **3.** *U.S. Informal* A timid person. **4.** *Slang* A black eye. —*v.i.* **moused, mous·ing 1.** To hunt or catch mice. **2.** To hunt for something cautiously and softly; prowl. [OE *mūs*]
mous·er (mou′zər) *n.* Any animal that catches mice.
mouse·trap (mous′trap′) *n.* A trap for catching mice.
mousse (mo͞os) *n.* Any of various light, frozen desserts made with whipped cream, egg white, etc., and sugar and flavoring. [< F < L *mulsus* sweetened with honey]
mous·tache (məs·tash′, mus′tash) See MUSTACHE.
Mous·te·ri·an (mo͞o·stir′ē·ən) *adj.* *Anthropol.* Pertaining to or describing a culture stage of the Paleolithic, represented in western Europe by artifacts of stone and generally found associated with Neanderthal men. [< F < *Le Moustier*, a village in France where such remains were found]
mous·y (mou′sē, -zē) *adj.* **mous·i·er, mous·i·est 1.** Of or resembling a mouse. **2.** Characterized by timidity, shyness, drabness, etc. **3.** Infested with mice. Also **mous′ey.**
mouth (*n.* mouth; *v.* mouth) *n. pl.* **mouths** (mouthz) **1.** The opening at which food is taken into the body; also, the cavity between the lips and throat containing the lingual and masticating structures. ◆ Collateral adjective: *oral.* **2.** One who needs food: so many *mouths* to feed. **3.** The organ or instrument of speech: to shut one's *mouth.* **4.** Something resembling a mouth; as: **a** The part of a stream where its waters are discharged into another body of water. **b** The entrance or opening of a cave, mine, etc. **c** The opening of a container: the *mouth* of a jar. —**down in** (or **at**) **the mouth** *Informal* Disconsolate; dejected. —**to have a big mouth** *Informal* **1.** To speak loudly or rudely. **2.** To talk too much. —*v.t.* **1.** To speak in a forced or affected manner. **2.** To seize or take in the mouth. **3.** To caress or rub with the mouth. **4.** To form (words, etc.) silently with the lips and tongue. —*v.i.* **5.** To speak in an affected manner. [OE *mūth*] —**mouth′er** (mou′thər) *n.*

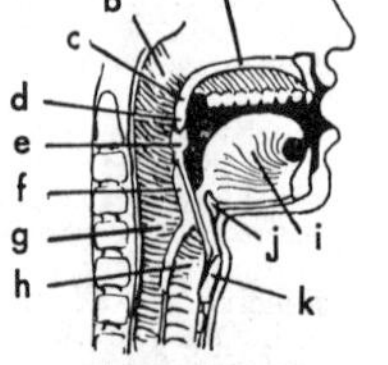

HUMAN MOUTH
a Hard palate. *b* Pharynx. *c* Soft palate. *d* Uvula. *e* Tonsil. *f* Epiglottis. *g* Esophagus. *h* Trachea. *i* Tongue. *j* Hyoid bone. *k* Larynx.

mouthed (mouthd, moutht) *adj.* **1.** Having a mouth or mouths. **2.** Having a (specified kind of) mouth or (a specified number of) mouths: used in combination: *evil-mouthed.*
mouth·ful (mouth′fo͝ol′) *n. pl.* **·fuls** (-fo͝olz′) **1.** As much as can be held in the mouth. **2.** As much as is usu. taken or put in the mouth at one time. **3.** A small quantity. **4.** *Slang* An important or perceptive remark: chiefly in the phrase **to say a mouthful.**
mouth organ **1.** A harmonica. **2.** A set of panpipes.
mouth·piece (mouth′pēs′) *n.* **1.** That part of a musical instrument, telephone, etc., that is used in or near the mouth. **2.** One who acts as spokesman for an individual, group, belief, etc. **3.** *Slang* A criminal lawyer. **4.** A rubber guard placed in the mouth of a boxer.
mouth·wash (mouth′wosh′, -wôsh′) *n.* An antiseptic and scented solution used for cleaning the mouth.
mouth·y (mou′thē, -thē) *adj.* **mouth·i·er, mouth·i·est** Garrulous; bombastic. —**mouth′i·ly** *adv.* —**mouth′i·ness** *n.*
mou·ton (mo͞o′ton) *n.* Sheepskin processed to simulate beaver or seal, used for women's coats, etc. [< F, sheep]
mov·a·ble (mo͞o′və·bəl) *adj.* **1.** Capable of being moved. **2.** *Eccl.* Varying in date from year to year: *movable* feast. **3.** *Law* Pertaining to personal property as distinguished from real property. —*n.* **1.** *Usu. pl.* Anything that can be moved; esp., an article of furniture. **2.** *pl. Law* Pe[rsonal] property. Also **move′a·ble.** —**mov′a·bil′i·ty, mov′[a·ble]ness** *n.* —**mov′a·bly** *adv.*
move (mo͞ov) *v.* **moved, mov·ing** *v.i.* **1.** To change pl[ace or] position; go to or from a place. **2.** To change one's resi[dence.] **3.** To make progress; advance. **4.** To live or carry on life: to *move* in cultivated circles. **5.** To operate, wor[k, re]volve, etc., as a machine. **6.** To take or begin to take a[ction;] act. **7.** To be disposed of by sale. **8.** To make an ap[plica]tion or proposal: to *move* for adjournment. **9.** To evac[uate:] said of the bowels. **10.** In checkers, chess, etc., to tr[ansfer] a piece from one position to another. **11.** *Informal* [To go] fast. —*v.t.* **12.** To change the place or position of, [as by] carrying, pushing, pulling, etc. **13.** To set or keep i[n mo]tion. **14.** To dislodge or force from a set position: to [move] him from his purpose. **15.** To couse, influence, or im[pel to] some action: to *move* her to agree. **16.** To affect or a[rouse] the emotions, sympathies, etc., of; touch. **17.** To pr[opose] for action, deliberation, etc. **18.** To cause (the bowe[ls) to] evacuate. **19.** In checkers, chess, etc., to transfer (a p[iece).] —*n.* **1.** An act of moving; movement. **2.** An actio[n for] some purpose or design; step; maneuver. **3.** A chan[ge of] residence. **4.** In checkers, chess, etc., the transfer [of a] piece. [< AF, OF < L *movere* to set in motion]
move·ment (mo͞ov′mənt) *n.* **1.** The act of moving[;] change of place or position. **2.** A specific instance or m[anner] of moving: a dance *movement.* **3.** A series of actions, [p...] etc., tending toward some end: the temperance *move[ment];* also, organizations, persons, etc., of a particular tend[ency:] the right-wing *movement.* **4.** An inclination or tend[ency.] **5.** *Mech.* A particular arrangement of related moving [parts.] **6.** *Music* **a** One of the sections of a work, as of a symp[hony,] string quartet, etc. **b** Tempo. **c** Rhythm. **7.** In pros[ody,] rhythm or meter; cadence. **8.** An emptying of the bo[wels.] **9.** *Mil.* A maneuver. [< OF < L *movere* to set in moti[on]]
mov·er (mo͞o′vər) *n.* One who or that which moves; one whose business is moving household goods.
mov·ie (mo͞o′vē) *Informal n.* **1.** A motion picture. [2. A] motion-picture theater. **3.** *pl.* The motion-picture indu[stry.] [Contr. of MOVING PICTURE]
mov·ing (mo͞o′ving) *adj.* **1.** Going or capable of going [from] place to place, position to position, etc. **2.** Causing or [pro]ducing motion or change. **3.** That actuates, impels, o[r in]fluences. **4.** Affecting, arousing, or touching the feelin[gs or] passions. **5.** Exciting or stirring up controversy, de[bate,] etc. —**mov′ing·ly** *adv.* —**mov′ing·ness** *n.*
moving picture A motion picture.
moving staircase An escalator.
mow[1] (mō) *v.* **mowed, mowed** or **mown, mow·ing** *v.t.* [1.] To cut down (grain, grass, etc.) with a scythe or mac[hine.] **2.** To cut the grain or grass of (a field, lawn, etc.). **3.** *I[nfor]mal* To cut down or kill rapidly or indiscriminately: [often with] *down.* —*v.i.* **4.** To cut down grass or grain. [OE *mā[wan]*] —**mow′er** *n.*
mow[2] (mou) *n.* Hay or grain stored in a barn; also [the] place of storage. —*v.t.* To store in a mow. [OE *mū[ga]*]
mowing machine A farm machine with cutting blades [used] for mowing hay, etc.
mox·ie (mok′sē) *n. Slang* Native shrewdness or common se[nse.]
moz·za·rel·la (môd′dzä·rel′lä) *n.* A soft Italian curd ch[eese] that is very stringy when cooked. [< Ital.]
Mrs. (mis′iz) *n.* A title prefixed to the name of a mar[ried] woman: a contracted form of *Mistress.*
mu (myo͞o, mo͞o) *n.* **1.** The twelfth letter in the Greek al[pha]bet (M, μ), corresponding to the English *m.* See ALPHA[BET.] **2.** The micron (symbol μ).
much (much) *adj.* **more, most** Great in quantity, amo[unt,] extent, etc.: *much* noise. —*n.* **1.** A considerable quan[tity] or amount; a great deal. **2.** A remarkable or impor[tant] thing: It isn't *much.* —**to make much of 1.** To treat as [very] important. **2.** To treat (someone) with great court[esy,] regard, etc. —*adv.* **1.** Greatly: *much* obliged. **2.** For [the] most part; almost. [ME < OE *mycel*] —**much′ness** *n.*
mu·ci·lage (myo͞o′sə·lij) *n.* **1.** An aqueous solution of v[ege]table gum or the like, used as an adhesive. **2.** Any of v[ari]ous gummy or gelatinous substances found in some pla[nts.] [< F < LL *mucilago* musty juice]
mu·ci·lag·i·nous (myo͞o′si·laj′ə·nəs) *adj.* **1.** Of, pertain[ing] to, or producing mucilage. **2.** Resembling or character[istic] of mucilage; slimy and viscid. —**mu′ci·lag′i·nous·ness**
muck (muk) *n.* **1.** Any wet and clinging material that so[ils,] esp., viscid mud. **2.** Moist dung mixed with decompo[sing] vegetable matter, used as a soil fertilizer; manure. **3** [A] dark brown to black soil consisting largely of decompos[ed] peat and other vegetable materials. **4.** A confusing or [un]certain state or condition; mess. —*v.t.* **1.** To fertilize w[ith] manure. **2.** *Informal* To make dirty; pollute. **3.** To rem[ove] manure, dirt, rocks, etc., from. [ME *muk*] —**muck′y** *adj.*
muck·rake (muk′rāk′) *v.i.* **·raked, ·rak·ing** To search [for] or expose real or alleged corruption on the part of polit[ical] officials, businessmen, etc. [Back formation < *muckra[ker]*]

g term in late 19th c. U.S. politics] —**muck′rak′er** *n.* **uck′rak′ing** *n.*
ous (myōō′kəs) *adj.* **1.** Secreting mucus. **2.** Perng to, consisting of, or resembling mucus. Also **mu′cose** s). —**mu·cos′i·ty** (-kos′ə·tē) *n.*
ous membrane *Anat.* A membrane secreting or prong mucus, that lines passages communicating with the rior, as the alimentary and respiratory passages, etc.
cus (myōō′kəs) *n. Biol.* A viscid substance secreted by mucous membranes. [< L]
l (mud) *n.* **1.** Soft and sticky wet earth. **2.** *Informal* most degrading place or situation: to drag one into the . —**clear as mud** Absolutely incomprehensible. — **mud·ded, mud·ding** To soil or cover with or as with mud. E < MLG *mudde* or MDu. *modde*]
·der (mud′ər) *n.* A race horse that runs well on a ldy track.
l·dle (mud′l) *v.* **·dled, ·dling** *v.t.* **1.** To mix in a cond or disordered way; jumble. **2.** To confuse or cond (the mind, speech, etc.). **3.** To mess up or misage; bungle. **4.** To make muddy or turbid. —*v.i.* To act or think in a confused or ineffective manner. — **muddle through** *Chiefly Brit.* To achieve one's object pite confusion or mistakes. —*n.* **1.** A state or condition onfusion, disorder, or uncertainty. **2.** A state of mental ntellectual disorder. [< MUD + freq. suffix *-le*]
l·dle·head·ed (mud′l·hed′id) *adj.* Mentally confused; lebrained; stupid. —**mud′dle·head′ed·ness** *n.*
l·dler (mud′lər) *n.* **1.** A stick for stirring liquids, esp. nks. **2.** One who muddles.
l·dy (mud′ē) *adj.* **·di·er, ·di·est** **1.** Covered, spattered, filled with mud. **2.** Not clear, bright, or distinct, as or, liquid, etc. **3.** Confused or obscure in thought, exssion, meaning, etc. —*v.t. & v.i.* **·died, ·dy·ing** To bene or cause to become muddy. —**mud′di·ly** *adv.* — **d′di·ness** *n.*
l eel An eel-shaped amphibian, with no hind legs, that abits swamps of the southern U.S.: also called *siren.*
l·fish (mud′fish′) *n. pl.* **·fish** or **·fish·es** Any of various es that inhabit mud or muddy waters.
l flat A low-lying strip of muddy ground, esp. one beeen high and low tide.
d puppy A tailed amphibian found in streams and lakes North America.
d·sling·er (mud′sling′ər) *n.* One who casts malicious rs, esp. at a political opponent. —**mud′sling′ing** *n.*
d·suck·er (mud′suk′ər) *n.* A fish of California, comnly used as bait.
d turtle Any of various turtles inhabiting muddy ters in North and Central America.
·ez·zin (myōō·ez′in) *n.* In Islam, a crier who calls the thful to prayer, as from a minaret of a mosque. Also **mu· ′din** (-ed′in). [< Arabic *mu'adhdhin* < *adhana* to call]
ff[1] (muf) *v.t. & v.i.* To perform (some act) clumsily; ., to fail to catch (a ball). —*n.* An awkward action. [< FF[2]; prob. to handle as if wearing a muff]
ff[2] (muf) *n.* **1.** A pillowlike or tubular case of fur or cloth, en at the ends, into which the hands are put for warmth. A tuft of feathers on the head or legs of certain birds. Du. < F *moufle* mitten]
f·fin (muf′in) *n.* A small, cup-shaped portion of light ead, usu. eaten hot with butter. [Origin uncertain]
f·fle (muf′əl) *v.t.* **·fled, ·fling** **1.** To wrap up in a blanket, arf, etc., as for warmth or concealment: often with *up.* **2.** deaden the sound of by or as by wrapping. **3.** To deaden sound). **4.** To prevent (someone) from seeing, hearing, ., by wrapping the head. —*n.* **1.** Something used for uffling. **2.** A chamber in a kiln or furnace that protects its ntents from flame, gases, etc. [< F < *moufle* mitten]
f·fler (muf′lər) *n.* **1.** A device to reduce noise, as from e exhaust of an engine. **2.** A heavy scarf worn about the ck for warmth. **3.** Anything that muffles. [< MUFFLE]
f·ti[1] (muf′tē) *n.* In Islam, an expounder of religious law. < Arabic, active participle of *aftā* to expound the law]
f·ti[2] (muf′tē) *n.* Civilian dress; plain clothes, esp. when orn by one who normally wears a uniform. [< MUFTI[1]]
ıg[1] (mug) *n.* **1.** A large drinking cup. **2.** As much as will l a mug. [Origin unknown]
ıg[2] (mug) *Slang n.* **1.** The face, esp. the mouth and chin. *U.S.* A photograph of the face. Also **mug shot.** **3.** *U.S.* man; guy. **4.** *U.S.* A criminal. —*v.* **mugged, mug·ging** *t.* **1.** *U.S.* To photograph (someone's face), esp. for police es. **2.** To assault viciously and rob. —*v.i.* **3.** To make nny faces; overact to win an audience. Also **mugg.** [< UG[1]] —**mug′ger** *n.*
ug·gy (mug′ē) *adj.* **·gi·er, ·gi·est** Warm, humid, and ose; sultry. [< dial. E *mug* drizzle] —**mug′gi·ness** *n.*
u·ghal (mōō′gəl) *n. & adj.* Mogul. Also **Mu′ghul.**

mug·wump (mug′wump′) *n. U.S.* **1.** *Usu. cap.* A Republican who bolted the party in the presidential election of 1884. **2.** Anyone who is independent, esp. in politics. [< Algonquian *mugquomp* great man, chief] —**mug′wump′·er·y, mug′wump′ism** *n.*
Mu·ham·ma·dan (mōō·ham′ə·dən) *adj. & n.* Mohammedan. Also **Mu·ham′me·dan.**
mu·jik (mōō·zhēk′, mōō′zhik) See MUZHIK.
mu·lat·to (mə·lat′ō, myōō-, -lä′tō) *n. pl.* **·toes** **1.** A person having one white and one Negro parent. **2.** Anyone having mixed white and Negro ancestry. —*adj.* Having the light brown color of a mulatto. [< Sp. < L *mulus* mule]
mul·ber·ry (mul′ber′ē, mul′bər·ē) *n. pl.* **·ries** **1.** Any of various trees whose leaves are valued for silkworm culture. **2.** The berrylike fruit of any of these trees. **3.** A purplish red color. [ME *mulberie,* var. of *murberie,* < OF < L *morum* mulberry + OE *berie* berry]
mulch (mulch) *n.* Any loose material, as straw, leaves, peat moss, etc., placed about the stalks of plants to protect their roots from drying, freezing, etc. —*v.t.* To cover with mulch. [ME *molsh* soft, OE *milisc*]
mulct (mulkt) *v.t.* **1.** To defraud or cheat (someone). **2.** To punish with a fine. —*n.* A fine or similar penalty. [< L *mulcta, multa* fine]
mule[1] (myōōl) *n.* **1.** A hybrid between the ass and horse; esp., a hybrid between a jackass and mare. **2.** *Biol.* Any hybrid or cross, esp. one that is sterile: said usu. of the hybrid between the canary and a related bird. **3.** *U.S. Informal* A stubborn person. **4.** A textile machine that spins fibers into yarn and winds it on spindles: also called *spinning mule:* also **mule′jen′ny.** [< OF < L *mulus*]
mule[2] (myōōl) *n.* A backless lounging slipper. [< F < L *mulleus* reddish (shoe)]
mule skinner *U.S. Informal* One who drives mules.
mu·le·teer (myōō′lə·tir′) *n.* A mule driver. [< F < MF *mulet,* dim. of OF *mul* mule] —**mu′le·tress** (-tris) *n.fem.*
mule train A train of mules carrying packs; also, a train of freight wagons drawn by mules.
mul·ish (myōō′lish) *adj.* Resembling a mule; stubborn. — **mul′ish·ly** *adv.* —**mul′ish·ness** *n.*
mull[1] (mul) *v.t.* To heat and spice, as wine or cider. [Origin uncertain]
mull[2] (mul) *v.t.* To ponder: usu. with *over.* [ME *mullen* to pulverize]
mul·lah (mul′ə, mōōl′ə) *n.* A Moslem religious leader or teacher, or any man of learned reputation: a title of respect. Also **mul′la.** [< Turkish, Persian, and Hind. < Arabic *mawlā* master, sir]
mul·lein (mul′ən) *n.* Any of various herbs of the figwort family; esp., the **great mullein** and the **moth mullein.** Also **mul′len.** [< AF *moleine,* prob. < OF *mol* soft < L *mollis*]
mul·let (mul′it) *n. pl.* **·lets** or **·let** Any of various marine and fresh-water fish, as the **striped mullet** of the Atlantic and Pacific. [< OF < L *mullus* red mullet]
mul·li·gan stew (mul′i·gən) *U.S. Slang* A stew, originally made by tramps, composed of odds and ends of meat, vegetables, etc. Also **mul′li·gan.** [? from personal name]
mul·li·ga·taw·ny (mul′i·gə·tô′nē) *n.* A strongly flavored soup of the East Indies, made of meat and curry. [< Tamil *milagutannir* pepper water]
mul·lion (mul′yən) *n. Archit.* A vertical dividing piece in an opening, esp. in a window. —*v.t.* To furnish with or divide by means of mullions. [? Var. of *monial* < OF < L *medianus* medial]
mul·lock (mul′ək) *n.* Waste rock or earth left from mining. [ME *mull* dust + -OCK] —**mul′lock·y** *adj.*
multi- *combining form* **1.** Much; many; consisting of many; as in:

multiangular	**multihued**	**multipurpose**
multiblade	**multimillion**	**multisection**
multicellular	**multimolecular**	**multistoried**
multicolor	**multipartisan**	**multisyllable**
multidirectional	**multipersonal**	**multivoiced**
multifaced	**multipointed**	**multivolumed**

2. Having more than two (or more than one); as in:

multicuspid	**multielectrode**	**multinucleate**
multicylinder	**multimammate**	**multispeed**

3. Many times over: *multimillionaire.* **4.** *Med.* Affecting many: *multiglandular.* Also, before vowels, sometimes **mult-.** [< L *multus* much]
mul·ti·col·ored (mul′ti·kul′ərd) *adj.* Having many colors.
mul·ti·far·i·ous (mul′tə·fâr′ē·əs) *adj.* Having great diversity or variety. [< LL *multifarius*] —**mul′ti·far′i·ous·ly** *adv.* —**mul′ti·far′i·ous·ness** *n.*
mul·ti·fold (mul′tə·fōld) *adj.* Many times doubled.
mul·ti·form (mul′tə·fôrm) *adj.* Having many forms or appearances. —**mul′ti·for′mi·ty** *n.*
mul·ti·lat·er·al (mul′ti·lat′ər·əl) *adj.* **1.** Having many

sides. **2.** *Govt.* Involving more than two nations: also *multipartite.* **—mul′ti·lat′er·al·ly** *adv.*

mul·ti·lin·gual (mul′ti·ling′gwəl) *n. & adj.* Polyglot.

mul·ti·mil·lion·aire (mul′ti·mil′yən·âr′) *n.* One having a fortune of many millions; a very rich person.

mul·ti·no·mi·al (mul′ti·nō′mē·əl) *adj.* Polynomial.

mul·tip·a·ra (mul·tip′ə·rə) *n. pl.* **·rae** (-rē) A woman who has borne more than one child, or who is bearing her second. [< NL < MULTI- + L *parere* to give birth]

mul·tip·a·rous (mul·tip′ə·rəs) *adj.* **1.** Giving birth to many at one time. **2.** Of or relating to a multipara.

mul·ti·par·tite (mul′ti·pär′tīt) *adj.* **1.** Divided into many parts. **2.** *Govt.* Multilateral (def. 2).

mul·ti·ple (mul′tə·pəl) *adj.* **1.** Having, consisting of, or relating to more than one part, aspect, individual, etc.; manifold. **2.** Happening more than once; repeated: *multiple* echoes. **3.** *Electr.* Denoting a circuit having two or more conductors arranged in parallel. **—***n. Math.* Any of the products of a given number and some other number: 8 and 12 are *multiples* of 4. [< F]

mul·ti·ple-choice (mul′tə·pəl·chois′) *adj.* Giving several answers from which the correct one is to be selected.

multiple sclerosis *Pathol.* Sclerosis occurring in various areas of the brain or spinal cord or both, and characterized by tremors, failure of coordination, etc.

mul·ti·plex (mul′tə·pleks) *adj.* **1.** Multiple; manifold. **2.** *Telecom.* Designating a system for the simultaneous transmission of two or more signals over the same wire or radio frequency channel. [< L < *multus* much + *plicare* to fold]

mul·ti·pli·cand (mul′tə·plə·kand′) *n. Math.* A number multiplied, or to be multiplied, by another. [< L *multiplicandus* to be multiplied]

mul·ti·pli·ca·tion (mul′tə·plə·kā′shən) *n.* **1.** The act of multiplying, or the state of being multiplied. **2.** *Math.* The process of finding the sum of a number repeated a given number of times.

multiplication sign The symbol (×) placed between two numbers or quantities to denote a multiplication of the first by the second, as $4 \times 2 = 8$.

mul·ti·plic·i·ty (mul′tə·plis′ə·tē) *n. pl.* **·ties 1.** The condition or quality of being manifold or various. **2.** A large number. [< OF < LL < L *multiplicare* to multiply]

mul·ti·pli·er (mul′tə·plī′ər) *n.* **1.** One who or that which multiplies or causes multiplication. **2.** *Math.* The number by which a quantity is multiplied.

mul·ti·ply[1] (mul′tə·plī) *v.* **·plied, ·ply·ing** *v.t.* **1.** To increase the quantity, amount, or degree of. **2.** *Math.* To determine the product of by multiplication. **—***v.i.* **3.** To become more in number, amount, or degree; increase. **4.** *Math.* To determine the product by multiplication. **5.** To grow in number by procreation; propagate. [< OF < L *multus* much + *plicare* to fold] **—mul′ti·pli′a·ble** *adj.*

mul·ti·ply[2] (mul′tə·plē) *adv.* So as to be multiple; in many ways.

mul·ti·pro·pel·lant (mul′ti·prə·pel′ənt) *Aerospace n.* A rocket propellant consisting of two or more chemicals separately fed into the combustion chamber.

mul·ti·stage (mul′ti·stāj) *adj.* **1.** Having or characterized by a number of definite stages in the completion of a process or action. **2.** *Aerospace* Having several sections, as in a rocket, each of which fulfills a given task before burnout.

mul·ti·tude (mul′tə·tōōd, -tyōōd) *n.* **1.** A great number. **2.** A large gathering of people. **3.** The quality of being many or numerous. **—the multitude** The common people. [< OF < L *multus* many]

mul·ti·tu·di·nous (mul′tə·tōō′də·nəs, -tyōō′-) *adj.* **1.** Existing in great numbers; numerous; myriad. **2.** Consisting of or exhibiting many parts, features, etc. **—mul′ti·tu′di·nous·ly** *adv.* **—mul′ti·tu′di·nous·ness** *n.*

mul·ti·va·lent (mul′ti·vā′lənt) *adj. Chem.* Having three or more valences: also *polyvalent.* **—mul′ti·va′lence** *n.*

mum[1] (mum) *adj.* Silent; saying nothing. **—***interj.* Hush! **—mum's the word** Keep silent; be secretive. [Imit.]

mum[2] (mum) *v.i.* **mummed, mum·ming** To play or act in a mask or disguise. Also **mumm.** [Prob. < MUM[1]]

mum[3] (mum) *n. Informal* A chrysanthemum.

mum·ble (mum′bəl) *v.t. & v.i.* **·bled, ·bling** To speak low and indistinctly; mutter. **—***n.* A low, indistinct speech or sound; mutter. [ME *momelen*] **—mum′bler** *n.*

mum·ble·ty-peg (mum′bəl·tē·peg′) *n.* A game played by manipulating a jackknife in various ways so as to stick it into the ground. Also **mum′ble-peg′, mum·ble-the-peg** (mum′bəl·thə·peg′).

mum·bo jum·bo (mum′bō jum′bō) **1.** Meaningless, complicated, or obscure ritual, observance, incantation, etc. **2.** *Usu. cap.* In certain African tribes, a village god or idol who opposes evil and terrifies the women into subjection. [< Mandingo *mama dyambo* a tutelary god]

mum·mer (mum′ər) *n.* **1.** One who acts or makes sport in a mask or disguise. **2.** An actor.

mum·mer·y (mum′ər·ē) *n. pl.* **·mer·ies 1.** A performance by mummers. **2.** A pretentious or hypocritical ritual [< MF *mommerie* dumb show]

mum·mi·fy (mum′ə·fī) *v.* **·fied, ·fy·ing** *v.t.* **1.** To m[ake a] mummy of; preserve by embalming, drying, etc. **2** [To] make dry and lifeless, as an idea, institution, etc. **—***v* To dry up; shrivel. **—mum′mi·fi·ca′tion** *n.*

mum·my (mum′ē) *n. pl.* **·mies 1.** A human or a[nimal] body embalmed in the ancient Egyptian manner. **2.** [A] corpse that has been well preserved, as by cold, s[pecial] preparation, etc. **3.** One who is lifeless, withered, or t[c] **—***v.t. & v.i.* **·mied, ·my·ing** To mummify. [< F < M < Arabic < Persian *mum* wax] **—mum′mi·form** *adj.*

mumps (mumps) *n.pl.* (*construed as sing.*) *Pathol.* A [con]tagious virus disease usu. occurring in childhood, chara[cter]ized by fever and swelling of the parotid and other [salivary] glands, and occasionally of the testicles. [Pl. of obs. *m* grimace]

munch (munch) *v.t. & v.i.* To chew steadily with a cr[unch]ing noise. [ME, ? < MF *manger*] **—munch′er** *n.*

mun·dane (mun′dān, mun·dān′) *adj.* **1.** Pertaining characterized by that which is practical, routine, or nary: *mundane* concerns. **2.** Of or relating to the wor earth; earthly. [< F < L *mundus* world] **—mun·da** *adv.* **—mun·dane′ness** *n.*

Munich Pact A pact, signed in 1938 by Nazi Gern Great Britain, France, and Italy, in which the Sudeter was ceded to Germany. Also **Munich Agreement.**

mu·nic·i·pal (myōō·nis′ə·pəl) *adj.* **1.** Of or pertaining town or city or its local government. **2.** Having local government. [< L < *municeps, -cipis* free citizen < *m* duties + *capere* to take] **—mu·nic′i·pal·ly** *adv.*

municipal borough See under BOROUGH.

mu·nic·i·pal·i·ty (myōō·nis′ə·pal′ə·tē) *n. pl.* **·ties** A corporated borough, town, or city.

mu·nic·i·pal·ize (myōō·nis′ə·pəl·īz′) *v.t.* **·ized, ·iz·ing 1** place within municipal authority or transfer to muni ownership. **2.** To make a municipality of. **—mu· pal′i·za′tion** *n.*

mu·nif·i·cent (myōō·nif′ə·sənt) *adj.* Extraordinarily erous or bountiful; liberal. [< L < *munus* gift + *face* make] **—mu·nif′i·cence** *n.* **—mu·nif′i·cent·ly** *adv.*

mu·ni·tion (myōō·nish′ən) *n. Usu. pl.* Ammunition all other necessary war materiel. **—***v.t.* To furnish munitions. [< F < L < *munire* to fortify]

mu·ral (myŏŏr′əl) *n.* A painting or decoration applied wall or ceiling. **—***adj.* **1.** Placed or executed on a wa *mural* painting. **2.** Of, pertaining to, or resembling a [< F < L < *murus* wall] **—mu′ral·ist** *n.*

mur·der (mûr′dər) *n.* **1.** The unlawful, malicious, an tentional killing of one human being by another. **2.** *Informal* Something exceedingly difficult, painful, or haz ous. **—to get away with murder** *U.S. Slang* To avoi elude punishment or responsibility. **—***v.t.* **1.** To ki human being) unlawfully and with deliberate malice. To kill or slaughter in a brutal manner, as in war. **3** spoil or mar by a bad performance, improper pronunciat etc. **—***v.i.* **4.** To commit murder. **—Syn.** See K [< OE *morthor*] **—mur′der·er** *n.* **—mur′der·ess** *n.fe*

mur·der·ous (mûr′dər·əs) *adj.* **1.** Of, pertaining to, or volving murder. **2.** Capable of or given to murder. **3.** H ing the characteristics of or resembling murder; bru deadly. **4.** Extremely difficult or dangerous. **—mur′ ous·ly** *adv.* **—mur′der·ous·ness** *n.*

mu·ri·at·ic acid (myŏŏr′ē·at′ik) *n.* Hydrochloric acid, an impure grade used commercially. [< L *muriat* pickled < *muria* brine]

mu·rine (myŏŏr′īn, -in) *adj.* Of or pertaining to a far or a subfamily of rodents that includes the true mice rats. **—***n.* A murine rodent. [< L *mus, muris* mouse]

murk (mûrk) *n.* Darkness; gloom. Also spelled *m* [OE *mirce*]

murk·y (mûr′kē) *adj.* **mur·ki·er, mur·ki·est 1.** D gloomy, or obscure: the *murky* depths. **2.** Hazy, thick, misty, as atmosphere, color, etc. **3.** Not clear or disti to the mind; confused; abstruse. Also *mirky.* **—murk′** *adv.* **—murk′i·ness** *n.*

mur·mur (mûr′mər) *n.* **1.** A low, indistinct, continuou repeated sound, as of many voices. **2.** An indistinct or mu bled complaint; grumbling. **3.** *Med.* A soft, low sound he on auscultation of certain organs; esp., an abnormal, rasp sound produced within the heart. **—***v.i.* **1.** To make a l indistinct sound. **2.** To complain in low, muttered ton grumble. **—***v.t.* **3.** To mutter. [< OF < L *murmur* ult. imit.] **—mur′mur·er** *n.* **—mur′mur·ing·ly** *adv.*

mur·mur·ous (mûr′mər·əs) *adj.* Characterized by, fi with, or making murmurs. **—mur′mur·ous·ly** *adv.* **—mu mur·ous·ness** *n.*

mur·rain (mûr′in) *n.* Any of various contagious disea affecting cattle. [< OF < L *mori* to die]

mur·rey (mûr′ē) *adj.* Of a purplish red color. **—***n.* dark purplish red. [< OF < L *morum* mulberry]

·a (mus′kə) *n.* A constellation, the Fly. [< NL]
·a·dine (mus′kə·din, -dīn) *n.* A North American
having a thick skin and a strong flavor. [Prob. <
ençal < LL *muscus* musk]
·at (mus′kat, -kət) *n.* **1.** Any of several varieties of
-flavored Old World grapes. **2.** A sweet wine made
such cultivated grapes. Also called *muscatel.* [< F<
ençal, smelling like musk < LL *muscus* musk]
·a·tel (mus′kə·tel′) *n.* **1.** A rich, sweet wine, made
the muscat grape. **2.** The muscat grape. Also **mus′·**
·l′ (-del′).
·cle (mus′əl) *n.* **1.** *Anat.* A contractile tissue composed
undles of elongated fibers that function to produce
y movements. **2.** An organ or structure consisting of
tissue. **3.** Muscular strength; brawn. **—** *v.i.* **·cled,**
U.S. Slang To force one's way by or as by sheer brawn:
with *in.* [< F < L *musculus,* lit., little mouse, dim. of
] **— mus′cled** *adj.*
·cle-bound (mus′əl·bound′) *adj.* Having enlarged and
stic muscles, as from excessive exercise.
·o·vite (mus′kə·vīt) *n.* An inhabitant of Muscovy or
oscow. **—** *adj.* **1.** Of or pertaining to Muscovy.
·co·vy (mus′kə·vē) Ancient Russia.
·ovy duck A large, greenish black duck of Central and
h America. [Alter. of MUSK DUCK]
·cu·lar (mus′kyə·lər) *adj.* **1.** Pertaining to or com-
d of muscle. **2.** Having strong muscles; brawny.
us′cu·lar′i·ty (-lar′ə·tē) *n.* **— mus′cu·lar·ly** *adv.*
·ular dystrophy *Pathol.* One of various diseases
acterized by a progressive degeneration of muscle tissue.
·cu·la·ture (mus′kyə·lə·choor) *n.* **1.** The disposition
rangement of muscles in a part or organ. **2.** The muscle
m as a whole. Also **mus′cu·la′tion.** [< F]
[1] (myōōz) *n.* A spirit or power regarded as inspiring
ts, poets, etc. [< MUSE]
[2] (myōōz) *v.t. & v.i.* **mused, mus·ing** To consider
ghtfully or at length; ponder; meditate. [< OF *muser*
flect] **— muse′ful** *adj.* **— muse′ful·ly** *adv.*
(myōōz) *n.* In Greek mythology, any of the nine
lesses who preside over the arts and sciences. [< F
< Gk. *Mousa* a Muse, eloquence, music]
·e·um (myōō·zē′əm) *n.* A place or building for preserv-
and exhibiting works of art, scientific objects, curiosi-
etc. [< L < Gk. *mouseion* shrine of the Muses]
·h[1] (mush) *n.* **1.** *U.S.* A thick porridge made with corn
boiled in water or milk. **2.** Anything soft and pulpy.
nformal Maudlin sentimentality. [Var. of MASH]
·h[2] (mush) *Chiefly Canadian* *v.i.* In arctic regions, to
el over snow with a dog sled. **—** *interj.* Get along!: a
mand to a dog team. [Prob. < F (Canadian) *marche,*
cry of voyageurs and trappers to their dogs]
·h·mel·on (mush′mel′ən) *n.* *U.S. Dial.* A muskmelon.
·h·room (mush′rōōm, -rŏŏm) *n.* **1.** Any of various
y, rapidly growing, umbrella-shaped fungi, esp., the
mon edible **field mushroom** and certain poisonous vari-
loosely called toadstools. **2.** Anything resembling a
hroom in shape or rapid growth. **—** *v.i.* To grow or
ad rapidly or in a mushroomlike shape. [ME *muscheron*]
·h·y (mush′ē) *adj.* **mush·i·er, mush·i·est** **1.** Soft; pulpy.
nformal Mawkishly sentimental. **— mush′i·ly** *adv.*
ush′i·ness *n.*
·sic (myōō′zik) *n.* **1.** The art of producing significant
ngements of sounds, usu. with reference to rhythm,
h, and tone color. **2.** A musical composition or body of
positions; also, a musical score. **3.** A succession or com-
ation of musical sounds, esp. if pleasing to the ear.
program music Music intended to be heard with reference
story, idea, situation, event, etc. **— to face the music**
accept the consequences of one's acts. [< OF < L < Gk.
usikē (*technē*), lit., the art of the Muse]
·si·cal (myōō′zi·kəl) *adj.* **1.** Of, pertaining to, or capa-
of creating music. **2.** Having the nature or characteris-
of music; melodious; harmonious. **3.** Fond of or versed
music. **4.** Set to music. **—** *n.* A musical comedy. **—**
′si·cal·ly *adv.* **— mu′si·cal′i·ty, mu′si·cal·ness** *n.*
·ical comedy A show with music, songs, dances, jokes,
orful staging, etc., often based on a tenuous plot.
·si·cale (myōō′zə·kal′) *n.* A private concert or recital,
n a home. [< F (*soirée*) *musicale*]
·ical saw A handsaw that is played with a violin bow
produces musical tones by being bent or flexed.
·ic box A mechanism that plays tunes, usu. by means of
that strike the tuned teeth of a comblike metal plate.
·ic hall **1.** A public building for musical performances.
Brit. A vaudeville theatre.
·si·cian (myōō·zish′ən) *n.* **1.** A professional performer
composer of music. **2.** One skilled in performing or coming music. **— mu·si′cian·ly** *adj.* **— mu·si′cian·ship** *n.*

mu·si·col·o·gy (myōō′zə·kol′ə·jē) *n. pl.* **·gies** The scientific and historical study of the forms, theory, methods, etc., of music. **— mu′si·col′o·gist** *n.*
music stand A rack to hold music for a performer.
musk (musk) *n.* **1.** A soft, powdery secretion with a penetrating odor, obtained from the sac (**musk bag**) of the male musk deer, and used in making perfumes and in medicine. **2.** Any similar substamce, either natural or synthetic. **3.** The odor of musk. [< OF < LL < LGk. *moskos*]
musk deer A small, hornless deer of Asia, of which the male has a musk-secreting gland.
mus·kel·lunge (mus′kə·lunj) *n. pl.* **·lunge** or **·lung·es** A large North American pike, valued as a game fish. Also **mus′kal·lunge, mus′kie** (-kē). [< Algonquian < *mas* great + *kinong* pike]
mus·ket (mus′kit) *n.* An archaic smoothbore, usually muzzleloading, firearm designed to be fired from the shoulder. [< MF < Ital. *moschetto* crossbow, dart]
mus·ket·eer (mus′kə·tir′) *n.* Formerly, a soldier armed with a musket. [< F *mousquetaire*]
mus·ket·ry (mus′kit·rē) *n.* **1.** Muskets collectively. **2.** The technique of firing small arms.
Mus·kho·ge·an (mus·kō′gē·ən, mus′kō·gē′ən) *n.* One of the principal North American Indian linguistic stocks formerly inhabiting the SE U.S. Also **Mus·ko′gi·an.**
musk·mel·on (musk′mel′ən) *n.* Any of several varieties of juicy, edible fruits of the gourd family, as the cantaloupe; also, the plant.
musk ox A shaggy, hollow-horned ruminant of arctic America and Greenland, emitting a strong odor of musk.
musk·rat (musk′rat) *n. pl.* **·rats** or **·rat** **1.** An aquatic rodent of North America, having dark, glossy brown fur and a musky odor: also called *water rat.* **2.** The valuable fur of this rodent. [< Algonquian *musquash*]
musk·y (mus′kē) *adj.* **musk·i·er, musk·i·est** Resembling musk in odor or taste. **— musk′i·ly** *adv.* **— musk′i·ness** *n.*
Mus·lim (muz′lim, mōōz′-, mōōs′-) *n. pl.* **·lims** or **·lim** A believer in Islam; Mohammedan. **—** *adj.* Of or pertainingto Islam. Also called *Moslem*: also **Mus′·lem.** [< Arabic, one who submits < *aslama* to surrender (to God)]

MUSKRAT
(About 12 inches long; tail 10 inches)

Mus·lim·ism (muz′ləm·iz′əm, mōōz′-, mōōs′-) *n.* Islam.
mus·lin (muz′lin) *n.* Any of several plain-weave cotton fabrics of varying fineness. [< F < Ital. < *Mussolo* Mosul, city in Iraq, where it was made]
muss (mus) *U.S. Informal* *n.* **1.** A state of disorder or untidiness; mess. **2.** A commotion or tumult. **—** *v.t.* To make messy or untidy; rumple: often with *up.* [Alter. of MESS]
mus·sel (mus′əl) *n.* **1.** A bivalve marine mollusk, esp. the edible **blue mussel. 2.** Any of several fresh-water mollusks. [OE < L *musculus,* dim. of *mus* mouse]
Mus·sel·man (mus′əl·mən) *n. pl.* **·mans** (-mənz) or **·men** (-mən) A Muslim. [< Persian and Turkish *musulmān*]
muss·y (mus′ē) *adj.* *U.S. Informal* **muss·i·er, muss·i·est** Rumpled; messy. **— muss′i·ly** *adv.* **— muss′i·ness** *n.*
must[1] (must) *v. Present 3rd person sing.* **must** A defective verb now used only as an auxiliary followed by the infinitive without *to,* or elliptically with the infinitive understood, to express: **a** Compulsion: *Must* you go? **b** Requirement: You *must* be healthy to be accepted. **c** Probability or supposition: You *must* be tired. **d** Conviction or certainty: War *must* follow. ◆ A past conditional is formed by placing the following verb in the perfect infinitive: *He must have gone.* **—** *n. Informal* Anything that is required or vital: Safety is a *must.* **—** *adj. Informal* Important and essential: a *must* book. [OE *mōtan* to be able, to be obliged to]
must[2] (must) *n.* Mustiness; mold. [< MUSTY]
must[3] (must) *n.* The expressed unfermented juice of the grape or other fruit. [OE < L *mustum* (*vinum*) new (wine)]
mus·tache (məs·tash′, mus′tash) *n.* **1.** The growth of hair on the upper lip. **2.** The hair or bristles growing near the mouth of an animal. Also **mus·ta·chio** (məs·tä′shō). Also, *Chiefly Brit., moustache.* [< F < Ital. *mostaccio* face] **— mus·tached** (məs·tasht′) *adj.*
mus·tang (mus′tang) *n.* A wild horse of the American plains. [< Sp. *mesteño* belonging to a cattlemen's association]
mus·tard (mus′tərd) *n.* **1.** A pungent condiment prepared as a paste or powder from the seed of the mustard plant. **2.** Any of several plants of a large family that includes broccoli, cabbage, cress, etc. **3.** The yellowish or brownish color of ground mustard. [< MF *moustarde*]
mustard gas *Chem.* An oily amber liquid, $C_4H_8Cl_2S$, having an odor of mustard or garlic, and used in warfare because of its powerful blistering effect.

mustard plaster A mixture of powdered black mustard and a suitable adhesive, used as a counterirritant.

mus·ter (mus′tər) *v.t.* **1.** To summon or assemble (troops, etc.), for service, review, roll call, etc. **2.** To collect, gather, or summon: often with *up.* — *v.i.* **3.** To gather or assemble, as troops for service, review, etc. — **to muster in** (or **out**) To enlist in (or leave) military service. — *n.* **1.** An assembling or gathering, as of troops. **2.** An assemblage or collection, as of troops. **3.** An official list of officers and men in a military unit or ship's crew: also **muster roll.** [< OF < L *monstrare* to show]

must·y (mus′tē) *adj.* **must·i·er, must·i·est 1.** Having a moldy odor or flavor, as a close room. **2.** Dull or stale with age. **3.** Without vigor; lifeless. [? Alter. of obs. *moisty* < MOIST] — **must′i·ly** *adv.* — **must′i·ness** *n.*

mu·ta·ble (myo͞o′tə·bəl) *adj.* **1.** Capable of or subject to change. **2.** Liable to frequent change. [< L < *mutare* to change] — **mu′ta·ble·ness, mu′ta·bil′i·ty** *n.* — **mu′ta·bly** *adv.*

mu·ta·gen·ic (myo͞o′tə·jen′ik) *adj. Genetics* Having the power to produce mutations in plant or animal organisms, as X-rays, certain chemicals, etc. [< L *mutare* to change]

mu·tant (myo͞o′tənt) *n.* A plant or animal organism differing from its parents in one or more characteristics that are inheritable; mutation; sport. — *adj.* Pertaining to, resulting from, or undergoing mutation. [< L *mutare* to change]

mu·tate (myo͞o′tāt) *v.t. & v.i.* **·tat·ed, ·tat·ing** To undergo or subject to change or mutation. [< L < *mutare* to change] — **mu′ta·tive** (-tə·tiv) *adj.*

mu·ta·tion (myo͞o·tā′shən) *n.* **1.** The act or process of changing; alteration. **2.** A change or modification in form, structure, function, etc. **3.** *Biol.* **a** A sudden, transmissible variation in a plant or animal. **b** An individual, species, etc., resulting from such a variation. [< OF < L < *mutare* to change] — **mu·ta′tion·al** *adj.*

mute (myo͞ot) *adj.* **1.** Not producing speech or sound; silent. **2.** Lacking the power of speech; dumb. **3.** Expressed or conveyed without speech; unspoken: a *mute* appeal. **4.** *Law* Deliberately refusing to plead on arraignment. **5.** *Phonet.* Not pronounced; silent, as the *e* in *gone.* — *n.* **1.** One who is unable to speak; esp. a deaf-mute. **2.** *Law* One who refuses to plead on arraignment. **3.** *Phonet.* **a** A silent letter. **b** A plosive. **4.** *Music* A device used to muffle the tone of an instrument. — *v.t.* **mut·ed, mut·ing 1.** To muffle or deaden the sound of (a musical instrument, etc.). **2.** In art, to soften (a color, a shade, etc.). [< L *mutus* dumb] — **mute′ly** *adv.* — **mute′ness** *n.*

mu·ti·late (myo͞o′tə·lāt) *v.t.* **·lat·ed, ·lat·ing 1.** To deprive (a person, animal, etc.) of a limb or essential part; maim. **2.** To damage or make imperfect: to *mutilate* a speech. [< L *mutilare* to maim] — **mu′ti·la′tion** *n.* — **mu′ti·la′tive** *adj.* — **mu′ti·la′tor** *n.*

mu·ti·neer (myo͞o′tə·nir′) *n.* One guilty of mutiny.

mu·ti·nous (myo͞o′tə·nəs) *adj.* **1.** Disposed to mutiny; seditious. **2.** Characterized by, expressing, or constituting mutiny. — **mu′ti·nous·ly** *adv.* — **mu′ti·nous·ness** *n.*

mu·ti·ny (myo͞o′tə·nē) *n. pl.* **·nies** Rebellion against constituted authority; insubordination; esp., a revolt of soldiers or sailors against their commanders. — *v.i.* **·nied, ·ny·ing** To take part in a mutiny. [< MF *mutin* rebellious < OF < Med.L < L *movere* to move]

mutt (mut) *n. Slang* **1.** A cur; mongrel dog. **2.** A stupid person; blockhead. Also **mut.** [< MUTT(ONHEAD)]

mut·ter (mut′ər) *v.i.* **1.** To speak in a low, indistinct tone, as in complaining. **2.** To complain; grumble. **3.** To make a low, rumbling sound. — *v.t.* **4.** To say in a low, indistinct tone. — *n.* A low, indistinct utterance or tone. [ME *muteren*] — **mut′ter·er** *n.* — **mut′ter·ing·ly** *adv.*

mut·ton (mut′n) *n.* The flesh of sheep used as food; esp. the flesh of mature sheep as distinguished from lambs. [< OF *molton* sheep] — **mut′ton·y** *adv.*

mutton chop A piece of mutton from the rib for broiling or frying.

mut·ton·chops (mut′n·chops′) *n.pl.* Side whiskers narrow at the temples and broad at the lower cheeks.

mut·ton·head (mut′n·hed′) *n. Slang* A stupid, dense person. — **mut′ton·head′ed** (-hed′id) *adj.*

mu·tu·al (myo͞o′cho͞o·əl) *adj.* **1.** Felt, expressed, or performed for or toward each other; reciprocal: *mutual* dislike. **2.** Having the same attitude toward or relationship with each other or others: *mutual* friends. **3.** Possessed in common. [< OF < L *mutuus* borrowed, exchanged, reciprocal] — **mu′tu·al·ly** *adv.* — **mu′tu·al′i·ty** *n.*

muu·muu (mo͞o′mo͞o′) *n.* A loose, flowing gown for women, gathered from the neckline. [< Hawaiian]

mu·zhik (mo͞o·zhēk′, mo͞o′zhēk) *n.* A Russian peasant in Czarist times. Also **mu·zjik′.** [< Russian]

muz·zle (muz′əl) *n.* **1.** The projecting part of an animal's head, including the jaws, mouth, and snout. **2.** A guard or covering for the snout. **3.** The front end of the barrel of a firearm. — *v.t.* **·zled, ·zling 1.** To put a muzzle on (an animal, etc.). **2.** To restrain from speaking, expr opinions, etc.; gag. [< OF < Med.L *musus* snout]

muz·zle·load·er (muz′əl·lō′dər) *n.* A gun loaded th the muzzle. — **muz′zle·load′ing** *adj.*

MVD The Ministry of Internal Affairs of the Soviet U the secret police. Also **M.V.D.**

my (mī) *pronominal adj.* The possessive case of the pr *I*, used attributively: also used in certain forms of ad *my* lord; *my* good man. — *interj.* An exclamation o prise, dismay, etc.: Oh, *my!* [OE *mīn*]

my- Var. of MYO-.

my·as·the·ni·a (mī′əs·thē′nē·ə) *n. Pathol.* Muscular ity, often accompanied by progressive exhaustion.

my·ce·li·um (mī·sē′lē·əm) *n. pl.* **·li·a** (-lē·ə) *Bot.* thallus or vegetative portion of a fungus, consisti hyphae. Also **my′cele** (-sēl). [< NL < Gk. *mykēs* fu — **my·ce′li·al, my·ce′li·an** *adj.* — **my·ce′li·oid, my·** (mī′sə·loid) *adj.*

My·ce·nae (mī·sē′nē) An ancient city in the NE Pel nesus, Greece; first excavated 1876–77. — **My′ce·n** *adj. & n.*

-mycete *combining form Bot.* A member of a class of corresponding in use to class names in *-mycetes.*

-mycetes *combining form Bot.* Used to form class na fungi. [< Gk. *mykētes*, pl. of *mykēs* fungus]

myco- *combining form* Fungus. Also, before vowels, [< Gk. *mykēs* fungus]

my·col·o·gy (mī·kol′ə·jē) *n. pl.* **·gies** The bran botany dealing with fungi. — **my·co·log·ic** (mī′kə· or **·i·cal** *adj.* — **my·col′o·gist** *n.*

my·co·sis (mī·kō′sis) *n. Pathol.* **1.** A fungous growth in the body. **2.** A disease caused by such a growth, as worm. — **my·cot′ic** (-kot′ik) *adj.*

my·e·len·ceph·a·lon (mī′ə·len·sef′ə·lon) *n. Anat.* posterior part of the rhombencephalon or that portion medulla oblongata lying behind the pons Varolii and ce lum.

my·e·li·tis (mī′ə·lī′tis) *n. Pathol.* **1.** Inflammation spinal cord. **2.** Inflammation of the bone marrow.

myelo- *combining form Anat.* The spinal cord or bone row. Also, before vowels, **myel-.** [< Gk. *myelos* marr

my·na (mī′nə) *n.* One of the various starlinglike Ori birds, some of which are taught to speak words: some spelled *mina.* Also **my′nah.** [< Hind. *mainā*]

myn·heer (mīn·hâr′, -hir′) *n.* **1.** *Cap.* The Dutch e alent of *Mr.* **2.** A title of courtesy, equivalent to *sir.* Du. < *mijn* my + *heer* lord, master]

myo- *combining form* Muscle. Also, before vowels, [< Gk. *mys, myos* muscle]

my·o·car·di·al (mī′ō·kär′dē·əl) *adj. Anat.* Of or perta to the heart muscle. [< MYO- + Gk. *kardia* heart]

my·o·car·di·um (mī′ō·kär′dē·əm) *n. Anat.* The mus tissue of the heart. [< MYO- + Gk. *kardia* heart]

my·o·pi·a (mī·ō′pē·ə) *n.* **1.** *Pathol.* A visual defect in w objects are seen clearly only when close to the eye; sightedness. **2.** Lack of insight or discernment; obtuse Also **my·o·py** (mī′ə·pē). [< NL] — **my·op′ic** (-op′ik)

myria- *combining form* **1.** Very many; of great nur **2.** In the metric system, ten thousand. Also, before vo **myri-.** [< Gk. *myrios* numberless]

myr·i·ad (mir′ē·əd) *adj.* Countless; innumerable. **1.** A vast indefinite number. **2.** A vast number of pe or things. **3.** Ten thousand. [< Gk. *myrios* numberl

myr·i·a·pod (mir′ē·ə·pod) *n. Zool.* One of a group o thropods whose bodies are made up of a certain numb segments, each of which bears one or two pairs of jo appendages, including the centipedes. — **myr·i·ap·o** (mir′ē·ap′ə·dən) *adj. & n.* — **myr′i·ap′o·dous** *adj.*

myr·mi·don (mûr′mə·don, -dən) *n.* A faithful, unques ing follower. [< MYRMIDON]

Myr·mi·don (mûr′mə·don, -dən) *n.* In Greek legend, of a warlike people of Thessaly, followers of Achilles ir Trojan War. [< L < Gk., pl. *Myrmidones*]

myrrh (mûr) *n.* **1.** An aromatic gum resin that exudes certain small trees of Arabia and eastern Africa, use incense, perfume, and in medicine. **2.** Any shrub or that yields this gum. [OE < L < Gk. *myrra* < Hebrew *mar* bitter]

myr·tle (mûr′təl) *n.* Any of a group of shrubs with e green leaves, white or rose-colored flowers, and black ries. **2.** One of various other plants, as the periwir [< F < Med.L *myrtillus* myrtle]

my·self (mī·self′) *pron.* A form of the first person sing pronoun, used: **1.** As a reflexive or as the object of a pr sition in a reflexive sense: I saw *myself* in the mirror. **2** an emphatic or intensive form of *I*: I *myself* invented yo-yo. **3.** Informally as part of a direct compound ob of a verb, or as an emphatic form of *me*: He asked John *myself* to come along; They saw *myself* on television. **4** a designation of a normal, proper, or usual state: Once of uniform, I was *myself* again in no time. [OE *mē* + s

:e·ri·ous (mis·tir′ē·əs) *adj.* **1.** Implying or charac- ›d by mystery. **2.** Unexplained; puzzling. **— mys· ous·ly** *adv.* **— mys·te′ri·ous·ness** *n.*
Syn. A *mysterious* occurrence contains something unknown, ›t necessarily unknowable, while something *obscure* is hidden nay be brought to light. *Inscrutable* refers to that which is beyond the power of perception; *abstruse*, to that which is ılt to understand because of its complexity or profundity. *ric* suggests something that is understood only by a small and ; group possessing special knowledge. *Occult* marks those s considered to belong to a realm beyond human experience.

ter·y (mis′tər·ē) *n. pl.* **·ter·ies 1.** Something that is ›r cannot be known, understood, or explained. **2.** Any n, affair, or thing that arouses curiosity or suspense ıse it is not fully revealed. **3.** A story, play, movie, etc., ating or dramatizing such an affair. **4.** Obscurity or ness: shrouded in *mystery.* **5.** Baffling character or ›erty, as of a glance, gesture, etc. **6.** *Theol.* A truth can be known only through divine revelation. **7.** **a** A sacrament, esp. the Eucharist. **b** *pl.* The Eucha- : elements. **c** Any of fifteen events in the life of Christ. *'su. pl.* In ancient times, one of certain religious cults. *ften pl.* A secret rite, doctrine, or practice. [< L < Gk. *erion* secret rite]

ery play A medieval dramatic representation dealing Scriptural events or characters and typically presented craft guild on a holiday. Compare MIRACLE PLAY.

tic (mis′tik) *adj.* **1.** Of the nature of or pertaining to teries. **2.** Of or designating an occult or esoteric rite, tice, belief, religion, etc. **3.** Of or pertaining to mystics nysticism. **4.** Baffling or enigmatic. **—** *n.* One who ›ves in mysticism, or professes to have had mystical ex- ences. [< L *mysticus* pertaining to secret rites]

·ti·cal (mis′ti·kəl) *adj.* **1.** Of the nature of a direct, itive, or subjective perception beyond the ordinary :e of human experience, esp. one of a religious character. **2.** Having a spiritual character or reality beyond human reason. **3.** Mystic (defs. 1, 2, & 3). **— mys′ti·cal′i·ty** (-kal′ə·tē), **mys′ti·cal·ness** *n.* **— mys′ti·cal·ly** *adv.*

mys·ti·cism (mis′tə·siz′əm) *n.* **1.** The doctrine or belief that through contemplation and love man can achieve a direct and immediate consciousness of God or of divine truth, etc., without the use of reason or of any of the ordinary senses. **2.** Any mystical theory. **3.** Vague thinking.

mys·ti·fy (mis′tə·fī) *v.t.* **·fied, ·fy·ing 1.** To confuse or perplex, esp. deliberately. **2.** To make obscure or mysterious. [< F < *mystique* mystic] **— mys′ti·fi·ca′tion** *n.* **— mys′ti·fi′er** *n.* **— mys′ti·fy′ing·ly** *adv.*

mys·tique (mis·tēk′) *n.* A body of attitudes, opinions, or ideas that become associated with a person, thing, institution, etc., and give it a superhuman or mythical status: the *mystique* of bullfighting. [< F]

myth (mith) *n.* **1.** A traditional story, usu. focusing on the deeds of gods or heroes, often in explanation of some natural phenomenon, as the origin of the sun, etc. **2.** A theme, motif, character type, etc., in modern literature. **3.** Myths collectively. **4.** An imaginary or fictitious person, thing, event, or story. **5.** A false opinion, belief, or ideal. [< LL *mythos* < Gk., word, speech, story]

myth·i·cal (mith′i·kəl) *adj.* **1.** Pertaining to or like a myth; **2.** Derived from or contained in a myth. **3.** Imaginary. fictitious. Also **myth′ic. — myth′i·cal·ly** *adv.*

mytho- *combining form* Myth. Also, before vowels, **myth-.** [< Gk. *mythos* story]

myth·o·log·i·cal (mith′ə·loj′i·kəl) *adj.* **1.** Of, pertaining to, or described in mythology. **2.** Imaginary. Also **myth′o·log′ic. — myth′o·log′i·cal·ly** *adv.*

my·thol·o·gy (mi·thol′ə·jē) *n. pl.* **·gies 1.** The collective myths and legends of a particular people, person, institution, etc. **2.** The scientific collection and study of myths. **3.** A volume of myths. [< F < LL < Gk. < *mythos* story + *logos* < *legein* to speak, tell] **— my·thol′o·gist** *n.*